THE TIMES

CONCISE
ATLAS
OF THE WORLD

Book Club Associates London

Contributors

John C Bartholomew
Editorial Director
John Bartholomew & Son Limited

Hugh Clayton
Agricultural Correspondent
The Times London

Charles Cotter
Department of Maritime Studies, Uwist
Cardiff

F W Dunning
Curator
The Geological Museum, London

John Gribbin
Science Policy Research Unit
University of Sussex

H A G Lewis OBE
Geographical Consultant

Kenneth Mellanby
Monks Wood Experimental Station
Institute of Terrestrial Ecology

Eric Rawstron
Professor of Geography
Queen Mary College
University of London

Ian Ridpath
Editor
Encyclopedia of Astronomy and Space

Alan Smith
Department of Geology
University of Cambridge

Peter J Smith
Department of Earth Sciences
The Open University

David Tennant
Travel Correspondent
Thomson Regional Newspapers, London

Roger Vielvoye
Formerly Energy Correspondent
The Times, London

Editorial direction
Barry Winkleman
Paul Middleton

Maps prepared and printed
in Great Britain by
John Bartholomew & Son Limited, Edinburgh

Conurbation maps compiled and drawn by
Fairey Surveys Limited, Maidenhead;
A W Gatrell; and Hunting Surveys Limited

Artwork by Ivan and Robin Dodd, Key Graphics
and Donald Shewan

Preliminary section cartography by
Fairey Surveys Limited, Maidenhead
and filmset by
Crawley Composition Ltd, Crawley, Sussex

Index prepared by
Geographical Research Associates, Maidenhead

Index data processing by
Computer Data Processing Ltd, Haywards Heath

Index set by Computaprint, London

Index printed by The Anchor Press Limited, England

Books bound by
Bookbinders Brandt, The Netherlands

First published 1972 by
Times Books Limited,
London

Reprinted with revisions 1973, 1974
Revised edition 1975
Reprinted 1976, 1978
Revised edition 1978
Reprinted with revisions 1979
Revised edition 1980
Reprinted with revisions 1982
Reprinted 1983

This edition published 1983 by
Book Club Associates
by arrangement with
Times Books

Contents

Acknowledgements

Academy of Sciences of the USSR and the National
Atlas Committee, Moscow

Aeronautical Chart and Information Center, United
States Air Force, St Louis, Missouri

American Geographical Society, New York

The British Petroleum Company Ltd, London

British Tourist Authority, London

Ceskoslovenské Akademie Ved, Prague

Department of Lands and Survey, Wellington,
New Zealand

The Department of the Environment, London

Food & Agriculture Organization of the
United Nations, Rome

French Railways, London

Freytag-Berndt und Artaria, Vienna

Mr P. J. M. Geelan

General Drafting Company Inc, Convent Station,
New Jersey

Dr R. Habel, VEB Hermann Haack,
Geographisch-Kartographische Anstalt, Gotha,
East Germany

The Controller, H.M. Stationery Office, London

Institut Géographique Militaire, Brussels

Le Directeur de l'Institut Géographique National, Paris

Instituto Brasiliero de Geografia e Estatistica,
Rio de Janeiro

International Hydrographic Bureau, Monaco

International Road Federation, London

International Union of Official Travel Organizations,
Geneva

Professor P. E. James, Syracuse University, New York

Mr P. Laffitte, Ecole des Mines, Paris

Dr E. Meynen, Bad Godesberg, West Germany

National Aeronautical and Space Administration,
Washington DC

National Geographic Society, Washington DC

National Library of Scotland, Edinburgh

Director of National Mapping, Department of National
Development, Canberra

Director-General, Ordnance Survey, Southampton

Palomar Observatory, California Institute of Technology

Petroleum Information Bureau, London

Dr B. B. Roberts, Antarctic Place-Names Committee,
London

Mr P. Rouveyrol, Bureau de Recherches Géologiques et
Minières, Paris

Royal Geographical Society, London

Royal Observatory, Edinburgh

Royal Scottish Geographical Society, Edinburgh

The Scientific American, San Francisco

Dr John Paxton, The Editor, The Statesman's Year
Book, London

Dr H. J. Störig, Lexikon-Redaktion, Munich

The Trigonometrical Survey Office, Pretoria

Touring Club Italiano, Milan

Under-Secretary of State, Foreign and Commonwealth
Office, London

Surveys and Mapping Branch, Department of Energy,
Mines, and Resources, Ottawa

United States Army Topographic Command,
Washington DC

United States Board on Geographic Names,
Washington DC

United States Department of State, Washington DC

United States Embassy Press Office, London

Introduction

In presenting a further revision of an atlas which has proved to be extremely popular, we draw attention to an important change in this edition. Place-names in China are given in their Pinyin spellings, a step likewise taken in our larger atlas, the Comprehensive Edition. More is said on the subject below.

The preliminary section of the atlas is concerned with geography in its widest sense: as a science that has much to contribute to the understanding of the contemporary world. In these pages we first describe the origin and geology of the Earth and its physical nature, its resources of climate, vegetation and minerals. Then we examine major features of the geography of man, particularly his settlements and population patterns, his trade and industry, his use of energy, the development of tourism, and the effect of all these activities on the balance of his natural environment. The complex techniques of navigation, which have been central to the development of human history, are described, and the Earth as a whole is placed into its context in the expanding Universe. The present state of our knowledge of the Universe is described; two pages are devoted to maps of the Moon and one to star charts.

In the main body of the atlas the maps, with the exception of those covering the conurbation areas, have been compiled by John Bartholomew & Son Limited of Edinburgh, who have been associated with *The Times* in atlas-publishing since 1922. Several map projections are used, each for its own special properties. Without some adaptation the surface of the spherical earth cannot be transferred to a flat sheet of paper, any more than an orange can be wrapped in a sheet of paper without cutting and folding. Map projections are the means of adapting the round globe to the flat map.

How best to spell place-names, a matter of great complexity, has always been considered carefully in the preparation of atlases published by *The Times*. Difficulties arise from the diversity of writing systems in use in the world and the great number of languages, hundreds of which are inadequately written or have no writing system. In the absence of a uniform and internationally accepted method of recording and writing geographical names, conventional spellings established by long usage furnish us with Athens (English), Athènes (French), Azine (Spanish), etc. *The Times Concise Atlas* gives transliterations in English, e.g. Athinai, with the English conventional name, where appropriate, in parentheses: Athinai (Athens). In general, *The Times Concise Atlas* follows the rules recommended by the United States Board on Geographical Names and the Permanent Committee on Geographical Names for British Official Use.

In all previous editions names in China have been transcribed in terms of the Wade-Giles readings of Chinese characters. With increasing use of Pinyin within China as a roman alphabet equivalent of the Han characters and the recent availability of sufficient sources for names, the publishers decided to replace Wade-Giles by Pinyin in mainland China. In Taiwan, Wade-Giles is still in use and so is retained in this atlas. Neither is Pinyin applicable in Hong Kong where a local system is in use. A special section on the Transcription of Chinese Place-Names has been added to this edition (p.88).

With regard to the sensitive political implications of maps, *The Times Atlas* has always considered its task to be to show facts as they are and not to pass judgements. When delineating a frontier this atlas shows which authority is administering the area at the time the map goes to press. Our wish is to help the traveller, businessman, student or teacher who we hope will buy it. It also follows that place-names are, as far as possible, spelt according to the usage of those administering the region concerned. An atlas can show where a frontier is disputed, but it strays beyond its proper sphere if it tries to adjudicate between the rights and wrongs of the dispute rather than to set down the facts as they are.

The index section contains over 90,000 entries. Not every name on the maps appears in that index, but all towns and physical features other than the smallest are indexed. Place-names and their descriptions (such as Lake or River) are listed in strict alphabetical order, so that Haig L. (Lake) does not immediately follow the town of Haig, but is interrupted by Haiger. Each name is accompanied by its country or location and by the page number and grid reference by letter and numeral.

The information on states and territories which precedes the index section has been revised to accord with the latest information available.

It is with pleasure that we issue this, our latest edition, and we hope the reader will find equal interest and pleasure from its use.

The Earth

The origin of the Earth

The Earth originated as part of the solar system about 4,700 million years ago, probably by the accretion of particles from a cloud of gas and dust (see *The origin of the planets*). Certainly it must have formed in a fairly cold state, for otherwise many of the more volatile elements still present in the Earth would never have been able to condense. On the other hand, the Earth must have warmed up quickly as it increased in size, heat being produced in three ways – by conversion of kinetic energy of the particles coming to rest on the surface of the new planet as the result of great compression in the body's interior, and from decay of radioactive elements.

This heat, which was produced more rapidly than it could escape, had a profound effect on the new Earth's structure. Without it, the Earth would have become a homogeneous globe of silicon compounds, iron and magnesium oxides and smaller quantities of all naturally-occurring elements. As it was, the planet very soon warmed up sufficiently to allow the separation of elements and compounds, to begin. The heavier materials such as iron sank towards the Earth's centre whereas the lighter ones, chiefly silicon compounds, rose towards the surface.

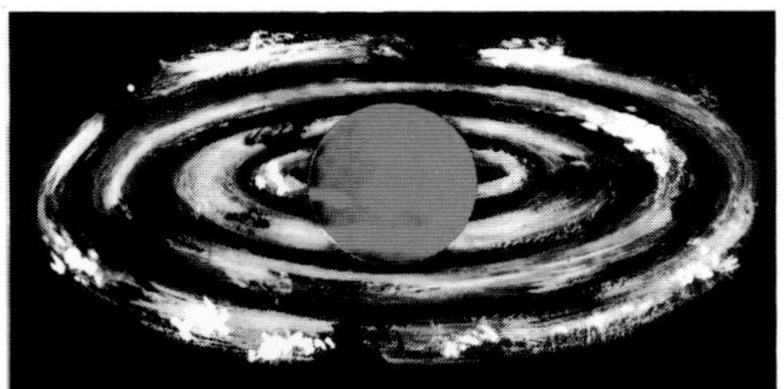

The origin of the planets

Most of the theories about the origin of the planets in the solar system may be divided into two broad types – those which attribute the creation of a solar system to gradual evolutionary processes and those which see it as the result of a catastrophic action.

Kant and Laplace *Nebular Theory*

The earliest theory of the first type was put forward in 1755 by Kant, who suggested that the solar system originated as a spinning disc of material which later separated out into the Sun and the planets. In 1796 this basic idea was developed by Laplace into the nebular theory. Laplace proposed that the Sun was originally a rotating gaseous nebula (1) which gradually contracted under gravitational forces and rotated more and more rapidly until gaseous material was thrown off at the edges to form a series of rings. Each ring then condensed into a separate planet.

Moulton, Chamberlin and Jeans *Tidal Theory*

By 1900 Laplace's theory in its original form had been abandoned, partly because it had proved to be inconsistent with the Sun's observed period of rotation and partly because scientists had shown that Laplace's rings would be too stable to coalesce into planets. So in 1905 Moulton and Chamberlin suggested a return to Buffon's idea of about 200 years before, namely, that the solar system resulted from the collision of the Sun with another body. Thirteen years later this proposal was modified by Jeans, who envisaged not a collision but a close encounter between the Sun and a star (2). As the star passed by the Sun its gravitational attraction drew out from the Sun's surface a long filament of gaseous matter which, being unstable, broke into separate zones. Each zone cooled and contracted into a planet.

Von Weizsäcker's Theory

By the 1930s, however, it had become clear that the sort of filament suggested by Jeans would be so unstable that it would be dispersed into space within a few hours. Moreover, planets such as the Earth are so different from the Sun in composition that they are unlikely to have formed directly from it. So in 1944 von Weizsäcker returned to, and modified, the nebular theory. He suggested that the Sun passed through a vast dense cloud of interstellar dust and gas which it attracted to itself in the form of a disc. The particles in the disc then gradually aggregated into larger and larger lumps which became the planets (3).

Hoyle's Theory

Although the broad outlines of von Weizsäcker's theory are now quite widely accepted, the theory is not entirely satisfactory in detail and so other scientists have proposed variations or even completely different theories. One of the most interesting of modern suggestions was put forward by Hoyle, who drew attention to the role of magnetism. Hoyle proposed that magnetic forces between the Sun and the dust-gas disc gradually move the disc outwards (4). As the disc spread away from the Sun it was capable of carrying smaller and smaller particles and so the larger particles gradually got left behind. This segregation into sizes also implies segregation into different compositions, which quite neatly explains why, when the particles aggregate into planets, the compositions of the planets vary considerably right across the solar system.

The position of the Earth in the Universe

The Earth is the third planet from the Sun and the largest of the group of inner, or terrestrial, planets, the other members of which are Mercury, Venus and Mars. The Sun, the inner planets and the group of outer planets (Jupiter, Saturn, Uranus, Neptune and Pluto – all of which, with the exception of Pluto, are much larger than the Earth) together make up most of the solar system. The solar system is completed by over 400,000 or so asteroids, or minor planets, most of whose orbits lie between Mars and Jupiter and the largest of which is Ceres with a diameter of 730 km. All the planets revolve around the Sun in the same direction and, with the exception of Pluto, their elliptical orbits lie almost in one plane.

Pluto, the outermost planet, is about 5,900 million kilometres, or about 5 light hours, away from the Sun. Yet vast as this distance is, the Sun and planets are but a speck in the universe. For a start, the solar system is but a very small part of the Milky Way, a lens-shaped galaxy which contains some 100,000 million stars like the Sun and vast clouds of hydrogen, helium and dust. The diameter of the Milky Way is about 100,000 light years and the Sun lies about two-thirds of the way from the centre.

The Milky Way, in turn, is only one of many thousands of millions of galaxies scattered throughout the universe. Galaxies tend to cluster; the Milky Way, for example, is but one galaxy in a local group of about 20 and is only about half the size of the largest galaxy in the group. The group itself has a spread of about 5 million light years.

Outside the local group, the furthest known ordinary galaxy is more than 8,000 million light years away, but beyond that are radio galaxies and quasars. Radio galaxies emit vast quantities of radio energy (more than a million times than that emitted by the Milky Way) and are believed to be the sites of gigantic explosions, possibly representing an early stage of galaxy formation. Quasars are very brilliant, but much smaller objects (less than 1 light year across), which are powerful emitters of radio waves and may be the nuclei of distant galaxies. The furthest known object, quasar OQ 172, lies 18,000 million light years away, at the very edge of the detectable universe.

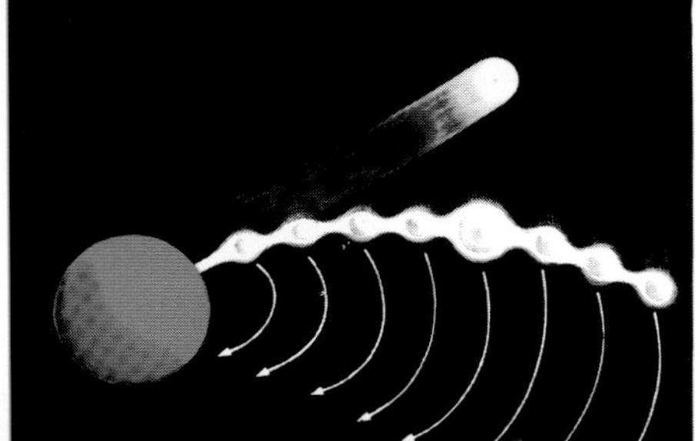

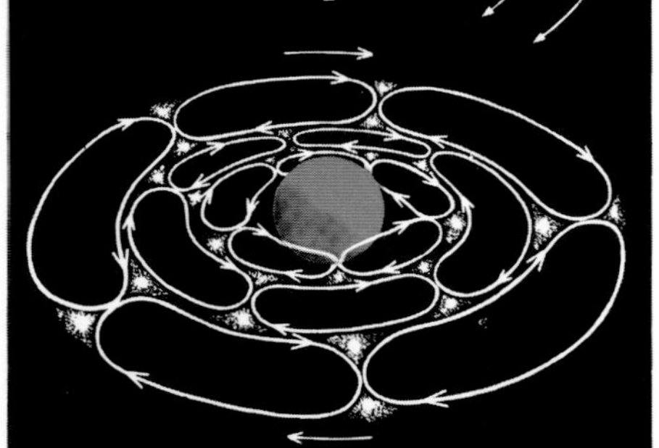

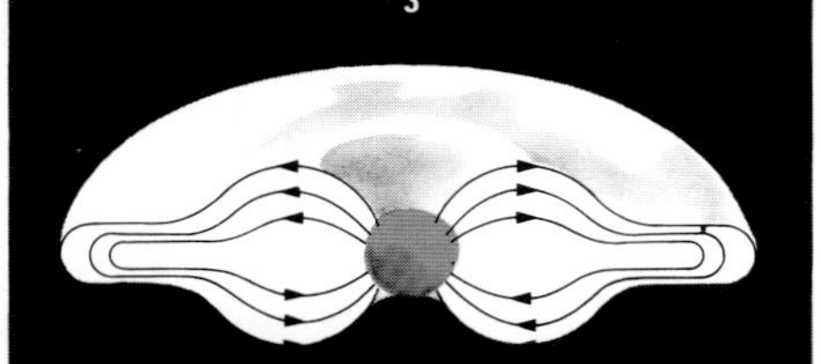

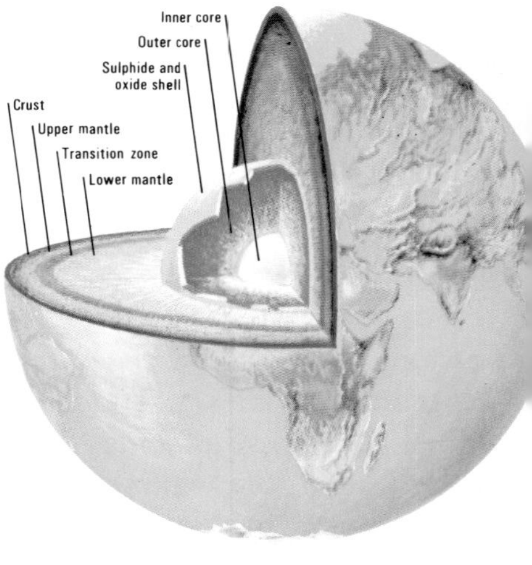

Structure of the solid Earth

The solid Earth consists of three shells: crust, mantle and core. The thin outer shell, the crust, is made up of different types of rock. Under continents it is about 40 km thick and is mostly granitic in composition. Under mountain ranges it may be thicker than 70 km. The oceanic crust is about 8 km thick and is basaltic. The mean crustal density is 2·8 (water = 1·0), and it is about 0·4% of the total mass of the Earth.

The base of the crust is marked by the Mohorovicic discontinuity (Moho or M−). At this level the velocity of the fastest seismic waves sent out by earthquakes rises rapidly from 6 km/sec to .8 km/sec. Below the Moho lies the mantle. Solid rocks brought up from the mantle by lava flows suggest that it is much less varied than the crust and consists mostly of the rock peridotite. The mantle has a thickness of 2,900 km, density of 4·5, and makes up 67·2% of the Earth's mass. The increase in pressure with depth causes the minerals in peridotite (mainly olivine and pyroxene) to change through a transition zone to new dense minerals unknown at the surface.

The innermost Earth shell is the core. The outer core, 2,200 km thick, is fluid. Motions in the fluid generate the Earth's magnetic field. The inner core, radius 1,270 km, is solid. The core density is 11·0 and contains 32·4% of the Earth's mass. Both cores are probably made of nickel-iron.

Physical characteristics of the Earth
The Earth is not perfectly spherical but has the shape of a spheroid, a sphere flattened at the poles. The average polar radius of 6,357 km is thus smaller than the average equatorial radius of 6,378 km. The overall average radius is 6,371 km, which is the radius of the sphere that has the same volume as the Earth.

The mass of the Earth is 6×10^{24} kg and its average density is about 5·5 grams/cm^3. But the average density of the surface rocks is only about 2·8 grams/cm^3. There must therefore be an increase in density towards the Earth's centre where the pressure exceeds that of $3\frac{1}{2}$ million atmospheres. The temperature at the centre is uncertain; but is probably no more than about 5,000°C.

More than 70 per cent of the Earth's surface is covered by ocean. Indeed, the Pacific Ocean alone, which with its adjacent seas accounts for more than 35 per cent of the Earth's surface, covers a larger area than that of all the continents combined. More than 65 per cent of the continental area lies in the northern hemisphere, although at the poles themselves this imbalance is reversed.

Metal-bearing rocks deep inside the Earth, contain crystals of ferro-magnetic materials revealed by production of local anomalous magnetism. As the rocks cooled and solidified, the magnetised molecules were aligned like small magnets in the direction of the magnetic poles, thus preserving as 'frozen magnetism' a permanent record of the magnetism at the place and time of their solidification.

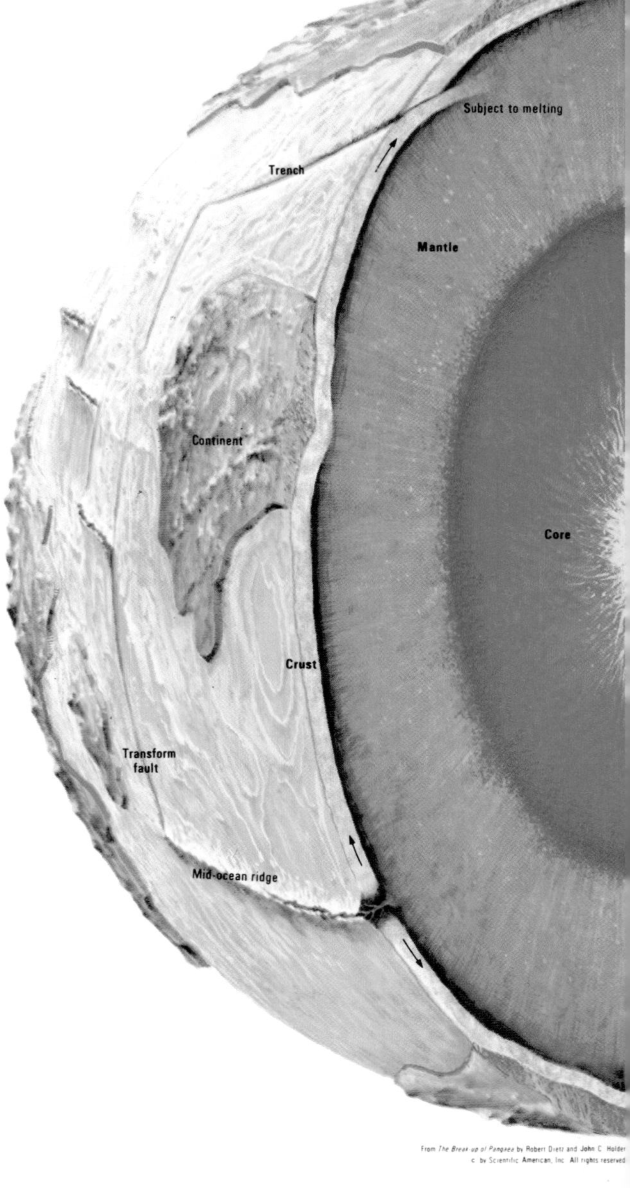

The magnetosphere

Ionized gas, or plasma, streams from the Sun in all directions, and is known as the 'solar wind'. The Earth's fluid iron-nickel core produces a magnetic field which extends beyond the Earth's surface into space. Where the solar wind comes into contact with this magnetic field there is a mutual interaction.

On the side of the Earth facing the Sun the solar wind compresses the Earth's magnetic field, whereas on the side of the Earth away from the Sun the field is greatly elongated. The field is thus confined to a zone known as the magnetosphere, the boundary of which is called the magnetopause. The position of the magnetopause changes a little as the intensity of the solar wind varies, but in the solar direction it lies at an average distance of about 10 Earth radii from the centre of the Earth, whilst in the anti-solar direction, it extends out to very large distances of at least 60 Earth radii.

The solar wind is travelling at almost

1000 km per second when it encounters the Earth's magnetic field. A shock wave is formed several Earth radii from the magnetopause in the direction of the Sun.

The region between the magnetopause and the shock wave front is known as the magnetosheath, or transition region of the magnetosphere.

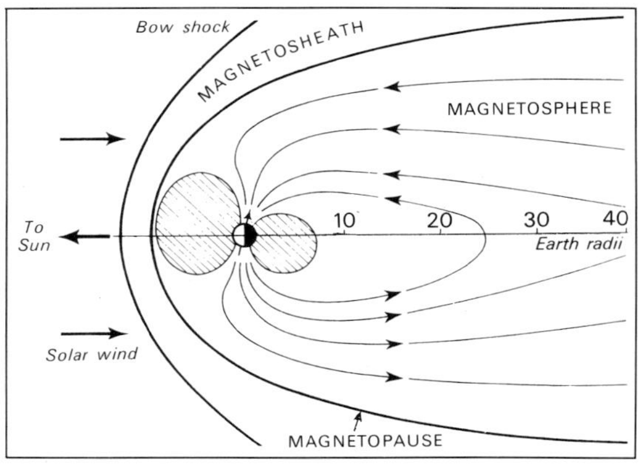

Earthquakes

An earthquake is a sudden release of strain energy at a point – or, more accurately, within a small zone – in the Earth's crust or upper mantle. Because many shallow earthquakes are obviously related to sudden fault movements, it was once thought that they were responsible for all earthquakes. But it seems likely that at depths greater than a few tens of kilometres the pressure would be too great to allow any fault slippage, whereas earthquakes are known to occur down to depths of about 700 km. The cause of the deeper shocks remains unknown.

Whatever their basic cause, however, most earthquakes are clearly related to plate tectonic processes and occur along plate boundaries – oceanic ridges, oceanic trenches and transform faults. The most intense belt of seismic activity lies around the margin of the Pacific Ocean where 75 per cent of all shallow earthquakes (0–70 km depth), 90 per cent of all intermediate earthquakes (70–300 km) and almost all deep earthquakes (greater than 300 km) occur. Most of the remaining large earthquakes take place along the Alpine-Himalayan chain. Earthquakes are also concentrated along the oceanic ridge system, but most of these are shallow and comparatively small.

There are two ways of specifying the size of an earthquake – by magnitude and intensity. Magnitude is denoted by a number on a logarithmic scale ranging up to about 9·0. It is an absolute measure of the energy released by the earthquake, and so each earthquake is specified by a single magnitude number. Intensity, on the other hand, is denoted by numbered grades on the Modified Mercalli Scale and is based on the damage caused by the earthquake at the Earth's surface as well as on people's reaction to the shock. As these effects decrease with distance from the focus, an earthquake is described by a series of decreasing intensity grades with the highest grade corresponding to the area immediately above the focus.

Earthquake waves

When an earthquake occurs, the shock gives rise to vibrations, or seismic waves, which radiate outwards in all directions from the earthquake's focus. Some of the waves, known as body waves, pass through the Earth's interior; but others, surface waves, travel close to the Earth's surface.

There are two distinct types of body wave. In P, or longitudinal waves the particles of the Earth vibrate backwards and forwards along the direction in which the wave is travelling. In S, or transverse waves the Earth particles move up and down at right angles to the direction of wave travel. Both P and S waves travel along the same paths, except that S waves do not pass through fluids. S waves therefore do not enter the Earth's fluid outer core. In solid materials, however, P waves travel about twice as fast as S waves; so where both P and S waves arrive at a distant measuring station, the P waves arrive first.

The velocities of body waves depend on the physical and chemical state of the material through which they are passing and they generally increase with depth in the Earth. Within any given zone (the mantle, for example), waves are refracted along curved paths which ultimately bring them to the surface. But where the physical properties in the Earth suddenly change, the waves change velocity and are refracted equally abruptly. This occurs chiefly at the crust-mantle and mantle-core boundaries at which there are sharp chemical changes; indeed, these discontinuities were first recognized from the study of seismic waves. The combined effect of refraction and the inability of S waves to travel through the outer core is to prevent most P and S waves reaching the Earth's surface at angles of 105°–142° from the earthquake, a region known as the "shadow zone"

Surface waves are slower than body waves, but they are responsible for most of the ground motion and hence most of the earthquake damage to buildings.

Seismic waves
Body waves, both Primary (P) and Secondary (S), pass through the interior of the Earth. Long waves are the slowest and the most damaging of waves, passing along the surface of the crust. The amplitude or strength of the waves is used to determine the magnitude of the earthquake. Magnitude is graded according to the Richter Scale which is logarithmic: a magnitude of 5 emits waves with a strength ten times that of 4 and one hundred times that of 3 etc.

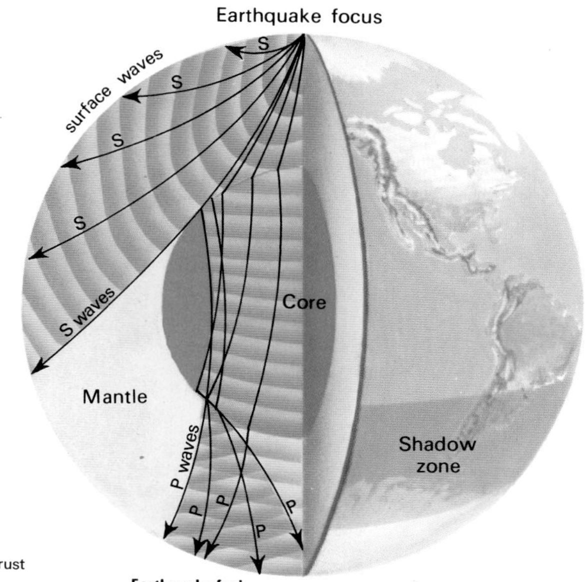

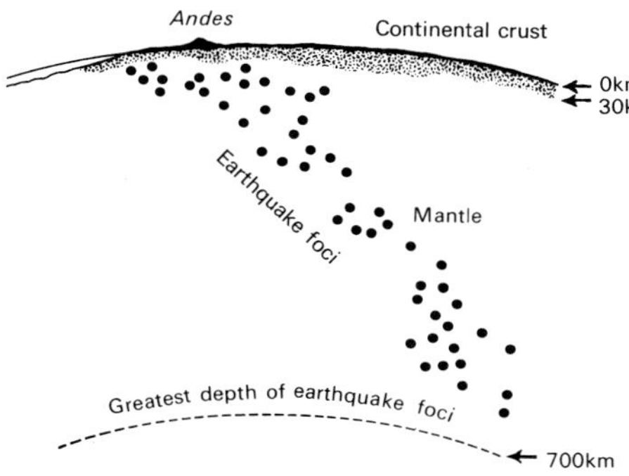

Earthquake foci
The focus of an earthquake is the small zone from which the seismic waves and energy are released. More than 70 per cent of all foci lie within the Earth's upper 70 km, but some earthquakes occur down to depths of about 700 km. Along deep ocean trenches, where the ocean plate descends into the mantle, the downward path of the plate may be traced by plotting the positions of the associated earthquake foci. Along other types of plate boundary the foci are usually much shallower; along the San Andreas fault, for example, they all lie in the upper 20 km or so.

Modified Mercalli Earthquake Intensity Scale
The 12-point scale designed in 1935 grades shocks according to the degree of disturbance felt by ordinary citizens. The numerals I to XII define the categories.

- I Shock not felt except by a few people under special circumstances.
- II Shock felt by few people at rest. Delicately suspended objects swing.
- III Shock felt noticeably indoors. Stationary cars may rock.
- IV Shock felt generally indoors. People awakened, cars rock and windows rattle.
- V Shock felt generally. Some plaster falls, dishes and windows break and pendulum clocks stop.
- VI Shock felt by all. Many frightened, chimneys and plaster damaged, furniture moves and objects upset.
- VII Shock felt in moving cars. People run outdoors. Moderate damage to buildings.
- VIII General alarm, shock very destructive. Damage to weak structures, but little to well-built structures. Furniture overturned.
- IX Panic. Total destruction of weak structures and considerable damage to well-built structures, foundations damaged, underground pipes break and ground fissures and cracks.
- X Panic. All but the very strongest buildings destroyed, foundations ruined, rails bend and water slops over river banks.
- XI Panic. Few buildings survive, broad fissures form and underground pipes out of service.
- XII Panic. Total destruction, waves seen in ground and objects thrown in air.

Volcanoes

There are about 500 active volcanoes situated on tectonic plate margins (see page 8 Plate tectonics). Volcanic belts are of two major types; those at the crest of mid-ocean ridges and those at the convergence of plate boundaries. The most recent eruptions include an eruption at Tristan Da Cunha (1956), the birth of a volcanic island at Surtsey near Iceland (1963), and eruption at Eldfjell, Heimaey in Iceland (1973). Other volcanoes are continuously active but with less dramatic results. They include Cotopaxi and Chimborazo in Ecuador, Popocatepetl in Mexico, and Lassen Peak and Katmai in the USA.

Cinder cone

This is the simplest form of volcano. Material is ejected through the central pipe and each eruption produces new deposits to overlay preceding layers. Gradually the cone is built up with larger fragments remaining near the summit at the steepest angle, around 30 degrees, and the smaller deposits moving to the base of the cone where the angle of rest may be as low as 10 degrees. Cinder cones rarely develop more than a kilometre in diameter.

Shield volcano

If much liquid or viscous lava is produced then deposits slowly build up a shallow-sloped volcano which may stretch up to 20 kilometres across. The gentle slopes are rarely steeper than 10 degrees.

Composite cone

This is the most common type of volcano formed by the vent emitting both rocks and lava at different times. The deposits therefore alternate to form a strong bonded structure resistant to erosion. Examples are Etna in Sicily, Vesuvius by Naples and Fujiyama in Japan.

Caldera

Calderas are formed either as the result of eruptions when the upper part of the cone is destroyed, or else by the collapse of the unsupported rim following the ejection of large quantities of lava. The cone is reduced in height but increased in circumference. Collapse occurs when the reservoir of molten magma issues through a side fissure instead of the central vent. The unsupported floor collapses with the crater rim, considerably enlarging the crater. Crater Lake, Oregon, 6–10 km in diameter, is an example of a caldera.

Flood basalt

Long narrow fissures in the Earth's crust may leak lava and heated rocks spreading them over a vast area. Fissure eruptions have produced the Deccan in India which covers half a million square kilometres.

Gas emission

In periods between eruptions, volcanoes release steam and various gases. As volcanic extinction approaches, lava and ashes are no longer ejected, the leaking gases are not under sufficient pressure to cause a fracture of the lava crust. This is called the solfatara stage after the large crater near Naples in Italy. The gases include sulphuretted hydrogen, sulphur dioxide, carbon dioxide, hydrochloric acid and ammonium chloride.

Explosive volcanoes sometimes eject material mixed with hot gas and this is known as *nuée ardente* or glowing cloud emission.

Volcanoes which emit chiefly steam are called fumaroles. The best example is the Valley of Ten Thousand Smokes near Katmai Volcano in Alaska. Carbon dioxide emitting volcanoes are termed mofettes.

Geysers and mud volcanoes

In certain parts of the world volcanic eruption expresses itself by the ejection of water at a high temperature. Geysers consist of clear water emission, but are called mud volcanoes if the water has a high content of solid matter. Both these mark the terminal phase of volcanic activity. The Waimangu geyser in New Zealand, active until 1904, had a jet fountain 500 feet high.

Volcanic prediction

The monitoring and prediction of volcanic activity is linked to earthquake detection on the site of recently active volcanoes. Most of those close to populated areas have permanently staffed observatories, such as at Mt Etna in Sicily and Mauna Loa in Hawaii. Transportable seismometers at selected locations record the small movements of the magma within the volcano which precede an eruption. The probable point of eruption can then be calculated. Tiltmeters and distance measuring equipment are used to map the changes to the landscape during and after an eruption. On many volcanoes, the slopes tilt downwards after an eruption and then build up slowly towards the next peak of activity. Volcanic movement sometimes produces a change in the local magnetic field caused by a rise in temperature of the underlying magma.

Cross-section through composite volcano

Volcanic activity
Volcanoes are formed when magma or molten material from the mantle or atmosphere, is extruded through weak or fractured points in the Earth's crust. Magma reaches the surface from the magma chamber through a volcanic pipe, but in some instances side vents leak magma through horizontal sills and vertical dykes. When magma reaches the surface it may be in liquid, solid or gaseous form. A lacolith is sometimes formed where molten rock is unable to reach the surface but is under enough pressure before solidifying to distort the overlying strata into a dome.

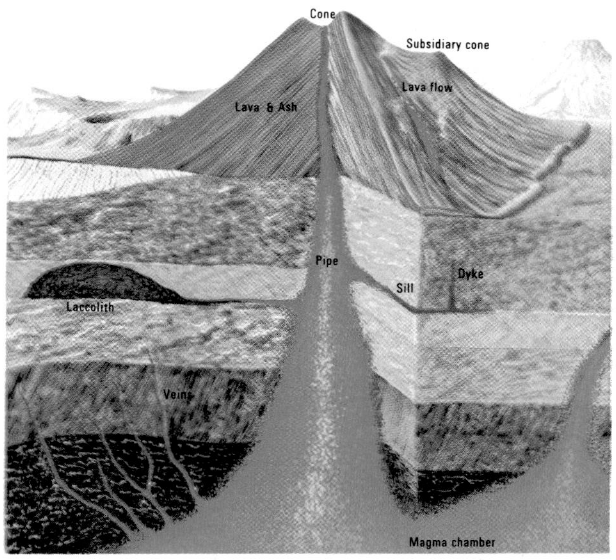

Caldera

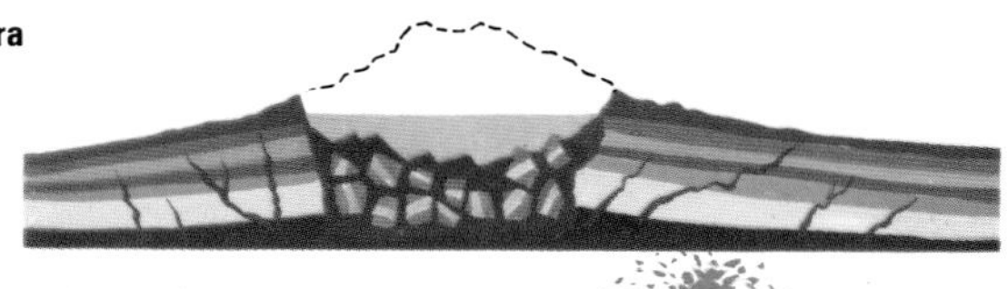

Calderas are large, basin-shaped depressions bounded by steep cliffs, like Crater Lake, Oregon, USA. They are usually formed when the magma chamber cannot support the cone above.

Shield volcano

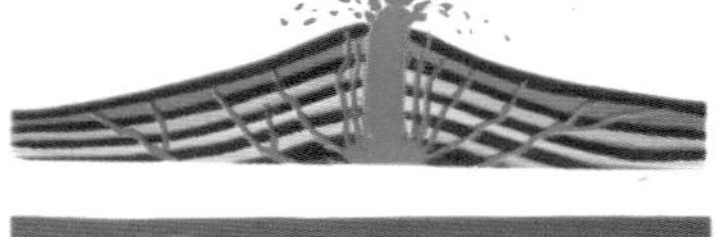

Shield volcanoes, like Kilauea, Hawaii, repeatedly erupt highly fluid basalt lava that spreads out sometimes tens of kilometres.

Flood basalt

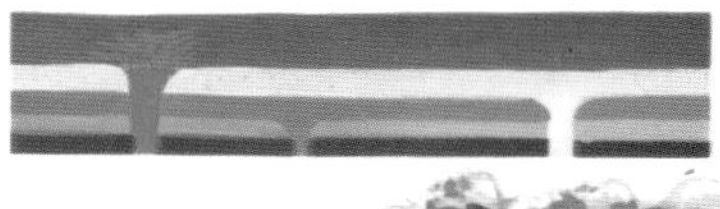

Flood basalt is an outflow of fluid lava from long and narrow fissures. The lava may spread out over vast areas to form extensive plateaux, like the Deccan in central India.

Nuée ardente

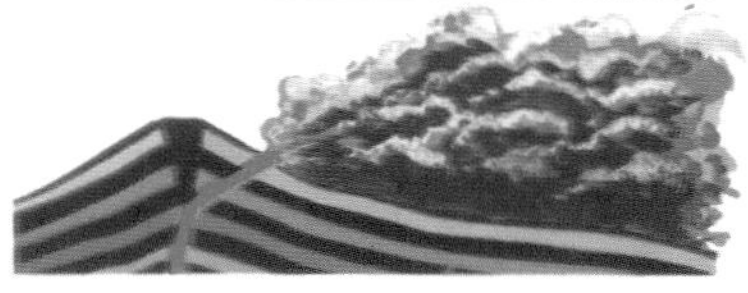

Nuée ardente (glowing cloud) eruptions are violent explosions of gas mixed with rock fragments which are ejected, sometimes to a considerable height, as at Mont Pelée in Martinique in 1902.

Plate tectonics

Earthquakes originate in well-defined zones of the Earth where rocks are actively being deformed. Earthquake zones separate large rigid areas free from active deformation known as tectonic plates. There are at least twelve such plates composing the Earth's outer shell, the lithosphere, and seven of them occupy a very large area, over 40 million square kilometres (see below Relative motions of tectonic plates). The lithosphere averages about 100 km in thickness and rests upon the asthenosphere, the semi-molten upper layer of the mantle. The detailed mechanism of plate movement is unknown but it is probably related to the transfer of heat energy deep within the Earth.

The idea of continual creation and destruction of the crust is seen in the movement of the ocean-floor plates forming mid-ocean ridges and deep trenches at the plate margins. Molten material from below the crust rises to the surface at the oceanic ridge where it forms new crust. To compensate for this additional material the leading edge of the moving plate is deflected downwards back into the mantle.

The theory of ocean-floor plate movement has been substantiated by dating of rock-core samples and comparison between magnetised rocks from either side of median ocean ridges. Deep ocean drilling has revealed that the oldest rock samples are in fact furthest away from the ocean ridge. Similarly, magnetised rock samples taken at an identical distance either side of a ridge show the same pattern of magnetic reversals. The oldest age of the rock samples appear to be about 200 million years, consistent with the estimate of the time when the Pangaea started to break up (see Continental drift).

There are three basic types of plate boundary identified by the differing movements of the plates in relation to one another.

Extensional plate boundary

At an extensional plate boundary new ocean floor is continuously created by the welling up of an oceanic ridge of hot basaltic crustal material from the underlying mantle. This material adheres to the plate edges as they move outwards from the median ridge. This process is known as ocean-floor spreading. The 40,000 km world-wide submarine mountain chain formed by ocean-floor spreading is the longest chain on Earth, but is visible only where exceptionally intense vulcanism, as in Iceland and Tristan da Cunha, raises it above sea-level. The usual ridge height is up to 5 km but widths may extend as far as 4,000 km. The forces of tension between the two diverging plates, cause rifts and transform faults where the fractured margins break up.

As the new ocean floor cools it acquires a weak magnetism. The older ocean floor moves away from the ridge at rates of between one and ten centimetres per year (see map below). The polarity of the Earth's magnetic field changes with time. Thus older ocean floors may be weakly magnetised in a differing direction to the present. The successive polarity changes or reversals, which occur at irregular intervals of a few hundred thousand years, give rise to a magnetic striping on the ocean floor by which older floors may be dated and the history of the oceans interpreted.

Translational plate boundaries

Crust is neither created nor destroyed at translational plate boundaries. The plates slide past each other along vertical faults or fractures known as transform or transcurrent faults. Best known as the San Andreas Fault in California (see diagram) and the Alpine Fault of New Zealand. Seismic activity is considerable along the numerous fracture zones which traverse the ocean ridge transform faults.

Compressional plate boundary

At compressional plate boundaries the older ocean floor sinks into the mantle at a subduction zone or steep zone of underthrust. This type of boundary is marked by ocean trenches where the edges of the crustal plates drop steeply into the mantle and become re-absorbed into the asthenosphere at depths of up to 600 or 700 km. Either plate could be pushed or subducted under the other, but usually, the less rigid and more flexible ocean-floor plate is deflected downwards by the continental plate. The descending plate carries crust material back into the under-lying mantle where it melts and breaks up. As it is less dense than the mantle it rises either towards the oceanic ridge and island arc or towards the continental lithosphere where it causes lava eruptions in a chain of volcanoes. The Aleutian, Japanese and Marianas islands are examples of such island arcs, and the South America Andes is an example of a subduction zone beneath a continental landmass. The sinking rate of one plate beneath its neighbour appears to be between 2 and 10 cm per year, resulting in intense seismic activity. The Earthquake foci in the subduction zone may be as deep as 700 km but they follow the subducted plate margin and give rise to severe disturbance.

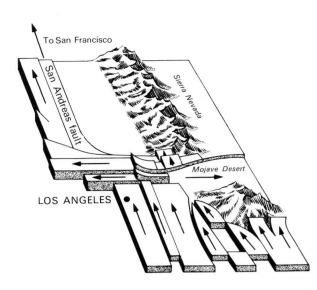

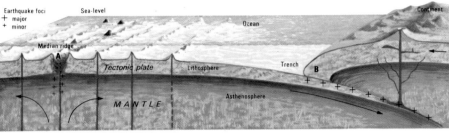
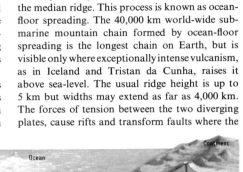

Volcanic activity and earthquakes are associated with plate tectonics. At A, an extensional boundary, magma from the upper mantle forms two parallel ridges. The rift between them broadens and new ridges are formed. At a compressional plate boundary, B, the ocean crust descends to perhaps 700 km, at which depth melting takes place.

Relative motions of tectonic plates

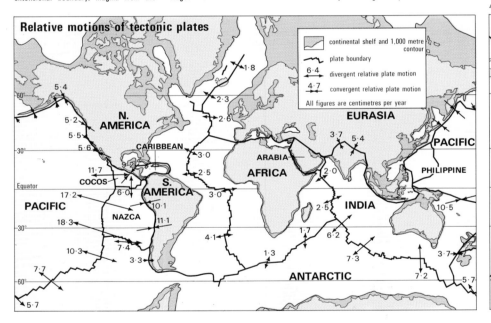

At mid-ocean ridges, plates are diverging at up to 18 centimetres per year. Where a continental plate meets an ocean plate the less dense continental material "floats" over the descending ocean plate and is pushed up to form a mountain range. Where two continental plates converge the continental material of both plates is forced upwards.

Ocean floors and orogenic belts 70 million years ago

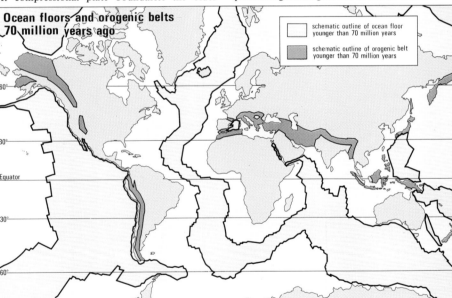

Ocean-floor spreading during the last 70 million years has been particularly apparent in the eastern Pacific and in the mid-Atlantic ridge which extends east of Africa across the south Indian Ocean. In the Americas the active orogenic belts are close up against the spreading plate boundaries. The mid-Atlantic ridge is passive in comparison.

Plate movement

Crustal plate movement occurs continuously in all parts of the globe but varies in type and rate of movement. This movement is generated by the complex interaction of a number of elements; the continental lithosphere plates themselves; the mid-ocean plate boundary ridges; micro-continental plates; island arcs; small enclosed ocean basins; and inland seas.

A variety of movements are therefore possible. The fastest rate of movement is the divergence of the Pacific plate from the Cocos, Nazca and Antarctic plates with a figure of 18·3 cms per year at latitude 30° South (see map above). The Mid-Atlantic Ridge marks the boundary between the American, African and Eurasian plates. This divergence remains fairly constant at between 2 and 4 cms per year. The African, Indian and Antarctic plates are diverging from each other at a rate between 2 and 7 cms per year.

The above map shows that convergent plate motion involves an ocean plate and a continental plate or two continental plates, but rarely two ocean plates. The fastest rate of convergence is between the Cocos and the Caribbean plate in Central America where the Guatemala Trench marks the edge where the Cocos plate is sliding downwards at over 9 cms per year. The Himalayas mark a collision zone between the Eurasian and the Indian plates; the rate of crustal compression here is over 5 cms per year.

Mountain building

Orogeny is the geological process of mountain-building. The two most important agents of orogeny are deformation of Earth's crust (diastrophism), which includes faulting and folding; and vulcanism. Orogeny usually occurs along narrow belts of the Earth's surface and can involve the uplift and deformation of great thicknesses of sedimentary and volcanic rocks. This process is called the orogenic cycle and is associated with the movement of an oceanic plate against a continental land-mass (see Compressional plate boundary above). At this margin many layers of sedimentary and volcanic rock deposited over millions of years become uplifted and deformed. Until recently mountain-building was thought to be more associated with ascending and descending currents within crustal rocks.

The Earth's orogenic belts lie between the stable continental plates and an ocean or inland sea (see map of orogenic belts above). The Andes and Rocky Mountains lie between the American plates and the Pacific Ocean; the Himalayas lie between the stable Eurasian plate and the Indian sub-continent.

The uplifted and deformed rocks formed as a result of plate collision may be mixed with molten igneous rock rising from the mantle as a result of the melting subducted crust. Younger fold mountains less than 500 million years old consist of these rocks thrust upward and over-folded as in the Alps, or simply uplifted as the central Andes. The rate of uplift may be as much as one centimetre a year. Over-fold mountain ranges are the remnants of earlier folding cycles which have been stranded away from active plate collision margins.

The map above was computed from the relative positions of dated sedimentary and metamorphic rocks plotted with reference to the trapped magnetism fields within them. Latest research reveals over one hundred and fifty magnetic field reversals during the last 70 million years. It is clear that the Earth's major orogenic belts have changed little during that time but the ocean floor areas have spread considerably.

Present-day plates		
Plate	Area	Continental area
	(millions of sq.km)	
Pacific	108	1·9
Eurasia	68	59·4
N. America	58·8	35·0
S. America	42·7	25·6
India	61	21·7
Africa	78·4	35·4
Antarctic	59·9	17·9
Nazca	16·4	
Cocos	3·1	
Philippine	5·7	
Caribbean	3·5	1·4
Arabia	4·9	4·2

Folding and faulting

When the Earth's crust bends under compression, folds develop. The simplest of these is the monocline, a one-sided fold, although downfolds (synclines) and upfolds (anticlines) are more usual. Increasing pressure steepens the side facing the pressure until one side is pushed under the other, forming a recumbent fold. Finally the fold may break along its axis, one limb being thrust over the other. Mountain chains often demonstrate intense folding, when sediments are crushed between converging plates.

Faults occur when the Earth's crust breaks, often causing earthquakes. When tension stretches the crust normal faulting occurs and the rocks on one side of the fault-plane override those on the other.

A horst is a block of the crust thrust up between faults; the reverse is called a graben or rift valley. Repeated horst and graben forms give basin and range topography as in Nevada, USA.

The upward movement of a roughly circular plug of salt, some thousands of feet in depth, may force up strata and the surface layers to form a salt dome. These are often associated with oil and gas.

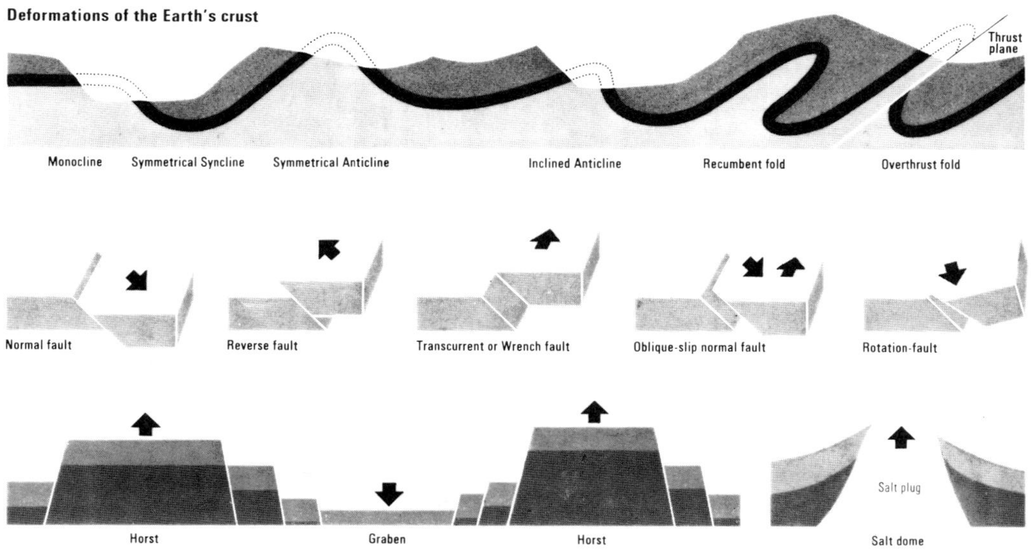

Deformations of the Earth's crust

Monocline   Symmetrical Syncline   Symmetrical Anticline   Inclined Anticline   Recumbent fold   Overthrust fold / Thrust plane

Normal fault   Reverse fault   Transcurrent or Wrench fault   Oblique-slip normal fault   Rotation-fault

Horst   Graben   Horst   Salt plug / Salt dome

Continental crust

A cross-section through the continental crust typically shows the following features: continental margins, younger and older-fold mountain chains, platforms and shields. The continental margin will either be passive as are most Atlantic margins, or active, as are the Pacific margins. Younger-fold mountains formed during the last 500 million years, such as the Rockies and Andes of America, and the Himalayas of Asia, mark the younger subduction zones and occur along most of the active continental margins. Older-fold mountains, like the Appalachians of eastern America and the Caledonian system of Britain and Scandinavia, are nearer to the older subduction zones across which two continents have been joined together. Platforms are areas on which flat-lying sediments have been laid down as in the central United States, Saharan Africa and the Arabian peninsula. Underneath the platforms are highly deformed pre-Cambrian rocks that emerge at the surface as shields. Most of north Canada, central Africa, South America east of the Andes, and Antarctica are shield areas.

The internal structure of the continental crust is known from monitoring seismic activity and from echo-sounding experiments. In most places the crust consists of an upper layer of less dense material over-lying a lower, more dense layer. The boundary between the two is termed the Conrad Discontinuity. The upper layer is 92 per cent igneous and metamorphic and 8 per cent sedimentary in composition. The lower layer is probably basaltic in character or a product of metamorphism called amphibolite, and is derived from partial melting of the mantle. The zone of transition between the continental crust and the underlying magma is called the Mohorovičić Discontinuity.

In comparison with the oceanic crust, the continental crust is less dense with a value of 2·7 as against 3·0; thicker reaching down to a depth of 70 km below mountain belts as opposed to 6 km; and older with some parts aged 3,500 million years and much over 1,500 million years compared with a maximum of 200 million years for the most ancient regions of the submerged oceanic crust.

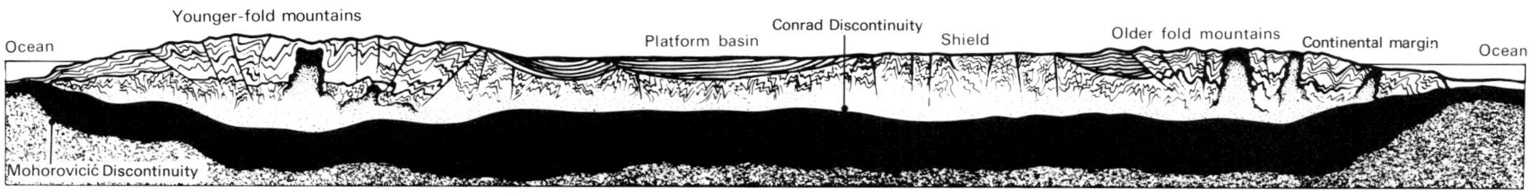

Folding and faulting

In unstable regions of the Earth's crust stresses may cause folding, fracturing and distortion of sedimentary and volcanic rocks. This is termed crust deformation and is most apparent in the European Alps, South American Andes and the Himalayas. The causes of instability are multiple. Orogenesis or mountain-building deforms the crust, but larger more gentle movements may be caused by isostasy or natural adjustment of crustal levels. A basin accumulating sedimentary deposits may slowly sink under their weight, and weathering may lighten a mountain chain causing it to rise.

The processes and extent of folding and faulting depend on the type and magnitude of the stress; fast or slow, regular or irregular application of stress; the period of time of the stress; the constituency and type of rock or rocks; and relationship with adjacent rock strata. The interrelationships of these factors are so complex that the deformation may range from micro-scopic waves to vast folds tens of kilometres across, and from displacement of single crystals to giant faults.

Folding

Folds are of many types, classified according to the severity and shape of the fold. Basically a fold consists of two limbs or sides with a bisecting axis. If the limbs dip in opposite directions and are divided into two equal halves, the fold is symmetrical; if the axis does not bisect the fold it is asymmetric. An overturned fold has one limb lying partly under the other, and a fold is termed recumbent when one limb is wholly under the other. Folds are usually formed well below the surface and are only exposed by erosion. Anticlinal or synclinal stumps are typical of eroded folds – the ridges of the Appalachian Mountains in the eastern USA are the exposed limbs of folds.

Faulting

A fault is a fracture of the Earth's crust in which the rock on one side of the fracture moves in a different direction to the rock on the opposing side. The fracture and movement along the plane of the fault may be vertical, inclined or horizontal. A normal fault has the inclined plane of fracture exposed as one part of the crust slips downwards and away from another. A reverse fault occurs when compression causes a slab of the crust to slide under an adjacent block. Faults with horizontal rock movement are termed transcurrent or wrench faults, the best-known example of which is the San Andreas fault (see page 8). A combination of movements can produce a highly complex fault structure which creates problems of interpretation for the geologist. The block on one side of a normal fault may slip sideways as well as downwards, it may rotate about a fixed point, or both blocks may move in the same direction but one faster than the other.

Rift valleys or grabens, are caused by the subsidence of elongated blocks of crust sometimes on such a scale that they are marked by chains of volcanoes. The East African Rift Valley System stretches from the coast of Africa opposite Madagascar northwards to the Red Sea and the Mediterranean. Crustal movements upwards produce horst scenery of uplifted blocks; typical examples are the Tien Shan mountains of central Asia, now heavily eroded, and the ranges of Nevada, USA.

Ocean   Younger-fold mountains   Conrad Discontinuity   Platform basin   Shield   Older fold mountains   Continental margin   Ocean
Mohorovičić Discontinuity

Continental crust
The chemical composition of the crust down to 16 kilometres is: oxygen 46 per cent, silicon 28 per cent, aluminium 8 per cent, iron 5 per cent, calcium 4 per cent, sodium 3 per cent, potassium 2 per cent and magnesium 2 per cent.

Continental drift

Continental drift is a term used to describe the relative motions of the continents.

The relative positions of the continents as far back as 200 million years may be found from the magnetic anomaly maps of the Atlantic and Indian Oceans. The position of the geographic pole of past time may be found from studies of ancient magnetism on continents. From a knowledge of the relative positions and the geographic pole a map of the former positions of continents may be drawn.

Four such maps, drawn by computer, are shown opposite; the Earth 50, 100, 150 and 200 million years ago. By comparing the maps against each other one can see how the Atlantic and Indian Oceans shrank in size as the continents came closer together. As they shrank, a space opened between Eurasia on the one hand and Africa, Arabia, Iran and India on the other. This space is assumed to represent an old ocean, known as the Tethys, that has been completely subducted in the region east of the Mediterranean. The Alpine-Himalayan mountain chain is assumed to represent the final phases of a plate tectonic cycle involving the collision of continents that once bordered the Tethyan Ocean.

About 80 million years ago, Eurasia, Greenland and North America formed a single continent known as Laurasia. One hundred and forty million years ago the southern continents were joined together to form a single continent known as Gondwanaland. About 180 million years ago all the major continents formed a single supercontinent known as Pangaea, first postulated by Wegener over half-a-century ago. Pangaea was itself formed some 250–300 million years ago by the collision of Gondwanaland with Laurasia west of the Urals and of Asia east of the Urals. It is not yet possible to draw maps of the continents prior to about 350 million years ago because the distance between the fragments that collided to form Pangaea prior to their collision cannot be estimated.

Continental drift
Early evidence of break-up and drift of the continents away from the single Pangaea landmass, has been confirmed by recent studies of ancient magnetism. The evidence consisted of matching continental shapes, for example the 'bulge' of Brazil fits closely to the coast of West Africa; and the joining of geological strata across the fit, for example the coal deposits of Uruguay and South Africa. The distribution of certain species of flora and fauna worldwide in the Palaeozoic and Mesozoic eras can only be satisfactorily explained by supporting the theory of continental drift. Animal fossils from Antarctica match those discovered in Argentina and South Africa, and climatic changes to the British Isles during the last 200 million years can be explained by continental movement.

Map 1
50 million years

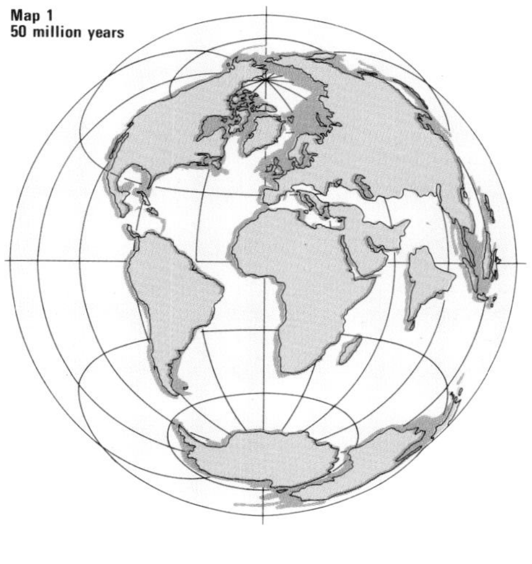

Map 2
100 million years
Laurasia

Map 3
150 million years
Laurasia
Gondwanala

Map 4
200 million years
Pangaea
Tethys

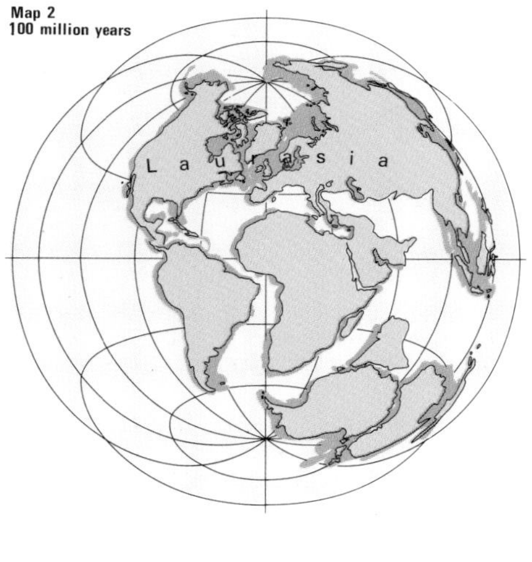

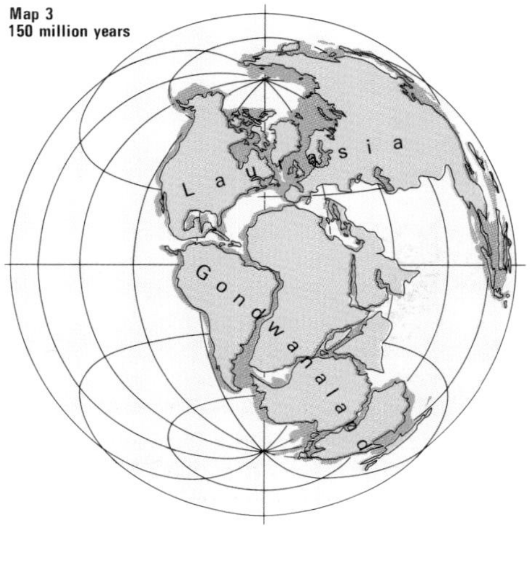

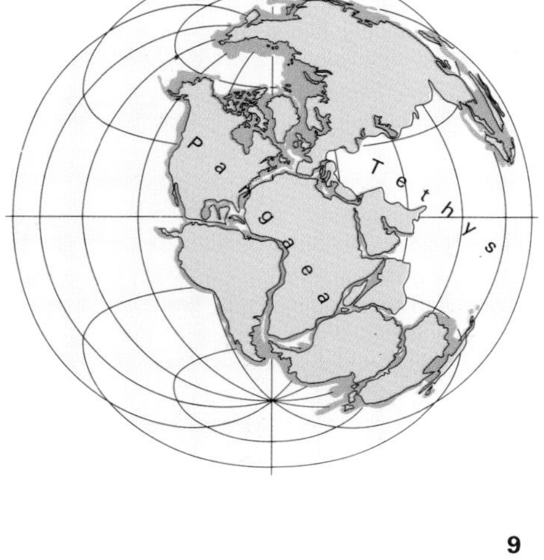

Land and sea forms

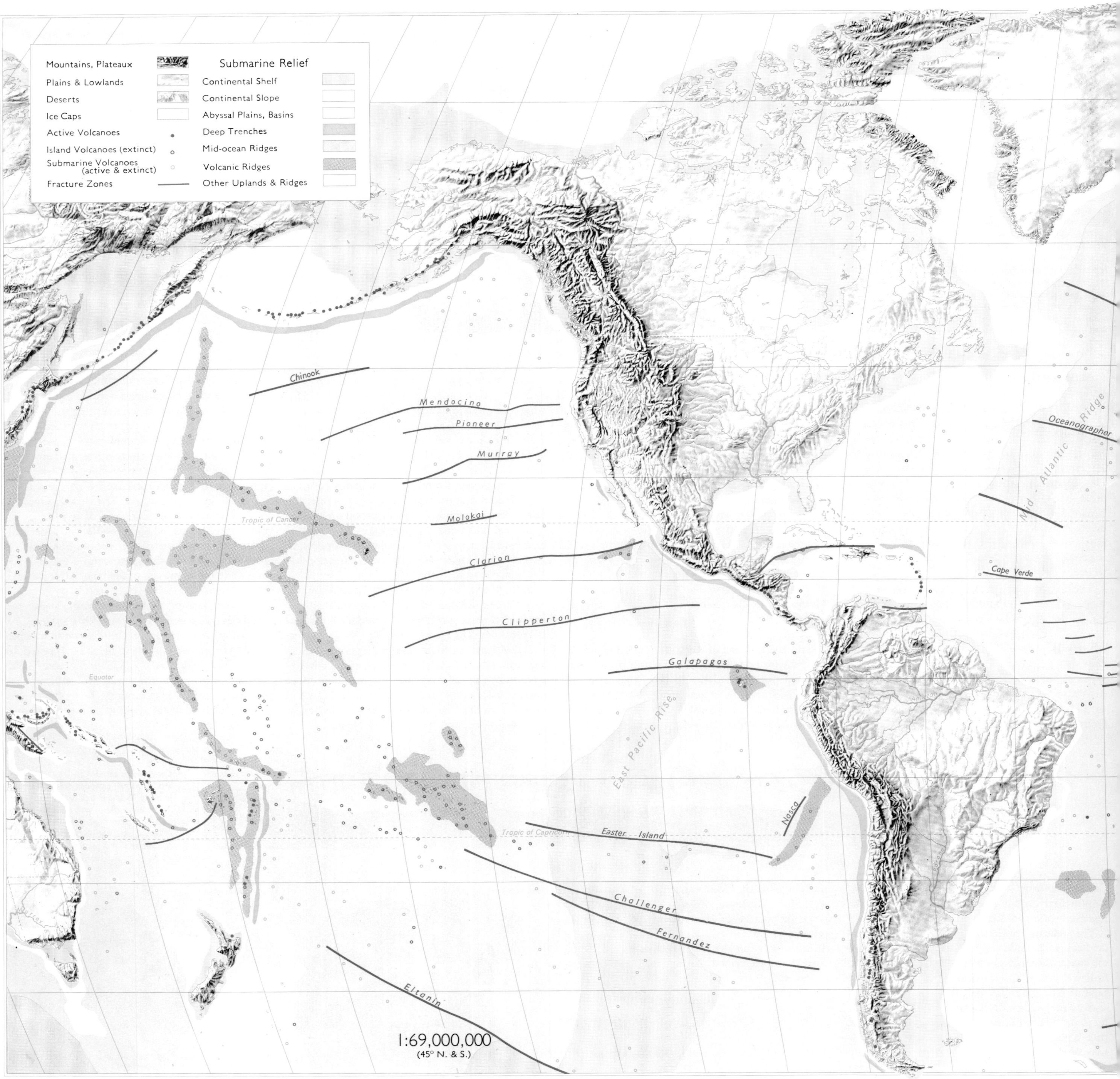

Legend:

Mountains, Plateaux ~ **Submarine Relief**

Plains & Lowlands	Continental Shelf
Deserts	Continental Slope
Ice Caps	Abyssal Plains, Basins
Active Volcanoes •	Deep Trenches
Island Volcanoes (extinct) ○	Mid-ocean Ridges
Submarine Volcanoes (active & extinct) ○	Volcanic Ridges
Fracture Zones ——	Other Uplands & Ridges

1:69,000,000
(45° N. & S.)

The simplest division of the surface of the Earth is into continents and oceans. All the evidence confirms that the ocean basins were never part of the continental areas and the oldest continental blocks were never part of the true ocean floor.

The rocks of the old continental blocks are markedly different from the young folded mountains. The former are the original blocks, granitic and among the oldest rocks formed in Pre-Cambrian times. The margins of the continents have been repeatedly covered by the sea and the true limit of the continents is the edge of the continental shelf, the physiography of the continents therefore consists basically of the old stable mountain masses, young folded mountain ranges and the coastal plains and continental shelf.

The fundamental difference between the physiography of the oceans and that of the continents arises from distinct geological processes involved in their formation. The granite rocks of the continental masses are lighter than the silica and magnesia (sima) rocks on which they rest, and thus 'float' on them. The floor of the ocean is

therefore composed of material denser than that of the surface rocks of the continents.

Different chemical processes operate in the continental and ocean rocks because of their different composition and also because of the atmospheric as opposed to the aqueous environment. The continents are subjected to the severe erosional forces of the weather and to more rapid chemical processes resulting from direct contact with the atmosphere. A wide temperature fluctuation ranging from intense heat to extreme cold has transformed the land forms; but of all the meteorological factors rain is the most destructive.

The Earth's surface features are produced by the interaction of internal and external forces. The former include mountain building, faulting, uplift, vulcanicity, and resistance, of the rocks. The external forces include the physical and chemical reactions that weather the surface rocks, and the main agents of erosion: running water, ice, sea and wind. Each of these gives rise to distinctive land forms, so that we can, for example, identify glaciated landscapes or desert landscapes,

but always reflects the interaction of structure and the erosional process.

Running water is the most important sculptor of land forms, and the results of its work can be seen even in desert areas. Valleys are the work of the rivers that flow, or have flowed, through them. Most river systems flow into the sea but some empty into interior lakes, such as the Dead Sea, where water is lost by evaporation.

Glacier ice produced very distinctive land forms, such as trough-shaped valleys, pyramidal peaks and moraines; in the Pleistocene period glaciers were much more widespread than now.

The wind is most effective in areas of sparse or absent vegetation. Only about 25 per cent of the area of the world's deserts are dune-covered. The rest is rocky or gravelly.

The oceans are not subject to the violent effects of heat and frost, wind and rain, only to the quiet forces of sedimentation and gravity. Near the continents the sediments are at their thickest; over the rest of the ocean floor they are seldom more than a few hundred metres thick.

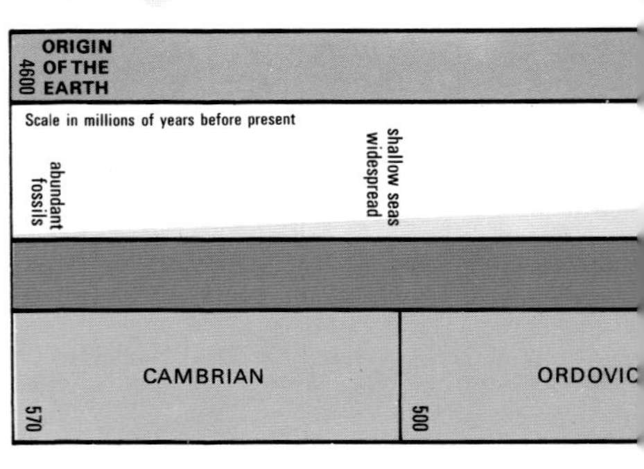

Like the continents, the oceans can be divided into main physiographic categories: continental shelf and slope, continental rises, abyssal plains, ocean ridges and rises and trenches. If we exclude the continental shelf and part of the continental slopes the area of the oceans at 2,000 metres below sea level is about 320 million sq km.

The abyssal plains extend over almost half this area and are below 2,500 metres. At this depth, temperature is never higher than 4°C (39°F).

Map labels: Jan Mayen · St. Helena · Owen · Vema · Chagos · Rodrigues · Amsterdam · Diamantina · Mid Indian Rise · Mozambique · Prince Edward · Malagasy · Tropic of Cancer · Equator · Tropic of Capricorn

			PRE-CAMBRIAN					PHANEROZOIC
early forms of life	3300	3000		2000	1000	570	abundant fossils	

Caledonian Mountains	rise of fishes	amphibians and trees	ancestral Atlantic closed	coal forests	Appalachian Mountains	conifers	rise of reptiles	Pangaea formed	opening of present Atlantic disruption of Pangaea	dinosaurs	birds and mammals	plants	dinosaurs extinct

PRIMARY (PALAEOZOIC)				SECONDARY (MESOZOIC)			TERTIARY & QUATERNARY (CAINOZOIC)				
SILURIAN	DEVONIAN	CARBONIFEROUS	PERMIAN	TRIASSIC	JURASSIC	CRETACEOUS	EOCENE	OLIGOCENE	MIOCENE	PLIOCENE	PLEISTOCENE
435	395	345	280	225	193	136	65	38	26		7

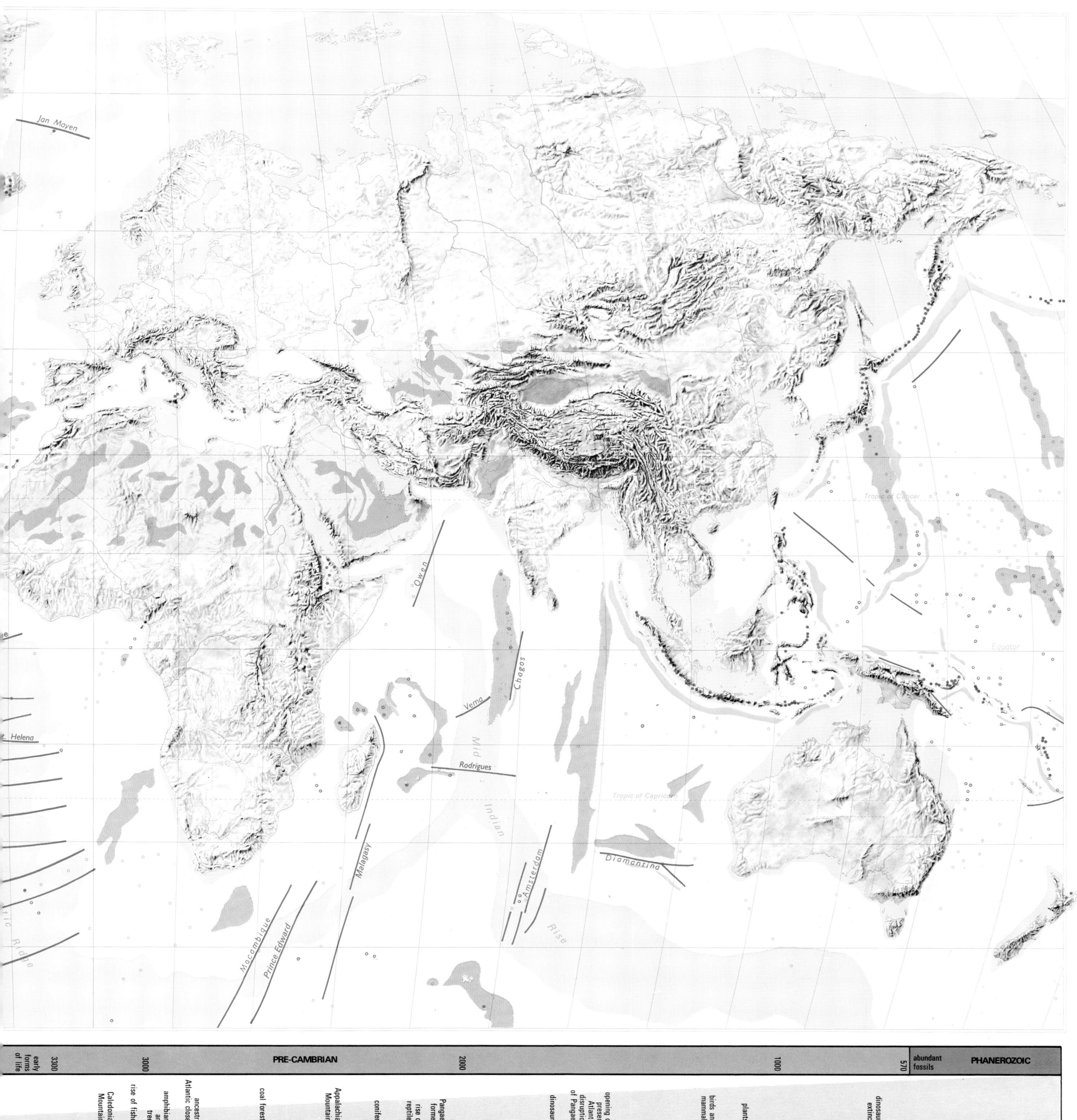

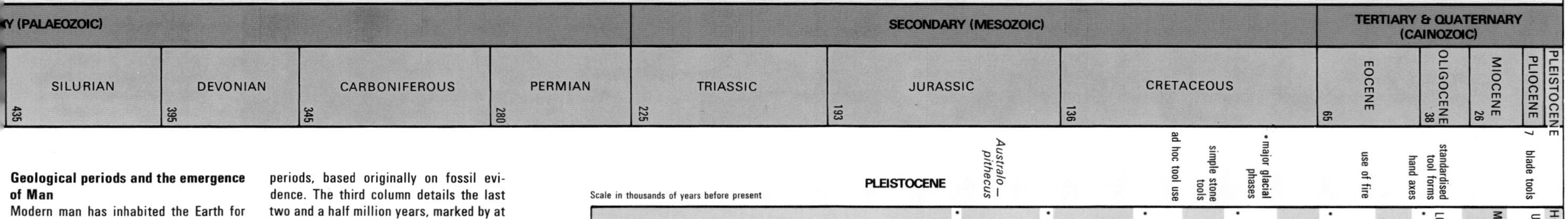

Geological periods and the emergence of Man

Modern man has inhabited the Earth for less than one millionth of the total period of its existence, now known to approach some 5,000 million years. Much of this enormous span of time (see top column) was the almost barren and relatively unknown Pre-Cambrian period. For only one eighth of its history has the Earth borne abundant life: the second column shows this Phanerozoic divided into stratigraphic periods, based originally on fossil evidence. The third column details the last two and a half million years, marked by at least seven ice ages and the period when many of the Earth's land forms were shaped. *Homo sapiens* appears only recently, and though he became a cultivator and developed urban living quite early in this final period covering the last 10,000 years, only in the last 250 years has he harnessed the world's power and mineral resources.

PLEISTOCENE

Scale in thousands of years before present

	Australopithecus	ad hoc tool use	simple stone tools	major glacial phases	use of fire	standardised tool forms hand axes	blade tools
2500	2000		1000		500	LOWER	MIDDLE · UPPER · HOLOCENE
domestication of plants and animals begins	earliest towns	postglacial rise in sea-level ends	Stonehenge first pyramid	Buddha Confucius	Birth of Christ	Norsemen reach America	Industrial Revolution

HOLOCENE

MESOLITHIC			NEOLITHIC			BRONZE AGE		IRON AGE		
10	9	8	7	6	5	4	3	2	1	0

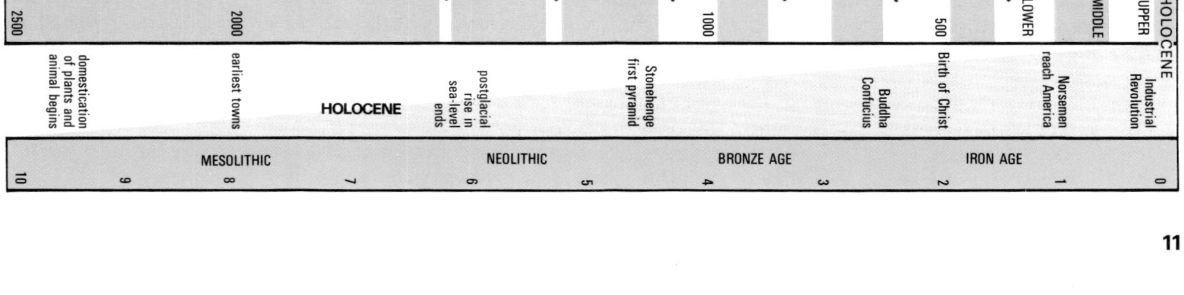

Atmosphere and climate

Annual rainfall distribution and ocean currents

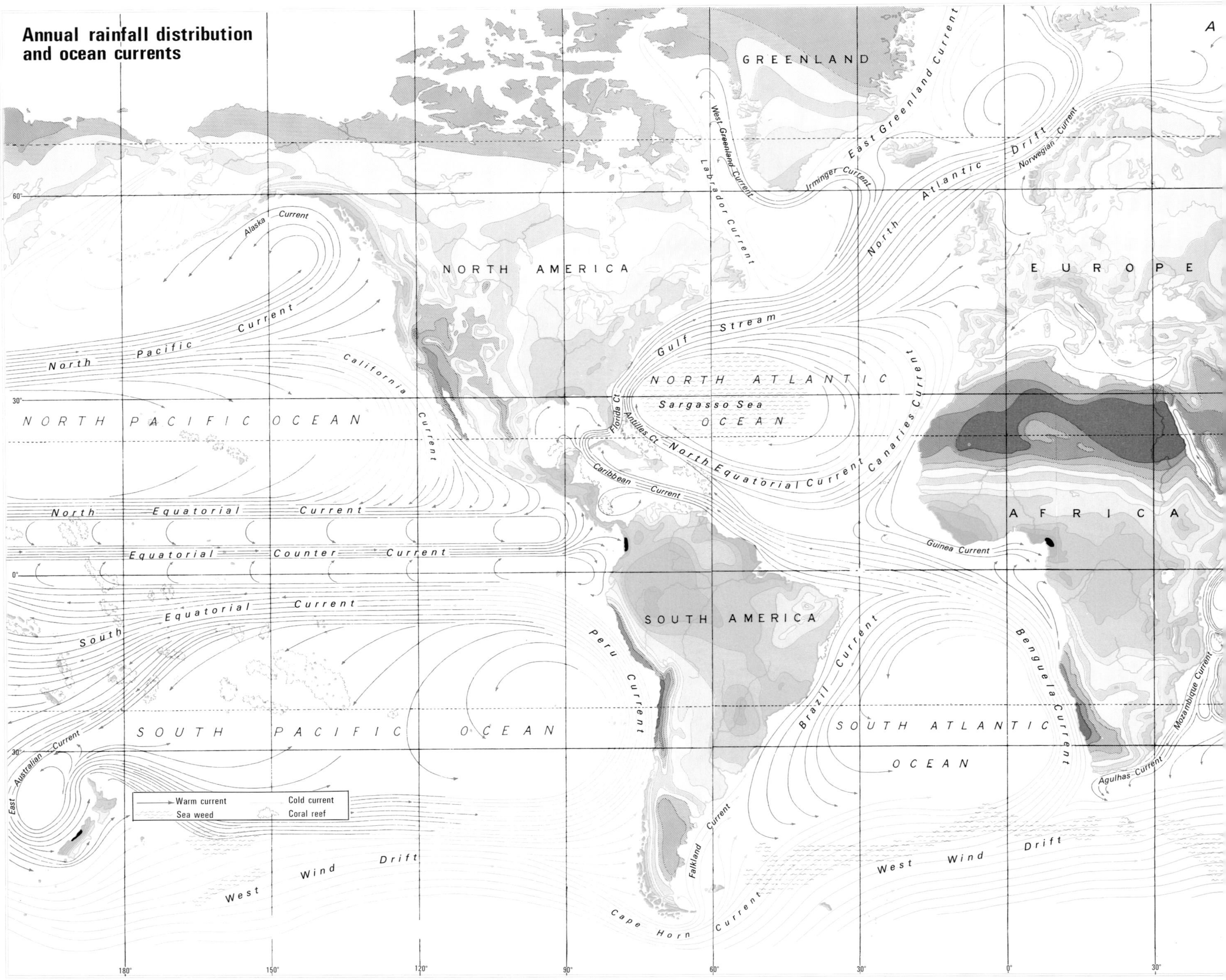

Warm current — Cold current
Sea weed — Coral reef

Evolution of the atmosphere

The Earth has an atmosphere because it is large enough for its gravitational pull to retain the gases surrounding it. Our present atmosphere is not the first. Most of the gases and probably all of the water in the oceans are the result of volcanic activity.

As the atmosphere lacks certain of the heavy gases it has been suggested that the Earth's original atmosphere was boiled away by a tremendous increase in the Sun's heat. At the same time the water and water vapour then present would also have evaporated. Studies of Mars from the Mariner and Viking spacecraft suggest that the same process happened there too, confirming the validity of this theory.

The Earth's atmosphere once largely consisted of hydrogen, combined with methane and ammonia. The hydrogen was gradually lost and free oxygen was slowly added.

In Cambrian times, between 570 and 500 million years ago, a much greater proportion of carbon dioxide was present in the atmosphere. Since life first appeared, the plants and rocks both on land and in the seas have competed for the carbon dioxide and the free oxygen. There is now a greater quantity of oxygen and carbon dioxide locked up in the rocks of the Earth than is to be found in the whole atmosphere. The balance of the atmosphere today is maintained by the constant erosion of limestone rocks and the decay of vegetable matter.

The composition by volume of the atmosphere is: nitrogen 78·09%, oxygen 20·95%, argon 0·93%, carbon dioxide, 0·03%, and smaller quantities of helium, krypton and hydrogen, 0·2% water vapour, traces of other gases and atmospheric dust.

Exactly what composition is necessary to support life and how far terrestial species can adapt by evolution to great changes in the composition of the atmosphere is not known. The basic essentials are oxygen, nitrogen, carbon dioxide and water.

The protective atmosphere

Apart from the atmosphere's role as the source of the gases necessary to life, it acts as a great shield against a perpetual bombardment of meteors and deadly rays and particles. Friction with the atmosphere causes all except the largest meteorites to burn themselves out before reaching the surface. Ultra-violet rays are absorbed in a layer of ozone present in the Stratosphere. Charged particles are prevented from reaching the Earth. Their contact with the atmosphere produces the aurora borealis and the aurora australis. Cosmic rays originating either from the Sun or from the outer reaches of space are likewise kept out.

Divisions of the atmosphere

For the first 80 kilometres above the Earth's surface the composition of the atmosphere is constant. Density decreases with height: at 16 kilometres it is only one-tenth of the density at sea level; at 32 kilometres it is one-tenth as dense as at 16 kilometres, and so on.

The terms Troposphere, Stratosphere, Mesosphere, Thermosphere and Exosphere have been used to describe the divisions of the atmosphere.

The Troposphere is the lowest division. Within it takes place nearly all the processes that produce weather and climate; evaporation, precipitation, movement of winds and air currents and the formation of the many types of storm etc.

Above 80 kilometres, oxygen and nitrogen molecules cannot remain associated and tend first to separate into atoms and then to be ionised into charged particles (ions) by the strong solar radiation. At the outermost limits of the atmosphere ionised helium and hydrogen dominate the very tenuous plasma (ionised gas), which, because of its electric charge, is controlled more by the Earth's magnetic field than by gravity.

The Ionosphere is the region of electrification which extends from the upper limit of the Stratosphere as far as the Thermosphere. It consists of a number of belts of radiation designated D, E, F_1 and F_2 which reflect radio waves back to Earth.

The outermost regions are now more commonly termed the Magnetosphere, the region dominated by magnetic fields. Beyond the Magnetosphere interplanetary space is dominated by the Sun's magnetic field and charged particles from the Sun – the solar wind.

Ultra-violet radiation produces concentrations of charged particles which are at their maximum in the upper part of the F_1 layer and the lower part of the F_2 layer.

The electrification belts are not fixed at particular altitudes: light and darkness and other physical factors cause them to move up or down. At night the F layers combine to form a single layer.

Atmosphere and the weather
Climate of the Troposphere close to the Earth's surface may be affected by changing influences high in the atmosphere. The amount of energy that penetrates the Stratosphere appears to follow the Sun's 11 year cycle of activity by altering the percentage of ozone in the Stratosphere. It is probable that energy in the form of ultra-violet waves from the Sun produces a swing in the ozone balance changing the effectiveness of heat absorption by the atmosphere.

At 3,000 and 15,000 kilometres, the two Van Allen radiation belts consist of electrically charged particles which occasionally migrate into the atmosphere. These particles react with atmospheric gases to produce the auroras. There is a strong likelihood that weather patterns are thus affected in the polar latitudes.

Changes in climate have been observed to coincide with changes in the Earth's magnetic field. The nature of the relationship is not known, but the extinction of species of fauna and changes in flora appear to have coincided with abrupt magnetic changes. These are identified by analysis of the direction of the magnetic field trapped within rocks on their formation.

Mean temperature January

Mean temperature July

Mean Annual Precipitation

| 0 | 25 | 100 | 200 | 300 | 400 | 500 | 750 | 1000 | 1500 | 2000 | 3000 | 5000 | Millimetres |
| 0 | 1 | 3.9 | 7.8 | 11.8 | 15.7 | 19.6 | 29.5 | 39.3 | 59 | 78.7 | 118 | 196.8 | Inches |

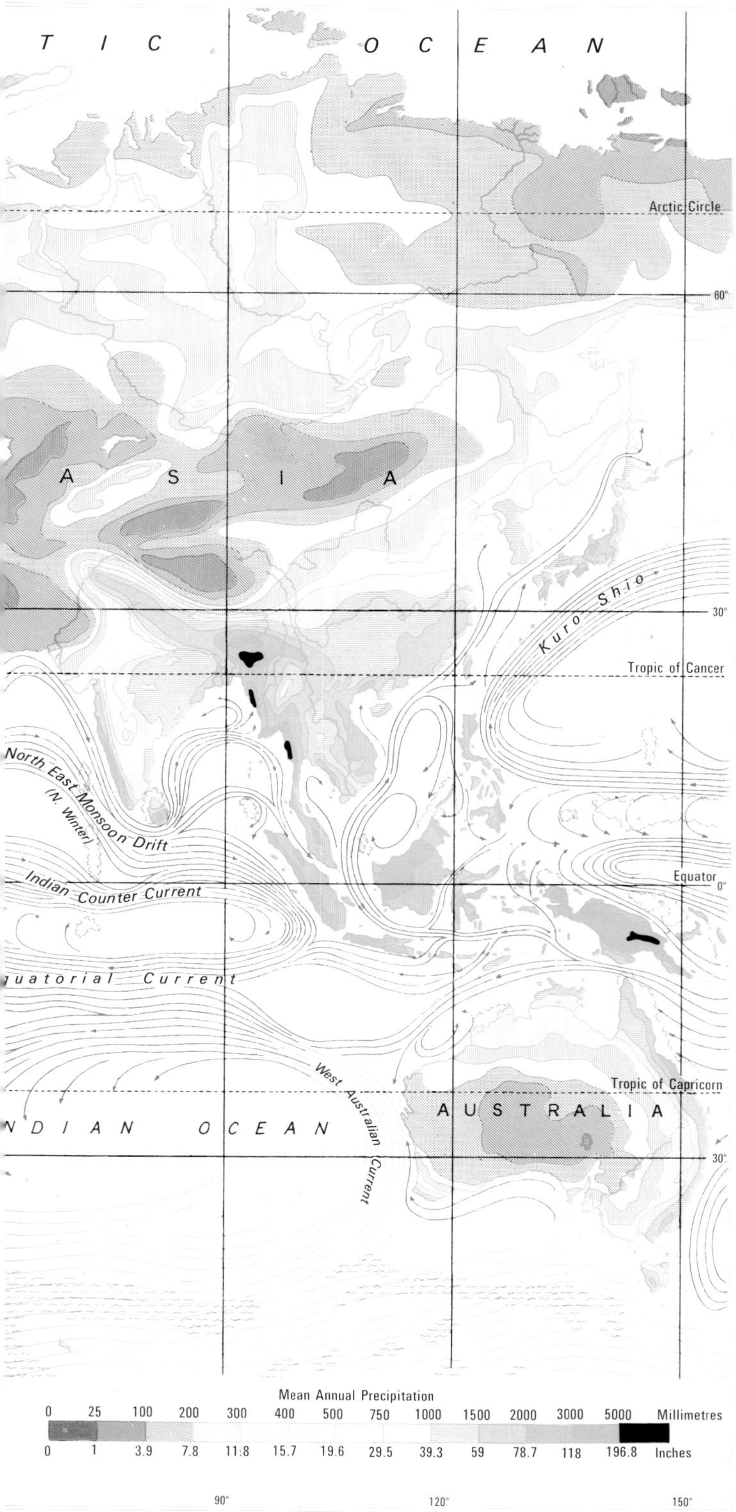

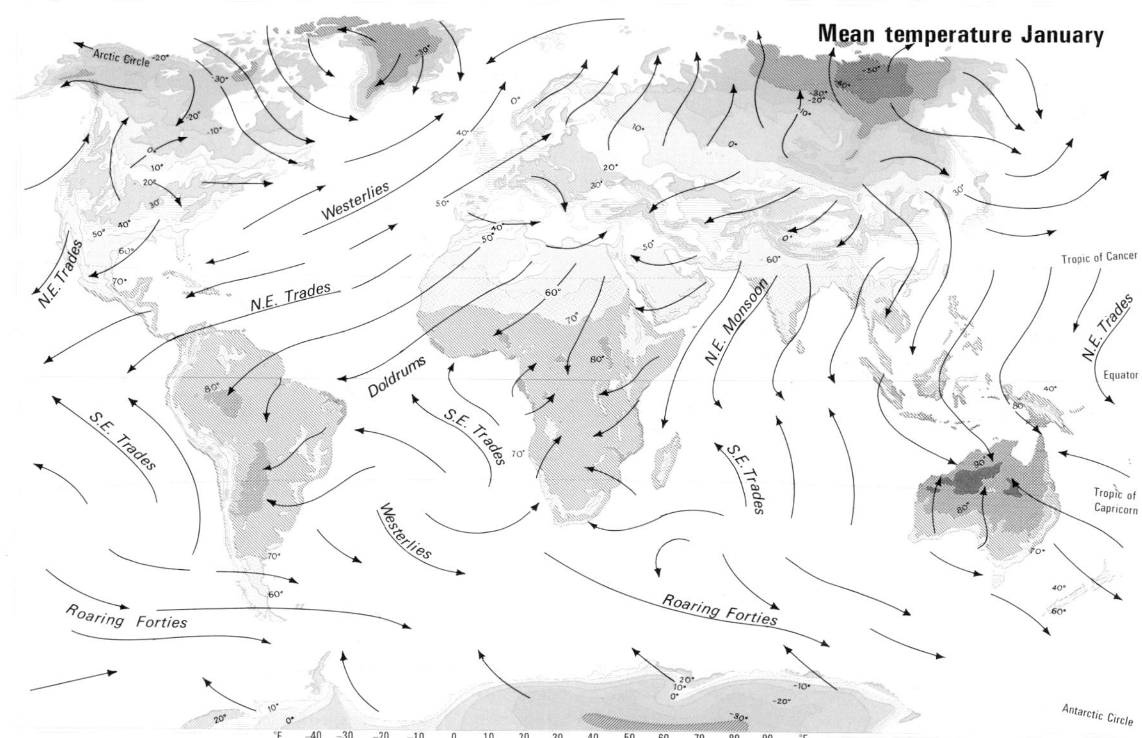

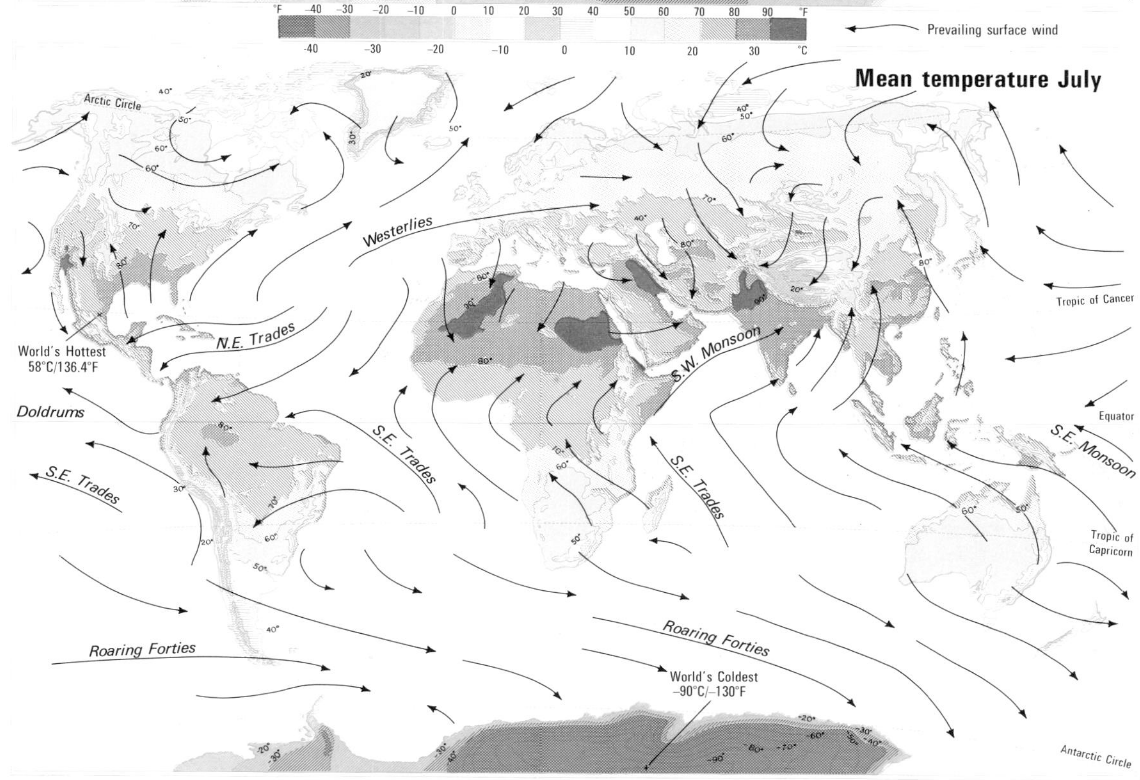

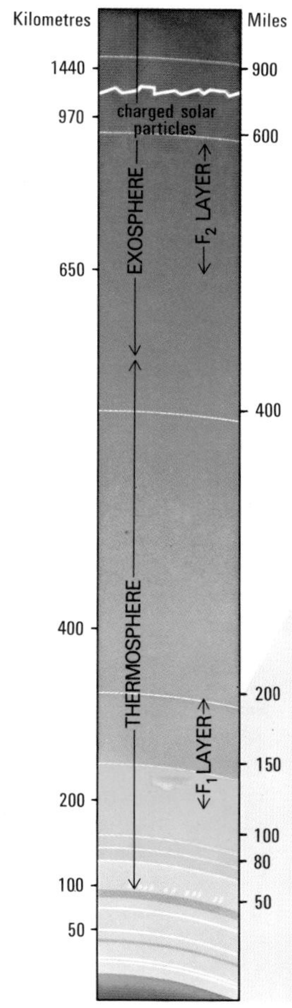

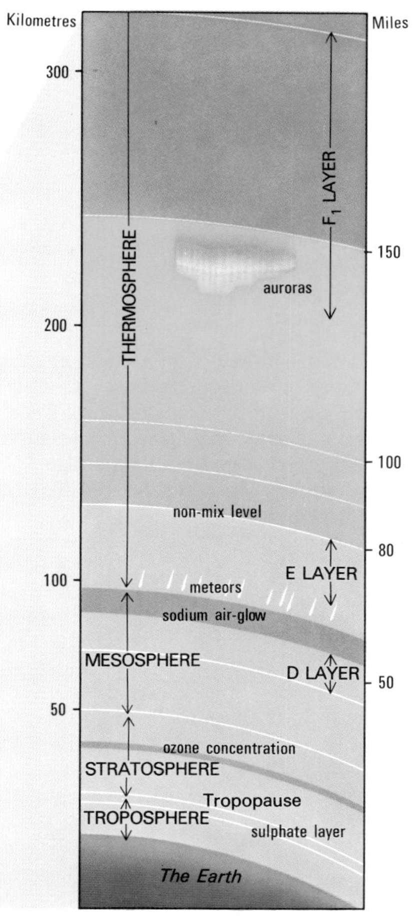

Monitoring the World's weather

International meteorology has made great advances in the last twenty-five years profiting from technological enterprise, notably artificial satellites, high-speed computers and methods of statistical analysis.

In 1961 the United Nations recommended that the World Meteorological Organisation (WMO), undertake a study of two measures. To advance the state of atmospheric science and technology so as to provide greater knowledge of basic physical forces affecting climate and the possibility of large-scale weather modification; and to develop existing weather-forecasting capabilities and to help Member States make effective use of such capabilities through regional meteorological centres. The WMO quickly produced a report on the advance of the atmospheric sciences and application in view of space developments. After four years of discussion and study this report was accepted in the form of the World Weather Watch plan.

The idea of monitoring a global weather system requires world-wide data collection on the condition of the atmosphere and associated geophysical phenomena, its processing to establish likely future weather activity, and a telecommunications network for collection and distribution of processed information. The WMO therefore set up the Global Observing System (GOS), the Global Data-processing System (GDPS), and the Global Telecommunications System (GTS) to carry out these functions.

Details of the activities of these organisations are impressive. In 24 hours the GOS makes about 110,000 observations from 9,000 land stations, 3,000 aircraft and 7,000 merchant ships throughout the world. In remote areas automatic weather stations are being built, and special-purpose ships are being constructed to traverse data-sparse areas. The GDPS has developed its System to manage this huge amount of input information. Giant computers are installed at Melbourne, Moscow and Washington DC, and a model of global weather for the following 24 hours is produced twice a day. These analyses and forecasts are distributed visually and digitally to the 23 Regional Meteorological Centres and 100 National Met. Centres. The GTS uses telegraph, telephone, radio, cable and landlines to distribute the material at speeds of up to 7,200 words per second.

The WMO has also instigated a Global Atmospheric Research Programme (GARP), to extend the scope and accuracy of weather forecasts, and to better understand the physical basis of climate and climatic fluctuations. To do this GARP has set up a series of regional experiments, such as the Atlantic Tropical, Air-Mass Transformation, Monsoon and Polar Experiments. In late 1978 the largest experimental programme will start. Named the First GARP Global Experiment (FGGE), it will monitor the atmospheric condition of the entire globe for one year, and apply world-wide tests of existing climatic models.

Polar-orbiting and geostationary satellites will be used to collect the extensive data for this global experiment.

Water resources and vegetation

Water is essential not only to practically all forms of life but is required in enormous quantities to support our modern industrial society. The average daily consumption for each individual in the UK is about 1 cubic metre, and in the USA the figure approaches ten times this quantity. Domestic use accounts for 20 per cent of this total in the UK and 10 per cent in the US. The need to husband water supplies is obvious in arid climates, but it is only in recent years that the need to conserve water resources in areas of more abundant rainfall, has been appreciated.

Hydrological cycle

Fresh water forms only 2 per cent of the water available on the Earth's surface. Even so, this amount would be more than adequate were not the greatest reserves locked, inaccessibly, in the polar ice caps. The problem therefore, is to provide water where and when it is needed and to ensure that it is not used faster than it can be replaced. The oceans are nature's reservoirs. From them water is evaporated to fall as rain or snow over the land. From the land it returns, mostly through rivers, to the sea. This process is known as the 'hydrological' cycle (see diagram). The maximum water potentially available is therefore dependent on the amount precipitated on the land. Water conservation aims to preserve for subsequent use as much of this water as possible.

Water conservation

When rain falls over land a proportion is quickly evaporated back into the atmosphere. Apart from limited and local measures, not a great deal can be done to conserve this water, nor that which is taken up by plants and returned to the atmosphere by transpiration. Some water 'runs off' and finds its way into rivers. Here control can be exercised, by adopting agricultural methods that will prevent too rapid run-off of surface water, retaining it in the soil for the benefit of crops, or alternatively by constructing drainage channels, dams and reservoirs in which water can be stored for later use. The remainder of the rainfall will sink deep into the earth, where a proportion will be held in rock strata. Rocks with a capacity to hold water are known as 'aquifers'; water is recovered by sinking wells to them.

Elementary though these measures are, they provide the foundation of proper control of water resources. Modern treatments increase the water supply still further by providing for water to be re-used. Water taken for industry can be cleansed and returned to the river from which it came. Further downstream it may be taken into the public water supply, and so into a sewage system from which it is discharged clean for further use.

Simple water conservation techniques can assure adequate supplies for large cities situated on rivers or lakes. Thus London, Washington and Chicago rarely suffer from water shortage. For other cities, not so fortunately situated, methods must be found to bring water from elsewhere. Birmingham in the UK, for example, is supplied with water from central Wales. New York City cannot use the brackish water of the Hudson estuary, but relies on supplies from catchment areas in New York State, some of which are over 160 km (100 miles) away. This water is brought to the metropolis from 27 reservoirs through 640 km (400 miles) of aqueducts and tunnels.

Techniques similar to those used to reclaim land allow arms of the sea to be isolated for conversion into freshwater lakes.

Further possibilities of increasing the water supply bring some hope for the arid regions of the world. For many decades rain has been induced by 'seeding' clouds with silver iodide crystals. This technique has achieved success, but it is extremely costly and uncertain. It cannot succeed unless there are clouds (i.e. water vapour) in the air. More promising are schemes to obtain fresh water from the sea by desalination and this is most commonly done by distillation and freezing. Distillation plants are currently in commercial use, particularly in the Middle East, but the cost is high and the quantity of water produced is small. The use of solar energy to support distillation processes is attractive in that fuel costs are abolished. However, while solar stills have proved successful on a small scale, larger versions have not worked efficiently. Experimental desalination plants based on freezing processes are in operation in the United States, and in Britain a pilot plant of this type is to be constructed in East Anglia.

Oil-rich but arid states have also considered seriously the possibility of towing icebergs from Antarctica to serve as a water supply. Recent estimates show this operation to be comparable in cost with desalination processes.

The Hydrological Cycle

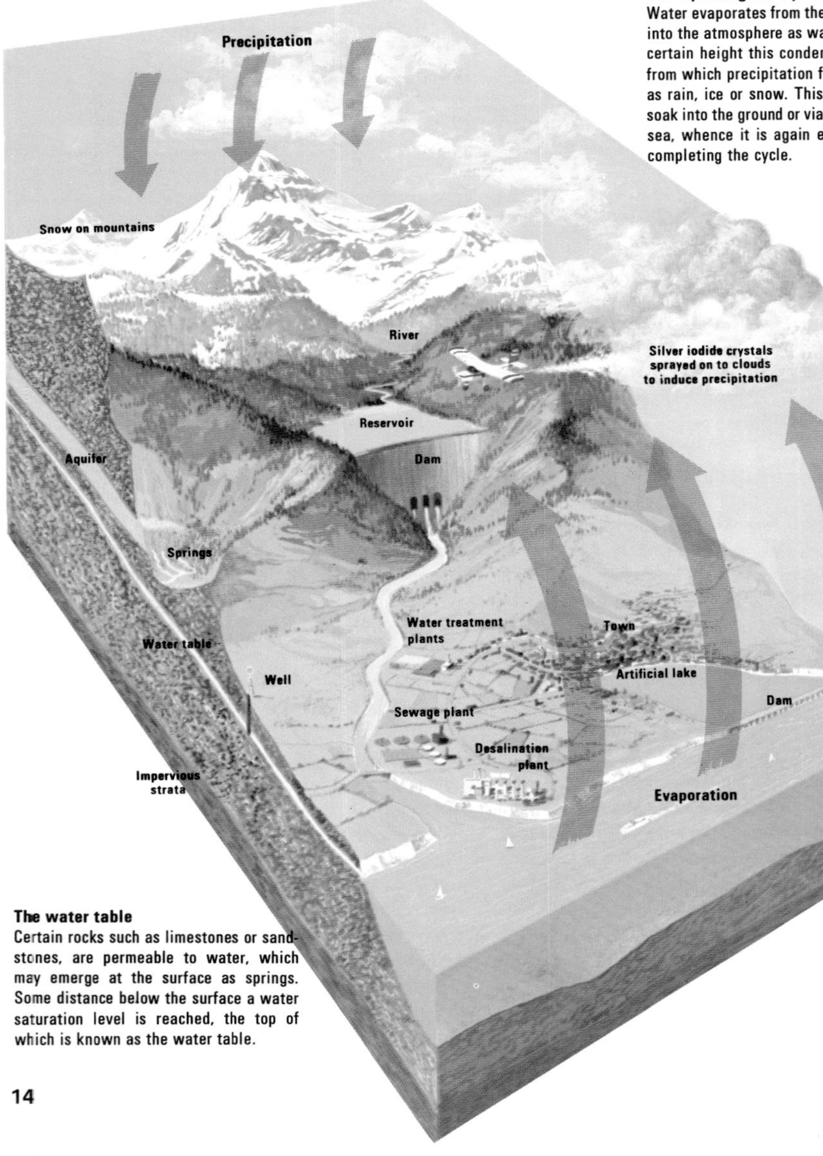

The Hydrological Cycle
Water evaporates from the sea and passes into the atmosphere as water vapour. At a certain height this condenses into clouds from which precipitation falls to the earth as rain, ice or snow. This will evaporate, soak into the ground or via rivers reach the sea, whence it is again evaporated, thus completing the cycle.

The water table
Certain rocks such as limestones or sandstones, are permeable to water, which may emerge at the surface as springs. Some distance below the surface a water saturation level is reached, the top of which is known as the water table.

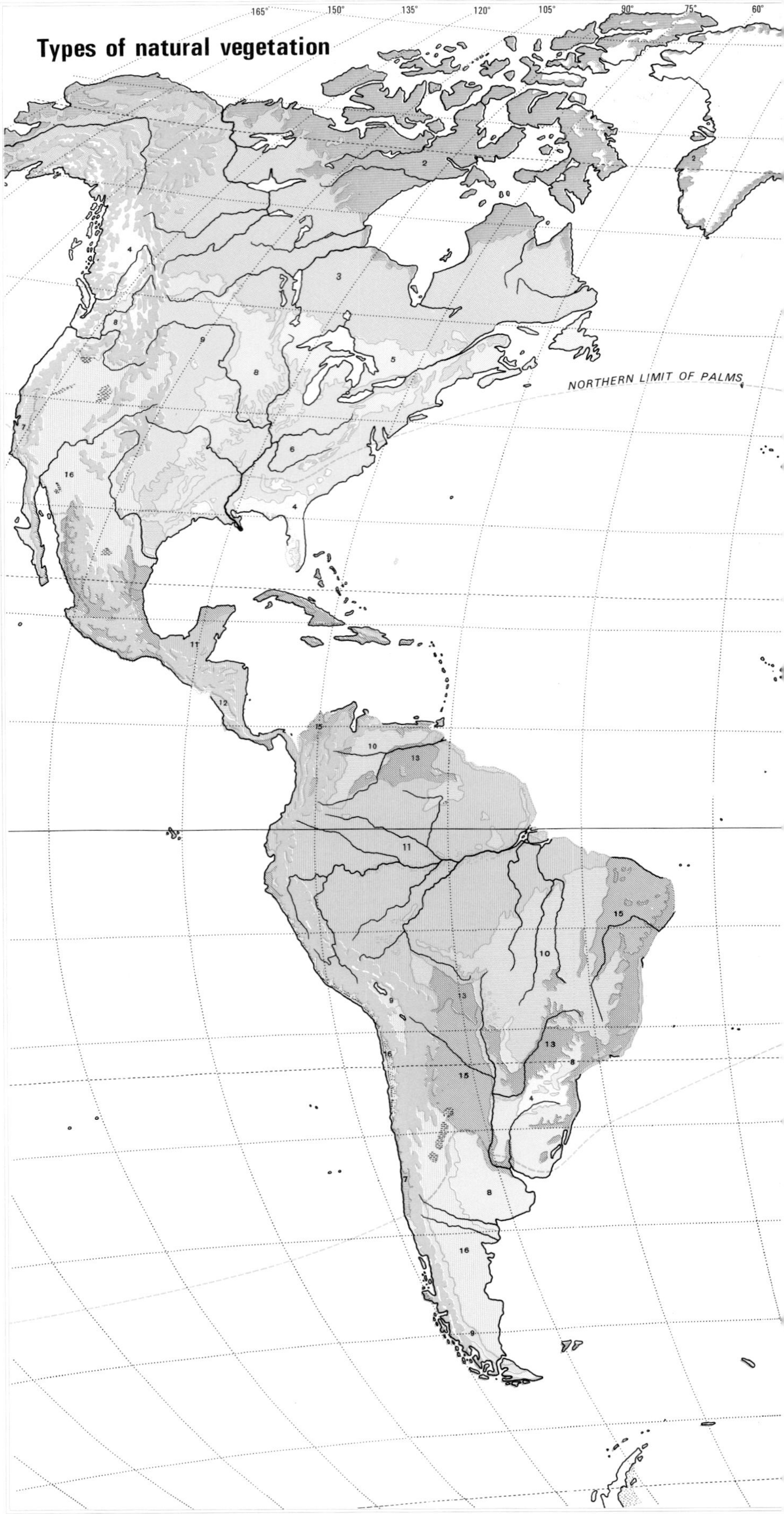

Types of natural vegetation

NORTHERN LIMIT OF PALMS

Natural vegetation

A remarkable feature of the earth's land surface is the extent to which it is covered with plant life. Though there are inhospitable areas – such as the peaks of great mountain ranges and polar ice caps – where plant life all but disappears, for the most part vegetation exists in great abundance. Natural vegetation means the type of plant cover that would occur naturally without man's interference. In western Europe, man's activities have over the centuries so altered the natural plant cover that practically nowhere does it exist in its original form. Yet there is no difficulty in defining the broad categories of plants that flourish in the conditions that prevail locally.

The map on this page displays the major categories of natural vegetation, each characterized by important features which transcend differences between individual species. These vegetation zones are in essence a response to climatic conditions, for although local conditions of soil, relief and micro-climate are all important in determining local particulars of plant cover, the temperature and rainfall conditions of climatic regions exercise substantial control over the nature of plant cover. Thus, since latitude largely determines climate, the vegetation regions north and south of the Equator tend to be a mirror image one of the other. The close relationship between climate and vegetation has provided geographers with a convenient division of the world into major regions, since the particular features of plant life of each region are distinctive.

Vegetation regions

Near the Equator climate varies little throughout the year with rainfall and temperature consistently high. The absence of seasons means that plants do not undergo a resting period, while the abundance of warmth and moisture ensures a particularly luxuriant growth. Thus the characteristic vegetation of areas such as the Amazon and Zaire basins and the islands of Indonesia is dense, almost impenetrable forest, with trees competing for light attaining great heights.

Further away from the Equator lie the tropical

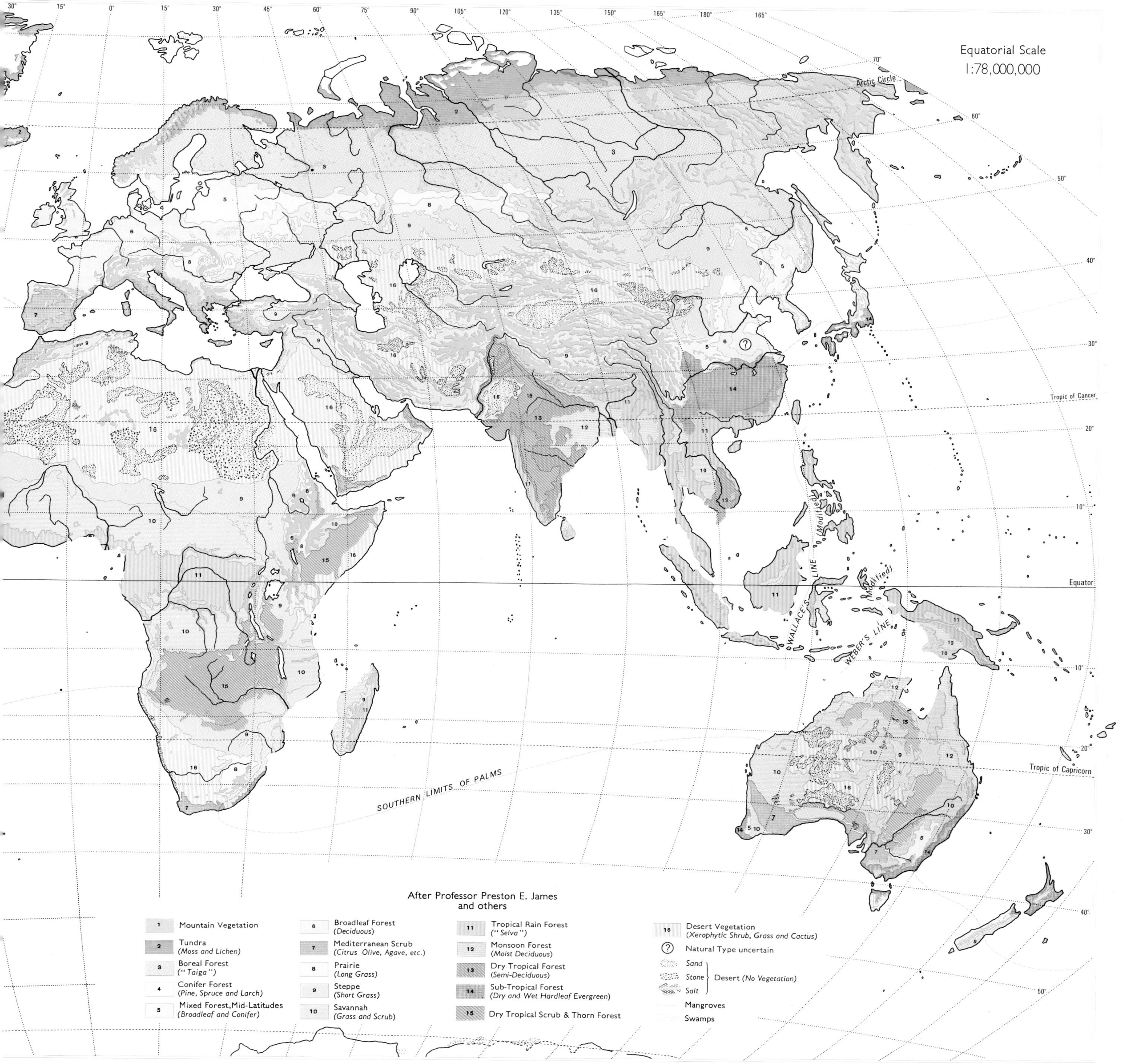

Equatorial Scale
1:78,000,000

Arctic Circle

Tropic of Cancer

Equator

Tropic of Capricorn

SOUTHERN LIMITS OF PALMS

WALLACE'S LINE

WEBER'S LINE

(Modified)

After Professor Preston E. James
and others

1	Mountain Vegetation	**6**	Broadleaf Forest (Deciduous)	**11**	Tropical Rain Forest ("Selva")
2	Tundra (Moss and Lichen)	**7**	Mediterranean Scrub (Citrus Olive, Agave, etc.)	**12**	Monsoon Forest (Moist Deciduous)
3	Boreal Forest ("Taiga")	**8**	Prairie (Long Grass)	**13**	Dry Tropical Forest (Semi-Deciduous)
4	Conifer Forest (Pine, Spruce and Larch)	**9**	Steppe (Short Grass)	**14**	Sub-Tropical Forest (Dry and Wet Hardleaf Evergreen)
5	Mixed Forest, Mid-Latitudes (Broadleaf and Conifer)	**10**	Savannah (Grass and Scrub)	**15**	Dry Tropical Scrub & Thorn Forest

16 Desert Vegetation (Xerophytic Shrub, Grass and Cactus)

(?) Natural Type uncertain

Sand
Stone } Desert (No Vegetation)
Salt

Mangroves

Swamps

grasslands. Here grass grows in abundance during the rainy season only to be withered by the sun in the ensuing drought. The sparse plant life of the world's deserts shows particular adaptations to drought conditions. Some species develop seeds which lie dormant for long periods and then, when rainfall comes, grow and complete their life cycle in the brief period in which moisture is retained in the soil. Many, including the cactus species' so typical of the arid regions of the western United States, are able to store water efficiently with little loss through transpiration.

The characteristic vegetation of much of Europe, including the British Isles, and the eastern half of the United States, is broad-leaved deciduous forest. In response to the clear climatic differences between summer and winter, trees have adapted to take fullest advantage of the favourable growing season. The broad leaf structure which allows maximum exposure to light and air means that the tree is an efficient starch-producing organ. This same adaptation renders the plant extremely sensitive to low temperatures and high

winds, and thus these plants lie dormant during winter months. So precise is their adaptation that their activity is not dependent on average climatic conditions but on the likely variations from this average. In Britain the oak and ash are not tempted to unfold their leaves early in a mild spring yet imported species like the horse chestnut will do so. Most cultivated plants are imported or are 'artificial' cross-breeds and lack precise adaptation to prevailing climatic conditions. They need protection by shelter or irrigation or removal of other competitive plants if they are to flourish.

North of the regions of the broad-leaved deciduous forest flourish the conifer forests. In the United States they are developed particularly well in the north-western states. The trees that form these forests are much better adapted to withstanding unfavourable conditions and include the world's most magnificent specimens, in particular the giant redwood trees, which grow to greater heights than any other tree except the eucalyptus. These forests are of substantial economic importance and provide over 30 per cent

of timber needed by the USA.

Climatic variations

We are now in an interglacial period within which minor climatic variations have occurred. Some 3,000 to 4,000 years ago climate in the British Isles was drier, with greater temperature variations between summer and winter so that hazel and birch flourished more than they do now. There is considerable evidence that land bordering the Sahara desert is drier now than it was 2,000 or so years ago, for plants grew more abundantly then, and in north Africa wheat was grown for the Roman Empire in regions which are now semi-desert. Some of this decline is undoubtably due to unwise farming methods, which have resulted in the loss of topsoil, or to clearance of the natural plant cover to grow crops. A wealth of evidence now shows that both Sahara and Gobi deserts spread towards the Equator when the climate cools slightly – as it has since the 1950s. This, plus overgrazing, is the cause of recent droughts in the Sahel (the region bordering the Sahara to the south), in Ethiopia, and in

Somalia and north-east Kenya.

Although we are concerned mainly with the broad characteristics of the plant life of the major vegetation zones, we should not ignore the strange variations that occur, as species adapt to local conditions. The vegetation of the Everglades in Florida displays a remarkable adaption to the swampy conditions that prevail there, while along tropical coasts mangroves grow and with their preponderance of stilt-like roots keep a firm hold on the shifting ground beneath. These roots, the upper parts of which are exposed at low tide, have pores through which the plant can take oxygen, since there is little oxygen in the muddy water below, where organic matter is decomposing.

Precise adaptation of particular species to local conditions has been turned to economic advantage. A few species flourish abnormally well where certain minerals are present, and by study of these 'indicator plants', deposits of copper and other ores have been traced in many parts of the world.

Minerals and their uses

Gold

Precious metal and principal international reserve asset underwriting the means of exchange. Used in manufacture, medicine and fabrication for its special corrosive resistant properties. It does not tarnish and is unaffected by most acids. It weighs about two and a half times as much as steel and is very malleable and ductile. Thus it can be hammered to an extremely thin sheet or drawn into the finest of metal wires. Gold is an excellent conductor of electricity. Applications vary from jewellery and coinage to dentistry and electronic circuitry. Over 70 per cent of free world production comes from South Africa. Other producers include North America, USSR, Australia and central Africa. Non-communist output totals over 1,027,000 kilograms annually. For every million parts of ore about 13 parts of gold are extracted.

Silver

Precious metal of wide industrial usage and reusage. Mine production is around 9,230 tonnes of new silver, to serve both speculative and industrial markets, which include photography and the decorative arts as well as coinage. Main producers include North America, Mexico, Peru and Australia.

Platinum

Often a by-product of copper-nickel mining, a precious metal of catalytic properties in, e.g., making nitric acid. Provides long-lasting protective coatings which are used in chemical, electrical, petroleum, glass and electronic industries. Main producer is South Africa, with 70 per cent of output, in meeting world demand of 1·4m troy oz. USSR and Canada also substantial producers. Platinum metals include Iridium, Rhodium, Palladium, Osmium, Ruthenium. Future demand may be affected by anti-pollution use in reforming petroleum.

Diamond

Precious stone of pure carbon formed at depth under pressure and temperature and then extruded in Kimberlitic rock pipes and dykes – coveted for rarity and qualities such as hardness, cutting and abrasive properties. World output of diamonds for industrial purposes 32,400 metric carats. Gemstone production is just over 13,500 metric carats. Over twenty countries produce diamonds with the bulk of output coming from Zaire, South Africa and the USSR. World synthetic diamond output is over 45 million metric carats.

Copper

One of the oldest known and most exploited metals, the mineral in refined form is used widely through the whole spectrum of industry, half going to electrical and telecommunication sectors. Other big areas of consumption are in general engineering and building components. Its main properties are its capacity as a conductor of heat or electricity, its ductile nature which allows it to be drawn into fine wire, and its value in alloys with zinc and tin. Bronzes are largely copper-tin alloys. Brasses are alloys of copper, zinc and tin. Copper deposits occur in the oceans and promise to extend the life of copper when continental deposits are nearing exhaustion. Total refined output varies because of volatile market conditions, but is now nearly 8 million tonnes. Top producers are USA, USSR, Chile, Zambia, Canada, Zaire, Peru and Australia, with about 20 other significant sources.

Tin

Soft silver-white corrosion-resistant metal used primarily as a coating for steel sheets used in food canning; has strong resistance to atmospheric tarnishing. Widely used in alloys, notably the brasses and bronzes, brazing materials and solder. World consumption is 197 million tonnes, mainly by USA, Japan, UK, Germany and France. Main sources are Malaysia, Bolivia, Thailand and Indonesia. Also mined in Australia, Nigeria, Zaire and Brazil. Total mined output is 181 million tonnes. Prices are subject to international marketing agreements because of importance of material (8 industrial countries account for 80 per cent of consumption).

Lead and Zinc

Major metals smelted from mines to meet consumption of more than 5·5 million tonnes of zinc and over 3·4 million tonnes of lead. Large stocks are kept in Europe, North America and USSR. Zinc is used in die castings for cars, and for brass and galvanizing iron and steel. Also used as a pigment in paints, chemical manufacture and metallurgical processes. Non-ferrous lead goes into production of batteries, and as additive for gasoline; main producers of refined lead are in North America and Europe, while mine production is led by the Americas, Oceania, USSR and Africa. Zinc production is dominated by North America, Europe and socialist countries.

Steel Metals

These include nickel, manganese, chromium, cobalt, molybdenum, tungsten, vanadium, columbium and tantalum, all offering specific qualities and properties for making special steels. Nickel, for example, is essential for making high quality stainless steel, which takes 40 per cent of consumption. Chromium is also necessary for the production of stainless steel. Tungsten is added to steel to produce high grade steels which can be hardened in air instead of water. Manganese is added to iron to produce castings which are not brittle. Base material of steel is iron ore, production of which rises steadily and in 1974 reached 507 million tonnes. The world's biggest producer of iron ore is USSR with around 123 million tonnes. Other big suppliers are Australia, Brazil, China, France, India, Liberia, Sweden and North America (90m tonnes). Ore is sold in lump, sinter and pellet forms for transportation to blast furnaces.

Aluminium

Primary aluminium (which, with titanium and magnesium, is a principal light weight metal) depends on production of bauxite amounting to 78 million tonnes annually. Nearly a fifth of bauxite comes from Jamaica. Other major sources are Australia, USSR, Surinam, Guyana, France, Guinea and Hungary. The USA accounts for about half of the Free World consumption; most primary aluminium goes into fabrication of industrial products made from plate, strip and wire. Alloyed with manganese or titanium, it offers tensile properties combined with lightness. World primary aluminium output is over 13 million tonnes led by North America, USSR, Japan and Norway.

Nuclear Metals

The most important of these is uranium. They include thorium, beryllium, zirconium and hafnium, caesium and ribidium, and rare earths. Development of nuclear power and related industries has expanded the search for and production of the various metals. Uranium production is around 18,500 tonnes a year.

Mercury

Liquid metal with volatile properties, known as quicksilver, derived from cinnabar. Mercury is used in scientific instruments and in chemicals, particularly in the production of chlorine and caustic soda. World mine output is 92 million tonnes. Leading sources are Spain, North America, Italy, Mexico, China, USSR and Yugoslavia.

Cadmium

A soft silvery-white metal occurs together with zinc. Mainly used in plating processes, as a pigment for plastics, for television phosphors and for nickel-cadmium batteries. It is also used for control rods in atomic nuclear reactors. The largest commercial producer is the USA. Total output is well over 10m lbs a year.

Rhenium

Derived from copper ores with molybdenite, this metal has a melting point exceeded only by tungsten. Its outstanding ductility, high temperature strength and corrosion resistance makes it an alternative for platinum as a petrochemical catalyst. Used for camera flash bulb filaments and for alloys. Main sources are Chile. USA, USSR and Sweden. Other electronic metals and minerals are indium, selenium, tellurium and mica.

Phosphate Rock

Universally mined phosphoric material with widespread usage in chemical processes. Output is in excess of 117 million tonnes.

Potash

An alkaline substance used for fertilizers and other chemical synthesis. World production is 24·2 million tonnes, with North America, USSR, Germany and France the leading sources.

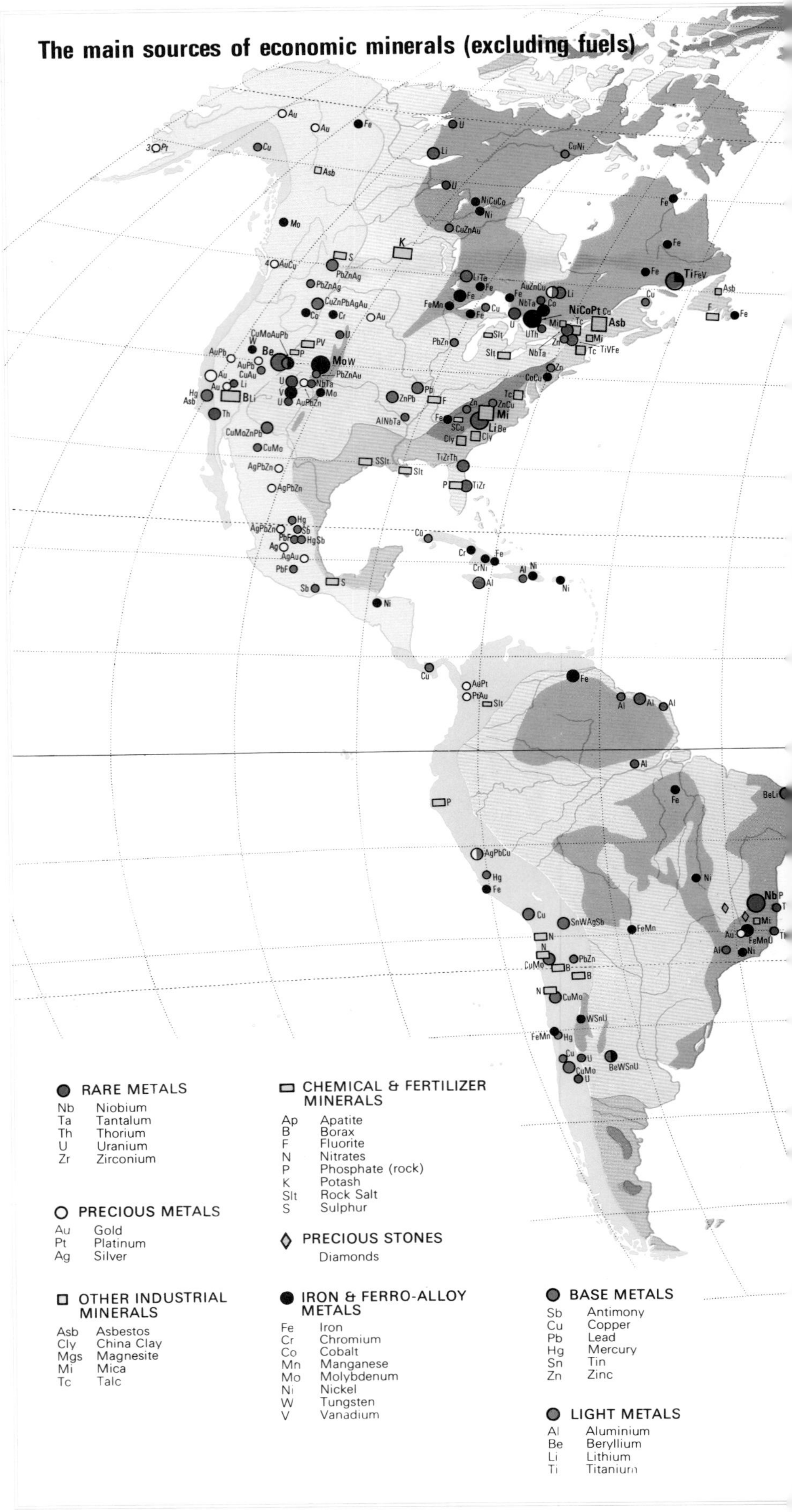

The main sources of economic minerals (excluding fuels)

● RARE METALS		□ CHEMICAL & FERTILIZER MINERALS	
Nb	Niobium	Ap	Apatite
Ta	Tantalum	B	Borax
Th	Thorium	F	Fluorite
U	Uranium	N	Nitrates
Zr	Zirconium	P	Phosphate (rock)
		K	Potash
○ PRECIOUS METALS		Slt	Rock Salt
Au	Gold	S	Sulphur
Pt	Platinum		
Ag	Silver	◇ PRECIOUS STONES	
			Diamonds

□ OTHER INDUSTRIAL MINERALS		● IRON & FERRO-ALLOY METALS		● BASE METALS	
Asb	Asbestos	Fe	Iron	Sb	Antimony
Cly	China Clay	Cr	Chromium	Cu	Copper
Mgs	Magnesite	Co	Cobalt	Pb	Lead
Mi	Mica	Mn	Manganese	Hg	Mercury
Tc	Talc	Mo	Molybdenum	Sn	Tin
		Ni	Nickel	Zn	Zinc
		W	Tungsten		
		V	Vanadium	● LIGHT METALS	
				Al	Aluminium
				Be	Beryllium
				Li	Lithium
				Ti	Titanium

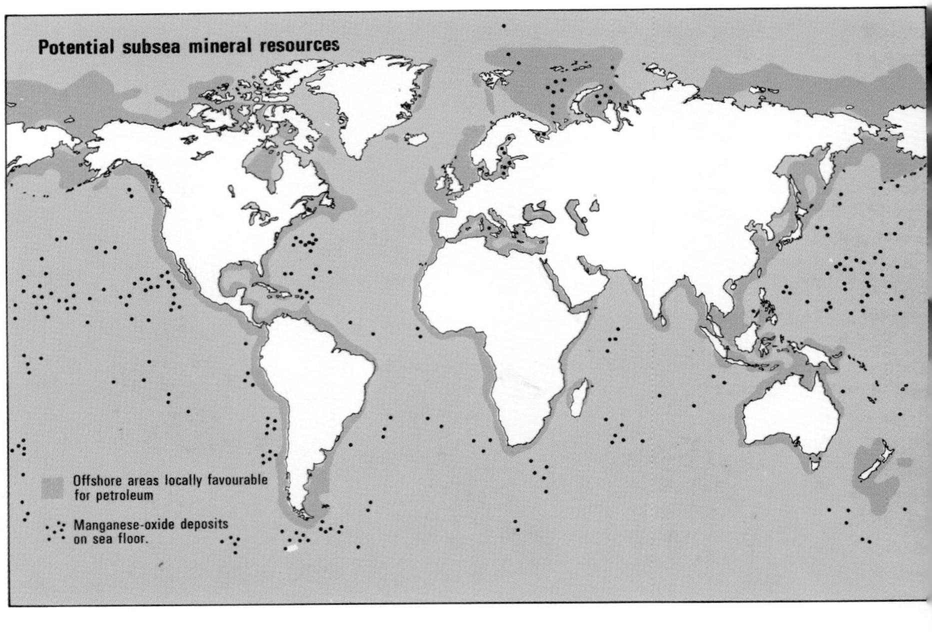

Potential subsea mineral resources

Offshore areas locally favourable for petroleum

Manganese-oxide deposits on sea floor.

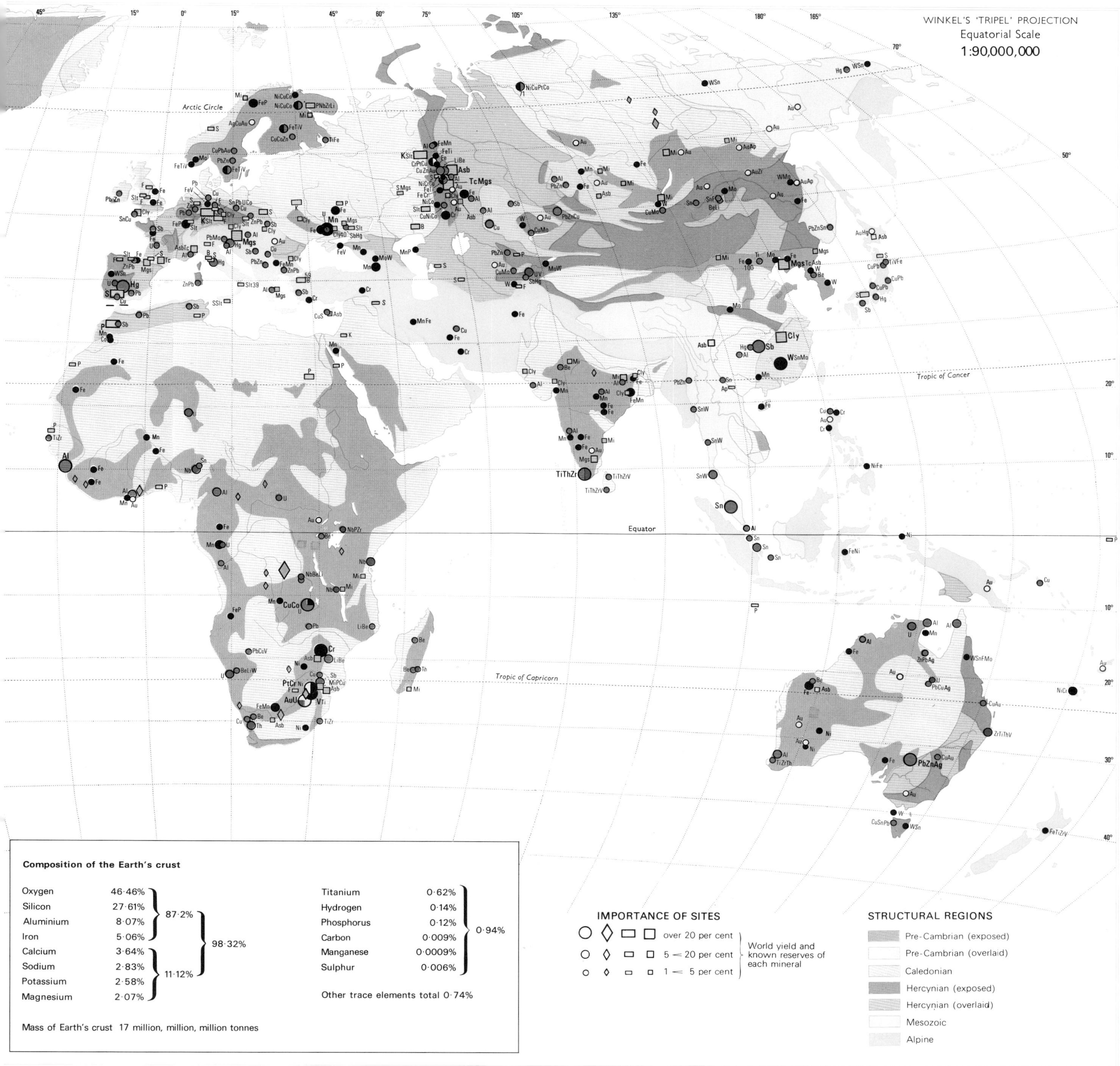

Composition of the Earth's crust

Oxygen	46·46%		
Silicon	27·61%		
Aluminium	8·07%	87·2%	
Iron	5·06%		98·32%
Calcium	3·64%		
Sodium	2·83%	11·12%	
Potassium	2·58%		
Magnesium	2·07%		

Titanium	0·62%	
Hydrogen	0·14%	
Phosphorus	0·12%	
Carbon	0·009%	0·94%
Manganese	0·0009%	
Sulphur	0·006%	

Other trace elements total 0·74%

Mass of Earth's crust 17 million, million, million tonnes

IMPORTANCE OF SITES

○ ◇ ▭ ☐ over 20 per cent
○ ◊ ▭ ☐ 5 — 20 per cent } World yield and known reserves of each mineral
○ ◊ ▭ ▫ 1 — 5 per cent

STRUCTURAL REGIONS

Pre-Cambrian (exposed)
Pre-Cambrian (overlaid)
Caledonian
Hercynian (exposed)
Hercynian (overlaid)
Mesozoic
Alpine

Sulphur

Pale yellow non-metallic element used for making sulphuric acid, gunpowder, matches and vulcanite. Also known as brimstone, the primary rock from which various sulphurs are recovered. World brimstone output is around 25 million tonnes. Derived also from natural gas, oil refining and iron pyrites. Chemicals industries are major consumers.

Lithium

Lightest metallic element produced from ore or natural brine in USA, USSR and Brazil for use in chemicals production.

Bismuth

Greyish-white metal mainly supplied by Peru, Bolivia, Mexico, USA, USSR and China. Important catalyst and is often recovered for secondary usage from other mining or smelting operations.

Barytes

The sulphate of barium; produced in 40 countries with output totalling 4 million tonnes. Usually used as weighting agent in drilling through mud for oil and gas. Also goes into making barium chemicals. USA is the largest producer.

Antimony

World output totals over 71,000 tonnes of this brittle metal substance derived from ores and concentrates. Leading suppliers are South Africa, Bolivia, China, Mexico, USSR and Yugoslavia, Thailand and Turkey. Used in battery, paint and oxide manufacture.

Boron

Dark brown non-metallic substance used to make fibreglass, vitreous enamel, heat-resistant glass, detergents and ceramics. Main source is USA borate mines; other supplies from Turkey, Argentina, France and Spain.

Fluorspar

Fusible gem-like mineral of varying quality needed for steel-making, aluminium, and fluorine based chemicals. World output is over 4 million tonnes. Leading producer is Mexico, but major sources also include USA, Argentina, Brazil, Chile, Europe, USSR, South Africa, Far and Middle East (Thailand dominant with China and North Korea).

Asbestos

A mined fibre which is best known of insulant and refractory materials, which also include perlite, sillimanite, vermiculite, graphite and magnesite. Over 5·2 million tonnes are produced annually mainly from Canada, Rhodesia, USSR, South Africa, China, Italy and USA.

Abrasives

A range of natural materials, apart from diamonds, used for abrasive and polishing purposes. Most common are emery (main sources Turkey, USA, Greece, USSR), corundum (USSR and Rhodesia), garnet (USA), tripoli (USA), pumice (USA, Germany and Italy). Finely ground and calcined clays are also used with lime, talc, feldspar and whiting. World usage of abrasives is beyond estimate.

Nickel

Element used for steel and other alloys. World consumption 750,500 tonnes, led by main steel producing countries. Main sources: Canada, New Caledonia, Australia, Rhodesia, USA, USSR, S. Africa and Japan. Latin America is a growing supplier. Biggest single use is in stainless steel.

Cobalt

Much used, like nickel, in special steels and alloys. World output is well over 22,000 million tonnes of ore bodies, often associated with copper deposits. Leading sources are Congo, Zambia, Canada, Finland and Germany.

Chromium

Chromium is derived from the ore chromite. Its main usages are in metallurgical (particularly stainless steel), refractory and chemicals industries. Output is 3·3 million tonnes. Largest producers are Rhodesia, South Africa, USSR, Turkey, Iran, Philippines, Albania and India.

Food and nutrition

Food sources

HIGH YIELD ZONES		LIVESTOCK		MAJOR SPECIALISED CROPS				LOW YIELD ZONES	
Wheat				Sugar beet/cane		Coffee		Tundra, Ice-cap	
Maize		Dairy farming		Apples		Cocoa		Forest	
Barley, Oats, Rye		Cattle		Bananas		Tea		Mountain	
Rice		Sheep		Citrus fruit		Soybeans/Groundnuts 1 2		Extensive grassland	
Millets		Pigs		Vine growing		Cottonseed/Sunflower 3 4		Desert, semi-desert	
Sea fishing									

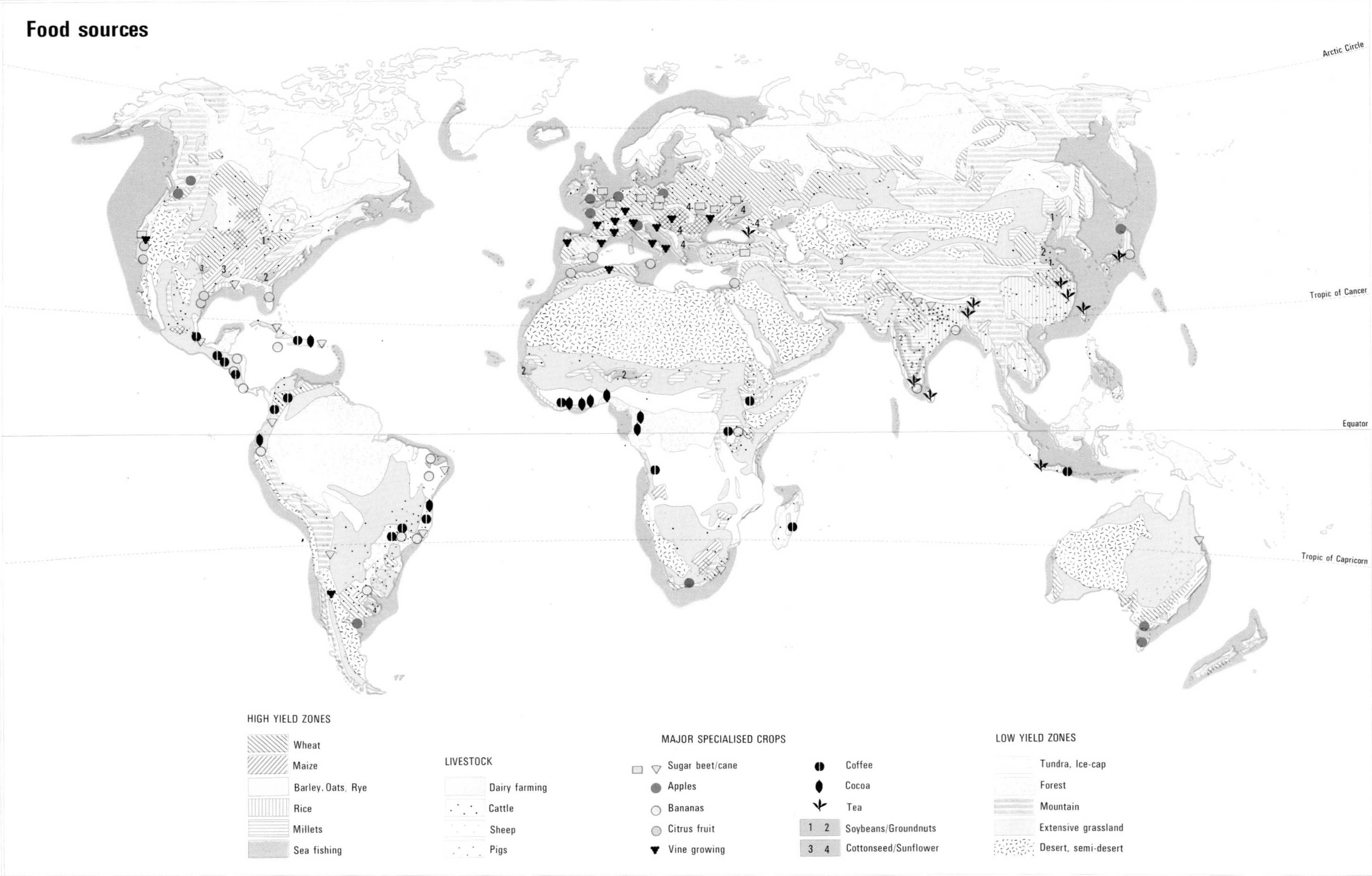

The provision of food from farms and factories depends on the most complex of all economic chains of supply. Basic foodstuffs pass from continent to continent, from temperate to tropical zones and vice versa. Foods are frozen, chilled, dehydrated, cooked and canned, pulped, or distributed fresh. Yet, in spite of better methods of preservation, storage and distribution, there is still not enough to go round. The greatest challenge to mankind is to cultivate and to process enough food to keep pace with the growth of world population, and to contrive efficient means of distribution world wide.

Poor harvests, natural disasters and civil disturbances complicate the task of agricultural scientists and economic planners who try to ease the worst problems. Their job, involving international collaboration, is formidable. In 1975 the world consumed 15,200 billion (i.e. thousand million) calories each day, but by the year 2050 the need will be 73,500 billion, with virtually all the increase concentrated on the regions of the world less well developed economically.

While the demand for food in less prosperous areas is based on grain, the raising of standards of living brings a demand for a higher consumption of animal foods. This implies great pressure to improve land crops, for only about 40 per cent of the world's crops are eaten directly by humans. The rest is fed to animals or represents waste. According to calculations, this means that six out of every seven calories are used to keep animals alive. As over half the Earth's fertile soil available for agriculture is devoted to the raising of animals, the supply of foodstuff to a world population of

possibly 16 billion people by 2050 will require new sources for food if a diet comparable to that of the richer nations is to be attained.

World consumption and production patterns

Roughly 98 per cent of all human food is produced by agriculture, including horticulture; the remaining 2 per cent comes from the oceans. To avoid excessive price increases and rationing, agricultural output must continually be expanded, demanding suitable land, capital, labour and scientific knowledge. The factors of production vary according to region; plant production (i.e. crops) representing the basis of agriculture. The raw materials for raising animals come from plant production, for livestock transforms plants into finished or semi-finished products in a way similar to that of other processing industries.

Food consumption

All supply depends upon the world-wide production of basic foodstuffs, essential for either direct consumption or processing. Among the most important primary agricultural products are grains, used for both human and animal consumption, the animals being reared both for human food (meat and drink) and for their by-products such as wool or hides. Present diets, inadequate in large parts of the world, annually require up to 350 million tonnes of wheat, 176 million tonnes of barley, over 300 million tonnes of maize, and about 265 million tonnes of rice.

Food production

In tonnage terms, the world produces 424 million tonnes of milk, 84 million tonnes of meat (including poultry) and something like 23 million

tonnes of eggs per year. Coffee output fluctuates around 5 million tonnes and wine near 32 million tonnes, while tea and cocoa production total about 3 million tonnes. To these must be added 38 million tonnes of vegetable oils and oil-seeds, and over 100 million tonnes of fresh fruit.

The United States slaughters around 39 million head of cattle annually to feed herself and others. Another 7 million sheep and lambs add to this huge supply of meat. Argentina, producing about 60 million head of cattle in 1976, is a major meat exporter, selling to Europe great quantities of chilled and frozen beef and various canned meats. Australian slaughterings of sheep amount to about 35 million head annually, some 5 million ahead of New Zealand which sells large quantities of lamb to Europe, beef to the USA and mutton to Japan. Nearly 8 million pigs form the stock for the famous Danish bacon industry.

The great dairy industry of Western Europe, is based on an average herd ranging from 5 head per herd in Italy to 22 in the Netherlands and 37 in the UK. With the trend to bigger farms the average herd size is growing each year.

Over the period 1967–77 the trend of food production per capita in the developing countries of the Far East (the world's most concentrated food deficit zone) and the Near East did not keep pace with the rise in population. There was a barely perceptible rise in Latin America, and a slight fall for the developing areas of Africa.

The introduction of new varieties of wheat has made Mexico virtually self-sufficient in this food commodity. Cereal yields have also advanced markedly in the Far East and India. The rising

volume of world agricultural exports, up about 10 per cent annually, reflects the growing interdependence of all nations in exchanging surplus food or co-operating to ease the impact of crop failures. The operation of various international commodity agreements and markets is intended to assist marketing of food.

Changes in food supply

Fishing is a vital industry. The economies of Peru and the Philippines have benefited greatly from substantial landings. In Japan, fish still provides two-thirds of animal protein and in south-east Asia fish is more commonly eaten than meat. About one-third of fish landings round the world go to the production of fish meal to feed poultry and cattle. Over the last three decades many new fishing grounds have been intensively developed, including the Bering Sea (exploited by Japan and the Soviet Union), the north-east Pacific, the north-west Atlantic, many areas around South America, and south-east Asia.

Drought, cyclone and civil disturbance are not the only factors to alter the geographical patterns of food supply year by year; political and economic difficulties sometimes arise as well. National farm policies and subsidies to food industries, have become important elements in the world economy. A decision taken in Europe to restrict imports of a certain food in order to expand indigenous production may have a profound effect on the populations of other continents. The European Community's common agricultural policy and the United States' farm support programmes are of constant importance to the distribution of world food production.

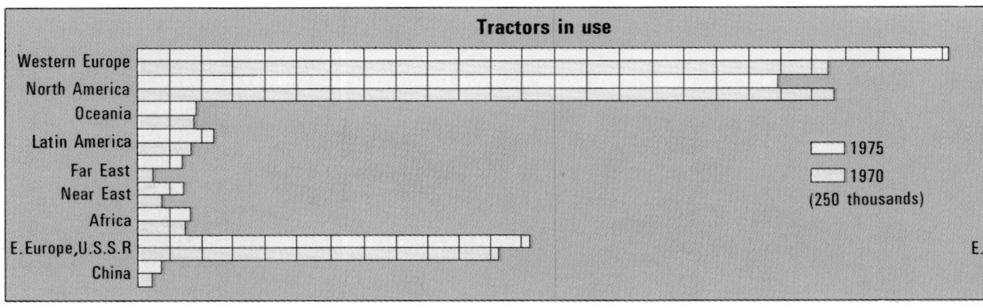

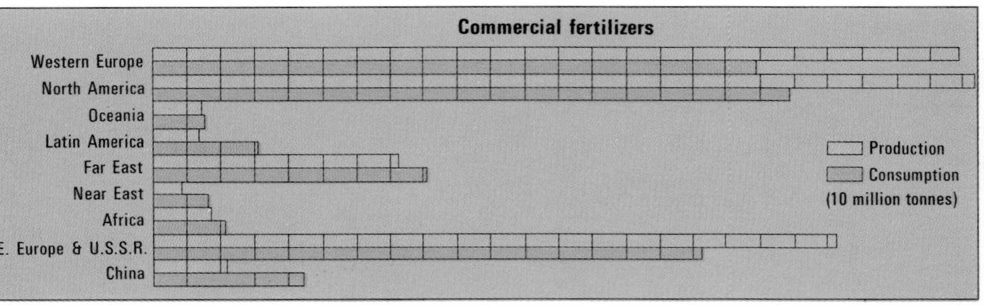

Calorie and protein consumption

Differences in calories and protein intake by different national populations need to be treated with caution. The average per capita difference in calorie intake between Canada and Brazil, for example, is around 550 calories and 35 grams of protein, yet the difference between income groups in urban areas within Brazil itself can be as high as 1,500 calories and 70 gms of protein. Some examples of calories per head per day are United States 3,330; Netherlands 3,320; West Germany 3,220; France 3,210; Italy 3,180; United Kingdom 3,180; Canada 3,180; and Japan 2,460.

To sustain their nutritional standards, nations vary greatly in their levels of consumption. Germany needs 92 kg per head per year of potatoes, compared with 36 kg for the United States. Japan consumes per head annually 90 kg of husked rice; in the UK the rice consumption is 2 kg. France and Italy drink between 100 and 105 litres of wine per head annually, whereas the consumption in the Netherlands is only 10 litres.

The importance of fish and rice in Japanese diets is demonstrated by the consumption of 25 kg per head per year of meat (measured by carcase weight) compared with 70 kg for the United Kingdom and 105 kg for the United States. The latter two nations are leading consumers of eggs in shell at 14 to 17 kg per head per year. Per capita, Finland consumes 258 kg of liquid milk annually, against 118 kg for the USA and 25 kg for Japan. Consumption of fats per head per year is 25 kg in Western Europe and North America, but in Japan the intake is 11 kg – half the level of consumption in Italy.

Innovations in food production

In recent years agricultural technologists have achieved profound changes to increase land yields by biological engineering in one form or another. Developed countries have contributed scientific skills to developing varieties of higher-yielding seed, precision fertilizers, and chemicals for pest control. As well as the 'Green Revolution', as this has become known, progress takes many other forms, such as conditioning the plants and animals of temperate zones to tropical agriculture. Desalination of sea water holds great promise for irrigation, while products unpalatable for human consumption are now being used for the enrichment of foodstuffs or for animal feeds.

There are twelve main categories of innovation in food production:

- high-yielding varieties of certain grains
- developing protein rich plants
- developing animal husbandry in less developed regions
- breeding plants and animals with high inbuilt resistance to pests and diseases
- providing more water
- providing more land
- new methods of getting food from the sea
- cultivation of algae
- producing single-cell protein
- getting food or feed from leaves
- extracting food or feed from wood
- synthetic industrial food production

Innovation in food production is taking an exciting new path in non-agricultural sectors. Fish and other sea foods offer valuable proteins. Their potential contribution to solving the world's food problems is beyond estimate. Fish protein concentrates can be used for either human or animal consumption. Mariculture in shallow waters of certain sea foods represents a major area of new research. The cultivation of algae, rich in proteins, in artificial surroundings to supplement the supply of animal feeding stuffs holds considerable promise.

One of the most dramatic recent developments has been the production of proteins by feeding single-cell organisms either bacteria or yeast on a petroleum base. The waste from various other materials or plants is being used to feed organisms. In the future, the greatest radical innovation is to produce food or feed, without the use of plants. The use of solar or other energy sources will allow amino-acids to be produced on an industrial scale, to be used to fortify foodstuffs. The consequence of the development of food without the use of plants could be enormous, reducing the world's total dependence on agriculture by a factor depending on the degree of scientific progress and scale of commercial exploitation.

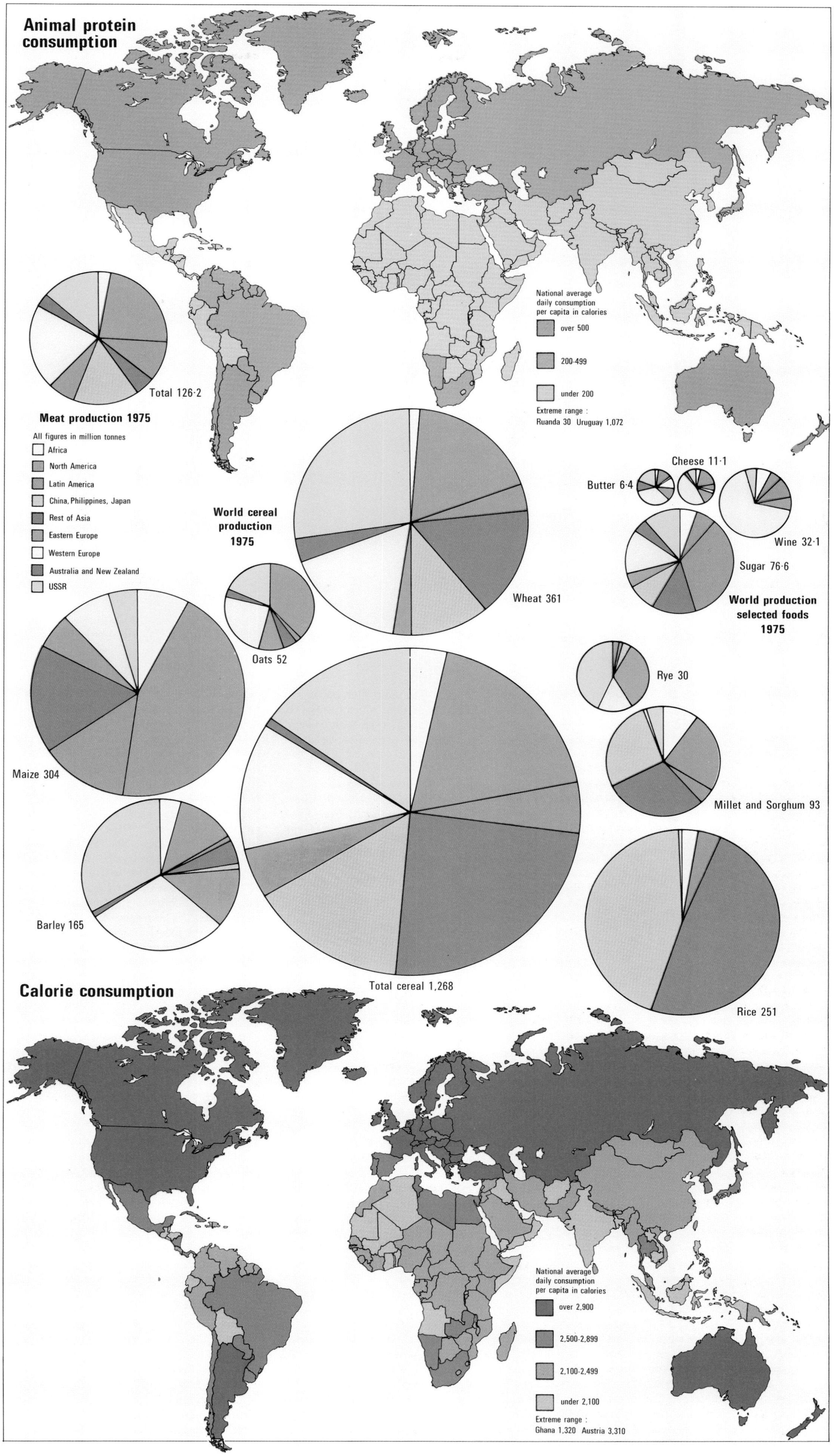

Animal protein consumption

National average daily consumption per capita in calories
- over 500
- 200-499
- under 200

Extreme range: Ruanda 30 Uruguay 1,072

Meat production 1975

All figures in million tonnes
- Africa
- North America
- Latin America
- China, Philippines, Japan
- Rest of Asia
- Eastern Europe
- Western Europe
- Australia and New Zealand
- USSR

Total 126·2

Cheese 11·1
Butter 6·4
Wine 32·1
Sugar 76·6

World production selected foods 1975

World cereal production 1975

Wheat 361
Oats 52
Maize 304
Barley 165
Rye 30
Millet and Sorghum 93
Rice 251
Total cereal 1,268

Calorie consumption

National average daily consumption per capita in calories
- over 2,900
- 2,500-2,899
- 2,100-2,499
- under 2,100

Extreme range: Ghana 1,320 Austria 3,310

Population variations

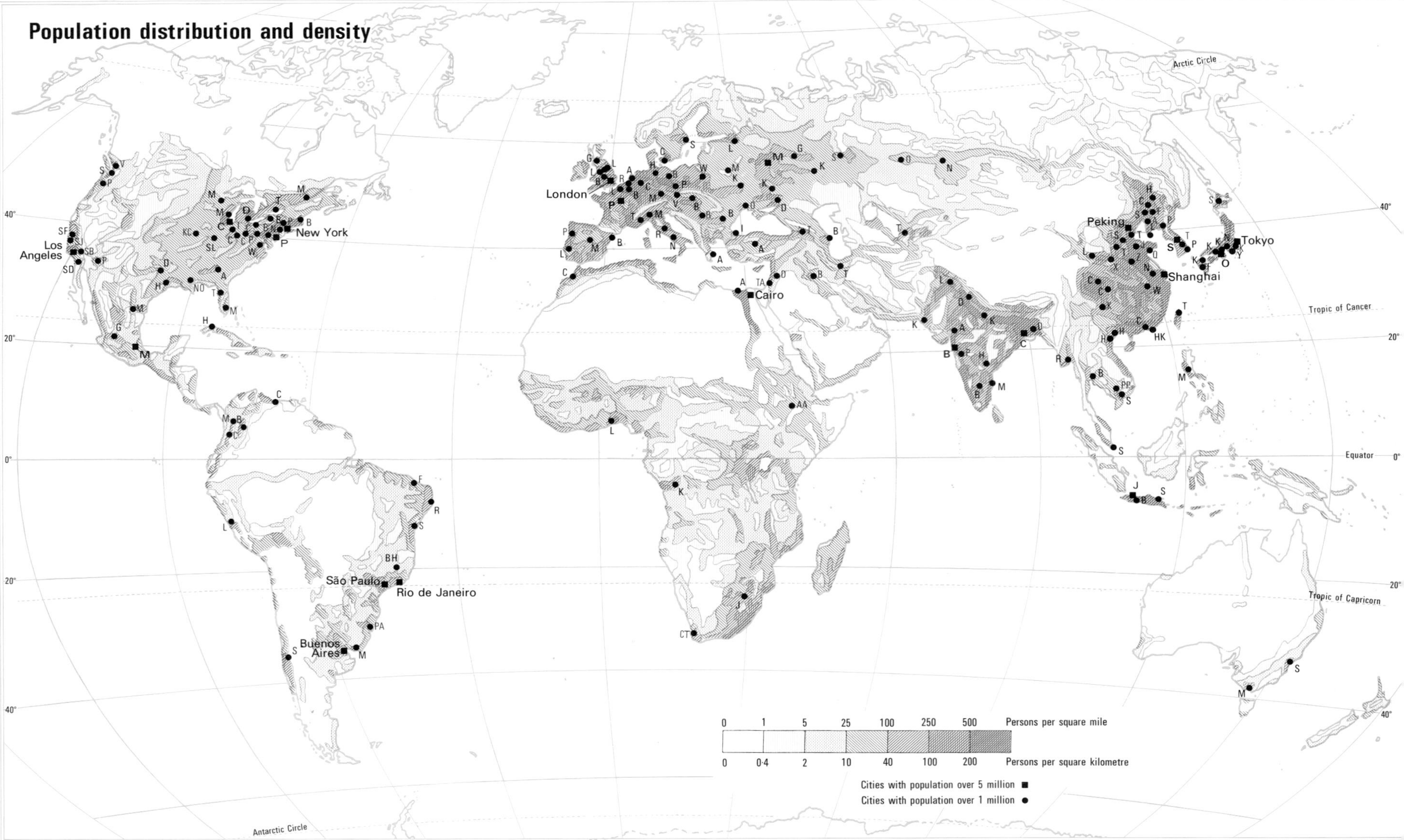

Population distribution and density

In the first 17 centuries AD world population increased by a mere 500 million. Then, largely through reduction in the death-rate rather than increase in fertility, the rate of growth accelerated so that by 1850 a further 500 million had been added, the population then being 1,300 million. A further 400 million was added to this figure in the next 50 years bringing the population in 1900 to 1,700 million.

Between 1930 and the beginning of 1975 the population of the world virtually doubled to about 3,900 million. If the growth rate of the last few decades (1·9%) were to continue there would be over 7,500 million people by AD 2010 representing an increase of 1,100 million in the decade following the end of the century. By 2050 this figure would have risen to 16,000 million and would attain 25,500 million by 2075. At this rate of growth the population doubles every 37 years.

Density and distribution

The mean density of population in 1975 was some 28 per square kilometre (about 73 per square mile). In other words each human being could have 9½ acres (or very nearly 4 hectares) to live on if the population were evenly distributed over all the land surface of the globe. But about 70 per cent of the land is either too cold or too high, too aird or too wet or else infertile and so presents mankind with conditions unfavourable for settlement by more than a very small proportion of even the world's present population. It is no wonder then, that the population is not evenly distributed over the Earth.

To this uneven distribution of population; imposed largely by nature, must be added maldistribution in relation to resources. Much of the land area (one third of the total) that could possibly be cultivated fairly intensively remains virtually unused. Economic efficiency in the actual areas under production varies greatly from one place to another. Less than 10 per cent (13,500,000 square km or 5,200,000 square miles) of the non-polar land surface is occupied by more than 95 per cent of the world's population. Within this proportionately small area, the patterns of distribution and density of population vary very greatly in response to many factors, none of which remains constant in its effect upon mankind save over areas where the pattern of

human culture itself is the same. Thus the map on this page shows a pattern which cannot be interpreted in global terms simply with reference either to the density of population or to the distribution of cities.

Asia

The greatest concentration of people is to be found in monsoon Asia, especially in China, India, Japan and Java. Here, apart from Japan and small localities such as Hong Kong, Singapore, and Shanghai, people are dependent for their livelihood mainly upon agriculture. When the scarcity of cultivable land in monsoon Asia and its huge agricultural population (certainly more than 1,000 million) are taken jointly into account, the distinctive feature of the population distribution over the area is seen to be the prevalence of high rural, agrarian, densities. Farms become small holdings, often of no more than one hectare (two and a half acres) in size; farms larger than ten hectares are very rare indeed, and rural densities of population of 500 per square km (1,300 per square mile) are commonplace. Such densities as these are to be found in, for example, the Ganges plain; the valleys of southern China; much of the Great Plain of China; the Yangtse basin; the rice lands of Honshu, and in Java. Similar rural densities could have developed in the Mississippi lowlands following the discovery of the New World had the Chinese settled there and not the Europeans. Instead it can be seen that neither in North nor South America are extensive Asian-type rural densities to be found. Likewise in Europe agrarian densities are far lower than in monsoon Asia because farms are larger. It should be noted, on the other hand, that agrarian densities in the fertile parts of Europe generally exceed those of similar areas in North America because farm sizes in the mainland of western Europe are small in comparison with those of North America, and are smaller even than those of the United Kingdom.

Europe

The second great concentration of population is to be found in Europe, as is seen from a comparison of maps C and D opposite. Agriculture first led to the dense settlement of population in many areas in Europe but the growth of manufacturing, mining and service industries augmented those densities and led to further concentrations of

people in areas not previously densely settled, e.g. the Ruhr and Lancashire. Unlike monsoon Asia, therefore, western Europe has become densely populated through urban growth and is now predominantly a land of town-dwellers, or town-workers. Nowhere is this fact more plainly visible than in Britain.

N.E. United States

The third great concentration comprises the north-eastern quarter of the USA and the adjacent strip of Canada. The total population of this highly urbanized area slightly exceeds that of Japan and is about equal to that of Indonesia. It is, therefore, much smaller than that of western Europe and is minute in comparison with the concentration in monsoon Asia. Yet this third concentration produces at least as much wealth as Western Europe and considerably more wealth than the whole of monsoon Asia (map E opposite).

In the rest of the world, population density is generally low but there are local pockets of high density in, for example, the Nile Valley of Egypt; California; some coastal areas of South America; central Mexico; parts of western and southern Africa, and in metropolitan Australia. The paramount fact of human geography is, therefore, the emptiness of the Earth. Very little of it is densely populated. Very little of it is overpopulated. Most of it is underpopulated.

Expectation of life

Lack of space may prove less of a problem than how to ensure a more uniform life-expectancy throughout the world. As map B on the opposite page shows, there is a large area including most of Africa, Arabia, Afghanistan, India, Bangladesh, Indo-China and Indonesia where the expectation of life at birth is less than 50 years, whereas in the United States, Canada, Cuba, Jamaica, most of Europe, Japan, and Australasia it is over 70 years. Latin America contrasts sharply with North America, but worst of all is the expectation of less than 40 years indicated for Bangladesh, Madagascar and several other African countries.

These and the other wide variations in life-expectancy illustrated on the map merit more immediate international concern than mere numbers of people or the numerical increase. Although effective measures to reduce the birth rate will contribute to the lowering of the death rate, some

nations with high rate of birth oppose reduction in national birth-rate. As with density of population, problems arising from life-expectancy are not the same the world over; nor can they be solved solely by global strategies; they are regional and local in occurrence and for the most part demand regional and local treatment.

Increase of population

Increase of population is a matter of world concern because of its impact on life-expectancy, the quality of life and local living conditions. The rate of increase (shown on map A above) is highest in parts of Africa and Latin America, and almost tropical and sub-tropical countries have rates greater than the mean (1·9 per cent) for the world as a whole. It should be noted, however, that whereas rates of increase generally diminished a little in a large part of South America during the decade to 1975 the converse is probably true for Africa. Temperate lands of the northern hemisphere show low increases in the period up to 1975 while several, including England and Wales, have most recently recorded small decreases. The trend is towards a numerically static population, the birth rate equating to the death rate.

Rates of change, whether up or down, are less crucial to human well-being and political action than absolute changes represented by the differences between birth-rate and death-rate. China and, even more so, the Indian subcontinent, face the greatest problems of population increase. Their natural resources including availability of land are modest in relation to the total number of people added annually. In India alone, the increase exceeds that in the whole of the Americas. China's population growth is greater than that of Europe and the USSR combined. Mexico's annual increase now exceeds that of the United States and by AD 2000 the population will approach half that of the USA in a land only one-fifth of the area. Indonesia's absolute increase exceeds those of all countries except China and India.

Absolute increase in the population of a given area is caused either by the birth rate exceeding the death rate or by immigration. Large-scale migration occurs where there is disparity between two areas. In the past it was towards areas where agriculture offered better prospects. Today it is towards countries of high technology

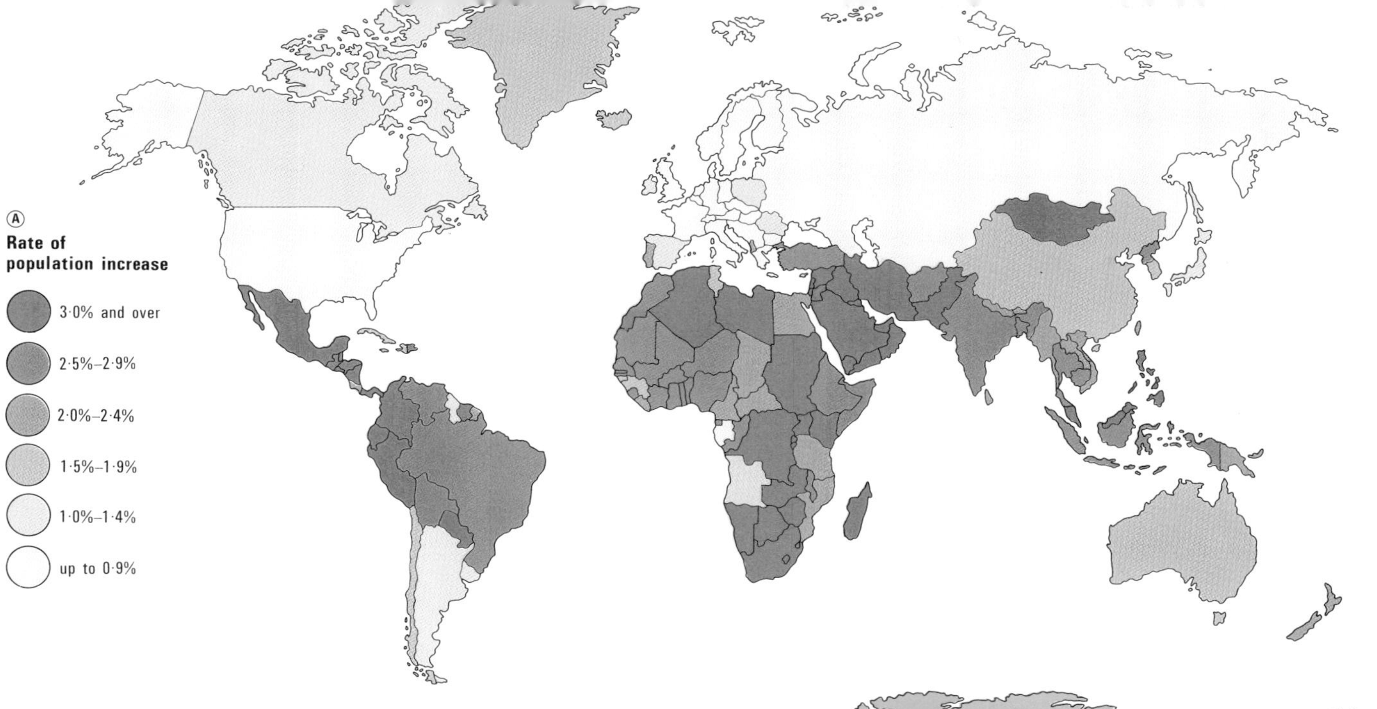

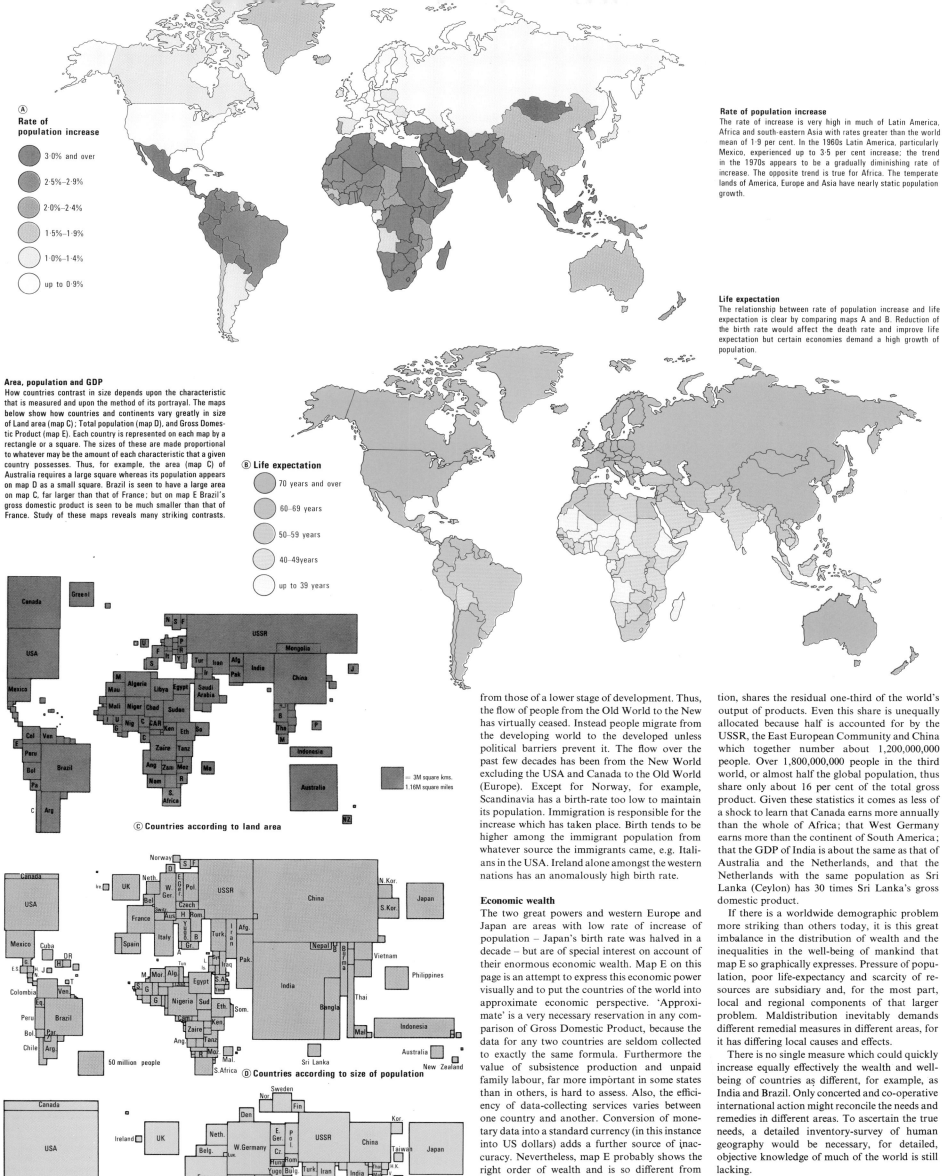

Rate of population increase

(A) **Rate of
population increase**

3·0% and over

2·5%–2·9%

2·0%–2·4%

1·5%–1·9%

1·0%–1·4%

up to 0·9%

Rate of population increase
The rate of increase is very high in much of Latin America, Africa and south-eastern Asia with rates greater than the world mean of 1·9 per cent. In the 1960s Latin America, particularly Mexico, experienced up to 3·5 per cent increase; the trend in the 1970s appears to be a gradually diminishing rate of increase. The opposite trend is true for Africa. The temperate lands of America, Europe and Asia have nearly static population growth.

Life expectation
The relationship between rate of population increase and life expectation is clear by comparing maps A and B. Reduction of the birth rate would affect the death rate and improve life expectation but certain economies demand a high growth of population.

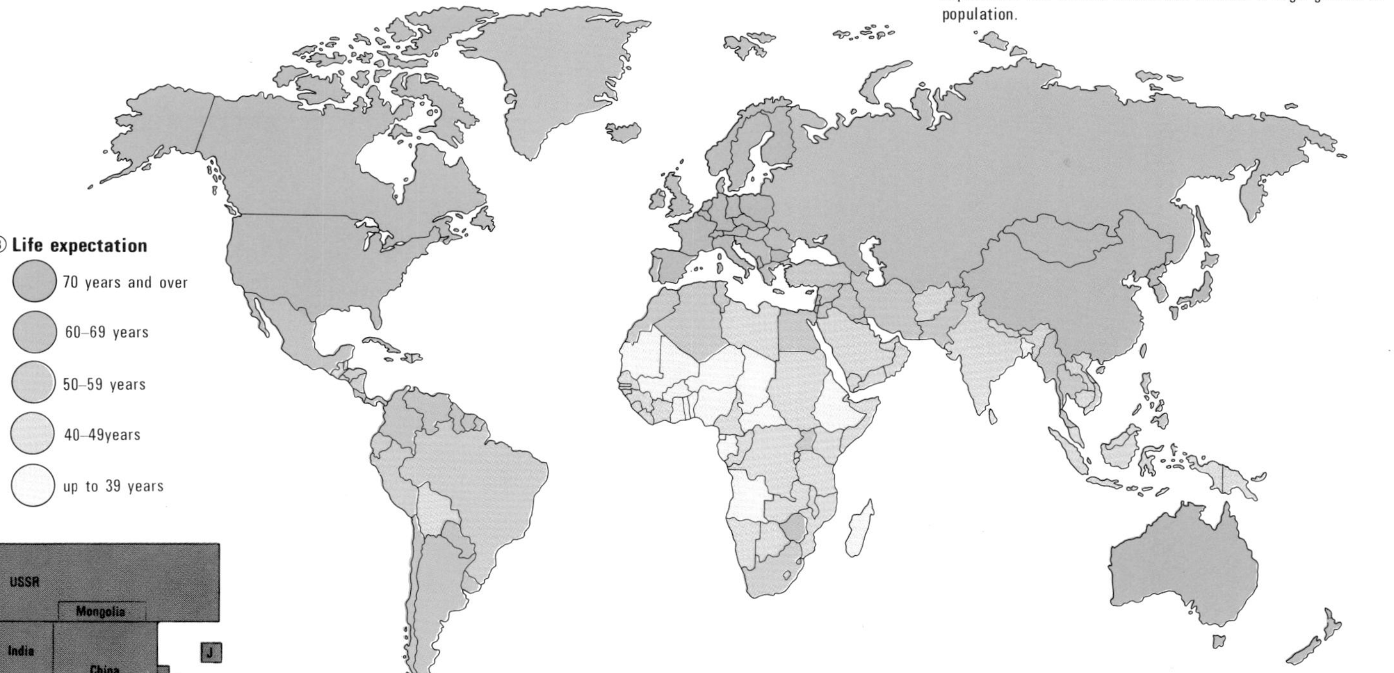

Area, population and GDP
How countries contrast in size depends upon the characteristic that is measured and upon the method of its portrayal. The maps below show how countries and continents vary greatly in size of Land area (map C); Total population (map D), and Gross Domestic Product (map E). Each country is represented on each map by a rectangle or a square. The sizes of these are made proportional to whatever may be the amount of each characteristic that a given country possesses. Thus, for example, the area (map C) of Australia requires a large square whereas its population appears on map D as a small square. Brazil is seen to have a large area on map C, far larger than that of France; but on map E Brazil's gross domestic product is seen to be much smaller than that of France. Study of these maps reveals many striking contrasts.

(B) **Life expectation**

70 years and over

60–69 years

50–59 years

40–49 years

up to 39 years

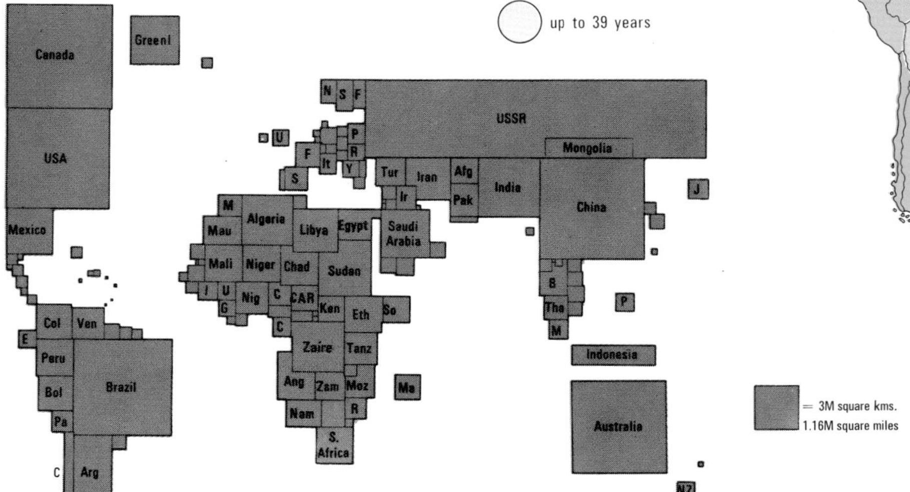

(C) **Countries according to land area**

= 3M square kms.
1.16M square miles

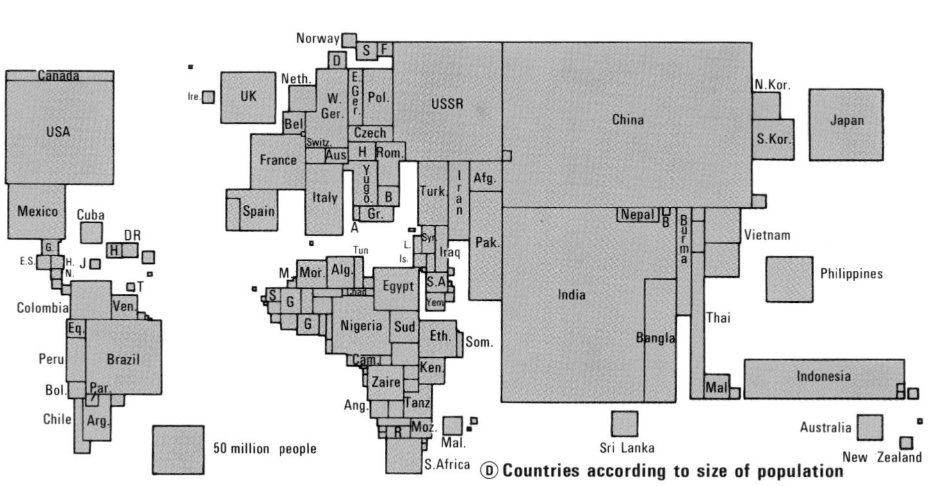

(D) **Countries according to size of population**

50 million people

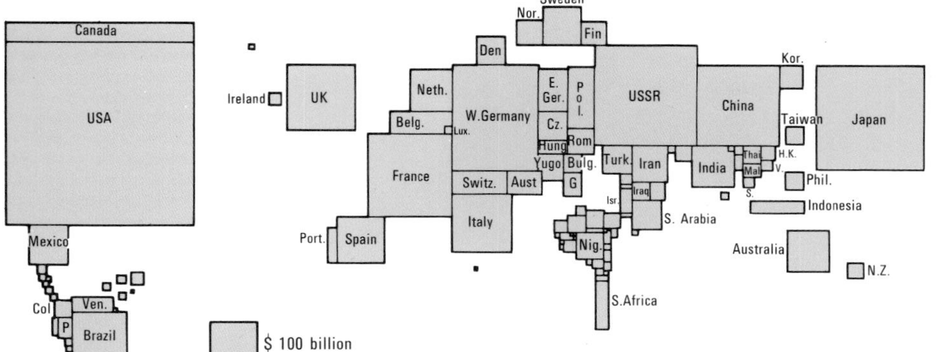

(E) **Countries according to Gross Domestic Product (1976)**

$ 100 billion

from those of a lower stage of development. Thus, the flow of people from the Old World to the New has virtually ceased. Instead people migrate from the developing world to the developed unless political barriers prevent it. The flow over the past few decades has been from the New World excluding the USA and Canada to the Old World (Europe). Except for Norway, for example, Scandinavia has a birth-rate too low to maintain its population. Immigration is responsible for the increase which has taken place. Birth tends to be higher among the immigrant population from whatever source the immigrants came, e.g. Italians in the USA. Ireland alone amongst the western nations has an anomalously high birth rate.

Economic wealth
The two great powers and western Europe and Japan are areas with low rate of increase of population – Japan's birth rate was halved in a decade – but are of special interest on account of their enormous economic wealth. Map E on this page is an attempt to express this economic power visually and to put the countries of the world into approximate economic perspective. 'Approximate' is a very necessary reservation in any comparison of Gross Domestic Product, because the data for any two countries are seldom collected to exactly the same formula. Furthermore the value of subsistence production and unpaid family labour, far more important in some states than in others, is hard to assess. Also, the efficiency of data-collecting services varies between one country and another. Conversion of monetary data into a standard currency (in this instance into US dollars) adds a further source of inaccuracy. Nevertheless, map E probably shows the right order of wealth and is so different from normal atlas maps in the size it ascribes to particular countries and continents that it invites examination in some detail.

The outstanding feature is the pre-eminence of North America, with about 40 per cent of the gross global product. Next comes Western Europe with about 25 per cent. These two areas, together with Japan, produces annually at least two-thirds of the world's wealth. The rest of the world, comprising about five-sixths of the total popula-

tion, shares the residual one-third of the world's output of products. Even this share is unequally allocated because half is accounted for by the USSR, the East European Community and China which together number about 1,200,000,000 people. Over 1,800,000,000 people in the third world, or almost half the global population, thus share only about 16 per cent of the total gross product. Given these statistics it comes as less of a shock to learn that Canada earns more annually than the whole of Africa; that West Germany earns more than the continent of South America; that the GDP of India is about the same as that of Australia and the Netherlands, and that the Netherlands with the same population as Sri Lanka (Ceylon) has 30 times Sri Lanka's gross domestic product.

If there is a worldwide demographic problem more striking than others today, it is this great imbalance in the distribution of wealth and the inequalities in the well-being of mankind that map E so graphically expresses. Pressure of population, poor life-expectancy and scarcity of resources are subsidiary and, for the most part, local and regional components of that larger problem. Maldistribution inevitably demands different remedial measures in different areas, for it has differing local causes and effects.

There is no single measure which could quickly increase equally effectively the wealth and well-being of countries as different, for example, as India and Brazil. Only concerted and co-operative international action might reconcile the needs and remedies in different areas. To ascertain the true needs, a detailed inventory-survey of human geography would be necessary, for detailed, objective knowledge of much of the world is still lacking.

Brazil is sparsely peopled, undeveloped and quite capable of absorbing a large number of immigrants provided they were used to develop and exploit the resources of the interior. India is, in contrast, densely populated, intensely but inefficiently developed and quite unsuited to receiving large numbers of immigrants. In Brazil, the key problem is how to organize development; in India, how to undertake redevelopment. Immigration could help Brazil. Emigration would help India.

Patterns of human settlement

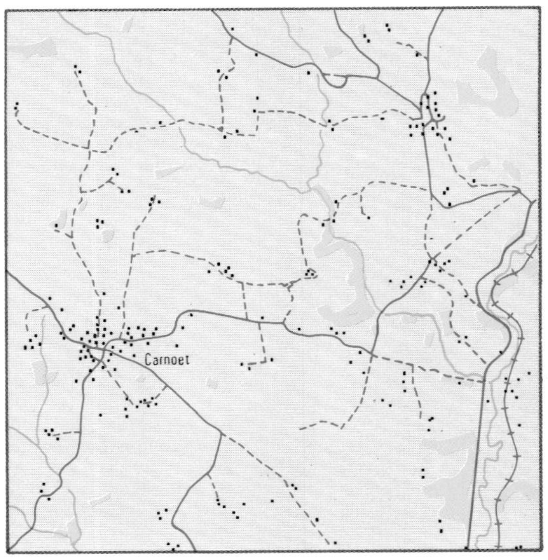

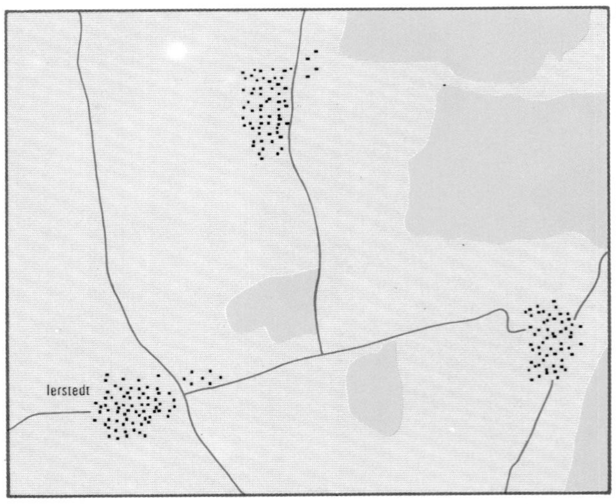

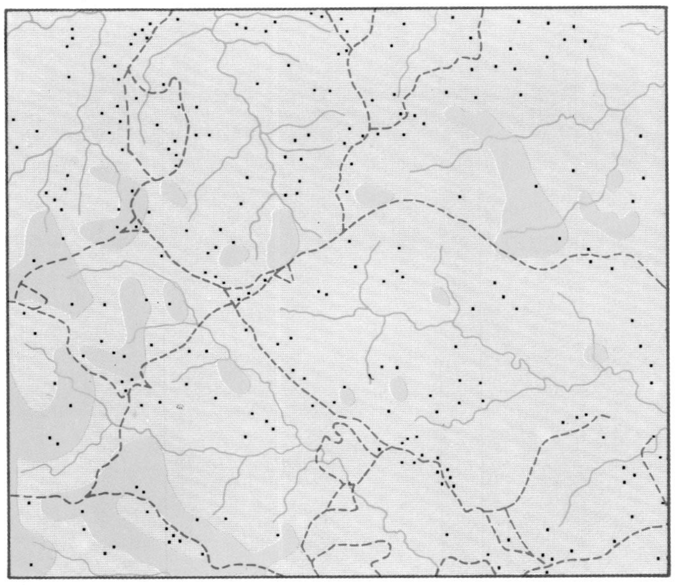

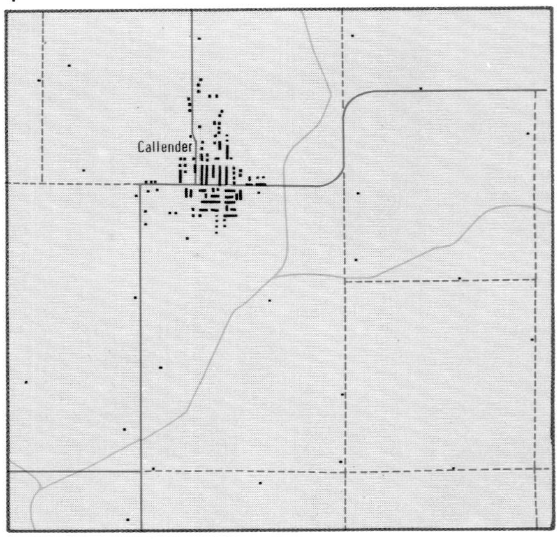

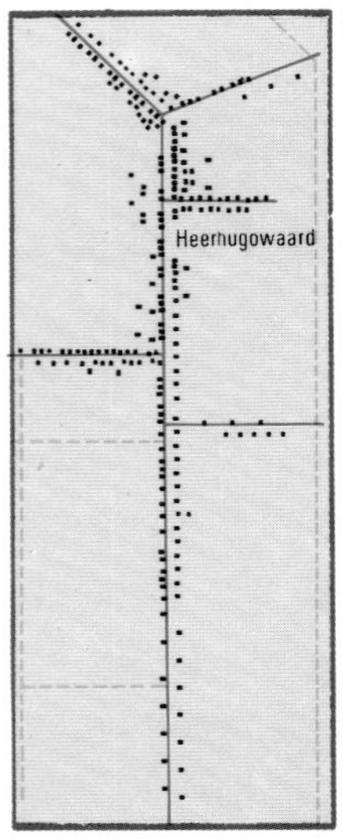

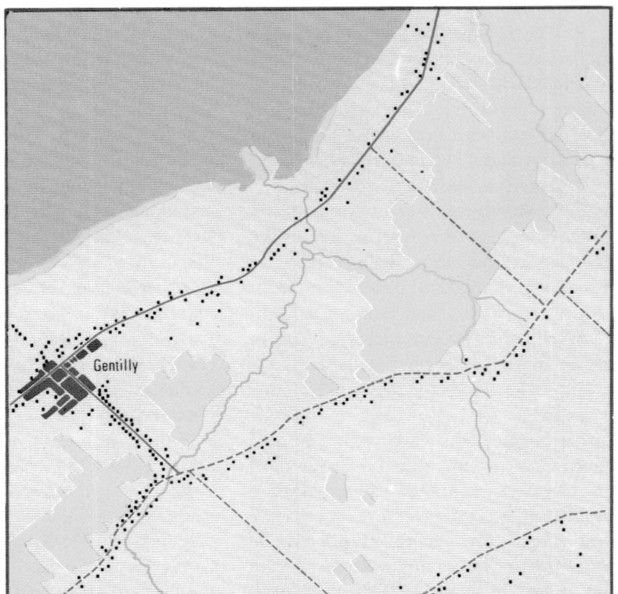

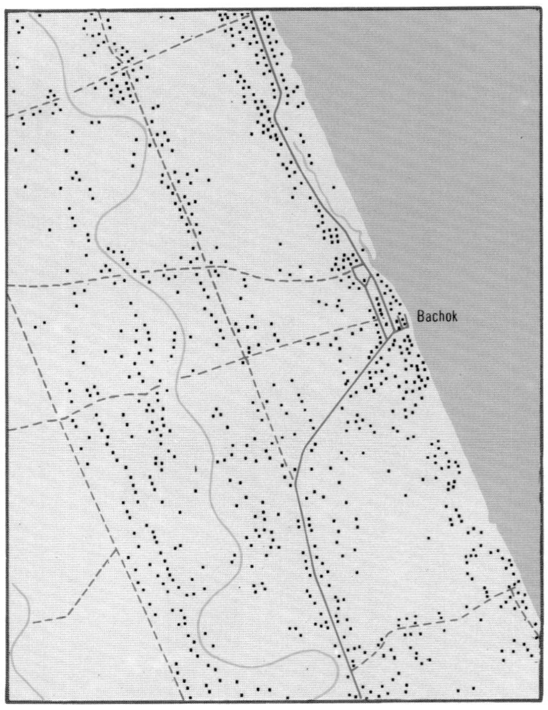

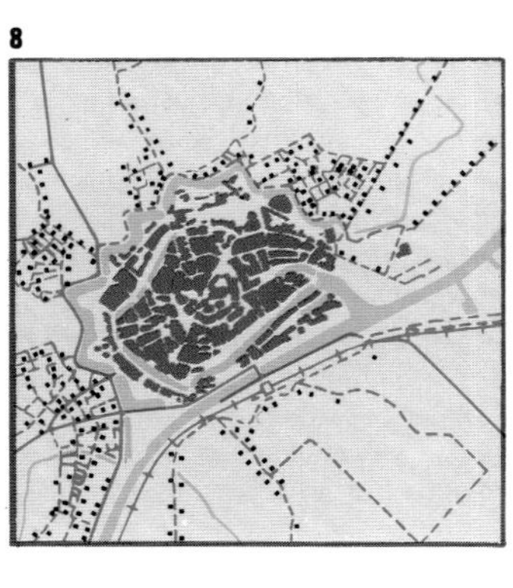

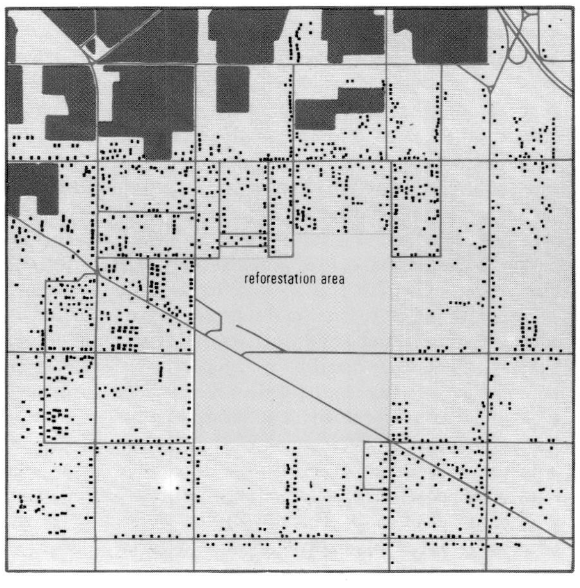

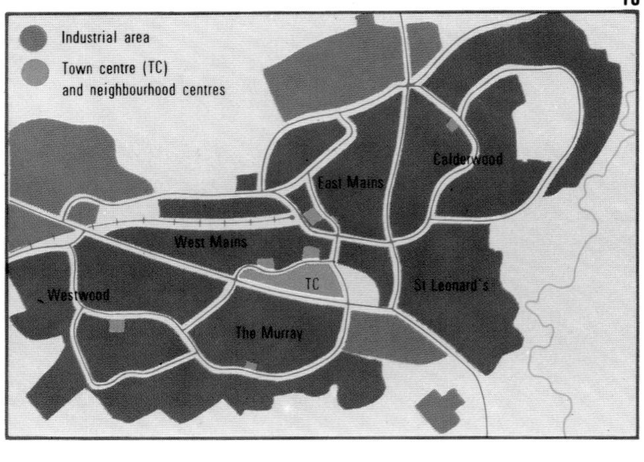

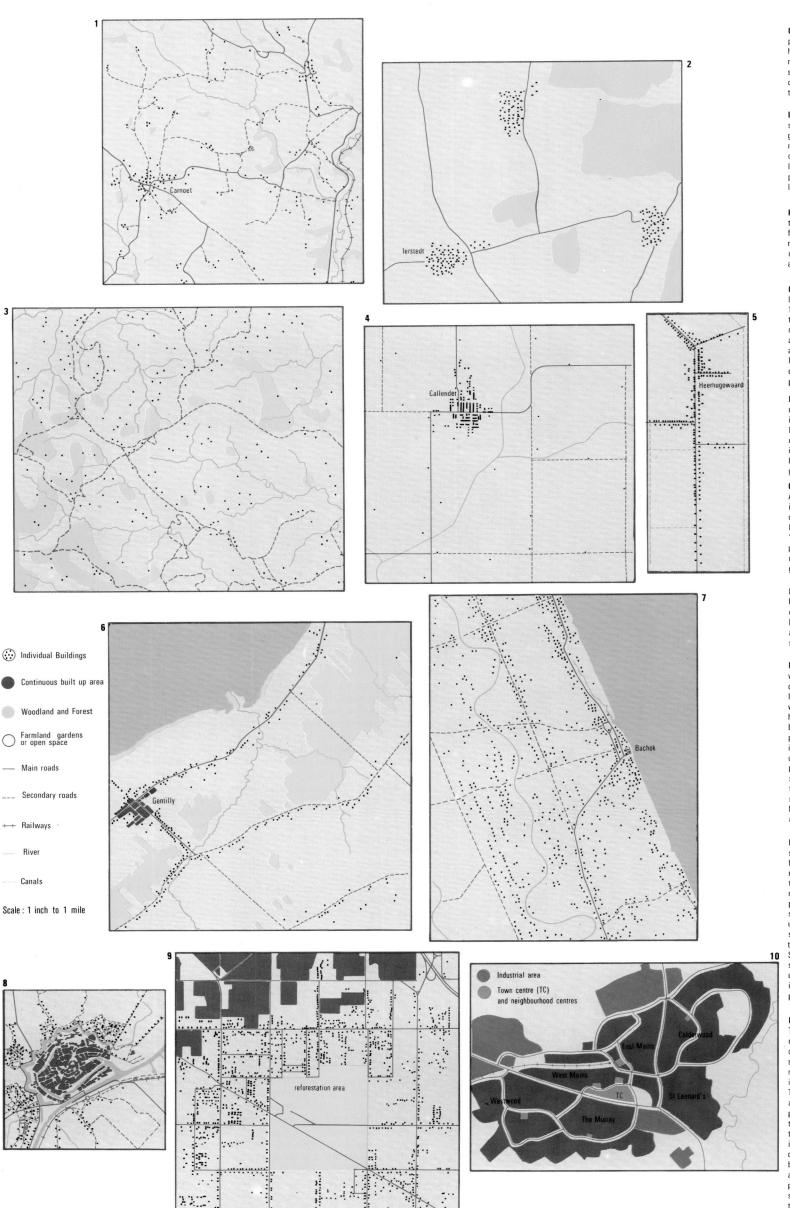

1

Carnoet, France Farmsteads are widely dispersed on compact holdings, with scattered hamlets and small villages containing community facilities like churches, schools and shops. In western Europe such a pattern occurs especially in regions where Celtic traditions survive.

2

Ierstedt, Germany Highly nucleated rural settlement, associated historically with regions of post-Roman Europe settled by Germanic tribes. Even today few farmsteads occur outside the large, rather formless villages, because traditionally farms are composed of separate scattered strips, although land consolidation is now widespread.

3

Kangundo, Kenya Moderately dense pattern of dispersed settlement in a tribal farming economy. Community facilities like markets and schools stand on isolated sites, not having formed, here at least, nuclei around which villages have evolved.

4

Callender, Iowa, USA To dispose of public land to settlers, US government surveys after 1785 created 1-mile square farm units ('sections'), though many have since been subdivided. Dispersed rural settlement thus appeared from the outset, with small nucleated villages at intervals throughout the area. Roads were built along most section boundaries, giving a characteristic checkerboard pattern.

5

Heerhugowaard, Holland Strongly linear rural settlement at high density in a region of intensive farming. Land reclamation confines building to the elevated dikes that line major drainage canals. Villages are large, extending considerable distances along roadsides, but with little opportunity for compact growth.

6

Gentilly, Québec French colonists in North America divided land into narrow plots, initially running back from rivers, with farms close together for safety, and along the river banks for access to water transport. This 'long lot' system later developed to incorporate other rows (rangs) of farms along roads, often parallel to the rivers. Villages grew up especially around churches.

7

Bachok, Malaya This linear arrangement of houses and villages has been strongly influenced by the existence of parallel sandy beach ridges. These are elevated slightly above the flat intervening tracts that are seasonally flooded for padi (rice) cultivation.

8

Middelburg, Holland Medieval towns in western Europe were small by modern standards and compact. Winding, narrow streets led to a central market square, around which were the town's chief public buildings (town hall, guildhall, the main church – in Middelburg, a 12th century abbey). Walls usually protected the town, but when later demolished, their line is often shown by roughly circular streets. In Middelburg, typical post-medieval fortifications were also constructed with moats and geometrical bastions. Many present-day large cities have such medieval towns as a historic core, but Middelburg has not expanded greatly due to a restricted economic basis.

9

Fort Mann, BC, Canada The characteristic sprawl of the North American 'rural-urban fringe'. Without tight control on development, and often with intense land speculation, sporadic growth of this kind occurs commonly around American cities. Housing appears in small clusters, or along roads, or on scattered individual lots. Non-residential uses develop, especially those needing ample space, e.g. shopping centres, modern factories, motels, drive-in cinemas or schools. Set among all these are recreational open spaces such as golf courses and country clubs. What is left of earlier farmsteads (often in a rundown condition) forms another component in this highly diversified area.

10

East Kilbride, Scotland The British New Towns, all established since 1946, are planned urban communities drawing population chiefly from conurbations (London and Clydeside especially), for which by intention they relieve housing pressures. Local employment is simultaneously created to make each New Town as independent as possible economically and socially. Earlier New Towns are composed of several neighbourhood units around the town centre, each neighbourhood containing facilities for the everyday needs of its residents (primary schools, shops, churches, doctors, meeting halls, etc.). East Kilbride (designated 1947) is an excellent example. Since 1952 somewhat more flexible plans are utilized, but all New Towns have segregated industrial areas and also sophisticated internal circulation systems, emphasising the separation of pedestrians from vehicular traffic.

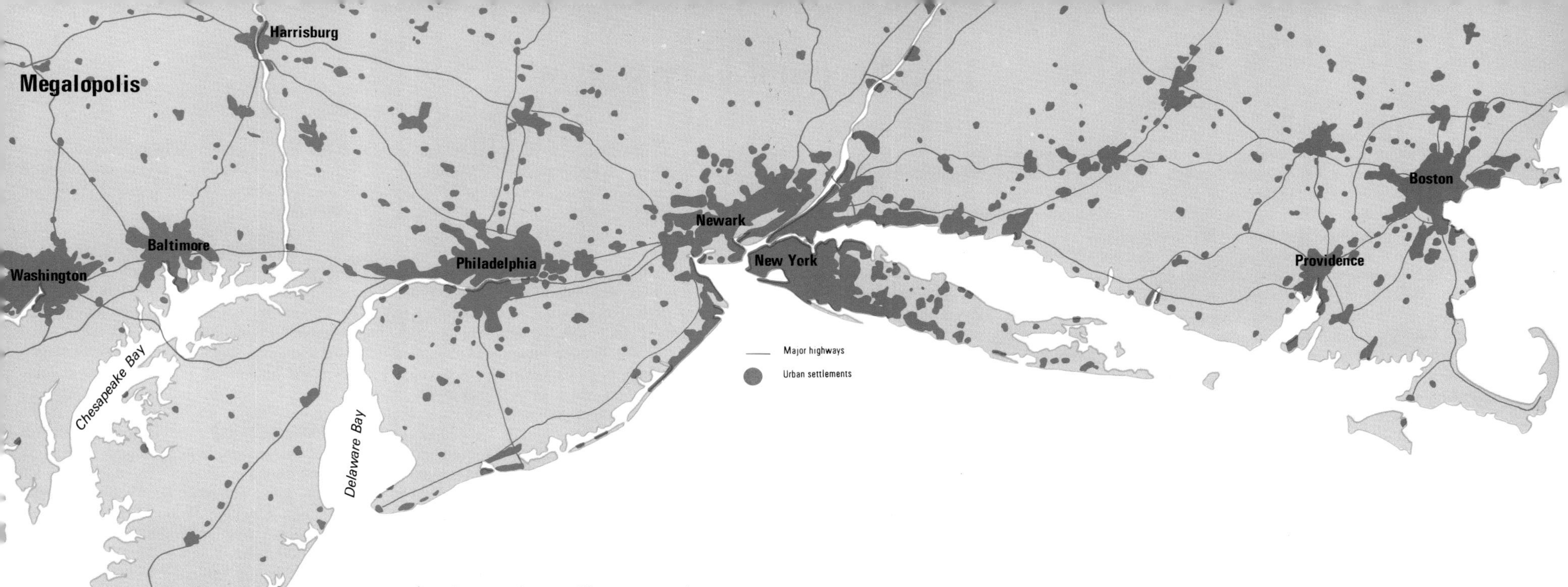

Megalopolis

Harrisburg · Boston · Newark · Baltimore · Philadelphia · New York · Providence · Washington

Chesapeake Bay · Delaware Bay

— Major highways
● Urban settlements

The distribution of homes and other buildings, constituting the settlement pattern of a region, is affected by a complex interplay of factors.

Rural settlement

Considering rural regions first, there are great differences in the *density* of settlement depending largely upon the carrying capacity of the land in terms of the particular types of agriculture practised, and upon the length of time the region has been settled. The disposition of buildings over the area, or the *form* of settlement, can vary from almost total dispersion to virtually complete clustering, though more often there will be a mixture of scattered farms and small nucleations (i.e. groupings of buildings). Such differences in form stem from variations in, for example, cultural tradition, land ownership systems, types of farming, the technological status of the society or the need for protection from external dangers, either human or environmental. Where an area has been occupied for very considerable periods, there are likely to be changes through time in some or all of these influences and thus the rural settlement pattern itself changes in response: for example, the enclosure movements that led to the consolidation of the earlier strip-field holdings into compact farm units over much of lowland Britain between the 16th and 18th centuries permitted farmers to move their homes from the highly

nucleated pre-enclosure villages on to the new compact units, thereby creating the present mixed form of rural settlement that characterizes this region. Thus a *primary*, or original, settlement pattern changes into a *secondary* one.

The rural nucleations, villages and hamlets exhibit a morphology, or layout, which also varies considerably throughout the world. Linear types, e.g. along roadsides or riversides, are extremely common, but so too are compact but irregular groupings, of which the French and German examples are but two types. More regular shapes occur in many regions, e.g. rectangular and roughly circular villages are found in several parts of central and eastern Europe, and a grid plan is normal in Anglo-America.

Urban settlement

The regional or national economy develops and elaborates itself by the expansion of trade and the growth of industry. Both activities require, and create, more sophisticated types of settlement than the village, and towns and cities evolve, supported by an intensifying network of routes. The *degree of urbanisation* in a country is measured by the proportion of its population that live in towns and cities, and this is high (generally well over 60%) in advanced countries.

Urban settlements act as service centres where increasingly specialised activities locate themselves as the towns become larger, and people from usually extensive areas nearby will depend on them to provide goods and services that are unobtainable in smaller settlements, especially the villages. Towns and cities, too, will exhibit their distinctive morphologies, influenced in their case by factors such as the age of the town (for

different historical periods tend to have their own characteristic standards and forms of street and building patterns) and by the cultural context in which the town has developed: compare, for example, the medieval and modern sections of European cities, or cities in Europe and India.

Conurbations

During the 19th century in advanced industrial nations, and especially on coalfields with their close grouping of thriving mining and manufacturing towns, continued growth produced the *conurbation*. Economic expansion was accompanied by increase in both population and the built-up areas of the towns, the latter outpacing the former very markedly by the late 1800s. Many urban activities came to require more spacious sites than their earlier counterparts (a trend that has become even more intense during the present century), housing in particular: the increasingly affluent populations in these countries demanded better standards in housing, and the drop in average family size generated an additional component since more homes were now required for a given size of population than when larger families were the rule.

Thus where these expansionist trends occurred in closely neighbouring towns, frequently the built-up areas of each merged with one another, obliterating most of the open spaces which had once separated them. This, then, was the conurbation, dominated by one main city, but composed of many towns, some at least quite sizeable entities in their own right. Generally, however, civic identity is retained for local administration and, especially, for local loyalties among the populace. In Britain, the West Midlands and South Lancashire (see page 11) are examples, and in Germany the Ruhr (see page 35), but all advanced nations contain conurbations.

London

London represents a rather different kind of conurbation, the 'super-city' (other examples being New York, Paris, Tokyo). This results from the surge of growth in one pre-eminent city, overwhelming in its expansion a very large number of villages and small towns which had always been completely overshadowed in size by comparison with the main urban centre.

Up to 1850, as the map shows, London was still reasonably compact, with its chief development on the north bank of the Thames: the paucity of crossing places had hampered development south of the river, away from London's Roman and medieval nucleus (which coincided approximately with the present City of London). Beyond the built-up area in 1850 were small communities which in some cases had already become the homes of wealthy commuters. During the next sixty years, however, growth was extensive.

London's rôle as capital of nation and empire added several millions to its population in this period. But the physical expansion which this necessitated was no longer compact. An intensifying network of railways attracted growth around suburban stations, and the beginnings of the Underground system towards the turn of the century added to these trends. Other forms of surface public transport were also improving, and larger segments of the city's population were becoming able to afford not inconsiderable daily journeys to their work. After 1918 motor buses and cars made

travel even easier, many industrial and commercial activities moved to the suburbs from congested inner city locations (generating residential development around their new sites), slum clearance and re-housing programmes created vast new low-density municipal estates at increasing distances from central London, and private housing developments also added great increments to the total built-up area. Meanwhile, dormitory communities were attaching themselves to many outlying towns and villages, before they too became absorbed by the constant progress of urban sprawl. Checks were introduced by the creation of the Green Belt in 1935, by the effects of the Town and Country Planning Acts after the Second World War, and by the establishment of New Towns after 1946, but the conurbation still possesses remarkable economic and social vitality, largely frustrating attempts to constrain it.

Megalopolis

The north-eastern seaboard of the USA, first landfall of most European colonists, became the country's chief centre of economic activity and urbanisation from the outset. Despite subsequent developments elsewhere, this seaboard region between Boston and Washington DC has retained its dominance, to such an extent that though it comprises less than one-twentieth of the area of the USA it contains approximately 42 million people, one in five of the nation's population.

In terms of settlements, it is characterised first by a series of great conurbations, but there is also a dense scatter of other cities of all sizes, as the map shows. What the scale of the map does not allow, however, is to show the smaller communities, quasi-rural in nature, that act essentially as dormitories for the urban centres due to the ease of communication conferred by a complex, highly developed network of roads and, in places, commuter railway services. But the map does indicate that within the boundaries of this region vast tracts of non-urban land occur. Some of these are agricultural, with intensive and prosperous farming, for the most part geared to serving the needs of the region's urban dwellers (especially in milk and fresh vegetables and fruit); but much of the rest of the open land in Megalopolis is devoted to the recreational needs of the region's population, particularly the extensive forested areas of the central and northern Appalachians.

It is the extremely large territorial extent that exhibits such intimate and complicated integration between town and country that led Professor J. Gottmann to identify the whole region as a new and special phenomenon of urbanisation, and to use the word *Megalopolis* to denote it. Yet similar characteristics have by now emerged elsewhere: Chicago – Detroit – Buffalo – Toronto; south-east England – the Midlands – South Lancashire – West Riding of Yorkshire; and Tokyo – Nagoya – Osaka are but three other examples where megalopolitan features are clearly recognisable. The phenomenon cannot fail to multiply, because its essential bases continue to emerge; even planned decentralisation policies will not halt the process, as the dispersion of population and economic activities from major cities and conurbations only relocates them at no great distance away, promoting growth in the smaller urban constituents of a proto-megalopolis or, by creating New Towns, introducing new urban settlements into the open spaces of the region.

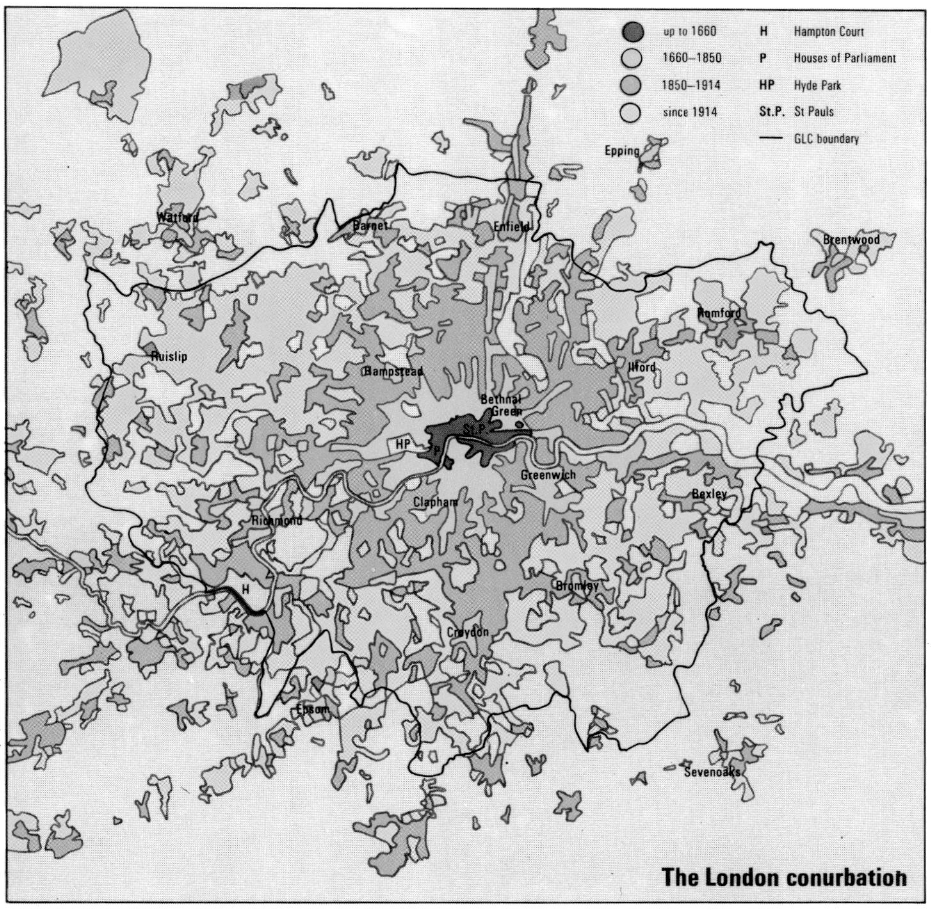

● up to 1660
● 1660–1850
● 1850–1914
● since 1914
H Hampton Court
P Houses of Parliament
HP Hyde Park
St.P. St Pauls
— GLC boundary

Epping · Watford · Barnet · Enfield · Brentwood · Ruislip · Hampstead · Ilford · Romford · Bethnal Green · St.P. · HP · Greenwich · Bexley · Clapham · Richmond · Bromley · Croydon · Cheam · Sevenoaks

The London conurbation

Fuel and Energy

The relentless increase in the demand of all nations for fuel and power raises important questions about the future security of world energy supplies. Energy consumption accelerates from decade to decade, driven onwards by the world's rising population, the industrialisation of more economies and improvements in living standards.

In the 30 years from 1970 the energy-producing industries will, on conservative estimates, be required to raise their output to four times the total world consumption from the start of the industrial era to the present day. Extra energy resources are almost as vital to world populations as the requirements for food. Indeed, increase in food production calls for increase in energy resources. Maintenance of present rates of economic growth necessitate increased supply of energy.

Energy output
Over the past two decades the increase in world output of energy has reflected both the dominant economic progress of the great industrialised countries and greater utilisation of mineral fuels and electrical power by developing nations.

Using the standard measure of million metric tons of coal equivalent (mtce), total world energy output in 1950 was a little over 2,600 mtce. Coal was the major primary energy source ahead of crude oil and natural gas. All three, supplemented by hydroelectric power, were used to make electricity. By the mid 1970s production had reached over 8,000 mtce and crude oil had taken over from coal as the most important energy source. Nuclear power and tiny amounts of geothermal power had

been introduced into the electricity generating systems. Most expert forecasters now project a global requirement of around 11,000 mtce by 1980 rising to over 20,000 mtce by the year 2000.

Energy consumption
The United States with her massive economic machine, is the largest single consumer of energy, aided by large resources of indigenous fossil fuels and the application of advanced technology to power production. By far the greater part of world energy resources is consumed by North America, the Soviet Union and Western Europe. In more recent years Japan has emerged as a leading consumer, multiplying her requirements six times since 1950 (see map).

Together, these areas account for over 80 per cent of world energy consumption but contain only 25 per cent of world population (see map on page 20). This imbalance, due to the concentration of manufacturing industry has occured over a long period during which the supply of fuel for energy has been relatively abundant.

Energy consumption per capita varies widely from country to country. Increasing industrialisation and application of new techniques to agriculture in the developing countries was, before 1974, beginning to disturb traditional patterns of energy use. However, the rapid increase in oil costs in the mid 1970s had made it difficult for the poorer nations to sustain the use of these new techniques.

Coal, oil, natural gas and water power are not always available in the areas where they are most needed. The result has been that fossil fuels

have had to be transported both within and between continents. This availability of fuel as an export commodity depends on those with indigenous resources – particularly crude oil – selling their surpluses.

Except for short periods of political crisis in the Middle East, supplies of crude oil have always matched or exceeded demand. By the mid-1980s, oil supply from the Middle East and Africa will have reached its peak. Unless the energy-importing nations develop alternative sources of power, an energy crisis with soaring prices could drastically reduce world economic growth.

Nearly all the large industrial countries are dependent on imported oil. The United States which was self-sufficient in the 1950s, imports half of its oil requirements. Higher energy costs make it economically feasible to explore for oil in the deep oceans and the polar regions and to develop the more expensive alternatives such as solar power, tidal and wind power and to consider the extraction of the oil locked in shale rocks and tar sands. The discovery of new sources of oil and the development of alternative forms of energy will not alone be enough to meet energy requirements. Nuclear power and coal are the only sources of energy which can serve as an alternative to oil in the 1980s should supply fall short of world demand.

Oil
The organic remains of the earliest plant, marine and animal life that existed between 400 million and 40 million years ago are the sources of the crude oil deposits now tapped by man to meet

over 40 per cent of the world's total energy requirements. Early civilisations made use of bitumen and lubricants, but it was not until the middle of the 19th century that the first oil wells were drilled.

Total world production of crude oil and natural gas liquids in 1976 amounted to 2,936 million tonnes, the equivalent of 59,555,000 barrels a day. The map of oil supply shows that the western hemisphere accounts for 26·3 per cent of total output compared with 73·7 per cent for the eastern hemisphere (including the 21 per cent share accounted for by the Soviet Union, Eastern Europe and China).

The Middle East, North America, Africa and the Soviet Union are the major producing regions. In recent years, a succession of discoveries has begun to widen the basis of supply. The newer sources of oil include Arctic Alaska, the northern part of the North Sea, the Spanish sector of the Mediterranean, Ecuador, Mexico, Australia, Indonesia, Turkey and parts of South America.

The present estimate of proven reserves is 90,066 million tonnes. The ratio between these reserves and annual production is falling as the rate of discovery of new oil reservoirs around the world slows down. Of the proven quantity, 56 per cent is in the Middle East, nearly 9 per cent in Africa, over 16 per cent in the USSR, Eastern Europe and China, and 6 per cent in North America. Western Europe, because of the oil discoveries in the North Sea, now has nearly 4 per cent of the total. The geographic balance of the proven reserves is 12 per cent for the western hemisphere and 88 per cent for the eastern.

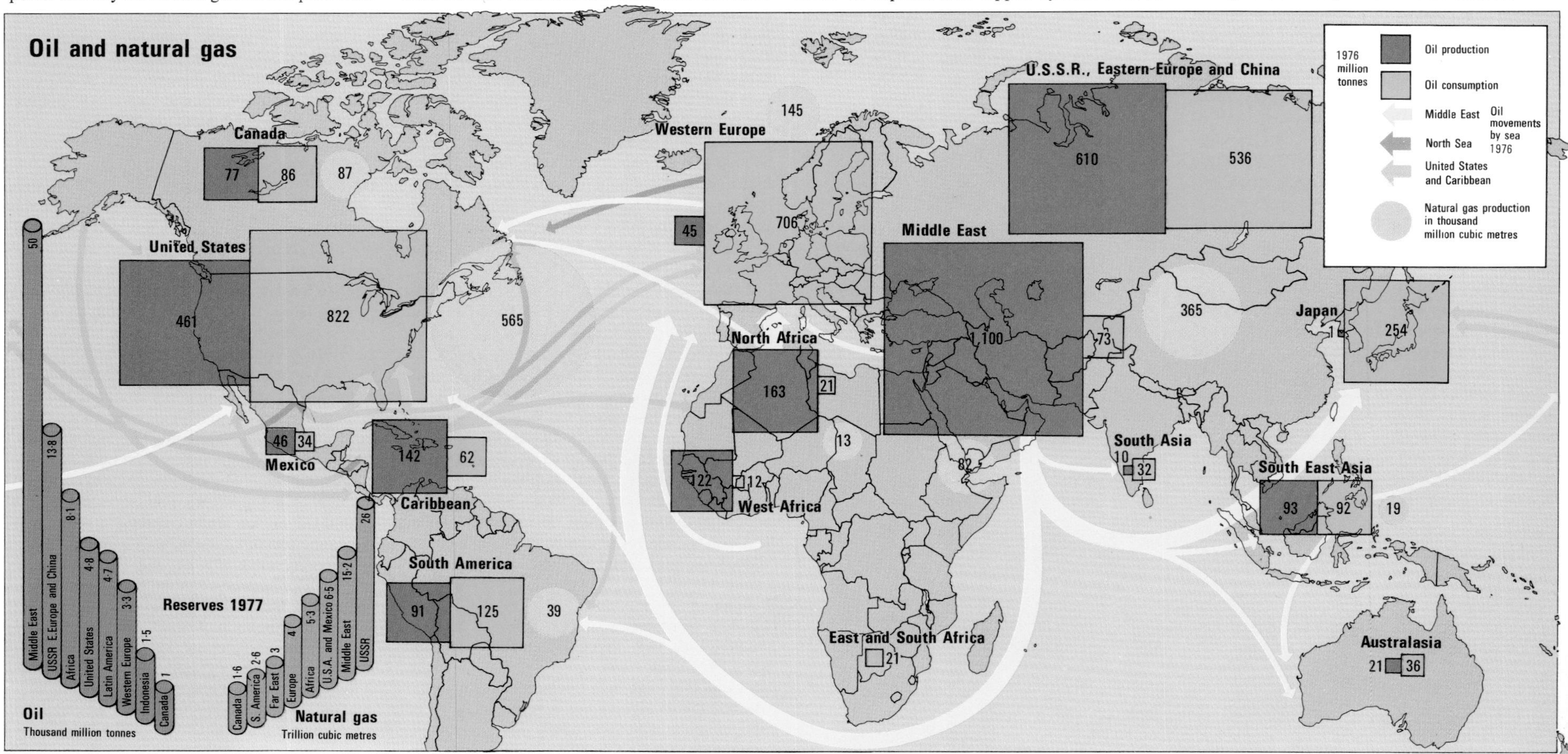

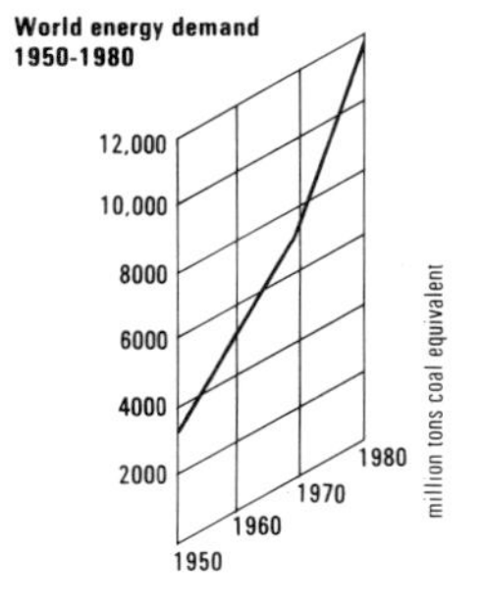

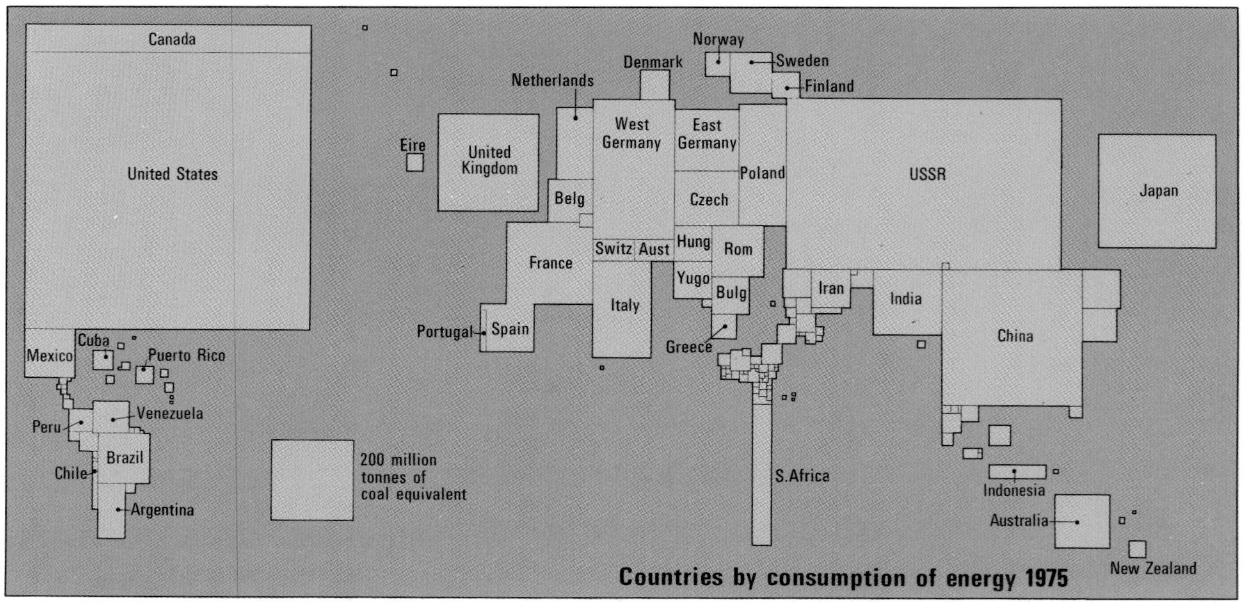

Countries by consumption of energy 1975

Energy consumption
Expressed in the standard measure of tonnes of coal equivalent, the world's demand for primary energy has attained a level of at least 7,000 million tce.

On current trends, projected future growth indicates a need for 11,000 million tce by the end of the present decade. All forms of energy will be required to make a high contribution, though oil is expected to remain the leading source. As the map illustrating the importance of oil to the world economy shows, annual consumption has reached over 2,936 million tonnes, and output more than 2,994 million tonnes; the balance represents stocks. This requires large-scale movements of crude oil and oil products between continents by sea and by pipeline.

More than \$550,000 million will be required by the world oil industry in the coming decade to pay for exploration and development. The search for new sources ranges from the Arctic to the Yellow Sea, South China Sea and from north Africa to offshore south America. The emergence of economic nationalism in the Middle East, and the use of the price of oil as a political weapon that has disturbed traditional marketing, has coincided with the transformation of the United States from the status of oil exporter to oil importer. As unlimited oil imports into the 1980s cannot be assured, the United States is trying to reduce its imports from 9 million barrels a day in 1977 to 6 million a day in 1985, by stimulating domestic production and converting from oil to coal in many power stations. Without these measures imports of over 12 million barrels a day would be required in the 1980s to meet a demand of about 20 million barrels a day. In Western Europe demand could also double over the same period to a similar amount and Japanese oil requirements could increase from under 4 million barrels a day to over 10 million barrels a day.

Coal

World output of coal amounts to over 2,200 million tonnes a year. The leading industrialised countries of Western Europe produce over 300 million tonnes a year – equivalent to the total power station requirements of the United States where coal production totals about 550 million tonnes a year. Production of lignite, is nearly 767,000 tonnes a year. The main producers are East and West Germany and the USSR.

Coal is the fuel on which the industrial base of Europe and America was built. Cheap oil supplies in the 1950s and 1960s brought a sharp decline in production particularly in the older mining areas of Europe and North America. The prospect of a shortfall in oil supplies, coupled with difficulties in the development of nuclear power has brought new life to the coal industry. Fresh reserves are being developed in the United States and Europe. There are massive reserves of coal in the Soviet Union, North America and China.

These coal reserves are extremely large and sufficient to sustain international needs for at least 250 years on present projections of productive activity. Known economic reserves amount to one million million tonnes of which about 430,000 million tonnes could be mined under the prices and technology that are likely to exist in the 1970s and 1980s. Rates of extraction could be stepped up by improvements in mining techniques.

Only deposits that have been drilled and sampled are included in known reserves. Estimates do not include coal possibly existing in areas geologically favourable for the presence of coal. Ultimate global coal reserves probably exceed eight million million tonnes.

Natural gas

Natural gas, of which methane is the main constituent, is a highly efficient fuel now making an increasing contribution to energy resources. It produces twice the heat of town gas, is generally free of sulphur, and offers clean combustion.

Natural gas was first used in the United States in centres of population close to the gas fields. In Europe most gas was manufactured from coal. The change-over to natural gas came in the 1950s and 1960s with the discovery of reserves in France, Italy and in Holland. Britain is supplied from fields off the coast of East Anglia and from reserves in the northern part of the North Sea.

For decades large quantities of gas produced in association with oil was burned off because there was no way of moving it to the industrial centres. Development of long distance pipelining techniques and the movement of gas in liquefied form has opened up a small world trade in gas.

At the end of 1976 it was estimated that natural gas reserves round the world amounted to 2,325 million million cubic feet, with heavy concentrations in North America, the USSR and Asia.

Nuclear power

High hopes have been placed in the development of nuclear energy to provide the world with a new source of cheap and abundant power. Problems associated with the initial heavy costs of proving the first nuclear power stations against stiff competition from coal and oil have been overcome. Development is now being checked by opposition from environmentalists concerned at the safety aspects of reactors and the possibility that wider sales of nuclear power stations and their associated fuel enrichment and reprocessing facilities could lead to the proliferation of nuclear weapons.

Opposition is strongest in the United States and is reflected in the long delays in obtaining the necessary Government permits for new reactors. In 1977 there were 66 reactors operating in the USA with a capacity of 41,544 megawatts (9·4 per cent of total capacity). There are a further 142 reactors either under construction or planned.

France has one of the most ambitious nuclear power programmes. It plans to augment its network of 11 reactors producing 9 per cent of the nation's electricity, with 26 new reactors to produce over 70 per cent by 1985.

Development of nuclear power requires new techniques of production and control and fresh supplies of uranium. In non-Communist bloc countries, annual demand for uranium could reach 53,500 tonnes by 1980, roughly in line with production facilities. Reserves are two million tonnes reasonably capable of being recovered on present estimates of prices and demand.

Hydro-Electricity

The building of great dams, tidal barriers and other forms of man-made controls over sea and fresh waters have assisted in the slow but steady development of hydro-electrical generation. Areas well endowed with water resources have already benefited from one of the cheapest sources of power but opportunities for new hydro-electrical projects are limited.

The world's hydro-electricity represents one quarter of total electrical energy supplied – nearly twice as much as output from nuclear power stations. The big producers are North America and the Soviet Union, but within Europe hydroelectric stations are a major source of electricity. Scandinavia and Switzerland have the most highly developed water-power resources, followed by Italy and France.

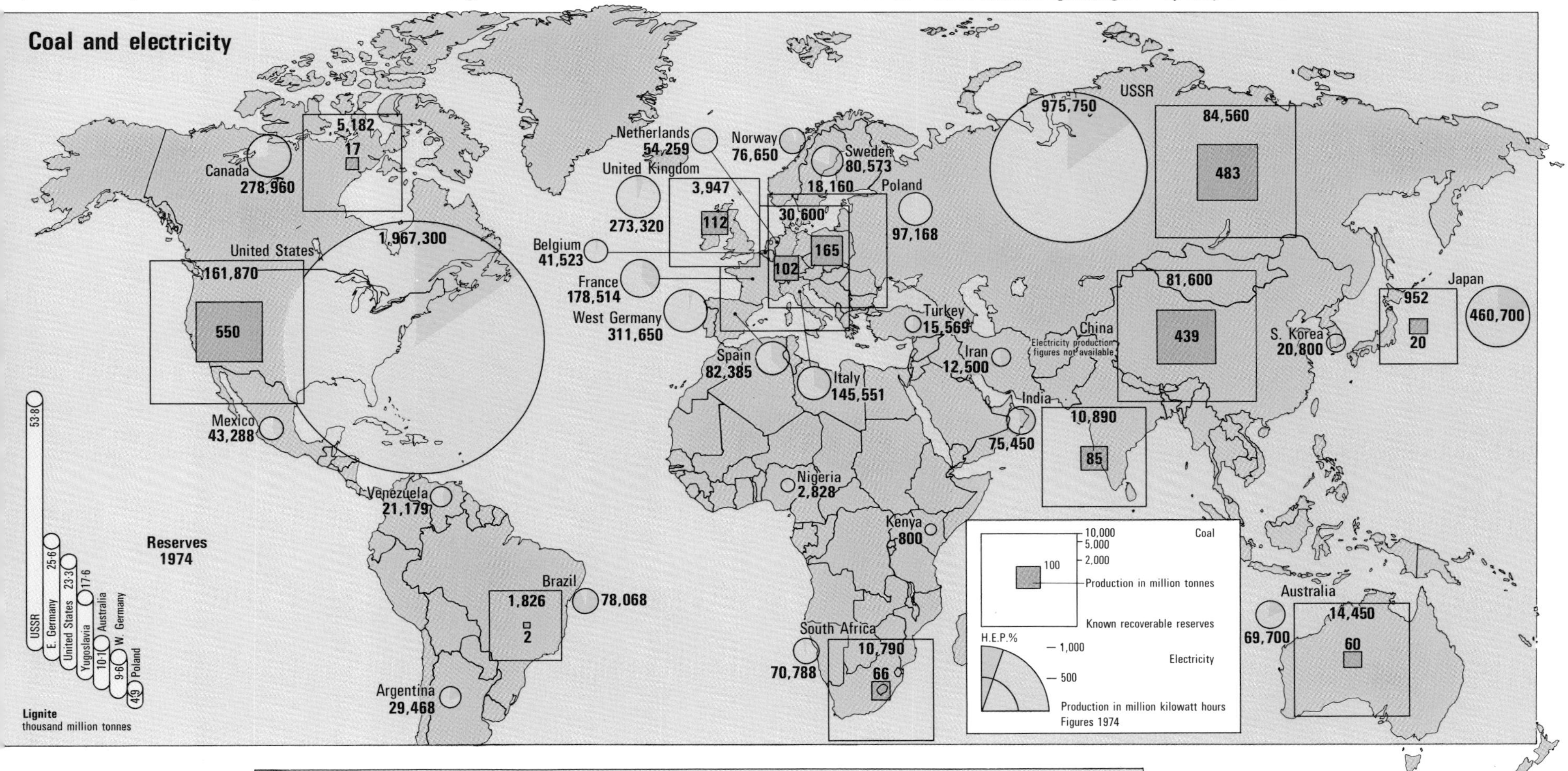

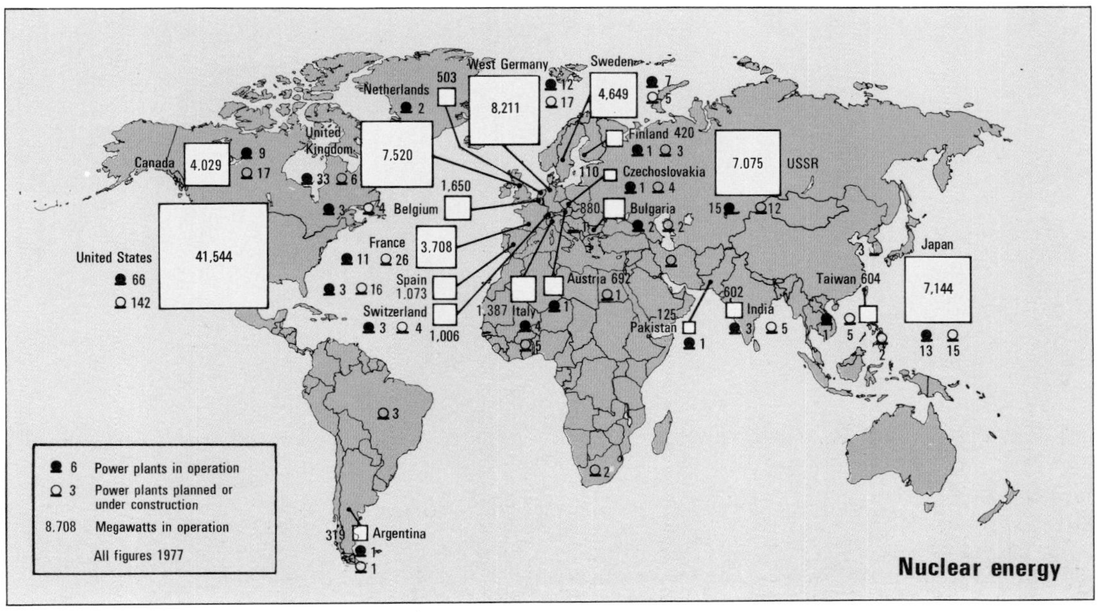

Nuclear energy

In 1977 there were 192 nuclear reactors in operation in 21 countries throughout the world with a capacity of 93,261 megawatts. A further seven countries have plans to become nuclear power producers. A total of 306 new reactors are either under construction or planned.

The quest for new forms of energy has also re-awakened interest in using geothermal power – hot steam from great depths below the earth's surface – to produce electricity. Italy leads the world in this field and has geothermal power stations with a capacity of 2,503 megawatts. There are also geothermal developments in the United States, Mexico, Japan and Iceland.

New needs, new sources

Great emphasis is now being placed on development of alternative sources of energy such as solar power, wind power and harnessing the energy contained in the tides. Although cheap to operate, the cost of developing efficient renewable energy systems is high and these sources are unlikely to make a significant contribution until the beginning of the next century.

Scientists are also working on prototype nuclear reactors that 'breed' more nuclear fuel than they consume, which would extend the life of world uranium reserves. Research is under way into the production of oil from coal, shale rocks and heavy tar sands, and into more effective and cleaner ways of burning coal in industry and in power stations. Even further into the future, scientists are working on ways to release energy from the hydrogen in sea water by the process of nuclear fusion. There is also a method of collecting solar energy by artificial satellite and transmitting it to Earth in the form of micro-waves.

Manufacturing industry

The wealth and economic influence of the world's richest nation, the United States of America, is derived from her factories and process plant. Although Europe has been the cradle of the industrial revolution, the New World has produced fresh concepts of manufacturing and the organisation of labour, establishing a chain of production and supply to which all advancing nations aspire, to raise their standards of material well-being. Whole new technologies have resulted from the constant application of the sciences to manufacturing. The consequence has been a worldwide urge to extract more materials to feed by mining or cultivation the industrial machines of all nations seeking to generate the economic wealth required to sustain their populations.

In the 20th century the determinants of economic power have been transformed. This transformation has been greatly affected by two world wars and periodic economic recessions. In the past few decades the rapid expansion in demand for material welfare and economic prosperity have brought an increase in world output of primary and secondary products to levels that have changed the living standards of whole populations. Wherever and however far back the roots of manufacturing, the fastest growth of production has taken place since the mid-fifties as nations embraced more productive concepts, selling their goods to each other and often specialising according to their indigenous skills or resources.

Manufacturing areas

The geographic concentration of world manufacturing power is well illustrated by the selected maps, which include crude steel production and motor vehicle engineering. The most striking development has been a significant shift of manufacturing power towards the Far East, related to the growth of industry in Japan and south-east Asia as well as the industrialisation of mainland China. However, this trend towards a wider distribution of industry has yet to show itself in Africa, the Middle East and to most of South America, areas which largely remain, in industrial terms, that of suppliers of raw materials and food.

Other important features reflected by the maps and in the closely related sections on world trade and energy supply are the re-emergence of Western Europe in the second half of this century, challenging the dominance of North America in global industry, and the establishment of the Soviet Union as a major industrialised nation. In steel manufacture, the Soviet Union and Japan have become main producers, though the former has yet to develop a substantial motor industry.

Textiles, electrical assembly, steel manufacturing, shipbuilding, and car production are now firmly established in the Far East, where output of certain goods has assumed dimensions of world importance in terms both of volume and commercial competitiveness.

Manufacturing growth

The most spectacular growth of production has taken place since the start of the 1960s, for by 1970 manufacturing output on a world basis had expanded by over 50 per cent, that for extractive industries by over 40 per cent, and these are to be compared with around 20 per cent for agricultural production.

Powering this industrial advance have been the factories and plant of North America, Western Europe and Japan. The installations grouped within the western trading nations have consequently lifted the gross domestic product by an average of nearly 5 per cent a year between 1960 and 1970.

The Western Nations, along with the Soviet Union, have made the major contribution to the world's increasing manufacturing capacity. That capacity, as reflected by actual output between 1960 and 1970, shows the following percentage rises in volume terms: light manufacturing 43 per cent; heavy manufacturing 58 per cent; food and drink 48 per cent; textiles 44 per cent; clothing and footwear 27 per cent; furniture and timber products 30 per cent; paper and printing 30 per cent; chemicals and fuel 95 per cent; basic metals 70 per cent; metal products 81 per cent.

Material possessions are greatest in the most industrialised nations. Using the measure of 1,000 inhabitants (taking no account of family groupings), there are over 523 telephones in the United States, 408 in Canada, and well over 200 in Japan and the United Kingdom, whereas Portugal has around 70 and Turkey only 12. With the same unit, there are around 400 television sets for the United States, over 260 for the United Kingdom, 200 in Japan and about 300 in Sweden, which enjoys one of the highest material standards of living.

The motor industry

The desire to own cars and replace them with new models has created one of the greatest and most economically important industries in the world consuming vast quantities of steel and other materials and providing the backbone to satellite engineering industries. World car output has now over 25 million units with North America's huge assembly lines producing nearly a quarter and Western Europe and Japan much of the remainder. Assembly plants using imported vehicle components have sprung up in the developing world where demand has yet to be matched by the personal affluence needed to attain widespread ownership.

The significance of the motor manufacturing industry is reflected in the fact that many of the production companies have become the biggest corporations in the world. The second largest, General Motors of America, commands sales of over 35 billion dollars per year and has assets worth $21 billion. The largest of all is an oil and petroleum refining group, the Exxon Corporation whose supplies of oil to manufacturing industry are as important as the petrol needed to power car engines. United States motorists buy over 8 million new cars each year attracting imports from Western Europe and Japan, which has now built itself into the second largest manufacturer in the world, and the largest exporter. Overseas sales by Japanese manufacturers in 1974 totalled 1·8 million vehicles worth $3·5 billion. Japan now dominates the market for the small and medium car in most developing countries and has begun to make similar inroads into the European markets. Japanese dominance of the motor cycle industry is even more pronounced and in some European countries domestic producers have gone out of business in the face of Japanese imports.

In addition to passenger cars, commercial vehicles of all kinds from giant railer trucks and earth-moving equipment to farm tractors and delivery vans are produced in growing quantities. Annually the United States alone makes over 6,700,000 passenger cars and over two million vehicles other than cars. In Western Europe, France was the largest producer of passenger cars in 1975 with 2,951,000 units.

Steel

Like motor manufacturing, steel is an industry that is largely confined to the developed countries of the world. Three countries, the USA, the USSR and Japan, account for over half world production which in 1976 topped 661 million tonnes. Most European countries have steel industries. In Japan the growth of the steel industry

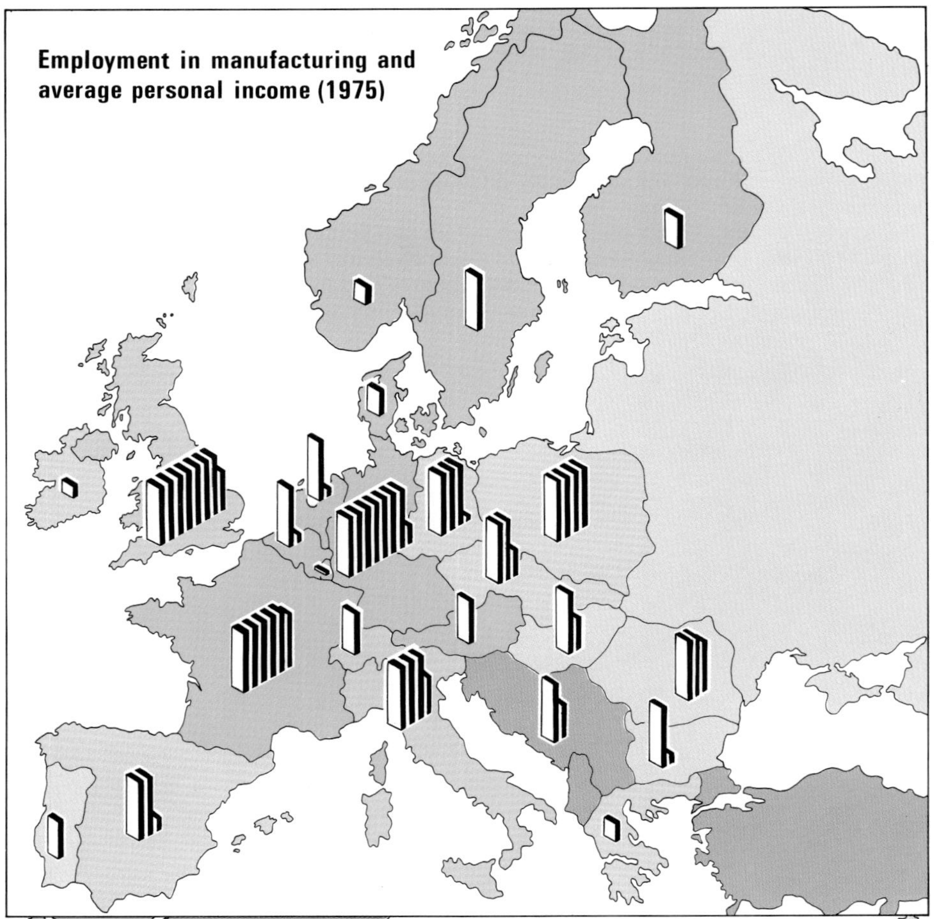

Employment in manufacturing and average personal income (1975)

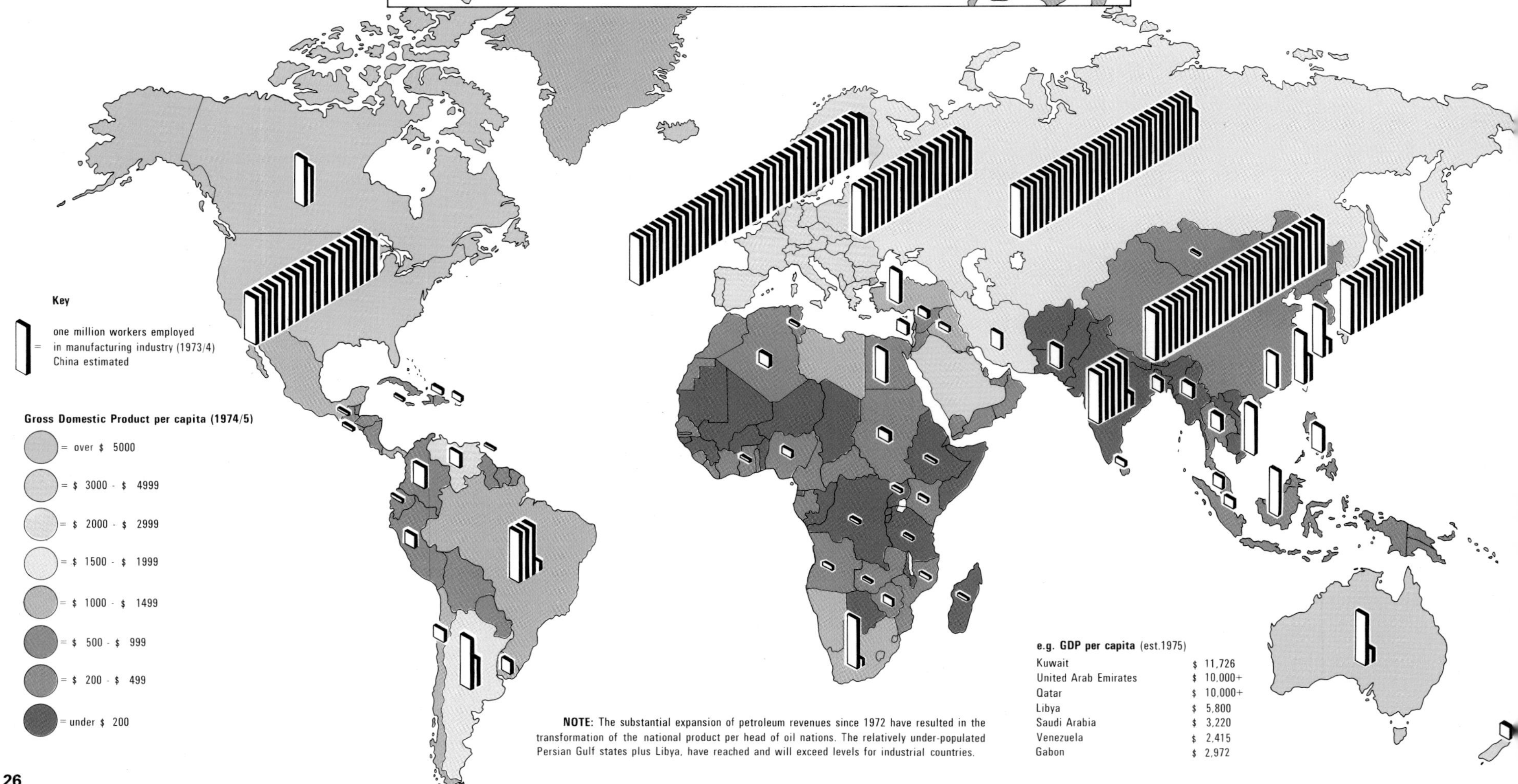

Key

= one million workers employed in manufacturing industry (1973/4) China estimated

Gross Domestic Product per capita (1974/5)

- = over $ 5000
- = $ 3000 - $ 4999
- = $ 2000 - $ 2999
- = $ 1500 - $ 1999
- = $ 1000 - $ 1499
- = $ 500 - $ 999
- = $ 200 - $ 499
- = under $ 200

NOTE: The substantial expansion of petroleum revenues since 1972 have resulted in the transformation of the national product per head of oil nations. The relatively under-populated Persian Gulf states plus Libya, have reached and will exceed levels for industrial countries.

e.g. GDP per capita (est.1975)	
Kuwait	$ 11,726
United Arab Emirates	$ 10,000+
Qatar	$ 10,000+
Libya	$ 5,800
Saudi Arabia	$ 3,220
Venezuela	$ 2,415
Gabon	$ 2,972

has paralleled that of its motor manufacturers. Since 1960 Japan has more than trebled its steel output using the very latest giant, continuous process mills and modern furnaces to make products so cheaply that they can be sold across oceans at prices keenly competitive with locally produced steel.

During the period 1970 to 1975 the regional share of world production changed significantly. North America's share decreased by 3½%, and that of Western Europe by 4%. Despite Japanese growth, Asia's share of world production increased by only 2¼% during the five years. The greatest increase was that of the USSR and Eastern Europe with over 7% growth.

World trade in steel products of all kinds has risen more than five-fold since the beginning of the 1950s with the pattern of supply shifting according to competitive conditions as well as to such factors as deep water ports to take the largest bulk ore carriers. These are now being constructed in many parts of the world.

Shipbuilding

Japanese shipbuilders have also benefitted from the availability of cheap steel just as a well organised steel industry led to the building of a thriving motor industry. Launchings from Japanese yards in 1973 totalled well over 16·5 million tonnes of shipping compared with about three million tonnes by each of the other main shipbuilding nations, Germany, Sweden and Norway. The fortunes of the world's shipbuilders were based on an apparently unending demand for more and larger oil tankers. But after oil prices quadrupled in 1973 and 1974 the world demand for oil declined sharply. Millions of tonnes of tankers left without cargoes were laid up indefinitely. The flow of orders for new tonnage practically ceased. As a response to these changing forces shipbuilders have drastically pruned their work forces and production facilities and are looking carefully at a variety of new uses for the shipyards such as building oil platforms or even prefabricated houses.

The world steel industry

Geographic shift in world production

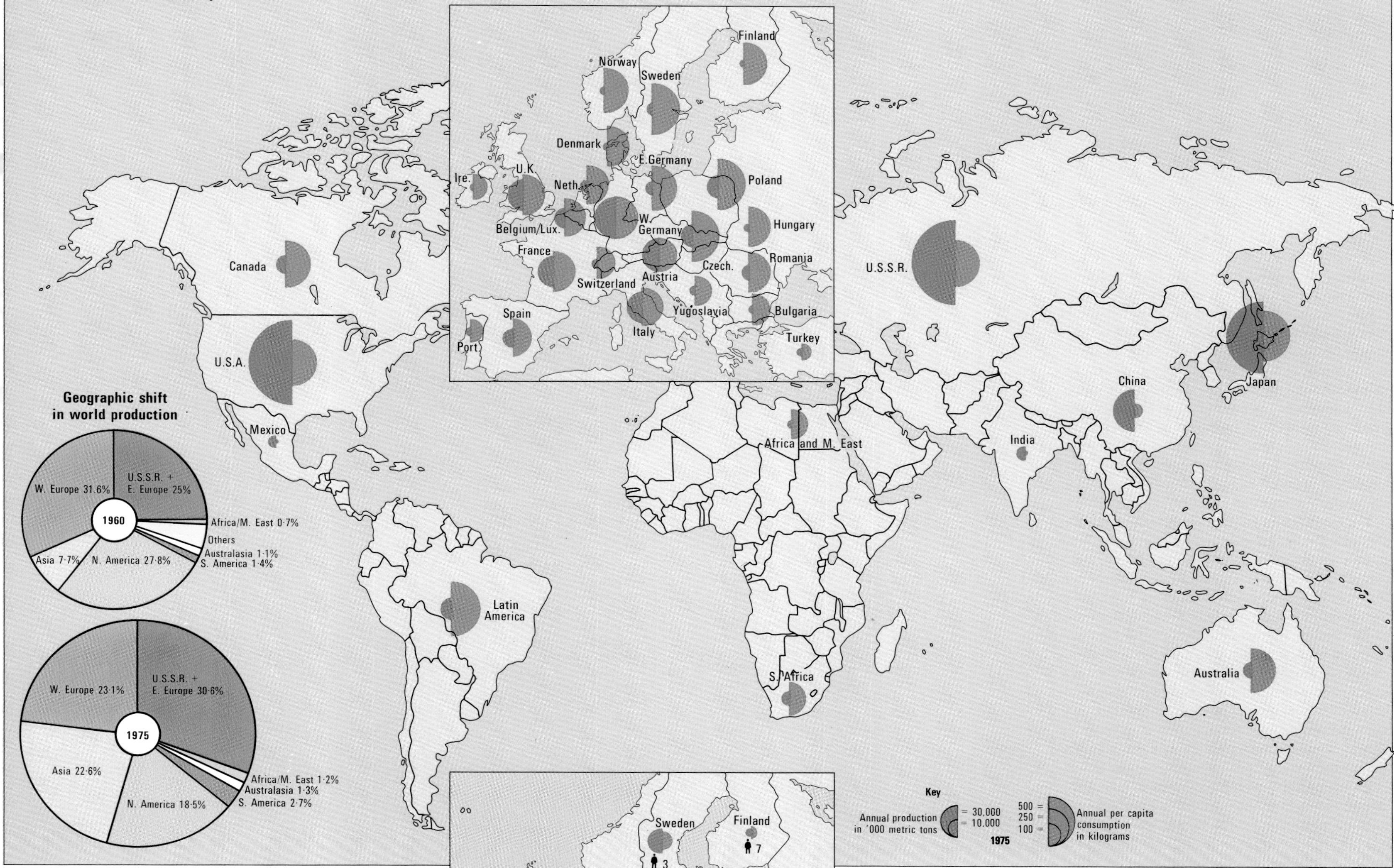

The world car industry

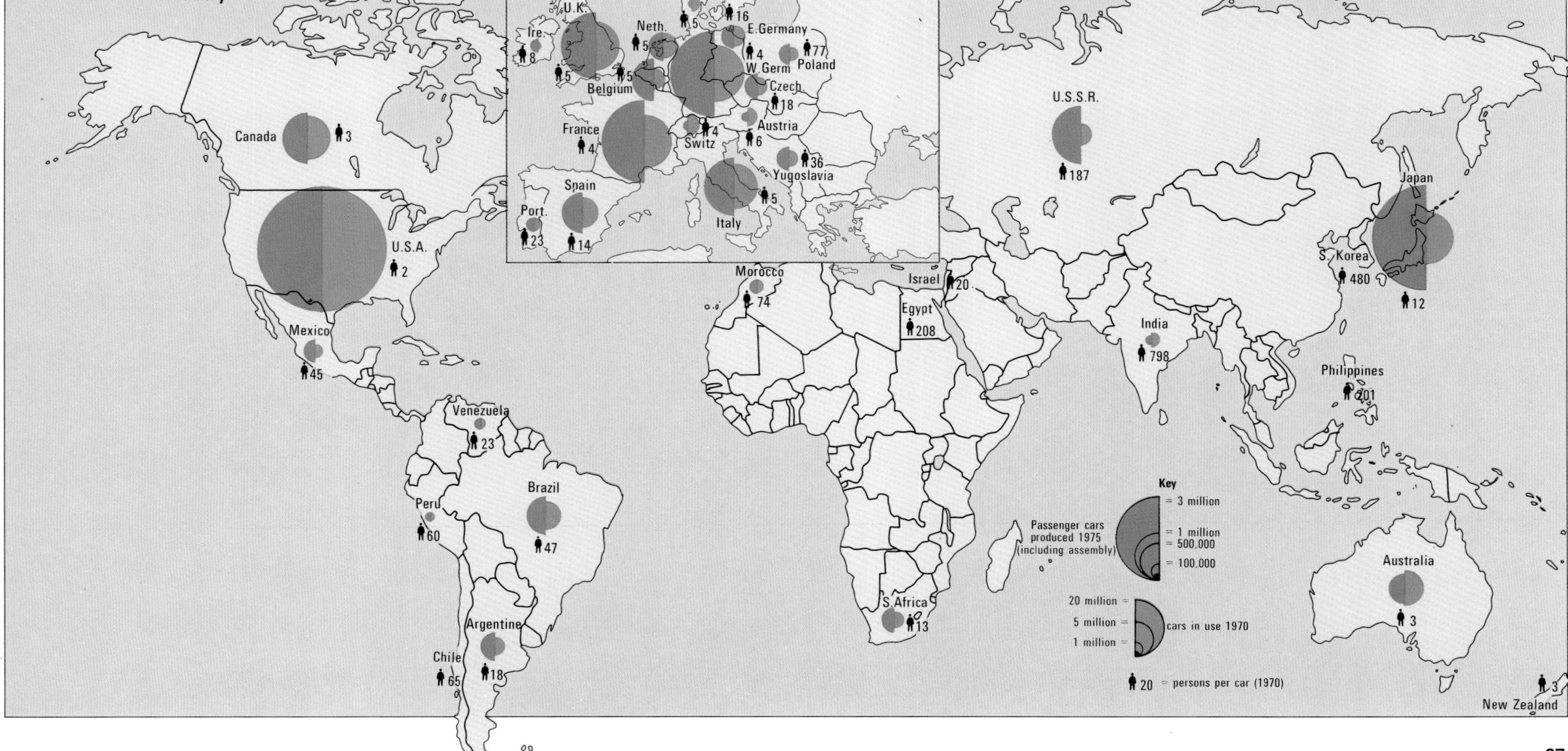

The trade of the U.S.A.

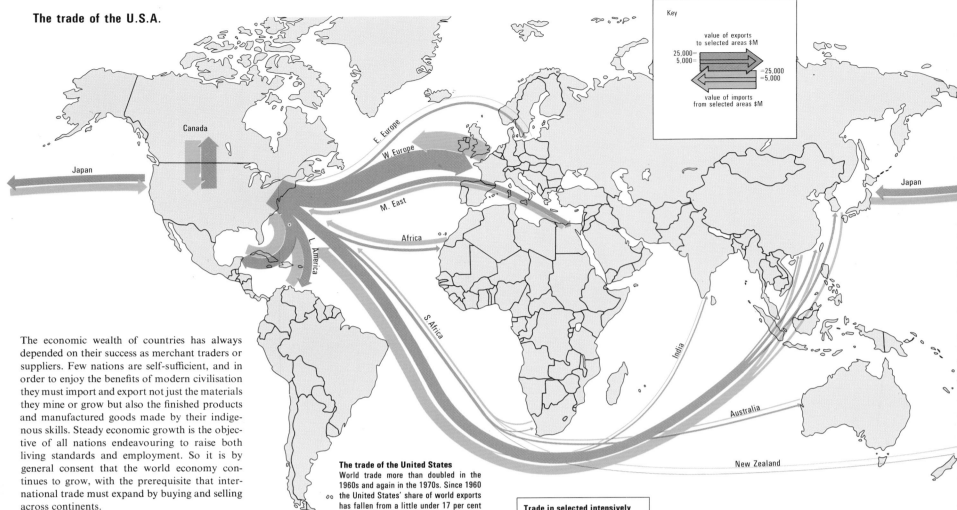

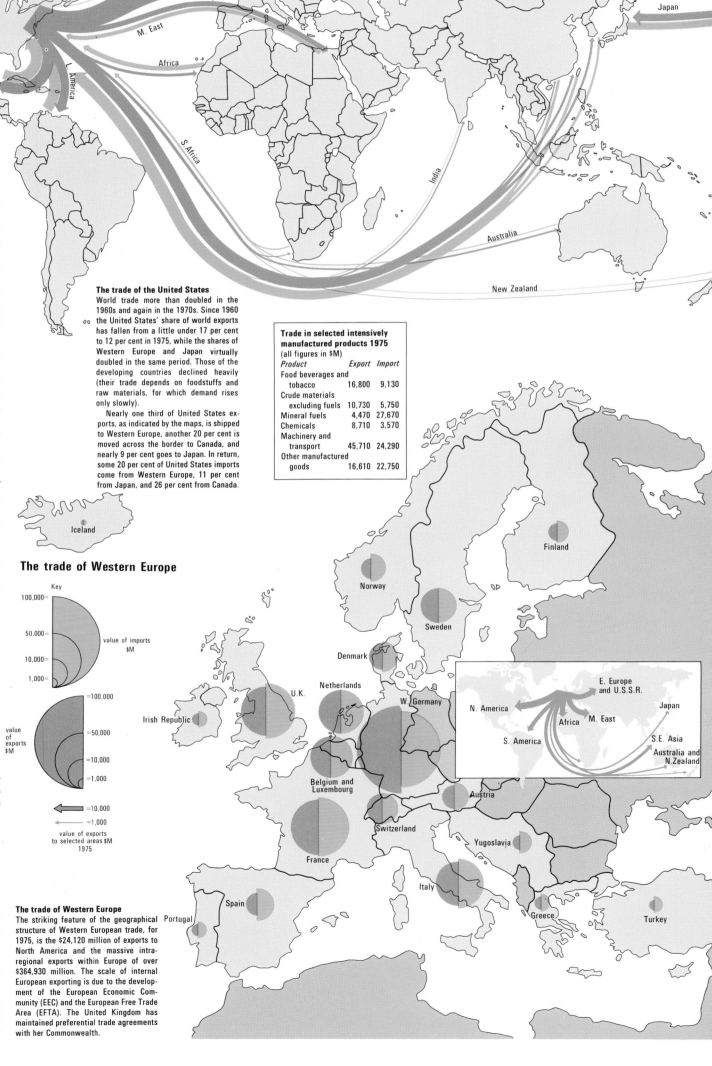

The economic wealth of countries has always depended on their success as merchant traders or suppliers. Few nations are self-sufficient, and in order to enjoy the benefits of modern civilisation they must import and export not just the materials they mine or grow but also the finished products and manufactured goods made by their indigenous skills. Steady economic growth is the objective of all nations endeavouring to raise both living standards and employment. So it is by general consent that the world economy continues to grow, with the prerequisite that international trade must expand by buying and selling across continents.

The mechanisms that move goods and materials farther, faster and in greater quantities year by year are highly complex. Vast sums of currency can be transmitted in seconds by a telephone call from one end of the world to the other, facilitating the shipment of iron ore from Western Australia to Rotterdam or ensuring that an oil or grain cargo on the high seas can be diverted to meet the emergency need of a customer. News of a crop failure in the Far East can send commodity markets into a turmoil of price changes that radically alter the pattern of demand. An expansion of mass production capacity in a major manufacture can transform sources of supply of materials.

Co-operation between governments and their merchant traders and manufacturers has not reduced the competitive spirit necessary for trade to flourish. The rapid rise in the volume of world trade in recent decades, the greater scale of capital movements from nation to nation and also the emergence of multinational companies and agencies have, nevertheless, made national economies more interdependent. Political sovereignty often masks the dependence of countries one on another as traders or suppliers. Technology, worldwide standardisation of man's material needs, a growing demand for the Earth's natural resources and the application of new agricultural and industrial methods have served to promote the expansion in world trade.

The capacity of nations to import to meet the requirements of their citizens, rises as living standards – measured in material possessions and services – improve. But nations that buy must have means to pay: an acceptable form of payment may be goods for barter or money that is convertible according to the importer's economic strength. All international trading nations need to balance their books, and the task of central bankers in keeping international trade flowing is crucial. The financial systems are as vital as communications. Their effectiveness is the preoccupation of economists and bankers round the world.

Industrialisation
The rebuilding of economies after the second world war has been characterised by rapid industrialisation, much under United States leadership, and the wider spread of economic nationalism created with the birth of many new nations once heavily dependent on American, British or French mercantile power and political rule. Efficiency in mass production and technological competence have a profound effect on the nature and routing of world trade. The rebuilding of

The trade of the United States
World trade more than doubled in the 1960s and again in the 1970s. Since 1960 the United States' share of world exports has fallen from a little under 17 per cent to 12 per cent in 1975, while the shares of Western Europe and Japan virtually doubled in the same period. Those of the developing countries declined heavily (their trade depends on foodstuffs and raw materials, for which demand rises only slowly).

Nearly one third of United States exports, as indicated by the maps, is shipped to Western Europe, another 20 per cent is moved across the border to Canada, and nearly 9 per cent goes to Japan. In return, some 20 per cent of United States imports come from Western Europe, 11 per cent from Japan, and 26 per cent from Canada.

Trade in selected intensively manufactured products 1975
(all figures in $M)

Product	Export	Import
Food beverages and tobacco	16,800	9,130
Crude materials excluding fuels	10,730	5,750
Mineral fuels	4,470	27,670
Chemicals	8,710	3,570
Machinery and transport	45,710	24,290
Other manufactured goods	16,610	22,750

The trade of Western Europe

The trade of Western Europe
The striking feature of the geographical structure of Western European trade, for 1975, is the $24,120 million of exports to North America and the massive intra-regional exports within Europe of over $364,930 million. The scale of internal European exporting is due to the development of the European Economic Community (EEC) and the European Free Trade Area (EFTA). The United Kingdom has maintained preferential trade agreements with her Commonwealth.

the Japanese and German economies has been accomplished by each country devoting a high proportion of its national efforts to selling their goods in world markets.

While the United States still accounts for 40 per cent of the non-communist world's production, the European Economic Community and Japan have become major centres of economic power and pace-setters for competition in international markets. Half the world's seaborne tanker and dry cargo shipments are now unloaded in Western Europe, and more than a quarter discharges in the Far East, with Japan at the centre of activity.

Japan

If present patterns of growth stay as they are, the Japanese may surpass the Soviet Union's output in the next 25 years and draw close to that of the United States. In the 15 years from 1960 she has doubled her share of world exports to reach over 7 per cent. Her rate of growth in world trade is about twice as fast as the international average. A substantial competitive endeavour in world markets – she is a leading exporter of ships, electrical goods, fish and motor vehicles – is vital to pay for heavy imports. Japan has to buy half her raw materials abroad to fuel her growth.

United States

With the largest economy in the world and a currency essential for the effective financing of continent-to-continent trade, the USA contributed a vast sum of her national wealth to rebuilding the war-torn countries of the western world. This has required running a balance of payments deficit in virtually every year since the end of the forties. These deficits are now growing to unmanageable proportions. Unlike the industrial countries of Europe and Japan, the United States until the late 1960s, had been self-sufficient in crude oil. The entry of the USA into the world oil markets has helped to trigger the huge increases in oil prices. With over 40 per cent of US oil requirements met from foreign sources in 1977, the true deficit suddenly rose to $40 billion from only $5 billion in the previous year.

The trade of Japan

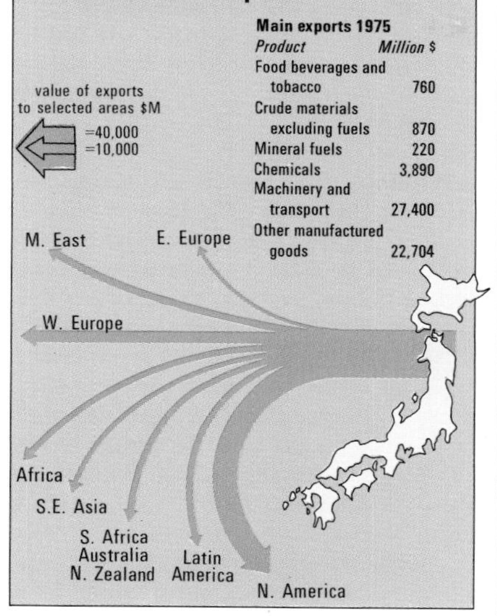

Main exports 1975

value of exports to selected areas $M

=40,000
=10,000

Product	Million $
Food beverages and tobacco	760
Crude materials excluding fuels	870
Mineral fuels	220
Chemicals	3,890
Machinery and transport	27,400
Other manufactured goods	22,704

The geographical distribution of Japan's exports is an interesting feature of contemporary world trade. She maintains a firm relationship with industrialised markets and developing regions.

About 22 per cent of Japanese exports by value were sent to the USA and Canada in 1975. A further 14·5 per cent went to the markets of South East Asia and the Middle East, 8 per cent to Africa and 8·5 per cent to Latin America. Western Europe took 14·5 per cent of her exports, while Australasia received 1·5 per cent, and Eastern Europe 4 per cent.

Japan's exports in 1975 were $55,844 million compared with $19,318 million in 1970 and $4,050 million in 1960.

In the 15 years from 1960 to 1975 United States imports from Japan surged from just over one billion dollars to over 11 billion dollars. Initially Japanese imports of US goods lagged well behind but now US exports in 1975 totalled $9·35 billion – halving the deficit of a few years previously.

For 35 years the USA has sought to reduce artificial barriers to international trade, culminating in the famous Kennedy Round of tariff reductions of the sixties. Her gross domestic product is now annually exceeding $1,000 billion, making the nation the richest in the world. Exports in 1976 totalled over $107 billion. Huge sums are transferred every year to developing countries in aid and investment along with human skills and technology. Additionally, the world's most powerful single economy carries a disproportionate share of western defence costs. The attainment of American accord with China and further development of trade with the USSR are seen as the most encouraging factors for the future of international economic co-operation.

Western Europe

The nations of Western Europe are the most potent force in world mercantile trade. Their exports have risen from $52 billion in 1960 to $295 billion by 1976, led during this period by the EEC founder members and the nations of the former European Free Trade Area.

Enlargement of the EEC to 9 nations has provided an economic grouping with a GDP of around $1,000 billion, fast approaching that of the United States ($1,295 billion in 1973). EEC exports in 1973, including intra-area trade, were valued as $210 billion, $149 billion going to countries outside the Community. Her merchant fleet is four times the size of the USA's, and vehicle output is nearly 10 million units annually.

The growth of European exporting power has been equally spectacular, assisted greatly by American-inspired reductions in import tariffs, direct financial aid for industrial reconstruction, and the transfer of technological know-how.

The result has been a transformation of monetary power as well as industrial strength. This has reduced the role of the American dollar and the British pound sterling in supplying the foreign exchange for the finance of world trade. The dollar, of course, remains the standard common currency for the convertibility of money. But this has required new alignments of exchange values to ensure that national monies reflect the strength of nations as international traders as well as the size of their gross national product and stocks of gold.

World trade

An International Monetary Fund helps central bankers to keep money working as hard as the aircraft and ships that ply between markets. United Nations agencies, organisations set up for economic co-operation, and a network of commodity arrangements framed for orderly marketing of essential materials have all been the means for averting chaos and correcting the economic disruption that market forces may create. Whatever the periodic difficulties, such as monetary and materials crises or unfair trade practices, the overall achievement has been the expansion of the volume of world trade by 10 per cent every year to the end of the sixties.

This growth, the aid to international economic development, has not corrected the imbalance between rich and poor countries. In the sixties, the export trade of industrialised countries grew by about 164 per cent, that of developing nations by only 99 per cent. This disparity reflects the rapid growth of trade between developed countries due to the creation of special groups of countries with mutually advantageous arrangements for economic expansion. The EEC and EFTA have been prime examples where intra-group exports have risen sharply.

Prior to enlargement, the EEC was assessed as supplying 29 per cent of world exports, but in fact, half the trade was conducted between the member nations. The disparity can be illustrated by the fact that trade among the main industrial countries of the world grew from $54 billion in 1960 to $161 billion in 1970, while that between developing countries and the industrial countries went up from $19 billion to $40 billion.

Record rates of inflation, higher oil payments and the demise of fixed exchange rates cast their shadow over world trade midway through the seventies. The total value of world exports in 1975 was $567 billion compared with $312 billion in 1970 and $128 billion in 1960. This impressive figure must be treated with caution, for it reflects a sustained world-wide rise in prices, in particular the huge increase in oil bills.

The trade of the developing areas

Key

value of imports $M 1975

=30,000
=10,000
=1,000

value of exports $M 1975

=20,000
=4,000

value of exports f.o.b. to selected trading areas from each region $M 1975

The trade of the developing areas

Less developed countries, though traditionally suppliers of raw materials and foodstuffs, are increasingly engaging in manufacturing. Manufactures still constitute less than a quarter of total exports of developing countries, but they are growing at the rate of about 15 per cent per year. However, suppliers of vital raw materials, such as oil or foodstuffs, are demanding higher prices to fund their industrial progress.

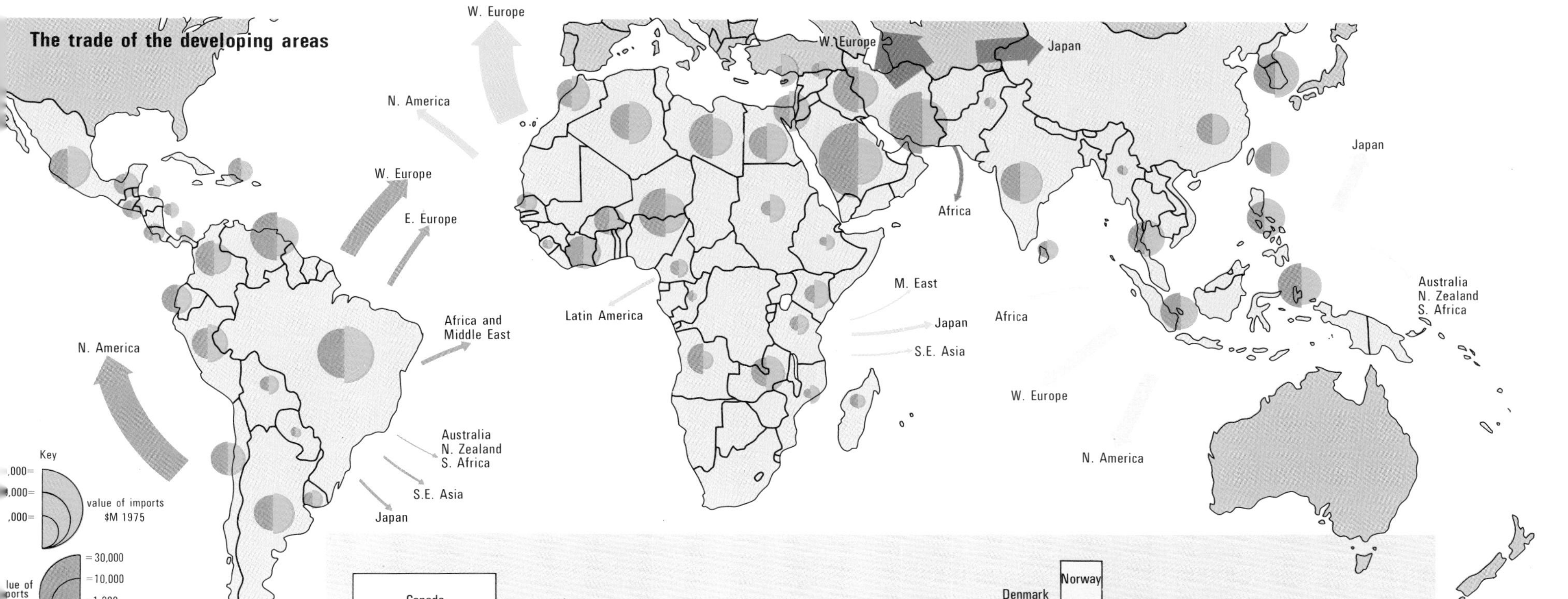

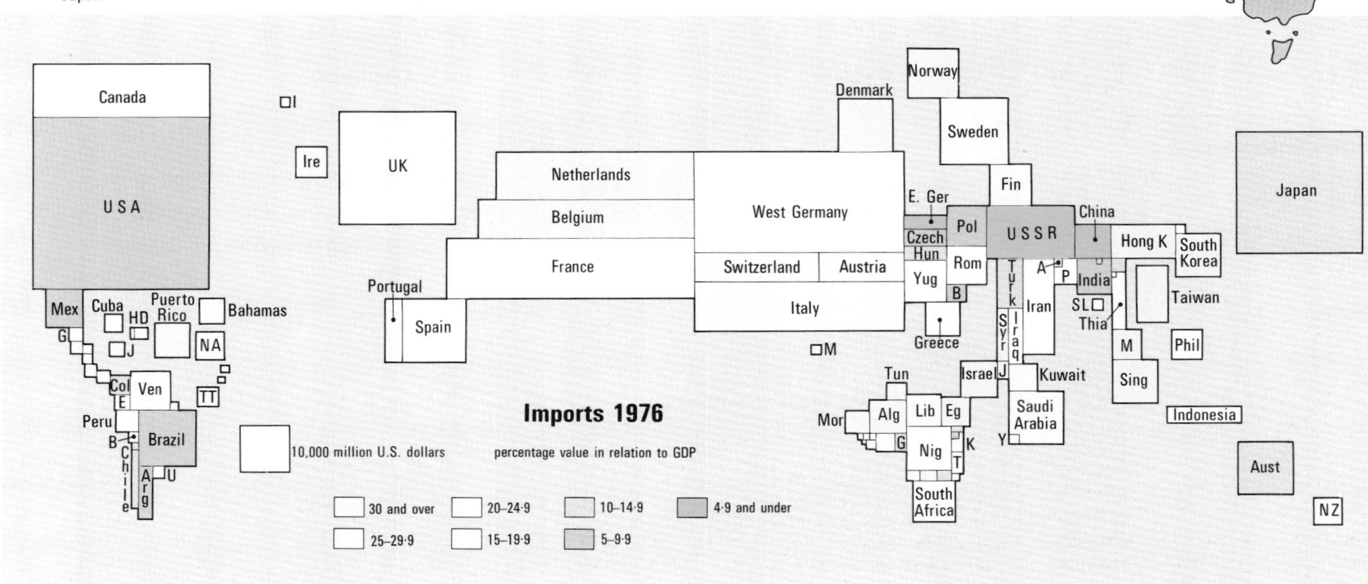

Imports 1976

10,000 million U.S. dollars   percentage value in relation to GDP

30 and over	20–24·9	10–14·9	4·9 and under
25–29·9	15–19·9	5–9·9	

World tourism

Travelling for pleasure provides the vast majority of people with their only experience of other countries. The number of such travellers is increasing so much that the tourist trade – which transports, accommodates, feeds and entertains them – is now one of the world's largest industries and is growing internationally at a very fast rate. By 1985, it is calculated that 320 million people will be travelling abroad for pleasure, spending approximately $60,000 million in the process.

Already, income from tourism is vital to the national economies of scores of countries. Spain, the most visited land, earned $3,083 million from her foreign visitors in 1976. Tourism has become the leading foreign currency earner for Kenya, bringing in more funds ($68·50 million) than the export of coffee. Canada earns more ($1,930 million) from tourism than from wheat exports.

The growth of tourism

For most of the last thirty years world tourism has grown steadily, other than where wars or major civil commotion has intervened. In 1973 some 200 million tourists grossed around $30,000 million. This fell in 1974 but by 1976 the recovery world-wide was complete and the numbers had risen to 222 million, grossing $45,000 million. That recovery has been maintained, and in many countries accelerated. Portugal is a good example of a country whose tourism was very badly affected by the political events of 1974 (and 1975) but by 1977 it had substantially recovered.

The maps which accompany these notes show clearly which countries receive most holiday visitors and, to a certain extent, who goes where. They cannot show why such pleasure journeys are made – why Spain stands well above all others, for example. One can appreciate that France and Italy are popular, but it takes more than guesswork to establish how Britain has managed to build up its tourist industry to such an extent that it now exceeds that of Switzerland, which has a much longer tradition in tourism.

Contemporary tourism

To some extent the present situation is a reflection of the past – those days of the Grand Tour when no man of substance could consider himself educated without the experience of that journey round selected European cities. It is reflected, too, from those times when travellers discovered the medicinal benefits of certain spas, or the climatic benefits of wintering on the French Riviera. There are small traces, in today's pattern, of those first organized holidays from Britain to the continent which bore the stamp of Mr Thomas Cook well over a century ago.

The current map of world tourist movement has, however, mainly been drafted by the post-war development of the travel industry, particularly within and from Europe. It is an industry which in the main sets out to sell a low cost 'package' of holiday pleasures, and the huge attraction of Spain is the most obvious symbol of its success. This overall success has continued in spite of the slump from the record breaking total of 30 million tourists of 1973 which resulted from the fuel and economic crises and of the political changes, which were followed by steep inflation. The upward curve was once more noticeable in 1976–77.

Spain's success as Europe's main tourist country stemmed from its low cost of living in the 1960s and early 1970s, its high sunshine record, its cheapness of land and subsequent building costs, an availability of inexpensive labour and the active encouragement of tourist investment by the government. The French provide the largest number of visitors to Spain, most coming on camping or caravan holidays, with the West Germans in second place, having overtaken the British in third place. However, holidaymakers from the UK constitute the largest number of foreigners visiting the country by air and indeed it was the British who 'invented' the air package holiday in the 1950s. Even with the rapidly increased costs in Spain which started in 1976 and accelerated in 1977, it remains the most popular country if for no other reason than that it is the only nation in Europe which can cope with the millions who seek the sun mostly on modest budgets.

Canadian tourism

The reasons behind Canada's high position in tourism tables are rather different. In 1976 some 32·2 million visitors (including a high proportion of day visitors) came from the USA. Although this was a drop from the previous year of about 2·4 million they actually brought in more money, largely because of rising costs, the total being $1,346 million. The proximity of the USA, the minimal border formalities and the lack of a language problem (even with the strong French-Canadian movement) 'sold' Canada to the leisure traveller from south of the 49th parallel.

Why do other nationals visit Canada? The next largest number (408,176) crossed the Atlantic from the UK, and clearly demonstrates the importance of historic ties as well as 'family' tourism. Travelling for a holiday with relatives, visiting sons or daughters who have married and moved away, usually means that one remains, in effect, within one's own country. In the case of the UK and countries such as Canada, Australia or New Zealand – and to a lesser extent the USA – such journeys show up on the international statistical tables.

United States tourism

Apart from its 'cross border' neighbours Canada and Mexico, which in 1976 accounted for over 12 million visitors to the country, the USA has only moved into the big international tourism league in the last ten years or so, largely due to two things – the development of cheap air travel and the active promotion of both government and private enterprise (the airlines in particular) to encourage foreigners to visit there. But the air fares motivation has been the greater, coupled with the increased affluence of Europe – and Japan. The USA is still well 'in the red' on her tourism account as her citizens in 1976 spent $1,076 million more on holidays and travel outside the country than incoming tourists earned for her.

A small example of how patterns can change is to be seen in the Caribbean, where for some time the tourist scene has been dominated by visitors from the USA and Canada. In Barbados for instance, nearly 130,000 of the island's 224,314 visitors in 1976 came from those two countries. However, the increasing availability of moderately-priced package holidays based on charter flights, from Britain and West Germany, are bringing more of a European influence to bear and changing the established tourist situation.

European tourism

The popularity of France and Italy lies in the history and cultural tradition of those countries and their great cities. Art treasures, architectural masterpieces and religious buildings are tremendous attractions, as are the gastronomic and wine-growing traditions. Italy and France have also sought to attract the mass market tourists, with such developments as the resorts of the Italian Adriatic coast and the grander projects in the south-west of France.

The UK has only comparatively recently achieved a high place in the list of 'Most visited countries' but in 1976 earned about $3,600 million from foreign visitors. This figure is over $500 million more than the total tourist income for Spain in the same year in spite of the fact that the number of visitors to that country was nearly 26 million while to the UK it was just over 10 million. In tourism, numbers alone do not by any means indicate the true economic effect.

One must keep in mind the fact that international tourism includes travel within the same region. A breakdown of statistics supplied by various European countries shows how large a part their immediate neighbours play in the flow of visitors. Such regional movements account for 88 per cent of the total international tourist traffic in Europe. The detailed 'Who goes where' statistics illustrate this vividly: the British travelling to Spain, France, Ireland, Italy and Germany; the French and the Germans preferring similar European destinations.

Motivation and fulfilment

Overall, the simple desire to take a holiday in totally different surroundings, preferably at low cost and quite often to some large resort on the sea coast, lies behind most tourist journeys. This is the basic reason why people go where they do. Although large functional and to some extent 'artificial' resorts will continue to be very popular and account for the majority of holiday destinations, there is a definite trend away from this by the more discriminating (and often the more frequently travelled) holidaymaker to seek his or her vacation in more genuine surroundings. And the younger generation are much less inclined to be 'packaged' than were the holidaymakers of the expansionist 1960s. Mass travel will undoubtedly continue to grow but along with it will be an increasing desire for independence and less regimentation.

It is clear that tourist travel will do more to shape the way we explore our world than anything else. It will also do more to shape the world we explore. Its future can be predicted, for the forces that control it are known. First, an increase in available leisure time will be matched by an increase of per capita income as well as improvements in transportation systems. Increased leisure time is already having an effect on the lives of the workers in the developed industrial societies. Throughout Europe, as well as North America, the growth of second holidays has been very rapid. As automation of the productive processes becomes more widespread one must pay great heed to predictions such as those of Herman Kahn of the Hudson Institute, who sees the post-industrial society requiring its citizens to work on just 147 days in a year – with a four-day working week and 13 weeks of annual holidays. Leisure in the form of earlier retirement is another inevitability.

Transport developments

Improvements in transport systems are already having an effect on tourism. The importance of the motoring holidaymaker is clearly appreciated by those responsible for the long-term planning of tourist facilities. In Europe one can point to the enormous growth in car ferry services between the UK and the continent as evidence of the importance of motoring, and to the highway construction programmes designed to speed holiday motorists to the pleasure areas.

Railway and road systems carry the largest amount of traffic on short and medium distances, and are being re-organized and expanded to cope with the demands of the next 20 years.

The next 20 years

The development and expansion of air transport will continue to be the most important influencing factor. The increasing use of larger aircraft purely for leisure travel will continue in spite of greatly increased fuel costs. The blurring of the lines between 'scheduled' and 'charter' services will accelerate and it could well be that by the mid-1980s the difference between the two, other than on certain business routes, will be academic.

The last 25 years have seen the industry of tourism grow in size and strength and, at the same time, a greater involvement by governments in the regulation of tourism. The day of 'laissez faire' in tourism is past. The World Tourism Organisation with its HQ in Madrid will increase its influence particularly with the developing nations. Without proper planning and safeguards for the environment in its widest sense, tourism can be a blight. But with the full co-operation on both governmental and private enterprise levels tourism can be of immense benefit financially, commercially, psychologically and also to understanding better the ways and nature of people the world over.

Where the British go		
1	Spain	2,170,000
2	France	2,036,000
3	Italy	690,000
4	West Germany	673,000
5	Netherlands	531,000
6	Belgium	472,000[1]
7	Greece	356,000
8	United States	346,000
9	Switzerland	252,000
10	Canada	200,000
11	Austria	197,000
12	Yugoslavia	196,000
13	Sweden	160,000
14	Norway	150,000
15	Malta	125,000
16	Denmark	109,000
17	Kenya	105,000
18	Morocco	95,000
19	Portugal	85,000
20	South Africa	55,000[2]
21	Cyprus	34,000

Where the Americans go		
1	Canada	11,641,000
2	Mexico	2,715,000
3	Italy	1,845,000
4	United Kingdom	1,490,000
5	West Germany	1,232,000
6	France	1,055,000
7	Switzerland	845,000
8	Spain	793,000
9	The Bahamas	667,000
10	Greece	493,000
11	Netherlands	424,000
12	Bermuda	391,000
13	Japan	277,000
14	Venezuela	266,000
15	Hong Kong	238,000
16	Ireland	231,000
17	Jamaica	229,000
18	Israel	214,000

19	Yugoslavia	189,000
20	Taiwan	125,000[3]
21	Singapore	122,000
22	Thailand	116,000
23	Turkey	114,000
24	Colombia	103,000
25	Korea	102,000
26	Morocco	97,000
27	Philippines	93,000
28	Malaysia	68,000
29	India	62,000
30	Portugal	56,000

Where the French go		
1	Spain	9,476,000
2	Italy	1,678,000
3	United Kingdom	1,171,000
4	Switzerland	644,000
5	West Germany	579,000
6	Austria	385,000
7	Yugoslavia	380,000
8	Tunisia	371,000
9	Greece	311,000
10	Netherlands	251,000
11	Morocco	225,000
12	United States	217,000
13	Portugal	114,000
14	Denmark	107,000
15	Algeria	83,000
16	USSR	71,000
17	Sweden	59,000

Where the West Germans go		
1	Denmark	13,307,000[4]
2	Austria	7,369,000
3	Spain	3,885,000
4	Italy	3,595,000
5	France	2,890,000
6	Switzerland	1,589,000
7	Yugoslavia	1,546,000

8	United Kingdom	1,104,000
9	Netherlands	683,000
10	Greece	519,000
11	United States	365,000
12	Czechoslovakia	325,000
13	Sweden	324,000
14	Norway	320,000
15	Hungary	275,000
16	Turkey	197,000
17	Bulgaria	162,000
18	Romania	149,000
19	Tunisia	139,000
20	USSR	129,000
21	Portugal	105,000

1976 figures in millions rounded to nearest thousand

1 also includes Luxembourg
2 provisional
3 rough estimate
4 includes all frontier crossings

Income from international tourism

1976 figures expressed in $US millions

United States	5,755
France	3,613
United Kingdom	3,600
West Germany	3,211
Austria	3,131
Spain	3,083
Italy	2,525
Switzerland	1,643
Canada	1,641
Netherlands	1,061
Belgium/Luxembourg	959
Greece	824
Portugal	317
Japan	312

The most visited countries

All figures are 1976

All figures are 1976

- over 20 million
- over 10 million
- over 5 million
- over 2 million
- over 1 million
- over 500 000
- over 300 000
- over 100 000
- over 50 000
- below 50 000

Canada

USA

Mexico

Bermuda

Bahamas

Jamaica

Costa Rica
Panama

Colombia

Venezuela

Trinidad & Tobago

Brazil

Argentina

Denmark
Sweden
Germany E.
Germany W.
Norway
Netherlands
Finland
Poland
Austria
Czechoslovakia
Hungary
USSR
Eire UK
Belgium
Luxembourg
Yugoslavia
Romania
Bulgaria
Greece
Switzerland
San Marino
Monaco
France
Italy
Syria
Lebanon
Israel
Jordan
Portugal
Malta
Cyprus
Turkey
Spain
Tunisia
Iraq
Iran
Afghanistan
Japan
Korea
Morocco
Algeria
Libya
Egypt
Kuwait
Pakistan
China
Hong Kong
India
Thailand
Vietnam
Philippines
Ethiopia
Malaysia
Singapore
Indonesia
Uganda
Kenya
Tanzania
Fiji
South Africa
Australia
New Zealand

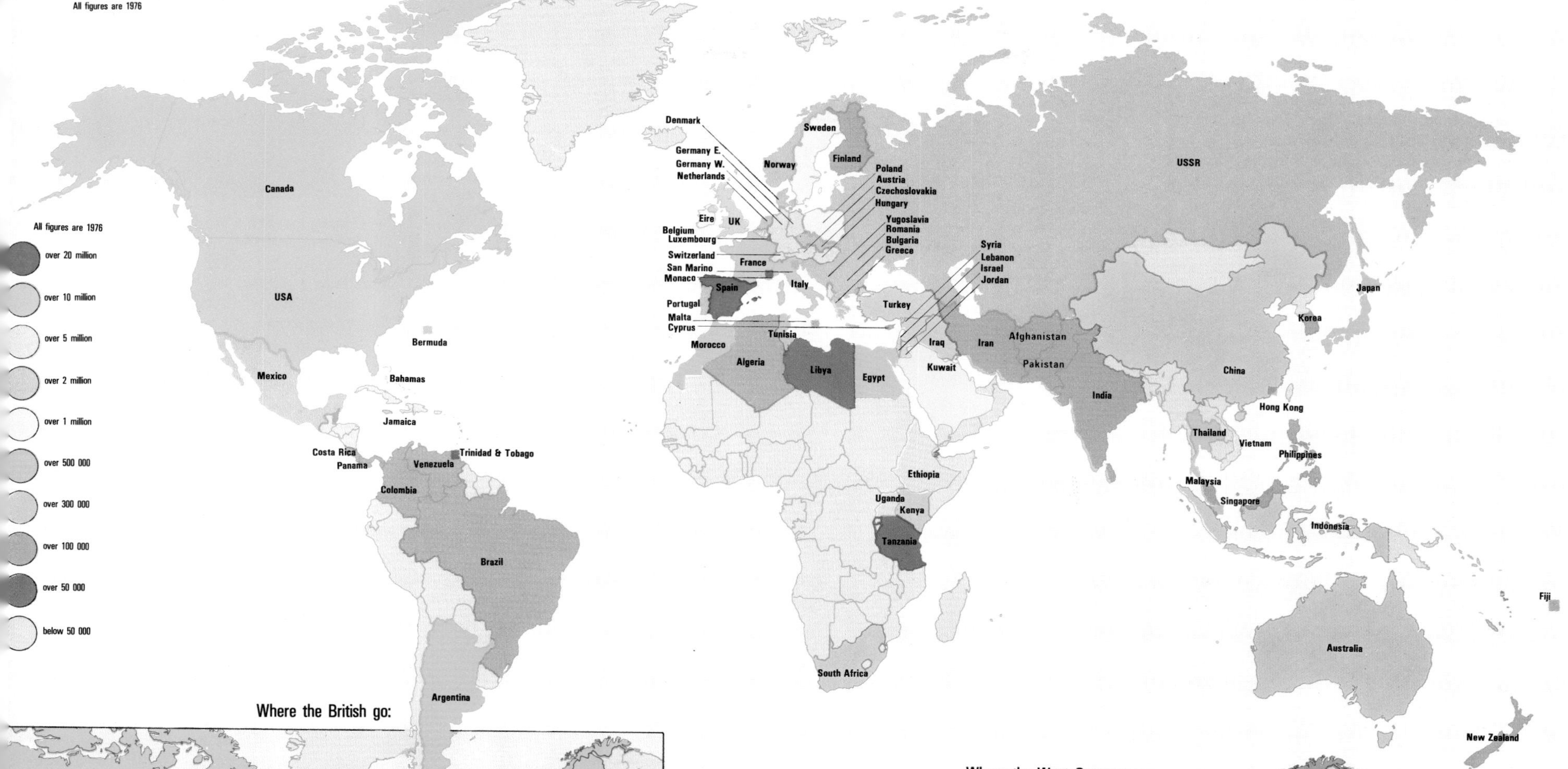

Where the British go:

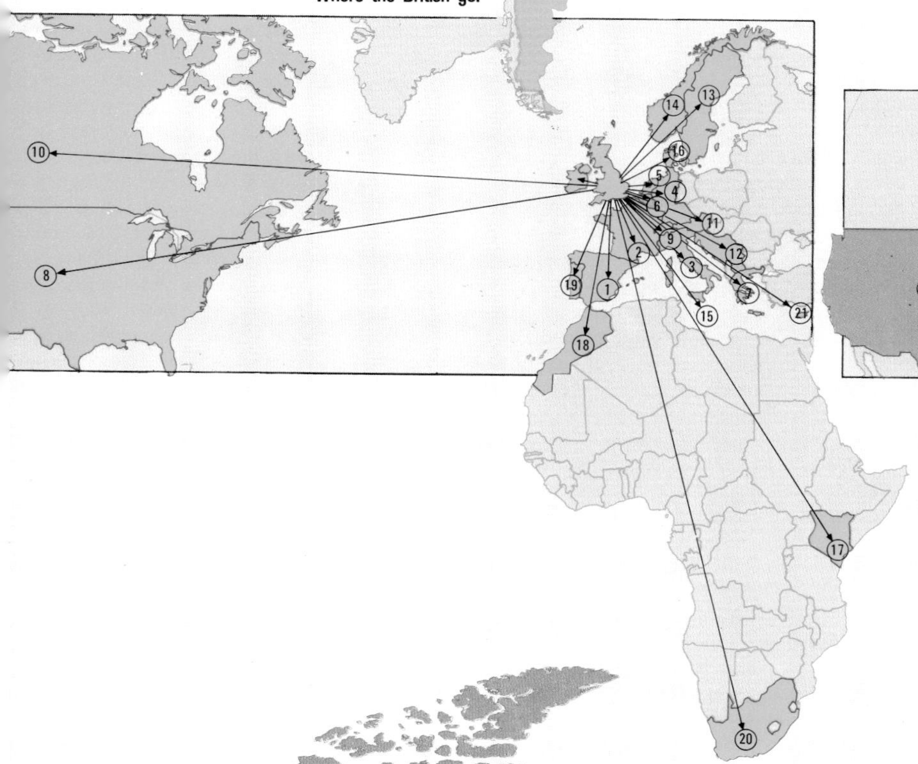

Where the West Germans go:

Where the French go:

Where the Americans go:

31

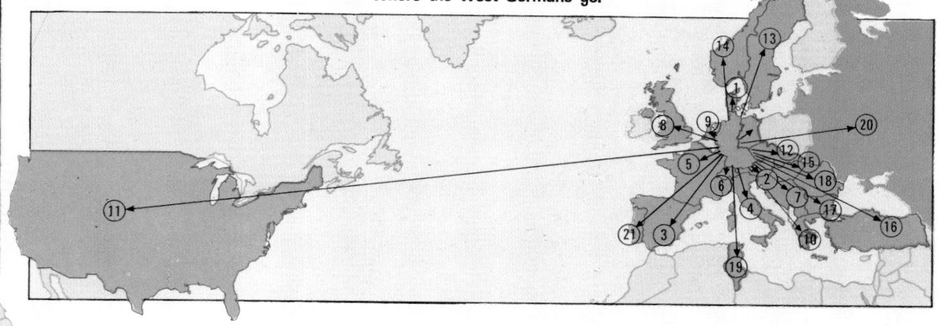

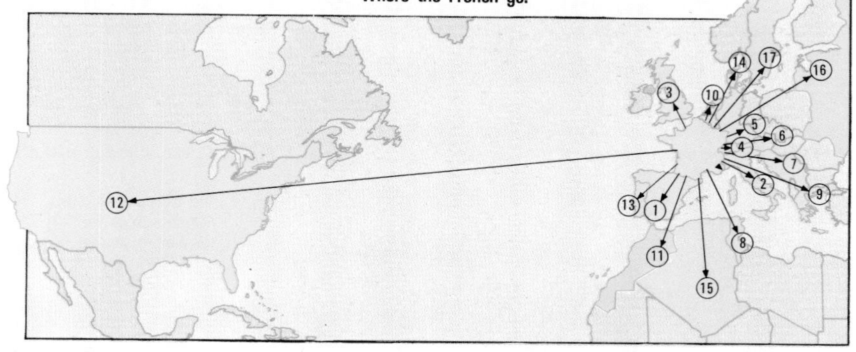

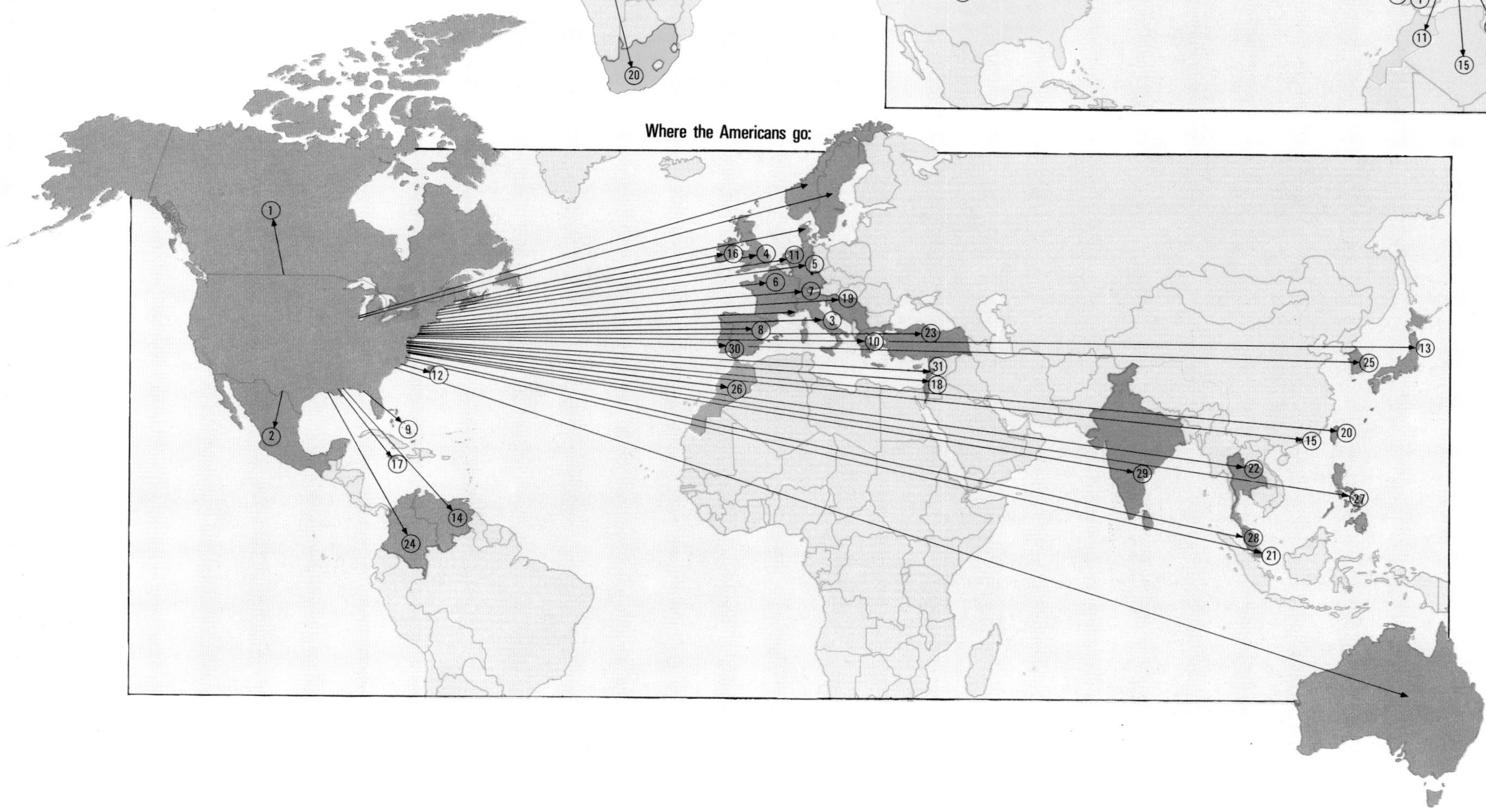

The balance of man's environment

The natural balance – gradual change

During the thousands of millions of years of its existence the Earth has undergone many changes. At first it had no atmosphere, then some gases were released from the interior. These were mainly carbon dioxide and water vapour, with a small amount of nitrogen and no free oxygen. The atmosphere's composition changed as the water vapour condensed to form the ocean, and as the carbon dioxide was taken up into carbonate rocks and as a constituent of growing plants. Ultimately some of the carbon was locked up in the fossil fuels produced from this vegetation, and it has remained so stored for millions of years until today, when it is being widely exploited by man. The oxygen in the atmosphere arose mainly as a result of the photosynthesis which reduced the carbon dioxide levels.

Thus throughout geological time the proportions of these gases have varied from epoch to epoch. Our present atmosphere is one stage in this process. Today the Earth is surrounded by a mixture of gases, consisting mainly of some four-fifths of nitrogen and one-fifth of oxygen, with other substances at much lower levels. These include the surprisingly small amount of carbon dioxide – only 0·03 to 0·04 per cent – on which all green plants depend, a varying amount of water vapour, small quantities of helium and other inert gases, and various additions and pollutants arising from man's activities as well as from natural processes. The balance of the atmosphere is maintained mainly by Earth's 'green mantle'. The vast areas of natural forest sustain the level of oxygen required by animal life. Any profound changes in vegetation would ultimately affect the atmosphere, and so affect all animal life also.

The scale of problems arising from interference by man with large natural regimes or ecosystems is perhaps well illustrated by the dilemma over the Brazilian rain forests. For some time there have been investigations and proposals to clear vast tracts of forest for agricultural development or the exploitation of potential mineral reserves. Latin America could certainly benefit socio-economically by some such successful development. Yet there is no clear understanding of what would happen to the climate and the fertility of the soil if a drastic change was attempted. Indeed, there is reason to believe that the decimation of the forests could easily lead to the creation of sterile deserts.

Effects of agriculture

The food for all animals is made by plants, which build up large molecules from the carbon dioxide in the air and water absorbed from the soil, using solar energy in the process. This process of photosynthesis is clearly vulnerable to direct and drastic alterations in the composition of the atmosphere, which in turn could interfere with the hydrological part of the natural cycle. Air pollution can screen radiation from the Sun, thus damaging plant life by reducing or inhibiting photosynthesis.

The changing oceans

Today land covers only about a third of the surface of the Earth; the rest is covered by the oceans. This enormous mass of water, weighing 1,428,000,000,000,000,000 tonnes, plays a big part in stabilizing the conditions of man's environment. Water temperatures fluctuate much less than those of air, and the oceans form a reservoir not only of water but also of carbon dioxide and oxygen, the gases on which life depends. The plant life in the oceans – the phytoplankton – makes an essential contribution to the balance of these gases, producing vast quantities of oxygen by its photosynthesis. The area and the composition of the seas have changed slowly over the whole period of the world's existence.

We tend to accept the world as it is now, or rather as it was before man had noticeably affected it, as the ideal environment both for man and for all animal and plant life. We forget that change has always occurred, and is likely to continue to occur whether or not man dominates the globe. If such changes are gradual, life will survive, and man may even be able to adapt. Man is now so powerful, however, that he could himself suddenly upset the whole balance, changing the climate and the composition of the atmosphere. If there were drastic changes, life in some form, would almost certainly survive. New forms suited to the new conditions would evolve, but man, ingenious as he is, might not be the species most able to adapt.

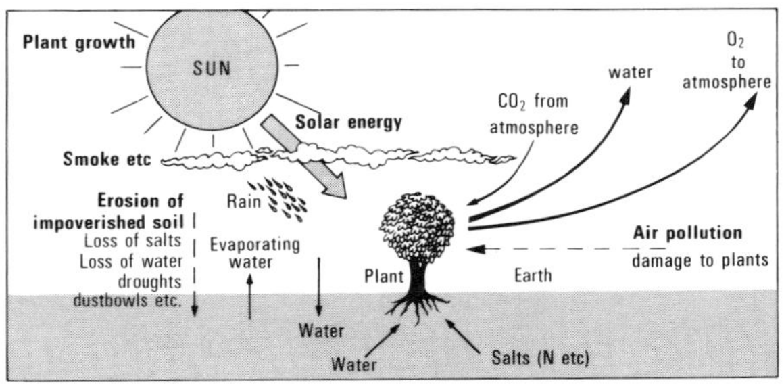

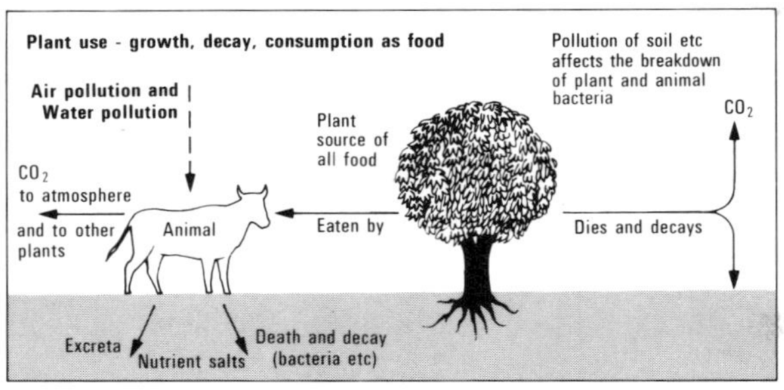

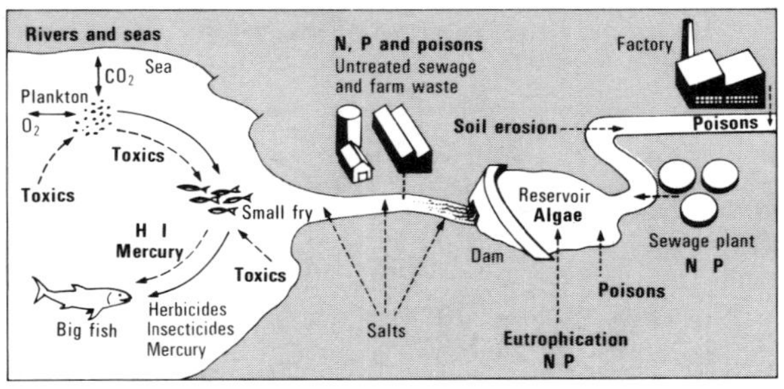

The essential cycles

All life on Earth depends on the essential cycle of energy, water and chemicals depicted here. The source of energy is radiation from the Sun. This radiation covers a wide range of wavelengths, some of which are essential for life, others harmful. The atmosphere filters out the most harmful rays, and admits those which are beneficial. Any atmospheric change alters the proportions of the various types of solar radiation which reach the Earth and the amounts which are lost. Any pollutant affects this balance.

Water, carbon dioxide and oxygen all go through these cycles. The rain falls on the land and sea alike. On land some is taken up by the soil, and is then absorbed by plant roots. A little of this water is used and retained by the plants, more is evaporated ('transpired') into the air. Water is also evaporated from the soil, and from the surface of streams, lakes and, most important, the sea. Solar energy is again involved in this evaporation. The water vapour eventually forms clouds and is deposited again as rain – and so the cycle continues.

The cycle in water is similar to that on land, except that aquatic animals are particularly susceptible to pollution. Pollutants are discharged into rivers, some of which run into lakes where excessive amounts of nutrient salts cause eutrophication. Poisons accumulate in the sea, are taken up by fish and other organisms and passed on (and concentrated) as predators eat their prey.

Man made changes

Man is the only animal to modify not only his immediate environment but also the appearance and the economy of the whole globe. He can cut down vast areas of natural forest and replace them with arable crops and, sometimes, by man-made desert. He drains the wet places, and irrigates the dry. His industry could alter the whole balance of the atmosphere and the climate of the Earth. He also consumes the Earth's resources, and moves substances from one place to another. The misuse of his powers, and the subsequent release of harmful substances, we call pollution. We must discover which forms of pollution are a danger to man's environment, and control them before they upset the natural balance irreversibly.

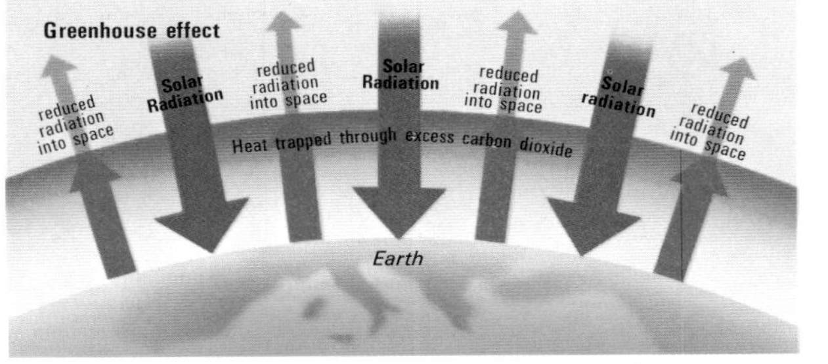

The Greenhouse Effect

Radiation from the Sun passes through space until it reaches the outer atmosphere of the Earth. Much of it is absorbed by the Earth's surface, causing the temperature to rise. The heat is then re-radiated. If the amount of CO_2 in the atmosphere increases, a larger amount of this radiation is trapped as in a glasshouse, instead of being lost into outer space. In the last fifty years the increase in the level of CO_2 in the Earth's atmosphere caused by the burning of fossil fuels has not been enough to raise the Earth's temperature.

Air pollution

Natural catastrophes, as well as human actions, can upset the balance. In 1883 Krakatoa blew up, and put so much dust into the atmosphere that the heat from the Sun was excluded and the average temperature of the Earth was significantly lowered for many months. Today man is polluting the air with dust and smoke, notwithstanding striking local improvements in Pittsburgh and other American cities and in Britain in places where the Clean Air Acts are operative. Air pollution, uncontrolled, could reduce sunlight at ground level and affect the world's climate, making it colder. An opposite effect, a warming of the Earth, could result from the increase in the level of carbon dioxide in the atmosphere. Carbon stored in fossil fuels (coal, oil, natural gas) is released as carbon dioxide gas when the fuels are burned; the levels of CO_2 in the atmosphere are rising slightly each year. This may produce the so-called 'greenhouse effect' (see diagram), and make the world warmer.

Such changes in climate would affect all forms of life. They would also affect the levels of the oceans. In former (natural) ice ages, so much water was immobilised as ice that the levels of the seas fell, to rise again and flood low-lying areas in the next warm epoch. A further rise in the temperature of the Earth could drown many of our cities and much of our most productive agricultural land. Scientists are not agreed on the probabilities of these changes, or on the magnitude of the likely effects, but they do agree that thorough monitoring of the atmosphere and climate is needed to detect the dangers at an early stage. The more optimistic scientists do also suggest that man-made changes in climate are likely to be less significant than the natural and inevitable fluctuations of temperature.

Green plants renew the supply of atmospheric oxygen. The destruction of forests may reduce the speed of renewal; the pollution of the oceans may affect the phytoplankton, which is equally important. This reduction in renewal is, at least in the short term, unlikely to endanger our oxygen supplies, which are probably sufficient for several hundred years, but the long-term composition of the atmosphere probably is being significantly affected, and will need to be safeguarded.

The atmosphere contains toxic gases, perhaps the most important being sulphur dioxide. Two thirds of the output of this gas is from natural sources, particularly the decay of vegetation in swamps, and from volcanoes. This natural SO_2 is just as toxic as that produced by man. It is harmful locally, but global levels are too low to have much effect. Man also raises the level of SO_2 in cities and where he is most numerous, often damaging trees and other plants which are particularly susceptible. These include lichens, mosses and liverworts, which are often absent from cities and from rural areas on the leeward side of cities. SO_2 pollu-

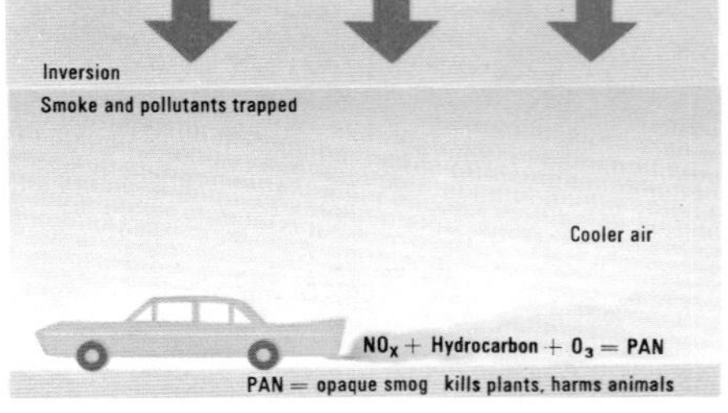

A toxic smog is produced by car exhaust when climatic factors trap the pollution at ground level.

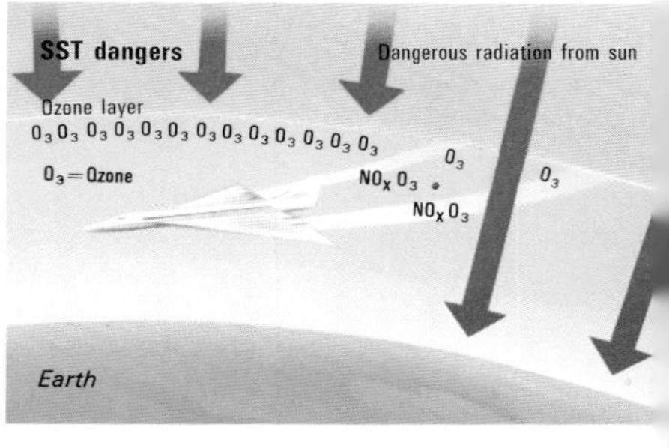

Exhausts from SST in the stratosphere may destroy the ozo layer which shields the earth from dangerous ultraviolet radiatio

tion is at present seldom serious enough to har man, except when its effects are combined wit those of smoke. Among other damaging gases pr duced by industry is fluorine, which harms veg tation and is particularly dangerous to cattle.

Automobiles and aircraft also pollute the atm sphere. Exhausts from internal combustion engin contain many potentially dangerous substance including carbon dioxide (CO_2), carbon monoxi (CO), oxides of nitrogen (NO), unburned hydro carbons and lead. All these pollute the air of citie often to a dangerous extent. In some areas whe this pollution is already serious its effects a exacerbated by climatic factors. A temperatu inversion traps the concentrated pollution ne to the ground, and if combined with brigh sunlight a photochemical reaction produces toxic smog as seen in California and Tokyo.

Aircraft cause ground level pollution similar t that of automobiles. Supersonic planes (SST flying in the thin atmosphere of the stratospher may impose a greater threat. The amount of wate vapour and of substances like oxides of nitrogen i likely to exceed, at least locally, the mass of th natural atmosphere, and some scientists are co cerned that this may upset the existing condition One risk is that levels of ozone (O_3) may be r duced. The ozone in these high levels acts as a filt to the dangerous radiation from the Sun; if th ozone layer is reduced, too much radiation coul reach the surface of the Earth. If too much ultra violet radiation did penetrate to Earth living thing would die. Calculations from measurements fro rockets fired into the atmosphere indicate th amount of ozone that has to be present. Remova of ozone would come through jet exhausts: nitro and hydrocarbon substances would modify th rate at which the chemical reaction takes place e couraging the separated two- and one-atom mol cules to recombine to reform ozone. These su stances would also steal some of the oxygen to for other compounds. The risk of this is probab small, but is one reason why environmentalis have opposed the operation of SST until th whole subject has been thoroughly studied.

In fact the possible changes of flying too man aircraft too high in the stratosphere is open to en less speculation, and will continue to be so unt very much more knowledge of the upper atm sphere is obtained from scientific satellite explora tion and allied investigations. Influences from th conditions 15 to 30 kilometres high have litt direct bearing on the short-term weather forecas Hence the amount of investigation of atmospher conditions at these rarified heights has been smal

A potentially greater threat to the ozone lay would be widespread use throughout the world fluoro-carbide aerosol sprays. The effect of thes sprays can be studied directly and there are amp grounds for concern.

Energy and the environment

Human civilisation depends on an increasin supply of energy. At present most of this come from burning fossil fuels: man is using at a fa rate the stored energy produced over millions years by photosynthesis. Even with economie oil reserves will be used up in a hundred years an

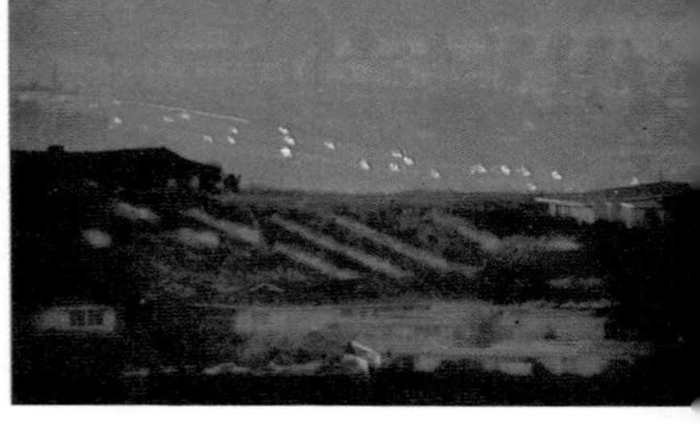

Traffic in Los Angeles

coal in two hundred. This will at least remove certain types of atmospheric pollution. Hydro-electric power is clean, but the amount attainable is limited. The energy of the Sun (solar energy) may be trapped directly and may make some contribution, but most future plans assume that nuclear power will play a greater, and ultimately a predominating, part in supplying man's needs. There are fears, however, concerning radiation hazards in spite of safeguards. Nuclear power stations are today very carefully controlled so that little radiation escapes to pollute the air or the sea, but as they increase in numbers the risk must grow. The greatest danger, however, is from the increasing amounts of radioactive waste, which are difficult to dispose of safely. Atmospheric testing of nuclear weapons imposes a further radiation risk whilst nuclear warfare of a global kind could lead to radiation levels so high as to threaten the existence of mankind.

Much of the energy man produces is lost as wasted heat. This too could eventually upset the climatic balance of the Earth. Already our large cities have a local climate measurably warmer than that of the surrounding country, though global effects are at present negligible. More serious 'thermal pollution' can occur locally when water from rivers and lakes is used for cooling purposes in industry as in large electrical generators, whether using fossil fuels or nuclear fuel. Water effluents from such power stations may be so hot that fish and invertebrates are killed; and even when heat pollution is less serious the water may be de-oxygenated so that aquatic life is asphyxiated. However, most electrical generating authorities are aware of the problem and try to guard against such damage to life.

Fresh water pollution

Rivers, lakes and the sea are all polluted by man. Limited amounts of sewage and other substances are disposed of by the process of self-purification in which nutrient salts are removed and used by living organisms – the normal process of biological cycling. Overloading prevents this from happening, and encourages organisms suited to living under polluted conditions. Man can reverse these processes by proper treatment of urban and industrial effluents but even in these, nutrient salts can cause damage by 'eutrophication', or excessive fertilisation of the water. Fortunately technology has developed methods – the tertiary treatment of effluents – which can obviate this danger, but only at a high cost. In Lake Tahoe in the USA, once very badly polluted, the problem has been overcome in this way.

In modern agriculture, with 'factory farming' where livestock is kept indoors in vast numbers, the animals' excreta, when not used as manure on the land, is often a source of pollution. Inorganic chemical fertilisers may also cause pollution when leached from the land into rivers and lakes.

Pesticides

Modern agriculture depends on chemical pesticides, particularly herbicides (weed-killers) and insecticides. These substances have contributed enormously to solving the problem of world starvation. Unfortunately some pesticides have also become contaminants, not usually at dangerous levels but sometimes in sufficient amounts to have harmful ecological effects locally. The organochlorine insecticides, including DDT and dieldrin, are of special concern. Although the dangers have often been exaggerated, there are many cases of contamination by those substances.

DDT and dieldrin are very stable, long-lasting substances, which is a great advantage in, for example, protecting a house from disease-bearing mosquitoes. However, this very property makes them dangerous because they become concentrated in a particular food chain: a predator like a hawk can eat a number of pigeons or voles containing small amounts of DDT, and retain the DDT until a dangerous level is reached. Fish and other aquatic animals can also cause the concentration of pesticides in rivers, by a factor of as much as 10,000 times. Scientists are trying

A river in Detroit, showing the effects of pollution.

to replace the more dangerous pesticides with other substances and to develop non-chemical methods of control. This will take time but, although chemical pesticides will be used for many years, with care global pollution will be avoided.

Some quantities of pesticides ultimately end up in the sea. Levels in estuaries and coastal areas can be high enough to damage fish and marine arthropods and even to affect plant life. In the open ocean, however, levels are very low, and there is at present no evidence that the phytoplankton is in danger of being damaged. Some scientists have suggested that levels are likely to increase in the future to danger point, but this does not seem to be happening yet. In fact levels in many marine fish and in the sea birds which eat them are decreasing and not increasing because better controls have been introduced in many countries.

Salt water pollution

The importance of the oceans in sustaining the natural balance cannot be over-stated; pollution of the oceans is therefore a very serious matter. The most obvious pollutant is oil including waste oil discharged by ships, or spilled when oil tankers ships are damaged or wrecked. Some oil is also spilled at terminals where it is pumped ashore from tankers. Leaks from underwater oil wells are difficult to control and can cause pollution more serious than that from the sinking of the largest tanker. Oil is dangerous because it floats on the surface of the ocean and most life, particularly plant life, is found near the surface. Fortunately the most toxic substances in oil are relatively volatile, and evaporate from the ocean's surface, but the tarry residues can damage fish and interfere with the life and photosynthesis of the phytoplankton.

1
Aerial spraying of pesticides, including DDT, is cheap and efficient, but may contaminate rivers, lakes and surrounding land.

2
Radiation escaping from nuclear power stations, and as fallout after testing atom bombs, is all harmful to life.

3
Chemical fertilizers have greatly increased crop production, but they may be washed off or leached out of the soil. They then cause eutrophication, which stimulates the production of harmful algal growth.

4
Rivers are particularly susceptible to pollution. Sewage, untreated or insufficiently treated, is one danger. Even properly treated sewage still contains nutrient salts – nitrogen and phosphorus – the latter coming increasingly from detergents used in domestic washing machines. Some detergents pass unchanged through sewage works, and cause massive amounts of foam on rivers.

5
Estuaries and coastal waters are particularly at risk from pollution, especially from oil.

6
Mining, both deep mining with its associated slag heaps and open cast mining, can destroy vast areas of the countryside. Many industries produce large areas of dereliction, particularly when they become obsolete.

7
Marine pollution from oil results from spillage from tankers and other ships, but underwater oil wells are now an even greater hazard.

8
Automobiles need vast motorways which deface countryside and town alike. They can also cause serious air pollution.

9
An increasing number of farm animals now live indoors ('factory farming') where their excreta, instead of being used as manure on the land, may pollute rivers.

10
Industrial factories and power stations pollute the air with sulphur, fluorine and smoke; they may also pass poisonous effluents and too much waste heat into the rivers.

11
Urban development is at the expense of living forests and agricultural land. Most cities pollute the air with smoke and toxic gases.

12
Large as the oceans are, they cannot absorb unharmed the increasing burden of waste.

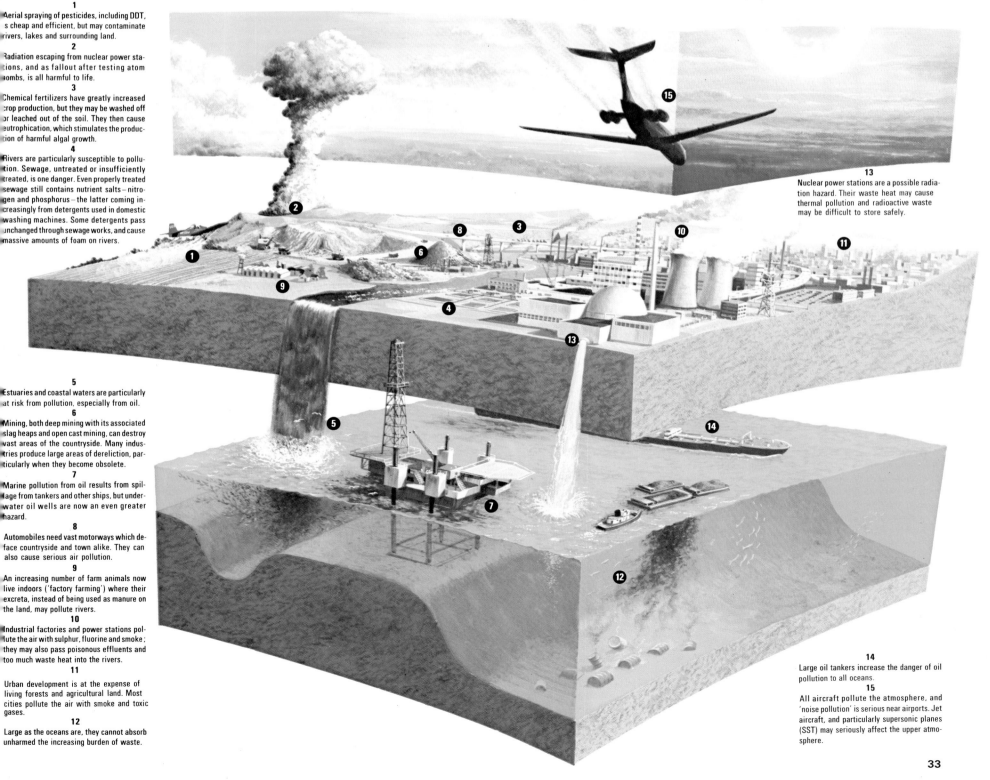

13
Nuclear power stations are a possible radiation hazard. Their waste heat may cause thermal pollution and radioactive waste may be difficult to store safely.

14
Large oil tankers increase the danger of oil pollution to all oceans.

15
All aircraft pollute the atmosphere, and 'noise pollution' is serious near airports. Jet aircraft, and particularly supersonic planes (SST) may seriously affect the upper atmosphere.

Techniques of navigation

Early maps were designed to show the spatial relationship between local geographical features, territorial boundaries, and routes. The early use of maps for finding the way (the essence of navigation) has persisted, first for travellers on land, later for mariners, and more recently for airmen and space travellers. Among the necessary instruments of marine navigation the chart – the seaman's name for a map – is important. In addition to the chart, the other basic navigational tools are 'sailing directions' which, in early times were passed down orally from master to apprentice, but which are now in printed form; the log, or device for measuring the speed of a ship; and, the most important instrument of all, the compass.

The Greeks

Anaximander of Miletus (6th century BC) is credited with having drawn the first map. Anaximander's map, which must have been crude and highly conjectural, marked an important epoch in the history of geography and navigation in particular, and in human progress in general. The first rectangular map was constructed by Democritus (5th century BC) who claimed that the habitable world was one and a half times as long in the east–west direction as it was broad in the north–south direction. It was this concept that led to the use of the terms 'latitude' and 'longitude', meaning respectively breadth and length, for defining terrestrial positions. Dicaearchus (4th century BC) constructed a map on which the first parallel of latitude was drawn through the Pillars of Hercules at the entrance to the Mediterranean Sea and the Island of Rhodes. Eratosthenes (3rd century BC), who made the first scientific attempt at measuring the Earth's size, constructed a map (according to the geographer Strabo) on which seven parallels of latitude and seven meridians or lines passing through the poles and any given place, irregularly spaced, were drawn; but the principles of Eratosthenes' division are not known. Hipparchus (2nd century BC) demanded that the positions of places to be mapped should be verified using astronomical observations. He suggested that parallels of latitude and meridians drawn on maps should be equidistantly spaced, and that to determine relative longitudes meridians should be regulated from eclipse observations.

Ptolemy of Alexandria (c AD 90–168), the 'Prince of Ancient Geographers', was the founder of scientific cartography. His monumental *Geographia* contains detailed explanations of mathematical geography and map projections. Ptolemy suggested that the Earth should be divided on the basis of climatic zones and that longitudes should be measured eastwards from a prime meridian through the 'Fortunate Isles' which he believed to be the westernmost part of the habitable globe. Ptolemy referred to Marinus, a Tyrian cartographer who employed a simple cylindrical projection for his maps.

Medieval navigation

The earliest charts extant are medieval maps of the Mediterranean world: the first record of a chart being used on a ship dating from 1270. By that time the Genoese, Venetians and Pisans had gained control of the maritime trade of the Mediterranean, and significant improvements in nautical science took place during the ascendancy of the Italian City States.

Portolan chart

The renaissance of scientific map-making began with the portolan charts of the thirteenth century to meet the needs of seamen. These charts were hand-drawn, each on a complete skin. The earlier examples are of the Mediterranean and Black Sea regions, but by the seventeenth century they embraced the whole of the known world, A characteristic feature of the portolan chart is the maze of intersecting straight lines which cover the sea area. These are systems of rhumb lines, each radiating from the centre of one of a series of compass roses. It is argued that each system of rhumb lines on a portolan chart denotes a magnetic compass, and that such charts, therefore, were based on compass bearings. If this be so, they must have made their first appearance after the invention of the magnetic compass.

There is no contemporary explanation of how the rhumb lines on a portolan chart were used; but it seems obvious that they were employed for finding the magnetic course to steer from one place to another. To find the course the navigator would place a straight-edge joining the plotted positions of departure and destination; and then, by means of dividers, he would seek the rhumb line most nearly parallel to the straight-edge. By tracing this line to the centre of the appropriate compass rose, he would readily ascertain the compass course to steer.

Magnetic compass

There is no strong evidence to suggest that the magnetic compass was not invented independently in the Mediterranean region; it is likely that it was invented in China perhaps before it made its first appearance, in the 12th century, in the Mediterranean. The 'natural' compass is the horizon of an observer, and in very early times, the horizon was divided into four quadrants by two rectangular diameters to indicate the four principal directions, North, East, South and West. The horizontal angle between the direction of North (or South) and that in which the ship is heading is the 'Course' of the ship. It is easy to see that when a ship is heading in a fixed direction on any given course, the line she traces out on the sea is one that cuts all meridians at the same angle. Such a line is a rhumb line, and because of the convenience of not having to change the ship's course when sailing from one given place to another, the normal navigational practice, especially for short distances, is to sail along a rhumb line.

The Golden Age of Discovery

When western Europeans first embarked on Atlantic voyages during the early phase of the Golden Age of Discovery, the need for scientifically constructed charts was pressing. Within the confines of the enclosed Mediterranean, where sailing distances between ports were relatively short, the portolan charts sufficed. But for ocean navigation, in which east–west distances of thousands of miles were common, something better was vitally necessary.

Although seamen must always have known that the Earth is spherical, the charts used by the Portuguese and Spanish mariners during the Age of Discoveries were based on the assumption that the Earth's surface was plane. The graticules or network of grid-lines drawn on the charts were simple rectangular networks in which equidistant parallels of latitude and meridians on the Earth were each projected as equidistant parallel lines forming a 'plane' projection. On such a map of the world every parallel of latitude is projected as a straight line of constant length. On the globe, however, the length of the parallels of latitude diminish from a maximum at the equator in latitude 0° to zero at either pole in latitude 90°.

Mercator chart

The most important step forward on the development of the navigational chart coincided with the publication of a world map in 1569 by the Flemish cartographer Gerhard Kremer, better known as Mercator. This map is the prototype of the modern chart.

On Mercator's world map equidistantly spaced meridians on the Earth are projected as equidistant parallel straight lines, and equidistantly spaced parallels of latitude are projected as parallel straight lines which cut the meridians at right angles. The graticule therefore, is rectangular like that of the 'plane' chart. The important difference is that the spacing of the parallels on a Mercator chart increases polewards in exactly the same proportion as the distortion of the east–west spacing of the meridians. In technical terms the Mercator projection is such that every line on the chart is distorted proportionally and therefore the projection is orthomorphic. In a cartographic sense, this means that angles are not distorted so that lines of constant course, or rhumb lines, are projected as straight lines. A mariner wishing to find the rhumb line course to steer from one place to another simply measures on a Mercator chart the angle which the rhumb line makes with any of the projected meridians.

Gnomonic chart

It was soon realised by early ocean navigators that long voyages could be substantially shortened, when wind and currents allowed, by practising what became known as 'Great Circle Sailing' instead of 'Rhumb Line Sailing'.

A great circle is a circle on a sphere on whose plane the centre of the sphere lies. The shortest route along the surface of a sphere between two points is along the shorter arc of the great circle on which the two points lie. In practising rhumb line sailing, although the navigator benefits in that a constant course is steered, his ship travels a greater distance than would be the case by practising great circle sailing. A major disadvantage of the latter however, is that the course along a great circle route constantly changes. Nevertheless, in the interests of economy of fuel and time, great circle sailing is commonly practised.

Mercator's projection shows all parallels of latitude as if equal in length to the Equator, although on the globe they are obviously progressively shorter towards the poles. Mercator increased his North–South scale on the meridians to match the increase in East–West scale, so that at any one point scale is equal in both directions and away from that point increases or decreases in equal proportions. Angles from the North–South meridians (i.e. bearings) can therefore be measured with a protractor without distortion. A straight line (rhumb line) thus has a constant bearing, but is not the shortest distance between its two end points. The Gnomonic chart has scale distortion outwards from its centre point, but the shortest distance between two points is the straight line joining them. The route required is therefore first plotted as a straight line on the Gnomonic chart and is then transferred to the Mercator chart as a series of straight lines, the bearing of each being measured with a protractor. A ship or aircraft does not follow the true Great Circle route, which would require continuous slow alteration of bearing, but steers on a constant bearing for a period of time and then changes to the new bearing at the next junction point along the series of straight lines drawn on the chart.

The Mercator map shows Great Circle routes and rhumb lines for three shipping routes and one air route. The latter is also shown on the Gnomonic map. The Great Circle route always lies on the poleward side of the rhumb line between the same points.

The Mercator chart need not be based on the Equator, but can be drawn at right-angles in the Transverse form, based on any meridian. This allows the polar areas to be charted, which is important for air routes although not for shipping. Likewise, the Gnomonic chart need not be centred on a pole but can be drawn centred on any point.

The navigator is, of course, constrained by many factors in laying out his route: the sailor may have to plan his voyage as a series of different Great Circle segments in order to avoid land, shallow water or ice hazards; sailing ships require routes planned with consideration of prevailing and seasonal winds and of ocean currents.

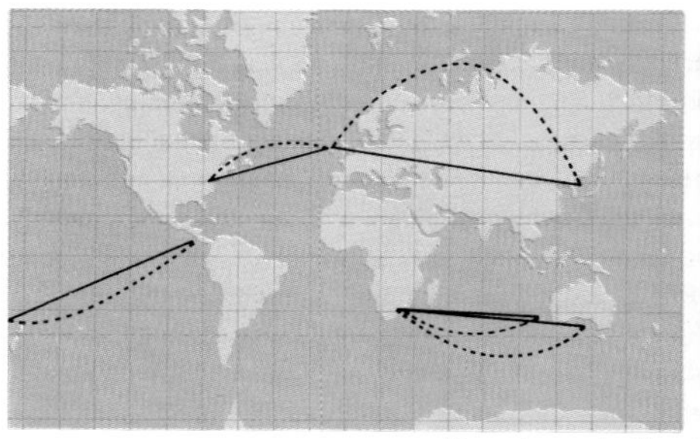

Mercator projection

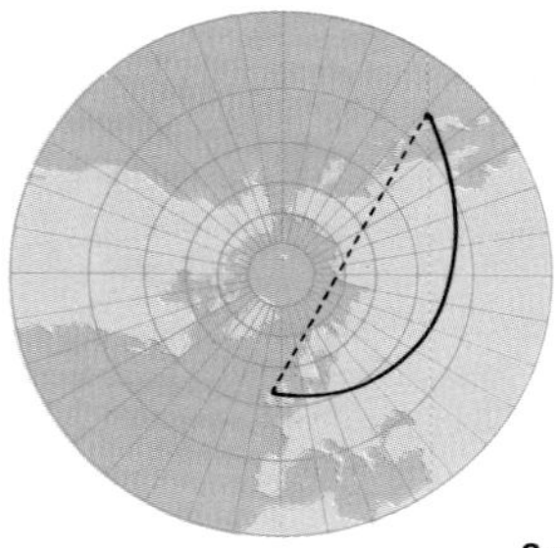

Gnomonic projection

On a Mercator chart a great circle is projected as a relatively complex curve. To plot a great circle route on a chart, a navigator employs a chart constructed on the gnomonic projection as an auxiliary to the Mercator chart. Unlike the conventional Mercator projection, the mathematical principles of which were first given by the eminent Elizabethan mathematician Edward Wright, the gnomonic projection is a geometrical or perspective projection in which points on a spherical surface are projected onto a plane touching the surface, by straight lines of projection which emanate from the centre of the sphere. It is clear that on a gnomonic projection great circle arcs are projected as straight lines. To plot a great circle route on a gnomonic chart the navigator simply joins the plotted positions of the points of departure and destination with a straight line. To transfer the great circle route onto a Mercator chart merely involves lifting positions of a series of points on the route as projected on the gnomonic chart and transferring them to the Mercator chart. A fair curve through these points delineates the great circle route on the Mercator chart. The navigator practising great circle sailing sails along a series of short rhumb lines which collectively approximate to the great circle arc described above.

Nautical Astronomy

A system of navigation in which the navigator relies wholly on compass and log to determine direction and distance travelled is known as 'Dead Reckoning' or 'DR Navigation'. Because compass and log are not without errors, and because their errors are cumulative, DR Navigation is unreliable and imperfect. It becomes necessary, in the interests of safety, for a navigator to be able to check his progress by some means other than by DR Navigation.

The defects of DR Navigation led to the development of 'Nautical Astronomy' by which a navigator may find his latitude and longitude from astronomical observations. The basic tools of a nautical astronomer are a *Nautical Almanac*, a sextant and a chronometer. The *Nautical Almanac* gives the celestial positions of the sun, moon, planets and stars used in nautical astronomy, against Greenwich Mean Time or GMT. The sextant is the instrument by which the navigator measures the elevations above his horizon of the sun, moon, planet or star he observes. The chronometer is merely an accurate timekeeper from which the GMT of an astronomical observation on 'sight' is obtained.

In the open sea a navigator may find his latitude from a sight of a celestial body on the celestial sphere bearing due north or south at which time the body reaches its greatest altitude during the day. Such an observation is known as a 'meridian altitude' sight. The celestial sphere is an imaginary sphere surrounding the Earth, on which celestial bodies are assumed to lie. The astronomical navigator constructs a network of guidelines on the celestial sphere like lines of latitude and longitude on the Earth. The equivalent of latitude is declination and that of longitude is called right ascension.

A mariner may find his ship's longitude from an observation of a celestial body provided that the observer knows his latitude. To find longitude it is necessary to solve a spherical triangle at the apexes of which are located, respectively, the celestial pole, the observer's zenith, and the observed body.

Radio and electronic navigation

The application of radio and electronic principles during the 20th century has revolutionised navigation. In the early decades of the century 'radio time signals' were made available for checking chronometers. Later, medium frequency radio direction finding (MF/DF) enabled a navigator to find his ship's position, even in fog when visual observations of the land or the celestial bodies rendered the traditional methods of navigation useless. This method of 'fixing' a position is exactly analogous to the method of taking bearings of lighthouses or other visible landmarks. Later still, the introduction of radar techniques facilitated coastal navigation in low visibility as well as providing efficient means for avoiding collision in fog. Radar, a contraction of 'radio detection and ranging' was developed between 1935 and 1940 independently in a number of countries. Range, direction and velocity are all displayed visually by means of a cathode-ray tube. After the Second World War refinements to radar techniques led in the direction of hyperbolic navigation.

Hyperbolic navigation

During the Second World War the need for sophisticated navigational systems for fast-flying military aircraft led to the introduction of hyper-

...olic navigation.

Hyperbolic navigation is based on the accurate measurement of the difference in times taken by simultaneous signals, transmitted from each of two fixed transmitting stations, to reach an observer.

If an observer receives radio signals transmitted simultaneously from each of two stations then he is able to measure the intervals of time taken for the radio energy to travel from the two stations to his position. Knowing the speed at which radio energy travels he can translate the difference of the two time intervals into a corresponding distance-difference. The position of constant distance-difference relative to the two stations is a hyperbola, which has the stations at its focal points. Such a hyperbola plotted on a chart gives the navigator a line somewhere on which his position is located. By plotting the second hyperbola from observations of a second pair of stations, the observer then locates his position at the point of intersection of the two hyperbolae. Systems of this nature, include the Decca Navigator, Loran and Omega, all of which are extensively used on aircraft and ships (see opposite for description of Decca Navigator System).

To facilitate hyperbolic navigation specially prepared charts, overprinted with families of hyperbolae, are used. Such a chart is called a 'lattice chart'. An example of a Decca Lattice Chart is illustrated.

The sophisticated technology of the Space Age has had a significant impact on navigation of ships and aeroplanes.

Inertial navigation

The system known as 'Inertial Navigation' is essentially, a sophisticated DR system in which the motion of an aircraft or ship is sensed, without compass or log, so that the position of the craft relative to its starting position is at all times known. It is a self-contained system that functions independently of weather conditions that can hamper the nautical astronomer, and of radio signals which may suffer natural or man-made interference. For this latter reason inertial navigation is of particular importance to naval vessels, especially nuclear submarines which attempt to avoid detection.

Satellite, VOR and DME navigation

Another advanced navigational technique of the Space Age is that which employs Earth satellites. By this system position finding to an accuracy of 0·1 miles is possible.

If a satellite is placed in polar orbit and can be tracked and plotted accurately, at a given instant of time its exact latitude, longitude and height is known. The distance of the satellite from a ship is obtained by utilising the Doppler principle that electromagnetic waves are modified by the motion of the source. As the satellite approaches the ship, its rapid motion shortens the wavelength of the signals. More waves therefore reach the ship per second than would be received from a stationary source. The wavelength leng-

thens as the satellite moves away from the ship and fewer waves per second are received. From the change in the number of signals received during transit of the satellite, range can be calculated.

A ship in motion fixes its position from more than one pass of a satellite; if stationary a greater number of fixes can be taken – these are called geodetic fixes and are often used by oil rigs and other off-shore installations such as large navigation beacons and lightships.

The navigation of aircraft is facilitated by VOR (VHF Omnidirectional Range) and DME (Distance Measuring Equipment). VOR allows an airman to navigate from any position directly towards or away from a fixed radio beacon, and DME enables him to measure the distance between his aircraft and the beacon using radio techniques.

Other electronic aids include the radio altimeter to measure the distance above ground, and the ground-speed indicator which uses the Doppler shift in reflected radio waves. Computers convert data to information capable of being instantly read by the pilot, and they are also capable of carrying out position-determining (dead-reckoning) by monitoring all speed and course changes of the aircraft. The automatic pilot can therefore carry out all the tasks necessary for piloting the aircraft.

Navigation, as has been stated, is essentially concerned with finding the way, but in certain instances, of more importance is the avoidance of collision. This becomes crucial in the vicinity of busy airports and seaways. The application of the concept of modern traffic control, in which aircraft are segregated and ships are routed, has marked an important epoch in the recent history of navigation. As far as the airman is concerned the role of the land-based traffic controller is vitally important in the navigation process. The Air Traffic Controller ensures that all the aircraft in his area follow carefully planned and prearranged routes. For certain defined points on these routes the controller identifies the height of each aircraft approaching it and the aircraft's arrival time at the point. By radio communication the controller is able to give directions to the pilots to ensure safe landings. The data for each aircraft is given on a 'flight strip', and it is the computerising of these data that will ultimately relieve controllers of much of their present onerous workload. (See Approach and Landing Chart for Heathrow Airport, and en route chart below).

The air and sea navigator is no longer limited to a small number of charts for use during a flight or voyage. He now has a wide variety at differing scales to back up his electronic aids. Coastal and land areas in particular are well mapped, and high-speed and multi-colour printing and symbol standardisation has now ensured that the navigator has information more readily available and more accurate than ever before.

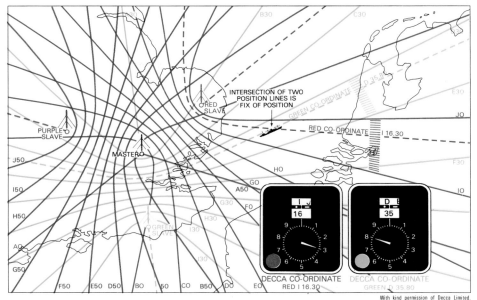

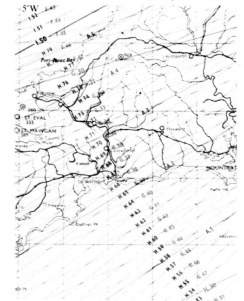

With kind permission of Decca Limited.

The Decca Navigator Sysytem fixes position using continuous radio waves from two transmitters. In the south-east of England the master transmitter is augmented by purple, red and green slave transmitters. The fix is given by the intersection of two hyperbolic position lines, and is obtained from the readings of two Decometer Indicators.

A Decca Lattice Chart used for location of aircraft position. The map shows only coast and rivers, railways, beacons and airfields (with their heights above sea level). The important part of the chart is the system of coloured lines, in purple, red and green, each colour representing directional signals from a fixed transmitter. It is possible to determine the aircraft's position on a line from each transmitter and so fix it on the map by the intersection of the corresponding coloured lines. For example, in the Bristol Channel a good fix can be obtained using the green transmitter with either the red or the purple; using only the latter two colours would give an uncertain fix.

Part of an aeronautical topographical chart. The relief of the land is shown by generalised contours at a 500-foot Vertical Interval, with layer-tinting to assist a quick appreciation of land form. Spot heights are given for the highest summits, which must obviously be avoided. Railways, main roads, towns and major settlements are shown, as these are easily identified from an aircraft. The pattern of runways on the airfield is shown diagrammatically to avoid confusion; note the second airport to the south of Edinburgh (Turnhouse) which has a distinctly different pattern of runways. Direction beacons and flashing lights are marked for night flights. More detailed charts than this one are used for approach and take-off, and for restricted areas or directed flight paths.

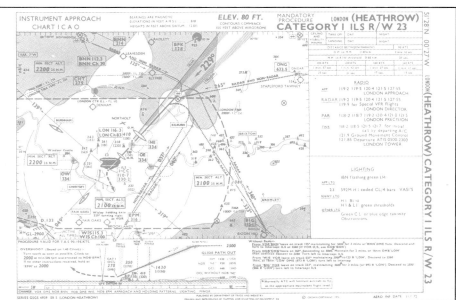

The Approach and Landing Chart for London (Heathrow) Airport illustrates the complexity of operation at a busy international centre. The higher land in the area is colour-tinted, and spot heights of topographical features and of towers, pylons and other obstructions are given not only

above sea level but also above airfield altitude as aircraft altimeters can be set to read height above the runway. Beacons, lights, radar information, etc., is given in detail, with routes for visual and instrumental approaches.

An en route chart gives the pilot the bearings and distances along his route from beacon to beacon, which allows a dead reckoning passage by compass and airspeed indicator, suitably corrected for wind strength and direction. The chart also indicates information such as the aircraft

control zones, radar transmitters, and lines of latitude and longitude. This is a specialised chart intended solely for aerial navigation purposes, and needs constant revision.

The Universe

No one knows how large the Universe is, or if indeed it has any limits. It stretches as far as our largest telescopes can see. Even a beam of light, which travels at the fastest known speed in the Universe, 186,000 miles per second, (i.e. the speed of light), takes 10,000 million years to reach the Earth from the remotest visible objects. Space is so vast that ordinary units of distance become insignificant. Distances in astronomy are usually described in light years, the distance that a beam of light covers in one year. This is equivalent to about six million million miles. The nearest star to our Sun, called Alpha Centauri, is 4·3 light years away, which means that we see it as it appeared 4·3 years ago. The remotest visible objects in the Universe are over 10,000 million light years away, which means that we see them as they appeared before the Earth was born.

Star magnitudes
The stars we see at night are relatively close to us in space. They are among the nearest of the estimated 100,000 million stars that make up our whirling star system called the Galaxy, the densest part of which is visible as the faint hazy band called the Milky Way. Stars appear different in brightness because some are genuinely bigger and hotter than others and also because they are all at different distances from the Earth. Astronomers grade star brightness in steps called magnitudes. The brightest-appearing stars are termed first magnitude, and the faintest visible to the naked eye are sixth magnitude. Still fainter stars, visible only through telescopes, are given progressively larger magnitude numbers. Each magnitude step corresponds to a change in brightness of approximately 2½ times.

The beginnings of the Universe
Astronomers speculate that originally the Universe was compressed into a single point from which it began to expand. The event which set off this expansion, and therefore marked the origin of the Universe as we know it, is termed the Big Bang. In this Big Bang, all the matter in the Universe was flung outwards in the form of a dense gas, which has since condensed into giant globules to form galaxies of stars, all of which continue to rush rapidly outwards as space expands.

When did the Big Bang occur? According to current measurements of the rate of expansion of the Universe, all the matter that we now see in space must have been compressed together into a superdense globule between 10,000 million and 20,000 million years ago – about two to four times the age of the Earth. Therefore, modern astronomy allows us to date the Creation with a fair degree of accuracy.

If this view is correct, we should be able to see the Universe as it appeared shortly after it was born by looking deep into space. This is equivalent to looking back in time, because we see objects whose light has taken thousands of millions of years to reach us. Certainly, as we look ever further into space, the Universe begins to change in appearance. Instead of normal-looking galaxies like our own or the Andromeda spiral, astronomers find strange galaxies with brilliant cores known as Seyfert galaxies. Most remote of all are the mysterious quasars, intense sources of light and radio waves which are believed to represent the violent birth of a galaxy. Seyfert galaxies mark a more recent stage than quasars in the evolution of galaxies.

Further confirmation of the Big Bang origin of the Universe has come in recent years with the discovery by radio astronomers of a weak background warmth pervading the Universe. This background radiation is believed to be heat left over from the intense fireball of the Big Bang, and it means that space is not entirely cold, but has a temperature 2·7° above absolute zero on the Centigrade scale.

What will happen to the Universe in the future? One possibility is that the expansion will slow down and the Universe will start to contract again until a further Big Bang. According to one theory, the Universe might continue with endless cycles of expansion and contraction. Astronomers can find no sign that the expansion of the Universe is markedly slowing down. They now think that the Universe will continue to expand forever, slowly thinning out, until all the stars are extinguished and the Universe runs down into eternal darkness.

Composition and structure of the Sun and planets
The **Sun** is a giant gaseous ball of hydrogen and helium with traces of heavier elements such as iron, carbon, calcium and sodium. There is uncertainty about the nature of its internal structure, but there is probably a large core in which thermonuclear reactions produce vast quantities of heat which is transmitted upwards by radiation and convection to the photosphere, the Sun's visible surface. Hydrogen is converted into helium and in the process 4,000,000 tons of matter are lost to the Sun every second. In spite of this staggering loss the supply of hydrogen at the core is sufficient for another 1,500 million years.

Mercury, Venus, Earth and **Mars,** the so-called terrestrial planets, consist largely of silicates (compounds of silicon and oxygen with various metals) and iron. They also include simpler compounds, such as oxides, some of which contain heat-producing radioactive elements. All four planets have undergone differentiation at some stage, with the heavier elements and compounds falling towards the centre. Thus each has a metallic core surrounded by a silicate mantle and topped with a crust of lighter silicates, although the relative sizes of these zones vary from planet to planet. The atmosphere of the Earth consists largely of oxygen and nitrogen, but those of Venus and Mars are predominantly carbon dioxide. Mercury has no atmosphere. The Moon has a composition similar to that of the terrestrial planets but with smaller concentrations of the more volatile elements.

The **Asteroids**, the thousands of small bodies revolving around the Sun mostly between Mars and Jupiter, vary in composition. About 80 per cent of them consist of silicates, 6–10 per cent are made of metal (chiefly iron with some nickel), and the rest are silicate-metal mixtures. Ceres, 429 miles in diameter, is the largest and Pallas (281 miles), is the second largest.

Jupiter is the largest of the planets, having a mass of about two and a half times greater than that of all the other planets combined. Because of its low density it must consist largely of light elements such as hydrogen and helium, although it probably also has a very small rocky core of silicates and iron. Surrounding this hypothetical core is a shell comprising mainly liquid atomic hydrogen, and above that is a surface layer of liquid molecular hydrogen. The atmosphere of Jupiter consists chiefly of hydrogen, helium, ammonia, methane and water. Apart from its great size, Jupiter is remarkable for the Red Spot and bands of clouds which sweep across its face.

Saturn, Uranus and **Neptune** are smaller than Jupiter but also have low densities and are similar in general composition and structure. Their rocky iron-silicate cores are proportionately larger, however, especially in the cases of Uranus and Neptune. All three planets have atmospheres in which the most abundant gas is hydrogen but in which there is little or no ammonia. Methane, on the other hand, is much more abundant than in the atmosphere of Jupiter. Titan, one of the 10 satellites of Saturn, is the largest satellite in the solar system (being larger even than the planet Mercury) and the only one known to have an atmosphere (mainly methane and hydrogen). It also appears to have a unique composition, for it comprises a rocky core surrounded by a wet rocky mantle, a layer of ammonia-water solution, and finally a surface layer of ice and methane. The rings of Saturn probably consist of small ice particles.

Pluto is an anomaly among the outer planets, although very little is really known about it. It is definitely very small, but its precise mass and density are uncertain. It would appear to have no atmosphere.

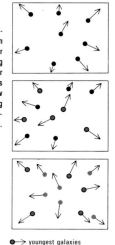

Pluto

Neptune

Uranus

Saturn

Jupiter

The asteroids

Mars

Earth

Venus

Mercury

The Sun

Planetary data	Mercury	Venus	Earth	Mars	Jupiter	Saturn	Uranus	Neptune	Pluto
Orbital revolution	87 days	224 days	365 days	1 year	10 years	29 years	84 years	164 years	249 years
	23 hours	17 hours	6 hours	322 days	318 days	168 days	4 days	292 days	330 days
Distance from Sun in miles	36M	67M	92M	141M	465M	886M	1,783M	2,791M	3,671M
Orbital inclination	7°	3°24'	0°	1°48'	1°18'	2°30'	0°48'	1°48'	17°12'
Equatorial diameter in miles	3,025	3,526	7,926·4	4,200	88,700	75,000	29,300	31,200	3,700
Rotation	59 days	243 days	23 hours	24 hours	9 hours	10 hours	10 hours	14 hours	153 hours
			56 mins	10 mins	50 mins	14 mins	48 mins		
Satellites	0	0	1	2	17	17	5	2	0
Orbital velocity in miles per second	29·8	21·8	18·5	15	8·1	6	4·2	3·4	3

Big Bang theory
Following initial explosion of exceedingly dense matter dispersal outward continues with simultaneous formation of galaxies. This event is estimated to have taken place between 10 and 20,000 million years ago.

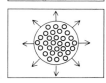

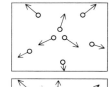

Steady State theory
The Universe did not originate at any one instant in time but all galaxies appear to be continually receding from each other. New matter is created to fill the spaces left and this forms new galaxies. There is strong evidence, particularly observational, against the theory.

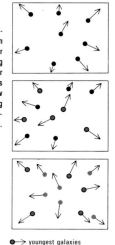

○→ galaxies
●→ oldest galaxies
→ youngest galaxies
→ subsequent galaxies

Bode's Law
If 4 is added to the sequence 0, 3, 6, 12, etc., the resulting numbers give the relative distances of the seven nearest planets to the Sun. The Law, first published in 1772 does not appear valid for Neptune and Pluto at the outer reaches of the solar system.

Mercury	Venus	Earth	Mars	Ceres (Asteroid)	Jupiter	Saturn	Uranus
0	3	6	12	24	48	96	192
4	4	4	4	4	4	4	4
4	7	10	16	28	52	100	196

Stars and galaxies
Stars are born from giant clouds of gas and dust in a galaxy. A typical cloud is the famous nebula in the constellation of Orion. The Orion nebula is lit up by stars that have formed within it during the past few million years. Such a cloud can eventually give rise to a whole cluster of perhaps a hundred stars or more, like the Pleiades cluster in Taurus (see photograph).

As the cloud collapses under the inward pull of its own gravity, it breaks up into smaller clumps from which individual stars will form. Each clump continues to get smaller and denser until the pressure and temperature at its centre becomes so extreme that nuclear reactions start to make the gas ball a true, self-luminous star. Sometimes two, three, or more stars come into being close to each other, and remain linked by gravity throughout their lives as a double or multiple star. In some cases, a star may be surrounded by a disc of material left over from its formation, from which a planetary system may grow. Planets are cold and non-luminous and shine only by reflecting the light of their parent stars.

Stars differ in size and temperature depending on how much matter they contain. The Sun, 865,000 miles in diameter, is an average star in its size and temperature. Some stars are smaller and cooler than the Sun; these are known as red dwarfs, and they are so faint that even the nearest is invisible without a telescope. Other stars are larger and hotter than the Sun, so they appear white like Sirius or even blue like Rigel. A star is powered throughout most of its active life by nuclear reactions that turn hydrogen into helium, as the process in a hydrogen bomb. Stars consist mostly of hydrogen, which is by far the most abundant element in the Universe, and of which gas clouds such as the Orion nebula are mostly made.

As a star ages, it begins to run out of hydrogen at its centre. The nuclear fires then move outwards into the layers surrounding the core, generating more energy as they do so. In response to this the star begins to swell up into a red giant, perhaps 100 times its former size. Stars several times heavier than the Sun then undergo a runaway series of nuclear reactions at their core, leading to their eventual eruption in a nuclear holocaust called a supernova. When a star erupts as a supernova, its brightness increases by millions of times for a few days or weeks before it fades away into obscurity.

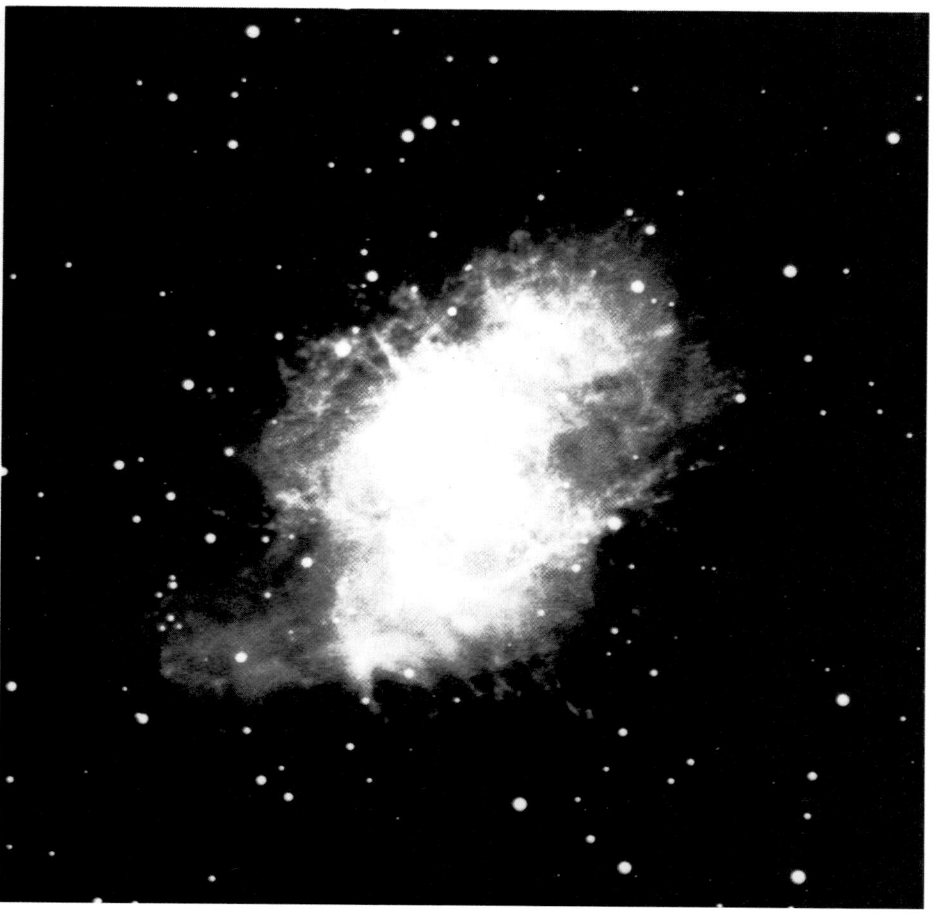

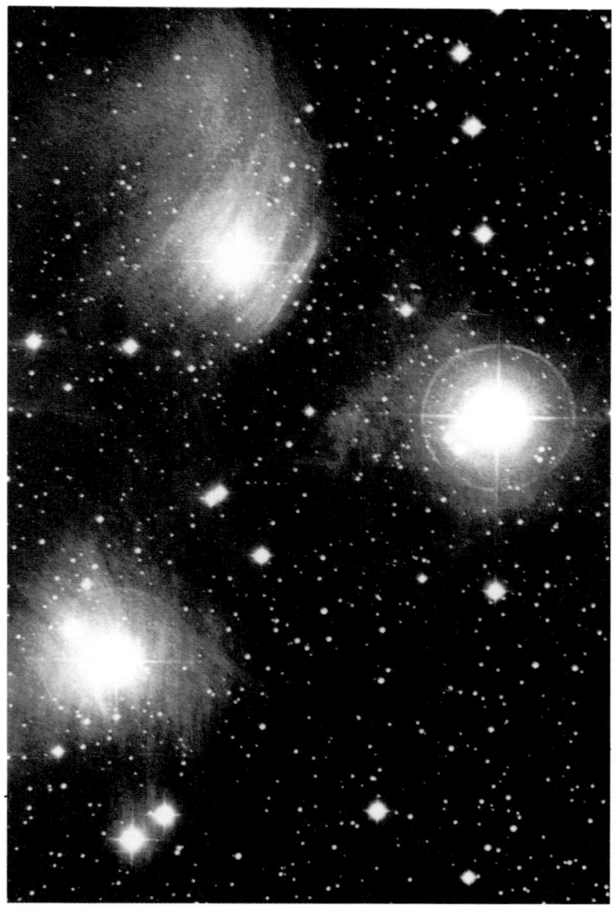

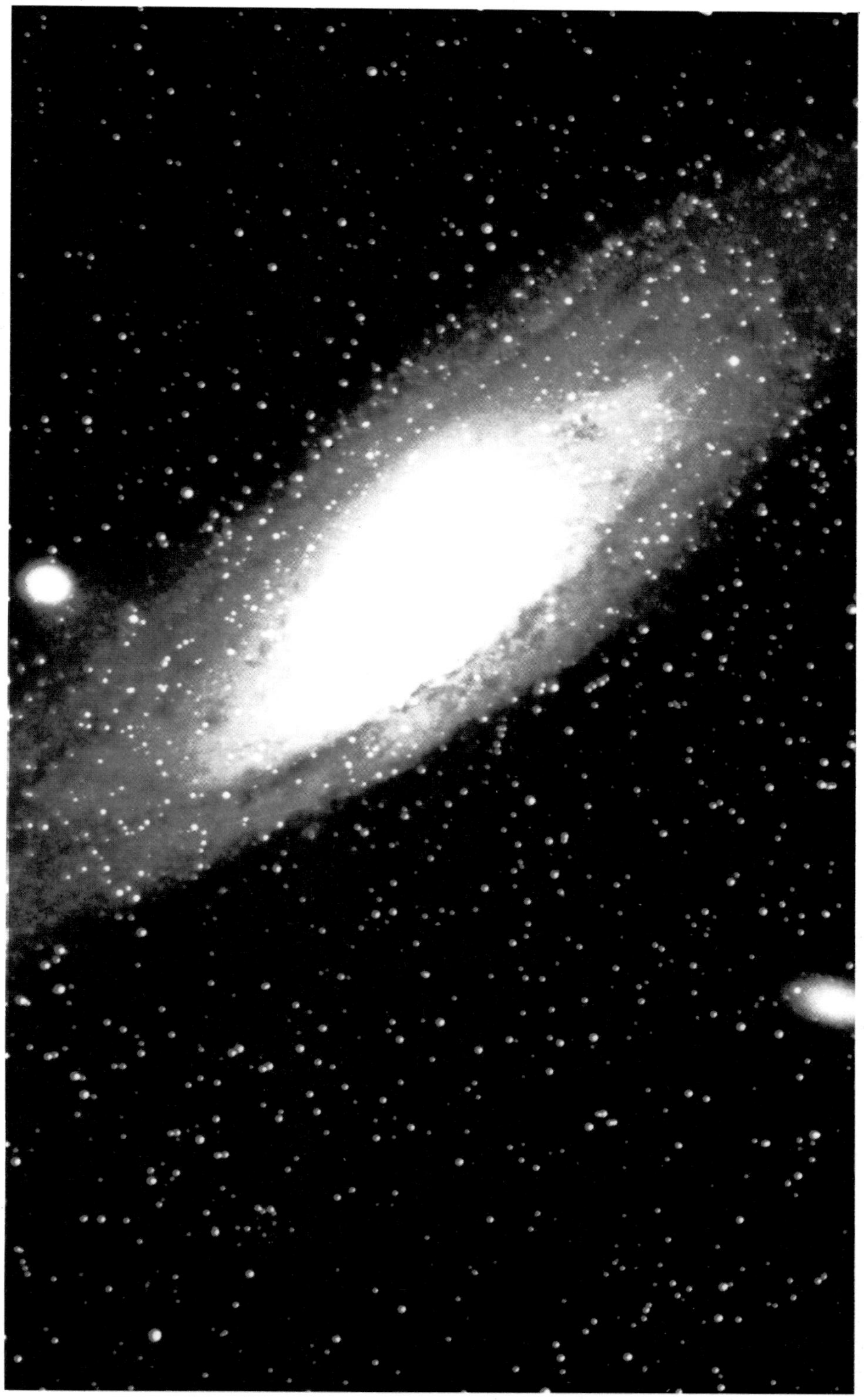

A supernova explosion throws the star's outer layers off into space, producing an object like the Crab nebula in Taurus (see photograph) which is the remains of a supernova observed by Oriental astronomers in AD 1054. During a supernova explosion the erupting star's central core is compressed into a small, dense object known as a neutron star, about 10 miles in diameter. Neutron stars were first detected by radio astronomers in 1967 as the rapidly flashing radio sources known as pulsars. Pulsars are actually fast-spinning neutron stars which emit a flash of energy every time they revolve.

Black holes
If the remnant core of a star weighs more than about three times the Sun, then the inward pull of its own gravity is so strong that it cannot remain as a neutron star. It continues to shrink ever smaller and denser until it vanishes from sight in a black hole. A black hole is formed once the object has reached a certain small size and high density and its gravitational pull is so great that nothing can escape, not even light. The centre of the black hole, the point where all matter is compressed to infinite density and zero volume is termed a 'singularity'. The hole therefore becomes truly black, and cannot be seen from outside. However, matter can fall into a black hole, and this gives a clue to the object's existence. Gas falling into the intense gravitational field around a black hole heats up to many millions of degrees, emitting X-rays which can be detected by satellites orbiting Earth. In this way, astronomers believe they have detected at least one black hole, known as the X-ray source Cygnus X-I, orbiting a visible star catalogued HDE 226868 in the constellation Cygnus about 6,500 light years distant.

Death of the Sun
An ordinary star such as the Sun dies much more quietly. The Sun is nearly 5,000 million years old, which means that it is halfway through its expected life. In about another 5,000 million years it will run out of hydrogen at the core and start to burn helium. It will then swell to 250 times its present size into a red giant star like Arcturus. As it does so it will engulf the planets Mercury, Venus, and perhaps also the Earth. Long before then, life on our planet will have become extinct. At its death, the Earth will be consumed by fire.

The nebulous outer layers of the red giant Sun will then slowly disperse into space, forming a giant smoke ring. This stage will last some fifty thousand years. The Sun's hot core will be left behind as a white dwarf star, about the size of the Earth. Over millions upon millions of years this white dwarf will slowly cool into invisibility by slowly releasing energy from its outer layers. Any charred remains of the Earth will be engulfed by ice as the white dwarf Sun fades away like a dying ember, leaving only memories of the human civilisation that once flourished around it.

Galaxies and the Universe
The Milky Way Galaxy in which the Solar System is situated probably started to form about 15,000 million years ago; the age of the oldest stars. This Galaxy is about 100,000 light years in diameter; the Sun and its system of nine planets lie about two-thirds of the way from the centre to the limit of the arm of the spiral. Large telescopes reveal countless other galaxies dotted throughout space. One of the nearest of these galaxies is the giant spiral in the constellation Andromeda (see photo) which lies over two million light years from the Earth. If we could see our own Galaxy from the outside, it would probably look much like Andromeda. All the Milky Way stars are orbiting around the centre of the Galaxy; the Sun takes 225 million years to complete the circuit.

Our own Galaxy and the Andromeda spiral are the two largest members of a cluster of about 30 galaxies called the Local Group. Many other galaxies are also bunched into groups like this, although there are plenty of individual galaxies dotted through space.

Two small galaxies, 160,000 light years away, are visible in the Southern Hemisphere. These are known as the Magellanic Clouds and are linked to our own Galaxy through a common envelope of hydrogen gas. Most galaxies are spiral in shape, but some are elliptical. The largest galaxies of all are giant ellipticals, containing a hundred times as many stars as our Milky Way.

As astronomers probed deep into the Universe with large telescopes half a century ago, they found an amazing fact: all galaxies, either individually or in groups, seemed to be rushing away from each other, as though the space between them was expanding. This fact was deduced from the red shift, or lengthening of the wavelength of light received from the galaxies, which would be caused by such a recession. The light waves are stretched out by the Doppler effect and at a given wavelength move towards the red end of the spectrum. The amount of the red shift is measured by the movement of the dark absorption line. This reveals the speed of recession of the galaxy and therefore its distance can be computed. Astronomers therefore began to compare the Universe to a continually inflating balloon. This provided a vital clue to the possible origin of the Universe, (see Big Bang theory).

Future scientific exploration of the centre of our Galaxy will rely on infra-red and radio observations which can penetrate the interstellar dust.

The Moon

The Moon is by far our nearest natural neighbour in space. It orbits the Earth every month at an average distance of 240,000 miles. The Moon is 2,160 miles in diameter, or roughly one-quarter the size of the Earth. No other natural satellite in the solar system is so close in size to its parent body, so astronomers often regard the Earth–Moon pairing as a double planet.

Roc. returned by American astronauts and Soviet automatic landers have confirmed that the Moon was born at the same time as the Earth, approximately 4,700 million years ago. Probably the two objects formed side by side, although it is possible that the Moon formed elsewhere in the solar system and was later captured. Most astronomers now think it unlikely that the Moon split away from the Earth.

The Moon's surface is pitted with craters of varying sizes, from vast basins more than 100 miles in diameter to microscopic pits. Astronomers argued over the origin of these for centuries, but it is now generally agreed that the majority of them were formed by the impact of meteorites long ago in the history of the solar system. This theory has been strengthened by the discovery that similar craters pockmark the surface of other bodies in the solar system, notably the planets Mercury and Mars.

Early in its history the Moon partially melted so that a rocky crust solidified at its surface. This crust has since been buffeted by meteorites which have produced the jumbled highlands. Several particularly large bodies have gouged out lowland basins which have since been flooded with dark lava. These dark lowlands are called the *maria*, or seas.

Unmanned space probes orbiting the Moon have made a complete photographic map of its front and back surface. As the Moon spins on its own axis in the same time as it takes to orbit the Earth (termed a *captured* rotation) no man had seen the far side of the Moon until the first space probes were sent to investigate. It has been found that there are no large *mare* regions on the far side of the Moon, evidently because the Moon's crust is about 25 miles thicker on the far side than on the Earth-turned hemisphere.

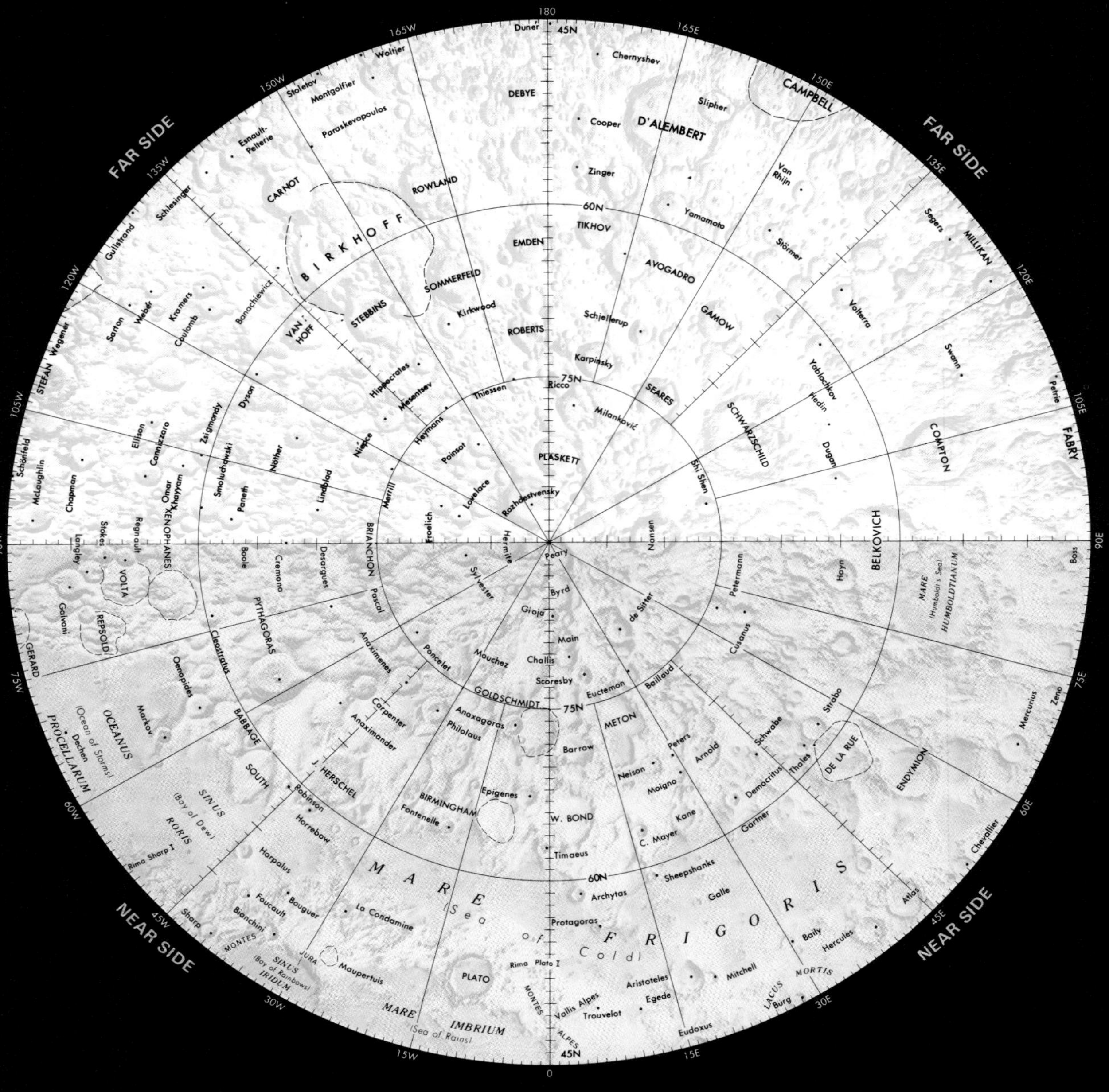

NORTH POLAR REGION

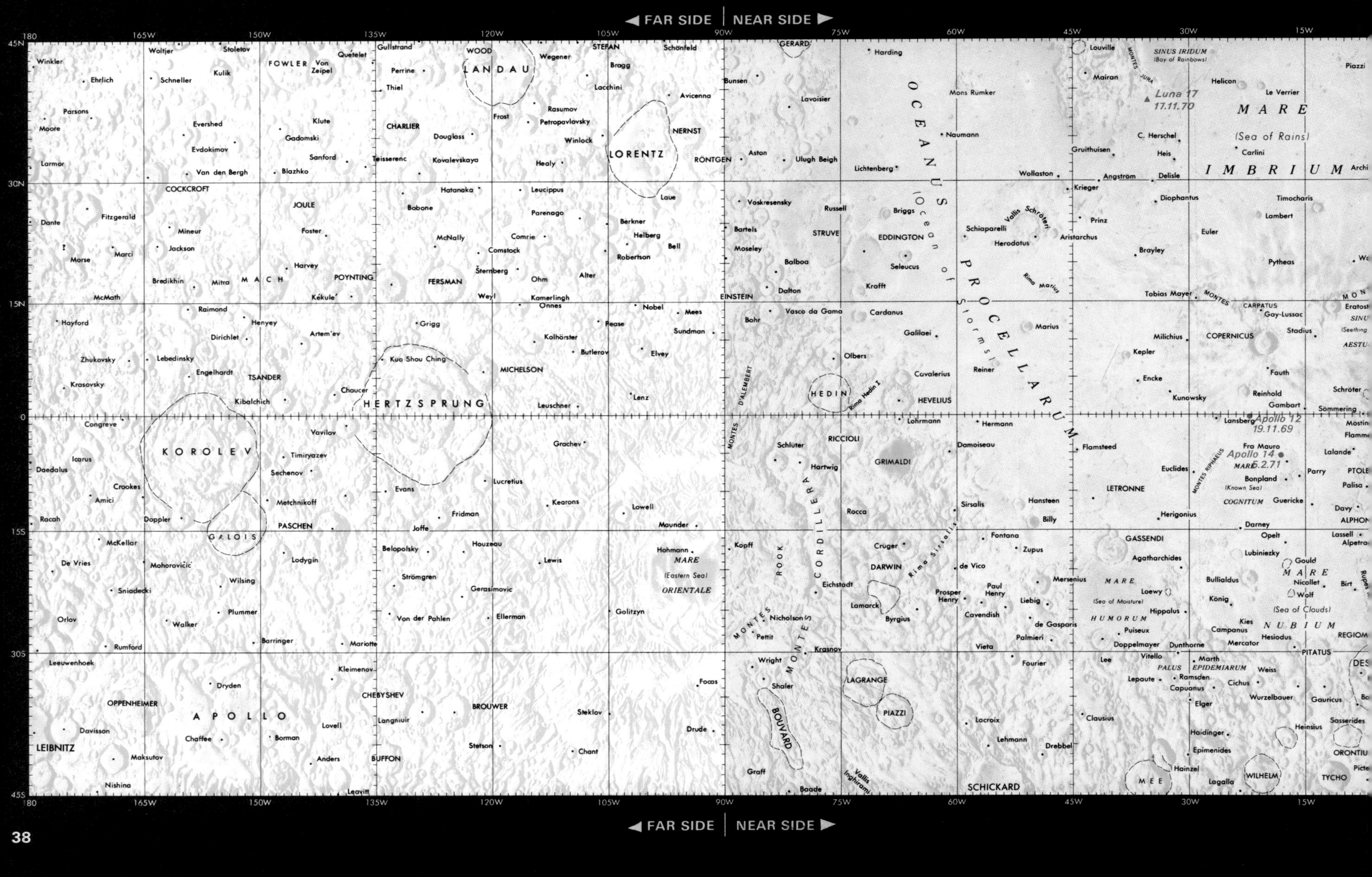

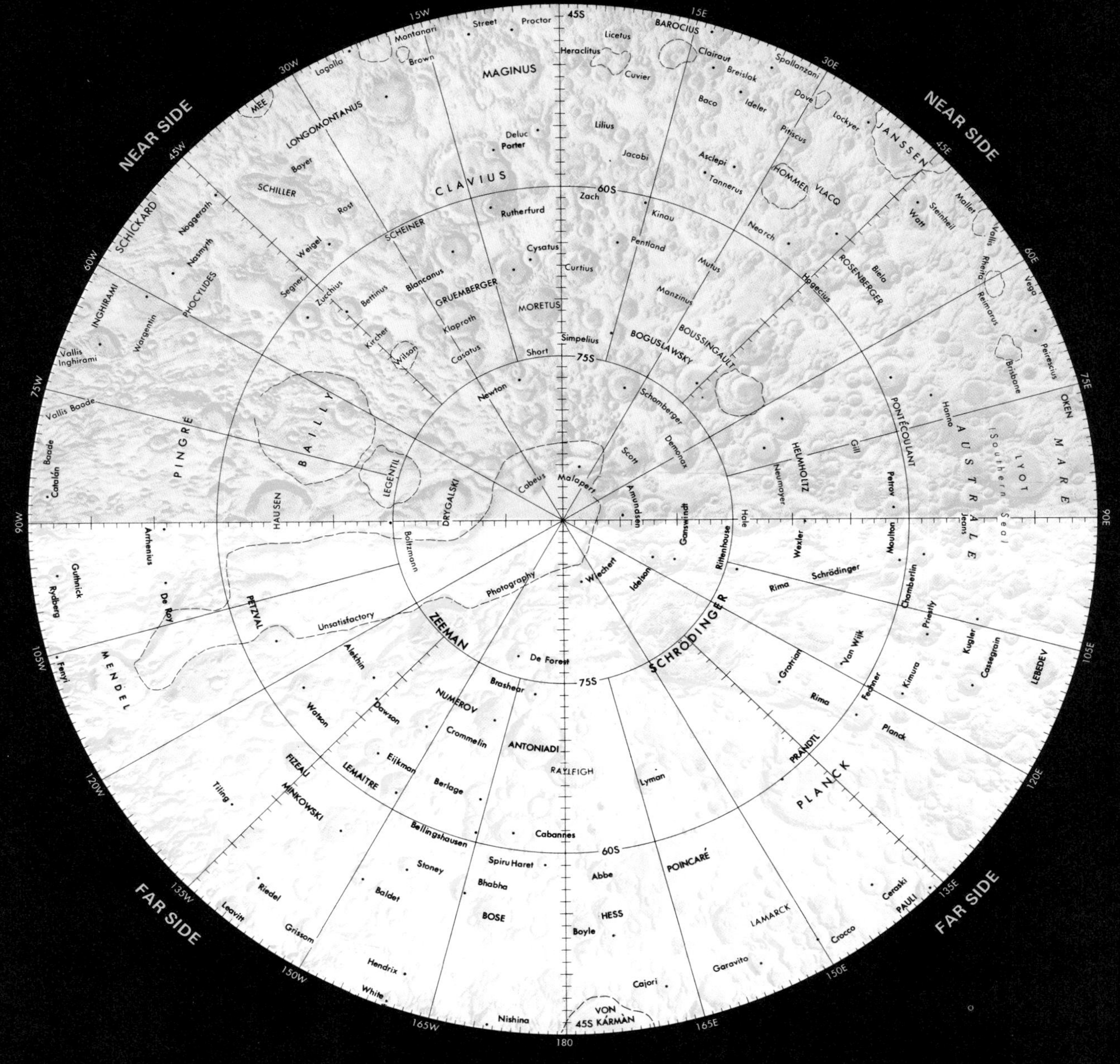

SOUTH POLAR REGION

LUNAR DATA

Earth/Moon Mass Ratio	M_e/M_m 81·3015
Density (mean)	3·34g/(cm)³
Synodic Month (new Moon to new Moon)	29·530, 588d
Sidereal Month (fixed star to fixed star)	27·321, 661d
Inclination of Lunar orbit to eclipse	5°8'43"
Inclination of equator to eclipse	1°40'32"
Inclination of Lunar orbit to Earth's equator	18°·5 to 28°·5
Distance from Moon to Earth (mean)	238·328M (384,400km)
Optical libration in longitude	±7°·6
Optical libration in latitude	±6°·7
Magnitude (mean of full Moon)	−12·7
Temperature	−244°F to +273°F (120°K to 407°K)
Escape velocity	1·48mi/sec (2·38km/sec)
Diameter of Moon 2,160mi (3,476km)	
Surface gravity	162·2 cm/sec²
Orbital velocity	0·64mi/sec (Moon) 1·024km/sec 18·5mi/sec (Earth) 29·6km/sec

◀ NEAR SIDE | FAR SIDE ▶

▲ Landing site of Soviet Moon vehicle "Lunokhod"
● Manned Spacecraft landing site

◀ NEAR SIDE | FAR SIDE ▶

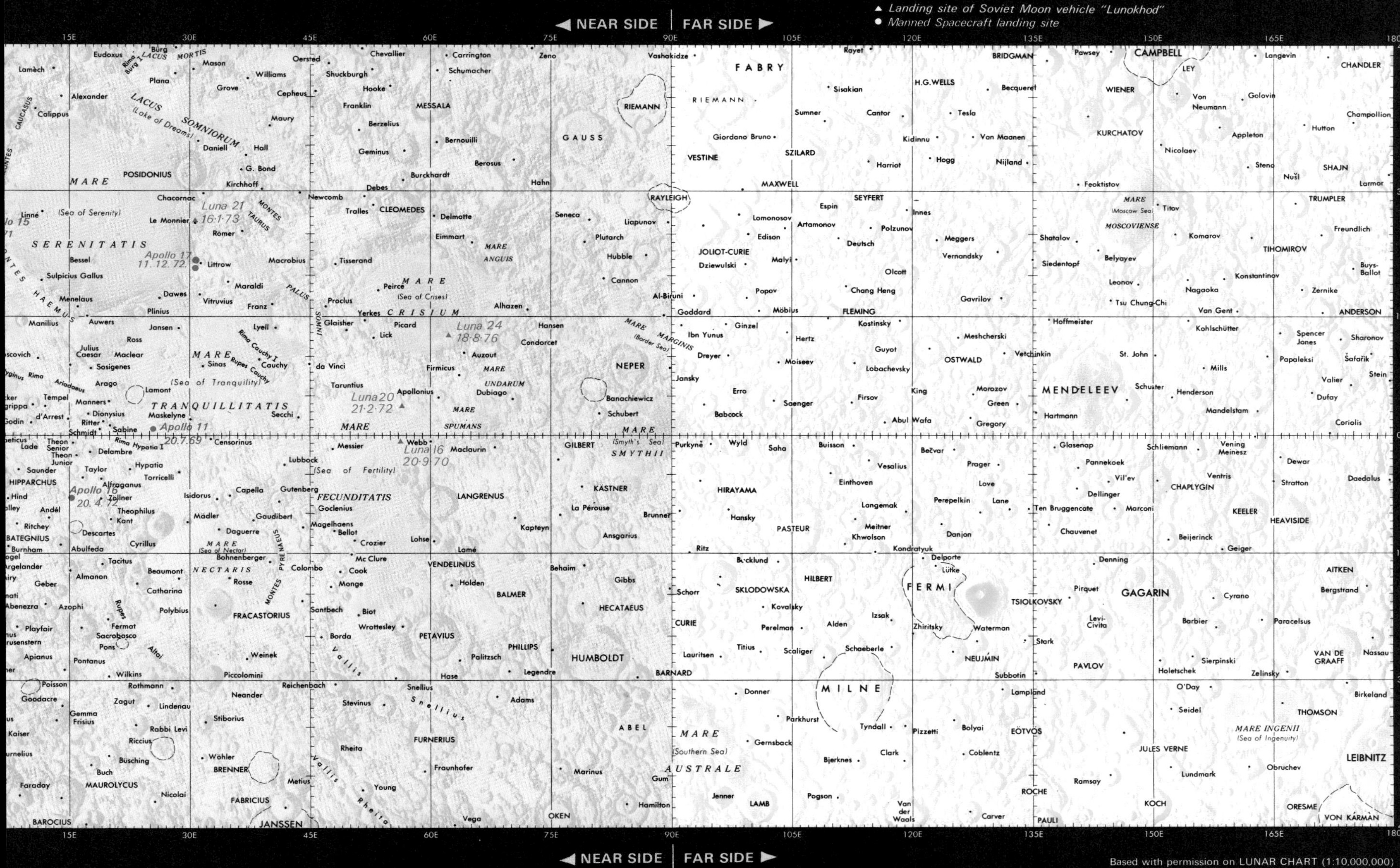

Based with permission on LUNAR CHART (1:10,000,000) by the Aeronautical Chart and Information Centre, United States Air Force.

The Stars

Northern Sky

Southern Sky

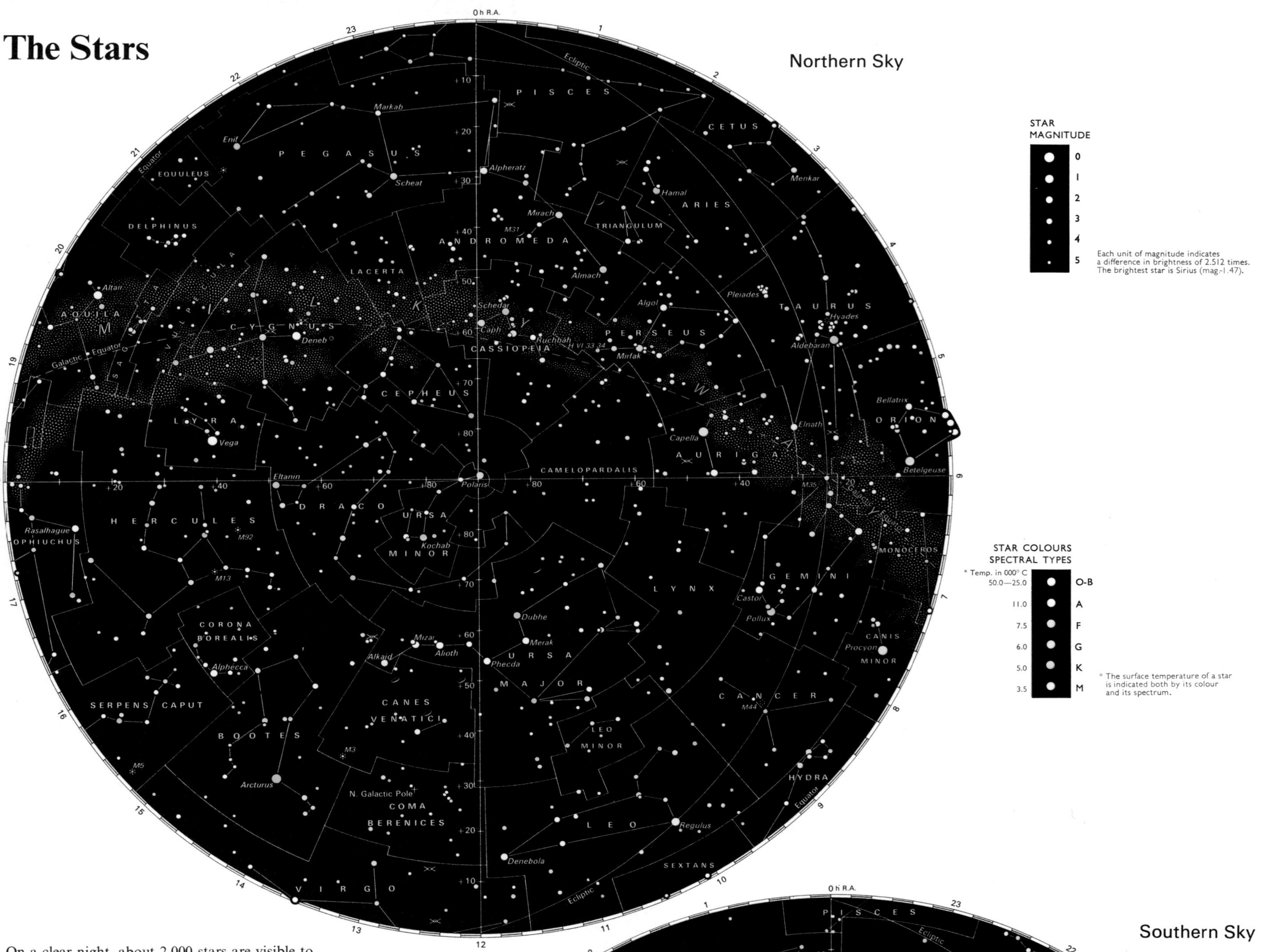

On a clear night, about 2,000 stars are visible to the naked eye at any one time. Countless thousands of others become visible with modest optical aid such as a pair of binoculars or a small telescope. The charts on this page show the main stars of the northern and southern hemisphere of the sky, along with the constellations into which they are grouped. Unless an observer is situated at the north or south pole, he will see some stars in both hemispheres. How far he sees into the opposite hemisphere depends on how close he is to the equator. The number of stars visible depends on the time and the season.

Some constellation figures go back thousands of years to ancient Mediterranean peoples, who placed their mythical beasts and heroes among the stars. Since then, more constellations have been added, particularly in the southern hemisphere which was invisible from the Mediterranean, so that a total of 88 constellations now cover the entire sky. They are useful for indicating the approximate locations of celestial objects. Precise locations are given by the celestial equivalents of longitude and latitude – Right Ascension (R.A., measured in hours, minutes, and seconds) and Declination (measured in degrees).

The size of the star images on the maps represents the perceived brightness of each star. Star brightnesses are measured in magnitudes, with the brightest stars first magnitude, and the faintest stars visible to the naked eye the sixth magnitude. A first magnitude star is 100 times brighter than a sixth magnitude star. Objects brighter than first magnitude are given increasingly large negative magnitudes, such as Sirius −1·47, the planet Venus at its brightest −4·4, the full Moon −12·7, and the Sun −26·8. Objects fainter than sixth magnitude are given progressively larger positive magnitudes. The faintest objects so far detected are around magnitude 24.

Although all stars appear white they are different colours, depending on their temperatures. The stars with coolest surface temperatures appear red, like the red giant Arcturus, while the hottest stars such as Sirius appears white or blue. The temperature of a star can be deduced from an examination of its spectrum; this classification is known as a star's spectral type.

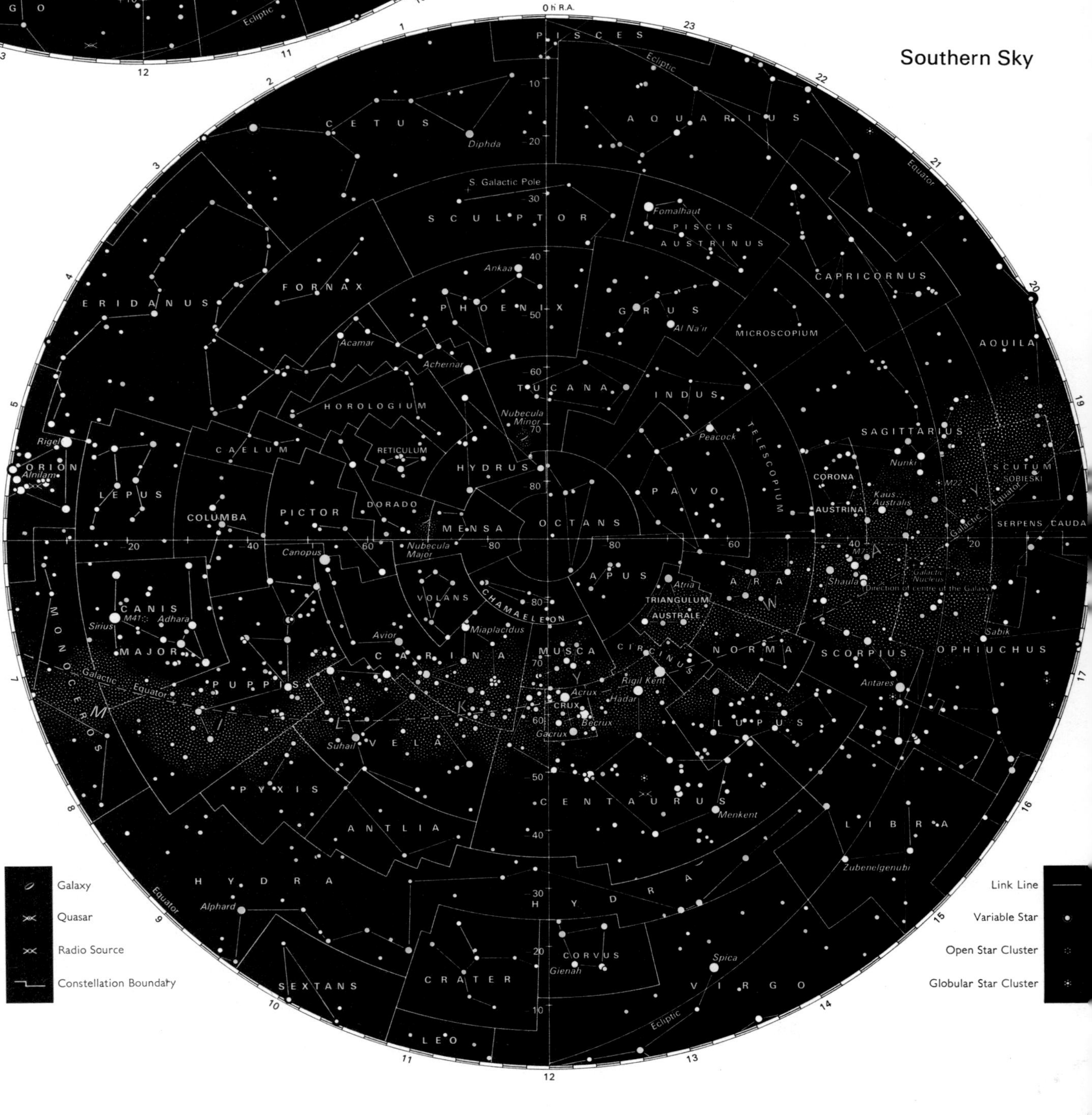

BOUNDARIES

- International
- International, Undefined or Alignment Uncertain
- Limits of Sovereignty across Water Areas
- Autonomous, Federal State
- Main Administrative
- Other Administrative
- Offshore Administrative
- Armistice, Cease-Fire Line
- Demilitarised Zone
- National Park
- Reserve, Reservation

COMMUNICATIONS

- Main Railways
- Other Railway
- Light Railway
- Projected Railways
- Railway Tunnels
- Road Tunnel
- Special Highway — *Projected*
- Main Road — *Projected*
- Other Road — *Projected*
- Tracks
- Car Ferries
- Rail Ferries
- Navigable Canals — *Locks*
- Projected or Disused Canal
- Drainage or Irrigation Canal
- Canal Tunnel
- Tunnel Aqueduct

LAKE TYPES

- Fresh-water
- Reservoir — *Dam*
- Seasonal Fresh
- Seasonal Brackish
- Salt-lake, Lagoon
- Perennial Salt-lake
- Seasonal Salt-lake
- Saline Mud-flat
- Salt-flat

LANDSCAPE FEATURES

- Ice-field and Glaciers
- Ice-cap, Ice-sheet
- Lava-fields
- Lava-fields
- Sand Desert, Dunes
- Saline Marsh, Salt Desert
- Marsh, Swamp
- Swamp, Flood-area
- Mangrove Swamp
- Tidal Area
- Atoll

OTHER FEATURES

- River, Stream
- Seasonal Watercourses
- Seasonal Flood-plain
- Undefined Course of River
- Pass; Gorges
- Waterfalls, Rapids
- Dam, Barrage
- Escarpments
- Flood Dyke
- Limits of Ice-shelf
- Reefs
- Rocks
- Spot Depth · 9650
- Lighthouse
- Lightship; Beacon
- Waterhole, Well
- Active Volcano
- Summit, Peak
- Oil Wells
- Oil or Natural Gas Pipeline
- Mine
- Site of Battle
- Historic Site
- Historic Ruin
- Ancient Walls
- Mosque, Sheikh's Tomb
- Cathedral, Monastery, Church
- International or Main Airport
- Airport, Airfield

CITY MAPS

- State Boundary
- County, Department Boundary
- City Limits
- Borough, District Boundary
- Main Railways — *Station*
- Other Railways — *Bridge*
- Projected Railways
- Underground Railway — *Station*
- Special Highway — *Projected*
- Main Road
- Secondary Road
- Other Road, Street
- Track
- Road Tunnel
- Bridge; Flyover
- Seaway — *Locks*
- Canals
- Drainage Canal
- Waterfalls, Rapids
- Historic Walls
- Airports
- Racecourses
- Stadium
- Cemetery; Churches
- Woodland, Park
- Built-up Area

STYLES OF LETTERING

T O G O	Country Name
A L B E R T A	-Major
KENT CHER	Administrative Divisions -Other
PARIS <u>Bern</u>	National Capitals
<u>Omsk</u>	
<u>Denver</u>	Administrative Centres
<u>Krakow</u>	
GANDER Gatwick	Airports

M O A B	Historic Region
D E C C A N	
S I N A I	Physical Regions
Mato Grosso	
ATLAS Nile	Physical Features
Mt Blanc Thames	
BASIN Ridge	Ocean Bottom Features
M A S A I	Tribal Name

PRINCIPAL MAP ABBREVIATIONS

A.	1. Alp, Alpen, Alpi. 2. Alt	Ch^lle	Chapelle	Hist.	Historic	M^gne	Montagne	Pr.	1. Proliv. 2. Przyladek. 3. Prince	S.S.R.	Sovétskaya Sotsialisticheskaya Respúblika
Abb^e	Abbaye	C^ma	Cima	H^n	Horn	Mkt.	Markt			
A.C.T.	Australian Capital Territory	C^mo	Corno	Hosp.	1. Hospice, Hospiz 2. Hospital	Mon.	Monasterio, Monastery	Prom^y	Promontory	S^t	Saint, Sint, Staryy
		C°	Cerro					Prop.	Proposed	St.	1. State. 2. Stor, Store
Aig.	Aiguille	Const^n	Construction	Ht.	Haut	Mont.	Monument	PROT.	Protectorate		
Akr.	Åkra, Akrotírion	Cord.	Cordillera	Hte.	Haute	Mt.	Mont, Mount, Mountain	PROV.	Provincial	Sta	Santa
Anch.	Anchorage	Cr.	Creek	H^ter	Hinter			P^so	Passo	Sta.	Station
A.O.	Avtonómnaya Oblast'	Cuch.	Cuchilla	H^y	Highway	Mte.	Monte	P^t.	1. Point. 2. Pont	Stby.	Staby, Statsjonsby
		Cuc^ru	Cuccuru (Sardinia)	I.	Île, Ilha, Insel, Isla, Island, Isle, Isola, Isole	Mtes	Montes	P^t.	1. Petit. 2. Point.	S^te	Sainte
App^no	Appennino	Cy.	City			Mti.	Monti, Munti		3. Pont	Ste.	Store
Aqued.	Aqueduct	Czo.	Cozzo			Mts.	Monts, Mountains	P^ta	1. Ponta, Punta.	Sten.	Stenon, Stenos
Ar.	Arroyo	D.	1. Da, Dag, Dagh, Dağ, Dağları. 2. Darreh. 3. Daryácheh	IJ.	IJssel	N.	1. Nam. 2. Neu, Ny. 2. Nevado, Nudo, 4. Noord, Nord, Nörre, Nørre, North. 5. Nos		2. Puente	S^to	Santo
Arch.	Archipel, Archipelago, Archipiélago			im.	imeni			P^te	1. Pointe. 2. Ponte. Puente	Str.	Strait
Arr.	Arrecife			In.	1. Inder, Indre, Inner, Inre. 2. Inlet			P^to	1. Porto, Puerto. 2. Ponto, Punto	S^tu	Stuvina (Sardinia)
A.S.S.R.	Avtonómnaya Sovétskaya Sotsialisticheskaya Respúblika	-d.	dake	IND.	India			P^zo	Pizzo	Sv.	Svaty, Sveti
		D.C.	District of Columbia	Inf.	Inferior, -e, Inférieure	N^a	Nuestra	Q.	1. Qala, Qara, Qarn. 2. Quang	S.W.	South West
		Den.	Denmark	Int.	International	Nat.	National			T.	1. Tal. 2. Tal, Tall, Tell. 3. Tepe, Tepesi
Ay.	Ayía, Ayíoi, Áyion, Ayios	Dists.	Districts	I^s	Îles, Ilhas, Islands, Islas, Isles	Nats.					
		Div.	Division	ISR.	Israel	Okr.	Natsionalnyy Okrug	Ra.	Range	Talsp.	Talsperre
B.	1. Baai, Bahía, Baía, Baie, Baja, Bay, Bucht, Bukhta, Bukt. 2. Bad, 3. Ban. 4. Barazh, Barrage, Barragem 5. Bayou. 6. Bir. 7. Boeloe, Bonto, Bulu	Dj.	Djebel	Isth.	Isthmus	N.D.	Notre Dame	Rap.	Rapids	Tel.	Teluk
		Dns.	Downs	J.	1. Jabal, Jebel, Jibāl. 2. Järvi, Jaure, Jazira, Jezero, Jezîoro. 3. Jökull	N^er	Neder, Nieder	R^ca	Rocca	Terr.	Terrace
		Dz.	Dzong			N.E.	North East	R^d	Road	Terr^y	Territory
		D^zg	Dzong			Neth.	Netherlands	REC.	Recreation	Thwy.	Throughway, Thruway
		E.	East			Nizh.	Nizhne, Nizhniy	Res.	Reservoir		
		E^il.	Eiland, Eilanden			Nizm.	Nizmennost	Reef	Reef		
		Emb.	Embalse	Jap.	Japan, Japanese	N.O.	Noord Oost, Nord Ost	R^ge	Ridge	Tk.	Teluk
		Escarp.	Escarpment	Jct.	Junction			Rib^a	Ribeira	T^mt	Tablemount
B°	1. Branch. 2. Bredning. 3. Bridge, Brücke. 4. Britain, British. 5. Burun	Est.	Estacion	K.	1. Kaap, Kap, Kapp. 2. Kaikyo. 3. Kato. 4. Kerang, Kering. 5. Kiang. 6. Kirke. 7. Ko. 8. Koh, Küh, Kühha. 9. Kolpos. 10. Kopf. 11. Kuala. 12. Kyst	Nor.	Norway, Norwegian	R^k	Rock	T°	Tando
B^ca	Boca	E^te	East			N^os	Nudos	Rly.	Railway	Tpk.	Turnpike
B^co	Banco	F.	Firth			Nov.	Novvy			Tr^c	Trench, Trough
Bel.	Belgium, Belgian	F.D.	Federal District			N^r	Nether	R.S.F.S.R.	Rossíyskaya Sovétskaya Federatívnaya Sotsialisticheskaya Respúblika	T^re	Torre
Bg.	Berg	Fj.	1. Fjell. 2. Fjord, Fjörður			N.W.	North West			Tun.	Tunnel
Bgt.	Bight, Bugt	F^k	Fork			N.Z.	New Zealand			U.	Uad
B^i	Bani, Beni	Fl.	Fleuve			O.	1. Old. 2. Oost, Ost. 3. Ostrov			U.A.E.	United Arab Emirates
B^j	Burj	F^r	France, French					R^te	Route		
B^k	Bank	Ft.	Fort	Kan.	Kanal, Kanaal	Ob.	Ober	Rom.	Romania, Romanian	Ug.	Ujung
Bk.	Boekoe, Buku	Fy.	Ferry	Kap.	Kapelle	O^de	Oude			U.K.	United Kingdom
B^n	Basin	G.	1. Gawa. 2. Gebel. 3. Ghedir. 4. Göl, Gölü, Göl. 5. Golfe, Golfo, Gulf. 6. Gompa. 7. Gora, Gory. 8. Guba. 9. Gunung	Kep.	Kepulauan	O^et	Oguilet	S.	1. Salar, Salina. 2. San. 3. Saw. 4. See. 5. Seto. 6. Sjö. 7. Sör, South, Syd. 8. Sung. 9. sur	Unt.	Unter
Bol.	Bol'shoy			Kg.	Kampong, Kompong, Kong	Ogl.	Oglat			Up^r	Upper
Bos.	Bosanski					O.L.V.	Onze Lieve Vrouw			U.S.A.	United States of America
Br.	1. Branch. 2. Bredning. 3. Bridge, Brücke. 4. Britain, British. 5. Burun			Kh.	1. Khawr. 2. Khirbet, Khiābān, -e. 3. Khowr	Or.	Ori, Oros			U.S.S.R.	Union of Soviet Socialist Republics
		G.D.&D.	Goa, Daman & Diu			Ormos	Ormos			V.	1. Val, Valle. 2. Väster, Vest, Vester. 3. Vatn. 4. Ville. 5. Vorder
		G^d	Grand			Ot.	Olet	S^a	Serra, Sierra		
Bt.	Bukit	G^de	Grande	Khr.	Khrebet	Öv.	Över, Övre	Sab.	Sabkhat		
Bü.	Büyük	Geb.	Gebergte, Gebirge	Kl.	1. Kechil. 2. Klein, -e	O^va	Ostrova	Sc.	Scoglio (Sardinia)	V^dkhr.	Vodokhranilishche
Bukh.	Bukhta	Geog^l	Geographical	Kör.	Körfez, -i	Oz.	Ozero	S^d	Sound, Sund	Vel.	Velikiy
C.	1. Cabo, Cap, Cape. 2. Cay. 3. Česká, -é, -y. 4. Col.	Gez.	Gezira	Kr.	Kangar	P.	1. Pass. 2. Pic, Pico, Piz. 3. Pulau	S.E.	South East	Ven.	Venezuela, Venezuelan
		Ghub.	Ghubba	Kü.	Küçük			Seb.	Sebjet, Sebkhat, Sebkra		
		Gl.	1. Gamle, Gammel. 2. Glacier	L.	1. Lac, Lago, Lagôa, Lake, Liman, Limni, Liqen, Loch, Lough. 2. Lom	Pal.	Palace, Palacio, Palais			Verkh.	Verkhniy
Cach.	Cachoeira, -o	Gp.	Group			Pass.	Passage	Sev.	Sever, Severnaya	Vol.	Volcán, Volcano, Vulkan
Can.	1. Canal. 2. Canale. 3. Canavese. 4. Cañon, Canyon	Gr.	1. Graben. 2. Gross, -e			Peg.	Pegunungan	S^ano	Stagno (Sardinia)		
		G^r	Gasr			Pen.	Peninsula, Penisola	Sh.	1. Sh'aib. 2. Sharif. 3. Shatt. 4. Shima	Vost.	Vostochnyy
Cas.	Castle	G^rtes	Grottes	Lag.	Lagoon, Laguna, -e	Per.	Pereval			Vozv.	Vozvyshennost'
Cat.	1. Cataract. 2. Catena (Sardinia)	Gt.	Great, Groot, -e	L^d	Land	P^gio	Poggio	S^i	Sidi	W.	1. Wadi. 2. Wald. 3. Wan. 4. Water. 5. Well. 6. West
Cath.	Cathedral	H.	1. Hawr. 2. Hill. 3. Hoch. 4. Hora, Hory	Ldg.	Landing	Pk.	1. Park. 2. Peak, Pik	S^knoll	Seaknoll		
C^ca	Cabeça, -o (Azores)			L.H.	Light House	Pkwy.	Parkway	S^kt	Sankt		
C^d	Ciudad	Halv.	Halvöy	Lit.	Little	Pl.	1. Planina, Planinski. 2. Plei	Sl.	Slieve		
Cerv.	Cervená, -é, -ý	H^b	Harbour	Ll.	Lille			S^mt	Seamount	W^r	Wester
Ch.	1. Chapel, Chapelle, Church. 2. Chaung. 3. Chott.	H^d	Head	M.	1. Mae, Me. 2. Meer. 3. Muang. 4. Muntil 5. Muong. 6. Mys	P^la	Playa	Snr^a	Senhora	Y.	Yama
		H.E.P.	Hydro-Electric Power			Plat.	Plateau	Snr^o	Senhoro	Y^t	Ytre, Ytter, Ytri
Chan.	Channel	H^g	Hegység	m.	metre/s	Plosk.	Ploskogor'ye	Sp.	1. Spain, Spanish. 2. Spitze	Yuzh.	Yuzhnaya, Yuzhno, Yuzhnyy
Ch^au	Château	H^ts	Heights	Mal.	Malyy	P^no	Pantano				
Ch°	Chaine	H^i	Hasi, Hasy	Mem.	Memorial	P^nte	Pointe	S^pk	Seapeak	Z.	Zaliv
				Mex.	Mexico, Mexican	Por.	Porog	Spr.	Spring	Zal.	Zaliv
				M^f	Massif	Port.	Portugal, Portuguese	S^r	Sönder, Sönder	Zap.	Zapadnyy, -aya, -o, -oye
				M^gna	Montagna	P^ov	Poluostrov	Sr.	Sredniy	Zem.	Zemlya

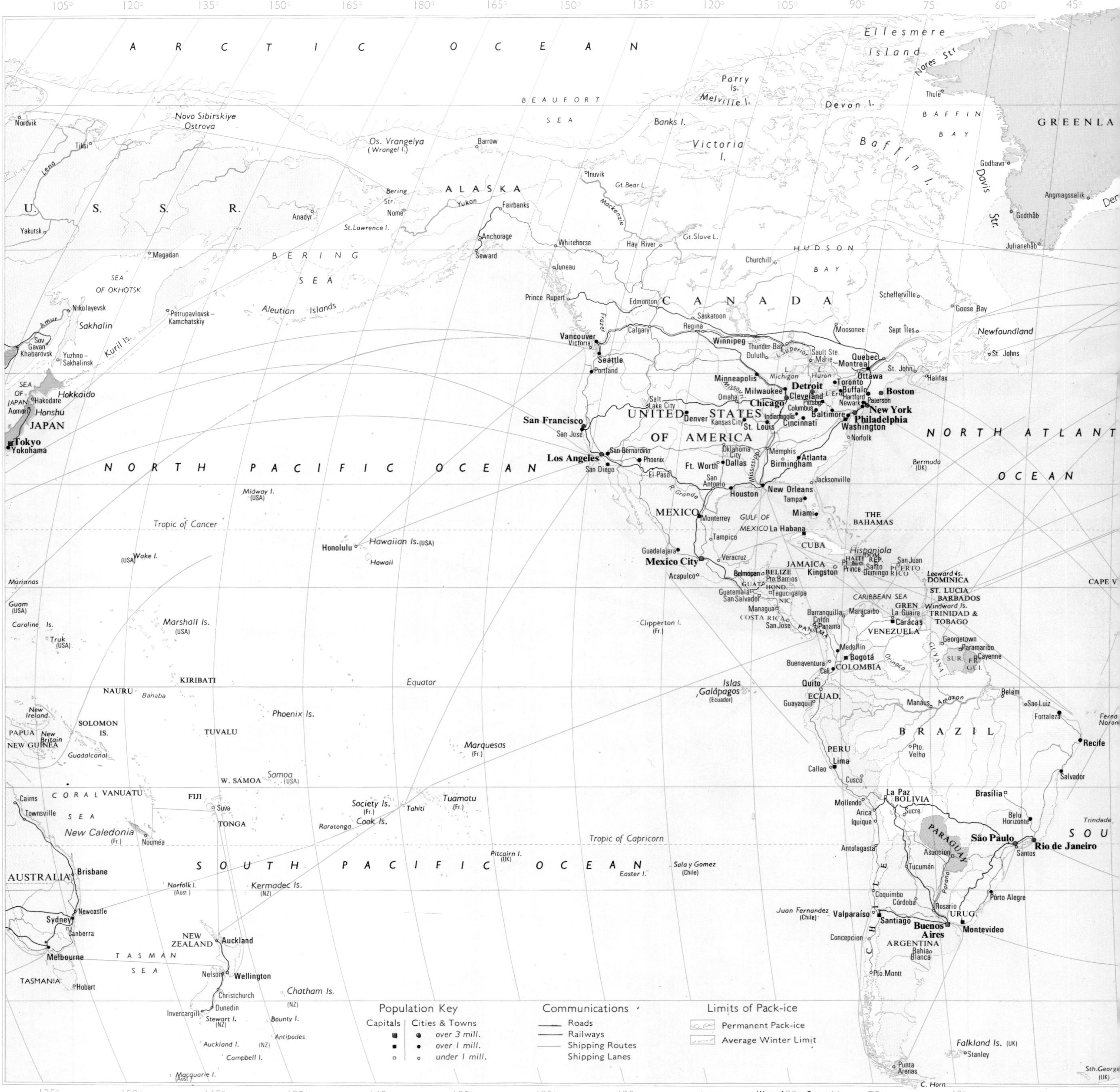

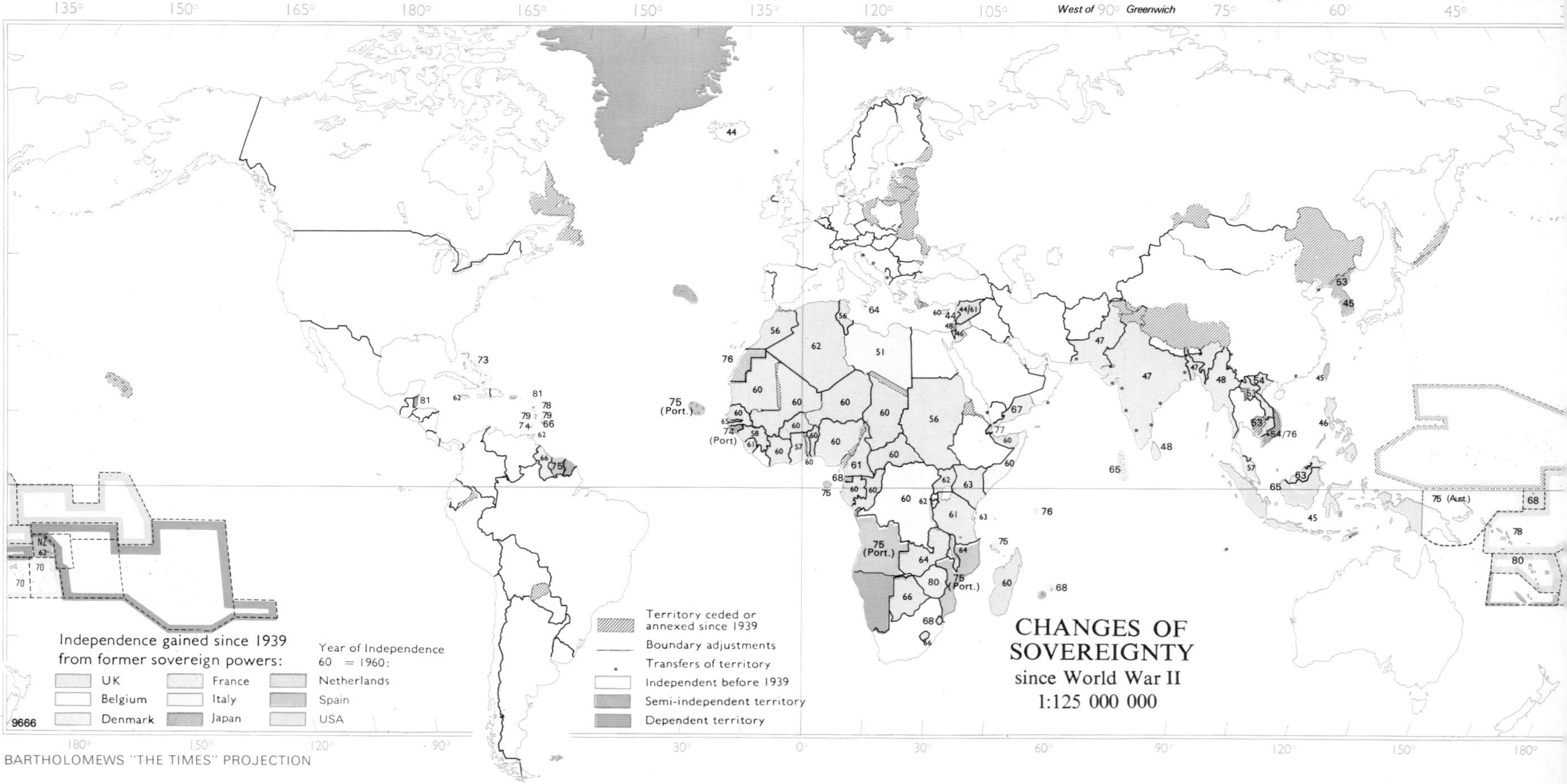

CHANGES OF SOVEREIGNTY
since World War II
1:125 000 000

BARTHOLOMEWS "THE TIMES" PROJECTION

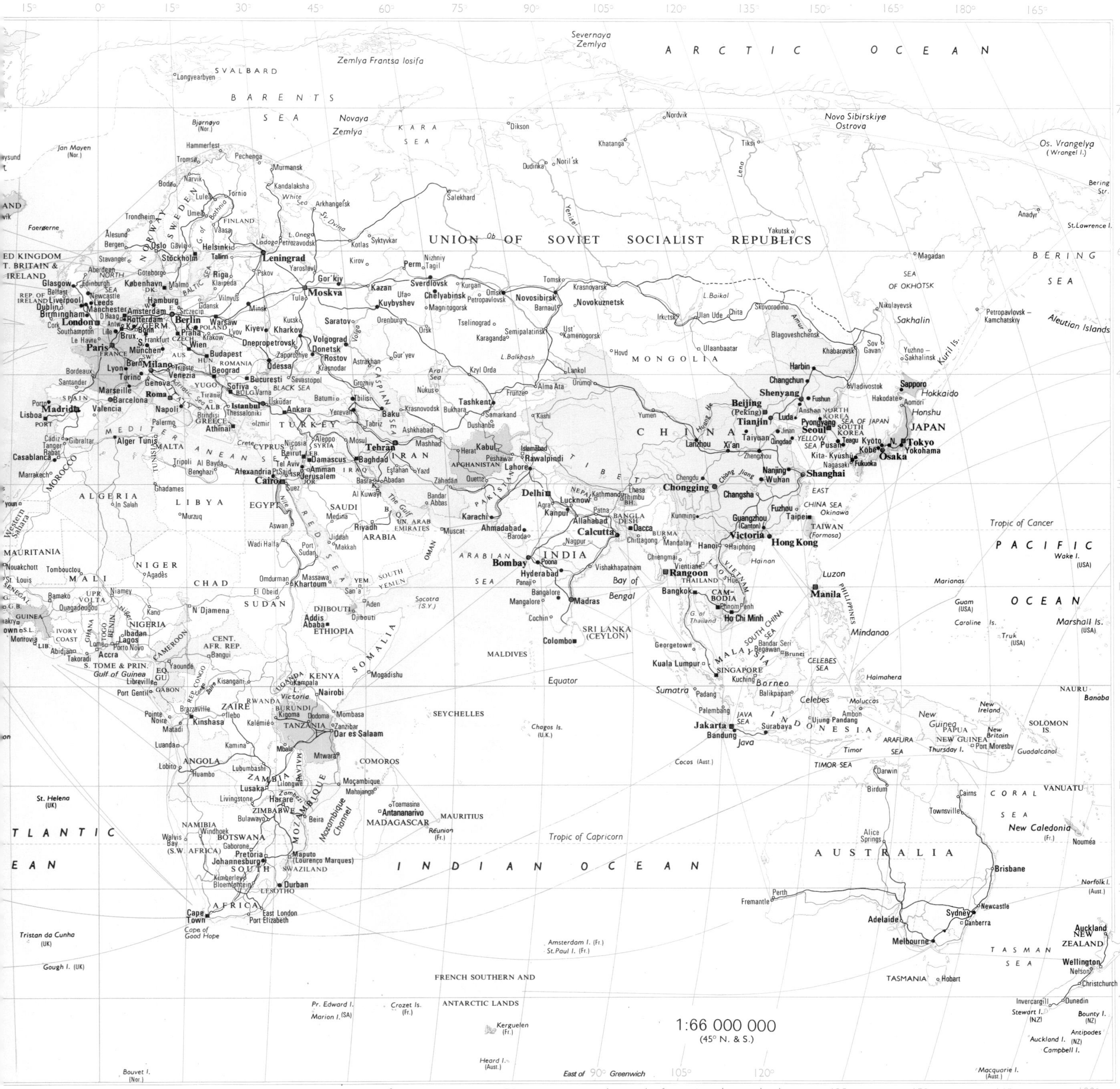

1:66 000 000
(45° N. & S.)

TIME ZONES
1:125 000 000

Zone Times are the Standard Times kept on land and sea compared with 12 hours (noon) Greenwich Mean Time. Daylight Saving Time (normally one hour in advance of local Standard Time), which is observed by certain countries for part of the year, is not shown on the map.

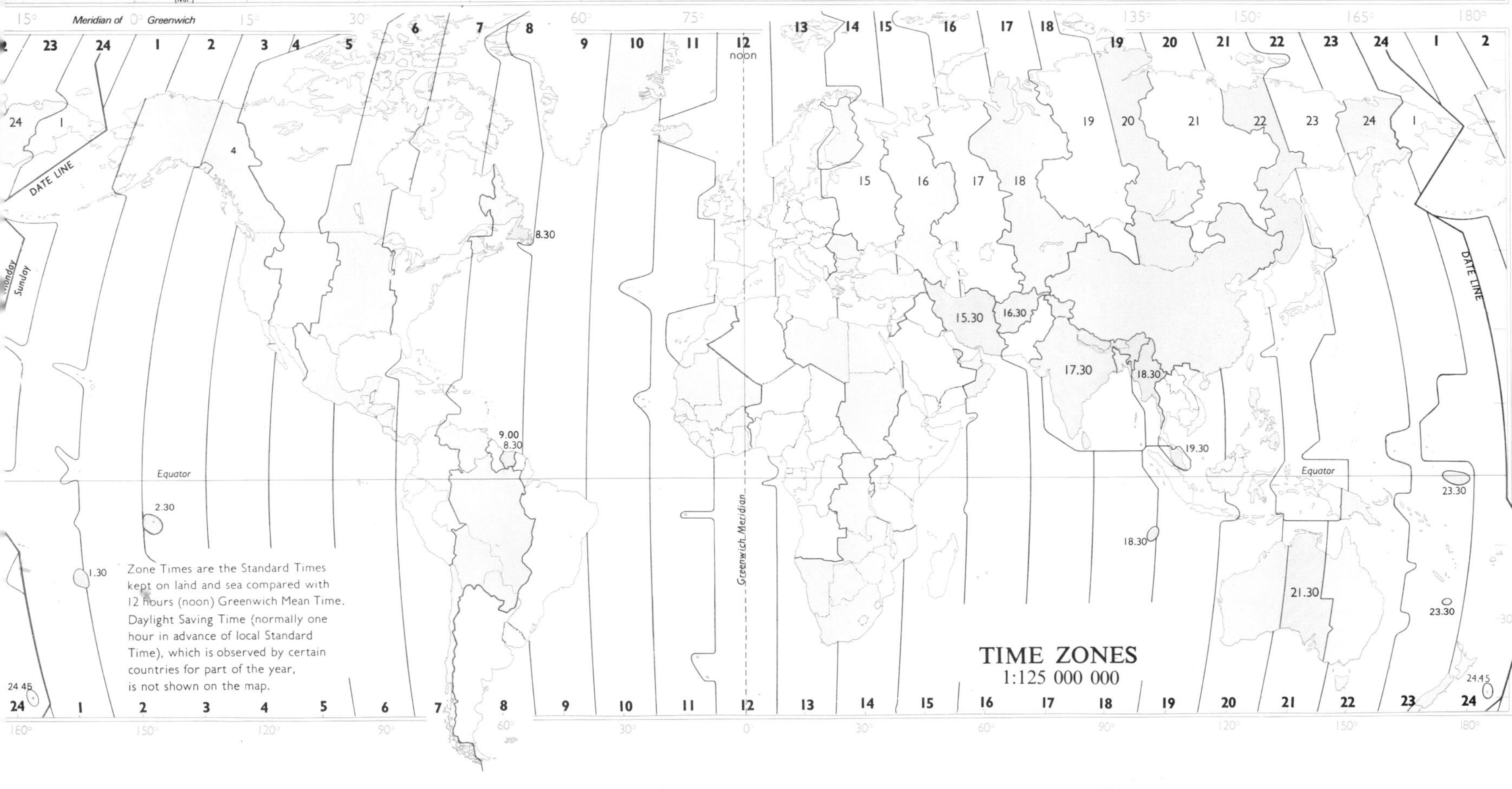

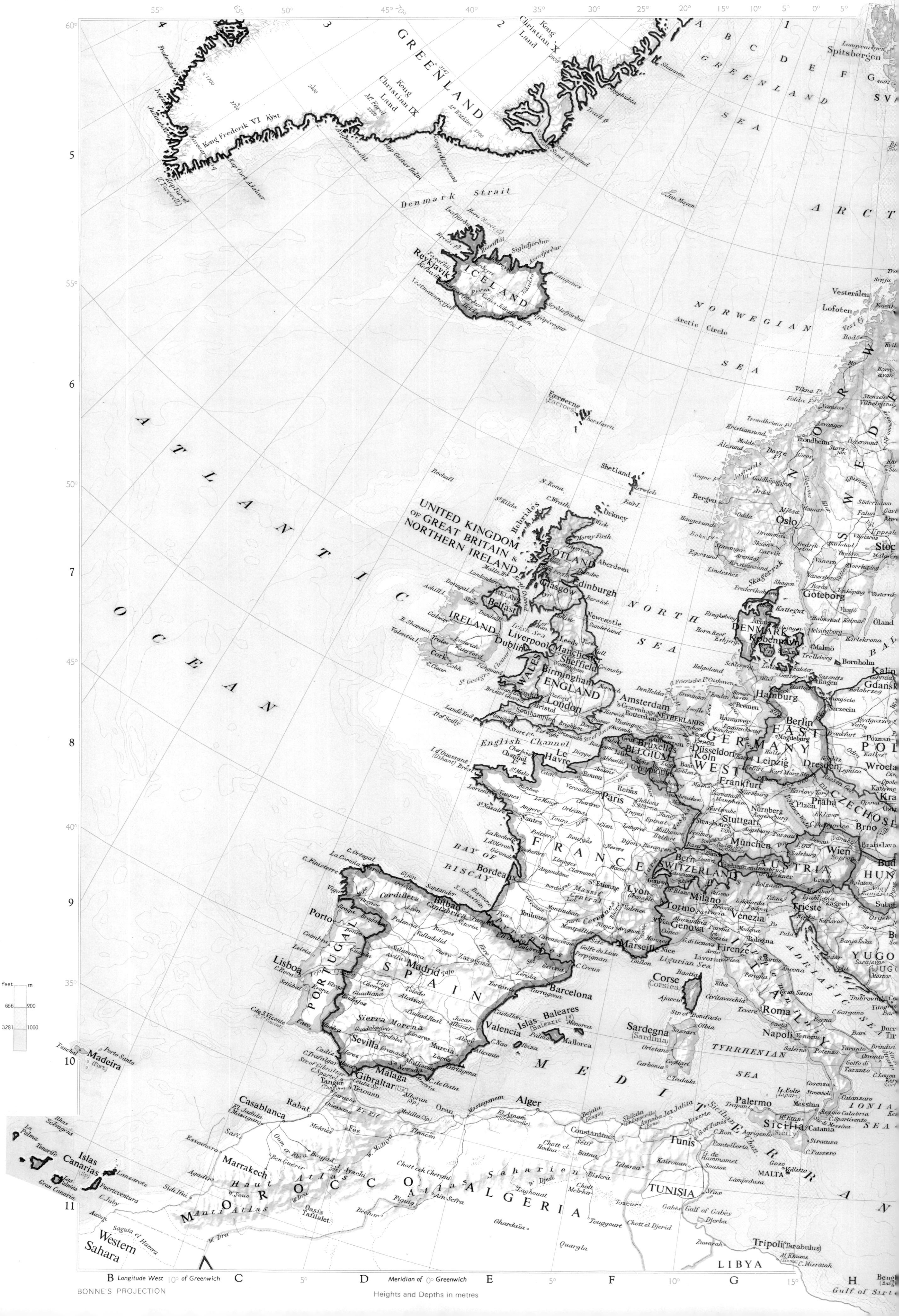

GREENLAND

Kong Christian X Land

Kong Christian IX Land

Kong Frederik VI Kyst

Denmark Strait

ICELAND
Reykjavik

ATLANTIC

OCEAN

NORWEGIAN

SEA

Arctic Circle

Spitsbergen

Jan Mayen

Shetland

Faerøerne (Faeroes)
Tórshavn

Rockall

N. Rona
Hebrides

Orkney

UNITED KINGDOM
OF GREAT BRITAIN &
NORTHERN IRELAND

SCOTLAND
Glasgow   Edinburgh
Aberdeen

Belfast
IRELAND
Dublin   Liverpool   Manchester
Cork   Sheffield
WALES   Birmingham
ENGLAND
London

Bergen
Oslo
Stavanger

NORTH
SEA

DENMARK
København

SWEDEN
Göteborg
Stockholm

NORWAY

Vesterålen
Lofoten

Trondheim

Hamburg
Amsterdam
NETHERLANDS   Berlin
BELGIUM   GERMANY
Bruxelles   WEST
Düsseldorf   Köln   EAST GERMANY
Leipzig   Dresden   POLAND
Frankfurt
LUXEMBOURG
Paris
FRANCE   Nürnberg
Stuttgart   München
SWITZERLAND   AUSTRIA
Bern   Wien
Lyon   Milano
Torino   Venezia
Genova   Trieste
Marseille   Firenze
ITALY   Roma
Corse   Napoli
(Corsica)
Sardegna
(Sardinia)

CZECHOSLOVAKIA
Praha
Brno
Bratislava
HUNGARY
YUGOSLAVIA

ENGLISH CHANNEL
Le Havre
Bordeaux
BAY OF BISCAY

PORTUGAL
Porto
Lisboa

SPAIN
Madrid
Cordillera Cantabrica
Bilbao
Zaragoza
Barcelona
Islas Baleares
Mallorca
Valencia
Sierra Morena
Sevilla
Malaga
Gibraltar

Madeira
(Port.)
Funchal

Islas Canarias
(Sp.)

Casablanca   Rabat
Marrakech   Fès
Haut Atlas
MOROCCO
Anti Atlas

Alger   Constantine   Tunis
Oran
ALGERIA
TUNISIA

Western Sahara

MEDITERRANEAN SEA

TYRRHENIAN SEA

Palermo
Sicilia (Sicily)
Catania
MALTA

LIBYA
Tripoli (Tarabulus)

TUNIS
Gulf of Sirte

feet   m
656   200
3281   1000

BONNE'S PROJECTION

B Longitude West 10° of Greenwich   C   5°   D Meridian of 0° Greenwich   E   5°   F   10°   G   15°

Heights and Depths in metres

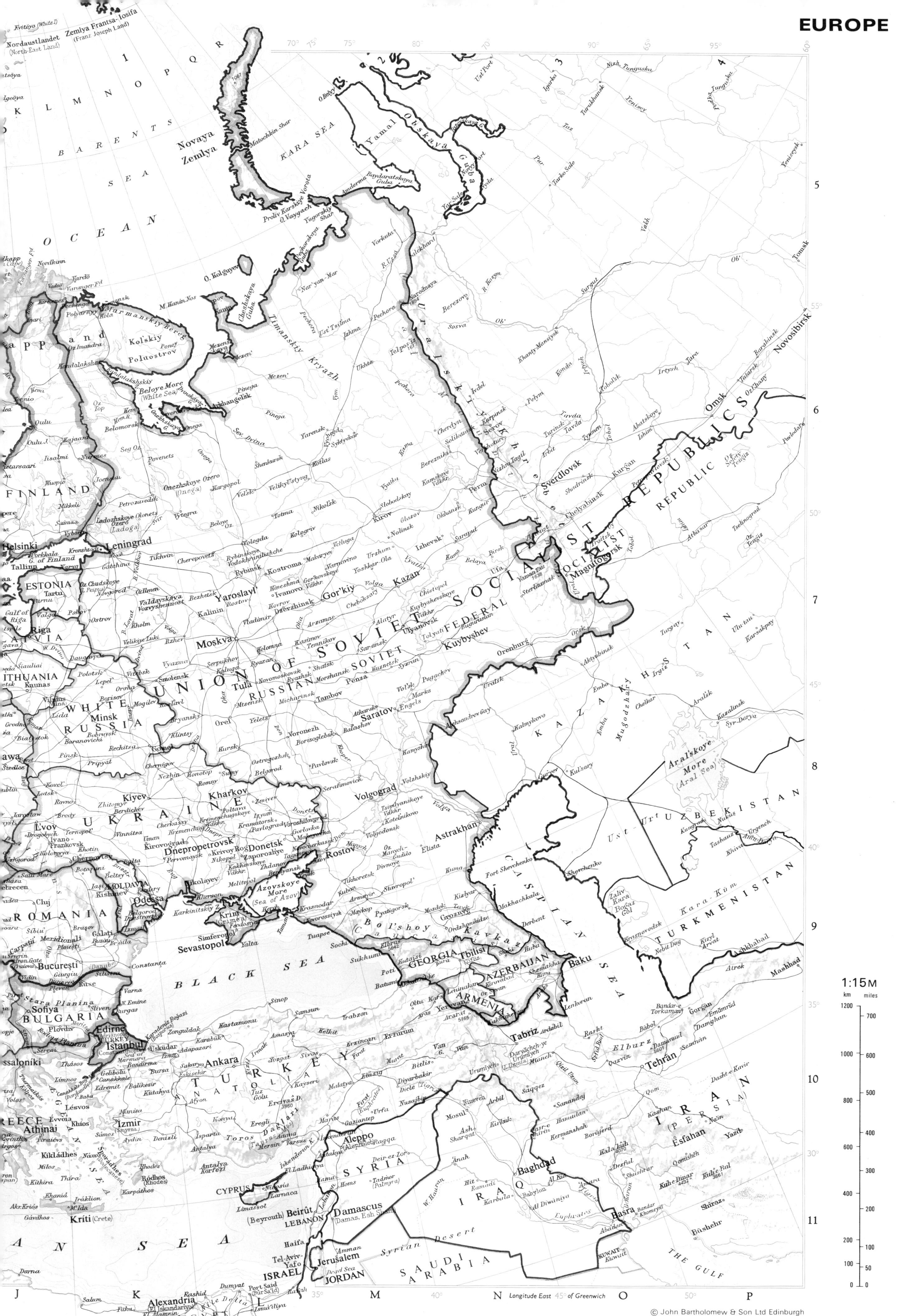

Map labels

Seas and Oceans:
BARENTS SEA
KARA SEA
OCEAN
Beloye More (White Sea)
BLACK SEA
Azovskoye More (Sea of Azov)
CASPIAN SEA
Aralskoye More (Aral Sea)
THE GULF

Countries/Regions:
UNION OF SOVIET SOCIALIST REPUBLICS
RUSSIAN SOVIET FEDERAL SOCIALIST REPUBLIC
FINLAND
ESTONIA
LATVIA
LITHUANIA
WHITE RUSSIA
UKRAINE
MOLDAVIA
ROMANIA
BULGARIA
TURKEY
GREECE
ANATOLIA
GEORGIA
ARMENIA
AZERBAIJAN
KAZAKHSTAN
UZBEKISTAN
TURKMENISTAN
IRAN (PERSIA)
IRAQ
SYRIA
LEBANON
ISRAEL
JORDAN
SAUDI ARABIA
CYPRUS
KUWAIT
EGYPT

Cities:
Novosibirsk, Omsk, Sverdlovsk, Chelyabinsk, Magnitogorsk, Kurgan
Leningrad, Helsinki, Tallinn, Tartu, Riga, Moskva, Yaroslavl', Gor'kiy, Kazan, Kuybyshev, Saratov, Volgograd, Astrakhan', Rostov, Kharkov, Kiev, Lvov, Odessa, Kishinev, Dnepropetrovsk, Donetsk, Minsk, Tula, Orel, Kursk, Voronezh, Penza, Ul'yanovsk, Orenburg, Uralsk, Orsk
Sofiya, Plovdiv, Edirne, Istanbul, Ankara, Izmir, Bucureşti
Tbilisi, Yerevan, Baku, Batumi
Tabriz, Tehran, Esfahan, Shiraz, Mashhad
Baghdad, Mosul, Basra, Damascus, Aleppo, Beirût (Beyrouth), Jerusalem, Amman, Tel-Aviv-Yafo, Haifa, Alexandria (El Iskandariya), Cairo

1:15M

km / miles
1200 — 700
1000 — 600
— 500
800 — 400
600 — 300
400 — 200
200 — 100
— 50
0 — 0

Longitude East of Greenwich

NORWAY

Bergen

Flora
Askvoll
Solund
Fedje
Fjære
Austrheim

O

N

Bergen or ODIN / Old Viking
Bank

Viking Bank

Bergen Bank

FRIGG

HEIMDAL

BALDER

GUDRUN

M

MURCHISON
STATFJORD
BRENT

MAGNUS

THISTLE
DUNLIN
TERN
CORMORANT
HUTTON
HEATHER
NINIAN
ALWYN

OIL

BRUCE
BERYL

BRAE

MAUREEN
ANDREW

FORTIES

TIFFANY
TONI/THELMA

PIPER

CLAYMORE
TARTAN

BUCHAN

MONTROSE

LOMOND

COD

NATURAL GAS
Great Fisher Bank

ALBUSKJELL
EKOFISK
ELDFISK
TOR
EDDA

JOSEPHINE
FILMAR
AUK

ARGYLL

N

L

OIL

NATURAL GAS

NATURAL GAS

OIL

Little Halibut Bank

BEATRICE

Buchan Deep

Long Forties

Devil's Hole

S

K

SHETLAND

Herma Ness
Unst.
Yell
Balta
Fetlar
Out Skerries
Whalsay
Bressay
Lerwick
Mousa
Scalloway
Sumburgh Hd.

Yell Sd.
Hillswick
S.Magnus Bay
Vidlin
Sullom Voe
Voe
The Faither
Papa Stour
Vaila
Foula
West Burra
Noss
Fair Isle

Fitful Hd.

J

ORKNEY

Papa Westray
Westray
Rousay
Eday
Sanday
Stronsay
Shapinsay
N.Ronaldsay
Birsay
Kirkwall
Scapa Flow
Hoy
Flotta
S.Ronaldsay
Stromness
Kirkwall
Mainland
Duncansby Hd.

Pentland Firth
Dunnet Hd.
Thurso
Wick

Sule Skerry

North Rona

Stack Skerry

H

SCOTLAND

GRAMPIAN
HIGHLAND
TAYSIDE
CENTRAL

Aberdeen
Peterhead
Fraserburgh
Kinnaird's Hd.
Buchan Ness
Stonehaven
Inverness
Moray Firth
Banff
Elgin
Lossiemouth

Montrose
Arbroath
Forfar
Dundee
FIFE
Firth of Forth
St Andrews
Bell Rock
Fife Ness

Inverness
Nairn
Forres
Tarbat Ness
Cromarty Firth
Helmsdale
Brora
Golspie
Dornoch Firth
Lybster
Latheron

GRAMPIAN MOUNTAINS
Cairngorms
Ben Macdui 1309
Aviemore
Kingussie

G

Ben Hope
C.Wrath
Durness
Loch Eriboll
Kinlochbervie
Scourie
Lochinver
Ben More Assynt

L.Shin
L.Loyal

Eddrachillis Bay
Egard Bay
L.Broom
Ullapool
Liag

Stornoway
Butt of Lewis

North Minch

F

Lewis
Harris
WESTERN ISLES
HEBRIDES
Flannan Is.
Scarp
Taransay
N.Uist
Benbecula
Monach Is.
S.Uist
Eriskay
Barra

Little Minch
Isle of Skye
Raasay
Broadford
Canna
Rum
Eigg
Muck
Coll
Tiree
Mull
Iona
Staffa
Colonsay
Oban

E

FÆRØERNE
(THE FAEROES)
(To Denmark)

Myggenæs
Eysturoy
Vaagø
Sandø
Streymoy
Bordø
Kalsø
Viderø
Svínø
Fugloy
Nólsoy
Skúvø
Store Dimon
Little Dimon
Suðurø
Skúgvur
Munken

Faeroe Bank

St Kilda

Stanton Banks

D

Rosemary Bank

Bill Baileys Bank

C

ATLANTIC

B

Outer Bailey or Lousy Bank

Rockall Bank
Rockall

A

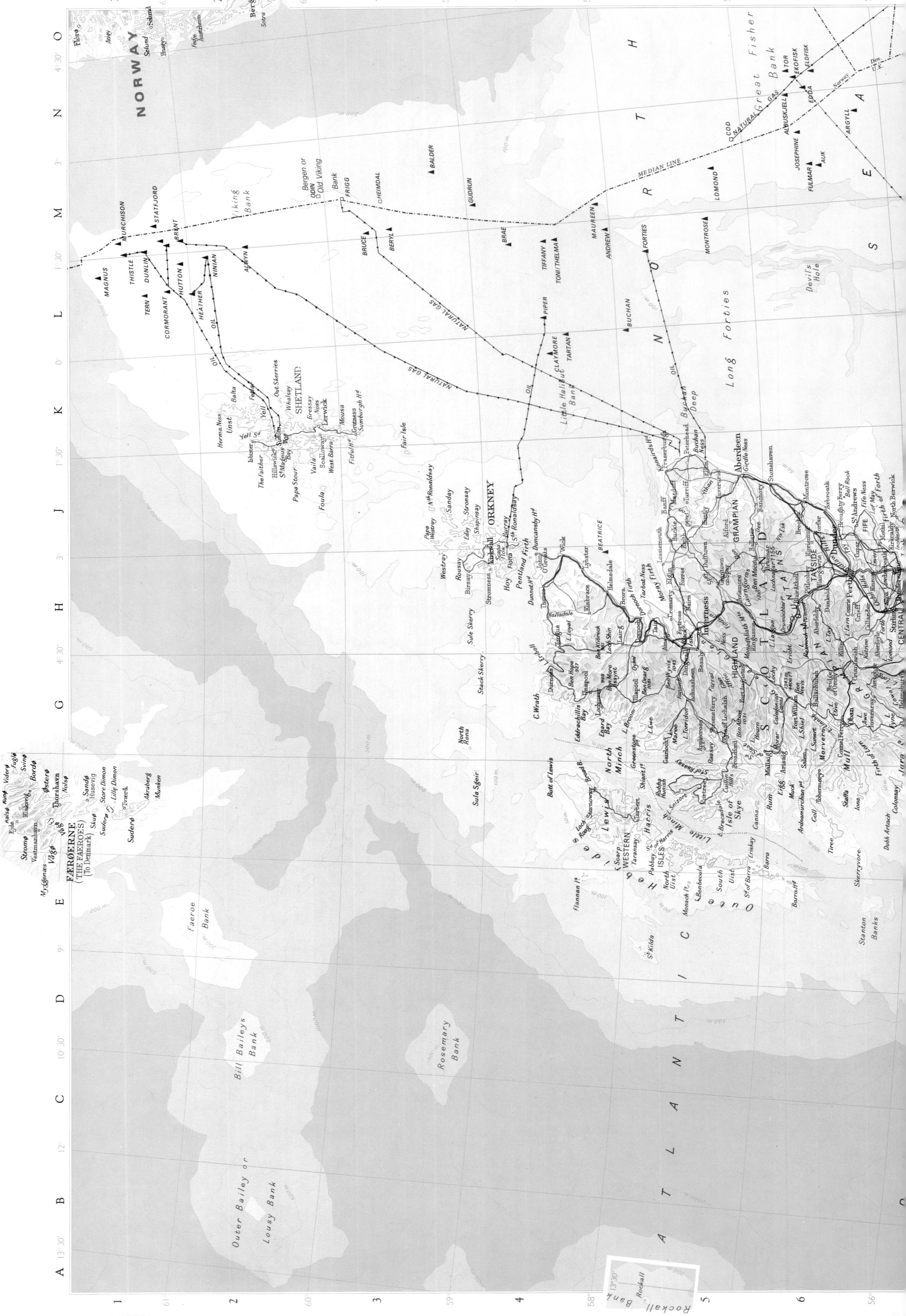

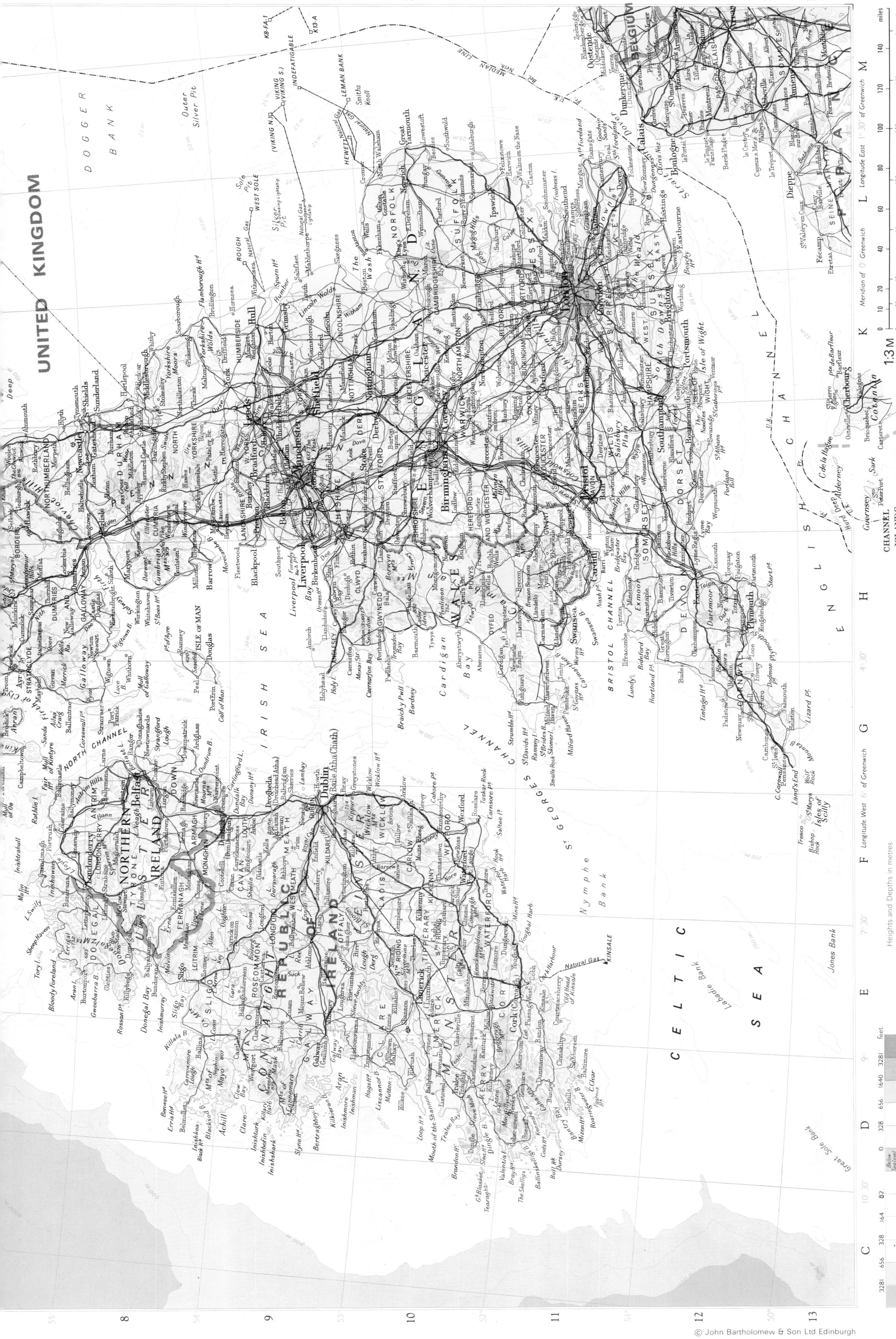
UNITED KINGDOM
BELGIUM
DOGGER BANK
IRISH SEA
CELTIC SEA
ENGLISH CHANNEL
BRISTOL CHANNEL
NORTH CHANNEL
ST GEORGE'S CHANNEL
NORTHERN IRELAND
REPUBLIC OF IRELAND
WALES
CHANNEL ISLANDS (U.K.)
London
Dublin
Belfast
Liverpool
Manchester
Birmingham
Bristol
Cardiff
Plymouth
Hull
Leeds
Sheffield
Nottingham
Calais
Dieppe
Cherbourg
1:3M
Heights and Depths in metres

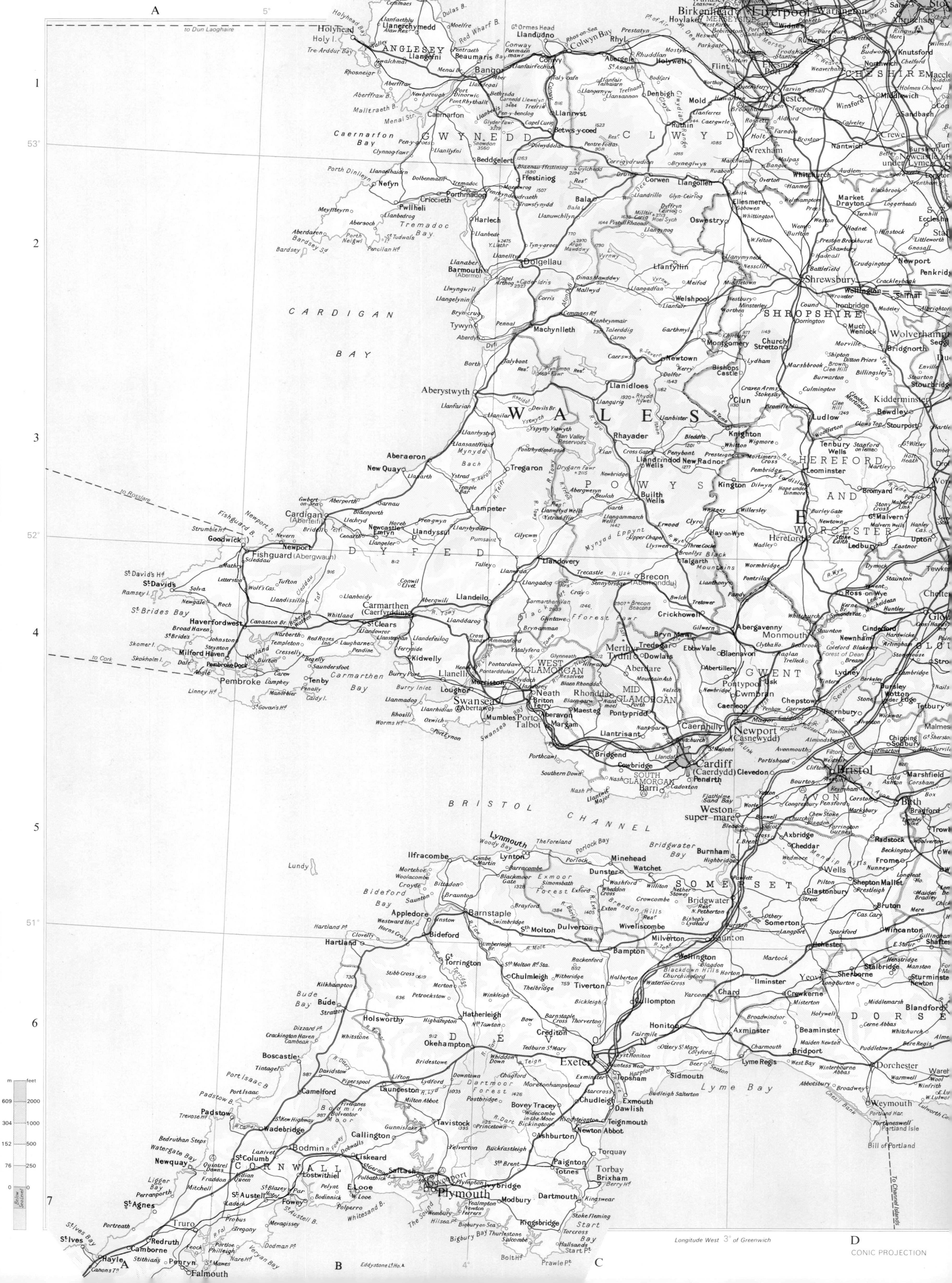
A
B
C
D
5°
4°
3°
53°
52°
51°
1
2
3
4
5
6
7
to Dun Laoghaire
to Rosslare
to Cork
to Channel Islands
ANGLESEY
Holyhead
Holy I.
Amlwch
Llangefni
Beaumaris
Bangor
Caernarfon
Caernarfon Bay
GWYNEDD
Snowdon 3560
Llandudno
Conwy
Colwyn Bay
Rhyl
Prestatyn
Betws-y-coed
Llanrwst
Denbigh
Ruthin
Mold
Flint
Holywell
CLWYD
Wrexham
Llangollen
Corwen
Bala
Ffestiniog
Blaenau-Ffestiniog
Porthmadog
Criccieth
Pwllheli
Nefyn
Harlech
Tremadoc Bay
Bardsey I.
Dolgellau
Barmouth
Tywyn
Machynlleth
Aberdyfi
Borth
CARDIGAN
BAY
Aberystwyth
WALES
Llanidloes
Newtown
Welshpool
Montgomery
Rhayader
Llandrindod Wells
Builth Wells
POWYS
Aberaeron
New Quay
Tregaron
Lampeter
Cardigan (Aberteifi)
Fishguard (Abergwaun)
Fishguard B.
Goodwick
Newport
St. David's
St. David's Hd
Ramsey I.
St. Brides Bay
Haverfordwest
Milford Haven
Pembroke Dock
Pembroke
Skomer I.
Skokholm I.
Tenby
Carmarthen Bay
DYFED
Carmarthen (Caerfyrddin)
St. Clears
Llandeilo
Llandovery
Brecon (Aberhonddu)
Brecon Beacons
Crickhowell
Abergavenny
Hay-on-Wye
Black Mountains
Llanelli
Swansea (Abertawe)
Gower
Mumbles
Port Talbot
Neath
WEST GLAMORGAN
MID GLAMORGAN
Merthyr Tydfil
Pontypridd
Bridgend
SOUTH GLAMORGAN
Cardiff (Caerdydd)
Barri
Penarth
Caerphilly
Newport (Casnewydd)
GWENT
Monmouth
Chepstow
Cwmbran
Pontypool
BRISTOL
CHANNEL
Lundy
Bristol
AVON
Bath
Weston-super-mare
Clevedon
Liverpool
Birkenhead
MERSEYSIDE
Wallasey
Chester
CHESHIRE
Crewe
Nantwich
Whitchurch
Ellesmere
Oswestry
Shrewsbury
SHROPSHIRE
Bridgnorth
Ludlow
Church Stretton
Bishops Castle
Knighton
Kington
Leominster
HEREFORD AND WORCESTER
Hereford
Ross-on-Wye
Ledbury
Kidderminster
Wolverhampton
Lynmouth
Lynton
Ilfracombe
Barnstaple
Bideford
Bideford Bay
Minehead
Exmoor
Bridgwater
Bridgwater Bay
SOMERSET
Taunton
Yeovil
DEVON
Exeter
Okehampton
Dartmoor Forest
Tiverton
Honiton
Exmouth
Teignmouth
Torquay
Paignton
Brixham
Dartmouth
Totnes
Newton Abbot
Plymouth
Kingsbridge
Salcombe
Tavistock
Launceston
Bodmin Moor
Bodmin
CORNWALL
Newquay
St. Austell
Truro
Falmouth
Penryn
Redruth
Camborne
St. Ives
St. Ives Bay
Hayle
Bude
Bude Bay
Lyme Bay
Lyme Regis
DORSET
Dorchester
Weymouth
Bridport
Chard
Portland Isle
Bill of Portland
Longitude West 3° of Greenwich
CONIC PROJECTION
m
feet
609
2000
304
1000
152
500
76
250
0
0
Below Sea Level

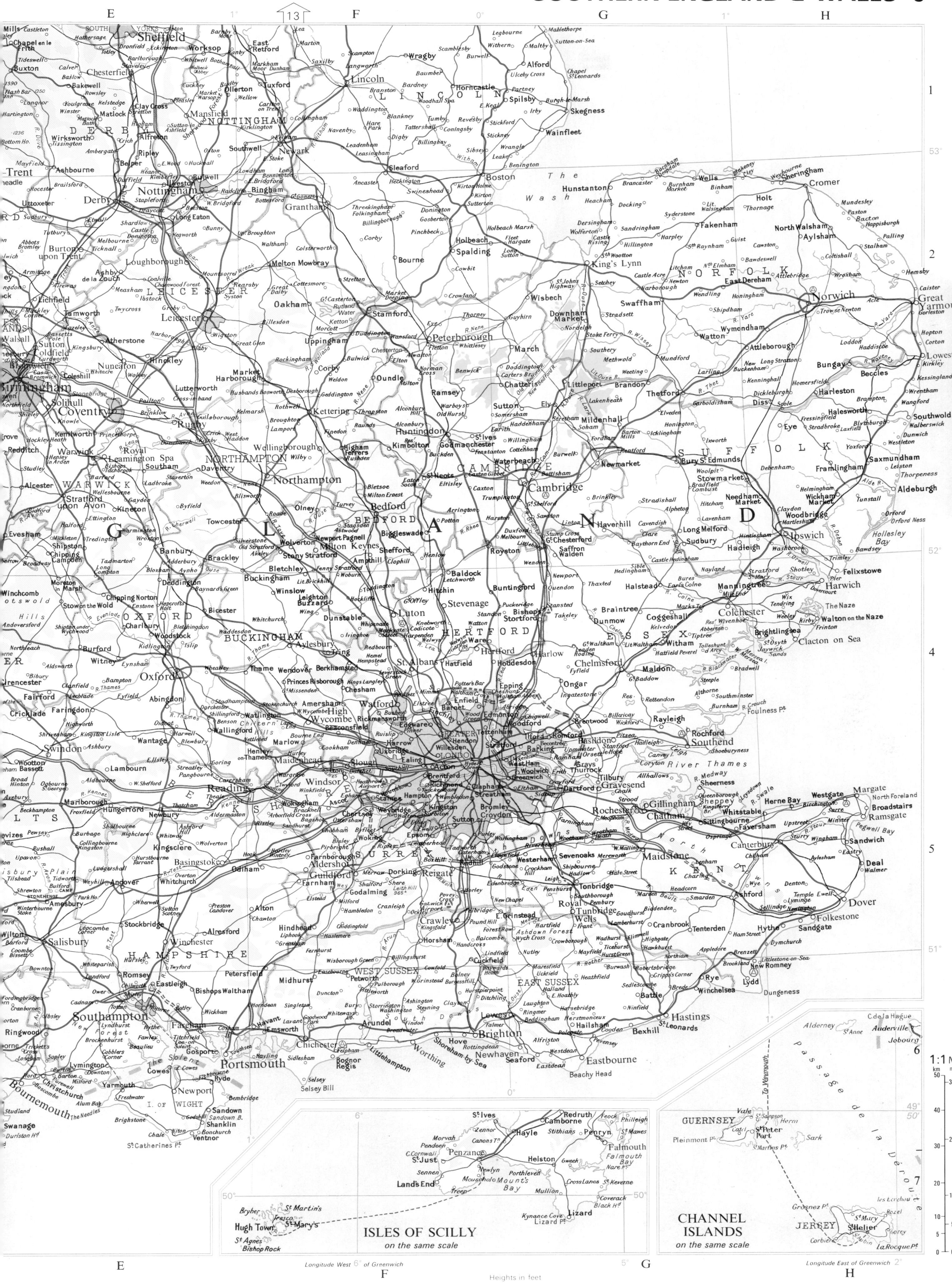

SOUTHERN ENGLAND & WALES

ISLES OF SCILLY
on the same scale

CHANNEL ISLANDS
on the same scale

1:1 M

Longitude West 6° of Greenwich

Longitude East of Greenwich 2°

Heights in feet

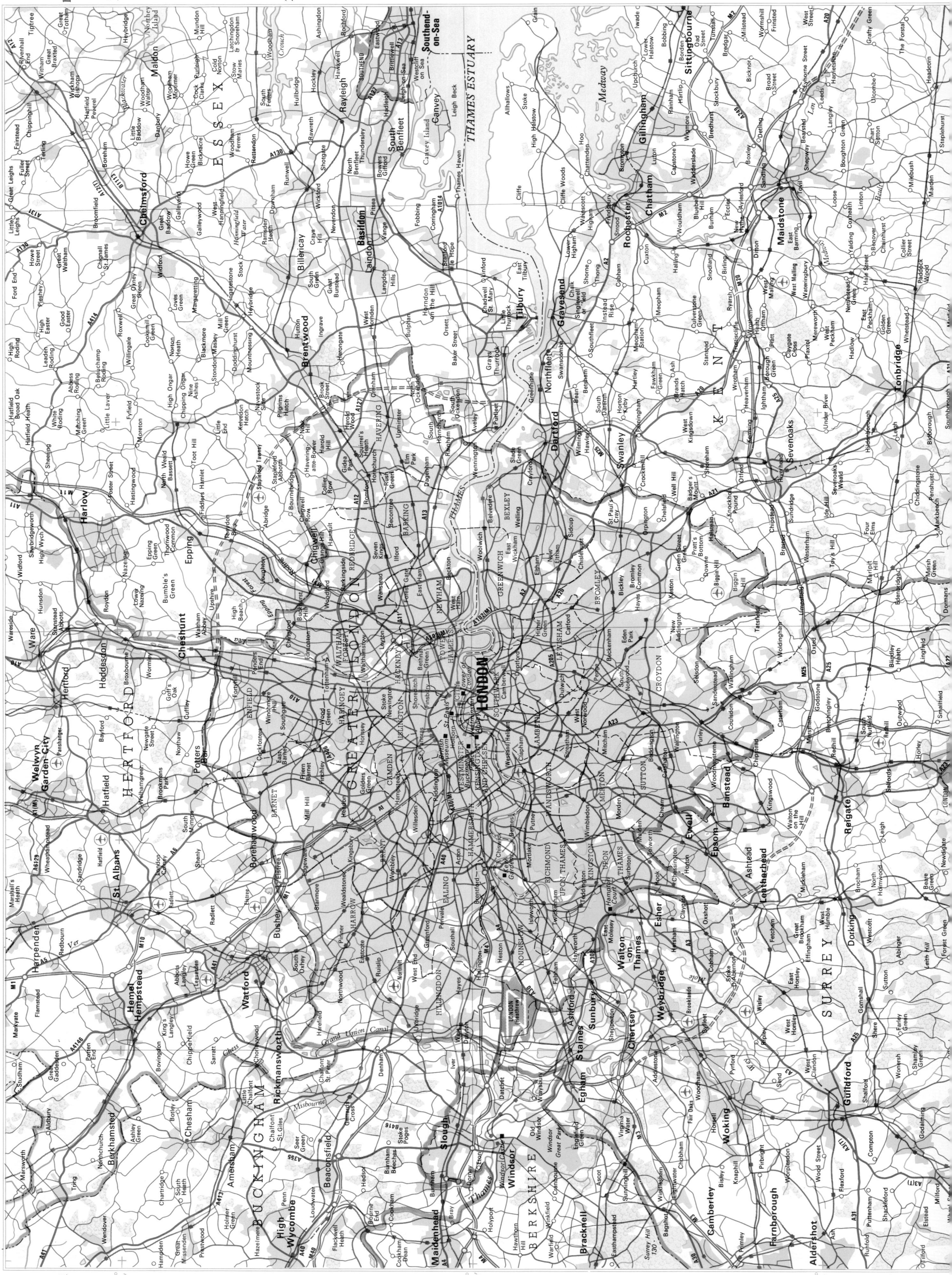

ESSEX

Tiptree
Great Totham
Maldon
Chelmsford
Billericay
Basildon
Laindon
Brentwood
Rayleigh
Southend-on-Sea
Canvey
THAMES ESTUARY
South Benfleet
Tilbury
Gravesend
Northfleet
Dartford
KENT
Gillingham
Chatham
Rochester
Sittingbourne
Maidstone
Tonbridge
Sevenoaks

HERTFORD
Welwyn Garden City
Hatfield
Hertford
Ware
Hoddesdon
Cheshunt
Harlow
Epping
Chigwell
REDBRIDGE
BARKING
HAVERING
NEWHAM
GREENWICH
BEXLEY
BROMLEY
Swanley
Harpenden
Hemel Hempstead
St Albans
Borehamwood
BARNET
Bushey
Watford
ENFIELD
WALTHAM FOREST
HARINGEY
CAMDEN
HACKNEY
GREATER LONDON
LONDON
Tower of London
St Paul's
Westminster
Buckingham Palace
CITY OF LONDON
SOUTHWARK
LEWISHAM
LAMBETH
CROYDON
SUTTON
MERTON
WANDSWORTH
RICHMOND UPON THAMES
KINGSTON UPON THAMES
HAMMERSMITH
EALING
HARROW
HILLINGDON
HOUNSLOW
LONDON Heathrow
Staines
Egham
Chertsey
Weybridge
Walton-on-Thames
Esher
Sunbury
Epsom
Ewell
Ashtead
Leatherhead
Banstead
Reigate
Dorking
SURREY
Guildford
Woking
Camberley
Farnborough
Aldershot

BUCKINGHAM
Amersham
High Wycombe
Beaconsfield
Maidenhead
Slough
Windsor
BERKSHIRE
Bracknell
Rickmansworth
Chesham
Berkhamsted
Tring

Grand Union Canal
THAMES

© Times Books Ltd

1:300000

0 5 10 15 km
0 5 10 miles

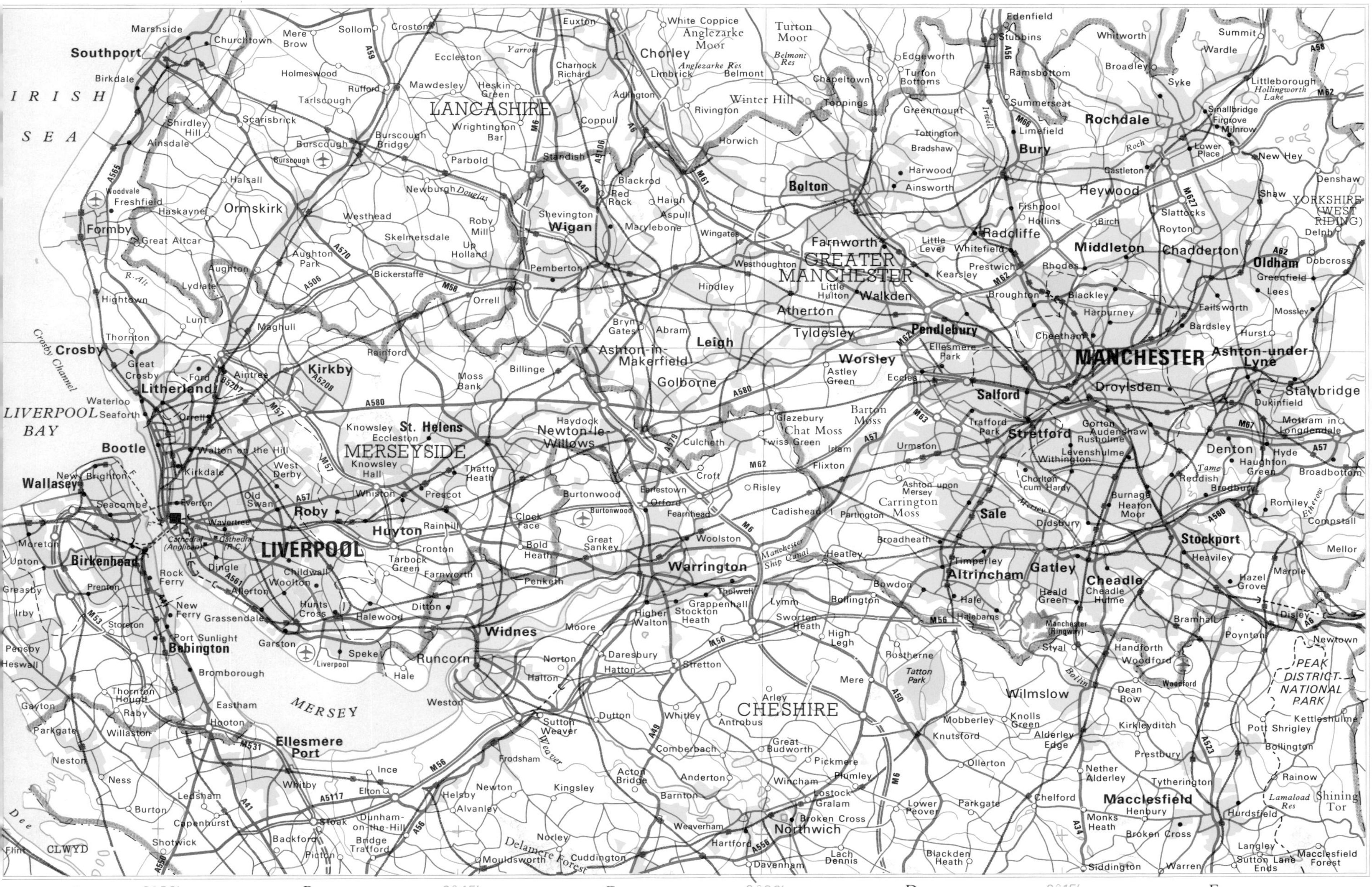

Map 1 — South Lancashire

Major labels and places include:

IRISH SEA · LIVERPOOL BAY · MERSEY · Dee · CLWYD

Southport · Birkdale · Ainsdale · Formby · Freshfield · Crosby · Waterloo · Seaforth · Bootle · Litherland · Wallasey · New Brighton · Seacombe · Birkenhead · Bebington · Port Sunlight · Bromborough · Eastham · Ellesmere Port · Neston · Heswall · Irby · Greasby · Upton · Moreton

LIVERPOOL · Huyton · Roby · Prescot · Whiston · Knowsley · Kirkby · St. Helens · Eccleston · Rainhill · Widnes · Runcorn · Frodsham · Helsby

Ormskirk · Skelmersdale · Up Holland · Wigan · Pemberton · Hindley · Leigh · Golborne · Ashton-in-Makerfield · Newton-le-Willows · Haydock · Warrington · Burtonwood

LANCASHIRE · Chorley · Coppull · Standish · Horwich · Rivington · Winter Hill · Bolton · Westhoughton · Atherton · Tyldesley · Worsley · Walkden · Farnworth · Kearsley

GREATER MANCHESTER · MANCHESTER · Salford · Stretford · Sale · Altrincham · Timperley · Gatley · Cheadle · Stockport · Wilmslow · Droylsden · Denton · Ashton-under-Lyne · Stalybridge · Hyde

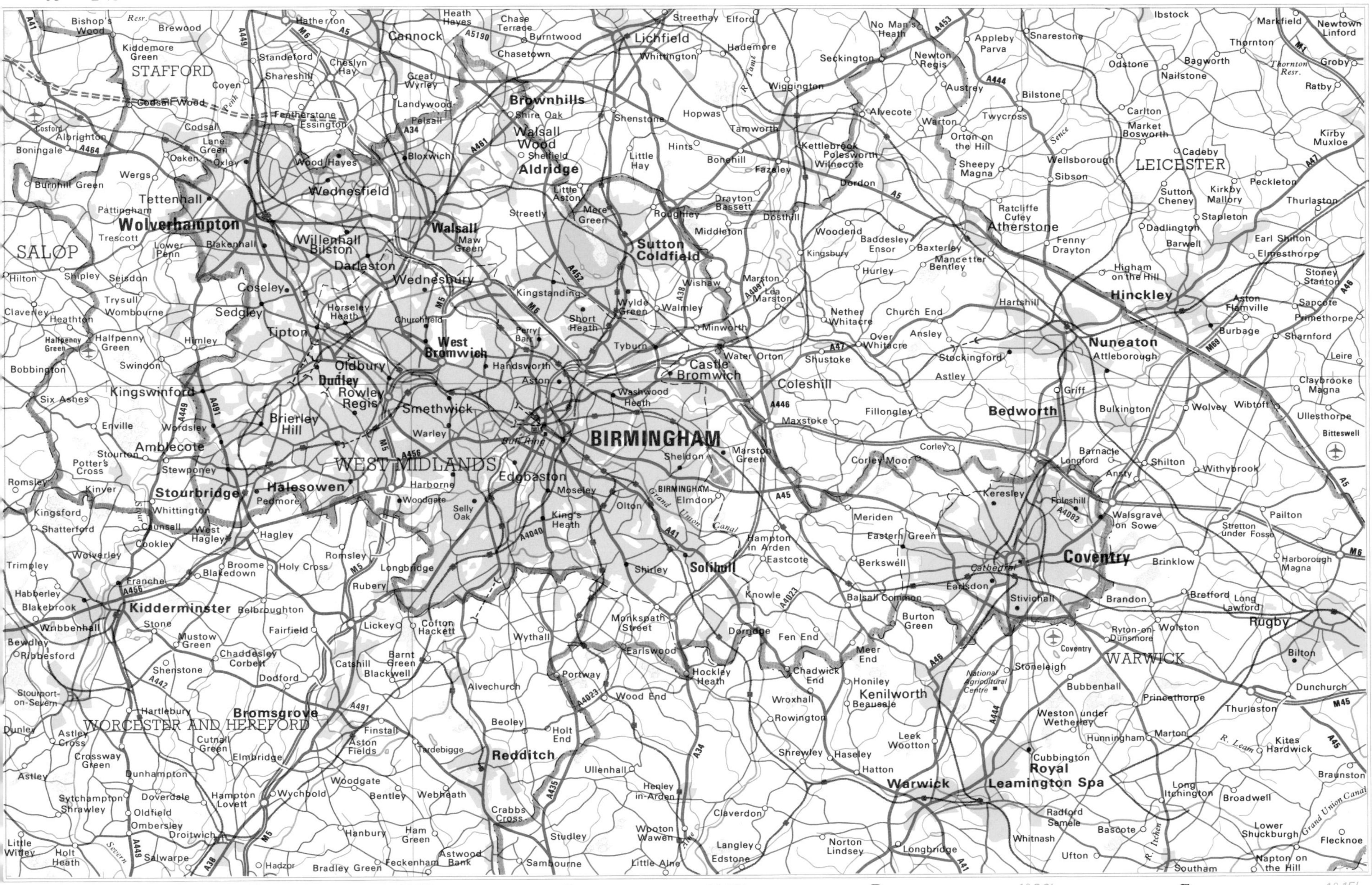

Bury · Radcliffe · Whitefield · Prestwich · Middleton · Heywood · Rochdale · Littleborough · Milnrow · Oldham · Chadderton · Mossley · Shaw · Delph

YORKSHIRE (WEST RIDING)

MERSEYSIDE

CHESHIRE · Warrington · Lymm · Knutsford · Northwich · Macclesfield · Prestbury · Alderley Edge · Mobberley · Tatton Park

PEAK DISTRICT NATIONAL PARK

Map 2 — West Midlands

Major labels and places include:

STAFFORD · Cannock · Brownhills · Walsall · Bloxwich · Aldridge · Wednesfield · Wolverhampton · Willenhall · Bilston · Darlaston · Wednesbury · Walsall Wood · Sutton Coldfield · Lichfield · Tamworth · Atherstone · Nuneaton · Bedworth

SALOP · WORCESTER AND HEREFORD

Kidderminster · Stourbridge · Halesowen · Brierley Hill · Dudley · Oldbury · Rowley Regis · Smethwick · West Bromwich · Tipton · Sedgley · Coseley · Kingswinford

WEST MIDLANDS · BIRMINGHAM · Edgbaston · Handsworth · Solihull · Shirley · Redditch · Bromsgrove

LEICESTER · Hinckley · Market Bosworth · Coalville

WARWICK · Coventry · Kenilworth · Royal Leamington Spa · Warwick · Rugby

---

Scale 1:300 000

0 · 5 · 10 · 15 km
0 · 5 · 10 miles

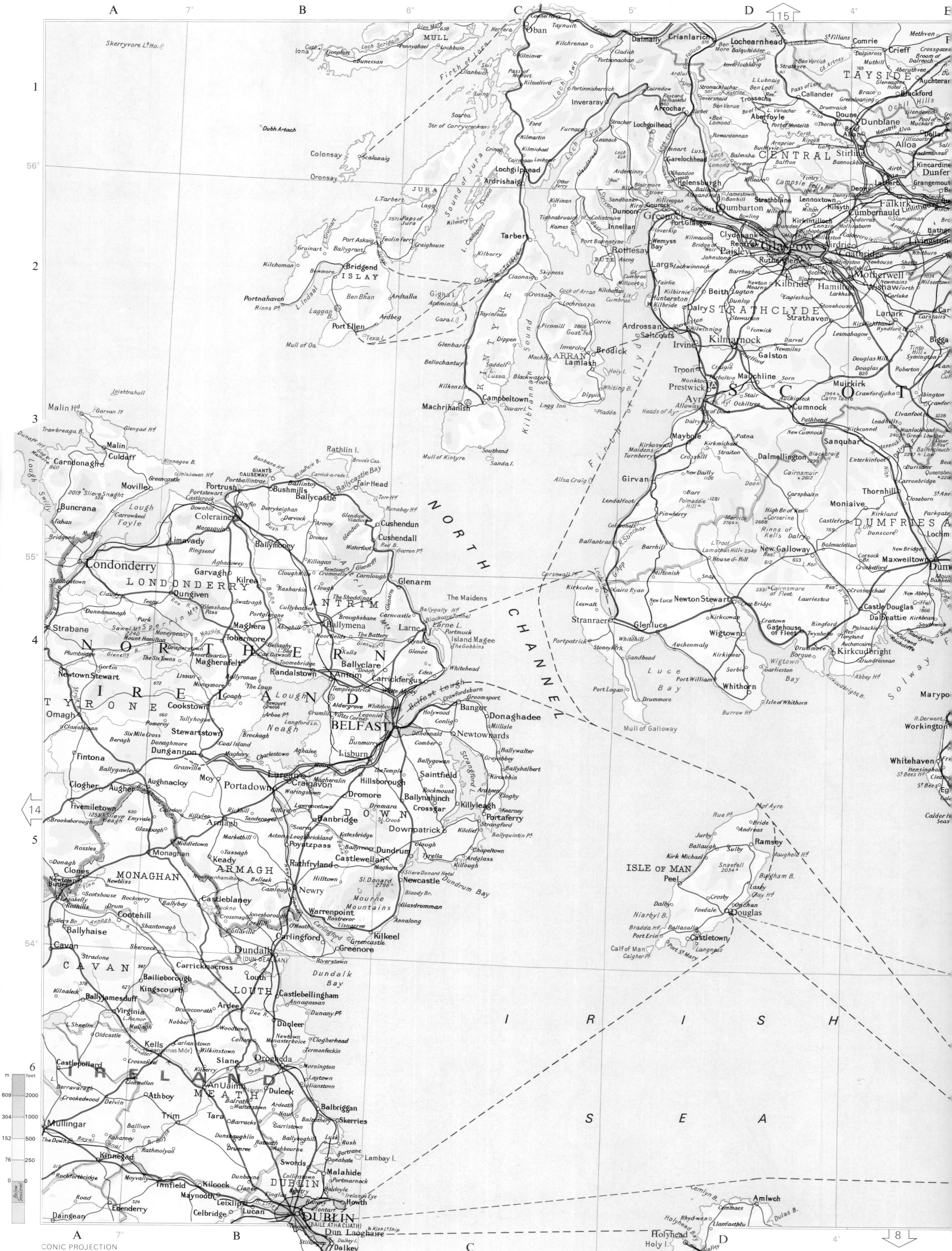

CONIC PROJECTION

NORTH CHANNEL
IRISH SEA
NORTHERN IRELAND
IRELAND
ISLE OF MAN
STRATHCLYDE
CENTRAL
TAYSIDE
DUMFRIES AND GALLOWAY
LONDONDERRY
ANTRIM
DOWN
ARMAGH
TYRONE
MONAGHAN
CAVAN
LOUTH
MEATH
DUBLIN
JURA
ISLAY
MULL
ARRAN
KINTYRE
BUTE
Londonderry
Belfast
Dublin
Glasgow
Oban
Ayr
Kilmarnock
Stranraer
Douglas
Newry
Dundalk
Drogheda
Larne
Coleraine
Firth of Clyde
Firth of Lorn
Belfast Lough
Dundalk Bay
Solway Firth
Luce Bay
Wigtown Bay
Mull of Kintyre
Mull of Galloway
Malin Hd
Holyhead
Holy I.
Amlwch
15
14
8
m feet
609 2000
304 1000
152 500
76 250
0 0
Below Sea Level

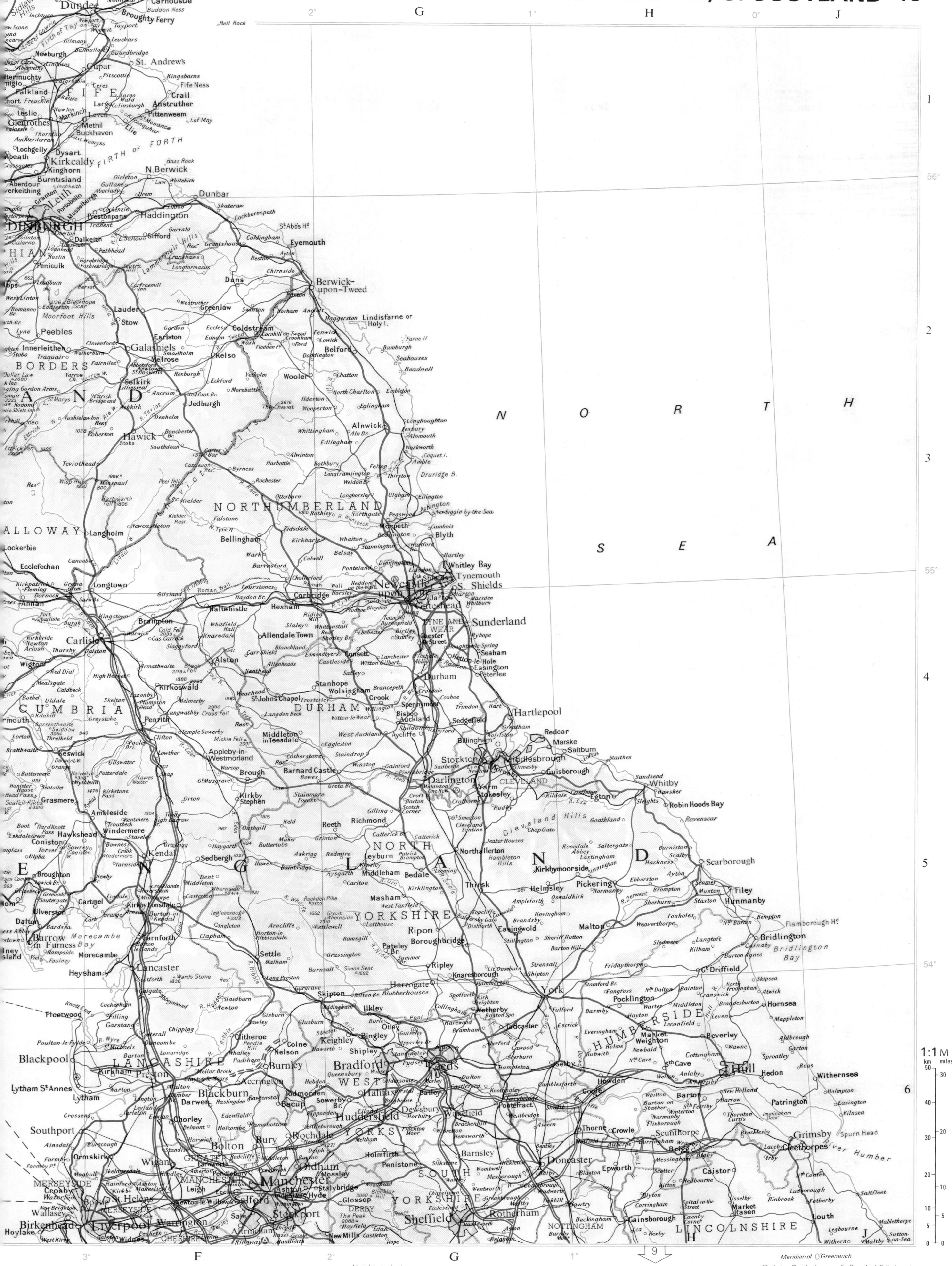
NORTH SEA
FIRTH OF FORTH
Firth of Tay
FIFE
BORDERS
LOTHIAN
NORTHUMBERLAND
TYNE AND WEAR
DURHAM
CUMBRIA
CLEVELAND
NORTH YORKSHIRE
WEST YORKS
SOUTH YORKSHIRE
HUMBERSIDE
LANCASHIRE
GREATER MANCHESTER
MERSEYSIDE
CHESHIRE
DERBY
NOTTINGHAM
LINCOLNSHIRE
ENGLAND
Morecambe Bay
Bridlington Bay
River Humber
Cleveland Hills
Dundee
St. Andrews
Kirkcaldy
EDINBURGH
Leith
Dunbar
Berwick-upon-Tweed
Newcastle upon Tyne
Sunderland
Durham
Hartlepool
Middlesbrough
Darlington
Whitby
Scarborough
Carlisle
Kendal
Lancaster
Blackpool
Preston
Blackburn
Bradford
Leeds
York
Hull
Grimsby
Cleethorpes
Manchester
Liverpool
Birkenhead
Sheffield
Doncaster
Heights in feet
Meridian of Greenwich
1:1M
km
miles

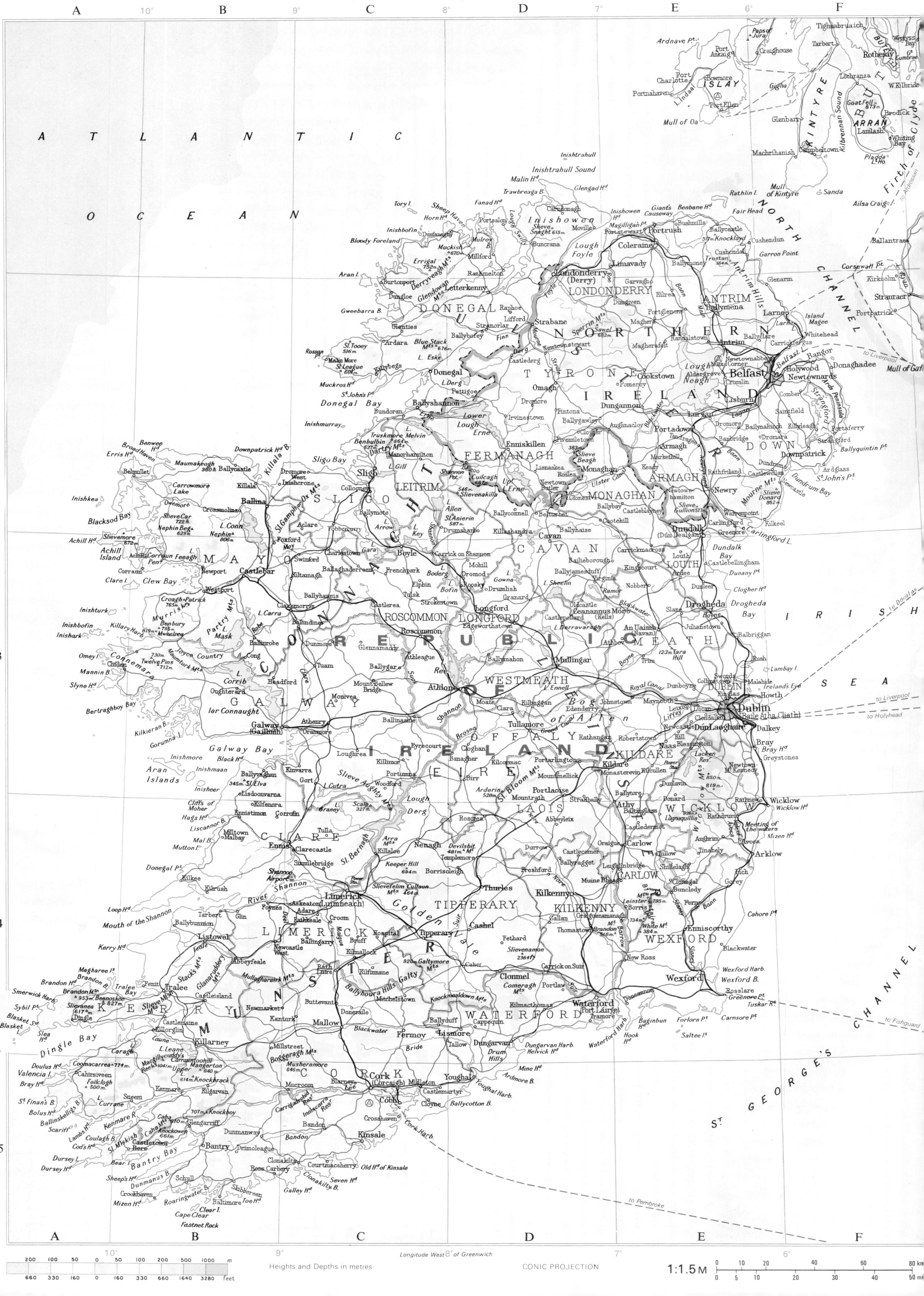

14 IRELAND

ATLANTIC OCEAN

NORTHERN IRELAND

REPUBLIC OF IRELAND (EIRE)

IRISH SEA

NORTH CHANNEL

ST. GEORGE'S CHANNEL

Heights and Depths in metres

CONIC PROJECTION

1:1.5 M

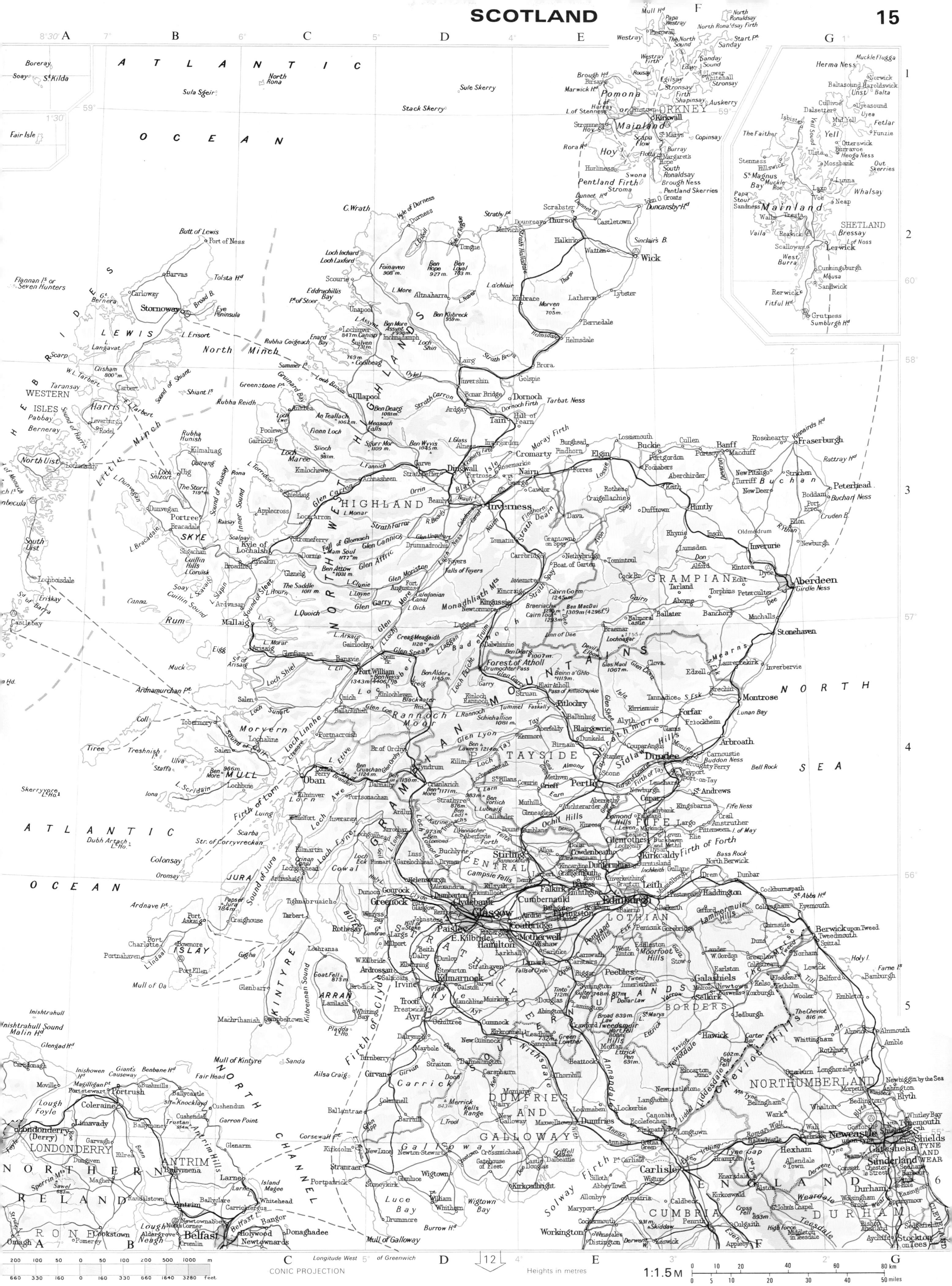

ATLANTIC

OCEAN

ORKNEY

SHETLAND

WESTERN ISLES

LEWIS

HARRIS

North Minch

Little Minch

SKYE

NORTH WEST HIGHLANDS

HIGHLAND

Inverness

GRAMPIAN

Aberdeen

GRAMPIAN MOUNTAINS

Fort William

TAYSIDE

Dundee

Perth

NORTH SEA

ATLANTIC OCEAN

MULL

JURA

ISLAY

KINTYRE

ARRAN

Glasgow

Paisley

Edinburgh

CENTRAL

STRATHCLYDE

LOTHIAN

SOUTHERN UPLANDS

BORDERS

DUMFRIES AND GALLOWAY

NORTHUMBERLAND

NORTHERN IRELAND

LONDONDERRY

ANTRIM

Belfast

ENGLAND

CUMBRIA

DURHAM

Newcastle upon Tyne

Carlisle

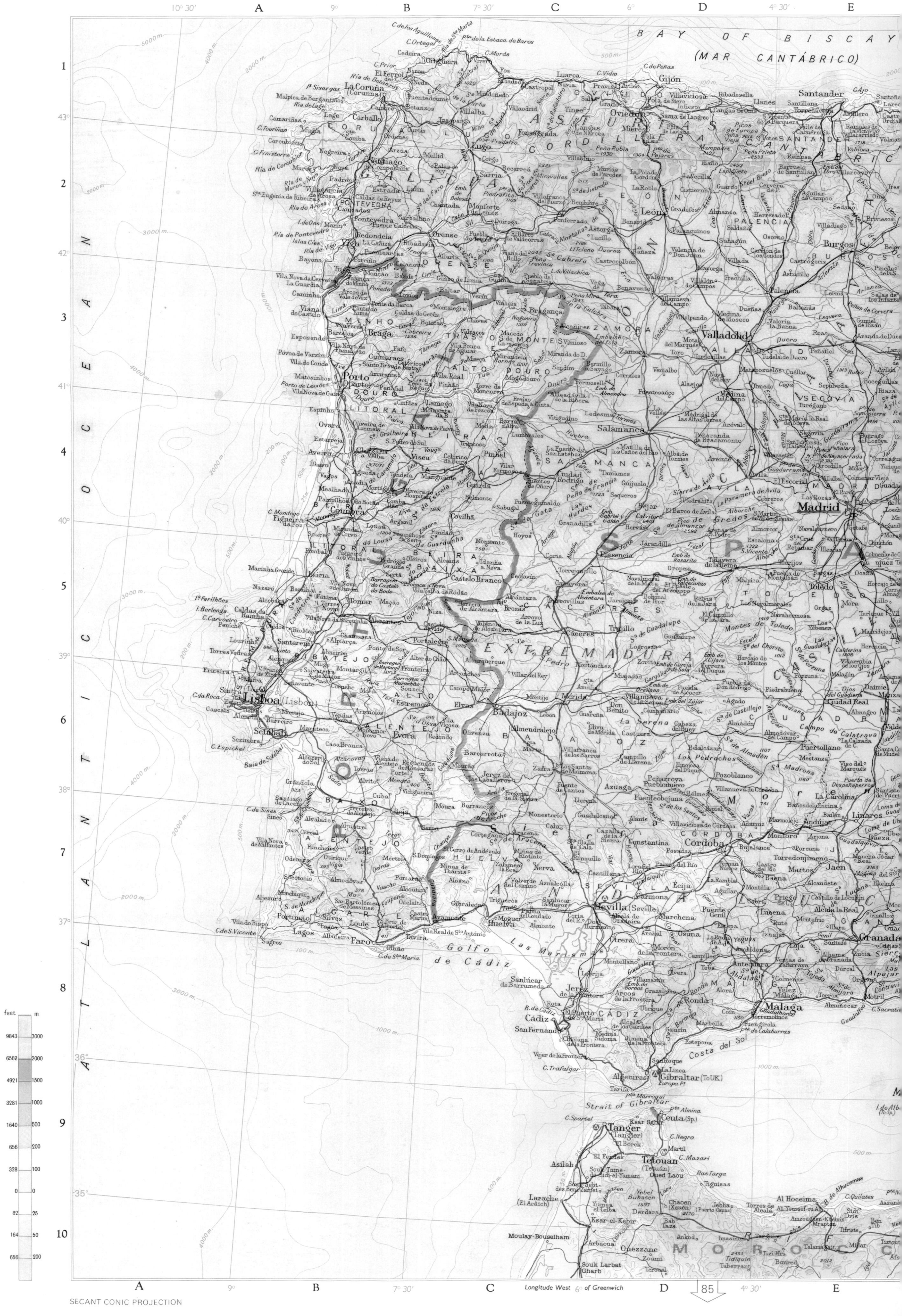

GOLFE DE GASCOGNE (GOLFO DE GASCUÑA)

FRANCE

PYRÉNÉES

GOLFE DU LION

Biarritz
Bayonne
San Sebastián
Pamplona
Logroño
Toulouse
Carcassonne
Narbonne
Perpignan
Andorra
Zaragoza (Zaragossa)
Huesca
Lérida
Gerona
Barcelona
Sabadell
Tarrasa
Badalona
Manresa
Calatayud
Tarragona
Reus
Tortosa
Teruel
Castellón de la Plana
Valencia
Golfo de Valencia
Sagunto
Albacete
Alcoy
Alicante
Elche
Murcia
Lorca
Cartagena
Almería
Golfo de Almería

ISLAS BALEARES (BALEARIC ISLANDS) (To Spain)

MALLORCA (MAJORCA)
Palma
Palma de Mallorca
Inca
Manacor
Felanitx
MENORCA (MINORCA)
Ciudadela
Mahón
IBIZA (IVIZA)
Ibiza
Formentera
Cabrera

MEDITERRANEAN SEA

Longitude East of Greenwich

Meridian of 0° Greenwich

ALGERIA
Oran
Mostaganem
Mascara
Sidi bel Abbès
Tlemcen

MADRID
1:60 000

CHAMARTIN
CIUDAD UNIVERSITARIA
Parque del Oeste
Casa de Campo
CHAMBERÍ
BUENAVISTA
SALAMANCA
Madrid Moderno
VENTAS
LATINA
CENTRO
RETIRO
Plaza de Toros
Puerta del Sol
Palacio Nacional
Atocha
ARGANZUELA
CARABANCHEL
PUENTE DE VALLECAS

1:3 M
km   miles

© John Bartholomew & Son Ltd Edinburgh

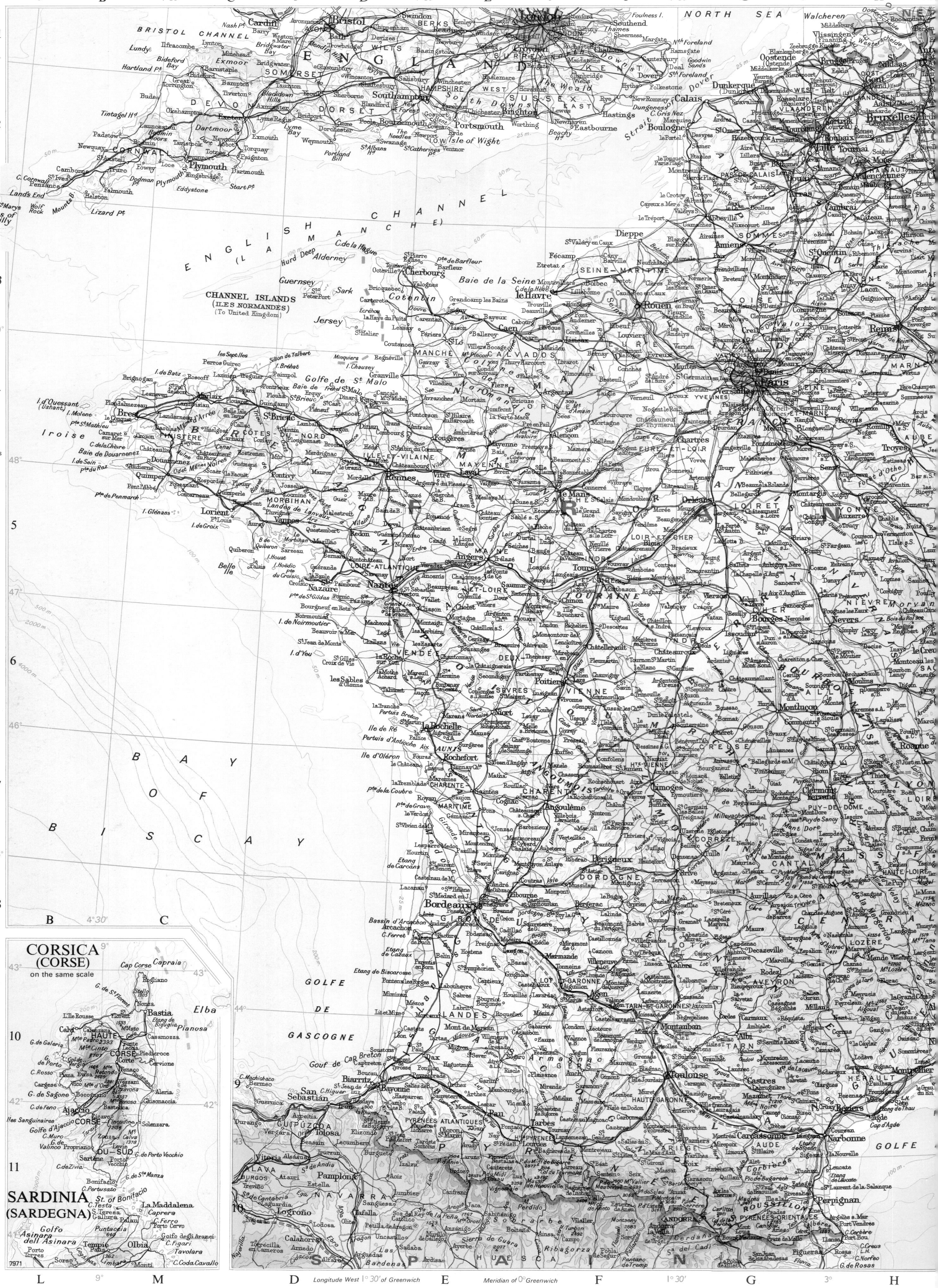

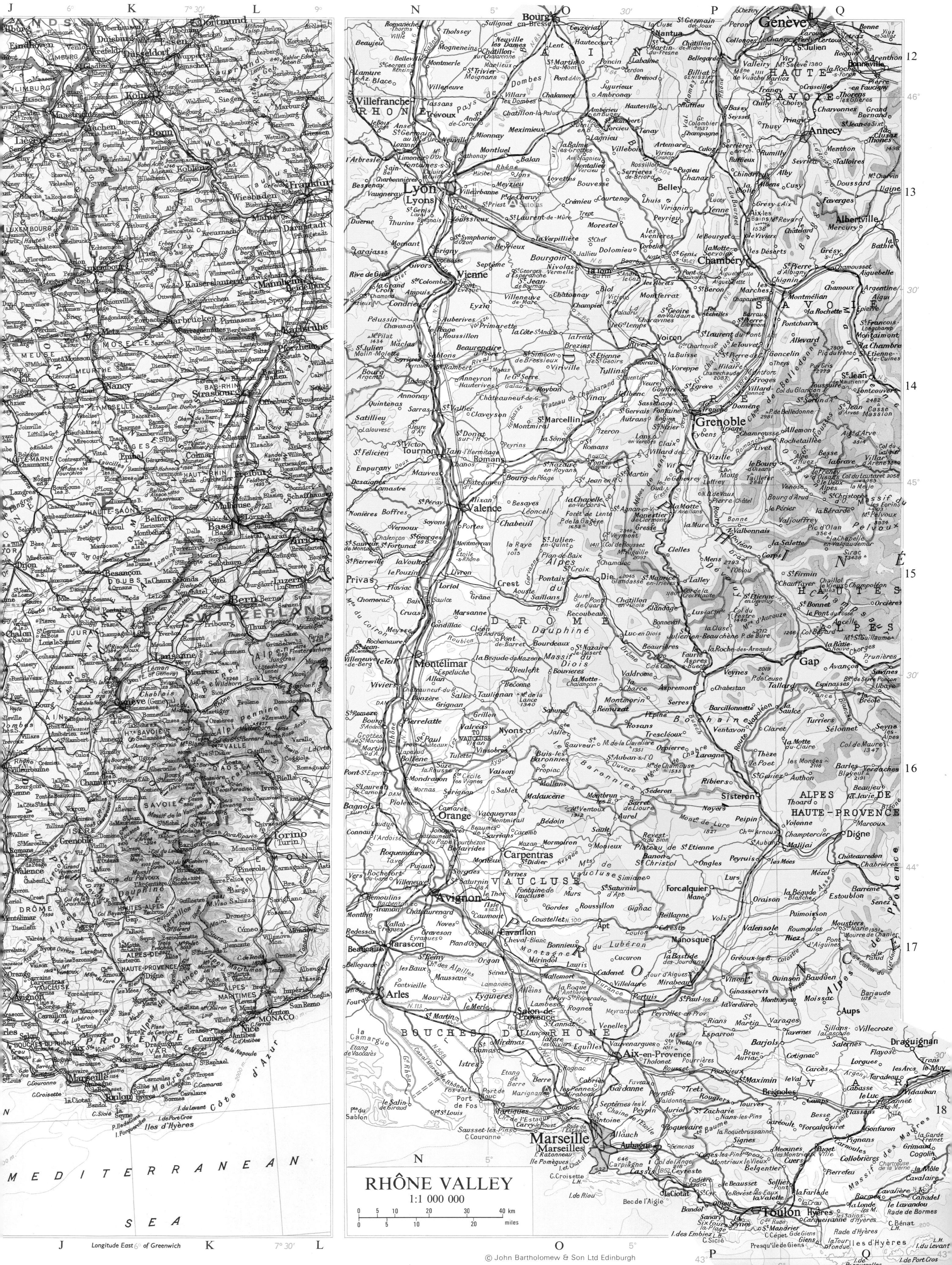

MEDITERRANEAN SEA

Longitude East of Greenwich

RHÔNE VALLEY
1:1 000 000

0 10 20 30 40 km
0 5 10 20 miles

© John Bartholomew & Son Ltd Edinburgh

W GERMANY
SWITZERLAND
LUXEMBOURG
FRANCE
ITALY
PROVENCE
SAVOIE
DAUPHINÉ
JURA

Köln
Bonn
Koblenz
Wiesbaden
Frankfurt
Mainz
Darmstadt
Mannheim
Heidelberg
Karlsruhe
Strasbourg
Saarbrücken
Trier
Nancy
Mulhouse
Basel
Bern
Lausanne
Genève (Geneva)
Annecy
Chambéry
Grenoble
Lyon (Lyons)
Vienne
Valence
Montélimar
Avignon
Arles
Marseille
Nice
MONACO
Toulon

Bourg-en-Bresse
Genève
Annecy
Albertville
Chambéry
Voiron
Grenoble
Gap
Digne
Carpentras
Orange
Avignon
Tarascon
Arles
Aix-en-Provence
Marseille
Toulon
Draguignan

HAUTE SAVOIE
SAVOIE
ISÈRE
DRÔME
Dauphiné
HAUTES ALPES
ALPES DE HAUTE-PROVENCE
VAUCLUSE
BOUCHES DU RHÔNE
AIN
RHÔNE

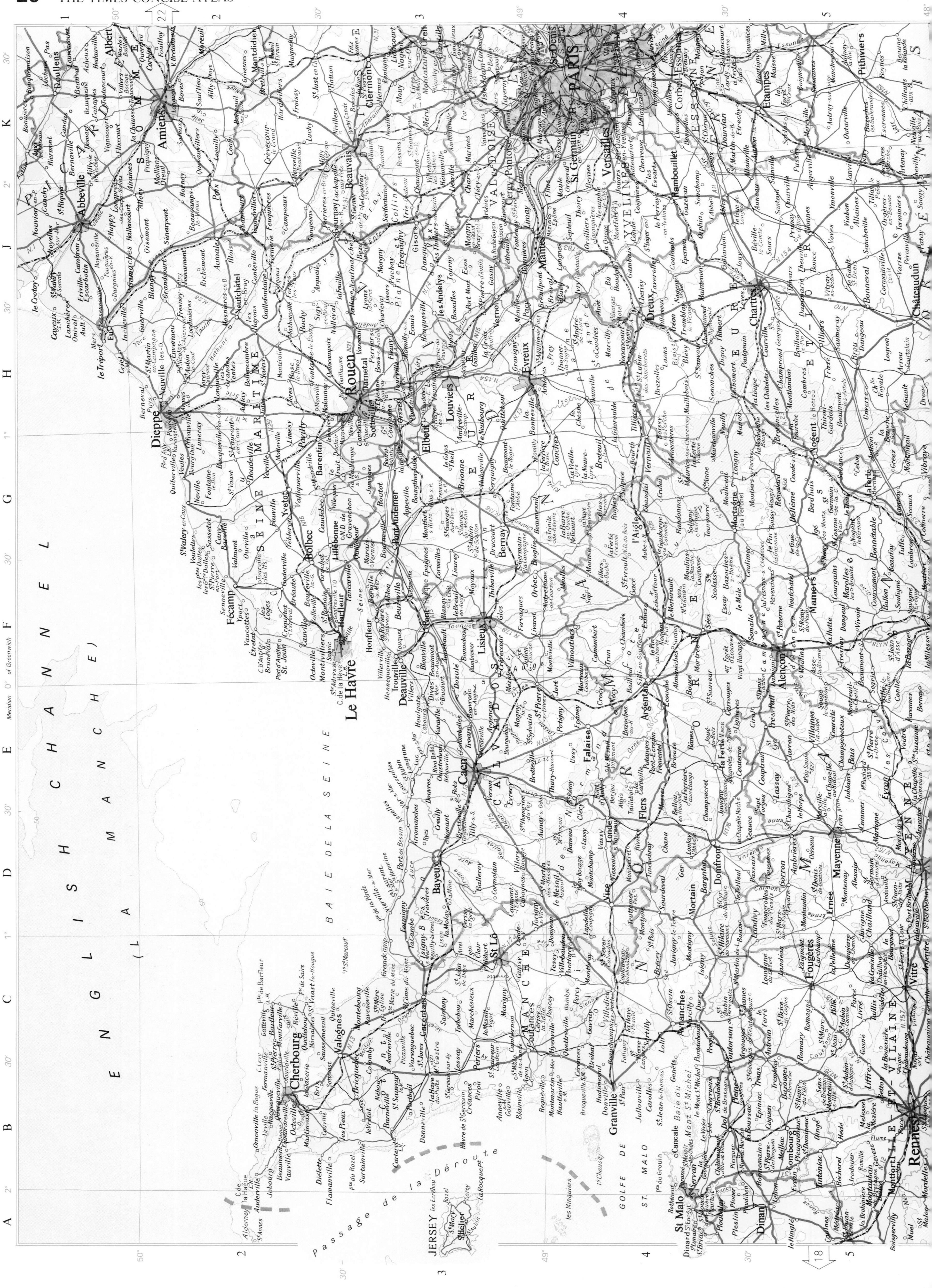

ENGLISH CHANNEL

LA MANCHE

(LA MANCHE)

Meridian 0° of Greenwich

BAIE DE LA SEINE

PARIS

Versailles

St-Denis

St-Germain

VAL-D'OISE

YVELINES

Cergy-Pontoise

Mantes

Dreux

Chartres

Évreux

EURE

Rouen

SEINE-MARITIME

Dieppe

Abbeville

Amiens

SOMME

Albert

Boulogne

PAS-DE-CALAIS

Beauvais

OISE

Clermont

Neufchâtel

Fécamp

Bolbec

Lillebonne

Yvetot

Barentin

Le Havre

Honfleur

Deauville

Trouville

Lisieux

Pont-Audemer

Bernay

Louviers

Elbeuf

Sotteville

Les Andelys

l'Aigle

Mortagne

Alençon

Mamers

Nogent

CALVADOS

Caen

Bayeux

Falaise

Argentan

ORNE

Flers

Domfront

Mayenne

MAYENNE

MANCHE

St-Lô

Coutances

Avranches

Granville

Cherbourg

Valognes

Carentan

Vitré

Fougères

Rennes

ILLE-ET-VILAINE

Dinan

St-Malo

GOLFE DE ST MALO

Passage de la Déroute

JERSEY

Étampes

Pithiviers

ESSONNE

EURE-ET-LOIR

Corbeil

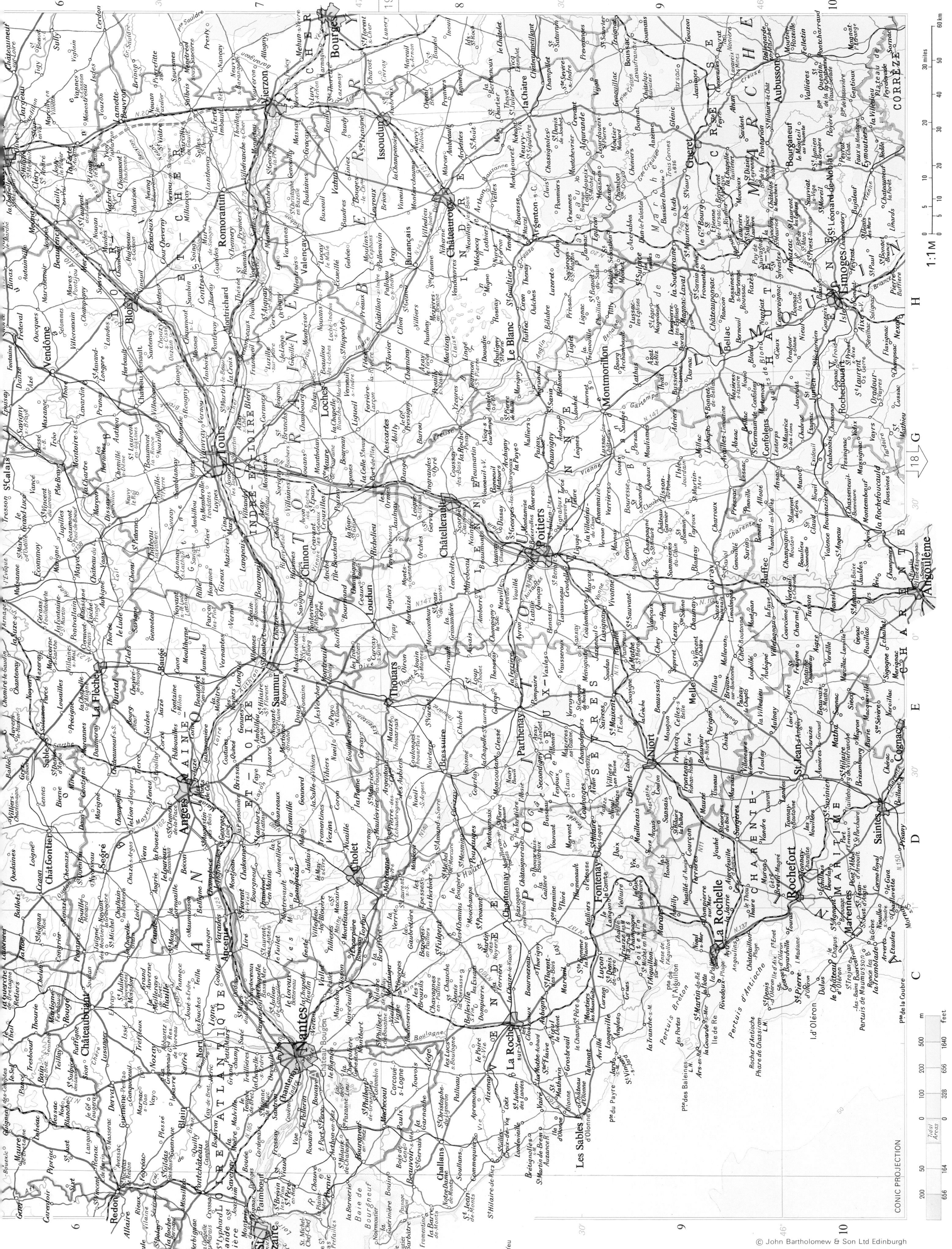

1.1 M

30 miles
60 km

CONIC PROJECTION

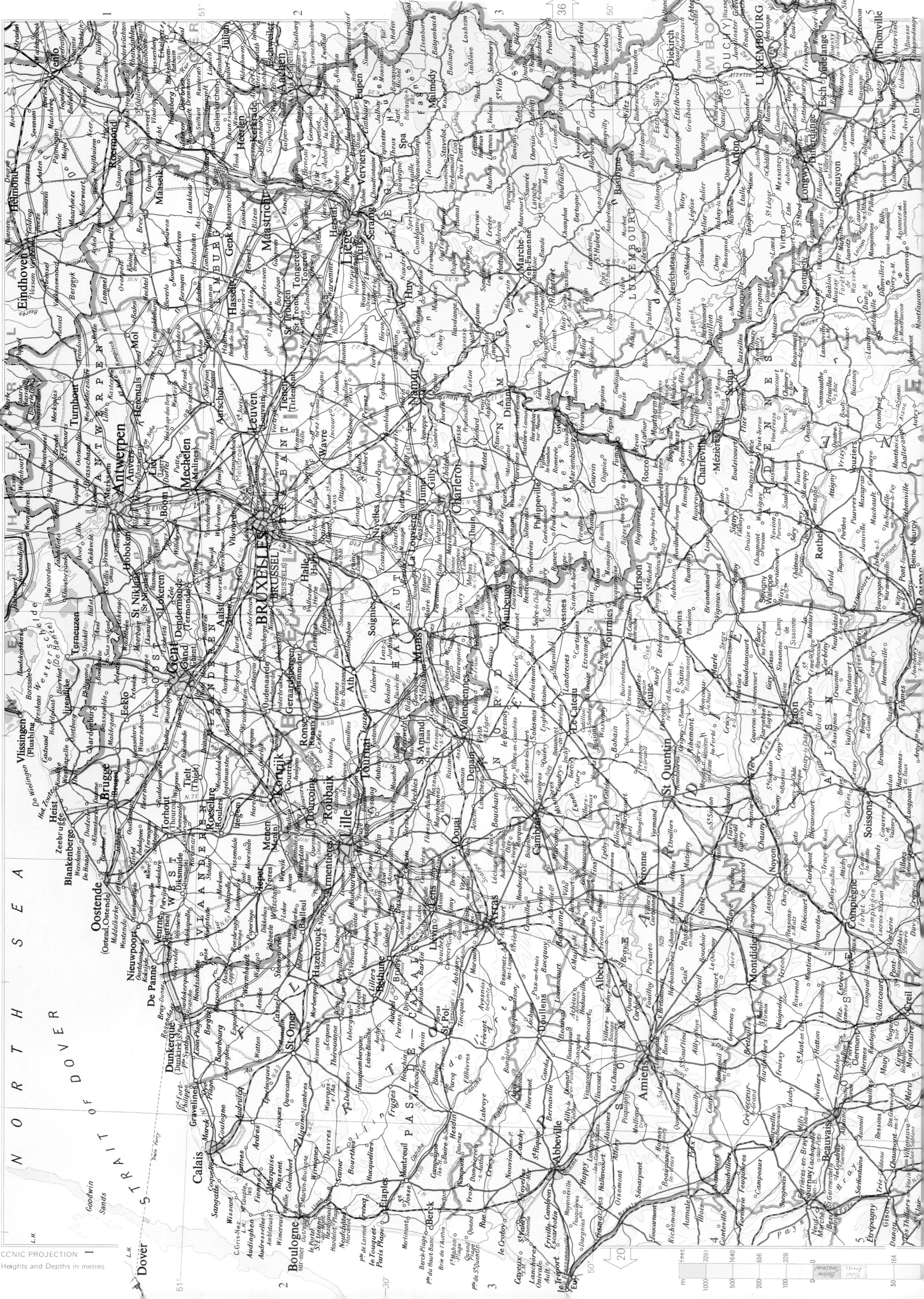
NORTH SEA
STRAIT OF DOVER
BRUXELLES (BRUSSEL)
Antwerpen
Gent
Brugge
Oostende
Liège
Namur
Charleroi
Mons
Lille
Roubaix
Tourcoing
Dunkerque
Calais
Boulogne
Amiens
Arras
Douai
Valenciennes
Cambrai
St Quentin
Laon
Reims
Soissons
Compiègne
Beauvais
Abbeville
Charleville
Mézières
Sedan
LUXEMBOURG
Thionville
Maastricht
Aachen
Eindhoven
Venlo
Dover
CCNIC PROJECTION
Heights and Depths in metres
1:1M

PARIS

Major labels and regions visible on the map:

OISE · SEINE-ET-MARNE · VAL-D'OISE · SEINE · MARNE · YVELINES · ESSONNE · EURE-ET-LOIRE

PARIS

Selected place names: Meaux · Melun · Versailles · St-Germain-en-Laye · Rambouillet · Corbeil-Essonnes · Mantes-la-Jolie · Poissy · Achères · Vernouillet · Maisons-Laffitte · St-Ouen-l'Aumône · Sarcelles · St-Denis · Neuilly · Montreuil · Bobigny · Bondy · Villemomble · Champigny-sur-Marne · Villeneuve-St-Georges · St-Maur-des-Fossés · Créteil · Choisy-le-Roi · Orly · Vitry-sur-Seine · Ivry · Montrouge · Clamart · Boulogne-Billancourt · Rueil · Malmaison · Suresnes · Nanterre · Courbevoie · Colombes · Argenteuil · Gennevilliers · Asnières · Clichy · Levallois · St-Cloud · Sèvres · Meudon · Issy-les-Moulineaux · Vanves · Cachan · Bagneux · Fontenay-aux-Roses · Charenton · Vincennes · Aubervilliers · Pantin · Noisy-le-Sec · Drancy · Stains · Pierrefitte · Chelles · Gonesse · AÉROPORT CHARLES DE GAULLE

Scale: 1:300 000

0 5 10 15 km
0 5 10 miles

© Times Books Ltd

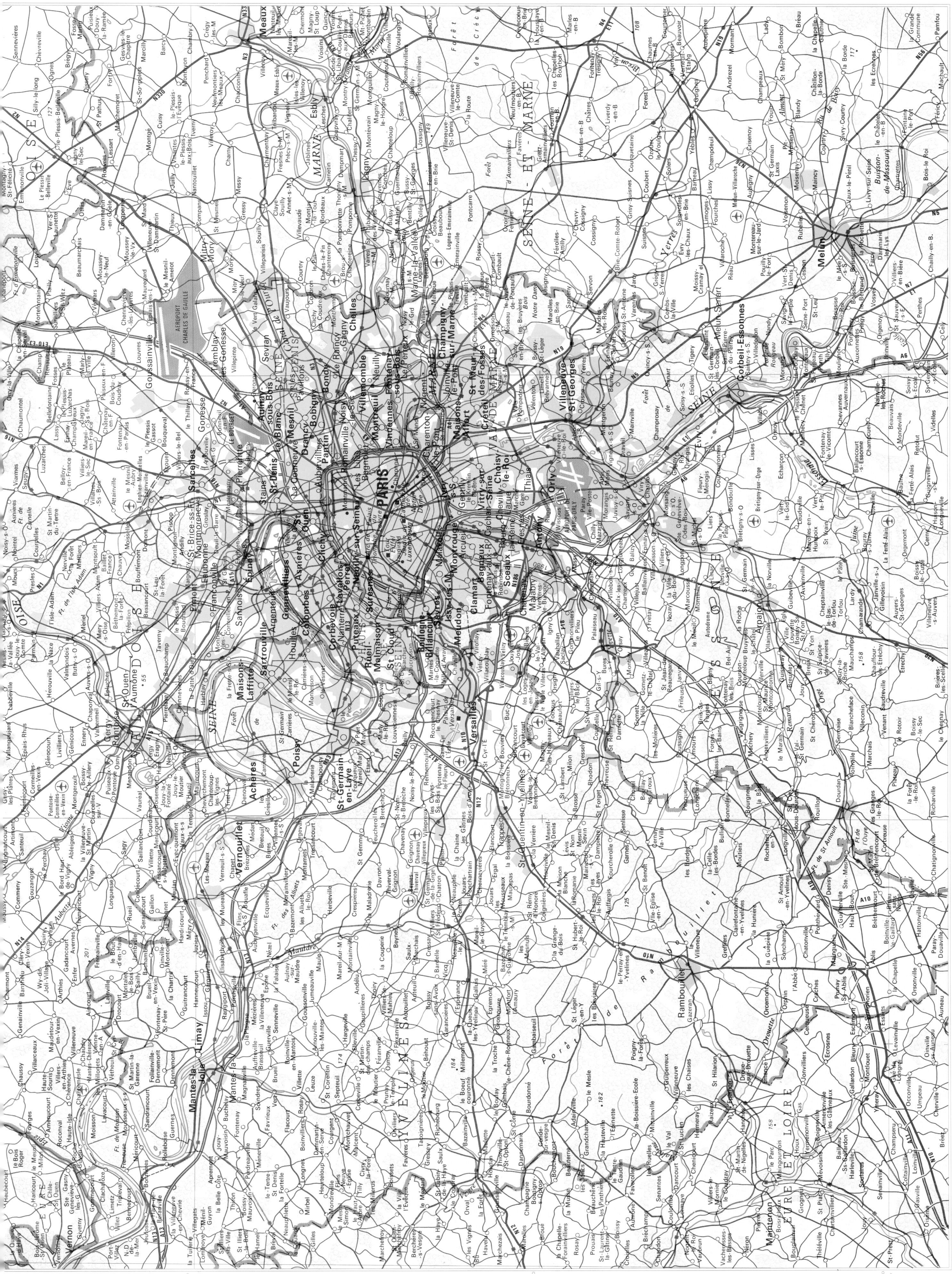

A   4°15'   B   4°30'   C   4°45'   D   5°00'   E   5°15'

NORTH SEA

Ijmuiden
Zaandam
MARKERWAARD
Marken

Haarlem
NOORDHOLLAND
AMSTERDAM

Zandvoort
Heemstede
Amstelveen
Weesp
Naarden
ZUIDELIJK - FLEVOLAND
GOOIMEER
IJMEER

Bloemendaal
Overveen
Aerdenhout
Hillegom

AMSTERDAM (Schiphol) Airport
Hoofddorp
Bussum
Huizen
Hilversum

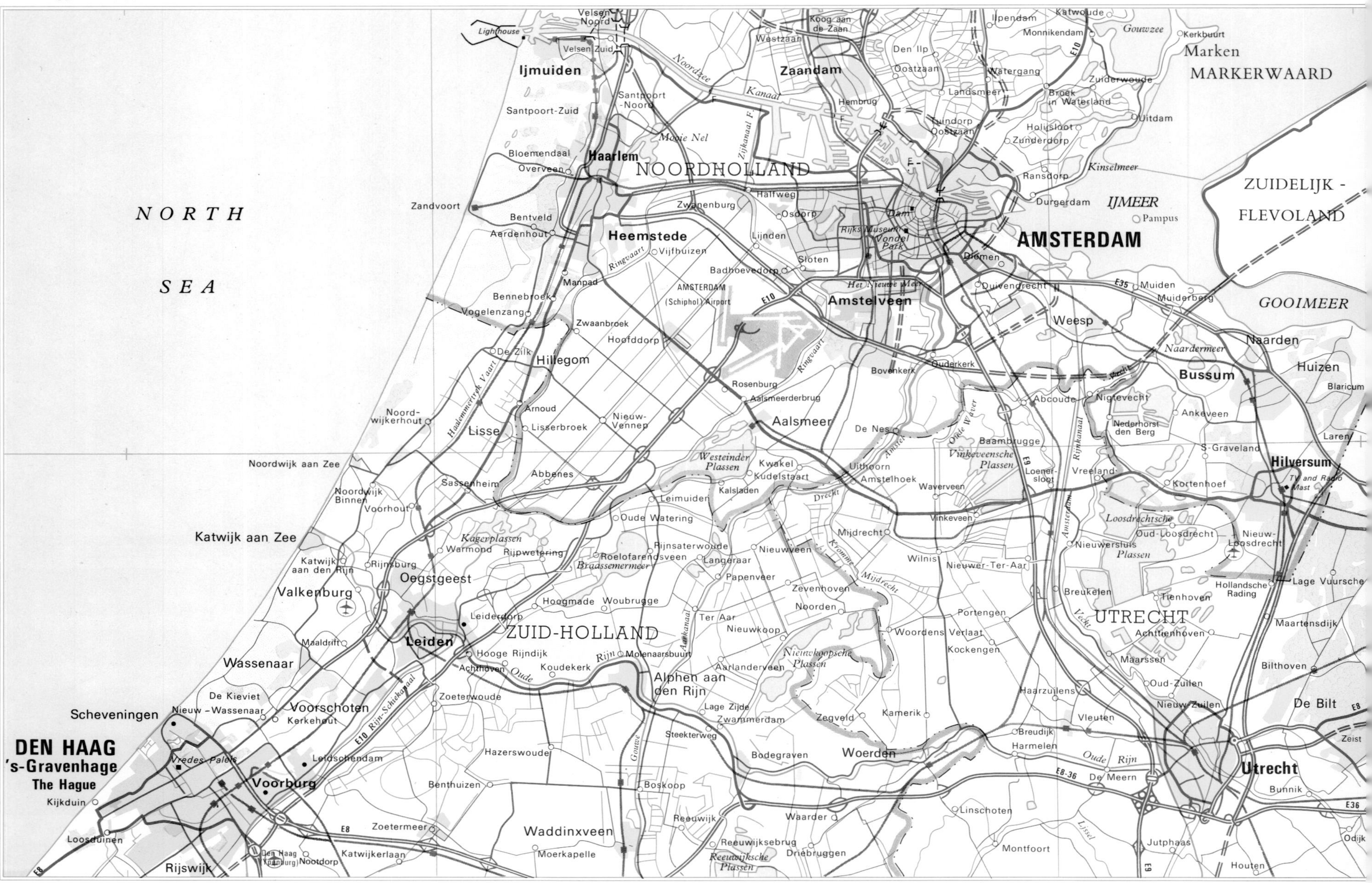

Lisse
Aalsmeer
Uithoorn

Noordwijk aan Zee
Sassenheim
UTRECHT

Katwijk aan Zee
Oegstgeest
Warmond

Leiden
ZUID-HOLLAND
Alphen aan den Rijn
Woerden

Wassenaar
Voorschoten
Utrecht

Scheveningen
DEN HAAG
's-Gravenhage
The Hague
Voorburg

Kijkduin
Rijswijk
Zoetermeer
Waddinxveen
Boskoop

Loosduinen

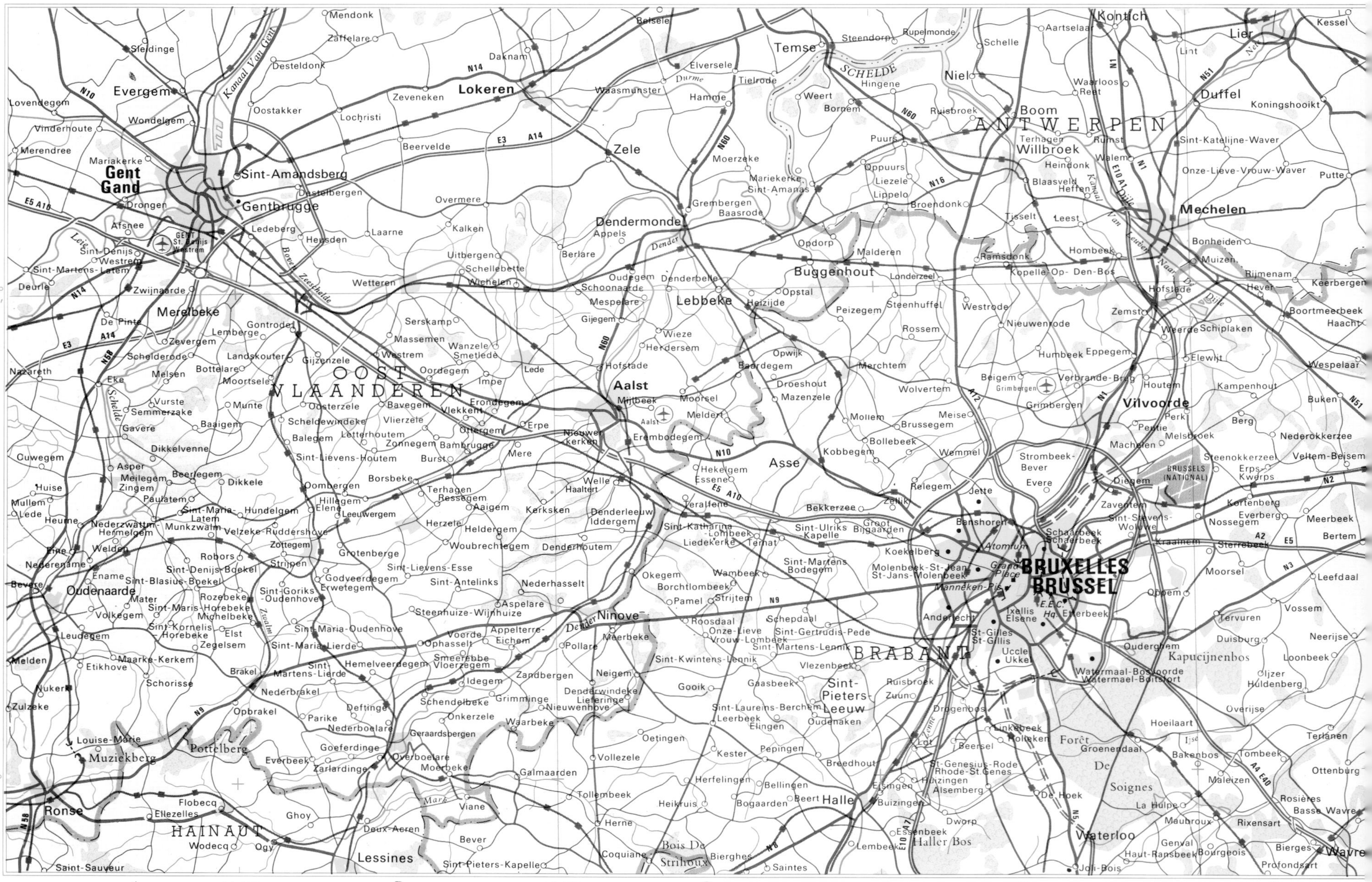

© Times Books Ltd   1:300 000

BRUSSELS

A   3°45'   B   4°00'   C   4°15'   D   4°30'   E

Temse
SCHELDE
Niel
Boom
ANTWERPEN
Duffel

Evergem
Lokeren
Willebroek

Gent Gand
Zele
Mechelen

Genthbrugge
Dendermonde
Buggenhout
Lebbeke

OOST VLAANDEREN
Aalst
Vilvoorde

Merelbeke
Asse
BRUSSELS NATIONAL

Oudenaarde
Ninove
BRUXELLES BRUSSEL
BRABANT

Ronse
Halle
Waterloo
Wavre
HAINAUT
Lessines

1:300 000   0   5   10   15 km

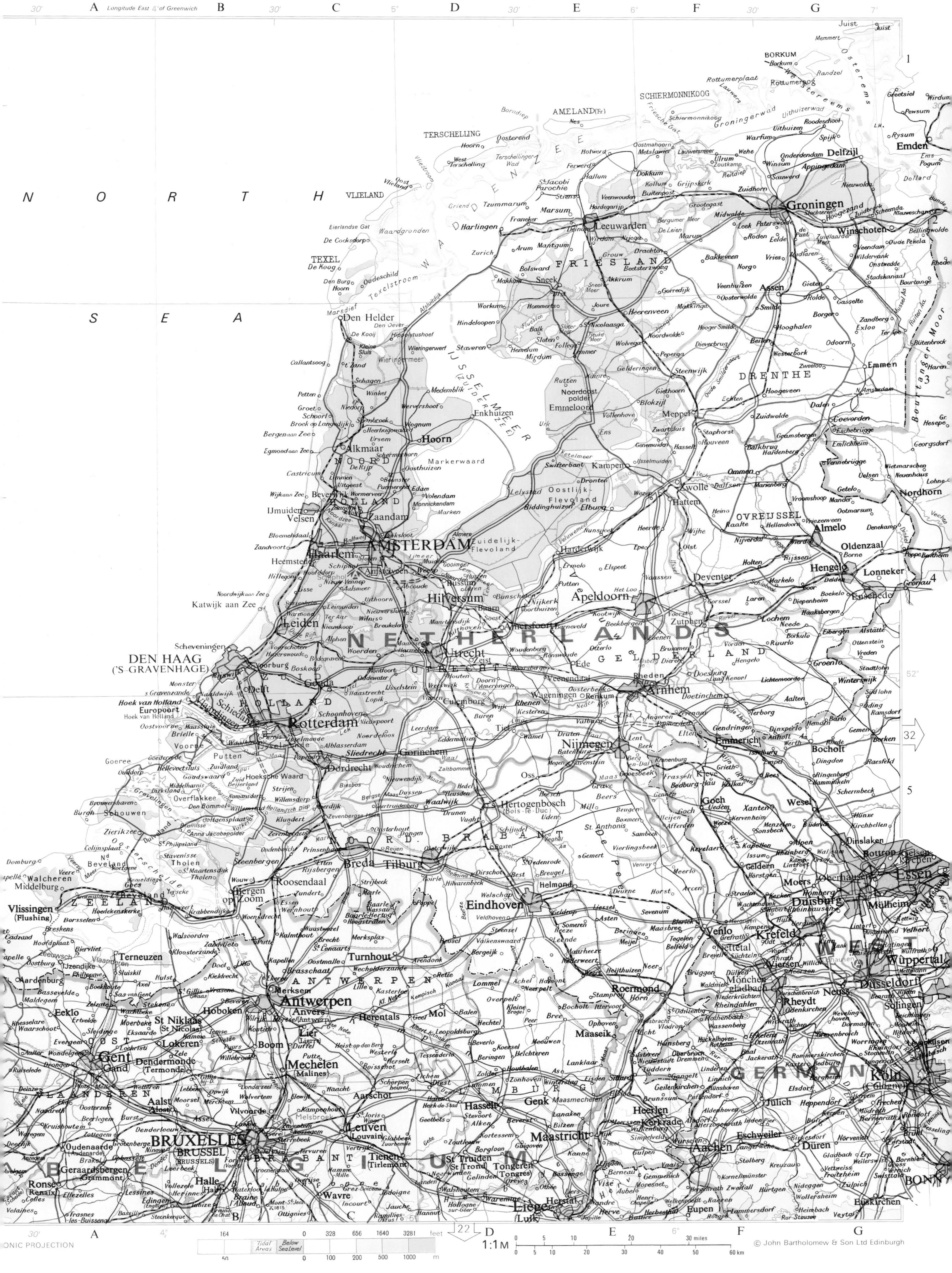
Longitude East 4° of Greenwich
N O R T H
S E A
W A D D E N Z E E
IJSSELMEER (ZUIDER ZEE)
Markerwaard
NETHERLANDS
FRIESLAND
DRENTHE
OVREIJSSEL
GELDERLAND
UTRECHT
NOORD HOLLAND
ZUID HOLLAND
ZEELAND
NOORD BRABANT
LIMBURG
ANTWERPEN
OOST VLAANDEREN
BRABANT
BELGIUM
GERMANY
WEST
TERSCHELLING
AMELAND
SCHIERMONNIKOOG
BORKUM
VLIELAND
TEXEL
Juist
Groningen
Leeuwarden
Emden
Delfzijl
Assen
Emmen
Den Helder
Alkmaar
Hoorn
Zwolle
Kampen
Meppel
Almelo
Hengelo
Enschede
Apeldoorn
Deventer
Zutphen
AMSTERDAM
Haarlem
Zaandam
Hilversum
Leiden
DEN HAAG ('S-GRAVENHAGE)
Delft
Rotterdam
Utrecht
Amersfoort
Arnhem
Nijmegen
Dordrecht
Gorinchem
's-Hertogenbosch
Breda
Tilburg
Eindhoven
Helmond
Venlo
Roermond
Maastricht
Heerlen
Aachen
Vlissingen (Flushing)
Middelburg
Antwerpen (Anvers)
Gent (Gand)
Mechelen (Malines)
Leuven (Louvain)
BRUXELLES BRUSSEL (BRUSSELS)
Liège (Luik)
Hasselt
Genk
Duisburg
Essen
Krefeld
Düsseldorf
Wuppertal
Mönchengladbach
Köln
BONN
32
22
ONIC PROJECTION
Tidal Areas
Below Sea Level
feet 164 0 328 656 1640 3281
m 50 0 100 200 500 1000
1:1M
0 5 10 20 30 miles
0 5 10 20 30 40 50 60 km
© John Bartholomew & Son Ltd Edinburgh

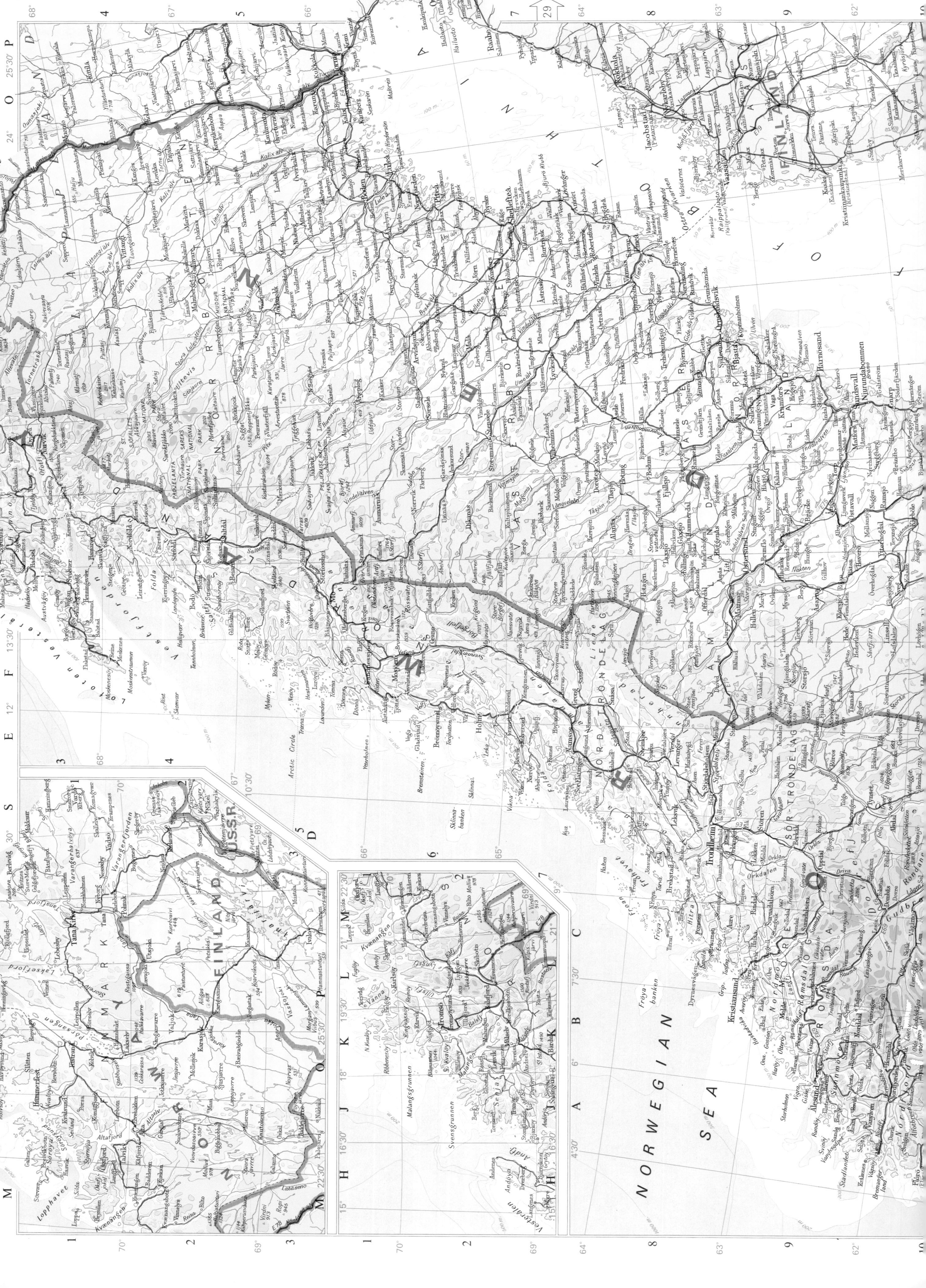
NORWEGIAN SEA
FINLAND
NORD-TRÖNDELAG
SÖR-TRÖNDELAG
Trondheim
Kristiansund
Ålesund
Östersund
Umeå
Luleå
Oulu
Hammerfest
Tromsø
Narvik
Bodø
Arctic Circle
FINNMARK
U.S.S.R.
29

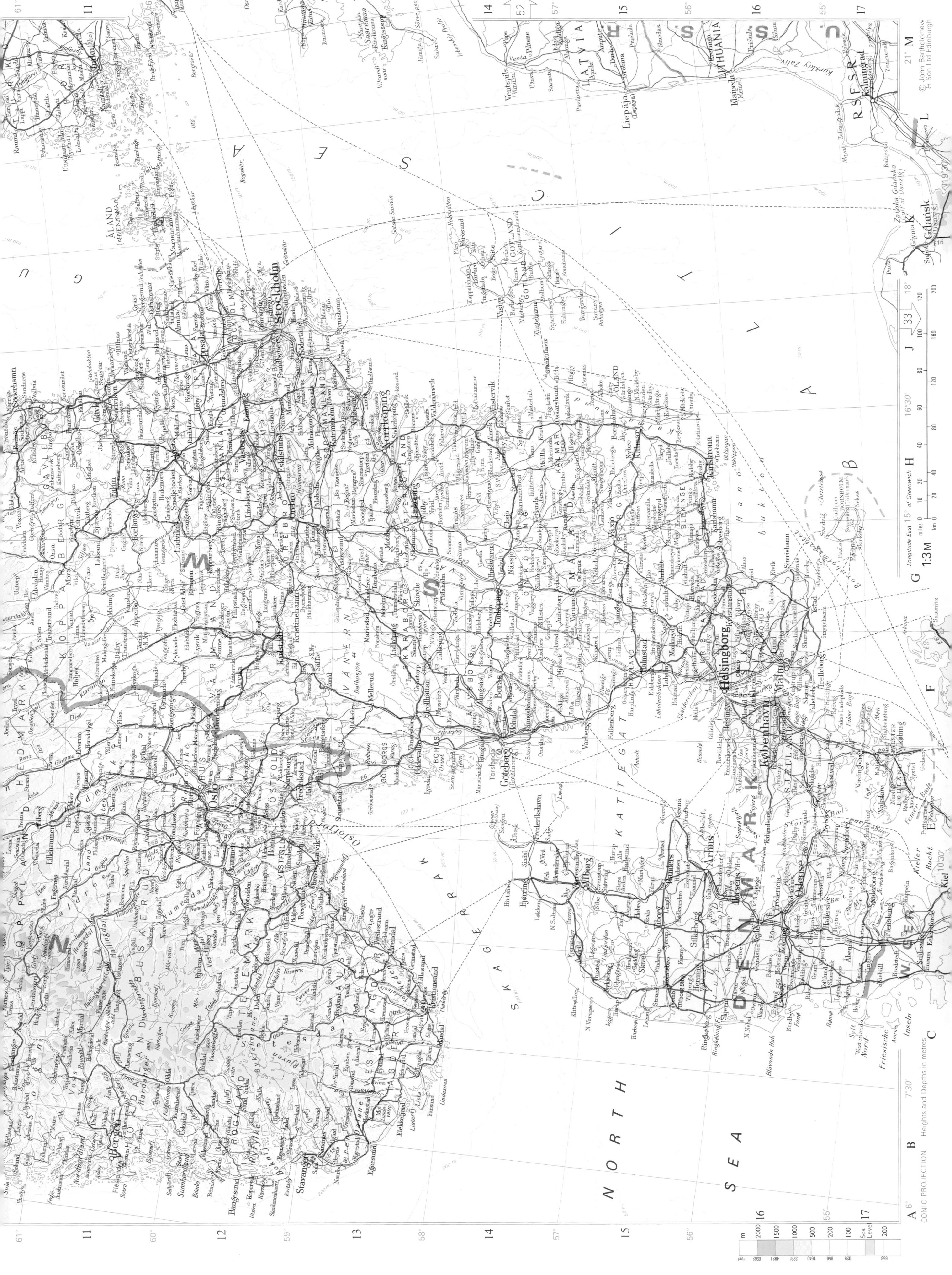

CONIC PROJECTION   Heights and Depths in metres

Longitude East 15° of Greenwich

1·3M

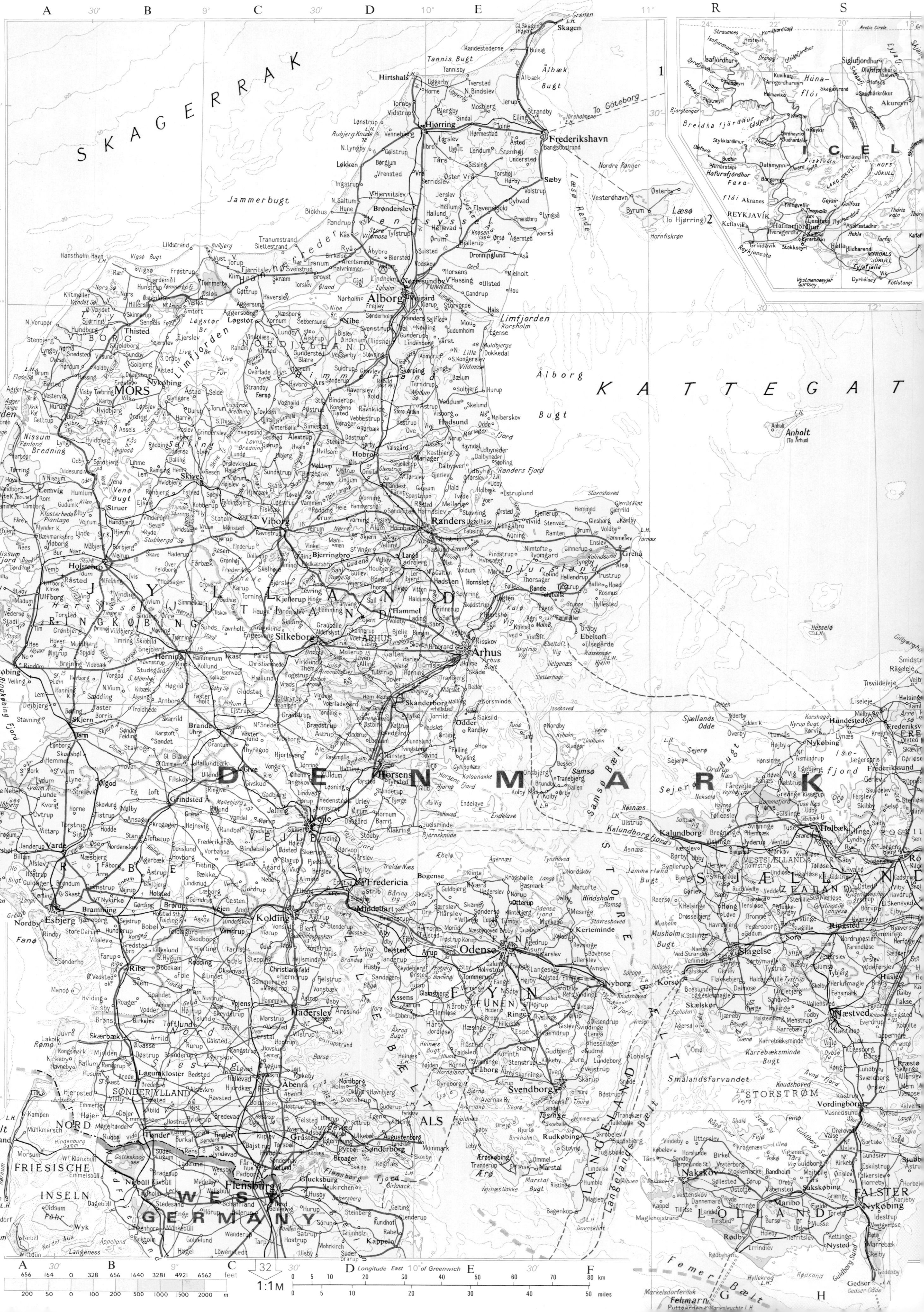
SKAGERRAK
KATTEGAT
DENMARK
ICELAND
Jammerbugt
Tannis Bugt
Ålbæk Bugt
Ålborg Bugt
Skagen
Grenen
Hirtshals
Hjørring
Frederikshavn
To Göteborg
Læsø
Læsø Rende
Sæby
Brønderslev
Vendsyssel
Ålborg
Nørresundby
Limfjorden
Thisted
Thy
Viborg
MORS
Nykøbing
Skive
Salling
Lemvig
Struer
Holstebro
Herning
Ringkøbing
Ringkøbing Fjord
Silkeborg
Randers
Randers Fjord
Hobro
Mariager Fjord
Grenå
Djursland
Anholt
Århus
Århus Bugt
Samsø
Samsø Bælt
Horsens
Skanderborg
Vejle
Fredericia
Kolding
Middelfart
Esbjerg
Fanø
Ribe
Varde
Skallingen
Rømø
Tønder
Haderslev
Åbenrå
Sønderborg
ALS
Lille Bælt
Odense
Nyborg
FYN (FÜNEN)
Svendborg
Fåborg
Ærø
Tåsinge
Langeland
Langelands Bælt
Store Bælt
Kalundborg
Holbæk
Sjælland (Zealand)
Sjællands Odde
Isefjord
Slagelse
Korsør
Sorø
Ringsted
Næstved
Smålandsfarvandet
Storstrøm
Vordingborg
Lolland
Nakskov
Maribo
Falster
Nykøbing
Gedser
Femer Bælt
Fehmarn
Sylt
Westerland
Friesische Inseln
Amrum
Föhr
Flensburg
West Germany
Reykjavík
Akureyri
Ísafjördhur
Húnaflói
Faxaflói
Breidha fjördhur
Hofs Jökull
Langjökull
Mýrdals Jökull
Eyjafjalla
Surtsey
Vestmannaeyjar
Longitude East 10° of Greenwich
1:1M
0 5 10 20 30 40 50 60 70 80 km
0 5 10 20 30 40 50 miles
656 164 0 328 656 1640 3281 4921 6562 feet
200 50 0 100 200 500 1000 1500 2000 m
32

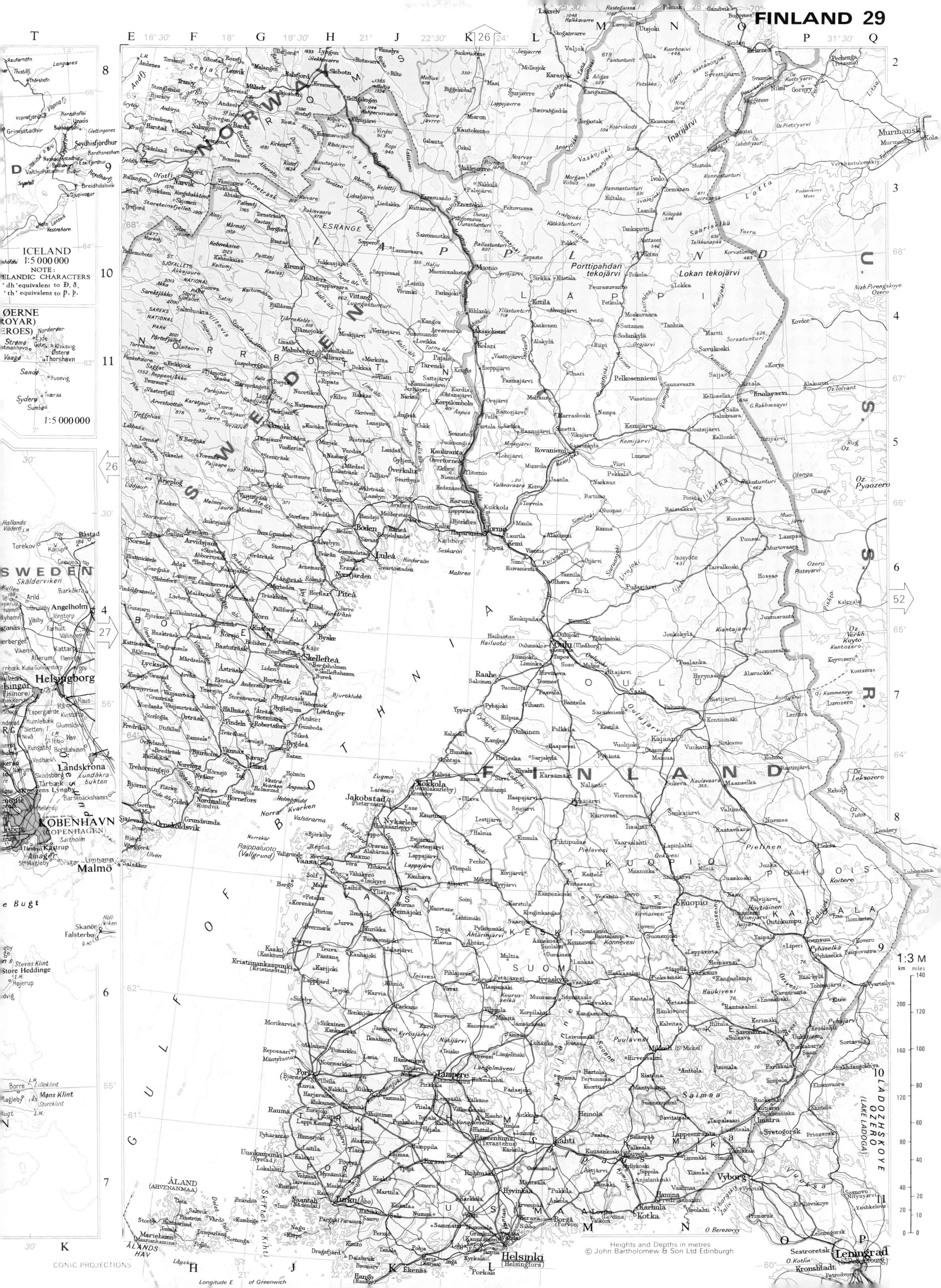
FINLAND
SWEDEN
NORWAY
U. S. S. R.
GULF OF BOTHNIA
LAPPI
OULU
VAASA
KESKI SUOMI
KUOPIO
POHJOIS KARJALA
MIKKELI
KYMI
HÄME
TURKU PORI
UUSIMAA
NORRBOTTEN
VÄSTERBOTTEN
ÅLAND (AHVENANMAA)
ÅLANDS HAV
LADOZHSKOYE OZERO (LAKE LADOGA)
Helsinki (Helsingfors)
Tampere
Turku (Åbo)
Oulu (Uleåborg)
Vaasa
Kuopio
Lahti
Jyväskylä
Pori
Kotka
Lappeenranta
Vyborg
Leningrad
Kronshtadt
Sestroretsk
Rovaniemi
Kemi
Tornio
Haparanda
Luleå
Piteå
Skellefteå
Umeå
Kiruna
Narvik
Murmansk
Kola
Inarijärvi
Porttipahdan tekojärvi
Lokan tekojärvi
Saimaa
Päijänne
Kemijärvi
Oulujärvi
Pielinen
ICELAND 1:5 000 000
NOTE: ICELANDIC CHARACTERS 'dh' equivalent to Ð, ð, 'th' equivalent to Þ, þ.
FÆRØERNE (FAROES) 1:5 000 000
Tórshavn
KØBENHAVN (COPENHAGEN)
Malmö
Helsingborg
Landskrona
1:3 M
Heights and Depths in metres
© John Bartholomew & Son Ltd Edinburgh
CONIC PROJECTIONS
Longitude E of Greenwich

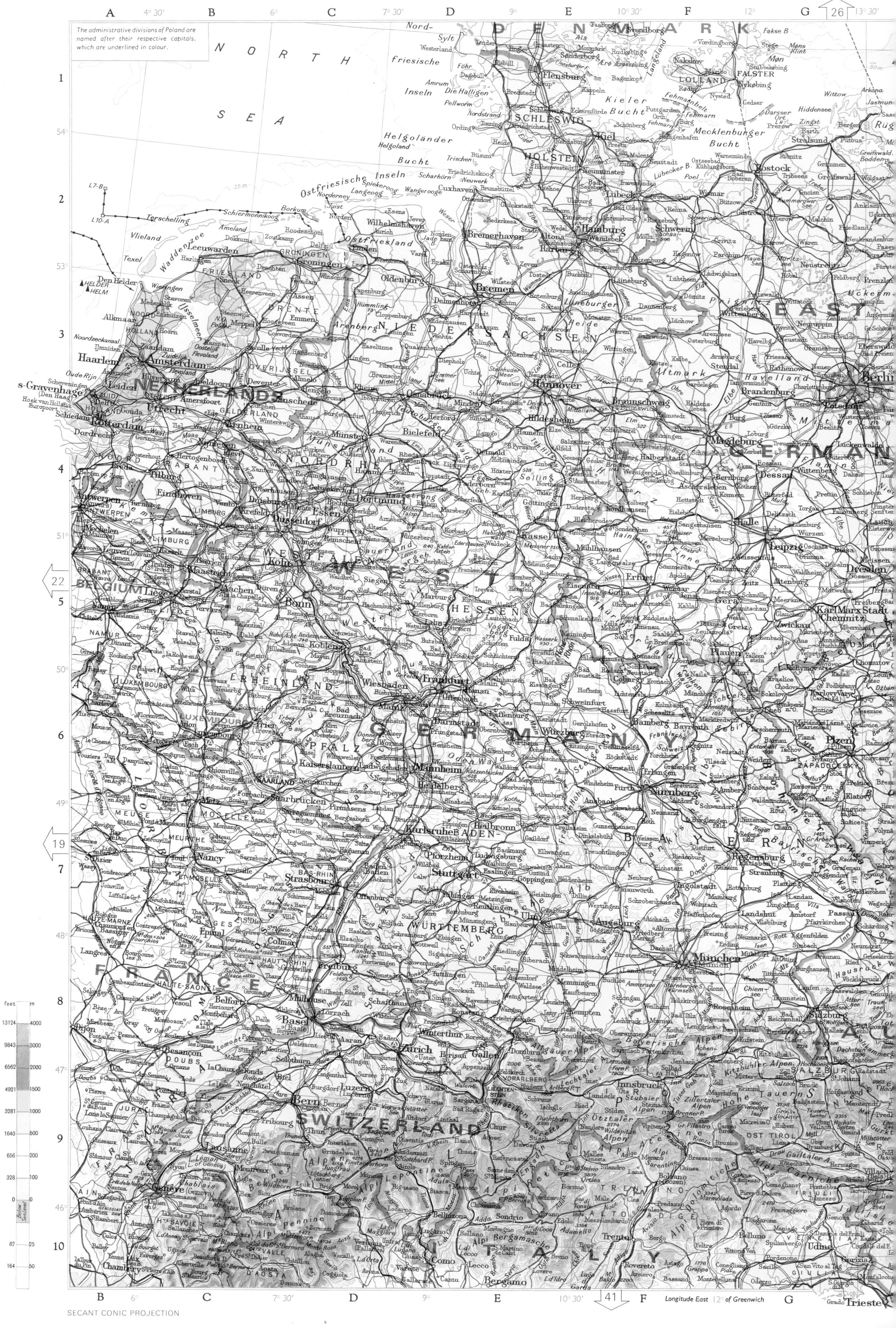
The administrative divisions of Poland are named after their respective capitals, which are underlined in colour.
NORTH SEA
DENMARK
NETHERLANDS
BELGIUM
LUXEMBOURG
FRANCE
SWITZERLAND
ITALY
WEST GERMANY
EAST GERMANY
SCHLESWIG-HOLSTEIN
NIEDERSACHSEN
NORDRHEIN-WESTFALEN
HESSEN
RHEINLAND-PFALZ
SAARLAND
BADEN-WÜRTTEMBERG
BAYERN
Longitude East 12° of Greenwich
SECANT CONIC PROJECTION

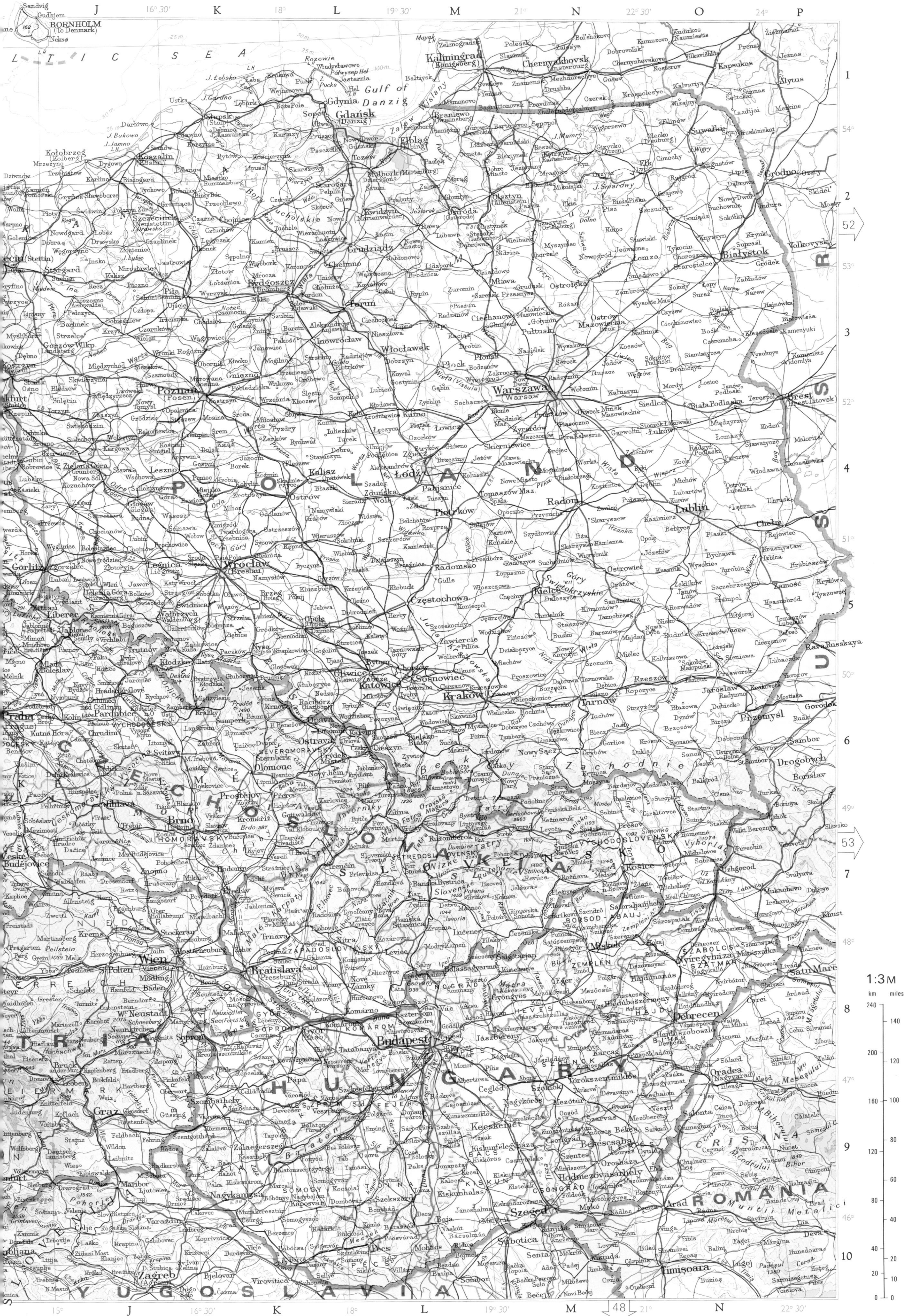

Heights and Depths in metres

© John Bartholomew & Son Ltd Edinburgh

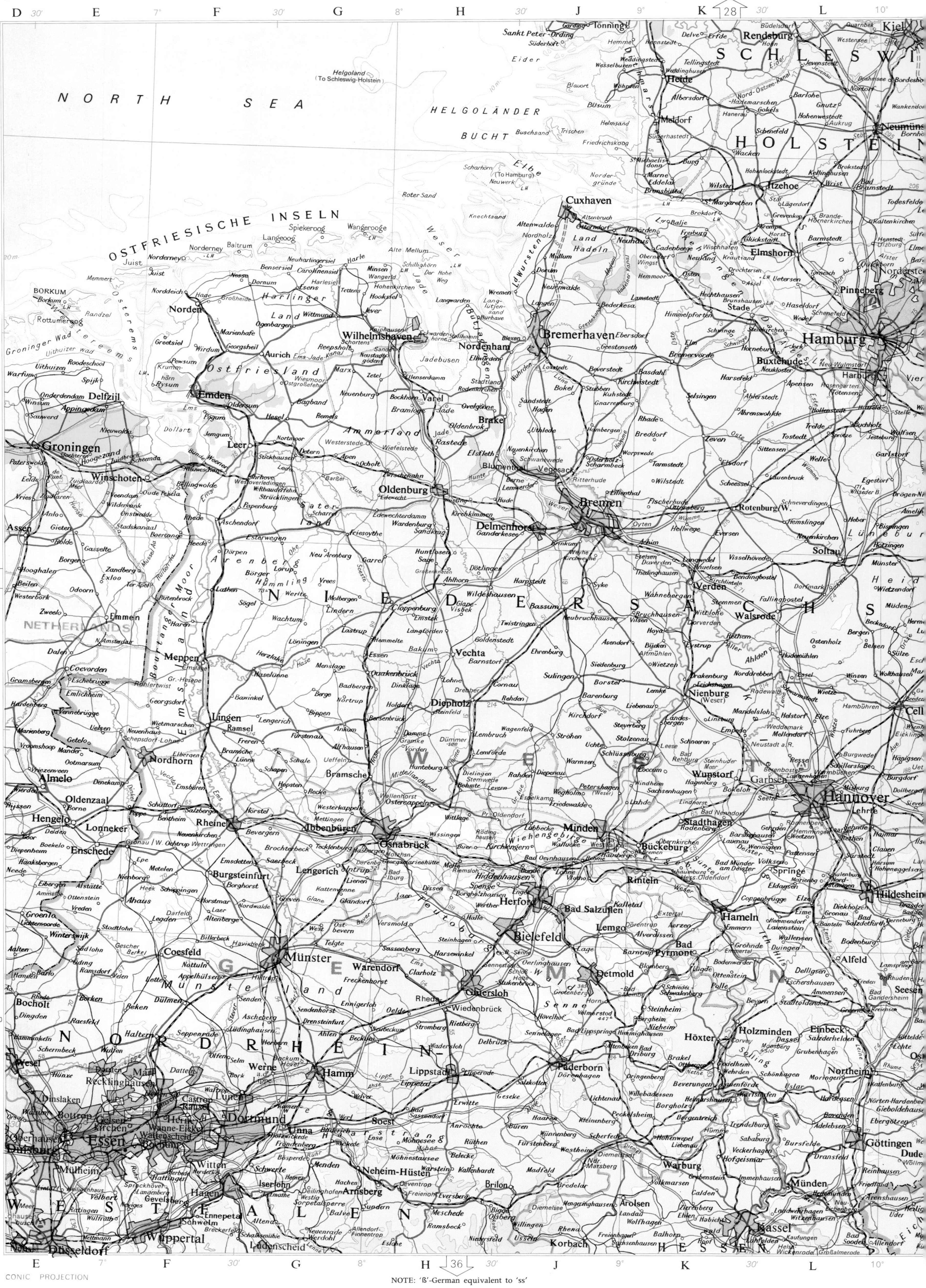

D E F 7° G 30' H 8° J 30' K 28 30' L 10°

NORTH SEA

SCHLESWIG

HOLSTEIN

HELGOLÄNDER BUCHT

Helgoland (To Schleswig-Holstein)

OSTFRIESISCHE INSELN

Cuxhaven

Rendsburg Kiel
Heide
Itzehoe
Elmshorn
Pinneberg
Stade
Hamburg
Harburg
Buxtehude

Norden
Emden
Wilhelmshaven
Aurich
Ostfriesland
Nordenham
Bremerhaven
Vegesack

Groningen
Winschoten
Leer
Oldenburg
Delmenhorst
Bremen
Verden

Assen
Emmen
Meppen
NIEDERSACHSEN
Cloppenburg
Vechta
Diepholz
Nienburg (Weser)
Walsrode
Celle

NETHERLANDS

Almelo
Nordhorn
Lingen
Quakenbrück
Osnabrück
Minden
Wunstorf
Garbsen
Hannover

Hengelo
Enschede
Rheine
Ibbenbüren
Bückeburg
Stadthagen

Münster
Burgsteinfurt
Lengerich
Herford
Bielefeld
Bad Salzuflen
Hameln
Hildesheim

Coesfeld
Warendorf
Gütersloh
Detmold
Bad Pyrmont

GERMANY

NORDRHEIN-WESTFALEN
Bocholt
Wesel
Hamm
Lippstadt
Paderborn
Höxter
Holzminden
Einbeck
Northeim

Recklinghausen
Dortmund
Unna
Soest
Warburg
Göttingen

Essen
Duisburg
Mülheim
Witten
Bochum
Hagen
Arnsberg
Brilon
Kassel

Wuppertal
Düsseldorf

HESSEN

CONIC PROJECTION

NOTE: 'ß'-German equivalent to 'ss'

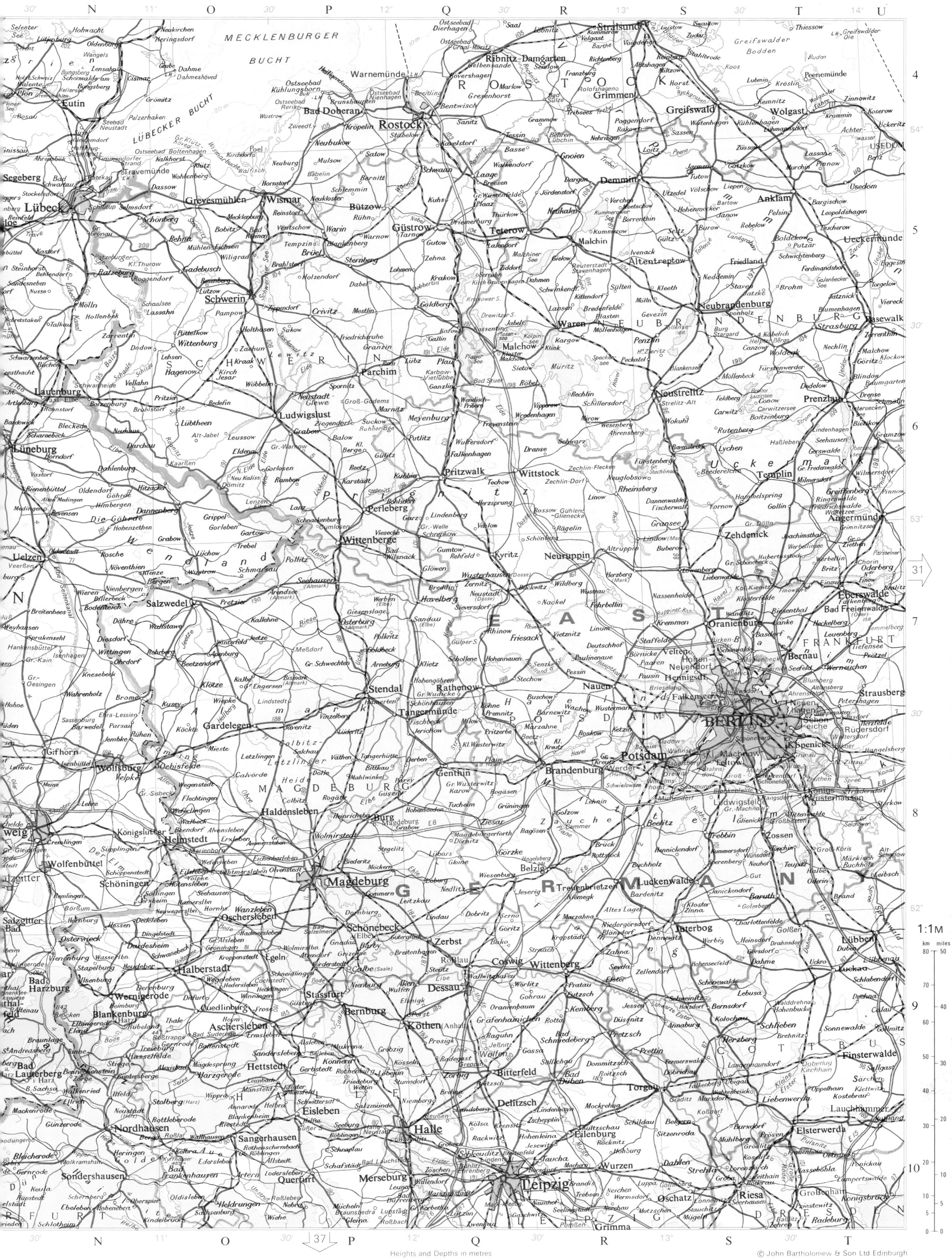

MECKLENBURGER BUCHT

LÜBECKER BUCHT

ROSTOCK
Rostock
Warnemünde
Ribnitz-Damgarten
Stralsund
Greifswald
Wolgast
USEDOM

Lübeck
Travemünde
Grevesmühlen
Wismar
Bützow
Güstrow
Teterow
Malchin
Demmin
Anklam
Uckermünde

Eutin
Segeberg
Schwerin
Parchim
Waren
Neubrandenburg
Friedland
Strasburg
Pasewalk

Lauenburg
Ludwigslust
Plau
Röbel
Neustrelitz
Prenzlau
Angermünde

Lüneburg
Uelzen
Wittenberge
Perleberg
Pritzwalk
Wittstock
Neuruppin
Templin
Zehdenick
Eberswalde
Bad Freienwalde

Salzwedel
Seehausen
Havelberg
Rathenow
Fehrbellin
Oranienburg
Bernau
FRANKFURT

Gardelegen
Stendal
Tangermünde
Genthin
Brandenburg
Nauen
Potsdam
BERLIN
Strausberg

Wolfsburg
Gifhorn
Helmstedt
Haldensleben
Burg
Wusterhausen

Braunschweig
Wolfenbüttel
Schöningen
Magdeburg
GERMAN
Belzig
Treuenbrietzen
Luckenwalde
Jüterbog
Zossen

Salzgitter
Osterwieck
Oschersleben
Schönebeck
Zerbst
Coswig
Wittenberg
Lübben
Luckau

Bad Harzburg
Halberstadt
Wernigerode
Blankenburg
Quedlinburg
Aschersleben
Stassfurt
Bernburg
Köthen
Dessau
Wörlitz
Bitterfeld
Bad Düben
Torgau
Finsterwalde
Elsterwerda

Nordhausen
Sangerhausen
Hettstedt
Eisleben
Delitzsch
Eilenburg
Wurzen

Sondershausen
Querfurt
Merseburg
Halle
Leipzig
Oschatz
Riesa

EAST GERMANY

Heights and Depths in metres

1:1M
km miles
80 / 50

© John Bartholomew & Son Ltd Edinburgh

HAMBURG

SCHLESWIG-HOLSTEIN

Steinburg · Pinneberg · Segeberg · Stormarn

Elmshorn · **Pinneberg** · **Norderstedt** · Ahrensburg · Grosshansdorf

HAMBURG

Stade · **Wedel** · Buxtehude

STADE

NIEDERSACHSEN

Harburg · LÜNEBURG · Herzogtum Lauenburg · Schwarzenbek · **Geesthacht**

ELBE

BERLIN

Potsdam · POTSDAM · FRANKFURT

Falkensee · **Spandau** · **Charlottenburg** · **Wittenau** · **Tegel** · **Pankow** · **Weissensee**

BERLIN · **Mitte** · **WEST-** · **EAST-** · **Wedding** · Prenzlauer Berg · Friedrichshain

Schöneberg · **Kreuzberg** · **Wilmersdorf** · **Tempelhof** · **Steglitz** · **Neukölln** · **Britz** · **Buckow**

Zehlendorf · Mariendorf · Lichterfelde · **Köpenick** · Oberschöneweide · Niederschöneweide

Klein-Machnow · **Teltow** · Lichtenrade · Johannisthal · Schöneiche · Rüdersdorf · Zeuthen

Checkpoint Charlie

© Times Books Ltd

1:300 000

0   5   10   15 km
0   5   10 mil

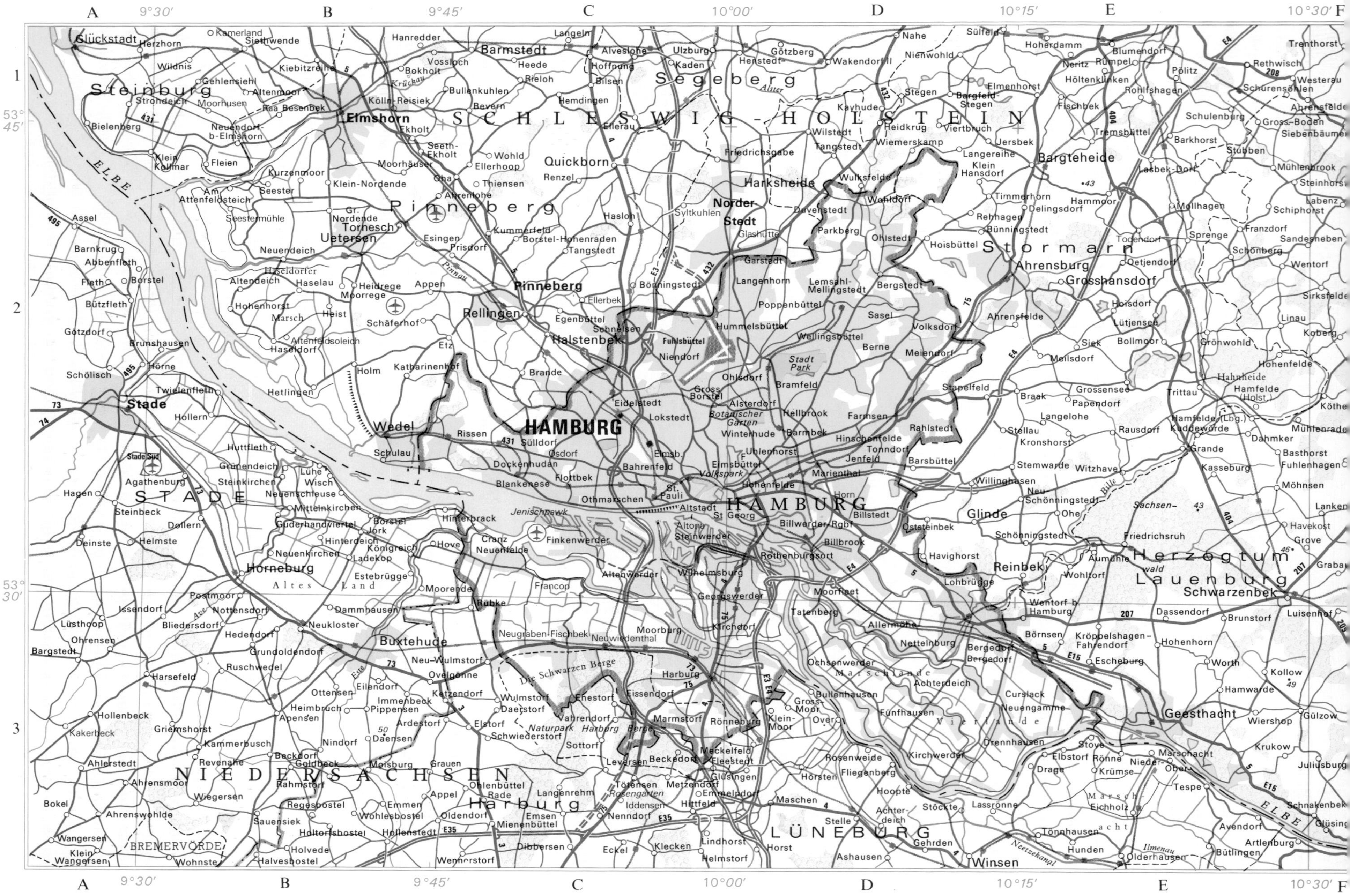

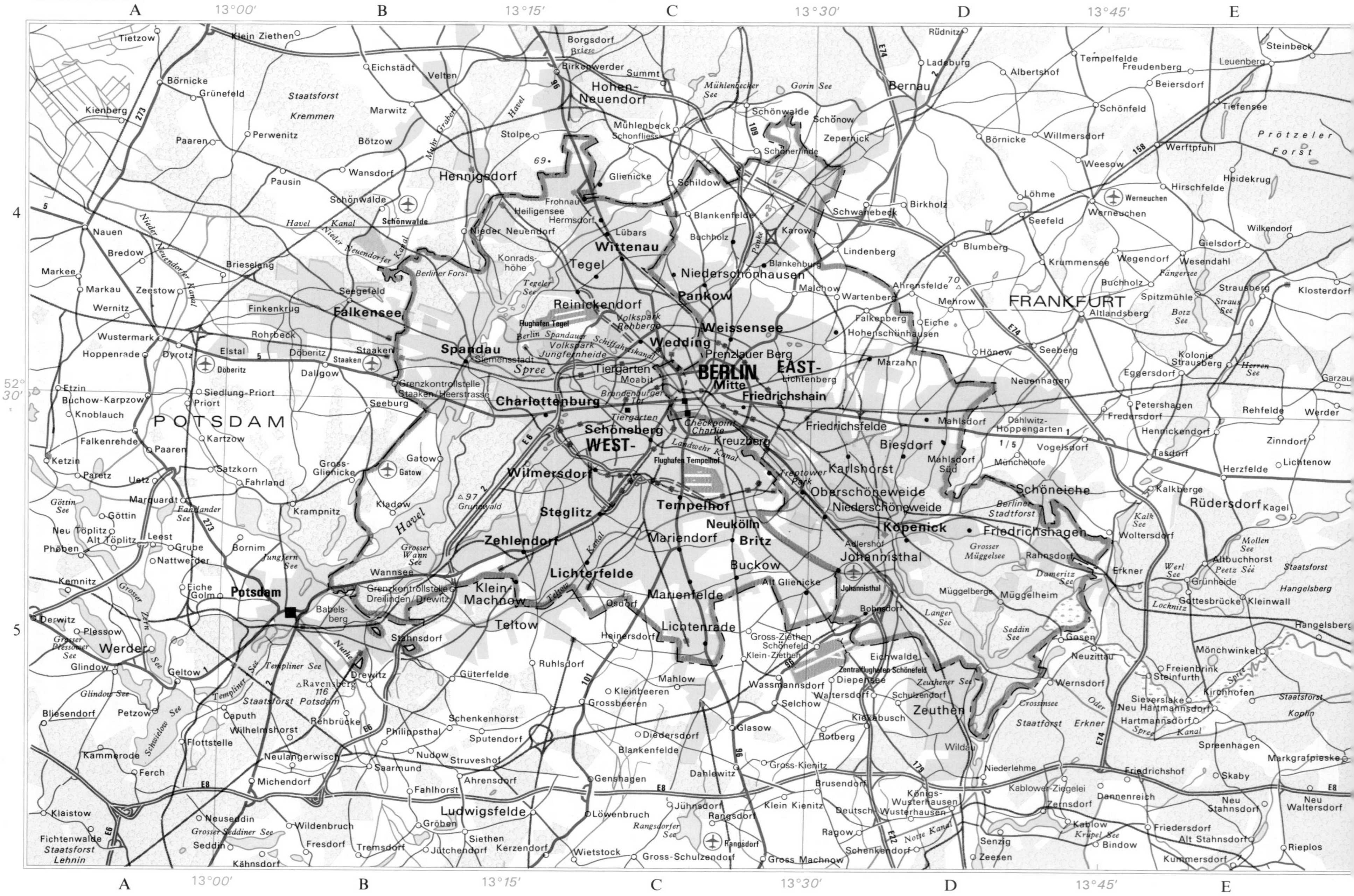

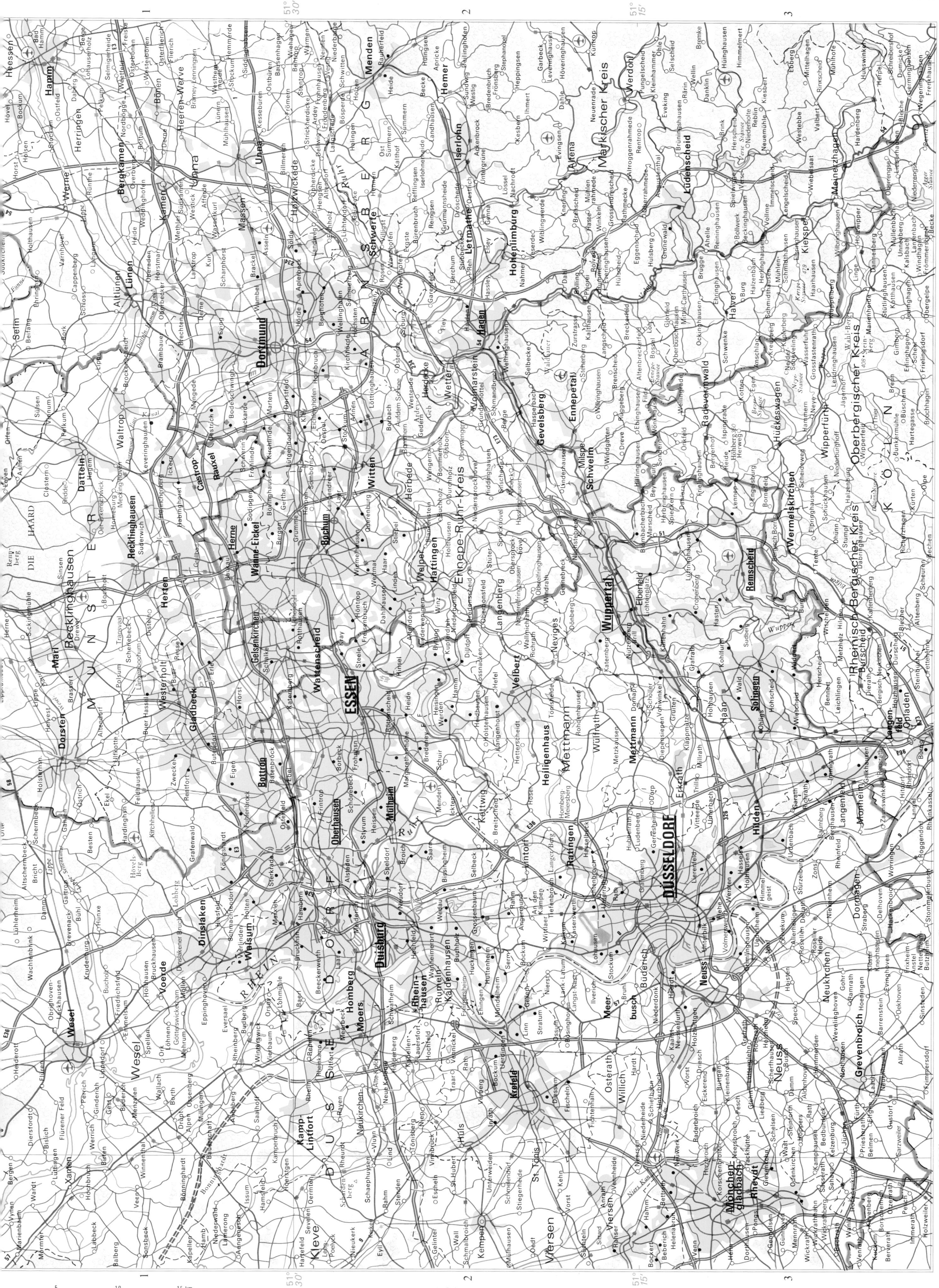

1:300 000

© Times Books Ltd

DÜSSELDORF
ESSEN
Dortmund
Duisburg
Bochum
Wuppertal
Gelsenkirchen
Oberhausen
Mülheim
Hagen
Remscheid
Solingen
Krefeld
Mönchengladbach
Rheydt
Neuss
Moers
Wesel
Dorsten
Recklinghausen
Herne
Bottrop
Gladbeck
Marl
Hamm
Unna
Iserlohn
Lüdenscheid
Witten
Velbert
Ratingen
Hilden
Mettmann
Viersen
Kempen
Dinslaken
Lünen
Kamen
Menden
Hemer
Schwelm
Gevelsberg
Ennepetal
Wattenscheid
Castrop-Rauxel
Wanne-Eickel
Herten
Datteln
Waltrop
Bergkamen
Schwerte
Langenfeld
Monheim
Dormagen
Grevenbroich
Willich
Xanten
Kamp-Lintfort
Ennepe-Ruhr-Kreis
Märkischer Kreis
Oberbergischer Kreis
Rheinisch-Bergischer Kreis
Mettmann
Wesel
Kleve
Viersen
Neuss
MÜNSTER
DÜSSELDORF
ARNSBERG
KÖLN
RHEIN
Ruhr
Lippe
Wupper
2
A
C
F
G
51° 30'
51° 15'
6°30'
6°45'
7°00'
7°15'
7°30'
7°45'

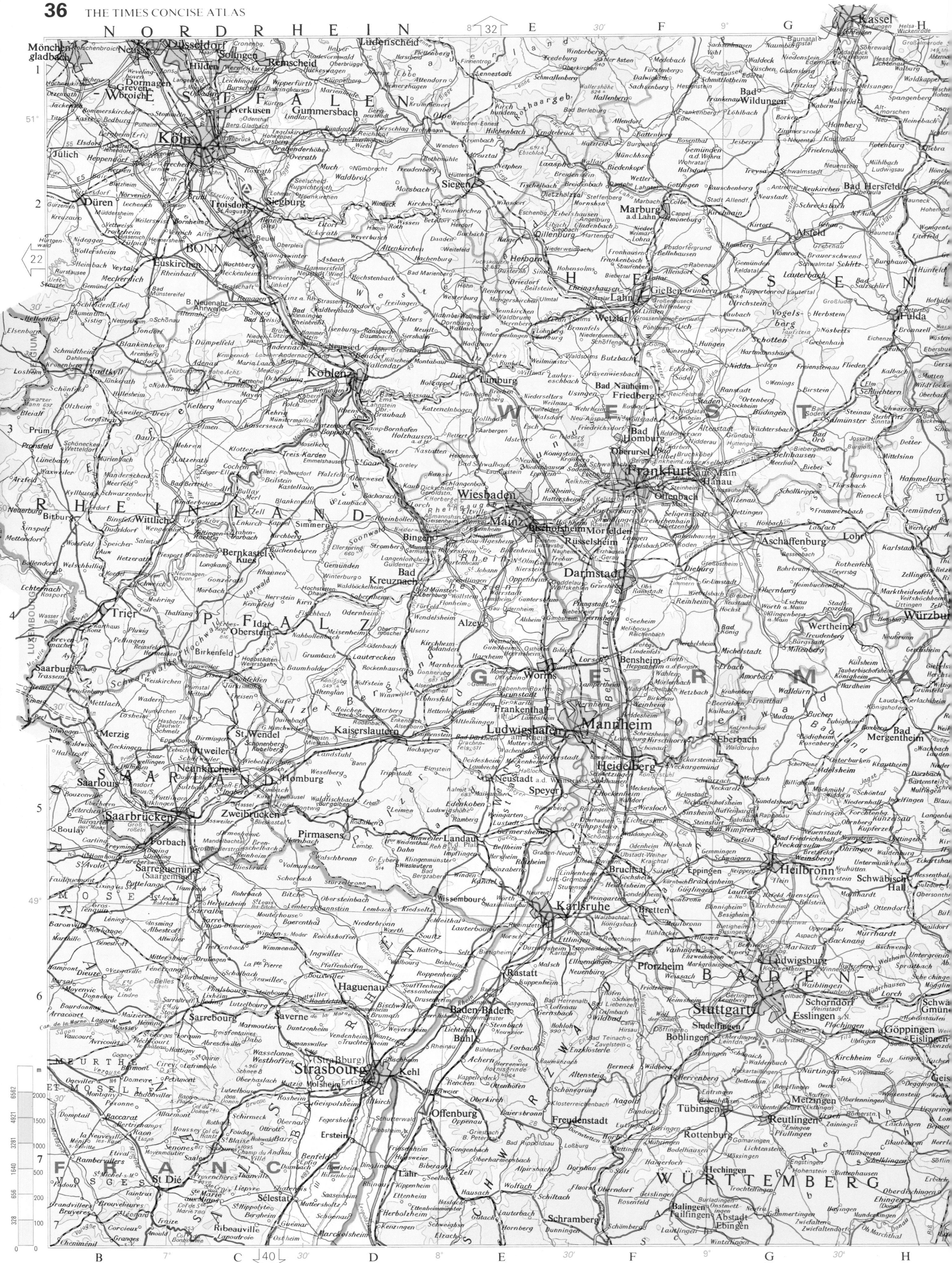

NORDRHEIN

WESTFALEN

HESSEN

RHEINLAND-PFALZ

SAARLAND

GERMANY

BADEN-WÜRTTEMBERG

FRANCE

Mönchengladbach · Neuss · Düsseldorf · Solingen · Remscheid · Hilden · Leverkusen · Köln · Jülich · Düren · Troisdorf · Siegburg · BONN · Euskirchen · Siegen · Ludenscheid · Gummersbach · Olpe · Marburg a.d. Lahn · Gießen · Wetzlar · Fulda · Kassel · Bad Wildungen · Bad Hersfeld · Alsfeld · Limburg · Koblenz · Neuwied · Bad Homburg · Friedberg · Bad Nauheim · Oberursel · Frankfurt am Main · Offenbach · Hanau · Aschaffenburg · Wiesbaden · Mainz · Bingen · Bad Kreuznach · Rüsselsheim · Mörfelden · Darmstadt · Würzburg · Wertheim · Bernkastel-Kues · Trier · Idar-Oberstein · Birkenfeld · Alzey · Worms · Frankenthal · Ludwigshafen · Mannheim · Eberbach · Bad Mergentheim · Saarbrücken · Saarlouis · Merzig · Neunkirchen · Homburg · Zweibrücken · Pirmasens · Kaiserslautern · Landau · Heidelberg · Neustadt a.d. Weinstrasse · Speyer · Heilbronn · Schwäbisch Hall · Forbach · Sarreguemines · Karlsruhe · Bretten · Pforzheim · Ludwigsburg · Stuttgart · Esslingen a.N. · Sindelfingen · Böblingen · Göppingen · Sarrebourg · Saverne · Haguenau · Baden-Baden · Bühl · Rastatt · Strasbourg · Kehl · Offenburg · Lahr · Freudenstadt · Tübingen · Reutlingen · Rottenburg · Metzingen · St Dié · Sélestat · Ribeauvillé · Schramberg · Balingen · Ebingen · WÜRTTEMBERG

MOSELLE · MEURTHE-ET-MOSELLE · VOSGES

SIMPLE CONIC PROJECTION

NOTE: ß =German equivalent to 'ss'

m 2000 1500 1000 500 200 100
6562 4921 3281 1640 656 328

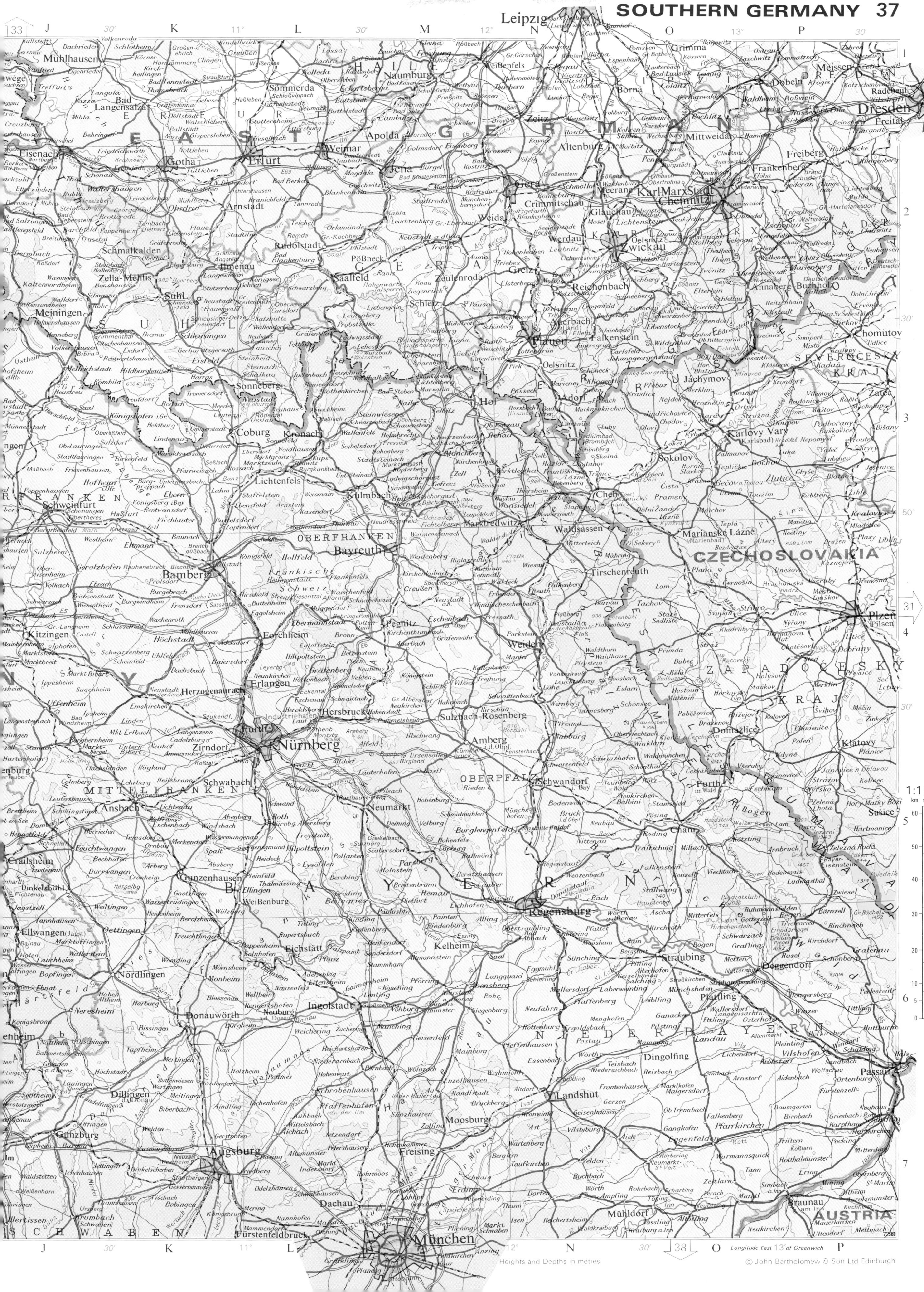
EAST GERMANY
CZECHOSLOVAKIA
AUSTRIA
HALLE
ERFURT
GERA
SUHL
KARL MARX STADT
DRESDEN
OBERFRANKEN
MITTELFRANKEN
OBERPFALZ
NIEDERBAYERN
SCHWABEN
BAYERN
ZAPADOČESKÝ KRAJ
SEVEROČESKÝ KRAJ
Leipzig
Dresden
Erfurt
Weimar
Jena
Gera
Gotha
Eisenach
Zwickau
Karl Marx Stadt
Chemnitz
Plauen
Hof
Coburg
Bamberg
Bayreuth
Schweinfurt
Nürnberg
Fürth
Erlangen
Ansbach
Regensburg
Ingolstadt
Augsburg
München
Landshut
Passau
Straubing
Deggendorf
Amberg
Weiden
Cheb
Karlovy Vary
Plzeň
Mariánské Lázně
Jáchymov
Chomutov
Domažlice
Klatovy
Sušice
Ulm
Nördlingen
Donauwörth
Eichstätt
Kelheim
Freising
Dachau
Braunau
Fränkische Schweiz
Heights and Depths in metres
Longitude East 13° of Greenwich
1:1 M
km
miles

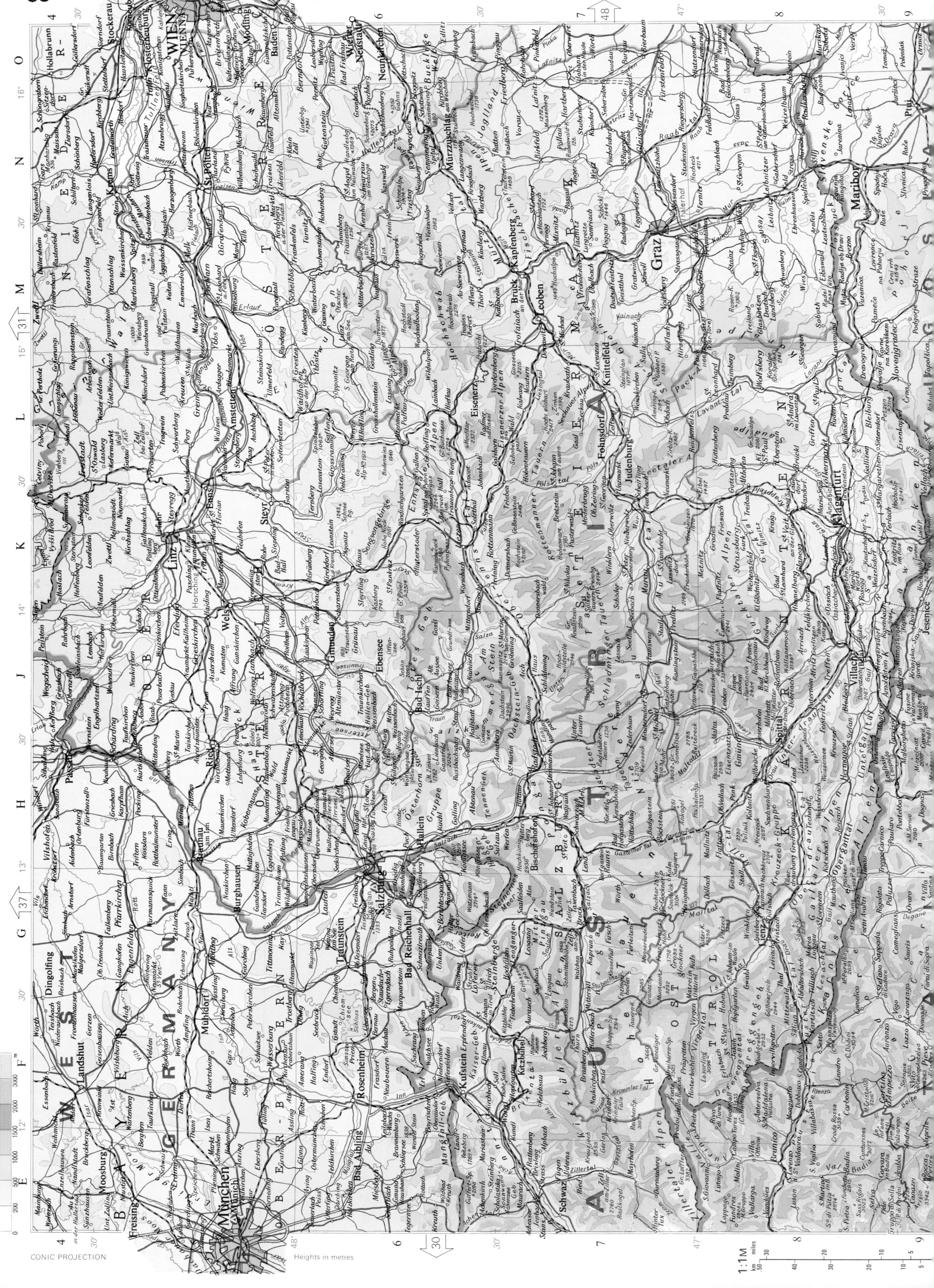
WIEN
Linz
Salzburg
Graz
Klagenfurt
Villach
Innsbruck
München
Maribor
Passau
St. Pölten
Steyr
Wels
Leoben
AUSTRIA
GERMANY
CONIC PROJECTION
Heights in metres
1:1M

MILAN

1:300 000

© Times Books Ltd

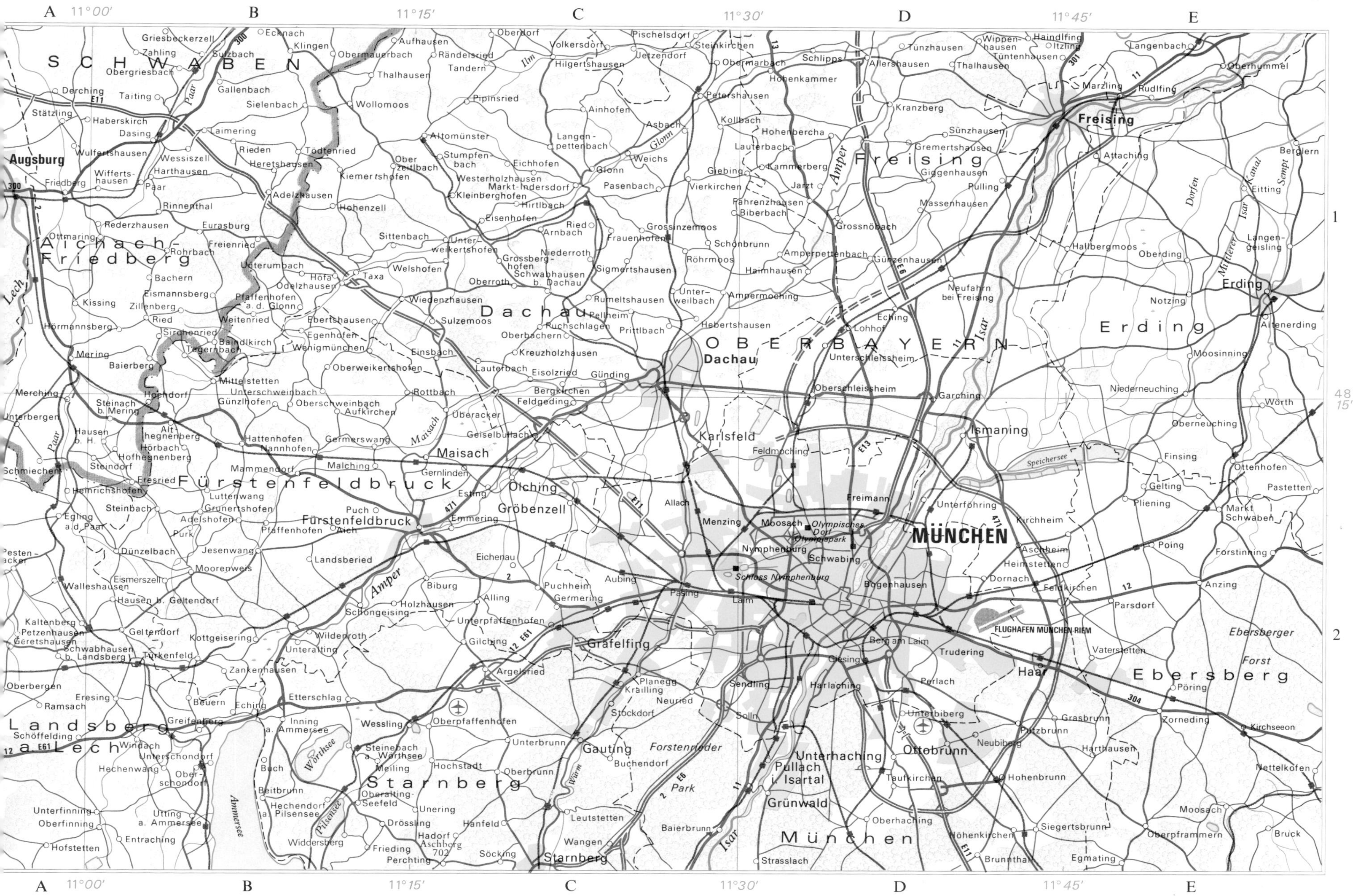

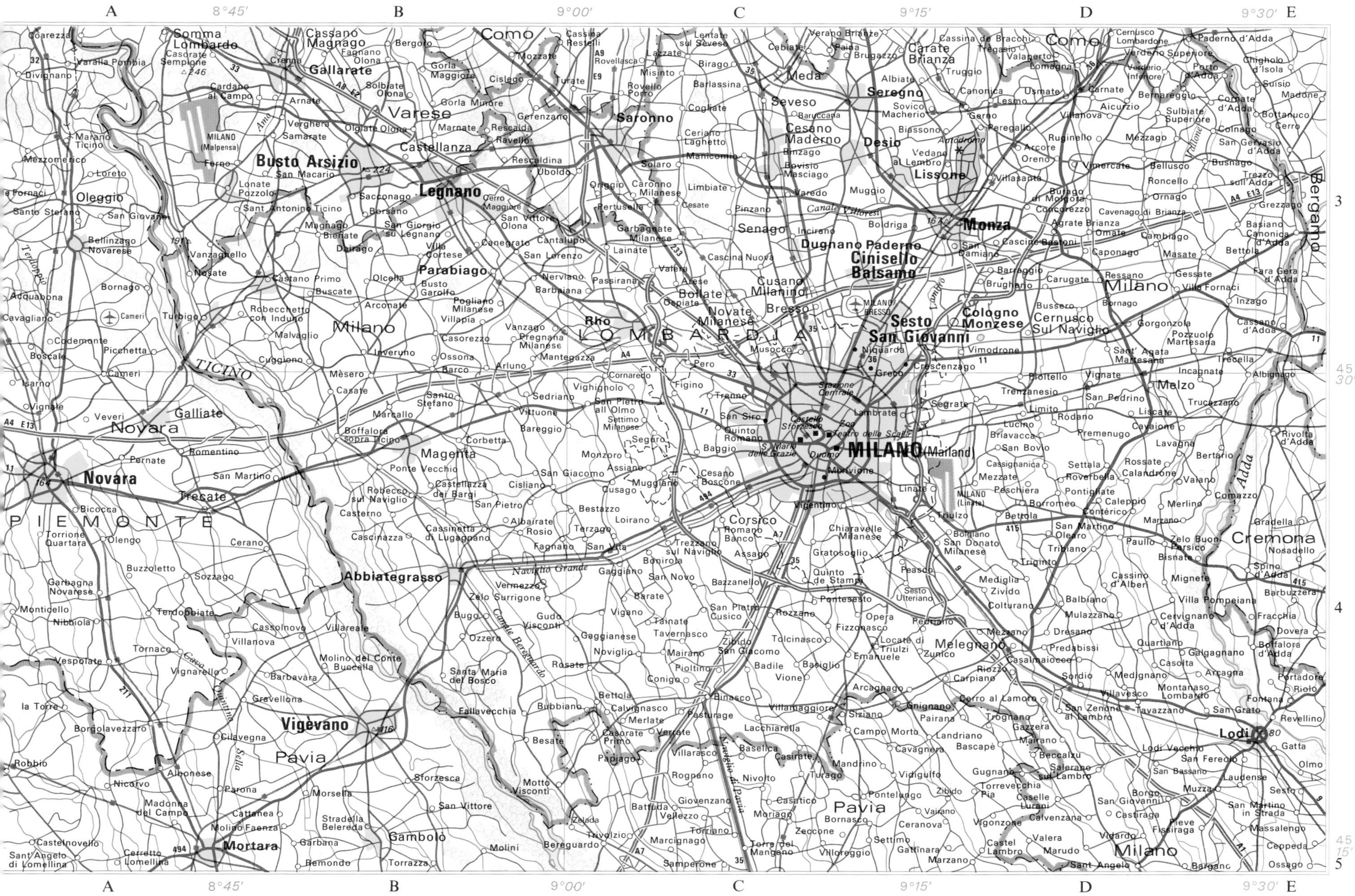

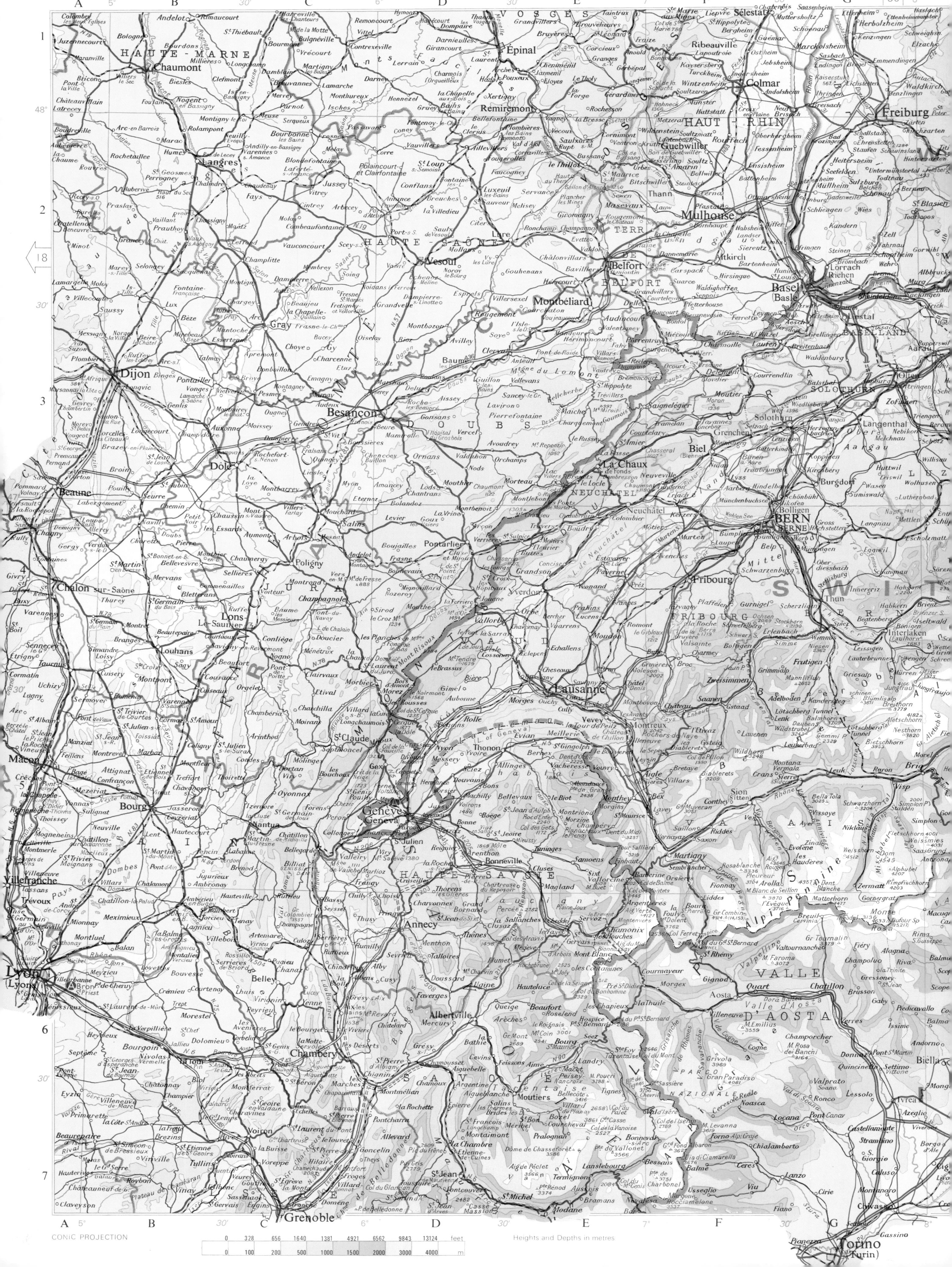

CONIC PROJECTION

Heights and Depths in metres

0	328	656	1640	1381	4921	6562	9843	13124	feet
0	100	200	500	1000	1500	2000	3000	4000	m

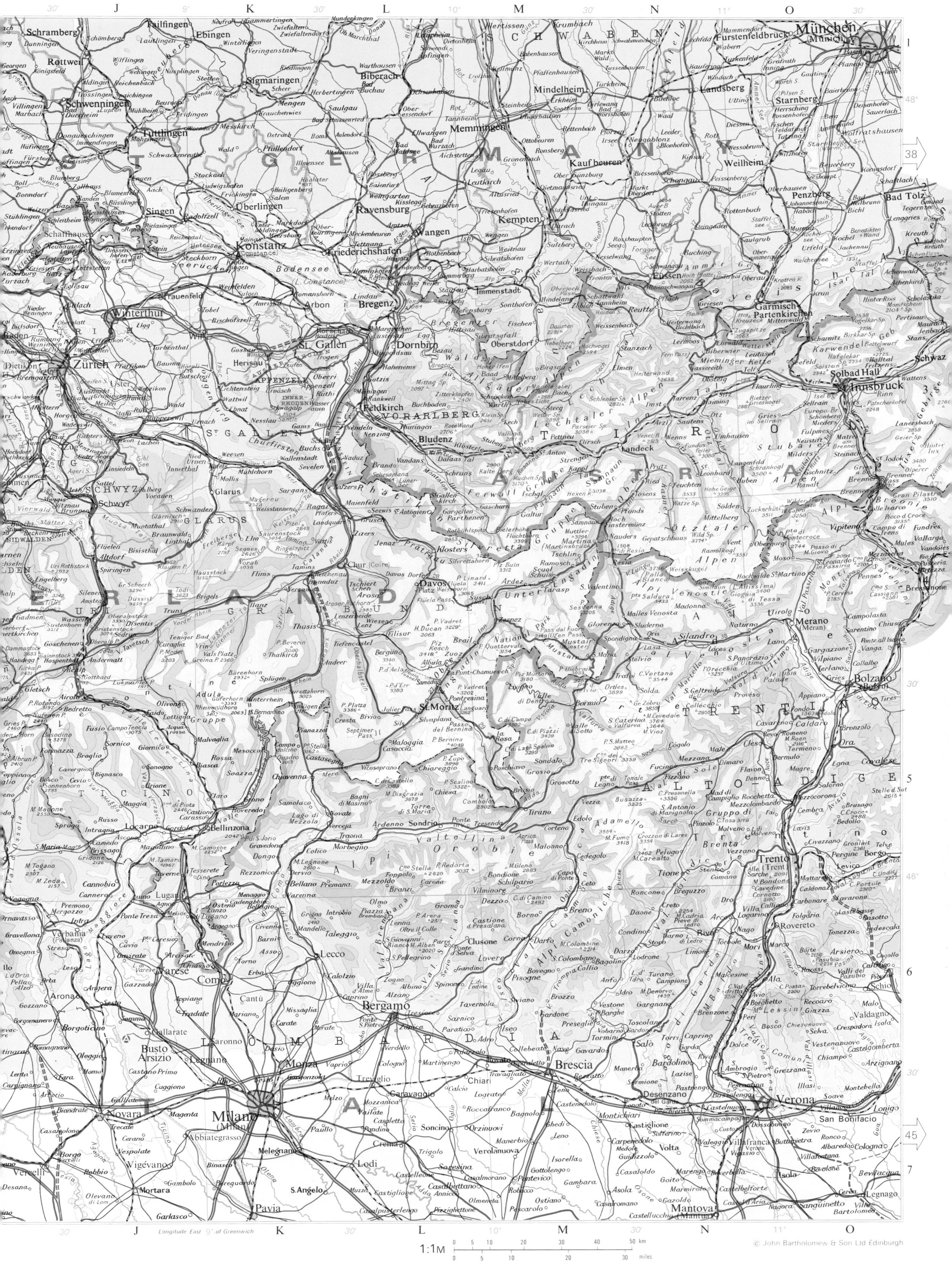
GERMANY
AUSTRIA
SWITZERLAND
ITALY
SCHWABEN
VORARLBERG
TIROL
GRAUBÜNDEN
TICINO
LOMBARDIA
TRENTINO
ALTO ADIGE
St. GALLEN
GLARUS
SCHWYZ
APPENZELL
Bodensee
(L. Constance)
Lago di Garda
Lago Maggiore
München
Innsbruck
Bolzano
Trento
Verona
Brescia
Bergamo
Milano
(Milan)
Como
Lugano
Bellinzona
Chur (Coire)
Davos
St. Moritz
Zürich
Winterthur
Konstanz
Bregenz
Dornbirn
Feldkirch
Bludenz
Kempten
Memmingen
Ravensburg
Friedrichshafen
Lindau
St. Gallen
Sondrio
Tirano
Merano
Novara
Varese
Lecco
Monza
Mantova
Garmisch-Partenkirchen
Landsberg
Kaufbeuren
Füssen
Sigmaringen
Schwenningen
Rottweil
Tuttlingen
Singen
Longitude East 9° of Greenwich
1:1M
0 5 10 20 30 40 50 km
0 5 10 20 30 miles
© John Bartholomew & Son Ltd Edinburgh

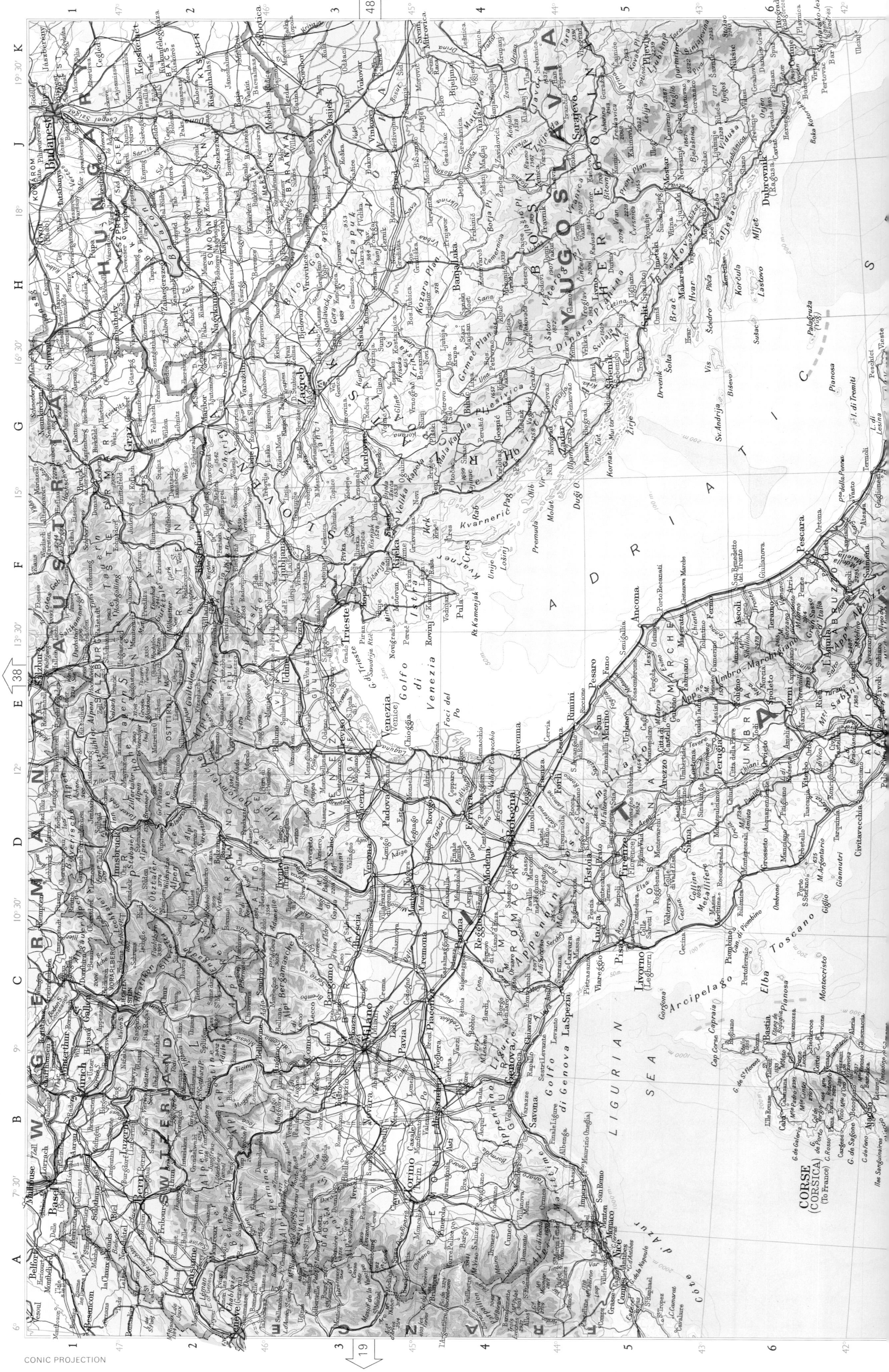

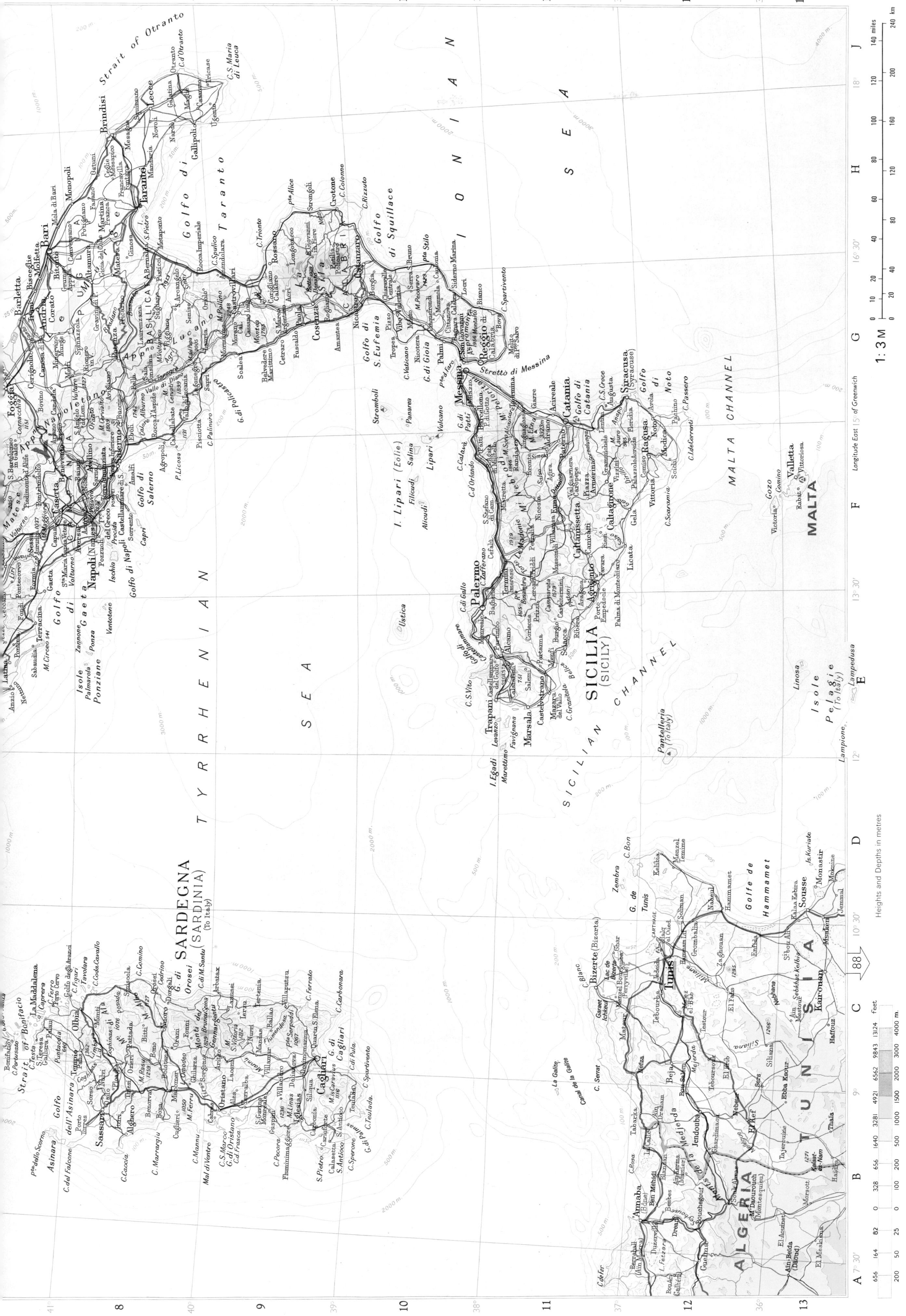
TYRRHENIAN SEA
IONIAN SEA
SICILIA (SICILY)
SARDEGNA (SARDINIA) (To Italy)
MALTA
TUNISIA
ALGERIA
SICILIAN CHANNEL
MALTA CHANNEL
Strait of Otranto
Golfo di Taranto
Golfo di Squillace
Stretto di Messina
Strait of Bonifacio
Golfe de Hammamet
G. de Tunis
I. Lipari (Eolie)
Isole Pelagie
Napoli
Bari
Taranto
Brindisi
Lecce
Foggia
Cosenza
Catanzaro
Messina
Reggio di Calabria
Palermo
Catania
Siracusa (Syracuse)
Ragusa
Marsala
Trapani
Agrigento
Cagliari
Sassari
Tunis
Bizerte (Bizerta)
Sousse
Valletta
Heights and Depths in metres
Longitude East of Greenwich
1:3M

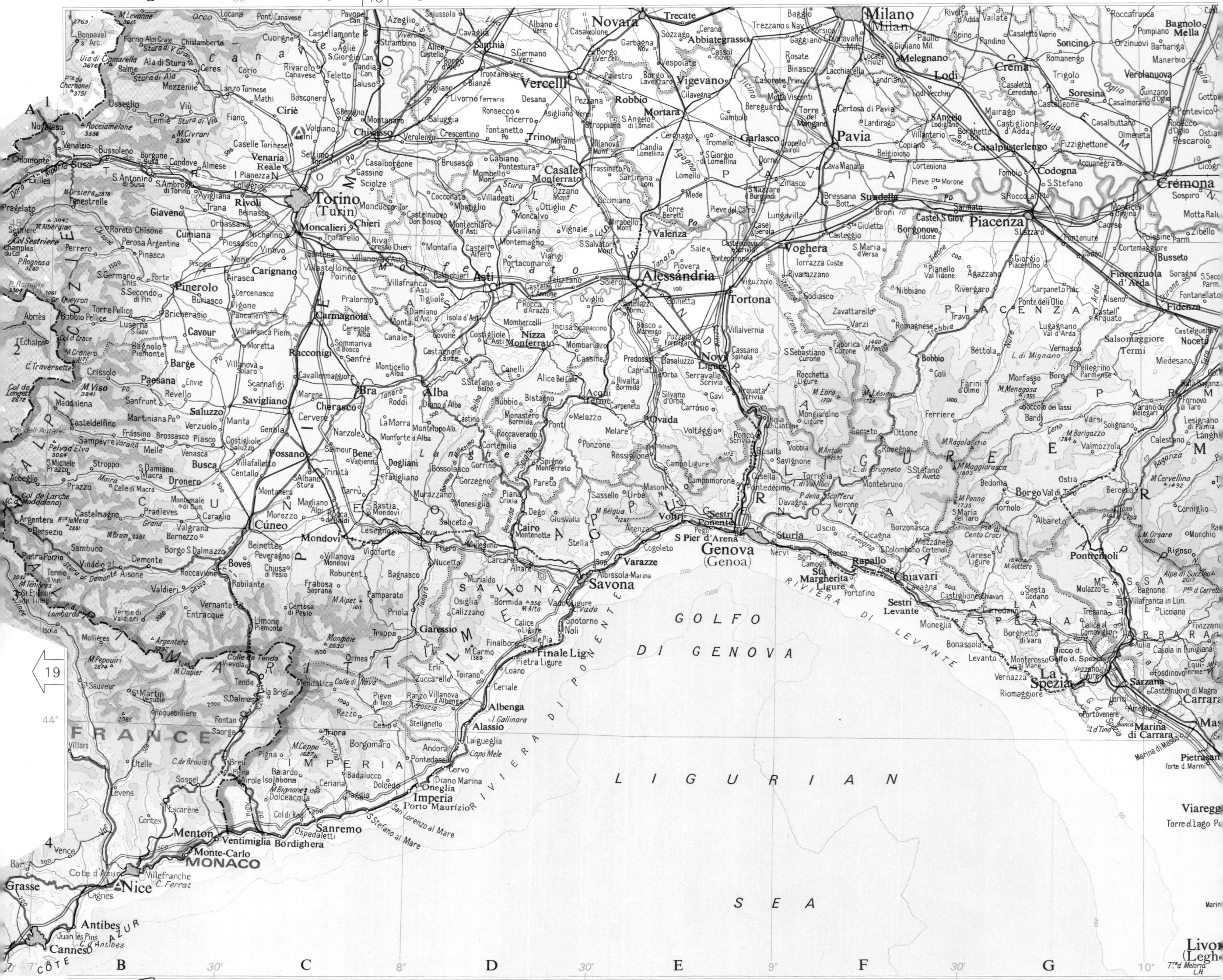

40

Milano
Milan
Novara
Vercelli
Vigevano
Torino
Turin
Asti
Alessandria
Tortona
Pavia
Piacenza
Cremona
Voghera
Nizza Monferrato
Novi Ligure
Pinerolo
Cúneo
Mondovi
Alba
Bra
Savigliano
Saluzzo
Fossano
Carmagnola
Racconigi
Bobbio
Fidenza
Salsomaggiore Terme
Genova
(Genoa)
Rapallo
Chiavari
Sestri
Levante
Savona
Varazze
Finale Lig.
Pietra Ligure
Loano
Albenga
Alassio
Oneglia
Imperia
Porto Maurizio
Sanremo
Bordighera
Ventimiglia
Menton
Monte-Carlo
MONACO
Nice
Antibes
Cannes
Grasse

La Spezia
Sarzana
Carrara
Marina di Carrara
Viareggio
Livorno
(Leghorn)

GOLFO
DI GENOVA

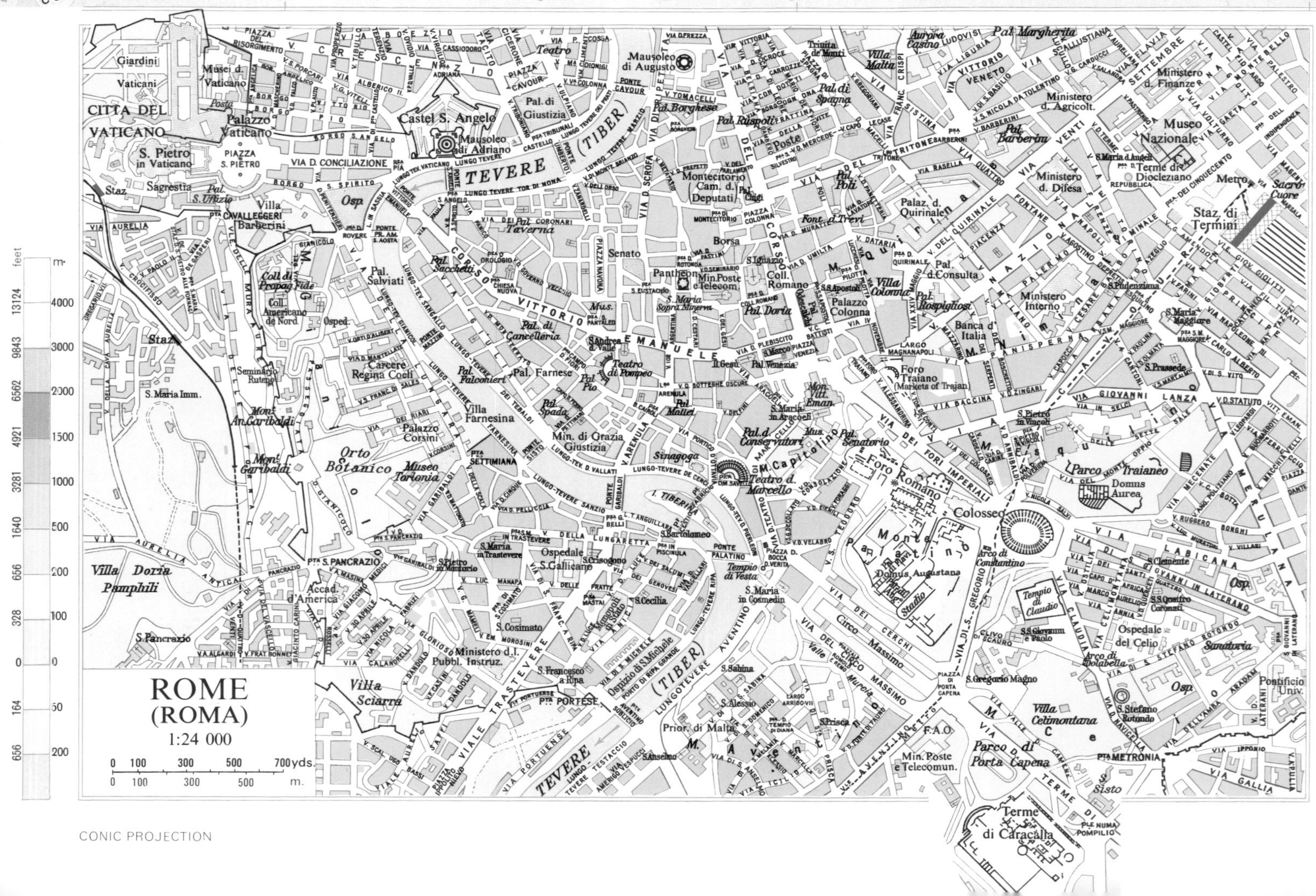

LIGURIAN

SEA

RIVIERA DI LEVANTE
RIVIERA DI PONENTE

FRANCE

CÔTE D'AZUR

CONIC PROJECTION

ROME
(ROMA)
1:24 000

CITTÀ DEL VATICANO
S. Pietro in Vaticano
Castel S. Angelo
TEVERE (TIBER)
Pantheon
Colosseo
Foro Romano
Staz. di Termini
Museo Nazionale
Villa Doria Pamphili
Orto Botanico

0 100 300 500 700yds.
0 100   300   500 m.

feet
13124 4000
9843   3000
6562   2000
4921   1500
3281   1000
1640   500
656   200
328   100
164   50
0   0
656   200

ROME
(ROMA)
on the same scale

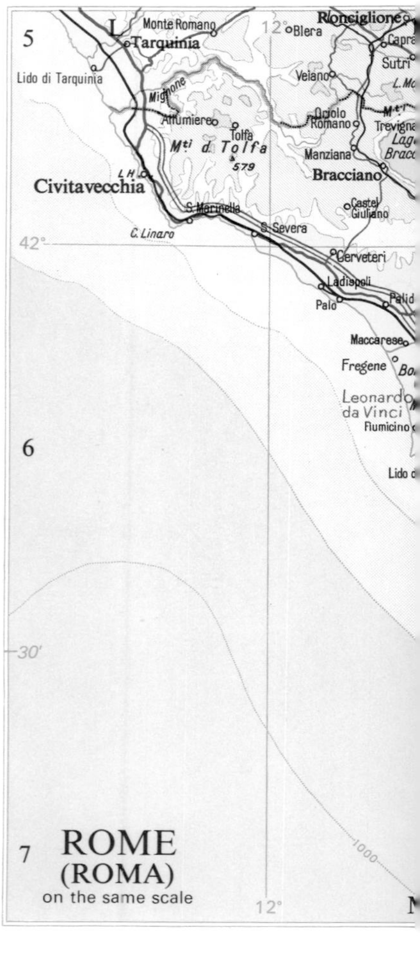

Tarquinia
Civitavecchia
Bracciano
Leonardo da Vinci
Fiumicino

NAPLES
(NAPOLI)
on the same scale

1:1M

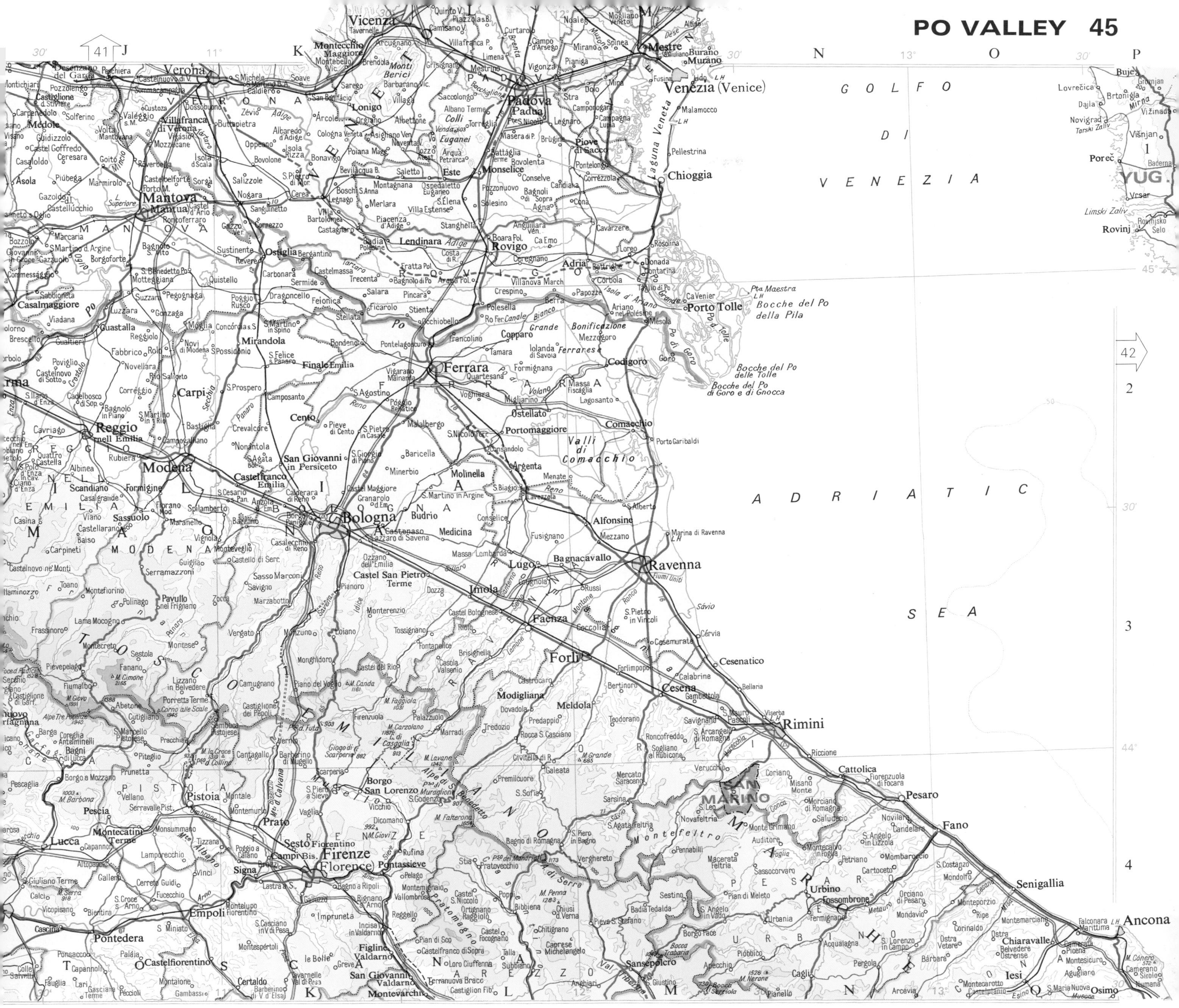

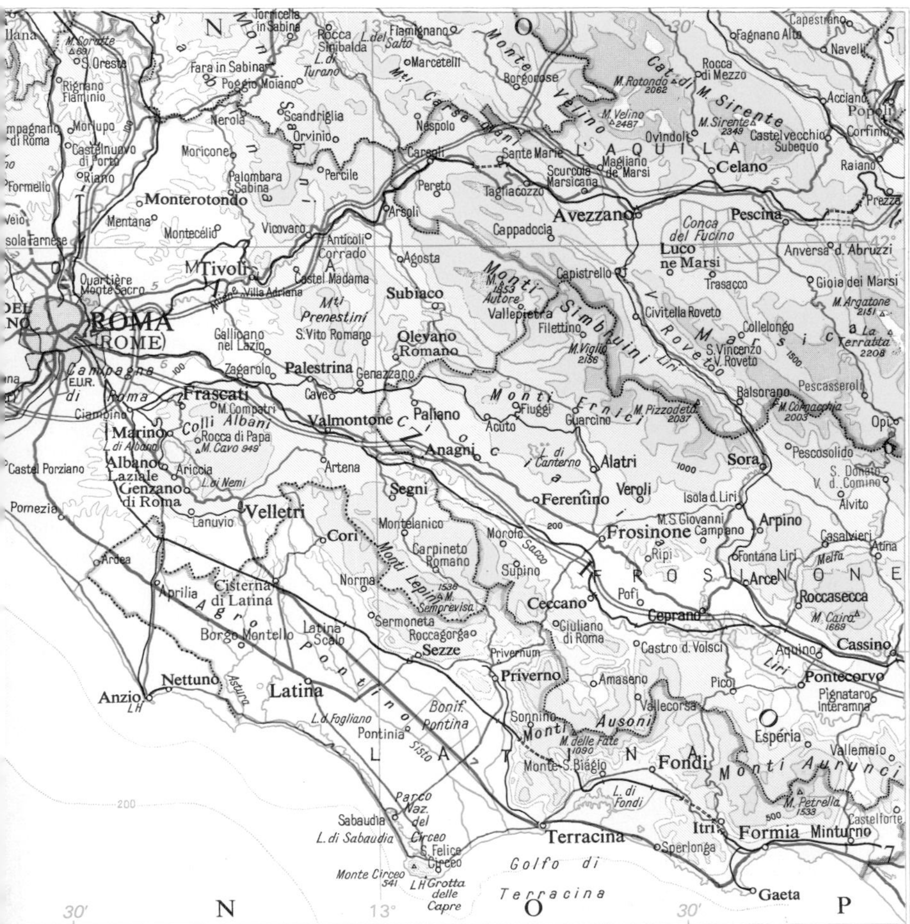

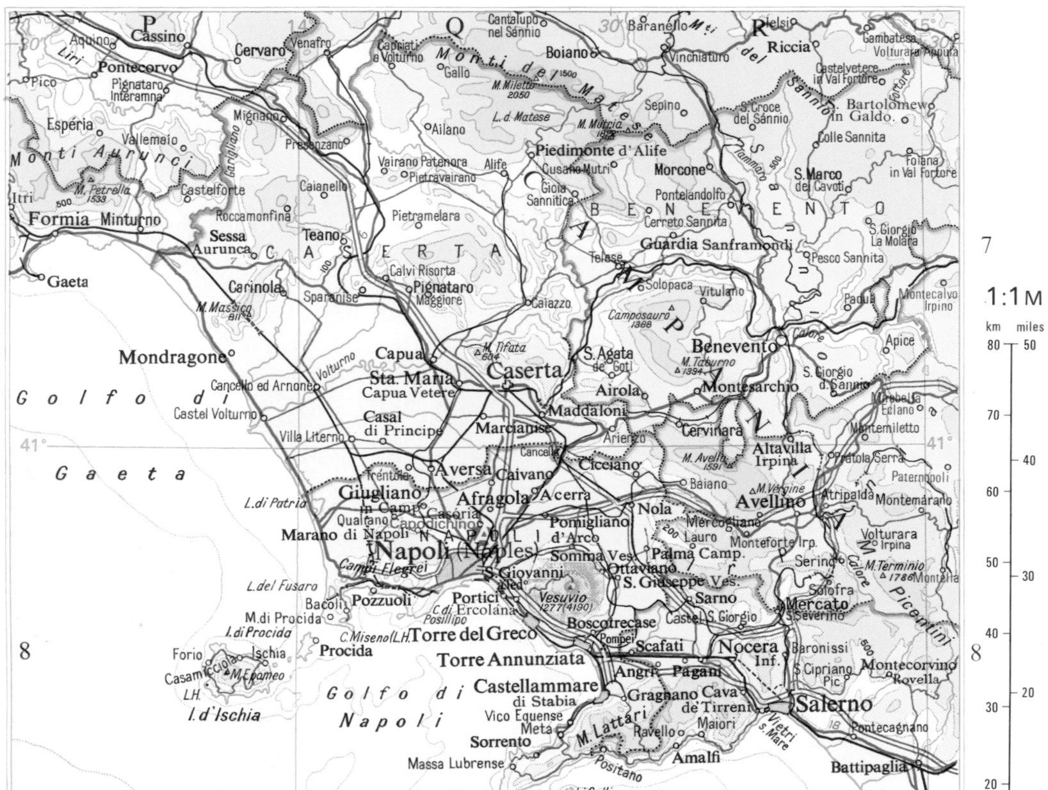

Heights and Depths in metres

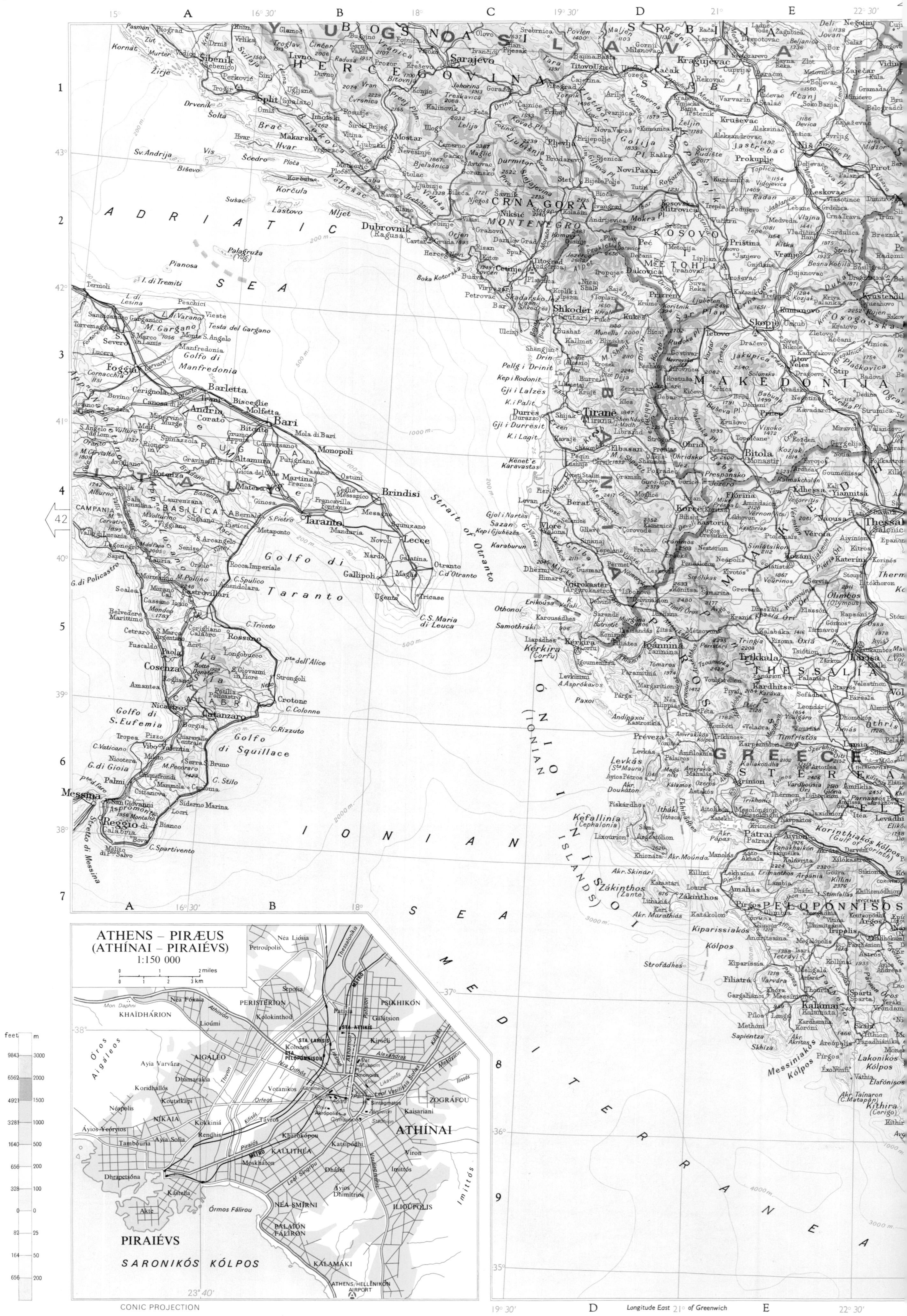

ATHENS – PIRAEUS
(ATHÍNAI – PIRAIÉVS)
1:150 000

PIRAIÉVS

SARONIKÓS KÓLPOS

CONIC PROJECTION

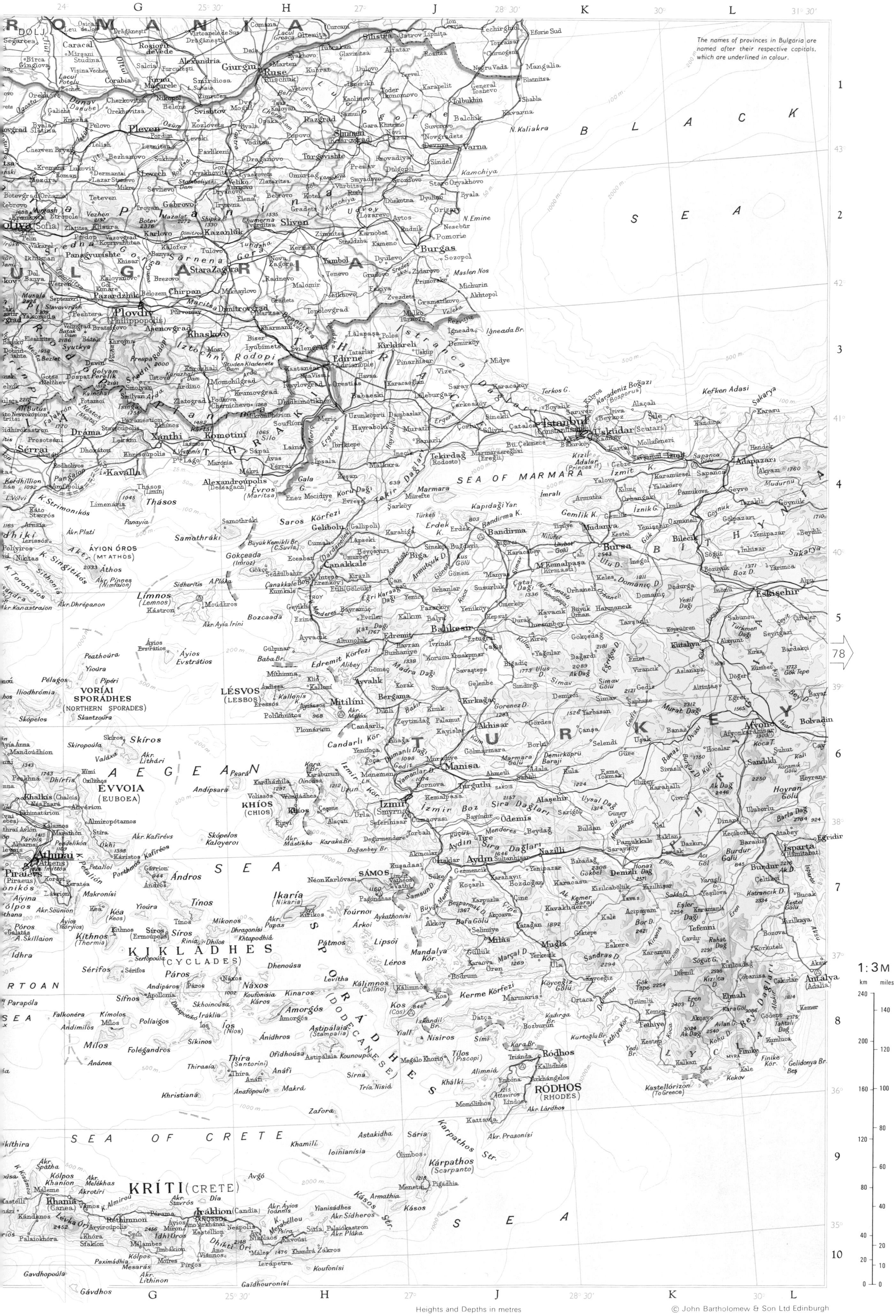

1:3M

km   miles

Heights and Depths in metres

© John Bartholomew & Son Ltd Edinburgh

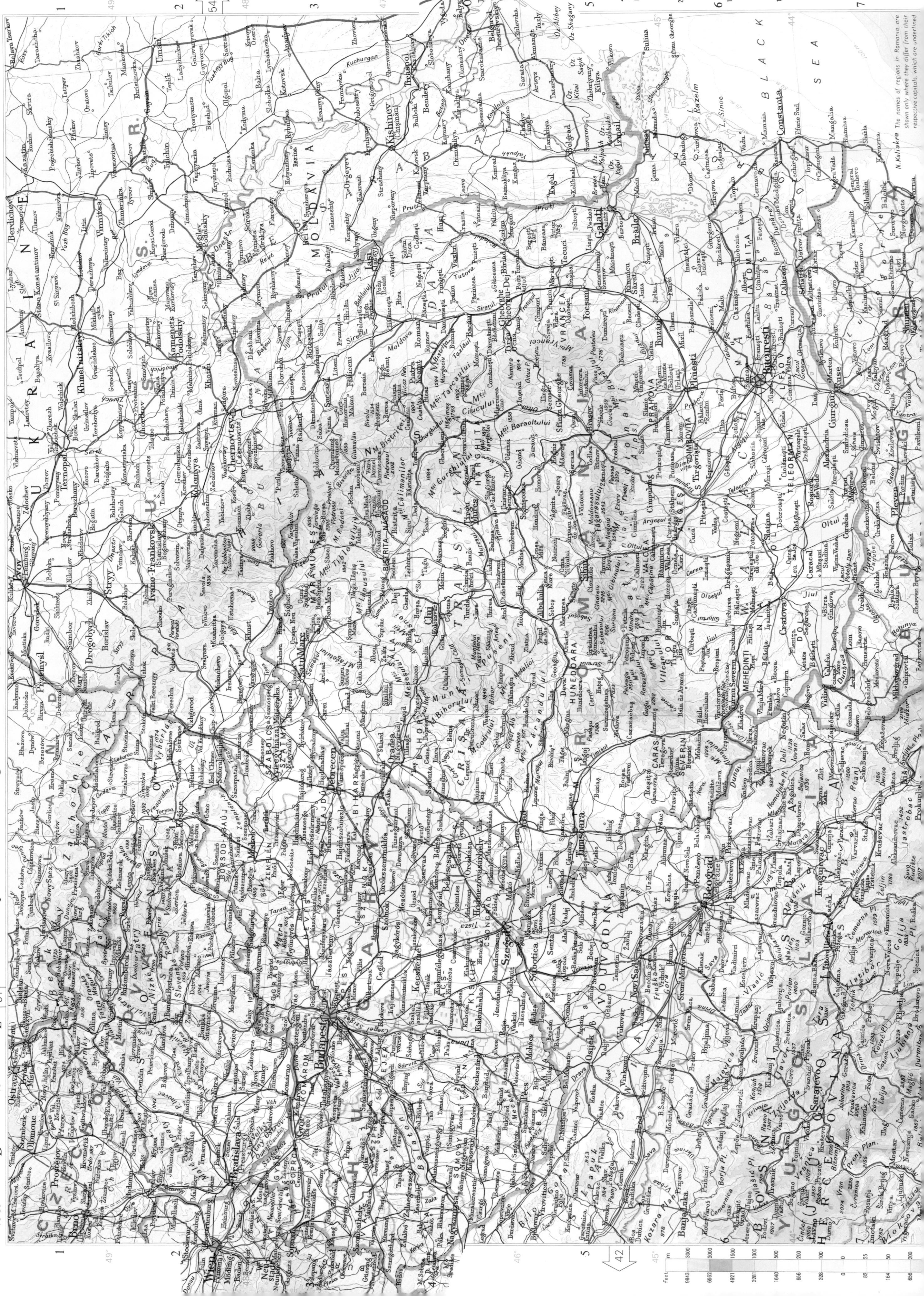
1:3M
BLACK SEA
Budapest
Bucureşti
Beograd
Debrecen
Cluj
Oradea
Timişoara
Szeged
Constanţa
Odessa
Kishinev
Iaşi
Galaţi
Brăila
Sarajevo
Bratislava
Wien
TRANSYLVANIA
MOLDAVIA
VOJVODINA
HUNGARY

LENINGRAD

GULF OF FINLAND

Kronshtadt
Ostrov Kotlin

LENINGRAD

GOROD LENINGRAD

LENINGRAD

Vsevolozhsk

Dubrovka

Kolpino

Pushkin
Sofiya
Pavlovsk

Ul'yanovka

Lomonosov
Petrodvorets
Krasnoye Selo
LENINGRAD AIRPORT
Fortress, Hermitage, Winter Palace, St Isaac's Cathedral
Ostrov Vasilyevskiy
Ostrov Krestovskiy
Sestroretsk

MOSCOW

Moskva
Kremlin, Red Square, Bolshoi Theatre

GOROD MOSKVA

MOSKVA

Mytishchi
Kaliningrad
Shchelkovo
Fryazino
Balashkha
Reutov
Lyubertsy
Zhukovskiy
Elektrougli
Ramenskoye
Krasnogorsk
Khimki
Tushino
Kuntsevo

Dedovsk
Kryukovo

1 : 300 000

5   10   15 km
5   10 miles

© Times Books Ltd

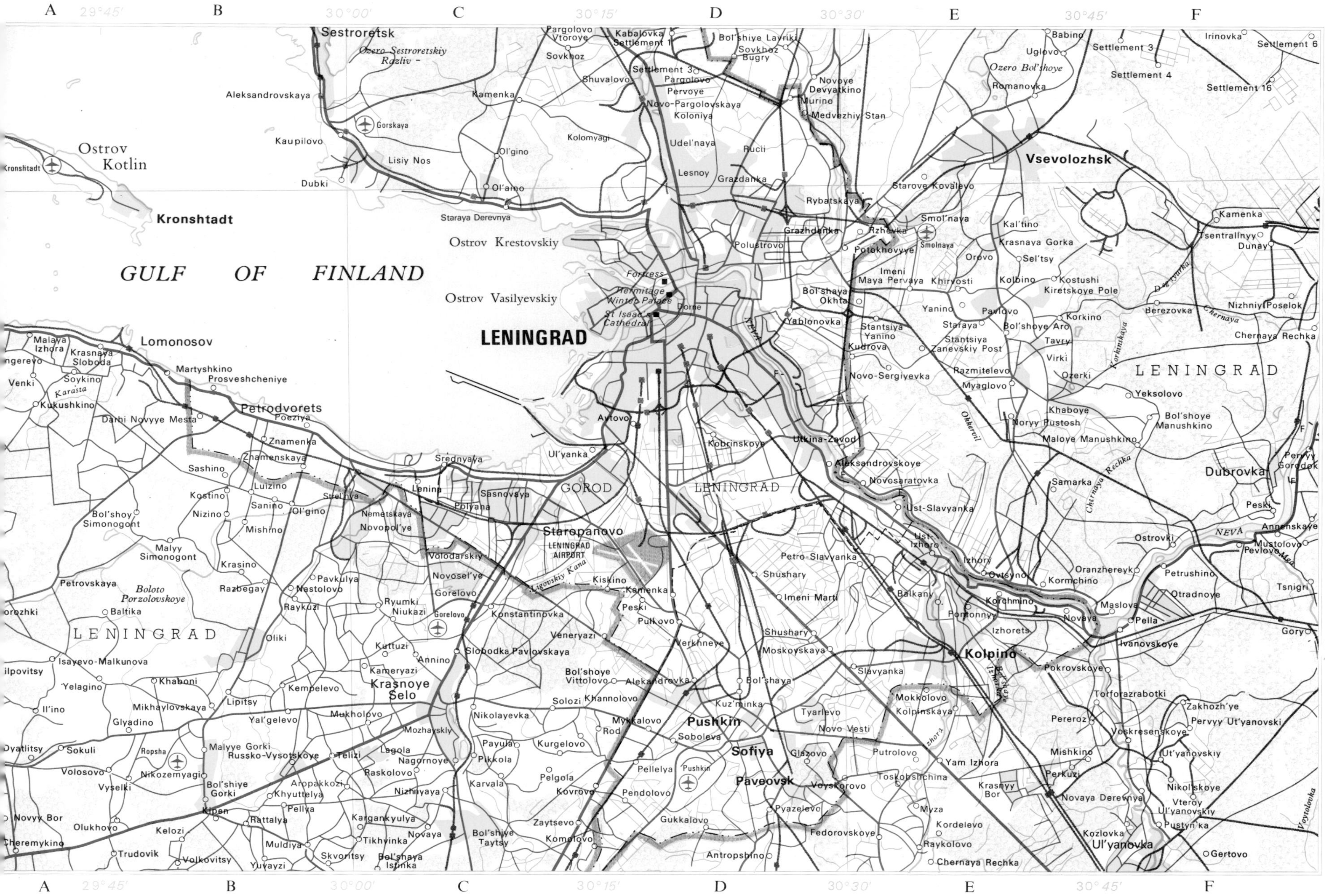

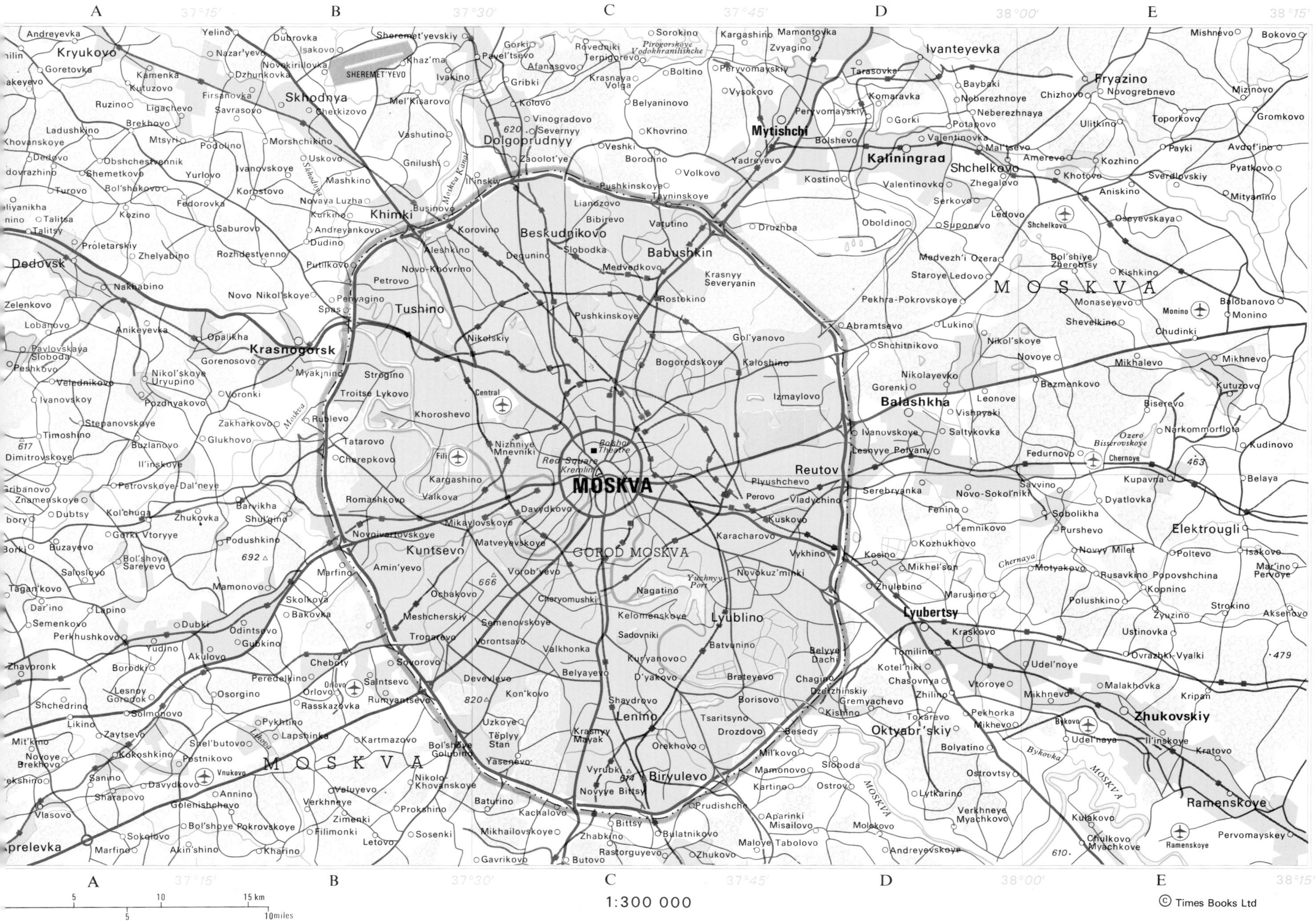

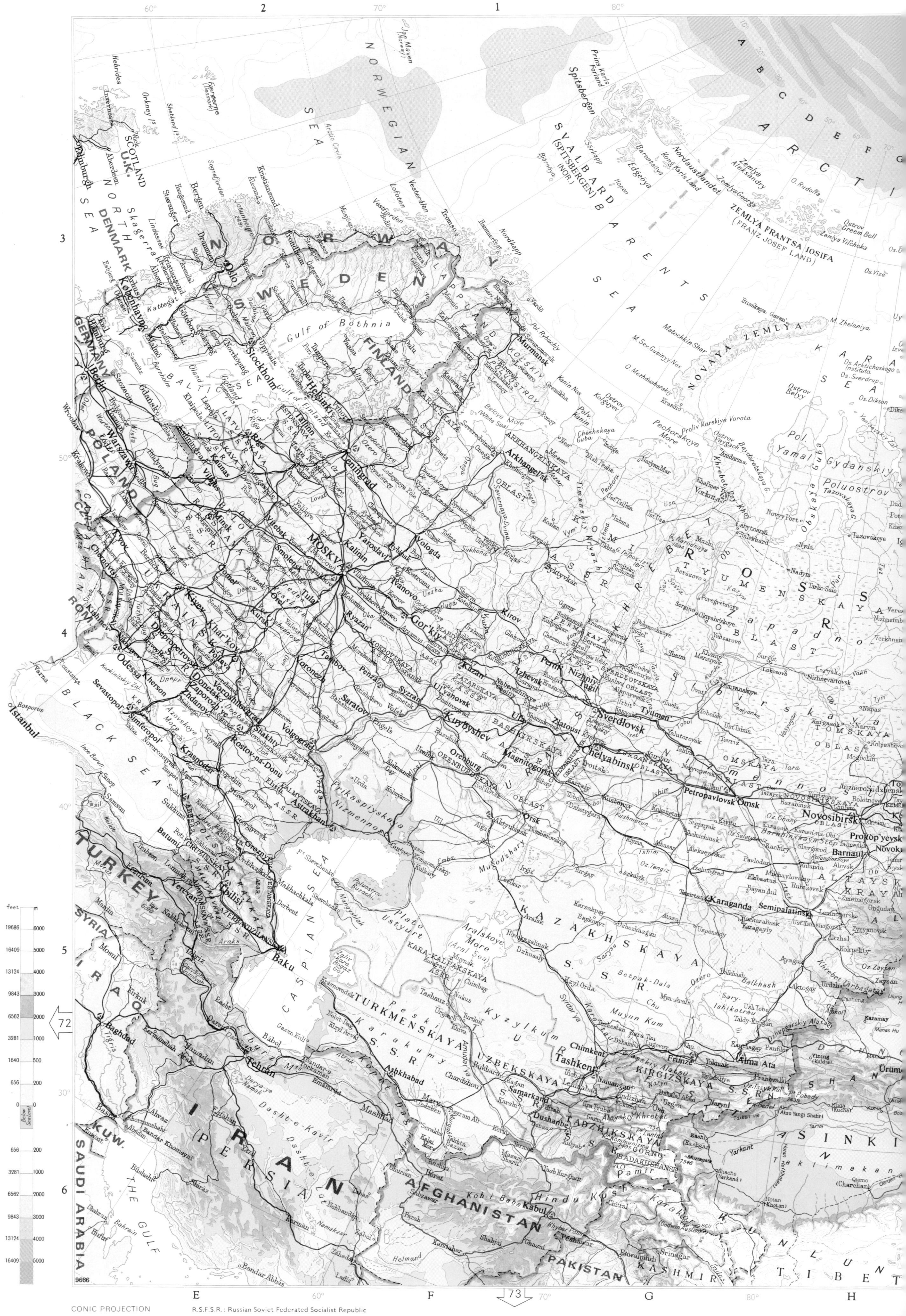

feet   m
19686   6000
16409   5000
13124   4000
9843   3000
6562   2000
3281   1000
1640   500
656   200
        Below Sea level
656   200
3281   1000
6562   2000
13124   4000
16409   5000

CONIC PROJECTION   R.S.F.S.R.: Russian Soviet Federated Socialist Republic

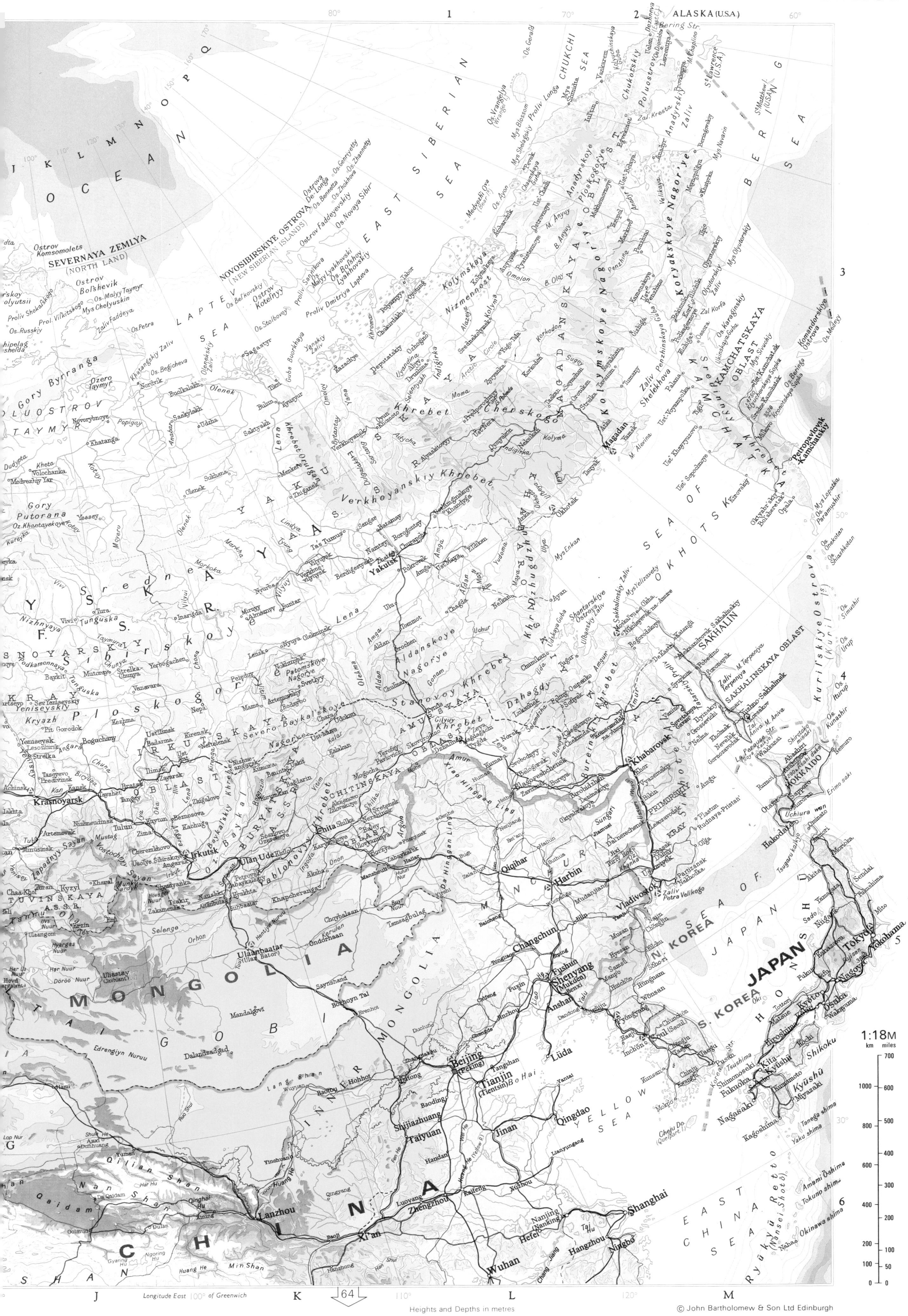

ALASKA (U.S.A.)

ARCTIC OCEAN

SEVERNAYA ZEMLYA (NORTH LAND)

EAST SIBERIAN SEA

CHUKCHI SEA

BERING SEA

LAPTEV SEA

NOVOSIBIRSKIYE OSTROVA (NEW SIBERIAN ISLANDS)

Gory Byrranga

POLUOSTROV TAYMYR

Gory Putorana

Yakutsk

SEA OF OKHOTSK

KAMCHATSKAYA OBLAST

Petropavlovsk-Kamchatskiy

SAKHALIN

Kuril'skiye Ostrova (Kuril Is.)

Magadan

Verkhoyanskiy Khrebet

Khrebet Cherskogo

Aldanskoye Nagorye

Stanovoy Khrebet

Krasnoyarsk

Irkutsk

Ulan-Ude

Chita

Khabarovsk

HOKKAIDO

Hakodate

Vladivostok

SEA OF JAPAN

TUVINSKAYA A.S.S.R.

Kyzyl

MANCHURIA

Qiqihar

Harbin

Changchun

Shenyang (Mukden)

Anshan

Fushun

JAPAN

Tokyo

Yokohama

Nagoya

Kyoto

Osaka

HONSHŪ

SHIKOKU

KYŪSHŪ

Hiroshima

Fukuoka

Nagasaki

MONGOLIA

Ulaanbaatar (Ulan Bator)

GOBI

INNER MONGOLIA

N. KOREA

S. KOREA

Seoul

Hohhot

Beijing (Peking)

Tianjin (Tientsin)

Bo Hai

Qingdao

YELLOW SEA

Jinan

Shijiazhuang

Taiyuan

Lüda

Lanzhou

Qilian Shan

Nan Shan

Qaidam

Xi'an

Zhengzhou

Luoyang

Kaifeng

Nanjing (Nanking)

Hefei

Shanghai

Hangzhou

Ningbo

EAST CHINA SEA

Ryūkyū Retto (Nansei Shotō)

CHINA

Wuhan

Huang He

1:18M

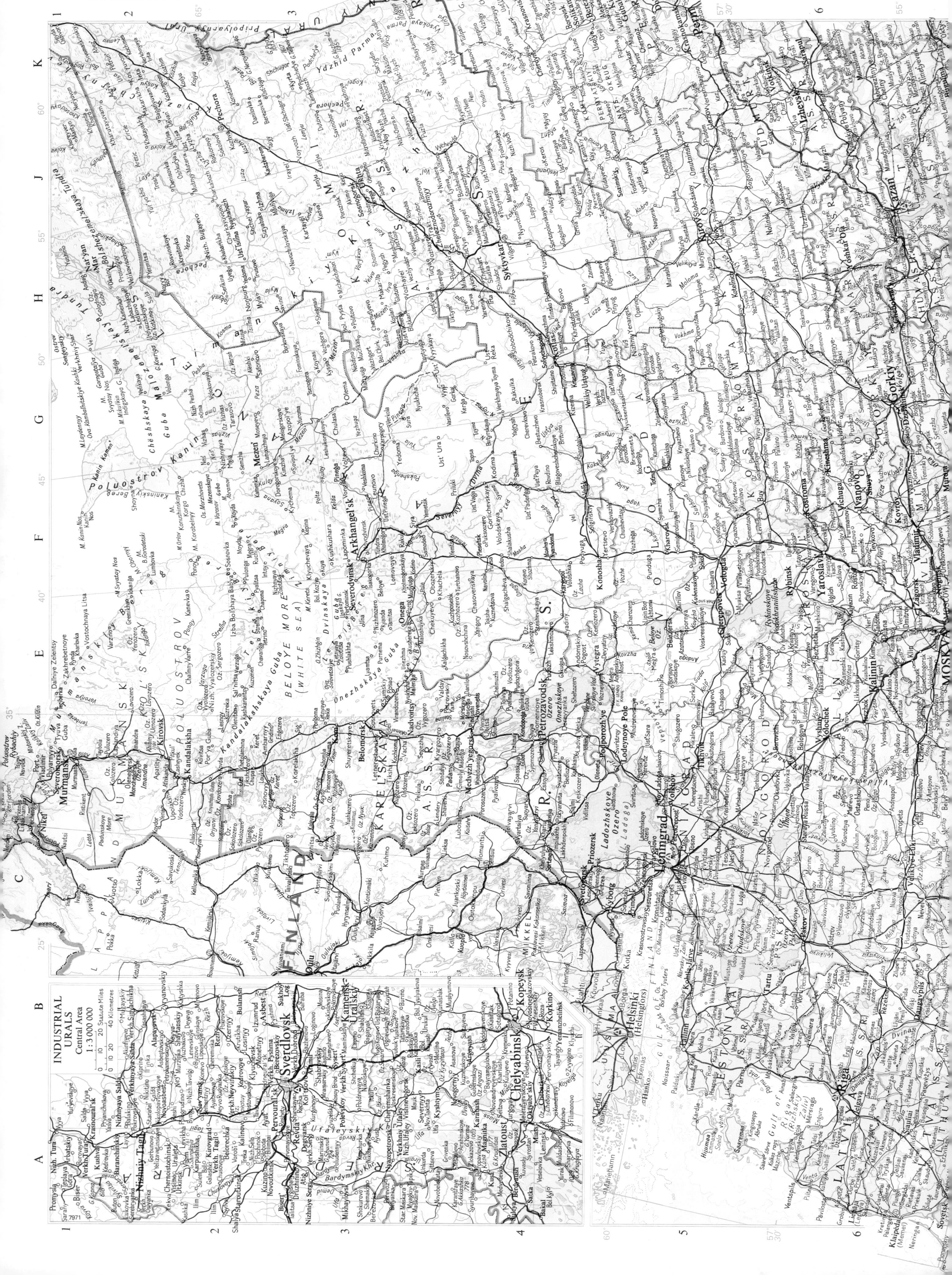
INDUSTRIAL URALS
Central Area
1:3 000 000
Statute Miles
Kilometres
BELOYE MORE (WHITE SEA)
Poluostrov Kanin
Leningrad
Arkhangel'sk
Murmansk
Sverdlovsk
Chelyabinsk
MOSKVA
Helsinki (Helsingfors)
Riga
FINLAND
ESTONIYA
LATVIYA

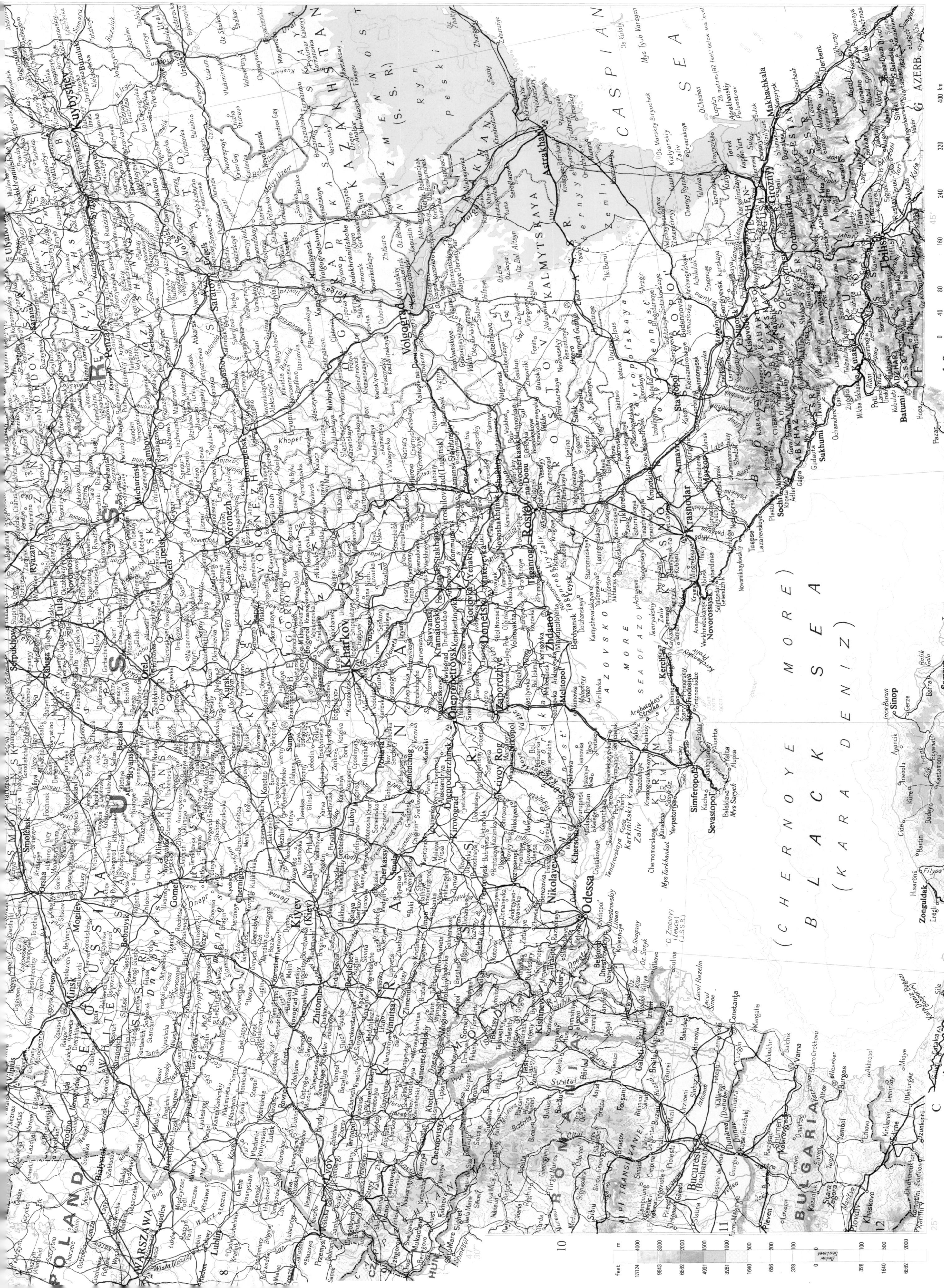

CONIC PROJECTION

1:6 M

C A S P I A N   S E A

C H E R N O Y E   M O R E
B L A C K   S E A
(K A R A   D E N I Z)

SEA OF AZOV
(AZOVSKOYE MORE)

POLAND

U K R A I N E

ROMANIA

BULGARIA

TURKEY

Longitude East 35° of Greenwich

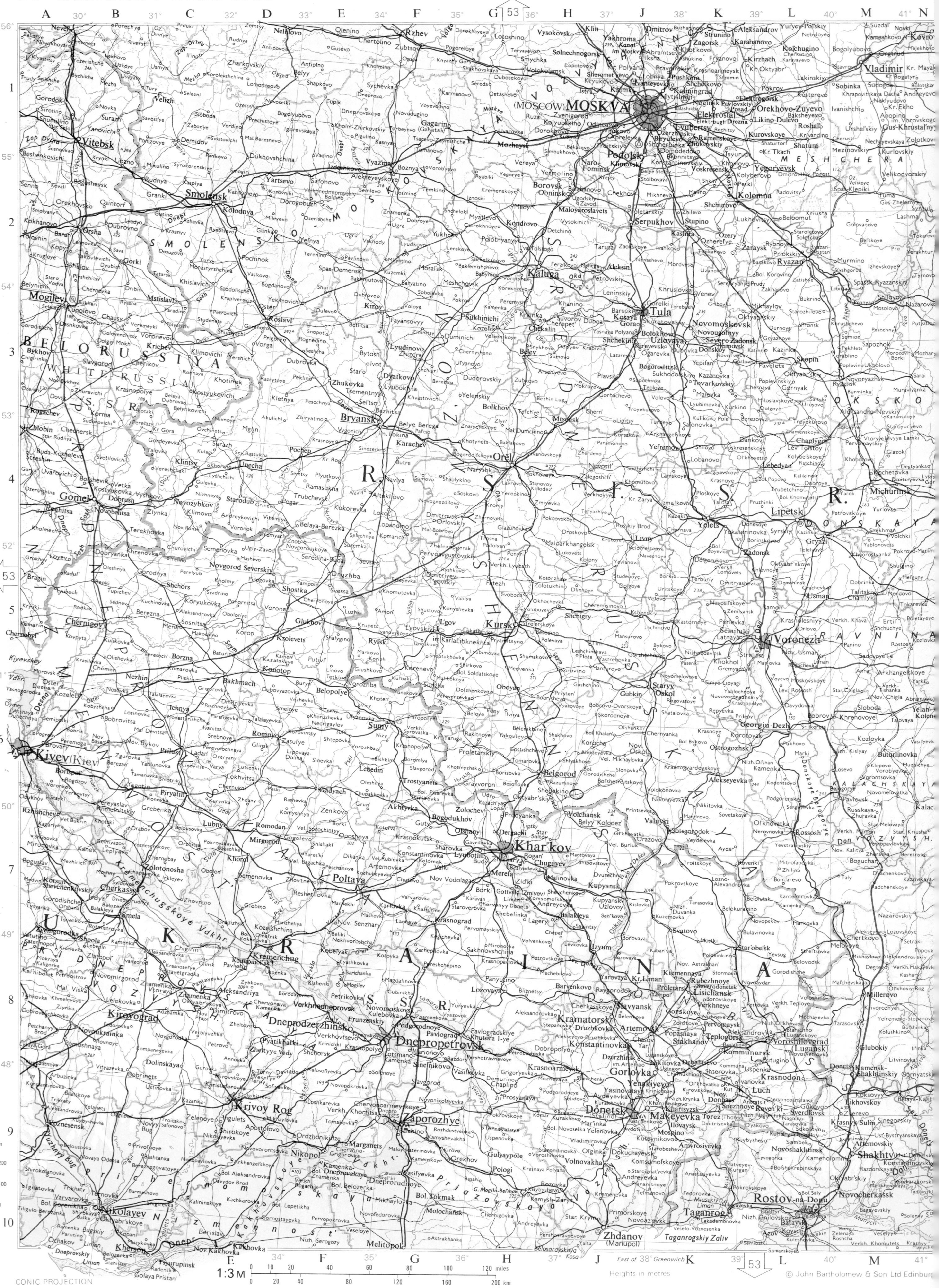

1:3 M
CONIC PROJECTION
East of 38° Greenwich
Heights in metres

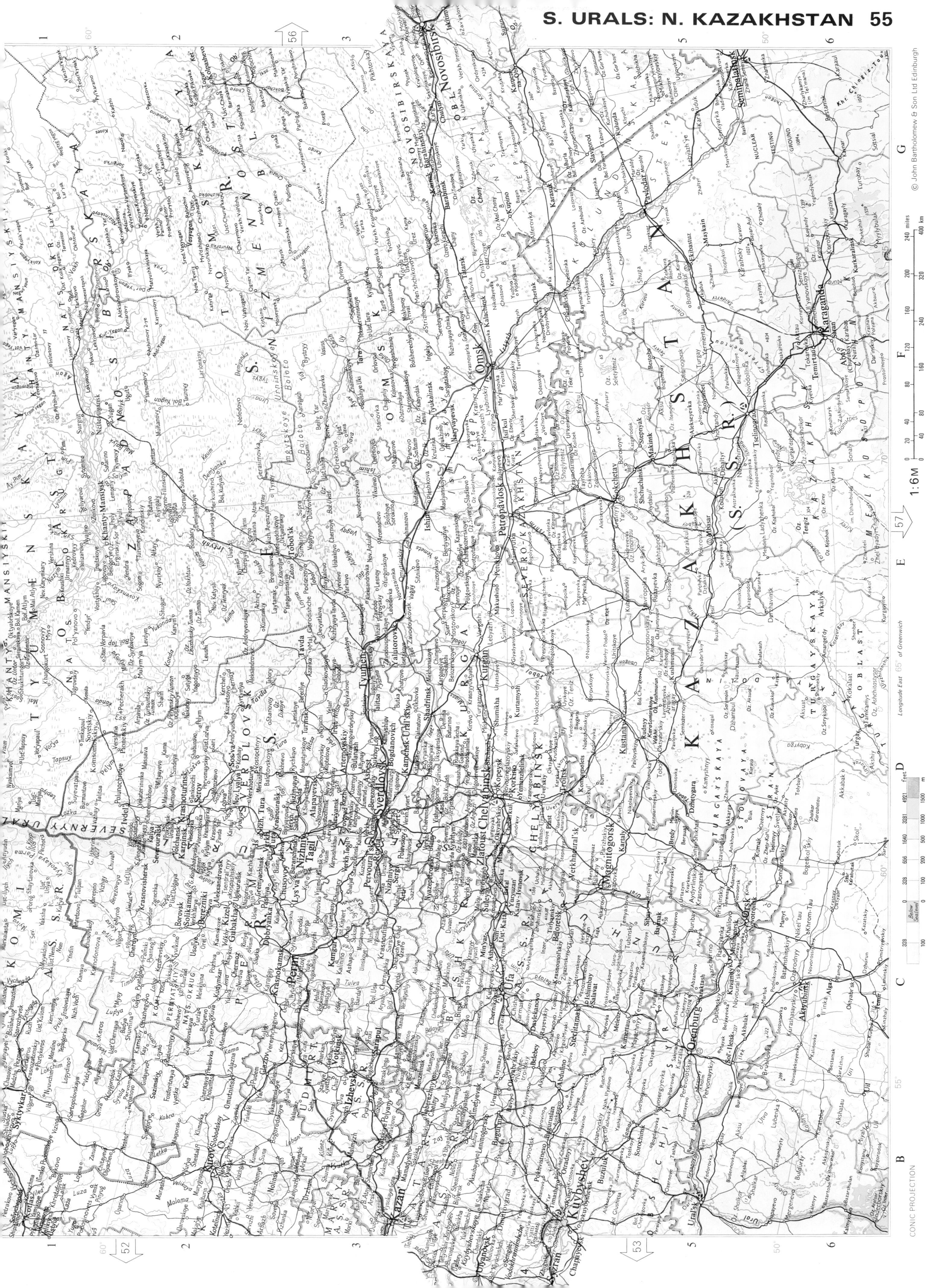

CONIC PROJECTION

1:6M

Longitude East 65 of Greenwich

1:6M

m 4000 3000 2000 1500 1000 500 200 0
feet 13124 9843 6562 4921 3281 1640 656 328 0

km miles
240 320 280 240 200 160 120 80 40 20 0

K R A S N O Y A R S K I Y   K R A Y

I R K U T S K A Y A   O B L A S T

R.S.F.S.R.

Z A P A D N O   S I B I R S K A Y A

T O M S K A Y A   O B L.

N O V O S I B I R S K A Y A   O B L.

A L T A Y S K I Y   K R A Y

K E M E R O V S K A Y A   O B L A S T

T U V I N S K A Y A   A.S.S.R.

B U R Y A T   A.S.S.R.

U S T-O R D Y N S K I Y   B U R Y A T   N A T.   O K R.

M O N G O L I A

C H I N A

K A Z A K H S T A N   (S.S.R.)

Tungusskiy

Novosibirsk
Tomsk
Kemerovo
Novokuznetsk
Prokopyevsk
Barnaul
Biysk
Irkutsk
Ulan-Ude
Bratsk
Kansk
Achinsk
Krasnoyarsk
Yeniseysk
Minusinsk
Abakan
Kyzyl
Anzhero-Sudzhensk
Cheremkhovo
Usol'ye-Sibirskoye
Angarsk
Leninogorsk
Semipalatinsk
Tayshet
Nizhneudinsk
Kuzel'sk
Gorno-Altaysk
Rubtsovsk

Vitim
Chuya
Yenisey
Angara
Ob'

Baykal

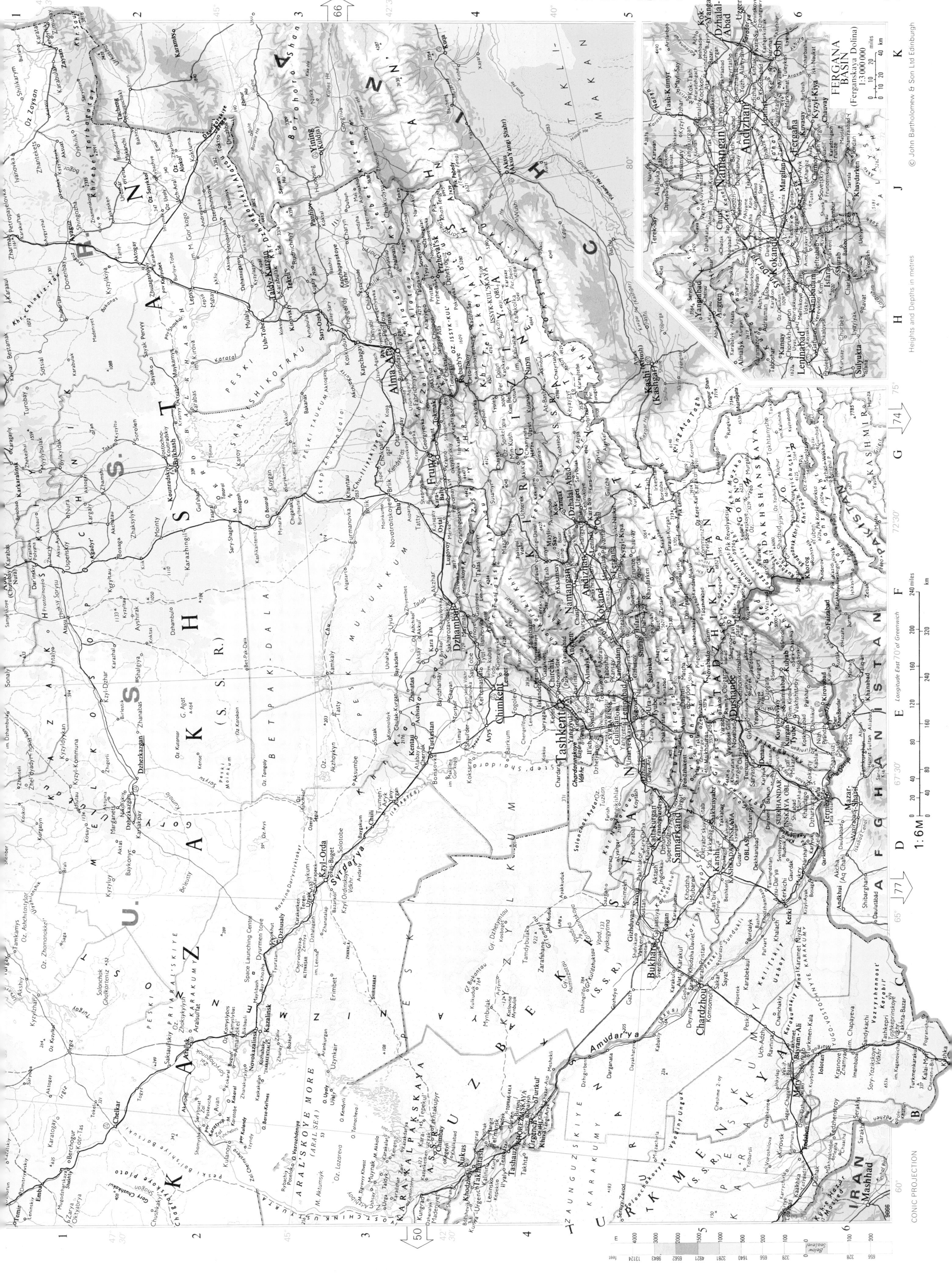

FERGANA BASIN
(Ferganskaya Dolina)
1:3 000 000

© John Bartholomew & Son Ltd Edinburgh

CONIC PROJECTION

1:6M

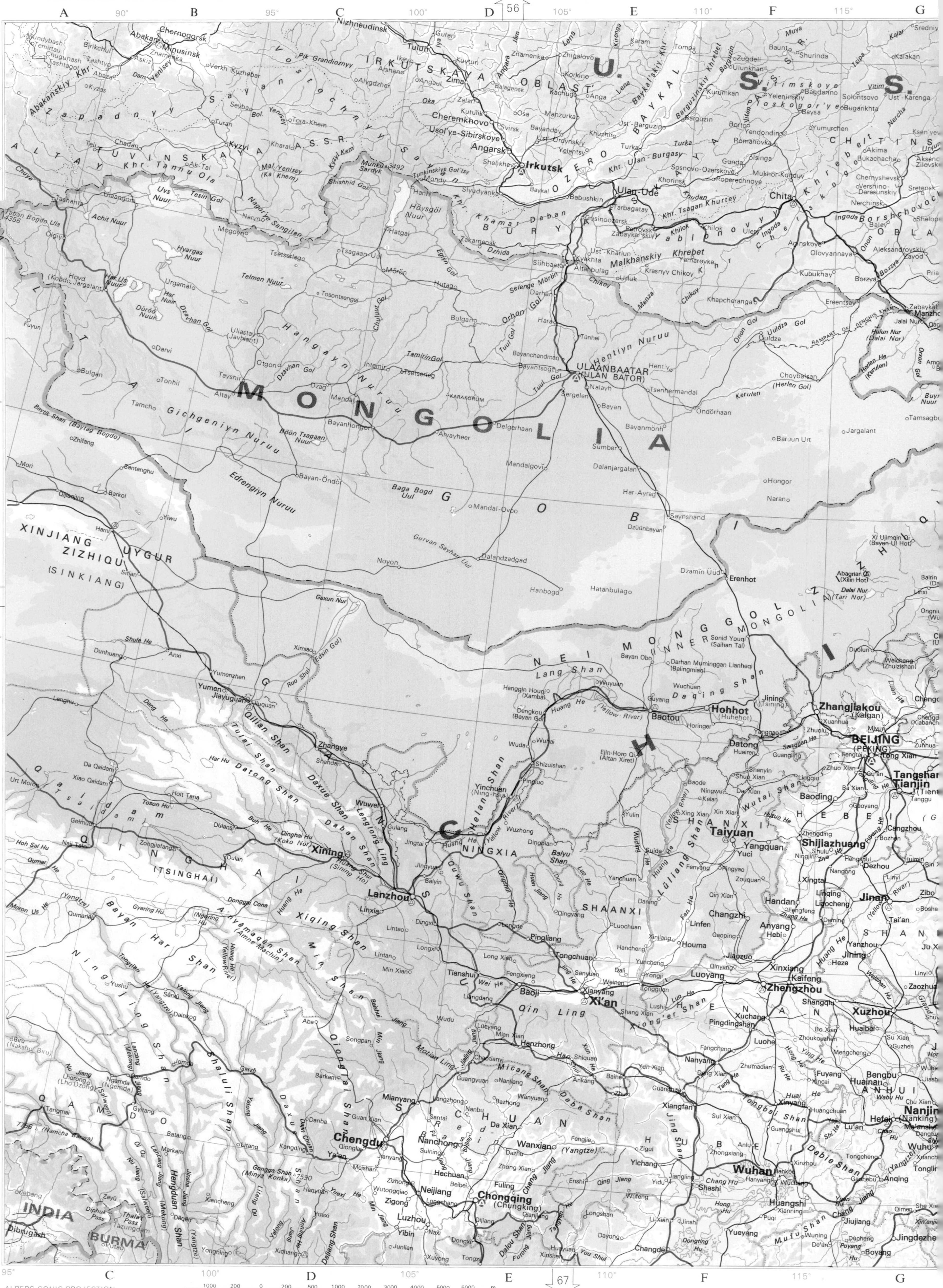

ALBERS CONIC PROJECTION

| 1000 | 200 | 0 | 200 | 500 | 1000 | 2000 | 3000 | 4000 | 5000 | 6000 | m |
| 3281 | 656 | 0 | 656 | 1640 | 3281 | 6562 | 9843 | 13124 | 16409 | 19686 | feet. |

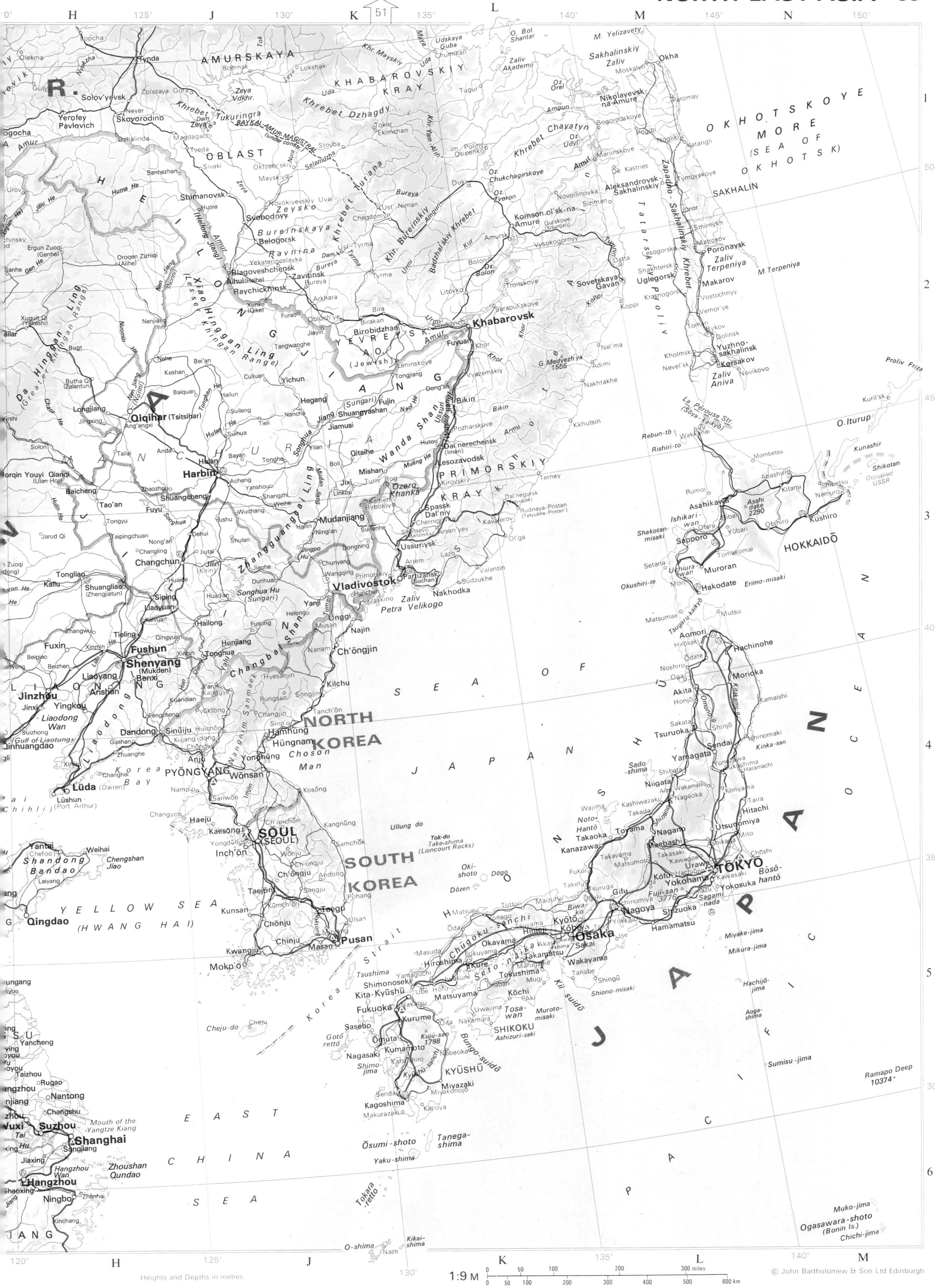

Heights and Depths in metres

© John Bartholomew & Son Ltd Edinburgh

SEA OF OKHOTSK

Continuation on the same scale

SEA OF JAPAN

U.S.S.R.

Occupied U.S.S.R.

HOKKAIDO

Sapporo
Asahikawa
Otaru
Muroran
Hakodate
Kushiro
Nemuro
Abashiri
Obihiro

SHIRIBESHI
SORACHI
ISHIKARI
ABASHIRI
TOKACHI
HIDAKA
NEMURO
KUSHIRO

Ishikari wan

Erimo-misaki

SOUTH KOREA

Pusan
Masan
Chinju

KOREA STRAIT

Tsushima

Matsue
Tottori
Hiroshima
Okayama
Kobe
Himeji
Fukuyama
Kurashiki
Kure
Matsuyama
Takamatsu
Tokushima
Kōchi

HIROSHIMA
YAMAGUCHI
OKAYAMA
HYŌGO
TOTTORI
HARIMA

SHIKOKU

Kita-Kyūshū
Fukuoka
Saga
Sasebo
Nagasaki
Kumamoto
Ōita
Beppu
Nobeoka
Miyazaki
Kagoshima
Kanoya
Kurume

FUKUOKA
SAGA
NAGASAKI
OITA

feet / m
9843 / 3000
6562 / 2000
4921 / 1500
3281 / 1000
1640 / 500
656 / 200
328 / 100
0 / 0
656 / 200
6562 / 2000
13124 / 4000
26248 / 8000

CONIC PROJECTION

Sata-misaki

OKINAWA
1:1 200 000

IWO JIMA
1:300 000

1:3M

Heights and Depths in metres

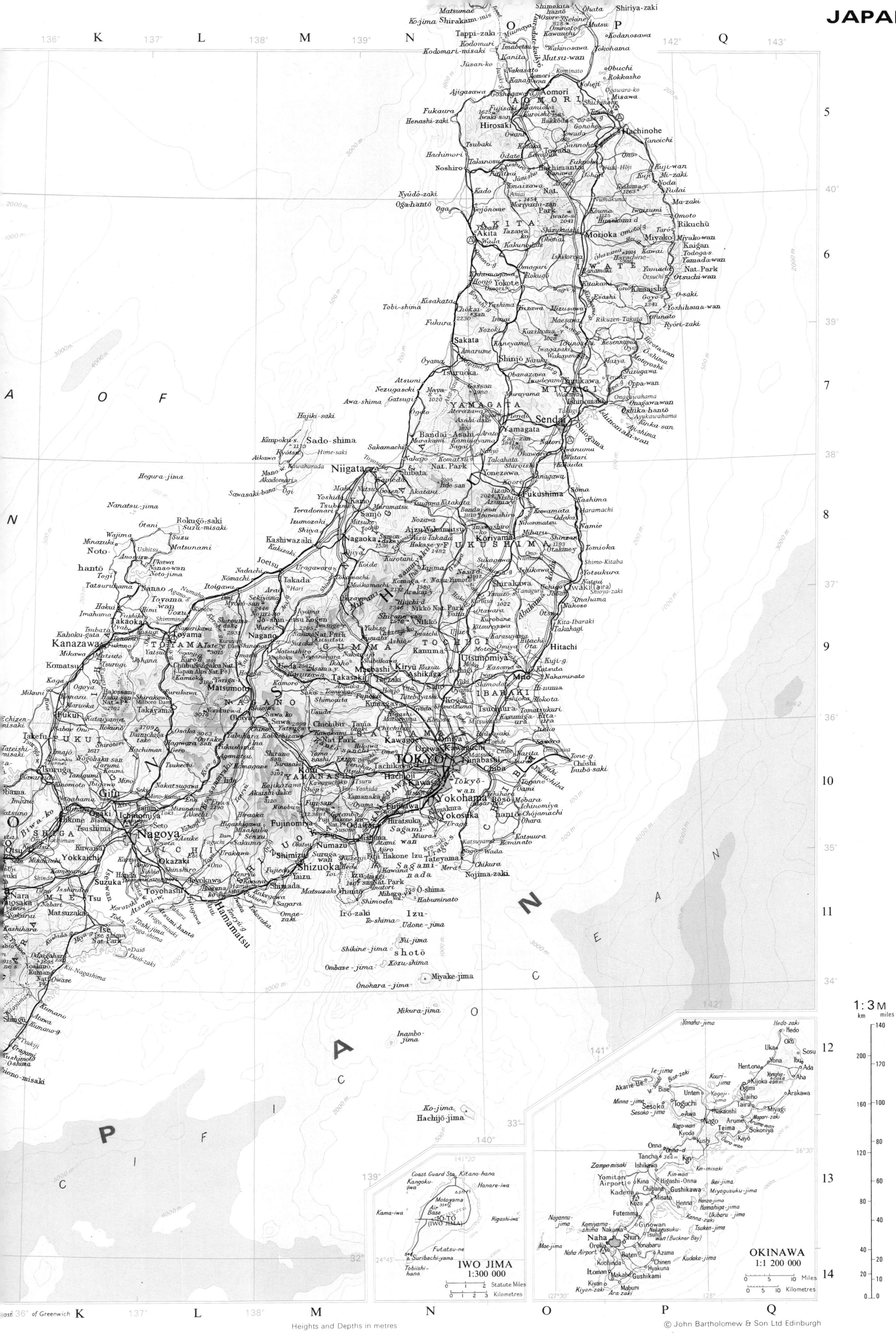

© John Bartholomew & Son Ltd Edinburgh

TOKYO (upper map)

Grid columns: A 139°30' B 139°45' C 140°00' D

Noda, Kurasu, Shimo-Shinden, Tsuruse-Danchi, Warabi, Hatogaya, Sōka, Misato, Izumi, Minowa, Ōmori

Kawahara, Kami-Hirose, Hongane, Miyoshi, Shimura, Kawaguchi, Yashio, Togasaki, Chiba, Funao

Iwasawa, Koyata, Minami-Irisō, Kitada, Kamegane, Naka-Tomi, Nobidome, Sakanoshita, Asaka, Kami-Bamba, Mabashi, Gokōmutsumi, Shimōsa, Shiroi

SAITAMA-KEN, **Iruma**, Fujisawa-Yaganuki, **Shiki**, Toda, Adachi, Gohono, Kanean, **Matsudo**, **CHIBA-KEN**, Yoshida

Minamimine, Nihongi, **Tokorozawa**, **Niiza**, **Wako**, Shimura-Akatsuka, Kita, Katsushika, **Ichikawa**, Ōmachi, **Kamagaya**, Yoshihashi

Takane, Hakonegasaki, Imokubo, **Higashi-Murayama**, **Hōya**, Nerima, Toshima, Arakawa, Edogawa, Tōkagi, Ōwada, Narashino, **Yachiyo**

Musashi-Murayama, Narahashi, **Kodaira**, **Tanashi**, Shimo-Hōya, **TŌKYŌ-TO**, Bunkyō, Hongō, Sumida, Kameido, **Funabashi**, Uchiyama

Fussa, Kokubunji, Nakano, **Shinjuku**, **TŌKYŌ**, Kōtō, Urayasu, **Narashino**

Hachiōji, **Tachikawa**, **Koganei**, **Mitaka**, **Musashino**, Suginami, Chiyoda, **Chūō**, Kasai

Hino, **Kunitachi**, **Fuchū**, **Chōfu**, Setagaya, Shibuya, Minato, Meguro, Shinagawa, Kasai, Kōtō

Tama, **Inagi**, **Komae**, Yōga, Komazawa Olympic Park, Koyama, Nakanobu, Ōta, **TŌKYŌ-WAN**, **Chiba**

Sagamihara, Midori, Nakahara, Hyoshi, Ōmori, TOKYO INTERNATIONAL AIRPORT HANEDA, **Ichihara**

Machida, Kami-Tsuruma, Takeshita, Katsuda, **Kawasaki**, Tsurumi, Kōhoku, Nagatsuda

KANAGAWA-KEN, **Yamato**, **Zama**, Asahi, Kanagawa, Kanagawa, Nakano, Sodegaura

Atsugi, **Ebina**, Fujisawa, Kitamura, Hodogaya, Nishi, **YOKOHAMA**, Naka, Minami-Isogo, Kōnan, Chōgo, Totsuka, Kisarazu, Shimo-Izumi

OSAKA (lower map)

Grid columns: A 135°15' B 135°30' C D

See Inset

Ushibuchi, Kitaura, Tokura, Sasao, Shimoda, Noma Naka, Yunohara, Ōharano, Kami-Ikoga, **SHIGA-KEN**, **Fushimi**, Daigo

Okawase, Yotsutsuji, Ōfuna-Yama, Hazukawa, Nomaguchi, Tōge, Ozakidani, Muko, **Biwa-ko Kokuritsu-Kōen Sotobatachō**

Kamo, Shidehara, Hazu, Uchibaba, Ōmori-dani cable car, **KYŌTO-FU**, Shakaga-dake, Oku-Keihinji, **Nagaoka**, Uji, Rokujizō

Inada, **Sanda**, Chikari Reservoir, Sakaino, **Inagawa**, Yūda, Akegatao-Yama, Izuhara, Hara, Ōyamazaki, Kumiyama, Ichida, Sako, Hirono, Zenjōji

Mino-gawa, Kōzutani, **Dōjō**, Ikuno, Muko-gawa, Kirihata, Todoromi, Ryōzenji, Shimamoto, Yodo, Kōtari, Odawara

HYŌGO-KEN, Nashio, Shimo-Yamaguchi, Tadain, **OSAKA-FU**, Ao, Fukui, Nariai, Saho, Matsui, Tanabe, **KYŌTO-FU**

Nose, Hata-Yama, **Kawanishi**, **Ikeda**, **Minoo**, **Senri**, Onohara, Hirao, **Ibaraki**, Tonda, **Takatsuki**, Nagao, Inooka, Taga, Tamura-Shinden

Taishaku-zan, **Karato**, **Arima**, Funasaka, Ishibashi, Hachō, Yamada, Karasaki, **Hirakata**, Tsuda, Sonenji, Ishitera, Monze, Chay

Jūrinji, Kami-Karato, **Takarazuka**, Machikaneyama, Kaizuka-Shinden, Senri-yama, **Neyagawa**, **Katano**, Kita-Inayazuma, **Yamashiro**, **Kamo**

Rokkō-san, **Itami**, **Toyonaka**, **Settsu**, Kōri, Bōji, Kita, Ikoma, **Yamato**

OSAKA INTERNATIONAL AIRPORT, Tsukaguchi, Hirata, **Suita**, Uzumasa, Hoshida, Takayama, Nimyō, Inudani, **Kizu**, Takata

KŌBE, **Nishinomiya**, Iwazono, Dainichi, **Shijōnawate**, Shimo-Tawara, Nozaki, Seika, **Ikoma**

Ashiya, **Nada**, **Higashi-Nada**, Nishinomiya, Mikage, Jusō, Asahi, **Moriguchi**, **Kadoma**, Ikoma-yama, Nakanokawa, Saidaiji

Maya-an 699, National Park, **Amagasaki**, Ōyodo, Miyakojima, **Daito**, Kawachi, Todaiji Temple, **Nara**

Kōbe-kō, Okamoto, Nishi-Yodogawa, **ŌSAKA**, Jōtō, Higashinari, **Yamato-Kōriyama**

Hyōgo, Fukushima, Konohana, Nishi, Ikuno, **Higashi-Ōsaka**, Kawachi, **NARA-KEN**, **Heguri**

Nagata, **Suma**, Nishi-Suma, Minato, Namiwa, Eishinji, Tennōji Park, **Abeno**, Kyūhōji, Ōze, Sango, **Ikaruga**, Nakate

Nishi-Suma, Ōsaka-kō, Lighthouse, Taishō, Nishinari, **Tao**, Takayasu-Yama, Kōrigawa, Ikoma, **Kashihara**, Kōkubu, Kita-kōga

Higashi-Sumiyoshi, Sumiyoshi, Yamato-gawa, Ōta, Karindōbata, Kashiba, Hashio, Kanmaki

Sakai, Natō, Mozu, **Matsubara**, Mihara, **Fujiidera**, Kokubu, **Kashiwara**, Samita, Yamato-Takada

Ōtori-Kita, Mukōshiba, Sekichaya, **Habikino**, Abe, **Yamato-Takada**

Ōtori-Minami, Ōmino, Hirao, Isokabe, Kasuga

Takaishi, Sukemasu, Kusabe, Natō

ŌSAKA-WAN

Inset (Kyoto)

Makinoo, **KYŌTO-FU**, Kita, Ginkaku Temp, Ukyō, Kamigyō, Sakyō, Nyoigō-Dake

KYŌTO, Nijō Castle, Imperial Palace, Higashiyama

Kawashima, Shimogyō, **Minami**, 136, Kami-katsura, Katsura-gawa

Muko, Kōtari, Yodo, 603, **Nagaoka**, Rokujizō, Fushimi

1:300 000

0 5 10 15 km
0 5 10 miles

© Times Books Ltd.

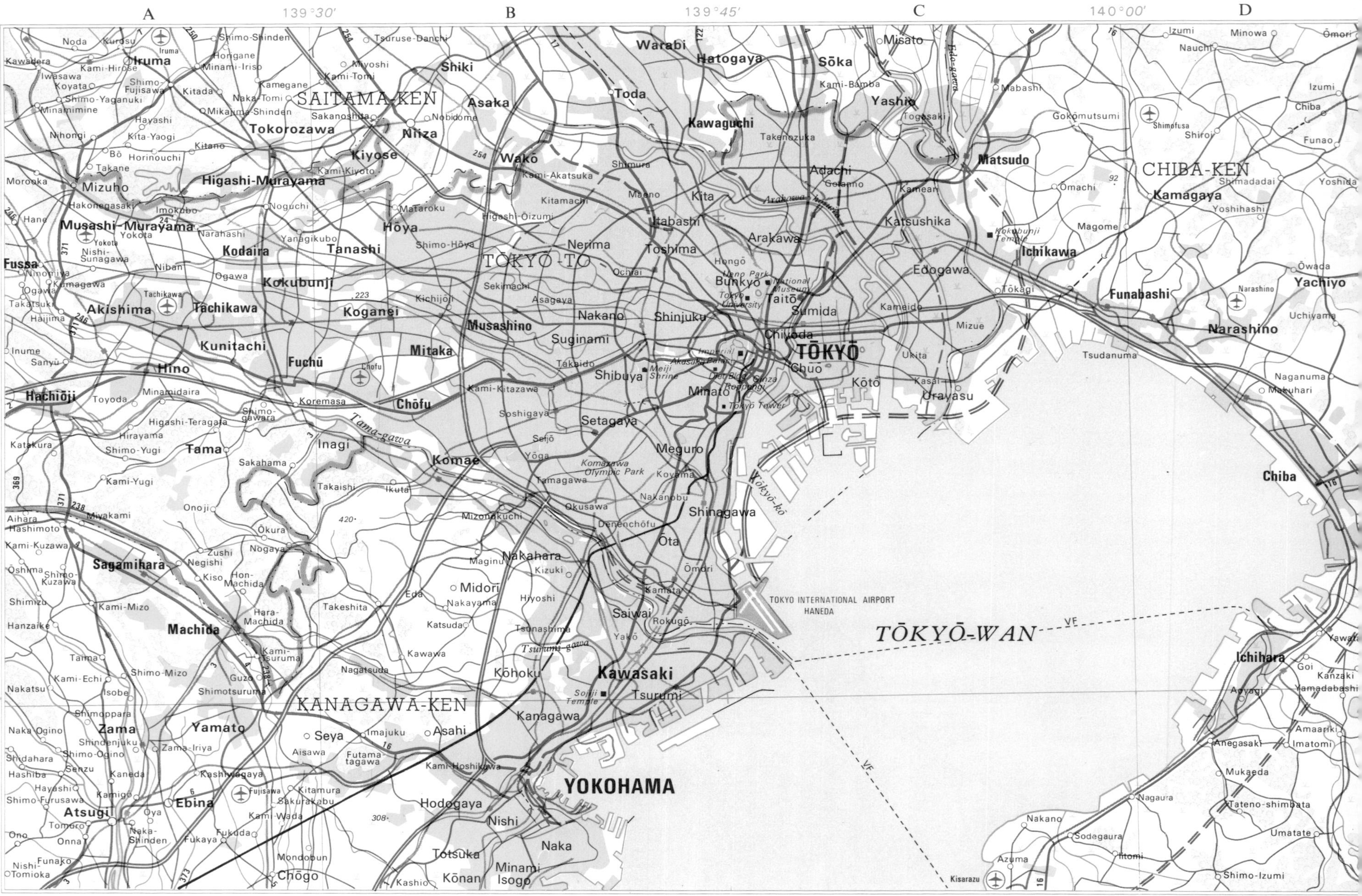

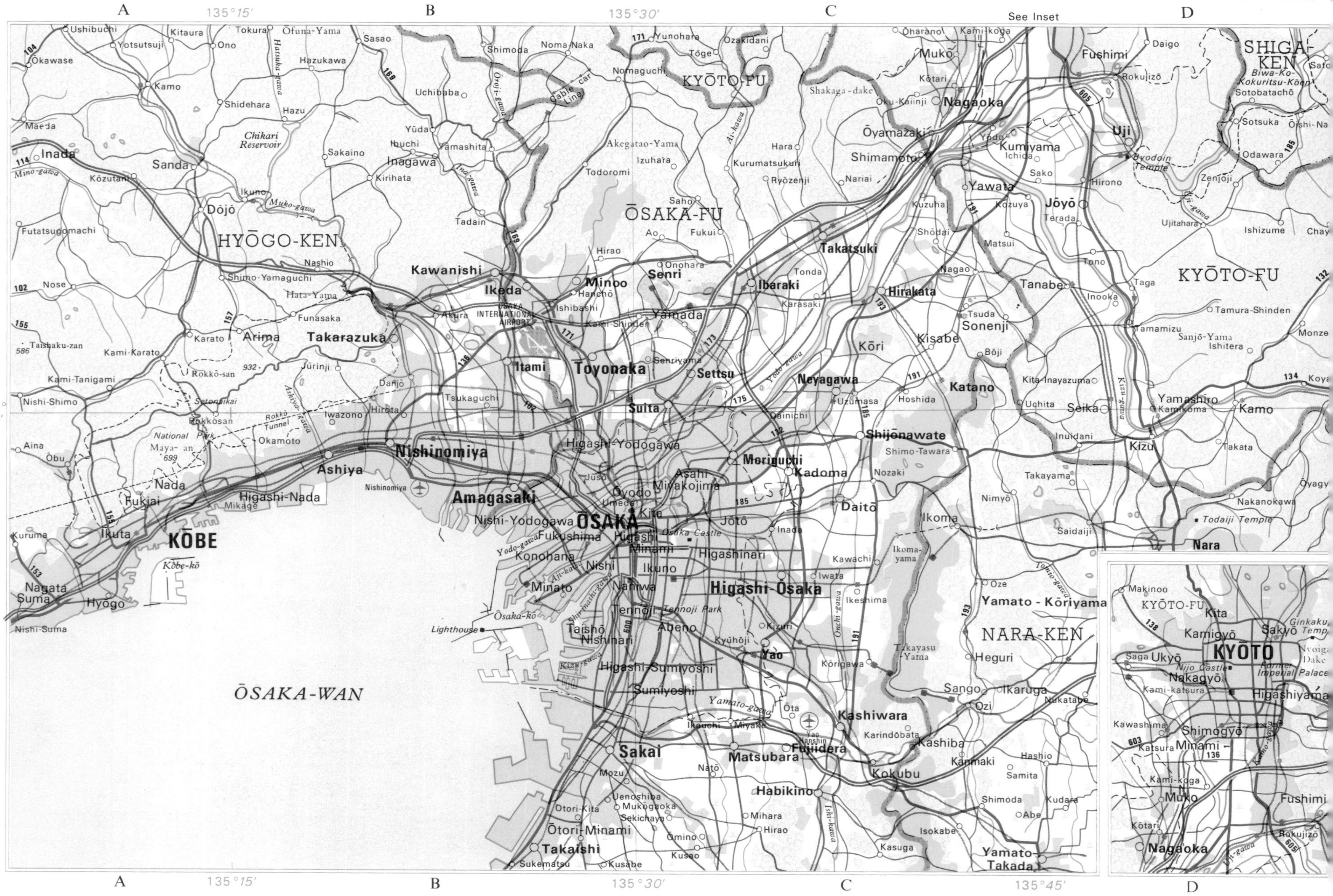

PEKING

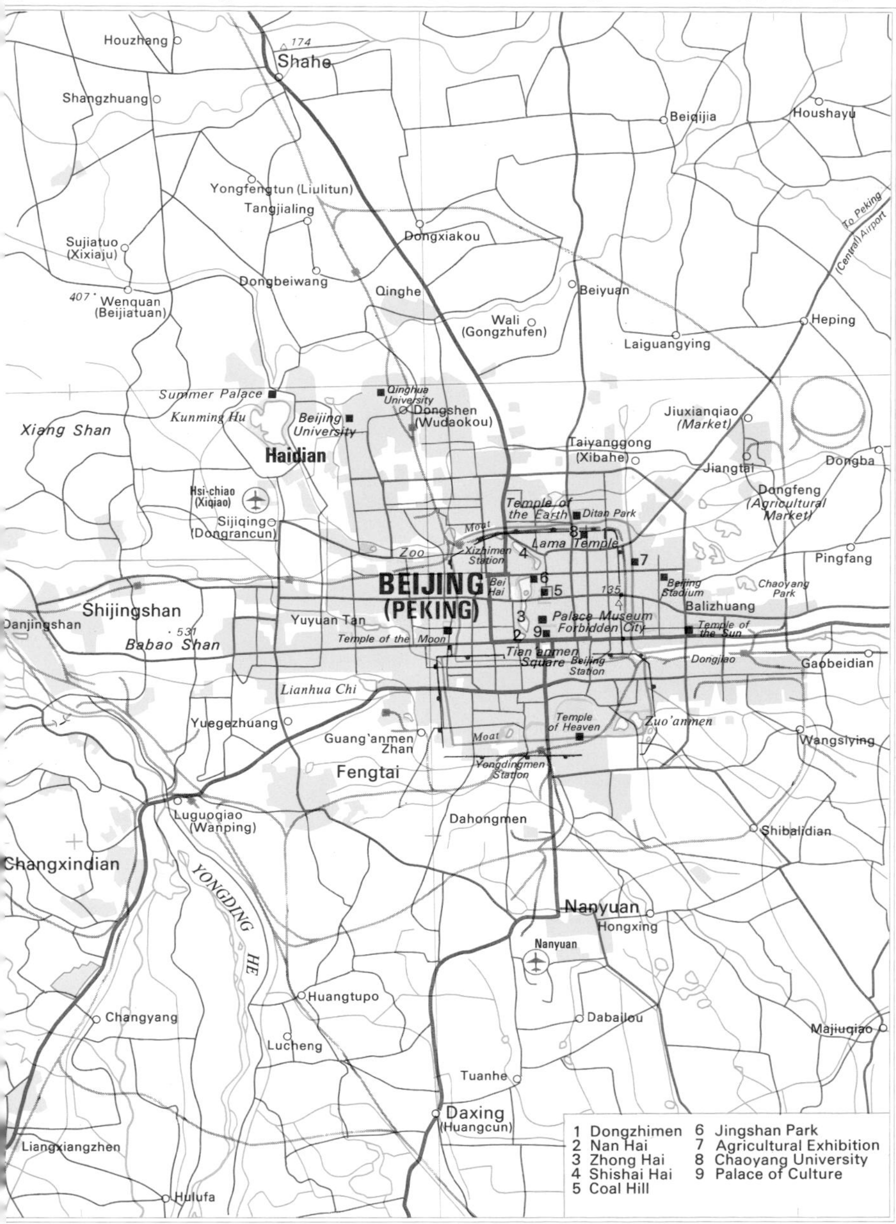

1:300000

SHANGHAI

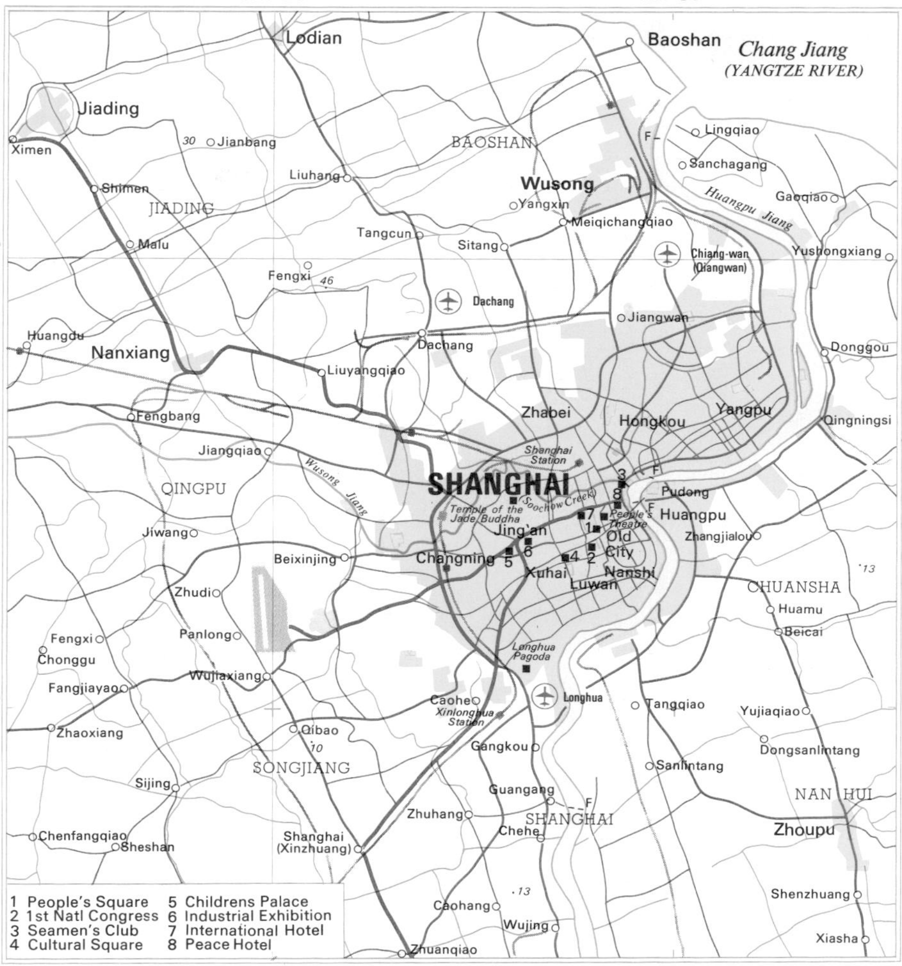

1:300000

CANTON

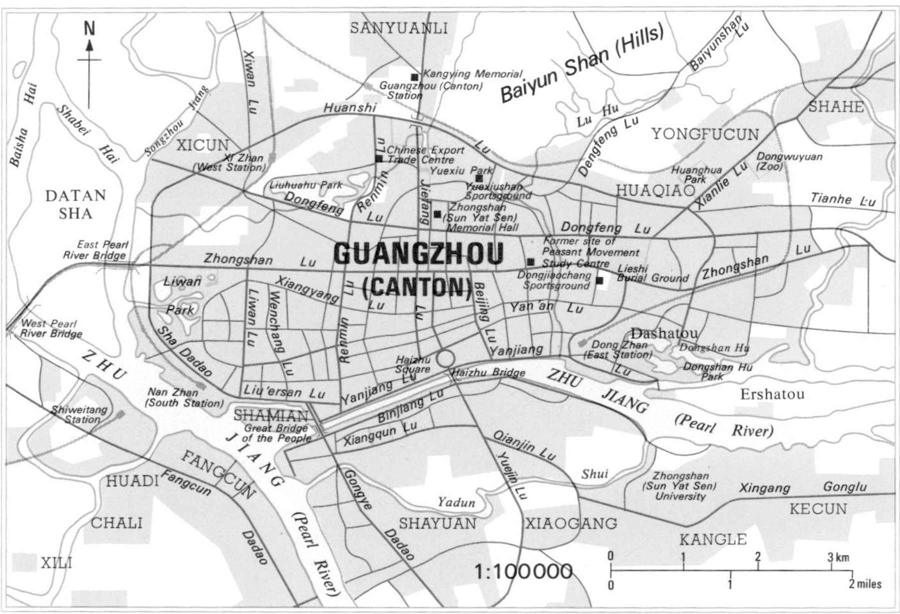

BANGKOK

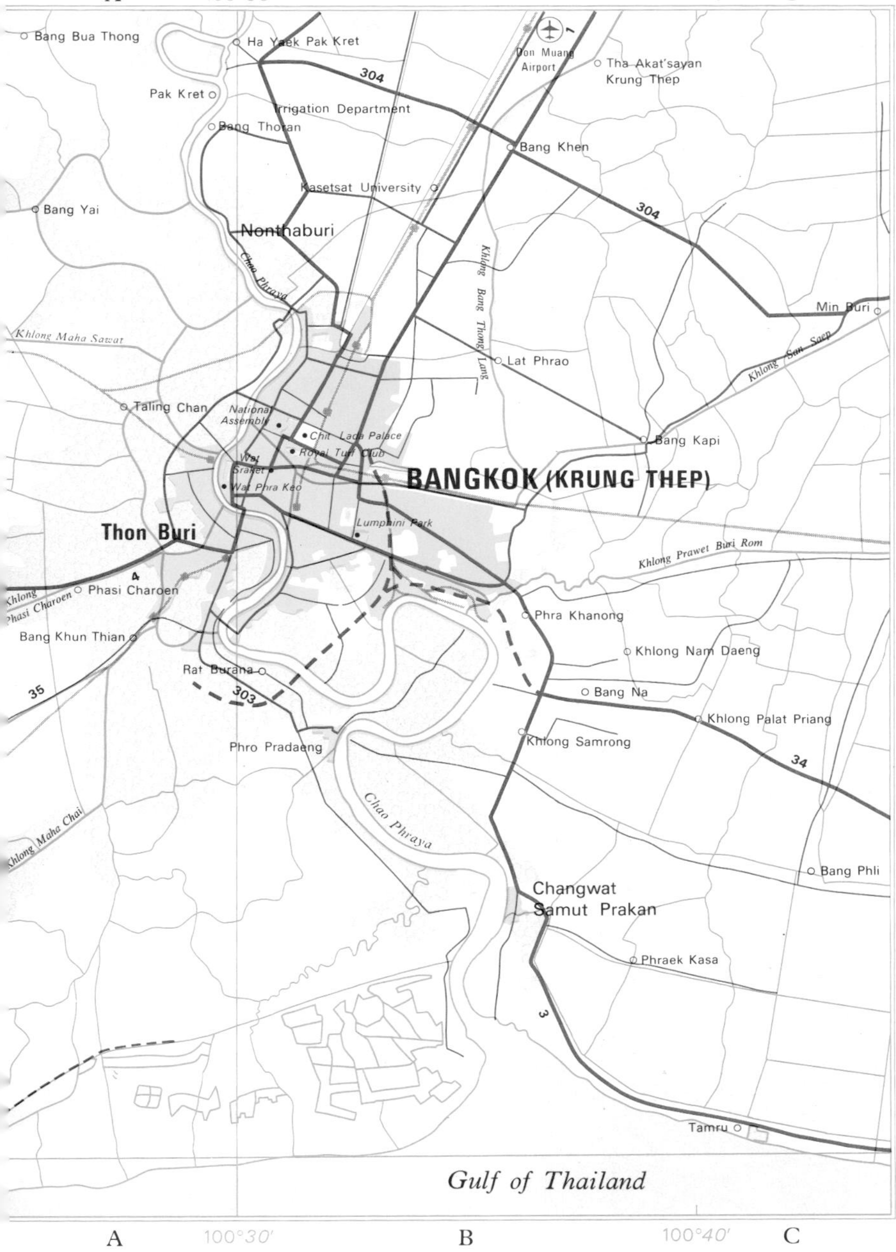

1:300000

JAKARTA

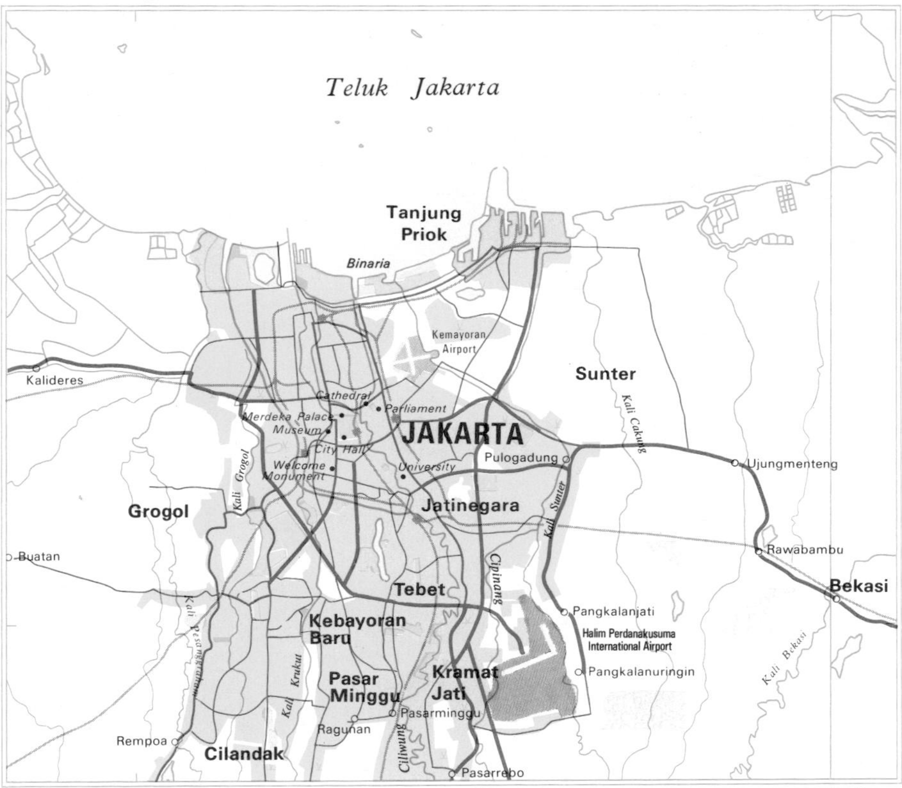

1:300000

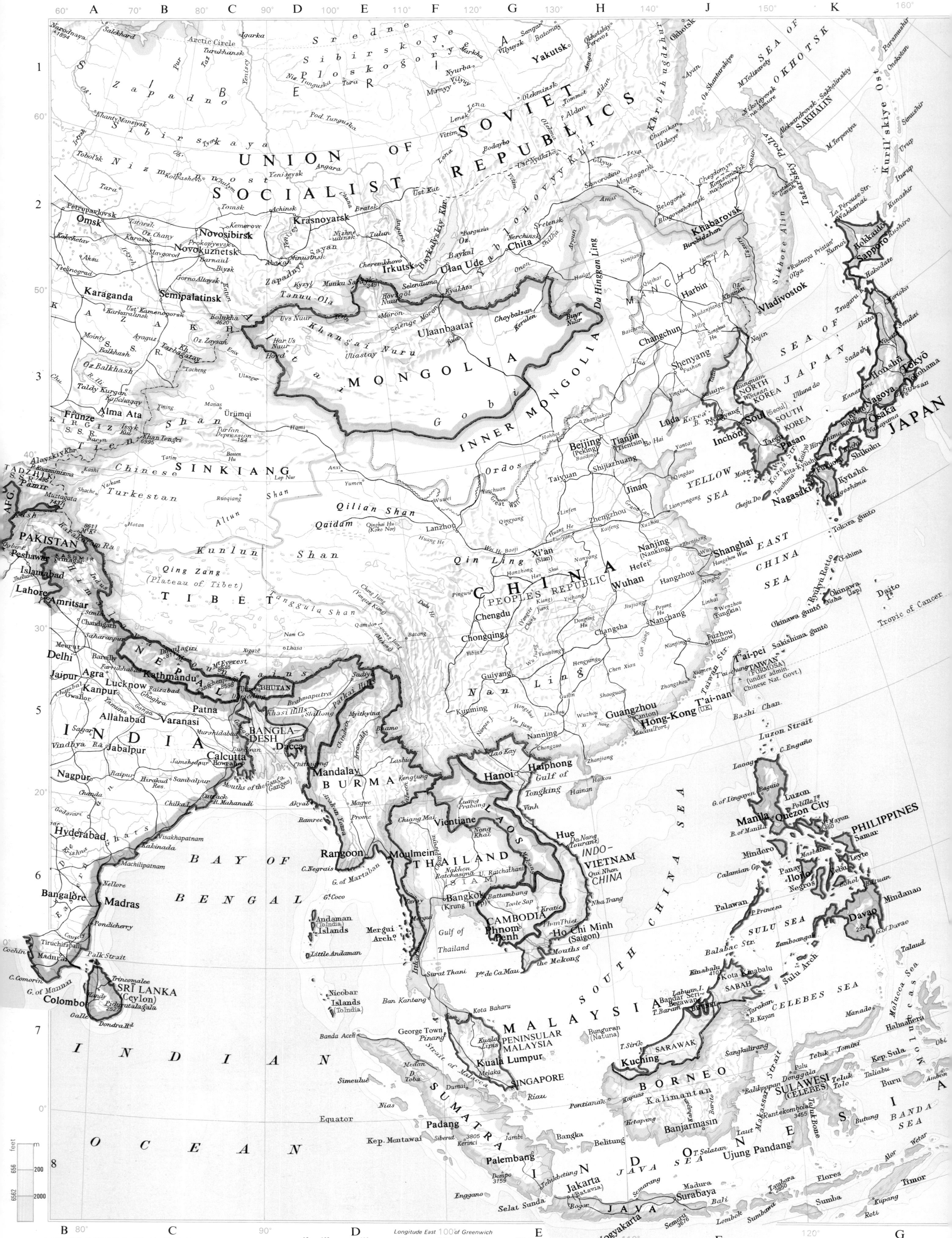

UNION OF SOVIET

SOCIALIST REPUBLICS

MONGOLIA

INNER MONGOLIA

MANCHURIA

SINKIANG

Chinese Turkestan

Kunlun Shan

TIBET

Qing Zang
(Plateau of Tibet)

CHINA
PEOPLES REPUBLIC

NEPAL

BHUTAN

INDIA

BANGLA-
DESH

BURMA

LAOS

THAILAND
(SIAM)

CAMBODIA

INDO-
CHINA

VIETNAM

PHILIPPINES

BAY OF BENGAL

SRI LANKA
(Ceylon)

INDIAN OCEAN

MALAYSIA

PENINSULAR
MALAYSIA

SARAWAK

BORNEO

SUMATRA

SOUTH
CHINA
SEA

SULU SEA

CELEBES SEA

SULAWESI
(CELEBES)

INDONESIA

JAVA SEA

JAVA

JAPAN

SEA OF JAPAN

SEA OF OKHOTSK

YELLOW SEA

EAST CHINA SEA

NORTH KOREA

SOUTH KOREA

TAIWAN
(FORMOSA)
(under admin.
Chinese Nat. Govt.)

PAKISTAN

AFG.

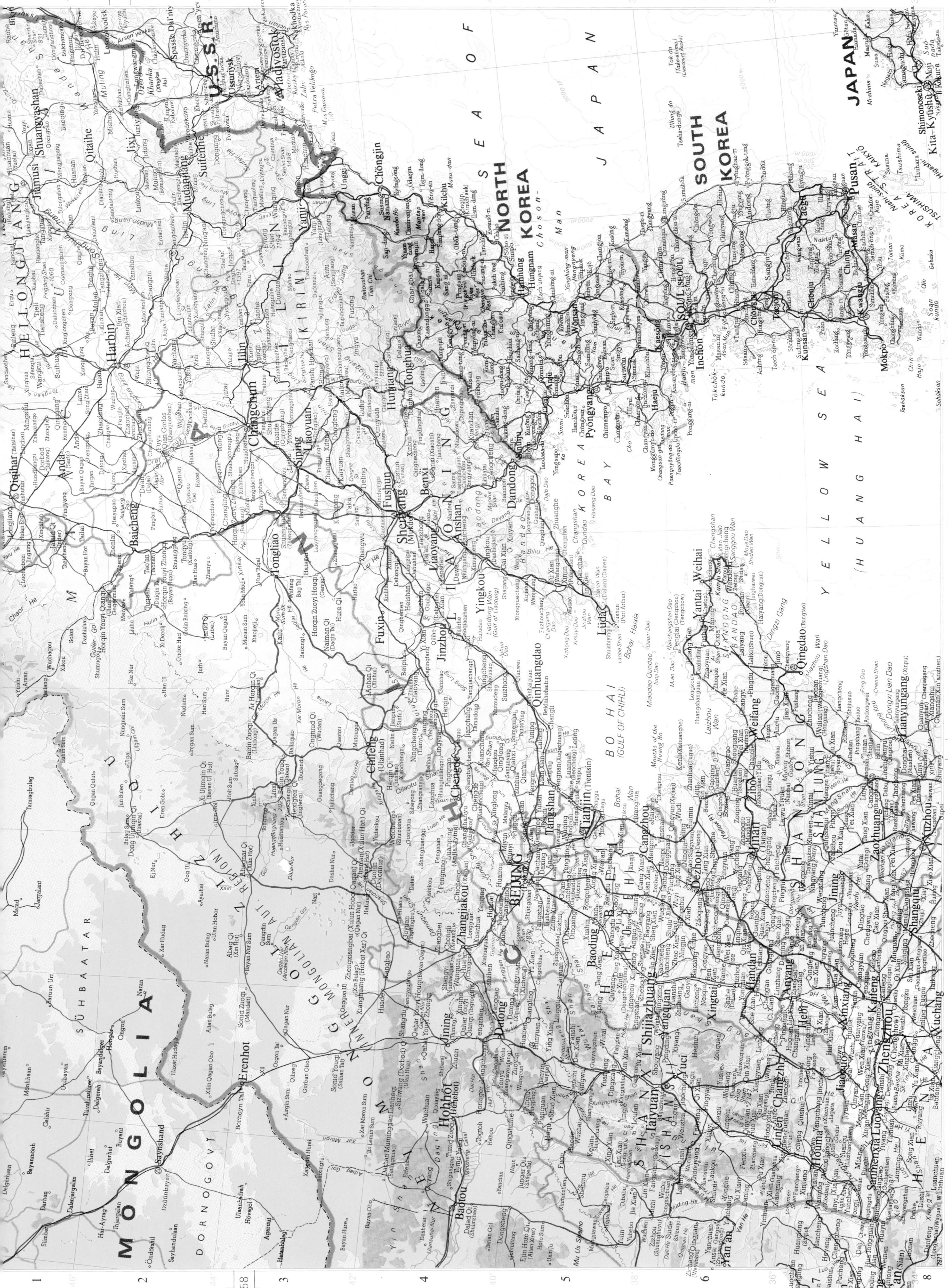

JAPAN

NORTH KOREA

SOUTH KOREA

U.S.S.R.

MONGOLIA

HEILONGJIANG

JILIN (KIRIN)

LIAONING

NEI MONGGOL ZIZHIQU (INNER MONGOLIA AUT. REGION)

HEBEI

SHANXI

SHANDONG

HENAN

SEA OF JAPAN

YELLOW SEA (HUANG HAI)

KOREA BAY

BO HAI (GULF OF CHIHLI)

KOREA STRAIT

Harbin

Changchun

Shenyang

Beijing

Tianjin (Tientsin)

Pyŏngyang

SŎUL (SEOUL)

Pusan

Qingdao

Dalian (Dairen) / Lüda

Qiqihar

Hohhot (Huhehot)

Taiyuan

Shijiazhuang

Zhengzhou

Jinan (Tsinan)

CONIC PROJECTION

1:6 M

Heights and Depths in metres

feet	m
6562	2000
4921	1500
3281	1000
1640	500
656	200
328	100
0	0

400 km

240 miles

© John Bartholomew & Son Ltd Edinburgh
Times Books Ltd

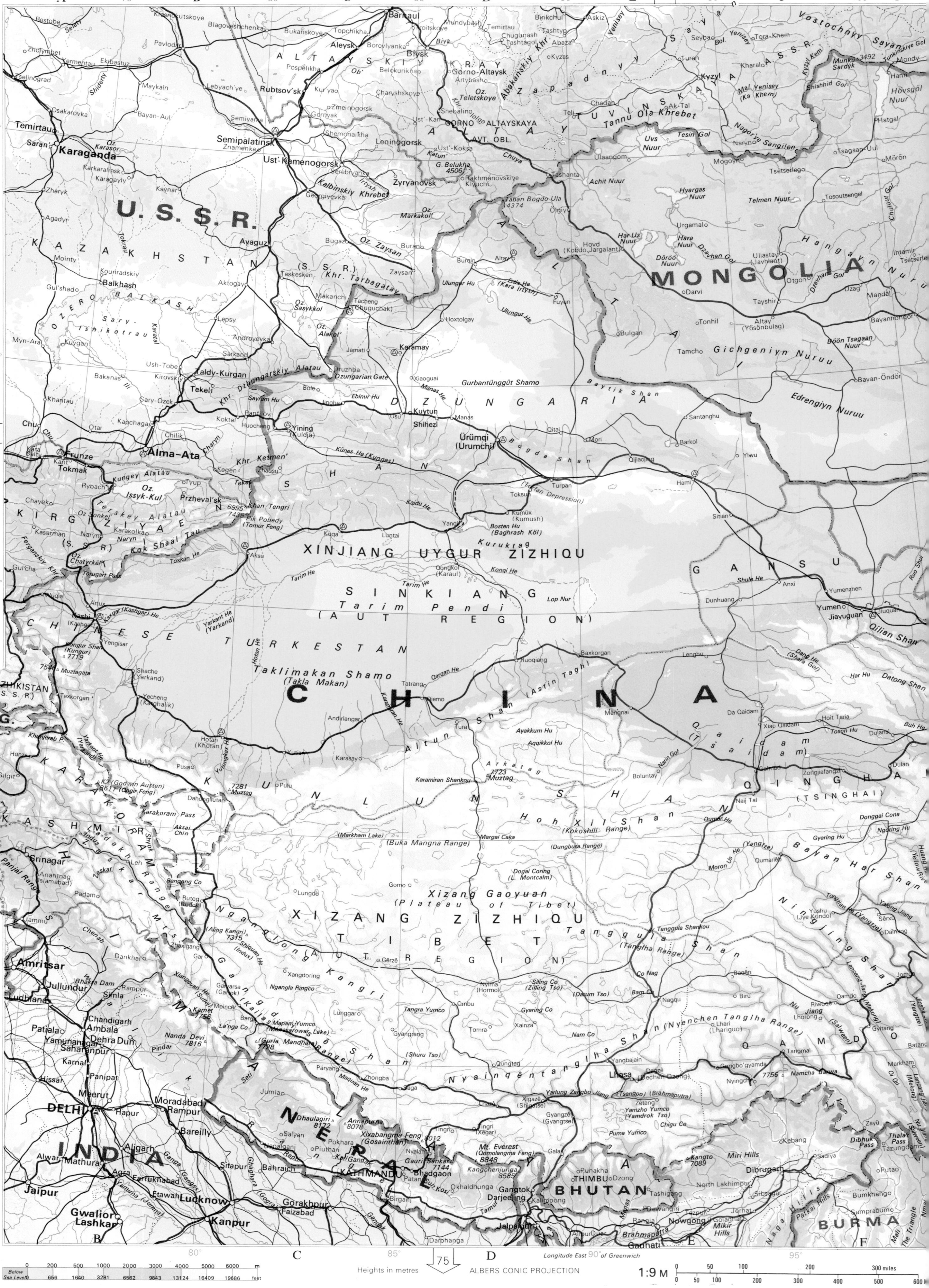

Heights in metres

Below Sea Level	0	200	500	1000	2000	3000	4000	5000	6000	m
	0	656	1640	3281	6562	9843	13124	16409	19686	feet

75

ALBERS CONIC PROJECTION

1:9 M

0 50 100 200 300 miles
0 50 100 200 300 400 500 600 km

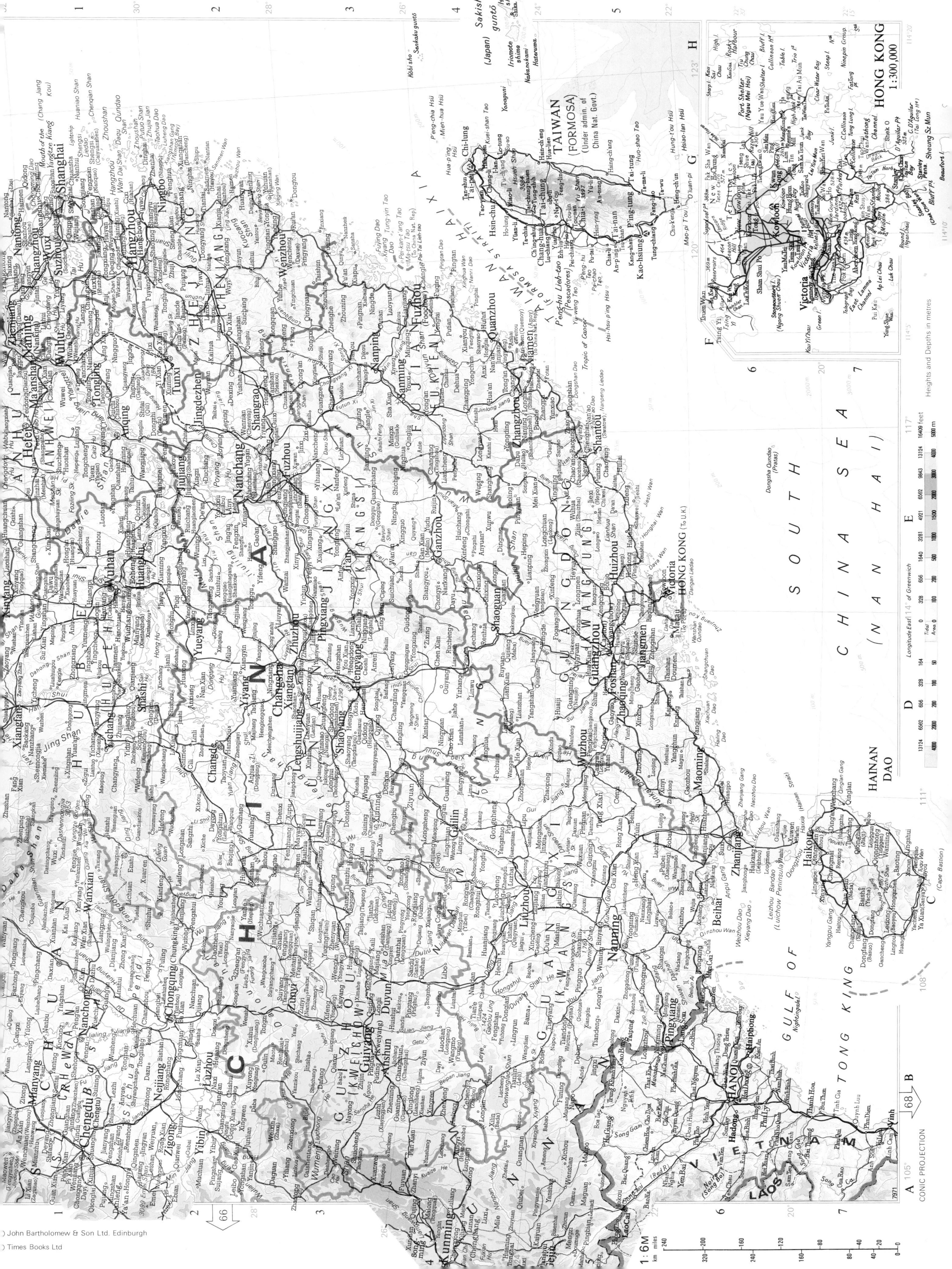

HONG KONG
1:300,000

TAIWAN (FORMOSA)
(Under admin. of China Nat. Govt.)

SOUTH CHINA SEA (NAN HAI)

GULF OF TONGKING

HAINAN DAO

VIETNAM

LAOS

1:6M

CONIC PROJECTION

© John Bartholomew & Son Ltd. Edinburgh
© Times Books Ltd

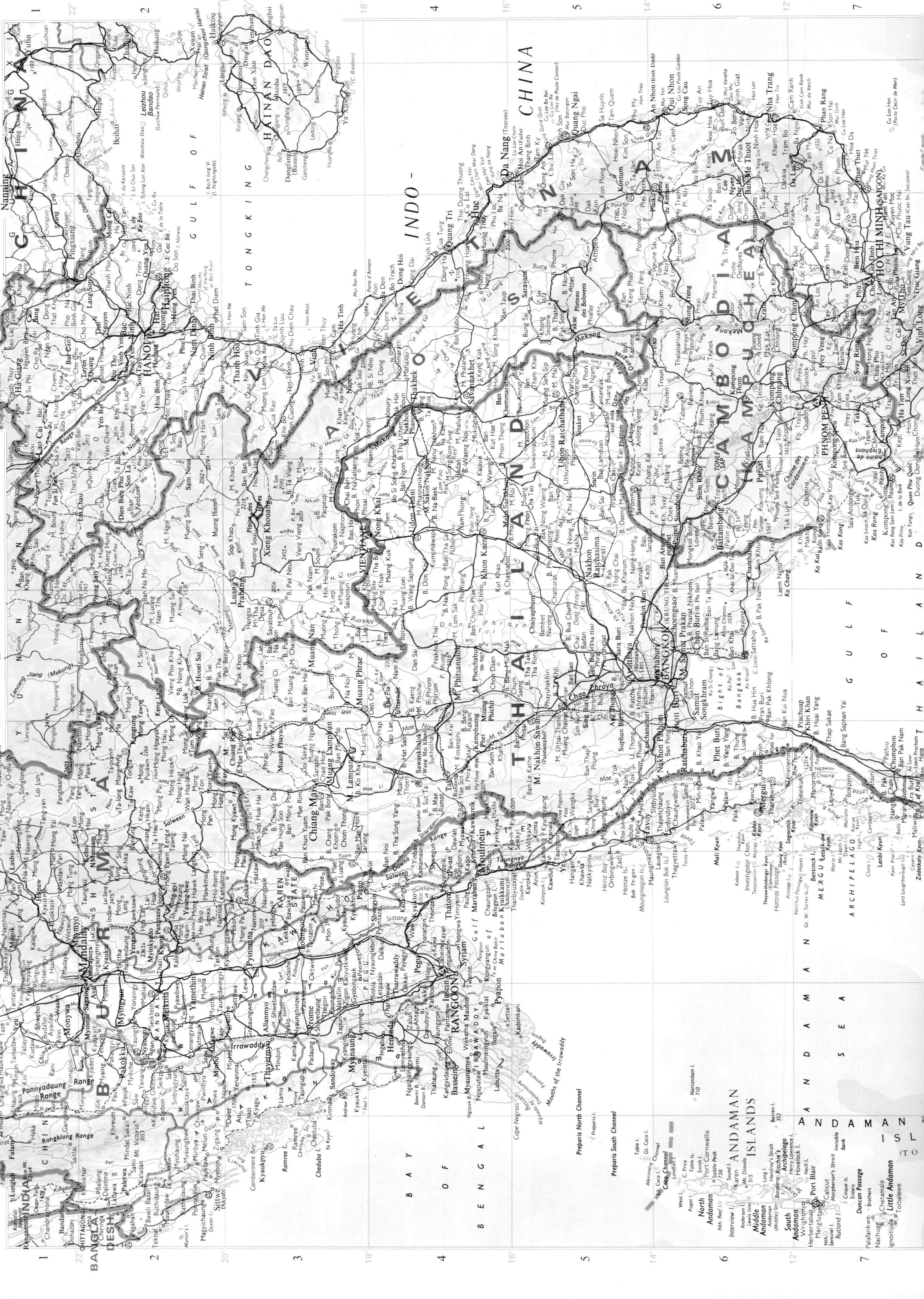
INDO-CHINA
THAILAND
BURMA
CAMBODIA
(KAMPUCHEA)
LAOS
VIETNAM
CHINA
GULF OF TONGKING
HAINAN DAO
BAY OF BENGAL
ANDAMAN SEA
GULF OF THAILAND
ANDAMAN ISLANDS
MERGUI ARCHIPELAGO
BANGKOK
RANGOON
HANOI
VIENTIANE
PHNOM PENH
HO CHI MINH (SAIGON)

67

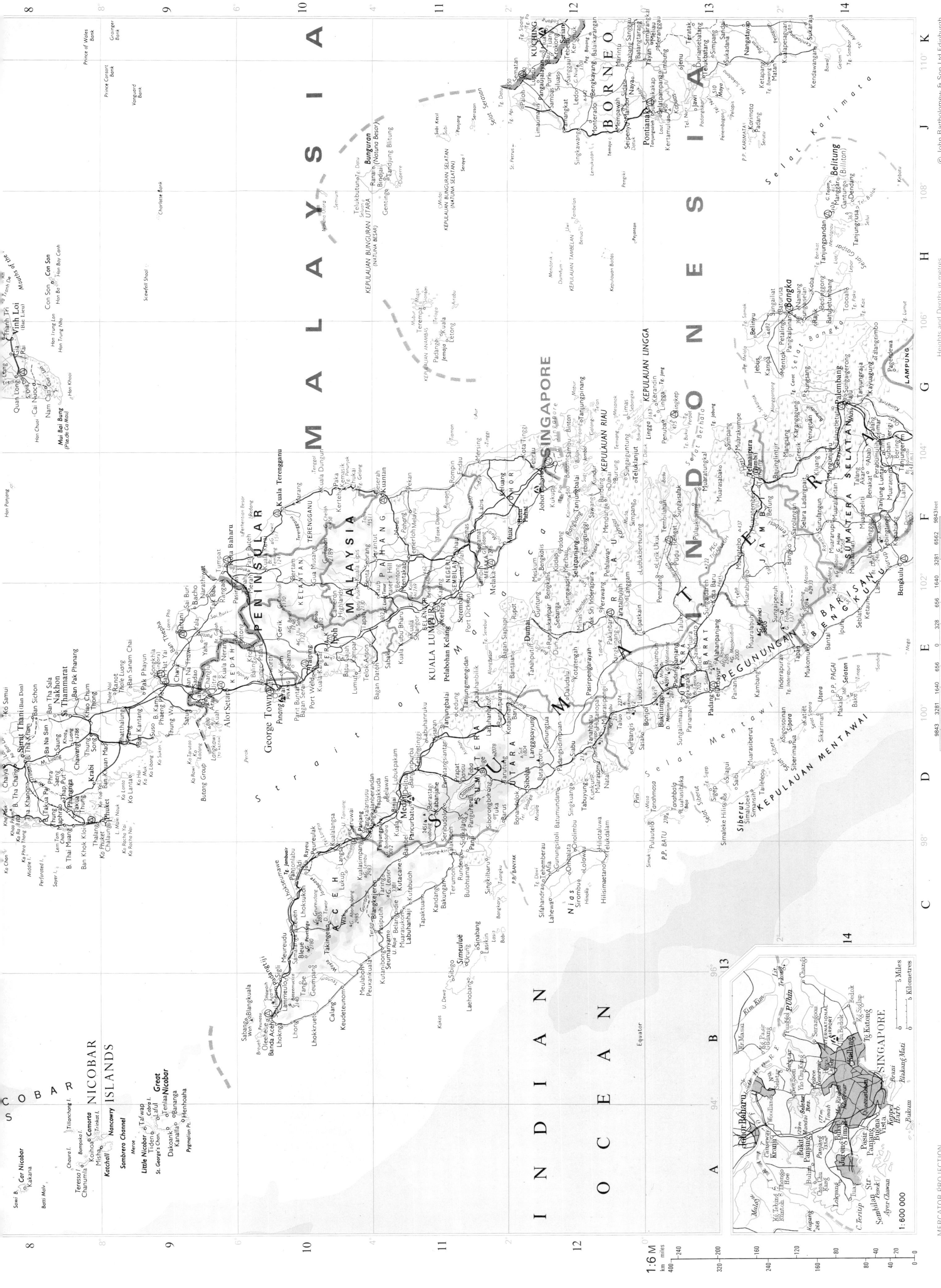

MERCATOR PROJECTION

© John Bartholomew & Son Ltd Edinburgh

Heights and Depths in metres

1:6 M

1:600 000

Major labels

MALAYSIA

INDONESIA

PENINSULAR MALAYSIA

SUMATERA

BORNEO

NICOBAR ISLANDS

INDIAN OCEAN

SINGAPORE

KUALA LUMPUR

George Town

Penang

Medan

Palembang

Bangka

Belitung (Billiton)

KEPULAUAN MENTAWAI

KEPULAUAN RIAU

KEPULAUAN LINGGA

KEPULAUAN BUNGURAN UTARA (NATUNA BESAR)

KEPULAUAN BUNGURAN SELATAN (NATUNA SELATAN)

Bunguran (Natuna Besar)

KUCHING

Pontianak

SUMATERA UTARA

SUMATERA BARAT

SUMATERA SELATAN

BENGKULU

JAMBI

RIAU

ACEH

KEDAH

PERAK

PAHANG

KELANTAN

TERENGGANU

NEGERI SEMBILAN

JOHOR

LAMPUNG

Nias

Simeulue

Siberut

Sipora

Selat Karimata

PEGUNUNGAN BARISAN

BORNEO & CELEBES

MALAYSIA

BRUNEI
BANDAR SERI BEGAWAN

SABAH

SARAWAK

KALIMANTAN TIMUR

KALIMANTAN BARAT

BORNEO

KALIMANTAN TENGAH

KALIMANTAN SELATAN

Pontianak

Kuching

Balikpapan

Samarinda

Banjarmasin

Palangkaraya

CELEBES SEA

SULAWESI (CELEBES)

SULAWESI TENGAH

SULAWESI SELATAN

Teluk Tomini

Donggala
Parigi
Palopo
Parepare
Watampone

Ujung Pandang (Makassar)
Sungguminasa

INDONE...

JAVA SEA

JAVA (JAWA)
(To Indonesia)

SUMATERA SELATAN

LAMPUNG

Palembang

JAKARTA (BATAVIA)
Serang
Bogor
Bandung
Sukabumi

JAWA BARAT

JAWA TENGAH

JAWA

Cirebon
Tegal
Pekalongan
Semarang
Surakarta
Magelang
Yogyakarta

Surabaya
Madura
Pamekasan
Madiun
Kediri
Malang
Probolinggo

BALI SEA

BALI
Singaraja
Denpasar

Longitude East of Greenwich

Heights and Depths in metres

MERCATOR PROJECTION

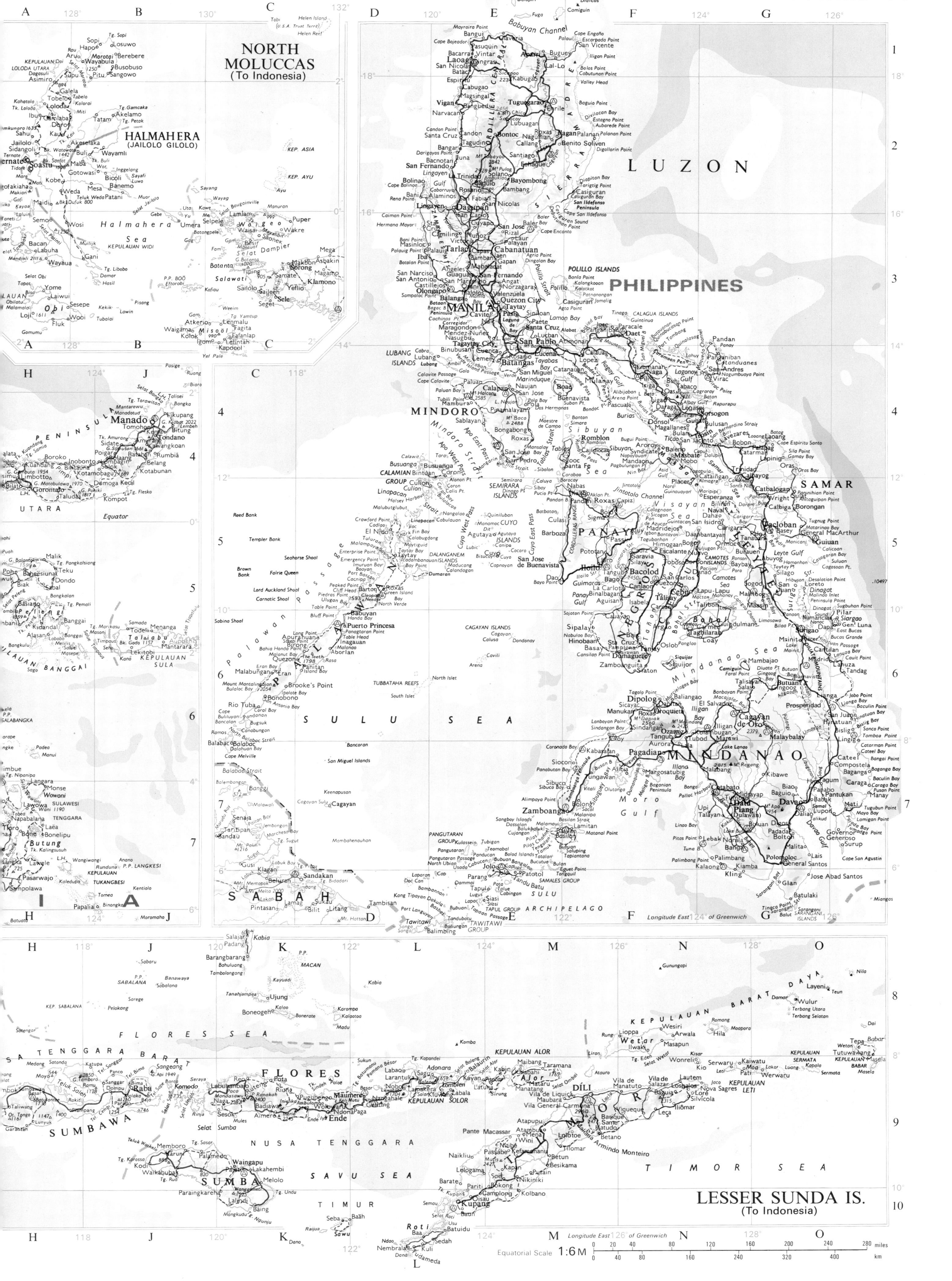
NORTH MOLUCCAS
(To Indonesia)
HALMAHERA
(JAILOLO GILOLO)
Halmahera Sea
LUZON
PHILIPPINES
MINDORO
SAMAR
PANAY
MINDANAO
SULU SEA
SULU ARCHIPELAGO
SABAH
Moro Gulf
Sibuyan Sea
Visayan Sea
Mindanao Sea
FLORES SEA
FLORES
SUMBAWA
SUMBA
TIMOR SEA
SAVU SEA
NUSA TENGGARA
LESSER SUNDA IS.
(To Indonesia)
Longitude East 124° of Greenwich
Longitude East 126° of Greenwich
Equatorial Scale 1:6M

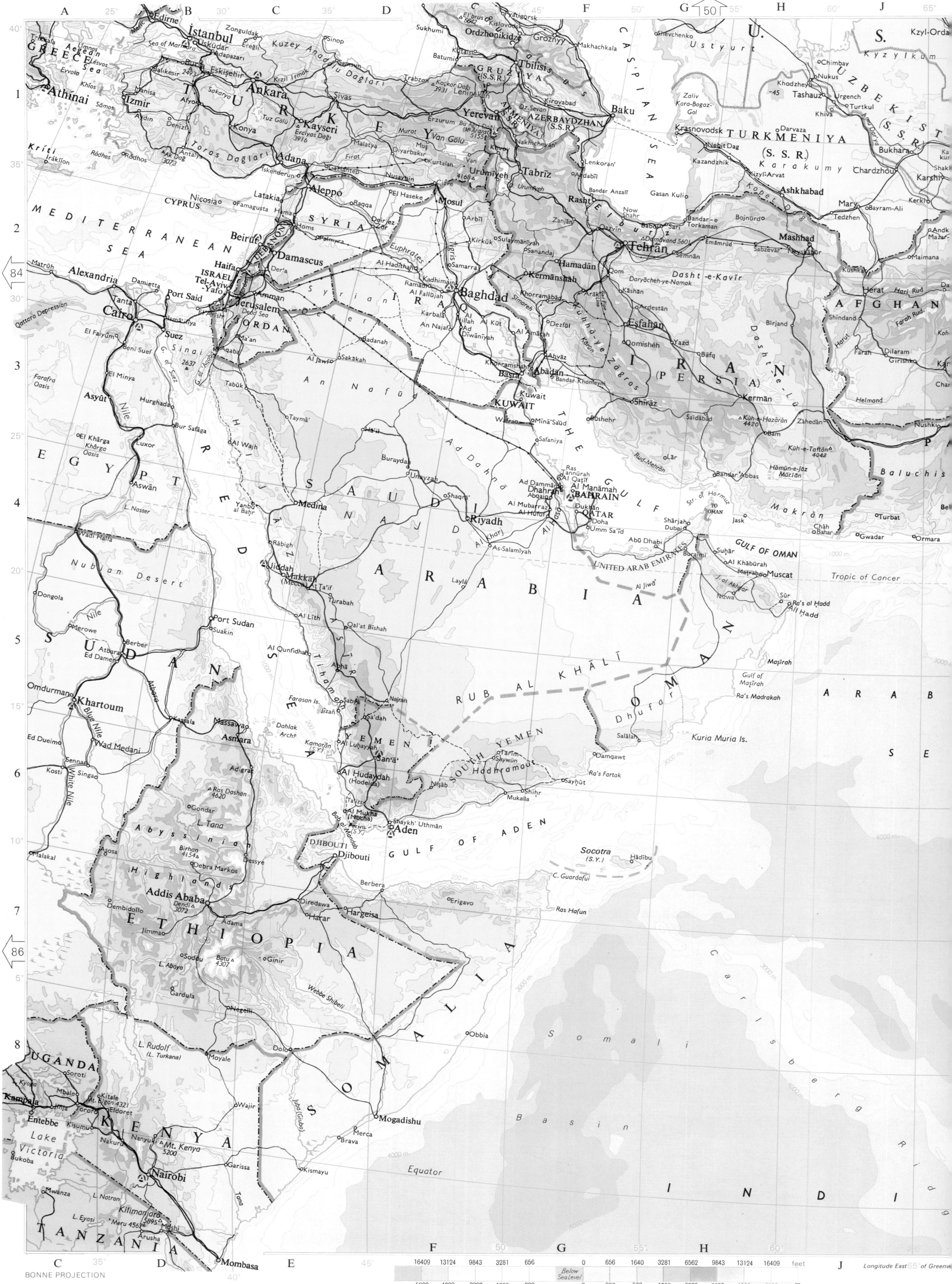

A
B
C
D
E
F
G
H
J
50
84
86
GREECE
Athinai
Aegean Sea
Kríti
Iráklion
Edirne
İstanbul
Üsküdar
Sea of Marmara
Zonguldak
Ereğli
Sinop
Bursa
Eskişehir
Izmir
Ankara
Kızıl Irmak
Konya
Kayseri
Erciyas Dağı 3916
Sivas
Trabzon
Erzurum
Malatya
Diyarbakır
Van Gölü
TURKEY
Toros Dağları
Antalya
Ródhos
Adana
Iskenderun
Gaziantep
Nusaybin
Aleppo
Latakia
Nicosia
CYPRUS
Famagusta
Hama
Homs
SYRIA
Raqqa
Deir ez Zor
El Haseke
Mosul
Arbil
Kirkuk
Sulaymaniyah
Beirut
LEBANON
Damascus
Haifa
ISRAEL
Tel-Aviv-Yafo
Amman
Jerusalem
Dead Sea
JORDAN
Palmyra
Euphrates
Tigris
Samarra
Al Hadithah
Ramadi
Al Fallujah
Kadhimain
Baghdad
IRAQ
Karbala
Al Hillah
Al Kut
An Najaf
Ad Diwaniyah
Al Amarah
Basra
Khorramshahr
Abadan
Ahvaz
Bandar Khomeyni
KUWAIT
Kuwait
Mina' Sa'ud
MEDITERRANEAN SEA
Matruh
Alexandria
Damietta
Port Said
Tanta
Cairo
Suez
Qattara Depression
El Faiyum
Beni Suef
Sinai
2637
El Minya
Farafra Oasis
Asyut
Hurghada
Nile
Bur Safaga
Luxor
El Khârga
Khârga Oasis
EGYPT
Aswan
L. Nasser
Wadi Halfa
Nubian Desert
Dongola
Merowe
Port Sudan
Suakin
Berber
Atbara
Ed Damer
SUDAN
Omdurman
Khartoum
Blue Nile
White Nile
Ed Dueim
Wad Medani
Kassala
Massawa
Asmara
Sennar
Singa
Kosti
Malakal
Aqaba
Ma'an
G. of Aqaba
G. of Suez
Tabuk
Al Jawf
Sakakah
Badanah
Syrian Desert
An Nafud
Tayma'
Ha'il
Al Wajh
Buraydah
Unayzah
Shaqra'
Ad Dahna
HIJAZ
NAJD
Medina
Yanbu' al Bahr
Riyadh
Al Kharj
As-Salamiyah
Rabigh
Jiddah
Makkah (Mecca)
Ta'if
Turabah
Layla
SAUDI ARABIA
RED SEA
Al Lith
Qal'at Bishah
Al Qunfidhah
ASIR
Abha
Tihama
Farasan Is.
Sabya
Jizan
Najran
Sa'dah
Dahlak Arch.
Kamaran (Y.)
Al Luhayyah
YEMEN
San'a'
Al Hudaydah (Hodeida)
Ta'izz
Al Mukha (Mocha)
Bab el Mandeb
Perim
Aden
Shaykh 'Uthman
SOUTH YEMEN
Tarim
Saywun
Hadhramaut
Nisab
Mukalla
Shihr
Sayhut
Ra's Fartak
Damqawt
Salalah
Dhufar
Kuria Muria Is.
RUB AL KHALI
OMAN
Muscat
Matrah
Al Khaburah
Suhar
Nizwa
J. al Akhdar
Sur
Ra's al Hadd
Al Hadd
Masirah
Gulf of Masirah
Ra's Madrakah
Tropic of Cancer
UNITED ARAB EMIRATES
Abu Dhabi
Sharjah
Dubai
Buraimi
Al Jiwa'
GULF OF OMAN
Str. of Hormuz
Ras Tannurah
Al Qatif
Ad Dammam
Al Manamah
Dhahran
BAHRAIN
Abqaiq
Al Mubarraz
Al Hufuf
Al Hasa
QATAR
Dukhan
Doha
Umm Sa'id
THE GULF
Safaniya
Wafrah
Bushehr
Shiraz
Lar
Bandar 'Abbas
Saidabad
IRAN (PERSIA)
Kerman
Kuh-e Hazaran 4420
Bam
Zahedan
Kuh-e Taftan 4042
Hamun-e Jaz Murian
Baluchistan
Makran
Jask
Chah Bahar
Gwadar
Ormara
Turbat
Esfahan
Qomisheh
Yazd
Bafq
Ardestan
Kashan
Qom
Arak
Dezful
Khorramabad
Kermanshah
Hamadan
Sanandaj
Zanjan
Qazvin
Tehran
Damavand 5601
Elburz
Rasht
Bandar Anzali
Now Shahr
Babol
Sari
Bandar-e Torkaman
Gorgan
Semnan
Emamrud
Sabzevar
Neyshabur
Mashhad
Bojnurd
Dasht-e-Kavir
Daryacheh-ye Namak
Dasht-e-Lut
Kuhha-ye Zagros
Birjand
Tabriz
Urumiyeh
Ardabil
Lenkoran'
Khoy
Nakhichevan
Yerevan
Ararat 5155
ARMENIYA (S.S.R.)
AZERBAYDZHAN (S.S.R.)
Kirovabad
Oz. Sevan
Leninakan
Kutaisi
Batumi
Tbilisi
GRUZIYA (S.S.R.)
Sukhumi
El'brus 5642
Kislovodsk
Pyatigorsk
Ordzhonikidze
Groznyy
Makhachkala
Baku
CASPIAN SEA
Shevchenko
Ustyurt
Zaliv Kara-Bogaz-Gol
Krasnovodsk
Nebit Dag
Kazandzhik
Kizyl-Arvat
Gasan Kuli
TURKMENIYA (S.S.R.)
Karakumy
Ashkhabad
Kopet Dag
Tedzhen
Mary
Bayram-Ali
Chardzhou
Bukhara
Karshi
Kerki
Chimbay
Nukus
Khodzheyli
Tashauz
Urgench
Khiva
Turtkul
Amu Darya
UZBEKISTAN (S.S.R.)
Kyzylkum
Kzyl-Orda
U. S. S. R.
Darvaza
AFGHANISTAN
Herat
Hari Rud
Shindand
Farah
Farah Rud
Dilaram
Girishk
Helmand
Kushka
Maimana
Nushki
Socotra (S.Y.)
Hadibu
C. Guardafui
GULF OF ADEN
DJIBOUTI
Djibouti
Berbera
Hargeisa
Erigavo
Ras Hafun
Diredawa
Harar
Addis Ababa
Dendi 3072
Dembidollo
Adama
Jimma
ETHIOPIA
Abyssinian Highlands
Ras Dashan 4620
Gondar
L. Tana
Birhan 4154
Debra Markos
Dessye
Adigrat
Gosa
Sodu
Botu 4307
Ginir
L. Abaya
Gardula
Negelli
Webbe Shibeli
SOMALIA
Obbia
Dolo
Moyale
L. Rudolf (L. Turkana)
Wajir
Juba (Giuba)
Mogadishu
Merca
Brava
Kismayu
Equator
UGANDA
Soroti
Kyoga
Mbale
Kampala
Jinja
Tororo
Kitale
Mt. Elgon 4321
Eldoret
Entebbe
Kisumu
Lake Victoria
Bukoba
KENYA
Nakuru
Nanyuki
Mt. Kenya 5200
Nairobi
Garissa
Tana
Mwanza
L. Natron
L. Eyasi
Kilimanjaro 5895
Meru 4567
Moshi
Arusha
TANZANIA
Mombasa
ARABIAN SEA
INDIAN OCEAN
Somali Basin
Carlsberg Ridge
Longitude East of Greenwich
feet
16409
13124
9843
3281
656
0
656
1640
3281
6562
9843
13124
16409
Below Sea Level
m
5000
4000
3000
1000
200
0
200
500
1000
2000
3000
4000
5000

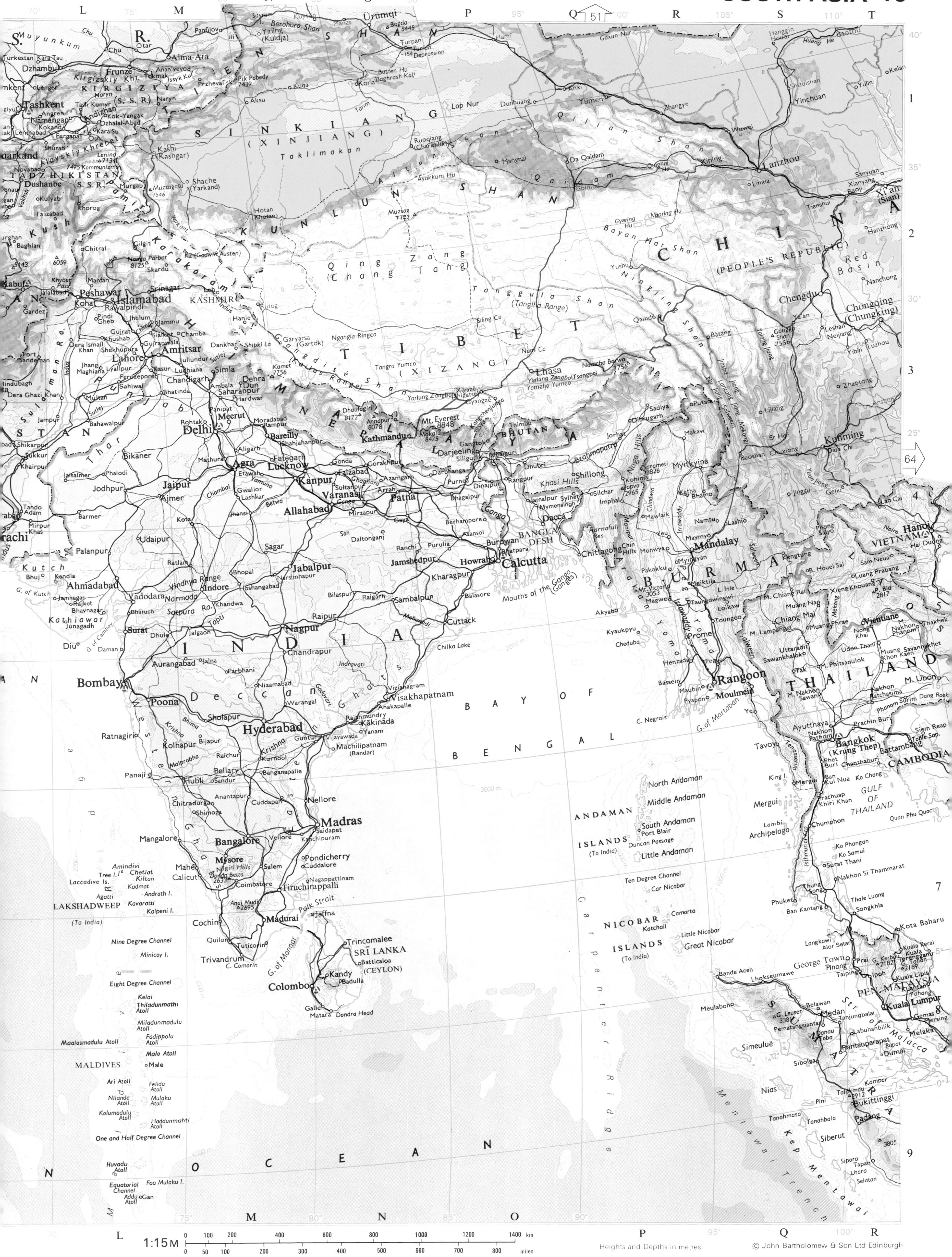

1:15M — 0 100 200 400 600 800 1000 1200 1400 km; 0 50 100 200 300 400 500 600 700 800 miles

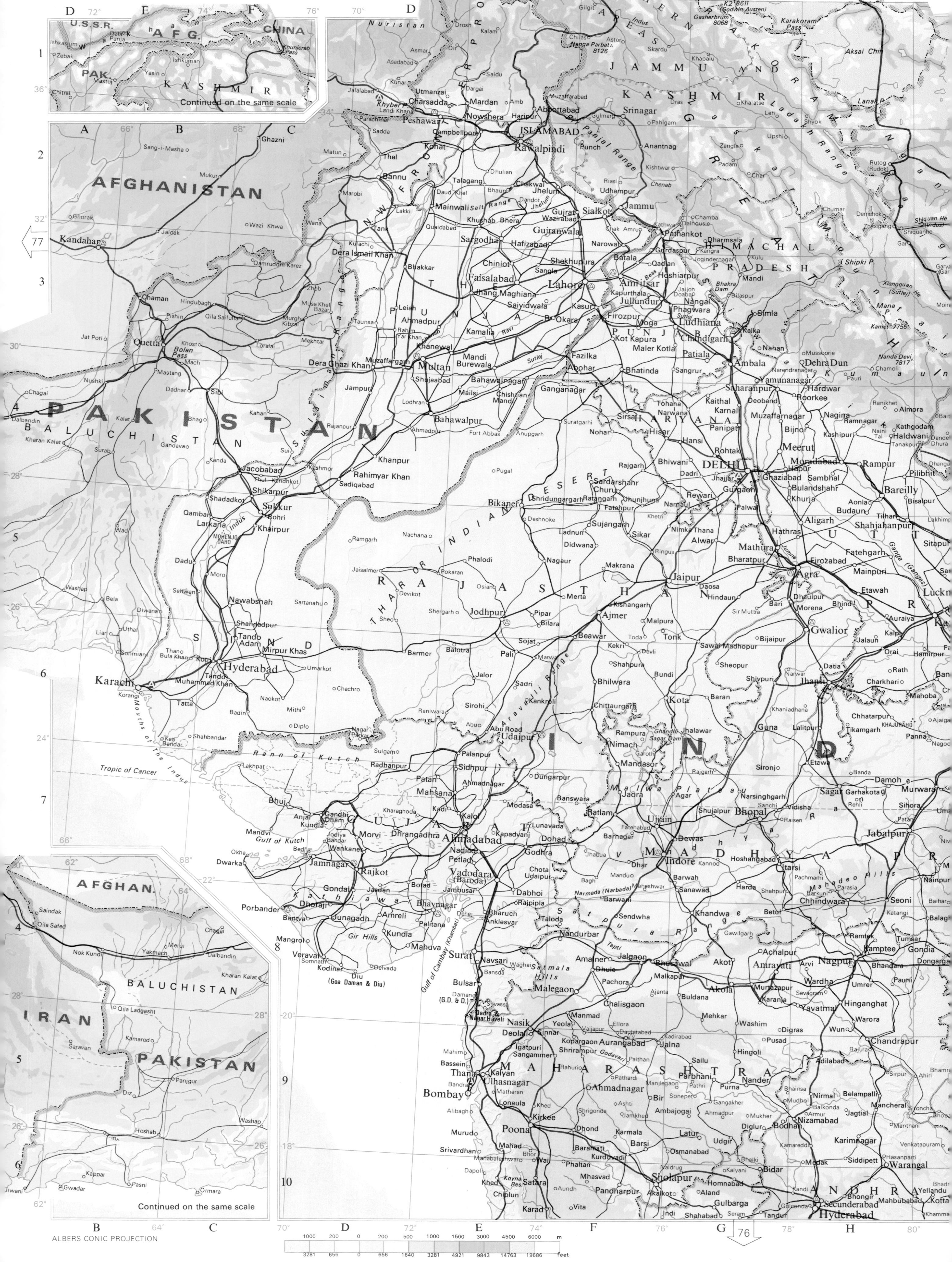

ALBERS CONIC PROJECTION

Continued on the same scale

Continued on the same scale

Tropic of Cancer

CHINA

XIZANG GAOYUAN
(PLATEAU OF TIBET)

XIZANG ZIZHIQU

QINGHAI
(TSINGHAI)

TIBET
(AUT. REGION)

NEPAL

KATHMANDU

BHUTAN

SIKKIM

ARUNACHAL PRADESH

THIMBU

ASSAM

NAGALAND

MEGHALAYA

BANGLADESH

DACCA

WEST BENGAL

BIHAR

Calcutta

TRIPURA

MIZORAM

MANIPUR

KACHIN STATE

SHAN STATE

CHIN STATE

ORISSA

BAY OF BENGAL

BURMA

Mouths of The Ganges (or Ganga)

Mandalay

Lhasa

Mt. Everest
(Qomolangma Feng)
8848 (29028ft)

Gorakhpur Patna Varanasi (Benares) Gaya Ranchi Jamshedpur Kharagpur Cuttack Bhubaneswar Puri Visakhapatnam

Chittagong Cox's Bazar Akyab

Heights and Depths in metres

1:6 M

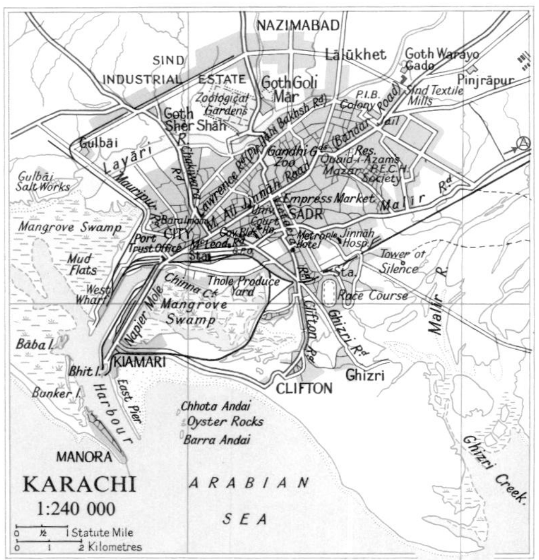

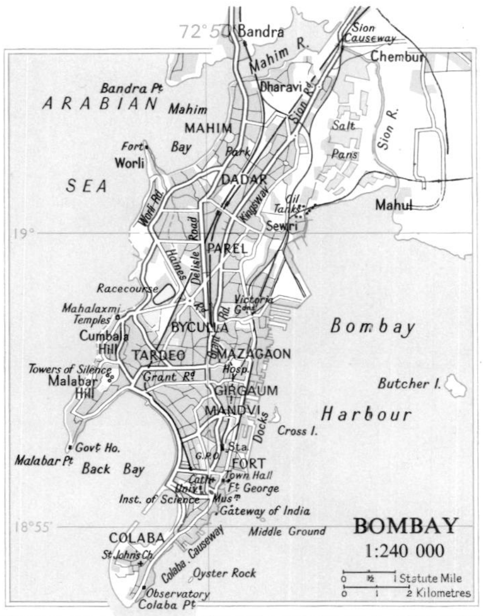

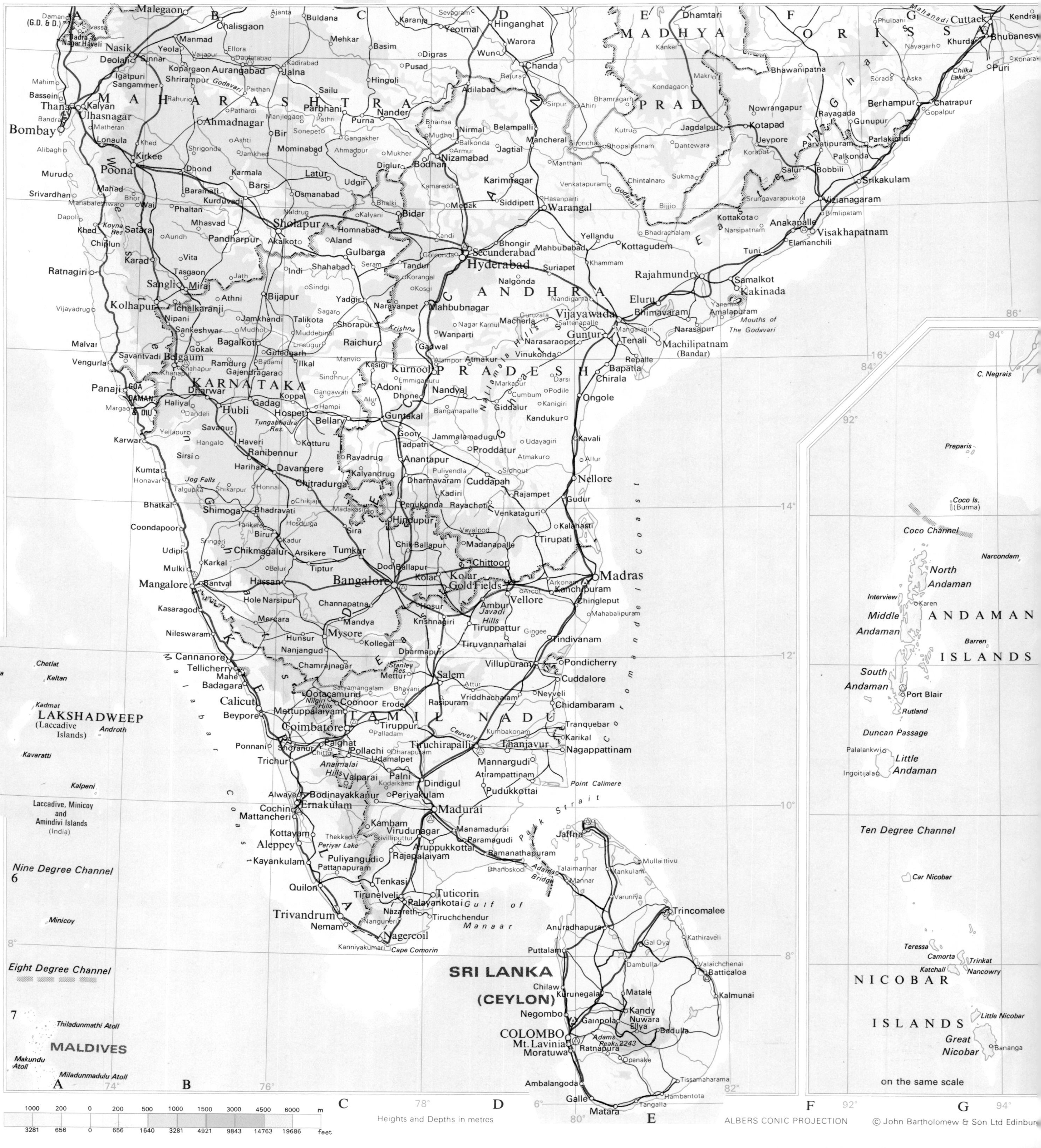

KARACHI
1:240 000

BOMBAY
1:240 000

DELHI
1:240 000

CALCUTTA
1:240 000

MAHARASHTRA

MADHYA PRADESH

ORISSA

ANDHRA PRADESH

KARNATAKA

TAMIL NADU

LAKSHADWEEP
(Laccadive Islands)

Laccadive, Minicoy and Amindivi Islands
(India)

Nine Degree Channel

Eight Degree Channel

MALDIVES

ANDAMAN ISLANDS

NICOBAR ISLANDS

North Andaman
Middle Andaman
South Andaman
Port Blair
Rutland
Duncan Passage
Little Andaman
Ten Degree Channel
Car Nicobar
Great Nicobar
Little Nicobar

Coco Channel

SRI LANKA
(CEYLON)

COLOMBO

on the same scale

1:6 M
miles km

Heights and Depths in metres

ALBERS CONIC PROJECTION

© John Bartholomew & Son Ltd Edinburgh

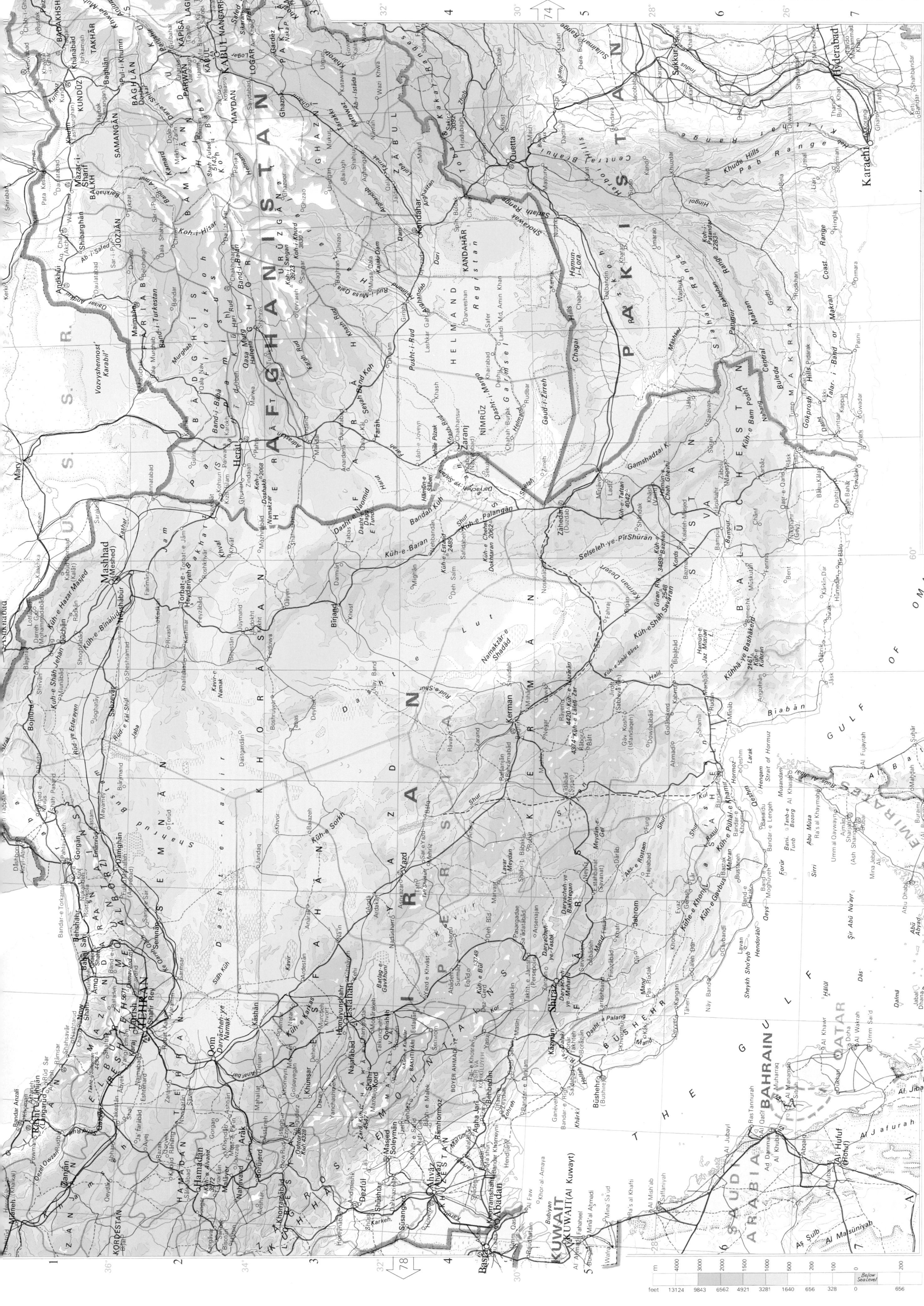

IRAN
AFGHANISTAN
PAKISTAN
TEHRAN
Mashhad (Meshed)
Herat
Kandahar
Quetta
Karachi
Hyderabad
Kerman
Yazd
Eşfahān
Shīrāz
Abadan
KUWAIT
BAHRAIN
QATAR
OMAN
UNITED ARAB EMIRATES
GULF OF OMAN
THE GULF
SAUDI ARABIA
Muscat
1:6M
CONIC PROJECTION
Heights in metres
Longitude East of Greenwich

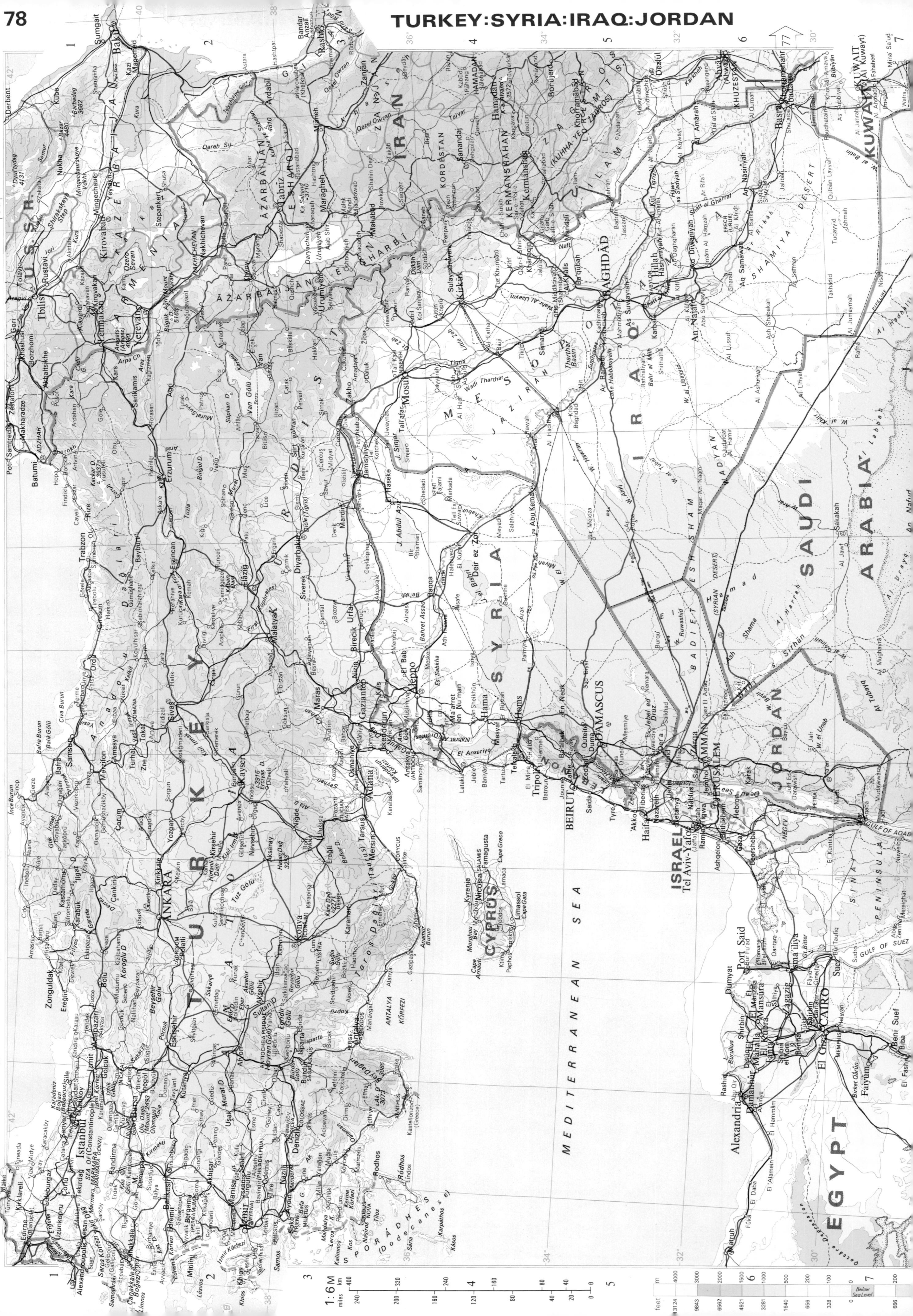

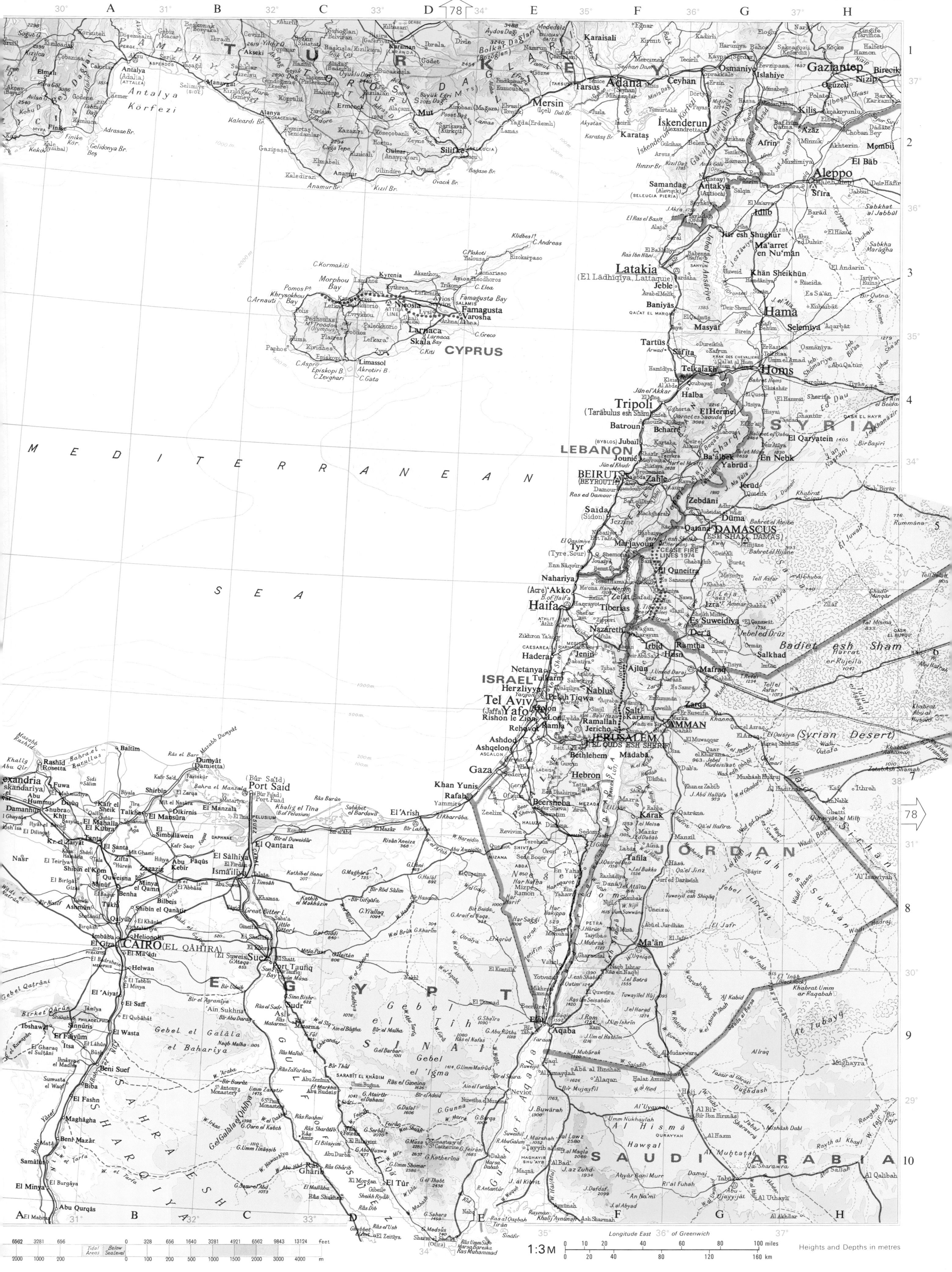
TURKEY
CYPRUS
LEBANON
ISRAEL
SYRIA
JORDAN
EGYPT
SAUDI ARABIA
M E D I T E R R A N E A N
S E A
SINAI
Adana
Mersin
Tarsus
Antalya
Gaziantep
İskenderun
Aleppo
Antakya
Latakia
Hama
Homs
Tripoli
Beirut
Damascus
Haifa
Tel Aviv Yafo
Jerusalem
Amman
Gaza
Port Said
Cairo (El Qahira)
Suez
Nicosia
Famagusta
Larnaca
Limassol
Akaba
Eilat
Ma'ān
Karak
Nablus
Hebron
Beersheba
El 'Arish
Bethlehem
Jericho
Es Suweidiya
Der'a
Irbid
Tiberias
Nazareth
Sidon
Tyr
Gulf of Suez
Gulf of Aqaba
Badiet esh Sham
(Syrian Desert)
1:3M
Longitude East 36° of Greenwich
Heights and Depths in metres

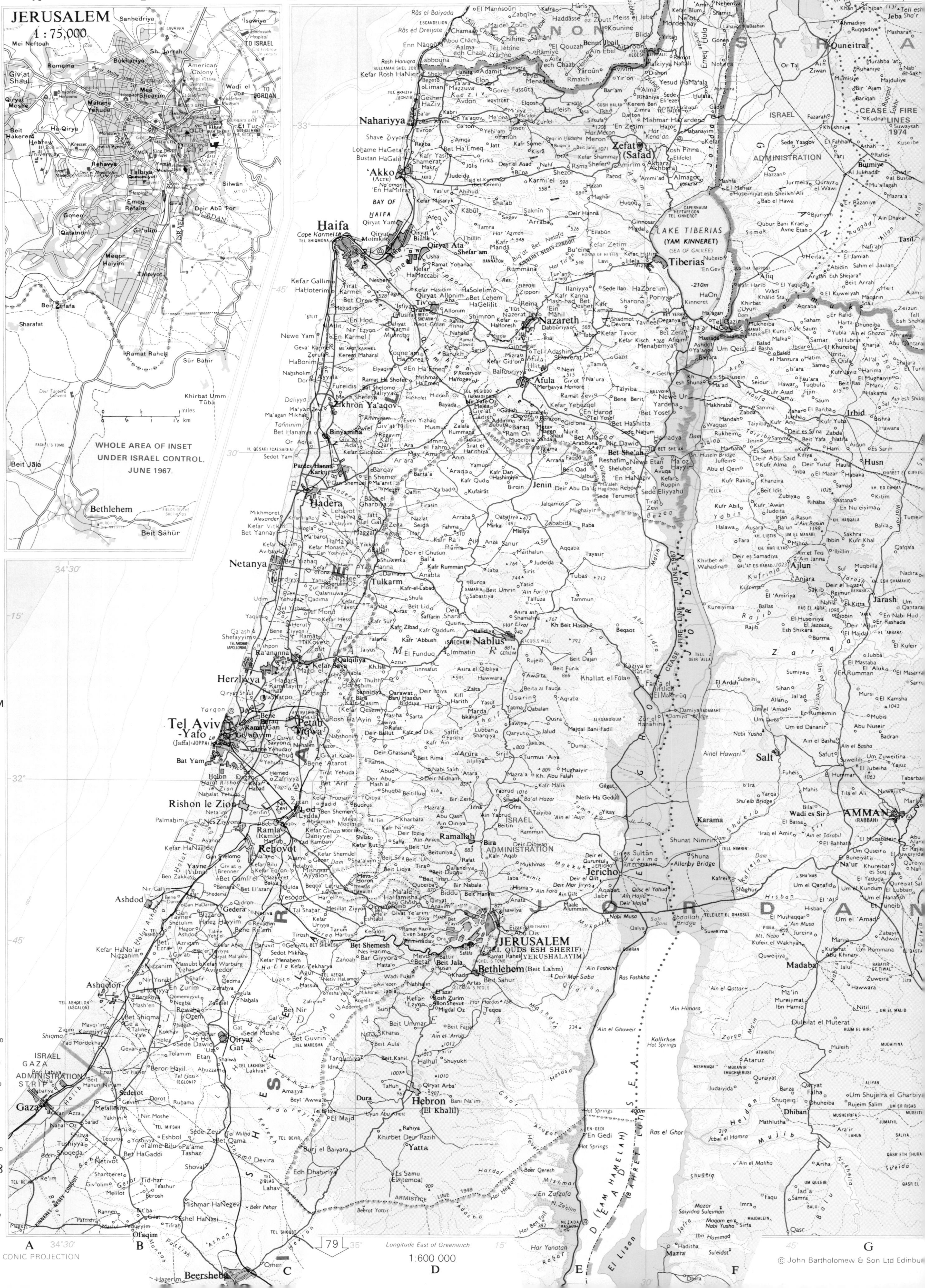
JERUSALEM
1 : 75,000
WHOLE AREA OF INSET UNDER ISRAEL CONTROL, JUNE 1967.
Mei Neftoah
Romema
Giv'at Shaul
Qiryat Moshe
Bukhariya
Mea Shearim
Mahane Yehuda
Sh. Jarrah
Wadi el Joz
Et Tur
Beit Hakerem
Ha-Qirya
Rehavya
Talbiya
Silwān
Gonen
(Qatamon)
Emeq Refaim
Deir Abū Tor
Ge'ulim
Meqor Haiyim
Talpiyot
Beit Zefafa
Sharafat
Ramat Rahel
Sūr Bāhir
Khirbat Umm Tūba
Beit Jāla
Bethlehem
Beit Sāhūr
TO ISRAEL
TO JORDAN
LEBANON
SYRIA
ISRAEL ADMINISTRATION
CEASE FIRE LINES 1974
DEMILITARIZED ZONE
Nahariyya
'Akko (Acre)
BAY OF HAIFA
Haifa
Cape Karmel
Qiryat Ata
Shefar'am
Zefat (Safad)
LAKE TIBERIAS (YAM KINNERET) (SEA OF GALILEE)
Tiberias
Nazareth
Afula
Beit She'an
Jenin
Hadera
Netanya
Tulkarm
Nablus
Herzliyya
Tel Aviv-Yafo
Bat Yam
Petah Tiqwa
Rishon le Zion
Lod
Ramla
Rehovot
Ashdod
Ashqelon
Gaza
ISRAEL GAZA ADMINISTRATION STRIP
Qiryat Gat
Ramallah
Jericho
JERUSALEM (EL QUDS ESH SHERIF) (YERUSHALAYIM)
Bethlehem (Beit Lahm)
Hebron (El Khalil)
Beersheba
Dimona
Irbid
Ajlun
Jarash
Salt
AMMAN (RABBAH)
Madaba
Dhiban
Karak
Mazra
JORDAN
En Gedi
BAHRET LUT (YAM HAMELAH)
1:0.6M
1:600 000
CONIC PROJECTION
Longitude East of Greenwich
© John Bartholomew & Son Ltd Edinburgh

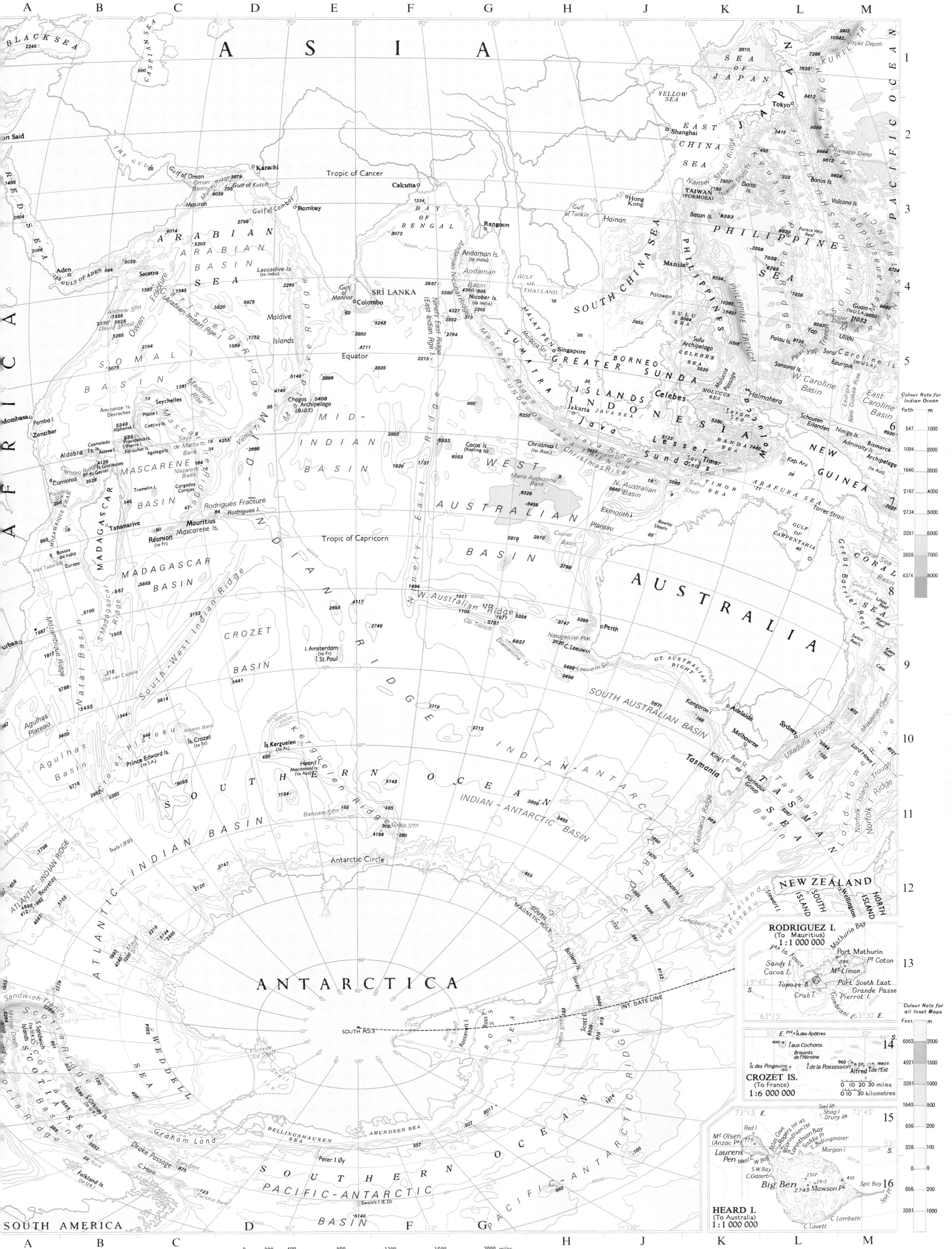

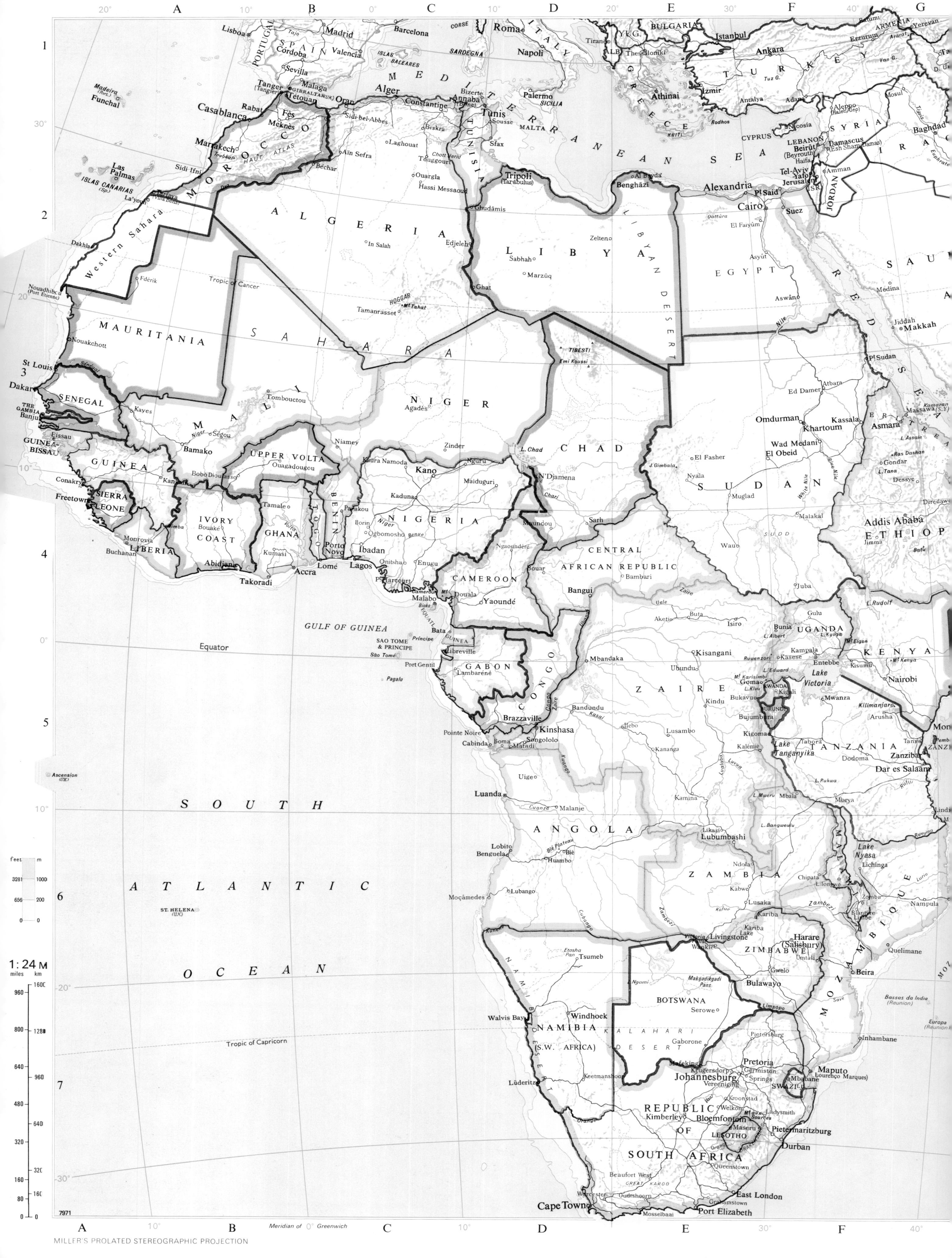

A map of Africa. Geographic labels visible include:

Grid columns (top): A 20° B 10° C 0° D 10° E 20° F 30° G 40°

Europe / Mediterranean:
Lisboa, Madrid, Barcelona, PORTUGAL, SPAIN, Valencia, CORSE, SARDEGNA, Roma, Napoli, ITALY, ALB, YUG, BULGARIA, Istanbul, Ankara, ARMENIA, Yerevan, Ararat, Erzurum, Tirano, Thessaloniki, GREECE, Athinai, Izmir, TURKEY, Van, Mosul, Córdoba, Sevilla, Málaga, Valencia, ISLAS BALEARES, Palermo, SICILIA, MALTA, Rodhos, KRITI, CYPRUS, Nicosia, Aleppo (Halab), SYRIA, Baghdad, Madeira, Funchal, Tanger (Tangier), Tétouan, Rabat, Casablanca, Fès, Meknès, Marrakech, Oran, Alger, Constantine, Annaba (Bône), Tunis, Bizerte, Sousse, Sfax, MALTA, Tripoli (Tarabulus), Benghazi, Al Bayda, Alexandria, Pt Said, Cairo, Suez, Beirût (Beyrouth), Haifa, Damascus (Esh Sham/Damas), Amman, Tel-Aviv, Yafo, Jerusalem, JORDAN, LEBANON, Medina, Jiddah, Makkah, SAUDI

North / West Africa:
Las Palmas, ISLAS CANARIAS (SP), Sidi Ifni, La'youn, Villa Bella, MOROCCO, HAUT ATLAS, Troubkal, Sidi bel-Abbès, Laghouat, Chott Melrhir, Touggourt, Béchar, Aïn Sefra, Ouargla, Ghudâmis, In Salah, Edjeleh, Ghat, Sabhah, Marzûq, LIBYA, Zelten, EGYPT, El Faiyûm, Asyût, Aswân, Qattâra, LIBYAN DESERT, Dakhla, Fdérik, Tropic of Cancer, MAURITANIA, Nouadhibou (Port Etienne), Nouakchott, SAHARA, HOGGAR, Mt Tahat, Tamanrasset, TIBESTI, Emi Koussi, NIGER, Agadès, L. Chad, CHAD, SUDAN, Pt Sudan, Jiddah, Massawa (S.Y), ERITREA, Asmara, L'Assale, Ras Dashan, Gondar, L. Tana, Dessye, Diredawa, Addis Abäba, ETHIOPIA, Jimma, Batu

Sahel / Sudan region:
St Louis, Dakar, SENEGAL, THE GAMBIA, Banjul, Bissau, GUINEA-BISSAU, Conakry, GUINEA, Freetown, SIERRA LEONE, Kindia, Monrovia, LIBERIA, Buchanan, IVORY COAST, Bouaké, GHANA, Kumasi, Abidjan, Takoradi, Accra, Lomé, TOGO, BENIN, Porto Novo, Kayes, Ségou, Bamako, MALI, Tombouctou, Niger, Bobo Dioulasso, UPPER VOLTA, Ouagadougou, Tamale, Niamey, Kaura Namoda, Kano, Zinder, Nguru, Maiduguri, Kaduna, Ibadan, Ogbomosho, Ilorin, Benue, NIGERIA, Lagos, Enugu, Onitsha, Port Harcourt, N'Djamena, Chari, Maundou, Sarh, Ed Damer, Atbara, Omdurman, Khartoum, Kassala, Wad Medani, El Obeid, El Fasher, Nyala, Muglad, Malakal, SUDD, Wau, Juba, Gulu

Central / Equatorial:
CAMEROON, Douala, Yaoundé, Mt Cameroun, Malabo, Bioko, EQ GUINEA, Bata, Libreville, GABON, Lambaréné, Port Gentil, Pagalu, SAO TOME & PRINCIPE, Principe, Sao Tomé, Equator, GULF OF GUINEA, Souar, Ngaoundéré, CENTRAL AFRICAN REPUBLIC, Bambari, Bangui, Uele, Aketi, Buta, Isiro, Mbandaka, Kisangani, ZAIRE, Ubundu, Kindu, CONGO, Brazzaville, Kinshasa, Pointe Noire, Cabinda, Boma, Matadi, Songololo, Uige, Bandundu, Kasai, Hebo, Lusambo, Kananga, Kamina, Mt Karisimbi, Goma, L. Kivu, RWANDA, Kigali, BURUNDI, Bujumbura, Kigoma, UGANDA, Kampala, Entebbe, Kasese, Ruwenzori, L. Albert, L. Edward, Mt Elgon, KENYA, Nairobi, Kisumu, Lake Victoria, Mwanza, Mt Kenya, Kilimanjaro, Arusha, TANZANIA, Tabora, Dodoma, Zanzibar, Dar es Salaam, L. Rudolf, Bunia

Southern Africa:
Luanda, Malanje, ANGOLA, Lubumbashi, Likasi, Kabwe, Lobito, Benguela, Bié Plateau, Huambo, Moçâmedes, Lubango, Kalémie, Lake Tanganyika, L. Mweru, Mbala, L. Bangweulu, Ndola, ZAMBIA, Lusaka, Kabwe, Kafue, Zambezi, Mbeya, Chipata, Lake Nyasa, Lichinga, MALAWI, Lilongwe, Zomba, Blantyre, Nampula, MOZAMBIQUE, Quelimane, Beira, Cabora, Kariba, Lake Kariba, Victoria Falls, Livingstone, Wankie, ZIMBABWE, Harare (Salisbury), Gwelo, Bulawayo, Umtali, Save, Inhambane, BOTSWANA, Serowe, Gaborone, Makgadikgadi Pans, Ngami, KALAHARI DESERT, Etosha Pan, Tsumeb, NAMIBIA (S.W. AFRICA), Walvis Bay, Windhoek, Lüderitz, Keetmanshoop, Tropic of Capricorn, Mafeking, Pietersburg, Pretoria, Johannesburg, Germiston, Springs, Krugersdorp, Vereeniging, Mbabane, SWAZILAND, Maputo (Lourenço Marques), Kroonstad, Welkom, Kimberley, Bloemfontein, LESOTHO, Maseru, Pietermaritzburg, Durban, REPUBLIC OF SOUTH AFRICA, GREAT KAROO, Beaufort West, Queenstown, Ladysmith, Oudtshoorn, Worcester, Mosselbaai, Cape Town, Port Elizabeth, East London, Grahamstown, Orange, Limpopo, Bassas da India (Réunion), Europa (Réunion)

Oceans:
SOUTH ATLANTIC OCEAN, Ascension (UK), ST. HELENA (UK), MEDITERRANEAN SEA, RED SEA

Scale / legend:
feet m, 3281 1000, 656 200, 0 0, 1:24 M, miles km, 960 1600, 800 1280, 640 960, 480, 320, 160, 80, 0

Grid (bottom): A 10° B C 0° Meridian of 0° Greenwich D 10° E 20° F 30° G 40°

MILLER'S PROLATED STEREOGRAPHIC PROJECTION

7971

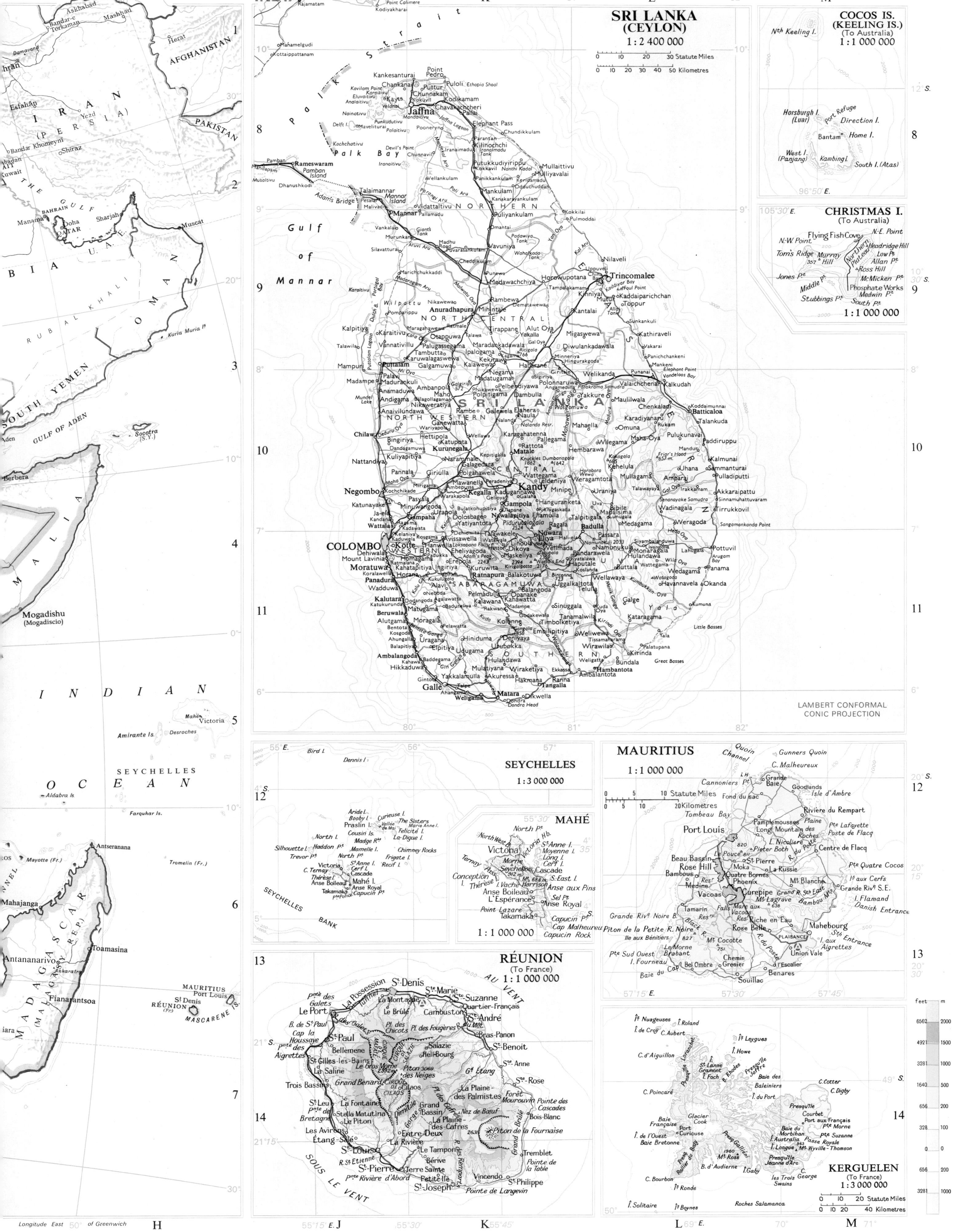

SRI LANKA
(CEYLON)
1:2 400 000

COCOS IS.
(KEELING IS.)
(To Australia)
1:1 000 000

CHRISTMAS I.
(To Australia)
1:1 000 000

LAMBERT CONFORMAL
CONIC PROJECTION

SEYCHELLES
1:3 000 000

MAHÉ
1:1 000 000

MAURITIUS
1:1 000 000

RÉUNION
(To France)
1:1 000 000

KERGUELEN
(To France)
1:3 000 000

Heights in metres

© John Bartholomew & Son Ltd Edinburgh

Longitude East of Greenwich

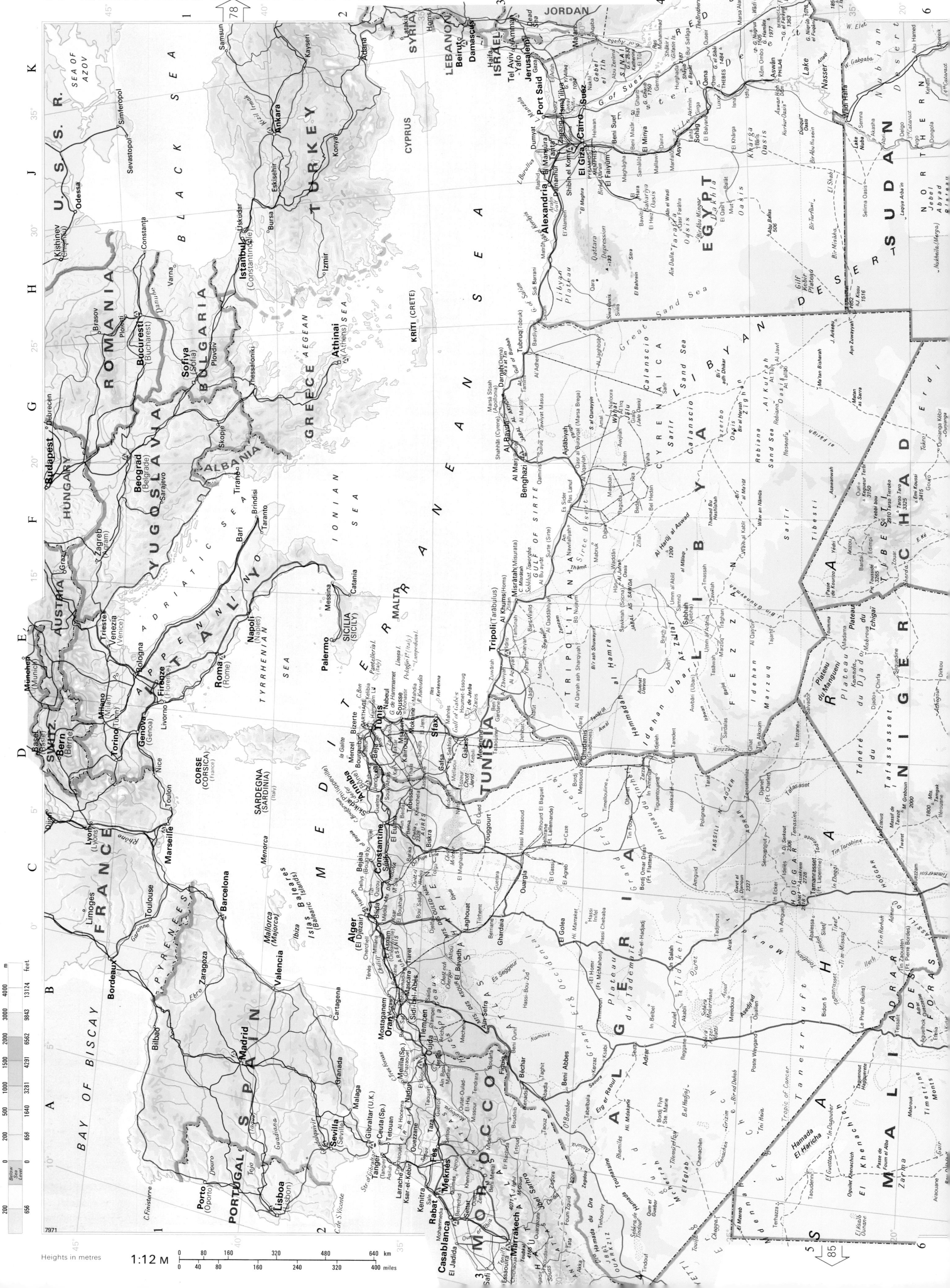
78
85
FRANCE
SPAIN
PORTUGAL
ITALY
SWITZ.
AUSTRIA
HUNGARY
YUGOSLAVIA
ROMANIA
BULGARIA
ALBANIA
GREECE
TURKEY
U.S.S.R.
CYPRUS
LEBANON
SYRIA
ISRAEL
JORDAN
MOROCCO
ALGERIA
TUNISIA
LIBYA
EGYPT
SUDAN
CHAD
NIGER
MALI
BAY OF BISCAY
MEDITERRANEAN SEA
BLACK SEA
SEA OF AZOV
ADRIATIC SEA
TYRRHENIAN SEA
IONIAN SEA
AEGEAN SEA
Madrid
Lisboa
Barcelona
Marseille
Roma (Rome)
Napoli (Naples)
Palermo
Alger (El Djezair)
Tunis
Tripoli
Benghazi
Cairo
Alexandria
Athinai (Athens)
Istanbul (Constantinople)
Ankara
Beograd (Belgrade)
Bucuresti (Bucharest)
Sofiya (Sofia)
Budapest
Heights in metres
1:12 M
km
miles

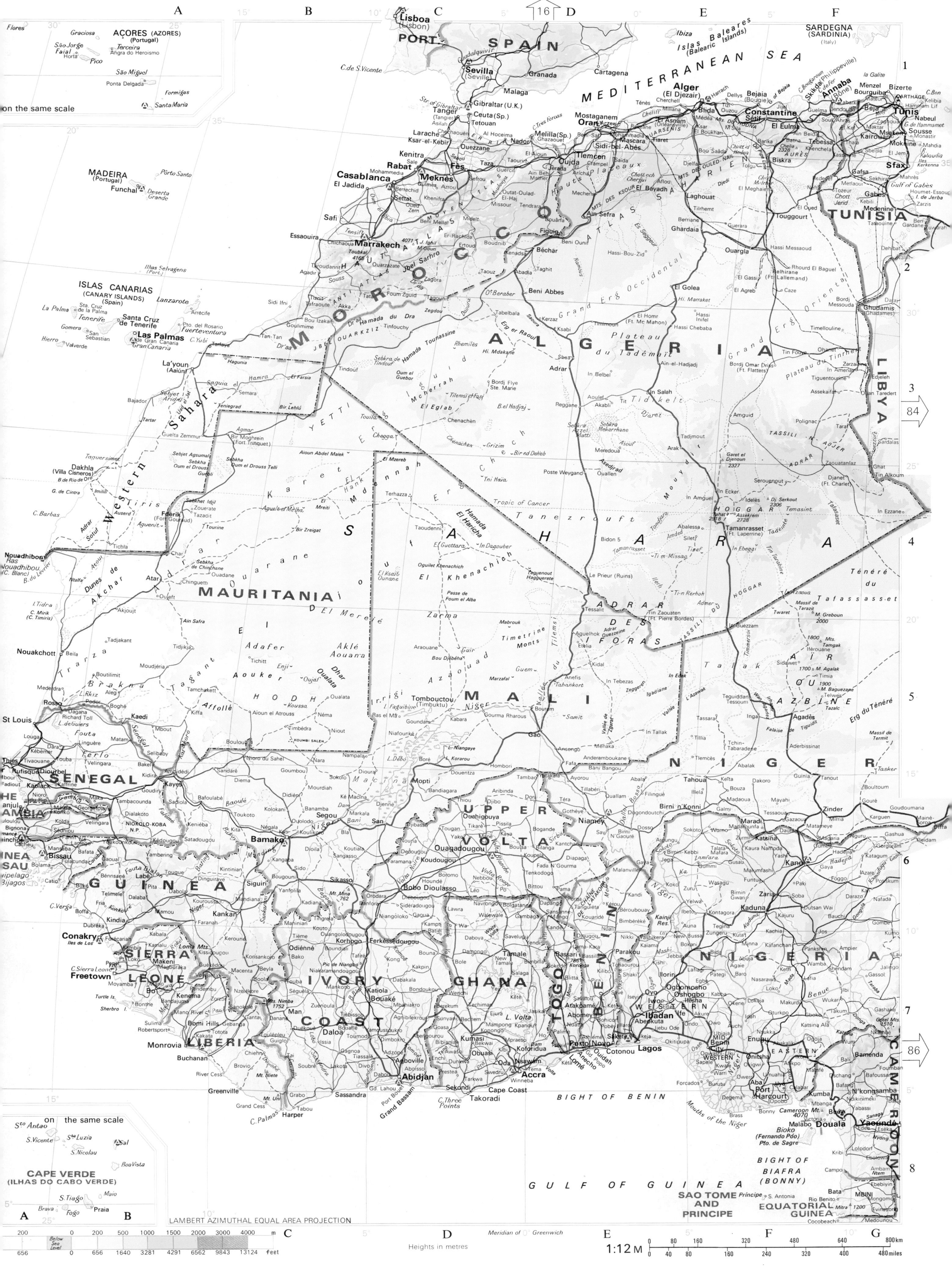
AÇORES (AZORES)
MADEIRA (Portugal)
ISLAS CANARIAS (CANARY ISLANDS) (Spain)
on the same scale
CAPE VERDE (ILHAS DO CABO VERDE)
PORT.
SPAIN
Lisboa (Lisbon)
Sevilla (Seville)
Granada
Cartagena
Ibiza
Islas Baleares (Balearic Islands)
SARDEGNA (SARDINIA) (Italy)
MEDITERRANEAN SEA
Alger (El Djezair)
Oran
Constantine
Annaba (Bône)
Tunis
Sfax
Gabès
TUNISIA
Rabat
Casablanca
Meknès
Fès
Marrakech
Tanger
Ceuta (Sp.)
Melilla (Sp.)
MOROCCO
ALGERIA
LIBYA
Western Sahara
La'youn (Aaiún)
Dakhla (Villa Cisneros)
Nouadhibou
Nouakchott
MAURITANIA
SAHARA
MALI
Tombouctou (Timbuktu)
Gao
NIGER
Niamey
Agadès
Zinder
SENEGAL
St Louis
Dakar
GAMBIA
GUINEA BISSAU
Bissau
GUINEA
Conakry
SIERRA LEONE
Freetown
LIBERIA
Monrovia
IVORY COAST
Abidjan
UPPER VOLTA
Ouagadougou
Bamako
GHANA
Accra
Kumasi
TOGO
Lomé
BENIN
Porto Novo
Cotonou
NIGERIA
Lagos
Ibadan
Kano
Kaduna
CAMEROON
Douala
Yaoundé
BIGHT OF BENIN
BIGHT OF BIAFRA (BONNY)
GULF OF GUINEA
SAO TOME AND PRINCIPE
EQUATORIAL GUINEA
Bioko (Fernando Póo)
Tropic of Cancer
Tanezrouft
Grand Erg Occidental
Grand Erg Oriental
HOGGAR
Tamanrasset
Ténéré
AÏR
Niger
L. Volta
84
86
16
LAMBERT AZIMUTHAL EQUAL AREA PROJECTION
Meridian of Greenwich
Heights in metres
1:12 M

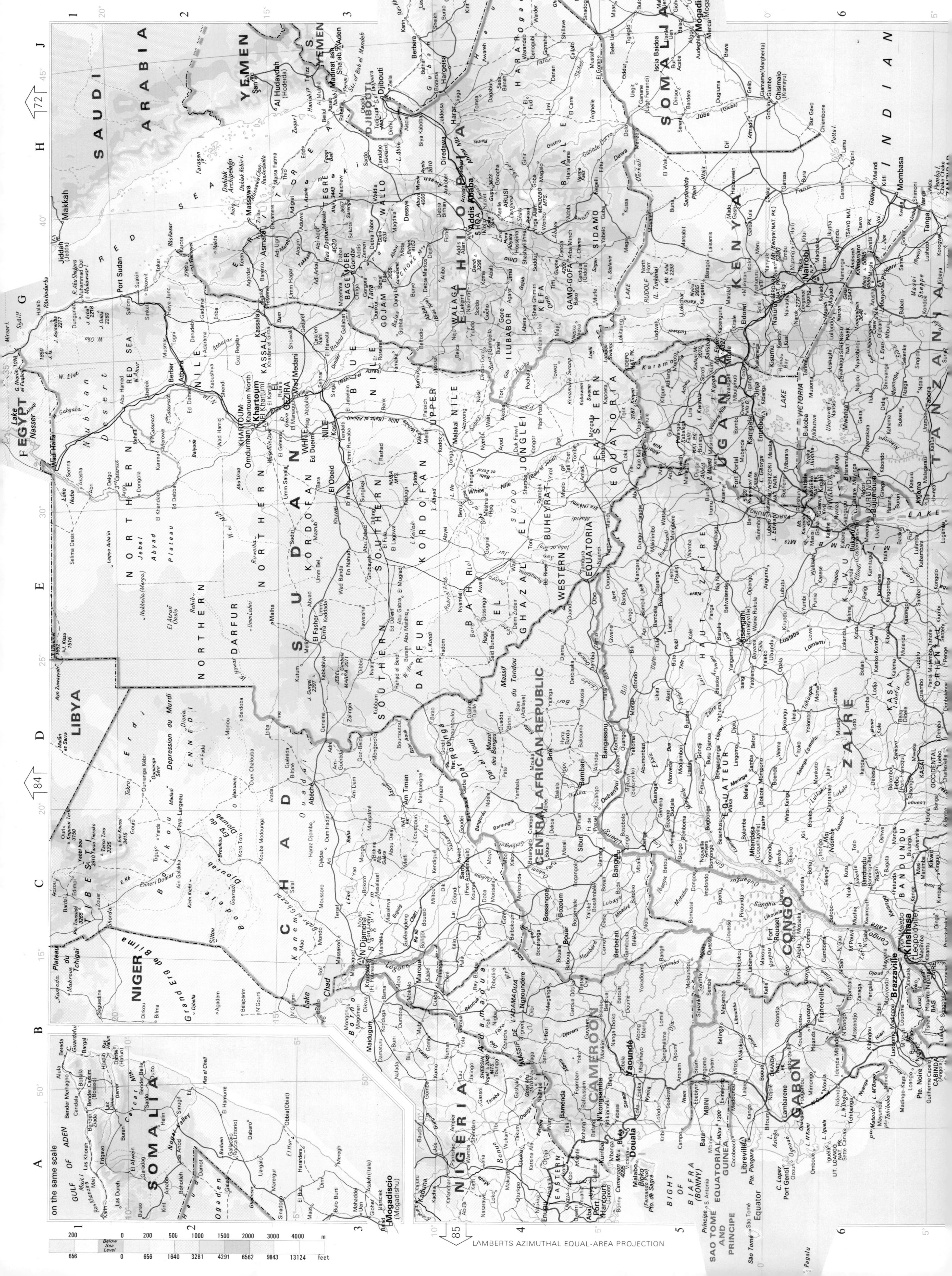
SAUDI ARABIA
YEMEN
S. YEMEN
DJIBOUTI
ETHIOPIA
SOMALIA
KENYA
UGANDA
RWANDA
BURUNDI
TANZANIA
INDIAN
SUDAN
CHAD
LIBYA
EGYPT
NIGER
NIGERIA
CAMEROON
CENTRAL AFRICAN REPUBLIC
ZAIRE
CONGO
GABON
CABINDA (Angola)
EQUATORIAL GUINEA
SAO TOME AND PRINCIPE
RED SEA
GULF OF ADEN
BIGHT OF BIAFRA (BONNY)
Lake Nasser
Lake Chad
LAKE VICTORIA
LAKE RUDOLF (L. Turkana)
Makkah
Jiddah (Jedda)
Port Sudan
Khartoum
Omdurman
Addis Ababa
Asmara
Djibouti
Hargeisa
Berbera
Mogadiscio (Mogadishu)
Nairobi
Mombasa
Kampala
Kigali
Bujumbura
Juba
El Obeid
Abéché
N'Djamena
Bangui
Yaoundé
Douala
Libreville
Brazzaville
Kinshasa
Malabo
Sao Tomé
on the same scale
SOMALIA
Below Sea Level
200 0 200 500 1000 1500 2000 3000 4000 m
656 0 656 1640 3281 4291 6562 9843 13124 feet
LAMBERTS AZIMUTHAL EQUAL-AREA PROJECTION

72
84
85

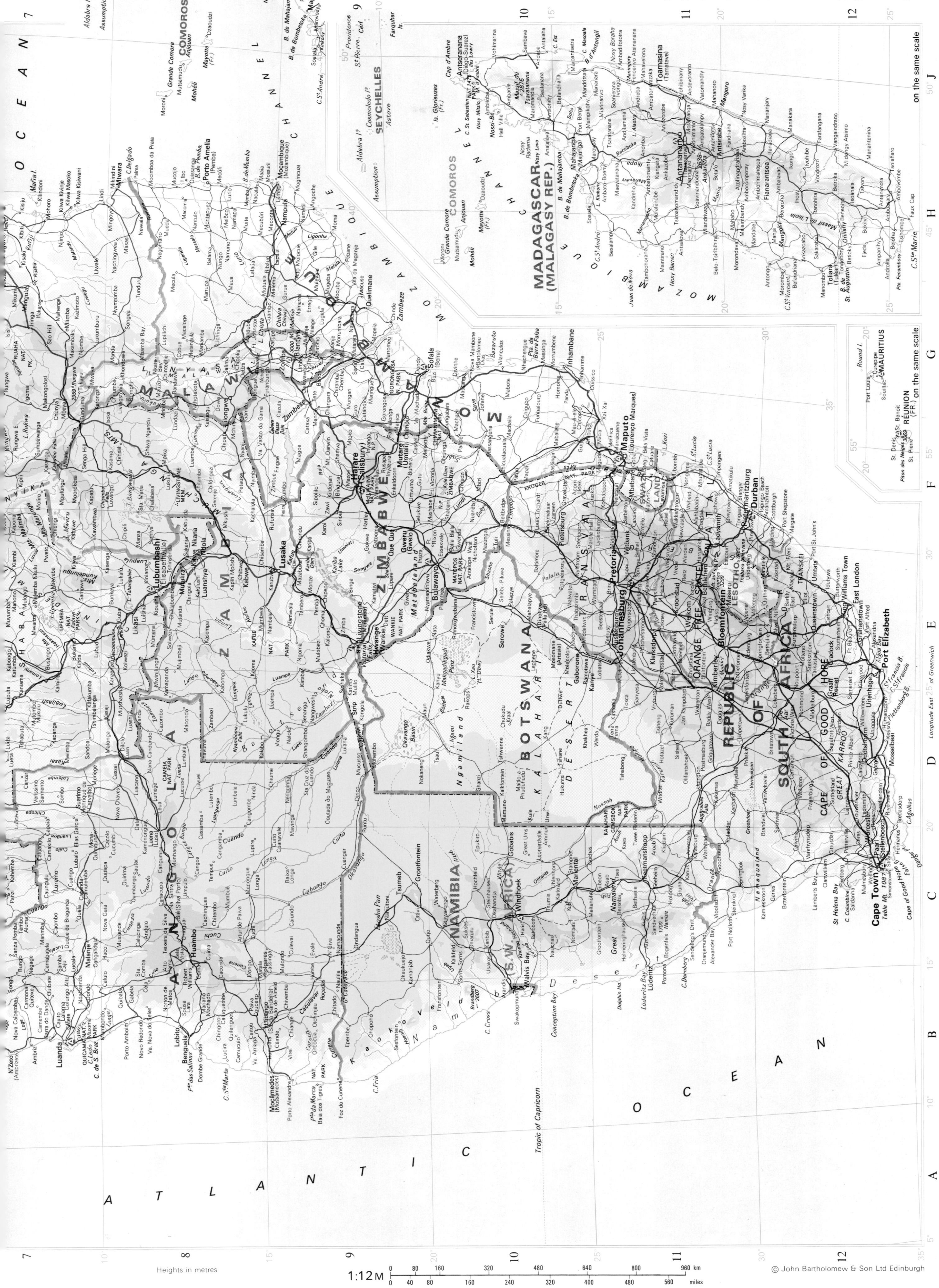

MADAGASCAR
(MALAGASY REP.)

COMOROS

SEYCHELLES

on the same scale

MAURITIUS
RÉUNION
(Fr.) on the same scale

ANGOLA

ZAMBIA

MALAWI

MOZAMBIQUE

ZIMBABWE

NAMIBIA
(S.W. AFRICA)

BOTSWANA

KALAHARI DESERT

REPUBLIC OF SOUTH AFRICA

TRANSVAAL

ORANGE FREE STATE

LESOTHO

SWAZILAND

NATAL

CAPE OF GOOD HOPE

Luanda
Benguela
Lobito
Huambo
Lusaka
Harare (Salisbury)
Bulawayo
Maputo (Lourenço Marques)
Windhoek
Gaborone
Pretoria
Johannesburg
Bloemfontein
Kimberley
Maseru
Durban
Pietermaritzburg
Port Elizabeth
East London
Cape Town
Nampula
Beira
Quelimane
Blantyre
Lilongwe
Antananarivo
Toamasina
(Tamatave)
Fianarantsoa
Toliara
(Tuléar)

ATLANTIC OCEAN

INDIAN OCEAN

MOZAMBIQUE CHANNEL

Tropic of Capricorn

Heights in metres

1:12 M

0 80 160 240 320 400 480 560 640 720 800 880 960 km

0 40 80 120 160 200 240 280 320 360 400 440 480 520 560 miles

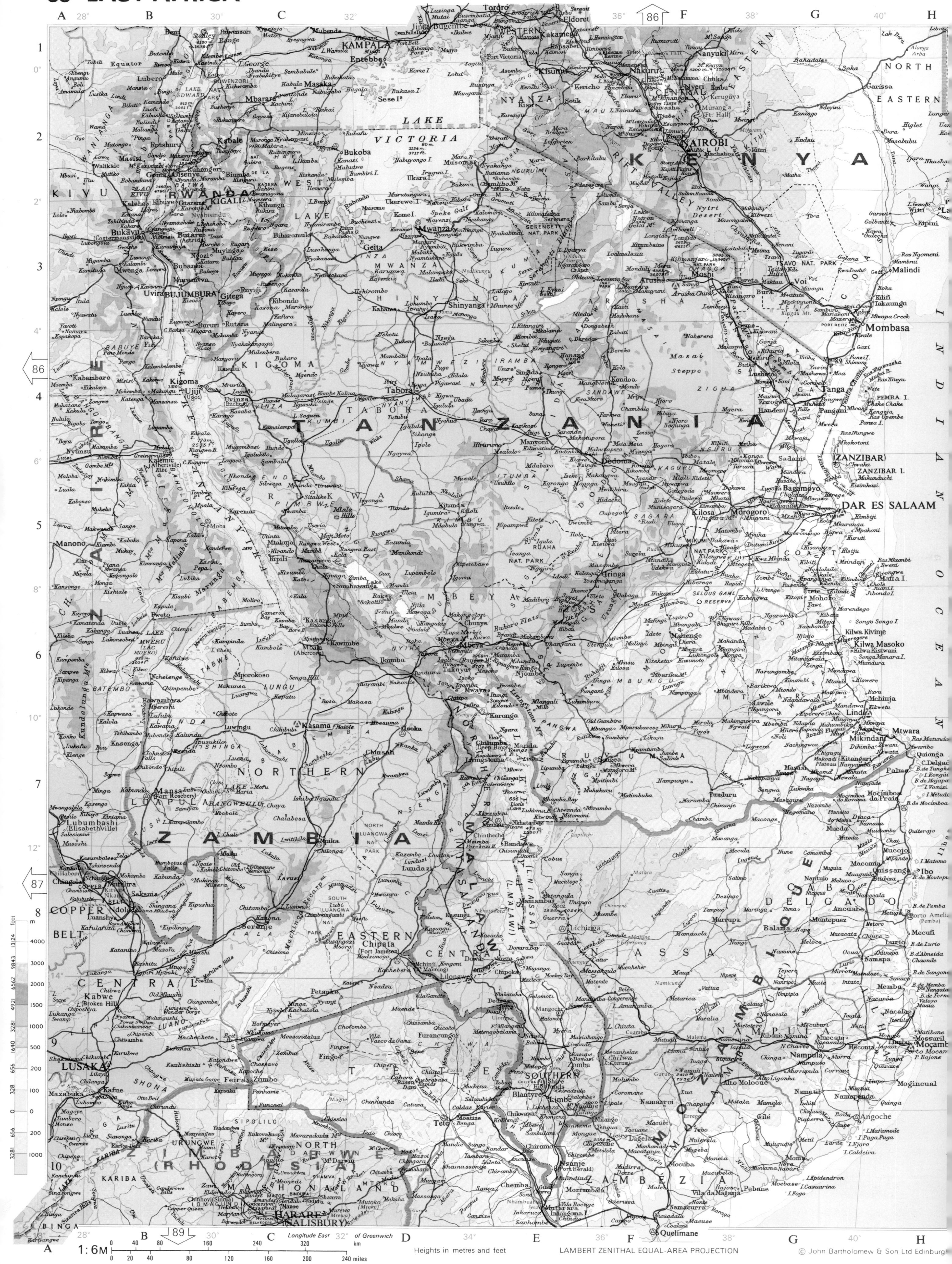

Heights in metres and feet

LAMBERT ZENITHAL EQUAL-AREA PROJECTION

© John Bartholomew & Son Ltd Edinburgh

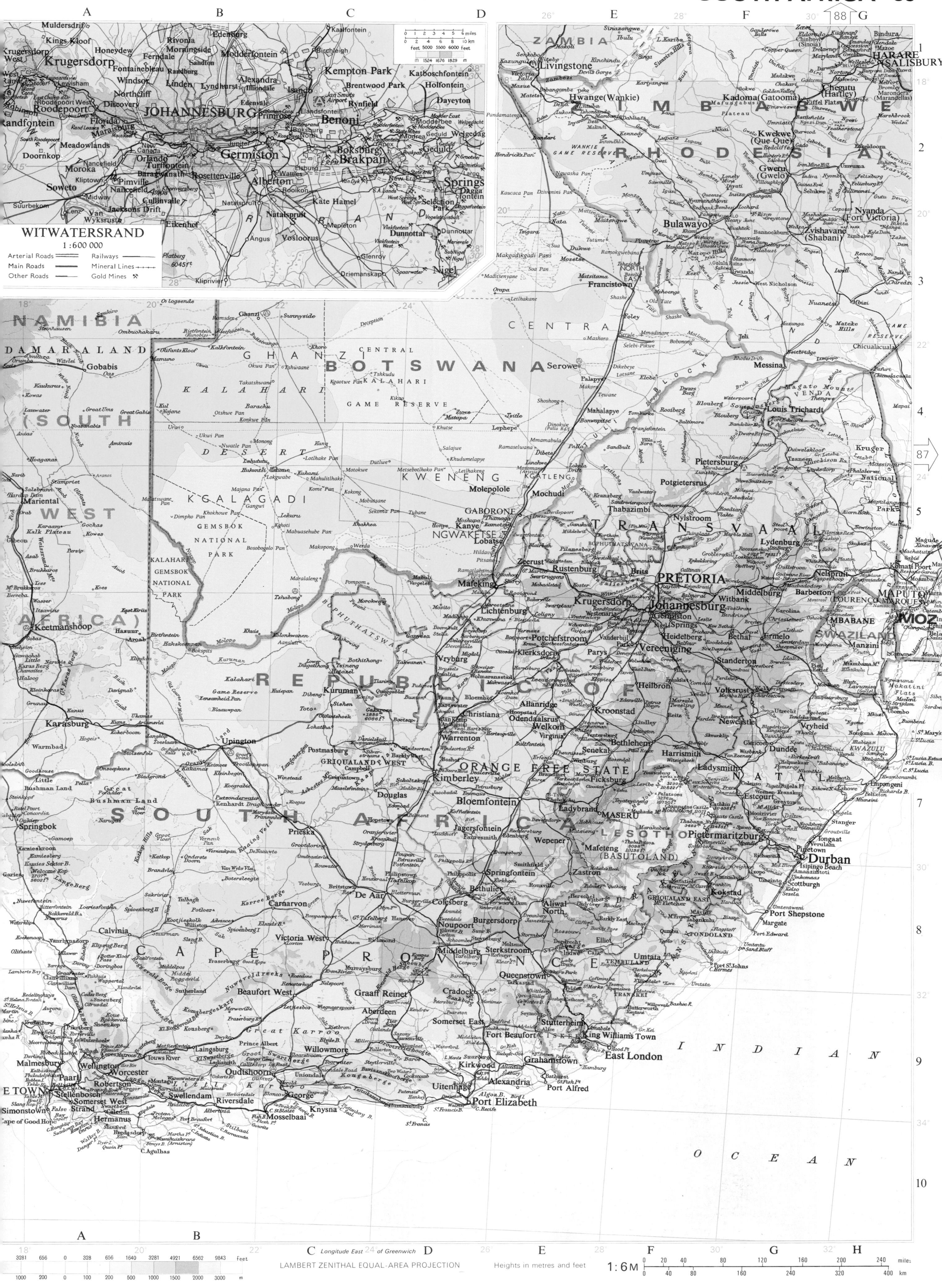

WITWATERSRAND
1:600 000

Arterial Roads ——— Railways ———
Main Roads ——— Mineral Lines ＋＋＋＋
Other Roads ——— Gold Mines ✕

LAMBERT ZENITHAL EQUAL-AREA PROJECTION

Longitude East of Greenwich

Heights in metres and feet

1:6 M

Feet 3281 656 3281 1640 3281 4921 6562 9843 feet
m 1000 200 0 100 500 1000 1500 2000 3000 m

miles 0 20 40 80 120 160 200 240
km 0 40 80 160 240 320 400 km

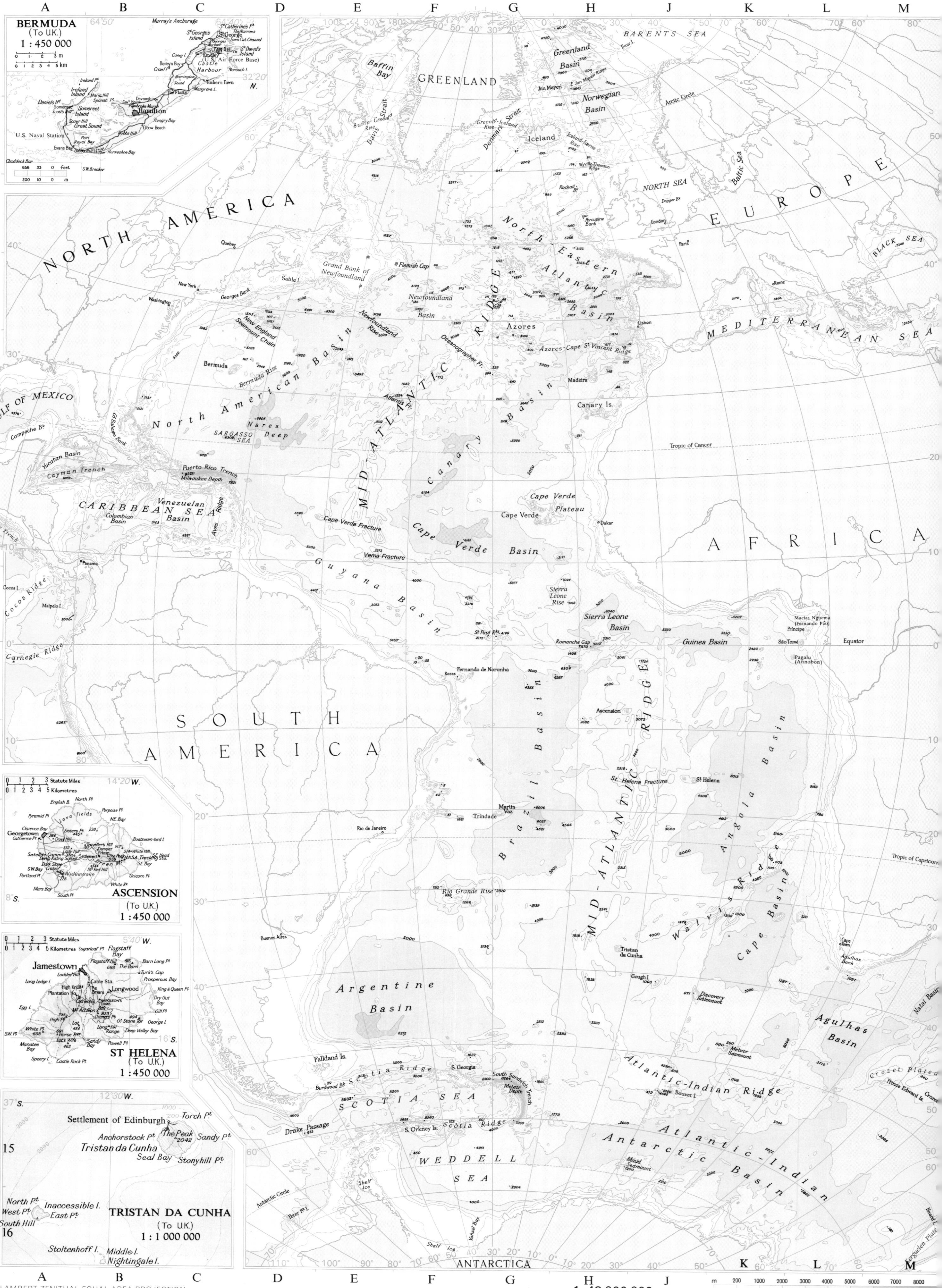

LAMBERT ZENITHAL EQUAL AREA PROJECTION

Heights and Depths in metres

1: 48 000 000

m	200	1000	2000	3000	4000	5000	6000	7000	8000
fathoms	109	547	1094	1640	2187	2734	3281	3828	4374

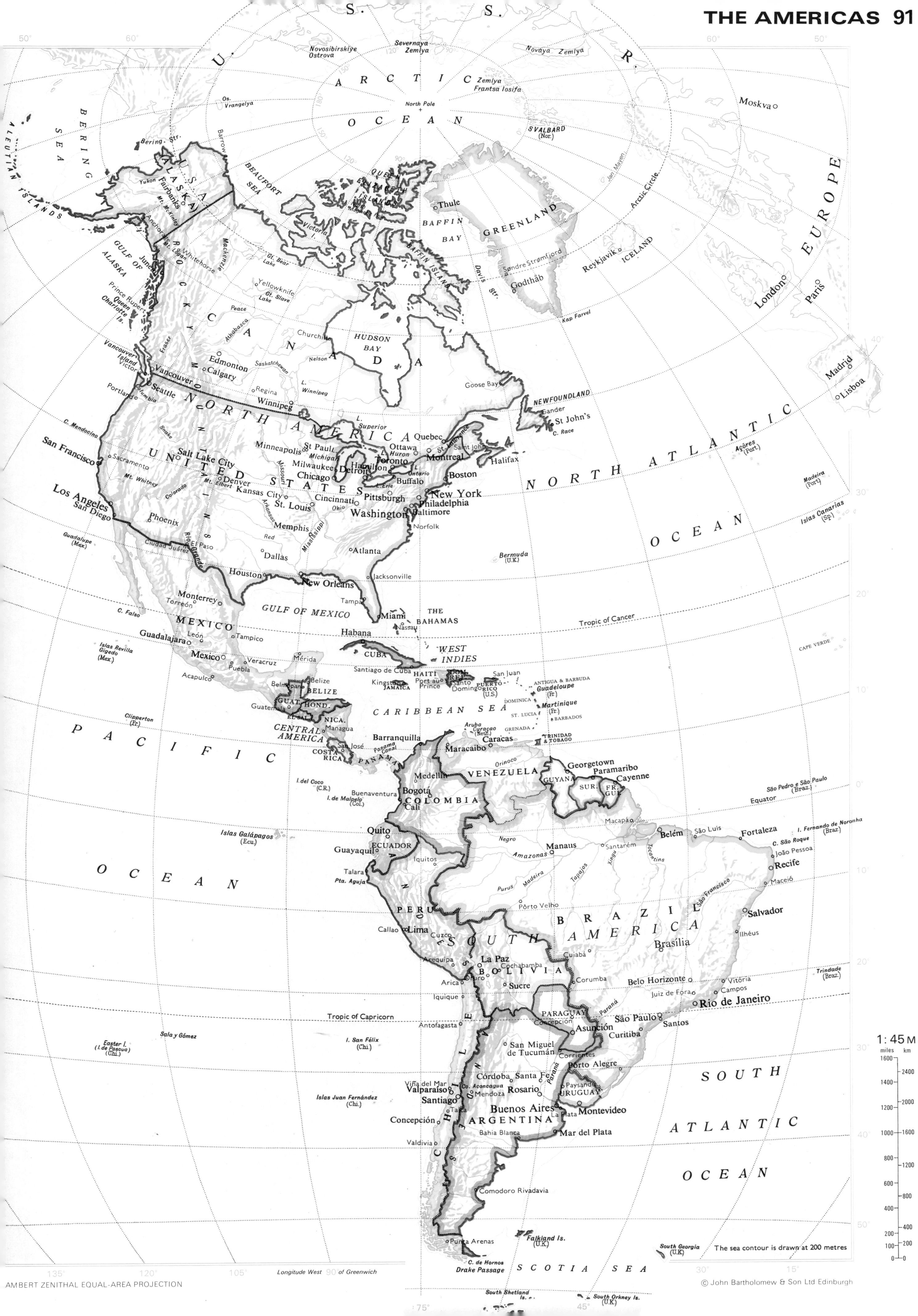

U. S. S. R.

ARCTIC OCEAN
North Pole +
Novosibirskiye Ostrova
Severnaya Zemlya
Zemlya Frantsa Iosifa
Novaya Zemlya
Moskva
Os. Vrangelya
SVALBARD (Nor.)

BERING SEA
ALEUTIAN ISLANDS
Bering Str.
BEAUFORT SEA
ALASKA
Barrow
Thule
GREENLAND
EUROPE
Fairbanks
Anchorage
Mt. McKinley
Juneau
GULF OF ALASKA
Yukon
R. Mackenzie
QUEEN ELIZABETH ISLANDS
BAFFIN BAY
Arctic Circle
Reykjavik
ICELAND
London
Paris
Gt. Bear L.
Whitehorse
Victoria I.
BAFFIN ISLAND
Søndre Strømfjord
Godthåb
Prince Rupert
Queen Charlotte Is.
Yellowknife
Gt. Slave L.
Davis Str.
Kap Farvel
Madrid
Lisboa
Vancouver Island
Vancouver
Victoria
Seattle
Portland
Fraser
Edmonton
Calgary
Peace
Athabasca
Saskatchewan
L. Athabasca
C A N A D A
Churchill
Nelson
HUDSON BAY
Goose Bay
NEWFOUNDLAND
Gander
St. John's
C. Race
NORTH ATLANTIC
Açores (Port.)
C. Mendocino
Regina
L. Winnipeg
Winnipeg
NORTH AMERICA
Quebec
Saint John
Halifax
Madeira (Port.)
San Francisco
Sacramento
Salt Lake City
UNITED STATES
Minneapolis
St. Paul
L. Superior
L. Michigan
L. Huron
Milwaukee
Chicago
Detroit
Hamilton
Toronto
L. Ontario
Montreal
L. Erie
Buffalo
Boston
New York
OCEAN
Mt. Whitney
Denver
Mt. Elbert
Kansas City
St. Louis
Cincinnati
Ohio
Pittsburgh
Philadelphia
Washington
Baltimore
Islas Canarias (Sp.)
Los Angeles
San Diego
Phoenix
Colorado
Memphis
Arkansas
Red
Mississippi
Norfolk
Guadalupe (Mex.)
Ciudad Juárez
El Paso
Rio Grande
Dallas
Atlanta
Jacksonville
Bermuda (U.K.)
Houston
New Orleans
Tampa
Monterrey
Torreón
GULF OF MEXICO
Miami
THE BAHAMAS
Nassau
Tropic of Cancer
CAPE VERDE
C. Falso
MEXICO
León
Tampico
Habana
CUBA
Islas Revilla Gigedo (Mex.)
Guadalajara
Mexico
Puebla
Veracruz
Mérida
Santiago de Cuba
HAITI
DOM. REP.
San Juan
ANTIGUA & BARBUDA
Acapulco
Belize
Kingston
JAMAICA
Port au Prince
Santo Domingo
PUERTO RICO (U.S.)
Guadeloupe (Fr.)
DOMINICA
Clipperton (Fr.)
BELMOPAN
BELIZE
GUAT.
HOND.
Guatemala
EL SAL.
NICA.
WEST INDIES
CARIBBEAN SEA
Martinique (Fr.)
ST. LUCIA
BARBADOS
CENTRAL AMERICA
Managua
Barranquilla
Aruba
Curaçao (Neth.)
GRENADA
TRINIDAD & TOBAGO
COSTA RICA
San José
Panama Canal
PANAMA
Caracas
PACIFIC
I. del Coco (C.R.)
Maracaibo
Medellín
VENEZUELA
GUYANA
Georgetown
Paramaribo
SUR.
Cayenne
FR. GUI.
Buenaventura
I. de Malpelo (Col.)
Bogotá
COLOMBIA
Cali
Orinoco
São Pedro e São Paulo (Braz.)
Equator
Islas Galápagos (Ecu.)
Quito
ECUADOR
Guayaquil
Iquitos
Negro
Macapá
Manaus
Amazonas
Santarém
Belém
São Luís
Fortaleza
C. São Roque
I. Fernando de Noronha (Braz.)
OCEAN
Talara
Pta. Aguja
P E R U
Purus
Madeira
Xingu
Tapajós
Tocantins
Pôrto Velho
João Pessoa
Recife
Maceió
Callao
Lima
Cuzco
BRAZIL
SOUTH AMERICA
São Francisco
Salvador
Ilhéus
Brasília
Belo Horizonte
Arequipa
La Paz
Cochabamba
Cuiabá
BOLIVIA
Sucre
Corumbá
Juiz de Fora
Vitória
Campos
Trindade (Braz.)
Arica
Oruro
Iquique
Tropic of Capricorn
PARAGUAY
Paraná
São Paulo
Rio de Janeiro
Santos
Antofagasta
Concepción
Asunción
Curitiba
Sala y Gómez
San Miguel de Tucumán
Corrientes
Pôrto Alegre
SOUTH
Easter I. (I. de Pascua) (Chi.)
I. San Félix (Chi.)
Córdoba
Santa Fe
Rosario
Paysandú
URUGUAY
Viña del Mar
Co. Aconcagua
Valparaíso
Santiago
Mendoza
Buenos Aires
La Plata
Montevideo
ATLANTIC
Islas Juan Fernández (Chi.)
Concepción
ARGENTINA
Mar del Plata
Valdivia
Bahía Blanca
OCEAN
Comodoro Rivadavia

1 : 45 M
miles   km
1600   2400
1400   2000
1200
1000   1600
800   1200
600   800
400
200   400
100   200
The sea contour is drawn at 200 metres

Punta Arenas
Falkland Is. (U.K.)
South Georgia (U.K.)
C. de Hornos
Drake Passage
SCOTIA SEA
South Shetland Is.
South Orkney Is. (U.K.)

AMBERT ZENITHAL EQUAL-AREA PROJECTION
Longitude West 90 of Greenwich

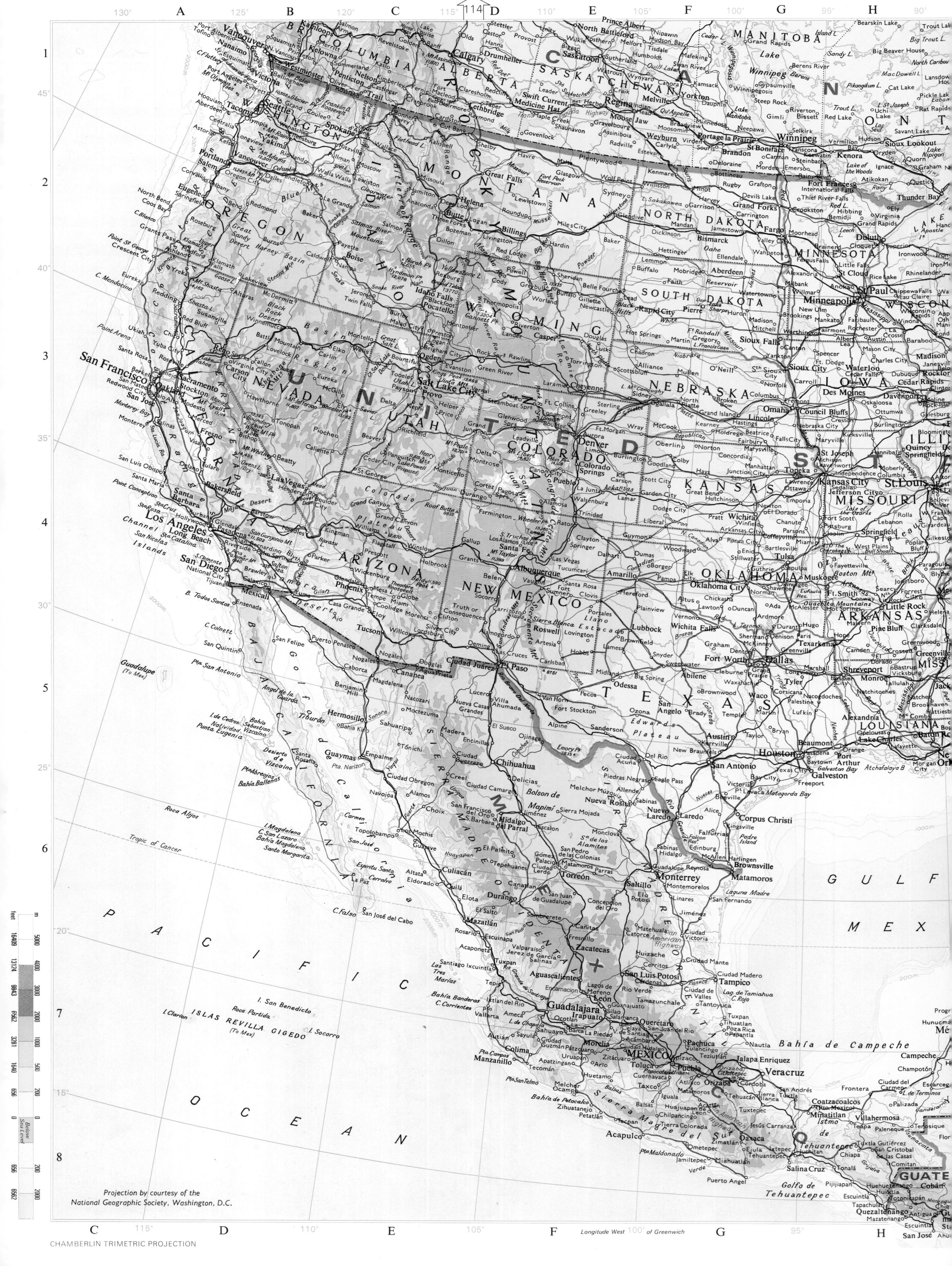

OCEAN

130°   125°   120°   115°   114°   110°   105°   100°   95°   90°

A   B   C   D   E   F   G   H

CANADA

BRITISH COLUMBIA   ALBERTA   SASKATCHEWAN   MANITOBA

WASHINGTON   MONTANA   NORTH DAKOTA   MINNESOTA

OREGON   IDAHO   WYOMING   SOUTH DAKOTA   WISCON

NEVADA   UTAH   NEBRASKA   IOWA

UNITED   COLORADO   KANSAS   MISSOURI   ILL

CALIFORNIA   ARIZONA   NEW MEXICO   OKLAHOMA   ARKANSAS   MISS

STATES   TEXAS   LOUISIANA

BAJA CALIFORNIA   SONORA   MEXICO

SIERRA MADRE OCCIDENTAL   SIERRA MADRE ORIENTAL

GULF MEX

PACIFIC   OCEAN

Tropic of Cancer

ISLAS REVILLA GIGEDO (To Mex)

Bahía de Campeche

GUATE

Projection by courtesy of the
National Geographic Society, Washington, D.C.

Longitude West of Greenwich

CHAMBERLIN TRIMETRIC PROJECTION

C   D   E   F   G   H
115°   110°   105°   100°   95°

feet   m
16409   5000
13124   4000
9843   3000
6562   2000
3281   1000
1640   500
656   200
0   Sea Level   0
656   200
6562   2000

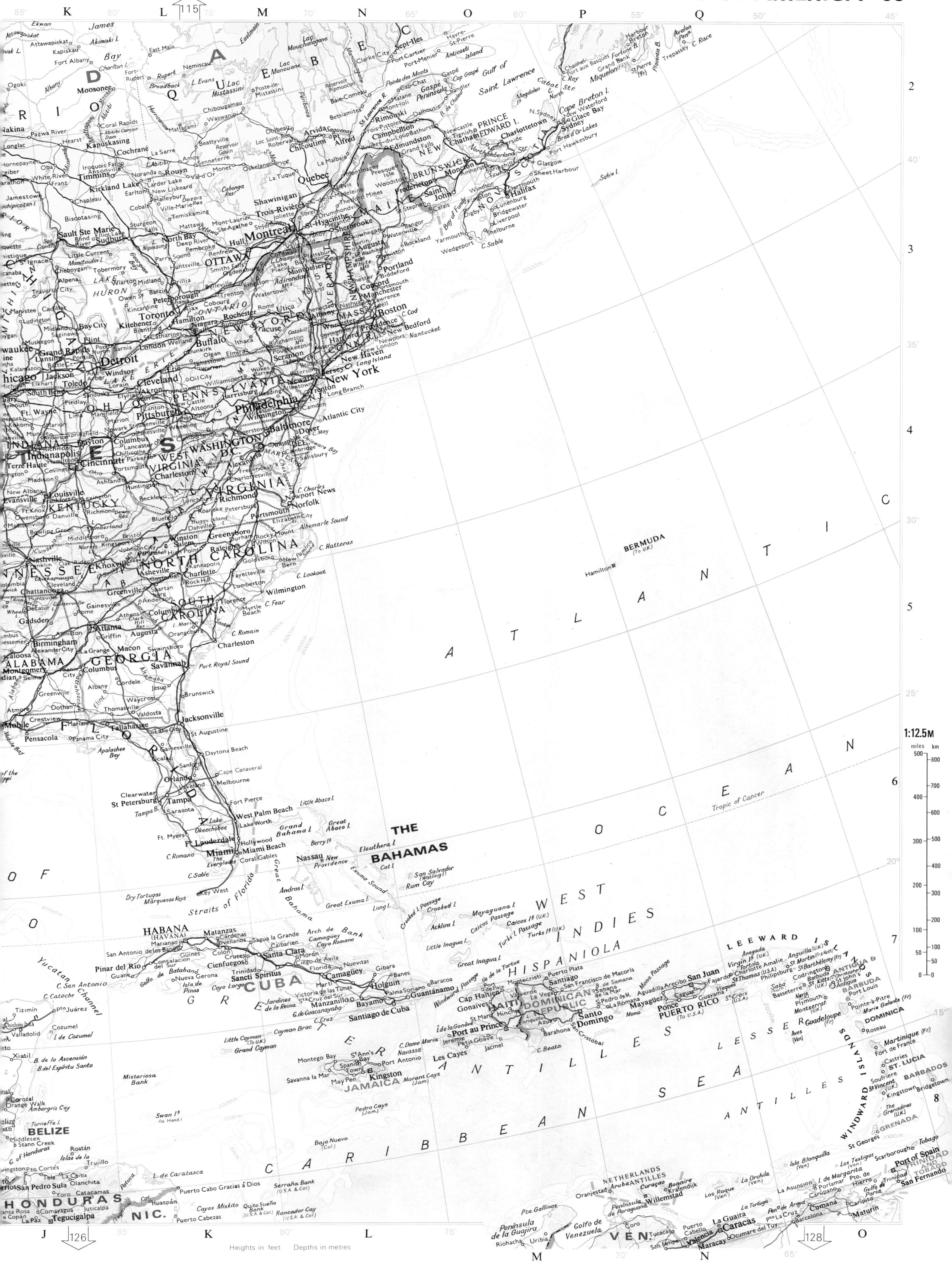
K
L
M
N
O
P
Q
115
2
3
4
5
6
7
8
C
I
T
N
A
L
T
A
N
A
E
C
O
BERMUDA (To U.K.)
Hamilton
Tropic of Cancer
1:12.5M
miles
km
THE BAHAMAS
Nassau
Eleuthera I.
Andros I.
Great Abaco I.
Grand Bahama I.
HABANA (HAVANA)
CUBA
Santiago de Cuba
Camagüey
Guantánamo
Cienfuegos
HISPANIOLA
HAITI
DOMINICAN REPUBLIC
Port au Prince
Santo Domingo
San Juan
PUERTO RICO (To U.S.A.)
JAMAICA
Kingston
W E S T
I N D I E S
G R E A T
A N T I L L E S
L E S S E R
A N T I L L E S
C A R I B B E A N
S E A
LEEWARD IS.
WINDWARD ISLANDS
Guadeloupe (Fr.)
DOMINICA
Martinique (Fr.)
ST. LUCIA
BARBADOS
GRENADA
TRINIDAD AND TOBAGO
Port of Spain
San Fernando
NETHERLANDS ANTILLES
Curaçao
Bonaire
Willemstad
Aruba
Caracas
La Guaira
Maracay
Valencia
VEN.
Golfo de Venezuela
Península de la Guajira
BELIZE
HONDURAS
Tegucigalpa
San Pedro Sula
NIC.
Yucatan Channel
Cozumel
Straits of Florida
Key West
Miami
Ft. Lauderdale
West Palm Beach
Tampa
St Petersburg
Orlando
Cape Canaveral
Jacksonville
Tallahassee
Pensacola
Mobile
Savannah
Charleston
Atlanta
Birmingham
Montgomery
ALABAMA
GEORGIA
FLORIDA
SOUTH CAROLINA
NORTH CAROLINA
Wilmington
C. Hatteras
C. Lookout
C. Fear
Raleigh
Greensboro
Charlotte
Nashville
Chattanooga
Knoxville
Asheville
Norfolk
Richmond
VIRGINIA
WEST VIRGINIA
Charleston
WASHINGTON D.C.
Baltimore
Philadelphia
Atlantic City
New York
Long Island
Pittsburgh
Cleveland
Columbus
Cincinnati
Dayton
Indianapolis
Louisville
KENTUCKY
Detroit
Toledo
Chicago
Milwaukee
LAKE HURON
LAKE ERIE
LAKE ONTARIO
Toronto
Hamilton
Buffalo
Rochester
NEW YORK
PENNSYLVANIA
Boston
C. Cod
Nantucket
Portland
Concord
Manchester
Providence
Hartford
New Haven
New Bedford
VERMONT
NEW HAMPSHIRE
MAINE
OTTAWA
Montreal
Quebec
Trois-Rivières
Sherbrooke
Sault Ste Marie
Sudbury
North Bay
Timmins
Kirkland Lake
Rouyn
Val d'Or
Chicoutimi
Saint Lawrence
Gulf of Saint Lawrence
Anticosti Island
PRINCE EDWARD I.
Charlottetown
NEW BRUNSWICK
Fredericton
Saint John
Moncton
Halifax
NOVA SCOTIA
Sydney
Cape Breton I.
Sable I.
C. Sable
Bay of Fundy
C. Race
Miquelon (Fr.)
St Pierre (Fr.)
Cabot Str.
James Bay
Moosonee
Hudson Bay
Great Exuma I.
Cat I.
San Salvador (Watling I.)
Rum Cay
Crooked I.
Acklins I.
Mayaguana I.
Caicos Is (U.K.)
Turks Is (U.K.)
Great Inagua I.
Little Inagua I.
Grand Cayman
Little Cayman (To U.K.)
Cayman Brac
Misteriosa Bank
Swan Is (to Hond.)
Pedro Cays (Jam.)
Bajo Nuevo (Col.)
Serrana Bank (U.S.A. & Col.)
Roncador Cay (U.S.A. & Col.)
Quito Sueño Bank (U.S.A. & Col.)
Cayos Miskito
Puerto Cabezas
Puerto Cabo Gracias á Dios
I. de Margarita
Cumaná
Barcelona
Maturín
Isla Blanquilla
Los Roques (Ven.)
La Orchila (Ven.)
Tobago
Scarborough
J
126
K
L
M
N
128
O
Heights in feet Depths in metres

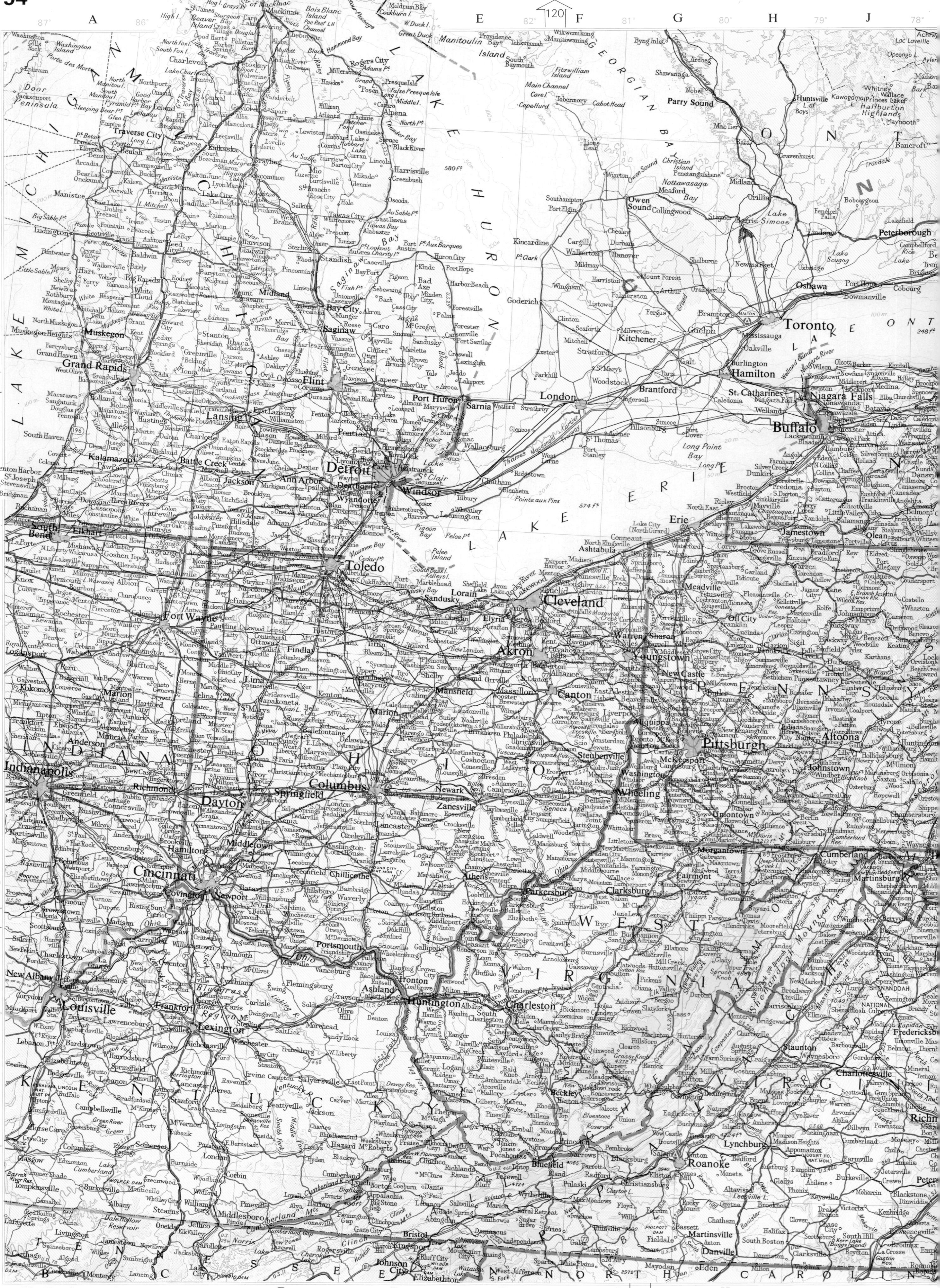

LAKE HURON

LAKE ERIE

LAKE ONTARIO

GEORGIAN BAY

MICHIGAN

ONTARIO

OHIO

INDIANA

PENNSYLVANIA

WEST VIRGINIA

KENTUCKY

TENNESSEE

NORTH CAROLINA

VIRGINIA

Toronto
Buffalo
Niagara Falls
Hamilton
Parry Sound
Owen Sound

Detroit
Windsor
Toledo
Cleveland
Akron
Youngstown
Pittsburgh
Altoona
Cincinnati
Columbus
Dayton
Indianapolis
Fort Wayne
Grand Rapids
Muskegon
Kalamazoo
Lansing
Flint
Saginaw
Bay City
Battle Creek
Ann Arbor
Jackson
Traverse City
South Bend
Elkhart
Mansfield
Canton
Wheeling
Parkersburg
Clarksburg
Cumberland
Morgantown
Johnstown
Louisville
Frankfort
Lexington
New Albany
Huntington
Ashland
Charleston
Beckley
Bluefield
Roanoke
Lynchburg
Charlottesville
Martinsburg
Staunton
Fredericksburg

CONFORMAL CONIC PROJECTION

3281 656   0   300 600 1500 3000 6000 feet
1000 200   0   91 183 457   914   1829 m

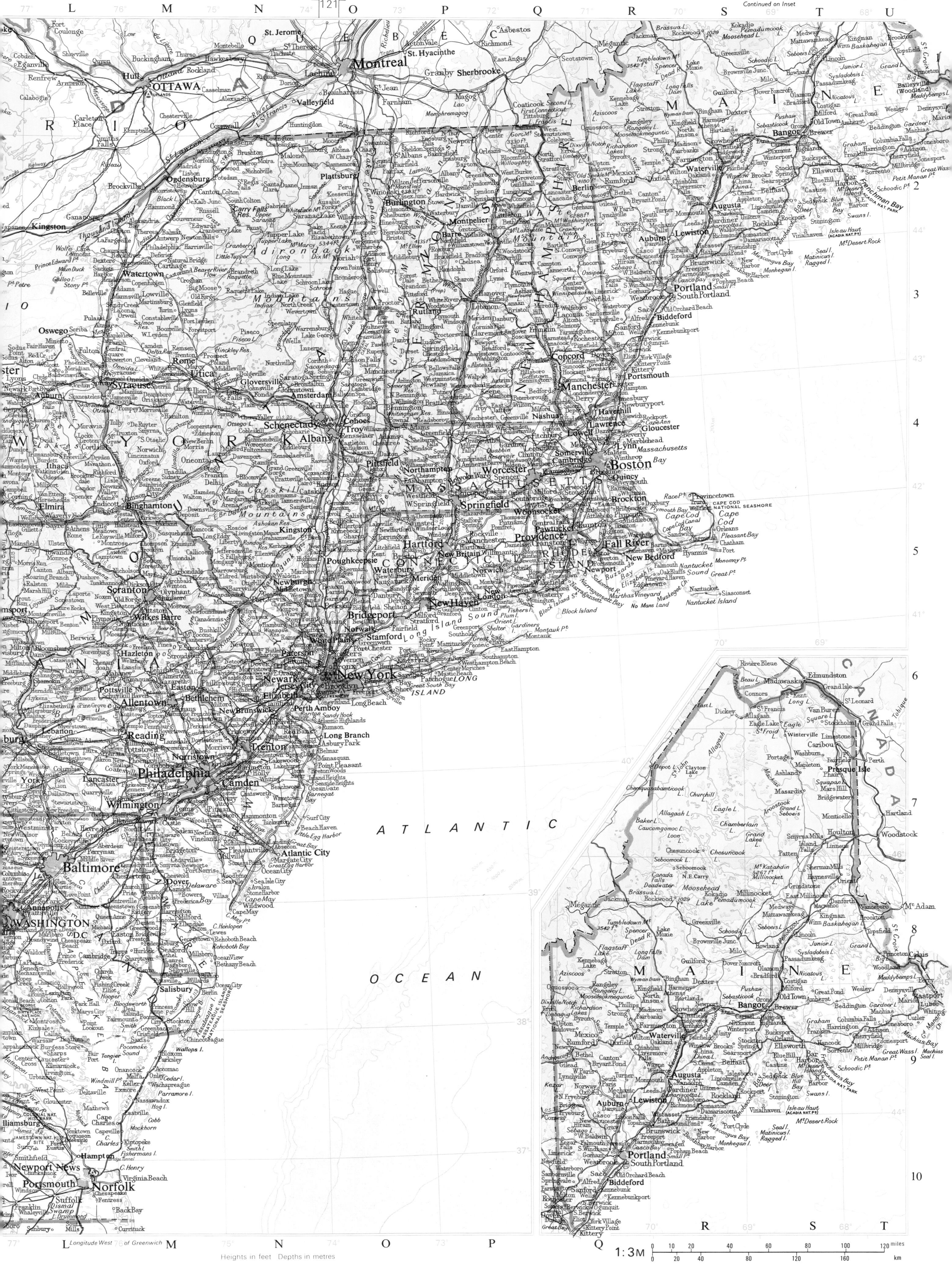

Continued on Inset
1:3M
Heights in feet Depths in metres

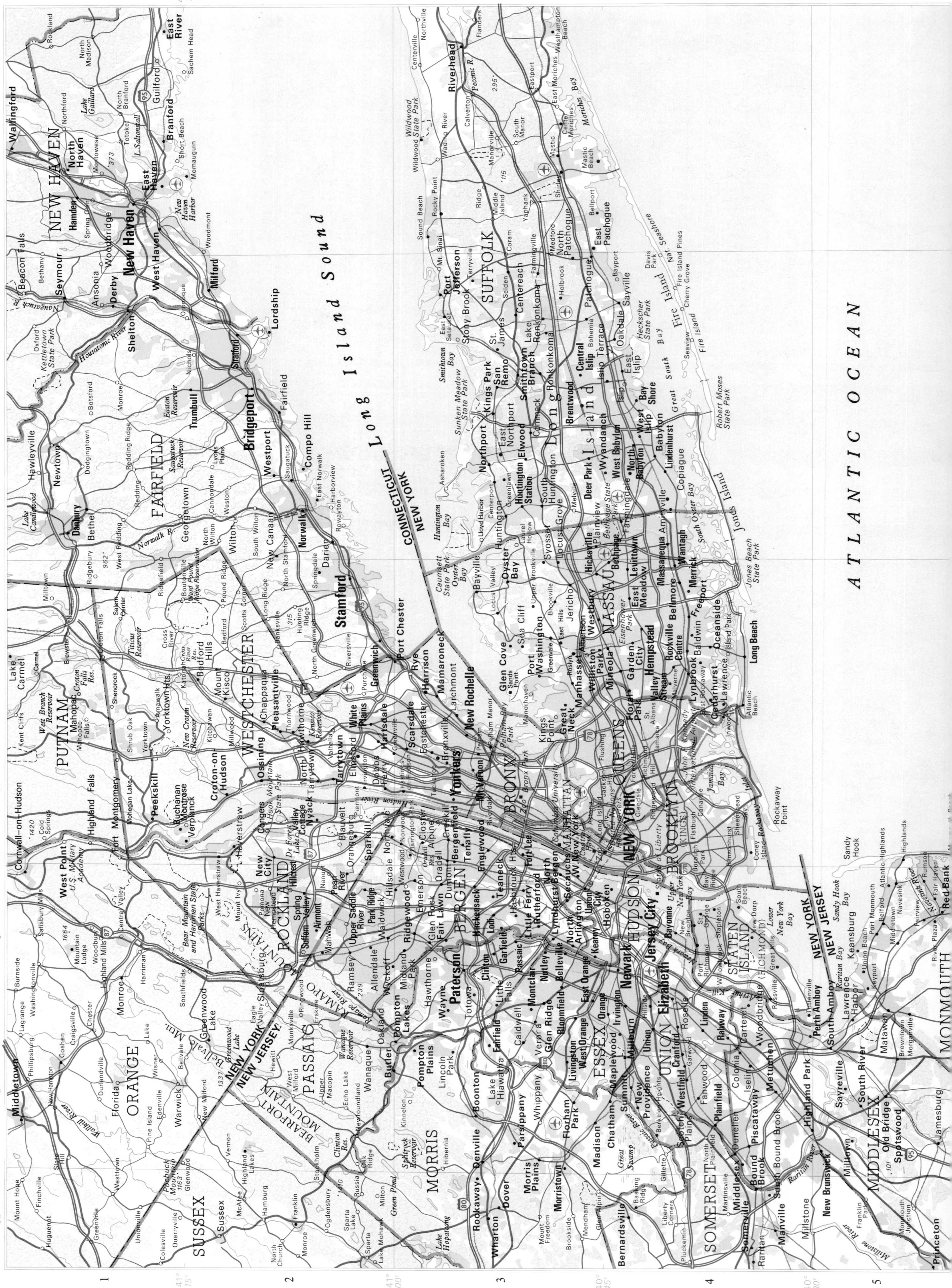
ATLANTIC OCEAN
Long Island Sound
Long Island
NEW YORK
CONNECTICUT
NEW JERSEY
NEW HAVEN
FAIRFIELD
PUTNAM
WESTCHESTER
ROCKLAND
ORANGE
SUSSEX
PASSAIC
MORRIS
BERGEN
ESSEX
HUDSON
UNION
SOMERSET
MIDDLESEX
MONMOUTH
SUFFOLK
NASSAU
QUEENS
BRONX
MANHATTAN
BROOKLYN
STATEN ISLAND (RICHMOND)
New Haven
Bridgeport
Stamford
Norwalk
Danbury
Yonkers
New Rochelle
Paterson
Newark
Jersey City
Elizabeth
Hempstead
Riverhead
New Brunswick
Princeton
Hudson River
Fire Island
Jones Beach State Park
RAMAPO MOUNTAINS
BEARFORT MOUNTAIN

1:500 000

PHILADELPHIA

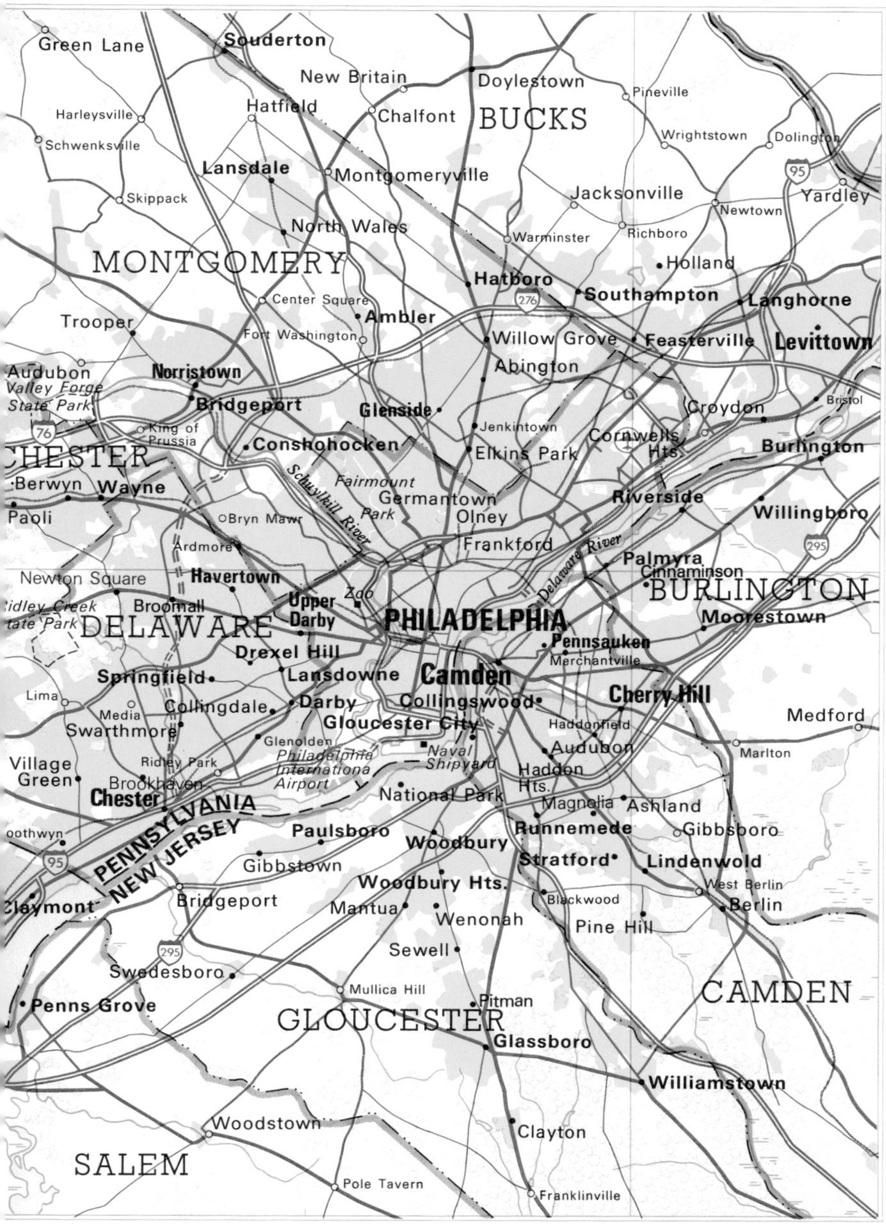

BOSTON

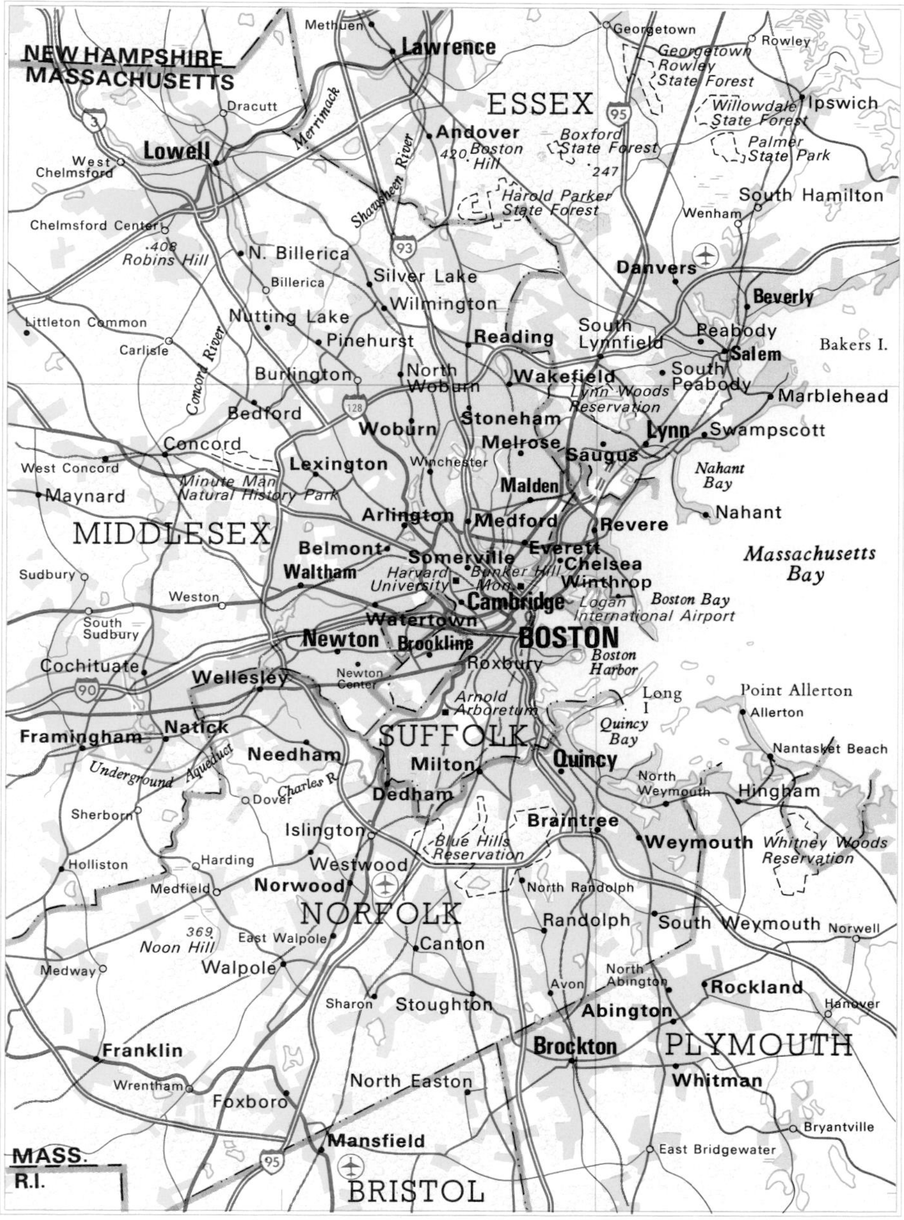

D 71°15' E 71°00' F

WASHINGTON

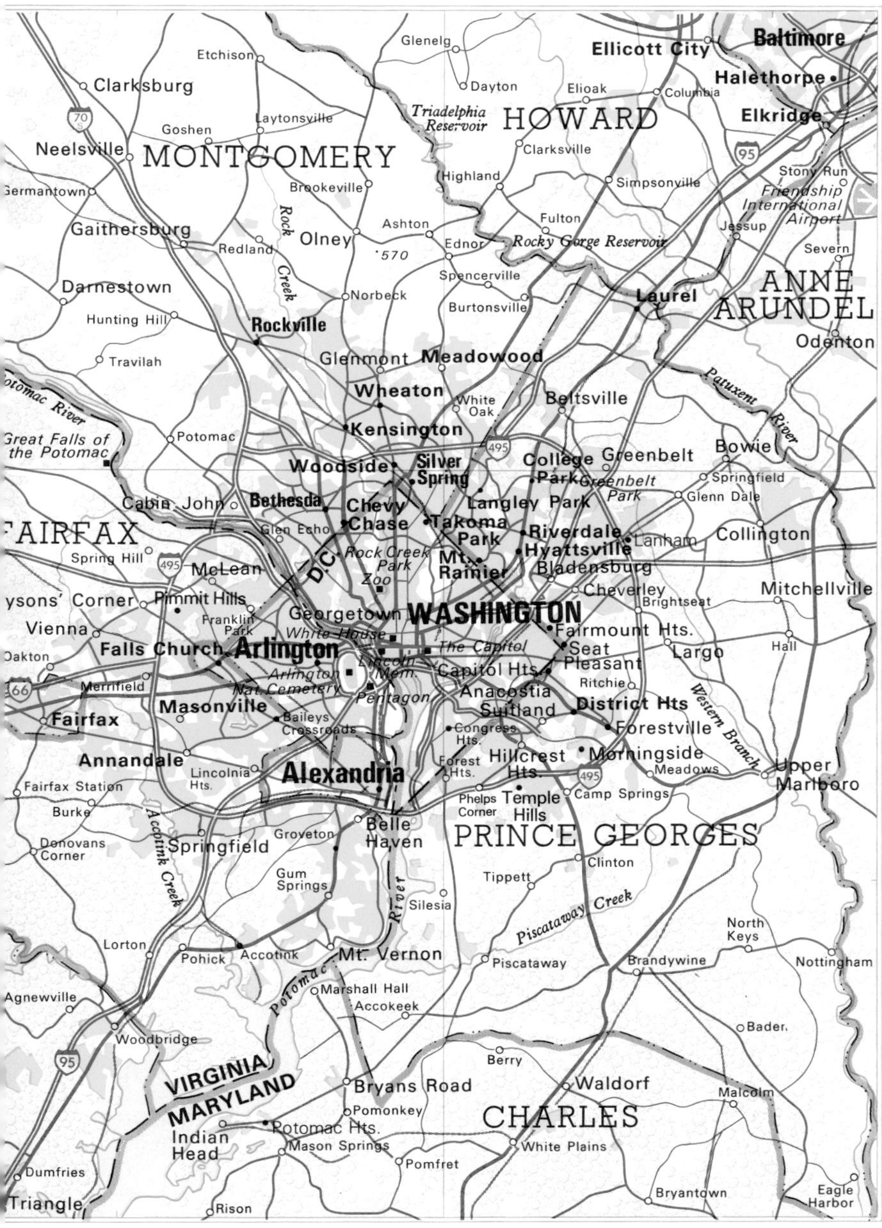

77°15' G 77°00' H 76°45'

BALTIMORE

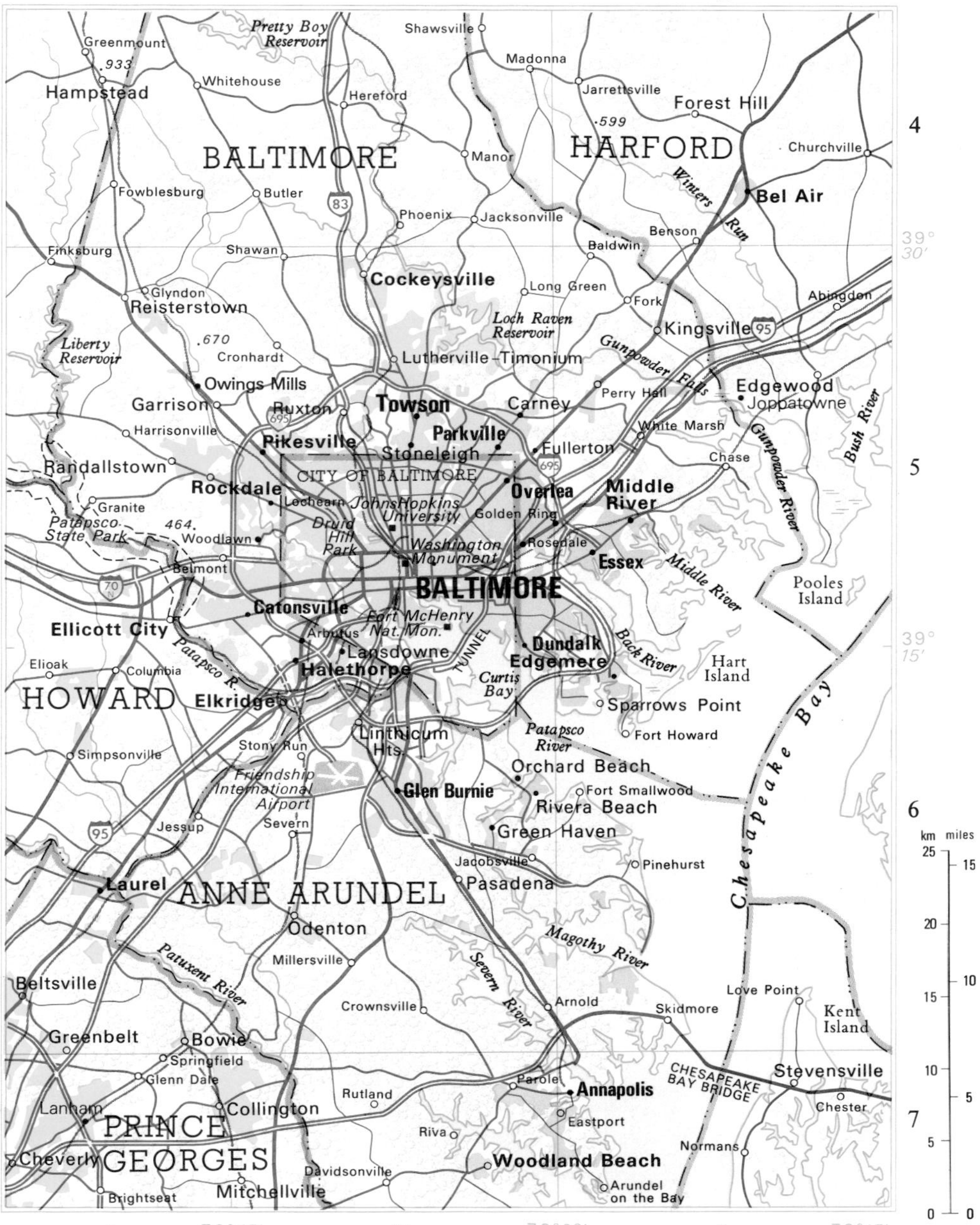

J 76°45' K 76°30' L

C A N A D A

MONTANA

NORTH DAKOTA

SOUTH DAKOTA

WYOMING

NEBRASKA

COLORADO

KANSAS

Williston · Minot · Grand Forks · Fargo · Bismarck · Mandan · Dickinson · Jamestown · Aberdeen · Pierre · Rapid City · Miles City · Gillette · Cheyenne · Fort Collins · Denver · Boulder · Laramie · Scottsbluff · North Platte · Grand Island · Lincoln · Columbus

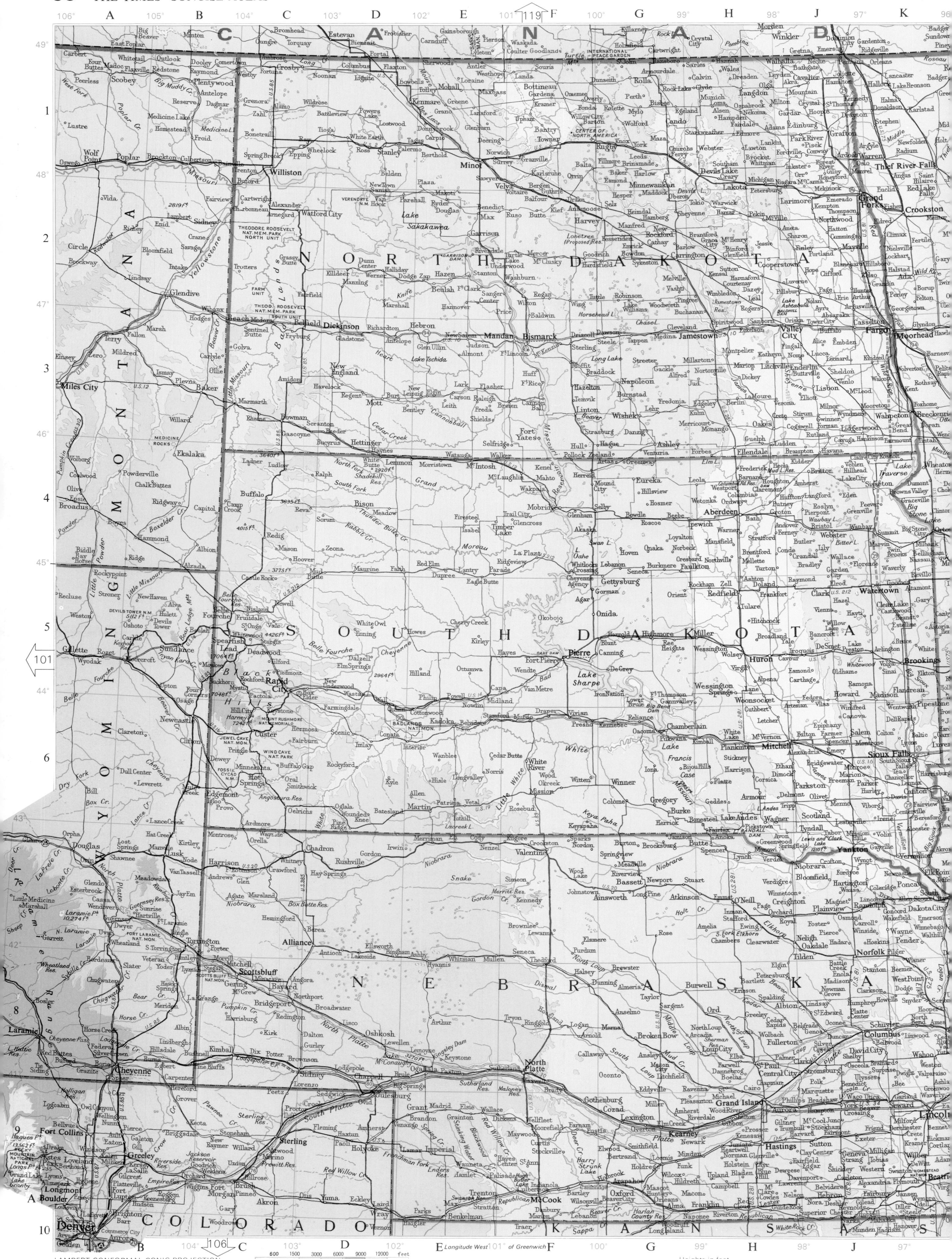

LAMBERT CONFORMAL CONIC PROJECTION

600 1500 3000 6000 9000 12000 feet
183 457 914 1829 2743 3658 m

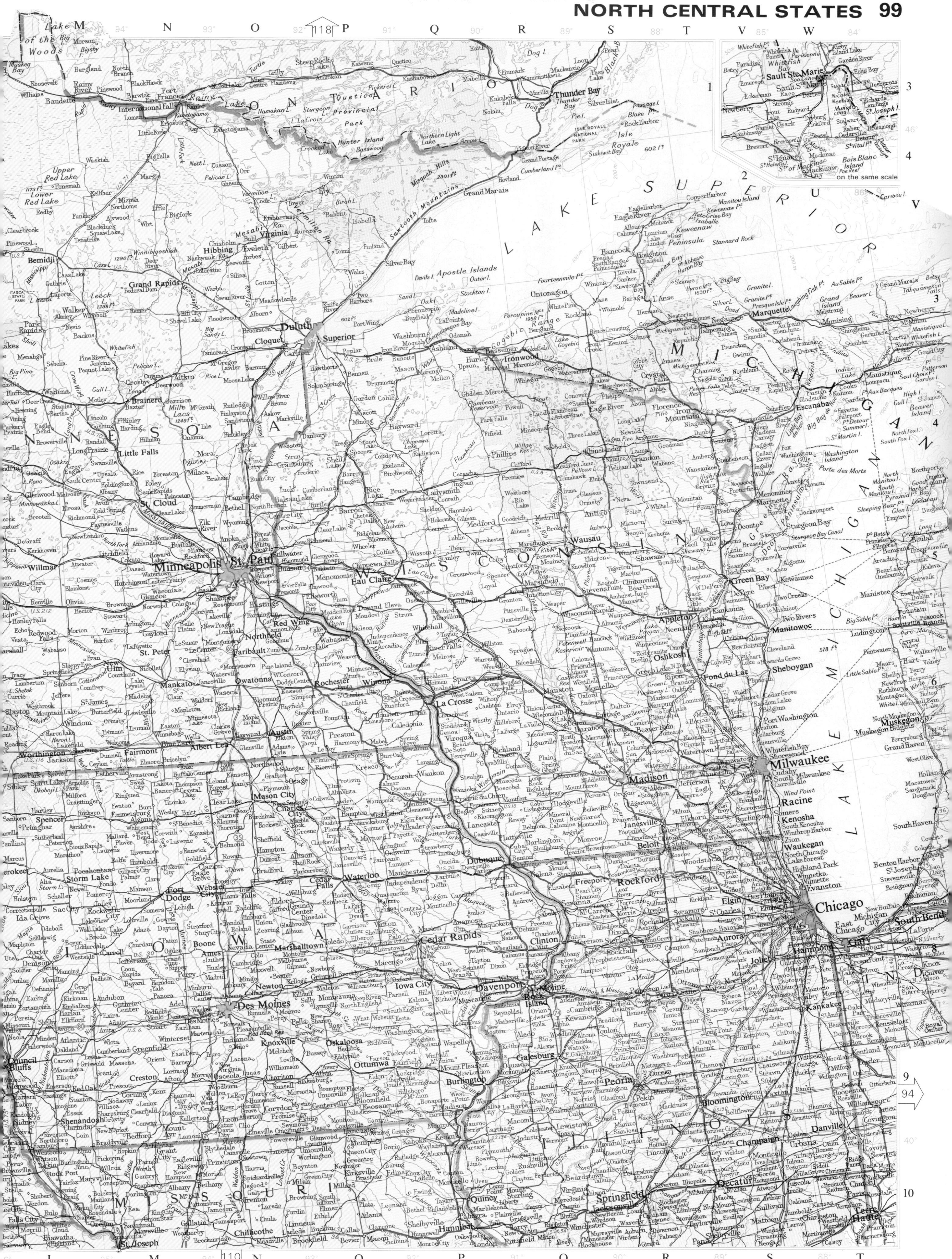

1:3M 0 10 20 40 60 80 100 miles
0 20 40 80 120 160 km

CANADA

VANCOUVER ISLAND

WASHINGTON

OREGON

CALIFORNIA

NEVADA

IDAHO

PACIFIC OCEAN

STRAIT OF JUAN DE FUCA

Vancouver · New Westminster · Bellingham · Victoria · Port Angeles · Everett · Seattle · Tacoma · Olympia · Aberdeen · Bremerton · Renton · Puyallup · Centralia · Chehalis · Wenatchee · Ellensburg · Yakima · Spokane · Coeur d'Alene · Moscow · Pullman · Astoria · Longview · Kelso · Vancouver · Portland · Oregon City · The Dalles · Pendleton · La Grande · Walla Walla · Kennewick · Pasco · Richland · Prosser · Salem · Albany · Corvallis · Eugene · Springfield · Bend · Baker · Boise · Nampa · Caldwell · Ontario · Coos Bay · Roseburg · Grants Pass · Medford · Ashland · Klamath Falls · Altamont · Burns · Lakeview · Eureka · Redding · Susanville · Alturas

Scale bar:
feet	3281	656	0	300	600	1500	3000	6000	9000	12000
m	1000	200	0	91	183	457	914	1829	2743	3658

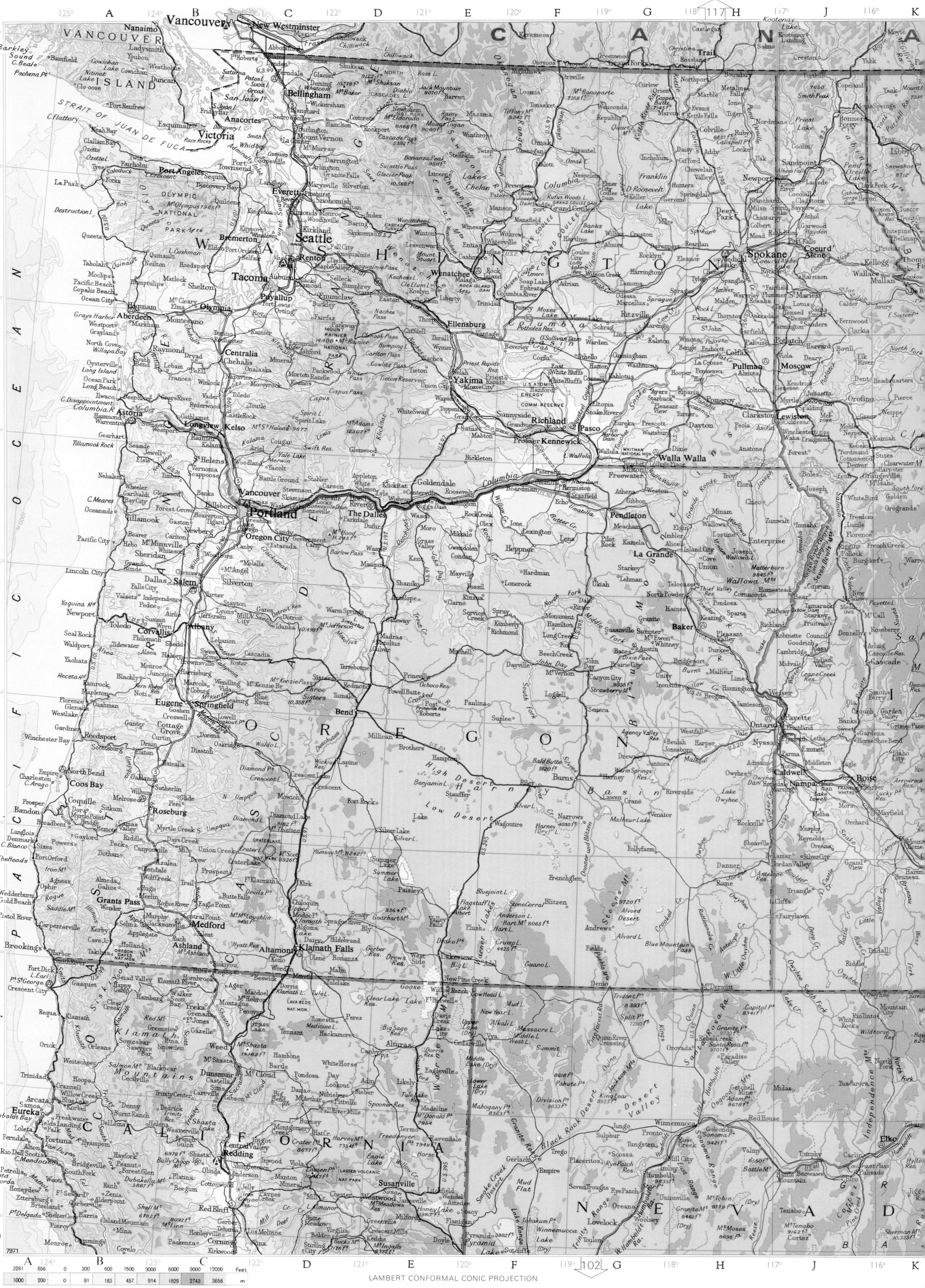

Heights in feet
Depths in metres

© John Bartholomew & Son Ltd Edinburgh

1:3M

miles 0 10 20 30 40 50 60 80 100 120
km 0 20 40 80 120 160 200

Long West of Greenwich

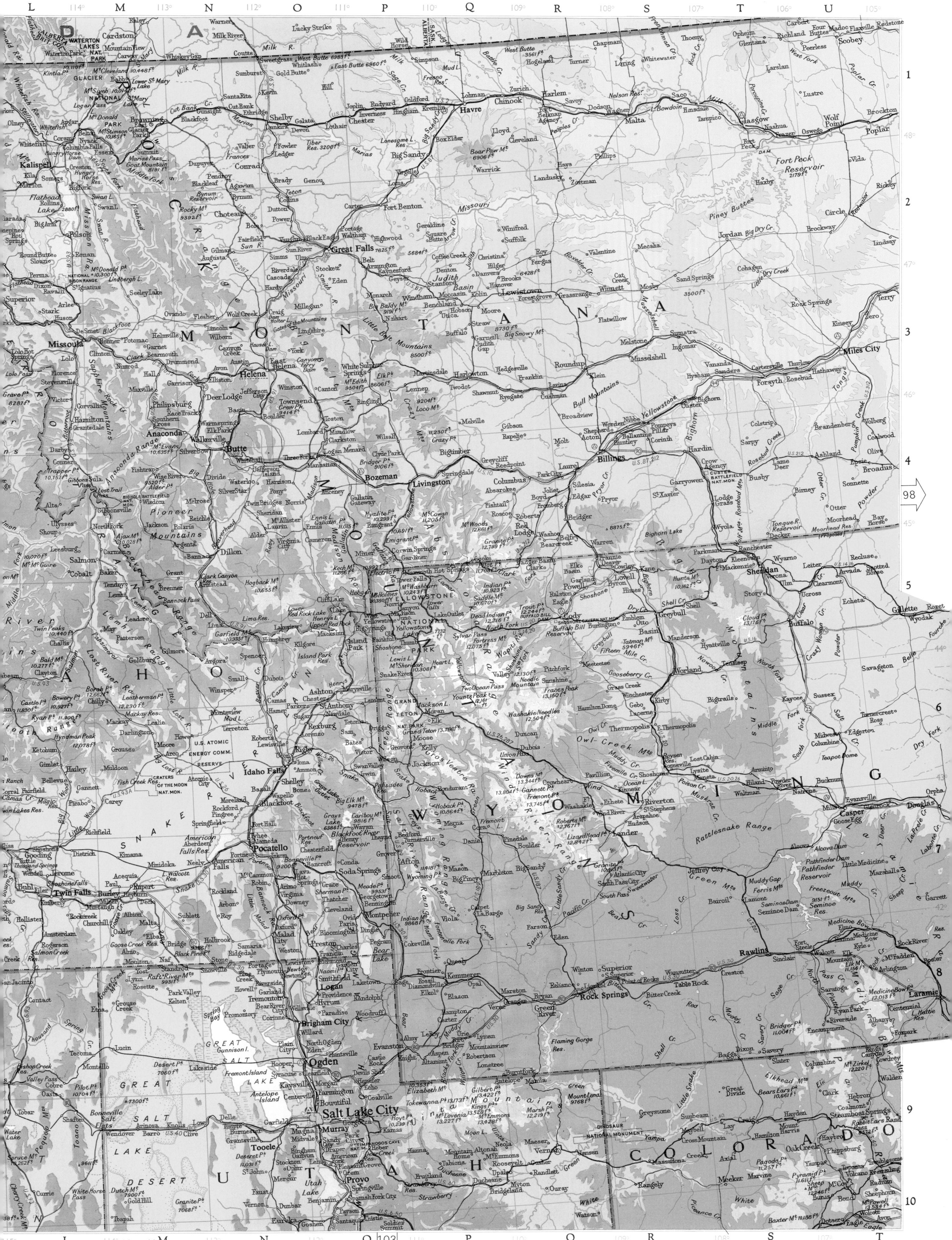

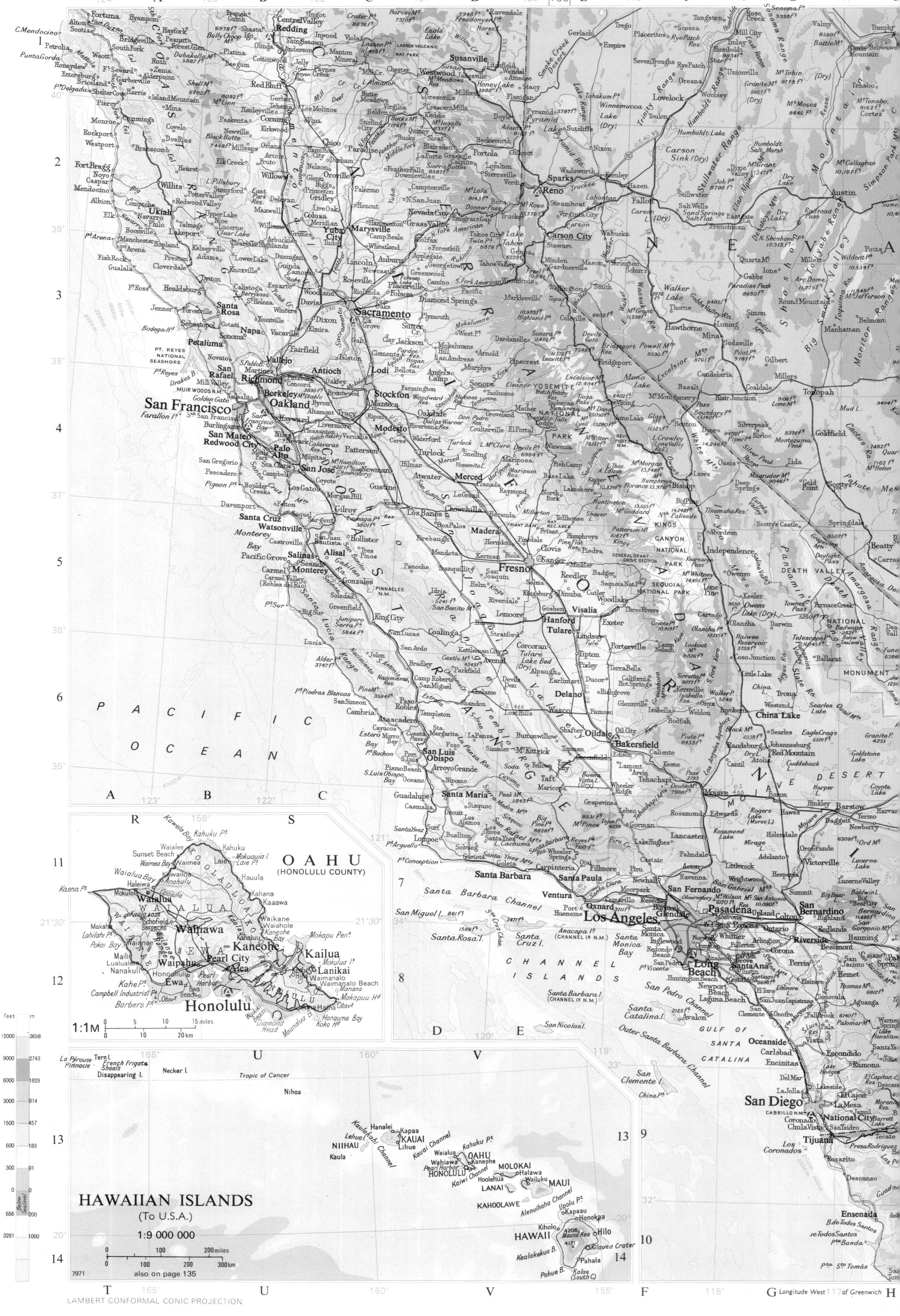

PACIFIC OCEAN

OAHU
(HONOLULU COUNTY)

1:1M

HAWAIIAN ISLANDS
(To U.S.A.)

1:9 000 000

also on page 135

LAMBERT CONFORMAL CONIC PROJECTION

G Longitude West 117° of Greenwich

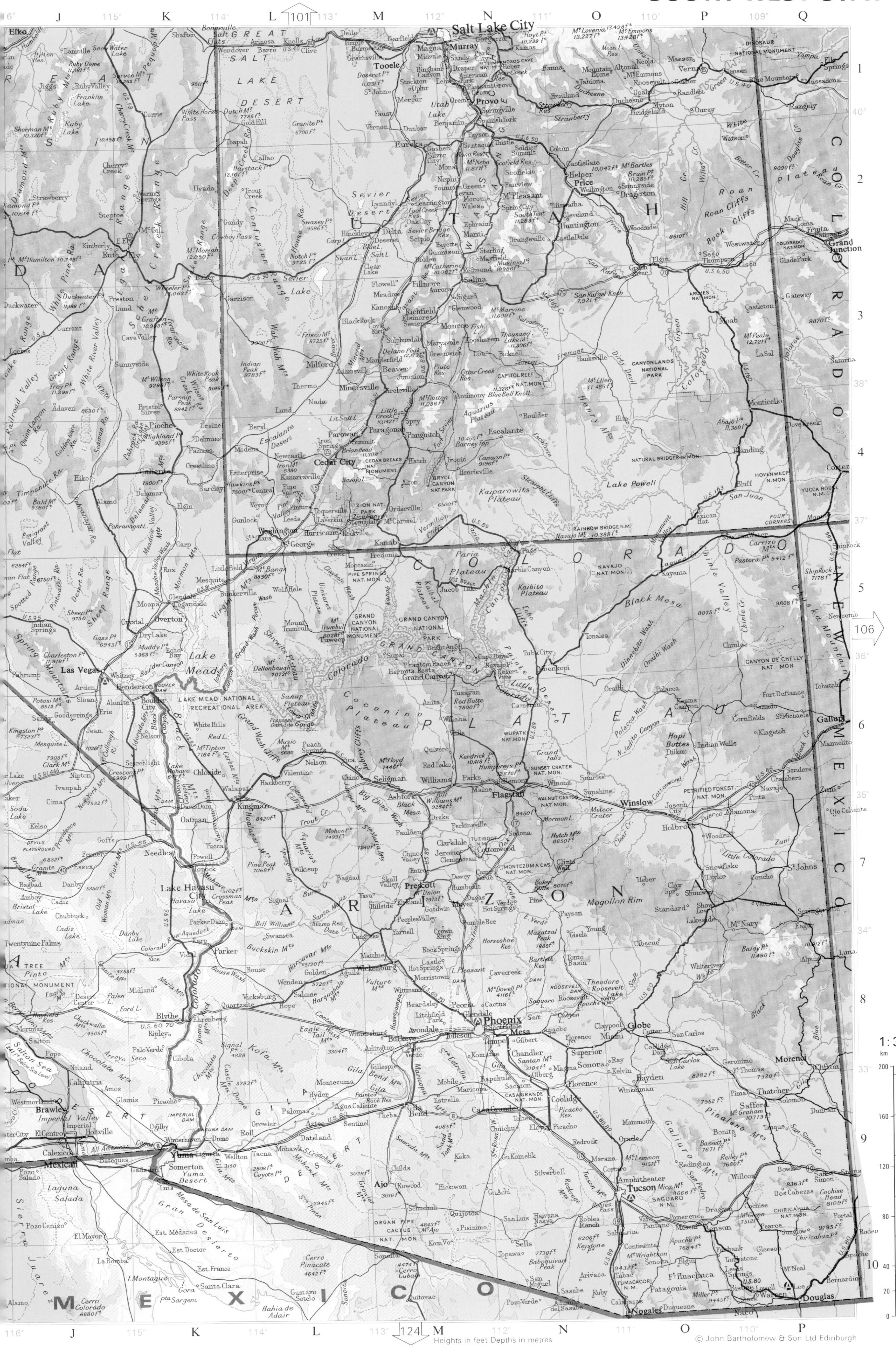

Heights in feet Depths in metres

1:3M

km miles

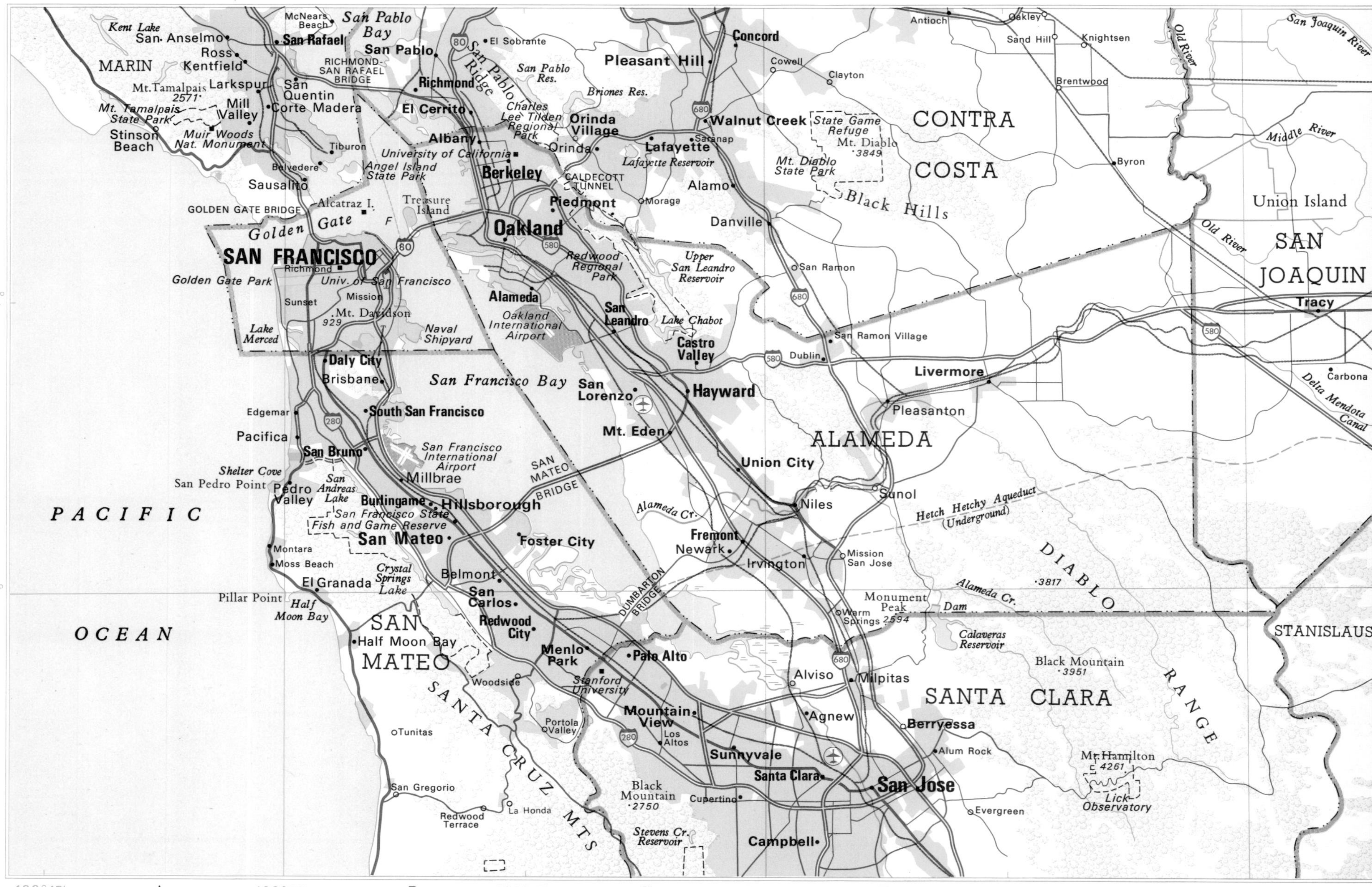

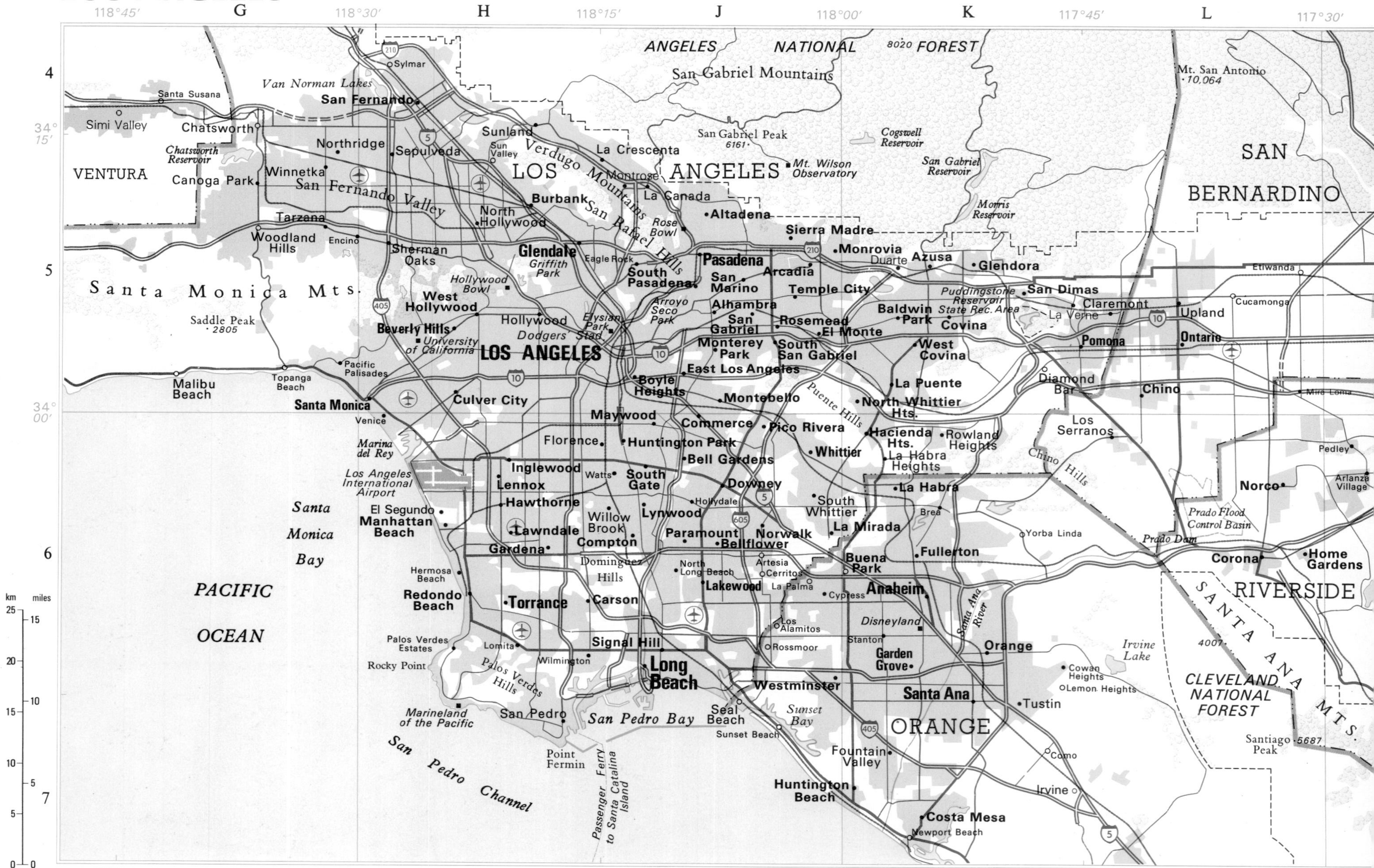

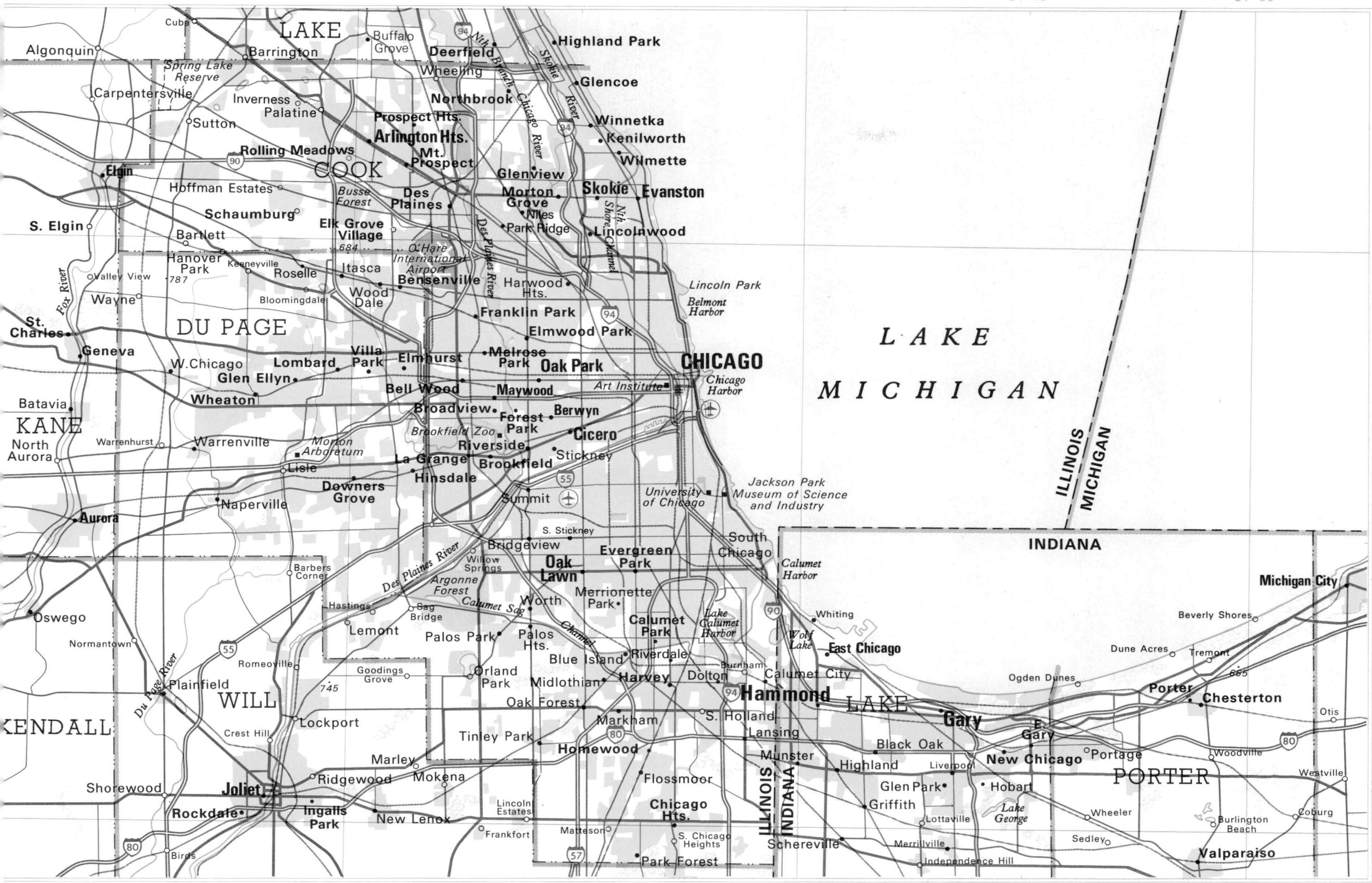

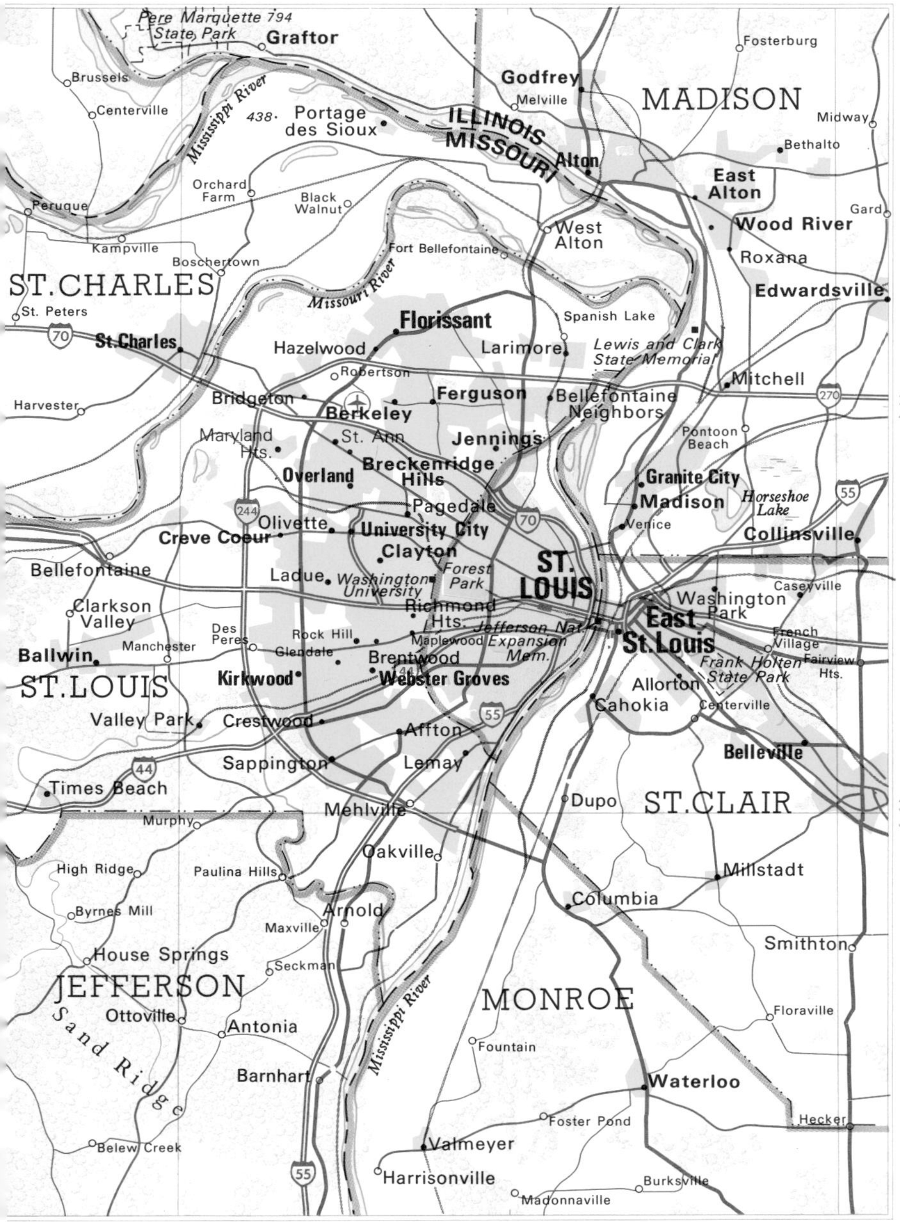

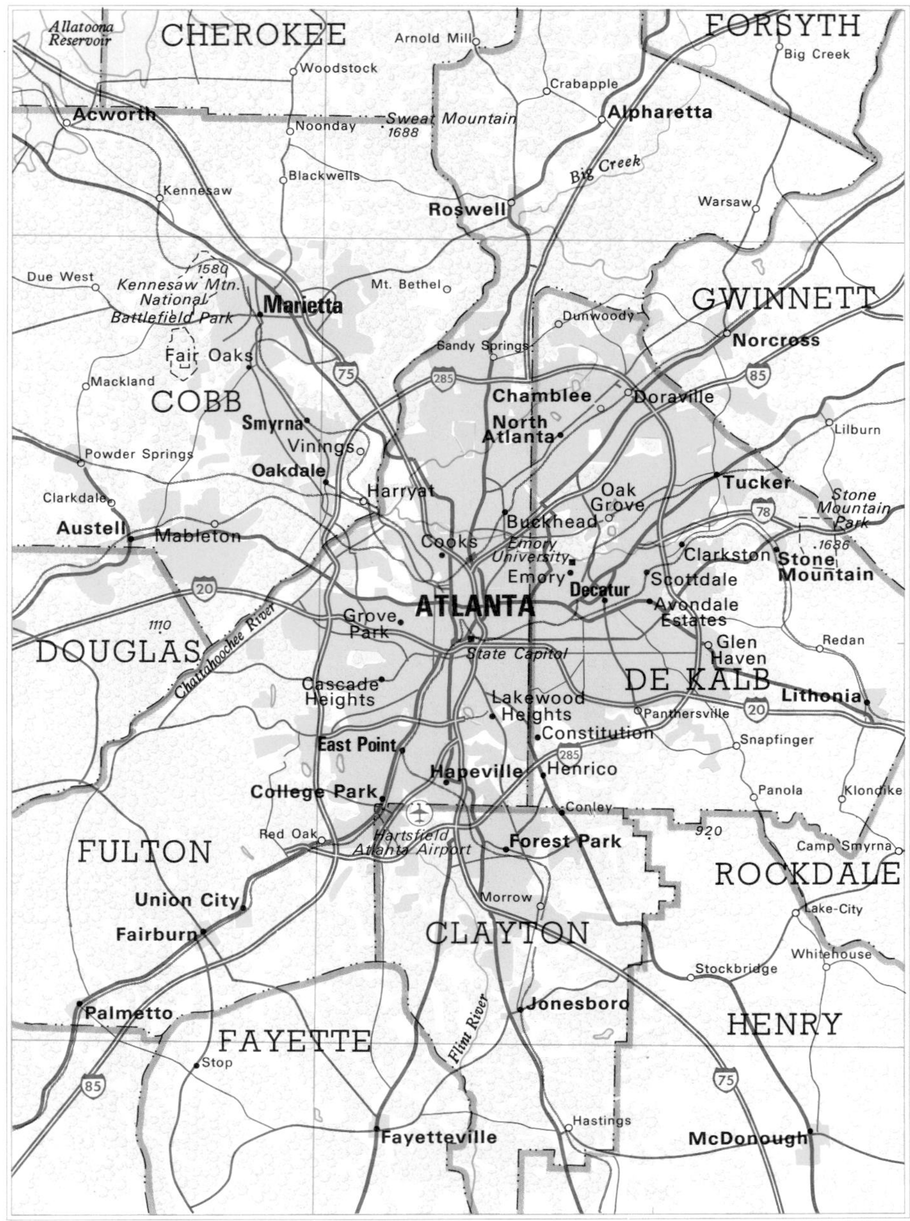

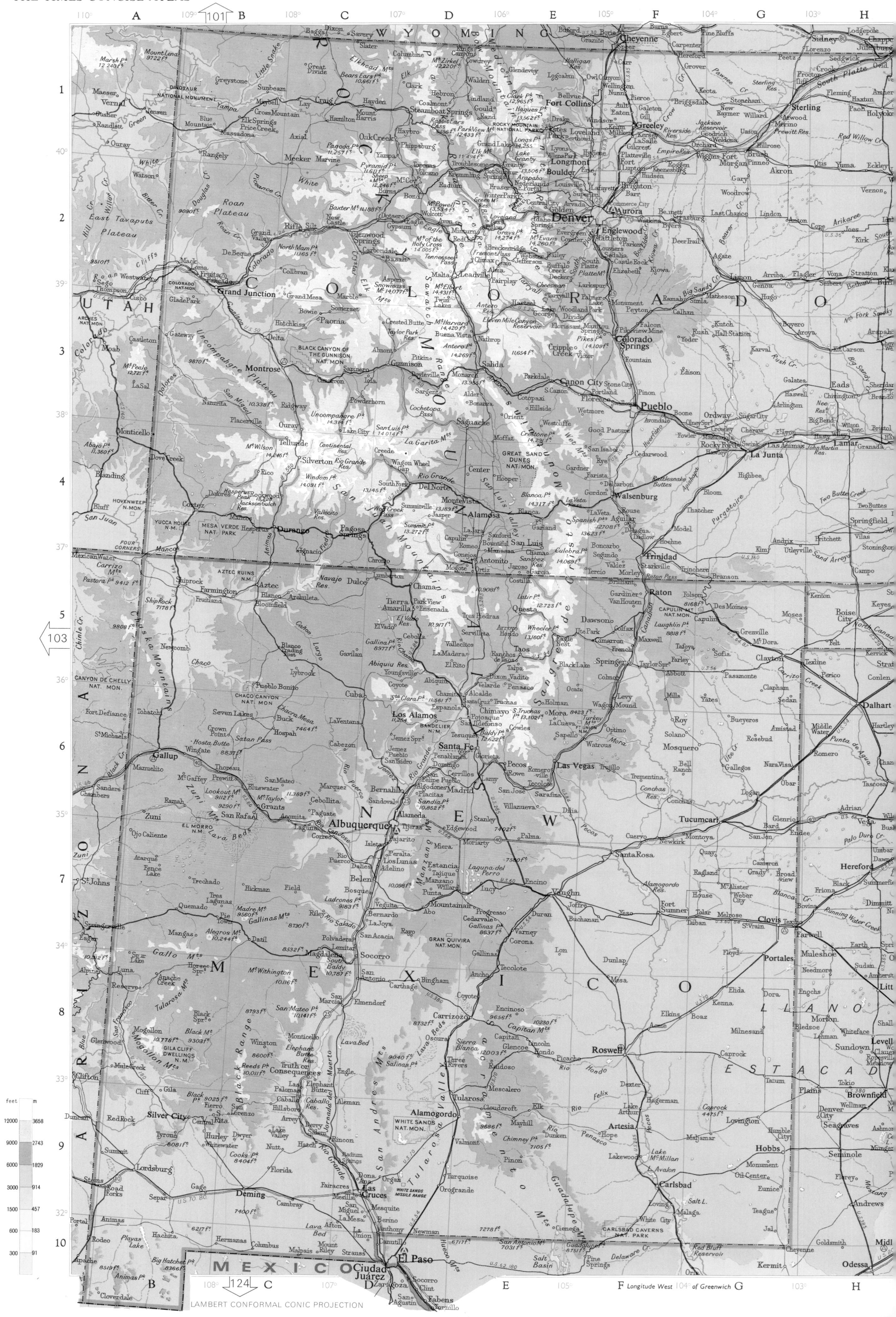

WYOMING
COLORADO
UTAH
ARIZONA
NEW MEXICO
MEXICO
ROCKY MOUNTAINS
LLANO ESTACADO
Cheyenne
Fort Collins
Greeley
Boulder
Longmont
Denver
Aurora
Englewood
Colorado Springs
Pueblo
Grand Junction
Montrose
Durango
Alamosa
Trinidad
La Junta
Lamar
Sterling
Raton
Santa Fe
Los Alamos
Taos
Gallup
Farmington
Albuquerque
Las Vegas
Tucumcari
Clovis
Roswell
Carlsbad
Hobbs
Alamogordo
Las Cruces
Deming
Silver City
El Paso
Ciudad Juárez
Odessa
Sangre de Cristo Mts
San Juan Mountains
Sacramento Mts
Guadalupe Mts
San Andres Mts
Black Range
Mogollon Mts
Chuska Mountains
Uncompahgre Plateau
Roan Plateau
East Tavaputs Plateau
Rio Grande
Pecos
Canadian
Arkansas
South Platte
Colorado
San Juan
GREAT SAND DUNES NAT. MON.
BLACK CANYON OF THE GUNNISON NAT. MON.
MESA VERDE NAT. PARK
ROCKY MOUNTAIN NATIONAL PARK
DINOSAUR NATIONAL MONUMENT
COLORADO NAT. MON.
ARCHES NAT. MON.
CHACO CANYON NAT. MON.
AZTEC RUINS N.M.
CANYON DE CHELLY NAT. MON.
EL MORRO N.M.
BANDELIER N.M.
GRAN QUIVIRA NAT. MON.
WHITE SANDS NAT. MON.
WHITE SANDS MISSILE RANGE
GILA CLIFF DWELLINGS N.M.
CARLSBAD CAVERNS NAT. PARK
CAPULIN MTN. NAT. MON.
FOUR CORNERS
Longitude West of Greenwich
LAMBERT CONFORMAL CONIC PROJECTION
feet m
12000 3658
9000 2743
6000 1829
3000 914
1500 457
600 183
300 91
101
103
124

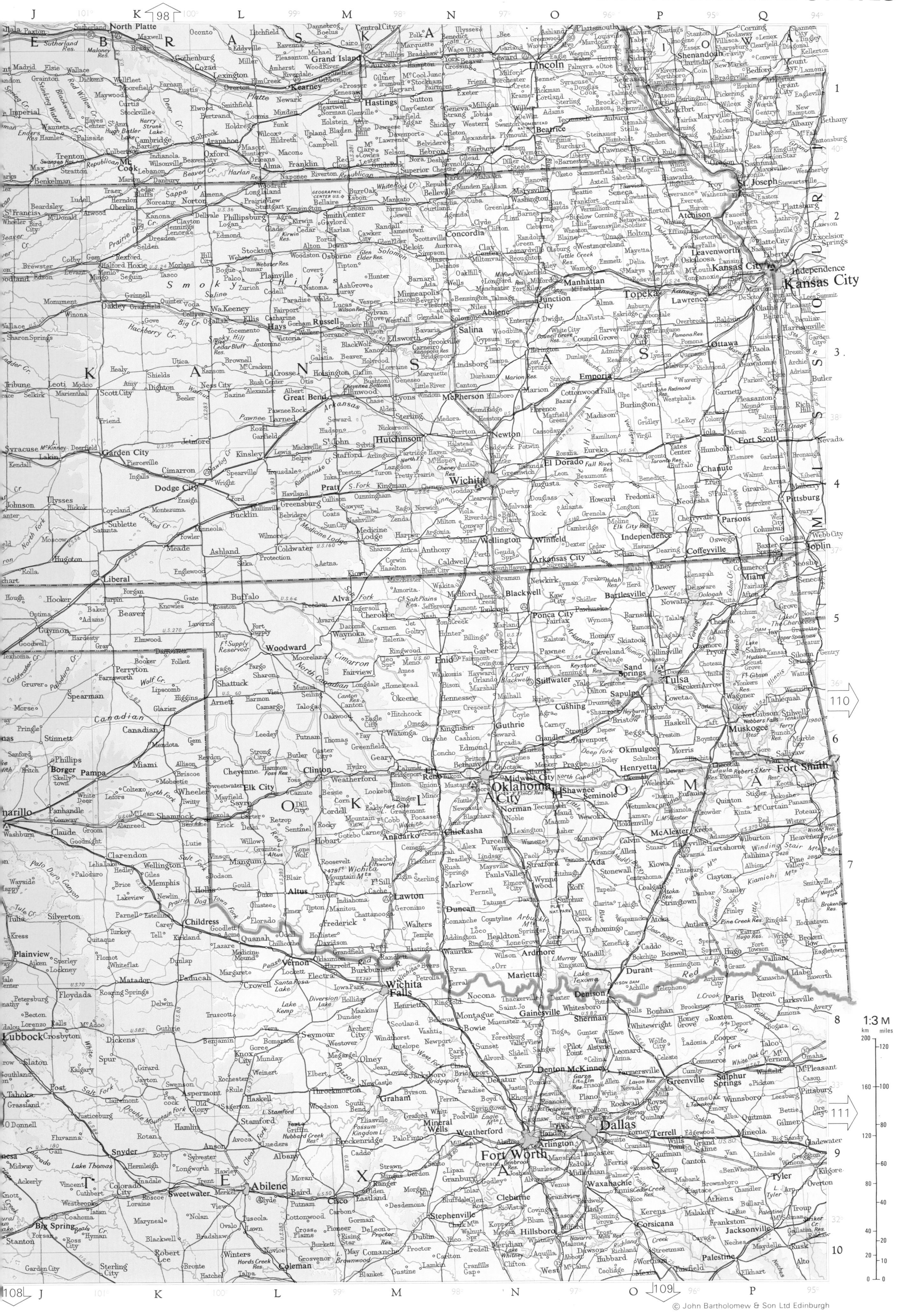
J
K
L
M
N
O
P
Q
1
2
3
4
5
6
7
8
9
10
98
110
111
108
109
1:3 M
km
miles
North Platte
Grand Island
Kearney
Hastings
Lincoln
Beatrice
St. Joseph
Atchison
Leavenworth
Kansas City
Independence
Topeka
Lawrence
Manhattan
Junction City
Salina
Abilene
Hays
Russell
Great Bend
Hutchinson
McPherson
Emporia
Newton
Wichita
Dodge City
Garden City
Liberal
Pittsburg
Coffeyville
Joplin
Bartlesville
Ponca City
Enid
Woodward
Tulsa
Muskogee
Fort Smith
Oklahoma City
Norman
Shawnee
McAlester
Lawton
Ardmore
Durant
Wichita Falls
Denison
Sherman
Amarillo
Lubbock
Abilene
Big Spring
Fort Worth
Dallas
Arlington
Corsicana
Tyler
Palestine
Denton
McKinney
Greenville
Paris
Lake Texoma
K A N S A S
O K L A H O M A
T E X A S
N E B R A S K A
I O W A
M I S S O U R I

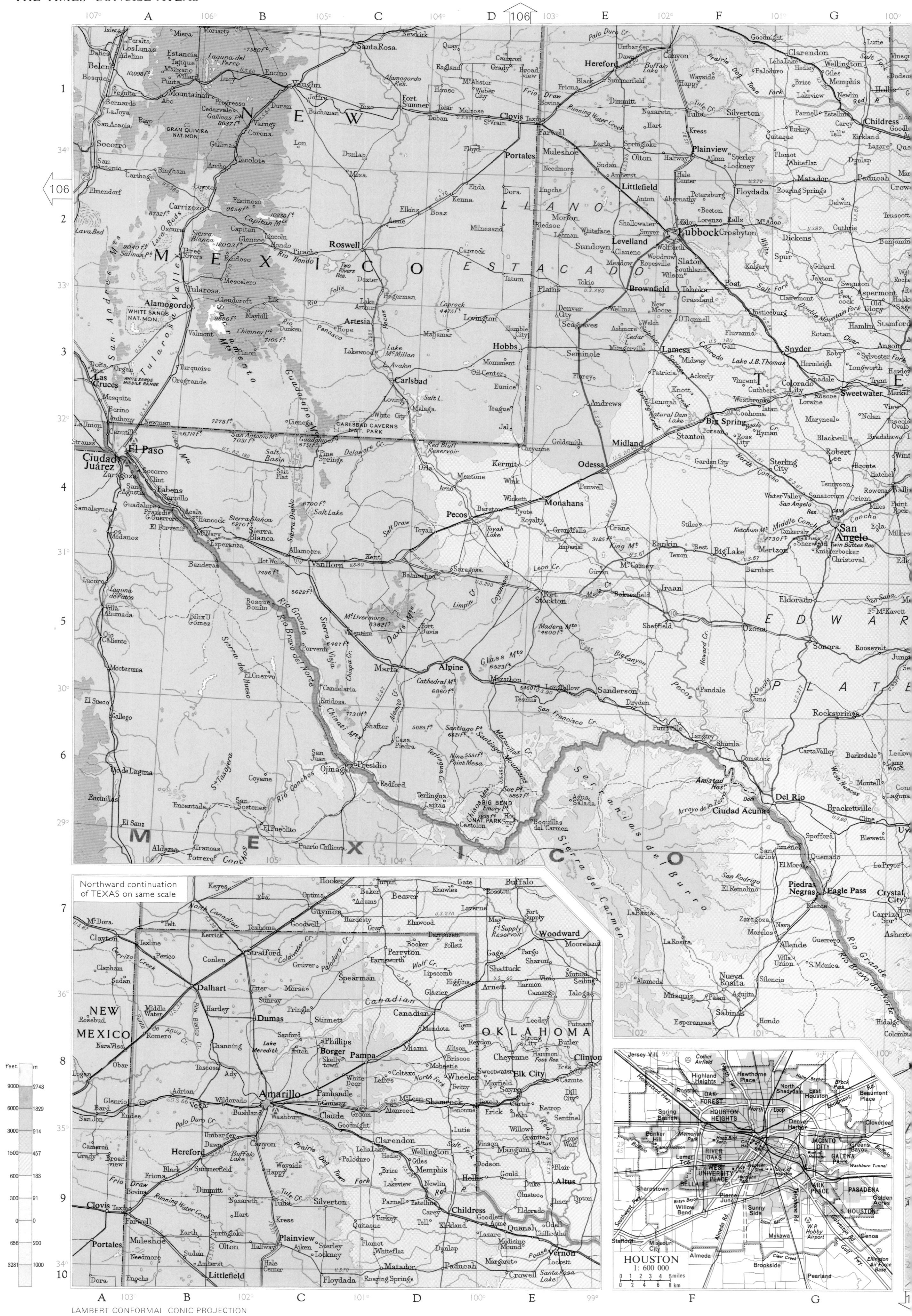

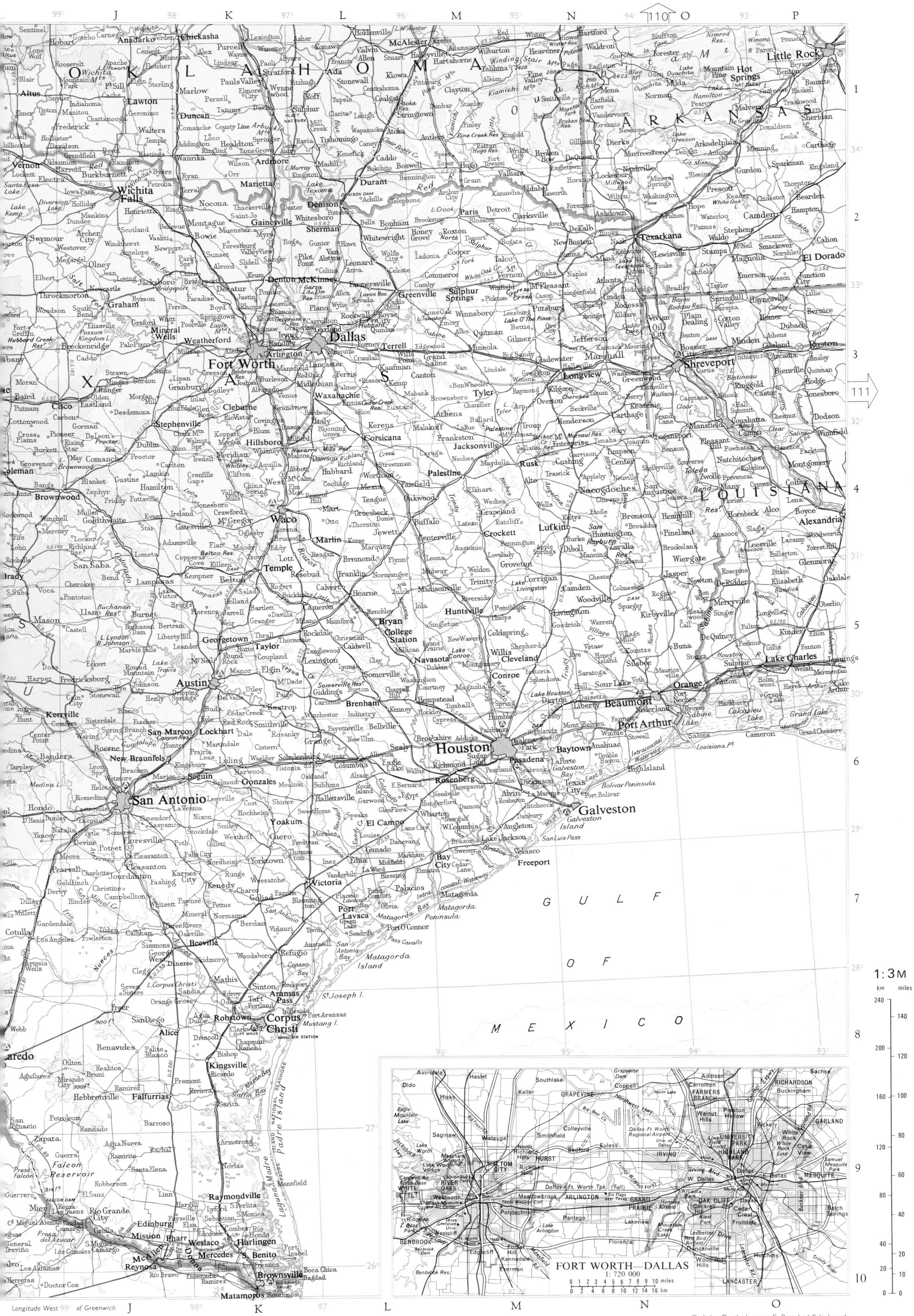

1:3M

FORT WORTH – DALLAS
1:720 000

Heights in feet
Depths in metres

© John Bartholomew & Son Ltd Edinburgh

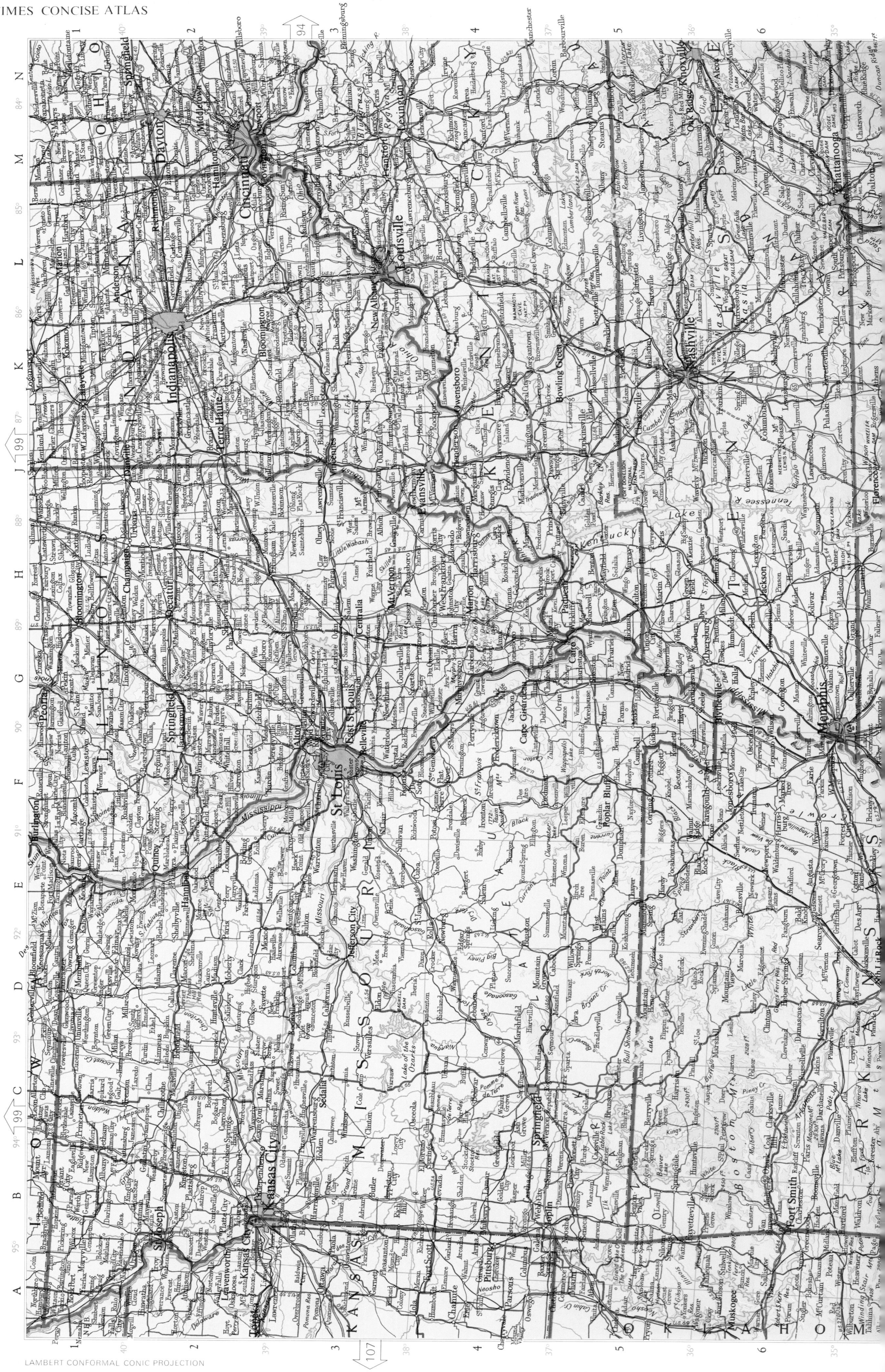

LAMBERT CONFORMAL CONIC PROJECTION

ST LOUIS
1: 300 000

1:3M

NEW ORLEANS
1: 300 000

LAKE PONTCHARTRAIN

GULF OF MEXICO

Heights in feet Depths in metres

© John Bartholomew & Son Ltd Edinburgh

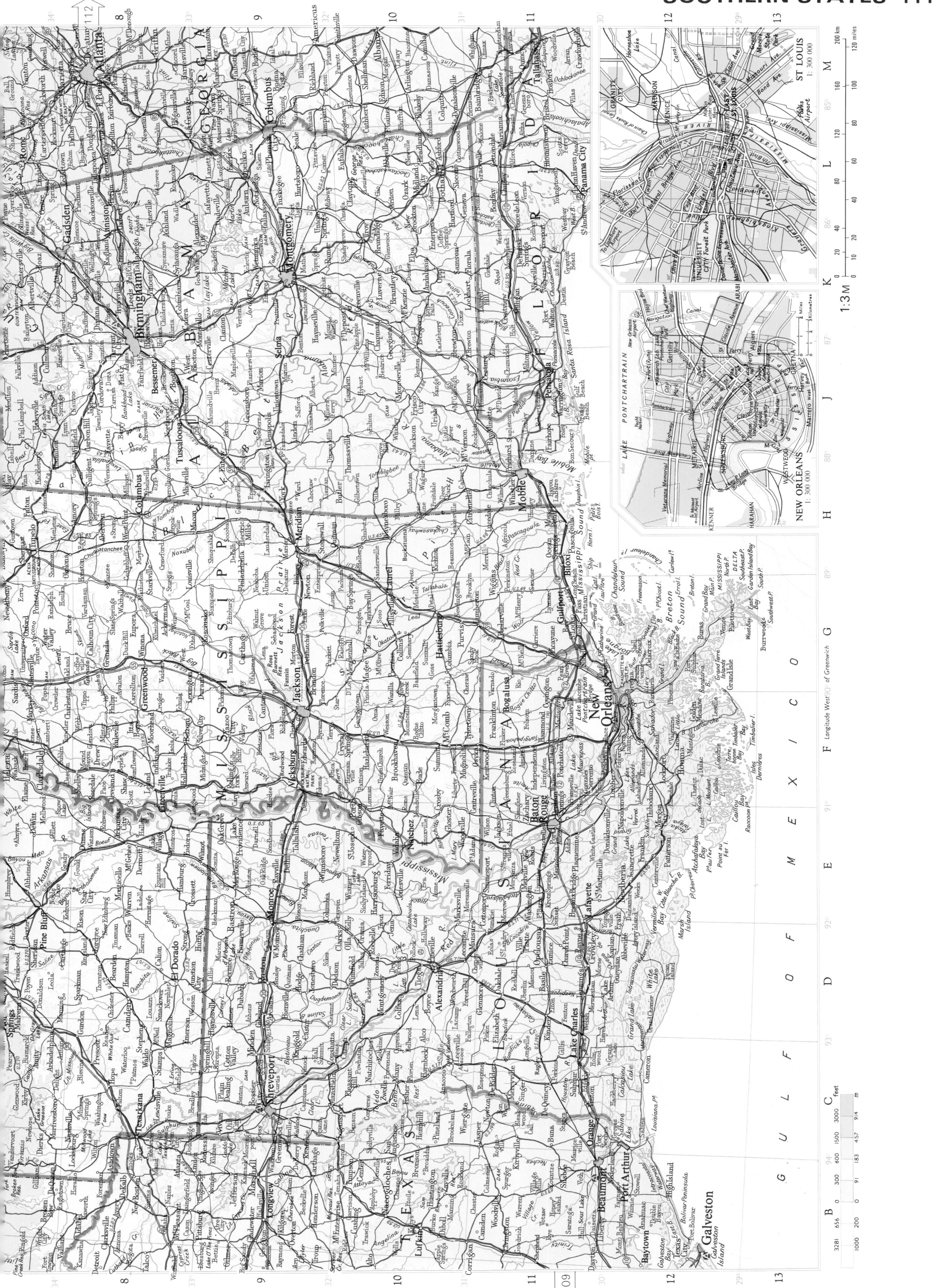

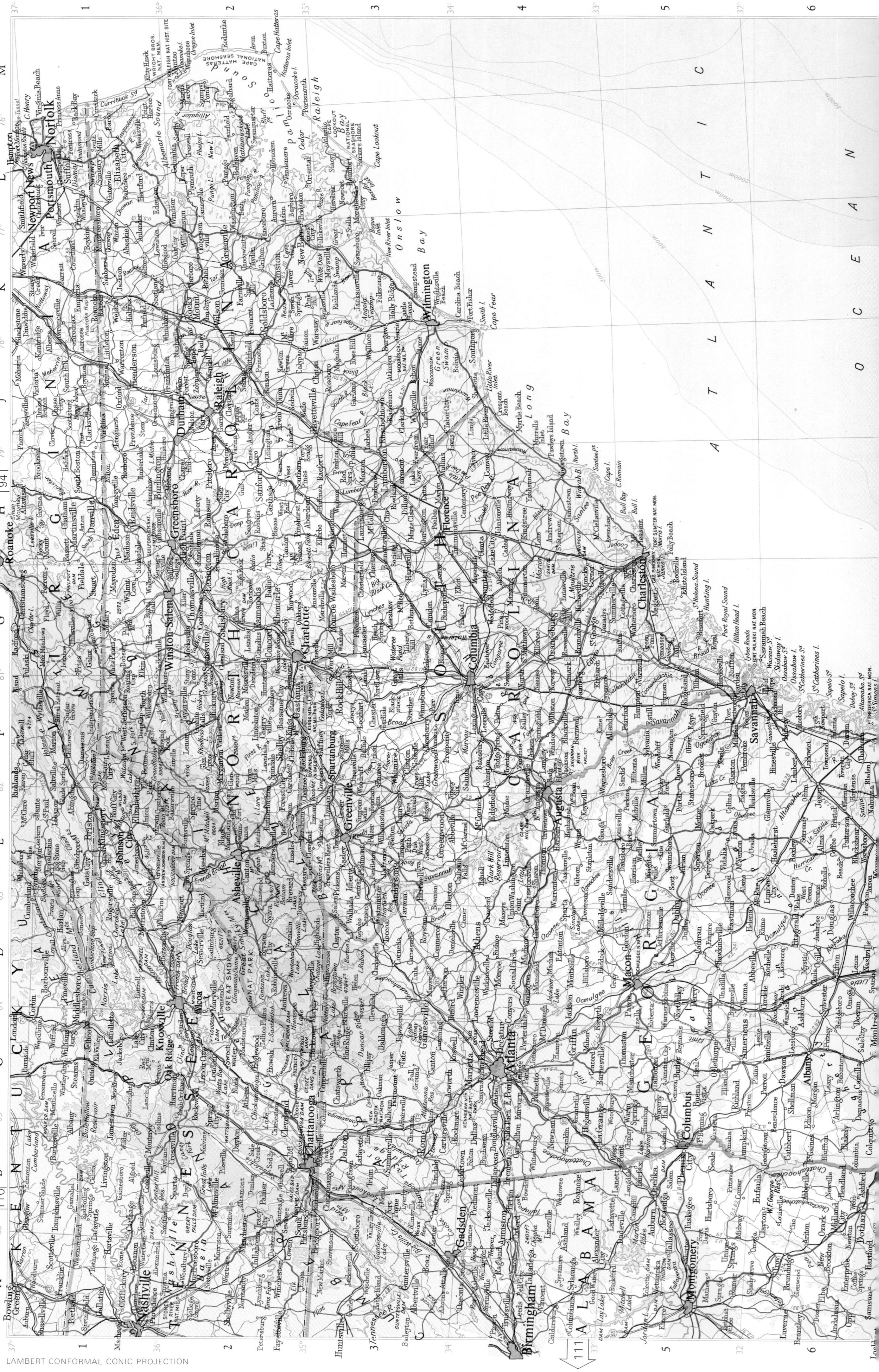

LAMBERT CONFORMAL CONIC PROJECTION

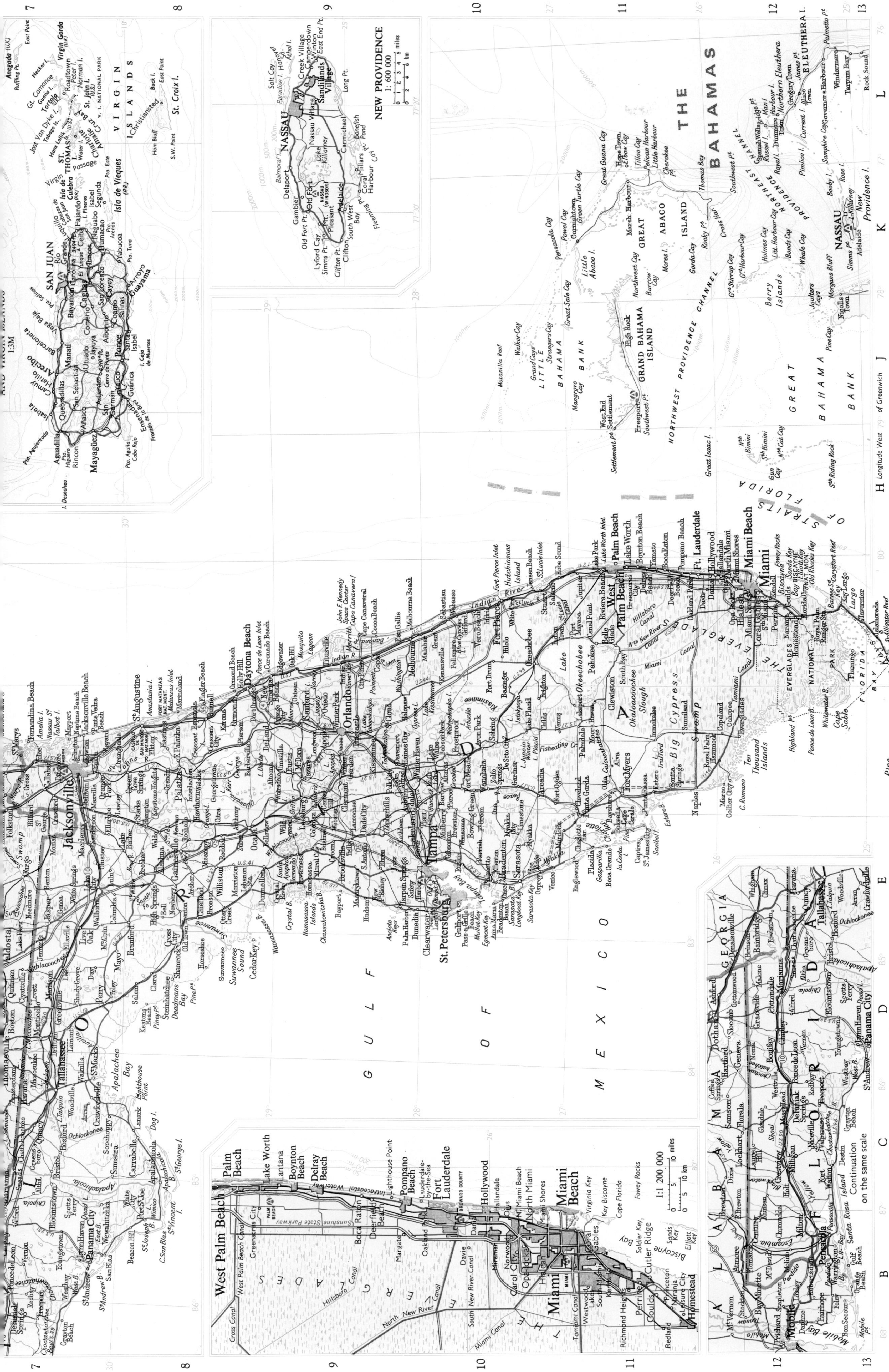

© John Bartholomew & Son Ltd Edinburgh

THE BAHAMAS
NEW PROVIDENCE
1: 600 000
NASSAU
GRAND BAHAMA ISLAND
GREAT ABACO ISLAND
ELEUTHERA I.
NORTHWEST PROVIDENCE CHANNEL
NORTHEAST PROVIDENCE CHANNEL
GREAT BAHAMA BANK
LITTLE BAHAMA BANK
STRAITS OF FLORIDA
1:3M
SAN JUAN
VIRGIN ISLANDS
Isla de Vieques
St. Croix I.
GULF OF MEXICO
FLORIDA
GEORGIA
ALABAMA
Jacksonville
Tallahassee
Orlando
Tampa
St. Petersburg
Miami
Miami Beach
Key West
West Palm Beach
Ft. Lauderdale
THE EVERGLADES
EVERGLADES NATIONAL PARK
Lake Okeechobee
1:1 200 000
Continuation on the same scale
Heights in feet
Depths in metres
Longitude West of Greenwich

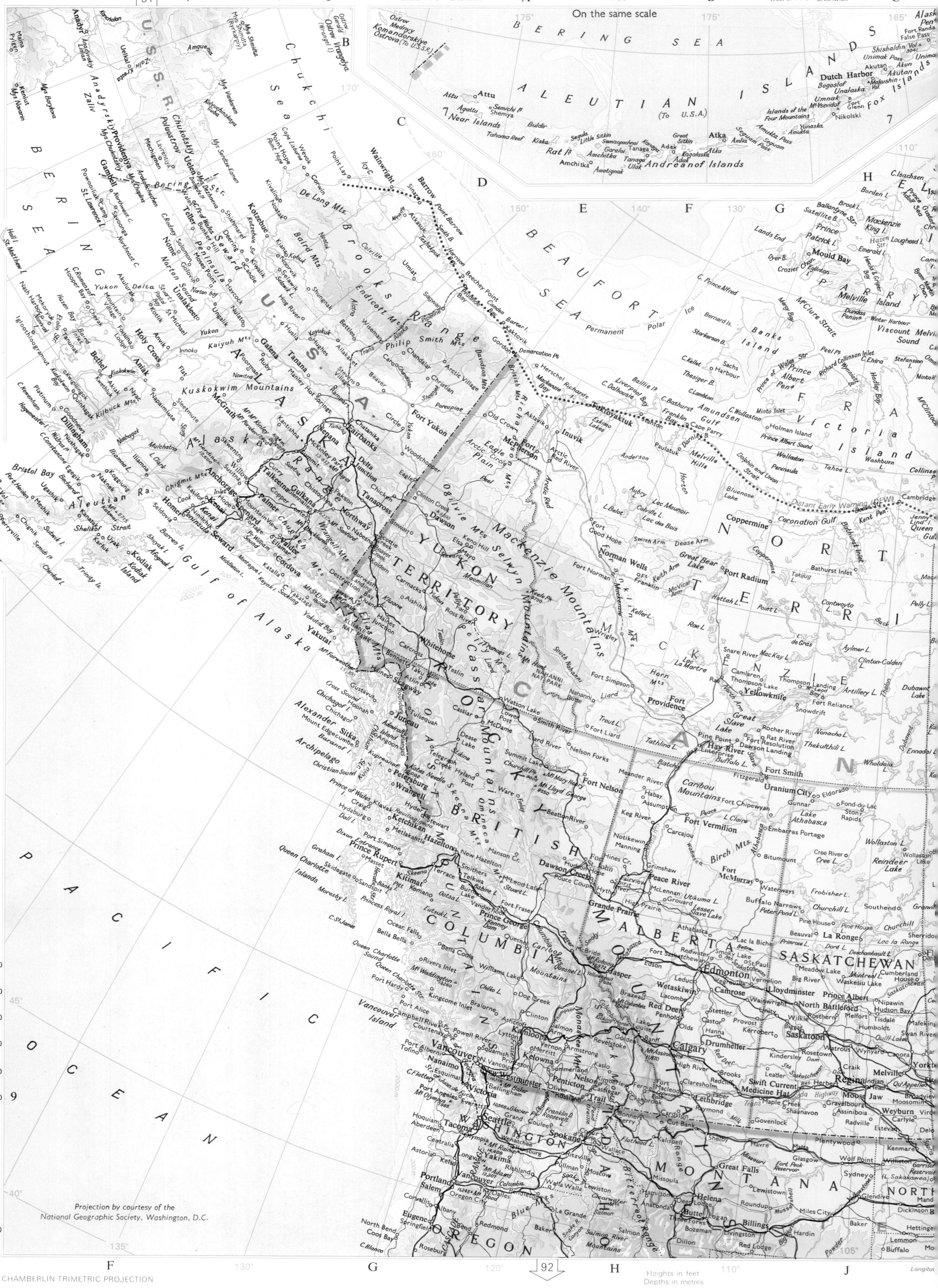

On the same scale

BERING SEA

ALEUTIAN ISLANDS

BEAUFORT SEA

U.S.S.R.

ALASKA

U.S.A.

YUKON TERRITORY

NORTHWEST TERRITORIES

MACKENZIE

BRITISH COLUMBIA

ALBERTA

SASKATCHEWAN

PACIFIC OCEAN

Gulf of Alaska

Bering Sea

Chukchi Sea

Brooks Range

Mackenzie Mountains

Selwyn Mountains

Rocky Mountains

Vancouver Island

Queen Charlotte Islands

WASHINGTON

OREGON

IDAHO

MONTANA

NORTH DAKOTA

Fairbanks
Anchorage
Juneau
Whitehorse
Dawson
Inuvik
Yellowknife
Edmonton
Calgary
Saskatoon
Regina
Vancouver
Victoria
Seattle
Tacoma
Portland
Salem

Projection by courtesy of the
National Geographic Society, Washington, D.C.

CHAMBERLIN TRIMETRIC PROJECTION

Heights in feet
Depths in metres

feet   m
19686   6000
16409   5000
13124   4000
9843   3000
6562   2000
3281   1000
1640   500
656   200
0   0
656   200
6562   2000

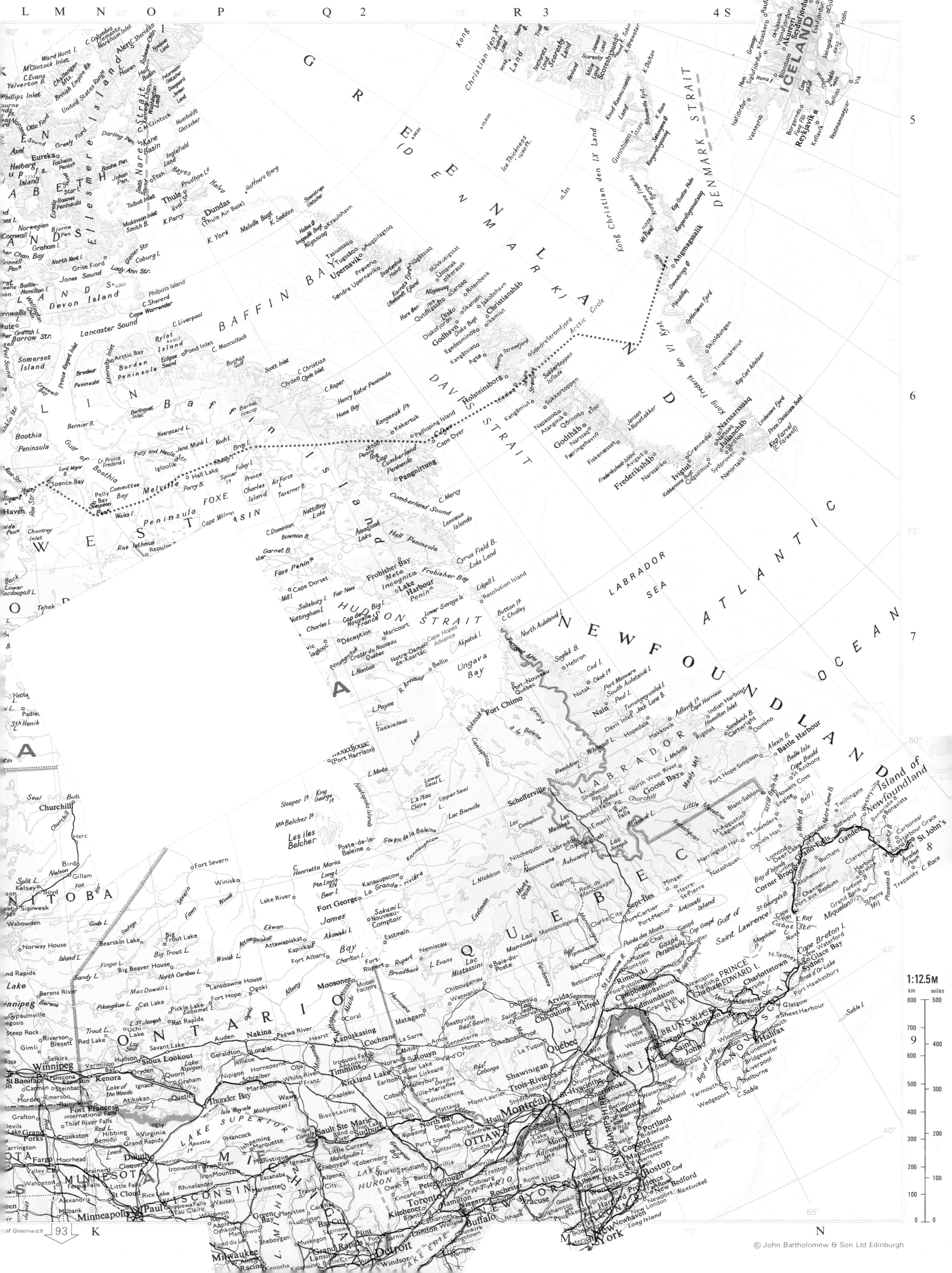
GREENLAND (KALAALLIT NUNAAT)
ICELAND
Reykjavík
DENMARK STRAIT
BAFFIN BAY
DAVIS STRAIT
Baffin Island
Devon Island
Ellesmere Island
Greenland Sea
Arctic Circle
LABRADOR SEA
ATLANTIC OCEAN
HUDSON STRAIT
Ungava Bay
Hudson Bay
LABRADOR
NEWFOUNDLAND
Island of Newfoundland
St John's
QUEBEC
ONTARIO
MANITOBA
NEW BRUNSWICK
NOVA SCOTIA
PRINCE EDWARD I.
Gulf of Saint Lawrence
LAKE SUPERIOR
LAKE HURON
LAKE ONTARIO
LAKE ERIE
MINNESOTA
WISCONSIN
MICHIGAN
NEW YORK
MAINE
MASS.
VERMONT
NEW HAMPSHIRE
Winnipeg
Thunder Bay
Sault Ste Marie
Sudbury
Ottawa
Montréal
Québec
Toronto
Hamilton
Buffalo
Detroit
Milwaukee
Minneapolis
St Paul
Duluth
Boston
New York
Halifax
Sydney
Charlottetown
Fredericton
Saint John
Moncton
Goose Bay
Schefferville
Churchill
Moosonee
Fort Chimo
Frobisher Bay
Godthåb
Angmagssalik
Thule
1:12.5M
km
miles
© John Bartholomew & Son Ltd Edinburgh

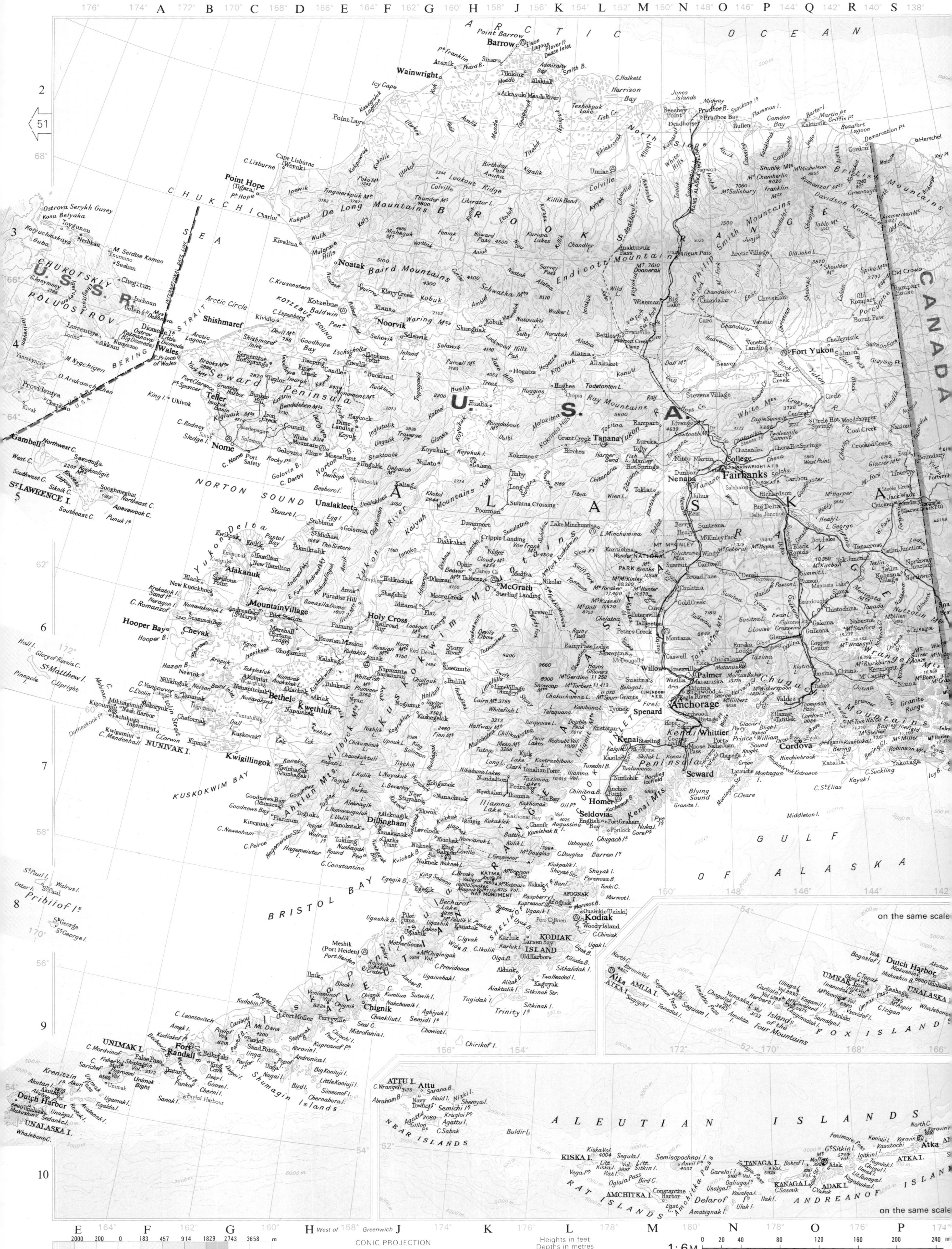

ARCTIC OCEAN

Point Barrow
Barrow
Wainwright

CHUKCHI SEA

Point Hope (Tigara)
Cape Lisburne

BROOKS RANGE
De Long Mountains
Baird Mountains
Endicott Mountains
Schwatka Mts
Philip Smith Mountains
Davidson Mountains
British Mountains

U.S.S.R.
CHUKOTSKIY POLUOSTROV

BERING STRAIT

Shishmaref
Wales
Kotzebue
Noorvik
Noatak
KOTZEBUE SOUND

Arctic Circle

CANADA
Fort Yukon
Old Crow

Seward Peninsula
Teller
Nome
ST LAWRENCE I.
Gambell

NORTON SOUND
Unalakleet

U. S. A.

Tanana
College
Fairbanks
Nenana

ALASKA RANGE
Mt McKINLEY
NATIONAL PARK

Yukon Delta
Alakanuk
Mountain Village
Holy Cross
McGrath
Bethel
Kwethluk

KUSKOKWIM BAY
Hooper Bay
Chevak
Kwigillingok
NUNIVAK I.

Dillingham
BRISTOL BAY

Willow
Palmer
Wasilla
Matanuska
Anchorage
Spenard
Kenai
Whittier
Valdez
Cordova
Seward
Homer
Seldovia
KENAI PENINSULA

GULF OF ALASKA

Pribilof Is.
St Paul I.
St George I.

Kodiak
KODIAK ISLAND
KATMAI NAT MONUMENT

UNIMAK I.
Fort Randall
Chignik
SHUMAGIN ISLANDS
ALASKA PENINSULA

Dutch Harbor
UNALASKA I.

ALEUTIAN ISLANDS
NEAR ISLANDS
ATTU I.
KISKA I.
AMCHITKA I.
RAT ISLANDS
ANDREANOF ISLANDS
Atka
ATKA I.
KANAGA I.
ADAK I.
FOX ISLANDS
UMNAK I.
UNALASKA
Dutch Harbor
Islands of the Four Mountains

on the same scale

CONIC PROJECTION
West of 158° Greenwich
Heights in feet
Depths in metres
1:6M

2000 200 0 183 457 914 1829 2743 3658 m
6562 656 0 600 1500 3000 6000 9000 12000 feet

0 20 40 80 120 160 200 km
0 40 80 160 240 320 miles

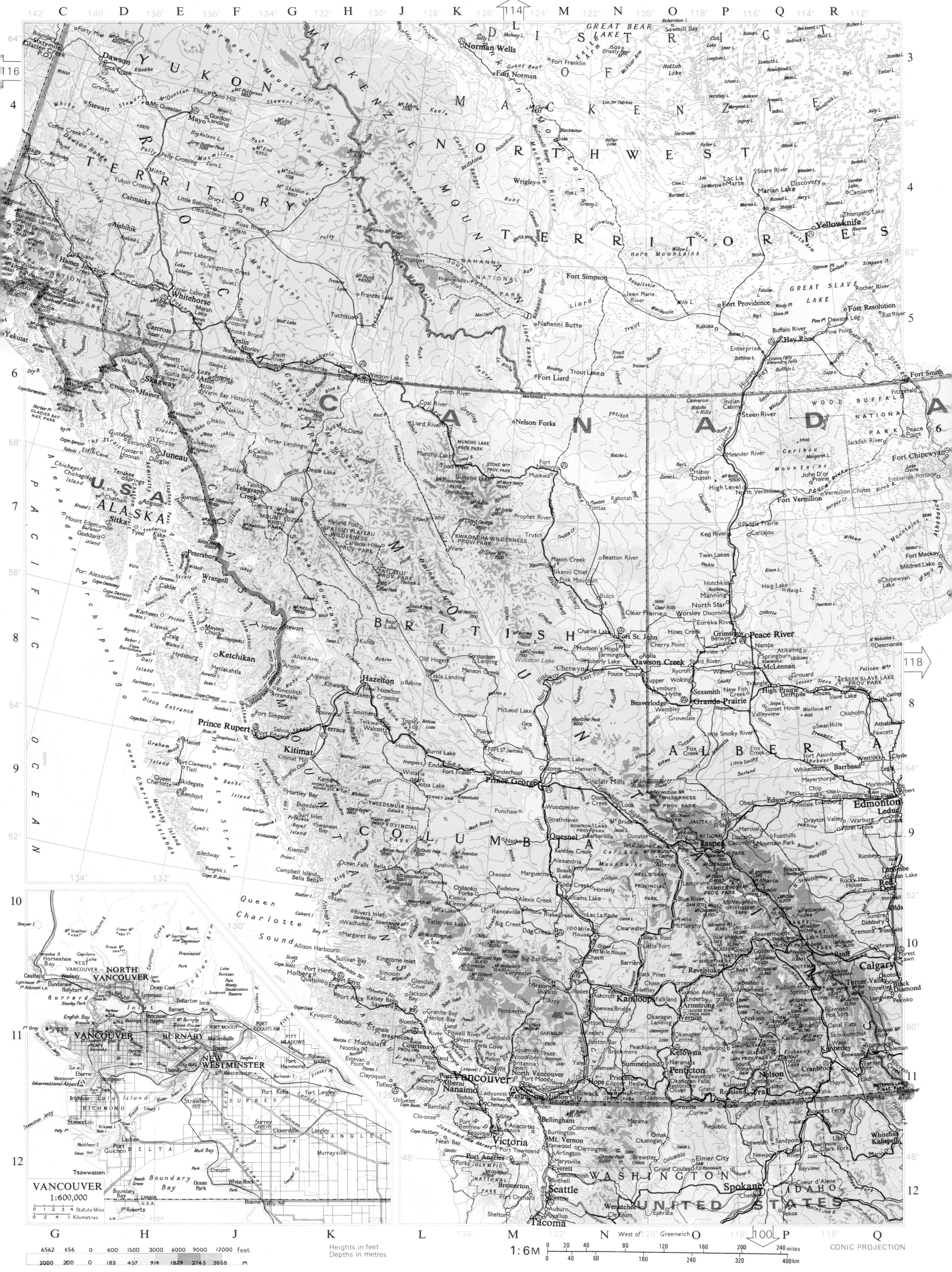

YUKON TERRITORY

NORTHWEST TERRITORIES

DISTRICT OF MACKENZIE

BRITISH COLUMBIA

ALBERTA

U.S.A. ALASKA

CANADA

PACIFIC OCEAN

UNITED STATES

GREAT BEAR LAKE

GREAT SLAVE LAKE

WOOD BUFFALO NATIONAL PARK

Queen Charlotte Sound

VANCOUVER
1:600,000

NORTH VANCOUVER
WEST VANCOUVER
BURNABY
NEW WESTMINSTER
VANCOUVER

Statute Miles
Kilometres

6562 656 0 600 1500 3000 6000 9000 12000 feet.
2000 200 0 183 457 914 1829 2743 3658 m

Heights in feet
Depths in metres

1:6M

0 20 40 80 120 160 200 240 miles
0 40 80 160 240 320 400 km

CONIC PROJECTION

West of Greenwich

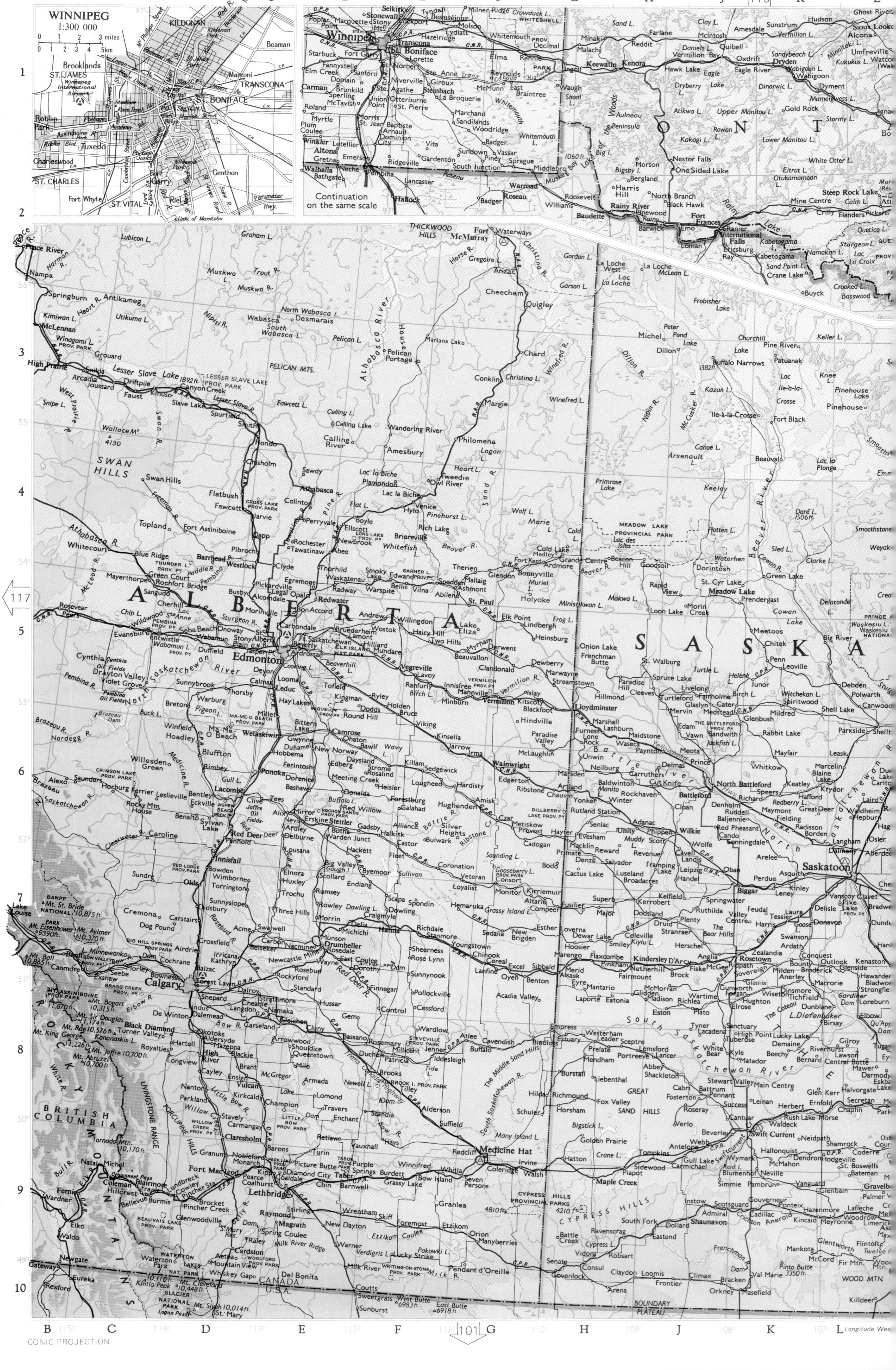
WINNIPEG
1:300 000
Continuation on the same scale
Winnipeg
St. Boniface
Kildonan
Transcona
St. James
Tuxedo
St. Vital
Fort Garry
Brooklands
Charleswood
St. Charles
Selkirk
Steinbach
Morris
Emerson
Altona
Winkler
Kenora
Dryden
Fort Frances
International Falls
Rainy River
Baudette
Roseau
Warroad
ONT
ALBERTA
SASKA
BRITISH COLUMBIA
ROCKY MOUNTAINS
SWAN HILLS
PELICAN MTS.
THICKWOOD HILLS
CYPRESS HILLS
GREAT SAND HILLS
LIVINGSTONE RANGE
PORCUPINE HILLS
MEADOW LAKE PROVINCIAL PARK
BANFF NATIONAL PARK
WATERTON LAKES NAT. PARK
GLACIER NATIONAL PARK
CANADA
U.S.A.
BOUNDARY PLATEAU
WOOD MTN.
Fort McMurray
Peace River
High Prairie
Lesser Slave Lake
Slave Lake
Athabasca
Lac la Biche
Cold Lake
St. Paul
Edmonton
St. Albert
Lloydminster
Vermilion
Vegreville
Camrose
Wetaskiwin
Ponoka
Red Deer
Innisfail
Olds
Drumheller
Calgary
Banff
Canmore
High River
Claresholm
Fort Macleod
Lethbridge
Medicine Hat
Brooks
Hanna
Coleman
Blairmore
Fernie
Wainwright
North Battleford
Battleford
Saskatoon
Kindersley
Rosetown
Swift Current
Maple Creek
Meadow Lake
Lake Louise
Mt. Assiniboine 11,870 ft.
Mt. Joffre 10,700 ft.
Mt. Cleveland 10,448 ft.
South Saskatchewan River
North Saskatchewan River
Athabasca River
Red Deer R.
Bow R.
Oldman R.
Milk River
Battle R.
Beaver R.
Lake of the Woods
Rainy Lake
CONIC PROJECTION
Longitude West
115
117
101

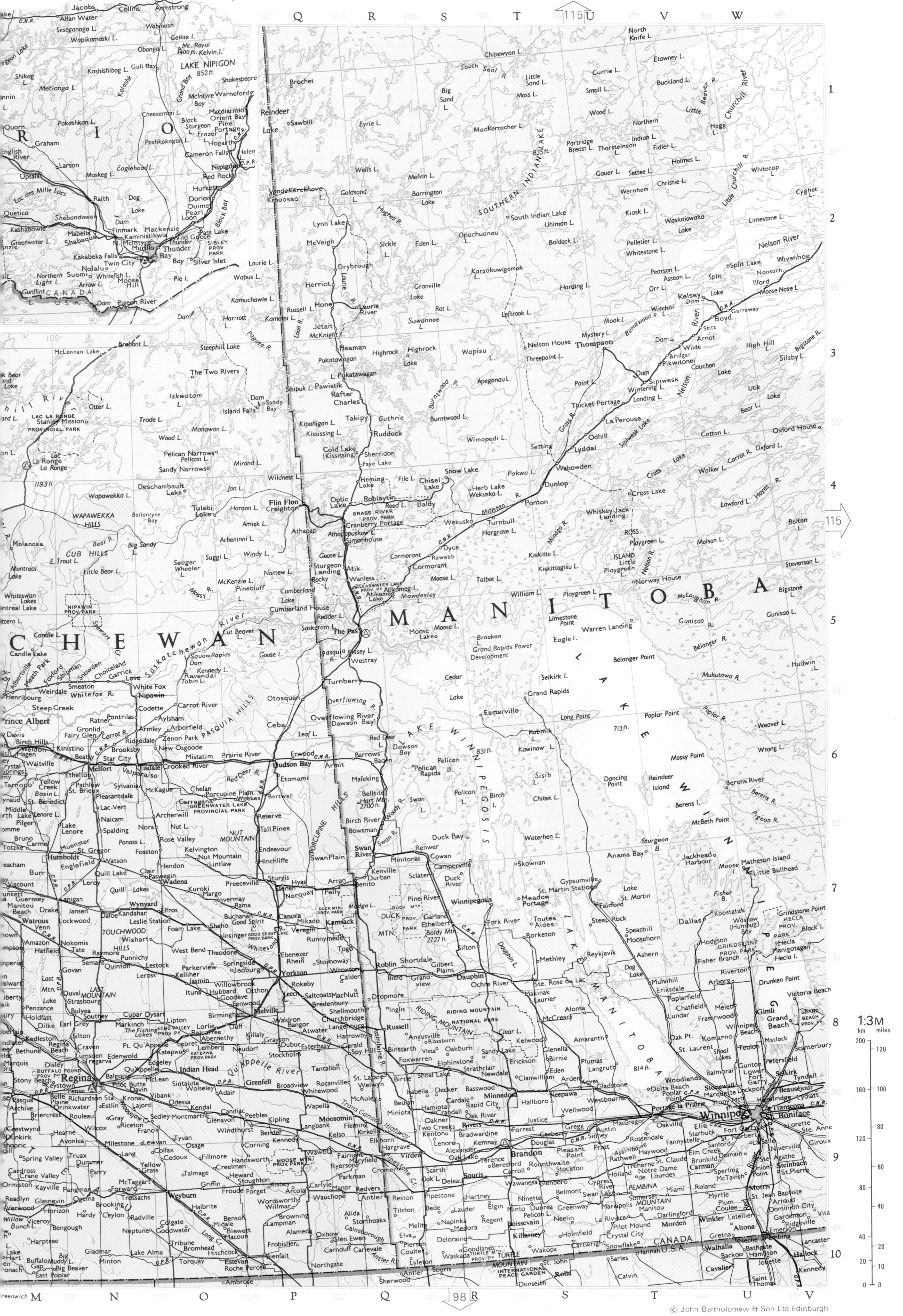

CHEWAN MANITOBA

LAKE NIPIGON 852ft.

Lake NIPIGON

SIBLEY PROV. PARK

LAC LA RONGE STANLEY MISSION PROVINCIAL PARK

WAPAPWEKKA HILLS

CUB HILLS

NIPAWIN PROV. PARK

PASQUIA HILLS

PORCUPINE HILLS

GREENWATER LAKE PROVINCIAL PARK

NUT MOUNTAIN

DUCK MTN. PROV. PARK

TOUCHWOOD HILLS

RIDING MOUNTAIN NATIONAL PARK

LAST MTN.

BUFFALO POUND PROV. PARK

QU'APPELLE RIVER

TRANS CANADA HIGHWAY

QU'APPELLE VALLEY

MOOSE MTN. PROV. PARK

TURTLE MOUNTAIN PROVINCIAL PARK

INTERNATIONAL PEACE GARDEN

LAKE WINNIPEG

LAKE WINNIPEGOSIS

LAKE MANITOBA

SOUTHERN INDIAN LAKE

Churchill River

Nelson River

Saskatchewan River

CANADA / U.S.A.

Thunder Bay

Flin Flon
Creighton
The Pas
Thompson
Nelson House
Cranberry Portage
Cumberland House
Prince Albert
Melfort
Humboldt
Nipawin
Hudson Bay
Swan River
Dauphin
Yorkton
Melville
Regina
Indian Head
Weyburn
Estevan
Brandon
Virden
Souris
Portage la Prairie
Winnipeg
St. Boniface
Transcona
Selkirk
Gimli
Morden
Winkler
Altona
Morris
Steinbach
Oxford House
Norway House
Grand Rapids
Reindeer Lake
Grass River PROV. PARK

1:3M
km   miles
200 — 120
160 — 100
120 — 80
80 — 60
40 — 40
20
0 — 0

© John Bartholomew & Son Ltd Edinburgh

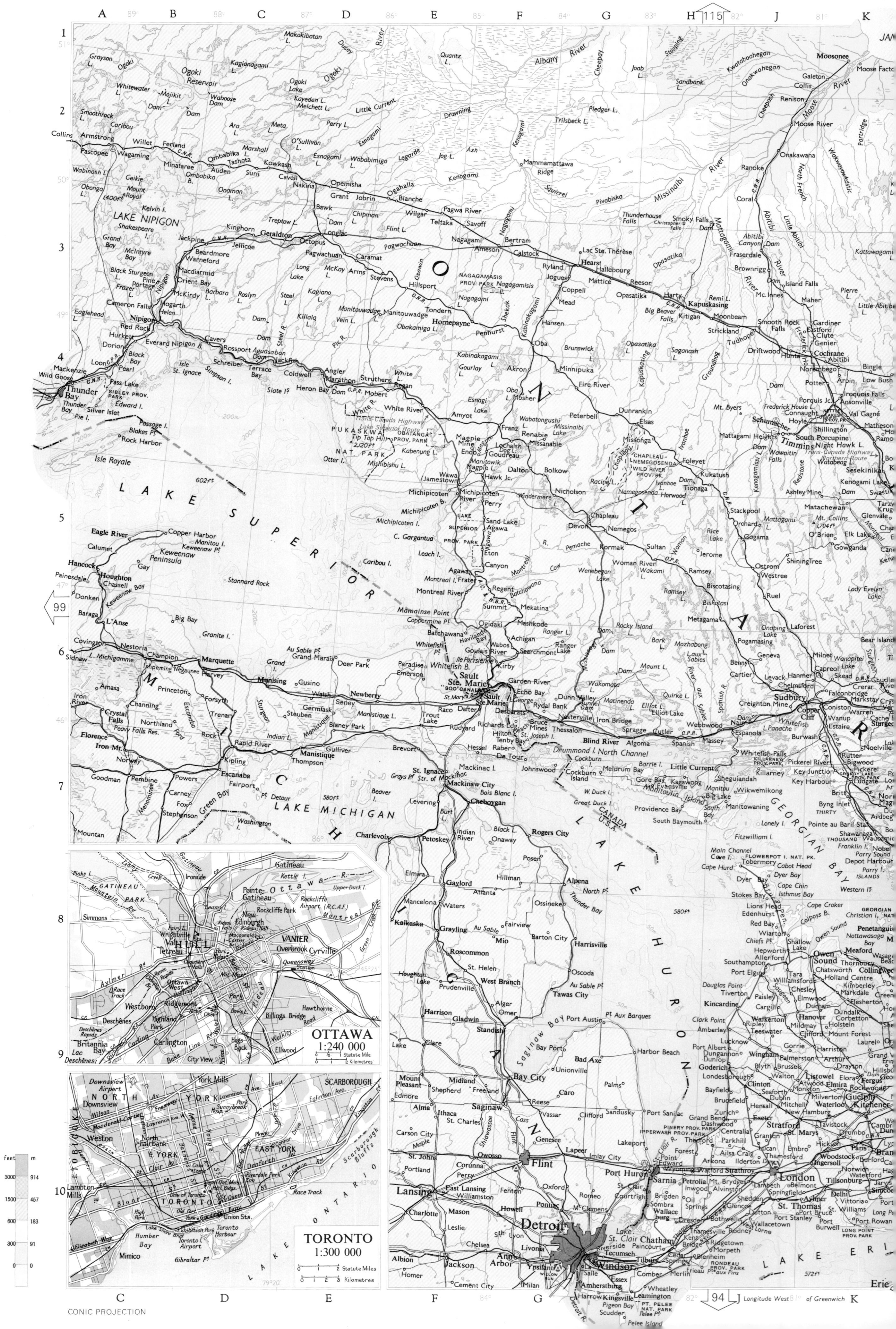

OTTAWA
1:240 000

TORONTO
1:300 000

CONIC PROJECTION

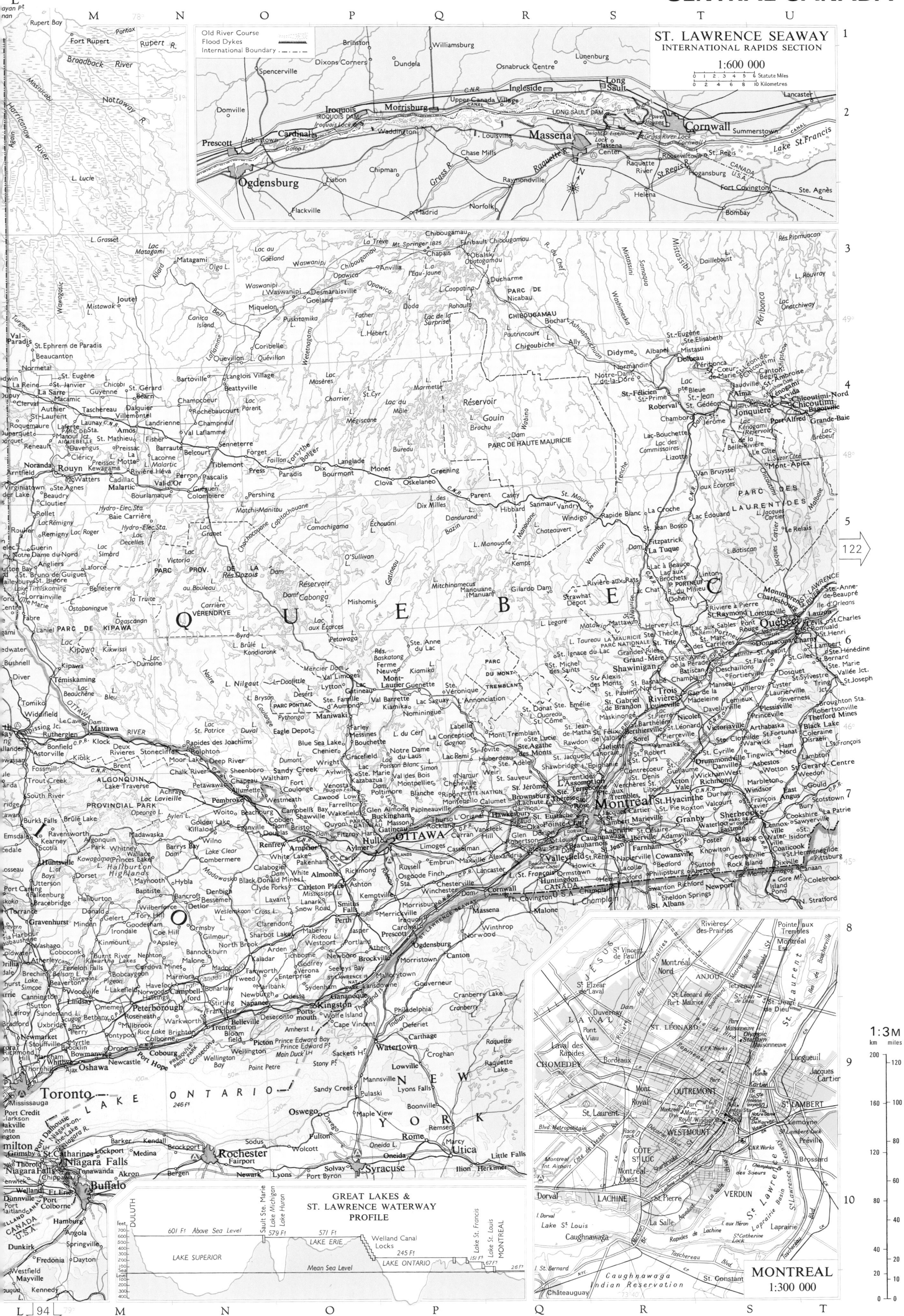

ST. LAWRENCE SEAWAY
INTERNATIONAL RAPIDS SECTION
1:600 000

Statute Miles 0 1 2 3 4 5
Kilometres 0 2 4 6 8 10

Old River Course
Flood Dykes
International Boundary

Brinston · Williamsburg · Lunenburg
Dixons Corners · Dundela · Osnabruck Centre · Long Sault · Lancaster
Spencerville · Morrisburg · Upper Canada Village · Ingleside · LONG SAULT DAM · Cornwall · Summerstown
Iroquois · IROQUOIS DAM · Iroquois Lock · Waddington · Massena · Dwight D. Eisenhower Lock · Massena Center · Roosevelt Br. · St. Regis · Ste. Agnès
Prescott · Johnstown · Cardinal · Chase Mills · Raquette R. · Raquette River · Hogansburg · U.S.A. · Ste. Agnès
Ogdensburg · Chipman · Grass R. · Raymondville · Helena · Fort Covington · Bombay
Domville · Lisbon · Flackville · Norfolk · Madrid

Lake St. Francis

QUEBEC

Rupert Bay · Fort Rupert · Pontax · Rupert R.
Broadback River · Nottaway R. · Harricana R. · Mistassibi

Chibougamau · Mt. Springer 1825 · Faribault · Chibougamau · Res. Pipmuacan
La Trève · Chapais · Obalski · Obatogamau · Daillebout · Rouvray
Anvilla · Opawica · Opawica · Ducharme · Mistassini · Péribonca · Lac Onatchiway
Waswanipi · L. Waswanipi · Desmaraisville · Goeland · Father · Doda · L'Eau-Jaune · Rohault · CHIBOUGAMAU · Washineka · St-Eugène · Ste-Elisabeth
Miquelon · Puskitamika · Lac de la Surprise · Pautricourt · Achouanipi R. · Didyme · Albanel · Dolbeau · Notre-Dame-de-la-Doré
Canica Island · Quévillon · L. Hébert · Bochart · Chigoubiche · Ally · Normandins · St-Félicien · St-Prime · Lac Bleue · Alma · Chicoutimi-Nord
Bartoville · Langlois Village · Lac Masères · Marmette · St-Cyr · Réservoir Gouin · Brochu · Dam · St-Coeur · St-Jean · St-Gédéon · Jonquière · Chicoutimi
Beattyville · Charrier · Lac du Mâle · Bureau · Mégiscane · PARC DE HAUTE MAURICIE · Lizotte · Chambord · St-Jérôme · Port-Alfred · Grande-Baie

PARC PROV. DE LA VÉRENDRYE
Rés. Dozois · Réservoir Cabonga
PARC DE KIPAWA

O N T A R I O

ALGONQUIN PROVINCIAL PARK · Lake Traverse · Achray

OTTAWA RIVER · Mattawa · Deep River · Chalk River · Petawawa · Pembroke

Hull · OTTAWA · Aylmer · Renfrew · Arnprior

Hawkesbury · Montreal · St-Hyacinthe · Granby · Sherbrooke
Valleyfield · Cornwall · Huntingdon

Smiths Falls · Perth · Brockville · Ogdensburg · Cornwall · Massena · Malone
Kingston · Gananoque · Watertown · NEW YORK · Lowville
Belleville · Picton · Prince Edward Bay · Oswego · Rome · Utica
Peterborough · Lindsay · Port Hope · Cobourg

Toronto
LAKE ONTARIO · 246 Ft
Hamilton · St. Catharines · Niagara Falls · Buffalo · Rochester · Syracuse

GREAT LAKES & ST. LAWRENCE WATERWAY PROFILE
Lake Superior · Sault Ste. Marie · Lake Michigan · Lake Huron · 601 Ft Above Sea Level · 579 Ft · LAKE ERIE · 571 Ft · Welland Canal Locks · 245 Ft · LAKE ONTARIO · Lake St. Francis · Lake St. Louis · MONTREAL · 26 Ft · Mean Sea Level

MONTREAL
1:300 000
1:3M

Ste-Rose · LAVAL · CHOMEDEY · Montréal Nord · ANJOU · Rivières-des-Prairies · Pointe aux Trembles
St-Léonard · St-Laurent · OUTREMONT · ST-LAMBERT · Longueuil · Jacques Cartier
WESTMOUNT · Mont Royal · Montréal · VERDUN · Côte St-Luc · LACHINE · LA SALLE · Caughnawaga · Lake St. Louis · St-Constant · Châteauguay · Caughnawaga Indian Reservation

Heights in feet · Depths in metres

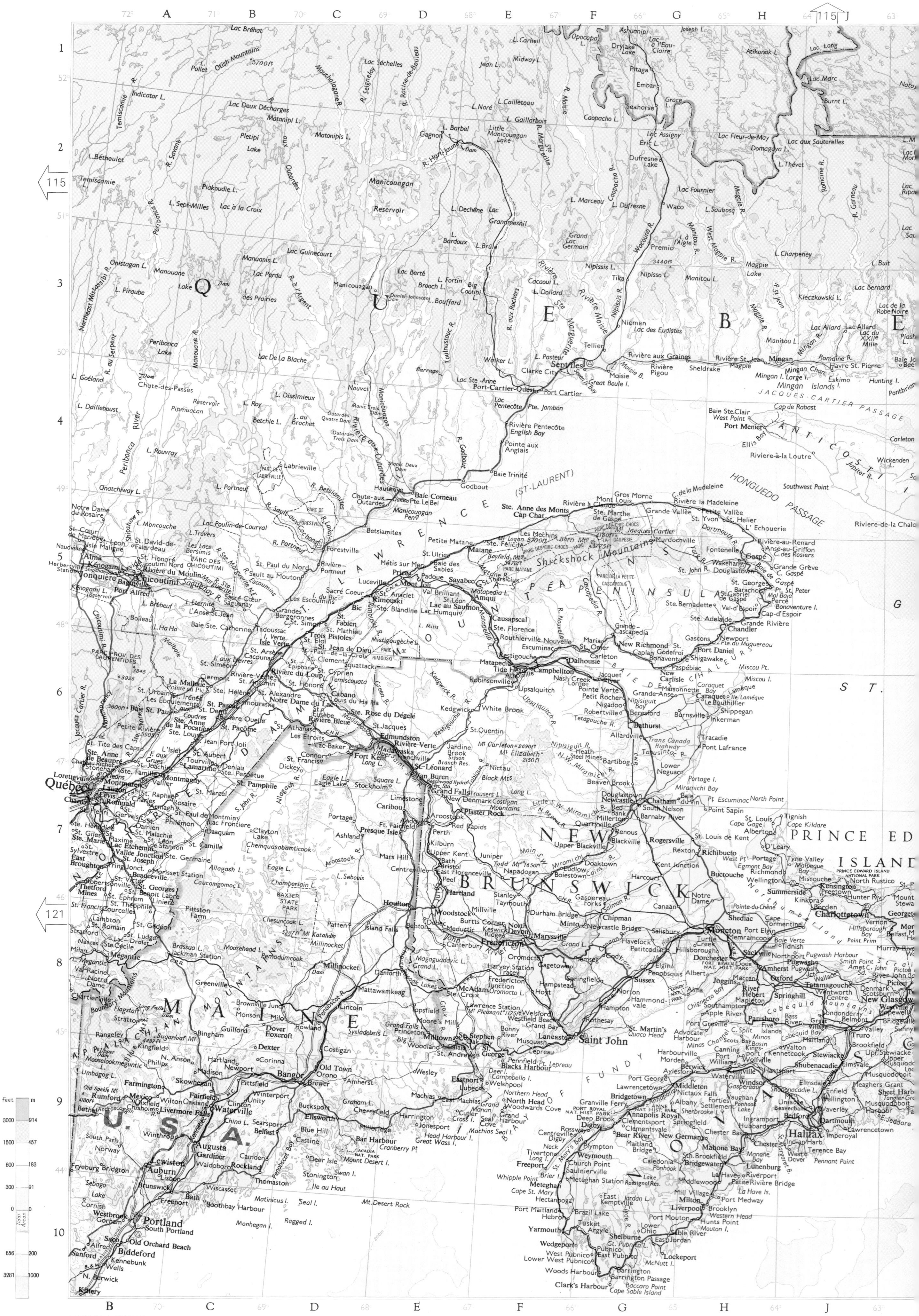

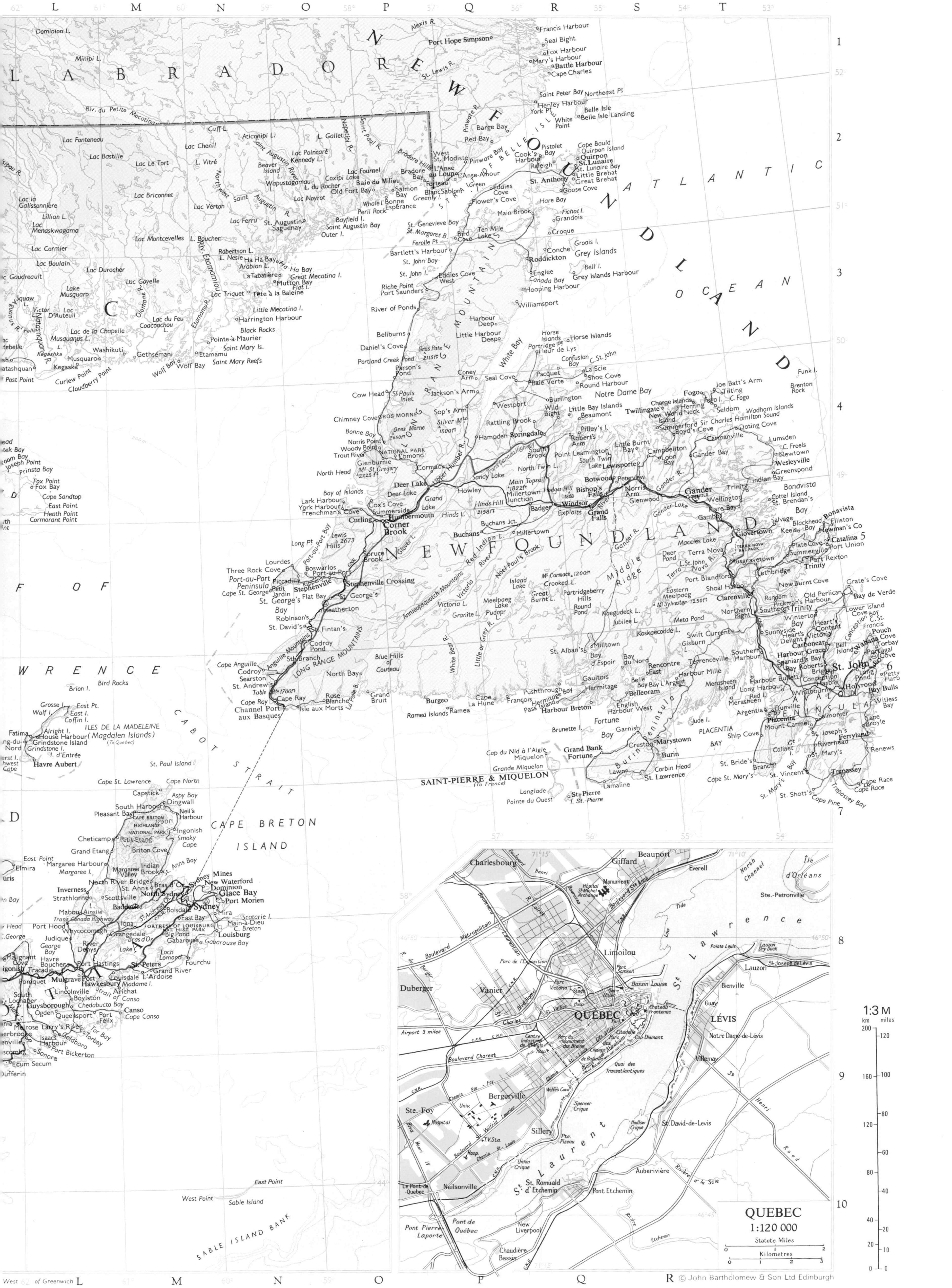

QUEBEC
1:120 000

Statute Miles
Kilometres

1:3 M
km   miles

West of Greenwich

MEXICO
CITY

1:250 000

0 1 2 3 4 5 km

PANAMA CANAL
1: 900 000

Statute Miles
0 2 4 6 8 10 12 14 16 Kilometres
feet 164 65 0 328 656 1640 feet
m 50 20 0 100 200 500 m

PACIFIC OCEAN

feet | m
13124 | 4000
9843 | 3000
6562 | 2000
3281 | 1000
1640 | 500
656 | 200
0 | Below Sea level
656 | 200
6562 | 2000

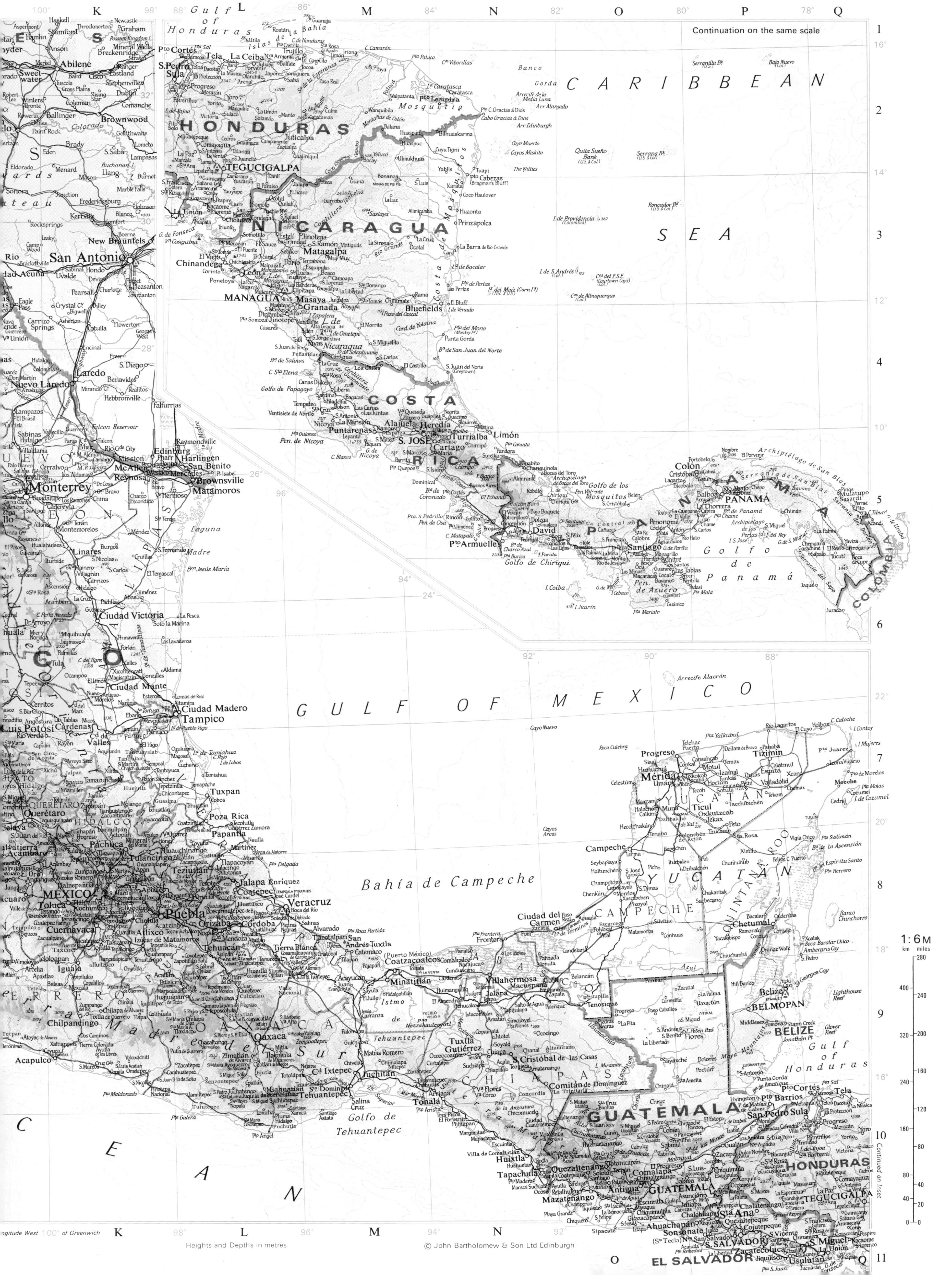

Continuation on the same scale

CARIBBEAN

SEA

GULF OF MEXICO

Bahía de Campeche

Golfo de Tehuantepec

Gulf of Honduras

HONDURAS

TEGUCIGALPA

NICARAGUA

MANAGUA

COSTA RICA

S. JOSÉ

PANAMA

PANAMÁ

Golfo de Panamá

Golfo de Chiriquí

COLOMBIA

MEXICO

Monterrey

San Antonio

Nuevo Laredo

Laredo

Ciudad Victoria

Tampico

Ciudad Madero

Veracruz

Puebla

México

Toluca

Cuernavaca

Oaxaca

Acapulco

Chilpancingo

Mérida

YUCATÁN

Campeche

CAMPECHE

QUINTANA ROO

Chetumal

BELIZE

BELMOPAN

GUATEMALA

Quezaltenango

Mazatenango

Tapachula

CHIAPAS

Tuxtla Gutiérrez

S. Cristóbal de las Casas

Comitán de Dominguez

Villahermosa

TABASCO

Coatzacoalcos

Minatitlán

EL SALVADOR

SAN SALVADOR

Sta Ana

HONDURAS

San Pedro Sula

Tela

La Ceiba

OAXACA

GUERRERO

Sierra Madre del Sur

OCEAN

1 : 6 M

km   miles

© John Bartholomew & Son Ltd Edinburgh

Heights and Depths in metres

Longitude West of Greenwich

Continued on Inset

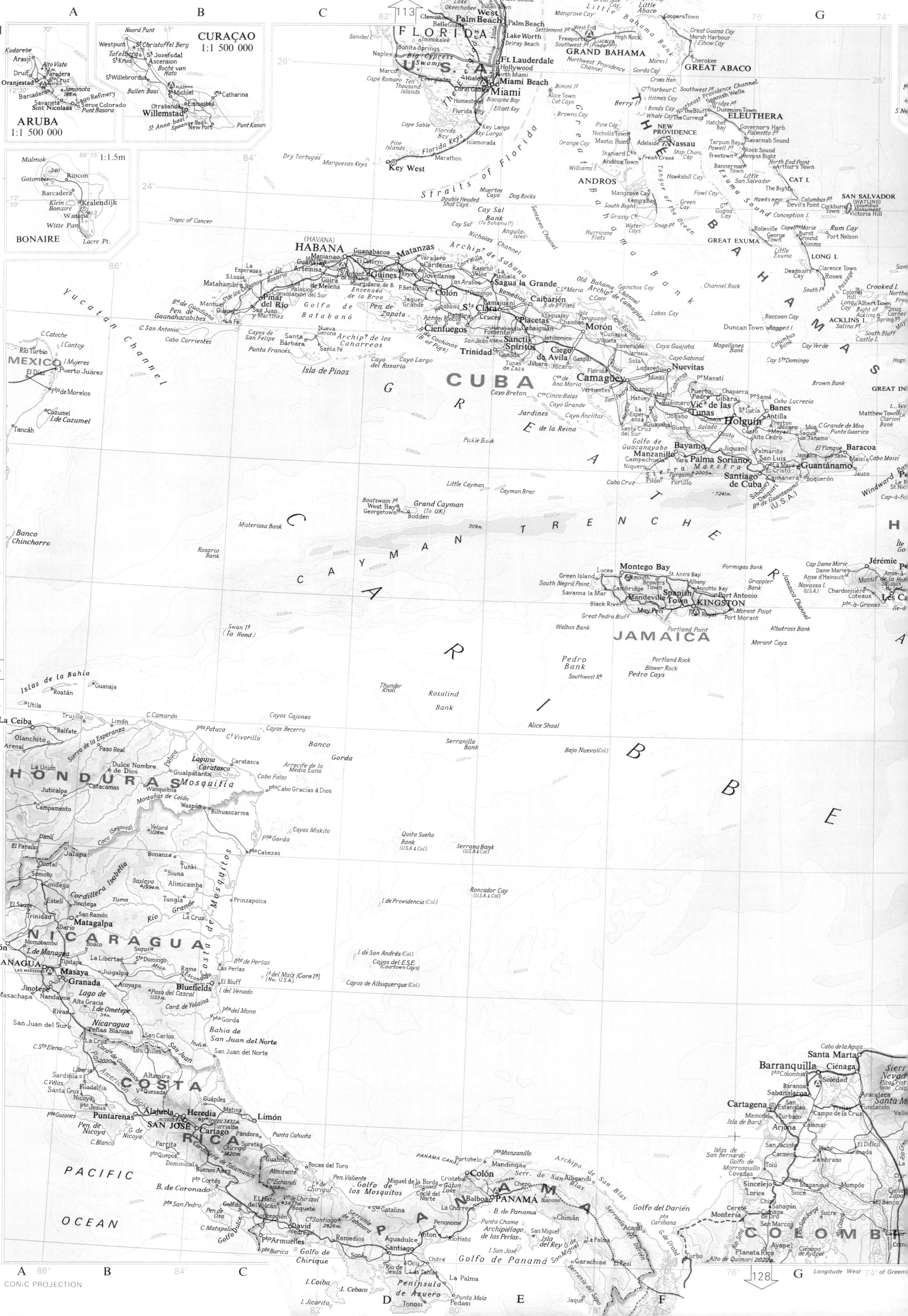
CURAÇAO
1:1 500 000
ARUBA
1:1 500 000
BONAIRE
1:1.5m
Oranjestad
Willemstad
Kralendijk
FLORIDA
U.S.A.
Miami
Miami Beach
Ft. Lauderdale
West Palm Beach
Key West
Straits of Florida
GRAND BAHAMA
GREAT ABACO
ELEUTHERA
NEW PROVIDENCE
Nassau
ANDROS
CAT I.
SAN SALVADOR (WATLING)
GREAT EXUMA
LONG I.
ACKLINS I.
THE BAHAMAS
Great Bahama Bank
Tropic of Cancer
(HAVANA)
HABANA
Matanzas
Pinar del Río
Cienfuegos
Trinidad
Sancti Spíritus
Ciego de Avila
Morón
Camagüey
Nuevitas
Holguín
Bayamo
Manzanillo
Santiago de Cuba
Guantánamo
Baracoa
Isla de Pinos
Golfo de Batabanó
CUBA
Yucatan Channel
MEXICO
I. de Cozumel
Cayman Trench
Grand Cayman
Little Cayman
Cayman Brac
Georgetown
Montego Bay
Mandeville
Spanish Town
KINGSTON
JAMAICA
Pedro Bank
Rosalind Bank
Serranilla Bank
Islas de la Bahía
La Ceiba
HONDURAS
Mosquitia
Cabo Gracias á Dios
Caratasca
NICARAGUA
Matagalpa
León
MANAGUA
Masaya
Granada
Lago de Nicaragua
Bluefields
San Juan del Norte
COSTA RICA
SAN JOSÉ
Cartago
Heredia
Alajuela
Puntarenas
Limón
PACIFIC OCEAN
PANAMA
PANAMÁ
Colón
Golfo de Panamá
Golfo de los Mosquitos
David
Santiago
Península de Azuero
Golfo de Chiriquí
Golfo del Darién
COLOMBIA
Barranquilla
Cartagena
Santa Marta
Montería
Sincelejo
CARIBBEAN SEA
Serrana Bank
Roncador Cay
I. de Providencia (Col.)
I. de San Andrés (Col.)
Windward Passage
Jérémie
Les Cayes
CONIC PROJECTION
Longitude West 74° of Greenwich

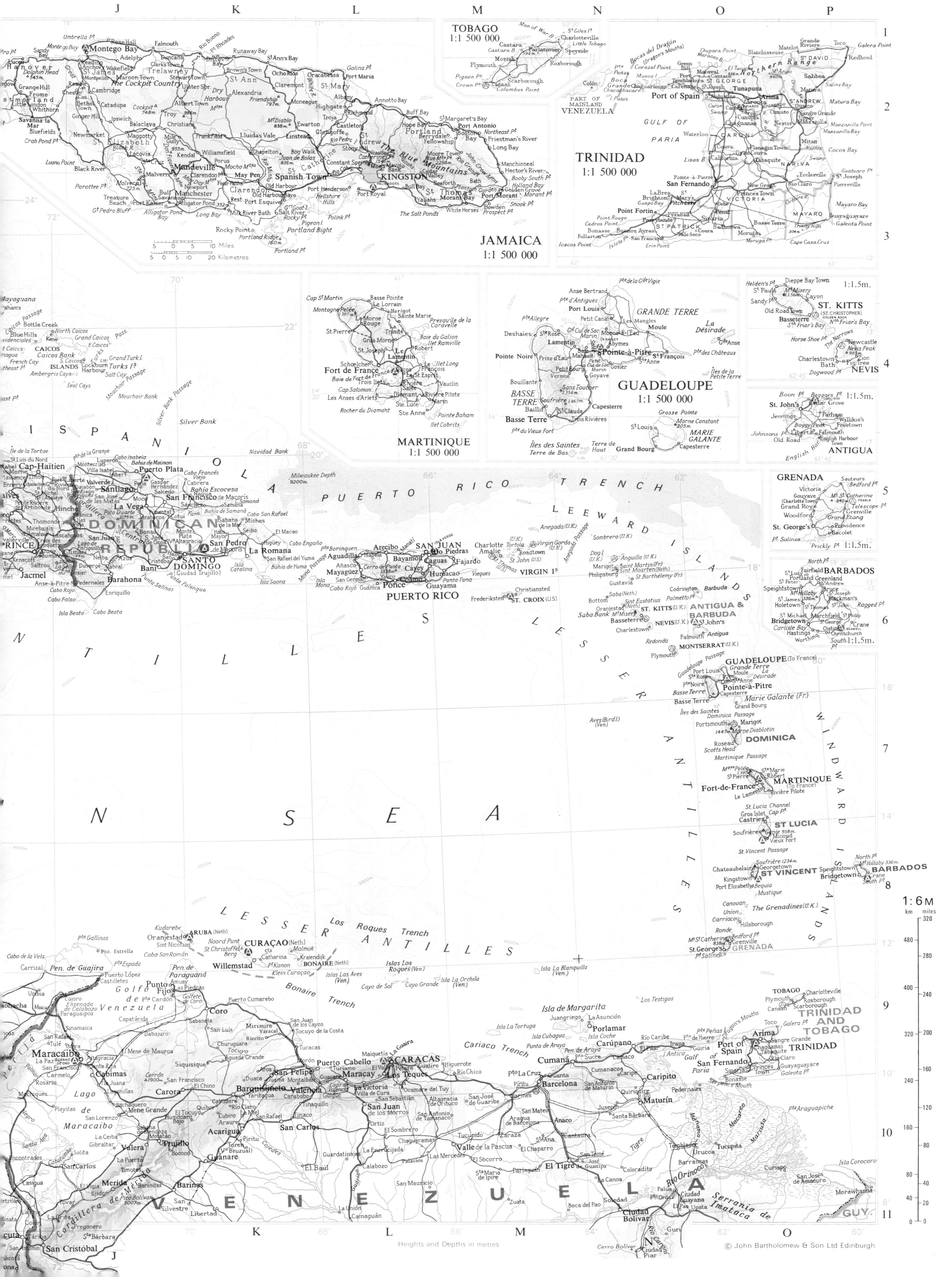

JAMAICA
1:1 500 000

Montego Bay · Falmouth · Rio Bueno · Runaway Bay · St Ann's Bay · Ocho Rios · Port Maria · Annotto Bay
Hanover · Adelphi · Duncans · Brown's Town · Claremont · St Mary · Port Antonio
Grange Hill · Lucea · Cambridge · The Cockpit Country · Albert Town · Moneague · Richmond · Hope Bay · Boston
Westmoreland · Catadupa · Cockpit 748m · Troy 985m · Ewarton · Troja · Buff Bay · Northeast's River
Savanna la Mar · Ginger Hill · Maggotty · Williamsfield · Frankfield · Bog Walk · Priestman's River · Long Bay
Bluefields · Newmarket · St Elizabeth · Kendal · Chapelton · Rio Cobre · Stony Hill · Manchioneal
Crab Pond Pt · Mandeville · Clarendon · Spanish Town · St Andrew · Hector's River · Booby South Pt
Malvern · Manchester · May Pen · Old Harbour · KINGSTON · The Blue Mountains 2256m · Bath
Luana Point · Bull Savanna · Porus · Old Harbour Bay · Port Henderson · Port Royal · Yallahs · Morant Bay
Treasure Beach · Gt Pedro Bluff · Alligator Pond · Milk River Bath · Salt River · Port Morant · Morant Pt
Portland Ridge · Portland Point · Rocky Point · Portland Bight · The Salt Ponds · White Horses · Snook Pt · Bowden

Scale: 5 0 5 10 Miles / 5 0 5 10 20 Kilometres

TOBAGO
1:1 500 000

Charlotteville · Little Tobago · Speyside · Castara · Parlatuvier · Roxborough · Plymouth · Scarborough · Columbus Point · Crown Pt · Canaan

TRINIDAD
1:1 500 000

PART OF MAINLAND VENEZUELA

Port of Spain · Tunapuna · Arima · Northern Range · Grande Riviere · Galera Point · Toco · Redhead
GULF OF PARIA · Waterloo · CARONI · Sangre Grande · Matura Bay · Manzanilla Bay · Cocos Bay
San Fernando · VICTORIA · Princes Town · St Joseph · Pierreville
La Brea · Brighton · Point Fortin · Fyzabad · Siparia · MAYARO · Mayaro Point
Cedros Point · ST PATRICK · Basse Terre · Guayaguayare · Galeota Point
Icacos Pt · Erin Point · Cape Casa Cruz

MARTINIQUE
1:1 500 000

Basse Pointe · Le Lorrain · Cap St Martin · Montagne Pelée 1397m · Marigot · Sainte Marie · Presqu'île de la Caravelle
St-Pierre · Gros Morne · Le Robert · Schoelcher · Le Lamentin · Îlet Long · François
Fort de France · Trois Ilets · Rivière Salée · Vauclin · St-Esprit · Le Diamant · Rivière Pilote · Ste Luce · Marin
Les Anses d'Arlets · Rocher du Diamant · Ste Anne · Pointe Baham · Îlet Cabrits

GUADELOUPE
1:1 500 000

Anse Bertrand · Pte de la Gde Vigie · Port Louis · GRANDE TERRE · La Désirade · Anse
Deshaies · Ste Rose · Moule · St François · Îles de la Petite Terre
Pointe Noire · Prise d'Eau · Baie-Mahault · Pointe-à-Pitre · Gosier · Ste Anne
BASSE TERRE · Soufrière 1467m · Capesterre · Bouillante · St Claude · Trois Rivières · MARIE GALANTE · Morne Constant 205m
Basse Terre · Îles des Saintes · Terre de Haut · Terre de Bas · Grand Bourg · St Louis · Capesterre · Grosse Pointe

ST KITTS
(ST CHRISTOPHER)
1:1.5m.

Dieppe Bay Town · St Misery · St Paul's · Cayon · Sandy Pt · Old Road Town · Basseterre · Sts Friar's Bay · Nds Friar's Bay

NEVIS
Horse Shoe Pt · The Narrows · Newcastle · Charlestown · Nevis Peak 985m · Bath · Fig Tree · Dogwood Pt

ANTIGUA
1:1.5m.

Boon Pt · Beggars Pt · Cedar Grove · St John's · Parham · Willikie's · Jennings · Boggy Peak · Liberta · Freetown · Johnsons Pt · Old Road · English Harbour

GRENADA
1:1.5m.

Sauteurs · Bedford Pt · Victoria · Gouyave · Mt St Catherine 840m · PEARLS · Grand Roy · Woodford · Grand Etang · St George's · Bacolet · Prickly Pt · St Salines

BARBADOS
1:1.5m.

Fairfield · St Lucy · Portland · St Peter · Greenland · St Andrew · Speightstown · Bruce · St James 336m · Blackman's · Holetown · St Thomas · St John · Ragged Pt · Bridgetown · St Michael · Marchfield · St Philip · Carlisle Bay · Oistins · Christchurch · Hastings · Crane · Worthing · South 1:1.5m.

ISPANIOLA · CAICOS ISLANDS · Grand Turk I. · Turks Is · Cockburn Harbour · Salt Cay · Mouchoir Bank · Silver Bank · Navidad Bank

DOMINICAN REPUBLIC · Cap-Haïtien · Puerto Plata · Santiago · La Vega · SANTO DOMINGO (Ciudad Trujillo) · San Pedro de Macoris · La Romana · San Juan · PUERTO RICO · Mayagüez · Ponce · Arecibo · San Juan · Caguas · Humacao · Fajardo

GREATER ANTILLES · PUERTO RICO TRENCH · 9200m · LEEWARD ISLANDS · VIRGIN Is · St Thomas (U.S.) · St Croix (U.S.) · Anguilla (U.K.) · St Martin (Neth.) · Saba (Neth.) · St Kitts (U.K.) · NEVIS (U.K.) · ANTIGUA & BARBUDA · Barbuda · MONTSERRAT (U.K.)

LESSER ANTILLES · CARIBBEAN SEA · GUADELOUPE (To France) · Basse Terre · Pointe-à-Pitre · Marie Galante (Fr.) · DOMINICA · Roseau · Morne Diablotin 1447m · MARTINIQUE (To France) · Fort-de-France · ST LUCIA · Castries · Soufrière · ST VINCENT · Kingstown · The Grenadines (U.K.) · BARBADOS · Bridgetown · GRENADA · St George's · WINDWARD ISLANDS

ARUBA (Neth.) · Oranjestad · CURAÇAO (Neth.) · Willemstad · BONAIRE (Neth.) · Los Roques (Ven.) · Islas Las Aves (Ven.) · Isla La Orchila (Ven.) · Isla La Blanquilla (Ven.) · Isla de Margarita · Porlamar · Isla La Tortuga (Ven.) · Los Testigos · TOBAGO · TRINIDAD AND TOBAGO · Port of Spain · TRINIDAD · San Fernando

VENEZUELA · Maracaibo · Lago de Maracaibo · Cabimas · Coro · Barquisimeto · Valencia · Maracay · CARACAS · Barcelona · Cumaná · Carúpano · Maturín · Ciudad Bolívar · Río Orinoco · GUY(ANA)

Heights and Depths in metres
© John Bartholomew & Son Ltd Edinburgh

1:6M
km miles

NICARAGUA

COSTA RICA

PANAMA

SOUTH

PACIFIC

OCEAN

COLOMBIA

VENEZUELA

ECUADOR

PERU

BOLIVIA

CHILE

ARG.

GUY

Bogotá

Medellín

Cali

Quito

Guayaquil

Lima

Callao

Caracas

Maracaibo

Barranquilla

Cartagena

La Paz

Trujillo

Manaus

Arequipa

Antofagasta

GALAPAGOS ISLANDS
(ARCHIPIÉLAGO DE COLÓN)
(To Ecuador)

On the same scale

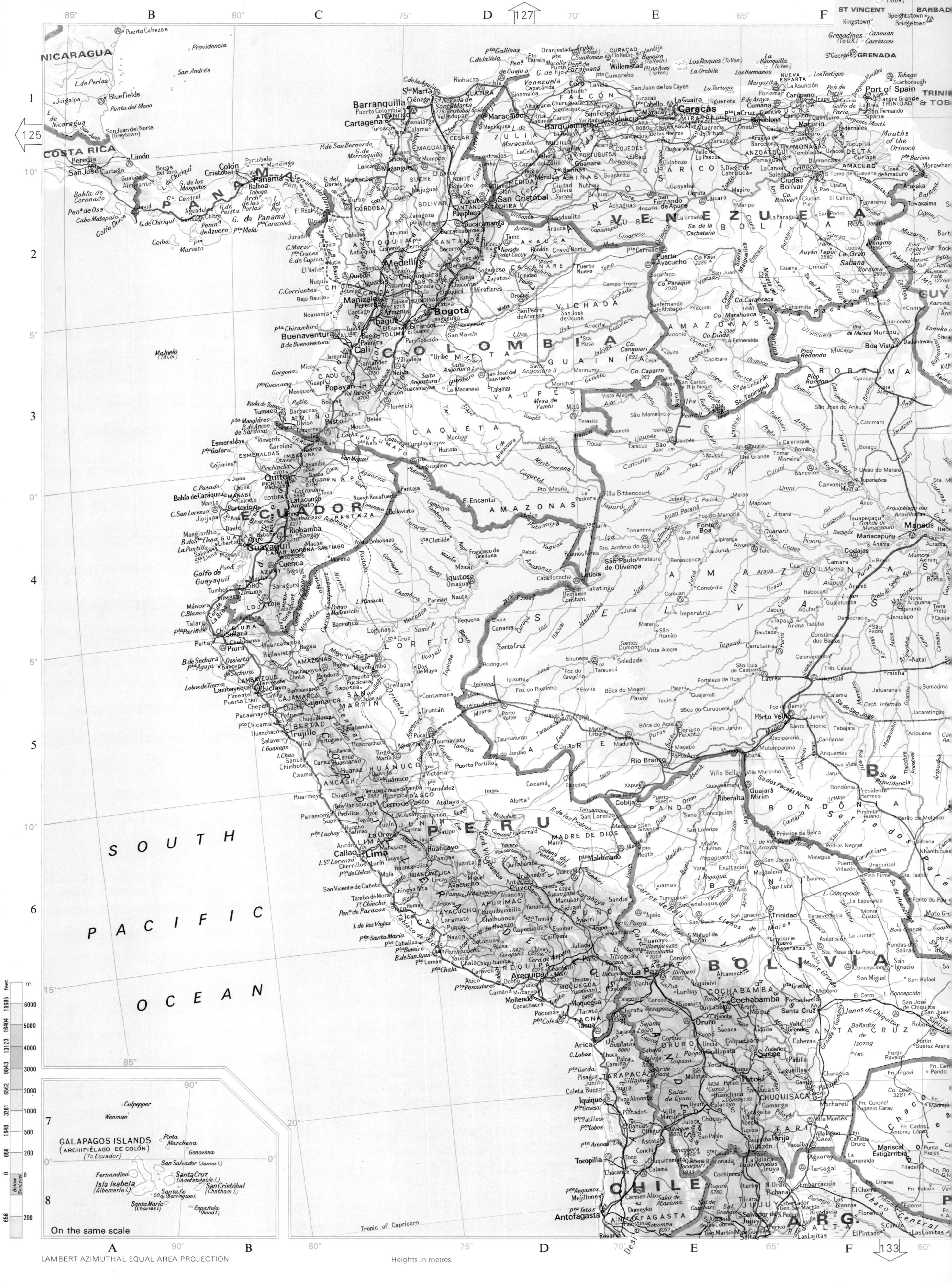

LAMBERT AZIMUTHAL EQUAL AREA PROJECTION

Heights in metres

Longitude West of Greenwich

N O R T H   A T L A N T I C

O C E A N

SURINAME
FRENCH GUIANA

Paramaribo
New Amsterdam
Nieuw Nickerie
Cayenne
I. du Salut
I. du Diable (Devils I.)
Cabo Orange
C. Cassiporé

A M A P Á
Macapá
Mouths of the Amazon
Equator

I. de Marajó
Belém (Pará)
Óbidos
Santarém
São Luís
Rosário
Parnaíba
Camocim
Fortaleza (Ceará)

P A R Á
M A R A N H Ã O
Teresina
Caxias
Sobral
Mossoró
Natal
RIO GRANDE DO NORTE

João Pessoa
Campina Grande
Caruaru
Recife (Pernambuco)
Jaboatão
Maceió

P I A U Í
C E A R Á
P A R A Í B A
P E R N A M B U C O
A L A G O A S

Imperatriz
Carolina
Juazeiro
Aracaju

B R A Z I L

B A H I A
Salvador (Bahia)
Valença
Jequié
Ilhéus
Itabuna
Vitória

S E R G I P E

Planalto de Mato Grosso
Cuiabá
M A T O   G R O S S O
M A T O   G R O S S O   D O   S U L
Corumbá
Campo Grande

G O I Á S
Brasília
Anápolis
Goiânia
Montes Claros
Diamantina
Governador Valadares

M I N A S   G E R A I S
Belo Horizonte
Uberlândia
Araguari

E S P Í R I T O   S A N T O

São Paulo
S Ã O   P A U L O
Ribeirão Prêto
Campinas
Sorocaba
Santos
Presidente Prudente
Marília
Bauru
Londrina
P A R A N Á

Juiz de Fora
Campos
Niterói
Rio de Janeiro
Petrópolis
Nova Friburgo
Cabo Frio

P A R A G U A Y
U R U G U A Y

Fernando de Noronha (To Brazil)
Rocas

1:12 M
km   miles
800 — 480
640 — 400
480 — 320
320 — 240
240 — 160
160 — 80
80

I. Martin Vaz
I. Trindade (To Brazil)

© John Bartholomew & Son Ltd Edinburgh

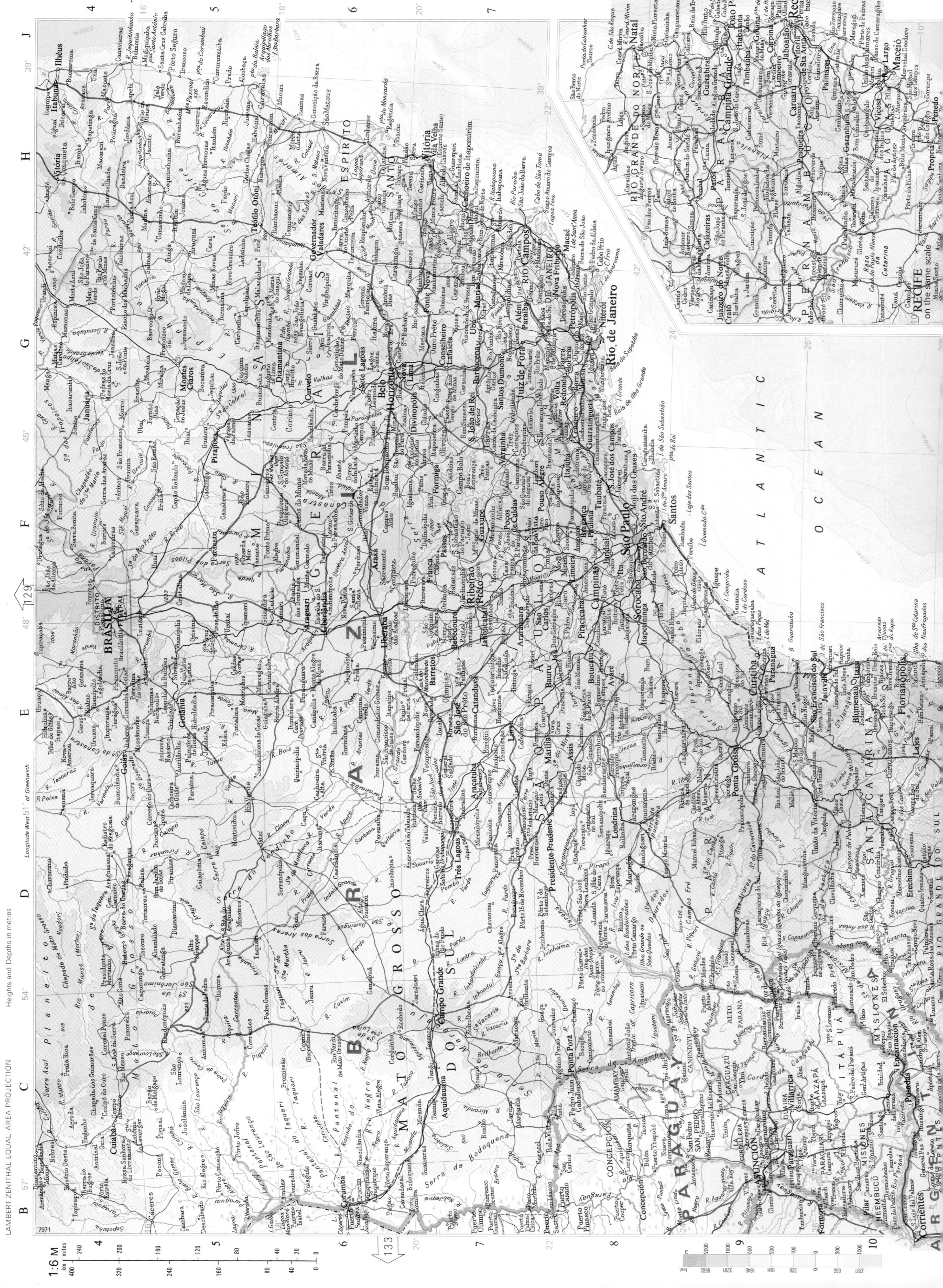

RECIFE
on the same scale

LAMBERT ZENITHAL EQUAL-AREA PROJECTION

Longitude West 51° of Greenwich

Heights and Depths in metres

1:6 M

7971

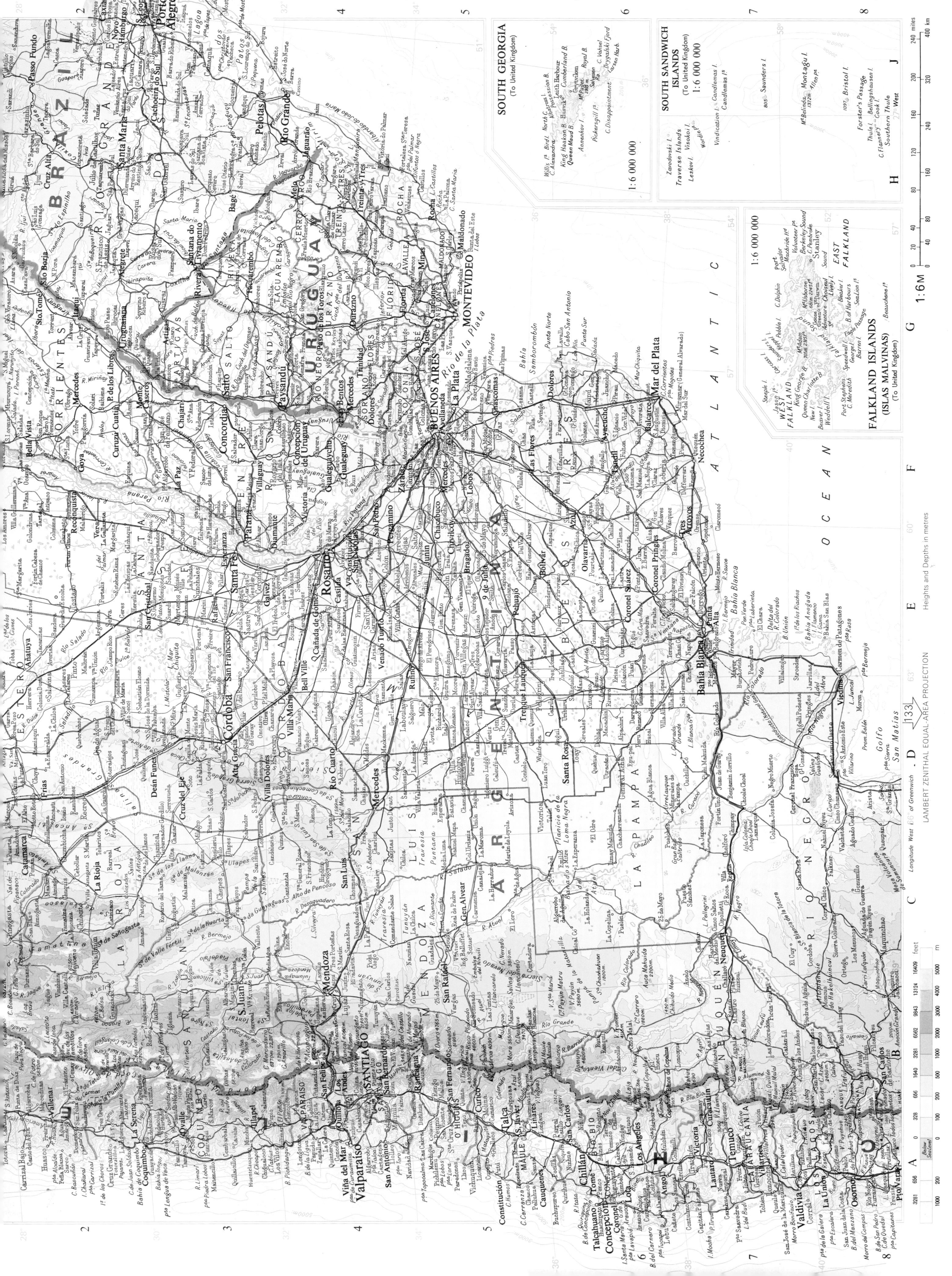

SOUTH GEORGIA
(To United Kingdom)

1:6 000 000

SOUTH SANDWICH
ISLANDS
(To United Kingdom)

1:6 000 000

1:6 000 000

FALKLAND ISLANDS
(ISLAS MALVINAS)
(To United Kingdom)

1:6M

LAMBERT ZENITHAL EQUAL-AREA PROJECTION

Heights and Depths in metres

RIO DE JANEIRO

43°30' · 43°15' · 43°00'

A · B · C · D

Teófilo Cunha · Aliézur · Caramujos · Rio d'Ouro · Cachoeiras · São Bernardino · Surui · Magé · Magé Mirim · Sernambitiba · Piedade

RIO DE JANEIRO · Carlos Sampaio · Santa Rita · Ambaí · Itaipu · Heliópolis · Amaral · Aiva · Cava · Figueira · Miguel Couto · Baby · DUQUE DE CAXIAS · Campos Elyseos · Olaria · São Francisco do Croará · ITABORAÍ · Itambi

Queimados · Austin · NOVA IGUAÇU · Morro Agudo · Andrade Araújo · Núcleo Colonial São Bento · Ipiranga · Guia de Pacobaiba

Sarapó · Nova Iguaçu · Belford Roxo · Coelho da Rocha · Gramacho · BAIA DE GUANABARA · Ilha do Boqueirão · Lighthouse · Morro do Itaúna 281

Cabuçu · Mesquita · Agostinho Pôrto · Duque de Caxias · Ponta Grossa · Ilha do Governador · Ilha de Paquetá · RIO DE GONÇALO · JANEIRO

Marapicu · Nilópolis · São João de Meriti · Tijuca · Ilha D'Agua · Ilha dos Tavares · São Gonçalo · Pacheco · Sacramento

Cosmos · Campo Grande · GUANABARA · Olinda · São Mateus · GALEÃO · Galeão · Cocotá · Ilha Santa Cruz · Sete Pontes · Neves · Cotubandé · S. Isabel

Inhoaiba · Serra de Madureira · Morro do Capim Melado 438 · Vila Pedro · Penha · Olaria · RIO DE JANEIRO · Niterói · Maria Paula · Vila Progresso · Rio d'Ouro

Serra da Pedra Branca · Padre Miguel · Campo dos Afonso · Deodoro · Rocha Miranda · Madureira · Bonsucesso · Cidade Universitária · Ponte Costa e Silva · Centro · Graçbata · Boa Vista · Vázzeas das Moças

Pedra Branca 1025 · Bangu · Realengo · Bastos · Cascadura · Meier · Eng. Novo · NITERÓI · Canto de Rio · Badu

Morro de Santa Bárbara 851 · Pico da Tijuca 1022 · Praça Sêca · Pechincha · Boca do Mato · Andaraí · Fab. das Chitas · Palacio de Guanabara · Pão de Açúcar (Sugar Loaf) 404 · Piratininga · Engenho do Mato

Vargem Grande · Taguara · Jacarépaguá · Floresta da Tijuca · Laranjeiras · Botafogo · Copacabana · Ilha do Veado · MARICÁ

Morro Amorim 125 · Lagoa de Jacarépaguá · Lagoa da Tijuca · Pedra da Gávea 845 · Gávea · Leblon · Ipanema · Ilha da Mãe · Ponta de Itaipu · Itaocaia

Baía de Sepetiba · Ilha · Portela · Lagoa de Marapendi · Praia dos Bandeirantes · São Conrado · Niemeyer · Ponta do Marisco · Ilha do Pontes

Ilha do Bom Jardim · Piraquê · Portinho · Ilha da Alfavaca · Ilha das Palmas · Ilha Pontuda · Ilha Comprida · Ilha Rasa · Lighthouse

Morro de Guaratiba 355 · Ponta da Praia Funda · Ilha Rasa da Guaratiba · Ponta de Sernambitiba · **ATLANTIC OCEAN** · Ilha Redonda · Lighthouse

BUENOS AIRES

58°45' · 58°30' · 58°15'

A · B · C · D

ESCOBAR · Villa Rosa · Benavidez · TIGRE · Tigre · San Fernando · RÍO DE

Pilar · PILAR · Garin · General Pacheco · SAN FERNANDO · Victoria · Beccar

Del Viso · El Talar · Don Torcuato · San Isidro · SAN ISIDRO · Juan Anchorena · LA PLATA

Presidente Derqui · Tortuguitas · Los Polvorines · Martínez · Olivos · Vicente López

Manzone · Piñero · GENERAL SARMIENTO · Villa de Mayo · Boulogne · VICENTE LÓPEZ · Florida

LUJAN · José C Paz · Muñiz · GENERAL SAN MARTIN · Saavedra · Aeroparque

General Sarmiento · Bella Vista · Villa Ballester · General San Martin · Belgrano · Hipódromo Argentino

GENERAL RODRIGUEZ · BUENOS · Hurlingham · TRES DE FEBRERO · Villa Lynch · Palermo · BUENOS AIRES

General Rodriguez · MORENO · El Palomar · Caseros · Villa Saenz Peña · Once · Boca

Francisco Alvarez · MORON · Ramos Mejia · DISTRITO FEDERAL · Constitución · Barracas

Moreno · Paso del Rey · Merlo · Castelar · Morón · Nueva Chicago · Avellaneda

MERLO · San Antonio de Pádua · San Justo · Parque Almirante Brown · Lanús · Quilmes

AIRES · Libertad · Rafael Castillo · Isidro Casanova · Tablada · Caraza · Don Bosco

Mariano Acosta · MARCOS · Laferrere · MATANZA · Cuidad General Belgrano · Florito · QUILMES · Berazategui

Elias Romero · Marcos Paz · Pontevedra · González Catán · LOMAS DE ZAMORA · Lomas de Zamora · BERAZATEGUI

PAZ · ESTEBAN ECHEVERRIA · EZEIZA · Esteban Echeverría · Temperley · ALMIRANTE BROWN · Burzaco · Florencio Varela · FLORENCIO VARELA

1:300 000 · © Times Books Ltd

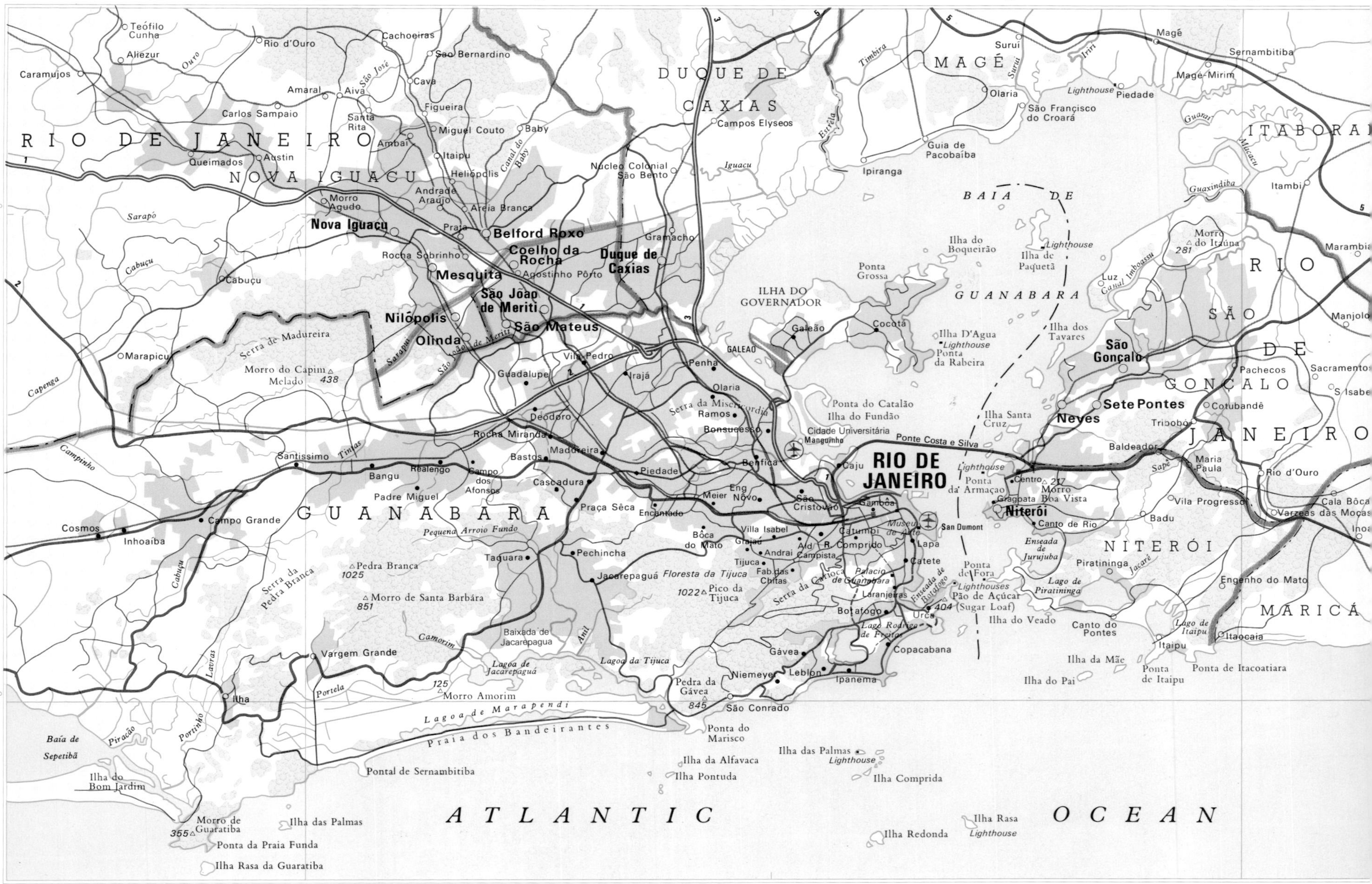

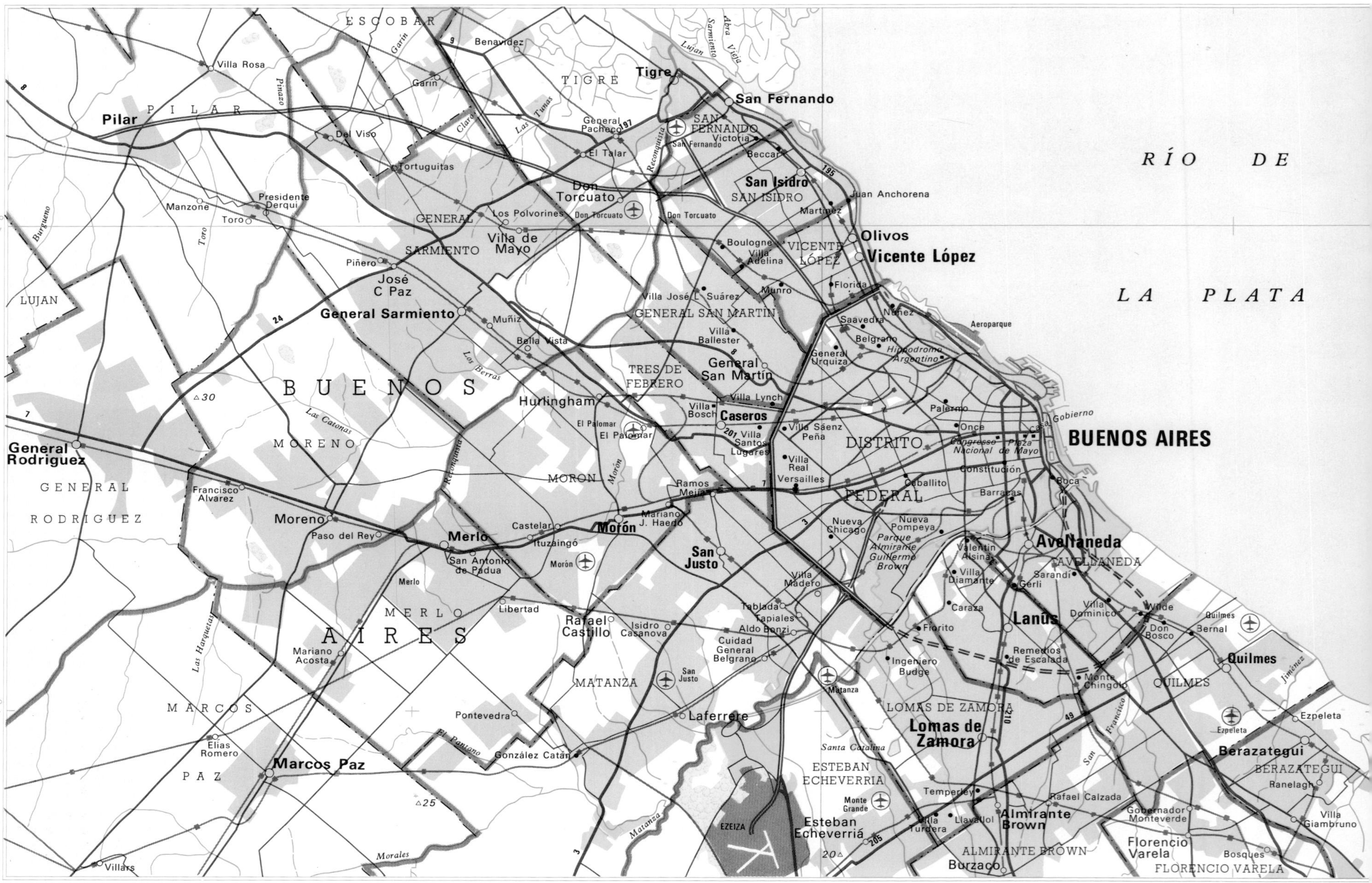

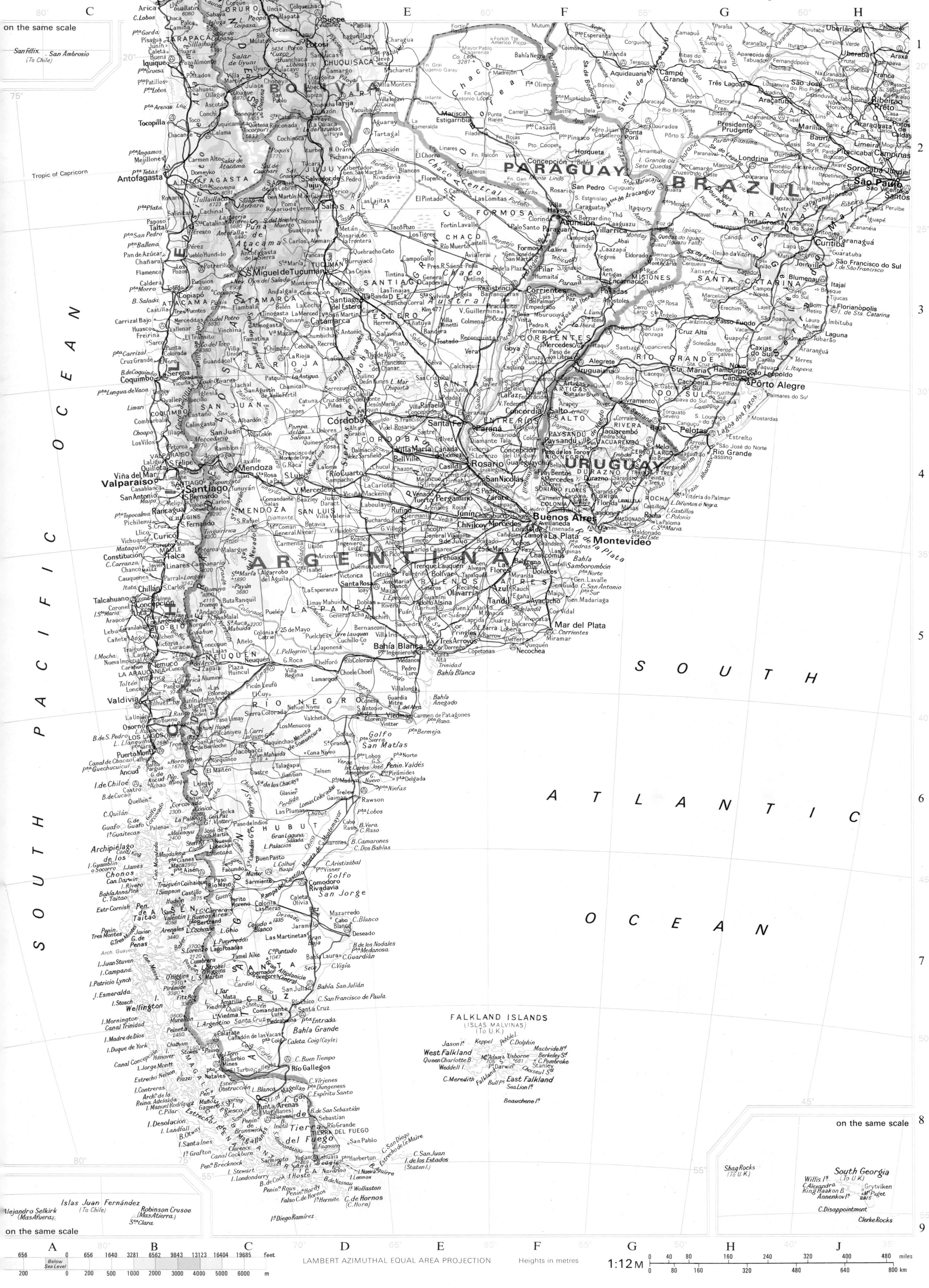
BOLIVIA
PARAGUAY
BRAZIL
URUGUAY
ARGENTINA
SOUTH PACIFIC OCEAN
SOUTH ATLANTIC OCEAN
FALKLAND ISLANDS
(ISLAS MALVINAS)
(To U.K.)
West Falkland
East Falkland
Tierra del Fuego
C. de Hornos
(C. Horn)
Tropic of Capricorn
Antofagasta
Santiago
Valparaíso
Concepción
Valdivia
Puerto Montt
Buenos Aires
Montevideo
Asunción
Córdoba
Rosario
Mendoza
La Plata
Mar del Plata
Bahía Blanca
Pôrto Alegre
Curitiba
São Paulo
Santos
S. Miguel de Tucumán
Salta
Corrientes
Resistencia
Santa Fe
Paraná
Comodoro Rivadavia
Río Gallegos
Punta Arenas
Golfo San Matías
Golfo San Jorge
Bahía Grande
Estrecho de Magallanes
Islas Juan Fernández
(To Chile)
Robinson Crusoe
(Mas Atierra)
Alejandro Selkirk
(Mas Afuera)
San Félix
San Ambrosio
(To Chile)
South Georgia
(To U.K.)
Shag Rocks
(To U.K.)
Clerke Rocks
on the same scale
on the same scale
on the same scale
LAMBERT AZIMUTHAL EQUAL AREA PROJECTION
Heights in metres
1:12 M
miles
km
feet
m
Below Sea Level

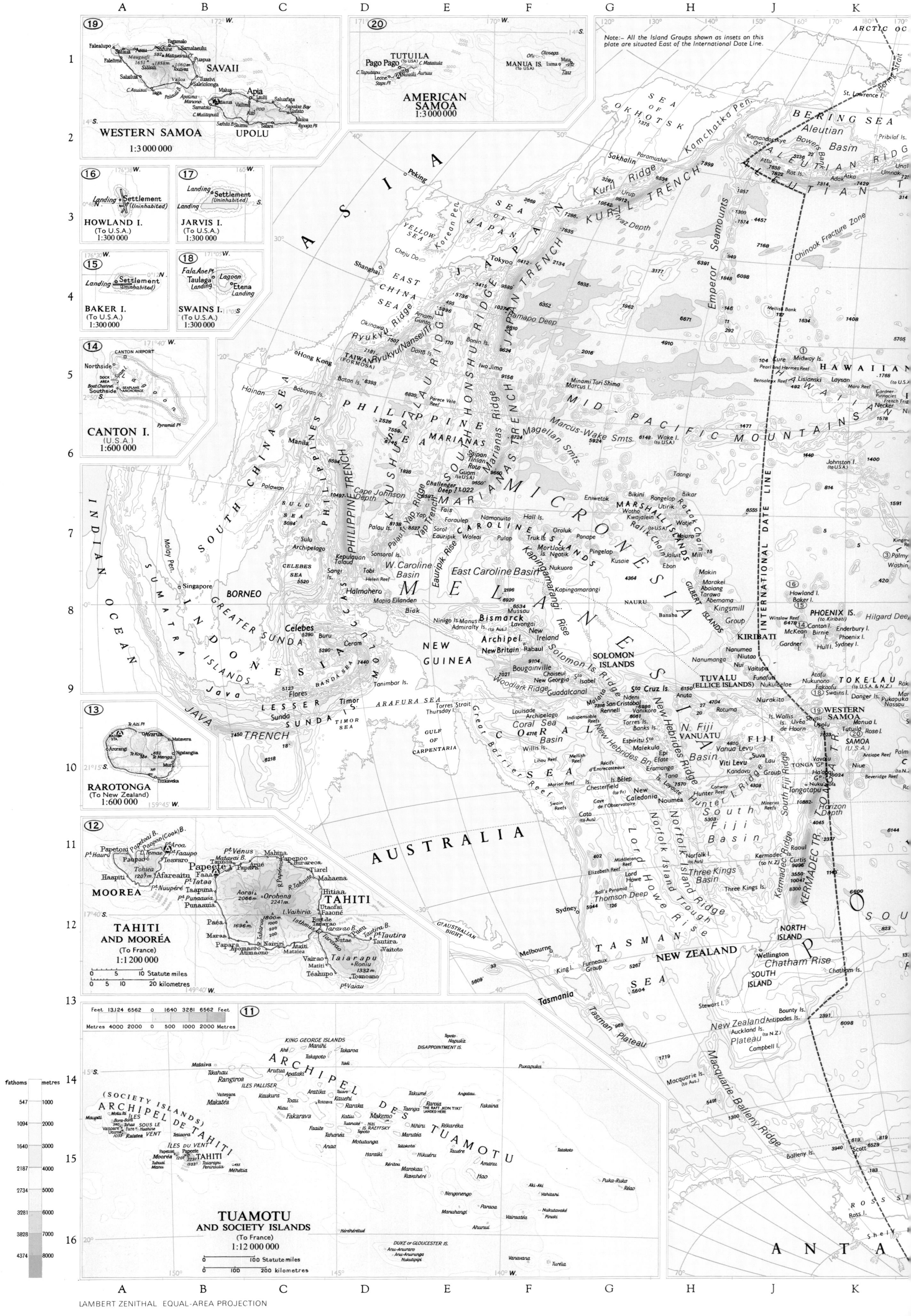

LAMBERT ZENITHAL EQUAL-AREA PROJECTION

Note:– All the Island Groups shown as insets on this plate are situated East of the International Date Line.
WESTERN SAMOA
1:3 000 000
SAVAII
UPOLU
Apia
AMERICAN SAMOA
1:3 000 000
TUTUILA
Pago Pago
MANUA IS.
HOWLAND I.
(To U.S.A.)
1:300 000
JARVIS I.
(To U.S.A.)
1:300 000
BAKER I.
(To U.S.A.)
1:300 000
SWAINS I.
(To U.S.A.)
1:300 000
CANTON I.
(U.S.A.)
1:600 000
RAROTONGA
(To New Zealand)
1:600 000
TAHITI AND MOORÉA
(To France)
1:1 200 000
MOOREA
TAHITI
Papeete
TUAMOTU AND SOCIETY ISLANDS
(To France)
1:12 000 000
ARCHIPEL DES TUAMOTU
(SOCIETY ISLANDS) ARCHIPEL DE TAHITI
ASIA
SEA OF OKHOTSK
BERING SEA
Aleutian Basin
ALEUTIAN TRENCH
KURIL TRENCH
Kuril Ridge
SEA OF JAPAN
JAPAN TRENCH
YELLOW SEA
EAST CHINA SEA
SOUTH CHINA SEA
PHILIPPINE SEA
PHILIPPINE TRENCH
MARIANAS TRENCH
Emperor Seamounts
Chinook Fracture Zone
MID-PACIFIC MOUNTAINS
HAWAIIAN
MICRONESIA
MARSHALL ISLANDS
CAROLINE ISLANDS
East Caroline Basin
MELANESIA
INDONESIA
BORNEO
SUMATRA
Java
JAVA TRENCH
INDIAN OCEAN
NEW GUINEA
Bismarck Archipel
SOLOMON ISLANDS
CORAL SEA
AUSTRALIA
TASMAN SEA
NEW ZEALAND
NORTH ISLAND
SOUTH ISLAND
Chatham Rise
Tasmania
Melbourne
Sydney
KIRIBATI
TUVALU (ELLICE ISLANDS)
TOKELAU
VANUATU
FIJI
South Fiji Basin
KERMADEC TR.
TONGA TR.
INTERNATIONAL DATE LINE
PHOENIX IS.
Lord Howe Rise
Macquarie-Balleny Ridge
ANTA
fathoms
metres

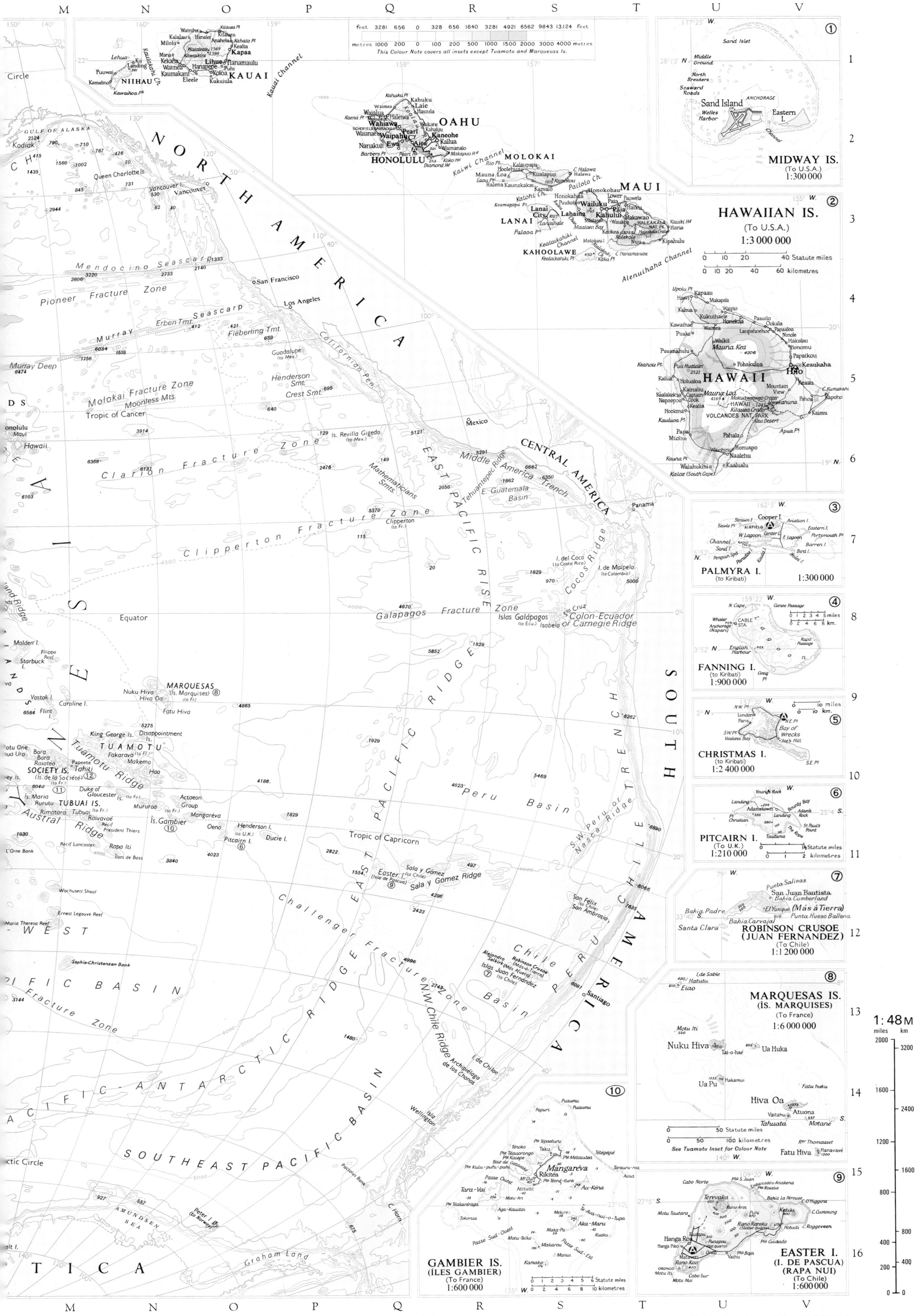
NORTH AMERICA
CENTRAL AMERICA
SOUTH AMERICA
Mendocino Seascarp
Pioneer Fracture Zone
Murray Seascarp
Molokai Fracture Zone
Clarion Fracture Zone
Clipperton Fracture Zone
Galapagos Fracture Zone
Challenger Fracture Zone
EAST PACIFIC RISE
EAST PACIFIC RIDGE
PACIFIC-ANTARCTIC RIDGE
SOUTHEAST PACIFIC BASIN
Peru Basin
Chile Basin
PERU-CHILE TRENCH
Middle America Trench
Cocos Ridge
Colon-Ecuador or Carnegie Ridge
S.W. Peru or Nasca Ridge
Sala y Gomez Ridge
Tuamotu Ridge
Austral Ridge
Tropic of Cancer
Equator
Tropic of Capricorn
San Francisco
Los Angeles
Mexico
Panama
Santiago
MARQUESAS (Is. Marquises)
TUAMOTU
SOCIETY IS.
TUBUAI IS.
Easter I. (Isla de Pascua)
Pitcairn I.
Ìs. Gambier
Heights and Depths in metres
1: 48 M
miles
km
① MIDWAY IS. (To U.S.A.) 1:300 000
② HAWAIIAN IS. (To U.S.A.) 1:3 000 000
NIIHAU
KAUAI
OAHU
HONOLULU
MOLOKAI
LANAI
MAUI
KAHOOLAWE
HAWAII
③ PALMYRA I. (to Kiribati) 1:300 000
④ FANNING I. (to Kiribati) 1:900 000
⑤ CHRISTMAS I. (to Kiribati) 1:2 400 000
⑥ PITCAIRN I. (To U.K.) 1:210 000
⑦ ROBINSON CRUSOE (JUAN FERNANDEZ) (To Chile) 1:1 200 000
⑧ MARQUESAS IS. (ÎS. MARQUISES) (To France) 1:6 000 000
⑨ EASTER I. (I. DE PASCUA) (RAPA NUI) (To Chile) 1:600 000
⑩ GAMBIER IS. (ÎLES GAMBIER) (To France) 1:600 000

MOLUCCAS

CERAM SEA

IRIAN JAYA

NEW GUINEA

PAPUA

NEW GUINEA

BISMARCK ARCHIPELAGO

BISMARCK SEA

Port Moresby

Gulf of Papua

BANDA SEA

SULAWESI (Celebes)

INDONESIA

FLORES SEA

TIMOR SEA

ARAFURA SEA

INDIAN OCEAN

Java Trough

Timor Trough

Darwin

Arnhem Land

Gulf of Carpentaria

Cape York Peninsula

CORAL SEA

Cairns

Townsville

NORTHERN TERRITORY

QUEENSLAND

Alice Springs

Macdonnell Ranges

Simpson Desert

Lake Eyre Basin

WESTERN AUSTRALIA

Gibson Desert

Great Sandy Desert

Great Victoria Desert

SOUTH AUSTRALIA

AUSTRALIA

NEW SOUTH WALES

Perth

Fremantle

Kalgoorlie

Nullarbor Plain

Great Australian Bight

Adelaide

Broken Hill

Sydney

CANBERRA A.C.T.

VICTORIA

Melbourne

SOUTH AUSTRALIAN BASIN

Bass Strait

TASMANIA

Hobart

Launceston

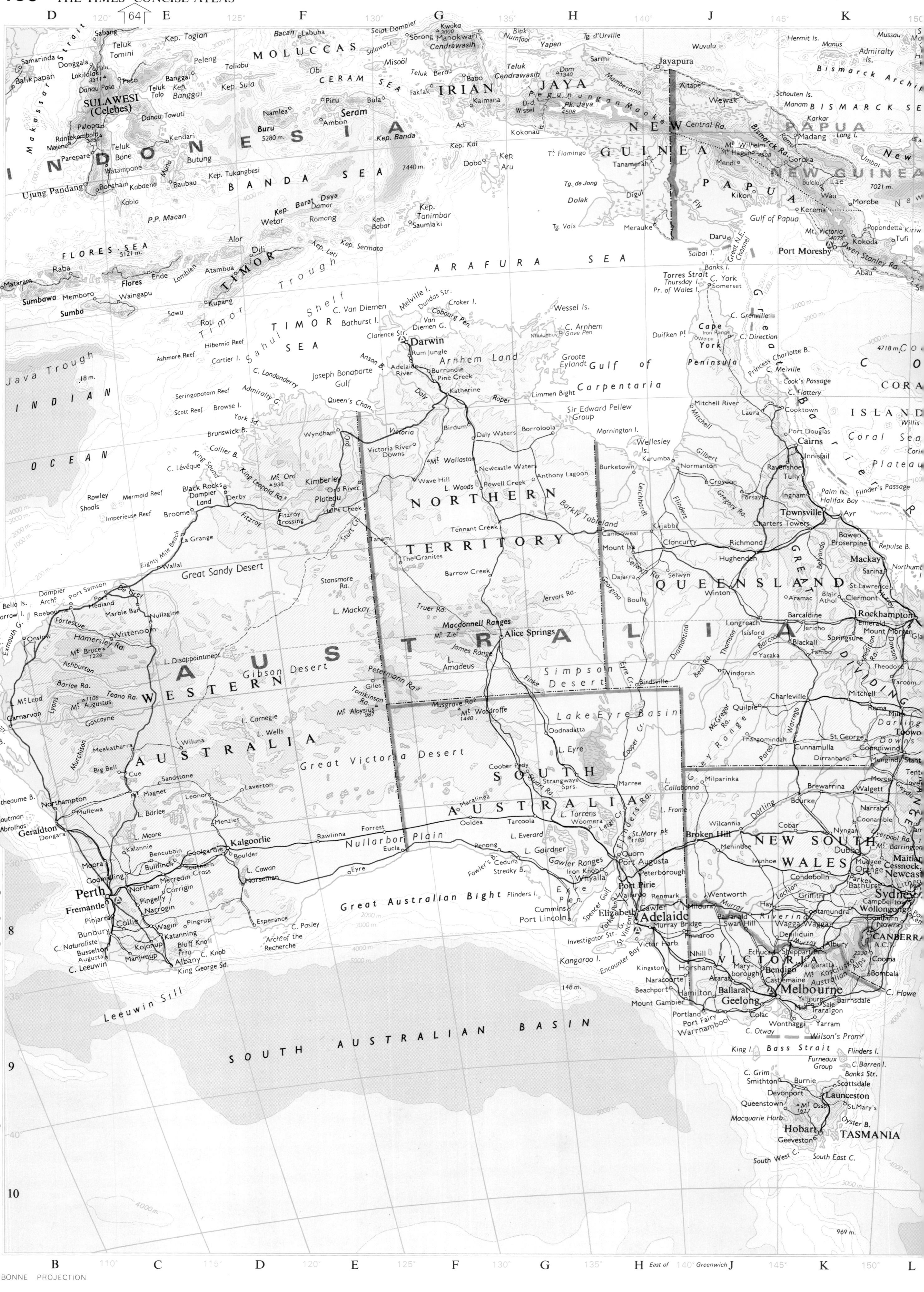

PACIFIC OCEAN

NAURU
Banaba (Ocean I.)

GILBERT ISLANDS
Maiana
Kuria Abemama
Tapiteuea Kingsmill Group
Nonouti Beru Nukunau
Onotoa Tamana
Arorae

KIRIBATI
Equator
Nanouti
(To U.S.A.)
Howland I.
Baker I.
Winslow Reef
McKean I.
Gardner I.
Carondelet Reef

Tabar Is.
Lihir Group
Lyra Reef
New Ireland
St. George's Chan.
Nuguria Is.
Tanga Is.
Green Is.
Kilinailau Is.
Tauu Is.
Nukumanu Is.
Ontong Java Is.
Ontong Java Rise

Buka
Sohano
Bougainville
Kieta
Buin
Planet Deep ·9140
Choiseul
SOLOMON ISLANDS
Vella Lavella
New Georgia
Kolombangaro
Vangunu
Russell Is.
Santa Isabel
Florida
Malaita
Stewart Is.
Maramasike

SOLOMON SEA
Woodlark
Louisiade Arch°
Rennell Ridge
Solomons Basin
Guadalcanal Honiara
San Cristobal
S. Cristobal Tr.
Rennell

Louisiade Rise
Santa Cruz Basin
Nupani Tinakula
Swallow Is.
Duff Is.
Santa Cruz Is.
Ndeni
Utupua
Vanikoro I. 6061
Torres Tr.
Cherry
Mitre
Tikopia

CORAL SEA
Mellish Rise
Mellish Reef
New Hebrides Basin
VANUATU
(NOUVELLES HÉBRIDES) (To U.K. & Fr.)
Espiritu Santo I.
Malo
Oba
Maewo
Pentecost I.
Malekula
Epi
Ambrim
Shepherd Is.
Émaé
Vila Éfaté

Melanesian Border Plateau
Nanomea
Niutao
Nanomana
Nui
Vaitupu
Nukufetau
Funafuti
TUVALU
(ELLICE IS.)
Nukulaelae

Pandora Bk 22
20 5064
Alexa Bk
Niulakita
Rotuma
Eaglestone Reef
Îles Wallis (To Fr.)
Uvea
Futuna Îles de Horn (To Fr.)
Alofi

WESTERN SAMOA
Palauli
Savaii
Apia
Upolu
Tutuila
Tafahi
Niuatoputapu

NTH. FIJI (PANDORA) BASIN

Vatganai
Ureparapara
Vanua Lava
Banks Islands
Santa Maria
C. Cumberland
Merig
Mera Lava

New Hebrides Basin

Récifs d'Entrecasteaux
Sable
Îles Belep
Éromanga
Tana
Aneityum
Is. Loyauté
Uvéa
Lifu (To Fr.)
Maré
7660

Chesterfield (To Fr.)
Îles
Marion Reef
Frederick Reef
Kenn Reef
Saumarez Reef
Wreck Reef
Cato
Caye de l'Observatoire
Bellona Plateau
Bellona Reefs
Mt. Panié
Koné
Bourail
NEW CALEDONIA
(NOUVELLE CALÉDONIE)
(To France)
Nouméa
Île des Pins
Thio
Walpole
Matthew
Hunter

4963 Yasawa Tr.
Yasawa Group
Vanua Levu
Lambasa
Taveuni
FIJI
Nadi
Viti Levu
Suva
Kandavu
Lakemba
Vatoa
Conway Reef
Ono-i-Lau
Tuvana-i-Tholo
Tuvana-i-Ra
Niuafo'ou
Tafahi
Niuatoputapu
Fonualei
Late
Neiafu
Vava'u Group
Kao
Tofua
Ha'apai Group
Nomuka
Nuku'alofa
Tongatapu
Group
'Eua
Ata
Minerva Reefs
Horizon Depth
S10,882

TONGA
Niue (To N.Z.)

Hunter Ridge
SOUTH FIJI BASIN
5303
SOUTH FIJI (LAU) RIDGE
Conway Reef
4770
Lau Basin
Tonga Trench
Tropic of Capricorn

Brisbane
Ipswich
Lismore
Casino
Grafton
Port Macquarie

Lord Howe Smts.
Lord Howe Rise
Middleton Reef
Elizabeth Reef
Lord Howe I. (To Aust.)
Ball's Pyramid
·402
·132
·732

Norfolk Ridge
Norfolk Basin
4021
Norfolk I. (To Aust.)
Philip I.

TASMAN SEA

Three Kings Basin
Three Kings Is.
C. Maria van Diemen
North Cape
Kaitaia

North Cape Rise

Kermadec Ridge
Colville Ridge
Havre Tr.
Kermadec Is. (To N.Z.)
Raoul
Macauley I. 9476
Curtis I.
L'Esperance Rock
Galathea Depth 9994
8600
KERMADEC TRENCH
·1280
2377
4045
·2103

INTERNATIONAL DATE LINE

NORTH ISLAND
Whangarei
Dargaville
Great Barrier I.
Hauraki Gulf
Auckland
Manukau
Thames
Hamilton
Tauranga
Bay of Plenty
East Cape
Rotorua
Whakatane
Gisborne
New Plymouth
Taupo
Ruapehu 2797
Mahia Peninsula
Hawke Bay
Hawera
Wanganui
Hastings
Napier
C. Farewell
Palmerston North
Masterton
Motueka
Picton
Nelson
Blenheim
WELLINGTON
Westport
Cook Strait
NEW ZEALAND
SOUTH ISLAND
Greymouth
Kaikoura
Hokitika
Otira
Southern Alps
Rangiora
Christchurch
Lyttelton
Cascade Pt.
Mt. Cook 3764
Fairlie
Ashburton
Milford Sd.
Queenstown
Timaru
L. Wakatipu
L. Te Anau
Alexandra
Oamaru
Resolution I.
Gore
Balclutha
Dunedin
Foveaux Strait
Bluff
Invercargill
Stewart I.
Snares Is.
Chatham Rise
Chatham Is. (To N.Z.)
Pitt I.

1:15M
km miles
1600 1000
900
1400 800
700
1200 600
1000 500
800 400
600 300
200
400
200 100
0 0

Heights and Depths in metres

© John Bartholomew & Son Ltd Edinburgh

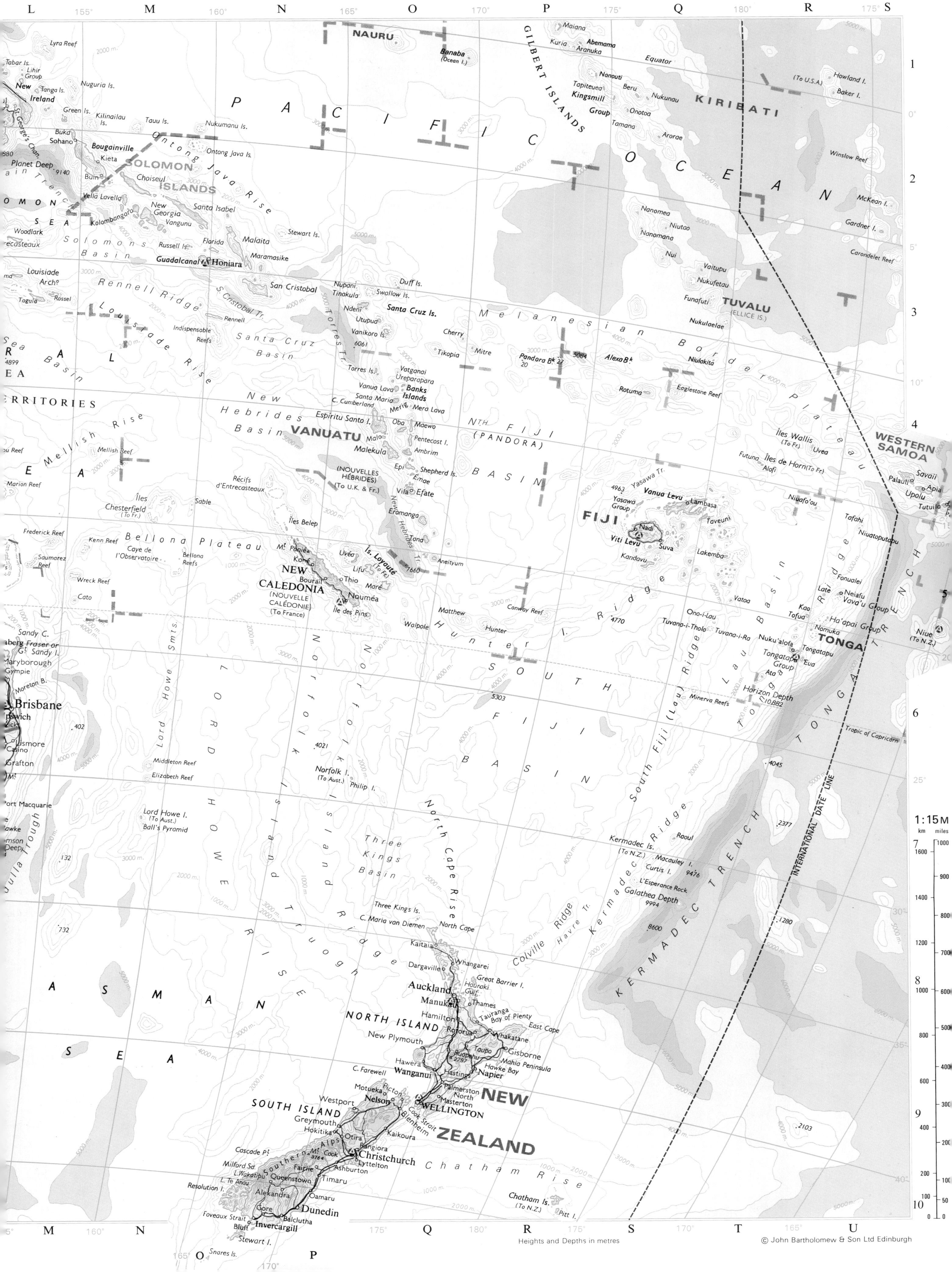

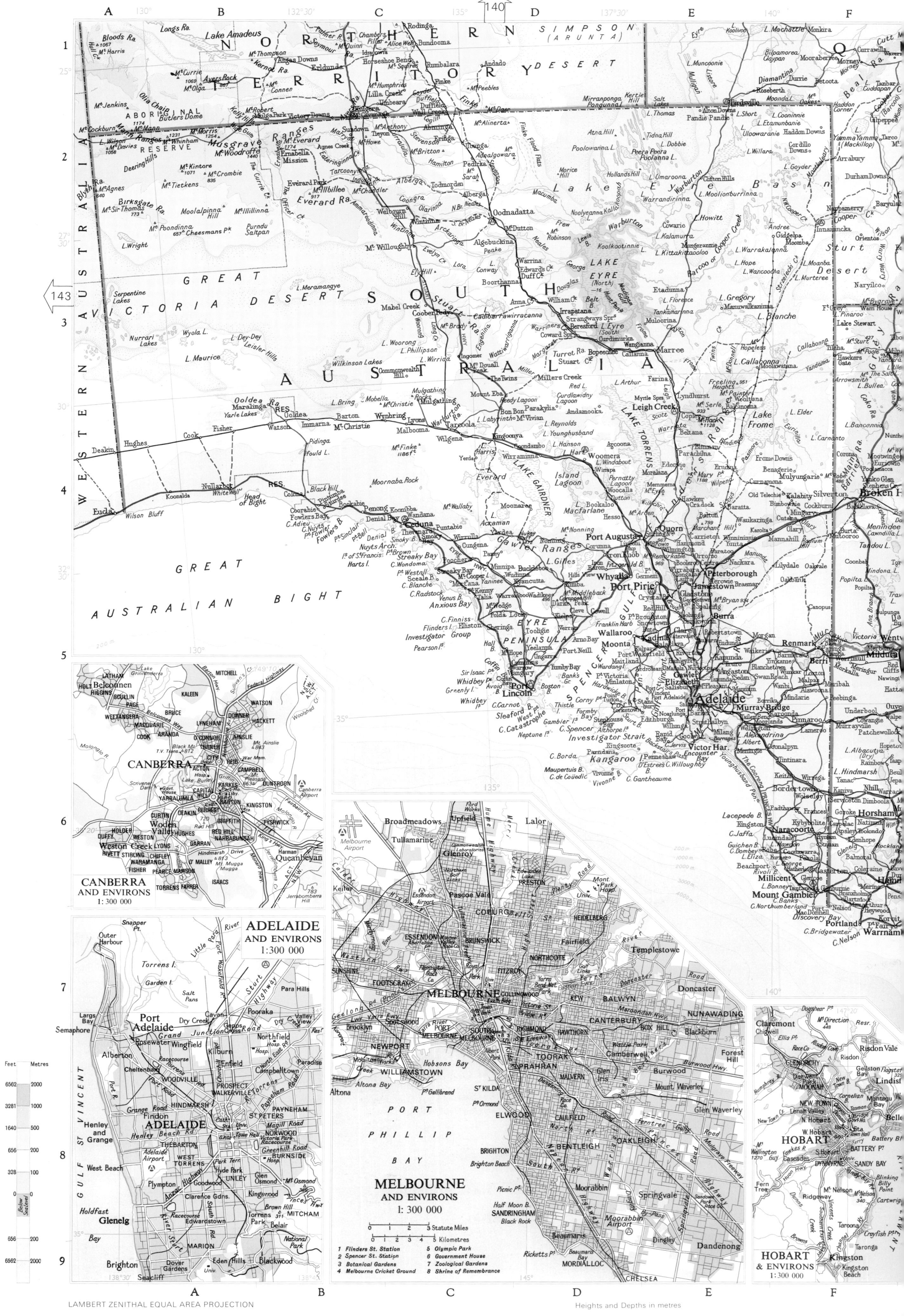

LAMBERT ZENITHAL EQUAL AREA PROJECTION

Heights and Depths in metres

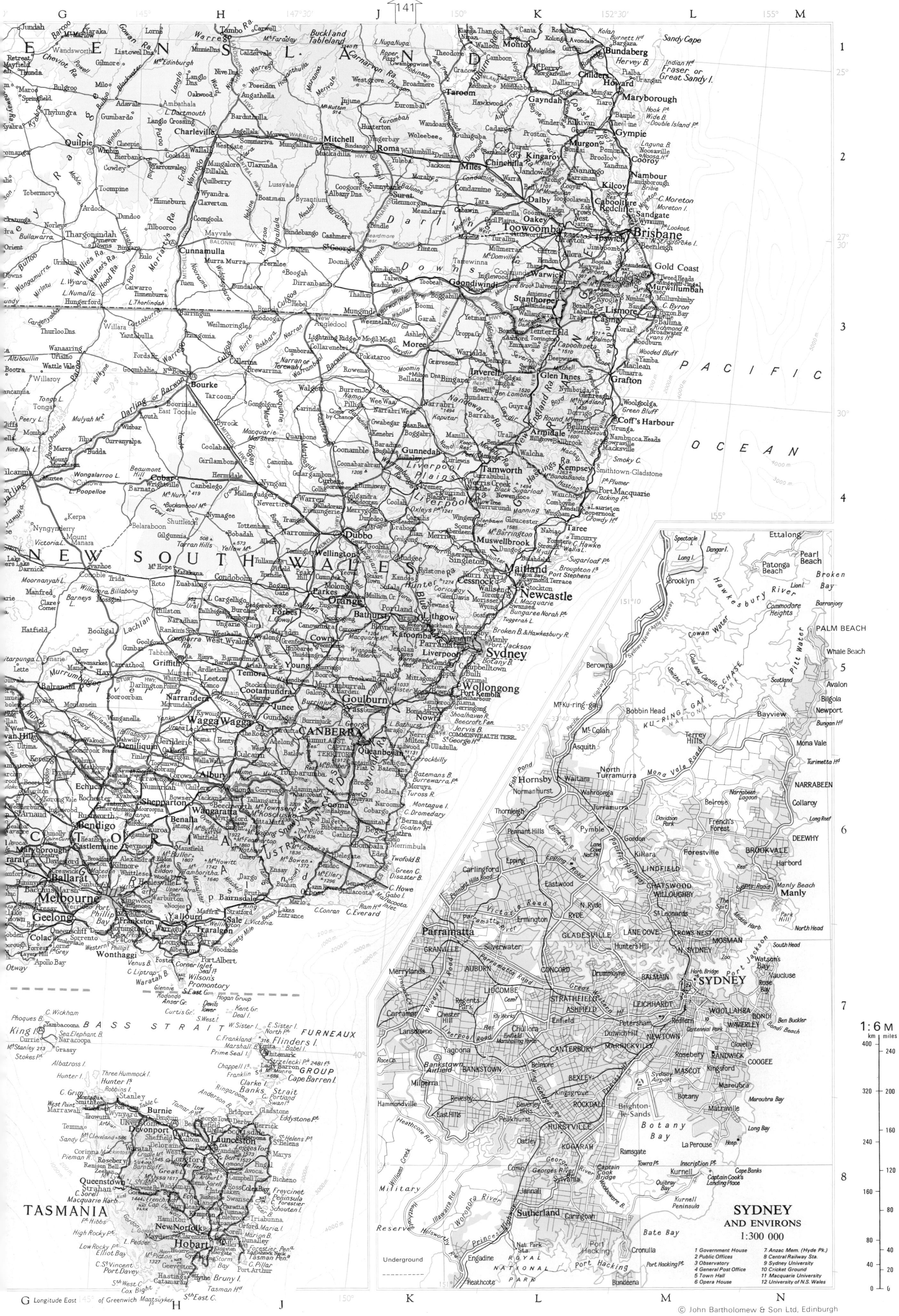

SYDNEY
AND ENVIRONS
1:300 000

1 Government House
2 Public Offices
3 Observatory
4 General Post Office
5 Town Hall
6 Opera House
7 Anzac Mem. (Hyde Pk.)
8 Central Railway Sta.
9 Sydney University
10 Cricket Ground
11 Macquarie University
12 University of N.S. Wales

1:6 M

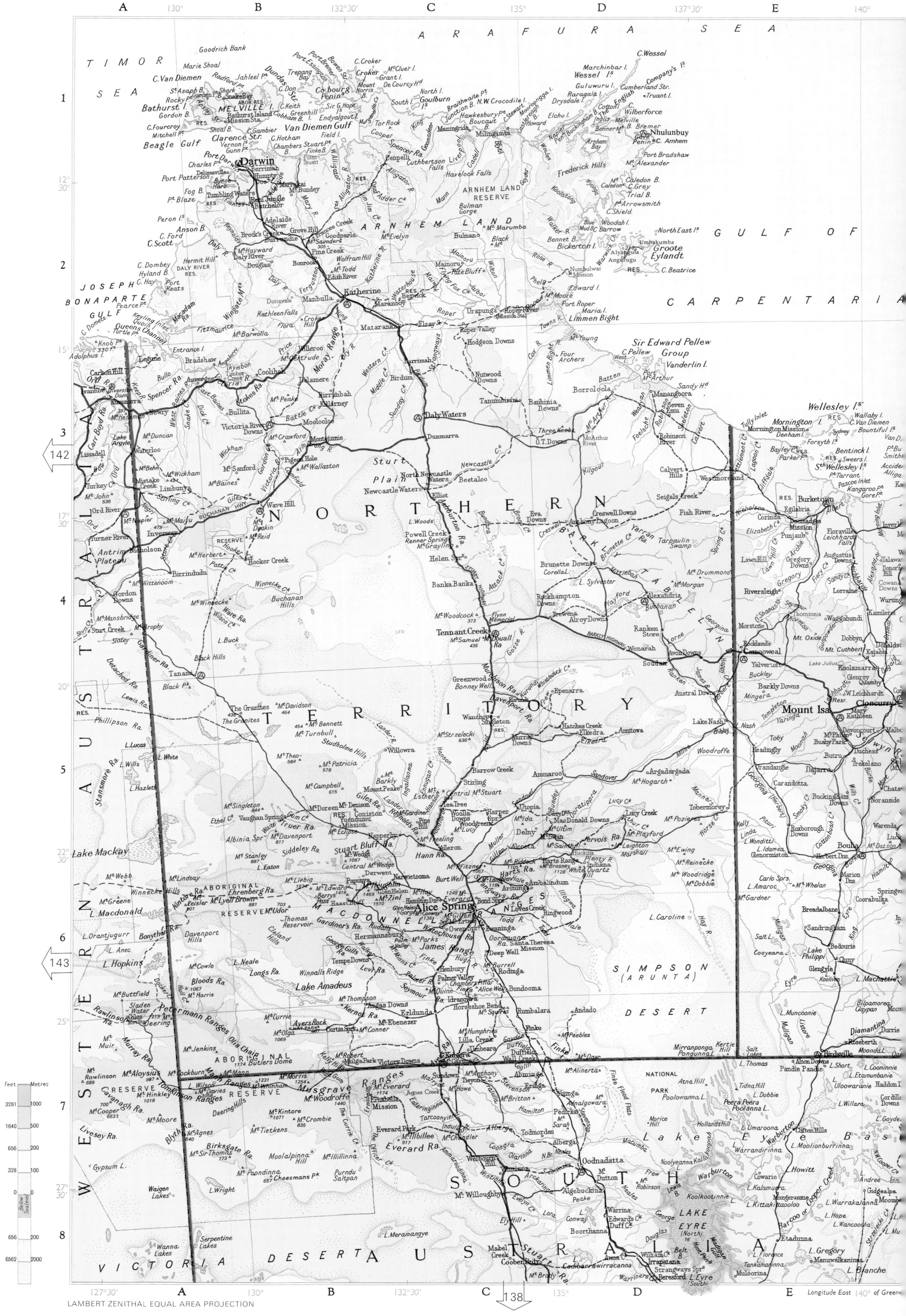
ARAFURA SEA
TIMOR SEA
GULF OF CARPENTARIA
JOSEPH BONAPARTE GULF
NORTHERN TERRITORY
WESTERN AUSTRALIA
SOUTH AUSTRALIA
ARNHEM LAND
ARNHEM LAND RESERVE
MELVILLE I.
Bathurst I.
Van Diemen Gulf
Beagle Gulf
Darwin
Katherine
Groote Eylandt
Wessel Is
Nhulunbuy
Sir Edward Pellew Group
Wellesley Is
Mornington I.
Daly Waters
Tennant Creek
Alice Springs
Mount Isa
Cloncurry
Camooweal
Burketown
Boulia
Birdsville
Oodnadatta
Coober Pedy
BARKLY TABLELAND
Sturt Plain
Lake Mackay
L. Amadeus
MACDONNELL RANGES
Musgrave Ranges
Petermann Ranges
SIMPSON (ARUNTA) DESERT
Lake Eyre Basin
LAKE EYRE (North)
VICTORIA DESERT
142
143
138
Feet
Metres
3281
1000
1640
500
656
200
328
100
0
0
Below Sea Level
656
200
6562
2000
Longitude East 140° of Greenwich

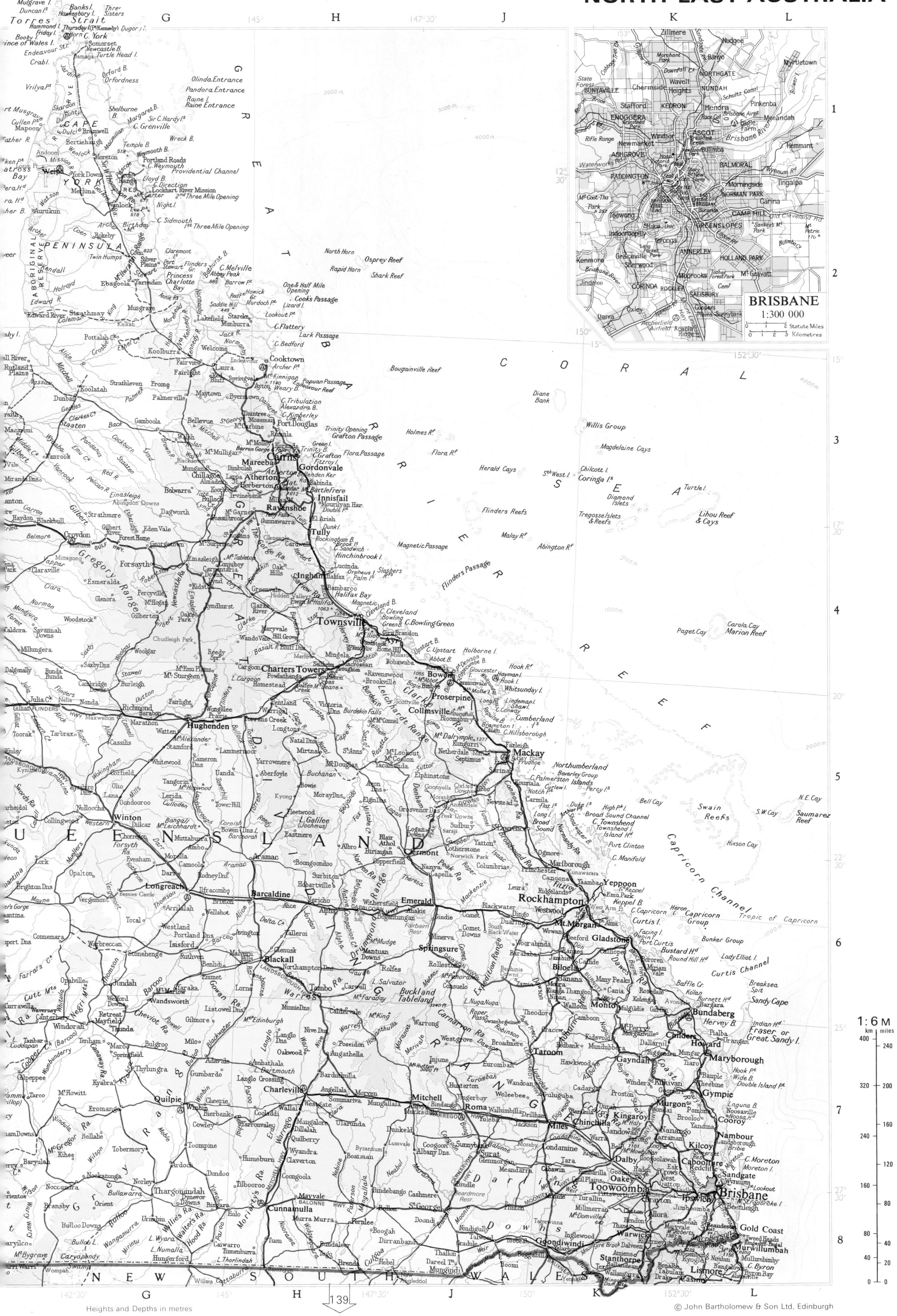

BRISBANE
1:300 000

Statute Miles
Kilometres

1:6 M
km miles

Heights and Depths in metres

© John Bartholomew & Son Ltd, Edinburgh

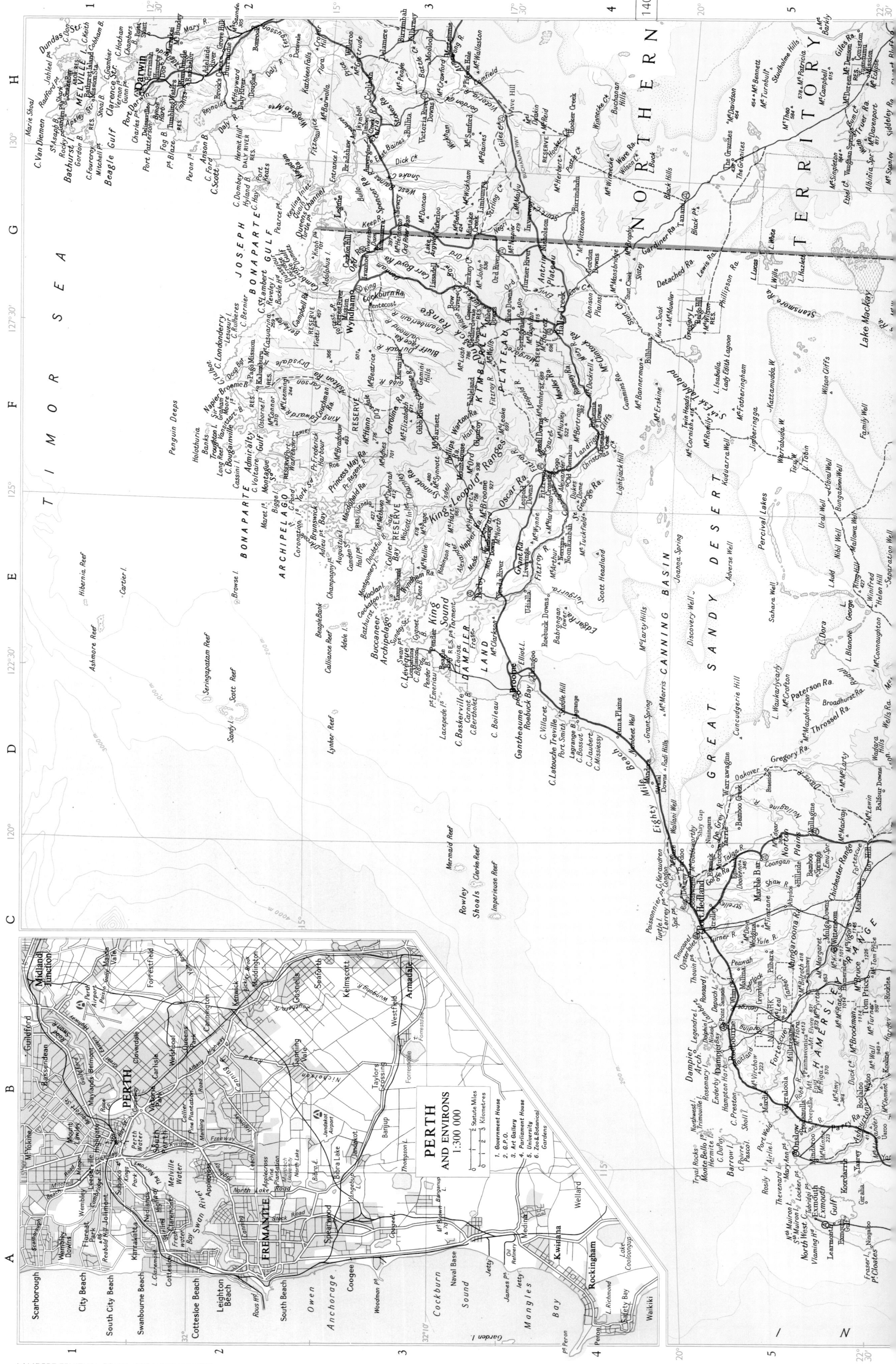

LAMBERT ZENITHAL EQUAL AREA PROJECTION

TIMOR SEA
JOSEPH BONAPARTE GULF
BONAPARTE ARCHIPELAGO
KIMBERLEY PLATEAU
DAMPIER LAND
CANNING BASIN
GREAT SANDY DESERT
NORTHERN TERRITORY
Darwin
Wyndham
Broome
Port Hedland
PERTH AND ENVIRONS
1:300 000
PERTH
FREMANTLE
Kwinana
Rockingham
1. Government House
2. G.P.O.
3. Art Gallery
4. Parliament House
5. University
6. Zoo & Botanical Gardens

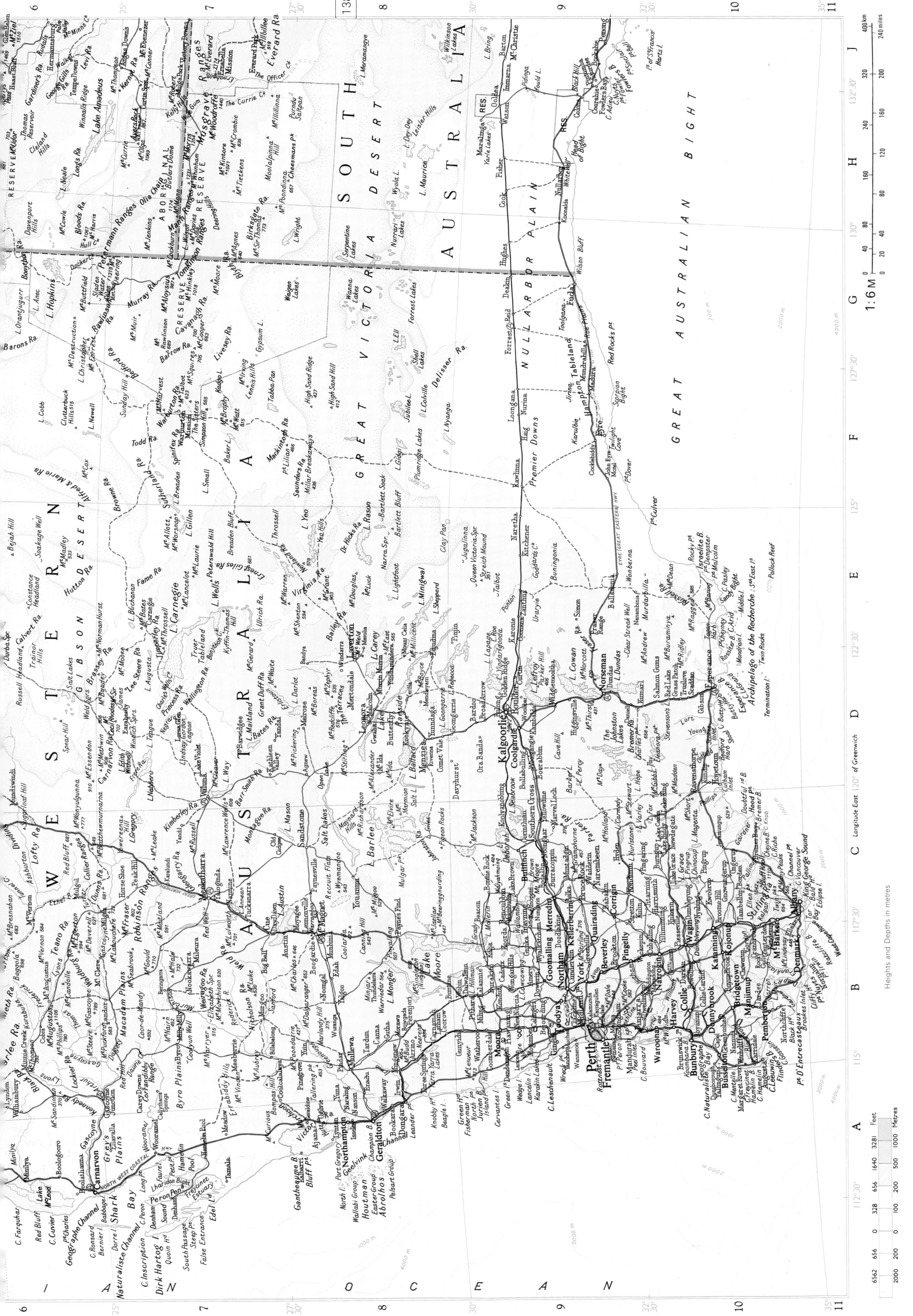

WESTERN AUSTRALIA

SOUTH AUSTRALIA

GREAT VICTORIA DESERT

GIBSON DESERT

GREAT SANDY DESERT

NULLARBOR PLAIN

GREAT AUSTRALIAN BIGHT

INDIAN OCEAN

Shark Bay

Perth
Fremantle
Kalgoorlie
Coolgardie
Norseman
Esperance
Geraldton
Carnarvon
Bunbury
Albany

1:6 M

Heights and Depths in metres

© John Bartholomew & Son Ltd, Edinburgh

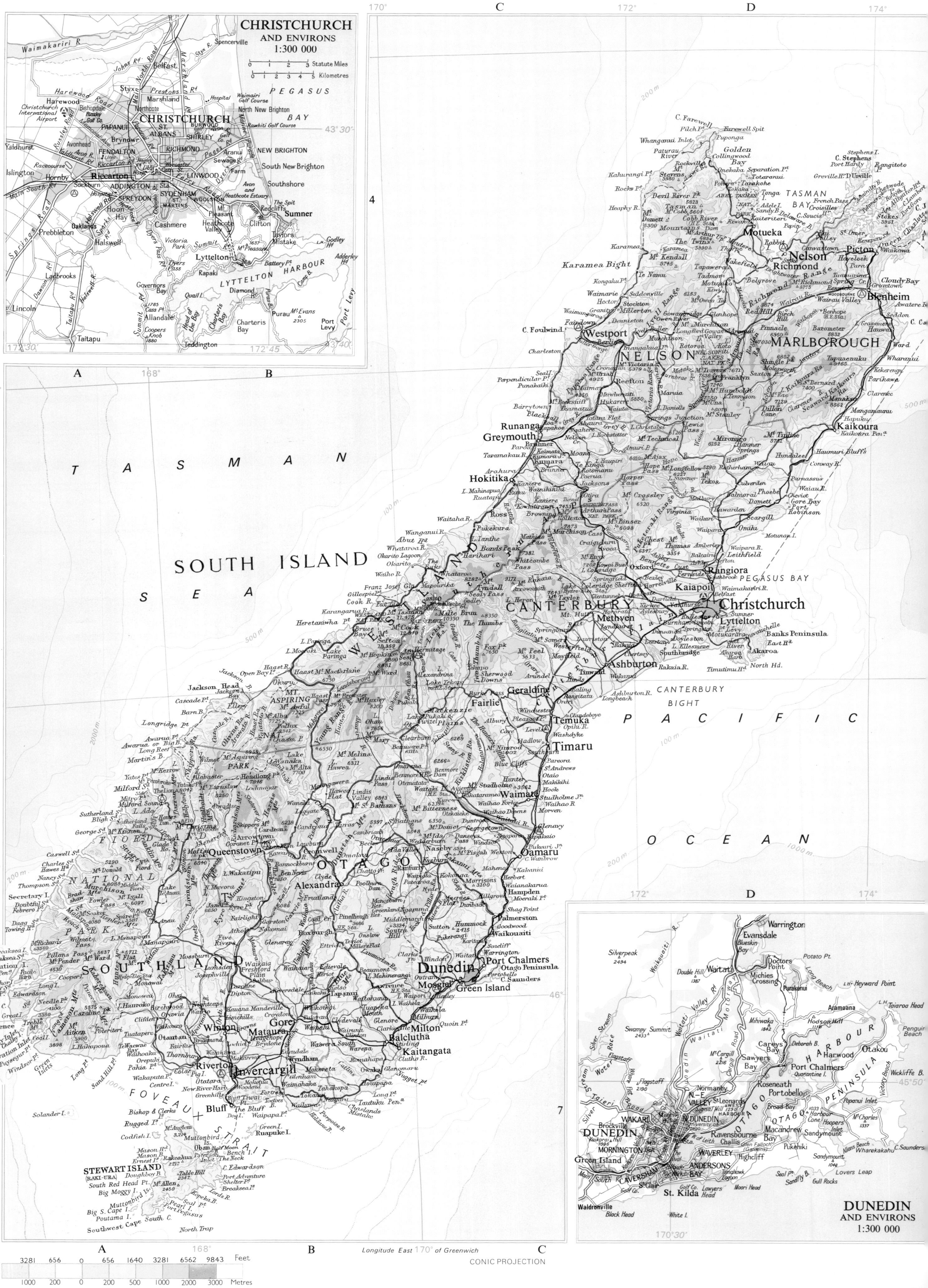

CHRISTCHURCH
AND ENVIRONS
1:300 000

DUNEDIN
AND ENVIRONS
1:300 000

SOUTH ISLAND

TASMAN SEA

PACIFIC OCEAN

Longitude East 170° of Greenwich

Conic Projection

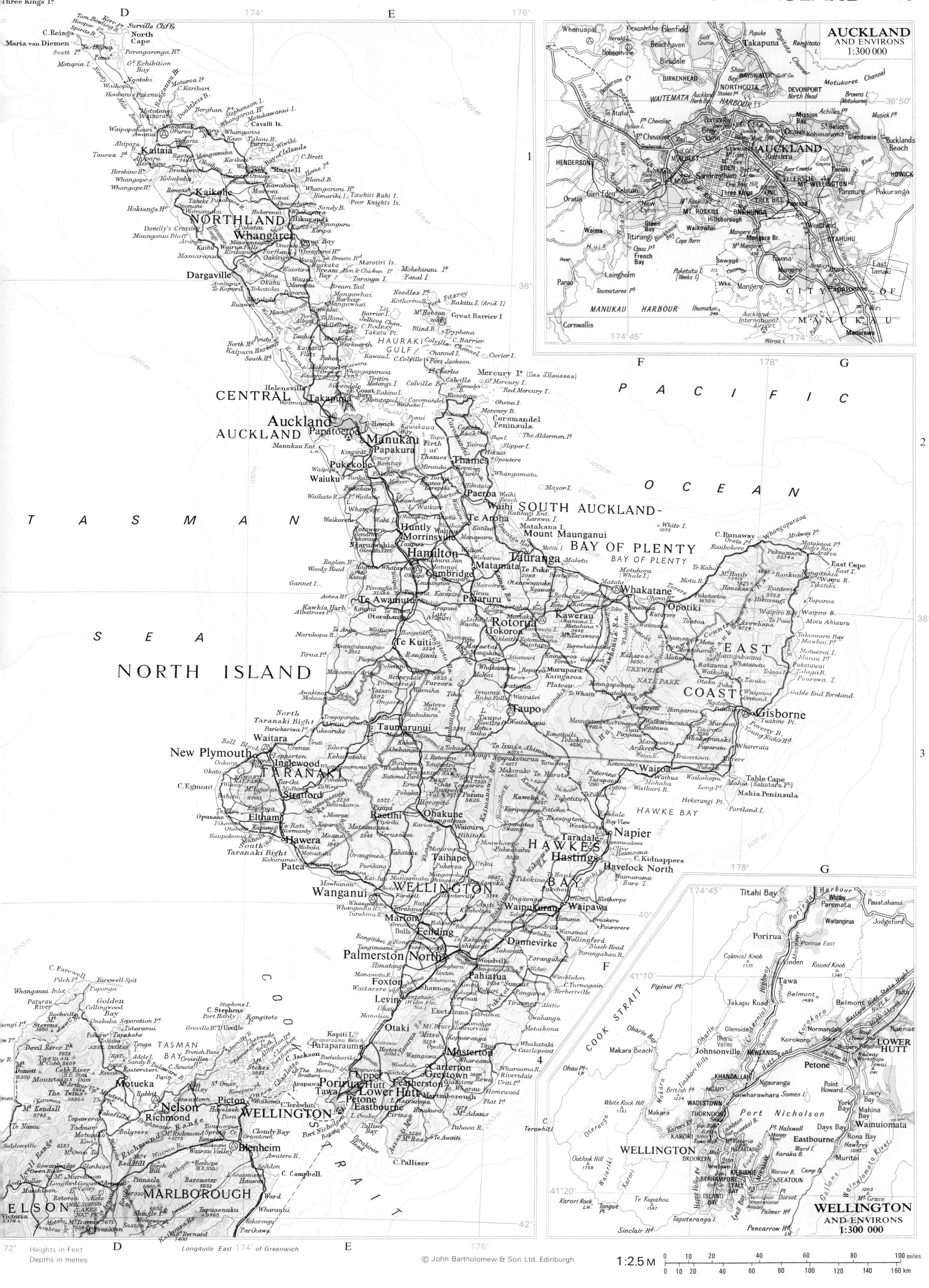

AUCKLAND
AND ENVIRONS
1:300 000

NORTHLAND

CENTRAL

AUCKLAND

SOUTH AUCKLAND-

BAY OF PLENTY

TASMAN

SEA

NORTH ISLAND

EAST

COAST

TARANAKI

WELLINGTON

HAWKE'S

BAY

MARLBOROUGH

NELSON

COOK   STRAIT

PACIFIC

OCEAN

WELLINGTON
AND ENVIRONS
1:300 000

Heights in feet
Depths in metres

Longitude East 174° of Greenwich

© John Bartholomew & Son Ltd, Edinburgh

1:2.5 M

Longitude East 90° of Greenwich

SOUTHERN OCEAN

WILKES LAND

QUEEN MARY LAND

Wilhelm II Land

PRINCESS ELIZABETH LAND

AUSTRALIAN ANTARCTIC TERRITORY

ANTARCTIC TERRITORY

MAC. ROBERTSON LAND

KEMP LAND

ENDERBY LAND

DRONNING MAUD LAND

GREATER ANTARCTICA

Pole of Inaccessibility ·3719 m.

South Polar Plateau

South Pole
Amundsen-Scott (U.S.A.) 2800 m.
(Depth of ice 2722 m.)
HILLARY 4th Jan. FUCHS 19th Jan. 1958

Vostok (U.S.S.R.)
3500 m. South Geomagnetic Pole (1975)

TERRE ADÉLIE

GEORGE V LAND

AUST. ANTARCTIC TERRITORY

VICTORIA LAND

Transantarctic Mts

ROSS Ice Shelf

ROSS DEPENDENCY (To N.Z.)

ROSS SEA

Roosevelt Island

Bay of Whales

KING EDWARD VII LAND

MARIE BYRD LAND

LESSER ANTARCTICA

Rockefeller Plateau

Ford Ranges

Hollick - Kenyon Plateau

ELLSWORTH LAND

Vinson Massif 5140 m.

Sentinel Ra.

Ellsworth Mountains

Ronne Ice Shelf

Filchner Ice Shelf

Berkner Island

COATS LAND

Pensacola Mountains

Neptune Ra.

WEDDELL SEA

BRITISH ANTARCTIC TERRITORY

Larsen Ice Shelf

ANTARCTIC PENINSULA

GRAHAM LAND

PALMER LAND

Alexander Island

Thurston Island

BELLINGHAUSEN SEA

AMUNDSEN SEA

Peter I Øy (To Norway)

Charcot I.

PACIFIC OCEAN

SOUTH SHETLAND Is (To U.K.)

SOUTH ORKNEY Is (To U.K.)

SOUTH SANDWICH Is (To U.K.)

SCOTIA SEA

Scotia Ridge

SOUTH GEORGIA (To U.K.)

DRAKE PASSAGE

Antarctic Circle

Longitude West 90° of Greenwich

Note. Under the Antarctic Treaty of 1959 all territorial claims are held in abeyance in the interest of international co-operation for scientific purposes.

Heights and Depths in metres

1:18 M

6000 5000 4000 3000 1000 m
19686 16409 13124 9843 3281 feet

0 50 100 200 300 400 500 600 miles
0 100 200 400 600 800 1000 km

ZENITHAL EQUIDISTANT PROJECTION

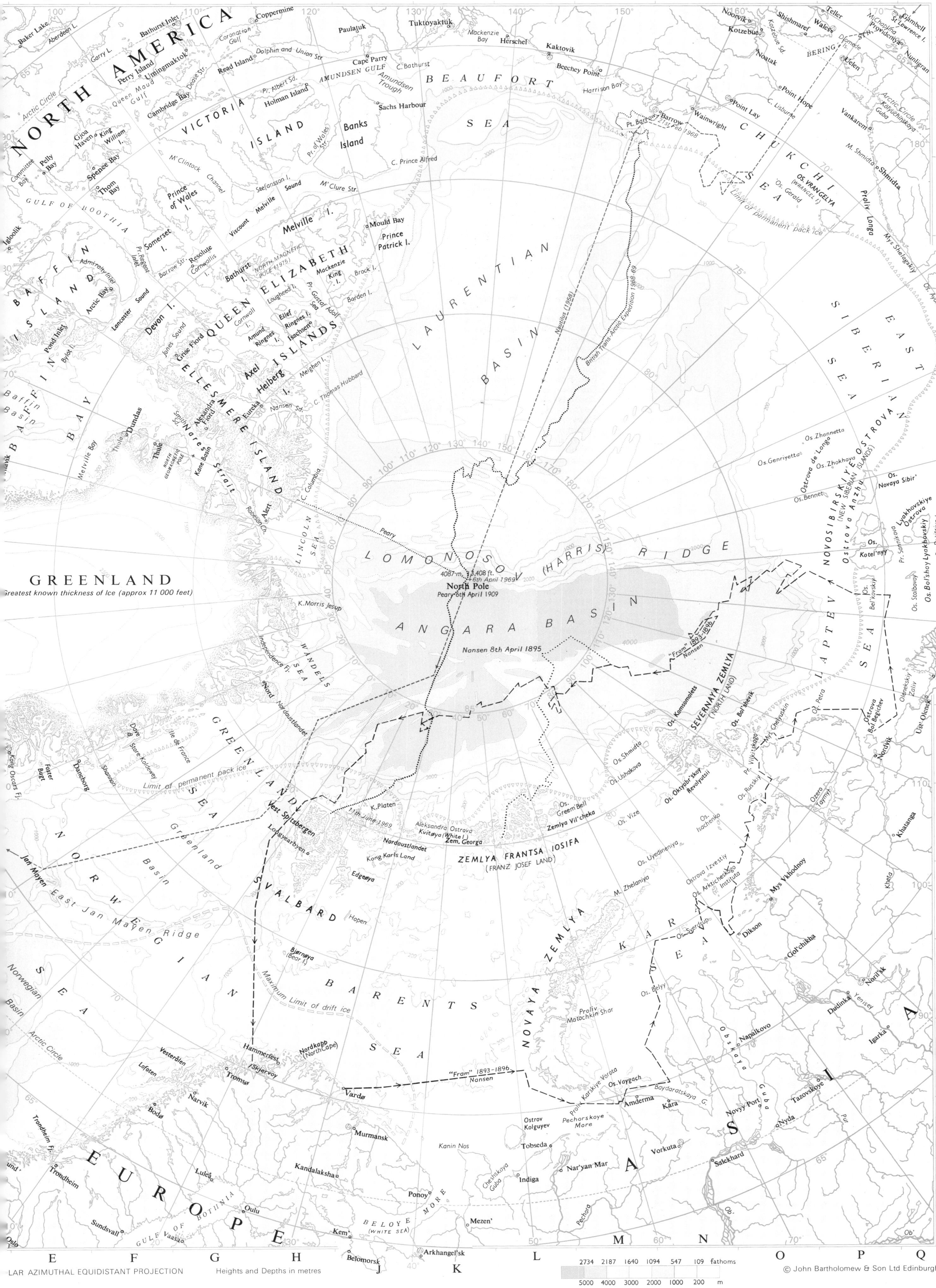

Geographical comparisons

Populations (estimated) of largest metropolitan areas

New York - N.E. New Jersey	16,678,818
Mexico City Mexico	11,943,050
Tokyo Japan	11,540,283
Shanghai China	11,300,000
Los Angeles - Long Beach Calif., USA	10,350,362
São Paulo Brazil	10,041,132
Paris France	9,878,524
Buenos Aires Argentina	8,925,000
Rio de Janeiro Brazil	8,328,800
Osaka Japan	8,279,000
Beijing (Peking) China	8,000,000
Moscow USSR	7,819,000
Seoul South Korea	7,800,000
Calcutta India	7,700,000
Chicago Illinois - N.W. Indiana, USA	7,658,335
Bombay India	7,450,000
London England, UK	7,110,000
Tianjin (Tientsin) China	7,000,000
Cairo Egypt	6,588,000
Chongqing (Chungking) China	6,000,000
Jakarta Indonesia	5,849,000
Philadelphia, Penn. - New Jersey USA	5,643,223
Guangzhou (Canton) China	5,000,000
Bangkok (Krung Thep) Thailand	4,870,509
Delhi - New Delhi India	4,700,000
Detroit Michigan, USA	4,669,106
San Francisco - Oakland Calif., USA	4,591,928
Hong Kong	4,514,000
Manila Philippines	4,500,000
Tehran Iran	4,498,159
Leningrad USSR	4,425,000
Shenyang (Mukden) China	4,400,000
Madras India	4,100,000
Karachi Pakistan	4,000,000
Santiago Chile	3,899,495
Istanbul Turkey	3,864,493
Boston Massachusetts, USA	3,553,203
Ho Chi Minh (Saigon) Vietnam	3,500,000
Wuhan China	3,500,000
Lima Peru	3,302,000
Madrid Spain	3,206,100
Baghdad Iraq	3,206,000
Washington DC, USA	3,021,801
Rome Italy	2,914,640
Cleveland Ohio, USA	2,902,461
Bogota Colombia	2,855,065
Montreal Canada	2,798,000
Sydney Australia	2,765,040
Toronto Canada	2,741,000
Birmingham England, UK	2,730,000
Manchester England, UK	2,675,000
Ankara Turkey	2,600,000
Athens-Piraeus Greece	2,540,241
Melbourne Australia	2,479,225
St. Louis Missouri - Illinois, USA	2,366,542
Pittsburgh Pennsylvania, USA	2,322,224
Alexandria Egypt	2,320,000
Singapore	2,308,000
Budapest Hungary	2,089,000
Kiev USSR	2,079,000
Bucharest Romania	1,934,025
Berlin W. Germany	1,909,706
Havana Cuba	1,861,442
Barcelona Spain	1,809,722
Casablanca Morocco	1,753,000
Johannesburg S. Africa	1,748,000
Glasgow Scotland, UK	1,727,625
Hamburg W. Germany	1,699,000

Lake Areas

Areas are average and some are subject to seasonal variations

	Sq. Miles	Sq. Km
Caspian USSR – Iran (salt)	143,240	371,000
Superior USA – Canada	32,150	83,270
Victoria Kenya – Uganda – Tanzania	26,560	68,800
Aral USSR (salt)	25,300	65,500
Huron USA – Canada	23,430	60,700
Michigan USA	22,400	58,020
Tanganyika Tanzania – Zambia – Zaire – Burundi	12,700	32,900
Great Bear Canada	12,270	31,790
Baykal USSR	11,800	30,500
Great Slave Canada	10,980	28,440
Erie USA – Canada	9,910	25,680
Winnipeg Canada	9,460	24,510
Nyasa (Malawi) Malawi – Mozambique	8,680	22,490
Ontario USA-Canada	7,430	19,230
Ladoga USSR	7,100	18,390
Balkhash USSR	6,700	17,400
Maracaibo Venezuela	6,300	16,300
Chad Nigeria – Niger – Chad – Cameroon	4-10,000	10-26,000
Onega USSR	3,710	9,600
Eyre Australia	0-3,430	0-8,900
Titicaca Peru – Bolivia	3,220	8,340
Nicaragua Nicaragua	3,190	8,270
Rudolf Kenya-Ethiopia	2,470	6,410
Torrens Australia	2,230	5,780
Vänern Sweden	2,160	5,580
Manitoba Canada	1,820	4,710
Loch Lomond Scotland, UK	27	70
Windermere England, UK	10	26

River Lengths

	Miles	Km
Nile Africa	4,160	6,695
Amazon South America	4,080	6,570
Yangtze Asia	3,964	6,380
Mississippi - Missouri N. America	3,740	6,020
Ob-Irtysh Asia	3,360	5,410
Huang He (Yellow) Asia	3,010	4,840
Zaïre (Congo) Africa	2,880	4,630
Paraná South America	2,796	4,500
Irtysh Asia	2,760	4,440
Amur Asia	2,745	4,416
Lena Asia	2,730	4,400
Mackenzie North America	2,630	4,240
Mekong Asia	2,600	4,180
Niger Africa	2,550	4,100
Yenisey Asia	2,540	4,090
Missouri North America	2,466	3,969
Mississippi North America	2,348	3,779
Murray-Darling Australia	2,330	3,750
Volga Europe	2,292	3,688
Madeira South America	2,013	3,240
Indus Asia	1,980	3,180
St Lawrence North America	1,900	3,058
Rio Grande North America	1,880	3,030
Yukon North America	1,870	3,020
Brahmaputra Asia	1,840	2,960
Danube Europe	1,770	2,850
Salween Asia	1,750	2,820
São Francisco South America	1,730	2,780
Ganges Asia	1,678	2,700
Zambezi Africa	1,650	2,650
Nelson - Saskatchewan North America	1,600	2,570
Euphrates Asia	1,510	2,430
Arkansas North America	1,450	2,330
Colorado North America	1,450	2,330
Dnepr Europe	1,370	2,200
Irrawaddy Asia	1,300	2,090
Orinoco South America	1,280	2,060
Negro South America	1,240	2,000
Don Europe	1,160	1,870
Orange Africa	1,155	1,859
Pechora Europe	1,118	1,799
Marañón South America	1,000	1,609
Dnestr Europe	876	1,410
Rhine Europe	820	1,320
Donets Europe	735	1,183
Elbe Europe	720	1,159
Gambia Africa	680	1,094
Yellowstone North America	671	1,080
Vistula Europe	630	1,014
Tagus Europe	625	1,006
Oder Europe	565	909
Seine Europe	473	761
Thames England, UK	209	336
Liffey Ireland	50	80

Populations 1981

China	985,000,000
India	688,600,000
USSR	268,000,000
USA	229,800,000
Indonesia	148,800,000
Brazil	121,400,000
Japan	117,800,000
Bangladesh	92,800,000
Pakistan	88,900,000
Nigeria	79,700,000
Mexico	69,300,000
West Germany	61,300,000
Italy	57,200,000
United Kingdom	55,900,000
Vietnam	54,900,000
France	53,900,000
Philippines	48,900,000
Thailand	48,600,000
Turkey	46,200,000
Egypt	43,500,000
Iran	39,800,000
South Korea	38,900,000
Spain	37,800,000
Poland	36,000,000
Burma	35,200,000

Mountain Heights

	Feet	Metres
Everest Tibet - Nepal	29,028	8,848
K2 (Godwin Austen) Kashmir - Sinkiang	28,250	8,611
Kangchenjunga Nepal - Sikkim	28,168	8,586
Makalu Tibet - Nepal	27,805	8,475
Dhaulagiri Nepal	26,810	8,172
Nanga Parbat Jammu/Kashmir	26,660	8,126
Annapurna Nepal	26,504	8,078
Gasherbrum Kashmir	26,470	8,068
Gosainthan (Xixabangma Feng) Tibet	26,291	8,013
Nanda Devi India	25,645	7,817
Rakaposhi Jammu/Kashmir	25,550	7,780
Kamet India - Tibet	25,447	7,756
Namcha Barwa Tibet	25,447	7,756
Gurla Mandhata Tibet	25,355	7,728
Ulugh Muztagh Tibet - Sinkiang	25,338	7,723
Kungur (Kongur Shan) Sinkiang	25,325	7,719
Tirich Mir Pakistan	25,230	7,690
Minya Konka (Gongga Shan) China	24,903	7,590
Muztagh Ata Sinkiang	24,757	7,546
Pik Kommunizma USSR	24,590	7,495
Pik Pobedy (Tomur Feng) USSR - Sinkiang	24,407	7,439
Chomo Lhari Bhutan - Tibet	23,993	7,313
Pik Lenina USSR	23,406	7,134
Ojos del Salado Chile - Argentina	23,240	7,084
Ancohuma Bolivia	23,012	7,014
Aconcagua Argentina	22,834	6,960
Bonete Argentina	22,541	6,870
Tupungato Argentina - Chile	22,310	6,800
Mercedario Argentina	22,211	6,770
Huascarán Peru	22,205	6,768
Llullaillaco Argentina - Chile	22,057	6,723
Kailas Tibet	22,028	6,714
Yerupaja Peru	21,765	6,634
Sajama Bolivia	21,463	6,542
Illampu Bolivia	21,276	6,485
Nudo Coropuna Peru	21,079	6,425
Illimani Bolivia	21,004	6,402
Chimborazo Ecuador	20,702	6,310
Mt McKinley USA	20,320	6,194
Logan Canada	19,850	6,050
Kilimanjaro Tanzania	19,340	5,895
Citlaltepetl Mexico	18,700	5,700
El'bruz USSR	18,510	5,642
Popocatepetl Mexico	17,887	5,452
Mt Kenya Kenya	17,058	5,200
Mt Ararat Turkey	16,946	5,165
Vinson Massif Antarctica	16,864	5,140
Stanley Zaire/Uganda	16,763	5,110
Jaya (Carstensz)	16,500	5,030
Mont Blanc France	15,781	4,810
Matterhorn Switzerland - Italy	14,688	4,477
Zugspitze Germany	9,721	2,963
Ben Nevis Scotland	4,406	1,343
Snowdon Wales	3,560	1,085
Carrantuohill Ireland	3,414	1,041
Scafell Pike England, UK	3,210	978

Areas

	Sq. Miles	Sq. Km
USSR	8,600,000	22,271,000
Canada	3,851,809	9,976,185
China	3,691,500	9,560,985
USA	3,615,123	9,363,169
Brazil	3,286,488	8,511,978
Australia	2,967,909	7,686,884
India	1,269,346	3,287,590
Argentina	1,072,067	2,776,654
Sudan	967,491	2,505,802
Algeria	919,591	2,381,741
UK	94,500	244,755

Oceans and Seas
Areas and greatest depths

	Sq. Miles	Sq. Km	Feet	Metres
Pacific Ocean	63,855,000	165,384,000	36,198	11,033
Atlantic Ocean	31,744,000	82,217,000	27,498	8,381
Indian Ocean	28,371,000	73,481,000	26,400	8,047
Arctic Ocean	5,427,000	14,056,000	17,880	5,450
Mediterranean Sea	967,000	2,505,000	15,900	4,846
South China Sea	895,000	2,318,000	18,090	5,514
Bering Sea	876,000	2,269,000	16,800	5,121
Caribbean Sea	750,000	1,943,000	24,580	7,492
Gulf of Mexico	596,000	1,544,000	14,360	4,377
Sea of Okhotsk	590,000	1,528,000	11,400	3,475
East China Sea	482,000	1,248,000	9,840	2,999
Yellow Sea	480,000	1,243,000	300	91
Hudson Bay	476,000	1,233,000	850	259
Sea of Japan	389,000	1,008,000	12,280	3,743
North Sea	222,000	575,000	2,170	661
Black Sea	178,000	461,000	7,360	2,243
Red Sea	169,000	438,000	7,370	2,246
Baltic Sea	163,000	422,000	1,400	439

Countries of the World

Country	Status or title	Capital	Sq. km.	Sq. miles	Population	Languages	Currency	Page numbers
Afghanistan	Democratic Republic	Kabul	636,266	(245,664)	17,050,000 (1976)*	Pushtu, Dari Persian	Afghani (Afs)	77
Albania	People's Socialist Republic	Tirana	28,748	(11,100)	2,590,600 (1979)	Albanian (Gheg, Tosk)	lek	46
Algeria	Democratic and Popular Republic	Algiers	2,381,745	(919,597)	18,250,000 (1979)*	Arabic, French, Berber	Algerian dinar (DA)	85
Andorra	Co-principality under French/Spanish sovereignty	Andorra la Vella	465	(180)	32,700 (1980)	Catalan, French, Spanish	French franc, Spanish peseta	17
Angola	People's Republic	Luanda	1,246,699	(481,353)	7,000,000 (1979)*	Portuguese, tribal dialects	kwanza	87
Antigua and Barbuda	Independent 1981	St John's	442	(171)	72,000 (1977)*	English	E Caribbean dollar (EC$)	127
Argentina	Republic	Buenos Aires	2,808,602	(1,084,407)	27,860,000 (1980)	Spanish	Arg. new peso	130–3
Australia	Commonwealth Nation	Canberra	7,682,300	(2,966,151)	14,421,900 (1979)*	English	Australian dollar ($A)	136,138–40
Austria	Republic	Vienna	83,853	(32,376)	7,508,400 (1978)*	German	schilling (sch)	38,41
Bahamas	Commonwealth Nation	Nassau	13,864	(5,353)	234,000 (1979)*	English	Bahamian dollar	113,126
Bahrain	State (Sheikhdom)	Manama	661	(255)	350,000 (1980)*	Arabic, English	Bahrain dinar (BD)	77
Bangladesh	People's Republic. Commonwealth Nation formerly East Pakistan	Dacca	144,020	(55,606)	88,704,000 (1980)	Bengali, Bihari, Hindi, English	Taka (Tk)	75
Barbados	Commonwealth Nation	Bridgetown	430	(166)	248,983 (1980)	English	Barbados dollar (BD$)	127
Belgium	Kingdom	Brussels	30,519	(11,784)	9,855,110 (1979)	French, Dutch, German	Belgian franc	22
Belize	Commonwealth Nation formerly British Honduras	Belmopan	22,963	(8,866)	151,607 (1978)*	English, Spanish ($B)	Belize dollar ($B)	125
Benin	People's Republic formerly Republic of Dahomey	Porto Novo	112,622	(43,484)	3,470,000 (1979)	French, Fon, Adja	CFA franc	85
Bhutan	Kingdom	Thimphu	46,600	(17,992)	1,100,000 (1979)*	Dzongkha, Nepali, English	Ngultrum, Indian rupee	75
Bolivia	Republic	La Paz	1,098,579	(424,164)	5,150,000 (1980)*	Spanish, Quechua, Aymará	Bolivian peso ($b)	128,133
Botswana	Republic. Commonwealth Nation	Gaborone	575,000	(222,009)	831,000 (1979)*	Setswana, English	pula (P)	87,89
Brazil	Federative Republic	Brasília	8,511,965	(3,286,487)	123,032,100 (1980)	Portuguese	Cruzeiro (Cr$)	128–131
Brunei	Due to become fully independent state at end of 1983	Bandar Seri Begawan	5,800	(2,239)	212,840 (1980)*	Malay, English, Chinese	Brunei dollar (B$)	70
Bulgaria	People's Republic	Sofia	110,912	(42,823)	8,880,000 (1980)	Bulgarian	lev	47
Burma	Socialist Republic of the Union of Burma	Rangoon	678,000	(261,777)	33,000,000 (1979)*	Burmese	kyat	68
Burundi	Republic	Bujumbura	27,834	(10,747)	4,280,000 (1978)*	French, Kirundi, Swahili	Burundi franc	88
Cambodia	Democratic Kampuchea formerly the Khmer Republic	Phnom Penh	181,036	(69,898)	7,735,279 (1976)	Khmer	riel	68–9
Cameroon	United Republic	Yaoundé	465,054	(179,558)	8,280,000 (1980)*	English, French	CFA franc	86
Canada	Commonwealth Nation	Ottawa	9,220,975	(3,560,237)	23,900,000 (1980)*	English, French	Canadian dollar (C$)	115,117–123
Cape Verde	Republic	Praia	4,033	(1,557)	306,046 (1978)*	Portuguese Creole	escudo Caboverdianos	85
Central African Rep.	Republic (1979) formerly Empire	Bangui	624,977	(241,305)	2,088,000 (1980)	French, Sango	CFA franc	86
Chad	Republic	N'Djaména	1,284,000	(495,755)	4,405,000 (1979)*	French, Arabic	CFA franc	86
Chile	Republic	Santiago	751,626	(290,204)	11,100,000 (1980)*	Spanish	Chilean peso	128,131,133
China	People's Republic	Beijing (Peking)	9,597,000	(3,705,421)	970,930,000 (1979)	Mandarin Chinese, regional languages	Renminbi or yuan	65–7
Colombia	Republic	Bogotá	1,138,914	(439,737)	26,400,000 (1979)*	Spanish, Indian languages	Colombian peso	126,128
Comoros	Federal and Islamic Republic	Moroni	1,862	(719)	385,000 (1979)*	Kiswahili, French, Arabic	CFA franc	87
Congo	People's Republic	Brazzaville	342,000	(132,047)	1,434,000 (1978)*	French, Kongo, Teke, Sanga	CFA franc	86
Costa Rica	Republic	San José	50,899	(19,652)	2,192,410 (1979)*	Spanish	colone (₡)	125
Cuba	Republic	Havana	114,525	(44,218)	9,730,000 (1978)*	Spanish	Cuban peso	126
Cyprus	Republic. Commonwealth Nation	Nicosia	9,251	(3,572)	624,600 (1979)*	Greek, Turkish, English	Cyprus pound (£C)	79
Czechoslovakia	Federal Socialist Republic	Prague	127,871	(49,371)	15,184,323 (1979)	Czech, Slovak	koruna (Kčs)	31,37,48
Dahomey	See Benin							
Denmark	Kingdom	Copenhagen	43,075	(16,631)	5,122,065 (1980)	Danish	krone	28–9
Djibouti	Republic (1977) formerly French Territory of Afars and Issas	Djibouti	23,000	(8,880)	300,000 (1980)*	French, Somali, Dankali, Arabic	Djibouti franc	86
Dominica	Commonwealth Nation	Roseau	728	(281)	83,000 (1978)	English, French patois	E Caribbean dollar (EC$)	127
Dominican Republic	Republic	Santo Domingo	48,441	(18,703)	5,660,000 (1978)	Spanish	Dominican peso	127
Ecuador	Republic	Quito	455,454	(175,852)	7,810,000 (1979)*	Spanish, Quechua, other Indian languages	sucre	128
Egypt	Arab Republic	Cairo	1,000,000	(386,102)	40,980,000 (1979)*	Arabic, Berber, Nubian, English, French	Egyptian pound (£E)	79,84
Eire	see Irish Republic							
El Salvador	Republic	San Salvador	21,393	(8,260)	4,364,539 (1979)	Spanish	colón (₡)	125
Equatorial Guinea	Republic	Malabo	28,051	(10,831)	325,000 (1978)*	Spanish, Fang, Bubi, other tribal languages	Ekuele	85–6
Ethiopia	Socialist Republic	Addis Ababa	1,000,000	(386,100)	30,400,000 (1979)*	Amharic, English, Arabic	Birr	86
Fiji	Commonwealth Nation	Suva	18,272	(7,055)	618,979 (1979)*	Fijian, English	Fiji dollar ($F)	137
Finland	Republic	Helsinki	337,032	(130,129)	4,787,784 (1980)	Finnish, Swedish	mark	29
Formosa	see Taiwan							
France	Republic	Paris	543,965	(210,026)	53,589,000 (1979)*	French	franc	18–22,40
Gabon	Republic	Libreville	267,667	(103,347)	1,300,200 (1978)*	French, Bantu dialects	CFA franc	86
Gambia, The	Republic. Commonwealth Nation	Banjul	10,689	(4,127)	592,000 (1980)*	English, Madinka	dalasi	85
Germany, East	German Democratic Republic	Berlin (East)	108,177	(41,767)	16,744,700 (1979)	German	Mark of the GDR (M)	30,32–3,36–7
Germany, West	Federal Republic of Germany	Bonn	248,667	(96,011)	61,439,300 (1979)	German	Deutsche Mark (DM)	30,32–9
Ghana	Republic. Commonwealth Nation	Accra	238,305	(92,010)	11,700,000 (1980)*	English, tribal languages	cedi (₡)	85
Gilbert Islands	see Kiribati							
Great Britain	see United Kingdom							
Greece	The Hellenic Republic	Athens	131,990	(50,962)	9,500,000 (1980)*	Greek	drachma	46–7
Grenada	Commonwealth Nation	St George's	344	(133)	110,394 (1978)*	English	E Caribbean dollar (EC$)	127
Guatemala	Republic	Guatemala City	108,889	(42,042)	7,050,000 (1979)*	Spanish, Indian languages	quetzal (Q)	125
Guinea	Republic	Conakry	245,856	(94,926)	5,130,000 (1978)*	French, Susu, Malinké	syli	85
Guinea-Bissau	Republic	Bissau	36,125	(13,948)	777,214 (1979)	Portuguese, Guinean Créole	peso	85
Guyana	Co-operative Republic. Commonwealth Nation	Georgetown	214,970	(83,000)	824,000 (1978)*	English, Hindu, Urdu, Amerindian dialects	Guyana dollar (G$)	128–9
Haiti	Republic	Port-au-Prince	27,749	(10,714)	5,530,000 (1978)*	French, Créole	gourde	126–7
Honduras	Republic	Tegucigalpa	112,087	(43,277)	3,691,027 (1980)*	Spanish, Indian dialects	lempira or peso	125
Hungary	People's Republic	Budapest	93,030	(35,919)	10,710,000 (1980)*	Hungarian	forint	48
Iceland	Republic	Reykjavík	103,000	(39,769)	226,724 (1978)	Icelandic	króna	115
India	Republic and Union of States. Commonwealth Nation	New Delhi	3,166,828	(1,222,719)	683,000,000 (1981)*	Hindi, English, regional languages	rupee (R)	73–6
Indonesia	Republic	Jakarta	1,903,650	(735,003)	148,500,000 (1979)*	Bahasa Indonesia	rupiah	69–71
Iran	Islamic Republic (1979) formerly Empire	Tehrán	1,648,190	(636,370)	34,000,000 (1977)*	Farsi, Kurdish, Arabic, Baluchi	rial	77
Iraq	Republic	Baghdad	438,446	(169,285)	12,171,480 (1977)	Arabic Kurdish	Iraqi dinar (ID)	78
Irish Republic	The Republic of Ireland	Dublin	70,282	(27,136)	3,368,000 (1979)	Irish, English	punt or Irish pound (IR£)	14
Israel	The State of Israel. Republic	Jerusalem	20,702	(7,993)	3,830,000 (1979)*	Hebrew, Arabic	shekel	79–80
Italy	Republic	Rome	301,191	(116,290)	56,999,047 (1980)*	Italian	lira	41–5
Ivory Coast	Republic	Abidjan	322,463	(124,504)	7,920,000 (1979)*	French, tribal languages	CFA franc	85
Jamaica	Commonwealth Nation	Kingston	10,991	(4,244)	2,160,000 (1979)*	English	Jamaican dollar (J$)	127
Japan	Democratic State with Emperor	Tokyo	369,699	(142,742)	116,133,000 (1979)	Japanese	yen	60–1
Jordan	Hashemite Kingdom	Amman	96,000	(37,066)	2,950,000 (1979)*	Arabic	Jordan dinar (JD)	80
Kampuchea	see Cambodia							
Kenya	Republic. Commonwealth Nation	Nairobi	582,646	(224,961)	15,320,000 (1979)	Swahili, English, Kikuya, other tribal langs	Kenya Shilling (Sh)	86,88
Khmer Republic	see Cambodia							
Kiribati	Republic (1979). Commonwealth Nation formerly Gilbert Is UK Dependent Territory	Tarawa	684	(264)	58,518 (1980)	Gilbertese, English	Australian dollar (A$)	137
Korea, North	Democratic People's Republic of Korea	Pyongyang	122,370	(47,247)	17,930,000 (1980)*	Korean	won	65
Korea, South	Republic of Korea	Seoul	98,447	(38,011)	37,019,000 (1978)*	Korean	won	65
Kuwait	Sovereign State	Kuwait	24,280	(9,375)	1,270,000 (1979)*	Arabic, English	Kuwait dinar (KD)	77
Laos	Lao People's Democratic Republic	Vientiane	236,792	(91,429)	3,500,000 (1979)*	Lao, French, tribal langs	kip (K)	68
Lebanon	Republic	Beirut	10,399	(4,015)	2,700,000 (1978)*	Arabic, French, English, Armenian	Lebanese pound (£Leb)	79
Lesotho	Kingdom. Commonwealth Nation	Maseru	30,344	(11,716)	1,279,000 (1978)	Sesotho, English	Loti	89
Liberia	Republic	Monrovia	112,600	(43,475)	1,800,000 (1979)*	English, tribal languages	Liberian dollar (L$)	85
Libya	Socialist People's Libyan Arab Jamahiriyah	Tripoli	1,759,537	(679,361)	2,940,000 (1978)*	Arabic, Italian	Libyan dinar (LD)	84

estimate*

Country	Status or title	Capital	Area Sq. km.	Sq. miles	Population	Languages	Currency	Page numbers
Liechtenstein	Principality	Vaduz	161	(62)	25,808 (1979)*	Alemannish, German	Swiss franc	41
Luxembourg	Grand Duchy	Luxembourg	2,587	(999)	363,700 (1979)	Luxemburgish, French, German	Luxembourg franc, Belgian franc	22
Madagascar	Democratic Republic	Antananarivo	594,180	(229,414)	8,047,044 (1978)*	Malagasy, French	Malagasy, franc (FMG)	87
Malawi	Republic. Commonwealth Nation	Lilongwe	94,527	(36,497)	5,800,000 (1979)*	Chichewa, English	kwacha (K)	88
Malaysia	Federation of States. Commonwealth Nation (comprising Peninsular Malaysia, Sabah and Sarawak)	Kuala Lumpur	332,318	(128,309)	13,300,000 (1978)*	Malay, English, Chinese, Tamil	Malaysian ringgit (M$)	69–70
Maldives	Republic	Malé	298	(115)	143,046 (1978)	Divehi	Maldivian rupee	73
Mali	Republic	Bamako	1,204,026	(464,877)	6,470,000 (1979)*	French, native languages	Mali franc (MF)	85
Malta	Republic. Commonwealth Nation	Valletta	316	(122)	316,850 (1980)*	Maltese, English	Maltese pound (£M)	43
Mauritania	Islamic Republic	Nouakchott	1,119,367	(432,190)	1,540,000 (1979)*	Arabic, French	ouguiya	85
Mauritius	Commonwealth Nation	Port Louis	1,865	(720)	924,243 (1979)*	English, French, Creole	Mauritius Rupee (R)	83
Mexico	The United Mexican States. Federal Republic	Mexico City	1,972,546	(761,604)	69,400,000 (1979)*	Spanish	peso	125
Monaco	Principality	Monaco	1.5	(0.6)	26,000 (1978)*	French, Monégasque	French franc	44
Mongolia	People's Republic	Ulaanbaatar	1,565,007	(604,252)	1,641,100 (1980)	Mongolian	tugrik	58
Morocco	Kingdom	Rabat	622,014	(240,161)	19,470,000 (1979)*	Arabic, French, Spanish	dirham (DH)	85
Mozambique	People's Republic	Maputo	784,964	(303,076)	19,750,000 (1979)*	Portuguese, tribal langs	metical	87–8
Namibia	United Nations Trust Territory	Windhoek	822,021	(317,384)	908,800 (1977)*	Afrikaans, German, Eng.	South African rand (R)	87,89
Nauru	Republic with special membership of the Commonwealth	Nauru	21	(8)	7,254 (1977)	Nauruan, English	Australian dollar ($A)	137
Nepal	Kingdom	Kathmandu	141,414	(54,600)	13,420,000 (1978)*	Nepali	Nepalese rupee (NR)	75
Netherlands, The	Kingdom	Amsterdam	41,160	(15,892)	14,091,014 (1980)*	Dutch	gulden (guilder, florin)	25
New Hebrides	*see Vanuatu*							
New Zealand	Commonwealth Nation	Wellington	268,676	(103,736)	3,100,000 (1980)*	English, Maori	New Zealand dollar (NZ$)	144–5
Nicaragua	Republic	Managua	148,006	(57,145)	2,568,000 (1980)*	Spanish	córdoba (C$)	125
Niger	Republic	Niamey	1,186,408	(458,075)	5,300,000 (1979)*	French, native languages	CFA franc	85
Nigeria	Federal Republic. Commonwealth Nation	Lagos	923,773	(356,671)	81,039,000 (1978)*	English, Hausa, Yoruba	Naira (₦)	85–6
Norway	Kingdom	Oslo	323,895	(125,057)	4,078,900 (1980)	Norwegian, (Bakmål and Landsmål), Lappish	Norwegian krone	26–7
Oman	Sultanate	Muscat	272,000	(105,020)	820,000 (1980)*	Arabic, English	Rial Omani (RO)	72,77
Pakistan	Islamic Republic	Islamabad	803,944	(310,404)	80,200,000 (1980)*	Punjabi, Sindhi, Urdu, Pushtu	Pakistan rupee (R)	74,77
Panama	Republic	Panama City	78,020	(30,124)	1,890,000 (1980)*	Spanish, English	balboa	125
Papua New Guinea	Commonwealth Nation	Port Moresby	462,840	(178,703)	3,080,000 (1979)*	Pidgin English, native languages	kina (K)	136
Paraguay	Republic	Asunción	406,752	(157,048)	3,000,000 (1980)*	Spanish, Guaraní	guaraní (G)	130
Peru	Republic	Lima	1,285,220	(496,226)	17,293,100 (1979)	Spanish, Quechua, Aymará	sol (S)	128
Philippines	Republic	Manila	299,767	(115,741)	47,914,017 (1980)	Pilipino Tagalog, English, Spanish	Philippine peso (P)	71
Poland	People's Republic	Warsaw	312,683	(120,728)	35,382,000 (1980)	Polish	zlotny	31
Portugal	Republic	Lisbon	91,631	(35,379)	9,862,700 (1979)*	Portuguese	escudo	16
Puerto Rico	Self governing commonwealth associated with the USA	San Juan	8,897	(3,433)	3,187,566 (1980)	English, Spanish	US dollar ($)	127
Qatar	State	Doha	11,000	(4,247)	over 200,000 (1978)*	Arabic, English	Qatar Riyal	77
Rhodesia	*see Zimbabwe*							
Romania	Socialist Republic	Bucharest	237,500	(91,699)	22,050,000 (1979)*	Romanian, Magyar	leu	48
Rwanda	Republic	Kigali	26,338	(10,169)	4,650,000 (1979)*	French, tribal languages, Kinyarwanda (Bantu)	Rwanda franc	88
St Lucia	Commonwealth Nation	Castries	616	(238)	113,000 (1979)	English, French patois	E Caribbean dollar (EC$)	127
St Vincent	Commonwealth Nation	Kingstown	389	(150)	117,646 (1978)	English	E Caribbean dollar (EC$)	127
San Marino	Republic	San Marino	61	(24)	21,000 (1978)	Italian	Italian lira, Papal coinage	45
São Tomé and Principe	Democratic Republic	São Tomé	963	(372)	82,750 (1977)*	Portuguese	dobra	86
Saudi Arabia	Kingdom	Riyadh	2,400,000	(926,645)	7,012,642 (1974)	Arabic	rial	72,86
Senegal	Republic	Dakar	196,722	(75,955)	5,660,000 (1980)*	French, native languages	CFA franc	85
Seychelles	Republic. Commonwealth Nation	Victoria	404	(156)	61,900 (1977)*	English, French	Seychelles rupee (R)	83
Sierra Leone	Republic. Commonwealth Nation	Freetown	73,326	(28,311)	3,470,000 (1978)*	English, (also Krio Temne, Mende)	leone	85
Singapore	Republic. Commonwealth Nation	Singapore	616	(238)	2,390,800 (1980)*	Malay, Chinese (Mandarin), Tamil, English	Singapore dollar (S$)	69
Solomon Islands	Commonwealth Nation	Honiara	29,785	(11,500)	215,000 (1978)*	English, native langs	Solomon Is dollar (SI$)	137
Somalia	The Somali Democratic Republic	Mogadishu	630,000	(243,244)	3,640,000 (1980)*	Somali, Arabic, English, Italian	Somali shilling (Som. Sh.)	86
South Africa	Republic	Pretoria	1,184,831	(457,466)	24,091,000 (1979)*	Afrikaans, English, various African langs	rand (R)	87,89
South West Africa	*see Namibia*							
South Yemen	The People's Democratic Republic of Yemen	Aden	160,300	(61,892)	2,000,000 (1980)*	Arabic	South Yemen dinar	72
Spain	The Spanish State. Kingdom	Madrid	504,879	(194,935)	37,700,000 (1977)*	Spanish, Catalan, Basque	peseta	16–7
Sri Lanka	Democratic Socialist Republic. Commonwealth Nation *formerly Ceylon*	Colombo	65,610	(25,332)	14,470,000 (1979)*	Sinhale, Tamil, English	Sri Lanka rupee (R)	83
Sudan	Democratic Republic	Khartoum	2,505,802	(967,495)	18,400,000 (1980)*	Arabic, tribal languages	Sudanese pound (£S)	86
Suriname	Republic	Paramaribo	163,265	(63,037)	384,900 (1979)*	Dutch, Spanish, Surinamese	Suriname guilder	129
Swaziland	Kingdom. Commonwealth Nation	Mbabane	17,366	(6,705)	563,733 (1979)*	English, SiSwati	emalangeni (E)	89
Sweden	Kingdom	Stockholm	449,792	(173,666)	8,303,010 (1979)*	Swedish, Finnish, Lappish	Swedish krona (kr)	26–7
Switzerland	Republic. Confederation	Bern	41,288	(15,941)	6,356,300 (1979)*	German, French, Italian, Romansch	Swiss franc	40–1
Syria	Arab Republic	Damascus	185,680	(71,691)	8,330,000 (1979)*	Arabic	Syrian pound (£Syr)	78–80
Taiwan	Republic of China	Taipei	35,989	(13,895)	17,480,000 (1979)	Mandarin Chinese	New Taiwan dollar (NT$)	67
Tanzania	United Republic. Commonwealth Nation	Dodoma	939,766	(362,846)	17,600,000 (1979)*	Swahili, English, tribal languages	Tanzanian shilling (Sh)	88
Thailand	Kingdom	Bangkok (Krung Thep)	514,000	(198,456)	45,221,625 (1979)	Thai	baht	68
Togo	Republic	Lomé	56,591	(21,850)	2,470,000 (1979)*	French, tribal languages	CFA franc	85
Tonga	Kingdom. Commonwealth Nation	Nuku'alofa	699	(270)	90,128 (1976)	Tongan, English	pa'anga (T$)	137
Trinidad and Tobago	Republic. Commonwealth Nation	Port of Spain	5,128	(1,980)	1,157,000 (1979)*	English	Trinidad and Tobago dollar (TT$)	127
Tunisia	Republic	Tunis	164,149	(63,378)	6,030,000 (1978)*	Arabic, French	Tunisian dinar	85
Turkey	Republic	Ankara	779,452	(300,948)	45,442,000 (1980)*	Turkish, Arabic, Kurdish	Turkish Lira (TL)	47,78
Tuvalu	Special membership of the Commonwealth *formerly Ellice Islands*	Funafuti	24.5	(9.5)	7,349 (1979)*	Tuvaluan, English	Australian dollar ($A)	134
Uganda	Republic. Commonwealth Nation	Kampala	236,860	(91,452)	13,220,000 (1979)*	English, tribal languages	Uganda shilling	86,88
USSR	Union of Soviet Socialist Republics	Moscow	22,402,200	(8,649,534)	264,500,000 (1980)*	Russian, regional langs	rouble	49–59
United Arab Emirates	Federal union of seven emirates *formerly Trucial States*	Abu Dhabi	92,100	(35,560)	1,040,275 (1980)	Arabic, English	UAE dirham (UD)	77
United Kingdom	United Kingdom of Great Britain and Northern Ireland. Commonwealth Nation	London	244,755	(94,500)	55,945,000 (1981)*	English, Welsh, Gaelic	Pound Sterling (£)	8–15
United States of America	Federal Republic	Washington DC	3,363,168	(3,615,138)	226,504,825 (1980)	English	US dollar ($)	91–116
Upper Volta	Republic	Ouagadougou	274,123	(105,839)	6,617,000 (1979)*	French, native languages	CFA franc	85
Uruguay	Republic	Montevideo	186,926	(72,173)	2,886,000 (1978)*	Spanish	Nuevo Peso (N$)	131,133
Vanuatu	Republic. Commonwealth Nation. *Formerly Anglo-French Condominium of The New Hebrides*	Vila	14,763	(5,700)	112,596 (1979)	Bislama, English, French, many Melanesian languages	Australian dollar and New Hebrides franc (NH franc)	137
Vatican City	Ecclesiastical State	Vatican City	0.44	(0.17)	about 1,000 (1980)*	Italian, Latin	Italian lira, Papal coinage	44
Venezuela	Republic	Caracas	912,050	(352,144)	14,539,000 (1979)*	Spanish	bolívar (B)	127–8
Vietnam	Socialist Republic	Hanoi	329,566	(127,246)	54,000,000 (1981)	Vietnamese, French, Chinese	dong	65
Western Sahara	Ceded to Morocco and Mauritania (1976) (disputed) *formerly Spanish Sahara*							
Western Samoa	Sovereign State. Commonwealth Nation	Apia	2,831	(1,093)	157,000 (1978)*	English, Samoan	talà dollar ($WS)	137
Yemen	Yemen Arab Republic	San'a	195,000	(75,290)	6,471,893 (1975)	Arabic	riyal	72
Yemen, South	*See South Yemen*							
Yugoslavia	Socialist Federal Republic	Belgrade	255,804	(98,766)	22,300,000 (1980)*	Serbo-Croat, Albanian Macedonian, Slovenian	dinar	42,46,48
Zaire	Republic	Kinshasa	2,345,409	(905,567)	29,270,000 (1979)*	French, Kiswahili Tshiluba, Kikongo	zaïre	86
Zambia	Republic. Commonwealth Nation	Lusaka	752,620	(290,588)	5,600,000 (1979)*	English, African langs	Kwacha (K)	87–8
Zimbabwe	Republic. Commonwealth Nation. Unilaterally independent as Rhodesia 1965 to 1980	Harare (Salisbury)	390,308	(150,699)	7,400,000 (1980)* *estimate**	English, native languages	Zimbabwe dollar (Z$)	88–9

INDEX

Abbreviations used in the Index

Afghan	Afghanistan	Conn	Connecticut	L	Lake
Afr	Africa, African	Czech	Czechoslovakia	Lincs	Lincolnshire
Ala	Alabama	Den	Denmark	Lt Ho	Light House
Amer	America, American	Dep	Département, department	Madhya Prad	Madhya Pradesh
Anc mon	Ancient monument	Des	Desert	Man	Manitoba
Anc site	Ancient site	Dist	District	Mich	Michigan
Arch	Archipel, archipelago, archipiélago	Div	Division	Minn	Minnesota
Arg	Argentina	E	East	Miss	Mississippi
Ariz	Arizona	Equat	Equatorial	Mon	Monument
Ark	Arkansas	Est	Estuary	Mont	Montana
A.S.S.R.	Autonomous Soviet Socialist Republic	Fed	Federal, federation	Moz	Mozambique
Aust	Australia	Fj	Fjord	Mt, Mte	Mountain
Aut	Autonomous	Fr	French	Mts	Mountains
B	Bay	G	Gulf	Mt ra	Mountain range
Berks	Berkshire	Ger	Germany	N	North
Br	British	Gla	Glacier	Nether	Netherlands
Br Col	British Columbia	Gt	Great	Nev	Nevada
C	Cape	Hbr	Harbor, harbour	New Bruns	New Brunswick
Cal	California	Hd	Head	New Hamps	New Hampshire
Can	Canal	H.E.	Hydro-electricity	Nex Mex	New Mexico
Cat(s)	Cataract(s)	Hist reg	Historical region	Nfld	Newfoundland
Cent	Central	I, isld	Island	Notts	Nottinghamshire
Chan	Channel	Ind	Indian	N Scotia	Nova Scotia
Co	County	Is, islds	Islands	N.S.W.	New South Wales
Coastal reg	Coastal region	Isld king	Island kingdom	Oc	Ocean
Colo	Colorado	Isth	Isthmus	Old prov	Old province
		Jct, junc, junct	Junction	Pass	Passage

Pen	Peninsula	S.S.R.	Soviet Socialist Republic
Penn	Pennsylvania	St, Ste	Saint, Sainte
People's Rep	People's Republic	Sta	Station
Physical reg	Physical region	Staffs	Staffordshire
Pk	Peak	Stat Area	Statistical Area
Port	Portuguese	Stony des	Stony desert
Pt, Pta, Pto	Point	Str	Strait
Prefect	Prefecture	Swtz	Switzerland
Princ	Principality	Terr	Territory
Prot	Protectorate	Tex	Texas
Prov	Province	Tribal dist	Tribal district
Qnsld	Queensland	U.A.E.	United Arab Emirates
R	Rio, River	U.K.	United Kingdom
Ra	Range	Union Terr	Union Territory
Rdg	Ridge	U.S.A.	United States of America
Reg	Region	U.S.S.R.	Union of Soviet Socialist Republics
Rep	Republic	V	Valley
Res	Reservoir	Ven	Venezuela
River mth	River mouth	Vict	Victoria
S	South	Virg	Virginia
Sa	Serra, Sierra	Vol	Volcano
Salt des	Salt desert	W	West
Sand des	Sand desert	Wash	Washington
Sask	Saskatchewan	Wilts	Wiltshire
Sd	Sound		
Sk	Shuiku (reservoir)		
Spr	Spring		

Aa — Aiguillon

Addenda and Errata see page 87

36 F3 Altenstadt Hessen W Germany
36 F6 Altensteig W Germany
33 S5 Altentreptow E Germany
32 J5 Altenwalde W Germany
16 B5 Alter do Chão Portugal
33 R8 Altes Lager E Germany
26 K3 Altevatn *L* Norway
111 L11 Altha Florida
37 J6 Altheim W Germany
111 E7 Altheimer Arkansas
38 K8 Althofen Austria
9 G4 Althorne England
13 H6 Althorpe England
138 D6 Althorpe Is S Australia
139 G3 Altiboullin, L New S Wales
45 M1 Altino Italy
47 L5 Altıntaş Turkey
33 O6 Alt-Jabel E Germany
19 K5 Altkirch France
33 T7 Altlandsberg E Germany
36 E5 Altleiningen W Germany
37 M6 Altmannstein W Germany
95 L3 Altmar New York
33 O7 Altmark *reg* E Germany
36 H1 Altmorschen W Germany
37 K5 Altmühl *R* W Germany
32 K7 Altmühlen W Germany
15 D2 Altnaharra Scotland
111 A10 Alto Texas
16 B6 Alto Alentejo *prov* Portugal
130 D5 Alto Araguaia Brazil
126 G4 Alto Cedro Cuba
130 C4 Alto Coité Brazil
130 D5 Alto Garças Brazil
87 C8 Alto Hama Angola
87 G9 Alto Molocue Mozambique
44 D3 Alto,Monte Italy
37 L7 Altomünster W Germany
102 A1 Alton California
9 F5 Alton Hampshire England
110 F3 Alton Illinois
95 L3 Alton New York
103 M4 Alton Utah
99 Q8 Altona Illinois
118 D1 Altona Manitoba
101 P9 Altonah Utah
138 E2 Alton Downs S Australia
111 K7 Altoona Alabama
113 F9 Altoona Florida
107 P4 Altoona Kansas
94 J6 Altoona Pennsylvania
128 G8 Alto Paraguay *dep* Paraguay
130 C9 Alto Paraná *dep* Paraguay
129 J5 Alto Parnaíba Brazil
45 J4 Altopascio Italy
129 H7 Alto Sucuriú Brazil
38 G5 Altötting W Germany
129 J4 Alto Turi Brazil
130 C10 Alto Uruguai Brazil
126 A1 Alto Vista *hill* Aruba W I
13 F6 Altrincham England
33 R7 Altruppin E Germany
33 T8 Alt-Schadow E Germany
54 F4 Altukhovo U.S.S.R.
78 K4 Altun Köprü Iraq
47 H5 Altunoluk Turkey
66 C4 Altun Shan *mts* China
99 O5 Altura Minnesota
100 E8 Alturas California
113 F10 Alturas Florida
107 L7 Altus Oklahoma
41 M2 Altusried W Germany
36 B6 Altwiller France
57 C2 Altynasar U.S.S.R.
55 D3 Altynay U.S.S.R.
52 C6 Alūksne U.S.S.R.
86 B1 Alula Somalia
28 D4 Alum Denmark
9 E6 Alum Bay England
133 C5 Aluminé Argentina
26 M6 Ålund Sweden
27 K11 Alunda Sweden
103 K6 Alunite Nevada
76 C3 Alur India
53 D11 Alushta U.S.S.R.
17 F4 Alustante Spain
83 J11 Alutgama Sri Lanka
83 K9 Alut Oya Sri Lanka
113 F11 Alva Florida
94 D10 Alva Kentucky
107 M5 Alva Oklahoma
12 E1 Alva Scotland
98 B5 Alva Wyoming
16 B4 Alva *R* Portugal
16 B7 Alvalade Portugal
125 M8 Alvarado Mexico
109 K3 Alvarado Texas
128 F4 Alvaraes Brazil
26 E9 Alvdal Norway
118 L6 Alvena Sask
33 O8 Alvensleben E Germany
32 K8 Alverdissen W Germany
117 D5 Alverstone Mt Alaska/Yukon Terr
27 A11 Alversund Norway
27 G15 Alvesta Sweden
8 D4 Alveston England
27 G10 Älvho Sweden
110 J1 Alvin Illinois
109 M6 Alvin Texas
99 S4 Alvin Wisconsin
45 P6 Alvito Italy
16 B6 Alvito Portugal
27 J11 Älvkarleby Sweden
98 K9 Alvo Nebraska
109 K2 Alvord Texas
100 G7 Alvord L Oregon
26 F10 Älvros Sweden
27 F14 Älvsborg *reg* Sweden
26 M6 Älvsbyn Sweden
27 F14 Älvsered Sweden
99 M2 Alvwood Minnesota
87 E12 Alwal Nth S Africa
74 G5 Alwar India
76 C5 Alwaye India
13 F3 Alwinton England
110 C7 Aly Arkansas
140 D2 Alyangula N Terr Aust
51 N2 Alyaskitovyy U.S.S.R.
55 E2 Alymka *R* U.S.S.R.
15 E4 Alyth Scotland
31 P1 Alytus U.S.S.R.
38 G5 Alz *R* W Germany
98 B4 Alzada Montana
36 G3 Alzenau W Germany
22 L4 Alzette *R* Luxembourg
36 E4 Alzey W Germany
128 F2 Amacuro Delta Venezuela
140 B6 Amadeus,L N Terr Aust
86 F4 Amadi Sudan
115 M4 Amadjuak L N W Terr
60 J11 Amagasaki Japan
28 K5 Amager *isld* Denmark
60 D12 Amagi Japan
61 N11 Amagi-san *mt* Japan
22 G5 Amagne France
20 F4 Amain,Mt.d' France
116 F9 Amak I Alaska
60 C13 Amakusa-nada *sea* Japan
60 D13 Amakusa-shotō *islds* Japan
84 G4 Amal Libya
27 F12 Åmål Sweden
76 F2 Amalapuram India
43 F8 Amalfi Italy
46 E7 Amaliás Greece
16 C5 Amalia,Sta Spain
74 F8 Amalner India
129 G8 Amambai Brazil
130 C8 Amambaí, Serra de *mts* Brazil/Paraguay
130 C8 Amambay *dep* Paraguay
133 F2 Amambay, Sa. de *mts* Brazil/Paraguay
128 F4 Amaná,L Brazil
40 D2 Amance France
40 D3 Amancey France
94 E7 Amanda Ohio
42 E6 Amandola Italy
55 E6 Amangel'dy U.S.S.R.
55 D4 Amankaragay U.S.S.R.
60 J10 Amano-hashidate *inlet* Japan
43 G9 Amantea Italy
87 F12 Amanzimtoti S Africa
129 H3 Amapa Brazil
72 F2 Amārah, Al Iraq
88 F9 Amaramba,L Mozambique
129 K5 Amarante Brazil
119 T8 Amaranth Manitoba
68 C2 Amarapura Burma
102 H5 Amargosa Ra California
106 D5 Amarilla New Mexico
108 C8 Amarillo Texas
131 B4 Amarillo,Cerro *peak* Argentina
75 J7 Amarkantah India
129 J6 Amaro Leite Brazil
140 E6 Amaroo,L Queensland
61 N7 Amarume Japan
99 S3 Amasa Michigan
45 O7 Amaseno Italy
78 D1 Amasra Turkey
78 F1 Amasya Turkey
128 E4 Amataura Brazil
125 N9 Amatenango Mexico
87 F11 Amatikulu S Africa
124 H7 Amatitán Mexico
125 L8 Amatlan Mexico
124 G7 Amatlán de Cañas Mexico
22 J2 Amay Belgium
119 M7 Amazon Sask
Amazon *R* see Amazonas *R*
128 C5 Amazonas *dep* Peru
128 D4 Amazonas *div* Colombia
129 H4 Amazonas *R* S America
128 E4 Amazonas *state* Brazil
128 E3 Amazonas *state* Venezuela
110 B2 Amazonia Missouri
129 J3 Amazon,Mouths of the Brazil
80 C7 Amazya Israel
74 E1 Amb Pakistan
74 G9 Ambajogai India
74 G3 Ambala India
83 J11 Ambalangodo Sri Lanka
87 H12 Ambalavao Madagascar
140 C6 Ambalindum N Terr Aust
85 G8 Ambam Cameroon
83 K10 Amban Ganga *R* Sri Lanka
87 H10 Ambanje Madagascar
70 N9 Ambarawa Java
51 Q2 Ambarchik U.S.S.R.
18 E8 Ambarès et Lagrave France
52 D2 Ambarnyy U.S.S.R.
139 H2 Ambathala Queensland
128 C4 Ambato Ecuador
87 H11 Ambato-Boeny Madagascar
87 H11 Ambatolampy Madagascar
131 C2 Ambato,Sa *ra* Argentina
18 F7 Ambazac France
107 N6 Amber Oklahoma
100 H2 Amber Washington
116 J8 Amber B Alaska
37 M5 Amberg W Germany
99 T4 Amberg Wisconsin
9 E1 Ambergate England
127 H4 Ambergris Cays *islds* Turks & Caicos Is
19 O13 Ambérieu-en-Bugey France
144 D5 Amberley New Zealand
120 J8 Amberley Ontario
22 K3 Amberloup Belgium
18 H7 Ambert France
18 G9 Ambialet France
85 B6 Ambidédi Mali
75 K7 Ambikapur India
71 E4 Ambil *isld* Philippines
21 F7 Ambillou France
87 H10 Ambilobe Madagascar
117 H7 Ambition,Mt Br Columbia
20 K3 Amblainville France
13 G3 Amble England
116 J3 Ambler *R* Alaska
13 F5 Ambleside England
22 B2 Ambleteuse France
22 L3 Amblève Belgium
141 G6 Ambo Queensland
87 H12 Amboasary Madagascar
87 H11 Ambodifototra Madagascar
87 H12 Ambohimahasoa Madagascar
21 H7 Amboise France
136 F2 Ambon Moluccas Indonesia
87 H12 Amborompotsy Madagascar
86 G6 Amboseli, L Kenya
87 H12 Ambositra Madagascar
87 H13 Ambovombe Madagascar
103 J7 Amboy California
99 R8 Amboy Illinois
95 N6 Amboy,S New Jersey
21 I8 Ambrault France
87 H10 Ambre, Cap d' Madagascar
94 G6 Ambridge Pennsylvania
20 D5 Ambrières France
137 O5 Ambrim *isld* New Hebrides
87 B7 Ambriz Angola
112 D6 Ambrose Georgia
98 C1 Ambrose N Dakota
71 E2 Ambuklao Dam Luzon Philippines
71 K9 Ambulombo Vol Indonesia
70 O10 Ambulu Java
70 O9 Ambunten Java
76 D4 Ambur India
141 J7 Amby Queensland
27 C12 Åmdal Norway
86 D3 Am Dam Chad
85 E4 Amded *watercourse* Algeria
50 F2 Amderma U.S.S.R.
75 O2 Amdo China
86 G3 Amedamit *mt* Ethiopia
102 D1 Amedee California
25 E2 Ameland *isld* Netherlands
42 E6 Amelia Italy
98 H7 Amelia Nebraska
94 K9 Amelia Virginia
113 F7 Amelia I Florida
32 M6 Amelinghausen W Germany
43 H9 Amendolara Italy
67 A5 Ameng China
17 J2 Amer Spain
102 D2 American *R* California
130 F8 Americana Brazil
101 N7 American Falls Idaho
103 N1 American Fork Utah
134 E1 American Samoa *islds* Pacific Oc
113 F13 American Shoal *lt ho* Florida
112 C5 Americus Georgia
25 D4 Amerongen Netherlands
25 D4 Amersfoort Netherlands
9 F4 Amersham England
143 B9 Amery W Australia
99 O4 Amery Wisconsin
146 C4 Amery Ice Shelf Antarctica
99 N7 Ames Iowa
98 K8 Ames Nebraska
107 M5 Ames Oklahoma
118 E3 Amesbury Alberta
9 E5 Amesbury England
95 R4 Amesbury Massachusetts
118 J1 Amesdale Ontario
120 F3 Ameson Ontario
94 F7 Amesville Ohio
122 J8 Amet Sound Nova Scotia
46 F6 Amfíklia Greece
46 E6 Amfilokhía Greece
47 F4 Amfípolis Greece
46 E6 Ámfissa Greece
20 C3 Amfreville France
20 G3 Amfreville-la-Campagne France
51 N2 Amga U.S.S.R.
51 M3 Amga *R* U.S.S.R.
58 G2 Amgalang Bulag China
51 N3 Amgan *R* U.S.S.R.
51 N4 Amgu U.S.S.R.
86 D3 Am Guéréda Chad
85 F3 Amguid Algeria
59 K1 Amgun *R* U.S.S.R.
86 G3 Amhara *reg* Ethiopia
Amherst *see* Kyaikkami
106 H1 Amherst Colorado
95 T2 Amherst Maine
95 P4 Amherst Massachusetts
98 G9 Amherst Nebraska
95 Q4 Amherst New Hampshire
115 N8 Amherst Nova Scotia
94 E5 Amherst Ohio
98 J4 Amherst S Dakota
94 H9 Amherst Virginia
120 G10 Amherstburg Ontario
94 F9 Amherstdale W Virginia
123 K6 Amherst I Madeleine Is, Quebec
121 O8 Amherst I Ontario
99 R5 Amherst Junction Wisconsin
142 F4 Amherst, Mt W Australia
42 D6 Amiata,Monte Italy
98 C3 Amidon N Dakota
20 K2 Amiens France
141 K8 Amiens Queensland
78 H5 Amij,Wadi Iraq
46 E4 Amíndaion Greece
73 L6 Amindivi Is Lakshadweep Indian Ocean
60 H10 Amino Japan
87 C10 Aminuis Namibia
79 F4 Amioune Lebanon
80 F1 'Amir Israel
83 H5 Amirante Is Indian Oc
118 F6 Amisk Alberta
119 P4 Amisk L Sask
106 G6 Amistad New Mexico
108 F6 Amistad Res Mexico
111 F11 Amite Louisiana
111 C7 Amity Arkansas
95 O6 Amityville Long I, N Y
75 L5 Amlekhganj Nepal
27 C13 Amli Norway
8 B1 Amlwch Wales
80 G6 'Amman Jordan
8 C4 Ammanford Wales
26 H5 Ammarfjallet *mt* Sweden
26 H6 Ammarnäs Sweden
140 D5 Ammaroo N Terr Aust
28 E4 Ammelhede Denmark
33 P10 Ammendorf E Germany
32 L9 Ammensen W Germany
41 O2 Ammer *R* W Germany
41 N2 Ammer Gebirge *mt* W Germany
41 O2 Ammerland W Germany
32 G6 Ammerland *reg* W Germany
116 R2 Ammerman Mt Yukon Terr
37 K5 Ammerndorf W Germany
41 O1 Ammer See *L* W Germany
80 F2 'Ammi 'ad Israel
101 O6 Ammon Idaho
Amne Machin *see* A'nyêmaqên Shan
77 C1 Āmol Iran
130 B6 Amolar Brazil
109 N9 Amon Carter Airfield Texas
36 F2 Amöneburg W Germany
36 G4 Amorbach W Germany
131 F2 Amores *R* Argentina
47 H8 Amorgós *isld* Greece
107 M5 Amorita Oklahoma
111 H8 Amory Mississippi
103 J8 Amos California
115 M8 Amos Quebec
28 G5 Åmose Å *R* Denmark
27 H11 Åmot Sweden
27 D12 Åmot Akershus Norway
27 C12 Åmotsdal Norway
Amoy *see* Xiamen
70 G5 Ampana Sulawesi Indonesia
87 G12 Ampanihy Madagascar
130 F8 Amparo Brazil
128 D7 Ampato, Cord. de *mts* Peru
70 Q10 Ampenan Indonesia
37 M7 Amper *R* W Germany
37 N7 Ampfing W Germany
103 O9 Amphitheater Arizona
85 F7 Ampier Nigeria
13 G5 Ampleforth England
17 H4 Amposta Spain
9 F3 Ampthill England
19 N14 Ampuis France
17 J2 Ampurdán *dist* Spain
80 D2 'Amqa Israel
122 E5 Amqui Quebec
74 G8 Amravati India
74 D8 Amreli India
74 F3 Amritsar India
30 D1 Amrum *isld* W Germany
26 K7 Åmsele Sweden
38 J7 Am Stein *mt* Austria
25 C4 Amstelveen Netherlands
113 C7 Amsterdam Georgia
101 L7 Amsterdam Idaho
25 C4 Amsterdam Netherlands
95 N4 Amsterdam New York
94 G6 Amsterdam Ohio
24 Amsterdam *conurbation* Netherlands
81 E9 Amsterdam,I Indian Oc
38 L5 Amstetten Austria
27 F12 Ämtervik, V Sweden
86 D3 Am Timan Chad
28 B2 Amtoft Denmark
41 L2 Amtzell W Germany
127 J9 Amuay Venezuela
57 D5 Amu-Dar'ya U.S.S.R.
57 B4 Amudar'ya *R* U.S.S.R.
147 H5 Amund Ringness I N W Terr
146 A5 Amundsen B Antarctica
146 G8 Amundsen Glacier Antarctica
147 J1 Amundsen Gulf N W Terr
146 E3 Amundsen, Mt Antarctica
146 J11 Amundsen Sea Antarctica
147 J2 Amundsen Trough Arctic Oc
27 H10 Amungen *L* Sweden
70 D6 Amuntai Kalimantan
51 N3 Amur *R* U.S.S.R.
59 J1 Amur *reg* U.S.S.R.
71 J4 Amurang Sulawesi Indonesia
71 J4 Amurang Teluk *B* Sulawesi Indonesia
144 D5 Amuri Pass New Zealand
17 F1 Amurrio Spain
59 L1 Amursk U.S.S.R.
51 M3 Amurskaya Oblast' *prov* U.S.S.R.
55 C4 Amurskiy U.S.S.R.
46 E6 Amvrakía, L Greece
46 D6 Amvrakikós Kólpos *gulf* Greece
54 K9 Amvrosiyevka U.S.S.R.
107 K3 Amy Kansas
56 D4 Amyl *R* U.S.S.R.
142 B5 Amy, Mt W Australia
120 F4 Amyot Ontario
16 E9 Amzoughen-Khémis-Mrapten Morocco
68 B3 An Burma
138 F5 Ana Branch *R* New S Wales
80 D4 Anabta Jordan
102 E7 Anacapa Is California
45 Q8 Anacapri Italy
127 M10 Anaco Venezuela
111 C10 Anacoco Louisiana
114 H8 Anaconda Montana
101 M4 Anaconda Range Montana
100 C1 Anacortes Washington
107 M6 Anadarko Oklahoma
130 H10 Anadia Brazil
16 B4 Anadia Portugal
78 F1 Anadolu Dağlari *mt* Turkey
51 R2 Anadyr U.S.S.R.
51 R2 Anadyrskoye Ploskogor'ye *tableland* U.S.S.R.
47 H8 Anáfi *isld* Greece
26 F9 Anafjället *mt* Sweden
47 H8 Anafópoulo *isld* Greece
130 H4 Anagé Brazil
45 O6 Anagni Italy
117 L9 Anahim Lake Br Columbia
135 O1 Anahola Hawaiian Is
125 J4 Anáhuac Mexico
111 B12 Anahuac Texas
102 R11 Anahulu *R* Hawaiian Is
76 C5 Anaimalai Hills India
75 K10 Anakapalle India
141 J6 Anakie Queensland
116 M2 Anaktuvuk Pass Alaska
87 H10 Analalava Madagascar
128 F4 Anama Brazil
119 T7 Anama Bay Manitoba
126 E4 Ana Maria, Cayos de *islds* Cuba
69 G11 Anambas, Kep *isld* Indonesia
61 L8 Anamizu Japan
98 F2 Anamoose N Dakota
129 G3 Anamu *R* Brazil
78 D3 Anamur Turkey
60 H12 Anan Japan
47 G8 Anánes *isld* Greece
71 J7 Anano *isld* Indonesia
76 C3 Anantapur India
74 F2 Anantnag Kashmir
48 M3 Anan'yev U.S.S.R.
53 E11 Anapa U.S.S.R.
43 G11 Anapo *R* Sicily
129 J7 Anápolis Brazil
129 H4 Anapú *R* Brazil
77 D4 Anār Iran
77 C3 Anārak Iran
77 G3 Anardarra Afghanistan
26 F8 Anaris Fjällen *mt* Sweden
26 O3 Anarjokka *R* Norway/Finland
127 L5 Añasco Puerto Rico
26 M7 Ånäset Sweden
113 F8 Anastasia I Florida
78 D2 Anatolia *reg* Turkey
100 H3 Anatone Washington
29 O7 Änättijärvi *L* Finland
131 E2 Añatuya Argentina
128 F3 Anauá *R* Brazil
69 G8 An Bien Vietnam
128 C5 Ancash *dep* Peru
9 F2 Ancaster England
101 O4 Anceney Montana
21 C7 Ancenis France
21 F7 Anché France
130 H7 Anchieta Brazil
106 E8 Ancho New Mexico
116 N6 Anchorage Alaska
94 B8 Anchorage Kentucky
94 E4 Anchor Bay Michigan
144 A6 Anchor I New Zealand
116 M7 Anchor Point Alaska
127 J2 Anchovy Jamaica
65 C5 Anci China
121 T6 Ancienne Lorette *airport* Quebec
113 E9 Anclote Keys *islds* Florida
128 E7 Ancohuma *mt* Bolivia
128 C6 Ancón Peru
45 O4 Ancona Italy
128 C3 Ancon de Sardinas B.de Ecuador
95 O4 Ancram New York
22 D4 Ancre *R* France
13 F2 Ancroft England
13 F3 Ancrum Scotland
88 G8 Ancuabe Mozambique
133 C6 Ancud Chile
59 J2 Anda China
65 F1 Anda China
133 C5 Andacollo Argentina
140 D7 Andado N Terr Aust
128 D6 Andahuaylas Peru
107 N4 Andale Kansas
133 D3 Andalgala Argentina
26 C9 Åndalsnes Norway
16 D7 Andalucia *reg* Spain
111 K10 Andalusia Alabama
68 A6 Andaman Islands Bay of Bengal
138 D4 Andamooka S Australia
52 G5 Andanga U.S.S.R.
129 K6 Andaria Brazil
67 B5 Ande China
41 K4 Andeer Switzerland
28 N1 Andefjord Faeroes
52 H1 Andeg U.S.S.R.
20 H3 Andelle *R* France
19 J4 Andelot France
20 H3 Andelys,les France
22 J3 Andenne Belgium
85 E5 Anderamboukane Mali
41 J4 Andermatt Switzerland
36 C3 Andernach W Germany
36 C3 Andernach-Land W Germany
57 F6 Anderov U.S.S.R.
26 L7 Andersfors Sweden
100 C9 Anderson California
94 B6 Anderson Indiana
110 B5 Anderson Missouri
112 E3 Anderson S Carolina
114 G4 Anderson *R* N W Terr
139 H8 Anderson Bay Tasmania
68 A6 Anderson I Andaman Is
100 F7 Anderson L Oregon
101 K6 Anderson Ranch Res Idaho
112 C5 Andersonville Georgia
110 L2 Andersonville Indiana
27 G14 Anderstorp Sweden
95 N4 Andes New York
133 D3 Andes, Cordillera de los *mts* S America
98 H6 Andes,L S Dakota
87 H11 Andevoranto Madagascar
26 H2 Andfjord *inlet* Norway
76 D2 Andhra Pradesh *prov* India
17 F2 Andía,Sierra de *mt* Spain
83 J10 Andigama Sri Lanka
47 F9 Andikíthira *isld* Greece
87 H11 Andilamena Madagascar
47 G8 Andímilos *isld* Greece
47 G7 Andipáros *isld* Greece
46 D5 Andípaxoi *isld* Greece
47 H6 Andípsara *isld* Greece
78 F3 Andirin Turkey
66 C4 Andirlangar China
47 H5 Ándissa Greece
53 G12 Andiyskoye Koysu *R* U.S.S.R.
57 F4 Andizhan U.S.S.R.
77 J1 Andkhūi Afghanistan
36 C7 Andlau France
40 F1 Andolsheim France
52 E4 Andomskiy Pogost U.S.S.R.
65 G6 Andong S Korea
65 D7 Andongwei China
141 F1 Andoom Queensland
44 D4 Andora Italy
26 J3 Andörja *isld* Norway
17 J2 Andorra Pyrenees
17 H2 Andorra la Vella Andorra
20 D5 Andouille France
9 E5 Andover England
95 R2 Andover Maine
122 E7 Andover New Brunswick
95 Q3 Andover New Hampshire
95 N6 Andover New Jersey
94 K4 Andover New York
94 G5 Andover Ohio
98 J4 Andover S Dakota
9 E4 Andoversford England
26 H2 Andöya *isld* Norway
130 D7 Andradina Brazil
116 F5 Andreafsky Alaska
116 O10 Andreanof Is Aleutian Is
52 D6 Andreapol' U.S.S.R.
12 D5 Andreas I of Man U.K.
79 E3 Andreas,C Cyprus
87 H11 Andreba Madagascar
138 F2 Andree,L S Australia
115 R3 Andrée Land Greenland
130 G7 Andre lándia Brazil
118 E5 Andrew Alberta
99 Q7 Andrew Iowa
68 B3 Andrew B Burma
143 E10 Andrew, Mt W Australia
94 B6 Andrews Indiana
112 D2 Andrews N Carolina
98 C7 Andrews Nebraska
100 G7 Andrews Oregon
112 H4 Andrews S Carolina
108 E3 Andrews Texas
53 H8 Andreyevka U.S.S.R.
54 N1 Andreyevo U.S.S.R.
53 D9 Andreyevo-Ivanovka U.S.S.R.
55 E2 Andreyevskoye, Oz *L* U.S.S.R.
53 D8 Andreykovichi U.S.S.R.
43 G7 Andria Italy
46 D2 Andrijevica Yugoslavia
46 E7 Andrítsaina Greece
106 G4 Andrix Colorado
87 G12 Androka Madagascar
116 G9 Andronica I Alaska
126 E2 Andros *isld* Bahamas
47 G7 Ándros *isld* Greece
95 R2 Androscogg *R* New Hamps/Maine
53 G7 Androsovka U.S.S.R.
126 F2 Andros Town Andros Bahamas
73 L6 Androth I Lakshadweep Indian Oc
53 C8 Andrushevka U.S.S.R.
31 L6 Andrychów Poland
55 D2 Andryushino U.S.S.R.
26 K2 Andselv Norway
16 E6 Andújar Spain
87 C8 Andulo Angola
18 H8 Anduze France
27 G14 Aneby Sweden
85 E7 Anecho Togo
143 G6 Anec, L W Australia
131 B8 Anecón Grande *peak* Argentina
85 E5 Anefis Mali
113 L7 Anegada *isld* Virgin Is
133 E6 Anegado, B Argentina
137 O6 Aneityum *isld* New Hebrides
118 K7 Anerley Sask
118 K9 Aneroid Sask
20 H4 Anet France
98 J2 Aneta N Dakota
67 E3 Anfu China
140 B3 Angalarri *R* N Terr Aust
133 C2 Angamos, Pta *C* Chile
125 J8 Angangue Mexico
59 H2 Ang'angxi China
147 K8 Angara Basin Arctic Oc
56 F4 Angarsk U.S.S.R.
140 B7 Angas Downs N Terr Aust
142 G6 Angas Ra W Australia
138 E5 Angaston S Australia
71 E3 Angat Luzon Philippines
130 E8 Angatuba Brazil
26 H9 Änge Sweden
26 H10 Ängebo Sweden
124 C3 Angel de la Guarda *isld* Mexico
71 E3 Angeles Luzon Philippines
128 F2 Angel Falls *waterfall* Venezuela
27 F15 Ängelholm Sweden
94 J4 Angelica New York
111 B10 Angelina *R* Texas
141 H7 Angellala Queensland
28 D7 Angeln *reg* W Germany
43 G8 Angelo de Lom,S Italy
27 H12 Ängelsberg Sweden
102 D3 Angels Camp California
38 N7 Anger Austria
41 J6 Angera Italy
26 K9 Ångermanälven *isld* Sweden
26 J8 Ångermanälven *R* Sweden
32 E10 Angermund W Germany
21 D7 Angers France
26 G10 Ängersjö Sweden
20 J5 Angerville France
26 M5 Ängeså Sweden
26 N5 Ängesan *R* Sweden
26 L8 Ängesön *isld* Sweden
70 G7 Anggowala, Bk *mt* Sulawesi Indonesia
45 M4 Anghiari Italy
112 J2 Angier N Carolina
115 K5 Angikuni L N W Terr
8 A4 Angle Wales
144 A7 Anglem, Mt New Zealand
120 D4 Angler Ontario
Anglesey *co see* Gwynedd
Anglesey *isld see* Môn
18 D9 Anglet France
109 M6 Angleton Texas
118 J7 Anglia Sask
21 F8 Angliers France
21 H8 Anglin *R* France
115 Q4 Angmagssalik Greenland
88 G10 Angoche Mozambique
77 E6 Angohrān Iran
131 A6 Angol Chile
87 C8 Angola Africa
94 B5 Angola Indiana
94 H4 Angola New York
90 K11 Angola Basin Atlantic Oc
112 K3 Angola Swamp N Carolina
117 F7 Angoon Alaska
98 C8 Angora Nebraska
124 E5 Angostura Mexico
125 J6 Angostura Mexico
128 D3 Angostura I, Salto *cataract* Colombia
124 E2 Angostura, Presa de la *res* Mexico
125 N9 Angostura, Psa. de la *res* Mexico
98 C6 Angostura Reserve S Dakota
18 F7 Angoulême France
18 F7 Angoumois *prov* France
129 K8 Angra dos Reis Brazil
45 R8 Angri Italy
21 D6 Angrie France
37 L2 Angstedt-Gräfinau E Germany
68 E5 Ang Thong Thailand
17 G2 Angués Spain
126 E3 Anguila Isles Bahamas
127 N5 Anguilla *isld* Lesser Antilles
45 L1 Anguillara Ven Italy
123 N6 Anguille, C Newfoundland
75 L8 Angul India
86 E6 Angumu Zaïre
65 C5 Anguo China
140 D2 Angurugu Northern Territory
98 K1 Angus Minnesota
Angus *co see* Tayside *reg*
119 Q8 Angusville Manitoba
88 C10 Angwa *R* Zimbabwe
129 H8 Anhandui *R* Brazil
28 R3 Anholt Denmark
28 H3 Anholt *isld* Denmark
68 G3 Anh Son Vietnam
67 D2 Anhua China
58 G5 Anhui *prov* China
Anhwei *prov see* Anhui
61 O5 Aniai Japan
116 H6 Aniak Alaska
116 H8 Aniakchak Vol. Crater Alaska
22 E3 Aniche France
130 E5 Anicuns Brazil
47 H8 Ánidhros *isld* Greece
85 E7 Anié Togo
45 N6 Aniene *R* Italy
18 E10 Anie, Pic d' *mt* Spain/France
55 D5 Anikhovka U.S.S.R.
52 F5 Anikovo U.S.S.R.
106 B10 Animas New Mexico
106 C4 Animas *R* Colorado
124 C3 Animas,Pta Las *C* Mexico
68 C5 Anin Burma
48 G5 Anina Romania
103 M6 Anita Arizona
99 M8 Anita Iowa
71 G5 Anitaguipan Pt Philippines
130 E10 Anitápolis Brazil
116 J2 Aniuk *R* Alaska
59 M2 Aniva, Zaliv *B* U.S.S.R.
99 R4 Aniwa Wisconsin
22 E4 Anizy-le-Chât France
29 M11 Anjalankoski Finland
74 D7 Anjar India
80 G4 'Anjara Jordan
70 K9 Anjer-Lor Java
67 F1 Anji China
65 G2 Anjia China
Anjiang *see* Qianyang
Anjiangying *see* Luanping
61 L11 Anjō Japan
21 C7 Anjou *prov* France
87 G10 Anjouan *isld* Comoros
87 H11 Anjozorobe Madagascar
59 J4 Anjŭ N Korea
77 L2 Anjuman *reg* Afghanistan
58 E5 Ankang China
78 D2 Ankara Turkey
87 H11 Ankaratra *mt* Madagascar
27 H14 Ankarsrum Sweden
26 J6 Ankarsund Sweden
87 G12 Ankazoabo Madagascar
99 N8 Ankeny Iowa
33 T5 Anklam E Germany
74 E8 Anklesvar India
86 G4 Ankober Ethiopia
16 D10 Ankod Morocco
38 H7 Ankogel *mt* Austria
87 E7 Ankoro Zaïre
52 E6 An'kovo U.S.S.R.
32 G7 Ankum W Germany
13 H6 Anlaby England
67 E3 Anle China
22 K4 Anlier Belgium
68 H7 An Loc Vietnam
67 B4 Anlong China
68 G5 Anlong Veng Cambodia
58 F5 Anlu China
26 F8 Ånn Sweden
110 G4 Anna Illinois
25 C3 Anna Netherlands
94 C6 Anna Ohio
109 L2 Anna Texas
53 F8 Anna U.S.S.R.
85 F1 Annaba Algeria
38 H7 Annaberg Austria
37 P2 Annaberg-Buchholz E Germany
33 S9 Annaburg E Germany
138 D3 Anna Creek S Australia
128 G3 Annai Guyana
25 B5 Anna Jacobapolder Netherlands
61 M9 Annaka Japan
68 G3 Annam *reg* Vietnam
113 E10 Anna Maria Florida
13 E4 Annan Scotland
99 M4 Annandale Minnesota
141 J5 Annandale Queensland
15 E5 Annandale Scotland
13 E3 Annan Water Scotland
133 C7 Anna Pink, B Chile
142 D4 Anna Plains W Australia
95 L8 Annapolis Maryland
122 G9 Annapolis R Nova Scotia
75 K4 Annapurna *mt* Nepal
94 D4 Ann Arbor Michigan
33 O9 Annarode E Germany
78 L7 An Nāsirīyah Iraq
99 R8 Annawan Illinois
146 H12 Annawan,C Antarctica
146 A5 Ann,C Antarctica
143 C7 Annean, L W Australia
20 F3 Annebault France
19 Q13 Annecy France
40 D6 Annecy,L.d' France
146 A15 Annenkov I Antarctica
133 J8 Annenkov Is S Georgia
141 K2 Annerley *dist* Brisbane, Qnsld
117 H8 Annette I Alaska
20 B3 Anneville-sur-Mer France
19 N14 Anneyron France
68 J6 An Nhon Vietnam
141 G2 Annie *R* Queensland
123 P5 Annieopsquotch Mts Newfoundland
58 D6 Anning He *R* China
28 J5 Annisse Denmark
111 L8 Anniston Alabama
140 D5 Annitowa N Terr Aust
40 G5 Anniviers Val d' Switzerland
Annobón *isld see* Pagalu *isld*
22 D2 Annœulin France
109 N2 Annona Texas
19 N14 Annonay France
127 L2 Annotto Bay Jamaica
36 D5 Annweiler W Germany
47 G9 Áno Arkhánai Crete Greece
99 N4 Anoka Minnesota
98 H7 Anoka Nebraska
54 M1 Anopino U.S.S.R.
22 G4 Anor France
36 B7 Anould France
47 G9 Áno Viánnos Crete Greece
68 J7 An Phuoc Vietnam
65 C5 Anping China
67 C6 Anpu China
67 C6 Anpu Gang *B* China
58 G5 Anqing China
65 D6 Anqiu China
25 F6 Anrath W Germany
67 D3 Anren China
32 H9 Anröchte W Germany
22 K2 Ans Belgium
21 G10 Ansac-sur-Vienne France
28 B5 Ansager Denmark
65 A6 Ansai China
79 G3 Ansārīye, Jebel el *mts* Syria
37 K5 Ansbach W Germany
40 A6 Anse France
127 H5 Anse-à-Galets Haiti
127 J5 Anse-à-Pitre Haiti
122 H5 Anse-au-Griffon Quebec
126 H5 Anse-à-Veau Haiti
127 N4 Anse Bertrand Guadeloupe W I
126 G5 Anse d'Hainault Haiti
98 G8 Anselmo Nebraska
22 H3 Anseremme Belgium
139 H7 Anser Gr *islds* Tasmania
122 B5 Anse St.Jean,L' Quebec
127 L4 Anses d'Arlets, Les Martinique W I
59 H3 Anshan China
67 B3 Anshun China
131 B3 Ansilta *peak* Argentina
131 B3 Ansilta, Cord. de *ra* Argentina
109 P3 Ansley Louisiana
98 G8 Ansley Nebraska
140 B2 Anson B N Terr Aust
85 E5 Ansongo Mali
94 C6 Ansonia Ohio
112 G2 Ansonville N Carolina
115 L8 Ansonville Ontario
28 C6 Anst Denmark
94 F8 Ansted W Virginia
15 F4 Anstruther Scotland
128 D6 Anta Peru
78 C3 Antalya Turkey
87 H11 Antananarivo Madagascar
87 H11 Antanifotsy Madagascar
87 H12 Antanimora Madagascar
90 D16 Antarctic Circle
146 E13 Antarctic Pen Antarctica
81 C10 Antares Bank Indian Oc
130 H11 Antas Brazil
130 D10 Antas,R das Brazil
15 C3 An Teallach *mt* Scotland
98 B1 Antelope Montana
98 D3 Antelope N Dakota
118 J8 Antelope Sask
109 J2 Antelope Texas
101 Q9 Antelope Utah
100 H7 Antelope Cr Oregon
130 H9 Antenor Navarro Brazil
16 D7 Antequera Spain
130 B9 Antequera,Pto Paraguay
106 D3 Antero Pk Colorado
106 E3 Antero Res Colorado
38 F8 Anterselva Italy
107 N4 Anthony Kansas
106 D9 Anthony New Mexico
108 A3 Anthony New Mex/Tex
136 H5 Anthony Lagoon N Terr Australia
138 C2 Anthony,Mt S Australia
85 C3 Anti Atlas *mts* Morocco
44 B4 Antibes France
44 B4 Antibes,C.d' France
127 N9 Antica, I Venezuela
45 N5 Anticoli Corrado Italy
122 J4 Anticosti I Quebec
20 F2 Antifer,C.d' France
123 K8 Antigonish Nova Scotia
125 O10 Antigua Guatemala
127 P4 Antigua *isld* Lesser Antilles
127 N4 Antigues Pte. d' Guadeloupe W I
118 B3 Antikameg Alberta
133 C5 Antilhue Chile
126 G4 Antilla Cuba
103 N3 Antimony Utah
102 C3 Antioch California
99 S7 Antioch Illinois
98 D7 Antioch Nebraska
21 C9 Antioche, Pertuis d' *str* France
43 B9 Antioco, S Sardinia
43 B9 Antioco,S *isld* Sardinia
128 C2 Antioquia *div* Colombia
80 C5 Antipatris Israel
52 D6 Antipovo U.S.S.R.
128 C4 Antisana *mt* Ecuador
98 E1 Antler N Dakota
119 Q9 Antler Sask
107 P7 Antlers Oklahoma
133 C2 Antofagasta Chile
133 D3 Antofagasta de la Sierra Argentina
133 D3 Antofalla *vol* Argentina
109 O1 Antoine Arkansas
22 E2 Antoing Belgium
44 F2 Antola,Monte Italy
106 G2 Anton Colorado
108 E2 Anton Texas
87 J11 Antongil, B.d' Madagascar
87 G12 Antongo Madagascar
130 E9 Antonina Brazil
107 L3 Antonino Kansas
48 K1 Antoniny U.S.S.R.
129 K7 Antônio *R* Brazil
130 G7 Antônio Carlos Brazil
130 G6 Antônio Dias Brazil
Antonio Enes *see* Angoche
130 C8 Antônio João Brazil
106 D4 Antonito Colorado
126 D3 Antón Recio Cuba
140 D4 Antony Lagoon N Terr Aust
20 C5 Antrain France
52 C4 Antrea U.S.S.R.
36 G5 Antrefftal W Germany
95 P3 Antrim New Hampshire
14 E2 Antrim N Ireland
95 K5 Antrim Pennsylvania
14 E2 Antrim *co* N Ireland
14 E2 Antrim Hills N Ireland
142 G4 Antrim Plat W Australia
87 G11 Antsalova Madagascar
87 H10 Antseranana Madagascar
52 D5 Antsiferovo U.S.S.R.
87 H11 Antsirabe Madagascar
52 C5 Antsla U.S.S.R.
87 H10 Antsohihy Madagascar
29 N10 Anttola Finland
65 G3 Antu China
68 J6 An Tuc Vietnam
Antwerp *see* Antwerpen
95 M2 Antwerp New York
94 C5 Antwerp Ohio
22 H1 Antwerpen Belgium
14 E3 An Uaimh Irish Rep
116 F6 Anukslak L Alaska
26 K8 Anundsjö Sweden
74 E4 Anupgarh India
83 K9 Anuradhapura Sri Lanka
Anvers *see* Antwerpen
45 P6 Anversa degli Abruzzi Italy
146 E14 Anvers I Antarctica
116 G5 Anvik Alaska
121 P3 Anvilla Quebec
22 C3 Anvin France
58 C3 Anxi China
67 F4 Anxi China
67 A1 An Xian China
67 D2 Anxiang China
65 C5 Anxin China
138 C5 Anxious B S Australia
58 F4 Anyang China
58 C5 A'nyêmaqên Shan *mts* China
65 B7 Anyi China
67 E2 Anyi China
67 D7 Anyou China
117 J8 Anyox Br Col
67 E4 Anyuan China
52 J3 An'yudin U.S.S.R.
67 B1 Anyue China
51 Q2 Anyuy *R* U.S.S.R.
42 B3 Anza *R* Italy
118 F2 Anzac Alberta
17 G2 Anzánigo Spain
40 H6 Anzasca, Valle Italy
18 F10 Anzat France
65 B6 Anze China
22 E2 Anzegem Belgium
21 I9 Anzème France
56 C3 Anzhero-Sudzhensk U.S.S.R.
147 P7 Anzhu Os *isld* U.S.S.R.
22 E3 Anzin France
38 E5 Anzing W Germany
45 N7 Anzio Italy
128 F2 Anzoátegui *state* Venezuela
45 K2 Anzola dell'Emilia Italy
59 L5 Aoga-shima *isld* Japan
65 D3 Aohan Qi China
18 E10 Aoiz Spain
61 O5 Aomori Japan
60 N3 Aonae Japan
145 E4 Aorangi Mts New Zealand
145 D4 Aorere R New Zealand
68 D7 Ao Sawi *B* Thailand
40 F6 Aosta Italy
145 E3 Aotea Harbour New Zealand
85 C5 Aouker *reg* Mauritania
85 E3 Aoulef Algeria
67 B3 Aoxi China
60 G10 Aoya Japan
86 C1 Aozou Chad
103 P10 Apache Arizona
109 J1 Apache Oklahoma
106 B8 Apache Creek New Mexico
103 N8 Apache Junct Arizona
103 O10 Apache Pk Arizona
113 C7 Apalachee B Florida
112 C2 Apalachia Dam N Carolina
113 C8 Apalachicola Florida
128 D3 Apaporis *R* Colombia
130 B8 Apa.R Brazil/Paraguay
130 D7 Aparecida do Tabuado Brazil
144 B7 Aparima R New Zealand
71 E1 Aparri Luzon Philippines
70 E6 Apar, Teluk *B* Kalimantan
48 E5 Apatin Yugoslavia
52 D1 Apatity U.S.S.R.
124 H8 Apatzingán Mexico
116 C5 Apavawook C St. Lawrence I, Alaska
52 C5 Ape U.S.S.R.
45 M4 Apecchio Italy
119 S3 Apeganau L Manitoba
25 E4 Apeldoorn Netherlands
32 G6 Apen W Germany
33 O7 Apenburg E Germany
32 L6 Apensen W Germany
128 E6 Apere *R* Bolivia
112 J2 Apex N Carolina
41 L1 Apfingen W Germany
101 L1 Apgar Montana

6
Aphek — Ata

80 C5 Aphek Israel
116 E6 Aphrewn R Alaska
86 E5 Api Zaïre
137 S4 Apia W Samoa
129 G5 Apiacás,Serra dos mts Brazil
130 E9 Apiaí Brazil
45 R7 Apice Italy
71 J9 Api,Gunung vol Indonesia
130 B10 Apipe Grande isld Argentina
106 F4 Apishapa R Colorado
70 G5 Api,Tg C Sulawesi Indonesia
145 E3 Apiti New Zealand
125 K8 Apizaco Mexico
124 H5 Apizolaya Mexico
56 F2 Aplinskiy Porog falls U.S.S.R.
129 L5 Apodi R Brazil
71 E4 Apo East Pass Philippines
37 M1 Apolda E Germany
Apollonia see Marsá Süsah
47 G8 Apollonía Greece
128 E6 Apolo Bolivia
113 F9 Apopka Florida
113 F9 Apopka,L Florida
133 G1 Aporé R Brazil
129 H3 Aporema Brazil
99 Q2 Apostle Is Michigan
133 F3 Apostoles Argentina
54 E9 Apostolovo U.S.S.R.
128 G3 Apoteri Guyana
71 E4 Apo West Pass Philippines
94 E10 Appalachia Virginia
94 F10 Appalachian Mts U.S.A.
27 G11 Äppelbo Sweden
32 F9 Appelhülsen W Germany
28 B7 Appelland isld W Germany
44 D3 Appenino Ligure mt Italy
42 E5 Appennino Umbro-Marchigiano mts Italy
36 D6 Appenweier W Germany
41 K3 Appenzell canton Switzerland
13 G6 Apperley Br England
20 G3 Appeville France
25 G2 Appingedam Netherlands
109 N4 Appleby Texas
13 F4 Appleby-in-Westmorland England
142 A2 Applecross dist Perth, W Aust
8 B5 Appledore England
102 D3 Applegate California
100 B7 Applegate Oregon
122 H8 Apple River Nova Scotia
109 N4 Apple Springs Texas
95 S2 Appleton Maine
100 D4 Appleton Washington
99 S5 Appleton Wisconsin
110 B3 Appleton City Missouri
94 J9 Appomattox Virginia
54 J1 Aprelevka U.S.S.R.
22 J5 Apremont France
27 M15 Apriki U.S.S.R.
43 E7 Aprilia Italy
53 E11 Apsheronsk U.S.S.R.
121 M8 Apsley Ontario
138 F6 Apsley Victoria
140 B1 Apsley Str N Terr Aust
19 O17 Apt France
45 H3 Apuane Italy
135 V6 Apua Pt Hawaiian Is
130 D8 Apucarana Brazil
130 D8 Apucarana, Serra Da mts Brazil
71 D6 Apurauan Philippines
128 E2 Apure state Venezuela
128 D6 Apurímac dep Peru
48 H4 Apuseni Muntii mt Romania
88 D6 Apwa Tanzania
79 F9 'Aqaba Jordan
84 J4 Aqaba,G.of Red Sea
77 J1 Aq Chah Afghanistan
66 D4 Aqqikkol Hu L China
80 G3 'Aqraba Jordan
103 L7 Aquarius Mts Arizona
103 N4 Aquarius Plat Utah
130 B8 Aquidabán,R Paraguay
130 C7 Aquidauana Brazil
130 C6 Aquidauana,R Brazil
124 G3 Aquiles Serdán Mexico
109 K4 Aquilla Texas
126 H5 Aquin Haiti
45 P7 Aquino Italy
17 G2 Ara R Spain
80 F3 Arab R Jordan
53 E10 Arabatskaya Strelka spit U.S.S.R.
38 E8 Arabba Italy
112 D6 Arabi Georgia
111 K12 Arabi New Orleans
123 N3 Arabian L Quebec
84 H3 Arabs Gulf Egypt
78 D1 Araç Turkey
128 F3 Araçá R Brazil
129 L6 Aracaju Brazil
130 C9 Aracanguy, Mt de Paraguay
126 G9 Aracataca Colombia
129 L4 Aracati Brazil
130 E7 Araçatuba Brazil
16 C7 Aracena Spain
16 C7 Aracena, Sa. de mts Spain
130 G5 Araçuaí Brazil
48 G4 Arad Romania
86 D2 Arada Chad
56 D5 Aradanskiy Khrebet mts U.S.S.R.
81 L7 Arafura Sea Aust/New Guinea
129 H7 Aragarças Brazil
78 J1 Aragats mt U.S.S.R.
61 M9 Ara-gawa R Japan
100 A6 Arago,Cape Oregon
17 G2 Aragón R Spain
17 G4 Aragon reg Spain
43 F11 Aragona Sicily
17 F4 Aragoncillo mt Spain
128 E2 Aragua state Venezuela
129 J6 Araguaçu Brazil
128 F2 Aragua de Barcelona Venezuela
129 J7 Araguari Brazil
129 H3 Araguari R Brazil
133 H1 Araguari R Brazil
129 J5 Araguatins Brazil
53 F12 Aragvi R U.S.S.R.
144 C5 Arahura New Zealand
61 M8 Arai Japan
79 E8 Araif el Naqa mt Egypt
80 G8 Ara'ir Jordan
85 E3 Arak Algeria
77 A2 Arāk Iran
78 G4 Arak Syria
61 N8 Arakai-yama mt Japan
128 G2 Arakaka Guyana
116 A4 Arakamchechen, Ostrov isld U.S.S.R.
68 A2 Arakan prov Burma
68 B2 Arakan Yoma ra Burma
46 F6 Arákhova Greece
46 D5 Árakhthos R Greece
120 C2 Ara L Ontario
57 B2 Aral'sk U.S.S.R.
57 A3 Aral'skoye More sea U.S.S.R.
55 B6 Aralsor, Oz L U.S.S.R.
26 A9 Åram Norway
141 H6 Aramac Queensland
141 G6 Aramac R Queensland
125 K5 Aramberri Mexico
19 N17 Aramon France
16 E3 Aranda de Duero Spain
17 F3 Aranda de Moncayo Spain
87 B10 Arandis Namibia
145 D1 Aranga New Zealand
128 E7 Arani Bolivia
14 C1 Aran I Irish Rep
16 E4 Aranjuez Spain
89 A5 Aranos Namibia
109 L7 Aransas B Texas
109 K8 Aransas Pass Texas
130 E6 Arantes,R Brazil
137 P1 Aranuka isld Kiribati
85 D5 Araouane Mali
106 E1 Arapaho mt Colorado
106 H3 Arapahoe Colorado
98 G9 Arapahoe Nebraska
101 R7 Arapahoe Wyoming
128 E7 Arapa,L Peru
145 E4 Arapawa I New Zealand
133 F4 Arapey Uruguay
130 H10 Arapiraca Brazil
78 G2 Arapkir Turkey
130 D8 Arapongas Brazil
145 E3 Arapuni New Zealand
130 E10 Araquari Brazil
80 D4 'Ar'Ara Israel
133 H3 Araranguá Brazil
129 J8 Araraquara Brazil
130 F8 Araras São Paulo Brazil
130 D6 Araras,Serra das Mato Grosso Brazil
130 D9 Araras, Serra das mts Paraná Brazil
139 G6 Ararat Victoria
Ararat,Mt see Bügük Ağri
129 K4 Arari Brazil
75 M5 Araria India
130 G8 Araruama L.de Brazil
78 H6 Arar,Wadi Saudi Arabia
80 D5 A-ras Jordan
78 J1 Aras R Turkey
17 G5 Aras de Alpuente Spain
126 A1 Arasji Aruba W I
145 D2 Aratapu New Zealand
145 F3 Aratiatia New Zealand
61 O7 Arato Japan
128 F5 Araua R Brazil
128 D2 Arauca Colombia
133 C5 Arauco Chile
127 K10 Araure Venezuela
80 E2 'Arav Israel
74 E6 Aravalli Range India
144 B6 Arawata R New Zealand
129 J7 Araxá Brazil
128 F1 Araya,P.de Venezuela
61 P14 Ara-zaki C Okinawa
17 G3 Arba R Spain
86 G4 Arba Minch Ethiopia
43 C9 Arbatax Sardinia
52 G5 Arbazh U.S.S.R.
40 C2 Arbecey France
37 K5 Arberg W Germany
27 H12 Arboga Sweden
27 H12 Arbogaån R Sweden
40 C4 Arbois France
101 N7 Arbon Idaho
41 K2 Arbon Switzerland
119 O5 Arborfield Sask
9 F5 Arborfield Cross England
119 U8 Arborg Manitoba
99 R4 Arbor Vitae Wisconsin
27 H10 Arbrå Sweden
13 F1 Arbroath Scotland
102 B2 Arbuckle California
113 F10 Arbuckle,L Florida
109 K1 Arbuckle Mts Oklahoma
110 F5 Arbyrd Missouri
19 J5 Arc France
19 O18 Arc R France
18 E8 Arcachon France
94 J4 Arcade New York
118 A3 Arcadia Alberta
113 F10 Arcadia Florida
94 A6 Arcadia Indiana
107 Q4 Arcadia Kansas
111 D9 Arcadia Louisiana
99 U5 Arcadia Michigan
110 F4 Arcadia Missouri
98 G8 Arcadia Nebraska
94 D5 Arcadia Ohio
107 N6 Arcadia Oklahoma
99 P5 Arcadia Wisconsin
95 T2 Arcadia Nat. Park Maine
43 G8 Arcangelo,S Italy
94 C7 Arcanum Ohio
102 G3 Arc Dome mt Nevada
45 P6 Arce Italy
125 J8 Arcelia Mexico
25 F6 Arcen Netherlands
45 N4 Arcévia Italy
46 F1 Archar Bulgaria
95 M5 Archbald Pennsylvania
94 C5 Archbold Ohio
112 H2 Archdale N Carolina
113 E8 Archer Florida
141 F2 Archer R Queensland
109 J2 Archer City Texas
141 K2 Archerfield Airfield Brisbane, Qnsld
141 H3 Archer Pt Queensland
119 O6 Archerwill Sask
40 E1 Arches France
103 P3 Arches Nat.Mon Utah
110 B3 Archie Missouri
21 G8 Archigny France
119 M8 Archive Sask
106 C5 Archuleta New Mexico
18 H4 Arcis sur Aube France
138 C2 Arckaringa R S Australia
101 M6 Arco Idaho
98 K5 Arco Minnesota
99 S10 Arcola Illinois
111 F8 Arcola Mississippi
119 P9 Arcola Sask
45 K1 Árcole Italy
18 H6 Arconce R France
138 D4 Arcoona S Australia
131 B7 Arco, Paso de Arg/Chile
130 F7 Arcos Brazil
16 D8 Arcos de la Frontera Spain
16 B3 Arcos de Vale de Vez Portugal
17 G3 Arcos,Sierra de mt Spain
76 D4 Arcot India
130 H10 Arcoverde Brazil
19 J5 Arc-Senans France
147 F4 Arctic Bay N W Terr
90 J2 Arctic Circle
116 D4 Arctic Lagoon Alaska
147 Arctic Ocean
114 F4 Arctic Red River N W Terr
116 P2 Arctic Village Alaska
45 L1 Arcugnano Italy
22 E5 Arcy-Ste. Restitue France
44 G2 Arda R Italy
78 M2 Ardabil Iran
38 L5 Ardagger Austria
78 J1 Ardahan Turkey
77 C3 Ardakan Esfahān Iran
77 C4 Ardakan Fārs Iran
77 B4 Ardal Iran
27 C10 Årdal Opland Norway
27 B12 Årdal Rogaland Norway
14 C2 Ardara Irish Rep
118 K7 Ardath Sask
52 F6 Ardatov U.S.S.R.
120 K7 Ardbeg Ontario
12 B2 Ardbeg Scotland
45 N6 Ardea Italy
48 H3 Ardead Romania
18 H8 Ardèche dep France
14 E3 Ardee Irish Rep
119 S8 Arden Manitoba
103 J5 Arden Nevada
121 O8 Arden Ontario
138 E4 Arden Mt S Australia
22 H4 Ardennes France
21 I8 Ardentes France
12 D1 Ardentinny Scotland
77 C3 Ardestān Iran
15 D3 Ardgay Scotland
14 F2 Ardglass N Ireland
46 E4 Ardhéa Greece
16 C6 Ardila,R Spain
119 M9 Ardill Sask
124 H6 Ardilla, Cerro La peak Mexico
47 G3 Ardino Bulgaria
18 E10 Ardisa Spain
70 P9 Ardjasa Java
70 O9 Ardjuna,G mt Java
145 F3 Ardkeen New Zealand
118 D6 Ardley Alberta
15 D4 Ardlui Scotland
12 C2 Ardminish Scotland
139 H6 Ardmona Victoria
118 G4 Ardmore Alberta
107 N7 Ardmore Oklahoma
98 C6 Ardmore S Dakota
110 K6 Ardmore Tennessee
14 D5 Ardmore B Irish Rep
15 B4 Ardnamurchan Pt Scotland
15 B5 Ardnave Pt Scotland
98 J1 Ardoch N Dakota
141 G7 Ardoch Queensland
22 B2 Ardres France
12 C1 Ardrishaig Scotland
118 D5 Ardrossan Alberta
138 E5 Ardrossan S Australia
15 D5 Ardrossan Scotland
14 F2 Ards Pen N Ireland
12 B2 Ardtalla Scotland
15 C3 Ardvasar Scotland
53 F7 Ardym U.S.S.R.
26 F8 Åre Sweden
26 N4 Areavaara Sweden
127 L5 Arecibo Puerto Rico
131 F5 Areco R Argentina
129 L4 Areia Branca Brazil
45 Q7 Areinzo Italy
118 K6 Arelee Sask
27 E12 Aremark Norway
36 B3 Aremberg W Germany
95 N4 Arena New York
71 E6 Arena Philippines
118 H9 Arena Sask
133 C7 Arenales mt Chile
130 C4 Arenápolis Brazil
71 F4 Arena Pt Luzon Philippines
124 E6 Arena, Pta C Mexico
16 D4 Arenas de S.Pedro Spain
128 D8 Arenas,Pta C Chile
32 F7 Arenberg reg W Germany
27 C13 Arendal Norway
22 J1 Arendonk Belgium
33 O7 Arendsee E Germany
32 L10 Arenshausen E Germany
19 Q12 Arenthon France
28 D2 Arentsminde Denmark
17 J3 Arenys de Mar Spain
46 E8 Areópolis Greece
128 D7 Arequipa Peru
129 H4 Arere Brazil
18 E8 Arés France
16 D3 Arévalo Spain
42 D5 Arezzo Italy
46 E7 Arfará Greece
17 F2 Arga R Spain
140 D5 Argadargada N Terr Aust
16 E5 Argamasilla de Alba Spain
16 E4 Arganda Spain
16 B4 Arganil Portugal
71 F6 Argao Philippines
45 P6 Argatone, M mt Italy
55 D3 Argayash U.S.S.R.
55 D3 Argazi L U.S.S.R.
55 D3 Argazi, Oz U.S.S.R.
18 H10 Argelès sur Mer France
41 L2 Argen R W Germany
20 E3 Argences France
19 Q18 Argens R France
117 P10 Argenta Br Columbia
45 L2 Argenta Italy
101 N4 Argenta Montana
20 E4 Argentan France
42 D6 Argentario,Monte Italy
18 G7 Argentat France
44 B3 Argentera Mt Italy
20 K4 Argenteuil France
123 S6 Argentia Newfoundland
40 E6 Argentières France
44 C4 Argentina R Italy
131 D5 Argentina rep S America
90 E13 Argentine Basin Atlantic Oc
133 C8 Argentino,L Argentina
21 E7 Argenton R France
21 I8 Argenton-sur-Creuse France
122 C3 Argent,R à l' Quebec
20 D5 Argentré France
20 C5 Argentré-du-Plessis France
18 G5 Argent sur Sauldre France
48 J5 Argeş reg Romania
48 J5 Argeşul R Romania
77 J4 Arghandab R Afghanistan
77 K4 Arghastan R Afghanistan
86 H4 Argheile Ethiopia
84 J6 Argo Sudan
46 F7 Argolikós Kólpos B Greece
107 N4 Argonia Kansas
99 S4 Argonne Wisconsin
22 J5 Argonne reg France
70 O9 Argopura G mt Java
101 N5 Argora Idaho
46 F7 Argos Greece
94 A5 Argos Indiana
46 E4 Árgos Orestikón Greece
20 C4 Argouges France
18 D10 Arguedas Spain
20 J2 Argueil France
Argun R China see Ergun He
51 L3 Argun R U.S.S.R.
85 E6 Argungu Nigeria
102 G6 Argus Ra California
98 J2 Argusville N Dakota
112 E6 Argyle Georgia
94 E3 Argyle Michigan
98 K1 Argyle Minnesota
122 G10 Argyle Nova Scotia
99 R7 Argyle Wisconsin
140 A3 Argyle, L W Australia
Argyll co see Strathclyde and Highland regions
6 M6 Argyll oil rig North Sea
Argyrokastron see Gjirokastër
65 E3 Ar Horquin Qi China
28 E4 Århus Denmark
28 D4 Århus co Denmark
145 E3 Aria New Zealand
139 H5 Ariah Pk New S Wales
60 D13 Ariake-kai gulf Japan
87 C11 Ariamsvlei Namibia
43 G7 Ariano Irpino Italy
45 M2 Ariano Nel Polésine Italy
128 D3 Ariari R Colombia
73 L8 Ari Atoll Maldives
85 D6 Aribinda Upper Volta
128 D7 Arica Chile
128 D4 Arica Colombia
45 N6 Ariccia Italy
123 M8 Arichat C Breton I, N Scotia
60 J11 Arida Japan
60 J11 Arida-gawa R Japan
143 E10 Arid, C W Australia
83 J12 Aride I Seychelles
Arid I see Rakitu I
18 G9 Ariège dep France
18 G10 Ariège R France
100 C4 Ariel Washington
48 H4 Arieşul R Romania
80 G8 Ariha Jordan
106 H2 Arikaree R Colorado
60 C13 Arikawa Japan
28 K4 Arild Sweden
48 F7 Arilje Yugoslavia
128 F5 Arima Brazil
60 J11 Arima Japan
127 O2 Arima Trinidad
101 N7 Arimo Idaho
128 G3 Arinda Guyana
129 J7 Arinos Brazil
129 G6 Arinos R Brazil
101 M9 Arinosa Utah
99 L8 Arion Iowa
127 P1 Aripo, Mt Trinidad
128 D2 Ariporo R Colombia
128 F5 Aripuana R Brazil
128 F5 Ariquemes Brazil
130 D5 Ariranha R Brazil
15 C4 Arisaig Scotland
79 D7 'Arîsh, El Egypt
117 J9 Aristazabal I Br Columbia
133 D7 Aristizábal, C Argentina
111 L10 Ariton Alabama
43 C9 Aritzo Sardinia
103 N10 Arivaca Arizona
87 H11 Arivonimamo Madagascar
17 F3 Ariza Spain
18 F9 Arize R France
133 D5 Arizona Argentina
103 M7 Arizona state U.S.A.
124 D2 Arizpe Mexico
27 F12 Årjäng Sweden
26 J5 Arjeplog Sweden
128 D1 Arjona Colombia
16 E7 Arjona Spain
51 O2 Arka U.S.S.R.
53 F8 Arkadak U.S.S.R.
109 O1 Arkadelphia Arkansas
50 F3 Arkalyk U.S.S.R.
110 C6 Arkansas R Arkansas
109 O1 Arkansas state U.S.A.
111 E8 Arkansas City Arkansas
107 O4 Arkansas City Kansas
84 G5 Arkanu Jebel mt Libya
66 D4 Arkatag mts China
117 F5 Arkell,Mt Yukon Terr
27 G15 Arkelstorp Sweden
47 J8 Arkhángelos Rhodes Greece
52 F3 Arkhangel'sk U.S.S.R.
53 F11 Arkhangel'skoye U.S.S.R.
59 K2 Arkhara U.S.S.R.
53 D7 Arkhipovka U.S.S.R.
53 D8 Arkino U.S.S.R.
14 E4 Arklow Irish Rep
47 H7 Árkoi isld Greece
30 H1 Arkona E Germany
120 J9 Arkona Ontario
76 D4 Arkonam India
27 J13 Arkösund Sweden
94 K4 Arkport New York
52 H6 Arkul' U.S.S.R.
95 N4 Arkville New York
27 J12 Ärla Sweden
18 H7 Arlanc France
16 E2 Arlanza R Spain
41 M3 Arlberg pass Austria
101 L2 Arlee Montana
19 N17 Arles Bouches du Rhône France
18 G10 Arles Pyrénées-Orientales France
22 E3 Arleux France
100 J5 Arling Idaho
8 D4 Arlingham England
103 M8 Arlington Arizona
102 G8 Arlington California
106 G3 Arlington Colorado
113 F7 Arlington Florida
112 C6 Arlington Georgia
99 P7 Arlington Iowa
107 M4 Arlington Kansas
110 G5 Arlington Kentucky
99 M5 Arlington Minnesota
98 K8 Arlington Nebraska
94 D6 Arlington Ohio
100 E4 Arlington Oregon
98 J5 Arlington S Dakota
110 G6 Arlington Tennessee
109 N9 Arlington Texas
95 O3 Arlington Vermont
117 M11 Arlington Washington
101 T8 Arlington Wyoming
99 S7 Arlington Heights Illinois
110 E4 Arlington Res Missouri
22 K4 Arlon Belgium
140 C6 Arltunga N Terr Aust
107 Q4 Arma Kansas
118 E8 Armada Alberta
12 E2 Armadale Scotland
143 B9 Armadale W Australia
14 E2 Armagh N Ireland
122 B7 Armagh Quebec
14 E2 Armagh co N Ireland
18 F9 Armagnac reg France
18 H5 Armançon R France
47 H9 Armathia isld Greece
13 F4 Armathwaite England
53 F10 Armavir U.S.S.R.
128 C3 Armenia Colombia
78 K1 Armenia reg U.S.S.R.
48 G5 Armeniş Romania
20 G4 Armentières Eure France
22 D2 Armentières France
101 P2 Armington Montana
101 S6 Arminto Wyoming
119 Q6 Armit Sask
9 E2 Armitage England
55 E3 Armizonskoye U.S.S.R.
119 N5 Armley Sask
98 H6 Armour S Dakota
98 G1 Armourdale N Dakota
120 D3 Arms Ontario
36 E4 Armsheim W Germany
101 N5 Armstead Montana
114 H7 Armstrong Br Columbia
99 T9 Armstrong Illinois
99 M6 Armstrong Iowa
110 D2 Armstrong Missouri
109 K9 Armstrong Texas
140 B3 Armstrong R N Terr Aust
59 L2 Armu R U.S.S.R.
74 H9 Armur India
47 J4 Armutçuk Dağ mt Turkey
47 K4 Armutlu Turkey
53 D10 Armyansk U.S.S.R.
28 B7 Arnå R Denmark
28 M2 Árnafjall mt Faeroes
47 F4 Arnaía Greece
118 D1 Arnaud Manitoba
115 M6 Arnaud,R Quebec
79 C3 Arnauti, C Cyprus
18 J5 Arnay le Duc France
28 B4 Arnborg Denmark
37 P5 Arnbruck W Germany
33 Q7 Arneburg E Germany
18 D10 Arnedo Spain
28 O9 Arnefjord Faeroes
98 C2 Arnegard N Dakota
22 C2 Arneke France
26 M6 Arnemark Sweden
25 A6 Arnemuiden Netherlands
27 E11 Årnes Norway
107 L5 Arnett Oklahoma
94 F9 Arnett W Virginia
25 E5 Arnhem Netherlands
140 D1 Arnhem,C N Terr Aust
140 C2 Arnhem Land reg N Terr Aust
140 C2 Arnhem Land Res N Terr Aust
20 H4 Arnières France
45 H4 Arno R Italy
138 D5 Arno Bay S Australia
102 D3 Arnold California
98 F8 Arnold Nebraska
94 H6 Arnold Pennsylvania
99 L6 Arnolds Park Iowa
38 J8 Arnoldstein Austria
21 J7 Arnon R France
119 V3 Arnot Manitoba
26 L1 Arnöy Norway
16 B2 Arnoya R Spain
12 D1 Arnprior Scotland
32 G10 Arnsberg W Germany
13 F5 Arnside England
37 K2 Arnstadt E Germany
37 L3 Arnstein W Germany
37 O6 Arnstorf W Germany
Arnswalde see Choszczno
121 L4 Arntfield Quebec
28 B6 Arnum Denmark
128 F2 Aro R Venezuela
127 K9 Aroa Venezuela
87 C11 Aroab Namibia
46 E7 Aroánia mt Greece
124 H4 Arocha Mexico
130 C7 Aroeira Brazil
32 K10 Arolsen W Germany
55 E3 Aromashevo U.S.S.R.
20 D5 Aron France
20 D5 Aron R France
42 B3 Arona Italy
122 E7 Aroostook New Brunswick
95 S7 Aroostook R Maine
116 E6 Aropuk L Alaska
137 Q2 Arorae isld Kiribati
71 F4 Aroroy Philippines
28 D6 Arøsund Denmark
127 O2 Arouca Trinidad
145 F3 Arowhana mt New Zealand
106 G3 Aroya Colorado
109 M3 Arp Texas
57 G4 Arpa U.S.S.R.
18 G8 Arpajon France
20 K4 Arpajon France
48 J5 Arpasu de Jos Romania
55 D1 Arpavla U.S.S.R.
120 K4 Arpin Ontario
45 P6 Arpino Italy
45 L1 Arquà Petrarca Italy
45 L1 Arquà Polesine Italy
22 C2 Arques Pas-de-Calais France
20 H2 Arques-la-Bataille France
80 E2 'Arraba Israel
138 F2 Arrabury Queensland
141 F7 Arrabury Queensland
36 B6 Arracourt France
131 D2 Arraga Argentina
16 C4 Arrago R Spain
75 L6 Arrah India
129 J6 Arraias Brazil
16 B6 Arraiolos Portugal
14 C4 Arra Mts Irish Rep
111 M11 Arran Florida
119 Q7 Arran Sask
15 C5 Arran isld Scotland
80 E4 'Arrana Jordan
117 H8 Arrandale Br Col
22 D3 Arras Pas-de-Calais France
18 F9 Arrats R France
28 B5 Arre Denmark
18 F10 Arreau France
128 E3 Arrecifal Colombia
85 B3 Arrecife Canary Is
18 C4 Arrée,Mgnes.d' mts France
28 J5 Arresø L Denmark
106 C9 Arrey New Mexico
45 L4 Arrezzo reg Italy
38 J8 Arriach Austria
125 N9 Arriaga Mexico
106 G2 Arriba Colorado
141 G6 Arrilalah Queensland
28 B6 Arrild Denmark
9 F3 Arrington England
143 B8 Arrino W Australia
12 D1 Arrochar Scotland
133 G4 Arroio Grande Brazil
20 D3 Arromanches France
16 C5 Arronches Portugal
44 M6 Arrone R Italy
18 F9 Arros R France
20 H5 Arrou France
18 H6 Arroux R France
101 Q2 Arrow Cr Montana
117 P10 Arrowhead Br Col
14 C2 Arrow,L Irish Rep
119 O2 Arrow L Ontario
117 O10 Arrow Park Br Col
110 D2 Arrow Rock Missouri
100 K6 Arrowrock Res Idaho
138 F4 Arrowsmith Mt New S Wales
144 C5 Arrowsmith, Mt New Zealand
140 D2 Arrowsmith Pt N Terr Aust
144 B6 Arrowtown New Zealand
118 D8 Arrow Wood Alberta
16 C5 Arroyo de la Luz Spain
108 F6 Arroyo de la Zorra R Mexico
102 D6 Arroyo Grande California
131 F6 Arroyo Grande R Argentina
106 E5 Arroyo Hondo New Mexico
131 F4 Arroyo Negro R Uruguay
103 J8 Arroyo Seco R California
128 F6 Arroyos,L de Los Bolivia
130 B9 Arroyos-y-Esteros Paraguay
130 C4 Arruda Brazil
28 D3 Års Denmark
77 C5 Arsenajan Iran
118 J3 Arsenault L Sask
117 Q3 Arseno L N W Terr
59 K3 Arsen'yev U.S.S.R.
55 C3 Arshinskoye U.S.S.R.
41 O6 Arsiero Italy
76 C4 Arsikere India
52 G6 Arsk U.S.S.R.
26 J9 Årskogen Sweden
45 O5 Arsoli Italy
19 K3 Ars-sur-Moselle France
27 J11 Årsunda Sweden
22 D5 Arsy France
46 D5 Árta Greece
17 K5 Artá Majorca
80 D7 Artas Jordan
98 G4 Artas S Dakota
17 K5 Artá,Sierra de,Mt Majorca
124 H8 Arteaga Mexico
59 K3 Artem U.S.S.R.
126 C3 Artemisa Cuba
51 J3 Artemovak U.S.S.R.
54 G7 Artemovka U.S.S.R.
56 D4 Artemovsk U.S.S.R.
53 F9 Artemovskiy U.S.S.R.
45 N6 Artena Italy
20 J5 Artenay France
33 O10 Artern E Germany
17 H3 Artesa de Segre Spain
Artesia see Mosomane
111 H8 Artesia Mississippi
98 J5 Artesian S Dakota
109 H7 Artesia Wells Texas
26 G6 Artfjallet mt Sweden
121 T6 Arthabaska Quebec
18 E9 Arthez France
110 H2 Arthur Illinois
98 J2 Arthur N Dakota
98 E8 Arthur Nebraska
139 H8 Arthur R Tasmania
109 M2 Arthur City Texas
138 E4 Arthur,L S Australia
139 H8 Arthur,L Tasmania
145 D4 Arthur, Mt New Zealand
142 E4 Arthur, Mt W Australia
141 K5 Arthur Pt Queensland
143 B6 Arthur, R W Australia
144 C5 Arthur's Pass New Zealand
126 G2 Arthur's Town Cat I Bahamas
55 C3 Arti U.S.S.R.
133 F4 Artigas Uruguay
114 J5 Artillery L N W Terr
29 M11 Artjärvi Finland
118 H6 Artland Sask
33 M6 Artlenburg W Germany
102 B2 Artois California
22 C3 Artois prov France
22 D3 Artois Collines d' France
46 E6 Artotína Greece
78 F1 Artova Turkey
Artsakan Nor see Qagan Nur
48 M5 Artsyz U.S.S.R.
87 C8 Artur de Paiva Angola
66 B4 Artux China
71 B1 Aru Halmahera Indonesia
86 F5 Aru Zaïre
129 H6 Aruanã Brazil
126 A2 Aruba isld W Indies
18 E9 Arudy France
80 E8 Arugot R Jordan
136 G3 Aru,Kep islds Moluccas Indonesia
25 D2 Arum Netherlands
128 F4 Arumá Brazil
61 Q12 Arume B Okinawa
75 Q4 Arunachal Pradesh prov India
9 F6 Arundel England
144 C5 Arundel New Zealand
9 F5 Arun,R England
28 E6 Årup Denmark
76 D6 Aruppukkottai India
80 D5 'Arūra Jordan
88 F3 Arusha Tanzania
86 G4 Arusi prov Ethiopia
70 G4 Arus,Tg C Sulawesi Indonesia
70 B5 Arut R Kalimantan
70 E6 Aru,Tg C Kalimantan
83 K9 Aruvi Aru R Sri Lanka
86 D5 Aruwimi R Zaïre
106 E2 Arvada Colorado
101 T5 Arvada Wyoming
26 K7 Arvån Sweden
58 D2 Arvayheer Mongolia
40 D5 Arve R France
26 K5 Arvestuottar mt Sweden
74 H8 Arvi India
115 M8 Arvida Quebec
26 K6 Arvidsjaur Sweden
27 F12 Arvika Sweden
102 F6 Arvin California
94 J9 Arvonia Virginia
65 E1 Arxan China
147 Q9 Ary U.S.S.R.
55 C3 Aryazh U.S.S.R.
47 G9 Aryiroúpolis Crete Greece
55 E4 Aryk-Balyk U.S.S.R.
57 E4 Arys' U.S.S.R.
57 E4 Arys' R U.S.S.R.
57 D2 Arys,Ozero L U.S.S.R.
18 D5 Arz R France
52 F6 Arzamas U.S.S.R.
37 N3 Arzberg W Germany
37 L5 Arzberg mt W Germany
32 K8 Ärzen W Germany
85 D1 Arzew Algeria
36 B3 Arzfeld W Germany
53 F10 Arzgir U.S.S.R.
41 O6 Arzignano Italy
41 N3 Arzl Austria
16 B2 Arzúa Spain
22 K1 As Belgium
37 N3 Aš Czechoslovakia
26 E8 Ås Norway
28 E2 Aså Denmark
27 F14 Åsa Sweden
87 C11 Asab Namibia
74 D1 Asadabad Afghanistan
69 D11 Asahan R Sumatra
61 O10 Asahi Chiba Japan
60 G10 Asahi R Japan
60 Q2 Asahi-dake mt Japan
61 N7 Asahi-dake mt Japan
60 Q2 Asahikawa Japan
61 M9 Asama yama vol Japan
65 G6 Asan Man B S Korea
75 M7 Asansol India
26 G9 Åsarna Sweden
84 F5 Asawanwah Libya
36 C2 Asbach W Germany
71 C3 Asbakin W Irian
55 D3 Asbest U.S.S.R.
121 T7 Asbestos Quebec
89 C7 Asbestos Mts S Africa
107 Q4 Asbury Kansas
110 B4 Asbury Missouri
128 F7 Ascensión Bolivia
124 E2 Ascensión Chihuahua Mexico
126 A1 Ascension Curaçao W I
90 B12 Ascension isld Atlantic Oc
37 O6 Ascha W Germany
38 L5 Aschbach Austria
32 G9 Ascheberg Nordrhein-Westfalen W Germany
33 M4 Ascheberg W Germany
32 F6 Aschendorf W Germany
20 J5 Aschères-le Marche France
33 O9 Aschersleben E Germany
17 H3 Asco Spain
12 C2 Ascog Scotland
42 F6 Ascoli Piceno Italy
9 F5 Ascot England
141 K1 Ascot dist Brisbane, Qnsld
133 D2 Ascotán Chile
27 H14 Åseda Sweden
85 E4 Asedjrad hills Algeria
53 H7 Asekeyevo U.S.S.R.
26 J7 Åsele Sweden
86 G4 Aselle Ethiopia
26 E8 Åsen Norway
27 G10 Åsen Sweden
32 K7 Asendorf W Germany
47 G3 Asenovgrad Bulgaria
27 B13 Åseral Norway
22 G5 Asfeld-la-ville France
27 D12 Asgårdstr Norway
55 C3 Asha U.S.S.R.
52 J5 Ashan U.S.S.R.
80 C8 Ashan R Israel
55 C3 Ashap U.S.S.R.
77 A4 Ashar Iran
9 E1 Ashbourne England
112 D6 Ashburn Georgia
8 C6 Ashburton England
144 C5 Ashburton New Zealand
142 B6 Ashburton R W Australia
143 C6 Ashburton, R W Australia
140 C4 Ashburton Ra N Terr Aust
9 E4 Ashbury England
95 N6 Ashbury Park New Jersey
99 L3 Ashby Minnesota
9 E2 Ashby de la Zouch England
57 D2 Ashchikol', Ozero L U.S.S.R.
57 C1 Ashchitastysor, Ozero L U.S.S.R.
114 G7 Ashcroft Br Columbia
80 B6 Ashdod Israel
109 N2 Ash Down Arkansas
9 G5 Ashdown Forest England
112 H2 Asheboro N Carolina
107 O7 Asher Oklahoma
119 T7 Ashern Manitoba
108 H7 Asherton Texas
112 E2 Asheville N Carolina
110 E5 Ash Flat Arkansas
113 D11 Ashford Alabama
9 G5 Ashford Kent England
100 C3 Ashford Washington
9 E5 Ashford Hill England
103 M6 Ashfork Arizona
107 M2 Ash Grove Kansas
110 C4 Ash Grove Missouri
141 K1 Ashgrove dist Brisbane, Qnsld
145 E4 Ashhurst New Zealand
60 Q2 Ashibetsu Japan
61 N9 Ashikaga Japan
9 F6 Ashington W Sussex England
61 N9 Ashio Japan
52 G6 Ashit R U.S.S.R.
60 J11 Ashiya Japan
60 G13 Ashizuri-misaki C Japan
77 D4 Ashkazar Iran
77 F1 Ashkhabad Iran
50 E5 Ashkhabad U.S.S.R.
13 F3 Ashkirk Scotland
99 T9 Ashkum Illinois
111 L8 Ashland Alabama
110 F2 Ashland Illinois
107 L4 Ashland Kansas
94 E8 Ashland Kentucky
95 S7 Ashland Maine
101 T4 Ashland Montana
98 K8 Ashland Nebraska
95 Q3 Ashland New Hampshire
94 E6 Ashland Ohio
100 C7 Ashland Oregon
95 L6 Ashland Pennsylvania
94 K9 Ashland Virginia
99 Q3 Ashland Wisconsin
110 J5 Ashland City Tennessee
110 G3 Ashley Illinois
94 C3 Ashley Michigan
98 G3 Ashley N Dakota
144 D5 Ashley New Zealand
120 K4 Ashley Mine Ontario
55 E3 Ashlyk R U.S.S.R.
118 F4 Ashmont Alberta
108 E3 Ashmore Texas
142 E1 Ashmore Reef Timor Sea
79 A8 Ashmûn Egypt
80 F1 Ashmura Syria
95 N5 Ashokan Res New York
60 R2 Ashorobuto Japan
80 B7 Ashqelon Israel
78 J4 Ash Sharqat Iraq
94 G5 Ashtabula Ohio
98 J2 Ashtabula,L N Dakota
74 F9 Ashti India
77 A2 Ashtiān Iran
101 O5 Ashton Idaho
99 R8 Ashton Illinois
94 B3 Ashton Michigan
121 O7 Ashton Ontario
98 H5 Ashton S Dakota
142 F3 Ashton Ra W Australia
13 F6 Ashton-under-Lyne England
115 N7 Ashuanipi,L Labrador
121 R3 Ashuapmuchuan R Quebec
78 J4 Ashur Iraq
78 J6 Ashuriyah, Al Iraq
111 K8 Ashville Alabama
79 G3 'Āsi R Syria/Lebanon
42 D3 Asiago Italy
71 C2 Asia Pulau Pulau islds Indonesia
71 F4 Asid Gulf Philippines
124 H6 Asientos Mexico
45 K1 Asigliano Ven Italy
85 C1 Asilah Morocco
71 A1 Asimiro Halmahera Indonesia
43 B7 Asinara isld Sardinia
43 B7 Asinara, Golfo dell' Sardinia
56 C3 Asino U.S.S.R.
75 L9 Aska India
53 D10 Askaniya Nova U.S.S.R.
55 C4 Askarovo U.S.S.R.
14 C4 Askeaton Adare Irish Rep
27 D12 Asker Norway
13 G6 Askern England
27 G13 Askersund Sweden
83 H1 Askhabad Iran
26 J7 Åskilje Sweden
27 E12 Askim Norway
112 K2 Askin N Carolina
55 C3 Askino U.S.S.R.
28 G7 Askø Denmark
29 M11 Askola Finland
65 J3 Askol'd, O isld U.S.S.R.
28 C6 Askov Denmark
99 O3 Askov Minnesota
13 F5 Askrigg England
27 A10 Askvoll Norway
79 C9 Asl Egypt
47 K5 Aslanapa Turkey
74 D1 Asmar Afghanistan
86 G2 Asmara Ethiopia
28 K5 Asminderød Denmark
28 G5 Asnæs Denmark
28 F5 Asnæs pen Denmark
85 E1 Asnam, El Algeria
20 D3 Asnelles France
27 G15 Åsnen Sweden
27 E11 Åsnes Norway
129 G3 Asoenangka Brazil
45 J1 Asola Italy
60 E13 Aso Nat. Park Japan
86 F3 Asosa Ethiopia
86 G1 Asoteriba, Jebel mt Sudan
100 H3 Asotin Washington
85 E3 Asouf watercourse Algeria
60 C11 Asō-wan B Japan
60 E13 Aso zan vol Japan
36 G6 Aspach W Germany
48 C3 Aspang Austria
26 G8 Aspås Sweden
13 E4 Aspatria England
17 G6 Aspe Spain
26 J8 Aspeå Sweden
106 D2 Aspen Colorado
101 P8 Aspen Wyoming
118 D6 Aspen Beach Prov. Park Alberta
36 G6 Asperg W Germany
28 D6 Asperup Denmark
144 B6 Aspiring, Mt New Zealand
19 P16 Aspremont France
46 D5 Asprókavos, Akr C Greece
43 G10 Aspromonte mts Italy
123 M7 Aspy B C Breton I, N Scotia
118 K6 Asquith Sask
86 H3 Assab Ethiopia
74 D1 Assad-Abad Afghanistan
86 H3 Assale, L Ethiopia
75 O5 Assam prov India
95 M8 Assateague I Maryland
22 G2 Asse Belgium
19 Q17 Asse R France
119 V2 Assean L Manitoba
89 G6 Assegai R Swaziland
85 F3 Assekaifaf Algeria
85 F4 Assekreme mt Algeria
32 K5 Assel W Germany
20 E5 Asse-la-Boisne France
22 K3 Asselborn Luxembourg
25 G3 Assen Netherlands
36 F3 Assenheim W Germany
28 E3 Assens Århus Denmark
28 D6 Assens Fyn Denmark
22 J3 Assesse Belgium
122 G2 Assigny,L Quebec
118 L9 Assinboia Sask
28 B4 Assing Denmark
114 J8 Assiniboia Sask
114 H7 Assiniboine,Mt Br Col/Alberta
119 Q8 Assiniboine R Manitoba/Sask
46 F4 Ássiros Greece
129 H8 Assis Brazil
42 E5 Assisi Italy
36 D3 Assmannshausen W Germany
41 K6 Asso Italy
110 G2 Assumption Illinois
87 H9 Assumption isld Seychelles
78 K5 As Suwayrah Iraq
36 C5 Assweiler W Germany
37 N7 Ast W Germany
27 E10 Asta R Norway
18 F8 Astaffort France
47 H9 Astakidha isld Greece
46 E6 Astakós Greece
77 A1 Astaneh Iran
28 E2 Åsted Nordjylland Denmark
28 B3 Åsted Viborg Denmark
25 E6 Asten Netherlands
77 C1 Asterabad Iran
44 D2 Asti Italy
16 E1 Astillero Spain
Astin Tagh mt ra see Altun Shan
47 H8 Astipálaia isld Greece
9 E1 Aston England
8 D3 Aston Cross England
74 F1 Astor Kashmir
16 C2 Astorga Spain
99 Q9 Astoria Illinois
114 G8 Astoria Oregon
98 K5 Astoria S Dakota
27 F15 Åstorp Sweden
121 L6 Astorville Ontario
87 H10 Astove isld Br Indian Oc Terr
53 G10 Astrakhan' U.S.S.R.
55 E5 Astrakhanka U.S.S.R.
26 L7 Åsträsk Sweden
46 F7 Astros Greece
28 E6 Astrup Fyn Denmark
28 B5 Åstrup Ribe Denmark
28 D6 Åstrup Sønderjylland Denmark
28 D5 Åstrup Vejle Denmark
28 J7 Åstrup isld Storstrøm Denmark
16 E2 Astudillo Spain
45 N7 Astura R Italy
16 C1 Asturias reg Spain
9 F3 Astwood England
28 E6 Åsum Denmark
133 F3 Asunción Paraguay
27 H14 Asunden L Sweden
28 E5 As Vig B Denmark
84 J5 Aswân Egypt
84 J5 Aswan High Dam Egypt
84 J4 Asyût Egypt
48 E3 Aszód Hungary
137 R6 Ata isld Pacific Oc

Atabay — Bagnolo San Vito 7

57 E3 **Atabay** U.S.S.R.
47 L7 **Atabey** Turkey
133 C3 **Atacama** *reg* Chile
128 E8 **Atacama, Des de** Chile
133 D3 **Atacama, Puna de** *plat* Argentina
48 L2 **Ataki** U.S.S.R.
85 E7 **Atakpamé** Togo
130 J10 **Atalaia** Brazil
46 F6 **Atalándi** Greece
128 D6 **Atalaya** Peru
86 J5 **Ataleh** Somalia
130 H6 **Ataléia** Brazil
71 M9 **Atambua** Timor Indonesia
61 N10 **Atami** Japan
115 O5 **Atangmik** Greenland
55 F4 **Atansor, Oz** *L* U.S.S.R.
71 M9 **Atapupo** Timor Indonesia
79 C9 **'Ataqa, G** *mt* Egypt
85 B4 **Atar** Mauritania
80 D5 **'Atara** Jordan
80 F7 **Ataroth** Jordan
106 B7 **Atarque** New Mexico
80 F7 **Ataruz** Jordan
Atas *isld see* **South I**
102 D6 **Atascadero** California
109 J6 **Atascosa** *R* Texas
57 F1 **Atasu** U.S.S.R.
68 C4 **Atatano** *R* Burma
17 F2 **Atauri** Spain
71 M9 **Atauro** *isld* Indonesia
86 F2 **Atbara** Sudan
86 G2 **Atbara** *R* Sudan
50 F3 **Atbasar** Kazakhstan U.S.S.R.
57 H4 **At-Bash** U.S.S.R.
111 E12 **Atchafalaya Bay** Louisiana
107 P2 **Atchison** Kansas
116 G5 **Atchueelinguk** *R* Alaska
112 C3 **Atco** Georgia
95 N7 **Atco** New Jersey
17 F3 **Ateca** Spain
79 G5 **Ateibe, Bahret el** *L* Syria
58 E4 **A-t'eng-hsi-lien** China
124 G7 **Atenguillo** Mexico
61 O7 **Aterazawa** Japan
42 F6 **Aterno** *R* Italy
42 D2 **Atesine,Alpi** Italy
42 F6 **Atessa** Italy
22 F2 **Ath** Belgium
114 H7 **Athabasca** Alberta
114 J6 **Athabasca, L** Alberta/Sask
119 Q4 **Athapap** Manitoba
119 Q4 **Athapapuskow L** Manitoba
28 C4 **Atheden** *reg* Denmark
110 B1 **Athelstan** Iowa
100 G4 **Athena** Oregon
14 C3 **Athenry** Irish Rep
112 D4 **Athens** Georgia
Athens Greece *see* **Athínai**
99 R10 **Athens** Illinois
109 O3 **Athens** Louisiana
95 S2 **Athens** Maine
94 B4 **Athens** Michigan
94 E7 **Athens** Ohio
121 P8 **Athens** Ontario
95 L5 **Athens** Pennsylvania
112 C2 **Athens** Tennessee
109 M3 **Athens** Texas
99 Q4 **Athens** Wisconsin
121 L8 **Atherley** Ontario
9 E2 **Atherstone** England
13 F6 **Atherton** England
141 H3 **Atherton** Queensland
141 H3 **Atherton Plateau** Queensland
85 E7 **Athiémé** Benin
22 F4 **Athies** Aisne France
22 D4 **Athies** Somme France
47 F7 **Athínai** Greece
20 K4 **Athis** Essonne France
20 E4 **Athis** Orne France
14 C3 **Athleague** Irish Rep
14 D3 **Athlone** Irish Rep
79 D3 **Athna** Cyprus
76 B2 **Athni** India
100 J2 **Athol** Idaho
95 P4 **Athol** Massachusetts
144 B6 **Athol** New Zealand
113 L9 **Athol I** New Providence I Bahamas
122 F6 **Atholville** New Brunswick
47 G4 **Áthos** *mt* Greece
Athos, Mt *see* **Áyion Óros**
78 G4 **Ath-Thawra** Syria
22 K4 **Athus** Belgium
14 E4 **Athy** Irish Rep
86 C3 **Ati** Chad
145 F3 **Atiamuri** New Zealand
130 F8 **Atibaia** Brazil
128 D7 **Atico** Peru
123 N2 **Aticonipi L** Quebec
17 F3 **Atienza** Spain
119 Q4 **Atik** Manitoba
117 Q8 **Atikameg** Alberta
119 R4 **Atikameg Lake** Manitoba
115 K8 **Atikokan** Ontario
115 N7 **Atikonak, L** Labrador
122 H1 **Atikonal L** Labrador
118 J1 **Atikwa L** Ontario
71 E3 **Atimonan** Philippines
45 P6 **Atina** Italy
76 D5 **Atirampattinam** India
116 P9 **Atka** Aleutian Is
51 P2 **Atka** U.S.S.R.
53 F8 **Atkarsk** U.S.S.R.
116 J1 **Atkasuk** Alaska
71 B3 **Atkerio** W Irian
110 D6 **Atkins** Arkansas
99 Q8 **Atkinson** Illinois
112 J3 **Atkinson** N Carolina
98 G7 **Atkinson** Nebraska
111 M8 **Atlanta** Georgia
101 K6 **Atlanta** Idaho
110 G1 **Atlanta** Illinois
94 A6 **Atlanta** Indiana
107 O4 **Atlanta** Kansas
110 D2 **Atlanta** Missouri
95 K4 **Atlanta** New York
109 N2 **Atlanta** Texas
105 **Atlanta** *conurbation* Georgia
99 L8 **Atlantic** Iowa
112 L3 **Atlantic** N Carolina
95 N7 **Atlantic City** New Jersey
101 R7 **Atlantic City** Wyoming
95 N6 **Atlantic Highlands** New Jersey
90 J15 **Atlantic-Indian Basin** Southern Oc
90 J14 **Atlantic-Indian Ridge** S Atlantic Oc
128 D1 **Atlántico** *div* Colombia
90 **Atlantic Oc**
90 E5 **Atlantis Fracture** Atlantic Oc
94 D4 **Atlas** Michigan
85 C2 **Atlas, Haut** *mts* Morocco
85 C2 **Atlas, Moyen** *mts* Morocco
85 E2 **Atlas Saharien** *mts* Algeria
118 G8 **Atlee** Alberta
114 F6 **Atlin** Br Columbia
80 C3 **'Atlit** Israel
125 K8 **Atlixco** Mexico
26 A10 **Atlöy** *isld* Norway
76 D3 **Atmakur** India
113 B11 **Atmore** Alabama
138 D2 **Atna Hill** S Australia
117 L9 **Atnarko** Br Columbia
26 D10 **Atnasjö** *L* Norway
55 E2 **Atnis** U.S.S.R.
87 H12 **Atofinandrahana** Madagascar
107 O7 **Atoka** Oklahoma
102 G6 **Atolia** California
101 N6 **Atomic City** Idaho
124 H7 **Atotonilco el Alto** Mexico
77 E1 **Atrak** *R* Iran
27 F14 **Atran** Sweden
26 L7 **Åträsk** Sweden
128 C2 **Atrato** *R* Colombia
42 F6 **Atri** Italy
45 R8 **Atripaida** Italy
61 N10 **Atsugi** Japan
61 N7 **Atsumi** Japan
61 L11 **Atsumi-hantō** *pen* Japan
61 L11 **Atsumi wan** *B* Japan
140 C4 **Attack Cr** N Terr Aust
111 K7 **Attalla** Alabama
47 J8 **Attaviros** *mt* Rhodes Greece
115 L7 **Attawapiskat** Ontario
36 D1 **Attendorn** W Germany
38 J6 **Attersee** Austria
110 J1 **Attica** Indiana
107 M4 **Attica** Kansas
94 D3 **Attica** Michigan
94 J4 **Attica** New York
94 E5 **Attica** Ohio
22 E5 **Attichy** France
40 B5 **Attignat** France
22 H5 **Attigny** France
95 Q5 **Attleboro** Massachusetts
9 H2 **Attleborough** England
9 H2 **Attlebridge** England
26 J9 **Attmar** Sweden
68 H5 **Attopeu** Laos
109 N4 **Attoyac Bayou** *R* Texas
116 J9 **Attu** Aleutian Is
76 D5 **Attur** India
133 D5 **Atuel** *R* Argentina
131 C6 **Atuel, Banados del** *swamps* Argentina
27 H13 **Åtvid** Sweden
27 H13 **Åtvidaberg** Sweden
102 D4 **Atwater** California
99 M4 **Atwater** Minnesota
119 P8 **Atwater** Sask
13 H6 **Atwick** England
106 G1 **Atwood** Colorado
110 H2 **Atwood** Illinois
107 J2 **Atwood** Kansas
94 F6 **Atwood Res** Ohio
53 G7 **Atyashevo** U.S.S.R.
38 N5 **Atzenbrugg** Austria
33 P9 **Atzendorf** E Germany
36 D2 **Au** Rheinland-Pfalz W Germany
128 E4 **Auati-Paraná** *R* Brazil
135 S3 **Auau Chan** Hawaiian Is
37 J4 **Aub** W Germany
19 P18 **Aubagne** France
22 K4 **Aubange** Belgium
71 F2 **Aubarede Pt** Luzon Philippines
18 H4 **Aube** *dep* France
18 H4 **Aube** *R* France
22 K2 **Aubel** Belgium
22 E3 **Aubencheul-Au-Bac** France
22 G4 **Aubenton** France
83 L13 **Aubert,C** Kerguelen Indian Ocean
20 G4 **Aube-sur-Risle** France
18 F7 **Aubeterre** France
21 E9 **Aubigné** Deux-Sèvres France
21 F6 **Aubigné** Sarthe France
21 C8 **Aubigny** France
22 D3 **Aubigny** Pas-de-Calais France
18 G5 **Aubigny sur Nère** France
18 G8 **Aubin** France
18 H8 **Aubrac, Mts d'** France
103 M6 **Aubrey Cliffs** Arizona
143 B7 **Aubrey, Mt** W Australia
114 G4 **Aubry L** N W Terr
111 L9 **Auburn** Alabama
102 C3 **Auburn** California
110 G2 **Auburn** Illinois
94 B5 **Auburn** Indiana
107 P3 **Auburn** Kansas
110 K5 **Auburn** Kentucky
95 R2 **Auburn** Maine
94 C3 **Auburn** Michigan
99 L9 **Auburn** Nebraska
95 L4 **Auburn** New York
138 E5 **Auburn** S Australia
117 M12 **Auburn** Washington
141 K7 **Auburn** *R* Queensland
113 F9 **Auburndale** Florida
99 R5 **Auburndale** Wisconsin
141 K7 **Auburn Ra** Queensland
18 G7 **Aubusson** France
133 D5 **Auca Mahuida,Sa** *mt* Argentina
52 B6 **Auce** U.S.S.R.
18 F9 **Auch** France
22 C3 **Auchel** France
12 E4 **Auchencairn** Scotland
12 D4 **Auchenmalg** Scotland
85 F7 **Auchi** Nigeria
12 D3 **Auchinleck** Scotland
12 E1 **Auchterarder** Scotland
13 E1 **Auchterderran** Scotland
13 E1 **Auchtermuchty** Scotland
22 C2 **Auchy-au-Bois** France
113 D7 **Aucilla** *R* Florida
145 F1 **Auckland** New Zealand
68 D6 **Auckland B** Burma
18 G9 **Aude** *dep* France
18 G9 **Aude** *R* France
18 G10 **Aude** *R* France
86 H5 **Audeghle** Somalia
115 L7 **Auden** Ontario
Audenarde *see* **Oudenaarde**
18 E8 **Audenge** France
20 B2 **Auderville** France
18 B4 **Audierne** France
83 L14 **Audierne,B** Kerguelen Indian Ocean
40 E3 **Audincourt** France
22 B2 **Audinghen** France
45 N4 **Auditore** Italy
8 D2 **Audlem** England
22 B2 **Audresselles** France
22 C2 **Audruicq** France
99 M8 **Audubon** Iowa
19 J3 **Audun le Roman** France
37 O2 **Aue** E Germany
32 G6 **Aue** *R* W Germany
84 E4 **Auenat Uennin** Libya
36 G5 **Auenstein** W Germany
37 N2 **Auerbach** E Germany
36 F4 **Auerbach** Hessen W Germany
41 N2 **Auer Berg** *mt* W Germany
37 O2 **Auerswalde** E Germany
111 E12 **Au Far, Point** Louisiana
20 H2 **Auffay** France
141 H7 **Augathella** Queensland
14 E2 **Aughnacloy** N Ireland
87 D11 **Aughrabies Falls** S Africa
14 E4 **Aughrim** Irish Rep
115 O3 **Augpilagtoq** Greenland
94 D2 **Au Gres** Michigan
37 K7 **Augsburg** W Germany
110 E6 **Augusta** Arkansas
112 E4 **Augusta** Georgia
110 F1 **Augusta** Illinois
107 O4 **Augusta** Kansas
94 C8 **Augusta** Kentucky
95 S2 **Augusta** Maine
94 B4 **Augusta** Michigan
101 N2 **Augusta** Montana
43 G11 **Augusta** Sicily
143 B10 **Augusta** W Australia
99 P5 **Augusta** Wisconsin
143 E7 **Augusta, L** W Australia
116 R6 **Augusta,Mt** Yukon Terr
94 H8 **Augusta Springs** Virginia
116 L7 **Augustine I** Alaska
130 G6 **Augusto de Lima** Brazil
130 H8 **Augusto Severo** Brazil
31 O2 **Augustów** Poland
140 E4 **Augustus Downs** Queensland
142 E3 **Augustus Island** W Australia
143 B6 **Augustus, Mt** W Australia
37 M6 **Au in der Hallertau** W Germany
40 B2 **Aujon** *R* France
32 L4 **Aukrug** W Germany
26 K6 **Auktsjaur** Sweden
112 K1 **Aulander** N Carolina
142 E5 **Auld, L** W Australia
21 E9 **Aulnay** France
18 E6 **Aulnay de Saintonge** France
20 K5 **Aulnay-la-Rivière** France
18 C4 **Aulne** *R* France
118 H1 **Aulneau Pen** Ontario
22 F3 **Aulnoye** France
106 F1 **Ault** Colorado
20 H1 **Ault** France
15 C3 **Aultbea** Scotland
54 F8 **Auly** U.S.S.R.
37 M2 **Auma** E Germany
37 M2 **Auma** *R* E Germany
20 J2 **Aumale** France
18 G6 **Aumance** *R* France
22 K5 **Aumetz** France
57 C4 **Auminzatau,Gory** *mt* U.S.S.R.
40 C4 **Aumont** France
18 H8 **Aumont** Lozère France
33 M5 **Aumühle** W Germany
20 D3 **Aunay-sur-Odon** France
74 F10 **Aundh** India
21 F6 **Aune** *R* France
20 J5 **Auneau** France
20 K3 **Auneuil** France
28 E4 **Aüning** Denmark
18 E6 **Aunis** *prov* France
21 C10 **Aunis** *reg* France
87 C11 **Auob** *R* Namibia
71 J5 **Auponhia** Moluccas Indonesia
19 Q17 **Aups** France
69 G11 **Aur** *isld* Malaysia
29 K11 **Aura** Finland
26 C9 **Aura** *R* Norway
37 K4 **Aurach** *R* W Germany
74 H5 **Auraiya** India
29 K11 **Aurajoki** *R* Finland
74 F9 **Aurangabad** India
18 C5 **Auray** France
26 C8 **Aure** Norway
20 D3 **Aure** *R* France
19 O16 **Aurel** France
99 L7 **Aurelia** Iowa
85 F1 **Aurès** *mts* Algeria
32 F6 **Aurich** W Germany
130 E5 **Aurilândia** Brazil
18 G8 **Aurillac** France
19 P18 **Auriol** France
27 B11 **Aurland** Norway
130 H9 **Aurora** Brazil
106 F2 **Aurora** Colorado
99 S8 **Aurora** Illinois
94 C7 **Aurora** Indiana
107 N2 **Aurora** Kansas
110 C5 **Aurora** Missouri
112 L2 **Aurora** N Carolina
98 H9 **Aurora** Nebraska
121 L9 **Aurora** Ontario
103 N3 **Aurora** Utah
19 P15 **Aurouze, Mt d'** France
26 C9 **Aursjöen** *L* Norway
27 E12 **Aurskog** Norway
26 E9 **Aursunden** *L* Norway
141 F2 **Aurukun** Queensland
45 P7 **Aurunci Monti** Italy
87 C11 **Aus** Namibia
94 C2 **Au Sable** *R* Michigan
95 O2 **Ausable Forks** New York
94 D2 **Au Sable Pt** Michigan
128 D6 **Ausangate** *mt* Peru
80 F4 **Ausara** Jordan
85 B4 **Auserd** Mauritania
88 B7 **Aushi** Zambia
15 F1 **Auskerry** Scotland
45 O7 **Ausoni, Monti** *mt* Italy
41 K3 **Ausser-Rhoden** *dist* Switzerland
8 D4 **Aust** England
27 C13 **Austad** Norway
27 C13 **Aust Agder Fylker** Norway
112 C4 **Austell** Georgia
Austerlitz *see* **Slavkov**
119 T9 **Austin** Manitoba
99 O6 **Austin** Minnesota
101 N3 **Austin** Montana
100 G5 **Austin** Oregon
94 J5 **Austin** Pennsylvania
109 K5 **Austin** Texas
143 C8 **Austin** W Australia
143 C8 **Austin, L** W Australia
109 M4 **Austonio** Texas
140 E5 **Austral Downs** N Terr Aust
136 **Australia**
139 J6 **Australian Alps** New S Wales/Victoria
146 C6 **Australian Antarctic Territory** Antarctica
135 M11 **Austral Ridge** Pacific Oc
26 D8 **Austråt** Norway
27 A11 **Austrheim** Norway
38 E7 **Austria** *rep*
26 G3 **Austvågöy** *isld* Norway
109 L7 **Austwell** Texas
21 H6 **Autainville** France
128 G4 **Autazes** Brazil
22 K4 **Autelbas** Belgium
18 G9 **Auterive** France
123 L3 **Auteuil, L. d'** Quebec
22 C3 **Authie** *R* France
121 M4 **Authier** Quebec
21 E7 **Authion** *R* France
21 G6 **Authon** France
20 G5 **Authon-du-Perche** France
20 J5 **Authon-la-Plaine** France
124 G8 **Autlán de Navarro** Mexico
45 O6 **Autore, M** *mt* Italy
99 U3 **Au Train** Michigan
19 P14 **Autrans** France
20 K5 **Autruy-sur-Juine** France
22 H5 **Autry** France
18 H6 **Autun** France
140 B3 **Auvergne** N Terr Aust
18 H7 **Auvergne** *prov* France
21 E6 **Auvers-le-Hamon** France
20 K3 **Auvers-sur-Oise** France
18 F7 **Auvezère** *R* France
22 G4 **Auvillers-les-Forges** France
94 E2 **Aux Barques, Pt** Michigan
18 H5 **Auxerre** France
20 K1 **Auxi-le-Château** France
40 B3 **Auxonne** France
110 E2 **Auxvasse** Missouri
128 F2 **Auyán Tepui** *mt* Venezuela
18 G6 **Auzances** France
68 B2 **Ava** Burma
110 G4 **Ava** Illinois
110 D5 **Ava** Missouri
26 M5 **Avafors** Sweden
18 F6 **Availles-Limouzine** France
116 H1 **Avalik** *R* Alaska
18 H5 **Avallon** France
102 F8 **Avalon** California
111 F8 **Avalon** Mississippi
95 N7 **Avalon** New Jersey
108 C3 **Avalon, L** New Mexico
115 O8 **Avalon Pen** Nfld
124 J5 **Avalos** Mexico
131 F2 **Avalos** *R* Argentina
57 B2 **Avan** U.S.S.R.
19 Q15 **Avançon** France
53 G12 **Avar** *R* U.S.S.R.
107 M5 **Avard** Oklahoma
129 J8 **Avaré** Brazil
47 H4 **Ávas** Greece
116 E9 **Avatanak I** Aleutian Is
26 H7 **Avaträsk** Sweden
26 L5 **Avaudden** Sweden
26 K6 **Avaviken** Sweden
102 H6 **Avawatz Mts** California
54 J8 **Avdeyevka** U.S.S.R.
9 E5 **Avebury** England
16 D4 **Aveinte** Spain
129 G4 **Aveiro** Brazil
16 B4 **Aveiro** Portugal
77 A2 **Avej** Iran
22 E2 **Avelgem** Belgium
94 G6 **Avella** Pennsylvania
133 F4 **Avellaneda** Argentina
45 R8 **Avellino** Italy
102 D6 **Avenal** California
40 F4 **Avenches** Switzerland
95 Q4 **Aver** Massachusetts
28 E6 **Avernak By** *B* Denmark
26 B8 **Averöy** *isld* Norway
45 Q8 **Aversa** Italy
100 K2 **Avery** Idaho
99 O8 **Avery** Iowa
109 N2 **Avery** Texas
111 E12 **Avery Island** Louisiana
22 F3 **Avesnes** France
22 D3 **Avesnes le Comte** France
22 E3 **Avesnes-les-Aubert** France
90 C7 **Aves Ridge** Atlantic Oc
27 H11 **Avesta** Sweden
28 O9 **Avevig** Faeroes
18 G8 **Aveyron** *dep* France
18 F8 **Aveyron** *R* France
45 O5 **Avezzano** Italy
46 F8 **Avgó** *isld* Greece
47 H9 **Avgó** *isld* Greece
46 E5 **Avgó** *mt* Greece
133 E3 **Aviá Terai** Argentina
15 E3 **Aviemore** Scotland
144 C6 **Aviemore Dam** New Zealand
115 P5 **Avigait** Greenland
80 B7 **Avigedor** Israel
43 G8 **Avigliano** Italy
19 N17 **Avignon** France
16 D4 **Avila** *prov* Spain
16 D4 **Ávila, Sa. de** *mts* Spain
16 D1 **Avilés** Spain
40 D3 **Avilley** France
109 N3 **Avinger** Texas
141 H6 **Avington** Queensland
22 D3 **Avion** France
95 K5 **Avis** Pennsylvania
41 O5 **Avisio** *R* Italy
80 E1 **Avivim** Israel
16 B5 **Aviz** Portugal
47 K8 **Avlan Gölü** *L* Turkey
47 F6 **Avlón** Greece
28 B4 **Avlum** Denmark
80 G2 **Avne Etan** Syria
28 H6 **Avnø Fjord** *inlet* Denmark
28 F6 **Avnslev** Denmark
14 E4 **Avoca** Irish Rep
94 E3 **Avoca** Michigan
95 K4 **Avoca** New York
144 C5 **Avoca** New Zealand
108 H3 **Avoca** Texas
139 G6 **Avoca** Victoria
14 E4 **Avoca,Vale of** Irish Rep
138 D5 **Avoid B** S Australia
117 O10 **Avola** Br Columbia
43 G12 **Avola** Sicily
106 D2 **Avon** Colorado
95 P5 **Avon** Connecticut
110 F1 **Avon** Illinois
99 M4 **Avon** Minnesota
101 N3 **Avon** Montana
112 M2 **Avon** N Carolina
94 K4 **Avon** New York
94 E5 **Avon** Ohio
98 H6 **Avon** S Dakota
8 D5 **Avon** *co* England
15 E3 **Avon** *R* Scotland
103 M8 **Avondale** Arizona
106 F3 **Avondale** Colorado
110 B2 **Avondale** Missouri
141 K6 **Avondale** Queensland
109 L8 **Avondale** Texas
140 D4 **Avon Downs** N Terr Aust
141 H5 **Avon Downs** Queensland
94 E5 **Avon Lake** Ohio
119 M8 **Avonlea** Sask
94 H6 **Avonmore** Pennsylvania
8 D4 **Avonmouth** England
113 F10 **Avon Park** Florida
9 E3 **Avon, R** Warwicks England
143 B9 **Avon, R** W Australia
9 E5 **Avon, R** Wilts/Hants England
130 E10 **Avoredo** *lt ho* Brazil
40 D3 **Avoudrey** France
20 C4 **Avranches** France
20 H4 **Avre** *R* Eure France
36 B6 **Avricourt** France
48 J5 **Avrig** Romania
22 K5 **Avril** France
21 C9 **Avrillé** France
48 E7 **Avtovac** Yugoslavia
80 F4 **Avuqa** Israel
61 P12 **Awa** Okinawa
60 H11 **Awaji-shima** *isld* Japan
145 E3 **Awakino** New Zealand
84 E4 **Awāl** *watercourse* Libya
70 Q10 **Awang** Indonesia
145 D1 **Awanui** New Zealand
86 H4 **Awarch** Ethiopia
144 B6 **Awarua Bay** New Zealand
86 H4 **Awash** Ethiopia
61 N7 **Awa-shima** *isld* Japan
85 D7 **Awaso** Ghana
57 K4 **Awat** China
86 G4 **Awata** *R* Ethiopia
145 E4 **Awatere R** New Zealand
84 E4 **Awbāri** Libya
12 C1 **Awe,L** Scotland
112 H4 **Awendaw** S Carolina
144 B6 **Awful, Mt** New Zealand
84 G4 **Awjilah** Libya
70 G6 **Awo** *R* Sulawesi Indonesia
117 Q4 **Awry L** N W Terr
116 J2 **Awuna** *R* Alaska
86 G4 **Awusa, L** Ethiopia
8 D5 **Axbridge** England
25 A6 **Axel** Netherlands
27 F14 **Axelfors** Sweden
146 G8 **Axel Heiberg Gl** Antarctica
147 H5 **Axel Heiberg I** N W Terr
106 C1 **Axial** Colorado
128 G4 **Axinim** Brazil
18 G10 **Ax-les-Thermes** France
8 D6 **Axminster** England
112 E6 **Axson** Georgia
107 O2 **Axtell** Kansas
27 G13 **Axvall** Sweden
18 H3 **Ay** France
128 C4 **Ayabaca** Peru
60 J10 **Ayabe** Japan
133 F5 **Ayacucho** Argentina
128 D6 **Ayacucho** Peru
68 B1 **Ayadaw** Burma
57 K1 **Ayaguz** U.S.S.R.
57 D4 **Ayakkuduk** U.S.S.R.
66 D4 **Ayakkum Hu** *L* China
16 C7 **Ayamonte** Spain
78 E1 **Ayancik** Turkey
80 C6 **Ayanot** Israel
126 G10 **Ayapel** Colombia
78 D1 **Ayaş** Turkey
128 D6 **Ayaviri** Peru
13 G4 **Aycliffe** England
55 E4 **Aydabul'** U.S.S.R.
54 L8 **Aydar** *R* U.S.S.R.
112 K2 **Ayden** N Carolina
47 J7 **Aydın** Turkey
78 A3 **Aydin** Turkey
47 J7 **Aydın Sıra Dağları** *mts* Turkey
55 C5 **Aydrlinskiy** U.S.S.R.
86 H3 **Ayelu** *mt* Ethiopia
40 G5 **Ayer** Switzerland
17 G2 **Ayerbe** Spain
100 G3 **Ayers** Washington
140 C7 **Ayers Ra** N Terr Aust
140 B7 **Ayers Rock** *mt* N Terr Aust
55 F3 **Ayev** *R* U.S.S.R.
19 O16 **Aygues** *R* France
56 C5 **Aygulaskiy Khrebet** *mts* U.S.S.R.
46 F5 **Ayiá** Greece
47 F6 **Ayía Ánna** Greece
47 G5 **Ayía Iríni Akra** *C* Greece
47 H5 **Ayiássos** Greece
47 G4 **Áyion Óros** *mt* Greece
47 F7 **Áyios** *isld* Greece
47 G5 **Áyios Evstrátios** *isld* Greece
47 G9 **Áyios Míron** Crete Greece
47 H9 **Ayios Nikólaos** Crete Greece
46 D6 **Ayios Pétros** Greece
79 D3 **Ayios Seryios** Cyprus
79 E3 **Ayios Theodhoros** Cyprus
116 L2 **Ayiyak** *R* Alaska
47 H7 **Aykathonisi** *isld* Greece
47 H7 **Ay Kírikos** Greece
36 B4 **Ayl** W Germany
121 N7 **Aylen,L** Ontario
9 F4 **Aylesbury** England
144 D5 **Aylesbury** New Zealand
119 M8 **Aylesbury** Sask
122 H8 **Aylesford** Nova Scotia
9 H5 **Aylesham** England
117 D6 **Aylesworth, Mt** Br Col/Alaska
16 E3 **Ayllón** Spain
16 E3 **Ayllón, Sa. de** *mts* Spain
121 P7 **Aylmer** Quebec
114 J5 **Aylmer L** N W Terr
118 B7 **Aylmer,Mt** Alberta
9 H2 **Aylsham** England
119 O5 **Aylsham** Sask
121 O7 **Aylwin** Quebec
17 F6 **Ayna** Spain
9 E3 **Aynho** England
112 H4 **Aynor** S Carolina
84 G5 **Ayn Zuwayyah** Libya
147 Q4 **Ayon,Ostrov** *isld* U.S.S.R.
17 G5 **Ayora** Spain
85 E6 **Ayorou** Niger
55 G2 **Aypolovo** U.S.S.R.
98 J2 **Ayr** N Dakota
98 H9 **Ayr** Nebraska
141 H4 **Ayr** Queensland
12 D3 **Ayr** Scotland
Ayr *co see* **Strathclyde** *reg*
21 F8 **Ayron** France
99 M6 **Ayrshire** Iowa
141 G5 **Ayrshire Downs** Queensland
55 F4 **Aysary** U.S.S.R.
13 G5 **Aysgarth** England
57 F1 **Ayshirak** U.S.S.R.
13 H5 **Ayton** N Yorks England
141 H3 **Ayton** Queensland
13 F2 **Ayton** Scotland
47 J2 **Aytos** Bulgaria
57 C4 **Aytym** U.S.S.R.
61 P7 **Ayukawahama** Japan
65 C2 **Ayulhai** China
124 G7 **Ayutla** Mexico
68 E5 **Ayutthaya** Thailand
78 A2 **Ayvacik** Turkey
47 H5 **Ayvalık** Turkey
78 A2 **Ayvalik** Turkey
22 K3 **Aywaille** Belgium
100 B7 **Azalea** Oregon
61 P13 **Azama** Okinawa
75 K5 **Azamgarh** India
55 C3 **Azangulovo** U.S.S.R.
55 D2 **Azanka** U.S.S.R.
22 J5 **Azannes-et-Soumazannes** France
78 K2 **Āzarbāījān-e Gharbī** Iran
78 L2 **Āzarbāījān-e Sharqi** Iran
85 G6 **Azare** Nigeria
52 E5 **Azatskoye, Oz** *L* U.S.S.R.
21 F7 **Azay-le-Rideau** France
21 G7 **Azay-sur-Cher** France
21 E8 **Azay-sur-Thouet** France
79 H2 **A'zāz** Syria
Azbine *reg* Niger *see* **Aïr ou Azbine**
21 H6 **Azé** France
40 G7 **Azeglio** Italy
78 L1 **Azerbaijan** U.S.S.R.
50 D4 **Azerbaydzhanskaya S.S.R** U.S.S.R.
19 N13 **Azergues** *R* France
53 F7 **Azeyevo** U.S.S.R.
55 G4 **Azhbulat, Oz** *L* U.S.S.R.
56 C5 **Azho-Tayga, Gora** *mt* U.S.S.R.
22 C3 **Azincourt** France
86 A6 **Azingo, L** Gabon
95 R1 **Aziscoos L** Maine
84 E3 **Aziziyan, Al** Libya
16 C7 **Aznàlcóllar** Spain
128 C4 **Azogues** Ecuador
52 G2 **Azopol'ye** U.S.S.R.
Azores *islds see* **Açores**
90 G5 **Azores-Cape St Vincent Ridge** Atlantic Oc
86 D3 **Azoum** *R* Chad
54 L9 **Azov** U.S.S.R.
Azov,Sea of *see* **Azovskoye More**
54 L9 **Azovskiy Kanal** U.S.S.R.
53 E10 **Azovskoye More** U.S.S.R.
17 F1 **Azpeitia** Spain
85 C2 **Azrou** Morocco
103 L9 **Aztec** Arizona
106 C5 **Aztec** New Mexico
106 B5 **Aztec Ruins Nat.Mon** New Mexico
127 J5 **Azua** Dominican Rep
16 D6 **Azuaga** Spain
17 G3 **Azuara** Spain
128 C4 **Azuay** *prov* Ecuador
17 F6 **Azuer** *R* Spain
125 O6 **Azuero,Pen.de** Panama
131 B3 **Azufre, P. del** Chile
133 F5 **Azul** Argentina
131 B5 **Azul** *peak* Chile
125 P9 **Azul** *R* Mexico
131 B8 **Azul, Cerro** *peak* Neuquén Argentina
130 E7 **Azul Paulista, Mte** Brazil
130 C4 **Azul,Serra** *mts* Mato Grosso Brazil
61 O8 **Azuma-yama** *mt* Japan
80 B8 **Azza** Israel
84 E4 **Az Zallaf** Libya
71 L10 **Baa** Indonesia
79 F5 **Ba'abda** Lebanon
41 M3 **Baad** Austria
71 K10 **Baäh** Indonesia
70 E4 **Baai** *R* Kalimantan
25 F6 **Baal** W Germany
79 G4 **Ba'albek** Lebanon
25 C6 **Baarle-Hertog** Netherlands
25 C6 **Baarle Nassau** Netherlands
25 D4 **Baarn** Netherlands
70 K8 **Baati, G** *mt* Sumatra Indonesia
60 D14 **Baba** Japan
46 E4 **Baba** *mt* Yugoslavia
47 H5 **Baba Burun** *C* Turkey
48 M6 **Babadag** Romania
47 J3 **Babaeski** Turkey
128 C4 **Babahoyo** Ecuador
71 G7 **Babak** Philippines
143 C9 **Babakin** W Australia
77 K2 **Bābā, Koh-i-** *mts* Afghanistan
72 E6 **Bab al Mandab** *str* Arabia/Djibouti
67 B5 **Babao** China
71 O8 **Babar** *isld* Indonesia
71 O9 **Babar,Kep** *islds* Indonesia
70 O9 **Babat** Java
57 E5 **Babatag, Khr** *mts* U.S.S.R.
88 E4 **Babati** Tanzania
80 G7 **Babayir et Tiwal** Jordan
101 M1 **Babb** Montana
116 S2 **Babbage** *R* Yukon Terr
143 A6 **Babbage I** W Australia
99 P2 **Babbitt** Minnesota
99 Q5 **Babcock** Wisconsin
79 H2 **Bāb, El** Syria
33 P5 **Babelin** E Germany
88 C7 **Babemba** *tribe* Zambia
88 C5 **Babemba** *tribe* Zaïre
36 F4 **Babenhausen** Hessen W Germany
79 G3 **Babenna** Syria
69 C11 **Babi** *isld* Indonesia
31 M6 **Babia Góra** *mts* Czech/Poland
124 E3 **Babícora** Mexico
124 F3 **Babícora, L. de** Mexico
141 H3 **Babinda** Queensland
114 G7 **Babine L** Br Columbia
117 K8 **Babine Ra** Br Columbia
136 G2 **Babo** W Irian
48 D4 **Babócsa** Hungary
77 C1 **Bābol** Iran
103 N10 **Baboquivari Pk** Arizona
142 E4 **Babrongan Tower** *mt* W Australia
113 F10 **Babson Park** Florida
36 G5 **Babstadt** W Germany
16 D9 **Bab Taza** Morocco
67 B3 **Babu** China
46 E3 **Babuna** *mt* Yugoslavia
56 G5 **Babushkin** U.S.S.R.
71 D6 **Babuyan** Philippines
71 E1 **Babuyan** *islds* Philippines
71 E1 **Babuyan Ch** Philippines
124 E4 **Baca** Mexico
124 E4 **Bacabáche** Mexico
129 G5 **Bacabal** Brazil
129 H4 **Bacaja** *R* Brazil
71 A3 **Bacan** Halmahera Indonesia
124 E3 **Bacanora** Mexico
71 E1 **Bacarra** Philippines
48 K4 **Bacău** Romania
68 G1 **Bac Can** Vietnam
19 K4 **Baccarat** France
122 G10 **Baccaro Pt** Nova Scotia
45 L1 **Bacchiglione** *R* Italy
41 H5 **Baceno** Italy
48 L4 **Băceşti** Romania
94 D3 **Bach** Michigan
37 N5 **Bach** W Germany
127 J10 **Bachaquero** Venezuela
36 D3 **Bacharach** W Germany
115 M2 **Bache Pen** N W Terr
124 F3 **Bachiniva** Mexico
68 J2 **Bach Long Vi** *isld* Vietnam
69 E9 **Bacho** Thailand
37 L1 **Bachra** E Germany
57 J5 **Bachu** China
115 K4 **Back** *R* N W Terr
48 E5 **Backa** *reg* Yugoslavia
27 G14 **Bäckaby** Sweden
48 E5 **Bačka Palanka** Yugoslavia
48 F5 **Bačka Petrovo Selo** Yugoslavia
48 F5 **Bačka Topola** Yugoslavia
95 L10 **Back Bay** Virginia
117 J4 **Backbone Ranges** N W Terr
27 F13 **Bäckefors** Sweden
27 G12 **Bäckhammar** Sweden
36 G6 **Backnang** W Germany
119 U10 **Backoo** N Dakota
138 E6 **Backstaiys Pass** S Australia
26 H6 **Bäckstrand** Sweden
99 M3 **Backus** Minnesota
Bac Lieu *see* **Vinh Loi**
68 H2 **Bac Ninh** Vietnam
71 E2 **Bacnotan** Luzon Philippines
127 P5 **Bacolet** Grenada
45 Q8 **Bacoli** Italy
71 F5 **Bacolod** Philippines
71 E4 **Baco, Mt** Philippines
112 C6 **Baconton** Georgia
68 G1 **Bac Quang** Vietnam
20 G2 **Bacqueville-en-Caux** France
48 E4 **Bácsalmás** Hungary
48 E4 **Bács-Kiskun** *co* Hungary
9 H2 **Bacton** England
124 F5 **Bacubirito** Mexico
71 G7 **Baculin Bay** Mindanao Philippines
13 F6 **Bacup** England
129 J4 **Bacuri,I de** Brazil
98 F5 **Bad** *R* S Dakota
Bada *see* **Xilin**
68 D7 **Bada** *isld* Burma
75 L7 **Bada Barabil** India
37 N6 **Bad Abbach** W Germany
76 B5 **Badagara** India
38 E6 **Bad Aibling** W Germany
129 J4 **Badajós** Brazil
16 C6 **Badajoz** Spain
16 C6 **Badajoz** *prov* Spain
128 F4 **Badajoz, L** Brazil
77 L1 **Badakhshan** Afghanistan
17 J3 **Badalona** Spain
76 B3 **Badami** India
75 M7 **Badampahar** India
72 E2 **Badanah** Saudi Arabia
56 E3 **Badan, Khrebet** *mts* U.S.S.R.
65 H3 **Badaohe** China
Badaojiang *see* **Hunjiang**
124 F5 **Badariguato** Mexico
70 D2 **Badas** Brunei
69 H12 **Badas,Kep** *isld* Indonesia
38 J6 **Bad Aussee** Austria
94 E3 **Bad Axe** Michigan
32 G7 **Badbergen** W Germany
36 D5 **Bad Bergzabern** W Germany
37 L2 **Bad Berka** E Germany
36 E1 **Bad Berleburg** W Germany
37 M3 **Bad Berneck** W Germany
36 B3 **Bad Bertrich** W Germany
37 M1 **Bad Bibra** Halle E Germany
37 L2 **Bad Blankenburg** E Germany
37 J3 **Bad Bocklet** W Germany
32 L5 **Bad Bramstedt** W Germany
123 M7 **Baddeck** C Breton I, N Scotia
32 M8 **Baddeckenstedt** W Germany
26 M2 **Badderen** Norway
33 P4 **Bad Doberan** E Germany
32 K9 **Bad Driburg** W Germany
33 R9 **Bad Düben** E Germany
36 E5 **Bad Dürkheim** W Germany
33 Q10 **Bad Dürrenberg** E Germany
37 N3 **Bad Elster** E Germany
36 D3 **Bad Ems** W Germany
48 C2 **Baden** Austria
119 Q6 **Baden** Manitoba
94 G6 **Baden** Pennsylvania
41 H3 **Baden** Switzerland
36 E6 **Baden-Baden** W Germany
15 D4 **Badenoch** Scotland
19 K4 **Badenviller** France
36 G6 **Baden-Württemberg** W Germany
45 P1 **Baderna** Yugoslavia
33 U7 **Bad Freienwalde** E Germany
36 G5 **Bad Friedrichshall** W Germany
32 M9 **Bad Gandersheim** W Germany
102 E5 **Badger** California
118 F1 **Badger** Manitoba
98 K1 **Badger** Minnesota
123 Q5 **Badger** Nfld
101 Q5 **Badger Basin** Wyoming
77 H2 **Bādghīs** Afghanistan
38 N8 **Bad Gleichenberg** Austria
36 C2 **Bad Godesberg** W Germany
30 H5 **Bad Gottleuba** E Germany
32 M9 **Bad Grund** W Germany
38 K5 **Bad Hall** Austria
33 N9 **Bad Harzburg** W Germany
36 E6 **Bad Herrenalb** W Germany
36 H2 **Bad Hersfeld** W Germany
38 H7 **Bad Hofgastein** Austria
36 F3 **Bad Homburg** W Germany
36 C2 **Bad Honnef** W Germany
45 K1 **Badia Polesine** Italy
45 M4 **Badia Tedalda** Italy
32 H8 **Bad Iburg** W Germany
79 H6 **Badiet esh Sham** *des* Jordan/Syria
112 G2 **Badin** N Carolina
74 C6 **Badin** Pakistan
112 G2 **Badin L** N Carolina
38 J6 **Bad Ischl** Austria
71 K9 **Badjawa** Flores Indonesia
70 G4 **Badjo** Sulawesi Indonesia
37 J3 **Bad Kissingen** W Germany
33 O5 **Bad Kleinen** E Germany
37 M2 **Bad Klosterlausnitz** E Germany
37 M1 **Bad Kösen** E Germany
36 D4 **Bad Kreuznach** W Germany
98 C2 **Bad Lands** *reg* N Dakota
98 E6 **Badlands Nat.Mon** S Dakota
37 K1 **Bad Langensalza** E Germany
33 P10 **Bad Lauchstädt** E Germany
37 O1 **Bad Lausik** E Germany
33 M9 **Bad Lauterberg** W Germany
38 K8 **Bad Leonhard** Austria
37 K2 **Bad Liebenstein** E Germany
36 F6 **Bad Liebenzell** W Germany
32 J9 **Bad Lippspringe** W Germany
32 J9 **Bad Meinberg** W Germany
36 H5 **Bad Mergentheim** W Germany
32 K8 **Bad Münder am Deister** W Germany
36 D4 **Bad Münster** W Germany
36 B2 **Bad Münstereifel** W Germany
36 F3 **Bad Nauheim** W Germany
32 K8 **Bad Nenndorf** W Germany
36 C2 **Bad Neuenahr** W Germany
36 C2 **Bad Neuenahr-Ahrweiler** W Germany
37 J3 **Bad Neustadt** W Germany
32 J8 **Bad Oeynhausen** W Germany
33 M5 **Bad Oldersloe** W Germany
68 H4 **Ba Don** Vietnam
67 C1 **Badong** China
69 H8 **Ba Dong** Vietnam
36 B6 **Badonviller** France
36 G3 **Bad Orb** W Germany
65 D6 **Badou** China
36 E7 **Bad Peterstal** W Germany
32 K9 **Bad Pyrmont** W Germany
36 G5 **Bad Rappenau** W Germany
38 G6 **Bad Reichenhall** W Germany
36 E7 **Bad Rippoldsau** W Germany
32 M8 **Bad Salzdetfurth** W Germany
33 P8 **Bad Salzelmen** E Germany
36 H2 **Bad Salzschlirf** W Germany
32 J8 **Bad Salzuflen** W Germany
37 J2 **Bad Salzungen** E Germany
32 H9 **Bad Sassendorf** W Germany
33 R9 **Bad Schmiedeberg** E Germany
36 E3 **Bad Schwalbach** W Germany
33 N5 **Bad Schwartau** W Germany
33 M5 **Bad Segeberg** W Germany
36 E3 **Bad Soden** W Germany
32 L10 **Bad Sooden** W Germany
37 M3 **Bad Steben** W Germany
33 Q6 **Bad Stuer** E Germany
33 O9 **Bad Suderode** E Germany
37 M1 **Bad Sulza** E Germany
33 R4 **Bad Sülze** E Germany
36 F6 **Bad Teinach-Zavelstein** W Germany
37 K1 **Bad Tennstedt** E Germany
41 P2 **Bad Tölz** W Germany
86 A2 **Baduen** Somalia
83 L10 **Badulla** Sri Lanka
36 F3 **Bad Vilbel** W Germany
38 O6 **Bad Voslau** Austria
102 H5 **Badwater** *L* California
36 G1 **Bad Wildungen** W Germany
33 P7 **Bad Wilsnack** E Germany
36 G5 **Bad Wimpfen** W Germany
37 J5 **Bad Windsheim** W Germany
59 K1 **Badzhal'skiy Khrebet** *mt* U.S.S.R.
26 O2 **Baeivašgiedde** Norway
28 C5 **Bække** Denmark
28 A4 **Bækmarksbro** Denmark
28 E3 **Bælum** Denmark
16 E7 **Baena** Spain
36 D6 **Baerenthal** France
128 C4 **Baeza** Ecuador
16 E7 **Baeza** Spain
47 J7 **Bafa Gölü** *L* Turkey
86 B4 **Bafang** Cameroon
85 B6 **Bafata** Guinea-Bissau
109 K8 **Baffin B** Texas
147 E6 **Baffin Basin** Arctic Oc
115 N3 **Baffin Bay** Greenland/Canada
90 E2 **Baffin-Greenland Rise** Atlantic Oc
115 M3 **Baffin I** N W Terr
141 K6 **Baffle Creek** Queensland
86 B5 **Bafia** Cameroon
85 B6 **Bafing** *R* Guinea/Mali
79 H2 **Bafliün** Syria
85 B6 **Bafoulabé** Mali
86 B4 **Bafoussam** Cameroon
77 D4 **Bāfq** Iran
78 E1 **Bafra** Turkey
86 E5 **Bafwasende** Zaïre
58 D3 **Baga Bogd Uul** *mt* Mongolia
71 E3 **Bagac Bay** Luzon Philippines
76 B2 **Bagalkot** India
88 G5 **Bagamoyo** Tanzania
71 G7 **Baganga** Mindanao Philippines
71 F7 **Baganian Peninsula** Mindanao Philippines
69 E10 **Bagan Serai** Malaysia
142 A3 **Baganup L** W Australia
44 H2 **Baganza** *R* Italy
57 K1 **Bagar** *R* U.S.S.R.
55 D3 **Bagaryak** U.S.S.R.
103 J7 **Bagbad** California
32 G6 **Bagband** W Germany
103 L7 **Bagdad** Arizona
110 L3 **Bagdad** Kentucky
109 K10 **Bagdad** Mexico
51 L3 **Bagdarin** U.S.S.R.
58 F1 **Bagdarino** U.S.S.R.
131 G3 **Bagé** Brazil
86 G3 **Bagemder** *prov* Ethiopia
28 F7 **Bagenkop** Denmark
101 S8 **Baggs** Wyoming
78 K5 **Baghdād** Iraq
77 A4 **Bāgh-e Malek** Iran
75 N7 **Bagherhat** Bangladesh
43 F10 **Bagheria** Sicily
77 E4 **Baghīn** Iran
77 L1 **Baghlān** Afghanistan
77 J3 **Baghran** Afghanistan
Baghrash Köl *see* **Bosten Hu**
14 E4 **Baginbun Hd** Irish Rep
99 L2 **Bagley** Minnesota
99 P7 **Bagley** Wisconsin
116 Q6 **Bagley Icefield** Alaska
45 L3 **Bagnacavallo** Italy
110 D3 **Bagnell Dam** Missouri
18 F9 **Bagnères de Bigorre** France
18 F10 **Bagnères de Luchon** France
40 F6 **Bagnes,Val De** Switzerland
21 E7 **Bagneux** France
45 J3 **Bagni di Lucca** Italy
41 L5 **Bagni di Masino** Italy
45 K4 **Bagno A Ripoli** Italy
45 L4 **Bagno di Romagna** Italy
20 E4 **Bagnoles-de-l'Orne** France
45 L1 **Bagnoli di Sopra** Italy
45 L1 **Bagnolo di Po** Italy
45 J2 **Bagnolo in Piano** Italy
44 H1 **Bagnolo Mella** Italy
45 J1 **Bagnolo San Vito** Italy

8
Bagnols-sur-Cèze — Baricella

19 N16 **Bagnols-sur-Cèze** France
28 D6 **Bågø** *isld* Denmark
85 C6 **Bagoe** *R* Ivory Co/Mali
Bagong *see* **Sansui**
121 U4 **Bagotville** Quebec
31 M1 **Bagrationovsk** U.S.S.R.
9 F5 **Bagshot** England
65 E3 **Bag Tal** China
128 C5 **Bagua** Peru
85 F5 **Baguezane, Mt** Niger
71 N9 **Baguia** Timor Indonesia
71 E2 **Baguio** Luzon Philippines
71 G7 **Baguio** Mindanao Philippines
71 F2 **Baguio Pt** Luzon Philippines
86 C3 **Baguirmi** *dist* Chad
126 E2 **Bahama Bank,Great** Bahamas
126 F1 **Bahama Bank, Little** Bahamas
126 F2 **Bahamas, The** W Indies
127 M4 **Baham, Pte** Martinique W I
86 G3 **Bahar Dar** Ethiopia
84 H4 **Baharîya Oasis** Egypt
70 D3 **Bahau** *R* Sarawak
74 E4 **Bahawalnagar** Pakistan
74 D4 **Bahawalpur** Pakistan
71 H5 **Baheësiuna** Sulawesi Indonesia
88 E4 **Bahi** Tanzania
129 K6 **Bahia** *state* Brazil
131 E7 **Bahia Blanca** Argentina
125 L1 **Bahía, Islas de la** Honduras
124 C3 **Bahia Kino** Mexico
133 D7 **Bahía Laura** Argentina
133 C6 **Bahía Pargua** Chile
124 B4 **Bahía Tortugas** Mexico
48 L3 **Bahluiul** *R* Romania
48 J4 **Bahnea** Romania
88 B5 **Baholoholo** *tribe* Zaïre
69 H8 **Ba,Hon** *isld* Vietnam
79 A7 **Bahra el Burullus** *lagoon* Egypt
79 B7 **Baḥra el Manzala** *lagoon* Egypt
75 J5 **Bahraich** India
77 B6 **Bahrain** *sheikhdom* The Gulf
86 C4 **Bahr Aouk** *R* Cent Afr Republic
86 D3 **Bahr Aouk** *R* Chad
86 F3 **Bahr el Abiad** *R* Sudan
86 E4 **Bahr el Arab** *watercourse* Sudan
86 F3 **Bahr el Azraq** *R* Sudan
86 E4 **Bahr el Ghazal** *prov* Sudan
86 E4 **Bahr el Ghazal** *R* Sudan
78 G4 **Bahret Assad** *L* Syria
86 F4 **Bahr ez Zeraf** *R* Sudan
77 G7 **Bāhu Kālat** Iran
71 H6 **Bahulu** *isld* Sulawesi Indonesia
71 K8 **Bahuluang** *isld* Indonesia
70 G6 **Bahu-Mbelu** Sulawesi Indonesia
129 J4 **Baiã** Brazil
48 H6 **Baia de Aramă** Romania
48 H4 **Baia de Cris** Romania
16 B6 **Baia de Setúbal** Portugal
87 B9 **Baia doz Tigres** Angola
128 F7 **Baia Grande,L** Brazil
48 H3 **Baia Mare** Romania
45 R8 **Baiano** Italy
48 H3 **Baia Spriei** Romania
77 D3 **Baiazeh** Iran
86 C4 **Baïbokoum** Chad
65 H3 **Baicaogou** China
57 K4 **Baicheng** China
65 F2 **Baicheng** China
48 K5 **Băicoi** Romania
121 N5 **Baie Carrière** Quebec
115 N8 **Baie-Comeau** Quebec
21 A7 **Baie de Bourgneuf** France
126 H5 **Baie de Henne** Haiti
122 E5 **Baie de Sables** Quebec
123 P2 **Baie-du-Milieu** Quebec
115 M7 **Baie-du-Poste** Quebec
122 G6 **Baie du Vin** New Brunswick
68 F7 **Baie,l.de la** Cambodia
122 K3 **Baie Johan Beetz** Quebec
127 N4 **Baie Mahault** Guadeloupe W I
36 E7 **Baiersbronn** W Germany
122 C5 **Baie Ste.Catherine** Quebec
122 H4 **Baie Ste.Clair** Quebec
122 B6 **Baie St.Paul** Quebec
122 E4 **Baie Trinité** Quebec
122 J7 **Baie Verte** New Brunswick
123 Q4 **Baie Verte** Newfoundland
67 D3 **Baifang** China
Baiguan *see* **Shangyu**
74 J7 **Baihar** India
58 F5 **Baihe** China
65 B6 **Baijiazhuang** China
Baikal *L see* **Baykal,Ozero** *L*
75 K7 **Baikunthpur** India
65 E1 **Bailang** China
Baile Átha *see* **Dublin**
48 G6 **Băile Herculane** Romania
16 E6 **Bailén** Spain
48 H6 **Băileşti** Romania
22 G3 **Baileux** Belgium
106 E2 **Bailey** Colorado
112 J2 **Bailey** N Carolina
143 D8 **Bailey Ra** W Australia
111 K7 **Baileyton** Alabama
95 U1 **Baileyville** Maine
14 D3 **Bailieborough** Irish Rep
67 D3 **Bailin** China
129 H3 **Bailique, I** Brazil
20 H5 **Bailleau-le-Pin** France
22 D2 **Bailleul** France
20 E4 **Bailleul** Orne France
22 D3 **Bailleul-Sire-Berthoult** France
115 K2 **Baillie Hamilton I** N W Terr
114 G3 **Baillie Is** N W Terr
127 M4 **Baillif** Guadeloupe W I
77 K3 **Bailugh** Afghanistan
48 L4 **Baimakliya** U.S.S.R.
111 M11 **Bainbridge** Georgia
95 M4 **Bainbridge** New York
94 D7 **Bainbridge** Ohio
21 B6 **Bain-de-Brét** France
140 B3 **Baines, Mt** N Terr Aust
127 H5 **Bainet** Haiti
71 K10 **Baing** Indonesia
Baini *see* **Yuqing**
19 K4 **Bains-les-Bains** France
13 H6 **Bainton** England
98 B1 **Bainville** Montana
59 J2 **Baiquan** China
109 H3 **Baird** Texas
116 E6 **Baird Inlet** Alaska
116 G3 **Baird Mts** Alaska
65 D3 **Bairin Youqi** China
58 G3 **Bairin Zuoqi** China
139 J7 **Bairnsdale** Victoria
101 S7 **Bairoil** Wyoming
21 C6 **Bais** France
20 E5 **Bais** Mayenne France
18 F8 **Baïse** *R* France
Baisha *see* **Jiande**
65 B7 **Baisha** China
67 B2 **Baisha** China
67 C7 **Baisha** China
65 B7 **Baisha Shuiku** *res* China
67 E3 **Baishi Feng** *mt* China
65 A7 **Baishui** China
58 D5 **Baishui Jiang** *R* China
22 E2 **Baisieux** France
45 J3 **Baiso** Italy
52 B6 **Baisogala** U.S.S.R.
74 J4 **Baitadi** Nepal
68 G3 **Bai Thoung** Vietnam
19 N15 **Baix** France
65 C6 **Baixiang** China
65 A3 **Baixingt** China
65 E3 **Baixingt** China
16 B6 **Baixo Alentejo** *prov* Portugal
130 H6 **Baixo Guandu** Brazil
87 C9 **Baixo Longa** Angola
65 C5 **Baiyang Dian** *L* China
67 C1 **Baiyangping** China
Baiyashi *see* **Dong'an**
58 D4 **Baiyin** China
86 F2 **Baiyuda** Sudan
67 E3 **Baiyun Shan** *mt* China
58 E4 **Baiyu Shan** *mts* China
67 B1 **Baizi** China
48 E4 **Baja** Hungary
124 B3 **Baja California** *state* Mexico
70 Q10 **Bajan** Indonesia
124 J4 **Baján** Mexico
124 B3 **Baja, Pta** *C* Mexico
48 F7 **Bajina Bašta** Yugoslavia
48 E5 **Bajmok** Yugoslavia
71 J9 **Bajo** Sumbawa Indonesia
128 C2 **Bajo Baudo** Colombia
126 E7 **Bajo Nuevo** Caribbean
141 K6 **Bajool** Queensland
28 C7 **Bajstrup** Denmark
48 D4 **Bak** Hungary
70 E3 **Bakajan, G** *mt* Kalimantan
55 C4 **Bakal** U.S.S.R.
86 D4 **Bakala** Cent Afr Republic
57 H3 **Bakanas** U.S.S.R.
57 J2 **Bakanas** *R* U.S.S.R.
56 B3 **Bakchar** *R* U.S.S.R.
69 E14 **Bake** Indonesia
85 B6 **Bakel** Senegal
103 H6 **Baker** California
101 M4 **Baker** Idaho
98 B3 **Baker** Montana
98 G1 **Baker** N Dakota
103 K2 **Baker** Nevada
100 H5 **Baker** Oregon
94 J7 **Baker** W Virginia
133 C7 **Baker** *R* Chile
103 N7 **Baker Butte** *mt* Arizona
117 G8 **Baker I** Alaska
137 R1 **Baker I** Pacific Oc
95 R7 **Baker L** Maine
115 K5 **Baker Lake** N W Terr
143 F7 **Baker Lake** W Australia
100 D1 **Baker,Mt** Washington
125 P9 **Bakers** Belize
102 F6 **Bakersfield** California
112 E1 **Bakersfield** N Carolina
108 E5 **Bakersfield** Texas
95 P2 **Bakersfield** Vermont
9 E1 **Bakewell** England
77 G2 **Bakharz** *reg* Iran
53 D11 **Bakhchisaray** U.S.S.R.
54 D5 **Bakhmach** U.S.S.R.
77 B4 **Bakhtiyāri** Iran
47 J5 **Bakır** *R* Turkey
47 K4 **Bakırköy** Turkey
25 F2 **Bakkeveen** Netherlands
47 K7 **Baklan** Turkey
86 G4 **Bako** Ethiopia
85 C7 **Bako** Ivory Coast
48 D4 **Bakony** *mts* Hungary
86 D4 **Bakouma** Cent Afr Republic
85 C6 **Bakoye** *R* Guinea/Mali
54 L1 **Baksheyevo** U.S.S.R.
26 K6 **Baktsjaure** Sweden
50 D4 **Baku** U.S.S.R.
71 G6 **Bakulin Pt** Mindanao Philippines
32 H7 **Bakum** W Germany
70 C5 **Bakumpai** Kalimantan
69 G12 **Bakung** *isld* Indonesia
69 C11 **Bakungan** Sumatra
142 J10 **Bakutis Coast** Antarctica
80 D4 **Bal'a** Jordan
121 L7 **Bala** Ontario
78 D2 **Bâlâ** Turkey
8 C2 **Bala** Wales
71 C7 **Balabac Str** Borneo/Philippines
70 E6 **Balabalangan, Kep** *islds* Indonesia
71 H8 **Balabalangan Pulau Pulau** *islds* Indonesia
54 H1 **Balabanovo** U.S.S.R.
71 C7 **Balabec** *isld* Palawan Philippines
54 G9 **Balabino** U.S.S.R.
128 E6 **Bala,Cerros de** *mts* Bolivia
48 H6 **Bălăciţa** Romania
127 J2 **Balaclava** Jamaica
138 F4 **Balaclava** New S Wales
86 J5 **Balad** Somalia
77 B1 **Baladeh** Iran
80 F3 **Balad el Basha** Jordan
80 F3 **Balad el Mansura** Jordan
146 F2 **Balæna Is** Antarctica
74 J8 **Balaghat** India
17 H3 **Balaguer** Spain
68 A2 **Balaing** Burma
70 B4 **Balaisepuac** Kalimantan
138 E5 **Balaklava** S Australia
54 H7 **Balakleya** U.S.S.R.
8 C2 **Bala, L** Wales
87 G8 **Balama** Mozambique
77 H2 **Bala Murghab** Afghanistan
40 B6 **Balan** France
125 O9 **Balancán** Mexico
71 E3 **Balanga** Luzon Philippines
71 H5 **Balantak, G** *mt* Sulawesi Indonesia
71 F5 **Balaring** Negros Philippines
86 G3 **Balas** *R* Ethiopia
75 M8 **Balasore** India
48 E2 **Balassagyarmat** Hungary
84 H4 **Balât** Egypt
99 L5 **Balaton** Minnesota
48 D4 **Balaton** *L* Hungary
48 D4 **Balatonfüred** Hungary
48 D4 **Balatonszentgyörgy** Hungary
71 L9 **Balaurin** Flores Indonesia
124 F10 **Balboa** Panama Can Zone
14 E3 **Balbriggan** Irish Rep
141 H8 **Balbuna** Queensland
13 G6 **Balby** England
144 D5 **Balcairn** New Zealand
138 E4 **Balcanoona** S Australia
131 F6 **Balcarce** Argentina
119 O8 **Balcarres** Sask
48 H6 **Bălceşti** Romania
47 J1 **Balchik** Bulgaria
109 O9 **Balch Springs** Texas
144 B7 **Balclutha** New Zealand
9 F5 **Balcombe** England
100 F6 **Bald Butte** *mt* Oregon
94 K6 **Bald Eagle Mt** Pennsylvania
41 H3 **Baldegg See** *L* Switzerland
143 C11 **Bald Hd** W Australia
110 E6 **Bald Knob** Arkansas
94 F9 **Bald Knob** W Virginia
101 L5 **Bald Mt** Idaho
103 J4 **Bald Mt** Nevada
9 F4 **Baldock** England
119 T2 **Baldock L** Manitoba
42 D3 **Baldo,Monte** Italy
113 F7 **Baldwin** Florida
110 A3 **Baldwin** Kansas
94 B3 **Baldwin** Michigan
98 F2 **Baldwin** N Dakota
99 O5 **Baldwin** Wisconsin
102 H7 **Baldwin L** California
116 F3 **Baldwin Pen** Alaska
118 H6 **Baldwinton** Sask
95 P4 **Baldwinville** Massachusetts
95 R3 **Baldwin, W** Maine
111 H7 **Baldwyn** Mississippi
119 R7 **Baldy Mt** Manitoba
103 P8 **Baldy Pk** Arizona
106 E6 **Baldy Pk** New Mexico
86 H4 **Bale** *prov* Ethiopia
Balearic Is *see* **Islas Baleares**
70 C4 **Baleh** *R* Sarawak
130 H5 **Baleia, Pta da** *C* Brazil
115 N6 **Baleine,à la** *R* Quebec
83 L14 **Baleiniers, Baie des** Kerguelen Indian Oc
71 C7 **Balembangan** *isld* Sabah
22 J1 **Balen** Belgium
48 K6 **Băleni Romîni** Romania
71 E3 **Baler** Luzon Philippines
71 E3 **Baler Bay** Luzon Philippines
15 E5 **Balerno** Scotland
51 L3 **Baley** U.S.S.R.
58 G1 **Baley** U.S.S.R.
141 H5 **Balfe's Creek** Queensland
48 D4 **Bal Földvár** Hungary
26 K7 **Bålforsen** Sweden
117 P11 **Balfour** Br Columbia
98 F2 **Balfour** N Dakota
144 B6 **Balfour** New Zealand
142 D6 **Balfour Downs** W Australia
12 D1 **Balfron** Scotland
77 F1 **Bālgirān** Iran
142 G5 **Balgo Hill** W Australia
119 N8 **Balgonie** Sask
32 K10 **Balhorn** W Germany
86 B4 **Bali** Cameroon
70 P10 **Bali** *isld* Indonesia
71 F6 **Baliangao** Mindanao Philippines
69 D11 **Balige** Sumatra
31 N6 **Baligród** Poland
65 D4 **Balihan** China
47 J5 **Balıkesir** Turkey
70 E5 **Balikpapan** Kalimantan
86 C3 **Bal Illi** *R* Chad
70 G2 **Balimbing Tawitaw** *isld* Philippines
69 E10 **Baling** Malaysia
70 C3 **Balingian** Sarawak
70 C3 **Balingian** *R* Sarawak
65 D3 **Balinqiao** China
48 G5 **Balint** Romania
70 P9 **Bali Sea** Indonesia
70 P10 **Bali,Selat** Bali/Java
70 G2 **Baliungan** Tawitawi Philippines
130 D5 **Baliza** Brazil
32 K5 **Balje** W Germany
118 K6 **Baljennie** Sask
25 E3 **Balk** Netherlands
48 G3 **Balkány** Hungary
55 C4 **Balkany** U.S.S.R.
55 E4 **Balkashino** U.S.S.R.
25 F3 **Balkbrug** Netherlands
77 K1 **Balkh** Afghanistan
57 G2 **Balkhash** U.S.S.R.
57 G2 **Balkhash, Ozero** *L* U.S.S.R.
74 H9 **Balkonda** India
87 E10 **Balla Balla** Zimbabwe
15 C4 **Ballachulish** Scotland
143 E9 **Balladonia** W Australia
14 C3 **Ballaghaderreen** Irish Rep
20 K4 **Ballancourt-sur-Essonne** France
141 K8 **Ballandean** Queensland
26 J3 **Ballangen** Norway
101 R4 **Ballantine** Montana
15 C5 **Ballantrae** Scotland
114 J7 **Ballantyne Bay** Sask
114 H2 **Ballantyne Str** N W Terr
43 C9 **Ballao** Sardinia
102 G5 **Ballarat** California
139 G6 **Ballarat** Victoria
143 D8 **Ballard, L** W Australia
80 F4 **Ballas** Jordan
15 E3 **Ballater** Scotland
12 D5 **Ballaugh** I of Man U.K.
28 F4 **Balle** Denmark
21 E6 **Ballée** France
28 F5 **Ballen** Denmark
133 C3 **Ballena,Pta** *C* Chile
33 O9 **Ballenstedt** E Germany
146 K5 **Balleny I** Antarctica
20 D3 **Balleroy** France
28 K5 **Ballerup** Denmark
112 C3 **Ball Ground** Georgia
75 L6 **Ballia** India
14 B2 **Ballina** Irish Rep
14 C3 **Ballinasloe** Irish Rep
14 C3 **Ballindine** Irish Rep
28 B3 **Balling** Denmark
14 C4 **Ballingarry** Irish Rep
108 H4 **Ballinger** Texas
15 E4 **Ballinluig** Scotland
14 B3 **Ballinrobe** Irish Rep
14 A5 **Ballinskelligs B** Irish Rep
37 J6 **Ballmertshofen** W Germany
118 B7 **Ball,Mt** Alberta
12 D1 **Balloch** Scotland
20 F5 **Ballon** France
19 K5 **Ballon d'Alsace** *mt* France
21 C6 **Ballots** France
137 M8 **Ball's Pyramid** *isld* Pacific Oc
37 K1 **Ballstädt** E Germany
95 O4 **Ballston Spa** New York
28 B6 **Ballum** Denmark
14 E2 **Ballybay** Irish Rep
14 D2 **Ballybofey** Irish Rep
14 B4 **Ballybunnion** Irish Rep
14 B2 **Ballycastle** Irish Rep
14 E1 **Ballycastle** N Ireland
14 E2 **Ballyclare** N Ireland
14 D2 **Ballyconnell** Irish Rep
14 D5 **Ballycotton B** Irish Rep
14 C4 **Ballyduff** Irish Rep
14 C3 **Ballygar** Irish Rep
14 D2 **Ballygawley** N Ireland
12 B2 **Ballygrant** Scotland
14 D2 **Ballyhaise** Irish Rep
14 C3 **Ballyhaunis** Irish Rep
14 C4 **Ballyhoura Hills** Irish Rep
14 D3 **Ballyjamesduff** Irish Rep
14 D3 **Ballymahon** Irish Rep
14 E2 **Ballymena** N Ireland
14 E1 **Ballymoney** N Ireland
14 C2 **Ballymote** Irish Rep
14 F2 **Ballynahinch** N Ireland
14 F2 **Ballyquintin Pt** N Ireland
14 D4 **Ballyragget** Irish Rep
14 C2 **Ballyshannon** Irish Rep
14 E3 **Ballytore** Irish Rep
14 B3 **Ballyvaghan** Irish Rep
12 D3 **Balmaclellan** Scotland
12 D1 **Balmaha** Scotland
95 M2 **Balmat** New York
48 G3 **Balmazújváros** Hungary
40 F7 **Balme** Italy
40 G5 **Balmhorn** *mt* Switzerland
119 U8 **Balmoral** Manitoba
144 D5 **Balmoral** New Zealand
138 F6 **Balmoral** Victoria
141 K1 **Balmoral** *dist* Brisbane, Qnsld
15 E3 **Balmoral Castle** Scotland
113 L9 **Balmoral I** *isld* New Providence I Bahamas
108 D5 **Balmorhea** Texas
13 F1 **Balmullo** Scotland
139 J2 **Balonne** *R* Queensland
141 J8 **Balonne R** Queensland
55 D2 **Balotovskoye** U.S.S.R.
74 E6 **Balotra** India
33 P6 **Balow** E Germany
12 D1 **Balquhidder** Scotland
75 K5 **Balrampur** India
48 J6 **Balş** Romania
99 O4 **Balsam L** Wisconsin
121 M8 **Balsam Lake** Ontario
129 J5 **Balsas** Brazil
124 H8 **Balsas** *R* Mexico
26 K2 **Balsfjord** Norway
26 K2 **Balsfjord** *inlet* Norway
45 P6 **Balsorano** Italy
26 G3 **Balstad** Norway
98 F1 **Balta** N Dakota
48 M3 **Balta** U.S.S.R.
16 E3 **Baltanás** Spain
16 B3 **Baltar** Spain
133 F4 **Baltasar Brum** Uruguay
98 K6 **Baltic** S Dakota
27 H16 **Baltic Sea** N Europe
79 B7 **Baltîm** Egypt
14 B5 **Baltimore** Irish Rep
95 L7 **Baltimore** Maryland
87 E10 **Baltimore** S Africa
97 **Baltimore** *conurbation* Maryland
14 E4 **Baltinglass** Irish Rep
Baltit *see* **Hunza**
31 M1 **Baltiysk** U.S.S.R.
32 F5 **Baltrum** W Germany
80 G8 **Balu** Jordan
80 G8 **Balu** *R* Jordan
77 G6 **Balūchestān va Sīstān** Iran
74 A4 **Baluchistan** *reg* Pakistan
70 C3 **Balui** *R* Sarawak
71 E7 **Balukbaluk** *isld* Philippines
75 N6 **Balurghat** India
71 G8 **Balut** *isld* Philippines
32 G10 **Balve** W Germany
52 C6 **Balvi** U.S.S.R.
47 J5 **Balya** Turkey
84 J4 **Balyana,El** Egypt
56 H4 **Bal Yeravnoye, Oz** *L* U.S.S.R.
56 C4 **Balyksa** U.S.S.R.
56 E5 **Balyktyg Khem** *R* U.S.S.R.
118 C7 **Balzac** Alberta
77 F5 **Bam** Iran
67 B4 **Bama** China
86 B3 **Bama** Nigeria
141 F1 **Bamaga** Queensland
85 C6 **Bamako** Mali
128 C5 **Bambamarca** Peru
71 E3 **Bamban** Luzon Philippines
71 E2 **Bambang** Luzon Philippines
71 E8 **Bambannan** *isld* Philippines
86 D4 **Bambari** Cent Afr Republic
141 H4 **Bambaroo** Queensland
69 C11 **Bambel** Sumatra
13 F6 **Bamber Br** England
112 F4 **Bamberg** S Carolina
37 K4 **Bamberg** W Germany
86 E5 **Bambesa** Zaïre
86 E5 **Bambili** Zaïre
86 C5 **Bambio** Cent Afr Republic
27 D13 **Bamble** Norway
142 D5 **Bamboo Creek** W Australia
142 C5 **Bamboo Springs** W Australia
83 M13 **Bambou Mt** Mauritius
130 F7 **Bambui** Brazil
13 G2 **Bamburgh** England
66 E5 **Bam Co** *L* China
86 B4 **Bamenda** Cameroon
117 L11 **Bamfield** Br Col
77 K2 **Bamian** Afghanistan
67 C4 **Bamian** China
65 F3 **Bamiancheng** China
Bamiantong *see* **Muling**
86 C4 **Bamingui** *R* Cent Afr Republic
77 K2 **Bāmīyān** Afghanistan
68 G6 **Bam Nak** Cambodia
68 E5 **Bamnet Narong** Thailand
124 E5 **Bamoa** Mexico
69 A8 **Bampoka I** Nicobar Is
77 H6 **Bam Posht, Kūh-e** *mts* Iran
8 C6 **Bampton** England
9 E4 **Bampton** Oxon England
77 G6 **Bampūr** Iran
77 G6 **Bampur** *R* Iran
68 H4 **Ba Na** Vietnam
137 O1 **Banaba** *isld* Pacific Oc
129 L5 **Banabuiu Açude** *res* Brazil
14 D3 **Banagher** Irish Rep
71 E4 **Banahao, Mt** Luzon Philippines
86 E5 **Banalia** Zaïre
68 G7 **Banam** Cambodia
85 C6 **Banamba** Mali
124 D2 **Banámichi** Mexico
68 G5 **Ban Amnat** Thailand
141 K6 **Banana** Queensland
129 H6 **Bananal, Ilha do** Brazil
113 G9 **Banana R** Florida
130 J9 **Bananeiras** Brazil
76 G7 **Bananga** Nicobar Is
68 F6 **Ban Aranyaprathet** Thailand
47 J3 **Banarlı** Turkey
69 D8 **Ba Na San** Thailand
48 F6 **Banat Novo Selo** Yugoslavia
15 C4 **Banavie** Scotland
71 J8 **Banawaja** *isld* Indonesia
78 B2 **Banaz** Turkey
68 E4 **Ban Bang Mun Nak** Thailand
68 E4 **Ban Bang Rakam** Thailand
71 G6 **Banbayan Pt** Mindanao Philippines
69 E10 **Ban Betong** Thailand
68 J6 **Ban Bik** Vietnam
14 E2 **Banbridge** N Ireland
68 E5 **Ban Bua Chum** Thailand
68 F5 **Ban Bua Yai** Thailand
68 E5 **Ban Bu Khanum** Thailand
68 H5 **Ban Bung Sai** Laos
9 E3 **Banbury** England
71 C6 **Bancalan** Palawan Philippines
138 F4 **Bancannia, L** New S Wales
68 D3 **Ban Chang Khoeng** Thailand
68 F4 **Ban Channabot** Thailand
68 D3 **Ban Chiang Dao** Thailand
15 F3 **Banchory** Scotland
68 E4 **Ban Chum Phae** Thailand
125 Q8 **Banco Chinchorro** *isld* Mexico
71 D7 **Bancoron** *isld* Philippines
101 O7 **Bancroft** Idaho
99 M6 **Bancroft** Iowa
121 N7 **Bancroft** Ontario
98 J5 **Bancroft** S Dakota
48 J4 **Band** Romania
74 J6 **Banda** India
69 B10 **Banda Aceh** Sumatra
69 C11 **Bandahara, Gunung** *mt* Sumatra
61 N7 **Bandai-Asahi Nat.Pk** Japan
61 O8 **Bandai-san** *mt* Japan
85 B7 **Bandajuma** Sierra Leone
27 C12 **Bandak** *L* Norway
136 G2 **Banda, Kep.** *isld* Indonesia
85 C7 **Bandama** *R* Ivory Coast
77 G4 **Bandan Kuh** *mt* Iran
Bandar *see* **Machilipatnam**
77 J2 **Bandar** Afghanistan
87 F9 **Bandar** Mozambique
75 J4 **Bandar** Nepal
77 E6 **Bandar 'Abbās** Iran
77 A1 **Bandar Anzalī** Iran
77 B4 **Bandar-e Deylam** Iran
77 D6 **Bandar-e Khoemir** Iran
77 D6 **Bandar-e Lengeh** Iran
77 A4 **Bandar-e Ma'shūr** Iran
77 B5 **Bandar-e Rīg** Iran
77 D1 **Bandar-e Shah** Iran
77 A4 **Bandar Khomeynī** Iran
70 D2 **Bandar Seri Begawan** Brunei
83 H1 **Bandar Shah** Iran
136 F3 **Banda Sea** Indonesia
71 C7 **Bandau** Sabah
88 E7 **Bandawe** Malawi
22 J3 **Bande** Belgium
16 B2 **Bande** Spain
129 K8 **Bandeira** *mt* Brazil
130 H7 **Bandeira** *mt* Brazil
130 E8 **Bandeirantes** Brazil
130 D8 **Bandeirantes, I. dos** Brazil
87 B8 **Bandeira, Sa da** Angola
106 D6 **Bandelier Nat.Mon** New Mexico
77 D6 **Band-e Moghūyeh** Iran
109 H6 **Bandera** Texas
108 B4 **Banderas** Mexico
124 G7 **Banderas,B de** Mexico
28 G7 **Bandholm** Denmark
85 D6 **Bandiagara** Mali
77 K2 **Band-i-Amur** *R* Afghanistan
77 J2 **Band-i-Balan** *mts* Afghanistan
78 B1 **Bandirma** Turkey
47 J4 **Bandirma Körfezi** *gulf* Turkey
77 J2 **Band-i-Turkestan** *mts* Afghanistan
70 M9 **Bandjar** Java
70 D6 **Bandjermasin** Kalimantan
70 M9 **Bandjarnegara** Java
19 P18 **Bandol** France
Ban Don *see* **Surat Thani**
14 C5 **Bandon** Irish Rep
100 A6 **Bandon** Oregon
68 H6 **Ban Don** Vietnam
14 C5 **Bandon** *R* Irish Rep
68 G4 **Ban Dong** Laos
68 F4 **Ban Don Khi** Thailand
74 E9 **Bandra** India
86 C6 **Bandundu** Zaïre
70 L9 **Bandung** Java
69 F12 **Bandung** Sumatra
68 G4 **Ban Dupre** Laos
94 F9 **Bandy** Virginia
143 D8 **Bandya** W Australia
48 K6 **Băneasa** Romania
48 L5 **Băneasa** Romania
78 K4 **Baneh** Iran
71 B2 **Banema** Halmahera Indonesia
17 G6 **Bañeras** Spain
126 G4 **Banes** Cuba
118 B7 **Banff** Alberta
15 F3 **Banff** Scotland
Banff *co see* **Grampian** *reg*
85 D6 **Banfora** Upper Volta
86 D7 **Banga** Zaïre
71 F7 **Bangaan** Mindanao Philippines
71 G7 **Bangai Pt** Mindanao Philippines
71 E7 **Bangalao** *isld* Philippines
76 C4 **Bangalore** India
71 E2 **Bangar** Luzon Philippines
70 D2 **Bangar** Sarawak
27 H12 **Bångbro** Sweden
86 C5 **Bangé** Cameroon
110 E4 **Bangert** Missouri
70 C4 **Bang,G** *mt* Kalimantan
71 H6 **Banggai, Kep** *islds* Indonesia
71 C7 **Banggi** *isld* Sabah
68 G4 **Bang Hieng** *R* Laos
70 O9 **Bangil** Java
71 J4 **Bangka** Sulawesi Indonesia
69 G14 **Bangka** *isld* Indonesia
70 C8 **Bangkal** Kalimantan
70 F7 **Bangkala** Sulawesi Indonesia
70 O9 **Bangkalan** Java
69 C11 **Bangkaru** *isld* Sumatra
69 G14 **Bangka,Selat** *str* Sumatra
70 G4 **Bangkir** Sulawesi Indonesia
69 F14 **Bangko** Sumatra
68 E6 **Bangkok** Thailand
63 **Bangkok** *conurbation* China
68 E6 **Bangkok,Bight of** Thailand
71 H5 **Bangkulu** Sulawesi Indonesia
75 N6 **Bangladesh** *rep* S Asia
68 E6 **Bang Lamung** Thailand
68 J7 **Ba Ngoi** Vietnam
66 B5 **Bangong Co** *L* China
95 T2 **Bangor** Maine
94 A4 **Bangor** Michigan
14 F2 **Bangor** N Ireland
95 M6 **Bangor** Pennsylvania
119 P8 **Bangor** Sask
8 B1 **Bangor** Wales
86 C4 **Bangoran** *R* Cent Afr Republic
109 H4 **Bangs** Texas
70 E5 **Bangsalsembera** Kalimantan
68 D7 **Bang Saphan Yai** Thailand
28 F2 **Bangsbostrand** Denmark
103 L5 **Bangs,Mt** Arizona
26 E7 **Bangsund** Norway
71 E2 **Bangued** Luzon Philippines
86 C5 **Bangui** Cent Afr Republic
71 E1 **Bangui** Luzon Philippines
69 D11 **Bangunpurba** Sumatra
88 B7 **Bangweulu, L** Zambia
68 F3 **Ban Hai** Laos
68 D4 **Ban Hat Sao** Thailand
69 E9 **Ban Hat Yai** Thailand
68 F3 **Ban Hin Heup** Laos
68 J6 **Ban Ho** Vietnam
68 E2 **Ban Houei Sai** Laos
68 D6 **Ban Hua Hin** Thailand
68 F3 **Ban Huai Kho** Thailand
68 D7 **Ban Huai Yang** Thailand
116 L7 **Ban I** Alaska
86 D4 **Bani** Cent Afr Republic
127 J5 **Baní** Dominican Rep
71 D2 **Bani** Luzon Philippines
85 C6 **Bani** *R* Mali
85 E5 **Bani Bangou** Niger
127 J5 **Bánica** Dominican Rep
31 H2 **Banie** Poland
71 D3 **Bani Pt** Luzon Philippines
94 H10 **Banister** *R* Virginia
77 D6 **Bani Tunb** *isld* Iran
84 E3 **Bani Walid** Libya
79 F3 **Bāniyās** Syria
80 F1 **Bāniyās** Syria
48 E6 **Banja Koviljača** Yugoslavia
42 H4 **Banja Luka** Yugoslavia
68 H6 **Ban Jeng Drom** Vietnam
85 A6 **Banjul** The Gambia
70 M9 **Banjumas** Java
142 B3 **Banjup** *dist* Perth, W Aust
70 P10 **Banjuwangi** Java
140 C4 **Banka Banka** N Terr Aust
68 G5 **Ban Kadiene** Laos
68 E4 **Ban Kaeng** Thailand
69 E9 **Ban Kam Phaeng Phet** Thailand
69 D9 **Ban Kantang** Thailand
89 D9 **Bankberg** *mts* S Africa
12 E3 **Bankend** Scotland
68 H5 **Ban Keng Phao** Cambodia
68 F2 **Ban Keo Lom** Vietnam
68 E6 **Ban Khai** Thailand
68 F1 **Ban Khang Kha** Vietnam
68 D6 **Ban Khao Yoi** Thailand
111 J8 **Bankhead L** Alabama
68 G4 **Ban Khemmarat** Thailand
68 E3 **Ban Khing** Laos
68 F6 **Ban Khlung** Thailand
69 D8 **Ban Khok Kloi** Thailand
69 D9 **Ban Khuan Mao** Thailand
68 E3 **Ban Khun Ban Hai** Thailand
68 F5 **Ban Khu Noi** Thailand
68 C3 **Ban Khun Yuam** Thailand
68 J6 **Ban Kniet** Vietnam
70 E7 **Bankobankoang** *isld* Indonesia
68 D4 **Ban Krai** Thailand
100 J5 **Banks** Idaho
100 B4 **Banks** Oregon
138 F7 **Banks,C** S Australia
138 D5 **Bank's Group** *isld* S Australia
117 H9 **Banks I** Br Columbia
147 J2 **Banks I** N W Terr
141 F1 **Banks I** Queensland
100 F2 **Banks L** Washington
144 D5 **Banks Peninsula** New Zealand
139 K7 **Bankstown Airfield** Sydney, New S Wales
68 D6 **Ban Kui Nua** Thailand
75 M7 **Bankura** India
68 G4 **Ban Kut Hae** Thailand
46 F2 **Bankya** Bulgaria
68 F5 **Ban Lamduan** Thailand
71 F3 **Banla Pt** Philippines
68 D5 **Ban Le Kathe** Thailand
68 E5 **Ban Len** Thailand
68 C3 **Ban Mae La Luang** Thailand
68 D3 **Ban Mae Mo** Thailand
68 D4 **Ban Mae Ramat** Thailand
68 C3 **Ban Mae Sariang** Thailand
68 D4 **Ban Mae Sot** Thailand
68 D3 **Ban Mae Suai** Thailand
68 D3 **Ban Mae Thalop** Thailand
68 J6 **Ban Me Thout** Vietnam
68 D3 **Ban Mong Pong** Thailand
68 E3 **Ban Muang** Thailand
68 F6 **Ban Muang** Thailand
68 F5 **Ban Muang Phon** Thailand
14 E4 **Bann** *R* Irish Rep
14 E2 **Bann** *R* N Ireland
71 E1 **Banna** Luzon Philippines
69 D8 **Ban Na** Thailand
68 F4 **Ban Na Baek** Thailand
68 H4 **Ban Nabo** Laos
101 N4 **Bannack** Montana
68 G4 **Ban Na Kae** Thailand
68 E3 **Ban Na Kon** Thailand
68 E2 **Ban Na Mo** Laos
68 E4 **Ban Nam Pong** Thailand
68 F1 **Ban Nam Sau** Vietnam
68 E3 **Ban Na Noi** Thailand
68 F3 **Ban Naphong** Laos
68 F3 **Ban Na Sabaeng** Thailand
69 E9 **Ban Na Thawi** Thailand
142 F4 **Bannerman, Mt** W Australia
126 F2 **Bannerman Town** Eleuthera Bahamas
68 F4 **Ban Ngon** Thailand
102 H8 **Banning** California
Banningville *see* **Bandundu**
40 H6 **Bannio** Italy
144 B6 **Bannockburn** New Zealand
121 N8 **Bannockburn** Ontario
12 E1 **Bannockburn** Scotland
101 M5 **Bannock Pass** Idaho/Montana
101 N7 **Bannock Ra** Idaho
68 C4 **Ban Noi** Thailand
68 E2 **Ban Nong Kha** Laos
68 F5 **Ban Nong Makha** Thailand
68 H5 **Ban Nong Met** Laos
68 F5 **Ban Nong Waeng** Thailand
74 D2 **Bannu** Pakistan
17 J2 **Bañolas** Spain
19 P16 **Banon** France
124 H6 **Bañón** Mexico
31 L7 **Bánovce** Czechoslovakia
68 F3 **Ban Pacpeup** Laos
68 D3 **Ban Pak Bong** Thailand
68 D7 **Ban Pak Chan** Thailand
68 D6 **Ban Pak Khlong** Thailand
68 D7 **Ban Pak Nam** Thailand
68 E6 **Ban Pak Nam** Thailand
68 E3 **Ban Pak Neun** Laos
69 E8 **Ban Pak Phanang** Thailand
68 F5 **Ban Pak Thong Chai** Thailand
68 E5 **Ban Phachi** Thailand
68 G4 **Ban Phaeng** Thailand
68 F5 **Ban Phai** Thailand
68 E6 **Ban Phanat Nikhom** Thailand
68 H5 **Ban Phone** Laos
68 G5 **Ban Phon Ngam** Thailand
68 F4 **Ban Phon Thong** Thailand
68 D5 **BanPhot Phisai** Thailand
68 D4 **Ban Phran Katai** Thailand
68 E4 **Ban Phrom Phirom** Thailand
68 F5 **Ban Phutthaisong** Thailand
Ban Pla Soi *see* **Chon Buri**
68 D6 **Ban Pong** Thailand
67 A3 **Banqiao** China
65 D7 **Banquan** China
68 D4 **Ban Saen To** Thailand
68 E2 **Ban Sai** Laos
68 F5 **Ban Sai** Thailand
68 D5 **Ban Sai Yok** Thailand
69 E9 **Ban Sanam Chai** Thailand
68 F5 **Ban Sangae** Thailand
68 E5 **Ban Sao** Thailand
68 D3 **Ban Saraphi Chae Hom** Thailand
68 E6 **Ban Sattahip** Thailand
68 D7 **Ban Sawi** Thailand
74 E8 **Bansda** India
75 K5 **Bansi** India
69 E8 **Ban Sichon** Thailand
68 E6 **Ban Si Racha** Thailand
31 L7 **Banská Bystrica** Czechoslovakia
31 L7 **Banská Stiavnica** Czechoslovakia
47 F3 **Bansko** Bulgaria
68 D3 **Ban Sop Huai Hai** Thailand
68 D4 **Ban Sop Prap** Thailand
68 G3 **Ban Sot** Laos
68 D4 **Ban Sut Ta** Thailand
74 F7 **Banswara** India
71 J9 **Banta** *isld* Sumbawa Indonesia
70 F7 **Bantaeng** Sulawesi Indonesia
69 E12 **Bantaian** Sumatra
68 E5 **Ban Ta Khli** Thailand
69 D8 **Ban Takua Pa** Thailand
69 E13 **Bantal** Sumatra
68 F5 **Ban Tan** Thailand
68 F6 **Ban Ta Ruang** Thailand
68 H4 **Ban Taup** Laos
68 F3 **Ban Ta Viang** Laos
71 F5 **Bantayan** *isld* Philippines
32 L8 **Banteln** W Germany
70 L9 **Banten** Java
69 D8 **Ban Tha Chang** Thailand
69 D8 **Ban Thai Muang** Thailand
69 D8 **Ban Tha Kham** Thailand
68 F4 **Ban Tha Lat** Thailand
68 G5 **Ban Tham Khae** Thailand
68 D5 **Ban Thap Phung** Thailand
69 E8 **Ban Tha Sala** Thailand
68 D4 **Ban Tha Song Yang** Thailand
68 E5 **Ban Tha Tako** Thailand
68 H5 **Ban Thateng** Laos
68 G4 **Ban Tha Uthen** Thailand
69 E9 **Ban Thepha** Thailand
22 J5 **Bantheville** France
68 D6 **Ban Thung Luang** Thailand
71 F4 **Banton** *isld* Philippines
68 H6 **Ban Treo** Cambodia
14 B5 **Bantry** Irish Rep
98 F1 **Bantry** N Dakota
14 B5 **Bantry B** Irish Rep
70 N9 **Bantul** Java
74 D8 **Bantva** India
76 B4 **Bantval** India
68 F4 **Ban Waeng Noi** Thailand
68 E4 **Ban Wang Saphong** Thailand
68 G4 **Ban Wang Ta Mua** Thailand
8 D5 **Banwell** England
47 G2 **Banya** Bulgaria
69 C11 **Banyak, Kep.** *isld* Indonesia
68 F4 **Ban Yang Talat** Thailand
68 D6 **Ban Yang Yong** Thailand
68 H6 **Ban Ya Soup** Vietnam
86 B4 **Banyo** Cameroon
141 K1 **Banyo** *dist* Brisbane, Qnsld
69 G14 **Banyuasin** *R* Sumatra
37 L3 **Banz** W Germany
146 G3 **Banzare Coast** Antarctica
81 E11 **Banzare Seamount** Southern Oc
67 B4 **Bao'an** China
67 E5 **Bao'an** China
58 F4 **Baode** China
65 D5 **Baodi** China
58 G4 **Baoding** China
65 B7 **Baofeng** China
67 A5 **Bao Ha** Vietnam
65 D4 **Bao He** *R* China
58 E5 **Baoji** China
67 C2 **Baojing** China
Baokang *see* **Horqin Zouyi Zhongqi**
67 D1 **Baokang** China
68 G1 **Bao Lac** Vietnam
65 F3 **Baolizhen** China
68 H7 **Bao Loc** Vietnam
65 J1 **Baoqing** China
67 G1 **Baoshan** China
68 J3 **Baoting** China
58 E3 **Baotou** China
85 C6 **Baoulé** *R* Mali
59 G5 **Baoying** China
Baoyou *see* **Ledong**
76 E3 **Bapatla** India
22 D3 **Bapaume** France
103 N8 **Bapchule** Arizona
121 M7 **Baptiste** Ontario
Bapu *see* **Liucheng**
70 D6 **Bapuju** Kalimantan
80 D4 **Bāqa el Gharbiya** Israel
66 E5 **Baqên** China
79 F9 **Bāqir, J** *mt* Jordan
78 K5 **Ba'Qūbah** Iraq
80 F3 **Baqura** Jordan
48 L1 **Bar** U.S.S.R.
42 J6 **Bar** Yugoslavia
22 H4 **Bar** *R* France
86 F3 **Bara** Sudan
70 D6 **Barabai** Kalimantan
55 G3 **Barabinsk** U.S.S.R.
50 G3 **Barabinskaya Step'** U.S.S.R.
141 G5 **Barabon** Queensland
99 R6 **Baraboo** Wisconsin
122 H5 **Barachois** Quebec
126 G4 **Baracoa** Cuba
47 L7 **Baradis** Turkey
99 S3 **Baraga** Michigan
86 G5 **Baragoi** Kenya
127 J5 **Barahona** Dom Rep
57 F6 **Barak** Afghanistan
88 B4 **Baraka** Zaïre
75 L8 **Barakot** India
141 K7 **Barakula** Queensland
141 J6 **Baralaba** Queensland
80 E1 **Bar'am** Israel
70 D3 **Baram** *R* Sarawak
128 G2 **Barama** *R* Guyana
74 F9 **Baramati** India
141 K7 **Barambah** *R* Queensland
70 C2 **Baram,Tg** *C* Sarawak
74 G6 **Baran** India
54 B2 **Baran'** U.S.S.R.
75 N7 **Baranagar** India
55 C2 **Baranchinskiy** U.S.S.R.
45 R6 **Baranello** Italy
86 E5 **Baranga** Zaïre
71 K8 **Barangbarang** Indonesia
21 J7 **Barangeon** *R* France
77 G4 **Baran, Kūh-e-** *mts* Iran
126 G9 **Baranoa** Colombia
117 F7 **Baranof I** Alaska
31 N5 **Baranów** Poland
48 E5 **Baranya** *co* Hungary
129 G6 **Barao de Capenema** Brazil
130 C5 **Barão de Melgaço** Mato Grosso Brazil
48 K4 **Baraolt** Romania
48 K4 **Baraoltului Munti** *mt* Romania
22 K3 **Baraque-le Fraiture** Belgium
22 L2 **Baraque Michel** Belgium
70 L9 **Barat** Java
70 B5 **Barat** Kalimantan
111 F12 **Barataria** Louisiana
111 G12 **Barataria B** Louisiana
71 N8 **Barat Daya, Kep** *islds* Philippines
71 L9 **Barate** Indonesia
138 E4 **Baratta** S Australia
75 M6 **Barauni** India
130 G7 **Barbacena** Minas Gerais Brazil
128 C3 **Barbacoas** Colombia
78 M1 **Barbadag** *mt* U.S.S.R.
127 P6 **Barbados** Lesser Antilles
130 G9 **Barbalha** Brazil
45 O4 **Bárbara** Italy
120 C3 **Barbara L** Ontario
45 L1 **Barbarano Vicentino** Italy
85 A4 **Barbas,C** Mauritania
21 A8 **Barbâtre** France
122 D2 **Barbel,L** Quebec
100 J6 **Barber** Idaho
45 K3 **Barberino di Mugello** Italy
45 K4 **Barberino di Val d'Elsa** Italy
102 R12 **Barbers Pt** Hawaiian Is
94 F5 **Barberton** Ohio
89 G5 **Barberton** S Africa
113 F8 **Barberville** Florida
18 E7 **Barbezieux** France
45 J4 **Barbona, M** *mt* Italy
128 D2 **Barbosa** Colombia
48 L5 **Barbosi** Romania
94 J8 **Barboursville** Virginia
110 N5 **Barbourville** Kentucky
127 O6 **Barbuda** *isld* Lesser Antilles
33 P9 **Barby** E Germany
16 C4 **Barca d'Alva** Portugal
126 A2 **Barcadera** Aruba W I
126 A2 **Barcadera** Bonaire W I
141 H6 **Barcaldine** Queensland
16 C6 **Barcarrota** Spain
17 J3 **Barcelona** Spain
127 M9 **Barcelona** Venezuela
17 J3 **Barcelona** *prov* Spain
128 F4 **Barcelos** Brazil
16 B3 **Barcelos** Portugal
37 J2 **Barchfeld** E Germany
19 P16 **Barcillonnette** France
31 K3 **Barcin** Poland
103 K4 **Barclay** Nevada
112 L1 **Barco** N Carolina
136 J6 **Barcoo** *R* Queensland
141 G6 **Barcoo Cr** Queensland/S Aust
141 H6 **Barcoorah, L** Queensland
48 D5 **Barcs** Hungary
106 G6 **Bard** New Mexico
84 F5 **Bardai** Chad
47 L5 **Bardakçi** Turkey
31 N6 **Bardejov** Czechoslovakia
33 R8 **Bardenitz** E Germany
86 H5 **Bardera** Somalia
28 M2 **Bardhidh** *C* Faeroes
139 J4 **Bardine** New S Wales
84 G3 **Bardiyah** Libya
9 F1 **Bardney** England
143 D9 **Bardoc** W Australia
41 N6 **Bardolino** Italy
122 E2 **Bardoux,L** Quebec
33 M6 **Bardowick** W Germany
13 E5 **Bardsea** England
8 B2 **Bardsey** *isld* Wales
110 L4 **Bardstown** Kentucky
26 K3 **Bardu** Norway
26 K3 **Barduelv** *R* Norway
141 H7 **Barduthulla** Queensland
110 G5 **Bardwell** Kentucky
109 L3 **Bardwell** Texas
145 F3 **Bare I** New Zealand
74 H4 **Bareilly** India
32 J7 **Barenburg** W Germany
37 O3 **Bärenstein** E Germany
20 G2 **Barentin** France
20 D4 **Barenton** France
22 F4 **Barenton-Bugny** France
50 B1 **Barentsöya** *isld* Spitzbergen
147 J13 **Barents Sea** Arctic Oc
86 G2 **Barentu** Ethiopia
70 D3 **Bareo** Sarawak
20 C2 **Barfleur** France
20 C2 **Barfleur, Pte. de** France
9 E3 **Barford** Warwicks England
9 E5 **Barford** Wilts England
66 C5 **Barga** China
45 H3 **Barga** Italy
86 B1 **Bargal** Somalia
141 K6 **Bargara** Queensland
75 K8 **Bargarh** India
16 E5 **Bargas** Spain
44 B2 **Barge** Italy
123 Q2 **Barge B** Labrador
33 T5 **Bargischow** E Germany
32 M5 **Bargteheide** W Germany
56 H3 **Barguzin** *R* U.S.S.R.
56 G4 **Barguzinskiy Khrebet** *mts* U.S.S.R.
56 G4 **Barguzinskiy Zaliv** *gulf* U.S.S.R.
95 T2 **Bar Harbor** Maine
75 L6 **Barhi** India
74 G5 **Bari** India
43 H7 **Bari** Italy
86 D4 **Bari** *R* Cent Afr Republic
128 E3 **Baria** *R* Venezuela
45 L2 **Baricella** Italy

Barielly — Bela 9

74 H4 Barielly India
44 G2 Barigazzo Monte Italy
85 F1 Barika Algeria
128 F2 Barima,Pta C Venezuela
127 J10 Barinas Venezuela
128 D2 Barinas Venezuela
110 D1 Baring Missouri
100 D2 Baring Washington
143 B6 Baring Downs W Australia
143 E10 Baring, Mt W Australia
28 D5 Båring Vig B Denmark
127 J10 Barinitas Venezuela
75 M8 Baripada India
130 E8 Bariri Brazil
84 J5 Bârîs Egypt
22 E4 Barisis France
70 D5 Barito R Kalimantan
19 Q17 Barjaude mt France
19 P17 Barjols France
84 E4 Barjuj watercourse Libya
28 K4 Barkåkra Sweden
58 D5 Barkam China
27 H11 Barken,N L Sweden
94 J3 Barker New York
143 D9 Barker L W Australia
117 N9 Barkerville Br Columbia
94 H5 Barkeyville Pennsylvania
9 G4 Barking England
120 H6 Bark L Ontario
110 J5 Barkley Res Kentucky
100 A1 Barkley Sound Br Columbia
140 E5 Barkly Downs Queensland
140 D4 Barkly Highway rd N Terr Aust
140 B5 Barkly, Mt N Terr Aust
136 H5 Barkly Tableland Qnsld/N Terr
89 D7 Barkly West S Africa
66 E3 Barkol China
99 T4 Bark River Michigan
108 G6 Barksdale Texas
47 L6 Barla Dağ mt Turkey
9 E1 Barlborough England
19 J4 Bar le Duc France
143 C8 Barlee L W Australia
143 B6 Barlee Ra W Australia
8 C5 Barle, R England
19 Q16 Barles France
43 G7 Barletta Italy
22 D3 Barlin France
31 J3 Barlinek Poland
27 K14 Barlingbo isld Gotland Sweden
32 E9 Barlo W Germany
32 L4 Barlohe W Germany
98 G2 Barlow N Dakota
100 D4 Barlow Pass Oregon
57 L2 Barlyk, Khr mts U.S.S.R.
13 H6 Barmby England
139 H5 Barmedman New S Wales
74 D6 Barmer India
138 F5 Barmera S Australia
8 B2 Barmouth Wales
32 L5 Barmstedt W Germany
122 G7 Barnaby River New Brunswick
74 F7 Barnagar India
107 N2 Barnard Kansas
98 H4 Barnard S Dakota
13 G4 Barnard Castle England
117 E6 Barnard,Mt Br Col/Alaska
37 N4 Bärnau W Germany
56 B4 Barnaul U.S.S.R.
56 B4 Barnaulka R U.S.S.R.
139 H8 Barn Bluff mt Tasmania
9 E1 Barnby Moor England
95 N7 Barnegat New Jersey
146 H7 Barne Inlet Antarctica
107 O2 Barnes Kansas
94 J6 Barnesboro Pennsylvania
115 M3 Barnes Icecap N W Terr
113 G12 Barnes Sd Florida
98 K9 Barneston Nebraska
112 C4 Barnesville Georgia
98 K3 Barnesville Minnesota
9 F4 Barnet England
25 E4 Barneveld Netherlands
20 B3 Barneville France
33 R7 Barnewitz E Germany
99 M8 Barney Iowa
103 N4 Barney Top mt Utah
108 F4 Barnhart Texas
33 T7 Barnim reg E Germany
122 F5 Barn Mtn Quebec
107 O5 Barnsdall Oklahoma
13 G6 Barnsley England
95 R5 Barnstable Massachusetts
8 B5 Barnstaple England
8 C6 Barnstaple Cross England
95 Q3 Barnstead New Hampshire
32 H7 Barnstorf W Germany
32 K9 Barntrup W Germany
99 O3 Barnum Minnesota
118 E9 Barnwell Alberta
112 F4 Barnwell S Carolina
37 P6 Bärnzell W Germany
85 F7 Baro Nigeria
86 F4 Baro R Ethiopia
Baroda see Vadodara
145 D4 Barometer mt New Zealand
22 K5 Baroncourt France
45 R8 Baronissi Italy
19 O16 Baronnies, Les reg France
118 D9 Barons Alberta
143 F6 Baron's Ra W Australia
36 B6 Baronville France
87 D8 Barotseland reg Zambia
75 O5 Barpeta India
80 D4 Barqay Israel
99 U4 Barques, Pt. Aux Michigan
127 K9 Barquisimeto Venezuela
98 B10 Barr Colorado
19 K4 Barr France
12 D3 Barr Scotland
129 K6 Barra Brazil
15 A3 Barra isld Scotland
130 E8 Barra Bonita Brazil
130 G5 Barracão Brazil
128 G5 Barracão do Barreto Brazil
89 B10 Barracouta,C S Africa
129 K6 Barra da Estiva Brazil
124 G8 Barra de Navidad Mexico
130 H8 Barra de sâ João Brazil
130 B4 Barra do Bugres Brazil
129 J5 Barra do Corda Brazil
130 H6 Barra do Cuieté Brazil
87 B7 Barra do Dande Angola
130 D4 Barra do Garças Brazil
130 F6 Barra do Paraopeba Brazil
130 G8 Barra do Pirai Brazil
129 G5 Barra do São Manuel Brazil
87 G10 Barra Falsa,Pta.da Mozambique
16 B5 Barragem de Maranhão res Portugal
16 B5 Barragem de Montargil Res Portugal
16 B5 Barragem do Castello do Bode Portugal
138 E6 Barrages S Australia
15 A4 Barra Head Scotland
129 K8 Barra Mansa Brazil
128 C4 Barranca Peru
128 D2 Barrancabermeja Colombia
127 H9 Barrancas Colombia
127 N10 Barrancas Venezuela
131 F2 Barrancas R Corrientes Argentina
131 B6 Barrancas,R Mendoza Argentina
130 B7 Barranco Branco Brazil
16 C6 Barrancos Portugal
133 F3 Barranqueras Argentina
126 G9 Barranquilla Colombia
13 F3 Barrasford England
121 N4 Barraute Quebec
19 P14 Barraux France
17 F5 Barrax Spain
95 P4 Barre Massachusetts
95 P2 Barre Vermont
20 G4 Barre-en-Ouche,la France
129 K6 Barreiras Brazil
129 G4 Barreirinha Brazil
129 K4 Barreirinhas Brazil
16 A6 Barreiro Portugal
130 D4 Barreiro R Brazil
130 J10 Barreiros Brazil
110 K5 Barren R Kentucky
68 A6 Barren I Andaman Is
116 L7 Barren Is Alaska
19 P16 Barret de Lioure France
129 J8 Barretos Brazil
102 H9 Barrett L California
142 F4 Barrett, Mt W Australia
118 C4 Barrhead Alberta
12 D2 Barrhead Scotland
15 D5 Barrhill Scotland
8 C5 Barri Wales
115 M9 Barrie Ontario
120 H7 Barrie I Ontario
145 E2 Barrier, C New Zealand
117 N10 Barrière Br Columbia
99 S7 Barrington Illinois
141 H8 Barrington New S Wales
122 G10 Barrington Nova Scotia
119 R1 Barrington L Manitoba
141 H8 Barringun New S Wales
129 L6 Barris R Brazil
28 D5 Barrit Denmark
101 M9 Barro Utah
130 E4 Barro Alto Brazil
100 E1 Barron Washington
99 P4 Barron Wisconsin
99 P4 Barronett Wisconsin
141 H3 Barron Falls & Gorge Queensland
109 J8 Barroso Texas
124 J4 Barroterán Mexico
21 G8 Barrou France
116 J1 Barrow Alaska
133 E5 Barrow Argentina
14 E4 Barrow R Irish Rep
140 D2 Barrow, C N Terr Aust
140 C5 Barrow Creek N Terr Aust
142 B5 Barrow I W Australia
13 E5 Barrow-in-Furness England
147 M2 Barrow,Pt Alaska
141 G2 Barrow Pt Queensland
143 F7 Barrow Ra W Australia
119 Q6 Barrows Manitoba
115 K3 Barrow Str N W Terr
143 D7 Barr Smith Ra W Australia
16 E2 Barruelo de Santullán Spain
110 E2 Barry Illinois
13 F1 Barry Scotland
121 N7 Barrys Bay Ontario
94 B3 Barryton Michigan
144 C5 Barrytown New Zealand
95 N5 Barryville New York
28 H6 Bårse Denmark
28 K5 Barsebäckshamn Sweden
76 B1 Barsi India
32 K8 Barsinghausen W Germany
28 D6 Barsø isld Denmark
32 G6 Barssel W Germany
102 G7 Barstow California
108 D4 Barstow Texas
54 J2 Barsuki U.S.S.R.
19 J4 Bar-sur-Aube France
18 H4 Bar-sur-Seine France
80 D4 Barta'a Jordan
36 H5 Bartenstein W Germany
116 Q1 Barter I Alaska
30 G1 Barth E Germany
146 B14 Barth Bank Antarctica
33 R4 Barthe R E Germany
81 B15 Barth Seamount S Atlantic Oc
122 G6 Bartibog New Brunswick
128 G2 Bartica Guyana
78 D1 Bartin Turkey
100 D8 Bartle California
141 H3 Bartle Frere,Mt Queensland
103 O2 Bartles,Mt Utah
107 P5 Bartlesville Oklahoma
98 H8 Bartlett Nebraska
95 Q2 Bartlett New Hampshire
109 K5 Bartlett Texas
143 E8 Bartlett Bluff W Australia
117 O4 Bartlett L N W Terr
103 N8 Bartlett Res Arizona
123 P3 Bartlett's Harbour Nfld
143 E8 Bartlett Soak L W Australia
98 F9 Bartley Nebraska
117 G8 Bartolome, C Alaska
87 G10 Bartolomeu Dias Mozambique
13 H6 Barton Humberside England
13 F6 Barton Lancs England
98 F1 Barton N Dakota
71 D5 Barton Palawan Philippines
138 C4 Barton S Australia
95 P2 Barton Vermont
94 D2 Barton City Michigan
9 G3 Barton Mills England
31 M1 Bartoszyce Poland
121 N4 Bartoville Quebec
33 S5 Bartow E Germany
113 F10 Bartow Florida
112 E5 Bartow Georgia
126 G9 Barú, I. de Colombia
69 E12 Barumun R Sumatra
70 O10 Barung isld Java
69 D11 Barus Sumatra
33 S8 Baruth E Germany
58 F2 Baruun Urt Mongolia
15 B2 Barvas Scotland
22 J3 Barvaux Belgium
54 J8 Barvenkovo U.S.S.R.
74 G7 Barwah India
74 F7 Barwani India
33 N7 Barwedel W Germany
113 D7 Barwick Georgia
99 N1 Barwick Ontario
143 D7 Barwidgee W Australia
140 B2 Barwolla, Mt N Terr Aust
141 F7 Baryulah Queensland
80 F7 Barza Jordan
77 D6 Basaidu Iran
106 D2 Basalt Colorado
101 N6 Basalt Idaho
102 F3 Basalt Nevada
141 H4 Basalt R Queensland
86 C5 Basankusu Zaïre
48 L6 Basarabi Romania
57 G2 Basaral, Ozero L U.S.S.R.
71 F6 Basay Negros Philippines
71 E8 Basbas Philippines
131 B2 Bascuñán,C Chile
32 K6 Basdahl W Germany
33 S7 Basdorf E Germany
22 F2 Basècles Belgium
40 G2 Basel Switzerland
40 G3 Baselland canton Switzerland
43 G8 Basento R Italy
48 K2 Başeul R Romania
71 G5 Basey Samar Philippines
77 F6 Bashākerd, Kūhhā-ye mts Iran
118 E6 Bashaw Alberta
56 B5 Bashchelakskiy Khrebet mts U.S.S.R.
89 F9 Bashee R S Africa
57 C5 Bashir U.S.S.R.
56 C5 Bashkaus R U.S.S.R.
50 E3 Bashkirskaya ASSR U.S.S.R.
71 F3 Basiad Bay Luzon Philippines
71 H5 Basiano Sulawesi Indonesia
71 F7 Basilan isld Mindanao Philippines
71 F7 Basilan Str Mindanao Philippines
9 G4 Basildon England
111 D11 Basile Louisiana
43 G8 Basilicata prov Italy
101 N3 Basin Montana
101 R5 Basin Wyoming
113 F10 Basinger Florida
9 E5 Basingstoke England
119 M6 Basin L Sask
95 U1 Baskahegan L Maine
78 K2 Başkale Turkey
121 P6 Baskatong, Rés Quebec
142 D3 Baskerville, C W Australia
Basle see Basel
9 E1 Baslow England
26 G5 Båsmoen Norway
41 H5 Basodino mt Switzerland
86 D5 Basoko Zaïre
86 D6 Basongo Zaïre
126 A2 Basora,Pt Aruba W I
77 A4 Basra Iran
83 G1 Basra Iraq
36 D6 Bas Rhin dep France
118 E8 Bassano Alberta
42 D3 Bassano Italy
85 E7 Bassari Togo
81 A8 Bassas da India isld Mozambique Chan
33 R5 Basse E Germany
22 D3 Bassée, la France
68 B4 Bassein Burma
76 A1 Bassein India
142 B1 Bassendean dist Perth, W Aust
22 K2 Bassenge Belgium
13 E4 Bassenthwaite L England
127 L4 Basse Pointe Martinique W I
127 M4 Basse Terre Guadeloupe W I
127 P4 Basseterre St Kitts W I
127 O3 Basse Terre Trinidad
98 G7 Bassett Nebraska
103 O9 Bassett Pk Arizona
22 F1 Bassevelde Belgium
111 G10 Bassfield Mississippi
85 E7 Bassila Benin
22 F2 Bassilly Belgium
102 E4 Bass Lake California
33 T10 Basslitz E Germany
122 J8 Bass River Nova Scotia
15 F4 Bass Rock Scotland
139 H7 Bass Strait Tasmania
32 J7 Bassum W Germany
119 R8 Basswood Manitoba
99 P1 Basswood L Ontario
19 P13 Bassy France
27 F15 Båstad Sweden
77 D6 Bastak Iran
77 D1 Bastam Iran
18 M10 Bastia Corsica
45 J2 Bastiglia Italy
123 M2 Bastille,L Quebec
22 K3 Bastogne Belgium
112 E4 Bastonville Georgia
111 E9 Bastrop Louisiana
109 K5 Bastrop Texas
26 L7 Bastuträsk Sweden
Basuo see Dongfang
Basutoland see Lesotho
55 D2 Bas'yanovskiy U.S.S.R.
86 B7 Bas Zaïre prov Zaïre
86 A5 Bata Equat Guinea
85 F8 Bata Mbini Eq Guinea
71 E3 Bataan Penin Luzon Philippines
126 C3 Batabanó, G. de Cuba
71 E1 Batac Luzon Philippines
71 G4 Batag isld Philippines
130 D7 Bataguaçu Brazil
47 G3 Batak Bulgaria
70 E5 Batakan Kalimantan
47 G3 Batak Dam Bulgaria
74 F3 Batala India
16 B5 Batalha Portugal
51 M2 Batamay U.S.S.R.
71 G4 Batan isld Philippines
58 C5 Batang China
70 M9 Batang Java
86 C4 Batangafo Cent Afr Republic
71 E4 Batangas Luzon Philippines
71 C3 Batangpele Waigeo Indonesia
69 D12 Batangtoru Sumatra
71 C3 Batanta isld W Irian
48 E4 Bataszék Hungary
130 F7 Batatais Brazil
Batavia see Jakarta
133 D4 Batavia Argentina
99 S8 Batavia Illinois
94 J3 Batavia New York
110 M2 Batavia Ohio
54 L9 Bataysk U.S.S.R.
71 E5 Batbatan Panay Philippines
120 F6 Batchawana Ontario
140 B2 Batchelor N Terr Aust
69 B10 Bateemucica, Gunung mt Sumatra
88 B6 Batembo Zaïre
61 P13 Baten Okinawa
25 E5 Batenburg Netherlands
56 D4 Batenevskiy Kryazh ridge U.S.S.R.
103 J9 Bateques Mexico
101 O6 Bates Idaho
100 G5 Bates Oregon
112 F4 Batesburg S Carolina
98 D6 Batesland S Dakota
143 E7 Bates,Mt W Australia
143 D7 Bates Ra W Australia
110 E6 Batesville Arkansas
110 L2 Batesville Indiana
111 G7 Batesville Mississippi
109 H7 Batesville Texas
52 D5 Batetskiy U.S.S.R.
8 D5 Bath England
110 F1 Bath Illinois
127 M3 Bath Jamaica
95 S3 Bath Maine
112 L2 Bath N Carolina
127 P4 Bath Nevis W I
122 E7 Bath New Brunswick
95 K4 Bath New York
112 F4 Bath S Carolina
98 H4 Bath S Dakota
86 C3 Batha R Chad
68 G6 Batheay Cambodia
98 J1 Bathgate N Dakota
12 E2 Bathgate Scotland
122 G6 Bathurst New Brunswick
139 J5 Bathurst New S Wales
Bathurst The Gambia see Banjul
141 G2 Bathurst Bay Queensland
114 G3 Bathurst,C N W Terr
136 G4 Bathurst I N Terr Australia
115 K2 Bathurst I N W Terr
114 J4 Bathurst Inlet N W Terr
142 E3 Bathurst Is W Australia
140 B1 Bathurst Island Mission Sta N Terr Aust
85 D7 Batié Upper Volta
70 G6 Batikala,Tg B Sulawesi Indonesia
48 E5 Batina Yugoslavia
78 L7 Batin, Wadi al Iraq
121 S6 Batiscan Quebec
121 T5 Batiscan,L Quebec
77 C3 Batlag-e-Gavkhuni Iran
13 G6 Batley England
85 F1 Batna Algeria
71 F4 Bato,L Luzon Philippines
111 E11 Baton Rouge Louisiana
86 B5 Batouri Cameroon
130 D4 Batovi Brazil
68 H7 Ba Tri Vietnam
42 H3 Batrina Yugoslavia
79 F4 Batroun Lebanon
26 R1 Båtsfjord Norway
80 D3 Bat Shelomo Israel
45 L1 Battáglia Terme Italy
68 F6 Battambang Cambodia
140 D3 Batten R N Terr Aust
36 F1 Battenberg W Germany
146 F12 Batterbee Mts Antarctica
143 C6 Batthewmurnarna mt W Aust
83 L10 Batticaloa Sri Lanka
22 K2 Battice Belgium
69 A8 Batti Malv isld Nicobar Is
45 R8 Battipaglia Italy
9 G6 Battle England
100 J7 Battle Cr Idaho
101 Q1 Battle Cr Montana
98 J8 Battle Cr Nebraska
140 B3 Battle Cr N Terr Aust
94 B4 Battle Creek Michigan
118 H9 Battle Creek Sask
118 J6 Battleford Sask
118 J5 Battlefords Prov.Park,The Sask
100 C4 Battle Ground Washington
115 O7 Battle Harbour Labrador
102 G1 Battle Mt Nevada
118 F6 Battle R Alberta
118 H6 Battle R Sask
98 D1 Battleview N Dakota
48 G4 Battonya Hungary
118 J8 Battrum Sask
70 D4 Batuajau, Bt mt Kalimantan
71 H8 Batuata isld Indonesia
69 H14 Batubetumbang Indonesia
70 D3 Batu Bora mt Sarawak
70 D4 Batubrok, Bt mt Kalimantan
70 G5 Batudaka Indonesia
70 C4 Batuensambang mt Kalimantan
69 E10 Batu Gajah Malaysia
71 H5 Batuhitam,Tg C Sulawesi Indonesia
71 L10 Batuidu Roti Indonesia
70 D4 Batuilangmebang, G mt Kalimantan
70 D4 Batukelau Kalimantan
70 P10 Batukou, Bt mt Bali Indonesia
70 D6 Batulitjin Kalimantan
70 D3 Batu Mabun mt Sarawak
78 H1 Batumi U.S.S.R.
69 D12 Batumundam Sumatra
69 F12 Batu Pahat Malaysia
69 C13 Batu,Pulaupulau isld Indonesia
70 F4 Batuputih Kalimantan
70 K8 Baturadja Sumatra Indonesia
70 N9 Baturetno Java
52 D6 Baturino U.S.S.R.
129 L4 Baturité Brazil
69 H14 Baturusa Indonesia
70 F3 Batu Tg B Kalimantan
70 C5 Batutinggi Kalimantan
80 B5 Bat Yam Israel
18 C4 Batz,I.de France
71 H7 Baubau Sulawesi Indonesia
86 A3 Bauchi Nigeria
18 C5 Baud France
75 L8 Baudh India
128 C2 Baudo, Sa. de mts Colombia
21 I7 Baudres France
19 Q17 Bauduen France
21 E6 Baugé France
19 Q13 Bauges dist France
140 D3 Bauhinia Downs N Terr Aust
141 J6 Bauhinia Downs Queensland
70 G7 Baula Sulawesi Indonesia
123 R2 Bauld,C Nfld
18 D5 Baule,la France
21 B6 Baulon France
41 J3 Bauma Switzerland
9 F1 Baumber England
19 K5 Baume les Dames France
33 T6 Baumgarten E Germany
37 O7 Baumgarten W Germany
36 C4 Baumholder W Germany
71 L10 Baun Timor Indonesia
37 K4 Baunach W Germany
37 K3 Baunach R W Germany
58 F1 Baunt U.S.S.R.
141 L7 Bauple Queensland
128 F6 Baures Bolivia
130 E8 Bauru Brazil
130 D6 Baús Brazil
52 B6 Bauska U.S.S.R.
31 H4 Bautzen E Germany
109 P1 Bauxite Arkansas
21 I8 Bauzanne R France
126 E10 Bavano L. Panama
107 N3 Bavaria Kansas
22 F3 Bavay France
89 C9 Baviaanskloofberge mts S Africa
124 E2 Bavispe Mexico
9 H2 Bawdeswell England
9 H3 Bawdsey England
70 O8 Bawean isld Java
32 F7 Bawinkel W Germany
84 H4 Bawîti Egypt
120 D3 Bawk Ontario
85 D6 Bawku Ghana
68 C3 Bawlake Burma
118 E6 Bawlf Alberta
68 A2 Bawli Bazar Burma
68 B4 Bawmi Burma
13 G6 Bawtry England
68 F1 Ba Xat Vietnam
58 G4 Ba Xian China
67 B2 Ba Xian China
66 D4 Baxkorgan China
112 E6 Baxley Georgia
99 N8 Baxter Iowa
99 M3 Baxter Minnesota
101 S10 Baxter Mt Colorado
110 B4 Baxter Springs Kansas
122 C7 Baxter State Park Maine
80 D3 Bayada Israel
126 F4 Bayamo Cuba
127 L5 Bayamón Puerto Rico
59 J2 Bayan China
58 E2 Bayan Mongolia
58 E2 Bayanchandman Mongolia
56 G4 Bayanday U.S.S.R.
Bayan Gol see Dengkou
58 C5 Bayan Har Shan China
58 D2 Bayanhongor Mongolia
65 E1 Bayan Hot China
65 A3 Bayan Hure China
Bayan Huxu see Horqin Youyi Zhongqi
58 E2 Bayanmönh Mongolia
65 C3 Bayan Nur Sum China
58 E3 Bayan Obo China
58 C3 Bayan-Öndör Mongolia
Bayan Qagan see Qahar Youyi Houqi
65 A1 Bayan Qagan China
65 E2 Bayan Qagan China
58 E2 Bayantsogt Mongolia
113 F7 Bayard Florida
99 M8 Bayard Iowa
98 C8 Bayard Nebraska
94 H7 Bayard W Virginia
19 Q15 Bayard, Col pass France
47 L6 Bayat Turkey
71 F6 Bayawan Negros Philippines
71 G5 Baybay Leyte Philippines
112 L2 Bayboro N Carolina
123 U6 Bay Bulls Nfld
78 H1 Bayburt Turkey
69 H8 Bay Canh, Hon isld Vietnam
94 D3 Bay City Michigan
100 B4 Bay City Oregon
109 M7 Bay City Texas
99 O5 Bay City Wisconsin
84 G3 Baydā,Al Libya
50 F2 Baydaratskaya Guba gulf U.S.S.R.
123 U5 Bay de Verde Nfld
123 R6 Bay du Nord Nfld
57 E3 Baydzhansay U.S.S.R.
37 P5 Bayer-Eisenstein W Germany
41 O2 Bayerische Alpen mt W Germany
37 K5 Bayern land W Germany
20 D3 Bayeux France
120 J9 Bayfield Ontario
99 Q3 Bayfield Wisconsin
123 O2 Bayfield I Quebec
122 E5 Bayfield Mtn Quebec
57 D3 Baygakum U.S.S.R.
55 D4 Baygara U.S.S.R.
98 A4 Bay Horse Montana
47 J6 Bayindır Turkey
55 D3 Baykalovo U.S.S.R.
56 G4 Baykal,Ozero L U.S.S.R.
56 G4 Baykal'skiy Khrebet mts U.S.S.R.
57 C2 Bay-Khozha U.S.S.R.
55 C3 Baykibashevo U.S.S.R.
56 E1 Baykit U.S.S.R.
57 D1 Baykonyr U.S.S.R.
71 E3 Bay, Laguna de Luzon Philippines
123 R6 Bay l'Argent Nfld
140 E3 Bayley Pt Queensland
55 C4 Baymak U.S.S.R.
111 J11 Bay Minette Alabama
9 E4 Baynard's Green England
71 E2 Bayombong Luzon Philippines
19 K4 Bayon France
16 B2 Bayona Spain
18 E9 Bayonne France
71 E5 Bayo Pt Panay Philippines
111 E7 Bayou Bartholomew R Arkansas
111 D9 Bayou D'Arbonne Louisiana
110 E6 Bayou de View R Arkansas
111 H11 Bayou La Batre Alabama
111 F12 Bayou Lafourche R Louisiana
111 E9 Bayou Macon R Louisiana
111 E7 Bayou Meto R Arkansas
111 F9 Bayou Pierre R Mississippi
128 B5 Bayovar Peru
113 E9 Bayport Florida
94 D3 Bay Port Michigan
99 O5 Bayport Minnesota
117 K10 Bay Pt Br Col
71 D5 Bay Pt Philippines
47 H5 Bayramiç Turkey
37 M4 Bayreuth W Germany
37 N5 Bayrischer Wald mts W Germany
123 T6 Bay Roberts Nfld
58 F1 Baysa U.S.S.R.
111 G11 Bay St.Louis Mississippi
113 F11 Bayshore Florida
95 O6 Bay Shore Long I, N Y
112 E1 Bays Mt Tennessee
111 G10 Bay Springs Mississippi
Baytag Bogdo see Baytik Shan
9 G3 Baythorn End England
66 E2 Baytik Shan mt ra China/Mongolia
109 N6 Baytown Texas
117 P12 Bayview Idaho
145 F3 Bay View New Zealand
17 F7 Baza Spain
48 K1 Bazaliya U.S.S.R.
22 G5 Bazancourt France
107 O3 Bazar Kansas
87 G10 Bazaruto, I Mozambique
18 E8 Bazas France
17 F7 Baza,Sierra de Spain
22 J4 Bazeilles France
67 B1 Bazhong China
48 G6 Baziaş Romania
18 G9 Baziége France
121 Q5 Bazin R Quebec
107 L3 Bazine Kansas
77 G5 Bazmām, Kūh-e mt Iran
77 F6 Bazman Iran
20 G5 Bazoche-Gouet,la France
22 F5 Bazoches France
20 E4 Bazoches-au-Houlme France
20 K5 Bazoches-les-Gallerandes France
20 F4 Bazoches-sur-Hoëne France
20 F5 Bazoge,la France
21 C8 Bazoges-en-Paillers France
20 D5 Bazougers France
20 B5 Bazouges la Perouse France
45 K3 Bazzano Italy
79 F4 Bcharre Lebanon
112 E6 Beach Georgia
98 C3 Beach N Dakota
95 N7 Beach Haven New Jersey
138 E6 Beachport S Australia
95 N7 Beachwood New Jersey
9 G6 Beachy Head England
95 O5 Beacon New York
143 C9 Beacon W Australia
113 B8 Beacon Hill Florida
118 H4 Beacon Hill Sask
9 F4 Beaconsfield England
139 H8 Beaconsfield Tasmania
13 G2 Beadnell England
142 E3 Beagle Bank W Australia
142 E3 Beagle Bay W Australia
133 D8 Beagle, Canal str Chile/Arg
140 A1 Beagle G N Terr Aust
143 A8 Beagle I W Australia
87 H10 Bealanana Madagascar
117 L11 Beale,C Br Col
94 K8 Bealeton Virginia
141 F7 Beal Ra Queensland
108 F3 Beals Cr Texas
118 C1 Beaman Manitoba
8 D6 Beaminster England
100 J4 Bear Idaho
101 O7 Bear R Idaho etc
111 J7 Bear Cr Alabama
107 J4 Bear Cr Kansas
99 S5 Bear Cr Wisconsin
98 B8 Bear Cr Wyoming
101 Q4 Bearcreek Montana
95 M5 Bear Cr.Res Pennsylvania
111 D8 Bearden Arkansas
120 C3 Beardmore Ontario
146 G7 Beardmore Gl Antarctica
139 J3 Beardmore Res. Queensland
103 M8 Beardsley Arizona
107 J2 Beardsley Kansas
110 F1 Beardstown Illinois
123 K4 Bear Head Anticosti I, Quebec
118 J7 Bear Hills,The Sask
90 H1 Bear I Arctic Oc
14 B5 Bear I Irish Rep
115 L7 Bear I N W Terr
120 K6 Bear Island Ontario
101 O7 Bear L Idaho/Utah
119 V3 Bear L Manitoba
117 K7 Bear Lake Br Col
94 A2 Bear Lake Michigan
98 B5 Bear Lodge Mts Wyoming
101 M3 Bearmouth Montana
121 M4 Béarn Quebec
18 E9 Béarn prov France
101 Q1 Bear Paw Mt Montana
119 N4 Bear R Sask
101 N8 Bear R.City Utah
12 D2 Bearsden Scotland
101 S9 Bears Ears Pk Colorado
115 K7 Bearskin L Ontario
74 F3 Beas R India
18 D9 Beasain Spain
17 F6 Beas de Segura Spain
127 J6 Beata, I Dom Rep
40 G4 Beatenberg Switzerland
117 P10 Beaton Br Col
111 J10 Beatrice Alabama
98 K9 Beatrice Nebraska
6 H4 Beatrice oil rig North Sea
140 D2 Beatrice,C Aust
142 F3 Beatrice,Mt W Australia
107 O2 Beattie Kansas
15 E5 Beattock Scotland
117 N7 Beatton River Br Col
102 H5 Beatty Nevada
100 D7 Beatty Oregon
119 N6 Beatty Sask
94 D9 Beattyville Kentucky
115 M8 Beattyville Quebec
19 N17 Beaucaire France
20 J2 Beaucamps-le-Vieux France
121 L3 Beaucanton Quebec
122 B7 Beauceville Quebec
20 C4 Beauchamps France
133 F8 Beauchene is Falkland Is
121 M6 Beauchêne, Lac Quebec
141 L8 Beaudesert Queensland
121 L4 Beaudry Quebec
20 F5 Beaufay France
40 E6 Beaufort France
22 L4 Beaufort Luxembourg
112 L3 Beaufort N Carolina
70 D2 Beaufort Sabah
112 G5 Beaufort S Carolina
21 E7 Beaufort-en-Vallée France
146 J6 Beaufort I Antarctica
112 L3 Beaufort Inlet N Carolina
116 R2 Beaufort Lag Alaska
147 K2 Beaufort Sea Arctic Oc
89 B9 Beaufort West S Africa
21 I6 Beaugency France
121 R7 Beauharnois Quebec
121 Q7 Beauharnois Power Canal Quebec
19 N12 Beaujeu France
19 Q16 Beaujeu France
18 H6 Beaujolais, Mts du France
95 S6 Beau L Maine/New Brunswick
9 E6 Beaulieu England
21 H7 Beaulieu-lès-Loches France
15 D3 Beauly Scotland
15 D3 Beauly, R Scotland
8 B1 Beaumaris Wales
22 D3 Beaumetz-les-Loges France
22 G3 Beaumont Belgium
102 H8 Beaumont California
107 O4 Beaumont Kansas
111 H10 Beaumont Mississippi
144 B6 Beaumont New Zealand
123 R4 Beaumont Nfld
111 B11 Beaumont Texas
146 H7 Beaumont B Antarctica
18 F9 Beaumont de Lomogne France
18 F8 Beaumont de Périgord France
22 J4 Beaumont-en-Argonne France
20 F3 Beaumont-en-Auge France
22 E3 Beaumont-en-Cambrésis France
20 B2 Beaumont-Hague France
21 G6 Beaumont la-Ronce France
20 G3 Beaumont-le-Roger France
20 G5 Beaumont-les-Autels France
20 K3 Beaumont-sur-Oise France
20 F5 Beaumont-sur-Sarthe France
19 J5 Beaune France
18 G4 Beaune la Rolande France
21 D7 Beaupréau France
20 K1 Beauquesne France
22 H3 Beauraing Belgium
40 B7 Beaurepaire d'Isère France
19 P15 Beaurières France
22 F5 Beaurieux France
118 E1 Beausejour Manitoba
21 E9 Beaussais France
139 H6 Beauty,Mt Victoria
20 K3 Beauvais France
118 C9 Beauvais Lake Prov. Park Alberta
21 E10 Beauvais sur Matha France
20 K1 Beauval France
118 K3 Beauval Sask
118 F5 Beauvallon Alberta
21 B8 Beauvoir-sur-Mer France
116 O3 Beaver Alaska
107 M3 Beaver Kansas
108 D7 Beaver Oklahoma
100 B4 Beaver Oregon
94 G6 Beaver Pennsylvania
103 M3 Beaver Utah
114 H7 Beaver R Alberta
98 F3 Beaver R N Dakota
103 L3 Beaver R Utah
117 L5 Beaver R Yukon Terr/Br Col
122 J9 Beaverbank Nova Scotia
122 G6 Beaver Brook New Brunswick
98 G9 Beaver City Nebraska
116 O4 Beaver Cr Alaska
106 G2 Beaver Cr Colorado
101 N5 Beaver Cr Idaho
107 J2 Beaver Cr Kansas
110 D5 Beaver Cr Missouri
98 B3 Beaver Cr Montana
98 F9 Beaver Cr Nebraska
98 B6 Beaver Cr Wyoming
114 E5 Beaver Creek Yukon Terr
117 C4 Beaver Creek Yukon Terr
98 J9 Beaver Crossing Nebraska
110 K4 Beaver Dam Kentucky
99 S6 Beaver Dam Wisconsin
117 O11 Beaverdell Falls Br Col
94 G6 Beaver Falls Pennsylvania
101 N4 Beaverhead R Montana
101 M4 Beaverhead Ra Idaho/Montana
118 E5 Beaverhill L Alberta
99 V4 Beaver I Michigan
123 N2 Beaver Island L Quebec
99 U3 Beaver L Michigan
117 N9 Beaver Lake Br Col
117 O8 Beaverlodge Alberta
117 P10 Beavermouth Br Col
116 J5 Beaver Mts Alaska
118 F4 Beaver R Alberta
118 H4 Beaver R Sask
118 K4 Beaver R Sask
110 C5 Beaver Res Arkansas
95 M3 Beaver R.Flow New York
94 C3 Beaverton Michigan
121 L8 Beaverton Ontario
100 C4 Beaverton Oregon
95 K6 Beavertown Pennsylvania
99 T9 Beaverville Illinois
74 F5 Beawar India
133 D4 Beazley Argentina
131 C4 Bebedero, Salina Argentina
129 J8 Bebedouro Brazil
36 G6 Bebenhausen W Germany
129 L4 Beberibe Brazil
36 H2 Bebra W Germany
47 H2 Bebrovo Bulgaria
9 H3 Beccles England
48 F5 Bečej Yugoslavia
48 K5 Beceni Romania
16 C2 Becerreá Spain
126 C7 Becerro,Cayos reefs Caribbean
85 D2 Béchar Algeria
116 J8 Becharof L Alaska
85 D7 Bechem Ghana
144 C5 Beche, Mt de la New Zealand
20 B5 Bécherel France
47 G1 Bechet Romania
116 F9 Bechevin B Alaska
37 K5 Bechhofen W Germany
Bechuanaland Prot see Botswana
31 H6 Bechyně Czechoslovakia
32 M7 Beckedorf W Germany
13 E4 Beckfoot England
9 E5 Beckhampton England
36 B5 Beckingen W Germany
8 D5 Beckington England
94 F9 Beckley W Virginia
144 B6 Becks New Zealand
32 H9 Beckum W Germany
109 N3 Beckville Texas
102 D2 Beckwourth California
48 J3 Beclean Romania
21 D7 Bécon France
19 O16 Béconne France
9 G4 Becontree England
37 O3 Bečov nad Teplou Czechoslovakia
108 F2 Becton Texas
31 K6 Bečva R Czechoslovakia
84 F4 Beda Libya
13 G5 Bedale England
18 H9 Bédarieux France
19 N16 Bedarrides France
36 B1 Bedburg W Germany
8 B1 Beddgelert Wales
9 G6 Beddingham England
119 R9 Bede Manitoba
20 B5 Bédée France
28 E4 Beder Denmark
32 J5 Bederkesa W Germany
55 C3 Bedeyeva Polyana U.S.S.R.
9 F3 Bedford England
110 K3 Bedford Indiana
99 M9 Bedford Iowa
94 B8 Bedford Kentucky
95 Q4 Bedford New Hampshire
122 J9 Bedford Nova Scotia
94 J6 Bedford Pennsylvania
121 S7 Bedford Quebec
94 H9 Bedford Virginia
101 P7 Bedford Wyoming
141 H3 Bedford C Queensland
142 F3 Bedford Downs W Australia
143 D10 Bedford Harb W Australia
127 P5 Bedford Pt Grenada
143 F7 Bedford Ra W Australia
9 F3 Bedfordshire co England
74 D7 Bedi India
69 H14 Bedinggong Indonesia
13 G3 Bedlington England
19 O16 Bédoin France
41 O5 Bedollo Italy
140 E6 Bedourie Queensland
8 A7 Bedruthan Steps England
28 C6 Bedsted Denmark
98 J8 Bee Nebraska
110 E6 Beebe Arkansas
98 G4 Beebe S Dakota
141 H7 Beechal R Queensland
94 K5 Beech Cr Pennsylvania
110 J4 Beech Creek Kentucky
100 F5 Beech Creek Oregon
99 T8 Beecher Illinois
110 H2 Beecher City Illinois
116 N1 Beechey Point Alaska
110 L4 Beech Fork R Kentucky
110 K2 Beech Grove Indiana
99 S3 Beechwood Michigan
139 H6 Beechworth Victoria
118 K8 Beechy Sask
32 M7 Beedenbostel W Germany
100 C9 Beegum California
25 E5 Beek Gelderland Netherlands
25 E4 Beekbergen Netherlands
111 E9 Beekman Louisiana
107 K3 Beeler Kansas
33 R8 Beelitz E Germany
98 K8 Beemer Nebraska
33 O8 Beendorf E Germany
141 L8 Beenleigh Queensland
37 K2 Beerberg mt E Germany
33 S8 Beeren E Germany
36 F4 Beerfelden W Germany
113 E10 Bee Ridge Florida
143 C8 Beeringgnurding, Mt W Aust
22 F2 Beerlegem Belgium
79 F8 Beer Menuha Israel
22 E1 Beernem Belgium
79 E9 Beer Ora Israel
80 C8 Be'er Pehar Israel
25 E5 Beers Netherlands
80 C8 Beersheba Israel
25 D6 Beerze R Netherlands
31 H3 Beeskow E Germany
87 E11 Beestekraal S Africa
9 E2 Beeston England
140 C3 Beetaloo N Terr Aust
146 G13 Beethoven Pen Antarctica
25 F2 Beetsterzwaag Netherlands
33 O7 Beetzendorf E Germany
33 R8 Beetz-see L E Germany
109 K7 Beeville Texas
86 D5 Befale Zaïre
87 H11 Befandriana Madagascar
86 D5 Befori Zaïre
18 C4 Begard France
8 B4 Begelly Wales
127 P4 Beggars Pt Antigua W I
107 O6 Beggs Oklahoma
51 L1 Begicheva, Ostrov isld U.S.S.R.
27 D11 Begna R Norway
57 E4 Begovat U.S.S.R.
28 E4 Begtrup Vig B Denmark
19 N15 Begude-de-Mazenc, la France
77 B4 Behbedān Iran
33 N5 Behlendorf W Germany
117 H8 Behm Can Alaska
140 A3 Behn, Mt N Terr Aust
22 L3 Beho Belgium
33 R4 Behren-Lübchin E Germany
37 L4 Behringersmühle W Germany
77 C1 Behshahr Iran
59 J2 Bei'an China
26 G4 Beiarn Norway
67 B2 Beibei China
86 F4 Beica Ethiopia
67 A1 Beichuan China
65 A6 Beichuan He R China
65 D5 Beidaihehaibin China
32 M10 Beienrode W Germany
37 O2 Beierfeld E Germany
68 J2 Beihai China
36 G6 Beihingen W Germany
67 D4 Bei Jiang R China
63 Beijing conurbation China
85 A5 Beila Mauritania
25 G3 Beilen Netherlands
68 J3 Beili China
68 K1 Beiliu China
37 L5 Beilngries W Germany
36 G5 Beilstein Baden-Württemberg W Germany
36 E2 Beilstein Hessen W Germany
36 C3 Beilstein Rheinland-Pfalz W Germany
86 H3 Beilul Ethiopia
67 B6 Beilun Ai pass China
36 H7 Beimerstetten W Germany
22 G5 Beine France
36 E6 Beinheim France
15 E4 Beinn a' Ghlo mt Scotland
40 H3 Beinwil Switzerland
67 B4 Beipan Jiang R China
65 E4 Beipiao China
Beira see Sofala
16 B4 Beira Alta prov Portugal
16 B5 Beira Baixa prov Portugal
16 B4 Beira Litoral prov Portugal
79 F5 Beirut Lebanon
118 D7 Beiseker Alberta
65 F2 Beitaolaizhao China
87 E10 Beitbridge Zimbabwe
79 F5 Beit ed Dine Lebanon
15 D5 Beith Scotland
80 D6 Beit Hanīnā Jordan
80 F4 Beit Idis Jordan
80 D7 Beit Jala Jordan
80 D7 Beit Kahil Jordan
80 A7 Beit Lahiya Israel
80 D7 Beit Lahm Jordan
80 G3 Beit Ras Jordan
80 D7 Beit Sahur Jordan
26 E7 Beitstad Norway
26 E8 Beitstadfjord inlet Norway
48 G4 Beius Romania
67 G2 Beiyandang Shan mt China
65 D6 Beizhen China
65 E4 Beizhen China
16 B6 Beja Portugal
43 C12 Beja Tunisia
143 E6 Bejah Hill W Australia
85 E1 Bejaia Algeria
16 D4 Béjar Spain
77 F2 Bejestān Iran
143 B9 Bejoording W Australia
70 L9 Bekasi Java
48 G4 Békés Hungary
48 F4 Békés co Hungary
48 G4 Békéscsaba Hungary
85 D7 Bekwai Ghana
Bela see Villach
74 B5 Bela Pakistan

86 B2 Bélabérim Niger
86 B4 Bélabo Cameroon
48 G6 Bela Crkva Yugoslavia
56 B5 Bel'Agach U.S.S.R.
95 L7 Bel Air Maryland
70 D4 Belajan R Kalimantan
70 D4 Belajan, G mt Kalimantan
16 D6 Belalcázar Spain
74 H9 Belampalli India
37 O4 Bélá nad Radbuzou Czechoslovakia
71 J4 Belang Sulawesi Indonesia
119 U5 Bélanger Pt Manitoba
119 U5 Bélanger R Manitoba
69 C11 Belanglie Downs
46 E1 Bela Palanka Yugoslavia
139 H4 Belaraboon New S Wales
87 C8 Bela Vista Angola
129 G8 Bela Vista Brazil
133 F2 Bela Vista Brazil
87 F11 Bela Vista Mozambique
130 C8 Bela Vista Paraguay
130 E5 Bela Vista de Goiás Brazil
69 D11 Belawan Sumatra
54 E4 Belaya-Berezka U.S.S.R.
54 M8 Belaya-Kalitva U.S.S.R.
48 N1 Belaya Tserkov U.S.S.R.
44 D2 Belbo R Italy
48 L3 Belceşti Romania
115 K2 Belcher Chan N W Terr
115 M6 Belcher, Les Iles N W Terr
17 G3 Belchite Spain
12 N4 Belcoo N Ireland
121 N4 Belcourt Quebec
102 C1 Belden California
98 D1 Belden N Dakota
94 B3 Belding Michigan
52 D5 Belebelka U.S.S.R.
55 B4 Belebey U.S.S.R.
129 J4 Belém Brazil
129 L5 Belém de São Francisco Brazil
128 C3 Belén Colombia
108 A1 Belen New Mexico
129 G8 Belén Paraguay
131 G3 Belén,Cuchilla de mt Uruguay
124 H7 Belén del Refugio Mexico
47 G1 Belene Bulgaria
137 N5 Belep,Îles New Caledonia
16 B2 Belesar, Embalse de res Spain
86 J5 Belet Uen Somalia
57 D2 Beleutty U.S.S.R.
54 H3 Belev U.S.S.R.
86 C5 Belézé Cent Afr Republic
100 C2 Belfair Washington
95 S2 Belfast Maine
144 M4 Belfast New Zealand
14 F2 Belfast N Ireland
122 K7 Belfast Pr Edward I
25 F6 Belfeld Netherlands
98 C3 Belfield N Dakota
86 F3 Belfodio Ethiopia
13 G2 Belford England
19 K5 Belfort France
40 E2 Belfort, Terr De France
101 Q4 Belfry Montana
76 B3 Belgaum India
19 P18 Belgentier France
33 S10 Belgern E Germany
146 B7 Belgica Fjella Antarctica
22 E2 Belgium
99 T6 Belgium Wisconsin
54 H6 Belgorod U.S.S.R.
48 N4 Belgorod Dnestrovskiy U.S.S.R.
107 M2 Belgrade Minnesota
(Belgrade see Beograd)
98 H8 Belgrade Nebraska
133 F5 Belgrano Argentina
131 E7 Belgrano,Pto Argentina
145 D4 Belgrove New Zealand
112 L2 Belhaven N Carolina
84 F4 Bel Hadam Libya
85 F2 Belhirane Algeria
20 H5 Belhomert France
43 E11 Belice R Sicily
78 G4 Belikh R Syria
47 H1 Beli Lom R Bulgaria
48 E5 Beli Manastir Yugoslavia
70 K8 Belimbing Indonesia
18 E8 Belin France
94 H7 Belington W Virginia
69 G13 Belinyu Indonesia
69 J14 Belitung isld Indonesia
125 P9 Belize Belize
125 P9 Belize Cent America
48 G6 Beljanica mt Yugoslavia
143 C9 Belka W Australia
99 O9 Belknap Iowa
100 K2 Belknap Montana
147 P8 Bel'kovskiy Os isld U.S.S.R.
113 E8 Bell Florida
141 K7 Bell Queensland
121 N3 Bell R Quebec
114 Q7 Bella Bella Br Col
18 F6 Bellac France
133 F4 Bellaco Uruguay
117 K9 Bella Coola Br Col
107 M2 Bellaire Kansas
94 B2 Bellaire Michigan
94 G6 Bellaire Ohio
141 G7 Bellalie Queensland
42 C2 Bellano Italy
76 C3 Bellary India
40 G5 Bella Tola mt Switzerland
131 E7 Bella Vista Argentina
128 C4 Bellavista Loreto Peru
128 C5 Bellavista San Martin Peru
139 J8 Bell B Tasmania
145 K5 Bell Block New Zealand
141 K5 Bell Cay isld Gt Barrier Reef Aust
110 E3 Belle Missouri
123 R6 Belle B Nfld
33 P9 Belleben E Germany
94 D6 Belle Center Ohio
40 E7 Bellecombe mt France
19 P4 Bellecombe, Pic de mt France
94 D6 Bellefontaine Ohio
94 K6 Bellefonte Pennsylvania
98 C5 Belle Fourche S Dakota
98 A5 Belle Fourche R Wyoming
18 G8 Bellegarde France
19 P12 Bellegarde France
21 J10 Bellegarde en-Marche France
113 G11 Belle Glade Florida
40 E3 Belleherbe France
18 C5 Belle Île France
110 O7 Belle Isle Nfld
18 C4 Belle Isle en Terre France
123 R2 Belle Isle Landing,
      Belle I, Nfld
123 Q2 Belle Isle,Strait of
      Labrador/Nfld
20 G5 Bellême France
110 K5 Belle Meade Tennessee
103 N6 Bellemont Arizona
20 H2 Bellencombre France
141 H3 Bellendon Ker Ra Queensland
22 C4 Bellengreville France
123 R6 Bellearam Nfld
107 N4 Belle Plaine Iowa
99 N5 Belle Plaine Kansas
119 M8 Belle Plaine Minnesota
119 H3 Belle Plaine Sask
139 H3 Bellerive Tasmania
121 T4 Belle-Rivière,Lac de la Quebec
121 M5 Belleterre Quebec
94 G6 Belle Valley Ohio
40 E5 Bellevaux France
40 B3 Bellevaure France
18 E3 Belleville France
113 E8 Belleville France
110 N2 Belleville Illinois
115 M8 Belleville Kansas
94 R7 Belleville New York
94 F7 Belleville Ontario
99 R7 Belleville Wisconsin
94 F7 Belleville W Virginia
101 P2 Benchland Montana

21 C8 Belleville-sur-Vie France
15 C4 Bellevue Alberta
118 C9 Bellevue Alberta
101 L6 Bellevue Idaho
99 Q7 Bellevue Iowa
94 B4 Bellevue Michigan
94 E5 Bellevue Ohio
141 G3 Bellevue Queensland
109 J2 Bellevue Texas
19 P13 Belley France
119 P8 Bell I Newfoundland
115 O7 Bell I Nfld
86 A1 Bellheim W Germany
12 D7 Bellingham England
98 E4 Bellingham Minnesota
114 G8 Bellingham Washington
146 G12 Bellingshausen Sea Antarctica
25 H2 Bellingwolde Netherlands
41 K5 Bellinzona Switzerland
118 E4 Bellis Alberta
36 F2 Bellochantuy Scotland
12 C2 Bellona Plateau Coral Sea
98 J8 Bellot California
41 O2 Bellota California
129 K5 Benedikitnos Brazil
87 H12 Benenitra Madagascar
31 H6 Benešov Czechoslovakia
19 K4 Bénestroff France
18 G6 Bénévent L'Abbaye France
9 9 Benevento Italy
112 C6 Benevolence Georgia
94 J5 Benezett Pennsylvania
80 C5 Bene Ziyyon Israel
19 L4 Benfeld France
94 F5 Berea Ohio
71 B1 Berebere Halmahera
      Beregomet U.S.S.R.
86 B1 Bereda Somalia
48 J2 Beregomet U.S.S.R.
48 H2 Beregovo U.S.S.R.
85 E6 Berekum Ghana
30 H6 Beremend Czechoslovakia
85 F7 Berenice Egypt
119 U6 Berens I Manitoba
119 U6 Berens River Manitoba
8 D5 Bere Regis England
119 R9 Bereslav Manitoba... etc.

107 P4 Benedict Kansas
98 L8 Benedict N Dakota
41 O2 Benediktbeuren mt
      W Germany
109 K7 Benavides Texas
56 B4 Berd' R U.S.S.R.
20 H2 Berck Plage France
111 D9 Berclair Texas
110 G5 Bernie Missouri
115 O3 Bernier B N W Terr
143 A6 Bernier I W Australia
41 L5 Bernina, Passo del
10 K5 Berhampur Quebec
89 D8 Bethulie S Africa
106 H2 Bethune Colorado
19 K5 Béthune France
119 R9 Bethune S Carolina
20 H2 Béthune R France
79 A10 Biba Egypt
42 D5 Bibbiena Italy
140 E5 Bibby R N Terr Aust
37 K5 Bibert R W Germany
16 C2 Bibey,R Spain
85 D7 Bibiania Ghana
37 J3 Biblis W Germany
142 A3 Bibra Lake
      Perth, W Aust
9 E4 Bibury England

<!-- (dense gazetteer index — remaining entries continue across nine columns in the same "grid-reference / place-name" format, alphabetically from Belleville-sur-Vie through Bigger,Mt Br Col) -->

117 E6 Bigger,Mt Br Col

110 F5 **Biggers** Arkansas
9 F3 **Biggleswade** England
102 C2 **Biggs** California
100 E4 **Biggs** Oregon
99 Q9 **Biggsville** Illinois
106 B10 **Big Hatchet Pk** New Mexico
118 C7 **Big Hill Sp.Prov.Pk** Alberta
101 N4 **Big Hole** *R* Montana
101 M4 **Big Hole Battlefield Nat. Mon** Montana
114 J8 **Big Horn** *R* Montana
101 S4 **Bighorn** *R* Wyo/Mont
101 S5 **Bighorn Mts** Wyo/Mont
126 G3 **Bight of Acklins Bahamas**
126 G2 **Bight,The** Cat I **Bahamas**
111 E8 **Big I** Arkansas
115 M5 **Big I** N W Terr
118 H1 **Big I** Ontario
94 H9 **Big Island** Virginia
117 F4 **Big Kalzas L** Yukon Terr
116 H9 **Big Koniuji I** Alaska
95 U1 **Big L** Maine
117 R3 **Big L** N W Terr
100 E7 **Big L** Oregon
116 N3 **Big Lake** Alaska
108 F4 **Big Lake** Texas
95 K7 **Biglerville** Pennsylvania
144 A7 **Big Moggy I New Zealand**
95 N3 **Big Moose** New York
110 G4 **Big Muddy** *R* Illinois
98 B1 **Big Muddy Cr** Montana
119 N9 **Big Muddy L** Sask
44 C4 **Bignone,Monte Italy**
94 H9 **Big Otter** *R* Virginia
102 F4 **Big Pine** California
99 L3 **Big Pine L** Minnesota
102 E7 **Big Pine Peak** California
101 P7 **Big Piney** Wyoming
110 D4 **Big Piney** *R* Missouri
123 M8 **Big Pond** C Breton I, N Scotia
94 B3 **Big Rapids** Michigan
99 Q4 **Big Rib** *R* Wisconsin
114 J7 **Big River** Sask
99 U5 **Big Sable Pt** Michigan
100 E8 **Big Sage Res** California
117 F5 **Big Salmon** *R* Yukon Terr
119 S1 **Big Sand L** Manitoba
101 P1 **Big Sandy** Montana
109 M3 **Big Sandy** Texas
101 Q7 **Big Sandy** Wyoming
103 L7 **Big Sandy** *R* Arizona
106 H3 **Big Sandy Cr** Colorado
99 N3 **Big Sandy L** Minnesota
119 N4 **Big Sandy L** Sask
118 H1 **Bigsby I** Ontario
98 K5 **Big Sioux** *R* S Dakota
102 G3 **Big Smoky Valley** Nevada
101 Q3 **Big Snowy Mt** Montana
144 A7 **Big South Cape I** New Zealand
108 F3 **Big Spring** Texas
101 O5 **Big Springs** Idaho
98 D8 **Big Springs** Nebraska
118 H8 **Bigstick L** Sask
98 K4 **Big Stone City** S Dakota
94 E10 **Big Stone Gap** Virginia
119 W5 **Bigstone L** Manitoba
98 K4 **Big Stone L** Minnesota
119 W3 **Bigstone R** Manitoba
102 C5 **Big Sur** California
109 M5 **Big Thicket L** Texas
101 Q4 **Bigtimber** Montana
101 S6 **Bigtrails** Wyoming
115 L7 **Big Trout Lake** Ontario
130 E10 **Biguacú** Brazil
118 E6 **Big Valley** Alberta
109 H7 **Big Wells** Texas
111 L7 **Big Wills Cr** Alabama
120 K6 **Bigwood** Ontario
101 L6 **Big Wood** *R* Idaho
42 G4 **Bihac** Yugoslavia
75 L6 **Bihar** *prov* India
48 G4 **Bihor** *reg* Romania
48 G4 **Bihorului Muntii** *mts* Romania
67 F2 **Bihu** China
85 A6 **Bijagós, Arquipélago dos** Guinea-Bissau
74 G5 **Bijaipur** India
76 B2 **Bijapur** India
77 A2 **Bijar** Iran
75 K4 **Bijauri** Nepal
42 F3 **Bijela Lasica** *mt* Yugoslavia
48 E6 **Bijeljina** Yugoslavia
46 D1 **Bijelo Polje** Yugoslavia
67 B3 **Bijie** China
76 E1 **Bijji** India
77 F6 **Bijnābād** Iran
74 H4 **Bijnor** India
98 G6 **Bijou Hills** S Dakota
74 E4 **Bikaner** India
79 F5 **Bikfaya** Lebanon
51 N4 **Bikin** U.S.S.R.
65 J1 **Bikin** U.S.S.R.
59 L2 **Bikin** *R* U.S.S.R.
134 G7 **Bikini** *atoll* Marshall Is Pacific Oc
31 L6 **Bílá** Czechoslovakia
71 G6 **Bilaa Pt** Mindanao Philippines
85 E6 **Bilanga** Upper Volta
70 F3 **Bilangbilangen** Kalimantan
74 E5 **Bilara** India
74 G3 **Bilaspur** India
70 F2 **Bilatan** *isld* Philippines
71 H4 **Bilato** Sulawesi Indonesia
68 D5 **Bilauktaung Range** Burma/Thailand
17 F1 **Bilbao** Spain
79 B8 **Bilbeis** Egypt
42 J6 **Bileća** Yugoslavia
78 B1 **Bilecik** Turkey
48 F5 **Biled** Romania
48 D2 **Bilé Karpaty** Czechoslovakia
31 O5 **Biłgoraj** Poland
125 N2 **Bilhuaskarma** Nicaragua
86 E5 **Bili** Zaïre
68 C4 **Bilin** Burma
30 H5 **Bílina** *R* Czechoslovakia
71 D8 **Bilit** Sabah
65 E5 **Biliu He** *R* China
98 A6 **Bill** Wyoming
143 B7 **Billabalong** W Australia
6 D2 **Bill Baileys Bank** N Atlantic Oc
20 C5 **Billé** France
33 M5 **Bille** *R* W Germany
32 F9 **Billerbeck** W Germany
9 G4 **Billericay** England
9 F2 **Billesdon** England
19 P12 **Billiat** France
36 G5 **Billigheim** W Germany
142 G4 **Billiluna** W Australia
9 F2 **Billingborough** England
27 F16 **Billinge** Sweden
9 F1 **Billinghay** England
114 J8 **Billings** Montana
107 N5 **Billings** Oklahoma
9 F5 **Billingshurst** England
8 D3 **Billingsley** England
Billiton *see* **Belitung** *I*
18 H7 **Billom** France
28 A5 **Billum** Denmark
28 C5 **Billund** Denmark
103 M6 **Bill Williams Mt** Arizona
56 G1 **Billyakh Porog** *falls* U.S.S.R.
22 K5 **Billy-sous-Mangiennes** France
86 B2 **Bilma** Niger
141 K6 **Biloela** Queensland
42 H3 **Bilo Gora** *dist* Yugoslavia
111 H11 **Biloxi** Mississippi
140 E7 **Bilpamorea Claypan** Queensland
142 C5 **Bilroth,Mt** W Australia
36 E1 **Bilstein** W Germany
25 D4 **Bilthoven** Netherlands
86 D3 **Biltine** Chad
26 M2 **Bilto** Norway
68 C4 **Bilugyun** *isld* Burma
22 K2 **Bilzen** Belgium
71 J9 **Bima,Teluk** *B* Sumbawa Indonesia
85 E6 **Bimbéréké** Benin
138 F4 **Bimbowrie** S Australia
126 E2 **Bimini Is** Bahamas
75 K10 **Bimlipatam** India
71 F5 **Binalbagan** Negros Philippines
77 F1 **Bīnālūd, Kūh-e-** *mts* Iran
70 B3 **Binatang** Sarawak
141 J5 **Binbee** Queensland
13 H6 **Binbrook** England
22 G3 **Binche** Belgium
141 J7 **Bindango** Queensland
28 C5 **Bindeballe** Denmark
139 H3 **Bindebango** Queensland
28 D3 **Binderup** Denmark
69 J11 **Bindjai** Indonesia
141 J8 **Bindle** Queensland
118 G8 **Bindloss** Alberta
89 G1 **Bindura** Zimbabwe
17 H3 **Binéfar** Spain
98 H2 **Binford** N Dakota
87 E9 **Binga** Zimbabwe
87 F9 **Binga,Mt** Mozambique/Zimbabwe
141 G8 **Bingara** Queensland
36 D4 **Bingen** W Germany
107 M6 **Binger** Oklahoma
9 F2 **Bingham** England
95 S1 **Bingham** Maine
99 V5 **Bingham** Michigan
108 A2 **Bingham** New Mexico
101 N9 **Bingham Canyon** Utah
95 M4 **Binghamton** New York
70 E2 **Bingkor** Sabah
120 K4 **Bingle** Ontario
13 G6 **Bingley** England
Bingmei *see* **Congjiang**
78 H2 **Bingol** Turkey
78 H2 **Bingol D** Turkey
9 G2 **Binham** England
Binh Dinh *see* **An Nhon**
68 G7 **Binh Minh** Vietnam
68 J5 **Binh Son** Vietnam
69 J11 **Binjai** Indonesia
69 D11 **Binjai** Sumatra
71 J7 **Binongka** *isld* Indonesia
119 Q8 **Binscarth** Manitoba
144 C5 **Binser, Mt** New Zealand
36 B4 **Binsfeld** W Germany
69 G12 **Bintan** *isld* Indonesia
71 H4 **Bintauna** Sulawesi Indonesia
71 E4 **Bintuan** Philippines
70 C3 **Bintulu** Sarawak
71 E4 **Binubusan** Philippines
58 G4 **Bin Xian** China
65 G2 **Bin Xian** China
80 C3 **Binyamina** Israel
67 C5 **Binyang** China
Binzhou *see* **Bin Xian**
133 C5 **Bio-Bio** *prov* Chile
46 D2 **Bioča** Yugoslavia
42 G5 **Biograd** Yugoslavia
85 F8 **Bioko** *isld* Eq Guinea
19 O14 **Biol** France
40 E5 **Biot, le** France
32 G7 **Bippen** W Germany
94 B6 **Bippus** Indiana
80 E2 **Biq'at Bet Netofa** Israel
74 F9 **Bir** India
80 D6 **Bira** Jordan
48 L3 **Bîra** Romania
59 K2 **Bira** U.S.S.R.
84 J5 **Bir Abu Husein** Egypt
84 H4 **Bir Abu Minqar** Egypt
71 E2 **Birac** Philippines
59 K2 **Birakan** U.S.S.R.
86 D3 **Birao** Cent Afr Republic
84 E4 **Bi'r Ash Shuwayrif** Libya
75 M5 **Biratnagar** Nepal
77 F7 **Bīr Bālo** Iran
78 G4 **Bir Btaiman** Syria
47 F1 **Bîrca Gîngiova** Romania
116 P3 **Birch Cr** Alaska
116 L4 **Birches** Alaska
145 D4 **Birch Hill New Zealand**
119 M5 **Birch Hills** Sask
119 S6 **Birch I** Manitoba
9 H5 **Birchington** England
48 G5 **Birchiş** Romania
118 F5 **Birch L** Alberta
99 P2 **Birch L** Minnesota
117 P4 **Birch L** N W Terr
118 J5 **Birch L** Sask
114 H6 **Birch Mts** Alberta
117 R6 **Birch R** Alberta
119 Q6 **Birch River** Manitoba
110 E5 **Birch Tree** Missouri
116 N6 **Birchwood** Alaska
144 A6 **Birchwood New Zealand**
99 P4 **Birchwood** Wisconsin
31 N6 **Bircza** Poland
115 K6 **Bird** Manitoba
107 J2 **Bird City** Kansas
116 H9 **Bird I** Alaska
83 J12 **Bird I** Seychelles
89 E9 **Bird I** *lt ho* S **Africa**
8 D4 **Birdlip** England
123 L6 **Bird Rocks** *lt ho* Madeleine Is, Quebec
110 K3 **Birdseye** Indiana
140 E7 **Birdsville** Queensland
140 C3 **Birdum** N Terr **Aust**
140 C3 **Birdum** *R* N Terr **Aust**
85 D3 **Bir ed Deheb** Algeria
79 G3 **Birein** Syria
85 D3 **Bir el Hadjaj** Algeria
69 C10 **Bireuën** Sumatra
79 H10 **Bi'r Fajr** Saudi Arabia
75 L5 **Birganj** Nepal
37 M5 **Birgland** W Germany
27 E11 **Biri** Norway
71 G4 **Biri** *isld* Philippines
89 G1 **Biri** *R* Zimbabwe
130 E7 **Birigüi** Brazil
56 D4 **Birikchul'** U.S.S.R.
141 H6 **Birimgan** Queensland
86 D4 **Birini** Cent Afr Republic
77 F3 **Bīrjand** Iran
28 B6 **Birkelev** Denmark
28 D2 **Birkelse** Denmark
36 F4 **Birkenau** W Germany
41 H2 **Birkendorf** W Germany
27 C13 **Birkenes** Norway
36 C4 **Birkenfeld** W Germany
13 E6 **Birkenhead** England
33 S7 **Birkenwerder** E Germany
28 K5 **Birkerød** Denmark
36 B2 **Birkesdorf** W Germany
28 G7 **Birket** Denmark
79 A9 **Birket Qârûn** *L* Egypt
38 N7 **Birkfeld** Austria
41 O3 **Birkkar Sp** Austria
28 D7 **Birknack** *C* W Germany
138 A2 **Birksgate Ra** S Australia
48 L4 **Bîrlad** Romania
48 L4 **Bîrladul** *R* Romania
79 D7 **Bîr Lahfân** Egypt
85 C3 **Bir Lehlú** Morocco
78 H5 **Bir Meloza** Iraq
111 K8 **Birmingham** Alabama
9 E3 **Birmingham** England
99 P9 **Birmingham** Iowa
94 D4 **Birmingham** Michigan
119 P8 **Birmingham** Sask
11 C5 **Birmingham** *conurbation* England
84 H5 **Bir Misâha** Egypt
85 B3 **Bir Moghrein** Mauritania
15 E4 **Birnam** Scotland
37 P7 **Birnbach** W Germany
101 T4 **Birney** Montana
134 K8 **Birnie I** Phoenix Is Pacific Oc
85 E6 **Birni N'Gaouré** Niger
85 F6 **Birnin Gwari** Nigeria
85 E6 **Birnin-Kebbi** Nigeria
85 F6 **Birni n'Konni** Niger
51 N3 **Birodidzhan** U.S.S.R.
71 D6 **Birong** Palawan **Philippines**
14 D3 **Birr** Irish Rep
140 B3 **Birrimbah** N Terr **Aust**
140 A4 **Birrindudu** N Terr **Aust**
118 K7 **Birsay** Sask
50 E3 **Birsk** U.S.S.R.
13 G6 **Birstal** W Yorks England
36 G3 **Birstein** W Germany
26 L2 **Birtavarre** Norway
141 G2 **Birthday Mt** Queensland
116 J2 **Birthday Pass** Alaska
13 G4 **Birtley** England
66 E5 **Biru** China
56 E3 **Biryusa** *R* U.S.S.R.
52 B6 **Biržai** U.S.S.R.
85 C4 **Bir Zreigat** Mauritania
88 C8 **Bisa** Zambia
61 K10 **Bisai** Japan
74 H4 **Bisalpur** India
103 P10 **Bisbee** Arizona
18 C7 **Biscay,B of** France/Spain
113 G12 **Biscayne Nat. Mon** Florida
43 G7 **Bisceglie** Italy
37 K4 **Bischberg** W Germany
36 H1 **Bischhausen** W Germany
36 D6 **Bischheim** France
37 M3 **Bischofsgrün** W Germany
37 J3 **Bischofsheim** W Germany
38 H7 **Bischofshofen** Austria
31 H4 **Bischofswerda** E Germany
19 L4 **Bischwiller** France
112 H2 **Biscoe** N Carolina
146 F14 **Biscoe I** Antarctica
115 L8 **Biscotasing** Ontario
61 P12 **Bise** Okinawa
45 K4 **Bisenzio** *R* Italy
47 H3 **Biser** Bulgaria
55 C2 **Biser** U.S.S.R.
55 C3 **Bisert'** U.S.S.R.
42 G6 **Biševo** *isld* Yugoslavia
61 P12 **Bise-zaki** *C* Okinawa
67 A5 **Bisezhai** China
67 B2 **Bishan** China
102 F4 **Bishop** California
112 D4 **Bishop** Georgia
95 M8 **Bishop** Maryland
109 K8 **Bishop** Texas
144 A7 **Bishop and Clerks Is** New Zealand
13 G4 **Bishop Auckland** England
12 D2 **Bishopbriggs** Scotland
101 L8 **Bishop Creek Res** Nevada
117 P3 **Bishop L** N W Terr
119 M8 **Bishopric** Sask
9 E7 **Bishop Rock** Isles of Scilly England
8 D3 **Bishops Castle** England
123 R4 **Bishop's Falls** Nfld
8 C5 **Bishop's Lydeard** England
9 G4 **Bishop's Stortford** England
9 E3 **Bishops Tachbrook** England
9 E6 **Bishops Waltham** England
112 G3 **Bishopville** S Carolina
80 G3 **Bishra** Jordan
85 F2 **Biskra** Algeria
31 M2 **Biskupiec** Poland
28 D3 **Bislev** Denmark
9 F5 **Bisley** England
71 G6 **Bislig** Mindanao **Philippines**
71 G6 **Bislig Bay** Mindanao Philippines
111 C7 **Bismarck** Arkansas
99 T9 **Bismarck** Illinois
110 F4 **Bismarck** Missouri
98 F3 **Bismarck** N Dakota
136 K2 **Bismarck Archipelago** Papua New Guinea
136 J3 **Bismarck Range** Papua New Guinea
136 K2 **Bismarck Sea** Papua New Guinea
146 E14 **Bismarck Str** Antarctica
33 P7 **Bismark** E Germany
78 H3 **Bismil** Turkey
107 N5 **Bison** Oklahoma
98 D4 **Bison** S Dakota
117 P7 **Bison L** Alberta
77 A2 **Bīsotūn** Iran
36 B6 **Bisping** France
32 L6 **Bispingen** W Germany
85 A6 **Bissau** Guinea-Bissau
115 K7 **Bissett** Manitoba
37 K6 **Bissingen** W Germany
114 H6 **Bistcho L** Alberta
47 F1 **Bistretu** Romania
48 J3 **Bistriţa** Romania
48 J3 **Bistrita Năsaud** *reg* Romania
48 K3 **Bistriţei, Muntii** *mt* Romania
71 E5 **Bisucay** *isld* **Philippines**
31 M1 **Bisztynek** Poland
86 B5 **Bitam** Gabon
36 B4 **Bitburg** W Germany
19 K3 **Bitche** France
80 B8 **Bit'ha** Israel
47 L4 **Bithynia** Turkey
71 B2 **Bitjoli** Halmahera **Indonesia**
86 C3 **Bitkine** Chad
78 H2 **Bitlis** Turkey
46 E3 **Bitola** Yugoslavia
43 H7 **Bitonto** Italy
42 H5 **Bitovnja** *mt* Yugoslavia
8 B5 **Bittadon** England
103 P2 **Bitter Cr** Utah
101 R8 **Bitter Creek** Wyoming
33 Q9 **Bitterfeld** E Germany
87 C12 **Bitterfontein** S Africa
84 J3 **Bitter L** Egypt
98 J4 **Bitter L** S Dakota
9 E6 **Bitterne** England
144 C6 **Bitterness, Mt** New Zealand
119 M5 **Bittern L** Sask
118 D5 **Bittern Lake** Alberta
101 L3 **Bitterroot** *R* Montana
114 H8 **Bitterroot Ra** Mont/Idaho
43 C8 **Bitti** Sardinia
33 P8 **Bittkau** E Germany
85 D6 **Bittou** Upper Volta
71 J4 **Bitung** Sulawesi Indonesia
86 B3 **Biu** Nigeria
48 L3 **Bivolari** Romania
48 K3 **Bivolu** *mt* Romania
59 L4 **Biwa Ko** *L* Japan
110 E4 **Bixby** Missouri
107 P6 **Bixby** Oklahoma
56 C5 **Biya** *R* U.S.S.R.
86 H3 **Biya Kaboba** Ethiopia
56 C4 **Biysk** U.S.S.R.
18 G9 **Bize** France
85 G1 **Bizerte** Tunisia
43 C11 **Bizerte, Lac de** Tunisia
80 B6 **Bizzaron** Israel
28 J6 **Bjæverskov** Denmark
27 H13 **BJärka-Säby** Sweden
26 J3 **Bjarköy** Norway
26 K8 **Bjästa** Sweden
48 E7 **Bjelašnica** *mt* Yugoslavia
27 C13 **Bjelland** Norway
42 H3 **Bjelovar** Yugoslavia
28 E1 **Bjergby** Denmark
28 G6 **Bjergby** Denmark
28 G5 **Bjerge** Denmark
28 G5 **Bjergsted** Denmark
27 G11 **Björbo** Sweden
27 A10 **Bjordal** Norway
27 B11 **Bjoreia** *R* Norway
26 D9 **Björgan** Norway
27 E12 **Björkelangen** Norway
27 F14 **Björketorp** Sweden
26 H5 **Björkfjall** *mt* Sweden
26 N6 **Björkfors** Sweden
26 K3 **Björkliden** Sweden
27 J11 **Björklinge** Sweden
27 K12 **Björkö** Sweden
29 J8 **Björköby** Finland
26 J8 **Björksele** Sweden
26 K7 **Björksele** Sweden
26 K8 **Björna** Sweden
27 M10 **Björneborg** Finland
27 G12 **Björneborg** Sweden
115 L2 **Bjorne Pen** N W Terr
27 C11 **Bjornesford** *L* Norway
27 J12 **Björnlunda** Sweden
28 E6 **Bjørnø** *isld* Denmark
147 H13 **Björnöya** *isld* Arctic Oc
28 C3 **Bjornsholm Å** *R* Denmark
26 H3 **Björnskinn** Norway
28 E5 **Bjørnsknude** *C* Denmark
27 H13 **Björsäter** Sweden
26 J10 **Bjuråker** Sweden
26 K8 **Bjurholm** Sweden
27 H11 **Bjursås** Sweden
27 G12 **Bjurtjärn** Sweden
26 K7 **Bjurträsk** Sweden
85 C6 **Bla** Mali
28 A5 **Blåbjerg** *hill* Denmark
9 E2 **Blaby** England
19 N12 **Blace** France
122 C3 **Blache,L.de la** Quebec
100 B5 **Blachly** Oregon
111 J8 **Black** *R* Alabama
116 R3 **Black** *R* Alaska/Yukon Terr
103 P8 **Black** *R* Arizona
110 F5 **Black** *R* Arkansas
111 E10 **Black** *R* Louisiana
94 E3 **Black** *R* Michigan
111 H11 **Black** *R* Mississippi
110 F4 **Black** *R* Missouri
112 J3 **Black** *R* N Carolina
112 H4 **Black** *R* S Carolina
99 Q5 **Black** *R* Wisconsin
141 H6 **Blackall** Queensland
144 C5 **Blackball New Zealand**
119 P2 **Black Bay** Ontario
100 B8 **Blackbear** California
119 M3 **Black Bear Island L** Sask
111 H8 **Black Belt** Miss/Ala
8 D2 **Blackbrook** England
141 F4 **Blackbull** Queensland
13 F6 **Blackburn** England
12 E2 **Blackburn** Scotland
116 Q6 **Blackburn,Mt** Alaska
103 K6 **Black Canyon** Nevada
106 C3 **Black Canyon of the Gunnison Nat.Mon** Colorado
146 E12 **Black Coast** Antarctica
103 P6 **Black Creek** Arizona
99 S5 **Black Creek** Wisconsin
118 C8 **Black Diamond** Alberta
100 C2 **Black Diamond** Washington
117 K9 **Black Dome** *mt* Br Col
121 O7 **Black Donald Mines** Ontario
141 G3 **Blackdown** Queensland
8 C6 **Blackdown Hills England**
99 M2 **Blackduck** Minnesota
101 O2 **Black Eagle** Montana
94 E9 **Blackey** Kentucky
13 F4 **Black Fell** England
118 G5 **Blackfoot** Alberta
101 N6 **Blackfoot** Idaho
101 N1 **Blackfoot** Montana
101 O6 **Blackfoot** *R* Idaho
12 E1 **Blackford** Scotland
118 J2 **Black Hawk** Ontario
14 B3 **Black Head** Irish Rep
145 F4 **Black Head New Zealand**
123 T5 **Blackhead B** Nfld
139 K5 **Blackheath** New S Wales
138 B4 **Black Hill** S Australia
140 A4 **Black Hills** N Terr **Aust**
98 C5 **Black Hills** S Dakota
146 H7 **Black I** Antarctica
119 V7 **Black I** Manitoba
15 D3 **Black I** Scotland
118 D8 **Blackie** Alberta
116 H8 **Black L** Alaska
111 C9 **Black L** Louisiana
94 C1 **Black L** Michigan
112 J3 **Black L** N Carolina
95 M2 **Black L** New York
106 E5 **Black Lake** New Mexico
121 T6 **Black Lake** Quebec
101 N1 **Blackleaf** Montana
127 P6 **Blackman's Barbados**
103 M6 **Black Mesa** *plat* Arizona
112 E2 **Black Mountain** N Carolina
102 G6 **Black Mt** California
106 B8 **Black Mt** New Mexico
140 C2 **Black Mt** N Terr **Aust**
103 K6 **Black Mts** Arizona
122 E6 **Black Mts** Quebec
8 C3 **Black Mts Wales/England**
101 M7 **Black Pine Pk** Idaho
117 N10 **Black Pines** Br Col
106 B9 **Black Pk** New Mexico
140 A5 **Black Pk** N Terr **Aust**
117 N10 **Black Pool** Br Col
13 E6 **Blackpool England**
83 L13 **Black R Mauritius**
143 B6 **Black Ra** W Australia
106 C8 **Black Range** New Mexico
94 D2 **Black River** Michigan
99 Q5 **Black River Falls** Wisconsin
110 E5 **Black Rock** Arkansas
103 M3 **Black Rock** Utah
100 F9 **Black Rock Desert** Nevada
112 F2 **Blacksburg** S Carolina
94 G9 **Blacksburg** Virginia
53 D11 **Black Sea** S E Europe
101 P8 **Blacks Fork** *R* Utah/Wyoming
122 F8 **Blacks Hbr** New Brunswick
112 E6 **Blackshear** Georgia
112 D6 **Blackshear, L** Georgia
14 A2 **Blacksod B** Irish Rep
106 B8 **Black Springs** New Mexico
27 H14 **Blackstad** Sweden
14 E4 **Blackstairs Mts** Irish Rep
112 F3 **Blackstock** S Carolina
94 J9 **Blackstone** Virginia
120 B3 **Black Sturgeon L** Ontario
94 G7 **Blacksville** W Virginia
94 H6 **Blackuck** Pennsylvania
122 G7 **Blackville** New Brunswick
112 F4 **Blackville** S Carolina
14 E4 **Blackwater** Irish Rep
110 D3 **Blackwater** Missouri
141 J6 **Blackwater** Queensland
113 C12 **Blackwater** *R* Florida
14 E3 **Blackwater** *R* Irish Rep
110 C3 **Blackwater** *R* Missouri
141 G7 **Blackwater** *R* Queensland
12 C3 **Blackwaterfoot** Scotland
117 M3 **Blackwater L** N W Terr
9 G4 **Blackwater,R** England
15 D4 **Blackwater Reservoir** Scotland
107 N5 **Blackwell** Oklahoma
108 G3 **Blackwell** Texas
107 M3 **Black Wolf** Kansas
98 E9 **Blackwood Cr** Nebraska
143 B10 **Blackwood, R** W Australia
112 F6 **Bladen** Georgia
98 H9 **Bladen** Nebraska
112 J3 **Bladenboro** N Carolina
118 L7 **Bladworth** Sask
8 C2 **Blaenau-Ffestiniog Wales**
8 C4 **Blaenavon Wales**
8 B3 **Blaenporth Wales**
8 C4 **Blaen Rhondda Wales**
28 C3 **Blære** Denmark
8 C6 **Blagdon** England
18 F9 **Blagnac** France
47 F2 **Blagoevgrad** Bulgaria
51 M3 **Blagoveshchensk** U.S.S.R.
28 B5 **Blåhøj** Denmark
21 B7 **Blain** France
94 K6 **Blain** Pennsylvania
107 O2 **Blaine** Kansas
117 M11 **Blaine** Washington
94 H7 **Blaine** W Virginia
118 L6 **Blaine Lake** Sask
20 B3 **Blainville** France
98 K8 **Blair** Nebraska
107 L7 **Blair** Oklahoma
99 P5 **Blair** Wisconsin
94 F9 **Blair** W Virginia
141 H6 **Blair Athol** Queensland
15 E4 **Blair Atholl** Scotland
15 E4 **Blairgowrie** Scotland
102 G3 **Blair Junction** Nevada
12 D1 **Blairmore** Scotland
143 B6 **Blair,Mt** W Australia
102 D2 **Blairsden** California
112 D3 **Blairsville** Georgia
94 H6 **Blairsville** Pennsylvania
20 H4 **Blaise** *R* Eure France
48 H4 **Blaj** Romania
112 C6 **Blakely** Georgia
9 H2 **Blakeney** England
99 S1 **Blake Pt** Michigan
99 O9 **Blakesburg** Iowa
26 K2 **Blåmannen** *mt* Norway
26 H4 **Blåmannsisen** *mt* Norway
36 B6 **Blâmont** France
43 C11 **Blanc** *C* Tunisia
131 E7 **Blanca,B** Argentina
106 G7 **Blanca Cr** New Mex/Tex
131 D7 **Blanca Grande,L** Argentina
133 C8 **Blanca,L** Chile
106 E4 **Blanca Pk** Colorado
106 E8 **Blanca, Sa** *mt* New Mexico
100 J1 **Blanchard** Idaho
94 B3 **Blanchard** Michigan
98 J2 **Blanchard** N Dakota
107 N6 **Blanchard** Oklahoma
120 E2 **Blanche** Ontario
121 P7 **Blanche** Quebec
138 C5 **Blanche,C** S Australia
138 F3 **Blanche,L** S Australia
142 E5 **Blanche, L** W Australia
94 D7 **Blanchester** Ohio
138 E5 **Blanchetown** S Australia
127 O1 **Blanchisseuse** Trinidad
13 F4 **Blanchland** England
106 C5 **Blanco** New Mexico
109 J5 **Blanco** Texas
128 F7 **Blanco** *R* Bolivia
128 D5 **Blanco** *R* Peru
114 G9 **Blanco,C** Oregon
128 B4 **Blanco,C** Peru
115 O7 **Blanc-Sablon** Quebec
94 F9 **Bland** Virginia
43 B12 **Blandan** Algeria
8 D6 **Blandford** England
103 P4 **Blanding** Utah
99 Q9 **Blandinsville** Illinois
17 J3 **Blanes** Spain
112 G3 **Blaney** S Carolina
99 V3 **Blaney Park** Michigan
69 C11 **Blangkejeren** Sumatra
69 B10 **Blangkuala** Sumatra
20 J2 **Blangy** France
20 F3 **Blangy-le-Château** France
22 C3 **Blangy-sur-Ternoise** France
30 H6 **Blanice** *R* Czechoslovakia
33 P5 **Blankenberg** E Germany
22 E1 **Blankenberge** Belgium
33 N9 **Blankenburg** E Germany
37 L2 **Blankenhain** Erfurt E Germany
37 N2 **Blankenhain** Karl-Marx-Stadt E Germany
33 O9 **Blankenheim** E Germany
36 B3 **Blankenheim** W Germany
36 C3 **Blankenrath** W Germany
33 S6 **Blankensee** E Germany
109 J4 **Blanket** Texas
9 F1 **Blankney** England
31 K6 **Blansko** Czechoslovakia
87 G9 **Blantyre** Malawi
12 D2 **Blantyre** Scotland
21 F9 **Blanzay** France
22 F3 **Blaregnies** Belgium
94 J4 **Blasdell** New York
26 G7 **Blåsjön** *L* Sweden
31 L4 **Błaszki** Poland
47 J1 **Blatnitsa** Bulgaria
37 P3 **Blatno** Czechoslovakia
22 F3 **Blaton** Belgium
26 J6 **Blattnicksele** Sweden
36 H7 **Blaubeuren** W Germany
36 H5 **Blaufelden** W Germany
32 J4 **Blauort** *isld* W Germany
18 C5 **Blavet** *R* France
13 H6 **Blaxton** England
13 G4 **Blaydon** England
18 E7 **Blaye** France
142 C5 **Blaze,Mt** W Australia
140 B2 **Blaze Pt** N Terr **Aust**
31 N6 **Błazowa** Poland
33 N6 **Bleckede** W Germany
42 F2 **Bled** Yugoslavia
8 C3 **Bleddfa** Wales
31 J3 **Bledzew** Poland
27 D12 **Blefjell** *mt* Norway
22 E3 **Bleharies** Belgium
36 B3 **Bleialf** W Germany
38 L8 **Bleiburg** Austria
33 N10 **Bleicherode** E Germany
37 M3 **Bleilochsperre** *res* E Germany
27 H15 **Blekinge** *reg* Sweden
99 L8 **Blencoe** Iowa
145 D4 **Blenheim** New Zealand
120 J10 **Blenheim** Ontario
21 G7 **Bléré** France
25 F6 **Blerick** Netherlands
19 J4 **Blesmes** France
109 L7 **Blessing** Texas
14 E3 **Blessington** Irish Rep
9 E4 **Bletchingdon** England
9 F3 **Bletchley** England
40 B4 **Bletterans** France
69 C10 **Bleuë** Sumatra
121 M6 **Bleu,L** Quebec
111 C8 **Blevins** Arkansas
20 H4 **Blévy** France
119 O9 **Blewett** Sask
108 G6 **Blewett** Texas
112 H2 **Blewett Falls L** N Carolina
32 J5 **Blexen** W Germany
85 E1 **Blida** Algeria
27 K12 **Blidö** Sweden
27 F14 **Blidsberg** Sweden
36 C5 **Blies** *R* W Germany
36 C5 **Blieskastel** W Germany
116 O6 **Bligh I** Alaska
38 L5 **Blindenmarkt** Austria
33 T6 **Blindow** E Germany
115 L8 **Blind River** Ontario
46 D3 **Blinisht** Albania
138 E4 **Blinman** S Australia
101 L7 **Bliss** Idaho
94 D5 **Blissfield** Michigan
9 F3 **Blisworth** England
70 O10 **Blitar** Java
85 E7 **Blitta** Togo
100 F7 **Blitzen** Oregon
37 O5 **Blížejov** Czechoslovakia
146 J9 **Block B** Antarctica
95 Q5 **Block I** Rhode I
117 L10 **Bloedel** Br Col
25 C4 **Bloemehdaal** Netherlands
89 E7 **Bloemfontein** S Africa
87 E11 **Bloemhof** S Africa
21 H6 **Blois** France
28 D2 **Blokhus** Denmark
25 E3 **Blokzijl** Netherlands
32 K9 **Blomberg** W Germany
99 L5 **Blomkest** Minnesota
21 H9 **Blond** France
21 G10 **Blond, Monts de** *mts* France
115 R4 **Blönduos** Iceland
70 Q10 **Blongas** Indonesia
31 M3 **Błonie** Poland
33 R9 **Blönsdorf** E Germany
20 F3 **Blonville** France
140 A6 **Bloods Ra** N Terr **Aust**
95 L8 **Bloodsworth I** Maryland
14 C1 **Bloody Foreland** Irish Rep
106 G4 **Bloom** Colorado
99 P4 **Bloomer** Wisconsin
110 K2 **Bloomfield** Indiana
110 D1 **Bloomfield** Iowa
94 B9 **Bloomfield** Kentucky
110 G5 **Bloomfield** Missouri
98 B2 **Bloomfield** Montana
98 J7 **Bloomfield** Nebraska
106 C5 **Bloomfield** New Mexico
121 N9 **Bloomfield** Ontario
95 Q2 **Bloomfield** Vermont
109 L3 **Blooming Grove** Texas
99 N6 **Blooming Prairie** Minnesota
101 O7 **Bloomington** Idaho
99 S9 **Bloomington** Illinois
110 K2 **Bloomington** Indiana
109 L7 **Bloomington** Texas
99 Q7 **Bloomington** Wisconsin
95 L5 **Bloomsburg** Pennsylvania
141 J5 **Bloomsbury** Queensland
110 F3 **Bloomsdale** Missouri
95 N4 **Bloomville** New York
94 D5 **Bloomville** Ohio
70 N9 **Blora** Java
37 K6 **Blosenau** W Germany
95 K5 **Blossburg** Pennsylvania
115 R4 **Blosseville Kyst** *coast* Greenland
109 M2 **Blossom** Texas
51 R2 **Blossom Mys** *C* U.S.S.R.
111 L11 **Blountstown** Florida
126 F6 **Blower Rock** Caribbean
112 F1 **Blowing Rock** N Carolina
9 E3 **Bloxham** England
95 M9 **Bloxom** Virginia
13 G6 **Blubberhouses** England
41 L3 **Bludenz** Austria
103 P8 **Blue** *R* Arizona
106 D2 **Blue** *R* Colorado
107 O7 **Blue** *R* Oklahoma
103 N3 **Blue Bell Knoll** *peak* Utah
117 N7 **Blueberry** *R* Br Col
144 C6 **Blue Cliffs New Zealand**
101 N8 **Blue Creek** Utah
113 G10 **Blue Cypress L** Florida
94 D9 **Blue Diamond** Kentucky
99 M6 **Blue Earth** Minnesota
99 M6 **Blue Earth** *R* Minnesota
110 C5 **Blue Eye** Missouri
94 F9 **Bluefield** W Virginia/Virg
125 N3 **Bluefields Nicaragua**
110 M3 **Bluegrass Reg** Kentucky
95 T2 **Blue Hill** Maine
98 H9 **Blue Hill** Nebraska
127 H4 **Blue Hills** Turks & Caicos Is
123 O6 **Blue Hills of Couteau** Nfld
100 F7 **Bluejoint L** Oregon
94 J6 **Blue Knob** *mt* Pennsylvania
103 M2 **Blue L** Utah
100 B9 **Blue Lake** California
99 T8 **Blue Lake** Illinois
94 K7 **Bluemont** Virginia
110 G2 **Blue Mound** Illinois
106 B1 **Blue Mountain** Colorado
110 B7 **Blue Mt** Arkansas
94 K6 **Blue Mt** Pennsylvania
95 L6 **Blue Mt** Pennsylvania
110 C6 **Blue Mt,L** Arkansas
95 N3 **Blue Mt. Lake** New York
100 H7 **Blue Mt. Pass** Oregon
127 M2 **Blue Mt.Pk** Jamaica
144 B6 **Blue Mts New Zealand**
114 H8 **Blue Mts** Oregon/Wash
127 L2 **Blue Mts, The Jamaica**
140 D2 **Blue Mud B** N Terr **Aust**
86 F3 **Blue Nile** *prov* Sudan
Blue Nile *R see* **Bahr el Azraq**
114 H4 **Bluenose L** N W Terr
117 J6 **Blue R** Br Col
107 O2 **Blue Rapids** Kansas
118 B4 **Blue Ridge** Alberta
112 C3 **Blue Ridge** Georgia
94 G10 **Blue Ridge** *mts* Virginia
112 C3 **Blue Ridge L** Georgia
117 O9 **Blue River** Br Col
100 C5 **Blue River** Oregon
121 O6 **Blue Sea Lake** Quebec
14 C2 **Blue Stack Mt** Irish Rep
106 C6 **Bluewater** New Mexico
144 B7 **Bluff New Zealand**
103 P4 **Bluff** Utah
107 N4 **Bluff City** Kansas
112 E1 **Bluff City** Tennessee
109 J3 **Bluffdale** Texas
141 H4 **Bluff Downs** Queensland
142 F3 **Bluff Face Ra** W Australia
143 C10 **Bluff Knoll** *mt* W Australia
71 D6 **Bluff Pt** Palawan Philippines
143 A8 **Bluff Pt** W Australia
110 F2 **Bluffs** Illinois
126 F2 **Bluff, The** Eleuthera Bahamas
118 C6 **Bluffton** Alberta
110 C7 **Bluffton** Arkansas
112 C6 **Bluffton** Georgia
94 B6 **Bluffton** Indiana
99 L3 **Bluffton** Minnesota
94 D6 **Bluffton** Ohio
112 G5 **Bluffton** S Carolina
109 K3 **Blum** Texas
130 E10 **Blumenau** Brazil
33 O8 **Blumenberg** E Germany
33 T5 **Blumenhagen** E Germany
118 K8 **Blumenhof** Sask
32 J6 **Blumenthal** W Germany
36 B3 **Blumenthal** W Germany
40 G4 **Blümlisalp** *mt* Switzerland
98 G5 **Blunt** S Dakota
100 D7 **Bly** Oregon
89 C9 **Blyde Berg** *mt* S Africa
116 N7 **Blying Sound** Alaska
13 G3 **Blyth** England
120 J9 **Blyth** Ontario
140 C1 **Blyth** *R* N Terr **Aust**
13 E2 **Blyth Br** Scotland
9 H3 **Blythburgh** England
110 C1 **Blythedale** Missouri
138 A2 **Blythe Ra** W Australia
110 G6 **Blytheville** Arkansas
143 G7 **Blyth Ra** S/W Australia
13 H6 **Blyton** England
55 G3 **Blyudtsy** U.S.S.R.
26 G3 **Bö** Norway
85 B7 **Bo** Sierra Leone
27 H13 **Bo** Sweden
71 E4 **Boac** *isld* Philippines
125 M3 **Boaco** Nicaragua
130 F7 **Bóa Esperança** Brazil
65 B7 **Bo'ai** China
120 K7 **Boakview** Ontario
67 D7 **Bo'ao** China
45 L1 **Boara Polesine** Italy
94 B2 **Boardman** *R* Michigan
141 H7 **Boatman** Queensland
15 E3 **Boat of Garten** Scotland
128 F3 **Boa Vista** Brazil
71 D5 **Boayan** *isld* Palawan Philippines
111 K7 **Boaz** Alabama
106 G8 **Boaz** New Mexico
68 J1 **Bobai** China
141 J4 **Bobawaba** Queensland
75 K9 **Bobbili** India
44 F2 **Bobbio** Italy
121 M8 **Bobcaygeon** Ontario
36 E4 **Bobenheim-Roxheim** W Germany
37 K7 **Bobingen** W Germany
33 O5 **Bobitz** E Germany
36 F6 **Böblingen** W Germany
85 D6 **Bobo Dioulasso** Upper Volta
31 K2 **Bobolice** Poland
71 G4 **Bobon** Philippines
128 C4 **Bobonaza** Ecuador
46 F2 **Bobov Dol** Bulgaria
31 J4 **Bóbr** *R* Poland
54 D8 **Bobrinets** U.S.S.R.
48 J1 **Bobrka** U.S.S.R.
54 M5 **Bobrov** U.S.S.R.
54 C6 **Bobrovitsa** U.S.S.R.
31 H4 **Bobrowice** Poland
94 H7 **Bobtown** Pennsylvania
109 K10 **Boca Chica** Texas
113 F13 **Boca Chica** *isld* Florida
127 M10 **Boca del Pao** Venezuela
128 E5 **Bôca do Acre** Brazil
128 E5 **Bôca do Curuquetê** Brazil
129 H4 **Bôca do Jari** Brazil
128 E5 **Bôca do Moaca** Brazil
21 D6 **Bocages** *reg* France
113 E11 **Boca Grande** Florida
127 N1 **Boca Grande** *chan* Trinidad/Ven
113 F13 **Boca Grande Key** *isld* Florida
129 K7 **Bocaiúva** Brazil
130 E9 **Bocaiúva do Sul** Brazil
130 C8 **Bocajá** Brazil
113 G11 **Boca Raton** Florida
127 N1 **Bocas del Dragon** *chan* Trinidad
125 M2 **Bocay** Nicaragua
45 M2 **Bocche del Po Della Pila** Italy
45 M2 **Bocche del Po Delle Tolle** Italy
45 M2 **Bocche del Po di Goro e di Gnocca** Italy
16 E3 **Boceguillas** Spain
19 P16 **Bochaine** *reg* France
121 R3 **Bochart** Quebec
31 M6 **Bochnia** Poland
22 K1 **Bocholt** Belgium
32 E9 **Bocholt** W Germany
37 P3 **Bochov** Czechoslovakia
32 F10 **Bochum** W Germany
37 O3 **Bockau** E Germany
32 M8 **Bockenem** W Germany
32 H6 **Bockhorn** W Germany
31 O3 **Boćki** Poland
38 H7 **Böckstein** Austria
33 T10 **Bockwitz** E Germany
127 J10 **Boconó** Venezuela
124 F4 **Bocoyna** Mexico
48 G5 **Bocsa Vasiovei** Romania
86 C5 **Boda** Cent Afr Republic
27 H10 **Boda** Sweden
27 J14 **Böda** Sweden
27 G14 **Bodafors** Sweden
143 C9 **Bodallin** W Australia
51 L3 **Bodaybo** U.S.S.R.
15 G3 **Boddam** Scotland
99 M7 **Bode** Iowa
102 A3 **Bodega Head** California
86 C2 **Bodele** *dist* Chad
36 F7 **Bodelhausen** W Germany
26 M6 **Boden** Sweden
32 L8 **Bodenburg** W Germany
36 E4 **Bodenheim** W Germany
37 J3 **Bodenlaube** W Germany
37 P5 **Bodenmais** W Germany
41 K2 **Bodensee** *L* Switzerland
33 N7 **Bodenteich** W Germany
32 L9 **Bodenwerder** W Germany
38 L6 **Bodenwies** *mt* Austria
37 N5 **Bodenwöhr** W Germany
14 C3 **Boderg,L** Irish Rep
102 F6 **Bodfish** California
74 G9 **Bodhan** India
70 G4 **Bodi** Sulawesi Indonesia
36 G5 **Bödigheim** W Germany
76 C5 **Bodinayakkanur** India
8 B7 **Bodinnick** England
70 O9 **Bodjonegoro** Java
8 B7 **Bodmin** England
8 B6 **Bodmin Moor** England
118 G6 **Bodo** Alberta
26 G4 **Bodö** Norway
25 C4 **Bodograven** Netherlands
130 C6 **Bodoquena** Brazil
78 A3 **Bodrum** Turkey
26 G9 **Bodsjö** Sweden
68 H7 **Bo Duc** Vietnam
26 H8 **Bodum** Sweden
48 F2 **Bodva** *R* Hungary
31 M3 **Bodzanów** Poland
40 D5 **Boëge** France
25 G4 **Boekelo** Netherlands
22 F1 **Boekhoute** Belgium
98 H8 **Boelus** Nebraska
18 H7 **Boën** France
86 D6 **Boende** Zaïre
68 G6 **Boeng Lovea** Cambodia
68 G6 **Boeng Me Alpa** Cambodia
109 J6 **Boerne** Texas
25 H2 **Boertange** Netherlands
28 G6 **Boeslunde** Denmark
111 E8 **Boeuf** *R* Arkansas
83 K14 **Bœuf, Nez de** *peak* Réunion
85 B6 **Boffa** Guinea
14 D3 **Bofin,L** Irish Rep
68 B4 **Bogale** Burma
68 B5 **Bogale** *R* Burma
111 F11 **Bogalusa** Louisiana
85 D6 **Bogande** Upper Volta
86 C4 **Bogangolo** Cent Afr Republic
141 H6 **Bogantungan** Queensland
17 F6 **Bogarra** Spain
118 B8 **Bogart,Mt** Alberta
109 M2 **Bogata** Texas
53 H7 **Bogatoye** U.S.S.R.
31 H5 **Bogatynia** Poland
86 C5 **Bogbonga** Zaïre
55 D3 **Bogdanovich** U.S.S.R.
66 D3 **Bogda Shan** *mts* China
27 K14 **Boge** *isld* Gotland **Sweden**
55 F4 **Bogembay** U.S.S.R.
37 O6 **Bogen** W Germany
87 C11 **Bogenfels** Namibia
28 E5 **Bogense** Denmark
14 C4 **Boggeragh Mts** Irish Rep
143 C6 **Boggola** *mt* W Australia
26 H8 **Boggsjö** Sweden
85 B5 **Boghé** Mauritania
141 J5 **Bogie** *R* Queensland
9 F6 **Bognor Regis** England
22 H4 **Bogny-sur-Meuse** France
71 F5 **Bogo** Cebu Philippines
28 J7 **Bogø** Denmark
54 G6 **Bogodukhov** U.S.S.R.
70 L9 **Bogor** Java
48 J2 **Bogorodchany** U.S.S.R.
51 O3 **Bogorodskoy** U.S.S.R.
128 D3 **Bogotá** Colombia
111 A8 **Bogota** Texas
56 C3 **Bogotol** U.S.S.R.
75 N6 **Bogra** Bangladesh
27 L12 **Bogskär** *lt ho* Finland
56 E2 **Boguchany** U.S.S.R.
54 M7 **Boguchar** U.S.S.R.
55 E4 **Bogudukhovka** U.S.S.R.
107 L2 **Bogue** Kansas
111 F10 **Bogue Chitto** Mississippi
112 K3 **Bogue Inlet** N Carolina
54 B2 **Bogushevsk** U.S.S.R.
54 B7 **Boguslav** U.S.S.R.
31 J5 **Boguszów** Poland
127 L2 **Bog Walk** Jamaica
65 D5 **Bo Hai** *gulf* China
65 E5 **Bohai Haixia** *str* China
22 E4 **Bohain** France
65 D5 **Bohai Wan** *B* China
119 M8 **Boharm** Sask
38 N5 **Böheimkirchen** Austria
30 H6 **Bohemia** *old region* Czech
142 F4 **Bohemia Downs** W Australia
85 E7 **Bohicon** Benin
42 F2 **Bohiniska Bistrica** Yugoslavia
37 N1 **Böhlen** W Germany
32 K7 **Böhme** W Germany
37 N4 **Böhmer Wald** *mts* W Germany
32 H8 **Bohmte** W Germany
33 Q7 **Böhne** E Germany
71 G6 **Bohol** *isld* Philippines
71 F6 **Bohol Str** Philippines
16 D5 **Bohonal de Ibor** Spain
48 D4 **Böhönye** Hungary
86 J4 **Bohotleh** Somalia
80 B8 **Bohu** Israel
128 F4 **Boiaçu** Brazil
43 F7 **Boiano** Italy
122 F7 **Boiestown** New Brunswick
20 K5 **Boigneville** France
122 B5 **Boileau** Quebec
130 C9 **Boi Preto,Serra de** *mts* Brazil
130 F8 **Boi, Pta. do** *C* Brazil
129 J7 **Bois** *R* Brazil
94 C1 **Bois Blanc I** Michigan
123 M7 **Boisdale** C Breton I, N Scotia
40 D4 **Bois d' Amont** France
18 H5 **Bois du Roi** *mt* France
100 J6 **Boise** Idaho
106 H5 **Boise City** Oklahoma
20 A5 **Boisgervilly** France
20 H3 **Bois Guillaume** France
114 G4 **Bois, Lac Des** *L* N W Terr
Bois-le-Duc *see* **'s-Hertogenbosch**
18 H7 **Bois Noirs** *hills* France
22 H1 **Boisschot** Belgium
119 R9 **Boissevain** Manitoba
20 G4 **Boissy-les-Perche** France
20 G5 **Boissy-Maugis** France
38 F9 **Boite** *R* Italy

130 F8 Boituva Brazil
33 T6 Boitzenburg E Germany
33 N6 Boize R E Germany
33 N6 Boizenburg E Germany
85 B3 Bojador Morocco
46 C3 Bojana R Albania
28 E6 Bøjden Denmark
71 E1 Bojeador,C Luzon Philippines
77 E1 Bojnūrd Iran
69 D13 Bojo isld Indonesia
48 F5 Boka Yugoslavia
42 J6 Boka Kotorska B Yugoslavia
85 F7 Bokani Nigeria
85 B6 Boké Guinea
113 E11 Bokeelia Florida
32 J6 Bokel W Germany
32 K8 Bokeloh W Germany
68 H6 Bo Kheo Cambodia
89 A8 Bokkeveld Berg mt S Africa
27 A12 Boknfjorden inlet Norway
56 B6 Boko Kazakhstan U.S.S.R.
86 C3 Bokoro Chad
107 Q6 Bokoshe Oklahoma
86 D6 Bokote Zaïre
59 H2 Bo-ko-tu China
68 D7 Bokpyin Burma
86 D6 Bokungu Zaïre
68 C5 Bok Ye-gan isld Burma
70 G5 Bolaäng Sulawesi Indonesia
71 J4 Bolaang Sulawesi Indonesia
86 D6 Bolaiti Zaïre
85 A6 Bolama Guinea-Bissau
75 K8 Bolangir India
124 H7 Bolaños Mexico
67 C5 Bolao China
20 F2 Bolbec France
55 E2 Bolchary U.S.S.R.
99 M9 Bolckow Missouri
48 E4 Bölcske Hungary
33 T5 Boldekow E Germany
28 C6 Bolderslev Denmark
48 K5 Boldeşti Romania
66 C3 Bole China
85 D7 Bole Ghana
101 N2 Bole Montana
48 H1 Bolekhov U.S.S.R.
86 D6 Boleko Zaïre
71 L9 Boleng,Selat Flores Indonesia
100 J4 Boles Idaho
31 J4 Bolesławiec Poland
107 O6 Boley Oklahoma
85 D6 Bolgatanga Ghana
121 O4 Bolger Quebec
48 M5 Bolgrad U.S.S.R.
59 K2 Boli China
86 C6 Bolia Zaïre
26 L7 Boliden Sweden
111 H9 Boligee Alabama
71 D2 Bolinao,C Luzon Philippines
48 K6 Bolintin Vale Romania
71 H4 Boliohutu,Gunung mt Sulawesi Indonesia
131 E6 Bolívar Argentina
128 C3 Bolivar Colombia
110 C4 Bolivar Missouri
94 J4 Bolivar New York
110 H6 Bolivar Tennessee
128 D2 Bolivar div Colombia
128 C4 Bolivar prov Ecuador
128 E2 Bolivar state Venezuela
128 F2 Bolivar,Cerro mt Venezuela
109 N6 Bolivar Pen Texas
112 J3 Bolivia N Carolina
128 E7 Bolivia rep S America
46 E1 Boljevac Yugoslavia
78 E3 Bolkar Dağları mts Turkey
27 D12 Bolkesjö Norway
120 G4 Bolkow Ontario
31 J5 Bolków Poland
36 H6 Boll W Germany
41 H2 Boll W Germany
45 K4 Bolle,Le Italy
36 B4 Bollendorf W Germany
19 N16 Bollène France
40 G4 Bolligen Switzerland
28 B5 Bølling Denmark
8 D1 Bollington England
27 H10 Bollnäs Sweden
141 H8 Bollon Queensland
27 G15 Bolmen L Sweden
9 F6 Bolney England
71 F5 Bolo Panay Philippines
86 C6 Bolobo Zaïre
71 E7 Bolod Islands Philippines
42 D4 Bologna Italy
19 J4 Bologne France
52 D6 Bologovo U.S.S.R.
54 J2 Bolokhovo U.S.S.R.
86 C5 Bolomba Zaïre
86 D6 Bolombo Zaïre
59 L2 Bolon U.S.S.R.
125 P7 Bolonchén de Rejón Mexico
71 F7 Bolong Mindanao Philippines
59 L2 Bolon,Oz L U.S.S.R.
71 F1 Bolos Pt Luzon Philippines
43 B8 Bolotana Sardinia
56 B3 Bolotnoye U.S.S.R.
68 H5 Bolovens, Plateau des Laos
131 C2 Bolsa,Cerro peak Argentina
42 D6 Bolsena,L.di Italy
31 N1 Bol'shakovo U.S.S.R.
54 F9 Bolshaya Belozerka U.S.S.R.
55 F3 Bol'shaya Tava R U.S.S.R.
56 G1 Bol'shaya Yerema R U.S.S.R.
55 F3 Bol'sherech'ye U.S.S.R.
51 P3 Bol'sheretsk U.S.S.R.
55 C3 Bolshe-ustikinskoye U.S.S.R.
54 B4 Bol'shevik U.S.S.R.
51 K1 Bol'shevik, Ostrov isld U.S.S.R.
55 F3 Bolshiye Uki U.S.S.R.
56 B1 Bolshoi Megtyg'yegan R U.S.S.R.
54 G9 Bolshoi Tokmak U.S.S.R.
48 J1 Bolshovtsy U.S.S.R.
55 E1 Bol'shoy Atlym U.S.S.R.
55 F1 Bol'shoy Balyk R U.S.S.R.
147 P10 Bol'shoy Begichev,Os isld U.S.S.R.
56 H2 Bol'shoy Chuya R U.S.S.R.
55 E3 Bol'shoye Sorokino U.S.S.R.
55 G4 Bol'shoye Topol'noye, Oz L U.S.S.R.
55 G4 Bol'shoye Yaravoye, Oz L U.S.S.R.
55 E1 Bol'shoy Kamen U.S.S.R.
55 F2 Bol'shoy Kun'yak U.S.S.R.
55 D3 Bol'shoy Kuyash U.S.S.R.
51 O1 Bolshoy Lyakhovskiy,O isld U.S.S.R.
56 D2 Bol'shoy Pit R U.S.S.R.
55 F1 Bolshoy Salym R U.S.S.R.
59 L1 Bol'shoy Shantar,Oz isld U.S.S.R.
55 E1 Bol'shoy Tap R U.S.S.R.
52 C5 Bol'shoy Tyuters, Os. isld U.S.S.R.
55 F3 Bol'shoy Uvat, Oz L U.S.S.R.
56 D5 Bolshoy Yenisey R U.S.S.R.
55 F2 Bol'shoy Yugan R U.S.S.R.
25 E2 Bolsward Netherlands
17 H2 Boltaña Spain
8 C7 Bolt Head England
13 F6 Bolton England
112 J3 Bolton N Carolina
121 L9 Bolton Ontario
13 G6 Bolton Br England
119 W4 Bolton L Manitoba
13 F5 Bolton le-Sands England
78 C1 Bolu Turkey
66 E4 Boluntay China
14 A5 Bolus Hd Irish Rep
54 F3 Bolva R U.S.S.R.
47 L6 Bolvadin Turkey
78 C2 Bolvadin Turkey
8 B6 Bolventor England
141 G4 Bolwarra Queensland
48 E5 Bóly Hungary
42 D2 Bolzano Italy
86 B7 Boma Zaïre
22 K3 Bomal Luxembourg/Belgium
86 B5 Bomandjokou Congo
109 H2 Bomarton Texas
86 C5 Bomassa Congo
74 E9 Bombay India
145 E2 Bombay New Zealand
87 H11 Bombetoka,B.de Madagascar
86 F5 Bombo Uganda
86 C5 Bomboma Zaïre
130 H10 Bom Conselho Brazil
129 J7 Bom Despacho Brazil
27 J11 Bomhus Sweden
85 B7 Bomi Hills Liberia
130 J9 Bom Jardim Brazil
130 D5 Bom Jardim de Goiás Brazil
128 E5 Bom Jardin Brazil
129 K5 Bom Jesus Brazil
129 K5 Bom Jesus da Gurgueia, Serra mts Brazil
129 K6 Bom Jesus da Lapa Brazil
130 H7 Bom Jesus do Itabapoana Brazil
130 H7 Bom Jesus do Norte Brazil
27 A12 Bömlafjorden inlet Norway
27 A12 Bömlo Norway
51 M3 Bomnak U.S.S.R.
86 E5 Bomokandi R Zaïre
86 C5 Bomongo Zaïre
143 B7 Bompas Hill W Australia
130 E10 Bom Retiro Brazil
130 G7 Bom Sucesso Brazil
118 D5 Bon Accord Alberta
94 K9 Bon Air Virginia
127 K8 Bonaire isld Lesser Antilles
127 K9 Bonaire Trench Caribbean
116 R6 Bona,Mt Alaska
69 D12 Bonandolok Sumatra
106 D3 Bonanza Colorado
125 M3 Bonanza Nicaragua
100 D7 Bonanza Oregon
127 J5 Bonao Dom Rep
99 P9 Bonaparte Iowa
142 E2 Bonaparte Arch W Australia
100 F1 Bonaparte,Mt Washington
15 D3 Bonar Bridge Scotland
121 N8 Bonarlaw Ontario
116 G5 Bonasila Dome mt Alaska
127 N3 Bonasse Trinidad
44 G3 Bonassola Italy
122 G5 Bonaventure Quebec
122 H5 Bonaventure I Quebec
115 O8 Bonavista Nfld
40 C3 Bonboillon France
138 D4 Bon Bon S Australia
85 G1 Bon,C Tunisia
106 F4 Boncarbo Colorado
20 J5 Bonce France
13 F3 Bonchester Br Scotland
9 E6 Bonchurch England
101 T10 Bond Colorado
28 C7 Bonden Au R W Germany
45 K2 Bondeno Italy
86 D5 Bondo Zaïre
71 F4 Bondoc Penin Luzon Philippines
71 F4 Bondoc Pt Luzon Philippines
36 F6 Bondorf W Germany
85 D7 Bondoukou Ivory Coast
70 O9 Bondowoso Java
126 F2 Bonds Cay isld Bahamas
144 C5 Bonds Peak mt New Zealand
140 C6 Bond Springs N Terr Aust
99 S5 Bonduel Wisconsin
101 P6 Bondurant Wyoming
Bône see Annaba
101 O6 Bone Idaho
113 L9 Bonefish Pond New Providence I Bahamas
71 H7 Bonelipu Indonesia
70 G7 Bonelohe Indonesia
68 G4 Boneng Laos
71 K8 Boneogeh Indonesia
71 K8 Bonerate isld Indonesia
26 K3 Bones Norway
15 E5 Boness Scotland
98 H6 Bonesteel S Dakota
131 C2 Bonete,Cerro peak Argentina
70 G7 Bone, Teluk B Sulawesi Indonesia
98 C1 Bonetraill N Dakota
121 L6 Bonfield Ontario
71 E4 Bongabong Philippines
86 D5 Bongandanga Zaïre
70 F2 Bongao Philippines
70 G5 Bongka Sulawesi Indonesia
70 M9 Bongkok mt Java
71 G7 Bongo isld Mindanao Philippines
86 C3 Bongor Chad
109 L2 Bonham Texas
118 L1 Bonheur Ontario
12 D2 Bonhill Scotland
36 C7 Bonhomme, Col du pass France
43 B7 Bonifacio,Str.of Corsica/Sardinia
111 L11 Bonifay Florida
Bonin Is see Ogasawara-shoto
103 P9 Bonita Arizona
111 E9 Bonita Louisiana
113 F11 Bonita Springs Florida
130 C7 Bonito Brazil
69 E13 Bonjol Sumatra
36 C2 Bonn W Germany
18 G6 Bonnat France
19 Q12 Bonne France
19 P15 Bonne R France
123 P4 Bonne Bay Nfld
20 F3 Bonnebosq France
22 G3 Bonne Esperance Belgium
123 P2 Bonne Espérance Quebec
20 K4 Bonnelles France
20 B5 Bonnemain France
101 M3 Bonner Montana
140 D1 Bonner Mt N Terr Aust
114 H8 Bonners Ferry Idaho
110 B2 Bonner Springs Kansas
28 A3 Bonnet Denmark
20 F5 Bonnétable France
110 F4 Bonne Terre Missouri
20 K2 Bonneuil-les-Eaux France
20 H5 Bonneval Eure-et-Loir France
40 F7 Bonneval-sur-Arc France
40 D4 Bonnevaux France
19 Q12 Bonneville France
100 D4 Bonneville Oregon
101 R6 Bonneville Wyoming
20 H3 Bonneville,la France
101 N7 Bonneville Pk Idaho
101 L9 Bonneville Salt Flats Utah/Nev
138 F6 Bonney,L S Australia
140 C5 Bonney Well N Terr Aust
20 K1 Bonnières Pas-de-Calais France
20 J3 Bonnières Yvelines France
143 C9 Bonnie Rock W Australia
19 O17 Bonnieux France
36 G5 Bönnigheim W Germany
36 H3 Bonnland W Germany
18 G5 Bonny France
85 F8 Bonny Nigeria
Bonny, Bight Of see Biafra, Bight Of
106 H2 Bonny Res Colorado
122 F8 Bonny River New Brunswick
118 G4 Bonnyville Alberta
110 F6 Bono Arkansas
43 C8 Bono Sardinia
71 C6 Bonobond Palawan Philippines
60 D14 Bōno-misaki C Japan
68 H7 Bonom Mhai mt Vietnam
43 B8 Bonorva Sardinia
140 B2 Bonrook N Terr Aust
111 J11 Bon Secour Alabama
70 E4 Bontang Kalimantan
89 A9 Bonteberg mts S Africa
85 B7 Bonthe Sierra Leone
71 E2 Bontoc Luzon Philippines
70 G7 Bontosunggu Sulawesi
109 O5 Bon Wier Texas
48 E4 Bonyhád Hungary
143 G6 Bonython Ra N Terr/W Aust
113 K12 Booby I Bahamas
141 F1 Booby I Queensland
127 M3 Booby South Pt Jamaica
36 D7 Boofzheim France
141 H8 Boogah Queensland
143 C8 Boogardie W Australia
138 C4 Bookabie S Australia
138 D4 Bookaloo,L S Australia
143 A8 Bookara W Australia
103 P2 Book Cliffs Utah
108 D7 Booker Texas
85 C7 Boola Guinea
142 B6 Boolaloo W Australia
143 A6 Boolathanna W Australia
138 E5 Booleroo Centre S Australia
143 A6 Boologooro W Australia
22 G1 Boom Belgium
94 B2 Boon Michigan
141 L8 Boonah Queensland
106 F3 Boone Colorado
99 N7 Boone Iowa
112 F1 Boone N Carolina
94 H9 Boones Mill Virginia
110 C6 Booneville Arkansas
110 N4 Booneville Kentucky
94 D9 Booneville Res Kentucky
141 H6 Boongoondoo Queensland
127 P4 Boon Pt Antigua W I
94 K7 Boonsboro Maryland
58 C2 Bööntsagaan Nuur L Mongolia
102 A2 Boonville California
110 J3 Boonville Indiana
110 D3 Boonville Missouri
95 M3 Boonville New York
71 B3 Boo,Pulau Pulau islds W Irian
143 D9 Boorabbin W Australia
138 D3 Boorthanna S Australia
20 H3 Boos-sur-Andelle France
13 E5 Boot England
146 A4 Boothby,C Antarctica
147 E3 Boothia, Gulf of N W Terr
115 K3 Boothia Pen N W Terr
111 J8 Boothton Alabama
13 E5 Bootle England
13 F6 Bootle England
37 J6 Bopfingen W Germany
89 C6 Bophuthatswana reg S Africa
65 C6 Boping China
36 D3 Boppard W Germany
129 K6 Boqueirão, Serra do mts Brazil
128 F8 Boquerón dep Paraguay
124 G4 Boquilla de Conchos Mexico
37 O4 Bor Czechoslovakia
86 E4 Bo R Sudan
78 E3 Bor Turkey
48 G6 Bor Yugoslavia
135 M10 Bora-Bora isld Society Is Pac Oc
101 M5 Borah Pk Idaho
86 H4 Borama Somalia
27 F14 Borås Sweden
77 B5 Borāzjān Iran
128 G4 Borba Brazil
28 B4 Borbjerg Denmark
71 G5 Borbon Cebu Philippines
130 H9 Borborema, Planalto da plat Brazil
48 K3 Borca Romania
48 L6 Borcea R Romania
78 H1 Borçka Turkey
138 D6 Borda,C S Australia
47 K7 Bor Dağı mt Turkey
18 E8 Bordeaux France
98 B8 Bordeaux Wyoming
122 J7 Borden Pr Edward I
118 K6 Borden Sask
143 C10 Borden W Australia
114 H2 Borden I N W Terr
115 L3 Borden Pen N W Terr
95 N6 Bordentown New Jersey
15 F5 Borders reg Scotland
138 F6 Bordertown S Australia
32 M4 Bordesholm W Germany
44 C4 Bordighera Italy
85 D3 Bordj Flye Ste Marie Algeria
85 F2 Bordj Messouda Algeria
85 F3 Bordj Omar Driss Algeria
28 O9 Bordø isld Faeroes
57 H4 Bordunskiy U.S.S.R.
85 D5 Boré Mali
143 D8 Boreas,Mt W Australia
31 K4 Borek Poland
29 M11 Borgå Finland
115 R5 Borgarnes Iceland
26 G3 Borge Norway
26 G6 Börgefjell mt Norway
32 K9 Borgentreich W Germany
25 G3 Borger Netherlands
108 C8 Borger Texas
32 G7 Börger W Germany
32 K9 Borgholz W Germany
32 H8 Borgholzhausen W Germany
32 F8 Borghorst W Germany
43 H10 Borgia Italy
28 N3 Borgin Faeroes
22 J2 Borgloon Belgium
28 D2 Børglum Denmark
40 G5 Borgne R Switzerland
41 O5 Borgo Italy
45 J4 Borgo a Mozzano Italy
45 J1 Borgoforte Italy
45 N6 Borgo Montello Italy
44 F1 Borgonovo Val Tidone Italy
45 M4 Borgo Pace Italy
45 K2 Borgo Panigale Italy
45 O5 Borgorose Italy
42 D5 Borgo S. Lorenzo Italy
41 J6 Borgoticino Italy
44 G3 Borgo Val di Taro Italy
42 D2 Borgo Valsugana Italy
41 H7 Borgo Vercelli Italy
26 H9 Borgsjö Sweden
27 F14 Borgstena Sweden
12 D4 Borgue Scotland
26 B9 Borgund Norway
27 C10 Borgund Norway
26 H8 Borgvattnet Sweden
98 B8 Borie Wyoming
68 F3 Borikhane Laos
31 O6 Borinya U.S.S.R.
26 S2 Boris Gleb U.S.S.R.
31 O6 Borislav U.S.S.R.
57 E3 Borisovka U.S.S.R.
55 F4 Borisovskiy U.S.S.R.
54 B6 Borispol U.S.S.R.
130 C9 Borja Paraguay
17 F3 Borja Spain
42 H4 Borja Planina Yugoslavia
17 H3 Borjas Blancas Spain
26 M6 Börjelslandet Sweden
32 F9 Bork W Germany
32 E9 Borken W Germany
36 G1 Borken W Germany
54 H7 Borki U.S.S.R.
28 D5 Børkop Denmark
86 C2 Borkou dist Chad
52 C6 Borkovichi U.S.S.R.
25 G4 Borkulo Netherlands
32 E5 Borkum W Germany
27 H11 Borlänge Sweden
47 J6 Borlu Turkey
44 D3 Bormida di Millésimo R Italy
44 D3 Bormida di Spigno R Italy
42 C2 Bormio Italy
37 O1 Borna E Germany
25 E2 Borndiep Netherlands
25 G4 Borne Netherlands
70 B4 Borneo isld E Indies
16 C3 Bornes mt Portugal
36 B2 Bornheim W Germany
27 H16 Bornholm isld Denmark
27 G16 Bornholmsgattet str Sweden/Denmark
32 M4 Bornhöved W Germany
33 R7 Börnicke E Germany
33 R8 Bornim E Germany
86 B3 Borno prov Nigeria
16 D8 Bornos, Embalse de res Spain
86 E4 Boro R Sudan
48 K3 Boroaia Romania
70 M9 Borobudur ruins Java
71 E5 Borocay isld Panay Philippines
51 N2 Borogontsy U.S.S.R.
57 L3 Borohoro Shan mt ra China
71 H4 Boroko Sulawesi Indonesia
85 D6 Boromo Upper Volta
102 G6 Boron California
141 K6 Bororen Queensland
13 G5 Boroughbridge England
56 B5 Borovlyanka U.S.S.R.
55 F4 Borovoye U.S.S.R.
54 H1 Borovsk U.S.S.R.
55 E3 Borovskiy U.S.S.R.
55 D4 Borovskoye U.S.S.R.
27 G16 Borrby Sweden
28 K6 Borre Denmark
33 R5 Borrenthin E Germany
138 E5 Borrika S Australia
28 B5 Borris Denmark
14 E4 Borris Irish Rep
14 D4 Borrisoleigh Irish Rep
140 D3 Borroloola N Terr Aust
27 J13 Börrum Sweden
48 J3 Borşa Romania
58 G1 Borsch Chovochnyy Khrebet mt U.S.S.R.
33 R10 Borsdorf E Germany
26 P1 Börselv Norway
48 H2 Borshava R U.S.S.R.
48 K2 Borshchev U.S.S.R.
48 F2 Borsod-Abaúj Zemplén Hungary
25 A6 Borsselen Netherlands
33 N8 Börssum W Germany
28 K5 Borstahusen Sweden
32 J7 Borstel W Germany
57 K3 Bortala He R China
8 B3 Borth Wales
18 G7 Bort-les-Orgues France
26 G9 Börtnan Sweden
58 F1 Borto U.S.S.R.
77 B4 Borūjen Iran
77 A3 Borūjerd Iran
28 E4 Borum Denmark
28 H5 Borup Denmark
98 K2 Borup Minnesota
56 D4 Borus,Khrebet mts U.S.S.R.
31 K2 Bory Tucholskie forest Poland
31 M5 Borzęcin Poland
78 J1 Borzhomi U.S.S.R.
54 D5 Borzna U.S.S.R.
51 L3 Borzya U.S.S.R.
58 G1 Borzya R U.S.S.R.
57 G1 Bosaga U.S.S.R.
Bosaso see Bender Cassim
33 M4 Bosau W Germany
8 B6 Boscastle England
95 Q3 Boscawen New Hampshire
45 K1 Boschi Santa Anna Italy
20 H2 Bosc-le-Hard France
99 Q6 Boscobel Wisconsin
9 E6 Boscombe England
45 Q8 Boscotrecase Italy
67 B5 Bose China
38 K7 Bosenstein,Gross mt Austria
65 D6 Boshan China
55 F5 Boshchekul' U.S.S.R.
89 D7 Boshof S Africa
77 E3 Boshruyeh Iran
46 E2 Bosiljgrad Yugoslavia
68 G4 Bo Si Song Khram Thailand
27 G12 Bosjön Sweden
25 C4 Boskoop Netherlands
98 A8 Bosler Wyoming
8 D1 Bosley England
42 H4 Bosna R Yugoslavia
86 C5 Bosobolo Zaïre
61 O10 Bōsō-hantō pen Japan
32 G10 Bösperde W Germany
Bosporus Turkey see Karadeniz Boğazı
106 D7 Bosque New Mexico
124 G2 Bosque Bonito Mexico
86 C4 Bossangoa Cent Afr Republic
86 C4 Bossèmbélé Cent Afr Republic
86 C4 Bossemtele Cent Afr Republic
111 C9 Bossier City Louisiana
86 B3 Bosso Niger
66 D3 Bosten Hu L China
9 F2 Boston England
113 D7 Boston Georgia
95 Q4 Boston Massachusetts
97 Boston conurbation Massachusetts
138 D5 Boston B S Australia
117 N11 Boston Bar Br Col
127 M2 Boston Bay Jamaica
110 C6 Boston Mts Arkansas
13 G6 Boston Spa England
28 F6 Bøstrup Fyn Denmark
28 D4 Bøstrup Viborg Denmark
48 E5 Bosut R Yugoslavia
123 O5 Boswarlos Nfld
117 P11 Boswell Br Col
99 T9 Boswell Indiana
107 P7 Boswell Oklahoma
94 H6 Boswell Pennsylvania
110 C2 Bosworth Missouri
74 D7 Botad India
139 K5 Botany B New S Wales
26 J8 Boteå Sweden
47 G2 Botev mt Bulgaria
47 F2 Botevgrad Bulgaria
118 E6 Botha Alberta
9 F1 Bothamsall England
87 E11 Bothaville S Africa
13 E4 Bothel England
117 M12 Bothell Washington
26 L8 Bothnia,Gulf of Sweden/Finland
120 J10 Bothwell Ontario
12 D2 Bothwell Scotland
139 H8 Bothwell Tasmania
86 B1 Botiala Somalia
16 B3 Boticas Portugal
87 D10 Botletle R Botswana
9 E6 Botley England
48 M4 Botna R U.S.S.R.
28 H7 Bøtø Denmark
71 D3 Botolan Pt Luzon Philippines
48 K3 Botoşani Romania
68 H4 Bo Trach Vietnam
22 L3 Botrange mt Belgium
26 L7 Botsmark Sweden
89 C4 Botswana rep Africa
43 G9 Botte Donato mt Italy
89 A8 Botter Kloof Pass S Africa
9 F2 Bottesford England
114 J8 Bottineau N Dakota
9 G3 Bottisham England
127 N6 Bottom Saba W I
9 E1 Bottom House England
45 M1 Bottrighe Italy
32 E9 Bottrop W Germany
47 F1 Botunya R Bulgaria
115 O8 Botwood Nfld
43 A12 Bou Aci Algeria
85 C7 Bouaflé Ivory Coast
20 H3 Bouafles France
85 D7 Bouaké Ivory Coast
86 C4 Bouala Cent Afr Republic
86 C4 Bouar Cent Afr Republic
85 D2 Bouârfa Morocco
21 B7 Bouaye France
30 H6 Boubín mt Czechoslovakia
86 C4 Bouca Cent Afr Republic
18 D9 Boucau France
140 C1 Boucaut B N Terr Aust
20 E4 Boucé France
22 E3 Bouchain France
22 D4 Bouchavesnes France
43 B12 Bouchegouf Algeria
123 N2 Boucher,L Quebec
19 N17 Bouches-du-Rhône dep France
121 P6 Bouchette Quebec
22 D4 Bouchoir France
85 D5 Bou Djébéha Mali
84 A3 Boudnib Morocco
40 A2 Boudreville France
40 E4 Boudry Switzerland
21 B7 Bouée France
122 E3 Bouffard,L Quebec
137 M3 Bougainville isld Solomon Is
142 F2 Bougainville, C W Australia
141 H3 Bougainville Reef Gt Barrier Reef Aust
71 C2 Bougainville,Selat W Irian
85 F1 Bougaroun,C Algeria
21 I7 Bouges-le-Château France
Bougie see Bejaia
85 C6 Bougouni Mali
43 C11 Bouhairet Benzart gulf Tunisia
17 G9 Bou Hanifa Algeria
17 G9 Bou Hanifa, Barrage de Algeria
127 M4 Bouillante Guadeloupe W I
20 G3 Bouille,la France
21 E7 Bouillé-Loretz France
21 D6 Bouillé-Ménard France
22 J4 Bouillon Belgium
85 C3 Bou Izakam Morocco
123 L3 Boulain,L Quebec
19 K3 Boulay France
98 A9 Boulder Colorado
101 N3 Boulder Montana
103 N4 Boulder Utah
143 D9 Boulder W Australia
101 Q7 Boulder Wyoming
103 K5 Boulder Can Nevada
103 K6 Boulder City Nevada
102 B4 Boulder Cr California
100 J7 Boulder Cr Idaho
121 N5 Bouleau, L. au Quebec
102 H9 Boulevard California
136 H6 Boulia Queensland
140 E6 Boulia Queensland
22 B2 Boulogne France
21 G6 Bouloire France
85 C5 Boulouli Mali
85 D6 Boulsa Upper Volta
22 H5 Boult-aux-Bois France
85 G6 Boultoum Niger
22 H4 Boulzicourt France
86 C5 Boumba R Cameroon
85 D7 Bouna Ivory Coast
117 C3 Boundary Alaska
116 R4 Boundary Yukon Terr
102 F4 Boundary Pk Nevada
118 J9 Boundary Plateau Mont/Sask
114 G7 Boundary Ranges Br Col
85 C7 Boundiali Ivory Coast
68 H6 Boung Long Cambodia
68 E2 Boun Neua Laos
106 E4 Bountiful Colorado
140 E3 Bountiful Is Queensland
118 K7 Bounty Sask
20 K1 Bouquemaison France
28 M2 Bøur Faeroes
110 E3 Bourbeuse R Missouri
94 A5 Bourbon Indiana
110 E3 Bourbon Missouri
83 L14 Bourbon,C Kerguelen Indian Oc
18 H6 Bourbon-Lancy France
18 H6 Bourbon l'Archambault France
18 H6 Bourbonnais prov France
40 C2 Bourbonne les Bains France
18 G7 Bourboule,la France
19 J5 Bourboune les Bassigny France
22 C2 Bourbourg France
19 O13 Bourbre R France
19 O15 Bourdeaux France
36 B6 Bourdonnay France
16 E10 Boured Morocco
85 D5 Bourem Mali
18 E7 Bourg Gironde France
20 G3 Bourg-Achard France
21 I10 Bourganeuf France
21 H9 Bourg Archambault France
18 H7 Bourg Argental France
19 Q15 Bourg d'Arud France
19 O14 Bourg-de-Péage France
21 B6 Bourg-des-Comptes France
20 G2 Bourg Dun France
19 O12 Bourg-en-Bresse Ain France
18 G5 Bourges France
22 F5 Bourg et Comin France
40 C6 Bourget,L.du France
20 K4 Bourget,le France
18 G10 Bourg-Madame France
21 D7 Bourgneuf Maine-et-Loire France
21 E6 Bourg-Neuf Maine-et-Loire France
21 B7 Bourgneuf-en-Retz France
20 D5 Bourgneuf,le France
22 G5 Bourgogne France
19 O13 Bourgoin France
40 E6 Bourg-St-Maurice France
20 G3 Bourgtheroulde France
20 E3 Bourguébus France
21 F7 Bourgueil France
120 K4 Bourkes Ontario
121 N4 Bourlamaque Quebec
22 E3 Bourlon France
40 C1 Bourmont France
121 P4 Bourmont Quebec
21 G7 Bournan France
21 F7 Bournand France
9 F2 Bourne England
115 K1 Bourne,C N W Terr
9 F4 Bourne End England
9 E6 Bournemouth England
20 G3 Bourneville France
21 C8 Bournezeau France
18 E8 Bourriot Bergonce France
32 F7 Bourtanger Moor W Germany
20 G4 Bourth France
22 B2 Bourthes France
8 D5 Bourton England
86 D3 Bourtoutou Chad
22 L4 Bous Luxembourg
85 E1 Bou Saâda Algeria
43 B12 Bou Salem Tunisia
103 K8 Bouse Arizona
103 K8 Bouse Wash R Arizona
36 B5 Bous/Saar W Germany
21 J9 Boussac France
20 B5 Boussac, la France
21 C7 Boussay France
22 L5 Bousse France
86 C3 Bousso Chad
20 K5 Boutigny France
85 B5 Boutilimit Mauritania
21 E9 Boutonne R France
143 B10 Bouvard,C W Australia
19 O13 Bouvesse France
90 J14 Bouvet isld S Atlantic Oc
81 A12 Bouvetøy isld S Atlantic Oc
21 B7 Bouvron France
36 C6 Bouxwiller France
85 F6 Bouza Niger
36 B5 Bouzonville France
28 C7 Bov Denmark
43 G11 Bova Italy
32 L9 Bovenden W Germany
70 C4 Boven Kapuas mts Sarawak
28 F6 Bovense Denmark
26 C10 Böverdal Norway
20 K2 Boves France
44 C3 Boves Italy
8 C6 Bovey Tracey England
22 K3 Bovigny Belgium
100 J3 Bovill Idaho
43 G7 Bovino Italy
28 A4 Bøvlingbjerg Denmark
45 L1 Bovolenta Italy
45 K1 Bovolone Italy
8 C6 Bow England
98 D1 Bowbells N Dakota
113 F7 Bowden Florida
127 M3 Bowden Jamaica
98 G4 Bowdle S Dakota
101 S1 Bowdoin,L Montana
112 B4 Bowdon Georgia
98 G2 Bowdon N Dakota
143 B10 Bowelling W Australia
110 E1 Bowen Illinois
141 J5 Bowen Queensland
141 J5 Bowen R Queensland
141 H5 Bowen Downs Queensland
117 M11 Bowen I Br Col
140 B1 Bowen Str N Terr Aust
95 M7 Bowers Delaware
94 D7 Bowersville Ohio
101 L5 Bowery Pk Idaho
13 F5 Bowes England
143 B8 Bowgada W Australia
103 P9 Bowie Arizona
106 C3 Bowie Colorado
141 H5 Bowie Queensland
109 K2 Bowie Texas
118 F9 Bow Island Alberta
78 L3 Bowkan Iran
12 D2 Bowling Scotland
113 F10 Bowling Green Florida
110 J2 Bowling Green Indiana
110 K4 Bowling Green Kentucky
110 E2 Bowling Green Missouri
94 D5 Bowling Green Ohio
95 K8 Bowling Green Virginia
141 H4 Bowling Green,C Queensland
112 D3 Bowman Georgia
98 C3 Bowman N Dakota
121 M9 Bowmanville Ontario
15 B5 Bowmore Scotland
118 C7 Bowness Alberta
13 F5 Bowness England
118 C7 Bow R Alberta
142 G3 Bow River W Australia
117 N9 Bowron Lake Prov. Park Br Columbia
117 J7 Bowser L Br Columbia
119 Q6 Bowsman Manitoba
118 B7 Bow Valley Prov. Park Alberta
36 H5 Boxberg W Germany
98 C7 Box Butte Res Nebraska
98 A6 Box Cr Wyoming
101 P1 Box Elder Montana
98 C5 Box Elder S Dakota
106 F2 Box Elder Cr Colorado
98 B4 Boxelder Cr Montana
101 R2 Boxelder Cr Montana
9 F5 Box Hill England
27 H13 Boxholm Sweden
58 G5 Bo Xian China
65 D6 Boxing China
25 E5 Boxmeer Netherlands
138 F4 Box Tank New S Wales
25 D5 Boxtel Netherlands
78 E1 Boyabat Turkey
128 D2 Boyacá div Colombia
86 C4 Boyali Cent Afr Republic
47 K3 Boyalık Turkey
58 G6 Boyang China
143 B10 Boyanup W Australia
111 D10 Boyce Louisiana
94 J7 Boyce Virginia
143 D8 Boyce,Mt W Australia
115 K6 Boyd Manitoba
101 Q4 Boyd Montana
109 K2 Boyd Texas
123 S4 Boyd's Cove Newfoundland
94 J10 Boydton Virginia
65 C5 Boye China
99 L7 Boyer Iowa
99 L7 Boyer R Iowa
106 G3 Boyero Colorado
95 M6 Boyertown Pennsylvania
98 A4 Boyes Montana
95 K10 Boykins Virginia
118 E4 Boyle Alberta
14 C3 Boyle Irish Rep
111 F8 Boyle Mississippi
123 L8 Boylston Nova Scotia
14 E3 Boyne R Irish Rep
141 K6 Boyne R Queensland
94 C1 Boyne City Michigan
94 C1 Boyne Falls Michigan
20 K5 Boynes France
110 C1 Boynton Missouri
107 P6 Boynton Oklahoma
113 G11 Boynton Beach Florida
86 E5 Boyoma Falls Zaire
101 R6 Boysen Res Wyoming
143 B10 Boyup Brook W Australia
47 J8 Bozburun Turkey
47 H5 Bozcaada isld Turkey
47 L5 Boz Dağ mt Turkey
47 J7 Bozdoğan Turkey
114 H8 Bozeman Montana
Bozen see Bolzano
86 C5 Bozene Zaïre
31 K1 Boże Pole Poland
65 C5 Bozhen China
37 O3 Boží Dar Czechoslovakia
78 D3 Bozkir Turkey
54 F1 Boznya U.S.S.R.
78 G3 Bozova Turkey
48 G6 Bozovici Romania
45 J1 Bozzolo Italy
44 C2 Bra Italy
22 G2 Brabançonne prov Belgium
22 G2 Brabant prov Belgium
146 E14 Brabant I Antarctica
119 O2 Brabant L Sask
28 E4 Brabrand Denmark
28 H6 Bråby Denmark
42 H5 Brač isld Yugoslavia
15 B3 Bracadale Scotland
129 H6 Braça Menor R Brazil
44 M5 Bracciano Italy
42 E6 Bracciano,Lago di Italy
44 M5 Bracciano, Lago di Italy
121 L7 Bracebridge Ontario
84 E4 Brach Libya
21 I6 Bracieux France
26 H9 Bräcke Sweden
118 J9 Bracken Sask
109 J6 Bracken Texas
36 G5 Brackenheim W Germany
13 G6 Brackenhill England
119 S5 Bracken L Manitoba
108 G6 Brackettville Texas
9 E3 Brackley England
9 F5 Bracknell England
32 J9 Brackwede W Germany
12 E1 Braco Scotland
43 G8 Bradano R Italy
98 F3 Braddock N Dakota
94 H6 Braddock Pennsylvania
99 L9 Braddyville Iowa
113 E10 Bradenton Florida
113 E10 Bradenton Beach Florida
28 B7 Braderup W Germany
110 E6 Bradford Arkansas
8 D5 Bradford England
13 G6 Bradford England
99 R8 Bradford Illinois
99 N7 Bradford Iowa
95 T1 Bradford Maine
95 P3 Bradford New Hampshire
94 C6 Bradford Ohio
121 L8 Bradford Ontario
94 J5 Bradford Pennsylvania
95 Q5 Bradford Rhode I
94 B9 Bradfordsville Kentucky
111 C8 Bradley Arkansas
102 D6 Bradley California
99 T8 Bradley Illinois
107 N7 Bradley Oklahoma
110 D5 Bradleyville Missouri
94 D5 Bradner Ohio
123 P2 Bradore Bay Quebec
123 P2 Bradore Hills Quebec
98 J9 Bradshaw Nebraska
140 B3 Bradshaw N Terr Aust
142 F3 Bradshaw,Mt W Australia
119 R9 Bradwardine Manitoba
9 G4 Bradwell England
118 L7 Bradwell Sask
98 F8 Brady Nebraska
109 H4 Brady Texas
117 E6 Brady Glacier Alaska
138 C3 Brady,Mt S Australia
28 D5 Brædstrup Denmark
138 E5 Braemar S Australia
15 E3 Braemar Scotland
15 E3 Braeriach mt Scotland
142 D5 Braeside W Australia
16 B3 Braga Portugal
131 E5 Bragado Argentina
129 J4 Bragança Brazil
16 C3 Bragança Portugal
130 F8 Bragança Paulista Brazil
112 E6 Braganza Georgia
110 G5 Bragg City Missouri
118 C7 Bragg Creek Prov. Park Alberta
54 B5 Bragin U.S.S.R.
99 N4 Braham Minnesota
33 N6 Brahlstorf Schwerin E Germany
75 O7 Brahmanbaria Bangladesh
75 P5 Brahmaputra R S Asia
32 L4 Brahmsee L W Germany
77 K5 Brahui,Cen reg Pakistan
99 S8 Braidwood Illinois
48 L5 Brăila Romania
9 E2 Brailsford England
98 J8 Brainard Nebraska
22 F5 Braine France
22 G2 Braine L'Alleud Belgium
22 G2 Braine-le Château Belgium
22 G2 Braine-le Comte Belgium
99 M3 Brainerd Minnesota
21 F7 Brain-sur-Allonnes France
9 G4 Braintree England
13 E4 Braithwaite England
111 G12 Braithwaite Louisiana
140 C1 Braithwaite Pt N Terr Aust
22 J2 Braives Belgium
89 F4 Brak R S Africa
32 H6 Brake W Germany
22 F2 Brakel Belgium
32 K9 Brakel W Germany
85 B5 Brakna reg Mauritania
57 D1 Brali U.S.S.R.
114 G7 Bralorne Br Columbia
107 N5 Braman Oklahoma
Brambach see Radiumbad-Brambach
38 F7 Bramberg Austria
13 G6 Bramham England
32 H6 Bramloge W Germany
28 B6 Bramming Denmark
44 B3 Bram,Monte Italy
26 J9 Brämö isld Sweden
9 H3 Brampton England
98 J3 Brampton N Dakota
141 J5 Brampton I Queensland
32 G8 Bramsche W Germany
141 G1 Bramwell Queensland
94 F9 Bramwell W Virginia
9 G2 Brancaster England
13 G4 Brancepeth England
99 U6 Branch Michigan
123 T7 Branch Nfld
95 K4 Branchport New York
112 G4 Branchville S Carolina
130 B7 Branco R Mato Grosso Brazil
128 F3 Branco R Roraima Brazil
130 J9 Branco,Cabo Brazil
131 B2 Branco,R Argentina
41 L3 Brand Austria
37 O3 Brand Czechoslovakia
87 B10 Brandberg mt Namibia
26 H9 Brändbo Sweden
28 C5 Brande Denmark
32 L5 Brande-Hörnerkirchen W Germany
101 T4 Brandenberg Montana
33 R8 Brandenburg E Germany
110 K4 Brandenburg Kentucky
37 P2 Brand-Erbisdorf E Germany
28 C6 Branderup Denmark
21 G9 Brandes reg France
13 H6 Brandesburton England
89 E7 Brandfort S Africa
33 R10 Brandis E Germany
29 J11 Brändö Finland
106 H3 Brandon Colorado
9 G3 Brandon England
119 S9 Brandon Manitoba
98 E9 Brandon Nebraska
141 H4 Brandon Queensland
95 O3 Brandon Vermont
99 S6 Brandon Wisconsin
14 A4 Brandon B Irish Rep
14 A4 Brandon Hd Irish Rep
14 A4 Brandon Mt Irish Rep
95 N3 Brandreth New York
13 G5 Brandsby England
133 F5 Brandsen Argentina
28 D6 Brandsø isld Denmark
110 E5 Brandsville Missouri
98 K5 Brandt S Dakota
27 F11 Brandval Norway
87 D12 Brandvlei S Africa
94 K8 Brandy Virginia
95 L8 Brandywine Maryland
48 K6 Braneşti Romania
95 P5 Branford Connecticut
113 E8 Branford Florida
31 M1 Braniewo Poland
27 L17 Braniewo U.S.S.R.
31 M6 Branisko mts Czechoslovakia
18 E8 Branne France
47 H3 Brannitsa Bulgaria
141 F8 Bransby Queensland
102 A2 Branscomb California
146 E14 Bransfield Str Antarctica
106 G4 Branson Colorado
110 C5 Branson Missouri
9 F1 Branston England
118 D8 Brant Alberta
70 O9 Brantas Java
70 O10 Brantas R Java
98 H2 Brantford N Dakota
115 L9 Brantford Ontario
111 K10 Brantley Alabama
18 F7 Brantôme France
138 F7 Branxholme Victoria
115 N8 Bras d'or L Nova Scotia
99 O9 Brashear Missouri
128 E6 Brasiléia Brazil
129 J7 Brasília Brazil
129 G4 Brasilia Legal Brazil
52 C6 Braslav U.S.S.R.
48 K5 Brasov Romania
85 F8 Brass Nigeria
22 G1 Brasschaat Belgium
140 C6 Brassey Mt N Terr Aust
143 D6 Brassey Ra W Australia
70 E2 Brassey Ra mts Sabah
139 G5 Brassi New S Wales
28 D4 Brassø L Denmark
95 R1 Brassua L Maine
48 H4 Bratca Romania
48 L5 Brates, L Romania
31 K7 Bratislava Czechoslovakia
47 G3 Bratsigovo Bulgaria
56 F3 Bratsk U.S.S.R.
48 M2 Bratslav U.S.S.R.

14 Bunger Hills — Campagne d'Alençon

146 E3 **Bunger Hills** Antarctica
141 J7 **Bungil** *R* Queensland
71 H6 **Bunginkela** *isld* Sulawesi Indonesia
70 G6 **Bungku** Sulawesi Indonesia
87 C7 **Bungo** Angola
60 G2 **Bungo-suido** *str* Japan
69 J11 **Bunguran Selatan Kep** *islds* Indonesia
70 H10 **Bunguran Utara, Kep** *isld* Indonesia
86 B3 **Buni** Nigeria
86 F5 **Bunia** Zaïre
143 E9 **Buningonia** W Australia
70 E3 **Bunju** *isld* Kalimantan
110 E4 **Bunker** Missouri
141 K6 **Bunker Grp** *islds* Gt Barrier Reef Aust
116 E4 **Bunker Hill** Alaska
110 G2 **Bunker Hill** Illinois
110 K1 **Bunker Hill** Indiana
107 M3 **Bunker Hill** Kansas
103 K5 **Bunkerville** Nevada
117 E8 **Bunkeya** Zaïre
111 D11 **Bunkie** Louisiana
113 F8 **Bunnell** Florida
9 E2 **Bunny** England
145 E4 **Bunnythorpe** New Zealand
68 H7 **Bu Noi** Vietnam
17 G5 **Buñol** Spain
25 D4 **Bunschoten** Netherlands
143 B8 **Buntine** W Australia
9 F4 **Buntingford** England
70 D5 **Buntok** Kalimantan
70 D6 **Buntui** Kalimantan
84 E3 **Bū Nujaym** Libya
70 C4 **Bunut** Kalimantan
141 K1 **Bunyaville** *dist* Brisbane, Qnsld
68 E3 **Bun Yun** Thailand
70 G4 **Buol** Sulawesi Indonesia
51 L1 **Buolkalakh** U.S.S.R.
51 N1 **Buorkhaya,Guba** *gulf* U.S.S.R.
28 A4 **Bur** Denmark
88 G3 **Bura** Kenya
77 D7 **Buraimi** U.A.E.
143 B9 **Burakin** W Australia
86 E3 **Buram** Sudan
143 E10 **Buraminya,Mt** W Australia
86 A1 **Buran** Somalia
141 K2 **Buranda** *dist* Brisbane, Qnsld
75 J3 **Burang** China
130 H5 **Buranhaém** Brazil
45 M1 **Burano** Italy
86 J4 **Burao** Somalia
111 G12 **Buras** Louisiana
71 G5 **Burauen** Leyte Philippines
72 E3 **Buraydah** Saudi Arabia
55 C3 **Burayevo** U.S.S.R.
36 E2 **Burbach** W Germany
9 E6 **Burbage** England
102 F7 **Burbank** California
98 K9 **Burchard** Nebraska
139 H5 **Burcher** New S Wales
96 N6 **Burchinal** Iowa
57 C5 **Burdalyk** U.S.S.R.
141 H5 **Burdekin** *R* Queensland
141 H5 **Burdekin Falls** Queensland
117 M7 **Burden,Mt** Br Col
118 F9 **Burdett** Alberta
95 L4 **Burdett** New York
48 K3 **Burdujeni** Romania
78 C3 **Burdur** Turkey
47 L7 **Burdur Gölü** *L* Turkey
75 M7 **Burdwan** India
90 E14 **Burdwood Bank** Atlantic Oc
26 M7 **Bureå** Sweden
121 P4 **Bureau, L** Quebec
86 G4 **Burei** Ethiopia
51 N4 **Bureinskiy Khrebet** *mts* U.S.S.R.
25 D5 **Buren** Netherlands
32 J9 **Büren** W Germany
51 N4 **Bureya** U.S.S.R.
59 K1 **Bureya** *R* U.S.S.R.
9 E4 **Burford** England
33 P8 **Burg** E Germany
32 K5 **Burg** W Germany
36 D5 **Burgalben** W Germany
77 A5 **Burgān** Kuwait
47 J2 **Burgas** Bulgaria
33 O7 **Burgau** Austria
37 J7 **Burgau** W Germany
86 H6 **Bur Gavo** Somalia
112 J3 **Burgaw** N Carolina
47 K6 **Burgaz Dağ** *mt* Turkey
37 J5 **Burgbernheim** W Germany
100 K4 **Burgdorf** Idaho
40 G3 **Burgdorf** Switzerland
32 M8 **Burgdorf** W Germany
37 K4 **Burgebrach** W Germany
37 M2 **Bürgel** E Germany
48 C3 **Burgenland** *prov* Austria
123 P6 **Burgeo** Nfld
87 E12 **Burgersdorp** S Africa
9 F6 **Burgess Hill** England
95 L9 **Burgess Store** Virginia
13 G2 **Burgh** England
25 A5 **Burgh** Netherlands
36 H2 **Burghaun** W Germany
38 G5 **Burghausen** W Germany
37 L6 **Burgheim** W Germany
9 G1 **Burgh-le-Marsh** England
43 E11 **Burgio** Sicily
36 H3 **Burgjoss** W Germany
37 L3 **Burgkunstadt** W Germany
37 N5 **Burglengenfeld** W Germany
16 E2 **Burgos** Spain
16 E2 **Burgos** *prov* Spain
37 K3 **Burgpreppach** W Germany
36 H3 **Burgsinn** W Germany
37 O2 **Burgstädt** E Germany
36 G4 **Bürgstadt** W Germany
33 S6 **Burg Stargard** E Germany
32 F8 **Burgsteinfurt** W Germany
27 K14 **Burgsvik** Sweden
17 G2 **Burguete** Spain
36 F2 **Burgwald** W Germany
32 L7 **Burgwedel** W Germany
37 K4 **Burgwindheim** W Germany
47 H5 **Burhaniye** Turkey
32 H5 **Burhave** W Germany
130 E8 **Buri** Brazil
71 F4 **Burias** *isld* Philippines
71 F4 **Burias Pass** Luzon Philippines
123 R6 **Burin** Nfld
55 D3 **Burino** U.S.S.R.
68 F5 **Buriram** Thailand
130 F7 **Buritama** Brazil
128 G6 **Buriti** *R* Brazil
130 E6 **Buriti Alegre** Brazil
129 K5 **Buriti Bravo** Brazil
130 F4 **Buritis** Brazil
80 C8 **Burj el Baiyara** Jordan
28 C7 **Burkal** Denmark
109 J1 **Burkburnett** Texas
100 K2 **Burke** Idaho
98 G6 **Burke** S Dakota
109 N4 **Burke** Texas
140 E6 **Burke** *R* Queensland
140 F5 **Burke** *R* Queensland
117 K9 **Burke Chan** Br Col
146 H11 **Burke I** Antarctica
144 C6 **Burke Pass** New Zealand
110 L5 **Burkesville** Kentucky
140 E4 **Burketown** Queensland
109 H4 **Burkett** Texas
94 J9 **Burkeville** Virginia
37 O2 **Burkhardtsdorf** E Germany
98 G4 **Burkmere** S Dakota
121 L7 **Burk's Falls** Ontario
55 G4 **Burla** U.S.S.R.
36 G7 **Burladingen** W Germany
141 G5 **Burleigh** Queensland
109 K3 **Burleson** Texas
13 G6 **Burley** England
101 M7 **Burley** Idaho
8 D3 **Burley Gate** England
55 D4 **Burli** U.S.S.R.
102 B4 **Burlingame** California
107 P3 **Burlingame** Kansas
106 H2 **Burlington** Colorado
99 P9 **Burlington** Iowa
107 P3 **Burlington** Kansas
112 H1 **Burlington** N Carolina
95 N6 **Burlington** New Jersey
123 Q4 **Burlington** Nfld
121 L9 **Burlington** Ontario
95 O2 **Burlington** Vermont
117 M11 **Burlington** Washington
101 R5 **Burlington** Wyoming
110 A1 **Burlington Junction** Missouri
8 D2 **Burlton** England
57 J2 **Burlyu-Tobe** U.S.S.R.
80 G5 **Burma** Jordan
68 B2 **Burma** *rep* S E Asia
139 H6 **Burmah Forest** Victoria
55 D1 **Burmantovo** U.S.S.R.
101 N9 **Burmester** Utah
118 C9 **Burmis** Alberta
144 D5 **Burnbrae** New Zealand
109 J5 **Burnet** Texas
141 K7 **Burnett** *R* Queensland
141 K6 **Burnett Hd** Queensland
100 D9 **Burney** California
143 C10 **Burngup** W Australia
8 C5 **Burnham** England
9 G4 **Burnham** Essex England
95 S2 **Burnham** Maine
144 D5 **Burnham** New Zealand
94 K6 **Burnham** Pennsylvania
9 G2 **Burnham Deepdale** England
9 G2 **Burnham Market** England
40 F2 **Burnhaupt** France
139 H8 **Burnie** Tasmania
13 H5 **Burniston** England
13 F6 **Burnley** England
13 G4 **Burnopfield** England
57 F3 **Burnoye** U.S.S.R.
101 T10 **Burns** Colorado
100 F6 **Burns** Oregon
98 B8 **Burns** Wyoming
13 G5 **Burnsall** England
110 M5 **Burnside** Kentucky
94 J6 **Burnside** Pennsylvania
114 G7 **Burns Lake** Br Col
98 G3 **Burnstad** N Dakota
112 E2 **Burnsville** N Carolina
122 G6 **Burnsville** New Brunswick
94 G8 **Burnsville** W Virginia
101 P8 **Burntfork** Wyoming
126 G3 **Burnt Ground** Long I Bahamas
15 E1 **Burntisland** Scotland
122 J1 **Burnt L** Labrador
116 Q3 **Burnt Paw** Alaska
100 H5 **Burnt R** Oregon
100 B9 **Burnt Ranch** California
121 M8 **Burnt River** Ontario
119 R3 **Burntwood L** Manitoba
33 S5 **Burow** E Germany
66 D2 **Burqin** China
119 M6 **Burr** Sask
138 E5 **Burra** S Australia
143 C9 **Burracoppin** W Australia
99 P6 **Burr Oak** Iowa
107 M2 **Burr Oak** Kansas
94 B5 **Burr Oak** Michigan
94 E7 **Burr Oak Res** Ohio
15 F2 **Burray** Scotland
46 D3 **Burrel** Albania
140 C6 **Burrell,Mt** N Terr Aust
13 E1 **Burrelton** Scotland
139 J5 **Burrendong Res.** New South Wales
17 G5 **Burriana** Spain
13 H6 **Burringham** England
124 J3 **Burro** Mexico
103 L7 **Burro Cr** Arizona
108 E6 **Burro, Serranias del** *mts* Mexico
113 K11 **Burrow Cay** Bahamas
140 F3 **Burrowes, Pt** Queensland
15 D6 **Burrow Head** Scotland
107 N3 **Burrton** Kansas
140 B2 **Burrundie** N Terr Aust
133 E3 **Burruyacú** Argentina
111 G13 **Burrwood** Louisiana
8 B4 **Burry Port** Wales
78 B1 **Bursa** Turkey
84 J4 **Bur Safâga** Egypt
36 C1 **Burscheid** W Germany
13 F6 **Burscough** England
32 L9 **Bursfelde** W Germany
8 D1 **Burslem** England
28 G7 **Bursø** Denmark
22 F2 **Burst** Belgium
118 H8 **Burstall** Sask
99 M6 **Burt** Iowa
98 D3 **Burt** N Dakota
138 F4 **Burta** New S Wales
94 C1 **Burt L** Michigan
9 E6 **Burton** England
98 G7 **Burton** Nebraska
109 L5 **Burton** Texas
8 B4 **Burton** Wales
13 H5 **Burton Agnes** England
13 F5 **Burton-in-Kendal** England
112 D3 **Burton L** Georgia
14 C2 **Burtonport** Irish Rep
9 E2 **Burton upon Trent** England
26 L7 **Burträsk** Sweden
122 F7 **Burtts Corner** New Brunswick
138 F5 **Burtundy** New S Wales
140 C6 **Burt Well** N Terr Aust
136 F2 **Buru** *isld* Moluccas Indonesia
84 J3 **Burullus** *L* Egypt
88 B3 **Burundi** *rep* Cent Africa
69 F12 **Burung** Sumatra
88 B3 **Bururi** Burundi
85 F7 **Burutu** Nigeria
8 D3 **Burwarton** England
9 G6 **Burwash** England
9 G1 **Burwell** England
98 G8 **Burwell** Nebraska
33 S10 **Burxdorf** E Germany
13 F6 **Bury** Greater Manchester England
121 T7 **Bury** Quebec
9 F6 **Bury** W Sussex England
56 F5 **Buryatskaya** U.S.S.R.
9 G3 **Bury St.Edmunds** England
43 E11 **Busambra, Rca** *mt* Sicily
71 F7 **Busan B** Mindanao Philippines
87 D7 **Busango** Zaïre
118 D5 **Busby** Alberta
101 T4 **Busby** Montana
44 B2 **Busca** Italy
33 R7 **Buschow** E Germany
32 J4 **Buschsand** *isld* W Germany
46 E3 **Buševa Planina** *mt* Yugoslavia
46 D3 **Bushat** Albania
77 B5 **Bushehr** Iran
88 C2 **Bushenyi** Uganda
95 M5 **Bushkill** Pennsylvania
108 B8 **Bushland** Texas
113 E9 **Bushnell** Florida
110 F1 **Bushnell** Illinois
98 C8 **Bushnell** Nebraska
121 L6 **Bushnell** Ontario
107 M3 **Bushton** Kansas
140 E5 **Bushy Park** Queensland
89 F1 **Busi** *R* Zimbabwe
88 E1 **Busia** Uganda
22 E3 **Busigny** France
86 D5 **Businga** Zaïre
86 C6 **Busira** *R* Zaïre
48 J1 **Busk** U.S.S.R.
27 C11 **Buskerud** *reg* Norway
31 M5 **Busko** Poland
55 D4 **Buskul'** U.S.S.R.
71 B1 **Busobuso** Halmahera Indonesia
19 K5 **Bussang** France
40 E2 **Bussang,Col.de** *pass* France
143 B10 **Busselton** W Australia
44 H2 **Busseto** Italy
99 O8 **Bussey** Iowa
21 G9 **Bussiere Poitevine** France
41 N7 **Bussolengo** Italy
25 D4 **Bussum** Netherlands
57 C4 **Bustan** U.S.S.R.
77 D6 **Bustaneh** Iran
80 D2 **Bustan Ha Galil** Israel
141 K6 **Bustard Hd** Queensland
48 K5 **Busteni** Romania
42 B3 **Busto Arsizio** Italy
71 D4 **Busuanga** Philippines
86 D5 **Busu Djanoa** Zaïre
32 J4 **Büsum** W Germany
86 D5 **Buta** Zaïre
131 G2 **Butai** *R* Brazil
70 O9 **Butak, G** *mt* Java
69 D9 **Butang Group** *isld* Thailand
133 D5 **Buta Ranquil** Argentina
88 B3 **Butare** Rwanda
71 F3 **Butauanan** *isld* Philippines
138 E5 **Bute** S Australia
Bute *co see* **Strathclyde** *reg*
15 C5 **Bute** *isld* Scotland
117 J9 **Butedale** Br Col
117 L10 **Bute Inlet** Br Col
88 B1 **Butembo** Zaïre
22 L3 **Bütgenbach** Belgium
59 H2 **Butha Qi** China
68 A2 **Buthidaung** Burma
86 F5 **Butiaba** Uganda
32 H5 **Butjadingen** *reg* W Germany
55 D3 **Butka** U.S.S.R.
68 B3 **Butle** *R* Burma
111 H9 **Butler** Alabama
112 C5 **Butler** Georgia
94 C5 **Butler** Indiana
110 M3 **Butler** Kentucky
110 B3 **Butler** Missouri
95 N6 **Butler** New Jersey
94 E6 **Butler** Ohio
107 L6 **Butler** Oklahoma
94 H6 **Butler** Pennsylvania
98 J4 **Butler** S Dakota
146 E12 **Butler I** Antarctica
138 B2 **Butlers Dome** *mt* N Terr Australia
80 G2 **Butmiye** Syria
70 D5 **Butong** Kalimantan
46 D5 **Butrintit, Liqen i** *L* Albania
140 E5 **Butru** Queensland
41 K3 **Bütschwil** Switzerland
45 K1 **Buttapietra** Italy
114 H8 **Butte** Montana
98 F2 **Butte** N Dakota
98 H7 **Butte** Nebraska
100 C7 **Butte Falls** Oregon
37 L1 **Buttelstedt** E Germany
102 C1 **Butte Meadows** California
32 L5 **Buttenhausen** W Germany
37 L4 **Buttenheim** W Germany
37 K6 **Buttenwiesen** W Germany
100 F4 **Butter Cr** Oregon
99 M6 **Butterfield** Minnesota
143 D8 **Butterfly** W Australia
13 E5 **Buttermere** England
87 E12 **Butterworth** S Africa
14 C4 **Buttevant** Irish Rep
143 G6 **Buttfield, Mt** W Australia
27 K14 **Buttle** Sweden
117 L11 **Buttle L** Br Col
15 B2 **Butt of Lewis** Scotland
115 K6 **Button B** Manitoba
115 N5 **Button Is** N W Terr
102 E6 **Buttonwillow** California
37 L1 **Buttstädt** E Germany
143 D10 **Butty Harb** W Australia
98 J3 **Buttzville** N Dakota
71 G6 **Butuan** Mindanao Philippines
71 G6 **Butuan B** Mindanao Philippines
71 H7 **Butung** *isld* Sulawesi Indonesia
54 M6 **Buturlinovka** U.S.S.R.
68 H6 **Bu Tu Suay** Vietnam
36 F3 **Butzbach** W Germany
33 P5 **Bützow** E Germany
26 E9 **Buvika** Norway
79 E10 **Buwārah, J** *mt* Saudi Arabia
21 I7 **Buxeuil** France
32 L6 **Buxtehude** W Germany
9 E1 **Buxton** England
112 M2 **Buxton** N Carolina
19 J6 **Buxy** France
55 C3 **Buy** *R* U.S.S.R.
58 G2 **Buyr Nuur** *L* Mongolia
47 H4 **Büyük Kemikli Br** *C* Turkey
47 J7 **Büyük Menderes** *R* Turkey
47 K5 **Büyük Orhan** Turkey
21 H8 **Buzançais** France
22 H5 **Buzancy** France
48 K5 **Buzau** Romania
48 K5 **Buzăul** *R* Romania
48 K5 **Buzăului Muntii** *mt* Romania
55 B4 **Buzdyak** U.S.S.R.
60 E12 **Buzen** Japan
89 F9 **Buzi** Mozambique
48 G5 **Buziaş** Romania
55 C4 **Buzov'yazy** U.S.S.R.
95 R5 **Buzzards B** Massachusetts
8 C4 **Bwlch** Wales
27 H11 **By** Sweden
47 H1 **Byala** Bulgaria
47 F1 **Byala Slatina** Bulgaria
114 J2 **Byam Martin I** N W Terr
109 K1 **Byars** Oklahoma
Byblos *see* **Jubail**
31 O4 **Bychawa** Poland
31 I4 **Byczyna** Poland
31 K2 **Bydgoszcz** Poland
106 F2 **Byers** Colorado
109 J1 **Byers** Texas
141 G3 **Byerstown** Queensland
94 F7 **Byesville** Ohio
9 E3 **Byfield** England
9 F5 **Byfleet** England
26 L7 **Bygdeå** Sweden
26 L7 **Bygdeträsk** Sweden
27 C10 **Bygdin** *L* Norway
26 L7 **Bygdsiljum** Sweden
28 D5 **Bygholm Å** *R* Denmark
27 C13 **Bygland** Norway
27 C13 **Byglandsfj** Norway
141 F8 **Bygrave, Mt** Queensland
54 B3 **Bykhov** U.S.S.R.
27 B12 **Bykle** Norway
27 B12 **Bykleheiane** Norway
52 M2 **Bykov** U.S.S.R.
27 C7 **Bylderup** Denmark
57 H1 **Bylkyldak** U.S.S.R.
115 M3 **Bylot I** N W Terr
140 F4 **Bynoe** *R* Queensland
140 B2 **Bynoe Harbour** N Terr Aust
101 N2 **Bynum Res** Montana
111 F9 **Byram** Mississippi
146 H7 **Byrd Gl** Antarctica
121 O5 **Byrd,L** Quebec
13 F3 **Byrness** England
143 B7 **Byro** W Australia
112 D5 **Byromville** Georgia
102 C4 **Byron** California
99 R7 **Byron** Illinois
95 R2 **Byron** Maine
101 R5 **Byron** Wyoming
139 L3 **Byron Bay** New S Wales
143 B7 **Byro Plains** W Australia
51 J1 **Byrranga,Gory** *mt* U.S.S.R.
109 J2 **Byrson** Texas
28 F2 **Byrum** Denmark
26 M7 **Byske** Sweden
26 L6 **Byske älv** *R* Sweden
48 F1 **Bystra** *mt* Czechoslovakia
55 F2 **Bystryy** U.S.S.R.
31 K5 **Bystrzyca Kłodzka** Poland
51 N2 **Bytantay** *R* U.S.S.R.
31 L6 **Bytča** Czechoslovakia
31 L5 **Bytom** Poland
54 F3 **Bytosh** U.S.S.R.
31 K1 **Bytów** Poland
141 J7 **Byzantium** Queensland
31 M3 **Bzura** *R* Poland
130 B9 **Caacupé** Paraguay
133 F3 **Caaguazu** Paraguay
130 C9 **Caaguazú** *dep* Paraguay
130 C9 **Caaguazú, Cord de** *mts* Paraguay
130 B10 **Caapucú** Paraguay
130 C8 **Caarapó** Brazil
130 F5 **Caatinga** Brazil
130 C10 **Caazapá** Paraguay
129 G7 **Cabacal** *R* Brazil
130 H9 **Cabaceiras** Brazil
126 E3 **Cabaiguán** Cuba
71 E3 **Cabalantian** Luzon Philippines
71 G5 **Cabalian** Leyte Philippines
106 C9 **Caballo** New Mexico
128 D4 **Caballococha** Peru
106 C9 **Caballo Res** New Mexico
124 G3 **Caballos Mesteños, Llano de los** Mexico
71 E3 **Cabanatuan** Luzon Philippines
122 D6 **Cabano** Quebec
71 E2 **Cabarruyan** *isld* Luzon Philippines
19 Q18 **Cabasse** France
141 K7 **Cabawin** Queensland
141 K1 **Cabbage Tree Cr** Brisbane, Qnsld
16 B2 **Cabe** *R* Spain
130 F4 **Cabeceiras** Brazil
130 J9 **Cabedelo** Brazil
99 S8 **Cabery** Illinois
16 D6 **Cabeza del Buey** Spain
128 F7 **Cabezas** Bolivia
106 C6 **Cabezon** New Mexico
71 F6 **Cabilao** *isld* Philippines
127 J9 **Cabimas** Venezuela
107 P5 **Cabin Creek** Oklahoma
86 B7 **Cabinda** Angola
100 J1 **Cabinet Gorge Dam** Idaho
100 J1 **Cabinet Mts** Idaho
71 E8 **Cabingan** *isld* Philippines
99 P3 **Cable** Wisconsin
133 D7 **Cabo Blanco** Argentina
17 F8 **Cabo de Gata,Sierra del** Spain
88 G8 **Cabo Delgado** *dist* Mozambique
130 G8 **Cabo Frio** Brazil
115 M8 **Cabonga, Rés** Quebec
110 D4 **Cabool** Missouri
141 L7 **Caboolture** Queensland
88 D9 **Cabora Bassa Dam** Mozambique
133 D6 **Cabo Raso** Argentina
110 E6 **Cabot** Arkansas
120 J7 **Cabot Head** *C* Ontario
115 O8 **Cabot Str** Nfld/Nova Scotia
20 E3 **Cabourg** France
85 A8 **Cabo Verde, Ilhas do** *islds* Atlantic Oc
71 E4 **Cabra** *isld* Philippines
16 E7 **Cabra del Santo Cristo** Spain
69 A9 **Cabra I** Nicobar Is
127 J5 **Cabral** Dominican Rep
130 G5 **Cabral,Serra do** *mts* Brazil
43 B9 **Cabras** Sardinia
19 P15 **Cabre, Col de** *pass* France
16 B3 **Cabreira** *mt* Portugal
127 K5 **Cabrera** Dominican Rep
17 J5 **Cabrera** *isld* Balearic Is
16 C2 **Cabrera** *R* Spain
126 F4 **Cabreras** *R* Cuba
16 C2 **Cabrera,Sierra** *mt* Spain
118 J8 **Cabri** Sask
17 F5 **Cabriel** *R* Spain
19 O18 **Cabriès** France
102 G9 **Cabrillo Nat Mon** California
127 M4 **Cabrits, I** Martinique W I
130 G10 **Cabrobó** Brazil
128 E2 **Cabruta** Venezuela
71 E7 **Cabucan** *isld* Philippines
71 E2 **Cabugao** Luzon Philippines
71 E5 **Cabulauan** *isld* Philippines
124 E2 **Cabullona** Mexico
71 G8 **Caburan** Mindanao Philippines
128 E1 **Cabure** Venezuela
71 F1 **Cabutunan Pt** Luzon Philippines
133 G3 **Caçador** Brazil
46 D1 **Čačak** Yugoslavia
122 F3 **Cacaoui L** Quebec
130 F8 **Cacapava** Brazil
133 G4 **Caçapava do Sul** Brazil
94 J7 **Cacapon** *R* W Virginia
68 H2 **Cac Ba** *isld* Vietnam
43 B8 **Caccia,C** Sardinia
133 G3 **Cacequi** Brazil
129 G7 **Cáceraes** Brazil
130 B5 **Cáceres** Brazil
16 C5 **Cáceres** Spain
16 C5 **Cáceres** *prov* Spain
107 M7 **Cache** Oklahoma
110 E6 **Cache** *R* Arkansas
110 G4 **Cache** *R* Illinois
120 K6 **Cache Bay** Ontario
102 B3 **Cache Cr** California
85 A6 **Cacheu** Guinea-Bissau
129 G5 **Cachimbo, Serra do** *mts* Brazil
133 D2 **Cachinal** Chile
87 C8 **Cachingues** Angola
129 L6 **Cachoeira** Brazil
130 E6 **Cachoeira Alta** Brazil
130 E5 **Cachoeira de Goiás** Brazil
131 H3 **Cachoeira do Sul** Brazil
130 F8 **Cachoeira Paulista** Brazil
130 H7 **Cachoeiro de Itapemirim** Brazil
102 E7 **Cachuma, L** California
16 E7 **Cacín** *R* Spain
42 H3 **Cačinci** Yugoslavia
71 D5 **Cacnipa** *isld* Philippines
87 C8 **Cacolo** Angola
87 C8 **Caconda** Angola
122 C6 **Cacouna** Quebec
103 M8 **Cactus** Arizona
109 H8 **Cactus** Texas
118 H6 **Cactus Lake** Sask
102 H4 **Cactus Ra** Nevada
130 D6 **Caçu** Brazil
87 B9 **Caculavar** *R* Angola
129 K6 **Caculé** Brazil
130 D5 **Caçununga** Brazil
141 K7 **Cadarga** Queensland
31 L6 **Čadca** Czechoslovakia
107 O7 **Caddo** Oklahoma
109 J3 **Caddo** Texas
111 C7 **Caddo** *R* Arkansas
111 B9 **Caddo L** Texas
109 L2 **Caddo Mills** Texas
45 J2 **Cadelbosco di Sopra** Italy
111 F12 **Cade,L.de** Louisiana
140 C1 **Cadell** *R* N Terr Aust
141 F5 **Cadell** *R* Queensland
128 D6 **Cadena del Pantiacolla** Peru
32 K5 **Cadenberge** W Germany
19 O17 **Cadenet** France
125 K5 **Cadereyta** Mexico
8 C2 **Cader Idris** *mt* Wales
112 H4 **Cades** S Carolina
138 D3 **Cadibarrawirracanna,L** S Australia
71 F3 **Cadig Mts** Philippines
18 E8 **Cadillac** France
94 B2 **Cadillac** Michigan
121 M4 **Cadillac** Quebec
118 K9 **Cadillac** Sask
18 G10 **Cadi, Sierra del** *mts* Spain
103 J7 **Cadiz** California
110 J5 **Cadiz** Kentucky
71 F5 **Cadiz** Negros Philippines
94 G6 **Cadiz** Ohio
16 C8 **Cádiz** Spain
16 D8 **Cádiz** *prov* Spain
16 C8 **Cádiz, B. de** Spain
103 J7 **Cadiz L** California
118 G6 **Cadogan** Alberta
117 P9 **Cadomin** Alberta
38 F9 **Cadore** *reg* Italy
99 P5 **Cadott** Wisconsin
117 P7 **Cadotte** *R* Alberta
143 B9 **Cadoux** W Australia
8 C5 **Cadoxton** Wales
41 N6 **Cadria,Monte** Italy
45 L1 **Ca Emo** Italy
20 E3 **Caen** France
13 H6 **Caenby Corner** England
8 C1 **Caergwrle** Wales
8 B1 **Caergybi** Wales
8 D4 **Caerleon** Wales
8 B1 **Caernarvon** Wales
Caernarvon *co see* **Gwynedd**
8 C4 **Caerphilly** Wales
8 C3 **Caersws** Wales
8 D4 **Caerwent** Wales
80 C3 **Caesarea** Israel
80 F1 **Caesarea Philippi** Syria
112 E2 **Caesars Head** S Carolina
130 G6 **Caete** Brazil
129 K6 **Caetite** Brazil
130 E7 **Cafelândia** Brazil
83 K14 **Cafres,Pl.des** Réunion Indian Oc
129 G3 **Cafuini** *R* Brazil
71 D7 **Cagayan** Philippines
71 E1 **Cagayan** *R* Luzon Philippines
71 G6 **Cagayan de Oro** Mindanao Philippines
71 E6 **Cagayan Is** Philippines
47 J5 **Çağiş** Turkey
42 E5 **Cagli** Italy
43 C9 **Cagliari** Sardinia
43 C9 **Cagliari,G.di** Sardinia
44 B4 **Cagnes** France
71 F4 **Cagraray** *isld* Philippines
127 L5 **Caguas** Puerto Rico
111 J9 **Cahaba** *R* Alabama
20 D3 **Cahagnes** France
14 B5 **Caha Mts** Irish Rep
14 D4 **Caher** Irish Rep
14 A5 **Cahirsiveen** Irish Rep
14 E4 **Cahore Pt** Irish Rep
18 G8 **Cahors** France
87 G9 **Caia** Mozambique
129 G6 **Caiabis, Serra dos** Brazil
87 D8 **Caianda** Angola
45 Q7 **Caianello** Italy
129 H7 **Caiapó** *R* Brazil
130 D5 **Caiapônia** Brazil
130 D5 **Caiapo, Serra do** *mts* Brazil
45 Q7 **Caiazzo** Italy
126 E3 **Caibarién** Cuba
68 H7 **Cai Be** Vietnam
128 E2 **Caicara** Bolívar Venezuela
130 J9 **Caicará** Brazil
128 F2 **Caicara** Monagas Venezuela
129 L5 **Caico** Brazil
127 H4 **Caicos Is** W Indies
Caidian *see* **Hanyang**
122 E1 **Cailleteau,L** Quebec
128 D7 **Cailloma** Peru
111 E12 **Caillou B** Louisiana
126 G5 **Caimanera** Cuba
71 D3 **Caiman Pt** Luzon Philippines
109 J5 **Cain City** Texas
87 B9 **Cainde** Angola
133 D1 **Caine** *R* Bolivia
122 G7 **Cains R** New Brunswick
99 N9 **Cainsville** Missouri
69 G8 **Cai Nuoc** Vietnam
45 P6 **Caira, M** *mt* Italy
146 C10 **Caird Coast** Antarctica
12 C1 **Cairnbaan** Scotland
94 J6 **Cairnbrook** Pennsylvania
139 G6 **Cairn Curran Dam** Victoria
15 E3 **Cairn Gorm** *mt* Scotland
116 K6 **Cairn Mt** Alaska
12 C4 **Cairn Ryan** Scotland
141 H3 **Cairns** Queensland
15 E3 **Cairn Toul** *mt* Scotland
79 B8 **Cairo** Egypt
113 C7 **Cairo** Georgia
110 G4 **Cairo** Illinois
44 D3 **Cairo** Italy
110 D2 **Cairo** Missouri
98 H8 **Cairo** Nebraska
95 N4 **Cairo** New York
94 C6 **Cairo** Ohio
94 F7 **Cairo** W Virginia
67 A3 **Caishenfang** China
67 F1 **Caishi** China
9 H2 **Caister** England
13 H6 **Caistor** England
Caithness *co see* **Highland** *reg*
87 B8 **Caitou** Angola
87 C9 **Caiundo** Angola
48 K4 **Căiuţi** Romania
45 Q8 **Caivano** Italy
141 G8 **Caiwarro** Queensland
22 D4 **Caix** France
Caiyuanzhen *see* **Shengsi**
67 F1 **Caizi Hu** China
128 C5 **Cajamarca** Peru
128 C5 **Cajamarca** *dep* Peru
18 G8 **Cajarc** France
130 H9 **Cajàzeiras** Brazil
48 F7 **Čajetina** Yugoslavia
71 F4 **Cajidiocan** Philippines
48 E7 **Čajniče** Yugoslavia
130 F7 **Cajuru** Brazil
47 L8 **Çakırlar** Turkey
47 K6 **Çal** Turkey
16 C7 **Cala** Spain
85 F7 **Calabar** Nigeria
103 O10 **Calabasas** Arizona
121 O7 **Calabogie** Ontario
127 L10 **Calabozo** Venezuela
43 G9 **Calabria** *prov* Italy
71 D5 **Calabugdong** Philippines
16 D8 **Calaburras, Pta. de** Spain
128 E7 **Calacoto** Bolivia
46 F1 **Calafat** Romania
133 C8 **Calafate** Argentina
71 F5 **Calagnaan** *isld* Philippines
71 F3 **Calagua** *islds* Philippines
17 F2 **Calahorra** Spain
22 B2 **Calais** France
95 T8 **Calais** Maine
115 N8 **Calais** New Brunswick
Calais,Pas de *see* **Dover,Str.of**
128 F5 **Calama** Brazil
133 D2 **Calama** Chile
126 G9 **Calamar** Colombia
71 D4 **Calamian Group** *islds* Philippines
99 Q7 **Calamine** Wisconsin
22 L2 **Calamine,la** Belgium
128 F4 **Calanaque** Brazil
17 G4 **Calanda** Spain
41 K4 **Calanda** *mt* Switzerland
71 E5 **Calandagan** *isld* Philippines
69 B10 **Calang** Sumatra
84 G4 **Calanscio Sand Sea** Libya
71 E4 **Calapan** Philippines
100 C5 **Calapooia** *R* Oregon
48 L6 **Călăraşi** Romania
43 B9 **Calasetta** Sardinia
17 F6 **Calasparra** Spain
43 E11 **Calatafimi** Sicily
17 F3 **Calatayud** Spain
48 H4 **Călăţele** Romania
33 T9 **Calau** E Germany
71 F4 **Calauag** Philippines
43 F10 **Calavà, C** Sicily
102 C4 **Calaveras Res** California
71 E4 **Calavite,Cape** Philippines
71 E1 **Calayan** *isld* Luzon Philippines
71 G4 **Calbayog** Philippines
33 P9 **Calbe** E Germany
71 G5 **Calbiga** Samar Philippines
131 A8 **Calbuco** *peak* Chile
129 L5 **Calcanhar, Pta. do** *C* Brazil
111 C12 **Calcasieu L** Louisiana
128 B4 **Calceta** Ecuador
133 E3 **Calchaqui** Argentina
45 J4 **Calci** Italy
45 J1 **Calcinato** Italy
129 H3 **Calcoene** Brazil
75 N7 **Calcutta** India
128 C2 **Caldas** *div* Colombia
16 A5 **Caldas da Rainha** Portugal
17 J3 **Caldas de Montbuy** Spain
16 B2 **Caldas de Reyes** Spain
16 B3 **Caldas do Gerês** Portugal
130 E5 **Caldas Novas** Brazil
13 E4 **Caldbeck** England
88 G10 **Caldeira** *isld* Mozambique
32 K10 **Calden** W Germany
117 G7 **Calder** Alaska
100 J2 **Calder** Idaho
133 C3 **Caldera** Chile
45 K2 **Calderara di Reno** Italy
12 E2 **Caldercruix** Scotland
12 E5 **Calder Hall** England
16 E5 **Calderina** *mt* Spain
141 H7 **Caldervale** Queensland
8 D4 **Caldicot** Wales
100 J6 **Caldwell** Idaho
107 N4 **Caldwell** Kansas
94 F7 **Caldwell** Ohio
109 L5 **Caldwell** Texas
8 B4 **Caldy I** Wales
89 A10 **Caledon** S Africa
89 E8 **Caledon** *R* S Africa
94 B4 **Caledonia** Michigan
99 P6 **Caledonia** Minnesota
94 K4 **Caledonia** New York
122 G9 **Caledonia** Nova Scotia
94 E6 **Caledonia** Ohio
15 D3 **Caledonian Canal** Scotland
140 D2 **Caledon,Mt** N Terr Aust
141 J5 **Calen** Queensland
111 K8 **Calera** Alabama
124 G3 **Calera** Mexico
124 H6 **Calera Victor Rosales** Mexico
128 D7 **Caleta Buena** Chile
133 D8 **Caleta Coig** *est* Argentina
133 D7 **Caleta Olivia** Argentina
131 B8 **Caleufu** *R* Argentina
103 J9 **Calexico** California
114 H7 **Calgary** Alberta
106 F2 **Calhan** Colorado
111 M7 **Calhoun** Georgia
110 J4 **Calhoun** Kentucky
111 G8 **Calhoun City** Mississippi
112 E3 **Calhoun Falls** S Carolina
128 C3 **Cali** Colombia
47 K4 **Çalı** Turkey
71 G5 **Calicoan** *isld* Samar Philippines
110 D5 **Calico Rock** Arkansas
68 A7 **Calicut** Andaman Is
76 B5 **Calicut** India
102 F6 **Caliente** California
103 K4 **Caliente** Nevada
110 D3 **California** Missouri
94 H6 **California** Pennsylvania
127 O2 **California** Trinidad
102 C1 **California** *state* U.S.A.
124 D4 **California,G.de** Mexico
102 F6 **California Hot Springs** California
48 J3 **Călimanilor Muntii** *mt* Romania
76 D5 **Calimere,Pt** India
48 J5 **Călinaneşti** Romania
48 J5 **Călinesti** Romania
133 D4 **Calingasta** Argentina
143 B9 **Calingiri** W Australia
Calino *isld see* **Kálimnos** *I*
111 D8 **Calion** Arkansas
103 J8 **Calipatria** California
100 H1 **Calispell Peak** Washington
71 E5 **Calis Pt** Philippines
102 B3 **Calistoga** California
87 D12 **Calitzdorp** S Africa
71 E4 **Calivite Passage** Philippines
109 O5 **Call** Texas
138 F3 **Callabonna** *R* S Australia
18 C4 **Callac** France
86 H4 **Callafo** Ethiopia
113 F7 **Callahan** Florida
14 D4 **Callan** Irish Rep
121 L6 **Callander** Ontario
12 D1 **Callander** Scotland
71 E2 **Callang** Luzon Philippines
138 E3 **Callanna** S Australia
25 C3 **Callantsoog** Netherlands
99 O10 **Callao** Missouri
128 C6 **Callao** Peru
103 L2 **Callao** Utah
95 L9 **Callao** Virginia
98 G8 **Callaway** Nebraska
43 B12 **Calle, la** Algeria
125 K6 **Calles** Mexico
142 E3 **Calliance Reef** W Australia
141 K6 **Callide** Queensland
109 J7 **Calliham** Texas
118 D3 **Calling L** Alberta
118 E3 **Calling River** Alberta
8 B7 **Callington** England
141 K6 **Calliope** Queensland
117 H6 **Callison Ranch** Br Col
17 G6 **Callosa de Ensarriá** Spain
143 B7 **Callytharra Springs** W Australia
118 D5 **Calmar** Alberta
99 P6 **Calmar** Iowa
36 F6 **Calmbach** W Germany
118 L2 **Calm L** Ontario
9 E5 **Calne** England
71 G4 **Calolbon** Philippines
71 F6 **Calolot** Mindanao Philippines
113 F11 **Caloosahatchee** *R* Florida
43 G8 **Calore** *R* Italy
17 H6 **Calpe** Spain
101 P7 **Calpet** Wyoming
102 D2 **Calpine** California
125 K8 **Calpulálpam** Mexico
120 F3 **Calstock** Ontario
43 F11 **Caltagirone** Sicily
43 F11 **Caltanissetta** Sicily
87 C7 **Caluango** Angola
87 C8 **Calucinga** Angola
87 B8 **Calulo** Angola
99 S2 **Calumet** Michigan
107 M6 **Calumet** Oklahoma
121 Q7 **Calumet** Quebec
87 B8 **Caluquembe** Angola
71 E6 **Calusa** *isld* Philippines
40 G7 **Caluso** Italy
71 E5 **Caluya** *isld* Philippines
103 O8 **Calva** Arizona
20 E3 **Calvados** *dep* France
45 K4 **Calvana,Monte Della** Italy
9 E1 **Calver** England
111 H10 **Calvert** Alabama
109 L5 **Calvert** Texas
140 D3 **Calvert** *R* N Terr Aust
110 H4 **Calvert City** Kentucky
140 D3 **Calvert Hills** N Terr Aust
117 J10 **Calvert I** Br Col
94 K8 **Calverton** Virginia
143 E6 **Calvert Ra** W Australia
124 H7 **Calvillo** Mexico
119 T10 **Calvin** N Dakota
107 O7 **Calvin** Oklahoma
89 A8 **Calvinia** S Africa
45 Q7 **Calvi Risorta** Italy
45 J1 **Calvisano** Italy
16 D4 **Calvitero** *mt* Spain
33 O8 **Calvörde** E Germany
36 F6 **Calw-Hirsau** W Germany
112 J2 **Calypso** N Carolina
87 C7 **Camabatela** Angola
129 L7 **Camacá** Brazil
124 H5 **Camacho** Mexico
121 O5 **Camachigama,L** Quebec
127 L10 **Camaguán** Venezuela
126 F4 **Camagüey** Cuba
126 E3 **Camagüey, Arch. de** *islds* Cuba
128 G5 **Camaitu** *R* Brazil
126 E3 **Camajuaní** Cuba
128 C5 **Camaña** Peru
71 G5 **Camandag** Samar Philippines
100 C1 **Camano I** Washington
100 C6 **Camapuã** Mato Grosso Brazil
133 G4 **Camaquã** Rio Grande do Sul Brazil
131 H3 **Camaquã,R** Brazil
128 F4 **Camara** Brazil
128 G6 **Camarare** *R* Brazil
17 H3 **Camarasa,Embalse de** Spain
18 G9 **Camarès** France
18 B4 **Camaret sur Mer** France
107 L5 **Camargo** Oklahoma
19 N17 **Camargue, La** *reg* France
102 E7 **Camarillo** California
16 A1 **Camariñas** Spain
124 F6 **Camaronero, L. del** Mexico
133 D6 **Camarones** Argentina
101 N5 **Camas** Idaho
100 C4 **Camas** Washington
101 L6 **Camas Cr** Idaho
100 B6 **Camas Valley** Oregon
Ca Mau, Pte De *see* **Mui Bai Bung**
87 C7 **Camaxilo** Angola
16 B2 **Cambados** Spain
130 B5 **Cambara** Brazil
Cambay, G. of *see* **Khambat, G. of**
8 B6 **Cambeak** England
20 C3 **Cambe,la** France
36 E3 **Camberg** W Germany
20 C3 **Cambernon** France
68 F6 **Cambodia** *rep* S E Asia
13 G3 **Cambois** England
18 E9 **Cambo les B** France
141 K7 **Camboon** Queensland
130 E10 **Camboriú** Brazil
8 A7 **Camborne** England
22 E3 **Cambrai** France
16 B1 **Cambre** Spain
20 F3 **Cambremer** France
102 C6 **Cambria** California
99 R6 **Cambria** Wisconsin
7 H10 **Cambrian Mts** Wales
144 B6 **Cambrians** New Zealand
9 G3 **Cambridge** England
100 J5 **Cambridge** Idaho
99 Q8 **Cambridge** Illinois
99 N8 **Cambridge** Iowa
127 J2 **Cambridge** Jamaica
107 O4 **Cambridge** Kansas
95 L8 **Cambridge** Maryland
95 Q4 **Cambridge** Massachusetts
99 N4 **Cambridge** Minnesota
98 F9 **Cambridge** Nebraska
95 O3 **Cambridge** New York
145 E2 **Cambridge** New Zealand
94 F6 **Cambridge** Ohio
120 K9 **Cambridge** Ontario
Cambridge and I of Ely *co see* **Cambridgeshire**
114 J4 **Cambridge Bay** N W Terr
141 G5 **Cambridge Downs** Queensland
142 G2 **Cambridge G** W Australia
9 F3 **Cambridgeshire** *co* England
94 G5 **Cambridge Springs** Pennsylvania
17 H3 **Cambrils** Spain
22 D3 **Cambrin** France
130 F7 **Cambuquira** Brazil
37 M1 **Camburg** E Germany
12 D2 **Cambuslang** Scotland
111 J10 **Camden** Alabama
111 D8 **Camden** Arkansas
95 M7 **Camden** Delaware
95 S2 **Camden** Maine
94 C5 **Camden** Michigan
95 N7 **Camden** New Jersey
139 K5 **Camden** New S Wales
95 M3 **Camden** New York
112 G3 **Camden** S Carolina
110 H5 **Camden** Tennessee
111 B11 **Camden** Texas
116 P1 **Camden B** Alaska
94 G8 **Camden on Gauley** W Virginia
142 E3 **Camden Sd** W Australia
110 D3 **Camdenton** Missouri
87 D8 **Cameia,Parque Nacional da** Angola
8 B6 **Camelford** England
8 B7 **Camel,R** England
145 E2 **Camels Back** *mt* New Zealand
87 B7 **Camembe** Angola
20 F4 **Camembert** France
45 O4 **Camerano** Italy
45 O4 **Camerata Picena** Italy
42 E5 **Camerino** Italy
103 N6 **Cameron** Arizona
99 Q9 **Cameron** Illinois
111 C12 **Cameron** Louisiana
110 B2 **Cameron** Missouri
101 O4 **Cameron** Montana
112 H2 **Cameron** N Carolina
106 G7 **Cameron** New Mexico
95 K4 **Cameron** New York
94 J5 **Cameron** Pennsylvania
109 L5 **Cameron** Texas
99 P4 **Cameron** Wisconsin
94 G7 **Cameron** W Virginia
88 C6 **Cameron B** Zambia
141 G5 **Cameron Downs** Queensland
120 B3 **Cameron Falls** Ontario
69 E10 **Cameron Highlands** Malaysia
117 O6 **Cameron Hills** Alberta
114 J2 **Cameron I** N W Terr
144 A7 **Cameron Mts** New Zealand
86 B4 **Cameroon** *rep* Africa
85 F8 **Cameroon Mt** Cameroon
129 J4 **Cameta** Brazil
140 B3 **Camfield** *R* N Terr Aust
71 E1 **Camiguin** *isld* Luzon Philippines
71 G6 **Camiguin** *isld* Philippines
71 E3 **Camiling** Luzon Philippines
111 M10 **Camilla** Georgia
133 D1 **Camiña** Chile
16 B3 **Caminha** Portugal
102 D3 **Camino** California
129 J4 **Camiranga** Brazil
133 E2 **Camiri** Bolivia
128 D6 **Camisea** *R* Peru
117 R4 **Camlaren** N W Terr
95 K5 **Cammal** Pennsylvania
43 F11 **Cammarata** *mt* Sicily
33 R8 **Cammer** E Germany
124 E4 **Camoa** Mexico
125 M3 **Camoapa** Nicaragua
129 K4 **Camocim** Brazil
41 K5 **Camoghe** *mt* Switzerland
44 F3 **Camogli** Italy
41 M6 **Camonica,Val** Italy
141 G6 **Camoola** Queensland
140 E4 **Camooweal** Queensland
129 H3 **Camopi** Fr Guiana
69 A8 **Camorta** Nicobar Is
71 G5 **Camotes Islands** Philippines
71 G5 **Camotes Sea** Philippines
124 G8 **Camotlán de Miraflores** Mexico
41 M6 **Camowiche,Alpi** *mt* Italy
42 E7 **Campagna** *reg* Italy
45 M1 **Campagna Lupia** Italy
45 M5 **Campagnano di Roma** Italy
20 F5 **Campagne d'Alençon** *reg* France

Campagne-lès-Hesdin — Castelfranco Emilia 15

22 B3 **Campagne-lès-Hesdin** France
125 L2 **Campamento** Honduras
133 F4 **Campana** Argentina
124 H4 **Campana** Mexico
133 B7 **Campana, I** Chile
130 C8 **Campanario** Mato Grosso Brazil
130 H6 **Campanário** Minas Gerais Brazil
16 D6 **Campanario** Spain
133 C5 **Campanario** *mt* Chile/Arg
45 Q8 **Campanella, Pta** *C* Italy
130 F7 **Campanha** Brazil
139 H8 **Campania** Tasmania
45 R7 **Campania** *reg* Italy
117 J9 **Campania I** Br Col
141 H5 **Campaspe** *R* Queensland
102 C2 **Camp Beale** California
102 C4 **Campbell** California
110 F5 **Campbell** Missouri
98 H9 **Campbell** Nebraska
95 K4 **Campbell** New York
94 G5 **Campbell** Ohio
141 J6 **Campbell** *R* Queensland
145 E4 **Campbell, C New Zealand**
121 N8 **Campbellford** Ontario
68 D7 **Campbell I** Burma
102 R12 **Campbell Industrial Pk** Hawaiian Is
117 J9 **Campbell Island** Br Col
140 B5 **Campbell, Mt** N Terr **Aust**
117 D3 **Campbell, Mt** Yukon Terr
74 E2 **Campbellpore** Pakistan
142 G2 **Campbell Ra** W Australia
81 K12 **Campbell Rise** S Pacific Oc
117 L10 **Campbell River** Br Col
121 O7 **Campbell's Bay** Quebec
99 S6 **Campbellsport** Wisconsin
110 L4 **Campbellsville** Kentucky
122 F6 **Campbellton** New Brunswick
123 S4 **Campbellton** Nfld
109 J7 **Campbellton** Texas
139 K5 **Campbelltown** New S Wales
139 J8 **Campbell Town** Tasmania
12 C3 **Campbeltown** Scotland
98 C4 **Camp Crook** S Dakota
99 Q6 **Camp Douglas** Wisconsin
20 J2 **Campeaux** France
125 O8 **Campeche Mexico**
90 A6 **Campeche Bank** Atlantic Oc
125 N8 **Campeche, B.de** Mexico
126 F4 **Campechuela** Cuba
48 H4 **Câmpeni** Romania
113 L9 **Camperdown** New Providence I **Bahamas**
139 G7 **Camperdown** Victoria
119 R7 **Camperville** Manitoba
111 L9 **Camp Hill** Alabama
141 K2 **Camphill** *dist* Brisbane, Qnsld
45 K4 **Campi Bisenzio** Italy
45 Q8 **Campi Flegrei** Italy
16 D6 **Campillo de Llerena** Spain
16 D7 **Campillos** Spain
130 H9 **Campina Grande** Brazil
130 F8 **Campinas** Brazil
130 E6 **Campina Verde** Brazil
102 F5 **Camp Nelson** California
86 A5 **Campo** Cameroon
106 H4 **Campo** Colorado
18 F10 **Campo** Spain
43 F7 **Campobasso** Italy
122 F9 **Campobello I** New Brunswick
130 F7 **Campo Belo** Brazil
130 E10 **Campo Belo do Sul** Brazil
45 L1 **Campo d'Arsego** Italy
16 E6 **Campo de Calatrava** *physical reg* Spain
16 E5 **Campo de Criptana** Spain
129 H6 **Campo de Diauarum** Brazil
126 G9 **Campo de la Cruz** Colombia
130 D10 **Campo Erê** Brazil
130 E6 **Campo Florido** Brazil
129 K6 **Campo Formoso** Brazil
45 J2 **Campogalliano** Italy
133 E3 **Campo Gallo** Argentina
133 G2 **Campo Grande** Brazil
130 C7 **Campo Grande** Mato Grosso Brazil
130 B9 **Campo Grande** *airport* Paraguay
130 E9 **Campo Largo** Brazil
129 K4 **Campo Maior** Brazil
130 D9 **Campo Mourão** Brazil
130 D10 **Campo Novo** Brazil
45 H3 **Camporgiano** Italy
130 H7 **Campos** Brazil
130 F6 **Campos Altos** Brazil
45 K2 **Camposanto** Italy
45 R7 **Camposauro** *mt* Italy
130 D10 **Campos de Palmas** *plains* Brazil
130 F8 **Campos do Jordão** Brazil
130 D9 **Campos Eré** Brazil
133 G3 **Campos Novos** Brazil
41 J5 **Campo Tencia** *mt* Switzerland
128 E3 **Campo Troco** Colombia
42 D2 **Campo Tures** Italy
99 P9 **Camp Point** Illinois
102 D6 **Camp Roberts** California
109 H5 **Camp San Saba** Texas
12 D1 **Campsie Fells** Scotland
111 C10 **Campti** Louisiana
94 D9 **Campton** Kentucky
95 Q3 **Campton** New Hampshire
102 C2 **Camptonville** California
103 N7 **Camp Verde** Arizona
68 J7 **Cam Ranh** Vietnam
118 E5 **Camrose** Alberta
45 L1 **Camsano Vicentino** Italy
117 M4 **Camsell Range** N W Terr
87 B8 **Camucuio** Angola
45 K3 **Camugnano** Italy
47 J4 **Çan** Turkey
95 O4 **Canaan** Connecticut
122 G7 **Canaan** New Brunswick
127 M2 **Canaan** Tobago
121 T8 **Canaan** Vermont
103 N4 **Canaan Pk** Utah
122 G8 **Canaan R** New Brunswick
130 F5 **Canabrava** Brazil
129 J6 **Cana Brava** *R* Brazil
71 C6 **Canabungan** *isld* Philippines
87 C8 **Canacupa** Angola
115 **Canada**
123 Q3 **Canada B** Nfld
131 E4 **Cañada de Gómez** Argentina
95 R8 **Canada Falls** Maine
95 M5 **Canadensis** Pennsylvania
108 D8 **Canadian** Texas
106 F5 **Canadian** *R* New Mexico
108 D8 **Canadian** *R* Texas etc
133 D8 **Cañadón de las Vacas** Argentina
133 D6 **Cañadón Grande, Sa** *ra* Argentina
112 G4 **Canadys** S Carolina
47 H4 **Canakkale** Turkey
47 H4 **Çanakkale Boğazi** *str* Turkey
43 B11 **Canal de la Galite** *str* Tunisia
127 H5 **Canal de St. Marc** Haiti
129 H3 **Canal do Norte** Brazil
129 J4 **Canal do Sul** Brazil
117 Q10 **Canal Flats** Br Col
110 G5 **Canalou** Missouri
113 G11 **Canal Point** Florida
94 E7 **Canal Winchester** Ohio
128 D5 **Canama** Brazil
95 K4 **Canandaigua L** New York
124 D2 **Cananea** Mexico
130 F9 **Cananéia** Brazil
128 E3 **Canapiari,Co** *mt* Colombia
20 K1 **Canaples** France
130 E6 **Canápolis** Brazil
128 C4 **Cañar** *prov* Ecuador
126 C4 **Canarreos,Arch.de los** Cuba
90 K10 **Canary Basin** Atlantic Oc
85 A3 **Canary Is** Atlantic Oc
94 K4 **Canaseraga** New York
130 E4 **Canastra, Serra da** *mts* Brazil
130 F7 **Canastra,Serra do** *mts* Minas Gerais Brazil
124 G5 **Canatlán** Mexico
44 B1 **Canave** Italy
16 C5 **Cañaveral** Spain
113 G9 **Canaveral, C** Florida
17 F4 **Cañaveras** Spain
129 L7 **Canavieiras** Brazil
141 G7 **Canaway Ra** Queensland
38 E9 **Canazei** Italy
139 H4 **Canbelego** New S Wales
139 J6 **Canberra** Aust Capital Terr
138 A6 **Canberra & Environs** Australia
100 E8 **Canby** California
98 K5 **Canby** Minnesota
100 C4 **Canby** Oregon
20 B4 **Cancale** France
45 Q8 **Cancello** Italy
45 Q7 **Cancello ed Arnone** Italy
22 B3 **Canche** *R* France
20 J1 **Canchy** France
18 F8 **Cancon** France
86 A1 **Candala** Somalia
45 K3 **Canda, M** *mt* Italy
47 H6 **Candarli** Turkey
47 H6 **Candarlı Körfezi** *gulf* Turkey
20 K1 **Candas** France
21 C6 **Candé** France
16 B5 **Candeeiros,Sa.de** Portugal
130 F7 **Candeias** Brazil
128 F5 **Candeias** *R* Brazil
43 G7 **Candela** Italy
45 N4 **Candelara** Italy
130 C10 **Candelaria** Argentina
124 F2 **Candelaria** Mexico
102 F3 **Candelaria** Nevada
108 C5 **Candelaria** Texas
139 J6 **Candelo** New S Wales
Candia Crete *see* **Iráklion**
119 O8 **Candiac** Sask
45 L1 **Candiana** Italy
130 D9 **Cândido de Abreu** Brazil
130 E8 **Cândido Mota** Brazil
116 F4 **Candle** Alaska
119 M5 **Candle L** Sask
146 A14 **Candlemas I** Antarctica
95 O5 **Candlewood,L** Connecticut
98 G1 **Cando** N Dakota
118 J6 **Cando** Sask
133 G3 **Candói** Brazil
143 B6 **Candolle, Mt** W Australia
71 E2 **Candon** Luzon **Philippines**
112 H2 **Candor** N Carolina
95 L4 **Candor** New York
120 K5 **Cane** Ontario
Canea Crete *see* **Khaniá**
94 J4 **Caneadea** New York
129 J6 **Canéia** Brazil
133 G3 **Canela** Brazil
133 F4 **Canelones** Uruguay
130 C9 **Canendiyu** *dep* Paraguay
133 C5 **Cañete** Chile
17 F4 **Cañete** Spain
128 C6 **Cañete** *R* Peru
107 P4 **Caney** Kansas
107 O7 **Caney** Oklahoma
110 L6 **Caney Fork** *R* Tennessee
110 K4 **Caneyville** Kentucky
111 C8 **Canfield** Arkansas
94 G5 **Canfield** Ohio
18 E10 **Canfranc** Spain
87 C8 **Cangamba** Angola
87 C7 **Cangandala** Angola
16 C1 **Cangas de Narcea** Spain
16 D1 **Cangas de Onís** Spain
21 H7 **Cangey** France
87 C8 **Cangoa** Angola
89 B9 **Cango Caves** S Africa
87 D8 **Cangombe** Angola
65 D7 **Cangshan** China
130 J9 **Canguaretama** Brazil
133 G4 **Canguçu** Brazil
131 H3 **Canguçu,Sa.do** *mt* Brazil
87 C8 **Cangumbe** Angola
67 D5 **Cangwu** China
67 B1 **Cangxi** China
65 C5 **Cang Xian** China
68 D1 **Cangyuan** China
65 C5 **Cangzhou** China
130 H10 **Canhotinho** Brazil
141 K6 **Cania** Queensland
115 N6 **Caniapiscau** *R* Quebec
115 N7 **Caniapiscau,Lac** Quebec
121 N3 **Canica I** Quebec
43 F11 **Canicatti** Sicily
71 G5 **Canigao Ch** Philippines
18 G10 **Canigou** *mt* France
17 F7 **Caniles** Spain
117 N10 **Canim L** Br Col
129 K5 **Caninde** *R* Brazil
71 E5 **Canipo** *isld* **Philippines**
15 C2 **Canisp Mt** Scotland
94 K4 **Canisteo** New York
95 K4 **Canisteo** *R* New York
20 C3 **Canisy** France
124 H6 **Cañitas** Mexico
17 F7 **Canjáyar** Spain
78 D1 **Çankiri** Turkey
71 E3 **Canlubang** Luzon Philippines
118 B7 **Canmore** Alberta
143 B8 **Canna** W Australia
15 B3 **Canna** *isld* Scotland
76 B5 **Cannanore** India
110 K4 **Cannelton** Indiana
41 J5 **Cannero** Italy
44 B4 **Cannes** France
45 J1 **Canneto s. Oglio** Italy
122 H8 **Canning** Nova Scotia
98 G5 **Canning** S Dakota
116 O2 **Canning** *R* Alaska
142 E4 **Canning Basin** W Australia
143 C8 **Canning Hill** W Australia
142 B2 **Canning River** W Australia
121 L8 **Cannington** Ontario
142 B2 **Cannington** *dist* Perth, W Aust
142 B2 **Canning Vale** W Australia
41 J5 **Cannobio** Italy
99 O5 **Cannon** *R* Minnesota
98 F3 **Cannon Ball** N Dakota
98 E3 **Cannonball** *R* N Dakota
99 O5 **Cannon Falls** Minnesota
141 J5 **Cannonsvale** Queensland
139 J7 **Cann R** Victoria
133 G3 **Canoas** Brazil
130 D10 **Canôas, R. das** Brazil
140 F4 **Canobie** Queensland
130 F6 **Canoeiros** Brazil
118 J3 **Canoe L** Sask
117 O9 **Canoe R** Br Col
130 E10 **Canoinhas** Brazil
139 H4 **Canonba** New S Wales
15 F5 **Canonbie** Scotland
106 E3 **Canon City** Colorado
106 C5 **Cañon Largo** *R* New Mexico
94 G6 **Canonsburg** Pennsylvania
112 F6 **Canoochia** *R* Georgia
141 K6 **Canoona** Queensland
138 F5 **Canopus** S Australia
119 P7 **Canora** Sask
43 G7 **Canosa di Puglia** Italy
127 O8 **Canouan** *isld* Lesser Antilles
98 J6 **Canova** S Dakota
139 J5 **Canowindra** New S Wales
47 K6 **Çanşa** Turkey
71 F6 **Cansilan Pt** Negros Philippines
123 M8 **Canso** Nova Scotia
123 L8 **Canso,Str.of** Nova Scotia
18 D10 **Cantabria,Sierra de** *mts* Spain
45 K3 **Cantagallo** Italy
18 G7 **Cantal** *dep* France
45 Q6 **Cantalupo nel Sánnio** Italy
127 O2 **Cantaro** Trinidad
127 M10 **Cantaura** Venezuela
20 H3 **Canteleu** France
9 H5 **Canterbury** England
122 E8 **Canterbury** New Brunswick
144 C5 **Canterbury** *stat area* New Zealand
144 D6 **Canterbury Bight** New Zealand
144 C6 **Canterbury Plains** New Zealand
45 O6 **Canterna, L. di** Italy
68 G7 **Can Tho** Vietnam
102 G6 **Cantil** California
71 G6 **Cantilan** Mindanao Philippines
16 D7 **Cantillana** Spain
129 K5 **Canto do Buriti** Brazil
Canton China *see* **Guangzhou**
112 C3 **Canton** Georgia
110 F1 **Canton** Illinois
107 N3 **Canton** Kansas
95 R2 **Canton** Maine
111 F9 **Canton** Mississippi
110 E1 **Canton** Missouri
101 O3 **Canton** Montana
112 E2 **Canton** N Carolina
121 P8 **Canton** New York
94 F6 **Canton** Ohio
107 M5 **Canton** Oklahoma
95 L5 **Canton** Pennsylvania
98 K6 **Canton** S Dakota
109 M3 **Canton** Texas
121 T4 **Canton-Bégin** Quebec
134 A5 **Canton I** Pacific Oc
110 D1 **Cantril** Iowa
41 K6 **Cantù** Italy
118 J8 **Cantuar** Sask
130 D9 **Cantú,R** Brazil
130 D9 **Cantú, Serra do** *mt* Brazil
130 G10 **Canudos** Brazil
133 F5 **Cañuelas** Argentina
128 G4 **Canuma** Brazil
128 F5 **Canutama** Brazil
107 L6 **Canute** Oklahoma
124 G4 **Canutillo** Mexico
108 A4 **Canutillo** Texas
145 D4 **Canvastown** New Zealand
9 G5 **Canvey I** England
118 L5 **Canwood** Sask
20 G2 **Cany-Barville** France
120 F5 **Canyon** Ontario
108 F1 **Canyon** Texas
101 P5 **Canyon** Wyoming
117 E5 **Canyon** Yukon Terr
100 G5 **Canyon City** Oregon
100 K6 **Canyon Cr** Idaho
118 C3 **Canyon Creek** Alberta
101 N3 **Canyon Creek** Montana
103 P5 **Canyon de Chelly Nat.Mon** Arizona
101 O3 **Canyon Ferry Dam** Montana
103 N8 **Canyon L** Arizona
103 O3 **Canyonlands Nat. Park** Utah
117 K4 **Canyon Ranges** N W Terr
109 J6 **Canyon Res** Texas
100 B7 **Canyonville** Oregon
87 D7 **Canzar** Angola
33 T6 **Canzow** E Germany
67 B5 **Cao Bang** Vietnam
65 C5 **Caogoubu** China
67 A3 **Cao Hai** *L* China
65 F4 **Cao He** *R* China
65 F4 **Caohekou** China
Caojiahe *see* **Qichun**
12 C2 **Caolisport, L** Scotland
87 C7 **Caombo** Angola
68 J6 **Cao Nguen Dar Lac** *plat* Vietnam
122 F1 **Caopacho L** Quebec
122 F2 **Caopacho R** Quebec
121 Q3 **Caopatina, L** Quebec
65 F3 **Caoshi** China
67 D3 **Caoshi** China
65 C7 **Cao Xian** China
98 F5 **Capa** S Dakota
87 D7 **Capaia** Angola
128 E2 **Capanaparo** *R* Venezuela
129 J4 **Capanema** Brazil
130 D9 **Capanema, R** Brazil
45 J4 **Capannoli** Italy
45 J4 **Capannori** Italy
130 F5 **Capão Redondo** Brazil
130 H7 **Caparaó,Sa do** *mts* Brazil
128 E3 **Caparro, Co** *mt* Colombia
71 E3 **Capas** Luzon Philippines
127 J9 **Capatárida** Venezuela
48 H5 **Căpăţîna, Muntii** *mt* Romania
71 D7 **Capayan Sulu** *isld* Philippines
18 D9 **Capbreton** France
122 F4 **Cap Chat** Quebec
121 S6 **Cap de la Madeleine** Quebec
18 G8 **Capdenac** France
122 H4 **Cap de Rabast** Quebec
122 H5 **Cap-d'Espoir** Quebec
95 R4 **Cape Ann** Massachusetts
139 J8 **Cape Barren I** Tasmania
90 K12 **Cape Basin Atlantic Oc**
67 C7 **Cape Bastion** China
123 M7 **Cape Breton Highlands Nat Pk** C Breton I, N Scotia
123 N7 **Cape Breton I** Nova Scotia
123 U6 **Cape Broyle** Nfld
113 G9 **Cape Canaveral** Florida
123 R1 **Cape Charles** Labrador
95 L9 **Cape Charles** Virginia
85 D7 **Cape Coast** Ghana
95 S5 **Cape Cod** Massachusetts
95 R5 **Cape Cod B** Massachusetts
95 R5 **Cape Cod Canal** Massachusetts
95 R5 **Cape Cod Nat.Seashore** Massachusetts
115 M5 **Cape Dorset** N W Terr
115 N4 **Cape Dyer** N W Terr
112 K4 **Cape Fear** N Carolina
110 G4 **Cape Girardeau** Missouri
112 M2 **Cape Hatteras** N Carolina
115 N5 **Cape Hopes Advance** Quebec
Cape Horn *see* **Hornos, C. de**
112 H4 **Cape I** S Carolina
143 B10 **Capel** W Australia
129 L6 **Capela** Brazil
123 P6 **Cape la Hune** Nfld
8 C1 **Capel Curig Wales**
130 G5 **Capelinha** Brazil
116 E2 **Cape Lisburne** Alaska
141 J6 **Capella** Queensland
22 F4 **Capelle-en-Thierache, la** France
22 K4 **Capellen** Luxembourg
95 N8 **Cape May** New Jersey
87 C7 **Capenda-Camulemba** Angola
89 A10 **Cape of Good Hope** S Africa
114 G3 **Cape Parry** N W Terr
89 B8 **Cape Province** S Africa
89 A10 **Cape Pt** S Africa
141 H5 **Cape R** Queensland
123 T7 **Cape Race** Nfld
123 N6 **Cape Ray** Nfld
80 F2 **Capernaum** Israel
112 H5 **Cape Romain** S Carolina
103 N5 **Cape Royal** Arizona
113 F12 **Cape Sable** *pen* Florida
122 G10 **Cape Sable I** Nova Scotia
122 F9 **Cape St.Mary** Nova Scotia
123 S7 **Cape St. Mary's** *lt ho* Nfld
127 N4 **Capesterre** Guadeloupe W I
127 N5 **Capesterre** Marie Galante W I
45 P5 **Capestrallo** Italy
89 A9 **Cape Town** S Africa
90 G7 **Cape Verde** *islds, rep* Atlantic Oc
90 E7 **Cape Verde Fracture** Atlantic Oc
90 H7 **Cape Verde Plateau** Atlantic Oc
95 M9 **Capeville** Virginia
95 L2 **Cape Vincent** New York
15 C2 **Cape Wrath** Scotland
141 F1 **Cape York Pen** Queensland
127 H5 **Cap-Haïtien** Haiti
130 B9 **Capiatá** Paraguay
128 E3 **Capibara** Venezuela
130 J9 **Capiberibe** *R* Brazil
133 F4 **Capilla** Argentina
133 E4 **Capilla del Monte** Argentina
129 J4 **Capim** *R* Brazil
128 E7 **Capinota** Bolivia
41 H6 **Capio, Monte** Italy
45 O6 **Capistrello** Italy
121 O5 **Capitachouane** *R* Quebec
106 E8 **Capitan** New Mexico
130 C8 **Capitán Bado** Paraguay
131 A8 **Capitanes, Pta** *C* Chile
106 E8 **Capitan Mts** New Mexico
42 E6 **Capitignano** Italy
98 B4 **Capitol** Montana
100 H8 **Capitol Peak** *mt* Nevada
103 N3 **Capitol Reef Nat.Mon** Utah
122 G5 **Caplan** Quebec
71 E5 **Capnoyan** *isld* Philippines
88 D9 **Capoche** *R* Mozambique
129 G5 **Capoeiras, Cachoeira das** *waterfall* Brazil
44 D4 **Capo Mele** Italy
139 K3 **Capoompeta** *mt* New S Wales
45 O5 **Cappadocia** Italy
36 F2 **Cappel** W Germany
14 D4 **Cappoquin** Irish Rep
127 O7 **Cap Pt** St Lucia
120 K6 **Capreol** Ontario
43 C7 **Caprera** *isld* Sardinia
45 L4 **Caprese Michelangelo** Italy
45 Q8 **Capri** Italy
45 Q7 **Capriati a Volturno** Italy
141 K5 **Capricorn Chan** Gt Barrier Reef Aust
141 K6 **Capricorn Grp** *islds* Gt Barrier Reef Aust
143 B6 **Capricorn Ra** W Australia
42 D3 **Caprino** Italy
87 D9 **Caprivi Strip** Namibia
108 D2 **Caprock** New Mexico
123 M7 **Capstick** C Breton I, N Scotia
135 U5 **Captain Cook** Hawaiian Is
139 J6 **Captain's Flat** New S Wales
18 E8 **Captieux** France
113 E11 **Captiva** Florida
45 Q7 **Capua** Italy
71 E7 **Capual** *isld* Philippines
83 K12 **Capucin Pt** Mahé I Indian Oc
71 G4 **Capul** Philippines
106 D4 **Capulin** Colorado
106 G5 **Capulin** New Mexico
128 D3 **Caqueta** *div* Colombia
128 D4 **Caquetá** *R* Colombia
71 E4 **Carabao** *isld* Philippines
128 D6 **Carabaya, Cord.de** *mts* Peru
128 F4 **Carabinani** *R* Brazil
128 E1 **Carabobo** *state* Venezuela
48 J6 **Caracal** Romania
127 L9 **Caracas** Venezuela
129 K5 **Caracol** Brazil
130 C7 **Caracol** Brazil
125 J8 **Caracuaro** Mexico
71 G7 **Caraga** Mindanao Philippines
14 B4 **Caragh,L** Irish Rep
131 G4 **Caraguatá** *R* Uruguay
130 F8 **Caraguata-tuba** Brazil
130 C9 **Caraĝuatay** Paraguay
133 C5 **Carahue** Chile
130 H5 **Caraí** Brazil
12 C2 **Cara I** Scotland
129 H5 **Carajás, Serra dos** *mts* Brazil
18 G9 **Caraman** France
120 D3 **Caramat** Ontario
71 F4 **Caramoan Pen** Philippines
128 F5 **Caranapatuba** Brazil
130 G7 **Carandaí** Brazil
130 B6 **Carandazal** Brazil
140 E5 **Carandotta** Queensland
129 K8 **Carangola** Brazil
128 F3 **Caransaca,Co** *mt* Venezuela
48 G5 **Caransebeş** Romania
130 B9 **Carapeguá** Paraguay
138 D5 **Carappee Hill** S Australia
122 H6 **Caraquet** New Brunswick
122 H6 **Caraquet Bay** New Brunswick
128 B4 **Caráquez,B.de** Ecuador
48 G5 **Carasova** Romania
48 G5 **Caras-Severin** *reg* Romania
125 N2 **Caratasca** Honduras
130 G6 **Caratinga** Brazil
69 G14 **Carat, Tanjung** *C* Indonesia
128 E4 **Carauari** Brazil
130 H8 **Caraúbas** Brazil
17 F6 **Caravaca** Spain
41 L7 **Caravaggio** Italy
130 H5 **Caravelas** Brazil
128 D7 **Caraveli** Peru
43 B9 **Caravius, M. is** *mt* Sardinia
128 C5 **Caraz** Peru
131 H2 **Carazinho** Brazil
16 B2 **Carballino** Spain
16 B1 **Carballo** Spain
16 B1 **Carba, Sa. de la** *mts* Spain
119 S9 **Carberry** Manitoba
101 U1 **Carbert** Montana
118 D7 **Carbon** Alberta
45 K1 **Carbonara** Italy
43 C9 **Carbonara,C** Sardinia
118 D5 **Carbondale** Alberta
106 C2 **Carbondale** Colorado
107 P3 **Carbondale** Kansas
95 M5 **Carbondale** Pennsylvania
123 T6 **Carbonear** Nfld
17 F8 **Carboneras** Spain
111 J8 **Carbon Hill** Alabama
43 B9 **Carbonia** Sardinia
38 F8 **Carbonin** Italy
130 G5 **Carbonita** Brazil
18 F9 **Carbonne** France
17 G5 **Carcagente** Spain
117 P7 **Carcajou** Alberta
18 E7 **Carcans, Etang de** *L* France
71 F5 **Carcar** Cebu **Philippines**
131 E4 **Carcaraña** *R* Argentina
86 A2 **Carcar Mts** Somalia
18 G9 **Carcassonne** France
128 C3 **Carchi** *prov* Ecuador
139 J5 **Carcoan** New S Wales
117 F5 **Carcross** Yukon Terr
47 K7 **Cardak** Turkey
119 R8 **Cardale** Manitoba
68 F7 **Cardamomes,Chaine des** *mts* Cambodia
125 K6 **Cárdenas** Mexico
139 G3 **Cardenyabba** *R* New S Wales
133 C7 **Cardiel,L** Argentina
8 C5 **Cardiff Wales**
8 B3 **Cardigan Wales**
Cardigan *co see* **Dyfed**
123 K7 **Cardigan B** Pr Edward I
8 B2 **Cardigan B Wales**
121 P8 **Cardinal** Ontario
94 E6 **Cardington** Ohio
17 J3 **Cardona** Spain
17 J3 **Cardoner,R** Spain
127 J9 **Cardón,Pta** Venezuela
130 E7 **Cardoso** Brazil
130 F9 **Cardoso,I.do** Brazil
144 B6 **Cardrona** New Zealand
144 B6 **Cardrona, Mt** New Zealand
119 M9 **Cardross** Sask
12 D2 **Cardross** Scotland
118 D9 **Cardston** Alberta
141 H4 **Cardwell** Queensland
48 G3 **Carei** Romania
127 O2 **Carenage** Trinidad
22 D3 **Carency** France
20 C3 **Carentan** France
21 A6 **Carentoir** France
8 B4 **Carew** Wales
101 M6 **Carey** Idaho
94 D6 **Carey** Ohio
108 G1 **Carey** Texas
143 B7 **Carey Downs** W Australia
143 D8 **Carey, L** W Australia
81 C7 **Cargados Carajos** *islds* Indian Oc
120 J8 **Cargill** Ontario
13 E1 **Cargill** Scotland
141 G5 **Cargoon** Queensland
18 C4 **Carhaix** France
122 E1 **Carheil,L** Quebec
130 H7 **Cariacica** Brazil
127 N9 **Cariaco** Venezuela
126 F10 **Caribana,Pta** Colombia
93 L7 **Caribbean Sea** Cent America
117 N9 **Cariboo Mts** Br Col
95 S7 **Caribou** Maine
122 K8 **Caribou** Nova Scotia
116 G9 **Caribou** *R* Alaska
117 K5 **Caribou** *R* N W Terr
117 K7 **Caribou Hide** Br Col
122 K8 **Caribou I** Nova Scotia
120 E5 **Caribou I** Ontario
117 R5 **Caribou Is** N W Terr
101 O6 **Caribou Mt** Idaho
117 Q6 **Caribou Mts** Alberta
124 F4 **Carichic** Mexico
119 Q9 **Carievale** Sask
71 G5 **Carigara** Leyte Philippines
22 J4 **Carignan** France
44 C2 **Carignano** Italy
121 Q7 **Carillon** Quebec
139 J4 **Carinda** New S Wales
17 G3 **Cariñena** Spain
129 K6 **Carinhanha** Brazil
45 P7 **Carinola** Italy
129 J6 **Caripare** Brazil
127 N9 **Caripe** Venezuela
127 N9 **Caripito** Venezuela
130 G9 **Caririaçu** Brazil
128 F5 **Caritianas** Brazil
130 G9 **Cariús** Brazil
107 N5 **Carl Blackwell, L** Oklahoma
22 E4 **Carlepont** France
17 G5 **Carlet** Spain
94 D4 **Carleton** Michigan
98 J9 **Carleton** Nebraska
122 F5 **Carleton** Quebec
122 F6 **Carleton,Mt** New Brunswick
121 O7 **Carleton Place** Ontario
122 K4 **Carleton Pt** Quebec
98 B5 **Carlile** Wyoming
103 H1 **Carlin** Nevada
36 B5 **Carling** France
14 E2 **Carlingford** Irish Rep
110 G2 **Carlinville** Illinois
110 E7 **Carlisle** Arkansas
13 F4 **Carlisle** England
110 J3 **Carlisle** Indiana
94 C8 **Carlisle** Kentucky
95 K6 **Carlisle** Pennsylvania
112 F3 **Carlisle** S Carolina
142 B2 **Carlisle** *dist* Perth, W Aust
127 P6 **Carlisle B** Barbados
18 G10 **Carlitte** *mt* France
43 B9 **Carloforte** Sardinia
13 E2 **Carlops** Scotland
133 E6 **Carlos Ameghino, Istmo** Argentina
133 E5 **Carlos Casares** Argentina
130 H5 **Carlos Chagas** Brazil
140 E6 **Carlo Springs** Queensland
131 G4 **Carlos Reyles** Uruguay
14 E4 **Carlow** Irish Rep
14 E4 **Carlow** *co* Irish Rep
15 B2 **Carloway** Scotland
102 G8 **Carlsbad** California
Carlsbad Czechoslovakia *see* **Karlovy Vary**
108 C3 **Carlsbad** New Mexico
108 C3 **Carlsbad Caverns Nat. Park** New Mexico
72 H7 **Carlsberg Ridge** Indian Oc
37 O3 **Carlsfeld** E Germany
99 T3 **Carlshend** Michigan
99 O3 **Carlton** Minnesota
100 B4 **Carlton** Oregon
118 L6 **Carlton** Sask
109 J4 **Carlton** Texas
142 G3 **Carlton Hill** W Australia
9 F1 **Carlton on Trent** England
100 D3 **Carlton Pass** Washington
12 E2 **Carluke** Scotland
110 G3 **Carlyle** Illinois
98 B3 **Carlyle** Montana
119 P9 **Carlyle** Sask
118 D1 **Carman** Manitoba
118 D8 **Carmangay** Alberta
123 S4 **Carmanville** Nfld
8 B4 **Carmarthen Wales**
Carmarthen *co see* **Dyfed**
8 C4 **Carmarthen Van** *mt* **Wales**
18 G8 **Carmaux** France
102 C5 **Carmel** California
95 O5 **Carmel** New York
119 M6 **Carmel** Sask
95 S2 **Carmell** Maine
80 D3 **Carmel,Mt** Israel
112 E3 **Carmel, Mt** S Carolina
133 F4 **Carmelo** Uruguay
127 J9 **Carmelo** Venezuela
102 C5 **Carmel Valley** California
126 G10 **Carmen** Colombia
101 M4 **Carmen** Idaho
107 M5 **Carmen** Oklahoma
71 G6 **Carmen** Philippines
124 D5 **Carmen** *isld* Mexico
124 F2 **Carmen** *R* Mexico
133 D2 **Carmen Alto** Chile
130 C10 **Carmen del Paraná** Paraguay
133 E6 **Carmen de Patagones** Argentina
131 B2 **Carmen,R.del** Chile
133 D5 **Carmensa** Argentina
108 E7 **Carmen, Sa del** *mts* Mexico
110 H3 **Carmi** Illinois
113 L9 **Carmichael** New Providence I **Bahamas**
118 J8 **Carmichael** Sask
141 J5 **Carmila** Queensland
109 L5 **Carmine** Texas
130 G7 **Carmo** Brazil
44 D3 **Carmo** *mt* Italy
130 F7 **Carmo da Cachoeira** Brazil
130 F6 **Carmo do Paranaiba** Brazil
143 C9 **Carmody, L** W Australia
16 D7 **Carmona** Spain
13 H5 **Carnaby** England
143 B8 **Carnamah** W Australia
138 F4 **Carnanto,L** S Australia
89 C8 **Carnarvon** S Africa
143 A6 **Carnarvon** W Australia
141 J7 **Carnarvon Ra** Queensland
143 D7 **Carnarvon Ra** W Australia
71 C5 **Carnatic Shoal** S China Sea
14 D1 **Carndonagh** Irish Rep
119 Q9 **Carnduff** Sask
8 C1 **Carnedd Llewelyn** *mt* Wales
107 M6 **Carnegie** Oklahoma
94 G6 **Carnegie** Pennsylvania
143 E7 **Carnegie** W Australia
143 E7 **Carnegie, L** W Australia
90 A9 **Carnegie Ridge** Pacific Oc
20 E4 **Carneille,la** France
107 N3 **Carneiro** Kansas
131 A6 **Carnero,B.del** Chile
112 D3 **Carnesville** Georgia
99 T4 **Carney** Michigan
107 O6 **Carney** Oklahoma
13 F5 **Carnforth** England
42 E2 **Carniche, Alpi** *mts* Italy
69 A8 **Car Nicobar** *isld* Nicobar Is
22 E3 **Carnieres** France
86 C5 **Carnot** Cent Afr Republic
138 D5 **Carnot,C** S Australia
19 Q18 **Carnoules** France
13 F1 **Carnoustie** Scotland
14 E4 **Carnsore Pt** Irish Rep
12 E2 **Carnwath** Scotland
116 N3 **Caro** Alaska
94 D3 **Caro** Michigan
141 K4 **Carola Cay** *isld* Gt Barrier Reef **Australia**
112 F2 **Caroleen** N Carolina
129 J5 **Carolina** Brazil
128 C3 **Carolina** Ecuador
87 F11 **Carolina** S Africa
112 K3 **Carolina Beach** N Carolina
118 C6 **Caroline** Alberta
144 B6 **Caroline New Zealand**
135 M9 **Caroline I Pacific Oc**
134 E7 **Caroline Is Pacific Oc**
140 D6 **Caroline, L** N Terr **Aust**
32 G5 **Carolinensiel** W Germany
144 A6 **Caroline Pk New Zealand**
142 F3 **Caroline Ra** W Australia
20 B4 **Carolles** France
119 M8 **Caron** Sask
137 S3 **Carondelet Reef** Phoenix Is Pacific Oc
127 O2 **Caroni** Trinidad
128 F2 **Caroni** *R* Venezuela
127 O2 **Caroni Swamp** Trinidad
127 J9 **Carora** Venezuela
103 K4 **Carp** Nevada
121 O7 **Carp** Ontario
53 B9 **Carpathian Mts** E Europe
48 H5 **Carpaţii Meridionali** *mts* Romania
41 M7 **Carpenèdolo** Italy
45 J1 **Carpenedolo** Italy
141 G4 **Carpentaria Downs** Queensland
136 H4 **Carpentaria,Gulf of** Australia
98 B8 **Carpenter** Wyoming
100 A7 **Carpenterville** Oregon
19 O16 **Carpentras** France
45 J2 **Carpi** Italy
19 P18 **Carpiâgne** *mt* France
130 J9 **Carpina** Brazil
45 J3 **Carpineti** Italy
45 O6 **Carpineto Romano** Italy
48 F5 **Cărpinis** Romania
102 E7 **Carpinteria** California
98 E1 **Carpio** N Dakota
117 M8 **Carp L** Br Col
103 M2 **Carp L** Utah
94 C1 **Carp Lake** Michigan
138 F6 **Carpolac** Victoria
21 C7 **Carquefou** France
19 Q18 **Carqueiranne** France
106 F1 **Carr** Colorado
113 C8 **Carrabelle** Florida
119 O6 **Carragana** Sask
14 B3 **Carra,L** Irish Rep
16 B4 **Carramulo, Sa. do** *mts* Portugal
131 A5 **Carranza,C** Chile
125 J4 **Carranza, Presa V.** *res* Mexico
128 F2 **Carrao** *R* Venezuela
44 H3 **Carrara** Italy
102 H5 **Carrara** Nevada
17 F4 **Carrascosa del Campo** Spain
17 G7 **Carrascoy,Sierra de** *mts* Spain
139 H5 **Carrathool** New S Wales
14 B5 **Carrauntoohil** *mt* Irish Rep
142 G3 **Carr Boyd Ra** W Australia
15 E3 **Carrbridge** Scotland
146 H3 **Carr,C** Antarctica
133 F2 **Carreria** Paraguay
131 B6 **Carrero,Cerro** *peak* Argentina
127 O8 **Carriacou** *isld* Lesser Antilles
15 D5 **Carrick** Scotland
14 F2 **Carrickfergus** N Ireland
14 E3 **Carrickmacross** Irish Rep
14 C3 **Carrick on Shannon** Irish Rep
14 D4 **Carrick on Suir** Irish Rep
111 G11 **Carriere** Mississippi
121 N5 **Carrière,L** Quebec
110 H4 **Carriers Mills** Illinois
138 E4 **Carrieton** S Australia
131 B8 **Carri Lafquén, L** Argentina
98 G2 **Carrington** N Dakota
16 D2 **Carrion** *R* Spain
16 D2 **Carrión de los Condes** Spain
127 H8 **Carrizal** Colombia
124 F2 **Carrizal** Mexico
133 C3 **Carrizal Bajo** Chile
131 B2 **Carrizal, Pta** *C* Chile
103 H9 **Carrizo Cr** California
106 G5 **Carrizo Cr** New Mex/Tex
103 P5 **Carrizo Mts** Arizona
108 H7 **Carrizo Springs** Texas
106 E8 **Carrizozo** New Mexico
99 M7 **Carroll** Iowa
119 R9 **Carroll** Manitoba
98 J7 **Carroll** Nebraska
146 G12 **Carroll Inlet** Antarctica
111 H8 **Carrollton** Alabama
112 B4 **Carrollton** Georgia
110 F2 **Carrollton** Illinois
94 B8 **Carrollton** Kentucky
111 G8 **Carrollton** Mississippi
110 C2 **Carrollton** Missouri
94 F6 **Carrollton** Ohio
109 O8 **Carrollton** Texas
94 J6 **Carrolltown** Pennsylvania
99 T7 **Carrollville** Wisconsin
141 F4 **Carron** *R* Queensland
12 E3 **Carronbridge** Scotland
119 V4 **Carrot R** Manitoba
119 O5 **Carrot River** Sask
20 E4 **Carrouges** France
14 B2 **Carrowmore L** Irish Rep
118 H6 **Carruthers** Sask
100 C8 **Carrville** California
95 N2 **Carry Falls Res** New York
19 O18 **Carry-le-Rouet** France
78 F1 **Çarşamba** Turkey
118 D8 **Carseland** Alberta
13 E1 **Carse of Gowrie** *dist* Scotland
45 O5 **Carseolani, Mti** Italy
45 O5 **Carsoli** Italy
99 L8 **Carson** Iowa
98 E3 **Carson** N Dakota
100 D4 **Carson** Washington
102 E2 **Carson** *R* Nevada
94 C3 **Carson City** Michigan
102 E2 **Carson City** Nevada
102 F2 **Carson L** Nevada
142 F3 **Carson, R** W Australia
102 F2 **Carson Sink** Nevada
94 E3 **Carsonville** Michigan
12 D3 **Carsphairn** Scotland
118 C7 **Carstairs** Alberta
12 E2 **Carstairs** Scotland
Carstensz, G *see* **Jaya Pk**
128 C1 **Cartagena** Colombia
17 G7 **Cartagena** Spain
102 F5 **Cartago** California
128 C3 **Cartago** Colombia
125 N5 **Cartago** Costa Rica
108 G6 **Carta Valley** Texas
101 P2 **Carter** Montana
107 L6 **Carter** Oklahoma
101 P8 **Carter** Wyoming
13 F3 **Carter Bar** England
20 B3 **Carteret** France
141 G2 **Carter, Mt** Queensland
9 G3 **Carters Bridge** England
111 M7 **Cartersville** Georgia
101 T3 **Cartersville** Montana
145 E4 **Carterton** New Zealand
109 P1 **Carthage** Arkansas
99 P9 **Carthage** Illinois
94 B7 **Carthage** Indiana
111 G9 **Carthage** Mississippi
110 B4 **Carthage** Missouri
112 H2 **Carthage** N Carolina
106 D8 **Carthage** New Mexico
95 M3 **Carthage** New York
98 J5 **Carthage** S Dakota
94 B10 **Carthage** Tennessee
109 N3 **Carthage** Texas
43 C12 **Carthage** Tunisia
85 G1 **Carthage** *ruins* Tunisia
120 J6 **Cartier** Ontario
142 E1 **Cartier I** Timor Sea
22 F3 **Cartignies** France
13 F5 **Cartmel** England
45 N4 **Cartoceto** Italy
48 J6 **Cărtojani** Romania
115 O7 **Cartwright** Labrador
119 S9 **Cartwright** Manitoba
98 C2 **Cartwright** N Dakota
129 L5 **Caruaru** Brazil
130 H10 **Caruarú** Brazil
128 F1 **Carúpano** Venezuela
129 J4 **Carutapera** Brazil
110 G5 **Caruthersville** Missouri
94 D9 **Carver** Kentucky
22 D3 **Carvin** France
16 A5 **Carvoeira,C** Portugal
128 F4 **Carvoeiro** Brazil
101 M1 **Carway** Alberta
141 H6 **Carwell** Queensland
33 S6 **Carwitz** E Germany
111 F9 **Cary** Mississippi
112 J2 **Cary** N Carolina
139 G3 **Caryapundy Swamp** Queensland
113 G12 **Carysfort Reef** Florida
45 K3 **Carzolano,Mt** Italy
133 C4 **Casablanca** Chile
85 C2 **Casablanca** Morocco
130 F7 **Casa Branca** Brazil
16 B6 **Casa Branca** Portugal
42 F7 **Casacalenda** Italy
41 L5 **Casaccia** Switzerland
127 P3 **Casa Cruz, C** Trinidad
124 E2 **Casa de János Mexico**
129 G8 **Casado** Paraguay
103 N9 **Casa Grande** Arizona
103 N9 **Casa Grande Nat. Mon** Arizona
17 G5 **Casa Ibáñez** Spain
41 L7 **Casalbuttano** Italy
45 Q7 **Casal di Principe** Italy
44 D1 **Casale** Italy
45 K3 **Casalecchio di Reno** Italy
45 J2 **Casalgrande** Italy
45 H2 **Casalmaggiore** Italy
45 J1 **Casaloldo** Italy
44 G1 **Casalpusterlengo** Italy
45 P6 **Casalvieri** Italy
45 P8 **Casamicciola** Italy
116 E4 **Casapedaga** Alaska
108 C6 **Casa Piedra** Texas
43 J8 **Casarano** Italy
124 F2 **Casas Grandes** Mexico
109 O9 **Casa View** Texas
100 J5 **Cascade** Idaho
101 O2 **Cascade** Montana
95 Q2 **Cascade** New Hampshire
100 D4 **Cascade Locks** Oregon
117 N11 **Cascade Mts** Br Col/Wash
100 D1 **Cascade Pass** Washington
100 C7 **Cascade Ra** U.S.A.
100 K5 **Cascade Res** Idaho
100 D2 **Cascade Tunnel** Washington
100 C5 **Cascadia** Oregon
16 A6 **Cascais** Portugal
122 G5 **Cascapedia** Quebec
122 F5 **Cascapedia R** Quebec
130 D9 **Cascavel** Brazil
45 J4 **Cascina** Italy
95 R2 **Casco** Maine
99 T5 **Casco** Wisconsin
95 R3 **Casco B** Maine
45 M3 **Casemurate** Italy
45 L4 **Casentina** Italy
133 E5 **Caseros** Argentina
45 Q7 **Caserta** Italy
94 D3 **Caseville** Michigan
99 T10 **Casey** Illinois
121 Q5 **Casey** Quebec
146 A5 **Casey B** Antarctica
14 D4 **Cashel** Irish Rep
87 F9 **Cashel** Zimbabwe
107 N6 **Cashion** Oklahoma
141 J8 **Cashmere** Queensland **Aust**
100 E2 **Cashmere** Washington
99 Q6 **Cashton** Wisconsin
71 F2 **Casiguran** Luzon Philippines
71 F2 **Casiguran B** Luzon Philippines
71 E3 **Casiguran Sound** Luzon Philippines
133 E4 **Casilda** Argentina
48 L6 **Casimcea** Romania
130 G8 **Casimiro de Abreu** Brazil
45 H2 **Casina** Italy
139 L3 **Casino** New S Wales
128 E3 **Casiquiare** *R* Venezuela
124 D2 **Casita** Mexico
31 J6 **Čáslav** Czechoslovakia
128 C5 **Casma** Peru
102 D7 **Casmalia** California
71 G5 **Casogoran B Philippines**
45 L3 **Casola Valsenio** Italy
109 N2 **Cason** Texas
45 Q8 **Casória** Italy
102 A2 **Caspar** California
17 G3 **Caspe** Spain
101 T7 **Casper** Wyoming
111 C9 **Caspiana** Louisiana
53 G10 **Caspian Sea**
110 C6 **Cass** Arkansas
144 C5 **Cass New Zealand**
94 H8 **Cass** W Virginia
94 D3 **Cass** *R* Michigan
144 C5 **Cass** *R* **New Zealand**
98 B7 **Cassa** Wyoming
18 G8 **Cassagnes-Bégonhès** France
87 D8 **Cassai** Angola
130 F7 **Cássai** Brazil
87 D8 **Cassamba** Angola
43 G9 **Cassano Ionio** Italy
94 D3 **Cass City** Michigan
121 P7 **Casselman** Ontario
98 J3 **Casselton** N Dakota
19 Q14 **Casse Massion** *mt* France
117 J6 **Cassiar** Br Col
117 H6 **Cassiar Mts** Br Col
130 D6 **Cassilândia** Brazil
139 J4 **Cassilis** New S Wales
141 G5 **Cassilis** Queensland
87 C9 **Cassinga** Angola
142 F2 **Cassini I** W Australia
133 G4 **Cassino** Brazil
43 F7 **Cassino** Italy
129 H3 **Cassiporé** *R* Brazil
19 P18 **Cassis** France
99 M2 **Cass L** Minnesota
107 O3 **Cassoday** Kansas
94 B5 **Cassopolis** Michigan
110 C5 **Cassville** Missouri
99 Q7 **Cassville** Wisconsin
45 K1 **Castagnaro** Italy
102 F7 **Castaic** California
129 J4 **Castanhal** Brazil
133 D4 **Castaño** Argentina
131 B3 **Castaño** *R* Argentina
124 J4 **Castaños** Mexico
127 M1 **Castara** Tobago
17 G3 **Castejón,Mt.de** Spain
45 J1 **Castelbelforte** Italy
45 L3 **Castel Bolognese** Italy
45 J1 **Castel d'Ario** Italy
42 D4 **Castel del Rio** Italy
42 F7 **Castel di Sangro** Italy
45 L4 **Castel Focognano** Italy
45 P7 **Castelforte** Italy
42 D3 **Castelfranco** Veneto Italy
45 L4 **Castelfranco di Sopra** Italy
45 K2 **Castelfranco Emilia** Italy

45 J1 Castel Goffredo Italy
18 F8 Casteljaloux France
109 J5 Castell Texas
37 J4 Castell W Germany
100 C8 Castella California
43 F8 Castellabate Italy
43 E10 Castellammare del Golfo Sicily
45 Q8 Castellammare di Stabia Italy
40 G7 Castellamònte Italy
45 J2 Castellarano Italy
133 F5 Castelli Argentina
45 K3 Castello di Serravalle Italy
17 G4 Castellón *prov* Spain
17 G5 Castellón de la Plana Spain
17 G4 Castellote Spain
45 J1 Castellucchio Italy
45 N6 Castel Madama Italy
45 K2 Castel Maggiore Italy
45 K1 Castelmassa Italy
18 G9 Castelnaudary France
18 E7 Castelnau de Médoc France
18 F8 Castelnau de Montratier France
18 F9 Castelnau-Magnoac France
45 J2 Castelnovo di Sotto Italy
45 H3 Castel novo ne'Monti Italy
45 H3 Castelnuovo di Garfagnana Italy
45 N5 Castelnuovo di Porto Italy
45 J1 Castelnuovo di Verona Italy
130 H7 Castelo Brazil
16 C5 Castelo de Vide Portugal
45 O4 Castelplanio Italy
45 M6 Castel Porziano Italy
45 R8 Castel San Giorgio Italy
45 L4 Castel San Niccolo Italy
45 L3 Castel San Pietro Terme Italy
18 F8 Castelsarrasin France
44 F1 Castel S.Giov Italy
43 F11 Casteltermini Sicily
45 P5 Castelvecchio Subequo Italy
43 E11 Castelvetrano Sicily
45 P7 Castel Volturno Italy
45 K3 Castenaso Italy
41 M7 Castenedolo Italy
138 F6 Casterton Victoria
18 E9 Castets France
122 F7 Castigan Mts New Brunswick
45 K3 Castiglione dei Pepoli Italy
45 J1 Castiglione delle Stiviere Italy
45 H3 Castiglione di Garfagnana Italy
45 L4 Castiglion Fibocchi Italy
42 D5 Castiglion Fiorentino Italy
94 K4 Castile New York
133 C3 Castilla Chile
16 D4 Castilla Lavieja *reg* Spain
71 E3 Castillejos Luzon Philippines
16 D6 Castillejo, Sa. de *mts* Spain
127 J9 Castilletes Venezuela
133 C7 Castillo *mt* Chile
131 B4 Castillo,Cerro del *peak* Argentina
113 F8 Castillo de San Marcos Nat. Mon Florida
124 H3 Castillón Mexico
18 F8 Castillon et Capitourlan France
18 F8 Castillonnès France
133 D7 Castillo,Pampa del *plain* Argentina
133 G4 Castillos Uruguay
95 T2 Castine Maine
9 G2 Castle Acre England
14 B3 Castlebar Irish Rep
15 A4 Castlebay Scotland
14 E3 Castlebellingham Irish Rep
111 J10 Castleberry Alabama
14 E2 Castleblayney Irish Rep
9 E3 Castle Bromwich England
13 F4 Castle Carrock England
8 D5 Castle Cary England
14 D4 Castlecomer Irish Rep
100 J7 Castle Cr Idaho
103 N2 Castle Dale Utah
14 D2 Castlederg N Ireland
14 E4 Castledermot Irish Rep
103 K8 Castle Dome Mts Arizona
9 E2 Castle Donington England
12 E4 Castle Douglas Scotland
12 E3 Castlefern Scotland
13 G6 Castleford England
101 L7 Castleford Idaho
100 H1 Castlegar Br Col
103 O2 Castle Gate Utah
90 C1 Castle Harbour Bermuda
112 K3 Castle Hayne N Carolina
103 M8 Castle Hot Sp Arizona
126 G3 Castle I Bahamas
14 B4 Castleisland Irish Rep
14 B4 Castlemaine Irish Rep
139 G6 Castlemaine Victoria
14 C5 Castlemartyr Irish Rep
102 D6 Castle Mt California
101 L5 Castle Peak Idaho
145 F4 Castlepoint New Zealand
14 D3 Castlepollard Irish Rep
14 C3 Castlerea Irish Rep
139 J4 Castlereagh *R* New S Wales
140 D1 Castlereagh B N Terr Aust
9 G2 Castle Rising England
106 F2 Castle Rock Colorado
98 C5 Castle Rock S Dakota
101 O8 Castle Rock Utah
100 C3 Castle Rock Washington
99 R6 Castle Rock Res Wisconsin
13 G4 Castleside England
9 E1 Castleton England
127 L2 Castleton Jamaica
103 P3 Castleton Utah
95 O3 Castleton Vermont
95 O4 Castleton on Hudson New York
12 D5 Castletown I of Man U.K.
14 B5 Castletown Bere Irish Rep
14 F2 Castlewellan N Ireland
98 J5 Castlewood S Dakota
108 D6 Castolon Texas
118 F6 Castor Alberta
111 C9 Castor Louisiana
111 D9 Castor *R* Louisiana
95 M3 Castorland New York
20 B3 Castre,Mt France
18 G9 Castres France
25 C3 Castricum Netherlands
127 O7 Castries St Lucia
133 C6 Castro Chile
16 D2 Castrocalbón Spain
45 L3 Castrocaro Italy
45 O6 Castro dei Volsci Italy
16 E2 Castrogeriz Spain
16 C1 Castropol Spain
32 F9 Castrop-Rauxel W Germany
16 E1 Castro Urdiales Spain
16 B7 Castro Verde Portugal
43 G9 Castrovillari Italy
102 C5 Castroville California
109 J6 Castroville Texas
16 D6 Castuera Spain
88 G10 Casuarina *isld* Mozambique
142 G2 Casuarina, Mt W Australia
116 N6 Caswell Alaska
144 A6 Caswell Sd New Zealand
48 E3 Čata Czechoslovakia
127 J2 Catadupa Jamaica
130 G7 Cataguases Brazil
111 D10 Catahoula L Louisiana
71 F4 Cataiñgan Philippines
78 J2 Çatak Turkey
130 F6 Catalão Brazil
47 J3 Çatalca Turkey
47 J5 Çatal Dağı *mt* Turkey
127 K5 Catalina, I Dominican Rep
139 H9 Catamaran Tasmania
131 D2 Catamarca Argentina
133 D3 Catamarca *prov* Argentina
71 F4 Catanauan Philippines
87 F9 Catandica Mozambique
71 G4 Catanduanes *isld* Philippines
130 E7 Catanduva Brazil
130 D9 Catanduvas Brazil
43 G11 Catania Sicily
43 G11 Catania,Golfo di Sicily
43 H10 Catanzaro Italy
111 F12 Cataouatche,L Louisiana
110 K2 Cataract L Indiana
71 G4 Catarman Philippines
71 G7 Catarman Pt Mindanao Philippines
17 G5 Catarroja Spain
95 M6 Catasauqua Pennsylvania
138 D6 Catastrophe, C S Australia
128 D2 Catatumbo *R* Venezuela/Colombia
111 M9 Cataula Georgia
129 G4 Catavara Brazil
99 Q4 Catawba Wisconsin
112 F2 Catawba L S Carolina
95 L6 Catawissa Pennsylvania
87 F9 Cataxa Mozambique
71 G5 Catbalogan Samar Philippines
126 E2 Cat Cays *islds* Bahamas
101 R2 Cat Creek Montana
22 F3 Cateau,Le France
71 G7 Cateel Mindanao Philippines
9 G6 Catel Channel Is
22 E3 Catelet, le France
125 M8 Catemaco Mexico
45 P5 Catena di Monte Sirente Italy
130 J10 Catende Brazil
118 J5 Cater Sask
9 F5 Caterham England
87 B7 Catete Angola
107 L3 Catharine Kansas
98 G2 Cathay N Dakota
139 J6 Cathcart New S Wales
87 E12 Cathcart S Africa
108 D5 Cathedral Mt Texas
109 P1 Catherine,L Arkansas
103 M2 Catherine, Mt Utah
127 L2 Catherine's Peak Jamaica
89 F7 Cathkin Pk *mt* Lesotho
100 B3 Cathlamet Washington
94 D1 Cathro Michigan
126 G2 Cat I Bahamas
111 G11 Cat I Mississippi
22 F3 Catillon-sur-Sambre France
85 A6 Catio Guinea-Bissau
128 F3 Catisimiña Venezuela
115 K7 Cat Lake Ontario
94 E8 Catlettsburg Kentucky
99 T9 Catlin Illinois
144 B7 Catlins *R* New Zealand
95 L3 Cato New York
137 M6 Cato *isld* Coral Sea
94 K7 Catoctin Mt Maryland/Virg
130 H9 Catolé do Rocha Brazil
42 E5 Catria,Monte Italy
133 E5 Catrilo Argentina
128 F3 Catrimani Brazil
95 O4 Catskill New York
95 N4 Catskill Mts New York
94 J4 Cattaraugus New York
22 L5 Cattenom France
13 F6 Catterall England
13 G5 Catterick England
45 N4 Cattolica Italy
87 F11 Catuane Mozambique
133 D4 Catuna Argentina
128 E3 Cauaburi *R* Brazil
45 M1 Cauárzera Italy
129 J4 Cauaxi *R* Brazil
71 F6 Cauayan Negros Philippines
128 C3 Cauca *div* Colombia
126 G10 Cauca,R Colombia
72 E1 Caucasus *mt ra* U.S.S.R.
119 V3 Cauchon L Manitoba
95 R7 Caucomgomoc L Maine
20 G2 Caudebec France
20 H3 Caudebec-les-Elbeuf France
17 G6 Caudete Spain
22 E3 Caudry France
88 C9 Cauese Mts Mozambique
121 R7 Caughnawaga Quebec
71 G6 Cauit Pt Philippines
20 A5 Caulnes France
43 G10 Caulonia Italy
19 N17 Caumont France
20 D3 Caumont-l'Eventé France
126 E4 Caunao *R* Cuba
18 G9 Caunes France
87 C7 Caungulu Angola
131 A5 Cauquenes Chile
133 C5 Cauquenes Chile
128 F2 Caura *R* Venezuela
122 E5 Causapscal Quebec
18 G8 Caussade France
128 F6 Cautário *R* Brazil
18 E10 Cauterets France
131 A7 Cautin *prov* Chile
126 F4 Cauto Cuba
76 D5 Cauvery *R* India
20 F2 Cauville France
45 R8 Cava Italy
16 B3 Cavado *R* Portugal
40 H7 Cavaglia Italy
19 O17 Cavaillon France
19 Q18 Cavalaire France
129 J6 Cavalcante Brazil
41 O5 Cavalese Italy
98 J1 Cavalier N Dakota
119 U10 Cavalier N Dakota
145 D1 Cavalli Is New Zealand
109 L7 Cavallo, Pass Texas
85 C7 Cavally *R* Ivory Co/Liberia
14 D3 Cavan Irish Rep
14 D3 Cavan *co* Irish Rep
143 G7 Cavanagh Ra W Australia
47 K7 Çavdır Turkey
45 N6 Cave Italy
144 C6 Cave New Zealand
110 E6 Cave City Arkansas
94 B9 Cave City Kentucky
103 N8 Cavecreek Arizona
143 D9 Cave Hill W Australia
110 H4 Cave in Rock Illinois
130 E10 Caveiras,R Brazil
100 B7 Cave Junction Oregon
120 C2 Cavell Ontario
118 J6 Cavell Sask
138 C2 Cavenagh,Mt N Terr Australia
118 G8 Cavendish Alberta
9 G3 Cavendish England
138 F6 Cavendish Victoria
45 M2 Ca Venier Italy
131 G3 Cavera *R* Brazil
131 G3 Cavera, Serra do *mts* Brazil
68 C7 Cavern I Burma
130 D9 Cavernoso, Serra do *mts* Brazil
120 C4 Cavers Ontario
9 F5 Caversham England
111 L7 Cave Spring Georgia
103 K3 Cave Valley Nevada
129 H3 Caviana *isld* Brazil
18 E7 Cavignac France
71 E6 Cavili Philippines
71 E3 Cavite Luzon Philippines
45 N6 Cavo, M *mt* Italy
44 B2 Cavour Italy
98 H5 Cavour S Dakota
45 J2 Cavriago Italy
42 J6 Cavtat Yugoslavia
15 E3 Cawdor Scotland
107 M2 Cawker City Kansas
138 F4 Cawndilla L New S Wales
Cawnpore *see* Kanpur
13 G6 Cawood England
121 P7 Cawood Low Quebec
9 H2 Cawston England
130 G7 Caxambu Brazil
128 D4 Caxias Amazonas Brazil
129 K4 Caxias Brazil
131 H2 Caxias do Sul Brazil
87 B7 Caxito Angola
9 F3 Caxton England
9 F3 Caxton Gibbet England
47 L6 Çay Turkey
128 C3 Cayambe *vol* Ecuador
112 F4 Cayce S Carolina
68 F8 Cay Dua *B* Vietnam
78 H1 Cayeli Turkey
129 H3 Cayenne Fr Guiana
20 H1 Cayeux-sur-Mer France
127 L5 Cayey Puerto Rico
18 H9 Caylar, le France
118 D8 Cayley Alberta
18 G8 Caylus France
126 E5 Cayman Brac *isld* W Indies
126 D5 Cayman, Grand *isld* W Indies
126 D5 Cayman, Little *isld* W Indies
90 A6 Cayman Trench Caribbean
68 G7 Cay Mit Vietnam
125 P9 Cayo Belize
127 P4 Cayon St Kitts W I
126 D3 Cay Sal Bank Bahamas
102 D6 Cayucos California
99 T10 Cayuga Indiana
98 J3 Cayuga N Dakota
109 M4 Cayuga Texas
95 L4 Cayuga L New York
16 D7 Cazalla de la Sierra Spain
48 L6 Căzăneşti Romania
18 E9 Cazaubon France
18 E8 Cazaux, Etang de *L* France
85 F2 Caze Algeria
95 M4 Cazenovia New York
18 F9 Cazères France
42 G4 Cazin Yugoslavia
42 H3 Čazma Yugoslavia
87 D8 Cazombo Angola
16 E7 Cazorla Spain
87 F9 Cazula Mozambique
16 D2 Cea *R* Spain
48 K3 Ceahlau Romania
48 K4 Ceahlău *mt* Romania
14 E3 Ceanannus Mór Irish Rep
130 J8 Ceará Mirim Brazil
20 D5 Ceauce France
21 F7 Ceaux France
119 P5 Ceba Sask
125 O6 Cebaco,I Panama
124 G4 Ceballos Mexico
106 D5 Cebolla New Mexico
133 D3 Cebollar Argentina
133 G4 Cebollati *R* Uruguay
17 F3 Cebollera *mt* Spain
106 C6 Cebollita New Mexico
16 E4 Cebreros Spain
71 F5 Cebu Philippines
71 F7 Cebuano Barracks Mindanao Philippines
43 E7 Ceccano Italy
48 E4 Cece Hungary
94 C5 Cecil Ohio
99 S5 Cecil Wisconsin
141 K8 Cecil Plains Queensland
143 D7 Cecil Rhodes, Mt *mt* W Australia
95 M7 Cecilton Maryland
100 B8 Cecilville California
42 D5 Cecina Italy
16 C5 Ceclavín Spain
107 M2 Cedar Kansas
99 O7 Cedar *R* Iowa
94 C2 Cedar *R* Michigan
98 H8 Cedar *R* Nebraska
111 H8 Cedarbluff Mississippi
94 F9 Cedar Bluff Virginia
107 L3 Cedar Bluff Res Kansas
107 K2 Cedar Bluffs Kansas
98 K8 Cedar Bluffs Nebraska
103 M4 Cedar Breaks Nat.Mon Utah
99 T6 Cedarburg Wisconsin
98 E6 Cedar Butte S Dakota
110 D3 Cedar City Missouri
103 L4 Cedar City Utah
98 D3 Cedar Cr N Dakota
109 K5 Cedar Creek Texas
109 O9 Cedar Crest Texas
101 L7 Cedar Cr.Res Idaho
109 L3 Cedar Cr.Res Texas
99 O7 Cedar Falls Iowa
127 P4 Cedar Grove Antigua W I
99 T6 Cedar Grove Wisconsin
94 F8 Cedar Grove W Virginia
112 L2 Cedar I N Carolina
95 M9 Cedar I Virginia
113 D8 Cedar Key Florida
119 R5 Cedar L Manitoba
108 E3 Cedar L Texas
99 T8 Cedar Lake Indiana
109 M7 Cedar Lane Texas
102 G3 Cedar Mts Nevada
94 D5 Cedar Pt Ohio
99 P8 Cedar Rapids Iowa
98 H8 Cedar Rapids Nebraska
95 K5 Cedar Run Pennsylvania
94 B3 Cedar Springs Michigan
120 H10 Cedar Springs Ontario
111 L7 Cedartown Georgia
107 O4 Cedar Vale Kansas
106 E7 Cedarvale New Mexico
127 L2 Cedar Valley Jamaica
100 E8 Cedarville California
95 M7 Cedarville New Jersey
110 N2 Cedarville Ohio
106 F4 Cedarwood Colorado
94 K8 Cedon Virginia
119 O9 Cedoux Sask
43 C8 Cedrino *R* Sardinia
130 G9 Cedro Brazil
124 E4 Cedros Mexico
124 B3 Cedros *isld* Mexico
127 N3 Cedros Pt Trinidad
138 C4 Ceduna S Australia
43 F10 Cefalù Sicily
16 E3 Cega *R* Spain
48 F3 Cegléd Hungary
43 H8 Ceglie Messapico Italy
17 F6 Cehegin Spain
67 B4 Ceheng China
48 H3 Cehu Silvaniei Romania
48 G4 Ceica Romania
128 E3 Cejal Colombia
87 C8 Cela Angola
45 P5 Celano Italy
16 B2 Celanova Spain
125 J7 Celaya Mexico
Celebes *isld see* Sulawesi
70 G3 Celebes Sea Indonesia
109 L2 Celeste Texas
94 C6 Celina Ohio
110 M1 Celina Ohio
94 B10 Celina Tennessee
109 L2 Celina Texas
17 G4 Cella Spain
48 D3 Celldömölk Hungary
32 M7 Celle W Germany
22 E2 Celles Belgium
21 H6 Cellettes France
16 B3 Celorico de Basto Portugal
7 E12 Celtic Sea British Isles/France
47 L7 Çeltikçi Turkey
41 O5 Cembra Italy
107 M7 Cement Oklahoma
94 C4 Cement City Michigan
46 D1 Čemerna Planina *mt* Yugoslavia
42 H4 Čemernica *mt* Yugoslavia
48 E7 Čemerno Yugoslavia
8 B1 Cemlyn B Wales
8 B1 Cemmaes Wales
17 F6 Cenajo,Embalso de *res* Spain
8 B3 Cenarth Wales
86 G4 Cencia Ethiopia
136 G2 Cendrawasih *pen* W Irian
44 G2 Ceno *R* Italy
133 C6 Cenoa *R* Argentina
86 C4 Cent.Afr.Rep Equat Africa
130 D8 Centenario do Sul Brazil
112 H3 Centenary S Carolina
101 T8 Centennial Wyoming
103 L8 Centennial Wash *R* Arizona
106 D4 Center Colorado
110 E2 Center Missouri
98 E2 Center N Dakota
111 B10 Center Texas
94 E6 Centerburg Ohio
99 O4 Center City Minnesota
95 L9 Center Cross Virginia
113 F9 Center Hill Florida
110 L5 Center Hill Res Tennessee
95 P6 Center Moriches Long I, N Y
95 Q3 Center Ossipee New Hampshire
109 H6 Center Point Texas
111 J9 Centerville Alabama
110 D1 Centerville Iowa
111 E12 Centerville Louisiana
94 H6 Centerville Pennsylvania
98 K6 Centerville S Dakota
110 J6 Centerville Tennessee
109 M4 Centerville Texas
101 O9 Centerville Utah
100 E4 Centerville Washington
124 H3 Centinela, Pico del *mt* Mexico
42 D4 Cento Italy
44 G3 Cento Croci, Passo di Italy
107 O7 Centrahoma Oklahoma
109 L1 Centrahoma Oklahoma
116 P4 Central Alaska
106 B9 Central New Mexico
112 E3 Central S Carolina
103 L4 Central Utah
130 B9 Central *dep* Paraguay
89 D3 Central *dist* Botswana
15 D4 Central *reg* Scotland
145 E2 Central Auckland *stat area* New Zealand
118 L8 Central Butt Sask
106 E2 Central City Colorado
99 P7 Central City Iowa
110 J4 Central City Kentucky
98 H8 Central City Nebraska
94 J6 Central City Pennsylvania
95 Q5 Central Falls Rhode I
110 G3 Centralia Illinois
107 O2 Centralia Kansas
110 D2 Centralia Missouri
100 C3 Centralia Washington
94 G8 Centralia W Virginia
94 B1 Central Lake Michigan
140 C5 Central Mt. Stewart N Terr Aust
100 C7 Central Point Oregon
136 J2 Central Ra Papua New Guinea
56 Central Siberia
95 L3 Central Square New York
102 B1 Central Valley California
111 L7 Centre Alabama
144 A7 Centre I New Zealand
95 L7 Centreville Maryland
94 B5 Centreville Michigan
111 E10 Centreville Mississippi
122 E7 Centreville New Brunswick
122 F9 Centreville Nova Scotia
111 J11 Century Florida
94 G7 Century W Virginia
67 B4 Cenwanglao Shan *mt* China
67 C5 Cenxi China
19 P18 Cépet,C France
Cephalonia *isld* Greece *see* Kefallinía *I*
44 C4 Ceppo Monte *mt* Italy
45 O6 Ceprano Italy
136 F2 Ceram Sea Indonesia
21 F6 Cérans-Foulletourte France
128 E2 Cerbatana, Sa. de la *mts* Venezuela
103 K6 Cerbat Mts Arizona
18 H10 Cerbère, C France
16 B7 Cercal Portugal
16 E4 Cercedilla Spain
37 O5 Čerchov *mt* Czechoslovakia
20 J6 Cercottes France
18 H6 Cercy la Tour France
18 G10 Cerdaña *dist* Spain
21 J6 Cerdon France
21 H7 Cere France
18 G8 Cère *R* France
45 K1 Cerea Italy
118 G7 Cereal Alberta
45 L1 Ceregnano Italy
20 C4 Cérences France
130 E4 Ceres Brazil
102 C4 Ceres California
40 F7 Ceres Italy
87 C12 Ceres S Africa
13 F1 Ceres Scotland
45 J1 Ceresara Italy
40 F7 Ceresole Reale Italy
18 G10 Céret France
126 G10 Cereté Colombia
87 J9 Cerf *isld* Br Indian Oc Terr
83 J12 Cerf I Mahé I Indian Oc
121 P6 Cerf. L du Quebec
22 G3 Cerfontaine Belgium
20 K3 Cergy-Pontoise France
44 D3 Ceriale Italy
43 G7 Cerignola Italy
Cerigo *isld* Greece *see* Kíthira *I*
18 G6 Cerilly France
20 D3 Cerisy-la Forêt France
20 C3 Cerisy-la-Salle France
47 J3 Çerkesköy Turkey
42 F3 Cerknica Yugoslavia
48 G4 Cermei Romania
48 L5 Cerna Romania
48 H5 Cerna *R* Romania
48 L6 Cernavodă Romania
19 K5 Cernay France
8 D6 Cerne Abbas England
42 H3 Cernik Yugoslavia
37 O4 Černošin Czechoslovakia
109 H9 Cerralvo Mexico
124 E5 Cerralvo *isld* Mexico
45 J4 Cerreto Guidi Italy
44 H3 Cerreto, Passo di Italy
45 R7 Cerreto Sannita Italy
8 C1 Cerrigydrudion Wales
46 D3 Cerrik Albania
106 D6 Cerrillos New Mexico
125 J6 Cerritos Mexico
130 E9 Cêrro Azul Brazil
128 C6 Cerro de Pasco Peru
127 L5 Cerro de Punta *peak* Puerto Rico
110 H2 Cerro Gordo Illinois
131 G4 Cerro Largo *dep* Uruguay
127 J9 Cerrón *mt* Venezuela
124 F4 Cerro Prieto Mexico
21 E7 Cersay France
45 K4 Certaldo Italy
143 B9 Cervantes I W Australia
45 P7 Cervaro Italy
43 G7 Cervaro *R* Italy
43 G8 Cervati, M *mt* Italy
44 H2 Cervellino *mt* Italy
17 H3 Cervera Spain
17 F2 Cervera del Rio Alhama Spain
16 D2 Cervera de P Spain
42 E4 Cervia Italy
43 G8 Cervialto, M *mt* Italy
45 R7 Cervinara Italy
44 D4 Cervo Italy
41 H7 Cervo *R* Italy
128 D2 César *div* Colombia
126 H10 César,R Colombia
42 E4 Cesena Italy
45 M3 Cesenatico Italy
52 C6 Cēsis U.S.S.R.
37 O5 Česká Kubice Czechoslovakia
31 H5 Česká Lípa Czechoslovakia
31 H7 Ceské Budějovice Czechoslovakia
31 H6 Českézemé *reg* Czechoslovakia
31 J6 Českomoravská Vysočina *mts* Czechoslovakia
31 H5 Český Brod Czechoslovakia
31 H7 Český Krumlov Czechoslovakia
37 O4 Český les Sumava *mts* Czechoslovakia
48 E1 Český Těšin Czechoslovakia
78 A2 Çesme Turkey
47 H6 Çeşnıe Turkey
139 K5 Cessnock New S Wales
48 H6 Cetate Romania
42 H5 Cetina *R* Yugoslavia
42 J6 Cetinje Yugoslavia
20 G5 Ceton France
43 G9 Cetraro Italy
19 P15 Ceuse, Pic de *mt* France
16 D9 Ceuta Spain
85 C1 Ceuta *Span exclave* Morocco
41 N5 Cevedale *mt* Italy
18 H8 Cevennes *mts* France
78 G3 Ceylânpinar Turkey
99 M6 Ceylon Minnesota
119 N9 Ceylon Sask
Ceylon *rep see* Sri Lanka *Rep*
19 P18 Ceyreste France
57 B6 Chaacha U.S.S.R.
21 G10 Chabanais France
19 P16 Chabestan France
19 O15 Chabeuil France
142 A6 Chabjuwardoo B W Australia
18 H5 Chablis France
19 P16 Chabre, Mt de France
19 Q16 Chabrières France
21 I7 Chabris France
133 C1 Chaca Chile
131 E5 Chacabuco Argentina
127 N1 Chacachacare I Trinidad
133 D2 Chacance Chile
133 C6 Chacao, Canal de Chile
133 D6 Chacays, Sa. de los *mts* Argentina
131 C6 Chachahuen,Sa *mt* Argentina
128 D7 Chachani *mt* Peru
128 C5 Chachapoyas Peru
68 E6 Chachoengsao Thailand
74 D6 Chachro Pakistan
128 F8 Chaco *dep* Paraguay
133 E3 Chaco *prov* Argentina
133 E3 Chaco Austral *reg* Argentina
128 F8 Chaco Boreal *plain* Paraguay
133 E2 Chaco Boreal *reg* Paraguay
106 B5 Chaco Canyon Nat. Mon New Mexico
133 E2 Chaco Central *reg* Argentina
117 H8 Chacon,C Pr of Wales I, Alaska
129 G5 Chacorãco, Cachoeira do *waterfall* Brazil
106 C6 Chacra Mesa *mt* New Mexico
86 C3 Chad *rep* Equat Africa
56 D5 Chadan U.S.S.R.
112 J3 Chadbourn N Carolina
131 C6 Chadileo,R Argentina
133 D5 Chadileuvú *R* Argentina
86 B3 Chad,L Equat Africa
56 F2 Chadobets *R* U.S.S.R.
98 D7 Chadron Nebraska
99 R7 Chadwick Illinois
48 M4 Chadyr Lunga U.S.S.R.
110 G4 Chaffee Missouri
94 J4 Chaffee New York
74 A4 Chagai Pakistan
77 H5 Chagai Hills Pakistan
53 H8 Chagan *R* U.S.S.R.
51 N3 Chagda U.S.S.R.
8 C6 Chagford England
55 E4 Chaglinka *R* U.S.S.R.
40 A4 Chagny France
52 E5 Chagoda U.S.S.R.
52 E5 Chagodoshcha *R* U.S.S.R.
81 E6 Chagos Arch Indian Oc
57 A2 Chagrayskoye Plato U.S.S.R.
94 F5 Chagrin Falls Ohio
127 O2 Chaguanas Trinidad
127 N1 Chaguaramas Trinidad
127 L10 Chaguaramas Venezuela
77 H4 Chahah Burjak Afghanistan
77 G7 Chāh Bahār Iran
77 G5 Chah Ghevhī, Hamún-e *L* Iran
77 L1 Chāh-i-Ghab Afghanistan
78 K4 Chah-I-Surkh Iraq
78 K2 Chai Iran
68 E5 Chai Badan Thailand
75 L7 Chaibassa India
68 F3 Chai Buri Thailand
Chaigoubu *see* Huai'an
20 D5 Chailland France
19 P14 Chaine de Belledonne *mts* France
85 E6 Chaîne de l'Atakora *mts* Benin
19 N17 Chaine des Alpilles *mts* France
18 H7 Chaise Dieu, la France
69 D8 Chaiya Thailand
68 E5 Chaiyaphum Thailand
131 F3 Chajari Argentina
116 L6 Chakachamna L Alaska
74 F2 Chak Amru Pakistan
88 G4 Chake Chake Tanzania
77 H4 Chakhansur Afghanistan
77 J2 Chakhcharan Afghanistan
74 E2 Chakwal Pakistan
128 D7 Chala Peru
87 F8 Chalabesa Zambia
40 C4 Chalain,L.de France
59 H2 Cha-lan-t'un China
128 D7 Chala,Pta Peru
125 P10 Chalatenango Honduras
69 D9 Chalaung Thailand
124 H6 Chalchihuites Mexico
125 P11 Chalchuapa El Salvador
Chalcis Greece *see* Khalkís
9 E6 Chale England
122 G6 Chaleurs, Baie des Quebec/New Bruns
128 D6 Chalhuanca Peru
133 C7 Chalía *R* Argentina
88 B7 Chali,L Zambia
19 J5 Chalindrey France
67 D3 Chaling China
74 F8 Chalisgaon India
9 G5 Chalk England
98 B4 Chalk Buttes Montana
109 K3 Chalk Mountain Texas
121 N6 Chalk River Ontario
144 A7 Chalky Inlet New Zealand
116 Q3 Chalkyitsik Alaska
21 C6 Challain-la-Potherie France
21 B8 Challans France
133 D1 Challapata Bolivia
115 M1 Challenger Mts N W Terr
22 H5 Challerange France
101 L5 Challis Idaho
111 G12 Chalmette Nat. Hist. Park Louisiana
52 E2 Chal'mny Varre U.S.S.R.
75 N7 Chalna Bangladesh
52 D4 Chalna U.S.S.R.
21 D7 Chalonnes France
18 H4 Chalons-sur-Marne France
19 J6 Chalon-sur-Saône France
65 J3 Chaluhe China
18 F7 Châlus France
57 B4 Chalysh U.S.S.R.
37 O5 Cham W Germany
37 O5 Cham *R* W Germany
106 E4 Chama Colorado
106 D5 Chama New Mexico
69 E10 Chamah, Gunung Malaysia
74 B3 Chaman Pakistan
68 E6 Chamao,Khao *mt* Thailand
106 D5 Chama, R New Mexico
128 C5 Chamaya *R* Peru
74 G2 Chamba India
73 M3 Chambal Madhya Prad/Rajasthan India
40 B7 Chambaran, Plat. de France
126 E3 Chambas Cuba
119 M8 Chamberlain Sask
98 G6 Chamberlain S Dakota
95 R7 Chamberlain L Maine
142 G3 Chamberlain R W Australia
116 P2 Chamberlin,Mt Alaska
103 P6 Chambers Arizona
98 H7 Chambers Nebraska
140 B1 Chambers B N Terr Aust
94 K7 Chambersburg Pennsylvania
99 T4 Chambers I Wisconsin
138 C1 Chambers Pillar *peak* N Terr Australia
19 P13 Chambéry France
88 C7 Chambeshi *R* Zambia
128 C4 Chambira *R* Peru
20 K3 Chambly France
20 F4 Chambois France
18 H7 Chambon, le Loire France
121 S4 Chambord Quebec
21 G7 Chambourg-sur-Indre France
66 E5 Chamdo *prov* China
124 G8 Chamela Mexico
77 B4 Cham-e Zeydun Iran
77 B3 Chamgordan Iran
133 D4 Chamical Argentina
106 D5 Chamita New Mexico
110 E3 Chamois Missouri
86 G4 Chamo, L Ethiopia
74 H3 Chamoli India
40 E6 Chamonix France
19 P16 Chamouse,Mt.de France
75 K7 Champa India
21 C9 Champagné Vendée France
89 F7 Champagne Castle *mt* Lesotho
21 F10 Champagne-Mouton France
40 C4 Champagnole France
142 E3 Champagny Is W Australia
99 S9 Champaign Illinois
131 D3 Champaqui *peak* Argentina
121 N4 Champcoeur Quebec
21 E9 Champdeniers France
36 C7 Champ du Feu *mt* France
20 E5 Champgeneteux France
19 O14 Champier France
21 D6 Champigné France
21 H6 Champigny France
21 F7 Champigny-sur-Veude France
21 J8 Champillet France
118 D8 Champion Alberta
22 J3 Champion Belgium
99 T3 Champion Michigan
94 G5 Champion Heights Ohio
95 O2 Champlain New York
121 R8 Champlain New York
121 S6 Champlain Quebec
95 O3 Champlain Canal New York
19 J5 Champlitte France
40 B2 Champlitte France
121 N4 Champneuf Quebec
40 G6 Champorcher Italy
20 H5 Champrond France
20 D4 Champsecret France
21 D7 Champtocé France
21 C7 Champtoceaux France
76 C5 Chamrajnagar India
19 P14 Chamrousse France
16 B5 Chamusca Portugal
69 E9 Chana Thailand
18 H8 Chanac France
133 C3 Chañaral Chile
131 B2 Chañaral *R* Chile
131 B2 Chañaral, I Chile
98 K6 Chancellor S Dakota
133 C5 Chanco Chile
116 N3 Chandalar Alaska
116 P2 Chandalar *R* Alaska
111 G11 Chandeleur Sound Louisiana
103 N8 Chandler Arizona
107 O6 Chandler Oklahoma
122 H5 Chandler Quebec
109 M3 Chandler Texas
116 M2 Chandler *R* Alaska
116 L2 Chandler L Alaska
138 C2 Chandler,Mt S Australia
99 Q9 Chandlerville Illinois
128 D6 Chandless *R* Peru/Brazil
75 O7 Chandpur Bangladesh
74 H9 Chandrapur India
77 G6 Chānf Iran
Chang'an *see* Rong'an
65 A7 Chang'an China
87 F9 Changara Mozambique
65 G4 Changbai China
65 G4 Changbai Shan *mt ra* China
67 B1 Changchi China
65 F3 Changchun China
65 F2 Changchunling China
67 F1 Changdang Hu *L* China
67 D2 Changde China
123 S4 Change I Nfld
65 B7 Changge China
65 E5 Changhai China
58 F5 Chang Hu *L* China
67 F1 Changhua China
67 G4 Chang-hua Taiwan
67 C7 Changhua Jiang *R* China
67 A4 Changjiang China
68 J3 Changjiang China
67 C1 Chang Jiang *R* China
67 E2 Chang Jiang *R* Jiangxi China
Chang Jiang Kou *see* Mouth of the Yangtze Kiang
65 G4 Changjin Res N Korea
68 F6 Chang,Ko *isld* Thailand
65 D6 Changle China
67 F4 Changle China
67 G2 Changle China
65 D5 Changli China
59 H3 Changling China
69 E9 Changlun Malaysia
67 A2 Changning China
67 D3 Changning China
65 C4 Changping China
Changpuzhen *see* Suining
65 C6 Changqing China
65 F5 Changsan-got *C* N Korea
67 D2 Changsha China
67 F2 Changshan China
65 E5 Changshan Qundao *islds* China
65 D4 Changshanyu China
67 B2 Changshou China
67 G1 Changshu China
67 B3 Changshun China
67 F4 Changtai China
65 G2 Changting China
67 E4 Changting China
65 F3 Changtu China
65 G2 Changwu China
67 F1 Changxing China
65 E5 Changxing Dao *isld* China
67 D1 Changyang China
65 D6 Changyi China
59 H4 Changyon N Korea
65 C7 Changyuan China
Changzhai *see* Changshun
65 B6 Changzhi China
67 G1 Changzhou Jiangsu China
67 E1 Changzhuyuan China
83 J8 Chankanai Sri Lanka
116 H8 Chankluit I Alaska
69 C8 Chan,Ko *isld* Thailand
21 F7 Channay-sur-Lathan France
145 E2 Channel I New Zealand
102 E8 Channel Is California
9 H7 Channel Is English Chan
123 N6 Channel Port aux Basques Nfld
143 C10 Channel Pt W Australia
126 F3 Channel Rock Bahamas
22 B1 Channel Tunnel
76 C4 Channiapatna India
99 S3 Channing Michigan
108 B8 Channing Texas
119 P4 Channing *airfield* Manitoba
16 B2 Chantada Spain
21 B7 Chantenay Loire-Atlantique France
21 E6 Chantenay Sarthe France
68 F6 Chanthaburi Thailand
18 G3 Chantilly France
21 C8 Chantonnay France
115 K4 Chantrey Inlet N W Terr
20 D4 Chanu France
69 A8 Chanumla Nicobar Is
107 P4 Chanute Kansas
110 A4 Chanute Kansas
55 G3 Chany U.S.S.R.
21 D7 Chanzeaux France
17 G10 Chanzy Algeria
67 E5 Chao'an China
65 C6 Chaocheng China
16 D9 Chaoen Morocco
58 G5 Chao Hu *L* China
128 C5 Chao, I Peru
68 E5 Chao Phraya Ra Thailand
65 E1 Chaor He *R* China
58 E5 Chaotianyi China
67 F1 Chao Xian China
Chaoyang *see* Huinan
59 K2 Ch'ao-Yang China
67 E5 Chaoyang Guangdong China
65 E4 Chaoyang Liaoning China
65 A7 Chaoyi China
Chaozhou *see* Chao'an
68 F1 Cha Pa Vietnam
129 J5 Chapada das Mangabeiras *mts* Brazil
129 K6 Chapada Diamantina *mts* Brazil
129 K5 Chapada do Araripe *mts* Brazil
130 C4 Chapada dos Guimarães Brazil
129 K4 Chapadinha Brazil
121 Q3 Chapais Quebec
124 H7 Chapala,L.de Mexico
129 K8 Chaparao,Serra do *mts* Brazil
126 F4 Chaparra Cuba
57 C6 Chapayeva, Imeni U.S.S.R.
53 G7 Chapayevsk U.S.S.R.
121 N7 Chapeau Quebec
130 D10 Chapecó Brazil
130 D10 Chapecózinho *R* Brazil
9 E1 Chapel en le Frith England
112 H2 Chapel Hill N Carolina
110 K6 Chapel Hill Tennessee
20 E5 Chapelle-au-Riboul,la France
18 G5 Chapelle d' Angillon,la France
22 J4 Chapelle, la France
123 L3 Chapelle,L. de la Quebec
20 E4 Chapelle Moche,la France
20 D5 Chapelle-Rainsouin,la France
20 H5 Chapelle-Royale France
9 G1 Chapel St Leonards England
127 K2 Chapelton Jamaica
13 G6 Chapeltown England
99 Q10 Chapin Illinois
110 F2 Chapin Illinois
115 L8 Chapleau Ontario
120 G4 Chapleau *R* Ontario
120 H4 Chapleau-Nemecosenda Wild R. Prov. Pk Ontario
118 L8 Chaplin Sask
147 P1 Chaplina,Mys *C* U.S.S.R.
54 H8 Chaplino U.S.S.R.
54 L3 Chaplygin U.S.S.R.
111 K10 Chapman Alabama
107 N3 Chapman Kansas
101 R1 Chapman Montana
98 H8 Chapman Nebraska
117 O10 Chapman,Mt Br Col
142 F3 Chapman R W Australia
109 K8 Chapman Ranch Texas
94 E9 Chapmanville W Virginia
52 E2 Chapoma U.S.S.R.
98 D8 Chappell Nebraska
109 L5 Chappell Hill Texas
139 J8 Chappell Is Tasmania
75 L6 Chapra India
95 L8 Chaptico Maryland
18 E7 Chapus, le France
120 K4 Chaput Ontario
128 E7 Chaqui Bolivia
133 D1 Chaqui Bolivia
74 G2 Char Kashmir
85 B4 Char Mauritania
51 L3 Chara U.S.S.R.
133 E1 Charagua Bolivia
124 E4 Charay Mexico
98 C2 Charbonneau N Dakota
40 C3 Charcenne France
20 E5 Charchigné France
109 K7 Charco Texas
146 F13 Charcot I Antarctica
118 G3 Chard Alberta
8 D6 Chard England
57 E4 Chardara U.S.S.R.
57 E4 Chardarinskoye Vdkhr *res* U.S.S.R.
94 F5 Chardon Ohio
126 G5 Chardonnière Haiti
57 C5 Chardzhou U.S.S.R.
21 E10 Charente *dep* France
21 D10 Charente *R* France
18 E7 Charente-Maritime *dep* France
20 G3 Charentonne *R* France
86 C3 Chari *R* Chad
77 L2 Charikar Afghanistan
9 G5 Charing England
116 D2 Chariot Alaska
18 H5 Charité, la France
99 N8 Chariton Iowa
99 N9 Chariton *R* Iowa
110 D2 Chariton *R* Missouri
128 G2 Charity Guyana
52 H2 Charkayuvom U.S.S.R.
74 H6 Charkhari India
57 F5 Charku U.S.S.R.
9 E4 Charlbury England
22 H3 Charleroi Belgium
94 H6 Charleroi Pennsylvania
119 Q3 Charles Manitoba
121 T6 Charlesbourg Quebec
95 M9 Charles,C Virginia
99 O6 Charles City Iowa
115 M5 Charles I N W Terr
143 B8 Charles,Mt W Australia
143 D10 Charles Pk W Australia
140 B1 Charles Pt N Terr Australia
144 A6 Charles Sd New Zealand
110 B6 Charleston Arkansas
99 S10 Charleston Illinois
111 F7 Charleston Mississippi
110 G5 Charleston Missouri
144 C4 Charleston New Zealand
100 A6 Charleston Oregon
112 H5 Charleston S Carolina
112 C2 Charleston Tennessee
94 F8 Charleston W Virginia
103 J5 Charleston Pk Nevada
94 B8 Charlestown Indiana
14 C3 Charlestown Irish Rep
127 P4 Charlestown Nevis W I
95 P3 Charlestown New Hampshire

Columbia — Craiova 19

95 L7 Columbia Maryland
111 G10 Columbia Mississippi
110 D3 Columbia Missouri
112 L2 Columbia N Carolina
95 L6 Columbia Pennsylvania
112 F3 Columbia S Carolina
98 H4 Columbia S Dakota
110 J6 Columbia Tennessee
94 J9 Columbia Virginia
117 O10 Columbia R Br Columbia
117 O11 Columbia R Wash/Br Col
100 E4 Columbia R Wash/Oregon
100 F2 Columbia Basin reg Washington
115 N1 Columbia, C N W Terr
94 B5 Columbia City Indiana
95 L8 Columbia, Dist. of (D.C.) U.S.A.
101 L1 Columbia Falls Montana
116 O6 Columbia Glacier Alaska
117 Q10 Columbia Lake Br Columbia
117 P9 Columbia, Mt Br Col/Alberta
114 G7 Columbia Mts Br Columbia
111 K8 Columbiana Alabama
94 G6 Columbiana Ohio
100 E2 Columbia River Washington
98 H4 Columbia Road Res S Dakota
95 O4 Columbiaville New York
106 D1 Columbine Colorado
101 T6 Columbine Wyoming
89 A9 Columbine, C S Africa
17 H5 Columbretes, I Spain
141 J6 Columbria Queensland
111 M9 Columbus Georgia
110 L2 Columbus Indiana
107 Q4 Columbus Kansas
111 H8 Columbus Mississippi
101 Q4 Columbus Montana
98 D1 Columbus N Dakota
98 J8 Columbus Nebraska
106 C10 Columbus New Mexico
94 D7 Columbus Ohio
109 L6 Columbus Texas
99 R6 Columbus Wisconsin
126 G3 Columbus Bank Bahamas
99 P8 Columbus Junction Iowa
126 G2 Columbus Mon San Salvador Bahamas
126 G2 Columbus Pt Cat I Bahamas
127 M2 Columbus Pt Tobago
102 B2 Colusa California
12 E4 Colvend Scotland
94 J6 Colver Pennsylvania
145 E2 Colville New Zealand
100 H1 Colville Washington
116 L2 Colville R Alaska
114 G4 Colville L N W Terr
143 F8 Colville, Lake W Australia
137 Q8 Colville Ridge sea feature Pacific Oc
13 F3 Colwell England
99 O6 Colwell Iowa
8 C1 Colwyn Bay Wales
8 C6 Colyford England
45 M2 Comacchio Italy
125 O10 Comalapa Guatemala
125 N8 Comalcalco Mexico
131 B8 Comallo R Argentina
48 K6 Comana Romania
107 N7 Comanche Oklahoma
109 J4 Comanche Texas
133 D7 Comandante Luis Piedrabuena Argentina
133 D4 Comandante Salas Argentina
48 K4 Comăneşti Romania
125 L2 Comayagua Honduras
16 B4 Comba Dão Portugal
112 G5 Combahee R S Carolina
133 C4 Combarbala Chile
40 C2 Combeaufontaine France
8 B5 Combe Martin England
14 F2 Comber N Ireland
120 H10 Comber Ontario
121 N7 Combermere Ontario
68 A3 Combermere B Burma
109 K9 Combes Texas
22 D3 Combles France
20 B5 Combourg France
139 L4 Comboyne New S Wales
20 H5 Combres France
94 D9 Combs Kentucky
131 D4 Comechingones, Sa. de ra Argentina
38 G8 Comeglians Italy
38 G8 Comelico Italy
130 E6 Comendador Gomes Brazil
111 L9 Comer Alabama
112 D3 Comer Georgia
14 D4 Comeragh Mts Irish Rep
130 H5 Comercinho Brazil
98 B1 Comertown Montana
141 J6 Comet Queensland
141 J6 Comet R Queensland
141 J6 Comet Downs Queensland
143 D8 Comet Vale W Australia
109 J6 Comfort Texas
99 M5 Comfrey Minnesota
75 O7 Comilla Bangladesh
22 E2 Comines France
43 F12 Comino isld Malta
43 C8 Comino, C Sardinia
94 C2 Comins Michigan
43 F12 Comiso Sicily
125 N9 Comitán de Domínguez Mexico
121 L7 Commanda Ontario
18 G6 Commentry France
20 D5 Commer France
112 D3 Commerce Georgia
107 Q5 Commerce Oklahoma
109 M2 Commerce Texas
106 F2 Commerce City Colorado
19 J4 Commercy France
45 J1 Commessaggio Italy
121 S4 Commissaires, Lac des Quebec
115 L4 Committee B N W Terr
146 J3 Commonwealth B Antarctica
138 C3 Commonwealth Hill S Australia
146 G7 Commonwealth Ra Antarctica
139 K6 Commonwealth Terr New S Wales
106 E2 Como Colorado
41 K6 Como Italy
111 G7 Como Mississippi
133 D7 Comodoro Rivadavia Argentina
41 K5 Como, Lago di Italy
124 D4 Comondú Mexico
125 J7 Comonfort Mexico
76 C6 Comorin, C India
81 B7 Comoro Ridge Indian Oc
87 G10 Comoros islds, rep Indian Oc
118 G7 Compeer Alberta
22 D5 Compiègne France
22 D5 Compiègne, Forêt de France
124 G7 Compostela Mexico
71 G7 Compostela Mindanao Philippines
21 H10 Compreignac France
130 F9 Comprida, I São Paulo Brazil
102 A2 Comptche California
102 F8 Compton California
99 R8 Compton Illinois
12 E1 Comrie Scotland
95 O3 Comstock New York
108 F6 Comstock Texas
45 O4 Cona Italy
66 E5 Co Nag L China
85 B7 Conakry Guinea
133 D6 Cona Niyeo Argentina
139 J8 Conara Junct Tasmania
112 C3 Conasauga R Georgia
98 D6 Conata S Dakota
45 N4 Conca R Italy
45 P5 Conca del Fucino Italy
108 H6 Concan Texas
18 C5 Concarneau France
130 H9 Conceição Paraíba Brazil
130 H6 Conceição da Barra Brazil
130 E6 Conceiçao das Alagoas Brazil
129 J5 Conceiçao do Araguaia Brazil
130 G6 Conceição do Mato Dentro Brazil
133 D3 Concepción Argentina
128 E6 Concepcíon Beni Bolivia
131 A6 Concepción Chile
130 B8 Concepción Paraguay
128 F7 Concepción Santa Cruz Bolivia
130 B8 Concepción dep Paraguay
124 C2 Concepcion R Mexico
131 A6 Concepción, B. del Chile
133 B8 Concepción, Can str Chile
130 C10 Concepción de la Sierra Argentina
124 J5 Concepción del Oro Mexico
131 F4 Concepción del Uruguay Argentina
128 F7 Concepción, L Bolivia
124 D4 Concepción, Pta C Mexico
99 M9 Conception Missouri
87 B10 Conception B Namibia
123 U6 Conception B Nfld
123 T6 Conception Harb Nfld
126 G3 Conception I Bahamas
83 K12 Conception I Mahé I Indian Oc
124 G6 Concha Mexico
130 E8 Conchas Brazil
106 F6 Conchas New Mexico
106 F6 Conchas Res New Mexico
20 G4 Conches France
133 D2 Conchi Chile
103 P7 Concho Arizona
124 G4 Concho Mexico
107 N6 Concho Oklahoma
108 G4 Concho R Texas
108 B7 Conchos, Rio Mexico
102 B4 Concord California
111 M8 Concord Georgia
94 C4 Concord Michigan
112 G2 Concord N Carolina
98 K7 Concord Nebraska
95 Q3 Concord New Hampshire
95 Q2 Concord Vermont
131 F3 Concordia Argentina
130 D10 Concórdia Brazil
107 N2 Concordia Kansas
124 F6 Concordia Mexico
110 C3 Concordia Missouri
45 J2 Concórdia sulla Secchia Italy
100 D1 Concrete Washington
68 G3 Con Cuong Vietnam
101 O7 Conda Idaho
141 K7 Condamine Queensland
141 K7 Condamine R Queensland
18 G7 Condat en Féniers France
129 L6 Cónde Brazil
98 H4 Conde S Dakota
88 E9 Condédzi R Mozambique
125 L3 Condega Nicaragua
20 G5 Condé-sur-Huîsne France
22 F3 Condé-sur-l'Escaut France
20 D4 Condé-sur-Noireau France
20 J4 Condé-sur-Vesgre France
20 C3 Conde-sur-Vire France
130 H4 Condeúba Brazil
139 H5 Condobolin New S Wales
18 F9 Condom France
100 E4 Condon Oregon
142 C5 Condon Creek B W Australia
128 C4 Condor, Cord. del mts Ecuador/Peru
12 D2 Condorrat Scotland
19 N14 Condrieu France
22 J3 Condroz Belgium
111 K10 Conecuh R Alabama
42 E3 Conegliano Italy
17 J5 Conejera isld Balearic Is
106 D4 Conejos Colorado
94 H6 Conemaugh R Pennsylvania
45 O4 Cónero, M mt Italy
133 E6 Conesa Argentina
94 K4 Conesus L New York
99 P8 Conesville Iowa
94 F6 Conesville Ohio
123 Q4 Coney Arm Nfld
90 C1 Coney I Bermuda
95 O6 Coney Island New York
40 D2 Conflans France
19 J3 Conflans-Jarny France
20 K3 Conflans-Ste. Honorine France
94 H7 Confluence Pennsylvania
21 G9 Confolens France
103 L2 Confusion Range Utah
130 B9 Confuso, R Paraguay
14 B3 Cong Irish Rep
112 G4 Congaree R S Carolina
67 D5 Conghua China
67 C4 Congjiang China
8 D1 Congleton England
82 D5 Congo rep W Africa
Congo (Brazzaville) rep see Congo Rep
Congo (Kinshasa) rep see Zaïre Rep
130 G7 Congonhas Brazil
8 D5 Congresbury England
103 M7 Congress Arizona
118 L9 Congress Sask
133 C6 Cónico mt Chile/Arg
20 J5 Conie R France
106 E2 Conifer Colorado
9 F1 Coningsby England
13 G6 Conisbrough England
13 E5 Coniston England
140 B5 Coniston N Terr Aust
120 K6 Coniston Ontario
141 G4 Conjuboy Queensland
118 F3 Conklin Alberta
108 B7 Conlen Texas
20 E5 Conlie France
40 C4 Conliège France
14 B3 Connacht prov Irish Rep
120 K4 Connaught Ontario
142 E6 Connaughton, Mt W Australia
19 N16 Connaux France
94 G5 Conneaut Ohio
94 G5 Conneautville Pennsylvania
95 P3 Connecticut R U.S.A.
95 O5 Connecticut state U.S.A.
15 C4 Connel Ferry Scotland
100 G3 Connell Washington
94 H6 Connellsville Pennsylvania
141 F6 Connemara Queensland
14 B3 Connemara dist Irish Rep
101 L4 Conner Montana
140 B7 Conner, Mt N Terr Aust
138 B2 Conner, Mt N Terr Australia
20 G5 Connerre France
94 B7 Connersville Indiana
14 B2 Conn, L Irish Rep
142 F2 Connor, Mt W Australia
122 D6 Connors New Brunswick
141 J5 Connors Ra mts Queensland
128 C4 Cononaco R Ecuador
112 F2 Conover N Carolina
99 R3 Conover Wisconsin
33 S6 Conow E Germany
118 K7 Conquest Sask
18 B4 Conquet, le France
130 F6 Conquista Brazil
101 O1 Conrad Montana
139 J7 Conran, C Victoria
99 Q4 Conrath Wisconsin
109 M5 Conroe Texas
109 M5 Conroe, L Texas
45 L2 Consandolo Italy
121 N9 Consecon Ontario
130 G7 Conselheiro Lafaiete Brazil
45 L3 Conselice Italy
45 L1 Conselve Italy
22 J5 Consenvoye France
13 G4 Consett England
95 M6 Conshohocken Pennsylvania
22 H4 Cons-la-Grandville France
126 C3 Consolación del Sur Cuba
69 H8 Con Son Vietnam
69 H8 Con Son isld Vietnam
118 G6 Consort Alberta
95 M3 Constableville New York
Constance see Konstanz
143 E6 Constance Headland hill W Aust
Constance, L see Bodensee
128 F5 Constância dos Baetas Brazil
48 M6 Constanţa Romania
16 D7 Constantina Spain
85 F1 Constantine Algeria
94 B5 Constantine Michigan
116 H7 Constantine, C Alaska
117 C5 Constantine, Mt Yukon Terr
Constantinople Turkey see İstanbul
127 N4 Constant, Morne hill Guadeloupe W I
127 L2 Constant Spring Jamaica
131 A5 Constitución Chile
141 J6 Consuelo Queensland
118 H9 Consul Sask
101 L8 Contact Nevada
130 G7 Contagalo Brazil
75 M8 Contai India
128 D5 Contamana Peru
128 F3 Contão Brazil
131 D4 Contara R Argentina
45 M1 Contarina Italy
129 K6 Cóntas R Brazil
20 J2 Conteville France
40 F5 Conthey Switzerland
103 O10 Continental Arizona
94 C5 Continental Ohio
106 C4 Continental Res Colorado
95 Q3 Contoocook New Hampshire
125 Q7 Contoy, I Mexico
16 E8 Contraviesa, Sa mts Spain
121 R7 Contrecoeur Quebec
133 C8 Contreras, I Chile
21 H7 Contres France
22 H5 Contreuve France
40 C1 Contrexéville France
130 G6 Contria Brazil
118 F7 Control Alberta
36 C5 Contwig W Germany
114 J4 Contwoyto L N W Terr
20 K2 Conty France
126 H10 Convención Colombia
43 H8 Conversano Italy
94 B6 Converse Indiana
111 C10 Converse Louisiana
94 C6 Convoy Ohio
110 D6 Conway Arkansas
99 M9 Conway Iowa
110 D4 Conway Missouri
112 K1 Conway N Carolina
98 J1 Conway N Dakota
95 Q3 Conway New Hampshire
112 H4 Conway S Carolina
141 J5 Conway, C Queensland
110 D6 Conway, L Arkansas
138 D3 Conway, L S Australia
140 C6 Conway, Mt N Terr Aust
95 Q2 Conway, N New Hampshire
144 D5 Conway R New Zealand
137 P6 Conway Reef Pacific Oc
107 N4 Conway Springs Kansas
8 B4 Conwil Elvet Wales
8 C1 Conwy Wales
112 C4 Conyers Georgia
22 K3 Coo Belgium
138 C3 Coober Pedy S Australia
9 G6 Cooden England
142 A3 Coogee dist Perth, W Aust
142 A3 Coogee L W Australia
141 J7 Coogoon Queensland
139 J2 Coogoon R Queensland
99 O2 Cook Minnesota
99 K9 Cook Nebraska
138 B4 Cook S Australia
133 C9 Cook, B.de Chile
117 K10 Cook, C Br Col
101 Q4 Cooke Montana
143 B9 Cooke, Mt W Australia
94 B10 Cookeville Tennessee
9 F4 Cookham England
146 A13 Cook I Antarctica
146 K4 Cook Ice Shelf Antarctica
118 D5 Cooking L Alberta
116 L7 Cook Inlet Alaska
117 D5 Cook, Mt Alaska/Yukon Terr
144 C5 Cook, Mt New Zealand
99 U4 Cooks Michigan
123 Q2 Cook's Hbr Nfld
121 T7 Cookshire Quebec
141 H2 Cook's Passage Queensland
106 C9 Cooks Pk New Mexico
14 E2 Cookstown N Ireland
121 L8 Cookstown Ontario
145 E4 Cook Strait New Zealand
141 H3 Cooktown Queensland
141 H7 Cooladdi Queensland
139 J4 Coolah New S Wales
139 H5 Coolamon New S Wales
143 C8 Coolarda hill W Australia
142 A2 Coolbellup, L W Australia
143 B8 Coolcalalaya W Australia
112 G2 Cooleemee N Carolina
143 D9 Coolgardie W Australia
140 B3 Coolibah N Terr Aust
103 N9 Coolidge Arizona
112 D6 Coolidge Georgia
109 L4 Coolidge Texas
127 P4 Coolidge airport Antigua W I
103 O8 Coolidge Dam Arizona
100 J1 Coolin Idaho
141 K8 Coolmunda Dam Queensland
142 A4 Cooloongup, L W Australia
94 F7 Coolville Ohio
143 B7 Coolyun Well W Australia
139 J6 Cooma New S Wales
14 A5 Coomacarrea mt Irish Rep
9 E5 Coombe Bissett England
8 D4 Coombe Hill England
143 B9 Coomberdale W Australia
139 J4 Coonabarabran New S Wales
138 F6 Coonalpyn S Australia
139 J4 Coonamble New S Wales
143 E9 Coonana W Australia
138 F6 Coonawarra S Australia
138 F5 Coonbah New S Wales
138 D4 Coondambo S Australia
76 B4 Coondapoor India
142 C5 Coongan, R W Australia
141 H8 Coongoola Queensland
138 C2 Coongra R S Australia
138 F2 Cooninnie, L S Australia
76 C5 Coonoor India
99 M8 Coon Rapids Iowa
129 G8 Cooper Paraguay
109 M2 Cooper Texas
140 C1 Cooper R N Terr Aust
141 F7 Cooper Cr Qnsld/S Aust
138 F2 Cooper Cr Queensland
144 A6 Cooper I New Zealand
138 C5 Cooper, Mt S Australia
143 G7 Cooper, Mt W Australia
139 L4 Coopernook New S Wales
141 K2 Coopers Plains dist Brisbane, Qnsld
126 F1 Coopers Town Great Abaco I Bahamas
98 H2 Cooperstown N Dakota
95 M4 Cooperstown New York
94 B3 Coopersville Michigan
127 O3 Coora Trinidad
138 B4 Coorabie S Australia
140 F6 Coorabulka Queensland
143 B7 Coor-de-Wandy mt W Australia
138 E6 Coorong, The L S Australia
143 B8 Coorow W Australia
141 L7 Cooroy Queensland
111 L7 Coosa R Alabama
112 C3 Coosawattee R Georgia
112 F5 Coosawhatchie R S Carolina
100 A6 Coos Bay Oregon
139 J5 Cootamundra New S Wales
14 E2 Cootehill Irish Rep
141 K7 Cooyar Queensland
140 E6 Cooyeana Queensland
133 C5 Copahue mt Chile/Arg
131 B6 Copahué peak Chile
100 A2 Copalis Beach Washington
109 K7 Copano B Texas
100 C8 Copco California
106 H2 Cope Colorado
128 F4 Copea, Paraná R Brazil
113 F12 Copeland Florida
100 J1 Copeland Idaho
107 K4 Copeland Kansas
94 B2 Copemish Michigan
Copenhagen see København
95 M3 Copenhagen New York
133 E5 Copetonas Argentina
139 K3 Copeton Res. New South Wales
133 C3 Copiapó Chile
15 F2 Copinsay Scotland
138 E4 Copley S Australia
128 D6 Coporaque Peru
45 L2 Copparo Italy
120 G3 Coppell Ontario
109 N8 Coppell Texas
129 G2 Coppename R Suriname
32 L8 Coppenbrügge W Germany
116 P5 Copper R Alaska
109 K4 Copperas Cove Texas
100 G1 Copper Butte mt Washington
116 P6 Copper Center Alaska
120 J6 Copper Cliff Ontario
141 J6 Copperfield Queensland
99 T2 Copper Hbr Michigan
114 H4 Coppermine N W Terr
120 F6 Coppermine Pt C Ontario
117 N11 Copper Mt Br Col
100 K8 Copper Mt Nevada
117 Q5 Copp L N W Terr
48 J4 Copşa Mică Romania
131 B6 Copulhue, Paso del Arg/Chile
75 L3 Coqên China
22 B2 Coquelles France
13 G3 Coquet I England
13 G3 Coquet, R England
Coquilhatville see Mbandaka
100 A6 Coquille Oregon
131 B2 Coquimbo Chile
101 P7 Cora Wyoming
47 G1 Corabia Romania
130 G5 Coração de Jesus Brazil
139 L3 Coraki New S Wales
120 J2 Coral Ontario
71 C6 Coral B Palawan Philippines
113 L9 Coral Harbour New Providence I Bahamas
115 L5 Coral Harbour N W Terr
137 K4 Coral Sea Islands Terr Australasia
99 P8 Coralville Res Iowa
101 L1 Coram Montana
139 G7 Corangamite, L Victoria
129 G3 Corantijn R Suriname
94 G6 Coraopolis Pennsylvania
43 G7 Corato Italy
20 K4 Corbeil-Essonnes France
19 P13 Corbelin France
22 F5 Corbény France
120 K8 Corbetton Ontario
20 K2 Corbie France
9 H7 Corbiere Channel Is
18 G10 Corbières reg France
18 H5 Corbigny France
94 C10 Corbin Kentucky
123 R7 Corbin Hd Nfld
45 M1 Córbola Italy
16 D7 Corbones R Spain
13 F4 Corbridge England
9 F2 Corby Lincs England
9 F2 Corby Northants England
Corcaigh see Cork
36 B7 Corcieux France
102 E5 Corcoran California
21 B8 Corcoué-sur-Logne France
133 C6 Corcovado mt Chile
133 C6 Corcovado, Golfo Chile
16 A2 Corcubion Spain
112 D6 Cordele Georgia
107 M6 Cordell Oklahoma
18 G8 Cordes France
129 J5 Cordilheiras, Serra das mts Brazil
16 D1 Cordillera Cantábrica mts Spain
128 C3 Cordillera Central mts Colombia
127 J5 Cordillera Central mts Dom Rep
71 E2 Cordillera Central mts Luzon Philippines
125 O5 Cordillera Central mts Panama
128 C5 Cordillera Central mts Peru
127 J10 Cordillera de Mérida mts Venezuela
128 C3 Cordillera Occidental mts Colombia
128 D2 Cordillera Oriental mts Colombia
71 F5 Cordilleras Ra Panay Philippines
138 F2 Cordillo Downs S Australia
130 G6 Cordisburgo Brazil
131 D3 Córdoba Argentina
125 L8 Cordoba Mexico
16 D7 Córdoba Spain
128 C2 Córdoba div Colombia
131 D4 Cordoba prov Argentina
16 D7 Córdoba prov Spain
131 D3 Cordoba, Sierra de ra Argentina
111 J8 Cordova Alabama
116 P6 Cordova Alaska
99 Q8 Cordova Illinois
128 C6 Córdova Peru
121 N8 Cordova Mines Ontario
116 P6 Cordova Pk Alaska
45 J3 Coreglia Antelminelli Italy
140 F4 Corella R Queensland
140 D4 Corella L N Terr Aust
141 G5 Corfield Queensland
45 P5 Corfinio Italy
94 J4 Corfu New York
100 F3 Corfu Washington
Corfu isld Greece see Kérkira I
16 C2 Corgo Spain
130 C6 Corguinho Brazil
45 N6 Cori Italy
16 C5 Coria Spain
16 C7 Coria del R Spain
45 N4 Coriano Italy
121 O3 Coribelle Quebec
139 K5 Coricudgy mt New S Wales
43 H9 Corigliano Calabro Italy
45 O4 Corinaldo Italy
140 E4 Corinda Queensland
141 K2 Corinda dist Brisbane, Qnsld
136 L5 Coringa Is Coral Sea
141 K3 Coringa Is Gt Barrier Reef Aust
139 H8 Corinna Tasmania
101 N8 Corinne Utah
Corinth see Kórinthos
101 S4 Corinth Montana
95 O3 Corinth New York
Corinth, Gulf of Greece see Korinthiakós Kólpos
143 C9 Corinthian W Australia
130 G6 Corinto Brazil
130 C6 Corixinha, R Brazil
14 C5 Cork Irish Rep
14 C5 Cork co Irish Rep
18 C4 Corlay France
43 E11 Corleone Sicily
47 J3 Çorlu Turkey
123 P4 Cormack Nfld
123 Q5 Cormack mt Nfld
20 J5 Cormainville France
20 F3 Cormeilles France
21 G7 Cormery France
22 F5 Cormicy France
123 L2 Cormier, L Quebec
20 D3 Cormolain France
119 R4 Cormorant Manitoba
123 L4 Cormorant Pt Anticosti I, Quebec
107 M6 Corn Oklahoma
41 M6 Corna Italy
45 P6 Cornacchia, M mt Italy
32 H7 Cornau W Germany
112 D3 Cornelia Georgia
133 G2 Cornélio Procópio Brazil
99 S9 Cornell Illinois
99 P4 Cornell Wisconsin
123 P5 Corner Brook Nfld
139 H7 Corner Inlet Victoria
110 K6 Cornersville Tennessee
111 D9 Corney L Louisiana
103 P6 Cornfields Arizona
13 F2 Cornhill-on-Tweed England
20 C5 Cornille France
40 E2 Cornimont France
110 F5 Corning Arkansas
99 M9 Corning Iowa
107 O2 Corning Kansas
99 L9 Corning Missouri
95 K4 Corning New York
94 E7 Corning Ohio
119 P9 Corning Sask
141 G5 Cornish R Queensland
95 P3 Cornish Flat New Hampshire
142 F5 Cornish, Mt W Australia
113 K11 Cornishtown Bahamas
45 J3 Corno alle Scale mt Italy
42 F6 Corno, M mt Italy
100 H4 Cornucopia Oregon
99 P3 Cornucopia Wisconsin
18 H9 Cornus France
121 Q7 Cornwall Ontario
8 B7 Cornwall co England
115 K2 Cornwallis I N W Terr
138 D5 Corny Pt S Australia
127 K9 Coro Venezuela
130 G6 Coroaci Brazil
129 K4 Coroatá Brazil
87 B9 Coroca R Angola
128 E7 Corocoro Bolivia
128 E7 Coroico Bolivia
130 F6 Coromandel Brazil
145 E2 Coromandel New Zealand
76 E5 Coromandel Coast India
145 E2 Coromandel Peninsula New Zealand
71 E4 Coron Philippines
102 G8 Corona California
106 E7 Corona New Mexico
138 F4 Corona N S Wales
119 M9 Coronach Sask
102 G9 Coronado California
71 F7 Coronado B Mindanao Philippines
125 N5 Coronado, B.de Costa Rica
113 G8 Coronado Beach Florida
118 F6 Coronation Alberta
114 H4 Coronation G N W Terr
146 C14 Coronation I S Orkney Is
142 E2 Coronation Is W Australia
71 E5 Coron B Philippines
71 E5 Coron Delian isld Philippines
131 A6 Coronel Chile
133 E5 Coronel Dorrego Argentina
130 G6 Coronel Fabriciano Brazil
130 C9 Coronel Oviedo Paraguay
130 C4 Coronel Ponce Brazil
131 E6 Coronel Pringles Argentina
131 E6 Coronel Suárez Argentina
133 F5 Coronel Vidal Argentina
144 B6 Coronet Pk New Zealand
128 D7 Coropuna mt Peru
46 D4 Çorovodë Albania
139 H6 Corowa New S Wales
126 G10 Corozal Colombia
127 O1 Corozal Pt Trinidad
130 C10 Corpus Argentina
109 K8 Corpus Christi Texas
133 D1 Corque Bolivia
101 L6 Corral Idaho
16 E5 Corralde Almaguer Spain
124 G5 Corrales Mexico
16 D3 Corrales Spain
133 F4 Corrales Uruguay
126 D3 Corralilla Cuba
124 F2 Corralitos Mexico
143 B7 Corrandibby Ra mts W Australia
14 B3 Corraun Irish Rep
14 B3 Corraun Pen Irish Rep
99 L7 Correctionville Iowa
71 E3 Corregidor Luzon Philippines
130 E5 Córrego do Ouro Brazil
129 J6 Corrente Brazil
130 D6 Corrente, R Goiás Brazil
43 F12 Correnti, C.I. de Sicily
129 K6 Correntina Brazil
106 C7 Correo New Mexico
21 I10 Corrèze dep France
18 G7 Corrèze R France
45 K1 Corezzo Italy
45 M1 Corrézzola Italy
14 B3 Corrib, L Irish Rep
12 C2 Corrie Scotland
130 B10 Corrientes Argentina
131 F2 Corrientes prov Argentina
133 F3 Corrientes R Argentina
128 C4 Corrientes R Peru
133 F5 Corrientes, C Argentina
126 B4 Corrientes, C Cuba
124 G7 Corrientes, C Mexico
109 N5 Corrigan Texas
143 C9 Corrigin W Australia
139 K5 Corrimal New S Wales
13 H6 Corringham England
14 B4 Corrofin Irish Rep
94 H5 Corry Pennsylvania
139 J6 Corryong Victoria
12 C1 Corryvreckan, Str.of Scotland
18 L11 Corse-du-Sud dep Corsica
12 C3 Corsewall Pt Scotland
8 D5 Corsham England
18 L10 Corsica France
98 H6 Corsica S Dakota
18 L10 Corsica isld Medit Sea
109 L3 Corsicana Texas
12 E3 Corsock Br Scotland
8 D5 Corston England
13 E2 Corstorphine Scotland
115 P5 Cort Adelaer, Kap C Greenland
103 N9 Cortaro Arizona
16 C7 Cortegana Spain
130 J10 Cortès Brazil
106 B4 Cortez Colorado
102 H1 Cortez Nevada
38 F8 Cortina d'Ampezzo Italy
98 K9 Cortland Nebraska
95 L4 Cortland New York
94 G5 Cortland Ohio
9 H2 Corton England
42 D5 Cortona Italy
85 B6 Corubal R Guinea/Guinea-Bissau
16 B6 Coruche Portugal
78 H1 Çoruh R Turkey
15 B3 Coruisk, L Scotland
78 E1 Çorum Turkey
130 B6 Corumbá Brazil
130 E4 Corumbá de Goiás Brazil
130 E6 Corumbaíba Brazil
130 E5 Corumbá, R Brazil
130 H5 Corumbaú, Pta. do C Brazil
128 F6 Corumbiara R Brazil
128 F2 Corumo R Venezuela
16 B1 Coruña prov Spain
16 B1 Coruña, Lá Spain
Corunna see Lá Coruña
94 C4 Corunna Michigan
138 D4 Corunna S Australia
130 H11 Coruripe Brazil
101 L3 Corvallis Montana
100 B5 Corvallis Oregon
38 E8 Corvara in Badia Italy
32 K9 Corvey W Germany
8 C2 Corwen Wales
107 M4 Corwin Kansas
116 E7 Corwin, C Alaska
101 P4 Corwin Springs Montana
94 A8 Corydon Indiana
99 N9 Corydon Iowa
110 J4 Corydon Kentucky
94 J5 Corydon Pennsylvania
9 G5 Coryton England
21 E6 Corzé France
Cos isld see Kos isld
124 F5 Cosalá Mexico
125 M8 Cosamaloapan Mexico
43 G9 Cosenza Italy
9 E6 Cosham England
94 F6 Coshocton Ohio
81 B6 Cosmoledo I Indian Oc
99 M5 Cosmos Minnesota
18 G5 Cosne France
18 G6 Cosne-d'Allier France
102 G5 Coso Junction California
133 E4 Cosquin Argentina
21 I6 Cosson R France
109 K6 Cost Texas
17 G7 Costa Blanca Spain
17 K3 Costa Brava Spain
45 L1 Costa di Rovigo Italy
113 E11 Costa I, La Florida
102 G8 Costa Mesa California
124 C2 Costa Rica Mexico
125 M4 Costa Rica rep Cent America
123 K3 Costebelle, L Quebec
94 J5 Costello Pennsylvania
Costermansville see Bukavu
48 J6 Costeşti Romania
95 T1 Costigan Maine
106 E5 Costilla New Mexico
33 Q9 Coswig E Germany
71 G7 Cotabato Mindanao Philippines
128 E8 Cotagaita Bolivia
128 D7 Cotahuasi Peru
102 B3 Cotati California
130 H6 Cotaxé, R Brazil
121 Q7 Côteau Station Quebec
118 K7 Coteau, The Sask
126 G5 Coteaux Haiti
20 G4 Coteaux-du-Perche reg France
111 E12 Cote Blanche B Louisiana
44 B4 Côte d'Azur France
19 J5 Côte d'Or France
20 B3 Cotentin reg France
18 C4 Côtes-du-Nord mts France
13 F4 Cotherstone England
141 J6 Cotherstone Queensland
19 Q18 Cotignac France
45 L3 Cotignola Italy
48 E7 Cotina R Yugoslavia
128 F3 Cotinga R Brazil
85 E7 Cotonou Benin
106 E3 Cotopaxi Colorado
128 C4 Cotopaxi vol Ecuador
9 E4 Cotswold Hills England
100 B6 Cottage Grove Oregon
112 G5 Cottageville S Carolina
94 F8 Cottageville W Virginia
31 H4 Cottbus E Germany
33 S9 Cottbus reg E Germany
123 T5 Cottel I Nfld
9 G3 Cottenham England
110 D5 Cotter Arkansas
83 M14 Cotter, C Mauritius
142 A2 Cottesloe Beach dist Perth, W Aust
9 F2 Cottesmore England
129 H3 Cottica Suriname
13 H6 Cottingham England
99 O2 Cotton Minnesota
140 E6 Cottonbush Cr Queensland
111 J8 Cottondale Alabama
111 L11 Cottondale Florida
140 D1 Cotton I N Terr Aust
119 V3 Cotton L Manitoba
110 E6 Cotton Plant Arkansas
111 D11 Cottonport Louisiana
109 O3 Cotton Valley Louisiana
111 L10 Cottonwood Alabama
103 N7 Cottonwood Arizona
100 C9 Cottonwood California
100 J3 Cottonwood Idaho
98 E6 Cottonwood S Dakota
109 H3 Cottonwood Texas
99 M5 Cottonwood R Minnesota
103 L6 Cottonwood Cliffs Arizona
107 O3 Cottonwood Falls Kansas
103 O6 Cottonwood Wash R Arizona
127 J5 Cotuí Dom Rep
109 H7 Cotulla Texas
21 C10 Coubre, Pte. de la France
142 F3 Couchman Ra W Australia
22 E4 Coucy-le-Château Auffrique France
21 H7 Couddes France
22 C1 Coudekerque-Branche France
99 P4 Couderay Wisconsin
94 J5 Coudersport Pennsylvania
20 J3 Coudray St. Germer, le France
20 G6 Coudrecieux France
20 H4 Coudres France
122 B6 Coudres, I.aux Quebec
138 D6 Couëdic, C.de S Australia
20 D5 Couesmes France
20 C5 Couesnon R France
21 C7 Couffé France
100 C3 Cougar Washington
18 F6 Couhé France
14 A5 Coulagh B Irish Rep
20 F5 Coulans France
15 C2 Coulbeag Mt Scotland
100 F2 Coulee City Washington
100 G1 Coulee Dam Washington
20 F5 Coulimer France
146 J6 Coulman I Antarctica
21 I6 Coulmiers France
22 B2 Coulogne France
21 F9 Coulombiers France
20 J4 Coulombs France
121 O6 Coulonge R Quebec
21 D9 Coulonges France
21 E8 Coulonges-Thouarsais France
20 C4 Coulouvray-Boisbenâtre France
119 R9 Coulter Manitoba
102 D4 Coulterville California
110 G3 Coulterville Illinois
116 F4 Council Alaska
100 J5 Council Idaho
99 L8 Council Bluffs Iowa
107 O3 Council Grove Kansas
8 D2 Cound England
107 N7 Countyline Oklahoma
15 E4 Coupar Angus Scotland
100 C1 Coupeville Washington
109 K5 Coupland Texas
22 B2 Couple, Mt France
20 E5 Couptrain France
117 S3 Courageous L N W Terr
20 K5 Courances France
122 B8 Courcelles Quebec
20 F5 Courcemont France
21 H7 Cour Cheverny France
20 E5 Courcité France
21 F10 Courcôme France
21 D9 Courçon France
20 F5 Courgains France
18 H7 Courpière France
22 D3 Courrières France
18 H9 Coursan France
20 E3 Courseulles France
18 H5 Courson les Carrières France
20 H5 Courtalain France
40 F3 Courtelary Switzerland
114 G8 Courtenay Br Columbia
98 H2 Courtenay N Dakota
18 G7 Courtine, la France
107 N2 Courtland Kansas
99 M5 Courtland Minnesota
95 K10 Courtland Virginia
14 C5 Courtmacsherry Irish Rep
109 L5 Courtney Texas
20 F4 Courtomer France
Courtrai see Kortrijk
22 H2 Court Saint-Etienne Belgium
118 L8 Courval Sask
20 H5 Courville France
109 O3 Coushatta Louisiana
83 J12 Cousin I Seychelles
22 G3 Cousolre France
87 D9 Coutada do Mucusso Angola
20 C3 Coutances France
20 E5 Couterne France
22 J2 Couthuin Belgium
18 E7 Coutras France
101 N1 Coutts Alberta
127 O2 Couva Trinidad
20 B2 Couville France
22 H3 Couvin Belgium
22 F4 Couvron-et-Aumencourt France
48 K5 Covasna Romania
109 N1 Cove Arkansas
100 H4 Cove Oregon
112 K2 Cove City N Carolina
103 M3 Cove Fort Utah
100 B10 Covelo California
94 K7 Cove Mt Pennsylvania
126 G10 Coveñas Colombia
9 E3 Coventry England
95 L8 Cove Point Maryland
107 M2 Covert Kansas
94 A4 Covert Michigan
94 J9 Covesville Virginia
16 B4 Covilhã Portugal
116 K7 Coville, L Alaska
112 D4 Covington Georgia
99 T9 Covington Indiana
94 C7 Covington Kentucky
111 F11 Covington Louisiana
99 S3 Covington Michigan
94 C6 Covington Ohio
107 N5 Covington Oklahoma
110 G6 Covington Tennessee
109 K3 Covington Texas
94 G9 Covington Virginia
120 G5 Cow R Ontario
15 C4 Cowal Scotland
139 J5 Cowal, L New S Wales
119 R6 Cowan Manitoba
110 K6 Cowan Tennessee
140 E4 Cowan Downs Queensland
138 F6 Cowangie Victoria
118 K4 Cowan L Sask
143 D9 Cowan, Lake W Australia
101 P4 Cowan, Mt Montana
121 S7 Cowansville Quebec
138 D3 Coward Springs S Australia
138 E2 Cowarie S Australia
9 F2 Cowbit England
103 L2 Cowboy Pass Utah
8 C5 Cowbridge Wales
143 B9 Cowcowing,L W Australia
100 G2 Cow Cr Washington
110 H2 Cowden Illinois
13 E1 Cowdenbeath Scotland
101 T9 Cowdrey Colorado
138 D5 Cowell S Australia
94 G8 Cowen W Virginia
9 E6 Cowes England
139 H7 Cowes Victoria
107 P6 Coweta Oklahoma
9 F6 Cowfold England
123 P4 Cow Head Nfld
100 E8 Cow Head L California
100 A1 Cowichan L Br Col
70 E2 Cowie Harb Kalimantan
140 A6 Cowle, Mt N Terr Australia
98 H9 Cowles Nebraska
106 E6 Cowles New Mexico
118 D9 Cowley Alberta
141 G7 Cowley Queensland
101 R5 Cowley Wyoming
100 C3 Cowlitz R Washington
100 D3 Cowlitz Pass Washington
94 H8 Cowpasture R Virginia
112 F2 Cowpens S Carolina
112 F2 Cowpens Nat.Bat.Site S Carolina
139 J5 Cowra New S Wales
130 G4 Coxa, R Brazil
139 H9 Cox Bight Tasmania
13 G4 Coxhoe England
130 C4 Coxibó do Ouro Brazil
130 C6 Coxim Brazil
123 O2 Coxipi L Quebec
130 C4 Coxipó da Ponté Brazil
143 F6 Cox,Mt W Australia
140 D3 Cox R N Terr Australia
95 O4 Coxsackie New York
75 O8 Cox's Bazar Bangladesh
123 P4 Cox's Cove Nfld
108 B6 Coyame Mexico
108 D5 Coyanosa Cr Texas
20 K3 Coye-la-Forêt France
107 N6 Coyle Oklahoma
102 C4 Coyote California
106 E8 Coyote New Mexico
102 H6 Coyote L California
102 F5 Coyote Peak California
103 L9 Coyote Pk Arizona
124 D5 Coyote, Pta C Mexico
124 F6 Coyotitán Mexico
98 G9 Cozad Nebraska
44 B2 Cozie Alpi mt Italy
124 C2 Cozón, Cerro mt Mexico
125 Q7 Cozumel, I.de Mexico
100 F3 Crab Cr Washington
141 F1 Crab I Queensland
139 J4 Craboon New S Wales
94 C9 Crab Orchard Kentucky
112 C2 Crab Orchard Tennessee
110 G4 Crab Orchard L Illinois
127 H2 Crab Pond Pt Jamaica
139 H7 Crab Pt Victoria
8 B6 Crackington Haven England
8 D2 Crackleybank England
Cracow see Kraków
141 K7 Cracow Queensland
139 H8 Cradle, Mt Tasmania
89 D9 Cradock S Africa
138 E4 Cradock S Australia
117 G8 Craig Alaska
101 S9 Craig Colorado
113 G13 Craig Florida
99 L9 Craig Missouri
101 O2 Craig Montana
98 K8 Craig Nebraska
15 E3 Craigellachie Scotland
13 E1 Craigend Scotland
15 C5 Craighouse Scotland
12 D2 Craigie Scotland
144 C5 Craigieburn New Zealand
100 J3 Craigmont Idaho
116 R6 Craig, Mt Alaska
118 E7 Craigmyle Alberta
13 E1 Craigrothie Scotland
141 K7 Craigs Ra mts Queensland
94 H8 Craigsville Virginia
14 D4 Craiguenamanagh Irish Rep
119 M7 Craik Sask
13 F1 Crail Scotland
37 J5 Crailsheim W Germany
48 H6 Craiova Romania

20 Cramond — Damville

13 E2 Cramond Scotland
85 D2 Crampel Algeria
86 C4 Crampel Cent Afr Republic
121 Q8 Cranberry, L New York
119 Q4 Cranberry Portage Manitoba
9 E6 Cranborne England
114 H8 Cranbrook Br Columbia
9 G5 Cranbrook England
143 C10 Cranbrook W Australia
119 R8 Crandall Manitoba
98 J4 Crandall S Dakota
109 L3 Crandall Texas
99 S4 Crandon Wisconsin
127 P6 Crane Barbados
110 C5 Crane Missouri
98 B2 Crane Montana
100 G6 Crane Oregon
108 E4 Crane Texas
100 J5 Crane Cr.Res Idaho
118 H8 Crane L Sask
119 M9 Crane Valley Sask
109 K4 Cranfills Gap Texas
9 F5 Cranleigh England
100 A8 Crannell California
13 F2 Cranshaws Scotland
95 Q5 Cranston Rhode I
13 H6 Cranswick England
21 D6 Craon France
22 F5 Craonne France
139 K2 Craoow Queensland
18 H7 Craponne-sur-Arzon France
98 H1 Crary N Dakota
146 H10 Crary Mts Antarctica
48 L4 Crasna Romania
48 H3 Crasna R Romania
48 H3 Crasnei, Muntii mt Romania
100 C7 Crater L Oregon
100 C7 Crater Lake Nat. Park Oregon
100 D9 Crater Peak mt California
101 M6 Craters of the Moon Nat.Mon Idaho
43 G9 Crati R Italy
130 G9 Crato Brazil
21 F8 Cravant les Coteaux France
119 N8 Craven Sask
130 F7 Cravinhos Brazil
128 D2 Cravo Norte R Colombia
145 D4 Crawford Georgia
111 H8 Crawford Mississippi
98 C7 Crawford Nebraska
12 E3 Crawford Scotland
109 K4 Crawford Texas
13 E3 Crawfordjohn Scotland
140 B3 Crawford,Mt N Terr Australia
95 Q2 Crawford Notch New Hampshire
71 D5 Crawford Pt Philippines
110 K1 Crawfordsville Indiana
111 M11 Crawfordville Florida
112 F4 Crawfordville Georgia
9 F5 Crawley England
8 C4 Cray Wales
9 G5 Crayford England
116 P4 Crazy Mts Alaska
101 P3 Crazy Mts Montana
101 P4 Crazy Pk Montana
101 T5 Crazy Woman Cr Wyoming
15 D4 Creag Meagaidh mt Scotland
20 B3 Créances France
118 L4 Crean L Sask
40 A5 Crêches France
22 B3 Crécy-en-Ponthieu France
22 F4 Crécy-sur-Serre France
8 C6 Crediton England
12 D4 Cree Bridge Scotland
106 D4 Creede Colorado
112 J1 Creedmoor N Carolina
101 R9 Creek Colorado
94 H6 Creekside Pennsylvania
113 L9 Creek Village New Providence I Bahamas
124 F4 Creel Mexico
114 J6 Cree L Sask
119 O9 Creelman Sask
120 K8 Creemore Ontario
114 J6 Cree River Saskatchewan
12 D4 Creetown Scotland
37 J5 Creglingen W Germany
98 H7 Creighton Nebraska
119 P4 Creighton Sask
120 J6 Creighton Mine Ontario
44 G1 Crema Italy
19 O13 Crémieu France
118 C7 Cremona Alberta
44 G1 Crémona Italy
111 F7 Crenshaw Mississippi
18 E8 Créon France
48 F5 Crepaja Yugoslavia
129 G5 Crepori R Brazil
22 D5 Crépy-en-Valois France
120 K6 Crerar Ontario
42 F4 Cres Yugoslavia
98 G4 Cresbard S Dakota
107 N6 Crescent Oklahoma
112 J4 Crescent Beach S Carolina
100 A8 Crescent City California
113 F8 Crescent L Florida
100 D6 Crescent L Oregon
100 B1 Crescent, L Washington
100 E9 Crescent Mills California
103 J6 Crescent Pk Nevada
99 O6 Cresco Iowa
45 L2 Crespino Italy
8 B4 Cresselly Wales
109 K3 Cresson Texas
139 H8 Cressy Tasmania
139 G7 Cressy Victoria
19 O15 Crest France
103 K4 Crestline Nevada
94 E6 Crestline Ohio
100 J1 Creston Br Col
99 M8 Creston Iowa
101 L1 Creston Montana
123 R6 Creston Nfld
100 G2 Creston Washington
101 S8 Creston Wyoming
106 E3 Crestone Pk Colorado
111 K11 Crestview Florida
110 J6 Crestview Tennessee
119 M8 Crestwynd Sask
112 L2 Creswell N Carolina
100 B6 Creswell Oregon
115 K3 Creswell B N W Terr
140 D4 Creswell Downs N Terr Australia
139 G7 Creswick Victoria
19 J6 Crêt de la Neige mt France
99 T8 Crete Illinois
98 H3 Crete N Dakota
98 K9 Crete Nebraska
Crete isld Greece see Kriti
47 G9 Crete, Sea of Greece
20 D3 Creully France
17 K2 Creus, C Spain
21 I9 Creuse dep France
18 G6 Creuse R France
37 M4 Creussen W Germany
37 J1 Creuzburg E Germany
45 K2 Crevalcore Italy
20 F3 Crèvecoeur France
20 K2 Crèvecoeur-le-Grand France
17 G6 Crevillente Spain
41 H5 Crevola Italy
8 D1 Crewe England
94 J9 Crewe Virginia
8 D6 Crewkerne England
12 D1 Crianlarich Scotland
8 B2 Criccieth Wales
9 E1 Crich England
118 K9 Crichton Sask
133 H3 Criciuma Brazil
9 E3 Crick England
8 C4 Crickhowell Wales
9 E4 Cricklade England
94 C6 Cridersville Ohio
12 E1 Crieff Scotland
20 H1 Criel-sur-Mer France
15 E6 Criffell mt Scotland
42 F3 Crikvenica Yugoslavia
117 E6 Crillon, Mt Alaska
99 O1 Crilly Ontario
Crimea see Krym
37 N2 Crimmitschau E Germany
12 C1 Crinan Scotland
15 C4 Crinan Canal Scotland
106 E3 Cripple Creek Colorado
116 J5 Cripple Landing Alaska
9 G6 Cripps's Corner England
20 F2 Criquetot-l'Esneval France
48 G4 Crişana Romania
130 F5 Cristalina Brazil
129 H6 Cristalino R Brazil
38 F8 Cristallo mt Italy
126 H10 Cristóbal Colón, Pico mt Colombia
48 J4 Cristuru Secuiesc Romania
48 G4 Crişul Alb R Romania
48 G4 Crişul Negru R Romania
48 H4 Crişul Repede R Romania
94 C8 Crittenden Kentucky
33 P5 Crivitz E Germany
99 S4 Crivitz Wisconsin
38 L9 Črna Yugoslavia
46 E3 Crna R Yugoslavia
46 E2 Crna Gora mt Yugoslavia
46 E2 Crna Trava Yugoslavia
46 D3 Crni Drim R Yugoslavia
38 M9 Crni-vrh mt Yugoslavia
14 B3 Croagh Patrick Mt Irish Rep
Croatia see Hrvatska
41 O5 Croce, C mt Italy
43 G11 Croce, S., C Sicily
110 D4 Crocker Missouri
70 D2 Crocker Ra Borneo
12 E3 Crocketford Scotland
109 M4 Crockett Texas
13 G6 Crockham Hill England
22 E5 Crocy France
38 F8 Croda Rossa mt Italy
110 J4 Crofton Kentucky
98 J7 Crofton Nebraska
142 D5 Crofton,Mt W Australia
95 M3 Croghan New York
19 O18 Croisette, C France
18 D5 Croisic, le France
22 D3 Croisilles France
145 D4 Croisilles Harbour New Zealand
127 H5 Croix des Bouquets Haiti
19 P15 Croix Haute, Col de la pass France
20 C5 Croixille, la France
122 B2 Croix, L.à la Quebec
122 E8 Croix R New Brunswick
20 H3 Croix-St.Leufroy, la France
22 D5 Croix-St.Ouen, la France
120 K8 Croker, Cape Ontario
140 B2 Croker Hill N Terr Australia
140 C1 Croker I N Terr Australia
15 D3 Cromarty Scotland
15 D3 Cromarty Firth Scotland
138 B2 Crombie, Mt S Australia
9 H2 Cromer England
119 Q9 Cromer Manitoba
99 O3 Cromwell Minnesota
144 B6 Cromwell New Zealand
144 C5 Cronadun New Zealand
37 K5 Cronheim W Germany
98 D9 Crook Colorado
13 F5 Crook Cumbria England
13 G4 Crook Durham England
107 K4 Crooked Cr Kansas
100 G7 Crooked Cr Oregon
126 G3 Crooked I Bahamas
126 G3 Crooked I.Passage Bahamas
113 F10 Crooked L Florida
123 Q5 Crooked L Nfld
117 M8 Crooked R Br Columbia
100 E5 Crooked R Oregon
119 O6 Crooked River Sask
13 F2 Crookham England
14 B5 Crookhaven Irish Rep
109 M2 Crook, L Texas
13 F5 Crooklands England
12 E1 Crook of Devon Scotland
98 K2 Crookston Minnesota
98 F7 Crookston Nebraska
94 E7 Crooksville Ohio
139 J5 Crookwell New S Wales
113 E9 Croom Florida
14 C4 Croom Irish Rep
139 K3 Croppa Cr New S Wales
123 R2 Croque Nfld
141 G3 Crosbie R Queensland
99 N3 Crosby Minnesota
111 E10 Crosby Mississippi
98 C1 Crosby N Dakota
109 M6 Crosby Texas
108 F2 Crosbyton Texas
8 D5 Cross England
85 F7 Cross R Nigeria
21 A7 Crossac France
12 C2 Crossaig Scotland
87 B10 Cross, C Namibia
113 D8 Cross City Florida
111 E8 Crossett Arkansas
13 F4 Cross Fell England
118 C7 Crossfield Alberta
13 E1 Crossgates Scotland
8 C3 Cross Gates Wales
8 B4 Cross Hands Wales
113 K12 Cross Harbour Bahamas
14 C5 Crosshaven Irish Rep
112 F3 Cross Hill S Carolina
12 D3 Crosshill Scotland
111 C9 Cross L Louisiana
121 O8 Cross, L Ontario
119 U4 Cross Lake Manitoba
144 D5 Crossley, Mt New Zealand
118 D4 Cross L. Prov. Park Alberta
12 B5 Crossmaglen N Ireland
103 K7 Crossman Pk Arizona
12 E4 Crossmichael Scotland
14 B2 Crossmolina Irish Rep
106 B1 Cross Mountain Colorado
109 H3 Cross Plains Texas
94 B1 Cross Village Michigan
110 L6 Crossville Tennessee
116 P5 Crosswind L Alaska
45 J2 Crostolo R Italy
94 E3 Croswell Michigan
110 J3 Crothersville Indiana
43 H9 Crotone Italy
20 J1 Crotoy, le France
37 O3 Crottendorf E Germany
100 K5 Crouch Idaho
9 G4 Crouch, R England
21 F8 Croutelle France
22 E5 Crouy France
21 F7 Crouzilles France
101 S4 Crow Agency Montana
139 H4 Crowal R New S Wales
9 G5 Crowborough England
8 C5 Crowcombe England
106 F1 Crow Cr Colorado
111 F7 Crowder Mississippi
107 P6 Crowder Oklahoma
118 F1 Crowduck L. Manitoba
139 L4 Crowdy Hd New S Wales
108 H2 Crowell Texas
139 G7 Crowes Victoria
101 Q6 Crowheart Wyoming
139 H4 Crowl R New S Wales
9 F2 Crowland England
13 H6 Crowle England
106 G3 Crowley Colorado
111 D11 Crowley Louisiana
102 F4 Crowley, L California
94 E8 Crown City Ohio
103 M7 Crown King Arizona
106 B6 Crown Point New Mexico
95 O3 Crown Point New York
115 L4 Crown Prince Frederick I N W Terr
99 T8 Crown Pt Indiana
127 M2 Crown Pt Tobago
101 O3 Crow Peak Montana
141 K7 Crow's Nest Queensland
118 C9 Crowsnest Pass Alberta/Br Col
99 M3 Crow Wing R Minnesota
13 G4 Croxdale England
8 B5 Croyde England
9 F5 Croydon England
144 B7 Croydon New Zealand
141 F4 Croydon Queensland
142 C5 Croydon W Australia
83 L13 Croy, Î de Kerguelen
21 I9 Crozant France
94 J8 Crozet Virginia
81 D9 Crozet Basin Indian Oc
81 C10 Crozet, Is Indian Oc
81 B10 Crozet Plateau Indian Oc
146 J7 Crozier, C Antarctica
114 G2 Crozier Chan N W Terr
18 B4 Crozon France
19 N15 Cruas France
103 H6 Crucero California
126 D3 Cruces Cuba
128 C2 Cruces, Pta point Colombia
22 L4 Cruchten Luxembourg
94 H7 Crucible Pennsylvania
15 G3 Cruden B Scotland
8 D2 Crudgington England
8 D4 Crudwell England
111 F8 Cruger Mississippi
20 G4 Crulai France
14 E2 Crumlin N Ireland
100 F7 Crump L Oregon
22 K5 Crusnes France
133 E4 Cruz Argentina
130 H4 Cruz Alta Brazil
131 D3 Cruz del Eje Argentina
130 G8 Cruzeiro Brazil
133 G2 Cruzeiro do Oeste Brazil
128 D5 Cruzeiro do Sul Brazil
146 K9 Cruzen I Antarctica
133 C3 Cruz Grande Chile
128 C3 Cruz, La Colombia
19 P13 Cruzy France
117 M8 Crysdale, Mt Br Columbia
98 J1 Crystal N Dakota
103 K5 Crystal Nevada
106 C2 Crystal R Colorado
113 E9 Crystal B Florida
138 E5 Crystal Brook S Australia
119 T9 Crystal City Manitoba
108 H7 Crystal City Texas
99 S3 Crystal Falls Michigan
99 S7 Crystal L Illinois
99 U5 Crystal L Michigan
99 N6 Crystal Lake Iowa
113 E9 Crystal River Florida
111 F9 Crystal Springs Mississippi
119 M6 Crystal Springs Sask
99 U6 Crystal Valley Michigan
48 F4 Csanytelek Hungary
48 E3 Csepel Sziget R Hungary
48 F4 Csongrád Hungary
48 F4 Csongrád co Hungary
48 D3 Csorna Hungary
48 F4 Csorvas Hungary
48 E3 Csóvánnyos mt Hungary
48 D4 Csurgo Hungary
127 L9 Cúa Venezuela
88 F9 Cuamba Mozambique
87 D9 Cuando R Angola
87 C9 Cuangar Angola
87 C7 Cuango Angola
86 C7 Cuango Zaire
87 B7 Cuanza R Angola
67 A7 Cua Rao Vietnam
133 F4 Cuareim Brazil
131 F3 Cuaro R Uruguay
133 E4 Cuarto R Argentina
124 H4 Cuatro Ciénegas de Carranza Mexico
68 H4 Cua Tung Vietnam
124 F3 Cuauhtémoc Mexico
124 G8 Cuautitlán Mexico
125 K8 Cuautla Mexico
110 F1 Cuba Illinois
107 N2 Cuba Kansas
110 E3 Cuba Missouri
106 D5 Cuba New Mexico
94 J4 Cuba New York
16 B6 Cuba Portugal
126 D4 Cuba rep W Indies
103 M10 Cubabi, Cerro peak Mexico
99 Q7 Cuba City Wisconsin
127 M9 Cubagua, I Venezuela
143 B10 Cuballing W Australia
87 C9 Cubango R Angola
129 K4 Cubatão Brazil
119 N4 Cub Hills Sask
127 K10 Cubiro Venezuela
48 J6 Cuca Romania
133 C6 Cucao, B.de Chile
133 F4 Cuchilla de Haedo hills Uruguay
9 F5 Cuckfield England
9 E1 Cuckney England
94 K9 Cuckoo Virginia
87 C8 Cucumbi Angola
124 D2 Cucurpe Mexico
128 D2 Cúcuta Colombia
99 T7 Cudahy Wisconsin
76 D5 Cuddalore India
76 D3 Cuddapah India
141 F7 Cuddapan,L Queensland
102 G6 Cuddeback L California
113 F13 Cudjoe Key isld Florida
119 M6 Cudworth Sask
143 C7 Cue W Australia
16 E3 Cuéllar Spain
128 C4 Cuenca Ecuador
71 E4 Cuenca Philippines
17 F4 Cuenca Spain
17 F5 Cuenca prov Spain
124 H5 Cuencamé de Ceniceros Mexico
17 F4 Cuenca, Serrania de Spain
125 K8 Cuernavaca Mexico
109 K6 Cuero Texas
19 Q18 Cuers France
106 F6 Cuervo New Mexico
102 D6 Cuesta Pass California
126 G4 Cueto Cuba
17 F7 Cuevas del Almanzora Spain
133 E2 Cuevo Bolivia
22 E5 Cuffies France
123 N2 Cuff L Quebec
19 P18 Cuges-les-Pins France
43 B8 Cuglieri Sardinia
20 B5 Cuguen France
130 C4 Cuiabá Brazil
14 D2 Cuilcagh mt N Ireland
15 B3 Cuillin Hills Scotland
87 C7 Cuilo R Angola
65 J2 Cuiluan China
87 C8 Cuima Angola
22 D2 Cuinchy France
36 B4 Cuint W Germany
22 E5 Cuise-la-Motte France
130 H9 Cuité Brazil
130 H6 Cuité, R Brazil
87 C9 Cuito R Angola
87 C9 Cuito Cuanavale Angola
128 F4 Cuiuni R Brazil
110 E2 Cuivre R Missouri
71 E7 Cujangan isld Philippines
48 H6 Cujmir Romania
78 J3 Cukurca Turkey
68 H4 Cu Lai Vietnam
18 G6 Culan France
68 J5 Cu Lao Bo Bai isld Vietnam
68 J5 Cu Lao Cham isld Vietnam
68 J7 Cu Lao Hon isld Vietnam
68 J5 Cu Lao Re isld Vietnam
71 F5 Culasi Panay Philippines
98 B1 Culbertson Montana
98 F9 Culbertson Nebraska
139 H6 Culcairn New S Wales
22 G4 Cul-des-Sarts Belgium
106 E4 Culebra Pk Colorado
16 C3 Culebra, Sa de la mts Spain
25 D5 Culemborg Netherlands
87 C9 Culevai Angola
141 H8 Culgoa R N S W/Qnsld
139 H3 Culgoa, R Australia
124 F5 Culiacán Mexico
124 F5 Culiacancito Mexico
71 D5 Culion Philippines
129 H6 Culiseu R Brazil
17 F7 Cúllar de Baza Spain
139 J5 Cullarin Rge New S Wales
15 F3 Cullen Scotland
17 G5 Cullera Spain
107 M4 Cullison Kansas
111 K7 Cullman Alabama
141 G5 Culloden R Queensland
8 C6 Cullompton England
125 M2 Culmi Honduras
8 D3 Culmington England
19 P13 Culoz France
94 J8 Culpeper Virginia
128 A7 Culpepper isld Galapagos Is
15 E5 Culter Fell Scotland
139 G4 Cultowa New S Wales
129 H6 Culuene R Brazil
99 U8 Culver Indiana
107 N3 Culver Kansas
100 D5 Culver Oregon
144 D5 Culverden New Zealand
143 E10 Culver,Pt W Australia
87 C8 Cuma Angola
129 K4 Cuma, B.de Brazil
47 H4 Cumalı Turkey
128 F1 Cumaná Venezuela
127 N9 Cumanacoa Venezuela
47 J6 Cumaovası Turkey
130 E6 Cumari Brazil
117 L11 Cumberland Br Columbia
99 M8 Cumberland Iowa
94 D9 Cumberland Kentucky
94 J7 Cumberland Maryland
94 F7 Cumberland Ohio
94 J9 Cumberland Virginia
99 O4 Cumberland Wisconsin
Cumberland co see Cumbria
110 J5 Cumberland R Tennessee
146 A15 Cumberland B Antarctica
137 O4 Cumberland, C New Hebrides
110 J5 Cumberland City Tennessee
94 D10 Cumberland Gap Tenn/Virg
119 P5 Cumberland House Sask
113 F7 Cumberland I Georgia
141 J5 Cumberland Is Queensland
94 B10 Cumberland, L Kentucky
110 L5 Cumberland, L Kentucky
119 P4 Cumberland L Sask
94 D10 Cumberland Mts Tennessee etc
115 N4 Cumberland Pen N W Terr
99 R2 Cumberland Pt Michigan
94 D10 Cumberland R Kentucky
94 J7 Cumberland Res Pennsylvania
115 N4 Cumberland Sound N W Terr
140 D1 Cumberland Str N Terr Australia
12 E2 Cumbernauld Scotland
139 J3 Cumborah New S Wales
133 C7 Cumbrera mt Chile
13 E4 Cumbria co England
76 D3 Cumbum India
109 M2 Cumby Texas
44 B2 Cumiana Italy
129 G4 Cumina R Brazil
129 G3 Cuminapanema R Brazil
13 E4 Cummertrees Scotland
112 C3 Cumming Georgia
102 A2 Cummings California
98 J2 Cummings N Dakota
138 D5 Cummins S Australia
142 F4 Cummins Ra W Australia
139 J5 Cumnock New S Wales
12 D3 Cumnock Scotland
48 J5 Cumpăna Romania
124 E2 Cumpas Mexico
78 D3 Çumra Turkey
124 E3 Cumuripa Mexico
130 H5 Cumuruxatiba Brazil
127 O2 Cumuto Trinidad
126 E3 Cunagua Cuba
129 H3 Cunani Brazil
124 D6 Cuñaño Mexico
131 G3 Cuñapiru R Uruguay
133 C5 Cunco Chile
142 D5 Cuncudgerie Hill W Australia
143 B9 Cunderdin W Australia
128 D3 Cundinamarca div Colombia
87 B9 Cunene R Angola
44 B3 Cúneo Italy
138 C4 Cungena S Australia
17 H6 Cunillera isld Balearic Is
18 H7 Cunlhat France
141 H8 Cunnamulla Queensland
107 M4 Cunningham Kansas
100 G3 Cunningham Washington
127 O2 Cunupia Trinidad
21 E7 Cuon France
119 N8 Cupar Sask
13 E1 Cupar Scotland
128 C2 Cupica, G.de Colombia
46 E1 Ćuprija Yugoslavia
100 J4 Cuprum Idaho
124 D5 Cupula, P Mexico
129 G7 Curabá R Brazil
129 L5 Curaçá Brazil
126 B1 Curaçao isld W Indies
133 C5 Curacautin Chile
131 D7 Curaco, R Argentina
131 E6 Cura Malal, Cerro peak Argentina
133 C5 Curanilahue Chile
128 C4 Curaray R Peru/Ecuador
131 B4 Curaumilla, Pta de C Chile
139 J4 Curban New S Wales
48 K6 Curcani Romania
21 E7 Curcay-sur-Dive France
138 D3 Curdimurka S Australia
138 D4 Curdlawidny Lagoon S Australia
9 E2 Curdworth England
18 H5 Cure R France
83 M13 Curepipe Mauritius
87 G12 Curepipe Mauritius
133 C5 Curepto Chile
127 O10 Curiapo Venezuela
131 B5 Curico Chile
131 D8 Curico, L Argentina
128 E4 Curicuriari R Brazil
83 J12 Curieuse I Seychelles
130 J9 Curimataú R Brazil
143 A7 Curious,Mt W Australia
128 D3 Curiplaya Colombia
133 H3 Curitiba Brazil
130 E10 Curitibanos Brazil
100 G1 Curlew Washington
141 J5 Curlew I Queensland
111 H12 Curlew Is Louisiana
139 K4 Curlewis New S Wales
116 F5 Curlew L Alaska
123 L3 Curlew Pt Quebec
123 O5 Curling Nfld
138 E4 Curnamona S Australia
44 F2 Curone R Italy
139 K4 Currabubula New S Wales
130 H9 Currais Novas Brazil
138 C2 Curralulla R S Australia
94 D2 Curran Michigan
121 Q7 Curran Ontario
103 J3 Currant Nevada
139 G4 Curranyalpa New S Wales
141 F7 Currawilla Queensland
110 E4 Current R Missouri
113 L12 Current I Bahamas
126 F2 Current, The Eleuthera Bahamas
99 L5 Currie Minnesota
112 J3 Currie N Carolina
103 K1 Currie Nevada
13 E2 Currie Scotland
139 G7 Currie Tasmania
138 B2 Currie Cr., The S Australia
119 U1 Currie L Manitoba
140 B7 Currie,Mt N Terr Australia
112 L1 Currituck N Carolina
112 M1 Currituck Sound N Carolina
139 K6 Currockbilly, Mt New S Wales
110 E2 Curryville Missouri
37 L2 Cursdorf E Germany
45 L1 Curtarolo Italy
48 J5 Curtea de Argeş Romania
100 B6 Curtin Oregon
143 D9 Curtin W Australia
140 B7 Curtin Springs N Terr Aust
111 C9 Curtis Louisiana
99 V3 Curtis Michigan
98 F9 Curtis Nebraska
16 B1 Curtis Spain
141 L6 Curtis Chan Gt Barrier Reef Australia
139 H7 Curtis Group islds Tasmania
137 R8 Curtis I Kermadec Is Pacific Oc
141 K6 Curtis I Queensland
94 D2 Curtisville Michigan
129 G4 Curuá Brazil
129 H5 Curuaés R Brazil
129 H3 Curuá, I Brazil
129 G3 Curuapanema R Brazil
129 J4 Curuca Brazil
128 D5 Curuçá R Brazil
133 F2 Curuguaty Paraguay
129 J4 Cururupu Brazil
131 F2 Curuzú Cuatiá Argentina
129 K7 Curvelo Brazil
94 J6 Curwensville Pennsylvania
14 E1 Cushendall N Ireland
14 E1 Cushendun N Ireland
99 M3 Cushing Minnesota
107 O6 Cushing Oklahoma
111 B10 Cushing Texas
110 E6 Cushman Arkansas
101 Q3 Cushman Montana
100 A6 Cushman Oregon
100 B2 Cushman, L Washington
124 F3 Cusihuiráchic Mexico
45 H3 Cusna, Mt Italy
18 H6 Cusset France
112 C5 Cusseta Georgia
99 O1 Cusson Minnesota
144 D5 Cust New Zealand
101 S3 Custer Montana
98 C6 Custer S Dakota
101 S4 Custer Battlefield Nat.Mon Montana
107 M6 Custer City Oklahoma
45 J1 Custoza Italy
138 F4 Cutana S Australia
101 N1 Cut Bank Montana
117 O8 Cutbank R Alberta
119 P5 Cut Beaver L Sask
111 A8 Cuthand Cr Texas
112 C6 Cuthbert Georgia
98 H6 Cuthbert S Dakota
108 F3 Cuthbert Texas
140 E4 Cuthbert, Mt Queensland
45 J3 Cutigliano Italy
118 H6 Cut Knife Sask
102 E5 Cutler California
95 T9 Cutler Maine
120 H6 Cutler Ontario
116 H3 Cutler R Alaska
14 C3 Cutra, L Irish Rep
22 E4 Cuts France
139 H3 Cuttaburra R New S Wales
75 L8 Cuttack India
103 O8 Cutter Arizona
141 F7 Cutts Mts Queensland
81 H7 Cuvier Basin Indian Oc
143 A6 Cuvier,C W Australia
145 E2 Cuvier I New Zealand
87 C8 Cuvo R Angola
32 J5 Cuxhaven W Germany
68 H2 Cu Xu isld Vietnam
94 F5 Cuyahoga R Ohio
94 F5 Cuyahoga Falls Ohio
102 E6 Cuyama R California
71 E3 Cuyapo Luzon Philippines
71 E5 Cuyo isld Philippines
71 E5 Cuyo East Passage Philippines
71 E5 Cuyo West Passage Philippines
99 N3 Cuyuna Minnesota
128 G2 Cuyuni R Guyana
125 N2 Cuyu Tigni Nicaragua
128 D6 Cuzco Peru
128 E8 Cuzco mt Bolivia
42 H5 Čvrsnica mt Yugoslavia
8 C4 Cwmbran Wales
88 B3 Cyangugu Rwanda
31 H3 Cybinka Poland
Cyclades islds see Kikládhes Is
139 H9 Cygnet Tasmania
119 W2 Cygnet L Manitoba
118 B5 Cynthia Alberta
110 M3 Cynthiana Kentucky
110 G4 Cypress Illinois
111 C10 Cypress Louisiana
109 M6 Cypress Texas
111 A8 Cypress Cr Texas
109 N3 Cypress Cr., Lit Texas
118 H9 Cypress Hills Sask
118 G9 Cypress Hills Prov. Park Alberta
113 F9 Cypress L Florida
119 S9 Cypress River Manitoba
79 D4 Cyprus rep Mediterranean Sea
84 G4 Cyrenaica reg Libya
Cyrene see Shahhât
115 N5 Cyrus Field B N W Terr
22 E2 Cysoing France
31 J2 Czaplinek Poland
118 G6 Czar Alberta
31 M4 Czarna R Poland
31 K2 Czarne Poland
31 K3 Czarnków Poland
31 M6 Czarny Dunajec Poland
31 M6 Czchów Poland
31 J6 Czechoslovakia rep Europe
31 K3 Czempin Poland
31 O3 Czeremcha Poland
Czernowitz see Chernovtsy
31 K2 Czersk Poland
31 J3 Czerwiensk Poland
31 L5 Czestochowa Poland
31 J2 Człopa Poland
31 K2 Człuchów Poland
31 N3 Czyżew Poland
36 D2 Daaden W Germany
65 F2 Da'an China
71 F5 Daanbantayan Cebu Philippines
122 B7 Daaquam Quebec
67 B2 Daba China
79 F7 Dabāb, J. Ed mt Jordan
127 J9 Dabajuro Venezuela
85 D7 Dabakala Ivory Coast
58 D4 Daban Shan mt China
86 A2 Dabaro Somalia
67 C1 Daba Shan mts China
86 G3 Dabat Ethiopia
128 C2 Dabeiba Colombia
68 C4 Dabein Burma
33 P5 Dabel E Germany
74 E7 Dabhoi India
31 H2 Dąbie Poland
67 E1 Dabie Shan mts China
36 C6 Dabo France
85 B6 Dabola Guinea
85 D7 Dabou Ivory Coast
85 D7 Daboya Ghana
36 C1 Dabringhausen W Germany
31 O2 Dąbrowa Poland
31 M2 Dąbrówno Poland
65 D7 Dabu China
67 E4 Dabu China
65 F2 Dabusu Pao L China
75 O7 Dacca Bangladesh
65 C5 Dachang China
37 L7 Dachau W Germany
37 L7 Dachauer Moos marshes W Germany
37 K4 Dachsbach W Germany
38 J7 Dachstein mt Austria
38 J7 Dachstein-Gebirge mts Austria
31 J6 Dačice Czechoslovakia
107 M5 Dacoma Oklahoma
128 G3 Dadanawa Guyana
79 H2 Dādāte Syria
78 D1 Daday Turkey
113 E9 Dade City Florida
111 L9 Dadeville Alabama
74 B4 Dadhar Pakistan
65 D7 Dadian China
65 G3 Dadianzi China
71 C3 Dadi, Tg C W Irian
68 J1 Dadong China
18 G9 Dadou R France
27 H11 Dådran Sweden
74 E8 Dadra & Nagar Haveli Union Terr India
74 G4 Dadri India
74 B5 Dadu Pakistan
68 H7 Da Dung R Vietnam
48 L6 Dăeni Romania
65 C4 Da'erhao China
140 D7 Daer,Mt N Terr Australia
71 F3 Daet Philippines
67 B3 Dafang China
80 F1 Dafna Israel
119 N7 Dafoe Sask
68 B4 Daga R Burma
86 H4 Dagabur Ethiopia
27 C11 Dagali Norway
85 A5 Dagana Senegal
47 K5 Dağardı Turkey
71 A1 Dagasuli Indonesia
30 D1 Dagebüll W Germany
9 G4 Dagenham England
53 G11 Dagestan A.S.S.R U.S.S.R.
102 H7 Daggett California
99 T4 Daggett Michigan
78 K5 Daghgharah, Al Iraq
27 G12 Daglösen Sweden
98 B1 Dagmar Montana
65 D5 Dagu China
67 A3 Daguan China
71 E2 Dagupan Luzon Philippines
94 J5 Dagus Mines Pennsylvania
68 C4 Dagwin Burma
141 G4 Dagworth Queensland
66 E6 Dagzê China
79 E10 Dahab Egypt
117 L4 Dahadinni R N W Terr
67 D5 Dahao Dao isld China
65 J1 Dahezhen China
59 H2 Da Hinggan Ling mt ra China
86 H2 Dahlak Arch Ethiopia
86 H2 Dahlak Kebir I Ethiopia
32 G10 Dahle W Germany
36 B3 Dahleim W Germany
33 R10 Dahlen E Germany
33 N6 Dahlenburg W Germany
33 S8 Dahlewitz E Germany
95 K8 Dahlgren Virginia
112 C3 Dahlonega Georgia
33 S9 Dahme E Germany
33 O4 Dahme W Germany
33 T8 Dahme R E Germany
33 R5 Dahmen E Germany
33 O4 Dahmeshöved W Germany
36 D5 Dahn W Germany
72 F3 Dahnā, Ad reg Saudi Arabia
78 J3 Dahok Iraq
Dahomey rep see Benin, Rep. of
66 B4 Dahongliutan China
65 E4 Dahongqi China
67 D1 Dahong Shan mts China
84 F4 Dahra Libya
33 N7 Dähre E Germany
78 J3 Dahuk Iraq
65 E4 Dahushan China
139 G5 Dahwilly New S Wales
71 O8 Dai isld Indonesia
48 K7 Daia Romania
65 C5 Daicheng China
65 B4 Dai Hai L China
68 C4 Daik-U Burma
75 J4 Dailekh Nepal
121 T3 Dailleboust, L Quebec
60 G9 Daimanji-san mt Japan
16 E5 Daimiel Spain
109 N2 Daingerfield Texas
61 K10 Dainichiga-take peak Japan
66 F5 Dainkog China
141 H3 Daintree Queensland
141 H3 Daintree R Queensland
61 K11 Daiō Japan
65 E2 Daiqin Tal China
126 G5 Daiquiri Cuba
Dairen see Lüda
84 J4 Dairût Egypt
100 D7 Dairy Oregon
60 G10 Daisen mt Japan
60 G10 Dai sen-Oki Nat. Park Japan
109 N5 Daisetta Texas
67 G1 Dai Shan isld China
129 K5 Dais Irmaos, Serra mts Brazil
100 G1 Daisy Washington
58 F4 Dai Xian China
Daiyue see Shanyin
67 F4 Daiyun Shan mts China
127 J5 Dajabón Dom Rep
140 E5 Dajarra Queensland
58 D5 Dajin Chuan R China
67 G2 Dajing China
45 P1 Dajla Yugoslavia
70 D5 Daju Kalimantan
85 A6 Dakar Senegal
67 D4 Dakengkou China
67 D5 Dakengkou China
68 H5 Dak Gle Vietnam
85 A4 Dakhla Mauritania
85 A4 Dakhla Western Sahara
84 H4 Dakhla Oasis Egypt
68 H5 Dak Kon Vietnam
69 A9 Dakoank Nicobar Is
85 F6 Dakoro Niger
99 R7 Dakota Illinois
99 P6 Dakota Minnesota
99 M7 Dakota City Iowa
98 K7 Dakota City Nebraska
46 D2 Dakovica Yugoslavia
48 E5 Dakovo Yugoslavia
28 D3 Dal Denmark
27 E11 Dal Norway
87 D8 Dala Angola
27 J11 Dalä L Sweden
41 L3 Dalaas Tal Austria
85 B6 Dalaba Guinea
65 A4 Dalad Qi China
Dalai see Da'an
Dalai Nor L see Hulun Nur
58 G3 Dalai Nur L China
65 C3 Dalai Nur L China
27 G11 Dala-Järna Sweden
78 B3 Dalaman R Turkey
58 D3 Dalandzadgad Mongolia
71 E5 Dalanganem islds Philippines
58 E2 Dalanjargalan Mongolia
27 K12 Dalarö Sweden
70 B3 Dalat Sarawak
68 J7 Da Lat Vietnam
71 C6 Dalawan B Philippines
77 J5 Dalbandin Pakistan
15 E6 Dalbeattie Scotland
27 F13 Dalbosjön L Sweden
28 F5 Dalby Denmark
12 D5 Dalby I of Man U.K.
141 K7 Dalby Queensland
27 F11 Dalby Sweden
28 E3 Dalbyneder Denmark
28 E3 Dalbyover Denmark
110 K3 Dale Indiana
27 A10 Dale Norway
27 A11 Dale Norway
100 G5 Dale Oregon
94 J6 Dale Pennsylvania
109 K6 Dale Texas
8 A4 Dale Wales
118 D8 Dalemead Alberta
143 B9 Dale,Mt W Australia
25 G3 Dalen Netherlands
28 B7 Daler Denmark
31 M5 Daleszyce Poland
68 A3 Dalet Burma
68 A2 Dalet R Burma
68 A2 Daletme Burma
110 L1 Daleville Indiana
27 H10 Dalfors Sweden
25 F4 Dalfsen Netherlands
143 B8 Dalgaranger,Mt W Australia
139 J6 Dalgety New S Wales
12 E1 Dalginross Scotland
141 F5 Dalgonally Queensland
108 B7 Dalhart Texas
114 G3 Dalhousie, C N W Terr
65 A7 Dali China
Dalian see Lüda
58 D6 Daliang Shan China
65 E5 Dalian Wan B China
71 G7 Daliao Philippines
106 D7 Dalies New Mexico
65 A6 Dali He R China
Dalinghe see Jin Xian
80 D3 Daliyat el Karmil Israel
65 G4 Dalizi China
48 E5 Dalj Yugoslavia
15 E5 Dalkeith Scotland
14 E3 Dalkey Irish Rep
141 K7 Dallarnil Queensland
111 M8 Dallas Georgia
119 U7 Dallas Manitoba
100 B5 Dallas Oregon
109 N10 Dallas Texas
99 P4 Dallas Wisconsin
99 N8 Dallas Center Iowa
99 P9 Dallas City Illinois
95 L7 Dallastown Pennsylvania
102 D4 Dallas Warner Res California
100 D4 Dalles, The Oregon
117 G8 Dall I Alaska
116 F6 Dall L Alaska
116 N3 Dall Mt Alaska
85 E6 Dallol Bosso watercourse Niger
77 C7 Dalmá isld U.A.E.
133 E4 Dalmacio Velez Sarsfield Argentina
12 D1 Dalmally Scotland
42 G4 Dalmatia reg Yugoslavia
55 D3 Dalmatovo U.S.S.R.
12 D3 Dalmellington Scotland
118 L6 Dalmeny Sask
28 G6 Dalmose Denmark
12 D2 Dalmuir Scotland
59 L3 Dal'negorsk U.S.S.R.
52 F6 Dal'ne-Konstantinovo U.S.S.R.
59 K2 Dal'nerechensk U.S.S.R.
52 E1 Dal'niye Zelentsy U.S.S.R.
85 C7 Daloa Ivory Coast
67 C5 Dalongdong Shuiku res China
67 B3 Dalou Shan mt ra China
121 M4 Dalquier Quebec
118 D7 Dalroy Alberta
15 D5 Dalry Dumfries & Galloway Scotland
15 D5 Dalry Strathclyde Scotland
141 H4 Dalrymple Queensland
15 D5 Dalrymple Scotland
141 J5 Dalrymple,Mt Queensland
29 K11 Dalsbruk Finland
13 F4 Dalston England
112 C3 Dalton Georgia
95 O4 Dalton Massachusetts
98 D8 Dalton Nebraska
120 F4 Dalton Ontario
95 M5 Dalton Pennsylvania
13 E3 Dalton Scotland
75 L6 Daltonganj India
146 G2 Dalton Iceberg Tongue Antarctica
115 R4 Dalton, Kap C Greenland
69 E12 Daludalu Sumatra
65 F5 Dalu Dao isld China
28 E6 Dalum Denmark
68 E2 Daluo China
65 H2 Daluolemi China
65 G1 Daluozhen China
71 G4 Dalupiri Philippines
71 E1 Dalupiri isld Philippines
141 K8 Dalveen Queensland
12 E3 Dalveen P Scotland
143 B9 Dalwallinu W Australia
15 D4 Dalwhinnie Scotland
36 F1 Dalwigksthal W Germany
136 G4 Daly R N Terr Australia
140 B2 Daly R N Terr Aust
140 B2 Daly River N Terr Aust
140 C3 Daly Waters N Terr Aust
98 D5 Dalzell S Dakota
74 E8 Daman India
79 A7 Damanhûr Egypt
65 C4 Damaqun Shan mt ra China
107 L2 Damar Kansas
71 B3 Damar isld Indonesia
71 O8 Damar isld Indonesia
86 C5 Damara Cent Afr Republic
89 A4 Damaraland reg Namibia
95 S2 Damariscotta L Maine
Damas see Damascus
110 D6 Damascus Arkansas
95 K7 Damascus Maryland
79 G5 Damascus Syria
94 F10 Damascus Virginia
131 B5 Damas, Paso de las Chile/Arg
86 B3 Damaturu Nigeria
77 C2 Damavand Iran
87 C7 Damba Angola
36 C7 Dambach France
83 K10 Dambulla Sri Lanka
68 J4 Dam Cau Hai Vietnam
126 G5 Dame Marie Haiti
77 D1 Dāmghān Iran
28 A4 Damhus Å R Denmark
65 D3 Damiao China
48 L4 Dămieneşti Romania
20 F5 Damigni France
65 C6 Daming China
67 C5 Daming Shan mts China
80 F5 Damiya Jordan
80 F5 Damiya Br Jordan
71 E8 Dammai isld Philippines
77 B6 Dammam, Ad Saudi Arabia
20 J5 Dammarie France
18 G3 Dammartin-en-Goële France
22 E1 Damme Belgium
32 H7 Damme W Germany
74 H7 Damoh India
109 M6 Damon Texas
85 D7 Damongo Ghana
86 A2 Damot Ethiopia
79 F5 Damour Lebanon
70 F4 Dampelas, Tg C Celebes
22 K4 Dampicourt Belgium
142 B5 Dampier W Australia
142 B5 Dampier Arch W Australia
142 E3 Dampier Land pen W Australia
40 C2 Dampierre-sur-Saône France
71 C3 Dampier, Selat str W Irian
70 O10 Dampit Java
28 J7 Damsholte Denmark
19 J3 Damvillars France
20 H4 Damville France

Dâmvillers — Devli 21

22 J5 Dâmvillers France
112 H1 Dan R N Carolina
94 J10 Dan R Virginia
99 S9 Dana Illinois
110 J2 Dana Indiana
79 F8 Danā Jordan
119 M6 Dana Sask
71 K10 Dana isld Indonesia
69 F12 Danai Sumatra
86 H3 Danakil tribal dist Ethiopia
86 H4 Danan Ethiopia
85 C7 Danané Ivory Coast
68 J4 Da Nang Vietnam
75 L6 Danapur India
116 G9 Dana Vol Alaska
58 D5 Danba China
95 O5 Danbury Connecticut
98 F9 Danbury Nebraska
95 Q3 Danbury New Hampshire
109 M6 Danbury Texas
99 O4 Danbury Wisconsin
103 J7 Danby California
103 J7 Danby L California
119 T6 Dancing Point Manitoba
143 B9 Dandaragan W Australia
74 J4 Dandel Dhura Nepal
76 B3 Dandeli India
139 H7 Dandenong Victoria
59 H3 Dandong China
74 E2 Dandot Pakistan
121 Q5 Dandurand, L Quebec
99 R6 Dane Wisconsin
147 E10 Daneborg Greenland
109 L6 Danevang Texas
65 A8 Danfeng China
67 E6 Dangan Liedao isld China
57 E5 Dangara U.S.S.R.
65 J2 Dangbizhen China
Dangcheng see Xiangshan
21 G8 Dangé France
20 H5 Dangeau France
89 A10 Danger Pt S Africa
20 F5 Dangeul France
66 F4 Dang He R China
86 G3 Dangila Ethiopia
68 G5 Dangrek, Chaine des mts Cambodia
65 C7 Dangshan China
67 F1 Dangtu China
20 J3 Dangu France
67 D1 Dangyang China
68 J7 Da Nhim R Vietnam
113 G11 Dania Florida
101 P7 Daniel Wyoming
42 E2 Daniele del Friuli, S Italy
122 D3 Daniel-Johnston Dam Quebec
143 D10 Daniell W Australia
144 D5 Daniells, L New Zealand
123 P3 Daniel's Cove Nfld
115 O7 Daniels Har Nfld
118 J1 Daniels L Ontario
95 Q5 Danielson Connecticut
112 D3 Danielsville Georgia
52 F5 Danilov U.S.S.R.
42 J6 Danilov Grad Yugoslavia
52 J3 Danilovka U.S.S.R.
55 F4 Danilovka U.S.S.R.
52 E3 Danilovo U.S.S.R.
58 F4 Daning China
67 C1 Daningchang China
Danjiang see Leishan
68 J6 Dankia Vietnam
67 A1 Danleng China
98 H8 Dannebrog Nebraska
115 Q4 Dannebrogs Ø isld Greenland
28 G7 Dannemare Denmark
95 O2 Dannemora New York
27 J11 Dannemora Sweden
33 O6 Dannenberg W Germany
33 S6 Dannenwalde E Germany
100 H7 Danner Oregon
145 F4 Dannevirke New Zealand
70 D4 Danompari Kalimantan
68 E4 Dan Sai Thailand
144 C6 Danseys Pass New Zealand
67 E5 Danshui China
68 B4 Danson B Burma
94 C4 Dansville Michigan
94 K4 Dansville New York
86 B1 Dante Somalia
94 E10 Dante Virginia
76 E1 Dantewara India
Dantu see Zhenjiang
Danube R Bulgaria/Yugoslavia see Dunav R
Danube R Czechoslovakia see Dunaj R
Danube R Hungary see Duna R
Danube R Romania see Dunărea R
Danube R W Germany/Austria see Donau R
68 B4 Danubyu Burma
110 G1 Danvers Illinois
99 L4 Danvers Minnesota
101 Q2 Danvers Montana
110 C6 Danville Arkansas
112 D5 Danville Georgia
99 T9 Danville Illinois
110 K2 Danville Indiana
95 R2 Danville Maine
94 E6 Danville Ohio
95 L6 Danville Pennsylvania
121 S7 Danville Quebec
95 P2 Danville Vermont
94 H10 Danville Virginia
94 F8 Danville W Virginia
20 D4 Danvou France
67 C7 Dan Xian China
67 F1 Danyang China
21 H6 Danzé France
67 B3 Danzhai China
67 C5 Danzhu China
Danzig see Gdańsk
98 G3 Danzig N Dakota
Danzig, G. of see Gdańska, Zatoka
71 E5 Dao Panay Philippines
16 B4 Dão R Portugal
67 B6 Dao Bach Long Vi isld Vietnam
Daokou see Hua Xian
21 D6 Daon France
74 G5 Daosa India
Daoud see Aïn Beïda
18 C4 Daoulas France
85 D3 Daoura watercourse Algeria/Morocco
67 D4 Dao Xian China
67 B2 Daozhen China
71 G6 Dapa Philippines
85 E6 Dapango Togo
111 J11 Daphne Alabama
71 F6 Dapiak, Mt Philippines
65 E4 Dapingfang China
71 F6 Dapitan Philippines
74 E10 Dapoli India
118 D4 Dapp Alberta
66 F4 Da Qaidam China
65 E5 Daqin Dao isld China
65 A4 Daqing Shan mt ra China
65 B4 Daqing Shan mts China
Daqin Tal see Naiman Qi
67 G1 Daqu Shan isld China
85 A5 Dara Senegal
77 D5 Dārāb Iran
48 K2 Dărăbani Romania
71 F5 Daraga Philippines
85 G2 Daraj Libya
71 G5 Daram isld Philippines
77 B3 Daran Iran
48 D5 Darány Hungary
70 C5 Darap Kalimantan
46 D2 Daravice mt Yugoslavia
85 G6 Darazo Nigeria
52 B6 Darbėnai U.S.S.R.
101 L3 Darby Montana
116 F4 Darby C Alaska
116 F4 Darby Mts Alaska
33 N6 Darchau E Germany
142 E3 D'Arcole Is W Australia
117 M10 D'Arcy Br Col
118 J7 D'Arcy Sask
110 C6 Dardanelle Arkansas
102 E3 Dardanelle California
Dardanelles Turkey see Çanakkale Boğazi
33 N9 Dardesheim E Germany
141 J8 Dareel Town Queensland
Dar el Beida see Casablanca
86 D4 Dar-el-Kouti dist Cent Afr Republic
88 G5 Dar es Salaam Tanzania
144 D5 Darfield New Zealand
Darfur prov Sudan see Northern and Southern Darfur provs
74 D1 Dargai Pakistan
57 B4 Darganata U.S.S.R.
145 D1 Dargaville New Zealand
20 J1 Dargnies France
139 H6 Dargo Victoria
33 R5 Dargun E Germany
58 E2 Darhan Mongolia
59 F3 Darhan Muminggan Lianheqi China
112 F6 Darien Georgia
126 F10 Darién, G.del Colombia/Panama
125 Q5 Darién, Serranía del ra Panama
71 E2 Darigayos Pt Luzon Philippines
125 L3 Darío Nicaragua
66 D6 Darjeeling India
143 B10 Darkan W Australia
138 D5 Darke Peak S Australia
77 A4 Darkhazineh Iran
138 F5 Darling R S Australia
139 J3 Darling Downs Queensland
141 J8 Darling Downs reg Queensland
119 T9 Darlingford Manitoba
115 M1 Darling Pen N W Terr
13 G5 Darlington England
101 M6 Darlington Idaho
99 M9 Darlington Missouri
112 H3 Darlington S Carolina
99 Q7 Darlington Wisconsin
139 H5 Darlington Pt New S Wales
143 D8 Darlot, L W Australia
31 J1 Darłowo Poland
48 K3 Dărmăneşti Romania
77 F3 Darmiān Iran
118 L8 Darmody Sask
36 F4 Darmstadt W Germany
84 G3 Darnah Libya
111 E9 Darnell Louisiana
20 H3 Darnetal France
139 G5 Darnick New S Wales
114 G4 Darnley B N W Terr
146 B4 Darnley, C Antarctica
17 G3 Daroda Spain
48 J1 Darokhov U.S.S.R.
52 G5 Darovskoye U.S.S.R.
141 G6 Darr Queensland
141 G6 Darr R Queensland
141 K2 Darra sub Brisbane, Qnsld
77 F1 Darreh Gaz Iran
100 D1 Darrington Washington
86 A1 Darror R Somalia
86 D4 Dar Rounga reg Cent Afr Republic
108 D7 Darrouzett Texas
76 D3 Darsi India
30 G1 Darsser Ort C E Germany
146 J10 Dart, C Antarctica
9 G5 Dartford England
138 F7 Dartmoor Victoria
8 C6 Dartmoor Forest England
8 C7 Dartmouth England
122 J9 Dartmouth Nova Scotia
141 H7 Dartmouth L Queensland
122 H4 Dartmouth R Quebec
8 C6 Dart, R England
14 C2 Dartry Mts Irish Rep
136 J3 Daru Papua New Guinea
66 E5 Darum Tso L China
42 H3 Daruvar Yugoslavia
15 D5 Darvel Scotland
70 F2 Darvel B Sabah
58 B2 Darvi Mongolia
13 F6 Darwen England
77 J4 Darweshan Afghanistan
102 G5 Darwin California
140 B1 Darwin N Terr Aust
88 C10 Darwin Zimbabwe
133 C7 Darwin, Can str Chile
77 G4 Daryacheh L Iran
56 A1 Dar'yegan R U.S.S.R.
77 C7 Dās isld U.A.E.
22 L3 Dasburg W Germany
67 C1 Dashennongjia mt China
65 A4 Dashetai China
Dashiqiao see Yingkou
65 E1 Dashizhai China
77 E1 Dasht Iran
77 H7 Dasht R Pakistan
77 C2 Dasht-e-Kavir Iran
77 G7 Dashtiari Iran
65 C3 Dashui Nur China
120 J9 Dashwood Ontario
37 L7 Dasing W Germany
71 E7 Dassalan isld Philippines
99 M4 Dassel Minnesota
32 L9 Dassel W Germany
33 N5 Dassow E Germany
77 E2 Dastgardān Iran
70 D4 Datagenojang Kalimantan
65 C4 Datan China
68 J1 Datang China
47 J8 Datça Turkey
9 F5 Datchet England
60 O3 Date Japan
103 L7 Date Cr Arizona
103 L9 Dateland Arizona
74 H6 Datia India
67 F4 Datian China
106 C7 Datil New Mexico
67 F1 Datong China
67 F1 Datong Heilongjiang China
65 B4 Datong Shanxi China
58 C4 Datong Shan mt ra China
140 F6 Datson,Mt Queensland
59 M2 Datta U.S.S.R.
32 F9 Datteln W Germany
70 E3 Datumakuta Kalimantan
65 J2 Daubikhe R U.S.S.R.
74 D2 Daud Khel India
32 K7 Dauelsen W Germany
115 N1 Daugaard Jensen Land Greenland
28 D5 Daūgård Denmark
52 C6 Daugav'pils U.S.S.R.
77 K1 Daulatabad Afghanistan
74 F9 Daulatabad India
77 J2 Daulat Yar Afghanistan
128 C4 Daule Ecuador
41 M3 Daumen mt W Germany
21 E6 Daumeray France
36 B3 Daun W Germany
68 C6 Daung Kyun isld Burma
119 R7 Dauphin Manitoba
95 L6 Dauphin Pennsylvania
19 O14 Dauphiné prov France
111 H11 Dauphin I Alabama
119 S7 Dauphin L Manitoba
85 F6 Daura Nigeria
15 E3 Dava Scotland
76 B3 Davangere India
71 G7 Davao Mindanao Philippines
71 G7 Davao Gulf Mindanao Philippines
12 C3 Davarr I Scotland
147 F10 Dave isld Greenland
121 S6 Daveluyville Quebec
22 D4 Davenescourt France
121 M4 Davengus Quebec
116 J5 Davenport Alaska
102 B4 Davenport California
113 F9 Davenport Florida
99 Q8 Davenport Iowa
98 J9 Davenport Nebraska
95 N4 Davenport New York
107 O6 Davenport Oklahoma
100 G2 Davenport Washington
141 F6 Davenport Downs Queensland
140 A6 Davenport Hills N Terr Aust
140 B5 Davenport,Mt N Terr Aust
140 C5 Davenport Ra N Terr Aust
9 E3 Daventry England
80 E3 Daverat Israel
32 K7 Daverden W Germany
125 N5 David Panama
146 E2 David isld Antarctica
98 J8 David City Nebraska
112 G2 Davidson N Carolina
107 L7 Davidson Oklahoma
119 M7 Davidson Sask
140 B5 Davidson,Mt N Terr Aust
116 Q2 Davidson Mts Alaska
8 B6 Davidstow England
113 G11 Davie Florida
138 A2 Davies, Mt S Australia
26 A10 Davik Norway
109 K5 Davilla Texas
119 N8 Davin Sask
102 C3 Davis California
99 R7 Davis Illinois
107 N7 Davis Oklahoma
119 M5 Davis Sask
98 K6 Davis S Dakota
94 H7 Davis W Virginia
146 H3 Davis B Antarctica
112 E5 Davisboro Georgia
99 N9 Davis City Iowa
100 E8 Davis Creek California
103 K6 Davis Dam Arizona
115 N6 Davis Inlet Labrador
94 H7 Davis, Mt Pennsylvania
108 C5 Davis Mts Texas
94 D3 Davison Michigan
146 D3 Davis Sea Antarctica
115 O4 Davis Str Greenland/Canada
110 E4 Davisville Missouri
55 C4 Davlekanovo U.S.S.R.
41 L4 Davos Switzerland
94 F9 Davy W Virginia
143 D9 Davyhurst W Australia
65 E4 Dawa China
65 F3 Dawa China
86 H5 Dawa R Ethiopia
65 C6 Dawenkou China
141 K6 Dawes Ra Queensland
68 D4 Dawlan Burma
8 C6 Dawlish England
110 C2 Dawn Missouri
108 E1 Dawn Texas
68 C4 Dawna Ra Burma
111 M10 Dawson Georgia
98 K5 Dawson Minnesota
98 G3 Dawson N Dakota
106 F5 Dawson New Mexico
107 P5 Dawson Oklahoma
109 L4 Dawson Texas
117 D3 Dawson Yukon Terr
141 J6 Dawson R Queensland
119 R6 Dawson Bay Manitoba
117 N8 Dawson Creek Br Columbia
114 H5 Dawson Landing N W Terr
117 Q5 Dawson Lodge N W Terr
117 P10 Dawson, Mt Br Columbia
117 D4 Dawson Range Yukon Terr
110 J4 Dawson Springs Kentucky
111 M7 Dawsonville Georgia
67 E1 Dawu China
18 E9 Dax France
67 B1 Da Xian China
68 H1 Daxin China
65 E6 Daxindian China
65 C5 Daxing China
59 J3 Daxinggou China
36 E5 Daxlanden W Germany
67 C4 Daxu China
67 C5 Daxuan China
Daxue see Wencheng
58 D4 Daxue Shan mt ra China
58 D5 Daxue Shan mt China
67 F3 Daxu Shan pass China
100 D8 Day California
113 D7 Day Florida
57 B4 Dayakhatyn U.S.S.R.
65 F4 Dayang He R China
67 C5 Dayao Shan mts China
67 E5 Daya Wan B China
143 C8 Day Dawn W Australia
67 E1 Daye China
67 A1 Dayi China
67 B4 Dayi China
Dayishan see Guanyun
139 G6 Daylesford Victoria
102 G5 Daylight Pass California
133 F4 Dayman R Uruguay
131 F3 Dayman, Cuchilla del mts Uruguay
143 D9 Day, Mt W Australia
67 C2 Dayong China
100 B7 Days Creek Oregon
118 E6 Daysland Alberta
99 M7 Dayton Iowa
94 J4 Dayton New York
94 C7 Dayton Ohio
94 H6 Dayton Pennsylvania
112 B2 Dayton Tennessee
109 N5 Dayton Texas
100 H3 Dayton Washington
101 S5 Dayton Wyoming
113 F8 Daytona Beach Florida
67 E4 Dayu China
67 E4 Dayu Ling mt China
100 F5 Dayville Oregon
98 H2 Dazey N Dakota
67 F4 Dazhang Xi R China
67 B1 Dazhu China
47 K7 Dazkırı Turkey
67 B2 Dazu China
89 D8 De Aar S Africa
99 T3 Dead R Michigan
116 N1 Deadhorse Alaska
101 Q5 Dead Indian Pk Wyoming
111 L11 Dead L Florida
103 H7 Deadman L California
113 D8 Deadmans B Florida
126 G3 Deadman's Cay Long I Bahamas
103 K6 Dead Mts Cal/Nev
95 R1 Dead R Maine
80 E8 Dead Sea Israel/Jordan
95 R8 Deadwater L Maine
98 C5 Deadwood S Dakota
100 K5 Deadwood Res Idaho
140 C2 Deaf Adder Cr N Terr Aust
143 G9 Deakin W Australia
140 B4 Deakin,Mt N Terr Aust
9 H5 Deal England
95 L8 Deale Maryland
139 H7 Deal I Tasmania
95 M8 Deal Island Maryland
58 G6 De'an China
110 D1 Dean Iowa
117 K9 Dean Ch Br Columbia
141 H5 Deane,Mt Queensland
8 D4 Dean, Forest of England
131 D3 Deán Funes Argentina
143 E10 Dean,Mt W Australia
117 L9 Dean R Br Columbia
95 M4 Deansboro New York
94 D4 Dearborn Michigan
110 B2 Dearborn Missouri
107 P4 Dearing Kansas
100 J3 Deary Idaho
114 G4 Dease Arm B N W Terr
116 K1 Dease Inlet Alaska
117 J6 Dease Lake Br Col
147 G2 Dease Str N W Terr
102 G5 Death Valley California
20 F3 Deauville France
101 R5 Deaver Wyoming
70 B4 Debak Sarawak
54 K8 Debal'tsevo U.S.S.R.
67 B5 Debao China
46 D3 Debar Yugoslavia
116 H4 Debauch Mt Alaska
84 J6 Debba, Ed Sudan
118 L5 Debden Sask
127 O3 Débé Trinidad
122 E7 Debec New Brunswick
9 H3 Debenham England
9 H3 Deben, R England
106 B2 De Beque Colorado
109 N3 De Berry Texas
52 H5 Debessy U.S.S.R.
31 N5 Dębica Poland
31 N4 Dęblin Poland
31 K1 Dębnica Kaszubska Poland
31 H3 Dębno Poland
85 D5 Débó, L Mali
143 C9 Deborah,L W Australia
116 O5 Deborah, Mt Alaska
142 F3 Deborah,Mt W Australia
100 K2 De Borgia Montana
86 G4 Debra Birhan Ethiopia
86 G3 Debra Markos Ethiopia
86 G3 Debra Tabor Ethiopia
48 F6 Debrc Yugoslavia
48 G3 Debrecen Hungary
71 E2 Debutunan Pt Luzon Philippines
86 G2 Decamere Ethiopia
46 D2 Dečani Yugoslavia
111 K7 Decatur Alabama
110 B5 Decatur Arkansas
111 M8 Decatur Georgia
99 S10 Decatur Illinois
110 H2 Decatur Illinois
94 C6 Decatur Indiana
99 N9 Decatur Iowa
94 B4 Decatur Michigan
111 G9 Decatur Mississippi
98 K7 Decatur Nebraska
109 K2 Decatur Texas
110 H6 Decaturville Tennessee
18 G8 Decazeville France
76 C4 Deccan plat India
121 M5 Decelles, Lac Quebec
115 M5 Déception Quebec
89 C3 Deception watercourse Botswana
Dechen Dzong see Dagzê
122 E2 Dechêne, L Quebec
110 K6 Decherd Tennessee
22 E3 Dechy France
118 F1 Decimal Manitoba
43 B9 Decimomannu Sardinia
31 H5 Děčin Czechoslovakia
117 F7 Decision, C Alaska
18 H6 Decize France
110 J3 Decker Indiana
119 R8 Decker Manitoba
101 T4 Decker Montana
106 E2 Deckers Colorado
25 C2 De Cocksdorp Netherlands
140 C1 De Courcy Hd N Terr Aust
48 E4 Decs Hungary
48 J4 Deda Romania
9 E4 Deddington England
Dedéagach see Alexandroúpolis
33 N8 Dedeleben E Germany
33 T6 Dedelow E Germany
99 M8 Dedham Iowa
46 E3 Dedino Yugoslavia
130 F9 Dedo de Deus mt Brazil
85 D6 Dedougou Upper Volta
52 C6 Dedovichi U.S.S.R.
100 B9 Dedrick California
83 J10 Deduru Oya R Sri Lanka
56 E1 Dedushka, Porog falls U.S.S.R.
88 E9 Dedza Malawi
15 F3 Dee R Scotland
141 K6 Deeford Queensland
14 C4 Deel R Irish Rep
112 H2 Deep R N Carolina
Deep Bay Malawi see Chilumba
122 G9 Deep Brook Nova Scotia
100 J7 Deep Cr Idaho
94 H7 Deep Creek L Maryland
103 L2 Deep Creek Ra Utah
142 B5 Deepdale Western Australia
107 O6 Deep Fork R Oklahoma
112 F1 Deep Gap N Carolina
95 P5 Deep River Connecticut
99 O8 Deep River Iowa
121 N6 Deep River Ontario
100 B3 Deep River Washington
102 G4 Deep Sp California
110 C3 Deepwater Missouri
139 K3 Deepwater New S Wales Australia
140 C6 Deep Well N Terr Aust
110 C6 Deer Arkansas
8 C1 Dee, R England/Wales
12 E4 Dee, R Scotland
100 D9 Deer Cr California
99 L3 Deer Cr Minnesota
98 F9 Deer Cr Nebraska
101 T7 Deer Cr Wyoming
107 N5 Deer Creek Oklahoma
103 N1 Deer Cr.Res Utah
107 J3 Deerfield Kansas
113 G11 Deerfield Beach Florida
116 F9 Deer I Alaska
95 T2 Deer I Maine
122 F9 Deer I New Brunswick
116 F3 Deering Alaska
98 E1 Deering N Dakota
138 A2 Deering Hills S Australia
143 G7 Deering,Mt W Australia
123 P4 Deer Lake Nfld
22 E2 Deerlijk Belgium
101 N3 Deer Lodge Montana
111 H10 Deer Park Alabama
100 H2 Deer Park Washington
117 O11 Deer Pk Br Columbia
123 S5 Deer Pond Nfld
99 N2 Deer River Minnesota
99 T3 Deerton Michigan
106 F2 Deer Trail Colorado
99 N3 Deerwood Minnesota
111 F7 Deeson Mississippi
100 K8 Deeth Nevada
Defeng see Liping
38 F8 Defereggengeb mt Austria
38 F8 Defereggental V Austria
95 M2 Deferiet New York
133 F5 Defferrari Argentina
99 L8 Defiance Iowa
94 C5 Defiance Ohio
111 K11 De Funiak Springs Florida
16 B6 Degebe R Portugal
85 F8 Degema Nigeria
27 G12 Degerfors Sweden
37 O6 Deggendorf W Germany
36 H6 Deggingen W Germany
47 J6 Degirmendere Turkey
99 L4 De Graff Minnesota
110 N1 Degraff Ohio
111 C7 De Gray Res Arkansas
98 G5 De Grey S Dakota
142 C5 De Grey W Australia
142 D5 De Grey R W Australia
55 D3 Degtyarsk U.S.S.R.
22 E1 De Haan Belgium
77 C4 Deh Bid Iran
74 E8 Dehej India
85 G2 Dehibat Tunisia
74 H3 Dehra Dun India
75 L6 Dehri India
36 E3 Dehrn W Germany
77 F4 Deh Salm Iran
67 F4 Dehua China
59 J3 Dehui China
36 E5 Deidesheim W Germany
86 E4 Deim Zubeir Sudan
37 M5 Deining W Germany
25 E2 Deinum Netherlands
22 F2 Deinze Belgium
80 F4 Deir Abu Said Jordan
79 G4 Deir el Ahmar Lebanon
80 F4 Deir es Samadiya Jordan
78 H4 Deir ez Zor Syria
80 D5 Deir Istiya Jordan
80 E6 Deir Mar Jiryis Jordan
80 D4 Deir Sharal Jordan
79 G3 Deir Shemil Syria
32 K8 Deister hills W Germany
48 H3 Dej Romania
46 D3 Dêja mt Albania
71 B2 Dejailolo, Selat str Indonesia
28 A5 Dejbjerg Denmark
27 F12 Deje Sweden
86 G3 Dejen Ethiopia
67 C2 Dejiang China
99 S8 De Kalb Illinois
111 H9 De Kalb Mississippi
109 N2 De Kalb Texas
95 M2 De Kalb Junc New York
51 O3 De Kastri U.S.S.R.
59 M1 De Kastries U.S.S.R.
86 D6 Dekese Zaïre
86 C4 Dekoa Cent Afr Republic
25 C2 De Koog Netherlands
25 C3 De Kooij Netherlands
111 G12 Delacroix Louisiana
106 F4 Delagua Colorado
100 J6 Delamar Idaho
103 K4 Delamar Mts Nevada
140 B3 Delamere N Terr Aust
113 F8 De Land Florida
102 E6 Delano California
103 M3 Delano Peak Utah
113 L9 Delaport New Providence I Bahamas
118 K4 Delaronde L Sask
110 G1 Delavan Illinois
99 S7 Delavan Wisconsin
94 D6 Delaware Ohio
107 P5 Delaware Oklahoma
107 P2 Delaware R Kansas
95 N5 Delaware R U.S.A.
95 M7 Delaware state U.S.A.
145 D4 Delaware B New Zealand
95 M7 Delaware B U.S.A.
95 M7 Delaware City Delaware
108 C4 Delaware Cr Texas/New Mex
94 D6 Delaware Res Ohio
118 E9 Del Bonita Alberta
32 J9 Delbrück W Germany
118 D6 Delburne Alberta
111 E12 Delcambre Louisiana
106 F4 Delcarbon Colorado
46 F3 Delčevo Yugoslavia
87 E8 Delcommune, L Zaïre
25 G4 Delden Netherlands
119 R9 Deleau Manitoba
139 J6 Delegate New S Wales
25 F2 De Leien Netherlands
40 F3 Delémont Switzerland
109 J3 De Leon Texas
29 H11 Delet Teili chan Finland
22 C2 Delettes France
102 B2 Delevan California
94 J4 Delevan New York
130 F7 Delfinópolis Brazil
25 B5 Delfshaven Netherlands
25 B4 Delft Netherlands
83 J8 Delft isld Sri Lanka
25 G2 Delfzijl Netherlands
100 A9 Delgada, Pt California
133 E6 Delgada, Pta Argentina
88 H7 Delgado, C Mozambique
58 D2 Delgerhaan Mongolia
86 F1 Delgo Sudan
74 G4 Delhi India
99 P7 Delhi Iowa
111 E9 Delhi Louisiana
107 L6 Delhi Oklahoma
120 K10 Delhi Ontario
70 K9 Deli isld Java
118 E7 Delia Alberta
107 P2 Delia Kansas
129 H3 Delices Fr Guiana
109 O1 Delight Arkansas
77 B3 Delijan Iran
46 E1 Deli Jovan mt Yugoslavia
118 K7 Delisle Sask
140 B2 Delissaville N Terr Aust
143 F8 Delisser Ra W Australia
69 D11 Delitua Sumatra
33 Q9 Delitzsch E Germany
110 F6 Dell Arkansas
101 N5 Dell Montana
36 C2 Dellbrück W Germany
40 E2 Delle France
101 N9 Delle Utah
103 L5 Dellenbaugh, Mt Arizona
26 J10 Dellen, N L Sweden
32 L9 Delligsen W Germany
100 B9 Del Loma California
98 K6 Dell Rapids S Dakota
107 L2 Dellvale Kansas
85 E1 Dellys Algeria
102 G9 Del Mar California
99 Q7 Delmar Iowa
95 M8 Delmar Maryland
118 J6 Delmas Sask
32 J6 Delmenhorst W Germany
130 H10 Delmiro Gouveia Brazil
98 H6 Delmont S Dakota
103 K4 Delmues Nevada
42 F3 Delnice Yugoslavia
106 D4 Del Norte Colorado
140 C6 Delny N Terr Aust
116 F2 De Long Mts Alaska
119 R9 Deloraine Manitoba
139 H8 Deloraine Tasmania
13 F6 Delph England
46 E6 Delphi Greece
110 K1 Delphi Indiana
107 N2 Delphos Kansas
94 C6 Delphos Ohio
113 G11 Delray Beach Florida
124 D2 Del Río Mexico
108 G6 Del Rio Texas
26 J10 Delsbo Sweden
106 B3 Delta Colorado
110 G4 Delta Missouri
94 C5 Delta Ohio
95 L7 Delta Pennsylvania
103 M2 Delta Utah
119 T8 Delta Beach Manitoba
141 F3 Delta Downs Queensland
116 O4 Delta Junction Alaska
102 C4 Delta Mendota Canal California
95 M3 Delta Res New York
95 L9 Deltaville Virginia
94 B4 Delton Michigan
139 K3 Delungra New S Wales
74 D8 Delvada India
109 K5 Del Valle Texas
32 K4 Delve W Germany
46 D5 Delvinákion Greece
46 D5 Delvinë Albania
108 G2 Delwin Texas
48 J2 Delyatin U.S.S.R.
55 B4 Dema R U.S.S.R.
118 K8 Demaine Sask
70 N9 Demak Java
16 E2 Demando, S. de la mts Spain
116 R2 Demarcation Pt Alaska
86 D7 Demba Zaïre
86 D4 Dembia Cent Afr Republic
86 F4 Dembi Dolo Ethiopia
74 H2 Demchok India
48 G2 Demecser Hungary
22 J2 Demer R Belgium
Demerara see Georgetown Guyana
54 C1 Demidov U.S.S.R.
55 D3 Demina U.S.S.R.
106 C9 Deming New Mexico
100 C1 Deming Washington
128 F3 Demini R Brazil
47 K5 Demirci Turkey
47 J6 Demirköprü Baraji L Turkey
47 J3 Demirköy Turkey
33 S5 Demmin E Germany
128 F5 Democracia Brazil
111 J9 Demopolis Alabama
143 E10 Dempster, Pt W Australia
50 G3 Dem'yanka R U.S.S.R.
52 D5 Demyansk U.S.S.R.
50 F3 Dem'yanskoye U.S.S.R.
22 E3 Denain France
116 O5 Denali Alaska
114 J7 Denare Beach Saskatchewan
57 E5 Denau U.S.S.R.
121 N7 Denbigh Ontario
8 C1 Denbigh Wales
Denbigh co see Clwyd and Gwynedd counties
116 G4 Denbigh, C Alaska
25 B5 Den Bommel Netherlands
25 C2 Den Burg Netherlands
68 E4 Den Chai Thailand
69 J14 Dendang Indonesia
22 G2 Dender R Belgium
22 G2 Denderleeuw Belgium
22 G1 Dendermonde Belgium
25 D3 Den Dever Netherlands
86 G4 Dendi mt Ethiopia
118 K8 Dendron Sask
25 H4 Denekamp Netherlands
55 C1 Denezhkin Kamen', G mt U.S.S.R.
65 B7 Dengfeng China
58 E3 Dengkou China
75 Q3 Dêngqen China
58 F5 Deng Xian China
65 C4 Dengyoufang China
65 E6 Dengzhou China
24 A2 Den Haag conurbation Netherlands
9 F4 Denham England
143 A7 Denham W Australia
142 G3 Denham R W Australia
140 E3 Denham I Queensland
141 J5 Denham Ra Queensland
143 A7 Denham Sd W Australia
111 F11 Denham Springs Louisiana
25 C3 Den Helder Netherlands
118 K6 Denholm Sask
13 F3 Denholm Scotland
17 G7 Denia Spain
138 C4 Denial Bay S Australia
122 C6 Deniau Quebec
139 G6 Deniliquin New S Wales
100 G7 Denio Oregon
99 L7 Denison Iowa
109 L2 Denison Texas
146 J3 Denison, C Antarctica
107 O8 Denison Dam Oklahoma
116 K7 Denison, Mt Alaska
142 G4 Denison Plains W Australia
141 J4 Denison Pt Queensland
55 D4 Denisovka Kazakhstan U.S.S.R.
52 J2 Denisovka Komi U.S.S.R.
83 K11 Deniyaya Sri Lanka
47 K7 Denizli Turkey
37 L6 Denkendorf W Germany
139 K4 Denman New S Wales
146 E3 Denman Gl Antarctica
122 J8 Denmark Nova Scotia
100 A7 Denmark Oregon
112 F4 Denmark S Carolina
143 B10 Denmark W Australia
99 T5 Denmark Wisconsin
28 Denmark kingdom N W Europe
115 R4 Denmark Str Greenland/Iceland
20 B3 Denneville France
33 S9 Dennewitz E Germany
83 J12 Dennis I Seychelles
94 F6 Dennison Ohio
95 R5 Dennis Port Massachusetts
144 C4 Denniston New Zealand
94 H10 Denniston Virginia
100 B9 Denny California
12 E1 Denny Scotland
12 E2 Dennyloanhead Scotland
95 U2 Dennysville Maine
70 P10 Denpasar Bali Indonesia
13 F5 Dent England
100 J3 Dent Idaho
48 G5 Denta Romania
40 G5 Dent Blanche mt Switzerland
40 E5 Dent du Midi mt Switzerland
9 H5 Denton England
112 E6 Denton Georgia
94 E8 Denton Kentucky
95 M8 Denton Maryland
109 K2 Denton Texas
137 L3 D'Entrecasteaux Is Papua New Guinea
106 E2 Denver Colorado
100 J4 Denver Idaho
94 A6 Denver Indiana
99 O7 Denver Iowa
95 L6 Denver Pennsylvania
108 E3 Denver City Texas
118 H6 Denzil Sask
86 B4 Déo R Cameroon
74 G4 Deoband India
75 M6 Deogarh India
68 J4 Deo Hai Van Vietnam
74 E9 Deolali India
68 J6 Deo Ma Vietnam
22 D1 De Panne Belgium
25 E5 De Peel Netherlands
99 S5 De Pere Wisconsin
94 J4 Depew New York
107 O6 Depew Oklahoma
65 C6 Deping China
22 F2 De Pinte Belgium
70 L9 Depok Java
109 M2 Deport Texas
95 M4 Deposit New York
128 F3 Depósito Brazil
95 Q4 Depot New Hampshire
120 K7 Depot Harbour Ontario
146 B5 Depot Pk Antarctica
86 D2 Depression du Murdi Chad
9 E5 Deptford England
142 C5 Depuch I W Australia
99 R8 Depue Illinois
25 G2 De Punt Netherlands
51 O2 Deputatskiy U.S.S.R.
58 C6 Dêqên China
67 D5 Deqing China
67 G1 Deqing China
111 B7 De Queen Arkansas
111 C11 De Quincy Louisiana
77 L5 Dera Bugti Pakistan
74 D3 Dera Ghazi Khan Pakistan
74 D3 Dera Ismail Khan Pakistan
48 L1 Derazhnya U.S.S.R.
33 Q8 Derben E Germany
78 M1 Derbent U.S.S.R.
52 H6 Derbeshkinskiy U.S.S.R.
86 D4 Derbisaka Cent Afr Republic
95 O5 Derby Connecticut
9 E2 Derby England
99 N9 Derby Iowa
107 N4 Derby Kansas
139 J8 Derby Tasmania
109 H7 Derby Texas
142 E3 Derby W Australia
95 P2 Derby Center Vermont
9 E1 Derbyshire co England
16 D9 Derdara Morocco
48 G3 Derecske Hungary
33 N8 Der Elm hills W Germany
33 N9 Derenburg E Germany
52 D4 Derevyanka U.S.S.R.
14 D2 Derg R N Ireland
54 H6 Dergachi U.S.S.R.
14 D2 Derg, L Irish Rep
32 H5 Der Hohe Weg sandbank W Germany
111 C11 De Ridder Louisiana
25 C3 De Rijp Netherlands
86 H5 Derkali Kenya
54 L8 Derkul R U.S.S.R.
47 G1 Dermantsi Bulgaria
37 J2 Dermbach E Germany
111 E8 Dermott Arkansas
Derna see Darnah
87 C11 Dernberg, C Namibia
32 M8 Derneburg W Germany
111 F12 Dernieres, Is Louisiana
138 C2 De Rose Hill S Australia
20 B3 Déroute, Passage de la France
14 D3 Derravaragh, L Irish Rep
Derry see Londonderry
95 Q4 Derry New Hampshire
106 C9 Derry New Mexico
94 H6 Derry Pennsylvania
140 D5 Derry Downs N Terr Aust
14 C2 Derryveagh Mts Irish Rep
36 D1 Derschlag W Germany
9 G2 Dersingham England
86 G2 Derudeb Sudan
95 M4 De Ruyter New York
21 B6 Derval France
46 E6 Dervéni Greece
42 H4 Derventa Yugoslavia
118 F5 Derwent Alberta
140 B6 Derwent N Terr Aust
139 H8 Derwent R Tasmania
139 H8 Derwent Bridge Tasmania
12 E4 Derwent, R England
13 E4 Derwent Water L England
55 E5 Derzhavinsk U.S.S.R.
133 D4 Desaguadero R Argentina
131 B5 Desague, Cerro peak Argentina
110 E7 Des Arc Arkansas
110 F4 Des Arc Missouri
102 G2 Desatoya Mts Nevada
9 F3 Desborough England
130 B5 Descalvado Mato Grosso Brazil
130 F7 Descalvado São Paulo Brazil
102 H9 Descanso California
124 A1 Descanso Mexico
21 G8 Descartes France
121 S6 Deschaillons Quebec
100 E4 Deschutes R Oregon
109 J3 Desdemona Texas
45 M1 Dese R Italy
133 P7 Deseado Argentina
41 N7 Desenzano del Garda Italy
103 M2 Deseret Utah
101 N9 Deseret Pk Utah
121 N8 Deseronto Ontario
103 J8 Desert Center California
102 H8 Desert Hot Springs California
121 O6 Desért, L Quebec
101 M8 Desert Pk Utah
103 J5 Desert Ra Nevada
100 G8 Desert Valley Nevada
103 N5 Desert View Arizona
127 M4 Deshaies Guadeloupe W I
67 A3 Deshengpo China
98 J9 Deshler Nebraska
94 D5 Deshler Ohio
74 E5 Deshnoke India
77 H4 Deshu Afghanistan
124 B1 Desierto de Altar des Mexico
17 H4 Desierto de las Palmas Spain
98 E1 Des Lacs R N Dakota
118 D3 Desmarais Alberta
100 J2 Desmet Idaho
101 L3 De Smet Montana
98 J5 De Smet S Dakota
130 B10 Desmochados Paraguay
99 N8 Des Moines Iowa
106 G5 Des Moines New Mexico
99 M7 Des Moines R Iowa
99 L6 Des Moines R Minnesota
54 B6 Desna R U.S.S.R.
133 C8 Desolación, I Chile
71 G5 Desolation Pt Philippines
110 G4 De Soto Illinois
107 Q3 De Soto Kansas
110 F3 De Soto Missouri
99 P6 De Soto Wisconsin
113 F10 De Soto City Florida
16 E6 Despeñaperros, Pto. de Spain
99 T7 Des Plaines Illinois
48 G6 Despotovac Yugoslavia
83 H5 Desroches isld Seychelles
33 Q9 Dessau E Germany
40 E3 Dessoubre R France
86 G3 Dessye Ethiopia
111 K11 Destin Florida
31 K5 Deštná mt Poland
138 E6 D'Estrees, B S Australia
117 D5 Destruction Bay Yukon Terr
100 A2 Destruction I Washington
143 G6 Destruction,Mt W Australia
22 B2 Desvres France
48 G5 Deta Romania
142 G4 Detached Ra W Australia
32 G6 Detern W Germany
121 N7 Detlor Ontario
32 J9 Detmold W Germany
94 D1 Detour Michigan
94 D1 Detour Passage Michigan
99 U4 Detour, Pt Michigan
94 D4 Detroit Michigan
109 M2 Detroit Texas
122 H4 Détroit d'Honguedo Quebec
99 L3 Detroit Lakes Minnesota
94 D4 Detroit R Michigan
100 C5 Detroit Res Oregon
87 E9 Dett Zimbabwe
37 J4 Dettelbach W Germany
36 G6 Dettenhausen W Germany
36 H3 Detter W Germany
36 F7 Dettingen Baden-Württemberg W Germany
36 G3 Dettingen Bayern W Germany
36 C6 Dettwiller France
68 G5 Det Udom Thailand
48 E2 Detva Czechoslovakia
25 E6 Deurne Netherlands
37 Q2 Deutsch-Einsiedel E Germany
33 R7 Deutschhof E Germany
48 D3 Deutschkreutz Austria
37 P2 Deutsch-Neudorf E Germany
122 B2 Deux Décharges, L Quebec
121 M6 Deux Rivieres Ontario
21 E9 Deux-Sèvres dep France
48 H5 Deva Romania
16 D1 Deva R Spain
110 E7 De Valls Bluff Arkansas
48 F3 Dévaványa Hungary
48 D3 Devecser Hungary
78 E2 Develi Turkey
25 F4 Deventer Netherlands
143 C6 Deverell,Mt W Australia
112 D4 Devereux Georgia
15 F3 Deveron R Scotland
46 E1 Devica mt Yugoslavia
74 D5 Devikot India
20 H3 Deville France
116 E3 Devil Mt Alaska
102 E4 Devil Post Pile Nat.Mon California
145 D4 Devil River Pk New Zealand
108 F5 Devils R Texas
14 D4 Devilsbit Mt Irish Rep
8 C3 Devils Bridge Wales
102 E6 Devils Den California
15 E4 Devil's Elbow Scotland
116 K5 Devils Elbow V Alaska
102 E3 Devils Gate California
89 E1 Devil's Gorge Zambia
6 L6 Devil's Hole North Sea
99 Q2 Devils I Michigan
110 H4 Devil's Kitchen L Illinois
98 H1 Devils Lake N Dakota
100 K8 Devils L. Res Nevada
117 G6 Devils Paw mt Br Col/Alaska
100 C7 Devils Peak mt Oregon
102 E4 Devils Pk California
103 J7 Devils Playground des California
126 G2 Devil's Point Cat I Bahamas
101 O8 Devils Slide Utah
98 B5 Devils Tower Wyoming
139 H7 Devils Tower isld Tasmania
47 G3 Devin Bulgaria
109 J6 Devine Texas
80 C8 Devira Israel
9 E5 Devizes England
74 F6 Devli India

22
Devnya — Douglas Mill

47 J1 **Devnya** Bulgaria
107 M7 **Devol** Oklahoma
46 D4 **Devoll** *R* Albania
118 D5 **Devon** Alberta
101 O1 **Devon** Montana
120 G5 **Devon** Ontario
8 C6 **Devon** *co* England
140 F5 **Devoncourt** Queensland
115 L2 **Devon I** N W Terr
8 B7 **Devonport** England
139 H8 **Devonport** Tasmania
80 E3 **Devora** Israel
78 D1 **Devrez** *R* Turkey
89 G2 **Devuli** *R* Zimbabwe
52 E4 **Devyatiny** U.S.S.R.
55 E2 **Devyatkova** U.S.S.R.
70 F7 **Dewakang Besar** *isld* Indonesia
70 F7 **Dewakang Ketjil** *isld* Indonesia
107 P6 **Dewar** Oklahoma
118 H7 **Dewar Lake** Sask
74 G7 **Dewas** India
69 B11 **Dewa, Udjung** *C* Indonesia
118 G5 **Dewberry** Alberta
98 H9 **Deweese** Nebraska
103 M7 **Dewey** Arizona
107 P5 **Dewey** Oklahoma
98 C6 **Dewey** S Dakota
94 E9 **Dewey Res** Kentucky
22 E1 **De Wielingen** Belgium/Neths
118 C8 **De Winton** Alberta
111 E7 **De Witt** Arkansas
94 C4 **De Witt** Michigan
110 C2 **De Witt** Missouri
98 K9 **De Witt** Nebraska
13 G6 **Dewsbury** England
67 F2 **Dexing** China
111 D7 **Dexter** Arkansas
99 M8 **Dexter** Iowa
107 O4 **Dexter** Kansas
95 S1 **Dexter** Maine
94 D4 **Dexter** Michigan
99 O6 **Dexter** Minnesota
110 G5 **Dexter** Missouri
108 C2 **Dexter** New Mexico
95 L2 **Dexter** New York
109 L2 **Dexter** Texas
113 F8 **Dexter, L** Florida
99 Q5 **Dexterville** Wisconsin
138 B3 **Dey-Dey, L** S Australia
22 L3 **Deyfeldt** Belgium
77 E3 **Deyhuk** Iran
57 C5 **Deynau** U.S.S.R.
77 B6 **Deyyer** Iran
117 E5 **Dezadeash L** Yukon Terr
72 F2 **Dezfūl** Iran
77 A3 **Dezfūl** Iran
77 B4 **Dez Gerd** Iran
65 C6 **Dezhou** China
78 L4 **Dezh Shahpur** Iran
41 M6 **Dezzo** Italy
46 E7 **Dháfni** Greece
79 G6 **Dhahab, Wādī** *watercourse* Syria
79 D3 **Dhali** Cyprus
75 J8 **Dhamtari** India
75 M7 **Dhanbad** India
74 J4 **Dhangarhi** Nepal
109 H6 **D'Hanis** Texas
75 M5 **Dhankuta** Nepal
76 D6 **Dhanuskodi** India
74 F7 **Dhar** India
76 C5 **Dharapuram** India
75 K7 **Dharmajaygarh** India
76 D4 **Dharmapuri** India
76 C3 **Dharmavaram** India
74 G2 **Dharmsala** India
85 C5 **Dhar Oualata** *plat* Mauritania
76 B3 **Dharwar** India
66 C6 **Dhaulagiri** *mt* Nepal
74 G5 **Dhaulpur** India
75 L8 **Dhenkanal** India
47 H7 **Dhenoúsa** *isld* Greece
46 D4 **Dhërmi** Albania
46 E5 **Dheskáti** Greece
47 G8 **Dhespotikó** *isld* Greece
40 A4 **Dheune** *R* France
80 G7 **Dhiban** Jordan
46 F7 **Dhídhimoi** Greece
47 H3 **Dhidhimótikhon** Greece
47 G9 **Dhíkti Ori** *mt* Crete Greece
47 G7 **Dhílos** *isld* Greece
46 E7 **Dhimitsána** Greece
80 F8 **Dhira** Jordan
47 F6 **Dhírfis** *mt* Greece
74 G5 **Dholpur** India
46 E5 **Dhomokós** Greece
74 F9 **Dhond** India
76 C3 **Dhone** India
74 D8 **Dhoraji** India
47 G3 **Dhoxáton** Greece
47 G7 **Dhragonísi** *isld* Greece
74 D7 **Dhrangadhra** India
47 F5 **Dhrépanon, Ákr** *C* Greece
46 D5 **Dhrin** *R* Albania
75 N5 **Dhubri** India
72 G5 **Dhufar** *prov* Oman
21 I6 **Dhuison** France
74 F8 **Dhule** India
74 E2 **Dhulian** Pakistan
47 G9 **Día** *isld* Crete Greece
129 H2 **Diable, I.du** Fr Guiana
40 F5 **Diablerets** *mt* Switzerland
100 D1 **Diablo L** Washington
127 K2 **Diablo, Mt** Jamaica
108 C4 **Diablo, Sa** *mts* Texas
127 O7 **Diablotin, Morne** *hill* Dominica
99 M9 **Diagonal** Iowa
85 B6 **Dialakoto** Senegal
131 E4 **Diamante** Argentina
133 D4 **Diamante** *R* Argentina
129 K7 **Diamantina** Brazil
130 G6 **Diamantina** Minas Gerais Brazil
141 F6 **Diamantina** *R* Queensland
141 F6 **Diamantina Lakes** Queensland
81 G9 **Diamantina Trench** Indian Oc
129 G6 **Diamantino** Brazil
130 C4 **Diamantino** Mato Grosso Brazil
130 D5 **Diamantino** Mato Grosso Brazil
110 B5 **Diamond** Missouri
118 E9 **Diamond City** Alberta
75 N7 **Diamond Harb** India
102 S12 **Diamond Hd** Hawaiian Is
141 K3 **Diamond Islets** Gt Barrier Reef Australia
100 C6 **Diamond L** Oregon
103 J2 **Diamond Mts** Nevada
100 C6 **Diamond Peak** *mt* Oregon
103 J2 **Diamond Pk** Nevada
102 D3 **Diamond Springs** California
101 P8 **Diamondville** Wyoming
94 G8 **Diana** W Virginia
141 J3 **Diana Bank** Gt Barrier Reef Aust
28 G5 **Dianaland** Denmark
67 C6 **Dianbai** China
Dianbu *see* **Feidong**
67 A4 **Dian Chi** *L* China
67 B1 **Dianjiang** China
44 D4 **Diano Marina** Italy
129 J6 **Dianópolis** Brazil
65 H2 **Diaoling** China
85 E6 **Diapaga** Upper Volta
71 F2 **Diapitan B** Luzon Philippines
46 F4 **Diavata** Greece
68 A6 **Diavolo, Mt** Andaman Is
65 A5 **Dibabu** China
87 D7 **Dibaya** Zaïre
86 D3 **Dibbis** Sudan
146 J3 **Dibble Iceberg Tongue** Antarctica
66 F6 **Dibhuk Pass** India/Burma
86 B4 **Dibi** Cameroon
109 N4 **Diboll** Texas
66 E6 **Dibrugarh** India
75 Q5 **Dibrugarh** India
71 E3 **Dicapanisan Pt** Luzon Philippines
Diciosănmărtin *see* **Tîrnăveni**
98 E9 **Dickens** Nebraska
108 G2 **Dickens** Texas
95 R6 **Dickey** Maine
98 H3 **Dickey** N Dakota
98 D3 **Dickinson** N Dakota
109 M6 **Dickinson** Texas
9 H3 **Dickleburgh** England
36 D3 **Dickscheid-Geroldstein** W Germany
110 J5 **Dickson** Tennessee
95 M5 **Dickson City** Pennsylvania
78 H3 **Dicle** *R* Turkey
45 L4 **Dicomano** Italy
71 F1 **Didacas** *isld* Luzon Philippines
9 E4 **Didcot** England
85 C6 **Didiéni** Mali
109 L8 **Dido** Texas
118 C7 **Didsbury** Alberta
74 F5 **Didwana** India
121 S4 **Didyme** Quebec
19 O15 **Die** France
89 G5 **Die Berg** *mt* S Africa
36 B5 **Diebling** France
85 D6 **Diébougou** Upper Volta
36 F4 **Dieburg** W Germany
118 K7 **Diefenbaker, L** Sask
33 N6 **Die Göhrde** *reg* W Germany
131 F3 **Diego Lamas** Uruguay
133 D9 **Diego Ramírez, Is** Chile
Diego Suarez *see* **Antseranana**
30 D1 **Die Halligen** *inlet* W Germany
32 L8 **Diekholzen** W Germany
22 L4 **Diekirch** Luxembourg
20 B2 **Diélette** France
32 H8 **Dielingen** W Germany
85 C6 **Diema** Mali
32 K9 **Diemel** *R* W Germany
36 C6 **Diemeringen** France
68 F2 **Dien Bien Phu** Vietnam
32 J8 **Diepenau** W Germany
25 G4 **Diepenheim** Netherlands
32 H7 **Diepholz** W Germany
20 H2 **Dieppe** France
127 P4 **Dieppe Bay Town** St Kitts W I
36 D2 **Dierdorf** W Germany
25 F4 **Dieren** Netherlands
33 Q4 **Dierhagen** E Germany
36 D2 **Dieringhausen** W Germany
109 N1 **Dierks** Arkansas
65 F2 **Di'er Songhua Jiang** *R* China
33 N7 **Diesdorf** E Germany
41 J2 **Diessenhofen** Switzerland
22 J2 **Diest** Belgium
110 H2 **Dieterich** Illinois
37 K3 **Dietersdorf** W Germany
37 M5 **Dietfurt** W Germany
41 H3 **Dietikon** Switzerland
101 L7 **Dietrich** Idaho
36 F3 **Dietzenbach** W Germany
19 O15 **Dieulefit** France
19 K4 **Dieuze** France
25 F3 **Dieverbrug** Netherlands
36 B2 **Die Ville** *reg* W Germany
36 E3 **Diez** W Germany
86 H5 **Dif** Somalia
65 D7 **Difang** China
22 K4 **Differdange** Luxembourg
131 H5 **Difuntos ó Negra, L** Uruguay
67 F1 **Digang** China
75 Q5 **Digboi** India
9 F1 **Digby** England
122 G9 **Digby** Nova Scotia
83 M14 **Digby, C** Kerguelen Indian Oc
122 F9 **Digby Neck** Nova Scotia
107 K3 **Dighton** Kansas
95 Q5 **Dighton** Massachusetts
94 B2 **Dighton** Michigan
74 G9 **Diglur** India
19 Q16 **Digne** France
20 H4 **Digny** France
18 H6 **Digoin** France
71 F2 **Digollorin Pt** Luzon Philippines
71 G7 **Digos** Mindanao Philippines
74 G8 **Digras** India
136 H3 **Digul** *R* W Irian
71 E5 **Diit** *isld* Philippines
22 H2 **Dijle** *R* Belgium
19 J5 **Dijon** France
86 C4 **Dik** Chad
26 H6 **Dikanäs** Sweden
86 H3 **Dikhil** Djibouti
47 H5 **Dikili** Turkey
79 B7 **Dîkirnis** Egypt
22 D2 **Dikkebus** Belgium
67 F3 **Dikou** China
83 K11 **Dikoya** Sri Lanka
55 D2 **Dikoye, Oz** *L* U.S.S.R.
22 D1 **Diksmuide** Belgium
50 H1 **Dikson** U.S.S.R.
50 G1 **Dikson, Ostrov** *isld* U.S.S.R.
86 B3 **Dikwa** Nigeria
77 H3 **Dilaram** Afghanistan
71 M9 **Dili** Timor
106 E6 **Dilia** New Mexico
68 A6 **Diligent Str** Andaman Is
68 J7 **Di Linh** Vietnam
119 M8 **Dilke** Sask
103 O6 **Dilkon** Arizona
36 E2 **Dill** *R* W Germany
141 H7 **Dillalah** Queensland
118 G6 **Dillberry L. Prov Park** Alberta
141 G5 **Dillcar** Queensland
107 L6 **Dill City** Oklahoma
36 E2 **Dillenburg** W Germany
98 K9 **Diller** Nebraska
109 H7 **Dilley** Texas
86 E3 **Dilling** Sudan
36 B5 **Dillingen** W Germany
116 H7 **Dillingham** Alaska
106 D2 **Dillon** Colorado
101 N4 **Dillon** Montana
118 H3 **Dillon** Sask
112 H3 **Dillon** S Carolina
144 D5 **Dillon Cone** *mt* New Zealand
94 E6 **Dillon Res** Ohio
95 K6 **Dillsburg** Pennsylvania
94 J9 **Dillwyn** Virginia
87 D8 **Dilolo** Zaïre
75 P6 **Dimapur** India
124 F6 **Dimas** Mexico
86 D7 **Dimbelenge** Zaïre
85 D7 **Dimbokro** Ivory Coast
138 F6 **Dimboola** Victoria
48 J5 **Dîmbo Viţa** *R* Romania
141 H3 **Dimbulah** Queensland
54 E8 **Dimitrova** U.S.S.R.
47 G2 **Dimitrov Dam** Bulgaria
47 H2 **Dimitrovgrad** Bulgaria
53 G7 **Dimitrovgrad** U.S.S.R.
46 F1 **Dimitrovgrad** Yugoslavia
108 E1 **Dimmitt** Texas
98 H6 **Dimock** S Dakota
79 F7 **Dīmona** Israel
71 G5 **Dinagat** *isld* Philippines
71 G5 **Dinagat Sound** Philippines
75 N6 **Dinajpur** Bangladesh
20 A5 **Dinan** France
22 H3 **Dinant** Belgium
47 L6 **Dinar** Turkey
42 G4 **Dinara Planina** Yugoslavia
20 A4 **Dinard St Enogat** France
86 F3 **Dinder** *R* Sudan
76 C5 **Dindigul** India
109 K7 **Dinero** Texas
86 C7 **Dinga** Zaïre
71 E3 **Dingalan B** Luzon Philippines
68 K3 **Ding'an** China
58 E4 **Dingbian** China
32 E9 **Dingden** W Germany
20 B5 **Dingé** France
33 M10 **Dingelstädt** E Germany
33 O9 **Dingelstedt** E Germany
48 K3 **Dîngem** Romania
75 M4 **Dinggyê** China
67 G1 **Dinghai** China
101 O7 **Dingle** Idaho
14 A4 **Dingle B** Irish Rep
67 E4 **Dingnan** China
141 J6 **Dingo** Queensland
37 O6 **Dingolfing** W Germany
71 E1 **Dingras** Luzon Philippines
65 C7 **Dingtao** China
85 B6 **Dinguiraye** Guinea
123 M7 **Dingwall** C Breton I, N S
15 D3 **Dingwall** Scotland
58 D4 **Dingxi** China
65 C5 **Ding Xian** China
65 B5 **Dingxiang** China
65 C5 **Dingxing** China
65 E6 **Dingzi Gang** *B* China
69 H8 **Dinh An, Cua** *river mth* Vietnam
67 B6 **Dinh Lap** Vietnam
25 H4 **Dinkel** *R* Netherlands
37 J5 **Dinkelsbühl** W Germany
37 K7 **Dinkelscherben** W Germany
32 H7 **Dinklage** W Germany
103 O5 **Dinnebito Wash** *creek* Arizona
13 G3 **Dinnington** England
87 E10 **Dinokwe** Botswana
118 K1 **Dinorwic L** Ontario
101 Q9 **Dinosaur Nat.Mon** Utah/Colo
32 E9 **Dinslaken** W Germany
113 F7 **Dinsmore** Florida
118 K7 **Dinsmore** Sask
86 H5 **Dinsor** Somalia
102 E5 **Dinuba** California
94 K9 **Dinwiddie** Virginia
25 F5 **Dinxperlo** Netherlands
27 G15 **Diö** Sweden
85 C6 **Dioila** Mali
116 C4 **Diomede Is** Bering Str
51 S2 **Diomida, Ostrova** *islds* U.S.S.R.
22 H3 **Dion** Belgium
86 D2 **Diona** Chad
130 D10 **Dionisio Cerqueira** Brazil
130 D5 **Diorama** Brazil
48 F2 **Diósgyör** Hungary
85 A6 **Diouloulou** Senegal
85 C6 **Dioura** Mali
85 A6 **Diourbel** Senegal
74 C6 **Diplo** Pakistan
71 F6 **Dipolog** Mindanao Philippines
22 L4 **Dippach** Luxembourg
12 C2 **Dippen** Scotland
12 C3 **Dippin** Scotland
144 B6 **Dipton** New Zealand
74 D1 **Dir** Pakistan
27 B13 **Dirdal** Norway
141 G2 **Direction,C** Queensland
83 M8 **Direction I** Cocos Is Indian Oc
86 H4 **Diredawa** Ethiopia
125 L4 **Diriamba** Nicaragua
87 D9 **Dirico** Angola
43 F11 **Dirillo** *R* Sicily
143 A7 **Dirk Hartog I** W Australia
84 E6 **Dirkou** Niger
25 B5 **Dirksland** Netherlands
13 F1 **Dirleton** Scotland
47 K8 **Dirmil** Turkey
36 C5 **Dirmingen** W Germany
86 E3 **Dirra** Sudan
141 J8 **Dirranbandi** Queensland
86 J5 **Dirri** Somalia
103 O3 **Dirty Devil** *R* Utah
102 T13 **Disappearing I** Hawaiian Is
146 E14 **Disappointment, C** Antarctica
133 J8 **Disappointment, C** S Georgia
100 A3 **Disappointment, C** Washington
135 N9 **Disappointment Is** Tuamotu Arch **Pac Oc**
143 E6 **Disappointment,L** W Australia
139 K6 **Disaster B** New S Wales
100 F1 **Disautel** Washington
37 J6 **Dischingen** W Germany
117 Q4 **Discovery** N W Terr
138 F7 **Discovery B** S Aust/Vict
127 K1 **Discovery Bay** Jamaica
100 C2 **Discovery Bay** Washington
100 C1 **Discovery I** Washington
90 K13 **Discovery Tablemount** S Atlantic Oc
142 E5 **Discovery Well** W Australia
41 J4 **Disentis** Switzerland
13 G5 **Dishforth** England
116 J5 **Dishkakat** Alaska
116 J5 **Dishna** *R* Alaska
80 F1 **Dishon** Israel
80 F1 **Dishon** *R* Israel
115 O4 **Diskofjord** Greenland
119 M8 **Disley** Sask
98 F8 **Dismal** *R* Nebraska
140 F4 **Dismal** *R* Queensland
95 L10 **Dismal Swamp** Virginia
52 C6 **Disna** U.S.S.R.
22 K2 **Dison** Belgium
95 K9 **Disputanta** Virginia
121 T7 **Disraëli** Quebec
9 H3 **Diss** England
21 F8 **Dissay** France
32 H8 **Dissen** W Germany
122 C4 **Dissimieux, L** Quebec
100 C6 **Disston** Oregon
95 L8 **District of Columbia (D.C.)** U.S.A.
79 A7 **Disûq** Egypt
9 F6 **Ditchling** England
33 O9 **Ditfurt** E Germany
32 K4 **Dithmarschen** *reg* W Germany
43 F11 **Dittaino** *R* Sicily
74 D8 **Diu** India
71 G6 **Diuata Mts** Mindanao Philippines
52 D5 **Divenskaya** U.S.S.R.
121 L6 **Diver** Ontario
110 G2 **Divernon** Illinois
142 G3 **Diversion Dam** W Australia
109 H2 **Diversion L** Texas
20 E3 **Dives** *R* France
20 E3 **Dives-sur-Mer** France
20 B2 **Divette** *R* France
26 L3 **Dividal** *R* Norway
106 E3 **Divide** Colorado
143 C6 **Dividing Ra** W Australia
141 H6 **Dividing Range** Queensland
71 F2 **Divilacan B** Luzon Philippines
87 F10 **Divinhe** Mozambique
130 G7 **Divinopólis** Brazil
22 C3 **Divion** France
100 F8 **Division Peak** *mt* Nevada
53 F10 **Divnoye** U.S.S.R.
85 C7 **Divo** Ivory Coast
78 G2 **Divrigi** Turkey
74 B5 **Diwana** Pakistan
72 F2 **Dīwānīyah, Ad** Iraq
98 C8 **Dix** Nebraska
121 O4 **Dix** Quebec
95 R2 **Dixfield** Maine
111 K8 **Dixiana** Alabama
111 K10 **Dixie** Alabama
113 D7 **Dixie** Georgia
100 K4 **Dixie** Idaho
100 G3 **Dixie** Washington
100 G5 **Dixie Pass** Oregon
102 F2 **Dixie Valley** Nevada
121 Q5 **Dix Milles, L.des** Quebec
95 S2 **Dixmont** Maine
95 O2 **Dix Mt** New York
Dixmude *see* **Diksmuide**
102 C3 **Dixon** California
99 R8 **Dixon** Illinois
110 D4 **Dixon** Missouri
101 L2 **Dixon** Montana
98 K7 **Dixon** Nebraska
106 E5 **Dixon** New Mexico
101 S8 **Dixon** Wyoming
117 G8 **Dixon Entrance** *str* Br Col/Alaska
111 J9 **Dixons Mills** Alabama
117 P7 **Dixonville** Alberta
94 H6 **Dixonville** Pennsylvania
146 J4 **Dixson I** Antarctica
67 A4 **Dixu** China
121 T7 **Dixville** Quebec
65 H3 **Diyingou** China
74 B9 **Diz** Pakistan
67 C2 **Dizhuang** China
8 B6 **Dizzard Pt** England
86 B5 **Dja** *R* Cameroon
84 E5 **Djado** Niger
84 E5 **Djado, Pl.du** Niger
71 A2 **Djailolo** Halmahera Indonesia
Djailolo Gilolo *isld see* **Halmahera** *isld*
Djajapura *see* **Jayapura**
86 B6 **Djambala** Congo
69 F13 **Djambi** *prov* Sumatra
70 L9 **Djampang-Kulon** Java
85 F4 **Djanet** Algeria
70 E6 **Djangeru** Kalimantan
70 D5 **Djangkang** Kalimantan
70 E3 **Djanlonong** Kalimantan
85 E3 **Djaret** *watercourse* Algeria
70 M9 **Djatibarang** Java
70 L9 **Djatinegara** Java
70 M9 **Djatiwangi** Java
86 B2 **Djbella** Niger
69 G13 **Djebus** Indonesia
86 C3 **Djédaa** Chad
85 E2 **Djedi** *watercourse* Algeria
85 E2 **Djelfa** Algeria
70 O10 **Djember** Java
70 E5 **Djempang** *L* Kalimantan
70 F7 **Djeneponto** Sulawesi
70 N9 **Djepara** Java
Djerba, I de *see* **Jerba, I de**
86 B4 **Djerem** *R* Cameroon
Djezair, El *see* **Alger**
85 D6 **Djibasso** Upper Volta
85 D6 **Djibo** Upper Volta
86 H3 **Djibouti** Djibouti
86 H3 **Djibouti** *rep* N E Africa
86 D5 **Djolu** Zaïre
70 O9 **Djombang** Java
70 D7 **Djorong** Kalimantan
86 B6 **Djoué** *R* Congo
85 C5 **Djouf, El** *reg* Mauritania/Mali
85 E7 **Djougou** Benin
86 B5 **Djoum** Cameroon
86 C2 **Djourab** *dist* Chad
86 F5 **Djugu** Zaïre
115 S5 **Djúpivogur** Iceland
27 H11 **Djura** Sweden
27 K12 **Djursholm** Sweden
28 E4 **Djursland** *reg* Denmark
70 N9 **Djuwono** Java
111 G10 **D'Lo** Mississippi
51 O1 **Dmitriya Lapteva, Proliv** *str* U.S.S.R.
55 G3 **Dmitriyevka** U.S.S.R.
54 G4 **Dmitriyev-L'govskiy** U.S.S.R.
54 J1 **Dmitrov** U.S.S.R.
54 G4 **Dmitrovsk-Orlovskiy** U.S.S.R.
54 B4 **Dnepr** *R* U.S.S.R.
54 F8 **Dneprodzerzhinsk** U.S.S.R.
54 G8 **Dnepropetrovsk** U.S.S.R.
54 F9 **Dneprorudnoye** U.S.S.R.
53 C7 **Dneprovskaya Nizmennost** *lowland* U.S.S.R.
54 C10 **Dneprovskiy Liman** *lagoon* U.S.S.R.
53 C9 **Dnestr** *R* Europe
48 N4 **Dnestrovskiy Liman** *lagoon* Ukraine **U.S.S.R.**
Dnieper *R see* **Dnepr** *R*
Dniester *R see* **Dnestr** *R*
52 C5 **Dno** U.S.S.R.
77 K2 **Doāb Mekh-i-Zarīn** Afghanistan
122 F7 **Doaktown** New Brunswick
70 E7 **Doangdoangan Besar** *isld* Indonesia
70 E7 **Doangdoangan Ketjil** *isld* Indonesia
67 B6 **Doan Hung** Vietnam
86 C4 **Doba** Chad
33 Q5 **Dobbertin** E Germany
138 E2 **Dobbie, L** S Australia
140 E6 **Dobbie,Mt** N Terr **Aust**
109 M5 **Dobbin** Texas
140 E4 **Dobbyn** Queensland
31 M6 **Dobczyce** Poland
52 B6 **Dobele** U.S.S.R.
37 P1 **Döbeln** E Germany
33 T9 **Doberlug Kirchhain** E Germany
31 J3 **Dobiegniew** Poland
133 E5 **Doblas** Argentina
136 G3 **Dobo** Moluccas **Indonesia**
48 E6 **Doboj** Yugoslavia
112 F6 **Doboy Sd** Georgia
31 J2 **Dobra** Poland
37 M3 **Döbraberg** *mt* **W Germany**
37 P4 **Dobřany** Czechoslovakia
38 J8 **Dobratsch** *mt* Austria
31 M2 **Dobre Miasto** Poland
48 G4 **Dobresti** Romania
38 J8 **Döbriach** Austria
33 S9 **Döbrichau** E Germany
47 F3 **Dobrinisnta** Bulgaria
31 H6 **Dobříš** Czechoslovakia
31 L5 **Dobrodzień** Poland
31 O6 **Dobromil** U.S.S.R.
54 J8 **Dobropol'ye** U.S.S.R.
48 J6 **Dobroteşti** Romania
54 C4 **Dobrush** U.S.S.R.
54 C4 **Dobryanka** U.S.S.R.
31 L3 **Dobrzyn** Poland
48 F2 **Dobšiná** Czechoslovakia
112 G1 **Dobson** N Carolina
144 B6 **Dobson** *R* New Zealand
8 B7 **Dobwalls** England
127 N1 **Docas del Dragón** *chan* Trinidad/Ven
71 D7 **Doc Can** *isld* Sulu Arch Philippines
130 G6 **Doce, R** Brazil
143 G6 **Docker Cr** W Australia
9 G2 **Docking** England
26 H9 **Dockmyr** Sweden
142 F4 **Dockrell, Mt** W Australia
36 B3 **Dockweiler** W Germany
109 H10 **Doctor Cos** Mexico
143 E8 **Doctor Hicks Ra** W Australia
48 G4 **Doctor Petru Croza** Romania
121 P3 **Doda, L** Quebec
76 C4 **Dod Ballapur** India
13 F2 **Doddington** England
109 O2 **Doddridge** Arkansas
118 E5 **Dodds** Alberta
Dodecanese *see* **Sporádhes** *Is*
98 D2 **Dodge** N Dakota
98 K8 **Dodge** Nebraska
99 O5 **Dodge Center** Minnesota
107 K4 **Dodge City** Kansas
99 Q7 **Dodgeville** Wisconsin
8 B7 **Dodman Pt** England
88 E5 **Dodoma** Tanzania
33 O6 **Dodow** E Germany
118 J7 **Dodsland** Sask
109 P3 **Dodson** Louisiana
101 R1 **Dodson** Montana
47 K5 **Dodurga** Turkey
22 G1 **Doel** Belgium
112 D6 **Doerun** Georgia
25 F4 **Doesburg** Netherlands
25 F5 **Doetinchem** Netherlands
36 F6 **Doffingen** W Germany
66 D5 **Dogai Coring** *L* China
47 H6 **Doğanbey Burun** *C* Turkey
117 M10 **Dog Creek** Br Columbia
47 L5 **Döğer** Turkey
7 M8 **Dogger Bank** North Sea
113 C8 **Dog I** Florida
127 N5 **Dog I** Lesser Antilles
144 B7 **Dog I** New Zealand
119 T7 **Dog L** Manitoba
99 R1 **Dog L** Ontario
44 C2 **Dogliani** Italy
38 H9 **Dogna** Italy
60 G9 **Dōgo** *isld* Japan
85 E6 **Dogondoutchi** Niger
60 G10 **Dōgo-yama** *mt* Japan
118 C7 **Dog Pound** Alberta
126 E2 **Dog Rocks** Bahamas
78 K2 **Doğubayazit** Turkey
141 K7 **Dogwood** *R* Queensland
127 P4 **Dogwood Pt** Nevis W I
77 B7 **Doha** Qatar
74 F7 **Dohad** India
75 P7 **Dohazar** Bangladesh
121 S5 **Doheny** Quebec
33 N4 **Döhnsdorf** W Germany
71 A1 **Doi** Indonesia
68 D3 **Doi Saket** Thailand
22 H3 **Doische** Belgium
130 E8 **Dois Córregos** Brazil
21 D9 **Doix** France
46 F3 **Dojran** Yugoslavia
46 F3 **Dojransko, Jez** *L* Yugoslavia
27 D11 **Dokka** Norway
26 M4 **Dokkas** Sweden
28 E3 **Dokkedal** Denmark
25 E2 **Dokkum** Netherlands
54 J9 **Dokuchayevsk** U.S.S.R.
136 H3 **Dolak** *isld* W Irian
98 H5 **Doland** S Dakota
121 S4 **Dolbeau** Quebec
32 G9 **Dolberg** W Germany
20 B4 **Dol-de-Bretagne** France
19 J5 **Dôle** France
125 N5 **Dolega** Panama
8 C3 **Dolfor** Wales
8 C2 **Dolgellau** Wales
95 N3 **Dolgeville** New York
116 G9 **Dolgoi I** Alaska
48 H2 **Dolgoye** U.S.S.R.
43 C9 **Dolianova** Sardinia
48 H2 **Dolina** U.S.S.R.
59 M2 **Dolinsk** U.S.S.R.
54 D8 **Dolinskaya** U.S.S.R.
75 K5 **Dolirighat** India
47 F1 **Dolj** Romania
46 E1 **Doljevac** Yugoslavia
38 G8 **Döllach** Austria
12 E1 **Dollar** Scotland
118 J9 **Dollard** Sask
122 F3 **Dollard, L** Quebec
15 E5 **Dollar Law** *mt* Scotland
32 F6 **Dollart** *inlet* W Germany/Neths
32 M8 **Dollbergen** W Germany
33 P8 **Dolle** E Germany
146 E13 **Dolleman I** Antarctica
28 C4 **Dollerup** Denmark
37 L6 **Dollnstein** W Germany
20 G5 **Dollon** France
37 K1 **Döllstädt** E Germany
46 E3 **Dolneni** Yugoslavia
37 Q2 **Dolní Jiřetín** Czechoslovakia
31 J6 **Dolní Královice** Czechoslovakia
37 O3 **Dolní Žandov** Czechoslovakia
86 H5 **Dolo** Ethiopia
45 M1 **Dolo** Italy
19 P13 **Dolomieu** France
42 D2 **Dolomitiche, Alpi** Italy
Dolonnur *see* **Duolun**
131 F6 **Dolores** Argentina
106 B4 **Dolores** Colorado
125 P9 **Dolores** Guatemala
17 G6 **Dolores** Spain
131 F4 **Dolores** Uruguay
106 B3 **Dolores** *R* Colorado
125 J7 **Dolores Hidalgo** Mexico
133 F8 **Dolphin, C** Falkland Is
87 B11 **Dolphin Hd** Namibia
127 H1 **Dolphin Hd** *hill* Jamaica
142 B5 **Dolphin I** W Australia
13 E2 **Dolphinton** Scotland
114 H4 **Dolphin & Union Str** N W Terr
38 G8 **Dölsach** Austria
31 K4 **Dolsk** Poland
21 G7 **Dolus-le-Sec** France
8 C1 **Dolwyddelan** Wales
136 H2 **Dom** *mt* W Irian
122 H2 **Domagaya L** Labrador
119 U9 **Domain** Manitoba
47 K5 **Domaniç** Turkey
47 K5 **Domaniç Daği** *mt* Turkey
20 K1 **Domart** France
37 O5 **Domažlice** Czechoslovakia
50 E3 **Dombarovskiy** U.S.S.R.
26 D9 **Dombås** Norway
19 K4 **Dombasle** France
87 B8 **Dombe Grande** Angola
140 A2 **Dombey,C** N Terr Aust
138 E6 **Dombey, C** S Australia
48 E4 **Dombóvár** Hungary
48 G2 **Dombrád** Hungary
37 J5 **Dombühl** W Germany
25 A5 **Domburg** Netherlands
103 K9 **Dome** Arizona
117 N9 **Dome Creek** Br Col
40 E7 **Dôme-de-Chasseforêt** France
103 K8 **Dome Rock Mts** Arizona
144 C6 **Domet, Mt** New Zealand
144 D5 **Domett** New Zealand
145 D4 **Domett, Mt** New Zealand
36 B6 **Domèvre** France
20 D4 **Domfront** France
106 D6 **Domingo** New Mexico
127 O7 **Dominica** *isld* Lesser Antilles
127 J5 **Dominican Rep** W Indies
123 M7 **Dominion** C Breton I, N Scotia
115 M4 **Dominion, C** N W Terr
119 U9 **Dominion City** Manitoba
123 L1 **Dominion L** Labrador
146 G7 **Dominion Ra** Antarctica
115 O7 **Domino** Labrador
33 O6 **Dömitz** E Germany
20 C4 **Domjean** France
130 G6 **Dom Joaquim** Brazil
41 K4 **Domleschg** *R* Switzerland
18 F8 **Domme** France
25 D6 **Dommel** *R* Netherlands
33 R9 **Dommitzsch** E Germany
54 J1 **Domodedovo** U.S.S.R.
41 H5 **Domodossola** Italy
40 D1 **Dompaire** France
20 C5 **Dompierre du-Chemin** France
22 B3 **Dompierre-sur-Authie** France
21 C9 **Dompierre-sur-Mer** France
36 B7 **Domptail** France
71 J9 **Dompu** Sumbawa Indonesia
119 M6 **Domremy** Sask
26 K8 **Domsjö** Sweden
88 E9 **Domue** *peak* Mozambique
131 B6 **Domuyo** *peak* Argentina
139 K3 **Domville** *mt* Queensland
141 K8 **Domville,Mt** Queensland
46 F6 **Domvraína** Greece
42 F2 **Domzale** Yugoslavia
22 D2 **Don** France
124 E4 **Don** Mexico
21 B6 **Don** *R* France
141 J5 **Don** *R* Queensland
15 F3 **Don** *R* Scotland
54 L5 **Don** *R* U.S.S.R.
106 D9 **Dona Ana** New Mexico
45 M1 **Donada** Italy
14 F2 **Donaghadee** N Ireland
121 M8 **Donald** Ontario
139 G6 **Donald** Victoria
118 E6 **Donalda** Alberta
144 A6 **Donald, Mt** New Zealand
109 P1 **Donaldson** Arkansas
98 K1 **Donaldson** Minnesota
140 F4 **Donaldson** Queensland
111 E11 **Donaldsonville** Louisiana
112 C6 **Donalsonville** Georgia
14 E3 **Donard** Irish Rep
124 G5 **Donato Guerra** Mexico
38 L5 **Donau** *R* Austria
37 L6 **Donau** *R* W Germany
41 J2 **Donaueschingen** W Germany
37 L6 **Donaumoos** *reg* W Germany
37 K6 **Donauried** *reg* W Germany
37 N5 **Donaustauf** W Germany
37 K6 **Donauwörth** W Germany
118 K7 **Donavon** Sask
38 M7 **Donawitz** Austria
54 J8 **Donbass (Donetskiy Ugol'nyy Basseyn)** U.S.S.R.
16 D6 **Don Benito** Spain
140 B1 **Don,C** N Terr Aust
13 G6 **Doncaster** England
95 K8 **Doncaster** Maryland
22 H4 **Donchery** France
22 K4 **Doncols** Luxembourg
87 B7 **Dondo** Angola
87 F9 **Dondo** Mozambique
71 H5 **Dondo** Sulawesi
71 E6 **Dondonay** *isld* Philippines
70 G4 **Dondo, Teluk** *B* Sulawesi
70 G4 **Dondo, Tg** *C* Sulawesi
73 N7 **Dondra Head** *C* Sri Lanka
48 L2 **Dondyushany** U.S.S.R.
14 C2 **Donegal** Irish Rep
14 D2 **Donegal** *co* Irish Rep
14 B4 **Donegal Pt** Irish Rep
145 D1 **Donelly's Crossing** New Zealand
110 K5 **Donelson** Tennessee
14 C4 **Doneraile** Irish Rep
54 J8 **Donetsk** U.S.S.R.
53 E9 **Donetskiy Kryazh** *mts* U.S.S.R.
127 J2 **Don Figuerero Mts** Jamaica
86 B4 **Donga** *R* Nigeria
59 K2 **Dong'an** China
67 D3 **Dong'an** China
68 J5 **Dong An** Vietnam
143 A8 **Dongara** W Australia
74 J8 **Dongargarh** India
Dongchangshou *see* **Xinle**
Dongcun *see* **Haiyang**
68 H2 **Dong Dang** Vietnam
65 C6 **Dong'e** China
25 C5 **Dongen** Netherlands
67 C7 **Dongfang** China
68 J3 **Dongfang** China
65 J1 **Dongfanghong** China
65 F3 **Dongfeng** China
58 C4 **Donggai Cona** *L* China
70 F5 **Donggala** Sulawesi
136 D2 **Donggala** Sulawesi
67 D1 **Donggong** China
65 F4 **Donggou** China
67 E3 **Donggu** China
67 E5 **Dongguan** China
65 C6 **Dongguang** China
68 H4 **Dong Ha** Vietnam
65 D7 **Donghai** China
67 C6 **Donghai Dao** *isld* China
58 E4 **Dong He** *R* China
68 H4 **Dong Hoi** Vietnam
Donghuang *see* **Xishui**
70 G6 **Dongi** Sulawesi
67 C4 **Dongjiang** China
67 B4 **Dong Jiang** *R* China
65 H2 **Dongjingcheng** China
70 G4 **Dongkalang** Sulawesi
68 H1 **Dong Khe** Vietnam
67 C3 **Dongkou** China
67 B4 **Donglan** China
Dongliao *see* **Liaoyuan**
65 F3 **Dongliao He** *R* China
67 B5 **Dongling** China
67 E1 **Dongliu** China
65 C7 **Dongming** China
68 H7 **Dong Nai** *R* Vietnam
59 K2 **Dongning** China
87 C8 **Dongo** Angola
41 K5 **Dongo** Italy
86 C5 **Dongo** Zaïre
84 J6 **Dongola** Sudan
86 C5 **Dongou** Congo
68 E4 **Dong Phraya Fai** *ra* Thailand
68 E5 **Dong Phraya Yen** Thailand
Dongping *see* **Anhua**
65 C7 **Dongping** China
65 C6 **Dongping Hu** *L* China
68 H7 **Dong Sai** Vietnam
67 F5 **Dongshan** China
67 F5 **Dongshan Dao** *isld* China
67 E6 **Dongsha Qundao** *isld* China
65 A5 **Dongsheng** China
67 B2 **Dongsheng** China
67 D2 **Dongting Hu** *L* China
67 G3 **Dongtou** China
67 B6 **Dong Trieu** Vietnam
65 D2 **Dong Ujimqin Qi** China
68 G1 **Dong Van** Vietnam
87 D8 **Dongwe** *R* Zambia
67 B2 **Dongxi** China
67 E2 **Dongxiang** China
65 D7 **Dongxi Lian Dao** *isld* China
65 G1 **Dongxing** China
67 B6 **Dongxing** China
67 G2 **Dongyang** China
67 F1 **Dongzhi** China
109 L4 **Donie** Texas
9 F2 **Donington** England
110 F5 **Doniphan** Missouri
117 D4 **Donjek** *R* Yukon Terr
48 G6 **Donji Milanovac** Yugoslavia
42 H4 **Donji Vakuf** Yugoslavia
18 H6 **Donjon, le** France
99 S3 **Donken** Michigan
109 J9 **Donna** Texas
26 F5 **Dönna** *isld* Norway
121 T6 **Donnacona** Quebec
42 B3 **Donnaz** Italy
36 B6 **Donnelay** France
110 G2 **Donnellson** Illinois
117 P8 **Donnelly** Alberta
100 J5 **Donnelly** Idaho
98 K4 **Donnelly** Minnesota
145 D1 **Donnelly's Crossing** New Zealand
102 D2 **Donner Pass** California
38 K7 **Donnersbach** Austria
38 K7 **Donnersbach Wald** Austria
36 D4 **Donnersberg** *mt* W Germany
100 G6 **Donner und Blitzen** *R* Oregon
26 F5 **Dönnes** Norway
98 E1 **Donnybrook** N Dakota
143 B10 **Donnybrook** W Australia
19 K4 **Donon** *mt* France
36 C7 **Donon, Col du** *pass* France
94 H6 **Donora** Pennsylvania
140 F4 **Donor's Hill** Queensland
99 T9 **Donovan** Illinois
102 D4 **Don Pedro Res** California
13 G6 **Don, R** England
54 K3 **Donskoy** U.S.S.R.
54 L6 **Donskoye Belogorye** U.S.S.R.
28 B5 **Donslund** Denmark
68 C4 **Donthami** *R* Burma
20 B4 **Donville** France
36 H6 **Donzdorf** W Germany
18 G7 **Donzenac** France
19 N16 **Donzère** France
18 H5 **Donzy** France
143 C9 **Doodlakine** W Australia
109 H4 **Doole** Texas
142 C5 **Dooleena** *mt* W Australia
98 B1 **Dooley** Montana
121 O6 **Doolittle, L** Quebec
140 E4 **Doomadgee Mission** Queensland
141 J8 **Doondi** Queensland
116 M3 **Doonerak, Mt** Alaska
12 D3 **Doon, L** Scotland
25 D4 **Doorn** Netherlands
99 T5 **Door Pen** Wisconsin
111 J8 **Dora** Alabama
44 B1 **Dora** Italy
106 G8 **Dora** New Mexico
42 B3 **Dora Baltea** *R* Italy
124 G4 **Dorado** Mexico
142 E5 **Dora,L** W Australia
113 F9 **Dora, Mt** Florida
98 K3 **Doran** Minnesota
27 G15 **Dörarp** Sweden
18 F6 **Dorat, le** France
Dorbod *see* **Siziwang Qi**
65 F1 **Dorbod** China
8 D6 **Dorchester** England
9 E4 **Dorchester** England
98 J9 **Dorchester** Nebraska
122 H8 **Dorchester** New Brunswick
99 Q4 **Dorchester** Wisconsin
115 M4 **Dorchester, C** N W Terr
18 F7 **Dordogne** *dep* France
18 E8 **Dordogne** *R* France
25 C5 **Dordrecht** Netherlands
18 H7 **Dore** *R* France
118 K4 **Doré L** Sask
18 G7 **Dore, Mont** *mt* France
100 C6 **Dorena** Oregon
32 H8 **Dörenberg** *mt* W Germany
32 J9 **Dörenhagen** W Germany
118 E6 **Dorenlee** Alberta
32 J8 **Dörentrup** W Germany
130 F6 **Dores do Indaiá** Brazil
37 N7 **Dorfen** W Germany
32 L7 **Dorfmark** W Germany
33 R6 **Dorf Zechlin** E Germany
43 C8 **Dorgali** Sardinia
85 D6 **Dori** Upper Volta
77 J4 **Dori** *R* Afghanistan
89 A8 **Doring** *R* S Africa
118 J4 **Dorintosh** Sask
120 B4 **Dorion** Ontario
121 Q7 **Dorion** Quebec
140 B2 **Dorisvale** N Terr **Aust**
9 F5 **Dorking** England
36 B1 **Dormagen** W Germany
18 H3 **Dormans** France
19 N13 **D'Or, Mt** France
41 L3 **Dornbirn** Austria
36 E2 **Dornburg** W Germany
37 J2 **Dorndorf** E Germany
37 M1 **Dorndorf** E Germany
48 K3 **Dorneşti** Romania
36 F7 **Dornhan** W Germany
15 C3 **Dornie** Scotland
48 J3 **Dornisoara** Romania
33 Q8 **Dörnitz** E Germany
15 D3 **Dornoch** Scotland
15 D3 **Dornoch Firth** Scotland
13 E4 **Dornock** Scotland
65 A2 **Dornogovĭ** *prov* Mongolia
36 F7 **Dornstetten** W Germany
32 F5 **Dornum** W Germany
71 A2 **Doro** Indonesia
54 E2 **Dorogobuzh** U.S.S.R.
52 F2 **Dorogorskoye** U.S.S.R.
48 K3 **Dorohoi** Romania
54 H1 **Dorokhovo** U.S.S.R.
26 H7 **Dorotea** Sweden
118 E7 **Dorothy** Alberta
52 G5 **Dorovitsa** U.S.S.R.
32 F7 **Dörpen** W Germany
107 M3 **Dorrance** Kansas
143 A7 **Dorre I** W Australia
139 L4 **Dorrigo** New S Wales
8 D2 **Dorrington** England
100 D8 **Dorris** California
100 E8 **Dorris Res** California
94 G5 **Dorset** Ohio
121 M7 **Dorset** Ontario
95 O3 **Dorset** Vermont
8 D6 **Dorset** *co* England
32 E9 **Dorsten** W Germany
32 G9 **Dortmund** W Germany
32 J5 **Dorum** W Germany
86 E5 **Doruma** Zaïre
121 R7 **Dorval** Quebec
36 H5 **Dörzbach** W Germany
133 D6 **Dos Bahías, C** Argentina
125 P9 **Dos Bocas** Belize
103 P9 **Dos Cabezas** Arizona
77 G2 **Doshakh, Koh-I** *mt* Afghanistan
16 D7 **Dos Hermanas** Spain
71 E4 **Dos Hermanas** *isld* Philippines
77 L2 **Doshi** Afghanistan
68 H2 **Do Son** Vietnam
102 D5 **Dos Palos** California
47 G3 **Dospat** Bulgaria
121 T6 **Dosquet** Quebec
102 A2 **Dos Rios** California
109 H5 **Doss** Texas
33 R6 **Dosse** *R* E Germany
85 E6 **Dosso** Niger
45 J1 **Dossobuono** Italy
50 E4 **Dossor** U.S.S.R.
28 D3 **Døstrup** Denmark
94 K9 **Doswell** Virginia
111 L10 **Dothan** Alabama
100 B7 **Dothan** Oregon
123 T4 **Doting Cove** Nfld
116 P5 **Dot Lake** Alaska
32 H7 **Dötlingen** W Germany
101 S10 **Dotsero** Colorado
36 H5 **Döttingen** W Germany
22 E3 **Douai** France
86 A5 **Douala** Cameroon
18 C4 **Douarnenez** France
18 B4 **Douarnenez,Baie de** France
109 N6 **Double Bayou** Texas
126 D3 **Double Headed Shot Cays** *islds* Bahamas
68 C5 **Double I** Burma
141 L7 **Double Island Pt** Queensland
108 G2 **Double Mountain Fork** *R* Texas
102 F6 **Double Mt** California
116 L6 **Double Peak** Alaska
141 H4 **Double Pt** *C* Queensland
111 J7 **Double Springs** Alabama
31 J6 **Doubrava** *R* Czechoslovakia
40 D3 **Doubs** *dep* France
19 J6 **Doubs** *R* France
40 F3 **Doubs** *R* Switzerland
142 E3 **Doubtful B** W Australia
143 C10 **Doubtful Island B** W Australia
144 A6 **Doubtful Sd** New Zealand
145 D1 **Doubtless B** New Zealand
40 C4 **Doucier** France
20 G2 **Doudeville** France
99 O9 **Douds** Iowa
21 E7 **Doué-la-Fontaine** France
85 D6 **Douentza** Mali
144 A7 **Doughboy Bay** New Zealand
117 F6 **Douglas** Alaska
103 P10 **Douglas** Arizona
112 E6 **Douglas** Georgia
12 D5 **Douglas** I of Man U.K.
119 S9 **Douglas** Manitoba
99 U7 **Douglas** Michigan
98 E2 **Douglas** N Dakota
98 K9 **Douglas** Nebraska
140 B2 **Douglas** N Terr **Aust**
121 O7 **Douglas** Ontario
89 C7 **Douglas** S Africa
12 E3 **Douglas** Scotland
100 E2 **Douglas** Washington
98 A7 **Douglas** Wyoming
138 D3 **Douglas** *R* S Australia
117 J9 **Douglas Chan** Br Columbia
106 B2 **Douglas Cr** Colorado
112 D1 **Douglas Dam** Tennessee
94 C1 **Douglas L** Michigan
112 D2 **Douglas L** Tennessee
12 E2 **Douglas Mill** Scotland

Douglas,Mount — Eceabat 23

143 E8 Douglas,Mount W Australia
116 L7 Douglas, Mt Alaska
120 J8 Douglas Pt Ontario
146 F13 Douglas Ra Antarctica
107 O4 Douglass Kansas
122 G6 Douglastown New Brunswick
122 H5 Douglastown Quebec
111 M8 Douglasville Georgia
22 F3 Doui Belgium
46 D6 Doukáton,Akr C Greece
19 J4 Doulevant le Château France
20 K1 Doullens France
14 A5 Doulus Hd Irish Rep
86 B5 Doumé Cameroon
67 D5 Doumen China
67 A5 Doumuge China
12 D1 Doune Scotland
12 E2 Dounreay Scotland
85 C7 Douobé R Liberia
37 P3 Doupov Czechoslovakia
23 F1 Dour France
130 E6 Dourada, Cachoeira rapids Brazil
129 J6 Dourada,Serra mts Brazil
130 E5 Dourada,Serra mts Brazil
130 B6 Dourados Brazil
130 C8 Dourados Brazil
133 F2 Dourados R Brazil
130 D8 Dourados,Serra dos mts Brazil
20 K4 Dourdan France
18 G9 Dourdou R France
22 B3 Douriez France
16 C3 Douro R Portugal
16 B3 Douro Litoral prov Portugal
Doushi see Gong'an
19 Q13 Doussard France
20 C3 Douve R France
20 E3 Douvres France
19 N14 Doux R France
18 E9 Douze R France
22 J4 Douzy France
45 L3 Dovadola Italy
106 B4 Dove Creek Colorado
142 C5 Dove,Mt W Australia
110 C6 Dover Arkansas
95 M7 Dover Delaware
28 D4 Dover Denmark
9 E1 Dove,R England
9 H5 Dover England
113 E9 Dover Florida
112 F5 Dover Georgia
110 N3 Dover Kentucky
112 K2 Dover N Carolina
95 Q3 Dover New Hampshire
95 N6 Dover New Jersey
94 F6 Dover Ohio
107 N6 Dover Oklahoma
139 H9 Dover Tasmania
110 J5 Dover Tennessee
95 S1 Dover Foxcroft Maine
143 F10 Dover,Pt W Australia
22 C1 Dover,Str.of France/England
38 J9 Dovje Yugoslavia
28 F7 Dovnsklint Denmark
26 D9 Dovre Norway
26 D9 Dovrefjell Norway
88 D8 Dowa Malawi
94 A5 Dowagiac Michigan
143 B9 Dowerin W Australia
Dow, L. see Xau, L.
8 C4 Dowlais Wales
77 E5 Dowlatābād Iran
117 F7 Dowling Alberta
14 F2 Down co N Ireland
99 T8 Downers Grove Illinois
101 N7 Downey Idaho
141 K1 Downfall Cr Brisbane, Qnsld
9 G2 Downham Market England
102 D2 Downieville California
99 O9 Downing Missouri
95 M6 Downingtown Pennsylvania
14 F2 Downpatrick N Ireland
14 B2 Downpatrick Hd Irish Rep
107 M2 Downs Kansas
101 Q6 Downs Mt Wyoming
95 M4 Downsville New York
9 E5 Downton England
117 L9 Downton,Mt Br Columbia
8 B6 Downtown England
99 N7 Dows Iowa
7 L9 Dowsing Lightship North Sea
69 C12 Dowu, Tanjung C Indonesia
102 D1 Doyle California
110 L6 Doyle Tennessee
144 D5 Doyleston New Zealand
95 M6 Doylestown Pennsylvania
106 D3 Doyleville Colorado
60 F9 Dōzen islds Japan
59 K4 Dōzen Nishi Jima isld Japan
111 K10 Dozier Alabama
121 N5 Dozois, Rés Quebec
20 E3 Dozulé France
45 L3 Dozza Italy
85 C2 Dr'aa R Morocco/Algeria
36 C2 Drabenderhöhe W Germany
28 F4 Dråby Denmark
19 P15 Drac R France
130 D7 Dracena Brazil
46 E3 Dračevo Yugoslavia
36 E5 Drachenfels mt W Germany
25 F2 Drachten Netherlands
95 Q4 Dracut Massachusetts
28 F6 Dræby Denmark
26 H7 Dragan L Sweden
48 J6 Drăgăneşti Romania
47 H1 Draganovo Bulgaria
48 J6 Drăgăşani Romania
103 O2 Dragerton Utah
46 E3 Dragoevo Yugoslavia
46 F2 Dragoman Bulgaria
45 K2 Dragoncello Italy
Dragon's Mouths chan see Bocas del Dragon
103 O9 Dragoon Arizona
28 K5 Dragør Denmark
46 F2 Dragovistica Yugoslavia
29 J11 Dragsfjärd Finland
28 B3 Dragstrup Denmark
19 Q17 Draguignan France
33 T9 Drahnsdorf E Germany
100 B6 Drain Oregon
22 G4 Draize France
103 M7 Drake Arizona
98 A9 Drake Colorado
98 F2 Drake N Dakota
139 K3 Drake New S Wales
119 M7 Drake Sask
32 K7 Drakenburg W Germany
89 F8 Drakensberg mts S Africa
89 G5 Drakensberg Garden S Africa
146 D15 Drake Passage S Atlantic Oc
100 E7 Drake Peak mt Oregon
102 B4 Drakes Bay California
110 J4 Drakesboro Kentucky
94 J10 Drakes Branch Virginia
47 G3 Dráma Greece
27 D12 Drammen Norway
27 D12 Dramsfj inlet Norway
40 F5 Drance R Switzerland
48 L4 Drânceni Romania
27 D12 Drangedal Norway
33 R6 Dranse E Germany
40 E5 Dranse R France
32 L9 Dransfeld W Germany
28 C5 Drantum Denmark
112 H1 Draper N Carolina
98 F6 Draper S Dakota
101 O9 Draper Utah
117 D6 Draper, Mt Alaska
74 F1 Dras Kashmir
38 G8 Drau R Austria
38 N9 Drava R Yugoslavia
42 G2 Dravograd Yugoslavia
31 J2 Drawa R Poland
31 J2 Drawsko Poland
98 J1 Drayton N Dakota
141 K8 Drayton Queensland
118 B5 Drayton Val Alberta
37 O5 Draženov Czechoslovakia
43 B12 Drean Algeria
37 P2 Drebach E Germany
32 H7 Drebber W Germany
48 E2 Drégelypalánk Hungary
33 M5 Dreggers W Germany
36 F3 Dreieichenhain W Germany
Dreihausen see Ebsdorfergrund
38 F7 Dreiherrn-Spitze mt Italy/Austria
36 B3 Dreis W Germany
40 G1 Dreisam R W Germany
37 P6 Dreitannenriegel mt W Germany
28 E7 Drejø Denmark
13 F1 Drem Scotland
47 F2 Dren Bulgaria
33 T6 Drense E Germany
32 G9 Drensteinfurt W Germany
25 G3 Drente prov Netherlands
37 Q1 Dresden E Germany
107 K2 Dresden Kansas
98 H1 Dresden N Dakota
94 E6 Dresden Ohio
120 H10 Dresden Ontario
110 H5 Dresden Tennessee
33 T10 Dresden reg E Germany
52 C6 Dretun' U.S.S.R.
20 H4 Dreux France
26 F10 Drevsjö Norway
111 F8 Drew Mississippi
100 C7 Drew Oregon
33 Q5 Drewitzer See L E Germany
100 G6 Drewsey Oregon
100 E7 Drews Res Oregon
110 B3 Drexel Missouri
52 E6 Drezna U.S.S.R.
54 K1 Drezna U.S.S.R.
36 E2 Driedorf W Germany
113 D7 Drifton Florida
118 B3 Driftpile Alberta
120 J3 Driftwood Ontario
94 J5 Driftwood Pennsylvania
101 O6 Driggs Idaho
141 J7 Drillham Queensland
46 D2 Drim R Yugoslavia
14 B5 Drimoleague Irish Rep
46 D2 Drin R Albania
48 E7 Drina R Yugoslavia
32 K9 Dringenberg W Germany
48 K2 Drinin U.S.S.R.
46 D3 Drinit, Pellg i B Albania
46 D3 Drin i zi R Albania
119 M8 Drinkwater Sask
109 J5 Dripping Springs Texas
109 K8 Driscoll Texas
52 C6 Drissa U.S.S.R.
26 D9 Driva R Norway
26 D9 Drivstua Norway
41 N6 Dro Italy
27 E12 Dröbak Norway
31 M3 Drobin Poland
55 F4 Drobyshevo U.S.S.R.
48 G4 Drocea mt Romania
32 K5 Drochtersen W Germany
22 D3 Drocourt France
32 M6 Drögen Nindorf W Germany
14 E3 Drogheda Irish Rep
14 E3 Drogheda B Irish Rep
48 H1 Drogobych U.S.S.R.
31 O3 Drohiczyn Poland
8 D3 Droitwich England
48 L2 Drokiya U.S.S.R.
36 D1 Drolshagen W Germany
139 H7 Dromana Victoria
14 F2 Dromara N Ireland
19 O15 Drôme dep France
20 D3 Drome R France
139 K6 Dromedary,C New S Wales
33 O8 Dromling E Germany
14 D3 Dromod Irish Rep
14 D2 Dromore N Ireland
14 C2 Dromore West Irish Rep
44 B3 Dronero Italy
9 E1 Dronfield England
22 F1 Drongen Belgium
18 F7 Dronne R France
146 B7 Dronning Fabiolafjella Antarctica
28 E2 Dronninglund Denmark
146 B7 Dronning Maude Ld Antarctica
119 Q7 Dropmore Manitoba
18 F8 Dropt R France
31 J7 Drosendorf Austria
74 D1 Drosh Pakistan
28 G6 Drøsselbjerg Denmark
20 H5 Droué France
120 E2 Drowning R Ontario
37 N1 Droyssig E Germany
20 F3 Drucourt France
118 J7 Druid Sask
8 C2 Druid Wales
126 A1 Druif Aruba W Indies
36 C6 Drulingen France
118 E7 Drumheller Alberta
14 D4 Drum Hills Irish Rep
14 D3 Drumlish Irish Rep
101 M3 Drummond Montana
144 B7 Drummond New Zealand
99 P3 Drummond Wisconsin
94 D1 Drummond I Michigan
95 L10 Drummond,L Virginia
140 D4 Drummond,Mt N Terr Aust
141 H6 Drummond Ra Queensland
121 S7 Drummondville Quebec
12 D4 Drummore Luce Bay Scotland
12 D4 Drummore Scotland
15 D3 Drumnadrochit Scotland
15 D4 Drumochter Pass Scotland
107 O6 Drumright Oklahoma
14 C2 Drumshanbo Irish Rep
12 D1 Drumvaich Scotland
25 D5 Drunen Netherlands
119 V8 Drunken Point C Manitoba
13 G3 Druridge B England
145 E2 Drury New Zealand
117 F4 Drury L Yukon Terr
36 D6 Drusenheim France
31 O1 Druskininkai U.S.S.R.
25 E5 Druten Netherlands
52 C6 Druya U.S.S.R.
54 E4 Druzhba U.S.S.R.
51 O2 Druzhina U.S.S.R.
55 C3 Druzhinino U.S.S.R.
54 J8 Druzhkovka U.S.S.R.
79 G6 Drūz, Jebel ed mts Syria
42 G4 Drvar Yugoslavia
42 G5 Drvenik isld Yugoslavia
100 B3 Dryad Washington
47 G2 Dryanovo Bulgaria
117 D6 Dry B Alaska
118 J1 Dryberry L Ontario
119 Q2 Drybrough Manitoba
101 R5 Dry Cr Wyoming
94 D4 Dryden Michigan
95 L4 Dryden New York
118 K1 Dryden Ontario
108 E5 Dryden Texas
110 E4 Dry Fork R Missouri
98 A6 Dry Fork R Wyoming
146 D2 Drygalski I Antarctica
8 C3 Drygarn Fawr mt Wales
127 K2 Dry Harbour Mts Jamaica
102 G6 Dry L California
102 G2 Dry L Nevada
122 F1 Drylake Labrador
103 K5 Dry Lake Nevada
103 K4 Dry Lake Valley Nevada
12 D1 Drymen Scotland
111 D10 Dry Prong Louisiana
141 G4 Dry R Queensland
140 D1 Drysdale I N Terr Aust
142 F2 Drysdale R W Australia
113 E13 Dry Tortugas islds Florida
85 G7 Dschang Cameroon
86 D5 Dua R Zaïre
127 K9 Duaca Venezuela
67 C4 Du'an China
Duancun see Wuxiang
95 N2 Duane New York
141 J6 Duaringa Queensland
127 J5 Duarte, Pico mt Dom Rep
130 E8 Duartina Brazil
130 D8 Duas Onças,Ilha das Brazil
109 P3 Dubach Louisiana
72 H3 Dubai U.A.E.
100 B9 Dubakella Mt California
114 J5 Dubawnt R N W Terr
139 J4 Dubbo New S Wales
56 C1 Dubches R U.S.S.R.
37 O4 Dubec Czechoslovakia
33 T9 Duben E Germany
55 C5 Dubenskiy U.S.S.R.
12 B1 Dubh Artach isld Scotland
48 G1 Dubiecko Poland
124 F2 Dublán Mexico
112 E5 Dublin Georgia
94 B7 Dublin Indiana
14 E3 Dublin Irish Rep
99 V5 Dublin Michigan
111 F7 Dublin Mississippi
94 D6 Dublin Ohio
120 J9 Dublin Ontario
109 J3 Dublin Texas
14 E3 Dublin co Irish Rep
54 H2 Dubna U.S.S.R.
52 E6 Dubna R U.S.S.R.
101 N5 Dubois Idaho
99 K9 Du Bois Nebraska
94 J5 Du Bois Pennsylvania
101 Q6 Dubois Wyoming
48 M3 Dubossary U.S.S.R.
54 K3 Dubovka U.S.S.R.
85 B7 Dubréka Guinea
54 E3 Dubrovka U.S.S.R.
42 J6 Dubrovnik Yugoslavia
54 B2 Dubrovno U.S.S.R.
55 E2 Dubrovnoye U.S.S.R.
119 P8 Dubuc Sask
99 Q7 Dubuque Iowa
52 G6 Dub'yazy U.S.S.R.
20 C4 Ducey France
67 E2 Duchang China
121 Q3 Ducharme Quebec
30 H5 Duchcov Czechoslovakia
33 T5 Ducherow E Germany
101 P9 Duchesne Utah
118 F8 Duchess Alberta
140 E5 Duchess Queensland
135 O11 Ducie I Pacific Oc
110 J6 Duck R Tennessee
119 R6 Duck Bay Manitoba
99 S5 Duck Cr Wisconsin
111 G8 Duck Hill Mississippi
118 L6 Duck Lake Sask
119 Q7 Duck Mt ra Manitoba
119 R7 Duck Mt. Prov. Park Manitoba
112 C2 Ducktown Tennessee
103 J3 Duckwater Nevada
103 J3 Duckwater Pk Nevada
20 G3 Duclair France
102 E6 Ducor California
127 L4 Ducos Martinique W I
68 J5 Duc Pho Vietnam
9 F2 Duddington England
22 L5 Dudelange Luxembourg
36 B4 Dudeldorf W Germany
32 M9 Duderstadt W Germany
109 P3 Dudgemona R Louisiana
7 L9 Dudgeon Lightship North Sea
50 H2 Dudinka U.S.S.R.
9 D3 Dudley England
112 D5 Dudley Georgia
110 F5 Dudley Missouri
86 B2 Dudo Somalia
54 G3 Dudorovskiy U.S.S.R.
36 C5 Dudweiler W Germany
51 J1 Dudypta R U.S.S.R.
22 E1 Dudzele Belgium
85 C7 Duékoué Ivory Coast
16 D3 Dueñas Spain
16 C2 Duerna R Spain
17 F3 Duero R Spain
112 E3 Due West S Carolina
146 G8 Dufek Coast Antarctica
119 O8 Duff Sask
138 D3 Duff Creek S Australia
22 H1 Duffel Belgium
118 C5 Duffield Alberta
140 C7 Duffield N Terr Aust
138 C2 Duffield R N Terr Australia
137 O3 Duff Is Santa Cruz Is
15 E3 Dufftown Scotland
122 F2 Dufresne,L Quebec
122 G2 Dufresne Lake Quebec
100 D4 Dufur Oregon
140 F5 Dugald R Queensland
103 N7 Dugas Arizona
111 D9 Dugdemona R Louisiana
110 J2 Dugger Indiana
42 F4 Dugi O Yugoslavia
86 H5 Dugiuma Somalia
54 H2 Dugna U.S.S.R.
141 G1 Dugong I Gt Barrier Reef Aust
118 E6 Duhamel Alberta
131 D2 Duice, R Argentina
128 E3 Duida, Co mt Venezuela
141 F2 Duifken Pt Queensland
32 L8 Duingen W Germany
32 E10 Duisburg W Germany
25 A5 Duiveland Netherlands
67 C4 Dujiang China
46 E2 Dukat Yugoslavia
107 L7 Duke Oklahoma
117 H8 Duke I Alaska
141 K5 Duke Is Queensland
135 N10 Duke of Gloucester Is Pacific Oc
142 F4 Dukes Dome mt W Australia
86 F4 Duk Faiwil Sudan
72 G3 Dukhān Qatar
54 D1 Dukhovshchina U.S.S.R.
59 L1 Duki U.S.S.R.
31 N6 Dukla Poland
52 C6 Dukstas U.S.S.R.
111 F12 Dulac Louisiana
58 C4 Dulan China
58 C4 Dulansi China
8 B1 Dulas B Wales
71 G7 Dulawan Mindanao Philippines
116 K4 Dulbi R Alaska
106 D5 Dulce New Mexico
141 F1 Dulcie R Queensland
80 G7 Duleilat el Muterat Jordan
51 N2 Dulgalakh R U.S.S.R.
47 J1 Dŭlgopol Bulgaria
141 F1 Dulhunty R Queensland
70 D3 Dulit Ra Sarawak
67 C4 Duliu Jiang R China
71 G5 Duljugan Pt Leyte Philippines
25 F6 Dülken W Germany
75 P6 Dullabchara India
98 B6 Dull Center Wyoming
32 F9 Dülmen W Germany
67 A5 Dulong China
47 J1 Dulovo Bulgaria
99 O3 Duluth Minnesota
8 C5 Dulverton England
79 G5 Dūma Syria
71 F6 Dumaguete Negros Philippines
69 E12 Dumai Sumatra
47 J6 Dumanlı Dağı mt Turkey
71 F7 Dumanquilas B Mindanao Philippines
71 D5 Dumaran isld Philippines
139 K3 Dumaresq R Queensland
70 F4 Dumaring Kalimantan
111 E8 Dumas Arkansas
108 C8 Dumas Texas
83 K10 Dumbanagala mt Sri Lanka
12 D2 Dumbarton Scotland
48 F2 Ďumbier mt Czechoslovakia
143 C10 Dumbleyung W Australia
143 C10 Dumbleyung, L W Australia
86 B3 Dumboa Nigeria
48 J4 Dumbrăveni Romania
69 H12 Dumdum isld Indonesia
79 G5 Dumeir,Jebel mts Syria
12 E3 Dumfries Scotland
Dumfries co see Dumfries and Galloway reg
15 D5 Dumfries and Galloway reg Scotland
54 G3 Duminichi U.S.S.R.
48 K5 Dumitreşti Romania
75 M6 Dumka India
119 N9 Dummer Sask
32 H7 Dümmersee L W Germany
71 H4 Dumoga Ketjil Sulawesi
121 N6 Dumoine, L Quebec
98 K4 Dumont Minnesota
121 O6 Dumont,L Quebec
36 B3 Dümpelfeld W Germany
65 J1 Dumune China
79 B7 Dumyât Egypt
48 E4 Duna R Hungary
48 K2 Dunaevtsy U.S.S.R.
48 D3 Dunaj R Czechoslovakia
31 M6 Dunajec R Poland
14 E3 Dunany Pt Irish Rep
48 E4 Dunapataj Hungary
48 L6 Dunărea R Romania
48 E4 Dunaujváros Hungary
48 F5 Dunav R S Europe
144 C6 Dunback New Zealand
107 P7 Dunbar Oklahoma
141 F3 Dunbar Queensland
13 F1 Dunbar Scotland
101 N9 Dunbar Utah
99 S4 Dunbar Wisconsin
94 F8 Dunbar W Virginia
Dunbarton co see Strathclyde reg
118 L7 Dunblane Sask
12 E1 Dunblane Scotland
14 E3 Dunboyne Irish Rep
103 P9 Duncan Arizona
100 B1 Duncan Br Columbia
98 J8 Duncan Nebraska
107 N7 Duncan Oklahoma
101 Q6 Duncan Wyoming
141 F1 Duncan Is Queensland
117 R4 Duncan L N W Terr
140 A3 Duncan, Mt N Terr Aust
14 E4 Duncannon Irish Rep
95 K6 Duncannon Pennsylvania
68 A7 Duncan Passage Andaman Is
112 C3 Duncan Ridge Georgia
127 K1 Duncans Jamaica
15 E2 Duncansby Hd Scotland
126 G3 Duncan Town Bahamas
109 N10 Duncanville Texas
9 E3 Dunchurch England
13 F6 Duncombe England
9 F6 Duncton England
52 B6 Dundaga U.S.S.R.
14 E2 Dundalk Irish Rep
120 K8 Dundalk Ontario
14 E3 Dundalk B Irish Rep
115 N2 Dundas Greenland
147 F6 Dundas N W Terr
94 E7 Dundas Ohio
117 H8 Dundas I Br Columbia
143 D9 Dundas L W Australia
136 G4 Dundas Str N Terr Australia
99 S7 Dundee Illinois
94 D5 Dundee Michigan
95 L4 Dundee New York
89 G7 Dundee S Africa
13 F1 Dundee Scotland
109 J2 Dundee Texas
146 D14 Dundee I Antarctica
26 G5 Dunderlands-dal V Norway
Dund Hot see Zhenlan Qi
141 G8 Dundoo Queensland
12 E4 Dundrennan Scotland
14 F2 Dundrum N Ireland
14 F2 Dundrum B N Ireland
118 L7 Dundurn Sask
113 E9 Dunedin Florida
144 C7 Dunedin New Zealand
139 J4 Dunedoo New S Wales
14 C1 Dunfanaghy Irish Rep
15 E4 Dunfermline Scotland
14 E2 Dungannon N Ireland
120 J9 Dungannon Ontario
74 E7 Dungarpur India
14 D4 Dungarvan Irish Rep
14 D4 Dungarvan Harb Irish Rep
66 D5 Dungbaree Range China
9 G6 Dungeness England
133 D8 Dungeness,Pta Arg/Chile
14 E2 Dungiven N Ireland
14 C2 Dungloe Irish Rep
139 K4 Dungog New S Wales
86 E5 Dungu Zaïre
86 G1 Dungunab Sudan
9 F1 Dunham England
59 J3 Dunhua China
58 B3 Dunhuang China
141 J7 Dunkeld Queensland
15 E4 Dunkeld Scotland
138 F6 Dunkeld Victoria
106 E9 Dunken New Mexico
22 C1 Dunkerque France
141 H4 Dunk I Queensland
Dunkirk see Dunkerque
110 L1 Dunkirk Indiana
101 O1 Dunkirk Montana
121 L10 Dunkirk New York
119 M8 Dunkirk Sask
86 G3 Dunkur Ethiopia
85 D7 Dunkwa Ghana
14 E3 Dún Laoghaire Irish Rep
99 L8 Dunlap Iowa
107 O3 Dunlap Kansas
106 F7 Dunlap New Mexico
108 G1 Dunlap Texas
14 E3 Dunlavin Irish Rep
109 J6 Dunlay Texas
14 E3 Dunleer Irish Rep
119 T4 Dunlop Manitoba
120 J9 Dunlop Ontario
12 D2 Dunlop Scotland
14 B5 Dunmanus B Irish Rep
14 B5 Dunmanway Irish Rep
140 C3 Dunmarra N Terr Aust
14 C3 Dunmore Irish Rep
95 M5 Dunmore Pennsylvania
113 L12 Dunmore Town Bahamas
126 F2 Dunmore Town Eleuthera Bahamas
9 G4 Dunmow England
112 J2 Dunn N Carolina
98 D2 Dunn Center N Dakota
99 M6 Dunnell Minnesota
113 E8 Dunnellon Florida
15 E2 Dunnet B Scotland
15 E2 Dunnet Hd Scotland
98 F8 Dunning Nebraska
12 E1 Dunning Scotland
36 E7 Dunningen W Germany
143 C6 Dunns Ra W Australia
120 G6 Dunn Valley Ontario
121 L10 Dunnville Ontario
139 G6 Dunolly Victoria
12 D2 Dunoon Scotland
100 J9 Dunphy Nevada
84 J5 Dunqul Oasis Egypt
120 G4 Dunrankin Ontario
119 S9 Dunrea Manitoba
13 F2 Duns Scotland
144 D5 Dunsandel New Zealand
143 B10 Dunsborough W Australia
12 E3 Dunscore Scotland
98 G1 Dunseith N Dakota
100 C8 Dunsmuir California
9 F4 Dunstable England
144 B6 Dunstan Mts New Zealand
117 O9 Dunster Br Col
8 C5 Dunster England
31 K7 Dun Streda Czechoslovakia
18 G6 Dun sur Auron France
22 J5 Dun-sur-Meuse France
144 C6 Duntroon New Zealand
120 K8 Duntroon Ontario
36 D6 Duntzenheim France
15 B3 Dunvegan Scotland
15 B3 Dunvegan,L Scotland
123 T6 Dunville Nfld
9 H3 Dunwich England
58 G3 Duolun China
68 F7 Duong Dong Vietnam
67 D4 Dupang Ling mts China
121 L4 Duparquet Quebec
69 J11 Duperre I Indonesia
94 B8 Dupont Indiana
95 M5 Dupont Pennsylvania
98 E4 Dupree S Dakota
121 L4 Dupuy Quebec
101 N1 Dupuyer Montana
87 C7 Duque de Braganca Angola
130 G8 Duque de Caxias Brazil
133 B8 Duque de York,I Chile
103 O10 Duquesne Arizona
94 H6 Duquesne Pennsylvania
110 G3 Du Quoin Illinois
80 D7 Dura Jordan
41 M2 Durach W Germany
142 F3 Durack,R W Australia
142 F3 Durack Ra W Australia
78 E1 Durağan Turkey
139 K2 Durah Queensland
141 K7 Durah Queensland
47 J5 Durak Turkey
106 E7 Duran New Mexico
19 Q16 Durance R France
99 R7 Durand Illinois
94 D4 Durand Michigan
99 P5 Durand Wisconsin
106 C4 Durango Colorado
124 G5 Durango Mexico
18 D9 Durango Spain
111 G8 Durant Mississippi
107 O8 Durant Oklahoma
16 E3 Duratón R Spain
131 G4 Durazno Uruguay
131 G4 Durazno dep Uruguay
Durazzo see Durrës
89 G7 Durban S Africa
143 E6 Durba Spring W Australia
27 M15 Durbe U.S.S.R.
94 H8 Durbin W Virginia
22 J3 Durbuy Belgium
16 E8 Dúrcal Spain
79 G4 Dureikish Syria
36 B2 Düren W Germany
75 J8 Durg India
75 M7 Durgapur India
102 C2 Durham California
13 G4 Durham England
107 N3 Durham Kansas
112 J2 Durham N Carolina
95 R3 Durham New Hampshire
120 K8 Durham Ontario
121 S7 Durham Quebec
13 G4 Durham co England
122 F7 Durham Br New Brunswick
141 F7 Durham Downs Queensland
12 E3 Durisdeer Scotland
100 H5 Durkee Oregon
36 E6 Durlach W Germany
9 E6 Durlston Hd England
36 E6 Durmersheim W Germany
42 J5 Durmitor mt Yugoslavia
15 D2 Durness Scotland
38 N5 Durnstein Austria
123 L3 Durocher,L Quebec
38 M6 Durrenstein mt Austria
46 C3 Durrës Albania
140 F7 Durrie Queensland
14 D4 Durrow Irish Rep
37 J5 Dürrwangen W Germany
14 A5 Dursey Hd Irish Rep
14 A5 Dursey I Irish Rep
8 D4 Dursley England
8 C5 Durston England
47 K5 Dursunbey Turkey
21 E6 Durtal France
Duru see Wuchuan
28 B3 Durup Denmark
145 D4 D'Urville New Zealand
77 J2 Durzab Afghanistan
120 D1 Dusey R Ontario
57 A6 Dushak U.S.S.R.
67 B4 Dushan China
57 E5 Dushanbe U.S.S.R.
65 C4 Dushikou China
95 L5 Dushore Pennsylvania
47 J2 Dŭskotna Bulgaria
144 A6 Dusky Sd New Zealand
32 E10 Düsseldorf W Germany
25 C5 Dussen Netherlands
41 J4 Düssist mt Switzerland
33 R9 Düssnitz E Germany
107 O6 Dustin Oklahoma
83 J9 Dutch B Sri Lanka
Dutch Guiana see Surinam
116 D10 Dutch Harbor Aleutian Is
101 M9 Dutch Mt Utah
89 C4 Dutlwe Botswana
52 J3 Dutovo U.S.S.R.
85 F6 Dutsan Wai Nigeria
101 O2 Dutton Montana
120 J10 Dutton Ontario
141 G5 Dutton R Queensland
138 D4 Dutton,L S Australia
103 M3 Dutton,Mt Utah
119 N7 Duval Sask
127 H5 Duvalierville Haiti
121 N6 Duval,L Quebec
55 C3 Duvan U.S.S.R.
144 D5 Duvauchelle New Zealand
26 F8 Duved Sweden
127 J5 Duvergé Dominican Rep
52 D3 Duvogero U.S.S.R.
22 D5 Duvy France
95 R4 Duxbury Massachusetts
9 G3 Duxford England
67 B4 Duyang Shan mts China
68 C4 Duyinzeik Burma
67 B3 Duyun China
78 C1 Düzce Turkey
43 B12 Duzerville Algeria
47 H1 Dve Mogili Bulgaria
26 H2 Dverberg Norway
52 F3 Dvina, Severnyy R U.S.S.R.
52 E2 Dvinskaya Guba B U.S.S.R.
54 C1 Dvin'ye,Oz L U.S.S.R.
31 K6 Dvorec Czechoslovakia
31 J5 Dvůr Králové Czechoslovakia
88 D8 Dwangwa R Malawi
143 B10 Dwarda W Australia
74 C7 Dwarka India
89 E5 Dwars Berg mts S Africa
143 B10 Dwellingup W Australia
99 S8 Dwight Illinois
107 O3 Dwight Kansas
98 J8 Dwight Nebraska
94 F9 Dwight Virginia
106 C9 Dwyer New Mexico
98 B7 Dwyer Wyoming
54 F3 Dyat'kovo U.S.S.R.
28 D7 Dybbøl Denmark
28 A3 Dybe Kirke Denmark
28 H6 Dybsø Fjord inlet Denmark
119 R4 Dyce Manitoba
15 F3 Dyce Scotland
99 T5 Dyckesville Wisconsin
110 H5 Dyer Tennessee
114 G2 Dyer B N W Terr
120 J7 Dyer Bay Ontario
110 G5 Dyersburg Tennessee
99 P7 Dyersville Iowa
8 B3 Dyfed co Wales
8 B2 Dyfi R Wales
31 J1 Dygowo Poland
31 J7 Dyje R Czechoslovakia
22 H2 Dyle R Belgium
9 G5 Dymchurch England
118 K1 Dyment Ontario
8 D4 Dymock England
141 G8 Dynevor Downs Queensland
31 N6 Dynów Poland
102 F4 Dyor Nevada
28 E6 Dyreborg Denmark
26 C8 Dyrnesvågen Norway
26 J2 Dyröy Norway
99 O7 Dysart Iowa
119 N8 Dysart Sask
13 E1 Dysart Scotland
47 J2 Dyulevo Bulgaria
47 J2 Dyulino Bulgaria
78 L1 Dyul'tydag mt U.S.S.R.
57 C2 Dyurmen'tove U.S.S.R.
58 C2 Dzag Mongolia
58 F3 Dzamïn Üüde Mongolia
87 H10 Dzaoudzi Comoros
58 C2 Dzavhan Gol R Mongolia
30 H5 Džban mt Czechoslovakia
54 J8 Dzerzhinsk U.S.S.R.
56 C4 Dzerzhinskiy U.S.S.R.
57 K2 Dzerzhinskoye U.S.S.R.
51 N3 Dzhagdy,Khrebet mts U.S.S.R.
55 E5 Dzhaksy U.S.S.R.
56 D5 Dzhakul', Gora mt U.S.S.R.
57 G4 Dzhalal-Abad U.S.S.R.
59 H1 Dzhalinda U.S.S.R.
55 E5 Dzhaltyr U.S.S.R.
55 B5 Dzhambeyty U.S.S.R.
55 D5 Dzhambul U.S.S.R.
57 J2 Dzhansugurov U.S.S.R.
56 D5 Dzhebashskiy Khrebet mts U.S.S.R.
55 D5 Dzhetygara U.S.S.R.
57 C4 Dzhetymtau, Gory mt U.S.S.R.
57 E4 Dzhetysay U.S.S.R.
57 E1 Dzhezkazgan U.S.S.R.
56 G5 Dzhida R U.S.S.R.
56 F5 Dzhidinskiy,Khrebet mts Mongolia/U.S.S.R.
57 B4 Dzhigirbent U.S.S.R.
57 E4 Dzhizak U.S.S.R.
56 D4 Dzhoyskiy Khrebet mts U.S.S.R.
57 D5 Dzhuma U.S.S.R.
57 K2 Dzhungarskiy Alatau, Khrebet mts U.S.S.R.
48 L2 Dzhurin U.S.S.R.
57 C2 Dzhusaly U.S.S.R.
31 M2 Działdowo Poland
31 M5 Działoszyce Poland
31 L4 Działoszyn Poland
31 L2 Dzierżgoń Poland
31 K5 Dzierżoniów Poland
125 O7 Dzitbalché Mexico
31 H1 Dziwnów Poland
52 B6 Džūkste U.S.S.R.
66 C3 Dzungaria reg China
66 C2 Dzungarian Gate pass U.S.S.R./China
58 E3 Dzüünbayan Mongolia
106 H3 Eads Colorado
103 P7 Eagar Arizona
101 T10 Eagle Colorado
100 J6 Eagle Idaho
98 K9 Eagle Nebraska
99 S7 Eagle Wisconsin
101 R5 Eagle Wyoming
110 M3 Eagle R Kentucky
98 E4 Eagle Butte S Dakota
107 M6 Eagle City Oklahoma
102 G6 Eagle Crags California
121 O6 Eagle Depot Quebec
141 K1 Eagle Farm dist Brisbane, Qnsld
99 N7 Eagle Grove Iowa
99 S2 Eagle Harbor Michigan
139 J9 Eaglehawk Neck Tasmania
119 O1 Eaglehead L Ontario
119 T5 Eagle I Manitoba
100 E9 Eagle L California
95 R7 Eagle L Maine
95 S6 Eagle L Maine
118 J1 Eagle L Ontario
113 F10 Eagle Lake Florida
109 L6 Eagle Lake Texas
109 K3 Eagle Mt. L Texas
103 J8 Eagle Mts California
106 E5 Eagle Nest New Mexico
108 G7 Eagle Pass Texas
114 F4 Eagle Plain Yukon Terr
100 C7 Eagle Point Oregon
99 S2 Eagle River Michigan
99 R4 Eagle River Wisconsin
94 H9 Eagle Rock Virginia
12 D2 Eaglesham Scotland
137 Q4 Eaglestone Reef Pacific Oc
116 O4 Eagle Summit Alaska
103 L8 Eagle Tail Mts Arizona
109 N1 Eagleton Arkansas
107 Q7 Eagletown Oklahoma
100 E8 Eagleville California
61 O7 Eai-gawa R Japan
68 H6 Ea Kan R Vietnam
9 F4 Ealing England
144 C6 Ealing New Zealand
143 D7 Earaheedy W Australia
8 D3 Eardisland England
117 L11 Ear Lakes Cove Br Col
110 F6 Earle Arkansas
99 M8 Earlham Iowa
102 E6 Earlimart California
99 L8 Earling Iowa
110 J4 Earlington Kentucky
100 A8 Earl,L California
144 A6 Earl Mts New Zealand
13 F2 Earlston Scotland
121 L5 Earlton Ontario
99 S8 Earlville Illinois
99 P7 Earlville Iowa
13 E1 Earn,Br.of Scotland
12 D1 Earn,L Scotland
117 F4 Earn L Yukon Terr
12 E1 Earn,R Scotland
144 B6 Earnslaw, Mt New Zealand
103 K7 Earp California
13 G3 Earsdon England
9 F6 Easebourne England
13 G4 Easington Durham England
13 J6 Easington Humberside England
13 G5 Easingwold England
112 E3 Easley S Carolina
110 F3 East Alton Illinois
121 T7 East Angus Quebec
123 M7 East B C Breton I, N Scotia
113 B7 East B Florida
111 G12 East B Louisiana
111 B12 East B Texas
112 G1 East Bend N Carolina
95 L7 East Berlin Pennsylvania
109 L6 East Bernard Texas
9 G6 Eastbourne England
145 G4 Eastbourne New Zealand
94 H6 East Brady Pennsylvania
8 D5 East Brent England
111 J10 East Brewton Alabama
71 G6 East Bucas Philippines
101 O1 East Butte mt Montana
145 G2 East Cape New Zealand
99 T8 East Chicago Indiana
64 G4 East China Sea
145 F3 East Coast stat area New Zealand
145 E2 East Coast Bays New Zealand
118 E7 East Coulee Alberta
9 G6 Eastdean England
9 G2 East Dereham England
99 Q7 East Dubuque Illinois
103 K2 East Ely Nevada
118 J9 Eastend Sask
143 A8 Easter Grp islds W Australia
135 U16 Easter I Pacific Oc
141 F5 Eastern Creek Queensland
84 J4 Eastern Desert Egypt
86 F4 Eastern Equatoria prov Sudan
76 C4 Eastern Ghats mts India
123 S5 Eastern Meelpaeg L Nfld
119 S5 Easterville Manitoba
122 E7 East Florenceville New Brunswick
120 J3 Eastford Ontario
99 Q9 East Galesburg Illinois
102 G2 Eastgate Nevada
30 G2 East Germany
101 M1 East Glacier Park Montana
9 F5 East Grinstead England
95 P6 East Hampton Long I, N Y
95 P4 Easthampton Massachusetts
101 O3 East Helena Montana
9 G6 East Hoathly England
123 L6 East I Madeleine Is, Quebec
9 E4 East Ilsley England
95 P4 East Jaffrey New Hampshire
147 F12 East Jan Mayen Rdg Norwegian Sea
122 J9 East Jeddore Nova Scotia
94 B1 East Jordan Michigan
122 G10 East Jordan Nova Scotia
9 G1 East Keal England
122 G9 East Kemptville Nova Scotia
95 R6 East L Maine
99 U5 East Lake Michigan
109 J3 Eastland Texas
94 C4 East Lansing Michigan
9 E6 Eastleigh England
110 N1 East Liberty Ohio
13 F2 East Linton Scotland
94 G6 East Liverpool Ohio
89 E9 East London S Africa
East Lothian co see Lothian reg
94 E8 East Lynn W Virginia
115 M7 Eastmain Quebec
112 D5 Eastman Georgia
141 H6 Eastmere Queensland
143 E8 East, Mt W Australia
8 D3 Eastnor England
99 R9 Easton Illinois
95 Q4 Easton Massachusetts
99 N6 Easton Minnesota
110 B2 Easton Missouri
95 M6 Easton Pennsylvania
100 D2 Easton Washington
112 G4 Eastover S Carolina
East Pakistan see Bangladesh
113 F8 East Palatka Florida
94 G6 East Palestine Ohio
102 B2 East Park Res California
99 N8 East Peru Iowa
117 N8 East Pine Br Col
111 M8 East Point Georgia
94 E9 East Point Kentucky
123 L6 East Point Madeleine Is, Quebec
121 L1 East Point Ontario
123 L7 East Point Pr Edward I
123 N10 East Point Sable I, N Scotia
119 M9 East Poplar Sask
106 E2 East Portal Colorado
110 G5 East Prairie Missouri
122 G10 East Pubnico Nova Scotia
94 G9 East Rainelle W Virginia
100 H9 East Range Nevada
9 F1 East Retford England
9 H5 Eastry England
110 F3 East St Louis Illinois
147 P5 East Siberian Sea Arctic Oc
139 J7 East Sister I Tasmania
100 K2 East Sister Peak mt Idaho
9 F1 East Stoke England
8 D5 East Stour England
9 G6 East Sussex co England
94 D2 East Tawas Michigan
139 H4 East Toorale New S Wales
119 N4 East Trout L Sask
99 S7 East Troy Wisconsin
103 N7 East Verde R Arizona
95 M9 Eastville Virginia
13 E1 East Wemyss Scotland
9 E1 East Wood England
138 C2 Eateringinna Cr S Australia
98 B9 Eaton Colorado
110 L1 Eaton Indiana
110 M2 Eaton Ohio
118 H7 Eatonia Sask
140 B6 Eaton L N Terr Aust
94 C4 Eaton Rapids Michigan
9 F3 Eaton Socon England
112 D4 Eatonton Georgia
100 C3 Eatonville Washington
99 U7 Eau Claire Michigan
99 P5 Eau Claire Wisconsin
99 P5 Eau Claire R Wisconsin
122 G1 Eau-Claire, L. à l' Labrador
115 M6 Eau Claire, L. à l' Quebec
113 G9 Eau Gallie Florida
121 Q3 Eau-Jaune, L. a l' Quebec
20 H2 Eaulne R France
134 E7 Eauripik Rise Pac Oc
18 F9 Eauze France
141 G2 Ebagoola Queensland
125 K6 Ebano Mexico
43 B13 Ebba Ksour Tunisia
36 D1 Ebbe mts W Germany
13 H5 Ebberston England
28 D6 Ebberup Denmark
8 C4 Ebbw Vale Wales
86 B5 Ebebiyin Equat Guinea
33 N10 Ebeleben E Germany
28 F4 Ebeltoft Denmark
119 P7 Ebenezer Sask
99 U3 Eben Junction Michigan
94 J6 Ebensburg Pennsylvania
38 J6 Ebensee Austria
37 K3 Ebensfeld W Germany
36 G5 Eberbach W Germany
78 C2 Eber Gölü Turkey
32 M9 Ebergötzen W Germany
37 L4 Ebermannstadt W Germany
37 K3 Ebern W Germany
36 D4 Ebernburg W Germany
110 M4 E Bernstadt Kentucky
36 H6 Ebersbach W Germany
36 H3 Ebersburg W Germany
37 L3 Ebersdorf W Germany
36 F4 Eberstadt W Germany
38 L8 Eberstein Austria
33 T7 Eberswalde E Germany
60 P2 Ebetsu Japan
55 F4 Ebeyty, Oz L U.S.S.R.
67 A2 Ebian China
36 G7 Ebingen W Germany
66 C3 Ebinur Hu L China
79 G3 Ebla anc site Syria
41 K3 Ebnat Switzerland
37 J6 Ebnat W Germany
86 D5 Ebola R Zaïre
43 G8 Eboli Italy
86 B5 Ebolowa Cameroon
37 K4 Ebrach W Germany
9 F2 E Bridgford England
44 F2 Ebro mt Italy
16 E2 Ebro R Spain
16 E2 Ebro, Embalse del res Spain
36 E2 Ebschloh mt W Germany
36 F2 Ebsdorfergrund W Germany
33 M6 Ebstorf W Germany
22 G2 Ecaussines Belgium
13 E3 Ecclefechan Scotland
13 F2 Eccles Scotland
94 F9 Eccles W Virginia
13 G6 Ecclesfield England
8 D2 Eccleshall England
127 P2 Ecclesville Trinidad
47 H4 Eceabat Turkey

24
Echallens — Endicott Arm

40 E4 Echallens Switzerland
20 F4 Echauffour France
67 E1 Echeng China
101 U5 Echeta Wyoming
61 J10 Echizen-misaki C Japan
99 L5 Echo Minnesota
100 F4 Echo Oregon
101 O9 Echo Utah
103 K5 Echo B Nevada
120 G6 Echo Bay Ontario
103 N5 Echo Cliffs Arizona
139 H8 Echo,L Tasmania
121 P5 Échouani L Quebec
122 H4 Echouerie, L' Quebec
119 O8 Echo Valley Prov. Park Sask
25 E6 Echt Netherlands
15 F3 Echt Scotland
32 M9 Echte W Germany
25 F3 Echten Netherlands
36 G6 Echterdingen W Germany
22 L4 Echternach Luxembourg
139 G6 Echuca Victoria
36 F3 Echzell W Germany
16 D7 Écija Spain
36 H5 Eckartshausen W Germany
98 H3 Eckelson N Dakota
37 L4 Eckental W Germany
30 E1 Eckernförde W Germany
109 J5 Eckert Texas
13 F3 Eckford Scotland
9 E1 Eckington Derby England
8 D3 Eckington Hereford & Worcester England
12 C1 Eck,L Scotland
98 D9 Eckley Colorado
94 F9 Eckman W Virginia
118 C6 Eckville Alberta
32 H5 Eckwarderhörne W Germany
111 K9 Eclectic Alabama
143 C11 Eclipse I W Australia
140 B5 Eclipse, Mt N Terr Aust
115 M3 Eclipse Sound N W Terr
21 F6 Écommoy France
110 L2 Economy Indiana
121 O5 Écorces,L.aux Quebec
20 J3 Ecos France
20 E4 Ecouché France
20 H3 Ecouis France
20 F4 Ecouves,Forêt d' France
22 J4 Ecouviez Belgium
22 C2 Ecques France
20 A3 Ecréhou,les English Chan
111 G7 Ecru Mississippi
128 C4 Ecuador rep S America
21 H7 Écueillé France
123 K9 Ecum Secum Nova Scotia
143 B8 Edah W Australia
25 D3 Edam Netherlands
118 J5 Edam Sask
15 F1 Eday Scotland
118 E6 Edberg Alberta
109 K9 Edcouch Texas
86 H3 Edd Ethiopia
6 N6 Edda oil rig North Sea
86 E3 Ed Da'ein Sudan
86 F2 Ed Damer Sudan
86 F2 Ed Debba Sudan
32 K5 Eddelak W Germany
123 Q2 Eddies Cove Nfld
13 E2 Eddleston Scotland
15 C2 Eddrachillis B Scotland
86 F3 Ed Dueim Sudan
100 K2 Eddy Montana
109 K4 Eddy Texas
8 B7 Eddystone Lt. Ho English Chan
139 J8 Eddystone Pt Tasmania
99 O8 Eddyville Iowa
110 H4 Eddyville Kentucky
98 G8 Eddyville Nebraska
25 E4 Ede Netherlands
85 E7 Ede Nigeria
86 B5 Edea Cameroon
27 G11 Edebäck Sweden
27 K11 Edebo Sweden
130 E5 Edéia Brazil
143 A7 Edel Land pen W Australia
119 S8 Eden Manitoba
101 O2 Eden Montana
94 H10 Eden N Carolina
112 H1 Eden N Carolina
139 J6 Eden New S Wales
94 J4 Eden New York
98 J4 Eden S Dakota
108 H4 Eden Texas
101 O8 Eden Utah
99 S6 Eden Wisconsin
101 Q7 Eden Wyoming
9 G5 Edenbridge England
89 D7 Edenburg S Africa
144 B7 Edendale New Zealand
14 D3 Edenderry Irish Rep
13 F6 Edenfield England
138 F6 Edenhope Victoria
120 J8 Edenhurst Ontario
36 E5 Edenkoben W Germany
119 R2 Eden L Manitoba
9 G5 Eden,R England
71 N9 Eden,Tg C Indonesia
112 L1 Edenton N Carolina
141 G4 Eden Vale Queensland
94 C3 Edenville Michigan
119 N8 Edenwold Sask
138 E4 Edeowie S Australia
36 E1 Eder R W Germany
36 G1 Edermünde W Germany
33 O10 Edersleben E Germany
36 F1 Ederstausee res W Germany
36 G1 Edertal W Germany
27 F13 Edet, L Sweden
32 G6 Edewecht W Germany
32 G6 Edewechterdamm W Germany
101 R4 Edgar Montana
98 J9 Edgar Nebraska
111 F11 Edgard Louisiana
142 D5 Edgar, Mt W Australia
142 E4 Edgar Ra W Australia
110 E4 Edgar Springs Missouri
95 R5 Edgartown Massachusetts
109 M9 Edgecliff Texas
145 F2 Edgecumbe New Zealand
141 J5 Edgecumbe B Queensland
112 F4 Edgefield S Carolina
98 H3 Edgeley N Dakota
119 O8 Edgeley Sask
115 N5 Edgell I N W Terr
110 D6 Edgemont Arkansas
98 C6 Edgemont S Dakota
50 B1 Edgeöya isld Spitzbergen
109 O5 Edgerly Louisiana
118 G6 Edgerton Alberta
94 C5 Edgerton Ohio
99 R7 Edgerton Wisconsin
101 T6 Edgerton Wyoming
113 G9 Edgewater Florida
117 O11 Edgewood Br Col
110 H3 Edgewood Illinois
95 L7 Edgewood Maryland
106 D6 Edgewood New Mexico
109 M3 Edgewood Texas
9 F4 Edgware England
80 C8 Edh Dhahiriya Jordan
46 E4 Édhessa Greece
144 B6 Edievale New Zealand
36 C3 Ediger-Eller W Germany
84 F5 Edimpi Chad
94 G5 Edinboro Pennsylvania
99 R10 Edinburg Illinois
110 L2 Edinburg Indiana
111 G9 Edinburg Mississippi
98 J1 Edinburg N Dakota
109 J9 Edinburg Texas
94 J8 Edinburg Virginia
13 E2 Edinburgh Scotland
141 H7 Edinburgh, Mt Queensland
22 F2 Edingen Belgium
47 H3 Edirne Turkey
102 F6 Edison California
106 F3 Edison Colorado
111 M10 Edison Georgia
112 G4 Edisto R S Carolina
112 G5 Edisto Island S Carolina
138 E6 Edithburgh S Australia
117 P9 Edith Cavell,Mt Alberta
101 O3 Edith, Mt Montana
140 B2 Edith River N Terr Aust
143 D7 Edith Withnell, L W Australia
85 F3 Edjeleh Algeria
143 D8 Edjudina W Australia
13 G3 Edlingham England
38 O6 Edlitz Austria
95 M4 Edmeston New York
107 L2 Edmond Kansas
107 N6 Edmond Oklahoma
100 C2 Edmonds Washington
114 H7 Edmonton Alberta
9 F4 Edmonton England
94 C3 Edmore Michigan
98 H1 Edmore N Dakota
122 D6 Edmundston New Brunswick
109 L7 Edna Texas
13 F2 Ednam Scotland
27 J13 Ed, O Sweden
61 N10 Edo-gawa R Japan
27 M14 Edole U.S.S.R.
42 C2 Edolo Italy
26 C8 Edoy isld Norway
47 J5 Edremit Turkey
47 H5 Edremit Körfezi B Turkey
58 C3 Edrengiyn Nuruu mt Mongolia
109 K8 Edroy Texas
27 K12 Edsbro Sweden
27 H13 Edsbruk Sweden
27 H10 Edsbyn Sweden
26 J8 Edsele Sweden
Edsin Gol see Ruo Shui
58 D3 Edsin Gol China
114 H7 Edson Alberta
107 J2 Edson Kansas
27 J14 Ed, V Sweden
118 E4 Edwand Alberta
139 G6 Edward R New S Wales
140 D2 Edward I N Terr Aust
120 B4 Edward I Ontario
88 B2 Edward, L Zaïre
140 B6 Edward, Mt N Terr Aust
141 F2 Edward River Queensland
102 G7 Edwards California
111 F9 Edwards Mississippi
95 M2 Edwards New York
99 Q8 Edwards R Illinois
94 A5 Edwardsburg Michigan
138 D3 Edwards Creek S Australia
144 B7 Edwardson, C New Zealand
144 A6 Edwardson Sd New Zealand
108 G5 Edwards Plateau Texas
110 G3 Edwardsville Illinois
146 A4 Edward VIII B Antarctica
15 F4 Edzell Scotland
117 H7 Edziza, Mt Br Col
22 F1 Eeklo Belgium
100 B9 Eel R California
94 B6 Eel R Indiana
25 G2 Eelde Netherlands
25 D4 Eem R Netherlands
25 D4 Eem Meer Netherlands
89 B6 Eenzamheid Pan salt lake S Africa
22 E1 Eernegem Belgium
137 O5 Efate isld New Hebrides
38 K5 Eferding Austria
99 N2 Effie Minnesota
110 H2 Effingham Illinois
107 P2 Effingham Kansas
78 D1 Eflani Turkey
48 M6 Eforie Sud Romania
71 B3 Ef Torobi isld W Irian
28 E4 Egå Denmark
18 D10 Ega R Spain
43 E10 Egadi, I Sicily
133 F5 Egaña Argentina
103 K2 Egan Range Nevada
121 N7 Eganville Ontario
85 F7 Egbe Nigeria
98 B8 Egbert Wyoming
28 H5 Egebjerg Denmark
115 O4 Egedesminde Greenland
116 J7 Egegik B Alaska
98 G1 Egeland N Dakota
33 O9 Egeln E Germany
36 F4 Egelsbach W Germany
28 D7 Egen Denmark
28 F4 Egens Denmark
28 E3 Egense Denmark
48 F3 Eger Hungary
37 J6 Eger R W Germany
28 D7 Egernsund Denmark
27 A13 Egersund Norway
143 C6 Egerton, Mt W Australia
32 M6 Egestorf W Germany
41 L3 Egg Austria
27 D11 Eggedal Norway
31 J7 Eggenburg Austria
37 O7 Eggenfelden W Germany
33 U5 Eggesin E Germany
28 G6 Eggeslevmagle Denmark
99 T4 Egg Harbor Wisconsin
95 N7 Egg Harbor City New Jersey
95 N7 Egg Harbor, Gt New Jersey
95 N7 Egg Harbor, Little New Jersey
116 G5 Egg I Alaska
13 G4 Eggleston England
37 N6 Eggmühl W Germany
37 L4 Eggolsheim W Germany
9 F5 Egham England
22 H2 Eghezee Belgium
28 G6 Egholm isld Denmark
28 D2 Egholm isld Nordjylland Denmark
140 E4 Egilabria Queensland
15 F1 Egilsay Scotland
142 C5 Eginbah W Australia
56 F3 Egirta R U.S.S.R.
85 D3 Eglab,El reg Algeria
18 G7 Egletons France
36 G1 Egling W Germany
13 G3 Eglingham England
144 B6 Eglinton R New Zealand
114 H2 Eglinton I N W Terr
41 J2 Eglisau Switzerland
37 L4 Egloffstein W Germany
25 C3 Egmond aan Zee Netherlands
122 H7 Egmont B Pr Edward I
113 E10 Egmont Key isld Florida
145 E3 Egmont, Mt New Zealand
28 J6 Egøje Denmark
118 D4 Egremont Alberta
47 L6 Eğret Turkey
47 L7 Eğridir Turkey
78 C2 Egridir Gölü Turkey
47 K5 Egrigöz Dağı mt Turkey
47 J5 Eğri Karaağaç Dağı mt Turkey
13 H5 Egton England
28 C5 Egtved Denmark
71 E7 Eguet Pt Philippines
19 O17 Eguilles France
28 C6 Egvad Denmark
48 F3 Egyek Hungary
112 F5 Egypt Georgia
111 H8 Egypt Mississippi
109 L6 Egypt Texas
84 H4 Egypt rep Africa
79 F4 Ehdene Lebanon
36 H7 Ehingen W Germany
33 Q8 Ehle R E Germany
32 K10 Ehlen W Germany
36 F6 Ehningen W Germany
33 N7 Ehra-Lessien W Germany
113 E9 Ehren Florida
103 K8 Ehrenberg Arizona
140 B6 Ehrenberg Ra N Terr Aust
36 D3 Ehrenbreitstein W Germany
32 J7 Ehrenburg W Germany
37 O2 Ehrenfriedersdorf E Germany
112 F4 Ehrhardt S Carolina
36 E2 Ehringshausen W Germany
60 D14 Ei Japan
36 E2 Eibach W Germany
36 E2 Eibelshausen W Germany
37 J4 Eibelstadt W Germany
37 O3 Eibenstock E Germany
25 G4 Eibergen Netherlands
38 M8 Eibiswald Austria
33 O8 Eichenbarleben E Germany
37 O6 Eichendorf W Germany
37 M5 Eichhofen W Germany
32 M10 Eichsfeld mts E Germany
37 L6 Eichstätt W Germany
40 G1 Eichstetten W Germany
36 F5 Eichtersheim W Germany
33 T8 Eichwalde E Germany
36 H2 Eichzell W Germany
32 M7 Eicklingen W Germany
27 D12 Eidanger Norway
26 B9 Eide Norway
32 J4 Eider W Germany
32 L4 Eider R W Germany
26 G3 Eidsfjord Norway
27 D12 Eidsfoss Norway
27 F11 Eidskog Norway
141 K7 Eidsvold Queensland
27 E11 Eidsvoll Norway
25 C2 Eierlandse Gat Netherlands
36 B3 Eifel mts W Germany
89 F2 Eiffel Flats Zimbabwe
37 J1 Eigenrieden E Germany
40 G4 Eiger mt Switzerland
15 B4 Eigg isld Scotland
146 G12 Eights Coast Antarctica
142 D4 Eighty Mile Beach W Australia
26 A10 Eikefjord Norway
27 D12 Eikeren R Norway
26 C9 Eikesdalsvatn L Norway
86 A2 Eil Somalia
139 H6 Eildon Victoria
33 R10 Eilenburg E Germany
129 G3 Eilerts de Haan Geb mts Suriname
33 O8 Eilsleben E Germany
32 L8 Eime W Germany
33 M7 Eimke W Germany
27 E11 Eina Norway
141 G4 Einasleigh Queensland
32 L9 Einbeck W Germany
25 D6 Eindhoven Netherlands
32 L4 Einfeld W Germany
68 B4 Einme Burma
36 C5 Einöd W Germany
37 P6 Einödriegel mt W Germany
Einsiedel see Deutsch-Einsiedel
79 F8 Ein Yahav Israel
Eire rep see Irish Republic
120 G4 Eire River Ontario
128 E5 Eirunepé Brazil
22 L4 Eisch R Luxembourg
22 H2 Eisden Belgium
25 E7 Eisden Netherlands
36 C4 Eisen W Germany
37 J2 Eisenach E Germany
37 M2 Eisenberg E Germany
36 E4 Eisenberg W Germany
38 L6 Eisenerz Austria
38 L7 Eisenerzer-Alpen mts Austria
118 B7 Eisenhower, Mt Alberta
38 J8 Eisenhut mt Austria
31 H3 Eisenhüttenstadt E Germany
38 L8 Eisenkappel Austria
48 D3 Eisenstadt Austria
38 J8 Eisentratten Austria
38 L5 Eisenwurzen reg Austria
36 D2 Eiserfeld W Germany
37 K3 Eisfeld E Germany
33 P9 Eisleben E Germany
36 H6 Eislingen W Germany
37 L6 Eitensheim W Germany
36 H2 Eiterfeld W Germany
36 C2 Eitorf W Germany
28 M1 Ejde Faeroes
17 G2 Ejea de los Caballeros Spain
87 G12 Ejeda Madagascar
28 D5 Ejer Bavnehoj hill Denmark
28 B3 Ejerslev Denmark
127 J10 Ejido Venezuela
65 A5 Ejin Horo Qi China
65 C2 Ej Nur China
28 B3 Ejsing Denmark
28 C5 Ejstrup Denmark
85 D7 Ejura Ghana
98 B4 Ekalaka Montana
27 J15 Ekby Sweden
22 F2 Eke Belgium
29 K12 Ekenäs Finland
22 G1 Ekeren Belgium
145 E4 Eketahuna New Zealand
26 N5 Ekfors Sweden
46 D6 Ekhinádhes isld Greece
47 G3 Ekhínos Greece
55 G5 Ekibastuz U.S.S.R.
59 K1 Ekimchan U.S.S.R.
116 N6 Eklutna Alaska
27 J12 Ekoln L Sweden
22 F1 Eksaarde Belgium
27 G11 Ekshärad Sweden
27 G14 Eksjö Sweden
26 L7 Ekträsk Sweden
115 L7 Ekwan R Ontario
116 J7 Ekwok Alaska
68 C3 Ela Burma
El Aaiún see La'youn
46 F8 Elafónisos isld Greece
86 J4 El Afwein Somalia
111 F7 Elaine Arkansas
80 E5 El 'Ajâjira Jordan
103 H10 El Alamo Mexico
75 K10 Elamanchili India
99 R5 Eland Wisconsin
89 E5 Elands R S Africa
89 C8 Elands Berg mt S Africa
8 C3 Elan Valley Reservoirs Wales
43 B13 El-Aouinet Algeria
16 D7 El Arahal Spain
El Arâich see Larache Morocco
124 C4 El Arco Mexico
80 F5 El Ardah Jordan
141 H4 El Arish Queensland
46 E5 Elassón Greece
79 E9 Elat Israel
46 F6 Elátia Greece
86 E2 El Atrun Oasis Sudan
80 D7 El 'Azar Jordan
78 G2 Elâzığ Turkey
111 K10 Elba Alabama
101 M7 Elba Idaho
98 H8 Elba Nebraska
94 J3 Elba New York
42 C6 Elba isld Italy
79 F3 El Bahlūlīye Syria
126 H10 El Banco Colombia
16 D4 El Barco de Avila Spain
46 D3 Elbasan Albania
127 K10 El Baúl Venezuela
32 J5 Elbe est W Germany
33 M6 Elbe R W Germany
33 N5 Elbe-Lübeck Kanal W Germany
79 G4 El Beqa'a R Lebanon
110 J3 Elberfield Indiana
32 F8 Elbergen W Germany
99 O7 Elberon Iowa
109 J2 Elbert Texas
99 U5 Elberta Michigan
106 D2 Elbert,Mt Colorado
112 E3 Elberton Georgia
20 H3 Elbeuf France
Elbing see Elblag
33 N9 Elbingerode E Germany
78 F2 Elbistan Turkey
31 L1 Elblag Poland
17 F6 El Bonillo Spain
16 D9 El Borck Morocco
124 H6 El Bordo Mexico
118 L7 Elbow Sask
113 L11 Elbow Cay isld Bahamas
98 K4 Elbow L Minnesota
118 C8 Elbow R Alberta
124 J6 El Bozal Mexico
53 F11 El'brus mt U.S.S.R.
86 E4 El Buheyrat prov Sudan
86 A3 El Bur Somalia
25 E4 Elburg Netherlands
16 E3 El Burgo de Osma Spain
100 K9 Elburz Nevada
77 B1 Elburz Mountains Iran
102 H9 El Cajon California
128 F2 El Callao Venezuela
16 D5 El Campillo de la Jara Spain
109 L6 El Campo Texas
102 H9 El Capitan Res California
128 C2 El Carmen Colombia
86 H4 El Carre Ethiopia
124 G5 El Casco Mexico
17 G3 El Castellar Spain
103 J9 El Centro California
128 F7 El Cerro Bolivia
16 C7 El Cerro de Andévalo Spain
124 F3 El Charco Mexico
17 G6 Elche Spain
17 F6 Elche de la Sierra Spain
127 K9 El Chino Venezuela
99 R4 Elcho Wisconsin
140 D1 Elcho I N Terr Aust
133 E2 El Chorro Argentina
124 H5 El Cobre Mexico
128 D2 El Cocuy Colombia
126 C3 El Cotorro Cuba
126 G4 El Cristo Cuba
108 B5 El Cuervo Mexico
32 L8 Eldagsen W Germany
124 C2 El Dátil Mexico
33 Q6 Elde R E Germany
33 O6 Eldena E Germany
138 F4 Elder,L S Australia
99 R5 Elderon Wisconsin
126 G10 El Difícil Colombia
33 M7 Eldingen W Germany
124 G8 El Divisadero Mexico
128 C3 El Diviso Colombia
124 B2 El Doctor Mexico
99 O9 Eldon Iowa
110 D3 Eldon Missouri
100 B2 Eldon Washington
99 N7 Eldora Iowa
130 C10 Eldorado Argentina
109 P2 El Dorado Arkansas
130 E9 Eldorado Brazil
110 H4 Eldorado Illinois
107 O4 El Dorado Kansas
124 F5 Eldorado Mexico
114 J6 Eldorado Sask
108 G5 Eldorado Texas
128 F2 El Dorado Venezuela
89 G1 Eldorado Zimbabwe
100 D1 Eldorado,Mt Washington
103 K6 Eldorado Mts Nevada
110 B4 El Dorado Springs Missouri
88 E1 Eldoret Kenya
98 K2 Eldred Minnesota
95 N5 Eldred New York
94 J5 Eldred Pennsylvania
27 F15 Eldsberga Sweden
100 H2 Eleanor Washington
143 D10 Eleanora Pk W Australia
102 E3 Eleanor, L California
89 E4 Elebe mt Botswana
109 J1 Electra Texas
101 P5 Electric Pk Mont/Wyoming
135 O1 Eleele Hawaiian Is
52 B6 Eleja U.S.S.R.
48 G4 Elek Hungary
54 K1 Elektrogorsk U.S.S.R.
54 K1 Elektrostal' U.S.S.R.
22 J2 Elemalle Belgium
47 H2 Elena Bulgaria
128 D4 El Encanto Colombia
33 N9 Elend E Germany
106 C8 Elephant Butte New Mexico
106 C8 Elephant Butte Res New Mexico
68 G7 Elephant, Chaine de l' mts Cambodia
146 D15 Elephant I S Shetland Is
83 K8 Elephant Pass Sri Lanka
116 G3 Elephant Point Alaska
16 E4 El Escorial Spain
47 F3 Eleshnitsa Bulgaria
128 E3 El Esmeralda Venezuela
128 C3 El Espinal Colombia
84 J5 Elet, Wadi watercourse Sudan
84 C2 El Eulma Algeria
113 L12 Eleuthera I Bahamas
99 P5 Eleva Wisconsin
106 E3 Eleven Mile Canyon Res Colorado
110 E5 Eleven Point R Missouri
47 F6 Elevsís Greece
22 H2 Elewijt Belgium
80 G2 El Fahham Syria
43 C12 El Fahs Tunisia
86 E3 El Fasher Sudan
16 D9 El Fendek Morocco
16 B1 El Ferrol del C Spain
117 E6 Elfin Cove Alaska
119 O7 Elfros Sask
86 H4 El Fud Ethiopia
124 E4 El Fuerte Mexico
86 E3 El Fula Sudan
80 D5 El Fundug Jordan
26 E9 Elgå Norway
26 E9 Elgepiggen mt Norway
37 K2 Elgersburg E Germany
86 F3 El Geteina Sudan
86 F3 El Gezira prov Sudan
80 F5 El Ghor Jordan
103 O10 Elgin Arizona
99 S7 Elgin Illinois
99 P7 Elgin Iowa
119 R9 Elgin Manitoba
98 E3 Elgin N Dakota
98 H8 Elgin Nebraska
103 K4 Elgin Nevada
122 G8 Elgin New Brunswick
107 M7 Elgin Oklahoma
100 H4 Elgin Oregon
15 E3 Elgin Scotland
109 K5 Elgin Texas
103 O3 Elgin Utah
141 H5 Elgin Downs Queensland
86 F5 Elgon, Mt Uganda
86 H4 El Goran Ethiopia
17 H2 El Grado Spain
124 G8 El Grullo Mexico
128 D3 El Guamo Colombia
78 G5 El Hamad Saudi Arabia
86 A2 El Hamurre Somalia
84 H4 El Harra Egypt
86 F3 El Hawata Sudan
85 E3 El Homr Algeria
86 A2 El Hur Somalia
87 D7 Elias Garcia Angola
127 J5 Elías Piña Dom Rep
109 J3 Eliasville Texas
108 D2 Elida New Mexico
119 U9 Elie Manitoba
13 F1 Elie Scotland
46 F6 Elikón mt Greece
29 M11 Elimäki Finland
47 F2 Elin Pelin Bulgaria
95 R3 Eliot Maine
29 O10 Elisenvaara U.S.S.R.
129 K5 Eliseu Martins Brazil
53 F10 Elista U.S.S.R.
106 F2 Elizabeth Colorado
99 Q7 Elizabeth Illinois
109 P5 Elizabeth Louisiana
95 N6 Elizabeth New Jersey
94 F7 Elizabeth W Virginia
112 L1 Elizabeth City N Carolina
95 R5 Elizabeth Is Massachusetts
122 F6 Elizabeth,Mt New Brunswick
101 P9 Elizabeth Mt Utah
142 F3 Elizabeth, Mt W Australia
137 M7 Elizabeth Reef Pacific Oc
143 B7 Elizabeth Spring W Australia
94 E10 Elizabethton Tennessee
94 B7 Elizabethtown Indiana
94 B9 Elizabethtown Kentucky
112 J3 Elizabethtown N Carolina
95 O2 Elizabethtown New York
95 L6 Elizabethtown Pennsylvania
Elizabethville see Lubumbashi
95 L6 Elizabethville Pennsylvania
138 E6 Eliza,L S Australia
18 D9 Elizondo Spain
124 G4 El Jaralito Mexico
86 F3 El Jebelein Sudan
102 A2 Elk California
108 B3 Elk New Mexico
31 N2 Elk Poland
101 P6 Elk Wyoming
110 B5 Elk R Missouri
95 M7 Elk R Penn/Maryland
110 K6 Elk R Tennessee
94 F8 Elk R W Virginia
99 P7 Elkader Iowa
86 F2 El Kamlin Sudan
101 R5 Elk Basin Wyoming
100 K4 Elk City Idaho
107 P4 Elk City Kansas
107 L6 Elk City Oklahoma
102 B2 Elk Creek California
140 D5 Elkedra N Terr Aust
43 B12 El Kef Tunisia
102 C3 Elk Grove California
86 F2 El Khandaq Sudan
79 E7 El Kharrûba Egypt
94 B5 Elkhart Indiana
107 J4 Elkhart Kansas
109 M4 Elkhart Texas
99 T6 Elkhart Lake Wisconsin
101 S9 Elkhead Mts Colorado
99 L8 Elk Horn Iowa
119 Q9 Elkhorn Manitoba
99 S7 Elkhorn Wisconsin
98 H7 Elkhorn R Nebraska
47 H2 Elkhovo Bulgaria
112 G1 Elkin N Carolina
118 E5 Elk I. Nat. Park Alberta
108 C2 Elkins New Mexico
94 H8 Elkins W Virginia
94 B2 Elk L Michigan
120 K5 Elk Lake Ontario
95 K4 Elkland Pennsylvania
106 D1 Elk Mt Colorado
101 T8 Elk Mt Wyoming
100 K1 Elko Br Col
100 K9 Elko Nevada
101 P8 Elkol Wyoming
101 N3 Elk Park Montana
112 F1 Elk Park N Carolina
118 G5 Elk Point Alberta
98 K7 Elk Pt S Dakota
118 C9 Elk R Br Col
99 N4 Elk R Minnesota
94 B2 Elk Rapids Michigan
43 C12 El Krib Tunisia
100 J3 Elk River Idaho
106 B1 Elk Springs Colorado
113 F8 Elkton Florida
110 J5 Elkton Kentucky
95 M7 Elkton Maryland
99 O6 Elkton Minnesota
100 B6 Elkton Oregon
98 K5 Elkton S Dakota
110 K6 Elkton Tennessee
94 J8 Elkton Virginia
79 E9 El Kuntilla Egypt
94 C10 Elk Valley Tennessee
110 G4 Elkville Illinois
79 G4 El Laboue Lebanon
86 E3 El Lagowa Sudan
83 K10 Ellamulla Sri Lanka
12 C1 Ellanbeich Scotland
13 G6 Elland England
143 A7 Ellavalla W Australia
113 D7 Ellaville Florida
111 M9 Ellaville Georgia
37 N3 Ellefeld W Germany
114 J2 Ellef Ringnes I N W Terr
143 C10 Elleker W Australia
95 O2 Ellenburg New York
95 M8 Ellendale Delaware
111 F12 Ellendale Louisiana
98 H3 Ellendale N Dakota
103 O3 Ellen,Mt Utah
95 P2 Ellen,Mt Vermont
143 C10 Ellen Pk W Australia
13 E4 Ellen,R England
114 G8 Ellensburg Washington
32 H6 Ellenserdamm W Germany
113 E10 Ellenton Florida
95 N5 Ellenville New York
36 C3 Ellenz-Poltersdorf W Germany
112 G2 Eller N Carolina
112 H2 Ellerbe N Carolina
113 E7 Ellerbee Florida
36 D4 Ellerspring mt W Germany
144 B6 Ellery, L New Zealand
139 J6 Ellery,Mt Victoria
8 D2 Ellesmere England
115 L2 Ellesmere I N W Terr
144 D5 Ellesmere, L New Zealand
8 D1 Ellesmere Port England
110 K2 Ellettsville Indiana
22 F2 Ellezelles Belgium
Ellice Is. see Tuvalu islds state
95 L7 Ellicott City Maryland
94 J4 Ellicottville New York
28 D3 Ellidshøj Denmark
112 C3 Ellijay Georgia
28 E2 Elling Denmark
28 F6 Ellinge Denmark
37 K5 Ellingen W Germany
13 G3 Ellington England
110 F4 Ellington Missouri
107 M3 Ellinwood Kansas
95 L8 Elliot Maryland
140 C3 Elliot N Terr Aust
89 E8 Elliot S Africa
112 G3 Elliot S Carolina
139 H9 Elliot B Tasmania
120 H6 Elliot Lake Ontario
142 E4 Elliot Lake W Australia
141 H4 Elliot, Mt Queensland
99 L8 Elliott Iowa
98 J3 Elliott N Dakota
113 G12 Elliott Key isld Florida
122 H4 Ellis B Quebec
101 N3 Elliston Montana
123 T5 Elliston Nfld
138 C5 Elliston S Australia
94 G9 Elliston Virginia
111 G10 Ellisville Mississippi
143 G8 Ell, L W Australia
38 F6 Ellmau Austria
36 F6 Ellmendingen W Germany
15 F3 Ellon Scotland
74 F8 Ellora India
112 G4 Elloree S Carolina
33 N9 Ellrich W Germany
118 E4 Ellscott Alberta
110 F5 Ellsinore Missouri
107 M3 Ellsworth Kansas
95 T2 Ellsworth Maine
99 L6 Ellsworth Minnesota
98 D7 Ellsworth Nebraska
99 O5 Ellsworth Wisconsin
109 J1 Ellsworth,L Oklahoma
146 G11 Ellsworth Land Antarctica
146 G10 Ellsworth Mts Antarctica
37 J6 Ellwangen W Germany
94 G6 Ellwood City Pennsylvania
32 H6 Ellwürden W Germany
41 K4 Elm Switzerland
32 K5 Elm W Germany
99 O6 Elma Iowa
100 B2 Elma Washington
79 G2 El Ma'arra Syria
133 C6 El Maitén Argentina
47 K8 Elmalı Turkey
78 B3 Elmali Turkey
86 F3 El Manaquil Sudan
124 A2 El Maneadero Mexico
124 G5 El Martínez Mexico
109 L7 Elmaton Texas
103 J9 El Mayor Mexico
79 D7 El Mazâr Egypt
112 K2 Elm City N Carolina
98 G9 Elm Cr Nebraska
118 D1 Elm Creek Manitoba
107 N6 Elm Cr.Res.,E Oklahoma
108 A2 Elmendorf New Mexico
127 J9 El Mene de Mauroa Venezuela
32 M5 Elmenhorst W Germany
99 O10 Elmer Missouri
95 M7 Elmer New Jersey
109 H1 Elmer Oklahoma
100 G1 Elmer City Washington
43 B13 El Meskiana Algeria
99 T8 Elmhurst Illinois
79 F4 El Mina Lebanon
102 C3 Elmira California
94 C1 Elmira Michigan
95 L4 Elmira New York
123 K7 Elmira Pr Edward I
98 H4 Elm L S Dakota
109 K4 Elm Mott Texas
107 N3 Elmo Kansas
99 L9 Elmo Missouri
101 T8 Elmo Wyoming
16 E4 El Molar Spain
108 G7 El Moral Mexico
111 K9 Elmore Alabama
99 M6 Elmore Minnesota
94 D5 Elmore Ohio
139 G6 Elmore Victoria
109 K1 Elmore City Oklahoma
106 B6 El Morro Nat.Mon New Mexico
122 J9 Elmsdale Nova Scotia
32 L5 Elmshorn W Germany
98 D5 Elm Springs S Dakota
36 D5 Elmstein W Germany
122 J8 Elmsvale Nova Scotia
86 E3 ElMuglad Sudan
110 G1 Elmwood Illinois
107 K5 Elmwood Oklahoma
120 J8 Elmwood Ontario
99 O5 Elmwood Wisconsin
18 G10 Elne France
71 D5 El Nido Philippines
118 D7 Elnora Alberta
110 J3 Elnora Indiana
86 F3 El Obeid Sudan
111 G12 Eloi Bay Louisiana
80 D1 Elon Israel
110 K6 Elora Tennessee
125 J8 El Oro Mexico
128 C4 El Oro prov Ecuador
124 F6 Elota Mexico
103 N9 Eloy Arizona
124 G5 El Palmito Mexico
128 F2 El Pao Venezuela
16 E4 El Pardo Spain
99 R9 El Paso Illinois
108 A4 El Paso Texas
131 B4 El Peñón peak Chile
14 C3 Elphin Irish Rep
119 R8 Elphinstone Manitoba
141 J5 Elphinstone Queensland
127 N9 El Pilar Venezuela
133 E2 El Pintado Argentina
83 K11 Elpitiya Sri Lanka
102 E4 El Portal California
128 C5 El Portugues Peru
108 B4 El Porvenir Mexico
16 D5 El Puente del Arzobispo Spain
16 C8 El Puerto de Sta. Maria Spain
79 G3 El Qadmūs Syria
80 E1 El Qouzah Lebanon
131 B2 Elqui R Chile
79 E8 El Quşeima Egypt
79 G4 El Quseir Syria
79 F9 El Quweira Jordan
124 G6 El Regocijo Mexico
108 F7 El Remolino Mexico
125 J6 El Retorno Mexico
106 D5 El Rito New Mexico
98 J5 Elrod S Dakota
16 C7 El Ronquillo Spain
99 M4 Elrosa Minnesota
118 J7 Elrose Sask
99 Q6 Elroy Wisconsin
124 H6 El Rucio Mexico
109 K9 Elsa Texas
114 F5 Elsa Yukon Terr
42 D5 Elsa R Italy
124 G6 El Salto Mexico
71 G6 El Salvador Mindanao Philippines
125 P11 El Salvador rep Cent America
120 H4 Elsas Ontario
108 A6 El Sauz Mexico
109 J9 El Sauz Texas
25 E4 Elsberg hill Netherlands
110 F2 Elsberry Missouri
32 K6 Elsdorf W Germany
32 H8 Else R W Germany
28 F4 Elsegørde Denmark
22 L3 Elsenborn Belgium
36 F5 Elsenz R W Germany
140 C2 Elsey N Terr Aust
26 G5 Elsfjord Norway
32 H6 Elsfleth W Germany
98 E9 Elsie Nebraska
100 B4 Elsie Oregon
102 G8 Elsinore California
103 M3 Elsinore Utah
102 G8 Elsinore L California
25 E7 Elsloo Netherlands
98 F7 Elsmere Nebraska
107 P4 Elsmore Kansas
33 Q9 Elsnigk E Germany
130 C10 El Soberbio Argentina
127 M10 El Socorro Venezuela
127 L10 El Sombrero Venezuela
116 K1 Elson Lagoon Alaska
25 E4 Elspeet Netherlands
25 E5 Elst Netherlands
9 F5 Elstead England
33 R9 Elster E Germany
33 Q10 Elster R E Germany
37 N2 Elsterberg E Germany
33 T10 Elsterwerda E Germany
145 F3 Elsthorpe New Zealand
9 F4 Elstree England
108 A6 El Sueco Mexico
124 G8 El Tabaco Mexico
16 C2 El Teleno mt Spain
25 F5 Elten W Germany
37 O2 Elterlein E Germany
9 G5 Eltham England
145 E3 Eltham New Zealand
79 E9 El Thamad Egypt
128 F2 El Tigre Venezuela
9 F3 Eltisley England
37 K4 Eltmann W Germany
128 E2 El Tocuyo Venezuela
109 P5 Elton Louisiana
100 G3 Eltopia Washington
102 G8 El Toro California
133 C3 El toro Chile
133 C3 El Tránsito Chile
124 C2 El Tren Mexico
124 D6 El Triunfo Mexico
118 K1 Eltrut L Ontario
127 O2 El Tucuche mt Trinidad
133 C8 El Turbio Argentina
36 E3 Eltville W Germany
76 E2 Eluru India
119 Q9 Elva Manitoba
106 D5 El Vado New Mexico
128 C2 El Valle Colombia
127 L9 El Valle Venezuela
12 E3 Elvanfoot Scotland
27 E10 Elvdal Norway
26 N2 Elvebakken Norway
27 E11 Elverum Norway
125 L3 El Viejo Nicaragua
128 D2 El Vigia Venezuela
128 D5 Elvira Brazil
114 J3 Elvira,C N W Terr
142 B5 Elvire, Mt W Australia
143 C8 Elvire, Mt W Australia
142 G4 Elvire, R W Australia
44 D1 Elvo R Italy
133 C4 El Volcán Chile
86 H5 El Wak Kenya
99 S8 Elwood Illinois
94 B6 Elwood Indiana
110 B2 Elwood Missouri
98 G9 Elwood Nebraska
9 G3 Ely England
99 P8 Ely Iowa
99 P2 Ely Minnesota
103 K2 Ely Nevada
80 D3 Elyaqim Israel
138 C3 Ely Hill S Australia
99 N5 Elysian Minnesota
36 E3 Elz W Germany
40 H1 Elz R W Germany
36 E7 Elzach W Germany
124 G5 El Zape Mexico
32 L7 Elze W Germany
27 G10 Emådalen Sweden
137 O5 Emae isld New Hebrides
77 D1 Emāmrūd Iran
27 H14 Emån R Sweden
57 A1 Emba U.S.S.R.
50 E4 Emba R U.S.S.R.
122 G1 Embar Labrador
133 E2 Embarcación Argentina
110 H2 Embarras R Illinois
114 H6 Embarras Portage Alberta
99 O2 Embarrass Minnesota
98 J3 Embden N Dakota
60 P1 Embetsu Japan
128 D5 Embira R Brazil
101 R5 Emblem Wyoming
13 G3 Embleton England
47 J8 Embóna Rhodes Greece
121 P7 Embrun Ontario
88 F2 Embu Kenya
99 R9 Emden Illinois
32 F6 Emden W Germany
67 A2 Emei China
67 A2 Emei Shan mt China
80 F1 Emeq Hula Israel
80 D2 'Emeq Zevulun Israel
98 J2 Emerado N Dakota
141 J6 Emerald Queensland
114 H2 Emerald I N W Terr
71 D5 Emergency Pt Philippines
115 N7 Emeril Labrador
99 L8 Emerson Iowa
119 U9 Emerson Manitoba
98 K7 Emerson Nebraska
98 J6 Emery S Dakota
47 K5 Emet Turkey
101 P4 Emigrant Montana
102 D2 Emigrant Gap California
100 J9 Emigrant Pass Nevada
101 P4 Emigrant Pk Montana
103 J4 Emigrant Valley Nevada
86 C2 Emi Koussi mt Chad
42 D4 Emilia-Romagna prov Italy
40 F6 Emilius, M Italy
47 J2 Emine,N Bulgaria
94 B8 Eminence Kentucky
110 E4 Eminence Missouri
47 K7 Emir R Turkey
78 C2 Emirdag Turkey
139 J7 Emita Flinders I, Tasmania
94 H5 Emlenton Pennsylvania
32 E7 Emlichheim W Germany
27 H15 Emmaboda Sweden
126 B1 Emmastad Curaçao
27 N13 Emmaste U.S.S.R.
95 M6 Emmaus Pennsylvania
139 K3 Emmaville New S Wales
40 G4 Emme R Switzerland
118 L3 Emmeline L Sask
25 E3 Emmeloord Netherlands
25 G3 Emmen Netherlands
41 H3 Emmen Switzerland
40 G4 Emmen Tal Switzerland
25 F5 Emmerich W Germany
28 B7 Emmerlev Denmark
32 K8 Emmern W Germany
38 M5 Emmersdorf Austria
28 B7 Emmerske Denmark
32 K9 Emmerthal W Germany
100 J6 Emmet Idaho
98 H7 Emmet Nebraska
141 G6 Emmet Queensland
99 M6 Emmetsburg Iowa
107 O2 Emmett Kansas
76 C3 Emmiganuru India
95 K7 Emmitsburg Maryland
103 O1 Emmons,Mt Utah
99 N1 Emo Ontario
48 F3 Emöd Hungary
109 M3 Emory Texas
108 D6 Emory Pk Texas
124 D4 Empalme Mexico
89 G7 Empangeni S Africa
32 K7 Empede W Germany
133 F3 Empedrado Argentina
25 F5 Empel W Germany
112 D5 Empire Georgia
99 U5 Empire Michigan
100 F9 Empire Nevada
100 A6 Empire Oregon
106 F1 Empire Res Colorado
42 D5 Empoli Italy
107 O3 Emporia Kansas
94 K10 Emporia Virginia
94 J5 Emporium Pennsylvania
118 G8 Empress Alberta
22 J3 Emptinne Belgium
19 N14 Empurany France
98 G2 Emrick N Dakota
32 F6 Ems R W Germany
32 F8 Emsbüren W Germany
32 F9 Emscher R W Germany
121 L7 Emsdale Ontario
32 G8 Emsdetten W Germany
32 G6 Ems-Jade Kanal W Germany
37 K4 Emskirchen W Germany
32 F7 Emslage W Germany
36 G1 Emstal W Germany
32 H7 Emstek W Germany
9 F6 Emsworth England
65 G3 Emu China
141 F3 Emu Ck Queensland
142 C5 Emu Spring W Australia
61 L10 Ena Japan
27 J10 Enånger Sweden
80 C3 'En Ayyala Israel
101 T8 Encampment Wyoming
17 H4 Encanade mt Spain
108 B6 Encantada Mexico
124 B2 Encantada, Cerro de la Mexico
131 H3 Encantadas,Sa mts Brazil
124 C4 Encantado, Cerro mt Mexico
71 E3 Encanto,C Luzon Philippines
124 H7 Encarnación Mexico
130 C10 Encarnación Paraguay
118 E8 Enchant Alberta
85 D7 Enchi Ghana
109 H7 Encinal Texas
108 A6 Encinillas Mexico
102 G8 Encinitas California
108 B1 Encino New Mexico
108 B2 Encinoso New Mexico
128 D2 Encontrados Venezuela
138 E6 Encounter B S Australia
133 G4 Encruzilhada do Sul Brazil
117 L8 Endako Br Col
69 F11 Endau Malaysia
69 F11 Endau R Malaysia
71 K9 Ende isld Flores Indonesia
99 R6 Endeavor Wisconsin
141 H3 Endeavour Queensland
119 P6 Endeavour Sask
141 F1 Endeavour Str Queensland
108 A8 Endee New Mexico
28 E5 Endelave Denmark
134 K8 Enderbury I Phoenix Is Pacific Oc
117 O10 Enderby Br Col
142 B5 Enderby I W Australia
146 B6 Enderby Land Antarctica
98 J3 Enderlin N Dakota
98 E9 Enders Res Nebraska
118 E7 Endiang Alberta
95 L4 Endicott New York
100 H3 Endicott Washington
117 G7 Endicott Arm pen Alaska

26 Fairview — Folsom L

94 G7 **Fairview** W Virginia
117 D6 **Fairweather,C** Alaska
117 E6 **Fairweather,Mt** Br Col/Alaska
119 N5 **Fairy Glen** Sask
74 E3 **Faisalabad** India
112 J2 **Faison** N Carolina
22 H4 **Faissault** France
98 D4 **Faith** S Dakota
79 A9 **Faiyûm,El** Egypt
57 F6 **Faizabad** Afghanistan
66 C6 **Faizabad** India
127 M5 **Fajardo** Puerto Rico
135 N10 **Fakarava** *atoll* Tuamotu Arch **Pacific Oc**
9 G2 **Fakenham** England
136 G2 **Fakfak** W Irian
47 J2 **Fakiya** Bulgaria
28 J6 **Fakse** Denmark
28 J6 **Fakse Ladeplads** Denmark
65 F3 **Faku** China
20 E4 **Falaise** France
117 P5 **Falaise L** N W Terr
47 F3 **Falakrón** *mt* Greece
68 A1 **Falam** Burma
80 D5 **Falama** Jordan
48 L4 **Fălciu** Romania
106 F3 **Falcon** Colorado
128 D1 **Falcón** *state* Venezuela
45 O4 **Falconara Marittima** Italy
120 K6 **Falconbridge** Ontario
17 G9 **Falcon,C** Algeria
43 B8 **Falcone,C.del** Sardinia
94 H4 **Falconer** New York
109 H9 **Falcon Res** Texas/Mexico
28 E6 **Faldsled** Denmark
85 B6 **Falémé** *R* **Senegal/Mali**
52 H5 **Falenki** U.S.S.R.
27 H13 **Falerum** Sweden
48 L3 **Faleshty** U.S.S.R.
109 J8 **Falfurrias** Texas
117 P8 **Falher** Alberta
100 A9 **Falk** California
33 S9 **Falkenberg** Cottbus E Germany
33 T7 **Falkenberg** Frankfurt E Germany
37 O7 **Falkenberg** Niederbayern W Germany
121 L7 **Falkenberg** Ontario
27 F15 **Falkenberg** Sweden
37 N4 **Falkenberg** W Germany
33 Q6 **Falkenhagen** E Germany
33 S7 **Falkensee** E Germany
37 N3 **Falkenstein** E Germany
37 O5 **Falkenstein** W Germany
12 E2 **Falkirk** Scotland
117 O10 **Falkland** Br Columbia
13 E1 **Falkland** Scotland
131 G8 **Falkland Is** Atlantic Oc
133 E8 **Falkland Sd** Falkland Is
47 F8 **Falkonéra** *isld* Greece
27 F13 **Falköping** Sweden
111 K7 **Falkville** Alabama
125 P9 **Fallabón** Guatemala
102 G8 **Fallbrook** California
100 D2 **Fall City** Washington
99 P5 **Fall Creek** Wisconsin
33 N8 **Fallersleben** W Germany
26 L6 **Fällfors** Sweden
28 E5 **Falling** Denmark
32 L7 **Fallingbostel** W Germany
15 C3 **Fall of Glomach** Scotland
98 A3 **Fallon** Montana
102 F2 **Fallon** Nevada
95 Q5 **Fall River** Massachusetts
100 D8 **Fall River Mills** California
107 O4 **Fall R.Res** Kansas
95 N5 **Fallsburg, S** New York
99 L9 **Falls City** Nebraska
100 B5 **Falls City** Oregon
109 J7 **Falls City** Texas
94 J5 **Falls Cr** Pennsylvania
15 E5 **Falls of Clyde** Scotland
15 D3 **Falls of Foyers** Scotland
72 E2 **Fallūjah, Al** Iraq
22 H3 **Falmagne** Belgium
9 F6 **Falmer** England
127 P4 **Falmouth** Antigua **W I**
8 A7 **Falmouth** England
127 J1 **Falmouth** Jamaica
94 C8 **Falmouth** Kentucky
95 R5 **Falmouth** Massachusetts
94 B2 **Falmouth** Michigan
94 K8 **Falmouth** Virginia
95 R3 **Falmouth-Foreside** Maine
8 B7 **Fal,R** England
89 A10 **False B** S Africa
116 F9 **False Pass** Aleutian Is
141 F2 **False Pera Hd** Queensland
94 D1 **False Presque I** Michigan
17 H3 **Falset** Spain
127 J5 **Falso, C** Dom Rep
124 E6 **Falso,C** Mexico
133 D9 **Falso C. de Hornos** Chile
28 H7 **Falster** *isld* Denmark
28 K6 **Falsterbo** Sweden
13 F3 **Falstone** England
42 D5 **Falterona, M** *mt* Italy
48 K3 **Fălticeni** Romania
27 H11 **Falun** Sweden
71 C3 **Fam** *isld* W Irian
79 D3 **Famagusta** Cyprus
86 F3 **Famaka** Sudan
133 D3 **Famatina** Argentina
133 D3 **Famatina, Sa. de** *mts* Argentina
22 J3 **Famenne** Belgium
143 E7 **Fame Ra** W Australia
143 F6 **Family Well** W Australia
28 N3 **Fámjin** Faeroes
102 E6 **Famoso** California
71 C2 **Fan** *isld* W Irian
14 D1 **Fanad Hd** Irish Rep
145 E1 **Fanal I** New Zealand
45 J3 **Fanano** Italy
67 F1 **Fanchang** China
110 H5 **Fancy Farm** Kentucky
87 H12 **Fandriana** Madagascar
86 F4 **Fangak** Sudan
58 F5 **Fangcheng** China
67 C6 **Fangcheng** China
67 C1 **Fangdou Shan** *mts* China
28 E6 **Fangel** Denmark
65 B5 **Fanglan** China
65 B6 **Fangshan** China
67 C1 **Fang Xian** China
65 G2 **Fangzheng** China
65 D6 **Fangzi** China
65 F3 **Fanjiatun** China
111 B12 **Fannett** Texas
111 G9 **Fannin** Mississippi
109 K7 **Fannin** Texas
135 U9 **Fanning I** *atoll* **Pac Oc**
77 F6 **Fannuj** Iran
117 L11 **Fanny Bay** Br Columbia
119 U9 **Fannystelle** Manitoba
42 E5 **Fano** Italy
28 A6 **Fanø** *isld* Denmark
65 B5 **Fanshi** China
68 F1 **Fan Si Pan** *mt* Vietnam
65 C7 **Fan Xian** China
18 C4 **Faouët,le** France
80 F8 **Faqu** Jordan
79 B8 **Fâqûs** Egypt
80 F4 **Fara** Jordan
141 H6 **Faraday, Mt** Queensland
86 E5 **Faradje** Zaïre
87 H12 **Farafangana** Madagascar
45 Q8 **Faraglioni** Italy
77 H3 **Farāh** Afghanistan
77 H3 **Farah Rud** *R* Afghanistan
45 N5 **Fara in Sabina** Italy
102 A4 **Farallon Is** California
85 D6 **Faramana** Upper Volta
85 B6 **Faranah** Guinea
86 H2 **Farasan I** Red Sea
84 J5 **Farâyid,G.El** *mt* Egypt
28 C4 **Fårbæk** Denmark
110 E2 **Farber** Missouri
26 J6 **Fårberg** Sweden
48 J3 **Farcaului** *mt* Romania
16 E7 **Fardes** *R* Spain
28 A4 **Fåre** Denmark
36 B5 **Farebersviller** France
9 E6 **Fareham** England
28 H6 **Farendløse** Denmark
28 G5 **Fårevejle** Denmark
116 L5 **Farewell** Alaska
Farewell, C Greenland *see* **Farvel,Kap**
145 D4 **Farewell, C** New Zealand
98 K3 **Fargo** N Dakota
107 L5 **Fargo** Oklahoma
28 K4 **Farhult** Sweden
28 C7 **Fårhus** Denmark
77 J2 **Fāriab** Afghanistan
80 F5 **Fari'a el Jiftlick** Jordan
99 N5 **Faribault** Minnesota
121 Q3 **Faribault** Quebec
75 N7 **Faridpur** Bangladesh
84 G3 **Farigh** *watercourse* Libya
16 A5 **Farilhões** *isld* Portugal
26 H10 **Färilla** Sweden
85 A6 **Farim** Guinea-Bissau
138 E4 **Farina** S Australia
9 E4 **Faringdon** England
27 K12 **Faringe** Sweden
106 E4 **Farista** Colorado
27 H15 **Färjestaden** Sweden
80 D5 **Farkha** Jordan
118 H1 **Farlane** Ontario
141 J5 **Farleigh** Queensland
99 P7 **Farley** Iowa
106 F5 **Farley** New Mexico
121 O6 **Farley** Quebec
98 J6 **Farmer** S Dakota
99 S9 **Farmer City** Illinois
109 O8 **Farmers Branch** Texas
99 T10 **Farmersburg** Indiana
99 P7 **Farmersburg** Iowa
109 L2 **Farmersville** Texas
111 D9 **Farmerville** Louisiana
95 N6 **Farmingdale** New Jersey
98 D6 **Farmingdale** S Dakota
117 N8 **Farmington** Br Col
102 D4 **Farmington** California
99 Q9 **Farmington** Illinois
99 P9 **Farmington** Iowa
95 R2 **Farmington** Maine
99 N5 **Farmington** Minnesota
110 F4 **Farmington** Missouri
95 Q3 **Farmington** New Hampshire
106 B5 **Farmington** New Mexico
101 O9 **Farmington** Utah
100 H2 **Farmington** Washington
94 G7 **Farmington** W Virginia
94 B6 **Farmland** Indiana
98 C2 **Farm Unit** N Dakota
112 K2 **Farmville** N Carolina
94 J9 **Farmville** Virginia
98 F9 **Farnam** Nebraska
9 F5 **Farnborough** England
8 D1 **Farndon** England
13 G2 **Farne Is** England
112 C2 **Farner** Tennessee
27 C10 **Farnes** Norway
9 F5 **Farnham** England
94 H4 **Farnham** New York
121 S7 **Farnham** Quebec
117 P10 **Farnham,Mt** Br Col
9 G5 **Farningham** England
13 F6 **Farnworth** England
129 G4 **Faro** Brazil
16 B7 **Faro** Portugal
117 G4 **Faro** Yukon Terr
28 H7 **Farø** *isld* Denmark
27 K14 **Fårö** *isld* Gotland **Sweden**
71 G6 **Farol Pt** Philippines
43 G10 **Faro,Pta d** Sicily
86 B4 **Faro R** Cameroon
16 B2 **Faro, Sa del** *mts* Spain
27 K14 **Fårösund** Gotland **Sweden**
81 B7 **Farquhar I** Indian Oc
87 J10 **Farquhar Is** Br Indian Oc Terr
141 F6 **Farrars Cr** Queensland
26 H5 **Farras** *mt* Sweden
77 C5 **Farrāshband** Iran
94 G5 **Farrell** Pennsylvania
121 P7 **Farrellton** Quebec
8 D5 **Farrington Gurney** England
28 C6 **Farris** Denmark
77 C5 **Fārs** Iran
46 E5 **Fársala** Greece
77 H3 **Farsi** Afghanistan
85 C3 **Farsia,El** Morocco
28 C3 **Farsø** Denmark
99 O8 **Farson** Iowa
101 Q7 **Farson** Wyoming
27 B13 **Farsund** Norway
130 D10 **Fartura,Serra da** *mts* Brazil
28 D4 **Fårvang** Denmark
115 P6 **Farvel,Kap** *C* Greenland
94 C3 **Farwell** Michigan
98 H8 **Farwell** Nebraska
108 D1 **Farwell** Texas
77 C5 **Fasā** Iran
43 H8 **Fasano** Italy
109 J7 **Fashing** Texas
79 A10 **Fashn,El** Egypt
28 B5 **Faster** Denmark
28 C4 **Fasterholt** Denmark
14 B5 **Fastnet Rock** Irish Rep
74 F7 **Fatehabad** India
74 H5 **Fatehgarh** India
45 O7 **Fate, Mt. delle** Italy
54 G4 **Fatezh** U.S.S.R.
78 J4 **Fathan,Al** Iraq
121 P3 **Father,L** Quebec
123 L6 **Fatima** Madeleine Is, Quebec
16 B5 **Fatina** Portugal
78 F1 **Fatsa** Turkey
135 N9 **Fatu Hiva** *isld* Marquesas Is Pac Oc
86 C6 **Fatunda** Zaïre
110 B2 **Faucett** Missouri
40 D6 **Faucigny** *dist* France
19 K4 **Faucilles, Mts** France
45 J4 **Fauglia** Italy
40 G4 **Faulhorn** *mt* Switzerland
98 G4 **Faulkton** S Dakota
111 J9 **Faunsdale** Alabama
22 C2 **Fauquembergues** France
117 O11 **Fauquier** Br Col
48 L5 **Făurei** Romania
89 D7 **Fauresmith** S Africa
26 H4 **Fauske** Norway
118 B3 **Faust** Alberta
95 N2 **Faust** New York
101 N9 **Faust** Utah
20 G2 **Fauville** France
87 H13 **Faux Cap** Madagascar
43 F11 **Favara** Sicily
19 Q13 **Faverges** France
20 J4 **Faverolles** Eure France
9 G5 **Faversham** England
43 E11 **Favignana** *isld* Sicily
28 C4 **Favrholt** Denmark
77 A5 **Faw, Al** Iraq
118 C4 **Fawcett** Alberta
118 D3 **Fawcett L** Alberta
9 E6 **Fawley** England
115 L7 **Fawn** *R* Ontario
115 R5 **Faxa Flói** *B* Iceland
26 J8 **Faxälven** *R* Sweden
27 F10 **Faxfj** *mt* Norway
107 M6 **Fay** Oklahoma
Faya *see* **Largeau**
86 C2 **Faya-Largeau** Chad
54 F2 **Fayansovyy** U.S.S.R.
21 B7 **Fay-de-Bret** France
119 Q3 **Faye Lake** Manitoba
21 F8 **Faye-la-Vineuse** France
111 J8 **Fayette** Alabama
99 P7 **Fayette** Iowa
99 U4 **Fayette** Michigan
111 E10 **Fayette** Mississippi
110 D2 **Fayette** Missouri
94 C5 **Fayette** Ohio
103 N2 **Fayette** Utah
110 B5 **Fayetteville** Arkansas
111 M8 **Fayetteville** Georgia
112 J2 **Fayetteville** N Carolina
110 N2 **Fayetteville** Ohio
110 K6 **Fayetteville** Tennessee
109 L6 **Fayetteville** Texas
94 F8 **Fayetteville** W Virginia
22 F3 **Fay le Franc** Belgium
109 J9 **Faysville** Texas
80 G1 **Fazarah** Syria
74 F3 **Fazilka** India
85 B4 **Fdérik** Mauritania
14 B4 **Feale** *R* Irish Rep
102 C3 **Feather** *R* California
102 C2 **Feather Falls** California
145 E4 **Featherston** New Zealand
139 H6 **Feathertop,Mt** Victoria
101 K6 **Featherville** Idaho
144 A6 **Febrero Pt** New Zealand
20 F2 **Fécamp** France
40 F1 **Fecht** *R* France
133 F4 **Federación** Argentina
98 A8 **Federal** Wyoming
99 M2 **Federal Dam** Minnesota
95 M8 **Federalsburg** Maryland
27 A11 **Fedje** *isld* Norway
98 J5 **Fedora** S Dakota
14 B3 **Feeagh,L** Irish Rep
36 D7 **Fegersheim** France
28 B3 **Feggesund** *chan* Denmark
30 F1 **Fehmarn** *isld* W Germany
33 R7 **Fehrbellin** E Germany
38 O8 **Fehring** Austria
130 H8 **Feia, Lagoa** *L* Brazil
65 C6 **Feicheng** China
67 F1 **Feidong** China
65 C7 **Fei Huang** *R* China
128 D5 **Feijó** Brazil
67 D5 **Feilai Xia** *R* China
145 E4 **Feilding** New Zealand
88 C9 **Feira** Zambia
129 L6 **Feira de Santana** Brazil
38 J8 **Feistritz** Austria
38 K8 **Feistritz-im-Ros** Austria
67 F1 **Feixi** China
65 D7 **Fei Xian** China
65 C6 **Feixiang** China
129 K8 **Feja, L** Brazil
48 E3 **Fejer** *co* Hungary
28 G7 **Fejø** *isld* Denmark
48 D5 **Fekete Viz** *R* Hungary
17 K5 **Felanitx** Majorca
9 F5 **Felbridge** England
99 T3 **Felch** Michigan
36 G2 **Feldatal** W Germany
38 N8 **Feldbach** Austria
28 F4 **Feldballe** Denmark
33 S6 **Feldberg** E Germany
40 H2 **Feldberg** *mt* W Germany
28 C3 **Feldingbjerg** Denmark
41 L3 **Feldkirch** Austria
131 F3 **Feliciano** *R* Argentina
83 J12 **Felicité I** Seychelles
94 C8 **Felicity** Ohio
73 L8 **Felidu Atoll** Maldives
130 G6 **Felixlândia** Brazil
106 F8 **Felix,R** New Mexico
108 C3 **Felix, Rio** New Mexico
9 H4 **Felixstowe** England
108 B5 **Félix U. Gómez** Mexico
36 B4 **Fell** W Germany
36 G6 **Fellbach** W Germany
21 J10 **Felletin** France
13 G4 **Felling** England
102 E6 **Fellows** California
127 M2 **Fellowship** Jamaica
113 G10 **Fellsmere** Florida
45 K2 **Felonica** Italy
9 F6 **Felpham** England
36 G1 **Felsberg** W Germany
28 C7 **Felsted** Denmark
108 B7 **Felt** Oklahoma
102 B4 **Felton** California
13 G3 **Felton** England
111 L8 **Felton** Georgia
98 K2 **Felton** Minnesota
42 D2 **Feltre** Italy
28 F4 **Femmøller** Denmark
28 H7 **Femø** *isld* Denmark
28 G7 **Femø Sund** *chan* Denmark
87 G13 **Fenambosy, Pte** Madagascar
106 B7 **Fence Lake** New Mexico
65 B7 **Fencheng** China
121 M8 **Fenelon Falls** Ontario
36 B6 **Fénétrange** France
21 D6 **Feneu** France
59 H3 **Fengcheng** China
67 E2 **Fengcheng** China
67 D5 **Fengchuan** China
67 B2 **Fengdu** China
58 F4 **Fengfeng** China
67 B3 **Fenggang** China
67 G2 **Fenghua** China
67 C3 **Fenghuang** China
67 C1 **Fengjie** *R* China
67 D5 **Fengkai** China
65 F2 **Fengle** China
67 D1 **Fengle** China
67 E5 **Fengliang** China
65 A7 **Fenglingdu** China
65 D5 **Fengnan** China
65 C4 **Fengning** China
67 G2 **Fengqiao** China
65 C7 **Fengqiu** China
65 D5 **Fengrun** China
65 D4 **Fengshan** China
67 B4 **Fengshan** China
58 G4 **Fengtai** China
67 F4 **Fengting** China
67 B5 **Fengwu** China
65 C7 **Feng Xian** China
67 G1 **Fengxian** China
58 E5 **Fengxiang** China
67 E2 **Fengxin** China
Fengyi *see* **Zheng'an**
Fengyizhen *see* **Maowen**
65 B4 **Fengzhen** China
65 B6 **Fen He** *R* China
116 H2 **Feniak L** Alaska
14 B4 **Fenit** Irish Rep
100 J4 **Fenn** Idaho
103 J7 **Fenner** California
99 Q7 **Fennimore** Wisconsin
94 A4 **Fennville** Michigan
9 F3 **Fenny Stratford** England
87 H11 **Fenoarivo Atsinanana** Madagascar
28 H6 **Fensmark** Denmark
9 F3 **Fenstanton** England
109 P5 **Fenton** Louisiana
94 D4 **Fenton** Michigan
119 M6 **Fenton** Sask
95 L10 **Fentress** Virginia
135 L10 **Fenua Ura** *isld* Society Is Pacific Oc
13 G2 **Fenwick** England
121 L9 **Fenwick** Ontario
12 D2 **Fenwick** Strathclyde Scotland
94 G8 **Fenwick** W Virginia
119 O7 **Fenwood** Sask
99 Q5 **Fenwood** Wisconsin
65 B6 **Fenxi** China
65 B6 **Fenyang** China
67 E3 **Fenyi** China
22 H3 **Fépin** France
26 E9 **Feragen** *L* Norway
85 F1 **Fer,C.de** Algeria
100 J3 **Ferdinand** Idaho
110 K3 **Ferdinand** Indiana
33 T5 **Ferdinandshof** E Germany
18 H4 **Fère-Champenoise** France
22 E4 **Fère,La** France
26 E8 **Feren** *L* Norway
45 O6 **Ferentino** Italy
57 F4 **Fergana** U.S.S.R.
57 K6 **Fergana Basin** U.S.S.R.
57 G4 **Ferganskiy Khr** *mts* U.S.S.R.
101 Q2 **Fergus** Montana
98 K3 **Fergus Falls** Minnesota
140 B2 **Fergusson** *R* N Terr **Aust**
118 E6 **Ferintosh** Alberta
85 C7 **Ferkéssédougou** Ivory Coast
120 B2 **Ferland** Ontario
14 D2 **Fermanagh** *co* N Ireland
20 C2 **Fermanville** France
121 P6 **Ferme Neuve** Quebec
33 S9 **Fermerswalde** E Germany
45 N4 **Fermignano** Italy
42 F5 **Fermo** Italy
16 C3 **Fermoselle** Spain
14 C4 **Fermoy** Irish Rep
128 A8 **Fernandina** *isld* Galapagos Is
113 F7 **Fernandina Beach** Florida
90 G9 **Fernando de Noronha** *isld* Atlantic Oc
130 E7 **Fernandópolis** Brazil
Fernando Póo *isld see* **Bioko**
16 D7 **Fernán Núñez** Spain
130 G5 **Fernão Dias** Brazil
100 C1 **Ferndale** Washington
98 H4 **Ferney** S Dakota
9 F5 **Fernhurst** England
118 B9 **Fernie** Br Col
141 H8 **Fernlee** Queensland
102 E2 **Fernley** Nevada
41 N3 **Fern Pass** Austria
100 B5 **Fern Ridge Res** Oregon
14 E4 **Ferns** Irish Rep
144 D5 **Fernside** New Zealand
36 F2 **Fernwald** W Germany
100 J2 **Fernwood** Idaho
111 F10 **Fernwood** Mississippi
123 P2 **Ferolle Pt** Nfld
47 H4 **Férrai** Greece
42 D4 **Ferrara** Italy
146 H6 **Ferrar Gl** Antarctica
17 G9 **Ferrat,C** Algeria
44 B4 **Ferrat,Cape** France
43 C9 **Ferrato,C** Sardinia
79 F4 **Ferraya** Lebanon
16 B6 **Ferreira do Alentejo** Portugal
129 H3 **Ferreira Gomes** Brazil
130 D7 **Ferreiros** Brazil
20 C5 **Ferré, le** France
128 C5 **Ferreñafe** Peru
18 E8 **Ferret,C** France
40 F6 **Ferret,Col** *pass* Switz/Italy
19 K5 **Ferreue** France
111 E10 **Ferriday** Louisiana
118 C6 **Ferrier** Alberta
20 E4 **Ferrière-aux-Étangs** France
21 G7 **Ferrière-Larçon** France
18 G4 **Ferrières** France
20 J3 **Ferrieres-en-Bray** France
20 G4 **Ferrière-sur-Risle, la** France
28 A3 **Ferring** Denmark
28 A3 **Ferring Sø** Denmark
99 P9 **Ferris** Illinois
109 L3 **Ferris** Texas
95 O2 **Ferrisburg** Vermont
101 S7 **Ferris Mts** Wyoming
28 F6 **Ferritslev** Denmark
43 C7 **Ferro,C** Sardinia
130 G6 **Ferros** Brazil
123 N2 **Ferru,L** Quebec
94 G10 **Ferrum** Virginia
43 B8 **Ferru, M** *mt* Sardinia
116 N5 **Ferry** Alaska
99 U6 **Ferry** Michigan
13 G6 **Ferrybridge** England
123 U6 **Ferryland** Nfld
107 P5 **Ferry Res** Oklahoma
99 U6 **Ferrysburg** Michigan
8 B4 **Ferryside** Wales
99 P6 **Ferryville** Wisconsin
55 C4 **Fershampenuaz** U.S.S.R.
28 H5 **Forslev** Denmark
20 G5 **Ferté-Bernard, la** France
20 G4 **Ferté Fresnel, la** France
18 H4 **Ferté Gaucher,La** France
22 F4 **Ferté, la** France
20 E4 **Ferté-Macé, la** France
18 H4 **Ferté sur Jouarre, la** France
20 G4 **Ferté-Vidame, la** France
98 K2 **Fertile** Minnesota
48 D3 **Fertöszentmiklos** Hungary
Fertö Tór *see* **Neusiedler See**
20 F3 **Fervaques** France
41 M3 **Ferwall Gruppe** *mt* Austria
25 E2 **Ferwerd** Netherlands
85 C2 **Fès** Morocco
86 C7 **Feshi** Zaïre
98 G2 **Fessenden** N Dakota
19 P15 **Festre, Col du** *pass* France
22 D2 **Festubert** France
110 F3 **Festus** Missouri
48 L6 **Feteşti** Romania
14 D4 **Fethard** Irish Rep
47 K8 **Fethiye** Turkey
47 K8 **Fethiye Körfezi** *B* Turkey
43 A12 **Fetzara, L** Algeria
37 L5 **Feucht** W Germany
41 N3 **Feuchten** Austria
37 J5 **Feuchtwangen** W Germany
118 K7 **Feudal** Sask
20 J3 **Feuillie, la** France
123 M3 **Feu, L. du** Quebec
20 J2 **Feuquieres** France
20 J1 **Feuquières-en-Vimeu** France
18 H7 **Feurs** France
77 F2 **Feyzābād** Iran
84 E4 **Fezzan** Libya
8 C2 **Ffestiniog** Wales
8 C4 **Fforest Fawr** *hills* Wales
86 H3 **Fgogi Bad** Ethiopia
133 D3 **Fiambalá** Argentina
45 O5 **Fiamignano** Italy
83 G7 **Fianarantsoa** Madagascar
86 C4 **Fianga** Chad
40 F7 **Fiano** Italy
48 G5 **Fibiş** Romania
45 K2 **Ficarolo** Italy
86 G4 **Fiche** Ethiopia
123 R2 **Fichot I** Nfld
37 M3 **Fichtelberg** W Germany
37 O3 **Fichtelberg** *mt* E Germany
37 M3 **Fichtelfebirge** *mts* W Germany
37 J5 **Fichtenau** W Germany
89 E7 **Ficksburg** S Africa
44 H2 **Fidenza** Italy
119 V1 **Fidler L** Manitoba
135 O4 **Fieberling Table Mt** Pacific Oc
106 C7 **Field** New Mexico
94 G10 **Fieldale** Virginia
140 B1 **Field I** N Terr **Aust**
118 K6 **Fielding** Sask
100 G7 **Fields** Oregon
100 A9 **Fields Landing** California
139 H8 **Field West Mt** Tasmania
22 B2 **Fiennes** France
46 D4 **Fier** Albania
19 P13 **Fier** *R* France
42 D2 **Fiera di Primiero** Italy
106 B9 **Fierro** New Mexico
109 H4 **Fife** Texas
13 E1 **Fife** *reg* Scotland
119 M9 **Fife L** Sask
13 F1 **Fife Ness** Scotland
139 J5 **Fifield** New S Wales
99 Q4 **Fifield** Wisconsin
101 R5 **Fifteen Mile Cr** Wyoming
17 G9 **Figalo,C** Algeria
43 C8 **Figari,C** Sardinia
18 G8 **Figeac** France
27 J14 **Figeholm** Sweden
45 K4 **Figline Valdarno** Italy
127 P4 **Fig Tree** Nevis **W I**
16 B4 **Figuera da Foz** Portugal
16 B5 **Figuera dos Vinhos** Portugal
18 G10 **Figueras** Spain
85 D2 **Figuig** Morocco
137 Q5 **Fiji** *islds* Pacific Oc
17 F7 **Filabres, Sierra de los** *mts* Spain
129 J5 **Filadélfia** Brazil
128 F8 **Filadelfia** Paraguay
48 F2 **Filakovo** Czechoslovakia
146 E10 **Filchner Ice Shelf** Antarctica
27 C10 **Filefj** *mt* Norway
119 R4 **File L** Manitoba
101 L7 **Filer** Idaho
45 O6 **Filettino** Italy
13 H5 **Filey** England
46 D5 **Filiátes** Greece
46 E7 **Filiatrá** Greece
43 F10 **Filicudi** *isld* Italy
85 E6 **Filingué** Niger
31 O1 **Filipów** Poland
27 G12 **Filipstad** Sweden
41 L4 **Filisur** Switzerland
48 H6 **Fillaşi** Romania
22 C3 **Fillièvres** France
102 F7 **Fillmore** California
98 G1 **Fillmore** N Dakota
94 J4 **Fillmore** New York
119 O9 **Fillmore** Sask
103 M3 **Fillmore** Utah
36 H6 **Fils** *R* W Germany
28 C5 **Filskov** Denmark
28 A5 **Filsø** Denmark
8 D4 **Filton** England
86 H4 **Filtu** Ethiopia
146 B9 **Fimbulheimen** *ra* Antarctica
42 D4 **Finale Emilia** Italy
44 D3 **Finale Ligure** Italy
17 F7 **Fiñana** Spain
94 H9 **Fincastle** Virginia
121 P7 **Finch** Ontario
9 F4 **Finchley** England
28 C4 **Finderup** Denmark
15 E3 **Findhorn** Scotland
15 E3 **Findhorn** *R* Scotland
119 M8 **Findlater** Sask
99 S10 **Findlay** Illinois
94 D5 **Findlay** Ohio
117 P10 **Findlay,Mt** Br Col
9 F6 **Findon** England
9 F3 **Finedon** England
98 J3 **Fingal** N Dakota
139 J8 **Fingal** Tasmania
110 H6 **Finger** Tennessee
115 K7 **Finger L** Ontario
95 L4 **Finger Lakes** New York
14 E3 **Finglas** Irish Rep
88 C9 **Fingoe** Mozambique
88 C9 **Fingoe** *mt* Mozambique
47 L8 **Finike** Turkey
18 C4 **Finistère** *dep* France
140 C7 **Finke** N Terr **Aust**
138 D2 **Finke** *R* N Terr **Australia**
138 D2 **Finke Flood Flats** S Australia
140 C6 **Finke Gorge** N Terr **Aust**
138 C4 **Finke,Mt** S Australia
140 D7 **Finke, R** N Terr **Aust**
99 P2 **Finland** Minnesota
29 L8 **Finland** N Europe
52 C5 **Finland, Gulf of** Finland/U.S.S.R.
114 G6 **Finlay** *R* Br Col
99 O3 **Finlayson** Minnesota
98 J2 **Finley** N Dakota
109 M1 **Finley** Oklahoma
119 O2 **Finmark** Ontario
14 D2 **Finn** *R* Irish Rep
12 D1 **Finnart** Scotland
118 E7 **Finnegan** Alberta
26 H4 **Finneid** Norway
36 D1 **Finnentrop** W Germany
16 A2 **Finnesterre,C** Spain
26 L7 **Finnforsfallet** Sweden
141 H3 **Finnigan, Mt** Queensland
140 B2 **Finniss** *R* N Terr **Aust**
138 C5 **Finniss,C** S Australia
26 O1 **Finnmark** *county* Norway
116 J6 **Finn Mt** Alaska
27 F11 **Finnskog** Norway
27 F11 **Finnskoga,S** Sweden
26 K2 **Finnsnes** Norway
26 M6 **Finnträsk** Sweden
33 T7 **Finow** E Germany
33 T7 **Finowfurt** E Germany
33 T7 **Finow Kanal** E Germany
27 H13 **Finspång** Sweden
40 H4 **Finsteraarhorn** *mt* Switzerland
33 T9 **Finsterwalde** E Germany
15 E1 **Finstown** Scotland
29 H11 **Finström** Finland
36 E4 **Finthen** W Germany
14 D2 **Fintona** N Ireland
12 D1 **Fintry** Scotland
142 C5 **Finucane I** W Australia
141 F5 **Finucane Ra** Queensland
40 F5 **Fionnay** Switzerland
15 C3 **Fionn Loch** *L* Scotland
12 B1 **Fionphort** Scotland
45 J2 **Fiorano Modenese** Italy
144 A6 **Fiordland Nat. Park** New Zealand
44 G2 **Fiorenzuola d'Arda** Italy
45 N4 **Fiorenzuola di Focara** Italy
88 C5 **Fip** Tanzania
78 G2 **Firat** *R* Turkey
102 D5 **Firebaugh** California
116 M6 **Fire I** Alaska
42 D5 **Firenze** Italy
42 D4 **Firenzuola** Italy
98 E4 **Firesteel** S Dakota
48 H3 **Firiza de Jos** Romania
133 E4 **Firmat** Argentina
18 H7 **Firminy** France
118 L9 **Fir Mt** Sask
74 H5 **Firozabad** India
77 H2 **Firozkoh** *reg* Afghanistan
74 F3 **Firozpur** India
112 F2 **First R** N Carolina
116 R2 **Firth** *R* Alaska/Yukon Terr
77 C5 **Fīrūzābād** Iran
37 K7 **Fischach** W Germany
36 C4 **Fischbach** W Germany
38 M7 **Fischbacher Alpen** *mts* Austria
33 Q7 **Fischbeck** E Germany
36 E2 **Fischelbach** W Germany
41 M3 **Fischen** W Germany
109 J6 **Fischer** Texas
32 K6 **Fischerhude** W Germany
33 S6 **Fischerwall** E Germany
89 A5 **Fish** *watercourse* Namibia
9 E6 **Fishbourne** England
102 E4 **Fish Camp** California
116 L1 **Fish Cr** Alaska
101 M6 **Fish Cr.Res** Idaho
113 F10 **Fisheating Cr** Florida
111 C10 **Fisher** Louisiana
98 K2 **Fisher** Minnesota
121 N4 **Fisher** Quebec
138 B4 **Fisher** S Australia
146 J4 **Fisher B** Antarctica
119 U7 **Fisher Branch** Manitoba
146 C5 **Fisher Gl** Antarctica
143 A9 **Fisherman I** W Australia
95 M9 **Fishermans I** Virginia
115 L5 **Fisher Str** N W Terr
116 E9 **Fisher Vol** Aleutian Is
8 B4 **Fishguard** Wales
95 L8 **Fishing Creek** Maryland
116 M4 **Fish L** Alaska
117 M4 **Fish L** N W Terr
103 N3 **Fish L** Utah
94 D3 **Fish Pt** Michigan
140 E4 **Fish River** N Terr **Aust**
102 A3 **Fish Rock** California
101 Q4 **Fishtail** Montana
101 M4 **Fishtrap** Montana
94 E9 **Fishtrap Res** Kentucky
46 D6 **Fiskárdho** Greece
28 C3 **Fiskbæk** Denmark
95 P4 **Fiskdale** Massachusetts
118 J7 **Fiske** Sask
146 E12 **Fiske,C** Antarctica
115 O5 **Fiskenæsset** Greenland
22 F5 **Fismes** France
95 Q4 **Fitchburg** Massachusetts
86 C3 **Fitri, L** Chad
28 C5 **Fitting** Denmark
9 F6 **Fittleworth** England
128 D6 **Fitzcarrald** Peru
114 H6 **Fitzgerald** Alberta
112 D6 **Fitzgerald** Georgia
109 L1 **Fitzhugh** Oklahoma
117 K10 **Fitzhugh Sd** Br Columbia
22 C5 **Fitz James** France
140 B2 **Fitzmaurice** *R* N Terr **Aust**
121 S5 **Fitzpatrick** Quebec
133 D7 **Fitz Roy** Argentina
133 C7 **Fitz Roy** *mt* Chile/Arg
141 K6 **Fitzroy** *R* Queensland
142 F4 **Fitzroy Crossing** W Australia
121 O7 **Fitzroy Harbour** Ontario
141 H3 **Fitzroy I** Queensland
142 E4 **Fitzroy R** W Australia
120 J7 **Fitzwilliam I** Ontario
42 E7 **Fiuggi** Italy
45 J3 **Fiumalbo** Italy
Fiume *see* **Rijeka**
42 E7 **Fiumicino** Italy
45 M3 **Fiumi Uniti** *R* Italy
144 A6 **Five Fingers Pen** New Zealand
122 H8 **Five Islands** Nova Scotia
101 R6 **Fivemile Cr** Wyoming
14 D2 **Fivemiletown** N Ireland
144 B6 **Five Rivers** New Zealand
88 B4 **Fizi** Zaïre
26 L4 **Fjällåsen** Sweden
26 G6 **Fjällfjällen** *mt* Sweden
26 F9 **Fjällnäs** Sweden
26 H8 **Fjällsjö** Sweden
28 H7 **Fjelde** Denmark
28 F3 **Fjellerup** Denmark
28 E6 **Fjelsted** Denmark
28 D6 **Fjelstrup** Denmark
28 C2 **Fjerritslev** Denmark
27 B10 **Fjordane** *reg* Norway
27 B13 **Fjotland** Norway
27 D11 **Flå** Norway
37 K5 **Flachslanden** W Germany
28 A3 **Flade Sø** Denmark
28 B6 **Fladså** *R* Denmark
37 J2 **Fladungen** W Germany
106 G2 **Flagler** Colorado
113 F8 **Flagler Beach** Florida
103 N6 **Flagstaff** Arizona
95 R1 **Flagstaff L** Maine
100 E7 **Flagstaff L** Oregon
100 K1 **Flagstone** Br Col
28 G6 **Flakkebjerg** Denmark
26 F3 **Flakstad** Norway
27 B11 **Flåm** Norway
20 B2 **Flamanville** France
99 Q4 **Flambeau** *R* Wisconsin
99 Q3 **Flambeau Res** Wisconsin
13 H5 **Flamborough Hd** England
133 C3 **Flamenco** Chile
131 E8 **Flamenco, I** Argentina
33 R9 **Fläming** *reg* E Germany
101 Q8 **Flaming Gorge Res** Utah/Wyoming
113 G12 **Flamingo** Florida
18 F10 **Flamisell** *R* Spain
36 C2 **Flammersfeld** W Germany
127 O2 **Flanagin Town** Trinidad
99 O1 **Flanders** Ontario
22 E3 **Flandre** France
22 D2 **Flandre** *prov* France
98 K5 **Flandreau** S Dakota
102 E1 **Flanigan** Nevada
38 H6 **Flankenmarkt** Austria
26 K8 **Flärke** Sweden
98 E3 **Flasher** N Dakota
26 H7 **Flåsjön** *L* Sweden
109 K4 **Flat** Texas
94 B3 **Flat** *R* Michigan
117 K5 **Flat** *R* N W Terr
123 O5 **Flat Bay** Nfld
118 C4 **Flatbush** Alberta
111 J8 **Flat Creek** Alabama
101 L2 **Flathead L** Montana
101 L1 **Flathead Mts** Montana
117 Q11 **Flathead R** Idaho
141 J5 **Flat I** Queensland
118 E4 **Flat L** Alberta
144 A6 **Flat Mt** New Zealand
109 K6 **Flatonia** Texas
110 F4 **Flat River** Missouri
110 J3 **Flat Rock** Illinois
94 B7 **Flat Rock** Indiana
141 H2 **Flattery, C** Queensland
100 A1 **Flattery,C** Washington
38 K8 **Flattnitz** Austria
94 F9 **Flat Top** W Virginia
101 R3 **Flatwillow** Montana
94 G8 **Flatwoods** W Virginia
41 O3 **Flaurling** Austria
27 C12 **Flåv** *L* Norway
28 E2 **Flavanskjold** Denmark
21 H10 **Flavignac** France
22 F4 **Flavigny le Grd. et Beaurain** France
22 E4 **Flavy le Martel** France
118 H7 **Flaxcombe** Sask
116 P1 **Flaxsman I** Alaska
98 D1 **Flaxton** N Dakota
98 A1 **Flaxville** Montana
33 O8 **Flechtingen** E Germany
113 K9 **Fleeming Pt** New Providence I **Bahamas**
118 F6 **Fleet** Alberta
9 G2 **Fleet Hargate** England
13 E6 **Fleetwood** England
95 M6 **Fleetwood** Pennsylvania
141 H5 **Fleetwood** Queensland
36 G5 **Flein** W Germany
95 N4 **Fleischmanns** New York
27 B13 **Flekkefjord** Norway
27 C13 **Flekkeröy** *isld* Norway
Flemhude *see* **Quarnbek**
98 D9 **Fleming** Colorado
119 Q8 **Fleming** Sask
94 D8 **Flemingsburg** Kentucky
95 N6 **Flemington** New Jersey
90 F4 **Flemish Cap** Atlantic Oc
28 E6 **Flemløse** Denmark
27 J12 **Flen** Sweden
28 K4 **Fleninge** Sweden
28 D7 **Flensborg Fjord** *inlet* Denmark/W Germany
28 C7 **Flensburg** W Germany
21 H7 **Fléré-le-Rivière** France
20 D4 **Flers** France
22 D3 **Flers** France
101 N2 **Flesher** Montana
120 K8 **Flesherton** Ontario
71 J4 **Flesko,Tg** *C* Sulawesi
112 E2 **Fletcher** N Carolina
107 M7 **Fletcher** Oklahoma
94 D2 **Fletcher Pond** Michigan
9 F2 **Fletton** England
18 F9 **Fleurance** France
123 Q3 **Fleur de Lys** Nfld
122 H2 **Fleur-de-May,L** Labrador
40 E4 **Fleurier** Switzerland
22 H3 **Fleurus** Belgium
20 H3 **Fleury** France
21 J6 **Fleury les Aubrais** France
68 G1 **Fleuve Rouge** *R* Vietnam
36 H3 **Flieden** W Germany
41 K4 **Flims** Switzerland
9 G5 **Flimwell** England
140 F4 **Flinders** *R* Queensland
143 B10 **Flinders B** W Australia
141 G2 **Flinders Group** *islds* Gt Barrier Reef **Aust**
139 J7 **Flinders I** Tasmania
136 K5 **Flinder's Passage** Australia
141 J4 **Flinders Reefs** Gt Barrier Reef **Aust**
138 E4 **Flinders Rge** S Australia
22 E3 **Flines-le-Râches** France
114 J7 **Flin Flon** Manitoba
20 J4 **Flins** France
94 D3 **Flint** Michigan
8 C1 **Flint** Wales
Flint *co see* **Clwyd**
111 M10 **Flint** *R* Georgia
107 O4 **Flint Hills** Kansas
135 M9 **Flint I** Pacific Oc
120 E3 **Flint L** Ontario
118 L9 **Flintoft** Sask
141 J8 **Flinton** Queensland
110 D5 **Flippin** Arkansas
112 C4 **Flirt** *R* Georgia
27 F11 **Flisa** Norway
27 H14 **Fliseryd** Sweden
17 H3 **Flix** Spain
13 H6 **Flixborough** England
20 K1 **Flixecourt** France
22 H4 **Flize** France
13 G6 **Flockton Moor** England
111 J11 **Flomaton** Florida
108 G1 **Flomot** Texas
36 E4 **Flonheim** W Germany
67 D1 **Flood Basin** *L* Hubei **China**
146 J10 **Flood Ra** Antarctica
99 O3 **Floodwood** Minnesota
110 H3 **Flora** Illinois
94 A6 **Flora** Indiana
111 F9 **Flora** Mississippi
100 H4 **Flora** Oregon
18 H8 **Florac** France
111 K10 **Florala** Alabama
113 E9 **Floral City** Florida
142 B5 **Flora, Mt** W Australia
141 H3 **Flora Pass** Gt Barrier Reef Aust
140 E4 **Floraville** Queensland
142 A1 **Floreat Park** *dist* Perth, W Aust
22 H3 **Floreffe** Belgium
Florence *see* **Firenze**
103 N8 **Florence** Arizona
106 E3 **Florence** Colorado
100 J4 **Florence** Idaho
107 O3 **Florence** Kansas
94 C8 **Florence** Kentucky
111 F9 **Florence** Mississippi
101 L3 **Florence** Montana
95 N6 **Florence** New Jersey
100 A6 **Florence** Oregon
112 H3 **Florence** S Carolina
98 J4 **Florence** S Dakota
109 K5 **Florence** Texas
99 S4 **Florence** Wisconsin
103 N8 **Florence Junc** Arizona
102 F4 **Florence L** California
128 F8 **Florencia** Argentina
128 C3 **Florencia** Colombia
22 H3 **Florennes** Belgium
22 J4 **Florenville** Belgium
130 H9 **Flores** Brazil
125 P9 **Flores** Guatemala
131 F4 **Flores** *dep* Uruguay
85 A1 **Flores** *isld* Azores Atlantic Oc
71 K9 **Flores** *isld* Indonesia
131 F5 **Flores** *R* Argentina
48 L3 **Floreshty** U.S.S.R.
117 K11 **Flores I** Br Col
71 J8 **Flores Sea** Indonesia
130 H10 **Floresta** Brazil
109 J6 **Floresville** Texas
108 E3 **Florey** Texas
129 K5 **Floriano** Brazil
128 E5 **Floriano Peixoto** Brazil
130 E10 **Florianopólis** Brazil
126 E4 **Florida** Cuba
106 C9 **Florida** New Mexico
94 C5 **Florida** Ohio
131 G5 **Florida** Uruguay
137 N3 **Florida** *isld* **Solomon Is**
113 B12 **Florida** *state* **U.S.A.**
113 G12 **Florida B** Florida
113 F13 **Florida Keys** *islds* Florida
113 H12 **Florida,Str.of** U.S.A./Bahamas
130 B10 **Florida,V** Paraguay
43 G11 **Floridia** Sicily
109 O4 **Florien** Louisiana
46 E4 **Flórina** Greece
99 O9 **Floris** Iowa
106 E3 **Florissant** Colorado
26 A10 **Flörö** Norway
142 B6 **Florry, Mt** W Australia
36 G3 **Flörsbach** W Germany
37 N4 **Floss** W Germany
37 N4 **Flossenbürg** W Germany
15 F2 **Flotta** Scotland
118 J4 **Flotten L** Sask
27 J12 **Flottsund** Sweden
103 M3 **Flowell** Utah
120 J7 **Flowerpot I. Nat. Park** Ontario
123 Q2 **Flower's Cove** Nfld
108 D1 **Floyd** New Mexico
98 K7 **Floyd** *R* Iowa
108 F2 **Floydada** Texas
103 M6 **Floyd,Mt** Arizona
27 D11 **Fluberg** Norway
41 L4 **Flüela Pass** Switzerland
25 E3 **Fluessen** *R* Netherlands
71 A3 **Fluk** Indonesia
111 F11 **Fluker** Louisiana
20 B5 **Flume** *R* France
17 G3 **Flumen** *R* Spain
43 B9 **Fluminimaggiore** Sardinia
36 F7 **Fluorn** W Germany
94 D3 **Flushing** Michigan
Flushing Netherlands *see* **Vlissingen**
94 F6 **Flushing** Ohio
108 F3 **Fluvanna** Texas
18 G10 **Fluvia** *R* Spain
28 C4 **Fly** Denmark
136 J3 **Fly** *R* Papua/W Irian
146 H12 **Flying Fish,C** Antarctica
83 M9 **Flying Fish Cove** Christmas I Ind Oc
140 C2 **Flying Fox Cr** N Terr **Aust**
28 A4 **Flynder Kirke** Denmark
28 B3 **Flynder Sø** *L* Denmark
109 L4 **Flynn** Texas
140 C4 **Flynn Mem** N Terr **Aust**
119 O7 **Foam Lake** Sask
73 L9 **Foa Mulaku I** Maldives
47 H6 **Foça** Turkey
22 J3 **Focant** Belgium
45 H3 **Foce d. Radici** *mt* Italy
15 E3 **Fochabers** Scotland
42 E4 **Foci del Po** Italy
48 L5 **Focşani** Romania
28 H6 **Fodby** Denmark
140 D3 **Foelsche** *R* N Terr **Aust**
67 D5 **Fogang** China
140 B2 **Fog B** N Terr **Aust**
43 G7 **Foggia** Italy
85 F6 **Foggo** Nigeria
42 E5 **Foglia** *R* Italy
45 N7 **Fogliano** *L* Italy
29 H11 **Föglö** Finland
123 S4 **Fogo** Nfld
88 G10 **Fogo** *isld* Mozambique
123 S4 **Fogo,C** Nfld
28 C4 **Fogstrup** Denmark
38 L7 **Fohnsdorf** Austria
28 A7 **Föhr** *isld* W Germany
45 R7 **Foiana in Val Fortore** Italy
14 A5 **Foilclogh** *mt* Irish Rep
15 D2 **Foinaven,Mt** Scotland
18 G10 **Foix** France
52 H6 **Foki** U.S.S.R.
54 F3 **Fokina, imeni** U.S.S.R.
26 D9 **Fokstua** Norway
26 G4 **Folda** *inlet* Norway
48 F4 **Földeák** Hungary
26 F7 **Foldereid** Norway
28 B6 **Foldingbro** Denmark
28 C6 **Folding Kirke** Denmark
28 B6 **Fole** Denmark
47 G8 **Folégandros** *isld* Greece
111 J11 **Foley** Alabama
89 E3 **Foley** Botswana
113 D7 **Foley** Florida
99 N4 **Foley** Minnesota
120 H4 **Foleyet** Ontario
115 M4 **Foley I** N W Terr
87 C9 **Folgares** Angola
27 B11 **Folgefonna** *gla* Norway
116 J5 **Folger** Alaska
42 E6 **Foligno** Italy
9 H5 **Folkestone** England
9 F2 **Folkingham** England
113 E7 **Folkston** Georgia
112 K3 **Folkstone** N Carolina
26 D9 **Folla** *R* Norway
26 D9 **Folldal** Norway
28 E4 **Følle** Denmark
25 E3 **Follega** Netherlands
28 G5 **Føllenslev** Denmark
20 C4 **Folligny** France
26 G8 **Föllinge** Sweden
27 E12 **Follo** Norway
42 D6 **Follonica** Italy
112 H5 **Folly Beach** S Carolina
100 G6 **Follyfarm** Oregon
102 C3 **Folsom** California
111 F11 **Folsom** Louisiana
106 G5 **Folsom** New Mexico
102 C3 **Folsom L** California

48 L5 **Folteşti** Romania
126 E3 **Fómento** Cuba
52 F6 **Fominki** U.S.S.R.
52 G2 **Fominskaya** U.S.S.R.
52 F5 **Fominskoye** U.S.S.R.
99 M7 **Fonda** Iowa
98 F1 **Fonda** N Dakota
95 N4 **Fonda** New York
114 J6 **Fond-du-Lac** Sask
99 S6 **Fond du Lac** Wisconsin
94 D10 **Fonde** Kentucky
43 E7 **Fondi** Italy
45 O7 **Fondi, L. di** Italy
26 E8 **Fongen** *mt* Norway
43 C8 **Fonni** Sardinia
16 C1 **Fonsagrada** Spain
28 D6 **Fønsskov** Denmark
22 G3 **Fontaine** Belgium
21 H6 **Fontaine** France
18 G4 **Fontainebleau** France
19 O17 **Fontaine-de-Vaucluse** France
40 B2 **Fontaine-Française** France
20 G3 **Fontaine-l'Abbé** France
20 H2 **Fontaine-le-Bourg** France
20 G2 **Fontaine-le-Dun** France
21 E7 **Fontaine Milon** France
133 C6 **Fontana,L** Argentina
112 D2 **Fontana L** N Carolina
45 P6 **Fontana Liri** Italy
45 L3 **Fontanelice** Italy
117 N6 **Fontas** Br Columbia
40 D7 **Fontcouvert** France
38 F7 **Fonte** Italy
128 E4 **Fonte Boa** Brazil
128 G6 **Fonte do Pau d'Água** Brazil
21 D9 **Fontenay-le Comte** France
20 J3 **Fontenay-St.Père** France
123 L2 **Fonteneau,L** Quebec
122 H5 **Fontenelle** Quebec
101 P7 **Fontenelle Fork** *R* Wyoming
22 E2 **Fontenoy** Belgium
21 F7 **Fontevrault-l'abbaye** France
8 D6 **Fontmell Magna** England
22 L5 **Fontoy** France
137 S5 **Fonualei** *isld* Tonga
48 D4 **Fonyód** Hungary
Foochow *see* **Fuzhou**
103 M2 **Fool Cr.Res** Utah
117 P9 **Foothills** Alberta
99 R7 **Footville** Wisconsin
41 H5 **Foppiano** Italy
27 J14 **Föra** Sweden
107 O5 **Foraker** Oklahoma
116 M5 **Foraker,Mt** Alaska
19 K3 **Forbach** France
36 E6 **Forbach** W Germany
99 O2 **Forbes** Minnesota
98 H4 **Forbes** N Dakota
139 J5 **Forbes** New S Wales
117 P10 **Forbes, Mt** Alberta
85 F7 **Forcados** Nigeria
19 Q18 **Forcalqueiret** France
19 P17 **Forcalquier** France
38 E8 **Forchetta** *mt* Italy
37 L4 **Forchheim** W Germany
36 H5 **Forchtenberg** W Germany
13 F2 **Ford** England
107 L4 **Ford** Kansas
94 C9 **Ford** Kentucky
99 T3 **Ford** *R* Michigan
140 A2 **Ford, C** N Terr Aust
102 E6 **Ford City** California
94 H6 **Ford City** Pennsylvania
26 A10 **Förde** Norway
145 E3 **Fordell** New Zealand
33 P9 **Förderstedt** E Germany
9 G3 **Fordham** England
9 E6 **Fordingbridge** England
103 J8 **Ford L** California
110 D4 **Fordland** Missouri
31 L2 **Fordon** Poland
146 J9 **Ford Rge** Antarctica
139 H3 **Ford's Br** New S Wales
110 K4 **Fordsville** Kentucky
109 K6 **Fordtran** Texas
98 J1 **Fordville** N Dakota
111 D8 **Fordyce** Arkansas
98 J7 **Fordyce** Nebraska
26 G5 **Fore** Norway
85 B7 **Forécariah** Guinea
8 C5 **Foreland,The** England
115 Q4 **Forel, Mt** Greenland
109 N2 **Foreman** Arkansas
118 F9 **Foremost** Alberta
22 G2 **Forest** Belgium
100 J3 **Forest** Idaho
111 G9 **Forest** Mississippi
94 D6 **Forest** Ohio
120 H9 **Forest** Ontario
141 F4 **Forest** *R* Queensland
118 E6 **Forestburg** Alberta
109 K2 **Forestburg** Texas
110 F6 **Forest City** Arkansas
99 N6 **Forest City** Iowa
112 F2 **Forest City** N Carolina
95 M5 **Forest City** Pennsylvania
95 O3 **Forest Dale** Vermont
142 B3 **Forestdale** *dist* Perth, W Aust
109 O1 **Forester** Arkansas
94 E3 **Forester** Michigan
100 B9 **Forest Glen** California
101 Q3 **Forestgrove** Montana
100 B4 **Forest Grove** Oregon
102 D2 **Foresthill** California
111 D10 **Forest Hill** Louisiana
109 M9 **Forest Hill** Texas
141 G4 **Forest Home** Queensland
139 J8 **Forestier, C** Tasmania
139 J9 **Forestier Pen** Tasmania
99 O4 **Forest Lake** Minnesota
118 D7 **Forest Lawn** Alberta
15 D4 **Forest of Atholl** Scotland
99 N4 **Foreston** Minnesota
95 M3 **Forestport** New York
98 J1 **Forest River** N Dakota
9 G5 **Forest Row** England
102 B3 **Forestville** California
94 E3 **Forestville** Michigan
94 H4 **Forestville** New York
122 C5 **Forestville** Quebec
122 C5 **Forestville, Parc de** Quebec
19 J3 **Forêt d'Argonne** France
20 K5 **Forêt Ste. Croix, la** France
18 H7 **Forez, Mts du** France
15 F4 **Forfar** Scotland
107 K5 **Forgan** Oklahoma
118 K7 **Forgan** Sask
20 J2 **Forges-les-Eaux** France
121 O4 **Forget** Quebec
119 P9 **Forget** Sask
41 N2 **Forggen See** *L* W Germany
45 P8 **Forio** Italy
110 G6 **Forked Deer** *R* Tennessee
119 R7 **Fork River** *R* Manitoba
100 A2 **Forks** Washington
144 C5 **Forks, The** New Zealand
94 J9 **Fork Union** Virginia
42 E4 **Forlì** Italy
45 M3 **Forlimpopoli** Italy
14 E4 **Forlorn Pt** Irish Rep
98 J3 **Forman** N Dakota
13 E6 **Formby** England
138 D6 **Formby B** S Australia
13 E6 **Formby Pt** England
45 M5 **Formello** Italy
17 H6 **Formentera** *isld* Balearic Is
20 J2 **Formerie** France
43 F7 **Formia** Italy
130 F7 **Formiga** Brazil
126 G5 **Formigas Bank** Caribbean
45 J2 **Formigine** Italy
45 L2 **Formignana** Italy
20 D3 **Formigny** France
26 F7 **Formofoss** Norway
Formosa *see* **Taiwan**
133 F3 **Formosa** Argentina
129 J7 **Formosa** Brazil
129 J6 **Formosa** *R* Brazil
129 J6 **Formosa do Rio Prêto** Brazil

129 G6 **Formosa, Serra** *mts* Brazil
130 F4 **Formoso** Brazil
107 M2 **Formoso** Kansas
28 F4 **Fornæs** *C* Denmark
17 K4 **Fornells** Menorca
38 G8 **Forni Avoltri** Italy
15 E3 **Forres** Scotland
99 S9 **Forrest** Illinois
119 S9 **Forrest** Manitoba
143 G9 **Forrest** W Australia
146 E10 **Forrestal Ra** Antarctica
117 G8 **Forrester I** Alaska
142 C2 **Forrestfield** *dist* Perth, W Aust
143 G8 **Forrest Lakes** W Australia
143 G6 **Forrest, Mt** W Australia
99 R7 **Forreston** Illinois
142 G3 **Forrest River Mission** W Aust
26 J9 **Fors** Sweden
26 J3 **Forsa** Norway
26 J10 **Forsa** Sweden
108 F3 **Forsan** Texas
27 B13 **Forsand** Norway
141 G4 **Forsayth** Queensland
27 J11 **Forsbacka** Sweden
27 F12 **Forshaga** Sweden
27 F13 **Forshem** Sweden
27 F15 **Förslöv** Sweden
27 K11 **Forsmark** Sweden
26 J8 **Forsmo** Sweden
26 K5 **Forsnäs** Sweden
26 C8 **Forsnes** Norway
29 K11 **Forssa** Finland
31 H4 **Forst** E Germany
139 L4 **Forster** New S Wales
146 A13 **Forster's Passage** Antarctica
112 D4 **Forsyth** Georgia
99 S10 **Forsyth** Illinois
101 T3 **Forsyth** Montana
121 O4 **Forsythe** Quebec
145 E4 **Forsyth I** New Zealand
140 E3 **Forsyth Is** Queensland
141 G6 **Forsyth Ra** Queensland
74 E4 **Fort Abbas** Pakistan
111 E10 **Fort Adams** Mississippi
115 L7 **Fort Albany** Ontario
129 L4 **Fortaleza** Brazil
128 E5 **Fortaleza de Ituxi** Brazil
122 G9 **Fort Anne Nat. Hist. Park** Nova Scotia
Fort Archambault *see* **Sarh**
94 J7 **Fort Ashby** W Virginia
118 C4 **Fort Assiniboine** Alberta
99 S7 **Fort Atkinson** Wisconsin
15 D3 **Fort Augustus** Scotland
87 E12 **Fort Beaufort** S Africa
122 H8 **Fort Beau Sejour Nat. Hist. Park** New Brunswick
101 R1 **Fort Belknap Agency** Montana
111 M9 **Fort Benning** Georgia
101 P2 **Fort Benton** Montana
100 E8 **Fort Bidwell** California
118 K3 **Fort Black** Sask
102 A2 **Fort Bragg** California
112 H2 **Fort Bragg** N Carolina
110 J3 **Fort Branch** Indiana
101 P8 **Fort Bridger** Wyoming
99 K8 **Fort Calhoun** Nebraska
Fort Carnot *see* **Ikongo**
Fort Charlet *see* **Djanet**
115 N6 **Fort Chimo** Quebec
114 H6 **Fort Chipewyan** Alberta
98 E2 **Fort Clark** N Dakota
107 M6 **Fort Cobb** Oklahoma
98 A9 **Fort Collins** Colorado
140 F5 **Fort Constantine** Queensland
121 O7 **Fort Coulonge** Quebec
95 N2 **Fort Covington** New York
Fort Dauphin *see* **Taolañaro**
111 L9 **Fort Davis** Alabama
108 D5 **Fort Davis** Texas
103 P6 **Fort Defiance** Arizona
127 L4 **Fort de France** Martinique W I
111 K10 **Fort Deposit** Alabama
100 A8 **Fort Dick** California
99 M7 **Fort Dodge** Iowa
110 J5 **Fort Donelson Nat Mil Park** Tennessee
113 G10 **Fort Drum** Florida
9 E3 **Fort Dunlop** England
123 P2 **Forteau** Labrador
130 B6 **Forte Coimbra** Brazil
44 H4 **Forte dei Marmi** Italy
121 L10 **Fort Erie** Ontario
142 B5 **Fortescue R** W Australia
142 C5 **Fortescue, R** W Australia
95 L9 **Fort Eustis** Virginia
95 T7 **Fort Fairfield** Maine
112 K4 **Fort Fisher** N Carolina
Fort Flatters *see* **Bordj Omar Driss**
99 N1 **Fort Frances** Ontario
114 G4 **Fort Franklin** N W Terr
114 G7 **Fort Fraser** Br Col
112 F6 **Fort Frederica Nat. Mon** Georgia
111 L10 **Fort Gaines** Georgia
Fort Garaud *see* **Fdérik**
106 E4 **Fort Garland** Colorado
118 B1 **Fort Garry** Manitoba
94 E8 **Fort Gay** W Virginia
115 M7 **Fort George** Quebec
15 D3 **Fort George** Scotland
107 P6 **Fort Gibson** Oklahoma
114 G4 **Fort Good Hope** N W Terr
113 F10 **Fort Green** Florida
138 F3 **Fort Grey** New S Wales
109 H3 **Fort Griffin** Texas
12 E2 **Forth** Scotland
Fort Hall *see* **Murango** Kenya
101 N6 **Fort Hall** Idaho
13 F1 **Forth, Firth of** Scotland
115 L7 **Fort Hope** Ontario
12 D1 **Forth, R** Scotland
103 O10 **Fort Huachuca** Arizona
121 S6 **Fortierville** Quebec
6 L5 **Forties** *oil rig* North Sea
122 H9 **Forties Settlement** Nova Scotia
103 K3 **Fortification Ra** Nevada
128 F8 **Fortin Carlos Antonio López** Paraguay
101 L1 **Fortine** Montana
128 G8 **Fortin Falcón** Paraguay
133 F2 **Fortin Gen. Caballero** Paraguay
128 F8 **Fortin General Eugenio Garay** Paraguay
128 F8 **Fortin Infante Rivarola** Paraguay
122 E3 **Fortin, L** Quebec
133 E3 **Fortin Lavalle** Argentina
128 F8 **Fortin Linares** Paraguay
133 F2 **Fortín Madrejón** Paraguay
128 F7 **Fortin Ravelo** Bolivia
128 G8 **Fortin Rojas Silva** Paraguay
128 F7 **Fortin Suárez Arana** Bolivia
128 G7 **Fortin Teniente Américo Picco** Paraguay
Fort Jameson Zambia *see* **Chipata**
113 E13 **Fort Jefferson Nat.Mon** Florida
Fort Johnston *see* **Mangoche**
100 C8 **Fort Jones** California
118 G4 **Fort Kent** Alberta
95 S6 **Fort Kent** Maine
100 C7 **Fort Klamath** Oregon
94 B9 **Fort Knox** Kentucky
Fort Lallemande *see* **Belhirane**
Fort Lamy *see* **N'Djamena**
Fort Laperrine *see* **Tamanrasset**
98 B7 **Fort Laramie** Wyoming

113 G11 **Fort Lauderdale** Florida
112 G3 **Fort Lawn** S Carolina
100 C2 **Fort Lewis** Washington
114 G5 **Fort Liard** N W Terr
127 J5 **Fort Liberté** Haiti
98 F3 **Fort Lincoln** N Dakota
112 C2 **Fort Loudon Lake** Tennessee
98 B9 **Fort Lupton** Colorado
106 G3 **Fort Lyon** Colorado
108 G5 **Fort McKavett** Texas
117 S7 **Fort MacKay** Alberta
101 S5 **Fort Mackenzie** Wyoming
118 D9 **Fort Macleod** Alberta
Fort McMahon *see* **El Homr**
118 F2 **Fort McMurray** Alberta
114 F4 **Fort McPherson** N W Terr
99 P9 **Fort Madison** Iowa
22 B3 **Fort Mahon Plage** France
Fort Manning *see* **Mchinji**
113 F8 **Fort Matanzas Nat.Mon** Florida
113 F10 **Fort Meade** Florida
112 G2 **Fort Mill** S Carolina
98 C9 **Fort Morgan** Colorado
106 G1 **Fort Morgan** Colorado
113 F11 **Fort Myers** Florida
114 G6 **Fort Nelson** Br Col
117 M6 **Fort Nelson** Br Col
114 G5 **Fort Norman** N W Terr
113 F10 **Fort Ogden** Florida
43 G7 **Fortore** *R* Italy
111 L7 **Fort Payne** Alabama
114 J8 **Fort Peck Res** Montana
113 G10 **Fort Pierce** Florida
98 F5 **Fort Pierre** S Dakota
Fort Pierre Bordes *see* **Tin Zaouaten**
95 N4 **Fort Plain** New York
86 F5 **Fort Portal** Uganda
114 H5 **Fort Providence** N W Terr
112 G5 **Fort Pulaski Nat. Mon** Georgia
119 O8 **Fort Qu' Appelle** Sask
112 M2 **Fort Raleigh Nat.Hist.Site** N Carolina
116 F9 **Fort Randall** Alaska
98 H6 **Fort Randall Dam** S Dakota
94 C6 **Fort Recovery** Ohio
114 J5 **Fort Reliance** N W Terr
114 H5 **Fort Resolution** N W Terr
101 Q5 **Fortress Mt** Wyoming
123 M8 **Fortress of Louisburg Nat. Hist. Park** C Breton I, N Scotia
98 F3 **Fort Rice** N Dakota
107 O2 **Fort Riley** Kansas
99 M3 **Fort Ripley** Minnesota
87 E10 **Fort Rixon** Zimbabwe
98 C7 **Fort Robinson** Nebraska
100 D6 **Fort Rock** Oregon
144 B7 **Fortrose** New Zealand
Fort Rosebery Zambia *see* **Mansa**
102 A3 **Fort Ross** California
86 C6 **Fort Rousset** Congo
121 M1 **Fort Rupert** Quebec
117 L8 **Fort St. James** Br Col
114 G6 **Fort St. John** Br Col
74 C3 **Fort Sandeman** Pakistan
114 H7 **Fort Saskatchewan** Alberta
107 Q4 **Fort Scott** Kansas
115 L6 **Fort Severn** Ontario
100 B9 **Fort Seward** California
107 M7 **Fort Sill** Oklahoma
114 G5 **Fort Simpson** N W Terr
107 Q6 **Fort Smith** Arkansas
114 H5 **Fort Smith** N W Terr
101 T8 **Fort Steele** Wyoming
108 E5 **Fort Stockton** Texas
108 C1 **Fort Sumner** New Mexico
112 H5 **Fort Sumter Nat.Mon** S Carolina
107 L5 **Fort Supply** Oklahoma
108 E7 **Fort Supply Res** Oklahoma
103 P8 **Fort Thomas** Arizona
98 G5 **Fort Thompson** S Dakota
107 P7 **Fort Towson** Oklahoma
27 C10 **Fortun** Norway
100 A9 **Fortuna** California
98 C1 **Fortuna** N Dakota
17 G6 **Fortuna** Spain
116 F6 **Fortuna Lodge** Alaska
123 R6 **Fortune** Nfld
106 E6 **Fort Union Nat.Mon** New Mexico
112 D5 **Fort Valley** Georgia
114 H6 **Fort Vermilion** Alberta
89 G3 **Fort Victoria** Zimbabwe
94 B7 **Fortville** Indiana
111 K11 **Fort Walton** Florida
101 R6 **Fort Washakie** Wyoming
94 B5 **Fort Wayne** Indiana
113 E8 **Fort White** Florida
118 A2 **Fort Whyte** Manitoba
15 C4 **Fort William** Scotland
109 M10 **Fort Worth** Texas
98 F3 **Fort Yates** N Dakota
116 R5 **Fortymile** *R* Alaska
116 P3 **Fort Yukon** Alaska
77 D6 **Forūr** *isld* Iran
22 J2 **Forville** Belgium
119 N9 **Forward** Sask
52 H5 **Fosforitnaya** U.S.S.R.
67 D5 **Foshan** China
115 L2 **Fosheim Pen** N W Terr
26 D8 **Fosna** Norway
26 E7 **Fosnes** Norway
107 L6 **Foss** Oklahoma
44 C2 **Fossano** Italy
22 H3 **Fosse** Belgium
100 E4 **Fossil** Oregon
101 P8 **Fossil** Wyoming
141 G4 **Fossilbrook** Queensland
98 C6 **Fossil Cycad Nat.Mon** S Dakota
142 F4 **Fossil Downs** W Australia
121 L6 **Fossmill** Ontario
42 E5 **Fossombrone** Italy
99 L2 **Fosston** Minnesota
119 O6 **Fosston** Sask
98 J7 **Foster** Nebraska
100 C5 **Foster** Oregon
121 S7 **Foster** Quebec
139 H7 **Foster** Victoria
147 E10 **Foster Bugt** Greenland
99 T4 **Foster City** Michigan
118 J8 **Fosterton** Sask
110 K6 **Fosterville** Tennessee
94 D5 **Fostoria** Ohio
109 M5 **Fostoria** Texas
67 F4 **Fotan** China
142 F5 **Fotheringham, Mt** W Australia
20 J2 **Foucarmont** France
36 C7 **Fouday** France
18 C5 **Fouesnant** France
86 B6 **Fougamou** Gabon
20 C5 **Fougères** France
83 K13 **Fougères,Pl.des** Réunion Indian Oc
20 D5 **Fougerolles-du-Plessis** France
20 K2 **Fouilloy** France
109 O2 **Fouke** Arkansas
68 B3 **Foul** *isld* Burma
84 K5 **Foul Bay** Egypt
9 G4 **Foulness Pt** England
13 E5 **Foulney** *isld* England
144 C4 **Foulwind, C** New Zealand
86 B4 **Foumban** Cameroon
85 C2 **Foum Zguid** Morocco
106 F3 **Fountain** Colorado
99 U5 **Fountain** Michigan
99 O6 **Fountain** Minnesota
112 K2 **Fountain** N Carolina
103 N2 **Fountain Grn** Utah
111 E8 **Fountain Hill** Arkansas
112 E3 **Fountain Inn** S Carolina
16 B7 **Foupana** *R* Portugal
140 D3 **Four Archers** *mt* N Terr Aust
18 E7 **Fouras** France

101 U1 **Four Buttes** Montana
20 G5 **Fourche, la** France
110 B7 **Fourche la Fave** *R* Arkansas
19 J4 **Fourchies, Mts des** France
123 M8 **Fourchu** C Breton I, N Scotia
103 P4 **Four Corners** Utah
98 B5 **Four Corners** Wyoming
140 A1 **Fourcroy, C** N Terr Aust
146 C3 **Four Ladies Bank** Antarctica
22 G3 **Fourmies** France
83 K14 **Fournaise, Piton de la** *vol* Réunion Indian Oc
46 E5 **Fournás** Greece
83 L13 **Fourneau** *isld* Mauritius
123 P2 **Fournel, L** Quebec
22 D2 **Fournes-en-Weppes** France
122 G2 **Fournier, L** Quebec
47 H7 **Foúrnoi** *isld* Greece
127 K3 **Four Paths** Jamaica
19 N17 **Fourques** France
13 F3 **Fourstones** England
99 R3 **Fourteenmile Pt** Michigan
85 B6 **Fouta Djalon** *mt reg* Guinea
85 B5 **Fouta Ferlo** *rég* Senegal
8 D5 **Fovant** England
144 A7 **Foveaux Strait** New Zealand
28 C3 **Fovlum** Denmark
8 B7 **Fowey** England
113 G12 **Fowey Rocks** Florida
126 F2 **Fowl Cay** *isld* Bahamas
106 F3 **Fowler** Colorado
99 T9 **Fowler** Indiana
107 K4 **Fowler** Kansas
94 C3 **Fowler** Michigan
101 O1 **Fowler** Montana
144 A6 **Fowler Pass** New Zealand
138 B4 **Fowler Pt** S Australia
138 B4 **Fowlers B** S Australia
109 J7 **Fowlerton** Texas
94 C4 **Fowlerville** Michigan
110 G6 **Fowlkes** Tennessee
111 M11 **Fowlstown** Georgia
77 A1 **Fowman** Iran
99 T4 **Fox** Michigan
100 F5 **Fox** Oregon
99 S8 **Fox** *R* Illinois
115 K6 **Fox** *R* Manitoba
99 U3 **Fox** *R* Michigan
99 P9 **Fox** *R* Missouri
99 S5 **Fox** *R* Wisconsin
123 L4 **Fox B** Anticosti I, Quebec
94 H5 **Foxburg** Pennsylvania
117 O8 **Fox Creek** Alberta
117 P8 **Fox Creek** Alberta
115 M4 **Foxe Basin** N W Terr
115 L4 **Foxe Chan** N W Terr
115 M5 **Foxe Pen** N W Terr
14 B3 **Foxford** Irish Rep
119 M5 **Foxford** Sask
123 R1 **Fox Harbour** Labrador
13 H5 **Foxholes** England
98 K3 **Foxhome** Minnesota
116 P8 **Fox Islands** *isld* Aleutian Is
143 C10 **Fox, L** W Australia
99 S6 **Fox Lake** Wisconsin
101 T8 **Foxpark** Wyoming
144 C5 **Fox Peak** *mt* New Zealand
123 L4 **Fox Pt** Anticosti I, Quebec
117 L7 **Fox R** Br Col
145 E4 **Foxton** New Zealand
118 H8 **Fox Valley** Sask
119 Q8 **Foxwarren** Manitoba
111 G10 **Foxworth** Mississippi
15 D3 **Foyers** Scotland
14 D2 **Foyle** *R* N Ireland
14 D1 **Foyle, L** Irish Rep
14 B4 **Foynes** Irish Rep
16 C1 **Foz** Spain
87 B9 **Foz do Cunene** Angola
128 D5 **Foz do Gregório** Brazil
130 C9 **Foz do Iguaçú** Brazil
128 F5 **Foz do Jamari** Brazil
128 D5 **Foz do Jordao** Brazil
128 E4 **Foz do Jutai** Brazil
128 E4 **Foz do Mamoriá** Brazil
128 D5 **Foz do Riozinho** Brazil
67 E1 **Foziling Shuiku** *res* China
128 E5 **Foz Tarauacá** Brazil
95 L6 **Frackville** Pennsylvania
8 B7 **Fraddon** England
17 H3 **Fraga** Spain
36 B7 **Fraize** France
146 C3 **Fram Bank** Antarctica
22 F3 **Frameries** Belgium
95 Q4 **Framingham** Massachusetts
9 H3 **Framlingham** England
36 G3 **Frammersbach** W Germany
146 B5 **Framnes Mts** Antarctica
31 O5 **Frampol** Poland
130 F7 **Franca** Brazil
43 H8 **Francavilla Fontana** Italy
18 **France** *rep* W Europe
20 K3 **France, Île de** *reg* France
147 G10 **France, Ile de** Greenland
138 F6 **Frances** S Australia
100 B3 **Frances** Washington
117 J5 **Frances** *R* Yukon Terr
140 B2 **Frances Creek** N Terr Aust
101 N1 **Frances, L** Montana
114 G5 **Frances L** Yukon Terr
127 K5 **Francés Viejo, C** Dominican Rep
99 U9 **Francesville** Indiana
86 B6 **Franceville** Gabon
19 J6 **Franche Comté** *prov* France
107 O7 **Francis** Oklahoma
119 O8 **Francis** Sask
146 E13 **Francis** *isld* Antarctica
98 G6 **Francis Case, L** S Dakota
128 D4 **Francisco de Orellana** Peru
124 H5 **Francisco I. Madero** Coahuila Mexico
124 G5 **Francisco I. Madero** Durango Mexico
130 C9 **Francisco, S** *R* Brazil
130 G5 **Francisco Sá** Brazil
123 R1 **Francis Harbour** Labrador
95 Q1 **Francis, L** New Hampshire
89 E3 **Francistown** Botswana
123 Q6 **François** Nfld
117 K8 **François L** Br Col
127 M4 **François, Le** Martinique W I
45 L2 **Francolino** Italy
22 K2 **Francorchamps** Belgium
101 Q6 **Francs Pk** Wyoming
21 H7 **Francueil** France
25 E2 **Franeker** Netherlands
118 C9 **Frank** Alberta
36 F1 **Frankenau** W Germany
36 F2 **Frankenbach** W Germany
37 P2 **Frankenberg** E Germany
36 F1 **Frankenberg/Eder** W Germany
37 J5 **Frankenhardt** W Germany
37 J5 **Frankenhöhe** *mts* W Germany
94 D3 **Frankenmuth** Michigan
36 D5 **Frankenstein** W Germany
36 E4 **Frankenthal** W Germany
37 M3 **Frankenwald** *mts* E & W Germany
127 K2 **Frankfield** Jamaica
110 E2 **Frankford** Missouri
121 N8 **Frankford** Ontario
94 G9 **Frankford** W Virginia
94 A6 **Frankfort** Indiana
107 O2 **Frankfort** Kansas
94 C8 **Frankfort** Kentucky
99 U5 **Frankfort** Michigan
95 M3 **Frankfort** New York
94 D7 **Frankfort** Ohio
98 H5 **Frankfort** S Dakota
33 T7 **Frankfurt** E Germany
36 F3 **Frankfurt am Main** W Germany

31 H3 **Frankfurt an der Oder** E Germany
37 K6 **Fränkische Alb** *mts* W Germany
37 L4 **Fränkische Schweiz** *reg* W Germany
139 J7 **Frankland, C** Tasmania
111 L8 **Franklin** Georgia
101 O7 **Franklin** Idaho
94 A7 **Franklin** Indiana
110 K5 **Franklin** Kentucky
111 E12 **Franklin** Louisiana
95 T2 **Franklin** Maine
95 Q4 **Franklin** Massachusetts
101 Q3 **Franklin** Montana
112 D2 **Franklin** N Carolina
98 H9 **Franklin** Nebraska
95 Q3 **Franklin** New Hampshire
95 N5 **Franklin** New Jersey
95 M4 **Franklin** New York
94 C7 **Franklin** Ohio
94 H5 **Franklin** Pennsylvania
110 K6 **Franklin** Tennessee
109 L4 **Franklin** Texas
95 L10 **Franklin** Virginia
94 H8 **Franklin** W Virginia
114 G3 **Franklin B** N W Terr
115 H3 **Franklin, Dist.of** N W Terr
100 G1 **Franklin D. Roosevelt L** Washington
99 R8 **Franklin Grove** Illinois
138 D5 **Franklin Harb** S Australia
146 J6 **Franklin I** Antarctica
120 K7 **Franklin I** Ontario
103 J1 **Franklin L** Nevada
116 P2 **Franklin Mts** Alaska
144 A6 **Franklin Mts** New Zealand
117 L3 **Franklin Mts** N W Terr
116 H1 **Franklin, Pt** Alaska
139 J8 **Franklin Snd** Tasmania
115 K3 **Franklin Str** N W Terr
111 F11 **Franklinton** Louisiana
112 J1 **Franklinton** N Carolina
112 H2 **Franklinville** N Carolina
94 J4 **Franklinville** New York
100 J6 **Franklin Whitney** *airport* Idaho
144 D5 **Franklyn, Mt** New Zealand
37 J3 **Fränk Saale** *R* W Germany
109 M3 **Frankston** Texas
139 H7 **Frankston** Victoria
99 T7 **Franksville** Wisconsin
144 B6 **Frankton** New Zealand
101 R5 **Frannie** Wyoming
87 B10 **Fransfontein** Namibia
9 G5 **Frant** England
37 N3 **Františkovy Lázně** Czechoslovakia
147 L11 **Frantsa Iosifa, Zemlya** Arctic Oc
115 L8 **Franz** Ontario
33 R4 **Franzburg** E Germany
144 C5 **Franz Josef Gla** New Zealand
Franz Josef Land *see* **Frantsa Iosifa, Zemlya**
38 G7 **Franz-Josefs Höhe** *mt* Austria
43 B9 **Frasca, C. d** Sardinia
42 E7 **Frascati** Italy
106 E2 **Fraser** Colorado
139 L2 **Fraser** *isld* Queensland
100 C1 **Fraser** *R* Br Col
87 D12 **Fraserburg** S Africa
15 F3 **Fraserburgh** Scotland
120 J3 **Fraserdale** Ontario
141 L7 **Fraser I** Queensland
142 A6 **Fraser I** W Australia
143 C7 **Fraser, Mt** W Australia
143 E9 **Fraser Range** W Australia
69 E11 **Fraser's Hill** Malaysia
145 F3 **Frasertown** New Zealand
119 U8 **Fraserwood** Manitoba
46 D4 **Frashër** Albania
48 K6 **Frasinet** Romania
19 K6 **Frasne** France
22 F2 **Frasnes-les-Buissenal** Belgium
25 F5 **Frasselt** W Germany
45 J3 **Frassinoro** Italy
120 F5 **Frater** Ontario
45 L1 **Fratta Polesine** Italy
41 J2 **Frauenfeld** Switzerland
33 S10 **Frauenhain** E Germany
37 O5 **Frauenstein** *mt* W Germany
37 K2 **Frauenwald** E Germany
28 E6 **Fraugde** Denmark
131 F4 **Fray Bentos** Uruguay
20 H5 **Frazé** France
99 L3 **Frazee** Minnesota
101 T1 **Frazer** Montana
120 B3 **Frazer L** Ontario
36 B2 **Frechen** W Germany
16 D2 **Frechilla** Spain
32 G9 **Freckenhorst** W Germany
99 S2 **Freda** Michigan
98 E3 **Freda** N Dakota
36 E1 **Fredeburg** W Germany
32 L9 **Freden** W Germany
28 K5 **Fredensborg** Denmark
94 C2 **Frederic** Michigan
99 O4 **Frederic** Wisconsin
95 M7 **Frederica** Delaware
28 D5 **Fredericia** Denmark
99 Q9 **Frederick** Illinois
95 K7 **Frederick** Maryland
107 L7 **Frederick** Oklahoma
98 H4 **Frederick** S Dakota
140 D2 **Frederick Hills** N Terr Aust
120 J3 **Frederick House** *R* Ontario
137 L6 **Frederick Reef** Coral Sea
99 O7 **Fredericksburg** Iowa
95 L6 **Fredericksburg** Pennsylvania
94 K8 **Fredericksburg** Virginia
117 F7 **Frederick Sd** Alaska
110 F4 **Fredericktown** Missouri
94 E6 **Fredericktown** Ohio
122 F8 **Fredericton** New Brunswick
122 F8 **Fredericton Junct** New Brunswick
28 C4 **Frederiks** Denmark
29 K5 **Frederiksberg** Denmark
28 C5 **Frederikshåb** Denmark
115 P5 **Frederikshåb** Greenland
28 F2 **Frederikshavn** Denmark
28 H5 **Frederikssund** Denmark
127 M5 **Frederiksted** Virgin Is
28 J5 **Frederiksværk** Denmark
103 M5 **Fredonia** Arizona
128 C2 **Fredonia** Colombia
107 P4 **Fredonia** Kansas
110 H4 **Fredonia** Kentucky
98 G3 **Fredonia** N Dakota
94 H4 **Fredonia** New York
109 J5 **Fredricksburg** Texas
26 K7 **Fredrika** Sweden
27 E12 **Fredrikstad** Norway
110 E3 **Freeburg** Missouri
95 K6 **Freeburg** Pennsylvania
100 J4 **Freedom** Idaho
110 K2 **Freedom** Indiana
107 L5 **Freedom** Oklahoma
100 E9 **Freedonyer Peak** *mt* California
95 N6 **Freehold** New Jersey
94 C3 **Freeland** Michigan
95 M5 **Freeland** Pennsylvania
138 E4 **Freeling Heights** *mt* S Australia
140 C6 **Freeling Mt** N Terr Aust
102 E3 **Freel Peak** California
123 T4 **Freels, C** Nfld
98 J6 **Freeman** S Dakota
118 B4 **Freeman** *R* Alberta
110 K1 **Freeman, L** Indiana
111 G12 **Freemason I** Louisiana
111 K11 **Freeport** Florida
113 J11 **Freeport** Grand Bahama I
99 R7 **Freeport** Illinois
95 R3 **Freeport** Maine
122 F9 **Freeport** Nova Scotia
94 F6 **Freeport** Ohio
94 H6 **Freeport** Pennsylvania
109 M7 **Freeport** Texas

109 J8 **Freer** Texas
99 U5 **Freesoil** Michigan
127 P4 **Freetown** Antigua W I
126 F2 **Freetown** Eleuthera Bahamas
94 A8 **Freetown** Indiana
122 J7 **Freetown** Pr Edward I
85 B7 **Freetown** Sierra Leone
95 L4 **Freeville** New York
100 G4 **Freewater** Oregon
101 T7 **Freezeout Mts** Wyoming
16 C6 **Fregenal de la Sierra** Spain
26 C8 **Frei** Norway
37 P2 **Freiberg** E Germany
36 G6 **Freiberg** W Germany
37 O1 **Freiberger Mulde** *R* E Germany
40 G1 **Freiburg** W Germany
32 K10 **Freienhagen** W Germany
32 H10 **Freienohl** W Germany
36 G3 **Freiensteinau** W Germany
37 M4 **Freihung** W Germany
36 D2 **Freilingen** W Germany
133 C3 **Freirina** Chile
36 C4 **Freisen** W Germany
37 M7 **Freising** W Germany
38 L4 **Freistadt** Austria
16 C3 **Freixo de Espada à Cinta** Portugal
28 D2 **Frejlev** Denmark
143 B9 **Fremantle** W Australia
94 C5 **Fremont** Indiana
99 V6 **Fremont** Michigan
112 K2 **Fremont** N Carolina
98 K8 **Fremont** Nebraska
94 D5 **Fremont** Ohio
103 O3 **Fremont** *R* Utah
101 N8 **Fremont I** Utah
101 Q7 **Fremont L** Wyoming
106 D2 **Fremont Pass** Colorado
101 Q6 **Fremont Pk** Wyoming
106 F5 **French** New Mexico
112 D2 **French Broad** *R* Tennessee
94 D9 **Frenchburg** Kentucky
94 G5 **French Cr** Pennsylvania
100 J4 **French Creek** Idaho
102 T13 **French Frigate Shoals** Hawaiian Is
100 G7 **Frenchglen** Oregon
129 H3 **French Guiana** S America
100 C9 **French Gulch** California
139 H7 **French I** Victoria
110 K3 **French Lick** Indiana
102 F2 **Frenchman** Nevada
95 T2 **Frenchman Bay** Maine
118 H5 **Frenchman Butte** Sask
139 H8 **Frenchman Cap** Tasmania
101 S1 **Frenchman Cr** Mont/Sask
103 J5 **Frenchman Flat** *dry lake* Nevada
98 E9 **Frenchman Fork** *R* Nebraska
118 J9 **Frenchman R** Sask
123 O4 **Frenchman's Cove** Nfld
14 C3 **Frenchpark** Irish Rep
145 D4 **French Pass** New Zealand
French Terr. of the Afars and the Issas (FTAI) *see* **Djibouti** *rep*
95 M6 **Frenchtown** New Jersey
22 B2 **Frencq** France
19 Q14 **Frêne, Pic du** *mt* France
20 G3 **Freneuse-sur-Risle** France
37 K4 **Frensdorf** W Germany
31 L6 **Frenštát** Czechoslovakia
32 G8 **Freren** W Germany
143 D7 **Frere Ra** W Australia
129 H5 **Fresco** *R* Brazil
146 K4 **Freshfield, C** Antarctica
14 D4 **Freshford** Irish Rep
144 B6 **Freshford Plain** New Zealand
100 A9 **Freshwater** California
9 E6 **Freshwater** England
20 F5 **Fresnay** France
20 F5 **Fresnaye-sur-Chédouet, la** France
40 C2 **Fresnes** France
22 F3 **Fresnes-sur-L'Escaut** France
124 H6 **Fresnillo de González Echeverría** Mexico
102 E5 **Fresno** California
102 E4 **Fresno** *R* California
101 P1 **Fresno Res** Montana
20 H2 **Fresnoy-Folny** France
22 E4 **Fresnoy-le-Grand** France
40 C4 **Fresse, Mt.de** France
20 J1 **Fressenneville** France
27 B10 **Fresvik** Norway
21 H6 **Fréteval** France
27 B11 **Fretheim** Norway
19 J5 **Fretigney** France
13 E1 **Freuchie** Scotland
36 G4 **Freudenberg** Baden-Württemberg W Germany
36 D2 **Freudenberg** Nordrhein-Westfalen W Germany
36 E7 **Freudenstadt** W Germany
22 C3 **Frévent** France
138 D2 **Frew** *R* S Australia
140 D4 **Frewena** N Terr Aust
94 H4 **Frewsburg** New York
37 M1 **Freyburg** E Germany
143 A10 **Freycinet, C** W Australia
143 A7 **Freycinet Estuary** *inlet* W Aust
139 J8 **Freycinet Pen** Tasmania
33 Q6 **Freyenstein** E Germany
36 B5 **Freyming** France
37 L5 **Freystadt** W Germany
30 H7 **Freyung** W Germany
85 B6 **Fria** Guinea
87 B9 **Fria, C** Namibia
102 E5 **Friant** California
102 E5 **Friant Dam** California
111 F7 **Friar Port** Mississippi
127 P4 **Friar's B., North** St Kitts W I
83 L10 **Friar's Hood** *mt* Sri Lanka
131 D2 **Frias** Argentina
40 F4 **Fribourg** Switzerland
36 E3 **Frickhofen** W Germany
22 D3 **Fricourt** France
100 B1 **Friday Harbour** Washington
141 F1 **Friday I** Queensland
13 H5 **Fridaythorpe** England
146 G8 **Fridtjof Nansen, Mt** Antarctica
38 O7 **Friedberg** Austria
37 K7 **Friedberg** Bayern W Germany
36 F3 **Friedberg** Hessen W Germany
33 P9 **Friedeburg** E Germany
38 M4 **Friedersbach** Austria
33 T8 **Friedersdorf** E Germany
33 T5 **Friedland** E Germany
32 L10 **Friedland** W Germany
37 K2 **Friedrichroda** E Germany
36 F3 **Friedrichsdorf** W Germany
33 T7 **Friedrichsfelde** E Germany
41 K2 **Friedrichshafen** W Germany
33 T8 **Friedrichshagen** E Germany
32 J4 **Friedrichskoog** W Germany
33 P5 **Friedrichsruhe** E Germany
30 E1 **Friedrichstadt** W Germany
33 T6 **Friedrichswalde** E Germany
37 K2 **Friedrichswerth** E Germany
36 G2 **Frielendorf** W Germany
107 K3 **Friend** Kansas
98 J9 **Friend** Nebraska
Friendly Is *see* **Tonga**
95 S3 **Friendship** Maine
94 J4 **Friendship** New York
94 D8 **Friendship** Ohio
99 R6 **Friendship** Wisconsin
127 K2 **Friendship** *peak* Jamaica

70 C2 **Friendship Shoal** S China Sea
94 H7 **Friendsville** Maryland
27 D12 **Frierfjord** *inlet* Norway
94 F10 **Fries** Virginia
38 K8 **Friesach** Austria
33 R7 **Friesack** E Germany
25 F2 **Friesche Gat** Netherlands
36 D7 **Friesenheim** W Germany
28 A7 **Friesische Inseln** *islds* W Germany
25 E2 **Friesland** Netherlands
32 G6 **Friesoythe** W Germany
83 J12 **Frigate** *isld* Seychelles
45 J3 **Frignano** Italy
9 H4 **Frinton** England
124 H6 **Frío** Mexico
109 J7 **Frio** *R* Texas
130 H8 **Frio, C** Brazil
15 F4 **Friockheim** Scotland
108 E1 **Frio Draw** *R* New Mex/Tex
36 F6 **Friolzheim** W Germany
22 L4 **Frisange** Luxembourg
109 L2 **Frisco** Texas
111 J10 **Frisco City** Alabama
103 L3 **Frisco Mt** Utah
108 C8 **Fritch** Texas
8 B6 **Frithelstock Stone** England
36 G1 **Fritzlar** W Germany
42 E2 **Friuli-Venezia-Giulia** *prov* Italy
20 J1 **Friville-Escarbotin** France
12 E5 **Frizington** England
26 D8 **Froan** *isld* Norway
119 P9 **Frobisher** Sask
115 N5 **Frobisher Bay** N W Terr
114 J6 **Frobisher L** Sask
19 P14 **Froges** France
118 G5 **Frog L** *L* Alberta
26 D8 **Frohavet** *inlet* Norway
37 O1 **Frohburg** E Germany
33 S7 **Frohnau** E Germany
33 P8 **Frohse** E Germany
98 B1 **Froid** Montana
22 G3 **Froid-Chapelle** Belgium
130 F5 **Fróis** Brazil
20 K2 **Froïssy** France
36 B2 **Froitzheim** W Germany
52 H4 **Frolovskaya** U.S.S.R.
55 E1 **Froly** U.S.S.R.
101 R4 **Fromberg** Montana
31 M1 **Frombork** Poland
8 D5 **Frome** England
127 H1 **Frome** Jamaica
141 G3 **Frome** Queensland
138 E3 **Frome** *R* S Australia
138 E4 **Frome Downs** S Australia
138 E4 **Frome, L** S Australia
22 D2 **Fromelles** France
32 G10 **Fröndenberg** W Germany
36 F2 **Fronhausen** W Germany
16 B5 **Fronteira** Portugal
18 E6 **Frontenay** France
21 D9 **Frontenay-Rohan-Rohan** France
37 O6 **Frontenhausen** W Germany
125 N8 **Frontera** Mexico
124 E2 **Fronteras** Mexico
118 J9 **Frontier** Sask
101 P8 **Frontier** Wyoming
18 H9 **Frontignan** France
106 E1 **Front Range** Colorado
94 J8 **Front Royal** Virginia
28 F6 **Frørup** Denmark
33 O9 **Frose** E Germany
43 E7 **Frosinone** Italy
28 B3 **Frøslev** Denmark
21 B7 **Frossay** France
109 L3 **Frost** Texas
26 E8 **Frosta** Norway
94 J7 **Frostburg** Maryland
113 F10 **Frostproof** Florida
28 B2 **Føstrup** Denmark
26 G7 **Frostviken** Sweden
37 K2 **Fröttstädt** E Germany
19 K4 **Frouard** France
119 O9 **Froude** Sask
27 H12 **Frövi** Sweden
9 E5 **Froxfield** England
26 C8 **Fröya** *isld* Norway
26 B8 **Fröyabanken** Norway
22 C3 **Fruges** France
106 B2 **Fruita** Colorado
111 H10 **Fruitdale** Alabama
98 C5 **Fruitdale** S Dakota
100 J5 **Fruitland** Idaho
106 B5 **Fruitland** New Mexico
101 P9 **Fruitland** Utah
144 B6 **Fruitlands** New Zealand
100 J5 **Fruitvale** Idaho
48 K3 **Frumuşica** Romania
57 G3 **Frunze** U.S.S.R.
54 F8 **Frunzenskiy** U.S.S.R.
48 M3 **Frunzovka** U.S.S.R.
48 F5 **Fruška Gora** *mt* Yugoslavia
130 E7 **Frutal** Brazil
40 G4 **Frutigen** Switzerland
102 B2 **Fruto** California
54 K1 **Fryanovo** U.S.S.R.
98 C3 **Fryburg** N Dakota
48 E1 **Frýdek Mistek** Czechoslovakia
95 R2 **Fryeburg** Maine
27 F11 **Fryksände** Sweden
46 E5 **Ftéri** *mt* Greece
67 F3 **Fu'an** China
45 J4 **Fucecchio** Italy
65 B7 **Fucheng** China
65 C6 **Fucheng** China
36 E2 **Fuchskauten** *mt* W Germany
60 G11 **Fuchū** Japan
67 D4 **Fuchuan** China
59 G6 **Fuchun Jiang** *R* China
42 F7 **Fucino, Alveo del L** Italy
61 P5 **Fudai** Japan
67 G3 **Fuding** China
16 D8 **Fuengirola** Spain
108 G7 **Fuente** Mexico
17 G7 **Fuente Alamo de Murcia** Spain
16 C6 **Fuente de Cantos** Spain
16 C4 **Fuenteguinaldo** Spain
16 D6 **Fuenteobejuna** Spain
16 D3 **Fuentesaúco** Spain
17 G3 **Fuentes de Ebro** Spain
16 C4 **Fuentes de Oñoro** Spain
130 B7 **Fuerte Olimpo** Paraguay
85 B3 **Fuerteventura** *isld* Canary Is
71 E1 **Fuga** *isld* Luzon **Philippines**
38 E7 **Fügen** Austria
28 M2 **Fuglebjærge** Faeroes
28 H6 **Fuglebjerg** Denmark
28 O9 **Fuglø** *isld* Faeroes
26 L1 **Fuglöy** *isld* Norway
28 F7 **Fuglsbølle** Denmark
65 C7 **Fugou** China
65 B5 **Fugu** China
Fuguo *see* **Zhanhua**
33 Q9 **Fuhne** *R* E Germany
32 L7 **Fuhrberg** W Germany
77 E7 **Fujayrah, Al** U.A.E.
67 B1 **Fu Jiang** *R* China
67 F3 **Fujian** *prov* China
61 M10 **Fuji Hakone Izu Nat. Park** Japan
61 M10 **Fuji-kawa** *R* Japan
59 K2 **Fujin** China
61 M10 **Fujinomiya** Japan
61 N9 **Fujioka** Japan
61 O5 **Fujisaki** Japan
59 L4 **Fuji San** *mt* Japan
61 M10 **Fuji-san** *vol* Japan
61 N10 **Fujisawa** Japan
61 M10 **Fujiyoshida** Japan
61 N5 **Fukaura** Japan
Fukien *prov see* **Fujian**
60 J10 **Fukuchiyama** Japan
60 B13 **Fukue** Japan
60 B13 **Fukue-jima** *isld* Japan
61 K9 **Fukui** Japan
60 D12 **Fukuma** Japan

28 Fukuno — Georgetown

61 K9 Fukuno Japan
60 D12 Fukuoka Japan
60 H11 Fukura Japan
61 L11 Fukuroi Japan
60 O4 Fukushima Hokkaido Japan
61 O8 Fukushima Honshu Japan
61 L10 Fukushima Nagano Japan
61 O8 Fukushima prefect Japan
60 G11 Fukuyama Honshu Japan
60 D14 Fukuyama Kyūshū Japan
60 H10 Fukuzaki Japan
85 B6 Fulacunda Guinea-Bissau
77 C1 Fulād Mahalleh Iran
99 L6 Fulda Minnesota
36 H2 Fulda W Germany
32 L10 Fulda R W Germany
36 H2 Fulda R W Germany
36 G1 Fuldabrück W Germany
13 G6 Fulford England
58 D6 Fulin China
67 B2 Fuling China
67 F3 Fuling China
127 N3 Fullarton Trinidad
141 F5 Fullarton R Queensland
102 G8 Fullerton California
94 E8 Fullerton Kentucky
109 P4 Fullerton Louisiana
98 H8 Fullerton Nebraska
65 F2 Fulongquan China
48 E4 Fülöpszállás Hungary
41 O3 Fulpmes Austria
111 J10 Fulton Alabama
111 C8 Fulton Arkansas
99 Q8 Fulton Illinois
94 A6 Fulton Indiana
107 Q3 Fulton Kansas
110 H5 Fulton Kentucky
111 C11 Fulton Louisiana
111 H7 Fulton Mississippi
110 E3 Fulton Missouri
95 L3 Fulton New York
94 E6 Fulton Ohio
98 J6 Fulton S Dakota
95 N4 Fultonham New York
95 N4 Fultonville New York
27 F10 Fuluälven R Sweden
27 F10 Fulufj mt Sweden
27 F10 Fulunäs Sweden
22 H4 Fumay France
18 F8 Fumel France
41 N5 Fumo, Mt Italy
61 N10 Funabashi Japan
137 Q3 Funafuti atoll Tuvalu
60 E14 Funahiki Japan
Funan see Fusui
65 F4 Funan China
26 F9 Funäsdalen Sweden
85 A2 Funchal Madeira
16 B7 Funcheira Portugal
126 G9 Fundación Colombia
130 H6 Fundão Brazil
124 E4 Fundición Mexico
28 N1 Funding Faeroes
38 E8 Fundres Italy
48 K6 Fundulea Romania
41 N3 Fundus Feiler mt Austria
122 G8 Fundy, B. of Nova Scotia/New Bruns
122 G8 Fundy Nat. Park New Brunswick
Funen isld see Fyn
102 H5 Funeral Peak California
87 F10 Funhalouro Mozambique
65 D5 Funing China
67 B5 Funing China
98 G9 Funk Nebraska
123 T4 Funk I Nfld
141 J5 Funnel R Queensland
117 F6 Funter Alaska
85 F6 Funtua Nigeria
65 A7 Fuping China
65 C5 Fuping China
67 F4 Fuqing China
112 J2 Fuquay Springs N Carolina
88 D9 Furancungo Mozambique
60 Q2 Furano Japan
59 J2 Furao China
47 G1 Furculeşti Romania
80 C3 Fureidis Israel
60 Q3 Furenai Japan
60 T2 Fūren ko L Japan
28 K5 Furesø L Denmark
36 G5 Fürfeld Baden-Württemberg W Germany
36 D4 Fürfeld Rheinland-Pfalz W Germany
77 D5 Furg Iran
112 F5 Furman S Carolina
52 F6 Furmanov U.S.S.R.
57 G3 Furmanovka U.S.S.R.
12 C1 Furnace Scotland
130 F7 Furnas Dam Brazil
139 J8 Furneaux Group islds Tasmania
138 F6 Furner S Australia
Furnes see Veurne
27 E11 Furnes Norway
118 H5 Furness Sask
67 B2 Furong Jiang R China
67 E3 Furong Shan mt China
32 G7 Fürstenau W Germany
33 S6 Fürstenberg E Germany
36 F1 Fürstenberg W Germany
38 O7 Fürstenfeld Austria
37 L7 Fürstenfeldbrück W Germany
30 H3 Fürstenwalde E Germany
33 T6 Fürstenwerder E Germany
37 P6 Fürstenzell W Germany
36 F4 Fürth W Germany
37 O5 Furth im Wald W Germany
41 H1 Furtwangen W Germany
60 O2 Furubira Japan
61 L9 Furukawa Japan
61 O7 Furukawa Japan
115 L4 Fury & Hecla Str N W Terr
27 A11 Fusa Norway
128 D3 Fusagasuga Colombia
45 Q8 Fusaro L Italy
43 G9 Fuscaldo Italy
38 G7 Fusch Austria
32 M8 Fuse R W Germany
65 B6 Fushan China
65 E6 Fushan China
68 J3 Fushan China
13 E2 Fushiebridge Scotland
61 K9 Fushiki Japan
60 P2 Fushiko-Uryū Japan
59 H3 Fushun China
67 A2 Fushun China
45 L3 Fusignano Italy
118 H7 Fusilier Sask
Fusin see Fuxin
45 M1 Fusina Italy
41 J5 Fusio Switzerland
59 J3 Fusong China
41 N2 Füssen W Germany
28 D4 Fussing Sø L Denmark
67 B5 Fusui China
61 L11 Futagawa Japan
60 E12 Futago-san mt Japan
60 D11 Futaoi-jima isld Japan
45 K3 Futa, Passo di Italy
61 O5 Futatsui Japan
61 N13 Futatsu-ne rocks Japan
61 P13 Futemma Okinawa
137 R4 Futuna isld Îles de Horn Pacific Oc
67 F3 Futun Xi R China
79 A7 Fuwa Egypt
65 A6 Fu Xian China
65 E5 Fu Xian China
67 A4 Fuxian Hu L China
65 E3 Fuxin China
Fuxing see Wangmo
58 G5 Fuyang China
67 F1 Fuyang China
67 F5 Fuyang China
58 G4 Fuyang He R China
67 G3 Fuying Dao isld China
59 H2 Fuyu China
59 K2 Fuyuan China
67 A4 Fuyuan China
66 D2 Fuyun China
48 F3 Füzesabony Hungary
48 G3 Füzesgyarmat Hungary
67 F3 Fuzhou Fujian China
67 E2 Fuzhou Jiangxi China
65 E5 Fuzhoucheng China
9 G4 Fyfield Essex England
9 E4 Fyfield Oxon England
28 E6 Fyn co Denmark
28 E6 Fyn isld Denmark
12 C1 Fyne, L Scotland
28 D7 Fynshav Denmark
28 F5 Fynshoved C Denmark
27 C12 Fyresv L Norway
127 O3 Fyzabad Trinidad
70 C4 Gaat R Sarawak
52 D4 Gabanova U.S.S.R.
123 M8 Gabarouse C Breton I, N Scotia
18 F9 Gabarret France
102 G3 Gabbs Nevada
102 F3 Gabbs Valley Ra Nevada
87 B8 Gabela Angola
Gaberones see Gaborone
85 F2 Gabes Tunisia
85 G2 Gabès, Gulf of Tunisia
84 J5 Gabgaba, Wadi watercourse Sudan
102 C5 Gabilan Ra California
31 M3 Gąbin Poland
145 G3 Gable End Foreland New Zealand
117 K9 Gable Mt Br Columbia
139 J7 Gabo isld Victoria
28 C6 Gabol Denmark
86 B6 Gabon rep Equat Africa
89 D5 Gaborone Botswana
95 N2 Gabriels New York
16 C4 Gabriel y Galán, Embalse res Spain
77 F7 Gābrik Iran
47 G2 Gabrovo Bulgaria
83 L14 Gaby isld Kerguelen Indian Oc
20 F4 Gacé France
77 B4 Gach Sārān Iran
98 G3 Gackle N Dakota
48 E7 Gacko Yugoslavia
76 B3 Gadag India
86 G2 Gadamai Sudan
28 C5 Gadbjerg Denmark
26 G7 Gäddede Sweden
32 J8 Gadderbaum W Germany
33 O5 Gadebusch E Germany
80 D3 Gadish Israel
17 F8 Gador, Sierra de Spain
80 F1 Gadot Israel
118 E6 Gadsby Alberta
111 L8 Gadsden Alabama
103 K9 Gadsden Arizona
28 J5 Gadstrup Denmark
76 C2 Gadwal India
54 F6 Gadyach U.S.S.R.
89 G2 Gadzema Zimbabwe
86 C5 Gadzi Cent Afr Republic
48 J6 Găeşti Romania
43 F7 Gaeta Italy
45 P8 Gaeta, Gulf of Italy
112 F2 Gaffney S Carolina
71 A2 Gafi isld Indonesia
38 L6 Gaflenz Austria
85 F2 Gafsa Tunisia
57 E4 Gafurov U.S.S.R.
71 B3 Gag isld Indonesia
54 F1 Gagarin U.S.S.R.
106 B9 Gage New Mexico
107 L5 Gage Oklahoma
122 H7 Gage, C Pr Edward I
99 R4 Gagen Wisconsin
19 O15 Gagère, P. de la mt France
122 F8 Gagetown New Brunswick
36 E6 Gaggenau W Germany
52 F6 Gagino U.S.S.R.
27 H11 Gagnef Sweden
85 C7 Gagnoa Ivory Coast
115 N7 Gagnon Quebec
121 P6 Gagnon, L Quebec
52 H4 Gagshor U.S.S.R.
38 N6 Gahns mt Austria
89 A6 Gaiab watercourse Namibia
130 B5 Gaiba L Bolivia/Brazil
75 N6 Gaibanda Bangladesh
48 L4 Găiceana Romania
47 H10 Gaïdhouronísi isld Crete Greece
38 J8 Gail R Austria
36 H6 Gaildorf W Germany
18 G9 Gaillac France
122 E1 Gaillarbois, L Quebec
20 J2 Gailléfontaine France
20 H3 Gaillon France
38 G8 Gailtaler Alpen mts Austria
133 D6 Gaiman Argentina
37 L6 Gaimersheim W Germany
94 B10 Gainesboro Tennessee
111 H9 Gainesville Alabama
113 E8 Gainesville Florida
109 K2 Gainesville Texas
13 G4 Gainford England
13 H6 Gainsborough England
119 Q9 Gainsborough Sask
138 D4 Gairdner Lake S Australia
15 C3 Gairloch Scotland
15 C4 Gairlochy Scotland
15 E3 Gairn R Scotland
38 L7 Gaishorn Austria
95 K7 Gaithersburg Maryland
65 E4 Gai Xian China
70 P9 Gajam Indonesia
76 B3 Gajendragara India
89 C6 Gakarosa mt S Africa
116 P5 Gakona Alaska
52 E4 Gakugsa U.S.S.R.
66 D6 Gala China
15 F5 Gala R Scotland
77 H2 GāLā, Band-i- mts Afghanistan
86 J4 Galadi Ethiopia
83 K10 Galagedara Sri Lanka
47 H4 Gala Gölü L Turkey
118 F6 Galahad Alberta
79 B9 Galâla el Baharîya, G. el mts Egypt
79 C10 Galâla el Qiblîya, G. el mts Egypt
17 G4 Galamocha Spain
88 G3 Galana R Kenya
69 G12 Galang isld Indonesia
26 N3 Galanito Norway
48 D2 Galanta Czechoslovakia
128 A7 Galapagos Is Pacific Oc
13 F2 Galashiels Scotland
101 O1 Galata Montana
47 F7 Galatás Greece
106 G3 Galatea Colorado
145 F3 Galatea New Zealand
137 R8 Galathea Depth Pacific Oc
48 L5 Galati Romania
110 H4 Galatia Illinois
107 M3 Galatia Kansas
43 J8 Galatina Italy
Galatz see Galati
19 O14 Galaure R France
94 G10 Galax Virginia
46 E6 Galaxídhion Greece
141 F3 Galbraith Queensland
124 J5 Gal. Cepeda Mexico
26 C10 Galdhöpiggen mt Norway
124 F2 Galeana Mexico
130 G8 Galeào Brazil
45 L4 Galeata Italy
77 C6 Galeh Dār Iran
71 A2 Galela Indonesia
116 J4 Galena Alaska
99 Q7 Galena Illinois
107 Q4 Galena Kansas
95 M7 Galena Maryland
110 C5 Galena Missouri
109 G9 Galena Park Texas
33 T5 Galenbecker See L E Germany
127 P3 Galeota Pt Trinidad
17 F7 Galera Spain
128 B3 Galera, Pta point Ecuador
131 A8 Galera, Pta. de la Chile
99 Q9 Galesburg Illinois
94 B4 Galesburg Michigan
99 P5 Galesville Wisconsin
98 B9 Galeton Colorado
120 K1 Galeton Ontario
94 K5 Galeton Pennsylvania
83 J13 Galets, Pte des Réunion Indian Oc
13 F6 Galgate England
83 K10 Galgiriya mt Sri Lanka
117 M11 Galiano I Br Columbia
19 Q14 Galibier, Col du pass France
100 B7 Galice Oregon
48 J1 Galich U.S.S.R.
47 F1 Galiche Bulgaria
52 F5 Galichskoye, Oz L U.S.S.R.
16 B2 Galicia Spain
99 U8 Galien Michigan
141 H5 Galilee L Queensland
80 F2 Galilee, Sea of Israel
127 L2 Galina Pt Jamaica
94 E6 Galion Ohio
127 M4 Galion, Baie du Martinique W I
123 O2 Galissonnière, L.la Quebec
43 C11 Galite, La Tunisia
103 O9 Galiurov Mts Arizona
55 D3 Galkino U.S.S.R.
86 G3 Gallabat Sudan
86 A2 Gallacaio Somalia
42 B3 Gallarate Italy
20 J4 Gallardon France
99 N10 Gallatin Missouri
110 K5 Gallatin Tennessee
109 M4 Gallatin Texas
101 O4 Gallatin R Montana
101 O4 Gallatin Gateway Montana
101 O4 Gallatin Pk Montana
101 P4 Gallatin Ra Mont/Wyoming
83 K11 Galle Sri Lanka
17 G3 Gállego R Spain
106 G6 Gallegos New Mexico
133 C8 Gallegos R Argentina
45 J4 Galleno Italy
123 O2 Gallet L Quebec
14 C5 Galley Hd Irish Rep
45 J3 Gallicano Italy
45 N6 Gallicano nel Lazio Italy
46 F4 Gallikós R Greece
33 Q5 Gallin E Germany
106 D5 Gallina Pk New Mexico
44 D3 Gallinara isld Italy
108 B1 Gallinas Peak New Mexico
128 D1 Gallinas, Pta C Colombia
43 H8 Gallipoli Italy
Gallipoli Turkey see Gelibolu
94 E8 Gallipolis Ohio
94 J6 Gallitzin Penn
26 L4 Gällivare Sweden
45 Q7 Gallo Italy
26 H9 Gällö Sweden
17 F4 Gallo R Spain
17 F4 Gallocanta, L.de Spain
43 E10 Gallo, C.di Sicily
106 B8 Gallo Mts New Mexico
95 L3 Galloo I New York
7 M11 Galloper Lightship North Sea
15 D6 Galloway Scotland
27 F14 Gällstad Sweden
106 B6 Gallup New Mexico
17 G3 Gallur Spain
45 K4 Galluzzo Italy
85 F6 Galmi Niger
139 J5 Galong New S Wales
83 L10 Gal Oya R Sri Lanka
124 H5 Gal. Simon Bolívar Mexico
28 C6 Galsted Denmark
12 D2 Galston Scotland
26 J9 Galström Sweden
102 C3 Galt California
99 N9 Galt Missouri
28 D4 Galten Denmark
26 N1 Galten Norway
124 F3 Gal. Trías Mexico
41 M4 Galtür Austria
14 C4 Galtymore mt Irish Rep
70 F6 Galumpang Sulawesi
99 R8 Galva Illinois
94 A6 Galveston Indiana
111 B12 Galveston Texas
131 E4 Galvez Argentina
14 B3 Galway Irish Rep
14 B3 Galway co Irish Rep
14 B3 Galway Bay Irish Rep
71 B3 Gam isld Indonesia
71 C3 Gam isld W Irian
20 J2 Gamaches France
61 L11 Gamagōri Japan
131 E8 Gama, I Argentina
94 B10 Gamaliel Kentucky
86 H3 Gamarri, L Ethiopia
71 G4 Gamay Bay Philippines
75 N4 Gamba China
85 D6 Gambaga Ghana
20 J4 Gambais France
45 J4 Gambassi Italy
45 R6 Gambatesa Italy
86 F4 Gambeila Ethiopia
116 B5 Gambell St Lawrence I, Alaska
45 M3 Gambettola Italy
85 A6 Gambia R The Gambia/Senegal
85 A6 Gambia, The rep W Africa
113 L9 Gambier New Providence I Bahamas
94 E6 Gambier Ohio
140 B1 Gambier, C N Terr Aust
135 R15 Gambier Is Pacific Oc
138 D6 Gambier Is S Australia
124 F9 Gamboa Panama Canal Zone
86 C6 Gamboma Congo
141 G3 Gamboola Queensland
86 C5 Gamboula Cent Afr Republic
71 H4 Gambuta mt Sulawesi
130 J10 Gameleira Brazil
71 A2 Gamkunoro Gunung mt Indonesia
71 A2 Gamlaba Indonesia
27 H14 Gamleby Sweden
26 M6 Gammelstad Sweden
36 G7 Gammertingen W Germany
16 D4 Gamo R Spain
86 G4 Gamo-Gofa prov Ethiopia
76 E7 Gampola Sri Lanka
77 G5 Gamshadzai K mts Iran
71 B2 Gamtjaka, Tg C Indonesia
26 Q1 Gamvik Norway
18 E9 Gan France
73 L9 Gan Maldives
37 O6 Ganacker W Germany
103 P6 Ganado Arizona
109 L6 Ganado Texas
86 H4 Ganale Dorya R Ethiopia
86 H5 Ganane Somalia
121 O8 Gananoque Ontario
67 C7 Gancheng China
Gand see Gent
70 F6 Gandadiwata G mt Sulawesi
87 D7 Gandajika Zaïre
74 B4 Gandava Pakistan
115 O8 Gander Nfld
123 S4 Gander Bay Nfld
32 J6 Ganderkesee W Germany
123 R5 Gander R Nfld
17 H3 Gandesa Spain
17 G6 Gandia Spain
28 E2 Gandrup Denmark
103 L2 Gandy Utah
77 B5 Ganēveh Iran
83 K10 Ganewatta Sri Lanka
74 H5 Ganga R India
74 G9 Gangakher India
133 D6 Gan Gan Argentina
74 E4 Ganganagar India
68 B1 Gangaw Burma
76 C3 Gangawati India
75 R6 Gangaw Range Burma
66 C5 Gangdisê Shan mt ra China
25 F7 Gangelt W Germany
18 H9 Ganges France
Ganges R see Ganga R
75 N8 Ganges, Mouths of the Bangladesh/India
27 F14 Gånghester Sweden
37 O7 Gangkofen W Germany
65 F4 Gangou China
75 N5 Gangtok India
65 A6 Ganguan China
65 A6 Ganguyi China
71 B3 Gani Indonesia
67 E3 Gan Jiang R China
Ganjig see Horqin Zuoyi Houqi
139 H5 Ganmam New S Wales
18 H6 Gannat France
145 E2 Gannet I New Zealand
101 L6 Gannett Idaho
101 Q6 Gannett Pk Wyoming
80 C5 Ganne Yehuda Israel
98 G5 Gannvalley S Dakota
80 C6 Gan Shelomo Israel
58 C3 Gansu prov China
Gantang see Taiping
143 A8 Gantheaume B W Australia
138 E6 Gantheaume, C S Australia
142 D4 Gantheaume Pt W Australia
69 J14 Gantung Indonesia
67 E4 Gan Xian China
80 B6 Gan Yavne Israel
87 D11 Ganyesa S Africa
65 D7 Ganyu China
65 D4 Ganzhao China
67 E4 Ganzhou China
33 Q6 Ganzlin E Germany
85 D5 Gao Mali
67 E2 Gao'an China
Gaobeidian see Xincheng
65 C5 Gaocheng China
67 F1 Gaochun China
Gaocun see Mayang
65 B5 Gaocun China
67 D5 Gaohe China
67 E1 Gaohebu China
65 A5 Gaojiabu China
65 A7 Gaoling China
67 B4 Gaolou Ling mt China
65 D6 Gaomi China
67 E4 Gaopi China
65 B7 Gaoping China
65 D6 Gaoqing China
67 C3 Gaosha China
65 B4 Gaoshan China
65 E3 Gaotaishan China
65 C6 Gaotang China
85 D6 Gaoua Upper Volta
85 B6 Gaoual Guinea
67 A2 Gao Xian China
65 C7 Gaoxianji China
58 G4 Gaoyang China
67 D5 Gaoyao China
65 C6 Gaoyi China
59 G5 Gaoyou China
59 G5 Gaoyou Hu L China
67 C6 Gaozhou China
19 Q15 Gap France
71 E3 Gapan Luzon Philippines
19 P18 Gapeau R France
66 C5 Gar China
86 A2 Garadag Somalia
43 C11 Garaet Ichkeul L Tunisia
139 J3 Garah New S Wales
47 H1 Gara Khitrino Bulgaria
14 C3 Gara, L Irish Rep
130 H10 Garanhuns Brazil
71 H9 Garantah Indonesia
130 F5 Garapuava Brazil
86 D4 Garba Cent Afr Republic
107 N5 Garber Oklahoma
100 B9 Garberville California
9 G3 Garboldisham England
130 E8 Garça Brazil
130 D4 Garças R Brazil
37 M7 Garching W Germany
106 E4 Garcia Colorado
16 D5 García de Sola, Embalse de res Spain
130 D7 Garcias Brazil
18 H8 Gard dep France
18 H9 Gard R France
41 N6 Garda, Lago di Italy
42 D3 Garda, Lago di Italy
19 O18 Gardanne France
98 J1 Gardar N Dakota
27 J15 Gårdby Sweden
33 O7 Gardelegen E Germany
99 U4 Garden Michigan
100 J6 Gardena Idaho
98 F1 Gardena N Dakota
111 K7 Garden City Alabama
107 K4 Garden City Kansas
110 B3 Garden City Missouri
112 F5 Garden City S Carolina
98 J5 Garden City S Dakota
108 F4 Garden City Texas
101 O8 Garden City Utah
109 H7 Gardendale Texas
102 G8 Garden Grove California
99 N9 Garden Grove Iowa
99 V4 Garden I Michigan
142 A3 Garden I W Australia
143 B9 Garden I W Australia
111 G12 Garden I Bay Louisiana
140 B1 Garden Point N Terr Aust
119 V9 Gardenton Manitoba
100 K5 Garden Valley Idaho
77 L3 Gardēz Afghanistan
95 S2 Gardiner Maine
101 P4 Gardiner Montana
106 F5 Gardiner New Mexico
120 J3 Gardiner Ontario
100 A6 Gardiner Oregon
118 L7 Gardiner Dam Sask
140 C5 Gardiner, Mt N Terr Aust
142 G4 Gardiner Ra Australia
95 P5 Gardiners I New York
140 B6 Gardiner's Range N Terr Aust
32 J4 Garding W Germany
106 E4 Gardner Colorado
113 F10 Gardner Florida
99 S8 Gardner Illinois
95 P4 Gardner Massachusetts
137 S2 Gardner I Phoenix Is Pacific Oc
146 E11 Gardner Inlet Antarctica
95 U2 Gardner L Maine
140 E6 Gardner, Mt N Terr Aust
102 E3 Gardnerville Nevada
31 K1 Gardno, Jezioro L Poland
86 A2 Gardo Somalia
27 G13 Gårdsjö Sweden
26 H6 Gardsjönas Sweden
27 J15 Gärdslösa Sweden
86 G4 Gardula Ethiopia
12 D1 Gare L Scotland
12 D1 Garelochhead Scotland
42 H3 Garešnica Yugoslavia
44 D3 Garessio Italy
85 F3 Garet el Djenoun mt Algeria
45 H3 Garfagnane R Italy
110 C5 Garfield Arkansas
112 E5 Garfield Georgia
107 L3 Garfield Kansas
101 N9 Garfield Utah
100 H2 Garfield Washington
101 N5 Garfield Mt Idaho/Montana
46 E7 Gargaliánoi Greece
16 D5 Gargáligas R Spain
42 G7 Gargano, M mt Italy
120 E5 Gargantua, C Ontario
26 N2 Gargia Norway
41 N6 Gargnano Italy
26 J6 Gargnäs Sweden
13 F6 Gargrave England
12 D1 Gargunnock Scotland
52 B6 Gargždai U.S.S.R.
74 H7 Garhakota India
55 D2 Gari U.S.S.R.
100 B4 Garibaldi Oregon
117 M11 Garibaldi Prov. Park Br Columbia
43 F7 Garigliano R Italy
70 G7 Garintjing Sulawesi
15 F3 Garioch Scotland
88 G2 Garissa Kenya
107 Q4 Garland Kansas
119 R7 Garland Manitoba
112 J3 Garland N Carolina
98 K9 Garland Nebraska
94 H5 Garland Pennsylvania
109 O9 Garland Texas
101 N8 Garland Utah
101 R5 Garland Wyoming
44 E1 Garlasco Italy
12 D4 Garlieston Scotland
18 E9 Garlin France
111 K10 Garlrand Alabama
32 M6 Garlstorf W Germany
57 F5 Garm U.S.S.R.
41 O3 Garmisch-Partenkirchen W Germany
77 H4 Garmsel reg Afghanistan
99 P7 Garnavillo Iowa
122 J2 Garneau, R Quebec
101 Q3 Garneill Montana
99 N6 Garner Iowa
112 J2 Garner N Carolina
118 E4 Garner Lake Prov. Park peak Alberta
101 M3 Garnet Montana
115 M4 Garnet Bay N W Terr
107 P3 Garnett Kansas
18 F9 Garonne R France
130 E11 Garopaba Brazil
74 F6 Garoth India
86 B4 Garoua Cameroon
86 B4 Garoua Doulai Cameroon
119 V3 Garraway Manitoba
32 H7 Garrel W Germany
98 K6 Garretson S Dakota
94 B5 Garrett Indiana
94 H7 Garrett Pennsylvania
101 U7 Garrett Wyoming
94 F5 Garrettsville Ohio
119 N5 Garrick Sask
99 O7 Garrison Iowa
94 D8 Garrison Kentucky
99 N3 Garrison Minnesota
101 N3 Garrison Montana
114 J8 Garrison N Dakota
95 O5 Garrison New York
109 N4 Garrison Texas
103 L3 Garrison Utah
98 E2 Garrison Dam N Dakota
16 C5 Garrovillas Spain
15 D4 Garry L Scotland
115 K4 Garry L N W Terr
101 S4 Garryowen Montana
88 H3 Garsen Kenya
28 D5 Gårslev Denmark
27 G16 Gärsnäs Sweden
118 G2 Garson L Alberta
32 M7 Garssen W Germany
38 F7 Garsstein mt Austria
13 F6 Garstang England
13 F6 Garston England
144 B6 Garston New Zealand
21 G9 Gartempe R France
8 C3 Garth Wales
8 C2 Garthmyl Wales
Gartok see Garyarsa
33 O6 Gartow W Germany
31 H2 Gartz E Germany
70 M9 Garut Java
13 F2 Garvald Scotland
15 D3 Garve Scotland
144 B6 Garvie Mts New Zealand
31 N4 Garwolin Poland
100 J2 Garwood Idaho
109 L6 Garwood Texas
98 C9 Gary Colorado
99 T8 Gary Indiana
98 K2 Gary Minnesota
98 K5 Gary S Dakota
109 N3 Gary Texas
94 F9 Gary W Virginia
66 C5 Garyarsa China
60 F11 Garyū zan mt Japan
33 Q6 Garz E Germany
109 L2 Garza Little Elm Res Texas
58 C5 Garzê China
128 C3 Garzón Colombia
50 E5 Gasan-Kuli U.S.S.R.
33 Q10 Gaschwitz E Germany
45 J4 Gasciana Terme Italy
94 B6 Gas City Indiana
18 E9 Gascogne prov France
Gascogne, Golfe de see Biscay, Bay of
110 E3 Gasconade R Missouri
122 H5 Gascons Quebec
98 C3 Gascoyne N Dakota
143 B7 Gascoyne Junction W Australia
143 B6 Gascoyne, Mt W Australia
143 A6 Gascoyne, R W Australia
86 G2 Gash R Ethiopia
85 G7 Gashaka Nigeria
74 G1 Gasherbrum mt Kashmir
85 G6 Gashua Nigeria
Gashuun Nuur L see Gaxu Nur
26 H4 Gaskacok mt Norway
20 J3 Gasny France
126 E4 Gaspar Cuba
127 J5 Gaspar Hernández Dominican Rep
113 E11 Gasparilla isld Florida
69 H14 Gaspar, Selat str Indonesia
115 N8 Gaspé Quebec
122 H5 Gaspé, B. de Quebec
122 H5 Gaspé, C Quebec
122 F5 Gaspé Pen Quebec
122 H9 Gaspereau L Nova Scotia
122 G7 Gaspereau Forks New Brunswick
122 F5 Gaspesie, Parc de la Quebec
100 B8 Gasquet California
61 O7 Gassan mt Japan
94 G8 Gassaway W Virginia
25 G3 Gasselte Netherlands
85 F2 Gassi, El Algeria
85 G7 Gassol Nigeria
103 J5 Gass Pk Nevada
28 E3 Gassum Denmark
38 H7 Gasteiner Tal Austria
100 B4 Gaston Oregon
112 F2 Gastonia N Carolina
94 J10 Gaston Res Virginia
133 D6 Gastre Argentina
17 F8 Gata, C.de Spain
117 K6 Gataga R Br Columbia
48 G5 Gataia Romania
16 C4 Gata, Sa. de mts Spain
52 D5 Gatchina U.S.S.R.
108 D7 Gate Oklahoma
94 E10 Gate City Virginia
12 D4 Gatehouse of Fleet Scotland
100 C5 Gates Oregon
13 G4 Gateshead England
101 O3 Gates of the Mts pass Montana
112 L1 Gatesville N Carolina
109 K4 Gatesville Texas
106 B3 Gateway Colorado
100 K1 Gateway Montana
100 D5 Gateway Oregon
21 F7 Gâtine reg France
121 P7 Gatineau Quebec
121 P5 Gatineau R Quebec
112 D2 Gatlinburg Tennessee
80 D1 Ga'ton Israel
89 F2 Gatooma Zimbabwe
33 S8 Gatow E Germany
61 N7 Gatsugi Japan
20 C2 Gatteville France
41 H6 Gattinara Italy
141 K8 Gatton Queensland
124 E9 Gatun Panama Canal Zone
9 F5 Gatwick Airport England
36 E4 Gau-Algesheim W Germany
16 D8 Gaucin Spain
16 D6 Gaudalmellato R Spain
77 H5 Gaud-I-Zirreh salt des Afghanistan
123 K3 Gaudreault, L Quebec
119 U1 Gauer L Manitoba
75 O5 Gauhati India
26 E9 Gauldalen R Norway
94 F8 Gauley Bridge W Virginia
20 G5 Gault, le France
123 R6 Gaultois Nfld
20 H5 Gault-St. Denis, le France
36 E4 Gau-Odernheim W Germany
66 D6 Gauri Sankar mt Nepal/China
27 D10 Gausdal, Ö Norway
27 D10 Gausdal, V Norway
27 C12 Gausta mt Norway
17 J3 Gavarras mt Spain
77 G7 Gavāter Iran
77 C6 Gāvbandī Iran
77 C6 Gavbus Kūh-e mt Iran
47 F10 Gavdhopoúla isld Crete Greece
47 G10 Gávdhos isld Crete Greece
18 E9 Gave de Pau R France
130 H4 Gavião, R Brazil
106 C5 Gavilan New Mexico
43 B9 Gavino Monreale, S Sardinia
102 D7 Gaviota California
77 E5 Gāv Koshī Iran
27 J11 Gävle Sweden
27 J11 Gävlebukten B Sweden
20 C4 Gavray France
52 E6 Gavrilov Yam U.S.S.R.
52 F5 Gavrino U.S.S.R.
47 G7 Gávrion Greece
78 F3 Gavur Dağları mts Turkey
74 G8 Gawilgarh India
138 E5 Gawler S Australia
138 D4 Gawler Ranges S Australia
26 H8 Gåxsjö Sweden
58 D3 Gaxun Nur L China
99 S2 Gay Michigan
75 L6 Gaya India
85 E6 Gaya Niger
85 F6 Gaya Nigeria
17 H3 Gaya R Spain
65 H3 Gaya He R China
9 E3 Gaydon England
107 M2 Gaylord Kansas
94 C1 Gaylord Michigan
99 M5 Gaylord Minnesota
100 A7 Gaylord Oregon
139 K2 Gayndah Queensland
141 K7 Gayndah Queensland
52 H4 Gayny U.S.S.R.
48 M2 Gaysin U.S.S.R.
99 Q6 Gays Mills Wisconsin
52 E5 Gayutino U.S.S.R.
98 J7 Gayville S Dakota
48 M2 Gayvoron U.S.S.R.
79 E7 Gaza Egypt
85 F6 Gazaoua Niger
80 A7 Gaza Strip Israel
100 C8 Gazelle California
20 J4 Gazeran France
57 D4 Gazgan U.S.S.R.
78 F3 Gaziantep Turkey
78 D3 Gazipaşa Turkey
57 C4 Gazli U.S.S.R.
45 J1 Gazoldo degli Ippoliti Italy
45 K1 Gazzo Veronese Italy
45 J1 Gazzuolo Italy
85 C7 Gbanga Liberia
85 F7 Gboko Nigeria
31 L1 Gdańsk Poland
27 K17 Gdańska, Zatoka Poland
52 C5 Gdov U.S.S.R.
31 L1 Gdynia Poland
80 B7 Ge'a Israel
100 B3 Gearhart Oregon
100 E7 Gearhart Mt Oregon
107 M6 Geary Oklahoma
71 B3 Gebe isld Indonesia
37 K1 Gebesee E Germany
47 K4 Gebze Turkey
86 G3 Gedaref Sudan
98 H6 Geddes S Dakota
141 F3 Geddes R Queensland
9 F3 Geddington England
36 G3 Gedern W Germany
28 H7 Gedesby Denmark
70 L9 Gede, Tg C Java
28 C4 Gedhus Denmark
22 H4 Gedinne Belgium
47 K5 Gediz Turkey
47 J6 Gediz R Turkey
Gedong see Fangshan
70 B4 Gedong Sarawak
28 H7 Gedser Denmark
28 C3 Gedsted Denmark
22 H1 Geel Belgium
139 G7 Geelong Victoria
143 A8 Geelvink Chan W Australia
89 A7 Geel Vloer S Africa
110 D6 Geers Ferry Res Arkansas
25 C5 Geertruidenberg Netherlands
32 J5 Geestekanal W Germany
32 J5 Geestenseth W Germany
33 M6 Geesthacht W Germany
22 J2 Geetbets Belgium
139 H9 Geeveston Tasmania
37 M3 Gefell E Germany
80 C7 Gefen Israel
37 M3 Gefrees W Germany
65 E2 Gegenmiao China
65 D5 Gegu China
65 G7 Gehaku lt ho S Korea
36 G2 Gehau W Germany
32 L8 Gehrden W Germany
67 F1 Ge Hu L China
85 G6 Geidam Nigeria
41 P3 Geierspitze mt Austria
120 B2 Geikie I Ontario
141 G2 Geikie Ra Queensland
25 F7 Geilenkirchen W Germany
27 C11 Geilo Norway
33 R5 Geilow E Germany
36 E5 Geinsheim W Germany
26 B9 Geiranger Norway
37 N6 Geiselhöring W Germany
37 J4 Geiselwind W Germany
37 M6 Geisenfeld W Germany
37 N7 Geisenhausen W Germany
36 D3 Geisenheim W Germany
41 J2 Geisingen W Germany
36 F7 Geislingen W Germany
36 H6 Geislingen an der Steige W Germany
37 J1 Geismar E Germany
36 D6 Geispolsheim France
88 D3 Geita Tanzania
37 O1 Geithain E Germany
27 D12 Geithus Norway
67 A5 Gejiu China
43 F11 Gela Sicily
43 F11 Gela R Sicily
88 F3 Gelai mt Tanzania
33 Q4 Gelbensande E Germany
37 J4 Gelchsheim W Germany
25 F3 Gelderingen Netherlands
25 F4 Gelderland Netherlands
25 D5 Geldermalsen Netherlands
25 F5 Geldern W Germany
25 E6 Geldrop Netherlands
37 O2 Gelenau E Germany
47 J5 Gelenbe Turkey
121 M8 Gelert Ontario
47 H4 Gelibolu Turkey
47 L8 Gelidonya Burun C Turkey
22 J2 Gelinden Belgium
67 F4 Geling China
71 L9 Geliting Indonesia
36 G3 Gelnhausen W Germany
28 C6 Gelså R Denmark
Gelsdorf see Grafschaft
32 F9 Gelsenkirchen W Germany
28 D6 Gelsted Denmark
28 D7 Gelting W Germany
118 E8 Gem Alberta
107 K2 Gem Kansas
69 F11 Gemas Malaysia
22 H2 Gembloux Belgium
32 E9 Gemen W Germany
86 C5 Gemena Zaïre
19 P18 Gémenos France
78 F2 Gemerek Turkey
25 E5 Gemert Netherlands
142 F3 Gemini Hills W Australia
47 K4 Gemlik Körfezi B Turkey
22 K2 Gemmenich Belgium
36 F5 Gemmingen W Germany
42 E2 Gemona Italy
18 E7 Gémozac France
84 J4 Gemsa Egypt
89 B5 Gemsbok Nat. Park Botswana
36 B2 Gemünd W Germany
36 H3 Gemünden Bayern W Germany
36 F2 Gemünden Hessen W Germany
36 D4 Gemünden Rheinland-Pfalz W Germany
70 E7 Gemuru Kalimantan
22 G2 Genappe Belgium
27 F16 Genarp Sweden
45 N6 Genazzano Italy
78 H2 Genç Turkey
18 F6 Gençay France
25 F5 Gendringen Netherlands
107 N7 Gene Autry Oklahoma
86 D3 Geneina Sudan
25 F3 Genemuiden Netherlands
133 E5 General Acha Argentina
133 E5 General Alvear Argentina
131 C5 General Alvear Mendoza Argentina
130 C9 General Aquvino Paraguay
133 E4 General Arenales Argentina
130 C10 General Artigas Paraguay
130 D4 General Caneiro Brazil
133 E3 General Capdevila Argentina
102 F5 General Grant Grove Sctn California
133 F5 General Guido Argentina
17 G5 Generalísimo, Emb. de Spain
48 L5 Generalisinnul Suverov Romania
133 F3 General José de San Martín Argentina
133 E5 General La Madrid Argentina
133 F5 General Lavalle Argentina
71 G6 General Luna Philippines
71 G5 General MacArthur Philippines
133 F5 General Madariaga Argentina
128 E8 General Martin M. de Güemes Argentina
130 B10 General Paz Argentina
133 C6 General Paz, L Argentina
71 G7 General Santos Philippines
47 J1 General Toshevo Bulgaria
109 H9 General Treviño Mexico
133 E5 General Viamonte Argentina
100 J3 Genesee Idaho
94 D3 Genesee Michigan
94 K4 Genesee R New York
99 Q8 Geneseo Illinois
107 M3 Geneseo Kansas
94 K4 Geneseo New York
20 C4 Genéts France
Geneva see Genève
111 L10 Geneva Alabama
111 M9 Geneva Georgia
99 S8 Geneva Illinois
94 C6 Geneva Indiana
98 J9 Geneva Nebraska
94 G5 Geneva Ohio
109 O4 Geneva Texas
Geneva, L see Léman, Lac
99 S7 Geneva, L Wisconsin
120 J6 Geneva Lake Mine Ontario
40 D5 Genève Switzerland
36 E7 Gengenbach W Germany
68 D1 Gengma China
Genhe see Ergun Zuoqi
59 H1 Gen He R China
120 J3 Genier Ontario
16 E7 Genil R Spain
21 H7 Génillé France
22 K2 Genk Belgium
60 D12 Genkai-nada sea Japan
40 B3 Genlis France
25 E5 Gennep Netherlands
28 C6 Genner Denmark
21 E7 Gennes France
21 C6 Gennes-sur-Seiche France
21 F6 Genneteil France
Genoa see Genova
106 G2 Genoa Colorado
113 E7 Genoa Florida
99 S7 Genoa Illinois
98 J8 Genoa Nebraska
102 E2 Genoa Nevada
94 D5 Genoa Ohio
139 J6 Genoa Victoria
99 P6 Genoa Wisconsin
99 S7 Genoa City Wisconsin
101 O1 Genou Montana
21 J9 Genouillac France
21 I7 Genouilly France
44 E3 Genova Italy
128 B7 Genovesa isld Galapagos Is
51 P1 Genriyetty, Ostrov isld U.S.S.R.
22 F1 Gent Belgium
70 P9 Genteng Indonesia
70 L9 Genteng Java
33 Q8 Genthin E Germany
111 K12 Gentilly New Orleans
69 H11 Genting isld Indonesia
21 J10 Gentioux France
118 B1 Gent Lon Manitoba
28 K5 Gentofte Denmark
110 B5 Gentry Arkansas
99 M9 Gentry Missouri
45 N6 Genzano di Roma Italy
48 H5 Geoagiu Romania
143 B10 Geographe B W Australia
143 A6 Geographe Chan W Australia
107 M2 Geographic Center of US Kansas
22 H3 Geopinnes Belgium
99 L6 George Iowa
89 C9 George S Africa
83 M14 George C Kerguelen Indian Oc
116 J5 George R Alaska
115 N6 George R Quebec
138 D3 George R S Australia
123 L8 George B Nova Scotia
123 K8 George, C Nova Scotia
140 B6 George Gills Ra N Terr Aust
116 N6 George, L Alaska
113 F8 George, L Florida
139 J6 George, L New S Wales
99 W3 George, L Ontario
138 F6 George, L S Australia
88 C1 George, L Uganda
142 E5 George, L W Australia
37 L5 Georgensgmünd W Germany
37 K2 Georgenthal E Germany
90 C4 Georges Bank Atlantic Oc
144 A6 George Sd New Zealand
110 E6 Georgetown Arkansas
90 A11 Georgetown Ascension I
102 D3 Georgetown California
95 M8 Georgetown Delaware
113 F8 Georgetown Florida

111 L10 Georgetown Georgia
129 G2 Georgetown Guyana
101 O7 Georgetown Idaho
99 T10 Georgetown Illinois
94 C8 Georgetown Kentucky
69 E10 Georgetown Malaysia
111 F10 Georgetown Mississippi
144 C6 Georgetown New Zealand
94 D8 Georgetown Ohio
122 K7 Georgetown Pr Edward I
141 G4 Georgetown Queensland
127 O8 Georgetown St Vincent
138 E5 Georgetown S Australia
112 H4 Georgetown S Carolina
139 H8 George Town Tasmania
109 K5 Georgetown Texas
85 B6 Georgetown The Gambia
121 S7 Georgeville Quebec
146 F12 George VI Snd Antarctica
146 J4 George V Land Antarctica
109 J7 George West Texas
Georgia S.S.R. U.S.S.R. see Gruziya
112 C5 Georgia state U.S.A.
111 K10 Georgiana Alabama
115 L8 Georgian B Ontario
114 G8 Georgia, St. of Br Columbia
140 E5 Georgina R N Terr/Queensland
136 H6 Georgina R Queensland
140 E4 Georgina Cr N Terr Aust
54 L6 Georgiu-Dezh U.S.S.R.
53 F11 Georgiyevsk U.S.S.R.
32 F7 Georgsdorf W Germany
32 F6 Georgsheil W Germany
32 H8 Georgsmarienhütte W Germany
41 N4 Gepatschhaus Austria
20 D4 Ger France
37 N2 Gera E Germany
28 E2 Gerå R Denmark
37 K2 Gera R E Germany
22 F2 Geraardsbergen Belgium
36 H5 Gerabronn W Germany
110 E3 Gerald Missouri
119 Q8 Gerald Sask
101 P2 Geraldine Montana
144 C6 Geraldine New Zealand
143 A8 Geraldine W Australia
51 S2 Gerald, Ostrov islds U.S.S.R.
115 L8 Geraldton Ontario
120 D3 Geraldton Ontario
143 A8 Geraldton W Australia
130 E10 Geral, Serra mts Brazil
80 B8 Gerar R Israel
19 K4 Gérardmer France
143 E7 Gerard, Mt W Australia
80 G4 Gerasa Jordan
55 F2 Gerasimovka U.S.S.R.
100 C9 Gerber California
100 D7 Gerber Res Oregon
33 P9 Gerbstedt E Germany
36 H4 Gerchsheim W Germany
78 H3 Gercuş Turkey
116 L6 Gerdine, Mt Alaska
21 D9 Gère R France
78 D1 Gerede Turkey
17 F7 Gérgal Spain
40 A4 Gergy France
37 K3 Gerhardtsgereuth E Germany
69 E10 Gerik Malaysia
98 C8 Gering Nebraska
37 O1 Geringswalde E Germany
100 F9 Gerlach Nevada
48 F1 Gerlachovsky mt Czechoslovakia
36 H4 Gerlachsheim W Germany
28 G6 Gerlev Denmark
36 G6 Gerlingen W Germany
86 H4 Gerlogubi Ethiopia
38 E7 Gerlostal R Austria
133 E4 Germania Argentina
117 L8 Germansen Landing Br Columbia
110 G3 Germantown Illinois
95 K7 Germantown Maryland
95 O4 Germantown New York
94 C7 Germantown Ohio
110 G6 Germantown Tennessee
47 J7 Germencik Turkey
37 L7 Germering W Germany
36 E5 Germersheim W Germany
89 F6 Germiston S Africa
28 C5 Gerndrup Denmark
36 E6 Gernsbach W Germany
36 F4 Gernsheim W Germany
61 L10 Gero Japan
36 B3 Gerolstein W Germany
37 J4 Gerolzhofen W Germany
100 G1 Gerome Washington
17 J3 Gerona Spain
17 J2 Gerona prov Spain
103 O8 Geronimo Arizona
107 M7 Geronimo Oklahoma
139 K5 Gerringong New S Wales
18 F9 Gers R France
36 H3 Gersfeld W Germany
36 F4 Gersprenz R W Germany
37 J6 Gerstetten Herbrechtingen W Germany
37 K7 Gersthofen W Germany
37 J2 Gerstingen E Germany
116 P5 Gerstle R Alaska
33 T6 Gerswalde E Germany
140 B3 Gertrude, Mt N Terr Aust
48 K2 Gertsa U.S.S.R.
80 C4 Gerulim Israel
19 O15 Gervanne R France
66 C5 Gêrzê China
78 E1 Gerze Turkey
37 N7 Gerzen W Germany
32 E9 Gescher W Germany
32 J9 Geseke W Germany
80 D1 Gesher HaZiv Israel
22 H4 Gespunsart France
37 K7 Gessertshausen W Germany
44 B3 Gesso R Italy
21 C7 Gesté France
28 C5 Gesten Denmark
86 H4 Gestro R Ethiopia
26 H8 Gesunden L Sweden
29 H11 Geta Finland
16 E4 Getafe Spain
100 H8 Getchell Mine Nevada
22 J2 Gete R Belgium
123 M3 Gethsémani Quebec
28 A3 Gettrup Denmark
95 K7 Gettysburg Pennsylvania
98 G5 Gettysburg S Dakota
67 B4 Getu He R China
130 D10 Getúlio Vargas Brazil
146 J10 Getz Ice Shelf Antarctica
107 N4 Geuda Springs Kansas
69 C10 Geumpang Sumatra
69 C10 Geureudong, Gunung mt Sumatra
139 J4 Geurie New S Wales
80 C3 Geva' Karmel Israel
32 F10 Gevelsberg W Germany
80 B7 Gever'am Israel
20 B5 Geveze France
33 S5 Gevezin E Germany
46 E3 Gevgelija Yugoslavia
19 K6 Gex France
Gexianzhuang see Qinghe
37 O2 Geyer E Germany
36 G4 Geyersberg mt W Germany
47 H5 Geyikli Turkey
101 P2 Geyser Montana
81 B7 Geyser, Banc du Madagascar
47 L4 Geyve Turkey
Ghadames see Ghudamis
80 G2 Ghadir al Bustan Syria
77 C1 Ghaem Shahr Iran
73 N3 Ghaghara R India
85 D7 Ghana rep W Africa
74 D7 Ghandi Dham India
89 B3 Ghanzi Botswana
89 C4 Ghanzi dist Botswana
43 C11 Ghar Tunisia
80 E7 Ghar R Jordan
78 K6 Gharab Iraq
85 E2 Ghardaia Algeria
43 B12 Ghardimaou Tunisia
84 J4 Gharib, Gebel Egypt
84 E3 Gharyan Libya
85 G4 Ghat Libya
75 M7 Ghatsila India
17 F9 Ghazaouet Algeria
74 G4 Ghaziabad India
77 L3 Ghaznī Afghanistan
77 K3 Ghazoor Afghanistan
99 O2 Gheen Minnesota
86 J4 Ghelinsor Somalia
Ghent see Gent
94 B8 Ghent Kentucky
99 L5 Ghent Minnesota
48 K4 Gheorgheni Romania
48 K4 Gherghiului Muntii mt Romania
48 H3 Gherla Romania
43 B8 Ghilarza Sardinia
48 H3 Ghilvaci Romania
48 K4 Ghimeş Făget Romania
133 C7 Ghio, L Argentina
22 F2 Ghislenghien Belgium
77 J3 Ghizao Afghanistan
77 J2 Ghor Afghanistan
118 L1 Ghost R Ontario
117 Q4 Ghost L N W Terr
117 P9 Ghost Mt Br Columbia
86 E3 Ghubaysh Sudan
85 G2 Ghudamis Libya
77 G2 Ghurian Afghanistan
22 D1 Ghyvelde France
68 H7 Gia Dinh Vietnam
84 G4 Gialo Libya
86 H5 Giamame Somalia
42 D6 Giannutri isld Italy
89 F7 Giants Castle mt S Africa
14 E1 Giant's Causeway N Ireland
83 K9 Giants Tank L Sri Lanka
69 G8 Gia Rai Vietnam
43 G11 Giarre Sicily
18 G7 Giat France
44 B1 Giaveno Italy
126 F4 Gibara Cuba
98 H9 Gibbon Nebraska
100 G4 Gibbon Oregon
101 M4 Gibbons Pass Montana
101 M4 Gibbonsville Idaho
142 F3 Gibb River W Australia
99 S3 Gibbs City Michigan
146 D15 Gibbs I S Shetland Is
143 C10 Gibbs, Mt W Australia
87 C11 Gibeon Namibia
26 K2 Gibostad Norway
16 C7 Gibraleón Spain
16 D8 Gibraltar S W Europe
127 J10 Gibraltar Venezuela
16 D9 Gibraltar, Str of Spain/Africa
111 C9 Gibsland Louisiana
100 C8 Gibson California
112 E4 Gibson Georgia
101 Q3 Gibson Montana
94 D5 Gibsonburg Ohio
99 S9 Gibson City Illinois
143 D6 Gibson Des W Australia
117 M11 Gibsons Br Columbia
143 D10 Gibson Soak W Australia
113 E10 Gibsonton Florida
112 H1 Gibsonville N Carolina
58 B2 Gichgeniyn Nuruu mt Mongolia
52 H5 Gidayevo U.S.S.R.
76 D3 Giddalur India
79 D8 Giddi, G el Egypt
109 L5 Giddings Texas
26 K8 Gideå Sweden
26 K8 Gideå R Sweden
110 G5 Gideon Missouri
141 F6 Gideon, Mt Queensland
138 F3 Gidgelpa S Australia
143 F8 Gidgi, L W Australia
31 L5 Gidle Poland
Gidole see Gardula
36 H4 Giebelstadt W Germany
32 M9 Gieboldehausen W Germany
18 G5 Gien France
37 J6 Giengen W Germany
19 Q18 Giens France
19 N13 Gier R France
33 P7 Giesenslage E Germany
36 F2 Giessen W Germany
25 G2 Gieten Netherlands
25 F3 Giethoorn Netherlands
84 J4 Gifatin I Egypt
113 G10 Gifford Florida
99 N7 Gifford Iowa
13 F2 Gifford Scotland
100 G1 Gifford Washington
33 N8 Gifhorn W Germany
61 K10 Gifu Japan
124 D5 Giganta, Sa de la Mexico
124 E9 Gigante Panama Canal Zone
124 G3 Gigantes, Llanos de los Mexico
15 C5 Gigha isld Scotland
42 D6 Giglio isld Italy
18 H9 Gignac France
19 P17 Gignac France
40 F6 Gignod Italy
17 F5 Giguela R Spain
16 D1 Gijón Spain
106 B9 Gila New Mexico
103 P9 Gila R Arizona
103 M9 Gila Bend Arizona
103 L8 Gila Bend Mts Arizona
106 B8 Gila Cliff Dwellings Nat.Mon New Mexico
103 K9 Gila Mts Arizona
77 A1 Gilān Iran
78 K4 Gilan Garb Iran
121 R5 Gilardo Dam Quebec
48 H4 Gilău Romania
103 N8 Gilbert Arizona
99 O2 Gilbert Minnesota
102 G3 Gilbert Nevada
94 F9 Gilbert W Virginia
141 F3 Gilbert R Queensland
137 P1 Gilbert Is Pacific Oc
116 O6 Gilbert, Mt Alaska
117 L10 Gilbert, Mt Br Columbia
141 G4 Gilberton Queensland
111 H10 Gilbertown Alabama
101 P9 Gilbert Pk Utah
119 R7 Gilbert Plains Manitoba
141 G4 Gilbert River Queensland
28 J4 Gilbjerghoved C Denmark
129 J5 Gilbués Brazil
98 J1 Gilby N Dakota
98 B9 Gilcrest Colorado
13 G6 Gildersome England
26 G4 Gildeskal Norway
101 P1 Gildford Montana
88 G10 Gilé Mozambique
95 R2 Gilead Maine
98 J9 Gilead Nebraska
108 G1 Giles Texas
136 F7 Giles W Australia
143 G7 Giles W Australia
143 C8 Giles, L W Australia
140 B5 Giles Ra N Terr Aust
84 H5 Gilf Kebir Plateau Egypt
139 K3 Gilgai New S Wales
139 J4 Gilgandra New S Wales
80 E6 Gilgat Jordan
88 F2 Gilgil Kenya
139 J3 Gil Gil R New S Wales
74 F1 Gilgit Kashmir
139 H4 Gilgunnia New S Wales
117 J9 Gil I Br Columbia
70 P10 Gilimanuk Bali Indonesia
46 D1 Giljeva Planina mt Yugoslavia
98 B9 Gill Colorado
115 K6 Gillam Manitoba
28 J4 Gilleleje Denmark
143 E7 Gillen, L W Australia
140 C6 Gillen, Mt N Terr Aust
138 D4 Gilles, L S Australia
103 M8 Gillespie Arizona
110 G2 Gillespie Illinois
144 B5 Gillespie Pt New Zealand
111 E7 Gillett Arkansas
95 L5 Gillett Pennsylvania
109 K6 Gillett Texas
99 S5 Gillett Wisconsin
98 A5 Gillette Wyoming
109 N1 Gillham Arkansas
26 G9 Gillhov Sweden
110 C2 Gilliam Missouri
141 F5 Gilliat Queensland
141 F5 Gilliat R Queensland
13 G5 Gilling England
8 D5 Gillingham Dorset England
9 G5 Gillingham Kent England
109 O5 Gillis Louisiana
14 C2 Gill, L Irish Rep
99 T4 Gills Rock Wisconsin
22 G3 Gilly Belgium
99 S9 Gilman Illinois
99 O8 Gilman Iowa
101 N2 Gilman Montana
99 Q4 Gilman Wisconsin
110 C1 Gilman City Missouri
109 N3 Gilmer Texas
101 M5 Gilmore Idaho
141 G7 Gilmore Queensland
99 M7 Gilmore City Iowa
121 N8 Gilmour Ontario
86 F4 Gilo R Ethiopia
48 H6 Gilortul R Romania
141 F7 Gilpeppee Queensland
117 N9 Gilpin Br Columbia
102 C4 Gilroy California
118 L8 Gilroy Sask
13 F3 Gilsland England
98 H9 Giltner Nebraska
8 C4 Gilwern Wales
51 M3 Gilyuy R U.S.S.R.
86 D3 Gimbala mt Sudan
127 O8 Gimie mt St Lucia
101 L6 Gimlet Idaho
115 K7 Gimli Manitoba
27 K11 Gimo Sweden
52 D3 Gimoly U.S.S.R.
18 F9 Gimone R France
18 F9 Gimont France
26 G3 Gimsöy Norway
80 C6 Gimzo Israel
19 P17 Ginasservis France
141 J6 Gindie Queensland
76 D4 Gingee India
36 H6 Gingen W Germany
127 J2 Ginger Hill Jamaica
141 K6 Gin Gin Queensland
143 B9 Gingin W Australia
71 G6 Gingoog B Philippines
86 H4 Ginir Ethiopia
80 E3 Ginnegar Israel
28 F4 Ginnerup Denmark
80 F2 Ginnosar Israel
43 H8 Ginosa Italy
61 P13 Ginowan Okinawa
16 B2 Ginzo de Limia Spain
45 K3 Giogo di Casaglia Italy
45 K3 Giogo di Scarperia Italy
86 J5 Gioher Somalia
45 P6 Gioia dei Marsi Italy
43 G10 Gioia,G.di Italy
45 Q7 Gioia Sannitica Italy
46 E6 Gióna mt Greece
41 J5 Giornico Switzerland
43 H9 Giovanni in Fiore, S Italy
45 K4 Giovi mt Italy
139 H7 Gippsland Victoria
142 A6 Giralia W Australia
31 N6 Giraltovce Czechoslovakia
40 D1 Girancourt France
77 F5 Giran Rig mt Iran
99 R10 Girard Illinois
107 Q4 Girard Kansas
94 G5 Girard Ohio
94 G4 Girard Pennsylvania
108 G2 Girard Texas
128 D3 Girardot Colombia
15 F3 Girdle Ness Scotland
78 G1 Giresun Turkey
84 J4 Girga Egypt
74 D8 Gir Hills India
86 C5 Giri R Zaïre
75 M6 Giridih India
139 H4 Girilambone New S Wales
77 J4 Girishk Afghanistan
83 K10 Giriulla Sri Lanka
19 K5 Giromagny France
18 E8 Gironde dep France
18 E7 Gironde R France
17 J2 Gironella Spain
18 G9 Girou R France
119 V9 Giroux Manitoba
141 H4 Giru Queensland
130 C11 Giruá Brazil
15 D5 Girvan Scotland
15 D5 Girvan R Scotland
119 M7 Girvin Sask
108 E4 Girvin Texas
116 H4 Gisasa R Alaska
145 G3 Gisborne New Zealand
13 F6 Gisburn England
123 S6 Gisburn L Nfld
117 M8 Giscome Br Columbia
103 N7 Gisela Arizona
88 B2 Gisenye Rwanda
26 A9 Giske isld Norway
28 F6 Gislev Denmark
28 H5 Gislinge Denmark
20 J3 Gisors France
37 K1 Gispersleben E Germany
57 E5 Gissar U.S.S.R.
57 E5 Gissarskiy Khr mts U.S.S.R.
22 D1 Gistel Belgium
88 B3 Gitega Burundi
32 M9 Gittelde W Germany
Giuba R see Juba R
41 N6 Giudicarie Val Italy
45 Q8 Giugliano in Campo Italy
45 O6 Giuliano di Roma Italy
42 F6 Giulianova Italy
48 J3 Giumalău mt Romania
86 H6 Giumbo Somalia
48 L6 Giurgeni Romania
47 H1 Giurgiu Romania
80 C3 Giv'at 'Ada Israel
80 C5 Giv'atayim Israel
22 D3 Givenchy-en-Gohelle France
22 H3 Givet Belgium
22 G3 Givry Belgium
19 J6 Givry France
40 A4 Givry France
28 C5 Givskud Denmark
79 B8 Gîza, El Egypt
21 F7 Gizeux France
57 C5 Gizhduvan U.S.S.R.
51 Q2 Gizhiga U.S.S.R.
22 F4 Gizy France
31 N1 Gizycko Poland
27 C10 Gjende L Norway
27 C10 Gjendesheim Norway
28 E3 Gjerlev Denmark
28 D4 Gjern Denmark
28 F3 Gjerrild Denmark
27 C13 Gjerstad Norway
26 F7 Gjersvik Norway
26 D9 Gjevil-vatn L Norway
46 D4 Gjirokastër Albania
115 K4 Gjoa Haven N W Terr
28 N1 Gjógv Faeroes
28 D2 Gjøl Denmark
28 C3 Gjørup Denmark
27 C13 Gjovdal Norway
27 E11 Gjövik Norway
46 C4 Gjuhëzës, Kep I C Albania
22 H2 Glabbeek Zuurbemde Belgium
115 O8 Glace B Nova Scotia
20 B2 Glacerie, la France
117 P10 Glacier Br Columbia
117 E6 Glacier B Alaska
117 E6 Glacier Bay Nat. Park Alaska
116 O6 Glacier I Alaska
116 Q4 Glacier Mt Alaska
117 O10 Glacier Nat. Park Br Columbia
101 M1 Glacier Nat. Park Montana
100 D1 Glacier Peak Washington
115 M2 Glacier Str N W Terr
36 B2 Gladbach W Germany
99 O7 Gladbrook Iowa
107 L2 Glade Kansas
36 F2 Gladenbach W Germany
106 B3 Glade Park Colorado
94 F10 Glade Spring Virginia
109 N3 Gladewater Texas
119 N9 Gladmar Sask
26 E6 Gladstad Norway
119 T8 Gladstone Manitoba
99 T4 Gladstone Michigan
98 D3 Gladstone N Dakota
145 E4 Gladstone New Zealand
141 K6 Gladstone Queensland
138 E5 Gladstone S Australia
139 J8 Gladstone Tasmania
94 C3 Gladwin Michigan
94 H8 Glady W Virginia
94 H9 Gladys Virginia
117 G6 Gladys L Br Columbia
28 G6 Glænø isld Denmark
27 F12 Glafsfj L Sweden
103 J8 Glamis California
118 K7 Glamis Sask
15 F4 Glamis Scotland
42 H4 Glamoe Yugoslavia
Glamorgan co see W., Mid & S.Glam. counties
28 E6 Glamsbjerg Denmark
71 G8 Glan Mindanao Philippines
27 H13 Glan L Sweden
38 K8 Glan R Austria
36 D4 Glan R W Germany
14 B4 Glanaruddery Mts Irish Rep
19 P15 Glandage France
19 Q14 Glandon, Col du pass France
32 G8 Glandorf W Germany
32 G8 Glane R W Germany
38 K8 Glanegg Austria
41 J4 Glärnisch mt Switzerland
41 K3 Glarus Switzerland
107 N2 Glasco Kansas
95 O4 Glasco New York
99 R9 Glasford Illinois
127 H1 Glasgow Jamaica
94 B10 Glasgow Kentucky
110 D2 Glasgow Missouri
114 J8 Glasgow Montana
12 D2 Glasgow Scotland
94 H9 Glasgow Virginia
38 M8 Glashutten Austria
133 D6 Glasier Argentina
118 J5 Glaslyn Sask
15 E4 Glas Maol mt Scotland
119 M9 Glasnevin Sask
95 M7 Glassboro New Jersey
108 D5 Glass Mts Texas
8 D5 Glastonbury England
41 J3 Glatt R Switzerland
Glatz see Kłodzko
37 N2 Glauchau E Germany
47 H1 Glavinitsa Bulgaria
108 D7 Glazier Texas
52 H5 Glazov U.S.S.R.
31 K2 Gła R Poland
110 H5 Gleason Tennessee
99 R4 Gleason Wisconsin
94 K5 Gleasonton Pennsylvania
103 P10 Gleeson Arizona
37 K3 Gleichberg mt E Germany
118 D8 Gleichen Alberta
33 P10 Gleina E Germany
38 L7 Glein Alpe mts Austria
38 N7 Gleisdorf Austria
Gleiwitz see Gliwice
28 B5 Glejbjerg Denmark
98 C7 Glen Nebraska
95 Q2 Glen New Hampshire
100 A6 Glenada Oregon
15 D3 Glen Affric Scotland
145 E2 Glen Afton New Zealand
121 P7 Glen Almond Quebec
112 F2 Glen Alpine N Carolina
18 C5 Glénans, Iles France
15 D5 Glen App Scotland
144 B6 Glenaray New Zealand
14 F2 Glenarm N Ireland
12 D1 Glen Artney Scotland
119 O8 Glenavon Sask
144 C6 Glenavy New Zealand
118 K9 Glenbain Sask
12 C2 Glenbarr Scotland
139 K4 Glenbawn Reservoir New S Wales
119 S9 Glenboro Manitoba
98 E1 Glenburn N Dakota
95 L7 Glen Burnie Maryland
123 P4 Glenburnie Nfld
138 F6 Glenburnie S Australia
118 K5 Glenbush Sask
15 D3 Glen Cannich Scotland
103 N5 Glen Canyon Arizona
15 C3 Glen Carron R Scotland
13 E1 Glencarse Scotland
15 E4 Glen Clova Scotland
111 L8 Glencoe Alabama
99 M5 Glencoe Minnesota
106 E8 Glencoe New Mexico
120 J10 Glencoe Ontario
89 G7 Glencoe S Africa
138 F6 Glencoe S Australia
98 F4 Glencross S Dakota
103 M8 Glendale Arizona
102 F7 Glendale California
111 K11 Glendale Florida
107 N3 Glendale Kansas
103 K5 Glendale Nevada
94 C7 Glendale Ohio
100 B7 Glendale Oregon
94 G7 Glendale W Virginia
117 L10 Glendale Cove Br Columbia
12 C1 Glendaruel Scotland
139 K5 Glen Davis New S Wales
106 E1 Glendevey Colorado
12 E1 Glendevon Scotland
114 J8 Glendive Montana
98 A7 Glendo Wyoming
118 F4 Glendon Alberta
111 F8 Glendora Mississippi
14 C2 Glendowan Mts Irish Rep
141 H4 Gleneagle Queensland
15 E4 Gleneagles Scotland
107 M2 Glen Elder Kansas
138 E5 Glenelg S Australia
15 C3 Glenelg Scotland
138 F6 Glenelg R Victoria
119 S8 Glenella Manitoba
119 P9 Glen Ewen Sask
12 D1 Glen Falloch Scotland
13 E1 Glenfarg Scotland
98 H2 Glenfield N Dakota
95 M3 Glenfield New York
15 C4 Glenfinnan Scotland
109 L6 Glen Flora Texas
142 B6 Glen Florrie W Australia
14 D1 Glengad Hd Irish Rep
14 B5 Glengariff Irish Rep
15 D4 Glen Garry Scotland
15 C3 Glen Garry R Scotland
143 C7 Glengarry Ra W Australia
127 L2 Glengoffe Jamaica
140 E6 Glengyle Queensland
144 B7 Glenham New Zealand
98 F4 Glenham S Dakota
140 C6 Glen Helen N Terr Aust
140 C6 Glen Helen Gorge N Terr Aust
145 D4 Glenhope New Zealand
139 K3 Glen Innes New S Wales
118 K8 Glen Kerr Sask
99 V5 Glen L Michigan
12 D4 Glenluce Scotland
139 G4 Glen Lyon New S Wales
95 L5 Glen Lyon Pennsylvania
15 D4 Glen Lyon Scotland
145 E2 Glen Massey New Zealand
109 P5 Glenmora Louisiana
15 D3 Glen More Scotland
141 J7 Glenmorgan Queensland
15 D3 Glen Moriston Scotland
102 B2 Glenn California
116 P5 Glennallen Alaska
14 C3 Glennamaddy Irish Rep
94 D2 Glennie Michigan
139 H7 Glennie isld Victoria
103 P9 Glenn, Mt Arizona
100 K7 Glenns Ferry Idaho
102 F6 Glennville California
112 F6 Glennville Georgia
12 D1 Glen Ogle Scotland
144 B7 Glenomaru New Zealand
117 H7 Glenora Br Columbia
141 G4 Glenora Queensland
144 B6 Glenorchy New Zealand
15 D4 Glen Orchy Scotland
144 B7 Glenore New Zealand
141 F4 Glenore Queensland
140 E6 Glenormiston Queensland
139 L4 Glenreagh New S Wales
108 A8 Glenrio New Mex/Tex
121 Q7 Glen Robertson Ontario
98 A7 Glenrock Wyoming
109 K3 Glen Rose Texas
13 E1 Glenrothes Scotland
140 E5 Glenroy Queensland
142 F3 Glenroy W Australia
95 O3 Glens Falls New York
15 E4 Glen Shee Scotland
118 L7 Glenside Sask
15 D4 Glen Spean Scotland
28 D3 Glenstrup Sø L Denmark
101 T1 Glentana Montana
14 C2 Glenties Irish Rep
144 C5 Glentunnel New Zealand
118 L9 Glentworth Sask
98 E3 Glen Ullin N Dakota
15 D3 Glen Urquhart Scotland
141 H6 Glenusk Queensland
120 K5 Glenvale Ontario
99 T7 Glenview Illinois
99 N6 Glenville Minnesota
98 H9 Glenville Nebraska
94 G8 Glenville W Virginia
112 D2 Glenville L N Carolina
111 K10 Glenwood Alabama
111 C7 Glenwood Arkansas
112 E5 Glenwood Georgia
94 B7 Glenwood Indiana
99 L8 Glenwood Iowa
99 L4 Glenwood Minnesota
99 O9 Glenwood Missouri
112 F2 Glenwood N Carolina
106 B8 Glenwood New Mexico
123 S5 Glenwood Nfld
100 B4 Glenwood Oregon
103 N3 Glenwood Utah
100 D3 Glenwood Washington
99 O4 Glenwood Wisconsin
94 E8 Glenwood W Virginia
106 C2 Glenwood Springs Colorado
118 D9 Glenwoodville Alberta
28 F4 Glesborg Denmark
33 N4 Gleschendorf W Germany
41 H4 Gletsch Switzerland
118 H7 Glidden Sask
99 Q3 Glidden Wisconsin
100 B6 Glide Oregon
33 S8 Glienick E Germany
33 S7 Glienicke E Germany
14 B4 Glin Irish Rep
32 M5 Glinde W Germany
31 M3 Glinojeck Poland
48 J1 Glinyany U.S.S.R.
26 G9 Glissjöberg Sweden
26 C10 Glittertind mt Norway
31 L5 Gliwice Poland
46 D4 Gllavë Albania
103 O8 Globe Arizona
Glogau see Głogów
48 C3 Gloggnitz Austria
31 J4 Głogów Poland
31 K5 Głogówek Poland
33 Q8 Gloine E Germany
26 G5 Glomfjord Norway
26 E9 Glomma R Norway
26 L6 Glommerstrask Sweden
27 J15 Glönminge Sweden
130 H10 Glória Brazil
106 E6 Glorieta New Mexico
87 H10 Glorieuses, Is Indian Oc
116 C6 Glory of Russia C Alaska
20 F3 Glos France
20 G4 Glos-la-Ferrière France
13 G6 Glossop England
146 G9 Glossopteris, Mt Antarctica
20 G3 Glos-sur-Risle France
111 E10 Gloster Mississippi
28 K5 Glostrup Denmark
52 G3 Glotovo U.S.S.R.
8 D4 Gloucester England
95 R4 Gloucester Massachusetts
95 M7 Gloucester New Jersey
139 K4 Gloucester New S Wales
95 L9 Gloucester Virginia
141 J4 Gloucester I Queensland
94 E7 Glouster Ohio
123 P5 Glover I Nfld
95 N3 Gloversville New York
33 Q7 Glöwen E Germany
31 M4 Głowno Poland
31 K5 Głubczyce Poland
54 M8 Glubokiy U.S.S.R.
56 B5 Glubokoye U.S.S.R.
28 D7 Glucksburg W Germany
32 K5 Glückstadt W Germany
28 D5 Glud Denmark
28 C4 Gludsted, L Denmark
28 N3 Gluggarnir mt Faeroes
54 E5 Glukhov U.S.S.R.
52 F6 Glukhovo U.S.S.R.
28 K5 Glumslöv Sweden
28 H6 Glumsø Denmark
13 F6 Glusburn England
55 E4 Glyadyanskoye U.S.S.R.
48 K2 Glyboka U.S.S.R.
8 B1 Glyder Fawr mt Wales
143 E6 Glynde Hill W Australia
95 L7 Glyndon Maryland
98 K3 Glyndon Minnesota
28 B3 Glyngøre Denmark
8 C4 Glynneath Wales
8 C4 Glyntawe Wales
31 J7 Gmünd Austria
38 J6 Gmunden Austria
33 P9 Gnadau E Germany
94 F6 Gnadenhutten Ohio
26 J9 Gnarp Sweden
32 K6 Gnarrenburg W Germany
38 N8 Gnas Austria
28 G4 Gniben C Denmark
31 L2 Gniew Poland
31 K3 Gniezno Poland
33 M4 Gnissau W Germany
46 E2 Gnjilane Yugoslavia
33 R5 Gnoien E Germany
8 D2 Gnosall England
37 K5 Gnotzheim W Germany
143 C10 Gnowangerup W Australia
143 B9 Gnuka W Australia
32 L4 Gnutz W Germany
76 A3 Goa, Daman & Diu terr India
139 K6 Goalen Head New S Wales
75 O5 Goalpara India
12 C2 Goat Fell mt Scotland
13 H5 Goathland England
101 M1 Goat Mt Montana
87 F11 Goba Mozambique
89 A4 Gobabis Namibia
58 D3 Gobi Desert Mongolia
60 J12 Gobō Japan
8 C2 Gobowen England
86 H6 Gobuin Somalia
25 F5 Goch W Germany
87 C10 Gochas Namibia
86 G4 Gocho Ethiopia
36 F5 Gochsheim W Germany
9 F5 Godalming England
74 J9 Godavari R India
76 F2 Godavari, Mouths of the India
122 E4 Godbout Quebec
122 E4 Godbout, R Quebec
117 E7 Goddard Alaska
107 N4 Goddard Kansas
36 F4 Goddelau-Wolfskehlen W Germany
46 F1 Godech Bulgaria
27 H13 Godegård Sweden
32 K9 Godelheim W Germany
47 L8 Gödene Turkey
120 J9 Goderich Ontario
20 F2 Goderville France
22 D2 Godewaersvelde France
110 F3 Godfrey Illinois
121 O8 Godfrey Ontario
115 O4 Godhavn Greenland
74 E7 Godhra India
109 K3 Godley Texas
144 C5 Godley Gl New Zealand
144 C5 Godley R New Zealand
9 F3 Godmanchester England
71 J5 Godo mt Indonesia
48 E3 Gödöllö Hungary
9 E6 Godshill England
115 K7 Gods L Manitoba
9 F5 Godstone England
115 O5 Godthåb Greenland
112 J2 Godwin N Carolina
Godwin Austen see K2 Mt
25 A5 Goedereede Netherlands
121 O3 Goeland Quebec
25 A5 Goeree Netherlands
25 A6 Goes Netherlands
107 P2 Goff Kansas
103 J7 Goffs Carolina
95 Q3 Goffstown New Hampshire
120 J5 Gogama Ontario
60 F10 Gō-gawa R Japan
99 R3 Gogebic Michigan
99 R3 Gogebic Range mts Michigan
37 K7 Goggingen W Germany
41 H5 Goglio Italy
7 L10 Gog Magog Hills England
36 B6 Gogney France
22 F3 Gognies-Chaussée Belgium
142 F4 Gogo W Australia
31 K5 Gogolin Poland
86 E4 Gogrial Sudan
33 Q9 Gohrau E Germany
33 N6 Göhrde W Germany
130 J9 Goiana Brazil
130 E6 Goiandira Brazil
130 E4 Goianésia Brazil
130 E5 Goiânia Brazil
130 J9 Goianinha It ho Brazil
130 E4 Goiás Brazil
130 E6 Goiatuba Brazil
12 D1 Goil, L Scotland
130 D9 Goio Erê Brazil
25 D5 Goirle Netherlands
45 J1 Goito Italy
86 G4 Gojab R Ethiopia
86 G3 Gojam prov Ethiopia
61 J11 Gojō Japan
61 O6 Gojōme Japan
47 K5 Gök R Turkey
76 B2 Gokak India
47 K7 Gökbel mt Turkey
47 H4 Gökçe Turkey
47 H4 Gökçeada isld Turkey
47 K5 Gökçedağ Turkey
32 K4 Gokels W Germany
77 H7 Gokprosh Hills Pakistan
78 D3 Goksu R Turkey
78 F2 Göksun Turkey
68 C1 Gokteik Burma
47 K7 Göktepe Turkey
47 K8 Gök Tepe mt Turkey
87 E9 Gokwe Zimbabwe
27 C11 Gol Norway
75 P5 Golaghat India
80 G2 Golan Syria
31 K3 Gołańcz Poland
77 E6 Golāshkerd Iran
38 G8 Gölbnerjoch mt Austria
50 H1 Gol'chikha U.S.S.R.
110 H4 Golconda Illinois
74 H10 Golconda India
100 H9 Golconda Nevada
Gölcük see Etili
94 K5 Gold Pennsylvania
31 N1 Gołdap Poland
100 A7 Gold Beach Oregon
33 P7 Goldbeck E Germany
33 Q5 Goldberg E Germany
123 L8 Goldboro Nova Scotia
101 M5 Goldburg Idaho
101 O1 Gold Butte Montana
141 L8 Gold Coast Queensland Australia
28 C7 Goldelund W Germany
103 L8 Golden Arizona
117 P10 Golden Br Columbia
98 A10 Golden Colorado
100 K4 Golden Idaho
110 E1 Golden Illinois
145 D4 Golden Bay New Zealand
110 B4 Golden City Missouri
100 E4 Goldendale Washington
33 N10 Goldene Aue E Germany
102 B4 Golden Gate California
103 J4 Golden Gate Ra Nevada
127 M3 Golden Grove Jamaica
121 N7 Golden Lake Ontario
111 F12 Golden Meadow Louisiana
110 H5 Golden Pond Kentucky
118 H8 Golden Prairie Sask
143 D9 Golden Ridge W Australia
127 P4 Golden Rock airport St Kitts W I
32 H7 Goldenstedt W Germany
14 C4 Golden Vale Irish Rep
123 K8 Goldenville Nova Scotia
99 N7 Goldfield Iowa
102 G4 Goldfield Nevada
109 J7 Goldfinch Texas
101 M9 Gold Hill Utah
102 G4 Gold Point Nevada
118 K1 Gold Rock Ontario
119 R1 Goldsand L Manitoba
95 M7 Goldsboro Maryland
112 K2 Goldsboro N Carolina
108 E4 Goldsmith Texas
102 H6 Goldstone L California
142 C5 Goldsworthy W Australia
142 C5 Goldsworthy, Mt W Australia
109 J4 Goldthwaite Texas
112 F3 Goldville S Carolina
78 J1 Göle Turkey
85 E2 Golea, El Algeria
31 H2 Goleniów Poland
102 E7 Goleta California
56 G5 Golets Davydov, Gora mt U.S.S.R.
56 G3 Golets-Inyaptuk, Gora mt U.S.S.R.
16 C7 Golfo de Cádiz Spain
43 C7 Golfo degli Aranci Sardinia
43 E10 Golfo di Castellammare Sicily
43 E7 Golfo di Gaeta Italy
44 E3 Golfo di Genova Italy
45 N1 Golfo di Venezia Adriatic Sea
138 F5 Gol Gol New S Wales
109 K7 Goliad Texas
46 D1 Golija Planina mt Yugoslavia
65 E2 Golin Baixing China
47 H1 Gol. Kamchiya R Bulgaria
47 G2 Gol. Konare Bulgaria
Gollel see Lavumisa
33 T6 Gollin E Germany
38 H6 Golling Austria
33 S10 Gollmberg peak E Germany
33 T9 Gollmitz E Germany
47 J6 Gölmarmara Turkey
33 S8 Golmberg peak E Germany
37 M2 Golmsdorf E Germany
66 E4 Golmud China
71 E4 Golo isld Philippines
86 H4 Golocha Ethiopia
52 H1 Golodnaya Guba, Oz L U.S.S.R.
57 E4 Golodnaya Step' U.S.S.R.
88 E9 Golomoti Malawi
48 N2 Golovanyevsk U.S.S.R.
116 F4 Golovin Alaska
60 T2 Golovnino Kuril Is U.S.S.R.
77 B3 Golpayegan Iran
47 L4 Gölpazarı Turkey
116 G5 Golsovia Alaska
15 E3 Golspie Scotland
33 T9 Golssen E Germany
28 D2 Gølstrup Denmark
107 M5 Goltry Oklahoma
31 L2 Gołub Poland
55 F4 Golubovka U.S.S.R.
89 F3 Golulu Ruins Zimbabwe
87 B7 Golungo Alto Angola
98 C3 Golva N Dakota
47 G3 Golyam Perelik mt Bulgaria
31 M3 Gołymin Poland
55 E3 Golyshmanovo U.S.S.R.
33 R8 Golzow E Germany
88 B2 Goma Zaïre
85 G6 Gombe Nigeria
44 H4 Gombo Italy
70 M9 Gombong Java
47 H5 Gömeç Turkey
54 B4 Gomel' U.S.S.R.
85 A3 Gomera isld Canary Is
124 H5 Gómez Palacio Mexico
125 K4 Gómez, Presa M.R. res Mexico
33 P8 Gommern E Germany
66 C5 Gomo China
71 A3 Gomumu isld Indonesia
127 H5 Gonaïves Haiti
51 M3 Gonam R U.S.S.R.
126 H5 Gonâve, Île de la Haiti
48 G2 Gönc Hungary
74 D8 Gondal India
86 G3 Gondar Ethiopia
36 F5 Gondelsheim W Germany
74 J8 Gondia India
19 J4 Gondrecourt France
80 F1 Gonen Israel
47 J4 Gönen Turkey
47 J4 Gönen R Turkey
20 K4 Gonesse France
19 Q18 Gonfaron France
20 F3 Gonfreville l'Orcher France
83 K11 Gongala mt Sri Lanka
67 D1 Gong'an China
66 E5 Gongbo'gyamda China
67 C4 Gongcheng China
75 O4 Gonggar China
58 D6 Gongga Shan mt China
57 K3 Gongliu China
Gonglüe see Donggu
85 G6 Gongola R Nigeria
139 H4 Gongolgon New S Wales
67 D3 Gongpingxu China
67 D2 Gongtian China
65 B7 Gong Xian China
65 D4 Gongyingzi China
Gongzhuling see Huaide
31 O2 Goniądz Poland
88 G4 Gonja Tanzania
36 G7 Gönningen W Germany
21 D7 Gonnord France
46 E5 Gónnos Greece
61 P5 Gonohe Japan
60 C12 Gōnoura Japan
40 D3 Gonsans France
99 L2 Gonvick Minnesota
45 J2 Gonzaga Italy
102 C5 Gonzales California
109 K6 Gonzales Texas
36 C4 Gonzerath W Germany
94 K9 Goochland Virginia
146 H2 Goodenough, C Antarctica
121 M8 Gooderham Ontario
119 O7 Goodeve Sask
94 B1 Good Hart Michigan
99 V4 Good Hbr. B Michigan
116 E4 Goodhope R Alaska
116 F3 Goodhope B Alaska
87 C12 Good Hope, C. of S Africa
117 L10 Good Hope, Mt Br Columbia
87 C11 Goodhouse S Africa
99 O5 Goodhue Minnesota
101 L7 Gooding Idaho
107 J2 Goodland Kansas
119 R9 Goodlands Manitoba
83 M12 Goodlands Mauritius
110 K5 Goodlettsville Tennessee
99 S4 Goodman Wisconsin
116 F7 Goodnews B Alaska
108 C8 Goodnight Texas
139 H3 Goodooga New S Wales
140 B2 Goodparla N Terr Aust
116 P4 Goodpaster R Alaska
106 F3 Good Pasture Colorado
98 B9 Goodrich Colorado
100 J5 Goodrich Idaho
98 F2 Goodrich N Dakota
111 B11 Goodrich Texas
99 Q4 Goodrich Wisconsin
140 B1 Goodrich Bank N Terr Aust
117 P10 Goodsir, Mt Br Columbia
118 H4 Goodsoil Sask
119 P7 Good Spirit L Sask
103 J6 Goodsprings Nevada
111 K8 Good Water Alabama
119 O9 Goodwater Sask
107 J5 Goodwell Oklahoma
8 B3 Goodwick Wales
103 M7 Goodwin Arizona
121 L4 Goodwin Ontario
98 K5 Goodwin S Dakota
7 M11 Goodwin Sands English Chan
144 C6 Goodwood New Zealand
9 F6 Goodwood Park England
13 H6 Goole England
139 H5 Goolgowi New S Wales
139 J4 Goolma New S Wales
139 J5 Gooloogong New S Wales
138 E6 Goolwa S Australia
140 C1 Goomadeer R N Terr Aust
143 B9 Goomalling W Australia
139 H3 Goombalie New S Wales
141 K7 Goombungee Queensland
141 K7 Goomeri Queensland
141 K8 Goondiwindi Queensland
143 D9 Goongarrie W Australia
143 D8 Goongarrie, L W Australia
141 J5 Goonyella Queensland
25 G4 Goor Netherlands
117 P8 Goose R Alberta
115 N7 Goose Bay Labrador
101 R5 Gooseberry Cr Wyoming
118 G6 Gooseberry L. Prov. Park Alberta
123 R2 Goose Cove Nfld
101 M7 Goose Cr Idaho
101 M8 Goose Cr. Mts Utah
101 T7 Goose Egg Wyoming
116 F9 Goose I Alaska
100 E8 Goose L California
119 Q4 Goose L Manitoba
76 C3 Gooty India
75 L9 Gopalpur India
31 L3 Gopło, Jezioro L Poland
36 H6 Göppingen W Germany
31 K4 Góra Poland
103 K10 Gora isld Mexico
31 N4 Gora Kalwaria Poland
75 K5 Gorakhpur India
42 J5 Goransko Yugoslavia
48 E7 Goražde Yugoslavia
113 K11 Gorda Cay isld Bahamas
128 D7 Gorda, Pta C Chile
19 O17 Gordes France
47 J6 Gördes Turkey
86 D4 Gordil Cent Afr Republic
28 B6 Gørding Denmark
111 J8 Gordo Alabama
116 R2 Gordon Alaska
106 F4 Gordon Colorado
112 D5 Gordon Georgia
98 D7 Gordon Nebraska
13 F2 Gordon Scotland
109 J3 Gordon Texas
99 P3 Gordon Wisconsin
139 H8 Gordon R Tasmania
13 E3 Gordon Arms Scotland
140 B1 Gordon B N Terr Aust

30

Gordon Cr — Grey's Plains

98 E7 Gordon Cr Nebraska
140 B3 Gordon Cr N Terr Aust
142 G4 Gordon Downs W Australia
118 G2 Gordon, L Alberta
117 R4 Gordon L N W Terr
139 H8 Gordon L. Tasmania
117 F4 Gordon Landing Yukon Terr
94 B10 Gordonsville Tennessee
94 J8 Gordonsville Virginia
141 H3 Gordonvale Queensland
15 F5 Gordon W Scotland
86 C4 Goré Chad
86 G4 Gore Ethiopia
144 B7 Gore New Zealand
107 P6 Gore Oklahoma
144 D5 Gore Bay New Zealand
120 H7 Gore Bay Ontario
13 E2 Gorebridge Scotland
109 H2 Goree Texas
54 J2 Gorelki U.S.S.R.
95 Q2 Gore Mt Vermont
47 J5 Gorenez Dağı mt Turkey
116 M7 Gore Pt Alaska
140 E4 Gore Pt Queensland
106 D2 Gore Ra Colorado
110 H4 Goreville Illinois
9 H7 Gorey Channel Is
14 E4 Gorey Irish Rep
77 D1 Gorgān Iran
147 K11 Gorga, Zemlya isld U.S.S.R.
83 K14 Gorge R Réunion Indian Oc
142 C5 Gorge Ra W Australia
141 H4 Gorge Ra., The Queensland
128 C3 Gorgona isld Colombia
41 K6 Gorgonzola Italy
86 G3 Gorgora Ethiopia
85 G6 Gorgoram Nigeria
101 O9 Gorgorza Utah
107 L3 Gorham Kansas
95 R3 Gorham Maine
95 Q2 Gorham New Hampshire
95 K4 Gorham New York
53 F12 Gori U.S.S.R.
46 D4 Goricë Albania
99 O9 Gorin Missouri
25 C5 Gorinchem Netherlands
9 E4 Goring Oxon England
27 H10 Göringen Sweden
78 L2 Goris U.S.S.R.
52 E6 Goritsy U.S.S.R.
42 F3 Gorizia Italy
52 G3 Gorka U.S.S.R.
48 N1 Gorki Tikich R U.S.S.R.
52 F6 Gor'kiy U.S.S.R.
52 F6 Gor'kovskoye Vodokhranilishche res U.S.S.R.
33 O6 Gorleben W Germany
9 H2 Gorleston England
28 G5 Gørlev Denmark
31 N6 Gorlice Poland
52 F3 Gorlichevskaya U.S.S.R.
31 H4 Görlitz E Germany
28 J5 Gørløse Denmark
33 O6 Gorlosen E Germany
98 F5 Gorman S Dakota
109 J3 Gorman Texas
94 H7 Gormania Maryland
139 H8 Gormanston Tasmania
43 F11 Gornalunga R Sicily
47 H1 Gorna Oryakhovitsa Bulgaria
55 E2 Gornaya Subbota U.S.S.R.
46 D1 Gornji Milanovac Yugoslavia
42 H5 Gornji Vakuf Yugoslavia
56 C5 Gorno-Altaysk U.S.S.R.
56 C5 Gorno-Altayskaya U.S.S.R.
57 G5 Gorno Badakhshanskaya Oblast' prov U.S.S.R.
56 H2 Gorno-Chuyskiy U.S.S.R.
55 E2 Gorno Slinkina U.S.S.R.
52 G1 Gornostal'ya Guba B U.S.S.R.
54 M8 Gornyatskiy U.S.S.R.
29 P2 Gornyy U.S.S.R.
45 M2 Goro Italy
48 J2 Gorodenka U.S.S.R.
52 F6 Gorodets U.S.S.R.
54 C7 Gorodishche U.S.S.R.
52 D6 Gorodnya U.S.S.R.
54 A1 Gorodok U.S.S.R.
136 K3 Goroka Papua New Guinea
138 F6 Goroke Victoria
52 F6 Gorokhovets U.S.S.R.
87 F9 Gorongosa Mozambique
71 H4 Gorontalo Sulawesi
31 M1 Górowo Iławeckie Poland
86 H4 Gorrahei Ethiopia
25 F2 Gorredijk Netherlands
120 J9 Gorrie Ontario
20 D5 Gorron France
33 S9 Görsdorf E Germany
54 K8 Gorskoye U.S.S.R.
25 F4 Gorssel Netherlands
14 C3 Gort Irish Rep
14 B3 Gorumna I Irish Rep
130 G4 Gorutuba, R Brazil
57 A2 Gory Chushkakul' mt U.S.S.R.
53 C8 Goryn' R U.S.S.R.
31 M5 Góry Świętokrzyskie mts Poland
42 E6 Gorzano, M mt Italy
33 Q8 Görzke E Germany
31 L4 Gorzów Poland
31 J3 Gorzów Wielkopolski Poland
Gosainthan mt see Xixabangma Feng
9 F2 Gosberton England
37 M2 Göschwitz E Germany
61 N8 Gosen Japan
139 K5 Gosford New S Wales
102 E5 Goshen California
94 B5 Goshen Indiana
95 N5 Goshen New York
100 B6 Goshen Oregon
101 O10 Goshen Utah
94 H9 Goshen Virginia
61 O5 Goshogawara Japan
127 N4 Gosier Guadeloupe W I
33 M9 Goslar W Germany
20 C5 Gosné France
142 C2 Gosnells dist Perth, W Aust
42 G4 Gospić Yugoslavia
9 E6 Gosport England
110 K2 Gosport Indiana
111 G10 Goss Mississippi
33 Q9 Gossa E Germany
41 K3 Gossau Switzerland
22 G3 Gosselies Belgium
26 B9 Gossen isld Norway
140 C4 Gosse R N Terr Aust
86 E4 Gossinga Sudan
38 J6 Gossl Austria
38 H8 Gössnitz Austria
37 N2 Gössnitz E Germany
46 D3 Gostivar Yugoslavia
38 L6 Göstling Austria
38 L6 Göstlinger Alpen mts Austria
31 K4 Gostyn Poland
31 L3 Gostynin Poland
27 H13 Göta Kanal Sweden
28 N2 Gøte Faeroes
107 M6 Gotebo Oklahoma
27 E14 Göteborg Sweden
27 E13 Göteborgs Och Bohus county Sweden
85 G7 Gotel Mts Nigeria
61 M10 Gotemba Japan
37 K2 Gotha E Germany
27 K14 Gothem Gotland Sweden
98 F9 Gothenburg Nebraska
85 E6 Gothéye Niger
27 K14 Gotland county Sweden
27 K14 Gotland isld Sweden
27 H12 Götlunda Sweden
60 B12 Gotō-rettō islds Japan
71 B2 Gotowasi Indonesia
47 F3 Gotse Delchev Bulgaria
27 K13 Gotska Sandön isld Sweden
60 F10 Gōtsu Japan
44 G3 Gottero mt Italy
37 O6 Gotteszell W Germany
36 F2 Göttingen Hessen W Germany
32 L9 Göttingen Niedersachsen W Germany
26 K8 Gottne Sweden
117 M10 Gott Pk Br Columbia
28 C2 Gøttrup Denmark
54 H7 Gottvald U.S.S.R.
31 K6 Gottwaldov Czechoslovakia
41 L3 Götzis Austria
65 E4 Goubangzi China
25 C4 Gouda Netherlands
86 C4 Goudeï Chad
22 F4 Goudelancourt France
9 G5 Goudhurst England
85 B6 Goudiry Senegal
85 G6 Goudoumaria Niger
120 F4 Goudreau Ontario
25 B5 Goudswaard Netherlands
20 B4 Gouesnière, la France
112 E4 Gough Georgia
90 J13 Gough I S Atlantic Oc
118 E6 Gough L Alberta
40 D2 Gouhenans France
115 M8 Gouin, Rés Quebec
120 F6 Goulais River Ontario
139 J5 Goulburn New S Wales
139 K4 Goulburn R New S Wales
140 C1 Goulburn Is N Terr Aust
111 E8 Gould Arkansas
106 D1 Gould Colorado
107 L7 Gould Oklahoma
121 T7 Gould Quebec
99 V3 Gould City Michigan
146 G8 Gould Coast Antarctica
143 B7 Gould, Mt W Australia
85 B3 Goulimime Morocco
85 C6 Goumbou Mali
46 E4 Gouménissa Greece
40 E3 Goumois France
85 D5 Goundam Mali
86 C4 Goundi Chad
46 E7 Goúra Greece
86 C2 Gouradi Chad
18 F8 Gourdon France
85 G6 Gouré Niger
120 F4 Gourlay L Ontario
85 D5 Gourma Rharous Mali
20 J3 Gournay-en-Bray France
84 F6 Gouro Chad
12 D2 Gourock Scotland
139 J6 Gourock Rge New S Wales
95 M2 Gouverneur New York
118 K9 Gouverneur Sask
20 K3 Gouvieux France
20 B3 Gouville France
22 K3 Gouvy Belgium
127 P5 Gouyave Grenada
22 E3 Gouzeaucourt France
18 G6 Gouzon France
119 N7 Govan Sask
12 D2 Govan Scotland
107 K3 Gove Kansas
140 D1 Gove N Terr Australia
20 B5 Goven France
114 J8 Govenlock Sask
140 D1 Gove Pen N Terr Aust
48 J2 Goverla mt U.S.S.R.
130 H6 Governador Valadares Brazil
100 D4 Government Camp Oregon
71 G7 Governor Generoso Philippines
122 K8 Governor, L Nova Scotia
113 L12 Governor's Harbour Bahamas
145 D4 Gowanbridge New Zealand
94 J4 Gowanda New York
141 G6 Gowan Ra Queensland
144 D4 Gowan Valley New Zealand
110 B2 Gower Missouri
8 B4 Gower Inn Wales
120 K5 Gowganda Ontario
77 E5 Gowk Iran
14 D3 Gowna, L Irish Rep
99 M7 Gowrie Iowa
131 F2 Goya Argentina
127 N4 Goyave Guadeloupe W I
140 D2 Goyder R N Terr Aust
138 C2 Goyder R N Terr Australia
123 M3 Goyelle, L Quebec
128 C6 Goyllarisquizga Peru
47 L4 Göynük Turkey
61 P6 Goyō-zan mt Japan
86 D3 Goz-Beïda Chad
43 F12 Gozo isld Malta
86 G2 Goz Regeb Sudan
89 D9 Graaff Reinet S Africa
36 E5 Graben-Neudorf W Germany
85 C8 Grabo Ivory Coast
47 F9 Graboúsa isld Crete Greece
55 F4 Grabovo U.S.S.R.
33 P8 Grabow Magdeburg E Germany
31 L4 Grabów Poland
33 P6 Grabow Schwerin E Germany
33 O6 Grabow W Germany
42 G4 Gračac Yugoslavia
48 E6 Gračanica Yugoslavia
21 I7 Graçay France
101 O7 Grace Idaho
98 H2 Grace City N Dakota
121 O6 Gracefield Quebec
122 G1 Grace L Labrador
143 C10 Grace, L W Australia
107 M6 Gracemont Oklahoma
111 L11 Graceville Florida
98 K4 Graceville Minnesota
141 K2 Graceville dist Brisbane, Qnsld
110 J5 Gracey Kentucky
38 O8 Grad Yugoslavia
48 E6 Gradačac Yugoslavia
129 H5 Gradaús, Serra dos mts Brazil
26 H5 Graddis Norway
16 D2 Gradefes Spain
46 E3 Gradeska Pl mt Yugoslavia
47 H2 Gradets Bulgaria
48 H5 Grădistea Muncelului Romania
33 S9 Graditz E Germany
70 P10 Gradjagan Java
42 E3 Grado Italy
16 C1 Grado Spain
46 E3 Gradsko Yugoslavia
141 J8 Gradule Queensland
111 E7 Grady Arkansas
108 D1 Grady New Mexico
28 A5 Grådyb chan Denmark
143 B9 Grady, L W Australia
102 D2 Graeagle California
28 C5 Græderup Denmark
28 H7 Grænge Denmark
28 J4 Græsted Denmark
99 M6 Graettinger Iowa
37 P6 Grafenau W Germany
37 L4 Gräfenberg W Germany
33 Q9 Gräfenhainichen E Germany
37 K2 Gräfenroda E Germany
38 M5 Grafenschlag Austria
37 L2 Gräfenthal E Germany
37 K1 Gräfentonna E Germany
37 M4 Grafenwöhr W Germany
38 N5 Grafenwörth Austria
36 D6 Graffenstaden W Germany
Gräfinau see Angstedt-Gräfinau
37 O6 Grafling W Germany
109 J3 Graford Texas
32 F10 Grafrath W Germany
36 C2 Grafschaft W Germany
110 F3 Grafton Illinois
98 J1 Grafton N Dakota
139 L3 Grafton New S Wales
95 O4 Grafton New York
94 E5 Grafton Ohio
99 T6 Grafton Wisconsin
94 G7 Grafton W Virginia
141 H3 Grafton, C Queensland
133 C8 Grafton, Is Chile
103 K3 Grafton, Mt Nevada
141 H3 Grafton Pass Gt Barrier Reef Australia
45 R8 Gragnano Italy
119 N1 Graham Ontario
109 J2 Graham Texas
117 M7 Graham R Br Columbia
114 F7 Graham I Br Columbia
115 K2 Graham I N W Terr
118 C2 Graham L Alberta
95 T2 Graham L Maine
146 E14 Graham Land Antarctica
103 P9 Graham, Mt Arizona
89 E9 Grahamstown S Africa
95 N5 Grahamsville New York
42 J6 Grahovo Yugoslavia
42 A3 Graie, Alpi Italy
14 E4 Graigue Irish Rep
107 K2 Grainfield Kansas
118 D7 Grainger Alberta
98 E9 Grainton Nebraska
129 J5 Grajau Brazil
31 N2 Grajewo Poland
52 H6 Grakhovo U.S.S.R.
16 B4 Gralheira, Sa mts Portugal
28 C6 Gram Denmark
46 F1 Gramada Bulgaria
18 G8 Gramat France
47 J2 Gramatikovo Bulgaria
32 H7 Gramke W Germany
43 F11 Grammichele Sicily
Grammont see Geraardsbergen
33 R4 Grammow E Germany
143 C9 Gramphorne, Mt W Australia
15 F3 Grampian reg Scotland
15 D4 Grampian Mt Scotland
138 F6 Grampians mts Victoria
25 G3 Gramsbergen Netherlands
46 D4 Gramsh Albania
33 U6 Gramzow E Germany
44 B3 Grana R Italy
126 G10 Granada Colombia
106 H3 Granada Colorado
125 M4 Granada Nicaragua
16 E7 Granada Spain
16 E7 Granada prov Spain
16 C4 Granadilla Spain
133 D7 Gran Altiplanicie Central plain Argentina
14 D3 Granard Irish Rep
45 K2 Granarolo dell'Emilia Italy
38 G7 Granat-Spitze mt Austria
133 D7 Gran Baja hills Argentina
131 C7 Gran Bajo Salitroso salt lake Argentina
109 K3 Granbury Texas
106 E1 Granby Colorado
110 B5 Granby Missouri
115 M8 Granby Quebec
98 A9 Granby, L Colorado
85 A3 Gran Canaria isld Canary Is
40 B2 Grancey France
133 E3 Gran Chaco reg Argentina
127 O2 Gran Couva Trinidad
111 E12 Grand R Louisiana
99 M9 Grand R Missouri
98 E4 Grand R S Dakota
21 C6 Grand Auverne France
119 P1 Grand B Ontario
113 J11 Grand Bahama isld Bahamas
115 O8 Grand Bank Nfld
90 E4 Grand Banks of Nfld Atlantic Oc
85 D8 Grand Bassam Ivory Coast
122 F8 Grand Bay New Brunswick
119 V8 Grand Beach Manitoba
119 V8 Grand Beach Prov. Park Manitoba
120 J9 Grand Bend Ontario
94 D4 Grand Blanc Michigan
19 Q13 Grand Bornand France
127 N5 Grand Bourg Guadeloupe W I
123 O6 Grand Bruit Nfld
20 C3 Grandcamp France
103 M5 Grand Can Arizona
65 D7 Grand Canal China
14 D3 Grand Canal Irish Rep
111 C9 Grand Cane Louisiana
19 Q17 Grand Cañon du Verdon France
113 J10 Grand Cays islds Bahamas
85 C8 Grand Cess Liberia
111 D12 Grand Cheniere Louisiana
19 P13 Grand Colombier mt France
100 F2 Grand Coulee Washington
20 H3 Grand Couronne France
20 J2 Grandcourt France
127 N4 Grand Cul de Sac Marin B Guadeloupe W I
128 C6 Grande R Peru
131 G3 Grande R Uruguay
127 O4 Grande Anse Guadeloupe W I
122 G6 Grande-Anse New Brunswick
133 D8 Grande, B Argentina
121 U4 Grande-Baie Quebec
45 M2 Grande Bonificazione Ferrarese Italy
21 A7 Grande Brière reg France
83 K14 Grande Brûlé Réunion Indian Oc
118 G4 Grande Centre Alberta
19 P14 Grande Chartreuse mts France
133 D5 Grande Colorado R Argentina
18 H8 Grande Combe, la France
87 G10 Grande Comore isld Comoros
131 H2 Grande, Coxilha mt Brazil
21 I9 Grande Creuse R France
131 G4 Grande, Cuchilla ra Uruguay
126 G4 Grande de Moa, C Cuba
129 G4 Grande do Curuai, L Brazil
122 H5 Grande Grève Quebec
129 K8 Grande, I Brazil
45 M3 Grande, M mt Italy
128 F7 Grande, Monte mts Bolivia
128 F7 Grande O'Guapay R Bolivia
114 H6 Grande Prairie Alberta
127 M2 Grande, R Jamaica
86 B2 Grand Erg de Bilma Niger
85 E2 Grand Erg Occidental des Algeria
122 H5 Grande Rivière Quebec
127 P1 Grande Riviere Trinidad
127 H5 Grande Rivière du Nord Haiti
100 H4 Grande Ronde R Oregon
21 J6 Grande Sauldre R France
122 C5 Grandes Bergeronnes Quebec
20 G2 Grandes Dalles, les France
129 K5 Grande, Serra mts Brazil
121 S6 Grandes Piles Quebec
20 H2 Grandes Ventes, les France
123 L7 Grand Etang C Breton I, N Scotia
127 P5 Grand Etang L Grenada
127 N4 Grande Terre isld Guadeloupe W I
122 G4 Grande Vallée Quebec
127 N3 Grande Vigie,Pte.de la Guadeloupe W I
103 N6 Grand Falls Arizona
115 N8 Grand Falls New Brunswick
115 O8 Grand Falls Nfld
108 E4 Grandfalls Texas
112 F1 Grandfather Mt N Carolina
107 M7 Grandfield Oklahoma
100 G1 Grand Forks Br Columbia
98 J2 Grand Forks N Dakota
22 C1 Grand Fort Philippe France
95 N4 Grand Gorge New York
127 J5 Grand Gosier Haiti
22 K3 Grand-Halleux Belgium
122 F9 Grand Harbour New Brunswick
99 U6 Grand Haven Michigan
111 G11 Grand I Louisiana
99 U3 Grand I Michigan
98 H9 Grand I Nebraska
121 M9 Grand I New York
113 F8 Grandin Florida
110 F5 Grandin Missouri
98 J2 Grandin N Dakota
117 O3 Grandin, Lac N W Terr
111 G12 Grand Isle Louisiana
95 O2 Grand Isle Vermont
99 M7 Grand Junct Iowa
106 B2 Grand Junction Colorado
94 A4 Grand Junction Michigan
110 G6 Grand Junction Tennessee
95 U1 Grand L Maine
94 D1 Grand L Michigan
122 E8 Grand L New Brunswick
123 P4 Grand L Nfld
94 C6 Grand L Ohio
122 F2 Grand Lac Germain Quebec
106 E1 Grand Lake Colorado
111 C11 Grand Lake Louisiana
95 S7 Grand Lakes L Maine
94 C4 Grand Ledge Michigan
28 H5 Grandløse Denmark
99 V3 Grand Marais Michigan
99 Q2 Grand Marais Minnesota
111 M13 Grand Marais State Park St Louis
121 S6 Grand-Mère Quebec
106 C2 Grand Mesa Colorado
122 E2 Grandmesnil, L Quebec
117 P10 Grand Mt Br Columbia
123 R2 Grandois Nfld
16 B6 Grândola Portugal
16 B6 Grândola, Sa. de mt Portugal
110 C2 Grand Pass Missouri
99 R2 Grand Portage Minnesota
109 N9 Grand Prairie Texas
22 H5 Grandpré France
20 H3 Grand Quevilly France
94 F5 Grand R Ohio
119 S5 Grand Rapids Manitoba
94 B4 Grand Rapids Michigan
99 N2 Grand Rapids Minnesota
22 G3 Grandrieu Belgium
18 H8 Grandrieu France
123 M8 Grand River C Breton I, N Scotia
99 N9 Grand River Iowa
100 B4 Grand Ronde Oregon
127 P5 Grand Roy Grenada
42 A3 Grand St. Bernard, Col du pass Switz/Italy
109 M3 Grand Saline Texas
129 H3 Grand Santi Fr Guiana
40 E4 Grandson Switzerland
111 G12 Grand Terre Is Louisiana
101 P6 Grand Teton mt Wyoming
101 P6 Grand Teton Nat. Park Wyoming
106 B2 Grand Valley Colorado
100 J7 Grand View Idaho
119 R7 Grandview Manitoba
109 K3 Grandview Texas
100 F3 Grandview Washington
94 B4 Grandville Michigan
36 B7 Grandvillers France
103 L5 Grand Wash creek Arizona
103 L6 Grand Wash Cliffs Arizona
19 N15 Grâne France
26 F6 Grane Norway
26 K7 Graned Sweden
17 G3 Grañén Spain
44 B2 Granero mt Italy
121 N5 Granet, L Quebec
14 C4 Graney, L Irish Rep
27 G11 Grangarde Sweden
27 H11 Grängeberg Sweden
127 H1 Grange Hill Jamaica
12 E1 Grangemouth Scotland
99 P9 Granger Missouri
109 K5 Granger Texas
100 E3 Granger Washington
101 Q8 Granger Wyoming
36 B7 Granges-sur-Vologne France
100 J4 Grangeville Idaho
26 J8 Graninge Sweden
107 L7 Granite Oklahoma
100 G5 Granite Oregon
98 A8 Granite Wyoming
117 L10 Granite Bay Br Columbia
110 F3 Granite City Illinois
111 M12 Granite City St Louis
99 L5 Granite Falls Minnesota
112 F2 Granite Falls N Carolina
100 D1 Granite Falls Washington
116 N7 Granite I Alaska
99 T3 Granite I Michigan
123 P5 Granite L Nfld
100 H9 Granite Mt Nevada
103 J7 Granite Mts California
102 H6 Granite Peak California
100 H8 Granite Peak mt Nevada
101 Q4 Granite Pk Montana
101 M9 Granite Pk Utah
101 R7 Granite Pk Wyoming
99 T3 Granite Pt Michigan
116 Q6 Granite Range Alaska
100 F9 Granite Range Nevada
140 B5 Granites, The peak N Terr Aust
112 F4 Graniteville S Carolina
130 G9 Granito Brazil
144 C4 Granity New Zealand
129 K4 Granja Brazil
127 J5 Granja, Pta. de la Dominican Rep
54 C2 Granki U.S.S.R.
29 L11 Grankulla Finland
27 J14 Grankullavik Sweden
133 D6 Gran Laguna Salada L Argentina
118 F9 Granlea Alberta
133 E6 Gran Lorenzo Argentina
26 G8 Granlunda Sweden
124 F3 Gran Morelos Mexico
27 G13 Gränna Sweden
111 B7 Grannis Arkansas
98 E1 Grano N Dakota
17 J3 Granollers Spain
42 A3 Gran Paradiso mt Italy
133 E5 Gran Pico Argentina
42 D2 Gran Pilastro mt Italy/Austria
133 E4 Gran Pinto Argentina
44 B2 Gran Queyron mt Italy/France
108 A1 Gran Quivira Nat.Mon New Mexico
133 D5 Gran Roca Argentina
42 F6 Gran Sasso d'Italia Italy
33 S6 Gransee E Germany
113 G10 Grant Florida
99 M8 Grant Iowa
94 B3 Grant Michigan
101 M4 Grant Montana
98 E9 Grant Nebraska
107 P8 Grant Oklahoma
120 D2 Grant Ontario
99 M9 Grant City Missouri
143 D7 Grant Duff Ra W Australia
9 F2 Grantham England
140 C1 Grant I N Terr Aust
117 P3 Grant L N W Terr
116 E4 Grantley Hbr Alaska
143 E8 Grant, Mt W Australia
120 J9 Granton Ontario
13 E2 Granton Scotland
99 Q5 Granton Wisconsin
15 E3 Grantown on Spey Scotland
103 J3 Grant Ra Nevada
142 E4 Grant Ra W Australia
26 K7 Granträsk Sweden
116 M6 Grants Alaska
106 C6 Grants New Mexico
99 O4 Grantsburg Wisconsin
101 L3 Grantsdale Montana
13 F2 Grantshouse Scotland
100 B7 Grants Pass Oregon
142 D4 Grant Spring W Australia
101 N9 Grantsville Utah
94 F8 Grantsville W Virginia
111 M8 Grantville Georgia
20 B4 Granville France
99 R8 Granville Illinois
99 L7 Granville Iowa
98 F1 Granville N Dakota
95 O3 Granville New York
94 E6 Granville Ohio
94 K6 Granville Pennsylvania
122 G9 Granville Ferry Nova Scotia
133 E5 Gran Villegas Argentina
119 R2 Granville L Manitoba
33 P6 Granzin E Germany
130 G5 Grão Mogol Brazil
109 M4 Grapeland Texas
102 F7 Grapevine California
109 N8 Grapevine Texas
109 K3 Grapevine Res Texas
42 D3 Grappa mt Italy
126 G5 Grappler Bk Caribbean
27 H11 Gräsberg Sweden
32 M8 Grasdorf W Germany
87 F10 Graskop S Africa
114 H5 Gras,L.de N W Terr
13 E5 Grasmere England
27 K11 Gräsö Sweden
95 M2 Grass R New York
101 R6 Grass Creek Wyoming
44 B4 Grasse France
121 M3 Grasset, L Quebec
13 G5 Grassington England
100 C8 Grass Lake California
108 F2 Grassland Texas
145 E4 Grassmere, L New Zealand
143 D10 Grass Patch W Australia
119 T3 Grass R Manitoba
101 R2 Grassrange Montana
119 Q4 Grass River Prov. Park Manitoba
102 C2 Grass Valley California
100 E4 Grass Valley Oregon
139 G8 Grassy Tasmania
98 C2 Grassy Butte N Dakota
126 F3 Grassy Cr Andros Bahamas
118 G7 Grassy Island L Alberta
94 G8 Grassy Knob mt W Virginia
118 F9 Grassy Lake Alberta
28 D7 Gråsten Denmark
27 F13 Grästorp Sweden
26 J3 Gratangen Norway
123 U5 Grate's Cove Nfld
99 R7 Gratiot Wisconsin
94 C7 Gratis Ohio
26 L6 Gråträsk Sweden
28 D4 Graûballe Denmark
41 K4 Graubünden canton Switzerland
18 H9 Grau-du-Roi,le France
17 H2 Graus Spain
131 H2 Gravata Brazil
25 E5 Grave Netherlands
114 J8 Gravelbourg Sask
22 C2 Gravelines France
20 C5 Gravelle,la France
87 F10 Gravelotte S Africa
20 G3 Gravenchon, N.D. de France
121 L8 Gravenhurst Ontario
36 F3 Grävenwiesbach W Germany
101 L3 Grave Pk Idaho
18 E7 Grave, Pte de C France
9 G5 Gravesend England
139 K3 Gravesend New S Wales
19 N17 Graveson France
110 B5 Gravette Arkansas
20 H3 Gravigny France
20 F3 Graville France
43 G8 Gravina di Puglia Italy
99 M9 Gravity Iowa
28 D3 Gravlev Denmark
26 E7 Gravvik Norway
99 V5 Grawn Michigan
19 J5 Gray France
112 D4 Gray Georgia
95 R3 Gray Maine
108 D7 Gray Oklahoma
119 N8 Gray Sask
100 A3 Grayland Washington
94 C2 Grayling Michigan
117 L6 Grayling R Br Columbia
116 R3 Grayling Fk. R Alaska
140 C4 Grayling, Mt N Terr Aust
13 F5 Grayrigg England
100 A3 Grays Harbor Washington
101 O6 Grays L Idaho
99 S7 Grays Lake Illinois
94 E8 Grayson Kentucky
111 D9 Grayson Louisiana
119 P8 Grayson Sask
120 A2 Grayson L Ontario
106 E2 Grays Pk Colorado
94 B1 Grays Reef Michigan
100 B3 Grays River Washington
9 G5 Grays Thurrock England
111 K11 Grayton Beach Florida
110 H3 Grayville Illinois
54 G6 Grayvoron U.S.S.R.
38 M7 Graz Austria
16 D8 Grazalema Spain
46 E2 Grdelica Yugoslavia
48 K6 Greaca Lacul L Romania
13 G6 Greasbrough England
117 M4 Greasy L N W Terr
138 B5 Great Australian Bight Australia
9 G4 Great Baddow England
113 J12 Great Bahama Bank Bahamas
145 E2 Great Barrier I New Zealand
136 Great Barrier Reef Australia
95 O4 Great Barrington Massachusetts
103 H1 Great Basin Nevada
117 L3 Great Bear R N W Terr
114 H4 Great Bear L N W Terr
107 M3 Great Bend Kansas
98 K3 Great Bend N Dakota
89 A9 Great Berg R S Africa
15 B2 Great Bernera isld Scotland
14 A4 Great Blasket I. Irish Rep
122 F3 Great Boule I Quebec
123 R2 Great Brehat Nfld
8 D1 Great Budworth England
123 Q5 Great Burnt L. Nfld
89 A7 Great Bushman Land reg S Africa
94 J7 Great Cacapon W Virginia
9 F2 Great Casterton England
9 G3 Great Chesterford England
123 T7 Great Colinet I. Nfld
12 D2 Great Cumbrae isld Scotland
9 F2 Great Dalby England
118 K6 Great Deer Sask
101 S9 Great Divide Colorado
139 Great Dividing Ra Australia
13 H5 Great Driffield England
120 H7 Great Duck I. Ontario
Greater Khingan Range see Da Hinggan Ling
13 F6 Greater Manchester co England
145 D1 Great Exhibition Bay New Zealand
126 F3 Great Exuma isld Bahamas
114 H8 Great Falls Montana
112 G3 Great Falls S Carolina
110 L6 Great Falls Dam Tennessee
110 L6 Great Falls L Tennessee
89 E9 Great Fish R S Africa
6 N6 Great Fisher Bank North Sea
89 E9 Great Fish Pt. lt ho S Africa
145 E4 Greatford New Zealand
127 K3 Great Goat I Jamaica
9 F2 Great Gonerby England
113 K11 Great Guana Cay isld Bahamas
9 F5 Greatham England
126 F2 Great Harbour Cay isld Bahamas
144 A6 Great I New Zealand
145 D1 Great I New Zealand
126 H4 Great Inagua isld Bahamas
Great Indian Desert see Thar
113 H11 Great Isaac I Bahamas
89 A6 Great Karas Berg mts Namibia
89 C9 Great Karroo reg S Africa
89 E9 Great Kei R S Africa
141 K6 Great Keppel isld Queensland
112 K3 Great L N Carolina
139 H8 Great L Tasmania
8 D3 Great Malvern England
145 E2 Great Mercury I New Zealand
9 F4 Great Missenden England
87 C11 Great Namaland reg Namibia
136 J3 Great NE Channel Qnsld/Papua New Guinea
69 A9 Great Nicobar isld Nicobar Is
9 F4 Great Offley England
8 C1 Great Ormes Head Wales
95 P6 Great Peconic B Long I, N Y
127 J3 Great Pedro Bluff Jamaica
95 T2 Great Pond Maine
95 R5 Great Pt Massachusetts
122 G10 Great Pubnico L Nova Scotia
127 J2 Great R Jamaica
88 E5 Great Ruaha R Tanzania
113 J11 Great Sale Cay Bahamas
101 N8 Great Salt L Utah
101 M9 Great Salt L.Des Utah
107 M5 Great Salt Plains Res Oklahoma
106 E4 Great Sand Dunes Nat.Mon Colorado
118 H8 Great Sand Hills Sask
142 D5 Great Sandy Desert W Australia
141 L7 Great Sandy I Queensland
9 G3 Great Shelford England
89 G4 Great Shingwidzi R S Africa
114 H5 Great Slave L N W Terr
112 D2 Great Smoky Mts Tenn/N Carolina
117 L7 Great Snow Mt Br Columbia
7 D13 Great Sole Bank Atlantic Oc
95 O6 Great South Bay Long I, N Y
113 K12 Great Stirrup Cay isld Bahamas
8 B6 Great Torrington England
87 C10 Great Ums Namibia
138 B3 Great Victoria Desert S Australia
122 J8 Great Village Nova Scotia
9 G4 Great Waltham England
95 U2 Great Wass I Maine
139 H8 Great Western Tiers Tasmania
68 C7 Great West Torres I Burma
13 G5 Great Whernside mt England
9 H2 Great Yarmouth England
27 E13 Grebbestad Sweden
36 G2 Grebenau W Germany
36 G3 Grebenhain W Germany
54 D6 Grebenka U.S.S.R.
32 K10 Grebenstein W Germany
38 K7 Grebenzen mt Austria
85 F4 Greboun, Mt Niger
43 F8 Greco, Torre del Italy
37 L5 Greding W Germany
16 D4 Gredos, Sa. de mts Spain
28 B6 Gredstedbro Denmark
46 E6 Greece rep S Europe
98 B9 Greeley Colorado
98 H8 Greeley Nebraska
115 L1 Greely Fiord N W Terr
50 F1 Greem Bell, Ostrov isld U.S.S.R.
107 O2 Green Kansas
112 E2 Green R N Carolina
113 G11 Greenacres City Florida
95 M8 Greenbackville Maryland
99 T5 Green Bay Wisconsin
139 L4 Green Bluff New S Wales
94 G8 Greenbrier R W Virginia
94 D2 Greenbush Michigan
98 K1 Greenbush Minnesota
143 B10 Greenbushes W Australia
139 K6 Green Cape New S Wales
110 K2 Greencastle Indiana
94 K7 Greencastle Pennsylvania
126 F2 Green Cay isld Bahamas
99 O9 Green City Missouri
118 B4 Green Court Alberta
113 F8 Green Cove Springs Florida
99 O7 Greene Iowa
98 E1 Greene N Dakota
95 M4 Greene New York
32 L9 Greene W Germany
143 G6 Greene, Mt W Australia
112 E1 Greeneville Tennessee
102 C5 Greenfield California
110 F2 Greenfield Illinois
94 B7 Greenfield Indiana
99 M8 Greenfield Iowa
95 P4 Greenfield Massachusetts
110 C4 Greenfield Missouri
94 D7 Greenfield Ohio
107 M6 Greenfield Oklahoma
110 H5 Greenfield Tennessee
110 C5 Green Forest Arkansas
127 O2 Green Hill Trinidad
140 B1 Greenhill I N Terr Aust
144 B7 Greenhills New Zealand
143 B9 Greenhills W Australia
102 F6 Greenhorn Mts California
116 O6 Green I Alaska
144 B7 Green I New Zealand
123 Q2 Green I Nfld
141 H3 Green I Queensland
143 B9 Green I W Australia
121 Q4 Greening Quebec
137 L2 Green Is Solomon Is
127 H1 Green Island Jamaica
144 C7 Green Island New Zealand
71 D5 Green Island B Philippines
144 A7 Green Islets New Zealand
117 N10 Green L Br Columbia
99 S6 Green L Wisconsin
118 K4 Green Lake Sask
109 L7 Green Lake Texas
115 P2 Greenland
127 P6 Greenland Barbados
90 H1 Greenland Basin Arctic Oc
90 G2 Greenland-Iceland Rise N Atlantic Oc
144 B6 Greenland Res New Zealand
147 H10 Greenland Sea Arctic Oc
13 F2 Greenlaw Scotland
107 O2 Greenleaf Kansas
12 E1 Greenloaning Scotland
15 E5 Green Lowther mt Scotland
123 P2 Greenly I Quebec
138 C5 Greenly I S Australia
145 F3 Greenmeadows New Zealand
106 D2 Green Mt Res Colorado
95 O3 Green Mts Vermont
101 S7 Green Mts Wyoming
12 D2 Greenock Scotland
14 E2 Greenore Irish Rep
14 E4 Greenore Pt Irish Rep
116 R2 Greenough, Mt Alaska
112 G5 Green Pond S Carolina
95 P5 Greenport Long I, N Y
122 D6 Green R New Brunswick
101 Q8 Green River Wyoming
94 B9 Green R. Res Kentucky
111 J9 Greensboro Alabama
111 M11 Greensboro Florida
112 D4 Greensboro Georgia
112 H1 Greensboro N Carolina
95 P2 Greensboro Vermont
94 B7 Greensburg Indiana
107 L4 Greensburg Kansas
94 B9 Greensburg Kentucky
111 F11 Greensburg Louisiana
94 H6 Greensburg Pennsylvania
141 K2 Greenslopes dist Brisbane, Qnsld
123 T4 Greenspond Nfld
94 J7 Green Spring W Virginia
94 D5 Green Springs Ohio
139 J5 Greenthorpe New S Wales
99 O9 Greentop Missouri
94 B6 Greentown Indiana
113 K11 Green Turtle Cay isld Bahamas
110 H2 Greenup Illinois
141 H4 Greenvale Queensland
142 G3 Greenvale W Australia
111 K10 Greenville Alabama
100 E9 Greenville California
113 D7 Greenville Florida
110 G3 Greenville Illinois
110 J4 Greenville Kentucky
85 C8 Greenville Liberia
95 S1 Greenville Maine
94 B3 Greenville Michigan
111 E8 Greenville Mississippi
110 F4 Greenville Missouri
112 K2 Greenville N Carolina
95 Q4 Greenville New Hampshire
95 N4 Greenville New York
94 C6 Greenville Ohio
94 G5 Greenville Pennsylvania
112 E3 Greenville S Carolina
109 L2 Greenville Texas
94 H8 Greenville Virginia
119 N2 Greenwater L Ontario
119 O6 Greenwater L. Prov. Park Sask
119 S9 Greenway Manitoba
98 G4 Greenway S Dakota
9 G5 Greenwich England
107 N4 Greenwich Kansas
95 O3 Greenwich New York
94 E5 Greenwich Ohio
103 N3 Greenwich Utah
146 E15 Greenwich I S Shetland Is
110 B6 Greenwood Arkansas
100 G1 Greenwood Br Columbia
102 D3 Greenwood California
95 M8 Greenwood Delaware
94 A7 Greenwood Indiana
94 C10 Greenwood Kentucky
111 C9 Greenwood Louisiana
111 F8 Greenwood Mississippi
98 K9 Greenwood Nebraska
140 C5 Greenwood N Terr Aust
112 E3 Greenwood S Carolina
98 H7 Greenwood S Dakota
99 Q5 Greenwood Wisconsin
111 H8 Greenwood Springs Mississippi
100 J3 Greer Idaho
112 E3 Greer S Carolina
111 C7 Greeson, L Arkansas
32 F5 Greetsiel W Germany
20 G5 Greez France
25 F6 Grefrath W Germany
119 S9 Gregg Manitoba
111 B9 Greggton Texas
118 F2 Gregoire L Alberta
128 D5 Gregório R Brazil
98 G6 Gregory S Dakota
140 E4 Gregory Downs Queensland
142 G5 Gregory L W Australia
143 C7 Gregory, L W Australia
141 G4 Gregory Ra Queensland
142 D5 Gregory Ra W Australia
113 L12 Gregory Town Bahamas
38 H8 Greifenburg Austria
41 J3 Greifensee L Switzerland
33 T6 Greiffenberg E Germany
33 S4 Greifswald E Germany
33 T4 Greifswalder Bodden E Germany
33 T4 Greifswalder Oie isld E Germany
38 K7 Greimberg mt Austria
38 L5 Grein Austria
41 J4 Greina Pass Switzerland
38 M5 Greinerwald woods Austria
37 L5 Greisselbach W Germany
37 N2 Greiz E Germany
52 E1 Gremikha U.S.S.R.
33 N4 Gremsmühlen W Germany
28 F4 Grenå Denmark
100 C8 Grenada California
111 G8 Grenada Mississippi
127 P5 Grenada isld Lesser Antilles
18 E9 Grenade France
18 F9 Grenade sur Garonne France
127 O8 Grenadines, The islds Lesser Antilles
40 F3 Grenchen Switzerland
28 C5 Grene Denmark
28 F1 Grenen C Denmark
139 J5 Grenfell New S Wales
119 P8 Grenfell Sask
19 P14 Grenoble France
107 O4 Grenola Kansas
98 C1 Grenora N Dakota
26 S2 Grense/Jakobselv Norway
127 P5 Grenville Grenada
106 G5 Grenville New Mexico
98 J4 Grenville S Dakota
141 G1 Grenville C Queensland
117 J9 Grenville Chan Br Columbia
117 L10 Grenville, Mt Br Columbia
19 P17 Gréoux-les-Bains France
33 Q9 Greppin E Germany
33 Q4 Gresenhorst E Germany
100 C4 Gresham Oregon
70 O9 Gresik Java
69 F14 Gresik Sumatra
19 P15 Gresse France
19 Q13 Grésy-sur-Isère France
139 K5 Greta New S Wales
13 G5 Greta Br England
111 G12 Gretna Louisiana
119 U9 Gretna Manitoba
111 J13 Gretna New Orleans
94 H10 Gretna Virginia
13 E3 Gretna Green Scotland
37 K1 Greussen E Germany
45 K4 Greve Italy
25 A5 Grevelingen Netherlands
32 G8 Greven W Germany
46 E4 Grevená Greece
36 B1 Grevenbroich W Germany
32 L5 Grevenkop W Germany
33 O5 Grevesmühlen E Germany
27 F16 Grevie Sweden
29 K4 Grevie Sweden
28 H5 Grevinge Denmark
101 R5 Greybull Wyoming
140 D2 Grey, C N Terr Aust
101 Q4 Greycliff Montana
99 M4 Grey Eagle Minnesota
117 F4 Grey Hunter Pk Yukon Terr
123 R3 Grey I Nfld
123 R3 Grey Is Nfld
144 C5 Greymouth New Zealand
139 G7 Grey, Pt Victoria
123 Q5 Grey R Nfld
141 G8 Grey Ra Queensland/N S W
141 G8 Grey Range Queensland
101 P6 Greys R Wyoming
143 A7 Grey's Plains W Australia

13 F4 **Greystoke** England
101 R9 **Greystone** Colorado
14 E3 **Greystones** Irish Rep
145 E4 **Greytown** New Zealand
89 G7 **Greytown** S Africa
22 H2 **Grez-Doiceau** Belgium
21 E6 **Grez-en-Bouère** France
46 D4 **Griba** *mt* Albania
81 F11 **Gribb Seamount** Southern Oc
86 C4 **Gribingui** *R* Cent Afr Republic
52 D2 **Gridino** U.S.S.R.
102 C2 **Gridley** California
99 S9 **Gridley** Illinois
107 P3 **Gridley** Kansas
25 D2 **Griend** Netherlands
37 P7 **Griesbach** W Germany
36 F4 **Griesheim** W Germany
41 O3 **Gries im Sellrain** Austria
Griessen *see* **Klettgau**
25 F5 **Grieth** W Germany
38 L8 **Griffen** Austria
111 M8 **Griffin** Georgia
113 F9 **Griffin, L** Florida
116 Q1 **Griffin Pt** Alaska
139 H5 **Griffith** New S Wales
115 K3 **Griffith I** N W Terr
110 E6 **Griffithville** Arkansas
112 K2 **Grifton** N Carolina
99 Q10 **Griggsville** Illinois
41 K6 **Grigna** *mt* Italy
19 N16 **Grignan** France
18 E8 **Grignols** France
48 M3 **Grigoriopol** U.S.S.R.
25 F2 **Grijpskerk** Netherlands
48 K1 **Grimailov** U.S.S.R.
86 C4 **Grimari** Cent Afr Republic
19 Q18 **Grimaud** France
139 G8 **Grim, C** Tasmania
102 C2 **Grimes** California
100 K5 **Grimes Pass** Idaho
33 R10 **Grimma** E Germany
33 S4 **Grimmen** E Germany
Grimmenthal *see* **Obermassfeld-Grimmenthal**
37 J2 **Grimmenthal** E Germany
33 T7 **Grimnitzsee** E Germany
13 H6 **Grimsby** England
121 L9 **Grimsby** Ontario
41 H4 **Grimsel** *mt* Switzerland
115 S4 **Grimsey** *isld* Iceland
114 H6 **Grimshaw** Alberta
27 C13 **Grimstad** Norway
28 B5 **Grimstrup** Denmark
40 H4 **Grindelwald** Switzerland
28 C3 **Grinderslev** Denmark
28 B5 **Grindsted Å** *R* Denmark
95 S8 **Grindstone** Maine
123 L6 **Grindstone Island** Quebec
119 U7 **Grindstone Prov. Park** Manitoba
119 V7 **Grindstone Pt** Manitoba
99 O8 **Grinnell** Iowa
107 K2 **Grinnell** Kansas
115 K2 **Grinnell Pen** N W Terr
42 F2 **Grintavec** *mt* Yugoslavia
13 G5 **Grinton** England
26 C8 **Grip** *lt ho* Norway
33 O6 **Grippel** W Germany
89 F8 **Griqualand E** *reg* S Africa
89 C7 **Griqualand W** *reg* S Africa
87 D11 **Griquatown** S Africa
40 F6 **Grisanche, Val** Italy
115 L2 **Grise Fiord** N W Terr
45 L1 **Grisignano** Italy
22 B2 **Gris Nez, C** France
18 F9 **Grisolles** France
27 K11 **Grisslehamn** Sweden
99 L8 **Griswold** Iowa
52 H4 **Griva** U.S.S.R.
20 K2 **Grivesnes** France
40 F6 **Grivola** *mt* Italy
33 P9 **Grizeline** E Germany
85 D3 **Grizim** Algeria
117 N3 **Grizzly Bear Mt** N W Terr
26 C9 **Grjotli** Norway
42 G4 **Grmeč Plan** Yugoslavia
123 R3 **Groais I** Nfld
33 S10 **Gröba** E Germany
33 O10 **Grobers** E Germany
27 M15 **Grobina** U.S.S.R.
9 E2 **Groby** England
33 P9 **Gröbzig** E Germany
31 O2 **Gródek** Poland
31 K5 **Gródków** Poland
33 S10 **Gröditz** E Germany
31 O2 **Grodno** U.S.S.R.
31 J3 **Grodzisk** Poland
31 M3 **Grodzisk Mazowiecki** Poland
89 C8 **Groen** *watercourse* S Africa
22 G2 **Groenendaal** Belgium
25 G4 **Groenlo** Netherlands
109 L4 **Groesbeck** Texas
25 E5 **Groesbeek** Netherlands
25 C3 **Groet** Netherlands
25 P10 **Grogak** Bali Indonesia
32 K8 **Grohnde** W Germany
22 F3 **Groise, la** France
37 N1 **Groitzsch** E Germany
18 C5 **Groix, I.de** France
31 M4 **Grójec** Poland
43 C12 **Gromballa** Tunisia
28 C7 **Grønå** *R* Denmark
32 L8 **Gronau** Niedersachsen W Germany
32 F8 **Gronau** Nordrhein-Westfalen W Germany
28 B4 **Grønbjerg** Denmark
26 F7 **Grong** Norway
28 C4 **Grønhøj** Denmark
33 O9 **Gröningen** E Germany
25 G2 **Groningen** Netherlands
25 F2 **Groningerwad** Netherlands
119 N5 **Gronlid** Sask
115 P5 **Grønnedal** Greenland
26 F5 **Grönöy** Norway
27 K12 **Grönskär** *lt ho* Sweden
27 H14 **Grönskåra** Sweden
28 F7 **Grønsund** *chan* Denmark
89 D9 **Groot** *R* S Africa
89 B7 **Groot Aughrabies Falls** Orange *R* S Africa
140 D2 **Groote Eylandt** *isld* N Terr Aust
25 F2 **Grootegast** Netherlands
87 C9 **Grootfontein** Namibia
89 B3 **Groot Laagte** *watercourse* Namibia
89 B9 **Groot Swartberge** *mts* S Africa
89 C8 **Groot Tafelberg** *mt* S Africa
89 B7 **Groot Vloer** S Africa
87 D11 **Grootvloer** *L* S Africa
89 E9 **Groot Winterberg** *mt* S Africa
22 K4 **Grosbous** Luxembourg
127 O7 **Gros Islet** St Lucia
27 G14 **Grosjö** Sweden
127 H5 **Gros Morne** Haiti
127 L4 **Gros Morne** Martinique W I
122 G4 **Gros Morne** Quebec
123 P4 **Gros Morne** *peak* Nfld
123 P4 **Gros Morne Nat. Park** Newfoundland
19 J6 **Grosne** *R* France
9 H7 **Grosnez Pt** Channel Is
41 M5 **Grosotto** Italy
123 P3 **Gros Pate** *peak* Nfld
113 F7 **Gross** Florida
37 M4 **Gross Albershof** W Germany
40 H4 **Gross Aletsch Gl** Switzerland
32 L10 **Grossalmerode** W Germany
33 O9 **Gross Alsleben** E Germany
33 P8 **Gross Ammensleben** E Germany
37 P5 **Gross Arber** *mt* W Germany
33 S8 **Grossbeeren** E Germany
33 T8 **Grossbesten** E Germany
33 M10 **Grossbodungen** E Germany
37 O1 **Gross Bothen** E Germany
36 G5 **Grossbottwar** W Germany
37 L2 **Gross-Breitenbach** E Germany
33 T7 **Gross-Dölln** E Germany
37 M2 **Gross Ebersdorf** E Germany
123 L6 **Grosse I** Madeleine Is, Quebec
36 F2 **Grossenbuseck** W Germany
37 K1 **Grossenehrich** E Germany
33 O7 **Gross Engersen** E Germany
33 T10 **Grossenhain** E Germany
32 H7 **Grossenkneten** W Germany
37 N2 **Grossenstein** E Germany
127 N4 **Grosse Pointe** Guadeloupe W I
33 S10 **Grosse Röder** *R* E Germany
42 D6 **Grosseto** Italy
51 N4 **Grossevichi** U.S.S.R.
36 D5 **Gross Eyberg** *mt* W Germany
36 E3 **Gross Feldberg** *mt* W Germany
33 T6 **Gross Fredenwalde** E Germany
36 E4 **Gross-Gerau** W Germany
33 M8 **Gross Gleidingen** W Germany
38 G7 **Gross-Glockner** Austria
33 P6 **Gross-Godems** E Germany
37 N1 **Gross Görschen** E Germany
33 N5 **Gross Gronau** W Germany
33 M5 **Gross Hansdorf** W Germany
37 P2 **Gross Hartmannsdorf** E Germany
32 F5 **Grossheide** W Germany
37 M1 **Gross Heringen** E Germany
33 M7 **Gross-Kain** W Germany
36 E4 **Gross Karlbach** W Germany
33 O4 **Gross Klütshöved** E Germany
37 L2 **Gross Kochberg** E Germany
33 Q10 **Gross Korbetha** E Germany
33 T8 **Gross Köris** E Germany
33 R8 **Gross Kreutz** E Germany
37 N6 **Gross Laaber** *R* W Germany
37 J4 **Gross-Langheim** W Germany
36 H2 **Grosslüder** W Germany
33 S8 **Gross-Machnow** E Germany
37 M6 **Grossmehring** W Germany
33 M7 **Gross-Oesingen** W Germany
36 G4 **Grossostheim** W Germany
33 M4 **Gross Plöner See** *L* W Germany
37 P6 **Gross Rachel** *mt* W Germany
38 L6 **Grossraming** Austria
32 M9 **Gross Rhüden** W Germany
36 B5 **Grossrosseln** W Germany
37 L1 **Gross Rudestedt** E Germany
33 T7 **Gross Schönebeck** E Germany
33 P7 **Gross Schwechten** E Germany
33 T8 **Gross Selchower See** *L* E Germany
33 N8 **Gross-Sisbeck** W Germany
33 S6 **Gross Stechlinsee** *L* E Germany
36 H6 **Gross Süssen** W Germany
36 F4 **Gross-Umstadt** W Germany
37 P2 **Gross Waltersdorf** E Germany
33 P6 **Gross-Warnow** E Germany
33 Q6 **Gross Welle** E Germany
33 Q7 **Gross Wudicke** E Germany
33 R5 **Gross Wüstenfelde** E Germany
33 Q8 **Gross Wusterwitz** E Germany
33 T7 **Gross Ziethen** E Germany
36 F4 **Gross-Zimmern** W Germany
36 B6 **Gros Tenquin** France
42 F3 **Grosuplje** Yugoslavia
141 J5 **Grosvenor Downs** Queensland
116 K7 **Grosvenor, L** Alaska
101 P6 **Gros Ventre Ra** Wyoming
32 J9 **Grotenburg** *mt* W Germany
22 F2 **Grotenberge** Belgium
22 H1 **Grote Nete** *R* Belgium
95 Q5 **Groton** Connecticut
95 Q4 **Groton** Massachusetts
95 L4 **Groton** New York
98 H4 **Groton** S Dakota
95 P2 **Groton** Vermont
26 G4 **Grötöy** Norway
45 Q8 **Grotta Azzurra** Italy
45 O7 **Grotta delle Capre** Italy
22 J3 **Grotte-de-Han** Belgium
19 N16 **Grottes de St. Marcel** France
94 J8 **Grottoes** Virginia
36 F5 **Grotzingen** W Germany
114 H6 **Grouard** Alberta
20 B4 **Grouin, Pte. du** France
120 H4 **Groundhog** *R* Ontario
101 M6 **Grouse** Idaho
101 M8 **Grouse Creek** Utah
25 E2 **Grouw** Netherlands
27 C13 **Grovane** Norway
107 Q5 **Grove** Oklahoma
94 E7 **Grove City** Ohio
94 G5 **Grove City** Pennsylvania
117 O8 **Grovedale** Alberta
111 J10 **Grove Hill** Alabama
140 B2 **Grove Hill** N Terr Aust
28 C4 **Grove Kirke** Denmark
102 D4 **Groveland** California
28 F9 **Grovelsjön** Sweden
146 D5 **Grove Mts** Antarctica
98 B9 **Grover** Colorado
101 P7 **Grover** Wyoming
111 C12 **Groves** Texas
109 M4 **Groveton** Texas
95 Q2 **Groveton** Vermont
112 E4 **Grovetown** Georgia
145 D4 **Grovetown** New Zealand
101 P6 **Grovont** Wyoming
103 L9 **Growler** Arizona
103 L9 **Growler Mts** Arizona
47 J1 **Grozd'ovo** Bulgaria
45 P1 **Groznjan** Yugoslavia
53 F3 **Groznoye** U.S.S.R.
53 G11 **Groznyy** U.S.S.R.
41 J4 **Gr. Scheerh** *mt* Switzerland
33 O4 **Grube** W Germany
32 L9 **Grubenhagen** W Germany
42 H3 **Grubišno Polje** Yugoslavia
37 P6 **Grubweg** W Germany
20 F2 **Gruchet-le-Valasse** France
42 J6 **Gruda** Yugoslavia
47 J2 **Grudovo** Bulgaria
31 M2 **Grudusk** Poland
31 L2 **Grudziadz** Poland
128 D8 **Gruesa, Pta** *C* Chile
122 B6 **Grues, I. aux** Quebec
12 B2 **Gruinart** Scotland
109 J9 **Grulla** Texas
36 D4 **Grumbach** W Germany
43 H7 **Grumo Appula** Italy
27 F12 **Grums** Sweden
37 O2 **Gruna** E Germany
15 C3 **Grunard Bay** Scotland
33 T8 **Grunau** E Germany
87 C11 **Grunau** Namibia
36 G6 **Grunbach** W Germany
36 F2 **Grünberg** W Germany
36 G3 **Gründau** W Germany
Gründelhardt *see* **Frankenhardt**
26 K8 **Grundsunda** Sweden
26 J8 **Grundtjärn** Sweden
99 O7 **Grundy Center** Iowa
120 K7 **Grundy Lake Prov. Park** Ontario
28 D7 **Grünholz** W Germany
124 J5 **Gruñidora** Mexico
33 Q8 **Grüningen** E Germany
36 F2 **Grüningen** W Germany
36 H4 **Grünsfeld** W Germany
36 E4 **Grünstadt** W Germany
38 E8 **Gruppo** *mt* Italy
41 L4 **Grüsch** Switzerland
108 C7 **Gruver** Texas
40 F4 **Gruyère, L. de la** Switzerland
52 B6 **Gruzdžiai** U.S.S.R.
53 F12 **Gruziya** *S.S.R.* U.S.S.R.
54 L4 **Gryazi** U.S.S.R.
52 F5 **Gryazovets** U.S.S.R.
31 M6 **Grybów** Poland
27 H11 **Grycksbo** Sweden
31 J2 **Gryfice** Poland
31 H2 **Gryfino** Poland
99 L1 **Grygla** Minnesota
27 G12 **Grythyttehed** Sweden
26 H3 **Grytöy** *L* Norway
26 C9 **Grytten** Norway
133 J8 **Grytviken** S Georgia
31 J2 **Grzmiąca** Poland
41 O2 **Gschnitz** Austria
36 H6 **Gschwend** W Germany
40 F5 **Gstaad** Switzerland
40 F5 **Gsteig** Switzerland
19 P15 **Guâ** France
75 L7 **Gua** India
41 O7 **Gua** *R* Italy
128 D3 **Guacamayas** Colombia
126 F4 **Guacanayabo, G.de** Cuba
127 L9 **Guacara** Venezuela
103 M9 **Gu Achi** Arizona
128 D2 **Guachiria** *R* Colombia
130 C8 **Guaçuí** Brazil
124 H7 **Guadalajara** Mexico
16 E4 **Guadalajara** Spain
17 F4 **Guadalajara** *prov* Spain
16 D6 **Guadalcanal** Spain
137 M3 **Guadalcanal** *isld* Solomon Is
16 E6 **Guadalén** *R* Spain
17 F7 **Guadalentín** *R* Spain
16 D8 **Guadalete** *R* Spain
16 E8 **Guadalfeo** *R* Spain
16 E8 **Guadalhorce** *R* Spain
16 E6 **Guadalimar** *R* Spain
17 F6 **Guadalmena** *R* Spain
16 D6 **Guadalmez** *R* Spain
16 D7 **Guadalquivir** *R* Spain
131 C5 **Guadal, Sa. de** Argentina
102 D7 **Guadalupe** California
71 F5 **Guadalupe** Cebu Philippines
108 A4 **Guadalupe** Mexico
124 H6 **Guadalupe** Mexico
109 J6 **Guadalupe** *R* Texas
108 B3 **Guadalupe Mts** New Mex/Tex
108 C4 **Guadalupe Pk** Texas
16 D5 **Guadalupe, Sa de** *mts* Spain
124 G5 **Guadalupe Victoria** Durango Mexico
124 F4 **Guadalupe y Calvo** Mexico
16 E4 **Guadarrama, Sa. de** *mts* Spain
17 F5 **Guadazaón** *R* Spain
127 N4 **Guadeloupe** *islds* Lesser Antilles
16 E6 **Guadiana** *R* Spain
126 B3 **Guadiana, B.de** Cuba
16 E7 **Guadiano Menor** *R* Spain
16 D6 **Guadiato** *R* Spain
17 F4 **Guadiela** *R* Spain
16 E7 **Guadix** Spain
133 C6 **Guafo** *isld* Chile
127 P2 **Guaico** Trinidad
130 C7 **Guaicuras** Brazil
128 E2 **Guaina** Venezuela
128 E3 **Guainia** *R* Colombia
130 C9 **Guaira** Brazil
130 C9 **Guaira** Paraguay
133 C6 **Guaitecas, Is** Chile
126 F4 **Guajaba, Cayo** *isld* Cuba
128 E6 **Guajará Mirim** Brazil
128 E5 **Guajaraã** Brazil
128 F5 **Guajaturaba** Brazil
124 H4 **Guaje, Llano de** *reg* Mexico
125 L2 **Guajiniquil** Honduras
128 D1 **Guajira** *div* Colombia
128 D1 **Guajira, Pena de** *pen* Colombia
102 A3 **Gualala** California
42 E5 **Gualdo Tadino** Italy
131 F4 **Gualeguay** Argentina
131 F4 **Gualeguay** *R* Argentina
133 F4 **Gualeguaychu** Argentina
131 D8 **Gualicho Salina** *salt pan* Argentina
128 E7 **Guallatiri** *mt* Chile
45 J2 **Gualtieri** Italy
134 E6 **Guam** *isld* Mariana Is Pacific Oc
129 J4 **Guamá** Brazil
127 K9 **Guama** Venezuela
129 J4 **Guamá** *R* Brazil
133 B6 **Guamblin, I** Chile
131 D4 **Guamini** Argentina
124 E5 **Guamúchil** Mexico
69 E10 **Gua Musang** Malaysia
65 C5 **Gu'an** China
126 C3 **Guanabacoa** Cuba
130 G8 **Guanabara** Brazil
128 F4 **Guanacasté, Cord. de** *ra* Costa Rica
124 G5 **Guanacevi** Mexico
126 B3 **Guanahacabibes, Pen. de** Cuba
126 C3 **Guanajay** Cuba
124 J7 **Guanajuato** Mexico
129 K6 **Guanambi** Brazil
128 C5 **Guañape, I** Peru
109 J9 **Guanare** Texas
127 O2 **Guanapo** Trinidad
128 E2 **Guanarito** Venezuela
65 B5 **Guancen Shan** *mt ra* China
67 C6 **Guanchang** China
133 D3 **Guandacol** Argentina
65 G3 **Guandi** China
67 C1 **Guandiankou** China
126 B3 **Guane** Cuba
67 B1 **Guang'an** China
67 E3 **Guangchang** China
67 F1 **Guangde** China
67 D5 **Guangdong** *prov* China
67 F2 **Guangfeng** China
67 G3 **Guangfu** China
67 A1 **Guanghan** China
67 E1 **Guanghua** China
65 B6 **Guanghua** China
67 E2 **Guangji** China
58 F4 **Guangling** China
98 H9 **Guangling Dao** *isld* China
67 F1 **Guangming Ding** *mt* China
67 B4 **Guangnan** China
67 D5 **Guangning** China
65 C6 **Guangping** China
67 B4 **Guangrao** China
67 E1 **Guangshan** China
67 B5 **Guangxi** *aut reg* China
67 F1 **Guangyang** China
58 E5 **Guangyuan** China
67 F3 **Guangze** China
67 D5 **Guangzhou** China
67 F2 **Guangzhou** China
65 D7 **Guanhães** Brazil
67 F4 **Guánica** Puerto Rico
67 D3 **Guanipa** *R* Venezuela
67 B4 **Guanjiazui** China
67 C1 **Guanling** China
67 C1 **Guanmian Shan** *mts* China
65 D7 **Guannan** China
100 F7 **Guano L** Oregon
65 G1 **Guansongzhen** China
Guansuo *see* **Guanling**
128 F1 **Guanta** Venezuela
126 G4 **Guantánamo** Cuba
126 G5 **Guantánamo, B. de** Cuba
65 C6 **Guantao** China
65 C4 **Guanting Shuiku** *res* China
65 C6 **Guan Xian** China
67 A1 **Guan Xian** China
67 D4 **Guanyang** China
65 D7 **Guanyun** China
130 F7 **Guapé** Brazil
128 C3 **Guapi** Colombia
133 G3 **Guaporé** Brazil
130 J9 **Guarabira** Brazil
130 D10 **Guarama** Brazil
130 F8 **Guarantinguetá** Brazil
130 H7 **Guarapari** Brazil
130 D9 **Guarapuava** Brazil
130 E9 **Guaraqueçaba** Brazil
130 E7 **Guararapes** Brazil
130 J10 **Guararapes** Brazil
17 G2 **Guara, Sa. de** Spain
18 E10 **Guara, Sierra de** *mts* Spain
130 E9 **Guaratuba** Brazil
45 O6 **Guarcino** Italy
16 C4 **Guarda** Portugal
88 B1 **Guardafui, C** Somalia
16 D3 **Guardal** *R* Spain
17 F7 **Guarda Mor** Brazil
130 F5 **Guardatinajas** Venezuela
127 L10 **Guardbridge** Scotland
13 F1 **Guardia Mitre** Argentina
133 E6 **Guardian, C** Argentina
133 E7 **Guardia Sanframondi** Italy
45 R7 **Guardo** Spain
16 D2 **Guardunha Sa.da** *mts* Portugal
16 B4 **Guariba** *R* Amazonas Brazil
128 F5 **Guárico** *R* Venezuela
127 L10 **Guárico** *state* Venezuela
128 E2 **Guarita** *R* Brazil
130 D10 **Guasave** Mexico
124 E5 **Guascama, Pta** *point* Colombia
128 C3 **Guasima** Mexico
125 K7 **Guasu, R** Brazil
130 C9 **Guastalla** Italy
42 D4 **Guatemala** Guatemala
125 O10 **Guatemala** *rep* Cent America
125 O10 **Guatire** Venezuela
127 L9 **Guatire** Venezuela
128 E3 **Guaviare** *R* Colombia
126 E4 **Guayabal** Cuba
128 E2 **Guayabal** Venezuela
128 D3 **Guayabero** *R* Colombia
131 C3 **Guayaguas, Sa. de** *ra* Argentina
127 P3 **Guayaguayare** Trinidad
127 L5 **Guayama** Puerto Rico
128 C4 **Guayaquil** Ecuador
128 B4 **Guayaquil, Golfo de** Ecuador
128 E6 **Guayaramerín** Bolivia
128 B4 **Guayas** *prov* Ecuador
133 B7 **Guayeco Arch** *islds* Chile
124 D4 **Guaymas** Mexico
131 F3 **Guayquiraró, R** Argentina
130 F7 **Guazupé** Brazil
86 G5 **Guba** Ethiopia
87 E8 **Guba** Zaïre
67 B3 **Gubai** China
52 J5 **Gubakha** U.S.S.R.
86 H3 **Guban** *dist* Somalia
71 G4 **Gubat** Philippines
86 G3 **Gubba** Ethiopia
42 E5 **Gubbio** Italy
53 F7 **Gubdor** U.S.S.R.
65 D4 **Gubeikou** China
Guben *see* **Wilhelm Pieck Stadt**
31 H4 **Gubin** E Germany
54 J5 **Gubkin** U.S.S.R.
65 D6 **Gucheng** China
67 D1 **Gucheng** China
17 G4 **Gudar, Sa. de** *mts* Spain
28 F6 **Gudbjerg** Denmark
26 C9 **Gudbrandsdalen** Norway
28 D5 **Gudenå** *R* Denmark
67 G1 **Gudensberg** W Germany
36 F4 **Gudernheim** W Germany
28 D6 **Gudhjem** Denmark
27 G16 **Gudhjem** Denmark
28 F6 **Gudme** Denmark
77 J6 **Gudri** *R* Pakistan
65 B7 **Gudui** China
28 G6 **Gudum** Denmark
28 E3 **Gudumholm** Denmark
28 A3 **Gudum Kirke** Denmark
76 D3 **Gudur** India
27 B11 **Gudvangen** Norway
18 D5 **Guebwiller** France
133 C6 **Guechucuicui, Pta** Chile
20 G5 **Gué-de-la-Chaîne, le** France
20 J5 **Gué-de-Longroi, le** France
121 N4 **Guéguen, L** Quebec
16 E7 **Guéjar Sierra** Spain
85 B7 **Guékédou** Guinea
86 C3 **Guélengdeng** Chad
85 F1 **Guelma** Algeria
98 H3 **Guelph** N Dakota
85 B3 **Guelta Zemmur** Morocco
85 D6 **Guém** Mali
36 C7 **Guémar** France
18 C4 **Guémené** France
21 B6 **Guémene-Penfao** France
121 R6 **Guenette** Quebec
133 C7 **Guenguel** *R* Argentina
21 B6 **Guenroue** France
21 A6 **Guer** France
16 C6 **Gueraña** Spain
86 C3 **Guéra, Pic de** *mt* Chad
85 E2 **Guerara** Algeria
18 G6 **Guerche-sur-l'Aubois, la** France
86 D3 **Guéréda** Chad
21 I9 **Gueret** France
121 L5 **Guerin** Quebec
36 B5 **Guermange** France
119 M7 **Guernsey** Sask
98 B7 **Guernsey** Wyoming
9 G6 **Guernsey** *isld* Channel Is
98 B7 **Guernsey Res** Wyoming
20 G4 **Guerouide, la** France
109 H9 **Guerra** Texas
20 J2 **Guerville** France
146 J9 **Guest** *pen* Antarctica
85 D4 **Guettara, El** Mali
18 H6 **Gueugnon** France
111 D12 **Gueydan** Louisiana
41 K4 **Güferhorn** *mt* Switzerland
38 E6 **Güffert-Spitze** *mt* Austria
86 G4 **Gughe** *mt* Ethiopia
42 F7 **Guglionesi** Italy
86 G4 **Gugu** *mt* Ethiopia
48 H5 **Gugu** *mt* Romania
33 R6 **Gühlen-Glienecke** E Germany
130 C4 **Guia** Brazil
21 B8 **Guichen** France
67 F1 **Guichi** China
125 M9 **Guichicovi** Mexico
86 B4 **Guider** Cameroon
98 H9 **Guide Rock** Nebraska
67 B3 **Guiding** China
45 J1 **Guidizzolo** Italy
67 D3 **Guidong** China
19 P13 **Guiers** *R* France
85 A5 **Guiers, L. de** Senegal
45 L3 **Guiglia** Italy
85 C7 **Guiglo** Ivory Coast
21 B6 **Guignen** France
22 J2 **Guigoven** Belgium
127 L9 **Güigüe** Venezuela
Guihua *see* **Mingxi**
87 F10 **Guija** Mozambique
67 C4 **Gui Jiang** *R* China
67 D4 **Guiji Shan** *mts* China
9 F5 **Guildford** England
143 B9 **Guildford** W Australia
95 O2 **Guildhall** Vermont
65 E1 **Guiler Gol** *R* China
95 P5 **Guilford** Connecticut
95 S1 **Guilford** Maine
112 H1 **Guilford Ct. Ho. Nat. Mil. Park** N Carolina
86 B7 **Guilherme Capelo** Angola
67 C4 **Guilin** China
16 B3 **Guimaraes** Portugal
71 F5 **Guimaras** *isld* Philippines
71 F5 **Guimaras Str** Philippines
111 J8 **Guin** Alabama
125 M3 **Guina** Nicaragua
71 F5 **Guinayan** *isld* Philippines
126 E3 **Guinchos Cay** *isld* Cuba
102 B3 **Guinda** California
71 G6 **Guindulman** Philippines
85 B6 **Guinea** *rep* W Africa
90 J8 **Guinea Basin** Atlantic Oc
85 A6 **Guinea-Bissau** *rep* W Africa
85 E8 **Guinea, Gulf of** W Africa
122 C3 **Guinecourt, L** Quebec
126 D3 **Güines** Cuba
22 B2 **Guines** France
21 C8 **Guingamp** France
85 F6 **Guinia** Niger
71 F5 **Guintacan** *isld* Philippines
71 F3 **Guintinua** *isld* Philippines
110 E6 **Guion** Arkansas
67 C5 **Guiping** China
17 F2 **Guipúzcoa** *prov* Spain
71 F5 **Guir** Mali
85 D5 **Güira de Melena** Cuba
126 C3 **Guiratinga** Brazil
130 D5 **Guisanbourg** Fr Guiana
129 H3 **Guisborough** England
13 G5 **Guiscard** France
22 D5 **Guise** France
22 F4 **Guiseley** England
13 G6 **Guist** England
9 G2 **Guiuan** Philippines
71 G5 **Guivry** France
22 E4 **Guixi** China
67 F2 **Gui Xian** China
67 C5 **Guizhou** *prov* China
67 B3 **Gujarat** *prov* India
74 D7 **Gujranwala** Pakistan
74 F2 **Gujrat** Pakistan
74 F2 **Gujunba** China
67 C1 **Gu Komelik** Arizona
103 N9 **Gukovo** U.S.S.R.
54 L8 **Gulang** China
58 D4 **Gulargambone** New S Wales
139 J4 **Gulbahar** Afghanistan
77 L2 **Gulbarga** India
74 G10 **Gulbene** U.S.S.R.
52 C6 **Gul'cha** U.S.S.R.
57 G4 **Guldager** Denmark
28 A5 **Guldbjerg** Denmark
28 E5 **Guldborg** Denmark
28 H7 **Guldental** W Germany
36 D4 **Guldsmedshyttan** Sweden
27 H12 **Guledgarh** India
76 B2 **Gulen** Norway
27 A10 **Gulf** N Carolina
112 H2 **Gulf Beach** Florida
111 J11 **Gulf Highway** *rd* Queensland
141 G4 **Gulfport** Florida
113 E10 **Gulfport** Mississippi
111 G11 **Gulf, The** S W Asia
77 A5 **Gulgong** New S Wales
26 R1 **Gulian** China
139 J4 **Gulin** China
67 B2 **Gulistan** U.S.S.R.
57 E4 **Gülitz** E Germany
33 P6 **Gulkana** Alaska
116 P5 **Gull** *L* Alberta
118 D6 **Gullabo** Sweden
27 H15 **Gullane** Scotland
13 F1 **Gull Bay** Ontario
119 O1 **Gullev** Denmark
28 D4 **Gull I** Michigan
99 V4 **Gulliver** Michigan
99 V3 **Gull L** Minnesota
99 M3 **Gull Lake** Sask
118 J8 **Gullön** Sweden
26 K6 **Gullspång** Sweden
27 G13 **Gullträsk** Sweden
26 M5 **Güllük** Turkey
98 F1 **Gülnar** Turkey
65 F2 **Gulpen** Netherlands
25 E7 **Gülper See** *L* E Germany
33 Q7 **Gülpınar** Turkey
47 H5 **Gulran** Afghanistan
77 G2 **Gülşehir** Turkey
78 E2 **Gulsele** Sweden
26 J8 **Gul'shad** U.S.S.R.
57 G2 **Gültz** E Germany
33 S5 **Gulu** Uganda
87 F5 **Guluguba** Queensland
141 J7 **Guluwuru I** N Terr Aust
141 H1 **Gulyaypole** U.S.S.R.
59 H1 **Gülzow** E Germany
54 H9 **Gumbardo** Queensland
33 S4 **Gumboda** Sweden
141 G7 **Gum Cr** N Terr Aust
26 M7 **Gumel** Nigeria
140 C3 **Gümez** Mexico
85 F6 **Gumiel de Hizán** Spain
125 K6 **Gumla** India
16 E3 **Gum Lake L** New S Wales
75 L7 **Gumma** *prefect* Japan
139 G5 **Gummersbach** W Germany
61 M9 **Gummi** Nigeria
36 D1 **Gümüşhane** Turkey
85 F6 **Guna** India
71 E2 **Guna** *mt* Ethiopia
69 C10 **Gunanya Spring** W Australia
94 K9 **Gunbar** New S Wales
33 Q7 **Gun Cay** Bahamas
67 A5 **Gunda** U.S.S.R.
78 G1 **Gundagai** New S Wales
74 G6 **Gundelfingen** W Germany
86 G3 **Gundelsheim** W Germany
142 E6 **Gundersted** Denmark
139 H5 **Gundheim** W Germany
113 F10 **Gundih** Java
58 F1 **Gundji** Zaïre
139 J6 **Gundlupet** India
37 J7 **Gundsølille** Denmark
36 G5 **Gunedidi** Zaïre
28 C3 **Güney** Turkey
36 E4 **Gunflint** Ontario
70 N9 **Gunisao** *L* Manitoba
86 D5 **Gunisao** *R* Manitoba
76 C5 **Gunnar** Sask
28 J5 **Gunnarn** Sweden
47 K6 **Gunnawarra** Queensland
119 V5 **Gunnebo** Sweden
119 U5 **Gunnedah** New S Wales
103 U5 **Gunnerus Bank** Antarctica
118 J6 **Gunning** New S Wales
26 J6 **Gunnislake** England
141 H4 **Gunnison** Colorado
27 J14 **Gunnison** *R* Colorado
139 K4 **Gunnison** Utah
146 A7 **Gunn Pt** N Terr Aust
139 J5 **Gunong Ayer** Sarawak
8 B7 **Gunpowder** *R* Queensland
106 D3 **Gunsight** Montana
106 B3 **Guntakal** India
101 N8 **Gunter** Oregon
140 B1 **Gunter** Texas
70 F6 **Güntersberge** E Germany
140 E4 **Guntersblum** W Germany
101 N1 **Guntersville** Alabama
76 C3 **Gunton** Manitoba
100 B6 **Guntown** Mississippi
109 L2 **Guntur** India
33 N9 **Gunung Sumatra** ...
36 E4 ...
111 K7 ...
119 U8 ...
111 H7 ...
69 E12 ...
76 E2 ...
71 N8 ...
69 C12 ...
70 K8 ...
69 D12 ...
76 E3 ...
118 J7 ...
143 B9 **Gunyidi** W Australia
37 J7 **Günz** *R* W Germany
37 J7 **Günzburg** W Germany
37 K5 **Gunzenhausen** W Germany
33 N9 **Gunzerode** E Germany
67 B5 **Guohua** China
65 C4 **Guojiatun** China
Guoluezhen *see* **Lingbao**
65 B5 **Guoyangzhen** China
65 D7 **Gupei** China
65 B3 **Gurban Obo** China
66 D2 **Gurbantünggüt Shamo** *des* China
138 E6 **Gurchen B** S Australia
74 F2 **Gurdaspur** India
111 C8 **Gurdon** Arkansas
47 K6 **Güre** Turkey
74 G4 **Gurgaon** India
86 D3 **Gurgei, Jebel** *mt* Sudan
129 K5 **Gurgueia** *R* Brazil
127 N11 **Guri** Venezuela
130 E6 **Gurinhatã** Brazil
46 D4 **Gur-i-Topit** *mt* Albania
38 J8 **Gurk** *R* Austria
75 L5 **Gurkha** Nepal
38 K8 **Gurktal** *V* Austria
38 J8 **Gurktaler Alpen** *mts* Austria
66 C5 **Gurla Mandhata** *mt* China
57 B4 **Gurlen** U.S.S.R.
98 D8 **Gurley** Nebraska
88 D10 **Guro** Mozambique
59 L1 **Gurskoye** U.S.S.R.
88 F9 **Guruè** Mozambique
48 K3 **Guru Humorului** Romania
78 F2 **Gürün** Turkey
129 H4 **Gurupá** Brazil
129 J6 **Gurupi** Brazil
129 J4 **Gurupi** *R* Brazil
129 J4 **Gurupi, C** Brazil
76 D2 **Guruzala** India
58 D3 **Gurvan Sayhan Uul** *mt* Mongolia
50 E4 **Gur'yev** U.S.S.R.
56 C4 **Gur'yevsk** U.S.S.R.
85 F6 **Gusau** Nigeria
33 P8 **Güsen** E Germany
31 N1 **Gusev** U.S.S.R.
65 A4 **Gushan** China
59 H4 **Gushan** China
101 Q9 **Gusher** Utah
67 E1 **Gushi** China
61 P14 **Gushikami** Okinawa
61 P13 **Gushikawa** Okinawa
70 E1 **Gusi** Sabah
52 G7 **Gusikha** U.S.S.R.
46 D2 **Gusinje** Yugoslavia
56 G5 **Gusinoozersk** U.S.S.R.
56 G5 **Gusinoye, Oz** *L* U.S.S.R.
52 F6 **Gus'Khrustal'nyy** U.S.S.R.
46 D4 **Gusmar** Albania
57 B2 **Gusong** China
43 B9 **Guspini** Sardinia
48 C3 **Güssing** Austria
45 J1 **Gussola** Italy
27 G11 **Gust Adolf** Sweden
115 Q4 **Gustav Holm, Kap** *C* Greenland
127 N6 **Gustavia** Lesser Antilles
124 C2 **Gustavo Sotelo** Mexico
117 F6 **Gustavus** Alaska
33 P9 **Güsten** E Germany
36 E2 **Gusternhain** W Germany
102 C4 **Gustine** California
109 J4 **Gustine** Texas
33 S4 **Gustow** E Germany
33 Q5 **Güstrow** E Germany
27 H13 **Gusum** Sweden
48 K1 **Gusyatin** U.S.S.R.
36 E7 **Gutach** W Germany
56 E4 **Gutarskiy Khrebet** *mts* U.S.S.R.
38 L5 **Gutau** Austria
37 M3 **Gutenfürst** E Germany
38 N6 **Gutenstein** Austria
32 J9 **Gütersloh** W Germany
32 H9 **Gütersloh** W Germany
143 B8 **Gutha** W Australia
110 J5 **Guthrie** Kentucky
99 M2 **Guthrie** Minnesota
98 F1 **Guthrie** N Dakota
107 N6 **Guthrie** Oklahoma
108 G2 **Guthrie** Texas
99 M8 **Guthrie Center** Iowa
119 R3 **Guthrie L** Manitoba
67 F3 **Gutian** China
Gutian *see* **Yutai**
33 S8 **Gut-Neuhof** E Germany
33 Q5 **Gutow** E Germany
38 L8 **Guttaring** Austria
99 P7 **Guttenberg** Iowa
87 F9 **Gutu** Zimbabwe
54 G6 **Gutyy** U.S.S.R.
53 H5 **Gützkow** E Germany
80 C7 **Guvrin** *R* Israel
36 G1 **Guxhagen** W Germany
65 B6 **Gu Xian** China
65 C4 **Guyan** China
48 F8 **Guyandotte** *R* W Virginia
58 F3 **Guyang** China
65 A4 **Guyang** China
121 M4 **Guyenne** Quebec
18 E8 **Guyenne** *prov* France
9 G2 **Guyhirn** England
Guyi *see* **Sanjiang**
107 J5 **Guymon** Oklahoma
116 R6 **Guyot Glacier** Alaska
139 K4 **Guyra** New S Wales
123 L8 **Guysborough** Nova Scotia
112 F5 **Guyton** Georgia
67 C2 **Guzhang** China
58 G5 **Guzhen** China
Guzhou *see* **Rongjiang**
124 F2 **Guzmán, L. de** Mexico
74 E1 **Gvardeyskoye** U.S.S.R.
48 J2 **Gvozdets** U.S.S.R.
68 B4 **Gwa** Burma
139 J4 **Gwabegar** New S Wales
38 G8 **Gwabl** Austria
74 B10 **Gwadar** Pakistan
89 E2 **Gwai** *R* Zimbabwe
8 B1 **Gwalchmai** Wales
143 D8 **Gwalia** W Australia
74 H5 **Gwalior** India
141 J7 **Gwambegwine** Queensland
89 F3 **Gwanda** Zimbabwe
86 E5 **Gwane** Zaïre
8 B3 **Gwbert-on-Sea** Wales
68 B2 **Gwebin** Burma
14 C2 **Gweebarra B** Irish Rep
89 F2 **Gweelo** Zimbabwe
89 F2 **Gwelo** *R* Zimbabwe
100 E4 **Gwendolen** Oregon
8 D4 **Gwent** *co* Wales
99 T3 **Gwinn** Michigan
98 J3 **Gwinner** N Dakota
139 J3 **Gwydir** *R* New S Wales
8 B1 **Gwynedd** *co* Wales
118 D6 **Gwynne** Alberta
19 J5 **Gy** France
66 C5 **Gyangrang** China
Gyangtse *see* **Gyangzê**
66 D6 **Gyangzê** China
67 D6 **Gyaring Co** *L* China
58 C5 **Gyaring Hu** *L* China
50 G1 **Gydanskiy Poluostrov** *pen* U.S.S.R.
75 L4 **Gyirong** China
66 F5 **Gyitang** China
8 C3 **Gylchedd** *mt* Wales
115 P5 **Gyldenløves Fjord** Greenland
28 H5 **Gyldenløves Høj** *hill* Denmark
26 N5 **Gyljen** Sweden
28 E5 **Gylling** Denmark
28 E5 **Gylling Næs** Denmark
141 L7 **Gympie** Queensland
68 B3 **Gyobingauk** Burma
61 N9 **Gyōda** Japan
48 F4 **Gyoma** Hungary
48 F3 **Gyöngyös** Hungary
48 F3 **Gyöngyös** *R* Hungary
48 E4 **Gyönk** Hungary
48 D3 **Györ** Hungary
48 D3 **Györ-Sopron** Hungary
106 D2 **Gypsum** Colorado
107 N3 **Gypsum** Kansas
143 F7 **Gypsum L** W Australia
117 Q5 **Gypsum Pt** N W Terr
119 T7 **Gypsumville** Manitoba
28 H5 **Gyrstinge** Denmark
27 J11 **Gysinge** Sweden
46 F2 **Gyueshovo** Bulgaria
48 G4 **Gyula** Hungary
52 D6 **Gzhat'** *R* U.S.S.R.
Gzhatsk *see* **Gagarin**
22 H2 **Haacht** Belgium
37 M4 **Haag** W Germany
25 G4 **Haaksbergen** Netherlands
137 S5 **Ha'apai Group** *islds* Tonga
29 L8 **Haapajärvi** Finland
29 L9 **Haapamäki** Finland
29 L7 **Haapavesi** Finland
52 B5 **Haapsalu** U.S.S.R.
25 C4 **Haarlem** Netherlands
32 G9 **Haarstrang** W Germany
144 B5 **Haast** New Zealand
140 B6 **Haast Bluff** N Terr Aust
25 C5 **Haastrecht** Netherlands
80 G4 **Habaka** Jordan
126 C3 **Habana** Cuba
83 K9 **Habarane** Sri Lanka
86 G5 **Habaswein** Kenya
114 H6 **Habay** Alberta
22 K4 **Habay-la-Neuve** Belgium
78 J5 **Habbamyah** Iraq
32 K10 **Habichtswald** *wood* W Germany
75 O6 **Habiganj** Bangladesh
65 C3 **Habirag** China
80 G7 **Habis** *R* Jordan
80 C5 **Habla** Israel
27 K14 **Hablingo** Sweden
27 G14 **Habo** Sweden
80 C3 **Ha Bonim** Israel
60 P1 **Hoboro** Japan
22 L3 **Habscheid** W Germany
61 N11 **Habuminato** Japan
131 B7 **Hachado, Paso de** Arg/Chile
32 G10 **Hachen** W Germany
36 D2 **Hachenburg** W Germany
59 L5 **Hachijō Jima** *isld* Japan
61 N5 **Hachimori** Japan
60 O2 **Hachinai dake** *mt* Japan
59 M3 **Hachinohe** Japan
59 L4 **Hachiōjio** Japan
106 B10 **Hachita** New Mexico
100 D8 **Hackamore** California
26 G9 **Hackås** Sweden
103 L6 **Hackberry** Arizona
111 C12 **Hackberry** Louisiana
107 K3 **Hackberry Cr** Kansas
118 E6 **Hackett** Alberta
110 B6 **Hackett** Arkansas
95 N6 **Hackettstown** New Jersey
111 J7 **Hackleburg** Alabama
138 E4 **Hack, Mt** S Australia
13 H5 **Hackness** England
87 C8 **Haco** Angola
68 H2 **Ha Coi** Vietnam
36 E3 **Hadamar** W Germany
80 C5 **Hadar** Israel
98 J7 **Hadar** Nebraska
72 H4 **Hadd, Al** Oman
107 N2 **Haddam** Kansas
9 G3 **Haddenham** England
13 F2 **Haddington** Scotland
146 D14 **Haddington, Mt** Antarctica
9 H2 **Haddiscoe** England
112 D4 **Haddock** Georgia
141 F7 **Haddon Corner** Qnsld/S Aust
138 F2 **Haddon Downs** S Australia
73 L8 **Haddunmahti Atoll** Maldives
85 F6 **Hadejia** *R* Nigeria
27 D11 **Hadeland** Norway
32 J5 **Hadeler Kanal** W Germany
32 K4 **Hademarschen** W Germany
141 K7 **Haden** Queensland
80 C4 **Hadera** Israel
80 C4 **Hadera** *R* Israel
38 N5 **Hadersdorf** Austria
28 C6 **Haderslev** Denmark
Haderslev *co see* **Sønderjylland**
28 B4 **Haderup** Denmark
72 F5 **Hadhramaut** *reg* S Yemen
72 G6 **Hadiboh** Socotra
72 E2 **Hadithah, Al** Iraq
9 G4 **Hadleigh** England
9 G3 **Hadleigh** Suffolk England
114 J3 **Hadley B** N W Terr
144 C6 **Hadlow** New Zealand
33 O9 **Hadmersleben** E Germany
26 G3 **Hadsel** Norway
26 G3 **Hadselöy** *isld* Norway
28 E4 **Hadsten** Denmark
28 E3 **Hadsund** Denmark
116 O3 **Hadweenzic** *R* Alaska
131 G3 **Haedo, Cuchilla de** *ra* Uruguay
65 F5 **Haeju** N Korea
80 C7 **Ha-Ela** Israel
28 E6 **Hæsinge** Denmark
41 O3 **Hafelekar Sp** *mt* Austria
80 C6 **Hafez Hayyim** Israel
33 N4 **Haffkrug-Scharbeutz** W Germany
115 N2 **Haffners Bjerg** *mt* Greenland
118 K6 **Hafford** Sask
43 C13 **Haffouz** Tunisia
78 F2 **Hafik** Turkey
74 E2 **Hafizabad** Pakistan
75 P6 **Haflong** India
38 H7 **Hafner** *mt* Austria
77 A4 **Haft Gel** Iran
77 H2 **Haftqala** *R* Afghanistan
Hafun *see* **Dante** Somalia
86 F3 **Hag Abdullah** Sudan
112 F5 **Hagan** Georgia
27 J11 **Hagaström** Sweden
22 L5 **Hage** W Germany
80 D3 **Ha Gelilit** Israel
33 R8 **Hagelsberg** *mt* E Germany
116 G7 **Hagemeister I** Alaska
119 M6 **Hagen** Sask
32 F10 **Hagen** W Germany
32 K8 **Hagenburg** W Germany
38 H6 **Hagen-Gebirge** *mts* Austria
33 O6 **Hagenow** E Germany
101 L7 **Hagerman** Idaho
106 F8 **Hagerman** New Mexico
27 H13 **Hagerstad** Sweden
94 B7 **Hagerstown** Indiana
94 K7 **Hagerstown** Maryland
120 K10 **Hagersville** Ontario
27 G11 **Hagfors** Sweden
26 G8 **Häggenås** Sweden
13 G2 **Haggerston** England
26 G8 **Häggsjön** Sweden
68 G1 **Ha Giang** Vietnam
48 K4 **Hăgimaș** *mt* Romania
61 L10 **Hagiwara** Japan
8 D3 **Hagley** England
20 K5 **Hagondage** France
112 G3 **Hagood** S Carolina
80 C5 **Hagor** Israel
80 F1 **Ha Goshrim** Israel
14 B4 **Hags Hd** Irish Rep
98 F3 **Hague** N Dakota
95 O3 **Hague** New York
118 L6 **Hague** Sask
20 B2 **Hague, C. de la** France

19	L4	**Haguenau** France
98	A9	**Hagues Pk** Colorado
		Hague, The *see* **Den Haag**
18	E9	**Haguetmau** France
85	B3	**Hagunia** Morocco
123	O3	**Haha Bay** Quebec
122	B5	**Ha Ha, L** Quebec
80	D6	**Ha Hamisha** Jordan
113	D7	**Hahira** Georgia
37	M4	**Hahnbach** W Germany
36	D2	**Hahnbei** W Germany
33	M9	**Hahnenklee-Bockswiese** W Germany
80	C3	**Ha Hoterim** Israel
67	C6	**Hai'an** China
67	G1	**Hai'an** China
65	E4	**Haicheng** China
67	F4	**Haicheng** China
37	N5	**Haidhof** W Germany
43	B13	**Haïdra** Tunisia
37	O5	**Haidstein** *mt* W Germany
68	H2	**Hai Duong** Vietnam
22	J2	**Haien** Belgium
80	C2	**Haifa** Israel
80	D2	**Haifa, Bay of** Israel
67	E5	**Haifeng** China
143	F9	**Haig** W Australia
36	E2	**Haiger** W Germany
36	F7	**Haigerloch** W Germany
117	P7	**Haig Lake** Alberta
98	E10	**Haigler** Nebraska
65	D5	**Hai He** *R* China
67	C6	**Haikang** China
60	C12	**Haiki** Japan
69	D9	**Hai,Ko** *isld* Thailand
68	K2	**Haikou** China
135	T3	**Haiku** Hawaiian Is
75	P6	**Hailakandi** India
59	G2	**Hailar** China
101	L6	**Hailey** Idaho
115	M8	**Haileybury** Ontario
107	P7	**Haileyville** Oklahoma
59	J3	**Hailin** China
67	D6	**Hailing Dao** *isld* China
65	J3	**Hailong** China
9	G6	**Hailsham** England
59	J2	**Hailun** China
29	L6	**Hailuoto** *isld* Finland
32	M8	**Haimar** W Germany
67	G1	**Haimen** China
67	G2	**Haimen** China
67	D7	**Hainan Dao** *isld* China
68	D2	**Hai-nang** Burma
		Hainan Strait *see* **Qiongzhou Haixia**
22	F2	**Hainaut** Belgium
22	F3	**Hainaut** France
31	K7	**Hainburg** Austria
117	F6	**Haines** Alaska
100	H5	**Haines** Oregon
22	G3	**Haine-St-Paul** Belgium
113	F9	**Haines City** Florida
114	F5	**Haines Junct** Yukon Terr
38	N5	**Hainfeld** Austria
68	B4	**Haing** *R* Burma
37	P2	**Hainichen** E Germany
67	G1	**Haining** China
33	N10	**Hainleite** E Germany
37	Q2	**Hainsberg** E Germany
94	D4	**Haintramck** Michigan
68	H2	**Haiphong** Vietnam
118	F5	**Hairy Hill** Alberta
65	E3	**Haisgai** China
127	H5	**Haiti** *rep* W Indies
68	J3	**Haitou** China
65	F2	**Haituo** China
103	N9	**Haivana Nakya** Arizona
102	G5	**Haiwee Res** California
65	D5	**Haixing** China
86	G2	**Haiya Junct** Sudan
65	E6	**Haiyang** China
65	F5	**Haiyang Dao** *isld* China
		Haiyou *see* **Sanmen**
67	B5	**Haiyuan** China
68	H1	**Haiyuan** China
48	G3	**Hajdú-Bihar** *co* Hungary
48	G3	**Hajdúböszörmény** Hungary
48	G3	**Hajdúdorog** Hungary
48	G3	**Hajdúhadház** Hungary
48	G3	**Hajdúnánás** Hungary
48	G3	**Hajdúszoboszlo** Hungary
61	M7	**Hajiki-saki** *C* Japan
79	G9	**Hājj** Saudi Arabia
31	O3	**Hajnówka** Poland
65	F7	**Hajo** *isld* S Korea
68	A1	**Haka** Burma
135	V5	**Hakalou** Hawaiian Is
80	G3	**Hakama** Jordan
87	E7	**Hakansson** *mts* Zaïre
27	F13	**Håkantorp** Sweden
144	A7	**Hakapoua, L** New Zealand
61	N8	**Hakase-yama** *mt* Japan
144	C6	**Hakataramea** New Zealand
60	G11	**Hakata shima** *isld* Japan
131	B8	**Hakelhuincul, Altiplanicie de** *plat* Argentina
78	J3	**Hakkari** Turkey
26	M5	**Hakkas** Sweden
61	O5	**Hakkōda san** Japan
60	Q1	**Hako dake** *mt* Japan
59	M3	**Hakodate** Japan
60	O4	**Hakodate wan** *B* Japan
61	K9	**Haku-san** *mt* Japan
61	K9	**Hakusan Nat. Park** Japan
		Hal *see* **Halle**
78	K4	**Halabja** Iraq
65	F2	**Halahai** China
86	G1	**Halaib** Sudan
79	D8	**Halâl, G** *mt* Egypt
48	G3	**Halasto** *L* Hungary
79	G9	**Halat 'Ammar** Saudi Arabia
48	K3	**Hălăuceşti** Romania
135	S2	**Halawa** Hawaiian Is Pacific Ocean
80	F4	**Halawa** Jordan
135	S2	**Halawa, C** Hawaiian Is
79	G4	**Halba** Lebanon
33	T8	**Halbe** E Germany
33	O9	**Halberstadt** E Germany
8	C6	**Halberton** England
119	O9	**Halbrite** Sask
145	E4	**Halcombe** New Zealand
71	E4	**Halcon, Mt** Philippines
117	P10	**Halcyon Hot Springs** Br Columbia
28	E3	**Hald** Århus Denmark
28	C3	**Hald** Viborg Denmark
28	H6	**Haldagerlille** Denmark
27	E12	**Halden** Norway
33	O8	**Haldensleben** E Germany
28	M1	**Haldersvig** Faeroes
28	C4	**Hald Sø** *L* Denmark
28	E4	**Haldum** Denmark
74	H4	**Haldwani** India
106	H2	**Hale** Colorado
94	D2	**Hale** Michigan
110	C2	**Hale** Missouri
140	D6	**Hale** *R* N Terr Aust
135	T3	**Haleakala Crater** Hawaiian Is
86	H3	**Haleb I** Red Sea
78	G4	**Halebiye** Syria
108	F1	**Hale Center** Texas
135	Q2	**Haleiwa** Hawaiian Is
143	B7	**Hale, Mt** W Australia
135	R2	**Halena** Hawaiian Is
112	B2	**Hales Bar Dam** Tennessee
9	D3	**Halesowen** England
9	G5	**Hale Street** England
9	H3	**Halesworth** England
111	J7	**Haleyville** Alabama
144	B7	**Half Moon B** New Zealand
9	E3	**Halford** England
107	K2	**Halford** Kansas
94	K7	**Halfway** Maryland
100	H5	**Halfway** Oregon
108	F1	**Halfway** Texas
117	M7	**Halfway** *R* Br Columbia
116	K6	**Halfway Mt** Alaska
25	C4	**Halfweg** Netherlands
80	B7	**Halib** Israel
121	M7	**Haliburton** Ontario
13	G6	**Halifax** England
112	K1	**Halifax** N Carolina
115	N9	**Halifax** Nova Scotia
95	L6	**Halifax** Pennsylvania
141	H4	**Halifax** Queensland
94	H10	**Halifax** Virginia
136	K5	**Halifax B** Queensland
141	H4	**Halifax, Mt** Queensland
29	K11	**Halikko** Finland
77	E5	**Halil** *R* Iran
79	G4	**Halimet el Qabu** *mt* Lebanon
70	L9	**Halimun, G** *mt* Java
86	A2	**Halin** Somalia
		Haliut *see* **Urad Zhonghou Lianheqi**
76	B3	**Haliyal** India
26	N4	**Halju** *mt* Sweden
28	D6	**Halk** Denmark
116	L1	**Halkett, C** Alaska
118	E6	**Halkirk** Alberta
15	E2	**Halkirk** Scotland
26	O2	**Halkkavarre** *mt* Norway
101	M3	**Hall** Montana
26	J8	**Hälla** Sweden
9	G6	**Halland** England
26	F8	**Håland** Sweden
27	F15	**Halland** *county* Sweden
113	G12	**Hallandale** Florida
27	F15	**Hallandsås** *hills* Sweden
28	K4	**Hallands Väderö** *isld* Sweden
138	D5	**Hall B** S Australia
115	N1	**Hall Basin** Canada/Greenland
119	S8	**Hallboro** Manitoba
22	G2	**Halle** Belgium
33	P10	**Halle** E Germany
32	H8	**Halle** W Germany
33	O9	**Halle** *reg* E Germany
27	H15	**Hälleberga** Sweden
120	G3	**Hallebourg** Ontario
28	G5	**Halleby Å** *R* Denmark
100	K9	**Halleck** Nevada
27	G12	**Hällefors** Sweden
38	H6	**Hallein** Austria
26	G8	**Hallen** Sweden
36	F1	**Hallenberg** W Germany
20	J2	**Hallencourt** France
28	F4	**Hallendrup** Denmark
26	H9	**Hällesjö** Sweden
109	L6	**Hallettsville** Texas
111	E8	**Halley** Arkansas
116	B6	**Hall I** Bering Sea
98	D2	**Halliday** N Dakota
98	A9	**Halligan Res** Colorado
27	D11	**Hallingdalselv** *R* Norway
27	C11	**Hallingskarvet** *mt* Norway
27	B11	**Hallingskeid** Norway
115	L4	**Hall Lake** *L* N W Terr
27	J11	**Hållnäs** Sweden
119	V10	**Hallock** Minnesota
118	K8	**Hallonquist** Sask
115	N5	**Hall Pen** N W Terr
110	G6	**Halls** Tennessee
8	C7	**Hallsands** England
27	H12	**Hallsberg** Sweden
142	G4	**Halls Creek** W Australia
37	K4	**Hallstadt** W Germany
27	H12	**Hallstahammar** Sweden
106	G3	**Hall Station** Colorado
38	J6	**Hallstatt** Austria
27	K11	**Hallstavik** Sweden
95	M5	**Hallstead** Pennsylvania
111	C9	**Hall Summit** Louisiana
110	D2	**Hallsville** Missouri
109	N3	**Hallsville** Texas
81	A8	**Hall Table Mt** Indian Oc
41	O3	**Halltal** Austria
94	J5	**Hallton** Pennsylvania
22	E2	**Halluin** France
25	E2	**Hallum** Netherlands
28	E2	**Hallund** Denmark
28	C5	**Hallundbæk** Denmark
26	H8	**Hallviken** Sweden
98	K1	**Halma** Minnesota
71	B2	**Halmahera** *isld* Indonesia
71	B3	**Halmahera** *sea* Indonesia
48	H3	**Halmeu** Romania
27	F15	**Halmstad** Sweden
43	C12	**Halq el Oued** Tunisia
28	E2	**Hals** Denmark
26	C8	**Halsa** Norway
37	P2	**Halsbrucke** E Germany
36	F2	**Halsdorf** W Germany
98	F8	**Halsey** Nebraska
100	B5	**Halsey** Oregon
71	D5	**Halsey Harbour** Philippines
28	H5	**Halsnæs** *pen* Denmark
28	G6	**Halsskov** Denmark
98	K2	**Halstad** Minnesota
9	G4	**Halstead** England
107	N4	**Halstead** Kansas
36	B5	**Halstroff** France
29	L8	**Halsua** Finland
26	E9	**Haltdalen** Norway
26	D7	**Halten** Norway
32	F9	**Haltern** W Germany
29	J2	**Haltia** *mt* Finland
109	M9	**Haltom City** Texas
13	F4	**Haltwhistle** England
77	C7	**Hālūl** *isld* Qatar
36	C1	**Halver** W Germany
118	L8	**Halvorgate** Sask
28	D2	**Halvrimmen** Denmark
141	K7	**Haly, Mt** Queensland
22	E4	**Ham** France
80	G3	**Ham** Jordan
60	F12	**Hama** Japan
79	G3	**Hama** Syria
60	F11	**Hamada** Japan
85	F3	**Hamada de Tinrhert** *stony des* Algeria
85	D4	**Hamada El Haricha** *reg* Mali
72	F2	**Hamadān** Iran
85	C3	**Hamada Tounassine** *stony des* Algeria
80	F3	**Hamadya** Israel
61	P13	**Hamahika-jima** *isld* Okinawa
61	L11	**Hamakita** Japan
60	P2	**Hamamasu** Japan
59	L5	**Hamamatsu** Japan
60	T2	**Hamanaka** Japan
61	L11	**Hamana ko** *L* Japan
80	C4	**Ha Ma 'Pil** Israel
98	H2	**Hamar** N Dakota
27	E11	**Hamar** Norway
26	H3	**Hamaröy** Norway
60	H10	**Hamasaka** Japan
84	J5	**Hamâta, Gebel** *mt* Egypt
80	F3	**Hamat Gader** Jordan
60	Q1	**Hama-Tombetsu** Japan
36	C5	**Hambach** France
83	L11	**Hambantota** Sri Lanka
98	G2	**Hamberg** N Dakota
32	J6	**Hambergen** W Germany
117	O9	**Hamber Prov. Park** Br Columbia
9	F5	**Hambledon** England
13	G6	**Hambleton** England
13	G5	**Hambleton Hills** England
100	D8	**Hambone** California
32	L7	**Hambühren** W Germany
111	E8	**Hamburg** Arkansas
100	B8	**Hamburg** California
99	L9	**Hamburg** Iowa
95	N5	**Hamburg** New Jersey
94	J4	**Hamburg** New York
95	M6	**Hamburg** Pennsylvania
34		**Hamburg** *conurbation* W Germany
20	C4	**Hambye** France
79	G3	**Hamdānīya** Syria
95	M4	**Hamden** New York
94	E7	**Hamden** Ohio
29	L10	**Hame** *prov* Finland
29	K10	**Hämeenkyrö** Finland
29	L11	**Hämeenlinna** Finland
143	A10	**Hamelin B** W Australia
143	A7	**Hamelin Pool** W Australia
32	K8	**Hameln** W Germany
101	N6	**Hamer** Idaho
33	O8	**Hamersleben** E Germany
142	C5	**Hamersley** W Australia
142	B5	**Hamersley Ra** W Australia
33	P7	**Hamerten** E Germany
65	G5	**Hamhŭng** N Korea
66	E3	**Hami** China
111	J7	**Hamilton** Alabama
90	B2	**Hamilton** Bermuda
101	S9	**Hamilton** Colorado
111	M9	**Hamilton** Georgia
99	P9	**Hamilton** Illinois
94	C5	**Hamilton** Indiana
107	O4	**Hamilton** Kansas
94	A4	**Hamilton** Michigan
114	H8	**Hamilton** Montana
119	U10	**Hamilton** N Dakota
95	M4	**Hamilton** New York
145	E2	**Hamilton New Zealand**
94	C7	**Hamilton** Ohio
115	M9	**Hamilton** Ontario
100	F5	**Hamilton** Oregon
140	F6	**Hamilton** Queensland
12	D2	**Hamilton** Scotland
139	H8	**Hamilton** Tasmania
109	J4	**Hamilton** Texas
138	F6	**Hamilton** Victoria
100	D1	**Hamilton** Washington
140	F6	**Hamilton** *R* Queensland
138	C2	**Hamilton** *R* S Australia
102	C2	**Hamilton City** California
101	R6	**Hamilton Dome** Wyoming
140	C6	**Hamilton Downs** N Terr Aust
115	O7	**Hamilton Inlet** Labrador
111	C7	**Hamilton,L** Arkansas
103	J2	**Hamilton, Mt** Nevada
29	N11	**Hamina** Finland
74	J6	**Hamirpur** India
		Hamitabat *see* **Isparta**
94	C5	**Hamler** Ohio
94	A5	**Hamlet** Indiana
112	H3	**Hamlet** N Carolina
98	E9	**Hamlet** Nebraska
142	B6	**Hamlet, Mt** W Australia
138	E5	**Hamley Bridge** S Australia
94	K3	**Hamlin** New York
108	G3	**Hamlin** Texas
94	E8	**Hamlin** W Virginia
94	A2	**Hamlin L** Michigan
32	G9	**Hamm** W Germany
84	E4	**Hammādāh Al Hamrā** *plat* Libya
17	G9	**Hammam Bou Hadjar** Algeria
43	D12	**Hammamet** Tunisia
85	G1	**Hammamet, G de** Tunisia
85	G1	**Hammam Lif** Tunisia
29	H11	**Hammarland** Finland
27	F11	**Hammarsbyn** Sweden
29	M3	**Hammastunturi** *mt* Finland
22	G1	**Hamme** Belgium
32	J6	**Hamme** *R* W Germany
28	D4	**Hammel** Denmark
36	H3	**Hammelburg** W Germany
28	C6	**Hammelev** Denmark
28	F4	**Hammelev** Denmark
33	S6	**Hammelspring** E Germany
22	H2	**Hamme-Mille** Belgium
26	H8	**Hammerdal** Sweden
147	H14	**Hammerfest** Norway
28	D3	**Hammershøj** Denmark
36	C3	**Hammerstein** W Germany
13	G6	**Hammerton** England
28	C4	**Hammerum** Denmark
100	K7	**Hammett** Idaho
32	E9	**Hamminkeln** W Germany
107	L6	**Hammon** Oklahoma
99	T8	**Hammond** Illinois
110	H2	**Hammond** Illinois
111	F11	**Hammond** Louisiana
98	B4	**Hammond** Montana
95	M2	**Hammond** New York
100	B3	**Hammond** Oregon
138	E4	**Hammond** S Australia
99	O5	**Hammond** Wisconsin
94	D1	**Hammond B** Michigan
141	F1	**Hammond I** Queensland
95	K4	**Hammondsport** New York
122	G8	**Hammond Vale** New Brunswick
102	C2	**Hammonton** California
95	N7	**Hammonton** New Jersey
26	O1	**Hamnbukt** Norway
26	L2	**Hamneidet** Norway
26	S1	**Hamningberg** Norway
68	G7	**Ham Ninh** Vietnam
121	T7	**Ham Nord** Quebec
26	L4	**Håmojokk** Sweden
22	K1	**Hamont** Belgium
86	G2	**Hamoyet, Jebel** *mt* Sudan
98	H1	**Hampden** N Dakota
144	C6	**Hampden New Zealand**
115	O8	**Hampden** Nfld
95	T2	**Hampden Highlands** Maine
28	C4	**Hampen** Denmark
36	B6	**Hampont** France
9	E5	**Hampshire** *co* England
95	K7	**Hampstead** Maryland
112	K3	**Hampstead** N Carolina
122	F8	**Hampstead** New Brunswick
111	D8	**Hampton** Arkansas
9	F5	**Hampton** England
113	E8	**Hampton** Florida
111	M8	**Hampton** Georgia
99	N7	**Hampton** Iowa
98	J9	**Hampton** Nebraska
122	G8	**Hampton** New Brunswick
95	R4	**Hampton** New Hampshire
100	E6	**Hampton** Oregon
112	F5	**Hampton** S Carolina
95	L9	**Hampton** Virginia
101	P8	**Hampton** Wyoming
95	P6	**Hampton Bays** Long I, N Y
142	B5	**Hampton Harb** W Australia
143	F9	**Hampton Tableland** W Australia
27	H10	**Hamra** Sweden
27	J11	**Hamrånge** Sweden
101	P7	**Hams Fork** *R* Wyoming
9	G5	**Ham Street** England
68	H7	**Ham Tan** Vietnam
135	T3	**Hana** Hawaiian Is
126	D3	**Hanábana** *R* Cuba
135	O1	**Hanalei** Hawaiian Is
135	T3	**Hanamanioa, C** Hawaiian Is
135	O1	**Hanamaulu** Hawaiian Is
135	O1	**Hanapepe** Hawaiian Is
61	N13	**Hanare-iwa** *islds* Japan
36	F3	**Hanau** W Germany
102	S12	**Hanauma B** Hawaiian Is
121	L5	**Hanbury** Ontario
111	K7	**Hanceville** Alabama
117	M10	**Hanceville** Br Col
58	F4	**Hancheng** China
67	D1	**Hanchuan** China
95	T2	**Hancock** Maine
94	J7	**Hancock** Maryland
99	S2	**Hancock** Michigan
99	L4	**Hancock** Minnesota
95	P4	**Hancock** New Hampshire
95	M5	**Hancock** New York
99	R5	**Hancock** Wisconsin
113	F10	**Hancock, L** Florida
61	K11	**Handa** Japan
58	F4	**Handan** China
28	B4	**Handbjerg** Denmark
9	F5	**Handcross** England
118	J6	**Handel** Sask
27	K12	**Handen** Sweden
88	G4	**Handeni** Tanzania
28	D3	**Handest** Denmark
70	C6	**Handjalipan** Kalimantan
109	K3	**Handley** Texas
119	P9	**Handsworth** Sask
32	K4	**Hanerau** W Germany
102	E5	**Hanford** California
100	F3	**Hanford** Washington
76	B3	**Hangal** India
68	C5	**Hangan** Burma
65	G6	**Hangang** *R* S Korea
145	F3	**Hangaroa New Zealand**
27	C11	**Hangastöl** Norway
145	E3	**Hangatiki New Zealand**
58	C2	**Hangayn Nuruu** *mt* Mongolia
		Hangchow *see* **Hangzhou**
33	T8	**Hangelsberg** E Germany
27	G14	**Hånger** Sweden
58	E3	**Hanggin Houqi** China
94	E8	**Hanging Rock** Ohio
89	A10	**Hangklip, C** S Africa
100	H2	**Hangman Cr** Washington
29	K12	**Hango** Finland
65	D5	**Hangu** China
67	D4	**Hanguang** China
59	H5	**Hangzhou** China
59	H5	**Hangzhou Wan** *B* China
32	M7	**Hänigsen** W Germany
86	H3	**Hanish I** Red Sea
80	D1	**Hanita** Israel
		Hanjiang *see* **Yangzhou**
67	F4	**Hanjiang** China
29	M9	**Hankasalmi** Finland
85	C4	**Hank, El** Mauritania
98	J3	**Hankinson** N Dakota
58	F5	**Hankou** China
103	O3	**Hanksville** Utah
8	D1	**Hanley** England
118	L7	**Hanley** Sask
99	L5	**Hanley Falls** Minnesota
144	D5	**Hanmer Springs** New Zealand
118	F7	**Hanna** Alberta
101	P9	**Hanna** Utah
101	T8	**Hanna** Wyoming
98	H2	**Hannaford** N Dakota
119	T10	**Hannah** N Dakota
120	K1	**Hannah B** Ontario
99	P10	**Hannibal** Missouri
99	Q4	**Hannibal** Wisconsin
28	A4	**Hanning Kirke** Denmark
142	F3	**Hann, Mt** W Australia
98	E2	**Hannover** N Dakota
32	L8	**Hannover** W Germany
140	C6	**Hann Ra** N Terr **Aust**
22	J2	**Hannut** Belgium
27	H16	**Hanöbukten** *B* Sweden
68	G2	**Hanoi** Vietnam
48	D4	**Hanót** Hungary
107	O2	**Hanover** Kansas
99	N4	**Hanover** Minnesota
101	Q2	**Hanover** Montana
95	P3	**Hanover** New Hampshire
120	J8	**Hanover** Ontario
89	D8	**Hanover** S Africa
127	H1	**Hanover** *parish* Jamaica
133	C8	**Hanover, I** Chile
48	E6	**Han Pijesak** Yugoslavia
48	D3	**Hanság** Hungary
117	N8	**Hansard** Br Columbia
98	G1	**Hansboro** N Dakota
120	F3	**Hansen** Ontario
146	B5	**Hansen Mt** Antarctica
67	F1	**Hanshan** China
67	D2	**Hanshou** China
58	E5	**Han Shui** *R* China
67	D1	**Han Shui** *R* China
74	F4	**Hansi** India
27	G10	**Hansjö** Sweden
140	C5	**Hanson** *R* N Terr **Aust**
119	P4	**Hanson L** Sask
138	D4	**Hanson, L** S Australia
28	D5	**Hansted** Vejle Denmark
28	B2	**Hanstholm Havn** *C* Denmark
65	D2	**Han Sum** China
22	J3	**Han-sur-Lesse** Belgium
25	B6	**Hansweert** Netherlands
		Hantan *see* **Handan**
		Hanting *see* **Wei Xian**
		Hants *co see* **Hampshire**
122	H8	**Hantsport** Nova Scotia
36	C7	**Hantz, Col du** *pass* France
65	D2	**Han Ul** China
67	A1	**Hanwang** China
83	K11	**Hanwella** Sri Lanka
58	F5	**Hanyang** China
58	D6	**Hanyuan** China
58	E5	**Hanzhong** China
65	D7	**Hanzhuang** China
135	N10	**Hao** *atoll* Tuamotu Arch Pacific Oc
65	H1	**Haolianghe** China
80	F3	**Ha On** Israel
26	N6	**Haparanda** Sweden
71	B1	**Hapo** Halmahera **Indonesia**
9	H2	**Happisburgh** England
100	B8	**Happy Camp** California
140	E5	**Happy Cr** N Terr Aust
144	D5	**Hapuku New Zealand**
83	L11	**Haputale** Sri Lanka
79	E9	**Haql** Saudi Arabia
58	E2	**Hara** Mongolia
26	M5	**Harads** Sweden
86	H4	**Hara Fanna** Ethiopia
111	H12	**Harahan** New Orleans
26	B9	**Haram** Norway
59	M4	**Haramachi** Japan
86	H4	**Harar** Ethiopia
86	A3	**Harardera** Somalia
		Harare *see* **Salisbury** Zimbabwe
58	E2	**Har-ayrag** Mongolia
86	C3	**Haraz Djombo** Chad
86	D3	**Haraze** Chad
80	E8	**Har Ben Yai'r** Israel
65	G2	**Harbin** China
27	J11	**Harbo** Sweden
77	K5	**Harboi Hills** Pakistan
28	J7	**Hårbølle** Denmark
22	D4	**Harbonnières** France
28	A3	**Harboør** Denmark
28	A3	**Harboør Tange** *pen* Denmark
100	A7	**Harbor** Oregon
94	E3	**Harbor Beach** Michigan
117	E6	**Harbor Pt** Alaska
94	B1	**Harbor Springs** Michigan
13	F3	**Harbottle** England
115	O8	**Harbour Breton** Nfld
123	S6	**Harbour Buffett** Nfld
113	K12	**Harbour Cay, Little** *isld* Bahamas
123	Q3	**Harbour Deep** Nfld
115	O8	**Harbour Grace** Nfld
113	L12	**Harbour I** Bahamas
123	S6	**Harbour Mille** Nfld
122	H8	**Harbourville** Nova Scotia
37	K6	**Harburg** Bayern W Germany
32	L6	**Harburg** Niedersachsen W Germany
28	E6	**Hårby** Denmark
122	G7	**Harcourt** New Brunswick
103	L7	**Harcuvar Mts** Arizona
74	G7	**Harda** India
27	B11	**Hardanger** Norway
27	B11	**Hardanger-fjorden** *inlet* Norway
27	C11	**Hardangervidda** *plat* Norway
89	A5	**Hardap Dam** Namibia
111	F9	**Hardee** Mississippi
112	F5	**Hardeeville** S Carolina
25	E2	**Hardegarijp** Netherlands
32	L9	**Hardegsen** W Germany
22	B2	**Hardelot-Plage** France
25	G3	**Hardenberg** Netherlands
70	D2	**Harden, Bt** *mt* Kalimantan
25	E4	**Harderwijk** Netherlands
107	J5	**Hardesty** Oklahoma
142	B6	**Hardey, R** W Australia
36	H4	**Hardheim** W Germany
110	F2	**Hardin** Illinois
110	C2	**Hardin** Missouri
114	J8	**Hardin** Montana
99	M3	**Harding** Minnesota
87	E12	**Harding** S Africa
116	M6	**Harding Icefield** Alaska
111	L9	**Harding, L** Georgia
119	T2	**Harding L** Manitoba
110	K4	**Hardinsburg** Kentucky
118	F6	**Hardisty** Alberta
117	P3	**Hardisty L** N W Terr
20	K2	**Hardivillers** France
100	F4	**Hardman** Oregon
142	E4	**Hardman, Mt** W Australia
80	D8	**Hardof** *R* Jordan
74	H4	**Hardwar** India
98	K6	**Hardwick** Minnesota
95	P2	**Hardwick** Vermont
8	D4	**Hardwicke** England
138	D5	**Hardwicke B** S Australia
110	E5	**Hardy** Arkansas
101	O2	**Hardy** Montana
119	N9	**Hardy** Sask
145	F2	**Hardy, Mt** New Zealand
133	D9	**Hardy, Pen** Chile
94	B3	**Hardy Res** Michigan
123	S5	**Hare B** Nfld
80	E4	**Hare Gilboa** Israel
26	B9	**Hareid** Norway
22	E2	**Harelbeke** Belgium
32	F7	**Haren** W Germany
115	O3	**Hare Øen** *isld* Greenland
9	F1	**Hare Park** England
13	G6	**Harewood** England
79	F5	**Harf el Mreffi** *mt* Lebanon
20	F3	**Harfleur** France
27	K11	**Harg** Sweden
36	B5	**Hargarten aux Mines** France
86	H4	**Hargeisa** Somalia
48	K4	**Harghitei Muntii** *mt* Romania
22	E4	**Hargicourt** France
109	J9	**Hargill** Texas
22	J3	**Hargimont** Belgium
22	H3	**Hargnies** France
119	Q9	**Hargrave** Manitoba
119	S4	**Hargrave L** Manitoba
79	E8	**Har Hakippa** *mt* Israel
79	E8	**Har Harif** Israel
80	D8	**Har Hezron** Israel
66	F4	**Har Hu** *L* China
61	M9	**Hari** Japan
76	B3	**Harihar** India
144	C5	**Harihari** New Zealand
60	H11	**Harima-nada** *sea* Japan
25	B5	**Haringvliet** Netherlands
74	E1	**Haripur** Pakistan
77	J2	**Hari Rud** *R* Afghanistan/Iran
79	G6	**Harir, Wādi** *watercourse* Syria
87	C10	**Haris** Namibia
26	G10	**Härjån** *R* Sweden
29	J10	**Harjavalta** Finland
26	F10	**Härjehågna** *mt* Sweden
80	F2	**Har Kena'an** *peak* Israel
112	L3	**Harkers I** N Carolina
99	L8	**Harlan** Iowa
107	M2	**Harlan** Kansas
94	D10	**Harlan** Kentucky
98	G9	**Harlan Co. Res** Nebraska
22	K4	**Harlange** Luxembourg
32	G5	**Harle** W Germany
8	B2	**Harlech** Wales
112	E4	**Harlem** Georgia
101	R1	**Harlem** Montana
32	L5	**Harlesiel** W Germany
9	H3	**Harleston** England
28	D4	**Harlev** Denmark
28	J6	**Hårlev** Denmark
112	G4	**Harleyville** S Carolina
25	D2	**Harlingen** Netherlands
109	K9	**Harlingen** Texas
32	G5	**Harlinger Land** W Germany
33	M9	**Harlingerode** W Germany
9	G4	**Harlow** England
98	G1	**Harlow** N Dakota
101	Q3	**Harlowton** Montana
94	H8	**Harman** W Virginia
47	K5	**Harmancık** Turkey
26	J10	**Harmånger** Sweden
25	C4	**Harmelen** Netherlands
80	E2	**Har Meron** *peak* Israel
107	L5	**Harmon** Oklahoma
118	A2	**Harmon R** Alberta
95	S2	**Harmony** Maine
99	O6	**Harmony** Minnesota
79	E8	**Har Natha** *mt* Israel
100	G6	**Harney** Oregon
100	F6	**Harney Basin** *reg* Oregon
113	F9	**Harney, L** Florida
100	F6	**Harney L** Oregon
98	C6	**Harney Pk** S Dakota
28	E6	**Harnorup** Denmark
26	J9	**Härnösand** Sweden
65	E2	**Har Nur** China
58	B2	**Har Nuur** *L* Mongolia
80	E3	**Harod** *R* Israel
26	B9	**Haröy** *isld* Norway
9	F4	**Harpenden** England
107	M4	**Harper** Kansas
85	C8	**Harper** Liberia
100	H6	**Harper** Oregon
109	H5	**Harper** Texas
116	L4	**Harper Bend** Alaska
117	Q6	**Harper Cr** Alberta
102	G6	**Harper L** California
116	Q4	**Harper, Mt** Alaska
144	C5	**Harper Pass** New Zealand
94	K7	**Harpers Ferry** W Virginia
140	C5	**Harper Springs** N Terr Aust
110	J5	**Harpeth** *R* Tennessee
8	C6	**Harpford** England
9	G2	**Harpley** England
27	F15	**Harplinge** Sweden
32	J7	**Harpstedt** W Germany
119	M9	**Harptree** Sask
65	D4	**Harqin** China
65	D4	**Harqin Qi** China
103	L8	**Harquahala Mts** Arizona
85	E1	**Harrach, El** Algeria
107	N6	**Harrah** Oklahoma
26	F7	**Harran** Norway
37	K3	**Harras** E Germany
28	B3	**Harre** Denmark
111	D8	**Harrell** Arkansas
144	D5	**Harrelville** New Zealand
115	M7	**Harricana** *R* Quebec
28	E3	**Harridslev** Denmark
94	B2	**Harrietta** Michigan
112	C2	**Harriman** Tennessee
95	M8	**Harrington** Delaware
95	U2	**Harrington** Maine
100	G2	**Harrington** Washington
115	O7	**Harrington Harbour** Quebec
119	P2	**Harriot L** Sask
100	B9	**Harris** California
99	N9	**Harris** Missouri
118	K7	**Harris** Sask
15	B3	**Harris** *div* Scotland
110	F6	**Harrisburg** Arkansas
110	H4	**Harrisburg** Illinois
98	C8	**Harrisburg** Nebraska
94	D7	**Harrisburg** Ohio
100	B5	**Harrisburg** Oregon
95	L6	**Harrisburg** Pennsylvania
98	K6	**Harrisburg** S Dakota
118	H2	**Harris Hill** Ontario
113	F9	**Harris, L** Florida
138	D4	**Harris, L** S Australia
89	F7	**Harrismith** S Africa
143	C10	**Harrismith** W Australia
140	A6	**Harris, Mt** N Terr Aust
144	B6	**Harris Mts New Zealand**
110	C5	**Harrison** Arkansas
112	E5	**Harrison** Georgia
100	J2	**Harrison** Idaho
94	C2	**Harrison** Michigan
101	O4	**Harrison** Montana
98	C7	**Harrison** Nebraska
98	H6	**Harrison** S Dakota
116	L1	**Harrison B** Alaska
111	E10	**Harrisonburg** Louisiana
94	J8	**Harrisonburg** Virginia
115	O7	**Harrison, C** Labrador
117	M11	**Harrison L** Br Columbia
83	K12	**Harrison, Mt** Mahé I Ind Oc
110	B3	**Harrisonville** Missouri
94	D2	**Harrisville** Michigan
95	M2	**Harrisville** New York
94	F7	**Harrisville** W Virginia
110	K2	**Harrodsburg** Indiana
94	C9	**Harrodsburg** Kentucky
13	G6	**Harrogate** England
98	G5	**Harrold** S Dakota
109	H1	**Harrold** Texas
9	F4	**Harrow** England
120	H10	**Harrow** Ontario
119	Q8	**Harrowby** Manitoba
26	H7	**Harrsjön** Sweden
27	F14	**Härryda** Sweden
98	F9	**Harry Strunk L** Nebraska
79	E8	**Har Saggi** *mt* Israel
32	K6	**Harsefeld** W Germany
32	H9	**Harsewinkel** W Germany
78	G1	**Harsit** Turkey
26	L5	**Harsprånget** Sweden
26	J3	**Harstad** Norway
32	L8	**Harsum** W Germany
28	A4	**Harsyssel** *reg* Denmark
13	G4	**Hart** England
99	U6	**Hart** Michigan
119	M9	**Hart** Sask
65	E3	**Hartao** China
89	B7	**Hartbees** *watercourse* S Africa
38	N7	**Hartberg** Austria
89	E5	**Hartebeespoort Dam** S Africa
27	B11	**Hårteigen** *mt* Norway
118	C8	**Hartell** Alberta
22	E5	**Hartennes-et-Taux** France
36	E2	**Hartenrod** W Germany
37	O2	**Hartenstein** E Germany
37	J5	**Hartershofen** W Germany
15	E5	**Hart Fell** Scotland
9	G5	**Hartfield** England
111	L10	**Hartford** Alabama
109	N1	**Hartford** Arkansas
95	P5	**Hartford** Connecticut
107	P3	**Hartford** Kansas
110	K4	**Hartford** Kentucky
94	A4	**Hartford** Michigan
94	E6	**Hartford** Ohio
112	D2	**Hartford** Tennessee
99	S6	**Hartford** Wisconsin
94	B6	**Hartford City** Indiana
95	P5	**Hartford, E** Connecticut
37	O1	**Hartha** E Germany
37	O2	**Harthau** E Germany
12	E2	**Harthill** Scotland
9	E1	**Hartington** England
98	J7	**Hartington** Nebraska
80	E2	**Har Tir'an** Israel
122	D2	**Hart-jaune, R** Quebec
138	D4	**Hart, L** S Australia
8	B6	**Hartland** England
95	S2	**Hartland** Maine
122	E7	**Hartland** New Brunswick
8	B5	**Hartland Pt** England
8	D3	**Hartlebury** England
13	G4	**Hartlepool** England
13	G3	**Hartley** England
99	L6	**Hartley** Iowa
108	B8	**Hartley** Texas
89	G2	**Hartley** Zimbabwe
117	J9	**Hartley Bay** Br Columbia
9	F5	**Hartley Wintney** England
100	F2	**Hartline** Washington
106	H3	**Hartman** Colorado
37	P5	**Hartmanice** Czechoslovakia
37	O2	**Hartmannsdorf** E Germany
36	G3	**Hartmannshain** W Germany
119	Q6	**Hart Mt** Manitoba
100	F7	**Hart Mt** Oregon
142	F3	**Hart, Mt** W Australia
119	R9	**Hartney** Manitoba
29	M10	**Hartola** Finland
13	G4	**Harton** England
106	E2	**Hartsel** Colorado
111	K7	**Hartselle** Alabama
37	J6	**Härtsfeld** *mts* W Germany
107	P7	**Hartshorne** Oklahoma
138	C4	**Harts I** S Australia
140	C6	**Harts Range** N Terr **Aust**
112	G3	**Hartsville** S Carolina
110	K5	**Hartsville** Tennessee
89	D6	**Hartswater** S Africa
80	C6	**Hartuv** Israel
110	D4	**Hartville** Missouri
98	B7	**Hartville** Wyoming
112	E3	**Hartwell** Georgia
112	D3	**Hartwell Res** S Carolina
120	H3	**Harty** Ontario
89	D6	**Hartz** *R* S Africa
84	F4	**Harūj al Aswad, Al** Libya
58	B2	**Har Us Nuur** *L* Mongolia
80	C7	**Haruvit** Israel
102	H7	**Harvard** California
100	J3	**Harvard** Idaho
99	S7	**Harvard** Illinois
98	H9	**Harvard** Nebraska
116	O6	**Harvard Gl** Alaska
106	D3	**Harvard, Mt** Colorado
143	F7	**Harvest, Mt** W Australia
99	T8	**Harvey** Illinois
99	O8	**Harvey** Iowa
98	F2	**Harvey** N Dakota
111	J13	**Harvey** New Orleans
143	B10	**Harvey** W Australia
102	C1	**Harvey Mt** California
122	F8	**Harvey Stn** New Brunswick
107	P3	**Harveyville** Kansas
110	F5	**Harviell** Missouri
9	E4	**Harwell** England
9	H4	**Harwich** England
109	K6	**Harwood** Texas
36	E4	**Harxheim** W Germany
74	F4	**Haryana** *prov* India
80	E8	**Har Yonatan** Israel
33	N9	**Harz** *mts* Germany
33	O9	**Harzgerode** E Germany
79	F8	**Hāsā** Jordan
72	F4	**Hasā, Al** *reg* Saudi Arabia
74	H9	**Hasanparti** India
80	E7	**Hasasa** *R* Jordan
79	F5	**Hâsbaiya** Lebanon
32	G8	**Hasbergen** W Germany
36	B5	**Hasborn-Dautweiler** W Germany
32	G7	**Hase** *R* W Germany
78	H3	**Haseke, El** Syria
37	K2	**Hasel** *R* E Germany
32	L5	**Haseldorf** W Germany
32	F7	**Haselünne** W Germany
80	D4	**Hashimiye** Jordan
61	J11	**Hashimoto** Japan
78	M2	**Hashtpar** Iran
77	A1	**Hashtrūd** Iran
71	B3	**Hasil** Indonesia
26	H8	**Håsjö** Sweden
111	D7	**Haskell** Arkansas
107	P6	**Haskell** Oklahoma
108	H2	**Haskell** Texas
38	K4	**Haslach** Austria
36	E7	**Haslach** W Germany
27	G16	**Hasle** Denmark
109	M8	**Haslet** Texas
28	H6	**Haslev** Denmark
13	F6	**Haslingden** England
41	H4	**Hasli Tal** Switzerland
28	E4	**Haslund** Denmark
28	E5	**Hasmark** Denmark
22	E3	**Hasnon** France
80	D3	**Ha Solelim** Israel
18	E9	**Hasparren** France
32	F10	**Haspe** W Germany
22	E3	**Haspres** France
76	C4	**Hassan** India
103	M8	**Hassayampa** *R* Arizona
37	K3	**Hassberge** *mts* W Germany
26	J9	**Hassela** Sweden
33	N9	**Hasselfelde** E Germany
115	K2	**Hassel Sd** N W Terr
22	J2	**Hasselt** Belgium
25	F3	**Hasselt** Netherlands
28	F4	**Hassensør** *C* Denmark
33	N9	**Hasserode** E Germany
37	K3	**Hassfurt** W Germany
85	E2	**Hassi-Bou-Zid** Algeria
85	E3	**Hassi Chebaba** Algeria
28	A3	**Hassing** Denmark
79	H3	**Hass, Jebel el** *mts* Syria
37	L3	**Hasslach** W Germany
33	T6	**Hassleben** E Germany
37	K1	**Hassleben** Erfurt E Germany
27	G15	**Hässleholm** Sweden
27	G13	**Hasslerör** Sweden
36	E5	**Hassloch** W Germany
22	H3	**Hastière-Lavaux** Belgium
127	P6	**Hastings** Barbados
9	G6	**Hastings** England
113	F8	**Hastings** Florida
99	L9	**Hastings** Iowa
94	B4	**Hastings** Michigan
99	O5	**Hastings** Minnesota
98	H9	**Hastings** Nebraska
145	F3	**Hastings New Zealand**
107	M7	**Hastings** Oklahoma
121	N8	**Hastings** Ontario
94	J6	**Hastings** Pennsylvania
139	H9	**Hastings** Tasmania
139	L4	**Hastings** *R* New S Wales
139	K4	**Hastings Ra** *mts* New S Wales
28	E6	**Håstrup** Denmark
27	G15	**Hästveda** Sweden
106	H3	**Hasty** Colorado
26	M1	**Hasvik** Norway
106	G3	**Haswell** Colorado
58	E3	**Hatanbulag** Mongolia
95	M6	**Hatboro** Pennsylvania
106	C9	**Hatch** New Mexico
103	M4	**Hatch** Utah
140	D5	**Hatches Cr** N Terr Aust
126	F2	**Hatchet Bay** Eleuthera Bahamas
110	G6	**Hatchie** *R* Tennessee
98	B7	**Hat Cr** Wyoming
100	D9	**Hat Creek** California
48	H5	**Haţeg** Romania
67	H4	**Haterumashima** Japan
111	B7	**Hatfield** Arkansas
9	F4	**Hatfield** Herts **England**
98	K6	**Hatfield** Minnesota
139	G5	**Hatfield** New S Wales
119	M7	**Hatfield** Sask
9	G4	**Hatfield Peverel** England
101	T3	**Hathaway** Montana
8	B6	**Hatherleigh** England
138	F6	**Hatherleigh** S Australia
9	E1	**Hathersage** England
74	H5	**Hathras** India
68	G7	**Ha Tien** Vietnam
80	G3	**Hatim** Jordan
68	G3	**Ha Tinh** Vietnam
127	K5	**Hato Mayor** Dominican Rep
56	C3	**Hatskiy** U.S.S.R.
60	F11	**Hatsukaichi** Japan
138	F5	**Hattah** Victoria
70	F2	**Hattan, Mt** Sabah
25	F4	**Hattem** Netherlands
36	D6	**Hatten** France
112	M2	**Hatteras** N Carolina
112	M2	**Hatteras Inlet** N Carolina
36	E3	**Hattersheim** W Germany
28	O9	**Hattervig** Faeroes
26	G6	**Hattfjelldal** Norway
111	G10	**Hattiesburg** Mississippi
36	B6	**Hattigny** France
28	D5	**Hatting** Denmark
32	F10	**Hattingen** W Germany
20	K3	**Hatton** France
98	J2	**Hatton** N Dakota
118	H8	**Hatton** Sask
100	G3	**Hatton** Washington
68	C6	**Hattras Passage** Burma
40	F1	**Hattstatt** France
29	L10	**Hattula** Finland
126	F4	**Hatuey** Cuba
145	F4	**Hatuma New Zealand**
48	F3	**Hatvan** Hungary
38	O8	**Hatzendorf** Austria
36	C3	**Hatzenport** W Germany
36	F2	**Hatzfeld** W Germany
68	J6	**Hau Bon** Vietnam
22	D2	**Haubourdin** France
86	A2	**Haud** *reg* Ethiopia
80	G4	**Haufa** Jordan
28	C4	**Hauge** Denmark
27	C10	**Hauge** Norway
99	P4	**Haugen** Wisconsin
27	A12	**Haugesund** Norway
111	C9	**Haughton** Louisiana
31	J7	**Haugsdorf** Austria
29	L10	**Hauho** Finland
145	E3	**Hauhungaroa Ra** New Zealand
27	B12	**Haukeliseter** Norway
29	L6	**Haukipudas** Finland
29	N9	**Haukivesi** *L* Finland
29	N9	**Haukivuori** Finland
145	F3	**Haumoana New Zealand**
36	H2	**Haune** *R* W Germany
36	H2	**Hauneck** W Germany
36	H2	**Haunetal** Hessen W Germany
37	K7	**Haunstetten** W Germany
144	C5	**Haupiri, L New Zealand**
37	O5	**Hauptenberg** *mt* W Germany
145	E2	**Hauraki Gulf New Zealand**
144	A6	**Hauroko, L New Zealand**
27	A11	**Haus** Norway
36	E7	**Hausach** W Germany
32	J8	**Hausberge** W Germany
101	O3	**Hauser L. Dam** Montana
38	H5	**Hausruck** *mts* Austria
		Haussez Iles d' *see* **Mercury Is**
41	K4	**Hausstock** *mt* Switzerland
22	B3	**Haut Banc, Pte du** France
40	B2	**Haut du Sec** *mt* France
18	L10	**Haute-Corse** *dep* Corsica
18	F7	**Hautefort** France
18	F9	**Haute-Garonne** *dep* France
18	H7	**Haute-Loire** *dep* France
40	E6	**Hauteluce** France
19	J4	**Haute-Marne** *dep* France
121	Q4	**Haute Mauricie, Parc de** Quebec
122	D4	**Hauterive** Quebec
19	Q15	**Hautes Alpes** *dep* France
19	J5	**Haute-Saône** *dep* France
40	D6	**Haute-Savoie** *dep* France
22	L2	**Hautes Fagnes** Belgium
22	H4	**Hautes Rivières** France
21	D8	**Hauteurs de Gâtine** *hills* France
21	H9	**Haute-Vienne** *dep* France
36	B5	**Haut-Hombourg** France
95	T2	**Haut, I. au** Maine
22	F3	**Hautmont** France
19	K5	**Haut-Rhin** *dep* France
85	D2	**Hauts Plateaux** Morocco/Algeria
20	B4	**Hautteville-sur-Mer** France
86	E5	**Haut-Zaïre** *prov* Zaire
135	Q2	**Hauula** Hawaiian Is
145	E4	**Hauwai New Zealand**
110	C6	**Havana** Arkansas
		Havana Cuba *see* **Habana**
111	M11	**Havana** Florida
99	R9	**Havana** Illinois
107	P4	**Havana** Kansas
98	J4	**Havana** N Dakota
9	F6	**Havant** England
103	K7	**Havasu L** Cal/Ariz
28	C3	**Havbro** Denmark
28	J5	**Havdrup** Denmark
33	R6	**Havel** E Germany
22	J3	**Havelange** Belgium
33	Q7	**Havelberg** E Germany
33	R7	**Havelland** *reg* E Germany
33	R7	**Havelland Grosse Haupt-kanal** E Germany
112	L3	**Havelock** N Carolina
98	D3	**Havelock** N Dakota
122	G8	**Havelock** New Brunswick
145	D4	**Havelock New Zealand**
121	N8	**Havelock** Ontario
140	C2	**Havelock Falls** N Terr **Aust**
68	A7	**Havelock I** Andaman Is
145	F3	**Havelock North** New Zealand
107	N4	**Haven** Kansas
107	O2	**Havensville** Kansas
8	B4	**Haverfordwest Wales**
9	G3	**Haverhill** England
95	Q4	**Haverhill** Massachusetts
95	Q3	**Haverhill** New Hampshire
76	B3	**Haveri** India
26	H9	**Haverö** Sweden
22	J3	**Haversin** Belgium
28	D3	**Haverslev** Nordjylland Denmark
95	N5	**Haverstraw** New York
107	L4	**Haviland** Kansas
94	C5	**Haviland** Ohio
120	F6	**Haviland Bay** Ontario

Havirna — Hindenburg 33

48 K2 Havirna Romania
31 J6 Havlíčkův Brod Czechoslovakia
28 D6 Havnbjerg Denmark
28 E3 Havndal Denmark
28 B6 Havneby Denmark
28 G5 Havnsø Denmark
28 B4 Havnstrup Denmark
26 O1 Havøysund Norway
47 J5 Havran Turkey
22 G3 Havre Belgium
114 J8 Havre Montana
123 L6 Havre Aubert Madeleine Is, Quebec
28 G6 Havrebjerg Denmark
123 L8 Havre Boucher Nova Scotia
95 L7 Havre de Grace Maryland
20 F3 Havre, Le France
115 N7 Havre-St-Pierre Quebec
137 Q8 Havre Trench sea feature Pacific Oc
28 A5 Havrvig Denmark
26 H7 Havsnäs Sweden
78 E1 Havza Turkey
135 U5 Hawaii isld Hawaiian Is
135 Hawaiian Is Pacific Oc
86 B3 Hawal R Nigeria
98 K6 Hawarden Iowa
144 D5 Hawarden New Zealand
118 L7 Hawarden Sask
8 C1 Hawarden Wales
138 F6 Hawdon, L S Australia
144 B6 Hawea Flat New Zealand
145 E3 Hawera New Zealand
102 G7 Hawes California
110 K4 Hawesville Kentucky
13 F5 Hawes Water England
135 U4 Hawi Hawaiian Is
13 F3 Hawick Scotland
144 B6 Hawkdun Range New Zealand
145 F3 Hawke Bay New Zealand
139 L4 Hawke, C New S Wales
138 E4 Hawker S Australia
138 F3 Hawker Gate New S Wales
145 F3 Hawke's Bay stat area New Zealand
141 F1 Hawkesbury I Queensland
140 C1 Hawkesbury Pt N Terr Aust
139 K5 Hawkesbury R New S Wales
146 F9 Hawkes, Mt Antarctica
9 G5 Hawkhurst England
103 L4 Hawkins Pk Utah
112 D5 Hawkinsville Georgia
120 F4 Hawk Junct Ontario
118 J1 Hawk Lake Ontario
110 E3 Hawk Point Missouri
94 D1 Hawks Michigan
126 F2 Hawksbill Cay isld Bahamas
13 E5 Hawkshead England
126 G2 Hawks Nest Pt Cat I Bahamas
98 B8 Hawk Springs Wyoming
141 K7 Hawkwood Queensland
106 G4 Hawley Colorado
98 K3 Hawley Minnesota
95 M5 Hawley Pennsylvania
108 H3 Hawley Texas
68 D2 Hawng Luk Burma
13 G6 Haworth England
107 Q8 Haworth Oklahoma
112 H2 Haw R N Carolina
78 H5 Hawran, Wadi Iraq
78 L5 Hawr as S'adiyah L Iraq
13 H5 Hawsker England
113 E8 Hawthorn Florida
102 F3 Hawthorne Nevada
99 P3 Hawthorne Wisconsin
80 D5 Hawwara Jordan
65 F2 Haxat China
65 B2 Haxat Hudag China
101 T2 Haxby Montana
101 Q9 Haxtun Colorado
139 G5 Hay New S Wales
100 H3 Hay Washington
117 N6 Hay R Br Columbia
99 P4 Hay R Wisconsin
61 P6 Hayachine-san mt Japan
60 P3 Hayakita Japan
19 K3 Hayange France
60 E12 Hayasui-seto str Japan
101 T9 Haybro Colorado
103 O8 Hayden Arizona
101 S9 Hayden Colorado
100 J2 Hayden L Idaho
141 F4 Hayden Queensland
13 F4 Haydon Br England
20 B3 Haye-du-Puits, la France
20 H3 Haye, la France
20 C4 Haye-Pesnel, la France
111 D11 Hayes Louisiana
98 E5 Hayes S Dakota
115 K6 Hayes R Manitoba
20 G4 Haye St. Sylvestre, la France
98 E9 Hayes Center Nebraska
116 L6 Hayes Glaciers Alaska
115 N2 Hayes Halvø pen Greenland
68 C7 Hayes I Burma
116 O5 Hayes, Mt Alaska
112 D2 Hayesville N Carolina
13 G6 Hayfield England
99 O6 Hayfield Minnesota
103 J8 Hayfield Res California
102 A1 Hayfork California
13 F5 Haygarth England
36 G7 Hayingen W Germany
117 O6 Hay L Alberta
117 Q6 Hay Lakes Alberta
8 A7 Hayle England
9 F6 Hayling England
113 E7 Haylow Georgia
141 J5 Hayman I Queensland
94 K8 Haymarket Virginia
140 C6 Hay, Mt N Terr Aust
109 O3 Haynesville Louisiana
95 T8 Haynesville Maine
111 K9 Hayneville Alabama
20 H2 Hayons, les France
9 G6 Hay-on-Wye England
141 J5 Hay Point Queensland
140 D6 Hay R N Terr Aust
47 J3 Hayrabolu Turkey
47 J3 Hayrabolu R Turkey
114 H5 Hay River N W Terr
118 F8 Hays Alberta
107 L3 Hays Kansas
101 R1 Hays Montana
98 D7 Hay Springs Nebraska
100 K8 Haystack Mt Nevada
103 L2 Haystack Pk Utah
118 G6 Hayter Alberta
110 G5 Hayti Missouri
98 J5 Hayti S Dakota
13 H6 Hayton England
102 B4 Hayward California
99 N6 Hayward Minnesota
107 N5 Hayward Oklahoma
99 P4 Hayward Wisconsin
140 B2 Hayward, Mt N Terr Aust
9 F6 Haywards Heath England
119 T9 Haywood Manitoba
80 E2 Hazan Israel
57 F6 Hazara Afghanistan
77 J3 Hazarajat reg Afghanistan
94 D9 Hazard Kentucky
95 P4 Hazardville Connecticut
75 L7 Hazaribagh India
77 F1 Hazar Masjed, Kuh-e mts Iran
22 D2 Hazebrouck France
98 K1 Hazel Minnesota
98 J5 Hazel S Dakota
119 V9 Hazelridge Manitoba
117 K8 Hazelton Br Col
107 M4 Hazelton Kansas
98 F3 Hazelton N Dakota
116 E7 Hazen Arkansas
98 E2 Hazen N Dakota
102 E2 Hazen Nevada
116 E6 Hazen B Alaska
115 N1 Hazen, L N W Terr
118 K9 Hazenmore Sask
114 H2 Hazen Str N W Terr
80 B8 Hazerim Israel
25 C4 Hazerswoude Netherlands
79 F8 Hazeva Israel
112 E2 Hazewood N Carolina
112 E6 Hazlehurst Georgia
111 F10 Hazlehurst Mississippi
95 M6 Hazleton Pennsylvania
142 G5 Hazlett, L W Australia
37 N3 Hazlov Czechoslovakia
80 F2 Hazor Israel
80 F3 HaZore'im Israel
80 C7 He Israel
9 G2 Heacham England
9 G5 Headcorn England
14 B3 Headford Irish Rep
140 E5 Headingly Queensland
111 L10 Headland Alabama
144 B6 Headlong Pk New Zealand
138 B4 Head of Bight B S Australia
100 K3 Headquarters Idaho
83 M9 Headridge Hill Christmas I Indian Oc
100 A7 Heads, The C Oregon
99 R4 Heafford Junct Wisconsin
102 B3 Healdsburg California
109 K1 Healdton Oklahoma
139 H7 Healesville Victoria
116 N5 Healy Alaska
107 K3 Healy Kansas
116 P4 Healy R Alaska
116 P5 Healy L Alaska
119 Q3 Heaman Manitoba
9 E1 Heanor England
90 M16 Heard I Southern Oc
119 M8 Hearne Sask
109 L5 Hearne Texas
117 R4 Hearne L N W Terr
102 A2 Hearst California
115 L8 Hearst Ontario
146 E13 Hearst I Antarctica
98 D3 Heart R N Dakota
118 F3 Heart L Alberta
101 P5 Heart L Wyoming
118 A3 Heart R Alberta
123 T6 Heart's Content Nfld
123 T6 Heart's Delight Nfld
98 H9 Heartwell Nebraska
128 E6 Heath R Bolivia/Peru
139 G6 Heathcote Victoria
6 L2 Heather oil rig North Sea
123 O5 Heatherton Nfld
9 G6 Heathfield England
123 L4 Heath Pt Anticosti I, Quebec
9 F5 Heathrow Airport England
112 G3 Heath Springs S Carolina
122 F6 Heath Steel Mines New Brunswick
95 L9 Heathsville Virginia
107 Q7 Heavener Oklahoma
109 J8 Hebbronville Texas
13 F6 Hebden Br England
65 C5 Hebei prov China
103 O7 Heber Arizona
101 O9 Heber Utah
32 L6 Heber W Germany
110 D6 Heber Springs Arkansas
121 P3 Hébert, L Quebec
20 C3 Hébert, Pt France
121 T4 Hébertville Station Quebec
101 O5 Hebgen L Montana
65 C7 Hebi China
100 B4 Hebo Oregon
101 T9 Hebron Colorado
99 S7 Hebron Illinois
99 T8 Hebron Indiana
80 D7 Hebron Jordan
115 N6 Hebron Labrador
98 E3 Hebron N Dakota
98 J9 Hebron Nebraska
122 F10 Hebron Nova Scotia
94 E7 Hebron Ohio
27 J12 Heby Sweden
114 F7 Hecate Str Br Columbia
100 A5 Heceta Head Oregon
117 G8 Heceta I Alaska
67 C4 Hechi China
36 F7 Hechingen W Germany
22 J1 Hechtel Belgium
32 K5 Hechthausen W Germany
36 E4 Hechtsheim W Germany
67 B1 Hechuan China
33 T7 Heckelberg E Germany
9 F2 Heckington England
33 P9 Hecklingen E Germany
98 H4 Hecla S Dakota
114 H2 Hecla & Griper B N W Terr
119 V7 Hecla I Manitoba
119 V7 Hecla Prov. Park Manitoba
122 F9 Hectanooga Nova Scotia
102 H7 Hector California
99 M5 Hector Minnesota
144 C4 Hector New Zealand
145 E4 Hector mt New Zealand
117 P10 Hector, Mt Alberta
127 M2 Hector's River Jamaica
27 H12 Hed Sweden
61 M11 Heda Japan
27 D11 Hedal Norway
20 K1 Hedauville France
26 K6 Hedberg Sweden
27 D12 Heddal Norway
36 F4 Heddesheim W Germany
13 G3 Heddon on-the-Wall England
20 B5 Hédé France
26 G9 Hede Sweden
25 D5 Hedel Netherlands
27 H11 Hedemora Sweden
32 L10 Hedemunden W Germany
28 E6 Heden Denmark
26 M6 Heden Sweden
26 N5 Hedenäset Sweden
28 D5 Hedensted Denmark
33 O9 Hedersleben E Germany
27 J11 Hedesunda Sweden
26 G9 Hedeviken Sweden
144 B7 Hedgehope New Zealand
101 Q3 Hedgesville Montana
94 J7 Hedgesville W Virginia
67 C6 Hedi Shuiku res China
117 N11 Hedley Br Columbia
27 E11 Hedmark Norway
27 E10 Hedmark county Norway
61 Q12 Hedo Okinawa
13 H6 Hedon England
83 L11 Hedo Oya R Sri Lanka
61 Q12 Hedo-zaki C Okinawa
99 O8 Hedrick Iowa
28 A4 Hee Denmark
32 F7 Heede W Germany
33 T7 Heegermühle E Germany
32 F8 Heek W Germany
25 C4 Heemstede Netherlands
32 J8 Heepen W Germany
22 H3 Heer Belgium
25 E7 Heer Netherlands
25 F4 Heerde Netherlands
25 E3 Heerenveen Netherlands
25 C3 Heerhugo-waard Netherlands
25 E7 Heerlen Netherlands
25 E5 Heesch Netherlands
25 E6 Heeze Netherlands
67 F1 Hefei China
67 C2 Hefeng China
117 N10 Heffley Br Columbia
111 L8 Heflin Alabama
59 K2 Hegang China
65 H1 Hegang China
61 K8 Hegura-jima isld Japan
88 E5 Hehe Tanzania
26 D10 Heidal Norway
80 F8 Heidan R Jordan
32 K4 Heide W Germany
37 L5 Heideck W Germany
111 H10 Heidelberg Mississippi
87 E11 Heidelberg S Africa
36 F5 Heidelberg W Germany
110 N4 Heidelburg Kentucky
36 F5 Heidelsheim W Germany
37 M4 Heide Naab R W Germany
37 J6 Heidenheim W Germany
36 D3 Heidenrod W Germany
94 B2 Heights, The Michigan
60 F12 Heigun-tō isld Japan
Heihe see Aihui
59 J1 Hei-ho China
25 E6 Heijthuizsen Netherlands
87 E11 Heilbron S Africa
36 G5 Heilbronn W Germany
38 G7 Heiligenblut Austria
33 P4 Heiligendamm E Germany
30 F1 Heiligenhafen W Germany
32 M10 Heiligenstadt E Germany
37 L4 Heiligenstadt W Germany
65 D7 Heilin China
59 H1 Heilongjiang prov China
59 J1 Heilong Jiang R China
37 K5 Heilsbronn W Germany
Heilungkiang prov see Heilongjiang
36 B2 Heimbach W Germany
36 G4 Heimbuchenthal W Germany
33 N9 Heimburg E Germany
98 G2 Heimdal N Dakota
26 D8 Heimdal Norway
146 C10 Heimefrontfjella ra Antarctica
36 F6 Heimsheim W Germany
29 O9 Heinävesi Finland
36 H1 Heinebach W Germany
22 L3 Heinerscheid Luxembourg
37 L3 Heinersdorf E Germany
36 C5 Heinitz W Germany
25 F4 Heino Netherlands
29 M10 Heinola Finland
33 P8 Heinrichsburg E Germany
25 F6 Heinsberg W Germany
118 G5 Heinsburg Alberta
33 S9 Heinsdorf E Germany
68 C5 Heinz B Burma
68 C5 Heinze I Burma
65 E4 Heishan China
65 C3 Heishantou China
67 C2 Heishui China
118 E6 Heisler Alberta
22 E1 Heist Belgium
22 H1 Heist-op-den-Berg Belgium
80 G3 Heit Syria
80 G2 Heital Syria
79 D8 Heitân, G mt Egypt
40 G2 Heitersheim W Germany
65 F2 Heiyupao China
84 H4 Heiz, El Egypt
65 A5 Hejialiang China
67 B2 Hejiang China
67 C6 Hejiang China
67 D5 He Jiang R China
67 D4 Hejie China
65 A7 Hejin China
28 D6 Hejls Denmark
28 C6 Hejlsminde Denmark
28 B5 Hejnsvig Denmark
28 D6 Hejsager Denmark
145 F3 Hekerangi Pt New Zealand
115 S5 Hekla vol Iceland
Hekou see Yanshan
65 B4 Hekou China
67 D5 Hekou Guangdong China
67 A5 Hekou Yunnan China
31 L1 Hel Poland
80 E2 Hela Israel
26 F9 Helagsfjället mt Sweden
58 E4 Helan Shan mt ra China
37 K1 Helbe R E Germany
28 E3 Helberskov Denmark
33 O9 Helbra E Germany
22 J1 Helchteren Belgium
37 K3 Heldburg E Germany
36 F3 Heldenbergen W Germany
127 P3 Helden's Pt St Kitts W I
33 O10 Heldrungen E Germany
112 D3 Helen Georgia
111 K8 Helena Alabama
111 F7 Helena Arkansas
100 B9 Helena California
112 E5 Helena Georgia
114 H8 Helena Montana
107 M5 Helena Oklahoma
102 G7 Helendale California
118 J5 Helénè L Sask
146 D3 Helen Gl Antarctica
142 E6 Helen Hill W Australia
71 C1 Helen I Pacific Oc
119 P1 Helen L Ontario
141 F5 Helen, Mt Queensland
15 D4 Helensburgh Scotland
140 C4 Helen Springs N Terr Aust
145 E2 Helensville New Zealand
33 P10 Helfta E Germany
26 F6 Helgeland reg Norway
27 D12 Helgen Norway
32 G4 Helgoländ isld W Germany
32 H4 Helgoländer Bucht W Germany
26 K1 Helgöy Norway
65 H1 Heli China
79 B8 Heliopolis Egypt
26 E8 Hell Norway
33 O7 Hellberg hills E Germany
28 K4 Hellebæk Denmark
77 B5 Helleh R Iran
26 J4 Hellemobotn Norway
25 F4 Hellendoorn Netherlands
36 B3 Hellenthal W Germany
28 K5 Hellerup Denmark
28 J6 Hellested Denmark
26 B9 Hellesylt Norway
28 E2 Hellevad Nordjylland Denmark
28 C6 Hellevad Sønderjylland Denmark
26 L2 Helligskogen Norway
26 G4 Helligvoer isld Norway
17 F6 Hellin Spain
Hell's Canyon see Snake River Canyon
127 L3 Hellshire Hills Jamaica
28 E2 Hellum Denmark
87 H10 Hell-Ville Madagascar
32 K6 Hellwege W Germany
102 D5 Helm California
72 J2 Helmand R Afghanistan
32 K9 Helmarshausen W Germany
37 M3 Helmbrechts W Germany
33 N10 Helme R E Germany
87 C11 Helmeringhausen Namibia
37 J2 Helmershausen E Germany
9 H3 Helmingham England
25 E6 Helmond Netherlands
32 J4 Helmsand sandbank W Germany
15 E2 Helmsdale Scotland
15 E2 Helmsdale R Scotland
13 G5 Helmsley England
36 F5 Helmstadt W Germany
33 O8 Helmstedt W Germany
101 N3 Helmville Montana
28 D6 Helnæs Denmark
28 E6 Helnæs Bugt B Denmark
26 P1 Helnes Norway
59 J3 Helong China
65 F2 Helong China
109 J6 Helotes Texas
103 O2 Helper Utah
33 T6 Helpter Berge peak E Germany
32 L10 Helsa-Wickenrode W Germany
29 K4 Helsingborg Sweden
28 J4 Helsinge Denmark
Helsingfors see Helsinki
28 K4 Helsingør Denmark
29 L11 Helsinki Finland
9 G6 Helston England
32 L7 Helstorf W Germany
28 O9 Heltnin Faeroes
110 K3 Heltonville Indiana
130 H5 Helvécia Brazil
14 D4 Helvick Hd Irish Rep
84 J4 Helwan Egypt
28 D4 Hem Vejle Denmark
28 B3 Hem Viborg Denmark
118 F7 Hemaruka Alberta
37 M5 Hemau W Germany
32 E9 Hemden W Germany
9 F4 Hemel Hempstead England
25 D3 Hemelum Netherlands
32 G10 Hemer W Germany
102 H8 Hemet California
36 B6 Héming France
98 C7 Hemingford Nebraska
119 Q4 Heming Lake Manitoba
112 H4 Hemingway S Carolina
141 L1 Hemmant dist Brisbane, Qnsld
32 J4 Hemme W Germany
28 F3 Hemmed Denmark
32 L8 Hemmendorf W Germany
28 A5 Hemmet Denmark
32 L8 Hemmingen W Germany
121 R7 Hemmingford Quebec
32 K5 Hemmoor W Germany
26 G5 Hemnesberget Norway
111 C10 Hemphill Texas
95 O6 Hempstead Long I, N Y
109 L5 Hempstead Texas
9 H2 Hemsby England
27 K14 Hemse isld Gotland Sweden
27 C11 Hemsedal Norway
27 C11 Hemsil R Norway
27 G15 Hemsjö Sweden
32 L6 Hemslingen W Germany
26 K9 Hemsö Sweden
13 G6 Hemsworth England
65 B7 Henan prov China
145 E1 Hen and Chicken Is New Zealand
16 E4 Henares R Spain
61 N5 Henashi-zaki C Japan
140 C6 Henbury N Terr Aust
18 D9 Hendaye France
22 D3 Hendecourt-lès Cagnicourt France
47 L4 Hendek Turkey
112 J1 Henderson N Carolina
103 K5 Henderson Nevada
95 L3 Henderson New York
110 H6 Henderson Tennessee
109 N3 Henderson Texas
94 E8 Henderson W Virginia
135 O11 Henderson I Pacific Oc
112 E2 Hendersonville N Carolina
77 A4 Hendījān Iran
9 F4 Hendon England
141 K8 Hendon Queensland
119 O6 Hendon Sask
77 C6 Hendorābī isld Iran
48 J4 Hendorf Romania
141 K1 Hendra dist Brisbane, Qnsld
98 K5 Hendricks Minnesota
94 H7 Hendricks W Virginia
129 G3 Hendrik Top mt Suriname
89 D8 Hendrik Verwoerd Dam S Africa
8 B4 Hendy Wales
101 O8 Henefer Utah
65 H2 Hengdaohezi China
65 G3 Hengdaozi China
67 D3 Hengdong China
58 C6 Hengduan Shan mts China
25 G4 Hengelo Netherlands
37 P6 Hengersberg W Germany
67 F2 Hengfeng China
67 A2 Heng Jiang R China
67 D2 Henglongqiao China
67 D3 Hengnan China
67 D3 Hengshan China
67 D3 Heng Shan mt China
58 G4 Hengshui China
37 J5 Hengstfeld W Germany
67 C5 Heng Xian China
69 A9 Henhoaha Nicobar Is
22 D3 Henin Lietard France
144 C6 Henley New Zealand
123 R2 Henley Hbr Labrador
9 E3 Henley in Arden England
9 F4 Henley-on-Thames England
100 C10 Henleyville California
9 F3 Henlow England
109 J5 Henly Texas
27 E12 Henmes Norway
61 P13 Henna Okinawa
26 H9 Hennan Sweden
28 A5 Henne Denmark
37 J3 Henneberg E Germany
18 C5 Hennebont France
36 C2 Hennef W Germany
37 K5 Hennenbach W Germany
99 R8 Hennepin Illinois
20 F3 Hennequeville France
107 N5 Hennessey Oklahoma
33 S8 Hennickendorf E Germany
33 S7 Hennigsdorf E Germany
95 Q3 Henniker New Hampshire
110 J1 Henning Illinois
99 L3 Henning Minnesota
110 G6 Henning Tennessee
26 G3 Henningsvaer Norway
32 K4 Hennstedt W Germany
20 K3 Hénonville France
77 D6 Henqam isld Iran
119 M5 Henribourg Sask
22 K2 Henri-Chapelle Belgium
109 J2 Henrietta Texas
115 L6 Henrietta Maria, C Ontario
103 N4 Henrieville Utah
117 L7 Henri, Mt Br Col
Henrique de Carvalho see Suarimo
101 O7 Henry Idaho
99 R8 Henry Illinois
95 M10 Henry, C Virginia
146 E15 Henryk Arckowski Poland
115 N4 Henry Kater Pen N W Terr
111 K8 Henry L Alabama
68 A6 Henry Lawrence I Andaman Is
100 K1 Henry, Mt Montana
103 O4 Henry Mts Utah
142 B6 Henry, R W Australia
101 O5 Henrys Fork R Idaho
110 L3 Henryville Indiana
120 J9 Hensall Ontario
110 H4 Henshaw Kentucky
102 H8 Henshaw, L California
12 E5 Hensingham England
142 G3 Hensman, Mt W Australia
32 L5 Henstedt-Ulzburg W Germany
8 D6 Henstridge England
58 E2 Hentiy Mongolia
58 E2 Hentiyn Nuruu mt Mongolia
139 H6 Henty New S Wales
68 B4 Henzada Burma
61 P13 Henza-jima isld Okinawa
118 L6 Hepburn Sask
67 E1 Hepeng China
112 E4 Hephzibah Georgia
Heping see Yanhe
67 E4 Heping China
Hepo see Jiexi
36 B2 Heppendorf W Germany
36 F4 Heppenheim W Germany
100 F4 Heppner Oregon
80 F2 Heptapegon Israel
68 J2 Hepu China
120 J8 Hepworth Ontario
65 B5 Hequ China
27 E11 Heradsbygd Norway
141 J3 Herald Cays islds Gt Barrier Reef Aust
72 J2 Herat Afghanistan
18 H9 Hérault R France
19 O14 Herbasse R France
21 H6 Herbault France
32 F10 Herbede W Germany
36 D3 Herberge, K mt W Germany
32 G9 Herbern W Germany
144 C6 Herbert New Zealand
114 J7 Herbert Sask
140 E5 Herbert R N Terr Aust
141 H4 Herbert R Queensland
68 A7 Herbertabad Andaman Is
140 E6 Herbert Downs Queensland
140 B4 Herbert, Mt N Terr Aust
142 F3 Herbert, Mt W Australia
141 H3 Herberton Queensland
145 F4 Herbertville New Zealand
22 K2 Herbesthal Belgium
22 J4 Herbeumont Belgium
21 A7 Herbignac France
36 C5 Herbitzheim France
119 S4 Herb L Manitoba
36 D7 Herbolzheim W Germany
36 E2 Herborn W Germany
36 G2 Herbstein W Germany
31 L5 Herby Poland
42 J6 Herceg Novi Yugoslavia
42 H5 Hercegovina reg Yugoslavia
115 K6 Herchmer Manitoba
36 H4 Herchsheim W Germany
107 O5 Herd Oklahoma
32 F10 Herdecke W Germany
125 M4 Heredia Costa Rica
98 B9 Hereford Colorado
8 D3 Hereford England
108 E1 Hereford Texas
Hereford co see Hereford and Worcester co
8 D3 Hereford and Worcester co England
145 D1 Herekino New Zealand
16 E5 Herencia Spain
40 F5 Herens, Val. d' Switzerland
22 H1 Herentals Belgium
144 B5 Heretaniwha Pt New Zealand
28 J6 Herfølge Denmark
32 J8 Herford W Germany
22 L2 Hergenrath Belgium
19 K5 Hericourt France
33 N10 Heringen E Germany
107 O3 Herington Kansas
22 G2 Herinnes Belgium
144 B6 Heriot New Zealand
13 F2 Heriot Scotland
117 L10 Heriot Bay Br Col
41 K3 Herisau Switzerland
146 F10 Heritage Rge Antarctica
22 J2 Herk-de-Stad Belgium
95 N3 Herkimer New York
121 Q9 Herkimer New York
146 J11 Herlacher, C Antarctica
37 N2 Herlasgrün E Germany
58 F2 Herlen Gol R Mongolia
58 G2 Herlen He R China
37 J1 Herleshausen W Germany
28 K5 Herlev Denmark
28 H6 Herlufmagle Denmark
9 H6 Herm isld Channel Is
38 H8 Hermagor Austria
99 S3 Herman Michigan
98 K4 Herman Minnesota
98 K8 Herman Nebraska
71 D3 Hermana Mayor isld Philippines
124 J4 Hermanas Mexico
106 C10 Hermanas New Mexico
110 E3 Hermann Missouri
32 M7 Hermannsberg W Germany
140 C6 Hermannsburg N Terr Aust
37 P4 Heřmanova Hut' Czechoslovakia
99 T4 Hermansville Michigan
89 A10 Hermanus S Africa
111 F10 Hermanville Mississippi
79 G4 Hermel, El Lebanon
20 K3 Hermes France
36 B4 Hermeskeil W Germany
22 H3 Hermeton-sur-Meuse Belgium
139 H4 Hermidale New S Wales
22 E3 Hermies France
100 F4 Hermiston Oregon
111 D8 Hermitage Arkansas
144 C5 Hermitage New Zealand
123 R6 Hermitage Nfld
123 Q3 Hermitage B Nfld
142 B5 Hermite I W Australia
133 D9 Hermite, Is Chile
140 B2 Hermit Hill N Terr Aust
136 K2 Hermit Is Bismarck Arch
103 M5 Hermits Rest Arizona
108 G3 Hermleigh Texas
Hermón, Mt see Sheikh, J. esh
22 F5 Hermonville France
98 C6 Hermosa S Dakota
124 D3 Hermosillo Mexico
Hermsdorf see Ottendorf-Okrilla
130 C9 Hernandarias Paraguay
113 E9 Hernando Florida
102 E5 Herndon California
99 M8 Herndon Iowa
107 K2 Herndon Kansas
110 J5 Herndon Kentucky
95 L6 Herndon Pennsylvania
94 K8 Herndon Virginia
94 F9 Herndon W Virginia
32 F9 Herne W Germany
9 H5 Herne Bay England
28 B4 Herning Denmark
124 C2 Heroica Caborca Mexico
37 L4 Heroldsberg W Germany
22 J2 Héron Belgium
100 K1 Heron Montana
120 D4 Heron Bay Ontario
25 F6 Herongen W Germany
141 K6 Heron I Gt Barrier Reef Aust
99 L6 Heron L Minnesota
144 C5 Heron, L New Zealand
26 A9 Heroy Norway
42 F3 Herpelje Kozina Yugoslavia
130 B10 Herradura Argentina
16 D5 Herrara del Duque Spain
98 F4 Herreid S Dakota
36 F6 Herrenberg W Germany
36 E6 Herrenwies W Germany
133 E3 Herrera Argentina
17 G3 Herrera mt Spain
16 C5 Herrera de Alcántara Spain
17 G3 Herrera de los Navarros Spain
124 G5 Herreras Mexico
28 F6 Herrested Denmark
98 G6 Herrick S Dakota
139 J8 Herrick Tasmania
110 G4 Herrin Illinois
123 S4 Herring Neck Nfld
94 C9 Herrington L Kentucky
119 Q2 Herriot Manitoba
28 H7 Herritslev Denmark
36 H7 Herrlingen W Germany
27 F13 Herrljunga Sweden
36 E4 Herrnsheim W Germany
36 C4 Herrstein W Germany
18 G9 Hers R France
37 L5 Hersbruck W Germany
36 D1 Herscheid W Germany
118 J7 Herschel Sask
116 S2 Herschel Yukon Terr
99 S8 Herscher Illinois
37 J3 Herschfeld W Germany
22 H1 Herselt Belgium
94 B3 Hersey Michigan
95 L6 Hershey Pennsylvania
28 D5 Herslev Denmark
28 D3 Hersom Denmark
22 K2 Herstal Belgium
9 G6 Herstmonceux England
22 E2 Hertain Belgium
32 F9 Herten W Germany
9 F4 Hertford England
112 L1 Hertford N Carolina
9 F4 Hertfordshire co England
80 C5 Herut Israel
16 D4 Hervas Spain
22 K2 Herve Belgium
141 L7 Hervey B Queensland
121 S6 Hervey Junction Quebec
141 H4 Hervey Ra Queensland
36 E5 Herxheim W Germany
33 S9 Herzberg E Germany
33 M9 Herzberg W Germany
33 T8 Herzfelde E Germany
32 G7 Herzlake W Germany
80 C5 Herzliyya Israel
37 K4 Herzogenaurach W Germany
38 N5 Herzogenburg Austria
25 F7 Herzogenrath W Germany
33 Q6 Herzsprung E Germany
22 B2 Hesdigneul-lès-Boulogne France
22 C3 Hesdin France
32 G6 Hesel W Germany
67 D5 Heshui China
65 B6 Heshun China
27 B13 Heskestad Norway
98 G2 Hesper N Dakota
22 L4 Hesperange Luxembourg
102 G7 Hesperia California
94 A3 Hesperia Michigan
106 B4 Hesperus Colorado
106 B4 Hesperus Pk Colorado
117 G4 Hess R Yukon Terr
116 N4 Hess Cr Alaska
28 F6 Hesselager Denmark
37 K5 Hesselberg mt W Germany
28 H4 Hesselø isld Denmark
33 N8 Hessen E Germany
36 F2 Hessen land W Germany
36 F1 Hessenstein W Germany
36 H5 Hessenthal W Germany
36 H1 Hessisch Lichtenau W Germany
117 H4 Hess Mts Yukon Terr
138 D4 Hesso S Australia
107 N3 Hesston Kansas
28 J7 Hestehoved C Denmark
26 F5 Hestmannen isld Norway
28 N2 Hestø isld Faeroes
27 G14 Hestra, N Sweden
22 G3 Hestrud France
102 C4 Hetch Hetchy California
94 C2 Hetherton Michigan
25 E4 Het Loo Netherlands
68 J2 Hetou China
22 L5 Hettange Gde France
Hettenhausen see Ebersburg
36 E4 Hettenleidelheim W Germany
114 J8 Hettinger N Dakota
13 G4 Hetton-le-Hole England
33 P9 Hettstedt E Germany
36 F4 Hetzbach W Germany
36 B4 Hetzerath W Germany
22 E1 Het Zoute Belgium
36 H6 Heubach W Germany
41 J1 Heuberg dist W Germany
22 C3 Heuchin France
33 N9 Heudeber E Germany
140 B6 Heughlin, Mt N Terr Aust
36 C2 Heumar W Germany
20 H3 Heuqueville France
25 D5 Heusden Netherlands
37 J3 Heustreu W Germany
95 M2 Heuvelton New York
20 F3 Hève, C. de la France
80 E8 Hever R Jordan
13 F5 Heversham England
48 F3 Heves Hungary
28 E3 Hevring Å R Denmark
80 C8 Hevron R Israel
119 O9 Heward Sask
7 M9 Hewett sea rig North Sea
13 F4 Hexham England
67 F4 Hexi China
67 D4 He Xian China
67 F1 He Xian China
65 D3 Hexigten Qi China
109 H5 Hext Texas
65 A7 Heyang China
101 M7 Heyburn Idaho
107 O6 Heyburn Res Oklahoma
13 F5 Heysham England
8 D5 Heytesbury England
67 E5 Heyuan China
13 F6 Heywood England
138 F7 Heywood Victoria
65 C7 Heze China
113 G12 Hialeah Florida
112 D3 Hiawassee Georgia
107 P2 Hiawatha Kansas
103 O2 Hiawatha Utah
121 Q5 Hibbard Quebec
99 O2 Hibbing Minnesota
142 E1 Hibernia Reef Timor Sea
60 D11 Hibiki-nada sea Japan
71 G5 Hibuson isld Philippines
103 M9 Hickiwan Arizona
13 G6 Hickleton England
110 G5 Hickman Kentucky
98 K9 Hickman Nebraska
106 C7 Hickman New Mexico
123 T5 Hickman's Hbr Nfld
107 J4 Hickok Kansas
111 G9 Hickory Mississippi
112 F2 Hickory N Carolina
112 F2 Hickory, L N Carolina
110 G6 Hickory Valley Tennessee
109 M8 Hicks Texas
145 G2 Hick's Bay New Zealand
125 P9 Hicks Cays islds Belize
94 C5 Hicksville Ohio
109 J4 Hico Texas
48 H3 Hida Romania
60 Q3 Hidaka Japan
60 J12 Hidaka R Japan
60 R3 Hidaka-sammyaku mts Japan
124 G4 Hidalgo de Parral Mexico
32 J8 Hiddenhausen W Germany
30 G1 Hiddensee isld E Germany
141 H4 Hidden Valley Queensland
32 J9 Hiddesen W Germany
130 E5 Hidrolândia Brazil
130 E4 Hidrolina Brazil
20 K1 Hiermont France
85 A3 Hierro isld Canary Is
127 N9 Hierro, Pto. de Venezuela
61 O13 Higashi-iwa islds Japan
61 N9 Higashi-Matsuyama Japan
61 P13 Higashi-Onna Okinawa
61 J11 Higashiosaka Japan
60 C12 Higashi-suidō str Japan
110 D2 Higbee Missouri
94 C2 Higgins L Michigan
110 C2 Higginsville Missouri
143 D9 Higginsville W Australia
9 E1 Higham England
9 F3 Higham Ferrers England
8 B6 Highampton England
106 G4 Highbee Colorado
8 D5 Highbridge England
95 N6 High Bridge New Jersey
12 D3 High Br. of Ken Scotland
9 E5 Highclere England
99 S5 High Cliff Wisconsin
100 E6 High Desert Oregon
99 S4 High Falls Reservoir Wisconsin
9 G5 Highgate England
127 L2 Highgate Jamaica
142 B1 Highgate dist Perth, W Aust
13 F4 High Hesket England
119 W3 High Hill L Manitoba
99 V4 High I Michigan
109 N6 High Island Texas
102 G7 Highland California
110 G3 Highland Illinois
107 P2 Highland Kansas
99 Q6 Highland Wisconsin
15 C3 Highland reg Scotland
99 T7 Highland Park Illinois
94 D4 Highland Park Michigan
109 O9 Highland Park Texas
102 E3 Highland Peak California
103 K4 Highland Pk Nevada
112 D2 Highlands N Carolina
109 M6 Highlands Texas
95 K9 Highland Springs Virginia
117 P6 High Level Alberta
98 G5 Highmore S Dakota
141 K5 High Peak I Queensland
112 H2 High Point N Carolina
118 K8 High Point Sask
114 H6 High Prairie Alberta
114 H7 High River Alberta
113 J11 High Rock Grand Bahama I
119 R3 Highrock Manitoba
112 G2 High Rock L N Carolina
139 H9 High Rocky Pt Tasmania
143 F8 High Sand Hill W Australia
143 F8 High Sand Ridge W Australia
113 E8 High Springs Florida
95 N6 Hightstown New Jersey
99 S7 Highwood Illinois
101 P2 Highwood Montana
9 E4 Highworth England
9 F4 High Wycombe England
124 E5 Higuera de Zaragoza Mexico
17 F1 Higuer, C Spain
127 L9 Higuerote Venezuela
127 K5 Higüey Dom Rep
145 E3 Hihitahi New Zealand
27 N13 Hiiumaa isld U.S.S.R.
79 G5 Hijāne, Bahret el L Syria
17 G3 Hijar Spain
69 F14 Hijau, Gunung mt Sumatra
60 E12 Hiji Japan
71 G7 Hijo Philippines
60 E12 Hikari Japan
60 H11 Hiketa Japan
60 J12 Hiki R Japan
83 J11 Hikkaduwa Sri Lanka
103 J4 Hiko Nevada
61 K10 Hikone Japan
60 D12 Hiko-san mt Japan
145 E2 Hikuai New Zealand
145 E1 Hikurangi New Zealand
145 G2 Hikurangi mt New Zealand
145 E2 Hikutaia New Zealand
71 N8 Hila Indonesia
101 S6 Hiland Wyoming
36 E1 Hilchenbach W Germany
118 G8 Hilda Alberta
37 K3 Hildburghausen E Germany
100 D7 Hildebrand Oregon
36 B1 Hilden W Germany
37 J2 Hilders W Germany
32 L8 Hildesheim W Germany
98 G9 Hildreth Nebraska
101 Q2 Hilger Montana
69 C12 Hiliotaluwa Indonesia
69 C12 Hilisimaetano Indonesia
101 O1 Hill Montana
127 P6 Hillaby, Mt Barbados
78 K5 Hillah, Al Iraq
98 E5 Hilland S Dakota
27 F14 Hillared Sweden
146 H6 Hillary Coast Antarctica
125 P9 Hill Bank Belize
101 K6 Hill City Idaho
107 L2 Hill City Kansas
99 N3 Hill City Minnesota
98 C6 Hill City S Dakota
103 P2 Hill Cr Utah
118 C9 Hillcrest Alberta
117 Q11 Hillcrest Creek Alberta
25 C4 Hillegom Netherlands
32 J8 Hillegossen W Germany
28 J5 Hillerød Denmark
28 B2 Hillerslev Denmark
28 E6 Hillerslev Denmark
28 C7 Hillerup W Germany
36 B3 Hillesheim W Germany
26 K2 Hillesöy Norway
139 K4 Hillgrove New S Wales
144 C6 Hillgrove New Zealand
141 H4 Hill Grove Queensland
98 J4 Hillhead S Dakota
118 E5 Hilliard Alberta
113 F7 Hilliard Florida
9 G2 Hillington England
94 D1 Hillman Michigan
99 N3 Hillman Minnesota
143 B9 Hillman, L W Australia
118 H5 Hillmond Sask
15 E3 Hill of Fearn Scotland
15 D5 Hill of Stake mt Scotland
98 C9 Hillrose Colorado
99 P8 Hills Iowa
98 K6 Hills Minnesota
112 D4 Hillsboro Georgia
110 G2 Hillsboro Illinois
99 P9 Hillsboro Iowa
107 N3 Hillsboro Kansas
110 F3 Hillsboro Missouri
112 H1 Hillsboro N Carolina
98 J2 Hillsboro N Dakota
95 Q3 Hillsboro New Hampshire
106 C9 Hillsboro New Mexico
110 N2 Hillsboro Ohio
100 C4 Hillsboro Oregon
109 K3 Hillsboro Texas
94 G8 Hillsboro W Virginia
113 G11 Hillsboro Can Florida
122 H8 Hillsborough New Brunswick
122 J7 Hillsborough B Pr Edward I
141 J5 Hillsborough, C Queensland
36 D3 Hillscheid W Germany
94 C5 Hillsdale Michigan
121 L8 Hillsdale Ontario
98 B8 Hillsdale Wyoming
103 M7 Hillside Arizona
106 E3 Hillside Colorado
142 C5 Hillside W Australia
120 E3 Hillsport Ontario
139 H5 Hillston New S Wales
138 D5 Hills View Queensland
98 G4 Hillsview S Dakota
94 G10 Hillsville Virginia
112 F5 Hilltonia Georgia
110 F2 Hillview Illinois
102 D4 Hilmar California
102 V14 Hilo Hawaiian Is
113 G10 Hilolo Florida
37 L5 Hilpoltstein W Germany
36 F5 Hilsbach W Germany
8 B7 Hilsea Pt England
36 D7 Hilsenheim France
94 K3 Hilton New York
112 G5 Hilton Head I S Carolina
146 E12 Hilton Inlet Antarctica
37 L4 Hiltpoltstein W Germany
32 G9 Hiltrup W Germany
100 C8 Hilts California
29 N10 Hiltula Finland
25 D6 Hilvarenbeck Netherlands
25 D4 Hilversum Netherlands
74 G2 Himachal Pradesh prov India
74 F1 Himalayan Mt.Ra.,Great Asia
29 K7 Himanka Finland
46 D4 Himarë Albania
145 E4 Himatangi New Zealand
33 N6 Himbergen W Germany
60 H11 Himeji Japan
61 P6 Himekami dake mt Japan
101 R5 Himes Wyoming
60 E12 Hime-shima isld Japan
61 K9 Himi Japan
32 K5 Himmelpforten W Germany
32 K9 Himmighausen W Germany
71 F5 Himugaan Philippines
60 D13 Hinagu Japan
69 C12 Hinako isld Indonesia
145 E4 Hinakura New Zealand
71 G6 Hinatuan Philippines
127 J5 Hinche Haiti
116 O6 Hinchinbrook Entrance str Alaska
116 O6 Hinchinbrook I Alaska
141 H4 Hinchinbrook I Queensland
119 P6 Hinchliffe Sask
9 E2 Hinckley England
99 O3 Hinckley Minnesota
103 M2 Hinckley Utah
95 N3 Hinckley Res New York
74 G5 Hindaun India
41 M2 Hindelang W Germany
25 D3 Hindeloopen Netherlands
Hindenburg see Lindenhagen

34

Hindenburg Damm — Huairen

28 A7 **Hindenburg Damm** *causeway* W Germany
26 N6 **Hinderson** *isld* Sweden
109 J7 **Hindes** Texas
9 F5 **Hindhead** England
13 F6 **Hindley** England
138 F6 **Hindmarsh, L** Victoria
8 D5 **Hindon** England
144 C6 **Hindon** New Zealand
144 C6 **Hinds** New Zealand
123 Q4 **Hinds Hill** *peak* Nfld
28 F5 **Hindsholm** Denmark
123 P5 **Hinds L** Nfld
74 B3 **Hindubagh** Pakistan
72 K1 **Hindu Kush** *mts* Afghanistan
76 C4 **Hindupur** India
118 G5 **Hindville** Alberta
68 G4 **Hine** Laos
95 O2 **Hinesburg** Vermont
117 O7 **Hines Creek** Alberta
112 F6 **Hinesville** Georgia
74 H8 **Hinganghat** India
28 D4 **Hinge** Denmark
101 P1 **Hingham** Montana
77 J7 **Hinglaj** Pakistan
20 A5 **Hinglé, le** France
77 K6 **Hingol** *R* Pakistan
74 G9 **Hingoli** India
102 G7 **Hinkley** California
143 G7 **Hinkley, Mt** W Australia
29 J11 **Hinnerjoki** Finland
28 E4 **Hinnerup** Denmark
26 H3 **Hinnöy** *isld* Norway
61 K9 **Hino** *R* Japan
71 F6 **Hinoba-an** Philippines
16 D6 **Hinojosa del Duque** Spain
60 E13 **Hinokage** Japan
60 F10 **Hinomi saki** *C* Japan
99 S8 **Hinsdale** Illinois
95 O4 **Hinsdale** Massachusetts
101 S1 **Hinsdale** Montana
94 J4 **Hinsdale** New York
8 D2 **Hinstock** England
38 F7 **Hinterbichl** Austria
36 E3 **Hintermeilingen** W Germany
41 K4 **Hinterrhein** Switzerland
41 O3 **Hinter Riss** Austria
38 K6 **Hinterstoder** Austria
41 P3 **Hinter Tux** Austria
36 D5 **Hinter Weidenthal** W Germany
9 H3 **Hintlesham** England
117 P9 **Hinton** Alberta
107 M6 **Hinton** Oklahoma
61 O9 **Hi-numa** Japan
129 J7 **Hiocolândia** Brazil
135 R2 **Hio Pt** Hawaiian Is
124 J5 **Hipólito** Mexico
25 C3 **Hippolytushoef** Netherlands
80 F2 **Hippos** Syria
60 C12 **Hirado** Japan
60 C12 **Hirado-jima** *isld* Japan
75 K8 **Hirakud Res** India
95 R3 **Hiram** Maine
60 C12 **Hira shima** *isld* Japan
60 F10 **Hirata** Japan
61 N10 **Hiratsuka** Japan
124 D5 **Hiray** Mexico
78 D2 **Hirfanli Dam** Turkey
48 K3 **Hirlău** Romania
61 O8 **Hirono** Japan
60 R3 **Hiroo** Japan
61 O5 **Hirosaki** Japan
60 G10 **Hirose** Japan
60 F11 **Hiroshima** Japan
61 P7 **Hirota-wan** *B* Japan
36 F6 **Hirsau** W Germany
37 M4 **Hirschau** W Germany
Hirschberg *see* **Jelenia Góra**
37 M3 **Hirschberg** E Germany
38 L7 **Hirschegg** Austria
37 O6 **Hirschenstein** *mt* W Germany
36 F5 **Hirschhorn** W Germany
28 F2 **Hirsholmene** *isld* Denmark
22 G4 **Hirson** France
48 L6 **Hîrşova** Romania
28 D1 **Hirtshals** Denmark
29 M10 **Hirvensalmi** Finland
29 L7 **Hirvineva** Finland
8 C4 **Hirwaun** Wales
60 B13 **Hisaka-shima** *isld* Japan
74 F4 **Hisar** India
77 J2 **Hisar, Koh-i-** *mts* Afghanistan
80 F6 **Hisban** *R* Jordan
27 F15 **Hishult** Sweden
98 E6 **Hisle** S Dakota
80 E6 **Hisma** Jordan
127 J5 **Hispaniola** *isld* W Indies
80 G1 **Hispin** Syria
79 G4 **Hisya** Syria
78 J5 **Hit** Iraq
60 D12 **Hita** Japan
61 O9 **Hitachi** Japan
61 O9 **Hitachi-Ōta** Japan
60 C11 **Hitakatsu** Japan
9 G3 **Hitcham** England
107 M6 **Hitchcock** Oklahoma
119 O9 **Hitchcock** Sask
98 H5 **Hitchcock** S Dakota
109 M6 **Hitchcock** Texas
9 F4 **Hitchin** England
107 P6 **Hitchita** Oklahoma
103 O4 **Hite** Utah
60 D13 **Hitoyoshi** Japan
26 C8 **Hitra** Norway
32 L6 **Hittfeld** W Germany
33 O6 **Hitzacker** W Germany
61 N9 **Hiuchi dake** *mt* Japan
60 G11 **Hiuchi-nada** *sea* Japan
135 N9 **Hiva Oa** *isld* Pacific Oc
60 H12 **Hiwasa** Japan
112 C2 **Hiwassee** *R* N Carolina/Tenn
112 C2 **Hiwassee Lake** N Carolina
141 L5 **Hixson Cay** *isld* Gt Barrier Reef **Aust**
60 O3 **Hiyama** *prefect* Japan
78 J2 **Hizan** Turkey
28 E2 **Hjallerup** Denmark
27 H12 **Hjälmaren** *L* Sweden
28 C3 **Hjarbæk** Denmark
28 B2 **Hjardemål** Denmark
26 G6 **Hjarfjell** *mt* Norway
28 E5 **Hjarnø** *isld* Denmark
27 C12 **Hjartdal** Norway
28 C6 **Hjarup** Denmark
26 B10 **Hjelle** Norway
28 F4 **Hjelm** *isld* Denmark
28 K7 **Hjelm Bugt** *B* Denmark
27 B12 **Hjelmeland** Norway
26 O1 **Hjelmsöy** *isld* Norway
28 G5 **Hjembæk** Denmark
26 D9 **Hjerkinn** Norway
28 B4 **Hjerm** Denmark
28 C6 **Hjerndrup** Denmark
28 B6 **Hjerpsted** Denmark
28 A5 **Hjerting** Denmark
27 G13 **Hjo** Sweden
28 C4 **Hjøllund** Denmark
28 C6 **Hjordkær** Denmark
28 D2 **Hjørring** Denmark
Hjørring *co see* **Nordjylland**
28 E7 **Hjortø** Denmark
28 E4 **Hjortshøj** Denmark
28 C5 **Hjortsvang** Denmark
26 B9 **Hjørundfjord** Norway
27 D12 **Hjuksebö** Norway
68 D2 **Hka** *R* Burma
68 D2 **Hkok** *R* Burma
68 C4 **Hlegu** Burma
37 P3 **Hlinec** *R* Czechoslovakia
31 K7 **Hlohovec** Czechoslovakia
28 A5 **Ho** Denmark
85 E7 **Ho** Ghana
67 B8 **Hoa Binh** Vietnam
68 J7 **Hoa Da** Vietnam
118 C5 **Hoadley** Alberta
98 F8 **Hoagland** Nebraska
68 J5 **Hoai Nhon** Vietnam
68 G1 **Hoang Su Phi** Vietnam
87 B9 **Hoanib** *R* Namibia
60 E12 **Hoashi** Japan
101 P6 **Hoback** *R* Wyoming
101 P6 **Hoback Pk** Wyoming
99 T8 **Hobart** Indiana
107 L6 **Hobart** Oklahoma
138 F8 **Hobart** Tasmania
141 H6 **Hobartville** Queensland
108 D3 **Hobbs** New Mexico
146 J10 **Hobbs Coast** Antarctica
111 K7 **Hobbs Island** Alabama
113 G10 **Hobe Sound** Florida
112 K1 **Hobgood** N Carolina
22 G1 **Hoboken** Belgium
112 E6 **Hoboken** Georgia
Hobot Xar *see* **Xianghuang Qi**
28 D3 **Hobro** Denmark
101 Q3 **Hobson** Montana
145 E2 **Hobson, Mt** New Zealand
112 L2 **Hobucken** N Carolina
28 A5 **Ho Bugt** *B* Denmark
27 K15 **Hoburgen** *lt ho* Sweden
71 D5 **Hoc** *isld* Philippines
47 K6 **Hocalar** Turkey
111 B7 **Hochatown** Oklahoma
38 N8 **Hocheck** *mt* Austria
87 C10 **Hochfeld** Namibia
36 D6 **Hochfelden** France
38 G7 **Hochfilzen** Austria
38 F8 **Hochgall** *mt* Italy
37 K2 **Hochheim** E Germany
109 K6 **Hochheim** Texas
36 E3 **Hochheim** W Germany
68 H7 **Ho Chi Minh** Vietnam
38 K8 **Hochobir** *mt* Austria
41 N2 **Hoch Platte** *mt* W Germany
38 M6 **Hochschwab** *mt* Austria
36 D5 **Hochspeyer** W Germany
37 K4 **Höchstädt** W Germany
37 K6 **Höchstädt** W Germany
36 D2 **Höchstenbach** W Germany
144 C5 **Hochstetter, L** New Zealand
38 K9 **Hochstuhl** *mt* Yugoslavia
36 F5 **Hockenheim** W Germany
94 E7 **Hocking** *R* Ohio
94 F7 **Hockingport** Ohio
109 M5 **Hockley** Texas
9 E3 **Hockley Heath** England
9 F4 **Hockliffe** England
28 B5 **Hodde** Denmark
13 F6 **Hodder, R** England
9 F4 **Hoddesdon** England
Hodeida *see* **Ḩudaydah, Al**
111 D9 **Hodge** Louisiana
110 L4 **Hodgenville** Kentucky
98 B3 **Hodges** Montana
112 E3 **Hodges** S Carolina
123 Q4 **Hodges Hill** *peak* Nfld
102 G8 **Hodges, L** California
118 L8 **Hodgeville** Sask
119 U7 **Hodgson** Manitoba
140 C3 **Hodgson Downs** N Terr Aust
85 C5 **Hodh** *reg* Mauritania
80 B7 **Hodiyya** Israel
48 F4 **Hódmezővásárhely** Hungary
85 E1 **Hodna, Mts. du** Algeria
31 K7 **Hodonin** Czechoslovakia
48 C4 **Hodos** Yugoslavia
28 B4 **Hodsager** Denmark
116 N3 **Hodzana, R** Alaska
28 F4 **Hoed** Denmark
25 A6 **Hoedekenskerke** Netherlands
18 D5 **Hoëdic, I** France
106 F4 **Hoehne** Colorado
25 B5 **Hoeksche Waard** Netherlands
25 B5 **Hoek van Holland** Netherlands
119 M6 **Hoey** Sask
37 M3 **Hof** W Germany
36 H2 **Hofbieber** W Germany
Hofei *see* **Hefei**
36 F6 **Hofen** W Germany
37 J6 **Hofen** W Germany
98 L4 **Hoffman** Minnesota
112 H2 **Hoffman** N Carolina
32 K10 **Hofgeismar** W Germany
36 E3 **Hofheim** W Germany
37 K3 **Hofheim** W Germany
37 P6 **Hofkirchen** W Germany
115 S5 **Höfn** Iceland
60 E11 **Hōfu** Japan
28 K4 **Höganäs** Sweden
139 H7 **Hogan Group** *islds* Tasmania Australia
102 D3 **Hogan Res** California
111 M8 **Hogansville** Georgia
141 H7 **Hoganthulla** *R* Queensland
119 P1 **Hogarth** Ontario
140 D5 **Hogarth, Mt** N Terr Aust
116 K3 **Hogatza** Alaska
116 K3 **Hogatza** *R* Alaska
101 N5 **Hogback Mt** Montana
27 F12 **Hogboda** Sweden
27 J14 **Högby** Sweden
28 C7 **Högel** W Germany
101 R1 **Hogeland** Montana
27 H12 **Högfors** Sweden
85 F4 **Hoggar** *mt reg* Algeria
119 V1 **Hogg L** Manitoba
48 J5 **Hoghiz** Romania
94 B1 **Hog I** Michigan
95 M9 **Hog I** Virginia
28 B4 **Høgild** Denmark
80 C4 **Hogla** Israel
27 H14 **Högsby** Sweden
26 J9 **Högsjö** Sweden
126 H4 **Hogsty Reef** Bahamas
26 G5 **Högtuvbre** *mt* Norway
100 A2 **Hoh** *R* Washington
33 R10 **Hohburg** E Germany
36 C3 **Hohe Acht** *mt* W Germany
41 N3 **Hohe Geige** *mt* Austria
37 K6 **Hohen-Altheim** W Germany
38 N6 **Hohenberg** Austria
37 M3 **Hohenberg** W Germany
33 S9 **Hohenbucke** E Germany
37 M5 **Hohenburg** W Germany
33 N10 **Hohenebra** E Germany
32 M8 **Hoheneggelsen** W Germany
36 H1 **Hoheneiche** W Germany
41 L3 **Hohenems** Austria
37 M5 **Hohenfels** W Germany
33 Q7 **Hohengöhren** E Germany
36 G6 **Hohenheim** W Germany
37 M7 **Hohenkammer** W Germany
33 Q10 **Hohenleina** E Germany
37 N2 **Hohenleuben** E Germany
32 G10 **Hohenlimburg** W Germany
32 L5 **Hohenlockstedt** W Germany
33 S5 **Hohenmocker** E Germany
37 N1 **Hohenmölsen** E Germany
33 Q7 **Hohennauen** E Germany
36 H2 **Hohenroda** W Germany
33 Q8 **Hohenseeden** E Germany
33 S9 **Hohenseefeld** E Germany
36 E2 **Hohensolms** W Germany
36 H6 **Hohenstaufen** W Germany
36 G7 **Hohenstein** W Germany
37 O2 **Hohenstein-Ernstthal** E Germany
110 J6 **Hohenwald** Tennessee
37 L6 **Hohenwart** W Germany
32 K9 **Hohenwepel** W Germany
32 L4 **Hohenwestedt** W Germany
33 N6 **Hohenzethen** W Germany
36 F7 **Hohenzollern** W Germany
41 M3 **Hoher Ifen** *mt* Austria
41 M3 **Hohes Licht** *mt* Austria
37 J5 **Hohe Steig** *mt* W Germany
38 F7 **Hohe Tauern** Austria
58 F3 **Hohhot** China
36 E6 **Hohloh** *mt* W Germany
33 M7 **Hohne** W Germany
19 K4 **Hohneck** *mt* France
33 N6 **Hohnstorf** W Germany
116 J6 **Hoholitna** *R* Alaska
32 K4 **Hohrr** W Germany
66 E4 **Hoh Sai Hu** *L* China
33 N4 **Hohwacht** W Germany
36 C7 **Hohwald** France
66 D4 **Hoh Xil Shan** *ra* China
68 J5 **Hoi An** Vietnam
107 M3 **Hoisington** Kansas
66 F4 **Hoit Taria** China
67 B6 **Hoi-Xuan** Vietnam
75 P6 **Hojai** India
28 E6 **Højby** Denmark
28 C5 **Højen** Denmark
28 B7 **Højer** Denmark
28 K6 **Højerup** Denmark
60 F12 **Hōjō** Japan
28 B6 **Højrup** Denmark
28 C3 **Højslev** Denmark
68 D2 **Hok** *R* Burma
99 P6 **Hokah** Minnesota
Hokang *see* **Hegang**
27 K11 **Hökhuvud** Sweden
61 N9 **Hōki** *R* Japan
145 D1 **Hokianga Harbour** New Zealand
144 C5 **Hokitika** New Zealand
60 Q2 **Hokkaido** *isld* Japan
27 D12 **Hokksund** Norway
61 O9 **Hokota** Japan
61 K10 **Hokunō** Japan
61 K10 **Hokuriku Tunnel** Japan
27 C11 **Hol** Norway
27 E12 **Höland** Norway
28 E3 **Holbæk** Denmark
28 H5 **Holbæk** Denmark
Holbæk *co see* **Vestsjælland**
9 G2 **Holbeach** England
117 K10 **Holberg** Br Col
28 C7 **Holbøl** Denmark
141 J4 **Holborne I** Queensland
103 O7 **Holbrook** Arizona
101 N7 **Holbrook** Idaho
98 F9 **Holbrook** Nebraska
139 H6 **Holbrook** New S Wales
13 F6 **Holcombe** England
99 P4 **Holcombe** Wisconsin
118 E5 **Holden** Alberta
95 Q4 **Holden** Massachusetts
110 C3 **Holden** Missouri
103 M2 **Holden** Utah
94 E9 **Holden** W Virginia
107 O6 **Holdenville** Oklahoma
119 M8 **Holdfast** Sask
99 M4 **Holdingford** Minnesota
32 H7 **Holdorf** W Germany
98 G9 **Holdrege** Nebraska
28 G7 **Holeby** Denmark
27 E12 **Holen** Norway
76 C4 **Hole Narsipur** India
31 K6 **Holešov** Czechoslovakia
127 P6 **Holetown** Barbados
94 C5 **Holgate** Ohio
126 F4 **Holguín** Cuba
48 D2 **Holíč** Czechoslovakia
116 H5 **Holikachuk** Alaska
116 J6 **Holitna** *R* Alaska
27 F11 **Höljes** Sweden
119 T9 **Holland** Manitoba
99 U7 **Holland** Michigan
98 K5 **Holland** Minnesota
94 J4 **Holland** New York
100 B7 **Holland** Oregon
109 K5 **Holland** Texas
9 F2 **Holland** *div* England
111 F8 **Hollandale** Mississippi
127 M3 **Holland B** Jamaica
120 K8 **Holland Centre** Ontario
143 C9 **Holland,Mt** W Australia
141 K2 **Holland Park** *dist* Brisbane, Qnsld
25 C5 **Hollandsch Diep** Netherlands
138 E2 **Hollands Hill** S Australia
22 K4 **Hollange** Belgium
32 M8 **Holle** W Germany
33 N5 **Hollenbek** W Germany
32 L6 **Hollenstedt** W Germany
38 N6 **Hollen-Tal** *V* Austria
38 F7 **Hollersbach** Austria
9 H3 **Hollesley B** England
94 J3 **Holley** New York
37 L4 **Hollfeld** W Germany
146 G10 **Hollick-Kenyon Pl** Antarctica
109 J2 **Holliday** Texas
94 J6 **Hollidaysburg** Pennsylvania
107 L7 **Hollis** Oklahoma
102 C5 **Hollister** California
101 L7 **Hollister** Idaho
110 C5 **Hollister** Missouri
107 M7 **Hollister** Oklahoma
22 J2 **Hollogne-sur-Geer** Belgium
111 D10 **Holloway** Louisiana
28 K6 **Höllviken** *C* Sweden
106 H3 **Holly** Colorado
94 D4 **Holly** Michigan
111 F9 **Holly Bluff** Mississippi
144 B6 **Hollyford** *R* New Zealand
111 E7 **Holly Grove** Arkansas
113 F8 **Holly Hill** Florida
112 G4 **Holly Hill** S Carolina
112 K3 **Holly Ridge** N Carolina
113 G11 **Hollywood** Florida
95 L8 **Hollywood** Maryland
28 D6 **Holm** Denmark
26 F6 **Holm** Norway
26 J9 **Holm** Sweden
106 E5 **Holman** New Mexico
114 H3 **Holman Island** N W Terr
28 B5 **Holme Å** *R* Denmark
146 B4 **Holme B** Antarctica
99 P6 **Holmen** Wisconsin
113 K12 **Holmes Cay** *isld* Bahamas
8 D1 **Holmes Chapel** England
119 V1 **Holmes L** Manitoba
101 P5 **Holmes, Mt** Wyoming
141 J3 **Holmes Reef** Great Barrier Reef **Aust**
27 D12 **Holmestr** Norway
119 S9 **Holmfield** Manitoba
13 G6 **Holmfirth** England
26 K6 **Holmfors** Sweden
26 L8 **Holmögadd** *lt ho* Sweden
26 L8 **Holmön** Sweden
13 J6 **Holmpton** England
27 D12 **Holmsbu** Norway
26 J8 **Holmsjö** Sweden
26 H9 **Holmsjön** *L* Sweden
28 A4 **Holmsland Klit** *sand spit* Denmark
115 O3 **Holms Ø** *isld* Greenland
28 E6 **Holmstrup** Fyn **Denmark**
28 G5 **Holmstrup** Vestsjælland Denmark
26 L8 **Holmsund** Sweden
27 K14 **Holmudden** *lt ho* Gotland Sweden
111 C11 **Holmwood** Louisiana
37 M5 **Holnstein** W Germany
27 J12 **Hölö** Sweden
88 C5 **Holoholo** Tanzania
80 C5 **Holon** Israel
87 C11 **Holoog** Namibia
113 F9 **Holopaw** Florida
80 B6 **Holot Ashdod** Israel
142 F2 **Holothuria Banks** W Australia
80 B6 **Holot Yavne** Israel
26 E9 **Holöydal** Norway
141 F2 **Holroyd** *R* Queensland
28 B4 **Holstebro** Denmark
28 B5 **Holsted** Denmark
99 L7 **Holstein** Iowa
98 H9 **Holstein** Nebraska
120 K8 **Holstein** Ontario
28 G6 **Holsteinborg** Denmark
115 O4 **Holsteinsborg** Greenland
112 E1 **Holston** *R* Tennessee
94 F10 **Holston R** Virginia
33 N4 **Holst Schweiz** W Germany
8 B6 **Holsworthy** England
111 J8 **Holt** Alabama
9 H2 **Holt** England
111 K11 **Holt** Florida
94 C4 **Holt** Michigan
98 K1 **Holt** Minnesota
8 D1 **Holt** Wales
98 G7 **Holt Cr** Nebraska
28 K5 **Holte** Denmark
33 O9 **Holtemme** *R* E Germany
25 F4 **Holten** Netherlands
101 O3 **Holter L. Dam** Montana
33 O5 **Holthusen** E Germany
94 B7 **Holton** Indiana
107 P2 **Holton** Kansas
94 B3 **Holton** Michigan
65 D2 **Holt Sum** China
28 C4 **Holtum Å** *R* Denmark
103 J9 **Holtville** California
120 K4 **Holtyre** Ontario
135 U5 **Holualoa** Hawaiian Is
27 C13 **Holum** Norway
25 E2 **Holwerd** Netherlands
116 H5 **Holy Cross** Alaska
Holyhead *see* **Caergybi**
Holy I *see* **Lindisfarne**
12 C3 **Holy I** Scotland
8 B1 **Holy I** Wales
118 G4 **Holyoke** Alberta
106 H1 **Holyoke** Colorado
95 P4 **Holyoke** Massachusetts
107 M3 **Holyrood** Kansas
123 T6 **Holyrood** Nfld
37 P4 **Holýšov** Czechoslovakia
8 D6 **Holywell** England
8 C1 **Holywell** Wales
14 F2 **Holywood** N Ireland
36 D3 **Holzappel** W Germany
33 S9 **Holzdorf** E Germany
33 P5 **Holzendorf** E Germany
32 H8 **Holzhausen** W Germany
36 D3 **Holzhausen** W Germany
37 K6 **Holzheim** W Germany
32 K9 **Holzminden** W Germany
32 G10 **Holzwickede** W Germany
28 H6 **Høm** Denmark
86 G6 **Homa Bay** Kenya
75 Q6 **Homalin** Burma
36 G1 **Homberg** W Germany
60 R2 **Hombetsu** Japan
22 E4 **Homblières** France
85 D5 **Hombori** Mali
Homburg *see* **Nümbrecht**
36 H4 **Homburg** Bayern W Germany
36 C5 **Homburg** Rheinland-Pfalz W Germany
115 N4 **Home B** N W Terr
100 J6 **Homedale** Idaho
141 H4 **Home Hill** Queensland
83 M8 **Home I** Cocos Is Indian Oc
116 M7 **Homer** Alaska
99 T9 **Homer** Illinois
111 C9 **Homer** Louisiana
94 C4 **Homer** Michigan
94 H6 **Homer City** Pennsylvania
9 H3 **Homersfield** England
144 A6 **Homer Tun** New Zealand
112 E6 **Homerville** Georgia
113 G12 **Homestead** Florida
99 P8 **Homestead** Iowa
98 B1 **Homestead** Montana
107 M5 **Homestead** Oklahoma
100 J4 **Homestead** Oregon
141 H5 **Homestead** Queensland
98 K9 **Homestead Nat Mon** Nebraska
111 K8 **Homewood** Alabama
145 E4 **Homewood** New Zealand
68 A6 **Homfray's Str** Andaman Is
107 O5 **Hominy** Oklahoma
26 E9 **Hommelfjell** *mt* Norway
26 E8 **Hommelvik** Norway
25 E3 **Hommerts** Netherlands
21 F7 **Hommes** France
74 G10 **Homnabad** India
89 H5 **Homoine** Mozambique
48 G6 **Homoljske Planina** *mt* Yugoslavia
71 G5 **Homonhon** Philippines
48 J4 **Homorod** Romania
113 E9 **Homosassa** Florida
Homs Libya *see* **Khums, Al**
79 G4 **Homs** Syria
60 F12 **Honai** Japan
Honan *prov see* **Henan**
76 B3 **Honavar** India
47 K7 **Honaz Dağ** *mt* Turkey
68 G7 **Hon Chong** Vietnam
102 C2 **Honcut** California
128 D2 **Honda** Colombia
71 D6 **Honda B** Palawan Philippines
118 D3 **Hondo** Alberta
60 D13 **Hondo** Japan
106 E8 **Hondo** New Mexico
109 H6 **Hondo** Texas
125 P8 **Hondo** *R* Belize
22 D2 **Hondschoote** France
125 L2 **Honduras** *rep* Cent America
119 Q2 **Hone** Manitoba
112 E3 **Honea Path** S Carolina
36 H2 **Hönebach** W Germany
27 D11 **Hönefoss** Norway
95 M5 **Honesdale** Pennsylvania
102 A1 **Honeydew** California
98 J1 **Honeyford** N Dakota
109 M2 **Honey Grove** Texas
109 N5 **Honey Island** Texas
100 E9 **Honey L** California
120 K8 **Honeywood** Ontario
20 F3 **Honfleur** France
28 G5 **Høng** Denmark
65 G2 **Hongai** China
68 H2 **Hon Gai** Vietnam
67 B6 **Hon Gay** Vietnam
67 E5 **Honghai Wan** *B* China
58 F5 **Hong He** *R* China
67 D2 **Honghu** China
67 C3 **Hongjiang** China
67 G6 **Hong Kong** *colony* E Asia
67 F4 **Honglai** China
68 G7 **Hong Ngu** Vietnam
Hongning *see* **Wulian**
58 F2 **Hongor** Mongolia
Hongqiao *see* **Qidong**
67 D7 **Hongqizhen** China
68 E3 **Hongsa** Laos
67 B4 **Hongshui He** *R* China
65 B6 **Hongtong** China
61 J12 **Hongū** Japan
122 H4 **Honguedo Passage** Canada
67 A2 **Hongya** China
58 G5 **Hongze Hu** *L* China
137 N3 **Honiara** Guadalcanal I Solomon Is
9 H2 **Honingham** England
8 C6 **Honiton** England
61 O6 **Honjō** Japan
29 J10 **Honkajoki** Finland
68 H3 **Hon Matt** *isld* Vietnam
68 G3 **Hon Me** *isld* Vietnam
76 B3 **Honnali** India
26 P1 **Honningsvåg** Norway
102 V13 **Honokaa** Hawaiian Is
135 S3 **Honokahua** Hawaiian Is
145 F2 **Honokawa** New Zealand
135 S3 **Honokohau** Hawaiian Is
102 S12 **Honolulu** Hawaiian Is
135 V5 **Honomu** Hawaiian Is
102 R12 **Honouliuli** Hawaiian Is
17 F5 **Honrubia** Spain
59 K4 **Honshū** *isld* Japan
28 H5 **Hønsinge** Denmark
135 U6 **Honuapo** Hawaiian Is
100 D4 **Hood, Mt** Oregon
143 C10 **Hood Pt** W Australia
141 G8 **Hood Ra** Queensland
100 D4 **Hood River** Oregon
100 B2 **Hoodsport** Washington
32 K10 **Hoof** W Germany
25 C4 **Hoofddorp** Netherlands
25 A6 **Hoofdplaat** Netherlands
25 F3 **Hooger Smilde** Netherlands
25 G3 **Hoogeveen** Netherlands
25 G2 **Hoogezand** Netherlands
25 G3 **Hooghalen** Netherlands
75 M8 **Hooghly** *R* India
22 D2 **Hoogstade** Belgium
22 H1 **Hoogstraten** Belgium
41 K2 **Höohster** *mt* W Germany
9 F5 **Hook** England
144 C6 **Hook** New Zealand
135 U5 **Hookena** Hawaiian Is
107 J5 **Hooker** Oklahoma
146 K6 **Hooker, C** Antarctica
140 B4 **Hooker Creek** N Terr **Aust**
14 E4 **Hook Hd** Irish Rep
141 J5 **Hook I** Queensland
141 L7 **Hook Pt** Queensland
141 J4 **Hook Reef** Gt Barrier Reef Aust
109 N2 **Hooks** Texas
95 Q3 **Hooksett** New Hampshire
32 H5 **Hooksiel** W Germany
102 V13 **Hoolehua** Hawaiian Is
117 F6 **Hoonah** Alaska
100 B8 **Hoopa** California
106 E4 **Hooper** Colorado
98 K8 **Hooper** Nebraska
101 N8 **Hooper** Utah
100 G3 **Hooper** Washington
116 D6 **Hooper Bay** Alaska
95 L8 **Hooper I** Maryland
99 T9 **Hoopeston** Illinois
123 Q3 **Hooping Hbr** Nfld
98 J1 **Hoople** N Dakota
89 D6 **Hoopstad** S Africa
27 G16 **Höör** Sweden
25 D3 **Hoorn** Noord **Netherlands**
25 C2 **Hoorn** Texel **Netherlands**
95 O4 **Hoosick Falls** New York
118 H7 **Hoosier** Sask
98 C4 **Hoover** S Dakota
103 K5 **Hoover Dam** Arizona
94 E6 **Hoover Res** Ohio
94 J6 **Hooversville** Pennsylvania
78 H1 **Hopa** Turkey
95 M5 **Hop Bottom** Pennsylvania
9 E4 **Hopcrofts Holt** England
103 L8 **Hope** Arizona
111 C8 **Hope** Arkansas
117 N11 **Hope** Br Col
94 B7 **Hope** Indiana
107 N3 **Hope** Kansas
98 J2 **Hope** N Dakota
127 M2 **Hope Bay** Jamaica
115 N6 **Hopedale** Labrador
Hopeh *prov see* **Hebei**
138 E3 **Hope, L** S Australia
138 E3 **Hopeless, Mt** S Australia
112 J3 **Hope Mills** N Carolina
138 D5 **Hope, Mt** S Australia
147 J12 **Hopen** *isld* Arctic Oc
144 D5 **Hope Pass** New Zealand
116 D2 **Hope, Pt** Alaska
138 F6 **Hopetoun** Victoria
143 D10 **Hopetoun** W Australia
113 L11 **Hope Town** Bahamas
89 D7 **Hopetown** S Africa
122 K8 **Hopewell** Nova Scotia
94 J6 **Hopewell** Pennsylvania
95 K9 **Hopewell** Virginia
115 M6 **Hopewell Is** N W Terr
103 O6 **Hopi Buttes** *mt* Arizona
67 E4 **Ho-p'ing** China
94 B4 **Hopkins** Michigan
99 M9 **Hopkins** Missouri
139 G7 **Hopkins** *R* Victoria
143 G6 **Hopkins,L** W Australia
144 B5 **Hopkins, Mt** New Zealand
110 J5 **Hopkinsville** Kentucky
102 A3 **Hopland** California
68 C2 **Hopong** Burma
33 T7 **Hoppegarten** E Germany
26 Q1 **Hopseidet** Norway
32 G8 **Hopsten** W Germany
9 H2 **Hopton** England
28 C6 **Hoptrup** Denmark
94 H7 **Hopwood** Pennsylvania
141 G5 **Hopwood,Mt** Queensland
114 G8 **Hoquiam** Washington
86 G4 **Hora Abyata** *dist* Ethiopia
107 J3 **Horace** Kansas
37 P2 **Hora Svatého Šebastiána** Czechoslovakia
37 P2 **Hora Svaté Katering** Czechoslovakia
111 B8 **Horatio** Arkansas
30 H6 **Horaždovice** Czechoslovakia
36 F7 **Horb** W Germany
28 J7 **Horbelev** Denmark
37 O7 **Horbering** W Germany
118 B6 **Horburg** Alberta
13 G6 **Horbury** England
28 D3 **Hørby** Nordjylland Denmark
28 E2 **Hørby** Nordjylland Denmark
27 G16 **Hörby** Sweden
16 D5 **Horcajo de los Montes** Spain
16 E5 **Horcajo de Santiago** Spain
124 G3 **Horcasitas** Mexico
36 E4 **Horchheim** W Germany
27 A11 **Hordaland** *reg* Norway
86 B1 **Hordio** Somalia
109 H4 **Hords Cr. Res** Texas
28 A3 **Hørdum** Denmark
8 B3 **Horeb** Wales
88 C6 **Hore B** Zambia
48 H5 **Horezu** Romania
48 F4 **Horgos** Yugoslavia
31 J5 **Hořice** Czechoslovakia
99 S6 **Horicon** Wisconsin
58 F3 **Horinger** China
22 J2 **Horion Hozémont** Belgium
119 M9 **Horizon** Sask
137 S6 **Horizon Depth** Pacific Oc
31 H4 **Horka** E Germany
9 F5 **Horley** England
146 G9 **Horlick Mts** Antarctica
28 E2 **Hørmested** Denmark
Hormo *see* **Nyima**
77 E6 **Hormoz** *isld* Iran
77 E6 **Hormuz, Strait of** Iran
31 J7 **Horn** Austria
25 E6 **Horn** Netherlands
27 H14 **Horn** Sweden
48 F2 **Hornad** *R* Czechoslovakia
26 J5 **Hornavan** *L* Sweden
36 C5 **Hornbach** W Germany
32 J9 **Horn-Bad Meinog** W Germany
28 K4 **Hornbæk** Denmark
111 C10 **Hornbeck** Louisiana
36 E7 **Hornberg** W Germany
27 G13 **Hornborgasjön** *L* Sweden
100 C8 **Hornbrook** California
33 N8 **Hornburg** W Germany
9 F1 **Horncastle** England
27 H11 **Horndal** Sweden
33 N6 **Horndorf** W Germany
28 D1 **Horne** Denmark
28 B5 **Horne** Ribe Denmark
32 L5 **Horneburg** W Germany
26 L8 **Hörnefors** Sweden
28 E6 **Horneland** Denmark
94 K4 **Hornell** New York
115 L8 **Hornepayne** Ontario
110 F5 **Hornersville** Missouri
27 C13 **Hornesund** Norway
28 G2 **Hornfiskrøn** *isld* Denmark
14 C1 **Horn Hd** Irish Rep
33 O8 **Hornhsleben** E Germany
111 H11 **Horn I** Mississippi
141 F1 **Horn I** Queensland
31 K6 **Horni Benešov** Czechoslovakia
137 R4 **Horn, Îles de** Îles Wallis Pacific Oc
124 E4 **Hornillos** Mexico
26 B10 **Hornindal** Norway
26 B10 **Hornindalsvatn** *L* Norway
36 E6 **Hornisgrinde** *mt* W Germany
37 O3 **Horní Slavkov** Czechoslovakia
41 J3 **Hörnli** *mt* Switzerland
116 H6 **Horn Mts** Alaska
114 G5 **Horn Mts** N W Terr
27 C13 **Hornnes** Norway
133 C6 **Hornopiren** *mt* Chile
124 H5 **Hornos** Mexico
133 D9 **Hornos, C. de** Chile
20 J2 **Hornoy** France
117 O4 **Horn R** N W Terr
139 K5 **Hornsby** New S Wales
110 H6 **Hornsby** Tennessee
8 B6 **Horns Cross** England
13 H6 **Hornsea** England
26 L8 **Hörnsjö** Sweden
28 E4 **Hornslet** Denmark
80 E2 **Horns of Hittin** Israel
37 K1 **Hornsömmern** E Germany
33 P5 **Hornstorf** E Germany
28 D5 **Hornstrup** Denmark
28 D5 **Hornum** Vejle Denmark
28 A7 **Hørnum** W Germany
33 S6 **Horn Zieritz** E Germany
60 T1 **Horobetsu** Japan
60 R3 **Horoizumi** Japan
60 Q1 **Horonai** Japan
145 E3 **Horopito** New Zealand
144 C5 **Hororata** New Zealand
60 Q3 **Horoshiri-dake** *mt* Japan
65 A5 **Horo Sum** China
30 H6 **Hořovice** Czechoslovakia
145 E4 **Horowhenua Plain** New Zealand
83 K9 **Horowupotana** Sri Lanka
20 E5 **Horps, le** France
59 H2 **Horqin Youyi Qianqi** China
65 E2 **Horqin Youyi Zhongqi** China
65 F2 **Horqin Zouyi Zhongqi** China
65 E3 **Horqin Zuoyi Houqi** China
129 G8 **Horqueta** Paraguay
133 F2 **Horqueta** Paraguay
28 H7 **Horreby** Denmark
27 F14 **Horred** Sweden
36 B2 **Horrem** W Germany
83 M8 **Horsburgh I** Cocos Is Indian Oc
37 J1 **Hörschel** E Germany
110 K4 **Horse Branch** Kentucky
9 G6 **Horsebridge** E Sussex England
94 B9 **Horse Cave** Kentucky
106 G3 **Horse Cr** Colorado
110 B4 **Horse Cr** Missouri
140 D6 **Horse Cr** N Terr **Aust**
98 A8 **Horse Cr** Wyoming
117 N9 **Horsefly** Br Col
98 F2 **Horsehead L** N Dakota
95 L4 **Horseheads** New York
123 R3 **Horse Is** Nfld
102 D1 **Horse L** California
37 J2 **Hörsel** *R* E Germany
37 J2 **Hörsel Berge** *mt* E Germany
28 D5 **Horsens** Vejle **Denmark**
28 E5 **Horsens Fjord** *inlet* Denmark
118 F2 **Horse, R** Alberta
113 D8 **Horseshoe** Florida
143 C7 **Horse Shoe** W Australia
100 J6 **Horse Shoe Bend** Idaho
140 C7 **Horseshoe Bend** N Terr Aust
138 C2 **Horseshoe Bend** N Terr Australia
127 P4 **Horse Shoe Pt** St Kitts **W I**
103 N7 **Horseshoe Res** Arizona
106 B8 **Horse Springs** New Mexico
9 F5 **Horsham** England
118 H8 **Horsham** Sask
138 F6 **Horsham** Victoria
28 K5 **Hørsholm** Denmark
13 G4 **Horsley** England
28 G7 **Horslunde** Denmark
37 O4 **Horšovský Týn** Czechoslovakia
33 S4 **Horst** E Germany
25 F6 **Horst** Netherlands
32 L5 **Horst** W Germany
32 G8 **Hörstel** W Germany
25 F6 **Hörstgen** W Germany
32 F8 **Horstmar** W Germany
48 E2 **Hor Stubňa** Czechoslovakia
27 D12 **Horten** Norway
112 F6 **Hortense** Georgia
26 M6 **Hortlax** Sweden
107 P2 **Horton** Kansas
114 G4 **Horton** *R* N W Terr
27 C10 **Horungane** Norway
28 C7 **Hörup** W Germany
28 G5 **Hørve** Denmark
27 G15 **Hörvik** Sweden
13 F6 **Horwich** England
120 H5 **Horwood L** Ontario
37 P5 **Hory Matky Boží** Czechoslovakia
31 J5 **Hory Orlické** *mts* Czechoslovakia
47 K7 **Horzom** *R* Turkey
36 G3 **Hösbach** W Germany
76 C4 **Hosdurga** India
70 C3 **Hose Mts** Sarawak
84 G5 **Hosenofu** Libya
77 A3 **Hoseynābad** Iran
111 M11 **Hosford** Florida
74 C10 **Hoshab** Pakistan
74 G7 **Hoshangabad** India
74 F3 **Hoshiarpur** India
98 J7 **Hoskins** Nebraska
98 G4 **Hosmer** S Dakota
60 E13 **Hososhima** Japan
106 C6 **Hospah** New Mexico
76 C3 **Hospet** India
14 C4 **Hospital** Irish Rep
131 G3 **Hospital, Cuchilla del** *mt* Uruguay
29 O6 **Hossa** Finland
86 G4 **Hosseina** Ethiopia
106 B6 **Hosta Butte** *mt* New Mexico
133 D9 **Hoste, I** Chile
18 E8 **Hostens** France
27 G13 **Höstholmen** Sweden
37 O4 **Hostouň** Czechoslovakia
28 A5 **Hostrup** Ribe **Denmark**
28 B7 **Hostrup** Sønderjylland Denmark
28 D7 **Hostrup** W Germany
28 C7 **Hostrup Sø** *L* Denmark
76 C4 **Hosur** India
26 G8 **Hotagen** Sweden
61 L9 **Hotaka** Japan
66 B4 **Hotan** China
66 C4 **Hotan He** *R* China
87 D11 **Hotazel** S Africa
117 P7 **Hotchkiss** Alberta
106 C3 **Hotchkiss** Colorado
102 H3 **Hot Creek Ra** Nevada
33 O8 **Hötensleben** E Germany
140 B1 **Hotham,C** N Terr **Aust**
116 F3 **Hotham Inlet** Alaska
139 H6 **Hotham, Mt** Victoria
26 H7 **Hoting** Sweden
111 C7 **Hot Springs** Arkansas
80 E8 **Hot Springs** Israel
101 L2 **Hot Springs** Montana
112 E2 **Hot Springs** N Carolina
98 C6 **Hot Springs** S Dakota
108 D6 **Hot Springs** Texas
94 H9 **Hot Springs** Virginia
109 O1 **Hot Springs** *nat park* Arkansas
106 D1 **Hot Sulphur Springs** Colorado
114 H4 **Hottah L** N W Terr
22 J3 **Hotton** Belgium
108 B5 **Hot Wells** Texas
32 L6 **Hötzingen** W Germany
28 E2 **Hou** Denmark
18 D5 **Houat, I** France
22 D3 **Houdain** France
20 J4 **Houdan** France
22 G3 **Houdeng** Belgium
18 E8 **Houeillès** France
22 K3 **Houffalize** Belgium
107 J5 **Hough** Oklahoma
99 S2 **Houghton** Michigan
94 J4 **Houghton** New York
98 H4 **Houghton** S Dakota
141 H4 **Houghton** *R* Queensland
94 C2 **Houghton L** Michigan
13 G4 **Houghton-le-Spring** England
145 D1 **Houhora** New Zealand
20 K4 **Houilles** France
144 B7 **Houipapa** New Zealand
20 E3 **Houlgate** France
111 G7 **Houlka** Mississippi
20 H3 **Houlme, le** France
95 T7 **Houlton** Maine
65 B7 **Houma** China
111 F12 **Houma** Louisiana
85 G2 **Houmet Essoug** Tunisia
85 D6 **Houndé** Upper Volta
9 F5 **Hounslow** England
18 E7 **Hourtin** France
95 O5 **Housatonic** *R* Connecticut
108 D1 **House** New Mexico
123 L6 **House Hbr** Madeleine Is, Quebec
12 D3 **House o'-Hill** Scotland
118 E3 **House R** Alberta
103 L2 **House Ra** Utah
117 K8 **Houston** Br Col
99 P6 **Houston** Minnesota
111 H8 **Houston** Mississippi
110 E4 **Houston** Missouri
109 F9 **Houston** Texas
110 C3 **Houstonia** Missouri
109 M5 **Houston, L** Texas
111 C11 **Houston R** Louisiana
89 F4 **Hout** *R* S Africa
89 A10 **Hout B** S Africa
25 D4 **Houten** Netherlands
22 J1 **Houthalen** Belgium
143 A8 **Houtman Abrolhos** *arch* W Aust
94 J6 **Houtzdale** Pennsylvania
22 J3 **Houyet** Belgium
28 E5 **Hov** Denmark
28 N3 **Hov** Faeroes
28 K4 **Hov** Sweden
27 G13 **Hova** Sweden
28 B5 **Hovborg** Denmark
58 B2 **Hovd** Mongolia
27 B12 **Hovden** Norway
26 H9 **Hovdsjö** Sweden
28 A3 **Hove** Denmark
9 F6 **Hove** England
28 G5 **Høve** Vestsjælland **Denmark**
28 D5 **Hovedgård** Denmark
32 J9 **Hövelhof** W Germany
28 B5 **Hoven** Denmark
98 G4 **Hoven** S Dakota
103 P4 **Hovenweep Nat. Mon** Utah
28 A4 **Hover** Denmark
28 A4 **Hover Å** *R* Denmark
77 A4 **Hoveyzeh** Iran
99 R2 **Hovland** Minnesota
53 F9 **Hovlya** U.S.S.R.
28 C6 **Hovslund** Denmark
107 O4 **Howard** Kansas
94 E6 **Howard** Ohio
94 K5 **Howard** Pennsylvania
141 L7 **Howard** Queensland
98 J5 **Howard** S Dakota
94 B3 **Howard City** Michigan
108 F5 **Howard Cr** Texas
140 D1 **Howard I** N Terr **Aust**
99 M4 **Howard L** Minnesota
116 J2 **Howard Pass** Alaska
99 T6 **Howards Grove** Wisconsin
86 D2 **Howar, Wadi** *watercourse* Sudan
13 H6 **Howden** England
101 M6 **Howe** Idaho
94 B5 **Howe** Indiana
109 N1 **Howe** Oklahoma
109 L2 **Howe** Texas
139 J6 **Howe, C** New S Wales
83 L13 **Howe, Î** Indian Oc
94 D4 **Howell** Michigan
139 K3 **Howell** New S Wales
101 N8 **Howell** Utah
98 J8 **Howells** Nebraska
138 C2 **Howe, Mt** S Australia
15 F4 **Howe of Mearns** Scotland
98 D5 **Howes** S Dakota
117 M11 **Howe Sound** Br Col
145 E2 **Howick** New Zealand
121 R7 **Howick** Quebec
141 H2 **Howick Group** *islds* Gt Barrier Reef **Aust**
138 E2 **Howitt, L** S Australia
139 H6 **Howitt, Mt** Victoria
95 T1 **Howland** Maine
137 R1 **Howland I** Pacific Oc
123 P4 **Howley** Nfld
75 N7 **Howrah** India
117 P10 **Howser** Br Col
14 E3 **Howth** Irish Rep
110 F5 **Hoxie** Arkansas
107 K2 **Hoxie** Kansas
32 K9 **Höxter** W Germany
66 D2 **Hoxtolgay** China
15 E2 **Hoy** Scotland
32 K7 **Hoya** W Germany
31 H4 **Hoyerswerda** E Germany
8 C1 **Hoylake** England
26 F7 **Höylandet** Norway
120 J4 **Hoyle** Ontario
110 G3 **Hoyleton** Illinois
33 O9 **Hoym** E Germany
16 C4 **Hoyos** Spain
47 L6 **Hoyran** Turkey
15 E2 **Hoy Snd** Scotland
107 P2 **Hoyt** Kansas
122 F8 **Hoyt** New Brunswick
29 O9 **Höytiäinen** *L* Finland
101 O9 **Hoyt Pk** Utah
68 C2 **Hpa Lai** Burma
37 P4 **Hracholuská Nádrž** *res* Czechoslovakia
31 J5 **Hradec Králové** Czechoslovakia
37 P3 **Hradiště** *mt* Czechoslovakia
Hranice Czechoslovakia *see* **Rossbach**
31 K6 **Hranice** Czechoslovakia
48 F2 **Hriňová** Czechoslovakia
31 L7 **Hron** *R* Czechoslovakia
37 O3 **Hroznětín** Czechoslovakia
31 O5 **Hrubieszów** Poland
31 J7 **Hrušovany** Czechoslovakia
42 G4 **Hrvatska** *reg* Yugoslavia
68 C2 **Hsa Mong Hkam** Burma
68 C3 **Hsataw** Burma
66 D5 **Hsia-ju Ts'o** *L* China
67 G6 **Hsiao-lan Hsü** *isld* Taiwan
68 C2 **Hsi Hkip** Burma
68 C2 **Hsi-hseng** Burma
58 F4 **Hsin-ch'iang** China
67 G4 **Hsin-chu** Taiwan
59 H3 **Hsin-min** China
68 C1 **Hsipaw** Burma
66 D5 **Hsi-tsang Kao-yüan** *reg* China
68 C1 **Hsumhsai** Burma
67 F4 **Hua'an** China
128 C6 **Huacho** Peru
65 H1 **Huachuan** China
128 C5 **Huacrachuco** Peru
65 C4 **Huade** China
59 J3 **Huadian** China
67 G2 **Huading Shan** *mt* China
68 F5 **Huai** *R* Thailand
65 C4 **Huai'an** China
58 G5 **Huaibei** China
65 F3 **Huaide** China
65 F3 **Huaidezhen** China
58 F5 **Huai He** *R* China
67 C3 **Huaihua** China
67 D5 **Huaiji** China
65 C4 **Huailai** China
68 F4 **Huai Luang** *R* Thailand
58 G5 **Huainan** China
67 E1 **Huaining** China
58 F4 **Huairen** China

Huairou — Inegöl 35

65 C4 Huairou China
68 F4 Huai Yang Res Thailand
67 C4 Huaiyuan China
125 L9 Huajuápan de León Mexico
103 L6 Hualapai Mts Arizona
67 E2 Hualin China
128 C5 Huallaga R Peru
128 C5 Huallanca Peru
65 H1 Huama China
65 H1 Huanan China
128 E7 Huanay Bolivia
128 C6 Huancabamba Pasco Peru
128 C5 Huancabamba Piura Peru
128 E7 Huancane Peru
128 C6 Huancavelica Peru
128 C6 Huancayo Peru
128 E8 Huanchaca Bolivia
128 F6 Huanchaca, Sa. de mts Bolivia
128 C5 Huanchaco Peru
Huang'an see Hong'an
67 G1 Huangang China
Huangcaoba see Xingyi
58 G5 Huangchuan China
67 E1 Huanggang China
65 D3 Huangganliang mt China
67 F3 Huanggang Shan mt China
58 D4 Huang He R China
67 E1 Huang He R China
65 D5 Huang Ho, Mouths of the China
65 D5 Huanghua China
65 C7 Huangkou China
67 E2 Huanglaomen China
65 A7 Huangling China
68 J3 Huangliu China
65 A7 Huanglong China
65 C7 Huanglongsi China
67 E1 Huangmei China
67 C4 Huangmian China
65 G3 Huangnihe China
67 E1 Huangpi China
67 B3 Huangpin China
67 C6 Huangpo China
67 D5 Huangpu China
67 E2 Huangshagang China
67 F1 Huang Shan mts China
65 E6 Huangshanguan China
58 D4 Huang Shui R China
65 G3 Huangsongdian China
65 D4 Huangtuliangzi China
65 E6 Huang Xian China
67 G2 Huangyan China
67 D3 Huangyangsi China
Huangzhou see Huanggang
67 C7 Huangzhu China
67 G1 Huaniao Shan isld China
67 A4 Huaning China
67 C4 Huanjiang China
58 E4 Huan Jiang R China
65 F4 Huanren China
Huanshan see Yuhuan
58 G5 Huanshi China
128 D6 Huanta Peru
65 D6 Huantai China
128 C5 Huánuco Peru
128 D6 Huanzo, Cord. de mts Peru
125 N3 Huaonta Nicaragua
67 G4 Hua-p'ing Hsü isld Taiwan
128 E7 Huara Chile
128 C5 Huaraz Peru
128 C6 Huariaca Peru
128 C6 Huarmey Peru
67 D2 Huarong China
128 C5 Huascarán mt Peru
133 C3 Huasco Chile
131 B2 Huasco, R Chile
67 D3 Huashi China
125 M2 Huaspuc Honduras
124 E4 Huatabampo Mexico
65 E3 Hua Tugal China
125 L8 Huatusco Mexico
125 K7 Huauchinango Mexico
65 A7 Hua Xian China
65 C7 Hua Xian China
67 D5 Hua Xian China
65 C7 Huaxiancheng China
65 A7 Huayin China
67 B1 Huaying Shan mts China
58 E6 Huayuan China
67 C2 Huayuan China
67 E1 Huayuan China
67 C6 Huazhou China
65 F4 Huazi China
99 N7 Hubbard Iowa
119 O7 Hubbard Sask
109 L4 Hubbard Texas
109 H3 Hubbard Cr. Res Texas
94 D2 Hubbard L Michigan
117 D5 Hubbard, Mt Alaska/Yukon Terr
122 H9 Hubbards Nova Scotia
98 J9 Hubbell Nebraska
58 F5 Hubei prov China
121 Q7 Huberdeau Quebec
33 T7 Hubertusstock E Germany
76 B3 Hubli India
32 J6 Huchting W Germany
25 F6 Hückelhoven-Ratheim W Germany
36 C1 Hückeswagen W Germany
140 D6 Huckitta N Terr Aust
9 E1 Hucknall England
22 B2 Hucqueliers France
72 E6 Hudaydah, Al N Yemen
13 G6 Huddersfield England
27 J12 Huddinge Sweden
32 H6 Hude W Germany
32 L7 Hudemühlen W Germany
26 J10 Hudiksvall Sweden
20 B4 Hudimesnil France
106 F1 Hudson Colorado
113 E9 Hudson Florida
110 G1 Hudson Illinois
94 B5 Hudson Indiana
99 O7 Hudson Iowa
107 M3 Hudson Kansas
94 C5 Hudson Michigan
95 O4 Hudson New York
94 F5 Hudson Ohio
115 K7 Hudson Ontario
101 R7 Hudson Wyoming
133 C7 Hudson mt Chile
95 O3 Hudson R New York
115 L6 Hudson Bay Canada
114 J7 Hudson Bay Sask
95 O3 Hudson Falls New York
107 P5 Hudson, L. Oklahoma
146 H11 Hudson Mts Antarctica
114 G6 Hudson's Hope Br Columbia
115 M5 Hudson Str Canada
94 B4 Hudsonville Michigan
119 W5 Hudwin L Manitoba
68 H4 Hue Vietnam
16 C4 Huebra R Spain
131 B7 Huechulafquén, L Argentina
108 B4 Hueco Mts Texas
48 H4 Huedin Romania
124 G5 Huehueto, Cerro mt Mexico
125 K7 Huejutla Mexico
18 C4 Huelgoat France
16 E7 Huelma Spain
16 C7 Huelva Spain
16 C7 Huelva prov Spain
16 C7 Huelva R Spain
68 G4 Huen Laos
131 B3 Huentelauquén Chile
124 D3 Huépac Mexico
133 C6 Huequi, Pen Chile
17 F7 Huércal Overa Spain
106 F3 Huerfano R Colorado
131 C3 Huerta, Sa. de la ra Argentina
17 G6 Huertas, C. de las Spain
124 J5 Huertecillas Mexico
17 G3 Huerva R Spain
17 G2 Huesca Spain
17 G2 Huesca prov Spain
17 F7 Huéscar Spain
16 D7 Huesna R Spain
108 B5 Hueso, Sierra del mts Mexico
125 J8 Huétamo Mexico
17 F4 Huete Spain
98 F3 Huff N Dakota
36 G5 Hüffenhardt W Germany
98 H4 Huffton S Dakota
77 A7 Hufuf, Al Saudi Arabia
116 K4 Huggins I Alaska
98 F9 Hugh Butler L Nebraska
118 F6 Hughenden Alberta
141 G5 Hughenden Queensland
110 F7 Hughes Arkansas
121 L4 Hughes Ontario
138 A4 Hughes S Australia
119 R2 Hughes R Manitoba
109 N3 Hughes Springs Texas
110 C3 Hughesville Missouri
140 C6 Hugh R N Terr Aust
118 K7 Hughton Sask
9 F7 Hugh Town Isles of Scilly England
106 G2 Hugo Colorado
99 N4 Hugo Minnesota
107 P7 Hugo Oklahoma
100 B7 Hugo Oregon
107 J4 Hugoton Kansas
36 D7 Hugsweier W Germany
65 B6 Huguan China
Huhehot see Hohhot
58 F3 Huhehot China
67 F4 Hui'an China
145 F3 Huiarau Range New Zealand
67 E4 Huichang China
Huicheng see She Xian
124 H7 Huicholes, Sa. de los mts Mexico
59 J3 Huichŏn N Korea
67 E5 Huidong China
65 G2 Huifaheng China
128 C3 Huila div Colombia
58 G4 Huimin China
65 G3 Huinan China
67 B3 Huishui China
21 F7 Huismes France
20 G5 Huîsne R France
21 I6 Huisseau-sur-Cosson France
65 C7 Huiting China
67 C3 Huitong China
29 K10 Huittinen Finland
125 K8 Huitzuco Mexico
65 B7 Hui Xian China
125 N10 Huixtla Mexico
Huiyang see Huizhou
25 D4 Huizen Netherlands
67 E5 Huizhou China
145 F3 Huka Falls New Zealand
145 E4 Hukanui New Zealand
144 C5 Hukarere New Zealand
75 R5 Hukawng Valley Burma
145 E1 Hukerenui New Zealand
67 E2 Hukou China
87 D10 Hukuntsi Botswana
107 O5 Hulah Oklahoma
59 J2 Hulan China
65 F1 Hulan Ergi China
65 G1 Hulan He R China
80 F1 Hulata Israel
98 B5 Hulett Wyoming
Huliao see Dabu
65 J2 Hulin China
65 E2 Hulin He R China
13 H6 Hull England
99 P10 Hull Illinois
98 K6 Hull Iowa
98 F3 Hull N Dakota
115 M8 Hull Quebec
109 N5 Hull Texas
140 A6 Hull Cr N Terr Aust
138 A1 Hull Cr N Terr Australia
146 J10 Hull Gl Antarctica
134 K9 Hull I Phoenix Is Pacific Oc
22 G2 Hulpe, la Belgium
28 E1 Hulsig Denmark
25 B6 Hulst Netherlands
27 H14 Hultsfred Sweden
65 E4 Huludao China
58 G2 Hulun Nur L China
59 J1 Huma China
127 M5 Humacao Puerto Rico
59 H1 Huma He R China
128 F5 Humaitá Brazil
130 B10 Humaitá Paraguay
87 D12 Humansdorp S Africa
110 C4 Humansville Missouri
128 C6 Humay Peru
87 C9 Humbe Angola
123 P5 Humbermouth Nfld
13 H6 Humber, R England
13 H6 Humberside co England
99 Q5 Humbird Wisconsin
28 F7 Humble Denmark
109 M6 Humble Texas
106 G9 Humble City New Mexico
103 M7 Humboldt Arizona
99 S10 Humboldt Illinois
99 M7 Humboldt Iowa
107 P4 Humboldt Kansas
102 F1 Humboldt Nevada
114 J7 Humboldt Sask
110 H6 Humboldt Tennessee
102 F1 Humboldt R Nevada
100 A9 Humboldt B California
115 N2 Humboldt Gletscher gla Greenland
102 F2 Humboldt L Nevada
144 D5 Humboldt, Mt New Zealand
144 B6 Humboldt Mts New Zealand
100 G9 Humboldt Range Nevada
102 F1 Humboldt Rge Nevada
102 G2 Humboldt Salt Marsh Nevada
94 J8 Hume Virginia
141 H7 Humeburn Queensland
77 F7 Hūmedān Iran
48 G2 Humenné Czechoslovakia
139 H6 Hume Res New S Wales
99 N9 Humeston Iowa
28 K5 Humlebæk Denmark
28 B3 Humlum Denmark
32 K9 Humme W Germany
95 L6 Hummelstown Pennsylvania
32 G7 Hümmling hills W Germany
144 C6 Hummock mt New Zealand
127 K10 Humocaro Bajo Venezuela
131 A5 Humos, C Chile
87 B9 Humpata Angola
111 E7 Humphrey Arkansas
101 N5 Humphrey Idaho
98 J8 Humphrey Nebraska
100 D2 Humphrey Washington
102 E5 Humphreys California
110 C1 Humphreys Missouri
103 N6 Humphreys Pk Arizona
140 C7 Humphries, Mt N Terr Aust
31 J6 Humpolec Czechoslovakia
29 K11 Humppila Finland
100 B2 Humptulips Washington
140 B2 Humpty Doo N Terr Aust
84 F4 Hūn Libya
115 R4 Huna Fjordhur Iceland
67 C3 Hunan prov China
65 H3 Hunchun China
144 D5 Hundalee New Zealand
28 A3 Hundborg Denmark
28 B6 Hunderup Denmark
28 H5 Hundested Denmark
117 N10 Hundred Mile House Br Col
26 M6 Hundsjö Sweden
28 E5 Hundslund Denmark
38 G7 Hundstein mt Austria
28 D2 Hune Denmark
48 H5 Hunedoara Romania
48 H5 Hunedoara reg Romania
36 H2 Hünfeld W Germany
36 E3 Hünfelden W Germany
48 D3 Hungary rep Europe
26 H9 Hunge Sweden
36 F3 Hungen W Germany
9 E5 Hungerford England
141 G8 Hungerford Queensland
65 G5 Hŭngnam N Korea
101 L1 Hungry Horse Dam Montana
101 M1 Hungry Horse Res Montana
68 H2 Hung Yen Vietnam
65 B4 Hun He R China
65 E4 Hun He R China
65 G4 Hunjiang China
65 F4 Hun Jiang R China
13 H5 Hunmanby England
99 P10 Hunnewell Missouri
25 G2 Hunse R Netherlands
25 F7 Hünshoven W Germany
9 G2 Hunstanton England
28 B2 Hunstrup Denmark
76 C4 Hunsur India
65 E2 Hunt China
109 H5 Hunt Texas
120 J3 Hunta Ontario
32 H8 Hunte R W Germany
32 H8 Hunteburg W Germany
110 E6 Hunter Arkansas
107 M2 Hunter Kansas
98 J2 Hunter N Dakota
144 C6 Hunter New Zealand
107 N5 Hunter Oklahoma
109 J6 Hunter Texas
137 P6 Hunter isld Pacific Oc
139 K4 Hunter R New S Wales
117 J10 Hunter I Br Col
99 P1 Hunter I Ontario
139 G8 Hunter I Tasmania
116 M5 Hunter, Mt Alaska
144 A6 Hunter Mts New Zealand
144 B6 Hunter R New Zealand
122 J7 Hunter River Pr Edward I
100 G1 Hunters Washington
68 A3 Hunter's B Burma
141 F6 Hunter's Gorge Queensland
144 C6 Hunter's Hills, The New Zealand
12 D2 Hunterston Scotland
112 G2 Huntersville N Carolina
94 G8 Huntersville W Virginia
141 J7 Hunterton Queensland
94 B5 Huntertown Indiana
145 E3 Hunterville New Zealand
110 K3 Huntingburg Indiana
9 F3 Huntingdon England
94 J6 Huntingdon Pennsylvania
121 Q7 Huntingdon Quebec
110 H6 Huntingdon Tennessee
Huntingdon and Peterborough co see Cambridgeshire
122 J3 Hunting I Quebec
112 G5 Hunting I S Carolina
94 B6 Huntington Indiana
95 O6 Huntington Long I, N Y
100 H5 Huntington Oregon
111 B10 Huntington Texas
103 O2 Huntington Utah
94 E8 Huntington W Virginia
102 F8 Huntington Beach California
102 E4 Huntington L California
8 D4 Huntley England
101 R4 Huntley Montana
98 G9 Huntley Nebraska
98 B8 Huntley Wyoming
32 H7 Huntlosen W Germany
145 E2 Huntly New Zealand
15 F3 Huntly Scotland
114 G5 Hunt, Mt Yukon Terr
138 D3 Hunt Pen S Australia
101 S5 Hunts Mt Wyoming
122 H10 Hunts Pt Nova Scotia
110 C5 Huntsville Arkansas
110 D2 Huntsville Missouri
115 M8 Huntsville Ontario
109 M5 Huntsville Texas
101 O8 Huntsville Utah
32 E9 Hünxe W Germany
89 G1 Hunyani R Zimbabwe
88 C10 Hunyani Rge mts Zimbabwe
65 B5 Hunyuan China
66 A4 Hunza Kashmir
66 C3 Huocheng China
65 F1 Huodifangzi China
65 B7 Huojia China
139 H9 Huon R Tasmania
68 H4 Huong Hoa Vietnam
68 G3 Huong Khe Vietnam
68 H8 Huong My Vietnam
68 G3 Huong Son Vietnam
68 H4 Huong Thuy Vietnam
139 H9 Huonville Tasmania
67 E1 Huoshan China
65 B6 Huo Shan mt China
67 G5 Huo-shao Tao isld Taiwan
65 B6 Huo Xian China
Hupeh prov see Hubei
20 J1 Huppy France
33 M10 Hüpstedt E Germany
48 E3 Hurbanovo Czechoslovakia
27 E11 Hurdals L Norway
120 J7 Hurd, Cape Ontario
110 D1 Hurdland Missouri
98 F2 Hurdsfield N Dakota
65 E3 Hure Qi China
80 E1 Hurfeish Israel
84 J4 Hurghada Egypt
18 G6 Huriel France
119 P2 Hurkett Ontario
9 F4 Hurley England
111 H11 Hurley Mississippi
106 B9 Hurley New Mexico
98 J6 Hurley S Dakota
99 Q3 Hurley Wisconsin
12 D2 Hurlford Scotland
15 E2 Hurliness Scotland
95 M8 Hurlock Maryland
143 C10 Hurlstone, L W Australia
102 D5 Huron California
94 E5 Huron Ohio
98 H5 Huron S Dakota
99 S3 Huron B Michigan
94 E2 Huron City Michigan
94 E2 Huron, L U.S.A./Canada
99 T3 Huron Mts Michigan
103 L4 Hurricane Utah
94 E8 Hurricane W Virginia
112 E6 Hurricane Cr Georgia
126 E3 Hurricane Flats Bahamas
110 J6 Hurricane Mills Tennessee
9 E5 Hursley England
109 M9 Hurst Texas
9 E5 Hurstbourne Tarrant England
9 G5 Hurst Green England
9 F6 Hurstpierpoint England
131 B3 Hurtado R Chile
36 B2 Hürtgen W Germany
36 B2 Hürth W Germany
111 L9 Hurtsboro Alabama
144 D5 Hurunui R New Zealand
28 E3 Hurup Denmark
28 D7 Hurup W Germany
115 S4 Húsavík Iceland
9 E3 Husbands Bosworth England
28 A4 Husby Denmark
80 F3 Husein Br Jordan
28 O10 Husevig Faeroes
Hushan see Cixi
65 H2 Hushan China
48 L4 Huşi Romania
80 D3 Husifa Israel
27 G14 Huskvarna Sweden
116 J4 Huslia Alaska
80 G4 Husn Jordan
101 L2 Huson Montana
27 A10 Husöy Norway
118 E7 Hussar Alberta
26 B9 Hustadvika Norway
28 B6 Husum Denmark
28 N1 Husum Faeroes
30 E1 Husum W Germany
58 D2 Hutag Mongolia
69 D12 Hutanopan Sumatra
109 O10 Hutchins Texas
107 N3 Hutchinson Kansas
99 M5 Hutchinson Minnesota
113 G10 Hutchinsons I Florida
103 N7 Hutch Mt Arizona
68 D4 Huthi Burma
59 K2 Hutou China
110 J2 Hutsonville Illinois
38 H7 Hüttau Austria
20 F5 Hutte, la France
37 L4 Hüttenbach W Germany
38 L8 Hüttenberg Austria
36 G3 Hüttengesäss W Germany
37 P6 Hutthurm W Germany
111 D8 Huttig Arkansas
109 K5 Hutto Texas
141 J7 Hutton, Mt Queensland
143 E6 Hutton Ra W Australia
94 G8 Huttonsville W Virginia
40 G3 Huttwil Switzerland
58 F4 Hutuo He R China
73 L8 Huvadu Atoll Maldives
65 A7 Hu Xian China
118 D7 Huxley Alberta
116 R6 Huxley, Mt Alaska
144 B6 Huxley, Mt New Zealand
142 F4 Huxley, Mt W Australia
22 J3 Huy Belgium
Huzhou see Wuxing
27 E12 Hvaler isld Norway
28 C3 Hvalpsund Denmark
115 M2 Hval Sound Greenland
28 C3 Hvam Denmark
42 G5 Hvar Yugoslavia
42 H5 Hvar isld Yugoslavia
28 B3 Hvidbjerg Denmark
28 N2 Hvidenæs Faeroes
28 B6 Hviding Denmark
28 E4 Hvilsager Denmark
28 D3 Hvilsom Denmark
28 E4 Hvilsted Denmark
27 E12 Hvitsten Norway
27 D12 Hvittingfoss Norway
Hwainan see Huainan
Hwang-hai see Huang Hai
61 P14 Hyakuna Okinawa
101 P4 Hyalite Pk Montana
100 B9 Hyampom California
95 R5 Hyannis Massachusetts
98 E8 Hyannis Nebraska
58 B2 Hyargas Nuur L Mongolia
100 C7 Hyatt Res Oregon
95 L8 Hyattsville Maryland
101 S5 Hyattville Wyoming
111 J10 Hybart Alabama
121 N7 Hybla Ontario
27 H14 Hycklinge Sweden
117 G8 Hydaburg Alaska
13 F6 Hyde England
144 C6 Hyde New Zealand
94 D9 Hyden Kentucky
143 C9 Hyden W Australia
117 H8 Hyder Br Col/Alaska
74 H10 Hyderabad India
77 L7 Hyderabad Pakistan
Hydra isld see Ídhra I
109 J5 Hye Texas
20 C4 Hyenville France
19 Q18 Hyères France
59 J3 Hyesanjin N Korea
98 A9 Hygiene Colorado
117 J5 Hyland R Yukon Terr
114 G6 Hyland Post Br Col
28 D5 Hylke Denmark
28 G7 Hyllekrog C Denmark
27 A10 Hyllestad Norway
28 F4 Hyllested Denmark
118 E4 Hylo Alberta
27 B12 Hylsfjorden inlet Norway
110 J2 Hymera Indiana
138 F6 Hynam S Australia
12 E2 Hyndford Br Scotland
139 L4 Hyndland, Mt New S Wales
94 J7 Hyndman Pennsylvania
101 L6 Hyndman Peak Idaho
94 K5 Hyner Pennsylvania
60 J10 Hyōgo prefect Japan
86 D4 Hyrra Banda Cent Afr Republic
101 O8 Hyrum Utah
52 C3 Hyrynsalmi Finland
101 S3 Hysham Montana
114 H6 Hythe Alberta
9 E6 Hythe Hampshire England
9 H5 Hythe Kent England
60 E13 Hyūga Japan
29 L11 Hyvinkää Finland
68 J6 Ia Ayun R Vietnam
128 E6 Iaco R Brazil
48 J3 Iacobeni Romania
129 K6 Iaçu Brazil
94 F9 Iaeger W Virginia
36 B7 Iaintrux France
48 K6 Ialomiţa R Romania
113 C7 Iamonia, L Florida
48 L5 Ianca Romania
144 C5 Ianthe, L New Zealand
48 H4 Iara Romania
14 B3 Iar Connaught Irish Rep
129 H3 Iaripo Brazil
53 C10 Iasi Romania
47 G3 Íasmos Greece
111 D10 Iatt, L Louisiana
128 E3 Iauareté Brazil
52 H4 Ib U.S.S.R.
71 D3 Iba Luzon Philippines
85 E7 Ibadan Nigeria
128 C3 Ibagué Colombia
130 E8 Ibaiti Brazil
101 M9 Ibapah Utah
46 D1 Ibar R Yugoslavia
60 G11 Ibara Japan
61 O9 Ibaraki prefect Japan
128 C3 Ibarra Ecuador
32 G8 Ibbenbüren W Germany
80 G4 Ibbin Jordan
86 C5 Ibenga R Congo
131 F2 Iberá, Esteros del marshes Argentina
131 F2 Iberá, L Argentina
110 D3 Iberia Missouri
121 R7 Iberville Quebec
26 J3 Ibestad Norway
85 F6 Ibeto Nigeria
85 F7 Ibi Nigeria
129 J7 Ibiá Brazil
130 G5 Ibiaí Brazil
129 K4 Ibiapaba, Serra da mts Brazil
131 G3 Ibicui da Cruz R Brazil
131 G2 Ibicuí, R Brazil
133 F4 Ibicuy Argentina
61 K10 Ibigawa Japan
80 D2 I'billin Israel
130 D8 Ibiporã Brazil
130 H6 Ibiraçu Brazil
130 E10 Ibirama Brazil
130 H5 Ibiranhém Brazil
131 G3 Ibirapuita R Brazil
130 E7 Ibitinga Brazil
17 H5 Ibiza isld Balearic Is
80 F8 Ibn Hammad Jordan
88 H8 Ibo Mozambique
129 K6 Ibotirama Brazil
86 D3 Ibra., Wadi watercourse Sudan
52 G6 Ibresi U.S.S.R.
47 H3 İbriktepe Turkey
79 A9 Ibshawâi Egypt
9 E6 Ibsley England
61 Q12 Ibu Okinawa
60 D14 Ibusuki Japan
128 C6 Ica Peru
128 E4 Içá R Brazil
128 F3 Icabaru R Venezuela
127 N3 Icacos Pt Trinidad
71 D5 Icadambanauan Philippines
131 G2 Icamaqua R Brazil
128 E3 Icana Brazil
103 K5 Iceberg Canyon Nev/Ariz
100 G3 Ice Harbor Dam Washington
115 S4 Iceland rep N Atlantic Oc
90 H2 Iceland-Faeroe Rise Atlantic Oc
56 B3 Icha R U.S.S.R.
76 B2 Ichalkaranji India
37 J7 Ichenhausen W Germany
60 G11 Ichi Japan
60 E13 Ichifusa-yama mt Japan
61 O10 Ichihara Japan
61 P5 Ichinohe Japan
59 L4 Ichinomiya Japan
54 D6 Ichnya U.S.S.R.
22 E1 Ichtegem Belgium
37 K2 Ichtershausen E Germany
130 H7 Iconha Brazil
Iconium see Konya
116 R6 Icy B Alaska
116 F1 Icy Cape Alaska
117 E6 Icy Pt Alaska
109 O3 Ida Louisiana
94 D5 Ida Michigan
109 N2 Idabel Oklahoma
99 L7 Ida Grove Iowa
85 F7 Idah Nigeria
101 M6 Idaho state U.S.A.
100 K6 Idaho City Idaho
101 N6 Idaho Falls Idaho
106 E2 Idaho Springs Colorado
106 H2 Idalia Colorado
140 E6 Idamea, L Queensland
140 C5 Ida, Mt N Terr Aust
143 D8 Ida, Mt W Australia
36 C4 Idar Oberstein W Germany
56 E4 Idarskoye Belogor'ye mts U.S.S.R.
36 C4 Idarwald mts W Germany
144 C6 Ida Valley New Zealand
27 E12 Idd Norway
118 F8 Iddesleigh Alberta
111 M9 Ideal Georgia
84 E5 Idehan Marzuq Libya
84 E4 Idehan Ubari Libya
52 D3 Idel' U.S.S.R.
85 F4 Idelès Algeria
86 B6 Idemba Gabon
28 H7 Idestrup Denmark
84 J5 Idfu Egypt
47 G9 Ídhi Óros mt Crete Greece
47 F7 Ídhra isld Greece
69 C10 Idi Sumatra
Idi Amin Dada, L see Edward, L
45 K3 Idice R Italy
116 H5 Iditarod Alaska
70 P10 Idjen Java
27 H11 Idkerberget Sweden
79 G3 Idlib Syria
80 C7 Idna Jordan
140 C6 Idracowra N Terr Aust
26 F10 Idre Sweden
102 D5 Idria California
84 E3 Idris Libya
52 C6 Idritsa U.S.S.R.
42 C3 Idro, L. d' Italy
36 E3 Idstein W Germany
28 A4 Idum Denmark
87 E12 Idutywa S Africa
61 P12 Ie-jima isld Okinawa
45 R6 Ielsi Italy
22 H3 Iemeppe Belgium
130 D8 Iepê Brazil
22 D2 Ieper Belgium
47 H9 Ierápetra Crete Greece
47 F8 Iérax, Akr C Greece
59 G2 I-erh-hsieh China
47 F4 Ierissós Greece
43 C9 Ierzu Sardinia
45 O4 Iesi Italy
61 P12 Ie-suidō str Okinawa
17 H6 Ifach, Pta Spain
87 H12 Ifanadiana Madagascar
85 E7 Ife Nigeria
85 F5 Iférouane Niger
141 F4 Iffley Queensland
138 B4 Ifould L S Australia
16 E10 Igá R Morocco
85 E5 Igadiane watercourse Mali
70 B3 Igan Sarawak
88 D1 Iganga Uganda
130 J9 Igaraçu Brazil
129 J4 Igarape-Açu Brazil
147 P14 Igarka U.S.S.R.
130 C9 Igatimi Paraguay
74 E9 Igatpuri India
71 F5 Igbon isld Philippines
20 G5 Igé France
36 B4 Igel W Germany
27 J10 Iggesund Sweden
85 C2 Ighil M'Goun, Jbel mt Morocco
133 D4 Iglesia Argentina
43 B9 Iglesias Sardinia
98 C6 Igloo S Dakota
147 E4 Igloolik N W Terr
41 O3 Igls Austria
79 D9 'Igma, Gebel el mts Egypt
115 K8 Ignace Ontario
106 C4 Ignacio Colorado
124 H5 Ignacio Allende Mexico
52 C6 Ignalina U.S.S.R.
47 J3 İgneada Turkey
68 A7 Ignoitijala Andaman Is
102 B1 Igo California
71 C3 Igom W Irian
87 F7 Igoma Tanzania
70 B3 Igon R Sarawak
46 D5 Igoumenitsa Greece
52 H5 Igra U.S.S.R.
130 E9 Iguaçu, R Brazil
130 H4 Iguaí Brazil
125 K8 Iguala Mexico
17 J3 Igualda Spain
129 J8 Iguapé Brazil
130 D8 Iguaraçu Brazil
130 F7 Iguatama Brazil
130 C8 Iguatemi Brazil
129 L5 Iguatu Brazil
86 A6 Iguéla Gabon
116 K8 Igvak, C Alaska
87 H12 Ihosy Madagascar
68 F6 Ihr Cambodia
22 L3 Ihren W Germany
32 F6 Ihrhove W Germany
40 G1 Ihringen W Germany
58 D2 Ihtamir Mongolia
29 L6 Ii Finland
61 L10 Iida Japan
61 N8 Iide-san mt Japan
29 N2 Iijärvi L Finland
29 N6 Iijoki R Finland
52 C5 Iisaku U.S.S.R.
29 N9 Iisvesi Finland
61 O8 Iizaka Japan
60 D12 Iizuka Japan
71 K9 Ija isld Indonesia
70 P9 Ijang isld Indonesia
85 E7 Ijebu Ode Nigeria
25 E2 IJlst Netherlands
25 D4 IJmeer Netherlands
25 C4 IJmuiden Netherlands
25 F3 Ijonger R Netherlands
25 C4 Ijsel R Netherlands
25 F4 IJssel R Netherlands
25 D3 IJsselmeer Netherlands
25 C5 IJsselmonde Netherlands
25 E3 IJsselmuiden Netherlands
25 D4 IJsselstein Netherlands
133 G3 Ijuí Brazil
131 G2 Ijuí, R Brazil
25 A6 IJzendijke Netherlands
22 D2 Ijzer R Belgium
52 H6 Ik R U.S.S.R.
29 K10 Ikaalinen Finland
144 C5 Ikamatua New Zealand
115 O4 Ikamiut Greenland
86 D6 Ikanda Zaïre
47 H7 Ikaría isld Greece
28 C4 Ikast Denmark
56 H4 Ikatskiy Khrebet mts U.S.S.R.
145 F3 Ikawhenua Range New Zealand
60 J11 Ikeda Japan
60 G12 Ikegawa Japan
61 P13 Ikei-jima isld Okinawa
85 E7 Ikeja Nigeria
86 D6 Ikela Zaïre
115 O3 Ikerasak Greenland
47 F2 Ikhtiman Bulgaria
60 C12 Iki isld Japan
88 C2 Ikimba L Tanzania
60 C12 Iki-suidō str Japan
116 K8 Ikolik, C Alaska
85 F7 Ikom Nigeria
88 D6 Ikomba Tanzania
87 H12 Ikongo Madagascar
87 H11 Ikopa R Madagascar
116 K1 Ikpikpuk R Alaska
56 B3 Iksa R U.S.S.R.
54 J1 Iksha U.S.S.R.
88 C1 Ikulwe Uganda
60 H10 Ikuno Japan
60 R2 Ikutahara Japan
140 B3 Ikymbon R N Terr Aust
71 E2 Ilagan Philippines
78 L5 Ilam Iran
75 M5 Ilam Nepal
56 E3 Ilanskiy U.S.S.R.
41 K4 Ilanz Switzerland
85 E7 Ilaro Nigeria
31 M2 Iława Poland
28 E2 Ilbro Denmark
138 D2 Ilbunga S Australia
8 D5 Ilchester England
13 G3 Ilderton England
120 J9 Ilderton Ontario
118 J3 Ile-à-la Crosse Sask
118 K3 Ile-à-la-Crosse L Sask
48 H3 Ileanda Romania
83 L13 Ile aux Bénitiers Mauritius
86 D6 Ilebo Zaïre
21 C10 Ile d'Oléron France
25 E5 Ileijen Netherlands
55 B5 Ilek U.S.S.R.
85 E4 Ilerh watercourse Algeria
127 N5 Îles des Saintes Guadeloupe W I
85 F7 Ilesha Nigeria
52 G6 Ilet' R U.S.S.R.
33 N9 Ilfeld E Germany
9 G4 Ilford England
119 W2 Ilford Manitoba
8 B5 Ilfracombe England
141 G6 Ilfracombe Queensland
56 F4 Ilga R U.S.S.R.
78 D1 Ilgaz Dağ Turkey
88 H9 Ilha Mozambique
130 F8 Ilhabela Brazil
128 F4 Ilha Grande Brazil
130 G8 Ilha Grande, B. de Brazil
130 D7 Ilha Solteira Brazil
16 B4 Ílhavo Portugal
130 H4 Ilhéus Brazil
48 H5 Ilia Romania
116 K7 Iliamna L Alaska
71 L9 Ili Boleng vol Indonesia
48 N4 Ilichevsk U.S.S.R.
98 C9 Iliff Colorado
71 G6 Iligan Philippines
71 G6 Iligan B Philippines
71 F1 Iligan Pt Philippines
47 F6 Ilikí, L Greece
56 F3 Ilim R U.S.S.R.
56 F1 Ilimpeya R U.S.S.R.
56 F3 Ilimskiy, Khrebet mts U.S.S.R.
71 E4 Ilin isld Philippines
55 C6 Il'inka U.S.S.R.
52 F5 Il'inskoye U.S.S.R.
71 E4 Ilin Str Philippines
48 M1 Ilintsy U.S.S.R.
47 F5 Iliodhrómia isld Greece
95 M3 Ilion New York
42 F3 Ilirska Bistrica Yugoslavia
76 C3 Ilkal India
13 G6 Ilkley England
36 D7 Ill R France
128 E7 Illampu mt Bolivia
17 F4 Illana Spain
71 F7 Illana B Philippines
131 B3 Illapel Chile
131 B3 Illapel, R Chile
54 G8 Illarionovo U.S.S.R.
41 O7 Illasi Italy
41 O6 Illasi, Val d' Italy
138 C2 Illbillee, Mt S Australia
20 B5 Ille-et-Vilaine dep France
37 J7 Iller R W Germany
37 J7 Illertissen W Germany
16 E4 Illescas Spain
20 H5 Illiers France
128 E7 Illimani mt Bolivia
36 F6 Illingen W Germany
110 G1 Illinois R Illinois
110 B5 Illinois R Oklahoma
100 B7 Illinois R Oregon
99 R9 Illinois state U.S.A.
99 R8 Illinois & Mississippi Canal Illinois
110 G2 Illiopolis Illinois
128 G3 Illiwa R Guyana
36 D6 Illkirch France
110 G4 Illmo Missouri
140 D6 Illogwa R N Terr Aust
16 E7 Illora Spain
37 M5 Illschwang W Germany
28 E6 Illumø isld Denmark
37 M6 Ilm R W Germany
29 K9 Ilmajoki Finland
37 K2 Ilmenau E Germany
33 M6 Ilmenau R W Germany
52 D5 Il'men', Ozero L U.S.S.R.
8 D6 Ilminster England
128 D7 Ilo Peru
71 F5 Iloilo Philippines
29 P9 Ilomantsi Finland
85 E7 Ilorin Nigeria
54 K9 Ilovaysk U.S.S.R.
116 L7 Oil Pt Alaska
33 N8 Ilse R E Germany
33 N9 Ilsenburg E Germany
36 G5 Ilsfeld W Germany
36 H5 Ilshofen W Germany
28 C4 Ilskov Denmark
86 F4 Ilubabor prov Ethiopia
88 D3 Ilula Tanzania
48 J3 Ilva Mică Romania
100 A3 Ilwaco Washington
71 N8 Ilwaki Indonesia
52 J4 Ilych R U.S.S.R.
52 D6 Il'yino U.S.S.R.
31 N4 Iłża Poland
31 N4 Iłżanka R Poland
59 K5 Imabari Japan
60 O4 Imabetsu Japan
61 N9 Imaichi Japan
61 K10 Imajō Japan
124 F5 Imala Mexico
78 K6 Imām al Ḩamzah Iraq
57 B6 Imambaba U.S.S.R.
Iman see Dal'nerechensk
52 D1 Imandra U.S.S.R.
130 C10 Iman, Sa. del ra Argentina
55 E4 Imantau, Oz L U.S.S.R.
60 C12 Imari Japan
128 F2 Imataca, Sa de mts Venezuela
29 O10 Imatra Finland
61 J10 Imazu Japan
79 B8 Imbâba Egypt
128 C3 Imbabura prov Ecuador
127 J5 Imbert Dom Rep
133 H3 Imbituba Brazil
130 E9 Imbituva Brazil
100 H4 Imbler Oregon
110 E5 Imboden Arkansas
52 F5 Imeni-Babushkina U.S.S.R.
52 F5 Imeni Kalinina U.S.S.R.
128 E3 Imeri, Sa mts Venezuela
113 F7 Imeson airport Florida
55 F2 Imgyt R U.S.S.R.
86 H4 Imi Ethiopia
47 F7 Imittós mt Greece
65 G5 Imjin R N Korea
102 F1 Imlay Nevada
98 D6 Imlay S Dakota
94 D3 Imlay City Michigan
138 B4 Immarna S Australia
32 K10 Immenhausen W Germany
41 M2 Immenstadt W Germany
113 F11 Immokalee Florida
100 J4 Imnaha Oregon
99 L9 Imogene Iowa
45 L3 Imola Italy
42 H5 Imotski Yugoslavia
128 E5 Imperatriz Brazil
44 D4 Imperia Italy
103 J9 Imperial California
98 E9 Imperial Nebraska
119 M7 Imperial Sask
103 K9 Imperial Dam Cal/Ariz
103 J9 Imperial Valley California
142 C4 Imperieuse Reef W Australia
122 J9 Imperoyal Nova Scotia
36 E5 Impflingen W Germany
86 C5 Impfondo Congo
75 P6 Imphal India
18 H6 Imphy France
52 D4 Impilakhti U.S.S.R.
45 K4 Impruneta Italy
80 F8 Imra Jordan
47 K4 İmralı isld Turkey
İmroz isld see Gökçeada isld
41 N3 Imst Austria
124 D2 Imuris Mexico
71 D5 Imuruan B Philippines
116 D4 Imuruk Basin Alaska
116 F4 Imuruk L Alaska
61 L10 Ina Japan
31 J2 Ina R Poland
90 A16 Inaccessible I Atlantic Oc
146 C14 Inaccessible I S Orkney Is
71 D6 Inagauan Philippines
61 N8 Ina-gawa R Japan
127 H4 Inagua I., Little Bahamas
61 N12 Inamba-jima isld Japan
128 D6 Inambiri R Peru
85 F3 In Amenas Algeria
85 E4 In Amguel Algeria
70 E1 Inanam Sabah
144 C4 Inangahua Junction New Zealand
51 K2 Inarigda U.S.S.R.
29 N3 Inarijärvi L Finland
61 N11 Inatori Japan
61 O8 Inawashiro Japan
61 O8 Inawashiro ko L Japan
85 F4 In Azaoua Algeria
85 E3 In Belbel Algeria
133 D3 Incahuasi mt Chile/Arg
14 E4 Inch Irish Rep
100 G1 Inchelium Washington
37 L6 Inchenhofen W Germany
20 H1 Incheville France
13 E1 Inchkeith isld Scotland
15 D2 Inchnadamph Scotland
65 G6 Inch'ŏn S Korea
116 B3 Inchoun U.S.S.R.
13 E1 Inchture Scotland
22 E3 Inchy France
45 K4 Incisa in Valdarno Italy
89 H5 Incomati R Mozambique
22 H2 Incourt Belgium
12 B2 Indaal, L Scotland
85 D4 In Dagouber Mali
130 D6 Indaia Grande, R Brazil
26 J9 Indal Sweden
26 H8 Indalsälven R Sweden
68 C2 Indaw Burma
75 R6 Indawgyi Lake Burma
124 G5 Indé Mexico
7 M9 Indefatigable sea rig North Sea
102 F5 Independence California
99 P7 Independence Iowa
107 P4 Independence Kansas
111 F11 Independence Louisiana
110 B2 Independence Missouri
100 B5 Independence Oregon
94 F10 Independence Virginia
99 P5 Independence Wisconsin
147 H9 Independence Fj Greenland
100 J8 Independence Mts Nevada
69 F13 Inderagiri R Sumatra
69 E13 Inderapura Sumatra
69 E13 Inderapura, Tg C Sumatra
55 B6 Inderborskiy U.S.S.R.
26 E8 Inderöy Norway
55 B6 Inder, Oz L U.S.S.R.
100 D2 Index Washington
74 G10 Indi India
74 India rep S Asia
107 M7 Indiahoma Oklahoma
95 M2 Indian R New York
117 D4 Indian R Yukon Terr
140 D6 Indiana N Terr Aust
94 H6 Indiana Pennsylvania
94 B6 Indiana state U.S.A.
81 G11 Indian-Antarctic Basin Southern Oc
81 J11 Indian-Antarctic Ridge Southern Oc
94 A7 Indianapolis Indiana
123 T4 Indian B Nfld
123 M7 Indian Brook Nova Scotia
117 P6 Indian Cabins Alberta
115 O7 Indian Hbr Labrador
122 J9 Indian Hbr Nova Scotia
141 L7 Indian Hd Queensland
95 K8 Indian Head Maryland
114 J7 Indian Head Sask
115 K6 Indian L Manitoba
95 N3 Indian L New York
101 P7 Indian Mt Wyoming
81 Indian Ocean
83 Indian Ocean Islands
99 N8 Indianola Iowa
111 F8 Indianola Mississippi
98 F9 Indianola Nebraska
107 P6 Indianola Oklahoma
130 F6 Indianópolis Brazil
103 L3 Indian Peak Utah
101 Q5 Indian Pk Wyoming
113 G10 Indian R Florida
94 C1 Indian River Michigan
113 G9 Indian River City Florida
103 J5 Indian Sp Nevada
113 G10 Indian Town Florida
100 J5 Indian Valley Idaho
103 O6 Indian Wells Arizona
122 A2 Indicator L Quebec
52 G1 Indiga U.S.S.R.
147 L15 Indiga U.S.S.R.
51 O2 Indigirka R U.S.S.R.
52 G1 Indigskaya Guba B U.S.S.R.
48 F5 Indija Yugoslavia
117 Q3 Indin L N W Terr
103 H8 Indio California
109 K9 Indios Mexico
137 N4 Indispensable Reefs Pacific Oc
70 D7 Indonesia rep S E Asia
141 K2 Indooroopilly dist Brisbane, Qnsld
74 F7 Indore India
70 M9 Indramaju Java
73 N5 Indravati R India
21 H8 Indre dep France
21 H7 Indre R France
21 F7 Indre-et-Loire dep France
113 G10 Indrio Florida
21 H7 Indrois R France
138 C2 Indulkana R S Australia
31 O2 Indura U.S.S.R.
118 D8 Indus Alberta
73 L2 Indus R S W Asia
74 B6 Indus, Mouths of Pakistan
110 F1 Industry Illinois
109 L6 Industry Texas
89 E8 Indwe S Africa
85 F4 In Ebeggi Algeria
78 D1 Inebolu Turkey
47 J4 İnecik Turkey
85 F4 In Ecker Algeria
85 E5 In Edek Niger
78 B1 Inegöl Turkey

36 Inerie — Jarmen

71 K9 **Inerie** *mt* Flores Indonesia
109 L7 **Inez** Texas
85 G4 **In Ezzane** Algeria
89 B10 **Infanta, C** S Africa
16 E6 **Infantes** Spain
128 F5 **Infernão, Cach** *rapids* Brazil
124 H8 **Infiernillo, L** Mexico
16 D1 **Infiesto** Spain
130 J9 **Ingá** Brazil
29 L11 **Inga** Finland
85 F5 **Inga** Niger
68 B4 **Ingabu** Burma
140 C5 **Ingallanna** *R* N Terr Aust
94 B7 **Ingalls** Indiana
107 K4 **Ingalls** Kansas
99 T4 **Ingalls** Michigan
100 E10 **Ingalls, Mt** California
55 F3 **Ingaly** U.S.S.R.
9 G4 **Ingatestone** England
36 H5 **Ingelfingen** W Germany
36 E4 **Ingelheim** W Germany
22 E2 **Ingelmunster** Belgium
86 C6 **Ingende** Zaïre
133 E5 **Ingeniero Luiggi** Argentina
131 E7 **Ingeniero, Pto** Argentina
117 L7 **Ingenika** *R* Br Col
116 E7 **Ingeramuit** Alaska
107 M5 **Ingersoll** Oklahoma
71 B2 **Inggelang** *isld* Halmahera Indonesia
141 H4 **Ingham** Queensland
83 K11 **Ingiriya** Sri Lanka
13 F5 **Ingleborough** *mt* England
140 F6 **Ingledoon** Queensland
115 N2 **Inglefield Land** Greenland
109 K8 **Ingleside** Texas
13 F5 **Ingleton** England
102 F8 **Inglewood** California
145 E3 **Inglewood** New Zealand
141 K8 **Inglewood** Queensland
139 G6 **Inglewood** Victoria
119 Q8 **Inglis** Manitoba
140 D1 **Inglis** *isld* N Terr Aust
116 G4 **Inglutalik** *R* Alaska
51 L3 **Ingoda** *R* U.S.S.R.
76 G5 **Ingoitijala** Andaman Is
118 F1 **Ingolf** Ontario
86 C7 **Ingololo** Zaïre
37 L6 **Ingolstadt** W Germany
101 S3 **Ingomar** Montana
138 C3 **Ingomar** S Australia
123 M7 **Ingonish** C Breton I, N Scotia
102 B1 **Ingot** California
26 N1 **Ingöy** Norway
109 H5 **Ingram** Texas
99 Q4 **Ingram** Wisconsin
122 J9 **Ingramport** Nova Scotia
21 D7 **Ingrandes** France
21 G8 **Ingrandes** France
117 P3 **Ingray L** N W Terr
146 C4 **Ingrid Christensen Coast** Antarctica
28 D2 **Ingstrup** Denmark
85 F5 **In Guezzam** Algeria
54 D9 **Ingul** *R* U.S.S.R.
54 E9 **Ingulets** U.S.S.R.
54 D10 **Ingulets** *R* U.S.S.R.
55 F1 **Inguyagun** *R* U.S.S.R.
19 K4 **Ingwiller** France
89 H6 **Inhaca Pen** Mozambique
87 G10 **Inhambane** Mozambique
130 C7 **Inhandui, R** Brazil
130 C7 **Inhanduizinho, R** Brazil
88 E10 **Inhangoma I** Mozambique
130 C10 **Inhanhora** *R* Brazil
130 G6 **Inhapim** Brazil
87 G10 **Inharrime** Mozambique
47 L4 **İnhisar** Turkey
130 H4 **Inhobim** Brazil
129 J7 **Inhumas** Brazil
116 L3 **Iniakuk** *R* Alaska
71 K9 **Inielika** *mt* Flores Indonesia
17 F5 **Iniesta** Spain
85 E3 **Inifel, Hassi** Algeria
27 M11 **Iniö** Finland
128 E3 **Inírida** *R* Colombia
14 A3 **Inishark** *isld* Irish Rep
14 A3 **Inishbofin** *isld* Irish Rep
14 C1 **Inishbofin** *isld* Irish Rep
14 B2 **Inishcrone** Irish Rep
14 B3 **Inisheer** *isld* Irish Rep
14 A2 **Inishkea** *isld* Irish Rep
14 B3 **Inishmaan** *isld* Irish Rep
14 B3 **Inishmore** *isld* Irish Rep
14 C2 **Inishmurray** *isld* Irish Rep
14 D1 **Inishowen** *dist* Irish Rep
14 E1 **Inishowen Hd** Irish Rep
14 D1 **Inishtrahull** *isld* Irish Rep
14 A3 **Inishturk** *isld* Irish Rep
65 D2 **Injgan Sum** China
141 J7 **Injune** Queensland
122 H6 **Inkerman** New Brunswick
141 F3 **Inkerman** Queensland
86 C7 **Inkis** *R* Zaïre
117 G6 **Inklin** Br Col
101 N7 **Inkom** Idaho
52 F5 **Inkovo** U.S.S.R.
98 J1 **Inkster** N Dakota
68 C2 **Inle, L** Burma
98 H7 **Inman** Nebraska
95 N2 **Inman** New York
112 E2 **Inman** S Carolina
41 O3 **Inn** *R* Austria
38 F6 **Inn** *R* W Germany
138 F2 **Innamincka** S Australia
15 E5 **Innerleithen** Scotland
Inner Mongolia *see* **Nei Monggol Zizhiqu**
Inner Mongolia *aut reg see* **Nei Monggol Zizhiqu**
41 K3 **Inner-Rhoden** *dist* Switzerland
15 C3 **Inner Sound** Scotland
32 M8 **Innerste** *R* W Germany
41 H4 **Innertkirchen** Switzerland
38 F8 **Innervillgraten** Austria
Innien *see* **Aukrug**
14 C5 **Inniscarra Res** Irish Rep
118 D6 **Innisfail** Alberta
141 H3 **Innisfail** Queensland
118 F5 **Innisfree** Alberta
116 J5 **Innoko** *R* Alaska
60 G11 **Inno-shima** Japan
41 O3 **Innsbruck** Austria
26 K3 **Innset** Norway
26 B10 **Innvik** Norway
116 A3 **Innymney, Gora** *mt* U.S.S.R.
71 H4 **Inobonto** Sulawesi
130 D6 **Inocência** Brazil
107 P5 **Inola** Oklahoma
47 L5 **İnönü** Turkey
141 G4 **Inorunie** Queensland
31 L3 **Inowrocław** Poland
128 E7 **Inquisivi** Bolivia
40 F3 **Ins** Switzerland
85 E3 **In Salah** Algeria
15 F3 **Insch** Scotland
143 A7 **Inscription,C** W Australia
68 B4 **Insein** Burma
37 J2 **Inselsberg** *mt* E Germany
119 O7 **Insinger** Sask
87 E9 **Insiza** Zimbabwe
89 F2 **Insiza** *R* Zimbabwe
31 J2 **Insko** Poland
36 B6 **Insming** France
Insterburg *see* **Chernyakhovsk**
8 B5 **Instow** England
118 J9 **Instow** Sask
48 L6 **Insurăţei** Romania
52 K2 **Inta** U.S.S.R.
98 B2 **Intake** Montana
85 E5 **In Tebezas** Mali
47 H4 **İntepe** Turkey
98 E6 **Interior** S Dakota
113 F8 **Interlachen** Florida
40 G4 **Interlaken** Switzerland
139 H8 **Interlaken** Tasmania
99 N1 **International Falls** Minnesota
119 R10 **International Peace Gdn** Canada/U.S.A.
117 O9 **Intersection Mt** Alberta/Br Col
68 A6 **Interview I** Andaman Is
48 K5 **Intorsura Buzăului** Romania
41 J5 **Intragna** Switzerland
32 G8 **Intrup** W Germany
52 F2 **Intsy** U.S.S.R.
70 D5 **Intu** Kalimantan
61 O10 **Inubō saki** Japan
115 O3 **Inugsulik Bugt** *B* Greenland
133 C8 **Inútil, B** Chile
114 F4 **Inuvik** N W Terr
128 D6 **Inuya** *R* Peru
52 J5 **In'va** *R* U.S.S.R.
15 C4 **Inveraray** Scotland
15 F4 **Inverbervie** Scotland
144 B7 **Invercargill** New Zealand
12 C2 **Invercloy** Scotland
139 K3 **Inverell** New S Wales
15 D3 **Invergordon** Scotland
15 E4 **Inverkeithing** Scotland
12 D2 **Inverkip** Scotland
140 F4 **Inverleigh** Queensland
12 D1 **Inverlochlarig** Scotland
119 O7 **Invermay** Sask
117 P10 **Invermere** Br Col
123 L7 **Inverness** C Breton I, N Scotia
113 E9 **Inverness** Florida
101 P1 **Inverness** Montana
121 T6 **Inverness** Quebec
15 D3 **Inverness** Scotland
Inverness *co see* **Highland** *reg*
15 D3 **Invershin** Scotland
15 F3 **Inverurie** Scotland
140 A4 **Inverway** N Terr Aust
68 C6 **Investigator Chan** Burma
138 C5 **Investigator Group** *islds* S Australia
138 D6 **Investigator Str** S Australia
68 A7 **Invisible Bank** Andaman Is
102 C1 **Inwood** California
120 J10 **Inwood** Ontario
56 B3 **Inya** *R* U.S.S.R.
98 B5 **Inyan Kara Cr** Wyoming
87 F9 **Inyazura** Zimbabwe
102 G6 **Inyokern** California
55 C4 **Inzer** U.S.S.R.
86 C7 **Inzia** *R* Zaïre
46 D5 **Ioánnina** Greece
47 H9 **Ioinianísia** *isld* Greece
52 E1 **Iokanga** U.S.S.R.
106 C3 **Iola** Colorado
107 P4 **Iola** Kansas
109 L5 **Iola** Texas
45 L2 **Iolanda di Savoia** Italy
57 B6 **Iolotan'** U.S.S.R.
123 M8 **Iona** C Breton I, N Scotia
101 O6 **Iona** Idaho
99 L6 **Iona** Minnesota
98 G6 **Iona** S Dakota
12 B1 **Iona** *isld* Scotland
47 J1 **Ion Corvin** Romania
102 G3 **Ione** Nevada
100 F4 **Ione** Oregon
100 H1 **Ione** Washington
48 J6 **Ioneşti** Romania
99 O6 **Ionia** Iowa
94 B3 **Ionia** Michigan
110 C3 **Ionia** Missouri
Ionian Is *see* **Iónioi Nísoi**
43 H10 **Ionian Sea** S Europe
46 D5 **Iónioi Nísoi** *islds* Greece
116 A4 **Ioniveen** *R* U.S.S.R.
78 K1 **Iori** *R* U.S.S.R.
47 G8 **Íos** *isld* Greece
52 H3 **Iosser** U.S.S.R.
61 N13 **Iō tō** *isld* Japan
111 C11 **Iowa** Louisiana
99 N7 **Iowa** *R* Iowa
99 N7 **Iowa** *state* U.S.A.
99 P8 **Iowa City** Iowa
99 N7 **Iowa Falls** Iowa
109 J2 **Iowa Park** Texas
124 G7 **Ipala** Mexico
83 K9 **Ipalogama** Sri Lanka
130 E5 **Ipameri** Brazil
130 H6 **Ipanema** Brazil
130 H10 **Ipanema** *R* Brazil
130 H8 **Ipanguacu** Brazil
99 Q9 **Ipava** Illinois
48 E2 **Ipel'** *R* Czechoslovakia
116 E2 **Ipewik** *R* Alaska
37 J4 **Iphofen** W Germany
128 C3 **Ipiales** Colombia
129 L6 **Ipiau** Brazil
Ipin *see* **Yibin**
128 E4 **Ipiranga** Amazonas Brazil
130 E9 **Ipiranga** Paraná Brazil
128 D5 **Ipixuna** Amazonas Brazil
128 F5 **Ipixuna** *R* Amazonas Brazil
69 E10 **Ipoh** Malaysia
130 J10 **Ipojuca** *R* Brazil
71 C6 **Ipolote B** Palawan Philippines
129 H7 **Iporá** Brazil
130 E9 **Iporanga** Brazil
120 J9 **Ipperwash Prov. Park** Ontario
37 J4 **Ippesheim** W Germany
86 D4 **Ippy** Cent Afr Republic
78 A1 **Ipsala** Turkey
9 H3 **Ipswich** England
127 J2 **Ipswich** Jamaica
95 R4 **Ipswich** Massachusetts
141 L8 **Ipswich** Queensland
98 G4 **Ipswich** S Dakota
129 K4 **Ipu** Brazil
54 C4 **Iput'** *R* U.S.S.R.
78 K2 **Iğdir** Turkey
128 D8 **Iquique** Chile
128 D4 **Iquitos** Peru
80 F6 **'Ira** Jordan
108 F5 **Iraan** Texas
61 L11 **Irago-misaki** Japan
130 D10 **Irai** Brazil
47 G8 **Iráklia** *isld* Greece
47 G9 **Iráklion** Crete
130 C9 **Irala** Paraguay
77 C4 **Iran** *empire* S W Asia
130 D10 **Irani** *R* Brazil
77 G6 **Irānshahr** Iran
128 F1 **Irapa** Venezuela
124 J7 **Irapuato** Mexico
78 H5 **Iraq** *rep* S W Asia
95 P2 **Irasburg** Vermont
129 H3 **Iratapuru** *R* Brazil
130 E9 **Iratí** Brazil
133 G3 **Irati** Brazil
17 G2 **Irati** *R* Spain
84 E4 **Irāwan** Libya
52 J3 **Irayel'** U.S.S.R.
27 M14 **Irbenskiy Proliv** *str* U.S.S.R.
80 G3 **Irbid** Jordan
50 F3 **Irbit** U.S.S.R.
55 D2 **Irbit** *R* U.S.S.R.
9 G1 **Irby** England
38 K7 **Irdning** Austria
54 C7 **Irdyn'** U.S.S.R.
109 K4 **Iredell** Texas
109 K4 **Ireland** Texas
90 A1 **Ireland I** Bermuda
14 **Ireland, Rep of**
14 E3 **Ireland's Eye** *isld* Irish Rep
55 C3 **Iren** *R* U.S.S.R.
98 J6 **Irene** S Dakota
98 K7 **Ireton** Iowa
57 B1 **Irgiz** *R* U.S.S.R.
85 F5 **Irhazer Wan Agadez** *V* Niger
86 D2 **Iriba** Chad
129 G3 **Iricoumé, Serra** *mts* Brazil
71 F4 **Iriga** Philippines
55 C5 **Iriklinskiy** U.S.S.R.
87 G7 **Iringa** Tanzania
67 H4 **Iriomote-shima** *isld* Japan
125 M2 **Iriona** Honduras
129 H5 **Iriri** *R* Brazil
14 C3 **Irish Republic**
139 H8 **Irishtown** Tasmania
47 K3 **İriva** Turkey
56 E2 **Irkineyeva** *R* U.S.S.R.
56 F5 **Irkutsk** U.S.S.R.
56 F3 **Irkutskaya Oblast'** U.S.S.R.
118 F6 **Irma** Alberta
99 R4 **Irma** Wisconsin
36 E2 **Irmgarteichen** W Germany
112 F3 **Irmo** S Carolina
20 B5 **Irodouer** France
18 B4 **Iroise** *gulf* France
86 C3 **Iro, L** Chad
138 D4 **Iron Baron** S Australia
8 D2 **Ironbridge** England
120 G6 **Iron Bridge** Ontario
100 C9 **Iron Canyon Res** California
110 J6 **Iron City** Tennessee
110 F4 **Irondale** Missouri
94 G6 **Irondale** Ohio
121 M8 **Irondale** Ontario
138 D4 **Iron Knob** S Australia
99 S4 **Iron Mountain** Michigan
100 A7 **Iron Mt** Oregon
103 L4 **Iron Mt** Utah
98 G5 **Iron Nation** S Dakota
141 G2 **Iron Range** Queensland
99 S6 **Iron Ridge** Wisconsin
99 S3 **Iron River** Michigan
99 P3 **Iron River** Wisconsin
94 B2 **Irons** Michigan
100 H5 **Ironside** Oregon
103 L4 **Iron Sp** Utah
94 B1 **Ironton** Michigan
110 F4 **Ironton** Missouri
94 E8 **Ironton** Ohio
99 Q3 **Ironwood** Michigan
98 J5 **Iroquois** S Dakota
99 T9 **Iroquois** *R* Illinois
120 K4 **Iroquois Falls** Ontario
71 G4 **Irosin** Philippines
61 M11 **Irō zaki** *C* Japan
45 R8 **Irpinia** Italy
138 D3 **Irrapatana** S Australia
68 B4 **Irrawaddy** *prov* Burma
68 B5 **Irrawaddy** *R* Burma
68 B5 **Irrawaddy, Mouths of** Burma
36 B4 **Irrel** W Germany
118 D7 **Irricana** Alberta
85 D5 **Irrigi** *reg* Mali/Mauritania
56 D3 **Irsha** U.S.S.R.
48 H2 **Irshava** U.S.S.R.
52 G4 **Irta** U.S.S.R.
13 F3 **Irthing, R** England
55 D3 **Irtyash, Oz** *L* U.S.S.R.
55 F4 **Irtysh** U.S.S.R.
55 E2 **Irtysh** *R* U.S.S.R.
55 F4 **Irtyshsk** U.S.S.R.
86 E5 **Irumu** Zaïre
18 D9 **Irun** Spain
17 F2 **Irurzun** Spain
18 D10 **Irurzun** Spain
128 E8 **Iruya** Argentina
52 G3 **Irva** *R* U.S.S.R.
118 G9 **Irvine** Alberta
110 N4 **Irvine** Kentucky
15 D5 **Irvine** Scotland
15 D5 **Irvine** *R* Scotland
141 H3 **Irvinebank** Queensland
14 D2 **Irvinestown** N Ireland
107 O2 **Irving** Kansas
109 N9 **Irving** Texas
143 F7 **Irving, Mt** W Australia
110 K4 **Irvington** Kentucky
95 L9 **Irvington** Virginia
94 J6 **Irvona** Pennsylvania
13 F6 **Irwell, R** England
101 O6 **Irwin** Idaho
99 L8 **Irwin** Iowa
98 D7 **Irwin** Nebraska
143 B8 **Irwin** W Australia
143 B11 **Irwin, Pt** W Australia
112 D5 **Irwinton** Georgia
141 J6 **Isaac** *R* Queensland
117 N9 **Isaac L** Br Col
123 L8 **Isaacs Hbr** Nova Scotia
17 G2 **Isaba** Spain
107 M4 **Isabel** Kansas
98 E4 **Isabel** S Dakota
71 F5 **Isabela** Negros Philippines
71 E7 **Isabela** Philippines
127 L5 **Isabela** Puerto Rico
128 A8 **Isabela, Isla** Galapagos Is
125 M3 **Isabelia, Cord** *ra* Nicaragua
102 F6 **Isabella** California
119 Q8 **Isabella** Manitoba
99 P2 **Isabella** Minnesota
142 F5 **Isabella, L** W Australia
147 N11 **Isachenko, Ostrov** *isld* U.S.S.R.
114 J2 **Isachsen** N W Terr
60 D13 **Isahaya** Japan
52 F3 **Isakogorka** U.S.S.R.
48 H6 **Işalniţat** Romania
86 D5 **Isangi** Zaïre
37 N7 **Isar** *R* W Germany
42 D2 **Isarco** *R* Italy
46 E7 **Isari** Greece
41 O2 **Isar Tal** W Germany
111 J7 **Isbell** Alabama
22 C2 **Isbergues** France
15 G1 **Isbister** Scotland
40 C1 **Isches** France
41 M3 **Ischgl** Austria
45 P8 **Ischia** Italy
86 H5 **Iscia Baidoa** Somalia
142 F3 **Isdell,R** W Australia
21 J6 **Isdes** France
59 L5 **Ise** Japan
28 H5 **Isefjord** *inlet* Denmark
41 O3 **Isel Berg** *mt* Austria
146 K7 **Iselin Bank** Antarctica
81 H14 **Iselin Seamount** Southern Oc
52 H6 **Isenbayevo** U.S.S.R.
36 D3 **Isenburg** W Germany
33 N8 **Isenbüttel** W Germany
33 N7 **Isenhagen** W Germany
28 C4 **Isenvad** Denmark
42 C3 **Iseo** Italy
42 C3 **Iseo, L. d'** Italy
19 P14 **Isère** *dep* France
19 O14 **Isère** *R* France
32 G10 **Iserlohn** W Germany
43 F7 **Isernia** Italy
61 K11 **Ise shima Nat. Park** Japan
55 E3 **Isetskoye** U.S.S.R.
61 K11 **Ise-wan** *B* Japan
85 E7 **Iseyin** Nigeria
61 N9 **Isezaki** Japan
Isfahan *see* **Eşfahān**
57 E5 **Isfana** U.S.S.R.
57 F4 **Isfara** U.S.S.R.
80 D3 **Isfiya** Israel
52 J4 **Isherim, Gora** *mt* U.S.S.R.
128 G3 **Isherton** Guyana
88 C7 **Ishiba Ngandu** Zambia
67 H4 **Ishigaki** Japan
67 H4 **Ishigaki-shima** *isld* Japan
61 K9 **Ishika** *prefect* Japan
60 P2 **Ishikari** Japan
60 R2 **Ishikari dake** *mt* Japan
59 M3 **Ishikari-wan** *B* Japan
50 F3 **Ishim** U.S.S.R.
55 C4 **Ishimbay** U.S.S.R.
55 F5 **Ishimo** *R* U.S.S.R.
55 F3 **Ishimskaya Step** *steppe* U.S.S.R.
55 E5 **Ishimskoye** U.S.S.R.
59 M4 **Ishinomaki** Japan
60 G12 **Ishizuchi-san** *mt* Japan
86 G6 **Isiolo** Kenya
87 F11 **Isipingo Bch** S Africa
86 E5 **Isiro** Zaire
141 G6 **Isisford** Queensland
86 G1 **Is, Jebel** *mt* Sudan
55 E3 **Iska** *R* U.S.S.R.
80 D5 **Iskāka** Jordan
57 E4 **Iskander** U.S.S.R.
47 J8 **İskandil Burun** *C* Turkey
78 F3 **Iskenderun** Turkey
57 G4 **Iski-Naukat** U.S.S.R.
56 B4 **Iskitim** U.S.S.R.
47 G1 **Iskŭr** *R* Bulgaria
117 J7 **Iskut** Br Columbia
117 H7 **Iskut** *R* Br Col
119 O3 **Iskwatam L** Sask
15 E4 **Isla** *R* Scotland
78 F3 **Islâhiye** Turkey
74 E2 **Islamabad** Pakistan
113 G13 **Islamorada** Florida
110 J4 **Island** Kentucky
117 N5 **Island** *R* N W Terr
71 D6 **Island B** Palawan Philippines
100 H4 **Island City** Oregon
95 S7 **Island Falls** Maine
120 J3 **Island Falls** Ontario
119 P3 **Island Falls** Sask
141 K5 **Island Hd** Queensland
95 N7 **Island Heights** New Jersey
115 K7 **Island L** Manitoba
123 Q5 **Island L** Nfld
120 K7 **Island L** Ontario
138 D4 **Island Lagoon** S Australia
99 W3 **Island Lake** Ontario
100 B9 **Island Mountain** California
101 O5 **Island Park** Idaho
95 Q2 **Island Pond** Vermont
143 B9 **Island Pt** W Australia
145 E1 **Islands, Bay of** New Zealand
115 O8 **Islands, Bay of** Nfld
17 J5 **Islas Baleares** Spain
16 B2 **Islas Cíes** Spain
127 M5 **Isla Verde** *airport* Puerto Rico
118 G5 **Islay** Alberta
15 B5 **Islay** *isld* Scotland
21 H10 **Isle** France
99 N3 **Isle** Minnesota
18 F7 **Isle** *R* France
20 K3 **Isle Adam, l'** France
123 O6 **Isle aux Morts** Nfld
95 T2 **Isleboro** Maine
18 F9 **Isle en Dodon, L'** France
18 F9 **Isle Jourdain, L'** Gers France
18 F6 **Isle Jourdain, L'** Vienne France
118 H4 **Isle, Lac des** Sask
122 A5 **Isle Maligne** Quebec
112 F6 **Isle of Hope** Georgia
15 G2 **Isle of Noss** Scotland
12 D4 **Isle of Whithorn** Scotland
99 S1 **Isle Royale** Michigan
22 G5 **Isles-sur-Suippes** France
18 H5 **Isle-sur-Serein, L'** France
106 D7 **Isleta** New Mexico
102 C3 **Isleton** California
122 C5 **Isle Verte** Quebec
9 E4 **Islip** England
127 N3 **Islote Pt** Trinidad
133 D1 **Isluga** *mt* Chile
128 E7 **Isluga** *vol* Chile
131 F4 **Ismael Cortinas** Uruguay
84 J3 **Ismâ'ilîya** Egypt
37 M7 **Ismaning** W Germany
98 B3 **Ismay** Montana
78 A2 **Ismir Körfezi** Turkey
84 J4 **Isna** Egypt
87 H12 **Isoanala** Madagascar
29 J9 **Isojoki** Finland
87 F8 **Isoka** Zambia
29 J8 **Isokyrö** Finland
41 O7 **Isola** Italy
111 F8 **Isola** Mississippi
45 P6 **Isola d. Liri** Italy
45 M5 **Isola Farnese** Italy
87 H12 **Isola, Massif de L'** *mts* Madagascar
45 K1 **Isola Rizza** Italy
110 L5 **Isoline** Tennessee
45 J1 **Isorella** Italy
29 N6 **Isosyöte** *mt* Finland
78 C3 **Isparta** Turkey
47 H1 **Isperikh** Bulgaria
78 H1 **Ispir** Turkey
80 **Israel** *rep* S W Asia
143 E10 **Israelite B** W Australia
28 F4 **Issehoved** *C* Denmark
143 A8 **Isseka** W Australia
25 F5 **Isselburg** W Germany
85 C7 **Issia** Ivory Coast
18 H7 **Issoire** France
21 I8 **Issoudun** France
25 F5 **Issum** W Germany
57 H4 **Issyk-Kul, Ozero** *L* U.S.S.R.
57 J4 **Issyk-Kul'skaya** *oblast* U.S.S.R.
77 L2 **Istalif** Afghanistan
47 K3 **İstanbul** Turkey
120 J7 **Isthmus Bay** Ontario
46 F6 **Istiaía** Greece
78 H3 **Istilil** Turkey
128 C2 **Istmina** Colombia
54 H1 **Istra** U.S.S.R.
42 F3 **Istra** *pen* Yugoslavia
47 J3 **Istranca Dağları** *mts* Turkey
19 N18 **Istres** France
61 M11 **Isu hantō** *pen* Japan
55 C5 **Isyangulovo** U.S.S.R.
130 B9 **Itá** Paraguay
129 L6 **Itabaiana** Brazil
130 H7 **Itabapoana** Brazil
130 E8 **Itaberá** Brazil
130 E5 **Itaberaí** Brazil
129 K7 **Itabira** Brazil
130 G7 **Itabirito** Brazil
128 F4 **Itaboca** Brazil
129 L6 **Itabuna** Brazil
129 J5 **Itacajá** Brazil
129 H5 **Itacajuna** *R* Brazil
130 G4 **Itacarambi** Brazil
129 L6 **Itacaré** Brazil
128 G4 **Itacoatiara** Brazil
128 D5 **Itacuai** *R* Brazil
130 C9 **Itacurubí del Rosario** Paraguay
130 H6 **Itaguaçu** Brazil
130 D8 **Itaguaje** Brazil
129 J6 **Itaguari** *R* Brazil
130 E8 **Itaí** Brazil
130 E10 **Itaiópolis** Brazil
129 G4 **Itaituba** Brazil
130 E10 **Itajai Acú, R** Brazil
129 J8 **Itajuba** Brazil
130 H4 **Itajuipe** Brazil
61 O10 **Itako** Japan
Itala *see* **Ataleh**
109 L3 **Italy** Texas
42 **Italy** *rep* S Europe
130 G5 **Itamarandiba** Brazil
129 J4 **Itamatare** Brazil
130 H6 **Itambacuri** Brazil
129 K7 **Itambé** Brazil
130 G6 **Itambe, P. de** *mt* Brazil
60 J11 **Itami** Japan
130 F9 **Itanhaém** Brazil
129 K7 **Itanhém** *R* Brazil
129 H3 **Itany** *R* Suriname
130 H5 **Itaobim** Brazil
129 J6 **Itapaci** Brazil
130 E6 **Itapajipe** Brazil
130 H4 **Itapebi** Brazil
130 F7 **Itapecerica** Brazil
129 K4 **Itapecuru Mirim** Brazil
130 H7 **Itapemirim** Brazil
129 K8 **Itaperuna** Brazil
129 K7 **Itapetinga** Brazil
129 J8 **Itapetininga** Brazil
129 J8 **Itapeva** Brazil
129 G3 **Itapi** *R* Brazil
129 K5 **Itapicura** *R* Brazil
129 J5 **Itapicuru, Serra do** *mts* Brazil
128 F5 **Itapinima** Brazil
129 L4 **Itapipoca** Brazil
128 G4 **Itapira** Brazil
130 E10 **Itapocu, R** Brazil
130 E7 **Itápolis** Brazil
130 H9 **Itaporanga** Brazil
130 C10 **Itapuá** *reg* Paraguay
129 H7 **Itapuranga** Brazil
131 G2 **Itaqui** Brazil
133 F2 **Itaquyry** Paraguay
129 J8 **Itararé** Brazil
74 G7 **Itarsi** India
130 D6 **Itarumã** Brazil
109 K3 **Itasca** Texas
99 L2 **Itasca State Park** Minnesota
131 A6 **Itata, R** Chile
130 F8 **Itatiba** Brazil
131 F2 **Itati, L** Argentina
130 E8 **Itatinga** Brazil
128 F5 **Itatuba** Brazil
130 E5 **Itauçu** Brazil
130 G7 **Itaúna** Brazil
129 L7 **Itaúnas** Brazil
130 H6 **Itaúnas** Brazil
9 E5 **Itchin, R** England
55 F4 **Itemgen, Oz** *L* U.S.S.R.
94 C3 **Ithaca** Michigan
95 L4 **Ithaca** New York
Ithaca *isld* Greece *see* **Itháki**
46 D6 **Itháki** *isld* Greece
8 C3 **Ithon, R** Wales
86 D5 **Itimbiri** *R* Zaïre
130 H5 **Itinga** Brazil
129 H7 **Itiquira** Brazil
129 K6 **Itiúba, Serra de** *mts* Brazil
115 O4 **Itivdleq** Greenland
116 M2 **Itkillik** *R* Alaska
61 N11 **Itō** Japan
61 L8 **Itoigawa** Japan
86 D6 **Itoko** Zaïre
61 P14 **Itoman** Okinawa
20 H4 **Iton** *R* France
45 P7 **Itri** Italy
79 A9 **Itsa** Egypt
111 F8 **Itta Bena** Mississippi
25 E6 **Ittervoort** Netherlands
43 B8 **Ittiri** Sardinia
130 F8 **Itu** Brazil
131 G2 **Itú** *R* Brazil
129 J7 **Ituiutaba** Brazil
88 A3 **Itula** Zaïre
88 E5 **Itumba** Tanzania
129 J7 **Itumbiara** Brazil
119 O7 **Ituna** Sask
128 G2 **Ituni** Guyana
130 E10 **Ituporanga** Brazil
128 E8 **Iturbe** Argentina
130 C10 **Iturbe** Paraguay
59 N3 **Iturup, Ostrov** *isld* U.S.S.R.
130 F7 **Ituverava** Brazil
130 C10 **Ituzaingo** Argentina
37 K3 **Itz** *R* W Germany
32 L5 **Itzehoe** W Germany
32 K5 **Itzwärden** W Germany
88 D6 **Iufira** *R* Malawi
110 H3 **Iuka** Illinois
107 M4 **Iuka** Kansas
130 H7 **Iúna** Brazil
112 E3 **Iva** S Carolina
129 H8 **Ivaí** *R* Brazil
29 N3 **Ivalo** Finland
29 N3 **Ivalojoki** *R* Finland
48 E7 **Ivančići** Yugoslavia
46 D2 **Ivangrad** Yugoslavia
98 K5 **Ivanhoe** Minnesota
139 G5 **Ivanhoe** New S Wales
94 G10 **Ivanhoe** Virginia
142 G3 **Ivanhoe** W Australia
120 H4 **Ivanhoe** *R* Ontario
54 M1 **Ivanishchi** U.S.S.R.
48 F7 **Ivanjica** Yugoslavia
53 B9 **Ivano-Frankovsk** U.S.S.R.
48 L1 **Ivanopol** U.S.S.R.
55 G3 **Ivanovka** Omsk U.S.S.R.
55 B4 **Ivanovka** U.S.S.R.
52 F6 **Ivanovo** U.S.S.R.
103 J6 **Ivanpah** California
54 J1 **Ivanteyvka** U.S.S.R.
47 H3 **Ivaylovgrad** Bulgaria
55 D1 **Ivdel'** U.S.S.R.
33 R5 **Ivenack** E Germany
99 S10 **Ivesdale** Illinois
17 H8 **Ivi, C** Algeria
115 P5 **Ivigtut** Greenland
86 B5 **Ivindo** *R* Gabon
9 F4 **Ivinghoe** England
129 H8 **Ivinheima** *R* Brazil
116 N2 **Ivishak** *R* Alaska
Iviza *see* **Ibiza**
95 L10 **Ivor** Virginia
85 C7 **Ivory Coast** *rep* W Africa
27 G15 **Ivösjön** Sweden
54 F3 **Ivot** U.S.S.R.
42 B3 **Ivrea** Italy
47 J5 **İvrindi** Turkey
20 J4 **Ivry-la-Bataille** France
115 M5 **Ivugivik** Quebec
8 C7 **Ivybridge** England
94 F8 **Ivydale** W Virginia
61 O7 **Iwadeyama** Japan
61 O7 **Iwai-gawa** *R* Japan
61 P6 **Iwaizumi** Japan
61 O9 **Iwaki** Japan
61 O5 **Iwaki** *R* Japan
61 O5 **Iwaki-san** *mt* Japan
59 K5 **Iwakuni** Japan
60 P2 **Iwamizawa** Japan
70 D3 **Iwan** *R* Kalimantan
60 O3 **Iwanai** Japan
61 O7 **Iwanuma** Japan
61 O9 **Iwase** Japan
61 M9 **Iwasuge-yama** *mt* Japan
61 L11 **Iwata** Japan
61 P6 **Iwate** Japan
60 H11 **Iwaya** Japan
85 E7 **Iwo** Nigeria
Iwo Jima *see* **Iō-tō**
61 N13 **Iwo Jima** *isld* Japan
22 E3 **Iwuy** France
128 E6 **Ixiamas** Bolivia
125 M9 **Ixtepec, Ciudad** Mexico
124 H8 **Ixtlahuacán** Mexico
124 G7 **Ixtlán del Río** Mexico
9 G3 **Ixworth** England
56 F4 **Iya** *R* U.S.S.R.
55 E3 **Iyevlevo** U.S.S.R.
60 G12 **Iyomishima** Japan
60 F12 **Iyo-nada** *sea* Japan
48 J3 **Iza** *R* Romania
125 P10 **Izabal, L. de** Guatemala
17 G2 **Izalzu** Spain
116 F6 **Izaviknek** *R* Alaska
31 O5 **Izbica** Poland
54 E1 **Izdeshkovo** U.S.S.R.
22 E2 **Izegem** Belgium
19 O14 **Izeron** France
52 H6 **Izhevsk** U.S.S.R.
52 H2 **Izhma** U.S.S.R.
53 C10 **Izmail** U.S.S.R.
78 A2 **Izmir** Turkey
47 J6 **İzmir Boz Sira Dağları** *mts* Turkey
78 C1 **Izmit** Turkey
47 K4 **İzmit Körfezi** *B* Turkey
16 E7 **Iznajar** Spain
16 E7 **Iznalloz** Spain
78 B1 **Iznik** Turkey
78 B1 **Iznik Gölü** Turkey
128 F7 **Izozog, Bañados de** Bolivia
79 G6 **Izra'** Syria
48 E4 **Izsák** Hungary
47 G3 **Iztochni Rodopi** Bulgaria
60 C11 **Izuhara** Japan
60 D13 **Izumi** Japan
60 J11 **Izumi-ōtsu** Japan
60 F10 **Izumo** Japan
61 M8 **Izumozaki** Japan
55 D3 **Izumrud** U.S.S.R.
61 N11 **Izu-shotō** *islds* Japan
147 N12 **Izvestiy, Os** *isld* U.S.S.R.
50 H1 **Izvestiy Tsik, Ostrova** *isld* U.S.S.R.
48 K4 **Izvorul Oltului** Romania
57 A2 **Izyndy** U.S.S.R.
54 J7 **Izyum** U.S.S.R.
29 M10 **Jaala** Finland
29 L5 **Jaatila** Finland
77 E2 **Jaba** *R* Iran
84 G3 **Jabal al Akhdar** *mts* Libya
77 C7 **Jabal Dhana** U.A.E.
16 E6 **Jabalón** *R* Spain
74 H7 **Jabalpur** India
22 E1 **Jabbeke** Belgium
33 R5 **Jabel** E Germany
46 D3 **Jablanica** Albania
46 E2 **Jablanica** *R* Yugoslavia
31 J5 **Jablonec nad Nisou** Czechoslovakia
31 K7 **Jablonica** Czechoslovakia
31 L2 **Jabłonowo** Poland
31 L6 **Jablunkov** Czechoslovakia
129 M5 **Jaboatão** Brazil
129 J8 **Jaboticabal** Brazil
69 G13 **Jabung, Tanjung** *C* Sumatra
128 F5 **Jaburu** Brazil
17 G2 **Jaca** Spain
130 B6 **Jacadigo** *L* Brazil
130 G4 **Jacaraci** Brazil
129 K6 **Jacaré** *R* Brazil
130 F8 **Jacareí** Brazil
128 G5 **Jacaretinga** Brazil
130 E8 **Jacarezinho** Brazil
133 D4 **Jachal** Argentina
37 O3 **Jáchymov** Czechoslovakia
130 H5 **Jacinto** Brazil
109 M5 **Jacinto, S** *R* Texas
128 F5 **Jaciparaná** Brazil
120 D4 **Jackfish** Ontario
118 J5 **Jackfish L** Sask
117 R6 **Jackfish River** Alberta
119 U7 **Jackhead Harbour** Manitoba
115 N6 **Jack Lane B** Labrador
95 R1 **Jackman** Maine
100 E1 **Jack Mt** Washington
120 C3 **Jackpine** Ontario
141 G3 **Jack R** Queensland
112 C1 **Jacksboro** Tennessee
109 J2 **Jacksboro** Texas
94 K6 **Jacks Mt** Pennsylvania
111 J10 **Jackson** Alabama
102 D3 **Jackson** California
112 D4 **Jackson** Georgia
94 D9 **Jackson** Kentucky
111 E11 **Jackson** Louisiana
111 F9 **Jackson** Mississippi
110 G4 **Jackson** Missouri
101 M4 **Jackson** Montana
112 K1 **Jackson** N Carolina
94 E7 **Jackson** Ohio
141 J7 **Jackson** Queensland
112 F4 **Jackson** S Carolina
110 H6 **Jackson** Tennessee
101 P6 **Jackson** Wyoming
94 H8 **Jackson** *R* Virginia
117 L10 **Jackson Bay** Br Col
144 B5 **Jackson Bay** New Zealand
145 E4 **Jackson, C** New Zealand
110 M1 **Jackson Cen** Ohio
106 B4 **Jackson Gulch Res** Colorado
113 C7 **Jackson, L** Florida
112 D4 **Jackson L** Georgia
101 P6 **Jackson L** Wyoming
143 C9 **Jackson, Mt** W Australia
100 G8 **Jackson Mts** Nevada
99 T5 **Jacksonport** Wisconsin
111 G9 **Jackson Prairie** Mississippi
106 F1 **Jackson Res** Colorado
144 C5 **Jacksons** New Zealand
123 Q4 **Jackson's Arm** Nfld
111 L8 **Jacksonville** Alabama
110 D7 **Jacksonville** Arkansas
113 F7 **Jacksonville** Florida
99 Q10 **Jacksonville** Illinois
110 D2 **Jacksonville** Missouri
112 K3 **Jacksonville** N Carolina
100 C7 **Jacksonville** Oregon
109 M4 **Jacksonville** Texas
113 F7 **Jacksonville Beach** Florida
127 H5 **Jacmel** Haiti
124 G4 **Jaco** Mexico
71 N9 **Jaco** *isld* Timor
74 C4 **Jacobabad** Pakistan
129 K6 **Jacobina** Brazil
103 M5 **Jacob L** Arizona
80 E5 **Jacob's Well** Jordan
124 H8 **Jacona** Mexico
121 T9 **Jacques Cartier** Quebec
121 T5 **Jacques Cartier, L** Quebec
122 G4 **Jacques Cartier, Mt** Quebec
122 F6 **Jacquet R** New Brunswick
130 J9 **Jacú** *R* Brazil
130 F7 **Jacuí** Minas Gerais Brazil
131 H2 **Jacui** Rio Grande do Sul Brazil
131 H2 **Jacui** *R* Rio Grande do Sul Brazil
129 L6 **Jacuípe** *R* Brazil
103 H9 **Jacumba** California
129 J4 **Jacundá** Brazil
129 H4 **Jacunda** *R* Brazil
130 F9 **Jacupiranga** Brazil
129 E4 **Jaçura** Brazil
80 G8 **Jad'a** Jordan
48 E6 **Jadar** *R* Yugoslavia
32 H6 **Jade** W Germany
32 H6 **Jade** *R* W Germany
85 C2 **Jadida, El** Morocco
87 E8 **Jadotville** Zaïre
31 N3 **Jadów** Poland
17 F4 **Jadraque** Spain
84 E3 **Jādū** Libya
28 H5 **Jægerspris** Denmark
22 F3 **Jaeibise** Belgium
143 C8 **Jaellan, Mt** W Australia
71 E3 **Jaen** Luzon Philippines
16 E7 **Jaén** Spain
16 E7 **Jaén** *prov* Spain
27 A13 **Jaeren** *R* Norway
26 F7 **Jaevsjo** Norway
77 A2 **Ja'farābād** Iran
80 C5 **Jaffa** Israel
138 E6 **Jaffa, C** S Australia
83 K8 **Jaffna** Sri Lanka
75 K9 **Jagdalpur** India
87 E11 **Jagersfontein** S Africa
84 G4 **Jaghbūb, Al** Libya
116 Q2 **Jago** *R* Alaska
36 H5 **Jagst** *R* W Germany
37 J5 **Jagstzell** W Germany
74 H9 **Jagtial** India
129 K6 **Jaguaquara** Brazil
131 H4 **Jaguarão** Brazil
131 G2 **Jaguari** *R* Brazil
129 H8 **Jaguariaiva** Brazil
129 L5 **Jaguaribe** *R* Brazil
131 C2 **Jagüe, R** Argentina
126 D3 **Jaguey Grande** Cuba
140 B1 **Jahleel Pt** N Terr Aust
78 K7 **Jahmah** Iraq
48 E7 **Jahorina** *mt* Yugoslavia
77 C5 **Jahrom** Iran
74 G3 **Jaijon Doaba** India
74 F5 **Jaipur** India
74 D5 **Jaisalmer** India
42 H4 **Jajce** Yugoslavia
75 M8 **Jajpur** India
70 L9 **Jakarta** Java
63 **Jakarta** *conurbation* Indonesia
26 J5 **Jäkkvik** Sweden
26 S2 **Jakobselv** *R* Norway/U.S.S.R.
29 K8 **Jakobstad** Finland
46 E3 **Jakupica** Yugoslavia
106 G9 **Jal** New Mexico
77 H6 **Jāla** Iran
58 G2 **Jalai Nur** China
77 L2 **Jalalabad** Afghanistan
125 L3 **Jalapa** Nicaragua
125 L8 **Jalapa Enríquez** Mexico
29 K9 **Jalasjärvi** Finland
74 H5 **Jalaun** India
140 C2 **Jalboi** *R* N Terr Aust
86 H4 **Jaldessa** Ethiopia
130 E7 **Jales** Brazil
75 M8 **Jaleswar** India
74 F8 **Jalgaon** India
22 K2 **Jalhay** Belgium
78 L6 **Jalibah** Iraq
86 B4 **Jalingo** Nigeria
124 G8 **Jalisco** *state* Mexico
21 D7 **Jallais** France
74 F9 **Jalna** India
17 F3 **Jalón** *R* Spain
Jalo Oasis *see* **Gialo**
74 E6 **Jalor** India
124 H7 **Jalostotitlán** Mexico
124 H7 **Jalpa** Mexico
75 N5 **Jalpaiguri** India
124 K7 **Jalpan** Mexico
77 L2 **Jalrez** Afghanistan
84 G4 **Jalu** Libya
78 K4 **Jalūlā** Iraq
77 G2 **Jam** *reg* Iran
128 B4 **Jama** Ecuador
126 G4 **Jamaica** Cuba
95 P3 **Jamaica** Vermont
127 K2 **Jamaica W I**
126 G5 **Jamaica Chan** Caribbean
27 M13 **Jämaja** U.S.S.R.
75 N6 **Jamalpur** Bangladesh
75 M6 **Jamalpur** India
126 A2 **Jamanota** *hill* Aruba W I
129 G5 **Jamanxim** *R* Brazil
128 F5 **Jamari** Brazil
66 C2 **Jamati** China
139 K5 **Jamberoo** New S Wales
Jambi *see* **Telanaipura**
69 F13 **Jambi** *dist* Sumatra
141 K6 **Jambin** Queensland
69 C10 **Jamboaye** *R* Sumatra
122 F4 **Jambon, Pte** Quebec
69 C10 **Jambuair, Tanjung** *C* Sumatra
110 C5 **James** *R* Missouri
98 H3 **James** *R* N Dakota
98 J6 **James** *R* S Dakota
115 L7 **James B** Canada
95 N6 **Jamesburg** New Jersey
112 K2 **James City** N Carolina
94 J5 **James City** Pennsylvania
112 F2 **James, L** N Carolina
99 N9 **Jameson** Missouri
115 R3 **Jameson Land** Greenland
99 N10 **Jamesport** Missouri
113 L12 **James Pt** Bahamas
140 D5 **James R** N Terr Aust
95 L9 **James R** Virginia
140 C6 **James Ra** N Terr Aust
146 D14 **James Ross I** Antarctica
115 K4 **James Ross Str** N W Terr
110 K2 **Jamestown** Indiana
107 N2 **Jamestown** Kansas
94 B4 **Jamestown** Michigan
98 H3 **Jamestown** N Dakota
94 H4 **Jamestown** New York
94 D7 **Jamestown** Ohio
94 G5 **Jamestown** Pennsylvania
95 Q5 **Jamestown** Rhode I
90 A13 **Jamestown** St Helena
138 E5 **Jamestown** S Australia
112 H4 **Jamestown** S Carolina
94 C10 **Jamestown** Tennessee
95 L9 **Jamestown Nat. Hist. Site** Virginia
112 L2 **Jamesville** N Carolina
95 L4 **Jamesville** New York
22 J5 **Jametz** France
100 H5 **Jamieson** Oregon
29 K10 **Jämijärvi** Finland
125 L9 **Jamilzepec** Mexico
98 G7 **Jamison** Nebraska
76 B2 **Jamkhandi** India
74 F9 **Jamkhed** India
76 D3 **Jammalamadugu** India
28 C2 **Jammerbugt** *B* Denmark
28 F5 **Jammerland Bugt** *B* Denmark
74 F2 **Jammu** Kashmir
Jammu and Kashmir *see* **Kashmir**
74 G1 **Jammu and Kashmir** India
74 D7 **Jamnagar** India
31 J1 **Jamno, Jezioro** *L* Poland
22 J4 **Jamoigne** Belgium
74 D4 **Jampur** Pakistan
29 L10 **Jämsä** Finland
29 L10 **Jämsänkoski** Finland
75 M7 **Jamshedpur** India
26 F8 **Jämtland** Sweden
26 H8 **Jämtl Sikås** Sweden
71 C3 **Jamtup, Tg** *C* W Irian
70 E3 **Jamuk, G** *mt* Kalimantan
102 H9 **Jamul** California
75 N6 **Jamuna** *R* Bangladesh
128 C3 **Jamundí** Colombia
75 M5 **Janakpur** Nepal
129 K7 **Janaúba** Brazil
129 H3 **Janaucu, I** Brazil
130 E5 **Jandaia** Brazil
142 B3 **Jandakot** *dist* Perth, W Aust
142 B3 **Jandakot, L** W Australia
77 D2 **Jandaq** Iran
28 A5 **Janderup** Denmark
128 E5 **Jandiatuba** *R* Brazil
141 K7 **Jandowae** Queensland
94 G7 **Jane Lew** W Virginia
144 B6 **Jane Pk** New Zealand
100 E9 **Janesville** California
99 O7 **Janesville** Iowa
99 N5 **Janesville** Minnesota
99 R7 **Janesville** Wisconsin
130 D10 **Jangada** Brazil
130 C7 **Jango** Brazil
69 G13 **Jang, Tanjung** *C* Indonesia
33 S8 **Jänickendorf** E Germany
46 E2 **Janjevo** Yugoslavia
89 D6 **Jan Kemp** S Africa
119 P4 **Jan L** Sask
90 H1 **Jan Mayen** *isld* Arctic Oc
90 H1 **Jan Mayen Ridge, E** Arctic Oc
77 G2 **Jannatabad** Iran
124 E2 **Janos** Mexico
48 E4 **Jánoshalma** Hungary
48 D3 **Jánosháza** Hungary
37 P5 **Janovice nad Uhlavou** Czechoslovakia
33 S5 **Janow** E Germany
31 K3 **Janowiec** Poland
31 N5 **Janów Lubelski** Poland
31 O3 **Janów Podlaski** Poland
98 K9 **Jansen** Nebraska
119 N7 **Jansen** Sask
130 G4 **Januária** Brazil
20 J5 **Janville** France
21 C6 **Janzé** France
130 G5 **Jaoquim Felício** Brazil
74 F7 **Jaora** India
61 **Japan** *empire* E Asia
59 K3 **Japan, Sea of** E Asia
29 N9 **Jäppilä** Finland
128 E4 **Japurá** Brazil
127 J5 **Jarabacoa** Dom Rep
129 J7 **Jaraguá** Brazil
130 E10 **Jaraguá do Sul** Brazil
130 C7 **Jaraguari** Brazil
130 E10 **Jaraguá Serra** *mts* Brazil
16 D5 **Jaraicejo** Spain
16 E4 **Jarama** *R* Spain
133 D7 **Jaramillo** Argentina
16 D4 **Jarandilla** Spain
129 H4 **Jarauçu** *R* Brazil
100 K8 **Jarbidge** Nevada
100 K7 **Jarbidge** *R* Idaho
27 J11 **Järbo** Sweden
143 B10 **Jardee** W Australia
130 G9 **Jardim** Ceará Brazil
130 C7 **Jardim** Mato Grosso Brazil
130 H9 **Jardim do Seridó** Brazil
141 F1 **Jardine** *R* Queensland
122 E6 **Jardine Brook** New Brunswick
126 E4 **Jardines de la Reina** *islds* Cuba
130 E6 **Jardinésia** Brazil
130 F7 **Jardinópolis** Brazil
21 B9 **Jard-sur-Mer** France
27 H14 **Järeda** Sweden
27 E11 **Jaren** Norway
38 N8 **Jarenina** Yugoslavia
58 G2 **Jargalant** Mongolia
21 J6 **Jargeau** France
129 H3 **Jari** *R* Brazil
128 F4 **Jari, L** Brazil
33 S5 **Jarmen** E Germany

Järna — Kahemba 37

27 J12 Järna Sweden
18 E7 Jarnac France
27 H13 Järnlunden *L* Sweden
71 F5 Jaro Panay Philippines
31 K4 Jarocin Poland
31 J5 Jaroměř Czechoslovakia
31 J6 Jaroměřice Czechoslovakia
126 F4 Jaronu Cuba
31 O5 Jaroslaw Poland
106 E4 Jaroso Colorado
26 F8 Järpen Sweden
80 F8 Jarra *R* Jordan
94 K10 Jarratt Virginia
26 K5 Jarre *mt* Sweden
109 K5 Jarrell Texas
68 F3 Jarres, Plaine des Laos
118 F6 Jarrow Alberta
13 G4 Jarrow England
128 F6 Jaru Brazil
65 E2 Jarud Qi China
52 C5 Järva-Jaani U.S.S.R.
118 D4 Jarvie Alberta
134 B3 Jarvis I Pacific Oc
26 H10 Järvsö Sweden
21 E6 Jarzé France
48 F5 Jaša Tomic Yugoslavia
74 D7 Jasdan India
33 T8 Jasdorf E Germany
85 E7 Jasikan Ghana
77 E7 Jāsk Iran
31 N6 Jasło Poland
119 O7 Jasmin Sask
30 H1 Jasmund *pen* E Germany
133 E8 Jason Is Falkland Is
146 E14 Jason Pen Antarctica
110 J2 Jasonville Indiana
111 J8 Jasper Alabama
114 H7 Jasper Alberta
110 C5 Jasper Arkansas
106 D4 Jasper Colorado
113 E7 Jasper Florida
111 M7 Jasper Georgia
110 K3 Jasper Indiana
94 C5 Jasper Michigan
98 K6 Jasper Minnesota
110 B4 Jasper Missouri
94 K4 Jasper New York
121 P8 Jasper Ontario
112 B2 Jasper Tennessee
111 C11 Jasper Texas
117 O9 Jasper Nat. Park Alberta
118 D5 Jasper Place Alberta
78 K5 Jassan Iraq
Jassy *see* Iasi
31 L1 Jastarnia Poland
46 E1 Jastrebac *mt* Yugoslavia
31 K2 Jastrowie Poland
48 F3 Jászapáti Hungary
48 F3 Jászarokszállás Hungary
48 F3 Jászberény Hungary
48 F3 Jászfényszaru Hungary
48 F3 Jászladány Hungary
129 H7 Jataí Brazil
128 G4 Jatapu *R* Brazil
76 B2 Jath India
126 E4 Jatibonico Cuba
17 G6 Játiva Spain
129 H4 Jatobá Brazil
129 J4 Jatobal Brazil
80 D4 Jatt Israel
128 F5 Jatuarana Brazil
33 T5 Jatzke E Germany
33 T5 Jatznick E Germany
129 J8 Jaú Brazil
128 F4 Jaú *R* Brazil
128 F3 Jauaperi *R* Brazil
22 H2 Jauche Belgium
126 G4 Jauco Cuba
128 C6 Jauja Peru
21 F10 Jauldes France
128 G5 Jauna *R* Brazil
21 F8 Jaunay-Clan France
52 B6 Jaunjelgava U.S.S.R.
52 C6 Jaunpiebalga U.S.S.R.
75 K6 Jaunpur India
38 L8 Jauntal *V* Austria
129 G7 Jauru *R* Brazil
130 D6 Jauru, R Brazil
22 D5 Jaux France
Java *isld* Indonesia *see* Jawa
76 D4 Javadi Hills India
129 J6 Javaés, Serra dos *mts* Brazil
17 G4 Javalambre, Sierra de *mts* Spain
128 D4 Javari *R* Brazil/Peru
70 M8 Java Sea Indonesia
136 D4 Java Trough Indian Oc
17 H6 Jávea Spain
Javhlant *see* Uliastay
133 C7 Javier *B* Chile
48 E6 Javor *mts* Yugoslavia
48 E2 Javoria *mt* Czechoslovakia
38 K9 Javornik Yugoslavia
48 E1 Javorniky *mt* Czechoslovakia
26 M6 Jävre Sweden
20 E5 Javron France
80 G6 Jawa Jordan
70 Jawa *isld* Indonesia
84 G5 Jawf, Al Libya
69 J13 Jawi Indonesia
31 J4 Jawor Poland
31 L5 Jaworzno Poland
107 Q5 Jay Oklahoma
136 H2 Jaya Pk *mt* W Irian
136 J2 Jayapura W Irian
98 B7 Jay Em Wyoming
33 P7 Jayenitz E Germany
9 H4 Jaywick Sands England
78 H4 Jazirah, Al Iraq
124 J5 Jazminal Mexico
77 F6 Jaz Murian, Hamun-e *L* Iran
78 G4 Jdaide Syria
103 J6 Jean Nevada
109 J2 Jean Texas
111 E12 Jeanerette Louisiana
122 E1 Jean L Quebec
117 N5 Jean Marie River N W Terr
94 H6 Jeannette Pennsylvania
127 H5 Jean Rabel Haiti
13 G5 Jeater Houses England
80 G1 Jeba Syria
77 F5 Jebāl Bārez, Kūh-e *mts* Iran
85 E7 Jebba Nigeria
86 E2 Jebel Abyad Plateau Sudan
16 D9 Jebha Morocco
28 B3 Jebjerg Denmark
79 F3 Jeble Syria
88 E8 Jeci *mt* Mozambique
119 P7 Jedburgh Sask
13 F2 Jedburgh Scotland
Jedda *see* Jiddah
94 E3 Jeddo Michigan
43 C12 Jedeida Tunisia
13 F3 Jedfoot Br Scotland
31 M5 Jędrzejów Poland
31 N2 Jedwabne Poland
117 H9 Jedway Br Col
29 M4 Jeesiö Finland
33 O7 Jeetze E Germany
33 O6 Jeetze *R* W Germany
99 L5 Jeffers Minnesota
106 E2 Jefferson Colorado
112 D3 Jefferson Georgia
94 K7 Jefferson Maryland
94 G5 Jefferson Ohio
107 N5 Jefferson Oklahoma
100 C5 Jefferson Oregon
98 K7 Jefferson S Dakota
111 B9 Jefferson Texas
99 S6 Jefferson Wisconsin
110 D3 Jefferson City Missouri
101 N3 Jefferson City Montana
112 D1 Jefferson City Tennessee
101 O4 Jefferson Island Montana
100 D5 Jefferson, Mt Oregon
94 B8 Jeffersontown Kentucky
110 L3 Jeffersontown Kentucky
112 D5 Jeffersonville Georgia
94 B8 Jeffersonville Indiana
95 N5 Jeffersonville New York
94 D7 Jeffersonville Ohio
95 P2 Jeffersonville Vermont
101 S7 Jeffrey City Wyoming
71 C3 Jef Lio W Irian
85 E6 Jega Nigeria
28 B3 Jegindø *isld* Denmark
18 F9 Jegun France
77 G4 Jehile Pūzak *L* Iran
28 B7 Jejsing Denmark
130 C9 Jejui Guazú, R Paraguay
52 C6 Jēkabpils U.S.S.R.
112 F6 Jekyll I Georgia
31 J5 Jelenia Góra Poland
52 B6 Jelgava U.S.S.R.
115 L8 Jellicoe Ontario
28 C5 Jelling Denmark
102 B1 Jelly California
31 L5 Jełowa Poland
27 E12 Jelöy *isld* Norway
28 C6 Jels Denmark
27 B12 Jelsa Norway
48 F2 Jelšava Czechoslovakia
69 G11 Jemaja Indonesia
22 F3 Jemappes Belgium
33 N8 Jembke W Germany
70 E1 Jembongan *isld* Sabah
85 G1 Jem, El Tunisia
22 J3 Jemelle Belgium
106 D6 Jemez *R* New Mexico
106 D6 Jemez Pueblo New Mexico
106 D6 Jemez Springs New Mexico
32 F6 Jemgum W Germany
43 D13 Jemmal Tunisia
31 J6 Jemnice Czechoslovakia
122 F8 Jemseg New Brunswick
37 M2 Jena E Germany
111 D10 Jena Louisiana
38 E7 Jenbach Austria
80 E4 Jenin Jordan
94 F9 Jenkinjones W Virginia
94 E9 Jenkins Kentucky
99 M3 Jenkins Minnesota
140 A7 Jenkins,Mt N Terr Aust
118 F8 Jenner Alberta
102 A3 Jenner California
127 O4 Jennings Antigua W I
113 D7 Jennings Florida
107 K2 Jennings Kansas
111 D11 Jennings Louisiana
107 O5 Jennings Oklahoma
117 H6 Jennings *R* Br Col
114 J4 Jenny Lind I N W Terr
139 K5 Jenolan Caves New S Wales
101 Q9 Jensen Utah
113 G10 Jensen Beach Florida
115 P5 Jensen Nunatakker *peak* Greenland
115 L4 Jens Munk I N W Terr
69 J13 Jenu Indonesia
138 F6 Jeparit Victoria
29 K8 Jeppo Finland
129 K6 Jequie Brazil
130 G5 Jequitai Brazil
129 K7 Jequitinhonha Brazil
85 D2 Jerada Morocco
69 F11 Jerantut Malaysia
85 G2 Jerba, I de Tunisia
126 G5 Jérémie Haiti
129 L6 Jeremoabo Brazil
124 H6 Jerez de García Salinas Mexico
16 C8 Jerez de la Frontera Spain
16 C6 Jerez de los Caballeros Spain
80 E6 Jericho Jordan
141 H6 Jericho Queensland
33 Q8 Jerichow E Germany
129 K4 Jericoaquara, Pta *C* Brazil
69 G14 Jerigi Sumatra
26 N5 Jerijärvi Sweden
70 B3 Jerijeh, Tg *C* Sarawak
139 H6 Jerilderie New S Wales
29 L4 Jerisjärvi *L* Finland
130 E4 Jeroaquara Brazil
103 M7 Jerome Arizona
101 L7 Jerome Idaho
120 H5 Jerome Ontario
129 H7 Jerônimo, Serra do *mts* Brazil
143 C10 Jerraymungup W Australia
9 H7 Jersey *isld* Channel Is
95 N6 Jersey City New Jersey
95 K5 Jersey Shore Pennsylvania
110 F2 Jerseyville Illinois
28 E2 Jerslev Denmark
28 C6 Jerstal Denmark
16 D4 Jerte *R* Spain
79 G5 Jerūd Syria
70 D2 Jerudong Brunei
129 K5 Jerumenha Brazil
28 E1 Jerup Denmark
80 D6 Jerusalem Israel
145 E3 Jerusalem New Zealand
136 H6 Jervais Ra N Terr Australia
139 K6 Jervis Bay New S Wales
138 E6 Jervis, C S Australia
117 M10 Jervis Inlet Br Col
140 D6 Jervois Ra N Terr Aust
33 N8 Jerxheim W Germany
36 G2 Jesberg W Germany
37 P3 Jesenice Czechoslovakia
42 F2 Jesenice Yugoslavia
31 K5 Jeseník Czechoslovakia
48 F2 Jesenské Czechoslovakia
33 Q8 Jeserig E Germany
33 R10 Jesewitz E Germany
Jesselton Sabah *see* Kota Kinabalu
27 E11 Jessheim Norway
98 H2 Jessie N Dakota
33 Q9 Jessnitz E Germany
113 F9 Jessup, L Florida
32 L6 Jesteburg W Germany
112 F6 Jesup Georgia
99 O7 Jesup Iowa
133 E4 Jesús María Argentina
124 H7 Jesús María Mexico
107 M5 Jet Oklahoma
119 Q2 Jetait Manitoba
94 J9 Jetersville Virginia
107 L3 Jetmore Kansas
37 J7 Jettingen W Germany
37 L7 Jetzendorf W Germany
22 G3 Jeumont France
32 L4 Jevenau *R* W Germany
32 L4 Jevenstedt W Germany
32 G5 Jever W Germany
48 D1 Jevičko Czechoslovakia
27 D11 Jevnaker Norway
98 C6 Jewel Cave Nat. Mon S Dakota
99 N7 Jewell Iowa
107 M2 Jewell Kansas
100 B4 Jewell Oregon
110 H2 Jewett Illinois
94 G6 Jewett Ohio
109 L4 Jewett Texas
95 Q5 Jewett City Connecticut
75 K9 Jeypore India
46 D2 Jezerce *mt* Albania
37 P5 Jezerni *mt* Czechoslovakia
42 H4 Jezero Yugoslavia
31 M2 Jeziorak, Jezioro *L* Poland
31 M2 Jeziorany Poland
31 P1 Jeznas U.S.S.R.
31 M4 Jeżów Poland
79 F5 Jezzine Lebanon
74 F7 Jhabua India
74 G4 Jhajjar India
74 G6 Jhalawar India
74 E3 Jhang Maghiana Pakistan
74 H6 Jhansi India
75 M5 Jhapa Nepal
74 E2 Jhelum India
74 E2 Jhelum *R* Pakistan
74 F4 Jhunjhuna India
65 E3 Jiade He *R* China
67 G1 Jiading China
67 C4 Jiagui China
67 D4 Jiahe China
Jiaji *see* Qionghai
67 A2 Jiajiang China
58 E5 Jialing Jiang *R* China
65 G4 Ji'an China
67 E3 Ji'an China
65 D4 Jianchang China
65 F4 Jianchang China
67 F2 Jiande China
67 B2 Jiang'an China
67 B2 Jiangbei China
68 E1 Jiangcheng China
67 C3 Jiangdong China
67 F1 Jiangdu China
67 C6 Jianghong China
67 D4 Jianghua China
67 B2 Jiangjin China
Jiangkou *see* Fengkai
67 C3 Jiangkou China
67 D1 Jiangkou China
67 F3 Jiangle China
67 D1 Jiangling China
67 D5 Jiangman China
58 G5 Jiangsu *prov* China
67 E3 Jiangxi *prov* China
65 B7 Jiang Xian China
67 F1 Jiangxiang China
67 G1 Jiangyin China
67 D4 Jiangyong China
67 A1 Jiangyou China
67 C3 Jianhe China
Jianjun *see* Yongshou
67 D2 Jianli China
67 E3 Jianning China
67 F3 Jian'ou China
65 D4 Jianping China
65 D5 Jianping China
67 C1 Jianshi China
67 A5 Jianshui China
58 D5 Jianyang China
67 F3 Jianyang China
65 B6 Jiaocheng China
59 J3 Jiaohe China
65 C5 Jiaohe China
65 B6 Jiaokou China
67 E4 Jiaoling China
65 E7 Jiaonan China
65 D6 Jiao Xian China
58 F4 Jiaozuo China
65 G3 Jiapigou China
58 G5 Jiashan China
67 G1 Jiashan China
57 H5 Jiashi China
65 D7 Jiawang China
65 A5 Jia Xian China
65 B7 Jia Xian China
59 H5 Jiaxing China
67 C4 Jiaya China
59 K2 Jiayin China
67 D2 Jiayu China
58 C4 Jiayuguan China
65 E6 Jiazhou Wan *B* China
77 B7 Jiban, Al Saudi Arabia
129 J7 Jibao, Serra do *mts* Brazil
126 E4 Jibaro Cuba
88 G6 Jibondo *isld* Tanzania
48 H3 Jibou Romania
67 B3 Jichang China
31 J5 Jičín Czechoslovakia
86 G1 Jiddah Saudi Arabia
65 H2 Jidong China
Jiehu *see* Yinan
26 L2 Jiekkevarre *mt* Norway
67 E5 Jieshi China
67 E5 Jieshi Wan *B* China
26 O2 Jiesjavrre *L* Norway
67 E5 Jiexi China
65 B6 Jiexiu China
143 D6 Jiggalong W Australia
100 K9 Jiggs Nevada
67 E1 Jigong Shan *mt* China
79 H4 Jihar, Wādi el *watercourse* Syria
31 J6 Jihlava Czechoslovakia
31 H6 Jihočesky *reg* Czechoslovakia
31 J6 Jihomoravský *reg* Czechoslovakia
85 F1 Jijel Algeria
48 L3 Jijia *R* Romania
86 H4 Jijiga Ethiopia
80 G3 Jijjin Jordan
17 G6 Jijona Spain
59 H2 Jilin *prov* China
65 G3 Jilin China
65 F3 Jilin Hada Ling *mt ra* China
59 H1 Jiliu He *R* China
17 G4 Jiloca *R* Spain
116 M3 Jim *R* Alaska
86 G4 Jimā Ethiopia
69 G14 Jimar Sumatra
142 F5 Jimberingga W Australia
48 F5 Jimbolia Romania
141 L8 Jimboomba Queensland
16 D8 Jimena de la Frontera Spain
124 G4 Jiménez Mexico
140 C2 Jim Jim Cr N Terr Aust
65 E6 Jimo China
65 C6 Jinan China
65 B7 Jincheng China
139 J6 Jindabyne New S Wales
37 O3 Jindřichovice Czechoslovakia
31 J6 Jindřichův Hradec Czechoslovakia
67 E2 Jing'an China
67 F1 Jingde China
67 F2 Jingdezhen China
Jingfeng *see* Hexigten Qi
65 D5 Jinghai China
65 E6 Jinghaiwei China
66 C3 Jinghe China
58 E5 Jing He *R* China
68 E2 Jinghong China
67 G1 Jingjiang China
65 B5 Jingle China
67 D1 Jingmen China
Jingping *see* Pinglu
65 G2 Jingpo China
65 G3 Jingpo Hu *L* China
67 D1 Jingshan China
58 F5 Jing Shan *mt ra* China
58 D4 Jingtai China
65 C6 Jing Xian China
67 C3 Jing Xian China
67 F1 Jing Xian China
59 H2 Jingxing China
67 A2 Jingyan China
65 A7 Jingyang China
65 G3 Jingyu China
58 D4 Jingyuan China
Jingzhou *see* Jiangling
67 F2 Jinhua China
65 C7 Jining China
65 B4 Jining Nei Monggol Zizhiqu China
88 D1 Jinja-Bugembe Uganda
67 F4 Jinjiang China
67 C3 Jin Jiang *R* China
67 E2 Jin Jiang *R* China
67 D2 Jinjing China
65 E6 Jinkou China
67 E1 Jinkou China
67 F4 Jinlong Jiang *R* China
125 M3 Jinotega Nicaragua
125 L4 Jinotepe Nicaragua
67 C3 Jinping China
68 F1 Jinping China
Jinsha *see* Nantong
67 B3 Jinsha China
58 C6 Jinsha Jiang *R* China
Jinshan *see* Harqin Qi
67 G1 Jinshan China
67 D2 Jinshi China
67 F1 Jintan China
67 A1 Jintang China
67 C5 Jintian Shuiku *res* China
71 F5 Jintotolo *isld* Philippines
71 F5 Jintotolo Ch Philippines
59 H3 Jinxi China
67 B5 Jinxi China
67 E3 Jinxi China
67 F3 Jin Xi China
65 C5 Jin Xian China
65 E4 Jin Xian China
65 E5 Jin Xian China
67 E2 Jinxian China
65 C7 Jinxiang China
67 G3 Jinxiang China
67 C4 Jinxiu China
67 G2 Jinyun China
67 E1 Jinzhai China
65 E4 Jinzhou China
65 E5 Jinzhou Wan *B* China
128 B4 Jipijapa Ecuador
126 F4 Jiquaní Cuba
130 H5 Jiquitaia Brazil
143 F9 Jirina W Australia
65 D2 Jirin Gol China
37 P3 Jirkov Czechoslovakia
48 L5 Jirlău Romania
65 A7 Jishan China
67 C2 Jishou China
67 E3 Jishui China
79 G3 Jisr esh Shughūr Syria
16 C2 Jistredo, Sa. de *mts* Spain
143 C10 Jitarning W Australia
69 E9 Jitra Malaysia
Jiucheng *see* Wucheng
67 A1 Jiuding Shan *mt* China
58 G6 Jiujiang China
67 E2 Jiujiang China
67 D1 Jiukou China
48 H6 Jiul *R* Romania
67 E4 Jiulian Shan *mts* China
67 E2 Jiuling Shan *mt ra* China
58 C4 Jiuquan China
65 E6 Jiurongcheng China
59 J3 Jiutai China
67 C4 Jiuwan Dashan *mts* China
65 C5 Jiuwuqing China
65 C5 Jiuxincheng China
67 B4 Jiuxu China
67 F1 Jiuyuhang China
67 B4 Jiuzhou China
72 G4 Jiwā', Al *oasis* U.A.E.
77 G7 Jiwani Iran
74 B10 Jiwani Pakistan
65 H2 Jixi China
67 F1 Jixi China
65 A6 Ji Xian China
65 C6 Ji Xian China
65 C7 Ji Xian China
65 D4 Ji Xian China
65 D6 Jiyang China
65 B7 Jiyuan China
65 D5 Jiyun He *R* China
80 G7 Jiza Jordan
65 C6 Jize China
31 H5 Jizera *R* Czechoslovakia
60 G10 Jizō zaki *C* Japan
86 E1 J. Kissu *mt* Sudan
120 G1 Joab L Ontario
130 D10 Joaçaba Brazil
33 T7 Joachimsthal E Germany
130 H5 Joaíma Brazil
85 A6 Joal-Fadiout Senegal
142 E5 Joanna Spring W Australia
129 L5 Joao Camara Brazil
129 J4 João Coelho Brazil
87 B9 João de Almeid Angola
131 H4 João Maria, Albardão do Brazil
130 E10 João Paulo *R* Brazil
129 M5 João Pessoa Brazil
130 J9 João Pessoa Brazil
130 F5 João Pinheiro Brazil
111 B10 Joaquin Texas
126 F4 Jobabo Cuba
61 O9 Jōban Japan
71 G6 Jobo Pt Mindanao Philippines
20 B2 Jobourg France
102 F2 Job Pk Nevada
120 D2 Jobrin Ontario
38 F7 Jochberg Austria
16 E7 Jódar Spain
74 E5 Jodhpur India
74 D7 Jodiya Bandar India
22 H2 Jodoigne Belgium
123 S4 Joe Batt's Arm Nfld
29 O9 Joensuu Finland
106 H2 Joes Colorado
26 G6 Joeström Sweden
19 K3 Jœuf France
87 F10 Jofane Mozambique
106 E7 Joffre New Mexico
117 Q10 Joffre, Mt Br Col
61 L9 Joganji *R* Japan
75 M5 Jogbani India
65 C3 Jogdor China
52 C5 Jõgeva U.S.S.R.
122 H8 Joggins Nova Scotia
74 G3 Jogindernagar India
120 E2 Jog L Ontario
38 N7 Joglland Austria
61 K9 Jōhana Japan
32 J9 Johannaberg W Germany
102 G6 Johannesburg California
89 A1 Johannesburg S Africa
37 O3 Johanngeorgenstadt E Germany
115 M2 Johan Pen N W Terr
60 F13 Jōhen Japan
116 L3 John *R* Alaska
122 J8 John, C Nova Scotia
127 M2 John Crow Mts Jamaica
100 G5 John Day Oregon
100 E4 John Day *R* Oregon
117 Q6 John d'Or Prairie Alberta
143 F9 John Eyre Motel W Australia
113 G9 John F. Kennedy Space Center Florida
106 H3 John Martin Res Colorado
142 G3 John,Mt W Australia
15 E2 John O'Groats Scotland
146 F3 John Quincey Adams Gl Antarctica
107 P3 John Redmond Res Kansas
107 J4 Johnson Kansas
99 K9 Johnson Nebraska
94 J5 Johnsonburg Pennsylvania
95 M4 Johnson City New York
94 E10 Johnson City Tennessee
109 J5 Johnson City Texas
99 S6 Johnson Cr Wisconsin
117 G5 Johnsons Crossing Yukon Terr
127 P4 Johnsons Pt Antigua W I
112 H4 Johnsonville S Carolina
112 F4 Johnston S Carolina
8 A4 Johnston Wales
110 H4 Johnston City Illinois
15 D5 Johnstone Scotland
117 K10 Johnstone Str Br Col
88 B7 Johnston Falls Zambia
143 D9 Johnston Ls.,The W Australia
143 C8 Johnston Ra W Australia
14 E3 Johnstown Irish Rep
98 F7 Johnstown Nebraska
95 N4 Johnstown New York
94 E6 Johnstown Ohio
94 J6 Johnstown Pennsylvania
94 E9 John W Flannagan Res Virginia
61 P5 Jōhōji Japan
69 F12 Johor Malaysia
69 F12 Johor Baharo Malaysia
37 P2 Jöhstadt E Germany
52 C5 Jōhvi U.S.S.R.
18 H5 Joigny France
110 F6 Joiner Arkansas
130 E10 Joinville Brazil
19 J4 Joinville France
146 D14 Joinville I Antarctica
48 L5 Joita Romania
125 K8 Jojutla Mexico
26 N5 Jokk Sweden
26 L5 Jokkmokk Sweden
27 C10 Jokuleggi *mt* Norway
78 K2 Jolfa Iran
99 S8 Joliet Illinois
101 Q4 Joliet Montana
119 U10 Joliette N Dakota
115 M8 Joliette Quebec
142 A1 Jolimont *dist* Perth, W Aust
99 M7 Jolley Iowa
117 S3 Jolly L N W Terr
71 E7 Jolo Philippines
102 C6 Jolon California
26 B10 Jölstervatn *L* Norway
26 G7 Joma *mt* Norway
29 H11 Jomala Finland
71 F3 Jomalig *isld* Luzon Philippines
69 F12 Jombol *isld* Indonesia
66 F5 Jomda China
71 A3 Jome Indonesia
27 D13 Jomfruland *isld* Norway
52 B6 Jonava U.S.S.R.
22 F5 Jonchery-sur-Vesle France
7 E13 Jones Bank Atlantic Oc
110 F6 Jonesboro Arkansas
111 M8 Jonesboro Georgia
110 G4 Jonesboro Illinois
109 P3 Jonesboro Louisiana
95 U2 Jonesboro Maine
112 H2 Jonesboro N Carolina
100 H6 Jonesboro Oregon
112 E1 Jonesboro Tennessee
109 K4 Jonesboro Texas
116 N1 Jones Is Alaska
146 G12 Jones Mts Antarctica
95 U2 Jonesport Maine
83 M9 Jones Pt Christmas I Indian Oc
115 L2 Jones Sound N W Terr
111 F7 Jonestown Mississippi
94 B7 Jonesville Indiana
111 E10 Jonesville Louisiana
94 C5 Jonesville Michigan
112 F3 Jonesville S Carolina
94 D10 Jonesville Virginia
86 F4 Jonglei *prov* Sudan
52 B6 Joniskis U.S.S.R.
27 G14 Jönköping Sweden
27 G14 Jönköping *county* Sweden
115 M8 Jonquière Quebec
28 K4 Jönstorp Sweden
18 E7 Jonzac France
110 B4 Joplin Missouri
101 P1 Joplin Montana
110 H4 Joppa Illinois
80 B5 Joppa Israel
99 N5 Jordan Minnesota
101 T2 Jordan Montana
95 L3 Jordan New York
80 Jordan *kingdom* S W Asia
80 F1 Jordan *R* Israel/Jordan
100 H7 Jordan *R* Oregon
141 H6 Jordan *R* Queensland
129 K7 Jordânia Brazil
111 K9 Jordan L Alabama
122 G9 Jordan L Nova Scotia
48 F1 Jordanow Poland
100 H7 Jordan Valley Oregon
130 D9 Jordão, R Brazil
28 C3 Jordbro Å *R* Denmark
33 R5 Jördenstorf E Germany
27 F10 Jordet Norway
28 E6 Jordløse Denmark
28 C5 Jordrup Denmark
28 B6 Jordsand *isld* Denmark
26 P2 Jorgastak Norway
133 B8 Jorge Montt, I Chile
75 Q5 Jorhat India
32 L5 Jork W Germany
26 L6 Jörn Sweden
106 C9 Jornada del Muerto *reg* New Mexico
27 B12 Jörpeland Norway
20 E4 Jort France
85 F7 Jos Nigeria
71 G8 Jose Abad Santos Mindanao Philippines
133 C6 José de San Martín Argentina
129 J8 José dos Campos Brazil
130 C5 Joselândia Brazil
133 E5 José Maria Blanco Argentina
27 B12 Josenfjord *inlet* Norway
71 F3 Jose Pañganiban Philippines
100 J4 Joseph Idaho
100 H4 Joseph Oregon
142 G2 Joseph Bonaparte G Australia
136 F4 Joseph Bonaparte Gulf Australia
103 O7 Joseph City Arizona
115 N7 Joseph L Labrador
123 K4 Joseph Pt Anticosti I, Quebec
144 B6 Josephville New Zealand
61 M9 Jōshin-etsu Kogen Nat. Park Japan
109 K3 Joshua Texas
102 H7 Joshua Tree California
21 I6 Josnes France
36 H3 Jossatal W Germany
18 D5 Josselin France
26 E7 Jössund Nord-Tröndelag Norway
26 D8 Jössund Sör-Tröndelag Norway
26 B10 Jostedal Norway
26 B10 Jostedalsbreen *gla* Norway
48 F2 Josvafö Hungary
26 N2 Jotkajavrre Norway
27 C10 Jotunheimen *mt* Norway
79 F5 Jouaiya Lebanon
20 J4 Jouars France
20 E4 Joué-du-Bois France
21 G7 Joué les Tours France
21 C7 Joué sur Erdre France
29 N6 Joukokylä Finland
113 J12 Joulters Cays *islds* Bahamas
79 F5 Jounié Lebanon
109 J7 Jourdanton Texas
25 E3 Joure Netherlands
118 B3 Joussard Alberta
121 M3 Joutel Quebec
29 M10 Joutsa Finland
29 N5 Joutsijärvi Finland
40 D4 Joux, L.de Switzerland
20 J5 Jouy France
21 I6 Jouy-le Potier France
126 D3 Jovellanos Cuba
75 P6 Jowai India
14 B3 Joyce Country Irish Rep
117 G4 Joy, Mt Yukon Terr
60 O3 Jōzankei Japan
31 N4 Józefów Poland
77 J1 Jozjān Afghanistan
71 B3 Ju *isld* Indonesia
124 H5 Juan Aldama Mexico
65 C7 Juancheng China
141 J7 Juandah *R* Queensland
127 K2 Juan de Bolas *peak* Jamaica
114 G8 Juan de Fuca, Str. of Canada/U.S.A.
87 G11 Juan de Nova *isld* Madagascar
133 A9 Juan Fernández, Is Pacific Oc
127 N9 Juangriego Venezuela
88 G6 Juani *isld* Tanzania
128 C5 Juanjui Peru
29 N8 Juankoski Finland
44 B4 Juan les Pins France
124 E2 Juan M. Ortíz Mexico
131 B2 Juan Soldado, C.de Chile
133 B7 Juan Stuven, I Chile
133 F5 Juárez Argentina
103 J9 Juárez, Sa *ra* Mexico
129 K5 Juazeiro Brazil
130 G9 Juàzeiro do Norte Brazil
86 F5 Juba Sudan
86 H5 Juba *R* Somalia
79 F4 Jubail Lebanon
77 A6 Jubayl, Al Saudi Arabia
80 G5 Jubba Jordan
123 R5 Jubilee L Nfld
143 F8 Jubilee Lake W Australia
102 H6 Jubilee Peak California
20 E5 Jublains France
17 F5 Júcar *R* Spain
36 B1 Jüchen W Germany
124 H7 Juchipila Mexico
125 M9 Juchitán Mexico
124 H7 Juchitlán Mexico
129 K7 Jucurucú *R* Brazil
98 H3 Jud N Dakota
99 R7 Juda Wisconsin
80 B7 Judaea Israel
123 S6 Jude I Nfld
80 D2 Judeida Israel
37 L3 Judenbach E Germany
38 L7 Judenburg Austria
123 L8 Judique C Breton I, N S
101 Q2 Judith *R* Montana
101 Q2 Judith Basin *reg* Montana
101 Q3 Judith Gap Montana
98 E3 Judson N Dakota
Juegang *see* Rudong
28 E5 Juelsminde Denmark
130 H5 Juerana Brazil
128 F4 Jufari *R* Brazil
84 F4 Jufrah Oasis, Al Libya
143 E9 Jugalinna W Australia
18 D4 Jugon France
65 E4 Juhua Dao *isld* China
18 F7 Juillac France
32 F5 Juist W Germany
32 E5 Juist *isld* W Germany
129 K8 Juiz de Fora Brazil
65 D3 Jujinchang China
69 E13 Jujuhan *R* Sumatra
128 E8 Jujuy *prov* Argentina
26 L7 Juken Sweden
26 L4 Jukkasjärvi Sweden
67 D3 Jukoupu China
26 H6 Juktån *R* Sweden
128 E8 Julaca Bolivia
98 D9 Julesburg Colorado
128 E7 Julí Peru
141 F5 Julia *R* Queensland
128 D7 Juliaca Peru
141 F5 Julia Creek Queensland
100 J3 Juliaetta Idaho
102 H8 Julian California
115 P5 Julianehåb Greenland
14 E3 Julianstown Irish Rep
36 B2 Jülich W Germany
42 E2 Julijske A *mts* Yugoslavia
124 G3 Julimes Mexico
80 D2 Jūlis Israel
27 H12 Julita Sweden
140 E5 Julius L. Queensland
20 B4 Jullouville France
28 D4 Julsø *L* Denmark
65 C6 Julu China
69 C10 Julu Rayeu Sumatra
80 G8 Jumaiyil Jordan
117 P10 Jumbo Mt Br Col
21 E7 Jumelles France
22 G3 Jumet Belgium
20 G3 Jumièges France
17 G6 Jumilla Spain
75 K4 Jumla Nepal
74 G5 Jumna *R* India
74 D8 Junagadh India
65 D7 Junan China
65 D2 Jun Bulen China
124 D5 Juncal Mexico
131 D8 Juncal, L Argentina
108 H5 Junction Texas
103 M3 Junction Utah
140 C1 Junction B N Terr Australia
111 D8 Junction City Arkansas
111 M9 Junction City Georgia
107 O2 Junction City Kansas
94 C9 Junction City Kentucky
110 M4 Junction City Kentucky
100 B5 Junction City Oregon
99 R5 Junction City Wisconsin
141 G6 Jundah Queensland
65 C4 Jundu Shan *mt ra* China
117 F6 Juneau Alaska
99 S6 Juneau Wisconsin
139 J5 Junee New S Wales
113 F10 June in Winter, L Florida
102 E4 June Lake California
79 F4 Jūn el 'Akkar Lebanon
65 A5 Jungar Qi China
40 G4 Jungfrau *mt* Switzerland
40 G4 Jungfraujoch Switzerland
22 L4 Junglinster Luxembourg
100 G9 Jungo Nevada
98 H9 Juniata Nebraska
95 K6 Juniata *R* Pennsylvania
131 E5 Junin Argentina
128 D7 Junín Chile
128 C6 Junin Peru
133 C5 Junín de los Andes Argentina
94 H8 Junior W Virginia
95 T1 Junior L Maine
122 E7 Juniper New Brunswick
103 L6 Juniper Mts Arizona
102 C5 Junipero Sierra Pk California
61 O5 Jūni sho Japan
22 G5 Juniville France
116 O2 Junjik *R* Alaska
36 B3 Jünkerath W Germany
26 H5 Junkerdal Norway
67 A2 Junlian China
108 F5 Juno Texas
118 K5 Junor Sask
26 M4 Junosuando Sweden
26 J8 Junsele Sweden
67 E2 Junshan Hu *L* China
16 A5 Junto *mt* Portugal
65 A5 Juntuliang China
100 G6 Juntura Oregon
29 O6 Juntusranta Finland
29 O9 Juojärvi *L* Finland
26 N5 Juoksengi Sweden
130 H6 Juparaña, Lagoa *L* Brazil
130 D7 Jupia Brazil
130 D7 Jupia Dam Brazil
22 K2 Jupille Belgium
21 F6 Jupilles France
113 G11 Jupiter Florida
122 J4 Jupiter R Quebec
129 J8 Juquiá Brazil
86 E4 Jur *R* Sudan
15 C4 Jura Scotland
40 F3 Jura *canton* Switzerland
40 C4 Jura *dep* France
128 C2 Jurado Colombia
31 L5 Jura Krakowska *reg* Poland
130 G5 Juramento Brazil
52 B6 Jurbarkas U.S.S.R.
12 D5 Jurby I of Man U.K.
79 F8 Jurf ed Darāwish Jordan
142 E4 Jurgurra,R W Australia
65 E2 Jurh China
143 B9 Jurien B W Australia
48 M6 Jurilovca Romania
57 F6 Jurm Afghanistan
52 B6 Jurmala U.S.S.R.
67 F1 Jurong China
38 N9 Juršinci Yugoslavia
128 E4 Juruá Brazil
128 D5 Juruá *R* Brazil
128 G6 Juruena Brazil
129 G4 Juruti Brazil
29 J9 Jurva Finland
61 O5 Jūsan-ko *L* Japan
127 N10 Jusepín Venezuela
79 G4 Jūsiya Syria
19 J5 Jussey France
119 S8 Justice Manitoba
108 F2 Justiceburg Texas
109 K2 Justin Texas
133 D4 Justo Daract Argentina
128 E5 Jutaí Brazil
33 S9 Jüterbog E Germany
130 C8 Juti Brazil
125 L2 Juticalpa Honduras
26 J5 Jutis Sweden
Jutland *see* Jylland
26 E10 Jutulhugget *pass* Norway
29 O8 Juuka Finland
29 N10 Juva Finland
20 C5 Juvigné France
20 C4 Juvigny-le-Tertre France
20 E4 Juvigny-sous-Andaine France
20 K4 Juvisy France
28 B6 Juvre Denmark
79 H5 Juwaīf, El Syria
65 D7 Ju Xian China
65 C7 Juye China
77 F2 Jūymand Iran
40 A1 Juzennecourt France
Jye Kundo *see* Yushu
28 B4 Jylland *reg* Denmark
29 M9 Jyväskylä Finland
66 B4 K2 *mt* Kashmir/China
85 E6 Ka *R* Nigeria
102 S11 Kaaawa Hawaiian Is
89 B7 Kaaing Veld *plat* S Africa
57 A5 Kaakhka U.S.S.R.
102 R11 Kaala *peak* Hawaiian Is
26 L4 Kaalasjarvi *L* Sweden
135 U6 Kaalualu Hawaiian Is
29 N2 Kaamanen Finland
89 C7 Kaap Plato S Africa
33 O6 Kaarssen E Germany
29 N9 Kaavi Finland
48 G3 Kaba Hungary
70 G7 Kabaena *isld* Sulawesi
85 B7 Kabala Sierra Leone
86 F5 Kabalega Falls Uganda
70 G5 Kabali Sulawesi
86 E7 Kabalo Zaïre
88 A4 Kabambare Zaïre
69 D11 Kabanjahe Sumatra
85 D5 Kabara Mali
53 F11 Kabardino Balkarskaya U.S.S.R.
88 B3 Kabare Zaïre
71 F7 Kabasalang Philippines
60 C13 Kaba shima *isld* Japan
68 C3 Kabaung *R* Burma
85 F7 Kabba Nigeria
26 G3 Kabelvåg *lt ho* Norway
120 E4 Kabenung L Ontario
70 G4 Kabetan. I Sulawesi
99 O1 Kabetogama Minnesota
99 N1 Kabetogama L Minnesota
71 L8 Kabia *isld* Indonesia
120 F3 Kabinakagami *R* Ontario
86 D7 Kabinda Zaïre
70 E2 Kabinu Kalimantan
71 M9 Kabir Indonesia
57 E5 Kabla U.S.S.R.
86 C4 Kabo Cent Afr Republic
87 D8 Kabompo *R* Zambia
70 B4 Kabong Sarawak
87 E7 Kabongo Zaïre
68 C6 Kabosa I. Burma
80 D1 Kabri Israel
77 F1 Kabūd Gonbad Iran
71 E2 Kabugao Philippines
77 L2 Kābul Afghanistan
80 D2 Kābūl Israel
88 C2 Kabula Uganda
88 B7 Kabunda Zambia
87 E8 Kabunda Zaïre
86 F2 Kabushiya Sudan
88 B9 Kabwe Zambia
55 F3 Kabyrdak U.S.S.R.
55 D5 Kabyrga *R* U.S.S.R.
46 E2 Kačanik Yugoslavia
87 F8 Kachalola Zambia
116 M7 Kachemak B Alaska
100 D2 Kachess L Washington
85 F7 Kachia Nigeria
75 R5 Kachin State *prov* Burma
55 G4 Kachiry U.S.S.R.
55 C2 Kachkanar U.S.S.R.
56 G4 Kachug U.S.S.R.
78 H1 Kackar D Turkey
60 J11 Kada Japan
68 C4 Kadaingti Burma
86 F5 Kadam Mt Uganda
37 P3 Kadaň Czechoslovakia
68 D6 Kadan Kyun *isld* Burma
70 D7 Kadapongan *isld* Indonesia
48 D4 Kadarkút Hungary
71 H7 Kadatuang *isld* Indonesia
41 H2 Kadelburg W Germany
61 P13 Kadena Okinawa
143 F7 Kadgo L W Australia
72 E2 Kadhimain Iraq
74 E7 Kadi India
85 C6 Kadiana Mali
46 F3 Kadijica *mt* Yugoslavia
47 K4 Kadıköy Turkey
138 E5 Kadina S Australia
74 F9 Kadirabad India
47 J8 Kadirga Burun *C* Turkey
76 D3 Kadiri India
78 F3 Kadirli Turkey
70 G7 Kadjang Sulawesi
77 F2 Kadkan Iran
73 L6 Kadmat *isld* Lakshadweep Indian Oc
52 F5 Kadnikov U.S.S.R.
68 C4 Kado Burma
60 E13 Kadogawa Japan
98 E6 Kadoka S Dakota
68 B5 Kadonkani Burma
46 E3 Kadrifakovo Yugoslavia
86 E3 Kadugli Sudan
86 A3 Kaduna Nigeria
76 C4 Kadur India
52 E5 Kaduy U.S.S.R.
56 E5 Kadyr-Egi-Tayga, Khrebet *mts* U.S.S.R.
52 F5 Kadyy U.S.S.R.
57 H4 Kadzhi-Say U.S.S.R.
85 B5 Kaedi Mauritania
123 R5 Kaegudeck L Nfld
86 B3 Kaélé Cameroon
145 D1 Kaeo New Zealand
28 D6 Kærum Denmark
65 G5 Kaesŏng N Korea
87 D7 Kāfakumba Zaïre
85 F7 Kafanchan Nigeria
85 A6 Kaffrine Senegal
47 G7 Kafiréos, Porthmós *str* Greece
47 G6 Kafirévs, Akr *C* Greece
26 N2 Kåfjord Norway
26 L2 Kåfjord *inlet* Norway
80 D5 Kafr 'Abbush Jordan
80 D5 Kafr 'Ain Jordan
79 G3 Kafr Behūm Syria
80 F6 Kafrein *R* Jordan
79 A7 Kafr el Dauwâr Egypt
80 D4 Kafr-el-Labad Jordan
79 A7 Kafr el Sheik Egypt
79 A8 Kafr el Zaiyât Egypt
80 D2 Kafr Mandā Israel
80 D4 Kafr Qud Jordan
80 D4 Kafr Ra'i Jordan
80 D4 Kafr Rumman Jordan
79 G4 Kafrun Syria
80 D5 Kafr Zibad Jordan
88 B9 Kafue Zambia
87 E8 Kafue Nat. Park Zambia
87 E7 Kafulwe Zambia
55 C4 Kaga U.S.S.R.
60 G10 Kagami Japan
57 C5 Kagan U.S.S.R.
116 G7 Kagati L Alaska
60 G11 Kagawa *prefect* Japan
120 H7 Kagawong Ontario
26 M7 Kåge Sweden
88 C2 Kagera National Park Rwanda
28 J5 Kagerup Denmark
120 C2 Kagianagami L Ontario
120 D3 Kagiano L Ontario
78 J1 Kagizman Turkey
60 D14 Kagoshima Japan
48 L5 Kagul Moldavia U.S.S.R.
48 L5 Kagul, Ozero *L* U.S.S.R.
116 L8 Kaguyak Alaska
70 D6 Kahajan *R* Kalimantan
135 O1 Kahala Pt Hawaiian Is
102 S12 Kahaluu Hawaiian Is
88 D3 Kahama Tanzania
74 C4 Kahan Pakistan
102 S11 Kahana Hawaiian Is
145 F3 Kaharoa *mt* New Zealand
71 A2 Kahatola *isld* Halmahera Indonesia
87 C7 Kahemba Zaire

102 R12 Kahe Pt Hawaiian Is
144 A6 Kaherekoau Mts
New Zealand
116 M5 Kahiltna Gl Alaska
36 G3 Kahl R W Germany
37 M2 Kahla E Germany
36 F1 Kahler-Asten mt
W Germany
100 G3 Kahlotus Washington
117 N6 Kahntah Br Columbia
77 E6 Kahnuj Iran
110 E1 Kahoka Missouri
61 K9 Kahoku-gata L Japan
102 V13 Kahoolawe isld Hawaiian Is
29 J2 Kahperusvaara mt Finland
135 U4 Kahua Hawaiian Is
135 Q1 Kahuku Hawaiian Is
102 S11 Kahuku Pt Hawaiian Is
135 T3 Kahului Hawaiian Is
Kahutara Pt see
Table Cape
85 E7 Kaiama Nigeria
144 D5 Kaiapoi New Zealand
119 O1 Kaiashk R Ontario
103 M5 Kaibab Plat Arizona
60 J10 Kaibara Japan
103 N5 Kaibito Plat Arizona
66 D3 Kaidu He R China
128 G2 Kaieteur Falls Guyana
65 C7 Kaifeng China
145 D1 Kaihu New Zealand
67 F2 Kaihua China
145 E3 Kai-Iwi New Zealand
67 B1 Kaijiang China
136 G3 Kai, Kep islds Moluccas
Indonesia
145 D1 Kaikohe New Zealand
67 B3 Kaikou China
144 D5 Kaikoura New Zealand
144 D5 Kaikoura Range
New Zealand
75 J3 Kailas mt Xizang Zizhiqu
Kailas Range see
Gangdisê Shan
36 G4 Kailbach W Germany
67 B3 Kaili China
65 E3 Kailu China
102 S12 Kailua Hawaiian Is
135 R2 Kailua Hawaiian Is
135 T5 Kailua Hawaiian Is
145 E2 Kaimai Ra New Zealand
46 E4 Kaimaktsalán mt Greece
136 G2 Kaimana W Irian
145 E3 Kaimata Mts
New Zealand
144 C5 Kaimata New Zealand
60 D14 Kaimon-dake peak Japan
135 V5 Kaimu Hawaiian Is
27 H13 Kaina U.S.S.R.
38 M7 Kainach R Austria
135 U5 Kainaliu Hawaiian Is
60 J11 Kainan Japan
47 G3 Kainchal mt Greece
57 G3 Kainda U.S.S.R.
68 B2 Kaing Burma
145 F3 Kaingaroa Forest
New Zealand
145 F3 Kaingaroa Plat.
New Zealand
38 J6 Kainisch Austria
85 E6 Kainji Res Nigeria
55 S3 Kainsk-Barabinskiy
U.S.S.R.
.71 H7 Kaioba Indonesia
145 E2 Kaipara Flats New Zealand
103 N4 Kaiparowits Plat Utah
65 D5 Kaiping China
67 D5 Kaiping China
43 C13 Kairouan Tunisia
38 F6 Kaiser-Gebirge mts Austria
102 E4 Kaiser Pk California
36 C3 Kaiserbasch W Germany
36 D5 Kaiserslautern W Germany
40 G1 Kaiserstuhl mt W Germany
32 E10 Kaiserswerth W Germany
60 F11 Kaita Japan
145 D1 Kaitaia New Zealand
144 B7 Kaitangata New Zealand
70 F6 Kai, Tanjung C Sulawesi
145 F3 Kaitawa New Zealand
145 D4 Kaiteriteri New Zealand
74 G4 Kaithal India
145 E4 Kaitoki New Zealand
Kaitong see Tongyu
26 K4 Kaitumälven R Sweden
26 K4 Kaitumj Sweden
26 L3 Kaivare mt Sweden
145 E2 Kaiwaka New Zealand
71 N9 Kaiwi Indonesia
102 V13 Kaiwi Ch Hawaiian Is
67 C1 Kai Xian China
67 B3 Kaiyang China
59 H3 Kaiyuan China
65 F2 Kaiyuan China
116 H5 Kaiyuh Mts Alaska
60 J11 Kaizuka Japan
70 E3 Kaka U.S.S.R.
29 N7 Kajaani Finland
141 F5 Kajabbi Queensland
77 J3 Kajaki Dam Afghanistan
71 K9 Kajan isld Indonesia
69 E11 Kajang Malaysia
88 F2 Kajiado Kenya
61 M10 Kajikazawa Japan
60 D14 Kajiki Japan
71 A2 Kajo Island Halmahera
Indonesia
86 F5 Kajo Kaji Sudan
71 K8 Kajuadi isld Indonesia
85 F6 Kajuru Nigeria
103 M9 Kaka Arizona
74 F4 Kaka Sudan
70 F3 Kakaban isld Kalimantan
119 O2 Kakabeka Falls Ontario
118 J1 Kakagi L Ontario
145 E3 Kakahi New Zealand
71 G7 Kakal R Mindanao
Philippines
70 F5 Kakali Sulawesi
87 D11 Kakamas S Africa
88 E1 Kakamega Kenya
69 A8 Kakana Nicobar Is
135 T3 Kakani Pt Hawaiian Is
135 T3 Kakani Pt Hawaiian Is
145 E3 Kakaramea New Zealand
85 B7 Kakata Liberia
145 E3 Kakatahi New Zealand
117 G7 Kake Alaska
60 F11 Kake Japan
42 F3 Kake Yugoslavia
61 M11 Kakegawa Japan
56 E5 Ka-Khem R U.S.S.R.
116 K7 Kakhonak Alaska
57 E10 Kakhovka U.S.S.R.
54 E10 Kakhovskoye Vdkhr res
U.S.S.R.
77 F2 Kakht Iran
77 B5 Käki Iran
76 F2 Kakinada India
117 P5 Kakisa L N W Terr
60 H11 Kakizaki Japan
60 H11 Kakogawa Japan
56 E4 Kak. Az. U.S.S.R.
85 D7 Kakpin Ivory Coast
116 Q1 Kaktovik Alaska
60 H6 Kakuda Japan
61 O6 Kakumagawa Japan
61 O6 Kakunodate Japan
70 C3 Kakusi R Sarawak
86 E7 Kakuyu Zaïre
117 O8 Kakwa R Alberta
48 F3 Kalá Hungary
43 D13 Kalaa Kebira Tunisia
83 J3 Kalaat-es-Nam mt Tunisia
71 H8 Kalabahi Indonesia
46 E5 Kalabáka Greece
70 E2 Kalabakan Sabah
138 F4 Kalabity S Australia
87 D8 Kalabo Zambia
54 N6 Kalach U.S.S.R.
55 F3 Kalachinsk U.S.S.R.
53 F9 Kalach-donu U.S.S.R.
54 N6 Kalachskaya
Vozvyshennost' uplands
U.S.S.R.
68 A2 Kaladan Burma

121 N8 Kaladar Ontario
70 G6 Kaladu R Sulawesi
102 V14 Kalae Hawaiian Is
70 G6 Kalaena R Sulawesi
68 C1 Kalagwe Burma
89 B4 Kalahari Desert Botswana
89 B6 Kalahari Game Res S Africa
89 B5 Kalahari Gemsbok Nat.
Park S Africa
76 D4 Kalahasti India
57 F5 Kalai-Khumb U.S.S.R.
57 B6 Kalai-Mor U.S.S.R.
29 L8 Kalajoki Finland
58 G1 Kalakan U.S.S.R.
69 C11 Kalakepen Sumatra
135 O1 Kalalau Hawaiian Is
74 E1 Kalam Pakistan
100 C3 Kalama Washington
46 E7 Kalámai Greece
Kalamáta Greece see
Kalámai
94 B4 Kalamazoo Michigan
70 D7 Kalambau isld Indonesia
87 F7 Kalambo Falls Tanzania
47 F6 Kálamos Greece
46 D6 Kálamos isld Greece
70 G6 Kalampising Kalimantan
143 B9 Kalamurra, L S Australia
143 B9 Kalamurra, L S Australia
29 K8 Kalanti Finland
25 L10 Kalao isld Indonesia
71 G7 Kalaong Mindanao
Philippines
71 K8 Kalaotoa isld Indonesia
83 K9 Kala Oya R Sri Lanka
58 G1 Kalar R U.S.S.R.
48 L3 Kalarash U.S.S.R.
26 H9 Kälarne Sweden
83 L9 Kal Aru R Sri Lanka
70 D4 Kalasin Kalimantan
74 B4 Kalat Pakistan
52 H5 Kalat R U.S.S.R.
86 B1 Kalateh-Masjed Iran
60 E13 Kalauepa Japan
61 P6 Kalaupapa Hawaiian Is
61 N13 Kalávrita Greece
135 S2 Kamakou peak Hawaiian Is
61 N10 Kamakura Japan
70 O9 Kamal Indonesia
74 E3 Kamalia Pakistan
135 S3 Kamalo Hawaiian Is
85 B7 Kamalu Sierra Leone
68 C4 Kamamaung Burma
78 D2 Kaman Turkey
87 D8 Kamapanda Zambia
72 E5 Kamaran isld S Yemen
77 K2 Kamard reg Afghanistan
74 H1 Kamareddi India
75 N9 Kamarhati India
76 D4 Kamarod Pakistan
101 O9 Kamas Utah
87 E9 Kamativi Zimbabwe
119 P2 Kamatsi L Sask
60 H11 Kamatsushima Japan
143 D9 Kambalda W Australia
52 G1 Kambal'nitskiye Koshki,
Ova islds U.S.S.R.
76 C6 Kamban India
69 E13 Kambang Sumatra
70 M9 Kambangan isld Java
94 E8 Kambarka U.S.S.R.
85 B7 Kambia Sierra Leone
83 M3 Kambing isld Cocos Is
Indian Oc
65 H4 Kambo Ho mt N Korea
70 F6 Kambuno mt Sulawesi
94 J2 Kamchatka Pen U.S.S.R.
51 Q3 Kamchatskaya Oblast'
prov U.S.S.R.
47 J1 Kamchiya R Bulgaria
61 N8 Kameda Japan
100 G4 Kamela Oregon
37 J2 Kamen W Germany
52 D6 Kamenets Podolskiy
U.S.S.R.
46 D4 Kamenicë Albania
42 F4 Kamenjak, Rt C
Yugoslavia
85 C6 Kamgaba Mali
78 F2 Kamgel Turkey
115 O4 Kamgeliut Greenland
77 C6 Kamgan Iran
69 E9 Kamgar Malaysia
138 D6 Kamgaroo I S Australia
140 E4 Kamgaroo Pt Queensland

28 E5 Kalsenakke Denmark
77 E1 Kal-Shur, Rüd-e R Iran
28 N1 Kalø isld Faeroes
116 H4 Kaltag Alaska
56 C4 Kaltan U.S.S.R.
41 M3 Kalte Berg mt Austria
37 M4 Kaltenbrunn W Germany
32 L5 Kaltenkirchen W Germany
37 J2 Kaltennordheim
E Germany
37 J2 Kaltensundheim
E Germany
46 E4 Kamvóunia, Óri mts
Greece
68 G5 Kamsack Sask
62 G6 Kamskoye Ust'ye U.S.S.R.
119 P2 Kamsuuma Zaïre
60 Q3 Kamtenkirchen W Germany
46 E4 Kamuchawie L Sask
60 Q3 Kamui-misaki mt Japan
46 E4 Kamvóunia, Óri mts
Greece
68 G5 Kamyak-Belorg'ye mts
U.S.S.R.
85 E6 Kamyshin U.S.S.R.
55 D3 Kamyshin U.S.S.R.
55 D5 Kamyshnyy U.S.S.R.
54 H9 Kamysh-Zarya U.S.S.R.
68 B1 Kan Burma
85 G6 Kan Nigeria
89 E2 Kan R Zimbabwe
56 G3 Kanaaupscow Quebec
61 N9 Kanana Japan
55 S11 Kanus Namibia
115 M7 Kanab Utah
116 M3 Kanab Cr Arizona
89 D5 Kana, Bt mt Sarawak
68 D5 Kanagi Japan
42 F2 Kanal Yugoslavia
61 Q5 Kanalla Greece
70 G6 Kanas Indonesia
137 R5 Kao isld Tonga
118 C6 Kananaskis L Alberta
86 D7 Kananga Zaïre
85 A6 Kaolack Senegal
70 E7 Kanarraville Utah
87 D8 Kaoma Zambia
52 G6 Kanash U.S.S.R.
47 F5 Kanastraion, Ákr C
Greece
74 K7 Kapadvanj India
57 J2 Kapal U.S.S.R.
71 Q9 Kapal isld Indonesia
57 H1 Kapanga Zaïre
81 D7 Kapanga Zaïre
95 F7 Kapatu Zambia
66 B3 Kapchagay U.S.S.R.
57 H3 Kapchagayskoye Vdkhr.
res U.S.S.R.
25 F5 Kapellen Belgium
25 F5 Kapellen W Germany
88 C6 Kapenguria Kenya
38 M7 Kapfenberg Austria
75 O5 Kapiding I Tarperi Turkey
70 G5 Kapinju, Tg C Sulawesi
87 E8 Kapiri Mposhi Zambia
77 L2 Kápisa Afghanistan
115 L7 Kapiskau Ontario
70 C4 Kapit Sarawak
145 E4 Kapiti I New Zealand
57 J2 Kapka U.S.S.R.

70 F5 Karang, Tg C Sulawesi
74 G8 Karang India
47 J7 Karaova Turkey
57 D3 Karaozek U.S.S.R.
57 D1 Karapinar Turkey
78 D3 Karapiro New Zealand
57 G2 Karasay China
47 J9 Kárpathos isld Greece
47 J9 Kárpathos Str Greece
147 N12 Kara Sea Arctic Oc
37 P7 Karpfham W Germany
55 C2 Karpinsk U.S.S.R.
52 F3 Karpogory U.S.S.R.
52 F3 Karpuselu Turkey
47 J7 Karpuzlu Turkey
143 B9 Karraguilen W Australia
142 A1 Karrakatta dist
Perth, W Aust
115 O3 Karrats Fjord Greenland
28 H6 Karrebek Denmark
28 G6 Karrebaeksminde Denmark
28 G6 Karrebaeksminde Bugt B
Denmark
89 B8 Karree Berge mts S Africa
143 B10 Karridale W Australia
78 J1 Kars Turkey
57 D1 Karsakpay U.S.S.R.
55 D5 Karsakuvigamak L
Manitoba
29 M8 Kärsämäki Finland
52 C6 Kärsava U.S.S.R.
57 D5 Karshi U.S.S.R.
57 A2 Karshinskaya Step'
U.S.S.R.
50 E1 Karakiye Vorota, Proliv str
U.S.S.R.
33 P6 Karstädt E Germany
28 B5 Karstoft Denmark
26 H10 Kärstula Finland
26 H10 Kärtet Finland
47 K4 Kartaba Lebanon
47 K4 Kartal Turkey
47 K4 Kártal mt Greece
50 F3 Kartaly U.S.S.R.
54 J5 Karthaus Pennsylvania
36 B4 Karthaus W Germany
31 L1 Karttula Finland
31 L1 Kartuzy Poland
61 M9 Karuizawa Japan
143 F9 Karuljevne Indonesia
142 G3 Karval Colorado
26 K9 Kärvik Norway
31 L6 Karviná Czechoslovakia
48 E1 Karvina Czechoslovakia
76 B3 Karwar India
41 O3 Karwendel Geb mts
Austria
55 E1 Karym U.S.S.R.
57 A3 Karzala U.S.S.R.
28 D2 Kás Denmark
71 J9 Kas R U.S.S.R.
88 C6 Kasa B Zambia
88 C6 Kasai R Zaïre
87 D7 Kasaji Zaïre
61 O9 Kasama Japan
88 B6 Kasama Zambia
88 C6 Kasama Tanzania
57 F4 Kasansay U.S.S.R.
87 D7 Kasai R Zaïre
33 P6 Kargow E Germany
31 J3 Kargowa Poland
75 O7 Kasba Bangladesh
114 J5 Kasba L N W Terr
2 G16 Käsebarga Sweden
60 D14 Kaseda Japan
116 F1 Kasegaluk Lag Alaska
77 E8 Kasempa Zambia
3 L3 Kasendorf W Germany
88 B7 Kasenga Zaïre
88 F5 Kasenyi Zaïre
88 D7 Kasenyi Zaïre
88 C1 Kasese Uganda
86 E6 Kasese Zaïre
119 N2 Kashabowie Ontario
77 B2 Kashan Iran
Kashgar see Kashi
66 B4 Kashgar China
61 J11 Kashihara Japan
60 D12 Kashima Japan
52 E6 Kashin U.S.S.R.
74 H4 Kashipur India
54 K2 Kashira U.S.S.R.
119 O1 Kashishibog L Ontario
57 M8 Kashiwazaki Japan
57 G2 Kashkadarin-skaya
Oblast' U.S.S.R.
57 D2 Kashkantengiz U.S.S.R.
57 H4 Kashkasu U.S.S.R.
57 H4 Kasmar Iran
66 B5 Kashmir India/Pakistan
136 B2 Kashmor Pakistan
71 A3 Kashiruts isld Indonesia
110 G2 Kaskaskia R Illinois
26 K6 Kasker Sweden
29 J8 Kaskö Finland
26 L6 Kas Kong Cambodia
55 D3 Kaskö Finland
117 P11 Kaslo Br Col
47 H9 Kásos isld Greece
47 H9 Kásos Str Greece
88 H6 Kas Prea Cambodia
68 H7 Kas Rong isld Cambodia
68 H7 Kas Rong Sam Lem isld
Cambodia
86 G2 Kassala Sudan
37 H4 Kassandra Greece
36 C2 Kassel W Germany
85 F7 Kasserine Tunisia
19 O5 Kas Smach isld Cambodia
26 O9 Kasson Minnesota
78 B1 Kastamonu Turkey
37 L4 Kastanéai Greece
28 C1 Kastbjerg Denmark
36 E3 Kastel W Germany
47 G3 Kastelli Crete Greece
28 F6 Kastellet Denmark
37 L7 Kastellorizon isld Greece
47 H9 Kastellorizon isld Greece
42 B4 Kaster W Germany
36 B1 Kastl W Germany
37 M5 Kastl W Germany
37 M5 Kastl W Germany
47 H4 Kastória Greece
47 H4 Kástron Límnos I Greece
28 G5 Kastron Nigríta Greece
47 K5 Kastrosikéli Greece
61 K10 Kasugai Japan
61 O9 Kasugai Japan
70 Q9 Kasungu Kalimantan
70 D9 Kasupe Malawi
74 F2 Kasur Pakistan
74 H7 Kata U.S.S.R.
85 S8 Katanga Nigeria
Mt. Maine
86 B7 Katako-Kombe Zaïre
46 E6 Kataoka U.S.S.R.
57 K9 Katanning W Australia
143 C10 Katanning W Australia
74 H4 Katanni Ghat India
46 D7 Katastári Greece

61 J10 Katata Japan
77 L3 Katáwáz-Urgan Afghanistan
55 D3 Kataysk U.S.S.R.
69 A9 Katchall isld Nicobar Is
38 J7 Katchberg Austria
116 H4 Kateel R Alaska
119 O8 Katepwa Sask
46 F4 Katerini Greece
25 F4 Katerveer Netherlands
114 F6 Kates Needle mt Br Col
75 K7 Katghora India
75 R6 Katha Burma
84 J4 Katherina, Gebel hill Egypt
140 B2 Katherine N Terr Aust
140 C2 Katherine R N Terr Aust
74 H4 Kathgodam India
74 D8 Kathiawar reg India
76 E6 Kathiraveli Sri Lanka
113 E9 Kathleen Florida
140 B2 Kathleen Falls N Terr Aust
143 D7 Kathleen Valley W Australia
75 L5 Kathmandu Nepal
118 D7 Kathryn Alberta
98 H3 Kathryn N Dakota
74 F2 Kathwa Kashmir
85 C6 Kati Mali
70 C4 Katibas R Sarawak
69 D14 Katiët Indonesia
75 M6 Katihar India
145 E2 Katikati New Zealand
87 D9 Katima Mulilo Namibia
119 S6 Katimik L Manitoba
85 C7 Katiola Ivory Coast
29 L3 Kätkätunturi mt Finland
89 A8 Katkop Hills S Africa
48 M5 Katlabukh, Oz L U.S.S.R.
32 M9 Katlenburg W Germany
116 K8 Katmai B Alaska
116 K7 Katmai Nat. Monument Alaska
116 K7 Katmai Vol., Mt Alaska
74 J7 Katni India
46 E6 Káto Akhaïa Greece
46 E6 Katokhí Greece
88 C9 Katondwe Zambia
47 F3 Káto Nevrokópion Greece
139 K5 Katoomba New S Wales
47 F4 Káto Stavrós Greece
31 L5 Katowice Poland
47 L7 Katrancık Dağ mt Turkey
27 H10 Katrineberg Sweden
27 H13 Katrineholm Sweden
12 D1 Katrine, L Scotland
85 F6 Katsina Nigeria
61 O9 Katsuta Japan
61 O10 Katsuura Japan
61 K9 Katsuyama Fukui Japan
61 N10 Katsuyama Japan
60 G10 Katsuyama Okayama Japan
57 D5 Kattakurgan U.S.S.R.
142 F5 Kattamudda Well W Australia
28 K4 Kattarp Sweden
47 J9 Kattavía Rhodes Greece
120 K3 Kattawagami L Ontario
28 E3 Kattegat str Denmark
32 G8 Kattenvenne W Germany
27 K14 Katthammarsvik isld Gotland Sweden
28 D5 Kattrup Denmark
88 A8 Katue R Zambia
87 E7 Katumba Zaïre
88 D7 Katumbi Malawi
56 C5 Katun' R U.S.S.R.
56 C6 Katunskiy Khr mts U.S.S.R.
71 J9 Katupa Sumbawa Indonesia
75 N7 Katwa India
88 B2 Katwe Uganda
25 B4 Katwijk aan Zee Netherlands
31 K4 Katy Wrocł Poland
36 G5 Katzenbuckel mt W Germany
36 D3 Katzenelnbogen W Germany
37 L2 Katzhütte E Germany
71 A2 Kau Halmahera Indonesia
102 V13 Kauai isld Hawaiian Is
102 V13 Kauai Ch Hawaiian Is
144 B7 Kauana New Zealand
36 D3 Kaub W Germany
135 U6 Kau Desert Hawaiian Is
41 N2 Kaufbeuren W Germany
41 N1 Kaufering W Germany
109 L3 Kaufman Texas
32 L10 Kaufungen W Germany
29 K8 Kauhava Finland
135 T3 Kauiki Hd Hawaiian Is
145 E2 Kaukapakapa New Zealand
99 S5 Kaukauna Wisconsin
102 U13 Kaula isld Hawaiian Is
102 U13 Kaulakahi Ch Hawaiian Is
135 U5 Kauluoa Pt Hawaiian Is
135 O1 Kaumakani Hawaiian Is
38 N5 Kaumberg Austria
135 R2 Kaunakakai Hawaiian Is
135 U6 Kauna Pt Hawaiian Is
53 B7 Kaunas U.S.S.R.
85 F6 Kaura Namoda Nigeria
48 M4 Kaushany U.S.S.R.
29 K8 Kaustinen Finland
22 L4 Kautenbach Luxembourg
71 A2 Kau, Tk B Halmahera Indonesia
26 N3 Kautokeino Norway
68 D7 Kau-ye Kyun isld Burma
47 K5 Kavacık Turkey
46 E3 Kavadarci Yugoslavia
46 D3 Kavajë Albania
47 J7 Kavaklıdere Turkey
59 K3 Kavalerov U.S.S.R.
76 E3 Kavali India
47 G4 Kaválla Greece
73 L6 Kavaratti isld Lakshadweep Indian Oc
47 J1 Kavarna Bulgaria
33 Q4 Kavelstorf E Germany
136 L2 Kavieng New Ireland
116 O2 Kavik R Alaska
27 F16 Kävlinge Sweden
47 H9 Kavoúsi Crete Greece
88 C5 Kavu R Tanzania
80 D2 Kavul Israel
129 H3 Kaw Fr Guiana
121 M7 Kawagama L Ontario
61 N10 Kawagoe Japan
61 N10 Kawaguchi Japan
60 H10 Kawahara Japan
61 M7 Kawaharada Japan
135 U4 Kawaihae Hawaiian Is
135 N1 Kawaihoa Pt Hawaiian Is
135 O1 Kawaikini peak Hawaiian Is
102 R11 Kawailoa Bch Hawaiian Is
61 M10 Kawakami Japan
145 E1 Kawakawa New Zealand
145 E2 Kawakawa B New Zealand
60 E13 Kawakita Japan
61 O8 Kawamata Japan
88 B6 Kawambwa Zambia
61 N11 Kawana Japan
71 J4 Kawangkoan Sulawesi
60 G11 Kawanoe Japan
144 B6 Kawarau R New Zealand
75 J7 Kawardha India
121 M8 Kawartha Lakes Ontario
61 N10 Kawasaki Japan
60 D11 Kawashiri-misaki C Japan
60 O4 Kawauchi Japan
145 E2 Kawau I New Zealand
107 O5 Kaw City Oklahoma
71 C2 Kawe isld Indonesia
102 E5 Kaweah R California
145 F3 Kaweka mt New Zealand
102 R11 Kawela B Hawaiian Is
145 F3 Kawerau New Zealand
145 E3 Kawhia New Zealand
102 H4 Kawich Ra Nevada
88 C6 Kawimbe Zambia
119 S6 Kawinaw L Manitoba
68 D4 Kawkareik Burma
68 C3 Kawludo Burma
68 D6 Kawmapyin Burma
68 D7 Kawthaung Burma
68 C3 Kawthoolei prov Burma
66 B4 Kaxgar He R China
52 H4 Kay U.S.S.R.
85 D6 Kaya Upper Volta
116 P7 Kayak I Alaska
68 C4 Kayan Burma
70 E3 Kayan R Kalimantan
76 C6 Kayankulam India
55 E4 Kaybagar, Oz L U.S.S.R.
101 T6 Kaycee Wyoming
120 D2 Kayedon L Ontario
103 O5 Kayenta Arizona
85 B6 Kayes Mali
94 F8 Kayford W Virginia
55 D5 Kaygy U.S.S.R.
47 J6 Kayislar Turkey
55 G4 Kaymanachikha U.S.S.R.
55 G2 Kaymysovy U.S.S.R.
37 N2 Kayna E Germany
48 M4 Kaynary U.S.S.R.
116 S2 Kay Pt Yukon Terr
129 G3 Kayser Geb mts Suriname
78 E2 Kayseri Turkey
101 O8 Kaysville Utah
69 G14 Kayuagung Sumatra
119 M9 Kayville Sask
121 P7 Kazabazua Quebec
78 K1 Kazakh U.S.S.R.
57 D1 Kazakhskiy Melkosopochnik region U.S.S.R.
57 Kazakhstan U.S.S.R.
57 B2 Kazalinsk U.S.S.R.
52 G6 Kazan' U.S.S.R.
115 K5 Kazan R N W Terr
52 G6 Kazanka R U.S.S.R.
47 G2 Kazanlŭk Bulgaria
54 K3 Kazanovka U.S.S.R.
55 E3 Kazanskoye U.S.S.R.
57 G4 Kazarman U.S.S.R.
48 M1 Kazatin U.S.S.R.
47 H5 Kaz Dağı mt Turkey
55 E5 Kazgorodok Kazakhstan U.S.S.R.
55 F4 Kazgorodok Kokchetav U.S.S.R.
52 H4 Kazhim U.S.S.R.
31 N4 Kazimierz Poland
48 F2 Kazincbarcika Hungary
54 L3 Kazinka U.S.S.R.
37 P4 Kaznějov Czechoslovakia
86 D7 Kazumba Zaïre
50 F2 Kazym R U.S.S.R.
56 D4 Kazyr R U.S.S.R.
77 G4 Kbash Afghanistan
31 K3 Kcynia Poland
37 P5 Kdyně Czechoslovakia
47 G7 Kéa isld Greece
135 V5 Keaau Hawaiian Is
14 E2 Keady N Ireland
135 T5 Keahole Pt Hawaiian Is
135 S3 Kealaikahiki Pt Hawaiian Is
102 V14 Kealakekue B Hawaiian Is
135 U5 Kealia Hawaiian Is
102 R11 Keamapapa Pt Hawaiian Is
103 O6 Keams Canyon Arizona
98 G9 Kearney Nebraska
121 L7 Kearney Ontario
102 F5 Kearsarge Pass California
109 O3 Keatchie Louisiana
100 H5 Keating Oregon
94 K5 Keating Pennsylvania
118 K6 Keatley Sask
113 D8 Keatons Beach Florida
135 V5 Keaukaha Hawaiian Is
70 L9 Kebajoran R Java
78 G2 Keban Turkey
68 H2 Ke Bao, I de Vietnam
85 A5 Kébémer Senegal
85 F2 Kebili Tunisia
79 F3 Kebīr R Syria/Lebanon
86 D3 Kebkabiya Sudan
26 K4 Kebnekaise Sweden
70 M9 Kebumen Java
48 E4 Kecel Hungary
60 C11 Kechi Japan
117 K6 Kechika R Br Col
47 L7 Keçiborlu Turkey
48 F4 Kecskemet Hungary
69 E9 Kedah prov Malaysia
52 B6 Kédainiai U.S.S.R.
100 E9 Keddie California
80 F1 Kedesh Naphtali Israel
122 E6 Kedgewick New Brunswick
70 O9 Kediri Java
85 B6 Kédougou Senegal
111 D7 Kedron Arkansas
141 K1 Kedron dist Brisbane, Qnsld
141 K1 Kedron Brook Brisbane, Qnsld
55 D3 Kedrovoye U.S.S.R.
55 E1 Kedrovyy U.S.S.R.
70 M9 Kedungwuni Java
52 H3 Kedva U.S.S.R.
117 N10 Keefers Br Col
117 J4 Keele Pk Yukon Terr
119 M8 Keeler Sask
118 J4 Keeley L Sask
Keeling Is see Cocos Is
123 T5 Keels Nfld
71 D7 Keenapusan Philippines
102 F6 Keene California
95 P4 Keene New Hampshire
95 O2 Keene New York
111 L7 Keener Alabama
98 B9 Keenesburg Colorado
14 C4 Keeper Hill Irish Rep
141 F2 Keer-weer,C Queensland
95 O2 Keeseville New York
89 A6 Keetmanshoop Namibia
99 N2 Keewatin Minnesota
118 H1 Keewatin Ontario
115 K5 Keewatin, Dist of N W Terr
86 G4 Kefa prov Ethiopia
46 D6 Kefallinía isld Greece
71 M9 Kefamenanu Timor Indonesia
80 C6 Kefar Bilu Israel
80 F1 Kefar Blum Israel
80 C6 Kefar Daniyyel Israel
80 D7 Kefar 'Ezyon Jordan
80 C2 Kefar Gallim Israel
80 C6 Kefar Habad Israel
80 D2 Kefar Ha Maccabi Israel
80 B6 Kefar Ha Nagid Israel
80 F2 Kefar HaNasi Israel
80 B7 Kefar Ha No'ar Nizzanim Israel
80 C5 Kefar Hess Israel
80 C5 Kefar Mallal Israel
80 C7 Kefar Menahem Israel
80 D1 Kefar Rosh HaNiqra Israel
80 F4 Kefar Ruppin Israel
80 D6 Kefar Rut Jordan
80 C5 Kefar Sava Israel
80 F1 Kefar Szold Israel
80 E3 Kefar Tavor Israel
80 C6 Kefar Uriyya Israel
80 C4 Kefar Vitkin Israel
80 C4 Kefar Ya'vetz Israel
80 C4 Kefar Yona Israel
80 C7 Kefar Zekharya Israel
80 C4 Kefer Monash Israel
85 F7 Keffi Nigeria
47 L3 Kefken Adasi isld Turkey
115 R5 Keflavík Iceland
83 K10 Kegalla Sri Lanka
123 L3 Kégashka, L Quebec
123 L3 Kegaska Quebec
28 D7 Kegnæs Denmark
117 P7 Keg River Alberta
84 F5 Kegueur Terbi mt Chad
52 B6 Kegums U.S.S.R.
9 E2 Kegworth England
32 K5 Kehdingen Das Alte Ld reg W Germany
84 J6 Keheili Sudan
77 C3 Kehi Iran
36 D6 Kehl W Germany
52 C5 Kehra U.S.S.R.
36 C3 Kehrig W Germany
13 G6 Keighley England
52 B5 Keila U.S.S.R.
86 E3 Keilak, L Sudan
85 F6 Keïta Niger
86 C4 Keita R Chad
29 M8 Keitele Finland
138 F6 Keith S Australia
117 M3 Keith Arm B N W Terr
117 N9 Keithley Creek Br Col
99 Q8 Keithsburg Illinois
109 O3 Keithville Louisiana
135 N1 Kekaha Hawaiian Is
145 E5 Kekerenga New Zealand
115 N4 Kekertuk N W Terr
48 F3 Kékes mt Hungary
71 B3 Kekik isld Indonesia
83 K9 Kekirawa Sri Lanka
47 K8 Kekov isld Turkey
74 F6 Kekri India
73 L7 Kelai isld Maldives
65 B5 Kelan China
69 E11 Kelang Malaysia
69 E10 Kelantan prov Malaysia
69 F9 Kelantan R Malaysia
70 F7 Kelara R Sulawesi
36 B3 Kelberg W Germany
33 O10 Kelbra E Germany
38 F7 Kelchsau Austria
13 F5 Keld England
52 F3 Kel'da R U.S.S.R.
28 K6 Keldby Denmark
80 C8 Kelekh R Israel
47 K5 Keles Turkey
57 E4 Keles U.S.S.R.
118 J7 Kelfield Sask
112 K1 Kelford N Carolina
37 M6 Kelheim W Germany
43 D12 Kelibia Tunisia
77 K1 Kelif U.S.S.R.
57 C5 Kelifskiy Uzboy U.S.S.R.
98 B9 Kelim Colorado
71 K9 Keli Mutu mt Flores Indonesia
36 E3 Kelkheim W Germany
78 G1 Kelkit Turkey
86 B6 Kellé Congo
95 M9 Keller Virginia
100 G1 Keller Washington
143 C9 Kellerberrin W Australia
117 N4 Keller L N W Terr
118 K2 Keller L Sask
33 N4 Kellersee W Germany
99 M9 Kellerton Iowa
114 G3 Kellet, C N W Terr
94 H5 Kellettville Pennsylvania
94 E5 Kelleys I Ohio
99 M2 Kelliher Minnesota
119 O7 Kelliher Sask
32 L5 Kellinghusen W Germany
41 M1 Kellmünz W Germany
100 J2 Kellogg Idaho
99 O8 Kellogg Iowa
29 O5 Kelloselkä Finland
15 D5 Kells Range Scotland
110 J5 Kelly Kentucky
111 D10 Kelly Louisiana
101 P6 Kelly Wyoming
116 F2 Kelly R Alaska
140 E6 Kelly R Queensland
140 B7 Kelly Hills N Terr Aust
117 K3 Kelly L N W Terr
9 F3 Kelmarsh England
52 B6 Kelme U.S.S.R.
48 K2 Kelmentsy U.S.S.R.
142 C3 Kelmscott dist Perth, W Aust
86 C4 Kélo Chad
26 M3 Kelottijarvi L Sweden
117 O11 Kelowna Br Col
8 D1 Kelsall England
36 F3 Kelsberbach W Germany
119 V2 Kelsey Manitoba
117 L10 Kelsey Bay Br Col
119 Q5 Kelsey L Manitoba
102 B3 Kelseyville California
103 J6 Kelso California
98 J2 Kelso N Dakota
144 B6 Kelso New Zealand
119 Q9 Kelso Sask
13 F2 Kelso Scotland
100 C3 Kelso Washington
9 E1 Kelstedge England
28 H5 Kelstrup Denmark
28 D6 Kelstrupstrand Denmark
101 M8 Kelton Utah
109 N4 Keltys Texas
69 F11 Keluang Malaysia
70 O9 Kelud G mt Java
9 G4 Kelvedon England
103 O8 Kelvin Arizona
119 O6 Kelvington Sask
119 P1 Kelvin I Ontario
119 S8 Kelwood Manitoba
52 D3 Kem' U.S.S.R.
71 J4 Kema Sulawesi
52 E4 Kema R U.S.S.R.
70 D2 Kemabong Sabah
78 G2 Kemah Turkey
78 G2 Kemaliye Turkey
47 J6 Kemalpasa Turkey
Kemalpaşa R Turkey see Kirmasti R
117 K9 Kemano Br Col
69 F10 Kemasik Malaysia
71 H5 Kembani Sulawesi
86 D5 Kembe Cent Afr Republic
33 R9 Kemberg E Germany
56 D3 Kemchug R U.S.S.R.
47 L8 Kemer Lycia Turkey
47 K8 Kemer Turkey
47 K7 Kemer Baraji L Turkey
56 C3 Kemerovo U.S.S.R.
56 C4 Kemerovskaya Oblast' prov U.S.S.R.
29 L6 Kemi Finland
29 N5 Kemijärvi Finland
29 M5 Kemijoki R Finland
101 P8 Kemmerer Wyoming
37 M4 Kemnath W Germany
119 R9 Kemnay Manitoba
33 T4 Kemnitz E Germany
109 L3 Kemp Texas
29 L7 Kempele Finland
25 F6 Kempen W Germany
36 C3 Kempenich W Germany
22 H1 Kempenland reg Belgium
36 C4 Kempfeld W Germany
22 J1 Kempisch Kan Belgium
109 H2 Kemp, L Texas
109 K4 Kempner Texas
146 E12 Kemp Pen Antarctica
126 F2 Kemp's Bay Andros Bahamas
139 L4 Kempsey New S Wales
36 D4 Kempten W Germany
41 M2 Kempten W Germany
121 Q5 Kempt, L Quebec
99 S9 Kempton Illinois
98 J2 Kempton N Dakota
139 H8 Kempton Tasmania
121 P7 Kemptville Ontario
70 N8 Kemudjan isld Indonesia
85 D2 Kenadsa Algeria
116 M6 Kenai Alaska
116 N6 Kenai L Alaska
116 N6 Kenai Pen Alaska
70 K8 Kenam, Tg C Sumatra
86 F4 Kenamuke Swamp Sudan
118 L7 Kenaston Sask
70 D3 Kenawang, Bt mt Sarawak
94 J10 Kenbridge Virginia
13 F5 Kendal England
127 K2 Kendal Jamaica
70 N9 Kendal Java
139 L4 Kendal New S Wales
119 O8 Kendal Sask
113 G12 Kendall Florida
107 J4 Kendall Kansas
94 J3 Kendall New York
141 F2 Kendall R Queensland
115 L5 Kendall, C N W Terr
145 D4 Kendall, Mt New Zealand
94 B5 Kendallville Indiana
71 H6 Kendari Sulawesi
143 C10 Kendenup W Australia
86 C3 Kendigué Chad
75 M8 Kendrapara Indiana
100 J3 Kendrick Idaho
103 N6 Kendrick Pk Arizona
57 L1 Kendyrlik U.S.S.R.
57 B3 Kendyrli, Ozero L U.S.S.R.
139 J4 Kenebri New S Wales
109 K7 Kenedy Texas
107 O7 Kenefick Oklahoma
98 F4 Kenel S Dakota
85 B7 Kenema Sierra Leone
70 B4 Kenepai mt Kalimantan
145 D4 Kenepuru Sound New Zealand
98 H9 Kenesaw Nebraska
56 B3 Kenga R U.S.S.R.
86 C6 Kenge Zaïre
57 A3 Kenges U.S.S.R.
26 N4 Kengis Sweden
68 G4 Keng Kabao Laos
68 G4 Keng Kok Laos
68 E2 Keng Lap Burma
68 D1 Keng Lon Burma
68 D2 Keng Tawng Burma
68 D2 Kengtung Burma
87 D11 Kenhardt S Africa
116 L6 Kenibuna L Alaska
85 B6 Keniéba Mali
9 E3 Kenilworth England
70 E2 Keningau Sabah
85 C2 Kenitra Morocco
12 D3 Ken, L Scotland
65 D6 Kenli China
112 J2 Kenly N Carolina
14 B5 Kenmare Irish Rep
98 E1 Kenmare N Dakota
14 A5 Kenmare, R Irish Rep
15 E4 Kenmore Scotland
141 K2 Kenmore dist Brisbane, Qnsld
108 D2 Kenna New Mexico
94 F8 Kenna W Virginia
95 R1 Kennebago Lake Maine
98 G6 Kennebec S Dakota
95 S2 Kennebec R Maine
95 R3 Kennebunk Maine
109 M10 Kennedale Texas
98 J1 Kennedy Minnesota
98 F7 Kennedy Nebraska
94 J4 Kennedy New York
119 P8 Kennedy Sask
115 N1 Kennedy Channel Canada/Greenland
141 G4 Kennedy Highway rd Queensland
119 P5 Kennedy L Sask
117 D5 Kennedy, Mt Yukon Terr
141 G3 Kennedy R Queensland
143 B6 Kennedy Ra W Australia
95 M7 Kennedyville Maryland
111 F11 Kenner Louisiana
111 H12 Kenner New Orleans
122 J8 Kennetcook Nova Scotia
143 B6 Kenneth Ra W Australia
9 E5 Kennet, R England
110 F5 Kennett Missouri
100 F3 Kennewick Washington
110 G1 Kenney Illinois
117 L9 Kenney Dam Br Col
116 Q6 Kennicott Alaska
9 H3 Kenninghall England
137 M6 Kenn Reef Coral Sea
100 D7 Keno Oregon
120 E2 Kenogami R Ontario
121 T4 Kénogami L res Quebec
120 J4 Kenogamissi L Ontario
117 F4 Keno Hill Yukon Terr
118 H1 Kenora Ontario
99 T7 Kenosha Wisconsin
94 E8 Kenova W Virginia
29 P7 Kenozero U.S.S.R.
52 E4 Kenozero, Oz L U.S.S.R.
98 H2 Kensal N Dakota
127 H5 Kenscoff Haiti
57 E2 Kense U.S.S.R.
110 E6 Kensett Arkansas
99 N6 Kensett Iowa
107 M2 Kensington Kansas
122 J7 Kensington Pr Edward I
95 O5 Kent Connecticut
99 M9 Kent Iowa
98 K3 Kent Minnesota
94 F5 Kent Ohio
100 E4 Kent Oregon
100 C2 Kent Washington
9 G5 Kent co England
57 E3 Kentau U.S.S.R.
120 H10 Kent Bridge Ontario
94 B3 Kent City Michigan
9 G3 Kentford England
139 H7 Kent Gr islds Tasmania
68 E4 Ken Thao Thailand
71 J7 Kentiolo isld Indonesia
122 G7 Kent Junction New Brunswick
99 T9 Kentland Indiana
13 F5 Kentmere England
119 R9 Kenton Manitoba
99 S3 Kenton Michigan
94 D6 Kenton Ohio
106 H5 Kenton Oklahoma
110 G5 Kenton Tennessee
114 J4 Kent Pen N W Terr
110 J4 Kentucky state U.S.A.
110 H5 Kentucky L Kentucky/Tenn
110 M3 Kentucky R Kentucky
122 H8 Kentville Nova Scotia
111 F11 Kentwood Louisiana
119 Q7 Kenville Manitoba
142 C2 Kenwick dist Perth, W Aust
86 G5 Kenya rep Africa
88 F2 Kenya Mt Kenya
88 F2 Kenya National Park Kenya
118 E9 Kenyon Alberta
61 N10 Ken-zaki C Japan
55 F6 Kenzharyk' U.S.S.R.
36 D7 Kenzingen W Germany
135 T3 Keokea Hawaiian Is
110 E1 Keokuk Iowa
102 S12 Keolu Hills Hawaiian Is
68 G3 Keo Neua, Col de mt Laos
75 L8 Keonjhargarh India
Keos isld Greece see Kéa I
110 D1 Keosauqua Iowa
98 B9 Keota Colorado
99 P8 Keota Iowa
107 Q6 Keota Oklahoma
68 G7 Kep Cambodia
52 D2 Kepa U.S.S.R.
57 A4 Këpekli U.S.S.R.
52 F2 Kepina U.S.S.R.
144 A6 Kepler Mts New Zealand
31 K4 Kępno Poland
133 E8 Keppel isld Falkland Is
141 K6 Keppel B Queensland
47 J5 Kepsut Turkey
69 D13 Kepulauan Mentawai island grp Indonesia
76 B5 Kerala prov India
69 G13 Kerandin Indonesia
139 G6 Kerang Victoria
47 F7 Keratéa Greece
142 C5 Keraudren,C W Australia
29 L11 Kerava Finland
100 B7 Kerby Oregon
53 E10 Kerch' U.S.S.R.
55 D2 Kerchel' U.S.S.R.
52 H4 Kerchem'ya U.S.S.R.
52 J5 Kerchevskiy U.S.S.R.
47 F4 Kerdhíllion mt Greece
136 K3 Kerema Papua New Guinea
100 F1 Keremeos Br Col
80 C3 Kerem Maharal Israel
86 G2 Keren Ethiopia
109 L3 Kerens Texas
145 E2 Kerepehi New Zealand
52 D2 Keret' U.S.S.R.
52 E2 Kerets, Mys C U.S.S.R.
52 G3 Kerga U.S.S.R.
90 M16 Kerguelen-Gaussberg Ridge Southern Oc
81 D10 Kerguelen Ridge Indian Oc
95 N5 Kerhonkson New York
46 D7 Kerí Greece
88 E2 Kerichot Kenya
145 D1 Kerikeri New Zealand
29 O10 Kerimäki Finland
69 E13 Kerinci, Danau L Sumatra
69 E13 Kerinci, Gunung mt Sumatra
48 D4 Kerka R Hungary
25 F6 Kerken W Germany
85 G2 Kerkenna, Is Tunisia
99 L4 Kerkhoven Minnesota
52 H3 Kerki U.S.S.R.
57 D5 Kerkichi U.S.S.R.
47 F3 Kerkinítis, L Greece
46 D5 Kérkira Greece
46 D5 Kérkira isld Greece
25 F7 Kerkrade Netherlands
137 R8 Kermadec Is Pacific Oc
102 D5 Kerman California
77 E4 Kerman Iran
77 F5 Kerman Desert Iran
78 L4 Kermānshāh Iran
78 A3 Kerme Körfezi Turkey
47 H2 Kermen Bulgaria
108 D4 Kermit Texas
94 E9 Kermit W Virginia
102 F6 Kern R California
36 B2 Kernen W Germany
112 G1 Kernersville N Carolina
140 B7 Kernot Ra N Terr Aust
102 F6 Kernville California
52 H4 Keros U.S.S.R.
85 C7 Kerouné Guinea
139 G4 Kerpa New S Wales
48 M4 Kerpineny U.S.S.R.
146 H7 Kerr, C Antarctica
12 C1 Kerrera isld Scotland
108 B7 Kerrick Texas
113 F8 Kerr, L Florida
94 J10 Kerr L N Carolina/Virg
118 H7 Kerrobert Sask
145 D1 Kerr Pt New Zealand
94 H9 Kerrs Creek Virginia
110 G6 Kerrville Tennessee
109 H5 Kerrville Texas
8 C3 Kerry Wales
14 A4 Kerry co Irish Rep
14 B4 Kerry Hd Irish Rep
68 J2 Kersaint, I. du Vietnam
106 F1 Kersey Colorado
112 G3 Kershaw S Carolina
69 F10 Kerteh Malaysia
28 F6 Kerteminde Denmark
140 E7 Kertie Hill N Terr Aust
70 O9 Kertosono Java
88 F2 Keruguya Kenya
Kerulen R see Herlen He
25 F5 Kervenheim W Germany
85 D3 Kerzaz Australia
36 H2 Kerzell W Germany
40 F4 Kerzers Switzerland
52 F6 Kerzhenets R U.S.S.R.
120 K2 Kesagami L Ontario
29 O10 Kesälahti Finland
78 A1 Kesan Turkey
41 L4 Kesch, Piz mt Switzerland
61 P7 Kesennuma Japan
59 J2 Keshan China
99 S5 Keshena Wisconsin
76 C3 Kesigi India
52 D4 Keskozero U.S.S.R.
52 E5 Kesova Gora U.S.S.R.
47 K4 Kestel Turkey
47 L7 Kestel Gölü L Turkey
52 D2 Kesten'ga U.S.S.R.
47 K8 Kestep Turkey
25 E5 Kesteren Netherlands
36 D3 Kestert W Germany
29 M7 Kestilä Finland
13 E4 Keswick England
122 F8 Keswick Rdg New Brunswick
48 D4 Keszthely Hungary
56 C2 Ket' R U.S.S.R.
85 E7 Kéta Ghana
70 O9 Ketapang Java
69 E13 Ketaun Sumatra
117 H8 Ketchikan Alaska
101 L6 Ketchum Idaho
107 P5 Ketchum Oklahoma
108 F4 Ketchum Mt Texas
85 D7 Kété Ghana
25 E3 Ketelmeer Netherlands
74 B6 Keti Bandar Pakistan
116 H2 Ketik R Alaska
66 C3 Ketmen', Khr mts U.S.S.R./China
85 E7 Kétou Benin
31 N1 Kętrzyn Poland
36 E3 Kettenbach W Germany
9 F3 Kettering England
28 D7 Ketting Denmark
28 H7 Kettinge Denmark
13 E1 Kettle Scotland
99 O3 Kettle R Minnesota
100 G1 Kettle R Washington
94 K5 Kettle Cr Pennsylvania
100 G1 Kettle Falls Washington
102 E5 Kettleman City California
100 G1 Kettle R. Range mts Washington
13 F5 Kettlewell England
9 F2 Ketton England
32 E10 Kettwig W Germany
70 B4 Ketungau R Kalimantan
33 R8 Ketzin E Germany
69 B10 Keudeteunom Sumatra
95 K4 Keuka L New York
33 N10 Keula E Germany
55 F2 Keum R U.S.S.R.
29 L9 Keurusselkä L Finland
55 E1 Keushki U.S.S.R.
25 F5 Kevelaer W Germany
110 H4 Kevil Kentucky
101 O1 Kevin Montana
121 M4 Kewagama Quebec
99 R8 Kewanee Illinois
111 H9 Kewanee Mississippi
94 A5 Kewanna Indiana
99 T5 Kewaunee Wisconsin
99 S3 Keweenaw B Michigan
99 S2 Keweenaw Pen Michigan
98 F6 Keyapaha S Dakota
98 F6 Keya Paha R S Dakota
119 S8 Keyes Manitoba
106 H5 Keyes Oklahoma
110 G3 Keyesport Illinois
98 B5 Keyhole Res Wyoming
120 K7 Key Junction Ontario
14 C2 Key, L Irish Rep
113 G12 Key Largo Florida
140 A2 Keyling Inlet N Terr Aust
95 K7 Keymar Maryland
8 D5 Keynsham England
100 C2 Keyport Washington
94 J7 Keyser W Virginia
99 O8 Keystone Iowa
98 E8 Keystone Nebraska
107 O5 Keystone Oklahoma
98 C6 Keystone S Dakota
94 F9 Keystone W Virginia
113 F8 Keystone Heights Florida
103 N10 Keystone Pk Arizona
119 M8 Keystown Sask
112 E4 Keysville Georgia
94 J9 Keysville Virginia
113 F13 Key West Florida
52 H5 Kez U.S.S.R.
95 R3 Kezar Falls Maine
95 R2 Kezar L Maine
31 M6 Kežmarok Czechoslovakia
89 B5 Kgalagadi dist Botswana
89 E5 Kgatleng reg Botswana
52 H2 Khabarikha U.S.S.R.
59 L2 Khabarovsk U.S.S.R.
55 E5 Khabay R U.S.S.R.
79 H5 Khabrat es Seiqal Syria
78 H4 Khabur R Syria
77 E7 Khābūrah, Al Oman
52 E3 Khachela U.S.S.R.
77 C5 Khafr Iran
77 H4 Khairabad Afghanistan
74 C5 Khairpur Pakistan
74 H6 Khajurāho anc site India
56 C4 Khakasskaya Aut. Oblast' U.S.S.R.
87 D10 Khakhea Botswana
57 C5 Khalach U.S.S.R.
77 A4 Khalafābād Iran
74 G1 Khalatse Kashmir
55 C5 Khalilovo U.S.S.R.
78 K5 Khālis, Al Iraq
46 F5 Khálki Greece
47 J8 Khálki isld Greece
47 F6 Khalkís Greece
80 E5 Khallat El Fūla Jordan
52 G5 Khalturin U.S.S.R.
75 J7 Khamaria India
74 E8 Khambat, Gulf of India
89 F2 Khami R Zimbabwe
47 H9 Khamilí isld Greece
68 G3 Kham Keut Laos
76 E2 Khammam India
68 H5 Khampho R Laos
56 E4 Khamsara R U.S.S.R.
77 A1 Khamseh Iran
57 F4 Khamza U.S.S.R.
77 L1 Khānābād Afghanistan
76 B3 Khanapur India
78 K4 Khānaqin Iraq
79 H4 Khanāzir, Jebel el mts Syria
139 J6 Khancoban New S Wales
84 J6 Khandaq, El Sudan
47 H9 Khandrá Crete Greece
74 G8 Khandwa India
74 D3 Khanewal Pakistan
55 D1 Khangokurt U.S.S.R.
68 J6 Khanh Hoa Vietnam
69 G8 Khanh Hung Vietnam
47 G9 Khaniá Crete Greece
74 H6 Khaniadhana India
54 H2 Khanino U.S.S.R.
47 F9 Khaníon, Kólpos B Crete Greece
74 D4 Khanpur Pakistan
79 G3 Khān Sheikhūn Syria
57 G3 Khantau U.S.S.R.
50 H2 Khantayka U.S.S.R.
51 J2 Khantayskoye, Ozero L U.S.S.R.
66 C3 Khan Tengri U.S.S.R.
57 J4 Khan Tengri, Pik mt U.S.S.R.
55 E1 Khanty-Mansiysk U.S.S.R.
68 D4 Khanu Thailand
79 E7 Khan Yunis Egypt
80 F4 Khanzira Jordan
69 D8 Khao Chum Thong Thailand
74 G1 Khapalu Kashmir
58 F2 Khapcheranga U.S.S.R.
75 M6 Kharagpur India
77 J5 Kharan Pakistan
74 A4 Kharan Kalat Pakistan
84 J4 Khârga, El Egypt
84 J5 Khârga Oasis Egypt
56 H4 Kharga, Oz L U.S.S.R.
79 D8 Kharîm, G mt Egypt
72 F4 Kharj, Al reg Saudi Arabia
77 B5 Khārk isld Iran
54 H6 Khar'kov U.S.S.R.
52 E1 Kharlovka U.S.S.R.
52 D4 Kharlu U.S.S.R.
47 H3 Kharmanli Bulgaria
77 L3 Kharoti reg Afghanistan
52 F5 Kharovsk U.S.S.R.
147 Q7 Kharstan U.S.S.R.
86 F2 Khartoum Sudan
54 K8 Khartsyzsk U.S.S.R.
52 J2 Kharutayuvam U.S.S.R.
65 H3 Khasan U.S.S.R.
77 H4 Khash Afghanistan
77 G5 Khāsh Iran
86 G2 Khashem el Girba Sudan
77 H4 Khash Rud R Afghanistan
78 J1 Khashusi U.S.S.R.
46 E5 Khasiá Óri Greece
75 O6 Khasi-Jaintia Hills India
47 H3 Khaskovo Bulgaria
51 K1 Khatanga U.S.S.R.
51 L1 Khatangskiy Zaliv gulf U.S.S.R.
52 J2 Khatayakha U.S.S.R.
57 D5 Khatyrchi U.S.S.R.
57 D5 Khaudag U.S.S.R.
68 C5 Khawsa Burma
57 F5 Khaydarken U.S.S.R.
57 B4 Khazar-Asp U.S.S.R.
68 G3 Khe Bo Vietnam
74 E10 Khed India
68 G2 Khe Long Vietnam
52 D4 Khelyulya U.S.S.R.
56 D5 Khemchik R U.S.S.R.
56 D5 Khemchikskiy, Khr mts U.S.S.R.
85 D4 Khenachich, El reg Mali
85 F1 Khenchela Algeria
68 A2 Khenkhar Burma
53 D10 Kherson U.S.S.R.
51 J1 Kheta R U.S.S.R.
52 D2 Khetolambina U.S.S.R.
74 F5 Khetri India
68 E5 Khiaw, Khao mt Thailand
52 D1 Khibiny mt U.S.S.R.
29 O10 Khiitola U.S.S.R.
46 F7 Khiliomódhion Greece
56 H5 Khilok U.S.S.R.
56 G5 Khilok R U.S.S.R.
52 E6 Khimki U.S.S.R.
56 C5 Khindiktig Khol', Oz L U.S.S.R.
46 D6 Khionáta Greece
47 H6 Khíos isld Greece
80 D8 Khirbet Deir Razih Jordan
80 G4 Khirbet el Kufeirat Jordan
80 F4 Khirbet el Wahadina Jordan
80 G4 Khirbet Harqala Jordan
80 D5 Khirbet Isla Jordan
80 F4 Khirbet Listib Jordan
80 F4 Khirbet Mar Ilyas Jordan
47 G2 Khisar Bulgaria
57 B4 Khiva U.S.S.R.
46 F6 Khlomón mt Greece
48 L1 Khmelnik U.S.S.R.
48 K1 Khmel'nitskiy U.S.S.R.
Khmer Rep see Cambodia
69 G8 Khoai, Hon isld Vietnam
48 J1 Khodorov U.S.S.R.
57 D5 Khodzha Mubarek U.S.S.R.
57 A4 Khodzheyli U.S.S.R.
54 K5 Khokhol U.S.S.R.
52 D6 Kholm U.S.S.R.
52 F3 Kholmogorskaya U.S.S.R.
52 F3 Kholmogory U.S.S.R.
59 M2 Kholmsk U.S.S.R.
56 B5 Kholzun, Khr mts U.S.S.R.
77 A1 Khoman Iran
87 C10 Khomas Hochland dist Namibia
77 B3 Khomeyn Iran
87 F8 Khondowe Malawi
68 G5 Khong Laos
68 G5 Khong Sedone Laos
88 E10 Khonjeni Malawi
77 C6 Khonj, Kūhe-e mt Iran
68 F4 Khon Kaen Thailand
53 F8 Khoper R U.S.S.R.
59 L2 Khor U.S.S.R.
59 L2 Khor R U.S.S.R.
46 E7 Khóra Greece
77 E2 Khorāsan Iran
47 G9 Khóra Sfakíon Crete Greece
52 J2 Khoreyver U.S.S.R.
57 B4 Khorezmskaya Oblast' prov U.S.S.R.
Khorgos see Huo ch eng
57 C2 Khorkhut U.S.S.R.
54 K1 Khorlovo U.S.S.R.
57 F6 Khorog U.S.S.R.
54 E7 Khorol U.S.S.R.
54 E7 Khorol R U.S.S.R.
55 G4 Khorosheye U.S.S.R.
77 A3 Khorramābād Iran
77 A4 Khorramshahr Iran
52 J2 Khoseda Khard U.S.S.R.
77 F3 Khosf Iran
74 B3 Khost Pakistan
77 L3 Khost reg Afghanistan
Khotan see Hotan
54 D3 Khotimsk U.S.S.R.
48 K2 Khotin U.S.S.R.
54 K1 Khot'kovo U.S.S.R.
116 H4 Khotol mt Alaska
53 F12 Khrami R U.S.S.R.
52 F6 Khrapovitskaya U.S.S.R.
54 M5 Khrenovoye U.S.S.R.
68 A2 Khreum Burma
47 G4 Khrisoúpolis Greece
47 G8 Khristianá isld Greece
48 M2 Khristinovka U.S.S.R.
52 G4 Khristoforovo U.S.S.R.
47 G3 Khrojna Bulgaria
55 C5 Khrom-Tau U.S.S.R.
79 C3 Khrysokhou B Cyprus
47 H7 Khtapodhiá isld Greece
77 B6 Khubar, Al Saudi Arabia
77 K6 Khude Hills Pakistan
56 G5 Khudunskiy Khr mts U.S.S.R.
68 G5 Khu Khan Thailand
77 K1 Khulm Afghanistan
75 N7 Khulna Bangladesh
84 E3 Khums, Al Libya
Khungari see Gurskoye
74 F1 Khunjerab Pass China/India
77 B3 Khunsar Iran
75 L7 Khunti India
75 L8 Khurda India
77 J3 Khurd, Koh-i- mt Afghanistan
74 G4 Khurja India
74 E2 Khushab Pakistan
48 H2 Khust U.S.S.R.
86 E3 Khuwei Sudan
77 A4 Khuzestan Iran
56 G4 Khuzhir U.S.S.R.
77 G2 Khvāf Iran
77 D3 Khvor Iran
78 K2 Khvoy Iran
52 D5 Khvoynaya U.S.S.R.
77 L1 Khwāja-i-Ghar Afghanistan
77 L1 Khwaja Muhammad Range Afghanistan
74 D1 Khyber Pass Pakistan/Afghan
48 H1 Khyrov U.S.S.R.
139 K5 Kiama New S Wales
71 G7 Kiamba Mindanao Philippines
88 F2 Kiambu Kenya
107 P7 Kiamichi Mts Oklahoma
121 P6 Kiamika Quebec
Kiamusze see Jiamusi
141 K6 Kianga Queensland
Kiangsi prov see Jiangxi
Kiangsu prov see Jiangsu
29 O6 Kiantajärvi L Finland
119 U2 Kiask L Manitoba
28 B4 Kibæk Denmark
86 F5 Kibanga Uganda
86 B6 Kibangou Congo
71 G7 Kibawe Mindanao Philippines
88 F4 Kibaya Tanzania
26 S1 Kiberg Norway
85 D7 Kibi Ghana
87 G7 Kibiti Tanzania
86 E6 Kibombo Zaïre
88 C3 Kibondo Tanzania
79 E10 Kibrīt, J. al Saudi Arabia
88 C3 Kibungu Rwanda
46 D3 Kičevo Yugoslavia
86 C2 Kichi Kichi Chad
52 G4 Kichmenga R U.S.S.R.
52 G5 Kichmengskiy Gorodok U.S.S.R.
52 H7 Kichuy U.S.S.R.
99 Q6 Kickapoo R Wisconsin
117 P10 Kicking Horse Pass Br Col
85 E5 Kidal Mali
71 H5 Kidandal Indonesia
98 J4 Kidder S Dakota
8 D3 Kidderminster England
86 F5 Kidepo Nat. Park Kenya
85 B6 Kidira Senegal
9 E4 Kidlington England
145 F3 Kidnappers, C New Zealand
141 G4 Kidston Queensland
70 C3 Kidurong, Tg C Sarawak
8 B4 Kidwelly Wales
98 F2 Kief N Dakota
32 M4 Kiel W Germany
99 S6 Kiel Wisconsin
31 M5 Kielce Poland
13 F3 Kielder England
13 F3 Kielder Res England
22 G1 Kieldrecht Belgium
30 E1 Kieler Bucht B W Germany
138 D5 Kielpa S Australia
67 B6 Kien An Vietnam
69 G8 Kien Hung Vietnam
37 N1 Kieritzsch E Germany
36 D1 Kierspe W Germany
109 N9 Kiest Park Texas
Kiev see Kiyev
139 H6 Kiewa R Victoria
85 B5 Kiffa Mauritania
46 F6 Kifissós R Greece
78 K5 Kifl, Al Iraq
88 C2 Kigali Rwanda
116 K2 Kigalik R Alaska
116 E4 Kigluaik Mts Alaska
88 B4 Kigoma Tanzania
88 C4 Kigoma dist Tanzania
141 F7 Kihee Queensland
27 M13 Kihelkonna U.S.S.R.
145 E3 Kihikihi New Zealand
29 K4 Kihlanki Finland
29 K9 Kihniö Finland
102 V14 Kiholo Hawaiian Is
29 K11 Kiikala Finland
29 K10 Kiikoinen Finland
135 N1 Kii Landing Hawaiian Is
29 M6 Kiiminki Finland
61 K11 Kii-Nagashima Japan
61 J12 Kii Sanchi mts Japan
60 H12 Kii suidō str Japan
116 K6 Kijik Alaska
61 Q12 Kijoka Okinawa
59 J6 Kikai-shima isld Japan
116 L2 Kikiakrorak R Alaska
48 F5 Kikinda Yugoslavia
47 G7 Kikladhes islds Greece
52 G6 Kiknur U.S.S.R.
60 O4 Kikonai Japan
136 J3 Kikori Papua New Guinea
60 D13 Kikuchi Japan
89 D8 Kikvors Berg S Africa
121 M6 Kikwissi, L Quebec
86 C7 Kikwit Zaïre
27 F12 Kil Sweden
101 L1 Kila Montana
27 J13 Kila Sweden
27 J10 Kilafors Sweden
113 L9 Kilarney, L New Providence I Bahamas
135 O1 Kilauea Hawaiian Is
102 V14 Kilauea Crater Hawaiian Is
14 D3 Kilbeggan Irish Rep
12 C2 Kilberry Scotland
15 C5 Kilbrennan Snd Scotland
12 D2 Kilbride Scotland
116 G6 Kilbuck Mts Alaska
122 E7 Kilburn New Brunswick
12 C2 Kilchattan Scotland
12 B2 Kilchoman Scotland
12 C1 Kilchrenan Scotland
65 H4 Kilchu N Korea
13 F1 Kilconquhar Scotland
14 D3 Kilcormac Irish Rep
141 K7 Kilcoy Queensland
14 E3 Kilcullen Irish Rep
117 K9 Kildala Arm R Br Columbia
13 G5 Kildale England
14 E3 Kildare Irish Rep
109 N3 Kildare Texas
14 E3 Kildare co Irish Rep
122 J7 Kildare, C Pr Edward I
28 J5 Kildebrønde Denmark
52 D1 Kil'din, Os isld U.S.S.R.
117 L11 Kildonan Br Col
118 B1 Kildonan Manitoba
87 F9 Kildonan Zimbabwe
86 C7 Kilembe Zaïre

40
Kilen — Konda

28 A3 Kilen L Denmark
14 B4 Kilfenora Irish Rep
12 C2 Kilfinan Scotland
14 C4 Kilfinnane Irish Rep
14 B5 Kilgarvan Irish Rep
101 O5 Kilgore Idaho
98 F7 Kilgore Nebraska
111 B9 Kilgore Texas
13 H5 Kilham England
85 E7 Kilibo Benin
88 G3 Kilifi Kenya
88 F3 Kilimanjaro mt Tanzania
137 M2 Kilinailau Is Solomon Is
47 K4 Kılınç Turkey
15 C4 Kilinelfort Scotland
52 B5 Kilingi-Nõmme U.S.S.R.
83 K8 Kilinochchi Sri Lanka
78 F3 Kilis Turkey
116 L8 Kiliuda B Alaska
48 M5 Kiliya U.S.S.R.
14 B4 Kilkee Irish Rep
14 F2 Kilkeel N Ireland
14 D4 Kilkenny Irish Rep
14 D4 Kilkenny co Irish Rep
12 C3 Kilkenzie Scotland
8 B6 Kilkhampton England
14 B3 Kilkieran B Irish Rep
46 F4 Kilkís Greece
141 K7 Kilkivan Queensland
14 E3 Kill Irish Rep
14 B2 Killala Irish Rep
14 B2 Killala B Irish Rep
120 D3 Killala L Ontario
14 C4 Killaloe Irish Rep
121 N7 Killaloe Ontario
119 P8 Killaly Sask
118 F6 Killam Alberta
14 B4 Killarney Irish Rep
119 S9 Killarney Manitoba
140 B3 Killarney N Terr Aust
120 J7 Killarney Ontario
141 K8 Killarney Queensland
120 J6 Killarney Prov. Park Ontario
14 A3 Killary Hbr Irish Rep
14 D2 Killashandra Irish Rep
98 D2 Killdeer N Dakota
118 L9 Killdeer Sask
99 O8 Killduff Iowa
12 D1 Killearn Scotland
109 K4 Killeen Texas
47 J5 Killer R Turkey
15 E4 Killiecrankie, Pass of Scotland
116 K2 Killik Bend Alaska
14 C3 Killimor Irish Rep
15 D4 Killin Scotland
26 E9 Killingdal Norway
46 E7 Killíni Greece
46 E7 Killíni mt Greece
14 B4 Killorglin Irish Rep
14 C2 Killybegs Irish Rep
14 F2 Killyleagh N Ireland
14 C4 Kilmallock Irish Rep
15 B3 Kilmaluag Scotland
13 F1 Kilmany Scotland
12 D2 Kilmarnock Scotland
95 L9 Kilmarnock Virginia
12 C1 Kilmartin Scotland
52 H6 Kil'mez U.S.S.R.
111 G8 Kilmichael Mississippi
139 G6 Kilmore Victoria
12 C2 Kilmory Scotland
12 D1 Kilmun Scotland
13 E4 Kilnhill England
12 C1 Kilninver Scotland
13 J6 Kilnsea England
88 F6 Kilombero R Tanzania
88 F5 Kilosa Tanzania
29 H2 Kilpisjärvi Finland
29 L7 Kilpua Finland
29 Q2 Kilp'yavr U.S.S.R.
14 E2 Kilrea N Ireland
14 B4 Kilrush Irish Rep
9 E3 Kilsby England
12 D2 Kilsyth Scotland
14 C3 Kiltamagh Irish Rep
73 L6 Kiltan isld Lakshadweep Indian Oc
26 M5 Kilvo Sweden
87 E7 Kilwa Zaïre
88 B6 Kilwa isld Zambia
88 G6 Kilwa Kisiwani Tanzania
88 G6 Kilwa Kivinje Tanzania
88 G6 Kilwa Masoko Tanzania
12 D2 Kilwinning Scotland
47 K3 Kilyos Turkey
106 G4 Kim Colorado
101 M7 Kimama Idaho
70 D2 Kimanis B Sabah
138 D5 Kimba S Australia
98 C8 Kimball Nebraska
98 H6 Kimball S Dakota
94 F9 Kimball W Virginia
116 P5 Kimball, Mt Alaska
99 L8 Kimballton Iowa
86 C7 Kimbao Zaïre
117 Q11 Kimberley Br Col
120 K8 Kimberley Ontario
89 D7 Kimberley S Africa
141 H3 Kimberley,C Queensland
142 E3 Kimberley Downs W Australia
142 F3 Kimberley Plateau W Australia
143 C7 Kimberley Ra W Australia
101 L7 Kimberly Idaho
103 J2 Kimberly Nevada
99 S5 Kimberly Wisconsin
9 F3 Kimbolton England
145 E4 Kimbolton New Zealand
88 D5 Kimbu Tanzania
47 G6 Kími Greece
29 K11 Kimito Finland
118 A3 Kimiwan Lake Alberta
110 F3 Kimmswick Missouri
47 G8 Kímolos isld Greece
61 M7 Kimpoku-san mt Japan
52 E6 Kimry U.S.S.R.
68 J5 Kim Son Vietnam
27 H13 Kimstad Sweden
52 F2 Kimzha U.S.S.R.
68 B1 Kin Burma
61 P13 Kin Okinawa
61 P13 Kina Okinawa
70 E1 Kinabalu mt Sabah
70 E2 Kinabatangan R Sabah
88 F2 Kinangop, Mt Kenya
47 H8 Kínaros isld Greece
70 D2 Kinarut Sabah
117 O10 Kinbasket Br Col
118 F8 Kinbrook I. Prov. Pk Alberta
107 P3 Kincaid Kansas
118 K9 Kincaid Sask
120 J8 Kincardine Ontario
12 E1 Kincardine Scotland
Kincardine co see Grampian reg
117 J8 Kincolith Br Col
15 E3 Kincraig Scotland
87 E7 Kinda Zaïre
94 E3 Kinde Michigan
33 O10 Kindelbrück E Germany
109 P5 Kinder Louisiana
36 C3 Kinderbeuern W Germany
118 J7 Kindersley Sask
85 B6 Kindia Guinea
98 J3 Kindred N Dakota
86 E6 Kindu Zaïre
116 G7 Kinegnak Alaska
53 H7 Kinelyu R U.S.S.R.
52 F6 Kineshma U.S.S.R.
140 C1 King R N Terr Aust
140 E6 King R Queensland
141 G2 King R Queensland
141 K7 Kingaroy Queensland
133 C6 King, Canal str Chile
114 J2 King Christian I N W Terr
102 C5 King City California
99 M9 King City Missouri
117 K10 Kingcome Inlet Br Col
116 F9 King Cove Alaska
142 F3 King Edward R W Australia
146 J8 King Edward V11 Land Antarctica
95 R2 Kingfield Maine
107 N6 Kingfisher Oklahoma
146 E15 King George 1 S Shetland Is
115 M6 King George Is N W Terr
135 N10 King George Is Tuamotu Arch Pacific Oc
118 B8 King George, Mt Br Col
117 D5 King George, Mt Yukon Terr
143 C11 King George Sd W Australia
133 J8 King Haakon B S Georgia
142 E6 King Hill W Australia
120 C3 Kinghorn Ontario
13 E1 Kinghorn Scotland
146 H11 King I Antarctica
117 K9 King I Br Col
73 Q6 King I Burma
139 G7 King I Tasmania
52 C5 Kingisepp U.S.S.R.
52 B5 Kingissepp U.S.S.R.
100 G8 King Lear mt Nevada
146 D3 King Leopold & Queen Astrid Coast Antarctica
142 E3 King Leopold Ra W Australia
118 E5 Kingman Alberta
103 K6 Kingman Arizona
107 M4 Kingman Kansas
95 T1 Kingman Maine
141 H7 King, Mt Queensland
108 E4 King Mt Texas
142 C5 King, Mt W Australia
86 E6 Kingombe Zaïre
138 D4 Kingoonya S Australia
139 H8 King, R Tasmania
142 G3 King, R W Australia
102 D5 Kings R California
100 G8 Kings R Nevada
116 J7 King Salmon Alaska
13 F1 Kingsbarns Scotland
8 C7 Kingsbridge England
102 E5 Kingsburg California
109 K6 Kingsbury Texas
106 D1 Kings Canyon Colorado
102 F4 Kings Canyon Nat Park California
9 E5 Kingsclere England
139 L3 Kingscliff-Fingal New S Wales
138 D6 Kingscote S Australia
14 E3 Kingscourt Irish Rep
145 E2 Kingseat New Zealand
9 G5 Kingsferry Bridge England
9 F5 Kingsfold England
109 P2 Kingsland Arkansas
113 F7 Kingsland Georgia
9 F4 Kings Langley England
99 L7 Kingsley Iowa
94 B2 Kingsley Michigan
98 E8 Kingsley Dam Nebraska
9 G2 King's Lynn England
137 P2 Kingsmill Group islds Kiribati
112 F2 Kings Mt N Carolina
95 O6 Kings Park Long I, N Y
101 P9 Kings Pks Utah
122 H8 Kingsport Nova Scotia
94 E10 Kingsport Tennessee
142 E3 Kings Sd W Australia
8 C6 Kingsteignton England
110 C5 Kingston Arkansas
9 F5 Kingston England
127 L3 Kingston Jamaica
110 B2 Kingston Missouri
95 R4 Kingston New Hampshire
95 N5 Kingston New York
144 B6 Kingston New Zealand
94 E7 Kingston Ohio
107 O7 Kingston Oklahoma
121 O8 Kingston Ontario
95 M5 Kingston Pennsylvania
138 E6 Kingston S Australia
139 H9 Kingston Tasmania
100 C2 Kingston Washington
94 F9 Kingston W Virginia
9 E4 Kingston Lisle England
103 J6 Kingston Pk California
13 F4 Kingstown England
127 O8 Kingstown St Vincent
112 H4 Kingstree S Carolina
94 G5 Kingsville Ohio
120 H10 Kingsville Ontario
109 K8 Kingsville Texas
8 C7 Kingswear England
8 C3 Kington England
86 C7 Kinguji Zaïre
15 D3 Kingussie Scotland
115 K4 King William I N W Terr
89 E9 King William's Town S Africa
94 H7 Kingwood W Virginia
87 E8 Kiniama Zaïre
47 J5 Kınık Turkey
119 M6 Kinistino Sask
61 P7 Kinka-san C Japan
87 H11 Kinkony, L Madagascar
122 J7 Kinkora Pr Edward I
145 E3 Kinleith New Zealand
118 K6 Kinley Sask
144 B6 Kinloch New Zealand
15 C3 Kinlochewe Scotland
15 D4 Kinlochleven Scotland
15 D4 Kinloch Rannoch Scotland
68 B3 Kinmaw Burma
61 P13 Kin-misaki C Okinawa
121 M8 Kinmount Ontario
110 H3 Kinmundy Illinois
27 F14 Kinna Sweden
117 P11 Kinnaird Br Col
15 F3 Kinnairds Hd Scotland
101 R6 Kinnear Wyoming
80 F3 Kinneret Israel
80 B8 Kinneret-Negev-Conduit Israel
83 L9 Kinniyai Sri Lanka
29 L8 Kinnula Finland
60 J11 Kino R Japan
61 K10 Kinomoto Japan
119 Q1 Kinoosa Manitoba
60 H10 Kinosaki Japan
13 E1 Kinqlassie Scotland
13 E1 Kinross Scotland
Kinross co see Tayside reg
14 C5 Kinsale Irish Rep
95 L8 Kinsale Virginia
7 E11 Kinsale oil rig Celtic Sea
14 C5 Kinsale, Old Hd of C Irish Rep
118 F5 Kinsella Alberta
101 U3 Kinsey Montana
86 C6 Kinshasa Zaïre
60 C11 Kin Shimo no-shima Japan
107 L4 Kinsley Kansas
94 G5 Kinsman Ohio
112 K2 Kinston N Carolina
107 P6 Kinta Oklahoma
70 P10 Kintamani, G mt Indonesia
70 D6 Kintap Kalimantan
85 C6 Kintinian Guinea
101 L1 Kintla Pk Montana
71 H5 Kintom Sulawesi
15 F3 Kintore Scotland
138 B2 Kintore, Mt S Australia
140 A6 Kintore Ra N Terr Aust
55 F1 Kintus U.S.S.R.
12 C2 Kintyre pen Scotland
68 B1 Kinu Burma
61 N9 Kinu R Japan
118 B3 Kinuso Alberta
14 C3 Kinvarra Irish Rep
61 P13 Kin wan B Okinawa
86 F5 Kinyeti mt Sudan
55 C6 Kinzhaly U.S.S.R.
36 D7 Kinzig R Baden-Württemberg W Germany
36 G3 Kinzig R Hessen W Germany
100 E5 Kinzua Oregon
94 J5 Kinzua Pennsylvania
71 N9 Kio Indonesia
100 F3 Kiona Washington
121 M6 Kiosk Ontario
106 F2 Kiowa Colorado
107 M4 Kiowa Kansas
107 P7 Kiowa Oklahoma
119 Q3 Kipahigan L Manitoba
135 T3 Kipahulu Hawaiian Is
46 E7 Kiparissia Greece
46 E7 Kiparissiakós Kolpos B Greece
121 M6 Kipawa Quebec
88 C5 Kipili Tanzania
86 H6 Kipini Kenya
119 P8 Kipling Sask
116 E7 Kipnuk Alaska
118 E9 Kipp Alberta
12 D1 Kippen Scotland
36 D7 Kippenheim W Germany
123 O5 Kippens Nfld
95 M9 Kiptopeke Virginia
87 E8 Kipushi Zaïre
60 H12 Kiragawa Japan
47 H4 Kirazh Turkey
Kirberg see Hünfelden
111 C7 Kirby Arkansas
9 H4 Kirby England
120 F6 Kirby Ontario
101 R6 Kirby Wyoming
111 C11 Kirbyville Texas
38 N8 Kirchbach Austria
38 M5 Kirchberg Austria
36 H5 Kirchberg Baden-Württemberg W Germany
37 O2 Kirchberg E Germany
36 C4 Kirchberg Rheinland-Pfalz W Germany
33 O5 Kirchdorf E Germany
37 P6 Kirchdorf W Germany
37 M4 Kirchenlaibach W Germany
37 M3 Kirchenlamitz W Germany
36 D2 Kirchen-Sieg W Germany
36 G6 Kirchentellinsfurt W Germany
37 M4 Kirchenthumbach W Germany
33 T9 Kirchhain E Germany
36 F2 Kirchhain W Germany
37 K1 Kirchheilingen E Germany
36 G5 Kirchheim W Germany
36 D4 Kirchheim Bolanden W Germany
32 E9 Kirchhellen W Germany
36 E1 Kirchhundem W Germany
33 O6 Kirch Jesar E Germany
32 H6 Kirchkimmen W Germany
37 K3 Kirchlauter W Germany
32 J8 Kirchlengern W Germany
32 K7 Kirchlinteln W Germany
38 K5 Kirchschlag Austria
32 J7 Kirchweyhe W Germany
32 J6 Kirchwistedt W Germany
47 J5 Kireç Turkey
33 Q5 Kireh Grubenhagen E Germany
56 G3 Kirenga R U.S.S.R.
47 K7 Kirenis R Turkey
56 G2 Kirensk U.S.S.R.
55 E6 Kirey R U.S.S.R.
54 J3 Kireyevsk U.S.S.R.
83 K11 Kirgalpotta mt Sri Lanka
55 G6 Kirgiziya U.S.S.R.
57 F4 Kirgiziya S.S.R rep U.S.S.R.
55 B4 Kirgiz-Miyaki U.S.S.R.
86 C6 Kiri Zaïre
78 F3 Kirikhan Turkey
78 D2 Kirikkale Turkey
145 E1 Kirikopuni New Zealand
29 O11 Kirillovskoye U.S.S.R.
Kirin see Jilin
Kirin prov see Jilin
83 L11 Kirindi Oya R Sri Lanka
145 E1 Kiripa New Zealand
52 D5 Kirishi U.S.S.R.
60 D14 Kirishima-yama mt Japan
86 A2 Kirit Somalia
136 L3 Kiriwina Is Papua New Guinea
106 H2 Kirk Colorado
98 C8 Kirk Nebraska
100 D7 Kirk Oregon
47 L5 Kırka Turkey
47 J5 Kırkağaç Turkey
12 E4 Kirkbean Scotland
13 E4 Kirkbride England
13 F5 Kirkby Lonsdale England
13 H5 Kirkbymoorside England
13 F5 Kirkby Stephen England
118 D8 Kirkcaldy Alberta
13 E1 Kirkcaldy Scotland
12 C4 Kirkcolm Scotland
12 D4 Kirkcowan Scotland
12 D4 Kirkcudbright Scotland
Kirkcudbright co see Dumfries and Galloway reg
12 D4 Kirkcudbright B Scotland
13 G6 Kirk Deighton England
28 N2 Kirkebø Faeroes
28 F6 Kirkeby Fyn Denmark
28 B6 Kirkeby Sønderjylland Denmark
28 G5 Kirke Helsinge Denmark
28 H5 Kirke Hvalsø Denmark
28 H5 Kirke Hyllinge Denmark
119 Q8 Kirkella Manitoba
36 C5 Kirkel-Neuhausel W Germany
26 R2 Kirkenes Norway
28 H5 Kirke Såby Denmark
28 G6 Kirke Stillinge Denmark
26 K3 Kirkestind mt Norway
12 E2 Kirkfieldbank Scotland
13 F6 Kirkham England
12 D4 Kirkinner Scotland
12 D2 Kirkintilloch Scotland
28 N2 Kirkjubønes Faeroes
103 M7 Kirkland Arizona
99 S7 Kirkland Illinois
12 E3 Kirkland Scotland
100 C2 Kirkland Washington
120 K4 Kirkland Lake Ontario
47 J3 Kirklareli Turkey
94 A6 Kirklin Indiana
9 F1 Kirklington Notts England
13 G5 Kirklington N Yorks England
12 E2 Kirkliston Scotland
144 C6 Kirkliston Range New Zealand
99 L8 Kirkman Iowa
12 D3 Kirkmichael Scotland
13 F4 Kirkoswald England
12 D3 Kirkoswald Scotland
13 E3 Kirkpatrick-Fleming Scotland
146 G7 Kirkpatrick, Mt Antarctica
13 F5 Kirkstone Pass England
110 D1 Kirksville Missouri
78 K4 Kirkūk Iraq
15 F2 Kirkwall Scotland
102 B2 Kirkwood California
95 M4 Kirkwood New York
89 D9 Kirkwood S Africa
98 E5 Kirley S Dakota
47 K5 Kirmasti R Turkey
12 D2 Kirn Scotland
36 C4 Kirn W Germany
54 F2 Kirov Kaluga U.S.S.R.
52 G5 Kirov Kirov U.S.S.R.
78 L1 Kirovabad Azerbaydzhan U.S.S.R.
57 E6 Kirovabad Tadzhik U.S.S.R.
78 K1 Kirovakan U.S.S.R.
55 D3 Kirovo U.S.S.R.
54 D8 Kirovograd U.S.S.R.
52 D1 Kirovsk U.S.S.R.
118 G7 Kirriemuir Alberta
15 E4 Kirriemuir Scotland
52 H5 Kirs U.S.S.R.
78 E2 Kirşehir Turkey
87 D11 Kirstonia S Africa
98 B7 Kirtley Wyoming
13 H6 Kirton England
9 F2 Kirton Holme England
36 G2 Kirtorf W Germany
26 L4 Kiruna Sweden
86 E6 Kirundu Zaïre
144 D5 Kirwee New Zealand
107 M2 Kirwin Kansas
61 N9 Kiryū Japan
54 K1 Kirzhach U.S.S.R.
27 H14 Kisa Sweden
61 N6 Kisakata Japan
87 G7 Kisaki Tanzania
47 F9 Kisámou, K B Crete Greece
86 E5 Kisangani Zaïre
71 N9 Kisar isld Indonesia
116 G6 Kisaralik R Alaska
69 D11 Kisaran Sumatra
61 N10 Kisarazu Japan
48 D3 Kisbér Hungary
119 P9 Kisbey Sask
56 C4 Kiselevsk U.S.S.R.
74 F5 Kishangarh India
85 E7 Kishi Nigeria
55 F4 Kishikaroy, Oz L U.S.S.R.
48 M3 Kishinev U.S.S.R.
60 J11 Kishiwada Japan
74 F2 Kishtwar Kashmir
Kisi see Jixi
88 G3 Kisigau Mt Kenya
88 E5 Kisigo R Tanzania
88 E2 Kisii Kenya
119 T4 Kiskittogisu L Manitoba
119 T4 Kiskitto L Manitoba
48 D4 Kiskomárom Hungary
48 E4 Kiskörei-viztárole L Hungary
48 F3 Kisköreiviztároló L Hungary
48 F4 Kiskundorozsma Hungary
48 F4 Kiskunfélegyháza Hungary
48 E4 Kiskunhalas Hungary
48 F4 Kiskunmajsa Hungary
53 F11 Kislovodsk U.S.S.R.
Kismayu see Chisimaio
61 L10 Kiso Japan
61 L10 Kiso-sammyaku mts Japan
48 E3 Kispest Hungary
117 J8 Kispiox R Br Col
28 H5 Kisserup Denmark
85 B7 Kissidougou Guinea
113 F9 Kissimmee Florida
113 F10 Kissimmee R Florida
119 Q3 Kississing L Manitoba
41 L2 Kisslegg W Germany
84 H5 Kissu, Jebel mt Sudan
26 L3 Kistefjell mt Norway
48 F4 Kistelek Hungary
48 F2 Kisterenye Hungary
26 O1 Kistrand Norway
48 F3 Kisújszállás Hungary
88 E2 Kisumu Kenya
48 G2 Kisvárda Hungary
50 E5 Kisyl Arvat U.S.S.R.
85 C6 Kita Mali
57 D5 Kitab U.S.S.R.
60 H12 Kitagawa Japan
61 O9 Kita-Ibaraki Japan
48 M5 Kitai, Ozero L U.S.S.R.
26 L5 Kitajaur Sweden
61 P6 Kitakami Japan
61 N8 Kitakata Japan
60 D12 Kita-Kyūshū Japan
86 G5 Kitale Kenya
60 R2 Kitami Japan
60 Q1 Kitami-sanchi mts Japan
88 G7 Kitangari Tanzania
61 N13 Kitano-hana C Japan
61 O9 Kita-ura L Japan
61 J12 Kitayama R Japan
106 H3 Kit Carson Colorado
115 L9 Kitchener Ontario
143 E9 Kitchener W Australia
112 E5 Kite Georgia
29 P9 Kitee Finland
86 F5 Kitgum Uganda
47 F6 Kithairón mt Greece
46 F8 Kíthira isld Greece
47 G7 Kíthnos isld Greece
120 H3 Kitigan Ontario
80 G4 Kitim Jordan
117 J8 Kitimat Br Col
117 J9 Kitimat Mill Alberta
29 M4 Kitinen R Finland
52 C1 Kitinen R Finland
46 E2 Kitka mt Yugoslavia
46 F4 Kítros Greece
118 G5 Kitscoty Alberta
48 K2 Kitsman U.S.S.R.
60 E12 Kitsuki Japan
61 O9 Kitsuregawa Japan
138 E3 Kittakittaooloo, L S Australia
94 H6 Kittanning Pennsylvania
95 N5 Kittatinny Mts New Jersey
33 R5 Kittendorf E Germany
95 R3 Kittery Maine
29 L4 Kittilä Finland
112 M1 Kitty Hawk N Carolina
88 G2 Kitui Kenya
88 D5 Kitunda Tanzania
117 J8 Kitwanga Br Col
88 B8 Kitwe-Nkana Zambia
38 F7 Kitzbühler Alpen mts Austria
37 J4 Kitzingen W Germany
27 M10 Kiukainen Finland
116 L7 Kiukpalik I Alaska
86 E7 Kiumbi Zaïre
29 M8 Kiuruvesi Finland
116 A4 Kivak U.S.S.R.
116 E3 Kivalina Alaska
116 E3 Kividlo Alaska
29 L8 Kivijärvi Finland
27 G17 Kivik Sweden
52 C5 Kiviõli U.S.S.R.
46 E4 Kivotós Greece
88 B2 Kivu, Lac Zaire/Rwanda
145 D4 Kiwi New Zealand
56 C3 Kiya R U.S.S.R.
55 E6 Kiyakty, Oz L U.S.S.R.
61 O14 Kiyan Okinawa
61 O14 Kiyan-zaki C Okinawa
54 B6 Kiyev U.S.S.R.
55 F5 Kiyevka U.S.S.R.
54 B5 Kiyevskoy Vdkr res U.S.S.R.
47 L5 Kıyır R Turkey
118 H7 Kiyiu L Sask
55 E5 Kiyma U.S.S.R.
52 J5 Kizel U.S.S.R.
52 F4 Kizema U.S.S.R.
47 K4 Kızıl Adalar islds Turkey
47 K7 Kızılcabölük Turkey
47 K7 Kızılcadağ Turkey
47 K8 Kızılca Dağ mt Turkey
78 D1 Kizilcahamam Turkey
47 K7 Kızılhişar Turkey
78 E2 Kizil Irmak R Turkey
77 G2 Kizil Islam Afghanistan
47 L7 Kızılkaya Turkey
55 C5 Kizil'skoye U.S.S.R.
56 D4 Kizir R U.S.S.R.
53 G11 Kizlyar U.S.S.R.
26 M2 Kjaekan Norway
28 C4 Kjellerup Denmark
26 P1 Kjelvik Norway
26 G4 Kjerringöy Norway
26 Q1 Kjöllefjord Norway
71 J4 Klabat mt Sulawesi
48 E6 Kladanj Yugoslavia
30 H5 Kladno Czechoslovakia
48 H6 Kladovo Yugoslavia
37 O4 Kladruby Czechoslovakia
70 E2 Klagan Sabah
38 K8 Klagenfurt Austria
103 P6 Klagetoh Arizona
27 M16 Klaipeda U.S.S.R.
52 B6 Klaipėda U.S.S.R.
28 D5 Klakring Denmark
28 O9 Klaksvig Faeroes
100 A8 Klamath California
100 B8 Klamath R California
100 D7 Klamath Falls Oregon
100 B8 Klamath Mts California
100 C8 Klamath River California
71 C3 Klamono W Irian
117 J7 Klappan R Br Col
27 F12 Klarä R Sweden
27 F11 Klarabro Sweden
27 F11 Klaräiven R Sweden
37 P3 Klášterec Czechoslovakia
70 N9 Klaten Java
37 P5 Klatovy Czechoslovakia
38 O5 Klausen-Leopoldsdorf Austria
41 J4 Klausen P mt Switzerland
117 G8 Klawak Alaska
31 K3 Kłecko Poland
31 L3 Kleczew Poland
122 J3 Kleczkowski L Quebec
117 L10 Kleena Kleene Br Col
101 S5 Kleenburn Wyoming
33 S5 Kleeth E Germany
25 F5 Klefe W Germany
79 F4 Kleiat Lebanon
101 R3 Klein Montana
33 P6 Kleinberge E Germany
22 J1 Kleine-Brogel Belgium
33 S9 Kleine Elster R E Germany
32 J9 Kleinenberg W Germany
22 H1 Kleine Nete R Belgium
33 R8 Klein Kreutz E Germany
37 N6 Klein Laaber R W Germany
36 F2 Klein Linden W Germany
89 B9 Klein Roggeveld Berge mts S Africa
89 B9 Klein Swartberge mts S Africa
33 N5 Klein Thurow E Germany
33 Q8 Klein Wusterwitz E Germany
38 N6 Klein Zell Austria
28 D3 Klejtrup Denmark
42 H4 Klekovača mt Yugoslavia
99 N6 Klemme Iowa
22 E1 Klemskerke Belgium
117 J9 Klemtu Br Col
48 F6 Klenak Yugoslavia
33 N7 Klenze W Germany
89 E6 Klerksdorp S Africa
116 G3 Klery Creek Alaska
54 E3 Kletnya U.S.S.R.
53 F9 Kletskiy U.S.S.R.
41 H2 Klettgau R W Germany
33 T9 Klettwitz E Germany
100 D3 Klickitat R Washington
79 E3 Klidhes Is Cyprus
33 Q7 Klietz E Germany
28 C2 Klim Denmark
31 N5 Klimontów Poland
54 C3 Klimovichi U.S.S.R.
52 H5 Klimovka U.S.S.R.
54 D4 Klimovo U.S.S.R.
54 J1 Klimovsk U.S.S.R.
26 G6 Klimpfjäll Sweden
54 H1 Klin U.S.S.R.
117 L10 Klinaklini R Br Col
112 F4 Kline S Carolina
71 G8 Kling Mindanao Philippines
37 Q2 Klingenberg E Germany
36 G4 Klingenberg W Germany
36 D5 Klingenmünster W Germany
37 N3 Klingenthal E Germany
70 B4 Klingkang Ra Sarawak
41 H2 Klingnau W Germany
33 R6 Klink E Germany
37 O3 Klínovec mt Czechoslovakia
28 E5 Klinte Denmark
27 K14 Klintehamn Sweden
54 D4 Klintsy U.S.S.R.
47 H5 Klió Greece
27 F15 Klippan Sweden
89 A8 Kliprug Berg mt S Africa
47 G2 Klisura Bulgaria
28 B2 Klitmøller Denmark
28 B7 Klixbüll W Germany
42 H4 Ključ Yugoslavia
31 L5 Kłobuck Poland
121 M6 Klock Ontario
33 U6 Klockow E Germany
31 L3 Kłodawa Poland
31 K5 Kłodzko Poland
27 E11 Klöfta Norway
103 H7 Klondike California
25 B6 Kloosterzande Netherlands
46 D3 Klos Albania
41 L3 Kloster R Austria
33 S7 Klosterfelde E Germany
28 A4 Klosterhede Plantage Denmark
41 M3 Klösterle Austria
33 Q6 Kloster Malchow E Germany
33 O9 Kloster Mansfeld E Germany
31 J7 Klosterneuburg Austria
36 E6 Klosterreichenbach W Germany
41 L4 Klosters Switzerland
33 S8 Kloster Zinna E Germany
27 H12 Kloten Sweden
36 C3 Klotten W Germany
33 O7 Klötze E Germany
28 C5 Klovborg Denmark
26 G9 Klövsjö Sweden
117 D5 Kluane Yukon Terr
117 D5 Kluane Nat. Park Yukon Terr
69 F14 Kluang Sumatra
31 L5 Kluczbork Poland
70 E6 Klumpeng, Teluk B Kalimantan
25 C5 Klundert Netherlands
70 P10 Klungkung Indonesia
36 C1 Kluppelberg W Germany
116 P6 Klutina L Alaska
26 L7 Klutmark Sweden
33 O5 Klütz E Germany
71 L9 Kluwang Indonesia
52 H7 Klyavlino U.S.S.R.
52 F6 Klyazma R U.S.S.R.
52 F2 Klyuchevaya U.S.S.R.
55 D2 Klyuchi U.S.S.R.
55 G4 Klyuchi U.S.S.R.
27 B13 Knabengruber Norway
38 J7 Knallstein, Gross mt Austria
99 O5 Knapp Wisconsin
13 G5 Knaresborough England
13 F4 Knarsdale England
37 M2 Knau E Germany
9 F4 Knebworth England
32 H5 Knechtsand sandbank W Germany
118 K3 Knee L Sask
33 N7 Knesebeck W Germany
22 E1 Knesselare Belgium
37 K4 Knetsgau W Germany
117 L9 Knewstubb L Br Col
47 G1 Knezha Bulgaria
98 D2 Knife R N Dakota
116 K7 Knife Pk Alaska
99 P3 Knife River Minnesota
101 P8 Knight Wyoming
116 O6 Knight I Alaska
117 K10 Knight Inlet Br Col
8 C3 Knighton Wales
94 B7 Knightstown Indiana
110 J2 Knightsville Indiana
42 G4 Knin Yugoslavia
32 H5 Kniphausen W Germany
109 H6 Knippa Texas
38 L7 Knittelfeld Austria
27 J12 Knivsta Sweden
46 E1 Knjaževac Yugoslavia
110 F5 Knobel Arkansas
142 G2 Knob Pk W Australia
14 B5 Knockboy mt Irish Rep
14 B5 Knockbrack mt Irish Rep
14 E1 Knocklayd mt N Ireland
14 D4 Knockmealdown Mts Irish Rep
14 B5 Knockowen mt Irish Rep
22 E1 Knokke Belgium
29 O5 Knolayarvi U.S.S.R.
101 M9 Knolls Utah
29 L10 Knorevesi Finland
28 E2 Knøsen hill Denmark
47 G9 Knossos Crete Greece
108 F3 Knott Texas
9 E3 Knowle England
107 K5 Knowles Oklahoma
121 S7 Knowlton Quebec
99 R5 Knowlton Wisconsin
99 U8 Knox Indiana
98 G1 Knox N Dakota
94 H5 Knox Pennsylvania
117 G8 Knox, C Graham I, Br Col
110 E1 Knox City Missouri
108 H2 Knox City Texas
146 F2 Knox Coast Antarctica
102 B3 Knoxville California
99 Q9 Knoxville Illinois
99 N8 Knoxville Iowa
111 E10 Knoxville Mississippi
94 K5 Knoxville Pennsylvania
112 C1 Knoxville Tennessee
83 K10 Knuckles mt Sri Lanka
115 R4 Knud Rasmussens Land Greenland
28 H6 Knudshoved C Denmark
36 G2 Knüllwald W Germany
8 D1 Knutsford England
52 D2 Knyazhaya Guba U.S.S.R.
52 F5 Knyazhevo U.S.S.R.
87 D12 Knysna S Africa
31 O2 Knyszyn Poland
29 M2 Koarvikods mt Finland
69 H14 Koba Indonesia
60 D14 Koba Japan
28 H6 Kobanke hill Denmark
42 F2 Kobarid Yugoslavia
60 D13 Kobayashi Japan
115 P5 Kobbermine Bugt B Greenland
28 C3 Kobberup Denmark
Kobdo Jargalant see Hovd
71 A2 Kobe Halmahera Indonesia
60 J11 Kōbe Japan
28 G7 Købelev Denmark
54 F7 Kobelyaki U.S.S.R.
89 A8 Kobe Mts S Africa
28 K5 København Denmark
38 H5 Kobernausser Wald reg Austria
36 C3 Kobern-Gondorf W Germany
67 H4 Kōbi-sho isld Japan
36 D3 Koblenz W Germany
86 F4 Kobowem Swamp Sudan
52 E5 Kobozha R U.S.S.R.
52 H5 Kobra R U.S.S.R.
61 M10 Kobuchizawa Japan
116 J3 Kobuk Alaska
116 H3 Kobuk R Alaska
31 K4 Kobylin Poland
47 K8 Koca R Turkey
47 J4 Kocabaş R Turkey
46 E3 Kočani Yugoslavia
47 J7 Koçarlı Turkey
47 L6 Koca Tepe mt Turkey
48 F6 Koceljevo Yugoslavia
42 F3 Kočevje Yugoslavia
73 R6 Ko Chang isld Thailand
52 F4 Kochen'ga U.S.S.R.
36 H5 Kocher R W Germany
54 M4 Kochetovka U.S.S.R.
52 H5 Kochevo U.S.S.R.
60 F11 Kōchi Japan
60 G12 Kōchi Japan
115 M4 Koch I N W Terr
60 G12 Kōchi prefect Japan
61 P14 Kochinda Okinawa
52 D3 Kochkoma U.S.S.R.
57 H4 Kochkorka U.S.S.R.
52 K2 Kochmes U.S.S.R.
101 O4 Koch Mt Montana
31 K4 Kocie Góry mts Poland
31 N4 Kock Poland
33 O7 Köckte E Germany
48 E4 Kocsola Hungary
52 J3 Kodachdikost U.S.S.R.
76 C5 Kodaikanal India
60 O4 Kodamari misaki C Japan
75 L6 Kodarma India
83 L9 Koddiyar B Sri Lanka
31 O4 Kodeń Poland
116 L8 Kodiak Alaska
116 L8 Kodiak I Alaska
83 K8 Kodikamam Sri Lanka
52 F4 Kodima U.S.S.R.
74 D8 Kodinar India
52 E3 Kodino U.S.S.R.
86 F4 Kodok Sudan
60 O4 Kodomari Japan
48 M2 Kodyma U.S.S.R.
22 D1 Koekelare Belgium
22 J1 Koersel Belgium
87 C11 Koes Namibia
60 P1 Koetoi Japan
103 L8 Kofa Mts Arizona
37 N6 Köfering W Germany
87 E11 Koffiefontein S Africa
71 C3 Kofiau isld W Irian
85 D7 Koforidua Ghana
61 M10 Kōfu Japan
61 N9 Koga Japan
141 K7 Kogan Queensland
28 J6 Køge Denmark
28 K6 Køge Bugt B Denmark
52 J3 Kogel' R U.S.S.R.
48 M4 Kogilnik R U.S.S.R.
116 H6 Kogrukluk R Alaska
60 D11 Kogushi Japan
74 D2 Kohat Pakistan
52 B5 Kohila U.S.S.R.
75 Q6 Kohima India
68 G6 Koh Ker Cambodia
146 H11 Kohler Ra Antarctica
37 O1 Kohren Sahlis E Germany
77 G2 Kohsun Afghanistan
68 F7 Koh Tang isld Cambodia
52 C5 Kohtla-Järve U.S.S.R.
47 K8 Kohu Dağ mt Turkey
145 E3 Kohuratahi New Zealand
61 M8 Koide Japan
114 E5 Koidern Yukon Terr
69 A8 Koihoa Nicobar Is
52 H3 Koin R U.S.S.R.
78 K3 Koi Sanjaq Iraq
29 P8 Koitere L Finland
29 L5 Koivu Finland
65 G7 Kōje isld S Korea
31 K6 Kojetín Czechoslovakia
60 N4 Ko jima isld Japan
143 B10 Kojonup W Australia
86 G4 Koka Dam Ethiopia
95 S1 Kokadjo Maine
83 L10 Kokagala mt Sri Lanka
55 D6 Kokalaat U.S.S.R.
57 F4 Kokand U.S.S.R.
117 P11 Kokanee Glacier Nat. Park Br Col
57 B2 Kokaral U.S.S.R.
48 F2 Kokava Czechoslovakia
60 J11 Kokawa Japan
57 D5 Kokayty U.S.S.R.
57 F6 Kokcha R Afghanistan
55 E4 Kokchetav U.S.S.R.
29 K10 Kokemäenjoki R Finland
29 J10 Kokemäki Finland
54 A2 Kokhanovo U.S.S.R.
80 B7 Kokhav Israel
29 K8 Kokkola Finland
85 E6 Koko Nigeria
136 K3 Kokoda Papua New Guinea
102 S12 Koko Head Hawaiian Is
116 F2 Kokolik R Alaska
94 A6 Kokomo Indiana
136 H2 Kokonau W Irian
144 C6 Kokonga New Zealand
Koko Nor see Qinghai Hu
52 C4 Kokonselka L Finland
54 F4 Kokorevka U.S.S.R.
69 B11 Kokos isld Indonesia
116 K4 Kokrines Hills Alaska
57 E4 Koksaray U.S.S.R.
66 B3 Kok Shaal Tau mts U.S.S.R.
52 G6 Kokshaga R U.S.S.R.
52 F4 Kokshen'ga R U.S.S.R.
22 D1 Koksijde Belgium
115 N6 Koksoak R Quebec
54 M8 Koksovyy U.S.S.R.
89 F8 Kokstad S Africa
60 D14 Kokubu Japan
60 D12 Kokura Japan
70 G7 Koku, Tg C Sulawesi
116 H7 Kokwok R Alaska
57 G4 Kok-Yangak U.S.S.R.
52 D1 Kola U.S.S.R.
70 G7 Kolaka Sulawesi
71 F6 Kolambugan Mindanao Philippines
139 K1 Kolan Queensland
141 K6 Kolan R Queensland
76 D4 Kolar India
76 D4 Kolar Gold Fields India
29 K4 Kolari Finland
Kolarovgrad Bulgaria see Shumen
48 D3 Kolárovo Czechoslovakia
26 F8 Kolåsen Sweden
46 D2 Kolašin Yugoslavia
27 H12 Kolbäck Sweden
71 M10 Kolbano Timor
Kolberg see Kołobrzeg
38 H8 Kölbnitz Austria
26 D9 Kolbotn Norway
31 N5 Kolbuszowa Poland
28 F5 Kolby Denmark
52 E6 Kol'chugino U.S.S.R.
85 A6 Kolda Senegal
28 B3 Koldby Denmark
28 C6 Kolding Denmark
86 E5 Kole Zaïre
135 T3 Kolekole peak Hawaiian Is
37 P5 Koleveč Czechoslovakia
52 B5 Kolga laht G U.S.S.R.
50 D2 Kolguyev Ostrov isld U.S.S.R.
76 B2 Kolhapur India
29 O8 Koli Finland
48 L5 Kolibash U.S.S.R.
116 J7 Koliganek Alaska
31 J5 Kolín Czechoslovakia
101 Q2 Kolin Montana
28 F4 Kolind Denmark
37 P5 Kolinec Czechoslovakia
28 C4 Kølkær Denmark
33 T7 Kol Kienitz E Germany
121 N7 Kol. Kienitz Ontario
37 L1 Kölleda E Germany
28 N2 Kollefjord Faeroes
76 C4 Kollegal India
46 E7 Kollínai Greece
25 F2 Kollum Netherlands
28 C4 Kollund Ringkøbing Denmark
28 C7 Kollund Sønderjylland Denmark
36 B2 Köln W Germany
31 N2 Kolno Poland
31 L3 Koło Poland
135 O1 Koloa Hawaiian Is
31 J1 Kołobrzeg Poland
33 S9 Kolochau E Germany
54 D2 Kolodnya U.S.S.R.
52 F5 Kologriv U.S.S.R.
71 B3 Kolok Indonesia
85 C6 Kolokani Mali
137 M3 Kolombangara isld Solomon Is
54 K1 Kolomna U.S.S.R.
48 J2 Kolomyya U.S.S.R.
141 K6 Kolonga Queensland
70 G6 Kolono Sulawesi
70 G6 Kolonodale Sulawesi
71 B2 Kolorai isld Halmahera Indonesia
55 F3 Kolosovka U.S.S.R.
Kolozsvar see Cluj
52 E5 Kolp' R U.S.S.R.
56 B2 Kolpashevo U.S.S.R.
33 R6 Kölpin-See L E Germany
33 Q10 Kölsa E Germany
26 G9 Kolsätt Sweden
52 D1 Kol'skiy Poluostrov pen U.S.S.R.
52 D1 Kol'skiy Zaliv gulf U.S.S.R.
28 F6 Kølstrup Denmark
27 H12 Kolsva Sweden
28 N2 Kolter Faeroes
52 A3 Kol'tsovo U.S.S.R.
48 F6 Kolubara R Yugoslavia
145 D1 Koluikohu New Zealand
73 L8 Kolumadulu Atoll Maldives
31 M4 Koluszki Poland
55 E5 Koluton U.S.S.R.
52 J1 Kolva R Komi U.S.S.R.
52 J4 Kolva R Perm U.S.S.R.
26 E7 Kolvereid Norway
26 O1 Kolvik Norway
52 D2 Kolvitsa U.S.S.R.
87 E8 Kolwezi Zaïre
54 K1 Kolyberovo U.S.S.R.
54 H1 Kolyubakino U.S.S.R.
147 P2 Kolyuchinskaya U.S.S.R.
116 A3 Kolyuchinskaya Guba gulf U.S.S.R.
56 B5 Kolyvan' U.S.S.R.
27 G14 Kölzby Sweden
46 F1 Kom mt Bulgaria
68 D5 Koma Burma
86 G4 Koma Ethiopia
61 P6 Kōma Japan
85 G6 Komadugu Gana R Nigeria
61 L10 Komagane Japan
60 O3 Komaga-take mt Hokkaido Japan
61 N8 Komaga-take mt Honshu Japan
26 N1 Komagfjord Norway
26 S1 Komagvaer Norway
48 E3 Komárno Czechoslovakia
119 U8 Komarno Manitoba
48 E3 Komárom Hungary
48 E3 Komárom co Hungary
89 G6 Komati R Swaziland
89 G5 Komati Poort S Africa
103 M8 Komatke Arizona
61 K9 Komatsu Ishikawa Japan
61 O7 Komatsu Yamagata Japan
71 L8 Komba isld Indonesia
46 E5 Kombóti Greece
28 E3 Komdrup Denmark
88 D2 Kome I Uganda
61 O5 Kominato Japan
48 E2 Komjatice Czechoslovakia
48 E4 Komló Hungary
53 E9 Kommunarsk U.S.S.R.
57 F5 Kommunizma, Pik mt U.S.S.R.
71 J9 Komodo isld Indonesia
85 D7 Komoé R Ivory Coast
84 J5 Kôm Ombo Egypt
61 M9 Komoro Japan
47 G3 Komotiní Greece
46 D2 Komovi mt Yugoslavia
89 D8 Kompas Berg mt S Africa
68 G7 Kompong Cham Cambodia
68 G6 Kompong Chhnang Cambodia
68 G6 Kompong Kleang Cambodia
68 F7 Kompong Som Cambodia
68 G7 Kompong Speu Cambodia
68 G6 Kompong Sralao Cambodia
68 G6 Kompong Thom Cambodia
68 G6 Kompong Trabek Cambodia
68 G7 Kompong Trach Cambodia
68 G7 Kompong Tralach Cambodia
71 J4 Kompot Sulawesi
48 M4 Komrat U.S.S.R.
89 B9 Komsbergeskarp mts S Africa
55 D4 Komsomolets U.S.S.R.
51 J1 Komsomolets, Ostrov isld U.S.S.R.
54 E8 Komsomol'sk Ukraine U.S.S.R.
52 F6 Komsomol'sk U.S.S.R.
55 D1 Komsomol'skiy U.S.S.R.
54 K9 Komsomol'skoye U.S.S.R.
59 L1 Komsomol'skoye-na-Amure U.S.S.R.
103 M10 Kom Vo Arizona
52 E6 Konakovo U.S.S.R.
77 B5 Konār Takhteh Iran
109 L1 Konawa Oklahoma
42 H3 Končanica Yugoslavia
71 C3 Konda W Irian

55 E2 Konda R U.S.S.R.
76 E1 Kondagaon India
121 O6 Kondiaronk, L Quebec
143 C10 Kondinin W Australia
88 E4 Kondoa Tanzania
52 D4 Kondopoga U.S.S.R.
48 F4 Kondoros Hungary
54 G2 Kondrovo U.S.S.R.
86 B3 Konduga Nigeria
143 B9 Kondut W Australia
56 D2 Konduyak U.S.S.R.
52 J3 Konetsbor U.S.S.R.
52 E4 Konevo U.S.S.R.
28 H6 Køng Denmark
85 D7 Kong Ivory Coast
116 R2 Kongakut R Alaska
115 Q4 Kong Christian den IX Land Greenland
115 R3 Kong Christian den X Land Greenland
28 B6 Kongeå R Denmark
28 K5 Kongens Lyngby Denmark
115 P5 Kong Frederik den VI Kyst coast Greenland
29 M9 Konginkangas Finland
68 F7 Kong Kaôh Kong Cambodia
50 B1 Kong Karls Land isld Spitzbergen
70 E4 Kong Kat mt Kalimantan
70 E4 Kongkemul mt Kalimantan
70 G6 Kongkong R Sulawesi
87 D9 Kongola Namibia
86 E7 Kongolo Zaïre
86 F4 Kongor Sudan
147 E10 Kong Oscars Fj Greenland
26 J3 Kongsbakktind mt Norway
27 D12 Kongsberg Norway
26 R1 Kongsfjord Norway
26 R1 Kongsfjord inlet Norway
28 B6 Kongsmark Denmark
26 F7 Kongsmoen Norway
28 J6 Kongsted Denmark
27 E11 Kongsvinger Norway
66 B4 Kongur Shan mt China
88 F5 Kongwa Tanzania
31 M5 Koniecpol Poland
36 H4 Königheim W Germany
36 F6 Königsbach W Germany
Königsberg see Kaliningrad
36 D4 Königsberg mt W Germany
37 J6 Königsbronn W Germany
33 T10 Königsbrück E Germany
37 K7 Königsbrunn W Germany
41 O2 Königsdorf W Germany
37 L2 Königsee E Germany
37 L4 Königsfeld W Germany
Königshofen see Lauda-Königshofen
36 H4 Königshofen W Germany
33 N8 Königslutter W Germany
36 F5 Königsstuhl mt W Germany
36 E3 Königstein W Germany
38 L5 Königswiesen Austria
36 C2 Königswinter W Germany
33 T8 Königs Wusterhausen E Germany
31 L3 Konin Poland
145 E4 Konini New Zealand
46 D5 Konispol Albania
42 H5 Konjic Yugoslavia
48 E6 Konjuh mt Yugoslavia
26 M3 Konkämä Älv R Sweden/Finland
88 A8 Konkola Zambia
85 B6 Konkouré R Guinea
33 P9 Könnern E Germany
37 N3 Konnersreuth W Germany
29 M9 Konnevesi Finland
85 D7 Konongo Ghana
88 C5 Konongo Tanzania
61 N9 Kōnosu Japan
54 E5 Konotop U.S.S.R.
66 D3 Konqi He R China
85 C7 Konsankoro Guinea
31 M4 Końskie Poland
53 F10 Konstantinovsk U.S.S.R.
41 K2 Konstanz W Germany
85 F6 Kontagora Nigeria
86 B4 Kontcha Cameroon
22 G1 Kontich Belgium
29 N7 Kontiomäki Finland
116 L6 Kontrashibuna L Alaska
68 J6 Kontum, Plat. du Vietnam
52 F2 Konushinskaya Korga C U.S.S.R.
78 D3 Konya Turkey
36 B4 Konz W Germany
88 F2 Konza Kenya
37 O5 Konzell W Germany
55 C2 Konzhakovskiy Kamen', G mt U.S.S.R.
25 C4 Koog Netherlands
116 C5 Kookooligit Mts St Lawrence I, Alaska
143 D8 Kookynie W Australia
140 F5 Koolamarra Queensland
141 F3 Koolatah Queensland
140 D2 Koolatong R N Terr Australia
102 S11 Koolauloa Hawaiian Is
102 S12 Koolaupoko Hawaiian Is
141 G3 Koolburra Queensland
142 B6 Kooline W Australia
140 E6 Koolivoo,L Queensland
143 C9 Koolyanobbing W Australia
143 G9 Koonalda S Australia
141 G3 Koorboora Queensland
143 B9 Koorda W Australia
142 B5 Koordarrie W Australia
144 A7 Kopeka B New Zealand
33 T8 Kopenick E Germany
26 K8 Köpmanholmen Sweden
27 F10 Kopparberg county Sweden
145 E2 Kopu New Zealand
145 E4 Kopuaranga New Zealand
77 C4 Kor R Iran
75 K7 Korba India
32 J10 Korbach W Germany
100 B9 Korbel California
69 E10 Korbu, G. mt Malaysia
46 D4 Korcë Albania
42 H6 Korčula Yugoslavia
36 B4 Kordel W Germany
77 A2 Kordestan Iran
77 D1 Kord Küv Iran
Kordofan prov Sudan see Northern and Southern Kordofan provs
77 G6 Kords reg Iran
59 H4 Korea Bay China/Korea
65 G4 Korea, North rep E Asia
65 H6 Korea, South rep E Asia
52 D2 Korelaksha U.S.S.R.
54 F5 Korenevo U.S.S.R.
26 G5 Korgen Norway
85 C7 Korhogo Ivory Coast
60 D14 Kori Japan
46 F4 Korinós Greece
28 E6 Korinth Denmark
46 E6 Korinthiakós Kólpos gulf Greece
46 F7 Kórinthos Greece
46 D2 Koritnik mt Yugoslavia
Koritsa see Korcë
61 O8 Kōriyama Japan
55 D4 Korkino U.S.S.R.
47 L7 Korkuteli Turkey
54 B3 Korma U.S.S.R.
120 G5 Kormak Ontario
48 D3 Körmend Hungary
55 F3 Kormilovka U.S.S.R.
42 G5 Kornat isld Yugoslavia
37 L5 Kornburg W Germany
25 F7 Kornelimünster W Germany
37 K1 Körner E Germany
48 L3 Korneshty U.S.S.R.
55 E4 Korneyevka U.S.S.R.
55 F5 Korneyevka U.S.S.R.
27 E13 Kornsjö Norway
28 C3 Kornum Denmark
36 G6 Kornwestheim W Germany
70 G5 Koro R Sulawesi
55 G6 Korobovskiy U.S.S.R.
54 J6 Korocha U.S.S.R.
78 C1 Köroglu D Turkey
88 G4 Korogwe Tanzania
138 F7 Koroit Victoria
113 F8 Korona Florida
85 E7 Koronga mt Togo
139 G6 Korong Vale Victoria
46 E8 Koróni Greece
47 F4 Korónia, L Greece
31 K2 Koronowo Poland
54 D5 Korop U.S.S.R.
48 J2 Koropets U.S.S.R.
47 F7 Koropí Greece
48 F4 Körös R Hungary
53 C8 Korosten U.S.S.R.
86 C2 Koro Toro Chad
54 L6 Korotoyak U.S.S.R.
116 G9 Korovin I Alaska
29 M9 Korpilahti Finland
26 N5 Korpilombolo Sweden
29 J11 Korpo Finland
59 M2 Korsakov U.S.S.R.
27 H14 Korsberga Sweden
36 B1 Korschenbroich W Germany
28 H5 Korshage C Denmark
48 J2 Korshev U.S.S.R.
28 E3 Korsholm isld Denmark
27 H11 Korsnäs Sweden
26 H3 Korsnes Norway
28 G6 Korsør Denmark
54 C7 Korsun' Shevchenkovskiy U.S.S.R.
22 E1 Kortemark Belgium
29 K8 Kortesjärvi Finland
22 J2 Kortessem Belgium
27 G12 Kortfors Sweden
25 A5 Kortgene Netherlands
52 H4 Kortkeros U.S.S.R.
22 E2 Kortrijk Belgium
52 F5 Kortsovo U.S.S.R.
47 J5 Korucu Turkey
47 H4 Koru Dağı mt Turkey
139 H7 Korumburra Victoria
29 O3 Korvatunturi mt Finland
29 O4 Korya U.S.S.R.
52 G4 Koryazhma U.S.S.R.
54 D5 Koryukovka U.S.S.R.
47 J8 Kos isld Greece
52 H5 Kosa U.S.S.R.
55 D5 Kosagal U.S.S.R.
61 O5 Kosaka Japan
73 R7 Ko Samui isld Thailand
57 D1 Kosay U.S.S.R.
54 J2 Kosaya Gora U.S.S.R.
56 E2 Kosaya, Shiv U.S.S.R.
57 C4 Kosboget U.S.S.R.
37 M6 Kösching W Germany
31 K3 Kościan Poland
31 K1 Kościerzyna Poland
111 G8 Kosciusko Mississippi
117 G7 Kosciusko I Alaska
139 J6 Kosciusko, Mt Victoria
33 S10 Koselitz E Germany
33 U4 Koserow E Germany
56 B1 Koses R U.S.S.R.
76 C2 Kosgi India
56 C6 Kosh Agach U.S.S.R.
55 D2 Koshay U.S.S.R.
60 S2 Koshikawa Japan
60 C14 Koshiki-kaikyō str Japan
60 C14 Koshiki-rettō islds Japan
110 E5 Koshkonong Missouri
57 B4 Kosh-Kupyr U.S.S.R.
61 M9 Koshoku Japan
48 G2 Košice Czechoslovakia
89 H6 Kosi L S Africa
55 C5 Kos-Istek U.S.S.R.
48 E5 Koška Yugoslavia
123 R6 Koskaecodde L Nfld
29 K11 Koski Finland
26 M5 Koskivaara Sweden
57 D1 Koskol' U.S.S.R.
57 H3 Koskuduk U.S.S.R.
26 L4 Koskullskulle Sweden
52 G3 Koslan U.S.S.R.
Köslin see Koszalin
52 G2 Kosma R U.S.S.R.
48 J2 Kosmach U.S.S.R.
100 C3 Kosmos Washington
59 J4 Kosŏng N Korea
48 J2 Kosov U.S.S.R.
46 E2 Kosovo Yugoslavia
46 D2 Kosovska Mitrovica Yugoslavia
33 S10 Kossdorf E Germany
109 L4 Kosse Texas
33 P9 Kössein E Germany
37 O1 Kössern E Germany
37 P7 Kösslarn W Germany
31 N3 Kossów Poland
27 H15 Kosta Sweden
52 D3 Kostamus U.S.S.R.
33 T9 Kostebrau E Germany
28 J7 Koster Denmark
54 L1 Kosterevo U.S.S.R.
86 F3 Kosti Sudan
52 F5 Kostroma U.S.S.R.
54 D3 Kostyukovichi U.S.S.R.
54 B4 Kostyukovka U.S.S.R.
61 L9 Kosugi Japan
50 H2 Kosuno U.S.S.R.
52 J2 Kos'yu U.S.S.R.
52 J2 Kos'yuvom U.S.S.R.
31 J1 Koszalin Poland
48 D3 Köszeg Hungary
75 K7 Kota India
70 K8 Kotaagung Sumatra
70 B5 Kotabaharu Kalimantan
69 F9 Kota Baharu Malaysia
69 E13 Kota Baru Sumatra
70 E1 Kota Belud Sabah
70 K8 Kotabumi Sumatra
71 J4 Kotabunan Sulawesi
70 E2 Kota Kinabalu Sabah
29 O4 Kotala Finland
71 J4 Kotamobagu Sulawesi
76 F1 Kotapad India
69 E12 Kotapinang Baru Sumatra
69 E12 Kotatengah Sumatra
69 F12 Kota Tinggi Malaysia
70 B6 Kotawaringin Kalimantan
117 N6 Kotcho R Br Col
47 H2 Kotel Bulgaria
53 F9 Kotel'nikovo U.S.S.R.
51 N1 Kotel'nyy, Ostrov isld U.S.S.R.
145 F3 Kotemaori New Zealand
33 P9 Köthen E Germany
74 F3 Kot Kapura India
52 H2 Kotkino U.S.S.R.
55 G2 Kotkino U.S.S.R.
52 G4 Kotlas U.S.S.R.
29 O11 Kotlin, O isld U.S.S.R.
52 C5 Kotly U.S.S.R.
60 G11 Kotohira Japan
60 P2 Kotoni Japan
42 J6 Kotor Yugoslavia
42 H4 Kotor Varoš Yugoslavia
53 C10 Kotovsk U.S.S.R.
74 C6 Kotri Pakistan
57 A1 Kotr-Tas U.S.S.R.
38 H8 Kötschach Austria
74 J10 Kottagudem India
75 K10 Kottakota India
76 C6 Kottayam India
83 J11 Kotte Sri Lanka
86 D4 Kotto R Cent Afr Republic
26 H8 Köttsjön Sweden
76 C3 Kotturu India
51 K1 Kotuy R U.S.S.R.
48 M3 Kotyuzhany U.S.S.R.
116 F3 Kotzebue Alaska
116 E3 Kotzebue Sd Alaska
37 Q1 Kötzschenbroda E Germany
37 O5 Kötzting W Germany
85 E6 Kouandé Benin
86 D4 Kouango Cent Afr Republic
86 C2 Kouba Modounga Chad
85 D6 Koudougou Upper Volta
89 A9 Koue Bokkeveld reg S Africa
89 D8 Koueveld Berge mts S Africa
47 H10 Koufonísi isld Crete Greece
47 H8 Koufonisia isld Greece
89 C9 Kougaberge mts S Africa
7 L9 Kough oil rig North Sea
86 B6 Koulamoutou Gabon
68 G6 Koulen Cambodia
85 C6 Koulikoro Mali
141 J5 Koumala Queensland
86 C4 Koumra Chad
86 C3 Koungouri Chad
48 C1 Kounice Czechoslovakia
47 H8 Kounoupói isld Greece
57 G2 Kounradskiy U.S.S.R.
111 B11 Kountze Texas
85 D6 Koupela Upper Volta
Kouqian see Yongji
61 Q12 Kouri-jima isld Okinawa
84 F5 Kourizo, Passe de Chad
129 H2 Kourou Fr Guiana
85 C6 Kouroussa Guinea
89 B9 Kousberg mt S Africa
85 C5 Koussa Mauritania
86 B3 Kousséri Cameroon
85 C6 Koutiala Mali
85 C7 Kouto Ivory Coast
46 F7 Koutsopódhi Greece
29 M11 Kouvola Finland
86 C6 Kouyou R Congo
56 F2 Kova R U.S.S.R.
48 F5 Kovačica Yugoslavia
46 C1 Kovač Planina mt Yugoslavia
52 D2 Kovda U.S.S.R.
52 D2 Kovdozero, Oz L U.S.S.R.
55 E1 Kovenskaya R U.S.S.R.
52 F6 Kovernino U.S.S.R.
29 P9 Kovero Finland
48 F6 Kovin Yugoslavia
52 G1 Kovriga, Gora mt U.S.S.R.
54 N1 Kovrov U.S.S.R.
52 E5 Kovzha R U.S.S.R.
52 E4 Kovzhskoye, Oz L U.S.S.R.
144 C5 Kowai Bush New Zealand
31 L3 Kowal Poland
31 L2 Kowalewo Poland
144 C5 Kowhitirangi New Zealand
120 C2 Kowkash Ontario
67 G6 Kowloon Hong Kong
55 G6 Koyandy U.S.S.R.
61 J11 Kōyasan Japan
47 K8 Koyceğiz Turkey
47 J8 Köyceğiz Gölü L Turkey
52 F2 Koyda U.S.S.R.
52 H4 Koygorodok U.S.S.R.
52 G3 Koynas U.S.S.R.
61 O6 Koyoshi-gawa R Japan
52 J4 Koyp, Gora mt U.S.S.R.
54 L9 Koysug U.S.S.R.
57 D4 Koytash U.S.S.R.
116 G4 Koyuk Alaska
116 L3 Koyukuk R Alaska
116 J4 Koyukuk I Alaska
78 F1 Koyulhisar Turkey
55 C2 Koyva R U.S.S.R.
29 P7 Koyvozero U.S.S.R.
61 P13 Koza Okinawa
61 J12 Koza R Japan
47 J5 Kozak Turkey
60 C11 Kō-zaki C Japan
60 G11 Kōzan Japan
78 E3 Kozan Turkey
46 E4 Kozáni Greece
42 H3 Kozara Plan Yugoslavia
48 E2 Kozárovce Czechoslovakia
54 C6 Kozelets U.S.S.R.
54 E7 Kozel'shchina U.S.S.R.
54 G2 Kozel'sk U.S.S.R.
55 E5 Kozhakol', Oz L U.S.S.R.
55 G3 Kozhevnikovo U.S.S.R.
52 J2 Kozhim U.S.S.R.
52 J3 Kozhim-Iz, Gora mt U.S.S.R.
52 J2 Kozhimvom U.S.S.R.
52 E3 Kozhozero, Oz L U.S.S.R.
52 E3 Kozhposelok U.S.S.R.
55 G3 Kozhurla U.S.S.R.
52 J2 Kozhva U.S.S.R.
31 N4 Kozienice Poland
46 E3 Kozjak mt Yugoslavia
31 L5 Koźle Poland
47 G1 Kozlovets Bulgaria
54 M6 Kozlovka U.S.S.R.
78 C1 Kozlu Turkey
31 K4 Koźmin Poland
48 J1 Kozovo U.S.S.R.
31 J4 Kozuchów Poland
61 N11 Kōzu-shima isld Japan
85 D7 Kpandu Ghana
89 E8 Kraai R S Africa
33 O6 Kraak E Germany
25 B6 Krabbendijke Netherlands
69 D8 Krabi Thailand
68 D7 Kra Buri Thailand
37 M2 Kraftsdorf E Germany
70 N9 Kragan Java
28 C4 Kragelund Denmark
28 G7 Kragenæs Denmark
27 D13 Kragerö Norway
48 F6 Kragujevac Yugoslavia
36 G4 Krahenberg W Germany
37 K2 Krahnberg mt E Germany
36 F5 Kraich R W Germany
36 F5 Kraichtal W Germany
73 Q7 Kra, Isthmus of Thailand
Krakatau isld see Rakata I
79 G4 Krak des Chevaliers Syria
26 A9 Kråkenes Norway
68 F6 Krakor Cambodia
48 H1 Krakovets U.S.S.R.
33 Q5 Krakow E Germany
31 M5 Kraków Poland
68 F6 Kralanh Cambodia
48 G2 Král Chlmec Czechoslovakia
31 K5 Králíky Czechoslovakia
46 D1 Kraljevo Vrnjacka Yugoslavia
48 E1 Kralovany Czechoslovakia
37 Q4 Kralovice Czechoslovakia
37 P3 Kralupy Czechoslovakia
98 F1 Kramer N Dakota
26 J9 Kramfors Sweden
68 E6 Kram, Ko isld Thailand
26 S1 Krampenes Norway
25 F5 Kranenburg W Germany
26 H8 Krångede Sweden
46 E5 Kraniá Greece
37 L2 Kranichfeld E Germany
46 F7 Kranídhion Greece
42 F2 Kranj Yugoslavia
38 J9 Kranjska-Gord Yugoslavia
31 K5 Krapkowice Poland
28 K4 Krapperup Sweden
52 G4 Krasavino U.S.S.R.
54 K1 Krashy Oktyabr' U.S.S.R.
48 K1 Krasilov U.S.S.R.
50 E1 Krasino U.S.S.R.
59 K3 Kraskino U.S.S.R.
52 C6 Krāslava U.S.S.R.
37 O3 Kraslice Czechoslovakia
31 N5 Krasnik Poland
37 O3 Krásno Czechoslovakia
55 E4 Krasnoarmeyesk U.S.S.R.
54 J8 Krasnoarmeysk U.S.S.R.
54 K1 Krasnoarmeysk U.S.S.R.
55 D4 Krasnoarmeyskiy Kustanay U.S.S.R.
52 G4 Krasnoborsk U.S.S.R.
31 O5 Krasnobród Poland
53 E11 Krasnodar U.S.S.R.
54 L8 Krasnodon U.S.S.R.
48 J1 Krasnoe U.S.S.R.
52 D5 Krasnofarfornyy U.S.S.R.
52 C6 Krasnogorodskoye U.S.S.R.
59 M2 Krasnogorsk U.S.S.R.
55 D4 Krasnogorskiy Chelyabinsk U.S.S.R.
52 H5 Krasnogorskoye U.S.S.R.
54 G7 Krasnograd U.S.S.R.
55 D3 Krasnogvardeyskiy U.S.S.R.
54 G6 Krasnokutsk U.S.S.R.
55 G4 Krasnokutskoye Pavlodar U.S.S.R.
54 L5 Krasnolesniyy U.S.S.R.
31 N1 Krasnoles'ye U.S.S.R.
52 C4 Krasnoostrovskiy U.S.S.R.
53 F9 Krasnoslobodsk U.S.S.R.
55 D2 Krasnotur'insk U.S.S.R.
55 C3 Krasnoufimsk U.S.S.R.
55 D2 Krasnoural'sk U.S.S.R.
55 C4 Krasnousol'skiy U.S.S.R.
52 J4 Krasnovishersk U.S.S.R.
50 E4 Krasnovodsk U.S.S.R.
55 F3 Krasnoyarka Omsk U.S.S.R.
55 D2 Krasnoyarka Sverdlovsk U.S.S.R.
56 D3 Krasnoyarsk U.S.S.R.
54 M1 Krasnoye Ekho U.S.S.R.
57 B6 Krasnoye Znamya U.S.S.R.
52 H4 Krasnozatonskiy U.S.S.R.
55 G4 Krasnozerskoye U.S.S.R.
55 E5 Krasnoznamenskiy Atbasar U.S.S.R.
55 C4 Krasnoznamenskiy Bashkirskaya U.S.S.R.
52 H6 Krasny Bor U.S.S.R.
48 M3 Krasnye Okny U.S.S.R.
54 J8 Krasny Liman U.S.S.R.
54 K8 Krasny Luch U.S.S.R.
54 N1 Krasny Mayak U.S.S.R.
31 O5 Krasnystaw Poland
54 L1 Krasny Tkach U.S.S.R.
54 C2 Krasnyy U.S.S.R.
52 G6 Krasnyye-Baki U.S.S.R.
52 E5 Krasnyye Tkachi U.S.S.R.
52 E5 Krasnyy Kholm Kalinin U.S.S.R.
55 B5 Krasnyy Kholm Orenburg U.S.S.R.
55 C3 Krasnyy-Klyuch U.S.S.R.
55 D3 Krasnyy Oktyabr U.S.S.R.
52 E5 Krasnyy Pereval U.S.S.R.
55 F3 Krasnyy Yar Omsk U.S.S.R.
55 D2 Krasnyy Yar Sverdlovsk U.S.S.R.
68 H6 Kratie Cambodia
38 L7 Kraubath Austria
41 K1 Krauchenwies W Germany
115 O3 Kraulshavn Greenland
36 H5 Krautheim W Germany
32 K5 Krautsand W Germany
107 P7 Krebs Oklahoma
25 G6 Krefeld W Germany
28 J5 Kregme Denmark
36 F4 Krehberg mt W Germany
32 L9 Kreiensen W Germany
116 D5 Krekatok I Alaska
47 F1 Kremena Bulgaria
54 E7 Kremenchug U.S.S.R.
54 D7 Kremenchugskoye Vdkhr res U.S.S.R.
54 K7 Kremennaya U.S.S.R.
47 F2 Kremikovtsi Bulgaria
101 P1 Kremlin Montana
33 N8 Kremlingen W Germany
33 S7 Kremmen E Germany
106 D1 Kremmling Colorado
32 K5 Krempe W Germany
38 N5 Krems Austria
38 M5 Krems R Austria
116 D9 Krenitzin Is Aleutian Is
33 Q10 Krensitz E Germany
48 E7 Kreševo Yugoslavia
108 F1 Kress Texas
52 D6 Kresti U.S.S.R.
52 H2 Krestovka U.S.S.R.
51 H1 Kresty U.S.S.R.
27 M16 Kretinga U.S.S.R.
41 P2 Kreuth W Germany
36 B2 Kreuzau W Germany
41 O3 Kreuzeck mt W Germany
38 H8 Kreuzeck-Gruppe mts Austria
38 L5 Kreuzen Austria
38 E7 Kreuzjoch mt Austria
41 K2 Kreuzlingen Switzerland
36 E2 Kreuztal W Germany
86 A5 Kribi Cameroon
54 C3 Krichev U.S.S.R.
28 A3 Krik Denmark
28 A3 Krik Vig B Denmark
38 F7 Krimml Austria
38 F7 Krimmler Fälle Austria
38 F7 Krimmler Tal R Austria
26 D10 Kringen Norway
46 E6 Krionéri Greece
47 F9 Kriós, Akr C Crete Greece
76 C2 Krishna R India
76 D4 Krishnagiri India
75 N7 Krishnanagar India
27 H14 Kristdala Sweden
17 G9 Kristel Algeria
27 H15 Kristianopel Sweden
27 C13 Kristiansand Norway
27 G15 Kristianstad Sweden
27 F15 Kristianstad county Sweden
26 C8 Kristiansund Norway
29 J9 Kristiinankaupunki Finland
27 G12 Kristinehamn Sweden
28 E4 Kristrup Denmark
47 G9 Kríti isld Greece
46 E2 Kriva R Yugoslavia
48 E6 Krivaja R Yugoslavia
46 E2 Kriva Palanka Yugoslavia
48 N3 Krivoye Ozero U.S.S.R.
54 E9 Krivoy Rog U.S.S.R.
52 G5 Krivyachka U.S.S.R.
42 F3 Krk Yugoslavia
31 J5 Krkonoše mts Czechoslovakia
31 K5 Krnov Czechoslovakia
31 K4 Krobia Poland
27 D11 Kröderen Norway
28 B5 Krogager Denmark
37 P1 Krögis E Germany
28 E5 Krogsbølle Denmark
69 E10 Kroh Malaysia
37 O6 Kröhstorf W Germany
70 M9 Kroja Java
27 H13 Krokek Sweden
26 G6 Kroken Norway
89 E5 Krokodil R S Africa
26 G8 Krokom Sweden
31 L1 Krokowa Poland
26 J7 Kroksjö Sweden
54 E5 Krolevets U.S.S.R.
36 D2 Krombach W Germany
48 D1 Kroměříž Czechoslovakia
25 D5 Kromme Rijn R Netherlands
37 L3 Kronach W Germany
119 N8 Kronau Sask
36 E3 Kronberg W Germany
37 P3 Krondorf Czechoslovakia
36 B3 Kronenberg W Germany
68 H5 Krong Poko R Vietnam
27 G15 Kronoberg county Sweden
29 K8 Kronoby Finland
146 B10 Kronprinsesse Märtha Kyst Antarctica
115 Q4 Kronprins Frederiks Bjerge mts Greenland
146 A6 Kronprins Olav Kyst Antarctica
29 O12 Kronshtadt U.S.S.R.
68 D5 Kronwa Burma
37 N7 Kronwinkl W Germany
89 E6 Kroonstad S Africa
55 C3 Kropachevo U.S.S.R.
33 P4 Kröpelin E Germany
53 F10 Kropotkin U.S.S.R.
28 K4 Kropp Sweden
33 O9 Kroppenstedt E Germany
33 R9 Kropstädt E Germany
33 T4 Kröslin E Germany
31 L3 Krośniewice Poland
37 M2 Krossen E Germany
31 K4 Krotoszyn Poland
41 O2 Krotten Kopf mt W Germany
111 E11 Krotz Springs Louisiana
46 F3 Kroúsia mt Greece
46 D2 Krrab mt Albania
36 C3 Kruft-Mendig W Germany
89 G4 Kruger Nat. Park S Africa
89 E6 Krugersdorp S Africa
70 K8 Krui Sumatra
22 F2 Kruishoutem Belgium
46 D3 Krujë Albania
109 K2 Krum Texas
38 O6 Krumbach Austria
37 J7 Krumbach W Germany
46 D2 Krume Albania
36 D1 Krummenerl W Germany
32 F6 Krummhörn W Germany
33 T4 Krummin E Germany
47 H3 Krumovgrad Bulgaria
41 O2 Krün W Germany
Krungkao see Ayutthaya
Krung Thep see Bangkok
68 E6 Krung Thep Thailand
48 E6 Krupanj Yugoslavia
48 E2 Krupina Czechoslovakia
116 F3 Krusenstern, C Alaska
46 E1 Kruševac Yugoslavia
Krušné Hory mts see Erzgebirge Mts
46 E3 Kruševo Yugoslavia
52 C6 Krustpils U.S.S.R.
52 H3 Krutaya U.S.S.R.
19 K5 Kruth France
55 D4 Krutoyarskiy U.S.S.R.
117 F7 Kruzof I Alaska
118 K6 Krydor Sask
27 H11 Krylbo Sweden
31 P5 Krylów Poland
53 D10 Krym reg U.S.S.R.
48 F1 Krynica Poland
31 O2 Krynki Poland
37 P3 Kryry Czechoslovakia
54 J1 Kryukovo U.S.S.R.
48 M3 Kryulyany U.S.S.R.
56 E4 Kryzhina, Khr mts U.S.S.R.
48 M2 Kryzhopol U.S.S.R.
31 L5 Krzepice Poland
31 N5 Krzeszów Poland
31 M5 Krzeszowice Poland
31 K4 Krzywin Poland
31 J3 Krzyż Poland
85 D3 Ksabi Algeria
85 C4 Ksaib Ounane, El Mali
85 E1 Ksar el Boukhari Algeria
16 D9 Ksar-el-Kebir Morocco
16 D9 Ksar Sghir Morocco
52 J4 Ksenofontova U.S.S.R.
85 E2 Ksour, Mts. des Algeria
79 C4 Ktima Cyprus
69 D9 Kuah Malaysia
67 A4 Kuaize He R China
69 G11 Kuala Indonesia
69 D11 Kuala Sumatra
69 F10 Kuala Dungun Malaysia
69 E10 Kuala Kangsar Malaysia
69 F10 Kuala Kerai Malaysia
70 C5 Kualakurun Kalimantan
69 C10 Kualalangsa Sumatra
69 F10 Kuala Lipis Malaysia
69 E11 Kuala Lumpur Malaysia
70 C5 Kualamandjual Kalimantan
69 E9 Kuala Nerang Malaysia
70 C6 Kualapembuang Kalimantan
70 D2 Kuala Penyu Sabah
69 F11 Kuala Pilah Malaysia
135 S2 Kualapuu Hawaiian Is
69 E11 Kuala Selangor Malaysia
69 F10 Kuala Terengganu Malaysia
70 E2 Kuamut Sabah
70 E2 Kuamut R Sabah
65 D4 Kuancheng China
71 H4 Kuandang Sulawesi
71 H4 Kuandang, Tk B Sulawesi Indonesia
59 H3 Kuandian China
69 F11 Kuantan Malaysia
145 E2 Kuaotunu New Zealand
87 C10 Kub Namibia
53 G12 Kuba U.S.S.R.
53 F11 Kuban' R U.S.S.R.
78 G4 Kubar, el Syria
26 K8 Kubbe Sweden
86 D3 Kubbum Sudan
52 F4 Kubena R U.S.S.R.
52 E5 Kubenskoye, Oz L U.S.S.R.
52 G6 Kubnya R U.S.S.R.
60 G12 Kubokawa Japan
79 A8 Kubra, El Egypt
47 H1 Kubrat Bulgaria
70 P10 Kubu Indonesia
58 F1 Kubukhay U.S.S.R.
70 D4 Kubumesaäi Kalimantan
55 E4 Kubyshevskiy U.S.S.R.
48 G6 Kučevo Yugoslavia
36 H6 Kuchen W Germany
41 M3 Kuchen Spitze mt Austria
70 B4 Kuching Sarawak
60 D13 Kuchinotsu Japan
60 F10 Kuchitagi Japan
55 G4 Kuchukskoye, Oz L U.S.S.R.
48 M3 Kuchurgan R U.S.S.R.
33 N5 Kücknitz W Germany
47 J6 Küçük Menderes R Turkey
83 K11 Kuda R Sri Lanka
61 P14 Kudaka-jima isld Okinawa
60 E11 Kudamatsu Japan
70 B5 Kudangan Kalimantan
69 F12 Kudap Sumatra
70 E1 Kudat Sabah
68 B1 Kudaw Burma
55 C4 Kudeyevskiy U.S.S.R.
116 F9 Kudiakof Is Alaska
31 O1 Kudirkos Naumiestis U.S.S.R.
80 G1 Kudnah Syria
116 G8 Kudobin Is Alaska
142 F5 Kuduarra Well W Australia
57 E5 Kuduk U.S.S.R.
70 N9 Kudus Java
52 H5 Kudymkar U.S.S.R.
Kueiyang see Guiyang
26 S2 Kuets'yarv, Oz L U.S.S.R.
80 D4 Kufairāt Jordan
47 K6 Kûfi R Turkey
84 G5 Kufrah Oasis,Al Libya
80 F4 Kufr Alma Jordan
80 F4 Kufrinja Jordan
80 F4 Kufrinja R Jordan
80 G3 Kufr Jayiz Jordan
80 G4 Kufr Khal Jordan
80 G3 Kufr Kifiya Jordan
80 F4 Kufr Rakib Jordan
80 G3 Kufr Saum Jordan
38 F6 Kufstein Austria
60 F11 Kuga Japan
57 D5 Kugitangtau, Khr mts U.S.S.R.
116 F4 Kugruk R Alaska
37 L7 Kühbach W Germany
33 Q6 Kuhbier E Germany
77 A2 Küh-e Alvand Iran
77 C4 Küh-e Bül mt Iran
77 B3 Küh-e Karkas Iran
78 L2 Kuhha-ye Sabalan mt Iran
33 T4 Kühlenhagen E Germany
29 L10 Kuhmalahti Finland
29 O7 Kuhmo Finland
77 F6 Kührān, Küh-e mt Iran
33 Q5 Kuhs E Germany
32 J6 Kuhstedt W Germany
87 C11 Kuibis Namibia
87 C10 Kuiseb R Namibia
117 F7 Kuiu I Alaska
29 L6 Kuivajoki R Finland
29 L6 Kuivaniemi Finland
59 J4 Kujang-dong N Korea
61 O9 Kuji-gawa Japan
60 E12 Kujū-san mt Japan
116 G1 Kuk R Alaska
116 M7 Kukak Alaska
116 K7 Kukaklek L Alaska
116 G6 Kukaklik L Alaska
120 H4 Kukatush Ontario
143 C10 Kukerin W Australia
46 D2 Kukës Albania
29 L5 Kukkola Finland
52 H6 Kukmor U.S.S.R.
52 E5 Kukoboy U.S.S.R.
116 F2 Kukpowruk R Alaska
116 E2 Kukpuk R Alaska
135 U4 Kukuihaele Hawaiian Is
135 O1 Kukuiula Hawaiian Is
118 K1 Kukukus L Ontario
83 K11 Kukulugala mt Sri Lanka
69 F12 Kukup Malaysia
70 D6 Kukusan, G mt Kalimantan
89 B4 Kul Botswana
46 F1 Kula Bulgaria
47 K6 Kula Turkey
48 F5 Kula Yugoslavia
69 D12 Kulabu, Gunung mt Sumatra
74 D3 Kulachi Pakistan
57 A2 Kulandy, Poluostrov pen U.S.S.R.
57 A2 Kulanoy U.S.S.R.
55 F6 Kulanutpes R U.S.S.R.
71 E7 Kulassein isld Philippines
47 F3 Kulata Bulgaria
27 M15 Kuldiga U.S.S.R.
Kuldja see Yining
117 K8 Kuldo Br Col
57 C4 Kul'dzhuktau, Gory mt U.S.S.R.
52 F6 Kulebaki U.S.S.R.
54 G8 Kulebovka U.S.S.R.
42 G4 Kulen Vakuf Yugoslavia
48 M4 Kulevcha U.S.S.R.
55 D4 Kulevchi U.S.S.R.
140 C7 Kulgera N Terr Aust
71 L10 Kuli Indonesia
52 H5 Kuligi U.S.S.R.
48 J1 Kulikov U.S.S.R.
69 E10 Kulim Malaysia
143 C10 Kulin W Australia
143 B9 Kulja W Australia
139 G4 Kulkyne R New S Wales
28 K4 Kulla Gunnarstorp Sweden
28 K4 Kullen mt Sweden
32 M10 Küllstedt E Germany
98 H3 Kulm N Dakota
37 M4 Kulmain W Germany
37 L3 Kulmbach W Germany
52 F3 Kuloy U.S.S.R.
52 F4 Kuloy R U.S.S.R.
138 E5 Kulpara S Australia
95 L6 Kulpmont Pennsylvania
38 G7 Kuls Austria
50 E4 Kul'sary U.S.S.R.
36 H4 Külsheim W Germany
29 M3 Kultala Finland
75 M7 Kulti India
26 H7 Kultsjöluspen Sweden
26 G6 Kultsjön L Sweden
33 R10 Kültzschau E Germany
78 D2 Kulu Turkey
55 G4 Kulunda U.S.S.R.
56 B4 Kulunda R U.S.S.R.
57 E5 Kulyab U.S.S.R.
47 J6 Kum R Turkey
60 F12 Kuma Japan
60 D13 Kuma R Japan
53 G11 Kuma R U.S.S.R.
61 N9 Kumagaya Japan
70 B6 Kumai Kalimantan
70 B6 Kumai, Teluk B Kalimantan
55 D5 Kumak U.S.S.R.
55 C5 Kumak R U.S.S.R.
60 D13 Kumamoto Japan
48 F7 Kumanica Yugoslavia
61 K12 Kumano Japan
46 E2 Kumanovo Yugoslavia
144 C5 Kumara New Zealand
51 M3 Kumara U.S.S.R.
143 D10 Kumarl W Australia
85 D7 Kumasi Ghana
74 H3 Kumaun reg India
86 A5 Kumba Cameroon
76 D5 Kumbakonam India
141 K7 Kumbarilla Queensland
47 L5 Kümbet Turkey
83 L11 Kumbukkan Oya R Sri Lanka
59 J4 Kümch'ŏn S Korea
50 E3 Kumertan U.S.S.R.
55 C4 Kumertau U.S.S.R.
86 F5 Kumi Uganda
60 H10 Kumihama Japan
55 E2 Kuminskiy U.S.S.R.
47 H5 Kumkale Turkey
27 H12 Kumla Sweden
29 H11 Kumlinge Finland
116 J8 Kumliun, C Alaska
47 L8 Kumluca Turkey
33 R5 Kummerow E Germany
33 R4 Kummerow Rostock E Germany
33 R5 Kummerower See L E Germany
37 M5 Kümmersbruck W Germany
33 S8 Kummersdorf E Germany
85 G7 Kumo Nigeria
65 G7 Kŭmo isld S Korea
57 D2 Kumola R U.S.S.R.
75 R5 Kumon Range Burma
68 F4 Kumphawapi Thailand
76 B3 Kumta India
135 V5 Kumukahi, C Hawaiian Is
Kumush see Küm üx
66 D3 Kümüx China
31 O1 Kumuzovo U.S.S.R.
68 C3 Kun R Burma
116 J2 Kuna R Alaska
143 E6 Kunanaggi Well W Australia
74 D1 Kunar Afghanistan
55 D3 Kunashak U.S.S.R.
60 T1 Kunashir O isld U.S.S.R.
141 K6 Kunawarara Queensland
52 C5 Kunda U.S.S.R.
88 A6 Kundelungu mt Zaïre
86 E3 Kundi, L Sudan
143 D10 Kundip W Australia
74 D7 Kundla India
55 D4 Kundravy U.S.S.R.
69 F12 Kundur isld Indonesia
77 L1 Kunduz Afghanistan
66 C3 Künes He R China
27 E14 Kungälv Sweden
Kunges see Künes He
57 H3 Kungey Alatau, Khr mts U.S.S.R.
117 H9 Kunghit I Br Col
57 K3 Kung-liu China
57 A3 Kungrad U.S.S.R.
27 F14 Kungsbacka Sweden
27 J11 Kungsgården Sweden
27 H12 Kungsör Sweden
86 C5 Kungu Zaïre
55 C2 Kungur U.S.S.R.
Kungur mt see Kongur Shan
141 J5 Kungurri Queensland
68 C4 Kungyangon Burma
48 F3 Kunhegyes Hungary
68 D2 Kunhing Burma
61 Q12 Kunigami Okinawa
60 E13 Kunimi-dake mt Japan
70 M9 Kuningan Java
67 C5 Kunlun Guan pass China
48 F3 Kunmadaras Hungary
67 A4 Kunming China
60 R2 Kunneppu Japan
25 E3 Kunnre Netherlands
60 O3 Kunnui R Japan
28 O9 Kunø Faeroes
65 G7 Kunsan S Korea
67 G1 Kunshan China
48 F4 Kunszentmárton Hungary
48 E3 Kunszentmiklós Hungary
52 E6 Kuntsevo U.S.S.R.
143 C9 Kununoppin W Australia
142 G3 Kununurra W Australia
52 D6 Kunya U.S.S.R.
52 J5 Kun'ya U.S.S.R.
57 A4 Kunya Urgench U.S.S.R.
65 E6 Kunyu Shan mts China
36 H5 Künzelsau W Germany
67 G2 Kuocang Shan mts China
52 C2 Kuolayarvi U.S.S.R.
29 N9 Kuopio Finland
29 N2 Kuorboaivi mt Finland
29 K9 Kuortane Finland
29 M10 Kuortti Finland
26 L5 Kuouka Sweden
26 L3 Kuoutatjärro mt Sweden
71 L10 Kupang Timor Indonesia
71 L10 Kupang, Tk B Timor Indonesia
116 N1 Kuparuk R Alaska
37 M3 Kupferberg W Germany
36 H5 Kupferzell W Germany
55 G4 Kupino U.S.S.R.
52 B6 Kupiškis U.S.S.R.
36 E6 Kuppenheim W Germany
117 G7 Kupreanof I Alaska
116 H9 Kupreanof Pt Alaska
116 L7 Kupreanof St Alaska
37 L3 Küps W Germany
42 G3 Kupu R Yugoslavia
54 J7 Kupyansk U.S.S.R.
54 J7 Kupyansk-Uzlovoy U.S.S.R.
66 C3 Kuqa China
59 L1 Kur R U.S.S.R.
57 G3 Kuragaty U.S.S.R.
60 F11 Kurahashi-jima isld Japan
53 G12 Kurakh R U.S.S.R.
57 E4 Kuramins'kiy Khr mts U.S.S.R.
60 C12 Kuramoto Japan
141 H3 Kuranda Queensland
55 C5 Kurashasayskiy U.S.S.R.
60 G11 Kurashiki Japan
142 G4 Kura Soak W Australia
60 G10 Kurayoshi Japan
56 C5 Kurayskiy Khr mts U.S.S.R.
47 G3 Kurazhali Dam Bulgaria
56 G5 Kurba R U.S.S.R.
56 B6 Kurchum R U.S.S.R.
57 H3 Kurday U.S.S.R.
78 G2 Kurdistan reg Turkey/Iraq/Iran
74 F9 Kurduvadi India
47 G3 Kürdzhali Bulgaria
60 F11 Kure Japan
80 F4 Kureiyima Jordan
51 H2 Kureyka U.S.S.R.
51 J2 Kureyka R U.S.S.R.
55 F5 Kurgal'dzhino U.S.S.R.
55 E3 Kurgan U.S.S.R.
50 F3 Kurganskaya Oblast' prov U.S.S.R.
57 E5 Kurgan-Tyube U.S.S.R.
57 D1 Kurgasyn U.S.S.R.
137 P1 Kuria isld Kiribati
83 H3 Kuria Muria isld Arabian Sea
43 D13 Kuriate Is. Tunisia
140 F5 Kuridala Queensland
29 J9 Kurikka Finland
61 O7 Kurikoma-yama mt Japan
Kuril Is see Kuril'skiye Ostrova
52 F5 Kurilovo U.S.S.R.
59 N2 Kuril'sk U.S.S.R.
51 O4 Kuril'skiye Ostrova U.S.S.R.
145 F3 Kuripapango New Zealand
60 P2 Kuriyama Japan
29 O10 Kurkieki U.S.S.R.
84 J5 Kurkur Oasis Egypt
52 F6 Kurlovskiy U.S.S.R.
86 F3 Kurmuk Sudan
36 F5 Kürnbach W Germany
76 D3 Kurnool India
61 O9 Kurobane Japan
61 L9 Kurobe Japan
61 O5 Kuroishi Japan
61 O9 Kuroiso Japan
119 O7 Kuroki Sask
60 O3 Kuromatsunai Japan
60 G10 Kurosaka Japan
54 K1 Kurovskoye U.S.S.R.
144 C6 Kurow New Zealand
31 N4 Kurów Poland
139 K5 Kurri Kurri New S Wales
54 H5 Kursk U.S.S.R.
27 M16 Kurškiy Zaliv U.S.S.R.
46 E1 Kuršumlija Yugoslavia
57 A4 Kurt U.S.S.R.
55 D4 Kurtamysh U.S.S.R.
36 C1 Kürten W Germany
47 K8 Kurtoğlu Burun C Turkey
56 D5 Kurtushibinskiy, Khr mts U.S.S.R.
29 K10 Kuru Finland
78 G2 Kuruçay Turkey
57 E6 Kuruk U.S.S.R.
66 D3 Kuruktag mts China
89 C6 Kuruman S Africa
60 D12 Kurume Japan
58 F1 Kurumkan U.S.S.R.
140 C5 Kurundi N Terr Aust
83 K10 Kurunegala Sri Lanka
116 K2 Kurupa Lakes Alaska
61 O10 Kururi Japan
52 J4 Kur'ya U.S.S.R.
68 G7 Kus Cambodia
47 J7 Kuşadasi Turkey
70 D6 Kusan, Peg mt Kalimantan
117 E5 Kusawa L Yukon Terr
60 G10 Kuse Japan
36 C4 Kusel W Germany
33 O7 Kusey E Germany
26 L7 Kusfors Sweden
47 J4 Kuş Gölü L Turkey
52 E6 Kushalino U.S.S.R.
52 E3 Kushereka U.S.S.R.
61 P12 Kushi Okinawa
61 K11 Kushida-gawa R Japan
60 D14 Kushikino Japan
60 E14 Kushima Japan
61 J12 Kushimoto Japan
60 S3 Kushiro Japan
60 R2 Kushiro prefect Japan
57 C6 Kushka U.S.S.R.
52 F3 Kushkushara U.S.S.R.
48 H2 Kushnitsa U.S.S.R.
57 D4 Kushrabat U.S.S.R.
116 P6 Kushtaka L Alaska
75 N7 Kushtia Bangladesh
53 H9 Kushum R U.S.S.R.
55 C2 Kushva U.S.S.R.
116 G6 Kuskokwim R Alaska
116 F7 Kuskokwim B Alaska
116 H6 Kuskokwim Mts Alaska
116 F6 Kuskovak Alaska
75 K4 Kusma Nepal
86 G5 Kussa Ethiopia
60 S2 Kussharo ko L Japan
29 L4 Küstala Finland
55 D4 Kustanay U.S.S.R.
26 J5 Kustarakaise mt Sweden
29 J11 Kustavi Finland
85 F7 Kuta Nigeria
56 G3 Kuta R U.S.S.R.
69 C11 Kutabuloh Sumatra
69 C11 Kutacane Sumatra
47 K5 Kütahya Turkey
70 E5 Kutai R Kalimantan
53 F12 Kutaisi U.S.S.R.
78 K5 Küt, Al Iraq
69 C11 Kutanibong Sumatra
57 E2 Kutansor, Ozero L U.S.S.R.
145 F3 Kutarere New Zealand
56 E5 Ku Tayga, Khr mts U.S.S.R.
106 G3 Kutch Colorado
60 O3 Kutchan Japan
74 C7 Kutch, Gulf of India
74 C6 Kutch, Rann of India
54 K9 Kuteynikovo U.S.S.R.
42 H3 Kutina Yugoslavia
68 F4 Kut Khao Thailand
68 F7 Kut, Ko isld Thailand
31 J6 Kutná Hóra Czechoslovakia
31 L3 Kutno Poland
70 M9 Kutoadjo Java
76 E1 Kutru India
26 N3 Kuttainen Sweden
110 H4 Kuttawa Kentucky
88 F5 Kutu Tanzania
86 C6 Kutu Zaïre
56 F4 Kutulik U.S.S.R.
86 D3 Kutum Sudan
56 D4 Kuturchinskoye Belog mt U.S.S.R.

42
Kuty — Langesundsfjord

48 J2 Kuty U.S.S.R.
37 J3 Kützberg W Germany
95 M6 Kutztown Pennsylvania
29 O6 Kuusamo Finland
29 M11 Kuusankoski Finland
52 H5 Kuva U.S.S.R.
55 C5 Kuvandyk U.S.S.R.
52 D6 Kuvshinovo U.S.S.R.
77 A5 Kuwait Kuwait
77 A5 Kuwait sheikhdom The Gulf
61 K10 Kuwana Japan
Kuwayt, Al see Kuwait
78 L5 Kuwayt, Al Iraq
52 F2 Kuya U.S.S.R.
53 H7 Kuybyshev U.S.S.R.
57 E5 Kuybyshevskiy U.S.S.R.
53 G7 Kuybyshev-skoye U.S.S.R.
55 C3 Kuyeda U.S.S.R.
65 A5 Kuye He R China
66 D3 Kuytun China
55 D5 Kuyukkol', Oz L U.S.S.R.
128 G3 Kuyuwini R Guyana
56 C3 Kuzbass basin U.S.S.R.
116 E4 Kuzitrin R Alaska
53 G7 Kuznetsk U.S.S.R.
56 C3 Kuznetskiy Alatau mt U.S.S.R.
55 D2 Kuznetsovo U.S.S.R.
52 E2 Kuzomen U.S.S.R.
26 H3 Kvaefjord Norway
26 M2 Kvaenangen Norway
26 M1 Kvaenangen inlet Norway
26 M2 Kvaenangsbotn Norway
28 H6 Kværkeby Denmark
28 F6 Kværndrup Denmark
28 C7 Kværs Denmark
28 N3 Kvalbø Faeroes
26 N1 Kvalöya isld Norway
26 K1 Kvalöy, N isld Norway
26 K2 Kvalöy, S isld Norway
26 N1 Kvalsund Norway
28 M2 Kvalvig Faeroes
26 D10 Kvam Norway
28 O9 Kvannesund Faeroes
55 C5 Kvarkeno U.S.S.R.
27 G15 Kvarnamåla Sweden
26 G7 Kvarnbergsvattnet L Sweden
42 F4 Kvarner chan Yugoslavia
42 F4 Kvarnerić chan Yugoslavia
27 J13 Kvarsebo Sweden
27 C11 Kvenna R Norway
26 C8 Kvernes Norway
26 L2 Kvesmenas Norway
29 J8 Kvevlax Finland
116 J7 Kvichak Alaska
26 G6 Kvigtind mt Norway
26 J5 Kvikkjock Sweden
26 D9 Kvikne Norway
27 B13 Kvina R Norway
27 B13 Kvinesdal Norway
27 B12 Kvinnherad Norway
27 G12 Kvistbro Sweden
28 K5 Kvistofta Sweden
26 C8 Kvisvik Norway
27 C12 Kviteseid Norway
26 R1 Kvitnes Norway
147 K11 Kvitöya isld Spitzbergen
27 A12 Kvitsöy isld Norway
28 M2 Kvivig Faeroes
28 A5 Kvong Denmark
28 D4 Kvorning Denmark
117 L7 Kwadacha Wilderness Prov. Park Br Columbia
134 G7 Kwajalein atoll Marshall Is Pacific Oc
129 G2 Kwakoegron Suriname
88 G4 Kwale Kenya
85 F7 Kwale Nigeria
86 C6 Kwamouth Zaïre
Kwangchow see Guangzhou
65 G7 Kwangju S Korea
86 C6 Kwango R Zaïre
Kwangsi aut reg see Guangxi
Kwangtung prov see Guangdong
86 F5 Kwania, L Uganda
120 H1 Kwataboahegan R Ontario
89 G7 Kwazulu reg S Africa
Kweichow prov see Guizhou
Kweilin see Guilin
89 D5 Kweneng dist Botswana
87 C7 Kwenge R Zaïre
116 G6 Kwethluk Alaska
31 L2 Kwidzyn Poland
116 D7 Kwigamiuk Alaska
116 F7 Kwigillingok Alaska
116 E5 Kwiguk Alaska
116 E5 Kwikpak Alaska
87 C7 Kwilu R Zaïre
142 A4 Kwinana W Australia
31 J4 Kwisa R Poland
128 G3 Kwitaro R Guyana
143 C10 Kwobrup W Australia
136 G2 Kwoka mt W Irian
26 D7 Kya isld Norway
86 C4 Kyabé Chad
141 G7 Kyabra Queensland
139 H6 Kyabram Victoria
68 B2 Kyadet Burma
68 B3 Kyagu Burma
68 C4 Kyaikkami Burma
68 B4 Kyaiklat Burma
68 C4 Kyaikto Burma
68 D5 Kya-in Seikkyi Burma
88 C2 Kyaka Tanzania
56 G5 Kyakhta U.S.S.R.
139 G5 Kyalite New S Wales
138 D5 Kyancutta S Australia
52 E3 Kyanda U.S.S.R.
52 D3 Kyargozero U.S.S.R.
68 C3 Kyaukhnyat Burma
68 B3 Kyaukkyi Burma
68 C1 Kyaukme Burma
68 B1 Kyaukmyaung Burma
68 A3 Kyaukpyu Burma
68 C2 Kyaukse Burma
68 A2 Kyauktaw Burma
68 B2 Kyaukyit Burma
68 B4 Kyaunggon Burma
138 F6 Kybybolite S Australia
52 F2 Kychema U.S.S.R.
26 G7 Kycklingvattnet Sweden
68 C3 Kyebogyi Burma
144 C6 Kyeburn New Zealand
68 D5 Kyeikdon Burma
68 D4 Kyeikywa Burma
68 B3 Kyeintali Burma
33 O10 Kyffhäuser mt E Germany
143 E7 Kyffin-Thomas Hill W Australia
28 F5 Kyholm isld Denmark
68 C3 Kyidaunggan Burma
68 A2 Kyindwe Burma
31 K6 Kyjov Czechoslovakia
118 J8 Kyle Sask
98 D6 Kyle S Dakota
109 K6 Kyle Texas
101 T8 Kyle Wyoming
15 C3 Kyleakin Scotland
87 F10 Kyle Dam Zimbabwe
15 D2 Kyle of Durness Scotland
15 C3 Kyle of Lochalsh Scotland
15 D2 Kyle of Tongue Scotland
12 C2 Kyles of Bute chan Scotland
36 B3 Kyll R W Germany
36 B3 Kyllburg W Germany
29 N10 Kymi prov Finland
29 M11 Kymijoki R Finland
55 C2 Kyn U.S.S.R.
139 G6 Kyneton Victoria
37 O3 Kynšperk nad Ohři Czechoslovakia
141 F5 Kynuna Queensland
61 P12 Kyoda Okinawa
86 F5 Kyoga, L Uganda
60 J10 Kyôga-misaki C Japan
139 L3 Kyogle New S Wales
65 F5 Kyŏmip'o N Korea
68 D4 Kyondo Burma
68 C2 Kyong Burma
141 H5 Kyong Queensland
62 Kyôto conurbation Japan
60 J10 Kyôto prefect Japan
55 E6 Kypshak, Oz L U.S.S.R.
79 D3 Kyrenia Cyprus
33 Q7 Kyritz E Germany
29 L11 Kyrkslätt Finland
29 J8 Kyröjoki R Finland
29 K10 Kyrösjärvi L Finland
52 J3 Kyrta U.S.S.R.
55 D2 Kyrtym'ya U.S.S.R.
55 C2 Kyr'ya U.S.S.R.
55 G3 Kyshtovka U.S.S.R.
55 D3 Kyshtym U.S.S.R.
52 G3 Kyssa U.S.S.R.
79 D3 Kythrea Cyprus
55 C2 Kytlym U.S.S.R.
68 D5 Kyungyaung Burma
68 C7 Kyun Pila islds Burma
117 K10 Kyuquot Br Col
60 D13 Kyûshû isld Japan
60 E13 Kyûshû-sanchi mts Japan
46 F2 Kyustendil Bulgaria
51 M1 Kyusyur U.S.S.R.
139 H6 Kywong New S Wales
29 L8 Kyyjärvi Finland
56 D5 Kyzyl U.S.S.R.
57 E1 Kyzyldyykan U.S.S.R.
56 E5 Kyzyl-Khem R U.S.S.R.
57 F4 Kyzyl-Kiya U.S.S.R.
57 J2 Kyzylkiya U.S.S.R.
57 E1 Kyzyl-Kommuna U.S.S.R.
57 C4 Kyzylkum, Peski des U.S.S.R.
55 F5 Kyzyltas U.S.S.R.
57 H1 Kyzyltu U.S.S.R.
57 D1 Kyzyluy U.S.S.R.
57 C1 Kyzylzhar U.S.S.R.
57 J3 Kyzylzhide U.S.S.R.
57 E1 Kzyl-Dzhar U.S.S.R.
57 D3 Kzyl-Orda U.S.S.R.
55 F4 Kzyltu U.S.S.R.
31 J7 Laa Austria
37 M5 Laaber W Germany
36 C3 Laacher See L W Germany
33 Q5 Laage E Germany
25 F4 Laag Keppel Netherlands
124 C4 La Angostura Mexico
29 N3 Laanila Finland
36 E2 Laasphe W Germany
127 N9 La Asunción Venezuela
135 R2 Laau Pt Hawaiian Is
108 E7 La Babia Mexico
110 F3 Labadie Missouri
7 E12 Labadie Bank Atlantic Oc
111 F12 Labadieville Louisiana
71 L9 Labala Indonesia
79 F8 Labān Jordan
16 D2 La Baneza Spain
71 L9 Labao Flores Indonesia
124 H7 La Barca Mexico
101 P7 La Barge Wyoming
21 A8 La Barre-de-Monts France
19 P17 La Bastide-des-Jourdans France
18 G8 Labastide Murat France
19 Q13 La Bathie France
19 Q15 La Bâtie-Neuve France
68 A2 Labawa Burma
52 H2 Labazhskoye U.S.S.R.
26 J5 Labbas Sweden
80 D1 Labbouna Lebanon
26 R3 Labdshy'aur, Oz L U.S.S.R.
85 B6 Labé Guinea
31 J5 Labe R Czechoslovakia
19 Q17 La Bégude Blanche France
99 P9 La Belle Missouri
121 Q6 Labelle Quebec
71 H6 Labengke isld Sulawesi
19 Q15 La Bérarde France
117 F5 Laberge, L Yukon Terr
131 E7 Laberinto, Pta Argentina
21 A7 La Bernerie France
21 J8 La Berthenoux France
37 N6 Laberweinting W Germany
70 D2 Labi Brunei
117 L5 La Biche R Yukon Terr/Br Col
42 F3 Labin Yugoslavia
69 F11 Labis Malaysia
127 M9 La Blanquilla, I Venezuela
71 F3 Labo Philippines
71 H5 Labobo isld Indonesia
103 J10 La Bomba Mexico
101 U7 Labonte Cr Wyoming
31 N6 Laborec R Czechoslovakia
48 G1 Laborec R Czechoslovakia
70 G6 Labota Sulawesi
143 C7 Labouchere, Mt W Australia
18 E8 Labouheyre France
133 E4 Laboulaye Argentina
115 N7 Labrador City Labrador
115 O6 Labrador Sea Nfld/Greenland
128 F5 Labrea Brazil
128 B4 La Brea, Cer. de hill Peru
124 E5 La Brecha Mexico
18 E8 Labrède France
122 C4 Labrieville Quebec
122 C4 Labrieville, Parc de Quebec
18 E8 Labrit France
118 E1 La Broquerie Manitoba
22 B3 Labroye France
21 C7 La Bruffière France
18 G9 Labruguière France
136 F2 Labuha Moluccas Indonesia
71 J9 Labuhanbadjo Sumba Indonesia
69 E11 Labuhanbatu Sumatra
69 E11 Labuhanbilik Sumatra
69 C11 Labuhanhaji Sumatra
69 D11 Labuhanruku Sumatra
70 K8 Labuhanwaiharu Sumatra
19 P14 La Buisse France
70 E2 Labuk R Sabah
70 E1 Labuk B Sabah
68 B4 Labutta Burma
138 D4 Labyrinth, L S Australia
50 F2 Labytnangi U.S.S.R.
46 D3 Laç Albania
124 G5 La Cadena Mexico
118 J8 Lacadena Sask
122 J3 Lac Allard Quebec
111 D10 Lacamp Louisiana
18 E8 Lacanau France
128 F2 La Canoa Venezuela
125 O9 Lacantum R Mexico
18 G8 Lacapelle-Marival France
131 B8 Lacar, L Argentina
133 E4 La Carlota Argentina
71 F5 La Carlota Negros Philippines
16 E6 La Carolina Spain
18 G9 Lacaune France
Laccadive Is see Lakshadweep
122 B8 Lac-Drolet Quebec
99 R4 Lac du Flambeau Wisconsin
13 H6 Laceby England
125 L2 La Ceiba Honduras
128 D2 La Ceiba Venezuela
21 G7 La Celle St Avant France
138 E6 Lacepede B S Australia
142 D3 Lacepede Is W Australia
21 C8 La Chaize-le-Vicomte France
19 Q14 La Chambre France
52 E4 Lacha, Oz L U.S.S.R.
20 J3 Lachapelle-aux-Pots France
21 C7 La Chapelle Basse Mer France
21 G7 La Chapelle-Blanche-St. Martin France
21 B6 La Chapelle-Bouexic France
21 E6 La Chapelle-d'Aligné France
19 O15 La Chapelle-en-Vercors France
21 C6 La Chapelle-Glain France
21 I6 La Chapelle St. Mesmin France
21 I9 La Chapelle-Taillefert France
21 G6 La Chartre France
21 J8 La Châtre France
128 C6 Lachay, Pta point Peru
41 J3 Lachen Switzerland
36 E5 Lachen W Germany
21 B7 La Chevroliere France
94 D1 Lachine Michigan
139 H5 Lachlan R New S Wales
125 P5 La Chorrera Panama
33 M7 Lachte R W Germany
121 Q7 Lachute Quebec
19 P18 La Ciotat France
94 J4 Lackawanna New York
14 E3 Lacken Res Irish Rep
71 M9 Lacla R Timor
114 H7 Lac la Biche Alberta
117 N10 Lac La Hache Br Columbia
119 M3 Lac la Ronge Sask
100 J1 Laclede Idaho
99 N10 Laclede Missouri
19 Q13 La Clusaz France
133 D3 La Cocha Argentina
8 D5 Lacock England
121 R7 Lacolle Quebec
124 D3 La Colorada Mexico
118 D6 Lacombe Alberta
111 G11 Lacombe Louisiana
99 R8 Lacon Illinois
99 N8 Lacona Iowa
95 L3 Lacona New York
43 C9 Laconi Sardinia
95 Q3 Laconia New Hampshire
113 E9 Lacoochee Florida
130 B9 La Cordillera dep Paraguay
121 N4 Lacorne Quebec
21 D7 La Cornuaille France
16 B1 La Coruña Spain
109 J6 Lacoste Texas
19 O14 La Côte St. André France
127 J2 Lacovia Jamaica
98 K4 Lac Qui Parle Minnesota
98 E6 Lacreek L S Dakota
126 A3 Lacre Pt Bonaire W Indies
99 P6 La Crescent Minnesota
21 H7 La Croix France
99 O1 La Croix,L Ontario
99 U8 La Crosse Indiana
107 L3 La Crosse Kansas
94 J10 La Crosse Virginia
99 P6 La Crosse Wisconsin
133 F3 La Cruz Argentina
125 M4 La Cruz Costa Rica
124 F6 La Cruz Mexico
124 G4 La Cruz Mexico
120 G3 Lac Ste. Thérèse Ontario
133 C5 La Cueva Chile
106 E6 La Cueva New Mexico
119 N6 Lac Vert Sask
107 Q3 La Cygne Kansas
21 E7 La Daguenière France
130 H5 Ladainha Brazil
74 G1 Ladakh Range Kashmir
54 D6 Ladan' U.S.S.R.
69 D9 Ladang, Ko isld Thailand
129 G7 Ladário Brazil
70 K9 Lada, Teluk B Java
9 E3 Ladbroke England
99 R8 Ladd Illinois
107 J3 Ladder Cr Kansas
110 E2 Laddonia Missouri
111 E8 Ladelle Arkansas
28 C7 Ladelund W Germany
36 F5 Ladenburg W Germany
127 O4 La Désirade isld Guadeloupe W I
Lādhiqīya, El see Latakia
46 E7 Ládhon R Greece
83 J12 La Digue isld Seychelles
28 D4 Lading Denmark
89 B9 Ladismith S Africa
77 G5 Ladīz Iran
98 C4 Ladner S Dakota
48 G6 Ladne Vode Yugoslavia
74 F5 Ladnun India
8 B7 Ladock England
110 K2 Ladoga Indiana
Ladoga L see Ladozhskoye Oz
109 M2 Ladonia Texas
128 D2 La Dorada Colombia
52 D4 Ladozhskoye Oz L U.S.S.R.
106 C7 Ladrones Pk New Mexico
116 R5 Ladue R Alaska/Yukon Terr
124 E3 La Dura Mexico
52 D4 Ladva Vetka U.S.S.R.
115 L2 Lady Ann Str N W Terr
15 E4 Ladybank Scotland
139 J8 Lady Barron Tasmania
89 E7 Ladybrand S Africa
142 F5 Lady Edith L W Australia
141 L6 Lady Elliot I Gt Barrier Reef Aust
120 K5 Lady Evelyn L Ontario
146 J6 Lady Newnes Ice Shelf Antarctica
100 B1 Ladysmith Br Columbia
89 F7 Ladysmith S Africa
99 P4 Ladysmith Wisconsin
55 E5 Ladyzhenka U.S.S.R.
136 K3 Lae Papua New Guinea
68 E3 Lae Thailand
71 H7 Laëa Indonesia
28 C5 Læborg Denmark
69 B11 Laehobang Indonesia
22 G2 Laeken Belgium
68 F6 Laem Ngop Thailand
17 G6 La Encina Spain
127 L10 La Encrucijada Venezuela
27 B10 Laerdalsöyri Norway
128 F8 La Esmeralda Paraguay
28 G2 Læsø isld Denmark
28 F2 Læsø Rende str Denmark
133 D5 La Esperanza Argentina
126 F4 La Esperanza Cuba
16 B2 La Estrada Spain
26 P2 Laevajoki Norway
131 D3 La Falda Argentina
95 M2 La Fargeville New York
19 Q18 La Farlède France
111 L9 Lafayette Alabama
106 E2 Lafayette Colorado
112 B3 Lafayette Georgia
110 K1 Lafayette Indiana
111 E11 Lafayette Louisiana
99 M5 Lafayette Minnesota
94 B10 Lafayette Tennessee
95 Q2 Lafayette, Mt New Hampshire
126 B3 La Fe Cuba
109 K9 La Feria Texas
21 E8 La Ferrière-en-Parthenay France
121 M4 Laferte Quebec
21 I7 La Ferte Imbault France
21 I6 La Ferté-St. Aubin France
21 I6 La Ferté St. Cyr France
85 F7 Lafia Nigeria
85 F7 Lafiagi Nigeria
121 N3 Laflamme R Quebec
21 E6 La Flèche France
118 L9 Lafleche Sask
38 O7 Lafnitz R Austria
94 C10 La Follette Tennessee
21 F6 La Fontaine-St. Martin France
121 M5 Laforce Quebec
120 J5 Laforest Ontario
18 F8 Lafrançaise France
112 E3 La France S Carolina
36 C6 Lafrimbole France
16 C4 La Fuente de San Esteban Spain
69 A9 Laful Nicobar Is
124 G5 La Gallega Mexico
14 E2 Lagan R N Ireland
27 G15 Lagan R Sweden
16 B2 La Gañiza Spain
36 B6 Lagarde France
41 N6 Lagarina, Val Italy
106 D4 La Garita Mts Colorado
21 B8 La Garnache France
129 H8 Lagarto, Serra do mts Brazil
21 C8 La Gaubretière France
32 J8 Lage W Germany
26 D10 Lågen R Norway
32 L5 Lägerdorf W Germany
54 H7 Lagery U.S.S.R.
12 C2 Lagg Scotland
15 D3 Laggan Scotland
12 B2 Laggan B Scotland
77 L2 Laghmān Afghanistan
85 E2 Laghouat Algeria
40 B6 Lagnieu France
16 B7 Lagôa Portugal
130 G6 Lagoa Santa Brazil
130 E4 Lagolândia Brazil
43 G8 Lagonegro Italy
71 F4 Lagonoy Gulf Philippines
133 C7 Lago Posadas Argentina
85 E7 Lagos Nigeria
16 B7 Lagos Portugal
45 M2 Lagosanto Italy
100 G4 La Grande Oregon
115 M7 La Grande-Riviére R Quebec
111 L8 La Grange Georgia
94 B5 Lagrange Indiana
94 B8 La Grange Kentucky
99 P9 La Grange Missouri
112 K2 La Grange N Carolina
94 E5 Lagrange Ohio
109 L6 La Grange Texas
142 D4 Lagrange W Australia
98 B8 La Grange Wyoming
128 F2 La Gran Sabana reg Venezuela
19 Q14 La Grave France
83 M13 Lagrave mt Mauritius
127 J10 La Grita Venezuela
27 L12 Lågskär Finland
29 H11 Lågskär lt ho Finland
127 L9 La Guaira Venezuela
133 D3 La Guardia Argentina
16 B3 La Guardia Portugal
17 F2 Laguardia Spain
16 C2 La Gudiña Spain
21 C6 La Guerche de Bretagne France
21 A8 La Guérinière France
18 G8 Laguiole France
133 H3 Laguna Brazil
42 E3 Laguna Italy
106 C6 Laguna New Mexico
141 L7 Laguna B Queensland
102 G8 Laguna Beach California
103 O5 Laguna Cr Arizona
103 K9 Laguna Dam Cal/Ariz
102 H9 Laguna Mts California
128 C5 Lagunas Peru
133 E1 Lagunillas Bolivia
127 J9 Lagunillas Venezuela
65 F4 Lagushao China
70 F2 Lahad Datu Sabah
68 F1 Lahadi China
135 S3 Lahaina Hawaiian Is
70 D4 Laham Kalimantan
99 Q9 La Harpe Illinois
70 K7 Lahat Sumatra
80 C8 Lahav Israel
122 H9 La Have Nova Scotia
80 F1 Lahavot HaBashan Israel
32 J8 Lahde W Germany
124 D4 La Higuera Mexico
77 B1 Lāhījān Iran
102 R12 Lahilahi Pt Hawaiian Is
37 K3 Lahm W Germany
30 D5 Lahn W Germany
36 E2 Lahn R W Germany
36 F2 Lahntal W Germany
27 F15 Laholm Sweden
27 F15 Laholmsbukten Sweden
71 F4 Lahong Philippines
102 E2 Lahontan Res Nevada
74 F3 Lahore Pakistan
36 D7 Lahr W Germany
73 L6 Lahshadweep islds Indian Oc
32 M8 Lahstedt W Germany
29 M11 Lahti Finland
124 G8 La Huerta Mexico
80 G8 Lahun Jordan
71 F4 Lahuy isld Philippines
86 C4 Lai Chad
67 F1 Lai'an China
133 F3 La Iberá L Argentina
67 C5 Laibin China
68 F2 Lai Chau Vietnam
36 H7 Laichingen W Germany
139 K3 Laidley Queensland
141 K8 Laidley Queensland
102 S11 Laie Hawaiian Is
67 C2 Laifeng China
22 H4 Laifour France
20 C5 Laignelet France
18 H5 Laignes France
44 D4 Laigueglia Italy
21 C9 L'Aiguillon-sur-Mer France
29 J9 Laihia Finland
68 C2 Lai-Hka Burma
68 C2 Lai-Hsak Burma
70 F7 Laikang, Tk B Sulawesi
21 I6 Lailly-en-Val France
71 E1 Lai-Lo Luzon Philippines
47 H3 Lainá Greece
38 L6 Lainbach Austria
94 C4 Laingsburg Michigan
89 B9 Laingsburg S Africa
26 K6 Lainijaur Sweden
26 M4 Lainio Sweden
26 M3 Lainio älv R Sweden
98 D9 Laird Colorado
118 L6 Laird Sask
15 D2 Lairg Scotland
71 G7 Lais Mindanao Philippines
70 G4 Lais Sulawesi
126 D3 La Isabela Cuba
86 G5 Laisamis Kenya
52 G6 Laishevo U.S.S.R.
65 C5 Laishui China
20 E3 Laison R France
18 G8 Laissac France
26 J5 Laisvall Sweden
26 K4 Laitaure L Sweden
29 J11 Laitila Finland
65 D6 Laiwu China
65 E6 Laixi China
71 E4 Laiya Philippines
59 H4 Laiyang China
65 C5 Laiyuan China
20 E3 Laize R France
65 D6 Laizhou Wan B China
133 C5 Laja, L Chile
131 B6 Laja, L. de Chile
133 D5 La Japonesa Argentina
131 A6 Laja, R Chile
106 E4 La Jara Colorado
70 E7 Lajar, Tg C Kalimantan
19 Q16 La Javie France
130 F9 Laje dos Santos isld Brazil
71 O8 Lajeni Indonesia
130 E10 Lajes Brazil
108 D6 Lajitas Texas
133 E2 Lajitas, Las Argentina
48 F6 Lajkovac Yugoslavia
102 G9 La Jolla California
119 N8 Lajord Sask
48 F3 Lajosmizse Hungary
124 F4 La Joya Mexico
106 D7 La Joya New Mexico
21 D7 La Jumellière France
128 F7 La Junta Bolivia
106 G4 La Junta Colorado
124 F3 La Junta Mexico
71 K9 Lakahembi Sumba Indonesia
26 J8 Lakasjö Sweden
26 M5 Lakaträsk Sweden
101 O5 Lake Idaho
94 B3 Lake Michigan
100 E6 Lake Oregon
113 F9 Lake Alfred Florida
119 N9 Lake Alma Sask
109 P5 Lake Arthur Louisiana
106 F8 Lake Arthur New Mexico
98 K5 Lake Benton Minnesota
143 C10 Lake Biddy W Australia
98 K1 Lake Bronson Minnesota
143 C9 Lake Brown W Australia
113 E7 Lake Butler Florida
143 C10 Lake Camm W Australia
109 O5 Lake Charles Louisiana
110 F6 Lake City Arkansas
100 E8 Lake City California
106 C3 Lake City Colorado
113 E7 Lake City Florida
99 M7 Lake City Iowa
94 B2 Lake City Michigan
99 O5 Lake City Minnesota
94 G4 Lake City Pennsylvania
112 H4 Lake City S Carolina
98 J4 Lake City S Dakota
94 C10 Lake City Tennessee
144 C5 Lake Coleridge New Zealand
100 J8 Lake Cr Nevada
99 M5 Lake Crystal Minnesota
99 R6 Lake Delton Wisconsin
118 F5 Lake Eliza Alberta
138 D2 Lake Eyre Basin S Australia
99 L6 Lakefield Minnesota
121 M8 Lakefield Ontario
141 G2 Lakefield Queensland
99 T7 Lake Forest Illinois
99 S7 Lake Geneva Wisconsin
106 E3 Lake George Colorado
95 O3 Lake George New York
115 N5 Lake Harbour N W Terr
101 U8 Lake Hattie Res Wyoming
103 K7 Lake Havasu City Arizona
102 F7 Lake Hughes California
95 N6 Lakehurst New Jersey
109 M6 Lake Jackson Texas
142 C10 Lake King W Australia
143 C10 Lake King W Australia
112 D6 Lakeland Georgia
119 N6 Lake Lenore Sask
99 S2 Lake Linden Michigan
117 P10 Lake Louise Alberta
137 R5 Lakemba isld Fiji
99 N6 Lake Mills Iowa
94 G5 Lake Milton Ohio
116 L5 Lake Minchumina Alaska
95 S1 Lake Moxie Maine
140 E5 Lake Nash N Terr Aust
37 P5 Laken Berg mt W Germany/Czech
9 G3 Lakenheath England
94 B4 Lake Odessa Michigan
99 M1 Lake of the Woods L Ontario
94 D4 Lake Orion Michigan
100 C4 Lake Oswego Oregon
107 Q5 Lake O' The Cherokees L Oklahoma
109 N3 Lake O'The Pines L Texas
101 P5 Lake Outlet Wyoming
144 B5 Lake Paringa New Zealand
113 G11 Lake Park Florida
113 D7 Lake Park Georgia
99 L6 Lake Park Iowa
113 F10 Lake Placid Florida
95 O2 Lake Placid New York
102 B2 Lakeport California
113 F11 Lakeport Florida
94 E3 Lakeport Michigan
98 J5 Lake Preston S Dakota
111 E9 Lake Providence Louisiana
144 C6 Lake Pukaki New Zealand
100 F9 Lake Range mts Nevada
115 L7 Lake River Ontario
139 J7 Lakes Entrance Victoria
102 E4 Lakeshore California
103 P7 Lakeside Arizona
102 H9 Lakeside California
98 D7 Lakeside Nebraska
101 N8 Lakeside Utah
120 F5 Lake Superior Prov. Park Ontario
144 C5 Lake Tekapo New Zealand
101 O8 Laketown Utah
121 M7 Lake Traverse Ontario
106 C9 Lake Valley New Mexico
118 L8 Lake Valley Sask
109 J5 Lake Victor Texas
99 L7 Lake View Iowa
94 B3 Lakeview Michigan
101 O5 Lakeview Montana
100 E7 Lakeview Oregon
112 H3 Lake View S Carolina
109 N9 Lakeview Texas
111 E8 Lake Village Arkansas
95 O5 Lakeville Connecticut
94 A5 Lakeville Indiana
99 N5 Lakeville Minnesota
94 K4 Lakeville New York
143 D7 Lake Violet W Australia
113 F10 Lake Wales Florida
98 G2 Lake Williams N Dakota
95 N6 Lakewood New Jersey
106 F9 Lakewood New Mexico
94 H4 Lakewood New York
94 F5 Lakewood Ohio
113 G11 Lake Worth Florida
52 D4 Lakhdenpokh'ya U.S.S.R.
74 J5 Lakhimpur India
80 B6 Lakhish Israel
80 C7 Lakhish Israel
80 C7 Lakhish R Israel
74 C7 Lakhpat India
107 J4 Lakin Kansas
54 L1 Lakinskiy U.S.S.R.
74 D2 Lakki Pakistan
28 A6 Lakoik Denmark
46 F8 Lakonikós Kólpos B Greece
71 O9 Lakor isld Indonesia
99 M6 Lakota Iowa
85 C7 Lakota Ivory Coast
98 H1 Lakota N Dakota
68 G3 Lak Sao Laos
26 P1 Lakse Fjord inlet Norway
26 O1 Lakselv Norway
26 F6 Laksfors Norway
76 A5 Lakshadweep islds terr India
71 F7 Lala Mindanao Philippines
88 C8 Lala Zambia
87 B7 Lalama Angola
47 H3 Lâlapaşa Turkey
86 B5 Lalare Gabon
87 G8 Lalaúa Mozambique
18 G8 Lalbenque France
77 E5 Lāleh Zar, Kūh-e mt Iran
33 Q5 Lalendorf E Germany
70 F5 Lalereh, Tg C Sulawesi
77 A3 Lāli Iran
128 B4 La Libertad Ecuador
125 O9 La Libertad Guatemala
133 C4 La Ligua Chile
71 H6 Lalimbuë Sulawesi
65 G2 Lalin China
16 B2 Lalin Spain
18 F8 Lalinde France
71 K10 Lalindi Sumba Indonesia
70 G6 Lalindu R Sulawesi
65 G2 Lalin He R China
74 H6 Lalitpur India
19 P15 Lalley France
70 G7 Laloa Sulawesi
118 H2 La Loche West Sask
71 A2 Laloda Halmahera Indonesia
52 G4 Lal'sk U.S.S.R.
124 H6 La Luz Mexico
46 C3 Lalzës, Gji i B Albania
37 P5 Lam W Germany
52 E6 Lama R U.S.S.R.
128 D3 La Macarena Colombia
43 C7 La Maddalena Sardinia
106 D5 La Madera New Mexico
65 D4 Lamadong China
124 J4 Lamadrid Mexico
70 E2 Lamag Sabah
68 C5 Lamaing Burma
85 E7 Lama-Kara Togo
71 L9 Lamakera Indonesia
115 M8 La Malbaie Quebec
123 R7 Lamaline Nfld
45 J3 Lama Mocogno Italy
124 H5 La Mancha Mexico
17 F5 La Mancha reg Spain
125 M4 La Mansión Costa Rica
110 C6 Lamar Arkansas
106 H3 Lamar Colorado
110 B4 Lamar Missouri
98 E9 Lamar Nebraska
107 O6 Lamar Oklahoma
112 G3 Lamar S Carolina
101 P5 Lamar R Wyoming
40 C1 Lamarche France
40 A2 Lamargelle France
133 D5 Lamarque Argentina
109 N6 La Marque Texas
122 B6 Lamartine Quebec
125 L2 La Masica Honduras
19 N15 Lamastre France
126 G4 La Maya Cuba
18 D4 Lamballe France
86 B6 Lambarene Gabon
130 F7 Lambari Brazil
137 Q5 Lambasa Vanua Levu Fiji
70 G7 Lambasina isld Sulawesi
28 O9 Lamba Vig inlet Faeroes
128 B5 Lambayeque dep Peru
14 E3 Lambay I Irish Rep
9 G5 Lamberhurst England
112 F6 Lambert Georgia
111 F7 Lambert Mississippi
98 B2 Lambert Montana
142 B5 Lambert, C W Australia
146 C5 Lambert Gl Antarctica
99 L5 Lamberton Minnesota
87 C12 Lamberts B S Africa
95 N6 Lambertville New Jersey
19 O17 Lambesc France
120 J10 Lambeth Ontario
73 Q6 Lambi isld Burma
46 E7 Lámbia Greece
9 E5 Lambourn England
36 E5 Lambrecht W Germany
41 K7 Lambro R Italy
94 G10 Lambsburg Virginia
14 A5 Lambs Hd Irish Rep
36 E4 Lambsheim W Germany
121 T7 Lambton Quebec
114 G3 Lambton, C N W Terr
68 F5 Lam Chi R Thailand
68 G5 Lam Dom Noi R Thailand
101 T4 Lame Deer Montana
16 B3 Lamego Portugal
21 C6 La Meilleraye-de-Bret France
21 G7 La Membrolle France
21 E7 La Ménitre France
127 N4 Lamentin Guadeloupe W I
122 H6 Lameque New Brunswick
122 H6 Lamèque, Ile New Brunswick
133 D3 La Merced Argentina
138 F6 Lameroo S Australia
102 G9 La Mesa California
106 D9 La Mesa New Mexico
108 F3 Lamesa Texas
43 F7 La Meta mt Italy
46 E6 Lamia Greece
127 K10 La Miel Venezuela
71 G7 Lamigan Pt Mindanao Philippines
15 E5 Lamington Scotland
124 D3 La Misa Mexico
71 F7 Lamitan Philippines
109 J4 Lamkin Texas
71 C3 Lamlam Indonesia
15 C5 Lamlash Scotland
144 B6 Lammerlaw Range New Zealand
141 G5 Lammermoor Queensland
15 F5 Lammermuir Hills Scotland
25 F7 Lammersdorf W Germany
69 B10 Lammeulo Sumatra
27 G14 Lammhult Sweden
29 L10 Lammi Finland
20 G5 Lamnay France
21 B7 La Moëre France
99 R8 La Moille Illinois
103 J1 Lamoille Nevada
95 P2 Lamoille R Vermont
110 F1 La Moine R Illinois
100 G2 Lamona Washington
71 E3 Lamon B Luzon Philippines
42 D4 Lamone R Italy
70 O9 Lamongan Java
110 C1 Lamoni Iowa
118 E5 Lamont Alberta
102 F6 Lamont California
113 D7 Lamont Florida
101 O6 Lamont Idaho
99 P7 Lamont Iowa
107 N5 Lamont Oklahoma
101 S7 Lamont Wyoming
124 G3 La Morita Mexico
19 P14 La Morte France
22 J4 Lamorteau Belgium
21 E9 La Mothe St. Héraye France
121 M4 La Motte Quebec
21 J6 Lamotte-Beuvron France
19 P15 La Motte d'Aveillans France
19 P13 La Motte-Servolex France
98 H3 La Moure N Dakota
68 F4 Lam Pao Res Thailand
109 J4 Lampasas Texas
109 K5 Lampasas R Texas
125 K4 Lampazos Mexico
36 E4 Lampertheim W Germany
33 T10 Lampërtswalde E Germany
8 B3 Lampeter Wales
8 B4 Lamphey Wales
47 F5 Lampinoú Greece
43 E13 Lampione isld Italy
68 F5 Lam Plai R Thailand
119 P9 Lampman Sask
45 J4 Lamporecchio Italy
9 F3 Lamport England
52 F2 Lampozhnya U.S.S.R.
29 O6 Lämpsä Finland
70 D5 Lampung Kalimantan
70 K8 Lampung Teluk B Sumatra
68 G5 Lam Si Bai R Thailand
32 M9 Lamspringe W Germany
32 K5 Lamstedt W Germany
68 B3 Lamu Burma
86 H6 Lamu Kenya
19 P15 La Mure France
19 N12 Lamure-sur-Azergues France
106 E6 Lamy New Mexico
42 D2 Lana Italy
141 G5 Lana Queensland
135 S3 Lanai isld Hawaiian Is
135 S3 Lanai City Hawaiian Is
135 S3 Lanaihale peak Hawaiian Is
22 K2 Lanaken Belgium
74 H1 Lanak Pass Kashmir/Xizang Zizhiqu
71 G7 Lanao L Mindanao Philippines
113 C8 Lanark Florida
99 R7 Lanark Illinois
121 O7 Lanark Ontario
12 E2 Lanark Scotland
Lanark co see Strathclyde reg
70 E2 Lanas Sabah
68 C7 Lanbi Kyun isld Burma
71 F6 Lanboyan Pt Mindanao Philippines
68 D1 Lancang China
Lancang Jiang R see Mekong
13 F6 Lancashire co England
102 F7 Lancaster California
13 F5 Lancaster England
110 M4 Lancaster Kentucky
98 K1 Lancaster Minnesota
110 D1 Lancaster Missouri
122 F8 Lancaster New Brunswick
95 Q2 Lancaster New Hampshire
94 J4 Lancaster New York
94 E7 Lancaster Ohio
121 Q7 Lancaster Ontario
95 L6 Lancaster Pennsylvania
112 G3 Lancaster S Carolina
109 L3 Lancaster Texas
95 L9 Lancaster Virginia
99 Q7 Lancaster Wisconsin
115 L3 Lancaster Sd N W Terr
98 B6 Lance Cr Wyoming
143 B9 Lancelin W Australia
143 B9 Lancelin I W Australia
143 E7 Lancelot, Mt W Australia
19 O16 Lance, Mt. de la France
118 J8 Lancer Sask
20 H1 Lanchères France
13 G4 Lanchester England
66 C5 Lan-chia Ts'o L China
48 J2 Lanchin U.S.S.R.
Lanchow see Lanzhou
42 F6 Lanciano Italy
94 C10 Lancing Tennessee
19 O17 Lançon France
31 N5 Łańcut Poland
27 D11 Land reg Norway
98 F1 Landa N Dakota
32 K10 Landau Hessen W Germany
36 E5 Landau Rheinland-Pfalz W Germany
20 C5 Landéan France
41 N3 Landeck Austria
26 G4 Landegode isld Norway
20 C4 Landelles-et-Coupigny France
22 J2 Landen Belgium
101 R7 Lander Wyoming
140 C5 Lander R N Terr Aust
18 C4 Landerneau France
140 B5 Lander R N Terr Aust
27 F14 Landeryd Sweden
94 H8 Landes W Virginia
18 D5 Landes de Lanvaux reg France
18 E8 Landes, Les reg France
28 G7 Landet Denmark
17 G5 Landete Spain
68 A6 Landfall I Andaman Is
133 C8 Landfall, I Chile
9 E6 Landford England
146 J9 Land Glacier Antarctica
33 S5 Landgraben R E Germany
32 J5 Land Hadeln W Germany
74 D1 Landi Khana Pakistan
77 H4 Landi Md. Amin Khan Afghanistan
119 U3 Landing L Manitoba
112 G2 Landis N Carolina
118 J6 Landis Sask
18 C4 Landivisiau France
20 C5 Landivy France
112 F3 Lando S Carolina
99 R3 Land O Lakes Wisconsin
143 B7 Landor W Australia
26 G8 Landösjön L Sweden
22 F3 Landrecies France
22 J5 Landres Ardennes France
22 K5 Landres Meurthe-et-Moselle France
121 N4 Landrienne Quebec
142 F4 Landrigan Cliffs W Australia
38 F8 Landro Italy
112 E2 Landrum S Carolina
40 E6 Landry France
26 M5 Landså Sweden
Landsberg see Gorzów Wielkopolski
33 Q9 Landsberg E Germany
41 N1 Landsberg W Germany
141 L7 Landsborough Queensland
144 B5 Landsborough R New Zealand
141 G5 Landsborough R Queensland
9 F7 Land's End England
114 G2 Lands End C N W Terr
37 N6 Landshut W Germany
28 K5 Landskrona Sweden
36 D5 Landstuhl W Germany
101 R2 Landusky Montana
32 L10 Landwehrhagen W Germany
37 N3 Landwüst E Germany
112 H4 Lane S Carolina
98 H5 Lane S Dakota
109 L6 Lane City Texas
22 G3 Laneffe Belgium
99 P6 Lanesboro Minnesota
111 L9 Lanett Alabama
22 D5 Laneuville-Roy France
22 J5 Laneuville-sur-Meuse France
Lanfeng see Lankao
118 G7 Lanfine Alberta
119 N9 Lang Sask
28 F6 Langå Denmark
66 C5 La'nga Co L China
16 E3 Langa de Duero Spain
47 F4 Langadhás Greece
46 E7 Langádhia Greece
86 G4 Langana, L Ethiopia
71 H7 Langara Sulawesi
117 G8 Langara I Br Columbia
77 A1 Langarūd Iran
119 P8 Langbank Sask
67 B6 Lang Chanh Vietnam
Lang-ch'u Ho see Sutlej
111 L9 Langdale Alabama
118 D8 Langdon Alberta
107 M4 Langdon Kansas
98 H1 Langdon N Dakota
13 F4 Langdon Beck England
18 H7 Langeac France
21 F7 Langeais France
89 A9 Langeberg mts S Africa
89 C7 Langebergen mts S Africa
19 P18 L'Ange, Col de France
28 F7 Langeland isld Denmark
29 L10 Längelmäki Finland
29 L10 Längelmävesi L Finland
33 M9 Langelsheim W Germany
22 D2 Langemark Belgium
36 F4 Langen Hessen W Germany
32 J5 Langen W Germany
37 P2 Langenau E Germany
37 J7 Langenau W Germany
37 N2 Langenberg Gera W Germany
32 F10 Langenberg W Germany
37 M4 Langenbruck W Germany
119 Q8 Langenburg Sask
36 H5 Langenburg W Germany
26 H2 Langenes lt ho Norway
28 B7 Langeness isld W Germany
32 L8 Langenhagen W Germany
28 B7 Langenhorn W Germany
37 O6 Langenisarhofen W Germany
38 N5 Langenlois Austria
36 D4 Langenlonsheim W Germany
33 S9 Langennaundorf E Germany
36 G3 Langenselbold W Germany
37 J5 Langensteinach W Germany
36 F6 Langensteinbach W Germany
40 G3 Langenthal Switzerland
38 N6 Langenwang Austria
37 K5 Langenzenn W Germany
32 F5 Langeoog W Germany
28 E2 Lange-Rak inlet Denmark
28 F6 Langeskov Denmark
28 H5 Langesø L Denmark
27 D12 Langesund Norway
27 D13 Langesundsfjord inlet Norway

Langevag — Lent 43

26 B9 **Langevag** Norway
37 K2 **Langewiesen** E Germany
20 H5 **Langey** France
Langfang *see* **Anci**
26 M1 **Langfjord** Norway
26 Q1 **Langfjord** *inlet* Finnmark Norway
26 C9 **Langfjord** *inlet* More og Romsdal Norway
98 J4 **Langford** S Dakota
32 H7 **Langförden** W Germany
69 E12 **Langgam** Sumatra
69 D12 **Langgapayung** Sumatra
118 L6 **Langham** Sask
44 D2 **Langhe** Italy
44 H2 **Langhirano** Italy
68 C2 **Langhko** Burma
15 F5 **Langholm** Scotland
115 R5 **Langjökull** *ice cap* Iceland
69 D9 **Langkawi** *isld* Malaysia
69 D8 **Lang Kha Toek, Khao** *mt* Thailand
70 E1 **Langkon** Sabah
121 P4 **Langlade** Quebec
123 Q7 **Langlade** *isld* Atlantic Oc
100 C1 **Langley** Washington
28 A5 **Langli** *isld* Denmark
139 H2 **Langlo** *R* Queensland
139 H2 **Langlo Crossing** Queensland
141 H7 **Langlo Downs** Queensland
100 A7 **Langlois** Oregon
121 N4 **Langlois Village** Quebec
32 H5 **Langlütjensand** *sandbank* W Germany
36 D4 **Langmeil** W Germany
40 G4 **Langnau** Switzerland
28 J7 **Langø** *isld* Denmark
18 H8 **Langogne** France
18 E8 **Langon** France
28 F5 **Langør** Denmark
26 G3 **Langöy** *isld* Norway
8 D5 **Langport** England
37 N6 **Langquaid** W Germany
40 B2 **Langres** France
40 B2 **Langres, Plat. de** France
20 E3 **Langrune** France
119 T8 **Langruth** Manitoba
69 C10 **Langsa** Sumatra
69 C10 **Langsa, Teluk** *B* Sumatra
26 J8 **Långsele** Sweden
26 H7 **Långseleån** *R* Sweden
58 E3 **Lang Shan** *mt ra* China
27 H11 **Långshyttan** Sweden
28 D5 **Langskov** Denmark
67 B6 **Lang Son** Vietnam
13 H5 **Langtoft** England
26 L6 **Långträsk** Sweden
108 F6 **Langtry** Texas
18 H8 **Languedoc** *prov* France
110 F6 **L'Anguille** *R* Arkansas
37 J1 **Langula** E Germany
32 H5 **Langwarden** W Germany
13 F4 **Langwathby** England
32 K7 **Langwedel** W Germany
9 F1 **Langworth** England
67 F1 **Langxi** China
67 F2 **Langxi** China
58 E5 **Langzhong** China
67 G5 **Lan Hsü** *isld* Taiwan
121 L5 **Laniel** Quebec
119 N7 **Lanigan** Sask
102 S12 **Lanikai** Hawaiian Is
133 C5 **Lanín** *mt* Argentina
131 B7 **Lanin, Vol** Arg/Chile
8 B7 **Lanivet** England
70 B4 **Lanjak, Bt** *mt* Sarawak
32 E10 **Lank** W Germany
65 C7 **Lankao** China
33 T7 **Lanke** E Germany
98 J1 **Lankin** N Dakota
22 K1 **Lanklaar** Belgium
26 M3 **Lannavaara** Sweden
18 F9 **Lannemezan** France
18 C4 **Lannion** France
22 E2 **Lannoy** France
17 H3 **La Noguera** *dist* Spain
121 R7 **Lanoraie** Quebec
124 F6 **La Noria** Mexico
48 K1 **Lanovtsy** U.S.S.R.
95 M6 **Lansdale** Pennsylvania
121 P8 **Lansdowne** Ontario
115 L7 **Lansdowne House** Ontario
99 S3 **L'Anse** Michigan
123 Q2 **L'Anse-Amour** Labrador
123 P2 **L'Anse au Loup** Quebec
33 R5 **Lansen** E Germany
19 P14 **Lans en Vercors** France
98 E1 **Lansford** N Dakota
95 M6 **Lansford** Pennsylvania
67 D4 **Lanshan** China
99 P6 **Lansing** Iowa
107 Q2 **Lansing** Kansas
94 C4 **Lansing** Michigan
112 F1 **Lansing** N Carolina
31 K6 **Lanškroun** Czechoslovakia
40 E7 **Lanslebourg** France
19 P14 **Lans, Mts de** France
69 D9 **Lanta Ko** Thailand
69 D9 **Lanta, Ko** *isld* Thailand
21 I7 **Lanthenay** France
Lantian *see* **Lianyuan**
65 A7 **Lantian** China
98 E4 **Lantry** S Dakota
43 C9 **Lanusei** Sardinia
71 G6 **Lanuza** Mindanao Philippines
65 G1 **Lanxi** China
67 E1 **Lanxi** China
65 B5 **Lan Xian** China
33 P6 **Lanz** E Germany
85 B3 **Lanzarote** *isld* Canary Is
58 D4 **Lanzhou** China
65 F2 **Lanzijing** China
71 E1 **Laoag** Luzon Philippines
71 G4 **Laoang** Philippines
67 A5 **Lao Cai** Vietnam
67 A4 **Laochang** China
65 D4 **Laoguo** China
59 G3 **Laoha He** *R* China
58 F5 **Lao-ho-k'ou** China
14 D4 **Laois** *co* Irish Rep
65 G4 **Laoling** China
Laolong *see* **Longchuan**
22 F4 **Laon** France
99 S4 **Laona** Wisconsin
20 H4 **Laons** France
127 L9 **La Orchila, I** Venezuela
128 C6 **La Oroya** Peru
68 F3 **Laos** *kingdom* S E Asia
65 E5 **Laotie Shan** *C* China
16 D9 **Laou** *R* Morocco
70 G6 **Laowu** Sulawesi
65 G2 **Laoye Ling** *mts* China
65 H3 **Laoye Ling** *mts* China
71 E8 **Lapac** *isld* Philippines
143 D9 **Lapage, L** W Australia
87 G8 **Lapala** Mozambique
18 H6 **Lapalisse** France
125 P9 **La Palma** Guatemala
85 A3 **La Palma** *isld* Canary Is
16 C7 **La Palma del Concado** Spain
131 C6 **La Pampa** *prov* Argentina
102 D6 **La Panza** California
102 D6 **La Panza Ra** California
128 F2 **La Paragua** Venezuela
17 F4 **La Paraleja** *L* Spain
16 D4 **La Paramera de Avila** Spain
71 D7 **Laparan** *isld* Sulu Arch
124 G6 **La Parilla** Mexico
133 D4 **La Paz** Argentina
128 E7 **La Paz** Bolivia
131 F3 **La Paz** Entre Rios Argentina
94 A5 **Lapaz** Indiana
124 D5 **La Paz** Mexico
127 H9 **La Paz** Venezuela
128 E7 **La Paz** *R* Bolivia
128 E4 **La Pedrera** Colombia
94 D3 **Lapeer** Michigan
94 B6 **Lapel** Indiana
133 E4 **La Pelada** Argentina
124 G3 **La Perla** Mexico
119 U3 **La Perouse** Manitoba
102 T13 **La Pérouse Pinnacle** Hawaiian Is
59 M2 **La Pérouse Strait** Japan/U.S.S.R.
124 H7 **La Piedad** Mexico
100 D6 **Lapine** Oregon
71 G5 **Lapinin** Bohol Philippines
29 N8 **Lapinlahti** Finland
79 D3 **Lapithos** Cyprus
111 F11 **Laplace** Louisiana
68 D4 **Lap Lae** Thailand
21 D7 **La Plaine** France
52 D1 **Laplandiya** U.S.S.R.
131 F5 **La Plata** Argentina
95 L8 **La Plata** Maryland
99 O9 **La Plata** Missouri
123 O6 **La Poile B** Nfld
99 Q3 **La Pointe** Wisconsin
16 D2 **La Pola de Gordón** Spain
52 F3 **Lapominka** U.S.S.R.
102 D2 **La Porte** California
99 U8 **La Porte** Indiana
99 M2 **Laporte** Minnesota
95 L5 **Laporte** Pennsylvania
118 H7 **Laporte** Sask
109 N6 **La Porte** Texas
99 O7 **La Porte City** Iowa
70 F7 **Laposa, Bk** *mt* Sulawesi
21 D6 **La Poueze** France
36 C7 **Lapoutroie** France
48 G6 **Lapovo** Yugoslavia
29 K8 **Lappajärvi** Finland
141 G3 **Lappa Junction** Queensland
29 N10 **Lappeenranta** Finland
29 J9 **Lappfjärd** Finland
27 M10 **Lappi** Finland
29 J10 **Lappi Kauttua** Finland
26 L3 **Lappland** Sweden/Finland
26 N2 **Lappojavrre** *L* Norway
26 N5 **Lappträsk** Sweden
121 R7 **Laprairie** Quebec
101 U7 **La Prele Cr** Wyoming
133 E5 **Laprida** Argentina
108 H7 **La Pryor** Texas
47 H4 **Lâpseki** Turkey
54 J2 **Laptevo** U.S.S.R.
51 M1 **Laptev Sea** U.S.S.R.
29 K9 **Lapua** Finland
29 K8 **Lapuanjoki** *R* Finland
16 E5 **La Puebla de Montalbán** Spain
127 J10 **La Puerta** Venezuela
128 B4 **La Puntilla** *point* Ecuador
124 C4 **La Purisima** Mexico
100 A2 **La Push** Washington
48 H3 **Lăpusului, Muntii** *mts* Romania
21 G8 **La Puye** France
31 O3 **Łapy** Poland
84 H5 **Laqiya Arba'in** Sudan
128 E8 **La Quiaca** Argentina
42 E6 **L'Aquila** Italy
77 D6 **Lār** Iran
16 C9 **Larache** Morocco
19 P16 **Laragne** France
77 E6 **Larak** *isld* Iran
128 D6 **Laramate** Peru
16 D7 **La Rambla** Spain
98 A8 **Laramie** Wyoming
98 A7 **Laramie** *R* Wyoming
98 A7 **Laramie Pk** *mt* Wyoming
130 F8 **Laranjal Paulista** Brazil
130 D9 **Laranjeiras do Sul** Brazil
130 E8 **Laranjinha, R** Brazil
71 L9 **Larantuka** Flores Indonesia
19 O15 **La Raye** *mt* France
15 E4 **Larbert** Scotland
19 N13 **L'Arbresle** France
127 H5 **L'Arcahaie** Haiti
20 D5 **Larchamp** France
121 L4 **Larder Lake** Ontario
47 J8 **Lárdhos, Akr** Rhodes Greece
123 M8 **L'Ardoise** C Breton I, N Scotia
20 K5 **Lardy a Ferte-Alais** France
99 N9 **Laredo** Missouri
16 E1 **Laredo** Spain
109 H8 **Laredo** Texas
121 L4 **La Reine** Quebec
48 K2 **Larga** U.S.S.R.
122 J3 **Large I** Quebec
18 H8 **Largentière** France
113 E10 **Largo** Florida
15 F4 **Largo** Scotland
126 D4 **Largo, Cayo** *isld* Cuba
13 F1 **Largo Ward** Scotland
15 D5 **Largs** Scotland
45 J4 **Lari** Italy
70 F5 **Lariang** Sulawesi
70 F5 **Lariang** *R* Sulawesi
47 F6 **Lárimna** Greece
98 J2 **Larimore** N Dakota
42 F7 **Larino** Italy
131 C2 **La Rioja** Argentina
46 E5 **Lárisa** Greece
77 D6 **Laristan** Iran
119 T9 **La Rivière** Manitoba
98 E3 **Lark** N Dakota
74 C5 **Larkana** Pakistan
12 E2 **Larkhall** Scotland
123 O4 **Lark Harb** Nfld
141 H3 **Lark Pass** Gt Barrier Reef Aust
9 G3 **Lark, R** England
106 F2 **Larkspur** Colorado
9 G3 **Larling** England
55 F2 **Larlomkiny** U.S.S.R.
79 D4 **Larnaca** Cyprus
14 F2 **Larne** N Ireland
107 L3 **Larned** Kansas
14 F2 **Larne L** N Ireland
16 D2 **La Robla** Spain
21 A6 **La Roche-Bernard** France
19 P15 **La Roche-des-Arnauds** France
21 F10 **La Rochefoucauld** France
21 C9 **La Rochelle** France
18 H5 **Laroche-Migennes** France
21 G8 **La Roche-Posay** France
21 C8 **La Roche-sur-Yon** France
19 Q14 **La Rochette** France
22 L4 **Larochette** Luxembourg
9 H7 **La Rocque Pt** Channel Is
17 F5 **La Roda** Spain
16 D7 **La Roda de A** Spain
21 C6 **La Roë** France
127 K5 **La Romana** Dominican Rep
70 G6 **Larompong** Sulawesi
70 G6 **Larona** Sulawesi
21 D9 **La Ronde** France
119 M3 **La Ronge** Sask
124 J5 **La Rosa** Mexico
111 F12 **La Rose** Louisiana
124 J3 **La Rosita** Mexico
142 C5 **Larrey Pt** W Australia
140 C3 **Larrimah** N Terr Aust
123 L8 **Larry's R** Nova Scotia
146 C4 **Lars Christensen Coast** Antarctica
146 E13 **Larsen Ice Shelf** Antarctica
101 T1 **Larslan** Montana
29 K8 **Larsmo** Finland
119 N1 **Larson** Ontario
109 M3 **La Rue** Texas
18 E10 **Laruns** France
27 D12 **Larvik** Norway
50 G2 **Laryak** U.S.S.R.
56 B1 **Lar'yak** U.S.S.R.
124 G6 **Las Adjuntas** Mexico
103 P3 **La Sal** Utah
98 B9 **La Salle** Colorado
99 R8 **La Salle** Illinois
119 U9 **La Salle** Manitoba
120 G10 **La Salle** Ontario
16 E8 **Las Alpujarras** *dist* Spain
70 D4 **Lasan** Kalimantan
124 D2 **La Sangre** Mexico
106 G3 **Las Animas** Colorado
86 A2 **Las Anod** Somalia
121 L4 **La Sarre** Quebec
19 Q16 **La Saulce** France
128 E1 **Las Aves, Is** Venezuela
38 L5 **Lasberg** Austria
28 D4 **Låsby** Denmark
127 J5 **Lascahobas** Haiti
133 E3 **Las Cejas** Argentina
123 R4 **La Scie** Nfld
133 C5 **Las Coloradas** Neuquén Argentina
124 F3 **Las Cruces** Mexico
106 D9 **Las Cruces** New Mexico
86 J3 **Las Dureh** Somalia
127 J5 **La Selle** *mt* Haiti
131 B2 **La Serena** Chile
16 D6 **La Serena** *reg* Spain
124 J4 **Las Esperancas** Mexico
19 P18 **La Seyne** France
131 F6 **Las Flores** Argentina
16 E5 **Las Guadalerzas** *reg* Spain
118 H5 **Lashburn** Sask
77 G4 **Lāsh-ē Joveyn** Afghanistan
68 C1 **Lashio** Burma
77 J4 **Lashkar Gah** Afghanistan
54 N2 **Lashma** U.S.S.R.
16 C4 **Las Hurdes** Spain
69 C11 **Lasia** *isld* Indonesia
69 C11 **Lasikin** Indonesia
43 G9 **La Sila** *dist* Italy
31 L2 **Łasin** Poland
31 L4 **Łask** Poland
86 A1 **Las Khoreh** Somalia
31 L2 **Laskowice** Poland
133 C5 **Las Lajas** Argentina
128 F8 **Las Lajitas** Argentina
128 F8 **Las Lomitas** Argentina
16 C7 **Las Marismas** *dist* Spain
133 D7 **Las Martinetas** Argentina
127 L10 **Las Mercedes** Venezuela
124 G3 **Las Mesteñas** Mexico
124 G4 **Las Nieves** Mexico
16 E6 **La Solana** Spain
70 G6 **Lasolo** Sulawesi
70 G6 **Lasolo** *R* Sulawesi
71 H6 **Lasolo, Tk** *B* Sulawesi
19 O14 **La Sône** France
38 F8 **Lasorling** *mt* Austria
21 H9 **La Souterraine** France
85 A3 **Las Palmas de Gran Canaria** Canary Is
106 C8 **Las Palomas** New Mexico
44 G3 **La Spezia** Italy
117 L11 **Lasqueti I** Br Col
16 E4 **Las Rozas** Spain
33 N5 **Lassahn** E Germany
33 T5 **Lassan** E Germany
130 G5 **Lassance** Brazil
20 E5 **Lassay** France
26 M5 **Lassbyn** Sweden
100 D9 **Lassen Peak** *mt* California
100 D9 **Lassen Vol. Nat. Park** California
22 D4 **Lassigny** France
38 L6 **Lassing** Austria
146 E12 **Lassiter Coast** Antarctica
38 K7 **Lassnitz-Dorf** Austria
38 N7 **Lassnitzhöhe** Austria
121 R7 **L'Assomption** Quebec
13 E2 **Lasswade** Scotland
20 D4 **Lassy** France
133 D3 **Lastarria** *mt* Chile/Arg
106 G2 **Last Chance** Colorado
13 H5 **Lastingham** England
119 N7 **Last Mountain** Sask
119 M7 **Last Mountain L** Sask
86 B6 **Lastoursville** Gabon
42 H6 **Lastovo** *isld* Yugoslavia
124 F7 **Las Tres Marías** *islds* Mexico
32 G7 **Lastrup** W Germany
21 F6 **La Suze-sur-Sarthe** France
124 E3 **Las Varas** Mexico
124 G3 **Las Varas** Mexico
124 G7 **Las Varas** Mexico
103 J5 **Las Vegas** Nevada
106 E6 **Las Vegas** New Mexico
128 C4 **Latacunga** Ecuador
146 F13 **Latady I** Antarctica
79 F3 **Latakia** Syria
29 J3 **Latäseno** *R* Finland
121 L5 **Latchford** Ontario
137 S5 **Late** *isld* Tonga
109 M4 **Latexo** Texas
99 R10 **Latham** Illinois
143 B8 **Latham** W Australia
21 F7 **Lathan** *R* France
32 F7 **Lathen** W Germany
15 E2 **Latheron** Scotland
110 B2 **Lathrop** Missouri
102 H5 **Lathrop Wells** Nevada
21 G9 **Lathus** France
26 J7 **Latikberg** Sweden
43 E7 **Latina** Italy
45 N6 **Latina Scalo** Italy
106 E5 **Latir Pk** New Mexico
54 K5 **Latnaya** U.S.S.R.
133 D4 **La Toma** Argentina
48 H2 **Latoritsa** *R* U.S.S.R.
128 E1 **La Tortuga** *isld* Venezuela
142 D4 **Latouche Treville, C** W Australia
19 O13 **La Tour du Pin** France
21 F7 **La Tour-St. Gélin** France
21 C10 **La Tremblade** France
121 P3 **La Trève, L** Quebec
127 L4 **La Trinité** Martinique W I
94 H6 **Latrobe** Pennsylvania
139 H8 **Latrobe** Tasmania
131 C2 **La Troya, R** Argentina
112 H3 **Latta** S Carolina
Lattaquie *see* **Latakia**
94 C5 **Latty** Ohio
71 M9 **Latuna** Indonesia
121 S5 **La Tuque** Quebec
74 G9 **Latur** India
27 M15 **Latvia** *S.S.R.* U.S.S.R.
85 G7 **Lau** Nigeria
36 G2 **Laubach** Hessen W Germany
36 D3 **Laubach** Rheinland-Pfalz W Germany
137 R6 **Lau Basin** Pacific Oc
21 C6 **Laubrières** France
36 E3 **Laubuseschbach** W Germany
128 E7 **Lauca** *R* Bolivia
37 M1 **Laucha** E Germany
33 T9 **Lauchhammer** E Germany
37 J6 **Lauchheim** W Germany
36 H4 **Lauda-Königshofen** W Germany
27 C13 **Laudal** Norway
36 H5 **Laudenbach** W Germany
119 R9 **Lauder** Manitoba
13 F2 **Lauder** Scotland
15 F5 **Lauder** Scotland
111 H9 **Lauderdale** Mississippi
19 N16 **Laudun** France
32 K8 **Lauenau** W Germany
32 L6 **Lauenbruck** W Germany
33 N6 **Lauenburg** W Germany
32 K9 **Lauenförde** W Germany
32 L8 **Lauenstein** W Germany
37 J3 **Lauer** *R* W Germany
37 L5 **Lauf** W Germany
36 G3 **Laufach** W Germany
40 F3 **Laufen** Switzerland
38 G6 **Laufen** W Germany
36 G5 **Lauffen** W Germany
8 B4 **Laugharne** Wales
99 U3 **Laughing Fish Pt** Michigan
140 C6 **Laughlen Mt** N Terr Aust
106 F5 **Laughlin Pk** New Mexico
9 G6 **Laughton** England
37 J6 **Lauingen** W Germany
29 M9 **Laukaa** Finland
18 H5 **Laumes, les** France
68 D7 **Laun** Thailand
121 M4 **Launay Sta** Quebec
8 B6 **Launceston** England
139 H8 **Launceston** Tasmania
14 B4 **Laune** *R* Irish Rep
68 C6 **Launglon Bok** *islds* Burma
131 A8 **La Unión** Chile
106 D10 **La Union** New Mexico
127 L10 **La Unión** Venezuela
22 H4 **Launois-sur-Vence** France
38 K8 **Launsdorf** Austria
135 V4 **Laupahoehoe** Hawaiian Is
36 H7 **Laupheim** W Germany
71 E3 **Laur** Luzon Philippines
141 G3 **Laura** Queensland
118 K7 **Laura** Sask
138 E5 **Laura** S Australia
128 E2 **La Urbana** Venezuela
28 D4 **Laurbjerg** Denmark
95 M8 **Laurel** Delaware
94 B7 **Laurel** Indiana
95 L7 **Laurel** Maryland
111 G10 **Laurel** Mississippi
101 R4 **Laurel** Montana
130 B10 **Laureles** Paraguay
111 K11 **Laurel Hill** Florida
94 H6 **Laurel Hill** Pennsylvania
94 E7 **Laurelville** Ohio
15 F4 **Laurencekirk** Scotland
99 M7 **Laurens** Iowa
95 M4 **Laurens** New York
112 E3 **Laurens** S Carolina
121 R7 **Laurentides** Quebec
121 T5 **Laurentides, Parc Prov. des** Quebec
43 G8 **Laurenzana** Italy
43 G8 **Lauria** Italy
146 C14 **Laurie I** S Orkney Is
119 P2 **Laurie L** Sask
143 E7 **Laurie, Mt** W Australia
119 Q2 **Laurie R** Manitoba
119 S8 **Laurier** Manitoba
121 T6 **Laurierville** Quebec
12 D4 **Laurieston** Scotland
139 L4 **Laurieton** New S Wales
29 L6 **Laurila** Finland
101 N4 **Laurin** Montana
112 H3 **Laurinburg** N Carolina
19 O17 **Lauris** France
144 C5 **Lauriston** New Zealand
29 N10 **Lauritsala** Finland
99 S2 **Laurium** Michigan
45 R8 **Lauro** Italy
43 F11 **Lauro, M** *mt* Sicily
133 H3 **Lauro Muller** Brazil
40 E4 **Lausanne** Switzerland
37 L3 **Lauscha** E Germany
70 E6 **Laut** *isld* Kalimantan
19 Q14 **Lautaret, Col du** *pass* France
131 A7 **Lautaro** Chile
33 M9 **Lautenthal** W Germany
37 O2 **Lauter** E Germany
36 D5 **Lauter** *R* W Germany
37 M5 **Lauterach** *R* W Germany
36 E7 **Lauterbach** Baden-Württemberg W Germany
36 G2 **Lauterbach** Hessen W Germany
37 O1 **Lauterbach** Leipzig E Germany
36 E6 **Lauterbourg** France
36 D4 **Lauterecken** W Germany
37 M5 **Lauterhofen** W Germany
36 G2 **Lautertal** W Germany
37 K3 **Lautertal** W Germany
41 J1 **Lautlingen** W Germany
18 G9 **Lautrec** France
70 D6 **Laut, Selat** *str* Kalimantan
26 E7 **Lauvsnes** Norway
25 F2 **Lauwers** Netherlands
25 F2 **Lauwers Zee** Netherlands
18 F8 **Lauzerte** France
121 T6 **Lauzon** Quebec
100 D8 **Lava Beds Nat. Mon** California
109 L6 **Lavaca** *R* Texas
109 **Lavaca B** Texas
22 J3 **Lavacherie** Belgium
44 F3 **Lavagna** Italy
44 F3 **Lavagna** *R* Italy
101 O7 **Lava Hot Springs** Idaho
20 D5 **Laval** France
19 P18 **La Valette** France
99 Q6 **La Valle** Wisconsin
131 G5 **Lavalleja** *dep* Uruguay
122 C5 **Laval, R** Quebec
38 L8 **Lavamünd** Austria
77 C6 **Lavan** Iran
45 L3 **Lavane, M** *mt* Italy
26 J3 **Lavangen** Norway
9 F6 **Lavant** England
121 O7 **Lavant** Ontario
38 L8 **Lavant** *R* Austria
38 L8 **Lavanttal** *V* Austria
131 A6 **Lavaplé, Pta** *C* Chile
18 F8 **Lavardac** France
21 G6 **Lavardin** France
20 G5 **Lavaré** France
77 D4 **Lavar Meydan** *salt lake* Iran
18 G9 **Lavaur** France
102 C5 **Laveaga Pk** California
16 D2 **La Vecilla** Spain
127 J5 **La Vega** Dom Rep
124 H7 **La Vega** Mexico
128 E1 **La Vela** Venezuela
18 G10 **Lavelanet** France
16 D3 **La Vellés** Spain
28 D4 **Laven** Denmark
9 G3 **Lavenham** England
41 J6 **Laveno** Italy
22 D2 **Laventie** France
130 B10 **La Verá** *L* Paraguay
133 F3 **La Vera** *L* Paraguay
103 L4 **La Verkin** Utah
107 L5 **Laverne** Oklahoma
109 J6 **La Vernia** Texas
143 D8 **Laverton** W Australia
106 E4 **La Veta** Colorado
71 G4 **Lavezares** Philippines
45 L2 **Lavezzola** Italy
29 K10 **Lavia** Finland
124 H4 **La Víbora** Mexico
121 M7 **Lavieille, L** Ontario
27 A10 **Lavik** Norway
21 H6 **La Ville aux Clèrcs** France
21 I10 **La Villedieu** France
21 F9 **La Villedieu-du-Clain** France
101 R3 **Lavina** Montana
128 C5 **La Viña** Peru
8 D5 **Lavington** England
112 D3 **Lavonia** Georgia
109 L2 **Lavon Res** Texas
118 F5 **Lavoy** Alberta
130 G7 **Lavras** Brazil
130 H9 **Lavras da Mangabeira** Brazil
55 D4 **Lavrent'yevka** U.S.S.R.
26 J7 **Lavsjö** Sweden
87 F11 **Lavumisa** Swaziland
88 C8 **Lavusi** *mt* Zambia
109 L7 **La Ward** Texas
70 D2 **Lawas** Sarawak
70 G6 **Lawato** Sulawesi
71 H7 **Lawele** Indonesia
100 G6 **Lawen** Oregon
119 V4 **Lawford L** Manitoba
141 K6 **Lawgi** Queensland
71 B3 **Lawin** *isld* Indonesia
70 C4 **Lawit, G** *mt* Sarawak
68 C2 **Lawksawk** Burma
99 N3 **Lawler** Minnesota
123 R7 **Lawn** Nfld
108 H3 **Lawn** Texas
112 F2 **Lawndale** N Carolina
140 E4 **Lawn Hill** Queensland
71 H7 **Lawowa** Sulawesi
146 C5 **Law Plat** Antarctica
85 D6 **Lawra** Ghana
94 A7 **Lawrence** Indiana
107 P3 **Lawrence** Kansas
95 Q4 **Lawrence** Massachusetts
98 H9 **Lawrence** Nebraska
144 B6 **Lawrence** New Zealand
94 B7 **Lawrenceburg** Indiana
94 C8 **Lawrenceburg** Kentucky
110 J6 **Lawrenceburg** Tennessee
122 E8 **Lawrence Stn** New Brunswick
122 G9 **Lawrencetown** Nova Scotia
122 J9 **Lawrencetown** Nova Scotia
112 D4 **Lawrenceville** Georgia
110 J3 **Lawrenceville** Illinois
95 L5 **Lawrenceville** Pennsylvania
94 K10 **Lawrenceville** Virginia
143 D7 **Lawrence Wells, Mt** W Australia
102 F4 **Laws** California
110 B2 **Lawson** Missouri
118 L8 **Lawson** Sask
113 E7 **Lawtey** Florida
94 B4 **Lawton** Michigan
98 H1 **Lawton** N Dakota
107 M7 **Lawton** Oklahoma
27 G12 **Laxå** Sweden
12 D5 **Laxey** I of Man U.K.
9 H3 **Laxfield** England
15 G2 **Laxo** Scotland
26 G8 **Laxsjö** Sweden
101 S9 **Lay** Colorado
21 C8 **Lay** *R* France
52 J2 **Laya** *R* U.S.S.R.
52 G1 **Laydennyy, Mys** *C* U.S.S.R.
20 K5 **Laye** *R* France
139 G7 **Layers Hill** Victoria
111 K9 **Lay L** Alabama
21 D7 **Layon** *R* France
85 B3 **La'youn** Western Sahara
55 E2 **Laytamak** U.S.S.R.
83 K12 **Lazare, Pt** Mahé I Indian Oc
48 F6 **Lazarevac** Yugoslavia
57 A3 **Lazareva, Oz** *isld* U.S.S.R.
124 B2 **Lázaro Cárdenas** Mexico
47 G1 **Lazar Stanevo** Bulgaria
86 A1 **Laz Daua** Somalia
31 O1 **Lazdijai** U.S.S.R.
21 J7 **Lazenay** France
42 E6 **Lazio** *prov* Italy
37 O3 **Lázně Kynžvart** Czechoslovakia
59 K3 **Lazo** U.S.S.R.
13 F4 **Lazonby** England
9 F1 **Lea** England
100 C5 **Leaburg** Oregon
68 F6 **Leach** Cambodia
110 F6 **Leachville** Arkansas
98 C5 **Lead** S Dakota
13 E2 **Leadburn** Scotland
9 F1 **Leadenham** England
9 G4 **Leaden Roding** England
118 H8 **Leader** Sask
15 E5 **Leadhills** Scotland
101 M5 **Leadore** Idaho
106 D2 **Leadville** Colorado
139 J4 **Leadville** New S Wales
115 M6 **Leaf** *R* Quebec
99 R7 **Leaf River** Illinois
146 J11 **Leahy,C** Antarctica
9 G1 **Leake** England
142 F4 **Leake, Mt** W Australia
143 C7 **Leake, Mt** W Australia
111 H10 **Leakesville** Mississippi
108 H6 **Leakey** Texas
98 H2 **Leal** N Dakota
111 G10 **Leal** *R* Mississippi
133 D3 **Leales** Argentina
142 B5 **Leal, Mt** W Australia
145 E2 **Leamington** New Zealand
120 H10 **Leamington** Ontario
103 M2 **Leamington** Utah
9 E3 **Leamington Spa, Royal** England
9 E3 **Leam,R** England
67 E3 **Le'an** China
12 C1 **Leanach** Scotland
109 K5 **Leander** Texas
130 C10 **Leandro N.Alem** Argentina
14 B4 **Leane,L** Irish Rep
67 F2 **Le'an Jiang** *R* China
9 F4 **Lea, R** England
142 A5 **Learmonth** W Australia
111 M10 **Leary** Georgia
9 F1 **Leasingham** England
118 L5 **Leask** Sask
9 F5 **Leatherhead** England
101 M5 **Leatherman Pk** Idaho
110 K3 **Leavenworth** Indiana
107 P2 **Leavenworth** Kansas
100 E2 **Leavenworth** Washington
102 E3 **Leavitt Pk** California
31 K1 **Łeba** Poland
36 B5 **Lebach** W Germany
70 L9 **Lebak** Java
71 G7 **Lebak** Mindanao Philippines
100 B3 **Lebam** Washington
46 E2 **Lebane** Yugoslavia
86 B5 **Lebango** Congo
110 G3 **Lebanon** Illinois
110 K1 **Lebanon** Indiana
107 M2 **Lebanon** Kansas
110 L4 **Lebanon** Kentucky
110 D4 **Lebanon** Missouri
98 F9 **Lebanon** Nebraska
95 Q3 **Lebanon** New Hampshire
94 C7 **Lebanon** Ohio
100 C5 **Lebanon** Oregon
95 L6 **Lebanon** Pennsylvania
98 G4 **Lebanon** S Dakota
110 K5 **Lebanon** Tennessee
94 E10 **Lebanon** Virginia
79 F4 **Lebanon** *rep* S W Asia
94 B9 **Lebanon Junc** Kentucky
113 E8 **Lebanon Stn** Florida
19 P18 **Le Beausset** France
102 F7 **Lebec** California
55 E3 **Lebedevka** U.S.S.R.
54 F6 **Lebedin** U.S.S.R.
54 L3 **Lebedyan'** U.S.S.R.
48 D3 **Lébény** Hungary
26 Q1 **Lebesby** Norway
21 H8 **Le Blanc** France
107 P3 **Lebo** Kansas
89 G4 **Lebombo Mts** Mozambique
68 A2 **Lebon** Burma
31 K1 **Lębórk** Poland
71 M9 **Lebos** Timor
19 Q14 **Le Bourg d'Oisans** France
19 P13 **Le Bourget** France
122 H6 **Le Bouthillier** New Brunswick
119 O8 **Lebret** Sask
16 C8 **Lebrija** Spain
31 K1 **Łebsko, Jezioro** *L* Poland
133 C5 **Lebu** Chile
33 S9 **Lebusa** E Germany
28 E7 **Leby** Denmark
55 G5 **Lebyazh'ye** Kazakhstan U.S.S.R.
52 G6 **Lebyazh'ye** Kirov U.S.S.R.
55 E3 **Lebyazh'ye** Kurgan U.S.S.R.
71 N9 **Leça** Timor
19 Q18 **Le Canadel** France
43 J8 **Lecce** Italy
41 K6 **Lecco** Italy
41 K6 **Lecco, Lago di** Italy
99 N5 **Le Center** Minnesota
37 K7 **Lech** *R* W Germany
67 D4 **Lechang** China
21 C10 **Le Château d'Oléron** France
21 J8 **Le Châtelet** France
41 N2 **Lechbruck** W Germany
19 J3 **Le Chesne** France
41 N1 **Lechfeld** *plain* W Germany
48 J3 **Lechința** Romania
9 E4 **Lechlade** England
41 M3 **Lech Tal** *V* Austria
41 M3 **Lechtaler Alpen** *mt* Austria
17 G3 **Leciñena** Spain
28 B7 **Leck** W Germany
146 B5 **Leckie Ra** Antarctica
22 E3 **Lecluse** France
111 D10 **Lecompte** Louisiana
13 H6 **Leconfield** England
18 H6 **Le Creusot** France
18 F9 **Lectoure** France
18 D9 **Lecumberri** Spain
31 O4 **Łęczna** Poland
31 L3 **Łęczyca** Poland
52 F4 **Led** *R* U.S.S.R.
32 G6 **Leda** *R* W Germany
69 F11 **Ledang, Gunung** Malaysia
8 D3 **Ledbury** England
16 C3 **Ledesma** Spain
143 C10 **Ledge Pt** W Australia
101 O1 **Ledger** Montana
87 B7 **Ledo, C** Angola
68 J3 **Ledong** China
21 H9 **Le Dorat** France
41 N6 **Ledro,L.di** Italy
118 D5 **Leduc** Alberta
69 D11 **Ledung** Sumatra
31 K2 **Lędyczek** Poland
103 P10 **Lee** Arizona
28 D4 **Lee** Denmark
113 D7 **Lee** Florida
99 S8 **Lee** Illinois
95 O4 **Lee** Massachusetts
94 H6 **Leechburg** Pennsylvania
99 M2 **Leech L** Minnesota
119 P7 **Leech L** Sask
41 N2 **Leeder** W Germany
142 B1 **Leederville** *dist* Perth, W Aust
108 E8 **Leedey** Oklahoma
111 K8 **Leeds** Alabama
13 G6 **Leeds** England
98 G1 **Leeds** N Dakota
103 L4 **Leeds** Utah
95 R2 **Leeds Junct** Maine
8 D1 **Leek** England
25 F2 **Leek** Netherlands
94 B2 **Leelanau L** Michigan
13 G5 **Leeming** England
142 F2 **Leeming,Mt** W Australia
25 E6 **Leende** Netherlands
9 E6 **Lee-on-Solent** England
110 F4 **Leeper** Missouri
94 H5 **Leeper** Pennsylvania
32 F6 **Leer** W Germany
22 G2 **Leerbeek** Belgium
25 D5 **Leerdam** Netherlands
113 F9 **Leesburg** Florida
112 C6 **Leesburg** Georgia
101 L4 **Leesburg** Idaho
94 D7 **Leesburg** Ohio
109 M3 **Leesburg** Texas
94 K7 **Leesburg** Virginia
32 K7 **Leese** W Germany
110 B3 **Lees Summit** Missouri
143 D7 **Lee Steere Ra** W Australia
144 D5 **Leeston** New Zealand
109 O4 **Leesville** Louisiana
112 F4 **Leesville** S Carolina
109 K6 **Leesville** Texas
94 H9 **Leesville L.** Virginia
94 F6 **Leesville Res** Ohio
139 H5 **Leeton** New S Wales
94 G6 **Leetonia** Ohio
94 B2 **Leetsville** Michigan
25 E2 **Leeuwarden** Netherlands
143 B10 **Leeuwin,C** W Australia
102 E4 **Lee Vining** California
127 N5 **Leeward Is** W Indies
32 M5 **Leezen** W Germany
22 D1 **Leffinge** Belgium
86 C6 **Lefini** *R* Congo
79 C3 **Lefka** Cyprus
79 D4 **Lefkara** Cyprus
79 D3 **Lefkoniko** Cyprus
71 C3 **Lef Pale** *isld* W Irian
121 L8 **Lefroy** Ontario
143 D9 **Lefroy,L** W Australia
119 T2 **Leftrook L** Manitoba
21 C7 **Le Fuilet** France
118 D5 **Legal** Alberta
120 E2 **Legarde** *R* Ontario
121 R6 **Legaré,L** Quebec
71 F4 **Legaspi** Philippines
21 B7 **Le Gavre** France
9 G1 **Legbourne** England
32 F8 **Legden** W Germany
21 B8 **Lége** France
142 B5 **Legendre I** W Australia
19 P14 **Le Genevrey** France
Leghorn *see* **Livorno**
121 T4 **Le Gîte** Quebec
22 K4 **Léglise** Belgium
45 K1 **Legnago** Italy
41 J6 **Legnano** Italy
45 L1 **Legnaro** Italy
31 J4 **Legnica** Poland
41 K5 **Legnone** *mt* Italy
56 B4 **Legostayevo** U.S.S.R.
48 D4 **Legrad** Yugoslavia
102 D4 **Le Grand** California
21 I9 **Le Grand Bourg** France
143 E10 **Le Grand,C** W Australia
21 F6 **Le Grand-Lucé** France
19 O14 **Le Grand Serre** France
140 A3 **Legune** N Terr Aust
74 G1 **Leh** Kashmir
37 L3 **Lehesten** E Germany
101 O9 **Lehi** Utah
107 O7 **Lehigh** Oklahoma
109 L1 **Lehigh** Oklahoma
95 M6 **Lehighton** Pennsylvania
48 K6 **Lehliu** Romania
100 G4 **Lehman** Oregon
33 R8 **Lehnin** E Germany
20 A5 **Lehon** France
98 G3 **Lehr** N Dakota
37 K5 **Lehrberg** W Germany
33 N8 **Lehre** W Germany
32 L8 **Lehrte** W Germany
33 O6 **Lehsen** E Germany
29 K9 **Lehtimäki** Finland
67 E2 **Lehua** China
102 U13 **Lehua I** Hawaiian Is
74 D3 **Leiah** Pakistan
37 O6 **Leiblfing** W Germany
38 N8 **Leibnitzer** Austria
67 A2 **Leibo** China
33 T8 **Leibsch** E Germany
9 E2 **Leicester** England
9 E2 **Leicestershire** *co* England
140 E4 **Leichhardt** *R* Queensland
140 E4 **Leichhardt Falls** Queensland
141 G5 **Leichhardt,Mt** Queensland
141 H5 **Leichhardt Ra** Queensland
36 C1 **Leichlingen** W Germany
68 K2 **Lei-chou** China
25 C4 **Leiden** Netherlands
22 E2 **Leie** *R* Belgium
33 M8 **Leiferde** W Germany
9 G5 **Leigh** England
145 E2 **Leigh** New Zealand
138 E4 **Leigh** *R* S Australia
138 E4 **Leigh Creek** S Australia
14 E4 **Leighlinbridge** Irish Rep
142 A2 **Leighton Beach** *dist* Perth, W Aust
9 F4 **Leighton Buzzard** England
140 D6 **Leighton,Mt** N Terr Aust
22 J3 **Leignon** Belgium
27 B10 **Leikanger** Norway
68 C3 **Leiktho** Burma
141 F5 **Leila Vale** Queensland
33 O9 **Leimbach** E Germany
36 D5 **Leimen** W Germany
25 C4 **Leimuiden** Netherlands
37 K2 **Leina** *R* E Germany
118 K8 **Leinan** Sask
32 M10 **Leine** *R* E Germany
32 L8 **Leine** *R* W Germany
33 M10 **Leinefelde** E Germany
36 G6 **Leinfelden** W Germany
14 E4 **Leinster** *mt* Irish Rep
14 D3 **Leinster** *prov* Irish Rep
37 J7 **Leipheim** W Germany
26 M4 **Leipojärvi** Sweden
94 D5 **Leipsic** Ohio
33 Q10 **Leipzig** E Germany
118 J6 **Leipzig** Sask
33 R10 **Leipzig** *reg* E Germany
26 G4 **Leiranger** Norway
26 N1 **Leirbotn** Norway
16 B5 **Leiria** Portugal
26 R1 **Leirpollen** Norway
27 A12 **Leirvik** Norway
22 D2 **Leisele** Belgium
67 C3 **Leishan** China
67 D3 **Lei Shui** *R* China
138 B3 **Leisler Hills** S Australia
140 A6 **Leisler,Mt** N Terr Aust
37 O1 **Leisnig** E Germany
9 H3 **Leiston** England
110 K4 **Leitchfield** Kentucky
101 T5 **Leiter** Wyoming
98 E3 **Leith** N Dakota
13 E2 **Leith** Scotland
48 C3 **Leitha** *R* Austria
144 D5 **Leithfield** New Zealand
9 F5 **Leith Hill** England
14 C2 **Leitrim** *co* Irish Rep
33 P8 **Leitzkau** E Germany
29 M10 **Leivonmäki** Finland
14 E3 **Leixlip** Irish Rep
67 D3 **Leiyang** China
Leizhou *see* **Haikang**
67 C6 **Leizhou Bandao** *pen* China
67 C6 **Leizhou Wan** *inlet* China
28 M2 **Lejnum** Faeroes
25 C5 **Lek** *R* Netherlands
26 E6 **Leka** *isld* Norway
47 G3 **Lekáni** Greece
86 G4 **Lekemti** Ethiopia
46 E7 **Lekhainá** Greece
46 E4 **Lékhovon** Greece
16 D10 **Lekkous** *R* Morocco
27 G11 **Leksand** Sweden
29 P8 **Leksozero, Ozero** *L* U.S.S.R.
26 E8 **Leksvik** Norway
127 L4 **Le Lamentin** Martinique W I
99 N6 **Leland** Iowa
99 V4 **Leland** Michigan
111 F8 **Leland** Mississippi
27 E12 **Lelången** *L* Sweden
19 Q18 **Le Lavandou** France
133 C6 **Leleque** Argentina
70 G6 **Lelewau** Sulawesi
Leli *see* **Tianlin**
108 G1 **Lelia Lake** Texas
21 H7 **Le Liège** France
48 E7 **Lelija** *mt* Yugoslavia
65 D6 **Leling** China
71 C3 **Lelintah** W Irian
21 D6 **Le Lion-d'Angers** France
28 J6 **Lellinge** Denmark
71 L9 **Lelogama** Timor Indonesia
21 C7 **Le Loroux-Bottereau** France
127 L4 **Le Lorrain** Martinique W I
21 D7 **Le Louroux-Beconnais** France
19 Q18 **Le Luc** France
21 F6 **Le Lude** France
25 D3 **Lelystad** Netherlands
28 A4 **Lem** Denmark
43 F11 **Le Madonie** *mts* Sicily
133 E8 **Le Maire, Estrecho de** *str* Argentina
7 M9 **Leman Bank** *sea rig* North Sea
40 D5 **Léman,Lac** Switz/France
20 F5 **Le Mans** France
94 K7 **Lemasters** Pennsylvania
21 D7 **Le May-sur-Evre** France
70 E4 **Lembac** Kalimantan
38 J5 **Lembach** Austria
36 D5 **Lembach** France
71 J4 **Lembeh** *isld* Sulawesi
Lemberg *see* **L'vov**
36 C5 **Lemberg** France
119 O8 **Lemberg** Sask
36 D5 **Lemberg** W Germany
32 H7 **Lembruch** W Germany
69 C10 **Lembu,Gunung** *mt* Sumatra
130 F8 **Leme** São Paulo Brazil
71 E4 **Lemery** Philippines
32 H8 **Lemforde** W Germany
32 J8 **Lemgo** W Germany
101 M5 **Lemhi** Idaho
101 M5 **Lemhi Ra** Idaho
121 S6 **Lemieux** Quebec
115 N5 **Lemieux Is** N W Terr
106 D7 **Lemitar** New Mexico
32 K7 **Lemke** W Germany
29 M3 **Lemmenjoki** *R* Finland
25 E3 **Lemmer** Netherlands
28 D4 **Lemming** Denmark
98 D4 **Lemmon** S Dakota
114 J8 **Lemmon** S Dakota
103 O9 **Lemmon, Mt** Arizona
Lemnos *isld* Greece *see* **Límnos** *I*
126 H5 **Le Môle St. Nicolas** Haiti
111 G9 **Lemon** Mississippi
102 E5 **Lemoore** California
127 L4 **Le Morne Rouge** Martinique W I
70 G5 **Lemoro** Sulawesi
98 E8 **Lemoyne** Nebraska
125 P11 **Lempa** *R* El Salvador
29 K10 **Lempäälä** Finland
18 H7 **Lempdes** France
117 O9 **Lempriere** Br Columbia
118 H8 **Lemsford** Sask
43 G7 **Le Murge** *dist* Italy
70 D3 **Lemutan** Kalimantan
19 Q18 **Le Muy** France
28 A3 **Lemvig** Denmark
32 J6 **Lemwerder** W Germany
68 B4 **Lemyethna** Burma
70 D4 **Len** *R* Kalimantan
99 R7 **Lena** Illinois
109 P4 **Lena** Louisiana
111 G9 **Lena** Mississippi
100 F4 **Lena** Oregon
27 J11 **Lena** Sweden
99 S5 **Lena** Wisconsin
56 G3 **Lena** *R* U.S.S.R.
101 Q9 **Lena, Mt** Utah
107 P5 **Lenapah** Oklahoma
38 H7 **Lend** Austria
12 D3 **Lendalfoot** Scotland
29 P8 **Lendery** U.S.S.R.
45 L1 **Lendinara** Italy
118 K6 **Leney** Sask
33 M8 **Lengede** W Germany
37 P2 **Lengefeld** E Germany
32 G8 **Lengerich** W Germany
66 E4 **Lenghu** China
58 D4 **Lenglong Ling** *mt ra* China
67 D3 **Lengshuijiang** China
131 B3 **Lengua de Vaca,Pta** Chile
65 E4 **Lengzipu** China
9 G5 **Lenham** England
27 H15 **Lenhovda** Sweden
78 J1 **Leninakan** U.S.S.R.
57 G5 **Lenina, Pik** *mt* U.S.S.R.
36 B6 **Léning** France
49 **Leningrad** *conurbation* U.S.S.R.
146 K5 **Leningradskaya** U.S.S.R.
Lenin I.V. Kanal *see* **Volgo Balt**
56 B5 **Leninogorsk** U.S.S.R.
55 C4 **Leninsk** Chelyabinsk U.S.S.R.
57 A4 **Leninsk** Turkmenia U.S.S.R.
52 G6 **Leninskiy** Mariy U.S.S.R.
54 J2 **Leninskiy** Tula U.S.S.R.
56 B4 **Leninsk-Kuznetskiy** U.S.S.R.
57 G4 **Leninskoye** Kirgiziya U.S.S.R.
52 G5 **Leninskoye** Kirov U.S.S.R.
88 B9 **Lenje** Zambia
55 H4 **Len'ki** U.S.S.R.
71 C3 **Lenmalu** W Irian
142 E3 **Lennard,R** W Australia
27 E12 **Lennartsfors** Sweden
36 E1 **Lenne** *R* W Germany
101 P3 **Lennep** Montana
36 E1 **Lennestadt** W Germany
143 F7 **Lennis Hills** W Australia
143 C8 **Lennonville** W Australia
98 K6 **Lennox** S Dakota
133 D9 **Lennox, I** Chile/Arg
12 D2 **Lennoxtown** Scotland
121 T7 **Lennoxville** Quebec
112 F2 **Lenoir** N Carolina
112 C2 **Lenoir City** Tennessee
107 K2 **Lenora** Kansas
119 R9 **Lenore** Manitoba
119 M6 **Lenore L** Sask
100 F2 **Lenore, L** Washington
112 D6 **Lenox** Georgia
99 M9 **Lenox** Iowa
95 O4 **Lenox** Massachusetts
22 F2 **Lens** Belgium
22 D3 **Lens** France
33 N4 **Lensahn** W Germany
26 D8 **Lensvik** Norway
25 E5 **Lent** Netherlands

110 M2 **Little Miami** *R* Ohio
15 B3 **Little Minch** *chan* Hebrides Scotland
98 B5 **Little Missouri** *R* Wyoming
69 A9 **Little Nicobar** *isld* Nicobar Is
107 Q3 **Little Osage** *R* Kansas/Missouri
112 H3 **Little Pee Dee R** S Carolina
9 G3 **Littleport** England
98 A5 **Little Powder** *R* Wyoming
123 Q5 **Little R** Nfld
111 J10 **Little River** Alabama
107 N3 **Little River** Kansas
144 D5 **Little River** New Zealand
112 J4 **Little River Inlet** N Carolina
110 D7 **Little Rock** Arkansas
102 G7 **Littlerock** California
88 E6 **Little Ruaha** *R* Tanzania
99 U6 **Little Sable Pt** Michigan
110 C4 **Little Sac** *R* Missouri
117 F4 **Little Salmon L** Yukon Terr
103 M4 **Little Salt L** Utah
119 T1 **Little Sand L** Manitoba
101 Q7 **Little Sandy Cr** Wyoming
112 E6 **Little Satilla** *R* Georgia
99 L7 **Little Sioux** *R* Iowa
117 P8 **Little Smoky River** Alberta
101 R9 **Little Snake** *R* Colorado
9 G6 **Littlestone-on-Sea** England
95 K7 **Littlestown** Pennsylvania
99 T5 **Little Suamico** Wisconsin
122 F7 **Little S.W. Miramichi R** New Brunswick
112 C2 **Little Tennessee** *R* Tennessee
127 N1 **Little Tobago** *isld* Tobago
106 E2 **Littleton** Colorado
99 Q9 **Littleton** Illinois
112 K1 **Littleton** N Carolina
95 Q2 **Littleton** New Hampshire
94 G7 **Littleton** W Virginia
95 N2 **Little Tupper L** New York
94 J4 **Little Valley** New York
100 K7 **Little Valley Cr** Idaho
111 J7 **Littleville** Alabama
110 H3 **Little Wabash** *R* Illinois
9 G4 **Little Waltham** England
98 E6 **Little White** *R* S Dakota
101 L6 **Little Wood** *R* Idaho
8 D2 **Littleworth** England
78 J4 **Little Zab** *R* Iraq
37 Q2 **Litvinov** Czechoslovakia
67 C4 **Liucheng** China
67 B3 **Liuchong He** *R* China
Liuchuan *see* **Jianhe**
67 B2 **Liudu** China
67 B3 **Liuguang** China
67 F3 **Liuhe** China
65 E3 **Liu He** *R* China
65 F3 **Liu He** *R* China
67 B1 **Liuhechang** China
67 G2 **Liuheng Dao** *isld* China
65 E2 **Liuhu** China
67 D1 **Liujiachang** China
67 C4 **Liu Jiang** *R* China
88 E7 **Liuli** Tanzania
65 C5 **Liulinzhen** China
67 B4 **Liuma** China
Liupai *see* **Tian'e**
67 D1 **Liushuigou** China
67 C4 **Liutang** China
67 D2 **Liuyang** China
67 D2 **Liuyang He** *R* China
67 B4 **Liuzhai** China
Liuzhangzhen *see* **Yuangu**
67 C4 **Liuzhou** China
65 C7 **Liuzhuang** China
48 H3 **Livada** Romania
52 C6 **Livani** U.S.S.R.
20 F3 **Livarot** France
118 J5 **Livelong** Sask
110 N4 **Livengood** Alaska
42 E3 **Livenza** *R* Italy
102 C2 **Live Oak** California
113 E7 **Live Oak** Florida
142 E4 **Liveringa** W Australia
102 C4 **Livermore** California
99 M7 **Livermore** Iowa
110 J4 **Livermore** Kentucky
95 R2 **Livermore Falls** Maine
108 C5 **Livermore, Mt** Texas
139 K5 **Liverpool** New S Wales
95 L3 **Liverpool** New York
122 H9 **Liverpool** Nova Scotia
11 B2 **Liverpool** *conurbation* England
140 C1 **Liverpool R** N Terr Aust
114 G3 **Liverpool B** N W Terr
115 M3 **Liverpool,C** N W Terr
139 K4 **Liverpool Plains** New S Wales
139 K4 **Liverpool Ra** *mts* New S Wales
143 F7 **Livesey Ra** W Australia
19 P14 **Livet** France
41 M4 **Livigno** Italy
111 H9 **Livingston** Alabama
125 P10 **Livingston** Guatemala
110 M4 **Livingston** Kentucky
111 F11 **Livingston** Louisiana
101 P4 **Livingston** Montana
15 E5 **Livingston** Scotland
109 N5 **Livingston** Texas
99 Q7 **Livingston** Wisconsin
89 D1 **Livingstone** Zambia
117 F5 **Livingstone Creek** Yukon Terr
88 C8 **Livingstone Memorial** Zambia
144 B6 **Livingstone Mts** New Zealand
88 E6 **Livingstone Mts** Tanzania
118 C8 **Livingstone Ra** Alberta
146 E15 **Livingston I** S Shetland Is
87 F8 **Livingstonia** Malawi
95 N5 **Livingston Manor** New York
42 H5 **Livno** Yugoslavia
54 J4 **Livny** U.S.S.R.
28 B3 **Livø** *isld* Denmark
29 M6 **Livojoki** *R* Finland
111 E11 **Livonia** Louisiana
94 D4 **Livonia** Michigan
99 Q9 **Livonia** Missouri
44 H4 **Livorno** Italy
18 H7 **Livradois,Mts.du** France
133 F4 **Livramento** Brazil
20 C5 **Livré** France
19 N15 **Livron** France
87 G7 **Liwale** Tanzania
88 G6 **Liwale** Tanzania
31 N3 **Liwiec** *R* Poland
67 E2 **Lixi** China
65 C5 **Li Xian** China
67 D2 **Li Xian** Hunan China
67 A1 **Li Xian** Sichuan China
36 B5 **Lixing les St.Avold** France
46 D6 **Lixourion** Greece
67 F1 **Liyang** China
67 C4 **Liyong** China
9 G7 **Lizard** *pen* England
129 J5 **Lizarda** Brazil
101 Q7 **Lizard Head Pk** Wyoming
141 H2 **Lizard I** Gt Barrier Reef Aust
112 D5 **Lizella** Georgia
94 F8 **Lizemores** W Virginia
52 D4 **Lizhma** U.S.S.R.
18 F7 **Lizonne** *R* France
121 S4 **Lizotte** Quebec
110 K2 **Lizton** Indiana
45 J3 **Lizzano in Belvedere** Italy
27 F10 **Ljåra** *R* Norway
42 H4 **Ljubija** Yugoslavia
42 J6 **Ljubinje** Yugoslavia
46 C1 **Ljubišnja** *mt* Yugoslavia
42 F2 **Ljubljana** Yugoslavia
46 E2 **Ljuboten** *mt* Yugoslavia
48 E6 **Ljubovija** Yugoslavia
42 H5 **Ljubuški** Yugoslavia
27 K14 **Ljugarn** Gotland Sweden
26 H9 **Ljunga** Sweden
26 H9 **Ljungan** *R* Sweden
26 H9 **Ljungaverk** Sweden
27 G15 **Ljungby** Sweden
27 G15 **Ljungby, Ö** Sweden
26 F9 **Ljungdalen** Sweden
26 H10 **Ljusdal** Sweden
26 H9 **Ljusnan** *R* Sweden
27 J10 **Ljusne** Sweden
27 K12 **Ljusterö** Sweden
133 C5 **Llaima** *mt* Chile
131 B7 **Llaima,Vol** Chile
8 B2 **Llanaelhaiarn** Wales
8 B3 **Llanarth** Wales
8 B2 **Llanbedr** Wales
8 B2 **Llanbedrog** Wales
8 B1 **Llanberis** Wales
8 C3 **Llanbister** Wales
131 B5 **Llancanelo, L** Argentina
131 C5 **Llancanelo,Salina** Argentina
8 C5 **Llandaf** Wales
8 C4 **Llandarcy** Wales
8 B4 **Llanddarog** Wales
8 B4 **Llandefeilog** Wales
8 B1 **Llandegai** Wales
8 B4 **Llandeilo** Wales
8 B4 **Llandissilio** Wales
8 C4 **Llandovery** Wales
8 B4 **Llandowror** Wales
8 C2 **Llandrillo** Wales
8 C3 **Llandrindod Wells** Wales
8 C1 **Llandudno** Wales
8 B3 **Llandyssul** Wales
8 B4 **Llanelli** Wales
8 B1 **Llanerchymedd** Wales
16 D1 **Llanes** Spain
8 B1 **Llanfaethlu** Wales
8 C1 **Llanfairfechan** Wales
8 C1 **Llanfair Talhaiarn** Wales
8 B3 **Llanfarian** Wales
8 C1 **Llanferres** Wales
8 C2 **Llanfyllin** Wales
8 C2 **Llangadfan** Wales
8 C4 **Llangadog** Wales
8 C3 **Llangammarch Wells** Wales
8 B1 **Llangefni** Wales
8 B3 **Llangeler** Wales
8 B2 **Llangelynin** Wales
8 C1 **Llangernyw** Wales
8 C2 **Llangollen** Wales
8 C2 **Llangurig** Wales
8 C2 **Llangynog** Wales
8 C3 **Llanidloes** Wales
8 B3 **Llanilar** Wales
8 B1 **Llanllyfni** Wales
8 B4 **Llanmadog** Wales
124 D2 **Llano** Mexico
109 J5 **Llano** Texas
109 H5 **Llano** *R* Texas
124 G6 **Llano Grande** Mexico
128 D2 **Llanos** *prairies* Colombia/Venezuela
131 C3 **Llanos,Sa.de los** *mts* Argentina
133 C6 **Llanquihue** *prov* Chile
131 A8 **Llanquihue,L** Chile
141 F5 **Llanrheidol** Queensland
8 B4 **Llanrhidian** Wales
8 C3 **Llanrhystyd** Wales
8 C1 **Llanrwst** Wales
18 H10 **Llansa** Spain
8 C1 **Llansannan** Wales
8 B3 **Llansantffraid** Wales
8 B4 **Llanstephan** Wales
8 C4 **Llanthony** Wales
8 C2 **Llantrisant** Wales
8 C4 **Llanwrda** Wales
8 C3 **Llanwrtyd Wells** Wales
8 B3 **Llanybydder** Wales
8 C2 **Llanymynech** England
77 E5 **Llazarán, Küh-e** *mt* Iran
8 B3 **Llechryd** Wales
17 H3 **Llena,Sierra de la** *mts* Spain
16 C6 **Llerena** Spain
133 C4 **Llico** Chile
17 J3 **Llobregat** *R* Spain
101 Q1 **Lloyd** Montana
141 G2 **Lloyd B** Queensland
117 L7 **Lloyd George, Mt** Br Columbia
118 H5 **Lloydminster** Alberta/Sask
127 K2 **Lluidas Vale** Jamaica
133 D2 **Llullaillaco** *mt* Arg/Chile
128 E7 **Lluta** *R* Chile
8 B2 **Llwyngwril** Wales
8 C3 **Llyswen** Wales
103 N3 **Loa** Utah
128 E8 **Loa** *R* Chile
70 E5 **Loakulu** Kalimantan
99 R10 **Loami** Illinois
130 D8 **Loanda** Brazil
86 D6 **Loange** *R* Zaïre
86 B6 **Loango** Congo
13 E2 **Loanhead** Scotland
110 G2 **Loami** Illinois
44 D4 **Loano** Italy
71 G6 **Loay** Philippines
52 H5 **Loban'** *R* U.S.S.R.
54 K3 **Lobanovo** U.S.S.R.
89 D5 **Lobatse** Botswana
36 F4 **Löbau** E Germany
86 C5 **Lobaye** *R* Cent Afr Republic
22 G3 **Lobbes** Belgium
37 M2 **Lobeda** E Germany
33 P9 **Löbejün** E Germany
37 M3 **Lobenstein** E Germany
133 F5 **Loberia** Argentina
31 J2 **Łobez** Poland
87 B8 **Lobito** Angola
33 R4 **Löbnitz** E Germany
54 J1 **Lobnya** U.S.S.R.
85 C7 **Lobo** *R* Ivory Coast
16 C6 **Lobón** Spain
27 H10 **Lobonäs** Sweden
131 F5 **Lobos** Argentina
124 D4 **Lobos** *isld* Mexico
128 D7 **Lobos,C** Chile
124 D3 **Lobos,C** Mexico
126 F3 **Lobos Cay** *isld* Cuba
128 B5 **Lobos de Tierra** *isld* Peru
133 D6 **Lobos,Pta** Argentina
131 A5 **Lobos,Pta** Colchagua Chile
37 N1 **Lobstädt** E Germany
115 N7 **Lobstick L** Labrador
33 Q8 **Loburg** E Germany
55 D2 **Lobva** U.S.S.R.
31 K2 **Łobżenica** Poland
40 G7 **Locana** Italy
41 J5 **Locarno** Switzerland
67 B6 **Loc Binh** Vietnam
32 K8 **Loccum** W Germany
15 D4 **Lochaber** Scotland
122 K8 **Lochaber Mines** Nova Scotia
15 C4 **Lochaline** Scotland
120 F4 **Lochalsh** Ontario
15 C2 **Loch Assynt** Scotland
15 C4 **Loch Awe** Scotland
15 A3 **Loch Boisdale** Outer Hebrides Scotland
15 C3 **Loch Broom** Scotland
15 C4 **Lochbuie** Scotland
15 C3 **Loch Cluanie** Scotland
15 D4 **Lochearnhead** Scotland
15 C4 **Loch Eil** Scotland
25 F4 **Lochem** Netherlands
15 D2 **Loch Eriboll** Scotland
15 D4 **Loch Ericht** Scotland
21 C7 **Loches** France
15 C4 **Loch Etive** Scotland
15 C4 **Loch Ewe** Scotland
15 E4 **Loch Faskally** Scotland
15 C4 **Loch Fyne** Scotland
12 C1 **Lochgilphead** Scotland
15 C4 **Lochgilphead** Scotland
15 D3 **Loch Glass** Scotland
12 D1 **Lochgoilhead** Scotland
15 C3 **Loch Hourn** Scotland
144 B7 **Lochie** New Zealand
15 C2 **Loch Inchard** Scotland
15 C2 **Lochinver** Scotland
15 C4 **Loch Laggan** Scotland
15 B2 **Loch Langavat** Scotland
15 C2 **Loch Laxford** Scotland
15 E4 **Loch Leven** Scotland
15 D4 **Loch Lochy** Scotland
15 D4 **Loch Long** Scotland
15 C3 **Loch Loyne** Scotland
12 E3 **Lochmaben** Scotland
15 E5 **Lochmaben** Scotland
15 A3 **Lochmaddy** Outer Hebrides Scotland
15 C3 **Loch Maree** Scotland
15 C3 **Loch Monar** Scotland
15 C4 **Loch Morar** Scotland
15 D2 **Loch More** Scotland
144 B6 **Lochnagar** *L* New Zealand
15 E4 **Lochnagar** *mt* Scotland
15 D2 **Loch Naver** Scotland
15 D3 **Loch Ness** Scotland
15 D3 **Loch Oich** Scotland
15 C3 **Loch Quoich** Scotland
15 D4 **Loch Rannoch** Scotland
12 C2 **Lochranza** Scotland
22 F1 **Lochristi** Belgium
15 C4 **Loch Sheil** Scotland
15 D2 **Loch Shin** Scotland
15 C4 **Loch Sunart** Scotland
15 D4 **Loch Tay** Scotland
15 C3 **Loch Torridon** Scotland
68 J2 **Lo Chuc San** *isld* Vietnam
15 D4 **Loch Vennacher** Scotland
12 D2 **Lochwinnoch** Scotland
138 D5 **Lock** S Australia
95 L4 **Locke** New York
100 H1 **Locke** Washington
122 G10 **Lockeport** Nova Scotia
109 J4 **Locker** Texas
15 E5 **Lockerbie** Scotland
142 A5 **Locker Pt** W Australia
103 J3 **Lockes** Nevada
111 B8 **Lockesburg** Arkansas
109 H1 **Lockett** Texas
111 K10 **Lockhart** Alabama
98 K2 **Lockhart** Minnesota
139 H6 **Lockhart** New S Wales
112 F3 **Lockhart** S Carolina
109 K6 **Lockhart** Texas
141 G2 **Lockhart River Mission** Queensland
94 K5 **Lock Haven** Pennsylvania
143 B6 **Lockier Ra** W Australia
108 F1 **Lockney** Texas
33 P6 **Löcknitz** *R* E Germany
99 S8 **Lockport** Illinois
111 F12 **Lockport** Louisiana
94 J3 **Lockport** New York
99 P9 **Lockridge** Iowa
110 C4 **Lockwood** Missouri
119 N7 **Lockwood** Sask
116 J3 **Lockwood Hills** Alaska
19 K5 **Locle, Le** France
18 D5 **Locminé** France
68 H7 **Loc Ninh** Vietnam
107 N7 **Loco** Oklahoma
101 P3 **Loco Mt** Montana
83 G10 **Locri** Italy
99 N9 **Locust Cr** *R* Missouri
111 K7 **Locust Fork** *R* Alabama
94 D8 **Locust Grove** Ohio
107 P5 **Locust Grove** Oklahoma
80 C6 **Lod** Israel
99 S9 **Loda** Illinois
26 B10 **Lodalskåpa** *mt* Norway
9 H2 **Loddon** England
139 G6 **Loddon** *R* Victoria
33 P10 **Lodersleben** E Germany
18 H9 **Lodève** France
52 D4 **Lodeynoye Pole** U.S.S.R.
101 Q1 **Lodge Cr** Mont/Sask
101 S4 **Lodge Grass** Montana
117 E6 **Lodge, Mt** Br Col/Alaska
98 D8 **Lodgepole** Nebraska
98 C8 **Lodgepole Cr** Nebraska
98 B8 **Lodgepole Cr** Wyoming
74 D4 **Lodhran** Pakistan
102 C3 **Lodi** California
41 L7 **Lodi** Italy
94 E5 **Lodi** Ohio
99 R6 **Lodi** Wisconsin
28 H3 **Lödingen** Norway
86 D6 **Lodja** Zaïre
88 F3 **Lodwar** Kenya
74 A3 **Lodi** Indonesia
88 E3 **Lodmalasin** *mt* Tanzania
18 D10 **Lodosa** Spain
40 D3 **Lods** France
86 G5 **Lodwar** Kenya
31 L4 **Łódź** Poland
16 E4 **Loeches** Spain
86 F4 **Loelli** Sudan
25 F4 **Loenen** Netherlands
26 B10 **Loenvatn** *L* Norway
20 K2 **Loeuilly** France
38 G6 **Lofer** Austria
38 G6 **Loferer St Ulrich** Austria
36 E6 **Loffenau** W Germany
15 E1 **L of Harray** Scotland
26 F3 **Lofoten** *islds* Norway
26 G8 **Lofsdalen** Sweden
28 B5 **Loft** Denmark
27 J14 **Loftahammar** Sweden
13 G5 **Lofthouse** England
13 H4 **Loftus** England
143 C6 **Lofty Ra** W Australia
99 L8 **Logan** Iowa
107 L2 **Logan** Kansas
101 Q4 **Logan** Montana
98 F8 **Logan** Nebraska
106 G6 **Logan** New Mexico
101 O8 **Logan** Utah
94 F9 **Logan** W Virginia
141 H5 **Logan** *R* Queensland
141 L8 **Logan** *R* Queensland
98 K8 **Logan Cr** Nebraska
103 K5 **Logandale** Nevada
141 L8 **Logan Downs** Queensland
116 R6 **Logan Glacier** Alaska/Yukon Terr
118 F3 **Logan L** Alberta
122 F5 **Logan,Mt** Quebec
100 E1 **Logan, Mt** Washington
117 C5 **Logan,Mt** Yukon Terr
117 K5 **Logan Mts** Yukon Terr/N W Terr
101 M1 **Logan Pass** Montana
94 A6 **Logansport** Indiana
111 B10 **Logansport** Louisiana
95 K5 **Loganton** Pennsylvania
99 Q6 **Loganville** Wisconsin
75 L2 **Logar** *R* Afghanistan
98 A9 **Logachin** Colorado
26 K8 **Lögde älv** *R* Sweden
100 F5 **Logdell** Oregon
87 B7 **Loge** *R* Angola
20 F2 **Loges, les** France
13 F6 **Loggerheads** England
55 D3 **Loginovo** U.S.S.R.
86 B3 **Logone** *R* Cameroon
20 H5 **Logron** France
17 F2 **Logroño** Spain
17 F2 **Logroño** *prov* Spain
16 D5 **Logrosán** Spain
28 C3 **Løgstør** Denmark
28 C3 **Løgstrup** Denmark
28 E4 **Løgten** Denmark
28 B6 **Løgumkloster** Denmark
28 F6 **Lohals** Denmark
80 D2 **Lohame HaGeta'ot** Israel
75 L7 **Lohardaga** India
36 B3 **Lohéac** France
32 L10 **Lohfelden** W Germany
37 M7 **Lohhof** W Germany
29 L5 **Lohijärvi** Finland
29 L11 **Lohja** Finland
101 Q1 **Lohman** Montana
33 Q5 **Lohmen** E Germany
109 H4 **Lohn** Texas
36 E3 **Löhnberg** W Germany
32 J8 **Löhne** W Germany
36 D4 **Lohnsfeld** W Germany
71 G6 **Loholoho** Sulawesi
36 H4 **Lohr** W Germany
36 F2 **Lohra** W Germany
99 M7 **Lohrville** Iowa
29 K7 **Lohtaja** Finland
68 C2 **Loi-ai** Burma
38 K8 **Loibl Pass** Austria/Italy
20 D6 **Loigné** France
68 C3 **Loikaw** Burma
68 C3 **Loi Lan** *mt* Burma
68 C2 **Loi-Lem** Burma
68 D1 **Loi Lun** Burma
29 K11 **Loimaa** Finland
18 G4 **Loing** *R* France
21 F6 **Loir** *R* France
21 E10 **Loiré** Charente-Maritime France
21 D6 **Loiré** Maine-et-Loire France
18 H7 **Loire** *R* France
21 B7 **Loire Atlantique** *dep* France
21 J6 **Loiret** *dep* France
21 H6 **Loir et Cher** *dep* France
20 D5 **Loiron** France
41 O2 **Loisach** *R* W Germany
68 C2 **Loi Sang** *mt* Burma
22 J5 **Loison** *R* France
40 B4 **Loisy** France
33 S5 **Loitz** E Germany
16 E7 **Loja** Spain
128 C4 **Loja** *prov* Ecuador
28 C6 **Lojt** Denmark
86 F5 **Loka** Sudan
29 J11 **Lokalahti** Finland
70 E2 **Lokan** *R* Sabah
86 E6 **Lokandu** Zaïre
29 N4 **Lokantekojärvi** *L* Finland
70 D6 **Lokbatu** Kalimantan
52 H4 **Lokchim** *R* U.S.S.R.
22 D2 **Loker** Belgium
22 F1 **Lokeren** Belgium
37 O3 **Loket** Czechoslovakia
54 E6 **Lokhvitsa** U.S.S.R.
86 G5 **Lokichar** Kenya
70 G5 **Lokilalaki, G** *mt* Sulawesi
86 G5 **Lokitaung** Kenya
59 K1 **Lokshak** U.S.S.R.
29 N4 **Lokka** Finland
28 D2 **Løkken** Denmark
26 D8 **Løkken** Norway
52 D6 **Loknya** U.S.S.R.
86 A4 **Loko** Nigeria
86 D6 **Lokolo** *R* Zaïre
86 C6 **Lokoro** *R* Zaïre
50 G2 **Lokosovo** U.S.S.R.
55 F1 **Lokosovo** U.S.S.R.
54 F4 **Lokot'** U.S.S.R.
52 C5 **Loksa** U.S.S.R.
59 K1 **Lokshak** U.S.S.R.
115 N5 **Loks Land** N W Terr
86 E4 **Lol** *R* Sudan
100 A9 **Loleta** California
20 C4 **Lolif** France
88 E3 **Loliondo** Tanzania
28 G7 **Lolland** *isld* Denmark
52 F2 **Lollar** W Germany
101 L3 **Lolo** Montana
101 L3 **Lolo Pass** Idaho/Montana
71 A2 **Loloda,Tk** *B* Halmahera Indonesia
71 A1 **Loloda Utara, Pulau Pulau** *islds* Halmahera Indonesia
86 B5 **Lolodorf** Cameroon
52 H4 **Lolog** *R* U.S.S.R.
101 L3 **Lolo Hot Springs** Montana
69 C12 **Lolowau** Indonesia
47 F1 **Lom** Bulgaria
37 O4 **Lom** Czechoslovakia
26 C10 **Lom** Norway
37 P4 **Lom** *mt* Czechoslovakia
106 B2 **Loma** Colorado
101 P2 **Loma** Montana
98 H1 **Loma** N Dakota
16 E6 **Loma de Chiclana** Spain
16 E6 **Loma de Úbeda** Spain
88 B10 **Lomagundi** Zimbabwe
86 E6 **Lomami** *R* Zaïre
85 B7 **Loma Mts** Sierra Leone/Guinea
99 N1 **Loman** Minnesota
131 D6 **Loma Negra,Planicie de la** *plain* Argentina
133 D6 **Lomas Coloradas** *hills* Argentina
130 B10 **Lomas de Vallejos** Argentina
133 F4 **Lomas de Zamora** Argentina
31 O4 **Łomazy** Poland
71 J4 **Lombagin** Sulawesi
101 O3 **Lombard** Montana
129 H3 **Lombard, Serra** *mts* Brazil
42 C3 **Lombardia** *prov* Italy
142 E3 **Lombardina Mission** W Australia
22 D1 **Lombardsijde** Belgium
18 F9 **Lombez** France
71 L9 **Lomblen** *isld* Indonesia
70 G10 **Lombok** *isld* Indonesia
70 P10 **Lombok,Selat** *str* Indonesia
20 F5 **Lombron** France
85 E7 **Lomé** Togo
86 D6 **Lomela** Zaïre
109 J4 **Lometa** Texas
86 B5 **Lomié** Cameroon
98 A9 **Lomira** Wisconsin
37 P1 **Lommatzsch** E Germany
20 D2 **Lomme** France
22 J1 **Lommel** Belgium
118 E8 **Lomond** Alberta
123 P4 **Lomond** Nfld
15 E4 **Lomond Hills** Scotland
12 D1 **Lomond, Loch L** Scotland
52 C5 **Lomonosov** U.S.S.R.
52 D6 **Lomonosovo** U.S.S.R.
55 E4 **Lomonosovskaya** U.S.S.R.
52 F3 **Lomovoye** U.S.S.R.
68 D6 **Lomphat** Cambodia
70 G7 **Lompobattang, G** *mt* Sulawesi
102 D7 **Lompoc** California
26 C10 **Lomseggja** *mt* Norway
26 H9 **Lomsjö** Sweden
31 N2 **Łomża** Poland
106 E7 **Lon** New Mexico
94 J7 **Lonaconing** Maryland
74 E9 **Lonavale** India
28 A5 **Lønborg** Denmark
133 C5 **Loncoche** Chile
133 C5 **Loncopue** Argentina
22 F2 **Londerzeel** Belgium
120 J9 **Londesborough** Ontario
110 C6 **London** Arkansas
94 C9 **London** Kentucky
94 D7 **London** Ohio
120 J10 **London** Ontario
109 H5 **London** Texas
10 **London** *conurbation* England
95 Q4 **Londonderry** New Hampshire
14 D1 **Londonderry** N Ireland
122 J8 **Londonderry** Nova Scotia
95 P3 **Londonderry** Vermont
14 D2 **Londonderry** *co* N Ireland
142 F2 **Londonderry, C** W Australia
133 C9 **Londonderry, I** Chile
Londorf *see* **Rabenau**
130 D8 **Londrina** Brazil
107 N7 **Lone Grove** Oklahoma
120 J7 **Lonely I** Ontario
103 J4 **Lone Mt** Nevada
109 M3 **Lone Oak** Texas
102 F5 **Lone Pine** California
101 L2 **Lonepine** Montana
100 F4 **Lonerock** Oregon
118 H5 **Lone Rock** Sask
99 Q6 **Lone Rock** Wisconsin
101 P1 **Lonesome L.Res** Montana
98 A8 **Lonetree** Wyoming
98 F2 **Lonetree Res** N Dakota
107 L7 **Lone Wolf** Oklahoma
87 C8 **Longa** Angola
46 E8 **Longá** Greece
129 K4 **Longa** *R* Brazil
70 D4 **Long Akah** Sarawak
65 C4 **Long'an** China
141 F5 **Longara** Queensland
42 E2 **Longarone** Italy
133 C5 **Longavi** *mt* Chile
127 K3 **Long B** Jamaica
70 D4 **Longbangan** Kalimantan
127 M2 **Long Bay** Jamaica
112 J4 **Long Bay** S Carolina
102 F8 **Long Beach** California
95 O6 **Long Beach** Long I, N Y
111 G11 **Long Beach** Mississippi
144 C6 **Longbeach** New Zealand
100 A3 **Long Beach** Washington
9 F2 **Long Bennington** England
70 E4 **Longbleh** Kalimantan
113 E10 **Longboat Key** *isld* Florida
95 N6 **Long Branch** New Jersey
8 D5 **Longbridge Deverill** England
145 E4 **Longburn** New Zealand
8 D6 **Long Burton** England
22 K3 **Longchamps** Belgium
67 B2 **Longchang** China
67 E4 **Longchuan** China
9 E3 **Long Compton** England
98 C1 **Long Cr** N Dakota
119 O9 **Long Cr** Sask
138 C3 **Long Cr** S Australia
100 F5 **Long Creek** Oregon
68 H4 **Long Dai** Vietnam
107 M5 **Longdale** Oklahoma
58 E4 **Longde** China
9 E2 **Longdon** England
126 G3 **Long Eaton** England
40 B3 **Longecourt** France
95 M5 **Long Eddy** New York
36 B1 **Longerich** W Germany
21 C9 **Longeville** France
95 R1 **Long Falls Dam** Maine
108 E5 **Longfellow** Texas
144 D5 **Longfellow, Mt** New Zealand
65 G2 **Longfengshan Shuiku** *res* China
14 D3 **Longford** Irish Rep
107 N2 **Longford** Kansas
145 D4 **Longford** New Zealand
139 H8 **Longford** Tasmania
14 D3 **Longford** *co* Irish Rep
13 F2 **Longformacus** Scotland
6 K5 **Long Forties** *bank* North Sea
13 G3 **Longframlington** England
65 G3 **Longgang Shan** *mt ra* China
70 E4 **Longgi** *R* Kalimantan
70 E3 **Longglat** Kalimantan
65 C4 **Longguan** China
65 C7 **Longguji** China
67 C7 **Longgun** China
70 C4 **Longguntur** Kalimantan
67 F4 **Longhai** China
9 E6 **Longham** England
123 T6 **Long Harbour** Nfld
13 G3 **Longhorsley** England
13 G3 **Longhoughton** England
65 D4 **Longhua** China
67 D3 **Longhui** China
112 J1 **Longhurst** N Carolina
68 A6 **Long I** Andaman Is
126 G3 **Long I** Bahamas
83 K12 **Long I** Mahé I Indian Oc
127 M4 **Long, I** Martinique W I
95 P6 **Long I** New York
144 A6 **Long I** New Zealand
122 F9 **Long I** Nova Scotia
115 M7 **Long I** N W Terr
136 K3 **Long I** Papua New Guinea
141 J5 **Long I** Queensland
100 A3 **Long I** Washington
70 D5 **Longiram** Kalimantan
95 P5 **Long I Sd** Conn/New York
107 L2 **Long Island** Kansas
59 H2 **Longjiang** China
Longjing *see* **Yanji**
20 K4 **Longjumeau** France
Longjuzhai *see* **Danfeng**
36 C4 **Longkamp** W Germany
65 E6 **Longkou** China
116 K6 **Long L** Alaska
95 S6 **Long L** Maine
94 B2 **Long L** Michigan
99 M3 **Long L** Minnesota
98 G3 **Long L** N Dakota
122 F7 **Long L** New Brunswick
95 N2 **Long L** New York
120 D3 **Long L** Ontario
122 J1 **Long, Lac** Labrador
120 D3 **Longlac** Ontario
95 N3 **Long Lake** New York
99 S4 **Long Lake** Wisconsin
70 D3 **Long Lama** Sarawak
8 D5 **Longleat House** England
70 E3 **Longledju** Kalimantan
67 B3 **Longli** China
22 J4 **Longlier** Belgium
67 B4 **Longlin** China
12 D1 **Long, Loch** *L* Scotland
118 E4 **Long L. Prov. Park** Alberta
100 F2 **Long L.Res** Washington
9 G3 **Long Melford** England
67 C6 **Longmen** China
65 A7 **Longmen Shan** *mts* China
98 A9 **Longmont** Colorado
70 D3 **Long Murum** Sarawak
67 E4 **Longnan** China
70 D4 **Longnawan** Kalimantan
20 J4 **Longnes** France
9 E1 **Longnor** England
67 G4 **Longny** France
43 H9 **Longobucco** Italy
88 F2 **Longonot,Mt** Kenya
69 H8 **Long Phu** Vietnam
98 F7 **Long Pine** Nebraska
Longping *see* **Luodian**
99 S8 **Long Point** Illinois
120 K10 **Long Point B** Ontario
123 U6 **Long Pond** Nfld
22 E5 **Longpont** France
99 M4 **Long Prairie** Minnesota
20 J1 **Longpré-les-Corps-Saints** France
119 T5 **Long Pt** Manitoba
144 A7 **Long Pt** New Zealand
123 O5 **Long Pt** Nfld
71 D6 **Long Pt** Philippines
Longquan *see* **Danzhai**
67 F2 **Longquan** China
67 E3 **Longquan Xi** *R* China
123 P4 **Long Range Mts** Nfld
141 G6 **Longreach** Queensland
142 F2 **Long Reef** W Australia
13 F6 **Longridge** England
112 J4 **Longs** S Carolina
144 A7 **Long Sd** New Zealand
70 E3 **Longsegah** Kalimantan
67 D2 **Longshan** China
67 C4 **Longsheng** China
67 D5 **Longsheng** China
Longshi *see* **Ninggang**
98 A9 **Longs Peak** *mt* Colorado
140 B6 **Longs Ra** N Terr Aust
13 F4 **Longtown** England
9 G2 **Long Sutton** England
67 B2 **Longtan** China
45 N6 **Longtan** China
67 C3 **Longtian** China
103 N4 **Long Teru** Sarawak
67 C3 **Longtian** China
79 ...

McMurdo Sound — Manito 47

146 H6 McMurdo Sound Antarctica
117 O10 McMurphy Br Col
100 C1 McMurray Washington
111 E10 McNair Mississippi
103 P7 McNary Arizona
108 B4 McNary Texas
100 F4 McNary Dam Oregon
117 O9 McNaughton, L Canada
103 P10 McNeal Arizona
111 C8 McNeil Arkansas
109 K5 McNeil Texas
111 G11 McNeill Mississippi
119 Q7 MacNutt Sask
122 G10 McNutt I Nova Scotia
128 D1 Macollo, Pta C Venezuela
110 F1 Macomb Illinois
107 O6 Macomb Oklahoma
43 B8 Macomer Sardinia
88 H8 Macomia Mozambique
22 G3 Maçon Belgium
19 J6 Mâcon France
112 D5 Macon Georgia
99 S10 Macon Illinois
111 H8 Macon Mississippi
99 O10 Macon Missouri
98 G9 Macon Nebraska
87 D8 Macondo Angola
119 O9 Macoun Sask
107 N3 McPherson Kansas
142 D5 Macpherson, Mt W Australia
141 L8 Macpherson Ra N S W/Qnsld
68 A7 Macpherson's Str Andaman Is
139 J4 MacQuarie R New S Wales
139 H8 Macquarie R Tasmania
139 H8 Macquarie Harbour Tasmania
81 J12 Macquarie I S Pacific Oc
139 K5 Macquarie, L New S Wales
139 J4 Macquarie Marshes New S Wales
139 J5 Macquarie, Mt New S Wales
22 G4 Macquenoise Belgium
117 E4 McQuesten Yukon Terr
117 E4 McQuesten R Yukon Terr
112 E5 McRae Georgia
144 D5 McRae, L New Zealand
142 C5 McRae, Mt W Australia
144 C6 Macraes Flat New Zealand
94 E9 McRoberts Kentucky
146 C5 MacRobertson Land Antarctica
14 C5 Macroom Irish Rep
118 K7 Macrorie Sask
141 H4 Macrossan Queensland
119 N9 McTaggart Sask
71 G5 Mactan isld Philippines
118 D1 McTavish Manitoba
128 D3 Macujer Colombia
71 G4 Maculiv Philippines
138 D2 Macumba R S Australia
95 M6 Macungie Pennsylvania
128 D6 Macusani Peru
87 G9 Macuse Mozambique
125 N9 Macuspana Mexico
124 E4 Macuzari, Presa res Mexico
94 E9 McVeigh Kentucky
119 Q2 McVeigh Manitoba
117 N3 McVicar Arm inlet N W Terr
98 H2 McVille N Dakota
121 M4 McWatters Quebec
111 J10 McWilliams Alabama
86 A4 Mada R Nigeria
80 G7 Madaba Jordan
86 D2 Madadi Chad
87 H11 Madagascar Indian Oc
81 C8 Madagascar Basin Indian Oc
76 C4 Madakasira India
70 E1 Madalon mt Sabah
84 E5 Madama Niger
76 D4 Madanapalle India
136 K3 Madang Papua New Guinea
85 F6 Madaoua Niger
75 O7 Madaripur Bangladesh
85 F6 Madarounfa Niger
95 S6 Madawaska Maine
121 M7 Madawaska Ontario
121 N7 Madawaska R Ontario
122 D6 Madawaska R Quebec
68 C1 Madaya Burma
45 Q7 Maddaloni Italy
143 C10 Madden, Mt W Australia
142 C2 Maddington dist Perth, W Aust
98 G2 Maddock N Dakota
85 A2 Madeira Atlantic Oc
128 F5 Madeira R Brazil
128 F5 Madeirinho R Brazil
41 M3 Madelegabel mt Austria
20 G5 Madeleine Bouvet, la France
123 L6 Madeleine, Iles de la Quebec
18 H6 Madeleine, Mts.de la France
99 M5 Madelia Minnesota
100 E8 Madeline California
99 Q3 Madeline I Wisconsin
57 J1 Madeniyet U.S.S.R.
102 D5 Madera California
124 E3 Madera Mexico
94 J6 Madera Pennsylvania
108 E5 Madera Mt Texas
32 J10 Madfeld W Germany
119 Q7 Madge L Sask
83 J12 Madge Rocks Seychelles
75 M5 Madhubani India
74 G7 Madhya Pradesh prov India
65 H3 Madida China
128 E6 Madidi R Bolivia
70 C4 Madi, Dtt Kalimantan
138 E3 Madigan Gulf S Australia
146 J3 Madigan Nunatak Antarctica
109 L1 Madill Oklahoma
86 C6 Madimba Zaïre
86 H3 Madinat ash Sha'ab S Yemen
81 C5 Madingley Rise Indian Oc
86 B6 Madingo-Kayes Congo
86 B6 Madingou Congo
110 F6 Madison Arkansas
113 D7 Madison Florida
112 D4 Madison Georgia
107 O3 Madison Kansas
98 K4 Madison Minnesota
110 D2 Madison Missouri
112 H1 Madison N Carolina
98 J8 Madison Nebraska
94 F5 Madison Ohio
111 M12 Madison St Louis
118 J7 Madison Sask
98 J5 Madison S Dakota
110 K5 Madison Tennessee
94 J8 Madison Virginia
99 R6 Madison Wisconsin
94 F8 Madison W Virginia
101 O4 Madison R Montana
94 H9 Madison Heights Virginia
101 P5 Madison Junct Wyoming
101 O4 Madison Ra Montana
110 J4 Madisonville Kentucky
111 F11 Madisonville Louisiana
112 C2 Madisonville Tennessee
109 M5 Madisonville Texas
70 N9 Madiun Java
8 D3 Madley England
143 E6 Madley, Mt W Australia
98 A1 Madoc Montana
121 N8 Madoc Ontario
86 G5 Mado Gashi Kenya
52 C6 Madona U.S.S.R.
100 B9 Mad R California
47 J5 Madra Dağı mt Turkey
76 E4 Madras India
100 D5 Madras Oregon
128 D6 Madre de Dios dep Peru
128 E6 Madre de Dios R Bolivia/Peru
133 B8 Madre de Dios, I Chile
125 L5 Madre. Laguna Mexico
109 K9 Madre, Laguna Texas
124 F4 Madre Occidental, Sierra mts Mexico
18 G10 Madrès mt France
71 F2 Madre, Sierra mts Luzon Philippines
99 N8 Madrid Iowa
71 G6 Madrid Mindanao Philippines
98 E9 Madrid Nebraska
106 D6 Madrid New Mexico
95 M2 Madrid New York
16 E4 Madrid Spain
16 E4 Madrid prov Spain
71 F5 Madridejos Philippines
16 E5 Madridejos Spain
16 D3 Madrigal de las Atlas Torres Spain
16 E6 Madrona, Sa mts Spain
128 G4 Madruba, L Brazil
126 D3 Madruga Cuba
79 E11 Madsûs, G mt Egypt
71 K8 Madu isld Indonesia
71 E5 Maducang isld Philippines
28 A4 Madum Denmark
28 D3 Madum Sø Denmark
143 F9 Madura W Australia
70 O9 Madura isld Indonesia
76 D6 Madurai India
70 O9 Madura, Selat str Java
83 L10 Maduru Oya R Sri Lanka
52 H4 Madzha U.S.S.R.
60 D12 Maebaru Japan
61 N9 Maebashi Japan
68 C3 Mae Hong Son Thailand
61 O13 Mae-jima isld Okinawa
68 D5 Mae Khlong R Thailand
69 D8 Mae Kirirath R Thailand
27 C12 Mael Norway
68 D3 Mae Lao R Thailand
68 D3 Mae Li R Thailand
17 H3 Maella Spain
69 D8 Mae Luang R Thailand
68 F4 Mae Nam R Thailand
68 E3 Mae Nam Ing R Thailand
68 F5 Mae Nam Mun R Thailand
68 E3 Mae Nam Nan R Thailand
68 D3 Mae Nam Ping R Thailand
68 E3 Mae Nam Yom R Thailand
68 D3 Mae Rim Thailand
48 K5 Măeruş Romania
103 P1 Maeser Utah
8 C4 Maesteg Wales
45 M2 Maestra, Pta Italy
126 F4 Maestra, Sierra mts Cuba
71 E4 Maestre de Campo isld Philippines
137 O5 Maewo isld New Hebrides
88 H10 Mafameda isld Mozambique
114 J7 Mafeking Manitoba
89 D5 Mafeking S Africa
89 E7 Mafeteng Lesotho
139 H7 Maffra Victoria
88 G5 Mafia Channel Tanzania
88 G5 Mafia,I Tanzania
88 E8 Mafinto Mozambique
67 E1 Ma-fou China
130 E10 Mafra Brazil
16 A6 Mafra Portugal
89 F2 Mafungabusi Plateau Zimbabwe
51 P3 Magadan U.S.S.R.
51 P2 Magadanskaya Oblast' U.S.S.R.
88 F2 Magadi Kenya
88 F2 Magadi L Kenya
122 E8 Magaguadavic L New Brunswick
71 F4 Magallanes Philippines
133 C8 Magallanes prov Chile
133 C8 Magallanes, Estrecho de chan Chile
71 F5 Magallon Negros Philippines
86 H4 Magalo Ethiopia
71 C3 Magamo W Irian
126 G10 Magangué Colombia
128 C2 Magangue Colombia
85 F6 Magaria Niger
61 Q12 Magari-zaki C Okinawa
71 E2 Magat R Luzon Philippines
89 G4 Magato Mts S Africa
110 C6 Magazine Mt Arkansas
85 B7 Magburaka Sierra Leone
59 J1 Magdagachi U.S.S.R.
37 L2 Magdala E Germany
86 G3 Magdala Ethiopia
128 F6 Magdalena Bolivia
106 C7 Magdalena New Mexico
124 D2 Magdalena Sonora Mexico
128 D2 Magdalena div Colombia
128 C3 Magdalena R Colombia
133 C6 Magdalena, I Chile
124 C5 Magdalena, I Mexico
70 E2 Magdalena, Mt Sabah
115 N8 Magdalen Is Quebec
33 P8 Magdeburg E Germany
33 P8 Magdeburg reg E Germany
33 Q8 Magdeburgerforth E Germany
141 K3 Magdelaine Cays islds Gt Barrier Reef Aust
33 O9 Mägdesprung E Germany
80 C5 Magdi'el Israel
111 G10 Magee Mississippi
14 F2 Magee, I N Ireland
116 K7 Mageik Vol Alaska
70 N9 Magelang Java
133 D8 Magellan, Str. of Chile
80 E3 Magen Shaul Israel
41 J7 Magenta Italy
143 C10 Magenta, L W Australia
41 K3 Magereu mt Switzerland
26 P1 Mageröya isld Norway
80 D4 Maggal Israel
41 J5 Maggia, Val Switzerland
44 F2 Maggiorasca mt Italy
41 J6 Maggiore, Lago Italy
43 F7 Maggiore, M mt Italy
127 J2 Maggotty Jamaica
79 A10 Maghâgha Egypt
79 D8 Maghâra, G mt Egypt
14 A4 Magharee Is Irish Rep
14 E2 Maghera N Ireland
14 E2 Magherafelt N Ireland
17 F10 Maghnia Algeria
84 H3 Maghra, El Egypt
13 F6 Maghull England
101 L6 Magic Res Idaho
14 E1 Magilligan Pt N Ireland
16 E7 Mágina mt Spain
56 G3 Magistral'niy U.S.S.R.
48 E6 Maglaj Yugoslavia
40 E5 Magland France
28 K6 Magleby Denmark
28 K7 Magleby isld Denmark
28 G7 Maglehöjstrand Denmark
45 M6 Magliana Italy
45 O5 Magliano de Marsi Italy
48 E7 Maglić mt Yugoslavia
43 J8 Maglie Italy
103 N8 Magma Arizona
21 H9 Magnac-Laval France
21 J10 Magnat-l'Etrange France
98 J7 Magnet Nebraska
121 L7 Magnetawan Ontario
146 A5 Magnet B Antarctica
141 H4 Magnetic I Queensland
55 C3 Magnitka U.S.S.R.
55 C4 Magnitogorsk U.S.S.R.
109 O2 Magnolia Arkansas
111 F10 Magnolia Mississippi
112 J3 Magnolia N Carolina
109 M5 Magnolia Texas
27 F12 Magnor Norway
6 L1 Magnus oil rig North Sea
20 J3 Magny-en-Vexin France
20 E3 Magny-la-Campagne France
88 C9 Magoe Mozambique
121 S7 Magog Quebec
8 D4 Magor Wales
120 F4 Magpie Ontario
122 H3 Magpie Quebec
122 H2 Magpie L Quebec
120 F4 Magpie Mine Ontario
122 H2 Magpie R Quebec
44 G3 Magra, R Italy
118 E9 Magrath Alberta
17 G5 Magro R Spain
102 G4 Magruder Mt Nevada
71 E2 Magsingal Luzon Philippines
28 C6 Magstrup Denmark
67 A5 Maguan China
129 J4 Maguari, C Brazil
89 H5 Magude Mozambique
67 D5 Magui China
86 B3 Magumeri Nigeria
68 B2 Magwe Burma
68 A2 Magyichaung Burma
78 K3 Mahābād Iran
74 E10 Mahabaleshwar India
87 G12 Mahabo Madagascar
74 E9 Mahad India
86 A3 Mahaddei Uen Somalia
74 H7 Mahadeo Hills India
94 J6 Mahaffey Penn
86 F5 Mahagl Zaïre
87 H11 Mahajamba, B.de Madagascar
87 H11 Mahajanga Madagascar
70 D4 Mahakam R Kalimantan
89 E4 Mahalapye Botswana
46 E6 Mahalás Greece
79 B8 Mahalla, El Egypt
77 B3 Maḩallat Iran
77 E4 Mahān Iran
75 K8 Mahanadi R India
71 G5 Mahanay isld Philippines
95 L6 Mahanoy City Pennsylvania
65 G3 Mahao China
83 J10 Maha Oya R Sri Lanka
74 E9 Maharashtra prov India
75 K8 Mahasamund India
68 F4 Maha Sarakham Thailand
98 J10 Mahaska Kansas
87 H11 Mahavavy R Madagascar
87 H11 Mahavelona Madagascar
83 K10 Mahaweli Ganga R Sri Lanka
68 G4 Mahaxay Laos
74 H10 Mahbubabad India
76 C2 Mahbubnagar India
77 D7 Maḩḑah Oman
85 G1 Mahdia Tunisia
76 B5 Mahe India
83 J12 Mahé isld Seychelles
83 M13 Mahebourg Mauritius
88 F6 Mahenge Tanzania
144 C6 Maheno New Zealand
120 J3 Maher Ontario
74 F7 Maheshwar India
145 F3 Mahia New Zealand
74 E9 Mahim India
144 C5 Mahinapua, L New Zealand
144 B6 Mahinerangi, L New Zealand
80 G6 Mahis Jordan
87 F11 Mahlabatini S Africa
68 B2 Mahlaing Burma
33 S8 Mahlow E Germany
33 P8 Mahlwinkel E Germany
75 J5 Mahmudabad India
48 M5 Mahmudia Romania
83 K10 Maho Sri Lanka
74 H6 Mahoba India
145 E3 Mahoenui New Zealand
100 F8 Mahogany Peak mt Nevada
99 S9 Mahomet Illinois
17 K5 Mahón Menorca
122 H9 Mahone Bay Nova Scotia
117 L3 Mahony L N W Terr
17 F5 Mahora Spain
85 G2 Mahrès Tunisia
74 E7 Mahsana India
98 F4 Mahto S Dakota
145 E4 Mahuri New Zealand
74 D8 Mahuva India
137 P1 Maiana atoll Kiribati
71 M9 Maibang Indonesia
61 K10 Maibara Japan
48 L5 Măicăneşti Romania
19 K5 Maich France
40 E3 Maiche France
68 J2 Maichen China
86 G3 Maichew Ethiopia
68 J2 Mai-ch'u China
129 H3 Maicuru R Brazil
142 C1 Maida Vale W Australia
112 F2 Maiden N Carolina
8 D5 Maiden Bradley England
9 F4 Maidenhead England
8 D6 Maiden Newton England
99 O5 Maiden Rock Wisconsin
12 D3 Maidens Scotland
71 A2 Maidi Halmahera Indonesia
9 G5 Maidstone England
118 H5 Maidstone Sask
86 B3 Maidugun Nigeria
42 F6 Maiella, M.della Italy
41 L3 Maienfeld Switzerland
20 K2 Maignelay France
128 E2 Maigualida, Sierra mts Venezuela
14 C4 Maigue R Irish Rep
74 J8 Maikala Range India
36 E5 Maikammer W Germany
102 R12 Maili Hawaiian Is
20 H4 Maillebois France
20 G3 Mailleraye-sur-Seine, la France
21 D9 Maillezais France
22 D3 Mailly Maillet France
74 E4 Mailsi Pakistan
144 C5 Maimai New Zealand
77 J2 Maimaña Afghanistan
127 J5 Maimon, B.de Dom Rep
80 F7 Ma'in Jordan
14 E2 Main R N Ireland
37 K3 Main R W Germany
123 N8 Main-à-Dieu C Breton I, N Scotia
37 J4 Mainbernheim W Germany
123 Q2 Main Brook Nfld
37 M6 Mainburg W Germany
118 K8 Main Centre Sask
120 J7 Main Channel Cave I Ontario
86 C6 Mai Ndombe, L Zaïre
Maindong see Coqên
121 O9 Main Duck I Ontario
103 N6 Maine Arizona
95 L4 Maine New York
21 C7 Maine R France
20 F5 Maine reg France
95 R1 Maine state U.S.A.
21 D7 Maine-et-Loire dep France
85 G6 Mainé-Soroa Niger
110 M2 Maineville Ohio
68 D6 Maingy isld Burma
36 H5 Mainhardt W Germany
71 G6 Mainit, L Mindanao Philippines
15 G2 Mainland Shetland Scotland
140 C2 Mainoru N Terr Aust
74 H5 Mainpuri India
138 F4 Main Range Barrier New S Wales
122 F7 Main S.W. Miramichi R New Brunswick
36 F3 Maintal W Germany
20 J4 Maintenon France
87 G11 Maintirano Madagascar
123 Q4 Main Topsail peak Newfoundland
29 N7 Mainua Finland
74 D2 Mainwali Pakistan
36 E3 Mainz W Germany
45 R8 Maiori Italy
133 D4 Maipo mt Chile/Arg
133 C4 Maipo R Chile
131 B5 Maipo, Vol peak Arg/Chile
133 F5 Maipu Argentina
127 L9 Maiquetia Venezuela
44 B3 Maira R Italy
75 P5 Mairabari India
37 L7 Maisach W Germany
21 C7 Maisdon France
126 G4 Maisí Cuba
122 G6 Maisonnette New Brunswick
20 K4 Maisons-Laffitte France
38 N4 Maissau Austria
20 K5 Maisse France
22 J4 Maissin Belgium
86 J3 Mait Somalia
99 L9 Maitland Missouri
139 K5 Maitland New S Wales
122 J8 Maitland Nova Scotia
138 D5 Maitland S Australia
122 G9 Maitland Br Nova Scotia
143 D7 Maitland, L W Australia
143 C7 Maitland, Mt W Australia
142 B5 Maitland, R W Australia
70 E2 Maitland Ra Sabah
140 C2 Maiwok R N Terr Aust
61 P7 Maiya Japan
140 A4 Maiyu, Mt N Terr Aust
75 O4 Maizhokunggar China
36 B6 Maizières-les-Vic France
60 J10 Maizuru Japan
128 D2 Majagual Colombia
128 F3 Majari R Brazil
26 F6 Majavatn L Norway
28 H7 Majbølle Denmark
80 E5 Majdal Bani Fadil Jordan
80 F8 Majdalein Jordan
31 N5 Majdan Poland
48 G6 Majdanpek Yugoslavia
80 D2 Majd el Kurum Israel
130 G8 Majé Brazil
70 F6 Majene Sulawesi
48 E6 Majevica mts Yugoslavia
86 G4 Maji Ethiopia
67 B3 Majiang China
67 D5 Majiang China
67 A4 Majie China
67 F2 Majin China
67 D2 Majitang China
118 H7 Major Sask
Majorca isld see Mallorca
89 F6 Majuba Hill S Africa
Majunga see Mahajanga
85 B6 Maka Senegal
61 P14 Makabe Okinawa
102 R12 Makaha Hawaiian Is
86 G3 Makale Ethiopia
70 F6 Makale Sulawesi
69 E14 Makalo Indonesia
75 M5 Makalu mt Xizang Zizhiqu/Nepal
87 F7 Makambako Tanzania
135 U4 Makapala Hawaiian Is
102 S12 Makapuu Hd Hawaiian Is
145 E2 Makarau New Zealand
144 B7 Makarewa New Zealand
52 G3 Makar-Ib U.S.S.R.
52 J2 Makarikha U.S.S.R.
144 B6 Makarora R New Zealand
59 M2 Makarov U.S.S.R.
42 H5 Makarska Yugoslavia
52 G5 Makar'ye U.S.S.R.
Makassar see Ujung Pandang
70 F5 Makassar Str Indonesia
89 H6 Makatini Flats reg S Africa
135 T3 Makawao Hawaiian Is
71 C3 Makbon W Irian
46 E4 Makedhonia Greece
46 E3 Makedonija Yugoslavia
135 N10 Makemo atoll Pac Oc
85 B7 Makeni Sierra Leone
145 F2 Maketu New Zealand
54 K8 Makeyevka U.S.S.R.
89 D3 Makgadikgadi Pans salt pans Botswana
78 J1 Makharadze U.S.S.R.
16 D9 Makhazen R Morocco
55 D2 Makhnevo U.S.S.R.
55 E4 Makhorovka U.S.S.R.
80 F3 Makhraba Jordan
61 M8 Maki Japan
71 A2 Makian Halmahera Indonesia
144 C6 Makikihi New Zealand
84 G3 Makilī Al Libya
119 S8 Makinak Manitoba
55 F4 Makinsk U.S.S.R.
115 M2 Makinson Inlet N W Terr
26 S1 Makkaur Norway
25 F3 Makkinga Netherlands
115 O6 Makkovik Labrador
25 D2 Makkum Netherlands
48 F4 Makó Hungary
120 C1 Makokibatan L Ontario
87 F7 Makongolosi Tanzania
145 F3 Makorako mt New Zealand
98 E2 Makoti N Dakota
145 F4 Makotuku New Zealand
86 C5 Makoua Congo
31 L6 Makov Czechoslovakia
31 M6 Maków Poland
31 N3 Maków Mazowiecki Poland
80 D2 Makr Israel
47 H8 Makrá isld Greece
74 F5 Makrana India
77 J7 Makran Coast Range Pakistan
47 H4 Mákri Greece
76 E1 Makri India
47 G7 Makronísi isld Greece
52 J3 Maksim U.S.S.R.
85 F1 Maktar Tunisia
78 K2 Maku Iran
70 C4 Makup, Bt mt Kalimantan
60 D14 Makurazaki Japan
86 A4 Makurdi Nigeria
55 E3 Makushino U.S.S.R.
116 D10 Makushin Vol Aleutian Is
88 D7 Makutu Mts Zambia
118 H4 Makwa L Sask
89 G1 Makwiro Zimbabwe
128 C6 Mala Peru
71 G7 Malabang Mindanao Philippines
113 G9 Malabar Florida
76 B5 Malabar Coast India
70 L9 Malabar, G mt Java
85 F8 Malabo Bioko Equat Guinea
85 F8 Malabo Fernando Póo Eq Guinea
71 C6 Malabuñgan Palawan Philippines
69 E11 Malacca, Str. of Malaysia
118 H1 Malachi Ontario
31 K7 Malacky Czechoslovakia
101 N7 Malad City Idaho
17 H2 Maladeta Spain
31 L6 Malá Fatra mts Czechoslovakia
16 E8 Málaga Spain
100 E2 Malaga Washington
16 D8 Málaga prov Spain
88 C4 Malagarasi Tanzania
Malagasy Rep see Madagascar
16 E5 Malagón Spain
14 E3 Malahide Irish Rep
87 G12 Malaimbandy Madagascar
137 N3 Malaita isld Solomon Is
71 J9 Malaka mt Sumbawa Indonesia
86 F4 Malakal Sudan
42 G4 Mala Kapela Yugoslavia
109 L3 Malakoff Texas
71 B2 Malaku islds Indonesia
45 L2 Malalbergo Italy
70 G6 Malamala Sulawesi
71 A3 Malamala isld Indonesia
71 E7 Malamaui isld Philippines
45 M1 Malamocco Italy
71 D5 Malampaya Snd Philippines
141 H3 Malanda Queensland
70 O10 Malang Java
88 E6 Malangali Tanzania
70 M9 Malangbong Java
26 K2 Malangen Norway
26 K2 Malangen inlet Norway
26 J2 Malangsgrunnen shoal Norway
75 L5 Malangwa Nepal
48 K3 Mălani Romania
71 F7 Malanipa isld Philippines
87 C7 Malanje Angola
71 D6 Malanut B Philippines
85 E6 Malanville Benin
65 D4 Malanyu China
131 C3 Malanzaán, Sa. de mts Argentina
27 J12 Mälaren L Sweden
133 D5 Malargue Argentina
131 B5 Malargue R Argentina
129 H3 Malaripo Brazil
121 M4 Malartic Quebec
70 F7 Malasoro, Tk B Sulawesi
117 C6 Malaspina Gl Alaska
144 A6 Malaspina Reach New Zealand
117 L11 Malaspina Str Br Col
26 K6 Malåtrask Sweden
78 G2 Malatya Turkey
19 O16 Malaucène France
20 H2 Malaunay France
70 E1 Malawali isld Sabah
88 D8 Malawi rep Africa
Malawi, L see Nyasa, L
29 J9 Malax Finland
55 D1 Malaya Sos'va R U.S.S.R.
52 D5 Malaya Vishera U.S.S.R.
77 A2 Malāyer Iran
141 J4 Malay Reef Gt Barrier Reef Aust
69 Malaysia S E Asia
69 E10 Malaysia, Peninsular S E Asia
14 B4 Mal B Irish Rep
122 H5 Mal Baie Quebec
122 B6 Malbaie R Quebec
131 B6 Malbarco, L Argentina
140 F5 Malbon Queensland
138 C4 Malbooma S Australia
38 J9 Malborghetto Italy
31 L1 Malbork Poland
41 N6 Malcesine Italy
33 R5 Malchin E Germany
33 Q6 Malchow E Germany
143 D8 Malcolm W Australia
116 R2 Malcolm R Yukon Terr
68 D7 Malcolm I Burma
143 E10 Malcolm,Pt W Australia
99 O8 Malcom Iowa
22 E1 Maldegem Belgium
95 Q4 Malden Massachusetts
110 G5 Malden Missouri
100 H2 Malden Washington
94 F8 Malden W Virginia
135 M8 Malden I Pacific Oc
73 L8 Maldive Is rep Indian Oc
43 B9 Mal di Ventre isld Sardinia
73 L9 Maldive Ridge Indian Oc
9 G4 Maldon England
131 G5 Maldonado Uruguay
131 G5 Maldonado dep Uruguay
41 N5 Male Italy
73 L8 Male Maldives
47 H5 Maléa, Akr Turkey
47 F8 Maléa, Akr C Greece
74 F8 Malegaon India
48 D2 Malé Karpaty Czechoslovakia
137 O5 Malekula isld New Hebrides
121 P4 Mâle, L.du Quebec
88 F9 Malema Mozambique
87 E7 Malemba Nkulu Zaïre
47 F9 Máleme Crete
52 E3 Malen'ga U.S.S.R.
33 N4 Malente W Germany
74 F3 Maler Kotla India
47 H9 Máles Crete Greece
18 G4 Malesherbes France
54 K3 Malevka U.S.S.R.
37 O6 Malgersdorf W Germany
86 E2 Malha Sudan
13 F5 Malham England
100 H5 Malheur Oregon
100 H6 Malheur R Oregon
83 K12 Malheureu, Cap Mahé I Indian Oc
100 G6 Malheur L Oregon
66 F6 Mali R Burma
85 D5 Mali rep W Africa
21 E6 Malicorne-sur-Sarthe France
71 F7 Maligoy B Mindanao Philippines
80 F4 Malih R Jordan
19 Q16 Malijai France
71 H5 Malik Sulawesi
68 D6 Mali Kyun isld Burma
70 G6 Malili Sulawesi
27 H14 Målilla Sweden
88 B5 Malimba mts Zaïre
100 D7 Malin Oregon
71 G5 Malinao Inlet Philippines
70 E3 Malinau Kalimantan
71 F6 Malindang, Mt Mindanao Philippines
88 H3 Malindi Kenya
48 F2 Malinec Czechoslovakia
Malines see Mechelen
70 G4 Maling, G mt Sulawesi
70 L9 Malingping Java
27 H12 Malingsbo Sweden
14 D1 Malin Hd Irish Rep
14 C2 Malin More Irish Rep
70 F7 Malino Sulawesi
54 H7 Malinovka U.S.S.R.
55 G5 Malinovoye Ozero U.S.S.R.
28 M2 Malinstindur mt Faeroes
68 G1 Malipo China
71 G7 Malita Mindanao Philippines
71 G5 Malitbog Leyte Philippines
68 D7 Maliwun Burma
106 G9 Maljamar New Mexico
48 F6 Maljen mt Yugoslavia
80 F3 Malka Jordan
53 F11 Malka R U.S.S.R.
74 G8 Malkapur India
47 H4 Malkara Turkey
56 G5 Malkhanskiy Khr mts U.S.S.R.
31 N3 Małkinia Poland
80 F1 Malkiyya Israel
47 J2 Malko Tŭrnovo Bulgaria
139 J7 Mallacoota Victoria
118 F4 Mallaig Alberta
15 C3 Mallaig Highland Scotland
99 M7 Mallard Iowa
84 J4 Mallawi Egypt
131 A7 Malleco prov Chile
19 O17 Mallemort France
37 N6 Mallersdorf W Germany
41 N4 Malles Venosta Italy
130 E9 Mallét Brazil
142 C5 Mallina W Australia
28 E4 Malling Denmark
38 H8 Mallnitz Austria
17 J5 Mallorca isld Balearic Is
94 F9 Mallory W Virginia
121 P8 Mallorytown Ontario
14 C4 Mallow Irish Rep
142 E5 Mallowa Well W Australia
8 B1 Malltraeth B Môn Wales
22 F5 Malmaison, la France
27 G14 Malmbäck Sweden
26 L4 Malmberget Sweden
22 L3 Malmédy Belgium
8 D4 Malmesbury England
89 A9 Malmesbury S Africa
26 K6 Malmesjaure L Sweden
27 J12 Malmköping Sweden
28 K5 Malmö Sweden
27 F16 Malmöhus county Sweden
126 A2 Malmok pt Bonaire W Indies
52 H6 Malmyzh U.S.S.R.
26 G3 Malnes Norway
137 O5 Malo isld New Hebrides
129 G3 Maloca Amapá Brazil
129 H5 Maloca Pará Brazil
41 L5 Maloggia Switzerland
71 E3 Malolos Luzon Philippines
55 C2 Malomal'sk U.S.S.R.
88 E9 Malombe,L Malawi
47 H2 Malomir Bulgaria
113 B7 Malone Florida
95 N2 Malone New York
121 N8 Malone Ontario
109 L4 Malone Texas
98 F8 Maloney Res Nebraska
67 A4 Malong China
87 D8 Malonga Zaïre
26 N6 Malören Sweden
31 P4 Malorita U.S.S.R.
52 E3 Maloshuyka U.S.S.R.
89 F7 Maloti Mts Lesotho
100 F1 Malott Washington
55 C4 Malouchalinskiy U.S.S.R.
26 A10 Målöy Norway
54 H1 Maloyaroslavets U.S.S.R.
55 E2 Maloye Gorodishche U.S.S.R.
52 H1 Malozemel'skaya Tundra plain U.S.S.R.
106 C10 Malpais New Mexico
8 D1 Malpas England
138 F5 Malpas S Australia
124 H6 Malpaso Mexico
90 A8 Malpelo I Pacific Oc
122 J7 Malpeque B Pr Edward I
16 D5 Malpica Spain
16 B1 Malpica de Bergantiños Spain
131 B4 Malpo R Chile
73 L5 Malprabha R India
74 F5 Malpura India
36 E6 Malsch W Germany
31 H7 Malše R Czechoslovakia
26 K2 Målselv Norway
26 K2 Målselv R Norway
36 H1 Malsfeld W Germany
77 A7 Malsūniyah, Al Saudi Arabia
38 J8 Malta Austria
106 D2 Malta Colorado
101 M7 Malta Idaho
101 S1 Malta Montana
94 F7 Malta Ohio
43 F13 Malta rep Mediterranean Sea
43 F12 Malta Ch Med Sea
87 C10 Maltahöhe Namibia
38 H7 Maltatel V Austria
9 G1 Maltby Lincs England
13 G6 Maltby S Yorks England
144 C5 Malte Brun mt New Zealand
13 H5 Malton England
121 L9 Malton airport Ontario
48 K6 Malu Romania
71 D5 Malubutglubut isld Philippines
85 F6 Malumfashi Nigeria
70 F6 Malunda Sulawesi
27 G11 Malung Sweden
41 K5 Malvaglia Switzerland
76 A2 Malvan India
109 P1 Malvern Arkansas
99 L9 Malvern Iowa
127 J2 Malvern Jamaica
94 F6 Malvern Ohio
127 J3 Malvern peak Jamaica
141 H6 Malvern Hills Queensland
8 D3 Malvern Wells England
21 B7 Malville France
Malvinas, Is see Falkland Is.
74 F7 Malwa Plateau India
83 K9 Malwatu Oya R Sri Lanka
78 K1 Maly Kavkaz mt U.S.S.R.
55 E1 Malyy Atlym U.S.S.R.
55 F1 Malyy Balyk R U.S.S.R.
55 G4 Malyye Chany, Oz L U.S.S.R.
52 G6 Malyy Kundysh R U.S.S.R.
51 O1 Malyy Lyakhovski,Ostrov isld U.S.S.R.
51 K1 Malyy Taymyr, Ostrov isld U.S.S.R.
55 G2 Malyy Yugan R U.S.S.R.
56 H2 Mama U.S.S.R.
56 H2 Mama R U.S.S.R.
52 H6 Mamadysh U.S.S.R.
48 M6 Mamaia Romania
120 F5 Mamainse Point Ontario
145 F3 Mamaku New Zealand
145 D1 Mamaranui New Zealand
70 F6 Mamasa Sulawesi
71 D7 Mambahenauhan isld Philippines
71 G6 Mambajao Philippines
89 F3 Mambala Cave Zimbabwe
86 E5 Mambasa Zaïre
136 H2 Mamberamo R W Irian
86 C4 Mambéré R Cent Afr Republic
71 E4 Mamburao Philippines
70 D4 Mamehaktebo Kalimantan
118 K1 Mameigwess L Ontario
83 J12 Mamelle isld Seychelles
118 D6 Ma-Me-O Beach Alberta
118 D5 Ma-Me-O Beach Prov. Park Alberta
22 K4 Mamer Luxembourg
20 F5 Mamers France
86 A4 Mamfé Cameroon
128 F4 Mamia, L Brazil
40 D3 Mamirolle France
55 E4 Mamlyutka U.S.S.R.
120 F2 Mammamattawa Ontario
28 D4 Mammen Denmark
37 L7 Mammendorf W Germany
37 O6 Mamming W Germany
43 G10 Mammola Italy
94 F8 Mammoth W Virginia
110 K4 Mammoth Cave Kentucky
101 P5 Mammoth Hot Springs Wyoming
110 E5 Mammoth Spring Arkansas
126 G9 Mamonal Colombia
130 G4 Mamonas Brazil
31 M1 Mamo-novo U.S.S.R.
128 E6 Mamore R Bolivia/Brazil
128 F4 Mamoré, L Brazil
85 B6 Mamou Guinea
111 D11 Mamou Louisiana
87 H11 Mampikohy Madagascar
16 D1 Mampodre mt Spain
85 D7 Mampong Ghana
83 J9 Mampuri Sri Lanka
31 N1 Mamry,Jezioro L Poland
15 C3 Mam Soul mt Scotland
70 F6 Mamudju Sulawesi
Mamuji see Yucheng
87 D10 Mamuno Botswana
55 C5 Mamyt U.S.S.R.
85 C7 Man Ivory Coast
94 F9 Man W Virginia
135 N1 Mana Hawaiian Is
129 H3 Mana R Fr Guiana
56 D3 Mana R U.S.S.R.
128 B4 Manabi Ecuador
128 F4 Manacapuru Brazil
128 F4 Manacapuru,L.Grande de Brazil
17 K5 Manacor Majorca
71 J4 Manado Sulawesi
71 J4 Manadotua isld Sulawesi
22 G3 Manage Belgium
140 D3 Managoora N Terr Aust
125 L3 Managua Nicaragua
145 E4 Mana I New Zealand
145 E3 Manaia New Zealand
87 H12 Manakara Madagascar
145 E4 Manakau New Zealand
144 D5 Manakau mt New Zealand
136 K2 Manam isld Papua New Guinea
76 D6 Manamadurai India
77 B6 Manamah,Al Bahrain
87 G11 Manambaho R Madagascar
127 N10 Mánamo R Venezuela
71 E5 Manamoc isld Philippines
102 S12 Manana Hawaiian Is
87 H11 Mananara Madagascar
139 G6 Manangatang Victoria
87 H12 Mananjary Madagascar
128 F2 Manano,Caño creek Venezuela
87 H12 Manantenina Madagascar
144 A6 Manapouri New Zealand
66 D3 Manas China
Manasarowar Lake see Mapam Yumco
66 D3 Manas He R China
75 L4 Manaslu mt Nepal
95 N6 Manasquan New Jersey
106 E4 Manassa Colorado
94 K8 Manassas Virginia
71 M9 Manatang Indonesia
127 L5 Manatí Puerto Rico
128 G4 Manaus Brazil
78 C3 Manavgat Turkey
99 S5 Manawa Wisconsin
119 P3 Manawan L Sask
145 E2 Manawaru New Zealand
145 E4 Manawatu R New Zealand
71 G7 Manay Mindanao Philippines
140 B2 Manbulla N Terr Aust
94 C2 Mancelona Michigan
16 E7 Mancha Real Spain
20 C3 Manche dep France
20 K5 Manchecourt France
Manche,la see English Channel
74 H9 Mancheral India
102 A3 Manchester California
95 P5 Manchester Connecticut
112 C5 Manchester Georgia
110 F2 Manchester Illinois
99 P7 Manchester Iowa
107 N2 Manchester Kansas
110 N4 Manchester Kentucky
94 C4 Manchester Michigan
95 Q4 Manchester New Hampshire
95 K4 Manchester New York
94 D8 Manchester Ohio
107 M5 Manchester Oklahoma
95 L6 Manchester Pennsylvania
110 K6 Manchester Tennessee
95 O3 Manchester Vermont
11 E2 Manchester conurbation England
127 K3 Manchester parish Jamaica
37 M6 Manching W Germany
127 M2 Manchioneal Jamaica
65 E1 Manchuria reg China
42 D6 Manciano Italy
128 B4 Máncora Peru
106 B4 Mancos Colorado
77 B5 Mand R Iran
87 F8 Manda Tanzania
130 D8 Mandaguari Brazil
80 F3 Mandah Jordan
88 D7 Manda Hd Zambia
77 G3 Mandal Afghanistan
58 D2 Mandal Mongolia
27 B13 Mandal Norway
68 C2 Mandalay Burma
78 A3 Mandalaya isld Turkey
58 E2 Mandalgovī Mongolia
78 K5 Mandalī Iraq
58 D3 Mandal-Ovoo Mongolia
27 B13 Mandalsâni R Norway
Mandalt see Sonid Zuoqi
47 J7 Mandalya Körfezi B Turkey
98 F3 Mandan N Dakota
36 C5 Mandelbachtal W Germany
127 K2 Mandeville Jamaica
111 F11 Mandeville Louisiana
144 B7 Mandeville New Zealand
146 B10 Mandheim Antarctica
130 B6 Mandioré, Lagoa L Bolivia/Brazil
74 J7 Mandla India
142 D4 Mandora W Australia
47 F6 Mandoúdhion Greece
143 B10 Mandurah W Australia
145 E4 Mangahao New Zealand
145 E3 Mangakino New Zealand
76 E2 Mangalagiri India
76 B4 Mangalore India
141 H7 Mangalore Queensland
145 E4 Mangamahoe New Zealand
145 E3 Mangamahu New Zealand
144 D5 Mangamaunu New Zealand
145 D1 Mangamuka New Zealand
145 E3 Mangapehi New Zealand
145 E4 Mangatainoka New Zealand
145 E3 Mangaweka New Zealand
145 E2 Mangawhai New Zealand
142 A4 Mangles B W Australia
66 E4 Mangnai China
88 E9 Mangoche Malawi
87 G12 Mangoky R Madagascar
145 D1 Mangonui New Zealand
87 H12 Mangoro Madagascar
74 D8 Mangrol India
126 F2 Mangrove Cay Andros Bahamas
113 J11 Mangrove Cay isld Bahamas
71 E4 Mangsoagui Pt Philippines
130 H10 Manguaba,L Brazil
16 B4 Mangualde Portugal
86 D3 Mangueigne Chad
131 H4 Mangueira, L Brazil
130 D9 Mangueirinha Brazil
84 E5 Mangueni,Pl.du Niger
87 G7 Mangula Tanzania
108 E9 Mangum Oklahoma
69 F14 Mangunjaya Sumatra
67 A5 Manhao China
99 T8 Manhattan Illinois
107 O2 Manhattan Kansas
101 O4 Manhattan Montana
102 G3 Manhattan Nevada
22 K3 Manhay Belgium
130 H7 Manhuaçu Brazil
130 H6 Manhuaçu,R Brazil
113 L12 Man I Bahamas
87 E7 Mani Zaïre
87 H11 Mania R Madagascar
42 E2 Maniago Italy
88 E8 Maniamba Mozambique
87 F9 Manica Mozambique
71 G5 Manicani isld Philippines
122 D4 Manic Deux Dam Quebec
128 F5 Manicoré R Brazil
122 D3 Manicouagan Quebec
122 D4 Manicouagan Pen Quebec
122 D4 Manicouagan R Quebec
122 D2 Manicouagan Res. Quebec
141 K6 Manifold, C Queensland
119 V7 Manigotagan Manitoba
110 F6 Manila Arkansas
71 E3 Manila Luzon Philippines
101 Q9 Manila Utah
71 E3 Manila B Luzon Philippines
139 J5 Manildra New S Wales
99 L8 Manilla Iowa
139 K4 Manilla New S Wales
70 F5 Manimbaja,Tg C Sulawesi
69 E13 Manindjan,Danau L Sumatra
87 H11 Maningory Madagascar
140 C1 Maningrida N Terr Aust
85 C6 Maninian Ivory Coast
69 E13 Maninjau Danau L Sumatra
75 P6 Manipur prov India
73 P4 Manipur R Burma
47 J6 Manisa Turkey
17 G5 Manises Spain
12 D5 Man,Isle of U.K.
99 U5 Manistee Michigan
94 B2 Manistee R Michigan
99 U4 Manistique Michigan
99 U3 Manistique R Michigan
99 V3 Manistique L Michigan
99 R9 Manito Illinois

119 **Manitoba** Canada
119 S7 **Manitoba, L** Manitoba
118 H6 **Manito L** Sask
119 T9 **Manitou** Manitoba
109 J1 **Manitou** Oklahoma
119 M7 **Manitou Bch** Sask
99 T2 **Manitou I** Michigan
120 J7 **Manitou L** Ontario
122 G3 **Manitou,L** Quebec
120 H7 **Manitoulin I** Ontario
122 G2 **Manitou R** Quebec
106 F3 **Manitou Springs** Colorado
120 E3 **Manitouwadge** Ontario
120 J7 **Manitowaning** Ontario
120 F4 **Manitowik L** Ontario
99 T5 **Manitowoc** Wisconsin
121 P6 **Maniwaki** Quebec
128 C2 **Manizales** Colombia
80 G6 **Manja** Jordan
87 G12 **Manja** Madagascar
143 B10 **Manjimup** W Australia
74 G9 **Manjlegaon** India
38 M5 **Mank** Austria
107 M2 **Mankato** Kansas
99 N5 **Mankato** Minnesota
86 B5 **Mankim** Cameroon
109 J2 **Mankins** Texas
85 C7 **Mankono** Ivory Coast
118 K9 **Mankota** Sask
48 N2 **Mankovka** U.S.S.R.
76 E6 **Mankulam** Sri Lanka
95 M3 **Manlius** New York
17 J2 **Manlleu** Spain
99 N6 **Manly** Iowa
139 K5 **Manly** New S Wales
74 F8 **Manmad** India
140 C2 **Mann** *R* N Terr **Aust**
138 F4 **Mannahill** S Australia
83 J9 **Mannar** Sri Lanka
73 M7 **Mannar,G.of** India/Sri Lanka
76 D5 **Mannargudi** India
83 J8 **Mannar I** Sri Lanka
36 F5 **Mannheim** W Germany
14 A3 **Mannin B** Irish Rep
117 P7 **Manning** Alberta
109 P1 **Manning** Arkansas
99 L8 **Manning** Iowa
98 D2 **Manning** N Dakota
112 G4 **Manning** S Carolina
109 N4 **Manning** Texas
139 K4 **Manning** *R* New S Wales
117 N11 **Manning Prov. Park** Br Col
94 G7 **Mannington** W Virginia
9 H4 **Manningtree** England
140 A7 **Mann, Mt** N Terr **Aust**
140 A7 **Mann Ranges** N Terr/S Aust
112 M2 **Manns Harbor** N Carolina
95 L3 **Mannsville** New York
43 C9 **Mannu** *R* Sardinia
43 B8 **Mannu,C** Sardinia
138 E5 **Mannum** S Australia
118 F5 **Mannville** Alberta
85 B7 **Mano** Sierra Leone
128 E5 **Manoa** Bolivia
80 B8 **Manoah** *R* Israel
127 N1 **Man of War B** Tobago
116 H7 **Manokotak** Alaska
136 G2 **Manokwari** W Irian
46 E6 **Manolás** Greece
87 G12 **Manombo** Madagascar
88 A5 **Manono** Zaïre
112 E6 **Manor** Georgia
119 Q9 **Manor** Sask
109 K5 **Manor** Texas
8 B4 **Manorbier** Wales
144 B6 **Manorburn Res** New Zealand
14 C2 **Manorhamilton** Irish Rep
85 B7 **Mano River** Liberia
68 D7 **Manoron** Burma
19 P17 **Manosque** France
21 G10 **Manot** France
20 G5 **Manou** France
121 Q5 **Manouane** Quebec
122 B3 **Manouane L** Quebec
61 M8 **Mano-wan** *B* Japan
68 C1 **Man Pan** Burma
17 J3 **Manresa** Spain
88 B7 **Mansa** Zambia
85 A6 **Mansaba** Guinea-Bissau
85 A6 **Mansa Konko** The Gambia
71 E4 **Mansalay B** Philippines
68 C1 **Man Sam** Burma
142 G4 **Mansbridge, Mt** W Australia
115 L5 **Mansel I** N W Terr
33 O9 **Mansfeld** E Germany
110 B6 **Mansfield** Arkansas
9 E1 **Mansfield** England
112 D4 **Mansfield** Georgia
99 S9 **Mansfield** Illinois
109 O3 **Mansfield** Louisiana
95 Q4 **Mansfield** Massachusetts
110 D4 **Mansfield** Missouri
94 E6 **Mansfield** Ohio
98 H4 **Mansfield** S Dakota
109 K3 **Mansfield** Texas
139 H6 **Mansfield** Victoria
100 F2 **Mansfield** Washington
95 P2 **Mansfield,Mt** Vermont
56 D4 **Manskoye Belogor'ye** *mts* U.S.S.R.
21 F10 **Mansle** France
99 M7 **Manson** Iowa
100 E2 **Manson** Washington
117 L8 **Manson Creek** Br Col
130 C4 **Manso,R** Brazil
8 D6 **Manston** England
71 C3 **Mansuar** *isld* W Irian
111 D10 **Mansura** Louisiana
79 B7 **Mansûra,El** Egypt
128 B4 **Manta** Ecuador
71 C6 **Mantalingajan, Mt** Palawan Philippines
70 E1 **Mantanani Besar** *isld* Sabah
86 D6 **Mantantale** Zaïre
65 H4 **Mantap-san** *mt* N Korea
71 J5 **Mantarara** Indonesia
118 H7 **Mantario** Sask
128 C6 **Mantaro** *R* Peru
102 C4 **Manteca** California
111 G8 **Mantee** Mississippi
37 N4 **Mantel** W Germany
130 H6 **Mantena** Brazil
99 T8 **Manteno** Illinois
112 M2 **Manteo** N Carolina
107 J4 **Manter** Kansas
71 J4 **Manterawo** *isld* Sulawesi
20 J4 **Mantes** France
25 E2 **Mantgum** Netherlands
74 H9 **Manthani** India
21 G7 **Manthelan** France
103 N2 **Manti** Utah
130 F8 **Mantiqueira,Serra da** *mts* Brazil
100 D9 **Manton** California
94 B2 **Manton** Michigan
65 B5 **Mantou Shan** *mt ra* China
45 J1 **Mantova** Italy
29 L11 **Mäntsälä** Finland
29 L10 **Mänttä** Finland
126 B3 **Mantua** Cuba
Mantua Italy *see* **Mantova**
94 F5 **Mantua** Ohio
141 H6 **Mantuan Downs** Queensland
52 F5 **Manturovo** U.S.S.R.
29 J10 **Mäntyluoto** Finland
128 D6 **Manú** Peru
Manuan *see* **Manouane**
122 B3 **Manuanis,L** Quebec
71 F6 **Manucan** Mindanao Philippines
129 J5 **Manuel Alves** *R* Brazil
106 B6 **Manuelito** New Mexico
130 D9 **Manuel Ribas** Brazil
133 C8 **Manuel Rodríguez, I** Chile
128 E5 **Manuel Urbano** Brazil
129 H5 **Manuelzinho** Brazil
71 H6 **Manui** *isld* Indonesia
77 E6 **Manūjān** Iran
145 G2 **Manukau** New Zealand
70 F2 **Manuk Manka** Philippines
138 E4 **Manunda** *R* S Australia
145 E3 **Manunui** New Zealand
71 C3 **Manuran** *isld* W Irian
128 E6 **Manuripe** *R* Bolivia/Peru
136 K2 **Manus** *isld* Bismarck Arch
145 E3 **Manutahi** New Zealand
138 E3 **Manuwalkaninna** S Australia
98 J1 **Manvel** N Dakota
76 C3 **Manvi** India
98 B7 **Manville** Wyoming
109 O4 **Many** Louisiana
52 K4 **Man'ya** U.S.S.R.
88 B10 **Manyangau** *mt* Zimbabwe
88 G3 **Manyara,L** Tanzania
47 J4 **Manyas** Turkey
118 G9 **Manyberries** Alberta
54 M9 **Manych** *R* U.S.S.R.
118 G8 **Many Island I** Alberta
88 E4 **Manyoni** Tanzania
141 K6 **Many Peaks** Queensland
143 C10 **Many Peaks, Mt** W Australia
79 B7 **Manzala,El** Egypt
84 J3 **Manzala, L** Egypt
89 E2 **Manzamnyama** *R* Zimbabwe
16 E5 **Manzanares** Spain
127 P2 **Manzanilla B** Trinidad
126 F4 **Manzanillo** Cuba
124 G8 **Manzanillo** Mexico
106 D7 **Manzano** New Mexico
131 A8 **Manzano,B del** Chile
106 G3 **Manzanola** Colorado
106 D7 **Manzano Mts** New Mexico
58 G2 **Manzhouli** China
79 G7 **Manzil** Jordan
89 G6 **Manzini** Swaziland
Manzovka *see* **Sibirtsevo**
86 C3 **Mao** Chad
65 G2 **Mao'ershan** China
136 H2 **Maoke, Pegunungan** *ra* W Irian
65 F4 **Maokui Shan** *mt* China
65 G3 **Maolin** China
67 C6 **Maoming** China
67 C1 **Maoping** China
67 G6 **Mao-pi T'ou** *C* Taiwan
67 B3 **Maotai** China
67 A1 **Maowen** China
65 F2 **Maoxing** China
80 F4 **Ma'oz** Israel
70 F5 **Mapaga** Sulawesi
87 F10 **Mapai** Mozambique
66 C5 **Mapam Yumco** *L* China
70 B6 **Mapan** Kalimantan
70 G5 **Mapane** Sulawesi
70 F5 **Mapida** Sulawesi
70 F6 **Mapili** Sulawesi
124 G4 **Mapimí, Bolson de** *dist* Mexico
67 D1 **Maping** China
128 F2 **Mapire** Venezuela
129 H3 **Mapireme** Brazil
128 E7 **Mapiri** *R* La Paz **Bolivia**
128 F4 **Mapixari, L** Brazil
99 L7 **Maple** *R* Iowa
94 C3 **Maple** *R* Michigan
118 H9 **Maple Creek** Sask
99 N6 **Maple Island** Minnesota
111 K9 **Maplesville** Alabama
99 L7 **Mapleton** Iowa
95 S7 **Mapleton** Maine
99 N6 **Mapleton** Minnesota
122 H8 **Mapleton** Nova Scotia
100 B5 **Mapleton** Oregon
100 C2 **Maple Valley** Washington
95 L3 **Maple View** New York
141 F1 **Mapoon** Queensland
144 C5 **Mapourika, L** New Zealand
13 H6 **Mappleton** England
129 G4 **Mapuera** *R* Brazil
69 G12 **Mapur** *isld* Indonesia
89 H5 **Maputo** Mozambique
89 H6 **Maputo** *R* Mozambique
80 F8 **Maqam en Nabi Yusha** Jordan
78 H6 **Maqar an Naam** Iraq
46 D3 **Maqellarë** Albania
65 H2 **Maqiaohe** China
79 E10 **Maqnā** Saudi Arabia
66 C6 **Maquan He** *R* China
71 G4 **Maqueda Chan** Philippines
122 H5 **Maquereau Pte.au** Quebec
133 D6 **Maquinchao** Argentina
131 B8 **Maquinchao, R** Argentina
99 Q7 **Maquoketa** Iowa
99 Q9 **Maquon** Illinois
70 E3 **Mara** Kalimantan
127 J9 **Mara** Venezuela
128 E4 **Maraa** Brazil
129 J5 **Marabá** Brazil
70 D6 **Marabahan** Kalimantan
40 B2 **Marac** France
127 J9 **Maracaibo** Venezuela
127 J9 **Maracaibo, L. de** Venezuela
129 H3 **Maracá, Ilha de** Amapá Brazil
128 F3 **Maracá, Ilha de** Roraima Brazil
133 F2 **Maracaju** Brazil
130 C7 **Maracaju,Serra de** *mts* Brazil
129 J4 **Maracana** Brazil
127 O2 **Maracas B** Trinidad
127 L9 **Maracay** Venezuela
84 F4 **Maradah** Libya
85 F6 **Maradi** Niger
145 E3 **Maraetai** New Zealand
78 L3 **Marāgheh** Iran
130 J10 **Maragogi** Brazil
128 E3 **Marahuaca,Co** *mt* Venezuela
65 E2 **Marain Sum** China
110 A3 **Marais des Cygnes** *R* Kansas/Missouri
20 F3 **Marais-Vernier** France
129 J4 **Marajó,I.de** Brazil
86 G5 **Maralal** Kenya
55 G4 **Maraldy** U.S.S.R.
86 C4 **Marali** Cent Afr Republic
137 N3 **Maramasike** *isld* Solomon Is
Maramba *see* **Livingstone** Zambia
48 H3 **Maramures** *old prov* Romania
69 F11 **Maran** Malaysia
103 N9 **Marana** Arizona
140 C2 **Maranboy** N Terr Aust
17 F3 **Maranchón** Spain
78 K2 **Marand** Iran
89 G2 **Marandellas** Zimbabwe
45 J2 **Maranello** Italy
68 D7 **Marang** Burma
69 F10 **Marang** Malaysia
129 L4 **Maranguape** Brazil
130 E4 **Maranhão** *R* Brazil
129 J4 **Maranhão** *state* Brazil
141 J7 **Maranoa** *R* Queensland
45 Q8 **Marano di Napoli** Italy
128 D4 **Marañón** *R* Peru
21 C9 **Marans** France
40 A1 **Maranville** France
16 B3 **Marão, Sa do** *mts* Portugal
129 G3 **Marapi** *R* Brazil
128 E5 **Marari** Brazil
144 B6 **Mararoa** *R* New Zealand
78 F3 **Maras** Turkey
70 F7 **Marasende** *isld* Indonesia
48 L5 **Mărăşeşti** Romania
71 C6 **Marasi B** Palawan Philippines
16 B6 **Marateca** Portugal
46 D7 **Marathiás,Akr** *C* Greece
113 F13 **Marathon** Florida
47 F6 **Marathón** Greece
95 L4 **Marathon** New York
120 D4 **Marathon** Ontario
141 G5 **Marathon** Queensland
108 D5 **Marathon** Texas
99 R5 **Marathon** Wisconsin
70 F3 **Maratua** *isld* Indonesia
129 L6 **Maraú** Brazil
128 E3 **Marauaí** *R* Brazil
127 O2 **Maraval** Trinidad
108 E6 **Maravillas Cr** Texas
71 G7 **Marawi** Mindanao Philippines
38 M5 **Marbach** Austria
36 F2 **Marbach** W Germany
22 K4 **Marbehan** Belgium
106 C2 **Marble** Colorado
100 H1 **Marble** Washington
142 C5 **Marble Bar** W Australia
103 N5 **Marble Canyon** Arizona
110 B6 **Marble City** Oklahoma
109 J5 **Marble Falls** Texas
87 E10 **Marble Hall** S Africa
99 P10 **Marblehead** Illinois
95 R4 **Marblehead** Massachusetts
94 E5 **Marblehead** Ohio
99 O7 **Marble Rock** Iowa
121 T7 **Marbleton** Quebec
101 P7 **Marbleton** Wyoming
36 F2 **Marburg** W Germany
95 K8 **Marbury** Maryland
26 G8 **Marby** Sweden
48 D3 **Marcal** *R* Hungary
47 J7 **Marçal Dağ** *mt* Turkey
48 D4 **Marcali** Hungary
45 J1 **Marcaria** Italy
21 F9 **Marçay** France
122 F2 **Marceau,L** Quebec
118 L6 **Marcelin** Sask
110 D2 **Marceline** Missouri
133 G3 **Marcelino Ramos** Brazil
110 E6 **Marcella** Arkansas
94 B4 **Marcellus** Michigan
100 G2 **Marcellus** Washington
45 O5 **Marcetelli** Italy
9 G2 **March** England
20 G4 **Marchainville** France
118 E2 **Marchand** Manitoba
138 E4 **Marchant Hill** S Australia
40 D3 **Marchaux** France
21 I9 **Marche** *reg* France
45 N4 **Marche** *reg* Italy
22 J3 **Marche-en-Famenne** Belgium
16 D7 **Marchena** Spain
128 A7 **Marchena** *isld* Galapagos Is
21 H6 **Marchenoir** France
70 E1 **Marchesa B** Sabah
20 C3 **Marchésieux** France
127 P6 **Marchfield** Barbados
22 E3 **Marchiennes-Ville** France
22 J3 **Marchin** Belgium
140 D1 **Marchinbar I** N Terr **Aust**
131 E3 **Mar Chiquita, L** Córdoba Argentina
45 Q7 **Marcianise** Italy
18 H6 **Marcigny** France
18 G8 **Marcillac** France
20 D5 **Marcille-la-Ville** France
20 H4 **Marcilly** France
21 I7 **Marcilly-en Gault** France
21 J6 **Marcilly-en Villette** France
40 G1 **Marckolsheim** France
122 J1 **Marc,L** Labrador
113 F12 **Marco** Florida
110 J3 **Marco** Indiana
43 G9 **Marco Argentano, S** Italy
22 E3 **Marcoing** France
100 C5 **Marcola** Oregon
21 G6 **Marçon** France
118 C1 **Marconi** Manitoba
22 K3 **Marcourt** Belgium
99 L7 **Marcus** Iowa
100 G1 **Marcus** Washington
116 O6 **Marcus Baker,Mt** Alaska
134 G5 **Marcus I** Pacific Oc
95 M3 **Marcy** New York
95 O2 **Marcy, Mt** New York
80 D5 **Marda** Jordan
74 E1 **Mardan** Pakistan
131 F6 **Mar del Plata** Argentina
9 G5 **Marden** England
142 B5 **Mardie** W Australia
78 H3 **Mardin** Turkey
26 M5 **Mårdsel** Sweden
26 K7 **Mårdsele** Sweden
26 J7 **Mardsjö** Sweden
26 H8 **Mårdsjön** Sweden
70 G7 **Mare** Sulawesi
71 A2 **Mare** *isld* Halmahera Indonesia
137 O6 **Maré** *isld* Îles Loyauté Pac Oc
86 G3 **Mareb** *R* Ethiopia
45 M3 **Marecchia** *R* Italy
130 J10 **Marechal Deodoro** Brazil
141 H3 **Mareeba** Queensland
110 K3 **Marengo** Indiana
99 P8 **Marengo** Iowa
41 N7 **Marengo** Italy
94 E6 **Marengo** Ohio
118 H7 **Marengo** Sask
100 G2 **Marengo** Washington
99 Q3 **Marengo** Wisconsin
99 R3 **Marenisco** Michigan
21 C10 **Marennes** France
145 E2 **Mareretu** New Zealand
86 A2 **Marergur** Somalia
9 G6 **Maresfield** England
43 E11 **Marettimo** *isld* Sicily
22 E3 **Maretz** France
21 C8 **Mareuil** France
21 J8 **Mareuil-sur-Arnon** France
108 C5 **Marfa** Texas
66 D4 **Margai Caka** *L* China
75 M1 **Margai Caka** *L* China
8 C4 **Margam** Wales
57 D1 **Marganets** U.S.S.R.
76 A3 **Margao** India
123 L7 **Margaree Harbour** C Breton I, N Scotia
123 L7 **Margaree I** Nova Scotia
123 M7 **Margaree Valley** C Breton I, N Scotia
108 H1 **Margaret** Texas
138 D3 **Margaret** *R* S Australia
117 K10 **Margaret Bay** Br Col
141 G1 **Margaret Bay** Queensland
117 Q6 **Margaret L** Alberta
117 P3 **Margaret L** N W Terr
142 C5 **Margaret, Mt** W Australia
143 B10 **Margaret R** W Australia
95 N4 **Margaretville** New York
130 C7 **Margarida** Brazil
127 N9 **Margarita I. de Venezuela**
46 D5 **Margarítion** Greece
9 H5 **Margate** England
89 G8 **Margate** S Africa
139 H9 **Margate** Tasmania
95 N7 **Margate City** New Jersey
18 H8 **Margeride, Mts de la** France
Margherita *see* **Giamame** Somalia
48 G3 **Marghita** Romania
118 F3 **Margie** Alberta
99 N1 **Margie** Minnesota
57 F4 **Margilan** U.S.S.R.
48 G5 **Mărgina** Romania
48 G5 **Margita** Yugoslavia
119 O7 **Margo** Sask
77 H4 **Margo, Dasht-i-** *des* Afghanistan
71 F7 **Margosatubig** Mindanao Philippines
94 C2 **Margrethe, L** Michigan
117 M9 **Marguerite** Br Columbia
146 F13 **Marguerite B** Antarctica
22 J4 **Margut** France
80 F3 **Marhaba** Jordan
122 F5 **Maria** Quebec
124 F7 **María Cleofas, I** Mexico
28 D3 **Mariager** Denmark
32 M7 **Mariaglück** W Germany
68 C7 **Maria I** Burma
140 D2 **Maria I** N Terr Aust
139 J8 **Maria I** Tasmania
36 C3 **Maria Laach** W Germany
38 G8 **Maria Luggau** Austria
124 F7 **María Madre, I** Mexico
124 F7 **María Magdalena, I** Mexico
103 K8 **Maria Mts** California
141 J5 **Marian** Queensland
130 G7 **Mariana** Brazil
118 E3 **Mariana Lake** Alberta
126 C3 **Marianao** Cuba
134 E6 **Marianas** *islds* Pacific Oc
75 Q5 **Mariani** India
117 P4 **Marian L** N W Terr
110 F7 **Marianna** Arkansas
113 B7 **Marianna** Florida
27 H14 **Mariannelund** Sweden
87 B8 **Mariano Machado** Angola
37 O4 **Marianské Lázně** Czechoslovakia
119 T9 **Mariapolis** Manitoba
101 N1 **Marias** *R* Montana
17 F7 **Maria,Sierra de** *mts* Spain
101 M1 **Marias Pass** Montana
38 F6 **Mariastein** Austria
135 M12 **Maria Theresa Reef** Pacific Oc
145 D1 **Maria van Diemen, C** New Zealand
38 M6 **Mariazell** Austria
99 T5 **Maribel** Wisconsin
28 G7 **Maribo** Denmark
Maribo *co see* **Storstrøm**
38 N8 **Maribor** Yugoslavia
71 E4 **Maricaban** *isld* Philippines
89 E5 **Marico** *R* Botswana
103 M8 **Maricopa** Arizona
102 E6 **Maricopa** California
103 M8 **Maricopa Mts** Arizona
115 M5 **Maricourt** Quebec
86 E5 **Maridi** Sudan
128 E4 **Marié** *R* Brazil
83 K12 **Marie Anne I** Seychelles
146 H10 **Marie Byrd Land** Antarctica
27 H13 **Mariedam** Sweden
27 J12 **Mariefred** Sweden
127 N5 **Marie Galante** *isld* Guadeloupe **W Indies**
27 L11 **Mariehamn** Finland
118 G4 **Marie L** Alberta
126 C3 **Mariel** Cuba
Marienbad *see* **Marianské Lázně**
37 P2 **Marienberg** E Germany
25 G3 **Marienberg** Netherlands
32 L8 **Marienberg** W Germany
22 H3 **Marienbourg** Belgium
Marienburg *see* **Malbork**
36 C2 **Marienburg** Nordrhein-Westfalen W Germany
37 N3 **Marieney** E Germany
32 F5 **Marienhafe** W Germany
36 C1 **Marienheide** W Germany
28 G7 **Marienleuchte** *C* W Germany
89 A5 **Mariental** Namibia
107 J3 **Marienthal** Kansas
94 H5 **Marienville** Pennsylvania
Marienwerder *see* **Kwidzyn**
140 B1 **Marie Shoal** N Terr **Aust**
27 G13 **Mariestad** Sweden
112 C4 **Marietta** Georgia
94 F7 **Marietta** Ohio
109 K2 **Marietta** Oklahoma
112 E2 **Marietta** S Carolina
121 R7 **Marieville** Quebec
19 O18 **Marignane** France
21 F6 **Marigné** France
20 C3 **Marigny** France
127 N5 **Marigot** Saint Martin **W I**
56 C3 **Mariinsk** U.S.S.R.
55 D4 **Mariinskoye** U.S.S.R.
52 G6 **Mariinsky Posad** U.S.S.R.
71 J5 **Marikasu,Tg** *C* Indonesia
130 D8 **Marila** Brazil
133 H2 **Marília** Brazil
142 C6 **Marillana** W Australia
130 E7 **Marimbondo Cachoeira** *rapids* Brazil
127 M4 **Marin** Martinique **W I**
16 B2 **Marín** Spain
44 H3 **Marina di Carrara** Italy
44 H3 **Marina di Massa** Italy
44 H4 **Marina di Pisa** Italy
45 M3 **Marina di Ravenna** Italy
128 G2 **Marina Fall** Guyana
70 B6 **Marindjahan** Kalimantan
71 E4 **Marinduque** *isld* Philippines
110 G3 **Marine** Illinois
113 F8 **Marineland** Florida
20 K3 **Marines** France
99 T4 **Marinette** Wisconsin
129 H8 **Maringá** Brazil
86 D5 **Maringa** *R* Zaïre
111 E11 **Maringouin** Louisiana
87 F9 **Maringue** Mozambique
16 B5 **Marinha Grande** Portugal
54 J9 **Mar'inka** U.S.S.R.
42 E7 **Marino** Italy
128 E3 **Marinuma** Colombia
111 J9 **Marion** Alabama
110 F6 **Marion** Arkansas
117 Q11 **Marion** Idaho
110 H4 **Marion** Illinois
94 B6 **Marion** Indiana
99 P7 **Marion** Iowa
107 O3 **Marion** Kansas
110 H4 **Marion** Kentucky
111 D9 **Marion** Louisiana
95 U2 **Marion** Maine
94 B2 **Marion** Michigan
111 H9 **Marion** Mississippi
101 L1 **Marion** Montana
112 E2 **Marion** N Carolina
98 H3 **Marion** N Dakota
98 F9 **Marion** Nebraska
94 D6 **Marion** Ohio
112 H3 **Marion** S Carolina
98 J6 **Marion** S Dakota
109 J6 **Marion** Texas
94 F10 **Marion** Virginia
99 S5 **Marion** Wisconsin
139 J8 **Marion B** Tasmania
140 E6 **Marion Downs** Queensland
111 J9 **Marion Junction** Alabama
137 L5 **Marion Reef** Coral Sea
141 K4 **Marion Reef** Gt Barrier Reef **Aust**
110 C4 **Marionville** Missouri
128 E2 **Maripa** Venezuela
71 G5 **Maripipi** *isld* Philippines
102 E4 **Mariposa** California
102 D4 **Mariposa** *R* California
70 G4 **Marisa** Sulawesi
133 E2 **Mariscal Estigarribia** Paraguay
110 G3 **Marissa** Illinois
47 H2 **Maritsa** Bulgaria
Maritsa *R see* **Évros** *R*
47 G2 **Maritsa** *R* Bulgaria
44 B3 **Marittime, Alpi** *mts* Italy/France
52 G6 **Mari Turek** U.S.S.R.
Mariupol *see* **Zhdanov**
127 O10 **Mariusa** *R* Venezuela
77 J4 **Marja** Afghanistan
84 G3 **Marj, Al** Libya
26 N5 **Marjärv** Sweden
79 F5 **Marjayoûn** Lebanon
25 C5 **Mark** *R* Netherlands
80 G6 **Marka** Jordan
26 E8 **Markabygd** Norway
78 H4 **Markada** Syria
56 C6 **Markakal', Oz** *L* U.S.S.R.
52 J4 **Markalasta** U.S.S.R.
58 C6 **Markam** China
76 D3 **Markapur** India
120 K8 **Markdale** Ontario
41 K2 **Markdorf** W Germany
110 F6 **Marked Tree** Arkansas
25 G4 **Markelo** Netherlands
28 G7 **Markelsdorfe Huk** *C* W Germany
25 D4 **Marken** Netherlands
25 D3 **Markerwaard** Netherlands
99 S6 **Markesan** Wisconsin
9 F2 **Market Deeping** England
8 D2 **Market Drayton** England
9 F3 **Market Harborough** England
14 E2 **Markethill** N Ireland
13 H6 **Market Rasen** England
9 E1 **Market Warsop** England
13 H6 **Market Weighton** England
36 G6 **Markgröningen** W Germany
121 L9 **Markham** Ontario
109 L7 **Markham** Texas
100 B3 **Markham** Washington
66 C4 **Markham Lake** China
9 F1 **Markham Moor** England
146 G7 **Markham,Mt** Antarctica
119 N8 **Markinch** Sask
15 E4 **Markinch** Scotland
33 T8 **Märkisch Buchholz** E Germany
26 M4 **Markitta** Sweden
102 E3 **Markleeville** California
37 O6 **Marklkofen** W Germany
37 N3 **Markneukirchen** E Germany
26 J4 **Markotjåkko** *mt* Sweden
33 Q10 **Markrapstädt** E Germany
111 F7 **Marks** Mississippi
8 D5 **Marksbury** England
120 K6 **Markstay** Ontario
9 G4 **Marks Tey** England
37 J2 **Marksuhl** E Germany
111 D10 **Marksville** Louisiana
37 J5 **Marktbergel** W Germany
37 J4 **Markt Bibart** W Germany
37 J4 **Marktbreit** W Germany
37 L3 **Marktgraitz** W Germany
36 H4 **Marktheidenfeld** W Germany
37 L7 **Markt Indersdorf** W Germany
37 O7 **Marktl** W Germany
37 M3 **Marktleugast** W Germany
37 J6 **Markttoffingen** W Germany
37 N3 **Marktredwitz** W Germany
37 M3 **Marktschorgast** W Germany
37 J4 **Marktsteft** W Germany
41 N1 **Markt Wald** W Germany
37 L3 **Marktzeuln** W Germany
99 O3 **Markville** Minnesota
32 F9 **Marl** W Germany
107 N5 **Marland** Oklahoma
143 B8 **Marlandy Hill** W Australia
121 N8 **Marlbank** Ontario
95 Q4 **Marlboro** Massachusetts
95 P4 **Marlboro** New Hampshire
9 E5 **Marlborough** England
128 G2 **Marlborough** Guyana
141 J6 **Marlborough** Queensland
145 D4 **Marlborough** *stat area* New Zealand
22 F4 **Marle** France
33 S8 **Marlendorf** E Germany
33 S8 **Marlenfelde** E Germany
94 D3 **Marlette** Michigan
109 L4 **Marlin** Texas
94 G8 **Marlinton** W Virginia
139 J7 **Marlo** Victoria
22 J3 **Marloie** Belgium
33 R4 **Marlow** E Germany
9 F4 **Marlow** England
95 P3 **Marlow** New Hampshire
109 K1 **Marlow** Oklahoma
141 H5 **Marlow** Queensland
22 F4 **Marly** France
20 K4 **Marly-le-Roi** France
27 J10 **Marma** Sweden
110 F5 **Marmaduke** Arkansas
18 F8 **Marmande** France
47 J4 **Marmara** Turkey
47 J4 **Marmaraereğlisi** Turkey
47 J6 **Marmara Gölü** *L* Turkey
47 J4 **Marmara,Sea of** Turkey
47 J8 **Marmaris** Turkey
98 C3 **Marmarth** N Dakota
26 K3 **Mårmatj** *mt* Sweden
94 E4 **Marme City** Michigan
16 B2 **Marmed,Sa des S** *mts* Spain
128 F5 **Marmelos** *R* Brazil
94 F8 **Marmet** W Virginia
121 P4 **Marmette,L** Quebec
118 L1 **Marmion L** *res* Ontario
143 C8 **Marmion, Mt** W Australia
45 J1 **Marmirolo** Italy
42 D2 **Marmolada** *mt* Italy
16 E6 **Marmolejo** Spain
116 L7 **Marmot B** Alaska
125 M9 **Mar Muerto** *B* Mexico
19 J5 **Marnay** France
32 K5 **Marne** W Germany
18 H4 **Marne** *dep* France
40 B1 **Marne** *R* France
36 B6 **Marne, Canal de la** France
36 D4 **Marnheim** W Germany
33 P6 **Marnitz** E Germany
139 G6 **Marnoo** Victoria
99 S9 **Maroa** Illinois
145 F3 **Maroa** New Zealand
87 H11 **Maroantsetra** Madagascar
74 C2 **Marobi** Pakistan
22 D3 **Marœuil** France
22 F3 **Maroilles** France
37 K3 **Maroldsweisach** W Germany
20 F5 **Marolles-les-Braults** France
87 H10 **Maromandia** Madagascar
20 H3 **Maromme** France
47 H4 **Marónia** Greece
18 G7 **Maronne** *R* France
141 G7 **Maroo** Queensland
143 B6 **Maroonah** W Australia
127 J2 **Maroon Town** Jamaica
70 F7 **Maros** Sulawesi
70 F7 **Maros** *R* Sulawesi
145 E1 **Marotiri Is** New Zealand
86 B3 **Maroua** Cameroon
121 L4 **Marouf Jct** Quebec
129 H3 **Marouini** *R* Fr Guiana
87 H11 **Marovoay** Madagascar
110 F4 **Marquano** Missouri
135 U13 **Marquesas Is** Pacific Oc
113 E13 **Marquesas Keys** *islds* Florida
130 G8 **Marquês de Valença** Brazil
99 P6 **Marquette** Iowa
107 N3 **Marquette** Kansas
118 D1 **Marquette** Manitoba
99 T3 **Marquette** Michigan
98 H8 **Marquette** Nebraska
99 U6 **Marquette** *R* Michigan
106 C6 **Marquez** New Mexico
109 L4 **Marquez** Texas
17 F1 **Marquina** Spain
22 E3 **Marquion** France
119 M8 **Marquis** Sask
22 B2 **Marquise** France
139 G4 **Marra** New S Wales
139 H4 **Marra** *R* New S Wales
89 H5 **Marracuene** Mozambique
45 L3 **Marradi** Italy
143 B10 **Marradong** W Australia
86 D3 **Marra, Jebel** *mts* Sudan
140 B2 **Marrakai** N Terr Aust
85 C2 **Marrakech** Morocco
85 E2 **Marraket, Hassi** Algeria
139 H5 **Marrar** New S Wales
43 B8 **Marrargiu, C** Sardinia
139 G8 **Marrawah** Tasmania
28 H7 **Marrebæk** Denmark
138 E3 **Marree** S Australia
111 J13 **Marrero** New Orleans
87 G9 **Marromeu** Mozambique
16 D8 **Marroqui,Pta** Spain
88 F8 **Marrupa** Mozambique
138 C2 **Marryat** *R* S Australia
94 G6 **Mars** Pennsylvania
84 K4 **Marsá Alam** Egypt
17 F9 **Marsa Ben Mehidi** Algeria
86 G5 **Marsabit** Kenya
Marsa Brega *see* **Qasr al Burayqal**
21 B6 **Marsac-sur-Don** France
130 F8 **Mar,Sa.do** *mts* Brazil
86 H3 **Marsa Fatma** Ethiopia
36 B6 **Marsal** France
43 E11 **Marsala** Sicily
19 N15 **Marsanne** France
84 G3 **Marsá Sūsah** Libya
13 G4 **Marsden** England
139 J5 **Marsden** New S Wales
118 H6 **Marsden** Sask
19 O18 **Marseille** France
20 J2 **Marseille-en-Beauvaisis** France
19 N18 **Marseille-Rhône, Canal** France
Marseilles France *see* **Marseille**
99 S8 **Marseilles** Illinois
94 D6 **Marseilles** Ohio
98 B3 **Marsh** Montana
79 E10 **Marshah, J** *mt* Saudi Arabia
110 D6 **Marshall** Arkansas
99 T10 **Marshall** Illinois
94 C4 **Marshall** Michigan
99 L5 **Marshall** Minnesota
110 C2 **Marshall** Missouri
112 E2 **Marshall** N Carolina
98 D2 **Marshall** N Dakota
107 N5 **Marshall** Oklahoma
118 H5 **Marshall** Sask
109 N3 **Marshall** Texas
94 K8 **Marshall** Virginia
101 U7 **Marshall** Wyoming
140 D6 **Marshall** *R* N Terr **Aust**
139 J7 **Marshall B** Tasmania
134 G7 **Marshall Is** Pacific Oc
120 C2 **Marshall L** Ontario
99 O7 **Marshalltown** Iowa
8 D3 **Marshbrook** England
8 D5 **Marshfield** England
110 D4 **Marshfield** Missouri
99 Q5 **Marshfield** Wisconsin
113 K11 **Marsh Harbour** Great Abaco I **Bahamas**
95 L5 **Marsh Hill** Pennsylvania
95 T7 **Mars Hill** Maine
111 D12 **Marsh Island** Louisiana
117 F5 **Marsh L** Yukon Terr
98 K4 **Marsh Lake** Minnesota
101 Q9 **Marsh Pk** Utah
112 G3 **Marshville** N Carolina
100 J6 **Marsing** Idaho
98 C7 **Marsland** Nebraska
19 J3 **Mars la Tour** France
28 E4 **Mårslet** Denmark
28 F6 **Marslev** Denmark
27 J12 **Märsta** Sweden
28 F7 **Marstal** Denmark
28 E7 **Marstal Bugt** *B* Denmark
101 Q8 **Marston** Wyoming
27 E14 **Marstrand** Sweden
28 C6 **Marstrup** Denmark
25 E2 **Marsum** Netherlands
55 D1 **Marsyaty** U.S.S.R.
109 L4 **Mart** Texas
42 D6 **Marta** *R* Italy
68 C4 **Martaban** Burma
73 Q5 **Martaban,G.of** Burma
21 F8 **Martaizé** France
70 D6 **Martapura** Kalimantan
70 K8 **Martapura** Sumatra
18 G8 **Martel** France
22 K4 **Martelange** Belgium
41 N4 **Martello, Val** Italy
47 H1 **Marten** Bulgaria
99 N8 **Martensdale** Iowa
17 G5 **Martés,Sierra** *mts* Spain
139 J4 **Marthaguy** *R* New S Wales
110 E3 **Marthasville** Missouri
95 R5 **Marthas Vineyard** Massachusetts
36 B6 **Marthille** France
126 F4 **Martí** Cuba
45 M5 **Martignano,L.di** Italy
20 D5 **Martigné** France
21 E7 **Martigné-Briand** France
21 C6 **Martigné-Ferchaud** France
40 F5 **Martigny** Switzerland
40 C1 **Martigny-les-Bains** France
19 O18 **Martigues** France
16 D9 **Martil** Morocco
116 N4 **Martin** Alaska
31 L6 **Martin** Czechoslovakia
94 E9 **Martin** Kentucky
94 B4 **Martin** Michigan
98 E6 **Martin** S Dakota
110 H5 **Martin** Tennessee
17 G4 **Martin** *R* Spain
41 M4 **Martina** Switzerland
43 H8 **Martina Franca** Italy
145 E4 **Martinborough** New Zealand
109 K6 **Martindale** Texas
102 B3 **Martinez** California
125 L7 **Martínez** Mexico
32 M10 **Martinfeld** E Germany
130 F6 **Martinho Campos** Brazil
127 L4 **Martinique** *isld* Lesser Antilles
111 L9 **Martin L** Alabama
130 D8 **Martinópolis** Brazil
146 H11 **Martin Pen** Antarctica
116 Q1 **Martin Pt** Alaska
144 A6 **Martin's B** New Zealand
38 M5 **Martinsberg** Austria
Martinsbrück *see* **Martina**
110 E2 **Martinsburg** Missouri
95 M3 **Martinsburg** New York
94 E6 **Martinsburg** Ohio
94 J6 **Martinsburg** Pennsylvania
94 K7 **Martinsburg** W Virginia
101 P3 **Martinsdale** Montana
94 G6 **Martins Ferry** Ohio
99 T10 **Martinsville** Illinois
94 A7 **Martinsville** Indiana
94 H10 **Martinsville** Virginia
20 B2 **Martinvast** France
21 H8 **Martizay** France
9 H3 **Martlesham** England
8 D6 **Martock** England
28 F5 **Martofte** Denmark
9 F1 **Marton** England
145 E4 **Marton** New Zealand
17 J3 **Martorell** Spain
16 E7 **Martos** Spain
117 O4 **Martre, Lac La** N W Terr
29 N4 **Martti** Finland
29 K11 **Marttila** Finland
55 C5 **Martuk** U.S.S.R.
52 J2 **Martyn** U.S.S.R.
80 G3 **Maru** Jordan
77 H2 **Maruchak** Afghanistan
70 D2 **Marudi** Sarawak
70 E1 **Marudu Bay** Sabah
77 K4 **Maruf** Afghanistan
60 G11 **Marugame** Japan
144 D5 **Maruia** New Zealand
129 L6 **Maruim** Brazil
28 J4 **Mårum** Denmark
25 F2 **Marum** Netherlands
145 F3 **Marumaru** New Zealand
140 C2 **Marumba Mt** N Terr **Aust**
88 B5 **Marungu** *mts* Zaïre
61 K9 **Maruoka** Japan
77 D4 **Marvast** Iran
27 C11 **Mår-vatn** *L* Norway
18 H8 **Marvejols** France
111 F7 **Marvell** Arkansas
143 C9 **Marvel Loch** W Australia
22 J5 **Marville** France
98 K4 **Marvin** S Dakota
106 C1 **Marvine** Colorado
103 N3 **Marvine,Mt** Utah
77 H2 **Marwa** Afghanistan
74 E6 **Marwar** India
118 G5 **Marwayne** Alberta
15 E1 **Marwick Hd** Orkney Scotland
32 G6 **Marx** W Germany
33 S9 **Marxdorf** E Germany
37 M3 **Marxgrün** W Germany
77 G1 **Mary** U.S.S.R.
142 B5 **Mary Ann Pt** W Australia
55 F3 **Mar'yanovka** U.S.S.R.
139 G6 **Maryborough** New S Wales
141 L7 **Maryborough** Queensland
87 D11 **Marydale** S Africa
55 E4 **Mar'yevka** U.S.S.R.
119 Q9 **Maryfield** Sask
117 L6 **Mary Henry,Mt** Br Col
12 D2 **Maryhill** Scotland
140 F5 **Mary Kathleen** Queensland
111 E10 **Mary,L** Mississippi
89 G1 **Maryland** Zimbabwe
95 K7 **Maryland** *state* U.S.A.
108 G3 **Maryneal** Texas
12 E4 **Maryport** England
141 K7 **Mary R** Queensland
123 R1 **Mary's Hbr** Labrador
100 K8 **Marys R** Nevada
123 R6 **Marystown** Newfoundland
103 M3 **Marysvale** Utah
101 O5 **Marysville** Idaho
107 O2 **Marysville** Kansas
94 E4 **Marysville** Michigan
122 F8 **Marysville** New Brunswick
94 D6 **Marysville** Ohio
100 C1 **Marysville** Washington
141 H4 **Maryvale** Queensland
141 K8 **Maryvale** Queensland
99 M9 **Maryville** Missouri
112 D2 **Maryville** Tennessee
45 K3 **Marzabotto** Italy
85 D5 **Marzafal** Mali
130 E5 **Marzagão** Brazil
33 R8 **Marzahna** E Germany
33 R7 **Marzahne** E Germany
128 C2 **Marzo,C** Colombia
84 E4 **Marzūq** Libya
70 O9 **Mas** *R* Java
69 D13 **Masa** *isld* Indonesia
Masada *see* **Meẓada**
80 F1 **Mas'ada** Syria
88 F4 **Masai Steppe** Tanzania
88 C2 **Masaka** Uganda
86 C3 **Masalasef** Chad
70 G6 **Masamba** Sulawesi
65 G7 **Masan** S Korea
71 N8 **Masapun** Indonesia
95 S7 **Masardis** Maine
113 E9 **Masaryktown** Florida
88 G7 **Masasi** Tanzania
Mas Atierra *isld see* **Robinson Crusoe I**
71 F4 **Masbate** *isld* Philippines
32 F9 **Masbeck** W Germany
17 H9 **Mascara** Algeria
81 C7 **Mascarene Basin** Indian Oc
81 C7 **Mascarene I** Indian Oc
81 C7 **Mascarene Rge** Indian Oc
98 G9 **Mascot** Nebraska
112 D1 **Mascot** Tennessee
130 H4 **Mascote** Brazil
110 G3 **Mascoutah** Illinois
18 F9 **Mas d'Azil, le** France
118 K9 **Masefield** Sask
70 E3 **Ma Sekatok** Kalimantan
71 O9 **Masela** *isld* Indonesia
38 N7 **Masenberg** *mt* Austria
45 L1 **Masera di P** Italy
121 P4 **Masères,L** Quebec
89 E7 **Maseru** Lesotho
40 E2 **Masevaux** France
87 F9 **Mashabe** Zimbabwe
13 G5 **Masham** England
65 H2 **Mashan** China
67 C5 **Mashan** China
80 G1 **Masharah** Syria
80 E7 **Mashash** *R* Jordan
80 F2 **Mashfa** Syria
77 F1 **Mashhad** Iran
85 E7 **Mashi** *R* Nigeria
60 P2 **Mashike** Japan
77 E5 **Mashīz** Iran
77 H6 **Mashkel** *R* Pakistan
120 F5 **Mashkode** Ontario
89 C6 **Mashowing** *watercourse* S Africa
95 R5 **Mashpee** Massachusetts
60 S2 **Mashū-ko** *L* Japan
26 N2 **Masi** Norway
124 E4 **Masiáca** Mexico
86 C6 **Masi-Manimba** Zaïre
70 F5 **Masimbu** Sulawesi
86 F5 **Masindi** Uganda
71 D3 **Masinloc** Luzon **Philippines**
72 H4 **Maşirah** *isld* Oman
77 B4 **Masiri** Iran
89 G5 **Masitonto** *R* S Africa
77 A4 **Masjed Soleymān** Iran
125 P9 **Maskall** Belize
121 R6 **Maskinongé** Quebec
14 B3 **Mask,L** Irish Rep
29 J11 **Masku** Finland
47 J2 **Maslen Nos** Bulgaria
55 D1 **Maslovo** U.S.S.R.
56 B4 **Maslyanino** U.S.S.R.
55 F3 **Maslyanskoye** U.S.S.R.
28 H7 **Masnedssund** Denmark
22 E3 **Masnieres** France
87 I11 **Masoala, C** Madagascar
110 H3 **Mason** Illinois
94 C4 **Mason** Michigan
102 E3 **Mason** Nevada
110 M2 **Mason** Ohio
98 C4 **Mason** S Dakota
110 G6 **Mason** Tennessee
109 H5 **Mason** Texas
99 P3 **Mason** Wisconsin
101 P7 **Mason** Wyoming
144 A7 **Mason Bay** New Zealand
99 R9 **Mason City** Illinois
99 N6 **Mason City** Iowa
98 G8 **Mason City** Nebraska
117 M7 **Mason Creek** Br Columbia
88 F3 **Masongaleni** Kenya
71 J5 **Masoni** *isld* Indonesia
143 C8 **Mason, L** W Australia
94 H7 **Masontown** Pennsylvania
94 H7 **Masontown** W Virginia
26 O1 **Måsöy** *isld* Norway
99 R3 **Mass** Michigan
44 H3 **Massa** Italy
95 P4 **Massachusetts** *state* U.S.A.
95 R4 **Massachusetts B** U.S.A.
45 H4 **Massaciuccoli,L.di** Italy
100 F8 **Massacre L** Nevada
80 F3 **Massada** Israel
106 B1 **Massadona** Colorado
45 M2 **Massa Fiscáglia** Italy
86 C3 **Massaguet** Chad
86 C3 **Massakoti** Chad
45 L3 **Massa Lombarda** Italy
45 Q8 **Massa Lubrense** Italy
42 D5 **Massa Marittima** Italy
87 F10 **Massanga** Mozambique
87 F10 **Massangena** Mozambique
94 J8 **Massanutten Mt** Virginia
129 K4 **Massape** Brazil
94 K8 **Massaponax** Virginia
45 H4 **Massarosa** Italy
18 F10 **Massat** France
55 D1 **Massava** U.S.S.R.
86 G2 **Massawa** Ethiopia
86 H2 **Massawa Chan** Ethiopia
21 I7 **Massay** France
37 J3 **Massbach** W Germany
99 M8 **Massena** Iowa
95 N2 **Massena** New York
86 C3 **Massénya** Chad
117 G9 **Masset** Br Col
18 F9 **Masseube** France
120 H6 **Massey** Ontario
18 H7 **Massiac** France
45 P7 **Massico, M** *mt* Italy
94 H9 **Massies Mill** Virginia
18 H7 **Massif Central** *plat* France
86 B4 **Massif de l'Adamaoua** *mt* Cameroon
18 F10 **Massif de Néouvieille** *mt* France
86 D4 **Massif des Bongos** *mts* Cent Afr Republic
19 Q18 **Massif des Maures** *mts* France
85 F4 **Massif de Tarazit** *mts* Niger
85 G5 **Massif de Termit** *mts* Niger
19 O15 **Massif du Diois** *mts* France
19 Q15 **Massif du Pelvoux** *mts* France
86 D4 **Massif du Tondou** *mts* Cent Afr Republic

94 F6 Massillon Ohio
87 G10 Massinga Mozambique
89 G4 Massingir Mozambique
121 P7 Masson Quebec
80 C7 Massu'a Israel
74 B4 Mastang Pakistan
27 K14 Mästerby Sweden
145 E4 Masterton New Zealand
95 P6 Mastic Beach Long I, N Y
126 E2 Mastic Point Andros Bahamas
47 H6 Mástikho,Akr C Greece
37 P3 Maštov Czechoslovakia
74 E1 Mastuj Pakistan
60 E11 Masuda Japan
79 G3 Masyāf Syria
46 D3 Mat R Albania
68 F5 Mat R Thailand
133 C7 Mata Amarilla Argentina
89 E2 Matabeleland reg Zimbabwe
71 H4 Matabulawa mt Sulawesi
88 F8 Mataca Mozambique
120 K5 Matachewan Ontario
86 B7 Matadi Zaïre
118 K8 Matador Sask
108 G1 Matador Texas
125 M3 Matagalpa Nicaragua
115 M8 Matagami Quebec
109 M7 Matagorda Texas
109 L7 Matagorda I Texas
130 H10 Mata Grande Brazil
126 C3 Matahambre Cuba
145 F3 Matahina New Zealand
134 C12 Mataiea Tahiti I Pac Oc
145 F4 Mataikona New Zealand
145 E3 Mataimoana mt New Zealand
69 H11 Matak isld Indonesia
139 H5 Matakana New S Wales
145 E2 Matakana New Zealand
145 F2 Matakana I New Zealand
145 G2 Matakaoa Pt New Zealand
144 D5 Matakitaki R New Zealand
145 E2 Matakohe New Zealand
87 C8 Matala Angola
85 B5 Matam Senegal
145 E2 Matamata New Zealand
145 F4 Matamau New Zealand
85 F6 Matameye Niger
95 N5 Matamoras Pennsylvania
124 H5 Matamoros Coahuila Mexico
125 L5 Matamoros Tamaulipas Mexico
71 F7 Matanal Pt Philippines
86 D1 Matan as Sarra Libya
84 G5 Ma'tan Bisharah Libya
88 G6 Matandu R Tanzania
115 N8 Matane Quebec
122 F5 Matane,Parc Quebec
122 E5 Matane R Quebec
145 E2 Matangi New Zealand
145 E2 Matangi I New Zealand
113 J10 Matanilla Reef Bahamas
116 O6 Matanuska mt Alaska
126 D3 Matanzas Cuba
113 F8 Matanzas Inlet Florida
131 C6 Matanzilla, Pampa de la plain Argentina
129 H5 Matão, Serra do mts Brazil
Matapán, C Greece see Tainaron, Akr
122 F6 Matapedia Quebec
122 E5 Matapedia L Quebec
122 E5 Matapedia R Quebec
16 D3 Matapozuelos Spain
131 B5 Mataquito R Chile
83 K12 Matara Sri Lanka
70 O10 Mataram Indonesia
128 D7 Matarani Peru
140 C2 Mataranka N Terr Aust
71 H6 Matarape,Tk B Sulawesi
17 J3 Mataró Spain
145 E3 Mataroa New Zealand
71 M9 Mataru Indonesia
17 F3 Mata,Sierra de la mts Spain
145 F2 Matata New Zealand
87 E12 Matatiele S Africa
144 B7 Mataura New Zealand
145 F3 Matawai New Zealand
121 R6 Matawin R Quebec
57 J2 Matay U.S.S.R.
57 E5 Matcha U.S.S.R.
121 N5 Matchi-Manitou, L Quebec
128 F6 Mategua Bolivia
125 J6 Matehuala Mexico
89 G3 Mateke Hills Zimbabwe
127 P1 Matelot Trinidad
145 E3 Matemateaonga Ra New Zealand
88 H8 Matemo isld Mozambique
43 H8 Matera Italy
45 Q7 Matese L Italy
45 Q7 Matese, Monti del mts Italy
48 G3 Mátészalka Hungary
43 C11 Mateur Tunisia
129 L7 Mateus Brazil
129 K7 Mateus R Brazil
94 E9 Matewan W Virginia
107 O3 Matfield Green Kansas
26 J9 Matfors Sweden
21 E10 Matha France
146 F14 Matha Strait Antarctica
102 E4 Mather California
94 G7 Mather Pennsylvania
74 E9 Matheran India
99 Q8 Matherville Illinois
106 G2 Matheson Colorado
120 K4 Matheson Ontario
119 V7 Matheson Island Manitoba
111 K9 Mathews Alabama
95 L9 Mathews Virginia
144 C5 Mathias Pass New Zealand
109 K7 Mathis Texas
108 G4 Mathis Field airport Texas
111 G8 Mathiston Mississippi
80 F8 Mathlutha Jordan
20 H2 Mathonville France
139 G6 Mathoura New S Wales
8 A4 Mathry Wales
74 G5 Mathura India
71 G7 Mati Mindanao Philippines
125 M9 Matías Romero Mexico
145 E3 Matiere New Zealand
22 E4 Matigny France
16 D4 Matilla de los Caños del Rio Spain
120 H6 Matinenda L Ontario
70 D7 Matisiri isld Indonesia
134 C13 Matiti Tahiti I Pac Oc
89 E5 Matlabas R S Africa
119 V8 Matlock Manitoba
100 B2 Matlock Washington
9 E1 Matlock Bath England
94 F9 Matoaka W Virginia
50 E1 Matochkin Shar U.S.S.R.
129 G6 Mato Grosso reg Brazil
130 D4 Mato Grosso,Chapada de hills Brazil
130 C7 Mato Grosso do Sul state Brazil
130 C4 Mato Grosso,Planalto de plat Brazil
122 C2 Matonipi L Quebec
122 C2 Matonipis L Quebec
89 F3 Matopo Hills Nat. Park Zimbabwe
87 E10 Matopos Nat. Park Zimbabwe
130 D10 Matos Costa Brazil
16 B3 Matosinhos Portugal
Matou see Qiu Xian
86 B6 Matouti, Pto Gabon
130 G4 Mato Verde Minas Gerais Brazil
48 F3 Mátra mts Hungary
72 H4 Maṭraḥ Oman
27 F11 Matrand Norway
83 K13 Mât, R. du Réunion Indian Ocean
27 A11 Matre Norway
41 O3 Matrei am Brenner Austria
89 A9 Matroos Berg mt S Africa
59 M2 Matrosov U.S.S.R.
84 H3 Matrûh Egypt
61 N10 Matsudo Japan
59 K4 Matsue Japan
60 O4 Matsumae Japan
61 L9 Matsumoto Japan
60 G11 Matsunaga Japan
61 M9 Matsushiro Japan
67 G3 Ma-tsu Tao isld Taiwan
61 K9 Matsuto Japan
60 C12 Matsuura Japan
61 P7 Matsuyama Honshu Japan
60 F12 Matsuyama Shikoku Japan
61 K11 Matsuzaka Japan
61 M11 Matsuzaki Japan
120 J4 Mattagami Heights Ontario
120 J5 Mattagami L Ontario
120 H2 Mattagami R Ontario
112 L2 Mattamuskeet L N Carolina
76 C6 Mattancheri India
95 K9 Mattaponi R Virginia
115 M8 Mattawa Ontario
95 T1 Mattawamkeag Maine
89 E3 Mattengwe R Botswana
100 H4 Matterhorn mt Oregon
40 G6 Matterhorn mt Switzerland
48 C3 Mattersburg Austria
137 P6 Matthew isld Pacific Oc
126 H4 Matthew Town Great Inagua I Bahamas
103 M7 Matthie Arizona
120 G3 Mattice Ontario
38 H5 Mattig R Austria
95 P6 Mattituck Long I, N Y
26 G8 Mattmar Sweden
102 A1 Mattole R California
99 S10 Mattoon Illinois
110 H4 Mattoon Kentucky
99 R4 Mattoon Wisconsin
113 E7 Mattox Georgia
115 K4 Matty I N W Terr
70 B3 Matu Sarawak
70 B6 Matua Kalimantan
128 C6 Matucana Peru
144 B6 Matukituki R New Zealand
77 L3 Matūn Afghanistan
145 D1 Matupia I New Zealand
127 P2 Matura Trinidad
127 N10 Maturín Venezuela
55 B4 Matveyevka U.S.S.R.
75 K6 Mau India
87 G8 Maua Mozambique
71 M9 Maubara Timor
18 F10 Mauberme, Pic de mt France/Spain
22 G4 Maubert-Fontaine France
22 F3 Maubeuge France
68 B4 Maubin Burma
18 E9 Maubourguet France
12 D3 Mauchline Scotland
94 A8 Mauckport Indiana
107 O6 Maud Oklahoma
109 N2 Maud Texas
146 B10 Maudheim Vidda Antarctica
101 O3 Maudlow Montana
90 J15 Maud Seamount S Atlantic Oc
87 F10 Mau-é-ele Mozambique
129 G4 Maués Brazil
134 A1 Maugaafi Western Samoa
94 K7 Maugansville Maryland
12 D5 Maughold Hd I of Man U.K.
135 T3 Maui isld Hawaiian Is
36 F6 Maulbronn W Germany
22 E3 Maulde France
20 J4 Maule France
131 A5 Maule prov Chile
131 B5 Maule R Chile
18 E9 Mauléon Licharre France
21 D7 Maulévrier France
14 B2 Maumakeogh mt Irish Rep
94 D5 Maumee Ohio
94 D5 Maumee Bay Michigan/Ohio
110 D7 Maumelle, L Arkansas
71 L9 Maumere Flores Indonesia
14 B3 Maumturk Mts Irish Rep
21 C7 Maumusson France
21 C10 Maumusson, Pertuis de str France
87 D9 Maun Botswana
135 U5 Mauna Kea peak Hawaiian Is
135 R2 Mauna Loa Hawaiian Is
135 U5 Mauna Loa vol Hawaiian Is
102 S12 Maunalua Bay Hawaiian Is
116 K3 Mauneluk R Alaska
145 F3 Maungahaumi mt New Zealand
145 E3 Maungamangero mt New Zealand
145 F3 Maungapohatu New Zealand
145 F3 Maungataniwha mt New Zealand
145 E1 Maungatapere New Zealand
145 E2 Maungaturoto New Zealand
144 B6 Maungawera New Zealand
68 A2 Maungdaw Burma
68 C5 Maungmagan islds Burma
114 G4 Maunoir,L N W Terr
138 D6 Maupertuis B S Australia
100 D4 Maupin Oregon
38 E7 Maurach Austria
19 Q16 Maure,Col de pass France
21 B6 Maure de-Bretagne France
111 F11 Maurepas,L Louisiana
18 G7 Mauriac France
145 E4 Mauriceville New Zealand
111 C11 Mauriceville Texas
19 Q14 Maurienne dist France
40 D7 Maurienne V France
98 D4 Maurine S Dakota
85 B4 Mauritania rep W Africa
83 L12 Mauritius Indian Oc
18 D4 Mauron France
18 G8 Maurs France
19 N17 Maussane France
99 Q6 Mauston Wisconsin
38 N5 Mautern Austria
38 J7 Mauterndorf Austria
38 L5 Mauthausen Austria
40 B2 Maûtz France
19 N14 Mauves France
18 F9 Mauvezin France
21 D9 Mauzé France
21 E8 Mauzé-Thouarsais France
128 E3 Mavaca R Venezuela
21 H6 Maves-Pontijou France
87 D9 Mavinga Angola
127 L2 Mavis Bank Jamaica
144 B6 Mavora L, N New Zealand
46 F5 Mavrovqúni mt Greece
88 D9 Mavudzi R Mozambique
88 C10 Mavuradonha Mts Zimbabwe
70 C4 Mawa, Bt mt Kalimantan
71 H7 Mawasangka Indonesia
68 C3 Mawchi Burma
68 D7 Mawdaung pass Burma/Thailand
119 R4 Mawdesley L Manitoba
118 L8 Mawer Sask
144 C5 Mawheraiti New Zealand
68 D4 Mawkhi Burma
68 C2 Mawkmai Burma
75 Q7 Mawlaik Burma
146 B4 Mawson Coast Antarctica
146 C5 Mawson Escarpment Antarctica
146 K4 Mawson Pen Antarctica
70 L9 Mawuk Java
98 E2 Max N Dakota
98 E9 Max Nebraska
98 E1 Maxbass N Dakota
21 A6 Maxent France
112 D4 Maxeys Georgia
117 M6 Maxhamish L Br Col
37 N5 Maxhütte-Haidof W Germany
36 E5 Maximiliansau W Germany
94 G10 Max Meadows Virginia
29 J8 Maxmo Finland
118 L9 Maxstone Sask
112 H3 Maxton N Carolina
113 E7 Maxville Florida
101 M3 Maxville Montana
121 Q7 Maxville Ontario
102 B2 Maxwell California
99 N8 Maxwell Iowa
98 F8 Maxwell Nebraska
106 F5 Maxwell New Mexico
12 E3 Maxwelltown Scotland
141 G5 Maxwelton Queensland
101 M5 May Idaho
108 E7 May Oklahoma
109 J4 May Texas
59 K1 Maya R U.S.S.R.
55 C4 Mayachnyy U.S.S.R.
126 H3 Mayaguana Passage Bahamas
127 L5 Mayagüez Puerto Rico
85 F6 Mayahi Niger
55 C5 Mayak U.S.S.R.
31 M1 Mayak lt ho U.S.S.R.
17 H3 Mayals Spain
77 D1 Mayamey Iran
80 D3 May 'Ami Israel
125 P9 Maya Mts Belize
67 C3 Mayang China
126 G4 Mayari Cuba
127 P3 Mayaro co Trinidad
94 D4 Maybee Michigan
106 B1 Maybell Colorado
12 D3 Maybole Scotland
77 L2 Maydan Afghanistan
127 K3 May Day Mts Jamaica
109 M4 Maydelle Texas
139 H9 Maydena Tasmania
36 C3 Mayen W Germany
20 D5 Mayenne France
20 D5 Mayenne dep France
103 M7 Mayer Arizona
118 B5 Mayerthorpe Alberta
112 G4 Mayesville S Carolina
21 F6 Mayet France
107 P2 Mayetta Kansas
118 K5 Mayfair Sask
9 G5 Mayfield E Sussex England
100 K6 Mayfield Idaho
110 H5 Mayfield Kentucky
144 C5 Mayfield New Zealand
107 L6 Mayfield Oklahoma
95 M5 Mayfield Pennsylvania
141 G7 Mayfield Queensland
9 E1 Mayfield Staffs England
103 N2 Mayfield Utah
110 D7 Mayflower Arkansas
111 H8 Mayhew Mississippi
106 E9 Mayhill New Mexico
65 G2 Mayi He R China
13 F1 May, I. of Scotland
55 G5 Maykain U.S.S.R.
57 H2 Maykamys U.S.S.R.
53 F11 Maykop U.S.S.R.
52 J5 Maykor U.S.S.R.
110 L5 Mayland Tennessee
142 B1 Maylands dist Perth, W Aust
57 C2 Maylibash U.S.S.R.
57 L2 Mayli, Khrebet mts U.S.S.R.
57 D2 Maylykum U.S.S.R.
57 F3 Maymak U.S.S.R.
118 K6 Maymont Sask
68 C1 Maymyo Burma
99 P7 Maynard Iowa
143 C8 Maynard Hills W Australia
141 F6 Mayne R Queensland
14 E3 Maynooth Irish Rep
121 N7 Maynooth Ontario
51 R2 Maynopilgyn U.S.S.R.
113 D7 Mayo Florida
95 L8 Mayo Maryland
117 F4 Mayo Yukon Terr
14 B3 Mayo co Irish Rep
128 C5 Mayo R Peru
71 G7 Mayo B Mindanao Philippines
86 B4 Mayo Daga Nigeria
94 G10 Mayodan N Carolina
71 F4 Mayon mt Philippines
17 F4 Mayor R Spain
16 D2 Mayorga Spain
145 F2 Mayor I New Zealand
133 E2 Mayor Pablo Lagerenza Paraguay
87 H10 Mayotte isld Comoros
127 K3 May Pen Jamaica
113 F7 Mayport Florida
142 E3 May R W Australia
71 E1 Mayraira Pt Luzon Philippines
38 E7 Mayrhofen Austria
79 F5 Mayrouba Lebanon
55 G2 Maysk U.S.S.R.
59 J1 Mayskiy U.S.S.R.
55 G5 Mayskoye U.S.S.R.
95 N7 Mays Landing New Jersey
112 D3 Maysville Georgia
94 D8 Maysville Kentucky
99 M10 Maysville Missouri
112 K3 Maysville N Carolina
107 N7 Maysville Oklahoma
71 D5 Maytiguid Philippines
141 G3 Maytown Queensland
68 A2 Mayu R Burma
86 B6 Mayumba Gabon
94 D3 Mayville Michigan
98 J2 Mayville N Dakota
94 H4 Mayville New York
100 E4 Mayville Oregon
99 S6 Mayville Wisconsin
98 F9 Maywood Nebraska
133 E5 Maza Argentina
98 G1 Maza N Dakota
88 A9 Mazabuka Zambia
129 H4 Mazagão Brazil
22 H5 Mazagram France
47 G2 Mazalat mt Bulgaria
100 E1 Mazama Washington
18 G9 Mazamet France
77 B1 Mazandaran Iran
124 J5 Mazapil Mexico
79 F7 Mazār Jordan
43 E11 Mazara del Vallo Sicily
16 D9 Mazari,C Morocco
77 K1 Mazar-i-Sharif Afghanistan
133 D7 Mazarredo Argentina
17 G7 Mazarrón Spain
80 F8 Mazar Saiyidna Suleiman Jordan
128 F2 Mazaruni R Guyana
124 D3 Mazatán Mexico
125 O10 Mazatenango Guatemala
124 F6 Mazatlán Mexico
103 N7 Mazatzal Pk Arizona
77 B3 Mazdaj Iran
52 B6 Mazeikiai U.S.S.R.
118 D8 Mazeppa Alberta
21 F7 Mazières France
21 E8 Mazieres-en-Gatine France
52 B5 Mazirbe U.S.S.R.
80 C6 Mazliaḥ Israel
89 G1 Mazoe Zimbabwe
88 C10 Mazoe R Zimbabwe
99 R6 Mazomanie Wisconsin
99 S8 Mazon Illinois
80 F8 Mazra' Jordan
86 E3 Mazrub Sudan
87 E10 Mazunga Zimbabwe
22 H4 Mazures, les France
31 M2 Mazury reg Poland
89 G6 Mbabane Swaziland
86 C5 Mbaéré R Cent Afr Republic
85 D7 Mbahiakro Ivory Coast
86 C5 Mbaïki Cent Afr Republic
88 C6 Mbala Zambia
86 F5 Mbale Uganda
86 B5 Mbalmayo Cameroon
86 B4 Mbam R Cameroon
87 F8 Mbamba B Tanzania
86 C5 Mbandaka Zaïre
85 F8 Mbanga Cameroon
86 B6 M'Banio, L Gabon
86 B7 Mbanza-Ngungu Zaïre
88 C2 Mbarara Uganda
88 F6 Mbarika mt Tanzania
88 G6 Mbemkuru R Tanzania
88 D6 Mbeya Tanzania
88 D6 Mbeya mt Tanzania
85 G8 Mbini prov Eq Guinea
87 F10 Mbizi Zimbabwe
86 C4 Mbo Cent Afr Republic
85 A6 Mbour Senegal
85 B5 Mbout Mauritania
87 B7 M'Bridge R Angola
86 D7 Mbuji Mayi Zaïre
86 F5 Mbulamuti Uganda
88 E3 Mbulu Tanzania
88 F6 Mbungu Tanzania
133 F3 Mburucuyá Argentina
88 G6 Mchinja Tanzania
88 D8 Mchinji Malawi
117 F5 M'Clintock Yukon Terr
115 M1 M'Clintock, C N W Terr
115 L1 M'Clintock Inlet N W Terr
85 C3 Mdakane, Hassi Algeria
43 B12 M'Daourouch Algeria
85 C4 Mdennah Mali/Mauritania
68 J6 Mdrak Vietnam
71 C3 Me isld Indonesia
100 G4 Meacham Oregon
119 M6 Meacham Sask
120 G3 Mead Ontario
100 H2 Mead Washington
107 K4 Meade Kansas
116 K1 Meade R Alaska
101 O7 Meade Pk Idaho
103 K5 Mead,L Nev/Ariz
103 K6 Mead, L. National Recreational Area Arizona
98 D4 Meadow S Dakota
108 E2 Meadow Texas
143 A7 Meadow W Australia
94 G9 Meadow Bridge W Virginia
109 M9 Meadowbrook Texas
94 G9 Meadow Creek W Virginia
98 B7 Meadowdale Wyoming
118 J4 Meadow Lake Sask
99 O2 Meadowlands Minnesota
118 H4 Meadow L. Prov. Park Sask
119 S7 Meadow Portage Manitoba
100 J5 Meadows Idaho
103 K4 Meadow Val.Mts Nevada
103 K5 Meadow Val.Wash R Nevada
110 C2 Meadville Missouri
98 G7 Meadville Nebraska
94 G5 Meadville Pennsylvania
120 K8 Meaford Ontario
122 J9 Meaghers Grant Nova Scotia
60 R2 Me-akan dake mt Japan
16 B4 Mealhada Portugal
13 E4 Mealsgate England
115 N7 Mealy Mts Labrador
141 J7 Meandarra Queensland
117 P6 Meander River Alberta
100 B4 Meares,Cape Oregon
80 C3 Me 'Arot Karmel Israel
99 U6 Mears Michigan
15 C3 Measach Falls Scotland
9 E2 Measham England
14 E3 Meath co Irish Rep
119 M5 Meath Park Sask
18 G4 Meaux France
112 H1 Mebane N Carolina
17 G9 Mebtoub R Algeria
70 P10 Mebulu,Tg C Bali Indonesia
101 S2 Mecaha Montana
123 O3 Mecatina I.,Gt Quebec
123 N3 Mecatina I.,Little Quebec
123 M1 Mecatina,Riv.du Petite Quebec
103 H8 Mecca California
86 G1 Mecca Saudi Arabia
95 R2 Mechanic Falls Maine
94 D6 Mechanicsburg Ohio
95 K6 Mechanicsburg Pennsylvania
95 L8 Mechanicsville Maryland
95 O4 Mechanicville New York
111 F12 Mechant,L Louisiana
22 G1 Mechelen Belgium
85 D2 Mecheria Algeria
36 B2 Mechernich W Germany
122 F5 Méchins,Les Quebec
37 Q3 Mecholupy Czechoslovakia
33 M6 Mechtersen W Germany
47 H4 Mecidiye Turkey
37 P5 Měčin Czechoslovakia
41 L2 Meckenbeuren W Germany
36 C2 Meckenheim W Germany
36 E5 Meckenheim W Germany
36 F5 Meckesheim W Germany
33 O5 Mecklenburg E Germany
30 F1 Mecklenburger Bucht B W Germany
88 G9 Meconta Mozambique
94 B3 Mecosta Michigan
48 E4 Mecsek mts Hungary
88 G9 Mecuburi R Mozambique
88 H8 Mecufi Mozambique
87 G8 Mecula Mozambique
16 C4 Meda Portugal
74 H9 Medak India
42 G4 Medak Yugoslavia
69 D11 Medan Sumatra
71 H9 Medang isld Indonesia
124 D4 Médano Mexico
133 E5 Médanos Argentina
133 D7 Medanosa,Pta Argentina
99 U8 Medaryville Indiana
17 K2 Medas isld Spain
83 K9 Medawachchiya Sri Lanka
144 D5 Medbury New Zealand
95 U1 Meddybemps L Maine
85 E1 Médéa Algeria
36 F1 Medebach W Germany
41 J4 Medel mt Switzerland
28 C7 Medelby W Germany
128 C2 Medellín Colombia
32 J5 Medem R W Germany
25 D3 Medemblik Netherlands
85 G2 Medenine Tunisia
85 A5 Mederdra Mauritania
22 L4 Medernach Luxembourg
95 Q4 Medford Massachusetts
107 N5 Medford Oklahoma
100 C7 Medford Oregon
99 Q4 Medford Wisconsin
116 K5 Medfra Alaska
48 L6 Medgidia Romania
99 P8 Mediapolis Iowa
48 J4 Mediaş Romania
100 H2 Medical Lake Washington
45 L3 Medicina Italy
101 T8 Medicine Bow Wyoming
101 T8 Medicine Bow R Wyoming
106 D1 Medicine Bow Mts Wyo/Colo
101 T8 Medicine Bow Pk Wyoming
118 G8 Medicine Hat Alberta
100 D8 Medicine L California
98 B1 Medicine L Montana
107 M4 Medicine Lodge Kansas
109 H1 Medicine Mound Texas
118 C6 Medicine R Alberta
98 B3 Medicine Rocks Montana
130 H5 Medina Brazil
98 G3 Medina N Dakota
94 J3 Medina New York
94 F5 Medina Ohio
72 D4 Medina Saudi Arabia
110 H6 Medina Tennessee
109 H6 Medina Texas
143 B9 Medina W Australia
17 F3 Medinaceli Spain
16 D3 Medina de Campo Spain
16 D3 Medina de Rioseco Spain
131 F2 Medina,L Argentina
16 D8 Medina Sidonia Spain
33 N6 Medingen W Germany
84 F2 Mediterranean Sea Europe/Africa
85 F1 Medjerda R Tunisia
43 B12 Medjerda, Monts de la Algeria/Tunisia
118 G4 Medley Alberta
55 C5 Mednogorsk U.S.S.R.
18 E7 Medoc reg France
45 J1 Médole Italy
110 H6 Medon Tennessee
110 F2 Medora Illinois
107 N3 Medora Kansas
119 R9 Medora Manitoba
98 C3 Medora N Dakota
86 B5 Medounou Gabon
20 A5 Médréac France
118 J5 Medstead Sask
122 E8 Meductic New Brunswick
Medu Kongkar see Maizhokunggar
46 E2 Medveda Yugoslavia
55 E2 Medvedchikovo U.S.S.R.
52 H6 Medvedok U.S.S.R.
51 J1 Medvezhiy Yar U.S.S.R.
59 L2 Medvezh'ya, Gora mt U.S.S.R.
55 F3 Medvezh'ye U.S.S.R.
52 D3 Medvezh'yegorsk U.S.S.R.
52 E6 Medvyeditsa R U.S.S.R.
95 T1 Medway Maine
9 G5 Medway,R England
83 M9 Medwin Pt Christmas I Indian Oc
54 G2 Medyn U.S.S.R.
48 L1 Medzhibozh U.S.S.R.
31 N6 Medzilaborce Czechoslovakia
141 L1 Meeandah dist Brisbane, Qnsld
143 B7 Meeberrie W Australia
37 K3 Meeder W Germany
143 C7 Meekatharra W Australia
106 C1 Meeker Colorado
107 O6 Meeker Oklahoma
123 Q5 Meelpaeg L Newfoundland
37 N2 Meerane E Germany
36 B3 Meerfeld W Germany
25 F5 Meerlo Netherlands
25 E7 Meerssen Netherlands
74 G4 Meerut India
101 R5 Meeteetse Wyoming
118 E6 Meeting Cr Alberta
14 E4 Meeting of the Waters Irish Rep
118 K5 Meetoos Sask
33 R5 Meetschow E Germany
22 K1 Meeuwen Belgium
80 B7 Mefallesim Israel
86 G5 Mega Ethiopia
71 C3 Mega W Irian
69 E14 Mega isld Indonesia
80 C3 Megadim Israel
18 H7 Megal mt France
47 J8 Megálo Khorió Tílos I Greece
46 E7 Megalópolis Greece
46 D6 Meganisi mt Greece
122 B8 Mégantic Quebec
122 B8 Megantic,L Quebec
47 F6 Mégara Greece
109 J2 Megargel Texas
46 E5 Mégdhova R Greece
25 E5 Megen Netherlands
40 E6 Megève France
36 E1 Meggen W Germany
112 G5 Meggett S Carolina
85 F2 Meghaiër, El Algeria
75 O6 Meghalaya prov India
75 O6 Meghna R Bangladesh
121 P4 Mégiscane, L Quebec
100 B3 Megler Washington
52 F2 Megra Arkhangelsk U.S.S.R.
52 E4 Megra Vologda U.S.S.R.
48 G6 Mehadia Romania
70 D6 Mehakit Kalimantan
26 Q1 Mehamn Norway
48 H6 Mehedinti reg Romania
94 J9 Meherrin Virginia
94 J10 Meherrin R Virginia
37 N2 Mehitheuer E Germany
74 G8 Mehkar India
75 K5 Mehndawal India
78 L5 Mehran Iran
36 B3 Mehren W Germany
36 B4 Mehring W Germany
77 D4 Mehriz Iran
21 J7 Mehun sur Yèvre France
130 E5 Meia Ponte,R Brazil
67 D2 Meichengzhen China
67 E1 Meichuan China
8 C2 Meifod Wales
86 B4 Meiganga Cameroon
114 K1 Meighen I N W Terr
112 C6 Meigs Georgia
25 E6 Meijel Netherlands
67 E5 Mei Jiang R China
117 O7 Meikle R Alberta
68 B2 Meiktila Burma
Meilin see Gan Xian
20 B5 Meillac France
117 L5 Meilleur Cr N W Terr
33 N8 Meine W Germany
33 M8 Meinersen W Germany
36 D1 Meinerzhagen W Germany
37 J2 Meiningen E Germany
16 C1 Meira, Sa. de mts Spain
41 H4 Meiringen Switzerland
80 C3 Me'ir Shefeya Israel
36 D4 Meisenheim W Germany
67 A1 Meisham China
Meishan see Jinzhai
67 E1 Meishan Shuiku res China
37 P1 Meissen E Germany
32 L7 Meissendorf W Germany
36 H1 Meissner mt W Germany
67 B3 Meitan China
37 K6 Meitingen W Germany
67 E4 Mei Xian China
65 E2 Meiyao China
43 C12 Mejerda R Tunisia
43 C12 Mejez el-Bab Tunisia
133 C2 Mejillones Chile
28 B4 Mejrup Denmark
86 B5 Mekambo Gabon
120 F5 Mekatina Ontario
55 D3 Mekhonskoye U.S.S.R.
74 C3 Mekhtar Pakistan
98 J1 Mekinock N Dakota
85 C2 Meknès Morocco
68 G6 Mekong R S E Asia
70 G6 Mekongga, G mt Sulawesi
70 G7 Mekongga, Tk B Sulawesi
69 H8 Mekong, Mouths of the Vietnam
116 D6 Mekoryuk Alaska
85 E6 Mekrou R Benin/Niger
69 F11 Melaka Malaysia
47 G9 Mélambes Crete Greece
134 E8 Melanesia Pac Oc
137 P4 Melanesian Border Plat Pacific Oc
70 D2 Melapap Sabah
70 E2 Melaut mt Sabah
118 L9 Melaval Sask
70 C5 Melawi R Kalimantan
21 D7 Melay France
100 J6 Melba Idaho
33 M6 Melbeck W Germany
9 G3 Melbourn England
9 E2 Melbourne England
113 G9 Melbourne Florida
99 N8 Melbourne Iowa
138 C7 Melbourne Victoria
113 G9 Melbourne Beach Florida
26 G3 Melbu Norway
28 H5 Melby Denmark
99 N8 Melcher Iowa
120 D2 Melchett L Ontario
124 J5 Melchor Ocampo Coahuila Mexico
124 H8 Melchor Ocampo Michigan Mexico
26 D8 Meldal Norway
26 M6 Melderstein Sweden
45 M3 Meldola Italy
32 K4 Meldorf W Germany
112 F5 Meldrim Georgia
120 G7 Meldrum Bay Ontario
80 D3 Melea Israel
119 U8 Meleb Manitoba
44 F1 Melegnano Italy
47 G9 Melékhas, Akr C Crete Greece
52 J5 Melekhina U.S.S.R.
87 G9 Melela R Mozambique
70 O10 Meleman Java
52 F6 Melenki U.S.S.R.
55 D3 Melent'yevskoye U.S.S.R.
20 B5 Melesse France
20 F5 Mêle-sur-Sarthe, le France
55 C4 Meleuz U.S.S.R.
95 M9 Melfa Virginia
45 P6 Melfa R Italy
86 C3 Melfi Chad
43 G8 Melfi Italy
114 J7 Melfort Sask
28 E2 Melholt Denmark
26 D8 Melhus Norway
36 F4 Melibocus mt W Germany
20 G4 Melicourt France
130 E9 Mel, I. do Brazil
46 E7 Meligalá Greece
71 H5 Melilis isld Indonesia
85 D1 Melilla Span exclave Morocco
133 C6 Melimoyu mt Chile
144 B6 Melina, Mt New Zealand
48 H6 Melineşti Romania
70 E5 Melintang, D L Kalimantan
133 C4 Melipilla Chile
119 R9 Melita Manitoba
43 G11 Melito di Porto Salvo Italy
54 G10 Melitopol' U.S.S.R.
38 M5 Melk Austria
8 D5 Melksham England
44 H1 Mella R Italy
26 H9 Mellansjö Sweden
22 F2 Melle Belgium
21 E9 Melle France
32 H8 Melle W Germany
43 B12 Mellégue R Tunisia
99 Q3 Mellen Wisconsin
32 L7 Mellendorf W Germany
27 F13 Mellerud Sweden
18 E6 Melle S. Bretonne France
98 H4 Mellette S Dakota
16 B2 Mellid Spain
22 K4 Mellier Belgium
37 L2 Mellingen E Germany
137 M5 Mellish Rise Coral Sea
86 E3 Mellit Sudan
13 F6 Mellor Brook England
32 H5 Mellun isld W Germany
111 E7 Mellwood Arkansas
13 F4 Melmerby England
47 F3 Melnik Bulgaria
31 H5 Mělník Czechoslovakia
48 K2 Melnitsa Podolskaya U.S.S.R.
131 G4 Melo Uruguay
52 G2 Melogorskoye U.S.S.R.
71 K9 Melolo Sumba Indonesia
102 D4 Melones Res California
54 M7 Melovoye U.S.S.R.
26 F5 Melöy Norway
116 K4 Melozitna R Alaska
22 J3 Melreux Belgium
17 G9 Melrir R Algeria
100 J3 Melrose Idaho
99 M4 Melrose Minnesota
101 N4 Melrose Montana
106 G7 Melrose New Mexico
123 K8 Melrose Nova Scotia
100 B6 Melrose Oregon
13 F2 Melrose Scotland
143 D8 Melrose W Australia
99 P5 Melrose Wisconsin
87 F9 Melsetter Zimbabwe
101 S3 Melstone Montana
99 U3 Melstrand Michigan
36 H1 Melsungen W Germany
70 E2 Melta, Mt Sabah
29 L5 Meltaus Finland
13 G6 Meltham England
9 F2 Melton Mowbray England
88 G10 Meluli R Mozambique
68 A2 Melun Burma
18 G4 Melun France
86 F3 Melut Sudan
107 P3 Melvern Kansas
15 E2 Melvich Scotland
111 E11 Melville Louisiana
101 Q3 Melville Montana
98 G2 Melville N Dakota
119 P8 Melville Sask
140 D1 Melville B N Terr Aust
115 N2 Melville Bugt B Greenland
141 G2 Melville, C Queensland
71 C6 Melville, Cape Philippines
114 G4 Melville Hills N W Terr
140 B1 Melville I N Terr Aust
114 H2 Melville I N W Terr
115 O7 Melville, L Labrador
115 L4 Melville Pen N W Terr
142 A1 Melville Water B Perth, W Aust
109 H4 Melvin Texas
14 C2 Melvin, L Irish Rep
119 R1 Melvin L Manitoba
48 E4 Mélykút Hungary
70 C5 Memala Kalimantan
68 H6 Meman Cambodia
88 H9 Memba Mozambique
79 H2 Membij Syria
71 J9 Memboro Sumba Indonesia
22 H4 Membre France
Memel see Klaipeda
32 E5 Memmert isld W Germany
41 M2 Memmingen W Germany
70 D2 Mempakul Sabah
99 O9 Memphis Missouri
110 G6 Memphis Tennessee
108 G1 Memphis Texas
84 J4 Memphis ruins Egypt
121 S8 Memphremagog, L Vermont
122 H7 Memramcook New Brunswick
60 R3 Memuro Japan
110 B7 Mena Arkansas
71 M9 Ména Timor Indonesia
54 D5 Mena U.S.S.R.
80 F3 Menaḥemya Israel
99 L3 Menahga Minnesota
8 B1 Menai Str Wales
85 E5 Menaka Mali
101 O4 Menard Montana
108 H5 Menard Texas
99 S5 Menasha Wisconsin
123 L2 Menaskwagama, L Quebec
45 M2 Menate Italy
70 C5 Menate Kalimantan
69 H14 Mendanau isld Indonesia
130 G6 Mendanha Brazil
69 H12 Mendarik Indonesia
70 C6 Mendawai Kalimantan
18 H8 Mende France
86 G4 Mendebo Mts Ethiopia
56 D3 Mendel' R U.S.S.R.
32 G10 Menden W Germany
111 G10 Mendenhall Mississippi
116 D7 Mendenhall, C Alaska
47 K6 Menderes R Turkey
55 E5 Mendesh U.S.S.R.
71 E3 Mendez-Nuñez Luzon Philippines
118 H8 Mendham Sask
136 J3 Mendi Papua New Guinea
8 D5 Mendip Hills England
143 D8 Mendleyarri W Australia
100 A9 Mendocino, C California
135 N4 Mendocino Seascarp Pacific Oc
94 B4 Mendon Michigan
110 M1 Mendon Ohio
139 J4 Mendooran New S Wales
102 D5 Mendota California
99 R8 Mendota Illinois
108 D8 Mendota Texas
99 R6 Mendota, L Wisconsin
131 C4 Mendoza Argentina
128 C5 Mendoza Peru
131 C5 Mendoza prov Argentina
16 B6 Mendro mt Portugal
69 F12 Mendung Sumatra
44 G2 Menegosa mt Italy
127 J10 Mene Grande Venezuela
47 J6 Menemen Turkey
22 E2 Menen Belgium
47 J9 Menetai Kárpathos I Greece
21 J7 Ménétréol-sous-Sancerre France
43 E11 Menfi Sicily
70 D1 Mengalum isld S China Sea
58 G5 Mengcheng China
65 D5 Mengcun China
41 K1 Mengen W Germany
32 J10 Mengeringhausen W Germany
36 E2 Mengerskirchen W Germany
70 K8 Menggala Sumatra
68 E2 Menghai China
65 H1 Mengjiagang China
67 C5 Mengjiang China
65 A5 Mengjiawan China
65 B7 Mengjin China
70 B4 Mengkiang R Kalimantan
37 N6 Mengkofen W Germany
68 E2 Mengla China
68 D1 Menglian China
68 E1 Meng man China
67 C4 Mengshan China
68 E1 Mengwang China
65 B7 Meng Xian China
65 D7 Mengyin China
68 E2 Mengyuan China
67 A5 Mengzi China
21 E9 Ménigoute France
115 N7 Menihek, Lac Labrador
83 L11 Menik Ganga R Sri Lanka
20 H3 Menilles France
36 B7 Ménil-sur-Bélvitte France
Menin see Menen
139 G4 Menindee New S Wales
138 E6 Meningie S Australia
70 E4 Menjapa, Gt mt Kalimantan
51 M2 Menkere U.S.S.R.
112 B3 Menlo Georgia
99 M8 Menlo Iowa
107 K2 Menlo Kansas
102 B4 Menlo Pk California
20 K4 Mennecy France
21 I7 Mennetou-sur-Cher France
98 J6 Menno S Dakota
12 E3 Mennock P Scotland
99 T4 Menominee R Michigan
99 S6 Menomonee Falls Wisconsin
99 P5 Menomonie Wisconsin
17 K4 Menorca isld Balearic Is
55 G3 Men'shchikovo U.S.S.R.
66 C5 Men-shih China
32 G7 Menslage W Germany
12 E1 Menstrie Scotland
28 H6 Menstrup Denmark
70 C5 Mentaja R Kalimantan
69 F11 Mentakab Malaysia
45 N5 Mentana Italy
70 E2 Mentapok Sabah
70 E3 Mentarang R Kalimantan
116 Q5 Mentasta Mts Alaska
73 Q9 Mentawai, Kep islds Indonesia
69 G14 Mentok Sumatra
44 B4 Menton France
94 A5 Mentone Indiana
108 D4 Mentone Texas
98 K2 Mentor Minnesota
94 F5 Mentor Ohio
70 C5 Mentubar R Kalimantan
89 D9 Mentz, L S Africa
58 E2 Menza R Mongolia
56 G5 Menza R U.S.S.R.
43 C11 Menzel Bourguiba Tunisia
52 H6 Menzelinsk U.S.S.R.
43 D12 Menzel Temime Tunisia
143 D8 Menzies W Australia
146 C5 Menzies, Mt Antarctica
Menzingen see Kraichtal
9 G5 Meopham England
124 G3 Meoqui Mexico
118 J5 Meota Sask
25 F3 Meppel Netherlands
32 F7 Meppen W Germany
17 H3 Mequinenza Spain
21 I6 Mer France
52 F5 Mera R U.S.S.R.
47 H9 Merabéllou, Kólpos B Crete Greece
70 E4 Merah Kalimantan
70 K8 Merak Java
26 E8 Meråker Norway
137 O4 Mera Lava isld New Hebrides
138 B3 Meramangye, L S Australia
110 F3 Meramec Park Missouri
Meran see Merano
41 O4 Merano Italy
70 P9 Merapi, G mt Java
123 S6 Merasheen Newfoundland
70 D6 Meratus, Peg mts Kalimantan
136 J3 Merauke W Irian
69 F12 Merbau Sumatra
138 F5 Merbein Victoria
22 G3 Merbes-le-Château Belgium
70 P10 Merbuk mt Indonesia
86 H5 Merca Somalia
76 B4 Mercara India
45 M4 Mercato Saraceno Italy
102 D4 Merced California
102 D4 Merced R California
131 B3 Mercedario, Cerro mt Chile/Arg
131 D4 Mercedes Argentina
131 F5 Mercedes Buenos Aires Argentina
131 F2 Mercedes Corrientes Argentina
109 K9 Mercedes Texas
131 F4 Mercedes Uruguay
133 C3 Merceditas Chile
99 N9 Mercer Missouri
98 F2 Mercer N Dakota
145 E2 Mercer New Zealand
94 G5 Mercer Pennsylvania
110 H6 Mercer Tennessee
99 Q3 Mercer Wisconsin
94 J7 Mercersburg Pennsylvania
22 G2 Merchtem Belgium
121 O6 Mercier Dam Quebec
117 P9 Mercoal Alberta
45 R8 Mercogliano Italy
103 M1 Mercur Utah
48 H5 Mercurea Romania
109 H4 Mercury Texas
19 Q13 Mercury-Gemilly France
145 E2 Mercury Is New Zealand
114 H3 Mercy B N W Terr
115 N5 Mercy, C N W Terr
20 C3 Merderet R France
18 D4 Merdrignac France
8 D5 Mere England
133 E8 Meredith, C Falkland Is
95 Q3 Meredith Hill New Hampshire
108 C8 Meredith, L Texas
99 Q10 Meredosia Illinois
85 E3 Meredoua Algeria
54 H7 Merefa U.S.S.R.
86 A3 Meregh Somalia
85 C5 Mereié, El reg Mauritania/Mali
36 E3 Merenberg W Germany
20 K5 Méréville France
9 G5 Mereworth England
Merga see Nukheila
68 D6 Mergui Burma
73 Q6 Mergui Arch Burma
138 F5 Meribah S Australia
47 H3 Meriç Turkey
47 H3 Meriç R Greece
118 H7 Merid Sask

50
Mérida — Misiones

125 P7 Mérida Mexico
16 C6 Mérida Spain
128 D2 Mérida Venezuela
95 O5 Meriden Connecticut
107 P2 Meriden Kansas
95 P3 Meriden New Hampshire
98 B8 Meriden Wyoming
102 C2 Meridian California
100 J6 Meridian Idaho
111 H9 Meridian Mississippi
95 L3 Meridian New York
109 K4 Meridian Texas
137 O4 Merig isld New Hebrides
29 J10 Merikarvia Finland
141 J4 Merinda Queensland
19 O17 Mérindol France
37 L7 Mering W Germany
138 F5 Meringur Victoria
106 G1 Merino Colorado
138 F6 Merino Victoria
Merioneth co see Gwynedd
70 C3 Merit Sarawak
139 J2 Merivale R Queensland
57 G3 Merke U.S.S.R.
22 D2 Merkem Belgium
37 K5 Merkendorf W Germany
26 H5 Merkenes Sweden
31 P1 Merkine U.S.S.R.
37 O3 Merklín Czechoslovakia
37 P4 Merklín Czechoslovakia
22 G1 Merksem Belgium
22 H1 Merksplas Belgium
55 D2 Merkushino Sverdlovsk U.S.S.R.
55 E2 Merkushino Tyumen U.S.S.R.
36 C3 Merl W Germany
45 K1 Merlara Italy
20 F4 Merlerault, le France
22 B3 Merlimont France
120 H10 Merlin Ontario
100 B7 Merlin Oregon
141 F2 Merluna Queensland
142 C3 Mermaid Reef Indian Oc
111 C12 Mermentau R Louisiana
28 J6 Mern Denmark
98 G8 Merna Nebraska
101 P7 Merna Wyoming
138 E4 Mernemerna S Australia
69 A9 Meroe isld Nicobar Is
143 D8 Merolia W Australia
80 E2 Meron Israel
86 F2 Merowe Sudan
143 C9 Merredin W Australia
110 B2 Merriam Kansas
15 D5 Merrick Mt Scotland
121 P8 Merrickville Ontario
98 H3 Merricourt N Dakota
98 K7 Merrill Iowa
94 C3 Merrill Michigan
111 H11 Merrill Mississippi
100 D7 Merrill Oregon
99 R4 Merrill Wisconsin
99 Q5 Merrillan Wisconsin
99 R6 Merrimac Wisconsin
95 Q3 Merrimack R New Hamps/Mass
98 E7 Merriman Nebraska
139 J6 Merrimbula New S Wales
117 N10 Merritt Br Col
98 F7 Merritt Res Nebraska
139 K4 Merriwa New S Wales
111 E9 Mer Rouge Louisiana
9 F5 Merrow England
139 J4 Merrygoen New S Wales
109 O5 Merryville Louisiana
20 H1 Mers France
22 L4 Mersch Luxembourg
9 G4 Mersea I England
33 P10 Merseburg E Germany
17 G9 Mers el Kebir Algeria
8 D1 Mersey, R England
13 F6 Merseyside co England
69 F11 Mersing Malaysia
52 B6 Mērsrags U.S.S.R.
74 F5 Merta India
8 C4 Merthyr Tydfil Wales
37 K6 Mertingen W Germany
16 B7 Mértola Portugal
8 B6 Merton England
143 D8 Mertondale W Australia
146 J4 Mertz Gl Antarctica
108 G4 Mertzon Texas
20 K3 Méru France
88 F1 Meru Kenya
88 F3 Meru mt Tanzania
74 C8 Merui Pakistan
70 E2 Merutai Sabah
22 D2 Merville France
118 J5 Mervin Sask
100 C4 Merwin, L Washington
18 H4 Méry-sur-Seine France
78 E1 Merzifon Turkey
36 B5 Merzig W Germany
103 N8 Mesa Arizona
71 B2 Mesa Halmahera Indonesia
100 J5 Mesa Idaho
106 F8 Mesa New Mexico
17 F3 Mesa R Spain
99 N2 Mesabi Ra mts Minnesota
43 H8 Mesagne Italy
117 Q3 Mesa L N W Terr
116 K6 Mesa Mt Alaska
69 G12 Mesanak isld Indonesia
21 C7 Mésanger France
70 D2 Mesapo Sabah
47 G10 Mesarás, Kólpos B Crete Greece
106 B4 Mesa Verde Nat. Park Colorado
103 O10 Mescal Arizona
106 E8 Mescalero New Mexico
32 H10 Meschede W Germany
68 C3 Mese Burma
26 J7 Meselefors Sweden
48 H3 Meseşului, Muntii mts Romania
128 F2 Meseta del Cerro Jaua mts Venezuela
52 G6 Mesha R U.S.S.R.
54 L1 Meshchera lowland U.S.S.R.
54 G2 Meshchovsk U.S.S.R.
52 H3 Meshchura U.S.S.R.
Meshed see Mashhad
57 B4 Meshekli U.S.S.R.
116 H8 Meshik Alaska
86 E4 Meshra er Req Sudan
94 B2 Mesick Michigan
117 L7 Mesilinka R Br Col
106 D9 Mesilla New Mexico
80 C6 Mesillat Ziyyon Israel
28 F5 Mesinge Denmark
69 F12 Meskum Sumatra
21 D6 Meslay-du-Maine France
27 E10 Mesna L Norway
20 H2 Mesnières-en-Bêthune France
20 D4 Mesnil Auzouf, le France
20 K2 Mesnil St. Firmin, le France
20 C3 Mesnil-Vigot, le France
20 E4 Mesnil-Villement, le France
41 K5 Mesocco Switzerland
45 M2 Mésola Italy
41 K5 Mesolcina, Valle Switzerland
46 E6 Mesolóngion Greece
78 J4 Mesopotamia Iraq
130 G6 Mesquita Brazil
103 K5 Mesquite Nevada
106 D9 Mesquite New Mexico
109 O9 Mesquite Texas
103 J6 Mesquite L California
21 B6 Messac France
Messalo R see Mualo R
87 G8 Messalo R Mozambique
22 K4 Messancy Belgium
85 F2 Messaoud, Hassi Algeria
33 P7 Messdorf E Germany
20 D4 Messei France
Messick see Poquoson
133 C7 Messie, Can str Chile
89 F4 Messina S Africa
43 G10 Messina Sicily
22 J4 Messincourt France
121 O6 Messines Quebec
13 H6 Messingham England
46 E7 Messíni Greece
46 E8 Messiniakós Kólpos B Greece
41 K2 Messkirch W Germany
Mesta R see Néstos R
47 F3 Mesta R Bulgaria
16 E6 Mestanza Spain
33 P5 Mestlin E Germany
42 G3 Mesto, N Yugoslavia
37 P4 Město-Touškov Czechoslovakia
42 E3 Mestre Italy
45 L1 Mestrino Italy
45 Q8 Meta Italy
110 D3 Meta Missouri
128 D3 Meta div Colombia
128 E2 Meta R Venezuela/Colombia
115 N5 Meta Incognita Pen N W Terr
111 H12 Metairie New Orleans
120 C2 Meta L Ontario
48 H4 Metalici, Muntii mts Romania
117 P11 Metaline Falls Washington
42 D5 Metallifere, Colline hills Italy
99 R9 Metamora Illinois
133 E3 Metán Argentina
87 F8 Metangula Mozambique
43 H8 Metaponto Italy
42 E5 Metauro R Italy
80 E3 Metav Israel
122 F9 Meteghan Nova Scotia
32 F8 Metelen W Germany
86 G3 Metemma Ethiopia
141 J6 Meteor R Queensland
90 G14 Meteor Depth S Atlantic Oc
90 K14 Meteor Seamount S Atlantic Oc
22 D2 Méteren France
47 F7 Méthana Greece
119 S7 Methley Manitoba
46 E8 Methóni Greece
100 E1 Methow R Washington
95 Q4 Methuen Massachusetts
142 E3 Methuen,Mt W Australia
144 C5 Methven New Zealand
12 E1 Methven Scotland
143 D7 Methwin,Mt W Australia
9 G2 Methwold England
119 N1 Metionga L Ontario
118 G6 Metiskow Alberta
122 E5 Metis L Quebec
42 H5 Metković Yugoslavia
117 H8 Metlakahtla Alaska
85 F2 Metlaoui Tunisia
38 K8 Metnitz Austria
46 D2 Metohija Yugoslavia
100 D5 Metolius Oregon
46 E1 Metovnica Yugoslavia
70 K8 Metro Sumatra
110 H4 Metropolis Illinois
25 F2 Metslawier Netherlands
46 E5 Métsovon Greece
37 O6 Metten W Germany
36 B4 Mettendorf W Germany
112 E5 Metter Georgia
22 H3 Mettet Belgium
32 G8 Mettingen W Germany
36 B4 Mettlach W Germany
32 E10 Mettmann W Germany
36 B4 Mettnich W Germany
76 C5 Mettuppalaiyam India
76 C5 Mettur India
88 H7 Metudo isld Mozambique
79 F5 Metulla Israel
19 K3 Metz France
40 F1 Metzeral France
22 L5 Metzervisse France
36 G6 Metzingen W Germany
20 A5 Meu R France
88 G9 Meucate Mozambique
36 D3 Meudt W Germany
69 C10 Meulaboh Sumatra
20 J3 Meulan France
22 E2 Meulebeke Belgium
20 F4 Meulles France
21 I6 Meung sur-Loire France
69 C10 Meureudu Sumatra
40 A4 Meursault France
19 K4 Meurthe R France
36 B6 Meurthe et Moselle dep France
19 J4 Meuse dep France
22 H3 Meuse R Belgium
19 J3 Meuse R France
37 N1 Meuselwitz E Germany
21 I7 Meusnes France
8 B7 Mevagissey England
80 D6 Meva Horon Jordan
80 C6 Meva Modiin Jordan
13 G6 Mexborough England
109 L4 Mexia Texas
129 J3 Mexiana isld Brazil
103 J9 Mexicali Mexico
103 P4 Mexican Hat Utah
124 F3 Mexicanos, Lago de los Mexico
103 P5 Mexican Water Arizona
94 A6 Mexico Indiana
95 R2 Mexico Maine
110 E2 Mexico Missouri
95 L3 Mexico New York
124 G6 Mexico rep N America
125 K8 Mexico City Mexico
125 M6 Mexico, G. of Mexico etc
40 B6 Meximieux France
71 E3 Meycawayan Luzon Philippines
77 D5 Meydān-e-Gel salt lake Iran
33 Q6 Meyenburg E Germany
117 G8 Meyers Chuck Alaska
94 H7 Meyersdale Pennsylvania
18 G7 Meymac France
77 B3 Meymeh Iran
118 L8 Meyronne Sask
18 H8 Meyrueis France
18 G7 Meyssac France
80 E8 Mezada Israel
125 N9 Mezcalapa R Mexico
47 F1 Mezdra Bulgaria
18 H9 Mèze France
19 Q17 Mézel France
52 F2 Mezen' Arkhangelsk U.S.S.R.
52 G3 Mezen' R U.S.S.R.
52 F2 Mezenskaya Guba B U.S.S.R.
80 D4 Mezer Israel
54 C1 Mezha R U.S.S.R.
56 C4 Mezhdurechensk U.S.S.R.
31 N1 Mezhdurech'ye U.S.S.R.
50 D1 Mezhdusharskiy Ostrov isld U.S.S.R.
42 F2 Mežica Yugoslavia
20 E3 Mézidon France
20 B5 Meziére, la France
20 J4 Mézières Yvelines France
21 H8 Mézières-en-Brenne France
31 H6 Mezimostí Czechoslovakia
18 F8 Mézin France
54 M1 Mezinovskiy U.S.S.R.
48 G4 Mezöberény Hungary
48 F3 Mezöcsát Hungary
48 F4 Mezöhegyes Hungary
48 F4 Mezökovacsháza Hungary
48 F3 Mezökövesd Hungary
18 E8 Mézos France
48 F3 Mezötúr Hungary
124 G6 Mezquital Mexico
124 G6 Mezquital R Mexico
124 H6 Mezquitic Mexico
41 N5 Mezzana Italy
45 M3 Mezzano Italy
41 O4 Mezzaselva Italy
45 M2 Mezzogoro Italy
41 K5 Mezzola, Lago di Italy
41 L5 Mezzoldo Italy
42 D2 Mezzolombardo Italy
52 D5 Mga U.S.S.R.
74 F10 Mhasvad India
125 L9 Miahuatián de Porfirio Diaz Mexico
16 D5 Miajadas Spain
103 O8 Miami Arizona
113 G12 Miami Florida
119 T9 Miami Manitoba
107 Q5 Miami Oklahoma
108 D8 Miami Texas
94 C7 Miami R Ohio
113 G12 Miami Beach Florida
113 G11 Miami Canal Florida
94 C6 Miami, Great R Ohio
94 C7 Miami, Little R Ohio
94 C7 Miamisburg Ohio
113 G12 Miami Shores Florida
113 G12 Miami Springs Florida
65 B7 Mianchi China
78 L3 Miandowab Iran
87 H11 Miandrivazo Madagascar
77 A1 Miāneh Iran
67 E4 Mian Shui R China
58 E5 Mian Xian China
58 D5 Mianyang China
67 D1 Mianyang China
67 A1 Mianzhu China
65 E6 Miao Dao isld China
65 E5 Miaodao Qundao islds China
65 H3 Miaoling China
67 B3 Miao Ling mt ra China
67 C4 Miaoping China
87 H11 Miarinarivo Madagascar
55 D3 Miass R U.S.S.R.
31 K1 Miastko Poland
103 O9 Mica Mt Arizona
58 E5 Micang Shan mt ra China
113 E8 Micanopy Florida
128 C3 Micay Colombia
113 C7 Miccosukee Florida
52 H3 Michaichmon' U.S.S.R.
48 G2 Michal'any Czechoslovakia
48 G2 Michalovce Czechoslovakia
118 C9 Michel Br Col
118 H3 Michel Sask
38 N5 Michelbach Austria
36 E3 Michelbach W Germany
116 Q2 Michelson, Mt Alaska
36 G4 Michelstadt W Germany
33 S8 Michendorf E Germany
127 K5 Miches Dominican Rep
118 E7 Michichi Alberta
112 J1 Michie, L N Carolina
99 S3 Michigamme Michigan
99 S3 Michigamme L Michigan
99 S3 Michigamme Res Michigan
98 H1 Michigan N Dakota
94 A1 Michigan state U.S.A.
94 C4 Michigan Center Michigan
99 U8 Michigan City Indiana
94 A4 Michigan, L U.S.A.
110 K1 Michigantown Indiana
120 F5 Michipicoten Ontario
31 N4 Michów Poland
47 J2 Michurin Bulgaria
54 M4 Michurinsk U.S.S.R.
13 F4 Mickle Fell mt England
9 E3 Mickleton Gloucs England
127 O8 Micoud St Lucia
134 F7 Micronesia Pac Oc
69 H11 Midai isld Indonesia
119 O9 Midale Sask
100 J8 Midas Nevada
90 E6 Mid-Atlantic Ridge Atlantic Oc
12 E2 Mid Calder Scotland
89 D8 Middelburg Cape Prov S Africa
25 A6 Middelburg Netherlands
87 D12 Middelburg S Africa
89 F5 Middelburg Transvaal S Africa
25 B5 Middelharnis Netherlands
22 D1 Middelkerke Belgium
89 B9 Middel Roggeveld reg S Africa
87 E10 Middelwit S Africa
90 A7 Middle America Trench Pacific Oc
68 A6 Middle Andaman isld Andaman Is
138 D5 Middleback, Mt S Australia
95 R5 Middleboro Massachusetts
94 G7 Middlebourne W Virginia
118 F1 Middlebro Manitoba
95 N4 Middleburg New York
95 K6 Middleburg Pennsylvania
94 K8 Middleburg Virginia
94 B5 Middlebury Indiana
95 O2 Middlebury Vermont
108 G4 Middle Concho R Texas
28 D5 Middlefart Denmark
144 A6 Middle Fiord New Zealand
13 G5 Middleham England
94 D1 Middle I Michigan
69 C8 Middle I Thailand
90 B16 Middle I Tristan da Cunha
143 E10 Middle I W Australia
100 F8 Middle L Nevada
119 M6 Middle Lake Sask
98 G8 Middle Loup R Nebraska
144 C6 Middlemarch New Zealand
8 D6 Middlemarsh England
94 J3 Middleport New York
94 E8 Middleport Ohio
83 M9 Middle Pt Christmas I Indian Oc
94 C6 Middle Pt Ohio
98 K1 Middle R Minnesota
123 R5 Middle Rge Newfoundland
95 L7 Middle River Maryland
118 G8 Middle Sand Hills, The Alberta
94 D10 Middlesboro Kentucky
13 G4 Middlesbrough England
125 P9 Middlesex Belize
95 K4 Middlesex New York
13 F5 Middleton Cumbria England
13 F6 Middleton Greater Manchester England
13 H6 Middleton Humberside England
100 J6 Middleton Idaho
94 C3 Middleton Michigan
122 G9 Middleton Nova Scotia
141 F5 Middleton Queensland
110 H6 Middleton Tennessee
99 R6 Middleton Wisconsin
116 P7 Middleton I Alaska
13 F4 Middleton in Teesdale England
95 P5 Middletown Connecticut
95 M7 Middletown Delaware
94 B6 Middletown Indiana
94 K7 Middletown Maryland
95 N5 Middletown New York
110 M2 Middletown Ohio
95 L6 Middletown Pennsylvania
8 D2 Middletown Wales
94 B4 Middleville Michigan
95 N3 Middleville New York
108 B8 Middle Water Texas
8 D1 Middlewich England
122 H9 Middlewood Nova Scotia
85 D2 Midelt Morocco
109 L7 Midfield Texas
8 C4 Mid Glamorgan co Wales
145 E3 Midhirst New Zealand
9 F6 Midhurst England
121 L8 Midhurst Ontario
18 G9 Midi, Canal du France
18 E10 Midi d'Ossau, Pic du mt France
18 F10 Midi du Bigorre, Pic du mt France
110 B6 Midland Arkansas
103 K8 Midland California
94 J7 Midland Maryland
94 C3 Midland Michigan
98 E5 Midland S Dakota
108 E4 Midland Texas
111 L10 Midland City Alabama
143 B9 Midland Junc W Australia
14 C5 Midleton Irish Rep
109 K3 Midlothian Texas
94 K9 Midlothian Virginia
Midlothian co see Lothian and Borders regions
32 J5 Midlum W Germany
75 M7 Midnapur India
111 F8 Midnight Mississippi
87 H12 Midongy Atsimo Madagascar
60 D13 Midori-kawa R Japan
18 E9 Midouze R France
134 G5 Mid-Pacific Mountains Pac Oc
71 G7 Midsayap Philippines
100 J5 Midvale Idaho
101 O9 Midvale Utah
112 E5 Midville Georgia
111 L9 Midway Alabama
117 O11 Midway Br Col
112 F6 Midway Georgia
94 C8 Midway Kentucky
109 M4 Midway Texas
116 O1 Midway Is Alaska
135 U2 Midway Is atoll Hawaiian Is
122 E1 Midway L Quebec
143 E6 Midway Well W Australia
101 T6 Midwest Wyoming
107 N6 Midwest City Oklahoma
25 F2 Midwolde Netherlands
78 H3 Midyat Turkey
47 J3 Midye Turkey
15 G1 Mid Yell Scotland
46 F1 Midžor mt Yugoslavia
61 K11 Mie prefect Japan
31 M5 Miechów Poland
40 F3 Miécourt Switzerland
31 J3 Międzychód Poland
31 K5 Międzylesie Poland
31 O4 Międzyrzec Poland
31 J3 Międzyrzecz Poland
31 K4 Miejska Gorka Poland
29 L5 Miekojärvi L Finland
18 F9 Miélan France
31 N5 Mielec Poland
41 N3 Mieminger Kette mt Austria
27 G15 Mien L Sweden
139 H8 Miena Tasmania
67 G4 Mien-hua Hsü isld Taiwan
109 H9 Mier Mexico
106 D7 Miera New Mexico
48 K4 Miercurea Cinc Romania
16 D1 Mieres Spain
26 N2 Mieron Norway
38 E6 Miesbach W Germany
86 H4 Miesso Ethiopia
33 O8 Mieste E Germany
31 H3 Mieszkowice Poland
94 K6 Mifflin Pennsylvania
95 K6 Mifflinburg Pennsylvania
95 K6 Mifflintown Pennsylvania
83 L9 Migaswewa Sri Lanka
80 F2 Migdal Israel
80 D7 Migdal Oz Jordan
77 F4 Mighān Iran
45 L2 Migliarino Italy
45 P7 Mignano Italy
44 G2 Mignano, L. di Italy
44 L5 Mignone R Italy
124 H5 Miguel Auza Mexico
88 H2 Migwani Kenya
68 B3 Migyaunye Burma
48 K3 Mihăileni Romania
60 G11 Mihara Japan
61 N11 Mihara-yama vol Japan
61 O8 Miharu Japan
37 J1 Mihla E Germany
60 G10 Miho wan B Japan
40 D5 Mijoux France
94 D2 Mikado Michigan
119 P7 Mikado Sask
60 P2 Mikasa Japan
61 K9 Mikawa Japan
48 L1 Mikhailovka U.S.S.R.
54 L2 Mikhaylov U.S.S.R.
47 F1 Mikhaylovgrad Bulgaria
146 D3 Mikhaylov I Antarctica
55 G4 Mikhaylovka Altay U.S.S.R.
47 H2 Mikhaylovo Bulgaria
55 C3 Mikhaylovsk U.S.S.R.
80 C4 Mikhmoret Israel
79 E9 Mikhrot Timna Israel
88 H7 Mikindani Tanzania
100 E4 Mikkalo Oregon
29 N10 Mikkeli Finland
117 Q7 Mikkwa R Alberta
31 N2 Mikołajki Poland
31 L5 Mikołow Poland
47 G1 Mikre Bulgaria
46 E4 Mikrï Préspa L Greece
47 H3 Mikrón Dhérion Greece
52 G1 Mikulkin, Mys C U.S.S.R.
48 D2 Mikulov Czechoslovakia
87 G7 Mikumi Tanzania
88 F5 Mikumi Nat. Park Tanzania
61 N8 Mikuni sammyaku mts Japan
61 N12 Mikura-jima isld Japan
99 N4 Milaca Minnesota
73 L7 Miladunmadulu Atoll Maldives
130 H9 Milagres Brazil
Milan see Milano
94 B7 Milan Indiana
107 N4 Milan Kansas
94 D4 Milan Michigan
99 L4 Milan Minnesota
99 N9 Milan Missouri
94 E5 Milan Ohio
122 A8 Milan Quebec
110 H6 Milan Tennessee
100 H2 Milan Washington
138 E6 Milang S Australia
88 E10 Milange Mozambique
70 G4 Milango R Sulawesi
109 L5 Milano Texas
39 Milano conurbation Italy
17 G4 Milares R Spain
47 J7 Milâs Turkey
43 G10 Milazzo Sicily
98 K4 Milbank S Dakota
94 A4 Milburg Michigan
144 B7 Milburn New Zealand
9 G3 Mildenhall England
120 J8 Mildmay Ontario
98 A3 Mildred Montana
95 L5 Mildred Pennsylvania
118 K5 Mildred Sask
117 R7 Mildred Lake Alberta
138 F5 Mildura Victoria
67 A4 Mile China
46 F5 Miléai Greece
127 J2 Mile Gully Jamaica
141 K7 Miles Queensland
100 G2 Miles Washington
101 U3 Miles City Montana
119 N9 Milestone Sask
43 G10 Mileto Italy
45 Q7 Miletto, M mt Italy
143 B7 Mileura W Australia
31 H6 Milevsko Czechoslovakia
102 D1 Milford California
95 O5 Milford Connecticut
95 M8 Milford Delaware
9 E6 Milford Hampshire England
99 T9 Milford Illinois
94 B5 Milford Indiana
99 L6 Milford Iowa
107 O2 Milford Kansas
95 T2 Milford Maine
95 Q4 Milford Massachusetts
94 D4 Milford Michigan
98 J9 Milford Nebraska
95 Q4 Milford New Hampshire
95 N4 Milford New York
9 F5 Milford Surrey England
109 L3 Milford Texas
103 L3 Milford Utah
94 K8 Milford Virginia
94 D6 Milford Center Ohio
8 A4 Milford Haven Wales
144 A6 Milford Sound New Zealand
140 F4 Milgarra Queensland
143 C8 Milgoo, Mt W Australia
143 C7 Milgun W Australia
85 E1 Miliana Algeria
43 C12 Miliane R Tunisia
31 K4 Milicz Poland
143 B9 Miling W Australia
140 C1 Milingimbi N Terr Aust
51 P3 Milkovo U.S.S.R.
118 F9 Milk R Alberta/Montana
127 K3 Milk River Bath Jamaica
86 E2 Milk, Wadi el watercourse Sudan
25 E5 Mill Netherlands
141 H4 Millaa Millaa Queensland
21 G9 Millac France
21 I7 Millançay France
143 F8 Millar Breakaways W Australia
99 O9 Millard Missouri
141 H4 Millaroo Queensland
98 H3 Millarton N Dakota
94 H9 Millboro Virginia
95 U2 Millbridge Maine
95 O5 Millbrook New York
121 M8 Millbrook Ontario
102 F1 Mill City Nevada
100 C5 Mill City Oregon
102 C1 Mill Creek California
109 L1 Mill Creek Oklahoma
94 H8 Mill Creek W Virginia
112 D4 Milledgeville Georgia
99 R8 Milledgeville Illinois
101 O2 Millegan Montana
99 N3 Mille Lacs L Minnesota
119 N2 Mille Lacs, Lac des Ontario
112 F5 Millen Georgia
110 C4 Miller Missouri
98 G9 Miller Nebraska
98 H5 Miller S Dakota
138 D3 Miller R S Australia
124 B3 Miller, Desembarcadero de Mexico
116 Q6 Miller, Mt Alaska
54 M8 Millerovo U.S.S.R.
103 O10 Miller Pk Arizona
102 G3 Millers Nevada
94 B5 Millersburg Indiana
110 M3 Millersburg Kentucky
94 D1 Millersburg Michigan
94 F6 Millersburg Ohio
95 L6 Millersburg Pennsylvania
138 D4 Millers Creek S Australia
95 P4 Millers Falls Massachusetts
111 J9 Millers Ferry Alabama
144 B6 Miller's Flat New Zealand
12 D2 Millerston Scotland
94 H6 Millerstown Pennsylvania
108 H4 Millersview Texas
122 G7 Millerton New Brunswick
95 O5 Millerton New York
144 C4 Millerton New Zealand
102 E4 Millerton L California
123 Q5 Millertown Newfoundland
123 Q4 Millertown Junct Newfoundland
118 D5 Millet Alberta
94 E9 Millet W Virginia
102 G2 Millett Nevada
109 H7 Millett Texas
18 G7 Millevaches, Plateau de France
14 D1 Millford Irish Rep
94 K5 Mill Hall Penn
146 E2 Mill I Antarctica
115 M5 Mill I N W Terr
100 E6 Millican Oregon
109 L5 Millican Texas
118 F8 Millicent Alberta
138 F6 Millicent S Australia
143 D8 Millicent,Mt W Australia
111 K11 Milligan Florida
98 J9 Milligan Nebraska
106 F1 Milliken Colorado
95 M7 Millington Maryland
94 D3 Millington Michigan
95 S8 Millinocket Maine
141 K8 Millmerran Queensland
13 E5 Millom England
111 H8 Millport Alabama
95 L4 Millport New York
12 D2 Millport Scotland
111 H10 Millry Alabama
106 F5 Mills New Mexico
101 T7 Mills Wyoming
141 G5 Mills R Queensland
109 J3 Millsap Texas
102 B2 Millsaps California
95 M8 Millsboro Delaware
94 G7 Millsboro Penn
117 O5 Mills L N W Terr
99 Q5 Millston Wisconsin
142 B5 Millstream W Australia
14 B4 Millstreet Irish Rep
8 C2 Milltir Cerig mt Wales
122 E8 Milltown New Brunswick
123 R6 Milltown Newfoundland
14 B4 Milltown Malbay Irish Rep
141 F4 Millungera Queensland
102 B4 Mill Valley California
122 H9 Mill Village Nova Scotia
122 E7 Millville New Brunswick
94 C7 Millville Ohio
95 L5 Millville Pennsylvania
109 N2 Millwood Res Arkansas
20 K5 Milly France
143 B7 Milly Milly W Australia
20 K3 Milly sur-Therain France
33 T6 Milmersdorf E Germany
13 E1 Milnathort Scotland
115 R3 Milne Land Greenland
112 C4 Milner Georgia
101 L7 Milner Idaho
118 E1 Milner Ridge Manitoba
120 K6 Milnet Ontario
12 D2 Milngavie Scotland
98 J3 Milnor N Dakota
13 F5 Milnthorpe England
118 E8 Milo Alberta
99 N8 Milo Iowa
95 S1 Milo Maine
100 B7 Milo Oregon
141 G7 Milo Queensland
88 E6 Milo Tanzania
135 U6 Milolii Hawaiian Is
31 M2 Miłomłyn Poland
47 G8 Mílos isld Greece
48 F5 Miloševo Yugoslavia
31 K3 Miłosław Poland
33 Q7 Milow E Germany
31 L6 Milówka Poland
138 F3 Milparinka New S Wales
102 C4 Milpitas California
110 L2 Milroy Indiana
94 K6 Milroy Pennsylvania
37 O5 Miltach W Germany
36 G4 Miltenberg W Germany
95 M8 Milton Delaware
111 J11 Milton Florida
99 Q10 Milton Illinois
110 D1 Milton Iowa
107 N4 Milton Kansas
95 R3 Milton Maine
94 H10 Milton N Carolina
98 J1 Milton N Dakota
139 K6 Milton New S Wales
144 B7 Milton New Zealand
122 H9 Milton Nova Scotia
100 G4 Milton Oregon
95 L5 Milton Pennsylvania
12 D2 Milton Scotland
95 O2 Milton Vermont
99 S7 Milton Wisconsin
94 E8 Milton W Virginia
8 B6 Milton Abbot England
139 J3 Milton Downs New S Wales
12 D3 Miltonish Scotland
9 F3 Milton Keynes England
107 N2 Miltonvale Kansas
86 C3 Miltou Chad
33 S4 Miltzow E Germany
67 D2 Miluo China
8 C5 Milverton England
99 T6 Milwaukee Wisconsin
127 K5 Milwaukee Depth Caribbean
60 E13 Mimitsu Japan
18 E8 Mimizan France
31 H5 Mimoň Czechoslovakia
86 B6 Mimongo Gabon
60 H10 Mimuro yama mt Japan
102 A2 Mina California
102 F3 Mina Nevada
77 A5 Mina' al Ahmadi Iran
77 E6 Mināb Iran
60 J12 Minabe Japan
124 F3 Miñaca Mexico
119 T4 Minago R Manitoba
71 H4 Minahassa Peninsula Sulawesi Indonesia
77 D7 Mina Jebel Ali United Arab Emirates
118 H1 Minaki Ontario
100 H4 Minam Oregon
60 D13 Minamata Japan
85 C6 Mina, Mt Mali
126 F4 Minas Cuba
69 E12 Minas Sumatra
131 G5 Minas Uruguay
77 A5 Mina' Sa'ud Kuwait
122 H8 Minas Basin Nova Scotia
16 C7 Minas de Riotinto Spain
16 C7 Minas de Tharsis Spain
130 F5 Minas Gerais state Brazil
129 K7 Minas Novas Brazil
130 G5 Minas Novas Brazil
125 P10 Minas, Sa. de las mts Guatemala
98 C8 Minatare Nebraska
120 B2 Minataree Ontario
125 M9 Minatitlán Mexico
68 B2 Minbu Burma
118 F5 Minburn Alberta
99 M8 Minburn Iowa
68 A2 Minbya Burma
116 M5 Minchumina, L Alaska
45 J1 Mincio R Italy
107 N6 Minco Oklahoma
31 M6 Minčol mt Czechoslovakia
71 G7 Mindanao Philippines
71 G6 Mindanao Sea Philippines
138 F5 Mindarie S Australia
68 A2 Mindat Sakan Burma
37 J7 Mindel R W Germany
41 M1 Mindelheim W Germany
111 C9 Minden Louisiana
98 G9 Minden Nebraska
102 E3 Minden Nevada
121 M8 Minden Ontario
32 J8 Minden W Germany
94 F9 Minden W Virginia
94 E3 Minden City Michigan
142 B5 Minderoo W Australia
68 B3 Mindon Burma
138 F5 Mindona L New S Wales
71 E4 Mindoro isld Philippines
71 E4 Mindoro Str Philippines
48 F4 Mindszent Hungary
55 C4 Mindyak U.S.S.R.
60 E11 Mine Japan
99 O1 Mine Centre Ontario
48 K5 Mineci-Ungureni Romania
14 D5 Mine Hd Irish Rep
8 C5 Minehead England
130 D5 Mineiros Brazil
20 D3 Mine, la France
99 L8 Mineola Iowa
109 M3 Mineola Texas
101 P4 Miner Montana
102 C1 Mineral California
109 K7 Mineral Texas
94 K8 Mineral Virginia
100 C3 Mineral Washington
125 K7 Mineral del Monte Mexico
103 M3 Mineral Mts Utah
99 Q7 Mineral Pt Wisconsin
109 O2 Mineral Springs Arkansas
109 J3 Mineral Wells Texas
45 K2 Minerbio Italy
103 M3 Minersville Utah
94 F6 Minerva Ohio
141 J6 Minerva Queensland
137 R6 Minerva Rfs Pacific Oc
43 G7 Minervino Murge Italy
95 L3 Minetto New York
94 E8 Minford Ohio
68 C4 Mingaladon Burma
122 H3 Mingan Quebec
122 J3 Mingan Chan Quebec
122 J3 Mingan Is Quebec
138 F4 Mingary S Australia
67 D5 Mingcheng China
78 L1 Mingechaur U.S.S.R.
78 L1 Mingechaurskoye Vdkhr res U.S.S.R.
141 H4 Mingela Queensland
143 B8 Mingenew W Australia
140 E5 Mingera R Queensland
68 B1 Mingin Burma
75 Q6 Mingin Range Burma
67 B5 Mingjiang China
58 G5 Ming-kuang China
17 G5 Minglanilla Spain
67 C4 Minglun China
99 N8 Mingo Iowa
107 K2 Mingo Kansas
94 G6 Mingo Junct Ohio
Mingolsheim see Bad Schönborn
87 G8 Mingoyo Tanzania
67 A1 Mingshan China
Mingshui see Zhangqiu
65 F1 Mingshui China
109 J3 Mingus Texas
67 F3 Mingxi China
68 G8 Minh Hoa, Hon isld Vietnam
68 B4 Minhla Burma
16 B3 Minho prov Portugal
16 B2 Minho R Spain/Portugal
127 K2 Minho, R Jamaica
20 B4 Miniac Morvan France
46 E1 Minićevo Yugoslavia
73 L7 Minicoy I Lakshadweep Indian Oc
101 M7 Minidoka Idaho
99 R9 Minier Illinois
143 E8 Minigwal,L W Australia
143 A6 Minilya W Australia
143 A6 Minilya R W Australia
110 K4 Mining City Res Kentucky
119 Q8 Miniota Manitoba
83 K10 Minipe Sri Lanka
123 L1 Minipi L Labrador
118 H4 Ministikwan L Sask
17 F3 Ministra, Sierra Spain
119 Q6 Minitonas Manitoba
143 B8 Minjar hill W Australia
58 D5 Min Jiang R China
67 F3 Min Jiang R China
102 E5 Minkler California
48 L2 Minkovtsy U.S.S.R.
57 G4 Min-Kush U.S.S.R.
138 D5 Minlaton S Australia
85 F7 Minna Nigeria
146 H7 Minna Bluff Antarctica
61 P12 Minna-jima isld Okinawa
107 N2 Minneapolis Kansas
99 N4 Minneapolis Minnesota
119 S8 Minnedosa Manitoba
98 C6 Minnekahta S Dakota
107 L4 Minneola Kansas
99 M5 Minnesota R Minnesota
99 N3 Minnesota state U.S.A.
99 P5 Minnesota City Minnesota
99 N6 Minnesota Lake Minnesota
27 E11 Minnesund Norway
118 B7 Minnewanka, L Alberta
99 L4 Minnewaska L Minnesota
98 G1 Minnewaukan N Dakota
68 D6 Min-Ngaw Burma
143 B6 Minnie Creek W Australia
141 H7 Minnie Downs Queensland
142 B5 Minnie,Mt W Australia
79 H2 Minnik Syria
138 D5 Minnipa S Australia
120 G4 Minnipuka Ontario
118 K1 Minnitaki L Ontario
61 K10 Mino Japan
16 B2 Miño R Spain
61 M10 Minobu Japan
99 R4 Minocqua Wisconsin
61 K10 Minokamo Japan
61 K11 Minokuchi Japan
99 P3 Minong Wisconsin
99 R9 Minonk Illinois
99 S8 Minooka Illinois
Minorca see Menorca
40 A2 Minot France
98 E1 Minot N Dakota
67 F3 Minqing China
65 C7 Minquan China
20 A4 Minquiers, les English Chan
32 G5 Minsen W Germany
65 A4 Minsheng Canal China
53 C7 Minsk U.S.S.R.
31 N3 Mińsk Mazowieckie Poland
9 H5 Minster England
94 C6 Minster Ohio
111 J9 Minter Alabama
111 F8 Minter City Mississippi
119 S9 Minto Manitoba
122 F7 Minto New Brunswick
117 E4 Minto Yukon Terr
114 J3 Minto Hd N W Terr
114 H3 Minto Inlet N W Terr
115 M6 Minto, L Quebec
98 B1 Minton Sask
106 D2 Minturn Colorado
45 P7 Minturno Italy
79 A8 Minûf Egypt
56 D4 Minusinsk U.S.S.R.
58 D5 Min Xian China
79 A10 Minya, El Egypt
79 B8 Minya el Qamn Egypt
Minya Konka mt see Gongga Shan
55 C3 Min'yar U.S.S.R.
138 F6 Minyip Victoria
68 B1 Minywa Burma
94 C2 Mio Michigan
83 J10 Mi Oya R Sri Lanka
78 K5 Miqdādiyah Iraq
121 O3 Miquelon Quebec
123 Q6 Miquelon, Grande, I Atlantic Oc
118 E5 Miquelon Prov. Park Alberta
123 N7 Mira C Breton I, N Scotia
45 M1 Mira Italy
17 G5 Mira Spain
16 B7 Mira R Portugal
19 P17 Mirabeau France
130 G5 Mirabela Brazil
45 R7 Mirabella Eclano Italy
130 G7 Miracema Brazil
128 D2 Miraflores Boyaca Colombia
124 E6 Miraflores Mexico
102 G7 Mirage L California
130 G7 Miraí Brazil
76 B2 Miraj India
130 G5 Miralta Brazil
19 O17 Miràmas France
18 E7 Mirambeau France
122 G6 Miramichi B New Brunswick
18 F8 Miramont de Guyenne France
133 F5 Miranda Argentina
145 E2 Miranda New Zealand
128 E1 Miranda state Venezuela
17 F2 Miranda de E.Haro Spain
16 C3 Miranda do D Portugal
141 F3 Miranda Downs Queensland
130 C6 Miranda, R Brazil
18 F9 Mirande France
16 C3 Mirandela Portugal
109 J8 Mirando City Texas
45 K2 Mirandola Italy
130 D7 Mirandópolis Brazil
45 M1 Mirano Italy
130 E8 Mirante Serra do mts Brazil
60 F11 Mirasaka Japan
17 G5 Mira, Sierra de mts Spain
130 E7 Mirassol Brazil
16 C2 Miravalles mt Spain
46 E3 Miravci Yugoslavia
77 L2 Mir Bachech Kūt Afghanistan
25 E3 Mirdum Netherlands
21 D6 Miré France
86 G1 Mirear I Egypt
127 H5 Mirebalais Haiti
19 J5 Mirebeau Côte-d'Or France
21 F8 Mirebeau Vienne France
18 G9 Mirepoix France
54 E7 Mirgorod U.S.S.R.
70 D2 Miri Sarawak
141 K6 Miriam Vale Queensland
85 A5 Mirik, C Mauritania
127 K9 Mirimire Venezuela
131 H4 Mirim, L Brazil/Uruguay
131 F2 Miriñay, R Argentina
141 G8 Mirintu R Queensland
128 D4 Miriti-Paraná R Colombia
77 G5 Mirjāveh Iran
80 D4 Mirka Jordan
45 P1 Mirna R Yugoslavia
56 H1 Mirnyy U.S.S.R.
40 E3 Miroir, Mt France
144 D5 Miromiro mt New Zealand
119 P3 Mirond L Sask
54 B7 Mironovka U.S.S.R.
48 J6 Miroşi Romania
31 J2 Mirosławiec Poland
33 R6 Mirow E Germany
77 L7 Mirpur Khas Pakistan
140 D7 Mirranponga Pongunna L N Terr Aust
85 F6 Mirria Niger
118 D6 Mirror Alberta
48 J6 Mîrşani Romania
56 D5 Mirskoy Khrebet mts U.S.S.R.
141 H5 Mirtna Queensland
47 F7 Mirtoan Sea Greece
59 J4 Miryang S Korea
56 E1 Miryuyginski Porog falls U.S.S.R.
57 B5 Mirzachiria U.S.S.R.
75 K6 Mirzapur India
45 O4 Misa R Italy
60 F12 Misaki Japan
60 G11 Mi-saki C Japan
61 L10 Misakubo Japan
45 N4 Misano Monte Italy
61 P13 Misato Okinawa
61 P5 Misawa Japan
32 L8 Misburg W Germany
40 G5 Mischabel mt Switzerland
122 J7 Miscouche Pr Edward I
122 H6 Miscou I New Brunswick
122 H5 Miscou, Pt New Brunswick
127 P4 Misery, Mt St Kitts W I
80 F1 Misgav 'Am Israel
69 A9 Misha Nicobar Is
77 A5 Mish'ab, Al U.A.E.
128 D6 Mishahua R Peru
65 H2 Mishan China
94 A5 Mishawaka Indiana
116 G2 Misheguk Mt Alaska
56 F4 Mishelevka U.S.S.R.
120 E4 Mishibishu L Ontario
99 T5 Mishicot Wisconsin
61 M10 Mishima Japan
60 E11 Mi shima isld Japan
55 C3 Mishkino Bashkirskaya U.S.S.R.
55 D3 Mishkino Sverdlovsk U.S.S.R.
80 F7 Mishmaqa Jordan
80 C6 Mishmar 'Ayyalon Israel
80 B8 Mishmar Ha Negev Israel
121 P5 Mishomis Quebec
52 J2 Mishvan' U.S.S.R.
80 E4 Misilya Jordan
137 L4 Misima isld Louisiade Arch
128 E6 Misión Cavinas Bolivia
130 B10 Misiones dep Paraguay
130 C10 Misiones prov Argentina

130 C10 Misiones, Sa.de ra Argentina
88 B4 Misisi Zaïre
125 N2 Miskito, Cayos islds Nicaragua
48 F2 Miskolc Hungary
60 G10 Misogu chi Japan
71 C3 Misoöl isld W Irian
99 Q2 Misquah Hills Minnesota
84 F3 Misrātah Libya
120 F4 Missanabie Ontario
130 G9 Missão Velhá Brazil
21 A7 Missillac France
120 G4 Missinaibi L Ontario
120 H2 Missinaibi R Ontario
100 C1 Mission Br Col
98 F6 Mission S Dakota
109 J9 Mission Texas
117 M11 Mission City Br Col
98 J7 Mission Hill S Dakota
101 M2 Mission Range Montana
121 L1 Missisicabi R Quebec
120 G6 Mississagi R Ontario
121 L9 Mississauga Ontario
111 E10 Mississippi R U.S.A.
92 J4 Mississippi state U.S.A.
111 G12 Mississippi Delta Louisiana
121 O7 Mississippi, L Ontario
111 H11 Mississippi Sound Mississippi
Missolonghi Greece see Mesolóngion
120 H4 Missonga Ontario
101 L3 Missoula Montana
110 C2 Missouri R Missouri
92 H3 Missouri state U.S.A.
109 O2 Missouri, Lit R Arkansas
98 F3 Missouri Res N Dakota
99 L8 Missouri Valley Iowa
141 H5 Mistake Cr Queensland
140 A3 Mistake Creek N Terr Aust
123 K2 Mistanipisipou R Quebec
121 S4 Mistassini Quebec
115 M7 Mistassini, Lac Quebec
119 O6 Mistatim Sask
121 M3 Mistawak L Quebec
31 K7 Mistelbach Austria
27 J14 Misterhult Sweden
126 C5 Misteriosa Bank Caribbean
8 D6 Misterton England
128 D7 Misti mt Peru
122 E5 Mistigougèche L Quebec
37 P3 Misto Czechoslovakia
131 D3 Mistolar, L Argentina
26 E10 Mistra R Norway
43 F11 Mistretta Sicily
60 E11 Misumi Japan
60 D13 Misumi-ura Japan
60 E13 Mitai Japan
127 P2 Mitan Trinidad
124 G7 Mita, Pta.de C Mexico
8 D4 Mitcheldean England
8 A7 Mitchell England
110 K3 Mitchell Indiana
98 C8 Mitchell Nebraska
120 J9 Mitchell Ontario
100 E5 Mitchell Oregon
141 J7 Mitchell Queensland
98 H6 Mitchell S Dakota
139 K3 Mitchell R New S Wales
111 K9 Mitchell L Alabama
94 B2 Mitchell, L Michigan
112 E2 Mitchell, Mt N Carolina
140 A1 Mitchell Pt N Terr Aust
141 F3 Mitchell River Queensland
14 C4 Mitchelstown Irish Rep
121 Q5 Mitchinamecus, L Quebec
74 C6 Mithi Pakistan
47 H5 Míthimna Greece
71 B2 Miti isld Halmahera Indonesia
47 H5 Mitilíni Greece
52 G2 Mitina U.S.S.R.
119 S4 Mitishto R Manitoba
117 G7 Mitkof I Alaska
79 C8 Mitla Pass Egypt
61 O9 Mito Japan
86 A5 Mitra mt Equat Guinea
137 P4 Mitre isld Santa Cruz Is
145 E4 Mitre, Mt New Zealand
144 A6 Mitre Pk New Zealand
116 H9 Mitrofania I Alaska
52 J3 Mitrofanovskaya U.S.S.R.
46 D5 Mitsikéli R Greece
60 F11 Mitsu Japan
60 F12 Mitsuhama Japan
60 H11 Mitsuishi Japan
60 Q3 Mitsuishi Japan
61 N9 Mitsukaidō Japan
61 M8 Mitsuke Japan
60 R2 Mitsumata Japan
139 K5 Mittagong New S Wales
141 F4 Mittagong Queensland
41 L3 Mittagspitze mt Austria
139 J6 Mitta Mitta Victoria
41 N4 Mittelberg Austria
37 J5 Mittelfranken dist Bayern W Germany
40 F4 Mittelland dist Switzerland
32 H8 Mittellandkanal W Germany
33 R8 Mittelmark reg E Germany
36 H3 Mittelsinn W Germany
41 O3 Mittenwald W Germany
33 T8 Mittenwalde E Germany
38 M6 Mitterbach Austria
37 O6 Mitterfels W Germany
38 G7 Mitter Pinzgau V Austria
36 B6 Mittersheim France
37 N4 Mitterteich W Germany
140 D4 Mittiebah R N Terr Aust
37 O2 Mittweida E Germany
128 D3 Mitú Colombia
88 B3 Mitumba mts Zaïre
87 E7 Mitwaba Zaïre
55 D1 Mityayevo U.S.S.R.
86 B5 Mitzic Gabon
60 O4 Miumaya Japan
61 N10 Miura Japan
54 K9 Mius R U.S.S.R.
54 K9 Miusskiy Liman lagoon U.S.S.R.
65 B7 Mi Xian China
38 M7 Mixnitz Austria
61 K11 Miya-gawa R Japan
61 Q12 Miyagi Okinawa
61 O7 Miyagi prefect Japan
61 P13 Miyagusuku-jima isld Okinawa
78 G4 Miyah, Wadi El Syria
61 N11 Miyake-jima isld Japan
61 P6 Miyako Japan
60 E14 Miyakonojō Japan
55 B6 Miyaly U.S.S.R.
60 E14 Miyazaki Japan
60 E13 Miyazaki prefect Japan
60 J10 Miyazu Japan
60 F11 Miyoshi Japan
65 C4 Miyun China
65 D4 Miyun Shuiku res China
86 G4 Mizan Teferi Ethiopia
84 E3 Mizdah Libya
111 G10 Mize Mississippi
14 B5 Mizen Hd Cork Irish Rep
14 E4 Mizen Hd Wicklow Irish Rep
65 A6 Mizhi China
48 K6 Mizil Romania
75 P7 Mizoram prov India
99 M2 Mizpah Minnesota
79 E7 Mizpe Ramon Israel
146 B6 Mizuho Japan
61 P6 Mizusawa Japan
88 C1 Mjanji Uganda
27 F14 Mjöbäck Sweden
27 H13 Mjölby Sweden
28 B6 Mjolden Denmark
27 D12 Mjöndalen Norway
27 F14 Mjörn L Sweden
27 E11 Mjösa L Norway
28 O9 Mjóvanes C Faeroes
88 C9 Mkokomo mt Zambia
88 G4 Mkokotoni Tanzania
88 B8 Mkuku Zambia
87 E8 Mkushi Zambia
88 B8 Mkushi R Zambia
31 H5 Mladá Boleslav Czechoslovakia
48 F6 Mladenovac Yugoslavia
37 P4 Mladotice Czechoslovakia
88 C5 Mlala Hills Tanzania
48 G6 Mlava R Yugoslavia
31 M2 Mława Poland
88 G10 M'lela R Mozambique
87 G7 Mlimba Tanzania
42 H6 Mljet isld Yugoslavia
88 E7 Mlowe Malawi
37 O3 Mnichov Czechoslovakia
31 H5 Mnichovo Hradiště Czechoslovakia
48 F2 Mnišek Czechoslovakia
26 K8 Mo Sweden
71 N9 Moa isld Indonesia
128 D5 Moa R Brazil
85 B7 Moa R Sierra Leone/Guinea
103 P3 Moab Utah
119 U3 Moak L Manitoba
139 G6 Moama New S Wales
89 H5 Moamba Mozambique
144 C5 Moana New Zealand
145 E3 Moana mt New Zealand
138 F3 Moanba, L S Australia
86 B6 Moanda Gabon
86 B7 Moanda Zaïre
103 K5 Moapa Nevada
71 N8 Moapora isld Indonesia
14 D3 Moate Irish Rep
88 D10 Moatize Mozambique
145 E3 Moawhango New Zealand
87 E7 Moba Zaïre
61 O10 Mobara Japan
77 B3 Mobārakeh Iran
86 D5 Mobaye Cent Afr Republic
86 D5 Mobayi Zaïre
138 C4 Mobella S Australia
110 D2 Moberly Missouri
117 N8 Moberly Lake Br Col
120 E4 Mobert Ontario
111 H11 Mobile Alabama
103 M8 Mobile Arizona
111 J11 Mobile Pt Alabama
141 G7 Moble R Queensland
71 F4 Mobo Philippines
28 A4 Møborg Denmark
98 F4 Mobridge S Dakota
Mobutu, L see Albert, L
127 J5 Moca Dom Rep
129 J4 Mocajuba Brazil
Moçambique see Mozambique
88 H9 Moçambique dist Mozambique
87 B9 Moçâmedes Angola
95 L5 Mocanaqua Pennsylvania
103 M5 Moccasin Arizona
101 Q2 Moccasin Montana
68 G2 Moc Chau Vietnam
125 Q7 Mocche Mexico
Mocha see Mukha, Al
131 A7 Mocha isld Chile
124 E5 Mochicahui Mexico
127 K2 Mocho Mts Jamaica
89 E5 Mochudi Botswana
88 H7 Mocímboa da Praia Mozambique
48 H4 Mociu Romania
27 G15 Möckeln L Sweden
33 P8 Möckern E Germany
95 M9 Mockhorn isld Virginia
27 J15 Möckleby, N Sweden
27 H15 Möckleby, S Sweden
36 G5 Mockmühl W Germany
33 R9 Mockrehna E Germany
112 G2 Mocksville N Carolina
100 A2 Moclips Washington
128 C3 Mocoa Colombia
130 F7 Mococa Brazil
131 F3 Mocoretá R Argentina
124 F5 Mocorito Mexico
124 F2 Moctezuma Chihuahua Mexico
124 E3 Moctezuma Sonora Mexico
88 F10 Mocuba Mozambique
40 E7 Modane France
83 K9 Modaragam Aru R Sri Lanka
74 E7 Modasa India
22 J3 Modave Belgium
8 C7 Modbury England
89 D7 Modder R S Africa
106 F4 Model Colorado
45 J2 Modena Italy
103 L4 Modena Utah
45 J3 Modena prov Italy
19 L4 Moder R France
38 K7 Moderbrugg Austria
102 C4 Modesto California
43 F12 Modica Sicily
45 L3 Modigliana Italy
80 C6 Modi'im Israel
86 D5 Modjamboli Zaïre
70 O9 Modjokerto Java
94 B6 Modoc Indiana
107 J3 Modoc Kansas
112 E4 Modoc S Carolina
100 D7 Modoc Point Oregon
36 B2 Mödrath W Germany
48 E6 Modriča Yugoslavia
48 E2 Modrý Kameň Czechoslovakia
139 H7 Moe Victoria
8 B1 Moelfre Môn Wales
8 C2 Moel Sych mt Wales
27 E11 Moelv Norway
129 H2 Moengo Suriname
103 N5 Moenkopi Arizona
144 B5 Moeraki, L New Zealand
22 F1 Moerbeke Belgium
25 C5 Moerdijk Netherlands
22 D1 Moere Belgium
145 E1 Moerewa New Zealand
145 E3 Moeroa New Zealand
Moero, Lac see Mweru, L
106 E3 Moffat Colorado
13 E3 Moffat Scotland
144 B6 Moffat Pk New Zealand
106 E2 Moffat Tunnel Colorado
98 F3 Moffit N Dakota
74 F3 Moga India
Mogadiscio see Mogadishu
72 F8 Mogadishu Somalia
94 F5 Mogadore Ohio
16 C3 Mogadouro Portugal
89 F4 Mogalakwena R S Africa
61 N7 Mogami-gawa R Japan
67 F1 Mogan Shan mt China
75 R6 Mogaung Burma
28 B7 Møgeltønder Denmark
17 G6 Mogente Spain
36 H6 Mögglingen W Germany
60 C13 Mogi Japan
129 J8 Mogi das Cruzes Brazil
31 M4 Mogielnica Poland
130 F7 Mogi Guaçu R Brazil
54 H9 Mogila-Bel'mak Gora mt U.S.S.R.
54 B3 Mogilev U.S.S.R.
48 L2 Mogilev Podolskiy U.S.S.R.
139 J3 Mogil-Mogil New S Wales
31 K3 Mogilno Poland
130 F8 Mogi Mirim Brazil
88 H9 Mogincual Mozambique
45 J2 Móglia Italy
42 E3 Mogliano Italy
45 M1 Mogliano Veneto Italy
46 D4 Moglicë Albania
19 N12 Mogneneins France
59 G1 Mogocha U.S.S.R.
68 C1 Mogok Burma
89 E4 Mogol R S Africa
106 B8 Mogollon New Mexico
106 B8 Mogollon Mts New Mexico
103 O7 Mogollon Rim tableland Arizona
106 D4 Mogote Colorado
58 C2 Mogoyn Mongolia
16 C7 Moguer Spain
143 B9 Mogumber W Australia
48 E5 Mohács Hungary
145 F3 Mohaka New Zealand
98 E1 Mohall N Dakota
17 H9 Mohammadia Algeria
85 C2 Mohammedia Morocco
103 K6 Mohave, L Nev/Ariz
103 K7 Mohave Mts Cal/Ariz
103 L9 Mohawk Arizona
99 S2 Mohawk Michigan
95 N4 Mohawk R New York
103 L9 Mohawk Mts Arizona
27 G14 Moheda Sweden
87 G10 Mohéli isld Comoros
87 D9 Mohembo Botswana
74 C5 Mohenjo Daro anc site Pakistan
14 B4 Moher, Cliffs of Irish Rep
116 D6 Mohican, C Alaska
14 D3 Mohill Irish Rep
100 J3 Mohler Idaho
32 H10 Möhne R W Germany
32 H10 Möhnesee W Germany
32 H10 Möhnestausee L W Germany
27 G13 Moholm Sweden
103 L7 Mohon Pk Arizona
70 O10 Mohoreru, G mt Java
88 G6 Mohoro Tanzania
124 H4 Mohovano Ranch Mexico
37 J2 Möhra E Germany
36 G6 Möhringen W Germany
28 D7 Mohrkirch W Germany
27 B13 Moi Norway
16 B4 Moimenta da Beira Portugal
66 C5 Moincêr China
57 G2 Mointy U.S.S.R.
95 N2 Moira New York
26 G5 Mo i Rana Norway
19 P14 Moirans France
47 G9 Moíres Crete Greece
52 C5 Mõisaküla U.S.S.R.
21 C6 Moisdon France
55 G2 Moiseyevka U.S.S.R.
122 F3 Moisie Quebec
19 Q17 Moissac France
86 C4 Moissala Chad
20 J3 Moisson France
21 H6 Moisy France
27 K12 Möja Sweden
17 F7 Mojácar Spain
102 F6 Mojave California
102 G7 Mojave R California
102 G6 Mojave Desert California
60 E12 Moji Japan
130 F8 Moji das Cruzes Brazil
120 B2 Mojikit L Ontario
86 G4 Mojjo Ethiopia
86 F5 Mojo Uganda
71 H9 Mojo isld Indonesia
128 E7 Mojos, Llanos de plain Bolivia
129 J4 Moju R Brazil
61 O9 Mōka Japan
145 E3 Mokai New Zealand
75 L6 Mokameh India
110 E3 Mokane Missouri
102 S12 Mokapu Pen Hawaiian Is
145 E3 Mokau New Zealand
102 D3 Mokelumne R California
89 F7 Mokhotlong mt Lesotho
55 F3 Mokhovoy Prival U.S.S.R.
27 J11 Möklinta Sweden
85 G1 Moknine Tunisia
145 E1 Mokohinau Is New Zealand
145 E3 Mokoia New Zealand
75 Q5 Mokokchung India
86 B3 Mokolo Cameroon
144 B7 Mokoreta New Zealand
144 B7 Mokotua New Zealand
65 G7 Mokp'o S Korea
46 D2 Mokra Pl mt Yugoslavia
48 F5 Mokrin Yugoslavia
55 E3 Mokrousovo U.S.S.R.
29 L8 Möksy Finland
102 S11 Mokuauia I Hawaiian Is
135 U5 Mokuaweoweo Crater Hawaiian Is
102 R11 Mokuleia Hawaiian Is
102 S12 Mokulua Is Hawaiian Is
22 J1 Mol Belgium
100 C4 Molalla Oregon
125 K7 Molango Mexico
46 F8 Moláoi Greece
42 F4 Molat isld Yugoslavia
20 D3 Molay, la France
32 G7 Molbergen W Germany
28 B5 Mølby Denmark
8 C1 Mold Wales
48 G2 Moldava nad Bodvon Czechoslovakia
48 K4 Moldavia reg Romania
26 B9 Molde Norway
48 K3 Moidova R Romania
48 J5 Moldoveanu mt Romania
48 K3 Moldoviţa Romania
28 D3 Møldrup Denmark
40 D5 Môle mt France
89 D5 Molepolole Botswana
8 C6 Mole, R England
9 F5 Mole, R England
144 D5 Molesworth New Zealand
43 H7 Molfetta Italy
133 C5 Molina Chile
17 F4 Molina de Aragón Spain
17 G6 Molina de Segura Spain
99 Q8 Moline Illinois
107 O4 Moline Kansas
94 B4 Moline Michigan
45 L2 Molinella Italy
38 E8 Molini Italy
111 J11 Molino Florida
124 D3 Molino Mexico
42 F7 Molise prov Italy
47 K4 Mollafeneri Turkey
40 D2 Mollans France
28 K4 Mölle Sweden
28 C5 Møllebjerg hill Denmark
33 S6 Möllenbeck E Germany
128 D7 Mollendo Peru
33 R5 Möllenhagen E Germany
143 C9 Mollerin, L W Australia
28 D4 Mollerup Denmark
17 H3 Mollerusa Spain
26 O2 Mollesjok Norway
20 K2 Molliens-Dreuil France
12 D2 Mollinsburn Scotland
26 M2 Mollius mt Norway
33 S5 Mölln E Germany
33 N5 Mölln W Germany
38 G8 Molltal V Austria
27 F14 Mölndal Sweden
54 G9 Molochansk U.S.S.R.
88 G10 Molocue R Mozambique
55 F4 Molodogvardeyskaya U.S.S.R.
52 D6 Molodoy-Tud U.S.S.R.
52 E5 Mologa R U.S.S.R.
102 V13 Molokai isld Hawaiian Is
135 S3 Molokini isld Hawaiian Is
52 E5 Molokovo U.S.S.R.
52 G5 Moloma R U.S.S.R.
139 J5 Molong New S Wales
89 B6 Molopo R S Africa
46 F6 Mólos Greece
86 C5 Moloundou Cameroon
28 F4 Mols B hill Denmark
36 D6 Molsheim France
118 E1 Molson Manitoba
119 V4 Molson L Manitoba
101 R4 Molt Montana
87 E12 Molteno S Africa
Moluccas see Malaku
88 G10 Moma Mozambique
86 D6 Moma Zaïre
51 O2 Moma R U.S.S.R.
139 G4 Momba New S Wales
88 D6 Momba R Tanzania
45 N4 Mombaroccio Italy
88 G4 Mombasa Kenya
60 Q3 Mombetsu Japan
60 R1 Mombetsu Japan
130 D6 Mombuca, Serra da mts Brazil
47 G3 Momchilgrad Bulgaria
99 T8 Momence Illinois
22 G3 Momignies Belgium
36 D6 Mommenheim France
71 F4 Mompog Passage Philippines
86 D5 Mompono Zaïre
126 G10 Mompós Colombia
68 C3 Mon Burma
28 K7 Møn isld Denmark
8 B1 Môn isld Wales
68 B2 Mon R Burma
127 L2 Mona Jamaica
103 N2 Mona Utah
94 G6 Monaca Pennsylvania
15 A3 Monach I Outer Hebrides Scotland
44 B4 Monaco princ
15 D3 Monadhliath Mts Scotland
29 J8 Monå Fjärd inlet Finland
128 F2 Monagas state Venezuela
14 E2 Monaghan Irish Rep
14 E2 Monaghan co Irish Rep
108 E4 Monahans Texas
127 L5 Mona, I Dom Rep
98 H3 Monango N Dakota
87 C7 Mona Quimbundo Angola
118 D9 Monarch Alberta
106 D3 Monarch Colorado
101 P2 Monarch Montana
117 L10 Monarch Mt Br Columbia
103 N2 Mona Res Utah
117 O10 Monashee Mts Br Col
14 D3 Monasterevin Irish Rep
18 H8 Monastier, le France
43 D13 Monastir Tunisia
48 J1 Monastyriska U.S.S.R.
55 D2 Monastyrskoye U.S.S.R.
44 C2 Moncalieri Italy
16 B2 Monção Portugal
17 F3 Moncayo, Sierra del Spain
22 F4 Monceau-le-Neuf France
38 L5 Mönchdorf Austria
52 D1 Monchegorsk U.S.S.R.
36 B1 Mönchengladbach W Germany
30 H1 Mönchgut pen E Germany
16 B7 Monchique Portugal
112 G4 Moncks Corner S Carolina
124 J4 Monclova Mexico
21 E8 Moncontour France
122 B5 Moncouche, L Quebec
122 H7 Moncton New Brunswick
130 D10 Mondai Brazil
99 L8 Mondamin Iowa
45 N4 Mondavio Italy
130 C9 Monday, R Paraguay
16 B4 Mondego R Portugal
16 B4 Mondego, C Portugal
16 E4 Mondéjar Spain
70 G6 Mondeodo Sulawesi
20 E3 Mondeville France
89 G3 Mondi R Zimbabwe
86 C3 Mondo Chad
45 O4 Mondolfo Italy
16 C1 Mondoñedo Spain
22 L4 Mondorf-les-Bains Luxembourg
20 G6 Mondoubleau France
44 C3 Mondovi Italy
99 P5 Mondovi Wisconsin
19 N16 Mondragon France
45 P7 Mondragone Italy
143 E10 Mondrain I W Australia
41 P3 Mondschein Spitze mt Austria
38 H6 Mondsee Austria
127 K2 Moneague Jamaica
44 F3 Moneglia Italy
18 E9 Monein France
46 F8 Monemvasía Greece
94 H9 Moneta Virginia
101 S6 Moneta Wyoming
110 C5 Monett Missouri
110 F6 Monette Arkansas
42 F3 Monfalcone Italy
68 D3 Mon Fang Thailand
44 C2 Monferrato dist Italy
86 D5 Monga Zaïre
95 N5 Mongaup Vall New York
68 H2 Mong Cai Vietnam
142 A1 Monger L Perth, W Aust
143 B8 Monger, L W Australia
68 D2 Mong Hai Burma
68 D2 Mong Hang Burma
45 K3 Monghidoro Italy
68 E2 Mong Hkan Burma
68 D2 Mong Hkok Burma
68 D2 Mong Hpayak Burma
68 D2 Mong Hsat Burma
68 C2 Mong Hsawk Burma
68 D2 Mong Hsu Burma
75 M6 Monghyr India
44 C3 Mongioie mt Italy
68 F6 Mongkol Borey Cambodia
68 D3 Mong Kyawt Burma
68 D2 Mong La Burma
68 C2 Mong Lang Burma
68 E2 Mong Lin Burma
68 E2 Mong Loi Burma
68 C1 Mong Long Burma
68 C3 Mong Mau Burma
68 C2 Mong Nai Burma
68 D2 Mong Nawng Burma
94 B5 Mongo Indiana
17 H6 Mongo mt Spain
58 C2 Mongolia People's Rep Asia
85 G8 Mongomo Mbini Eq Guinea
86 B3 Mongonu Nigeria
68 C3 Mong Pai Burma
68 D2 Mong Pan Burma
68 D1 Mong Pat Burma
68 D1 Mong Pawk Burma
68 C2 Mong Pawn Burma
68 D2 Mong Ping Burma
68 D2 Mong Pu Burma
68 D2 Mong Pu-awn Burma
124 H9 Mongrove, Pta C Mexico
68 D2 Mong Ton Burma
68 D2 Mong Tum Burma
68 C1 Mong Tung Burma
87 D9 Mongu Zambia
38 F8 Monguelfo Italy
68 E2 Mong Un Burma
68 D1 Mong Yai Burma
68 D2 Mong Yang Burma
68 D2 Mong Yawn Burma
68 E2 Mong Yawng Burma
95 S3 Monhegan I Maine
37 K6 Monheim Bayern W Germany
36 B1 Monheim Nordrhein-Westfalen W Germany
113 E7 Moniac Georgia
12 E3 Moniaive Scotland
19 O16 Monieux France
13 F1 Monifieth Scotland
18 H7 Monistrol-sur-Loire France
118 G7 Monitor Alberta
102 H3 Monitor peak Nevada
14 C3 Monivea Irish Rep
28 B7 Mönkebüll W Germany
140 F6 Monkira Queensland
86 D6 Monkoto Zaire
120 J9 Monkton Ontario
12 D3 Monkton Scotland
99 Q9 Monmouth Illinois
95 R2 Monmouth Maine
8 D4 Monmouth Wales
Monmouth co see Gwent
117 M10 Monmouth, Mt Br Col
20 F4 Monnai France
21 G7 Monnaie France
24 E1 Monnickendam Netherlands
85 E7 Mono R Togo
102 F3 Mono L California
47 J8 Monólithos Rhodes Greece
95 S5 Monomoy Pt Massachusetts
99 U9 Monon Indiana
99 P6 Monona Iowa
94 G7 Monongah W Virginia
94 H6 Monongahela Pennsylvania
43 H8 Monopoli Italy
48 E3 Monor Hungary
127 N1 Monos I Trinidad
86 D2 Monou Chad
17 G6 Monóvar Spain
144 A6 Monowai New Zealand
98 H7 Monowi Nebraska
18 F8 Monpont France
36 C3 Monreal W Germany
17 G4 Monreal del Campo Spain
43 E10 Monreale Sicily
102 A2 Monroe California
112 D4 Monroe Georgia
94 C6 Monroe Indiana
99 N8 Monroe Iowa
111 D9 Monroe Louisiana
94 D5 Monroe Michigan
112 G3 Monroe N Carolina
95 N5 Monroe New York
100 B5 Monroe Oregon
95 L5 Monroe Pennsylvania
98 J6 Monroe S Dakota
103 M3 Monroe Utah
94 H9 Monroe Virginia
100 D2 Monroe Washington
99 R7 Monroe Wisconsin
99 P10 Monroe City Missouri
113 F9 Monroe, L Florida
110 K2 Monroe Res Indiana
111 J10 Monroeville Alabama
94 C6 Monroeville Indiana
94 E5 Monroeville Ohio
102 G7 Monrovia California
85 B7 Monrovia Liberia
17 G4 Monroyo Spain
22 F3 Mons Belgium
16 C4 Monsanto Portugal
130 H6 Monsarás, Pta. de Brazil
22 L2 Monschau W Germany
71 H7 Monse Indonesia
42 D3 Monselice Italy
36 E4 Monsheim W Germany
95 P4 Monson Massachusetts
28 C4 Mønsted Denmark
25 B4 Monster Netherlands
27 H14 Mönsterås Sweden
45 J4 Monsummano Italy
22 K3 Mont Belgium
36 D3 Montabaur W Germany
41 L3 Montafon V Austria
45 K1 Montagnana Italy
89 B9 Montagu S Africa
100 C8 Montague California
94 A3 Montague Michigan
122 K7 Montague Pr Edward I
109 K2 Montague Texas
116 O6 Montague I Alaska
103 K10 Montague, I Mexico
139 K6 Montague I New S Wales
143 C7 Montague Ra W Australia
142 F2 Montague Sd W Australia
116 N7 Montague Str Alaska
146 A13 Montagu I Antarctica
21 C8 Montaigu France
18 F8 Montaigu-de-Quercy France
40 D7 Montaimont France
45 J4 Montaione Italy
70 D5 Montalat R Kalimantan
17 G4 Montalbán Spain
127 K9 Montalbán Venezuela
45 K4 Montale Italy
16 B3 Montalegre Portugal
40 B6 Montalieu France
19 O13 Montalieu Vercieu France
43 G10 Montalto mt Italy
21 F8 Montamise France
116 N5 Montana Alaska
101 P3 Montana state U.S.A.
40 G7 Montanaro Italy
16 C5 Montánchez Spain
121 T5 Mont-Apica Quebec
18 G5 Montargis France
38 H9 Montasio mt Italy
20 K3 Montataire France
18 F9 Montauban France
20 A5 Montauban-de-Bretagne France
20 D5 Montaudin France
18 H5 Montbard France
40 C3 Montbarrey France
21 G7 Montbazon France
40 E2 Montbéliard France
109 N6 Mont Belvieu Texas
40 D4 Montbenoit France
21 C7 Montbert France
40 E6 Mont Blanc mt France
17 H3 Montblanch Spain
40 D3 Montbozon France
20 C4 Montbray France
18 H7 Montbrison France
Montcalm, L see Dogai Coring
18 F10 Montcalm, Pic mt France
20 D4 Montchamp France
22 G4 Montcornet France
18 E9 Mont de Marsan France
22 D4 Montdidier France
43 G9 Montea mt Italy
110 L6 Monteagle Tennessee
129 H4 Monte Alegre Brazil
17 G6 Montealegre del Castillo Spain
130 E6 Monte Alegre de Minas Brazil
130 G4 Monte Azul Brazil
121 Q7 Montebello Quebec
142 B5 Monte Bello Is W Australia
45 K1 Montebello Vic Italy
42 E3 Montebelluna Italy
20 C3 Montebourg France
45 N4 Montecalvo in Foglia Italy
45 S7 Montecalvo Irpino Italy
133 G3 Montecarlo Argentina
44 B4 Monte-Carlo Monaco
129 J7 Monte Carmelo Brazil
45 O4 Montecarotto Italy
131 F3 Monte Caseros Argentina
45 J4 Montecatini Terme Italy
45 K1 Montecchio Maggiore Italy
45 H2 Montecchio nell'Emilia Italy
45 N5 Montecélio Italy
18 F9 Montech France
112 H3 Monte Clare S Carolina
45 R8 Montecorvino Rovella Italy
45 J3 Montecreto Italy
127 J5 Montecristi Dom Rep
128 F6 Monte Cristo Bolivia
42 C6 Montecristo isld Italy
41 O4 Montecroce, Pta di mt Italy
124 H6 Monte Escobedo Mexico
45 M4 Montefeltro Italy
45 J3 Montefiorino Italy
45 R8 Monteforte Irpina Italy
16 E7 Montefrio Spain
127 J1 Montego Bay Jamaica
45 M4 Monte Grimano Italy
130 H9 Monteiro Brazil
140 B3 Montejinnie N Terr Aust
45 O6 Montelanico Italy
131 E6 Monte, L.del Argentina
19 N15 Montélimar France
129 G8 Monte Lindo Paraguay
108 G6 Montell Texas
45 S8 Montella Italy
16 D8 Montellanto Spain
101 L8 Montello Nevada
99 R6 Montello Wisconsin
45 K4 Montelupo Fiorentino Italy
45 R8 Montemárano Italy
45 O4 Montemarciano Italy
133 D6 Montemayor, Meseta de hills Argentina
21 G10 Montemboeuf France
45 L4 Montemignaio Italy
45 R7 Montemiletto Italy
125 K5 Montemorelos Mexico
45 K4 Montemurio Italy
20 D5 Montenay France
18 E7 Montendre France
46 C2 Montenegro hist reg Yugoslavia
42 D6 Montepescali Italy
127 K5 Monte Plata Dom Rep
45 O4 Monteporzio Italy
88 G8 Montepuez Mozambique
42 D5 Montepulciano Italy
18 G4 Montereau France
45 K3 Monterenzio Italy
102 C5 Monterey California
99 U8 Monterey Indiana
110 L5 Monterey Tennessee
94 H8 Monterey Virginia
102 B5 Monterey B California
126 G10 Montería Colombia
128 F7 Montero Bolivia
20 H2 Montérolier France
45 M5 Monterosi Italy
44 M5 Monterosi, L Italy
45 N5 Monterotondo Italy
125 J5 Monterrey Mexico
42 G7 Monte S. Angelo Italy
100 B3 Montesano Washington
130 G11 Monte Santo Brazil
130 F7 Monte Santo de Minas Brazil
45 R7 Montesarchio Italy
45 O7 Monte S. Biágio Italy
129 K7 Montes Claros Brazil
45 J3 Montese Italy
45 O4 Montesicuro Italy
45 K4 Montespértoli Italy
18 F9 Montesquieu-Volvestre France
18 H6 Montet, le France
111 K8 Montevallo Alabama
42 D5 Montevarchi Italy
45 K3 Monteveglio Italy
45 O5 Monte Velino Italy
99 L5 Montevideo Minnesota
131 G5 Montevideo Uruguay
101 N6 Monteview Idaho
106 D4 Monte Vista Colorado
103 L8 Montezuma Arizona
112 C5 Montezuma Georgia
99 T10 Montezuma Indiana
99 O8 Montezuma Iowa
107 K4 Montezuma Kansas
103 N7 Montezuma Castle Nat.Mon Arizona
102 G4 Montezuma Pk Nevada
20 C2 Montfarville France
21 C7 Montfaucon Maine-et-Loire France
22 J5 Montfaucon Meuse France
19 P14 Montferrat France
20 J4 Montfort l'Amaury France
20 F5 Montfort-le-Rotrou France
20 B5 Montfort-sur-Meu France
20 G3 Montfort-sur-Risle France
19 N17 Montfrin France
111 K9 Montgomery Alabama
111 D10 Montgomery Louisiana
94 C5 Montgomery Michigan
99 N5 Montgomery Minnesota
109 M5 Montgomery Texas
8 C2 Montgomery Wales
94 F8 Montgomery W Virginia
Montgomery co see Powys
110 E3 Montgomery City Missouri
100 D9 Montgomery Creek California
142 E3 Montgomery I W Australia
18 E7 Montguyon France
22 H4 Monthermé France
40 E5 Monthey Switzerland
22 H5 Monthois France
40 C1 Monthureux-sur-Saône France
43 C8 Monti Sardinia
111 E8 Monticello Arkansas
113 D7 Monticello Florida
112 D4 Monticello Georgia
110 H1 Monticello Illinois
110 K1 Monticello Indiana
99 P7 Monticello Iowa
110 M5 Monticello Kentucky
95 T7 Monticello Maine
99 N4 Monticello Minnesota
111 F10 Monticello Mississippi
110 E1 Monticello Missouri
106 C8 Monticello New Mexico
95 N5 Monticello New York
103 P4 Monticello Utah
99 R7 Monticello Wisconsin
45 J1 Montichiari Italy
43 C8 Monti del Gennargentu Sardinia
131 F3 Montiel, Cuchilla de mts Argentina
19 J4 Montier en Der France
22 D5 Montiers France
18 F7 Montignac France
20 C4 Montigny Manche France
36 B6 Montigny Meurthe-et-Moselle France
40 B2 Montigny-le-Roi France
16 B6 Montijo Portugal
16 C6 Montijo Spain
125 O6 Montijo, G.de Panama
16 D7 Montilla Spain
45 N5 Monti Sabini Italy
130 D5 Montividiu Brazil
20 F2 Montivilliers France
21 D7 Montjean France
70 F7 Montjobalang Sulawesi
20 C4 Montjoie France
115 N8 Mont-Joli Quebec
70 F7 Montjonglowe Sulawesi
138 F2 Montkeleary R S Australia
20 H5 Montlandon France
115 M8 Mont-Laurier Quebec
40 E3 Montlebon France
20 K4 Montlhéry France
18 E7 Montlieu France
18 G10 Mont Louis France
122 G4 Mont Louis Quebec
18 G6 Montluçon France
19 O13 Montluel France
122 B7 Montmagny Quebec
20 B4 Montmartin-sur-Mer France
119 O8 Montmartre Sask
22 J4 Montmédy France
19 Q14 Montmélian France
40 A5 Montmerle France
19 Q17 Montmeyan France
19 N15 Montmeyran France
18 H4 Montmirail Marne France
20 G5 Montmirail Sarthe France
18 F7 Montmoreau France
20 K4 Montmorency France
121 T6 Montmorency Quebec
122 A6 Montmorency, R Quebec
21 G9 Montmorillon France
19 P16 Montmorin France
141 K6 Monto Queensland
21 A7 Montoir de Bretagne France
21 G6 Montoire-sur-Loir France
45 M3 Montone R Italy
16 E6 Montoro Spain
99 O8 Montour Iowa
95 L4 Montour Falls New York
95 L5 Montoursville Pennsylvania
106 F6 Montoya New Mexico
101 O7 Montpelier Idaho
110 L1 Montpelier Indiana
127 J2 Montpelier Jamaica
98 H3 Montpelier N Dakota
94 C5 Montpelier Ohio
95 P2 Montpelier Vermont
18 H9 Montpellier France
121 P7 Montpellier Quebec
40 B4 Montpont France
18 G9 Montréal France
121 R7 Montréal Quebec
99 Q3 Montreal Wisconsin
120 K5 Montreal R Ontario
120 F5 Montreal I Ontario
119 M4 Montreal Lake Sask
119 M4 Montreal R Sask
120 F5 Montreal River Ontario
18 G9 Montredon Labessonié France
18 F9 Montrejeau France
21 H7 Montrésor France
22 B3 Montreuil France
21 E7 Montreuil-Bellay France
20 E5 Montreuil-le-Chetif France
20 B5 Montreuil-sur-Ille France
40 E5 Montreux Switzerland
21 C7 Montrevault France
21 H7 Montrichard France
111 E8 Montrose Arkansas
106 C3 Montrose Colorado
110 H2 Montrose Illinois
99 P9 Montrose Iowa
98 C7 Montrose Nebraska
95 L5 Montrose Pennsylvania
15 F4 Montrose Scotland
98 J6 Montrose S Dakota
95 L8 Montross Virginia
22 G3 Mont. St.Christophe Belgium
22 G2 Mont-St.Jean Belgium
22 K4 Mont St.Martin France
20 B4 Mont St.Michel, B.du France
20 B4 Mont St. Michel, le France
20 D4 Montsecret France
17 H2 Montseny mt Spain
17 J3 Montseny, Sierra de mts Spain
17 J3 Montserrat dist Spain
127 N6 Montserrat isld Lesser Antilles
129 H3 Montsinery Fr Guiana
21 F7 Montsoreau France
20 K3 Montsoult France
115 N8 Monts, Pointe des Quebec
21 F8 Monts-sur-Guesnes France
22 H2 Mont.St.Guibert Belgium
20 D5 Montsûrs France
121 Q6 Mont Tremblant Quebec
20 F4 Montviette France
95 P5 Montville Connecticut
106 F2 Monument Colorado
107 J2 Monument Kansas
108 D3 Monument New Mexico
100 F5 Monument Oregon
116 F4 Monument Mt Alaska
103 O4 Monument V Utah/Ariz
86 D5 Monveda Zaïre
20 H2 Monville France
68 B1 Monywa Burma
41 K6 Monza Italy
87 E9 Monze Zambia
17 H3 Monzón Spain
45 K3 Monzuno Italy
109 K4 Moody Texas
95 O2 Mooers New York
138 B2 Moolalpinna Hill S Australia
138 E3 Moolawatana S Australia
138 E2 Moolionburrinna, L S Australia
140 B3 Moolooloo N Terr Aust
139 J3 Moomin R New S Wales
138 D4 Moonaree S Australia
120 H3 Moonbeam Ontario
140 F7 Moonda L Queensland
141 K8 Moonie Queensland
141 J8 Moonie R Queensland
103 O1 Moon L.Res Utah
139 K4 Moonoi Ra mts New S Wales
138 D5 Moonta S Australia
143 B9 Moora W Australia
140 F7 Mooraberree Queensland
98 B5 Moorcroft Wyoming
101 M6 Moore Idaho
101 Q3 Moore Montana
107 N6 Moore Oklahoma
109 H6 Moore Texas
134 A11 Moorea isld Society Is Pacific Oc
146 H7 Moore B Antarctica
116 J5 Moore Creek Alaska
98 F9 Moorefield Nebraska
94 J7 Moorefield W Virginia
113 F11 Moore Haven Florida
143 C8 Moore, L W Australia
108 E7 Mooreland Oklahoma
140 D2 Moore, Mt N Terr Aust
143 C9 Moore, Mt W Australia
143 E7 Moore, Mt W Australia
143 G7 Moore, Mt W Australia
95 Q2 Moore Res Vermont
112 J3 Moores Cr. Nat. Mil. Park N Carolina
122 E8 Moore's Mills New Brunswick
110 K2 Mooresville Indiana
112 G2 Mooresville N Carolina
98 J3 Mooreton N Dakota
127 M2 Moore Town Jamaica
13 E2 Moorfoot Hills Scotland
98 K3 Moorhead Minnesota
111 F8 Moorhead Mississippi
101 U4 Moorhead Montana
109 O3 Mooringsport Louisiana
121 N6 Moor Lake Ontario
99 M7 Moorland Iowa
110 J4 Moorman Kentucky
138 C4 Moornaba Rock S Australia
139 G5 Moornanyah L New S Wales
87 F7 Moorokosa Zambia
141 K2 Moorooka dist Brisbane, Qnsld
140 D1 Mooroongga I N Terr Aust
139 H6 Mooroopna Victoria
102 F7 Moorpark California
22 G2 Moorsel Belgium
22 E2 Moorslede Belgium
89 F5 Moos R S Africa
37 N4 Moosbach W Germany
32 L9 Moosberg mt W Germany
37 M7 Moosburg W Germany
101 P6 Moose Wyoming
115 L7 Moose R Ontario
120 K1 Moose Factory Ontario
95 S1 Moosehead L Maine
119 O2 Moose Hill Ontario
119 T7 Moosehorn Manitoba
119 U7 Moose I Manitoba
119 M8 Moose Jaw Sask
119 N8 Moosejaw Cr Sask
99 O3 Moose L Minnesota
119 R5 Moose Lake Manitoba
95 R2 Mooselookmeguntic L Maine
119 P9 Moose Mt. Prov. Park Sask
119 W2 Moose Nose L Manitoba
116 N6 Moose Pass Alaska
120 J2 Moose River Ontario
37 N6 Moosham W Germany
38 M8 Mooskirchen Austria
119 Q8 Moosomin Sask
120 K1 Moosonee Ontario
95 Q5 Moosup Connecticut
89 G7 Moot R S Africa
138 F4 Mootwingee New S Wales
87 G9 Mopeia Mozambique
85 D6 Mopti Mali
99 P3 Moquah Wisconsin
128 D7 Moquegua Peru
128 D7 Moquegua dep Peru
48 E3 Mór Hungary
86 B3 Mora Cameroon
100 J6 Mora Idaho
99 N4 Mora Minnesota
106 E6 Mora New Mexico
16 B6 Mora Portugal
16 E5 Mora Spain
27 G10 Mora Sweden
141 J7 Moraby Queensland
46 C2 Morača R Yugoslavia
131 B5 Mora, Cerro peak Arg/Chile
74 H4 Moradabad India
16 B5 Moradal, Sa. do mts Portugal
130 F6 Morada Nova de Minas Brazil
17 H3 Mora de Ebro Spain
17 G4 Mora de Rubielos Spain
87 G11 Morafenobe Madagascar
31 M2 Morąg Poland
83 K11 Moragala Sri Lanka
133 C6 Moraleda, Canal str Chile
109 L6 Morales Texas
87 H11 Moramanga Madagascar
110 A4 Moran Kansas
109 H3 Moran Texas

Mulyah,Mt — Narvik 53

139 G4 Mulyah,Mt New S Wales
55 D1 Mulym'ya U.S.S.R.
55 E1 Mulym'ya R U.S.S.R.
138 F4 Mulyungarie S Australia
8 C4 Mumbles Wales
87 B8 Mumbondo Angola
87 C8 Mumbué Angola
87 E8 Mumbwa Zambia
87 E8 Mumena Zaïre
109 L5 Mumford Texas
69 D9 Mum Nauk,Laem C Thailand
125 P7 Muna Mexico
71 H7 Muna isld Indonesia
67 B5 Munankwan Lin pass Vietnam/China
143 B8 Munbinia W Australia
141 G2 Munburra Queensland
37 M3 Münchberg W Germany
30 H3 Müncheberg E Germany
39 München conurbation W Germany
37 M2 Münchenbernsdorf E Germany
36 F2 Münchhausen W Germany
117 L6 Muncho Lake Br Col
37 N5 Münchshofen W Germany
37 O6 Münchshofen W Germany
37 M6 Münchsmünster W Germany
110 L1 Muncie Indiana
140 E7 Muncoonie, L Queensland
95 L5 Muncy Pennsylvania
118 E5 Mundare Alberta
109 H2 Munday Texas
99 S7 Mundelein Illinois
83 J10 Mundel L Sri Lanka
98 J10 Munden Kansas
32 L10 Münden W Germany
36 H7 Munderkingen W Germany
9 H2 Mundesley England
9 G2 Mundford England
143 D6 Mundiwindi W Australia
141 F4 Mundjuro R Queensland
17 F6 Mundo R Spain
129 K6 Mundo Nôvo Brazil
143 G9 Mundrabilla W Australia
141 K7 Mundubbera Queensland
56 C4 Mundybash U.S.S.R.
46 D3 Munella mt Albania
17 F5 Munera Spain
110 L4 Munfordville Kentucky
141 J7 Mungallala Queensland
141 H8 Mungallala R Queensland
141 G3 Mungana Queensland
141 L7 Mungar Queensland
87 F9 Mungari Mozambique
142 C5 Mungaroona Ra W Australia
56 D5 Mungash-Kul', Gora mt U.S.S.R.
86 E5 Mungbere Zaïre
75 J7 Mungeli India
94 D3 Munger Michigan
138 E3 Mungerannie S Australia
141 J8 Mungindi Queensland
87 C8 Munhango Angola
98 H1 Munich N Dakota
Munich W Germany see München
88 B8 Muniengashi R Zaïre
17 G3 Muniesa Spain
130 H7 Muniz Freire Brazil
28 H5 Munke Bjergby Denmark
28 F6 Munkebo Denmark
27 E13 Munkedal Sweden
26 G8 Munkflohögen Sweden
27 G12 Munkfors Sweden
28 A7 Munkmarsch W Germany
26 M6 Munksund Sweden
56 F5 Munku-Sardyk,Gora mt Mongolia/U.S.S.R.
37 J3 Münnerstadt W Germany
22 J4 Muno Belgium
71 E3 Muñoz Luzon Philippines
133 C8 Muñoz Gamero, Pen Chile
139 J8 Munro,Mt Tasmania
36 H7 Münsingen W Germany
118 E7 Munson Alberta
111 K11 Munson Florida
40 F1 Munster France
32 M7 Münster Niedersachsen W Germany
32 G9 Münster Nordrhein-Westfalen W Germany
41 H5 Münster Switzerland
14 B4 Munster prov Irish Rep
36 C3 Münstermaifeld W Germany
143 C9 Muntadgin W Australia
70 F4 Munte Sulawesi
48 H4 Muntelui Mare mt Romania
70 P10 Muntjar Java
36 F3 Münzenberg W Germany
29 O6 Muojärvi L Finland
68 F1 Muong Boum Vietnam
68 F2 Muong Hiem Laos
68 F2 Muong Hun Xieng Hung Laos
68 F3 Muong Khao Laos
68 F2 Muong Khoua Laos
68 G1 Muong Khuong Vietnam
68 E3 Muong Ki Laos
68 G3 Muong Lam Vietnam
68 E3 Muong Liep Laos
68 E2 Muong Luong Nam Tha Laos
68 H7 Muong Man Vietnam
68 F3 Muong May Laos
68 F3 Muong Moc Laos
68 F2 Muong Ngoi Laos
68 F1 Muong Nhie Vietnam
68 H4 Muong Nong Laos
68 E3 Muong Oua Laos
68 E1 Muong ou Neua Laos
68 E1 Muong ou Tay Laos
68 E3 Muong Pa Laos
68 G4 Muong Phalane Laos
68 E3 Muong Phieng Laos
68 E2 Muong Sai Laos
68 E3 Muong Saiapoun Laos
68 G3 Muong Sen Vietnam
68 E2 Muong Sing Laos
68 F2 Muong Son Laos
68 G4 Muong Song Khone Laos
68 F3 Muong Soui Laos
68 F3 Muong Soum Laos
68 F1 Muong Te Vietnam
68 E3 Muong Tha Deua Laos
68 E3 Muong Thong Laos
68 F2 Muong Va Laos
29 K4 Muonio Finland
26 N3 Muonio älv R Sweden/Finland
29 K4 Muoniojoki R Finland
26 N4 Muonionalusta Sweden
71 B2 Muor isld Halmahera Indonesia
41 J4 Muotathal Switzerland
88 B9 Mupata Gorge Zambia
65 E6 Muping China
80 G4 Muqbilla Jordan
130 H7 Muqui Brazil
18 D4 Mûr France
38 J7 Mur R Austria
56 E2 Mura R U.S.S.R.
48 C4 Mura R Yugoslavia
47 J6 Muradiye Turkey
45 L4 Muraglione,Pso.di pass Italy
61 N7 Murakami Japan
48 D4 Murakeresztúr Hungary
133 C7 Murallón mt Chile/Arg
61 N8 Muramatsu Japan
88 F2 Murang'a Kenya
45 M1 Murano Italy
52 G5 Murashi U.S.S.R.
18 G7 Murat France
78 H2 Murat R Turkey
47 K6 Murat Dağı Turkey
47 J3 Muratlı Turkey
78 J2 Murat Suyu R Turkey
38 K7 Murau Austria
77 C7 Mur'ban U.A.E.
16 C3 Murça Portugal
77 B3 Murcheh Khvort Iran
33 T5 Murchin E Germany
145 D4 Murchison New Zealand
139 H6 Murchison Victoria
6 M1 Murchison oil rig North Sea
Murchison Falls Uganda see Kabalega Falls
144 C5 Murchison, Mt New Zealand
145 D4 Murchison, Mt New Zealand
143 B7 Murchison, Mt W Australia
144 A6 Murchison Mts New Zealand
143 A8 Murchison, R W Australia
140 C5 Murchison Ra N Terr Aust
89 G4 Murchison Ra S Africa
88 E9 Murchison Rapids Malawi
17 G7 Murcia Spain
17 F7 Murcia prov Spain
71 F6 Murcielagos B Mindanao Philippines
143 E10 Murdarbilla W Australia
18 G8 Mur-de-Barrez France
21 I7 Mur de-Sologne France
98 F6 Murdo S Dakota
141 G2 Murdoch Pt Queensland
122 G5 Murdochville Quebec
113 E10 Murdock Florida
38 N8 Mureck Austria
47 J4 Mürefte Turkey
61 M9 Murei Japan
48 J4 Muresul R Romania
18 F9 Muret France
111 C7 Murfreesboro Arkansas
95 K10 Murfreesboro N Carolina
110 K6 Murfreesboro Tennessee
36 E6 Murg R W Germany
57 G5 Murgab U.S.S.R.
57 G5 Murgab R U.S.S.R.
46 D5 Murgána mt Greece
47 F2 Murgash mt Bulgaria
140 C1 Murgenella Cr N Terr Aust
48 L4 Murgeni Romania
77 H2 Murghab R Afghanistan
74 C3 Murgha Kibzai Pakistan
48 K4 Murgociu mt Romania
141 K7 Murgon Queensland
143 B7 Murgoo W Australia
75 L7 Muri India
130 G7 Muriaé Brazil
16 C2 Murias de Paredes Spain
87 D7 Muriege Angola
118 G4 Muriel L Alberta
60 R2 Murii-dake mt Japan
119 O2 Murill Ontario
17 G2 Murillo de Gállego Spain
33 R6 Müritz L E Germany
145 F3 Muriwai New Zealand
26 L5 Murjek Sweden
70 N9 Murjo, G mt Java
86 G4 Murle Ethiopia
36 B3 Mürlenbach W Germany
52 D1 Murmansk U.S.S.R.
52 D1 Murmashi U.S.S.R.
54 M2 Murmino U.S.S.R.
41 O2 Murnau W Germany
102 G7 Muroc L California
52 F6 Murom U.S.S.R.
55 G3 Muromtsevo U.S.S.R.
21 D9 Muron France
60 O3 Muroran Japan
16 A2 Muros Spain
60 H12 Muroto Japan
60 N3 Murotsu-shima isld Japan
48 L2 Murovano Kurilovtsy U.S.S.R.
31 K3 Murowana Goslina Poland
60 E12 Murozumi Japan
100 J6 Murphy Idaho
112 C2 Murphy N Carolina
100 B7 Murphy Oregon
146 H11 Murphy,Mt Antarctica
102 D3 Murphys California
110 G4 Murphysboro Illinois
141 H8 Murra Murra Queensland
99 N8 Murray Iowa
110 H5 Murray Kentucky
99 K9 Murray Nebraska
103 N1 Murray Utah
139 G6 Murray R New S Wales
138 E6 Murray Bridge S Australia
94 E7 Murray City Ohio
135 M5 Murray Deep Pacific Oc
140 C5 Murray Downs N Terr Aust
122 K7 Murray Hbr Pr Edward I
123 K8 Murray Hd Pr Edward I
83 M9 Murray Hill peak Christmas I Indian Oc
107 N7 Murray,L Oklahoma
112 F3 Murray, L S Carolina
146 B4 Murray Monolith Antarctica
117 N8 Murray R Br Col
143 B10 Murray, R W Australia
143 G7 Murray Ra W Australia
122 K7 Murray River Pr Edward I
89 C8 Murraysburg S Africa
135 M5 Murray Seascarp Pacific Oc
99 Q10 Murrayville Illinois
138 F6 Murrayville Victoria
112 H4 Murrells Inlet S Carolina
40 G4 Mürren Switzerland
36 H6 Murrhardt W Germany
139 J5 Murringo New S Wales
143 D8 Murrin Murrin W Australia
14 B3 Murrisk mts Irish Rep
139 G5 Murrumbidgee R New S Wales
139 J5 Murrumburrah & Harden New S Wales
139 K4 Murrurundi New S Wales
19 O17 Murs France
38 O8 Murska Sobota Yugoslavia
38 K7 Mur Tal V Austria
41 M4 Murtarol,Piz mt Italy
101 L7 Murtaugh Idaho
74 G8 Murtazapur India
139 G4 Murtee New S Wales
40 F4 Murten See L Switzerland
138 F3 Murteree,L S Australia
117 O9 Murtle L Br Col
138 F6 Murtoa Victoria
29 O6 Murtovaara Finland
74 E9 Murud India
70 D3 Murud mt Kalimantan
65 E3 Muruin Sum Shuiku res China
70 D5 Murui,R Kalimantan
70 D4 Murung,R Kalimantan
145 F3 Murupara New Zealand
128 F3 Murupu Brazil
109 N3 Murvaul Res Texas
22 K5 Murville France
74 J7 Murwara India
139 L3 Murwillumbah New S Wales
52 G5 Murygino U.S.S.R.
38 M6 Mürzsteg Austria
38 M7 Murz Tal V Austria
38 N6 Mürzzuchlag Austria
78 H2 Muş Turkey
86 D6 Musadi Zaïre
79 D10 Mûsa, G mt Egypt
74 C3 Musa Khel Bazar Pakistan
69 D12 Musala isld Sumatra
47 F2 Musala mt Bulgaria
59 J3 Musan N Korea
77 E6 Musandam pen Oman
77 J3 Musa Qala Afghanistan
77 F7 Muscat Oman
99 P8 Muscatine Iowa
Muscat & Oman sultanate see Oman
99 Q6 Muscoda Wisconsin
95 S3 Muscongus B Maine
88 C9 Muse R Mozambique
80 G8 Museitiba Jordan
141 G2 Musgrave Queensland
138 B2 Musgrave Ranges S Australia
123 S5 Musgravetown Newfoundland
89 G3 Mushandike Dam Zimbabwe
80 G8 Musheirifa Jordan
14 C5 Musheramore mt Irish Rep
86 C6 Mushie Zaïre
28 G6 Musholm isld Denmark
103 L6 Music Mt Arizona
103 N2 Musinia Pk Utah
117 M5 Muskeg R N W Terr
99 L1 Muskeg B Minnesota
95 R5 Muskeget Chan Massachusetts
119 O1 Muskeg L Ontario
94 A3 Muskegon Michigan
94 A3 Muskegon R Michigan
94 A3 Muskegon Heights Michigan
26 H4 Musken Norway
94 F7 Muskingum R Ohio
27 K13 Muskö Sweden
110 A6 Muskogee Oklahoma
121 L7 Muskoka,L Ontario
101 S6 Muskrat Cr Wyoming
77 F6 Mūskutān Iran
118 C2 Muskwa R Alberta
52 H6 Muslyumovo U.S.S.R.
86 G2 Musmar Sudan
80 D3 Musmus Israel
88 D2 Musoma Tanzania
45 O4 Musone Italy
45 M1 Musone R Italy
123 L3 Musquanus L Quebec
123 L3 Musquaro Quebec
122 F8 Musquash New Brunswick
122 J8 Musquodoboit Nova Scotia
122 J9 Musquodoboit Hbr Nova Scotia
28 H7 Musse Denmark
25 H3 Mussel Aa R Netherlands
13 E2 Musselburgh Scotland
101 R3 Musselshell Montana
101 S3 Musselshell R Montana
87 C8 Mussende Angola
18 F7 Mussidan France
43 F11 Mussomeli Sicily
47 K4 Mustafa Kemalpaşa Turkey
86 H4 Mustahil Ethiopia
75 K4 Mustang Nepal
107 N6 Mustang Oklahoma
108 E3 Mustang Cr Texas
109 K8 Mustang I Texas
55 B5 Mustayevo U.S.S.R.
133 D7 Muster,L Argentina
98 K4 Mustinka R Minnesota
127 O8 Mustique isld Lesser Antilles
27 M13 Mustjala Estonia U.S.S.R.
52 C5 Mustla U.S.S.R.
29 N3 Mustola Finland
13 H5 Muston England
52 C5 Mustvee U.S.S.R.
65 H4 Musu-dan C N Korea
139 K4 Muswellbrook New S Wales
48 F1 Muszyna Poland
84 H4 Mut Egypt
78 D3 Mut Turkey
38 M8 Muta Yugoslavia
88 C1 Mutai Uganda
89 G4 Mutale R S Africa
87 E8 Mutanda Zambia
Mutankiang see Mudanjiang
88 E10 Mutarara Mozambique
37 O4 Mutĕnín Czechoslovakia
12 E1 Muthill Scotland
71 M9 Mutis mt Timor Indonesia
52 J2 Mutnyy-Materik U.S.S.R.
87 D7 Mutombo Mukulu Zaïre
138 F4 Mutooroo S Australia
65 D4 Mutoudeng China
65 D3 Mutougou China
45 R7 Mutria, M mt Italy
87 G10 Mutsamudu Comoros
87 D8 Mutshatsha Zaïre
60 P4 Mutsu Japan
61 O5 Mutsu-wan B Japan
141 G6 Muttaburra Queensland
40 G1 Muttersholtz France
36 E5 Mutterstadt W Germany
41 M4 Muttler mt Switzerland
123 O3 Mutton Bay Quebec
144 B7 Muttonbird Is. New Zealand
14 B4 Mutton I Irish Rep
107 L5 Mutual Oklahoma
87 G8 Mutuala Mozambique
129 H7 Mutum Mato Grosso Brazil
130 H6 Mutum Minas Gerais Brazil
128 F5 Mutumparaná Brazil
83 L9 Mutur Sri Lanka
36 C6 Mutzig France
33 R10 Mutzschen E Germany
29 M9 Muurame Finland
29 L5 Muurola Finland
58 F1 Muya R U.S.S.R.
88 C3 Muyinga Burundi
125 M3 Muy Muy Nicaragua
57 A3 Muynak U.S.S.R.
87 E7 Muyumba Zaïre
67 C1 Muyuping China
74 E1 Muzaffarabad Kashmir
74 D3 Muzaffargarh Pakistan
74 G4 Muzaffarnagar India
75 L5 Muzaffarpur India
130 F7 Muzambinho Brazil
57 K4 Muzat He R China
50 F2 Muzhi U.S.S.R.
18 D5 Muzillac France
40 A3 Muzin R France
117 G8 Muzon, C Alaska
108 F8 Múzquiz Mexico
66 D4 Muztag China
66 C4 Muztag mt China
66 B4 Muztagata mt China
88 E8 Mvera Malawi
86 E4 Mvolo Sudan
87 G7 Mvomero Tanzania
86 B6 M'Vouti Congo
88 D7 Mwambwa R Zambia
88 D3 Mwanza Tanzania
88 D6 Mwaya Tanzania
14 B3 Mweelrea mts Irish Rep
86 D6 Mweka Zaïre
87 D7 Mwene Ditu Zaïre
88 B3 Mwenga Zaïre
88 G6 Mwera Tanzania
89 G2 Mwerihari R Zimbabwe
88 B6 Mweru, L Zaire/Zambia
88 B6 Mweru Wantipa Zambia
89 F3 Mwewe R Zimbabwe
87 D7 Mwimba Zaïre
87 D8 Mwinilunga Zambia
68 B2 Myaing Burma
113 E10 Myakka Florida
113 E10 Myakka City Florida
52 E5 Myaksa U.S.S.R.
31 H3 Myálibórz Poland
139 K4 Myall L New S Wales
68 B3 Myanaung Burma
52 D3 Myanduselga U.S.S.R.
54 G2 Myatlevo U.S.S.R.
68 A2 Myaungbwe Burma
68 B4 Myaungmya Burma
68 D4 Myawadi Burma
46 F7 Mycenae Greece
68 A2 Myebon Burma
95 L6 Myerstown Pennsylvania
28 L1 Myggenæs Faeroes
28 N1 Mygledal Faeroes
68 B2 Myingyan Burma
68 C2 Myinkyado Burma
68 D6 Myinmoletkat mt Burma
68 B2 Myinmu Burma
68 B2 Myitche Burma
68 D5 Myitta Burma
68 C2 Myittha Burma
48 D2 Myjava Czechoslovakia
26 F5 Myken lt ho Norway
52 H2 Myla U.S.S.R.
37 N2 Mylau E Germany
29 M11 Myllykoski Finland
98 G1 Mylo N Dakota
75 O6 Mymensingh Bangladesh
29 J11 Mynämäki Finland
57 G2 Mynaral U.S.S.R.
57 C4 Mynbulak U.S.S.R.
8 B3 Mynydd Bach hills Wales
8 C3 Mynydd Eppynt mts Wales
68 A2 Myohaung Burma
68 B2 Myohla Burma
68 B2 Myotha Burma
68 B2 Myothit Burma
109 K2 Myra Texas
47 K8 Myra Turkey
141 F3 Myra Vale Queensland
27 B11 Myrdal Norway
26 H3 Myre Norway
27 G14 Myresjö Sweden
26 L6 Myrheden Sweden
118 F5 Myrnam Alberta
100 J3 Myrtle Idaho
119 U9 Myrtle Manitoba
111 G7 Myrtle Mississippi
121 M8 Myrtle Ontario
112 J4 Myrtle Beach S Carolina
100 B6 Myrtle Cr Oregon
139 H6 Myrtleford Victoria
100 A6 Myrtle Point Oregon
138 E4 Myrtle Springs S Australia
141 L1 Myrtletown Queensland
65 H3 Mys Gamova lt ho U.S.S.R.
52 E5 Myshkino U.S.S.R.
56 C4 Myski U.S.S.R.
31 M6 Myślenice Poland
76 C4 Mysore India
26 G9 Myssjo Sweden
119 U3 Mystery L Manitoba
112 D6 Mystic Georgia
99 O9 Mystic Iowa
98 C5 Mystic S Dakota
52 H4 Mysy Perm U.S.S.R.
31 N2 Myszyniec Poland
52 F6 Myt U.S.S.R.
68 H7 My Tho Vietnam
54 J1 Mytishchi U.S.S.R.
101 P9 Myton Utah
68 J6 My Trach Vietnam
57 H1 Myylybulak U.S.S.R.
37 O4 Mže R Czechoslovakia
85 C4 Mzereb,El Mali
88 D7 Mzimba Malawi
88 E7 Mzuzu Malawi
37 M5 Naab R W Germany
25 B5 Naaldwijk Netherlands
135 U6 Naalehu Hawaiian Is
80 C6 Na'an Israel
86 E4 Naandi Sudan
29 J11 Naantali Finland
25 D4 Naarden Netherlands
14 E3 Naas Irish Rep
29 N2 Näätämönjoki R Finland
16 B5 Nabaõ R Portugal
61 K11 Nabari Japan
71 F5 Nabas Panay Philippines
79 F5 Nabatîyet Ett Tahta Lebanon
143 D7 Nabberu, L W Australia
71 E2 Nabbuan Luzon Philippines
37 N5 Nabburg W Germany
52 H6 Naberezhnyye Chelny U.S.S.R.
116 Q5 Nabesna Gl Alaska
43 D12 Nabeul Tunisia
139 K4 Nabiac New S Wales
130 B7 Nabileque,R Brazil
123 K3 Nabisipi R Quebec
80 E5 Nablus Jordan
79 E10 Nabq Egypt
71 F6 Nabulao B Negros Philippines
68 D5 Nabule Burma
88 H9 Nacala Mozambique
125 L3 Nacaome Honduras
67 B5 Nacham Vietnam
74 D5 Nachana India
100 E3 Naches Washington
100 D2 Naches Pass Washington
87 G8 Nachingwea Tanzania
66 E5 Na Ch'u R China
68 A7 Nachuge Andaman Is
102 C6 Nacimiento R California
102 C6 Nacimiento Res California
138 E4 Nackara S Australia
33 R7 Nackel E Germany
103 P10 Naco Mexico
111 B10 Nacogdoches Texas
68 B6 Nacondam I Andaman Is
124 E2 Nacozari de García Mexico
20 B2 Nacqueville France
Nada see Dan Xian
103 L3 Nada Utah
61 M8 Nadachi Japan
124 J4 Nadadores Mexico
67 B6 Nadang China
99 T4 Nadeau Michigan
Nådendal see Naantali
55 D4 Nadezhdinskiy U.S.S.R.
137 Q5 Nadi Viti Levu Fiji
74 E7 Nadiad India
48 F4 Nădlac Romania
85 D1 Nador Morocco
48 G3 Nádudvar Hungary
77 C3 Nadūshan Iran
52 D3 Nadvoitsy U.S.S.R.
48 J2 Nadvornaya U.S.S.R.
50 G2 Nadym U.S.S.R.
27 A13 Naerbö Norway
26 E7 Naeröy Norway
28 K5 Nærum Denmark
28 N9 Næs Faeroes
28 N10 Næs Faeroes
28 B5 Næsbjerg Denmark
28 C3 Næsborg Denmark
28 H6 Næsby Denmark
28 E6 Næsbyhoved Denmark
28 A3 Næs Sund inlet Denmark
28 H6 Næstelsø Denmark
28 H6 Næstved Denmark
101 M7 Naf Idaho
68 A2 Naf R Burma
85 G6 Nafada Nigeria
84 G4 Nafoora Libya
77 A4 Naft-e Safīd Iran
78 K4 Naft-e Shāh Iran
71 F4 Naga Philippines
120 F3 Nagagami Ontario
120 F3 Nagagamisis L Ontario
60 F12 Nagahama Japan
75 Q5 Nagaland prov India
139 H6 Nagambie Victoria
61 O13 Nagannu-jima isld Okinawa
61 M9 Nagano Japan
61 L9 Nagano prefect Japan
61 M9 Naganohara Japan
61 M8 Nagaoka Japan
76 D5 Nagappattinam India
76 D2 Nagar Karnul India
74 D6 Nagar Parkar Pakistan
60 C13 Nagasaki Japan
60 C12 Nagasaki prefect Japan
60 D14 Nagasaki-bana Japan
60 D13 Naga shima isld Japan
60 F12 Naga-shima isld Japan
60 E12 Nagasu Japan
60 E11 Nagato Japan
74 E5 Nagaur India
Nagchu Dzong see Nagqu
76 C6 Nagercoil India
26 H9 Naggen Sweden
74 H4 Nagina India
61 P12 Nago Okinawa
74 J6 Nagod India
36 F6 Nagold W Germany
36 F6 Nagold R W Germany
52 H5 Nagorsk U.S.S.R.
61 P13 Nago-wan B Okinawa
61 K10 Nagoya Japan
74 H8 Nagpur India
66 E5 Nagqu China
29 J11 Nagu Finland
127 K5 Nagua Dom Rep
71 E2 Naguilian Luzon Philippines
71 G4 Nagumbuaya Pt Philippines
48 D4 Nagybajom Hungary
48 G3 Nagyecsed Hungary
48 G3 Nagykálló Hungary
48 D4 Nagykanizsa Hungary
48 F3 Nagykáta Hungary
48 F3 Nagykörös Hungary
48 G3 Nagyléta Hungary
Nagyvárad see Oradea
61 P13 Naha Okinawa
70 D4 Nahabuan Kalimantan
80 D3 Nahalal Israel
80 C7 Nahalat Israel
74 G3 Nahan India
114 G5 Nahanni Butte N W Terr
117 M5 Nahanni Butte N W Terr
117 L5 Nahanni Nat. Park N W Terr
80 D1 Nahariyya Israel
77 A2 Nahāvand Iran
36 C4 Nahbollenbach W Germany
36 C4 Nahe R W Germany
80 G4 Nahla Jordan
21 I7 Nahon R France
80 C3 Nahsholim Israel
131 B8 Nahuel Huapi, L Argentina
133 D6 Nahuel Niyeu Argentina
112 E6 Nahunta Georgia
71 E3 Naic Luzon Philippines
124 G4 Naica Mexico
119 N6 Naicam Sask
66 E4 Naij Tal China
71 L9 Naikliu Timor Indonesia
37 M3 Naila W Germany
65 D4 Nailin China
8 D4 Nailsworth England
65 E3 Naiman Qi China
77 C3 Nā'īn Iran
115 N6 Nain Labrador
74 J7 Nainpur India
21 F8 Naintré France
120 J6 Nairn Ontario
15 E3 Nairn Scotland
Nairn co see Highland reg
143 B7 Nairn, Mt W Australia
15 D3 Nairn,R Scotland
88 F2 Nairobi Kenya
52 B5 Naissaar isld U.S.S.R.
88 F2 Naivasha Kenya
77 B3 Najafābād Iran
78 K6 Najaf, An Iraq
126 F4 Najasa R Cuba
17 F2 Nájera Spain
17 F2 Najerilla R Spain
65 H3 Najin N Korea
77 B2 Najmabad Iran
72 F5 Najran Saudi Arabia
60 H12 Naka R Japan
60 C13 Nakadōri shima isld Japan
60 C12 Nakagumi Japan
61 P13 Nakagusuku-wan B Okinawa
61 N7 Nakajō Japan
60 C14 Naka koshiki jima isld Japan
60 D12 Nakama Japan
61 P13 Nakama Okinawa
61 O9 Nakaminato Japan
Nakamti see Lekemti Ethiopia
60 E14 Nakamura Japan
60 F13 Nakamura Japan
61 M9 Nakano Japan
61 M9 Nakanojō Japan
60 G9 Nakano-shima isld Japan
67 H4 Nakanougan-jima isld Japan
61 Q12 Nakaoshi Okinawa
77 L3 Naka Pass Afghanistan
61 O5 Nakasato Japan
60 R3 Nakasatsunai Japan
60 T2 Naka-shibetsu Japan
55 D2 Nakatay U.S.S.R.
60 Q1 Naka-Tombetsu Japan
60 E12 Nakatsu Japan
61 L10 Nakatsugawa Japan
60 G10 Naka-umi Japan
116 J8 Nakchamik I Alaska
116 O6 Naked I Alaska
86 G2 Nakfa Ethiopia
78 K2 Nakhichevan U.S.S.R.
84 J4 Nakhl Egypt
65 J3 Nakhodka U.S.S.R.
68 E5 Nakhon Nayok Thailand
68 D6 Nakhon Pathom Thailand
68 F5 Nakhon Ratchasima Thailand
69 E8 Nakhon Si Thammarat Thailand
68 E4 Nakhon Thai Thailand
59 L2 Nakhtakhe U.S.S.R.
61 P12 Nakijin Okinawa
117 G6 Nakina Br Col
115 L7 Nakina Ontario
29 K3 Näkkälä Finland
29 J10 Nakkila Finland
28 O10 Nakkur Fjord inlet Faeroes
31 K2 Nakło Poland
116 J7 Naknek Alaska
61 O9 Nakoso Japan
67 F3 Nakou China
Naksho Biru see Biru
28 G7 Nakskov Denmark
26 G9 Näkten L Sweden
65 G7 Naktong R S Korea
88 F2 Nakuru Kenya
88 E2 Nakuru, L Kenya
117 P10 Nakusp Br Col
68 C1 Na-lang Burma
58 E2 Nalayh Mongolia
53 F11 Nal'chik U.S.S.R.
74 G10 Naldrug India
76 D2 Nalgonda India
22 G3 Nalinnes Belgium
76 D3 Nallamala Hills India
94 G8 Nallen W Virginia
78 C1 Nallihan Turkey
87 D9 Nalolo Zambia
68 C1 Nam R Burma
68 F3 Nam R Laos
65 G5 Nam R N Korea
60 C12 Nama Japan
87 C9 Namacunde Angola
88 F10 Namacurra Mozambique
118 D8 Namaka Alberta
118 K2 Namakan L Minn/Ontario
77 F4 Namakiār-e Shadād salt lake Iran
77 E2 Namak, Kavīr-e salt waste Iran
69 H14 Namang Indonesia
57 F4 Namangan U.S.S.R.
88 G8 Namapa Mozambique
88 G9 Namaponda Mozambique
87 C12 Namaqualand dist S Africa
88 F9 Namarroi Mozambique
86 F5 Namasagali Uganda
87 E9 Nambala Zambia
142 D4 Nambeet Well W Australia
68 E2 Nam Beng R Laos
141 L7 Nambour Queensland
139 L4 Nambucca Heads New S Wales
68 G3 Nam Ca Dinh R Laos
69 G8 Nam Can Vietnam
66 E6 Namcha Barwa mt China
66 E5 Nam Co L China
26 F7 Namdalen V Norway
26 E7 Namdalseid Norway
68 H2 Nam Dinh Vietnam
88 G8 Namecala Mozambique
70 E3 Nameh Kalimantan
99 P3 Namekagon R Wisconsin
61 L9 Namerikawa Japan
48 E1 Námestovo Czechoslovakia
88 G9 Nametil Mozambique
119 P4 Namew L Sask
68 F2 Nam Het R Laos
68 D2 Nam Hsin R Burma
87 B10 Namib Des Namibia
87 C10 Namibia terr Africa
88 F9 Namicunde Mozambique
61 O8 Namie Japan
61 O5 Namioka Japan
87 C11 Namiziz mt Namibia
68 F3 Nam Khan R Laos
68 D2 Nam Kok R Thailand
68 C1 Namlan Burma
68 C2 Namlang R Burma
68 E2 Nam Loi R Burma
68 E2 Nam Ma R Laos
68 C3 Nammekon Burma
68 G3 Nam Muone R Laos
68 F1 Nam Na R Vietnam
68 G4 Nam One R Laos
68 E2 Nam Ngaou R Laos
68 F2 Nam Noud R Vietnam
70 F5 Namo Sulawesi Indonesia
139 J4 Namoi R New S Wales
68 E1 Nam Ou R Laos
85 D2 Namous watercourse Algeria
118 A2 Nampa Alberta
29 M5 Nampa Finland
100 J6 Nampa Idaho
85 C5 Nampala Mali
68 E4 Nam Pa Sak R Thailand
68 E4 Nam Pat Thailand
68 F4 Nam Phong Thailand
22 B3 Nampont France
88 G9 Nampula Mozambique
68 G4 Nam Pung Res Thailand
68 C2 Namsang Burma
26 F7 Namsen R Norway
68 F2 Nam Seng R Laos
26 E7 Namsos Norway
68 F2 Nam Suong R Laos
26 G7 Namsvatn L Norway
68 C2 Nam Teng Burma
68 E2 Nam Tha Laos
68 G4 Nam Theun R Laos
68 C2 Namtok Burma
68 D5 Nam Tok Thailand
68 D1 Namton Burma
51 M2 Namtsy U.S.S.R.
88 F9 Namuli mt Mozambique
83 L11 Namunakuli mt Sri Lanka
87 G8 Namuno Mozambique
22 H3 Namur Belgium
121 Q7 Namur Quebec
117 R7 Namur L Alberta
87 C9 Namutoni Namibia
87 E9 Namwala Zambia
68 D4 Nam Wang R Thailand
88 E9 Namwera Malawi
31 L4 Namysłaki Poland
31 K4 Namysłów Poland
87 D8 Nana Candundo Angola
100 B1 Nanaimo Br Col
102 R12 Nanakuli Hawaiian Is
65 H4 Nanam N Korea
143 E10 Nanambinia W Australia
67 B6 Nanan China
67 F4 Nan'an China
141 K7 Nanango Queensland
67 F5 Nan'ao China
61 K8 Nanao Japan
67 F5 Nan'ao Dao isld China
61 L8 Nanao wan B Japan
61 K8 Nanatsu-jima isld Japan
67 B3 Nanbai China
67 B1 Nanbazhen China
67 B1 Nanbu China
21 J7 Nançay France
59 J2 Nancha China
67 E2 Nanchang China
65 E6 Nanchangshan Dao isld China
67 E3 Nancheng China
67 B1 Nanchong China
69 A9 Nancowry isld Nicobar Is
19 K4 Nancy France
144 A6 Nancy Sd New Zealand
74 H3 Nanda Devi mt India
67 B4 Nandan China
74 G9 Nander India
139 K4 Nandewar Ra mts New S Wales
37 M6 Nandlstadt W Germany
22 J3 Nandrin Belgium
67 C7 Nandu Jiang R China
74 F8 Nandurbar India
76 D3 Nandyal India
36 D4 Nane R W Germany
65 F4 Nanfen China
67 D5 Nanfeng China
67 E3 Nanfeng China
75 P4 Nang China
70 C4 Nangabadau Kalimantan
86 B5 Nanga Eboko Cameroon
71 L9 Nangahale Flores Indonesia
70 C4 Nangakelawit Kalimantan
74 G3 Nangal India
70 B5 Nangalanki Kalimantan
71 E5 Nangalao isld Philippines
70 B5 Nangamau Kalimantan
70 C5 Nangamuntatai Kalimantan
70 C4 Nangaobat Kalimantan
74 F1 Nanga Parbat mt Kashmir
70 B5 Nangapinoh Kalimantan
70 C4 Nangaraun Kalimantan
77 L2 Nangarhār Afghanistan
70 C4 Nangasuruk Kalimantan
69 K13 Nangatayap Indonesia
68 D7 Nangin Burma
18 G4 Nangis France
65 G5 Nangnim Sanmaek mts N Korea
65 C6 Nangong China
76 C6 Nanguneri India
87 D9 Nangweshi Zambia
67 D5 Nanhai China
Nanhaoqian see Shangyi
65 C6 Nanhe China
67 D1 Nan He R China
67 G1 Nanhui China
76 C4 Nanjangud India
58 E5 Nanjiang China
67 D2 Nanjiangqiao China
Nanjie see Guangning
67 F1 Nanjing China
67 F4 Nanjing China
67 C6 Nankang China
67 E4 Nankang China
Nanking see Nanjing
65 C4 Nankouzhen China
65 C6 Nanle China
67 F1 Nanling China
67 C4 Nan Ling mts China
Nanma see Yiyuan
67 G2 Nanma China
67 E3 Nanmiao Jiangxi China
37 L7 Nannhofen W Germany
143 C7 Nannine W Australia
67 C5 Nanning China
143 B10 Nannup W Australia
137 Q3 Nanomana isld Tuvalu
137 Q3 Nanomea isld Tuvalu
115 P5 Nanortalik Greenland
67 A4 Nanpan Jiang R China
75 J5 Nanpara India
67 F5 Nanpeng Liedao islds China
65 C5 Nanpi China
65 H3 Nanping China
68 E3 Nan Poui R Laos
65 D5 Nanpu China
67 F3 Nanpu Xi R China
Nanqiao see Fengxian
67 F4 Nanri Dao isld China
51 J5 Nan Shan mt ra China
88 D3 Nansio Tanzania
143 A8 Nanson W Australia
18 H8 Nant France
112 D2 Nantahala L N Carolina
115 M5 Nantais,L Quebec
75 K5 Nantanwa India
21 B7 Nantes France
122 A8 Nantes Quebec
8 C4 Nant-garw Wales
70 K8 Nanti mt Sumatra
67 G2 Nantian China
18 F6 Nantiat France
95 L5 Nanticoke Pennsylvania
95 M8 Nanticoke R Delaware/Maryland
8 C4 Nant Moel Wales
118 D8 Nanton Alberta
67 G1 Nantong China
40 C5 Nantua France
95 R5 Nantucket I Massachusetts
146 E12 Nantucket Inlet Antarctica
88 G8 Nantulo Mozambique
8 D1 Nantwich England
94 J6 Nanty Glo Pennsylvania
130 H5 Nanuque Brazil
116 M2 Nanushuk R Alaska
65 B6 Nanweiquan China
67 A2 Nanxi China
67 D2 Nan Xian China
67 C5 Nanxiang China
67 E4 Nanxiong China
141 J6 Nanya Queensland
58 F5 Nanyang China
67 C2 Nanyaojie China
65 C7 Nanyi China
67 F1 Nanyi Hu China
61 O7 Nanyō Japan
65 C5 Nanyuan China
88 F1 Nanyuki Kenya
65 F4 Nanzamu China
67 D1 Nanzhang China
67 G3 Nanzhen China
17 H6 Nao,C.de la Spain
115 M7 Naococane,L Quebec
61 M8 Naoetsu Japan
75 N6 Naogaon Bangladesh
74 C6 Naokot Pakistan
59 K2 Naol He R China
77 G3 Naomid, Dasht-e des Iran
101 O8 Naomi Pk Utah
46 E4 Náousa Greece
67 C6 Naozhou Dao isld China
102 B3 Napa California
71 H7 Napabalana Indonesia
122 F7 Napadogan New Brunswick
70 D3 Napaku Kalimantan
121 O8 Napanee Ontario
115 O4 Napassoq Greenland
100 C3 Napavine Washington
71 F4 Napayauan Philippines
68 G3 Nape Laos
99 S8 Naperville Illinois
123 O2 Napetipi R Quebec
40 G4 Napf mt Switzerland
99 L9 Napier Missouri
145 F3 Napier New Zealand
142 F2 Napier Broome B W Australia
140 A4 Napier, Mt N Terr Aust
146 A5 Napier Mts Antarctica
140 D1 Napier Pen N Terr Aust
142 E3 Napier Ra W Australia
121 R7 Napierville Quebec
119 R9 Napinka Manitoba
Naples see Napoli Italy
113 F11 Naples Florida
95 K4 Naples New York
109 N2 Naples Texas
67 B5 Napo China
68 G1 Napo China
128 C4 Napo R Peru/Ecuador
94 B7 Napoleon Indiana
98 G3 Napoleon N Dakota
94 C5 Napoleon Ohio
111 E12 Napoleonville Louisiana
43 G7 Napoletano, Appennino mts Italy
45 Q8 Napoli Italy
98 G9 Naponee Nebraska
135 U5 Napoopoo Hawaiian Is
131 E7 Naposta R Argentina
141 F8 Nappamerry Queensland
94 A5 Nappanee Indiana
140 C6 Napperby N Terr Aust
110 C2 Napton Missouri
78 K3 Naqadeh Iran
79 F8 Naqb Ishtar Jordan
79 C9 Naqb Malba mt Egypt
61 J11 Nara Japan
85 C5 Nara Mali
139 G7 Naracoopa Tasmania
138 F6 Naracoorte S Australia
139 H5 Naradhan New S Wales
143 A8 Naraling W Australia
117 O11 Naramata Br Col
65 C2 Naran Bulag China
113 G12 Naranja Florida
124 E5 Naranjo Mexico
76 E2 Naraspur India
69 E9 Narathiwat Thailand
106 G6 Nara Visa New Mexico
75 O7 Narayanganj Bangladesh
76 C2 Narayanpet India
Narbada R see Narmada R
18 H9 Narbonne France
9 G2 Narborough England
16 C1 Narcea R Spain
43 J8 Nardò Italy
8 B7 Nare Head England
143 C9 Narembeen W Australia
74 H3 Narendranagar India
90 D6 Nares Deep Atlantic Oc
115 M2 Nares Str Canada/Greenland
143 E9 Naretha W Australia
31 O3 Narew Poland
65 G3 Narhong China
65 A5 Narin China
66 E4 Narin Gol R China
128 C3 Nariño div Colombia
61 O10 Narita Japan
127 P2 Nariva co Trinidad
127 P2 Nariva Swamp Trinidad
60 G11 Nariwa Japan
124 D4 Narizon pt Mexico
107 N2 Narka Kansas
26 N5 Narken Sweden
74 F7 Narmada R India
42 E6 Narni Italy
71 F5 Naro isld Philippines
52 K2 Narodnaya, Gora mt U.S.S.R.
54 H1 Naro-Fominsk U.S.S.R.
88 E2 Narok Kenya
16 B1 Naron Spain
139 K6 Narooma New S Wales
74 F2 Narowal Pakistan
29 J9 Närpes Finland
139 K4 Narrabri New S Wales
139 J4 Narrabri West New S Wales
95 Q5 Narragansett Rhode I
139 J3 Narran R New S Wales
139 H5 Narrandera New S Wales
139 H3 Narran,L New S Wales
143 E8 Narra Spring W Australia
117 N8 Narraway R Br Col
141 H6 Narrien Ra Queensland
143 B10 Narrogin W Australia
139 J4 Narromine New S Wales
100 G6 Narrows Oregon
94 G9 Narrows Virginia
95 M5 Narrowsburg New York
127 P4 Narrows,The chan St Kitts W I
142 B1 Narrows, The str Perth, W Aust
143 B7 Narryer, Mt W Australia
37 O1 Narsdorf E Germany
74 G7 Narsinghgarh India
75 K10 Narsipatnam India
115 P5 Narssalik Greenland
115 O5 Narssaq Greenland
115 P5 Narssarssuaq Greenland
65 C3 Nart China
46 C4 Nartës,Gjol i isld Albania
61 O7 Naruko Japan
131 F2 Narunjito, L Argentina
60 B13 Naru-shima isld Japan
61 O10 Narutō Japan
60 H11 Naruto-kaikyō str Japan
52 C5 Narva U.S.S.R.
71 E2 Narvacan Luzon Philippines
52 C5 Narva-Jõesuu U.S.S.R.
26 J3 Narvik Norway

54 Narvskiy Zaliv — Newton Stewart

52 C5 Narvskiy Zaliv gulf U.S.S.R.
74 G4 Narwana India
74 G6 Narwar India
140 C6 Narwietooma N Terr Aust
52 H1 Nar'yan Mar U.S.S.R.
141 F8 Naryilco Queensland
56 B6 Narymskiy Khrebet mts U.S.S.R.
57 H4 Naryn U.S.S.R.
57 G4 Naryn Ugyut R U.S.S.R.
54 G4 Naryshkino U.S.S.R.
27 G11 Nås Sweden
85 F7 Nasarawa Nigeria
48 J3 Năsăud Romania
26 M5 Näsberg Sweden
18 H8 Nasbinals France
144 C6 Naseby New Zealand
107 M5 Nash Oklahoma
8 C5 Nash Wales
122 F6 Nash Cr New Brunswick
116 D6 Nash Harbor Alaska
140 E5 Nash, L Queensland
8 C5 Nash Pt Wales
99 O7 Nashua Iowa
101 T1 Nashua Montana
95 Q4 Nashua New Hampshire
111 C8 Nashville Arkansas
112 D6 Nashville Georgia
110 G3 Nashville Illinois
94 A7 Nashville Indiana
107 M4 Nashville Kansas
94 B4 Nashville Michigan
112 J2 Nashville N Carolina
94 E6 Nashville Ohio
110 K5 Nashville Tennessee
99 N2 Nashwauk Minnesota
48 E5 Našice Yugoslavia
29 K10 Näsijärvi L Finland
74 E8 Nasik India
86 F4 Nasir Sudan
79 A8 Nasr Egypt
79 H4 Naşrānī, Jebel an mts Syria
117 J8 Nass R Br Col
98 K4 Nassau Minnesota
113 L9 Nassau New Providence I Bahamas
95 O4 Nassau New York
36 D3 Nassau W Germany
141 F3 Nassau R Queensland
133 D9 Nassau,B.de Chile
113 F7 Nassau Sd Florida
95 M9 Nassawadox Virginia
33 T10 Nasseböhla E Germany
37 L6 Nassenfels W Germany
33 S7 Nassenheide E Germany
84 J5 Nasser, L Egypt
27 G14 Nässjö Sweden
22 J3 Nassogne Belgium
38 N6 Nasswald Austria
115 M6 Nastapoka Is N W Terr
36 D3 Nastätten W Germany
71 E3 Nasugbu Luzon Philippines
61 N8 Nasu-Yumoto Japan
52 D6 Nasva U.S.S.R.
26 J10 Näsviken Sweden
87 E10 Nata Botswana
89 E3 Nata R Botswana
128 F5 Natal Brazil
118 C9 Natal Br Col
69 D12 Natal Sumatra
89 F7 Natal prov S Africa
141 H5 Natal R Queensland
90 M13 Natal Basin Indian Oc
141 H5 Natal Downs Queensland
109 J6 Natalia Texas
55 C3 Natalinsk U.S.S.R.
77 B3 Nątanz Iran
123 L3 Natashquan Quebec
123 L3 Natashquan R Quebec/Labrador
116 K3 Natavukti L Alaska
116 R6 Natazhat Mt Alaska
111 E10 Natchez Mississippi
111 C10 Natchitoches Louisiana
139 H6 Nathalia Victoria
115 R3 Nathorsts Land Greenland
106 D3 Nathrop Colorado
124 J5 Natillas Mexico
138 F6 Natimuk Victoria
116 R4 Nation Alaska
101 L2 National Bison Ra Montana
102 G9 National City California
86 C3 National Park Chad
117 L8 Nation R Br Col
123 K4 Natiskotek B Anticosti I, Quebec
141 H6 Native Companion Cr Queensland
124 B4 Natividad isld Mexico
129 J6 Natividade Brazil
68 C5 Natkyizin Burma
107 M2 Natoma Kansas
124 E3 Nátora Mexico
61 O7 Natori Japan
22 J3 Natoye Belgium
101 T6 Natrona Wyoming
88 F3 Natron L Tanzania
68 B3 Nattalin Burma
83 J10 Nattandiya Sri Lanka
29 N3 Nattaset mt Finland
68 C3 Nattaung mt Burma
26 L5 Nattavaara Sweden
37 O6 Natternberg W Germany
37 J6 Nattheim W Germany
27 H15 Nättraby Sweden
Natuna Besar see Bunguran Utara, Kep. I
Natuna Selatan see Bunguran Selatan Kep I
69 H10 Natuna Utara Indonesia
95 M2 Natural Bridge New York
94 H9 Natural Bridge Virginia
103 O4 Natural Br.Nat.Mon Utah
108 F3 Natural Dam L Texas
143 B10 Naturaliste, C W Australia
143 A7 Naturaliste Chan W Australia
81 H9 Naturaliste Plateau Indian Oc
106 B3 Naturita Colorado
99 V3 Naubinway Michigan
87 C10 Nauchas Namibia
121 T4 Naudville Quebec
33 R7 Nauen E Germany
130 E10 Naufragados, Pta Dos C Brazil
95 O5 Naugatuck Connecticut
71 E4 Naujan Philippines
29 N8 Naulavaara mt Finland
87 B9 Naulila Angola
37 M1 Naumburg E Germany
36 G1 Naumburg W Germany
68 C4 Naunglon Burma
68 C3 Naungpale Burma
33 R10 Naunhof E Germany
80 G6 Na'ur Jordan
36 D2 Nauroth W Germany
137 O2 Nauru rep Pacific Oc
55 D5 Naurzum U.S.S.R.
26 A10 Naustdal Norway
26 C9 Nauste Norway
128 D4 Nauta Peru
26 R3 Nautsi U.S.S.R.
111 J8 Nauvoo Alabama
99 P9 Nauvoo Illinois
108 G7 Nava Mexico
16 D3 Nava de Rey Spain
16 E5 Navahermosa Spain
103 P6 Navajo Arizona
103 M4 Navajo L Utah
103 O4 Navajo Mt Utah
103 O5 Navajo Nat.Mon Arizona
103 N5 Navajo Pt Arizona
106 C5 Navajo Res Colo/New Mex
16 E4 Navalcarnero Spain
16 D5 Navalmoral de la Mata Spain
86 E5 Nava R Zaïre
133 D9 Navarino, I Chile
17 F2 Navarra prov Spain
94 F6 Navarre Ohio
139 G6 Navarre Victoria
102 A2 Navarro California
102 A2 Navarro R California
109 L4 Navarro Mills Res Texas
109 L5 Navasota Texas
126 G5 Navassa I Caribbean
45 P5 Navelli Italy
9 F1 Navenby England
16 C1 Navia Spain
16 C1 Navia R Spain
109 L6 Navidad R Texas
127 K4 Navidad Bank Caribbean
130 H10 Navio R Brazil
54 F4 Navlya U.S.S.R.
54 F4 Navlya R U.S.S.R.
57 D4 Navoi U.S.S.R.
124 E4 Navojoa Mexico
124 F5 Navolato Mexico
52 E3 Navolok U.S.S.R.
52 F5 Navoloki U.S.S.R.
46 E6 Návpaktos Greece
46 F7 Návplion Greece
28 B4 Navr Denmark
85 D6 Navrongo Ghana
74 E8 Navsari India
75 N6 Nawabganj Bangladesh
75 J5 Nawabganj India
74 C5 Nawabshah Pakistan
75 L6 Nawada India
77 K3 Nāwah Afghanistan
83 K10 Nawalapitiya Sri Lanka
84 F3 Nawfalīyah,an Libya
138 F5 Nawingi Victoria
68 D1 Nawng-Hpa Burma
68 C1 Nawngkio Burma
68 D1 Nawngleng Burma
67 B2 Naxi China
47 G7 Náxos Greece
47 H7 Náxos isld Greece
18 E9 Nay France
69 J12 Naya Indonesia
16 E4 Nayacerrada, Pto. de peak Spain
75 L8 Nayagarh India
124 G6 Nayar Mexico
124 G7 Nayarit state Mexico
77 E3 Nay Band Iran
9 G4 Nayland England
113 D7 Naylor Georgia
110 F5 Naylor Missouri
67 B3 Nayong China
59 M3 Nayoro Japan
129 L6 Nazaré Brazil
16 A5 Nazaré Portugal
130 J9 Nazaré da Mata Brazil
22 F2 Nazareth Belgium
Nazareth Ethiopia see Adama
76 C6 Nazareth India
80 E3 Nazareth Israel
95 M6 Nazareth Pennsylvania
130 E5 Nazário Brazil
54 N2 Nazarovka U.S.S.R.
56 D3 Nazarovo Krasnoyarskiy Kray U.S.S.R.
55 F3 Nazarovo Tyumenskaya U.S.S.R.
124 G5 Nazas Mexico
128 D6 Nazca Peru
59 J6 Naze Japan
9 H4 Naze,The C England
47 J7 Nazilli Turkey
56 A1 Nazinskaya R U.S.S.R.
75 Q5 Nazira India
75 O7 Nazir Hat Bangladesh
117 M9 Nazko Br Col
80 A7 Nazla Israel
80 D4 Nazlat Jordan
86 G4 Nazret Ethiopia
67 B4 Nazuo China
55 E1 Nazym R U.S.S.R.
55 F3 Nazyvayevsk U.S.S.R.
37 J1 Nazza E Germany
89 F3 Ncema Dam Zimbabwe
88 A8 Nchanga Zambia
88 E9 Ncheu Malawi
87 B7 Ndalakanda Angola
85 E6 Ndali Benin
71 L10 Ndao isld Indonesia
86 D4 Ndele Cent Afr Republic
86 B6 Ndendé Gabon
137 O4 Ndeni isld Santa Cruz Is
86 B5 Ndikiniméki Cameroon
86 B6 Ndindi Gabon
86 C3 N'Djamena Chad
86 B6 Ndjolé Gabon
86 B6 N'Dogou, L Gabon
88 B8 Ndola Zambia
71 K9 Ndona Flores Indonesia
86 B6 N'Dongo Congo
26 E8 Nea Norway
139 J3 Neabul R Queensland
46 D5 Néa Filippías Greece
14 E2 Neagh,L N Ireland
107 O4 Neal Kansas
140 B6 Neale,L N Terr Aust
138 D3 Neales R S Australia
47 F4 Neá Moudhaniá Greece
21 I6 Néant R France
15 G2 Neap Shetland Scotland
47 H9 Néapolis Crete Greece
46 E4 Neápolis Makedhonia Greece
46 F8 Neápolis Pelopónnisos Greece
47 F6 Néa Psará Greece
116 J9 Near Is Aleutian Is
8 C4 Neath Wales
20 J4 Neauphle-le-Château France
47 H3 Néa Víssi Greece
85 D6 Nebbou Upper Volta
52 G3 Nebdino U.S.S.R.
28 A7 Nebel W Germany
33 Q5 Nebel R E Germany
41 M3 Nebelhorn mt W Germany
43 B12 Nebeur Tunisia
43 C12 Nebhana R Tunisia
141 H8 Nebine R Queensland
50 E5 Nebit-Dag U.S.S.R.
141 J5 Nebo Queensland
52 D5 Nebolchi U.S.S.R.
80 F6 Nebo, Mt Jordan
103 N2 Nebo,Mt Utah
33 P10 Nebra E Germany
98 G8 Nebraska state U.S.A.
99 L9 Nebraska City Nebraska
43 F11 Nebrodi,Monti Sicily
99 Q5 Necedah Wisconsin
117 L9 Nechako R Br Col
98 J1 Neche N Dakota
109 M4 Neches R Texas
128 D2 Nechi R Colombia
33 T6 Nechlin E Germany
36 F7 Neckar R W Germany
36 F5 Neckarbischofsheim W Germany
36 G5 Neckarelz W Germany
36 F5 Neckargemünd W Germany
36 F5 Neckarsteinach W Germany
36 G5 Neckarsulm W Germany
102 U13 Necker I Hawaiian Is
144 B7 Neck, The New Zealand
131 F7 Necochea Argentina
37 P4 Nečtiny Czechoslovakia
86 B6 Necuto Angola
20 E4 Nécy France
16 B1 Neda Spain
33 S5 Neddemin E Germany
121 L5 Nedelec Quebec
106 E2 Nederland Colorado
109 N6 Nederland Texas
25 E5 Neder Rijn R Netherlands
25 E6 Nederweert Netherlands
142 A2 Nedlands dist Perth, W Aust
33 Q8 Nedlitz E Germany
17 F9 Nedroma Algeria
31 L5 Nedza Poland
25 G4 Neede Netherlands
9 H3 Needham Market England
101 Q5 Needle Mt Wyoming
144 A6 Needle Pk New Zealand
103 K7 Needles California
145 E2 Needles Pt New Zealand
9 E6 Needles, The rocks England
109 M6 Needville Texas
119 S9 Neelin Manitoba
101 N7 Neely Idaho
110 F5 Neelyville Missouri
130 B10 Neembucú dep Paraguay
99 S5 Neenah Wisconsin
119 S8 Neepawa Manitoba
25 E6 Neer Netherlands
143 B8 Neereno hill W Australia
106 H3 Nee Res Colorado
115 M3 Neergaard L N W Terr
22 J1 Neerpelt Belgium
22 J2 Neerwinden Belgium
28 A4 Nees Denmark
112 F4 Neeses S Carolina
55 F2 Nefedovo U.S.S.R.
85 F2 Nefta Tunisia
57 F4 Nefteabad U.S.S.R.
8 B2 Nefyn Wales
43 C12 Nefza Tunisia
87 C7 Negage Angola
85 C6 Negala Mali
83 K10 Negama Sri Lanka
70 P10 Negara Bali Indonesia
70 D6 Negara Kalimantan
70 D6 Negara R Kalimantan
99 T3 Negaunee Michigan
80 B7 Negba Israel
86 G4 Negelli Ethiopia
69 F11 Negeri Sembilan Malaysia
79 E8 Negev mt reg Israel
130 C8 Negla R Paraguay
48 J5 Negoiu mt Romania
87 G8 Negomano Mozambique
83 J10 Negombo Sri Lanka
48 H6 Negotin Yugoslavia
46 E3 Negotino Yugoslavia
73 P5 Negrais,C Burma
143 D7 Negrara,R W Australia
130 G6 Negra,Serra mts Brazil
16 B2 Negreira Spain
48 J6 Negreni Romania
18 G8 Nègrepelisse France
48 L4 Negreşti Romania
127 H1 Negril Pt.N Jamaica
141 F7 Negri Mts Queensland
16 E9 Negri,Pta Morocco
128 F4 Negro R Brazil
16 D9 Negro,C Morocco
94 H7 Negro Mt Penn/Maryland
131 C7 Negro,R Argentina
130 B9 Negro,R Paraguay
131 F4 Negro,R Uruguay
71 F5 Negros isld Philippines
47 J1 Negru Vadă Romania
100 B4 Nehalem Oregon
80 C5 Nehalim Israel
77 G4 Nehbandān Iran
59 H2 Nehe China
32 G10 Neheim-Hüsten W Germany
48 K5 Nehoiaşu Romania
20 B3 Néhou France
33 R4 Nehringen E Germany
137 S5 Neiafu Tonga
127 J5 Neiba Dom Rep
33 R10 Neichen E Germany
52 C1 Neiden Norway
118 K8 Neidpath Sask
101 P3 Neihart Montana
65 C7 Neihuang China
67 B2 Neijiang China
Neikiang see Neijiang
16 E2 Neila,Sa.de mts Spain
118 H6 Neilburg Sask
68 A7 Neill I Andaman Is
99 Q5 Neillsville Wisconsin
123 M7 Neil's Harbour C Breton I, N Scotia
100 B2 Neilton Washington
58 E3 Nei Monggol Zizhiqu aut reg China
33 N8 Neindorf W Germany
36 G5 Neipperg W Germany
65 C6 Neiqiu China
Neisse see Nysa
31 H4 Neisse R E Ger/Poland
128 C3 Neiva Colombia
37 O3 Nejdek Czechoslovakia
86 G4 Nejo Ethiopia
98 H1 Nekoma N Dakota
99 R5 Nekoosa Wisconsin
28 G5 Nekselø isld Denmark
51 O2 Neksikan U.S.S.R.
27 H16 Neksø Denmark
27 C13 Nelaug Norway
141 F5 Nelia Queensland
52 D6 Nelidovo U.S.S.R.
54 D1 Nelidovo U.S.S.R.
98 J7 Neligh Nebraska
142 E3 Nellie,Mt W Australia
139 K6 Nelligen New S Wales
76 D3 Nellore India
59 L2 Nel'ma U.S.S.R.
52 F5 Nel'sha U.S.S.R.
103 L6 Nelson Arizona
117 P11 Nelson Br Col
102 C2 Nelson California
13 F6 Nelson England
112 J2 Nelson N Carolina
98 H9 Nelson Nebraska
103 K6 Nelson Nevada
145 D4 Nelson New Zealand
95 K5 Nelson Pennsylvania
138 F7 Nelson Victoria
8 C4 Nelson Wales
99 P5 Nelson Wisconsin
144 C4 Nelson stat area New Zealand
138 F7 Nelson,C Victoria
144 C5 Nelson Cr New Zealand
133 C8 Nelson,Estrecho chan Chile
117 M6 Nelson Forks Br Col
119 T3 Nelson House Manitoba
116 E6 Nelson I Alaska
146 E15 Nelson I S Shetland Is
145 D4 Nelson Lakes Nat. Park New Zealand
119 V3 Nelson R Manitoba
101 S1 Nelson Res Montana
94 E7 Nelsonville Ohio
89 G5 Nelspruit S Africa
52 J4 Nem R U.S.S.R.
85 C5 Néma Mauritania
52 H5 Nema U.S.S.R.
99 O3 Nemadji R Minnesota
99 L9 Nemaha Nebraska
76 C6 Nemam India
31 O2 Neman R U.S.S.R.
71 L10 Nembrala Indonesia
52 F5 Nemda R U.S.S.R.
52 H3 Nemed U.S.S.R.
120 G5 Nemegos Ontario
120 G4 Nemegosenda L Ontario
119 M3 Nemeiban Sask
46 D4 Nëmerçkë Albania
45 N6 Nemi L Italy
48 K4 Nemira mt Romania
48 M2 Nemirov U.S.S.R.
115 M7 Nemiscau Quebec
18 G4 Nemours France
60 T2 Nemuro Japan
60 S2 Nemuro prefect Japan
60 T1 Nemuro-kaikyō str Japan/Kuril Is
14 C4 Nenagh Irish Rep
116 N4 Nenana Alaska
41 L3 Nendeln Liechtenstein
9 F2 Nene, R England
59 J2 Nenjiang China
59 H2 Nen Jiang R China
36 B4 Nennig W Germany
36 H1 Nentershausen W Germany
13 F4 Nenthead England
98 E7 Nenzel Nebraska
41 L3 Nenzing Austria
107 P4 Neodesha Kansas
99 S10 Neoga Illinois
99 L8 Neola Iowa
103 O1 Neola Utah
47 H7 Néon Karlóvasi Greece
99 S5 Neopit Wisconsin
130 H11 Neópolis Brazil
99 S6 Neosho Wisconsin
107 P4 Neosho R Kansas/Okla
80 D3 Neot Golan Israel
80 F1 Ne'ot Mordekhay Israel
56 G2 Nepa R U.S.S.R.
75 K4 Nepal kingdom S Asia
75 J5 Nepalganj India
103 N2 Nephi Utah
14 B2 Nephin mt Irish Rep
14 B2 Nephin Beg mt Irish Rep
121 N8 Nephton Ontario
45 M5 Nepi Italy
37 P3 Nepomyšl Czechoslovakia
119 N9 Neptune Sask
113 F7 Neptune Beach Florida
138 D6 Neptune Is S Australia
146 F10 Neptune Rge Antarctica
52 F6 Ner' U.S.S.R.
31 L4 Ner R Poland
42 E6 Nera R Italy
48 G6 Nera R Romania
18 F8 Nérac France
116 D6 Neragon I Alaska
58 G1 Nercha R U.S.S.R.
33 R10 Nerchau E Germany
58 G1 Nerchinsk U.S.S.R.
59 G1 Nerchinsky Zavod U.S.S.R.
68 C7 Nerchus Passage Burma
52 J5 Nerdva U.S.S.R.
21 E10 Néré France
52 F5 Nerekhta U.S.S.R.
37 J6 Neresheim W Germany
42 H5 Neretva R Yugoslavia
87 D9 Neriquinha Angola
116 H7 Nerka,L Alaska
52 E6 Nerl' U.S.S.R.
45 N5 Nerola Italy
18 G5 Nerondes France
45 N4 Nerone, M mt Italy
130 E5 Nerópolis Brazil
52 J3 Neroyka, Gora mt U.S.S.R.
17 F6 Nerpio Spain
139 K6 Nerriga New S Wales
142 E4 Nerrima W Australia
54 E4 Nerussa R U.S.S.R.
16 C7 Nerva Spain
44 F3 Nervi Italy
52 K2 Ner'yuvom U.S.S.R.
25 E2 Nes Netherlands
27 D11 Nesbyen Norway
95 L5 Nescopeck Pennsylvania
47 J2 Nesebŭr Bulgaria
52 C6 Neshcherdo Oz L U.S.S.R.
80 D2 Nesher Israel
116 A3 Neshkan Alaska
99 R6 Neshkoro Wisconsin
111 G9 Neshoba Mississippi
27 D13 Neslandsvatn Norway
22 D4 Nesle France
123 N3 Nesle,L Quebec
26 F5 Nesna Norway
26 F5 Nesöy isld Norway
100 G1 Nespelem Washington
45 O5 Nespolo Italy
19 O16 Nesque R France
107 L3 Ness City Kansas
37 K1 Nesse R E Germany
26 R1 Nesseby Norway
117 F6 Nesselrode,Mt Br Col/Alaska
18 F10 Neste R France
31 O1 Nesterov U.S.S.R.
120 G6 Nesterville Ontario
52 G6 Nestiary U.S.S.R.
127 P2 Nestor Trinidad
118 J1 Nestor Falls Ontario
99 S3 Nestoria Michigan
46 E4 Nestórion Greece
47 G3 Néstos R Greece
27 A11 Nesttun Norway
80 C6 Nes Ziyyona Israel
80 C4 Netanya Israel
107 P2 Netawaka Kansas
95 N6 Netcong New Jersey
32 K9 Nethe R W Germany
141 J5 Netherdale Queensland
118 H7 Netherhill Sask
25 Netherlands kingdom Europe
8 C5 Nether Stowey England
145 E2 Netherton New Zealand
15 E3 Nethy Bridge Scotland
80 C6 Netiva Israel
80 C7 Netiv HaLamed Israel
80 B8 Netivot Israel
43 H9 Neto R Italy
36 E2 Netphen W Germany
37 J1 Netra W Germany
75 O6 Netrakona Bangladesh
36 C3 Nette R W Germany
36 B3 Nettersheim W Germany
25 F6 Nettetal W Germany
115 M4 Nettilling L N W Terr
99 N1 Nett L Minnesota
9 F4 Nettlebed England
120 K4 Nettle Lakes Prov. Park Ontario
110 F6 Nettleton Arkansas
111 H7 Nettleton Mississippi
45 N7 Nettuno Italy
125 N9 Netzahaulcoyotl, Presa res Mexico
37 N2 Netzschkau E Germany
36 H1 Neu W Germany
32 G7 Neu Arenberg W Germany
37 N5 Neubäu W Germany
32 H9 Neubeckum W Germany
20 G3 Neubourg,le France
33 S5 Neubrandenburg E Germany
33 R5 Neubrandenburg reg E Germany
32 J7 Neubruchhausen W Germany
36 H4 Neubrunn W Germany
33 P4 Neubukow E Germany
33 P5 Neuburg E Germany
37 L6 Neuburg W Germany
40 E3 Neuchâtel canton Switzerland
40 E4 Neuchâtel, Lac de Switzerland
32 M9 Neuckrug W Germany
119 P8 Neudorf Sask
37 M3 Neudrossenfeld W Germany
32 L10 Neu-Eichenberg W Germany
36 F6 Neuenburg Baden-Württemberg W Germany
32 G6 Neuenburg Niedersachsen W Germany
32 E7 Neuenhaus W Germany
32 J6 Neuenkirchen Niedersachsen W Germany
32 F8 Neuenkirchen Nordrhein-Westfalen W Germany
32 G10 Neuenrade W Germany
36 G5 Neuenstadt W Germany
36 H5 Neuenstein W Germany
36 G2 Neuental W Germany
32 J5 Neuenwalde W Germany
37 M7 Neufahrn W Germany
40 G1 Neuf Brisach France
22 J4 Neufchateau Belgium
19 J4 Neufchâteau France
20 F5 Neufchâtel France
20 H2 Neufchâtel-en-Bray France
22 B2 Neufchâtel-Hardelot France
22 F5 Neufchâtel-sur-Aisne France
38 K5 Neufelden Austria
36 G6 Neuffen W Germany
20 J3 Neufmarche France
36 G7 Neufra W Germany
41 N2 Neugablonz W Germany
33 S6 Neuglobsow E Germany
32 G5 Neuharlingersiel W Germany
37 M4 Neuhaus Bayern W Germany
33 N6 Neuhaus E Germany
32 K5 Neuhaus Niedersachsen W Germany
37 P2 Neuhausen E Germany
36 G6 Neuhausen W Germany
33 S8 Neuhof E Germany
38 K5 Neuhofen Austria
36 G5 Neuhütten W Germany
21 G6 Neuillé-Pt. Pierre France
20 G4 Neuilly France
20 K3 Neuilly-en-Thelle France
20 C3 Neuilly-la-Fôret France
36 F3 Neu-Isenburg W Germany
33 R5 Neukalen E Germany
33 O6 Neu Kaliss E Germany
38 F7 Neukirchen Austria
37 O2 Neukirchen E Germany
33 O4 Neukirchen Schleswig-Holstein W Germany
37 N5 Neukirchen Balbini W Germany
33 P5 Neukloster E Germany
32 L6 Neukloster W Germany
37 N2 Neumark E Germany
38 H6 Neumarkt Salzburg Austria
38 K7 Neumarkt Steiermark Austria
37 L5 Neumarkt W Germany
37 O7 Neumarkt-St Veit W Germany
32 L4 Neumünster W Germany
37 N5 Neunburg W Germany
21 I6 Neung sur-Beuvron France
38 O6 Neunkirchen Austria
36 D2 Neunkirchen Nordrhein-Westfalen W Germany
36 E2 Neunkirchen Rheinland-Pfalz W Germany
36 C5 Neunkirchen Saarland W Germany
36 C2 Neunkirchen W Germany
37 O7 Neuötting W Germany
131 C7 Neuquén Argentina
131 B7 Neuquén terr Argentina
131 B7 Neuquén, R Argentina
33 R7 Neuruppin E Germany
37 K7 Neusäss W Germany
112 L3 Neuse R N Carolina
48 D3 Neusiedla Austria
48 D3 Neusiedler See Austria
36 B1 Neuss W Germany
18 H7 Neussargues France
48 C3 Neustadt Austria
37 M2 Neustadt Gera E Germany
36 G2 Neustadt Hessen W Germany
36 G4 Neustadt Hessen W Germany
36 H3 Neustadt Hessen W Germany
33 Q7 Neustadt Potsdam E Germany
36 E5 Neustadt Rheinland-Pfalz W Germany
37 K2 Neustadt Suhl E Germany
37 K4 Neustadt an der Aisch W Germany
37 N4 Neustadt an der Waldnaab W Germany
37 L3 Neustadt bei Coburg W Germany
33 P6 Neustadt-Glewe E Germany
32 G6 Neustadt-gödens W Germany
Neustettin see Szczecinek
37 M7 Neustift W Germany
33 S6 Neustrelitz E Germany
37 J7 Neu Ulm W Germany
22 D2 Neuve Chapelle France
20 G4 Neuve-Lyre, la France
40 F3 Neuveville Switzerland
18 G7 Neuvic France
109 N4 Neuville Texas
20 K5 Neuville-aux-Bois France
21 F8 Neuville-de-Poitou France
22 G5 Neuville-en-Tourne-à-Fuy France
19 O12 Neuville-les-Dames France
20 H2 Neuville-lès-Dieppe France
21 I8 Neuvy-St. Sépulchre France
21 J7 Neuvy sur Barangeon France
33 O8 Neuwegersleben E Germany
36 E6 Neuweier W Germany
32 H5 Neuwerk isld W Germany
36 C3 Neuwied W Germany
36 C6 Neuwiller France
32 L6 Neu-Wulmstorf W Germany
27 G11 Neva Sweden
99 R4 Neva Wisconsin
52 D5 Neva R U.S.S.R.
99 N7 Nevada Iowa
110 B4 Nevada Missouri
109 L2 Nevada Texas
92 C3 Nevada state U.S.A.
102 C2 Nevada City California
128 D2 Nevada de Cocuy,Sa mts Colombia
124 H8 Nevada de Colima Mexico
16 E7 Nevada, Sierra mts Spain
131 C5 Nevado, Cerro peak Argentina
131 B6 Nevados Chillán mt Chile
131 C5 Nevado, Sierra del ra Argentina
54 A1 Nevel' U.S.S.R.
59 M2 Nevel'sk U.S.S.R.
59 H1 Never U.S.S.R.
8 B3 Nevern Wales
26 F6 Nevernes Norway
18 H5 Nevers France
139 J4 Nevertire New S Wales
48 E7 Nevesinje Yugoslavia
45 H2 Neviano d'Arduini Italy
32 F10 Neviges W Germany
20 G2 Neville France
118 K9 Neville Sask
112 F5 Nevils Georgia
53 F11 Nevinnomyssk U.S.S.R.
79 E9 Neviot Egypt
118 D6 Nevis Alberta
99 M3 Nevis Minnesota
127 P4 Nevis isld Lesser Antilles
127 P4 Nevis Pk Nevis W I
80 E6 Nevit HaGedud Jordan
78 E2 Nevşehir Turkey
65 J2 Nevskoye U.S.S.R.
55 D2 Nev'yansk U.S.S.R.
103 J9 New R California
112 F1 New R N Carolina
94 F9 New R Virginia/W Virginia
12 E4 New Abbey Scotland
95 S3 Newagen Maine
87 G8 Newala Tanzania
94 B8 New Albany Indiana
111 G7 New Albany Mississippi
95 L5 New Albany Pennsylvania
99 P6 New Albin Iowa
99 S4 Newald Wisconsin
141 J8 New Angledool New S Wales
110 E6 Newark Arkansas
102 B4 Newark California
95 M7 Newark Delaware
9 F1 Newark England
99 S8 Newark Illinois
98 G9 Newark Nebraska
95 N6 Newark New Jersey
95 K3 Newark New York
94 E6 Newark Ohio
95 L4 Newark Valley New York
110 G3 New Athens Illinois
99 P4 New Auburn Wisconsin
111 G10 New Augusta Mississippi
94 E4 New Baltimore Michigan
94 J7 New Baltimore Pennsylvania
95 R5 New Bedford Massachusetts
146 E12 New Bedford Inlet Antarctica
100 C4 Newberg Oregon
99 Q10 New Berlin Illinois
95 M4 New Berlin New York
111 J9 Newbern Alabama
112 K2 New Bern N Carolina
110 G5 Newbern Tennessee
102 H7 Newberry California
113 E8 Newberry Florida
110 J3 Newberry Indiana
99 V3 Newberry Michigan
112 F3 Newberry S Carolina
94 H5 New Bethlehem Pennsylvania
13 G3 Newbiggin by-the-Sea England
13 E3 Newbigging Scotland
110 D3 New Bloomfield Missouri
99 R4 Newbold Wisconsin
121 O8 Newboro Ontario
8 B1 Newborough Môn Wales
99 Q8 New Boston Illinois
109 N2 New Boston Texas
109 J6 New Braunfels Texas
94 C6 New Bremen Ohio
12 E3 New Bridge Scotland
8 C3 Newbridge Wales
118 G7 New Brigden Alberta
95 P5 New Britain Connecticut
111 L10 New Brockton Alabama
95 N6 New Brunswick New Jersey
115 N8 New Brunswick prov Canada
9 H3 New Buckenham England
99 U8 New Buffalo Michigan
99 O8 Newburg Iowa
110 E4 Newburg Missouri
94 K6 Newburg Pennsylvania
94 H7 Newburg W Virginia
15 E4 Newburgh Fife Scotland
15 F3 Newburgh Grampian Scotland
110 J4 Newburgh Indiana
95 N5 Newburgh New York
121 O8 Newburgh Ontario
123 T5 New Burnt Cove Nfld
9 E5 Newbury England
95 R4 Newburyport Massachusetts
85 E6 New Bussa Nigeria
137 N6 New Caledonia isld Pacific Oc
95 O5 New Canaan Connecticut
99 P10 New Canton Illinois
94 C7 New Carlisle Ohio
122 G5 New Carlisle Quebec
102 C3 Newcastle California
106 C2 New Castle Colorado
94 B7 New Castle Indiana
14 E3 Newcastle Irish Rep
127 L2 Newcastle Jamaica
110 L3 New Castle Kentucky
98 K7 Newcastle Nebraska
127 P4 Newcastle Nevis W I
122 G6 Newcastle New Brunswick
95 M7 New Castle New Jersey
139 K5 Newcastle New S Wales
14 F2 Newcastle N Ireland
107 N6 Newcastle Oklahoma
121 M9 Newcastle Ontario
94 G6 New Castle Pennsylvania
89 F6 Newcastle S Africa
109 J2 Newcastle Texas
103 L4 Newcastle Utah
94 G9 New Castle Virginia
98 B6 Newcastle Wyoming
141 G1 Newcastle B Queensland
122 F7 Newcastle Br New Brunswick
8 B3 Newcastle Emlyn Wales
118 E7 Newcastle Mine Alberta
141 G4 Newcastle Ra Queensland
15 F5 Newcastleton Scotland
8 D1 Newcastle Under Lyme England
13 G4 Newcastle-upon-Tyne England
140 C3 Newcastle Waters N Terr Aust
14 B4 Newcastle West Irish Rep
9 F5 New Chapel England
106 B5 Newcomb New Mexico
94 F6 Newcomerstown Ohio
94 F7 New Concord Ohio
12 D3 New Cumnock Scotland
12 D3 New Dailly Scotland
101 O6 Newdale Idaho
119 R8 Newdale Manitoba
118 E9 New Dayton Alberta
15 F3 New Deer Scotland
143 C10 Newdegate W Australia
76 New Delhi India
117 P11 New Denver Br Col
111 M7 New Echota Nat.Mon Georgia
111 D8 New Edinburg Arkansas
113 E7 Newell Georgia
99 L7 Newell Iowa
112 G2 Newell N Carolina
98 C5 Newell S Dakota
112 F4 New Ellenton S Carolina
118 E8 Newell L Alberta
143 F6 Newell,L W Australia
111 E9 Newellton Louisiana
98 D3 New England N Dakota
139 K4 New England Ra mts New S Wales
90 D4 New England Seamount Chain Atlantic Oc
116 F7 Newenham,C Alaska
8 D4 Newent England
94 A3 New Era Michigan
80 F3 Newe Ur Israel
80 C3 Newe Yam Israel
94 J3 Newfane New York
95 P3 Newfane Vermont
141 K1 New Farm dist Brisbane, Qnsld
95 R3 Newfield Maine
95 M7 Newfield New Jersey
117 P8 New Fish Creek Alberta
110 E3 New Florence Missouri
98 K1 Newfolden Minnesota
9 E6 New Forest England
95 Q3 Newfound L New Hampshire
95 M5 Newfoundland Pennsylvania
123 P1 Newfoundland prov Canada
90 F5 Newfoundland Basin Atlantic Oc
90 E4 Newfoundland Rise Atlantic Oc
110 D2 New Franklin Missouri
95 L7 New Freedom Pennsylvania
8 A4 Newgale Wales
12 D3 New Galloway Scotland
118 B9 Newgate Br Col
137 M3 New Georgia isld Solomon Is
122 H9 New Germany Nova Scotia
99 R7 New Glarus Wisconsin
122 K8 New Glasgow Nova Scotia
95 R3 New Gloucester Maine
127 O3 New Grant Trinidad
136 J3 New Guinea isld S E Asia
109 M6 Newgulf Texas
100 D1 Newhalem Washington
116 K7 Newhalen Alaska
102 F7 Newhall California
116 F5 New Hamilton Alaska
95 Q4 New Hampshire state U.S.A.
99 O6 New Hampton Iowa
99 M9 New Hampton Missouri
95 S3 New Harbor Maine
110 J3 New Harmony Indiana
95 O5 New Hartford Connecticut
95 P5 New Haven Connecticut
9 G6 Newhaven England
94 B5 New Haven Indiana
110 E3 New Haven Missouri
94 F8 New Haven W Virginia
98 B5 New Haven Wyoming
117 K8 New Hazelton Br Col
137 O5 New Hebrides islds Pacific Oc
13 F6 New Hey England
13 H6 New Holland England
99 R9 New Holland Illinois
99 S6 New Holstein Wisconsin
109 O1 Newhope Arkansas
12 E2 Newhouse Scotland
111 E12 New Iberia Louisiana
9 H5 Newington England
112 F5 Newington Georgia
137 L2 New Ireland isld Bismarck Arch
95 N7 New Jersey state U.S.A.
94 H6 New Kensington Pennsylvania
95 L9 New Kent Virginia
106 F6 Newkirk New Mexico
107 N5 Newkirk Oklahoma
143 E8 Newland Ra W Australia
98 E3 New Leipzig N Dakota
94 E7 New Lexington Ohio
99 Q6 New Lisbon Wisconsin
121 L5 New Liskeard Ontario
99 P9 New London Iowa
99 M4 New London Minnesota
99 P10 New London Missouri
94 E5 New London Ohio
99 S5 New London Wisconsin
12 D4 New Luce Scotland
110 G5 New Madrid Missouri
12 E2 Newmains Scotland
102 C4 Newman California
99 T10 Newman Illinois
106 D9 Newman New Mexico
145 E4 Newman New Zealand
143 C6 Newman W Australia
98 J8 Newman Gr Nebraska
142 C6 Newman,Mt W Australia
123 T5 Newman's Cove Nfld
9 G3 Newmarket England
99 M9 New Market Iowa
14 B4 Newmarket Irish Rep
127 J2 Newmarket Jamaica
95 Q3 Newmarket New Hampshire
139 G5 Newmarket New S Wales
121 L8 Newmarket Ontario
94 J8 New Market Virginia
141 K1 Newmarket dist Brisbane, Qnsld
94 E7 New Marshfield Ohio
94 G7 New Martinsville W Virginia
94 F7 New Matamoras Ohio
100 J5 New Meadows Idaho
106 D6 New Mexico state U.S.A.
94 C7 New Miami Ohio
95 O5 New Milford Connecticut
95 M5 New Milford Pennsylvania
12 D2 Newmilns Scotland
108 E2 New Moore Texas
111 M8 Newnan Georgia
113 E8 Newnan L Florida
139 K5 Newnes New S Wales
8 D4 Newnham England
143 B9 New Norcia W Australia
139 H8 New Norfolk Tasmania
118 E6 New Norway Alberta
111 F11 New Orleans Louisiana
119 O6 New Osgoode Sask
95 K7 New Oxford Pennsylvania
95 N5 New Paltz New York
94 C7 New Paris Ohio
94 A8 New Pekin Indiana
94 F6 New Philadelphia Ohio
100 E7 New Pine Creek Oregon
15 F3 New Pitsligo Scotland
100 J6 New Plymouth Idaho
145 E3 New Plymouth New Zealand
110 E6 Newport Arkansas
126 B2 New Port Curaçao
8 B3 Newport Dyfed Wales
9 G4 Newport Essex England
8 D4 Newport Gwent Wales
99 T10 Newport Indiana
9 E6 Newport I of Wight England
14 B3 Newport Irish Rep
127 K3 Newport Jamaica
110 M2 Newport Kentucky
94 D5 Newport Michigan
99 O5 Newport Minnesota
112 L3 Newport N Carolina
98 G7 Newport Nebraska
95 P3 Newport New Hampshire
95 M7 Newport New Jersey
100 A5 Newport Oregon
95 K6 Newport Pennsylvania
122 H5 Newport Quebec
95 Q5 Newport Rhode I
8 D2 Newport Salop England
112 D2 Newport Tennessee
109 J2 Newport Texas
95 P2 Newport Vermont
100 H1 Newport Washington
102 G8 Newport Beach California
95 L10 Newport News Virginia
13 F1 Newport-on-Tay Scotland
9 F3 Newport Pagnell England
113 E9 New Port Richey Florida
112 D1 New Powell Tennessee
99 N5 New Prague Minnesota
113 L9 New Providence isld Bahamas
8 A7 Newquay England
8 B3 New Quay Wales
113 E8 New R Florida
8 C3 New Radnor Wales
106 G1 New Raymer Colorado
99 N6 New Richland Minnesota
94 C8 New Richmond Ohio
122 G5 New Richmond Quebec
99 O4 New Richmond Wisconsin
110 M5 New River Tennessee
112 K3 New River Inlet N Carolina
111 E11 New Roads Louisiana
98 G2 New Rockford N Dakota
9 G6 New Romney England
110 K2 New Ross Indiana
14 E4 New Ross Irish Rep
95 R2 Newry Maine
14 E2 Newry N Ireland
140 A3 Newry N Terr Aust
94 J6 Newry Pennsylvania
14 E2 Newry Canal N Ireland
98 E3 New Salem N Dakota
94 H7 New Salem Pennsylvania
13 E1 New Scone Scotland
99 O8 New Sharon Iowa
New Siberian Is see Novosibirskiye Os
113 G8 New Smyrna Beach Florida
139 New South Wales state Australia
141 J5 Newstead Queensland
94 E7 New Straitsville Ohio
85 D7 New Tamale Ghana
94 D10 New Tazewell Tennessee
116 E6 Newtok Alaska
111 L10 Newton Alabama
9 G2 Newton England
110 H3 Newton Illinois
99 N8 Newton Iowa
107 N3 Newton Kansas
95 Q4 Newton Massachusetts
111 G9 Newton Mississippi
112 F2 Newton N Carolina
13 E3 Newton Scotland
109 O5 Newton Texas
8 C6 Newton Abbot England
13 E4 Newton Arlosh England
95 M2 Newton Falls New York
94 G5 Newton Falls Ohio
8 B7 Newton Ferrers England
112 J2 Newton Grove N Carolina
94 K6 Newton Hamilton Pennsylvania
13 F6 Newton-le-Willows England
12 D2 Newton Mearns Scotland
15 D3 Newtonmore Scotland
101 O8 Newton Res Utah
12 D4 Newton Stewart Scotland

Newtown — North Uist 55

110 C1 Newtown Missouri
123 T4 Newtown Nfld
95 K9 Newtown Virginia
8 C3 Newtown Wales
14 E2 Newtownabbey N Ireland
14 F2 Newtownards N Ireland
14 D2 Newtown Butler N Ireland
14 E2 Newtownhamilton N Ireland
14 E3 Newtown Mt.Kennedy Irish Rep
98 D2 New Town Sanish N Dakota
14 D2 Newtown Stewart N Ireland
99 M5 New Ulm Minnesota
109 L6 New Ulm Texas
98 D5 New Underwood S Dakota
111 L10 Newville Alabama
102 B2 Newville California
94 K6 Newville Pennsylvania
99 N8 New Virginia Iowa
94 E6 New Washington Ohio
123 M7 New Waterford C Breton I, N S
109 M5 New Waverly Texas
117 J11 New Westminster Br Col
95 K7 New Windsor Maryland
123 S4 New World I Nfld
100 F8 New Year L Nevada
96 New York conurbation
95 K4 New York state U.S.A.
103 J6 New York Mts California
144 New Zealand state S W Pacific
21 H10 Nexon France
94 C5 Ney Ohio
52 F5 Neya U.S.S.R.
8 B4 Neyland Wales
77 D5 Neyriz Iran
77 F1 Neyshābūr Iran
55 D2 Neyvo Shaytanskiy U.S.S.R.
31 H6 Nežárka R Czechoslovakia
54 C5 Nezhin U.S.S.R.
100 J3 Nezperce Idaho
61 N7 Nezugaseki Japan
86 C6 N'Gabé Congo
68 D5 Nga Chong,Khao mt Burma/Thailand
68 H5 Ngac Linh mt Vietnam
68 A2 Ngahan Burma
144 C5 Ngahere New Zealand
145 F3 Ngamatea Swamp New Zealand
66 F5 Ngamda China
87 D10 Ngami, L Botswana
70 N9 Ngandjuk Java
66 C5 Ngangla Ringco L China
Nganglaring Tso see Ngangla Ringco
66 C5 Nganglong Kangri China
74 J2 Nganglong Kangri mt ra China
75 M3 Ngangzê Co L China
68 G3 Ngan Pha R Vietnam
68 G3 Ngan Sau R Vietnam
68 G1 Ngan Son Vietnam
86 C6 N'Gao Congo
86 B4 Ngaoundére Cameroon
144 C6 Ngapara New Zealand
68 B2 Ngape Burma
145 F3 Ngapuketurua mt New Zealand
144 C6 Ngapuna New Zealand
145 E3 Ngaroma New Zealand
145 E2 Ngaruawahia New Zealand
145 F3 Ngaruroro R New Zealand
145 D1 Ngataki New Zealand
145 F3 Ngatapo New Zealand
145 E2 Ngatea New Zealand
68 B4 Ngathainggyaung Burma
145 E3 Ngatira New Zealand
145 E3 Ngauruhoe vol New Zealand
68 D7 Ngawan Chaung R Burma
145 F2 Ngawaro New Zealand
70 N9 Ngawi Java
68 B4 Ngayok B Burma
Ngemda see Ngamda
89 G2 Ngezi R Zimbabwe
89 G2 Ngezi Dam Zimbabwe
Nghia Hung see Phu Qui
70 O9 Ngimbang Java
88 F6 Ngindo Tanzania
87 C9 N'Giva Angola
86 C5 Ngoko R Congo
87 E9 Ngoma Zambia
88 F2 Ngong Kenya
145 F3 Ngongotaha New Zealand
88 D7 Ngoni Malawi
86 F5 Ngoring Hu L China
88 E3 Ngorongoro Crater Tanzania
71 A2 Ngotakiaha Halmahera Indonesia
86 B6 N'Gounié R Gabon
86 B2 N'Gourti Niger
88 B3 Ngozi Burundi
86 B3 N'Guigmi Niger
68 F3 Ngum R Laos
71 K10 Ngundju,Tg C Sumba Indonesia
145 E1 Ngunguru New Zealand
88 E7 Ngunja Tanzania
70 O10 Ngunut Java
85 G6 Nguru Nigeria
67 B5 Nguyen Binh Vietnam
89 D5 Ngwaketse dist Botswana
87 G10 Nhachengue Mozambique
128 G6 Nhambiquara Brazil
129 G4 Nhamunda Brazil
67 A6 Nhan Nghia Vietnam
68 J6 Nha Trang Vietnam
128 C6 Nhecolândia Brazil
67 B5 Nhiep R Laos
138 F6 Nhill Victoria
68 G4 Nhommarath Laos
140 D1 Nhulunbuy N Terr Aust
68 G3 Nhu Xuan Vietnam
98 H1 Niagara N Dakota
144 B7 Niagara New Zealand
99 S4 Niagara Wisconsin
94 J3 Niagara Falls New York
121 L9 Niagara Falls Ontario
121 L9 Niagara-on-the-Lake Ontario
70 C3 Niah Sarawak
85 C7 Niakaramandougou Ivory Coast
85 E6 Niamey Niger
86 E5 Niangara Zaïre
85 D5 Niangaye,L Mali
85 C7 Niangbo,Pic de mt Ivory Coast
85 D6 Niangoloko Upper Volta
110 D4 Niangua R Missouri
Niangxi see Xinshao
86 E5 Nia Nia Zaïre
95 P5 Niantic Connecticut
65 E1 Nianzishan China
70 E4 Niapa, G mt Kalimantan
101 L2 Niarada Montana
86 B6 Niari R Congo
69 C12 Nias isld Indonesia
88 F8 Niassa Mozambique
46 F8 Niata Greece
101 R4 Nibbe Montana
28 D3 Nibe Denmark
28 D2 Nibe Bredning B Denmark
142 E5 Nibil Well W Australia
121 R3 Nicabau Quebec
125 L3 Nicaragua rep Cent America
95 T1 Nicatous L
102 B2 Nice California
44 B4 Nice France
111 K11 Niceville Florida
115 M7 Nichicun, L Quebec
60 E11 Nichihara Japan
112 E6 Nicholls Georgia
99 P8 Nichols Iowa
95 L4 Nichols New York
142 G4 Nicholson W Australia
140 E4 Nicholson R Queensland
143 B7 Nicholson Ra W Australia
95 N2 Nicholville New York
99 O1 Nickel L Ontario
129 G2 Nickerie R Suriname
107 M3 Nickerson Kansas
142 B5 Nickol B W Australia
122 F3 Nicman Quebec
69 A8 Nicobar Is Bay of Bengal
117 N10 Nicola Br Col
121 S6 Nicolet Quebec
99 M5 Nicollet Minnesota
78 D4 Nicosia Cyprus
43 F11 Nicosia Sicily
43 G10 Nicotera Italy
125 M4 Nicoya Costa Rica
125 M5 Nicoya,Pen.de Costa Rica
122 E8 Nictau New Brunswick
31 M5 Nida R Poland
76 C5 Nidadavole India
123 Q6 Nid à L'Aigle,C.du Miquelon I Atlantic Oc
40 F3 Nidau Switzerland
36 G3 Nidda W Germany
36 F3 Nidda R W Germany
36 F3 Niddatal W Germany
36 F3 Niddeggen W Germany
27 C13 Nidelv R Norway
41 H4 Nidwalden canton Switzerland
31 M2 Nidzica Poland
30 D1 Niebüll W Germany
36 G1 Niedenstein W Germany
37 N6 Niederaichbach W Germany
37 L6 Niederarnbach W Germany
36 H2 Nieder Aula W Germany
37 N6 Niederbayern dist W Germany
36 C3 Niederbieber Germany
19 L4 Niederbronn France
33 O6 Nieder Elde R E Germany
36 G2 Nieder Gemünden W Germany
33 R9 Niedergörsdorf E Germany
25 F6 Niederkrüchten W Germany
36 D3 Nieder Lahnstein W Germany
32 J10 Nieder Marsberg W Germany
33 M6 Nieder Marschacht W Germany
36 H5 Niedernhall W Germany
36 E3 Niederneisen W Germany
36 E4 Nieder Olm W Germany
36 E3 Nieder Ouembach W Germany
32 J7 Niedersachsen land W Germany
36 D2 Nieder Schelden W Germany
36 E3 Niederselters W Germany
32 J10 Niedersfeld W Germany
36 H5 Niederstetten W Germany
37 J6 Niederstotzingen W Germany
36 D4 Niederwald W Germany
36 E2 Nieder Weidbach W Germany
36 F2 Nieder Weimar W Germany
37 P2 Niederwiesa E Germany
36 F3 Nieder Wöllstadt W Germany
36 C3 Nieder Zissen W Germany
33 T8 Nieder Zittau E Germany
32 K6 Nieheim W Germany
98 K2 Nielsville Minnesota
88 B4 Niemba Zaïre
88 B5 Niemba R Zaïre
33 Q9 Niemberg E Germany
31 K5 Niemcza Poland
33 R8 Niemegk E Germany
26 N5 Niemis Sweden
31 K5 Niemodlin Poland
33 N7 Nienbergen W Germany
32 F8 Nienborg W Germany
33 P9 Nienburg E Germany
32 K7 Nienburg W Germany
33 N5 Niendorf W Germany
31 M5 Niepołomice Poland
22 D2 Nieppe France
25 F5 Niers R W Germany
36 E4 Nierstein W Germany
31 L3 Nieszawa Poland
85 C7 Niete, Mt Liberia
33 P10 Nietleben E Germany
21 H10 Nieul France
129 G2 Nieuw Amsterdam Suriname
25 B5 Nieuwe Maas Netherlands
25 C5 Nieuwendijk Netherlands
25 D4 Nieuwersluis Netherlands
25 H2 Nieuweschans Netherlands
32 F6 Nieuweschans W Germany
22 D2 Nieuwkerke Belgium
25 C4 Nieuwkoop Netherlands
129 G2 Nieuw Nickerie Suriname
25 G2 Nieuwolda Netherlands
22 D1 Nieuwpoort Belgium
25 C5 Nieuwpoort Netherlands
25 E6 Nieuwstadt Netherlands
25 C4 Nieuw-Vennep Netherlands
18 H5 Nièvre dep France
122 G6 Nigadoo New Brunswick
78 E3 Niğde Turkey
85 B6 Niger R W Africa
85 F5 Niger rep W Africa
85 F7 Nigeria rep W Africa
85 F8 Niger,Mouths of the Nigeria
144 B6 Nightcaps New Zealand
100 F1 Nighthawk Washington
141 G2 Night I Great Barrier Reef Aust
Nightingale I see Dao Bach Long Vi
90 B16 Nightingale I Atlantic Oc
116 K2 Nigu R Alaska
102 U13 Nihoa Hawaiian Is
131 C5 Nihuili, Embalse del res Argentina
61 N8 Niigata Japan
60 G12 Niihama Japan
135 N1 Niihau isld Hawaiian Is
61 N11 Nii-jima isld Japan
60 Q3 Niikappu R Japan
60 G10 Niimi Japan
60 D4 Niitomi Japan
61 N8 Niitsu Japan
17 F8 Níjar Spain
25 F2 Nijega Netherlands
60 S2 Nijibetsu Japan
79 F8 Nijil Jordan
25 D4 Nijkerk Netherlands
25 E5 Nijmegen Netherlands
25 F4 Nijverdal Netherlands
116 K6 Nikabuna Lakes Alaska
Nikaria isld see Ikaría I Greece
26 S2 Nikel U.S.S.R.
55 C5 Nikel'tau U.S.S.R.
71 M9 Nikiniki Timor Indonesia
47 F4 Nikitas Greece
52 D6 Nikitinka U.S.S.R.
54 K8 Nikitovka U.S.S.R.
85 E7 Nikki Benin
61 N9 Nikkō Japan
61 N9 Nikkō Nat. Park Japan
40 G5 Niklaus Switzerland
48 H1 Nikolaev U.S.S.R.
116 K5 Nikolai Alaska
54 D10 Nikolayev U.S.S.R.
55 E4 Nikolayevka U.S.S.R.
53 G8 Nikolayevsk U.S.S.R.
55 D4 Nikolayevskiy U.S.S.R.
59 M1 Nikolayevsk-na-Amure U.S.S.R.
52 G5 Nikol'sk U.S.S.R.
52 F5 Nikolskoye U.S.S.R.
55 C5 Nikol'skoye U.S.S.R.
88 C3 Nikonga R Tanzania
47 G1 Nikopol Bulgaria
54 F9 Nikopol U.S.S.R.
77 G6 Nīkshahr Iran
42 J6 Nikšić Yugoslavia
78 F1 Niksir Turkey
71 O8 Nila isld Indonesia
103 J8 Niland California
73 L8 Nilande Atoll Maldives
83 L9 Nilaveli Sri Lanka
86 F2 Nile prov Sudan
84 J4 Nile R N E Africa
102 B4 Niles California
107 N3 Niles Kansas
94 A5 Niles Michigan
94 G5 Niles Ohio
121 N6 Nilgaut, L Quebec
76 C5 Nilgiri Hills India
116 E6 Niliklugauk Alaska
57 K3 Nilka China
146 B4 Nilsen B Antarctica
29 N8 Nilsiä Finland
47 K4 Nilüfer R Turkey
83 K11 Nilwala R Sri Lanka
28 D5 Nim Denmark
74 F6 Nimach India
85 C7 Nimba, Mts Guinea/Liberia/Ivory Co
142 E6 Nimberra Well W Australia
139 L3 Nimbin New S Wales
18 H9 Nîmes France
74 F5 Nimka Thana India
139 J6 Nimmitabel New S Wales
101 M3 Nimrod Montana
Nimrod Bay see Xiangshan Gang
146 G7 Nimrod Gl Antarctica
110 C7 Nimrod L Arkansas
144 C6 Nimrod, Mt New Zealand
109 O1 Nimrod Res Arkansas
77 H4 Nīmrūz reg Afghanistan
28 F4 Nimtofte Denmark
42 G4 Nin Yugoslavia
71 F4 Nin Bay Philippines
87 D8 Ninda Angola
139 J3 Nindigully Queensland
141 J8 Nindigully Queensland
73 L7 Nine Degree Chan Lakshadweep Indian Ocean
13 E2 Nine Mile Burn Scotland
139 G4 Nine Mile L New S Wales
103 H2 Ninemile Pk Nevada
108 D6 Nine Point Mesa mt Texas
119 S9 Ninette Manitoba
145 D1 Ninety Mile Beach New Zealand
139 J7 Ninety Mile Beach Victoria
112 E3 Ninety Six S Carolina
94 G7 Ninevah Pennsylvania
133 E6 Ninfas,Pta Argentina
9 G6 Ninfield England
143 A6 Ningaloo W Australia
59 J3 Ning'an China
67 G2 Ningbo China
65 D4 Ningcheng China
67 F3 Ningde China
67 E3 Ningdu China
67 D3 Ninggang China
67 F1 Ningguo China
67 G2 Ninghai China
Ninghan mt see Singleton,Mt
65 D5 Ninghe China
Ning-hsia see Yinchuan
67 E3 Ninghua China
58 F4 Ningjin China
65 C6 Ningjin China
66 F5 Ningjing Shan ra China
65 C7 Ningling China
67 B5 Ningming China
Ningpo see Ningpo
Ningsia aut reg see Ningxia
58 E4 Ningxia Hui Aut Reg China
58 D4 Ningxia aut reg China
67 D2 Ningxiang China
65 C7 Ningyang China
67 D4 Ningyuan China
67 B6 Ninh Binh Vietnam
68 J6 Ninh Hoa Vietnam
116 M6 Ninilchik Alaska
142 C5 Niningarra W Australia
107 N7 Ninnekah Oklahoma
107 N4 Ninnescah R Kansas
146 J4 Ninnis Gl Antarctica
111 C9 Ninock Louisiana
60 E14 Ninokata Japan
22 G2 Ninove Belgium
130 C7 Nioaque Brazil
94 H4 Niobe New York
98 J7 Niobrara Nebraska
98 E7 Niobrara R Nebraska
86 C6 Nioki Zaïre
85 B6 Niokolo-koba,Parc Nat.du Senegal
85 A6 Nioro du Rip Senegal
85 C5 Nioro du Sahel Mali
18 E6 Niort France
21 D9 Niortaise R France
21 E9 Niort St.Florent France
Nios isld see Íos I Greece
99 P9 Niota Illinois
112 C2 Niota Tennessee
85 C5 Niout Mauritania
139 K1 Nipan Queensland
76 B2 Nipani India
71 H6 Nipanipa,Tg C Sulawesi
119 N5 Nipawin Sask
119 N4 Nipawin Prov.Park Sask
120 B3 Nipigon Ontario
120 C4 Nipigon B Ontario
120 B3 Nipigon, Lake Ontario
118 H3 Nipin R Sask
118 C3 Nipisi R Alberta
122 G6 Nipisquit,B New Brunswick
121 L6 Nipissing Junc Ontario
115 L8 Nipissing,L Ontario
122 F3 Nipissis L Quebec
122 F3 Nipissis R Quebec
122 G3 Nipisso L Quebec
102 D6 Nipomo California
103 J6 Nipton California
84 J5 Niqrûb el Fuqâni, Gebel mt Egypt
126 F4 Niquero Cuba
61 M10 Nirasaki Japan
80 C3 Nir 'Ezyon Israel
80 B6 Nir Gallim Israel
80 B7 Nir Hen Israel
74 H9 Nirmal India
75 M5 Nirmali India
80 B8 Nir Moshe Israel
94 B3 Nirvana Michigan
80 C6 Nir Zevi Israel
46 E1 Niš Yugoslavia
16 B5 Nisa Portugal
72 F6 Nişāb S Yemen
46 F1 Nisava R Yugoslavia
95 K5 Nisbet Pennsylvania
60 O3 Niseko Japan
67 C2 Nishi China
61 P5 Nishi-Hōji Japan
60 J11 Nishinomiya Japan
60 F9 Nishino-shima isld Japan
61 L11 Nishio Japan
60 C13 Nishi-Sonogi-hantō pen Japan
60 C11 Nishi-suidō str Japan
60 H10 Nishiwaki Japan
116 H6 Nishlik L Alaska
99 L8 Nishnabotna, E R Iowa
99 L8 Nishnabotna, W R Iowa
130 J9 Nísia Floresta Brazil
48 J3 Nisipitul Romania
47 J8 Nísíros isld Greece
31 N5 Nisko Poland
98 C5 Nisland S Dakota
117 D4 Nisling R Yukon Terr
48 L3 Nisporeny U.S.S.R.
100 C3 Nisqually R Washington
27 F15 Nissan R Sweden
27 C12 Nissedal Norway
27 C12 Nisserv L Norway
28 A3 Nissum Bredning B Denmark
28 A4 Nissum Fjord inlet Denmark
117 G5 Nisutlin R Yukon Terr
115 M7 Nitchequon Quebec
130 G8 Niterói Brazil
15 E5 Nith,R Scotland
15 E5 Nithsdale* Scotland
71 M9 Nitibe Timor
80 G7 Nitil Jordan
100 A1 Nitinat L Br Col
9 E6 Niton England
48 E2 Nitra Czechoslovakia
31 L7 Nitra R Czechoslovakia
94 F8 Nitro W Virginia
55 D2 Nitsa R U.S.S.R.
29 N2 Nitsjärvi L Finland
37 N5 Nittenau W Germany
37 M5 Nittendorf W Germany
29 P11 Nityuyarvi U.S.S.R.
137 R5 Niuafo'ou isld Pacific Oc
137 S5 Niuatoputapu isld Pacific Oc
137 T5 Niue isld Pacific Oc
137 Q4 Niulakita isld Tuvalu
65 F4 Niumaowu China
Niushan see Donghai
137 Q3 Niutao isld Tuvalu
65 E4 Niuzhuang China
28 K5 Nivå Denmark
29 L8 Nivala Finland
18 E9 Nive R France
139 H2 Nive R Queensland
139 H2 Nive Downs Queensland
141 H7 Nive Downs Queensland
22 G2 Nivelles Belgium
18 H5 Nivernais prov France
118 D1 Niverville Manitoba
20 K3 Nivillers France
102 G4 Nivloc Nevada
40 B6 Nivolas-Vermelle France
52 D2 Nivskiy U.S.S.R.
74 J7 Niwas India
102 E2 Nixon Nevada
109 K6 Nixon Texas
74 H9 Nizamabad India
52 E3 Nizhmozero U.S.S.R.
56 G3 Nizhneangarsk U.S.S.R.
52 H2 Nizhne Bugayevo U.S.S.R.
54 L9 Nizhne Gnilovskoy U.S.S.R.
50 H2 Nizhneimbatskoye U.S.S.R.
52 H1 Nizhne Kamenka U.S.S.R.
55 B4 Nizhne-troitskiy U.S.S.R.
56 E4 Nizhneudinsk U.S.S.R.
50 G2 Nizhnevartovsk U.S.S.R.
55 B4 Nizhneye Il'yasovo U.S.S.R.
52 D2 Nizhneye Kuyto, Oz L U.S.S.R.
55 C3 Nizhni Irginski U.S.S.R.
Nizhniy Novgorod see Gor'kiy
55 C2 Nizhniy Tagil U.S.S.R.
52 E2 Nizhniy Vyalozerskiy U.S.S.R.
52 G4 Nizhniy Yenangsk U.S.S.R.
55 E2 Nizhnyaya Aremzyan U.S.S.R.
55 F3 Nizhnyaya Omka U.S.S.R.
52 J3 Nizhnyaya-Omra U.S.S.R.
52 G2 Nizhnyaya Pesha U.S.S.R.
56 E3 Nizhnyaya Pomya U.S.S.R.
55 D2 Nizhnyaya Salda U.S.S.R.
55 G4 Nizhnyaya Suyetka U.S.S.R.
55 E2 Nizhnyaya Tavda U.S.S.R.
52 F3 Nizhnyaya Toyma R U.S.S.R.
56 G1 Nizhnyaya Tunguska R U.S.S.R.
55 C2 Nizhnyaya Tura U.S.S.R.
52 H4 Nizhnyaya Voch' U.S.S.R.
52 F2 Nizhnyaya Zolotitsa U.S.S.R.
29 Q4 Nizh Pirengskoye Ozero L U.S.S.R.
56 G2 Nizh Tunguska R U.S.S.R.
116 Q6 Nizina Alaska
78 F3 Nizip Turkey
31 L7 Nízké Tatry mts Czechoslovakia
48 F2 Nižm Medzev Czechoslovakia
72 H4 Nizwa Oman
22 G4 Nizy-le-Comte France
44 D2 Nizza Italy
80 C4 Nizzane 'Oz Israel
80 B7 Nizzanim Israel
70 D4 Njaän mt Kalimantan
42 J6 Njegoš mt Yugoslavia
87 G7 Njinjo Tanzania
87 D9 Njoko R Zambia
88 E6 Njombe Tanzania
88 E5 Njombe R Tanzania
88 G10 Njoro isld Mozambique
26 J9 Njurundabommen Sweden
27 J10 Njutånger Sweden
88 D7 Nkanka R Zambia
88 E7 Nkhata B Malawi
88 E8 Nkhotakota Malawi
86 A6 N'komi L Gabon
86 B5 N'kongsamba Cameroon
88 D5 Nkululu R Tanzania
28 A4 No Denmark
20 K3 Noailles France
75 O7 Noakhali Bangladesh
45 M1 Noale Italy
128 C3 Noanama Colombia
95 Q5 Noank Connecticut
26 O3 Noarvas mt Norway
40 F7 Noasca Italy
116 F3 Noatak Alaska
14 E3 Nobber Irish Rep
120 K7 Nobel Ontario
60 E13 Nobeoka Japan
110 H3 Noble Illinois
107 N6 Noble Oklahoma
118 D9 Nobleford Alberta
111 E7 Noble Lake Arkansas
94 A6 Noblesville Indiana
71 L9 Nobo Flores Indonesia
60 P3 Noboribetsu Japan
130 C4 Nobres Brazil
141 G8 Noccundra Queensland
20 G5 Noce France
41 O5 Noce R Italy
45 R8 Nocera Inferiore Italy
44 H2 Noceto Italy
124 H7 Nochistlán Mexico
141 G8 Nockatunga Queensland
109 K2 Nocona Texas
48 J5 Nocrich Romania
61 P5 Noda Japan
133 D7 Nodales,B.de los Argentina
99 M9 Nodaway Iowa
99 M8 Nodaway R Iowa
98 B7 Node Wyoming
21 B6 Noé Blanche France
130 D4 Noedori R Brazil
110 B5 Noel Missouri
123 Q5 Noel Paul's Brook Nfld
120 K6 Noelville Ontario
22 D3 Noeux les Mines France
103 O10 Nogales Arizona
124 D2 Nogales Sonora Mexico
125 L8 Nogales Vera Cruz Mexico
86 A2 Nogal Valley Somalia
116 J6 Nogamut Alaska
45 K1 Nogara Italy
18 E9 Nogaro France
31 L1 Nogat R Poland
60 D12 Nōgata Japan
40 B1 Nogent en Bassigny France
20 F5 Nogent-le-Bernard France
20 J4 Nogent-le-Roi France
20 G5 Nogent le Rotrou France
20 K3 Nogent-sur-Oise France
18 H4 Nogent-sur-Seine France
54 K1 Noginsk U.S.S.R.
59 M1 Nogliki U.S.S.R.
40 C4 Nogno France
141 K7 Nogo R Queensland
141 J6 Nogoa R Queensland
61 K10 Nōgōhaku san mt Japan
131 F4 Nogoya R Argentina
48 E3 Nograd co Hungary
16 C3 Nogueira mt Portugal
17 H2 Noguera Pallarésa R Spain
17 H2 Noguera Ribagorzana R Spain
74 F4 Nohar India
61 P5 Noheji Japan
36 C4 Nohfelden W Germany
36 B3 Nohn W Germany
121 N6 Noire R Quebec
67 A6 Noire R Vietnam
86 B6 Noire,Pte Congo
18 C4 Noires, Mgnes mts France
18 D6 Noirmoutier Île de France
17 H9 Noisy les Bains Algeria
61 N11 Nojima-zaki C Japan
61 M9 Nojiri-ko L Japan
87 D9 Nokaneng Botswana
29 K10 Nokia Finland
74 B8 Nok Kundi Pakistan
144 B6 Nokomai New Zealand
110 G2 Nokomis Illinois
119 N7 Nokomis Sask
86 C5 Nola Cent Afr Republic
45 R8 Nola Italy
119 O2 Nolalu Ontario
98 J2 Nolan N Dakota
108 G3 Nolan Texas
28 E5 Nølev Denmark
44 D3 Noli Italy
112 E1 Nolichucky R Tennessee
112 E1 Nolichucky Dam Tennessee
52 G5 Nolinsk U.S.S.R.
20 H3 Nolléval France
28 O10 Nølsø isld Faeroes
69 E9 Nol,Thale L Thailand
111 L11 Noma Florida
60 D14 Noma-misaki C Japan
95 R5 No Mans Land isld Massachusetts
116 E4 Nome Alaska
98 J3 Nome N Dakota
116 E4 Nome C Alaska
19 K4 Nomeny France
121 P6 Nominingue Quebec
60 C13 Nomo-zaki C Japan
87 C10 Nomtsas Namibia
137 S6 Nomuka isld Tonga
114 J5 Nonacho L N W Terr
20 H4 Nonancourt France
20 D3 Nonant France
20 F4 Nonant-le-Pin France
45 K2 Nonantola Italy
52 H2 Nonburg U.S.S.R.
65 F2 Nong'an China
68 F3 Nong Het Laos
68 F5 Nong Hong Thailand
68 F4 Nong Khai Thailand
87 F11 Nongoma S Africa
19 N15 Nonières France
Nonni R see Nen Jiang R
138 D4 Nonning S Australia
138 D4 Nonning,Mt S Australia
36 B4 Nonnweiler W Germany
130 D10 Nonoaí Brazil
124 F4 Nonoava Mexico
71 G6 Nonoc isld Philippines
137 P2 Nonouti atoll Kiribati
119 W2 Nonsuch Manitoba
68 E6 Nonthaburi Thailand
18 F7 Nontron France
116 K7 Nonvianuk L Alaska
139 H7 Noojee Victoria
143 B7 Nookawarra W Australia
138 D2 Noolyeanna,L S Australia
98 C1 Noonan N Dakota
143 C9 Noongaar W Australia
143 B8 Noongal W Australia
142 E4 Noonkanbah W Australia
139 H3 Noorama R Queensland
25 A5 Noord-Beveland Netherlands
25 D5 Noord Brabant Netherlands
25 C5 Noordeloos Netherlands
25 C3 Noord-Holland Netherlands
25 E3 Noordoost Polder Netherlands
126 A1 Noord Pt Curaçao
25 B4 Noordwijk aan zee Netherlands
7 N9 Noordwinning oil rig North Sea
25 F3 Noordwolde Netherlands
25 C4 Noordzee-Kanaal Netherlands
29 J10 Noormarkku Finland
116 G3 Noorvik Alaska
139 L2 Noosa Head Queensland
141 L7 Noosaville Queensland
117 K11 Nootka Br Col
117 K11 Nootka I Br Col
103 H5 Nopah Ra California
99 T4 Noquebay,L Wisconsin
98 J9 Nora Nebraska
119 O6 Nora Sask
27 H12 Nora Sweden
27 J11 Nora Sweden
59 J1 Nora R U.S.S.R.
28 D3 Nørager Denmark
86 G2 Nora I Ethiopia
71 G7 Norala Mindanao Philippines
121 L4 Noranda Quebec
140 F5 Noranside Queensland
99 O6 Nora Springs Iowa
98 G4 Norbeck S Dakota
27 H11 Norberg Sweden
110 C2 Norborne Missouri
107 K2 Norcatur Kansas
42 E6 Norcia Italy
143 D9 Norcott,Mt W Australia
111 M8 Norcross Georgia
27 D12 Nordaguta Norway
26 K7 Nordanås Sweden
27 D11 Nord-Aurdal Norway
50 B1 Nordaustlandet isld Spitzbergen
28 D6 Nordborg Denmark
28 A6 Nordby Denmark
26 B9 Norddal Norway
28 O9 Norddeble Faeroes
32 F5 Norddeich W Germany
28 A7 Norddorf W Germany
32 L7 Norddrebber W Germany
118 B6 Nordegg R Alberta
9 G2 Nordelph England
32 F5 Norden W Germany
37 K6 Nordendorf W Germany
32 H5 Nordenham W Germany
51 J1 Nordenshel'da Arkhipelag U.S.S.R.
117 E5 Nordenskiold R Yukon Terr
28 A7 Norder Aue chan W Germany
32 J5 Nordergründe sandbank W Germany
32 F5 Norderney W Germany
32 F5 Norderney isld W Germany
26 A10 Nordfjord inlet Norway
26 A10 Nordfjord reg Norway
26 B10 Nordfjordeid Norway
26 H4 Nordfold Norway
28 B7 Nordfriesand reg W Germany
30 D1 Nord-friesische Inseln islds W Germany
37 M3 Nordhalben W Germany
33 N10 Nordhausen E Germany
109 K7 Nordheim Texas
32 J5 Nordholz W Germany
27 A11 Nordhordland reg Norway
32 F8 Nordhorn W Germany
26 K9 Nordingrå Sweden
80 C4 Nordiyya Israel
28 C3 Nordjylland co Denmark
26 P1 Nordkapp C Norway
26 Q1 Nordkinn Norway
26 L2 Nordkjosbotn Norway
26 F6 Nordland Fylker Norway
26 G7 Nordli Norway
37 K6 Nördlingen W Germany
26 K8 Nordmaling Sweden
100 J1 Nordman Idaho
27 G12 Nordmark Sweden
27 D11 Nordmarka reg Norway
26 B9 Nordmöre reg Norway
98 F7 Nordon Nebraska
28 O9 Nordöre Faeroes
32 K4 Nord-Ostsee Kanal W Germany
28 F2 Nordre Rønner isld Denmark
115 O4 Nordre Strömfjord inlet Greenland
32 E9 Nordrhein Westfalen land W Germany
28 C7 Nord Schleswig W Germany
28 B6 Nord Slesvig reg Denmark
32 L8 Nord-Stemmen W Germany
30 D1 Nordstrand isld W Germany
26 E7 Nord-Tröndelag Fylker Norway
51 L1 Nordvik U.S.S.R.
32 F8 Nordwalde W Germany
27 C11 Nore Norway
14 D4 Nore R Irish Rep
27 D11 Norefjell mt Norway
122 E1 Nore,L Quebec
120 K4 Norembego Ontario
17 K2 Norfeo,C Spain
110 D5 Norfolk Arkansas
95 O5 Norfolk Connecticut
98 J7 Norfolk Nebraska
95 L10 Norfolk Virginia
9 H2 Norfolk co England
137 O7 Norfolk I Pacific Oc
110 D5 Norfolk L Arkansas
25 F2 Norg Netherlands
13 F2 Norham England
109 K9 Norias Texas
61 L9 Norikura-dake mt Japan
51 H2 Noril'sk U.S.S.R.
141 G8 Norley Queensland
112 J1 Norlina N Carolina
45 N6 Norma Italy
111 C7 Norman Arkansas
98 H9 Norman Nebraska
107 N6 Norman Oklahoma
141 F4 Norman R Queensland
13 H5 Normanby England
145 E3 Normanby New Zealand
141 G2 Normanby R Queensland
141 K5 Normanby Ra Queensland
20 F4 Normandie reg France
121 S4 Normandin Quebec
110 K6 Normandy Tennessee
109 L4 Normangee Texas
143 E7 Norman Hurst,Mt W Australia
112 F2 Norman, L N Carolina
109 K7 Normanna Texas
141 K2 Norman Park dist Brisbane, Qnsld
141 F4 Normanton Queensland
114 G4 Norman Wells N W Terr
121 L4 Normetal Quebec
143 B10 Nornalup W Australia
124 F4 Norogachic Mexico
111 D8 Norphlet Arkansas
119 Q7 Norquay Sask
133 C5 Norquin Argentina
133 C6 Norquinco Argentina
29 J8 Norra Kvarken chan Finland/Sweden
27 J10 Norrala Sweden
27 G15 Norraryd Sweden
26 J4 Norrbotten reg Sweden
28 D4 Nørreå R Denmark
28 C5 Nørre Bramdrup Denmark
28 A5 Nørre Nebel Denmark
22 C2 Norrent-Fontès France
28 D2 Nørre Saltum Denmark
28 D2 Nørresundby Denmark
26 M6 Norrfjärden Sweden
26 K8 Norrfors Sweden
26 J9 Norrhassel Sweden
95 S2 Norridgewock Maine
99 Q9 Norris Illinois
101 O4 Norris Montana
98 E6 Norris S Dakota
112 C1 Norris Tennessee
101 P5 Norris Wyoming
123 R4 Norris Arm Nfld
110 H4 Norris City Illinois
112 C1 Norris Dam Tennessee
112 D1 Norris Lake Tennessee
123 P4 Norris Point Newfoundland
95 M6 Norristown Pennsylvania
27 H13 Norrköping Sweden
29 H8 Norrskär lt ho Finland
27 J11 Norrsundet Sweden
27 K12 Norrtälje Sweden
26 H6 Norrvik Sweden
28 B2 Nors Denmark
27 F12 Norsä R Sweden
143 D9 Norseman W Australia
145 F4 Norsewood New Zealand
27 H13 Norsholm Sweden
26 K7 Norsjö Sweden
27 D12 Norsjö L Norway
26 Q1 Norskholmen Norway
21 B7 Nort France
129 H3 Norte,C Brazil
128 D2 Norte de Santander div Colombia
32 L9 Nörten Hardenburg W Germany
133 E6 Norte,Pta Argentina
131 D3 Norte,Sa de ra Argentina
128 G6 Norte,Serra do mts Brazil
112 F4 North S Carolina
111 J8 North R Alabama
94 C5 North Adams Michigan
13 G5 Northallerton England
143 B9 Northam W Australia
98 F1 North America, Center of N Dakota
90 C6 North American Basin Atlantic Oc
9 F3 Northampton England
95 P4 Northampton Massachusetts
143 A8 Northampton W Australia
141 H6 Northampton Downs Queensland
9 F3 Northamptonshire co England
68 A6 North Andaman isld Andaman Is
94 K8 North Anna R Virginia
95 S2 North Anson Maine
Northants co see Northamptonshire co
117 Q4 North Arm inlet N W Terr
112 E4 North Augusta Georgia
115 N6 North Aulatsivik I Labrador
94 D5 North Baltimore Ohio
118 J6 North Battleford Sask
123 O6 North Bay Nfld
121 L6 North Bay Ontario
98 K8 North Bend Nebraska
100 A6 North Bend Oregon
13 F1 North Berwick Scotland
99 L9 Northboro Iowa
139 H4 North Bourke New S Wales
94 D3 North Branch Michigan
99 O4 North Branch Minnesota
118 H2 North Branch Ontario
121 N8 North Brook Ontario
13 H5 North Burton England
123 M6 North,C C Breton I, N Scotia
108 B7 North Canadian R Oklahoma etc
145 D1 North Cape New Zealand
137 P8 North Cape Rise sea feature Pacific Oc
115 L7 North Caribou L Ontario
112 E2 North Carolina state U.S.A.
100 D1 North Cascades Nat. Park Washington
113 H12 North Cat Cay isld Bahamas
14 F1 North Chan N Ireland/Scotland
120 G6 North Channel Ontario
112 H5 North Charleston S Carolina
13 G2 North Charlton England
99 T7 North Chicago Illinois
143 B10 Northcliffe W Australia
108 F4 North Concho R Texas
100 A3 North Cove Washington
95 N3 North Creek New York
98 F2 North Dakota state U.S.A.
122 F8 North Devon New Brunswick
9 F5 North Downs England
94 H4 North East Pennsylvania
95 R8 North East Carry Maine
141 L5 North-East Cay isld Gt Barrier Reef Aust
90 G3 North Eastern Atlantic Basin Atlantic Oc
122 A3 Northeast Mistassibi R Quebec
126 F2 Northeast Providence Chan Bahamas
123 R1 Northeast Pt Belle Isle, Nfld
83 M9 North East Pt C Christmas I Indian Oc
32 L9 Northeim W Germany
99 O8 North English Iowa
123 T5 Northern Bight Nfld
86 E2 Northern Darfur prov Sudan
113 L12 Northern Eleuthera dist Bahamas
122 F9 Northern Hd New Brunswick
119 U1 Northern Indian L Manitoba
12 A4 Northern Ireland U.K.
86 E2 Northern Kordofan prov Sudan
99 Q1 Northern Light L Ontario
83 M9 Northern Plateau Christmas I Indian Oc
127 O2 Northern Range Trinidad
Northern Sporades islds see Voríai Sporádhes Is
138 B1 Northern Territory Australia
139 H8 North Esk R Tasmania
9 E3 Northfield England
95 P4 Northfield Massachusetts
99 N5 Northfield Minnesota
95 P2 Northfield Vermont
144 A6 North Fiord New Zealand
99 S6 North Fond du Lac Wisconsin
9 H5 North Foreland head England
102 E4 North Fork California
101 M4 North Fork Idaho
100 K8 North Fork Nevada
94 B1 North Fox I Michigan
99 R6 North Freedom Wisconsin
120 J2 North French R Ontario
13 H6 North Frodingham England
13 G3 Northgate England
119 P9 Northgate Sask
141 K1 Northgate dist Brisbane, Qnsld
North Girard see Lake City
95 P5 North Haven Connecticut
144 D5 North Hd. New Zealand
122 F9 North Head New Brunswick
123 O4 North Head Nfld
141 H2 North Horn C Gt Barrier Reef Aust
86 G5 North Horr Kenya
112 H4 North I S Carolina
83 J12 North I Seychelles
9 G6 Northiam England
145 E3 North Island New Zealand
71 E6 North Islet Philippines
103 O6 North Jadito Canyon R Arizona
83 M8 North Keeling I Cocos Is Indian Oc
115 L2 North Kent I N W Terr
94 G5 North Kingsville Ohio
119 V1 North Knife L Manitoba
59 J3 North Korea People's Rep E Asia
North Land see Severnaya Zemlya
99 T3 Northland Michigan
145 D1 Northland stat area New Zealand
9 E4 Northleach England
99 U8 North Liberty Indiana
110 D7 North Little Rock Arkansas
98 H8 North Loup Nebraska
98 H8 North Loup R Nebraska
88 D7 North Luangwa Nat. Park Zambia
70 C2 North Luconia Shoals S China Sea
106 C2 North Mam Pk Colorado
94 B5 North Manchester Indiana
99 U4 North Manitou I Michigan
88 C10 North Mashonaland Zimbabwe
113 G12 North Miami Florida
15 B2 North Minch Scotland
142 E4 North, Mt W Australia
94 A3 North Muskegon Michigan
117 L4 North Nahanni R N W Terr
113 G11 North New River Can Florida
99 M2 Northome Minnesota
8 C1 Northop Wales
102 F4 North Palisade peak California
98 F8 North Platte Nebraska
98 D8 North Platte R Nebraska
101 T8 North Platte R Wyoming
111 J8 Northport Alabama
99 V4 Northport Michigan
98 C8 Northport Nebraska
122 J8 Northport Nova Scotia
100 H1 Northport Washington
100 H4 North Powder Oregon
99 S7 North Prairie Wisconsin
139 J7 North Pt Flinders I, Tasmania
83 J12 North Pt Mahé I Indian Oc
94 D1 North Pt Michigan
122 H6 North Pt Pr Edward I
100 B3 North R Washington
68 A6 North Reef I Andaman Is
109 M9 North Richland Hills Texas
123 M7 North River Bridge C Breton I, N Scotia
15 C1 North Rona Scotland
15 F1 North Ronaldsay Orkney Scotland
15 F1 North Ronaldsay Firth Orkney Scotland
122 J7 North Rustico Pr Edward I
102 C2 North San Juan California
100 C5 North Santiam R Oregon
118 B6 North Sask R Alberta
90 J3 North Sea W Europe
68 A7 North Sentinel I Andaman Is
13 G3 North Shields England
102 G2 North Shoshone Pk Nevada
99 O8 North Skunk R Iowa
116 M1 North Slope Alaska
117 P7 North Star Alberta
110 M1 North Star Ohio
141 L8 North Stradbroke I Queensland
109 M2 North Sulphur R Texas
123 M7 North Sydney C Breton I, N Scotia
8 C6 North Tawton England
144 A7 North Trap islds New Zealand
71 E7 North Ubian isld Philippines
15 A3 North Uist isld Scotland

13 F3 Northumberland co England
141 J5 Northumberland islds Queensland
138 F7 Northumberland,C S Australia
115 N8 Northumberland Str Nova Scotia
117 G10 North Vancouver Br Col
71 D5 North Verde Philippines
117 P6 North Vermilion Alberta
94 B7 North Vernon Indiana
95 N3 Northville New York
98 H4 Northville S Dakota
9 H2 North Walsham England
116 R5 Northway Junc Alaska
116 B5 Northwest C. St Lawrence I, Alaska
113 K11 Northwest Cay isld Bahamas
74 D2 North West Frontier Prov Pakistan
126 E1 Northwest Providence Chan Bahamas
83 M9 North-West Pt C Christmas I Indian Oc
115 N7 North West River Labrador
123 N2 Northwest St.Augustin R Quebec
114 H4 North West Territories prov Canada
8 D1 Northwich England
112 F1 North Wilkesboro N Carolina
99 N6 Northwood Iowa
98 J2 Northwood N Dakota
72 E5 North Yemen rep Arabia
13 G5 North Yorkshire co England
109 L5 North Zulch Texas
32 G6 Nortmoor W Germany
122 G8 Norton New Brunswick
94 E10 Norton Virginia
89 G1 Norton Zimbabwe
116 G4 Norton B Alaska
87 B8 Norton de Matos Angola
142 C5 Norton Plains W Australia
116 E5 Norton Sound Alaska
107 P2 Nortonville Kansas
98 H3 Nortonville N Dakota
32 L4 Nortorf W Germany
32 G7 Nortrup W Germany
28 E5 Norup Denmark
116 K3 Norutak L Alaska
36 B2 Nörvenich W Germany
102 F8 Norwalk California
95 O5 Norwalk Connecticut
99 N8 Norwalk Iowa
99 U5 Norwalk Michigan
94 E5 Norwalk Ohio
99 Q6 Norwalk Wisconsin
99 P8 Norway Iowa
95 R2 Norway Maine
99 T4 Norway Michigan
112 F4 Norway S Carolina
68 H2 Norway isld Vietnam
26 Norway kingdom W Europe
119 U5 Norway House Manitoba
115 K2 Norwegian B N W Terr
147 E13 Norwegian Basin Arctic Oc
147 F12 Norwegian Sea Arctic Oc
95 P5 Norwich Connecticut
9 H2 Norwich England
107 N4 Norwich Kansas
95 M4 Norwich New York
120 K10 Norwich Ontario
141 J6 Norwich Park Queensland
15 G1 Norwick Scotland
95 Q4 Norwood Massachusetts
112 G2 Norwood N Carolina
95 N2 Norwood New York
121 N8 Norwood Ontario
71 E3 Norzagaray Luzon Philippines
60 T2 Nosappu-misaki C Japan
36 G2 Nösberts W Germany
61 N5 Noshiro Japan
52 G4 Noshul' U.S.S.R.
55 E2 Noska R U.S.S.R.
52 E3 Nosovshchina U.S.S.R.
77 F5 Nosratābād Iran
130 H11 Nossa Senhora das Dores Brazil
130 C4 Nossa Senhora do Livramento Brazil
27 F13 Nossebro Sweden
22 H2 Nossegem Belgium
37 P1 Nossen E Germany
33 Q5 Nossentin E Germany
87 H10 Nossi-Bé isld Madagascar
89 B5 Nossop R Botswana
87 G11 Nosy Barren Madagascar
87 H10 Nosy Lava Madagascar
87 H10 Nosy Mitsio isld Madagascar
87 H10 Nosy Radamà Madagascar
87 H11 Nosy Radamà Madagascar
87 H12 Nosy Varika Madagascar
111 L9 Notasulga Alabama
103 L2 Notch Pk Utah
141 J5 Notch Pt Queensland
31 K2 Noteć R Poland
80 F1 Notera Israel
21 I9 Noth France
100 B5 Noti Oregon
46 E3 Notia Greece
114 H6 Notikewin Alberta
117 O7 Notikewin R Alberta
43 G12 Noto Sicily
27 D12 Notodden Norway
43 G12 Noto, Golfo di Sicily
61 K8 Noto-hantō pen Japan
61 L8 Noto-jima isld Japan
60 S1 Notoro-ko L Japan
60 S1 Notoro-misaki C Japan
Notozero, Oz. see Padunskoye More
122 H7 Notre Dame New Brunswick
122 A8 Notre Dame Quebec
123 R4 Notre Dame B Nfld
20 F4 Notre Dame-de Courson France
115 M5 Notre Dame de Koartáo Quebec
121 S4 Notre-Dame-de-la-Doré Quebec
119 T9 Notre Dame de Lourdes Manitoba
121 P6 Notre Dame du Laus Quebec
121 L5 Notre Dame du-Nord Quebec
122 A5 Notre Dame du Rosaire Quebec
60 T2 Notsuke-saki C Japan
60 T2 Notsuke-suidō str Japan/Kuril Is
120 K8 Nottawasaga Bay Ontario
121 M2 Nottaway R Quebec
27 H14 Nottebäck Sweden
112 C3 Nottely L Georgia
27 E12 Nötteröy isld Norway
9 E2 Nottingham England
9 E1 Nottingham co England
115 M5 Nottingham Island N W Terr
27 G15 Nöttja Sweden
37 K2 Nottleben E Germany
94 K10 Nottoway R Virginia
100 J6 Notus Idaho
85 A4 Nouadhibou Mauritania
85 A5 Nouakchott Mauritania
21 H7 Nouans-les-Fontaines France
21 I6 Nouan sur-Loire France
22 J5 Nouart France
137 O6 Nouméa New Caledonia
85 D6 Nouna Upper Volta
89 D8 Noupoort S Africa
115 M7 Nouveau-Comptoir Quebec
115 M5 Nouveau Québec, Cratèr du Quebec
122 D4 Nouvel,L Quebec
86 C5 Nouvelle Anvers Zaïre
Nouvelle Calédonie isld see New Caledonia
115 M5 Nouvelle-France,Cap de Quebec
18 H9 Nouvelle, la France
122 F5 Nouvelle,R Quebec
Nouvelles Hébrides islds see New Hebrides
20 J1 Nouvion-en-Ponthieu France
22 F3 Nouvion-en-Thiérache,Le France
21 G6 Nouzilly France
22 H4 Nouzonville France
71 M9 Nova Anadia Timor
57 E5 Novabad U.S.S.R.
48 E2 Nová Baňa Czechoslovakia
87 B7 Nova Caipemba Angola
87 D8 Nova Chaves Angola
45 M4 Novafeltria Italy
130 G8 Nova Friburgo Brazil
87 C8 Nova Gaia Angola
42 H3 Nova Gradiška Yugoslavia
130 G8 Nova Iguaçu Brazil
129 K5 Nova Iorque Brazil
130 G6 Nova Lima Brazil
87 C8 Nova Lisboa Angola
87 F10 Nova Mambone Mozambique
128 G4 Nova Olinda do Norte Brazil
41 J7 Novara Italy
129 K4 Nova Russas Brazil
71 N9 Nova Sagres Timor
122 G9 Nova Scotia prov Canada
41 K5 Novate Italy
102 B3 Novato California
130 E10 Nova Trento Brazil
48 F7 Nova Varš Yugoslavia
128 F6 Nova Vida Brazil
55 C5 Novaya Akkermanovka U.S.S.R.
55 E3 Novaya Aptula U.S.S.R.
54 E10 Novaya Kakhovka U.S.S.R.
55 D2 Novaya Lyala U.S.S.R.
51 O1 Novaya Sibir,Ostrov isld U.S.S.R.
50 E1 Novaya Zemlya isld U.S.S.R.
47 H2 Nova Zagora Bulgaria
45 J2 Novellara Italy
110 D1 Novelty Missouri
45 L1 Noventa V Italy
33 N7 Növenthien W Germany
48 E3 Nové Zámky Czechoslovakia
52 D5 Novgorod U.S.S.R.
54 E5 Novgorod Severskiy U.S.S.R.
47 J1 Novgradets Bulgaria
44 E2 Novi Italy
42 F3 Novi Yugoslavia
109 H4 Novice Texas
45 J2 Novi di Modena Italy
42 F3 Novigrad Yugoslavia
42 G4 Novigrad Yugoslavia
48 F4 Novi Kneževac Yugoslavia
59 M2 Novikovo U.S.S.R.
45 N4 Novilara Italy
124 G6 Novillero Mexico
99 O9 Novinger Missouri
22 G4 Novion-Porcien France
47 J1 Novi Pazar Bulgaria
46 D1 Novi Pazar Yugoslavia
48 F5 Novi Sad Yugoslavia
54 N1 Novki U.S.S.R.
129 H4 Nôvo Acôrdo Brazil
53 F10 Novoaleksandrovsk U.S.S.R.
55 C5 Novoalekseyevka U.S.S.R.
56 B4 Novoaltaysk U.S.S.R.
128 F5 Novo Aripuana Brazil
53 D9 Novo Arkhangelsk U.S.S.R.
55 D2 Novoasbest U.S.S.R.
54 K9 Novoazovsk U.S.S.R.
54 C4 Novobelitsa U.S.S.R.
55 C3 Novobelokatay U.S.S.R.
55 E3 Novoberezovka U.S.S.R.
54 M9 Novocherkassk U.S.S.R.
55 F5 Novodolinka U.S.S.R.
52 D6 Novo Dugino U.S.S.R.
52 F3 Novodvinsk Arkhangelsk U.S.S.R.
53 C7 Novogrudok U.S.S.R.
131 H2 Novo Hamburgo Brazil
59 L1 Novoilinovka U.S.S.R.
55 F5 Novoishimskiy U.S.S.R.
57 B2 Novokazalinsk U.S.S.R.
59 J1 Novokiyevskiy Uval U.S.S.R.
55 D4 Novokocherdyk U.S.S.R.
56 C4 Novokuznetsk U.S.S.R.
129 H3 Novo, L Brazil
43 J8 Novoli Italy
71 M9 Novo Luso Timor
53 E11 Novomikhaylovskiy U.S.S.R.
54 C8 Novomirgorod U.S.S.R.
54 G8 Novomoskovsk U.S.S.R.
54 K2 Novomoskovsk U.S.S.R.
55 E3 Novonikolskoye U.S.S.R.
55 C5 Novoorsk U.S.S.R.
52 C6 Novopolotsk U.S.S.R.
87 B8 Novo Redondo Angola
53 E11 Novorossiysk U.S.S.R.
55 C5 Novorossiyskiy U.S.S.R.
54 M3 Novoryazhsk U.S.S.R.
55 F5 Novorybinka U.S.S.R.
51 K1 Novorybnoye U.S.S.R.
52 C6 Novorzhev U.S.S.R.
52 H7 Novo Sakhcha U.S.S.R.
48 K2 Novoselitsa U.S.S.R.
55 B5 Novosergiyevka U.S.S.R.
54 L9 Novoshakhtinsk U.S.S.R.
52 H6 Novo Sheshminsk U.S.S.R.
56 B4 Novosibirsk U.S.S.R.
50 G3 Novosibirskaya Oblast' prov U.S.S.R.
51 O1 Novosibirskiye Ostrova islds U.S.S.R.
54 J4 Novosil' U.S.S.R.
55 D3 Novosineglazovskiy U.S.S.R.
52 D6 Novosokol'niki U.S.S.R.
55 C5 Novotroitsk U.S.S.R.
57 G3 Novotroitskoye Kazakhstan U.S.S.R.
55 G3 Novotroitskoye Novosibirsk U.S.S.R.
54 K2 Novougol'nyy U.S.S.R.
54 C8 Novoukrainka U.S.S.R.
55 C5 Novoursal'sk U.S.S.R.
48 L2 Novo Ushitsa U.S.S.R.
53 G8 Novo Uzensk U.S.S.R.
55 F4 Novovarshavka U.S.S.R.
55 G2 Novovaya Vasyugan U.S.S.R.
52 G5 Novo-Vyatsk U.S.S.R.
56 D2 Novoyeniseysk U.S.S.R.
55 E3 Novozaimka U.S.S.R.
52 E6 Novozavidovskiy U.S.S.R.
52 H3 Novozhilovskaya U.S.S.R.
42 H3 Novska Yugoslavia
31 L6 Novy Bohumin Czechoslovakia
31 J5 Nový Bydžov Czechoslovakia
22 G4 Novy-Chevrières France
54 K8 Novy Donbass U.S.S.R.
54 F7 Novye Senzhary U.S.S.R.
48 J1 Novye Strelishcha U.S.S.R.
48 D1 Nový Jičín Czechoslovakia
54 J6 Novy Oskol U.S.S.R.
52 D1 Novyy U.S.S.R.
52 H2 Novyy Bor U.S.S.R.
54 D9 Novyy Bug U.S.S.R.
55 E1 Novyy Karymkary U.S.S.R.
55 E2 Novyy Katysh U.S.S.R.
50 G2 Novyy Port U.S.S.R.
52 G6 Novyy Tor'yal U.S.S.R.
31 J5 Nowa Ruda Poland
31 J4 Nowa Sól Poland
107 P5 Nowata Oklahoma
77 A2 Nowbarān Iran
31 L2 Nowe Poland
31 M2 Nowe Miasto Poland
139 K4 Nowendoc New S Wales
75 P5 Nowgong India
116 K4 Nowitna R Alaska
98 E5 Nowlin S Dakota
31 J2 Nowógard Poland
31 N2 Nowogród Poland
31 J4 Nowogrodziec Poland
101 S5 Nowood Cr Wyoming
139 K5 Nowra New S Wales
75 K9 Nowrangapur India
77 B1 Now Shahr Iran
74 E1 Nowshera Pakistan
31 M3 Nowy Dwor Poland
31 O2 Nowy Dwór Poland
31 L1 Nowy Dwór Gdański Poland
31 M5 Nowy Korczyn Poland
48 F1 Nowy Sącz Poland
48 F1 Nowy Targ Poland
31 J3 Nowy Tomysl Poland
111 G9 Noxapater Mississippi
95 L5 Noxen Pennsylvania
100 K2 Noxon Montana
111 H8 Noxubee R Mississippi
16 B2 Noya Spain
17 J3 Noya R Spain
20 B5 Noyal-sur-Vilaine France
21 C6 Noyant la Gravoyère France
21 E7 Noyant-la-Plaine France
21 F7 Noyant sur-le Lude France
20 K2 Noye R France
20 J1 Noyelles-sur-Mer France
21 E6 Noyen France
21 H7 Noyers-sur-Cher France
117 G8 Noyes I Alaska
102 A2 Noyo California
22 E4 Noyon France
58 D3 Noyon Mongolia
123 O2 Noyrot,L Quebec
21 B6 Nozay France
86 C6 N'Sah Congo
88 E10 Nsanje Malawi
85 D7 Nsawam Ghana
88 C9 Nsenga Zambia
86 B5 Ntem R Cameroon
83 L13 Nuageuses isld Kerguelen Indian Ocean
21 D7 Nuaillé France
21 D9 Nuaillé-d'Aunis France
87 F10 Nuanetsi Zimbabwe
89 G3 Nuanetsi R Zimbabwe
52 C3 Nuasjärvi L Finland
85 E7 Nuatja Togo
84 J5 Nuba, L Sudan
86 F3 Nuba Mts Sudan
84 J5 Nubian Des Sudan
100 D8 Nubieber California
131 B6 Nuble prov Chile
131 B6 Nuble R Chile
48 H4 Nucet Romania
65 D2 Nudam China
141 K1 Nudgee dist Brisbane, Qnsld
109 J7 Nueces R Texas
21 E7 Nueil France
115 K5 Nueltin L N W Terr
65 E4 Nü'erhe China
128 F8 Nueva Asunción dep Paraguay
124 F2 Nueva Casas Grandes Mexico
128 F1 Nueva Esparta state Venezuela
128 F7 Nueva Esperanza Bolivia
130 C8 Nueva Germania Paraguay
126 C4 Nueva Gerona Cuba
133 D9 Nueva, I Chile/Arg
133 C5 Nueva Imperial Chile
133 C6 Nueva Lubecka Argentina
124 J4 Nueva Rosita Mexico
133 E5 Nueve de Julio Argentina
126 F4 Nuevitas Cuba
71 F5 Nuevo Cebu Philippines
133 E6 Nuevo,G Argentina
109 H9 Nuevo Guerrero Mexico
124 G5 Nuevo Ideal Mexico
125 K4 Nuevo Laredo Mexico
125 J5 Nuevo Leon state Mexico
128 C4 Nuevo Rocafuerte Ecuador
141 J6 Nuga Nuga, L Queensland
84 J5 Nugrus,Gebel mt Egypt
115 O3 Nûgssuaq Greenland
137 L2 Nuguria Is Bismarck Arch
145 F3 Nuhaka New Zealand
137 Q3 Nui atoll Tuvalu
68 H5 Nui Ti On mt Vietnam
18 H5 Nuits France
19 J5 Nuits St.Georges France
66 E5 Nu Jiang R China
116 M7 Nuka I Alaska
138 D4 Nukey Bluff S Australia
84 H6 Nukheila Sudan
80 G8 Nukheila R Jordan
137 R6 Nuku'alofa isld Tonga
137 Q3 Nukufetau atoll Tuvalu
135 N9 Nuku Hiva isld Marquesas Is Pacific Oc
137 Q3 Nukulaelae atoll Tuvalu
137 M2 Nukumanu Is Solomon Is
137 Q2 Nukunau isld Kiribati
57 A4 Nukus U.S.S.R.
17 G5 Nules Spain
142 D5 Nullagine W Australia
142 D5 Nullagine R W Australia
138 B4 Nullarbor S Australia
143 F9 Nullarbor Plain S/W Australia
141 F5 Nulloocha Queensland
65 D4 Nulu'erhu Shan mt ra China
43 B8 Nulvi Sardinia
61 L8 Numaho Japan
61 P6 Numakunai Japan
141 G8 Numalla, L Queensland
86 B4 Numan Nigeria
45 O4 Numana Italy
17 F3 Numancia Spain
25 B5 Numansdorp Netherlands
60 P2 Numata Japan
86 E4 Numatinna R Sudan
61 M10 Numazu Japan
36 D2 Nümbrecht Nordrhein-Westfalen W Germany
140 D2 Numbulwar Mission N Terr Aust
27 D11 Numedal V Norway
27 D12 Numedalsågen R Norway
29 K11 Nummi Finland
139 H6 Numurkah Victoria
116 J7 Nunachuak Alaska
116 F6 Nunapitchuk Alaska
116 E6 Nunavakanuk L Alaska
94 K4 Nunda New York
141 K1 Nundah dist Brisbane, Qnsld
139 K4 Nundle New S Wales
9 E2 Nuneaton England
143 C9 Nungarin W Australia
65 D2 Nungnain Sum China
87 G8 Nungo Mozambique
116 E7 Nunivak I Alaska
106 F1 Nunn Colorado
110 J6 Nunnelly Tennessee
8 D5 Nunney England
25 E4 Nunspeet Netherlands
138 F4 Nuntherungie New S Wales
70 E3 Nunukan Timur Kalimantan
59 H2 Nuomin He R China
43 C8 Nuoro Sardinia
26 L5 Nuortikon Sweden
137 O4 Nupani Santa Cruz Is
128 C2 Nuquí Colombia
57 G1 Nura U.S.S.R.
57 G1 Nura R U.S.S.R.
57 D5 Nuratau, Khr mts U.S.S.R.
36 B3 Nürburg W Germany
44 G2 Nure R Italy
57 E5 Nurek Vdkhr. U.S.S.R.
Nuremberg see Nürnberg
95 L6 Nuremburg Pennsylvania
124 E3 Nuri Mexico
138 E5 Nuriootpa S Australia
74 D1 Nuristan reg Afghanistan
52 H7 Nurlat U.S.S.R.
52 G6 Nurlaty U.S.S.R.
29 O8 Nurmes Finland
29 K9 Nurmo Finland
37 L5 Nürnberg W Germany
71 G7 Nuro Mindanao Philippines
138 A3 Nurrari Lakes S Australia
43 C9 Nurri Sardinia
36 G6 Nürtingen W Germany
31 O3 Nurzec R Poland
71 K9 Nusa Tenggara Timur Indonesia
78 H3 Nusaybin Turkey
116 J6 Nushagak R Alaska
116 H7 Nushagak B Alaska
116 H7 Nushagak Pen Alaska
66 F6 Nu Shan mt ra China
74 B4 Nushki Pakistan
33 N5 Nusse W Germany
115 N6 Nutak Labrador
33 S8 Nuthe R E Germany
119 O6 Nut L Sask
9 G5 Nutley England
128 E2 Nutrias Venezuela
106 C9 Nutt New Mexico
14 E2 Nutts Corner N Ireland
140 C3 Nutwood Downs N Terr Aust
116 Q5 Nutzotin Mts Alaska
135 T3 Nuu Hawaiian Is
29 M5 Nuupas Finland
75 K4 Nuwakot Nepal
83 K11 Nuwara Eliya Sri Lanka
89 B9 Nuweveldreeks mts S Africa
116 J7 Nuyakuk R Alaska
116 H7 Nuyakuk,L Alaska
138 C4 Nuyts Arch S Australia
138 B4 Nuyts,C S Australia
143 B11 Nuyts, Pt W Australia
122 F6 N.W. Miramichi R New Brunswick
143 C10 Nyabing W Australia
88 B3 Nyabisindu Rwanda
101 M1 Nyack Montana
88 D10 Nyaderi R Zimbabwe
88 D10 Nyagadsi R Zimbabwe
139 G6 Nyah Victoria
88 F1 Nyahururu Falls Kenya
66 D6 Nyainqêntanglha Shan ra China
88 D3 Nyakabindi Tanzania
26 K8 Nyåker Sweden
55 D1 Nyaksimvol' U.S.S.R.
86 D3 Nyala Sudan
66 D6 Nyalam China
88 D3 Nyalikungu Tanzania
55 E1 Nyalino U.S.S.R.
87 E9 Nyamandhlovu Zimbabwe
88 C10 Nyamanji mt Zimbabwe
87 D8 Nyamboma Falls Zambia
86 E4 Nyamlell Sudan
87 G8 Nyamtumba Tanzania
52 F4 Nyandoma U.S.S.R.
143 F8 Nyanga, L W Australia
88 E10 Nyanja Malawi
87 F8 Nyanji Zambia
52 H4 Nyanyayel' U.S.S.R.
117 R5 Nyarling R N W Terr
88 E7 Nyasa tribe Tanzania
88 E7 Nyasa,L Malawi/Moz
Nyasaland see Malawi
52 H2 Nyashabozh U.S.S.R.
68 B3 Nyaungbinzeik Burma
68 C4 Nyaunglebin Burma
68 B2 Nyaungu Burma
55 C3 Nyazepetrovsk U.S.S.R.
89 G2 Nyazvidzi R Zimbabwe
28 F6 Nyborg Denmark
26 R1 Nyborg Norway
27 H15 Nybro Sweden
50 G2 Nyda U.S.S.R.
27 G14 Nydala Sweden
115 O1 Nyeboes Land Greenland
Nyenchen Tanglha Range see Nyainqêntanglha Shan
86 F4 Nyerol Sudan
27 G11 Nyhammar Sweden
28 K4 Nyhamn Sweden
26 H9 Nyhem Sweden
88 D6 Nyiha Tanzania
66 D5 Nyima China
87 F8 Nyimba Zambia
66 E6 Nyingchi China
48 G3 Nyíradony Hungary
48 G3 Nyírbátor Hungary
48 G3 Nyíregyháza Hungary
88 F3 Nyiri Desert Kenya
86 G5 Nyiru mt Kenya
29 K8 Nykarleby Finland
27 H13 Nykil Sweden
28 J5 Nykøbing Denmark
28 H7 Nykøbing Falster Denmark
28 B3 Nykøbing Mors Denmark
27 J13 Nyköping Sweden
27 G12 Nykroppa Sweden
89 F5 Nyl R S Africa
26 J8 Nyland Sweden
89 F5 Nylstroom S Africa
26 K6 Nylund Sweden
139 H4 Nymagee New S Wales
139 L3 Nymboida New S Wales
139 L3 Nymborda R New S Wales
31 J5 Nymburk Czechoslovakia
7 F11 Nymphe Bank Atlantic Oc
27 J13 Nynäshamn Sweden
139 H4 Nyngan New S Wales
139 G4 Nyngynderry New S Wales
21 D6 Nyoiseau France
86 B5 Nyong R Cameroon
19 O16 Nyons France
37 P4 Nýřany Czechoslovakia
52 J4 Nyrob U.S.S.R.
37 P5 Nýrsko Czechoslovakia
31 K5 Nysa Poland
27 F11 Nyskoga Sweden
100 H6 Nyssa Oregon
Nystad see Uusikaupunki
61 N5 Nyūdō zaki C Japan
52 G3 Nyukhcha Arkhangelsk U.S.S.R.
52 E3 Nyukhcha Karelskaya A.S.S.R. U.S.S.R.
52 D3 Nyuk, Oz L U.S.S.R.
52 F4 Nyuksenitsa U.S.S.R.
59 H1 Nyukzha R U.S.S.R.
51 L2 Nyurba U.S.S.R.
55 E1 Nyurkoy U.S.S.R.
52 H4 Nyuvchim U.S.S.R.
56 H1 Nyuya R U.S.S.R.
88 D4 Nzega Tanzania
85 C7 Nzerékore Guinea
87 B7 N'Zeto Angola
98 G6 Oacoma S Dakota
98 F4 Oahe, L S Dakota
114 J8 Oahe Res S Dakota
102 S11 Oahu isld Hawaiian Is
103 N7 Oak R Arizona
60 S2 O-akan-dake mt Japan
122 E8 Oak B New Brunswick
138 F5 Oakbank S Australia
95 R5 Oak Bluffs Massachusetts
112 G2 Oakboro N Carolina
119 R8 Oakburn Manitoba
112 K2 Oak City N Carolina
103 M2 Oak City Utah
109 N9 Oak Cliff Texas
101 T9 Oak Creek Colorado
102 D4 Oakdale California
111 D11 Oakdale Louisiana
98 J7 Oakdale Nebraska
98 H3 Oakes N Dakota
100 H2 Oakesdale Washington
140 F7 Oakes, Mt Queensland
141 K7 Oakey Queensland
99 S6 Oakfield Wisconsin
99 R9 Oakford Illinois
111 E9 Oak Grove Louisiana
9 F2 Oakham England
94 D5 Oak Harbor Ohio
113 G9 Oak Hill Florida
107 N2 Oak Hill Kansas
94 E8 Oak Hill Ohio
94 F9 Oak Hill W Virginia
141 H4 Oak Hills Queensland
119 R9 Oak Lake Manitoba
102 B4 Oakland California
99 S10 Oakland Illinois
99 L8 Oakland Iowa
95 S2 Oakland Maine
94 H7 Oakland Maryland
111 G7 Oakland Mississippi
98 K8 Oakland Nebraska
100 B6 Oakland Oregon
95 M5 Oakland Pennsylvania
110 G6 Oakland Tennessee
109 L6 Oakland Texas
110 J3 Oakland City Indiana
113 G11 Oakland Park Florida
139 H6 Oaklands New S Wales
145 E1 Oakleigh New Zealand
102 C4 Oakley California
101 M7 Oakley Idaho
107 K2 Oakley Kansas
94 C3 Oakley Michigan
112 C3 Oakman Georgia
94 H6 Oakmont Penn
119 R8 Oakner Manitoba
142 D5 Oakover, R W Australia
112 E5 Oakpark Georgia
141 G4 Oak Park Queensland
119 T8 Oak Pt Manitoba
111 E9 Oak Ridge Louisiana
110 G4 Oak Ridge Missouri
100 C6 Oakridge Oregon
112 C1 Oak Ridge Tennessee
119 R8 Oak River Manitoba
145 D3 Oakura New Zealand
138 F5 Oakvale S Australia
119 T9 Oakville Manitoba
121 L9 Oakville Ontario
109 J7 Oakville Texas
110 J1 Oakwood Illinois
110 E2 Oakwood Missouri
94 C5 Oakwood Ohio
107 M6 Oakwood Oklahoma
141 H7 Oakwood Queensland
144 C6 Oamaru New Zealand
61 O10 Ōami Japan
71 F4 Oas Philippines
60 F11 Ōasa Japan
102 G4 Oasis California
101 L8 Oasis Nevada
146 J5 Oates Land Antarctica
139 H8 Oatlands Tasmania
103 K6 Oatman Arizona
125 L9 Oaxaca de Juárez Mexico
56 B4 Ob' R U.S.S.R.
120 F3 Oba Ontario
137 O5 Oba isld New Hebrides
120 E3 Obakamiga L Ontario
120 F4 Oba L Ontario
86 B5 Obala Cameroon
121 Q3 Obalski Quebec
61 J10 Obama Japan
144 B7 Oban New Zealand
118 J6 Oban Sask
15 C4 Oban Scotland
61 O7 Obanazawa Japan
106 G6 Obar New Mexico
120 E4 Obatanga Prov. Park Ontario
121 Q3 Obatogamau L Quebec
38 L7 Obdach Austria
117 P9 Obed Alberta
38 J5 Ober dist Austria
40 G3 Ober Aargau dist Switzerland
30 F8 Oberammergau W Germany
37 Q1 Oberau E Germany
41 O2 Oberau W Germany
36 H2 Oberaula W Germany
36 H3 Oberbach W Germany
38 E5 Oberbayern dist W Germany
25 F6 Oberbruch-Dremmen W Germany
39 C2 Oberbrunn W Germany
36 H7 Oberdischingen W Germany
38 H8 Ober-Drau-Tal V Austria
37 J4 Obereisenheim W Germany
37 J2 Oberellen E Germany
41 L4 Oberengadin dist Switzerland
38 K7 Oberenns Tal Austria
37 K3 Oberessfeld W Germany
37 P1 Ober Eula E Germany
37 L4 Oberfranken dist W Germany
Oberfrohna see Limbach-Oberfrohna
38 H8 Obergailtal V Austria
41 O4 Obergurgl Austria
41 L4 Oberhalbstein R Switzerland
36 E7 Oberharmersbach W Germany
36 C6 Oberhaslach France
32 E10 Oberhausen W Germany
36 E4 Ober Hilbersheim W Germany
37 K2 Oberhof E Germany
36 E6 Oberkirch W Germany
36 F3 Oberkleen W Germany
37 J6 Ober-Kochen W Germany
37 M3 Ober Kotzau W Germany
37 J3 Ober Lauringen W Germany
36 H6 Oberlenningen W Germany
107 K2 Oberlin Kansas
111 D11 Oberlin Louisiana
94 E5 Oberlin Ohio
36 H7 Ober Marchthal W Germany
32 J10 Ober Marsberg W Germany
36 D4 Ober Moschel W Germany
36 C7 Obernai France
36 G4 Obernburg W Germany
32 K8 Obernkirchen W Germany
98 G2 Oberon N Dakota
139 J5 Oberon New S Wales
39 C2 Oberpfaffenhofen W Germany
37 M5 Oberpfalz dist W Germany
37 N4 Oberpfelzer Wald mts W Germany
36 C2 Oberpleis W Germany
36 F4 Ober Ramstadt W Germany
41 K3 Oberri Switzerland
37 O3 Ober Rittersgrün E Germany
33 P10 Ober Röblingen E Germany
36 F4 Ober-Roden W Germany
36 F3 Ober Rosbach W Germany
36 G5 Ober Schefflenz W Germany
40 F4 Ober Simmen Tal Switzerland
36 H5 Obersontheim W Germany
33 N10 Oberspier E Germany
41 M3 Oberstdorf W Germany
36 D5 Obersteinbach France
37 J3 Obertheres W Germany
37 N6 Obertraubling W Germany
37 O7 Ober Trennbach W Germany
33 T6 Oberueckersee L E Germany
36 F3 Oberursel W Germany
37 N5 Oberviechtach W Germany
41 H4 Oberwald Switzerland
38 O7 Oberwart Austria
36 D3 Oberwesel W Germany
37 O3 Oberwiesenthal E Germany
36 C2 Oberwinter W Germany
38 K7 Oberwölz Austria
60 E14 Obi Japan
71 A3 Obi isld Indonesia
129 G4 Obidos Brazil
16 A5 Obidos Portugal
60 R3 Obihiro Japan
71 A3 Obi,Kep isld Indonesia
71 A3 Obilatu isld Indonesia
38 F5 Obing W Germany
110 G5 Obion Tennessee
110 J3 Oblong Illinois
59 K2 Obluch'ye U.S.S.R.
54 H1 Obninsk U.S.S.R.
86 H3 Obock Djibouti
54 A1 Obol' R U.S.S.R.
120 A3 Obonga L Ontario
70 D2 Obong, G mt Sarawak
31 K3 Oborniki Poland
52 F1 Obornyy, Mys C U.S.S.R.
86 C6 Obouya Mossaka Congo
54 H5 Oboyan' U.S.S.R.
52 F3 Obozerskiy U.S.S.R.
124 E4 Obregón, Presa res Mexico
120 K5 O'Brien Ontario
33 Q8 Oobritz E Germany
42 G4 Obrovac Yugoslavia
57 E4 Obruchevo U.S.S.R.
137 M6 Observatoire, Caye de l' islds Coral Sea
117 H8 Observatory Inlet Br Col
54 D1 Obsha R U.S.S.R.
55 B5 Obshciy Syrt reg U.S.S.R.
101 L5 Obsidian Idaho
50 G2 Obskaya Guba gulf U.S.S.R.
85 D7 Obuasi Ghana
52 J5 Obva R U.S.S.R.
41 H4 Obwalden canton Switzerland
52 G4 Ob'yachevo U.S.S.R.
16 E2 Oca R Spain
113 E8 Ocala Florida
124 E3 Ocampo Chihuahua Mexico
124 H4 Ocampo Coahuila Mexico
16 E2 Oca,Mt.de Spain
126 H10 Ocaña Colombia
16 E5 Ocaña Spain
106 E5 Ocate New Mexico
45 L2 Occhiobello Italy
95 M8 Ocean City Maryland
95 N7 Ocean City New Jersey
100 A2 Ocean City Washington
117 K9 Ocean Falls Br Columbia
95 N7 Ocean Gate New Jersey
Ocean Is. see Banaba
101 R6 Ocean L Wyoming
102 D6 Oceano California
90 F5 Oceanographer Fracture Atlantic Oc
100 A3 Ocean Park Washington
102 G8 Oceanside California
100 B4 Oceanside Oregon
111 H11 Ocean Springs Mississippi
95 M8 Ocean View Delaware
16 E3 Ocejón,Pass Spain
54 C10 Ochakov U.S.S.R.
56 H1 Ochchuguy Botuobuya R U.S.S.R.
52 H5 Ocher U.S.S.R.
60 C12 Ōchi Japan
60 G10 Ochiai Japan
60 T2 Ochiishi-misaki C Japan
15 E4 Ochil Hills Scotland
15 D5 Ochiltree Scotland
113 C7 Ochlocknee Georgia
111 M11 Ochlockonee R Florida
100 E5 Ochoco Res Oregon
32 G6 Ocholt W Germany
113 F12 Ochopee Florida
127 K2 Ocho Rios Jamaica
119 S7 Ochre River Manitoba
40 F4 Ochsen mt Switzerland
37 J4 Ochsenfurt W Germany
41 L1 Ochsenhausen W Germany
37 M3 Ochsenkopf mt W Germany
32 L5 Ochsenzoll W Germany
36 C3 Ochtendung W Germany
33 O8 Ochtmersleben E Germany
32 F8 Ochtrup W Germany
112 D6 Ocilla Georgia
27 J11 Ockelbo Sweden
28 B7 Ockholm W Germany
9 F5 Ockley England
48 J4 Ocland Romania
112 D4 Ocmulgee R Georgia
112 D5 Ocmulgee Nat Mon Georgia
48 J5 Ocna Sibiului Romania
48 H3 Ocna Sugătag Romania
48 J5 Ocnele Mari Romania
113 F9 Ocoee Florida
112 C2 Ocoee Tennessee
128 D7 Ocoña Peru
110 G2 Oconee Illinois
98 J8 Oconee Nebraska
112 E5 Oconee R Georgia
141 G5 O'Connell R Queensland
98 G8 Oconto Nebraska
99 T5 Oconto Wisconsin
99 S5 Oconto Falls Wisconsin
124 E5 Ocoroni Mexico
125 M3 Ocotal Nicaragua
124 H7 Ocotlán Mexico
125 N9 Ocozocoautla Mexico
22 J3 Ocquier Belgium
112 M2 Ocracoke N Carolina
48 E3 Ocsa Hungary
48 F4 Öcsöd Hungary
20 B2 Octeville France
120 D3 Octopus Ontario
127 L9 Ocumare del Tuy Venezuela
71 M9 Ocussi Ambeno Timor
27 F14 Od Sweden
85 D7 Oda Ghana
60 F10 Ōda Japan
61 K11 Odaigahara-zan mt Japan
61 O8 Odaka Japan
27 E11 Odal,N Norway
27 E11 Odal,S Norway
99 Q3 Odanah Wisconsin
61 O5 Ōdate Japan
61 N10 Odawara Japan
27 B11 Odda Norway
86 G1 Odda,Jebel mt Sudan
28 E5 Odder Denmark
27 C13 Oddernes Norway
86 H5 Oddur Somalia
99 L7 Odebolt Iowa
16 B7 Odeleite Portugal
99 S8 Odell Illinois
98 K9 Odell Nebraska
109 H1 Odell Texas
37 L7 Odelzhausen W Germany
109 K8 Odem Texas
16 B7 Odemira Portugal
47 J6 Ödemis Turkey
110 C7 Oden Arkansas
36 D4 Odenbach W Germany
89 E6 Odendaalsrus S Africa
36 F5 Odenheim W Germany
36 B1 Odenkirchen W Germany
28 E6 Odense Denmark
Odense co see Fyn
28 F5 Odense Fjord inlet Denmark
36 G4 Odenwald mts W Germany
Oder R see Odra R
33 U7 Oderberg E Germany
33 T8 Oderin E Germany
36 E4 Odernheim W Germany
33 T8 Oder-Spree-Kanal E Germany
42 E3 Oderzo Italy
27 G13 Ödeshög Sweden
110 C3 Odessa Missouri
95 L4 Odessa New York
121 O8 Odessa Ontario
119 O8 Odessa Sask
108 E4 Odessa Texas
48 N4 Odessa U.S.S.R.
100 G2 Odessa Washington
55 F4 Odesskoye U.S.S.R.
18 C4 Odet R France
119 T3 Odhill Manitoba
87 E10 Odiakwe Botswana
85 C7 Odiénné Ivory Coast
9 F5 Odiham England
110 G3 Odin Illinois
32 E9 Öding W Germany
54 J1 Odintsovo U.S.S.R.
48 L5 Odobeşti Romania
31 K4 Odolanów Poland
146 E12 Odom Inlet Antarctica
110 K3 Odon Indiana
20 D3 Odon R France
108 F3 O'Donnell Texas
25 G3 Odoorn Netherlands
48 J4 Odorhei Romania
31 J4 Odra R Poland
16 E2 Odra R Spain
25 F6 Odt W Germany
112 E6 Odum Georgia
48 E5 Odžaci Yugoslavia
33 O8 Oebisfelde E Germany
37 J2 Oechsen E Germany
22 E1 Oedelem Belgium
37 P2 Oederan E Germany
36 E1 Oedingen W Germany
129 K5 Oeiras Brazil
16 A6 Oeiras Portugal
16 B7 Oeiras R Portugal
32 H9 Oelde W Germany
98 C6 Oelrichs S Dakota
37 N3 Oelsnitz E Germany
99 P7 Oelwein Iowa
37 L2 Oelze E Germany
135 O11 Oeno atoll Pacific Oc
140 C1 Oenpelli N Terr Aust
32 J9 Oerlinghausen W Germany
37 L3 Oeslau W Germany
71 M9 Oessilo Timor
36 E3 Oestrich-Winkel W Germany
133 E3 Oetling Argentina
37 K6 Oettingen W Germany
32 H10 Oeventrop W Germany
111 G9 Ofahoma Mississippi
43 G7 Ofanto R Italy
80 B8 Ofaqim Israel
80 C3 Ofer Israel
14 D3 Offaly co Irish Rep
36 F3 Offenbach am Main W Germany
36 D7 Offenburg W Germany
26 G8 Offerdal Sweden
112 E6 Offerman Georgia
138 B2 Officer Cr.,The S Australia
37 J7 Offingen W Germany
20 H2 Offranville France
36 E4 Offstein W Germany
47 H8 Ofidhoúsa isld Greece
79 E11 Ofira Egypt
26 J3 Ofotfjord inlet Norway
80 D6 Ofra Jordan
61 N6 Oga Japan
86 J4 Ogaden reg Ethiopia
120 E2 Ogahalla Ontario
61 N6 Oga-hantō pen Japan
61 K10 Ōgaki Japan
107 L3 Ogallah Kansas
98 E8 Ogallala Nebraska
54 J3 Ogarevka U.S.S.R.
59 M6 Ogasawara-shoto Japan
121 M5 Ogascanan, L Quebec
61 P5 Ogawara ko L Japan
85 E7 Ogbomosho Nigeria
9 E5 Ogbourne St.George England
110 J1 Ogden Illinois
99 M7 Ogden Iowa
107 O2 Ogden Kansas
123 L8 Ogden Nova Scotia
101 O8 Ogden Utah
117 G6 Ogden,Mt Br Col/Alaska
95 M2 Ogdensburg New York
115 M9 Ogdensburg Ontario
112 F5 Ogeechee R Georgia
98 K2 Ogema Minnesota
119 N9 Ogema Sask
32 G5 Ogenbargen W Germany
36 B6 Ogéviller France
41 K6 Oggiono Italy
61 M8 Ogi Japan
120 F6 Ogidaki Ontario
103 K9 Ogilby California
99 N4 Ogilvie Minnesota
143 A8 Ogilvie W Australia
114 F5 Ogilvie Mts Yukon Terr
61 Q12 Ōgimi Japan
98 D6 Oglala S Dakota
99 R8 Oglesby Illinois
109 K4 Oglesby Texas
112 C5 Oglethorpe Georgia
55 F3 Oglukhino U.S.S.R.
141 J6 Ogmore Queensland
55 G2 Ognev Yar U.S.S.R.
19 J5 Ognon R France
70 G4 Ogoamas, G mt Celebes
85 F7 Ogoja Nigeria
120 C2 Ogoki L Ontario
120 D2 Ogoki R Ontario
120 B2 Ogoki Res Ontario
86 A6 Ogooué R Gabon
47 F1 Ogosta R Bulgaria
70 G4 Ogotomubu Sulawesi
61 K9 Ogoya Japan
46 F3 Ograzden Planina mt Yugoslavia
52 B6 Ogre U.S.S.R.
28 N3 Øgrum Faeroes
61 N10 Oguchi Dam Japan
85 D4 Oguilet Khenachich Mali
124 F4 Oguivo Mexico
85 E7 Ogun R Nigeria
60 E12 Oguni Japan
95 R3 Ogunquit Maine
85 F7 Ogwashi-Uku Nigeria
145 D1 Ohaeawai New Zealand
144 A6 Ohai New Zealand
145 E3 Ohakune New Zealand
85 F3 Ohanet Algeria
86 D2 O Haouach dist Chad
61 O10 Ōhara Japan
60 P4 Ōhata Japan
118 E6 Ohaton Alberta
145 E4 Ohau New Zealand
144 B6 Ohau, L New Zealand
145 E2 Ohaupo New Zealand
61 P6 Ōhazama R Japan
32 G7 Ohe R W Germany
145 E2 Ohena I New Zealand
22 J3 Ohey Belgium
133 C4 O'Higgins prov Chile
133 C7 O'Higgins, L Chile/Arg
133 C7 O'Higgins Pirámide mt Chile
145 E2 Ohinewai New Zealand
145 E3 Ohingaiti New Zealand
99 R8 Ohio Illinois
94 C8 Ohio R Indiana
110 H4 Ohio R U.S.A.
94 C6 Ohio state U.S.A.
94 C6 Ohio City Ohio
32 G10 Ohle W Germany
36 F2 Ohm R W Germany
33 M8 Ohof W Germany
116 G6 Ohogamiut Alaska
112 E5 Ohoopee R Georgia
87 B9 Ohopoho Namibia
33 N7 Ohrdorf W Germany
37 K2 Ohrdruf E Germany
37 O3 Ohře R Czechoslovakia
33 O8 Ohre R E Germany
46 D3 Ohrid Yugoslavia
46 D3 Ohridsko Jez L Yugoslavia
36 H5 Öhringen W Germany
36 G5 Ohrnberg W Germany
26 N5 Ohtanajärvi Sweden
145 E3 Ohura New Zealand
129 H3 Oiapoque Fr Guiana
22 H3 Oignies Belgium
29 M6 Oijärvi Finland
106 G9 Oil Center New Mexico
102 F6 Oil City California

32 L7 Ostenholz W Germany
41 K6 Osteno Italy
54 D3 Oster R U.S.S.R.
33 P7 Osterburg E Germany
94 J6 Osterburg Pennsylvania
36 G5 Osterburken W Germany
27 J11 Österby Sweden
27 H14 Österbymo Sweden
32 H8 Ostercappeln W Germany
27 G10 Osterdalälven R Sweden
32 E5 Osterems est W Germany
27 H13 Östergotland county Sweden
37 P6 Osterhofen W Germany
32 J6 Osterholz-Scharmbeck W Germany
38 H6 Osterhorn Gruppe mts Austria
28 D3 Øster Hornum Nordjylland Denmark
27 J11 Österlövsta Sweden
26 J7 Östernoret Sweden
28 N2 Østerø isld Faeroes
Osterode Poland see Ostróda
32 M9 Osterode W Germany
27 A11 Osteröy isld Norway
38 H5 Osterreich dist Austria
26 G8 Östersund Sweden
28 H7 Øster Ulslev Denmark
27 J11 Östervåla Sweden
33 N9 Osterwieck E Germany
36 G6 Ostfildern W Germany
27 E12 Östfold reg Norway
32 F5 Ostfriesische Inseln islds W Germany
32 F6 Ostfriesland reg W Germany
32 G6 Ostgrossefehn W Germany
27 K11 Östhammar Sweden
36 C7 Ostheim France
37 J3 Ostheim W Germany
45 M6 Ostia Italy
45 K1 Ostiglia Italy
27 F11 Östmark Sweden
33 R5 Ost Peene R E Germany
45 O4 Ostra Italy
94 D6 Ostrander Ohio
37 P1 Ostrau E Germany
31 L6 Ostrava Czechoslovakia
45 O4 Ostra Vetere Italy
31 M2 Ostróda Poland
31 N2 Ostrołęka Poland
120 J5 Ostrom Ontario
37 O3 Ostrov Czechoslovakia
48 L6 Ostrov Romania
52 C6 Ostrov U.S.S.R.
55 F3 Ostrovnaya U.S.S.R.
51 Q2 Ostrovnoye U.S.S.R.
65 J3 Ostrov Russkiy isld U.S.S.R.
31 K4 Ostrów Poland
31 N5 Ostrowiec Poland
31 O4 Ostrów Lubelski Poland
31 N3 Ostrów Mazowieckia Poland
28 C3 Østrup Denmark
37 P5 Ostrý mt Czechoslovakia
31 K4 Ostrzeszów Poland
33 O5 Ostseebad Boltenhagen E Germany
33 Q4 Ostseebad Graal-Müritz E Germany
33 P4 Ostseebad Kühlungsborn E Germany
33 P4 Ostseebad Nienhagen E Germany
33 P4 Ostseebad Rerik E Germany
43 H8 Ostuni Italy
52 D6 Osuga R U.S.S.R.
100 F3 O'Sullivan Dam Washington
120 D2 O'Sullivan, L Ontario
121 P5 O'Sullivan, L Quebec
46 D4 Osum R Albania
47 G1 Osŭm R Bulgaria
60 D14 Ōsumi-hantō pen Japan
16 D7 Osuna Spain
52 J2 Os'van' U.S.S.R.
52 C6 Osveya U.S.S.R.
13 G5 Oswaldkirk England
94 J5 Oswayo Pennsylvania
95 M2 Oswegalchie R New York
99 S8 Oswego Illinois
107 P4 Oswego Kansas
101 U1 Oswego Montana
95 L3 Oswego New York
8 C2 Oswestry England
31 L5 Oświęcim Poland
111 F10 Osyka Mississippi
61 N9 Ōta Japan
60 F11 Ōta R Japan
144 B6 Otago stat area New Zealand
144 D7 Otago Peninsula New Zealand
144 C6 Otaio New Zealand
60 F11 Ōtake Japan
145 E3 Otakeho New Zealand
61 M10 Ōtaki Japan
145 E4 Otaki New Zealand
61 O8 Ōtakine-yama mt Japan
145 F3 Otane New Zealand
145 F2 Otanewainuku New Zealand
29 N7 Otanmäki Finland
83 K9 Otappuwa Sri Lanka
57 H3 Otar U.S.S.R.
60 O2 Otaru Japan
144 B7 Otatara New Zealand
144 B7 Otautau New Zealand
30 H6 Otava R Czechoslovakia
128 C3 Otavalo Ecuador
87 C9 Otavi Namibia
87 B9 Otchinjau Angola
95 M4 Otego New York
144 C6 Otekaieke New Zealand
48 F5 Otelec Romania
144 C6 Otematata New Zealand
52 C5 Otepää U.S.S.R.
58 C2 Otgon Mongolia
22 K5 Othain R France
22 J2 Othée Belgium
18 H4 Othe, Forêt d' France
100 F3 Othello Washington
27 K14 Othem Sweden
8 D5 Othery England
46 C5 Othonoí isld Greece
46 F5 Óthris mt Greece
70 F5 Oti Sulawesi
85 E7 Oti R W Africa
124 G5 Otinapa Mexico
144 C5 Otira New Zealand
106 H1 Otis Colorado
107 L3 Otis Kansas
95 O4 Otis Massachusetts
95 L4 Otisco L New York
122 B1 Otish Mts Quebec
95 N5 Otisville New York
87 C10 Otjiwarongo Namibia
60 O3 Otobe-dake mt Japan
42 G4 Otočac Yugoslavia
99 K9 Otoe Nebraska
60 R2 Otofuke Japan
60 Q1 Otoineppu Japan
145 F3 Otoko New Zealand
145 E3 Otorohanga New Zealand
119 P5 Otosquen Sask
27 C13 Otra R Norway
126 B1 Otrabanda Curaçao
43 J8 Otranto Italy
43 J8 Otranto, C.d' Italy
46 C4 Otranto, Str of Adriatic Sea
94 C2 Otsego Michigan
95 N4 Otsego I New York
94 C2 Otsego Lake Michigan
95 M4 Otselic, South New York
60 R3 Ōtsu Hokkaido Japan
61 J10 Ōtsu Honshu Japan
61 P6 Ōtsuchi-wan B Japan
61 M10 Ōtsuki Japan
26 D10 Otta Norway
26 C10 Otta R Norway
22 L5 Ottange France
27 F16 Ottarp Sweden
45 Q8 Ottaviano Italy
99 S8 Ottawa Illinois
107 P3 Ottawa Kansas
94 C5 Ottawa Ohio
120 D9 Ottawa Ontario
115 L6 Ottawa Is N W Terr
121 M6 Ottawa, R Quebec
32 K9 Ottbergen W Germany
27 H15 Ottenby Sweden
36 H5 Ottendorf W Germany
37 M2 Ottendorf-Okrilla E Germany
36 E6 Ottenhöfen W Germany
38 M5 Ottenshlag Austria
32 K9 Ottenstein Niedersachsen W Germany
32 E8 Ottenstein Nordrhein-Westfalen W Germany
101 T4 Otter Montana
110 J1 Otterbein Indiana
36 D4 Otterberg W Germany
13 F3 Otterburn England
118 D1 Otterburne Manitoba
113 E8 Otter Creek Florida
103 N3 Otter Cr Res Utah
38 E6 Otterfing W Germany
120 D4 Otter I Ontario
116 D8 Otter I Pribilof Is Bering Sea
119 N3 Otter L Sask
94 D3 Otter Lake Michigan
25 E4 Otterlo Netherlands
32 J5 Otterndorf W Germany
26 E7 Otteröy Norway
26 B9 Otteröy isld Norway
32 K6 Ottersberg W Germany
9 F5 Ottershaw England
33 P8 Ottersleben E Germany
15 G1 Otterswick Scotland
98 K3 Otter Tail R Minnesota
99 L3 Otter Tail L Minnesota
28 E5 Otterup Denmark
8 B6 Ottery, R England
8 C6 Ottery St. Mary England
119 P7 Otthon Sask
22 H2 Ottignies Belgium
109 L4 Otto Texas
101 R5 Otto Wyoming
37 M7 Ottobrunn W Germany
115 L1 Otto Fiord N W Terr
94 C6 Ottoville Ohio
36 C7 Ottrott France
99 O8 Ottumwa Iowa
98 E5 Ottumwa S Dakota
36 C5 Ottweiler W Germany
118 K2 Otukamanoan L Ontario
144 B6 Oturehua New Zealand
85 F7 Oturkpo Nigeria
94 D8 Otway Ohio
133 C8 Otway, B Chile
139 G7 Otway, C Victoria
31 N3 Otwock Poland
48 J2 Otynya U.S.S.R.
41 N3 Ötz Austria
36 B1 Otzenrath W Germany
41 N3 Ötztal Austria
41 N4 Ötztaler Alpen mt Austria
111 D8 Ouachita R Arkansas
110 C7 Ouachita, L Arkansas
109 N1 Ouachita Mts Ark/Okla
86 D3 Ouadai dist Chad
85 B4 Ouadane Mauritania
86 D4 Ouadda Cent Afr Republic
85 D6 Ouagadougou Upper Volta
85 D6 Ouahigouya Upper Volta
86 D4 Ouaka R Cent Afr Republic
85 C5 Oualata Mauritania
85 E4 Ouallen Algeria
86 D5 Ouango Cent Afr Republic
85 C7 Ouangolodougou Ivory Coast
18 H5 Ouanne R France
85 F3 Ouan Taredert Algeria
129 H3 Ouaqui Fr Guiana
85 C4 Ouarane reg Mauritania
121 Q6 Ouareau, L Quebec
85 F2 Ouargla Algeria
85 C3 Ouarkziz, Jbel mt reg Morocco/Algeria
20 J5 Ouarville France
85 C2 Ouarzazate Morocco
86 D5 Oubangui R Cent Afr Republic/Zaire
40 B3 Ouche R France
21 H6 Oucques France
25 A5 Ouddorp Netherlands
25 B5 Oude R Netherlands
25 F5 Oude Ijssel R Netherlands
22 D1 Oudekapelle Belgium
22 F2 Oudenaarde Belgium
25 C5 Oudenbosch Netherlands
25 H2 Oude Pekela Netherlands
25 C4 Oude Rijn Netherlands
25 C2 Oudeschild Netherlands
25 F3 Oude Smildervaart R Netherlands
25 C4 Oudewater Netherlands
22 L3 Oudler Belgium
21 C7 Oudon France
21 D6 Oudon R France
68 G7 Oudong Cambodia
89 C9 Oudtshoorn S Africa
85 F2 Oued, El Algeria
16 D9 Oued Laou Morocco
17 H9 Oued Taria Algeria
85 C2 Oued Zem Morocco
85 E7 Ouémé R Benin
18 B4 Ouessant, I. d' France
86 C5 Ouesso Congo
83 L14 Ouest, î de l' Kerguelen Indian Oc
123 Q7 Ouest, Pte du Miquelon I Atlantic Oc
71 F5 Ouezon Negros Philippines
85 C2 Ouezzane Morocco
22 J3 Ouffet Belgium
14 B3 Oughterard Irish Rep
40 C3 Ougney France
86 C4 Ouham R Cent Afr Republic
85 E7 Ouidah Benin
119 P2 Ouimet Ontario
124 E4 Ouiriego Mexico
18 H9 Ouissac France
20 E3 Ouistreham France
85 C5 Oujaf Mauritania
85 D2 Oujda Morocco
29 L7 Oulainen Finland
85 E2 Ouled-Nail, Mts. des Algeria
85 C2 Oulmès Morocco
13 G6 Oulton England
29 L6 Oulu Finland
29 M7 Oulujoki R Finland
86 D2 Oum Chalouba Chad
85 C3 Oum el Guebor Algeria
85 C2 Oum er Rbia R Morocco
86 C3 Oum Hadjer Chad
29 K3 Ounasjärvi L Finland
29 L4 Ounasjoki R Finland
29 K3 Ounastunturi mt Finland
9 F3 Oundle England
98 C1 Oungre Sask
84 G6 Ounianga Kébir Chad
84 G6 Ounianga Sérir Chad
85 C6 Ouolodo Mali
61 Q12 Oura-wan B Okinawa
106 C3 Ouray Colorado
103 P1 Ouray Utah
28 F6 Oure Denmark
84 F5 Ouri Chad
129 K5 Ouricuri Brazil
130 H9 Ouricuri, R Brazil
130 E8 Ourinhos Brazil
16 B7 Ourique Portugal
130 F8 Ouro Fino Brazil
130 G7 Ouro Prêto Brazil
22 K3 Ourthe R Belgium
20 G2 Ourville France
139 H8 Ouse Tasmania
9 G2 Ouse, R Norfolk England
13 G6 Ouse, R N Yorks England
18 D5 Oust R France
122 D4 Outardes, R. aux Quebec
122 D4 Outardes Trois Dam Quebec
20 K5 Outarville France
85 D2 Outat-Oulad-El-Haj Morocco
6 B2 Outer Bailey N Atlantic Oc
15 A3 Outer Hebrides Scotland
102 F8 Outer Santa Barbara Chan California
13 F5 Outhgill England
87 C10 Outjo Namibia
101 V1 Outlook Montana
118 K7 Outlook Sask
29 O9 Outokumpu Finland
144 C6 Outram New Zealand
22 B2 Outreau France
15 G2 Out Skerries isld Scotland
19 O16 Ouveze R France
138 F6 Ouyen New S Wales
21 I6 Ouzouer-le-Marché France
44 E2 Ovada Italy
131 B3 Ovalle Chile
108 H3 Ovalo Texas
101 M2 Ovando Montana
16 B4 Ovar Portugal
38 G9 Ovaro Italy
32 H6 Ovelgönne W Germany
139 H6 Ovens R Victoria
36 C2 Overath W Germany
107 P3 Overbrook Kansas
25 B5 Overflakkee Netherlands
119 Q5 Overflowing R Manitoba
26 G9 Överhogdal Sweden
22 H2 Overijse Belgium
26 N5 Överkalix Sweden
107 Q3 Overland Park Kansas
98 F1 Overly N Dakota
29 J9 Övermark Finland
131 B5 Overo, Vol Argentina
22 J1 Overpelt Belgium
9 E5 Overton England
98 G9 Overton Nebraska
103 K5 Overton Nevada
109 N3 Overton Texas
8 D2 Overton Wales
26 N5 Övertorneå Sweden
27 H14 Överum Sweden
26 G5 Over-uman L Sweden
111 G10 Ovett Mississippi
106 H1 Ovid Colorado
101 O7 Ovid Idaho
94 C3 Ovid Michigan
95 L4 Ovid New York
113 F9 Oviedo Florida
16 D1 Oviedo Spain
16 C1 Oviedo prov Spain
26 G9 Oviken Sweden
45 P5 Ovindoli Italy
52 E5 Ov'nishche U.S.S.R.
26 K8 Öv Nyland Sweden
27 B13 Övrebygd Norway
26 L6 Övre Grundsel Sweden
25 F4 Ovreijssel prov Netherlands
27 B13 Öv-Sirdal Norway
26 H8 Övsjö Sweden
145 F4 Owahanga New Zealand
144 B7 Owaka New Zealand
61 O5 Ōwani Japan
95 L4 Owasco L New York
61 K11 Owase Japan
107 P5 Owasso Oklahoma
99 N5 Owatonna Minnesota
95 L4 Owego New York
14 B2 Owemore R Irish Rep
36 G6 Owen W Germany
99 Q5 Owen Wisconsin
142 A3 Owen Anchorage W Australia
86 F5 Owen Falls D Uganda
68 C7 Owen I Burma
145 D4 Owen, Mt New Zealand
145 D4 Owen River New Zealand
94 F8 Owens W Virginia
102 F4 Owens R California
110 J4 Owensboro Kentucky
102 G5 Owens L California
120 K8 Owen Sound Ontario
140 C6 Owen Springs N Terr Aust
136 K3 Owen Stanley Ra Papua New Guinea
110 J3 Owensville Indiana
110 E3 Owensville Missouri
110 M3 Owenton Kentucky
102 F5 Owenyo California
9 E6 Ower England
85 F7 Owerri Nigeria
145 E3 Owhango New Zealand
117 K10 Owikeno L Br Col
94 D8 Owingsville Kentucky
36 F5 Öwisheim W Germany
106 E1 Owl Canyon Colorado
101 R6 Owl Cr Wyoming
101 R6 Owl-Creek Mts Wyoming
118 F4 Owl R Alberta
85 F7 Owo Nigeria
94 C3 Owosso Michigan
100 J8 Owyhee Nevada
100 H6 Owyhee Oregon
27 G10 Oxberg Sweden
119 P9 Oxbow Sask
100 J5 Oxbow Dam Oregon
111 F7 Oxbow L Mississippi
118 K1 Oxdrift Ontario
27 J13 Oxelösund Sweden
111 L8 Oxford Alabama
9 E4 Oxford England
101 N7 Oxford Idaho
110 J1 Oxford Indiana
99 P8 Oxford Iowa
107 N4 Oxford Kansas
95 R2 Oxford Maine
95 L8 Oxford Maryland
95 Q4 Oxford Massachusetts
94 D4 Oxford Michigan
111 G7 Oxford Mississippi
112 J1 Oxford N Carolina
98 G9 Oxford Nebraska
95 M4 Oxford New York
144 D5 Oxford New Zealand
122 J8 Oxford Nova Scotia
94 C7 Oxford Ohio
99 R6 Oxford Wisconsin
141 J5 Oxford Downs Queensland
119 W4 Oxford House Manitoba
101 N7 Oxford Pk Idaho
9 E4 Oxfordshire co England
46 E5 Oxiá mt Greece
140 E4 Oxide, Mt Queensland
47 G6 Oxílithos Greece
125 P7 Oxkutzcab Mexico
139 G5 Oxley New S Wales
141 K2 Oxley sub Brisbane, Qnsld
139 K4 Oxleys Pk New S Wales
14 C2 Ox Mts Irish Rep
102 E7 Oxnard California
Oxon co see Oxfordshire
9 E1 Oxton England
8 B4 Oxwich Wales
70 B3 Oya Sarawak
70 C3 Oya R Sarawak
56 D4 Oya R U.S.S.R.
61 K9 Oyabe Japan
61 M10 Oyama Shizuoka Japan
61 N9 Oyama Tochigi Japan
61 N7 Ōyama Yamagata Japan
60 D13 Ōyano shima isld Japan
129 H3 Oyapock, B. d' Fr Guiana
86 B5 Oyem Gabon
118 G7 Oyen Alberta
22 C2 Oye Plage France
27 E12 Oyeren L Norway
56 B3 Oyesh R U.S.S.R.
26 J3 Öyjord Norway
15 D3 Oykel R Scotland
51 O2 Oymyakon U.S.S.R.
85 E7 Oyo Nigeria
128 C6 Oyón Peru
40 C5 Oyonnax France
21 G8 Oyré France
109 M6 Oyster Cr Texas
68 A2 Oyster I Burma
142 C5 Oyster Inlet W Australia
100 A3 Oysterville Washington
57 G3 Oytal U.S.S.R.
32 K6 Oyten W Germany
51 N2 Oyun Khomoto U.S.S.R.
71 F6 Ozamiz Mindanao Philippines
111 L10 Ozark Alabama
110 C6 Ozark Arkansas
110 C4 Ozark Missouri
110 C5 Ozark Plateau Missouri
110 C3 Ozarks, L. of the Missouri
48 F2 Ozd Hungary
80 B7 Ozem Israel
55 F3 Ozernoye U.S.S.R.
55 D4 Ozernyy Kustanay U.S.S.R.
54 D1 Ozernyy Smolensk U.S.S.R.
55 D3 Ozernyy Sverdlovsk U.S.S.R.
55 G3 Ozero Karachi U.S.S.R.
65 J2 Ozero Khanka L China/U.S.S.R.
46 E6 Ozerós, L Greece
31 N1 Ozersk U.S.S.R.
54 K2 Ozery U.S.S.R.
100 A1 Ozette L Washington
54 K2 Ozherel'ye U.S.S.R.
51 O2 Ozhogino U.S.S.R.
43 C8 Ozieri Sardinia
31 L5 Ozimek Poland
108 F5 Ozona Texas
48 E4 Ozora Hungary
31 L4 Ozorków Poland
55 C5 Ozorodnyy U.S.S.R.
86 A6 Ozouri Gabon
60 F12 Ōzu Japan
60 D13 Ōzu R Japan
60 E11 Ozuki Japan
48 K5 Ozun Romania
45 K3 Ozzano dell'Emilia Italy
80 B8 Pa'ame Tashaz Israel
68 C4 Pa-an Burma
37 L6 Paar R W Germany
33 R7 Paaren E Germany
89 A9 Paarl S Africa
29 O3 Paatsjoki R Finland
135 U4 Paauilo Hawaiian Is
29 L7 Paavola Finland
15 A3 Pabbay isld Outer Hebrides Scotland
70 P9 Pabean Indonesia
31 L4 Pabjanice Poland
77 K6 Pab Range Pakistan
128 F6 Pacaás Novos, Sa. dos mts Brazil
129 H4 Pacajá R Brazil
128 F3 Pacaraima, Sa mts Brazil/Venezuela
128 C5 Pacasmayo Peru
111 F8 Pace Mississippi
67 F5 Pa'-chao Hsü isld Taiwan
124 E2 Pacheco Chihuahua Mexico
124 H5 Pacheco Zacatecas Mexico
100 A1 Pachena Pt Br Col
124 F3 Pachera Mexico
43 G12 Pachino Sicily
128 D5 Pachitea R Peru
125 K7 Pachuca Mexico
111 H9 Pachuta Mississippi
102 D3 Pacific California
110 F3 Pacific Missouri
135 L14 Pacific Antarctic Ridge Pac Oc
100 A2 Pacific Beach Washington
100 B4 Pacific City Oregon
101 Q7 Pacific Cr Wyoming
102 C5 Pacific Grove California
135 Pacific Ocean
71 G5 Pacijan isld Philippines
145 E4 Packakariki New Zealand
38 L7 Pack Alpe mts Austria
111 D10 Packton Louisiana
99 O8 Packwood Iowa
100 D3 Packwood Washington
112 E2 Pacolet R S Carolina
112 F3 Pacolet Mills S Carolina
31 J6 Pacov Czechoslovakia
123 R4 Pacquet Newfoundland
98 C5 Pactola S Dakota
135 Q15 Pactolus Bank Pacific Oc
130 G5 Pacui R Brazil
20 H3 Pacy France
31 K5 Paczków Poland
71 H6 Padabale isld Sulawesi
71 G7 Padada Mindanao Philippines
70 G7 Padamarang isld Sulawesi
69 G11 Padang Indonesia
69 F12 Padang Riau Arch Indonesia
69 E13 Padang Sumatra
69 E13 Padangpanjang Sumatra
69 D12 Padangsidimpuan Sumatra
69 B10 Padangtiji Sumatra
52 D3 Padany U.S.S.R.
70 D2 Padas R Sabah
29 L10 Padasjoki Finland
128 F3 Padauiri R Brazil
68 B3 Padaung Burma
83 K9 Padawiya Tank Sri Lanka
141 K1 Paddington dist Brisbane, Qnsld
117 P7 Paddle Prairie Alberta
119 M5 Paddockwood Sask
71 H6 Padea isld Indonesia
94 G7 Paden City W Virginia
32 J9 Paderborn W Germany
70 D3 Paderongan Kalimantan
48 G5 Padeşu mt Romania
13 F6 Padiham England
128 F7 Padilla Bolivia
48 L6 Padina Romania
26 J4 Padjelanta Nat. Park Sweden
115 K5 Padlei N W Terr
115 N4 Padloping Island N W Terr
122 E5 Padoue Quebec
36 B7 Padoux France
45 L1 Padova Italy
109 K9 Padre I Texas
16 B2 Padrón Spain
8 B6 Padstow England
138 F6 Padthaway S Australia
Padua see Padova
110 H4 Paducah Kentucky
108 G1 Paducah Texas
45 R7 Paduli Italy
52 D1 Padunskoye More L U.S.S.R.
145 F2 Paengaroa New Zealand
65 F6 Paengnyŏng-do isld S Korea
145 E2 Paeroa New Zealand
44 B2 Paesana Italy
45 R8 Paestum Italy
71 E3 Paete Luzon Philippines
87 F10 Pafuri Mozambique
42 G4 Pag Yugoslavia
42 F4 Pag isld Yugoslavia
71 L9 Paga Flores Indonesia
129 H4 Paga Centa Brazil
71 F7 Pagadian Mindanao Philippines
69 E14 Pagai, Pulau isld Indonesia
90 L9 Pagalu isld Equat Guinea
68 B2 Pagan Burma
45 R8 Pagani Italy
70 K7 Pagaralam Sumatra
46 F5 Pagasitikós, Kólpos B Greece
70 D6 Pagatan Kalimantan
119 P2 Pagato R Sask
71 F4 Pagbulungan Pt Philippines
103 N5 Page Arizona
98 J2 Page N Dakota
98 H7 Page Nebraska
107 Q7 Page Oklahoma
52 B6 Pagėgiai U.S.S.R.
112 G3 Pageland S Carolina
142 E3 Page, Mt W Australia
69 G14 Pagerdewa Sumatra
141 K4 Paget Cay isld Gt Barrier Reef Australia
68 A6 Paget I Andaman Is
133 J8 Paget, Mt S Georgia
77 L2 Paghman Afghanistan
42 D6 Paglia R Italy
101 S9 Pagoda Pk Colorado
142 F2 Pago Mission W Australia
47 H7 Pagóndhas Greece
70 D2 Pagonprick, G mt Sarawak
137 S4 Pago Pago Amer Samoa
106 C4 Pagosa Springs Colorado
106 C6 Paguate New Mexico
71 H4 Pagujaman R Sulawesi
120 D3 Pagwachuan Ontario
120 E3 Pagwachuan R Ontario
120 E2 Pagwa River Ontario
116 K3 Pah R Alaska
102 V14 Pahala Hawaiian Is
70 C6 Pahandut Kalimantan
73 R8 Pahang R Malaysia
69 F11 Pahang, S R Malaysia
145 E4 Pahaoa R New Zealand
144 A7 Pahia Pt New Zealand
145 E4 Pahiatua New Zealand
135 V5 Pahoa Hawaiian Is
77 G2 Pahra Afghanistan
103 J4 Pahranagat L Nevada
103 J4 Pahranagat Ra Nevada
103 K4 Pahrock Ra Nevada
103 J5 Pahrump Nevada
101 M5 Pahsimeroi R Idaho
102 H4 Pahute Mesa Nevada
100 F8 Pahute Peak mt Nevada
135 T3 Paia Hawaiian Is
130 B6 Paiaguás Brazil
52 C5 Paide U.S.S.R.
109 K5 Paige Texas
8 C7 Paignton England
145 E1 Paihia New Zealand
29 M10 Päijänne reg Finland
68 F6 Pailin Cambodia
Pailing see Chun'an
135 S3 Pailolo Ch Hawaiian Is
9 E3 Pailton England
21 A7 Paimboeuf France
116 G5 Paimiut Alaska
18 C4 Paimpol France
69 E13 Painan Sumatra
120 H10 Paincourt Ontario
133 C8 Paine mt Chile
99 S2 Painesdale Michigan
94 F5 Painesville Ohio
103 N5 Painted Des Arizona
103 L8 Painted Rock Res Arizona
37 M6 Painten W Germany
138 E4 Painter, Mt S Australia
119 T3 Paint L Manitoba
120 J8 Paisley Ontario
100 E7 Paisley Oregon
12 D2 Paisley Scotland
29 M2 Paistunturit mt Finland
128 B5 Paita Peru
67 G4 Pai-tai Lieh-tao islds Taiwan
70 E1 Paitan B Sabah
70 O9 Paiton Java
26 K4 Paittasjärbi L Sweden
16 B4 Paiva R Portugal
87 B8 Paiva Couceiro Angola
21 G8 Paizay le-Sec France
69 E13 Pajakumbuh Sumatra
26 N4 Pajala Sweden
16 D1 Pajares, Pto. de Spain
106 D7 Pajarito New Mexico
131 B2 Pajaros isld Chile
71 K9 Pajeti Sumba Indonesia
129 L5 Pajeu Brazil
130 H10 Pajeú, R Brazil
48 D4 Páka Hungary
69 F10 Paka Malaysia
69 E12 Pakanbaru Sumatra
68 B2 Pakangyi Burma
128 F2 Pakaraima Mts Guyana
119 N1 Pakashkhan L isld Ontario
68 E3 Pak Beng Laos
121 O7 Pakenham Ontario
145 D1 Pakenui New Zealand
70 E3 Pakerajan R Kalimantan
68 G4 Pak Hin Boun Laos
57 D4 Pakhtakor U.S.S.R.
85 F6 Paki Nigeria
74 A4 Pakistan rep Asia
68 E3 Pak Khop Laos
68 E3 Pak Lay Laos
Paknampho see Muang Nakhon Sawan
68 E3 Pak Niam Laos
68 B2 Pakokku Burma
145 D1 Pakotai New Zealand
69 E9 Pak Phayun Thailand
42 H3 Pakrac Yugoslavia
48 E4 Paks Hungary
68 F3 Pak Sane Laos
68 G5 Pakse Laos
68 E2 Pak Tha Laos
77 L3 Paktīā Afghanistan
70 C3 Paku R Sarawak
119 T4 Pakwa L Manitoba
89 F4 Pakwe R Botswana
86 F5 Pakwich Uganda
68 D6 Pala Burma
102 G8 Pala California
86 C4 Pala Chad
109 L7 Palacios Texas
127 L10 Palacios Venezuela
133 D6 Palacios, L Argentina
17 K3 Palafrugell Spain
42 G6 Palagruža isld Yugoslavia
46 F7 Palaiá Greece
45 J4 Paláia Italy
47 H9 Palaiókastron Crete Greece
47 F9 Palaiokhóra Crete Greece
46 D6 Pálairos Greece
20 K4 Palaiseau France
18 C5 Palais, le France
89 F4 Palala R S Africa
68 A7 Palalankwe Andaman Is
46 E5 Palamás Greece
71 J9 Palamedo Sumba Indonesia
17 K3 Palamós Spain
47 J6 Palamut Turkey
71 F2 Palanan Luzon Philippines
17 G5 Palancia R Spain
52 B6 Palanga U.S.S.R.
77 G4 Palangān, Kūh-e- mts Iran
70 C6 Palangka Raya Kalimantan
16 D2 Palanquinos Spain
70 F7 Palanro Sulawesi
135 S3 Palaoa Pt Hawaiian Is
71 G4 Palapag Philippines
89 E4 Palapye Botswana
16 B2 Palas de Rey Spain
113 F8 Palatka Florida
56 B6 Palattsy U.S.S.R.
108 F8 Palau Mexico
43 C7 Palau Sardinia
71 F1 Palaui isld Luzon Philippines
71 D3 Palauig Luzon Philippines
68 D6 Palauk Burma
83 J10 Palavi Sri Lanka
68 D6 Palaw Burma
71 D6 Palawan isld Philippines
71 C6 Palawan Passage Philippines
41 L6 Palazzolo Italy
43 F11 Palazzolo Acreide Sicily
45 L3 Palazzuolo Italy
133 D1 Palca Chile
52 B5 Paldiski U.S.S.R.
68 B2 Pale Burma
70 G4 Paleleh Sulawesi
69 G14 Palembang Sumatra
38 K6 Palen R Austria
16 D2 Palencia prov Spain
103 J8 Palen L California
79 D4 Paleokhorio Cyprus
102 C2 Palermo California
98 D1 Palermo N Dakota
43 E10 Palermo Sicily
128 E8 Palestina Chile
110 J3 Palestine Illinois
109 M4 Palestine Texas
110 M1 Palestine Hill Ohio
109 M3 Palestine, L Texas
45 N6 Palestrina Italy
68 A2 Paletwa Burma
143 B6 Palgrave, Mt W Australia
45 O6 Paliano Italy
83 K8 Pali Aru R Sri Lanka
70 P9 Paliat isld Indonesia
71 G7 Palimbang Mindanao Philippines
85 E7 Palime Togo
70 E1 Palin, Mt Sabah
43 G8 Palinuro, C Italy
106 B2 Palisade Colorado
98 E9 Palisade Nebraska
103 H1 Palisade Nevada
101 O6 Palisades Res Idaho
127 L3 Palisadoes airport Jamaica
22 J4 Paliseul Belgium
109 J8 Palito Blanco Texas
26 K5 Paljaape mt Sweden
29 L10 Pälkäne Finland
83 J8 Palk Bay Sri Lanka
52 F5 Palkino U.S.S.R.
83 J8 Palk Str India/Sri Lanka
83 K8 Pallai Sri Lanka
Pallanza see Verbania
Palla Rd see Dinokwe Botswana
18 F10 Pallaresa R Spain
29 L3 Pallastunturi mt Finland
83 K10 Pallegama Sri Lanka
26 K3 Pallemtjåkko mt Sweden
18 E6 Pallice, la France
36 B4 Pallien W Germany
70 G7 Pallima Sulawesi
9 H2 Palling England
Pallíni Greece see Kassándra
143 C10 Pallinup, R W Australia
145 E4 Palliser Bay New Zealand
21 H8 Palluau-sur-Indre France
88 H7 Palma Mozambique
106 E6 Palma New Mexico
17 J5 Palma, B. de Majorca
45 R8 Palma Camp Italy
17 J5 Palma de Mallorca Majorca
43 F11 Palma di Montechiaro Sicily
80 B6 Palmaḥim Israel
127 H9 Palmar R Venezuela
133 G4 Palmares do Sul Brazil
126 G4 Palmarito Cuba
43 E8 Palmarola isld Italy
85 C8 Palmas, C Liberia
43 B10 Palmas, G. di Sardinia
128 E1 Palma Sola Venezuela
126 G4 Palma Soriano Cuba
87 B7 Palmas, Pta. das Angola
113 G11 Palm Beach Florida
142 A4 Palm Beach W Australia
102 H8 Palm Canyon Nat. Mon California
102 F7 Palmdale California
113 F11 Palmdale Florida
133 G3 Palmeira Brazil
116 N6 Palmer Alaska
99 R10 Palmer Illinois
99 M7 Palmer Iowa
99 T3 Palmer Michigan
98 H8 Palmer Nebraska
118 L9 Palmer Sask
110 L6 Palmer Tennessee
109 L3 Palmer Texas
141 G3 Palmer R Queensland
146 F14 Palmer Arch Antarctica
146 H12 Palmer, C Antarctica
140 C6 Palmer R N Terr Aust
144 C6 Palmerston New Zealand
141 J5 Palmerston, C Queensland
145 E4 Palmerston North New Zealand
95 M6 Palmerton Pennsylvania
140 C6 Palmer Valley N Terr Aust
141 G3 Palmerville Queensland
113 E10 Palmetto Florida
112 C4 Palmetto Georgia
127 N6 Palmetto Pt Barbuda W I
126 F2 Palmetto Pt Eleuthera Bahamas
113 E9 Palm Harbor Florida
43 G10 Palmi Italy
128 C3 Palmira Colombia
126 D3 Palmira Cuba
141 H4 Palm Is Queensland
124 G6 Palmito del Verde, I Mexico
94 E3 Palms Michigan
102 H8 Palm Springs California
141 J7 Palm Tree Cr Queensland
140 C6 Palm Valley N Terr Aust
110 G2 Palmyra Illinois
99 P10 Palmyra Missouri
98 K9 Palmyra Nebraska
95 N7 Palmyra New Jersey
95 K3 Palmyra New York
95 L6 Palmyra Pennsylvania
72 D2 Palmyra Syria
110 J5 Palmyra Tennessee
94 J9 Palmyra Virginia
99 S7 Palmyra Wisconsin
135 U7 Palmyra I atoll Pacific Oc
12 E4 Palnackie Scotland
52 J4 Pal'niki U.S.S.R.
99 P7 Palo Iowa
42 E7 Palo Italy
71 G5 Palo Leyte Philippines
70 F5 Palo Sulawesi
102 B4 Palo Alto California
108 B8 Palo Duro Cr Texas
108 C7 Paloduro Cr Texas/Okla
71 K9 Paloe isld Flores Indonesia
70 B3 Paloh Sarawak
86 F3 Paloich Sudan
29 K3 Palojärvi Finland
29 K3 Palojoensuu Finland
29 K3 Palojoki R Finland
102 H8 Palomar Mt California
103 L9 Palomas Arizona
45 N5 Palombara Sabina Italy
17 G4 Palomera, Sa mts Spain
109 J3 Palo Pinto Texas
70 G6 Palopo Sulawesi
133 F3 Palo Santo Argentina
17 G7 Palos, C. de Spain
127 O3 Palo Seco Trinidad
100 H3 Palouse Washington
103 M8 Palo Verde Arizona
103 K8 Palo Verde California
141 F6 Palparara Queensland
27 H12 Pålsboda Sweden
29 N7 Paltamo Finland
38 H5 Palting Austria
70 F5 Palu R Sulawesi
127 N10 Palúa Venezuela
71 E4 Paluan Philippines
83 K9 Palugassegama Sri Lanka
57 C5 Pal'vart U.S.S.R.
85 E6 Pama Upper Volta
70 E5 Pamaluan Kalimantan
70 L9 Pamanukan Java
83 J8 Pamban isld India
70 F4 Pambero Sulawesi
118 K9 Pambrun Sask
139 J6 Pambula New S Wales
38 M8 Pameče Yugoslavia
70 O9 Pamekasan Java
70 L9 Pameungpeuk Java
18 G9 Pamiers France
46 E7 Pámisos R Greece
112 L2 Pamlico R N Carolina
68 E4 Pamong D.Site Thailand
133 D4 Pampa de las Salinas Argentina
70 G7 Pampanua Sulawesi
128 D6 Pampas Peru
133 E5 Pampas, Plains Argentina
16 B4 Pampilhosa da Serra Portugal
16 B4 Pampilhosa do Botão Portugal
94 J9 Pamplin City Virginia
128 D2 Pamplona Colombia
71 F6 Pamplona Negros Philippines
17 F2 Pamplona Spain
33 O5 Pampow E Germany
70 E6 Pamukan, Teluk B Kalimantan
47 K7 Pamukkale Turkey
47 L4 Pamukova Turkey
95 K9 Pamunkey R Virginia
99 R10 Pana Illinois
71 F7 Panabutan B Mindanao Philippines
103 K4 Panaca Nevada
120 J6 Panache, L Ontario
83 J11 Panadura Sri Lanka
71 D6 Panagtaran point Palawan Philippines
47 G2 Panagyurishte Bulgaria
70 B5 Panahan Kalimantan
70 K9 Panaitan isld Java
76 A3 Panaji India
46 E6 Panakhaikón mt Greece
94 H4 Panama New York
107 Q6 Panama Oklahoma
125 P5 Panamá Panama
125 O5 Panama rep Cent America
124 E10 Panama Canal Cent America
124 E9 Panama Canal Zone Central America
113 B7 Panama City Florida
125 P5 Panamá, Golfo de Panama
102 G5 Panamint V California
71 G6 Panaon isld Philippines
43 G10 Panarea isld Italy
45 K2 Panaro R Italy
70 O9 Panarukan Java
71 G4 Panay Philippines
71 F5 Panay isld Philippines
71 F5 Panay Gulf Philippines
47 G4 Panayía Greece
103 J3 Pancake Ra Nevada
21 B6 Pancé France
48 F6 Pančevo Yugoslavia
48 L5 Panciu Romania
69 D11 Pancurbatu Sumatra
87 F10 Panda Mozambique
108 F5 Pandale Texas
71 G3 Pandan Catanduanes Philippines
71 F5 Pandan Panay Philippines
70 C3 Pandan Sarawak
71 C6 Pandanan isld Palawan Philippines
71 F5 Pandan Bay Panay Philippines
70 K8 Pandan, Bt mt Sumatra
141 F3 Pandanus R Queensland
87 F10 Pande Mozambique
133 C3 Pan de Azúcar Chile
71 F5 Pan de Azucar Philippines
70 L9 Pandeglang Java
130 G4 Pandeiros R Brazil
138 E2 Pandie Pandie S Australia
70 F3 Pandjang isld Kalimantan
70 G4 Pandjang, Tg C Sulawesi
133 F4 Pando Uruguay
128 E6 Pando dep Bolivia
125 N5 Pandora Costa Rica
141 G1 Pandora Ent Gt Barrier Reef Aust
71 E7 Panducan isld Philippines
8 D4 Pandy Wales
52 B6 Panevėžys U.S.S.R.
138 D4 Paney S Australia
66 C3 Panfilov U.S.S.R.
57 H3 Panfilova, Imeni U.S.S.R.
86 E5 Panga Zaïre
47 F4 Pangaion mt Greece
70 M9 Pangandaran Java
88 G4 Pangani Tanzania
88 F4 Pangani R Tanzania
71 F4 Panganiran Philippines
69 J12 Pangaujalayan Indonesia
9 E5 Pangbourne England
110 E6 Pangburn Arkansas
70 F5 Pangean Sulawesi
70 N10 Panggul Java
68 D1 Panghsang Burma
86 E6 Pangi Zaïre
70 F7 Pangkadjene Sulawesi
70 O9 Pangkah, Tg C Java
70 B6 Pangkalanbuun Kalimantan
69 D10 Pangkalansusu Sumatra
69 H14 Pangkalpinang Sumatra
71 H5 Pangkalsiang, Tg C Sulawesi
71 F6 Panglao isld Philippines
68 C2 Panglong Burma
119 N9 Pangman Sask
115 N4 Pangnirtung N W Terr
70 L9 Pangrongo, G mt Java
68 C2 Pangtara Burma
133 C5 Panguipulli mt Chile
131 A7 Panguipulli, L Chile
103 M4 Panguitch Utah
71 E7 Pangutaran isld Philippines
71 E7 Pangutaran Group islds Philippines
88 E7 Pangwa Tanzania
68 D1 Pang Yang Burma
87 F9 Panhalonga Zimbabwe
108 C8 Panhandle Texas
65 A7 Panhe China
86 D7 Pania Mutembo Zaïre
137 N6 Panié, Mt New Caledonia
71 G5 Paninihian Pt Samar Philippines
71 D6 Panitan Palawan Philippines
69 D10 Panjang Sumatra
Panjang isld Cocos Is see West I
69 J11 Panjang isld Indonesia
69 F8 Panjang, Hon isld G of Thailand
77 H6 Panjgur reg Pakistan
69 C11 Panji Sumatra
77 L2 Panjshir reg Afghanistan
60 Q1 Panke-zan mt Japan
116 F9 Pankof, C Aleutian Is
33 S7 Pankow E Germany
85 F7 Pankshin Nigeria
65 H3 Pan Ling mts China
25 F5 Pannerden Netherlands
102 D5 Panoche California
70 B5 Panopah Kalimantan
99 M8 Panora Iowa
133 G2 Panorama Brazil
141 J6 Panorama, Mt Queensland
55 F3 Panovo U.S.S.R.
52 D2 Panozero U.S.S.R.
65 E4 Panshan China
65 G3 Panshi China
70 E6 Pantai Kalimantan
129 G7 Pantanal de São Lourénço swamp Brazil
68 B4 Pantanaw Burma
103 O9 Pantano Arizona
18 F10 Pantano de Tremp L Spain
71 M9 Pantar isld Indonesia
112 L2 Pantego N Carolina
109 M9 Pantego Texas
43 E12 Pantelleria isld Italy
41 N6 Pantena, Val Italy
110 J4 Panther R Kentucky
71 J9 Pantjo Sumbawa Indonesia
70 D4 Pantjungapang, Bt mt Kalimantan
128 C4 Pantoja Peru
69 C10 Pantonlabu Sumatra
125 K6 Pánuco Mexico
67 A4 Pan Xian China
67 D5 Panyu China
54 H8 Panyutino U.S.S.R.
87 C7 Panzi Zaïre
Paoki see Baoji
43 G9 Paola Italy
107 Q3 Paola Kansas
98 D9 Paoli Colorado
110 K3 Paoli Indiana
107 N7 Paoli Oklahoma

106 C3 **Paonia** Colorado
134 A11 **Paopao** Tahiti Pacific Ocean
Paotow *see* **Baotou**
135 U6 **Papa** Hawaiian Is
48 D3 **Pápa** Hungary
135 V4 **Papaaloa** Hawaiian Is
46 F8 **Papadhiánika** Greece
125 M4 **Papagayo, Golfo de** Costa Rica
135 V5 **Papaikou** Hawaiian Is
144 C6 **Papakaio** New Zealand
145 E2 **Papakura** New Zealand
71 H7 **Papalia** Indonesia
43 G8 **Papa, Monte del** Italy
125 L7 **Papantla** Mexico
70 D2 **Papar** Sabah
145 F3 **Paparatu** New Zealand
145 E2 **Paparoa** New Zealand
144 C5 **Paparoa Range** New Zealand
46 E6 **Pápas, Akr** Greece
15 G2 **Papa Stour** *isld* Scotland
145 G2 **Papatoetoe** New Zealand
15 F1 **Papa Westray** Orkney Scotland
135 M10 **Papeete** Tahiti I Pac Oc
32 F6 **Papenburg** W Germany
25 C5 **Papendrecht** Netherlands
79 C4 **Paphos** Cyprus
124 E3 **Papigochic** *R* Mexico
121 P7 **Papineauville** Quebec
133 C3 **Paposo** Chile
45 M2 **Papozze** Italy
37 J2 **Pappenheim** E Germany
37 K6 **Pappenheim** W Germany
15 C5 **Paps of Jura** *mt* Scotland
136 K3 **Papua** *terr* Papua New Guinea
136 J3 **Papua, G. of** Papua New Guinea
136 K3 **Papua New Guinea** *state* S W Pacific
141 H3 **Papuan Passage** Gt Barrier Reef Aust
42 H3 **Papuk** *mt* Yugoslavia
68 C3 **Papun** Burma
140 B6 **Papunya** N Terr Aust
128 E3 **Papuri** *R* Brazil/Colombia
48 J5 **Papusa** *mt* Romania
8 B7 **Par** England
145 D4 **Para** New Zealand
129 J4 **Pará** *R* Brazil
129 H4 **Para** *state* Brazil
56 B2 **Parabel'** *R* U.S.S.R.
143 B6 **Paraburdoo** W Australia
71 F3 **Paracale** Philippines
128 C6 **Paracas, Pena de** *pen* Peru
130 F5 **Paracatu** Brazil
138 E4 **Parachilna** S Australia
46 E1 **Paraćin** Yugoslavia
98 E4 **Parade** S Dakota
130 G6 **Pará de Minas** Brazil
126 A1 **Paradera** Aruba W Indies
121 O4 **Paradis** Quebec
102 C2 **Paradise** California
107 M2 **Paradise** Kansas
101 L2 **Paradise** Montana
144 B6 **Paradise** New Zealand
109 K2 **Paradise** Texas
101 O8 **Paradise** Utah
116 H5 **Paradise Hill** Alaska
118 H5 **Paradise Hill** Sask
113 L9 **Paradise I.** New Providence I Bahamas
102 G3 **Paradise Pk** Nevada
118 G5 **Paradise Valley** Alberta
100 H8 **Paradise Valley** Nevada
71 J9 **Parado** Sumbawa Indonesia
110 K2 **Paragon** Indiana
103 M4 **Paragonah** Utah
110 F5 **Paragould** Arkansas
128 F6 **Paraguá** *R* Bolivia
128 F2 **Paragua** *R* Venezuela
130 E8 **Paraguaca Paulista** Brazil
129 L6 **Paraguaçu** *R* Brazil
133 F2 **Paraguai** *R* Paraguay etc
127 J9 **Paraguaipoa** Venezuela
127 J9 **Paraguaná, Pen. de** Venezuela
130 B10 **Paraguari** *dep* Paraguay
133 F3 **Paraguay** *R* Paraguay
133 F2 **Paraguay** *rep* S America
130 H9 **Paraiba** *state* Brazil
130 G8 **Paraiba do Sul** Brazil
130 H7 **Paraíba, R** Brazil
Parainen *see* **Pargas**
71 K10 **Paraingkareha** Sumba Indonesia
133 G1 **Paraísa** Brazil
85 E7 **Parakou** Benin
138 D4 **Parakylia** S Australia
129 G2 **Paramaribo** Suriname
20 B4 **Paramé** France
131 B4 **Paramillos, Sa. de los** *mts* Argentina
129 K6 **Paramirim** Brazil
46 D5 **Paramithiá** Greece
128 C6 **Paramonga** Peru
133 E4 **Paraná** Argentina
133 G2 **Paraná** *R* Brazil
130 D9 **Paraná** *state* Brazil
130 E9 **Paranaguá** Brazil
133 G1 **Paranaíba** Brazil
130 E6 **Paranaiba, R** Brazil
131 F4 **Paraná Ibicuy** *R* Argentina
131 F2 **Paraná, L** Argentina
129 G2 **Paranam** Suriname
129 H8 **Paranapanema** *R* Brazil
133 G2 **Paranapanema** *R* Brazil
131 F3 **Paraná, R** Argentina
133 G2 **Paranaval** Brazil
47 G3 **Paranéstion** Greece
71 E8 **Parang** Philippines
70 N8 **Parang** *isld* Indonesia
86 F5 **Paranga** Uganda
83 K8 **Parangi Aru** *R* Sri Lanka
130 G6 **Paraopeba** Brazil
145 E4 **Paraparaumu** New Zealand
128 F8 **Parapeti** *R* Bolivia
47 F8 **Parapóla** *isld* Greece
128 E2 **Paraque, Cerro** *mt* Venezuela
70 G6 **Parara** Sulawesi
71 G5 **Parasan** *isld* Philippines
138 E4 **Paratoo** S Australia
139 H8 **Parattah** Tasmania
129 H5 **Parauapebas** *R* Brazil
18 H6 **Paray-le-Monial** France
56 B3 **Parbig** *R* U.S.S.R.
21 F7 **Parçay-les-Pins** France
20 C5 **Parcé** France
55 E5 **Parchevka** U.S.S.R.
33 P6 **Parchim** E Germany
45 O7 **Parco Naz. del Circeo** Italy
22 C3 **Parcq, le** France
31 O4 **Parczew** Poland
102 D3 **Pardee Res** California
99 R6 **Pardeeville** Wisconsin
80 C4 **Pardes Hanna-Karkur** Israel
129 H8 **Pardo** *R* Brazil
130 F4 **Pardo** *R* Minas Gerais Brazil
131 H2 **Pardo** *R* Rio Grande do Sul Brazil
142 C5 **Pardoo** W Australia
130 D7 **Pardo, R** Mato Grosso Brazil
31 J5 **Pardubice** Czechoslovakia
70 O9 **Pare** Java
129 G6 **Parecis** Brazil
128 F6 **Parecis, Sa. dos** *mts* Brazil
133 D3 **Pareditas** Argentina
145 D1 **Parengarenga Harbour** New Zealand
20 E5 **Parennes** France
121 Q5 **Parent** Quebec
18 E8 **Parentis en Born** France
121 O4 **Parent L** Quebec
144 C6 **Pareora** New Zealand
70 F7 **Parepare** Sulawesi
33 P8 **Parey** E Germany
52 F5 **Parfen'yevo** U.S.S.R.
46 D5 **Párga** Greece
29 J11 **Pargas** Finland
52 D4 **Pargolovo** U.S.S.R.
127 P4 **Parham** Antigua W Indies
103 N4 **Paria** *R* Utah
128 F1 **Paria, G. de** Venezuela/Trinidad
128 F2 **Pariaguán** Venezuela
69 E13 **Pariaman** Sumatra
128 F1 **Paria, Pen. de** Venezuela
103 N5 **Paria Plat** Arizona
128 E4 **Paricá, L** Brazil
70 G5 **Parigi** Sulawesi
21 F6 **Parigné-l'Evêque** France
128 G2 **Parika** Guyana
144 D5 **Parikawa** New Zealand
145 E3 **Parikino** New Zealand
29 O10 **Parikkala** Finland
128 F3 **Parima, Sa** *mts* Brazil/Venezuela
128 D7 **Parinacocha, L** Peru
128 D4 **Parinari** Peru
128 B4 **Pariñas, Pta** Peru
48 L4 **Părincea** Romania
138 F5 **Paringa** S Australia
129 G4 **Parintins** Brazil
110 C6 **Paris** Arkansas
101 O7 **Paris** Idaho
99 T10 **Paris** Illinois
110 M3 **Paris** Kentucky
110 E2 **Paris** Missouri
110 H5 **Paris** Tennessee
109 M2 **Paris** Texas
23 **Paris** *conurbation* France
95 L3 **Parish** New York
99 W3 **Parisienne, Ile** Ontario
69 E10 **Parit Buntar** Malaysia
71 L10 **Pariti** Timor Indonesia
55 D4 **Parizhskiy** U.S.S.R.
26 N4 **Parkajoki** Sweden
29 K9 **Parkano** Finland
118 L8 **Parkbeg** Sask
110 K4 **Park City** Kentucky
101 R4 **Park City** Montana
103 N1 **Park City** Utah
106 E3 **Parkdale** Colorado
100 D4 **Parkdale** Oregon
103 K7 **Parker** Arizona
106 F2 **Parker** Colorado
101 O6 **Parker** Idaho
107 Q3 **Parker** Kansas
98 J6 **Parker** S Dakota
110 L1 **Parker City** Indiana
94 H5 **Parker City** Pennsylvania
103 K7 **Parker Dam** California
143 D9 **Parker Hill** W Australia
140 E3 **Parker Pt** Queensland
143 C9 **Parker Range** W Australia
99 O7 **Parkersburg** Iowa
94 F7 **Parkersburg** W Virginia
99 L3 **Parkers Prairie** Minnesota
119 O7 **Parkerview** Sask
139 J5 **Parkes** New S Wales
95 M6 **Parkesburg** Pennsylvania
99 Q4 **Park Falls** Wisconsin
102 D6 **Parkfield** California
12 E3 **Parkgate** Scotland
95 L8 **Park Hall** Maryland
57 E5 **Parkhar** U.S.S.R.
120 J9 **Parkhill** Ontario
26 K5 **Parkijaur** *L* Sweden
110 F6 **Parkin** Arkansas
118 E9 **Park Lake Prov. Park** Alberta
118 D8 **Parkland** Alberta
119 Q9 **Parkman** Sask
101 S5 **Parkman** Wyoming
101 T9 **Park Ra** Colorado
99 L3 **Park Rapids** Minnesota
99 T8 **Park Ridge** Illinois
98 J1 **Park River** N Dakota
103 N6 **Parks** Arizona
98 E9 **Parks** Nebraska
111 L13 **Parks Airport** St Louis
118 L5 **Parkside** Sask
95 M9 **Parksley** Virginia
140 C6 **Parks, Mt** N Terr Aust
109 K2 **Park Springs** Texas
37 N4 **Parkstein** W Germany
98 J6 **Parkston** S Dakota
95 L7 **Parkton** Maryland
112 H3 **Parkton** N Carolina
101 M8 **Park Valley** Utah
106 D5 **Park View** New Mexico
106 D1 **Park View Mt** Colorado
100 D3 **Parkway** Washington
26 K5 **Pärlälven** *R* Sweden
127 M1 **Parlatuvier** Tobago
100 J6 **Parma** Idaho
45 H2 **Parma** Italy
94 C4 **Parma** Michigan
110 G5 **Parma** Missouri
94 F5 **Parma** Ohio
45 H2 **Parma** *R* Italy
21 H9 **Parnac** France
129 K6 **Parnaguá** Brazil
129 K4 **Parnaiba** Brazil
129 J5 **Parnaíba** *R* Brazil
46 F6 **Parnassós** *mt* Greece
144 D5 **Parnassus** New Zealand
99 O8 **Parnell** Iowa
99 M9 **Parnell** Missouri
108 G1 **Parnell** Texas
47 F6 **Párnis** *mt* Greece
46 F7 **Párnon Óros** *mts* Greece
52 B5 **Pärnu** U.S.S.R.
52 B5 **Pärnu laht** *G* U.S.S.R.
144 C5 **Paroa** New Zealand
59 M1 **Paromay** U.S.S.R.
110 D7 **Paron** Arkansas
141 G8 **Paroo** *R* Queensland
139 G4 **Paroo Chan** New S Wales
77 G2 **Paropamisus** *mts* Afghanistan
70 F6 **Paroreang, Bk** *mt* Sulawesi
47 G7 **Páros** *isld* Greece
127 J3 **Parottee Pt** Jamaica
103 M4 **Parowan** Utah
99 T8 **Parr** Indiana
112 F3 **Parr** S Carolina
8 C5 **Parracombe** England
133 C5 **Parral** Chile
139 K5 **Parramatta** New S Wales
95 M9 **Parramore I** Virginia
124 H5 **Parras de la Fuente** Mexico
8 D5 **Parrett, R** England
111 J8 **Parrish** Alabama
113 E10 **Parrish** Florida
111 M10 **Parrott** Georgia
112 C6 **Parrott** Georgia
94 G9 **Parrott** Virginia
122 H8 **Parrsboro** Nova Scotia
119 N9 **Parry** Sask
115 L4 **Parry B** N W Terr
120 K7 **Parry I** Ontario
114 H2 **Parry Is** N W Terr
115 M2 **Parry, Kap** Greenland
127 N3 **Parrylands** Trinidad
142 B5 **Parry Ra** W Australia
33 N7 **Parsau** W Germany
37 M5 **Parsberg** W Germany
41 M3 **Parseier Spitze** *mt* Austria
98 D2 **Parshall** N Dakota
103 K3 **Parsnip Pk** Nevada
107 P4 **Parsons** Kansas
110 H6 **Parsons** Tennessee
94 H7 **Parsons** W Virginia
123 P3 **Parson's Pond** Nfld
43 E11 **Partanna** Sicily
26 J4 **Pårtefjället** *mt* Sweden
36 E4 **Partenheim** W Germany
21 E8 **Parthenay** France
46 F7 **Parthénion** Greece
124 D5 **Partida** *isld* Mexico
43 E10 **Partinico** Sicily
59 K3 **Partizansk** U.S.S.R.
107 M4 **Partridge** Kansas
120 K2 **Partridge** *R* Ontario
123 R5 **Partridgeberry Hills** Newfoundland
119 U1 **Partridge Breast L** Manitoba
123 Q3 **Partridge Pt** Newfoundland
129 H4 **Paru** *R* Brazil
145 E1 **Parua Bay** New Zealand
77 L2 **Parwān** Afghanistan
66 C6 **Paryang** China
27 H15 **Påryd** Sweden
89 E6 **Parys** S Africa
102 G7 **Pasadena** California
109 G9 **Pasadena** Texas
128 B4 **Pasado, C** Ecuador
124 H5 **Pasaje** Mexico
133 E3 **Pasaje** *R* Argentina
106 G5 **Pasamonte** New Mexico
70 F5 **Pasangkaiu** Sulawesi
77 C4 **Pasargadae** Iran
71 H7 **Pasarwadjo** Indonesia
68 C3 **Pasawng** Burma
111 H11 **Pascagoula** *R* Mississippi
121 N4 **Pascalis** Quebec
48 K3 **Paşcani** Romania
100 F3 **Pasco** Washington
128 C6 **Pasco** *dep* Peru
95 Q5 **Pascoag** Rhode I
130 H5 **Pascoal, Mte** Brazil
140 E3 **Pascoe Inlet** Queensland
141 G2 **Pascoe, R** Queensland
142 B5 **Pasco I** W Australia
120 A2 **Pascopee** Ontario
133 C7 **Pascua** *R* Chile
22 C3 **Pas en Artois** France
33 T5 **Pasewalk** E Germany
52 J3 **Pashnya** U.S.S.R.
52 D4 **Pashskiy-Perevoz** U.S.S.R.
71 E3 **Pasig** Luzon Philippines
71 J4 **Pasige** *isld* Indonesia
78 H1 **Pasinler** Turkey
69 C11 **Pasiputih** Sumatra
70 O10 **Pasirian** Java
69 E12 **Pasirpengarayan** Sumatra
69 F10 **Pasir Puteh** Malaysia
27 H14 **Påskallavik** Sweden
102 B2 **Paskenta** California
57 B2 **Paskevicha, Zaliv** *gulf* U.S.S.R.
31 M1 **Pasłęk** Poland
143 E10 **Pasley, C** W Australia
29 L4 **Pasmajärvi** Finland
42 G5 **Pasman** *isld* Yugoslavia
138 E4 **Pasmore** *R* S Australia
77 H7 **Pasni** Pakistan
133 D6 **Paso de Indios** Argentina
125 M4 **Paso del Cascal** *mt* Nicaragua
133 F3 **Paso de los Libres** Argentina
133 F4 **Paso de los Toros** Uruguay
130 B10 **Paso de Patria** Paraguay
68 B2 **Pasok** Burma
133 C6 **Paso Limay** Argentina
125 M2 **Paso Reál** Honduras
133 C7 **Paso Rio Mayo** Argentina
102 D6 **Paso Robles** California
122 G5 **Paspébiac** Quebec
119 M8 **Pasqua** Sask
119 O5 **Pasquia Hills** Sask
119 Q5 **Pasquia R** Manitoba
112 L1 **Pasquotank R** N Carolina
77 C5 **Pas Rūdak** Iran
95 T1 **Passadumkeag** Maine
9 H7 **Passage de la Déroute** Channel Is
99 S1 **Passage I** Michigan
120 B4 **Passage I** Ontario
113 E10 **Pass-a-Grille Beach** Florida
95 N6 **Passaic** New Jersey
20 D5 **Passais** France
38 H4 **Passau** W Germany
40 D2 **Passavant** France
111 G11 **Pass Christian** Mississippi
101 T8 **Pass Cr** Wyoming
22 E2 **Passendale** Belgium
43 G12 **Passero, C** Sicily
123 Q6 **Pass I** Newfoundland
71 F5 **Passi** Philippines
41 O4 **Passiria, Val** Italy
99 S1 **Pass L** Ontario
120 B4 **Pass Lake** Ontario
15 C4 **Pass of Brander** Scotland
133 H2 **Passos** Brazil
128 C4 **Pastaza** *prov* Ecuador
122 F3 **Pasteur, L** Quebec
128 C3 **Pasto** Colombia
116 F5 **Pastol B** Alaska
9 H2 **Paston** England
103 P5 **Pastora Pk** Arizona
129 K5 **Pastos Bons** Brazil
71 E1 **Pasuquin** Luzon Philippines
70 O9 **Pasuruan** Java
52 B6 **Pasvalys** U.S.S.R.
52 C1 **Pasvikelv** *R* Norway
119 O6 **Paswegin** Sask
31 M2 **Pasym** Poland
48 F3 **Pásztó** Hungary
86 D4 **Pata** Cent Afr Republic
71 E8 **Pata** *isld* Philippines
103 O10 **Patagonia** Arizona
133 C7 **Patagonia** *terr* Chile/Arg
100 H3 **Pataha** *R* Washington
77 K1 **Pata Kesar** Afghanistan
130 G10 **Patamuté** Brazil
75 L5 **Patan** Nepal
71 B2 **Patani** Indonesia
95 L7 **Patapsco** *R* Maryland
20 J5 **Patay** France
138 F6 **Patchewollock** Victoria
95 P6 **Patchogue** Long I, N Y
145 E3 **Patea** New Zealand
144 C6 **Patearoa** New Zealand
70 G6 **Patedong** Sulawesi
85 F7 **Pategi** Nigeria
43 F11 **Paternò** Sicily
45 R8 **Paternopoli** Italy
100 F1 **Pateros** Washington
95 N6 **Paterson** New Jersey
100 F4 **Paterson** Washington
141 H8 **Paterson** *R* Queensland
144 B7 **Paterson Inlet** New Zealand
142 D5 **Paterson Ra** W Australia
25 G2 **Paterswolde** Netherlands
74 F2 **Pathankot** India
74 F9 **Pathardi** India
101 T7 **Pathfinder Res** Wyoming
13 F2 **Pathhead** Lothian Scotland
12 D3 **Pathhead** Strathclyde Scotland
68 D7 **Pathiu** Thailand
119 N6 **Pathlow** Sask
74 G9 **Pathri** India
68 E5 **Pathum Thani** Thailand
71 N9 **Pati** Indonesia
70 N9 **Pati** Java
70 B5 **Pati** Kalimantan
128 C3 **Patia** *R* Colombia
74 G3 **Patiala** India
143 F6 **Patience Well** W Australia
70 G7 **Patiro Tg** *C* Sulawesi
128 C6 **Pativilca** Peru
70 P9 **Patjinan Tg** *C* Java
70 N10 **Patjitan** Java
75 Q5 **Patkai Bum** *reg* India
111 C8 **Patmos** Arkansas
47 H7 **Pátmos** *isld* Greece
75 L6 **Patna** India
12 D3 **Patna** Scotland
75 K8 **Patnagarh** India
71 F3 **Patnanongan** *isld* Luzon Philippines
78 J2 **Patnos** Turkey
110 G3 **Patoka** Illinois
145 F3 **Patoka** New Zealand
110 K3 **Patoka** *R* Indiana
99 M7 **Paton** Iowa
130 H9 **Patos** Brazil
129 J7 **Patos de Minas** Brazil
127 N1 **Patos, I** Trinidad
100 C1 **Patos I** Washington
131 H3 **Patos, Lagoa dos** Brazil
108 A5 **Patos, Laguna de** Mexico
131 E3 **Patos, L. de los** Santa Fé Argentina
131 B3 **Patos, R. de los** Argentina
133 D4 **Patquía** Argentina
46 E6 **Pátrai** Greece
Patras Greece *see* **Pátrai**
118 F8 **Patricia** Alberta
98 E6 **Patricia** S Dakota
140 B5 **Patricia, Mt** N Terr Aust
133 B7 **Patricio Lynch, I** Chile
13 G5 **Patrick Brompton** England
121 T7 **Patrie, La** Quebec
110 M3 **Patriot** Indiana
133 H1 **Patrocinio** Brazil
111 K10 **Patsaliga** *R* Alabama
41 O3 **Patscherkofel** *mt* Austria
52 C1 **Patsoyoki** *R* U.S.S.R.
86 H6 **Patta** *isld* Kenya
43 C8 **Pattada** Sardinia
70 F7 **Pattallassang** Sulawesi Indonesia
76 C6 **Pattanapuram** India
69 E9 **Pattani** Thailand
69 E9 **Pattani** *R* Thailand
95 S7 **Patten** Maine
32 L8 **Pattensen** W Germany
13 F5 **Patterdale** England
102 C4 **Patterson** California
112 E6 **Patterson** Georgia
101 M5 **Patterson** Idaho
111 E12 **Patterson** Louisiana
94 H7 **Patterson Cr** W Virginia
102 E5 **Patterson Mt** California
117 F3 **Patterson, Mt** Yukon Terr
99 V4 **Patterson, Pt** Michigan
43 F10 **Patti** Sicily
140 B4 **Pattie Cr** N Terr Aust
43 G10 **Patti, G. di** Sicily
80 B8 **Pattish** *R* Israel
111 F10 **Pattison** Mississippi
94 J6 **Patton** Pennsylvania
99 M9 **Pattonsburg** Missouri
130 H9 **Patu** Brazil
78 H2 **Patu** Turkey
75 O7 **Patuakhali** Bangladesh
118 K3 **Patuanak** Sask
48 H6 **Pătuele** Romania
70 L9 **Patuha, G** *mt* Java
117 J7 **Patullo, Mt** Br Col
144 D4 **Paturau River** New Zealand
145 F3 **Patutahi** New Zealand
145 E3 **Patutu** *mt* New Zealand
95 L8 **Patuxent** *R* Maryland
18 E9 **Pau** France
145 D1 **Paua** New Zealand
129 J5 **Pau D'Arco** Brazil
121 O7 **Paugan Falls** Quebec
18 E7 **Pauillac** France
128 E5 **Pauini** Brazil
68 B2 **Pauk** Burma
68 A2 **Pauktaw** Burma
101 M7 **Paul** Idaho
38 H8 **Paularo** Italy
114 G4 **Paulatuk** N W Terr
103 M7 **Paulden** Arizona
94 C5 **Paulding** Ohio
146 G2 **Paulding B** Antarctica
18 H9 **Paulhan** France
116 H9 **Paul I** Alaska
115 N6 **Paul I** Labrador
100 F5 **Paulina** Oregon
33 R7 **Paulinenaue** E Germany
Paulis *see* **Isiro**
130 J9 **Paulista** Brazil
129 K5 **Paulistana** Brazil
99 L7 **Paullina** Iowa
41 K7 **Paullo** Italy
21 H8 **Paulnay** France
130 H10 **Paulo Alfonso, Cachoeira de** *falls* Brazil
25 C3 **Paulowna** Netherlands
107 N7 **Pauls Valley** Oklahoma
37 M5 **Paulushofen** W Germany
21 B8 **Paulx** France
68 C4 **Paung** Burma
68 B3 **Paungde** Burma
74 H8 **Pauni** India
74 H3 **Pauri** India
37 M2 **Pausa** E Germany
128 D7 **Pausa** Peru
33 S7 **Pausin** E Germany
128 D2 **Pauto** *R* Colombia
26 J7 **Pauträsk** Sweden
22 G5 **Pauvres** France
135 T3 **Pauwela** Hawaiian Is
103 M3 **Pavant Ra** Utah
55 C2 **Pavda** U.S.S.R.
54 L3 **Pavelets** U.S.S.R.
44 F1 **Pavia** Italy
117 N10 **Pavilion** Br Col
94 K4 **Pavilion** New York
101 R6 **Pavillion** Wyoming
20 G2 **Pavilly** France
27 M15 **Pāvilosta** U.S.S.R.
52 G5 **Pavino** U.S.S.R.
47 G1 **Pavlikeni** Bulgaria
55 G4 **Pavlodar** U.S.S.R.
116 G9 **Pavlof** Alaska
116 F9 **Pavlof Harbour** Aleutian Is
116 G9 **Pavlof Vol** Alaska
54 G8 **Pavlograd** U.S.S.R.
55 F4 **Pavlogradka** U.S.S.R.
54 G8 **Pavlogradskiye Khutora I-ye** U.S.S.R.
55 C3 **Pavlovka** Bashkirskaya U.S.S.R.
55 F5 **Pavlovka** Kazakhstan U.S.S.R.
52 F6 **Pavlovo** U.S.S.R.
56 B4 **Pavlovsk** Altay U.S.S.R.
52 D5 **Pavlovsk** Leningrad U.S.S.R.
55 D4 **Pavlovskiy** Kazakhstan U.S.S.R.
52 H5 **Pavlovskiy** Perm U.S.S.R.
113 D7 **Pavo** Georgia
45 J3 **Pavullo nel Frignano** Italy
107 O5 **Pawhuska** Oklahoma
119 Q3 **Pawistik** Manitoba
95 O3 **Pawlet** Vermont
8 D5 **Pawlett** England
112 H4 **Pawleys Island** S Carolina
68 C3 **Pawn** *R* Burma
99 R10 **Pawnee** Illinois
107 O5 **Pawnee** Oklahoma
109 K7 **Pawnee** Texas
99 L9 **Pawnee City** Nebraska
98 C9 **Pawnee Cr** Colorado
107 L3 **Pawnee Rock** Kansas
94 B4 **Paw Paw** Michigan
94 J7 **Paw Paw** W Virginia
95 Q5 **Pawtucket** Rhode I
47 G9 **Paximádhia** *isld* Crete Greece
46 D5 **Paxoi** *isld* Greece
116 P5 **Paxson** Alaska
116 P5 **Paxson L** Alaska
99 S9 **Paxton** Illinois
98 E8 **Paxton** Nebraska
68 C4 **Payagyi** Burma
58 E3 **Pa-yen-kao-le** China
40 E4 **Payerne** Switzerland
100 J5 **Payette** Idaho
100 J5 **Payette** *R* Idaho
109 L3 **Pay Hubbard, L** Texas
50 F2 **Pay-Khoy, Khrebet** *mt* U.S.S.R.
112 D5 **Payne** Georgia
94 C5 **Payne** Ohio
115 M6 **Payne, L** Quebec
102 C1 **Paynes Cr** California
143 C8 **Payne's Find** W Australia
99 M4 **Paynesville** Minnesota
143 C8 **Paynesville** W Australia
118 J5 **Paynton** Sask
70 C3 **Payong Tg** *C* Sarawak
131 F4 **Paysandu** Uruguay
20 F3 **Pays d'Auge** *reg* France
20 J3 **Pays de Bray** *reg* France
19 N13 **Pays de Dombes** *reg* France
40 F5 **Pays d'Enhaut** Switzerland
103 N7 **Payson** Arizona
103 N1 **Payson** Utah
131 B6 **Payún** *vol* Argentina
131 B6 **Payún Matru, Cerros** *hills* Argentina
77 A4 **Pāzanūn** Iran
47 G2 **Pazardzhik** Bulgaria
47 J5 **Pazarköy** Turkey
124 D5 **Paz, B. de la** Mexico
128 D2 **Paz de Rio** Colombia
42 F3 **Pazin** Yugoslavia
41 M3 **Paznauntal** Austria
52 D5 **Pchevzha** U.S.S.R.
31 M6 **Pcim** Poland
46 E2 **Pčinja** *R* Yugoslavia
68 D6 **Pe** Burma
111 L10 **Pea** *R* Alabama
117 R6 **Peace Point** Alberta
118 A2 **Peace R** Alberta
117 M7 **Peace R** Br Col/Alberta
113 F10 **Peace R** Florida
114 H6 **Peace River** Alberta
117 O11 **Peachland** Br Col
103 L6 **Peach Sp** Arizona
94 B2 **Peacock** Michigan
141 J5 **Peak Downs** Queensland
138 D3 **Peake** *R* S Australia
71 D5 **Peaked Pt** Philippines
140 B3 **Peake, Mt** N Terr Aust
143 C7 **Peak Hill** W Australia
102 E7 **Peak Mt** California
141 J6 **Peak Ra** Queensland
146 H12 **Peale Inlet** Antarctica
103 P3 **Peale, Mt** Utah
100 B9 **Peanut** California
118 D9 **Pearce** Alberta
103 P10 **Pearce** Arizona
140 A2 **Pearce Pt** N Terr Aust
111 C7 **Pearcy** Arkansas
116 H1 **Peard B** Alaska
110 F2 **Pearl** Illinois
119 P2 **Pearl** Ontario
111 G11 **Pearl** *R* Miss/Louisiana
109 G10 **Pearland** Texas
102 S12 **Pearl City** Hawaiian Is
99 R7 **Pearl City** Illinois
102 S12 **Pearl Hbr** Hawaiian Is
144 A7 **Pearl I** New Zealand
109 H7 **Pearsall** Texas
112 E6 **Pearson** Georgia
138 C5 **Pearson Is** S Australia
119 V2 **Pearson L** Manitoba
114 J2 **Peary Ch** N W Terr
109 H1 **Pease** *R* Texas
47 G5 **Peathoúra** *isld* Greece
21 A6 **Péaule** France
99 S3 **Peavy Falls Res** Michigan
142 C5 **Peawah, R** W Australia
88 G10 **Pebane** Mozambique
128 D4 **Pebas** Peru
133 F8 **Pebble I** Falkland Is
46 D2 **Peć** Yugoslavia
111 D12 **Pecan Island** Louisiana
130 E9 **Peças, I. das** Brazil
99 R7 **Pecatonica** Illinois
99 R7 **Pecatonica** *R* Illinois
45 J4 **Péccioli** Italy
48 L5 **Pechea** Romania
48 J2 **Pechenezhin** U.S.S.R.
29 P2 **Pechenga** U.S.S.R.
55 D1 **Pecherakh** U.S.S.R.
52 J2 **Pechora** U.S.S.R.
52 J3 **Pechora** *R* U.S.S.R.
50 E2 **Pechorskoy More** *sea* U.S.S.R.
52 C5 **Pechory** U.S.S.R.
48 G4 **Pecica** Romania
100 B7 **Peck** Oregon
33 S5 **Peckatel** E Germany
32 K9 **Peckelsheim** W Germany
144 C5 **Pecksniff, Mt** New Zealand
43 B9 **Pecora, C** Sardinia
43 G10 **Pecoraro, M** *mt* Italy
106 E6 **Pecos** New Mexico
108 D4 **Pecos** Texas
106 F6 **Pecos** *R* New Mexico
108 F5 **Pecos** *R* Texas/Mexico
48 E4 **Pécs** Hungary
48 E4 **Pécsvárad** Hungary
110 B3 **Peculiar** Missouri
125 O6 **Pedasí** Panama
139 H9 **Pedder, L** Tasmania
100 B5 **Pedee** Oregon
127 J5 **Pedernales** Dom Rep
124 F3 **Pedernales** Mexico
127 N10 **Pedernales** Venezuela
28 H6 **Pedersborg** Denmark
79 C4 **Pedhoulas** Cyprus
138 D2 **Pedirka** S Australia
129 K7 **Pedra Azul** Brazil
130 J9 **Pedra, Pta. de** *C* Brazil
128 F6 **Pedras Negras** Brazil
124 H5 **Pedriceña** Mexico
129 J5 **Pedro Afonso** Brazil
126 E6 **Pedro Bank** Caribbean
116 K7 **Pedro Bay** Alaska
126 F6 **Pedro Cays** *reefs* Caribbean
Peebles *co see* **Borders** *reg*
140 D7 **Peebles, Mt** N Terr Aust
142 B5 **Peedamulla** W Australia
144 C5 **Peel, Mt** New Zealand
103 M7 **Peeples Valley** Arizona
117 Q7 **Peerless L** Alberta
118 A5 **Peers** Alberta
139 G4 **Peery, L** New S Wales
106 G1 **Peetz** Colorado
98 K4 **Peever** S Dakota
144 D5 **Pegasus Bay** New Zealand
37 N1 **Pegau** E Germany
38 M7 **Peggau** Austria
44 E3 **Pegli** Italy
37 M4 **Pegnitz** W Germany
17 G6 **Pego** Spain
45 J2 **Pegognaga** Italy
101 O7 **Pegram** Idaho
13 G3 **Pegswood** England
69 F13 **Peg Tigabuluh** *mt* Sumatra
68 C4 **Pegu** Burma
69 E13 **Pegunungan Barisan** *mt* Sumatra
69 K12 **Pegunungan Bayang** *mt* Indonesia
68 B3 **Pegu Yoma** *ra* Burma
9 H5 **Pegwell B** England
52 H3 **Pegysh** U.S.S.R.
46 F3 **Pehčevo** Yugoslavia
67 B1 **Peijiangchang** China
67 G3 **Pei-Kan-t'ang Tao** *isld* Taiwan
38 M5 **Peilstein** *mt* Austria
32 M8 **Peine** W Germany
133 C8 **Peineta** *mt* Chile
68 B2 **Peinwa** Burma
19 P16 **Peipin** France
Peipus, L *see* **Chudskoye, Ozero**
41 N2 **Peiting** W Germany
133 G2 **Peixe** *R* Brazil
130 C5 **Peixe de Couro, R** Brazil
65 C7 **Pei Xian** China
65 D7 **Pei Xian** China
69 H12 **Pejantan** *isld* Indonesia
48 G6 **Pek** *R* Yugoslavia
70 M9 **Pekalongan** Java
69 F11 **Pekan** Malaysia
99 R9 **Pekin** Illinois
110 G1 **Pekin** Illinois
98 H2 **Pekin** N Dakota
Peking *see* **Beijing**
117 Q10 **Pekisko** Alberta
29 M5 **Pekkala** Finland
68 C3 **Pekon** Burma
69 E11 **Pelabohan Kelang** Malaysia
70 L9 **Pelabuanratu** Java
43 E13 **Pelagie, Isole** Italy
45 L4 **Pelago** Italy
47 G5 **Pélagos** *isld* Greece
111 G9 **Pelahatchee** Mississippi
69 F12 **Pelalawan** Sumatra
70 D6 **Pelampai** Kalimantan
17 G4 **Pelarda, Sa** *mts* Spain
46 F6 **Pelasyía** Greece
89 F7 **Pelatsoeu** *mt* Lesotho
31 J2 **Pełczyce** Poland
48 H5 **Peleaga** *mt* Romania
56 H2 **Peleduy** *R* U.S.S.R.
120 H10 **Pelee Island** Ontario
127 L4 **Pelée, Mt** Martinique W I
48 L3 **Peleney** U.S.S.R.
71 H5 **Peleng** *isld* Indonesia
71 H5 **Peleng, Selat** *str* Sulawesi
71 H5 **Peleng, Tk** *B* Indonesia
112 C6 **Pelham** Georgia
31 J6 **Pelhřimov** Czechoslovakia
119 R6 **Pelican B** Manitoba
113 L11 **Pelican Harbour** Bahamas
118 D3 **Pelican L** Alberta
119 S9 **Pelican L** Manitoba
99 O1 **Pelican L** Minnesota
119 O3 **Pelican L** Sask
99 R4 **Pelican L** Wisconsin
118 E3 **Pelican Portage** Alberta
141 G3 **Pelican R** Queensland
119 R6 **Pelican Rapids** Manitoba
98 K3 **Pelican Rapids** Minnesota
59 L1 **Peliny Osipenko, imeni** U.S.S.R.
112 F4 **Pelion** S Carolina
26 J5 **Peljekaise Nat. Park** Sweden
42 H6 **Pelješac** *pen* Yugoslavia
29 N4 **Pelkosenniemi** Finland
52 D3 **Pelkula** U.S.S.R.
32 G9 **Pelkum** W Germany
99 O8 **Pella** Iowa
43 G8 **Pella** Italy
80 F4 **Pella** Jordan
111 K8 **Pell City** Alabama
133 E5 **Pellegrini** Argentina
133 D5 **Pellegrini, L** Argentina
20 C5 **Pellerine, la** France
45 M1 **Pellestrina** Italy
119 U2 **Pelletier L** Manitoba
140 D3 **Pellew C** N Terr Aust
36 B4 **Pellingen** W Germany
29 L5 **Pello** Finland
21 E7 **Pellouailles** France
94 C1 **Pellston** Michigan
30 D1 **Pellworm** *isld* W Germany
119 Q7 **Pelly** Sask
117 E4 **Pelly** *R* Yukon Terr
115 L4 **Pelly Bay** N W Terr
117 E4 **Pelly Crossing** Yukon Terr
114 J4 **Pelly L** N W Terr
117 G5 **Pelly Mts** Yukon Terr
71 J8 **Pelokang** *isld* Indonesia
46 E7 **Pelopónnisos** Greece
43 G11 **Peloritani, Mi** *mts* Sicily
145 D4 **Pelorus Sound** New Zealand
131 H3 **Pelotas** Brazil
130 D10 **Pelotas, R.das** Brazil
47 G1 **Pelovo** Bulgaria
31 L2 **Pelplin** Poland
143 A8 **Pelsart Group** *islds* W Australia
33 T5 **Pelsin** E Germany
110 C6 **Pelsor** Arkansas
29 L3 **Peltovuoma** Finland
44 B2 **Pelvo d'Elva** *mt* Italy
19 Q15 **Pelvoux, Mt** France
55 D2 **Pelym** U.S.S.R.
55 D1 **Pelym** *R* U.S.S.R.
55 D1 **Pelymskiy Tuman, Oz** *L* U.S.S.R.
8 B7 **Pelynt** England
112 E3 **Pelzer** S Carolina
33 N4 **Pelzerhaken** W Germany
120 G5 **Pemache, R** Ontario
95 S1 **Pemadumcook L** Maine
70 M9 **Pemalang** Java
70 M9 **Pemalang, Tg** *C* Java
71 H5 **Pemali, Tg** *C* Sulawesi
70 C5 **Pemarunan** Kalimantan
70 E5 **Pemarung, P** Kalimantan
69 D11 **Pematangsiantar** Sumatra
88 H8 **Pemba** Mozambique
87 E9 **Pemba** Zambia
87 H8 **Pemba, B.de** Mozambique
88 G4 **Pemba I** Tanzania
117 M10 **Pemberton** Br Col
143 B10 **Pemberton** W Australia
119 U10 **Pembina** N Dakota
98 H1 **Pembina** *R* Manitoba
118 B5 **Pembina Oil Fields** Alberta
119 T9 **Pembina Mt** Manitoba
118 C5 **Pembina Prov. Park** Alberta
118 C4 **Pembina R** Alberta
99 T4 **Pembine** Wisconsin
112 F5 **Pembroke** Georgia
110 J5 **Pembroke** Kentucky
112 H3 **Pembroke** N Carolina
121 N7 **Pembroke** Ontario
94 G9 **Pembroke** Virginia
8 B4 **Pembroke** Wales
Pembroke *co see* **Dyfed**
133 F8 **Pembroke, C** Falkland Is
144 A6 **Pembroke, Mt** New Zealand
9 G5 **Pembury** England
127 J5 **Peña** Dom Rep
106 D6 **Penablanca** New Mexico
95 Q3 **Penacook** New Hampshire
17 G2 **Peña de Oroel** *mt* Spain
16 B3 **Penafiel** Portugal
16 E3 **Peñafiel** Spain
17 G4 **Peñagolosa** *mt* Spain
127 O3 **Penal** Trinidad
8 B4 **Penally** Wales
70 D3 **Penambo Ra** Kalimantan
16 C3 **Peña Mira** *mt* Spain
70 E2 **Penampang** Sabah
131 B2 **Peña Negra, Pasco de** Arg/Chile
125 K6 **Peña Nevada, Cerro** *mt* Mexico
Penang *see* **Pinang** *I*
130 E7 **Penápolis** Brazil
16 D1 **Peña Prieta** *mt* Spain
16 D4 **Peñaranda de Bracamonte** Spain
95 M6 **Pen Argyl** Pennsylvania
139 G5 **Penarie** New S Wales
17 G4 **Peñarroya** *mt* Spain
16 D6 **Peñarroya-Pueblonuevo** Spain
8 C5 **Penarth** Wales
16 C1 **Peña Rubia** *mt* Spain
17 G2 **Peña, Sa. de la** *mts* Spain
124 M4 **Peñas Blancas** Nicaragua
16 D1 **Peñas, C. de** Spain
106 E5 **Penasco** New Mexico
108 C3 **Penasco, Rio** *R* New Mexico
16 E3 **Peñas de Cervera** Spain
17 F6 **Peñas de San Pedro** Spain
133 C7 **Penas, G.de** Chile
127 N9 **Peñas, Pta** Venezuela
16 C2 **Peña Trevinca** *mt* Spain
16 D1 **Peña Vieja** *mt* Spain
100 H3 **Penawawa** Washington
65 F4 **Pen-ch'i** China
146 D3 **Penck, C** Antarctica
131 C4 **Pencoso, Alto de** *mt* Argentina
46 E4 **Pendálofon** Greece
118 F9 **Pendant d'Oreille** Alberta
86 C4 **Pende** *R* Cent Afr Republic
47 F6 **Pendelikón** *mt* Greece
85 B7 **Pendembu** Sierra Leone
130 H8 **Pendencia** Brazil
98 K7 **Pender** Nebraska
142 E3 **Pender** W Australia
142 E3 **Pender Bay** W Australia
144 A6 **Pender, Mt** New Zealand
8 B4 **Pendine** Wales
13 F6 **Pendlebury** England
13 F6 **Pendle Hill** England
94 B7 **Pendleton** Indiana
100 G4 **Pendleton** Oregon
112 E3 **Pendleton** S Carolina
117 J6 **Pendleton, Mt** Br Col
100 H1 **Pend Oreille** *R* Washington
117 P11 **Pend Oreille L** Idaho
101 N1 **Pendroy** Montana
16 B3 **Peneda** *mt* Portugal
129 L6 **Penedo** Brazil
94 J5 **Penfield** Pennsylvania
70 L9 **Pengalengan** Java
67 B1 **Peng'an** China
67 G4 **P'eng-chia Hsü** *isld* Taiwan
86 D7 **Penge** Zaïre
67 F5 **P'eng-hu Lieh-tao** *isld* Taiwan
67 F5 **P'eng-hu Tao** *isld* Taiwan
69 J12 **Pengiki** *isld* Indonesia
67 E4 **Pengkou** China
65 E6 **Penglai** China
58 G5 **Peng-pu** China
67 A1 **Pengshan** China
67 C2 **Pengshui** China
70 B6 **Pengudjan, Tg** *C* Kalimantan
139 H8 **Penguin** Tasmania
142 F2 **Penguin Deeps** Timor Sea
67 B1 **Pengxi** China
67 A1 **Peng Xian** China
67 E2 **Pengze** China
130 E10 **Penha** Brazil
118 D6 **Penhold** Alberta
8 D4 **Penhow** Wales
120 F3 **Penhurst** Ontario
44 F2 **Penice** *mt* Italy
16 A5 **Peniche** Portugal
13 E2 **Penicuik** Scotland
70 P10 **Penida** *isld* Indonesia
37 O2 **Penig** E Germany
71 G5 **Peninsula Pt** Philippines
69 E10 **Peninsular Malaysia** S E Asia
17 H4 **Peñíscola** Spain
13 G6 **Penistone** England
70 M9 **Penju, Teluk** *B* Java
78 K4 **Penjwin** Iran
38 H8 **Penk** Austria
Penki *see* **Benxi**
8 D2 **Penkridge** England
18 C5 **Penmarch, Pte.de** *C* France
118 K5 **Penn** Sask
45 M4 **Pennabilli** Italy
45 L4 **Penna, M** *mt* Italy
118 J8 **Pennant** Sask
122 J9 **Pennant Pt** Nova Scotia
42 F6 **Penna, Pta. della** Italy
42 F6 **Penne** Italy
18 F8 **Penne d'Agenais** France
146 J7 **Pennell Bank** Antarctica
138 E6 **Penneshaw** S Australia
122 F8 **Pennfield** New Brunswick
40 G5 **Pennine, Alpi** *mts* Switzerland
7 J8 **Pennine Chain** *mts* England
26 G7 **Penningkejsen** *mt* Norway/Sweden
95 N6 **Pennington** New Jersey
109 M4 **Pennington** Texas
94 D10 **Pennington Gap** Virginia
42 E5 **Pennino, M** *mt* Italy
95 M6 **Pennsburg** Pennsylvania
95 M7 **Penns Grove** New Jersey
94 H6 **Pennsylvania** *state* U.S.A.
95 K4 **Penn Yan** New York
12 B1 **Pennyghael** Scotland
115 N4 **Penny Ice Cap** N W Terr
115 K2 **Penny Str** N W Terr
52 D6 **Peno** U.S.S.R.
95 T1 **Penobscot** *R* Maine
95 T2 **Penobscot B** Maine
122 G8 **Penobsquis** New Brunswick
138 F6 **Penola** S Australia
124 G5 **Peñón Blanco** Mexico
138 C4 **Penong** S Australia
125 O5 **Penonomé** Panama
100 C8 **Penoyar** California
8 B2 **Penrhyndeudraeth** Wales
13 F4 **Penrith** England
139 K5 **Penrith** New S Wales
8 A7 **Penryn** England
111 J11 **Pensacola** Florida
113 K10 **Pensacola Cay** Bahamas
146 E10 **Pensacola Mts** Antarctica
119 N8 **Pense** Sask
8 D5 **Pensford** England
9 G5 **Penshurst** England
138 F7 **Penshurst** Victoria
70 E2 **Pensiangan** Sabah
137 O5 **Pentecost I** New Hebrides
142 G3 **Pentecost, R** W Australia
122 E4 **Pentecôte, L** Quebec
48 K5 **Penteleu** *mt* Romania
117 O11 **Penticton** Br Col
141 H5 **Pentland** Queensland
15 E2 **Pentland Firth** Scotland
13 E2 **Pentland Hills** Scotland
15 F2 **Pentland Skerries** Orkney Scotland
8 C1 **Pentre-Foelas** Wales
94 A3 **Pentwater** Michigan
131 E5 **Penuajo** Argentina
69 G13 **Penuba** Indonesia
69 G14 **Penuguan** Sumatra
68 C3 **Penwegon** Burma
8 C3 **Penybont** Wales
53 F7 **Penza** U.S.S.R.
9 F6 **Penzance** England
119 M7 **Penzance** Sask
41 O2 **Penzberg** W Germany
51 Q2 **Penzhino** U.S.S.R.
51 Q2 **Penzhinskaya Guba** *gulf* U.S.S.R.
33 S6 **Penzlin** E Germany
100 H3 **Peola** Washington
101 R1 **Peoples Cr** Montana
103 M8 **Peoria** Arizona
99 R9 **Peoria** Illinois
99 T8 **Peotone** Illinois
89 C6 **Pepani** *watercourse* S Africa
85 B7 **Pepel** Sierra Leone
25 F3 **Peperga** Netherlands
145 D4 **Pepin I** New Zealand
99 O5 **Pepin, L** Wisconsin
22 K2 **Pepinster** Belgium
130 D10 **Pepiri Guaçu. R** Brazil
44 B3 **Pepouiri, Mt** Italy
46 D3 **Peqin** Albania
131 H3 **Pequena, L** Brazil
124 C4 **Pequeña, Pta** *C* Mexico
103 K1 **Pequop Mts** Nevada
99 M3 **Pequot Lakes** Minnesota
37 O7 **Perach** W Germany
141 F2 **Pera Hd** Queensland
69 E10 **Perai** Malaysia
69 D10 **Perak** *isld* Malaysia
69 E10 **Perak** *prov* Malaysia
46 F6 **Perakhóra** Greece
38 G8 **Peralba** *mt* Italy
106 D7 **Peralta** New Mexico
47 G9 **Pérama** Crete Greece
29 K9 **Peräseinäjoki** Finland
69 E12 **Perawang** Sumatra
80 E3 **Perazon** Israel
122 H5 **Percé** Quebec
20 D3 **Pércée, Pte de la** France
18 G10 **Perche, Col de la** *pass* France
45 N5 **Percile** Italy
99 L9 **Percival** Iowa
142 E5 **Percival Ls** W Australia
20 C4 **Percy** France
110 G3 **Percy** Illinois
99 N8 **Percy** Iowa
141 K5 **Percy Is** Queensland
143 D9 **Percy, L** W Australia
141 G4 **Percyville** Queensland
17 H2 **Perdido** *mt* Spain
111 J11 **Perdido** *R* Alabama/Florida
133 D6 **Perdido** *R* Argentina
18 F10 **Perdido, M** *mt* Spain
130 B7 **Perdido, R** Brazil
118 K6 **Perdue** Sask
122 B3 **Perdu, L** Quebec
99 U6 **Pere** *R* Michigan
48 G2 **Perechin** U.S.S.R.
48 J2 **Pereginsko** U.S.S.R.
50 F2 **Peregrebnoye** U.S.S.R.
128 C3 **Pereira** Colombia
130 D7 **Pereira Barreto** Brazil
Pereira de Eça *see* **N'Giva**
129 G5 **Pereirinha** Brazil
17 H4 **Perello** Spain
94 A3 **Pere Marquette** *R* Michigan
146 E2 **Peremennyy, C** Antarctica
48 J1 **Peremyshlyany** U.S.S.R.
143 B8 **Perenjori** W Australia
116 L7 **Perenosa B** Alaska
52 E6 **Pereslavl' Zalesskiy** U.S.S.R.
45 O5 **Pereto** Italy
48 H2 **Pereval Veretski** *mt* U.S.S.R.
55 B5 **Perevolotskiy** U.S.S.R.
54 C6 **Pereyaslav Khmel'nitskiy** U.S.S.R.
100 D8 **Perez** California
133 D3 **Pérez** Chile

60 Perforated I — Plainview

69 C8 Perforated I Thailand
131 E4 Pergamino Argentina
Pergamum see Bergama
45 N4 Pergola Italy
52 E4 Perguba U.S.S.R.
99 L3 Perham Minnesota
69 F10 Perhentian Besar isld Malaysia
29 L8 Perho Finland
29 L8 Perhojoki R Finland
48 F4 Periam Romania
121 S4 Péribonca Quebec
121 T3 Péribonca R Quebec
122 A3 Peribonca L Quebec
133 D2 Perico Argentina
124 F5 Pericos Mexico
20 C3 Périers France
21 E9 Périgne France
129 J3 Perigoso, Can Brazil
18 F7 Périgueux France
127 H9 Perijá, Sa. de mts Colombia/Venezuela
123 P2 Peril Rock Quebec
117 F7 Peril Str Alaska
72 E6 Perim isld S Yemen
118 C2 Perimeter Highway Manitoba
130 H10 Periquito, Sa do mts Brazil
48 K6 Periş Romania
46 E5 Peristéri mt Greece
133 C7 Perito Moreno Argentina
76 C5 Periyakulam India
95 M6 Perkasie Pennsylvania
112 F5 Perkins Georgia
111 C11 Perkins Louisiana
99 T4 Perkins Michigan
111 G11 Perkinston Mississippi
103 M7 Perkinsville Arizona
22 L5 Perl W Germany
41 P1 Perlach W Germany
125 P5 Perlas, Arch. de las islds Panama
33 P6 Perleberg E Germany
37 P6 Perlesreut W Germany
54 K5 Perlevka U.S.S.R.
98 K2 Perley Minnesota
48 F5 Perlez Yugoslavia
69 E9 Perlis prov Malaysia
52 J5 Perm' U.S.S.R.
101 L2 Perma Montana
52 G5 Permas U.S.S.R.
46 D4 Përmet Albania
Pernambuco see Recife
130 H9 Pernambuco state Brazil
138 D4 Pernatty Lagoon S Australia
107 N7 Pernell Oklahoma
46 F2 Pernik Bulgaria
29 K11 Perniö Finland
25 B5 Pernis Netherlands
40 C5 Peron France
143 A7 Peron, C W Australia
140 B2 Peron Is N Terr Aust
22 D4 Péronne France
22 G3 Peronnes Belgium
143 A7 Peron Pen W Australia
143 B9 Peron, Pt W Australia
20 J5 Péronville France
18 G10 Perpignan France
112 L1 Perquimans R N Carolina
8 A7 Perranporth England
20 J4 Perray-en-Yvelines, le France
109 J2 Perrin Texas
113 G12 Perrine Florida
102 G8 Perris California
40 B2 Perrogney France
108 B1 Perro, Laguna del New Mexico
121 N4 Perron Quebec
18 C4 Perros Guirec France
110 D6 Perry Arkansas
113 D7 Perry Florida
112 D5 Perry Georgia
110 F2 Perry Illinois
99 M8 Perry Iowa
94 C4 Perry Michigan
110 E2 Perry Missouri
94 K4 Perry New York
107 N5 Perry Oklahoma
120 F5 Perry Ontario
116 O6 Perry I Alaska
120 D2 Perry L Ontario
95 L7 Perryman Maryland
110 A2 Perry Res Kansas
94 D5 Perrysburg Ohio
108 D7 Perryton Texas
118 D4 Perryvale Alberta
110 D6 Perryville Arkansas
110 G4 Perryville Missouri
20 K3 Persan France
Persepolis see Takht-e Jamshid
128 F6 Perseverancia Bolivia
121 O4 Pershing Quebec
8 D3 Pershore England
Persia see Iran
99 L8 Persia Iowa
Persian Gulf see Gulf, The
27 J14 Persnäs Sweden
107 N4 Perth Kansas
98 G1 Perth N Dakota
122 E7 Perth New Brunswick
121 O8 Perth Ontario
12 E1 Perth Scotland
139 H8 Perth Tasmania
143 B9 Perth W Australia
Perth co see Central and Tayside regions
95 N6 Perth Amboy New Jersey
38 L4 Pertholz Austria
41 P3 Pertisau Austria
52 E3 Pertominsk U.S.S.R.
42 J6 Pertovac Yugoslavia
20 C5 Pertre, le France
29 M10 Pertunmaa Finland
52 G5 Pertyugskiy U.S.S.R.
99 R8 Peru Illinois
94 A6 Peru Indiana
99 L9 Peru Nebraska
95 O2 Peru New York
128 D6 Peru rep S America
135 S12 Peru-Chile Trench Pacific Oc
42 E5 Perugia Italy
129 J8 Peruíbe Brazil
42 G4 Perušić Yugoslavia
22 F3 Peruwelz Belgium
78 J3 Pervari Turkey
20 F5 Pervencheres France
54 G4 Pervoavgustovskiy U.S.S.R.
55 F5 Pervomayka U.S.S.R.
54 K8 Pervomaysk U.S.S.R.
52 H4 Pervomayskaya U.S.S.R.
55 B5 Pervomayskiy Orenburg U.S.S.R.
55 D2 Pervomayskiy Serov U.S.S.R.
55 C4 Pervomayskiy Ufa U.S.S.R.
55 C3 Pervoural'sk U.S.S.R.
22 H2 Perwez Belgium
52 D5 Pes' R U.S.S.R.
45 K4 Pesa R Italy
45 N4 Pesaro Italy
102 B4 Pescadero California
Pescadores islds see P'eng-hu Lieh-tao
128 D7 Pescadores, Pta C Peru
45 H4 Pescaglia Italy
42 F6 Pescara Italy
42 F6 Pescara R Italy
45 P6 Pescasseroli Italy
42 G7 Peschici Italy
45 J1 Peschiera Italy
45 J4 Pescia Italy
45 P5 Pescina Italy
45 R7 Pesco Sannita Italy
45 P6 Pescosolido Italy
52 G2 Pesha R U.S.S.R.
74 D1 Peshawar Pakistan
46 D3 Peshkopi Albania
47 G2 Peshtera Bulgaria
99 T4 Peshtigo Wisconsin
99 S4 Peshtigo R Wisconsin
26 J5 Peskehaure Sweden
50 E5 Peski Karakumy U.S.S.R.
57 B2 Peski Priaral'skiye Karkumy U.S.S.R.
57 C5 Peski Sundukli U.S.S.R.
52 H5 Peskovka U.S.S.R.
38 N8 Pesnica R Yugoslavia
16 B3 Péso de Regua Portugal
110 H2 Pesotum Illinois
129 L5 Pesqueira Brazil
18 E8 Pessac France
33 R7 Pessin E Germany
48 E3 Pest co Hungary
48 H6 Peşteana Jiu Romania
52 E5 Pestovo U.S.S.R.
52 F6 Pestyaki U.S.S.R.
46 E5 Péta Greece
80 C5 Petah Tiqwa Israel
29 L9 Petäjävesi Finland
71 B2 Petak, Tg C Halmahera Indonesia
111 G10 Petal Mississippi
29 J9 Petalax Finland
69 G14 Petaling Sumatra
47 G7 Petalioí isld Greece
47 G7 Petalión Kólpos gulf Greece
102 B3 Petaluma California
22 K4 Petange Luxembourg
127 L9 Petare Venezuela
88 C9 Petauke Zambia
121 P6 Petawaga, L Quebec
121 N7 Petawawa Ontario
125 P9 Petén Itzá, L Guatemala
99 R5 Petenwell Res Wisconsin
120 G4 Peterbell Ontario
9 F2 Peterborough England
95 Q4 Peterborough New Hampshire
121 M8 Peterborough Ontario
138 E5 Peterborough S Australia
15 F3 Peterculter Scotland
15 G3 Peterhead Scotland
135 O16 Peter I. Øy Antarctica
13 G4 Peterlee England
115 O1 Petermann Gletscher gla Greenland
143 G6 Petermann Ra N Terr/W Aust
131 B5 Peteroa, Vol peak Arg/Chile
118 H2 Peter Pond L Sask
36 H2 Petersberg W Germany
117 G7 Petersburg Alaska
110 G1 Petersburg Illinois
110 J3 Petersburg Indiana
94 D5 Petersburg Michigan
98 H1 Petersburg N Dakota
98 H8 Petersburg Nebraska
94 J6 Petersburg Pennsylvania
110 K6 Petersburg Tennessee
108 F2 Petersburg Texas
94 K9 Petersburg Virginia
94 H7 Petersburg W Virginia
116 M5 Peters Creek Alaska
9 F5 Petersfield England
119 V8 Petersfield Manitoba
33 T7 Petershagen E Germany
32 J8 Petershagen W Germany
37 L7 Petershausen W Germany
99 L7 Peterson Iowa
90 D16 Peter 1st I Antarctica
116 M5 Petersville Alaska
143 E7 Peterswald Hill W Australia
123 R4 Peterview Nfld
43 H9 Petilia Policastro Italy
17 G2 Petilla de Aragón Spain
111 H11 Petit Bois I Mississippi
127 N4 Petit Bourg Guadeloupe W I
127 N4 Petit Canal Guadeloupe W I
122 G8 Petitcodiac New Brunswick
127 N4 Petit Cul de Sac Marin B Guadeloupe W I
122 G5 Petite Cascapedia, Parc de la Quebec
122 E5 Petite Matane Quebec
121 Q7 Petite-Nation, Parc Quebec
122 B6 Petite Rivière Quebec
122 H9 Petite Rivière Bridge Nova Scotia
127 H5 Petite Rivière de l'Artibonite Haiti
21 J7 Petite Sauldre R France
20 G2 Petites Dalles, les France
123 M7 Petit Etang C Breton I, N Scotia
127 O4 Petite Terre, Îles de la Guadeloupe W I
122 G4 Petite Vallèe Quebec
127 H5 Petit Goâve Haiti
123 N5 Petit Jardin Nfld
110 C6 Petit Jean R Arkansas
95 U2 Petit Manan Pt Maine
36 B6 Petitmont France
117 N6 Petitot R Br Col
122 G6 Petit Rocher New Brunswick
29 M4 Petkula Finland
74 E7 Petlad India
125 P7 Peto Mexico
145 G4 Petone New Zealand
133 C4 Petorca Chile
94 C1 Petoskey Michigan
52 G4 Petrakovo U.S.S.R.
43 F11 Petralia Sicily
51 L1 Petra, Ostrov isld U.S.S.R.
65 H3 Petra Velikogo, Zaliv B U.S.S.R.
45 P7 Petrella, M mt Italy
121 N9 Petre, Pt Ontario
52 J4 Petretsovo U.S.S.R.
45 N4 Petriano Italy
47 F3 Petricn Bulgaria
141 L2 Petrie, Mt Brisbane, Qnsld
103 O6 Petrified Forest Nat Mon Arizona
54 F8 Petrikovka U.S.S.R.
48 H5 Petrila Romania
8 B6 Petrockstow England
52 C5 Petrodvorets U.S.S.R.
47 F1 Petrokhanski P Bulgaria
52 D5 Petrokrepost' U.S.S.R.
129 L5 Petrolândia Brazil
109 J8 Petroleum Texas
100 A9 Petrolia California
120 H10 Petrolia Ontario
109 J2 Petrolia Texas
129 K5 Petrolina Brazil
46 F6 Petromagoúla Greece
55 E3 Petropavlosk U.S.S.R.
56 G5 Petropavlovka U.S.S.R.
51 P3 Petropavlovsk-Kamchatskiy U.S.S.R.
129 K8 Petrópolis Brazil
112 C1 Petros Tennessee
48 H5 Petroseni Romania
48 G6 Petrovac Yugoslavia
48 F5 Petrovaradin Yugoslavia
55 E4 Petrovka U.S.S.R.
52 E3 Petrovskiy Yam U.S.S.R.
55 C4 Petrovskoye Bashkirskaya U.S.S.R.
52 E6 Petrovskoye Yaroslavl' U.S.S.R.
56 G5 Petrovsk-Zabaykal'skiy U.S.S.R.
52 D4 Petrozavodsk U.S.S.R.
52 K2 Petrun' U.S.S.R.
Petsamo see Pechenga
29 N2 Petsikko mt Finland
25 C3 Petten Netherlands
38 K6 Pettenbach Austria
14 D2 Pettigoe Irish Rep
110 C6 Pettigrew Arkansas
109 K7 Pettus Texas
123 U6 Petty Hbr Nfld
55 E3 Petukhovo U.S.S.R.
9 F6 Petworth England
38 L8 Petzen mt Austria
38 J5 Peuerbach Austria
69 C10 Peuetsagu, Gunung mt Sumatra
69 C10 Peukankuala Sumatra
116 J8 Peulik, Mt Alaska
69 B10 Peunasu isld Sumatra
29 M4 Peurasuvanto Finland
26 J5 Peuraure Sweden
69 C10 Peureulak Sumatra
9 G6 Pevensey England
94 C3 Pewamo Michigan
99 S6 Pewaukee Wisconsin
9 E5 Pewsey England
32 F6 Pewsum W Germany
36 B7 Pexonne France
19 P18 Peynier France
19 P18 Peypin France
21 I10 Peyrat-le Chateau France
18 E9 Peyrehorade France
18 H8 Peyreleau France
19 P17 Peyrolles-en-Provence France
19 P16 Peyruis France
106 F2 Peyton Colorado
52 G2 Peza R U.S.S.R.
18 H9 Pézenas France
31 K7 Pezinok Czechoslovakia
52 H4 Pezmog U.S.S.R.
37 N6 Pfaffenberg W Germany
37 L6 Pfaffenhofen an der Ilm W Germany
36 D6 Pfaffenhoffen France
41 J3 Pfäffikon Switzerland
37 P2 Pfaffroda E Germany
36 C4 Pfälzer Bergland reg W Germany
36 D5 Pfalzer Wald mts W Germany
36 D3 Pfalzfeld W Germany
36 F6 Pfalzgrafenweiler W Germany
37 L6 Pfalzpaint W Germany
37 O7 Pfarrkirchen W Germany
37 K3 Pfarrweisach W Germany
37 N6 Pfatter W Germany
36 E4 Pfeddersheim W Germany
37 M6 Pfeffenhausen W Germany
36 F6 Pfinztal W Germany
140 C6 Pfitzner, Mt N Terr Aust
41 N2 Pflach Austria
37 M6 Pförring W Germany
36 F6 Pforzheim W Germany
37 N5 Pfreimd W Germany
36 D4 Pfrimm R W Germany
41 K2 Pfullendorf W Germany
36 G7 Pfullingen W Germany
41 N4 Pfunds Austria
36 F4 Pfungstadt W Germany
37 L6 Pfünz W Germany
74 F3 Phagwara India
95 T7 Phair Maine
74 E5 Phalodi India
88 E9 Phalombe Malawi
36 C6 Phalsbourg France
76 B2 Phaltan India
69 D8 Pha Luai, Ko isld Thailand
69 E8 Phangan, Ko isld Thailand
69 D8 Phangnga Thailand
68 G5 Phanom Dang Raek mt Thailand
68 D5 Phanom Thuan Thailand
68 J7 Phan Rang Vietnam
68 J7 Phan Thiet Vietnam
103 M5 Phantom Ranch Arizona
109 J9 Pharr Texas
68 H2 Phat Diem Vietnam
69 D9 Phatthalung Thailand
69 D8 Phayam, Ko isld Thailand
68 E5 Phayuhakhiri Thailand
140 D2 Phelp R N Terr Aust
94 E9 Phelps Kentucky
95 K4 Phelps New York
109 M5 Phelps Texas
99 R3 Phelps Wisconsin
112 L2 Phelps L N Carolina
68 F4 Phen Thailand
94 J9 Phenix Virginia
111 L9 Phenix City Alabama
68 D6 Phet Buri Thailand
68 H5 Phiafay Laos
111 G9 Philadelphia Mississippi
99 P10 Philadelphia Missouri
95 M2 Philadelphia New York
97 Philadelphia conurbation Pennsylvania
84 J5 Philae ruins Egypt
111 J7 Phil Campbell Alabama
98 E5 Philip S Dakota
137 O7 Philip I Pacific Oc
111 F8 Philipp Mississippi
Philippeville see Skikda
22 G3 Philippeville Belgium
94 G7 Philippi W Virginia
140 E6 Philippi, L Queensland
25 A6 Philippine Netherlands
71 Philippines rep E Indies
89 D8 Philippolis S Africa
Philippopolis Bulgaria see Plovdiv
36 E5 Philippsburg W Germany
101 M3 Philipsburg Montana
94 J6 Philipsburg Pennsylvania
121 R7 Philipsburg Quebec
116 O2 Philip Smith Mts Alaska
139 H7 Phillip I Victoria
95 R2 Phillips Maine
101 R1 Phillips Montana
98 H9 Phillips Nebraska
108 C8 Phillips Texas
99 Q4 Phillips Wisconsin
107 L2 Phillipsburg Kansas
115 L1 Phillips Inlet N W Terr
143 B6 Phillips, Mt W Australia
138 C3 Phillipson, L S Australia
142 G5 Phillipson Ra W Australia
142 F3 Phillips Ra W Australia
95 O4 Philmont New York
102 A2 Philo California
100 B5 Philomath Oregon
118 F3 Philomena Alberta
115 M3 Philpots Island N W Terr
94 G10 Philpott Dam Virginia
68 G5 Phimun Mangsahan Thailand
118 J6 Phippen Sask
106 D1 Phippsburg Colorado
68 G7 Phnom Penh Cambodia
67 B6 Pho Binh Gia Vietnam
144 D5 Phoebe New Zealand
95 N4 Phoenicia New York
103 M8 Phoenix Arizona
111 G12 Phoenix Louisiana
95 L3 Phoenix New York
134 K8 Phoenix Is Pacific Oc
95 M6 Phoenixville Pennsylvania
68 G1 Pho Lu Vietnam
68 H4 Phong Nha Vietnam
68 F2 Phong Saly Laos
73 R4 Phong Saly Thailand
68 F1 Phong Tho Vietnam
68 F3 Phon Phisai Thailand
139 G7 Phoques B Tasmania
68 H7 Phouc Le Vietnam
68 D3 Phrao Thailand
68 E5 Phra Phutthabat Thailand
69 D8 Phra Saeng Thailand
69 C8 Phra Thong, Ko isld Thailand
68 E5 Phrom Buri Thailand
47 L6 Phrygia Turkey
68 H7 Phu Cuong Vietnam
68 G2 Phuc Yen Vietnam
67 B7 Phu Dien Vietnam
68 G3 Phu Dien Chau Vietnam
69 D9 Phuket, Ko isld Thailand
68 F4 Phu Khieo Thailand
67 B6 Phulang Thuong Vietnam
75 L8 Phulbani India
68 H4 Phu Loc Vietnam
68 G2 Phu Ly Vietnam
68 F6 Phum Bavel Cambodia
68 G7 Phum Hay Cambodia
68 G6 Phum Khvao Cambodia
68 F6 Phum Siem Cambodia
68 F6 Phum Svai Cambodia
68 F6 Phum Treng Cambodia
68 F6 Phum Troy Toch Cambodia
68 J5 Phu My Vietnam
68 G2 Phu Nho Quan Vietnam
75 N5 Phuntsholing Bhutan
69 G8 Phuoc Long Vietnam
68 G3 Phu Qui Vietnam
68 G2 Phu Tho Vietnam
129 J5 Piaca Brazil
44 G1 Piacenza Italy
44 F2 Piacenza prov Italy
45 L1 Piacenza d'Adige Italy
45 J1 Piadena Italy
122 B2 Piakoudie L Quebec
141 L7 Pialba Queensland
139 J4 Pian R New S Wales
41 K5 Pianazzo Italy
130 H9 Piancó R Brazil
45 L4 Pian de Sco Italy
45 M4 Pian di Meleto Italy
45 N4 Pianello Italy
139 G6 Piangil Victoria
45 M1 Pianiga Italy
45 K3 Piano del Voglio Italy
42 G6 Pianosa isld Adriatic Sea
42 C6 Pianosa isld Italy
65 B5 Pianquan China
118 H9 Piapot Sask
127 O2 Piarco airport Trinidad
31 M3 Piaseczno Poland
122 K3 Piashti, L Quebec
31 O4 Piaski Poland
31 L3 Piątek Poland
48 K4 Piatra Neamt Romania
129 K5 Piauí state Brazil
129 K5 Piaui, Sa. do mts Brazil
42 E2 Piave R Italy
143 B9 Piawaning W Australia
45 H3 Piazza al Serchio Italy
43 F11 Piazza Armerina Sicily
133 C8 Piazzi isld Chile
45 L1 Piazzolas B Italy
86 F4 Pibor Post Sudan
118 D4 Pibroch Alberta
103 L6 Pica Arizona
101 L6 Picabo Idaho
103 N9 Picacho Arizona
103 K8 Picacho California
106 E8 Picacho New Mexico
103 N9 Picacho Res Arizona
124 B3 Picachos, Cerro dos mt Mexico
22 D4 Picardie France
20 K1 Picardie reg
20 C3 Picauville France
111 G11 Picayune Mississippi
123 O5 Piccadilly Nfld
106 B2 Piceance Cr Colorado
45 R8 Picentini, Mti mt Italy
124 F3 Picháchic Mexico
133 E2 Pichanal Argentina
131 B4 Pichidangul, B Chile
133 C4 Pichilemu Chile
128 C4 Pichincha prov Ecuador
52 G6 Pichkasy U.S.S.R.
118 D4 Pickardville Alberta
111 F9 Pickens Mississippi
112 E3 Pickens S Carolina
94 G8 Pickens W Virginia
120 K7 Pickerel Ontario
99 P1 Pickerel L Ontario
13 H5 Pickering England
110 B1 Pickering Missouri
143 D8 Pickering, Mt W Australia
126 D4 Pickle Bank Caribbean
115 K7 Pickle Lake Ontario
98 H6 Pickstown S Dakota
109 M2 Pickton Texas
110 H6 Pickwick L Tennessee
45 P7 Pico Italy
16 D4 Pico de Almanzor mt Spain
16 E4 Pico Penalara mt Spain
129 K5 Picos Brazil
16 C2 Picos de Ancares, Sa. de mts Spain
16 C6 Picos de Aroche mt Spain
20 K2 Picquigny France
120 D4 Pic R Ontario
139 K5 Picton New S Wales
145 E4 Picton New Zealand
121 N8 Picton Ontario
139 H9 Picton, Mt Tasmania
122 K8 Pictou Nova Scotia
122 K8 Pictou I Nova Scotia
118 E9 Picture Butte Alberta
95 L5 Picture Rocks Pennsylvania
130 H9 Picuí Brazil
131 B7 Picún Leufú Argentina
138 B4 Pidinga S Australia
45 Q7 Piedimonte d'Alife Italy
111 L8 Piedmont Alabama
110 F4 Piedmont Missouri
112 E3 Piedmont S Carolina
98 C5 Piedmont S Dakota
94 F6 Piedmont Res Ohio
102 E5 Piedra California
106 C4 Piedra R Colorado
17 F3 Piedra R Spain
16 E5 Piedrabuena Spain
16 C2 Piedrafita, Pto. de pass Spain
16 D4 Piedrahita Spain
131 B3 Piedra Lobos, Pta Chile
125 J3 Piedras Negras Mexico
71 D5 Piedras Point Philippines
133 F5 Piedras, Pta Argentina
128 D6 Piedras, R.de las R Peru
99 R1 Pie I Ontario
29 N9 Pieksämäki Finland
38 M5 Pielach R Austria
29 M8 Pielavesi L Finland
29 O8 Pielinen L Finland
29 O9 Pielisjoki R Finland
139 H8 Pieman R Tasmania
31 M1 Pieniężno Poland
22 K5 Piennes France
36 B2 Pier W Germany
106 F1 Pierce Colorado
113 F10 Pierce Florida
100 K3 Pierce Idaho
98 J7 Pierce Nebraska
13 G4 Piercebridge England
110 B5 Pierce City Missouri
94 B5 Pierceton Indiana
107 K4 Pierceville Kansas
102 A2 Piercy California
46 E4 Piéria Óri Greece
15 F1 Pierowall Orkney Scotland
98 J4 Pierpont S Dakota
19 J6 Pierre France
98 F5 Pierre S Dakota
21 H10 Pierre-Buffiere France
19 P15 Pierre-Châtel France
22 D5 Pierrefonds France
120 K3 Pierre L Ontario
19 N16 Pierrelatte France
22 K5 Pierrepont France
121 S6 Pierreville Quebec
127 P3 Pierreville Trinidad
113 F8 Pierson Florida
119 Q9 Pierson Manitoba
36 B4 Piesport W Germany
143 B10 Piesseville W Australia
31 K7 Piešt'any Czechoslovakia
Pietarsaari see Jakobstad
89 G7 Pietermaritzburg S Africa
89 F4 Pietersburg S Africa
22 G3 Piéton Belgium
106 B7 Pie Town New Mexico
44 D3 Pietra Ligure Italy
45 Q7 Pietramelara Italy
44 H4 Pietrasanta Italy
45 Q7 Pietravairano Italy
87 F11 Piet Retief S Africa
43 B9 Pietro, S isld Sardinia
48 J5 Pietroşiţa Romania
48 J3 Pietrosu mt Romania
48 J3 Pietrosul mt Romania
29 P2 Piets'yarvi, Oz L U.S.S.R.
20 B2 Pieux, les France
38 F9 Pieve Italy
42 E2 Pieve di Cadore Italy
45 K2 Pieve di Cento Italy
45 J3 Pievepelago Italy
45 M4 Pieve S. Stefano Italy
47 J9 Pigádhia Kárpathos I Greece
94 D3 Pigeon Michigan
94 C1 Pigeon R Michigan
120 H10 Pigeon B Ontario
111 K10 Pigeon Cr Alabama
140 B3 Pigeon Hole N Terr Aust
127 K3 Pigeon I Jamaica
118 C5 Pigeon L Alberta
121 M8 Pigeon L Ontario
102 B4 Pigeon Pt California
127 M2 Pigeon Pt Tobago
119 V6 Pigeon R Manitoba
119 O2 Pigeon River Ontario
143 C8 Pigeon Rocks W Australia
94 H10 Pigg R Virginia
110 F5 Piggott Arkansas
89 G8 Pigg's Peak Swaziland
19 Q18 Pignans France
45 P7 Pignataro Interamna Italy
45 Q7 Pignatoro Maggiore Italy
133 E5 Pigüe Argentina
145 D3 Pihaina New Zealand
67 E1 Pi He R China
29 L9 Pihlajavesi Finland
56 E4 Pik Grandioznyy mt U.S.S.R.
31 K2 Piła Poland
129 K6 Pilao Arcado Brazil
19 N14 Pilat, Mt France
142 C5 Pilbara W Australia
48 F3 Pilis Hungary
48 E3 Pilisvörösvár Hungary
144 A6 Pillans Pass New Zealand
98 J2 Pillsbury N Dakota
102 B2 Pillsbury, L California
52 G6 Pil'na U.S.S.R.
8 D4 Pilning England
130 F5 Pilões, Sa. dos mts Brazil
46 E8 Pílos Greece
119 N8 Pilot Butte Sask
110 D3 Pilot Grove Missouri
119 T9 Pilot Mound Manitoba
112 G1 Pilot Mountain N Carolina
102 G3 Pilot Pk Nevada
101 Q5 Pilot Pk Wyoming
116 J8 Pilot Point Alaska
109 L2 Pilot Point Texas
100 G4 Pilot Rock Oregon
116 F5 Pilot Station Alaska
139 J6 Pilot, The mt New S Wales
133 E2 Piloya R Bolivia
37 M5 Pilsach W Germany
Pilsen see Plzeň
99 T5 Pilsen Wisconsin
41 O1 Pilsen See L W Germany
37 O6 Pilsting W Germany
55 F1 Pil'tan-Lor, Oz L U.S.S.R.
27 M14 Piltene U.S.S.R.
8 D5 Pilton England
52 J4 Pil'va R U.S.S.R.
31 N6 Pilzno Poland
55 F1 Pim U.S.S.R.
103 P9 Pima Arizona
129 G4 Pimenta Brazil
128 F6 Pimenta Bueno Brazil
127 J5 Pimental Dom Rep
128 C5 Pimentel Peru
113 L12 Pimlico I Bahamas
71 H4 Pimpi Sulawesi
86 D5 Pimu Zaïre
17 G3 Pina Spain
103 L10 Pinacate, Cerro peak Mexico
124 C2 Pinacate, Sa. del mt Mexico
103 O9 Pinaleno Mts Arizona
71 E4 Pinamalayan Philippines
69 E10 Pinang isld Malaysia
70 E2 Pinangah Sabah
78 F2 Pinarbaşi Turkey
126 C3 Pinar del Río Cuba
47 J3 Pinarhisar Turkey
138 F3 Pinaroo, L New S Wales
133 D4 Piñas Argentina
45 L2 Pincara Italy
9 F2 Pinchbeck England
118 D9 Pincher Creek Alberta
117 L8 Pinchi Br Col
128 C4 Pinchincha mt Ecuador
94 D4 Pinckney Michigan
110 G3 Pinckneyville Illinois
20 D4 Pinçon, Mt France
94 C3 Pinconning Michigan
48 G4 Pîncota Romania
31 M5 Pińczów Poland
129 H6 Pindaiba Brazil
110 D5 Pindall Arkansas
143 B8 Pindar W Australia
129 J4 Pindaré R Brazil
70 G4 Pindjang Sulawesi
28 E4 Pindstrup Denmark
103 N7 Pine Arizona
100 K6 Pine Idaho
94 B2 Pine R Michigan
138 F4 Pine R New S Wales
99 Q6 Pine R Wisconsin
111 K10 Pine Apple Alabama
111 D7 Pine Bluff Arkansas
119 P4 Pinebluff L Sask
98 B8 Pine Bluffs Wyoming
123 T7 Pine, C Nfld
113 F9 Pinecastle Florida
126 E2 Pine Cay isld Bahamas
111 E7 Pine City Arkansas
99 O4 Pine City Minnesota
103 H1 Pine Cr Nevada
94 K5 Pine Cr Pennsylvania
140 B2 Pine Creek N Terr Aust
102 E3 Pinecrest California
107 P7 Pine Cr. Res Oklahoma
16 E2 Pineda de la S Spain
117 P9 Pinedale Alberta
102 E5 Pinedale California
101 Q7 Pinedale Wyoming
102 E5 Pine Flat Res California
100 G8 Pine Forest Range Nevada
52 F3 Pinega U.S.S.R.
52 G3 Pinega R U.S.S.R.
95 L6 Pine Grove Pennsylvania
143 B8 Pinegrove W Australia
140 C5 Pine Hill N Terr Aust
141 H6 Pinehill Queensland
114 J6 Pine House Saskatchewan
118 L3 Pine House L Sask
112 H2 Pinehurst N Carolina
100 C2 Pinehurst Washington
118 F4 Pinehurst L Alberta
113 E11 Pine I Florida
99 O5 Pine Island Minnesota
99 S4 Pine L Wisconsin
109 O4 Pineland Texas
146 H11 Pinel B Antarctica
144 B6 Pinelheugh mt New Zealand
113 E10 Pinellas airport Florida
102 C6 Pine Mt California
107 P7 Pine Mt Oklahoma
103 L7 Pine Pk Arizona
117 Q5 Pine Point N W Terr
119 P1 Pine Portage Ontario
113 D8 Pine Pt Florida
114 H5 Pine Pt N W Terr
118 D4 Pine R Alberta
117 M8 Pine R Br Col
98 D6 Pine Ridge S Dakota
119 R7 Pine River Manitoba
99 M3 Pine River Minnesota
118 K3 Pine River Sask
44 B2 Pinerolo Italy
120 J9 Pinery Prov. Park Ontario
111 B9 Pines, L. O'The Texas
108 C4 Pine Springs Texas
89 G7 Pinetown S Africa
110 B7 Pine Valley Oklahoma
103 L4 Pine Valley Utah
103 L4 Pine Valley Mts Utah
94 D10 Pineville Kentucky
111 D10 Pineville Louisiana
110 B5 Pineville Missouri
112 G2 Pineville N Carolina
94 F9 Pineville W Virginia
99 L2 Pinewood Minnesota
99 M1 Pinewood Ontario
112 G4 Pinewood S Carolina
98 K1 Piney Manitoba
101 T2 Piney Buttes hills Montana
110 C6 Piney Cr Arkansas
113 D8 Piney Pt Florida
65 F2 Ping'an China
143 C10 Pingaring W Australia
67 A5 Pingbian China
67 B1 Pingchang China
65 D7 Ping Dao isld China
67 C3 Pingdeng China
65 B6 Pingding China
Pingdingbu see Guyan
58 F5 Pingdingshan China
65 F4 Pingdingshan China
65 G1 Pingding Shan mt China
65 D6 Pingdu China
143 B10 Pingelly W Australia
65 C7 Pinggang China
65 F3 Pinggang China
65 D4 Pinggu China
67 B5 Pingguo China
67 F4 Pinghai China
67 F4 Pinghe China
Pinghu see Pingtang
67 G1 Pinghu China
67 D2 Pingjiang China
67 C4 Pingle China
58 E4 Pingliang China
67 D1 Pinglin China
65 B5 Pinglu China
65 B7 Pinglu China
58 E4 Pingluo China
Pingma see Tiandong
75 N6 Pingna Bangladesh
67 C5 Pingnan China
67 F3 Pingnan China
Pingqiao see Xinyang
65 D4 Pingquan China
101 N6 Pingree Idaho
98 G2 Pingree N Dakota
143 C10 Pingrup W Australia
65 C5 Pingshan China
67 A2 Pingshan China
65 D7 Pingshang China
67 D4 Pingshi China
67 E4 Pingshi China
65 B6 Pingshun China
67 F4 Pingtan China
67 F4 Pingtan Dao isld China
67 B4 Pingtang China
67 G5 P'ing-tung Taiwan
67 B5 Pingxiang China
67 D3 Pingxiang China
65 F1 Pingyang China
67 G3 Pingyang China
65 B6 Pingyao China
65 D7 Pingyi China
65 C6 Pingyin China
67 C3 Pingyong China
65 C6 Pingyuan China
67 E4 Pingyuan China
67 A5 Pingyuanjie China
130 F8 Pinhal Brazil
16 B3 Pinhão Portugal
129 J4 Pinheiro Brazil
16 C4 Pinhel Portugal
69 D12 Pini isld Indonesia
46 E5 Piniós R Greece
46 E7 Piniós R Greece
143 B10 Pinjarra W Australia
143 E9 Pinjin W Australia
38 O7 Pinka R Austria
38 O7 Pinkafeld Austria
141 K1 Pinkenba dist Brisbane, Qnsld
118 H7 Pinkham Sask
112 K2 Pink Hill N Carolina
117 M7 Pink Mountain Br Col
20 G5 Pin la Garenne, le France
68 C2 Pinlaung Burma
145 D4 Pinnacle mt New Zealand
116 C6 Pinnacle I Bering Sea
102 C5 Pinnacles Nat. Mon California
138 F6 Pinnaroo S Australia
32 L5 Pinn Au R W Germany
32 L5 Pinneberg W Germany
106 G1 Pinneo Colorado
9 F4 Pinner England
33 T5 Pinnow E Germany
70 B5 Pinoh R Kalimantan
111 F10 Pinola Mississippi
106 F3 Pinon Colorado
106 E9 Pinon New Mexico
112 H4 Pinopolis Dam S Carolina
126 C4 Pinos, I. de Cuba
102 E7 Pinos, Mt California
17 G6 Pinoso Spain
125 K9 Pinotepa Nacional Mexico
70 F6 Pinrang Sulawesi
137 O6 Pins, Île Des New Caledonia
53 C8 Pinsk U.S.S.R.
111 K8 Pinson Alabama
110 H6 Pinson Tennessee
120 J10 Pins, Pte. aux Ontario
103 P6 Pinta Arizona
128 A7 Pinta isld Galapagos Is
133 D2 Pintados Chile
103 L9 Pinta, Sa Arizona
70 E2 Pintasan Sabah
133 E3 Pinto Argentina
118 K9 Pinto Butte peak Sask
103 J8 Pinto Mts California
138 B4 Pintumba S Australia
103 L4 Pintura Utah
103 J5 Pintwater Ra Nevada
123 Q2 Pinware R Labrador
12 D3 Pinwherry Scotland
143 B8 Pinyalling mt W Australia
52 G4 Pinyug U.S.S.R.
41 N5 Pinzolo Italy
45 M4 Pióbbico Italy
103 K4 Pioche Nevada
19 N16 Piolenc France
42 D6 Piombino Italy
94 C5 Pioneer Ohio
109 H3 Pioneer Texas
101 M4 Pioneer Mts Montana
56 C3 Pioner U.S.S.R.
51 J1 Pioner, Ostrova islds U.S.S.R.
55 D1 Pionerskiy U.S.S.R.
145 E3 Piopio New Zealand
128 F4 Piorini L Brazil
31 L3 Piotrków Bydgoszcz Poland
31 M4 Piotrków Trybunalski Łódź Poland
45 M1 Piove di Sacco Italy
65 G3 Pipa Dingzi mt China
74 E5 Pipar India
102 G4 Piper Pk Nevada
103 M5 Pipe Sp. Nat. Mon Arizona
119 R9 Pipestone Manitoba
98 K6 Pipestone Minnesota
119 Q9 Pipestone Cr Manitoba
98 K5 Pipestone Nat. Mon Minnesota
145 E3 Pipipi mt New Zealand
145 E3 Pipiriki New Zealand
121 U3 Pipmuacan, Rés Quebec
122 B4 Pipmuacan, Res Quebec
60 Q2 Pippu Japan
21 B6 Pipriac France
107 P4 Piqua Kansas
110 M1 Piqua Ohio
17 F2 Piqueras, Pto. de Spain
130 C5 Piquiri, R Mato Grosso Brazil
130 D9 Piquiri, R Paraná Brazil
85 E7 Pira Benin
130 E5 Piracanjuba Brazil
129 J7 Piracanjuba R Brazil
129 J8 Piracicaba Brazil
130 G6 Piracicaba R Brazil
133 F3 Piracuacito Argentina
130 F7 Piraçununga Brazil
129 K4 Piraeuruca Brazil
47 F7 Piraiévs Greece
56 E4 Piramida, G mt U.S.S.R.
42 F3 Piran Yugoslavia
129 L5 Piranhas Alagoas Brazil
129 H7 Piranhas Goiás Brazil
130 D5 Piranhas Goiás Brazil
130 D8 Pirapó, R Brazil
129 K7 Pirapora Brazil
122 A3 Piraube, L Quebec
130 C10 Piray R Argentina
128 F7 Piray R Bolivia
9 F5 Pirbright England
47 G2 Pirdop Bulgaria
20 C5 Piré France
129 J7 Pires do Rio Brazil
47 G9 Pírgos Crete Greece
46 E7 Pírgos Greece
130 B9 Piribebuy Paraguay
17 G2 Pirineos mt Spain
145 E4 Pirinoa New Zealand
145 F3 Piripaua New Zealand
129 K4 Piripiri Brazil
127 M9 Píritu Anzoátegui Venezuela
127 K10 Piritu Miranda Venezuela
37 N3 Pirk E Germany
29 K10 Pirkkala Finland
36 D5 Pirmasens W Germany
30 H5 Pirna E Germany
12 C2 Pirnmill Scotland
145 E2 Pirongia New Zealand
46 F1 Pirot Yugoslavia
20 B3 Pirou France
74 F2 Pir Panjal Rge Kashmir
102 F7 Piru California
136 F2 Piru Moluccas Indonesia
54 D6 Piryatin U.S.S.R.
47 H6 Piryí Greece
77 J4 Pirzada Afghanistan
45 H4 Pisa Italy
133 C1 Pisagua Chile
71 B3 Pisang isld Indonesia
44 H3 Pisanino mt Italy
21 D10 Pisany France
144 B6 Pisa Range New Zealand
70 F1 Pisau, Tg C Sabah
43 G8 Pisciotta Italy
128 C6 Pisco Peru
Piscopi isld see Tílos
95 N3 Piseco New York
30 H6 Písek Czechoslovakia
98 J1 Pisek N Dakota
80 F6 Pisga Jordan
99 L8 Pisgah Iowa
112 E2 Pisgah, Mt N Carolina
144 C6 Pisgah, Mt New Zealand
77 G6 Pishin Iran
74 B3 Pishin Pakistan
29 P6 Pishta R U.S.S.R.
70 G7 Pising Sulawesi
103 M9 Pisinimo Arizona
102 D6 Pismo Bch California
128 F6 Piso Firme Bolivia
41 M6 Pisogne Italy
85 D6 Pissila Upper Volta
29 P6 Pistayarvi L U.S.S.R.
43 H8 Pisticci Italy
45 J4 Pistoia Italy
123 R2 Pistolet B Nfld
100 A7 Pistol River Oregon
52 F6 Pistsovo U.S.S.R.
8 C2 Pistyll Rhaeadr mt Wales
16 E3 Pisuerga R Spain
31 N2 Pisz Poland
100 D8 Pit R California
85 B6 Pita Guinea
122 G1 Pitaga Labrador
70 D6 Pitap, R Kalimantan
139 G5 Pitarpunga L New S Wales
71 G7 Pitas Pt Mindanao Philippines
135 U11 Pitcairn I Pacific Oc
101 Q5 Pitchfork Wyoming
127 O3 Pitch L Trinidad
26 M6 Piteå Sweden
26 L6 Piteälv R Sweden
45 J3 Piteglio Italy
48 J6 Piteşti Romania
143 B9 Pithara W Australia
20 K5 Pithiviers France
42 D6 Pitigliano Italy
124 C2 Pitiquito Mexico
106 D3 Pitkin Colorado
111 D11 Pitkin Louisiana
52 D1 Pitkul' U.S.S.R.
52 D4 Pitkyaranta U.S.S.R.
15 E4 Pitlochry Scotland
95 M7 Pitman New Jersey
87 G12 Piton des Neiges mt Réunion
111 G11 Pitre, I. au Louisiana
13 F1 Pitscottie Scotland
9 G4 Pitsea England
13 F1 Pittenweem Scotland
117 J9 Pitt I Br Col
137 R10 Pitt I Chatham Is Pacific Oc
112 H2 Pittsboro N Carolina
102 C3 Pittsburg California
110 B4 Pittsburg Kansas
110 M4 Pittsburg Kentucky
121 T7 Pittsburg New Hampshire
107 P7 Pittsburg Oklahoma
109 N3 Pittsburg Texas
94 H6 Pittsburgh Pennsylvania
110 E2 Pittsfield Illinois
95 S2 Pittsfield Maine
95 O4 Pittsfield Massachusetts
95 Q3 Pittsfield New Hampshire
94 C5 Pittsford Michigan
94 K3 Pittsford New York
95 O3 Pittsford Vermont
95 M5 Pittston Pennsylvania
111 L9 Pittsview Alabama
95 M8 Pittsville Maryland
110 C3 Pittsville Missouri
99 Q5 Pittsville Wisconsin
141 K8 Pittsworth Queensland
100 D8 Pittville California
71 B1 Pitu Halmahera Indonesia
88 E6 Pitu R Tanzania
140 E6 Pituri R Queensland
41 N3 Pitz Tal Austria
45 J1 Piú bega Italy
19 Q17 Piumoisson France
128 B5 Piura Peru
128 B4 Piura dep Peru
103 J7 Piute Mts California
102 F6 Piute Pk California
103 M3 Piute Res Utah
75 K4 Piuthan Nepal
42 J5 Piva R Yugoslavia
120 G2 Pivabiska R Ontario
126 G9 Pivijay Colombia
31 M6 Piwniczna Poland
102 E6 Pixley California
46 E5 Piyaí Greece
60 Q1 Piyashiri yama mt Japan
128 E7 Pizacoma Peru
52 G5 Pizhanka U.S.S.R.
52 G5 Pizhma U.S.S.R.
41 K4 Pizol mt Switzerland
43 G10 Pizzo Italy
45 O6 Pizzodeta, M mt Italy
33 Q5 Plaaz E Germany
109 L7 Placedo Texas
123 T6 Placentia Nfld
71 G6 Placer Mindanao Philippines
102 F1 Placeritos Nevada
102 D3 Placerville California
106 B3 Placerville Colorado
126 E3 Placetas Cuba
113 E11 Placida Florida
113 F10 Placid, L Florida
106 D6 Placitas New Mexico
46 E3 Plačkovica mt Yugoslavia
12 C3 Pladda I Scotland
15 C5 Pladda Lt. Ho Scotland
40 F4 Plaffeien Switzerland
99 Q6 Plain Wisconsin
94 D6 Plain City Ohio
101 N8 Plain City Utah
111 C9 Plain Dealing Louisiana
20 J3 Plaine et Collines reg France
94 A7 Plainfield Indiana
99 O7 Plainfield Iowa
95 N6 Plainfield New Jersey
99 R5 Plainfield Wisconsin
112 C5 Plains Georgia
101 L2 Plains Montana
108 E2 Plains Texas
94 K8 Plains, The Virginia
110 C6 Plainview Arkansas
99 O5 Plainview Minnesota
98 J7 Plainview Nebraska
108 F1 Plainview Texas

Plainville — Portree 61

95 P5 **Plainville** Connecticut
110 E2 **Plainville** Illinois
107 L2 **Plainville** Kansas
94 B4 **Plainwell** Michigan
18 F9 **Plaisance** France
127 H5 **Plaisance** Haiti
69 G14 **Plaju** Sumatra
47 G4 **Pláka, Akr** *C* Greece
47 H9 **Pláka, Akra** *C* Crete Greece
46 D3 **Plakenska Pl** *mt* Yugoslavia
118 E4 **Plamondon** Alberta
71 H9 **Plampang** Indonesia
37 O4 **Planá** Czechoslovakia
102 D4 **Planada** California
129 L5 **Planalto da Borborema** *plat* Brazil
129 H7 **Planalto de Mato Grosso** *plat* Brazil
17 G6 **Plana Ó Nueva Tabarca** *isld* Spain
40 E2 **Plancher les Mines** France
40 D4 **Planches-en-Montagne, Les** France
131 B5 **Planchon, Paso de** Chile/Arg
18 D4 **Plancoët** France
19 O15 **Plan-de-Baix** France
19 N17 **Plan d'Orgon** France
17 G9 **Plane** *isld* Algeria
33 R8 **Plane, R** E Germany
126 G10 **Planeta Rica** Colombia
137 L3 **Planet Deep** Solomon Sea
37 P5 **Plánice** Czechoslovakia
37 L4 **Plankenfels** W Germany
98 H6 **Plankinton** S Dakota
109 L2 **Plano** Texas
127 M3 **Plantain Garden R** Jamaica
113 E9 **Plant City** Florida
111 K9 **Plantersville** Alabama
111 E11 **Plaquemine** Louisiana
16 C4 **Plasencia** Spain
27 F10 **Plassen** Norway
55 D4 **Plast** U.S.S.R.
33 R5 **Plasten** E Germany
103 J9 **Plaster City** California
37 P4 **Plasy** Czechoslovakia
43 E11 **Platani** *R* Sicily
133 C2 **Plata, Puerta** Chile
131 G5 **Plata, Rio de la** Arg/Uruguay
19 O14 **Plateau de Chambarand** France
19 J15 **Plateau de Langres** France
21 K10 **Plateau de Peyrelevade** France
19 P16 **Plateau de St. Etienne** France
86 B1 **Plateau du Tchigaï** Niger
85 C3 **Plateau du Tinrhert** *stony des* Algeria
Plateau of Tibet *see* **Xizang Gaoyuan**
21 H9 **Plateaux de la Marche** France
123 T5 **Plate Cove** Nfld
124 H6 **Plateros** Mexico
46 F4 **Platí** Greece
47 G4 **Platí Ákra** *C* Greece
46 F5 **Platíkambos** Greece
102 B1 **Platina** California
116 G7 **Platinum** Alaska
126 G10 **Plato** Colombia
110 D4 **Plato** Missouri
118 J7 **Plato** Sask
56 D5 **Plato Alash** U.S.S.R.
79 C4 **Platres** Cyprus
98 H6 **Platte** S Dakota
37 N4 **Platte** *mt* W Germany
99 M9 **Platte** *R* Missouri
98 G9 **Platte** *R* Nebraska
98 J8 **Platte Center** Nebraska
110 B2 **Platte City** Missouri
106 E2 **Platte Mt** Colorado
98 B9 **Platteville** Colorado
99 Q7 **Platteville** Wisconsin
36 E6 **Plättig** W Germany
37 O6 **Plattling** W Germany
107 O7 **Platt Nat. Park** Oklahoma
110 B2 **Plattsburg** Missouri
95 O2 **Plattsburg** New York
99 K8 **Plattsmouth** Nebraska
33 Q6 **Plau** E Germany
33 Q8 **Plaue** E Germany
37 K2 **Plaue** Erfurt **E Germany**
37 N3 **Plauen** E Germany
46 D2 **Plav** Yugoslavia
52 C6 **Pļaviņas** U.S.S.R.
42 J6 **Plavnica** Yugoslavia
54 J3 **Plavsk** U.S.S.R.
128 B4 **Playas** Ecuador
106 B10 **Playas L** New Mexico
140 D4 **Playford** *R* N Terr **Aust**
140 D6 **Playford Mt** N Terr **Aust**
119 U4 **Playgreen L** Manitoba
124 E5 **Playón** Mexico
98 E1 **Plaza** N Dakota
133 D5 **Plaza Huincul Argentina**
12 E1 **Plean** Scotland
110 M1 **Pleasant** Ohio
95 S5 **Pleasant B** Massachusetts
123 M7 **Pleasant Bay** C Breton I, N S
94 F7 **Pleasant City** Ohio
119 N6 **Pleasantdale** Sask
94 K6 **Pleasant Gap** Pennsylvania
101 O9 **Pleasant Grove** Utah
110 F2 **Pleasant Hill** Illinois
111 C10 **Pleasant Hill** Louisiana
110 B3 **Pleasant Hill** Missouri
94 E6 **Pleasant Hill Res** Ohio
103 M8 **Pleasant, L** Arizona
122 F8 **Pleasant, Mt** New Brunswick
112 H5 **Pleasant, Mt** S Carolina
102 C4 **Pleasanton** California
110 B3 **Pleasanton** Kansas
98 G9 **Pleasanton** Nebraska
109 J7 **Pleasanton** Texas
110 E6 **Pleasant Plains** Arkansas
119 S9 **Pleasant Pt** Manitoba
144 C6 **Pleasant Pt New Zealand**
100 H5 **Pleasant Valley** Oregon
100 G3 **Pleasant View** Washington
99 N8 **Pleasantville** Iowa
95 N7 **Pleasantville** New Jersey
94 H5 **Pleasantville** Pennsylvania
9 E1 **Pleasley** England
110 L3 **Pleasureville** Kentucky
18 G7 **Pleaux** France
37 L4 **Plech** W Germany
120 G2 **Pledger L** Ontario
133 F4 **Pledra Sola** Uruguay
70 D3 **Pleieran** *R* Sarawak
70 D6 **Pleihari** Kalimantan
68 J5 **Plei Herel** Vietnam
68 J6 **Plei Kly** Vietnam
68 J6 **Pleiku** Vietnam
20 B4 **Pleine Fougères** France
37 L5 **Pleinfeld** W Germany
9 G6 **Pleinmont Pt** Channel Is
37 P6 **Pleinting** W Germany
37 N1 **Pleisse** *R* E Germany
68 H5 **Plei Ta Uan** Vietnam
20 A5 **Plélan-le-Grand** France
17 F1 **Plencia** Spain
18 D4 **Pléneuf** France
48 H6 **Plenţiţa** Romania
118 J7 **Plenty** Sask
145 F2 **Plenty, Bay of** New Zealand
140 D6 **Plenty R** N Terr **Aust**
98 B1 **Plentywood** Montana
20 B4 **Plerguer** France
52 F3 **Plesetsk** U.S.S.R.
55 E3 **Pleshkova** U.S.S.R.
48 F2 **Plešivec** Czechoslovakia
20 A4 **Pleslin** France
21 B6 **Plessé** France
121 T6 **Plessisville** Quebec
122 B2 **Pletipi L** Quebec
36 D1 **Plettenberg** W Germany
89 C10 **Plettenberg B** S Africa
20 B4 **Pleudihen** France
20 B5 **Pleugueneuc** France
20 A4 **Pleurtuit** France
47 G1 **Pleven** Bulgaria
98 B3 **Plevna** Montana
18 C4 **Pleyben** France
37 N4 **Pleystein** W Germany
145 E4 **Plimmerton** New Zealand
48 M1 **Pliskov** U.S.S.R.
42 G4 **Pljesivica** *dist* Yugoslavia
48 E7 **Pljevlja** Yugoslavia
43 B8 **Ploaghe** Sardinia
36 D7 **Plobsheim** France
42 H5 **Ploča** *lt ho* Yugoslavia
42 H5 **Ploče** Yugoslavia
36 G6 **Plochingen** W Germany
31 M3 **Płock** Poland
30 H7 **Plöckenstein** *mt* Czechoslovakia
22 D2 **Ploegsteert** Belgium
18 D5 **Ploërmel** France
48 K6 **Ploieşti** Romania
47 H6 **Plomárion** Greece
18 G7 **Plomb du Cantal** *mt* France
40 A3 **Plombières** France
19 K5 **Plombières-les-Bains** France
22 G4 **Plomion** France
33 M4 **Plön** W Germany
31 J2 **Płona** *R* Poland
31 M3 **Płońsk** Poland
48 H6 **Plopi** Romania
52 D6 **Ploskosh'** U.S.S.R.
37 N4 **Plössberg** W Germany
31 J2 **Płoty** Poland
18 C4 **Plouaret** France
18 C5 **Plouay** France
20 A4 **Ploubalay** France
31 H5 **Ploučnice** *R* Czechoslovakia
18 B4 **Ploudalmezeau** France
20 B4 **Plouer** France
18 D4 **Plouguenast** France
18 D4 **Plouha** France
47 G2 **Plovdiv** Bulgaria
99 M7 **Plover** Iowa
99 R5 **Plover** Wisconsin
99 R5 **Plover** *R* Wisconsin
116 K1 **Plover Is** Alaska
36 H6 **Plüderhausen** W Germany
119 S8 **Plumas** Manitoba
99 O5 **Plum City** Wisconsin
118 D1 **Plum Coulee** Manitoba
139 L4 **Plumer, Pt** New S Wales
95 P5 **Plum I** New York
100 J2 **Plummer** Idaho
116 H6 **Plummer, Mt** Alaska
110 D6 **Plummerville** Arkansas
13 F4 **Plumpton Hd** England
143 F8 **Plumridge Lakes** W Australia
87 E10 **Plumtree** Zimbabwe
52 B6 **Plunge** U.S.S.R.
119 M7 **Plunkett** Sask
100 F7 **Plush** Oregon
18 D5 **Pluvigner** France
36 B4 **Pluwig** W Germany
102 D3 **Plymouth** California
8 B7 **Plymouth** England
94 A5 **Plymouth** Indiana
99 N6 **Plymouth** Iowa
95 R5 **Plymouth** Massachusetts
127 O6 **Plymouth** Montserrat W Indies
98 K9 **Plymouth** Nebraska
95 Q3 **Plymouth** New Hampshire
94 E6 **Plymouth** Ohio
95 M5 **Plymouth** Pennsylvania
127 M2 **Plymouth** Tobago
101 N8 **Plymouth** Utah
95 P3 **Plymouth** Vermont
99 T6 **Plymouth** Wisconsin
8 B7 **Plympton** England
122 G9 **Plympton** Nova Scotia
8 C3 **Plynlimon Fawr** *mt* Wales
52 C5 **Plyusa** U.S.S.R.
52 C5 **Plyussa** *R* U.S.S.R.
37 P4 **Plzeň** Czechoslovakia
31 J3 **Pniewy** Poland
85 D6 **Po** Upper Volta
44 C1 **Po** *R* Italy
45 J2 **Po** *R* Italy
139 H8 **Poatina** Tasmania
85 E7 **Pobé** Benin
66 C3 **Pobedy, Pik** *mt* U.S.S.R./China
37 O5 **Poběžovice** Czechoslovakia
31 K3 **Pobiedziska** Poland
17 J2 **Pobla de Lilleta, L** Spain
17 H2 **Pobla de Segur** Spain
110 F5 **Pocahontas** Arkansas
99 M7 **Pocahontas** Iowa
94 F9 **Pocahontas** Virginia
107 N6 **Pocasse** Oklahoma
94 F8 **Pocatalico** *R* W Virginia
101 N7 **Pocatello** Idaho
31 J6 **Počátky** Czechoslovakia
131 D3 **Pocha, Sa. de** *mts* Argentina
54 E4 **Pochep** U.S.S.R.
54 D2 **Pochinok** U.S.S.R.
38 M5 **Pochlarn** Austria
125 L10 **Pochutla** Mexico
37 P5 **Pocinovice** Czechoslovakia
37 P2 **Pockau** E Germany
37 P7 **Pocking** W Germany
13 H6 **Pocklington** England
70 F2 **Pock, Mt** Sabah
128 D7 **Pocoma** Peru
95 M8 **Pocomoke City** Maryland
95 M9 **Pocomoke Sd** Virginia
129 G7 **Poconé** Brazil
95 M6 **Pocono Mts** Pennsylvania
95 M5 **Pocono Pines** Pennsylvania
129 J8 **Pocos de Caldas** Brazil
125 O6 **Pocrí** Panama
125 P9 **Poctún** Guatemala
103 L5 **Pocum Wash** *creek* Arizona
138 F4 **Podamacca** New S Wales
37 P3 **Podbořany** Czechoslovakia
52 J3 **Podcher'ye** U.S.S.R.
31 L4 **Poddębice** Poland
118 C4 **Poddle R** Alberta
52 D5 **Poddor'ye** U.S.S.R.
31 J5 **Poděbrady** Czechoslovakia
45 M2 **Po delle Tolle** *R* Italy
18 E8 **Podensac** France
48 J1 **Podgaits** U.S.S.R.
Podgorica *see* **Titograd**
54 G8 **Podgorodnoye** U.S.S.R.
45 M2 **Po di Goro** *R* Italy
76 D3 **Podile** India
45 L2 **Po di Volano** *R* Italy
51 Q2 **Podkagernoye** U.S.S.R.
56 D1 **Podkamennay** *R* U.S.S.R.
38 J9 **Podkoren** Yugoslavia
47 G3 **Podkova** Bulgaria
55 C5 **Podnikovskiy** U.S.S.R.
48 F1 **Podolinec** Czechoslovakia
54 J1 **Podolsk** U.S.S.R.
85 B5 **Podor** Senegal
52 G4 **Podosinovets** U.S.S.R.
42 H4 **Podovi** Yugoslavia
52 D4 **Podporozh'ye** U.S.S.R.
55 E2 **Podrezovo** U.S.S.R.
56 D2 **Podtesovo** U.S.S.R.
48 L3 **Podu Iloaiei** Romania
46 E2 **Podujevo** Yugoslavia
48 L4 **Podu Turcului** Romania
52 F4 **Podyuga** U.S.S.R.
33 O4 **Poel** *isld* E Germany
22 D2 **Poelkapelle** Belgium
94 C1 **Poe Reef Lt. Ho** Michigan
144 C5 **Poerua** New Zealand
87 C11 **Pofadder** S Africa
45 O6 **Pofi** Italy
120 J6 **Pogamasing** Ontario
54 E4 **Pogar** U.S.S.R.
33 S4 **Poggendorf** E Germany
42 D5 **Poggibonsi** Italy
45 K4 **Poggio a Caiano** Italy
45 N5 **Poggio Moiano** Italy
45 K2 **Pôggio Renatico** Italy
45 K2 **Póggio Rusco** Italy
59 M1 **Pogibi** U.S.S.R.
48 L6 **Pogoanele** Romania
46 D4 **Pogradec** Albania
45 M2 **Po Grande** *R* Italy
59 K3 **Pogranichnyy** U.S.S.R.
48 M1 **Pogrebishchenskiy** U.S.S.R.
116 E9 **Pogromni Vol** Aleutian Is
32 F6 **Pogum** W Germany
71 H5 **Poh** Sulawesi
135 U5 **Pohakuloa** Hawaiian Is
59 J4 **Pohang** S Korea
145 E4 **Pohangina New Zealand**
145 D4 **Pohara** New Zealand
29 K11 **Pohja** Finland
29 O8 **Pohjois-Karjala** *prov* Finland
36 F3 **Pohl-Göns** W Germany
36 F2 **Pohlheim** W Germany
145 E3 **Pohokura New Zealand**
145 F3 **Pohokura** *mt* **New Zealand**
48 F2 **Pohorelá** Czechoslovakia
31 K7 **Pohořelice** Czechoslovakia
38 M9 **Pohorje** *mt* Yugoslavia
102 V14 **Pohue B** Hawaiian Is
45 K1 **Poiana Magg** Italy
46 F1 **Poiana Mare** Romania
48 K3 **Poiana Teiului** Romania
71 J4 **Poigar** Sulawesi
29 M4 **Poikela** Finland
123 O2 **Poincaré, L** Quebec
146 F2 **Poinsett, C** Antarctica
113 G9 **Poinsett, L** Florida
102 D7 **Point Arguello** California
109 M5 **Pointblank** Texas
138 E5 **Point Broughton** S Australia
102 D6 **Point Buchon** California
139 G7 **Point Campbell** Victoria
109 L7 **Point Comfort** Texas
102 D7 **Point Conception** California
123 N3 **Pointe-à Maurier** Quebec
127 O3 **Pointe-à-Pierre** Trinidad
127 N4 **Pointe-à-Pitre** Guadeloupe W I
120 K7 **Pointe au Baril Station** Ontario
122 E4 **Pointe aux Anglais** Quebec
121 R7 **Pointe aux Trembles** Quebec
121 S4 **Pointe Bleue** Quebec
122 H7 **Pointe du Chêne** New Brunswick
120 H9 **Point Edward** Ontario
122 D4 **Pointe le Bel** Quebec
127 M4 **Pointe Noire** Guadeloupe W I
22 C1 **Pointe Synthe** France
122 G6 **Pointe Verte** New Brunswick
138 F7 **Point Fairy** S Australia
127 N3 **Point Fortin** Trinidad
112 M1 **Point Harbor** N Carolina
139 H8 **Point Hills** Tasmania
116 D2 **Point Hope** Alaska
117 R3 **Point L** N W Terr
116 F2 **Point Lay** Alaska
95 L8 **Point Lookout** Maryland
139 L4 **Point Lookout** *mt* New S Wales
94 H7 **Point Marion** Pennsylvania
94 K7 **Point of Rocks** Maryland
101 R8 **Point of Rocks** Wyoming
120 H10 **Point Pelee Nat Park** Ontario
102 C6 **Point Piedras Blancas** California
95 N6 **Point Pleasant** New Jersey
94 E8 **Point Pleasant** W Virginia
142 B5 **Point Samson** W Australia
140 B1 **Point Stuart** N Terr **Aust**
102 C5 **Point Sur** California
138 D5 **Point Turton** S Australia
145 E2 **Point Waikato** New Zealand
68 F6 **Poipet** Cambodia
52 H6 **Poisevo** U.S.S.R.
101 S6 **Poison Cr** Wyoming
142 B1 **Poison Gully** *R* Perth, W Aust
121 P6 **Poisson Blanc, L** Quebec
142 C5 **Poissonnier Pt** W Australia
20 K4 **Poissy** France
21 F8 **Poitiers** France
21 D8 **Poitou** *reg* France
142 B5 **Poivre, C** W Australia
20 J2 **Poix** France
22 J3 **Poix St. Hubert** Belgium
22 H4 **Poix-Terron** France
46 D4 **Pojan** Albania
106 D6 **Pojoaque** New Mexico
102 R12 **Pokai Bay** Hawaiian Is
145 E3 **Pokaka New Zealand**
74 D5 **Pokaran** India
139 J3 **Pokataroo** New S Wales
52 J3 **Pokcha** U.S.S.R.
145 E2 **Pokeno New Zealand**
75 L4 **Pokhara** Nepal
29 M3 **Pokka** Finland
86 E5 **Poko** Zaïre
31 K5 **Pokój** Poland
116 F2 **Poko Mt** Alaska
54 L1 **Pokrov** U.S.S.R.
55 E5 **Pokrovka** Atbasar U.S.S.R.
55 G3 **Pokrovka** Novosibirsk U.S.S.R.
55 B5 **Pokrovka** Orenburg U.S.S.R.
55 E3 **Pokrovskoye** U.S.S.R.
52 F3 **Pokshen'ga** *R* U.S.S.R.
71 E4 **Pola** Philippines
71 E4 **Pola B** Philippines
103 O6 **Polacca** Arizona
103 O6 **Polacca Wasa** *R* Arizona
16 D1 **Pola de Laviana** Spain
16 D1 **Pola de Lena** Spain
16 D1 **Pola de Siero** Spain
95 M3 **Poland** New York
31 K4 **Poland** *rep* Europe
31 K1 **Polanow** Poland
99 S4 **Polar** Wisconsin
101 M4 **Polaris** Montana
78 D2 **Polatli** Turkey
8 B7 **Polbathick** England
36 C3 **Polch** W Germany
133 C5 **Polcura** Chile
31 J2 **Połczyn Zdrój** Poland
138 D5 **Polda** S Australia
52 E3 **Pole** U.S.S.R.
70 G7 **Poleang** Sulawesi
37 P5 **Poledník** *mt* Czechoslovakia
80 C5 **Poleg** *R* Israel
9 G6 **Polegate** England
68 H5 **Polei Monu** Vietnam
37 P5 **Poleň** Czechoslovakia
146 D7 **Pole of Inaccessibility** Antarctica
45 L2 **Polesella** Italy
31 N1 **Polessk** U.S.S.R.
53 C8 **Polesye** *marsh* U.S.S.R.
55 D3 **Polevskoy** U.S.S.R.
70 F6 **Polewali** Sulawesi
48 G3 **Polgár** Hungary
48 E3 **Polgárdi** Hungary
55 E3 **Polgovskoye** U.S.S.R.
86 B4 **Poli** Cameroon
47 G8 **Políaigos** *isld* Greece
43 G8 **Policastro, G. di** Italy
31 H2 **Police** Poland
31 J6 **Polička** Czechoslovakia
85 F3 **Polignac** Algeria
19 J6 **Poligny** France
46 F3 **Políkastron** Greece
47 H5 **Políkhnitos** Greece
71 E3 **Polillo** *isld* Luzon Philippines
45 J3 **Polinago** Italy
38 H8 **Polinik** *mt* Austria
127 L3 **Polink Pt** Jamaica
79 C3 **Polis** Cyprus
52 D5 **Polist'** *R* U.S.S.R.
52 G3 **Politovo** U.S.S.R.
98 J8 **Polk** Nebraska
94 H5 **Polk** Pennsylvania
56 D1 **Polkan, Gora** *mt* U.S.S.R.
113 F9 **Polk City** Florida
33 P7 **Polkritz** E Germany
76 C5 **Pollachi** India
37 L5 **Pollanten** W Germany
110 F5 **Pollard** Arkansas
38 N7 **Pöllau** Austria
32 K9 **Polle** W Germany
122 A1 **Pollet, L** Quebec
43 G9 **Pollino, M** *mt* Italy
33 P7 **Pollitz** E Germany
100 J4 **Pollock** Idaho
111 D10 **Pollock** Louisiana
98 F4 **Pollock** S Dakota
143 E10 **Pollock Reef** W Australia
112 K3 **Pollocksville** N Carolina
118 F7 **Pollockville** Alberta
144 B6 **Pollux** *mt* New Zealand
29 N2 **Polmak** Finland
26 Q1 **Polmak** Norway
12 E2 **Polmont** Scotland
31 J6 **Polná** Czechoslovakia
52 C5 **Polna** U.S.S.R.
99 R8 **Polo** Illinois
110 B2 **Polo** Missouri
54 H9 **Pologi** U.S.S.R.
71 G7 **Polomoloc** Mindanao Philippines
47 J3 **Polos** Turkey
54 G2 **Polotnanyy** U.S.S.R.
52 C6 **Polotsk** U.S.S.R.
55 E4 **Polovinnoye** U.S.S.R.
52 H3 **Polovniki** U.S.S.R.
8 B7 **Polperro** England
83 K10 **Polpitigama** Sri Lanka
38 L7 **Pöls** *R* Austria
101 L2 **Polson** Montana
38 K7 **Pöls-Tal** *V* Austria
52 F2 **Polta** *R* U.S.S.R.
48 F2 **Poltár** Czechoslovakia
54 F7 **Poltava** U.S.S.R.
55 F4 **Poltavka** U.S.S.R.
121 P7 **Poltimore** Quebec
52 C5 **Põltsamaa** U.S.S.R.
55 E4 **Poludino** U.S.S.R.
55 D1 **Polunochnoye** U.S.S.R.
50 E4 **Poluostrov Buzachi** *pen* U.S.S.R.
106 D7 **Polvadera** New Mexico
29 O9 **Polvijärvi** Finland
118 L5 **Polwarth** Sask
31 L1 **Półwysep Hel** *pen* Poland
55 E1 **Pol'yanovo** U.S.S.R.
52 D1 **Polyarnyy** U.S.S.R.
116 N5 **Polychrome Pass** Alaska
47 F4 **Polýiros** Greece
56 C4 **Polysayevo** U.S.S.R.
37 N2 **Pölzig** E Germany
133 D2 **Poma** Argentina
144 B6 **Pomahaka** *R* **New Zealand**
133 D3 **Poman** Argentina
71 L9 **Pomana Besar** *isld* Flores Indonesia
16 B7 **Pomarão** Portugal
112 F3 **Pomaria** S Carolina
29 J10 **Pomarkku** Finland
130 G7 **Pomba** *R* Brazil
129 L5 **Pombal** Brazil
16 B5 **Pombal** Portugal
130 D7 **Pombo, R** Brazil
19 O18 **Pomègues, Île** France
31 G2 **Pomerania** *reg* E Germany/Poland
99 M7 **Pomercy** Iowa
103 O9 **Pomerene** Arizona
14 E2 **Pomeroy** N Ireland
94 E7 **Pomeroy** Ohio
100 H3 **Pomeroy** Washington
45 M6 **Pomezia** Italy
95 P5 **Pomfret** Connecticut
45 Q8 **Pomigliano d'Arco** Italy
110 C4 **Pomme de Terre** *R* Missouri
37 M5 **Pommelsbrunn** W Germany
107 P3 **Pomoma** Kansas
125 P9 **Pomona** Belize
102 G7 **Pomona** California
110 E5 **Pomona** Missouri
87 C11 **Pomona** Namibia
141 L7 **Pomona** Queensland
47 J2 **Pomorie** Bulgaria
52 E3 **Pomorskiy Bereg** *coast* U.S.S.R.
48 J1 **Pomoryany** U.S.S.R.
54 C8 **Pomoshnaya** U.S.S.R.
21 E8 **Pompaire** France
113 G11 **Pompano Beach** Florida
45 Q8 **Pompei** Italy
95 L4 **Pompey** New York
101 S4 **Pompeys Pillar** Montana
95 N5 **Pompton Lakes** New Jersey
88 D10 **Pompué** *R* **Mozambique**
123 L8 **Pomquet** Nova Scotia
33 R10 **Pomssen** E Germany
119 N6 **Ponass L** Sask
98 K7 **Ponca** Nebraska
107 N5 **Ponca City** Oklahoma
127 L5 **Ponce** Puerto Rico
111 L11 **Ponce de Leon** Florida
113 F12 **Ponce de Leon B** Florida
113 F8 **Ponce de Leon Inlet** Florida
111 F11 **Ponchatoula** Louisiana
124 H7 **Poncitlán** Mexico
107 N5 **Pond Creek** Oklahoma
109 K2 **Ponder** Texas
76 D5 **Pondicherry** India
115 M3 **Pond Inlet** N W Terr
89 F8 **Pondoland** *reg* S Africa
100 D8 **Pondosa** California
100 H4 **Pondosa** Oregon
99 M1 **Ponemah** Minnesota
44 E3 **Ponente** Italy
94 B6 **Poneto** Indiana
16 C2 **Ponferrada** Spain
86 A5 **Pongara, Pte** Gabon
145 F4 **Pongaroa New Zealand**
38 H7 **Pongau** *reg* Austria
70 G7 **Pongkolaero** Sulawesi
52 D2 **Pon'goma** U.S.S.R.
122 H9 **Ponhook L** Nova Scotia
33 T10 **Ponickau** E Germany
31 K4 **Poniec** Poland
71 H4 **Poniki, Mt** Sulawesi
70 G5 **Ponindilisa, Tg** *C* Sulawesi
68 A2 **Ponnagyun** Burma
68 B1 **Ponnyadaung** *ra* Burma
118 D6 **Ponoka** Alberta
55 B4 **Ponomarevka** U.S.S.R.
70 N9 **Ponorogo** Java
52 F2 **Ponoy** U.S.S.R.
52 E2 **Ponoy** *R* U.S.S.R.
18 E7 **Pons** France
17 H3 **Pons** Spain
45 J4 **Ponsacco** Italy
71 G5 **Ponson** *isld* Philippines
18 E9 **Pontacq** France
130 E9 **Ponta Grossa** Brazil
40 B3 **Pontailler** France
19 J5 **Pontailler-sur-Saône** France
19 O15 **Pontaix** France
22 E3 **Pont-à-Marcq** France
19 J4 **Pont à Mousson** France
129 G8 **Ponta Porá** Brazil
8 C4 **Pontardawe** Wales
8 B4 **Pontarddulais** Wales
19 K6 **Pontarlier** France
45 K4 **Pontassieve** Italy
20 C4 **Pontaubault** France
20 G3 **Pont Audemer** France
18 G7 **Pontaumur** France
22 F5 **Pontavert** France
121 M1 **Pontax** *R* Quebec
122 K3 **Pontbriand B** Quebec
40 G7 **Pont-Canav** Italy
19 Q14 **Pontcharra** France
21 J10 **Pontcharraud** France
111 F11 **Pontchartrain, L** Louisiana
21 A7 **Pontchâteau** France
19 O12 **Pont d'Ain** France
19 O15 **Pont-de-Barret** France
40 C4 **Pont-de-Poitte** France
19 J6 **Pont de Vaux** France
19 J6 **Pont de Veyle** France
20 E4 **Pont d'Ouilly** France
129 J6 **Ponte Alta do Norte** Brazil
42 E2 **Pontebba** Italy
45 R8 **Pontecagnano** Italy
45 P7 **Pontecorvo** Italy
20 E4 **Pont-Ecrepin Fromentel** France
16 B3 **Ponte da Barca** Portugal
129 G6 **Ponte de Pedra** Brazil
45 J4 **Pontedera** Italy
16 B5 **Ponte de Sor** Portugal
16 B3 **Ponte do Lima** Portugal
13 G6 **Pontefract** England
118 K9 **Ponteix** Sask
45 L2 **Pontelagoscuro** Italy
13 G3 **Ponteland** England
45 R7 **Pontelandolfo** Italy
45 M1 **Pontelongo** Italy
130 G7 **Ponte Nova** Brazil
18 E8 **Pontenx les Forges** France
16 B2 **Pontevedra** Spain
16 B2 **Pontevedra** *prov* Spain
113 F7 **Ponte Vedra Beach** Florida
41 M7 **Pontevico** Italy
20 C4 **Pontfarcy** France
22 G5 **Pont Faverger** France
20 H5 **Pontgouin** France
99 S9 **Pontiac** Illinois
94 D4 **Pontiac** Michigan
70 A5 **Pontianak** Kalimantan
43 E7 **Pontinia** Italy
18 D4 **Pontivy** France
18 C5 **Pont l'Abbé** France
122 H6 **Pont Lafrance** New Brunswick
40 A1 **Pont la Ville** France
20 F3 **Pont-l'Evêque** France
21 H7 **Pontlevoy** France
60 S2 **Pônto** Japan
119 S4 **Ponton** Manitoba
20 B4 **Pontorson** France
111 G7 **Pontotoc** Mississippi
109 J5 **Pontotoc** Texas
44 G3 **Pontremoli** Italy
41 L4 **Pontresina** Switzerland
8 C3 **Pontrhydfendigaid Wales**
18 C4 **Pontrieux** France
8 D4 **Pontrilas** England
119 N5 **Pontrilas** Sask
121 T6 **Pont Rouge** Quebec
19 N16 **Pont-St. Esprit** France
22 D5 **Pont-Ste. Maxence** France
22 F3 **Pont-sur-Sambre** France
18 H4 **Pont-sur-Yonne** France
21 F6 **Pontvallain** France
121 M8 **Pontypool** Ontario
8 C4 **Pontypool** Wales
8 C4 **Pontypridd** Wales
145 E2 **Ponui I** New Zealand
101 O4 **Pony** Montana
43 E8 **Ponza** *lt ho* Italy
43 E8 **Ponziane, Isole** *isld* Italy
138 C4 **Poochera** S Australia
13 G6 **Pool** England
138 D2 **Poolawanna L** S Australia
144 B6 **Poolburn Dam** New Zealand
9 E6 **Poole** England
138 F3 **Poole, Mt** New S Wales
112 F5 **Pooler** Georgia
95 K7 **Poolesville** Maryland
15 C3 **Poolewe** Scotland
12 E1 **Pool of Muckart** Scotland
109 K3 **Poolville** Texas
76 A1 **Poona** India
139 G5 **Pooncarie** New S Wales
143 B8 **Poondarrie,Mt** W Australia
139 G4 **Poopelloe, L** New S Wales
128 E7 **Poopó** Bolivia
145 E1 **Poor Knights Is** New Zealand
116 K4 **Poorman** Alaska
86 C7 **Popakabaka** Zaïre
129 G3 **Popakai** Suriname
54 K8 **Popasnaya** U.S.S.R.
128 C3 **Popayan** Colombia
103 J8 **Pope** California
111 G7 **Pope** Mississippi
27 M14 **Pope** U.S.S.R.
99 N7 **Popejoy** Iowa
58 F1 **Poperechnoye** U.S.S.R.
22 D2 **Poperinge** Belgium
95 L8 **Popes Creek** Maryland
95 S3 **Popham Beach** Maine
51 K1 **Popigay** *R* U.S.S.R.
138 F5 **Popiltah** New S Wales
98 A1 **Poplar** Montana
99 P3 **Poplar** Wisconsin
110 F5 **Poplar Bluff** Missouri
101 U1 **Poplar Cr** Montana
119 U6 **Poplar Pt** Manitoba
111 G11 **Poplarville** Mississippi
125 K8 **Popocatepetl** *vol* Mexico
116 G9 **Popof I** Alaska
70 N10 **Popoh** Java
45 P5 **Popoli** Italy
136 K3 **Popondetta** Papua New Guinea
47 H1 **Popovo** Bulgaria
37 M5 **Poppberg** *mt* W Germany
25 H4 **Poppe** Netherlands
22 J1 **Poppel** Belgium
37 J3 **Poppenhausen** W Germany
45 L4 **Poppi** Italy
31 M6 **Poprad** Czechoslovakia
48 F1 **Poprad** *R* Czechoslovakia
128 E8 **Poquis** *mt* Chile/Arg
95 L9 **Poquoson** Virginia
145 F4 **Porangahau New Zealand**
74 C8 **Porbander** India
117 H9 **Porcher I** Br Col
133 D1 **Porco** Bolivia
16 E7 **Porcuna** Spain
116 R3 **Porcupine** *R* Alaska/Yukon Terr
141 G5 **Porcupine** *R* Queensland
90 H3 **Porcupine Bank** Atlantic Oc
101 T1 **Porcupine Cr** Montana
118 C8 **Porcupine Hills** Alberta
119 Q6 **Porcupine Hills** Man/Sask
99 R3 **Porcupine Mts** Michigan
119 O6 **Porcupine Plain** Sask
42 E3 **Pordenoné** Italy
47 G1 **Pordim** Bulgaria
42 F3 **Poreč** Yugoslavia
130 D8 **Porecatu** Brazil
55 D2 **Porech'ye** U.S.S.R.
52 G6 **Poretskoye** U.S.S.R.
145 E4 **Porewa** New Zealand
85 E6 **Porga** Benin
29 J10 **Pori** Finland
145 F4 **Porirua** New Zealand
80 F3 **Poriyya** Israel
26 L5 **Porjus** Sweden
29 L12 **Porkala** Finland
28 N3 **Porkere** Faeroes
52 C5 **Porkhov** U.S.S.R.
128 F1 **Porlamar** Venezuela
41 K5 **Porlezza** Italy
8 C5 **Porlock** England
37 L6 **Pörnbach** W Germany
21 A7 **Pornic** France
71 G5 **Poro** *isld* Philippines
52 E3 **Porog** Arkhangelsk **U.S.S.R.**
52 J4 **Porog** Komi U.S.S.R.
59 M2 **Poronaysk** U.S.S.R.
68 G6 **Porong** *R* Cambodia
60 Q1 **Poronupuri yama** *mt* Japan
145 E3 **Porootarao** New Zealand
47 F7 **Póros** *isld* Greece
60 Q1 **Poroshiri yama** *mt* Japan
52 D3 **Porosozero** U.S.S.R.
52 H3 **Porozhsk** U.S.S.R.
56 F3 **Porozhskiy** U.S.S.R.
146 H3 **Porpoise B** Antarctica
19 Q18 **Porquerolles, I. de** France
120 K4 **Porquis Junct** Ontario
40 F3 **Pörrentruy** Switzerland
45 J3 **Porretta Terme** Italy
16 B2 **Porriño** Spain
26 N1 **Porsa** Norway
26 O1 **Pôrsangen** *inlet* Norway
27 D12 **Porsgrunn** Norway
33 Q9 **Porst** E Germany
47 L5 **Porsük** *R* Turkey
78 C2 **Porsuk** *R* Turkey
128 F7 **Portachuelo** Bolivia
138 E5 **Port Adelaide** S Australia
14 E2 **Portadown** N Ireland
144 B7 **Port Adventure** New Zealand
14 F2 **Portaferry** N Ireland
116 N6 **Portage** Alaska
95 S7 **Portage** Maine
101 O2 **Portage** Montana
94 J6 **Portage** Pennsylvania
122 H7 **Portage** Pr Edward I
101 N8 **Portage** Utah
94 D5 **Portage** *R* Ohio
110 F3 **Portage des Sioux** Missouri
122 G6 **Portage I** New Brunswick
119 T9 **Portage la Prairie** Manitoba
110 G5 **Portageville** Missouri
94 J4 **Portageville** New York
103 P10 **Portal** Arizona
112 F5 **Portal** Georgia
98 D1 **Portal** N Dakota
14 D3 **Portalaoise** Irish Rep
117 L11 **Port Alberni** Br Col
145 E2 **Port Albert New Zealand**
120 J9 **Port Albert** Ontario
139 H7 **Port Albert** Victoria
16 C5 **Portalegre** Portugal
106 G7 **Portales** New Mexico
117 F7 **Port Alexander** Alaska
121 U4 **Port Alfred** Quebec
89 E9 **Port Alfred** S Africa
117 K10 **Port Alice** Br Col
94 J5 **Port Allegany** Pennsylvania
111 E11 **Port Allen** Louisiana
141 K6 **Port Alma** Queensland
117 M11 **Port Angeles** Washington
109 K8 **Port Aransas** Texas
102 A3 **Port Arena** California
14 D3 **Portarlington** Irish Rep
Port Arthur *see* **Lüshun**
139 J9 **Port Arthur** Tasmania
109 N6 **Port Arthur** Texas
12 B2 **Port Askaig** Scotland
138 D4 **Port Augusta** S Australia
123 O5 **Port-au-Port** Nfld
123 N5 **Port-au-Port** *pen* Nfld
127 H5 **Port-au-Prince** Haiti
94 D2 **Port Austin** Michigan
32 J8 **Porta Westfalica** W Germany
20 B3 **Portbail** France
12 C2 **Port Bannatyne** Scotland
111 E11 **Port Barre** Louisiana
71 D5 **Port Barton** Palawan Philippines
87 H11 **Port Bergé** Madagascar
123 L8 **Port Bickerton** Nova Scotia
68 A7 **Port Blair** Andaman Is
109 N6 **Port Bolivar** Texas
17 K2 **Port Bou** Spain/France
85 D8 **Port Bouet** Ivory Coast
140 D2 **Port Bradshaw** *inlet* N Terr Aust
140 B1 **Port Bremer** *inlet* N Terr Aust
20 D5 **Port Brillet** France
120 J10 **Port Bruce** Ontario
120 K10 **Port Burwell** Ontario
99 Q8 **Port Byron** Illinois
95 L3 **Port Byron** New York
75 N7 **Port Canning** India
121 L7 **Port Carling** Ontario
13 E4 **Port Carlisle** England
122 F3 **Port Cartier** Quebec
144 D7 **Port Chalmers** New Zealand
145 E2 **Port Charles New Zealand**
15 B5 **Port Charlotte** Scotland
95 O6 **Port Chester** New York
111 G12 **Port Chicot I** Louisiana
116 D4 **Port Clarence** *hbr* Alaska
117 G9 **Port Clements** Br Col
94 E5 **Port Clinton** Ohio
141 K5 **Port Clinton** *inlet* Queensland
95 S3 **Port Clyde** Maine
121 L10 **Port Colborne** Ontario
117 M11 **Port Coquitlam** Br Col
68 A6 **Port Cornwallis** Andaman Is
121 L9 **Port Credit** Ontario
19 Q18 **Port Cros, I. de** France
141 K6 **Port Curtis** *inlet* Queensland
121 L9 **Port Dalhousie** Ontario
122 H5 **Port Daniel** Quebec
133 F8 **Port Darwin** Falkland Is
139 H9 **Port Davey** Tasmania
19 N18 **Port de Bouc** France
102 A1 **Port Delgada** California
127 H5 **Port-de-Paix** Haiti
21 G7 **Port-de-Piles** France
69 E11 **Port Dickson Malaysia**
141 H3 **Port Douglas** Queensland
120 K10 **Port Dover** Ontario
123 K9 **Port Dufferin** Nova Scotia
111 G12 **Porte a la Hache** Louisiana
99 U4 **Porte des Morts** Wisconsin
117 H8 **Port Edward** Br Col
89 G8 **Port Edward S Africa**
130 G4 **Porteirinha** Brazil
129 H4 **Portel** Brazil
16 B6 **Portel** Portugal
130 H7 **Portela** Brazil
122 H7 **Port Elgin** New Brunswick
120 J8 **Port Elgin** Ontario
127 O8 **Port Elizabeth** Lesser Antilles
89 D9 **Port Elizabeth S Africa**
22 B2 **Portel, le** France
12 B2 **Port Ellen** Scotland
130 B9 **Porteña** *R* Argentina
20 D3 **Port-en-Bessin** France
98 K5 **Porter** Minnesota
98 C7 **Porter** Nebraska
107 P6 **Porter** Oklahoma
112 D4 **Porterdale** Georgia
99 T4 **Porterfield** Wisconsin
12 D5 **Port Erin** I of Man U.K.
117 H6 **Porter Landing** Br Col
15 G3 **Port Errol** Scotland
102 E5 **Porterville** California
87 C12 **Porterville** S Africa
127 K3 **Port Esquivel** Jamaica
140 B1 **Port Essington** *inlet* N Terr Aust
8 B4 **Port Eynon Wales**
123 L8 **Port Felix** Nova Scotia
145 E2 **Port Fitzroy New Zealand**
Port Francqui *see* **Ilebo**
86 A6 **Port Gentil** Gabon
122 G9 **Port George** Nova Scotia
111 E10 **Port Gibson** Mississippi
12 D2 **Port Glasgow** Scotland
14 E2 **Portglenone** N Ireland
15 E3 **Portgordon** Grampian Scotland
145 E4 **Port Gore New Zealand**
116 M7 **Port Graham** Alaska
143 A8 **Port Gregory** *B* W Australia
122 H8 **Port Greville** Nova Scotia
8 C4 **Porth** Wales
85 F8 **Port Harcourt** Nigeria
117 K10 **Port Hardy** Br Col
145 D4 **Port Hardy New Zealand**
123 L8 **Port Hastings** C Breton I, N Scotia
123 L8 **Port Hawkesbury** C Breton I, N Scotia
8 C5 **Porthcawl Wales**
142 C5 **Port Hedland** W Australia
127 L3 **Port Henderson** Jamaica
95 O3 **Port Henry** New York
Port Herald *see* **Nsanje**
100 J1 **Porthill** Idaho
8 B2 **Porth Neigwl Wales**
123 L8 **Port Hood** C Breton I, N Scotia
94 E3 **Port Hope** Michigan
121 M9 **Port Hope** Ontario
123 Q1 **Port Hope Simpson** Labrador
102 E7 **Port Hueneme** California
94 E4 **Port Huron** Michigan
120 H10 **Port Huron** Ontario
45 Q8 **Portici** Italy
16 B7 **Portimão** Portugal
29 M5 **Portimo** Finland
12 C1 **Portinnisherrich** Scotland
107 M2 **Portis** Kansas
8 B6 **Port Isaac** England
109 K9 **Port Isabel** Texas
99 T2 **Port Isabelle** Michigan
8 D5 **Portishead** England
139 K5 **Port Jackson** New S Wales
145 E2 **Port Jackson New Zealand**
95 O6 **Port Jefferson** Long I, N Y
95 N5 **Port Jervis** New York
127 J3 **Port Kaiser** Jamaica
140 A2 **Port Keats** N Terr **Aust**
139 K5 **Port Kembla** New S Wales
127 P6 **Portland** Barbados
106 E3 **Portland** Colorado
94 C6 **Portland** Indiana
95 R3 **Portland** Maine
94 C4 **Portland** Michigan
98 J2 **Portland** N Dakota
139 J5 **Portland** New S Wales
145 E1 **Portland** New Zealand
121 O8 **Portland** Ontario
100 C4 **Portland** Oregon
110 K5 **Portland** Tennessee
109 K8 **Portland** Texas
138 F7 **Portland** Victoria
127 M2 **Portland** *parish* Jamaica
127 K3 **Portland Bight** Jamaica
8 D7 **Portland, Bill of** *head* England
139 J8 **Portland, C** Tasmania
117 H8 **Portland Canal** Br Col/Alaska
123 P3 **Portland Cr. Pond** Nfld
141 G6 **Portland Downs** Queensland
8 D6 **Portland Hbr** England
145 F3 **Portland I New Zealand**
117 H8 **Portland Inlet** Br Col
127 K3 **Portland Ridge** Jamaica
141 G2 **Portland Roads** Queensland
126 F6 **Portland Rock** Caribbean
71 E8 **Port Languyan Philippines**
139 H8 **Port Latta** Tasmania
109 L7 **Port Lavaca** Texas
14 D4 **Portlaw** Irish Rep
144 B4 **Port Levy New Zealand**
95 M3 **Port Leyden** New York
138 D5 **Port Lincoln** S Australia
12 D4 **Port Logan** Scotland
120 K7 **Port Loring** Ontario
18 C5 **Port Louis** France
127 N4 **Port Louis** Guadeloupe **W I**
83 L14 **Port Louis** Kerguelen
83 L12 **Port Louis** Mauritius
140 D3 **Port McArthur** *B* N Terr Aust
138 F7 **Port MacDonnell** S Australia
121 L8 **Port McNicoll** Ontario
139 L4 **Port Macquarie** New S Wales
8 B2 **Portmadog Wales**
122 F10 **Port Maitland** Nova Scotia
121 L10 **Port Maitland** Ontario
109 K9 **Port Mansfield** Texas
115 N6 **Port Manvers** Labrador
127 L2 **Port Maria** Jamaica
146 J3 **Port Martin** Antarctica
94 J6 **Port Matilda** Pennsylvania
113 G11 **Port Mayaca** Florida
122 H9 **Port Medway** Nova Scotia
117 M11 **Port Mellon** Br Col
122 H4 **Port Menier** Quebec
116 G8 **Port Moller** Alaska
117 M11 **Port Moody** Br Col
127 M3 **Port Morant** Jamaica
136 K3 **Port Moresby** Papua New Guinea
123 N7 **Port Morien** C Breton I, N Scotia
20 H3 **Port Mort** France
122 H10 **Port Mouton** Nova Scotia
141 F1 **Port Musgrave** *inlet* Queensland
15 C4 **Portnacroish** Scotland
12 B2 **Portnahaven** Scotland
109 O6 **Port Neches** Texas
138 D5 **Port Neill** S Australia
126 G3 **Port Nelson** Bahamas
101 N7 **Portneuf** Idaho
121 S5 **Portneuf, Parc** Quebec
122 C5 **Portneuf, R** Quebec
145 G4 **Port Nicholson** New Zealand
138 E6 **Port Noarlunga** S Australia
87 C11 **Port Nolloth** S Africa
95 M7 **Port Norris** New Jersey
115 N6 **Port-Nouveau Québec** Quebec
129 K4 **Pôrto** Brazil
16 B3 **Porto** Portugal
128 E5 **Pôrto Acre** Brazil
130 D7 **Pôrto Alegre** Mato Grosso Brazil
131 H3 **Pôrto Alegre** Rio Grande do Sul **Brazil**
87 B9 **Porto Alexandre** Angola
87 B8 **Porto Amboim** Angola
Porto Amelia *see* **Pemba** Mozambique
129 G6 **Porto Artur** Brazil
144 D7 **Portobello New Zealand**
13 E2 **Portobello** Scotland
130 E10 **Pôrto Belo** Brazil
116 L8 **Port O'Brian** Alaska
130 C9 **Pôrto Britânia** Brazil
43 C7 **Porto Cervo** Sardinia
109 L7 **Port O'Connor** Texas
16 B3 **Porto de Leixões** Portugal
129 H4 **Pôrto de Mos** Brazil
129 H6 **Pôrto dos Meinacos** Brazil
43 F11 **Porto Empedocle** Sicily
128 G7 **Pôrto Espiridião** Brazil
42 C6 **Portoferraio** Elba Italy
44 F3 **Portofino** Italy
12 D1 **Port of Menteith** Scotland
15 B2 **Port of Ness** Scotland
127 O2 **Port of Spain** Trinidad
45 M2 **Porto Garibaldi** Italy
129 H3 **Pôrto Grande** Brazil
42 E3 **Portogruaro** Italy
129 G7 **Pôrto Jofre** Brazil
102 D2 **Portola** California
29 J9 **Pörtom** Finland
45 L2 **Portomaggiore** Italy
44 D4 **Porto Maurizio** Italy
88 H9 **Porto Mocambo** Mozambique
129 G8 **Pôrto Murtinho** Brazil
129 J6 **Pôrto Nacional** Brazil
85 E7 **Porto Novo** Benin
113 G8 **Port Orange** Florida
117 M12 **Port Orchard** Washington
42 F5 **Porto Recanati** Italy
100 A7 **Port Orford** Oregon
133 G2 **Pôrto San José** Brazil
42 D6 **Porto San Stefano** Italy
85 A2 **Pôrto Santo** *isld* Madeira
129 H8 **Pôrto São José** Brazil
130 H5 **Pôrto Seguro** Brazil
45 M2 **Porto Tolle** Italy
43 B8 **Porto Torres** Sardinia
133 G3 **Pôrto União** Brazil
128 F5 **Pôrto Velho** Brazil
44 G3 **Portovenere** Italy
128 B4 **Portoviejo** Ecuador
12 C4 **Portpatrick** Scotland
140 B2 **Port Patterson** *inlet* N Terr Aust
144 A7 **Port Pegasus New Zealand**
121 M8 **Port Perry** Ontario
139 G7 **Port Phillip B** Victoria
138 E5 **Port Pirie** S Australia
114 H4 **Port Radium** N W Terr
8 A7 **Portreath** England
15 B3 **Portree** Scotland

62 Portreeve — Pyaozero, Oz

118 J8 **Portreeve** Sask
83 M8 **Port Refuge** Cocos Is Indian Oc
100 A1 **Port Renfrew** Br Col
123 T5 **Port Rexton** Nfld
102 A4 **Port Reyes** California
100 B1 **Port Roberts** Washington
144 D5 **Port Robinson** New Zealand
140 D2 **Port Roper** *inlet* N Terr Aust
120 K10 **Port Rowan** Ontario
127 L3 **Port Royal** Jamaica
112 G5 **Port Royal** S Carolina
95 K8 **Port Royal** Virginia
122 G9 **Port Royal Nat. Hist. Park** Ontario
14 E1 **Portrush** N Ireland
79 C7 **Port Said** Egypt
113 B8 **Port St. Joe** Florida
89 F8 **Port St Johns** S Africa
19 N18 **Port St. Louis** France
18 F8 **Port St. Marie** France
21 B7 **Port St. Père** France
14 D1 **Portsalon** Irish Rep
94 E3 **Port Sanilac** Michigan
102 D6 **Port San Luis** California
123 P3 **Port Saunders** Nfld
38 K8 **Pörtschach** Austria
89 G8 **Port Shepstone** S Africa
117 H8 **Port Simpson** Br Col
142 D4 **Port Smith** *B* W Australia
127 O7 **Portsmouth** Dominica
9 E6 **Portsmouth** England
99 L8 **Portsmouth** Iowa
112 L2 **Portsmouth** N Carolina
95 R3 **Portsmouth** New Hampshire
94 E8 **Portsmouth** Ohio
121 O8 **Portsmouth** Ontario
95 Q5 **Portsmouth** Rhode I
95 L10 **Portsmouth** Virginia
12 C1 **Portsonachan** Scotland
15 F3 **Portsoy** Scotland
120 J10 **Port Stanley** Ontario
139 K5 **Port Stephens** New S Wales
14 E1 **Port Stewart** N Ireland
141 G2 **Port Stewart** *inlet* Queensland
86 G2 **Port Sudan** Sudan
8 C4 **Port Talbot** Wales
71 F4 **Port Tambang** Philippines
79 C9 **Port Taufiq** Egypt
127 O2 **Port Tembladora** Trinidad
29 M3 **Porttipahdan tekojärvi** *L* Finland
114 G8 **Port Tofino** Br Col
117 M11 **Port Townsend** Washington
16 B7 **Portugal** *rep*
83 J9 **Portugal B** Sri Lanka
123 U6 **Portugal Cove** Nfld
17 F1 **Portugalete** Spain
128 E2 **Portuguesa** *state* Venezuela
Portuguese Guinea *see* **Guinea-Bissau** *rep*
14 C3 **Portumna** Irish Rep
123 T5 **Port Union** Nfld
18 H10 **Port Vendres** France
102 F8 **Port Vicente** California
88 D1 **Port Victoria** Kenya
94 J4 **Portville** New York
138 E5 **Port Vincent** S Australia
52 D1 **Port Vladimir** U.S.S.R.
138 E5 **Port Wakefield** S Australia
142 F2 **Port Warrender** *inlet* W Australia
99 T6 **Port Washington** Wisconsin
142 B5 **Port Weld** *B* W Australia
116 N6 **Port Wells** *inlet* Alaska
112 F5 **Port Wentworth** Georgia
12 D4 **Port William** Scotland
122 H8 **Port Williams** Nova Scotia
99 P3 **Port Wing** Wisconsin
107 P6 **Porum** Oklahoma
127 K2 **Porus** Jamaica
133 C8 **Porvenir** Chile
108 C5 **Porvenir** Texas
52 D2 **Por'ya Guba** U.S.S.R.
36 C2 **Porz** W Germany
16 E5 **Porzuna** Spain
16 E5 **Porzuna, Sa. de** *mts* Spain
43 C8 **Posada** *R* Sardinia
133 F3 **Posadas** Argentina
16 D7 **Posadas** Spain
41 M5 **Poschiavo** Switzerland
141 H7 **Poseidon** Queensland
94 D1 **Posen** Michigan
110 J3 **Poseyville** Indiana
52 E5 **Poshekhonye** U.S.S.R.
119 O1 **Poshkokagan L** Ontario
47 F5 **Posídhion, Ákr** *C* Greece
41 O6 **Posina** *R* Italy
37 O5 **Pösing** W Germany
29 N5 **Posio** Finland
45 Q8 **Positano** Italy
70 G5 **Poso** Sulawesi
78 J1 **Posof** Turkey
129 J6 **Posse** Brazil
37 N3 **Posseck** E Germany
146 K6 **Possession I** Antarctica
37 M2 **Pössneck** E Germany
38 M8 **Possruck** Yugoslavia
109 J3 **Possum Kingdom L** Texas
100 E5 **Post** Oregon
37 N6 **Postau** W Germany
37 L5 **Postbauer-Heng** W Germany
8 C6 **Postbridge** England
115 M6 **Poste-de-la-Baleine** Quebec
68 H6 **Poste Deshayes** Cambodia
83 M12 **Poste, R du** Mauritius
85 E4 **Poste Weygand** Algeria
100 J2 **Post Falls** Idaho
114 J7 **Posthern** Sask
71 J8 **Postiljon Pulau** *isld* Indonesia
89 C7 **Postmasburg** S Africa
129 H6 **Pôsto Alto Manissaua** Brazil
128 C4 **Posto Bobonazo** Peru
42 F3 **Postojna** Yugoslavia
99 P6 **Postville** Iowa
42 H5 **Posušje** Yugoslavia
71 K9 **Pota** Indonesia
124 D4 **Pótam** Mexico
47 G3 **Potamoí** Greece
46 F8 **Potamós** Greece
50 H2 **Potapovo** U.S.S.R.
128 G2 **Potaro** *R* Guyana
89 E6 **Potchefstroom** S Africa
48 J6 **Potcoava** Romania
130 H5 **Poté** Brazil
107 Q6 **Poteau** Oklahoma
107 Q7 **Poteau** *R* Okla/Ark
109 J6 **Poteet** Texas
47 G1 **Potelu Lacul** *L* Romania
130 J8 **Potengi** *R* Brazil
43 G8 **Potenza** Italy
144 A7 **Poteriteri, L** New Zealand
16 D1 **Potes** Spain
89 F5 **Potgietersrus** S Africa
109 J6 **Poth** Texas
100 F2 **Potholes Res** Washington
129 K5 **Poti** *R* Brazil
20 E4 **Potigny** France
85 G6 **Potiskum** Nigeria
71 K9 **Potjo Mandasawu** *mt* Indonesia
100 J3 **Potlatch** Idaho
89 B8 **Potloer** *mt* S Africa
48 K6 **Potlogi** Romania
101 M3 **Potomac** Montana
94 J7 **Potomac S. Branch** *R* W Virginia
133 D1 **Potosí** Bolivia
110 F4 **Potosi** Missouri
133 D2 **Potosí** *dep* Bolivia
103 J6 **Potosi Mt** Nevada
71 F5 **Pototan** Panay Philippines
133 D3 **Potrerillos** Chile
131 B2 **Potro, Cerro de** *peak* Chile
33 S8 **Potsdam** E Germany
95 N2 **Potsdam** New York
33 R7 **Potsdam** *reg* E Germany
141 G3 **Pottalah Cr** Queensland
37 L4 **Pottenstein** W Germany
98 C8 **Potter** Nebraska
120 K4 **Potter** Ontario
9 E5 **Potterne** England
9 F4 **Potter's Bar** England
102 A2 **Potter Valley** California
94 C4 **Potterville** Michigan
37 L6 **Pottmes** W Germany
9 F3 **Potton** England
109 L2 **Pottsboro** Texas
111 G7 **Potts Camp** Mississippi
95 M6 **Pottstown** Pennsylvania
95 L6 **Pottsville** Pennsylvania
109 J4 **Pottsville** Texas
83 L11 **Pottuvil** Sri Lanka
107 N4 **Potwin** Kansas
21 C6 **Pouancé** France
68 F3 **Pou Bia** *mt* Laos
117 N8 **Pouce Coupé** Br Col
123 U6 **Pouch Cove** Nfld
95 O5 **Poughkeepsie** New York
18 H5 **Pougues les Eaux** France
21 H7 **Pouillé** France
18 E9 **Pouillon** France
18 J5 **Pouilly en Auxois** France
21 I7 **Poulaines** France
122 B5 **Poulin de Courval, L** Quebec
68 J5 **Poulo Canton, Is de** Vietnam
69 G8 **Poulo Dama, Iles** Vietnam
68 J6 **Poulo Gambir, Cu Lao** *isld* Vietnam
95 O3 **Poultney** Vermont
13 E6 **Poulton-le-Fylde** England
68 E4 **Pou Miang** *mt* Thailand
99 S4 **Pound** Wisconsin
9 F5 **Pound Hill** England
19 P18 **Pourcieux** France
145 F4 **Pourerere** New Zealand
145 G3 **Pourewa I** New Zealand
146 F13 **Pourquoi Pas I** Antarctica
40 E6 **Pourri, Mont** France
20 G2 **Pourville** France
68 F3 **Pou San** *mt* Laos
68 F3 **Pou Sao** *mt* Laos
68 H5 **Pou Set** *mt* Laos
129 G6 **Pouso Alegre** Mato Grosso Brazil
130 F8 **Pouso Alegre** Minas Gerais Brazil
29 O6 **Poussu** Finland
144 A7 **Poutama I** New Zealand
145 E2 **Pouto** New Zealand
121 Q3 **Poutrincourt, L** Quebec
40 D1 **Pouxeux** France
21 D8 **Pouzauges** France
48 E1 **Pov Bystrica** Czechoslovakia
52 D3 **Povenets** U.S.S.R.
145 F3 **Poverty Bay** New Zealand
9 F5 **Povey Cross** England
45 J2 **Poviglio** Italy
48 F6 **Povlen** *mt* Yugoslavia
16 B3 **Póvoa de Varzim** Portugal
65 J3 **Povorotnyy, Mys** *C* U.S.S.R.
115 M5 **Povungnituk** Quebec
121 L6 **Powassan** Ontario
101 T5 **Powder** *R* Wyo/Mont
106 C3 **Powderhorn** Colorado
100 H5 **Powder R** Oregon
98 A4 **Powderville** Montana
113 K11 **Powel Cay** *isld* Bahamas
103 K7 **Powell** Arizona
98 E5 **Powell** S Dakota
99 R3 **Powell** Wisconsin
101 R5 **Powell** Wyoming
139 G2 **Powell** *R* Queensland
94 D10 **Powell** *R* Tenn/Virg
100 D5 **Powell Butte** Oregon
140 C4 **Powell Creek** N Terr **Aust**
146 C14 **Powell I** S Orkney Is
103 O4 **Powell, L** Ariz/Utah
106 D2 **Powell, Mt** Colorado
102 F3 **Powell Mt** Nevada
126 F2 **Powell Pt** Eleuthera Bahamas
117 L10 **Powell River** Br Col
94 F8 **Powellton** W Virginia
101 O2 **Power** Montana
99 T4 **Powers** Michigan
100 A7 **Powers** Oregon
98 D1 **Powers L** N Dakota
110 C1 **Powersville** Missouri
111 C10 **Powhatan** Louisiana
94 K9 **Powhatan** Virginia
107 P2 **Powhattan** Kansas
8 D3 **Powick** England
141 H5 **Powlathanga** Queensland
95 O4 **Pownal** Vermont
8 C3 **Powys** *co* Wales
130 C5 **Poxoreu** *R* Brazil
67 E2 **Poyang Hu** *L* China
111 D7 **Poyen** Arkansas
99 S5 **Poygan, L** Wisconsin
31 K7 **Poysdorf** Austria
124 C5 **Poza Grande** Mexico
78 E3 **Pozanti** Turkey
48 G6 **Požarevac** Yugoslavia
125 L7 **Poza Rica** Mexico
59 K2 **Pozharskoye** U.S.S.R.
52 J5 **Pozhva** U.S.S.R.
22 D3 **Pozières** France
140 D5 **Pozieres,Mt** N Terr **Aust**
31 K3 **Poznań** Poland
102 D6 **Pozo** California
17 F7 **Pozo Alcón** Spain
133 D2 **Pozo Almonte** Chile
16 D6 **Pozoblanco** Spain
103 J9 **Pozo Cenizo** Mexico
17 F6 **Pozohondo** Spain
103 J9 **Pozo Salado** Mexico
103 N10 **Pozo Verde** Mexico
52 H4 **Poztykeros** U.S.S.R.
133 D2 **Pozuelos, L. de** Argentina
45 J1 **Pozzolengo** Italy
45 L1 **Pozzonuovo** Italy
45 Q8 **Pozzuoli** Italy
68 F2 **P. Phac Mo** *mt* Vietnam
85 D7 **Pra** *R* Ghana
31 L2 **Prabuty** Poland
45 J3 **Pracchia** Italy
68 D7 **Pracham Hiang, Laem** Thailand
30 H7 **Prachatice** Czechoslovakia
68 E5 **Prachin Buri** Thailand
68 D7 **Prachuap Khiri Khan** Thailand
16 C1 **Pradairo** Spain
31 K5 **Praděd** *mt* Czechoslovakia
18 G10 **Prades** France
70 P9 **Pradjekan** Java
28 E2 **Præstbro** Denmark
28 J6 **Præsto** Denmark
Præstø *co see* **Storstrøm and Roskilde** *counties*
38 N9 **Pragersk** Yugoslavia
38 F7 **Prägraten** Austria
Prague *see* **Praha**
107 O6 **Prague** Oklahoma
31 H5 **Praha** Czechoslovakia
21 E9 **Prahecq** France
48 K5 **Prahova** Romania
48 H6 **Prahova** Yugoslavia
48 K6 **Prahova** *R* Romania
133 G4 **Praia Albardão** *beach* Brazil
48 J4 **Praid** Romania
129 H4 **Prainha** Brazil
122 B3 **Praires, L. des** Quebec
109 K6 **Prairia Lea** Texas
100 K6 **Prairie** Idaho
141 G5 **Prairie** Queensland
110 F1 **Prairie City** Illinois
100 G5 **Prairie City** Oregon
107 K2 **Prairie Dog Cr** Kansas
108 F1 **Prairie Dog Town Fork** *R* Texas
99 P6 **Prairie du Chien** Wisconsin
99 R6 **Prairie du Sac** Wisconsin
110 B6 **Prairie Grove** Arkansas
109 L4 **Prairie Hill** Texas
119 P6 **Prairie River** Sask
110 J2 **Prairieton** Indiana
107 L2 **Prairie View** Kansas
111 F11 **Prairieville** Louisiana
94 E9 **Praise** Kentucky
70 Q10 **Praja** Indonesia
68 F5 **Prakhon Chai** Thailand
40 E7 **Pralognan** France
42 E2 **Pramaggiore** *mt* Italy
70 N9 **Prambanan** Java
37 O3 **Prameny** Czechoslovakia
69 D8 **Pram, Khao** *mt* Thailand
68 D6 **Pran** *R* Thailand
68 D6 **Pran Buri** Thailand
38 K7 **Prankerhöhe** *mt* Austria
69 D11 **Prapat** Sumatra
40 B2 **Praslay** France
83 J12 **Praslin** *isld* Seychelles
47 J9 **Prasonísi, Akr** *C* Rhodes Greece
31 L4 **Praszka** Poland
129 J7 **Prata** *R* Brazil
Pratas *isld see* **Dongsha Qundao**
33 R9 **Pratau** E Germany
17 J3 **Prat de Llobregat** Spain
41 L4 **Prätigau** *V* Switzerland
45 K4 **Prato** Italy
45 R8 **Prátola Serra** Italy
45 L4 **Pratomagno** Italy
42 D5 **Pratomagno** *mt* Italy
45 H3 **Prato, Mt** Italy
45 L4 **Pratovecchio** Italy
18 G10 **Prats-de-Mollo** France
107 M4 **Pratt** Kansas
119 T9 **Pratt** Manitoba
95 N4 **Prattsville** New York
111 K9 **Prattville** Alabama
40 B2 **Prauthoy** France
31 N1 **Pravdinsk** U.S.S.R.
54 J1 **Pravdinskiy** U.S.S.R.
70 M9 **Prav, G** *mt* Java
16 C1 **Pravia** Spain
8 C7 **Prawle Pt** England
21 H7 **Préaux** France
37 O3 **Přebuz** Czechoslovakia
20 C4 **Precey** France
52 D6 **Prechistoye** U.S.S.R.
20 K3 **Précy-sur-Oise** France
45 L3 **Predappio** Italy
42 D2 **Predazzo** Italy
37 O5 **Predigtstuhl** *mt* W Germany
38 M8 **Preding** Austria
38 J7 **Predlitz** Austria
38 F7 **Predoi** Italy
44 E2 **Predosa** Italy
51 O2 **Predporozhnyy** U.S.S.R.
119 P7 **Preeceville** Sask
20 E5 **Pré-en-Pail** France
33 M4 **Preetz** W Germany
31 M1 **Pregolya** *R* U.S.S.R.
127 J10 **Pregonero** Venezuela
18 E8 **Preignac** France
52 C6 **Preiļi** U.S.S.R.
121 M4 **Preissac** Quebec
68 G6 **Prek Kak** Cambodia
68 H6 **Prek Preas** *R* Cambodia
68 G7 **Prek Sandek** Cambodia
68 F7 **Prek Taley** *R* Cambodia
143 F9 **Premier Downs** W Australia
8 B3 **Pren-gwyn** Wales
46 D4 **Prenjas** Albania
33 T6 **Prenzlau** E Germany
144 A7 **Preservation Inlet** New Zealand
130 D8 **Presidente Prudente** Brazil
108 C6 **Presidio** Texas
13 F6 **Preston** England
101 O7 **Preston** Idaho
95 M8 **Preston** Maryland
99 O6 **Preston** Minnesota
110 C4 **Preston** Missouri
103 J3 **Preston** Nevada
107 P6 **Preston** Oklahoma
9 E5 **Preston Candover** England
109 O9 **Preston Hollow** Texas
13 F2 **Prestonpans** Scotland
94 E9 **Prestonsburg** Kentucky
13 F6 **Prestwich** England
12 D3 **Prestwick** Scotland
129 K6 **Preto** *R* Bahia **Brazil**
129 J7 **Prêto** *R* Minas Gerais **Brazil**
128 F4 **Prêto do Igapó Açu** *R* Brazil
89 F5 **Pretoria** S Africa
33 R9 **Prettin** E Germany
95 L7 **Prettyboy Res** Maryland
107 M4 **Pretty Prairie** Kansas
33 O7 **Pretzier** E Germany
33 R9 **Pretzsch** E Germany
21 G8 **Preuilly-sur-Claise** France
38 L8 **Prevalje** Yugoslavia
46 D6 **Préveza** Greece
106 B6 **Prewitt** New Mexico
106 G1 **Prewitt Res** Colorado
20 H4 **Prey** France
68 G7 **Prey Lovea** Cambodia
68 G7 **Prey Veng** Cambodia
45 P5 **Prezza** Italy
54 H9 **Priazovskaya Vozvyshenost'** *uplands* U.S.S.R.
116 D8 **Pribilof Is** Bering Sea
30 H6 **Příbram** Czechoslovakia
95 M7 **Price** Maryland
98 F2 **Price** N Dakota
122 D5 **Price** Quebec
103 O2 **Price** Utah
103 O2 **Price** *R* Utah
68 A6 **Price, C** Andaman Is
106 B1 **Price Creek** Colorado
117 J9 **Price I** Br Col
111 H11 **Prichard** Alabama
100 K2 **Prichard** Idaho
54 E9 **Prichernomorskaya Nizmennost'** *lowland* U.S.S.R.
37 J4 **Prichsenstadt** W Germany
127 P5 **Prickly Pt** Grenada
109 J4 **Priddy** Texas
54 D7 **Pridneprovskaya Nizmennost'** *lowland* U.S.S.R.
54 C8 **Pridneprovskaya Vozvyshennost'** *uplands* U.S.S.R.
17 F4 **Priego** Spain
16 E7 **Priego de C** Spain
27 M15 **Priekule** Latvia U.S.S.R.
27 M16 **Priekulė** Lithuania U.S.S.R.
33 Q5 **Priemerburg** E Germany
89 C7 **Prieska** S Africa
37 M1 **Priessnitz** E Germany
33 T10 **Priestewitz** E Germany
100 J1 **Priest L** Idaho
127 M2 **Priestman's River** Jamaica
100 F3 **Priest Rapids** Washington
100 J1 **Priest River** Idaho
117 P11 **Priest River** Idaho
31 L7 **Prievidza** Czechoslovakia
33 Q6 **Prignitz** *reg* E Germany
56 C4 **Priiskovyy** U.S.S.R.
42 H4 **Prijedor** Yugoslavia
53 G9 **Prikaspiyskaya Nizmennost** *lowlands* U.S.S.R.
46 E3 **Prilep** Yugoslavia
54 D6 **Priluki** U.S.S.R.
40 B7 **Primarette** France
118 H6 **Primate** Sask
37 O4 **Přimda** Czechoslovakia
131 D3 **Primero, R** Argentina
139 J8 **Prime Seal I** Tasmania
99 L6 **Primghar** Iowa
52 C4 **Primorsk** U.S.S.R.
59 K3 **Primorskiy** U.S.S.R.
56 F5 **Primorskiy Khrebet** *mts* U.S.S.R.
59 K2 **Primorskiy Kray** *reg* U.S.S.R.
47 J2 **Primorsko** Bulgaria
54 J9 **Primorskoye** U.S.S.R.
122 J7 **Prim, Pt** Pr Edward I
117 F5 **Primrose** *R* Br Col/Yukon Terr
118 H4 **Primrose L** Sask
36 B5 **Prims** *R* W Germany
36 C4 **Primstal** W Germany
118 J6 **Prince** Sask
89 C9 **Prince Albert** S Africa
119 M5 **Prince Albert** Sask
118 L5 **Prince Albert Nat. Park** Sask
114 H3 **Prince Albert Pen** N W Terr
114 G3 **Prince Alfred, C** N W Terr
115 M4 **Prince Charles I** N W Terr
146 C5 **Prince Charles Mts** Antarctica
146 D15 **Prince Charles Str** S Shetland Is
121 O9 **Prince Edward B** Ontario
90 M14 **Prince Edward I** Indian Oc
115 N8 **Prince Edward I** *prov* Canada
122 J7 **Prince Edward I. Nat. Park** Canada
95 L8 **Prince Frederick** Maryland
142 F3 **Prince Frederick Harb** W Australia
117 M9 **Prince George** Br Col
114 J2 **Prince Gustaf Adolf Sea** N W Terr
116 C4 **Prince of Wales, C** Alaska
117 G8 **Prince of Wales I** Alaska
115 J3 **Prince of Wales I** N W Terr
141 F1 **Prince of Wales I** Queensland
114 H3 **Prince of Wales Str** N W Terr
146 G8 **Prince Olav Mts** Antarctica
114 H2 **Prince Patrick I** N W Terr
115 K3 **Prince Regent Inlet** N W Terr
142 F3 **Prince Regent R** W Australia
117 H8 **Prince Rupert** Br Col
130 H9 **Princesa Isabel** Brazil
Princes Is *see* **Kızıl Adalar**
Princes Lake Ontario *see* **Wallace**
9 F4 **Princes Risborough** England
95 M8 **Princess Anne** Maryland
141 G2 **Princess Charlotte B** Queensland
146 D4 **Princess Elizabeth Land** Antarctica
142 F3 **Princess May Ra** W Australia
144 A6 **Princess Mts** New Zealand
143 D7 **Princess Ra** W Australia
117 J9 **Princess Royal I** Br Col
127 O3 **Prince's Town** Trinidad
9 E3 **Princethorpe** England
117 N11 **Princeton** Br Col
102 B2 **Princeton** California
99 R8 **Princeton** Illinois
110 J3 **Princeton** Indiana
110 J4 **Princeton** Kentucky
95 U1 **Princeton** Maine
99 T3 **Princeton** Michigan
99 N4 **Princeton** Minnesota
99 N9 **Princeton** Missouri
112 J2 **Princeton** N Carolina
95 N6 **Princeton** New Jersey
99 R6 **Princeton** Wisconsin
94 F9 **Princeton** W Virginia
8 C6 **Princetown** England
99 R9 **Princeville** Illinois
121 T6 **Princeville** Quebec
116 O6 **Prince William Sound** Alaska
141 J6 **Princhester** Queensland
86 A5 **Príncipe** *isld* G of Guinea
128 F6 **Principe da Beira** Brazil
100 E5 **Prineville** Oregon
98 C6 **Pringle** S Dakota
108 C8 **Pringle** Texas
19 Q13 **Pringy** France
115 P5 **Prins Christians Sund** Greenland
25 C5 **Prinsenhage** Netherlands
68 C6 **Prinsep I** Burma
146 A9 **Prinsesse Astrid Kyst** Antarctica
146 A8 **Prinsesse Ragnhild Kyst** Antarctica
146 A7 **Prins Harald Kyst** Antarctica
50 A1 **Prins Karls Forland** Spitzbergen
123 L4 **Prinsta B** Anticosti I, Quebec
125 N3 **Prinzapolca** Nicaragua
54 L2 **Priokskiy** U.S.S.R.
16 B1 **Prior, C** Spain
52 D4 **Priozersk** U.S.S.R.
52 K3 **Pripolyarnyy Ural** *mts* U.S.S.R.
53 C8 **Pripyat** *R* U.S.S.R.
29 P3 **Prirechnyy** U.S.S.R.
37 P3 **Přísečnice** Czechoslovakia
48 J3 **Prislop Pass** Romania
46 E2 **Priština** Yugoslavia
106 H4 **Pritchett** Colorado
33 Q8 **Pritzerbe** E Germany
33 O6 **Pritzier** E Germany
33 Q6 **Pritzwalk** E Germany
19 N15 **Privas** France
45 O7 **Priverno** Italy
45 O6 **Privernum** Italy
42 F3 **Privka** Yugoslavia
52 F6 **Privolzhsk** U.S.S.R.
53 G7 **Privolzhskaya Vozvyshennost** *uplands* U.S.S.R.
46 D2 **Prizren** Yugoslavia
43 E11 **Prizzi** Sicily
70 O9 **Probolinggo** Java
37 L2 **Probstzella** E Germany
8 B7 **Probus** England
31 J4 **Prochowice** Poland
45 Q8 **Procida** Italy
43 F8 **Procida** *isld* Italy
106 H1 **Proctor** Colorado
109 J4 **Proctor** Texas
95 O3 **Proctor** Vermont
109 J3 **Proctor Res** Texas
95 P3 **Proctorsville** Vermont
16 B5 **Proènca a Nova** Portugal
37 N1 **Profen** E Germany
22 H3 **Profondeville** Belgium
125 L2 **Progreso** Honduras
125 P7 **Progreso** Mexico
106 E7 **Progresso** New Mexico
56 B6 **Prokhladnoye** U.S.S.R.
46 D2 **Prokletije** Yugoslavia
56 C4 **Prokop'yevsk** U.S.S.R.
46 E1 **Prokuplje** Yugoslavia
52 D5 **Proletariy** U.S.S.R.
54 K8 **Proletarsk** U.S.S.R.
54 G6 **Proletarskiy** U.S.S.R.
54 J1 **Proletarskiy** U.S.S.R.
59 N2 **Proliv Frizi** *str* U.S.S.R.
37 K4 **Prolsdorf** W Germany
68 B3 **Prome** Burma
99 N9 **Promise City** Iowa
101 N8 **Promontory** Utah
56 C3 **Promyshlennaya** U.S.S.R.
52 F5 **Pronino** U.S.S.R.
100 G9 **Pronto** Nevada
54 M2 **Pronya** *R* U.S.S.R.
117 M6 **Prophet River** Br Col
99 R8 **Prophetstown** Illinois
130 H11 **Propriá** Brazil
46 D3 **Prosek** Albania
33 S10 **Prösen** E Germany
141 J5 **Proserpine** Queensland
33 Q9 **Prosigk** E Germany
31 K3 **Prosna** *R* Poland
52 H5 **Prosnitsa** U.S.S.R.
47 F3 **Prosotsáni** Greece
95 M3 **Prospect** New York
94 D6 **Prospect** Ohio
100 C7 **Prospect** Oregon
94 G6 **Prospect** Pennsylvania
127 M3 **Prospect Pt** Jamaica
100 A6 **Prosper** Oregon
112 F3 **Prosperity** S Carolina
98 H9 **Prosser** Nebraska
100 F3 **Prosser** Washington
48 D1 **Prostějov** Czechoslovakia
141 K7 **Proston** Queensland
52 H2 **Prosunduy** U.S.S.R.
54 H8 **Prosyanaya** U.S.S.R.
31 M5 **Proszowice** Poland
107 L4 **Protection** Kansas
99 O6 **Protivin** Iowa
54 J2 **Protva** *R* U.S.S.R.
33 T7 **Prötzel** E Germany
47 J1 **Provadiya** Bulgaria
115 O3 **Prøven** Greenland
111 C10 **Provencal** Louisiana
19 O17 **Provence** *prov* France
36 C7 **Provenchères-sur-Fave** France
127 P5 **Providence** Grenada
110 J4 **Providence** Kentucky
112 J1 **Providence** N Carolina
95 Q5 **Providence** Rhode I
101 O8 **Providence** Utah
120 H7 **Providence Bay** Ontario
116 J8 **Providence, C** Alaska
144 A7 **Providence, C** New Zealand
87 J9 **Providence I** Br Indian Oc Terr
103 J7 **Providence Mts** California
127 H4 **Providenciales** *isld* Turks & Caicos Is
128 F6 **Providencia, Sa. da** *mts* Brazil
116 A4 **Provideniya** U.S.S.R.
141 G2 **Providential Chan** Gt Barrier Reef **Aust**
95 R4 **Provincetown** Massachusetts
18 H4 **Provins** France
98 C6 **Provo** S Dakota
103 N1 **Provo** Utah
118 G6 **Provost** Alberta
22 D4 **Proyart** France
42 H5 **Prozor** Yugoslavia
52 H4 **Prub** *R* U.S.S.R.
130 E9 **Prudentópolis** Brazil
94 C2 **Prudenville** Michigan
13 G4 **Prudhoe** England
116 O1 **Prudhoe Bay** Alaska
141 J5 **Prudhoe I** Queensland
115 N2 **Prudhoe Land** Greenland
119 M6 **Prud'homme** Sask
31 K5 **Prudnik** Poland
54 H6 **Prudyanka** U.S.S.R.
36 B3 **Prüm** W Germany
21 G6 **Prunay** France
45 J3 **Prunetta** Italy
19 Q15 **Prunières** France
21 I7 **Pruniers** Cher France
21 J8 **Pruniers** Indre France
31 K2 **Pruszcz** Poland
31 M3 **Pruszków** Poland
48 L4 **Prut** *R* U.S.S.R.
48 L3 **Prutul** *R* Romania
41 N3 **Prutz** Austria
52 D4 **Pryazha** U.S.S.R.
31 L6 **Prýdek Mistek** Czechoslovakia
146 C4 **Prydz B** Antarctica
101 R4 **Pryor** Montana
107 P5 **Pryor** Oklahoma
31 M2 **Przasnysz** Poland
31 K2 **Przechlewo** Poland
31 M4 **Przedbórz** Poland
31 O6 **Przemyśl** Poland
31 N5 **Przeworsk** Poland
31 H4 **Przewóz** Poland
57 J4 **Przheval'sk** U.S.S.R.
31 M4 **Przysucha** Poland
47 F6 **Psakhná** Greece
47 H6 **Psará** *isld* Greece
31 K4 **Psie Pole** Poland
47 H9 **Psíra** *isld* Greece
52 C5 **Pskov** U.S.S.R.
52 C5 **Pskovskoye, Ozero** *L* U.S.S.R.
42 H3 **Psunj** *mt* Yugoslavia
31 L1 **Pszczółki** Poland
31 L6 **Pszczyna** Poland
53 C7 **Ptich'** *R* U.S.S.R.
46 E4 **Ptolemaïs** Greece
38 N9 **Ptuj** Yugoslavia
71 H5 **Puah** *isld* Sulawesi
135 U4 **Puako** Hawaiian Is
116 K8 **Puale B** Alaska
133 E5 **Puán** Argentina
67 C5 **Pubei** China
122 G10 **Pubnico** Nova Scotia
128 C5 **Pucacaca** Peru
128 D5 **Pucallpa** Peru
20 J3 **Puchay** France
38 N6 **Puchberg** Austria
65 A7 **Pucheng** China
65 C7 **Pucheng** China
67 F3 **Pucheng** China
52 F6 **Puchezh** U.S.S.R.
31 L6 **Puchov** Czechoslovakia
71 E5 **Pucio Pt** Panay Philippines
31 L1 **Puck** Poland
99 R6 **Puckaway L** Wisconsin
9 G4 **Puckeridge** England
111 G9 **Puckett** Mississippi
143 B7 **Puckford,Mt** W Australia
29 M6 **Pudasjärvi** Finland
8 D6 **Puddletown** England
52 H5 **Pudem** U.S.S.R.
67 B3 **Puding** China
123 Q5 **Pudops L** Nfld
52 E4 **Pudozh** U.S.S.R.
52 E4 **Pudozhgora** U.S.S.R.
13 G6 **Pudsey** England
125 K8 **Puebla** Mexico
16 D5 **Puebla de Alcocer** Spain
17 F7 **Puebla de Don Fadrique** Spain
16 D5 **Puebla de Don Rodrigo** Spain
16 C2 **Puebla de Sanabria** Spain
16 C2 **Puebla de Trives** Spain
106 F3 **Pueblo** Colorado
106 C5 **Pueblo Bonito** New Mexico
133 C3 **Pueblo Hundido** Chile
100 G7 **Pueblo Mts** Oregon
124 G6 **Pueblo Nuevo** Mexico
125 N9 **Pueblo Viejo** Mexico
125 L6 **Pueblo Viejo, L. de** Mexico
133 D5 **Puelches** Argentina
133 D5 **Puelén** Argentina
16 B2 **Puenteareas** Spain
16 B2 **Puente Caldelas** Spain
16 D7 **Puente Genil** Spain
103 P7 **Puerco** *R* Arizona
106 C6 **Puerco, R** New Mexico
128 C2 **Puerta Mutis** Colombia
133 C7 **Puerto Aisén** Chile
125 N5 **Puerto Armuelles** Panama
128 C3 **Puerto Asis** Colombia
128 E2 **Puerto Ayacucho** Venezuela
125 P10 **Puerto Barrios** Guatemala
128 D6 **Puerto Bermúdez** Peru
128 D2 **Puerto Berrio** Colombia
133 C7 **Puerto Bertrand** Chile
128 C6 **Puerto Caballas** Peru
128 E1 **Puerto Cabello** Venezuela
125 N2 **Puerto Cabezas** Nicaragua
Puerto Capaz Morocco *see* **El Jebha**
128 E2 **Puerto Carreño** Colombia
130 B8 **Puerto Casado** Paraguay
128 C5 **Puerto Chicama** Peru
124 G3 **Puerto Chilicote** Mexico
133 C6 **Puerto Cisnes** Chile
133 D8 **Puerto Coig** Argentina
128 D1 **Puerto Colombia** Colombia
125 Q10 **Puerto Cortés** Honduras
128 E1 **Puerto Cumarebo** Venezuela
127 J8 **Puerto Estrella** Colombia
128 C5 **Puerto Eten** Peru
133 C5 **Puerto Fuy** Chile
128 F7 **Puerto Grether** Bolivia
133 D8 **Puerto Harberton** Argentina
128 E6 **Puerto Heath** Bolivia
128 D3 **Puerto Huitoto** Colombia
133 E5 **Puerto Ingeniero White** Argentina
127 M9 **Puerto La Cruz** Venezuela
128 D4 **Puerto Leguizamo** Colombia
125 N2 **Puerto Lempira** Honduras
16 E6 **Puertollano** Spain
128 D7 **Puerto Lomas** Peru
127 J9 **Puerto López** Colombia
17 F7 **Puerto Lumbreras** Spain
133 D6 **Puerto Madryn** Argentina
128 E6 **Puerto Maldonado** Peru
126 F4 **Puerto Manatí** Cuba
128 D4 **Puerto Miraña** Colombia
133 C6 **Puerto Montt** Chile
133 C8 **Puerto Natales** Chile
128 E2 **Puerto Nuevo** Colombia
133 F3 **Puerto Ocampo** Argentina
128 F2 **Puerto Ordaz** Venezuela
126 F4 **Puerto Padre** Cuba
133 C2 **Puerto Patillos** Chile
124 C2 **Puerto Penasco** Mexico
133 F2 **Puerto Pinasco** Paraguay
133 E6 **Puerto Pirámides** Argentina
128 F1 **Puerto Piritu** Venezuela
127 J5 **Puerto Plata** Dom Rep
128 D5 **Puerto Portillo** Peru
71 D6 **Puerto Princesa** Palawan Philippines
125 M5 **Puerto Quepos** Costa Rica
128 E6 **Puerto Rico** Bolivia
113 J7 **Puerto Rico** *terr* Caribbean
127 L5 **Puerto Rico Trench** Caribbean
126 G4 **Puerto Samá** Cuba
130 B8 **Puerto Sastre** Paraguay
128 E6 **Puerto Siles** Bolivia
130 C9 **Puerto Strossner** Paraguay
130 B6 **Puerto Suárez** Bolivia
124 G7 **Puerto Vallarta** Mexico
133 C6 **Puerto Varas** Chile
128 F7 **Puerto Velarde** Bolivia
128 D5 **Puerto Victoria** Peru
128 D2 **Puerto Villamizar** Colombia
133 D7 **Puerto Visser** Argentina
128 D2 **Puerto Wilches** Colombia
133 C7 **Pueyrredón, L** Chile/Arg
25 F7 **Puffendorf** W Germany
124 G7 **Puga** Mexico
52 H6 **Pugachevo** U.S.S.R.
74 E4 **Pugal** India
88 G10 **Puga Puga** *isld* Mozambique
70 O10 **Puger** Java
100 C2 **Puget Sound** Washington
19 P13 **Pugieu** France
43 G8 **Puglia** *prov* Italy
71 K9 **Pugubengo** Flores Indonesia
70 K8 **Pugung, G** *mt* Sumatra
122 J8 **Pugwash** Nova Scotia
145 F3 **Puha** New Zealand
135 O1 **Puhi** Hawaiian Is
145 E2 **Puhoi** New Zealand
48 H5 **Pui** Romania
48 L4 **Puieşti** Romania
17 J2 **Puigcerda** Spain
71 G7 **Pujada B** Mindanao Philippines
65 G4 **Pujan Res** N Korea
19 N16 **Pujaut** France
67 A1 **Pujiang** China
67 F2 **Pujiang** China
119 Q3 **Pukatawagan** Manitoba
46 D2 **Pukë** Albania
145 G2 **Pukeamaru** *mt* New Zealand
145 E3 **Pukearuhe** New Zealand
145 F3 **Pukehou** New Zealand
145 E2 **Pukekawa** New Zealand
145 E2 **Pukekohe** New Zealand
144 C5 **Pukekura** New Zealand
145 E2 **Pukemiro** New Zealand
145 D1 **Pukenui** New Zealand
145 F3 **Pukeokahu** New Zealand
144 C6 **Pukerangi** New Zealand
144 B7 **Pukerau** New Zealand
145 E3 **Pukeroa** New Zealand
145 G3 **Puketawai** New Zealand
144 D5 **Puketeraki Range** New Zealand
145 F3 **Puketitiri** New Zealand
145 F2 **Puketoetoe** *mt* New Zealand
145 F4 **Puketoi Range** New Zealand
145 E3 **Puketutu** New Zealand
145 F2 **Puketutu I** New Zealand
144 C6 **Pukeuri Junction** New Zealand
29 M11 **Pukkila** Finland
67 F1 **Pukou** China
52 F3 **Puksa** U.S.S.R.
52 F3 **Puksoozero** U.S.S.R.
52 H5 **Puksub** U.S.S.R.
98 G6 **Pukwana** S Dakota
42 F4 **Pula** Yugoslavia
128 E8 **Pulacayo** Bolivia
43 C9 **Pula, C. di** Sardinia
Pulandian *see* **Xinjin**
71 G6 **Pulangi** *R* Mindanao Philippines
70 D6 **Pulangpisau** Kalimantan
70 K8 **Pulao Seribu** *isld* Sumatra
70 K9 **Pulasari** *mt* Java
99 O9 **Pulaski** Iowa
95 L3 **Pulaski** New York
110 J6 **Pulaski** Tennessee
94 G9 **Pulaski** Virginia
99 S5 **Pulaski** Wisconsin
69 F13 **Pulaukidjang** Sumatra
70 B4 **Pulaumadjang** Kalimantan
69 D13 **Pulautelo** Indonesia
31 N4 **Puławy** Poland
9 F6 **Pulborough** England
77 L2 **Pul-i-Khumri** Afghanistan
76 D3 **Pulivendla** India
76 C6 **Puliyangudi** India
83 K9 **Puliyankulam** Sri Lanka
29 M7 **Pulkkila** Finland
100 H3 **Pullman** Washington
71 E2 **Pulog, Mt** Luzon Philippines
83 K8 **Puloli** Sri Lanka
52 F2 **Pulonga** U.S.S.R.
52 D1 **Pulozero** U.S.S.R.
124 D4 **Púlpito, Pta** *C* Mexico
33 T10 **Pulsnitz** *R* E Germany
31 M3 **Pułtusk** Poland
66 C4 **Pulu** China
70 P10 **Pulukan** Bali Indonesia
66 E6 **Puma Yumco** *L* China
Pumiao *see* **Yongning**
98 A4 **Pumpkin Cr** Montana
98 C8 **Pumpkin Cr** Nebraska
108 F6 **Pumpville** Texas
8 C3 **Pumsaint** Wales
128 B4 **Puná** *isld* Ecuador
70 G5 **Puna** *R* Sulawesi
144 C5 **Punakaiki** New Zealand
145 D1 **Punakitere R** New Zealand
70 D4 **Punan** Kalimantan
74 F2 **Punch** Kashmir
117 M9 **Punchaw** Br Col
70 C6 **Pundu** Kalimantan
52 F4 **Punduga** U.S.S.R.
55 D1 **Punga** *R* U.S.S.R.
112 L2 **Pungo** N Carolina
59 J3 **Pungsan** N Korea
86 E6 **Punia** Zaïre
70 Q10 **Punikan, G** *mt* Indonesia
131 B2 **Punilla, Sa. de la** *mts* Chile
74 F3 **Punjab** *prov* India
74 D3 **Punjab, The** *prov* Pakistan
140 E4 **Punjaub** Queensland
29 O10 **Punkaharju** Finland
29 K10 **Punkalaidun** Finland
119 N7 **Punnichy** Sask
128 D7 **Puno** Peru
128 D6 **Puno** *dep* Peru
106 D7 **Punta** New Mexico
131 E7 **Punta Alta** Argentina
133 C8 **Punta Arenas** Chile
43 C7 **Puntaccia** *mt* Sardinia
133 C3 **Punta Colorada** Chile
108 B8 **Punta de Agua Cr.** *R* Texas/New Mex
17 H4 **Punta de la Baña** Spain
125 P9 **Punta Gorda** Belize
100 A9 **Punta Gorda** California
113 E11 **Punta Gorda** Florida
125 N4 **Punta Gorda** Nicaragua
131 G6 **Punta Norte** Argentina
127 J5 **Punta Palenque** Dom Rep
124 B3 **Punta Prieta** Mexico
125 M5 **Puntarenas** Costa Rica
128 G8 **Punta Rieles** Paraguay
125 N5 **Punta San Pedrillo** Costa Rica
127 M5 **Punta Tuna** Puerto Rico
128 D1 **Punto Fijo** Venezuela
47 G4 **Punto Lágo** Greece
133 D7 **Puntudo, Cerro** *mt* Argentina
116 C5 **Punuk Is** Bering Sea
94 J6 **Punxsutawney** Pennsylvania
68 F6 **Puok** Cambodia
29 N7 **Puolanka** Finland
26 L5 **Puottaure** Sweden
128 E6 **Puoya** *mt* Bolivia
145 D4 **Puponga** New Zealand
58 F6 **Puqi** China
128 D6 **Puquio** Peru
133 D3 **Puquios** Chile
50 G2 **Pur** *R* U.S.S.R.
128 C3 **Puracé** *vol* Colombia
70 M9 **Purbolinggo** Java
107 N7 **Purcell** Oklahoma
116 J3 **Purcell Mt** Alaska
117 P10 **Purcell Mts** Br Col
100 K1 **Purcell Range** Montana
94 K7 **Purcellville** Virginia
17 F7 **Purchena** Spain
99 N10 **Purdin** Missouri
98 F7 **Purdum** Nebraska
110 C5 **Purdy** Missouri
145 E3 **Pureora** *mt* New Zealand
124 H8 **Purépero** Mexico
145 E1 **Purerua** New Zealand
9 E6 **Purewell** England
106 G4 **Purgatoire** *R* Colorado
116 N3 **Purgatory** Alaska
38 M5 **Purgstall** Austria
75 L9 **Puri** India
128 D3 **Purificación** Colombia
145 E2 **Puriri** New Zealand
9 F5 **Purley** England
25 C3 **Purmerend** Netherlands
74 G9 **Purna** India
138 B2 **Purndu Saltpan** S Australia
75 M6 **Purnea** India
52 E3 **Purnema** U.S.S.R.
118 F9 **Purple Springs** Alberta
68 F6 **Pursat** Cambodia
128 E4 **Purué** *R* Brazil
70 D5 **Puruktjahu** Kalimantan
128 F4 **Purus** *R* Brazil
29 O10 **Puruvesi** *L* Finland
111 G10 **Purvis** Mississippi
47 G2 **Pŭrvomay** Bulgaria
70 N9 **Purwodadi** Java
70 M9 **Purwokerto** Java
70 M9 **Purworedjo** Java
110 H5 **Puryear** Tennessee
66 B4 **Pusa** China
70 B4 **Pusa** Sarawak
52 C6 **Puša** U.S.S.R.
74 G9 **Pusad** India
52 B6 **Pušalotas** U.S.S.R.
65 H7 **Pusan** S Korea
71 G7 **Pusan Pt** Mindanao Philippines
65 D6 **Pushang** China
95 T2 **Pushaw L** Maine
52 D5 **Pushkin** U.S.S.R.
54 J1 **Pushkino** U.S.S.R.
52 E3 **Pushlakhta** U.S.S.R.
123 Q6 **Pushthrough** Nfld
77 H4 **Pusht-i-Rud** *reg* Afghanistan
120 E4 **Puskaskwa Nat. Park** Ontario
121 O3 **Puskitamika L** Quebec
48 G3 **Püspökladány** Hungary
20 J5 **Pussay** France
22 H4 **Pussemange** Belgium
38 K7 **Pusterwald** Austria
52 C6 **Pustoshka** U.S.S.R.
102 B3 **Putah Cr** California
67 G5 **Pu-tai** Taiwan
71 M9 **Putain** Timor **Indonesia**
20 E4 **Putanges** France
75 R5 **Putao** Burma
145 E3 **Putaruru** New Zealand
30 G1 **Putbus** E Germany
70 P9 **Puteran** *isld* Indonesia
67 F4 **Putian** China
43 H8 **Putignano** Italy
48 J3 **Putila** U.S.S.R.
52 F5 **Putilovo** U.S.S.R.
70 B6 **Puting Tg** *C* Kalimantan
54 E5 **Putivl'** U.S.S.R.
33 Q6 **Putlitz** E Germany
48 K3 **Putna** Romania
95 Q5 **Putnam** Connecticut
108 E8 **Putnam** Oklahoma
109 H3 **Putnam** Texas
112 C6 **Putney** Georgia
98 H4 **Putney** S Dakota
95 P4 **Putney** Vermont
51 J2 **Putorana, Gory** *mt* U.S.S.R.
145 F3 **Putorino** New Zealand
83 J9 **Puttalam** Sri Lanka
83 J9 **Puttalam Lag** Sri Lanka
22 G1 **Putte** Belgium
36 B5 **Puttelange** France
33 O5 **Püttelkow** E Germany
25 E4 **Putten** Netherlands
28 G7 **Puttgarden** W Germany
36 B5 **Püttlingen** W Germany
54 L8 **Putugino** U.S.S.R.
83 K8 **Putukkudiyirippu** Sri Lanka
128 C3 **Putumayo** *div* Colombia
128 D4 **Putumayo** *R* Peru/Colombia
67 G1 **Putuo Shan** *isld* China
70 C4 **Putussibau** Kalimantan
33 T5 **Putzar** E Germany
135 U5 **Puuanahulu** Hawaiian Is
135 U5 **Puu Hualalei** *crater* Hawaiian Is
135 S3 **Puukoli** Hawaiian Is
29 M10 **Puulavesi** *L* Finland
29 N10 **Puumala** Finland
22 G1 **Puurs** Belgium
135 N1 **Puuwai** Hawaiian Is
Puxian *see* **Pucheng**
65 A6 **Pu Xian** China
117 M12 **Puyallup** Washington
65 C7 **Puyang** China
18 G7 **Puy de Dôme** *dep* France
18 G7 **Puy-de-Sancy** *mt* France
131 A8 **Puyehue, L de** Chile
131 B8 **Puyehue, P. de** Argentina
131 A8 **Puyehue, V** Chile
19 Q14 **Puy Gris** *mt* France
18 G9 **Puylaurens** France
18 H7 **Puy, le** France
18 F8 **Puy l'Evêque** France
18 G7 **Puy Mary** *mt* France
20 H2 **Puys** France
52 H4 **Puzla** U.S.S.R.
88 B6 **Pweto** Zaïre
68 B2 **Pwinbyu** Burma
8 B2 **Pwllheli** Wales
52 E2 **Pyalitsa** U.S.S.R.
52 E4 **Pyal'ma** U.S.S.R.
68 B3 **Pyalo** Burma
68 B5 **Pyamalaw** *R* Burma
52 F6 **Pyana** *R* U.S.S.R.
57 E6 **Pyandzh** *R* U.S.S.R./Afghanistan
52 J4 **Pyanteg** U.S.S.R.
52 D2 **Pyaozero, Oz** *L* U.S.S.R.

Pyapalli — Rath
63

76 C3 Pyapalli India
68 B4 Pyapon Burma
51 H1 Pyasina R U.S.S.R.
53 F11 Pyatigorsk U.S.S.R.
54 E8 Pyatikhatki U.S.S.R.
52 H4 Pyatiqory U.S.S.R.
110 D5 Pyatt Arkansas
52 H6 Pychas U.S.S.R.
116 M7 Pye Is Alaska
29 M8 Pyhäjärvi Finland
27 M11 Pyhajärvi L Finland
29 L7 Pyhäjoki Finland
29 J11 Pyhäranta Finland
29 O9 Pyhäselkä Finland
38 N5 Pyhra Austria
68 C3 Pyinmana Burma
8 C4 Pyle Wales
29 L9 Pylkönmäki Finland
94 G5 Pymatuning Res Ohio/Penn
69 A9 Pymgalion Pt Nicobar Is
59 J3 Pyŏktong N Korea
65 F5 Pyŏngyang N Korea
100 F9 Pyramid Nevada
103 K6 Pyramid Canyon Ariz/Nev
139 G6 Pyramid Hill Victoria
106 C1 Pyramid Pk Colorado
94 A2 Pyramid Pt Michigan
102 E2 Pyramid Rge Nevada
18 F9 Pyrénées mts France/Spain
18 E9 Pyrénées Atlantiques dep France
18 G10 Pyrénées-Orientales dep France
142 B5 Pyrton,Mt W Australia
31 H2 Pyrzyce Poland
52 G5 Pyshchug U.S.S.R.
55 D3 Pyshma U.S.S.R.
52 C6 Pytalovo U.S.S.R.
121 O6 Pythonga, L Quebec
68 C3 Pyu Burma
68 C3 Pyu R Burma
68 C4 Pyuntaza Burma
31 K3 Pyzdry Poland

84 E3 Qaddāhīyah, Al Libya
74 F3 Qadian India
80 G4 Qafqafa Jordan
58 G2 Qagan China
Qagan Nur see Zhengxiangbai Qi
65 B3 Qagan Nur China
65 B4 Qagan Nur L China
65 C3 Qagan Nur L China
65 F2 Qagan Nur L China
65 D1 Qagan Qulut China
65 D3 Qagan Us China
115 P5 Qagssimiut Greenland
65 B4 Qahar Youyi Houqi China
65 B4 Qahar Youyi Qianqi China
65 B4 Qahar Youyi Zhongqi China
Qâhira, El see Cairo
66 E4 Qaidam Pendi reg China
77 J4 Qala Bist Afghanistan
86 G3 Qala'en Nahl Sudan
77 J3 Qala-i-Ghor Afghanistan
77 H3 Qala-i-Kāl Afghanistan
77 K3 Qalāt Afghanistan
79 F3 Qal'at el Marqab Syria
80 F4 Qal'at er Rabad Jordan
78 L6 Qal'at Sālih Iraq
80 C5 Qalqiliya Israel
80 E6 Qalya Jordan
79 B8 Qalyûb Egypt
80 G3 Qam Jordan
74 C5 Qambar Pakistan
66 F5 Qamdo reg China
84 F3 Qaminis Libya
78 H3 Qamishliye, El Syria
74 C3 Qamruddin Karez Pakistan
80 D5 Qana Jordan
65 C3 Qangdin Gol China
65 C3 Qangdin Sum China
79 C8 Qanṭara, El Egypt
84 H4 Qara Egypt
80 D5 Qarawat Bani Ḥassan Jordan
79 G3 Qardāha Syria
78 L2 Qareh Su R Iran
79 C10 Qarn el Kabsh, G mt Egypt
66 D4 Qarqan He R China
84 E3 Qaryahash Sharqiyah Libya
79 H4 Qaryatein, El Syria
80 G7 Qaryat Falha Jordan
77 H2 Qasa Murg Afghanistan
80 F8 Qasr Jordan
84 G3 Qasr al Burayqal Libya
79 F8 Qasr ed Deir, J mt Jordan
84 H4 Qasr, El Egypt
79 H4 Qasr el Hayr Syria
78 K4 Qasr-e-Shirin Iran
80 G8 Qasr eth Thuraiyat Jordan
84 H4 Qasr Farâfra Egypt
79 G5 Qatana Syria
77 B7 Qatar sheikhdom The Gulf
77 B6 Qatīf, Al Saudi Arabia
79 G7 Qatrāna Jordan
84 E5 Qaṭrūn, Al Libya
84 H4 Qattara Depression Egypt
77 F3 Qāyen Iran
78 J4 Qayyarah Iraq
77 A1 Qazvīn Iran
84 J4 Qena Egypt
77 E6 Qeshm Iran
77 A1 Qeydār Iran
77 C6 Qeys isld Iran
77 A1 Qezel Owzan R Iran
65 D4 Qian'an China
65 F2 Qian'an China
67 C3 Qiancheng China
65 F2 Qian Gorlos China
67 C3 Qiangu'ao China
Qianguozhen see Qian Gorlos
65 D7 Qiangwei He R China
67 C5 Qianjiang China
67 D1 Qianjiang China
67 C2 Qianjiang R China
67 E1 Qianshan China
65 F4 Qian Shan mt ra China
65 E4 Qianwei China
67 A2 Qianwei China
65 D4 Qianxi China
67 B3 Qianxi China
67 C3 Qianyang China
65 D3 Qiaotou China
67 E3 Qiaotou China
67 E1 Qichun China
67 D3 Qidong China
67 G1 Qidong China
66 D4 Qiemo China
67 C2 Qifeng Guan pass China
65 C6 Qihe China
65 B3 Qihreg China
58 E6 Qijiang China
66 E3 Qijiaojing China
Qike see Xunke
65 D5 Qikou China
74 B9 Qila Ladgasht Pakistan
65 D4 Qilaotu Shan mt ra China
74 A8 Qila Safed Pakistan
74 C3 Qila Saifullah Pakistan
Qili see Shitai
66 F4 Qilian Shan mt ra China
65 E4 Qilihe China
67 F2 Qimen China
65 D6 Qingcheng China
65 E6 Qingdao China
65 E5 Qingduizi China
65 C7 Qingfeng China
67 A2 Qingfu China
65 G1 Qinggang China
66 E4 Qinghai prov China
58 D4 Qinghai Hu L China
65 C6 Qinghe China
65 H1 Qinghe China
65 F4 Qinghecheng China
65 E4 Qinghemen China
65 F3 Qinghe Shuiku res China
67 F2 Qinghu China
65 A6 Qingjian China
59 G5 Qingjiang China
67 E2 Qingjiang China
67 C1 Qing Jiang R China
65 A6 Qingjian He R China
Qingkou see Ganyu
67 C7 Qinglan China
67 D7 Qinglan Gang inlet China
67 D4 Qinglian China
67 E3 Qingliu China
65 D4 Qinglong China
67 B4 Qinglong China
65 D4 Qinglong He R China
65 C6 Qingping China
68 J2 Qingping China
67 G1 Qingpu China
67 A2 Qingshen China
65 B5 Qingshuihe China
58 E4 Qingshui He R China
67 C3 Qingshui Jiang R China
67 G2 Qingtian China
65 C5 Qing Xian China
65 B6 Qingxu China
Qingyang see Jinjiang
58 E4 Qingyang China
67 F1 Qingyang China
Qingyuan see Yishan
59 J3 Qingyuan China
67 D5 Qingyuan China
67 F3 Qingyuan China
65 D6 Qingyun China
65 B7 Qin He R China
65 D5 Qinhuangdao China
67 C6 Qin Jiang R China
58 E5 Qin Ling mt ra China
65 B7 Qinshui China
67 C5 Qintang China
58 F4 Qin Xian China
58 F4 Qinyang China
67 G3 Qinyu China
65 B6 Qinyuan China
67 C6 Qinzhou China
68 J2 Qinzhou Wan B China
68 K3 Qionghai China
58 D5 Qionglai China
58 D5 Qionglai Shan mt ra China
68 K3 Qiongshan China
67 C7 Qiongzhong China
Qiongzhou see Qiongshan
68 J2 Qiongzhou Haixia China
67 B1 Qiping China
59 H2 Qiqihar China
77 C5 Qīr Iran
80 D7 Qiryat Arba' Jordan
80 D2 Qiryat Ata Israel
80 D2 Qiryat Bialik Israel
80 C7 Qiryat Gat Israel
80 D2 Qiryat Motmkin Israel
80 D3 Qiryat Tiv'on Israel
80 D2 Qiryat Yam Israel
80 D6 Qiryat Yearim Israel
67 C6 Qisha China
80 D3 Qishon 'Eneq Yizre'el Israel
68 J2 Qishui China
66 D3 Qitai China
65 H2 Qitaihe China
67 A4 Qiubei China
65 C6 Qiu Xian China
65 E6 Qixia China
65 B6 Qi Xian China
65 C7 Qi Xian China
65 B4 Qixiaying China
65 J1 Qixing He R China
65 H1 Qixingpao China
67 D3 Qiyang China
67 E1 Qizhou China
65 C2 Qog Ul China
Qogur Feng mt see K2
77 B2 Qom Iran
Qomolangma Feng mt see Everest, Mt
66 D3 Qongkol China
115 O5 Qôrnoq Greenland
77 A2 Qorveh Iran
79 G4 Qoubayat Lebanon
95 P4 Quabbin Res Massachusetts
122 G8 Quaco Hd New Brunswick
74 D2 Quaidabad Pakistan
102 H6 Quail Mts California
143 B9 Quairading W Australia
32 G7 Quakenbrück W Germany
95 M6 Quakertown Pennsylvania
45 Q8 Qualiano Italy
85 E6 Quallam Niger
139 G6 Quambatook Victoria
139 J4 Quambone New S Wales
140 F5 Quamby Queensland
108 H1 Quanah Texas
128 F4 Quanaru, Ilha Brazil
68 J5 Quang Nam Vietnam
68 J5 Quang Ngai Vietnam
68 H4 Quang Tri Vietnam
67 B6 Quang Yen Vietnam
67 F1 Quanjiao China
69 G8 Quan Long Vietnam
67 E4 Quannan China
68 F7 Quan Phu Quoc isld Vietnam
94 K8 Quantico Virginia
120 E1 Quantz L Ontario
67 C4 Quanzhou China
119 O8 Qu'Appelle Sask
119 P8 Qu'Appelle R Sask
118 L7 Qu'Appelle R. Dam Sask
133 F4 Quaraí Brazil
131 G3 Quarai, R Brazil
32 L4 Quarnbek W Germany
122 G7 Quarryville New Brunswick
95 L7 Quarryville Pennsylvania
40 F6 Quart Italy
45 L2 Quartesana Italy
45 N6 Quartière Mt. Sacro Italy
43 C9 Quartu S. Elena Sardinia
102 H4 Quartzite Mt Nevada
102 G2 Quartz Mt Nevada
100 G1 Quartz Mt Washington
103 K8 Quartzsite Arizona
99 P7 Quasqueton Iowa
22 G2 Quatre Bras Belgium
22 H5 Quatre-Champs France
117 K10 Quatsino Br Columbia
45 H2 Quattro Castella Italy
106 G7 Quay New Mexico
77 F1 Qūchān Iran
101 P8 Quealy Wyoming
139 J6 Queanbeyan New S Wales
121 T6 Québec Quebec
130 F6 Quebra Anzol R Brazil
88 D9 Quebrabasa Rapids Mozambique
133 E3 Quebracho Coto Argentina
131 A8 Quedal, C. de Chile
133 G3 Quedas do Iguaçu falls Brazil
33 O9 Quedlinburg E Germany
17 G9 Qued Tlélat Algeria
95 L8 Queen Anne Maryland
117 L10 Queen Bess, Mt Br Columbia
9 G5 Queenborough England
115 M5 Queen, C N W Terr
133 E8 Queen Charlotte B Falkland Is
117 G9 Queen Charlotte Is Br Columbia
117 J10 Queen Charlotte Sd Br Columbia
145 E4 Queen Charlotte Sound New Zealand
117 K10 Queen Charlotte Str Br Columbia
99 O9 Queen City Missouri
109 N2 Queen City Texas
115 K2 Queen Elizabeth Is N W Terr
146 D3 Queen Mary Land Antarctica
117 D5 Queen Mary, Mt Yukon Terr
114 J4 Queen Maud Gulf N W Terr
146 G8 Queen Maud Ra Antarctica
13 G6 Queensbury England
140 A2 Queens Chan N Terr Australia
115 K2 Queens Chan N W Terr
139 G7 Queenscliff Victoria
13 E2 Queensferry Scotland
139 Queensland state Australia
142 B2 Queens Park dist Perth, W Aust
123 L8 Queensport Nova Scotia
118 E8 Queenstown Alberta
95 L8 Queenstown Maryland
144 B6 Queenstown New Zealand
89 E8 Queenstown S Africa
139 H8 Queenstown Tasmania
143 E9 Queen Victoria Spring W Australia
100 A2 Queets Washington
131 F4 Queguay Grande R Uruguay
36 E5 Queich R W Germany
16 C2 Queija, S. de mts Spain
129 L6 Queimadas Brazil
87 C7 Quela Angola
21 D6 Quelaines France
87 B7 Quele Angola
88 F10 Quelimane Mozambique
124 F6 Quelite Mexico
133 C6 Quellen Chile
106 B7 Quemado New Mexico
108 G7 Quemado Texas
Quemoy see Chin-men
133 E5 Quemu Quemu Argentina
22 B3 Quend France
9 G4 Quendon England
22 B3 Quend Plage France
107 P3 Quenemo Kansas
111 F10 Quentin Mississippi
89 F2 Que Que Zimbabwe
133 F5 Quequén Argentina
22 C2 Quercamps France
130 D8 Querência do Norte Brazil
125 J7 Querétaro Mexico
33 P10 Querfurt E Germany
124 D2 Querobabi Mexico
20 B2 Querqueville France
20 K2 Querrieu France
117 M9 Quesnel Br Columbia
117 N9 Quesnel L Br Columbia
22 D4 Quesnoy France
22 F3 Quesnoy, le France
22 E2 Quesnoy-sur-Deule, le France
106 E5 Questa New Mexico
18 D5 Questembert France
133 D2 Quetena Bolivia
99 Q1 Quetico Ontario
118 L2 Quetico L Ontario
99 P1 Quetico Provincial Park Ontario
74 B3 Quetta Pakistan
20 C2 Quettehou France
20 F3 Quetteville France
20 C4 Quettreville France
111 D11 Queue de Tortue R Louisiana
20 J4 Queue-lez-Yvelines, la France
20 K2 Quevauvillers France
121 O3 Quévillon Quebec
125 O10 Quezaltenango Guatemala
79 E8 Queziot Israel
71 C6 Quezon Palawan Philippines
71 E3 Quezon City Luzon Philippines
65 D7 Qufu China
87 B8 Quibala Angola
87 B7 Quibate Angola
128 C2 Quibdó Colombia
118 J1 Quibell Ontario
18 C5 Quiberon France
20 G2 Quiberville France
127 K10 Quíbor Venezuela
87 B7 Quicama Nat. Park Angola
68 G3 Qui Chau Vietnam
32 L5 Quickborn W Germany
36 C5 Quierschied W Germany
117 G5 Quiet L Yukon Terr
22 F3 Quievrain Belgium
22 E3 Quiévy France
118 G2 Quigley Alberta
133 F3 Quiindy Paraguay
103 M9 Quijotoa Arizona
124 F5 Quilá Mexico
133 C6 Quilán, C Chile
16 E9 Quilates, C Morocco
141 H7 Quilberry Queensland
128 D7 Quilca Peru
100 C2 Quilcene Washington
87 B8 Quilengues Angola
133 E4 Quilino Argentina
128 D6 Quillabamba Peru
128 E7 Quillacollo Bolivia
18 G10 Quillan France
20 G3 Quillebeuf France
131 B7 Quillén, L Argentina
119 N6 Quill Lake Sask
131 B4 Quillota Chile
119 N7 Quillsks L Sask
21 B7 Quilly France
141 G7 Quilpie Queensland
87 C8 Quimbango Angola
18 C5 Quimper France
18 C5 Quimperle France
71 F3 Quinabucasan Pt Philippines
71 F4 Quinalasag isld Philippines
100 B2 Quinault Washington
100 A2 Quinault R Washington
20 H2 Quincampoix France
128 D6 Quince Mil Peru
102 D2 Quincy California
111 M11 Quincy Florida
99 P10 Quincy Illinois
95 R4 Quincy Massachusetts
110 N1 Quincy Ohio
100 B3 Quincy Oregon
100 F2 Quincy Washington
20 C2 Quineville France
68 F2 Quinh Nhai Vietnam
68 J6 Qui Nhon Vietnam
128 E3 Quinigua, Cerro mts Venezuela
71 E5 Quiniluban isld Philippines
109 L3 Quinlan Texas
98 D6 Quinn S Dakota
103 J4 Quinn Canyon Ra Nevada
140 C6 Quinn, Mt N Terr Aust
100 G8 Quinn River Crossing Nevada
19 Q17 Quinson France
16 E5 Quintanar de la Orden Spain
125 P8 Quintana Roo terr Mexico
107 K2 Quinter Kansas
18 D4 Quintin France
17 G3 Quinto Spain
131 D5 Quinto R Argentina
107 P6 Quinton Oklahoma
119 N7 Quinton Sask
45 L1 Quinto Vicentino Italy
8 A7 Quintrel Downs England
94 G8 Quinwood W Virginia
88 H7 Quionga Mozambique
130 J10 Quipapá Brazil
15 B3 Quirang Scotland
87 C8 Quirima Angola
139 K4 Quirindi New S Wales
131 A6 Quiriquina isld Chile
127 N10 Quiriquire Venezuela
120 H6 Quirke L Ontario
36 C5 Quirnbach W Germany
16 C2 Quiroga Spain
123 R2 Quirpon Nfld
88 H8 Quissanga Mozambique
87 F10 Quissico Mozambique
45 J1 Quistello Italy
87 C8 Quitapa Angola
126 D7 Quita Sueño Bank Caribbean
130 D6 Quitéria R Brazil
87 B7 Quitexe Angola
110 D6 Quitman Arkansas
113 D7 Quitman Georgia
109 P3 Quitman Louisiana
111 H9 Quitman Mississippi
109 M3 Quitman Texas
128 C4 Quito Ecuador
103 M10 Quitovac Mexico
20 H3 Quittebeuf France
103 M6 Quivero Arizona
128 C5 Quivilla Peru
129 L4 Quixadá Brazil
67 D4 Qujiang China
67 B1 Qu Jiang R China
67 C6 Qujie China
67 A4 Qujing China
46 D3 Qukës-Shkumbin Albania
80 G6 Quleib R Jordan
66 E4 Qumar He R China
58 C5 Qumarlêb China
89 F8 Qumbu S Africa
84 G4 Qunayyin, S. al Libya
80 G1 Quneitra Syria
72 E5 Qunfidhah, Al Saudi Arabia
66 D5 Qungtag China
83 M12 Quoin Chan Mauritius
140 A2 Quoin I N Terr Aust
141 K6 Quoin I Queensland
89 A10 Quoin Pt S Africa
119 N1 Quorn Ontario
138 E4 Quorn S Australia
129 J4 Qurem Brazil
84 J4 Qus Egypt
84 J4 Quseir Egypt
77 G6 Quṣr-e-Qand Iran
67 C1 Qutang Xia Wu Xia China
87 E12 Quthing Lesotho
79 H2 Quweiq R Syria
79 B8 Quweisna Egypt
65 B7 Quwo China
58 E4 Quwu Shan mt ra China
67 A5 Quxi China
67 B1 Qu Xian China
67 F2 Qu Xian China
75 O4 Qüxü China
65 C5 Quyang China
67 E3 Quyang China
67 B7 Quynh Luu Vietnam
121 O7 Quyon Quebec
65 C6 Quzhou China

28 K5 Rå Sweden
27 F16 Råå Sweden
Raab see Györ
31 J7 Raabs Austria
38 N7 Raab Tal V Austria
29 L7 Raahe Finland
29 O9 Rääl-kylä Finland
25 F4 Raalte Netherlands
115 L2 Raanes Pen N W Terr
29 L5 Raanujärvi Finland
70 P9 Raas isld Indonesia
77 A5 Ra'as Al Khafti Saudi Arabia
15 B3 Raasay, Sd of Scotland
42 F4 Rab isld Yugoslavia
80 E4 Raba Jordan
71 J9 Raba Sumbawa Indonesia
48 D3 Rába R Hungary
48 F1 Raba R Poland
16 C3 Rabaçal R Portugal
18 F9 Rabastens de Bigorre Hautes-Pyrénées France
85 C2 Rabat Morocco
137 L2 Rabaul New Britain
Rabbah see 'Amman
117 K6 Rabbit R Br Columbia
98 D4 Rabbit Cr S Dakota
106 D1 Rabbit Ears Pass Colorado
145 D4 Rabbit I New Zealand
118 K5 Rabbit Lake Sask
117 N5 Rabbitskin R N W Terr
28 D7 Rabel W Germany
36 F2 Rabenau W Germany
77 E5 Rābor Iran
52 F6 Rabotki U.S.S.R.
37 P3 Rabštejn Czechoslovakia
112 D3 Rabun, L Georgia
46 D1 Rača Yugoslavia
44 C2 Racconigi Italy
99 M8 Raccoon R Iowa
126 G3 Raccoon Cay Bahamas
94 E8 Raccoon Cr Ohio
38 N9 Rače Yugoslavia
115 O8 Race, C Nfld
94 E8 Raceland Kentucky
111 F12 Raceland Louisiana
95 R4 Race Pt Massachusetts
100 B1 Race Rocks Br Columbia
101 N3 Race Track Montana
109 J9 Rachal Texas
69 D9 Racha Noi, Ko isld Thailand
79 F5 Rāchaya Lebanon
69 D9 Racha Yai, Ko isld Thailand
68 G8 Rach Gia Vietnam
31 L5 Racibórz Poland
37 P3 Račic Czechoslovakia
94 F8 Racine Ohio
99 T7 Racine Wisconsin
122 D1 Racine-de-Bouleau, R Quebec
120 G4 Racine L Ontario
33 Q10 Rackwitz E Germany
37 O4 Racovský mt Czechoslovakia
46 E1 Radan mt Yugoslavia
48 K3 Rădăuţi Romania
37 P4 Radbuza R Czechoslovakia
13 F6 Radcliffe England
99 N7 Radcliffe Iowa
27 E12 Råde Norway
30 H4 Radeberg E Germany
37 Q1 Radebeul E Germany
33 T10 Radeburg E Germany
19 Q18 Rade d'Hyères B France
33 Q9 Radegast E Germany
38 M8 Radel Pass Austria
36 C1 Radevormwald W Germany
94 G9 Radford Virginia
140 B1 Radford Pt N Terr Australia
74 D7 Radhanpur India
142 D4 Radi Hills W Australia
118 K6 Radisson Sask
99 P4 Radisson Wisconsin
101 T10 Radium Colorado
98 K1 Radium Minnesota
37 N3 Radium-Brambach E Germany
138 F4 Radium Hill peak S Australia
117 P10 Radium Hot Springs Br Columbia
106 D9 Radium Springs New Mexico
70 K8 Radjabasa Sumatra
70 O9 Radja, I Indonesia
77 F1 Rādkān Iran
Radldorf see Bergsdorf
38 L6 Radmer-an-dem-Hasel Austria
47 H2 Radnevo Bulgaria
30 H6 Radnice Czechoslovakia
Radnor co see Powys
41 J2 Radolfzell W Germany
31 N4 Radom Poland
86 D4 Radom Sudan
46 F2 Radomir Bulgaria
31 L4 Radomsko Poland
37 P3 Radonice Czechoslovakia
31 K7 Radošina Czechoslovakia
31 M4 Radoszyce Poland
46 E3 Radoviš Yugoslavia
42 F2 Radovljica Yugoslavia
38 H7 Radstadt Austria
8 D5 Radstock England
38 L9 Raduha mt Yugoslavia
42 H5 Radusa mt Yugoslavia
52 B6 Radviliškis U.S.S.R.
119 N9 Radville Sask
118 E4 Radway Alberta
31 O6 Radymno Poland
31 M3 Radzanów Poland
31 L3 Radziejów Poland
31 N3 Radzymin Poland
31 O4 Radzyń Podlaski Poland
117 P4 Rae N W Terr
75 J5 Rae Bareli India
112 H3 Raeford N Carolina
115 L4 Rae Isthmus N W Terr
114 H5 Rae L N W Terr
118 B8 Rae, Mt Br Columbia
22 L2 Raeren Belgium
32 E9 Raesfeld W Germany
143 D8 Raeside, L W Australia
115 K4 Rae Str N W Terr
145 D1 Raetea mt New Zealand
145 E3 Raetihi New Zealand
131 E3 Rafaela Argentina
79 E7 Rafah Egypt
86 D5 Rafai Cent Afr Republic
80 D5 Rafat Jordan
17 G5 Rafelbūnol Spain
78 J7 Rafha Saudi Arabia
77 E4 Rafsanjān Iran
101 M7 Raft R Idaho
119 Q3 Rafter Manitoba
101 M8 Raft R. Mts Utah
26 H3 Raftsund Norway
86 E4 Raga Sudan
71 G7 Ragang, Mt Philippines
71 F4 Ragay G Philippines
28 J4 Rågeleje Denmark
33 R6 Rägelin E Germany
126 G3 Ragged I Bahamas
143 E10 Ragged,Mt W Australia
127 P6 Ragged Pt Barbados
145 E2 Raglan New Zealand
8 D4 Raglan Wales
111 K8 Ragland Alabama
108 D1 Ragland New Mexico
145 D4 Raglan Range New Zealand
107 M4 Rago Kansas
44 G2 Ragola Monte Italy
33 R8 Ragösen E Germany
28 G7 Rågø Sund chan Denmark
84 F4 Raguba Libya
33 Q9 Raguhn E Germany
26 H8 Ragunda Sweden
Ragusa see Dubrovnik
43 F12 Ragusa Sicily
71 H7 Raha Indonesia
86 G3 Rahad R Sudan
86 D3 Rahad el Berdi Sudan
Rahaeng see Tak
80 E8 Raḥaf Israel
27 J11 Råhällan Sweden
47 K7 Rahat Dağ mt Turkey
32 J8 Rahden W Germany
86 H3 Raheita Ethiopia
86 E2 Rahib Sudan
80 D8 Rahiya Jordan
145 D3 Raholu New Zealand
74 F9 Rahuri India
16 B6 Raia R Portugal
45 P5 Raiano Italy
76 C2 Raichur India
71 K10 Raidjua isld Indonesia
75 K8 Raigarh India
102 G2 Railroad Pass Nevada
103 J3 Railroad Valley Nevada
139 H8 Railton Tasmania
37 K6 Rain W Germany
37 N6 Rain W Germany
37 J6 Rainau W Germany
138 F6 Rainbow Victoria
103 O4 Rainbow Br. Nat. Mon Utah
124 E9 Rainbow City Panama Canal Zone
141 G1 Raine I Gt Barrier Reef Aust
9 G4 Rainham England
100 C3 Rainier Oregon
100 C3 Rainier Washington
100 D3 Rainier, Mt Washington
100 B5 Rainrock Oregon
94 J7 Rainsburg Pennsylvania
94 C1 Rainy R Michigan
99 M1 Rainy R Minnesota
118 J2 Rainy L Minn/Ontario
99 N1 Rainy Lake Ontario
100 E1 Rainy Pass Washington
116 L5 Rainy Pass Lodge Alaska
118 H2 Rainy R Ontario
115 K8 Rainy River Manitoba
29 J8 Raippaluoto isld Finland
75 J8 Raipur India
74 G7 Raisen India
27 M11 Raisio Finland
22 E3 Raismes France
29 N5 Raistakka Finland
119 O2 Raith Ontario
145 D4 Rai Valley New Zealand
70 F4 Raja Kalimantan
70 B5 Raja, Bt mt Kalimantan
70 C5 Raja, Bt mt Kalimantan
76 E2 Rajahmundry India
76 D3 Rajampet India
70 B3 Rajang Sarawak
74 D4 Rajanpur Pakistan
76 C6 Rajapalaiyam India
74 D5 Rajasthan prov India
69 C11 Raja, Ujung C Sumatra
46 D2 Rajë Albania
75 L6 Rajgir India
31 O2 Rajgród Poland
80 F5 Rajib Jordan
80 F5 Rajib R Jordan
69 G14 Rajik Bangka Indonesia
75 J8 Rajim India
42 F4 Rajinac mt Yugoslavia
74 D7 Rajkot India
75 J8 Raj Nandgaon India
74 E8 Rajpipla India
75 N6 Rajshahi Bangladesh
76 D1 Rajura India
88 C2 Rakai Uganda
144 D5 Rakaia New Zealand
70 K9 Rakata isld Sumatra
145 F3 Rakauroa New Zealand
99 N6 Rake Iowa
144 A7 Rakeahua mt New Zealand
56 C6 Rakhmanoviskoye U.S.S.R.
77 J6 Rakhshan R Pakistan
145 E2 Rakino I New Zealand
26 L3 Rakisvaara mt Sweden
70 M8 Rakit isld Indonesia
145 E2 Rakitu I New Zealand
55 C5 Rakityanka U.S.S.R.
Raki-ura isld see Stewart I
27 E12 Rakkestad Norway
69 D8 Ra, Ko isld Thailand
31 J3 Rakoniewice Poland
87 D10 Rakops Botswana
30 H5 Rakovník Czechoslovakia
46 F2 Rakovo Bulgaria
33 S4 Rakow E Germany
52 F3 Rakula U.S.S.R.
52 G4 Rakulka U.S.S.R.
52 B5 Rakvere Estonia U.S.S.R.
111 G9 Raleigh Mississippi
112 J2 Raleigh N Carolina
98 E3 Raleigh N Dakota
112 L3 Raleigh B N Carolina
101 M1 Raley Alberta
108 F2 Ralls Texas
99 T3 Ralph Michigan
98 C4 Ralph S Dakota
107 O5 Ralston Oklahoma
95 L5 Ralston Pennsylvania
100 G3 Ralston Washington
101 R5 Ralston Wyoming
79 F9 Ram Jordan
117 M5 Ram R N W Terr
80 D4 Rāma Jordan
125 M3 Rama Nicaragua
119 P7 Rama Sask
72 E2 Ramādi Iraq
106 F2 Ramah Colorado
106 B6 Ramah New Mexico
16 E1 Ramales de la Victoria Spain
129 K6 Ramalho, Sa. do mts Brazil
133 E4 Ramalio Argentina
80 D6 Ramallah Jordan
76 D6 Ramanathapuram India
89 E3 Ramaquabane R Zimbabwe
54 E4 Ramasukha U.S.S.R.
80 C5 Ramatayim Israel
80 C5 Ramat Gan Israel
80 C5 Ramat Ha Kovesh Israel
80 C5 Ramat Ha Sharon Israel
80 D3 Ramat HaShofet Israel
80 D2 Ramat Yoḥanan Israel
83 K10 Rambe Sri Lanka
36 E5 Ramberg W Germany
36 B7 Rambervillers France
83 K9 Rambewa Sri Lanka
127 J2 Ramble Jamaica
133 D4 Ramblon Argentina
20 J4 Rambouillet France
33 P6 Rambow E Germany
76 B3 Ramdurg India
123 P6 Ramea Nfld
52 E6 Ramenskoye U.S.S.R.
111 K9 Ramer Alabama
52 E6 Rameshki U.S.S.R.
83 J8 Rameswaram India
75 L7 Ramgarh India
139 J7 Ram Hd Victoria
77 A4 Rāmhormoz Iran
44 B2 Ramière, Punta mt Italy/France
22 H2 Ramillies-Offus Belgium
109 K10 Ramirez Mexico
109 J8 Ramirez Texas
109 J9 Ramirito Texas
86 H4 Ramis R Ethiopia
80 E1 Râmîye Lebanon
27 G14 Ramkvilla Sweden
80 C6 Ramla Israel
80 C6 Ramle Israel
27 G11 Rämmen Sweden
75 K6 Ramnagar India
27 H12 Ramnäs Sweden
48 J5 Râmnicu Vâlcea Romania
89 E3 Ramokgwebana Botswana
80 E3 Ram On Israel
54 L5 Ramon' U.S.S.R.
102 H8 Ramona California
94 B3 Ramona Michigan
107 P5 Ramona Oklahoma
98 J5 Ramona S Dakota
120 K4 Ramore Ontario
124 G5 Ramos Mexico
71 C6 Ramos isld Philippines
80 F1 Ramot Naftali Israel
87 E10 Ramotsua Botswana
116 M4 Rampart Alaska
116 R3 Rampart House Yukon Terr
13 E5 Rampside England
74 H4 Rampur India
75 L8 Rampur India
74 F6 Rampura India
68 A3 Ramree Burma
77 B1 Rāmsar Iran
142 F4 Ramsay Ra W Australia
32 H10 Ramsbeck W Germany
27 H12 Ramsberg Sweden
13 F6 Ramsbottom England
32 E9 Ramsdorf W Germany
32 F7 Ramsel W Germany
26 H8 Ramsele Sweden
112 H2 Ramseur N Carolina
9 F3 Ramsey England
110 G2 Ramsey Illinois
12 D5 Ramsey I of Man U.K.
95 N5 Ramsey New Jersey
120 H5 Ramsey Ontario
8 A4 Ramsey I Wales
9 H5 Ramsgate England
13 G5 Ramsgill England
28 B3 Ramsing Denmark
26 H9 Ramsjö Sweden
22 D1 Ramskapelle Belgium
74 H8 Ramtek India
79 G6 Ramtha Jordan
71 J9 Ramu mt Sumbawa Indonesia
136 K3 Ramu R Papua New Guinea
52 B6 Ramygala U.S.S.R.
26 G5 Rana inlet Norway
16 C1 Rañadoiro, Sa. de mts Spain
26 F5 Ranafjord inlet Norway
75 N7 Ranaghat India
69 J10 Ranai Indonesia
27 K12 Rånäs Sweden
27 E11 Rånåsfoss Norway
70 K8 Ranau, D L Sumatra
131 B5 Rancagua Chile
22 G3 Rance Belgium
20 A5 Rance R France
133 G2 Rancharia Brazil
117 F5 Rancheria Yukon Terr
101 S5 Ranchester Wyoming
75 L7 Ranchi India
129 G6 Rancho de Caça dos Tapiúnas Brazil
124 H6 Rancho Grande Mexico
106 E5 Ranchos de Taos New Mexico
126 D3 Rancho Veloz Cuba
131 A8 Ranco, L. de Chile
106 D1 Rand Colorado
109 J8 Randado Texas
99 N7 Randall Iowa
107 M2 Randall Kansas
99 M3 Randall Minnesota
14 E2 Randalstown N Ireland
43 F11 Randazzo Sicily
28 E4 Randers Denmark
Randers co see Århus
37 J4 Randersacker W Germany
26 L5 Randijaur L Sweden
100 D3 Randle Washington
112 H2 Randleman N Carolina
109 J1 Randlett Oklahoma
103 P1 Randlett Utah
28 E5 Randlev Denmark
99 L9 Randolph Iowa
107 O2 Randolph Kansas
95 S2 Randolph Maine
111 G7 Randolph Mississippi
98 J7 Randolph Nebraska
94 J4 Randolph New York
101 O8 Randolph Utah
95 P3 Randolph Vermont
99 S6 Randolph Wisconsin
123 T5 Random I Nfld
99 T6 Random Lake Wisconsin
20 G4 Randonnai France
102 G6 Randsburg California
27 D11 Randsfjord Norway
32 E5 Randzel sandbank W Germany
26 N6 Råneå Norway
20 E4 Rânes France
118 F5 Ranfurly Alberta
144 C6 Ranfurly New Zealand
69 E9 Rangae Thailand
70 C5 Rangantamiang Kalimantan
70 F6 Rangasa, Tg C Sulawesi
145 E3 Rangataua New Zealand
145 D1 Rangaunu Harbour New Zealand
111 J10 Range Alabama
95 R2 Rangeley Maine
101 R9 Rangely Colorado
109 J3 Ranger Texas
94 E8 Ranger W Virginia
120 G6 Ranger L Ontario
75 O5 Rangia India
145 E3 Ranginui mt New Zealand
144 D5 Rangiora New Zealand
145 F3 Rangitaiki New Zealand
145 F3 Rangitaiki R New Zealand
144 C6 Rangitata New Zealand
145 E4 Rangitikei R New Zealand
145 E2 Rangitoto I New Zealand
145 E3 Rangitoto Ra New Zealand
145 G2 Rangitukia New Zealand
69 D10 Rangkalanberandan Sumatra
70 L9 Rangkasbitung Java
68 C4 Rangoon Burma
68 C4 Rangoon R Burma
75 N6 Rangpur Bangladesh
69 F12 Rangsang isld Sumatra
33 S8 Rangsdorf W Germany
28 C6 Rangstrup Denmark
76 B3 Ranibennur India
99 N1 Ranier Minnesota
75 M7 Raniganj India
37 M2 Ranis E Germany
74 E6 Raniwara India
140 D5 Ranken R N Terr Aust
140 D4 Ranken Store N Terr Aust
110 J1 Rankin Illinois
108 F4 Rankin Texas
115 K5 Rankin Inlet N W Terr
139 H5 Rankin's Springs New S Wales
80 B8 Rannen Israel
141 K6 Rannes Queensland
55 B5 Ranniy U.S.S.R.
15 D4 Rannoch Moor Scotland
87 H12 Ranohira Madagascar
120 J2 Ranoke Ontario
68 D7 Ranong Thailand
69 E9 Ranot Thailand
26 G6 Ransaren L Sweden
36 D3 Ransel W Germany
99 S8 Ransom Illinois
107 L3 Ransom Kansas
94 K7 Ranson W Virginia
36 G3 Ranstadt W Germany
29 N9 Rantasalmi Finland
70 D6 Rantau Kalimantan
69 E12 Rantaukampar Sumatra
70 E3 Rantaupandjang Kalimantan
69 D11 Rantauparapat Sumatra
70 F6 Rantekombola, Bk mt Sulawesi
70 F6 Rantepao Sulawesi
20 K3 Rantigny France
110 H1 Rantoul Illinois
102 H1 Rant Pass Nevada
29 M7 Rantsila Finland
29 M6 Ranua Finland
131 A8 Ranue, R Chile
28 C3 Ranum Denmark
78 K3 Ranya Iraq
68 G3 Rao Go mt Laos
65 J1 Raohe China
36 B7 Raon-l'Etape France
36 C6 Raon-sur-Plaine France
67 E5 Raoping China
41 O6 Raossi Italy
137 R7 Raoul isld Kermadec Is Pacific Oc
65 C5 Raoyang China
144 C5 Rapahoe New Zealand
44 F3 Rapallo Italy
131 B4 Rapel R Chile
101 Q4 Rapelje Montana
115 N4 Raper, C N W Terr
94 H9 Raphine Virginia
14 D2 Raphoe Irish Rep
116 R3 Rapid R Alaska
99 M1 Rapid R Minnesota
94 J8 Rapidan Virginia
94 K8 Rapidan R Virginia
138 E6 Rapid B S Australia
119 R8 Rapid City Manitoba
98 C5 Rapid City S Dakota
121 R5 Rapide Blanc Quebec
121 N6 Rapides des Joachims Quebec
141 H2 Rapid Horn C Gt Barrier Reef Aust
99 U4 Rapid River Michigan
118 H4 Rapid View Sask
52 C5 Räpina U.S.S.R.
52 B5 Rapla U.S.S.R.
95 K8 Rappahannock R Virginia
70 F6 Rappang Sulawesi
41 J3 Rapperswil Switzerland
46 F5 Rapsáni Greece
128 E6 Rapulo R Bolivia
71 G4 Rapu Rapu Philippines
78 G4 Raqqa Syria
95 N2 Raquette R New York
95 N3 Raquette Lake New York
140 D1 Raragala I N Terr Aust
71 K9 Rarakah mt Flores Indonesia
95 N6 Raritan B New Jersey
40 G5 Raron Switzerland
134 A10 Rarotonga isld Pacific Oc
42 F3 Raša Yugoslavia
71 D6 Rasa isld Palawan Philippines
77 D7 Ra's al Khaymah U.A.E.
86 H2 Ras Andadda C Ethiopia
133 E6 Rasa, Pta Argentina
131 E8 Rasa, Pta C Argentina
86 G3 Ras Dashan mt Ethiopia
52 B6 Raseiniai U.S.S.R.
80 G4 Ras el Aqra Jordan
86 A2 Ras el Cheil Somalia
80 F8 Ras el Ghor Jordan
84 H3 Râs el Kenâyis C Egypt
85 D5 Ras el Ma Mali
72 G5 Ra's Fartak C S Yemen
79 D10 Râs Ghârib Egypt
86 F3 Rashad Sudan
86 G1 Râs Hadarba C Egypt
79 F8 Rashādīya Jordan
86 B1 Ras Hafun Somalia
79 A7 Rashîd Egypt
77 A1 Rasht Iran
76 D5 Rasipuram India
77 G6 Rāsk Iran
46 D1 Raška Yugoslavia
86 G2 Râs Kasar C Sudan
86 A1 Ras Khanzira Somalia
28 D5 Raskmølle Denmark
77 J5 Raskoh reg Pakistan
31 N6 Raslavice Czechoslovakia
72 H5 Ra's Madrakah C Oman
79 C9 Râs Matarma Egypt
84 J4 Ras Muhammad C Egypt
85 A4 Ras Nouadhibou Western Sahara
133 D6 Raso, C Argentina
130 H10 Raso da Catarina Brazil
143 E8 Rason,L W Australia
47 F1 Rasovo Bulgaria
116 L7 Raspberry I Alaska
79 D10 Râs Shukheir Egypt
53 F7 Rasskazov U.S.S.R.
77 B6 Ras Tannurah Saudi Arabia
16 D9 Ras Targa Morocco
36 E6 Rastatt W Germany
28 A4 Råsted Denmark
32 H6 Rastede W Germany
Rastenburg see Kętrzyn
38 M4 Rastenfeld Austria
26 P1 Rastigaissa mt Norway
38 E7 Rastkogel mt Austria
26 M3 Råsto Sweden
26 M3 Råstoätno R Sweden
43 B8 Rasu, M mt Sardinia
80 G4 Rasun Jordan
145 E3 Rata New Zealand
71 J4 Ratahan Sulawesi
31 H6 Rataje Czechoslovakia
53 C8 Ratalovka U.S.S.R.
26 G9 Rätan Sweden
26 L8 Ratan Sweden
74 F4 Ratangarh India
68 D6 Ratchaburi Thailand
55 B4 Ratchino U.S.S.R.
110 C6 Ratcliff Arkansas
109 M4 Ratcliff Texas
143 B10 Ratcliff B W Australia
33 N5 Ratekau W Germany
74 H6 Rath India

100 J2 **Rathdrum** Idaho
14 E4 **Rathdrum** Irish Rep
68 A2 **Rathedaung** Burma
33 Q7 **Rathenow** E Germany
14 E2 **Rathfriland** N Ireland
14 C4 **Ráth Luire** Irish Rep
14 D1 **Rathmelton** Irish Rep
14 E4 **Rathnew** Irish Rep
119 T9 **Rathwell** Manitoba
Ratibor *see* **Racibórz**
32 E10 **Ratingen** W Germany
116 L10 **Rat Is** Aleutian Is
Ratisbon *see* **Regensburg**
119 S2 **Rat L** Manitoba
74 F7 **Ratlam** India
116 C4 **Ratmenova, Ostrov** *isld* U.S.S.R.
76 A2 **Ratnagiri** India
83 K11 **Ratnapura** Sri Lanka
119 N5 **Ratner** Sask
106 F5 **Raton** New Mexico
19 O18 **Ratonneau, I** France
106 F4 **Raton Pass** Colorado
115 K7 **Rat Rapids** Ontario
117 R5 **Rat River** N W Terr
109 M1 **Rattan** Oklahoma
37 K3 **Rattelsdorf** W Germany
38 N7 **Ratten** Austria
38 E7 **Rattenberg** Austria
106 F4 **Rattlesnake Buttes** *mts* Colorado
107 L4 **Rattlesnake Cr** Kansas
100 H7 **Rattlesnake Cr** Oregon
101 S7 **Rattlesnake Ra** Wyoming
123 Q4 **Rattling Brook** Nfld
15 G3 **Rattray Head** Scotland
27 H11 **Rättvik** Sweden
33 N5 **Ratzeburg** W Germany
33 N5 **Ratzeburger See** *L* W Germany
71 B1 **Rau** Halmahera Indonesia
69 E11 **Raub** Malaysia
133 F5 **Rauch** Argentina
22 H4 **Raucourt** France
29 M5 **Raudanjoki** *R* Finland
115 S4 **Raufarhöfn** Iceland
27 E11 **Raufoss** Norway
36 G7 **Rauhe Alb** *mts* W Germany
37 K4 **Rauhe Ebrach** *R* W Germany
37 K4 **Rauhenebrach** W Germany
145 F2 **Raukokore** New Zealand
145 G2 **Raukumara** New Zealand
145 F3 **Raukumara Range** New Zealand
27 C12 **Rauland** Norway
27 M10 **Rauma** Finland
26 C9 **Rauma** *R* Norway
145 E4 **Raumati** New Zealand
36 E6 **Raumünzach** W Germany
52 C6 **Rauna** U.S.S.R.
27 B11 **Raundal** *R* Norway
70 P10 **Raung, G** *mt* Java
145 E3 **Raurimu** New Zealand
28 K4 **Reus** Sweden
36 F2 **Rauschenberg** W Germany
60 T1 **Rausu** Japan
29 M9 **Rautalampi** Finland
26 K3 **Rautasjaure** *L* Sweden
29 N8 **Rautavaara** Finland
29 O10 **Rautjärvi** Finland
101 L2 **Ravalli** Montana
31 O5 **Rava Russkaya** U.S.S.R.
45 R8 **Ravello** Italy
94 F9 **Raven** Virginia
95 O4 **Ravena** New York
119 O5 **Ravendal** Sask
102 D1 **Ravendale** California
22 C4 **Ravenel** France
13 E5 **Ravenglass** England
102 F7 **Ravenna** California
45 M3 **Ravenna** Italy
110 N4 **Ravenna** Kentucky
98 H8 **Ravenna** Nebraska
94 F5 **Ravenna** Ohio
45 L3 **Ravenna** *reg* Italy
20 C3 **Ravenoville** France
141 H6 **Ravensbourne** *R* Queensland
33 S6 **Ravensbrück** E Germany
41 L2 **Ravensburg** W Germany
13 H5 **Ravenscar** England
118 H9 **Ravenscrag** Sask
141 H4 **Ravenshoe** Queensland
25 E5 **Ravenstein** Netherlands
143 D10 **Ravensthorpe** W Australia
141 H5 **Ravenswood** Queensland
94 F8 **Ravenswood** W Virginia
121 L7 **Ravensworth** Ontario
74 E3 **Ravi** *R* Pakistan
109 L1 **Ravia** Oklahoma
18 H5 **Ravières** France
46 E1 **Ravna Reka** Yugoslavia
38 L8 **Ravne Na Koroškem** Yugoslavia
57 C2 **Ravnina Dar'yalytakyr** U.S.S.R.
115 K4 **Ravn, Kap** Greenland
28 D3 **Ravnkilde** Denmark
42 H6 **Ravno** Yugoslavia
48 E6 **Ravno** *mt* Yugoslavia
74 E2 **Rawalpindi** Pakistan
117 Q3 **Rawalpindi L** N W Terr
31 M4 **Rawa Mazowiecka** Poland
78 K3 **Rawandiz** Iraq
70 L9 **Rawauntjal** Java
121 R6 **Rawdon** Quebec
119 R4 **Rawebb** Manitoba
145 D1 **Rawene** New Zealand
98 B7 **Rawhide Cr** Wyoming
31 K4 **Rawicz** Poland
69 D9 **Rawi, Ko** *isld* Thailand
143 F9 **Rawlinna** W Australia
101 S8 **Rawlins** Wyoming
143 F7 **Rawlinson, Mt** W Australia
143 G7 **Rawlinson Ra** W Australia
133 D6 **Rawson** Argentina
94 D6 **Rawson** Ohio
38 N6 **Raxalpe** *mts* Austria
103 O8 **Ray** Arizona
99 N1 **Ray** Minnesota
98 C1 **Ray** N Dakota
116 M4 **Ray** *R* Alaska
76 D3 **Rayachoti** India
76 C3 **Rayadrug** India
75 K9 **Rayagada** India
79 G5 **Rayak** Lebanon
115 O8 **Ray, C** Nfld
59 J2 **Raychickhinsk** U.S.S.R.
112 D6 **Ray City** Georgia
77 E5 **Rāyen** Iran
55 B4 **Rayevskiy** U.S.S.R.
54 J8 **Raygorodok** U.S.S.R.
9 G4 **Rayleigh** England
118 E9 **Raymond** Alberta
102 E4 **Raymond** California
110 G2 **Raymond** Illinois
111 F9 **Raymond** Mississippi
98 B1 **Raymond** Montana
98 J5 **Raymond** S Dakota
109 N3 **Raymond** Texas
100 B3 **Raymond** Washington
139 K5 **Raymond Terrace** New S Wales
109 K9 **Raymondville** Texas
119 N7 **Raymore** Sask
116 L4 **Ray Mts** Alaska
111 D11 **Rayne** Louisiana
101 P2 **Raynesford** Montana
108 A1 **Rayo** New Mexico
68 E6 **Rayong** Thailand
111 E9 **Rayville** Louisiana
77 A2 **Razan** Iran
56 D2 **Razdolinsk** U.S.S.R.
48 M6 **Razelm, L** Romania
21 H9 **Razès** France
47 H1 **Razgrad** Bulgaria
47 F3 **Razlog** Bulgaria
18 B4 **Raz, Pte. du** France
110 B1 **Rea** Missouri
142 A1 **Reabold Hill** W Australia
117 D6 **Reaburn, Mt** Alaska
109 O2 **Reader** Arkansas
119 Q5 **Reader L** Manitoba
9 F5 **Reading** England
127 J2 **Reading** Jamaica
94 C5 **Reading** Michigan
99 L6 **Reading** Minnesota
95 M6 **Reading** Pennsylvania
119 M9 **Readlyn** Sask
95 P4 **Readsboro** Vermont
99 Q6 **Readstown** Wisconsin
109 L4 **Reagan** Texas
128 E7 **Real, Cord** *mts* Bolivia
128 C4 **Real, Cord** *mts* Ecuador
44 C1 **Reale** Italy
133 E5 **Realico** Argentina
109 J8 **Realitos** Texas
68 F7 **Ream** Cambodia
100 H2 **Reardan** Washington
15 G2 **Reawick** Scotland
112 D6 **Rebecca** Georgia
143 D9 **Rebecca, L** W Australia
100 H8 **Rebel Creek** Nevada
33 T5 **Rebelow** E Germany
117 P3 **Rebesca L** N W Terr
84 G5 **Rebiana** Libya
28 D3 **Rebild** Denmark
26 J5 **Rebnesjaure** *L* Sweden
128 G5 **Reboja, Cachoeira de** Brazil
29 P8 **Reboly** U.S.S.R.
47 F2 **Rebrovo** Bulgaria
60 P1 **Rebun-suidō** *str* Japan
60 P1 **Rebun-tō** *isld* Japan
133 E5 **Recalde** Argentina
48 G5 **Recaş** Romania
44 F3 **Recco** Italy
40 A2 **Recey** France
19 J5 **Recey-sur-Ource** France
143 D10 **Recherche, Arch.of the** W Australia
36 B6 **Réchicourt le Château** France
54 B4 **Rechitsa** U.S.S.R.
33 R6 **Rechlin** E Germany
22 L3 **Recht** Belgium
130 J10 **Recife** Brazil
89 D10 **Recife, C** S Africa
83 J12 **Recif I** Seychelles
32 G8 **Recke** W Germany
32 F9 **Recklinghausen** W Germany
101 U5 **Recluse** Wyoming
22 J4 **Recogne** Belgium
131 F2 **Reconquista** Argentina
19 O15 **Recoubeau** France
146 E10 **Recovery Gl** Antarctica
133 D3 **Recreo** Argentina
143 C8 **Recruit Flats** *salt pan* W Aust
31 J2 **Recz** Poland
110 E6 **Red** *R* Arkansas
98 K2 **Red** *R* Minnesota
69 F10 **Redang** *isld* Malaysia
22 K4 **Redange** Luxembourg
122 G7 **Red Bank** New Brunswick
95 N6 **Red Bank** New Jersey
141 K7 **Redbank** Queensland
Red Basin *see* **Sichuan Pendi**
111 H7 **Red Bay** Alabama
113 B7 **Redbay** Florida
123 Q2 **Red Bay** Labrador
120 J8 **Red Bay** Ontario
118 K6 **Redberry L** Sask
109 N10 **Red Bird Airfield** Texas
102 B1 **Red Bluff** California
141 G3 **Red Bluff** Queensland
143 C6 **Red Bluff** *mt* W Australia
108 D4 **Red Bluff Res** Texas/New Mex
9 F4 **Redbourn** England
110 G3 **Red Bud** Illinois
103 M6 **Red Butte** *mt* Arizona
98 A8 **Red Buttes** Wyoming
99 M2 **Redby** Minnesota
13 G4 **Redcar** England
106 D2 **Red Cliff** Colorado
141 L7 **Redcliffe** Queensland
89 F2 **Redcliffe** Zimbabwe
143 D8 **Redcliffe, Mt** W Australia
138 F5 **Red Cliffs** Victoria
111 H11 **Red Cr** Mississippi
101 R8 **Red Cr** Wyoming
95 L3 **Red Creek** New York
118 D6 **Red Deer** Alberta
119 Q6 **Red Deer L** Manitoba
119 P6 **Red Deer R** Sask
111 D11 **Reddell** Louisiana
13 E4 **Red Dial** England
113 E8 **Reddick** Florida
102 B1 **Redding** California
118 H1 **Reddit** Ontario
9 E3 **Redditch** England
33 O6 **Redefin** E Germany
98 E4 **Red Elm** S Dakota
129 K5 **Redenção** Brazil
85 F2 **Redeyef** Tunisia
111 D7 **Redfield** Arkansas
99 M8 **Redfield** Iowa
98 H5 **Redfield** S Dakota
101 L5 **Redfish L** Idaho
108 C6 **Redford** Texas
99 R5 **Redgranite** Wisconsin
9 F5 **Redhill** England
145 D4 **Red Hill** *mt* New Zealand
143 B7 **Red Hill** *peak* W Australia
111 K10 **Red Hills** Alabama
95 O5 **Red Hook** New York
100 H8 **Red House** Nevada
123 S6 **Red I** Nfld
98 C4 **Redig** S Dakota
123 Q5 **Red Indian L** Nfld
103 O9 **Redington** Arizona
98 C8 **Redinqton** Nebraska
110 L1 **Red Key** Indiana
52 E6 **Redkino** U.S.S.R.
117 O5 **Redknife** *R* N W Terr
103 K6 **Red L** Arizona
138 D4 **Red L** S Australia
103 M6 **Red Lake** Arizona
115 K7 **Red Lake** Ontario
143 D10 **Red Lake** W Australia
102 G7 **Redlands** California
98 K2 **Red L. Falls** Minnesota
95 L7 **Red Lion** Pennsylvania
101 Q4 **Red Lodge** Montana
118 C7 **Red Lodge Prov. Park** Alberta
145 E2 **Red Mercury I** New Zealand
13 G5 **Redmire** England
110 J2 **Redmon** Illinois
100 D5 **Redmond** Oregon
103 N2 **Redmond** Utah
102 G6 **Red Mt** California
112 C1 **Red Mt** Tennessee
37 L5 **Rednitz** *R* W Germany
99 L8 **Red Oak** Iowa
110 A7 **Red Oak** Oklahoma
109 L3 **Red Oak** Texas
21 A6 **Redon** France
16 B2 **Redondela** Spain
16 B6 **Redondo** Portugal
102 F8 **Redondo Beach** California
128 F3 **Redondo, Pico** *mt* Brazil
116 L6 **Redoubt Vol** Alaska
117 O9 **Red Pass** Br Columbia
118 J6 **Red Pheasant** Sask
141 G2 **Red Pt** Queensland
117 J6 **Red R** Br Columbia
111 D10 **Red R** Louisiana
119 U9 **Red R** Manitoba
109 J1 **Red R** Texas
Red R Vietnam *see* **Song-koi**
122 E7 **Red Rapids** New Brunswick
101 K4 **Red R. Hot Springs** Idaho
103 N9 **Redrock** Arizona
106 B9 **Red Rock** New Mexico
107 N5 **Red Rock** Oklahoma
119 P2 **Red Rock** Ontario
109 K6 **Red Rock** Texas
117 Q3 **Redrock L** N W Terr
99 N8 **Red Rock Res** Iowa
143 G9 **Red Rocks Pt** W Australia
8 A7 **Redruth** England
86 G1 **Red Sea** Africa/Arabian Pen
112 H3 **Red Springs** N Carolina
117 M9 **Redstone** Br Columbia
101 V1 **Redstone** Montana
117 K4 **Redstone** *R* N W Terr
120 J4 **Redstone** *R* Ontario
124 E9 **Red Tank** Panama Canal Zone
22 J4 **Redu** Belgium
119 Q9 **Redvers** Sask
118 D5 **Redwater** Alberta
121 L6 **Redwater** Ontario
109 N2 **Redwater** Texas
98 A2 **Redwater** *R* Montana
143 C7 **Red Well** W Australia
8 B1 **Red Wharf B** Wales
118 E6 **Red Willow** Alberta
98 E9 **Red Willow Cr** Nebraska
99 O5 **Red Wing** Minnesota
102 B4 **Redwood City** California
99 L5 **Redwood Falls** Minnesota
102 A2 **Redwood Valley** California
71 C5 **Reed Bank** S China Sea
94 B3 **Reed City** Michigan
98 D3 **Reeder** N Dakota
102 E5 **Reedley** California
101 Q4 **Reedpoint** Montana
106 C8 **Reeds Pk** New Mexico
100 A6 **Reedsport** Oregon
94 F8 **Reedy** W Virginia
112 E3 **Reedy** *R* S Carolina
138 D4 **Reedy Lagoon** S Australia
141 G4 **Reedy Springs** Queensland
144 C5 **Reefton** New Zealand
98 G5 **Ree Heights** S Dakota
14 C3 **Ree, L** Irish Rep
110 G5 **Reelfoot L** Tennessee
32 G6 **Reepsholt** W Germany
28 G5 **Reersø** Denmark
25 F5 **Rees** W Germany
94 D3 **Reese** Michigan
100 H9 **Reese** *R* Nevada
120 G3 **Reesor** Ontario
33 P6 **Reetz** E Germany
146 J6 **Reeves Gl** Antarctica
78 G2 **Refahiye** Turkey
111 J8 **Reform** Alabama
133 D3 **Refresco** Chile
28 F6 **Refs** Denmark
27 G14 **Reftele** Sweden
109 K7 **Refugio** Texas
31 J2 **Rega** *R* Poland
120 E4 **Regan** Ontario
80 D3 **Regavim** Israel
37 N5 **Regen** *R* W Germany
37 N5 **Regensburg** W Germany
37 N5 **Regenstauf** W Germany
119 R9 **Regent** Manitoba
120 F5 **Regent** Ontario
85 E3 **Reggane** Algeria
45 L4 **Reggello** Italy
43 G10 **Reggio di Calabria** Italy
45 J2 **Reggiolo** Italy
45 J2 **Reggio nell Emilia** Italy
129 H3 **Regina** Brazil
119 N8 **Regina** Sask
37 N1 **Regis** E Germany
77 J4 **Registan** Afghanistan
22 G4 **Régniowez** France
37 K4 **Regnitz** *R* W Germany
16 B6 **Reguengos de Monsaraz** Portugal
37 N3 **Rehau** W Germany
36 D5 **Rehberg** *mt* W Germany
32 H7 **Rehden** W Germany
33 Q7 **Rehfeld** E Germany
74 H7 **Rehli** India
32 J8 **Rehme** W Germany
33 O5 **Rehna** E Germany
87 C10 **Rehoboth** Namibia
95 M8 **Rehoboth Beach** Delaware
80 C6 **Rehovot** Israel
36 F3 **Reichelshausen** W Germany
37 N2 **Reichenbach** E Germany
38 L7 **Reichenfels** Austria
37 J1 **Reichensachsen** W Germany
38 F5 **Reichertsheim** W Germany
37 L6 **Reichertshofen** W Germany
101 N4 **Reichle** Montana
36 D2 **Reichshof** W Germany
36 D6 **Reichshoffen** France
143 G9 **Reid** W Australia
118 J8 **Reid L** Saskatchewan
140 B4 **Reid, Mt** N Terr Aust
141 H4 **Reid R** Queensland
112 E5 **Reidsville** Georgia
112 H1 **Reidsville** N Carolina
9 F5 **Reigate** England
27 N13 **Reigi** U.S.S.R.
25 C5 **Reijen** Netherlands
21 C9 **Ré, Ile de** France
103 O9 **Reiley Pk** Arizona
36 F5 **Reilingen** W Germany
19 P17 **Reillanne** France
80 A8 **Re'im** Israel
22 G5 **Reims** France
18 H3 **Reims, Mt de** France
133 C8 **Reina Adelaida, Arch. de la** *islds* Chile
99 O7 **Reinbeck** Iowa
32 M5 **Reinbek** W Germany
33 S4 **Reinberg** E Germany
119 U6 **Reindeer I** Manitoba
119 Q1 **Reindeer L** Man/Sask
26 F4 **Reine** Norway
140 D6 **Reinecke, Mt** N Terr Aust
27 C11 **Reineskarvet** *mt* Norway
33 M5 **Reinfeld** W Germany
145 D1 **Reinga, C** New Zealand
32 L10 **Reinhausen** W Germany
36 C5 **Reinheim** W Germany
33 S7 **Reinickendorf** E Germany
33 T7 **Reinickendorf** W Germany
16 E1 **Reinosa** Spain
26 L2 **Reinöy** *isld* Norway
37 P1 **Reinsberg** E Germany
36 B4 **Reinsfeld** W Germany
33 P5 **Reinstorf** E Germany
26 M2 **Reisa** *R* Norway
37 O6 **Reisbach** W Germany
29 L8 **Reisjärvi** Finland
38 H8 **Reisseck** *mt* Austria
25 F2 **Reitdiep** *R* Netherlands
38 G6 **Reiter Alpen** *mt* Austria
38 J7 **Reitereck** *mt* Austria
87 E11 **Reitz** S Africa
37 P2 **Reitzenhain** E Germany
27 H13 **Rejmyra** Sweden
31 O4 **Rejowiec** Poland
28 B6 **Rejsby** Denmark
27 H12 **Rekarne** Sweden
32 F9 **Reken** W Germany
60 R3 **Rekifune-gawa** *R* Japan
109 N4 **Reklaw** Texas
46 E1 **Rekovac** Yugoslavia
112 E6 **Relee** Georgia
98 G6 **Reliance** S Dakota
101 Q8 **Reliance** Wyoming
85 E1 **Relizane** Algeria
124 G4 **Rellano** Mexico
36 C2 **Remagen** W Germany
20 G5 **Rémalard** France
129 K5 **Remanso** Brazil
138 E4 **Remarkable, Mt** S Australia
70 N9 **Rembang** Java
36 F6 **Remchingen** W Germany
37 L2 **Remda** E Germany
126 E3 **Remedios** Cuba
124 F5 **Remedios** Mexico
32 G6 **Remels** W Germany
77 F6 **Remeshk** Iran
22 L4 **Remich** Luxembourg
121 L5 **Rémigny** Quebec
120 H3 **Remi L** Ontario
22 J4 **Remilly-Allicourt** France
99 T9 **Remington** Indiana
94 K8 **Remington** Virginia
40 E1 **Remiremont** France
33 N8 **Remlingen** W Germany
100 B6 **Remote** Oregon
22 K3 **Remouchamps** Belgium
19 N17 **Remoulins** France
83 K14 **Remparts, R. des** Réunion Indian Oc
36 H6 **Rems** *R* W Germany
36 C1 **Remscheid** W Germany
99 L7 **Remsen** Iowa
121 P9 **Remsen** New York
94 B3 **Remus** Michigan
19 O16 **Rémuzat** France
27 E10 **Rena** Norway
120 G4 **Renabie** Ontario
21 B6 **Renac** France
Renaix *see* **Ronse**
71 D2 **Rena Pt** Luzon Philippines
128 E4 **Renascença** Brazil
21 C6 **Renazé** France
36 E6 **Renchen** W Germany
26 E10 **Rendal** Norway
28 A5 **Renderne** Denmark
32 L4 **Rendsburg** W Germany
121 L4 **Reneault** Quebec
123 U7 **Renews** Nfld
121 O7 **Renfrew** Ontario
12 D2 **Renfrew** Scotland
Renfrew *co see* **Strathclyde** *reg*
69 F13 **Rengat** Sumatra
67 C1 **Ren He** *R* China
67 D4 **Renhua** China
67 B3 **Renhuai** China
48 L5 **Reni** U.S.S.R.
94 G9 **Renick** W Virginia
120 J2 **Renison** Ontario
139 H8 **Renison Bell** Tasmania
86 F3 **Renk** Sudan
29 L11 **Renko** Finland
25 E5 **Renkum** Netherlands
115 R3 **Renland** *reg* Greenland
138 F5 **Renmark** S Australia
65 F1 **Renmin** China
26 D9 **Rennebu** Norway
137 N4 **Rennell** *isld* Solomon Is
36 E2 **Rennerod** W Germany
140 C4 **Renner Springs** N Terr Aust
37 L6 **Rennertshafen** W Germany
20 B5 **Rennes** France
27 A12 **Rennesöy** *isld* Norway
118 F1 **Rennie** Manitoba
38 J7 **Rennweq** Austria
102 E2 **Reno** Nevada
45 K3 **Reno** *R* Italy
99 L4 **Reno, L** Minnesota
122 G7 **Renous** New Brunswick
94 K5 **Renovo** Pennsylvania
119 M7 **Renown** Sask
65 C5 **Renqiu** China
28 C7 **Rens** Denmark
67 E5 **Renshan** China
67 A2 **Renshou** China
99 T9 **Rensselaer** Indiana
95 O4 **Rensselaer** New York
95 N4 **Rensselaerville** New York
25 E4 **Renswoude** Netherlands
100 C2 **Renton** Washington
37 K3 **Rentweinsdorf** W Germany
37 J3 **Rentwertshausen** E Germany
99 L5 **Renville** Minnesota
119 R6 **Renwer** Manitoba
22 H4 **Renwez** France
99 N7 **Renwick** Iowa
145 D4 **Renwick** New Zealand
65 C6 **Ren Xian** China
67 D7 **Renxing** China
18 E8 **Réole, la** France
76 E2 **Repalle** India
129 G4 **Repartição** Brazil
129 G4 **Repartimento** Brazil
40 E3 **Repentis, Mt** France
29 J8 **Replot** Finland
55 E1 **Repolovo** U.S.S.R.
145 F3 **Reporoa** New Zealand
40 E6 **Reposoir, Chaine de** *mt* France
26 J5 **Reppentjåkko** *mt* Sweden
111 J10 **Repton** Alabama
107 N2 **Republic** Kansas
94 D5 **Republic** Ohio
100 G1 **Republic** Washington
98 H9 **Republican** *R* Nebraska/Kansas
115 L4 **Repulse Bay** N W Terr
141 J5 **Repulse Bay** Queensland
26 P1 **Repvåg** Norway
98 F2 **Reqan** N Dakota
130 H6 **Reqência** Brazil
98 D3 **Reqent** N Dakota
20 B3 **Reqnéville** France
25 G4 **Reqqe** *R* Netherlands
100 A8 **Requa** California
128 D5 **Requena** Peru
17 G5 **Requena** Spain
18 G8 **Réquista** France
21 J7 **Rère** *R* France
145 F3 **Rerewhakaaitu L** New Zealand
15 G2 **Rerwick** Scotland
70 K8 **Resag, G** *mt* Sumatra
102 F7 **Reseda** California
26 J8 **Resele** Sweden
28 C3 **Resen** Denmark
28 C4 **Resen** Denmark
46 E3 **Resen** Yugoslavia
111 F11 **Reserve** Louisiana
98 B1 **Reserve** Montana
106 B8 **Reserve** New Mexico
119 P6 **Reserve** Sask
54 F7 **Reshetilovka** U.S.S.R.
41 N4 **Resia** Italy
133 F3 **Resistencia** Argentina
48 G5 **Reşiţa** Romania
122 E6 **Resitgouche R** New Brunswick
115 K3 **Resolute** N W Terr
144 A6 **Resolution I** New Zealand
115 N5 **Resolution Island** N W Terr
115 N6 **Resolution L** Quebec
32 L7 **Resse** W Germany
20 K3 **Ressons** France
22 D4 **Ressons-sur-Matz** France
127 K3 **Rest** Jamaica
12 D1 **Rest and be Thankful** *hill* Scotland
122 F5 **Restigouche** Quebec
119 Q9 **Reston** Manitoba
13 F2 **Reston** Scotland
121 L6 **Restoule** Ontario
31 N1 **Reszel** Poland
48 H5 **Retezatului, Munti** *mts* Romania
22 G5 **Rethel** France
32 K7 **Rethem** W Germany
32 L8 **Rethen** W Germany
47 G9 **Réthimnon** Crete Greece
42 C2 **Retiche, Alpi** *mts* Italy
22 J1 **Retie** Belgium
21 C6 **Retiers** France
118 E8 **Retlaw** Alberta
141 G7 **Retreat** Queensland
108 E8 **Retrop** Oklahoma
9 G4 **Rettendon** England
36 D3 **Rettert** W Germany
31 J7 **Retz** Austria
21 B7 **Retz** *reg* France
36 H4 **Retzbach** W Germany
21 G7 **Reugny** France
22 L3 **Reuland** Belgium
83 K13 **Réunion** *isld* Indian Oc
17 H3 **Reus** Spain
25 D6 **Reusel** Netherlands
41 J4 **Reuss** *R* Switzerland
33 Q10 **Reussen** E Germany
48 L3 **Reut** *R* U.S.S.R.
33 R5 **Reuterstadt Stavenhagen** E Germany
37 M3 **Reuth** E Germany
37 N4 **Reuth** W Germany
36 G7 **Reutlingen** W Germany
41 N3 **Reutte** Austria
98 C4 **Reva** S Dakota
80 C6 **Revadim** Israel
40 C6 **Revard** *mt* France
103 H4 **Reveille Pk** Nevada
18 G9 **Revel** France
142 G2 **Reveley I** W Australia
117 O10 **Revelstoke** Br Columbia
118 J6 **Revenue** Sask
45 K1 **Revere** Italy
9 F1 **Revesby** England
19 J4 **Revigny** France
117 H8 **Revillagigedo I** Alaska
20 C2 **Réville** France
98 K5 **Revillo** S Dakota
22 H4 **Revin** France
79 E7 **Revivim** Israel
28 F6 **Revninge** Denmark
26 O1 **Revsbotn** Norway
26 H9 **Revsund** Sweden
88 D9 **Revubué** *R* Mozambique
94 J5 **Rew** Pennsylvania
75 J6 **Rewa** India
145 E4 **Rewa** *mt* New Zealand
80 B7 **Rewaha** Israel
118 H6 **Reward** Sask
74 G4 **Rewari** India
99 Q7 **Rewey** Wisconsin
101 O6 **Rexburg** Idaho
107 K2 **Rexford** Kansas
100 K1 **Rexford** Montana
22 D2 **Rexpoede** France
122 H7 **Rexton** New Brunswick
80 D2 **Reyba** Israel
86 B4 **Rey-Bouba** Cameroon
28 N2 **Reydhafells Tindur** *mt* Faeroes
107 L6 **Reydon** Oklahoma
102 E7 **Reyes Pk** California
115 R5 **Reykjavík** Iceland
119 T7 **Reykjavik** Manitoba
119 M6 **Reynaud** Sask
112 C5 **Reynolds** Georgia
100 J6 **Reynolds** Idaho
99 Q8 **Reynolds** Illinois
110 K1 **Reynolds** Indiana
98 J9 **Reynolds** Nebraska
140 B2 **Reynolds** *R* N Terr Aust
138 D4 **Reynolds, L** S Australia
140 C5 **Reynolds Ra** N Terr Aust
94 J5 **Reynoldsville** Pennsylvania
109 J9 **Reynosa** Mexico
40 B5 **Reyssouze** *R* France
78 K3 **Rezaiyeh** Iran
37 K5 **Rezat** *R* W Germany
52 C6 **Rēzekne** U.S.S.R.
55 D3 **Rezh** U.S.S.R.
48 M3 **Rezina** U.S.S.R.
47 J3 **Rezvaya** *R* Turkey
41 K5 **Rezzonico** Italy
32 K6 **Rhade** W Germany
98 C3 **Rhame** N Dakota
41 L3 **Rhätikon** *mt* Switzerland
36 C4 **Rhaunen** W Germany
8 C3 **Rhayader** Wales
79 F4 **Rhazir** Lebanon
32 H9 **Rheda-Wiedenbrück** W Germany
32 F6 **Rhede** Niedersachsen W Germany
32 E9 **Rhede** Nordrhein-Westfalen W Germany
25 F4 **Rheden** Netherlands
9 F3 **Rhee, R** England
119 P7 **Rhein** Sask
36 E6 **Rhein** *R* W Europe
36 D6 **Rheinau** W Germany
36 B2 **Rheinbach** W Germany
36 D3 **Rheinböllen** W Germany
36 C3 **Rheinbrohl** W Germany
25 F6 **Rheindahlen** W Germany
32 F8 **Rheine** W Germany
41 J2 **Rheinfall** Switzerland
40 G2 **Rheinfeldon** Switzerland
32 E10 **Rheinhausen** W Germany
36 B3 **Rheinland-Pfalz** *land* W Germany
36 E6 **Rheinmünster** W Germany
33 R6 **Rheinsberg** E Germany
36 E6 **Rheinstetten** W Germany
41 L3 **Rhein Tal** *V* Switzerland
36 E5 **Rheinzabern** W Germany
40 F6 **Rhêmes, Val de** Italy
85 D3 **Rhemilès** Algeria
32 J10 **Rhena** W Germany
25 E5 **Rhenen** Netherlands
36 D3 **Rhens** W Germany
36 B1 **Rheydt** W Germany
33 R6 **Rhin** *R* E Germany
40 G2 **Rhin** *R* France
36 D7 **Rhinau** France
112 D6 **Rhine** Georgia
Rhine *R* France *see* **Rhin** *R*
Rhine *R* Germany/Switzerland *see* **Rhein** *R*
95 O5 **Rhinebeck** New York
99 R4 **Rhinelander** Wisconsin
33 R7 **Rhinkanal** E Germany
33 Q7 **Rhinow** E Germany
16 E10 **Rhis** *R* Morocco
41 K6 **Rho** Italy
127 K1 **Rhoades, Pt** Jamaica
95 Q5 **Rhode I** *state* U.S.A.
94 F9 **Rhodell** W Virginia
32 K10 **Rhoden** W Germany
94 C3 **Rhodes** Michigan
83 L13 **Rhodes** *B* Kerguelen Indian Oc
Rhodes *isld see* **Ródhos**
Rhodesia *see* **Zimbabwe**
112 F2 **Rhodhiss L** N Carolina
109 K2 **Rhome** Texas
8 C4 **Rhondda** Wales
19 O13 **Rhône** *R* France
41 H5 **Rhône** *R* Switzerland
19 N18 **Rhône, Grand** *R* France
19 **Rhône Valley** France
8 B4 **Rhosili** Wales
8 B1 **Rhosneigr** Môn Wales
8 C1 **Rhos-on-Sea** Wales
85 F2 **Rhourd El Baguel** Algeria
18 G7 **Rhue** *R* France
32 M9 **Rhume** *R* W Germany
18 D9 **Rhune, la** *mt* France/Spain
8 C1 **Rhyl** Wales
32 G9 **Rhynern** W Germany
15 F3 **Rhynie** Scotland
131 E8 **Riachos, I de los** Argentina
16 B2 **Ría de Arosa** Spain
16 A2 **Ría de Corcubion** Spain
16 A1 **Ria de Lage** Spain
16 A2 **Ría de Murosa y Noya** Spain
16 B2 **Ría de Pontevedra** Spain
16 B1 **Ria de Sta. Marta** Spain
16 B2 **Ría de Vigo** Spain
21 C7 **Riaillé** France
70 B5 **Riam** Kalimantan
45 N5 **Riano** Italy
16 D2 **Riaño** Spain
19 P17 **Rians** France
16 E5 **Riansares** *R* Spain
74 F2 **Riasi** Kashmir
69 F12 **Riau, Kep** *islds* Indonesia
16 E3 **Riaza** Spain
16 B2 **Ribadavia** Spain
16 C1 **Ribadeo** Spain
16 D1 **Ribadesella** Spain
17 H2 **Ribagorza** *dist* Spain
129 K4 **Ribamar** Brazil
17 H3 **Ribarroja, Emb. de** *res* Spain
17 J2 **Ribas de Fresser** Spain
130 D7 **Ribas do Rio Pardo** Brazil
16 B5 **Ribatejo** *prov* Portugal
88 G9 **Ribauè** Mozambique
26 K1 **Ribbenesöy** *isld* Norway
13 F6 **Ribble, R** England
28 B6 **Ribe** Denmark
28 B6 **Ribe Å** *R* Denmark
40 F1 **Ribeauville** France
22 D4 **Ribécourt** France
133 H2 **Ribeira** *R* Brazil
133 H2 **Ribeirão Prêto** Brazil
129 J5 **Ribeiro Gonçalves** Brazil
22 E4 **Ribemont** France
43 E11 **Ribera** Sicily
18 F7 **Ribérac** France
128 E6 **Riberalta** Bolivia
19 P16 **Ribiers** France
121 L5 **Rib Lake** Ontario
99 Q4 **Rib Lake** Wisconsin
99 R5 **Rib Mt** Wisconsin
42 F3 **Ribnica** Yugoslavia
33 Q4 **Ribnitz-Damgarten** E Germany
118 G6 **Ribstone** Alberta
118 F6 **Ribstone Cr** Alberta
109 K8 **Ricardo** Texas
45 M3 **Riccione** Italy
103 K7 **Rice** California
109 L3 **Rice** Texas
112 F6 **Riceboro** Georgia
99 N3 **Rice L** Minnesota
121 M8 **Rice L** Ontario
120 H5 **Rice Lake** Ontario
99 P4 **Rice Lake** Wisconsin
119 N8 **Riceton** Sask
99 O6 **Riceville** Iowa
18 H5 **Riceys, les** France
118 K6 **Richard** Sask
114 H3 **Richard Collinson Inlet** N W Terr
89 H7 **Richards B** S Africa
114 F4 **Richards I** N W Terr
144 A6 **Richards, Mt** New Zealand
116 N6 **Richardson** Alaska
109 O8 **Richardson** Texas
117 O3 **Richardson I** N W Terr
95 R2 **Richardson Lakes** Maine
143 C8 **Richardson, Mt** W Australia
144 B6 **Richardson Mts** New Zealand
114 F4 **Richardson Mts** Yukon Terr/N W Terr
119 N8 **Richardson Sta** Sask
85 A5 **Richard Toll** Senegal
98 D3 **Richardton** N Dakota
94 J4 **Richburg** New York
118 F7 **Richdale** Alberta
143 C10 **Riche, C** W Australia
21 F7 **Richelieu** France
121 R7 **Richelieu** *R* Quebec
20 J2 **Richemont** France
123 P3 **Riche Pt** Nfld
101 U2 **Richey** Montana
101 L6 **Richfield** Idaho
107 J4 **Richfield** Kansas
103 M3 **Richfield** Utah
95 L4 **Richford** New York
121 S8 **Richford** Vermont
102 E6 **Richgrove** California
110 B3 **Rich Hill** Missouri
122 H7 **Richibucto** New Brunswick
118 F4 **Rich Lake** Alberta
112 C5 **Richland** Georgia
94 B4 **Richland** Michigan
110 D4 **Richland** Missouri
101 T1 **Richland** Montana
95 N7 **Richland** New Jersey
100 H5 **Richland** Oregon
100 F3 **Richland** Washington
99 Q6 **Richland Center** Wisconsin
109 L4 **Richland Cr** Texas
112 K3 **Richlands** N Carolina
94 F9 **Richlands** Virginia
109 J4 **Richland Springs** Texas
118 J7 **Richlea** Sask
102 B4 **Richmond** California
9 F5 **Richmond** Greater London England
110 M2 **Richmond** Indiana
127 L2 **Richmond** Jamaica
110 M4 **Richmond** Kentucky
95 S2 **Richmond** Maine
99 M4 **Richmond** Minnesota
139 K5 **Richmond** New S Wales
145 D4 **Richmond** New Zealand
13 G5 **Richmond** North Yorkshire England
121 P7 **Richmond** Ontario
100 F5 **Richmond** Oregon
122 H7 **Richmond** Pr Edward I
121 S7 **Richmond** Quebec
141 G5 **Richmond** Queensland
89 C8 **Richmond** S Africa
139 H8 **Richmond** Tasmania
109 M6 **Richmond** Texas
101 O8 **Richmond** Utah
94 K9 **Richmond** Virginia
112 F6 **Richmond Hill** Georgia
121 L9 **Richmond Hill** Ontario
142 A4 **Richmond, L** W Australia
139 L3 **Richmond R** New S Wales
139 L3 **Richmond Ra** *mts* New S Wales
95 N4 **Richmondville** New York
118 H8 **Richmound** Sask
110 B7 **Rich Mt** Arkansas
33 R4 **Richtenberg** E Germany
111 H10 **Richton** Mississippi
99 L3 **Richville** Minnesota
94 D6 **Richwood** Ohio
99 S6 **Richwood** Wisconsin
94 G8 **Richwood** W Virginia
110 F3 **Richwoods** Missouri
32 M4 **Rickling** W Germany
9 F4 **Rickmansworth** England
17 G3 **Ricla** Spain
106 B4 **Rico** Colorado
40 F5 **Riddes** Switzerland
100 J7 **Riddle** Idaho
100 B7 **Riddle** Oregon
140 C6 **Riddock, Mt** N Terr Aust
121 P7 **Rideau** *R* Ontario
121 P8 **Rideau Canal** Ontario
121 O8 **Rideau, L** Ontario
98 B4 **Ridge** Montana
120 F2 **Ridge** *R* Ontario
101 N7 **Ridgedale** Idaho
119 N5 **Ridgedale** Sask
99 T10 **Ridge Farm** Illinois
95 O5 **Ridgefield** Connecticut
111 F9 **Ridgeland** Mississippi
112 F5 **Ridgeland** S Carolina
99 P4 **Ridgeland** Wisconsin
141 K6 **Ridgelands** Queensland
94 J7 **Ridgeley** W Virginia
95 M8 **Ridgely** Maryland
112 F4 **Ridge Spring** S Carolina
120 J10 **Ridgetown** Ontario
110 L1 **Ridgeville** Indiana
118 E1 **Ridgeville** Manitoba
112 G4 **Ridgeville** S Carolina
110 C1 **Ridgeway** Missouri
112 G3 **Ridgeway** S Carolina
99 Q6 **Ridgeway** Wisconsin
110 G5 **Ridgley** Tennessee
106 C3 **Ridgway** Colorado
110 H4 **Ridgway** Illinois
98 B4 **Ridgway** Montana
94 J5 **Ridgway** Pennsylvania
119 R8 **Riding Mt** Manitoba
143 D10 **Ridley, Mt** W Australia
142 C5 **Ridley, R** W Australia
118 J7 **Ridpath** Sask
98 F4 **Ridqeview** S Dakota
13 F3 **Ridsdale** England
38 H5 **Ried** Austria
37 M5 **Rieden** W Germany
37 M6 **Riedenburg** W Germany
36 D5 **Riedseltz** France
40 G2 **Riehen** Switzerland
118 B2 **Riel** Manitoba
32 H8 **Riemsloh** W Germany
36 H3 **Rieneck** W Germany
33 S10 **Riesa** E Germany
133 C8 **Riesco, I** Chile
43 F11 **Riesi** Sicily
33 O10 **Riestedt** E Germany
89 D7 **Riet** *R* S Africa
52 B6 **Rietavas** U.S.S.R.
32 H9 **Rietberg** W Germany
89 B3 **Rietfontein** Botswana
42 E6 **Rieti** Italy
41 O3 **Rietzer Grieskogel** *mt* Austria
18 G8 **Rieupeyroux** France
19 Q17 **Riez** France
22 G4 **Riezes** Belgium
16 E10 **Rif** *dist* Morocco
106 C2 **Rifle** Colorado
94 C2 **Rifle** *R* Michigan
52 B5 **Riga, G of** U.S.S.R.
142 B5 **Riga, Mt** W Australia
77 F5 **Rigān** Iran
121 Q7 **Rigaud** Quebec
19 J6 **Rigaud, Mt** France
101 O6 **Rigby** Idaho
110 F2 **Riggston** Illinois
37 M4 **Riglasreuth** W Germany
45 K4 **Rignano sull'Arno** Italy
21 F7 **Rigny-Ussé** France
115 O7 **Rigolet** Labrador
80 G4 **Rihaba** Jordan
29 M4 **Riipi** Finland
146 A7 **Riiser-Larsenhalvøya** *pen* Antarctica
42 F3 **Rijeka** Yugoslavia
25 C5 **Rijsbergen** Netherlands
25 G4 **Rijssen** Netherlands
25 R4 **Rijswijk** Netherlands
48 H2 **Rika** *R* U.S.S.R.
60 R2 **Rikubetsu** Japan
61 Q6 **Rikuchū Kaigan Nat. Park** Japan
61 P6 **Rikuzen Takata** Japan
110 J2 **Riley** Indiana
107 O2 **Riley** Kansas
106 C7 **Riley** New Mexico
100 F6 **Riley** Oregon
21 F7 **Rillé** France
47 F2 **Rilski Manastir** Bulgaria
128 C4 **Rimachi, L** Peru
145 E1 **Rimariki I** New Zealand
40 B1 **Rimaucourt** France
48 F2 **Rimava** *R* Czechoslovakia
118 C6 **Rimbey** Alberta
27 K12 **Rimbo** Sweden
94 H5 **Rimersburg** Pennsylvania
27 H13 **Rimforsa** Sweden
45 N3 **Rimini** Italy
80 E2 **Rimmon** Israel
48 K5 **Rîmnicul** *R* Romania
22 H4 **Rimoqne** France
122 D5 **Rimouski R** Quebec
36 H4 **Rimpar** W Germany
40 G5 **Rimpfischhorn** *mt* Switzerland
75 N4 **Rinbung** China
37 P6 **Rinchnach** W Germany
126 A2 **Rincon** Bonaire **W Indies**
106 C9 **Rincon** New Mexico
133 D2 **Rinconada** Argentina
124 H6 **Rincón de Romos** Mexico
28 A6 **Rindby** Denmark
70 K8 **Rindingan, Bt** *mt* Sumatra
71 J9 **Rindja** *isld* Indonesia
70 Q10 **Rindjani,G** *mt* Indonesia
28 B4 **Rind Kirke** Denmark
139 J8 **Ringarooma** Tasmania
28 E6 **Ringe** Denmark
27 D10 **Ringebu** Norway
41 K4 **Ringelspitz** *mt* Switzerland
32 E9 **Ringenberg** W Germany
33 T6 **Ringenwalde** E Germany
27 D11 **Ringerike** *L* Norway
12 D4 **Ringford** Scotland
37 J1 **Ringgau** W Germany
109 O3 **Ringgold** Louisiana
109 K2 **Ringgold** Texas
28 C5 **Ringive** Denmark
28 A4 **Ringkøbing** Denmark
101 P3 **Ringling** Montana
109 K1 **Ringling** Oklahoma
9 G6 **Ringmer** England
109 M1 **Ringold** Oklahoma
27 E11 **Ringsaker** Norway
28 H6 **Ringsted** Denmark
99 M6 **Ringsted** Iowa
27 H13 **Ringstorp** Sweden
74 F5 **Ringus** India
26 K2 **Ringvassöy** *isld* Norway
9 E6 **Ringwood** England
140 C6 **Ringwood** N Terr Aust
107 M5 **Ringwood** Oklahoma
139 H7 **Ringwood** Victoria
47 G7 **Rinía** *isld* Greece
133 C5 **Rinihue** Chile
131 A7 **Riñihue, L** Chile
28 D7 **Rinkenæs** Denmark
41 O3 **Rinn** Austria
12 B2 **Rinns Pt** Scotland
27 G16 **Ringsjön** *L* Sweden
32 K8 **Rinteln** W Germany
22 B2 **Rinxent** France
99 Q8 **Rio** Illinois
111 G11 **Rio** Louisiana
99 R6 **Rio** Wisconsin
125 P5 **Río Abajo** Panama
130 C5 **Rio Aleqre** Brazil
124 G4 **Rio Arreola** Mexico
128 C4 **Riobamba** Ecuador
85 F8 **Rio Benito** Mbini Eq Guinea
128 E5 **Rio Branco** Brazil
133 G4 **Rio Branco** Uruguay
130 E9 **Rio Branco do Sul** Brazil
109 J10 **Río Bravo** Mexico
108 B5 **Rio Bravo del Norte** *R* Mexico
133 C6 **Rio Bueno** Chile
127 K1 **Rio Bueno** Jamaica
127 N9 **Río Caribe** Venezuela
133 D7 **Río Chico** Argentina
127 M9 **Río Chico** Venezuela
130 F8 **Rio Claro** Brazil
127 P3 **Rio Claro** Trinidad
127 K10 **Río Claro** Venezuela
131 D4 **Río Cuarto** Argentina
132 **Rio de Janeiro** *conurbation* Brazil
100 A9 **Rio Dell Scotia** California
128 D2 **Rio de Oro** Colombia
85 B4 **Rio de Oro** *terr* Mauritania/Morocco
85 A4 **Rio de Oro, B. de** Mauritania
131 E2 **Rio Dulce** Argentina
133 D8 **Río Gallegos** Argentina
131 H4 **Rio Grande** Brazil
124 H6 **Río Grande** Mexico
131 B6 **Rio Grande** *R* Argentina
125 M3 **Rio Grande** *R* Nicaragua
106 D4 **Rio Grande** *R* U.S.A./Mexico
109 J9 **Rio Grande City** Texas
130 H8 **Rio Grande do Norte** Brazil
131 G2 **Rio Grande do Sul** *state* Brazil
106 C4 **Rio Grande Res** Colorado
90 F12 **Rio Grande Rise** Atlantic Oc
109 K10 **Rio Grande Valley** *airport* Texas
127 H9 **Ríohacha** Colombia
109 K9 **Rio Hondo** Texas
108 B2 **Rio Hondo** *R* New Mexico
128 C5 **Rioja** Peru
102 C3 **Rio Landa** California
130 J10 **Rio Largo** Brazil
102 C3 **Rio Linda** California
16 B5 **Rio Maior** Portugal
109 J6 **Riomedina** Texas
18 G7 **Riom ès Montagne** France
133 E3 **Río Muerto** Argentina
133 D1 **Río Mulatos** Bolivia
Rio Muni *see* **Mbini**
130 E10 **Rio Negro** Brazil
131 F4 **Rio Negro** *dep* Uruguay
131 C8 **Rio Negro** *prov* Argentina
131 G4 **Rio Negro, Embalse del** *res* Uruguay
130 C6 **Rio Negro, Pantanal do** *swamp* Brazil
43 G8 **Rionero in Vulture** Italy
124 F3 **Rio Palacio** Mexico
17 F6 **Riópar** Spain
133 G4 **Rio Pardo** Brazil
127 M5 **Rio Piedras** Puerto Rico
130 F5 **Rio Prêto, Sa. do** *mts* Brazil
128 E8 **Rio Quetena** *R* Bolivia
129 L6 **Rio Real** Brazil
45 J2 **Rio Saliceto** Italy
130 J9 **Rio Tinto** Brazil
100 K8 **Rio Tinto** Nevada
71 C6 **Rio Tuba** Philippines
133 C8 **Río Turbio Mines** Argentina
19 O18 **Riou, I. de** France
128 C3 **Rioverde** Ecuador
125 J7 **Río Verde** Mexico
130 C6 **Rio Verdi de Mato Grosso** Brazil

66
Rovuma — St. Germain au Mt D'Or

87 G8 Rovuma *R* Mozambique
99 N7 Rowan Iowa
118 J1 Rowan L Ontario
106 E6 Rowe New Mexico
139 J3 Rowena New S Wales
108 G4 Rowena Texas
112 G4 Rowesville S Carolina
100 K8 Rowland Nevada
94 H7 Rowlesburg W Virginia
118 E7 Rowley Alberta
115 M4 Rowley I N W Terr
142 C3 Rowley Shoals W Australia
103 M9 Rowood Arizona
9 E1 Rowsley England
103 K5 Rox Nevada
71 E2 Roxas Luzon Philippines
71 E4 Roxas Mindoro Philippines
71 D5 Roxas Palawan Philippines
71 F5 Roxas Panay Philippines
112 H1 Roxboro N Carolina
127 N2 Roxborough Tobago
140 E6 Roxborough Downs Queensland
144 B6 Roxburgh New Zealand
Roxburgh *co see* Borders *reg*
95 N4 Roxbury New York
95 P2 Roxbury Vermont
27 H13 Roxen *L* Sweden
111 E10 Roxie Mississippi
121 S7 Roxton Quebec
109 M2 Roxton Texas
101 N7 Roy Idaho
101 R2 Roy Montana
106 F6 Roy New Mexico
100 C2 Roy Washington
98 H7 Royal Nebraska
14 E3 Royal Canal Irish Rep
99 U9 Royal Center Indiana
70 C1 Royal Charlotte Reef S China Sea
113 L12 Royal I Bahamas
120 B3 Royal, Mount Ontario
119 P1 Royal, Mt Ontario
89 F7 Royal Natal Nat. Park S Africa
94 D4 Royal Oak Michigan
113 F12 Royal Palm Hammock Florida
113 G12 Royal Palm Ranger Sta Florida
146 H6 Royal Society Rge Antarctica
118 C8 Royalties Alberta
18 E7 Royan France
19 O14 Roybon France
22 D4 Roye France
95 M6 Royersford Pennsylvania
142 C6 Roy Hill W Australia
27 D11 Röykenvik Norway
122 C4 Roy, L Quebec
26 G7 Röyrvik Norway
109 L3 Royse City Texas
26 C10 Röysheim Norway
9 F3 Royston England
112 D3 Royston Georgia
29 L6 Röytta Finland
31 N3 Rózan Poland
46 E3 Rožden Yugoslavia
20 A3 Rozel Jersey, Channel Is
107 L3 Rozel Kansas
20 B3 Rozel, Pte.du France
98 A5 Rozet Wyoming
31 L1 Rozewie *C* Poland
55 F5 Rozhdestvenka U.S.S.R.
52 G5 Rozhdestvenskoye U.S.S.R.
22 G4 Rozoy France
31 M4 Rozprza Poland
31 N5 Rozwadów Poland
46 E1 Rtanj *mt* Yugoslavia
87 G7 Ruaha, Gt *R* Tanzania
88 E5 Ruaha Nat. Park Tanzania
145 F4 Ruahine Range New Zealand
145 E1 Ruakaka New Zealand
145 E2 Ruakura Jun New Zealand
71 J4 Ruang *isld* Indonesia
145 E3 Ruapehu *vol* New Zealand
144 B7 Ruapuke I New Zealand
145 F3 Ruatahuna New Zealand
144 C5 Ruatapu New Zealand
71 J9 Rua, Tg *C* Sumba Indonesia
145 F3 Ruatoki New Zealand
145 G2 Ruatoria New Zealand
145 E2 Ruawai New Zealand
77 C7 Ru'ays U.A.E.
83 G3 Rub al Khali *des* Saudi Arabia
33 N9 Rübeland E Germany
60 R2 Rubeshibe Japan
54 K7 Rubezhnoye U.S.S.R.
15 C2 Rubha Coigeach Scotland
15 B3 Rubha Hunish Scotland
15 C3 Rubha Reidh Scotland
86 E5 Rubi *R* Zaïre
102 D3 Rubicon *R* California
45 J2 Rubiera Italy
133 G2 Rubinéia Brazil
124 F3 Rubio Mexico
16 E3 Rubio *mt* Spain
28 D2 Rubjerg Knude *hill* Denmark
56 B5 Rubtsovsk U.S.S.R.
116 K4 Ruby Alaska
103 N10 Ruby Arizona
100 H1 Ruby Washington
101 N4 Ruby *R* Montana
103 J1 Ruby Dome *peak* Nevada
103 J1 Ruby L Nevada
103 J1 Ruby Mts Nevada
103 J1 Ruby Valley Nevada
100 B7 Ruch Oregon
52 H4 Ruch' U.S.S.R.
67 D4 Rucheng China
52 F2 Ruch'i U.S.S.R.
Ruchugi *see* Uvinza
27 H14 Ruda Sweden
143 E6 Rudall, R W Australia
140 B6 Rudalls *R* N Terr Aust
77 E6 Rudan Iran
75 J5 Rudauli India
77 H4 Rudbar Afghanistan
77 A1 Rudbār Iran
28 B7 Rudbøl Denmark
118 K6 Ruddell Sask
22 E1 Ruddervoorde Belgium
119 R3 Ruddock Manitoba
116 P6 Rude *R* Alaska
38 L8 Ruden Austria
33 T4 Ruden *isld* E Germany
36 H6 Rudersberg W Germany
33 T8 Rudersdorf E Germany
36 D4 Rüdesheim W Germany
31 O6 Rudki U.S.S.R.
28 F7 Rudkøbing Denmark
31 J4 Rudna Poland
59 L3 Rudnaya Pristan' U.S.S.R.
52 H5 Rudnichnyy U.S.S.R.
47 J2 Rudnik Bulgaria
31 N5 Rudnik Poland
54 C2 Rudnya U.S.S.R.
55 D4 Rudnyy U.S.S.R.
Rudok *see* Rutog
46 D3 Rudoka Planina *mt* Yugoslavia
50 E1 Rudol'fa, O *isld* U.S.S.R.
86 G5 Rudolf, L Kenya
37 L2 Rudolstadt E Germany
67 G1 Rudong China
77 B1 Rūd Sar Iran
28 G5 Ruds Vedby Denmark
101 P1 Rudyard Montana
22 B3 Rue France
120 J5 Ruel Ontario
20 K3 Rue St. Pierre, la France
86 F3 Rufa'a Sudan
21 F9 Ruffec Charente France
21 H8 Ruffec Indre France
21 C6 Ruffigne France
112 G4 Ruffin S Carolina
88 F6 Rufiji *R* Tanzania
45 K4 Rufina Italy
131 E5 Rufino Argentina
85 A6 Rufisque Senegal
88 C9 Rufunsa *R* Zambia
100 F1 Rufus Woods L Washington
67 G1 Rugao China
9 E3 Rugby England
98 G1 Rugby N Dakota
9 E2 Rugeley England
30 H1 Rügen *isld* E Germany
144 A7 Rugged Is New Zealand
37 K5 Rügland W Germany
20 G4 Rugles France
29 P5 Rug Oz *L* U.S.S.R.
52 D3 Rugozero U.S.S.R.
80 B7 Ruhama Israel
75 N5 Ruhea Bangladesh
33 N7 Rühen W Germany
29 L11 Rühimäki Finland
37 J2 Ruhla E Germany
33 T10 Ruhland E Germany
33 S7 Ruhleben E Germany
37 O6 Ruhmannsfelden W Germany
33 P5 Rühn E Germany
33 P6 Ruhner Bge *mt* E Germany
32 F10 Ruhr *R* W Germany
35 Ruhr, The *reg* W Germany
88 E6 Ruhudji *R* Tanzania
88 E7 Ruhuhu *R* Tanzania
88 C10 Ruia *R* Zimbabwe
67 G3 Rui'an China
67 E2 Ruichang China
65 A7 Ruicheng China
108 C6 Ruidosa Texas
106 E8 Ruidoso New Mexico
108 B2 Ruidoso New Mexico
67 E4 Ruijin China
80 G7 Ruim el Hiri Jordan
22 E1 Ruiselede Belgium
9 F4 Ruislip England
25 H3 Ruiten Aa *R* Netherlands
124 G7 Ruiz Mexico
80 G7 Rujeim Salim Jordan
46 E2 Rujen *mt* Yugoslavia
52 C5 Rūjiena U.S.S.R.
29 O5 Rukatunturi *mt* U.S.S.R.
88 C10 Rukovakuona Mts Zimbabwe
88 D7 Rukuru *R* Malawi
88 C5 Rukwa *reg* Tanzania
88 D5 Rukwa, L Tanzania
107 J2 Ruleton Kansas
111 F8 Ruleville Mississippi
26 G10 Rullbo Sweden
99 L9 Rulo Nebraska
36 E5 Rülzheim W Germany
15 B3 Rum *isld* Scotland
48 F5 Ruma Yugoslavia
Rumania *see* Romania
140 C7 Rumbalara N Terr Aust
86 E4 Rumbek Sudan
71 J4 Rumbiā Sulawesi
31 H5 Rumburk Czechoslovakia
126 G3 Rum Cay *isld* Bahamas
22 E3 Rumegies France
22 L5 Rumelange Luxembourg
95 R2 Rumford Maine
22 G4 Rumigny France
22 E2 Rumillies Belgium
140 B2 Rum Jungle N Terr Aust
80 E2 Rummāna Israel
Rummelsburg *see* Miastko
60 P2 Rumoi Japan
88 D7 Rumphi Malawi
118 E7 Rumsey Alberta
95 N6 Rumson New Jersey
144 C5 Rumu New Zealand
141 H3 Rumula Queensland
144 C5 Runanga New Zealand
127 K1 Runaway Bay Jamaica
8 D1 Runcorn England
69 C11 Rundeng Sumatra
36 C1 Ründeroth W Germany
28 D7 Rundhof W Germany
26 A9 Rundöy Norway
71 J7 Runduma *isld* Indonesia
29 G8 Rundvik Sweden
71 M8 Rung *isld* Indonesia
70 C6 Rungan *R* Kalimantan
109 K7 Runge Texas
28 K5 Rungsted Denmark
88 D5 Rungwa *R* Tanzania
88 D6 Rungwe *peak* Tanzania
27 J11 Runhällen Sweden
36 E3 Runkel W Germany
27 H11 Runn *L* Sweden
99 N8 Runnells Iowa
108 E1 Running Water Cr Texas/Okla
119 Q7 Runnymede Sask
143 E6 Runton Ra W Australia
87 C9 Runtu Namibia
29 O10 Ruokolahti Finland
66 D4 Ruoqiang China
58 D3 Ruo Shui *R* China
29 L10 Ruovesi Finland
131 A8 Rupanco, L Chile
139 G6 Rupanyup Victoria
69 E12 Rupat *isld* Sumatra
101 M7 Rupert Idaho
95 O3 Rupert Vermont
94 G9 Rupert W Virginia
141 F5 Rupert *R* Queensland
121 L1 Rupert B Quebec
121 N1 Rupert, R Quebec
37 L6 Rupertsbuch W Germany
146 J9 Ruppert Coast Antarctica
36 G2 Ruppertenrod W Germany
36 F2 Ruppertsberg W Germany
36 C2 Ruppichteroth W Germany
33 S7 Ruppiner Kanal E Germany
128 G3 Rupununi *R* Guyana
80 G2 Ruqqād *R* Syria
80 G1 Ruqqād Sakhr Syria
25 F6 Rur *R* W Germany
112 G1 Rural Hall N Carolina
94 F10 Rural Retreat Virginia
128 E6 Rurrenabaque Bolivia
28 C6 Rurup Denmark
17 F5 Rus *R* Spain
87 F9 Rusape Zimbabwe
Ruschuk *see* Ruse Bulgaria
47 H1 Ruse Bulgaria
38 M8 Ruše Yugoslavia
37 P6 Rusel W Germany
106 F3 Rush Colorado
14 E3 Rush Irish Rep
9 E5 Rushall England
65 E6 Rushan China
57 F5 Rushanskiy Khrebet *mts* U.S.S.R.
107 L3 Rush Center Kansas
99 O4 Rush City Minnesota
106 G3 Rush Cr Colorado
9 F3 Rushden England
99 P6 Rushford Minnesota
94 J4 Rushford New York
118 K8 Rush Lake Sask
107 N7 Rush Springs Oklahoma
110 F1 Rushville Illinois
110 L2 Rushville Indiana
98 D7 Rushville Nebraska
139 H6 Rushworth Victoria
109 M4 Rusk Texas
113 E10 Ruskin Florida
26 K7 Rusksele Sweden
26 K7 Ruskträsk Sweden
98 F2 Ruso N Dakota
129 L4 Russas Brazil
38 H6 Russbachsaag Austria
113 L12 Russel I Bahamas
99 N9 Russell Iowa
107 M3 Russell Kansas
94 E8 Russell Kentucky
119 Q8 Russell Manitoba
99 L5 Russell Minnesota
95 M2 Russell New York
145 E1 Russell New Zealand
121 P7 Russell Ontario
94 H5 Russell Pennsylvania
143 E6 Russell Headland *mt* W Aust
115 K3 Russell I N W Terr
137 M3 Russell Is Solomon Is
119 Q2 Russell L Manitoba
117 Q4 Russell L N W Terr
116 M5 Russell, Mt Alaska
143 C7 Russell,Mt W Australia
143 E10 Russell Ra W Australia
110 L4 Russell Springs Kentucky
110 N1 Russells Pt Ohio
111 J7 Russellville Alabama
110 D6 Russellville Arkansas
110 K5 Russellville Kentucky
110 D3 Russellville Missouri
94 D8 Russellville Ohio
45 M3 Russi Italy
116 G6 Russian Mission Alaska
116 H6 Russian Mts Alaska
Russian Soviet Federated Socialist Republic *see* Rossiyskaya SFSR
50 F1 Russkaya Gavan' U.S.S.R.
55 F4 Russkaya-Polyana U.S.S.R.
55 D3 Russkaya-Techa U.S.S.R.
54 M6 Russkaya-Zhuravka U.S.S.R.
51 J1 Russkiy, Ostrova *islds* U.S.S.R.
77 L1 Rustak Afghanistan
78 K1 Rustavi U.S.S.R.
94 H9 Rustburg Virginia
89 E5 Rustenburg S Africa
32 H5 Rustersiel W Germany
109 P3 Ruston Louisiana
88 C3 Rutana Burundi
16 E7 Rute Spain
27 K14 Rute Sweden
33 S6 Rutenberg E Germany
32 F7 Rütenbrock W Germany
71 K9 Ruteng Flores Indonesia
102 A1 Ruth California
103 K2 Ruth Nevada
32 H10 Rüthen W Germany
112 F2 Rutherfordton N Carolina
121 L6 Rutherglen Ontario
12 D2 Rutherglen Scotland
94 K9 Ruther Glen Virginia
116 M5 Ruth Glacier Alaska
118 J7 Ruthilda Sask
8 C1 Ruthin Wales
98 K5 Ruthton Minnesota
99 M6 Ruthven Iowa
141 G6 Ruthven Queensland
88 E7 Rutikira *R* Tanzania
52 G6 Rutka *R* U.S.S.R.
99 R9 Rutland Illinois
98 J3 Rutland N Dakota
94 E7 Rutland Ohio
95 P3 Rutland Vermont
Rutland *co see* Leicestershire
68 A7 Rutland I Andaman Is
141 F3 Rutland Plains Queensland
118 H6 Rutland Station Sask
9 F2 Rutland Water *L* England
99 O3 Rutledge Minnesota
110 D1 Rutledge Missouri
66 B5 Rutog China
25 E3 Rutten Netherlands
120 K6 Rutter Ontario
25 F4 Ruurlo Netherlands
87 G7 Ruvu Tanzania
88 G5 Ruvu *R* Tanzania
88 E7 Ruvuma Tanzania
88 G7 Ruvuma *R* Tanzania
86 E2 Ruweiba Sudan
88 C1 Ruwenzori Rge *mts* Uganda
36 B4 Ruwer W Germany
65 B7 Ruyang China
67 D4 Ruyuan China
55 E4 Ruzayevka U.S.S.R.
48 M1 Ruzhin U.S.S.R.
48 E1 Ružomberok Czechoslovakia
88 B2 Rwanda *rep* Cent Africa
28 D4 Ry Denmark
28 D2 Ryå Denmark
47 H1 Ryakhovo Bulgaria
99 P7 Ryan Iowa
109 K1 Ryan Oklahoma
12 C4 Ryan, Loch Scotland
101 T8 Ryan Park Wyoming
101 L6 Ryan Pk Idaho
53 E7 Ryazan' U.S.S.R.
54 M3 Ryazhsk U.S.S.R.
57 H4 Rybach'ye U.S.S.R.
37 O3 Rybáře Czechoslovakia
52 E5 Rybinsk U.S.S.R.
52 E5 Rybinskoye Vdkhr *res* U.S.S.R.
31 L5 Rybnik Poland
48 M3 Rybnitsa U.S.S.R.
54 L2 Rybnoye U.S.S.R.
55 D2 Rychkovo U.S.S.R.
31 J5 Rychnov Czechoslovakia
31 L3 Rychwał Poland
33 S4 Ryckgraben *R* E Germany
117 O8 Rycroft Alberta
120 G6 Rydal Bank Ontario
28 B4 Ryde Denmark
28 G7 Ryde Denmark
9 E6 Ryde England
98 E2 Ryder N Dakota
100 B3 Ryderwood Washington
27 H14 Ryd, V Sweden
106 F4 Rye Colorado
28 D4 Rye Denmark
28 H5 Rye Denmark
9 G6 Rye England
95 R3 Rye New Hampshire
109 N5 Rye Texas
77 B5 R-ye Dalaki *R* Iran
101 Q3 Ryegate Montana
100 G9 Rye Patch Nevada
102 F1 Rye Patch Res Nevada
119 Q9 Ryerson Sask
20 D3 Ryes France
27 A12 Ryfylke Norway
13 G4 Ryhope England
31 N4 Ryki Poland
120 G3 Ryland Ontario
118 E5 Ryley Alberta
54 F5 Ryl'sk U.S.S.R.
139 J5 Rylstone New S Wales
31 N6 Rymanow Poland
31 K6 Rýmařov Czechoslovakia
55 F1 Rymovy U.S.S.R.
31 N2 Ryn Poland
52 E1 Rynda U.S.S.R.
53 G9 Ryn Peski *des* U.S.S.R.
28 F4 Ryomgard Denmark
61 P7 Ryōri-zaki *C* Japan
61 M7 Ryōtsu Japan
31 L2 Rypin Poland
48 L3 Ryshkany U.S.S.R.
28 F6 Ryslinge Denmark
32 F6 Rysum W Germany
61 O10 Ryūgasaki Japan
134 D4 Ryukyu Ridge Pac Oc
134 D5 Ryukyu Tr Pac Oc
31 H3 Rzepin Poland
31 N5 Rzeszów Poland
52 D6 Rzhev U.S.S.R.
77 C4 Sa'ādatābād Iran
33 R4 Saal E Germany
37 J3 Saal W Germany
36 F5 Saal *R* W Germany
38 G7 Saalach *R* Austria
37 M3 Saalburg E Germany
36 F3 Saalburg W Germany
33 P9 Saale *R* E Germany
37 M3 Saale *R* W Germany
36 C7 Saales France
37 L2 Saalfeld E Germany
40 F5 Saanen Switzerland
117 M11 Saanich Br Col
36 B5 Saar *R* W Germany
19 K3 Saarbrücken France
36 B5 Saarbrücken W Germany
36 B4 Saarburg W Germany
27 M14 Sääre U.S.S.R.
27 M13 Saaremaa U.S.S.R.
29 M5 Saarenkylä Finland
29 O10 Saari Finland
29 L9 Saarijärvi Finland
29 N3 Saariselkä *mts* Finland
36 B5 Saarland *land* W Germany
36 B5 Saarlouis W Germany
33 S8 Saarmund E Germany
36 B5 Saar-Wellingen W Germany
36 D7 Saasenheim France
40 G5 Saas Tal Switzerland
70 E3 Saätan Kalimantan
133 E5 Saavedra Argentina
131 A7 Saavedra, Pto Chile
125 L2 Sabá Honduras
127 N6 Saba *isld* Lesser Antilles
32 L9 Sababurg W Germany
48 F6 Sabac Yugoslavia
17 J3 Sabadell Spain
70 E2 Sabah *state* Borneo
69 E11 Sabak Malaysia
71 H5 Sabal Sulawesi
71 J8 Sabalana *isld* Indonesia
44 M5 Saba, Mt Italy
126 D3 Sabana, Arch. de *islds* Cuba
127 K5 Sabana de la Mar Dominican Rep
127 J10 Sabana de Mendoza Venezuela
128 D1 Sabanalarga Colombia
127 K9 Sabaneta Venezuela
70 F4 Sabang Sulawesi
69 B10 Sabang Sumatra
70 C6 Sabangan Teluk *B* Kalimantan
83 K11 Sabaragamuwa *reg* Sri Lanka
71 J8 Sabaru *isld* Indonesia
80 D4 Sabastiya Jordan
45 O7 Sabaudia Italy
128 E7 Sabaya Bolivia
41 M6 Sabbia, V Italy
45 H2 Sabbioneta Italy
77 G4 Şāberi, Hāmūn-e *L* Iran
107 P2 Sabetha Kansas
84 E4 Sabhah Libya
87 F10 Sabi *R* Zimbabwe
89 G5 Sabie *R* S Africa
52 B6 Sabile U.S.S.R.
45 N5 Sabina Italy
94 D7 Sabina Ohio
124 F2 Sabinal Mexico
109 H6 Sabinal Texas
17 G2 Sabiñánigo Spain
108 F8 Sabinas Mexico
125 J4 Sabinas Hidalgo Mexico
111 C11 Sabine *R* Louisiana/Texas
146 K6 Sabine, Mt Antarctica
42 E6 Sabini, Monti Italy
79 H2 Sabkhat al Jabbūl Syria
79 D7 Sabkhet el Bardawîl Egypt
71 E4 Sablayan Philippines
137 M5 Sable *isld* Coral Sea
115 N9 Sable, C Nova Scotia
123 N10 Sable I Nova Scotia
122 G10 Sable River Nova Scotia
120 H6 Sables, L. aux Ontario
120 H6 Sables, River Aux Ontario
19 O16 Sablet France
19 N18 Sablon, Pte. du France
19 N14 Sablons France
16 C3 Sabor *R* Portugal
131 G2 Sã Borja Brazil
94 H7 Sabraton W Virginia
18 E8 Sabres France
146 G3 Sabrina Coast Antarctica
28 E4 Sabro Denmark
16 C4 Sabugal Portugal
99 Q7 Sabula Iowa
47 L5 Sabuncu Turkey
70 P9 Sabunting *isld* Indonesia
77 E1 Sabzevār Iran
110 C4 Sac *R* Missouri
128 E7 Sacaca Bolivia
95 N3 Sacandaga Res New York
103 N8 Sacaton Arizona
99 L7 Sac City Iowa
43 E7 Sacco *R* Italy
45 L1 Saccolongo Italy
17 F4 Sacedón Spain
115 K7 Sachigo *R* Ontario
109 O8 Sachse Texas
36 F1 Sachsenberg W Germany
38 H8 Sachsenburg Austria
33 O10 Sachsenburg E Germany
32 K8 Sachsenhagen W Germany
32 K10 Sachsenhausen W Germany
114 G3 Sachs Harbour N W Terr
42 E3 Sacile Italy
95 L3 Sackets Harbor New York
122 H8 Sackville New Brunswick
110 B3 Sac, L Missouri
20 K5 Saclas France
95 R3 Saco Maine
101 S1 Saco Montana
71 F7 Sacol *isld* Philippines
40 B2 Sacquenay France
102 C3 Sacramento California
102 B2 Sacramento *R* California
108 B3 Sacramento Mts New Mexico
102 B1 Sacramento V California
103 K6 Sacramento Wash *R* Arizona
16 E8 Sacratif, C Spain
122 D5 Sacré Coeur Quebec
122 C5 Sacré-Coeur Saguenay Quebec
130 F6 Sacremento Brazil
48 G3 Săcueni Romania
18 E10 Sadaba Spain
77 B5 Sa'dabad Iran
72 E5 Şa'dah N Yemen
60 F12 Sada-misaki Japan
69 E9 Sadao Thailand
13 G4 Sadberge England
74 D2 Sadda Pakistan
141 G2 Saddle Hill Queensland
142 D4 Saddle Hill W Australia
100 A7 Saddle Mt Oregon
101 Q5 Saddle Mt Wyoming
68 A6 Saddle Pk Andaman Is
68 G7 Sa Dec Vietnam
48 K2 Sadgora U.S.S.R.
127 O3 Sadhoowa Trinidad
94 C8 Sadieville Kentucky
85 B6 Sadiola Mali
74 D4 Sadiqabad Pakistan
16 B6 Sado *R* Portugal
61 M7 Sado-shima *isld* Japan
74 E6 Sadri India
26 H5 Sadvajaur *L* Sweden
28 F2 Sæby Nordjylland Denmark
28 G5 Sæby Vestjælland Denmark
28 J6 Sædder Denmark
28 B4 Sædding Denmark
60 E13 Saeki Japan
60 E13 Saeki-wan *B* Japan
17 F5 Saelices Spain
32 G8 Saerbeck W Germany
28 E5 Særslev Denmark
22 K4 Saeul Luxembourg
Safad *see* Zefat
55 D4 Safakulevo U.S.S.R.
48 F2 Sáfárikovo Czechoslovakia
57 F5 Safed Khirs *reg* Afghanistan
77 L2 Safed Koh *mt* Afghanistan
38 O7 Safen *R* Austria
77 J4 Safer Afghanistan
142 A4 Safety Bay *dist* W Aust
80 D5 Saffārin Jordan
79 B9 Şaff, El Egypt
27 F12 Säffle Sweden
111 J9 Safford Alabama
103 P9 Safford Arizona
21 B7 Saffré France
9 G3 Saffron Walden England
85 C2 Safi Morocco
77 G4 Safidabeh Iran
77 A1 Safid Rud *R* Iran
41 K4 Safier Tal Switzerland
130 H6 Safiras, Sa. das *mts* Brazil
79 G4 Şāfita Syria
54 K3 Safonovka U.S.S.R.
52 G2 Safonovo U.S.S.R.
78 D1 Safronbolu Turkey
27 G11 Säfsnäs Sweden
80 G5 Safut Jordan
66 D6 Saga China
60 D12 Saga Kyūshū Japan
60 G12 Saga Shikoku Japan
60 C11 Saga Tsushima Japan
57 C1 Saga U.S.S.R.
60 D12 Saga *prefect* Japan
61 O7 Sagae Japan
68 B2 Sagaing Burma
59 L5 Sagami-nada *B* Japan
61 N10 Sagami-wan *B* Japan
94 H6 Sagamore Pennsylvania
86 G4 Sagan *watercourse* Ethiopia
119 N2 Saganaga L Ontario
120 H3 Saganash L Ontario
60 E12 Saganoseki Japan
68 D6 Saganthit Kyun *isld* Burma
76 C2 Sagar India
61 M11 Sagara Japan
88 F5 Sagara Tanzania
57 B5 Sagar-Chaga U.S.S.R.
116 N2 Sagavanirkok *R* Alaska
32 H7 Sage W Germany
101 P8 Sage Wyoming
101 P1 Sage Cr Montana
101 S8 Sage Cr Wyoming
27 G11 Sågen Sweden
26 H4 Sagfjord Norway
26 J5 Saggat *L* Sweden
95 P6 Sag Harbor Long I, N Y
94 D3 Saginaw Michigan
109 L9 Saginaw Texas
94 D3 Saginaw Bay Michigan
88 D2 Sagitu *isld* Uganda
115 N6 Saglek B Labrador
71 H6 Sago *isld* Indonesia
99 S3 Sagola Michigan
17 F7 Sagra, La *mt* Spain
85 F8 Sagre, Pto.de Bioko Eq Guinea
16 B7 Sagres Portugal
71 L9 Sagu Indonesia
106 D3 Saguache Colorado
126 G4 Sagua de Tánamo Cuba
126 D3 Sagua la Grande Cuba
103 N8 Saguaro L Arizona
103 O9 Saguaro Nat.Mon Arizona
115 M8 Saguenay *R* Quebec
85 B3 Saguia el Hamra *terr* Morocco
17 G5 Sagunto Spain
114 E4 Sagwan Alaska
80 G3 Saham Jordan
85 C4 Sahara *des* N Africa
79 E10 Sahara, G *mt* Egypt
74 G4 Saharanpur India
142 E5 Sahara Well W Australia
75 L5 Sahibganj India
28 D4 Sahl Denmark
71 A2 Sahu Halmahera Indonesia
124 E3 Sahuaripa Mexico
103 O10 Sahuarita Arizona
124 H7 Sahuayo Mexico
136 F4 Sahul Shelf Timor Sea
19 O16 Sahune France
68 J5 Sa Huynh Vietnam
61 L9 Sai *R* Japan
136 J3 Saibai I Papua New Guinea
69 D13 Saibi Indonesia
69 E9 Sai Buri Thailand
69 E9 Sai Buri *R* Thailand
85 E2 Saïda Algeria
79 F5 Saïda Lebanon
77 D5 Sa'īdābād Iran
68 F6 Sai Dao Tai, Khao *mt* Thailand
86 D4 Said Bundas Sudan
75 N6 Saidpur Bangladesh
74 E1 Saidu Pakistan
40 E3 Saignelégier Switzerland
60 G9 Saigō Japan
Saigon *see* Ho Chi Minh
68 H7 Saigon *R* Vietnam
29 O4 Saija Finland
60 G12 Saijō Japan
60 C13 Saikai Nat. Park Japan
71 C3 Saileen W Irian
19 O15 Saillans France
71 C3 Sailolof W Irian
100 K7 Sailor Cr Idaho
76 C1 Sailu India
65 F4 Saima China
29 N10 Saimaa *L* Finland
29 N11 Saimaa Canal Finland/U.S.S.R.
124 H6 Sain Alto Mexico
74 A8 Saindak Pakistan
22 D2 Sainghin-en-Weppes France
22 G3 Sains-du-Nord France
22 F4 Sains-Richaumont France
15 F5 St. Abb's Head Scotland
122 H5 Ste. Adelaide Quebec
121 Q7 Ste.Adèle Quebec
20 F3 Ste.Adresse France
38 N6 St.Aegyd Austria
18 G9 St.Affrique France
121 T6 St.Agapit Quebec
119 U9 Ste.Agathe Manitoba
121 Q6 Ste.Agathe des Monts Quebec
20 G5 St.Agil France
8 A7 St.Agnes England
121 L4 Ste.Agnes Quebec
9 F7 St.Agnes *isld* Isles of Scilly England
21 H7 St.Aignan-la-Ronde France
21 C6 St. Aignan sur Roë France
28 D3 Ste. Ajstrup Denmark
9 F4 St.Albans England
123 R6 St.Alban's Nfld
95 P2 St.Albans Vermont
94 F8 St.Albans W Virginia
118 D5 St.Albert Alberta
122 C6 St.Alexandre Quebec
121 R6 St.Alexis des Monts Quebec
22 E3 St.Amand-les-Eaux France
21 H6 St.Amand-Longpre France
18 G6 St. Amand Mont Rond France
21 D8 St.Amand-sur-Sevre France
21 F10 St. Amant de Boixe France
40 F2 St.Amarin France
121 T4 St.-Ambroise Quebec
21 J8 St.Ambroix France
122 D5 St.Anaclet Quebec
38 L8 St. Andra-im-Lavanttal Austria
83 K13 St.André Réunion Indian Oc
33 M9 St. Andreasberg W Germany
87 G11 St.André, C Madagascar
19 N13 St.André-de-Corcy France
18 E8 St.André-de-Cubzac France
20 H4 St.André-de-l'Eure France
20 H4 St.André, Plaine de France
111 L11 St.Andrew Florida
127 P2 St.Andrew *co* Trinidad
127 L2 St.Andrew *parish* Jamaica
144 C6 St. Andrews New Zealand
123 N6 St.Andrew's Nfld
13 F1 St.Andrews Scotland
123 M7 St.Andrew's Chan Nova Scotia
113 F7 St.Andrew Sd Georgia
21 F10 St.Angeau France
98 F9 St.Ann Nebraska
127 K2 St.Ann *parish* Jamaica
126 B2 St. Anna-Baai *B* Curaçao
9 H6 St.Anne Channel Is
20 G4 Ste.Anne France
127 N4 Ste.Anne Guadeloupe W Indies
99 T8 St.Anne Illinois
119 V9 Ste.Anne Manitoba
127 L4 Ste.Anne Martinique W Indies
121 U5 Ste.-Anne-de-Beaupré Quebec
121 S6 Ste. Anne de la Pérade Quebec
122 B6 Ste.Anne de la Pocatière Quebec
122 F4 Ste.Anne des Monts Quebec
121 P6 Ste.Anne du Lac Quebec
122 E3 Ste.Anne, L Quebec
118 C5 Ste. Anne, Lac Alberta
122 B6 Ste.Anne, R Quebec
20 A2 St.Annes Alderney, Channel Is
117 Q9 St.Ann, L Alberta
123 M7 St. Anns Nova Scotia
141 H5 St.Anns Queensland
127 K2 St. Ann's Bay Jamaica
12 E3 St Ann's Bridge Scotland
99 O6 St.Ansgar Iowa
25 E5 St.Anthonis Netherlands
101 O6 St.Anthony Idaho
115 O7 St.Anthony Nfld
19 O18 St.Antoine France
41 M3 St.Anton Austria
18 G8 St.Antonin France
122 C6 St.Antonin Quebec
21 I8 St.Août France
20 H3 St.Aquilin-de-Pacy France
145 D4 St. Arnaud New Zealand
139 G6 St.Arnaud Victoria
20 J4 St.Arnoux France
122 C6 St.Arsène Quebec
140 B1 St.Asaph B N Terr Aust
18 F7 St.Astier France
122 C6 St.Athanase Quebec
122 B6 St.Aubert Quebec
20 E3 St.Aubin France
20 A3 St.Aubin Jersey, Channel Is
20 B5 St. Aubin-d'Aubigné France
20 C4 St.Aubin-de-Terregatte France
20 C5 St.Aubin-du-Cormier France
20 H2 St.Aubin-le-Cauf France
123 O2 St.Augustin Quebec
36 C2 St. Augustin W Germany
123 O2 St.Augustin B Quebec
87 G12 St.Augustin, B.de Madagascar
21 D7 St.Augustin-des-Bois France
113 F8 St.Augustine Florida
127 O2 St.Augustine Trinidad
123 N2 St.Augustin R Quebec
18 F7 St.Aulaye France
8 B7 St. Austell England
19 K3 St.Avold France
121 S6 St.Barnabé Nord Quebec
121 R6 St.Barthélémi Quebec
18 G10 St.Barthélemy France
127 N5 St. Barthélemy *isld* Lesser Antilles
144 B6 St. Bathans New Zealand
19 P18 Ste.Baume France
18 F10 St. Béat France
12 E5 St.Bees England
99 M6 St.Benedict Iowa
119 M6 St.Benedict Sask
21 H9 St.Benoit-du-Sault France
122 B7 St.Benoit Labre Quebec
122 H5 Ste.Bernadette Quebec
121 T6 St.Bernard Quebec
144 D5 St. Bernard *mt* New Zealand
40 F6 St. Bernard, Col du Gd. Switz/Italy
42 A3 St. Bernard, Petit *pass* Italy/France
110 J2 St.Bernice Indiana
19 P13 St.Beron France
20 D5 St.Berthevin France
36 C7 St.Blaise France
122 D5 Ste.Blandine Quebec
8 B7 St.Blazey England
118 D1 St.Boniface Manitoba
21 H10 St. Bonnet-Briance France
118 L8 St.Boswells Sask
13 F2 St. Boswells Scotland
21 G7 St.Branchs France
123 T5 St.Brendan's Nfld
21 A7 St. Brévin les Pins France
20 A4 St.Briac France
20 C5 St.Brice-en-Cogles France
118 B7 St.Bride, Mt Alberta
123 S7 St.Bride's Nfld
8 A4 St. Bride's Wales
18 D4 St. Brieuc France
119 N6 St.Brieux Sask
20 B4 St.Broladre France
121 L5 St. Bruno de Guiques Quebec
21 G6 St.Calais France
119 T9 St.Calude Manitoba
122 B7 Ste.Camille Quebec
121 S6 St.Casimir Quebec
18 D4 St.Cast France
115 M9 St. Catharines Ontario
127 K2 St. Catherine *parish* Jamaica
127 P5 St.Catherine, Mt Grenada
112 F6 St.Catherines I Georgia
9 E6 St.Catherines Pt England
122 B8 Ste.Cécile Quebec
18 G8 St. Céré France
18 G7 St.Cernin France
121 R7 St.Césaire Quebec
18 H7 St.Chamond France
101 O7 St.Charles Idaho
99 S8 St.Charles Illinois
118 A1 St.Charles Manitoba
94 C3 St.Charles Michigan
99 O6 St.Charles Minnesota
110 F3 St.Charles Missouri
18 H8 St. Chély l'Apcher France
20 K4 St.Chéron France
18 G9 St.Chinian France
126 A1 St.Christoffel Berg *mt* Curaçao
19 Q15 St.Christophe d'Oisans France
St. Christopher *isld see* St Kitts
121 T4 St.-Cîour-de-Marie Quebec
20 C3 St. Clair France
94 E4 St.Clair Michigan
99 N5 St.Clair Minnesota
110 F3 St.Clair Missouri
94 E4 St. Clair, L U.S.A./Canada
120 H9 St.Clair R Ontario/Mich
20 J3 St.Clair-sur-Epte France
19 J6 St.Claude France
127 N4 St.Claude Guadeloupe W I
8 B4 St.Clears Wales
122 C6 St.Clement Quebec
21 D7 St. Clement-de-la-Place France
121 S7 Ste.Clothilde Quebec
113 F9 St.Cloud Florida
20 K4 St.Cloud France
99 M4 St.Cloud Minnesota
8 B7 St.Columb England
121 R6 St.Côme Quebec
20 C3 St.Côme-du-Mont France
20 F5 St.Cosme-de-Vair France
122 E8 Ste.Croix New Brunswick
40 D4 Ste.Croix Switzerland
95 T8 St. Croix *R* Maine/New Brunswick
99 O4 St. Croix *R* Wisconsin
36 C7 Ste.Croix aux Mines France
113 L8 St.Croix I Virgin Is
18 E7 St. Cybard Chalais France
18 F8 St.Cyprien France
122 C6 St.Cyprien Quebec
19 P18 St.Cyr France
20 D4 St.Cyr-du-Bailleul France
21 I6 St. Cyr-en Val France
121 S7 St.Cyrille Quebec
121 P4 St.Cyr, L Quebec
118 J4 St. Cyr Lake Sask
122 B7 St.Damien Quebec
110 F1 St.David Illinois
127 P1 St.David *co* Trinidad
122 A5 St.David-de-Falardeau Quebec
123 O5 St. David's Nfld
8 A4 St. David's Wales
90 D1 St.Davids I Bermuda
22 G3 St.Denis Belgium
20 K4 St. Denis France
121 R7 St.Denis Quebec
83 J13 St.Denis Réunion Indian Oc
21 E6 St.Denis d'Anjou France
20 D5 St.Denis-de-Gastines France
21 C9 St.Denis-d'Oléron France
20 E5 St. Denis-d'Orques France
20 E5 St.Denis-sur-Sarthon France
19 O16 St.Didier France
36 B7 St. Dié France
19 J4 St.Dizier France
20 B5 St. Domineuc France
19 N14 St.Donat sur l'Herbasse France
98 J8 St.Edward Nebraska
116 P7 St.Elias, C Alaska
117 D5 St. Elias Mts Alaska/Yukon Terr
121 S4 Ste.Elisabeth Quebec
127 J2 St.Elizabeth *parish* Jamaica
110 H2 St.Elmo Illinois
122 C5 St.Eloi Quebec
18 G6 St Éloy-les-Mines France
121 R6 Ste.Emélie Quebec
18 H8 Ste.Enimie France
20 C3 Sainteny France
21 G7 St.Epain France
122 B7 St.Ephrem Quebec
121 L3 St.Ephrem de Paradis Quebec
122 C6 St.-Epiphane Quebec
20 B5 St.Erblon France
22 F5 St.Erme-Outre-et-Ramecourt France
21 D10 Saintes France
127 L4 St. Ésprit, Le Martinique W Indies
22 B2 St.Étienne-au-Mont France
18 E9 St. Étienne de Baïgorry France
19 O14 St.Étienne de St.Geoirs France
20 H3 St.Étienne-du-Rouvray France
121 M4 St. Eugène Quebec
121 S4 St.-Eugène Quebec
122 D6 St.Eusèbe Quebec
121 R7 St.Eustache Quebec
20 F4 St.Evroult Notre Dame-du-Bois France
122 D5 St.Fabien Quebec
122 B7 Ste.Familie Quebec
121 P6 Ste.Famille d'Aumond Quebec
18 H5 St.Fargeau France
121 S4 St.Félicien Quebec
122 E5 Ste.Félicité Quebec
121 R6 St. Félix de Valois Quebec
12 D1 St.Fillans Scotland
14 A5 St. Finan's B Irish Rep
123 O5 St.Fintan's Nfld
121 T6 St.Flavien Quebec
122 E5 Ste.Florence Quebec
21 C8 St.Florent-des-Bois France
18 H4 St.Florentin France
18 G6 St.Florent-sur-Cher France
18 H7 St.Flour France
21 H8 St.Flovier France
19 N15 St.Fortunat France
121 T7 St.Fortunat Quebec
18 F8 Ste.Foy-la-Grande France
107 J2 St.Francis Kansas
95 R6 St. Francis *R* Maine/New Brunswick
110 F5 St. Francis *R* Missouri/Ark
89 D10 St. Francis B S Africa
123 U6 St.Francis, C Nfld
89 D10 St. Francis C S Africa
138 C4 St.Francis, I.of S Australia
110 J3 St. Francisville Illinois
111 E11 St.Francisville Louisiana
127 N4 St.François Guadeloupe W Indies
121 S7 St. François *R* Quebec
121 T7 St. François, L Quebec
110 F4 St. Francois Mts Missouri
121 S7 St.François Xavier Quebec
95 S7 St.Froid L Maine
21 C8 St.Fulgent France
111 E11 St.Gabriel Louisiana
121 R6 St.Gabriel de Brandon Quebec
122 H5 St.Gabriel de Gaspé Quebec
41 K3 St. Gallen Switzerland
20 F4 Ste.Gauburge-Ste. Colombe France
18 F9 St.Gaudens France
21 H8 St.Gaultier France
122 B8 St.Gédéon Quebec
20 K3 St. Genevieve France
110 F4 Ste.Genevieve Missouri
123 P2 St.Genevieve B Quebec
18 G8 St.Geniez France
19 P14 St Geoire-en-Valdaine France
90 C1 St.George Bermuda
113 E7 St.George Georgia
122 F8 St.George New Brunswick
141 J8 St.George Queensland
112 G4 St.George S Carolina
103 L4 St.George Utah
127 O2 St.George *co* Trinidad
127 P6 St.George *parish* Barbados
141 G3 St. George *R* Queensland
123 N5 St.George, C Nfld
139 K6 St.George Hd New S Wales
113 C8 St.George I Florida
116 D8 St. George I Pribilof Is Bering Sea
41 H1 St.Georgen W Germany
100 A8 St.George, Pt California
142 E4 St.George Ra W Australia
36 B6 St.Georges France
129 H3 St.Georges Fr Guiana
127 P5 St.George's Grenada
123 O5 St.George's Nfld
122 B7 St.Georges Quebec
123 N5 St.George's B Nfld
125 P9 St. Georges Cay *isld* Belize
7 F11 St Georges Chan U.K.
137 L2 St.George's Channel Bismarck Arch
14 E5 St. Georges Channel Ireland/U.K.
69 A9 St.George's Channel Nicobar Is
20 C5 St. Georges-de-Reintembault France
21 C10 St. Georges-d'Oléron France
20 G3 St.Georges-du-Mesnil France
20 G3 St.Georges-du-Vièvre France
90 C1 St.George's, I Bermuda
21 F8 St. Georges-les-Baillargeaux France
20 H4 St.Georges Motel France
20 H5 St.Georges-sur-Eure France
21 I7 St. Georges-sur-la Prée France
21 D7 St.Georges-sur-Loire France
22 H3 St.Gérard Belgium
121 M4 St. Gerard-Centre Quebec
19 N13 St. Germain au Mt D'Or France

St.Germain d'Anxure — Sambapolulu, G
67

20 D5 St.Germain d'Anxure France
20 G5 St. Germain-de-la-Coudre France
18 H6 St.Germain-des-Fosses France
19 J6 St.Germain du Bois France
122 B7 Ste.Germaine Quebec
20 K4 St.Germain-en-Laye France
20 B3 St.Germain, Hâvre de France
20 F3 St. Germain-la Campagne France
18 G7 St.Germain-les-Belles France
20 B3 St.Germain-sur-Ay France
8 B7 St.Germans England
20 J3 St.Germer-de-Fly France
22 F3 St.Ghislain Belgium
21 B6 St.Gildas des Bois France
18 D5 St.Gildas, Pte.de C France
121 T6 St.Giles Quebec
127 N1 St. Giles Is Tobago
22 G1 St. Gillis-bij-Dendermonde Belgium
22 G1 St.Gillis-Waas Belgium
18 F10 St.Girons France
27 F12 St.Gla L Sweden
36 D3 St.Goar W Germany
22 E4 St.Gobain France
122 G5 St.Godefroi Quebec
41 J4 St.Gotthard P Switzerland
8 B4 St.Govan's Hd Wales
119 N6 St.Gregor Sask
123 O4 St.Gregory, Mt Nfld
121 S7 St. Guillaume Quebec
19 Q15 St. Guillaume, Mt France
94 C2 St.Helen Michigan
102 B3 St.Helena California
90 B14 St. Helena isld Atlantic Oc
89 A9 St.Helena B S Africa
90 J10 St Helena Fracture Atlantic Oc
94 B1 St.Helena I Michigan
112 G5 St.Helena Sd S Carolina
18 E8 Ste.Hélène France
122 B6 Ste.Hélène Quebec
13 F6 St.Helens England
100 C4 St.Helens Oregon
139 J8 St.Helens Tasmania
100 C3 St.Helens, Mt Washington
139 J8 St.Helens Pt Tasmania
20 A3 St.Hélier Jersey, Channel Is
122 H4 St.Helier Quebec
121 U6 Ste.Hénédine Quebec
121 T6 St.Henri Quebec
121 T7 St.Herménégilde Quebec
18 G9 St.Hilaire France
98 K1 St.Hilaire Minnesota
21 B7 St. Hilaire-de-Chaleons France
21 C7 St.Hilaire de Loulay France
21 D9 St.Hilaire-des-Loges France
20 C4 St. Hilaire du-Harcouet France
21 I10 St. Hilaire-le Château France
21 E7 St. Hilaire-St. Florent France
140 D6 Sainthill,Mt N Terr Aust
19 K5 St.Hippolyte Doubs France
21 H7 St.Hippolyte Indre-et-Loire France
18 H9 St.Hippolyte du Fort France
122 A5 St.Honoré Quebec
122 C6 St.Honoré Quebec
20 D3 Ste.Honorine France
20 E3 Ste.Honorine-du-Fay France
22 J3 St.Hubert Belgium
25 F6 St.Hubert W Germany
115 M8 St-Hyacinthe Quebec
28 K5 St Ibb Sweden
94 C1 St.Ignace Michigan
121 R6 St.Ignace du Lac Quebec
120 C4 St. Ignace, Isle Ontario
101 L2 St.Ignatius Montana
40 E3 St.Imier Switzerland
36 C5 St.Ingbert W Germany
122 B6 St.Irénée Quebec
121 L5 St.Isidore Quebec
121 T7 St.Isidore Quebec
26 K3 St.Istind mt Norway
9 F3 St.Ives Cambridge England
8 A7 St.Ives Cornwall England
25 E2 St.Jacobi Parochie Netherlands
122 D6 St.Jacques New Brunswick
20 B5 St.Jacques-de-la-Lande France
38 F8 St.Jakob Austria
20 C4 St.James France
118 A1 St.James Manitoba
99 V4 St.James Michigan
99 M5 St.James Minnesota
110 E3 St.James Missouri
127 J2 St.James parish Jamaica
117 H10 St.James, C Br Columbia
113 E11 St.James City Florida
121 L4 St.Janvier Quebec
20 E5 St.Jean France
121 R7 St.Jean Quebec
119 U9 St.Jean Baptiste Manitoba
121 S5 St.Jean Bosco Quebec
21 E10 St. Jean d'Angély France
21 D10 St. Jean-d'Angle France
20 F5 St.Jean-d'Asse France
19 O13 St.Jean-de-Bournay France
20 C3 St.Jean-de-Daye France
122 C5 St.Jean de Dieu Quebec
19 J5 St.Jean de Losne France
18 D9 St.Jean-de-Luz France
121 R6 St. Jean-de-Matha Quebec
19 Q14 St.Jean-de-Maurienne France
21 A8 St.Jean-de-Monts France
21 F8 St.Jean-de-Sauves France
18 H8 St.Jean du Gard France
19 O14 St.Jean-en-Royans France
115 M8 Saint-Jean, Lac Quebec
20 B4 St.Jean-le-Thomas France
18 E9 St.Jean Pied de Port France
122 B6 St.Jean Port Joli Quebec
122 H3 St.Jean, R Quebec
36 B5 St.Jean Rohrbach France
20 C5 St.Jean-sur-Couesnon France
121 Q7 St.Jérôme Quebec
19 N14 St. Jeure D'Ay France
109 K2 St.Jo Texas
21 A7 St.Joachim France
122 B6 St.Joachim Quebec
41 O3 St.Jodok Austria
110 D5 St.Joe Arkansas
100 J2 St.Joe Idaho
94 C5 St.Joe Indiana
36 E4 St.Johann W Germany
38 G8 St. Johann-im-Walde Austria
107 M3 St.John Kansas
119 S10 St.John N Dakota
115 N8 St.John New Brunswick
103 M1 St.John Utah
100 H2 St.John Washington
127 P6 St.John parish Barbados
95 R7 St. John R Maine
123 P3 St John B Nfld
123 R3 St.John, C Nfld
113 L7 St.John I Virgin Is
123 S5 St.John, L Nfld
122 E7 St. John R New Brunswick
122 G5 St. John R Quebec
127 P4 St.John's Antigua W Indies
103 P7 St.Johns Arizona
94 C3 St.Johns Michigan
115 O8 St. John's Nfld
95 P2 St.Johnsbury Vermont
13 F4 St.John's Chapel England
14 C2 St.John's Pt Irish Rep
113 F7 St.Johns R Florida
95 N3 St.Johnsville New York
20 C3 St.Jores France
22 H2 St.Joris-Winge Belgium
111 E10 St.Joseph Louisiana
127 L4 St.Joseph Martinique W Indies
127 P2 St.Joseph Mayoro Trinidad
99 U7 St.Joseph Michigan
99 M10 St.Joseph Missouri
121 U6 St.Joseph Quebec
83 K14 St.Joseph Réunion Indian Oc
127 O2 St.Joseph St George Trinidad
127 P6 St.Joseph parish Barbados
94 A5 St. Joseph R Michigan
113 B8 St. Joseph Bay Florida
120 G6 St. Joseph I Ontario
109 L8 St. Joseph I Texas
115 K7 St. Joseph, L Ontario
123 T6 St.Joseph's Nfld
22 B3 St.Josse France
20 A5 St. Jouan-de-l'Isle France
20 A4 St. Jouan des-Guerets France
20 F2 St.Jouin France
121 Q6 St. Jovite Quebec
126 A1 St. Jozefsdal Curaçao
19 N14 St.Julian Molin-Molette France
40 D5 St.Julien France
21 C7 St. Julien-de-Concelles France
21 C6 St. Julien de-Vouvantes France
19 O15 St.Julien en Quint France
20 F3 St. Julien-le-Faucon France
18 F7 St.Junien France
9 F7 St.Just England
20 K2 St.Just-en-Chausée France
18 H7 St.Just-en-Chevalet France
38 M7 St.Katherein Austria
127 P3 St.Kitts isld Lesser Antilles
126 A1 St.Kruis Curaçao
121 R7 St.Lambert Quebec
121 T6 St.Lambert Quebec
142 G2 St.Lambert,C W Australia
21 E7 St. Lambert-des-Levées France
21 D7 St. Lambert-du-Lattay France
111 D11 St.Landry Louisiana
19 J6 St. Laurent France
129 H2 St.Laurent Fr Guiana
119 U8 St.Laurent Manitoba
121 L4 Saint-Laurent Quebec
18 G10 St.Laurent de la Salanque France
19 O13 St.Laurent-de-Mûre France
21 I6 St. Laurent-des Eaux France
19 P14 St.Laurent-du-Pont France
20 G2 St.Laurent-en-Caux France
21 G6 St. Laurent-en-Gâtines France
18 E7 St.Laurent-et-Benon France
121 U5 St.Laurent, R Quebec
21 G10 St.Laurent-sur-Gorre France
20 D3 St.Laurent-sur-Mer France
22 K5 St.Laurent-sur-Othain France
123 R7 St.Lawrence Nfld
141 J5 St.Lawrence Queensland
95 M2 St. Lawrence R Canada/U.S.A.
115 N8 St.Lawrence, G.of Canada
116 B5 St.Lawrence I Bering Sea
121 O8 St. Lawrence I Nat. Park Ontario
121 P8 St.Lawrence Seaway Canada/U.S.A.
119 Q8 St.Lazare Manitoba
22 K4 St.Léger Belgium
20 J4 St. Léger-en-Yvelines France
22 H1 St.Lenaarts Belgium
122 E5 St.Léon Quebec
36 B7 St. Léonard France
122 E6 St.-Léonard New Brunswick
121 S6 St.Léonard Quebec
21 I10 St. Léonard-de-Noblat France
9 G6 St.Leonards England
121 T4 St.-Léon-de-Chicoutimi Quebec
122 B7 St.Léon de Standon Quebec
38 L8 St.Leonhard Kärnten Austria
38 N4 St.Leonhard Nieder Österreich Austria
20 K3 St.Leu-la-Forêt France
123 Q1 St.Lewis R Labrador
121 S7 St.Liboire Quebec
18 F8 Ste. Livrade France
18 F9 St.Lizier France
20 C3 St.Lô France
127 N4 St.Louis Marie Galante W Indies
85 A5 St.Louis Mauritania
94 C3 St.Louis Michigan
122 H7 St.Louis Pr Edward I
83 J14 St.Louis Réunion Indian Oc
119 M6 St.Louis Sask
105 St.Louis conurbation Missouri
99 O2 St. Louis R Minnesota
122 H7 St.Louis de Kent New Brunswick
122 D6 St.Louis du Ha Ha Quebec
126 H5 St.Louis du Sud Haiti
122 B6 Ste.Louise Quebec
121 R7 St.Louis, L Quebec
36 C5 St. Louis-lès-Bitche France
94 E6 St.Louisville Ohio
40 D2 St. Loup-sur-Semoise France
19 K5 St.Loup-sur-Semouse France
20 H4 St.Lubin-des-Joncherets France
127 L4 Ste.Luce Martinique W Indies
141 K2 St.Lucia dist Brisbane, Qnsld
127 O8 St. Lucia isld Lesser Antilles
87 F11 St. Lucia, C S Africa
121 Q6 Ste.Lucie Quebec
113 G10 St. Lucie Canal Florida
127 P6 St.Lucy parish Barbados
122 B8 St.Ludger Quebec
127 H5 St.Luis du Nord Haiti
20 A4 St.Lunaire France
123 R2 St Lunaire Nfld
21 A7 St. Lyphard France
25 B5 St.Maartens-dijk Netherlands
18 E8 St. Macaire Gironde France
21 D7 St.Macaire Maine-et-Loire France
15 G2 St.Magnus B Scotland
21 E9 St.Maixent-l'Ecole France
122 B7 St.Malachie Quebec
20 A4 St.Malo France
20 B3 St. Mâlo-de-la-Lande France
20 B4 St.Malo, G.de France
20 A5 St.Malon-sur-Mel France
19 P18 St.Mandrier France
127 H5 St.Marc Haiti
121 S6 St.Marc des Carrières Quebec
122 B7 St.Marcel Quebec
19 O14 St.Marcellin France
20 C3 St. Marcouf, I France
20 C5 St.Marc-sur-Couesnon France
22 K4 St.Mard Belgium
123 P2 St.Margaret B Nfld
122 J9 St.Margaret B Nova Scotia
38 K8 St.Margarethen Austria
32 K5 St.Margarethen W Germany
15 F2 St.Margarets Hope Scotland
122 B5 Ste.Marguerite, R Quebec
122 F3 Ste.Marguerite, R Quebec
110 H3 Ste.Marie Illinois
127 L4 Ste.Marie Martinique W Indies
121 T6 Ste.Marie Quebec
83 K13 Ste.Marie Réunion Indian Oc
19 K4 Ste.Marie aux Mines France
36 C7 Ste. Marie, Col de pass France
20 C3 Ste.Marie-du-Mont France
19 Q17 St Marie Mourre de Chanier mt France
100 J2 St.Maries Idaho
113 C7 St.Marks Florida
21 F6 St. Mars-d'Outillé France
21 C7 St. Mars-du-Désert France
20 F5 St.Mars-la-Brière France
21 C7 St.Mars la Jaille France
20 C5 St.Mars-sur-la-Futaie France
122 F4 Ste.Marthe de Gaspé Quebec
18 E6 St.Martin France
127 N5 St.Martin isld Lesser Antilles
22 B2 St.Martin-Boulogne France
127 L4 St. Martin, C Martinique W Indies
89 A9 St.Martin, C S Africa
20 J5 St.Martin-de-Bretencourt France
19 N17 St.Martin-de-Crau France
20 C4 St.Martin-de-Landelle France
21 C9 St.Martin-de-Ré France
20 D3 St.Martin-des-Besaces France
16 E4 St.Martin de Valdeiglesias Spain
19 P12 St.Martin-du-Fresne France
19 O12 St.Martin-du-Mont France
40 B4 St.Martin en Bresse France
20 H2 St.Martin-en-Campagne France
99 U4 St.Martin I Michigan
119 T7 St. Martin, L Manitoba
122 G8 St. Martin's New Brunswick
9 F7 St. Martin's isld Isles of Scilly England
68 A2 St.Martin's I Burma
119 T7 St. Martin Station Manitoba
111 E11 St.Martinville Louisiana
9 H7 St.Mary Channel Is
127 L2 St.Mary parish Jamaica
101 M1 St. Mary R Mont/Alberta
123 N3 St. Mary Is Quebec
101 M1 St.Mary L Montana
117 P11 St. Mary, Mt Br Columbia
144 B6 St. Mary, Mt New Zealand
123 N3 St.Mary Reefs Quebec
118 D9 St.Mary Res Alberta
113 F7 St. Marys Georgia
107 O2 St Marys Kansas
110 G4 St.Marys Missouri
123 T7 St.Marys Nfld
94 C6 St.Marys Ohio
94 J5 St.Marys Pennsylvania
15 F2 St. Marys Scotland
139 J8 St.Marys Tasmania
127 O3 St. Mary's Trinidad
94 F7 St.Marys W Virginia
9 F7 St.Mary's isld Isles of Scilly England
94 B6 St. Marys R Indiana
123 T7 St.Mary's B Nfld
122 F9 St.Mary's B Nova Scotia
95 L8 St. Marys City Maryland
89 H6 St.Mary's Hill S Africa
15 E5 St. Marys Loch Scotland
113 F7 St.Marys R Florida/Georgia
123 K8 St.Mary's, R Nova Scotia
112 G4 St. Mathews S Carolina
21 G10 St.Mathieu France
121 M4 St.Mathieu Quebec
18 B4 St. Mathieu, Pte France
116 C6 St.Matthew I Bering Sea
136 K2 St. Matthias Group islds Bismarck Arch
21 G7 Ste. Maure de-Touraine France
40 E2 St.Maurice France
21 D7 St.Maurice-la-Fougereuse France
20 G4 St. Maurice-les-Charencey France
121 R5 St-Maurice, Parc Quebec
8 A7 St. Mawes England
122 B7 St. Maxime Quebec
19 P18 St.Maximin France
22 J4 St. Médard Belgium
18 E8 St Medard en Jalles France
110 K3 St.Meinrad Indiana
8 C4 St.Mellons Wales
20 B4 St. Meloir-des-Ondes France
19 J3 St. Menehould France
22 H4 St.Menges France
20 C3 Ste. Mère-Eglise France
98 H8 St.Michael Nebraska
127 P6 St.Michael parish Barbados
32 K5 St.Michaelisdonn W Germany
103 P6 St.Michaels Arizona
95 L8 St.Michaels Maryland
22 G4 St.Michel Aisne France
21 C6 St.Michel Maine-et-Loire France
127 H5 St.Michel de L'Atalaye Haiti
121 R6 St.Michel des Saints Quebec
36 B7 St.Michel-sur-Meurthe France
126 B1 St.Michiel Curaçao
19 J4 St Mihiel France
22 C2 St.Momelin France
13 F1 St.Monance Scotland
41 L5 St.Moritz Switzerland
21 A7 St.Nazaire France
19 O14 St.Nazaire-en-Royans France
9 F3 St.Neots England
St.Nicolas see St.Niklaas
20 H2 St.Nicolas-d'Aliermont France
22 G1 St.Niklaas Belgium
119 U9 St.Norbert Manitoba
25 F6 St.Odilienberg Netherlands
25 D5 St.Oedenrode Netherlands
22 C2 St.Omer France
145 D4 St. Omer New Zealand
122 F5 St.Omer Quebec
98 C5 St.Onge S Dakota
18 E7 Saintonge prov France
20 C4 St.Osvin France
20 D5 St.Ouen-des-Toits France
20 K3 St.Ouen-l'Aumône France
121 R7 St.Ours Quebec
122 C6 St.Pacôme Quebec
20 B4 St.Pair France
18 E9 St.Palais France
122 C7 St.Pamphile Quebec
18 F7 St.Pardoux la Rivière France
94 D6 St.Paris Ohio
122 C6 St.Pascal Quebec
20 F5 St.Paterne France
121 N6 St.Patrice, L Quebec
127 O3 St.Patrick co Trinidad
114 H7 St.Paul Alberta
110 C6 St.Paul Arkansas
38 L8 St.Paul Austria
18 E9 St.Paul France
94 B7 St.Paul Indiana
107 P4 St.Paul Kansas
99 N4 St.Paul Minnesota
98 H8 St.Paul Nebraska
83 J13 St.Paul Réunion Indian Oc
112 G4 St.Paul S Carolina
94 E10 St.Paul Virginia
85 C7 St. Paul R Guinea/Liberia
18 G10 St. Paul de Fenouillet France
122 C6 St.-Paul-de-la-Croix Quebec
122 B7 St.Paul de Montriny Quebec
122 C5 St.Paul du Nord Quebec
123 M6 St.Paul I C Breton I, N S
81 E9 St. Paul, Î Indian Oc
116 D8 St. Paul I Pribilof Is Bering Sea
18 H7 St.Paulien France
121 R6 St.Paulin Quebec
19 P17 St.Paul-les-Durance France
123 P2 St.Paul R Quebec
90 G8 St.Paul Rocks Atlantic Oc
112 H3 St.Pauls N Carolina
127 P4 St.Pauls St Kitts W Indies
123 P4 St.Paul's Inlet Nfld
19 N16 St Paul-Trois-Châteaux France
18 E9 St.Pé de B France
20 J5 St. Peravy-la-Colombe France
21 A7 St. Père-en-Retz France
122 C6 Ste.Perpétue Quebec
110 H3 St.Peter Illinois
38 K7 St.Peter-am-Kammersberg Austria
123 R1 St.Peter B Labrador
32 J4 St Peter-Ording W Germany
9 G6 St.Peter Port Channel Is
122 H5 St.Peter, Pt Quebec
123 M8 St.Peters C Breton I, N S
122 K7 St.Peters Pr Edward I
St.Petersburg see Leningrad
113 E10 St.Petersburg Florida
69 J12 St.Petrus isld Indonesia
21 B7 St.Philbert de Grandlieu France
122 B7 St.Philémon Quebec
127 P6 St. Philip parish Barbados
25 B5 St.Philipsland Netherlands
121 S7 St.Pie Quebec
123 Q7 St. Pierre Atlantic Oc
119 V9 St.Pierre Manitoba
127 L4 St.Pierre Martinique W Indies
83 J14 St.Pierre Réunion Indian Oc
19 Q13 St Pierre d'Albigny France
20 H3 St.Pierre-d'Autils France
20 B5 St.Pierre-de-Plesguen France
21 D8 St.Pierre-des-Echaubrognes France
20 E5 St. Pierre-des-Nids France
21 C10 St. Pierre-d'Oléron France
20 H3 St.Pierre-du-Vauvray France
20 C2 St. Pierre Eglise France
20 F2 St.Pierre-en-Port France
81 C6 St.Pierre I Indian Oc
121 S6 St.Pierre, L Quebec
20 C5 St.Pierre-la-Cour France
20 B4 St.Pierre-Langers France
18 H6 St. Pierre le Môutier France
20 H3 St. Pierre-les-Elbeuf France
20 E3 St.Pierre-sur-Dives France
20 E5 St.Pierre-sur-Orthe France
20 C4 St.Pois France
21 C6 St.Poix France
22 C1 St.Pol France
22 C3 St.Pol France
18 C4 St.Pol-de-Léon France
38 N5 St.Pölten Austria
19 K6 St.Pon, L.de France
18 G9 St Pons France
18 H6 St.Pourcain-sur-Sioule France
121 S4 St.-Prime Quebec
22 E4 St.Quentin Aisne France
21 D6 St.Quentin Maine-et-Loire France
122 E6 St.Quentin New Brunswick
20 K4 St. Quentin-en-Yvelines France
22 B3 St.Quentin, Pte.de France
36 C6 St.Quirin France
18 H7 St.Rambert France
122 B7 St.Raphaël Quebec
121 T6 St.Raymond Quebec
101 L2 St.Regis Montana
95 N2 St. Regis Falls New York
121 R7 St.Rémi Quebec
19 N17 St. Rémy Bouches du Rhône France
20 E4 St.Rémy Calvados France
20 F5 St.Rémy-des-Monts France
20 F5 St.Rémy-du-Plain France
20 B5 St. Remy-du-Plein France
20 H4 St. Remy-sur-Avre France
18 H7 St. Rémy-sur-Durolle France
40 F6 St.Rhémy Italy
20 J1 St.Riquier France
121 R7 St.Robert Quebec
122 A8 St.Romain Quebec
20 F2 St.Romain-de-Colbosc France
21 H7 St.Romain-sur-Cher France
121 T6 St.Romuald Quebec
141 G4 St. Ronans Queensland
127 N4 Ste.Rose Guadeloupe W Indies
121 R7 Ste.Rose Quebec
119 S7 Ste.Rose de Lac Manitoba
122 D6 Ste.Rose du Dégelé Quebec
38 N7 St.Ruprecht-an-der-Raab Austria
20 H2 St.Saëns France
31 O6 St.Sambor U.S.S.R.
9 G6 St.Sampson Channel Is
19 O17 St.Saturnin d'Apt France
19 N17 St Saturnin-lès-Avig-non France
20 K2 St.Sauflieu France
20 E4 St.Sauveur France
121 Q7 St.Sauveur Quebec
20 C3 St. Sauveur Lendelin France
20 B3 St.Sauveur-le-Vicomte France
18 E7 St.Savin France
21 D10 St.Savinien France
20 F4 Ste.Scolasse France
87 H10 St.Sebastien, C Madagascar
18 G9 St.Sernin-sur-Rance France
20 A4 St.Servan France
18 E9 St.Sever France
20 C4 St.Sever-Calvados France
21 E10 Ste Sévère France
123 T7 St.Shott's Nfld
22 E4 St.Simon France
122 C5 St.Simon Quebec
112 F6 St. Simons Georgia
26 J4 St. Sjöfallets Nat. Park Sweden
115 N8 St.Stephen New Brunswick
112 H4 St.Stephen S Carolina
101 R7 St.Stephens Wyoming
18 G9 St.Sulpice France
20 G4 St.Sulpice France
21 B6 St.Sulpice des Landes France
18 G6 St. Sulpice Laurière France
21 H9 St.Sulpice les Feuilles France
20 E5 Ste.Suzanne France
83 K13 Ste.Suzanne Réunion Indian Oc
20 E3 St.Sylvain France
121 T6 St.-Sylvestre Quebec
18 E8 St.Symphorien France
117 F6 St. Terese Alaska
122 E5 St.Tharsicius Quebec
121 S6 Ste.Thècle Quebec
122 B8 St. Théophile Quebec
121 R7 Ste.Thérèse Quebec
117 N3 Ste. Thérèse, Lac N W Terr
40 C1 St.Thiébault France
98 J1 St.Thomas N Dakota
120 J10 St.Thomas Ontario
127 P6 St.Thomas parish Barbados
127 M3 St.Thomas parish Jamaica
113 K7 St.Thomas I Virgin Is
121 S6 St.Tite Quebec
122 B6 St.Tite des Caps Quebec
40 B5 St.Trivier de Courtes France
19 N12 St. Trivier-Moignans France
St.Trond see St.Truiden
22 J2 St.Truiden Belgium
8 B2 St. Tudwal's Is Wales
27 H11 St.Tuna Sweden
122 E5 St.Ulric Quebec
122 B6 St.Urbain Quebec
20 G2 St.Vaast France
20 C2 St.Vaast-la-Hougue France
20 G2 St.Valery-en-Caux France
20 J1 St. Valéry-sur-Somme France
122 B7 St.Vallier Quebec
38 H7 St.Veit Austria
38 K8 St.Veit-an-der-Glan Austria
22 D2 St.Venant France
121 Q6 Ste.Véronique Quebec
21 I6 St. Viâtre France
19 P17 Ste Victoire, Mt France
21 A6 St.Vincent France
127 O8 St. Vincent isld Lesser Antilles
87 G12 St.Vincent, C Madagascar
139 H9 St.Vincent, C Tasmania
18 E9 St.Vincent-de-Tyrosse France
138 E5 St.Vincent, G S Australia
113 B8 St. Vincent I Florida
123 T7 St.Vincent's Nfld
21 B9 St.Vincent-sur-Jard France
118 A2 St.Vital Manitoba
94 C1 St. Vital Pt Michigan
22 L3 St.Vith Belgium
18 E7 St.Vivien-de-Médoc France
106 G7 St.Vrain New Mexico
118 H5 St.Walburg Sask
20 G2 St.Wandrille France
36 C5 St.Wendel W Germany
126 A1 St. Willebrordus Curaçao
120 K10 St.Williams Ontario
101 S4 St.Xavier Montana
18 F7 St. Yrieix France
122 H4 St.Yvon Quebec
19 P18 St.Zacharie France
20 J5 Sainville France
134 E6 Saipan isld Mariana Is Pacific Oc
20 C2 Saire R France
20 C2 Saire, Pte. de France
18 E9 Saison R France
61 M10 Saitama prefect Japan
68 A1 Saitlai Burma
60 E13 Saito Japan
26 N3 Saivomuotka Sweden
21 E9 Saivres France
77 L2 Saiydabad Afghanistan
77 L1 Saiyid Afghanistan
74 E3 Saiyidwala Pakistan
71 B2 Sajafi isld Indonesia
128 E7 Sajama Bolivia
71 B2 Sajang isld Indonesia
48 F2 Sajó R Hungary
89 B7 Sak watercourse S Africa
88 G2 Saka Kenya
Saka Dzong see Saga
59 L5 Sakai Japan
60 G11 Sakaide Japan
60 G10 Sakai Minato Japan
72 E2 Sakākah Saudi Arabia
78 H7 Sakakah Saudi Arabia
98 E2 Sakakawea, L N Dakota
70 Q9 Sakala isld Indonesia
61 N7 Sakamachi Japan
115 M7 Sakami L Quebec
88 B8 Sakania Zaïre
Sakar see Brannitsa Bulgaria
57 C5 Sakar U.S.S.R.
87 G12 Sakaraha Madagascar
78 C1 Sakarya R Turkey
78 C2 Sakarya R Turkey
59 L4 Sakata Japan
111 H8 Sakatonchee R Mississippi
85 E7 Sakete Benin
51 O3 Sakhalin isld U.S.S.R.
51 O4 Sakhalinskaya Oblast' U.S.S.R.
51 O3 Sakhalinskiy Zaliv B U.S.S.R.
54 G7 Sakhnovshchina U.S.S.R.
52 B7 Šakiai U.S.S.R.
80 G4 Sakib Jordan
60 H12 Sakihama Japan
67 H4 Sakishima-guntō islds Japan
55 C5 Sakmara U.S.S.R.
68 C3 Sa-koi Burma
95 Q5 Sakonnet R Rhode I
86 G3 Sakota Ethiopia
87 D12 Sakrivier S Africa
28 E5 Saksild Denmark
28 H7 Sakskøbing Denmark
75 K7 Sakti India
51 M1 Saktyakh U.S.S.R.
61 M9 Saku Japan
61 L10 Sakuma Japan
61 J11 Sakurai Japan
60 D14 Sakura jima isld Japan
27 M10 Säkylä Finland
80 G3 Sal Jordan
53 F9 Sal R U.S.S.R.
48 D2 Šala Czechoslovakia
27 J12 Sala Sweden
68 F7 Sala Andong Tuk Cambodia
71 H6 Salabangka isld Sulawesi
52 B5 Salacgriva U.S.S.R.
43 G8 Sala Consilina Italy
109 K5 Salad Texas
133 C3 Salada, B Chile
131 G6 Salada, L Buenos Aires Argentina
131 F2 Salada, L Corrientes Argentina
124 B1 Salada, L Mexico
103 J9 Salada, Laguna L Mexico
131 E4 Saladillo R Argentina
131 B2 Salado R La Rioja Argentina
106 C7 Salado, R New Mexico
131 E2 Salado, R Santa Fé Argentina
85 D7 Salaga Ghana
68 F7 Sala Hintoun Cambodia
78 H4 Salahiye Syria
56 C4 Salair U.S.S.R.
56 C4 Salairskiy Kryazh ridge U.S.S.R.
48 H3 Šalaj prov Romania
71 K8 Salajar Indonesia
70 G7 Salajar, Selat str Sulawesi
70 L9 Salak, G mt Java
86 C3 Salal Chad
72 G5 Salālah Oman
125 O10 Salamá Guatemala
94 J4 Salamanca New York
16 D4 Salamanca Spain
16 C4 Salamanca prov Spain
86 C4 Salamat R Chad
128 C2 Salamina Colombia
79 D3 Salamis Cyprus
47 F7 Salamís Greece
94 B6 Salamonie R Indiana
70 E2 Salang Kalimantan
26 J3 Salangen Norway
52 B6 Salantai U.S.S.R.
45 K2 Salara Italy
48 G3 Sălard Romania
133 D2 Salar de Arizaro salt pan Argentina
133 D2 Salar de Atacama salt pan Chile
133 D2 Salar de Cauchari salt pan Argentina
133 D1 Salar de Coipasa salt pan Bolivia
133 D3 Salar del Hombre Muerto salt pan Argentina
133 D2 Salar de Uyuni salt pan Bolivia
16 C1 Salas Spain
46 E1 Salaš Yugoslavia
16 E2 Salas de los Infantes Spain
18 F9 Salat R France
70 N9 Salatiga Java
18 F10 Salau, Pont de pass France/Spain
52 H6 Salaushi U.S.S.R.
55 C4 Salavat U.S.S.R.
128 C5 Salaverry Peru
133 E3 Salavina Argentina
71 C3 Salawati isld W Irian
71 G6 Salay Mindanao Philippines
135 Q11 Sala y Gómez isld Pacific Oc
Salazar see Ndalatanda
21 J7 Salbris France
126 D3 Sal, Cay isld Bahamas
127 J5 Salcedo Dominican Rep
116 P4 Salcha R Alaska
116 O4 Salchaket Alaska
33 P8 Salchau E Germany
37 O6 Salching W Germany
47 G1 Salcia Romania
8 C7 Salcombe England
47 K7 Salda Gölü L Turkey
16 D2 Saldaña Spain
87 C12 Saldanha S Africa
41 N4 Saldura, Pta mt Italy
52 B6 Saldus U.S.S.R.
68 B2 Sale Burma
8 D1 Sale England
85 C2 Sale Morocco
139 H7 Sale Victoria
112 C6 Sale City Georgia
112 B2 Sale Creek Tennessee
77 A2 Sālehābad Iran
71 H9 Saleh, Teluk B Indonesia
147 N15 Salekhard U.S.S.R.
111 L9 Salem Alabama
110 E5 Salem Arkansas
113 D8 Salem Florida
110 H3 Salem Illinois
76 D5 Salem India
110 K3 Salem Indiana
95 R4 Salem Massachusetts
110 E4 Salem Missouri
95 Q4 Salem New Hampshire
95 M7 Salem New Jersey
106 C9 Salem New Mexico
95 O3 Salem New York
94 G6 Salem Ohio
100 B5 Salem Oregon
112 E3 Salem S Carolina
98 J6 Salem S Dakota
94 G9 Salem Virginia
99 S7 Salem Wisconsin
70 D7 Salembu Besar isld Indonesia
43 E11 Salemi Sicily
15 C4 Salen Scotland
27 F10 Sälen Sweden
142 E3 Sale, R W Australia
19 Q17 Salernes France
113 G10 Salerno Florida
43 F8 Salerno Italy
43 F8 Salerno, Golfo di Italy
45 L1 Saletto Italy
20 K2 Saleux France
19 Q12 Salève, Mt France
13 F6 Salford England
130 H9 Salgado R Brazil
131 H2 Salgado Filho airport Brazil
48 F2 Salgótarján Hungary
130 G10 Salgueiro Brazil
79 C8 Sâlhîya, El Egypt
127 P2 Salibea Trinidad
106 D3 Salida Colorado
18 E9 Salies de Béarn France
18 F9 Salies du Salat France
47 J6 Salihli Turkey
87 F8 Salima Malawi
70 E3 Salimbatu Kalimantan
68 B2 Salin Burma
68 B2 Salin R Burma
107 N3 Salina Kansas
110 A5 Salina Oklahoma
103 N3 Salina Utah
43 F10 Salina isld Italy
125 M9 Salina Cruz Mexico
133 D4 Salina La Antigua salt pan Argentina
126 G3 Salina Pt Acklins I Bahamas
129 K7 Salinas Brazil
102 C5 Salinas California
128 B4 Salinas Ecuador
128 C6 Salinas Peru
102 C5 Salinas R California
133 D4 Salinas Grandes Argentina
131 C3 Salinas, Pampa de la Argentina
106 D8 Salinas Pk New Mexico
87 B8 Salinas, Pte. das Angola
94 D4 Saline Michigan
12 E1 Saline Scotland
111 D8 Saline R Arkansas
110 H4 Saline R Illinois
107 L2 Saline R Kansas
127 P2 Saline B Trinidad
109 P3 Saline Bayou R Louisiana
109 P4 Saline L Louisiana
127 P5 Salines, Pt Grenada
102 G5 Saline V California
94 G6 Salineville Ohio
68 B1 Salingyi Burma
133 C3 Salinitas Chile
129 J4 Salinópolis Brazil
70 F6 Salipolo Sulawesi
95 O4 Salisbury Connecticut
9 E5 Salisbury England
95 M8 Salisbury Maryland
110 D2 Salisbury Missouri
112 G2 Salisbury N Carolina
122 G7 Salisbury New Brunswick
94 H7 Salisbury Pennsylvania
138 E5 Salisbury S Australia
95 O3 Salisbury Vermont
88 C10 Salisbury Zimbabwe
141 K2 Salisbury dist Brisbane, Qnsld
115 M5 Salisbury I N W Terr
86 F5 Salisbury, L Uganda
116 O2 Salisbury, Mt Alaska
9 E5 Salisbury Plain England
48 H5 Săliste Romania
129 K6 Salitre R Brazil
80 G8 Saliya Jordan
45 K1 Salizzole Italy
112 F4 Salkehatchie R S Carolina
79 G6 Salkhad Syria
28 D4 Sall Denmark
38 L7 Salla Austria
29 O5 Salla Finland
17 G2 Sallent de G Spain
19 N16 Salles France
18 G8 Salles-Curan France
112 F4 Salley S Carolina
33 T9 Sallgast E Germany
28 B3 Salling reg Denmark
107 Q6 Sallisaw Oklahoma
86 G2 Sallom Sudan
78 K6 Salman, As Iraq
78 K2 Salmas Iran
17 F4 Salmerón Spain
29 N5 Salmivaara Finland
100 H1 Salmo Br Columbia
116 Q3 Salmon Alaska
101 M4 Salmon Idaho
117 M8 Salmon R Br Columbia
114 H7 Salmon Arm Br Columbia
123 P2 Salmon Bay Quebec
101 L7 Salmon Cr.Res Idaho
142 F3 Salmond R W Australia
101 L7 Salmon Falls Idaho
116 R4 Salmon Fork R Alaska
143 D10 Salmon Gums W Australia
123 T6 Salmonier Nfld
100 B8 Salmon Mt California
122 G7 Salmon R New Brunswick
122 K4 Salmon, R Quebec
95 M3 Salmon Res New York
114 H9 Salmon River Mts Idaho
36 G3 Salmünster W Germany
52 E2 Sal'nitsa U.S.S.R.
42 D3 Salò Italy
52 G6 Salobelyak U.S.S.R.
130 C7 Salobra, R Brazil
29 L7 Saloinen Finland
99 L1 Salol Minnesota
103 L8 Salome Arizona
127 L4 Salomon, C Martinique W Indies
40 C2 Salon R France
19 O17 Salon-de-Provence France
Salonica see Thessaloníki
48 G4 Salonta Romania
8 D2 Salop co England
17 H3 Salou, C Spain
29 M11 Salpausselkä reg Finland
26 K9 Salsåker Sweden
53 F10 Sal'sk U.S.S.R.
43 F11 Salso R Sicily
44 G2 Salsomaggiore Terme Italy
80 F5 Salt Jordan
103 N8 Salt R Arizona
110 L3 Salt R Kentucky
110 E2 Salt R Missouri
133 D2 Salta Argentina
55 F3 Saltaim, Oz L U.S.S.R.
8 B7 Saltash England
28 G5 Saltbæk Vig lagoon Denmark
108 B4 Salt Basin Texas
13 H4 Saltburn England
119 P7 Saltcoats Sask
12 D2 Saltcoats Scotland
110 G1 Salt Cr Illinois
94 E7 Salt Cr Ohio
101 T6 Salt Cr Wyoming
99 R9 Salt Cr R Illinois
26 H4 Saltdal Norway
108 C4 Salt Draw R Texas
14 E4 Saltee Is Irish Rep
26 H5 Saltelv R Norway
26 G4 Salten reg Norway
28 D4 Salten Langsø L Denmark
26 G4 Saltfjord inlet Norway
108 B4 Salt Flat Texas
13 J6 Saltfleet England
107 M5 Salt Fork R Oklahoma
108 F2 Salt Fork R Texas
109 H4 Salt Gap Texas
28 K5 Saltholm isld Denmark
125 J5 Saltillo Mexico
94 J6 Saltillo Pennsylvania
110 H6 Saltillo Tennessee
106 G9 Salt L New Mexico
108 C4 Salt L Texas
140 E6 Salt Lake Queensland
101 O9 Salt Lake City Utah
143 C8 Salt Lakes W Australia
94 D8 Salt Lick Kentucky
143 D6 Salt Ls W Australia
133 E4 Salto Argentina
130 F8 Salto Brazil
131 F3 Salto Uruguay
131 F3 Salto dep Uruguay
42 E6 Salto R Italy
130 C9 Salto das Sete Quedas falls Paraguay
130 D7 Salto do Urubupungá falls Brazil
45 O5 Salto, L. del Italy
26 K4 Saltoluokta Sweden
103 J8 Salton California
103 J8 Salton Sea California
127 L3 Salt Ponds, The Jamaica
74 E2 Salt Range Pakistan
127 K3 Salt River Jamaica
127 H5 Saltrou Haiti
101 P7 Salt R. Ra Wyoming
27 K12 Saltsjöbaden Sweden
27 L11 Saltvik Finland
94 F10 Saltville Virginia
102 F2 Salt Wells Nevada
112 F3 Saluda S Carolina
112 E3 Saluda R S Carolina
71 H5 Salue isld Indonesia
71 H5 Salue Timpaus, Selat str Indonesia
84 H3 Salûm Egypt
45 N4 Saluoecio Italy
71 F7 Saluping isld Philippines
76 F1 Salur India
110 C6 Salus Arkansas
129 H2 Salut, I.du Fr Guiana
44 B2 Saluzzo Italy
129 L6 Salvador Brazil
84 E5 Salvador Niger
118 H6 Salvador Sask
111 F12 Salvador, L Louisiana
123 T5 Salvage Nfld
16 B5 Salvaterra de Magos Portugal
125 J7 Salvatierra Mexico
103 N3 Salvation Cr Utah
141 H6 Salvator, L Queensland
18 G8 Salvetat, la Aveyron France
18 G9 Salvetat, la Hérault France
117 J8 Salvus Br Columbia
73 Q5 Salween R Burma/Thailand
75 K4 Salyan Nepal
94 D9 Salyersville Kentucky
38 L6 Salza R Austria
32 F8 Salzbergen W Germany
38 H6 Salzburg Austria
38 H7 Salzburg prov Austria
32 L9 Salzderhelden W Germany
33 M8 Salzgitter W Germany
33 M8 Salzgitter-Bad W Germany
38 J6 Salzkammer-gut res Austria
32 J9 Salzkotten W Germany
33 P9 Salzmünde E Germany
33 O7 Salzwedel E Germany
101 O6 Sam Idaho
80 G3 Sama Jordan
80 G4 Samad Jordan
71 J5 Samada isld Indonesia
16 D1 Sama de Langreo Spain
56 E5 Samagaltay U.S.S.R.
80 F2 Samak Syria
71 G7 Samal isld Mindanao Philippines
69 C10 Samalanga Sumatra
108 A4 Samalayuca Mexico
71 E7 Samales Group islds Philippines
76 F2 Samalkot India
84 J4 Samâlût Egypt
127 K5 Samaná Dominican Rep
126 H3 Samana Cay isld Bahamas
78 E3 Samandag Turkey
60 Q3 Samani Japan
121 S3 Samaqua R Quebec
80 G3 Samar Jordan
71 G5 Samar isld Philippines
53 H7 Samara R U.S.S.R.
136 L4 Samarai Papua New Guinea
101 N7 Samaria Idaho
80 D4 Samaria Jordan
46 E4 Samarína Greece
70 E5 Samarinda Kalimantan
57 D5 Samarkand U.S.S.R.
78 J4 Sāmarrā' Iraq
71 G5 Samar Sea Philippines
71 C3 Samate W Irian
78 K6 Samāwah, Aq Iraq
86 D5 Samba Equateur Zaïre
86 E6 Samba Kasai Oriental Zaïre
70 C5 Samba R Kalimantan
87 C7 Samba Caju Angola
71 A3 Sambaki, Selat Indonesia
70 F4 Sambaliung mts Kalimantan
75 L8 Sambalpur India
70 G7 Sambapolulu, G mt Sulawesi

70
Sebkra Azzel Matti — Shenmu

85 E3 Sebkra Azzel Matti salt flats Algeria
85 C3 Sebkra de Tindouf salt flats Algeria
17 G9 Sebkra d'Oran Algeria
85 E3 Sebkra Mekerrhane salt flats Algeria
69 E14 Seblat Sumatra
31 H5 Sebnitz E Germany
95 T1 Seboeis L Maine
95 R8 Seboomook L Maine
85 C2 Sebou R Morocco
110 J4 Sebree Kentucky
95 K10 Sebrell Virginia
113 F10 Sebring Florida
94 F6 Sebring Ohio
70 E2 Sebuku Kalimantan
70 E6 Sebuku isld Kalimantan
70 B4 Sebuyau Sarawak
37 Q4 Seč Czechoslovakia
42 C4 Secchia R Italy
112 E3 Secession L S Carolina
68 G4 Se Cham R Laos
122 C1 Séchelles, L Quebec
128 B5 Sechura, B. de Peru
128 B5 Sechura, Des. de des Peru
38 L7 Seckau Austria
38 L7 Seckauer Alpen mts Austria
22 E2 Seclin France
133 D7 Seco R Argentina
17 H4 Seco R Spain
21 E8 Secondigny France
118 L8 Secretan Sask
144 A6 Secretary I New Zealand
76 D2 Secunderabad India
128 E7 Sécure R Bolivia
48 E3 Séd R Hungary
52 B6 Seda U.S.S.R.
16 B5 Seda R Portugal
71 L10 Sedah Indonesia
118 G7 Sedalia Alberta
106 F2 Sedalia Colorado
94 D7 Sedalia Ohio
19 J3 Sedan France
107 O4 Sedan Kansas
106 G5 Sedan New Mexico
138 E5 Sedan S Australia
56 F3 Sedannavskaya, Shiver falls U.S.S.R.
16 E2 Sedano Spain
13 F5 Sedbergh England
145 E4 Seddon New Zealand
115 O2 Seddon, Kap C Greenland
144 C4 Seddonville New Zealand
47 H4 Seddülbahir Turkey
79 E8 Sede Boqer Israel
80 B7 Sede Dawid Israel
80 F1 Sede Eli'ezer Israel
80 F4 Sede Eliyyahu Israel
55 G3 Sedel'nikovo U.S.S.R.
80 C7 Sede Moshe Israel
80 F1 Sede Neemya Israel
19 P16 Séderon France
80 B7 Sederot Israel
80 G2 Sede Yaaqov Syria
80 B8 Sede Zevi Israel
9 E3 Sedgeberrow England
13 G4 Sedgefield England
8 D2 Sedgley England
106 H1 Sedgwick Colorado
107 N4 Sedgwick Kansas
95 T2 Sedgwick Maine
70 E6 Sedjaka Kalimantan
31 H6 Sedlčany Czechoslovakia
9 G6 Sedlescombe England
119 O8 Sedley Sask
79 F7 Sedom Israel
103 N7 Sedona Arizona
68 G5 Se Done R Laos
80 C7 Sedot Mikha Israel
80 C4 Sedot Yam Israel
100 C1 Sedro Woolley Washington
52 B6 Šeduva U.S.S.R.
20 C4 See R France
33 O4 Seebad Heringsdorf W Germany
118 C7 Seebe Alberta
37 K2 Seebergen E Germany
33 P10 Seeburg E Germany
41 O3 Seefeld Austria
33 T7 Seefeld E Germany
40 G2 Seefelden W Germany
33 O8 Seehausen E Germany
87 C11 Seeheim Namibia
36 F4 Seeheim W Germany
36 D7 Seelbach W Germany
101 M2 Seeley Lake Montana
121 O8 Seeleys Bay Ontario
146 G10 Seelig, Mt Antarctica
33 R10 Seelingstädt E Germany
36 C2 Seelscheid W Germany
70 P10 Seemanandjung Java
33 S10 Seerhausen E Germany
41 J2 Seerücken mt Switzerland
20 F4 Sées France
32 M9 Seesen W Germany
41 O2 Seeshaupt W Germany
38 L7 Seetaler Alpen mts Austria
41 K3 Seez R Switzerland
47 H6 Seferihisar Turkey
17 G9 Sefioun R Algeria
85 D2 Sefrou Morocco
144 D5 Sefton New Zealand
144 C5 Sefton, Mt New Zealand
70 F2 Segama R Sabah
69 F11 Segamat Malaysia
70 M9 Segara Anakan Java
47 F1 Segarcea Romania
70 F7 Segeri Sulawesi
43 E11 Segesta Sicily
71 C3 Seget W Irian
52 D3 Segezha U.S.S.R.
57 D3 Segiz, Ozero L U.S.S.R.
41 K4 Segnes Pass Switzerland
45 O6 Segni Italy
103 P2 Sego Utah
17 G5 Segorbe Spain
85 C6 Segou Mali
16 E4 Segovia Spain
108 H5 Segovia Texas
16 E3 Segovia prov Spain
52 D3 Segozero, Oz L U.S.S.R.
21 D6 Segré France
17 H2 Segre R Spain
84 E5 Séguedine Niger
85 C7 Séguéla Ivory Coast
107 K2 Seguin Kansas
124 J5 Seguín Mexico
109 K6 Seguin Texas
106 F4 Segundo Colorado
133 E4 Segundo R Argentina
70 E4 Seguntur Kalimantan
17 F6 Segura R Spain
17 F6 Segura, Sa de mts Spain
32 L8 Sehnde W Germany
71 J5 Seho isld Indonesia
74 B5 Sehwan Pakistan
100 B8 Seiad Valley California
37 L3 Seibelsdorf W Germany
106 H2 Seibert Colorado
127 K5 Seibo Dom Rep
21 C6 Seiche R France
21 E6 Seiches France
80 D4 Seidā Jordan
80 F3 Seidur Jordan
140 E4 Seigals Creek N Terr Aust
122 C1 Seignelay, R Quebec
68 B2 Seikpyu Burma
68 B2 Seiktein Burma
12 C1 Seil isld Scotland
26 N1 Seiland isld Norway
18 G7 Seilhac France
107 M5 Seiling Oklahoma
19 K4 Seille R France
29 K9 Seinäjoki Finland
20 H3 Seine R France
20 D2 Seine, B. de la France
18 H4 Seine-et-Marne dep France
20 G2 Seine-Maritime dep France
18 B4 Sein, I. de France
69 J12 Seipenyu Indonesia
38 L5 Seitenstetten Austria
18 F10 Seix France
28 G5 Sejerø isld Denmark
28 B3 Sejerslev Denmark
28 E3 Sejflod Denmark
31 O1 Sejny Poland
28 D4 Sejs Denmark
28 B6 Sejstrup Denmark
70 B5 Sekadau Kalimantan
69 G13 Sekanak, Teluk B Sumatra
69 F14 Sekayu Sumatra
88 E4 Sekenke Tanzania
61 K10 Seki Japan
70 B5 Sekima Kalimantan
70 K8 Sekintjau mt Sumatra
85 D7 Sekondi Ghana
68 H6 Se Kong R Laos/Cambodia
77 G4 Sekuheh Iran
69 E14 Selagan R Sumatra
100 E3 Selah Washington
70 B4 Selalang Sarawak
69 E10 Selama Malaysia
69 E11 Selangor Malaysia
68 H4 Se La Nong R Laos
29 M10 Selänpää Finland
69 F14 Selara Ladangpait Sumatra
70 D7 Selatan, Tg C Kalimantan
69 F12 Selatpanjang Sumatra
69 F12 Selat Panjang R Sumatra
69 D13 Selat Siberut str Sumatra
69 D14 Selat Sipora str Indonesia
116 H3 Selawik Alaska
116 G3 Selawik L Alaska
37 N3 Selb W Germany
37 M3 Selbitz W Germany
27 A12 Selbjörnfj inlet Norway
26 E8 Selbusjö L Norway
13 G6 Selby England
98 F4 Selby S Dakota
116 K3 Selby, L Alaska
95 M8 Selbyville Delaware
28 C3 Selde Denmark
107 K2 Selden Kansas
123 S4 Seldom Nfld
116 M7 Seldovia Alaska
71 C3 Sele W Irian
43 G8 Sele R Italy
87 E10 Selebi-Pikwe Botswana
59 K1 Selemdzha R U.S.S.R.
79 H3 Selemiya Syria
47 K6 Selendi Turkey
56 G5 Selenga R U.S.S.R.
86 C6 Selenge Zaïre
58 E2 Selenge Mörön R Mongolia
46 D4 Selenicë Albania
51 O2 Selennyakh R U.S.S.R.
33 M4 Selent W Germany
33 M4 Selenter See L W Germany
71 C3 Sele, Selat str W Irian
40 F1 Sélestat France
55 F4 Selety R U.S.S.R.
50 G3 Seletyteniz, Ozero L U.S.S.R.
115 R5 Selfoss Iceland
98 F3 Selfridge N Dakota
52 G3 Selib U.S.S.R.
85 B5 Selibaby Mauritania
36 F3 Seligenstadt W Germany
52 D6 Seliger, Oz L U.S.S.R.
103 M6 Seligman Arizona
110 C5 Seligman Missouri
84 H5 Selima Oasis Sudan
70 C4 Selimbau Kalimantan
47 J7 Selimiye Turkey
46 E7 Selinoús Greece
95 L6 Selinsgrove Pennsylvania
55 F1 Seliyarovo U.S.S.R.
52 D6 Selizharovo U.S.S.R.
33 O9 Selke R E Germany
107 J3 Selkirk Kansas
115 K7 Selkirk Manitoba
94 C2 Selkirk Michigan
13 F2 Selkirk Scotland
Selkirk co see Borders reg
114 H7 Selkirk Mts Br Col/Idaho
119 S5 Selkirk T Manitoba
20 K2 Selle R France
100 D2 Selleck Washington
94 B8 Sellersburg Indiana
21 I7 Selles-St Denis France
21 I7 Selles-sur-Cher France
141 H5 Sellheim R Queensland
40 C4 Sellières France
9 G5 Sellindge England
41 O3 Sellrain Austria
103 N10 Sells Arizona
32 F9 Selm W Germany
111 J9 Selma Alabama
111 D10 Selma Louisiana
112 J2 Selma N Carolina
100 B7 Selma Oregon
110 H6 Selmer Tennessee
33 N5 Selmsdorf E Germany
21 H6 Selommes France
70 Q10 Selong Indonesia
40 B2 Selongey France
88 F6 Selous Game Res Tanzania
117 G4 Selous, Mt Yukon Terr
71 C3 Selpele Indonesia
83 K12 Sel Pt Mahé I Indian Ocean
9 F6 Selsey England
32 K6 Selsingen W Germany
36 D2 Selters W Germany
54 F3 Sel'tso U.S.S.R.
52 H6 Selty U.S.S.R.
33 S5 Seltz E Germany
36 E6 Seltz France
69 H10 Seluan isld Indonesia
87 E9 Selukwe Zimbabwe
20 C4 Selune R France
133 E3 Selva Argentina
38 E8 Selva Italy
128 D5 Selvas forests Brazil
140 F5 Selwyn Queensland
117 H4 Selwyn Mts Yukon Terr
140 F5 Selwyn Ra Queensland
98 G2 Selz N Dakota
36 E4 Selz R W Germany
40 F3 Selzach Switzerland
38 K6 Selzthal Austria
70 E5 Semajang, D L Kalimantan
20 F5 Semallé France
46 D4 Seman R Albania
70 K8 Semang Ka, Teluk B Sumatra
79 G2 Semān, Jebel mts Syria
119 N7 Semans Sask
70 N10 Semanu Java
85 B3 Semara Morocco
70 N9 Semarang Java
71 L10 Semau isld Timor Indonesia
88 C2 Sembabule Uganda
70 E3 Sembakung R Kalimantan
86 B5 Sembé Congo
21 G7 Semblancay France
52 F6 Semenov U.S.S.R.
54 D4 Semenovka Chernigov U.S.S.R.
54 E7 Semenovka Poltava U.S.S.R.
52 G6 Semenovo U.S.S.R.
52 F5 Semenovskoye Kostroma U.S.S.R.
52 F5 Sementsovo U.S.S.R.
70 O10 Semeru Java
116 J8 Semidi Is Alaska
52 F5 Semigorodnyaya U.S.S.R.
31 J5 Semily Czechoslovakia
111 G10 Seminary Mississippi
101 T7 Seminoe Dam Wyoming
101 T7 Seminoe Res Wyoming
107 O6 Seminole Oklahoma
108 E3 Seminole Texas
111 M11 Seminole, L Georgia
56 C5 Seminsky Khrebet mts U.S.S.R.
55 D4 Semiozernoye U.S.S.R.
56 B5 Semipalatinsk U.S.S.R.
55 E4 Semipolka U.S.S.R.
71 E5 Semirara isld Philippines
77 B4 Semīrom Iran
70 C4 Semitau Kalimantan
69 H10 Semium isld Indonesia
55 G5 Semiyarka U.S.S.R.
55 F5 Semiz-Bugu U.S.S.R.
33 R4 Semlow E Germany
33 T7 Semmelberg mt E Germany
38 N6 Semmering Austria
84 J5 Semna Sudan
86 F1 Semna Sudan
77 C2 Semnān Iran
71 A3 Semo Indonesia
22 J4 Semois R Belgium
89 F3 Semokwe R Zimbabwe
70 E1 Sempang Mangayau, Tg C Sabah
70 F2 Semporna Sabah
45 O6 Semprevisa mt Italy
70 O10 Sempu isld Java
26 H5 Semskefjell mt Norway
129 H4 Sem Tripa Brazil
88 E3 Semu R Tanzania
70 C6 Semuda Kalimantan
18 H5 Semur-en-Auxois France
89 F2 Semwe R Zimbabwe
52 F2 Semzha U.S.S.R.
128 E6 Sena Bolivia
88 E10 Sena Mozambique
129 L5 Senador Pompeu Brazil
70 E1 Senaja Sabah
128 E5 Sena Madureira Brazil
87 D9 Senango Zambia
20 J2 Sénarpont France
19 O17 Sénas France
118 H9 Senate Sask
110 F5 Senath Missouri
111 G7 Senatobia Mississippi
61 O7 Sendai Honshu Japan
60 D14 Sendai Kyūshū Japan
87 C11 Sendeling's Drift Namibia
37 J7 Senden W Germany
32 G9 Sendenhorst W Germany
16 C3 Sendim Portugal
70 B5 Senduruhan Kalimantan
74 F8 Sendwha India
69 E11 Senebui, Tg C Sumatra
99 S8 Seneca Illinois
107 O2 Seneca Kansas
110 B5 Seneca Missouri
98 F7 Seneca Nebraska
100 G5 Seneca Oregon
112 E3 Seneca S Carolina
98 G4 Seneca S Dakota
95 L4 Seneca L New York
94 F7 Seneca Lake Ohio
94 F7 Senecaville Ohio
22 G2 Seneffe Belgium
85 B5 Sénégal R W Africa
85 B6 Senegal rep W Africa
87 E11 Senekal S Africa
99 V3 Seney Michigan
30 H4 Senftenberg E Germany
87 F7 Senga Hill Zambia
52 H1 Sengeyskiy, Ostrov isld U.S.S.R.
70 G7 Sengkang Sulawesi
38 K6 Sengsengebirge mts Austria
133 C7 Senguerr R Argentina
88 B10 Sengwa R Zimbabwe
32 H5 Sengwärden W Germany
87 E9 Sengwe R Zimbabwe
129 K6 Senhor do Bonfim Brazil
45 O4 Senigallia Italy
45 L3 Senio R Italy
80 F1 Senir Israel
43 G8 Senise Italy
42 F4 Senj Yugoslavia
26 J2 Senja isld Norway
67 H4 Senkaku-shotō isld Japan
52 H2 Sen'kina U.S.S.R.
118 H6 Senlac Sask
65 H3 Senlin Shan mt China
68 H6 Senmonorom Cambodia
86 F3 Sennar Sudan
32 J9 Senne reg W Germany
40 A4 Sennecey le Grand France
32 J9 Sennelager W Germany
28 B3 Sennels Denmark
115 M8 Senneterre Quebec
20 F2 Senneville France
54 A2 Senno U.S.S.R.
8 C4 Sennybridge Wales
133 C8 Seno Almirantazgo gulf Chile
68 G4 Se Noi R Laos
111 M8 Senoia Georgia
20 H4 Senonches France
19 K4 Senones France
133 C8 Seno Otway gulf Chile
133 C8 Seno Skyring gulf Chile
18 H4 Sens France
20 B5 Sens-de-Bretagne France
40 F4 Sense R Switzerland
48 F5 Senta Yugoslavia
70 B4 Sentarum L Kalimantan
18 F10 Sentem France
86 E7 Sentery Zaïre
103 L9 Sentinel Arizona
109 H1 Sentinel Oklahoma
98 C3 Sentinel Butte N Dakota
117 N8 Sentinel Pk Br Columbia
146 G11 Sentinel Rge Antarctica
124 G7 Sentispac Mexico
129 K5 Sento Sé Brazil
22 H5 Senuc France
78 H3 Şenyurt Turkey
33 R7 Senzke E Germany
74 H7 Seoni India
Seoul see Sŏul
70 C5 Sepandan Kalimantan
70 P9 Sepandjang Indonesia
70 C5 Sepang Kalimantan
106 B9 Separ New Mexico
142 E6 Separation Well W Australia
70 E4 Sepasu Kalimantan
130 G8 Sepetiba, B. de Brazil
70 D3 Seping R Sarawak
45 R7 Sepino Italy
21 G7 Sepmes France
31 K2 Sępolno Poland
68 H4 Sepone Laos
31 N1 Sępopol Poland
130 B4 Sepotuba R Brazil
32 F9 Seppenrade W Germany
19 O18 Septêmes les Valdonne France
47 G2 Septemvri Bulgaria
20 J4 Septeuil France
20 D5 Sept Forges France
122 F3 Sept Îles Quebec
18 C4 Sept Iles, les France
141 J5 Septimus Queensland
122 B2 Sept-Milles, L Quebec
70 O9 Sepulu Java
16 E3 Sepúlveda Spain
70 K8 Seputih R Sumatra
112 B2 Sequatchie R Tennessee
16 D3 Sequillo R Spain
100 B1 Sequim Washington
102 F5 Sequoia Nat. Park California
79 F3 Serai Syria
22 G4 Seraincourt France
22 K2 Seraing Belgium
71 J9 Seraja isld Indonesia
70 P10 Seraja, G mt Indonesia
70 M9 Seraju R Java
57 B6 Serakhs U.S.S.R.
76 C2 Seram India
136 F2 Seram isld Moluccas Indonesia
70 L9 Serang Java
69 J11 Serasan isld Indonesia
69 J11 Seraya Indonesia
46 D1 Serbia hist reg Yugoslavia
45 H4 Serchio R Italy
70 K8 Serdang, Tg C Sumatra
53 F7 Serdobsk U.S.S.R.
55 F3 Serebryanoye U.S.S.R.
56 B6 Serebryansk U.S.S.R.
88 F5 Serebu mt Tanzania
52 F5 Sereda U.S.S.R.
52 C5 Seredka U.S.S.R.
78 D2 Şereflikoçhisar Turkey
18 H5 Serein R France
69 E11 Seremban Malaysia
71 C3 Seremuk R W Irian
88 E3 Serengeti Nat. Park Tanzania
88 C8 Serenje Zambia
86 H5 Serenli Somalia
48 K1 Seret R U.S.S.R.
52 F6 Serezha R U.S.S.R.
47 G7 Serfopoúla isld Greece
52 G6 Sergach U.S.S.R.
98 K7 Sergeant Bluff Iowa
58 E2 Sergelen Mongolia
87 E7 Serge Tshimbo Zaïre
55 E4 Sergeyevka Kokchetav U.S.S.R.
55 G3 Sergeyevka Novosibirsk U.S.S.R.
50 F2 Sergino U.S.S.R.
129 L6 Sergipe state Brazil
52 E2 Sergozero, Oz L U.S.S.R.
70 D2 Seria Brunei
41 L6 Seriana, Val Italy
69 D11 Seribudolok Sumatra
130 H9 Seridó R Brazil
20 J3 Sérifontaine France
47 G7 Sérifos isld Greece
19 N16 Sérignan France
68 D5 Serim Burma
142 D2 Seringapatam Reef Indian Oc
129 H5 Seringa, Serra da mts Brazil
45 R8 Serino Italy
41 L7 Serio R Italy
85 F4 Serkout, Dj mt Algeria
138 E4 Serle, Mt S Australia
20 K5 Sermaises France
71 O9 Sermata isld Indonesia
45 K1 Sermide Italy
45 N6 Sermoneta Italy
38 H9 Sernio mt Italy
33 U6 Sernitz R E Germany
33 Q8 Serno E Germany
60 T2 Sernovodsk U.S.S.R.
57 A5 Sernyy-Zavod U.S.S.R.
31 N3 Serock Poland
126 A2 Seroe Colorado Aruba W I
17 F7 Serón Spain
85 F4 Serouenout Algeria
55 D2 Serov U.S.S.R.
89 E4 Serowe Botswana
16 B7 Serpa Portugal
87 C8 Serpa Pinto Angola
43 C9 Serpeddi, Pta mt Sardinia
116 E4 Serpentine Hot Springs Alaska
138 A3 Serpentine Lakes S Australia
143 B9 Serpentine, R W Australia
122 A3 Serpent, R. au Quebec
128 F1 Serpents Mouth str Venezuela
17 G6 Serpis R Spain
54 J2 Serpukhov U.S.S.R.
20 J2 Serqueux France
20 G3 Serquigny France
130 H7 Serra Brazil
45 L4 Serra, Alpe di mts Italy
130 E10 Serra Alta Brazil
130 F4 Serra Bonita Brazil
130 F4 Serra das Araras Brazil
129 H3 Serra do Navio Brazil
33 Q5 Serrahn E Germany
47 F3 Sérrai Greece
45 J3 Serramazzoni Italy
125 O2 Serrana Bank Caribbean
125 P2 Serranilla Bank Caribbean
43 G10 Serra San Bruno Italy
43 C11 Serrat, Cape C Tunisia
45 J4 Serravalle Pistojese Italy
22 F4 Serre R France
18 G10 Serrére, Pic de mt France
19 P16 Serres France
133 D4 Serrezuela Argentina
129 L6 Serrinha Brazil
45 M4 Serriola, Bocca pass Italy
43 B12 Sers Tunisia
16 B5 Sertã Portugal
130 F7 Sertãozinho Brazil
70 K9 Sertung isld Sumatra
70 C6 Serujan R Kalimantan
89 E3 Serule Botswana
69 D10 Seruwai Sumatra
40 E2 Servance France
46 E4 Sérvia Greece
100 E5 Service Creek Oregon
138 F6 Serviceton Victoria
106 E5 Servilleta New Mexico
71 N9 Serwaro Indonesia
66 F5 Sêrxü China
22 G4 Séry France
22 E4 Séry-les-Mezières France
68 G4 Se Sang Soi R Laos
70 E3 Sesatap Kalimantan
88 D2 Sese Is Uganda
120 K4 Sesekinika Ontario
71 A3 Sesepe Indonesia
87 B9 Sesfontein Namibia
87 D9 Sesheka Zambia
41 H7 Sesia R Italy
70 E2 Sesibu Kalimantan
26 N6 Seskarön isld Sweden
61 P12 Sesoko-jima isld Okinawa
43 F7 Sessa Aurunca Italy
36 D6 Sessenheim France
110 G3 Sesser Illinois
37 K3 Sesslach W Germany
71 K9 Sessok Flores Indonesia
45 M4 Sestino Italy
45 K4 Sesto Fiorentino Italy
31 O1 Seštokai U.S.S.R.
45 J3 Sestola Italy
52 E6 Sestra R U.S.S.R.
44 E3 Sestri Italy
44 F3 Sestri Levante Italy
29 O11 Sestroretsk U.S.S.R.
60 D12 Setaka Japan
60 N3 Setana Japan
9 G2 Setchey England
18 H9 Sète France
130 G6 Sete Lagoas Brazil
130 D8 Sete Quedas, Ilha Grande ou isld Brazil
27 B12 Setesdal Norway
94 F8 Seth W Virginia
85 F1 Sétif Algeria
60 C13 Seto Japan
59 K5 Seto-naika sea Japan
60 G11 Seto Naikai str Japan
68 B4 Setsan Burma
85 C2 Settat Morocco
86 A6 Sette Cama Gabon
119 U1 Settee L Manitoba
119 T3 Setting L Manitoba
13 F5 Settle England
140 E3 Settlement Cr Queensland
90 C15 Settlement of Edinburgh Tristan da Cunha
113 H11 Settlement Pt Bahamas
16 B6 Setúbal Portugal
37 M5 Seubersdorf W Germany
37 K5 Seukendorf W Germany
55 E1 Seul' R U.S.S.R.
99 V4 Seul Choix Pt Michigan
69 B10 Seulimeum Sumatra
115 K7 Seul, Lac Ontario
20 D3 Seulles R France
69 C11 Seumanyam Sumatra
40 B3 Seurre France
78 K1 Sevan, Ozero U.S.S.R.
53 D11 Sevastopol' U.S.S.R.
54 H6 Sev Donets R U.S.S.R.
28 B4 Sevel Denmark
100 J4 Seven Devils Mts Idaho
140 D3 Seven Emu N Terr Aust
14 C5 Seven Hd Irish Rep
122 F3 Seven Is. Bay Quebec
106 C6 Seven Lakes New Mexico
9 G5 Sevenoaks England
118 G9 Seven Persons Alberta
109 J7 Seven Sisters Texas
112 K2 Seven Springs N Carolina
102 F1 Seven Troughs Nevada
117 N10 Seventy Mile House Br Columbia
25 F6 Sevenum Netherlands
18 H8 Séverac-le-Château France
107 P2 Severance Kansas
139 K3 Severn R New S Wales
121 L8 Severn R Ontario
52 J4 Severnaya Mylva R U.S.S.R.
51 K1 Severnaya Zemlya arch Arctic Oc
55 G3 Severnoye U.S.S.R.
8 D4 Severn, R England
55 D3 Severnyy U.S.S.R.
52 J3 Severnyy Ural mts U.S.S.R.
51 L3 Severo-Baykal'skoye Nagor'ye uplands U.S.S.R.
37 P3 Severocesky Kraj reg Czechoslovakia
52 E3 Severodvinsk U.S.S.R.
31 K6 Severomoravský reg Czechoslovakia
52 D1 Severomorsk U.S.S.R.
55 C1 Severouralsk U.S.S.R.
54 K2 Severo Zadonsk U.S.S.R.
107 O4 Severy Kansas
29 O2 Sevettijarvi Finland
103 M3 Sevier Utah
103 M2 Sevier R Utah
103 M2 Sevier Bridge Res Utah
103 M2 Sevier Des Utah
112 D2 Sevierville Tennessee
22 G4 Sevigny France
16 D7 Sevilla Spain
16 D7 Sevilla prov Spain
126 F4 Sevilla R Cuba
Seville see Sevilla
47 G2 Sevlievo Bulgaria
48 J2 Sevola mt U.S.S.R.
53 F11 Sev. Osetinsk. A.S.S.R U.S.S.R.
18 E6 Sèvre-Niortaise R France
20 K4 Sevres France
40 B5 Sevron R France
54 F4 Sevsk U.S.S.R.
85 B7 Sewa R Sierra Leone
110 L6 Sewanee Tennessee
116 N6 Seward Alaska
107 M3 Seward Kansas
98 J9 Seward Nebraska
107 N6 Seward Oklahoma
94 H6 Seward Pennsylvania
116 R6 Seward Glacier Yukon Terr/Alaska
146 F12 Seward Mts Antarctica
116 E4 Seward Pen Alaska
133 C4 Sewell Chile
40 E2 Sewen France
94 G6 Sewickley Pennsylvania
117 O8 Sexsmith Alberta
124 G4 Sextín Mexico
77 H3 Seyah Band Koh mts Afghanistan
43 B12 Seybouse R Algeria
83 J12 Seychelles islds, rep Indian Oc
33 R9 Seyda E Germany
52 K2 Seyda U.S.S.R.
115 S4 Seydhisfjördhur Iceland
28 O9 Seydhtorva C Faeroes
78 C3 Seydişehir Turkey
20 B3 Seye R France
78 E3 Seyhan R Turkey
47 L5 Seyit R Turkey
47 L5 Seyitgazi Turkey
54 D5 Seym R U.S.S.R.
95 O5 Seymour Connecticut
94 B8 Seymour Indiana
110 C1 Seymour Iowa
110 D4 Seymour Missouri
109 H2 Seymour Texas
139 H6 Seymour Victoria
99 S5 Seymour Wisconsin
140 C6 Seymour Ra N Terr Aust
19 Q16 Seyne-les-Alpes France
42 F3 Sežana Yugoslavia
18 H4 Sezanne France
52 D6 Sezha R U.S.S.R.
16 A6 Sezimbra Portugal
45 O6 Sezze Italy
85 G2 Sfax Tunisia
47 F9 Sfinári Crete Greece
48 K5 Sfîntu Gheorghe Romania
48 M6 Sfîntu Gheorghe R Romania
79 H2 Sfira Syria
's-Gravenhage see Den Haag
25 B5 's-Gravenzande Netherlands
15 D3 Sgurr Mor mt Scotland
58 Shaanxi prov China
80 F3 Sha'ar Israel
79 H4 Sha'ar, Jebel mts Syria
Sha'av see Sha'ab
87 E7 Shaba reg Zaïre
89 G3 Shabani Zimbabwe
119 O2 Shabaqua Ontario
99 S8 Shabbona Illinois
84 H5 Shab, El Egypt
78 K2 Shabestar Iran
79 F9 Shabibī, J. esh mt Jordan
47 J1 Shabla Bulgaria
86 E6 Shabunda Zaïre
55 D2 Shaburovo U.S.S.R.
67 B3 Shachang China
66 B4 Shache China
118 J8 Shackleton Sask
146 G7 Shackleton Coast Antarctica
146 G8 Shackleton Glacier Antarctica
146 D2 Shackleton Ice Shelf Antarctica
146 H7 Shackleton Inlet Antarctica
146 D10 Shackleton Rge Antarctica
74 B5 Shadadkot Pakistan
98 D4 Shadehill Res S Dakota
67 E3 Shadi China
55 D3 Shadrinsk U.S.S.R.
111 K10 Shady Grove Alabama
113 D7 Shady Grove Florida
55 C4 Shafranovo U.S.S.R.
102 E6 Shafter California
101 L9 Shafter Nevada
108 C6 Shafter Texas
8 D5 Shaftesbury England
55 G5 Shagan R U.S.S.R.
65 E4 Shagang China
48 M5 Shagany, Oz L U.S.S.R.
Shagedu see Jungar Qi
55 F4 Shaglyteniz, Oz L U.S.S.R.
56 D5 Shagonar U.S.S.R.
144 C6 Shag R New Zealand
133 H8 Shag Rocks S Georgia
76 C2 Shahabad India
78 L4 Shahabad Iran
76 B3 Shahapur India
80 B7 Shahar Israel
74 C6 Shahbadpur Pakistan
74 B6 Shahbandar Pakistan
75 J7 Shahdol India
65 C6 Shahe China
65 D6 Shahe China
67 E2 Shahezhen China
Shahezi see Wan Xian
77 K2 Shah Fuladi mt Afghanistan
84 G3 Shahhāt Libya
78 L3 Shahin Dezh Iran
74 H5 Shahjahanpur India
77 E1 Shāh Jehān, Kuh-e mts Iran
77 K3 Shahjui Afghanistan
65 E4 Shahousuo China
74 G7 Shahpur India
74 F6 Shahpura India
77 J2 Shahrak Afghanistan
77 G3 Shāhrakht Iran
77 D4 Shahr-e Bābak Iran
77 B3 Shahr Kord Iran
77 B2 Shahr Rey Iran
77 D2 Shahrud Bustam Iran
77 B1 Shahsavār Iran
77 F5 Shāh Savāran, Kūh-e mts Iran
50 F2 Shaim U.S.S.R.
80 G3 Shajara Jordan
65 F4 Shajianzi China
52 E6 Shakhovskaya U.S.S.R.
59 M2 Shakhtersk U.S.S.R.
54 M9 Shakhty U.S.S.R.
52 G5 Shakhun'ya U.S.S.R.
85 E7 Shaki Nigeria
84 J4 Shâkir isld Egypt
99 N5 Shakopee Minnesota
60 O2 Shakotan dake mt Japan
59 L3 Shakotan misaki C Japan
55 C4 Shaksha U.S.S.R.
116 G4 Shaktolik Alaska
52 F4 Shalakusha U.S.S.R.
86 G4 Shala, L Ethiopia
117 M10 Shalalth Br Columbia
65 G2 Shalan China
67 D6 Shalang China
55 G4 Shalday U.S.S.R.
52 F6 Shaldezh U.S.S.R.
9 F5 Shalford England
52 E4 Shalgachëva U.S.S.R.
57 F2 Shalgiya U.S.S.R.
77 E4 Shalidab Iran
55 D5 Shalkar Karashatau L U.S.S.R.
55 D5 Shalkar-Yega-Kara L U.S.S.R.
80 G3 Shallala Jordan
112 J4 Shallotte N Carolina
108 E2 Shallowater Texas
120 J8 Shallow Lake Ontario
80 C7 Shalwa Israel
55 C3 Shalya U.S.S.R.
56 C4 Shalym U.S.S.R.
88 D5 Shama R Tanzania
56 G5 Shaman, Khrebet mts U.S.S.R.
55 C3 Shamary U.S.S.R.
86 F4 Shambe Sudan
80 D2 Shamerat Israel
75 O5 Shamgong Bhutan
77 E6 Shamīl Iran
80 F1 Shamir Israel
78 K6 Shamiya Des Iraq
95 L6 Shamokin Pennsylvania
113 D8 Shamrock Florida
107 O6 Shamrock Oklahoma
118 L8 Shamrock Sask
108 D8 Shamrock Texas
88 C10 Shamva Zimbabwe
68 C2 Shan prov Burma
80 G6 Sha'nab Jordan
Shanchengzhen see Nanjing
77 G5 Shāndak Iran
58 D4 Shandan China
65 C3 Shandian He R China
102 D6 Shandon California
12 D1 Shandon Scotland
65 C6 Shandong prov China
67 E6 Shandong Bandao pen China
52 F4 Shangaly U.S.S.R.
87 E9 Shangani R Zimbabwe
65 D4 Shangbancheng China
67 E1 Shangcheng China
65 F3 Shangchengzhen China
67 D6 Shangchuan Dao isld China
65 B4 Shangdu China
Shangdundu see Linchuan
67 E2 Shangfu China
67 E2 Shanggao China
67 G1 Shanghai China
63 Shanghai conurbation China
67 E4 Shanghang China
65 D6 Shanghe
65 C4 Shanghuangqi China
67 C1 Shangkan China
67 C5 Shanglin China
87 D9 Shangombo Zambia
Shangpaihe see Feixi
58 G5 Shangqiu China
67 F2 Shangrao China
67 B5 Shangsi China
58 E5 Shang Xian China
65 B5 Shangyangwu China
65 C4 Shangyi China
67 E4 Shangyou China
67 G1 Shangyu China
59 J2 Shangzhi China
65 D5 Shanhaiguan China
65 G2 Shanhetun China
100 E4 Shaniko Oregon
9 E6 Shanklin England
67 E2 Shankou China
94 J6 Shanksville Penn
112 B3 Shannon Georgia
99 R7 Shannon Illinois
111 H7 Shannon Mississippi
145 E4 Shannon New Zealand
14 C4 Shannon Airport Irish Rep
99 M9 Shannon City Iowa
14 D2 Shannon Pot Irish Rep
14 C2 Shannon R Irish Rep
Shansi prov see Shanxi
65 G3 Shansonggang China
80 G4 Shantana Jordan
51 N3 Shantarskiye, Ostrova islds U.S.S.R.
67 E5 Shantou China
Shantung prov see Shandong
Shantung Peninsula see Shandong Bandao
58 F4 Shanxi prov China
65 C7 Shan Xian China
67 F4 Shanyao China
58 F4 Shanyin China
67 F1 Shaobo China
67 D3 Shaodong China
67 D3 Shaoshan China
67 F3 Shaowu China
59 H5 Shaoxing China
67 D3 Shaoyang China
15 F1 Shapinsay Scotland
52 H2 Shapkina R U.S.S.R.
56 C5 Shapshal'skiy Khrebet mts U.S.S.R.
Shara Gol see Dang He
52 H7 Sharan U.S.S.R.
52 G6 Sharanga U.S.S.R.
121 O8 Sharbot Lake Ontario
48 L2 Shargorodo U.S.S.R.
60 S2 Shari Japan
77 D7 Sharjah U.A.E.
52 H6 Sharkan U.S.S.R.
71 D5 Shark Fin B Philippines
52 C6 Sharkovshchina U.S.S.R.
141 H2 Shark Reef Gt Barrier Reef Aust
55 B4 Sharlyk U.S.S.R.
95 O5 Sharon Connecticut
112 E4 Sharon Georgia
107 M4 Sharon Kansas
94 B2 Sharon Michigan
98 J2 Sharon N Dakota
108 E7 Sharon Oklahoma
110 H5 Sharon Tennessee
95 P3 Sharon Vermont
99 S7 Sharon Wisconsin
80 C5 Sharon, Plain of Israel
107 J3 Sharon Springs Kansas
54 G6 Sharovka U.S.S.R.
98 F5 Sharpe, L S Dakota
95 L9 Sharps Virginia
99 M9 Sharpsburg Iowa
94 K7 Sharpsburg Maryland
94 A6 Sharpsville Indiana
79 F5 Sharqi, Jebel esh mts Lebanon
52 G5 Shar'ya U.S.S.R.
86 G4 Shashamanna Ethiopia
89 F3 Shashani R Zimbabwe
89 E3 Shashe Botswana
89 G2 Shashe R Zimbabwe
87 E10 Shashe R Zimbabwe/Botswana
67 D1 Shashi China
100 C9 Shasta L California
100 C8 Shasta, Mt California
67 D4 Shatian China
52 F6 Shatki U.S.S.R.
55 D3 Shatrovo U.S.S.R.
108 E7 Shattuck Oklahoma
54 L1 Shatura U.S.S.R.
79 F8 Shaubak Jordan
80 G3 Shaumar Jordan
118 J9 Shaunavon Sask
52 D3 Shaverki U.S.S.R.
102 E4 Shaver L California
94 H8 Shavers Fork R W Virginia
80 D2 Shave Ziyyon Israel
111 F8 Shaw Mississippi
120 K7 Shawanaga Ontario
95 N5 Shawangunk Mts New York
99 S5 Shawano Wisconsin
99 S5 Shawano L Wisconsin
121 R7 Shawbridge Quebec
8 D2 Shawbury England
141 J5 Shaw I Queensland
115 M8 Shawinigan Quebec
101 Q3 Shawmut Montana
94 E7 Shawnee Ohio
107 O6 Shawnee Oklahoma
98 A7 Shawnee Wyoming
110 H4 Shawneetown Illinois
121 O7 Shawville Quebec
67 F3 Sha Xi R China
67 F3 Sha Xian China
67 D1 Shayang China
84 J4 Shayib el Banât, Gebel mt Egypt
72 F6 Shaykh' Uthmān S Yemen
52 J4 Shaytanovka U.S.S.R.
67 G1 Shazhou China
54 J3 Shchekino U.S.S.R.
54 K1 Shchelkovo U.S.S.R.
52 H2 Shchel'yayur U.S.S.R.
55 G4 Shcherbakty U.S.S.R.
54 J1 Shcherbinka U.S.S.R.
54 H5 Shchigry U.S.S.R.
54 C5 Shchors U.S.S.R.
54 F8 Shchorsk U.S.S.R.
50 G3 Shchuchinsk U.S.S.R.
55 D3 Shchuch'ye U.S.S.R.
55 C3 Shchuch'ye Ozero U.S.S.R.
54 K1 Shchurovo U.S.S.R.
128 G3 Shea Guyana
86 G4 Shea Ghimirri Ethiopia
100 H6 Sheaville Oregon
119 O2 Shebandowan L Ontario
54 H6 Shebekino U.S.S.R.
99 T6 Sheboygan Wisconsin
86 B4 Shebshi Mts Nigeria
80 E5 Shechem Jordan
78 H3 Shedadi Syria
100 B5 Shedd Oregon
120 J10 Shedden Ontario
122 H7 Shediac New Brunswick
14 D3 Sheelin, L Irish Rep
121 N7 Sheenboro Quebec
116 Q2 Sheenjek R Alaska
117 O9 Sheep Cr Alberta
101 U7 Sheep Cr Wyoming
14 D1 Sheep Haven Irish Rep
101 T10 Sheephorn Colorado
106 C2 Sheep Mt Colorado
103 J5 Sheep Pk Nevada
103 J5 Sheep Ra Nevada
14 B5 Sheep's Hd Irish Rep
118 F7 Sheerness Alberta
9 G5 Sheerness England
115 N9 Sheet Harbour Nova Scotia
80 D2 Shefar'am Israel
80 C7 Shefela Israel
13 G6 Sheffield England
99 R8 Sheffield Illinois
99 N7 Sheffield Iowa
95 O4 Sheffield Massachusetts
144 D5 Sheffield New Zealand
94 H5 Sheffield Pennsylvania
139 H8 Sheffield Tasmania
108 F5 Sheffield Texas
94 E5 Sheffield Lake Ohio
56 B3 Shegarka R U.S.S.R.
52 G3 Shegmas U.S.S.R.
120 J7 Sheguiandah Ontario
119 O7 Sheho Sask
67 B1 Shehong China
133 C7 Shehuén R Argentina
86 J4 Sheikh Somalia
79 F5 Sheikh, J. esh mt Lebanon/Syria
120 F3 Shekak R Ontario
Shekar Dzong see Tingri
74 F3 Shekhupura Pakistan
53 G12 Sheki U.S.S.R.
52 E5 Sheksna R U.S.S.R.
94 E9 Shelbiana Kentucky
110 D2 Shelbina Missouri
110 J2 Shelburn Indiana
115 N9 Shelburne Nova Scotia
120 K8 Shelburne Ontario
95 O2 Shelburne Vermont
141 G1 Shelburne B Queensland
95 P4 Shelburne Falls Massachusetts
99 T8 Shelby Indiana
99 L8 Shelby Iowa
99 U6 Shelby Michigan
111 F8 Shelby Mississippi
101 O1 Shelby Montana
112 F2 Shelby N Carolina
98 J8 Shelby Nebraska
94 E6 Shelby Ohio
110 H2 Shelbyville Illinois
110 L2 Shelbyville Indiana
110 L3 Shelbyville Kentucky
110 E2 Shelbyville Missouri
110 K6 Shelbyville Tennessee
109 N4 Shelbyville Texas
99 T9 Sheldon Illinois
99 L6 Sheldon Iowa
110 B4 Sheldon Missouri
98 J3 Sheldon N Dakota
117 H4 Sheldon, Mt Yukon Terr
95 P2 Sheldon Springs Vermont
122 H3 Sheldrake Quebec
56 F5 Shelekhov U.S.S.R.
90 F16 Shelf Ice Antarctica
116 K8 Shelikof Str Alaska
101 S5 Shell Wyoming
99 L3 Shell R Minnesota
111 G12 Shell Beach Louisiana
118 L5 Shellbrook Sask
101 R8 Shell Cr Wyoming
101 N6 Shelley Idaho
139 K5 Shellharbour New S Wales
99 P4 Shell L Wisconsin
118 K5 Shell Lake Sask
143 F8 Shell Lakes W Australia
111 M10 Shellman Georgia
119 Q8 Shellmouth Manitoba
102 A1 Shell Mt California
99 O7 Shell Rock Iowa
99 O7 Shellrock R Iowa
99 P7 Shellsburg Iowa
80 D1 Shelomi Israel
58 G1 Shelopugino U.S.S.R.
102 A1 Shelter Cove California
95 P5 Shelter I Long I, New York
144 B7 Shelter Pt New Zealand
95 O5 Shelton Connecticut
98 H9 Shelton Nebraska
117 M12 Shelton Washington
52 E4 Sheltozero U.S.S.R.
78 M1 Shemakha U.S.S.R.
56 B5 Shemonaikha U.S.S.R.
52 H6 Shemordan U.S.S.R.
52 G6 Shemursha U.S.S.R.
99 L9 Shenandoah Iowa
95 L6 Shenandoah Pennsylvania
94 J8 Shenandoah Virginia
94 K7 Shenandoah Junc W Virginia
94 H8 Shenandoah Mts W Virginia/Virginia
94 J8 Shenandoah Nat. Park Virginia
94 G5 Shenango Res Ohio/Penn
57 D1 Shenber U.S.S.R.
65 B5 Shenchi China
86 A4 Shendam Nigeria
86 F2 Shendi Sudan
65 J1 Shending Shan mt China
46 D3 Shëngjin Albania
65 F1 Shengping China
67 G1 Shengsi China
67 G1 Shengsi Liedao islds China
67 G2 Sheng Xian China
52 F4 Shenkursk U.S.S.R.
65 A5 Shenmu China

Shennongjia — Siyitang 71

67 C1 Shennongjia China
Shensi prov see Shaanxi
58 E4 Shensi prov China
52 H7 Shentala U.S.S.R.
143 E8 Shenton, Mt W Australia
Shentza Dzong see Xainza
65 C5 Shen Xian China
65 C6 Shen Xian China
59 H3 Shenyang China
65 C5 Shenze China
Shenzhen see Bao'an
74 D5 Sheo India
74 G6 Sheopur India
118 D7 Shepard Alberta
146 J10 Shepard I Antarctica
94 C3 Shepherd Michigan
101 R4 Shepherd Montana
109 M5 Shepherd Texas
137 O5 Shepherd Is New Hebrides
94 K7 Shepherdstown W Virginia
94 B9 Shepherdsville Kentucky
117 G7 Sheppard, Mt Br Columbia
139 H6 Shepparton Victoria
143 E8 Shepperd, L W Australia
9 G5 Sheppey isld England
8 D5 Shepton Mallet England
115 M3 Sherard, C N W Terr
55 F4 Sherbakul' U.S.S.R.
8 D6 Sherborne England
85 B7 Sherbro I Sierra Leone
115 M8 Sherbrooke Quebec
122 H9 Sherbrooke L Nova Scotia
13 G6 Sherburn England
13 H5 Sherburn England
99 M6 Sherburn Minnesota
95 M4 Sherburne New York
86 C1 Sherda Chad
9 F5 Shere England
84 J6 Shereik Sudan
54 J1 Sheremet'yevo airport U.S.S.R.
74 E5 Shergarh India
111 D7 Sheridan Arkansas
94 A6 Sheridan Indiana
94 B3 Sheridan Michigan
101 N4 Sheridan Montana
100 B4 Sheridan Oregon
101 T5 Sheridan Wyoming
115 N1 Sheridan, C N W Terr
106 H3 Sheridan L Colorado
101 P5 Sheridan, Mt Wyoming
138 D5 Sheringa S Australia
9 H2 Sheringham England
111 H7 Sherman Mississippi
94 H4 Sherman New York
109 L2 Sherman Texas
95 S8 Sherman Mills Maine
103 J1 Sherman Mt Nevada
101 O7 Sherman Pk Idaho
98 H8 Sherman Res Nebraska
77 L2 Sherpur Afghanistan
119 Q3 Sherridon Manitoba
95 M3 Sherrill New York
25 D5 's-Hertogenbosch Netherlands
98 E1 Sherwood N Dakota
108 G4 Sherwood Texas
141 K2 Sherwood dist Brisbane, Qnsld
144 C5 Sherwood Downs New Zealand
9 E1 Sherwood Forest England
52 H6 Sheshma R U.S.S.R.
77 E1 Sheshtamad Iran
67 E1 She Shui R China
117 H6 Sheslay Br Columbia
52 H5 Shestaki U.S.S.R.
99 L5 Shetek, L Minnesota
15 G2 Shetland reg Scotland
50 E4 Shevchenko U.S.S.R.
99 L2 Shevlin Minnesota
58 G6 She Xian China
65 B6 She Xian China
67 F2 She Xian China
98 G2 Sheyenne N Dakota
98 J3 Sheyenne R N Dakota
77 C6 Sheykh Sho'eyb isld Iran
80 E2 Shezor Israel
15 B3 Shiant isld Scotland
94 C3 Shiawassee R Michigan
77 J1 Shibarghān Afghanistan
61 N8 Shibata Japan
65 B4 Shibatai China
60 S2 Shibecha Japan
86 H4 Shibeli R Ethiopia
60 T2 Shibetsu Japan
84 J3 Shibîn el Kom Egypt
79 B8 Shibîn el Qanâtir Egypt
67 C3 Shibing China
61 M9 Shibukawa Japan
60 E14 Shibushi-wan Japan
65 D6 Shibuzi China
67 B3 Shichang China
67 E3 Shicheng China
61 P5 Shichinohe Japan
98 J9 Shickley Nebraska
95 L5 Shickshinny Pennsylvania
122 F5 Shickshock Mts Quebec
Shicun see Xiangfen
65 E6 Shidao China
65 E6 Shidao Wan B China
55 F5 Shiderty R U.S.S.R.
107 O5 Shidler Oklahoma
60 H11 Shido Japan
15 C3 Shieldaig Scotland
140 D2 Shield, C N Terr Aust
107 K3 Shields Kansas
98 E3 Shields N Dakota
67 A1 Shifang China
8 D2 Shifnal England
61 K10 Shiga prefect Japan
Shigatse see Xigazê
122 G5 Shigawake Quebec
65 A4 Shiguaigou China
67 F1 Shih-chiu Hu L China
58 G5 Shi He R China
66 D3 Shihezi China
Shihkiachwang see Shijiazhuang
72 F6 Shihr S Yemen
61 M8 Shiiya Japan
46 D3 Shijak Albania
67 A1 Shijiaba China
Shijiao see Fogang
65 B5 Shijiazhuang China
65 C5 Shijiazhuang China
65 C5 Shijingshan China
67 F1 Shijiu Hu China
65 D7 Shijiusuo China
60 O3 Shikabe Japan
119 N1 Shikag L Ontario
60 H11 Shikama Japan
68 J2 Shikang China
77 L2 Shikar, Darya-i- R Afghanistan
76 B3 Shikarpur India
74 C5 Shikarpur Pakistan
61 N11 Shikine-jima isld Japan
60 G12 Shikoku isld Japan
60 F12 Shikoku-sanchi mts Japan
59 N3 Shikotan isld Japan
60 O3 Shikotsu Toya Nat. Park Japan
52 G4 Shilador U.S.S.R.
80 D6 Shilat Jordan
Shiliu see Changjiang
59 G1 Shilka R U.S.S.R.
86 H4 Shillave Ethiopia
14 E4 Shillelagh Irish Rep
9 E4 Shillingford England
120 K4 Shillington Ontario
95 M6 Shillington Pennsylvania
75 O6 Shillong India
110 H6 Shiloh Nat. Mil. Park Tennessee
67 C5 Shilong China
67 D5 Shilong China
65 A6 Shilou China
54 M2 Shilovo U.S.S.R.
Shima see Longhai
67 E3 Shima China
60 D13 Shimabara Japan
61 M11 Shimada Japan
60 F10 Shimane prefect Japan
59 J1 Shimanovsk U.S.S.R.
60 F13 Shimanto Japan
67 D2 Shimen China
65 D4 Shimenzhai China
61 M11 Shimizu Japan
61 L9 Shimminato Japan
61 M11 Shimoda Japan
61 O9 Shimodate Japan
60 P4 Shimofuro Japan
76 B4 Shimoga India
60 E11 Shimogo Japan
60 D13 Shimo-jima isld Japan
60 Q1 Shimokawa Japan
61 O8 Shimo-kitaba Japan
60 O4 Shimokita-hantō pen Japan
60 C14 Shimo koshiki jima isld Japan
61 M9 Shimonita Japan
59 K5 Shimonoseki Japan
60 D14 Shimo-Taniguchi Japan
60 E13 Shimo-Tashima Japan
61 N9 Shimotsuma Japan
80 D3 Shimron Israel
52 D5 Shimsk U.S.S.R.
67 C5 Shinan China
59 L4 Shinano R Japan
77 H3 Shindand Afghanistan
61 K11 Shindō Japan
109 K6 Shiner Texas
94 J5 Shinglehouse Pennsylvania
145 D4 Shingle Pk New Zealand
99 U3 Shingleton Michigan
100 D9 Shingletown California
61 J12 Shingū Japan
120 J5 Shining Tree Ontario
61 O7 Shinjō Japan
60 E11 Shin-Nanyō Japan
94 G7 Shinnston W Virginia
61 M9 Shinonoi Japan
79 G4 Shinshār Syria
61 L11 Shinshiro Japan
60 Q2 Shintoku Japan
88 D3 Shinyanga Tanzania
61 P7 Shiogama Japan
61 L9 Shiojiri Japan
59 L5 Shiono-misaki C Japan
61 J12 Shiono-misaki C Japan
Shipai see Huaining
126 F2 Ship Chan. Cay isld Bahamas
123 S6 Ship Cove Nfld
9 G2 Shipdham England
111 H11 Ship I Mississippi
52 G4 Shipitsino U.S.S.R.
47 G2 Shipka P Bulgaria
74 H3 Shipki Pass India/Xizang Zizhiqu
13 G6 Shipley England
119 N5 Shipman Sask
94 K6 Shippensburg Pennsylvania
106 B5 Shiprock New Mexico
121 T4 Shipshaw Dam Quebec
111 E13 Ship Shoal Lt. Hse Louisiana
13 G5 Shipton N Yorks England
9 E4 Shipton under Wychwood Gloucs England
Shipu see Huanglong
67 G2 Shipu China
67 C3 Shiqian China
Shiqiao see Panyu
67 D5 Shiqiao China
80 A7 Shiqma Israel
80 C8 Shiqma R Israel
58 E5 Shiquan China
74 H2 Shiquanhe China
66 C5 Shiquan He R China
77 K1 Shirabad U.S.S.R.
60 J12 Shirahama Japan
60 O4 Shirakami-misaki C Japan
61 O8 Shirakawa Fukushima, Honshu Japan
61 K9 Shirakawa Toyama, Honshu Japan
78 L1 Shirakskaya Step' U.S.S.R.
61 N9 Shirane-san mt Tochigi, Honshu Japan
61 M10 Shirane san mt Yamanashi, Honshu Japan
60 S3 Shiranuka Japan
60 P3 Shiraoi Japan
146 B6 Shirasbreen Antarctica
146 J8 Shirase Coast Antarctica
77 C5 Shīrāz Iran
79 B7 Shirbîn Egypt
88 E9 Shire R Malawi
88 E9 Shire Highlands Malawi
65 G4 Shiren China
60 T1 Shiretoko misaki C Japan
60 O3 Shiribeshi prefect Japan
57 C3 Shirikrabat U.S.S.R.
60 O4 Shiriuchi Japan
60 P4 Shiriya-zaki C Japan
110 D6 Shirley Arkansas
9 E6 Shirley Hampshire England
9 E3 Shirley W Midlands England
61 O8 Shiroishi Japan
54 E9 Shirokoye U.S.S.R.
61 K10 Shirotori Japan
61 L9 Shirouma-dake mt Japan
77 E1 Shīrvān Iran
116 E9 Shishaldin Vol Aleutian Is
60 H12 Shishikui Japan
60 C11 Shishimi Japan
116 D3 Shishmaref Alaska
116 E3 Shishmaref Inlet Alaska
67 D2 Shishou China
67 F1 Shitai China
61 L10 Shitara Japan
74 G6 Shivpuri India
103 L5 Shivwits Plat Arizona
67 B6 Shiwan Dashan mts China
87 F8 Shiwa Ngandu Zambia
67 E4 Shixing China
67 B2 Shiyangchang China
67 C2 Shiye China
Shizhaihe see Zhenping
67 C2 Shizhu China
Shizilu see Junan
67 A4 Shizong China
61 P7 Shizugawa Japan
58 E4 Shizuishan China
65 A6 Shizuiyi China
61 O6 Shizukuishi Japan
60 Q3 Shizunai Japan
59 L5 Shizuoka Japan
61 M10 Shizuoka prefect Japan
54 B2 Shklov U.S.S.R.
46 D2 Shkodër Albania
46 D3 Shkumbin R Albania
52 D5 Shlino R U.S.S.R.
147 P3 Shmidta U.S.S.R.
51 J1 Shmidta, Ostrova islds U.S.S.R.
61 L9 Shō R Japan
86 G4 Shoa prov Ethiopia
113 A7 Shoal R Florida
140 B1 Shoal B N Terr Aust
123 T5 Shoal Harb Nfld
139 K5 Shoalhaven R New S Wales
119 U8 Shoal L Manitoba
118 F1 Shoal L Ontario
110 K3 Shoals Indiana
141 K5 Shoalwater B Queensland
60 F11 Shōbara Japan
60 H11 Shōdo-shima isld Japan
9 G4 Shoeburyness England
123 R4 Shoe Cove Nfld
145 E2 Shoe I New Zealand
77 F1 Shoghlābād Iran
51 K1 Shokal'skogo, Proliv str U.S.S.R.
60 P2 Shokambetsu dake mt Japan
60 R1 Shokotsu Japan
52 E4 Shola R U.S.S.R.
55 D5 Sholaksay U.S.S.R.
55 F5 Sholakshalkar, Oz L U.S.S.R.
76 B2 Sholapur India
142 B5 Sholl I W Australia
52 D2 Shomba U.S.S.R.
80 E1 Shomera Israel
52 H3 Shomvukva U.S.S.R.
57 A2 Shomyshkol' U.S.S.R.
88 B9 Shona Zambia
55 G5 Shoptykul' U.S.S.R.
52 G6 Shora R U.S.S.R.
76 C5 Shoranur India
76 C2 Shorapur India
77 J5 Shorawak reg Afghanistan
9 F6 Shoreham-by-Sea England
99 T6 Shorewood Wisconsin
55 F5 Shortandy U.S.S.R.
103 M5 Short Cr Arizona
119 Q7 Shortdale Manitoba
111 L9 Shorter Alabama
138 E2 Short, L S Australia
143 C10 Short, Mt W Australia
95 K4 Shortsville New York
102 H6 Shoshone California
101 L7 Shoshone Idaho
101 R5 Shoshone R Wyoming
101 Q5 Shoshone Cavern Nat. Mon Wyoming
101 P5 Shoshone L Wyoming
102 G2 Shoshone Mts Nevada
102 H5 Shoshone Pk Nevada
101 R6 Shoshoni Wyoming
54 E5 Shostka U.S.S.R.
9 H4 Shotley England
144 B6 Shotover R New Zealand
67 F2 Shouchang China
67 C4 Shoucheng China
65 D6 Shouguang China
116 Q3 Shoulder Mt Alaska
118 E8 Shouldice Alberta
67 F3 Shouning China
101 L4 Shoup Idaho
65 B6 Shouyang China
80 B8 Shoval Israel
99 N3 Shovel L Minnesota
86 G3 Showak Sudan
60 O3 Shōwa-Shinzan mt Japan
103 O7 Show Low Arizona
52 F1 Shoyna U.S.S.R.
52 F4 Shozhma U.S.S.R.
54 C7 Shpola U.S.S.R.
94 F6 Shreve Ohio
111 C9 Shreveport Louisiana
8 D2 Shrewsbury England
111 H12 Shrewsbury New Orleans
9 E5 Shrewton England
74 F4 Shridungargarh India
76 B1 Shrigonda India
76 B1 Shrirampur India
9 E4 Shrivenham England
Shropshire co see Salop
54 K8 Shterovka U.S.S.R.
65 G2 Shuang-ch'eng China
65 F2 Shuangchengpu China
67 D3 Shuangfeng China
65 E2 Shuanggang China
67 D1 Shuanggou China
65 G3 Shuanghezhen China
Shuanghuyu see Zizhou
Shuangjiang see Tongdao
59 H3 Shuangliao China
67 A1 Shuangliu China
65 F3 Shuangshan China
65 F3 Shuangyang China
59 K2 Shuangyashan China
55 C6 Shubar-Kuduk U.S.S.R.
79 H3 Shubeit, Jebel mts Syria
122 J8 Shubenacadie Nova Scotia
122 J9 Shubenacadie L Nova Scotia
99 L9 Shubert Nebraska
116 P2 Shublik Mts Alaska
79 A7 Shubra Khît Egypt
111 H10 Shubuta Mississippi
67 E1 Shucheng China
80 F6 Shu'eib R Jordan
80 F6 Shu'eib Br Jordan
80 D4 Shufa Jordan
57 H5 Shufu China
55 G4 Shuga U.S.S.R.
57 F5 Shugnan U.S.S.R.
57 F5 Shugnanskiy Khr mts U.S.S.R.
52 D5 Shugozero U.S.S.R.
55 E1 Shugur U.S.S.R.
52 H6 Shugurovo U.S.S.R.
65 D7 Shu He R China
67 B2 Shuibatang China
67 A3 Shuicheng China
Shuiji see Laixi
67 F3 Shuiji China
67 C4 Shuikou China
67 D5 Shuikou China
67 F3 Shuikou China
65 G2 Shuiquliu China
65 E5 Shuishiying China
74 D4 Shujaabad Pakistan
74 G7 Shujalpur India
55 D1 Shukhtungort U.S.S.R.
100 D1 Shuksan, Mt Washington
59 J3 Shulan China
57 H5 Shule China
58 C3 Shule He R China
Shulinzhao see Dalad Qi
99 Q7 Shullsburg Wisconsin
65 C6 Shulu China
116 G9 Shumagin Is Alaska
116 Q3 Shuman House Alaska
60 Q1 Shumarinai Japan
56 C6 Shumek U.S.S.R.
55 D5 Shumekty U.S.S.R.
47 H1 Shumen Bulgaria
52 G6 Shumerlya U.S.S.R.
55 D3 Shumikha U.S.S.R.
54 A1 Shumilino U.S.S.R.
52 H4 Shumina U.S.S.R.
108 F6 Shumla Texas
56 E4 Shumskiy U.S.S.R.
65 E1 Shumugou China
103 O7 Shumway Arizona
80 F6 Shunat Nimrin Jordan
67 F3 Shunchang China
67 D5 Shunde China
52 D3 Shunga U.S.S.R.
65 C4 Shunyi China
67 B5 Shuolong China
58 F4 Shuo Xian China
80 F8 Shuqeiq R Jordan
111 H9 Shuqualak Mississippi
77 G4 Shur R Iran
57 F4 Shurab U.S.S.R.
52 G6 Shuran U.S.S.R.
61 P13 Shuri Okinawa
58 F1 Shurinda U.S.S.R.
52 H6 Shurma U.S.S.R.
66 D5 Shuru Tso L China
78 L2 Shusa U.S.S.R.
77 A3 Shūsh Iran
46 D4 Shushicë R Albania
77 A3 Shūshtar Iran
117 O10 Shuswap L Br Columbia
139 H4 Shuttleton New S Wales
80 B8 Shuva Israel
52 F6 Shuya Ivanovo U.S.S.R.
52 D4 Shuya Karelskaya A.S.S.R. U.S.S.R.
116 L7 Shuyak I Alaska
65 D8 Shuyang China
52 D3 Shuyeretskoye U.S.S.R.
55 G4 Shuyreksor, Oz L U.S.S.R.
52 F5 Shuyskoye U.S.S.R.
61 M11 Shuzenji Japan
68 B3 Shwebandaw Burma
68 B1 Shwebo Burma
68 B3 Shwedaung Burma
68 C4 Shwegun Burma
68 C4 Shwegyin Burma
68 C2 Shwenyaung Burma
74 H1 Shyok Kashmir
69 D12 Siabu Sumatra
77 H6 Siahan Range Pakistan
69 E12 Siak Sri Inderapura Sumatra
74 F2 Sialkot Pakistan
Siam see Thailand
Sian see Xi'an
Siangtan see Xiangtan
31 J1 Sianów Poland
69 H11 Siantan isld Indonesia
69 D8 Si Ao Ban Don, Laem Thailand
128 E3 Siapa R Venezuela
71 G6 Siargao isld Philippines
95 S5 Siasconset Massachusetts
71 E8 Siasi Philippines
71 F6 Siaton Negros Philippines
52 B6 Siauliai U.S.S.R.
84 J4 Sibâi, Gebel mt Egypt
126 F4 Sibanicú Cuba
55 C4 Sibay U.S.S.R.
71 E5 Sibay isld Philippines
89 H6 Sibayi L S Africa
118 G7 Sibbald Alberta
29 L11 Sibbo Finland
69 D14 Siberimanua Indonesia
69 D13 Siberut isld Indonesia
74 B4 Sibi Pakistan
69 B11 Sibigo Indonesia
42 E6 Sibillini, Monti Italy
59 K3 Sibirtsevo U.S.S.R.
86 B6 Sibiti Congo
48 J5 Sibiu Romania
9 G4 Sible Hedingham England
99 S9 Sibley Illinois
99 L6 Sibley Iowa
109 O3 Sibley Louisiana
120 B4 Sibley Prov. Park Ontario
70 G4 Siboa Sulawesi
69 D12 Sibolga, Tel B Sumatra
71 E4 Sibolon isld Philippines
126 G5 Siboney Cuba
69 D11 Siborongborong Sumatra
41 M3 Sibratsgfäll Austria
75 Q5 Sibsagar India
9 G1 Sibsey England
70 B3 Sibu Sarawak
71 F7 Sibuco Mindanao Philippines
71 F7 Sibuguey Bay Mindanao Philippines
86 C4 Sibut Cent Afr Republic
70 C2 Sibuti Sarawak
71 F4 Sibuyan isld Philippines
48 H4 Sic Romania
71 E1 Sicapoo mt Luzon Philippines
128 E7 Sicasica Bolivia
71 F6 Sicayac Mindanao Philippines
138 E4 Siccus R S Australia
67 A1 Sichuan prov China
67 B1 Sichuan Pendi China
43 E11 Sicilia isld Italy
43 D11 Sicilian Chan S Europe
Sicily see Sicilia
111 E10 Sicily Island Louisiana
119 R2 Sickle L Manitoba
71 F5 Sicogon isld Philippines
128 D6 Sicuani Peru
48 E5 Šid Yugoslavia
71 A2 Sidangoli Halmahera Indonesia
71 J4 Sidate Sulawesi
85 F5 Sidawet Niger
8 D5 Sidcot England
9 G5 Sidcup England
140 B6 Siddeley Ra N Terr Aust
8 D1 Siddington England
76 D1 Siddipett India
29 J9 Sideby Finland
99 T10 Sidell Illinois
70 F6 Sidenreng, D L Sulawesi
26 K8 Sidensjö Sweden
85 D6 Sidéradougou Upper Volta
84 F3 Sider, Es Libya
43 H10 Siderno Marina Italy
118 H8 Sidewood Sask
47 G4 Sidherítis isld Greece
47 H9 Sídheros, Akra C Crete Greece
75 J6 Sidhi India
47 F3 Sidhirókastron Greece
74 E7 Sidhpur India
17 H8 Sidi Alio Algeria
84 H3 Sidi Barrani Egypt
85 D1 Sidi-bel-Abbès Algeria
43 C13 Sidi bou Ali Tunisia
16 E9 Sidi Dris Morocco
85 B3 Sidi Ifni Morocco
69 D11 Sidikalang Sumatra
13 E1 Sidlaw Hills Scotland
146 H10 Sidley, Mt Antarctica
8 C6 Sidmouth England
141 G2 Sidmouth, C Queensland
99 S3 Sidnaw Michigan
117 M11 Sidney Br Columbia
99 S9 Sidney Illinois
99 L9 Sidney Iowa
119 S9 Sidney Manitoba
98 B2 Sidney Montana
98 D8 Sidney Nebraska
95 M4 Sidney New York
110 M1 Sidney Ohio
85 C6 Sido Mali
70 G4 Sidoan Sulawesi
70 O9 Sidoardjo Java
68 B2 Sidoktaya Burma
70 F5 Sidole, Bk mt Sulawesi
Sidon see Saïda
130 C7 Sidrolândia Brazil
36 C2 Siebengebirge mt W Germany
37 P1 Siebenlehn E Germany
21 E10 Siecq France
32 J7 Siedenburg W Germany
31 N3 Siedlce Poland
36 D2 Sieg R W Germany
36 E2 Siegbach W Germany
36 C2 Siegburg W Germany
Siegelsdorf see Seukendorf
37 M6 Siegenburg W Germany
31 O3 Siemiatycze Poland
68 H5 Siem Pang Cambodia
68 F6 Siem Reap Cambodia
42 D5 Siena Italy
31 O5 Sieniawa Poland
20 C4 Sienne R France
29 K4 Sieppijärvi Finland
31 L4 Sieradz Poland
31 J3 Sieraków Poland
22 L5 Sierck France
40 F2 Sierentz France
31 M3 Sierpc Poland
108 B4 Sierra Blanca Texas
102 D2 Sierra Buttes peak California
133 D6 Sierra Colorada Argentina
133 D6 Sierra Grande Argentina
124 J6 Sierra Hermosa Mexico
85 B7 Sierra Leone rep W Africa
90 H8 Sierra Leone Basin Atlantic Oc
90 H8 Sierra Leone Rise Atlantic Oc
125 J9 Sierra Madre del Sur mts Mexico
102 D7 Sierra Madre Mts California
125 J5 Sierra Madre Oriental mts Mexico
124 H4 Sierra Mojada Mexico
102 D2 Sierraville California
36 D3 Siershahn W Germany
130 B8 Siete Puntas, R Paraguay
33 R6 Sietow E Germany
48 J4 Sieu Romania
45 K4 Sieve R Italy
33 Q7 Sieversdorf E Germany
32 M8 Sievershausen W Germany
29 L8 Sievi Finland
69 C12 Sifahandra Indonesia
67 C5 Sifang Ling mts China
65 G1 Sifangtai China
80 E1 Sifsufa Israel
119 R7 Sifton Manitoba
117 K7 Sifton Pass Br Columbia
17 G9 Sig Algeria
28 B5 Sig Denmark
52 D2 Sig U.S.S.R.
27 D11 Sigdal Norway
18 G9 Sigean France
110 H2 Sigel Illinois
94 H5 Sigel Pennsylvania
69 D13 Sigep Indonesia
26 H3 Sigerfjord Norway
53 B9 Sighet Romania
48 J4 Sighişoara Romania
47 J4 Sığırcı Turkey
69 B10 Sigli Sumatra
115 S4 Siglufjördhur Iceland
71 F5 Sigma Panay Philippines
41 K1 Sigmaringen W Germany
45 K4 Signa Italy
103 L7 Signal Arizona
18 G7 Signal du Luguet mt France
112 B2 Signal Mt Tennessee
103 K8 Signal Pk Arizona
19 P18 Signes France
22 G4 Signy-l'Abbaye France
22 G4 Signy-le-petit France
21 E10 Sigogne France
69 D14 Sigoisoinan Indonesia
99 O8 Sigourney Iowa
128 C4 Sigsig Ecuador
27 J12 Sigtuna Sweden
125 L2 Siguatepeque Honduras
17 F3 Sigüenza Spain
85 C6 Siguiri Guinea
103 N3 Sigurd Utah
20 H2 Sigy-en-Bray France
68 B1 Sihaung Myauk Burma
65 D4 Siheyong China
41 J3 Sihl R Switzerland
41 J3 Sihl See L Switzerland
74 J7 Sihora India
67 D5 Sihui China
29 J10 Siikainen Finland
52 C3 Siikajoki R Finland
29 N8 Siilinjärvi Finland
78 H3 Siirt Turkey
117 M7 Sikanni Chief Br Columbia
74 F5 Sikar India
77 L2 Sikaram mt Afghanistan
69 D14 Sikariman Indonesia
85 C6 Sikasso Mali
70 G7 Sikeli Sulawesi
110 G5 Sikeston Missouri
51 N4 Sikhote Alin' mts U.S.S.R.
47 G8 Síkinos isld Greece
46 F6 Sikionía Greece
75 N5 Sikkim prot India
48 E5 Siklós Hungary
116 B5 Siknik C Alaska
71 A2 Siko isld Halmahera Indonesia
70 E1 Sikuati Sabah
70 G4 Sikutu Sulawesi
16 C2 Sil R Spain
69 D13 Silagui Indonesia
52 B6 Šilale U.S.S.R.
41 N4 Silandro Italy
70 B4 Silantek, G mt Sarawak/Kalimantan
71 G4 Sila Pt Philippines
111 H10 Silas Alabama
70 B4 Silat Kalimantan
69 B10 Silawaih Agam vol Sumatra
71 F5 Silay Negros Philippines
75 P6 Silchar India
26 M1 Silda isld Norway
47 K3 Şile Turkey
22 G3 Silenrieux Belgium
27 F12 Silen, V L Sweden
112 H2 Siler City N Carolina
101 R4 Silesia Montana
31 K4 Silesia reg Poland/Czech
85 E4 Silet Algeria
74 J4 Silgarhi Nepal
83 J12 Silhouette I Seychelles
67 C4 Silian China
43 C12 Siliana Tunisia
99 N2 Silica Minnesota
75 N5 Siliguri India
66 D5 Siling Co L China
43 B9 Siliqua Sardinia
47 J1 Silistra Bulgaria
47 J3 Silivri Turkey
27 G11 Siljan L Sweden
28 C4 Silkeborg Denmark
13 G6 Silkstone England
128 E7 Sillajhuay mt Chile/Bolivia
45 H3 Sillano Italy
45 L3 Sillaro R Italy
20 E5 Sillé-le-Guillaume France
38 F8 Sillian Austria
20 F4 Silli-en-Gouffern France
18 C4 Sillon-de-Talbert C France
47 H3 Sílo mt Greece
110 B5 Siloam Springs Arkansas
109 N5 Silsbee Texas
119 W3 Silsby L Manitoba
106 C2 Silt Colorado
119 N8 Silton Sask
86 C2 Siltou Chad
70 Q10 Silungblanak Indonesia
111 K8 Siluria Alabama
52 B6 Šilutė U.S.S.R.
78 H2 Silvan Turkey
130 E5 Silvânia Brazil
Silva Porto see Bié
74 E8 Silvassa India
127 K4 Silver Bank Caribbean
99 P2 Silver Bay Minnesota
103 N9 Silverbell Arizona
101 N3 Silver Bow Montana
121 L5 Silver Centre Ontario
100 J6 Silver City Idaho
111 F8 Silver City Mississippi
106 B9 Silver City New Mexico
103 M2 Silver City Utah
98 J8 Silver Cr Nebraska
100 F6 Silver Cr Oregon
111 F10 Silver Creek Mississippi
94 H4 Silver Creek New York
98 A8 Silver Crown Wyoming
107 O4 Silverdale Kansas
145 E2 Silverdale New Zealand
118 F6 Silver Heights Alberta
120 B4 Silver Islet Ontario
103 H6 Silver L California
99 T3 Silver L Michigan
123 P4 Silver Mt Nfld
102 G4 Silverpeak Nevada
141 G2 Silver Plains Queensland
94 J4 Silver Springs New York
101 N4 Silver Star Montana
117 O10 Silver Star Prov. Park Br Columbia
117 K10 Silverthrone Mt Br Columbia
106 C4 Silverton Colorado
100 C5 Silverton Oregon
108 F1 Silverton Texas
100 D1 Silverton Washington
128 G4 Silves Brazil
16 B7 Silves Portugal
131 C4 Silveyra, L Argentina
71 N9 Silvícola Timor
100 F6 Silvies R Oregon
41 M4 Silvretta Gruppe mt Switzerland
41 M4 Silvrettahorn mt Switz/Austria
80 D6 Silwād Jordan
36 B5 Silwingen W Germany
55 C3 Sim U.S.S.R.
69 D13 Simaleke Hilir Indonesia
70 B4 Simanggang Sarawak
68 E1 Simao China
71 F4 Simara isld Philippines
121 M5 Simàrd, Lac Quebec
70 G4 Simatang isld Sulawesi
48 H3 Simăul Silvaniei Romania
47 K5 Simav Turkey
47 J4 Simav R Turkey
47 K5 Simav Gölü L Turkey
37 O6 Simbach W Germany
71 E7 Simbahan Philippines
79 B8 Simbillâwein, El Egypt
45 O6 Simbruini, Monti mt Italy
120 K10 Simcoe Ontario
98 F7 Simeon Nebraska
116 H9 Simeonof I Alaska
28 D3 Simested Denmark
43 F11 Simeto R Sicily
69 C11 Simeuluë isld Indonesia
53 D11 Simferopol' U.S.S.R.
47 J8 Sími isld Greece
46 F3 Simitli Bulgaria
106 F2 Simla Colorado
74 G3 Simla India
37 L4 Simmelsdorf W Germany
40 G4 Simmental R Switzerland
36 C4 Simmer R W Germany
22 L2 Simmerath W Germany
36 D4 Simmern W Germany
111 E11 Simmesport Louisiana
118 J9 Simmie Sask
102 E6 Simmler California
109 J7 Simmons Texas
126 G3 Simms Long I Bahamas
101 O2 Simms Montana
111 B8 Simms Texas
113 K9 Simms Pt New Providence I Bahamas
31 O1 Simnas U.S.S.R.
29 L6 Simo Finland
27 D12 Simoa R Norway
29 M6 Simojoki R Finland
29 N11 Simola Finland
102 G3 Simon Nevada
143 E9 Simon W Australia
117 O8 Simonette R Alberta
119 Q4 Simonhouse Manitoba
121 P7 Simon, L Quebec
13 G5 Simon Seat mt England
27 H13 Simonstorp Sweden
89 A10 Simonstown S Africa
117 K10 Simoom Sd Br Columbia
69 G13 Simpang Sumatra
29 O10 Simpele Finland
25 E7 Simpelveld Netherlands
129 K5 Simplício Mendes Brazil
40 H5 Simplon Tunnel Italy/Switz
107 N2 Simpson Kansas
99 O6 Simpson Minnesota
101 P1 Simpson Montana
119 M7 Simpson Sask
140 D6 Simpson Des N Terr Aust
143 F7 Simpson Hill W Australia
133 C7 Simpson, I Chile
120 C4 Simpson I Ontario
117 R5 Simpson Is N W Terr
115 L4 Simpson Pen N W Terr
102 H2 Simpson Pk Mts Nevada
112 E3 Simpsonville S Carolina
27 G16 Simrishamn Sweden
100 C8 Sims California
100 D5 Simtustus, L Oregon
69 C13 Simuk isld Indonesia
70 B4 Simunjan Sarawak
70 F2 Simunul isld Philippines
69 C11 Sinabang Indonesia
69 D11 Sinabung mt Sumatra
42 G4 Sinac Yugoslavia
86 J4 Sinadogo Somalia
98 J5 Sinai S Dakota
84 J4 Sinai pen Egypt
48 K5 Sinaia Romania
124 F5 Sinaloa state Mexico
42 D5 Sinalunga Italy
127 J9 Sinamaica Venezuela
67 C3 Sinan China
46 D4 Sinanaj Albania
55 D3 Sinara R U.S.S.R.
68 B3 Sinbaungwe Burma
75 R6 Sinbo Burma
68 D6 Sinbyubyin Burma
68 D6 Sinbyudaing Burma
68 B2 Sinbyugyun Burma
126 G10 Sincé Colombia
126 G10 Sincelejo Colombia
22 E4 Sinceny France
101 S8 Sinclair Wyoming
112 D4 Sinclair L Georgia
117 N9 Sinclair Mills Br Columbia
138 C4 Sinclair, Pt S Australia
15 E2 Sinclairs B Scotland
94 H4 Sinclairville New York
74 C6 Sind reg Pakistan
28 E2 Sindal Denmark
71 F6 Sindañgan Mindanao Philippines
70 L9 Sindangbarang Java
71 K9 Sindeh, Tk B Flores Indonesia
47 J1 Sindel Bulgaria
36 G6 Sindelfingen W Germany
55 D1 Sindeya U.S.S.R.
76 C2 Sindgi India
76 C3 Sindhnur India
52 B5 Sindi U.S.S.R.
47 J5 Sındırgı Turkey
70 G7 Sindjai Sulawesi
52 H3 Sindor U.S.S.R.
75 M7 Sindri India
36 G5 Sindringen W Germany
54 M9 Sinegorskiy U.S.S.R.
52 H5 Sinegor'ye U.S.S.R.
47 J4 Sinekçi Turkey
47 J3 Sinekli Turkey
54 G8 Sinel'nikoyo U.S.S.R.
16 B7 Sines Portugal
29 L5 Sinettä Finland
Sinfu see Jianping
68 D2 Sing Burma
86 F3 Singa Sudan
68 C2 Singaingmyo Burma
69 B14 Singapore city Singapore
69 G12 Singapore state S E Asia
69 F12 Singapore, Str. of S E Asia
70 P10 Singaradja Indonesia
68 E5 Sing Buri Thailand
41 J2 Singen W Germany
111 C11 Singer Louisiana
88 E4 Singida Tanzania
47 F4 Singitikós, Kólpos gulf Greece
75 Q5 Singkaling Hkamti Burma
69 E13 Singkarak Sumatra
69 G13 Singkep Indonesia
69 C11 Singkilbaru Sumatra
69 D12 Singkuang Sumatra
9 F6 Singleton England
139 K4 Singleton New S Wales
140 C5 Singleton N Terr Aust
109 M5 Singleton Texas
140 B5 Singleton, Mt N Terr Aust
143 B8 Singleton, Mt W Australia
67 A4 Singming China
Singora see Songkhla
68 B1 Singu Burma
46 E4 Siniátsikon mt Greece
71 E3 Siniloan Luzon Philippines
Sining see Xining
Sining Ho R see Huang Shui
43 C8 Siniscola Sardinia
55 D5 Siniy-Shikhan U.S.S.R.
46 C2 Sinjajevina mt Yugoslavia
86 G2 Sinkat Sudan
Sinkiang see Xinjiang Uygur Zizhiqu
Sinkiang-Uighur aut reg see Xinjiang Uygur Zizhiqu
94 D7 Sinking Spring Ohio
65 F5 Sinmi isld N Korea
36 E2 Sinn W Germany
36 H3 Sinn R W Germany
129 H2 Sinnamary Fr Guiana
76 B1 Sinnar India
94 J5 Sinnemahoning Pennsylvania
43 H8 Sinni R Italy
13 H5 Sinnington England
36 H3 Sinntal W Germany
79 A9 Sinnûris Egypt
48 M6 Sinoe, L Romania
88 C10 Sinoia Zimbabwe
78 E1 Sinop Turkey
124 D2 Sinoquipe Mexico
131 H2 Sinos R Brazil
59 J3 Sinp'o N Korea
36 F5 Sinsheim W Germany
36 B4 Sinspelt W Germany
119 O8 Sintaluta Sask
70 B4 Sintang Kalimantan
127 N6 Sint Eustatius isld Lesser Antilles
22 D2 Sint Jan Belgium
127 N5 Sint Maarten isld Lesser Antilles
126 A2 Sint Nicolaas Aruba W I
109 K7 Sinton Texas
16 A6 Sintra Portugal
86 A2 Sinugif Somalia
59 H3 Sinŭiju N Korea
126 G10 Sinú, R Colombia
52 C6 Sinyaya R U.S.S.R.
36 E6 Sinzheim W Germany
36 C2 Sinzig W Germany
28 F7 Siø isld Denmark
48 E4 Sió R Hungary
71 F7 Siocon Mindanao Philippines
40 F5 Sion Switzerland
18 G6 Sioule R France
98 K6 Sioux Center Iowa
98 K7 Sioux City Iowa
98 K6 Sioux Falls S Dakota
118 L1 Sioux Lookout Ontario
99 L7 Sioux Rapids Iowa
71 F6 Sipalay Negros Philippines
127 O3 Siparia Trinidad
Siping see Huangpin
59 H3 Siping China
70 D2 Sipitang Sabah
119 U3 Sipiwesk Manitoba
146 G11 Siple U.S.A.
146 H8 Siple Coast Antarctica
146 J10 Siple, Mt Antarctica
87 F9 Sipolilo Zimbabwe
69 D14 Sipora isld Indonesia
29 N11 Sippola Finland
111 J7 Sipsey Alabama
111 J8 Sipsey R Alabama
71 F6 Siquijor Philippines
128 E1 Siquisique Venezuela
80 G6 Sir R Jordan
76 C4 Sira India
128 D5 Sira mt Peru
27 B13 Sira R Norway
77 D7 Şir Abū Nu'ayr isld U.A.E.
19 Q15 Sirac mt France
43 G11 Siracusa Sicily
117 N9 Sir Alexander, Mt Br Columbia
85 E6 Sirba watercourse Niger/Upper Volta
123 S4 Sir Charles Hamilton Sd Nfld
141 G1 Sir Charles Hardy Is Gt Barrier Reef Aust
27 B13 Sirdalsvatn L Norway
118 B8 Sir Douglas, Mt Alberta
140 D3 Sir Edward Pellew Group islds N Terr Aust
99 O4 Siren Wisconsin
45 P5 Sirente, M mt Italy
48 K3 Siretul R Romania
80 F8 Sirfa Jordan
140 B1 Sir George Hope Is N Terr Aust
142 F2 Sir Graham Moore Is W Aust
79 H7 Sirhān, Wādi watercourse Saudi Arabia
68 E4 Siri Kit Dam Thailand
70 B3 Sirik, Tg C Sarawak
138 D5 Sir Isaac Pt S Australia
117 J4 Sir James McBrien, Mt N W Terr
143 D7 Sir James, Mt W Australia
29 L4 Sirkka Finland
74 G5 Sir Muttra India
47 H8 Sírna isld Greece
78 J3 Sirnak Turkey
74 E6 Sirohi India
42 H5 Široki Brijeg Yugoslavia
45 O4 Sirolo Italy
69 C12 Sirombu Indonesia
76 E1 Sironcha India
74 G6 Sironj India
47 G7 Síros Greece
76 D1 Sirpur India
102 F6 Sirretta Pk California
74 F4 Sirsa India
117 P10 Sir Sandford Mt Br Columbia
117 P10 Sir Sanford, Mt Br Columbia
76 B3 Sirsi India
Sirte see Surte
84 F3 Sirte Desert Libya
84 F3 Sirte, G. of Libya
138 A2 Sir Thomas, Mt S Australia
71 M9 Sirung isld Indonesia
117 O9 Sir Wilfrid Laurier, Mt Br Col
141 G2 Sir William Thompson Ra Queensland
68 G5 Sisaket Thailand
16 B1 Sisargas isld Spain
87 D11 Sishen S Africa
65 D7 Sishui China
119 S6 Sisib L Manitoba
56 D4 Sisim R U.S.S.R.
119 Q3 Sisipuk L Manitoba
99 S2 Siskiwit B Michigan
100 C7 Siskiyou Oregon
100 B8 Siskiyou Mts Cal/Oregon
124 F4 Sisogúichic Mexico
68 F6 Sisophon Cambodia
102 D7 Sisquoc California
40 G3 Sissach Switzerland
98 J4 Sisseton S Dakota
122 E6 Sisson Branch Res New Brunswick
22 F4 Sissonne France
77 G4 Sistan, Daryacheh ye L Afghanistan
109 J6 Sisterdale Texas
19 P16 Sisteron France
100 D5 Sisters Oregon
68 A7 Sisters islds Andaman Is
83 J12 Sisters, The isld Seychelles
116 G5 Sisters, The mt Alaska
143 F7 Sisters, The mt W Australia
94 G7 Sistersville W Virginia
36 B3 Sistig W Germany
45 O7 Sisto R Italy
52 E5 Sit R U.S.S.R.
75 L5 Sitamarhi India
70 F2 Si Tangkay Philippines
74 J5 Sitapur India
26 J3 Sitasjaure L Sweden
47 F4 Sithoniá Greece
47 H9 Sitía Crete Greece
66 E3 Sitian China
130 F4 Sítio da Abadia Brazil
129 K6 Sítio de Mato Brazil
117 F7 Sitka Alaska
107 L4 Sitka Kansas
116 L8 Sitkalidak I Alaska
116 L8 Sitkinak I Alaska
100 B6 Sitkum Oregon
46 D2 Sitnica R Yugoslavia
55 E3 Sitnikovo U.S.S.R.
26 K4 Sitojaure L Sweden
84 H4 Sitra oasis Egypt
77 B6 Sitrah Bahrain
68 C4 Sittang R Burma
25 E7 Sittard Netherlands
Sitten see Sion
32 K6 Sittensen W Germany
9 G5 Sittingbourne England
68 A2 Sittwe Burma
70 P9 Situbondo Java
33 R10 Sitzenroda E Germany
70 G6 Siumbatu Sulawesi
71 H7 Siumpu isld Indonesia
29 M6 Siuruanjoki R Finland
59 J1 Sivaki U.S.S.R.
78 F2 Sivas Turkey
47 K6 Sivash Turkey
78 G3 Siverek Turkey
52 D5 Siverskiy U.S.S.R.
52 K2 Sivomaskinskiy U.S.S.R.
78 C2 Sivrihisar Turkey
22 G3 Sivry Belgium
22 J5 Sivry-sur-Meuse France
84 H4 Siwa Egypt
70 G6 Siwa Sulawesi
100 A7 Sixes Oregon
19 P18 Six Fours-la-Plage France
14 C4 Sixmilebridge Irish Rep
111 E12 Six Mile L Louisiana
21 A6 Sixt France
40 E5 Sixt Vallorcine France
52 F3 Siya U.S.S.R.
86 G1 Siyâl I Egypt
52 G6 Siyava U.S.S.R.
101 M1 Siyeh, Mt Montana
65 A4 Siyitang China

89 E1 Sizarira Hills Zimbabwe
59 M1 Siziman U.S.S.R.
65 B4 Siziwang Qi China
52 H2 Sizyabsk U.S.S.R.
28 G5 Sjælland isld Denmark
28 G5 Sjællands Odde C Denmark
26 K8 Själevad Sweden
46 D1 Sjenica Yugoslavia
26 D10 Sjoa R Norway
27 G16 Sjöbo Sweden
127 M10 S. José de Guanipa Venezuela
26 G7 Sjoutnäs Sweden
27 F14 Sjövik Sweden
26 G7 Sjulsåsen Sweden
26 M6 Sjulsmark Sweden
26 O2 Sjusjavrre Norway
26 F8 Skäckerfjällen mt Sweden
42 J6 Skadarsko Jez L Yugoslavia
28 G6 Skælskør Denmark
27 J14 Skaftet Sweden
27 K11 Skäfthammar Sweden
27 C10 Skagastölstindane mt Norway
28 F1 Skagen Denmark
27 G13 Skagern L Sweden
27 C14 Skagerrak chan Den/Norway
27 D10 Skaget mt Norway
100 D1 Skagit R Washington
117 F6 Skagway Alaska
79 D4 Skala Cyprus
46 F8 Skála Greece
27 F15 Skälderviken B Sweden
28 O10 Skålevig Faeroes
26 K5 Skalka L Sweden
26 S1 Skallelv Norway
28 A5 Skallingen pen Denmark
27 F14 Skallsjö Sweden
27 J13 Skällvik Sweden
31 K4 Skalmierzyce Poland
37 N3 Skalná Czechoslovakia
28 G7 Skalø isld Denmark
28 C3 Skals Å R Denmark
100 C4 Skamania Washington
28 E5 Skamby Denmark
28 D6 Skamlingsbanken hill Denmark
Skanderborg co see Vejle
99 T3 Skandia Michigan
27 F16 Skåne physical reg Sweden
95 L4 Skaneateles New York
99 S3 Skanee Michigan
26 J3 Skånland Norway
28 D4 Skennerup Denmark
27 F16 Skanör Sweden
115 O4 Skansen Greenland
26 H7 Skansholm Sweden
26 J6 Skansnäs Sweden
47 G5 Skantzoúra isld Greece
27 F13 Skara Sweden
27 F13 Skaraborg reg Sweden
26 F9 Skardörfjell mt Norway
74 F1 Skardu Kashmir
27 E11 Skarnes Norway
28 E6 Skarø isld Denmark
28 F6 Skårop Denmark
28 B5 Skarrild Denmark
26 F9 Skarsfjället mt Sweden
31 L1 Skarszewy Poland
28 N2 Skarvanes Faeroes
26 J7 Skarvsjö Sweden
31 N4 Skaryszew Poland
31 M4 Skarżysko-Kamienna Poland
28 B5 Skast Denmark
26 H10 Skästra Sweden
27 G15 Skatelöv Sweden
13 F2 Skateraw Scotland
27 G12 Skattkärr Sweden
27 G10 Skattungen L Sweden
52 B6 Skaudvilė U.S.S.R.
28 B4 Skave Denmark
31 M6 Skawina Poland
120 K6 Skead Ontario
117 J8 Skeena R Br Columbia
117 K8 Skeena Crossing Br Columbia
114 G6 Skeena Mts Br Columbia
9 G1 Skegness England
28 H6 Skelby Denmark
28 H7 Skelby Storstrøm Denmark
28 D7 Skelde Denmark
140 D3 Skeleton R N Terr Aust
28 C4 Skelhøje Denmark
26 L7 Skellefteå Sweden
26 L6 Skellefte älv R Sweden
26 M7 Skelleftehamm Sweden
13 F6 Skelmersdale England
28 E3 Skelund Denmark
27 F14 Skene Sweden
28 J5 Skensved Denmark
47 F6 Skhimatárion Greece
46 E8 Skhíza isld Greece
47 G8 Skhoinoúsa isld Greece
27 E12 Ski Norway
47 F5 Skíathos isld Greece
107 O5 Skiatook Oklahoma
14 B5 Skibbereen Irish Rep
28 B4 Skibbild Denmark
28 H5 Skibby Denmark
28 C5 Skibet Denmark
28 J6 Skibinge Denmark
26 L2 Skibotn Norway
28 A3 Skibsted Fjord Denmark
112 F6 Skidaway I Georgia
114 F7 Skidegate Br Columbia
31 P2 Skidel' U.S.S.R.
95 L8 Skidmore Maryland
109 K7 Skidmore Texas
27 D12 Skien Norway
31 M4 Skierniewice Poland
118 F9 Skiff Alberta
29 J11 Skiftet Kihti Finland
85 F1 Skikda Algeria
116 M6 Skilak L Alaska
47 F7 Skillaion, Akra C Greece
27 G14 Skillengaryd Sweden
110 H3 Skillet R Illinois
46 D7 Skinári, Akra C Greece
28 B3 Skinnerup Denmark
27 H12 Skinnskatteberg Sweden
12 C2 Skipness Scotland
144 B6 Skippers New Zealand
144 B6 Skippers Range New Zealand
13 H6 Skipsea England
13 F6 Skipton England
139 G6 Skipton Victoria
47 G6 Skíros isld Greece
28 C3 Skive Denmark
28 C3 Skive Fj inlet Denmark
26 C10 Skjåk Norway
26 G5 Skjelåtind mt Norway
28 D3 Skjellerup Denmark
28 A5 Skjern Ringkøbing Denmark
28 D4 Skjern Viborg Denmark
28 C5 Skjern Å R Denmark
26 H4 Skjerstad Norway
26 L1 Skjervöy Norway
28 D4 Skjød Denmark
27 A12 Skjold Norway
28 B3 Skjoldborg Denmark
27 C10 Skjolden Norway
28 E7 Skjoldnæs C Denmark
115 P5 Skjoldungen Greenland
26 J3 Skjomen Norway
26 H4 Skjönstå Norway
26 E6 Sklinna lt ho Norway
26 D6 Sklinnabanken Norway
48 E1 Skoczow Poland
28 C6 Skodborg Denmark
28 A5 Skodsbøl Denmark
28 K5 Skodsborg Denmark
28 E4 Skødstrup Denmark
42 F2 Skofja Loka Yugoslavia
26 K9 Skog Sweden
26 O2 Skoganvarre Norway
26 R2 Skogeröy Norway
27 F12 Skoghall Sweden
8 A4 Skokholm I Wales
55 D6 Skol' U.S.S.R.
31 O6 Skole U.S.S.R.
48 H1 Skole U.S.S.R.
27 H12 Sköllersta Sweden
8 A4 Skomer I Wales
26 F4 Skomvoer Norway
117 Q11 Skookumchuk Br Columbia
47 F5 Skópelos isld Greece
47 G6 Skópelos Kaloyeroi isld Greece
28 N2 Skopen Faeroes
54 L3 Skopin U.S.S.R.
46 E2 Skopje Yugoslavia
31 L2 Skórcz Poland
55 F2 Skorodum U.S.S.R.
26 F7 Skorovatn Norway
26 J8 Skorped Sweden
28 D3 Skørping Denmark
28 G7 Skørringe Denmark
27 D12 Skotselv Norway
28 F7 Skovballe Denmark
28 D4 Skovby Århus Denmark
28 E5 Skovby Fyn Denmark
28 D7 Skovby Sønderjylland Denmark
27 G13 Skövde Sweden
28 B5 Skovlund Denmark
59 H1 Skovorodino U.S.S.R.
95 S2 Skowhegan Maine
119 S7 Skownan Manitoba
28 C2 Skræm Denmark
27 E11 Skreia Norway
28 F7 Skrøbelev Denmark
26 M5 Skröven Sweden
28 C6 Skrydstrup Denmark
27 A12 Skudeneshavn Norway
27 E12 Skulerud Norway
103 H5 Skull Pk Nevada
103 M7 Skull V Arizona
48 L3 Skulyany U.S.S.R.
111 G8 Skuna R Mississippi
110 E1 Skunk R Iowa
28 N2 Skuø isld Faeroes
27 M15 Skuodas U.S.S.R.
27 F16 Skurup Sweden
31 J6 Skuteč Czechoslovakia
27 J11 Skutskär Sweden
26 H3 Skutvik Norway
28 N2 Skúvoyar Bjørg mt Faeroes
48 M1 Skvira U.S.S.R.
116 M6 Skwentna Alaska
31 J3 Skwierzyna Poland
15 B3 Skye, I. of Scotland
100 D2 Skykomish Washington
143 G6 Sladen Water W Australia
55 D2 Sladkovskoye U.S.S.R.
28 N1 Slættaratindur mt Faeroes
28 G6 Slagelse Denmark
13 F4 Slaggyford England
111 C10 Slagle Louisiana
28 H5 Slaglille Denmark
26 K6 Slagnäs Sweden
13 F6 Slaidburn England
12 E2 Slamannan Scotland
70 M9 Slamet, G mt Java
116 P5 Slana Alaska
48 F2 Slana R Czechoslovakia
14 E3 Slane Irish Rep
14 E4 Slaney R Irish Rep
89 B8 Slang Berg mt S Africa
28 J5 Slangerup Denmark
89 A10 Slang Kop Pt S Africa
48 K5 Slănic Romania
42 H6 Slano Yugoslavia
52 C5 Slantsy U.S.S.R.
30 H5 Slaný Czechoslovakia
37 N3 Slapany Czechoslovakia
15 B3 Slapin, L Scotland
141 H4 Slashers Reefs Gt Barrier Reef Aust
120 D4 Slate I Ontario
101 S9 Slater Colorado
110 C2 Slater Missouri
98 B8 Slater Wyoming
102 G6 Slate Ra California
111 G8 Slate Springs Mississippi
48 J6 Slatina Romania
42 H3 Slatina, P Yugoslavia
108 F2 Slaton Texas
27 H11 Slättberg Sweden
26 O1 Slåtten Norway
94 G8 Slatyfork W Virginia
111 E11 Slaughter Louisiana
70 N10 Slaung Java
118 C3 Slave Lake Alberta
117 Q5 Slave Pt N W Terr
117 R5 Slave R N W Terr
54 C3 Slavgorod Belorussiya U.S.S.R.
54 G8 Slavgorod Dneprodzerzhinsk U.S.S.R.
31 N1 Slavinek U.S.S.R.
48 D1 Slavkov Czechoslovakia
52 C5 Slavkovichi U.S.S.R.
42 H3 Slavonia reg Yugoslavia
47 F2 Slavovvrŭkh mt Bulgaria
42 H3 Slav Požega Yugoslavia
48 H2 Slavsko U.S.S.R.
54 J8 Slavyansk U.S.S.R.
31 J4 Sława Poland
31 O4 Sławatycze Poland
31 K1 Sławno Poland
31 J2 Sławoborze Poland
99 L6 Slayton Minnesota
9 F1 Sleaford England
138 D6 Sleaford B S Australia
116 D4 Sledge I Alaska
118 K4 Sled L Sask
13 H5 Sledmere England
115 M6 Sleeper Is N W Terr
94 A2 Sleeping Bear Pt Michigan
99 M5 Sleepy Eye Minnesota
116 J6 Sleetmute Alaska
22 F1 Sleidinge Belgium
52 C5 Slepino U.S.S.R.
31 L3 Ślesin Poland
146 D10 Slessor Glac Antarctica
28 M2 Slettenæs Faeroes
28 F4 Sletterhage C Denmark
28 C2 Slettestrand Denmark
26 Q1 Slettnes Norway
111 G11 Slidell Louisiana
109 K2 Slidell Texas
27 D10 Slidre Norway
25 C5 Sliedrecht Netherlands
14 D2 Slieve Anierin mt Irish Rep
14 C3 Slieve Aughty mts Irish Rep
14 D2 Slieve Beagh mt Irish Rep
14 C4 Slieve Bernagh Irish Rep
14 D3 Slieve Bloom Mts Irish Rep
14 B2 Slieve Car mt Irish Rep
14 F2 Slieve Donard mt N Ireland
14 B3 Slieve Elva mt Irish Rep
14 C4 Slievefelim Cullaun Mts Irish Rep
14 B2 Slieve Gamph mt Irish Rep
14 E2 Slieve Gullion mt N Ireland
14 C2 Slieve League mt Irish Rep
14 B4 Slieve Mish mts Irish Rep
14 B5 Slieve Miskish mt Irish Rep
14 A3 Slievemore mt Irish Rep
14 D2 Slievenakilla hill Irish Rep
14 D4 Slievenamon mt Irish Rep
14 D1 Slieve Snaght mt Irish Rep
14 C2 Slieve Tooey mt Irish Rep
15 B3 Sligachan Scotland
14 C2 Sligo Irish Rep
94 H5 Sligo Pennsylvania
14 C2 Sligo co Irish Rep
28 H6 Slimminge Denmark
99 S6 Slinger Wisconsin
15 C3 Slioch Mt Scotland
145 E2 Slipper I New Zealand
94 G5 Slippery Rock Pennsylvania
27 K14 Slite Sweden
47 H2 Sliven Bulgaria
46 F2 Slivnitsa Bulgaria
98 K7 Sloan Iowa
101 L2 Sloan Montana
103 J6 Sloan Nevada
102 D2 Sloat California
54 M5 Sloboda U.S.S.R.
52 G4 Slobodchikovo U.S.S.R.
48 M3 Slobodka U.S.S.R.
52 H5 Slobodskoy U.S.S.R.
48 M4 Slobodzeya U.S.S.R.
48 L6 Slobozia Ialomita Romania
48 J6 Slobozia Teleorman Romania
117 P11 Slocan Br Columbia
25 G2 Slochteren Netherlands
111 L10 Slocomb Alabama
117 G6 Sloko R Br Columbia
27 F15 Slömge Sweden
31 H3 Słońsk Poland
25 E3 Sloten Netherlands
25 E3 Sloter Meer Netherlands
28 G6 Slots Denmark
81 B9 Slot van Capelle Indian Oc
9 F4 Slough England
48 F2 Slovakia Czechoslovakia
42 F3 Slovenija reg Yugoslavia
38 N8 Slovenske Gorice mts Yugoslavia
48 E2 Slovenské Pravno Czechoslovakia
31 L7 Slovenské Rudohorie mts Czechoslovakia
48 F2 Slovensko aut reg Czechoslovakia
116 L5 Slow Fork R Alaska
12 D1 Sloy, L Scotland
31 H3 Słubice Poland
53 C8 Sluch' R U.S.S.R.
52 H4 Sludka Komi U.S.S.R.
25 A6 Sluis Netherlands
25 A6 Sluiskil Netherlands
31 H4 Sluknov Czechoslovakia
31 K3 Słupca Poland
31 K1 Słupsk Poland
14 A3 Slyne Hd Irish Rep
111 D8 Smackover Arkansas
15 E4 Sma Glen Scotland
13 F2 Smailholm Scotland
27 G15 Småland physical reg Sweden
28 G6 Smålandsfarvandet Denmark
27 F14 Smål Burseryd Sweden
101 N5 Small Idaho
119 U1 Small L Manitoba
143 F7 Small, L W Australia
95 S3 Small Pt Maine
115 N7 Smallwood Res Labrador
9 G5 Smarden England
119 N5 Smeaton Sask
48 F6 Smederevo Yugoslavia
48 F6 Smederevska Palanka Yugoslavia
27 H11 Smedjebacken Sweden
54 C7 Smela U.S.S.R.
26 S1 Smelror Norway
94 J5 Smethport Pennsylvania
59 K2 Smidovich U.S.S.R.
28 J4 Smidstrup Denmark
31 K3 Śmigiel Poland
118 H7 Smiley Sask
109 K6 Smiley Texas
52 C6 Smiltene U.S.S.R.
47 G3 Smilyan Bulgaria
47 G1 Smîrdiosa Romania
31 J5 Smiřice Czechoslovakia
55 E4 Smirnovo U.S.S.R.
59 M2 Smirnykh U.S.S.R.
117 O8 Smith Alberta
102 E3 Smith Nevada
94 H10 Smith R Virginia/N Carolina
114 G4 Smith Arm B N W Terr
116 K1 Smith B Alaska
115 M2 Smith B N W Terr
110 G3 Smithboro Illinois
140 F3 Smithburne R Queensland
107 M2 Smith Center Kansas
117 K8 Smithers Br Columbia
112 J2 Smithfield N Carolina
98 G9 Smithfield Nebraska
94 H7 Smithfield Pennsylvania
89 E8 Smithfield S Africa
109 M9 Smithfield Texas
101 O8 Smithfield Utah
95 L9 Smithfield Virginia
94 G7 Smithfield W Virginia
68 A6 Smith I Andaman Is
95 M8 Smith I Maryland
112 K4 Smith I N Carolina
115 M5 Smith I N W Terr
146 E15 Smith I S Shetland Is
95 M9 Smith I Virginia
100 C1 Smith I Washington
146 K6 Smith Inlet Antarctica
100 J1 Smith Pk mt Idaho
122 J8 Smith Pt Nova Scotia
101 O2 Smith R Montana
114 G6 Smith River Br Columbia
100 A8 Smith River California
115 M9 Smiths Falls Ontario
100 J5 Smiths Ferry Idaho
110 K4 Smiths Grove Kentucky
115 M2 Smith Sound N W Terr
139 H8 Smithton Australia
110 C3 Smithton Missouri
139 L4 Smithtown-Gladstone New S Wales
111 M10 Smithville Georgia
110 B2 Smithville Missouri
107 O7 Smithville Oklahoma
110 L6 Smithville Tennessee
109 K6 Smithville Texas
94 F7 Smithville W Virginia
98 C6 Smithwick S Dakota
46 D4 Smlikas mt Greece
102 E1 Smoke Creek Desert Nevada
94 H8 Smoke Hole W Virginia
117 O8 Smoky R Alberta
138 C4 Smoky B S Australia
139 L4 Smoky C New S Wales
123 M7 Smoky C Nova Scotia
120 H2 Smoky Falls Ontario
106 H2 Smoky Hill R Colo/Kansas
107 L2 Smoky Hills Kansas
118 E4 Smoky Lake Alberta
26 C8 Smöla isld Norway
54 D2 Smolensk U.S.S.R.
54 E2 Smolensko-Moskovskaya Vozvyshennost' upland U.S.S.R.
47 G3 Smolyan Bulgaria
101 P7 Smoot Wyoming
120 J3 Smooth Rock Falls Ontario
120 A2 Smooth Rock L Ontario
118 L3 Smoothstone R Sask
48 K2 Smotrich U.S.S.R.
47 J1 Smyadovo Bulgaria
54 G1 Smychka U.S.S.R.
27 F16 Smygehamn Sweden
146 G12 Smyley, C Antarctica
Smyrna see Izmir
95 M7 Smyrna Delaware
112 C4 Smyrna Georgia
95 M4 Smyrna New York
110 K6 Smyrna Tennessee
95 S7 Smyrna Mills Maine
139 H9 Snag Tasmania
68 G7 Snaipol Cambodia
13 G6 Snaith England
101 O6 Snake R Idaho/Wyoming
98 E7 Snake R Nebraska
100 G3 Snake R Washington
140 B1 Snake Bay N Terr Aust
103 K2 Snake Ra Nevada
100 J4 Snake R. Canyon Idaho/Oregon
101 N6 Snake R. Plain Idaho
126 F3 Snap Pt Andros Bahamas
117 Q3 Snare L N W Terr
114 H5 Snare River N W Terr
26 F7 Snåsa Norway
26 F8 Snasahógarna mt Sweden
26 E7 Snåsavatn L Norway
111 M11 Sneads Florida
25 E2 Sneek Netherlands
25 E2 Sneeker Meer Netherlands
14 B5 Sneem Irish Rep
89 D8 Sneeuberg mts S Africa
89 A9 Sneeukop mt S Africa
28 K4 Snekkersten Denmark
102 D4 Snelling California
28 B5 Sneum Å R Denmark
54 L8 Snezhnoye U.S.S.R.
31 J5 Sněžka mt Czechoslovakia
42 F3 Snežnik mt Yugoslavia
31 N2 Śniadowo Poland
31 N2 Sniardwy, Jezioro L Poland
31 N7 Snina Czechoslovakia
118 A3 Snipe L Alberta
15 B3 Snizort, Loch Scotland
28 F6 Snøde Denmark
28 D5 Snoghøj Denmark
26 D9 Snöhetta mt Norway
100 C2 Snohomish Washington
28 J5 Snoldelev Denmark
127 M3 Snook Pt Jamaica
100 D2 Snoqualmie Pass Washington
26 G10 Snössvallen Sweden
68 H6 Snoul Cambodia
54 D4 Snov R U.S.S.R.
94 D3 Snover Michigan
116 L6 Snowcap Mt Alaska
100 B8 Snowden California
119 N5 Snowden Sask
8 B1 Snowdon mt Wales
114 H5 Snowdrift N W Terr
103 O7 Snowflake Arizona
119 T9 Snowflake Manitoba
95 M8 Snow Hill Maryland
112 K2 Snow Hill N Carolina
146 E15 Snow I S Shetland Is
111 E7 Snow Lake Arkansas
114 J7 Snow Lake Manitoba
106 C2 Snowmass Mt Colorado
121 O8 Snow Road Ontario
94 K5 Snow Shoe Pennsylvania
100 K1 Snowshoe Pk mt Montana
138 E5 Snowtown S Australia
101 N8 Snowville Utah
103 K1 Snow Water L Nevada
139 J6 Snowy Mts Vict/N S W
48 K2 Snyatyn U.S.S.R.
98 K8 Snyder Nebraska
107 M7 Snyder Oklahoma
108 G3 Snyder Texas
27 H12 Snyten Sweden
143 E6 Soakage Well W Australia
144 A6 Soaker, Mt New Zealand
87 H11 Soalala Madagascar
40 G7 Soana, Val di Italy
87 H11 Soanierana Ivongo Madagascar
65 G7 Soan kundo isld S Korea
89 D3 Soa Pan Botswana
100 F2 Soap Lake Washington
48 J5 Soarş Romania
71 A2 Soasiu Halmahera Indonesia
45 K1 Soave Italy
15 B3 Soay Scotland
41 K5 Soazza Switzerland
85 F6 Soba Nigeria
86 F4 Sobat R Sudan
36 D4 Sobernheim W Germany
31 H6 Soběslav Czechoslovakia
54 M1 Sobinka U.S.S.R.
60 E13 Sobo-san mt Japan
38 M8 Soboth Austria
31 K5 Sobótka Poland
129 K4 Sobral Brazil
48 G2 Sobrance Czechoslovakia
18 F10 Sobrarbe dist Spain
68 H1 Soc Bang Giang R Vietnam
68 H1 Soc Giang Vietnam
31 M3 Sochaczew Poland
53 E11 Sochi U.S.S.R.
112 D4 Social Circle Georgia
112 H3 Society Hill S Carolina
135 M10 Society Is Pacific Oc
Socna see Sawknah
128 E8 Socompa vol Chile/Arg
130 F8 Socorro Brazil
108 A1 Socorro New Mexico
133 B6 Socorro, I Chile
83 H3 Socotra isld Indian Oc
17 F5 Socuéllamos Spain
117 M9 Soda Creek Br Columbia
103 H6 Soda L California
29 M4 Sodankylä Finland
101 O7 Soda Springs Idaho
102 F3 Sodaville Nevada
86 G4 Soddo Ethiopia
112 B2 Soddy Tennessee
36 F3 Södel W Germany
27 K12 Söderby-Karl Sweden
26 J9 Söderfjärden Sweden
27 J11 Söderfors Sweden
27 J10 Söderhamn Sweden
27 H13 Söderköping Sweden
27 H12 Södermanland reg Sweden
27 J12 Södertälje Sweden
86 E3 Sodiri Sudan
95 K3 Sodus New York
71 M9 Soë Timor Indonesia
60 D12 Soeda Japan
87 E10 Soekmekaar S Africa
52 B5 Soela Väin chan U.S.S.R.
25 D4 Soest Netherlands
32 H9 Soest W Germany
32 G7 Soeste R W Germany
46 E5 Sofádhes Greece
87 F9 Sofala Mozambique
139 J5 Sofala New S Wales
79 F5 Sofar Lebanon
Sofia see Sofiya
106 G5 Sofia New Mexico
87 H11 Sofia R Madagascar
46 F7 Sofikón Greece
47 F2 Sofiya Bulgaria
36 H7 Söflingen W Germany
52 D2 Sofporog U.S.S.R.
75 P3 Sog China
128 D2 Sogamoso Colombia
32 G7 Sögel W Germany
45 M3 Sogliano al Rubicone Italy
27 B10 Sogn reg Norway
27 C13 Søgne Norway
27 B10 Sognefjorden inlet Norway
26 B10 Sogn og Fjordane Norway
71 G5 Sogod Philippines
55 E1 Sogom U.S.S.R.
78 C1 Söğüt Turkey
47 K7 Söğüt Gölü L Turkey
84 J4 Sohâg Egypt
75 J7 Sohagpur India
9 G3 Soham England
137 L3 Sohano Bougainville I Solomon Is
68 D5 Sohng Gwe, Khao mt Burma/Thailand
36 H1 Söhrewald W Germany
65 F7 Sohüksan isld S Korea
22 G2 Soignies Belgium
21 I7 Soings-en-Sologne France
29 L9 Soini Finland
22 E5 Soissons France
60 G11 Sōja Japan
74 E6 Sojat India
71 F6 Sojoton Pt Philippines
53 H7 Sok R U.S.S.R.
78 A3 Soke Turkey
115 R4 Søkengens Ø isld Greenland
47 F4 Sokhós Greece
46 E1 Soko Banja Yugoslavia
85 E7 Sokodé Togo
52 F5 Sokol U.S.S.R.
31 O2 Sokółka Poland
52 H6 Sokolka U.S.S.R.
31 L4 Sokolniki Poland
85 C6 Sokolo Mali
37 O3 Sokolov Czechoslovakia
55 E3 Sokolovka U.S.S.R.
52 J2 Sokolovo U.S.S.R.
31 N5 Sokołów Małopolski Poland
31 N3 Sokołów Podlaski Poland
52 D2 Sokolozero U.S.S.R.
52 F6 Sokol'skoye U.S.S.R.
31 O3 Sokoły Poland
61 Q12 Sokoniya Okinawa
85 F6 Sokoto Nigeria
85 F6 Sokoto R Nigeria
126 F4 Sola Cuba
27 A13 Sola Norway
88 F1 Solai Kenya
144 A7 Solander I New Zealand
71 E2 Solano Luzon Philippines
106 F6 Solano New Mexico
45 Q8 Solaro, M mt Italy
41 O3 Solbad Hall Austria
26 J8 Solberg Sweden
26 J2 Solbergfjord inlet Norway
27 E12 Solbergfoss Norway
28 D4 Solbjerg Sø L Denmark
48 K3 Solca Romania
41 O4 Sölden Austria
99 L8 Soldier Iowa
107 P2 Soldier Kansas
94 D8 Soldier Kentucky
31 L2 Solec Kujawski Poland
102 C5 Soledad California
126 G9 Soledad Colombia
124 C5 Soledad Mexico
127 N10 Soledad Venezuela
128 E5 Soledade Brazil
100 A1 Soleduck R Washington
125 M4 Solentiname, Is. de Nicaragua
9 E6 Solent, The chan England
45 L1 Solesino Italy
22 F3 Solesmes Nord France
21 E6 Solesmes Sarthe France
41 N5 Sole, Val. di Italy
29 J8 Solf Finland
45 J1 Solferino Italy
52 F4 Solginskiy U.S.S.R.
56 D3 Solgonskiy Kryzah ra U.S.S.R.
27 A11 Solheim Norway
52 F5 Soligalich U.S.S.R.
20 G4 Soligny-la-Trappe France
9 E3 Solihull England
52 J5 Solikamsk U.S.S.R.
43 C12 Soliman Tunisia
128 E4 Solimões R Brazil
36 C1 Solingen W Germany
127 J10 Solita Venezuela
17 H3 Solivella Spain
38 F7 Söll Austria
26 J8 Sollefteå Sweden
27 J12 Sollentuna Sweden
26 D10 Sollia Norway
33 R9 Söllichau E Germany
32 K9 Solling hills W Germany
33 N8 Söllingen W Germany
50 E3 Sol'lletsk U.S.S.R.
36 E3 Solms W Germany
26 E10 Söln mt Norway
27 J12 Solna Sweden
54 H1 Solnechnogorsk U.S.S.R.
37 K6 Solnhofen W Germany
26 D10 Sölnkletten mt Norway
70 N9 Solo R Java
45 R8 Solofra Italy
71 J4 Solok Sulawesi
69 E13 Solok Sumatra
52 D4 Solomennoye U.S.S.R.
103 P9 Solomon Arizona
107 N3 Solomon Kansas
107 M2 Solomon R Kansas
137 M3 Solomon Is Pacific Oc
137 L3 Solomon Sea Pacific Oc
80 D7 Solomon's Pools Jordan
59 H2 Solon China
99 P8 Solon Iowa
94 F5 Solon Ohio
55 F5 Solonichki U.S.S.R.
99 P3 Solon Springs Wisconsin
58 G1 Solontsovo U.S.S.R.
45 R7 Solopaca Italy
71 L9 Solor isld Indonesia
17 F3 Solorio, Sa. del mts Spain
71 L9 Solor, Kepulauan isld Indonesia
40 F3 Solothurn Switzerland
57 D3 Solotobe U.S.S.R.
52 E2 Solovetskiye Ostrova islds U.S.S.R.
59 H1 Solov'yevsk U.S.S.R.
22 G3 Solre-le-Château France
28 J5 Solrød Strand Denmark
41 O3 Solstein mt Austria
42 G5 Šolta isld Yugoslavia
32 L7 Soltau W Germany
52 D5 Soltsy U.S.S.R.
27 A10 Solund Norway
46 E3 Solunska mt Yugoslavia
102 D7 Solvang California
95 L3 Solvay New York
27 G15 Sölvesborg Sweden
52 G4 Sol'vychegodsk U.S.S.R.
15 E6 Solway Firth Scotland
87 E8 Solwezi Zambia
61 O8 Sōma Japan
47 J5 Soma Turkey
22 E3 Somain France
86 H5 Somalia rep E Africa
72 G7 Somali Basin Indian Oc
87 D7 Sombo Angola
48 E5 Sombor Yugoslavia
120 H10 Sombra Ontario
22 H2 Sombreffe Belgium
124 H6 Sombrerete Mexico
127 N5 Sombrero isld Lesser Antilles
69 A9 Sombrero Chan Nicobar Is
113 F13 Sombrero Key isld Florida
48 H3 Şomcuţa Mare Romania
25 E6 Someren Netherlands
29 K11 Somero Finland
99 M7 Somers Iowa
101 L1 Somers Montana
99 T7 Somers Wisconsin
106 C3 Somerset Colorado
94 C9 Somerset Kentucky
119 T9 Somerset Manitoba
95 Q5 Somerset Massachusetts
94 E7 Somerset Ohio
94 H6 Somerset Pennsylvania
141 G1 Somerset Queensland
139 H8 Somerset Tasmania
109 J6 Somerset Texas
8 C5 Somerset co England
87 E12 Somerset East S Africa
90 B2 Somerset I Bermuda
147 F4 Somerset I N W Terr
141 L7 Somerset Res Queensland
95 P4 Somerset Res Vermont
89 A10 Somerset West S Africa
95 N7 Somers Point New Jersey
95 Q3 Somersworth New Hampshire
103 K9 Somerton Arizona
8 D5 Somerton England
95 Q4 Somerville Massachusetts
95 N6 Somerville New Jersey
110 G6 Somerville Tennessee
109 L5 Somerville Res Texas
100 B8 Somesbar California
48 H3 Someşul R Romania
48 H4 Someşul Cald R Romania
48 J3 Someşul Mare R Romania
45 J1 Sommacompagna Italy
141 H7 Sommariva Queensland
22 H5 Sommauthe France
45 Q8 Somma Vesuvio Italy
20 K2 Somme dep France
22 D4 Somme R France
22 J3 Somme-Leuze Belgium
27 G13 Sommen Sweden
27 H13 Sommen L Sweden
37 L1 Sömmerda E Germany
18 H4 Sommesous France
18 H9 Sommières France
68 G2 Som Mong Vietnam
48 D4 Somogy co Hungary
48 D4 Somogyszob Hungary
48 D4 Somogyvár Hungary
99 S8 Somonauk Illinois
16 E3 Somosierra, Pto. de Spain
31 L3 Sompolno Poland
131 C8 Somuncurá, Mesa Vol. de mt Argentina
22 G3 Somzée Belgium
27 E12 Son Norway
73 N4 Son R India
20 J4 Sonchamp France
44 G1 Soncino Italy
41 M5 Sondalo Italy
52 D3 Sondaly U.S.S.R.
70 E3 Sondang, G mt Kalimantan
28 C7 Sønderå R Denmark
28 D7 Sønderborg Denmark
28 A6 Sønderjylland co Denmark
28 D3 Sønder Onsild Denmark
33 N10 Sondershausen E Germany
28 E6 Søndersø Denmark
111 E9 Sondheimer Louisiana
115 O4 Söndre Strömfjord Greenland
115 O3 Søndre Upernavik Greenland
42 C2 Sondrio Italy
76 C1 Sonepet India
128 E8 Sonequera mt Bolivia
95 L5 Sonestown Pennsylvania
70 C4 Song Sarawak
65 J2 Song'acha He R China/U.S.S.R.
88 G6 Songa Manara isld Tanzania
27 B12 Songa Totak R Norway
68 J6 Song Ba R Vietnam
68 H2 Song Ba Che R Vietnam
67 D3 Songbai China
Song Bo R see Noire R
68 G2 Song Boi R Vietnam
67 E1 Songbu China
67 A7 Song Ca R Vietnam
68 J6 Song Cai R Vietnam
68 J6 Song Cau Vietnam
68 G2 Song Chay R Vietnam
67 A7 Song Chu R Vietnam
69 H8 Song Co Chien R Vietnam
69 G8 Song Cua Lon R Vietnam
88 E7 Songea Tanzania
20 J2 Songeons France
67 B5 Song Gam R Vietnam
68 J5 Song Ha Giao R Vietnam
65 G3 Songhua Hu res China
59 J2 Songhua Jiang R China
65 F2 Songhua Jiang R China
Songjiachuan see Wubu
Songjiang see Antu
67 G1 Songjiang China
59 J3 Sŏngjin N Korea
67 B2 Songkan China
69 E9 Songkhla Thailand
68 F4 Song Khram R Thailand
67 A5 Song-koi R Vietnam
67 E4 Songkou China
68 H2 Song Ky Cung R Vietnam
65 E4 Song Ling mts China
68 D1 Songlong Burma
68 J7 Song Luy R Vietnam
68 G2 Song Ma R Vietnam
68 H7 Song Nha Be R Vietnam
87 B7 Songo Angola
86 B7 Songololo Zaïre
69 G8 Song Ong Doc R Vietnam
58 D5 Songpan China
88 G6 Song Songo isld Tanzania
67 C2 Songtao China
68 J5 Song Tra Khuc R Vietnam
68 H7 Song Vam Co Dong R Vietnam
68 H7 Song Vam Co Tay R Vietnam
88 D6 Songwe R Tanzania
67 F3 Songxi China
67 F3 Song Xi R China
65 B7 Song Xian China
65 F1 Song Zhan China
67 D1 Songzi China
68 J5 Son Ha Vietnam
68 J7 Son Hai Vietnam
68 J6 Son Hoa Vietnam
65 B3 Sonid Youqi China
65 B3 Sonid Zuoqi China
29 N8 Sonkajärvi Finland
57 G4 Sonkel', Oz U.S.S.R.
68 F2 Son La Vietnam
74 B6 Sonmiani Pakistan
38 H7 Sonnblick, Gross mt Austria
37 L3 Sonneberg E Germany
37 L3 Sonnefeld W Germany
37 P6 Sonnen Wald mts W Germany
33 T9 Sonnewalde E Germany
118 K6 Sonningdale Sask
45 O7 Sonnino Italy
129 J5 Sono R Brazil
60 J10 Sonobe Japan
41 J5 Sonogno Switzerland
103 O10 Sonoita Arizona
103 M10 Sonoita Mexico
103 M1 Sonoita R Utah
103 L10 Sonoita R Mexico
102 B3 Sonoma California
100 H9 Sonoma Range Nevada
103 O8 Sonora Arizona
102 D4 Sonora California
123 L8 Sonora Nova Scotia
108 G5 Sonora Texas
124 D3 Sonora state Mexico
102 E3 Sonora Pk California
25 F5 Sonsbeck W Germany
56 D4 Sonskiy U.S.S.R.
128 C2 Sonsón Colombia
125 P11 Sonsonate El Salvador
67 B6 Son Tay Vietnam
37 J6 Sontheim W Germany
41 M2 Sonthofen W Germany
36 H1 Sontra W Germany
94 K4 Sonyea New York
21 F7 Sonzay France
Soochow see Suzhou
116 C5 Sooghmeghat Alaska
117 M11 Sooke Br Columbia
36 D4 Soonwald mts W Germany
131 G3 Sopas R Uruguay
113 C7 Sopchoppy Florida
107 P7 Soper Oklahoma
112 E5 Soperton Georgia
135 M12 Sophie-Christensen Bank Pacific Oc
71 B1 Sopi Halmahera Indonesia
68 F3 Sop Khao Laos
9 E6 Sopley England
86 E4 Sopo R Sudan
31 L1 Sopot Poland
26 M3 Soppero Sweden
48 D3 Sopron Hungary
123 Q4 Sop's Arm Nfld
71 J4 Soputan, G Sulawesi
102 C5 Soquel California
16 B5 Sor R Portugal
42 F7 Sora Italy
27 G14 Söraby Sweden
60 Q2 Sorachi R Japan
75 L9 Sorada India
45 N5 Soratte, M mt Italy
17 F7 Sorbas Spain
16 E3 Sorbe R Spain
27 F10 Sörberget Sweden
12 D4 Sorbie Scotland
45 H2 Sorbolo Italy
26 H9 Sörbygden Sweden
28 G6 Sørbymagle Denmark
28 B3 Sørdbjerg Denmark
89 H6 Sordwana B S Africa
70 L9 Soreang Java
115 M8 Sorel Quebec
139 J8 Sorell Tasmania
139 H8 Sorell, C Tasmania
80 B6 Soreq R Israel
44 G1 Soresina Italy
27 B11 Sörfjorden Norway
26 E7 Sör Flatanger Norway
26 H4 Sörfold Norway
26 H7 Sörfors Sweden
45 J1 Sorgà Italy
43 C8 Sorgono Sardinia
19 N17 Sorgues France
18 G9 Sorgues R France
44 F3 Sori Italy
17 F3 Soria Spain
17 F3 Soria prov Spain
133 F4 Soriano dep Uruguay
21 G7 Sorigny France
69 D12 Sorikmerapi mt Sumatra
52 E5 Sorka U.S.S.R.
50 A1 Sörkapp isld Svalbard
26 G7 Sörli Norway
26 L8 Sörmjöle Sweden
12 D3 Sorn Scotland
21 J10 Sornac France
41 J5 Sornico Switzerland
28 H6 Sorø Denmark
Sorø co see Vestjælland
130 F8 Sorocaba Brazil
52 H6 Soroch'i Gory U.S.S.R.
55 B5 Sorochinsk U.S.S.R.
48 L2 Soroki U.S.S.R.
48 E3 Soroksár Hungary
57 H2 Sorolen U.S.S.R.
43 F11 Soro, M mt Sicily
71 C3 Sorong W Irian
86 F5 Soroti Uganda
26 N1 Söröya isld Norway
26 N1 Söröysund chan Norway
32 G10 Sorpetalsperre L W Germany
16 B6 Sorraia R Portugal
26 K2 Sörreisa Norway
117 O10 Sorrento Br Col
45 Q8 Sorrento Italy
111 F11 Sorrento Louisiana
95 T2 Sorrento Maine
139 G7 Sorrento Victoria
87 B10 Sorris-Sorris Namibia
146 B8 Sør Rondane mt Antarctica
29 O4 Sorsatunturi mt Finland
26 J6 Sorsele Sweden
27 F10 Sörsjön Sweden
43 B8 Sorso Sardinia
71 G4 Sorsogon Philippines
18 F10 Sort Spain
29 P10 Sortavala U.S.S.R.
26 H3 Sortland Norway
52 H4 Sortopolovskaya U.S.S.R.
26 E9 Sör-Tröndelag reg Norway
28 H7 Sortsø Denmark
98 D4 Sorum S Dakota
28 G7 Sørup Denmark
28 D7 Sörup W Germany
28 B4 Sørvad Denmark
26 M1 Sörvaer Norway
28 M2 Sörvåg Faeroes
26 F9 Sörvattnan Sweden
52 G5 Sorvizhi U.S.S.R.
17 G2 Sos del Rey Catolico Spain
32 M9 Sose R W Germany
131 B5 Sosneado peak Argentina
54 D5 Sosnitsa U.S.S.R.
52 H3 Sosnogorsk U.S.S.R.
52 D3 Sosnovets U.S.S.R.
52 G6 Sosnovka Chuvashskaya A.S.S.R. U.S.S.R.
52 F2 Sosnovka U.S.S.R.
29 P11 Sosnovo U.S.S.R.
58 F1 Sosnovo-Ozerskoye U.S.S.R.
55 E1 Sosnovyy Mys U.S.S.R.
31 L5 Sosnowiec Poland
29 M7 Soso Finland
111 G10 Soso Mississippi
42 G2 Šoštanj Yugoslavia
61 Q12 Sosu Okinawa
50 F3 Sos'va U.S.S.R.
53 E10 Sosyka R U.S.S.R.
78 H2 Sothan Turkey
29 N7 Sotkamo Finland
125 K6 Soto la Marina Mexico
27 A11 Sotra isld Norway
54 K6 Sotsgorodok U.S.S.R.
20 B2 Sottevast France
20 H3 Sotteville France
27 L11 Sottunga Finland
20 G5 Souance France
86 B5 Souanké Congo
85 C7 Soubré Ivory Coast
22 D3 Souchez France
140 D5 Soudan N Terr Aust
95 M6 Souderton Pennsylvania
21 J7 Souesmes France
86 B5 Soufflay Congo
36 D6 Soufflenheim France
47 H3 Souflíon Greece
127 O8 Soufrière St Lucia
127 O8 Soufrière mt St Vincent
127 N4 Soufrière peak Guadeloupe W Indies
20 E5 Sougé-le-Ganelon France
20 J5 Sougy France
18 G8 Souillac France
83 L13 Souillac Mauritius
85 F1 Souk Ahras Algeria
16 D10 Souk-el-Arba-du-Rharb Morocco
16 D9 Souk-Sebt-des-Beni-Zarfeto Morocco
16 D9 Souk-Tnine-de-Sidi-el-Yamani Morocco
65 G6 Sŏul S Korea
121 Q7 Soulanges Canal Quebec
20 D5 Soulgé-le-Bruant France
20 F5 Souligné France
21 F6 Souligne France
36 D6 Soultz France
68 A6 Sound I Andaman Is
118 G6 Sounding L Alberta
15 A3 Sound of Barra Scotland
15 A3 Sound of Harris Outer Hebrides Scotland
15 C3 Sound of Sleat Scotland
47 F7 Soúnion, Akra Greece
89 F7 Sources, Mt. aux Lesotho
20 D4 Sourdeval France
129 J4 Soure Brazil
16 B4 Souré Portugal
119 R9 Souris Manitoba
119 R10 Souris N Dakota
123 K7 Souris Pr Edward I
46 F5 Soúrpi Greece
20 J5 Sours France
130 H9 Sousa Brazil
87 B8 Sousa Lara Angola
129 H4 Sousel Brazil
85 C2 Souss R Morocco
43 D13 Sousse Tunisia
18 E9 Soustons France
18 G6 Souterraine, la France
89 South Africa, Republic of
9 F5 Southall England
9 E3 Southam England
98 H1 Southam N Dakota
9 E6 Southampton England
95 P6 Southampton Long I, New York
122 H8 Southampton Nova Scotia
120 J8 Southampton Ontario
115 L5 Southampton I N W Terr
68 A6 South Andaman isld Andaman Is
94 K9 South Anna R Virginia
102 C6 South Antonio R California
146 G2 Southard, C Antarctica
145 F2 South Auckland stat area New Zealand
138 South Australia state Australia
120 J7 South B Ontario
106 C8 South Baldy mt New Mexico
94 E5 South Bass I Ohio
113 G11 South Bay Florida
120 H7 South Baymouth Ontario
142 A2 South Beach dist Perth, W Aust
142 B2 South Belmont dist Perth, W Aust
99 S7 South Beloit Illinois
99 U8 South Bend Indiana
109 J3 South Bend Texas
100 B3 South Bend Washington
126 F2 South Bight Andros Bahamas
141 J6 South Blackwater Queensland
126 G3 South Bluff Acklins I Bahamas
94 B2 South Boardman Michigan
9 G5 Southborough England
94 H10 South Boston Virginia
94 D2 South Branch Michigan
123 N6 South Branch Nfld
8 C7 South Brent England
95 P4 Southbridge Massachusetts
144 D5 Southbridge New Zealand

74

Stonewall — Svir'

118 D1 **Stonewall** Manitoba
111 H9 **Stonewall** Mississippi
109 L1 **Stonewall** Oklahoma
109 J5 **Stonewall** Texas
121 L9 **Stoney Creek** Ontario
12 D4 **Stoneykirk** Scotland
26 J2 **Stonglandet** Norway
106 H4 **Stonington** Colorado
95 Q5 **Stonington** Connecticut
99 R10 **Stonington** Illinois
95 T2 **Stonington** Maine
119 M8 **Stony Beach** Sask
94 K10 **Stony Creek** Virginia
102 B2 **Stonyford** California
127 L2 **Stony Hill** Jamaica
118 D1 **Stony Mountain** Manitoba
118 D5 **Stony Plain** Alberta
112 F2 **Stony Point** N Carolina
95 N5 **Stony Point** New York
144 C6 **Stony R** New Zealand
114 J6 **Stony Rapids** Sask
116 J6 **Stony River** Alaska
9 F3 **Stony Stratford** England
120 H1 **Stooping** *R* Ontario
32 L4 **Stör** *R* W Germany
27 H12 **Storå** Sweden
28 C4 **Storå** *R* Denmark
26 G8 **Storåbränna** Sweden
28 O10 **Stórafjall** *mt* Faeroes
27 E12 **Stora Le** *L* Sweden
26 L5 **Stora Lule älv** *R* Sweden
26 K4 **Stora Lulevatten** *L* Sweden
26 F9 **Storån** *R* Sweden
26 J4 **Stora Sjoffallet** *L* Sweden
26 K6 **Storavan** *L* Sweden
26 K6 **Storberg** Sweden
27 L11 **Storby** Finland
27 A12 **Stord** Norway
26 B9 **Stordal** Möre og Romsdal Norway
26 E8 **Stordal** Sör-Tröndelag Norway
28 D3 **Store Arden** Denmark
28 F5 **Store Bælt** *chan* Denmark
26 G6 **Store Börgefjeld** *mt* Norway
27 H14 **Storebro** Sweden
28 B6 **Store Darum** Denmark
28 N3 **Store Dimon** *isld* Faeroes
28 G5 **Store Fuglede** Denmark
28 K6 **Store Heddinge** Denmark
28 C7 **Store Jyndevad** Denmark
28 K7 **Storeklint** *cliffs* Denmark
147 F10 **Store Koldewey** *isld* Greenland
26 P1 **Storelv** *R* Norway
27 E10 **Stor-Elvdal** Norway
28 K5 **Store Magleby** Denmark
28 H5 **Store Merløse** Denmark
26 R1 **Store Molvik** Norway
26 D8 **Stören** Norway
28 E7 **Store Rise** Denmark
28 J6 **Store Spjellerup** Denmark
28 J6 **Store Tårnby** Denmark
28 D2 **Store Vildmose** Denmark
26 H6 **Storfjellet,N** *mt* Sweden
26 G6 **Storfjellet,S** *mt* Sweden
26 B9 **Storfjord** *inlet* Norway
26 L6 **Storfors** Sweden
26 G5 **Storfosshei** Norway
26 H8 **Storhögen** Sweden
26 A9 **Storholmen** Norway
26 G7 **Storjorm** *L* Sweden
33 P5 **Störkanal** E Germany
114 G3 **Storkerson B** N W Terr
26 F8 **Storlien** Sweden
26 K7 **Storlögda** Sweden
32 L5 **Stormarn** *reg* W Germany
139 J9 **Storm B** Tasmania
89 E8 **Stormberge** *mts* S Africa
99 L7 **Storm L** Iowa
118 K1 **Stormy L** Ontario
119 P7 **Stornoway** Sask
15 B2 **Stornoway** Scotland
52 H4 **Storozhevsk** U.S.S.R.
48 K2 **Storozhinets** U.S.S.R.
26 F8 **Storrensjön** *L* Sweden
9 F6 **Storrington** England
15 B3 **Storr,The** *mt* Scotland
27 E11 **Stor-s** *L* Norway
26 L7 **Storsävarträsk** Sweden
26 F9 **Storsjö** Sweden
27 E10 **Stor-sjöen** *L* Norway
27 J11 **Storsjön** *L* Gävleborg Sweden
26 F9 **Storsjön** *L* Jämtland Sweden
28 H6 **Storstrøm** *co* Denmark
28 H7 **Storstrømmen** *chan* Denmark
119 Q9 **Storthoaks** Sask
26 J6 **Storuman** Sweden
27 G10 **Storvarden** *mt* Sweden
26 F9 **Storvigelen** *mt* Norway
27 J11 **Storvik** Sweden
26 J6 **Stor-vindein** *L* Sweden
28 E2 **Storvorde** Denmark
101 T5 **Story** Wyoming
99 N7 **Story City** Iowa
133 B7 **Stosch, I** Chile
37 M1 **Stössen** E Germany
26 F5 **Stött** Norway
41 N2 **Stotten** W Germany
37 L1 **Stotternheim** E Germany
28 D5 **Stouby** Denmark
121 L9 **Stouffville** Ontario
95 Q4 **Stoughton** Massachusetts
119 O9 **Stoughton** Sask
99 R7 **Stoughton** Wisconsin
22 K3 **Stoumont** Belgium
46 E4 **Stoupí** Greece
8 D3 **Stourbridge** England
8 D3 **Stourport** England
9 H5 **Stour,R** England
8 D3 **Stourton** England
94 E7 **Stoutsville** Ohio
28 D3 **Støvring** Denmark
28 E3 **Støvring** Denmark
13 F2 **Stow** Scotland
95 P2 **Stowe** Vermont
109 N6 **Stowell** Texas
9 G3 **Stowmarket** England
9 E4 **Stow on the Wold** England
28 E6 **Stoy** Denmark
59 K1 **Stoyba** U.S.S.R.
46 C2 **Stožac** *mt* Yugoslavia
45 M1 **Stra** Italy
33 R9 **Straach** E Germany
14 D2 **Strabane** N Ireland
12 C1 **Strachur** Scotland
14 D3 **Stradbally** Irish Rep
139 L3 **Stradbroke,I** Queensland Australia
44 F1 **Stradella** Italy
38 N8 **Straden** Austria
9 G2 **Stradsett** England
25 F6 **Straelen** W Germany
110 C4 **Strafford** Missouri
139 H8 **Strahan** Tasmania
103 N4 **Straight Cliffs** Utah
22 J4 **Straimont** Belgium
12 D3 **Straiton** Scotland
30 H6 **Strakonice** Czechoslovakia
47 H2 **Straldzha** Bulgaria
33 S4 **Stralsund** E Germany
27 E10 **Strand** Hedmark Norway
27 A12 **Strand** Rogaland Norway
89 A10 **Strand** S Africa
26 B9 **Stranda** Norway
28 C3 **Strandby** Nordjylland Denmark
28 F2 **Strandby** Vendsyssel Denmark
98 J9 **Strang** Nebraska
113 J10 **Strangers Cay** *isld* Bahamas
14 F2 **Strangford** N Ireland
14 F2 **Strangford L** N Ireland
27 J12 **Strängnäs** Sweden
27 H13 **Strångsjö** Sweden
140 C3 **Strangways** *R* N Terr Aust
140 C6 **Strangways Ra** N Terr Aust
138 D3 **Strangways Spr** S Australia
14 D2 **Stranorlar** Irish Rep
118 J7 **Stranraer** Sask
12 C4 **Stranraer** Scotland
36 D6 **Strasbourg** France
119 N7 **Strasbourg** Sask
106 F2 **Strasburg** Colorado
33 T5 **Strasburg** E Germany
110 H2 **Strasburg** Illinois
98 F3 **Strasburg** N Dakota
94 F6 **Strasburg** Ohio
94 J8 **Strasburg** Virginia
48 M3 **Strasheny** U.S.S.R.
38 N8 **Strass** Steiermark Austria
38 E7 **Strass** Tirol Austria
27 H12 **Stråssa** Sweden
38 K8 **Strassburg** Austria
36 C2 **Strassenhaus** W Germany
38 M7 **Strassgang** Austria
37 O6 **Strasskirchen** W Germany
38 H6 **Strasswalchen** Austria
95 O5 **Stratford** Connecticut
99 N7 **Stratford** Iowa
95 Q2 **Stratford** New Hampshire
145 E3 **Stratford** New Zealand
109 L1 **Stratford** Oklahoma
122 A8 **Stratford** Quebec
98 H4 **Stratford** S Dakota
108 B7 **Stratford** Texas
139 H7 **Stratford** Victoria
99 Q5 **Stratford** Wisconsin
9 H4 **Stratford St. Mary** England
9 E3 **Stratford upon Avon** England
138 E6 **Strathalbyn** S Australia
15 D5 **Strathaven** Scotland
12 D2 **Strathblane** Scotland
15 D2 **Strath Brora** Scotland
15 D3 **Strath Carron** Scotland
119 R8 **Strathclair** Manitoba
15 D5 **Strathclyde** *reg* Scotland
117 L11 **Strathcona Prov. Park** Br Columbia
15 E3 **Strath Dearn** Scotland
15 D3 **Strath Farrar** Scotland
15 E2 **Strath Halladale** Scotland
141 G3 **Strathleven** Queensland
123 L7 **Strathlorne** Nova Scotia
13 E1 **Strathmiglo** Scotland
118 D7 **Strathmore** Alberta
141 G4 **Strathmore** Queensland
15 E4 **Strathmore** *dist* Scotland
117 M9 **Strathnaver** Br Columbia
15 D3 **Strathpeffer** Scotland
120 J10 **Strathroy** Ontario
15 D2 **Strathy Pt** Scotland
12 D1 **Strathyre** Scotland
106 H2 **Stratton** Colorado
8 B6 **Stratton** England
95 R1 **Stratton** Maine
98 E9 **Stratton** Nebraska
37 O6 **Straubing** W Germany
26 G4 **Straumen** Norway
30 H3 **Strausberg** E Germany
108 A3 **Strauss** New Mexico
37 K1 **Straussfurt** E Germany
101 O3 **Straw** Montana
103 J2 **Strawberry** Nevada
110 E5 **Strawberry** *R* Arkansas
100 G5 **Strawberry Mt** Oregon
99 P7 **Strawberry Pt** Iowa
101 P9 **Strawberry Res** Utah
121 R5 **Strawhat Depot** Quebec
99 S9 **Strawn** Illinois
109 J3 **Strawn** Texas
37 O4 **Stráž** Czechoslovakia
38 M9 **Straze** Yugoslavia
31 K7 **Strážnice** Czechoslovakia
31 M6 **Štrba** Czechoslovakia
138 C5 **Streaky B** S Australia
118 G5 **Streamstown** Alberta
9 F5 **Streatham** England
9 E4 **Streatley** England
99 S8 **Streator** Illinois
31 H6 **Středočeský** *reg* Czechoslovakia
31 L7 **Strêdoslovenský** *reg* Czechoslovakia
8 D5 **Street** England
98 G3 **Streeter** N Dakota
109 H5 **Streeter** Texas
109 L4 **Streetman** Texas
48 H6 **Strehaia** Romania
33 S10 **Strehla** E Germany
143 E9 **Streich Mound** W Australia
37 L4 **Streitberg** W Germany
48 H5 **Streiul** *R* Romania
48 J6 **Strejeştii de Jos** Romania
37 P4 **Střela** *R* Czechoslovakia
54 K5 **Strelitsa** U.S.S.R.
33 S6 **Strelitz-Alt** E Germany
56 D2 **Strelka** U.S.S.R.
28 B5 **Strellev Kirke** Denmark
142 C5 **Strelley** W Australia
142 C5 **Strelley R** W Australia
52 E2 **Strel'na** U.S.S.R.
52 E2 **Strel'na** *R* U.S.S.R.
52 C5 **Strenči** U.S.S.R.
41 M3 **Strengen** Austria
27 C12 **Strengen** Norway
13 G5 **Strensall** England
46 E2 **Strešer** *mt* Yugoslavia
54 B4 **Streshin** U.S.S.R.
9 G3 **Stretham** England
43 G10 **Stretto di Messina** Sicily
9 E1 **Stretton** Derby England
8 D1 **Stretton** England
9 F2 **Stretton** Leicester England
143 C10 **Stretton** W Australia
37 J3 **Streu** *R* W Germany
37 K3 **Streufdorf** E Germany
28 D5 **Strib** Denmark
37 P4 **Stříbro** Czechoslovakia
15 F3 **Strichen** Scotland
120 J3 **Strickland** Ontario
25 C5 **Strijen** Netherlands
109 N4 **Striker Cr.Res** Texas
26 G5 **Strimasund** Sweden
47 F3 **Strimón** *R* Greece
47 F4 **Strimonikós,Kólpos** *gulf* Greece
109 L1 **Stringtown** Oklahoma
12 C2 **Striven,L** Scotland
55 F3 **Strizhovo** U.S.S.R.
48 E5 **Strižívojna** Yugoslavia
38 H6 **Strobl** Austria
46 D7 **Strofádhes** *isld* Greece
32 J7 **Ströhen** W Germany
14 C3 **Strokestown** Irish Rep
26 J10 **Ström** Sweden
33 T6 **Strom** *R* E Germany
15 E2 **Stroma** *isld* Orkney Scotland
32 H9 **Stromberg** Nordrhein-Westfalen W Germany
36 D4 **Stromberg** Rheinland-Pfalz W Germany
43 G10 **Stromboli** *isld* Italy
118 E6 **Strome** Alberta
15 C3 **Stromeferry** Scotland
26 L7 **Strömfors** Sweden
15 E2 **Stromness** Orkney Scotland
28 M2 **Strømø** *isld* Faeroes
98 J8 **Stromsburg** Nebraska
27 E13 **Strömstad** Sweden
26 H8 **Strömsund** Sweden
26 H8 **Stromsvattudal** *L* Sweden
12 D1 **Stronachlachar** Scotland
98 A5 **Stroner** Wyoming
111 D8 **Strong** Arkansas
95 R2 **Strong** Maine
111 H8 **Strong** Mississippi
107 O3 **Strong City** Kansas
107 L6 **Strong City** Oklahoma
118 L7 **Strongfield** Sask
99 Q9 **Stronghurst** Illinois
43 H9 **Strongoli** Italy
94 F5 **Strongsville** Ohio
15 F1 **Stronsay** Scotland
15 F1 **Stronsay Firth** Scotland
9 G5 **Strood** England
31 N6 **Stropkov** Czechoslovakia
112 F3 **Strother** S Carolina
8 D4 **Stroud** England
107 O6 **Stroud** Oklahoma
139 K4 **Stroud Road** New S Wales
95 M6 **Stroudsburg** Pennsylvania
138 F6 **Struan** S Australia
15 E4 **Struan** Scotland
32 G6 **Strücklingen** W Germany
38 L5 **Strudengau** *V* Austria
28 B3 **Struer** Denmark
46 D3 **Struga** Yugoslavia
52 C5 **Strugi Krasnye** U.S.S.R.
14 D2 **Strule** *R* N Ireland
99 P5 **Strum** Wisconsin
47 F3 **Struma** *R* Bulgaria
8 A3 **Strumble Head** Wales
46 F3 **Strumica** Yugoslavia
46 F3 **Strumitsa** *R* Yugoslavia
54 K1 **Strunino** U.S.S.R.
94 G5 **Struthers** Ohio
120 E4 **Struthers** Ontario
89 B10 **Struys B** S Africa
37 P3 **Stružná** Czechoslovakia
47 G2 **Stryama** *R* Bulgaria
101 L1 **Stryker** Montana
94 C5 **Stryker** Ohio
31 M4 **Stryków** Poland
28 F7 **Strynø** Denmark
26 B10 **Strynvatn** *L* Norway
48 H1 **Stryy** U.S.S.R.
31 J5 **Strzegom** Poland
31 L5 **Strzelce** Poland
31 J3 **Strzelce** Poland
138 F3 **Strzelecki Cr** S Australia
140 C5 **Strzelecki, Mt** N Terr Aust
139 J8 **Strzelecki Pk** Tasmania
31 K5 **Strzelin** Poland
31 L3 **Strzelno** Poland
31 N6 **Strzyżów** Poland
113 G10 **Stuart** Florida
99 M8 **Stuart** Iowa
98 G7 **Stuart** Nebraska
109 L1 **Stuart** Oklahoma
94 G10 **Stuart** Virginia
141 K7 **Stuart** *R* Queensland
140 B6 **Stuart Bluff Ra** N Terr Aust
138 D3 **Stuart Creek** S Australia
116 F5 **Stuart I** Alaska
117 L8 **Stuart L** Br Col
100 E2 **Stuart, Mt** Washington
144 A6 **Stuart Mts** New Zealand
140 B1 **Stuart Pt** N Terr Aust
138 C3 **Stuart Rge** S Australia
139 J5 **Stuart Town** New S Wales
41 O3 **Stubaier Alpen** *mt* Austria
41 O3 **Stubai Tal** Austria
38 L7 **Stub Alpe** *mts* Austria
28 J7 **Stubbekøbing** Denmark
32 J6 **Stubben** W Germany
28 B4 **Stubbergd Sø** *L* Denmark
28 F4 **Stubbe Sø** *L* Denmark
83 M9 **Stubbings Pt** Christmas I Indian Oc
41 M3 **Stuben** Austria
38 N7 **Stubenberg** Austria
38 M6 **Stübming** *R* Austria
47 H3 **Studen Kladenets Dam** Bulgaria
38 N7 **Studenzen** Austria
140 B5 **Studholme Hills** N Terr Aust
144 C6 **Studholme Junction** New Zealand
144 C6 **Studholme, Mt** New Zealand
47 G1 **Studina** Romania
9 E6 **Studland** England
28 E6 **Studsgård** Denmark
26 H8 **Stugun** Sweden
36 H5 **Stukenbrock** W Germany
9 G3 **Stump Cross** England
112 M2 **Stumpy Point** N Carolina
33 Q9 **Stumsdorf** E Germany
68 G6 **Stung Sen** *R* Cambodia
68 H6 **Stung Treng** Cambodia
26 N2 **Stuorrajavrre** *L* Norway
117 L9 **Stupendous Mt** Br Columbia
54 K2 **Stupino** U.S.S.R.
40 G7 **Stura** *R* Italy
44 B1 **Stura di Ala** *R* Italy
44 B3 **Stura di Demonte** *R* Italy
44 B1 **Stura di V,Grande** *R* Italy
44 B1 **Stura di Viu** *R* Italy
138 B4 **Sturdee** S Australia
146 K5 **Sturge I** Antarctica
110 D2 **Sturgeon** Missouri
94 C1 **Sturgeon** *R* Michigan
120 K6 **Sturgeon** *R* Ontario
119 U6 **Sturgeon B** Manitoba
94 B1 **Sturgeon B** Michigan
99 T5 **Sturgeon Bay** Wisconsin
99 T5 **Sturgeon Bay Canal** Wisconsin
115 M8 **Sturgeon Falls** Ontario
117 P8 **Sturgeon L** Alberta
121 M8 **Sturgeon L** Ontario
119 Q4 **Sturgeon Landing** Manitoba
118 C5 **Sturgeon R** Alberta
118 L5 **Sturgeon R** Sask
110 J4 **Sturgis** Kentucky
94 B5 **Sturgis** Michigan
111 G8 **Sturgis** Mississippi
109 M2 **Sturgis** Oklahoma
119 P7 **Sturgis** Sask
98 C5 **Sturgis** S Dakota
44 E3 **Sturla** Italy
8 D6 **Sturminster Newton** England
48 E3 **Štúrovo** Czechoslovakia
9 H5 **Sturry** England
138 D6 **Sturt B** S Australia
140 A4 **Sturt Cr** N Terr Aust
136 F5 **Sturt Cr** *R* W Australia
142 G4 **Sturt Creek** W Australia
141 F8 **Sturt Des** Qnsld/S Aust
99 T7 **Sturtevant** Wisconsin
138 F3 **Sturt, Mt** New S Wales
140 C3 **Sturt Plain** N Terr Aust
36 D5 **Stürzelbronn** France
36 E5 **Stutensee** W Germany
89 E9 **Stutterheim** S Africa
111 E7 **Stuttgart** Arkansas
107 L2 **Stuttgart** Kansas
36 G6 **Stuttgart** W Germany
37 K2 **Stützerbach** E Germany
26 H9 **Styggberg** Sweden
130 G6 **Suaçuí Grande, R** Brazil
70 C3 **Suai** Sarawak
86 G2 **Suakin** Sudan
99 T5 **Suamico** Wisconsin
124 E3 **Suaqui** Mexico
128 D2 **Suárez** *R* Colombia
87 D7 **Suarimo** Angola
71 F4 **Suban Pt** Philippines
52 C6 **Subate** U.S.S.R.
45 L4 **Subbiano** Italy
80 F5 **Subeihi** Jordan
69 J11 **Subi** *isld* Indonesia
42 E7 **Subiaco** Italy
142 A1 **Subiaco** *dist* Perth, W Aust
69 J1 **Subi Kecil** *isld* Indonesia
101 M7 **Sublett** Idaho
99 R8 **Sublette** Illinois
107 K4 **Sublette** Kansas
109 L6 **Sublime** Texas
48 F4 **Subotica** Yugoslavia
65 D2 **Subrag** China
110 D4 **Success** Missouri
118 J8 **Success** Sask
44 H3 **Succiso,Alpe di** *mt* Italy
48 F1 **Sucha** Poland
Suchan *see* **Partizansk**
31 J2 **Suchan** Poland
31 H7 **Suchdol** Czechoslovakia
31 M4 **Suchedniów** Poland
Süchow *see* **Xuzhou**
31 O2 **Suchowola** Poland
25 F6 **Süchteln** W Germany
100 C1 **Sucia I** Washington
14 C3 **Suck** *R* Irish Rep
100 H6 **Sucker Cr** Oregon
116 Q7 **Suckling,C** Alaska
33 P6 **Suckow** E Germany
128 E7 **Sucre** Bolivia
126 G10 **Sucre** Colombia
128 G5 **Sucunduri** *R* Brazil
130 D7 **Sucuriu** *R* Brazil
52 E5 **Suda** U.S.S.R.
108 E1 **Sudan** Texas
86 E3 **Sudan** *rep* Africa
52 F5 **Suday** U.S.S.R.
55 B5 **Sud'bodarovka** U.S.S.R.
9 G3 **Sudbury** England
120 J6 **Sudbury** Ontario
141 J5 **Sudbury** Queensland
86 E4 **Sudd** *dist* Sudan
128 G2 **Suddie** Guyana
33 O6 **Sude** *R* E Germany
28 D7 **Süderbrarup** W Germany
33 M7 **Suderburg** W Germany
32 K4 **Süderhastedt** W Germany
32 J4 **Süderhöft** W Germany
28 B7 **Süder Lügum** W Germany
52 E6 **Sudilova** U.S.S.R.
52 F5 **Sudislavl'** U.S.S.R.
32 E9 **Südlohn** W Germany
52 F6 **Sudogda** U.S.S.R.
54 E4 **Sudost'** *R* U.S.S.R.
83 L13 **Sud Ouest, Pte** Mauritius
79 C9 **Sudr** Egypt
54 G5 **Sudzha** U.S.S.R.
59 K3 **Sudzukhe** U.S.S.R.
17 G5 **Sueca** Spain
80 G8 **Su'eida** *R* Jordan
80 F8 **Su'eidat** Jordan
117 G8 **Suemez I** Alaska
108 D6 **Sue Pk** Texas
55 E3 **Suer'** *R* U.S.S.R.
21 H6 **Suèvres** France
84 J3 **Suez** Egypt
79 C8 **Suez Canal** Egypt
84 J4 **Suez,G.of** Egypt
80 G4 **Suf** Jordan
118 F8 **Suffield** Alberta
101 Q2 **Suffolk** Montana
95 L10 **Suffolk** Virginia
9 H3 **Suffolk** *co* England
61 K11 **Suga-jima** *isld* Japan
101 O6 **Sugar** Idaho
99 R7 **Sugar** *R* Wisconsin
106 G3 **Sugar City** Colorado
94 H5 **Sugar Grove** Pennsylvania
94 F10 **Sugar Grove** Virginia
109 M6 **Sugar Land** Texas
132 C2 **Sugarloaf** *mt* Brazil
143 C6 **Sugarloaf Hill** W Australia
113 F13 **Sugarloaf Key** *isld* Florida
139 L4 **Sugarloaf Pt** New S Wales
90 A13 **Sugar Loaf Pt** St Helena
71 G5 **Sugbuhan Pt** Philippines
37 J4 **Sugenheim** W Germany
119 P4 **Suggi L** Sask
69 F12 **Sugi** Indonesia
60 J10 **Sugi** Japan
78 D3 **Suğla Gölü** *L* Turkey
51 P2 **Sugoy** *R* U.S.S.R.
70 E1 **Sugut** *R* Sabah
47 G1 **Suhaia, L** Romania
70 B4 **Suhaid** Kalimantan
77 E7 **Şuḩār** Oman
37 K2 **Suhl** E Germany
42 H3 **Suhopolje** Yugoslavia
40 H3 **Suhr** *R* Switzerland
47 L6 **Suhut** Turkey
74 C4 **Sui** Pakistan
129 H6 **Suiá-Missu** *R* Brazil
100 E1 **Suiattle Pass** Washington
67 F2 **Suichang** China
67 E3 **Suichuan** China
58 F4 **Suide** China
65 H2 **Suifenhe** China
65 H3 **Suifen He** China
74 D6 **Suigam** India
65 G1 **Suihua** China
67 A2 **Suijang** China
67 D5 **Sui Jiang** *R* China
59 J2 **Suileng** China
58 E5 **Suining** China
67 C3 **Suining** China
128 E8 **Suipacha** Bolivia
22 G5 **Suippe** *R* France
14 D4 **Suir** *R* Irish Rep
60 T2 **Suishō tō** *isld* U.S.S.R.
95 L8 **Suitland** Maryland
68 K2 **Suixi** China
65 C7 **Sui Xian** China
67 D1 **Sui Xian** China
67 B2 **Suiyanchang** China
67 B3 **Suiyang** China
40 B2 **Suize** *R* France
59 H3 **Suizhong** China
74 F5 **Sujangarh** India
Suji *see* **Haixing**
70 L9 **Sukabumi** Java
70 K8 **Sukadana** Sumatra
61 O8 **Sukagawa** Japan
70 B6 **Sukamara** Kalimantan
70 L9 **Sukanegara** Java
69 K14 **Sukaraja** Indonesia
70 F2 **Sukau** Sabah
29 N8 **Sukeva** Finland
51 L2 **Sukhana** U.S.S.R.
65 J1 **Sukhanovka** U.S.S.R.
47 H2 **Sukhindol** Bulgaria
54 G2 **Sukhinichi** U.S.S.R.
54 K3 **Sukhodol'skiy** U.S.S.R.
52 F5 **Sukhona** *R* U.S.S.R.
68 D4 **Sukhothai** Thailand
50 E4 **Sukhoy Log** U.S.S.R.
53 F11 **Sukhumi** U.S.S.R.
115 O4 **Sukkertoppen Isflade** Greenland
74 C5 **Sukkur** Pakistan
76 E1 **Sukma** India
70 N9 **Sukoharjo** Java
69 D9 **Sukon,Ko** *isld* Thailand
33 P5 **Sukow** E Germany
87 C10 **Sukses** Namibia
55 C3 **Suksun** U.S.S.R.
60 F13 **Sukumo** Japan
60 F13 **Sukumo-wan** *B* Japan
71 L9 **Sukun** *isld* Indonesia
117 N8 **Sukunka** *R* Br Col
26 F8 **Sul** Norway
101 M4 **Sula** Montana
27 A10 **Sula** *isld* Norway
54 D7 **Sula** *R* U.S.S.R.
125 L2 **Sulaco** Honduras
74 C4 **Sulaiman Range** Pakistan
53 G11 **Sulak** U.S.S.R.
71 J6 **Sula,Kep** *isld* Indonesia
52 F4 **Sulanda** *R* U.S.S.R.
15 B1 **Sula Sgeir** *isld* Scotland
71 G5 **Sulat** Samar Philippines
70 Q10 **Sulat** *isld* Indonesia
116 K4 **Sulatna** Alaska
116 K4 **Sulatna** *R* Alaska
70 **Sulawesi** *isld* Indonesia
70 G7 **Sulawesi Selatan** Sulawesi
71 H4 **Sulawesi Utara** Sulawesi
78 K4 **Sulaymānīyah** Iraq
77 A7 **Şulb, Aş** *plain* Saudi Arabia
27 B12 **Suldal** Norway
27 B12 **Suldalsvatn** Norway
28 D3 **Suldrup** Denmark
31 J3 **Sulechów** Poland
31 J3 **Sulęcin** Poland
77 C1 **Suledeh** Iran
31 M3 **Sulejów** Poland
27 B12 **Suleskar** Norway
15 D1 **Sule Skerry** *isld* Scotland
32 M5 **Sülfeld** W Germany
69 E13 **Suliki** Sumatra
85 B7 **Sulima** Sierra Leone
48 M5 **Sulina** Romania
48 M5 **Sulina** *R* Romania
32 J7 **Sulingen** W Germany
48 K3 **Sulita** Romania
26 H4 **Sulitjelma** Norway
29 N10 **Sulkava** Finland
128 B4 **Sullana** Peru
111 H8 **Sulligent** Alabama
99 S10 **Sullivan** Illinois
110 E3 **Sullivan** Missouri
117 K10 **Sullivan Bay** Br Columbia
118 F6 **Sullivan L** Alberta
21 J6 **Sully** France
99 O8 **Sully** Iowa
20 K6 **Sully-la-Chapelle** France
18 G5 **Sully-sur-Loire** France
38 N8 **Sulm** *R* Austria
42 F6 **Sulmona** Italy
109 O5 **Sulphur** Louisiana
100 G9 **Sulphur** Nevada
109 L1 **Sulphur** Oklahoma
109 N2 **Sulphur** *R* Texas/Louisiana
103 M3 **Sulphurdale** Utah
109 M2 **Sulphur Springs** Texas
108 E3 **Sulphur Springs Cr** Texas
28 D2 **Sulsted** Denmark
120 H5 **Sultan** Ontario
78 C2 **Sultan Dağları** *mts* Turkey
47 J7 **Sultanhisar** Turkey
75 K5 **Sultanpur** India
33 R5 **Sülten** E Germany
71 G5 **Suluan** *isld* Philippines
70 G1 **Sulu Arch** *islds* Philippines
116 K5 **Sulukna** *R* Alaska
84 G3 **Suluq** Libya
55 E4 **Suly** U.S.S.R.
57 E5 **Sulyukta** U.S.S.R.
36 F7 **Sulz** W Germany
38 H7 **Sulzau** Austria
36 H5 **Sulzbach** Baden-Württemberg W Germany
36 C5 **Sulzbach** Saarland W Germany
37 M5 **Sulzbach-Rosenberg** W Germany
41 L2 **Sulzberg** Austria
41 M2 **Sulzberg** W Germany
146 J9 **Sulzberger B** Antarctica
37 L5 **Sulzbürg** W Germany
37 K3 **Sulzdorf** W Germany
32 M7 **Sülze** W Germany
117 C5 **Sulzer, Mt** Alaska
36 F5 **Sulzfeld** W Germany
37 J4 **Sulzheim** W Germany
37 J3 **Sulzthal** W Germany
71 H4 **Sumalata** Sulawesi Indonesia
100 C1 **Sumas** Washington
69 E13 **Sumatera Barat** *prov* Sumatra
69 F14 **Sumatera Selatan** *prov* Sumatra
69 D11 **Sumatera Utara** *prov* Sumatra
113 C7 **Sumatra** Florida
101 S3 **Sumatra** Montana
64 E8 **Sumatra** *isld* Indonesia
128 G5 **Sumaúma** Brazil
71 J9 **Sumba** *isld* Indonesia
70 F4 **Sumbang Teluk** *B* Kalimantan
71 J9 **Sumba,Selat** *str* Indonesia
71 H9 **Sumbawa** *isld* Indonesia
71 H9 **Sumbawa Besar** Indonesia
88 C5 **Sumbawanga** Tanzania
58 E2 **Sümber** Mongolia
70 N9 **Sumbing, G** *mt* Java
69 E13 **Sumbing Gunung** *mt* Sumatra
28 N3 **Sumbø** Faeroes
15 G2 **Sumburgh Hd** Scotland
117 G7 **Sumdum** Alaska
130 H9 **Sumé** Brazil
70 L9 **Sumedang** Java
48 D4 **Sümeg** Hungary
70 O9 **Sumenep** Indonesia
78 M1 **Sumgait** U.S.S.R.
29 M9 **Sumiainen** Finland
40 G3 **Sumiswald** Switzerland
111 J8 **Sumiton** Alabama
55 E3 **Sumki** U.S.S.R.
55 E2 **Sumkino** U.S.S.R.
98 K10 **Summerfield** Kansas
94 F7 **Summerfield** Ohio
108 E1 **Summerfield** Texas
123 S4 **Summerford** Nfld
99 U4 **Summer I** Michigan
15 C2 **Summer I** Scotland
100 E7 **Summer L** Oregon
114 H8 **Summerland** Br Columbia
94 B10 **Summer Shade** Kentucky
123 P4 **Summerside** Nfld
122 J7 **Summerside** Pr Edward I
146 B5 **Summers Pk** Antarctica
110 E4 **Summersville** Missouri
94 G8 **Summersville** W Virginia
112 G4 **Summerton** S Carolina
112 E5 **Summertown** Georgia
112 B3 **Summerville** Georgia
123 T5 **Summerville** Nfld
94 H5 **Summerville** Pennsylvania
112 G4 **Summerville** S Carolina
116 N5 **Summit** Alaska
102 G7 **Summit** California
101 M1 **Summit** Montana
106 B9 **Summit** New Mexico
120 F5 **Summit** Ontario
100 B5 **Summit** Oregon
98 J4 **Summit** S Dakota
103 M4 **Summit** Utah
145 F4 **Summit** *mt* New Zealand
94 B2 **Summit City** Michigan
116 P5 **Summit L** Alaska
100 F8 **Summit L** Nevada
114 G6 **Summit Lake** Br Columbia
102 H2 **Summit Mt** Nevada
106 D4 **Summit Pk** Colorado
106 D4 **Summitville** Colorado
94 B6 **Summitville** Indiana
110 L6 **Summitville** Tennessee
110 J3 **Sumner** Illinois
99 O7 **Sumner** Iowa
110 C2 **Sumner** Missouri
144 B4 **Sumner** New Zealand
144 D5 **Sumner, L** New Zealand
117 G7 **Sumner Str** Alaska
61 N8 **Sumon-dake** *mt* Japan
48 D5 **Sumony** Hungary
60 H11 **Sumoto** Japan
70 F7 **Sumpangbinangae** Sulawesi
31 K6 **Šumperk** Czechoslovakia
100 G5 **Sumpter** Oregon
111 G10 **Sumrall** Mississippi
52 E3 **Sumskiy Posad** U.S.S.R.
112 G4 **Sumter** S Carolina
54 F6 **Sumy** U.S.S.R.
88 C4 **Suna** Tanzania
52 H5 **Suna** U.S.S.R.
60 P2 **Sunagawa** Japan
101 R9 **Sunbeam** Colorado
101 L5 **Sunbeam** Idaho
94 C10 **Sunbright** Tennessee
101 O1 **Sunburst** Montana
95 L10 **Sunbury** N Carolina
94 E6 **Sunbury** Ohio
95 L6 **Sunbury** Pennsylvania
139 G7 **Sunbury** Victoria
37 N6 **Sünching** W Germany
133 E3 **Suncho Corral** Argentina
107 M4 **Sun City** Kansas
95 Q3 **Suncook** New Hampshire
28 N2 **Sund** Faeroes
98 B5 **Sundance** Wyoming
70 D2 **Sundar** Sarawak
75 N8 **Sundarbans** *tidal forest* India/Bangladesh
70 K9 **Sunda,Selat** *str* Sumatra
140 C3 **Sunday Cr** N Terr Aust
143 F7 **Sunday Hill** W Australia
89 D9 **Sundays** *R* S Africa
142 E3 **Sunday Str** W Australia
28 B3 **Sundby** Denmark
27 J12 **Sundbyberg** Sweden
28 M1 **Sundene** *inlet* Faeroes
13 G4 **Sunderland** England
121 L8 **Sunderland** Ontario
32 H10 **Sundern** W Germany
28 D7 **Sundeved** *reg* Denmark
40 F2 **Sundgau** *reg* France
70 N9 **Sundoro, G** *mt* Java
118 E1 **Sundown** Manitoba
138 C2 **Sundown** S Australia
108 E2 **Sundown** Texas
118 C7 **Sundre** Alberta
27 K15 **Sundre** Sweden
121 L7 **Sundridge** Ontario
28 C4 **Sunds** Denmark
26 H8 **Sundsjö** Sweden
27 C12 **Sundsli** Norway
28 C3 **Sundstrup** Denmark
26 J9 **Sundsvall** Sweden
32 G10 **Sundwig** W Germany
94 B4 **Sunfield** Michigan
111 F8 **Sunflower** Mississippi
70 E6 **Sungaianjar** Kalimantan
69 E12 **Sungaiapit** Sumatra
70 B4 **Sungaibatu** Kalimantan
69 E13 **Sungaidareh** Sumatra
69 G14 **Sungaigerong** Sumatra
69 F12 **Sungaiguntung** Sumatra
69 E13 **Sungailimau** Sumatra
70 D5 **Sungaipinang** Kalimantan
69 F13 **Sungaisalak** Sumatra
69 G14 **Sungaiselan** Indonesia
70 E5 **Sungaitiram** Kalimantan
Sungari *R see* **Songhua Jiang**
69 E10 **Sungei Patani** Malaysia
70 F7 **Sungguminasa** Sulawesi
86 E3 **Sungikai** Sudan
103 P10 **Sunglow** Arizona
67 D3 **Sung-pai** China
69 G14 **Sungsang** Sumatra
78 E1 **Sungurlu** Turkey
120 C2 **Suni** Ontario
70 E2 **Suniatan Besar, G** *mt* Sabah
65 C5 **Suning** China
37 P3 **Suniperk** Czechoslovakia
42 H3 **Sunja** Yugoslavia
94 B7 **Sunman** Indiana
26 C9 **Sunndal** *R* Norway
26 C9 **Sunndalsöra** Norway
27 F12 **Sunne** Sweden
27 A10 **Sunnfjord** Norway
27 A12 **Sunnhordland** *reg* Norway
113 F11 **Sunniland** Florida
26 B9 **Sunnmöre** Norway
141 J7 **Sunnybank** Queensland
141 K2 **Sunnybank** *dist* Brisbane, Qnsld
122 K8 **Sunnybrae** Nova Scotia
118 C5 **Sunnybrook** Alberta
26 B9 **Sunnylven** Norway
118 F7 **Sunnynook** Alberta
103 J3 **Sunnyside** Nevada
123 T6 **Sunnyside** Nfld
103 O2 **Sunnyside** Utah
100 E3 **Sunnyside** Washington
99 R6 **Sun Prairie** Wisconsin
108 C7 **Sunray** Texas
116 N6 **Sunrise** Alaska
103 O6 **Sunrise** Arizona
98 B7 **Sunrise** Wyoming
101 O2 **Sun River** Montana
111 D11 **Sunset** Louisiana
109 K2 **Sunset** Texas
102 R11 **Sunset Beach** Hawaiian Is
103 N6 **Sunset Crater Nat.Mon** Arizona
117 P8 **Sunset House** Alberta
103 N6 **Sunshine** Arizona
101 Q5 **Sunshine** Wyoming
118 K1 **Sunstrum** Ontario
51 L2 **Suntar** U.S.S.R.
32 K8 **Süntel** *hills* W Germany
85 D7 **Sunyani** Ghana
37 M7 **Sünzhausen** W Germany
67 B6 **Suoi Rut** Vietnam
29 M9 **Suolahti** Finland
26 N2 **Suolovuobme** Norway
29 N10 **Suomenniemi** Finland
119 O2 **Suomi** Ontario
29 O7 **Suomussalmi** Finland
60 E12 **Suō-nada** *sea* Japan
29 N9 **Suonenjoki** Finland
29 M10 **Suonne** *L* Finland
29 N3 **Suorsapää** *mt* Finland
26 K4 **Suorva** Sweden
52 D4 **Suoyarvi** U.S.S.R.
Suozhen *see* **Huantai**
103 M5 **Supai** Arizona
75 M5 **Supaul** India
128 C6 **Supe** Peru
118 H7 **Superb** Sask
57 D5 **Superfosfatnyy** U.S.S.R.
103 N8 **Superior** Arizona
106 E2 **Superior** Colorado
101 L2 **Superior** Montana
98 J9 **Superior** Nebraska
99 O3 **Superior** Wisconsin
101 R8 **Superior** Wyoming
45 J1 **Superiore,L** Italy
115 L8 **Superior,L** U.S.A./Canada
68 E5 **Suphan Buri** Thailand
78 J2 **Süphan D** *mt* Turkey
45 O6 **Supino** Italy
100 F5 **Suplee** Oregon
54 C7 **Supoy** *R* U.S.S.R.
33 N8 **Süpplingen** W Germany
31 O2 **Supraśl** Poland
71 A1 **Supu** Halmahera Indonesia
48 H3 **Supuru de Jos** Romania
27 H12 **Sura** Sweden
52 G3 **Sura** U.S.S.R.
52 G6 **Sura** *R* U.S.S.R.
74 B4 **Surab** Pakistan
70 O9 **Surabaja** Java
77 F7 **Sūrak** Iran
70 N9 **Surakarta** Java
70 F5 **Suramana** Sulawesi
79 G3 **Sūrān** Syria
40 B5 **Suran** *R* France
48 E2 **Šurany** Czechoslovakia
74 E8 **Surat** India
141 J7 **Surat** Queensland
74 E4 **Suratgarhi** India
69 D8 **Surat Thani** Thailand
31 O3 **Suraż** Poland
52 D6 **Surazh** U.S.S.R.
54 D4 **Surazh** U.S.S.R.
9 F5 **Surbiton** England
141 H6 **Surbiton** Queensland
48 F6 **Surčin** Yugoslavia
78 K4 **Sūrdāsh** Iraq
20 F4 **Surdon** France
48 H3 **Surduc** Romania
46 E2 **Surdulica** Yugoslavia
22 L4 **Sure** *R* Luxembourg
41 K4 **Surettahorn** *mt* Switzerland
102 D7 **Surf** California
95 N7 **Surf City** New Jersey
117 J9 **Surf Inlet** Br Col
18 E6 **Surgères** France
126 C3 **Surgidero de Batabanó** Cuba
50 G2 **Surgut** U.S.S.R.
76 D2 **Suriapet** India
61 N13 **Suribachi-yama** *mt* Japan
71 G6 **Surigao** Mindanao Philippines
71 G5 **Surigao Str** Philippines
21 F9 **Surin** France
68 F5 **Surin** Thailand
129 G2 **Suriname** Suriname
129 G3 **Suriname** *state* S America
99 S4 **Suring** Wisconsin
128 D2 **Suripá** *R* Venezuela
57 D5 **Surkhandar'inskaya Oblast** *prov* U.S.S.R.
77 C4 **Surmāq** Iran
26 C9 **Surnadalsöra** Norway
47 G2 **Sŭrnena Gora** Bulgaria
117 G6 **Surprise** Br Columbia
98 J8 **Surprise** Nebraska
121 Q3 **Surprise,L.de la** Quebec
133 F5 **Sur,Pta** Argentina
112 E6 **Surrency** Georgia
98 E1 **Surrey** N Dakota
9 F5 **Surrey** *co* England
95 L9 **Surry** Virginia
40 H3 **Sursee** Switzerland
20 B3 **Surtainville** France
84 F3 **Surte** Libya
71 N9 **Surubec,Danau** *L* Timor
78 G3 **Suruç** Turkey
61 M11 **Suruga-wan** *B* Japan
69 F14 **Surulangun** Sumatra
71 G7 **Surup** Mindanao Philippines
44 B1 **Susa** Italy
60 E11 **Susa** Japan
28 H6 **Susā** *R* Denmark
42 G6 **Sušac** *isld* Yugoslavia
42 F3 **Sušak** Yugoslavia
60 G12 **Susaki** Japan
60 J12 **Susami** Japan
57 G4 **Susamyr** U.S.S.R.
102 D1 **Susan** *R* California
77 A4 **Sūsangerd** Iran
52 F5 **Susanino** U.S.S.R.
102 D1 **Susanville** California
100 G5 **Susanville** Oregon
78 F1 **Suşehri** Turkey
33 N4 **Süsel** W Germany
37 Q5 **Sušice** Czechoslovakia
80 F2 **Susitha** Syria
116 M6 **Susitna** Alaska
116 O5 **Susitna L** Alaska
69 D9 **Suso** Thailand
61 M10 **Susono** Japan
95 M5 **Susquehanna** Pennsylvania
95 L5 **Susquehanna** *R* Pennsylvania
33 P10 **Süsser See** *L* E Germany
122 G8 **Sussex** New Brunswick
95 N5 **Sussex** New Jersey
101 T6 **Sussex** Wyoming
Sussex *co see* **West and East Sussex** *counties*
25 E6 **Susteren** Netherlands
45 K1 **Sustinente** Italy
117 K7 **Sustut Pk** Br Columbia
70 E2 **Susul** Sabah
116 K5 **Susulatna** *R* Alaska
47 J5 **Susurluk** Turkey
69 D12 **Sut** *mt* Sumatra
100 F10 **Sutcliffe** Nevada
48 L5 **Suţeşti** Romania
99 L7 **Sutherland** Iowa
98 E8 **Sutherland** Nebraska
87 D12 **Sutherland** S Africa
Sutherland *co see* **Highland** *reg*
143 F7 **Sutherland Ra** W Australia
98 E8 **Sutherland Res** Nebraska
144 A6 **Sutherland Sd** New Zealand
100 B6 **Sutherlin** Oregon
74 E3 **Sutlej** *R* Pakistan
102 D3 **Sutter Cr** California
9 F2 **Sutterton** England
9 G3 **Sutton** Cambridge England
9 F5 **Sutton** Greater London England
98 H2 **Sutton** N Dakota
98 J9 **Sutton** Nebraska
144 C6 **Sutton** New Zealand
121 L8 **Sutton** Ontario
121 S7 **Sutton** Quebec
94 G8 **Sutton** W Virginia
121 L5 **Sutton Bay** Ontario
9 E2 **Sutton Coldfield** England
9 E1 **Sutton-in-Ashfield** England
94 G8 **Sutton Res** W Virginia
9 E5 **Sutton Scotney** England
141 H5 **Suttor** *R* Queensland
116 J8 **Sutwik I** Alaska
89 D9 **Suurberge** *mts* S Africa
52 C5 **Suure-Jaani** U.S.S.R.
137 Q5 **Suva** Viti Levu Fiji
46 E1 **Suva Pl** *mt* Yugoslavia
46 D2 **Suva Reka** Yugoslavia
29 N9 **Suvasvesi** *L* Finland
Suvla, C *see* **Büyük Kemikli Br.**
54 H2 **Suvorov** U.S.S.R.
47 J1 **Suvorovo** Bulgaria
48 M5 **Suvorovo** U.S.S.R.
46 D1 **Suvo Rudište** *mt* Yugoslavia
61 M9 **Suwa** Japan
61 M9 **Suwa ko** *L* Japan
31 O1 **Suwałki** Poland
68 F5 **Suwannaphum** Thailand
113 D8 **Suwannee** Florida
119 R2 **Suwannee L** Manitoba
113 E7 **Suwanoochee Cr** Georgia
70 E4 **Suwaran, G** *mt* Kalimantan
80 G2 **Suwaysah** Syria
79 G6 **Suweidiya, Es** Syria
80 F6 **Suweima** Jordan
Suweis,El *see* **Suez**
58 G5 **Su Xian** China
88 A9 **Suye,L** Zambia
55 D1 **Suyevatpaul** U.S.S.R.
57 E3 **Suzak** U.S.S.R.
83 M14 **Suzanne,Pte** Kerguelen Indian Oc
52 F6 **Suzdal'** U.S.S.R.
19 N16 **Suze la Rousse** France
59 H5 **Suzhou** China
40 B3 **Suzon** *R* France
121 T4 **Suzor Côté** Quebec
61 L8 **Suzu** Japan
61 K11 **Suzuka** Japan
61 L8 **Suzu-misaki** *C* Japan
56 B4 **Suzun** U.S.S.R.
45 J2 **Suzzara** Italy
27 H10 **Svabensverk** Sweden
28 H6 **Sværdborg** Denmark
26 P1 **Svaerholtklubben** *C* Norway
26 H9 **Svågan** *R* Sweden
26 H5 **Svaipa** *mt* Sweden
147 H12 **Svalbard** Arctic Oc
28 G5 **Svallerup** Denmark
48 H2 **Svalyava** U.S.S.R.
27 H16 **Svaneke** Denmark
28 E6 **Svanninge** Denmark
27 F12 **Svanskog** Sweden
26 N5 **Svanstein** Sweden
26 R2 **Svanvik** Norway
54 F5 **Svapa** *R* U.S.S.R.
26 M4 **Svappavaara** Sweden
29 K11 **Svartå** Finland
27 G12 **Svartå** Sweden
26 N5 **Svartbyn** Sweden
115 O3 **Svartenhuk Halvö** *pen* Greenland
28 N1 **Svarthakstindur** *mt* Faeroes
26 G5 **Svartisen** *mt* Norway
26 M6 **Svartlå** Sweden
27 H11 **Svartnäs** Sweden
26 M6 **Svartöstaden** Sweden
54 K7 **Svatovo** U.S.S.R.
27 D10 **Svatsum** Norway
68 G7 **Svay Rieng** Cambodia
52 G5 **Svecha** U.S.S.R.
27 F16 **Svedala** Sweden
26 L7 **Svedun** Sweden
26 G9 **Sveg** Sweden
26 A10 **Svelgen** Norway
27 D12 **Svelvik** Norway
52 C6 **Švenčionėliai** U.S.S.R.
28 F6 **Svendborg** Denmark
Svendborg *co see* **Fyn**
27 F14 **Svenljunga** Sweden
146 C4 **Svenner I** Antarctica
27 H12 **Svennevad** Sweden
26 F6 **Svenningdal** Norway
100 B3 **Svensen** Oregon
26 J2 **Svensgrunnen** *shoal* Norway
28 D6 **Svenstrup** Sønderjylland Denmark
50 F3 **Sverdlovsk** U.S.S.R.
50 F3 **Sverdlovskaya Oblast'** *prov* U.S.S.R.
115 K1 **Sverdrup Chan** N W Terr
50 G1 **Sverdrup, Ostrov** *isld* U.S.S.R.
42 G5 **Sveti Andrija** *isld* Yugoslavia
46 E3 **Sveti Nikole** Yugoslavia
31 M1 **Svetloye** U.S.S.R.
51 L3 **Svetlyy** U.S.S.R.
52 C4 **Svetogorsk** U.S.S.R.
46 E1 **Svetozarevo** Yugoslavia
37 P5 **Švihov** Czechoslovakia
48 G6 **Svilajnac** Yugoslavia
47 H3 **Svilengrad** Bulgaria
28 F6 **Svindinge** Denmark
28 G5 **Svinninge** Denmark
28 O9 **Svinø** Faeroes
Svinoy *isld see* **Svinø**
52 D4 **Svir'** *R* U.S.S.R.

Sviritsa — Tarija 75

52 D4 Sviritsa U.S.S.R.
56 F4 Svirsk U.S.S.R.
52 D4 Svir'stroy U.S.S.R.
47 G1 Svishtov Bulgaria
53 C7 Svisloch' R U.S.S.R.
31 J6 Svitavy Czechoslovakia
52 G6 Sviyaga R U.S.S.R.
51 M3 Svobodnyy U.S.S.R.
28 J5 Svogerslev Denmark
37 O4 Svojšín Czechoslovakia
26 G3 Svolvaer Norway
31 J6 Svratka R Czechoslovakia
46 E1 Svrljig Yugoslavia
46 E1 Svrljiške Pl mt Yugoslavia
52 F5 Svyatogor'ye U.S.S.R.
52 E1 Svyatoy Nos, Mys C U.S.S.R.
52 D4 Svyatozero U.S.S.R.
68 C3 Swa R Burma
9 G2 Swaffham England
141 K5 Swain Reefs Gt Barrier Reef Aust
112 E5 Swainsboro Georgia
134 B4 Swains I Pacific Oc
81 E16 Swain's I S Pacific Oc
87 B10 Swakopmund S Africa
9 G5 Swale,R England
137 O4 Swallow Is Santa Cruz Is
70 C1 Swallow Reef S China Sea
106 F3 Swallows Colorado
118 D7 Swalwell Alberta
9 E6 Swanage England
142 A2 Swanbourne Beach dist Perth, W Aust
139 G6 Swan Hill Victoria
118 B4 Swan Hills Alberta
139 J8 Swan Is Tasmania
126 C6 Swan Is W Indies
117 J8 Swan, L Br Columbia
98 G4 Swan L S Dakota
103 M2 Swan L Utah
119 T9 Swan Lake Manitoba
101 M2 Swan Lake Montana
112 E2 Swannanoa N Carolina
119 Q6 Swan Plain Sask
142 E3 Swan Pt W Australia
112 L2 Swanquarter N Carolina
118 B3 Swan R Alberta
143 B9 Swan R W Australia
138 E5 Swan Reach S Australia
114 J7 Swan River Manitoba
99 N2 Swan River Minnesota
112 K3 Swansboro N Carolina
103 L7 Swansea Arizona
139 K5 Swansea New S Wales
112 F4 Swansea S Carolina
139 J8 Swansea Tasmania
8 C4 Swansea Wales
95 T2 Swans I Maine
118 K7 Swanson Sask
117 J9 Swanson Bay Br Col
98 E9 Swanson Res Nebraska
98 J9 Swanton Nebraska
94 D5 Swanton Ohio
121 R8 Swanton Vermont
33 S4 Swantow E Germany
139 K5 Swan Vale New S Wales
101 O6 Swan Valley Idaho
99 M4 Swanville Minnesota
89 A10 Swartberg mt S Africa
103 L2 Swasey Pk Utah
120 K4 Swastika Ontario
81 H9 S. W. Australian Ridge Indian Oc
89 G6 Swaziland kingdom Africa
99 M6 Swea City Iowa
26 Sweden kingdom W Europe
95 M7 Swedesboro New Jersey
85 D7 Swedru Ghana
12 C2 Sween, L Scotland
109 M6 Sweeny Texas
140 E3 Sweers I Queensland
100 J6 Sweet Idaho
101 O1 Sweetgrass Montana
111 D7 Sweet Home Arkansas
100 C5 Sweet Home Oregon
109 L6 Sweet Home Texas
110 C3 Sweet Springs Missouri
107 L6 Sweetwater Oklahoma
112 C2 Sweet Water Tennessee
108 G3 Sweetwater Texas
101 R7 Sweetwater R Wyoming
87 D12 Swellendam S Africa
108 G2 Swenson Texas
31 J5 Świdnica Poland
31 J2 Świdwin Poland
31 H3 Świebodzin Poland
31 L2 Świecie Poland
116 K6 Swift R Alaska
95 R2 Swift R Maine
123 S6 Swift Current Nfld
118 K8 Swiftcurrent Sask
116 L5 Swift Fork R Alaska
110 E6 Swifton Arkansas
100 C3 Swift Res Washington
117 H5 Swift River Yukon Terr
100 A1 Swiftsure Bank Lightship Br Col
14 D1 Swilly,L Irish Rep
8 C5 Swimbridge England
9 E4 Swindon England
Swinemünde see Swinoujście
9 F2 Swineshead England
14 C3 Swinford Irish Rep
106 G3 Swink Colorado
31 H2 Swinoujście Poland
13 F2 Swinton Scotland
40 F4 Switzerland rep Europe
15 E2 Swona isld Orkney Scotland
14 E3 Swords Irish Rep
141 F5 Swords Ra Queensland
52 D4 Syamozero, Oz L U.S.S.R.
52 F4 Syamzha U.S.S.R.
52 D5 Syas' R U.S.S.R.
52 G5 Syava U.S.S.R.
98 A6 Sybille Cr Wyoming
14 A4 Sybil Pt Irish Rep
111 K8 Sycamore Alabama
99 S8 Sycamore Illinois
94 D6 Sycamore Ohio
112 F4 Sycamore S Carolina
52 D6 Sychevka U.S.S.R.
31 K4 Syców Poland
56 D4 Syda R U.S.S.R.
121 O8 Sydenham Ontario
28 N3 Sydero isld Faeroes
9 G2 Syderstone England
28 O9 Sydhritangi C Faeroes
114 J8 Sydney Montana
139 K5 Sydney New S Wales
123 M7 Sydney Nova Scotia
134 K9 Sydney I Phoenix Is Pacific Oc
140 E3 Sydney I Queensland
123 M7 Sydney Mines Nova Scotia
115 P5 Sydproven Greenland
32 J7 Syke W Germany
98 G2 Sykeston N Dakota
94 J5 Sykesville Pennsylvania
52 H4 Syktyvkar U.S.S.R.
111 K8 Sylacauga Alabama
110 D6 Sylamore Arkansas
26 F8 Sylene mt Norway
75 O6 Sylhet Bangladesh
28 A7 Sylt isld W Germany
26 B9 Sylte Norway
26 E1 Sylterfjord inlet Norway
112 D2 Sylva N Carolina
55 C3 Sylva U.S.S.R.
94 J7 Sylvan Pennsylvania
107 M2 Sylvan Grove Kansas
112 F5 Sylvania Georgia
94 D5 Sylvania Ohio
119 N6 Sylvania Sask
143 D6 Sylvania W Australia
118 C6 Sylvan Lake Alberta
101 P5 Sylvan Pass Wyoming
112 D6 Sylvester Georgia
140 D4 Sylvester, L N Terr Aust
123 R5 Sylvester,Mt Nfld
107 M4 Sylvia Kansas
117 L6 Sylvia,Mt Br Col
56 C1 Sym R U.S.S.R.
15 E5 Symington Scotland
124 H5 Symon Mexico
8 D4 Symonds Yat England
71 F4 Syndicate Philippines
142 F3 Synnott Ra W Australia
56 H3 Synnyr, Khrebet mts U.S.S.R.
54 N2 Syntul U.S.S.R.
55 E1 Syn'yakha R U.S.S.R.
56 C4 Synzas U.S.S.R.
48 L3 Synzhereya U.S.S.R.
94 B5 Syracuse Indiana
Syracuse Italy see Siracusa
107 J3 Syracuse Kansas
98 K9 Syracuse Nebraska
121 O9 Syracuse New York
101 N8 Syracuse Utah
57 E4 Syrdarinsk. Obl U.S.S.R.
57 E4 Syrdar'ya U.S.S.R.
57 D3 Syrdar'ya R U.S.S.R.
57 D4 Syr Dar'ya Oblast' prov U.S.S.R.
79 G4 Syria rep S W Asia
68 C4 Syriam Burma
Syrian Desert see Badiet esh Sham
55 E1 Syrkovoye, Oz L U.S.S.R.
28 G2 Syr Odde C Denmark
54 L4 Syrskiy U.S.S.R.
55 D3 Sysert' U.S.S.R.
95 T1 Sysladobsis L Maine
52 H4 Sysola R U.S.S.R.
9 E2 Syston England
52 D6 Syt'kovo U.S.S.R.
55 F1 Sytomino U.S.S.R.
52 F4 Syuma R U.S.S.R.
52 H6 Syumsi U.S.S.R.
52 H6 Syun' R U.S.S.R.
47 F3 Syutkya mt Bulgaria
53 G7 Syzran' U.S.S.R.
48 E4 Szabadszállás Hungary
48 G2 Szabolcsszatmár co Hungary
31 L4 Szadek Poland
31 K2 Szamocin Poland
48 G2 Szamosszeg Hungary
31 K3 Szamotuły Poland
48 D3 Szany Hungary
48 F4 Szarvas Hungary
31 O5 Szczebrzeszyn Poland
31 H2 Szczecin Poland
31 K2 Szczecinek Poland
31 M5 Szczekociny Poland
31 L4 Szczerców Poland
31 N5 Szczucin Poland
31 N2 Szczuczyn Poland
31 M2 Szczytno Poland
Szechwan prov see Sichuan
48 F2 Szécsény Hungary
48 F4 Szeged Hungary
48 G3 Szeghalom Hungary
48 E3 Székesfehérvár Hungary
48 F2 Szendrö Hungary
48 E3 Szentendre Hungary
48 F4 Szentes Hungary
48 C4 Szentgotthárd Hungary
48 D4 Szentlörinc Hungary
48 G2 Szerencs Hungary
48 D3 Szigetköz dist Hungary
48 D4 Szigetvár Hungary
48 F2 Szikszó Hungary
31 N2 Szkwa R Poland
31 J4 Szlichtyngowa Poland
48 E3 Szob Hungary
48 F3 Szolnok Hungary
48 D3 Szombathely Hungary
31 J4 Szprotawa Poland
31 K2 Szreńsk Poland
31 M2 Sztum Poland
31 K2 Szubin Poland
31 M4 Szydłowiec Poland
71 E3 Taal,L Luzon Philippines
48 E4 Tab Hungary
71 F4 Tabaco Philippines
128 F4 Tabajara Brazil
70 P16 Tabanan Bali Indonesia
85 E5 Tabankort Mali
89 F8 Tabankulu S Africa
127 O2 Tabaquite Trinidad
137 L2 Tabar Is Bismarck Arch
43 B12 Tabarka Tunisia
77 E3 Tabas Iran
77 G3 Tabas Iran
124 H7 Tabasco Mexico
125 N8 Tabasco state Mexico
52 G6 Tabashino U.S.S.R.
123 N3 Tabatière,La Quebec
128 E4 Tabatinga Brazil
68 B1 Tabayin Burma
71 E2 Tabayoa, Mt Philippines
143 F7 Tabbe Pan W Australia
68 G6 Tabeng Cambodia
118 E9 Taber Alberta
27 G14 Taberg Sweden
17 F7 Tabernas Spain
17 G5 Tabernes de Valldigna Spain
16 D10 Taberrant Morocco
17 G9 Tabia Algeria
101 P9 Tabiona Utah
69 F13 Tabir R Sumatra
71 F4 Tablas isld Philippines
131 B3 Tablas,C Chile
71 E4 Tablas Strait Philippines
89 A9 Table B S Africa
139 H8 Table C Tasmania
145 G3 Table Cape New Zealand
71 D6 Table Hd Philippines
144 A7 Table Hill New Zealand
68 A6 Table I Andaman Is
68 H2 Table,I.de la Vietnam
142 F3 Tableland W Australia
116 Q2 Table Mt Alaska
87 C12 Table Mt S Africa
71 D5 Table Pt Philippines
83 L14 Table Pt.de la Réunion Indian Oc
108 F2 Table Rock Wyoming
110 C5 Table Rock Res Missouri
141 G4 Tabletop, Mt Queensland
130 C6 Taboco,R Brazil
31 H6 Tábor Czechoslovakia
99 L9 Tabor Iowa
98 J7 Tabor S Dakota
51 P1 Tabor U.S.S.R.
88 D4 Tabora Tanzania
88 D4 Tabora reg Tanzania
112 J3 Tabor City N Carolina
79 F7 Tabor, Mt Israel
118 E9 Tabor Prov. Park Alberta
55 D2 Tabory U.S.S.R.
85 C8 Tabou Ivory Coast
77 B1 Tabriz Iran
68 G2 Ta Bu Vietnam
72 D3 Tabūk Saudi Arabia
60 E12 Tabuka Japan
139 L3 Tabulam New S Wales
129 G5 Tabuleiro Brazil
55 G4 Tabuny U.S.S.R.
45 R7 Taburno, M mt Italy
122 G6 Tabusintac R New Brunswick
69 D12 Tabuyung Sumatra
88 B6 Tabwe Zambia
27 K12 Täby Sweden
130 H10 Tacaratú Brazil
67 C2 Tacheng China
66 C4 Ta-chia Taiwan
60 C13 Tachibana-wan B Japan
61 N10 Tachikawa Japan
128 D2 Táchira state Venezuela
37 O4 Tachov Czechoslovakia
139 L4 Tacking Pt New S Wales
71 G5 Tacloban Philippines
103 K9 Tacna Arizona
133 C1 Tacna Peru
20 J4 Tacoignières France
117 M12 Tacoma Washington
133 E3 Tacó Pozo Argentina
128 E7 Tacora mt Chile
130 E7 Tacquaritinga Brazil
130 B10 Tacuaras Paraguay
131 G3 Tacuarembó Uruguay
131 G3 Tacuari,R Uruguay
130 C8 Tacuati Paraguay
124 E3 Tacupeto Mexico
61 N8 Tadami R Japan
13 G6 Tadcaster England
85 F4 Tadeinte watercourse Algeria
85 E3 Tademait,Pl.du Algeria
85 B5 Tadjakant Mauritania
85 E3 Tadjmout Algeria
86 H3 Tadjoura Djibouti
9 E3 Tadmarton England
145 D4 Tadmor New Zealand
60 Q2 Tadoshi Japan
60 G11 Tadotsu Japan
122 C5 Tadoussac Quebec
76 D3 Tadpatri India
57 E5 Tadzhikistan S.S.R U.S.S.R.
65 F6 Taech'ŏngdo isld S Korea
65 G5 Taedong R N Korea
65 G7 Taegu S Korea
65 F7 Taehūksan isld S Korea
65 G6 Taejon S Korea
28 J7 Tæro isld Denmark
137 S5 Tafahi isld Pacific Oc
17 F2 Tafalla Spain
85 F4 Tafasaset watercourse Algeria
126 A1 Tafelberg mt Curaçao
8 C4 Taff,R Wales
79 F8 Tafila Jordan
85 C7 Tafiré Ivory Coast
26 B9 Tafjord Norway
17 F9 Tafna R Algeria
106 F5 Tafoya New Mexico
85 C3 Tafraoute Morocco
102 E6 Taft California
107 P6 Taft Oklahoma
109 K8 Taft Texas
77 G5 Taftan, Kūh-e- mt Iran
95 P5 Taftville Connecticut
69 A9 Tafwap Nicobar Is
75 N5 Tag Bhutan
77 L2 Tagab Afghanistan
116 H4 Tagagawik R Alaska
143 E10 Tagan Harb W Australia
53 E10 Taganrog U.S.S.R.
54 K9 Taganrogskiy Zaliv gulf U.S.S.R.
71 E3 Tagaytay City Philippines
71 F6 Tagbilaran Philippines
85 D2 Taghit Algeria
117 F6 Tagish L Br Col
45 O5 Tagliacozzo Italy
42 E2 Tagliamento R Italy
45 M1 Taglio di Po Italy
22 G5 Tagnon France
71 F6 Tagolo Pt Philippines
26 J8 Tågsjöberg Sweden
48 J4 Tagu Romania
129 J6 Taguatinga Brazil
71 F5 Tagubanhan isld Philippines
61 L11 Taguchi Japan
71 E2 Tagudin Philippines
85 A4 Taguersimet Morocco
137 L4 Tagula isld Louisiade Arch
98 E1 Tagus N Dakota
Tagus R Portugal see Tejo R
Tagus R Spain see Tajo R
144 B7 Tahakopa New Zealand
73 R8 Tahan, Gunung Malaysia
61 L11 Tahara Japan
85 F4 Tahat mt Algeria
145 D1 Taheke New Zealand
77 C6 Tāheri Iran
117 G6 Tahi R Br Col
135 M10 Tahiti isld Pacific Oc
110 B6 Tahlequah Oklahoma
117 H6 Tahltan Br Col
102 D2 Tahoe City California
102 D2 Tahoe L California
114 J4 Tahoe L N W Terr
102 D3 Tahoe Valley California
108 F2 Tahoka Texas
100 A2 Taholah Washington
145 E3 Tahora New Zealand
145 F4 Tahoraiti New Zealand
85 F6 Tahoua Niger
99 V3 Tahquamenon Falls Michigan
59 H2 Ta-hsing-an Ling China
59 H2 Ta Hsing-an-Ling Shan-mo ra China
117 K11 Tahsis Br Columbia
57 F6 Ta Hsü isld Taiwan
84 J4 Tahta Egypt
47 L8 Tahtali Dağ mt Turkey
117 K9 Tahtsa R Br Col
128 D6 Tahuamanu R Peru
145 E2 Tahuna New Zealand
85 C7 Tai Ivory Coast
65 C6 Tai'an China
65 E4 Tai'an China
67 F2 Taibai China
106 F7 Taiban New Mexico
17 F6 Taibilla,Sa de mts Spain
67 G1 Taicang China
67 G4 T'ai-chung Taiwan
144 C6 Taieri airport New Zealand
Taigong see Taijiang
65 B6 Taigu China
65 B6 Taihang Shan mt ra China
65 B7 Taihang Shan ra China
145 E3 Taihape New Zealand
67 E3 Taihe China
61 Q12 Taiho Okinawa
67 E1 Taihu China
67 G1 Tai Hu L China
67 C3 Taijiang China
Taijiang see Dorbod
67 F5 Taikang China
65 F2 Taikang China
60 R3 Taiki Japan
68 B4 Taikkyi Burma
59 H2 Tailai China
69 D13 Taileleo Indonesia
138 E6 Tailem Bend S Australia
36 G7 Tailfingen W Germany
20 E4 Taillebois France
19 P14 Taillefer mt France
20 C5 Taillis France
15 D3 Tain Scotland
46 E8 Taínaron, Akr C Greece
67 F3 Taining China
19 N14 Tain l'Hermitage France
67 G5 T'ain-nan Taiwan
130 G4 Taiobeiras Brazil
29 O9 Taipale Finland
29 N10 Taipalsaari Finland
67 G4 T'ai-pei Taiwan
67 B5 Taiping China
67 C5 Taiping China
67 F1 Taiping China
69 E10 Taiping Malaysia
59 H3 Taipingchuan China
65 G3 Taipingchuan China
65 F4 Taipingshao China
130 J8 Taipu Brazil
61 O8 Taira Japan
61 Q12 Taira Okinawa
60 O4 Tairadate kaikyō Japan
145 E2 Tairua New Zealand
60 N3 Taisei Japan
60 Q2 Taisetsuzan Nat.Park Japan
60 F10 Taisha Japan
67 D5 Taishan China
67 F3 Taishun China
133 C7 Taitao, Pen. de Chile
65 D4 Taitouying China
52 C2 Taivalkoski Finland
27 M11 Taivassalo Finland
67 G5 Taiwan rep E Asia
67 G1 Tai Xian China
67 G1 Taixing China
46 E7 Ta'iyetos mt Greece
80 D4 Taiyiba Israel
80 E3 Taiyiba Israel
80 F3 Taiyiba R Jordan
65 B6 Taiyuan China
65 B6 Taiyue Shan mt China
Taizhao see Linhai
67 G1 Taizhou China
67 G2 Taizhou Wan B China
65 F4 Taizi He R China
72 E6 Ta'izz N Yemen
86 H3 Ta'izz Yemen
84 E5 Tajarhi Libya
84 G5 Taj, At Libya
43 B13 Tajerouine Tunisia
61 N8 Tajima Japan
61 L10 Tajimi Japan
106 D7 Tajique New Mexico
124 C2 Tajito Mexico
16 E4 Tajo R Spain
70 N9 Taju Java
17 F4 Tajuna R Spain
68 D4 Tak Thailand
61 M8 Takada Japan
61 P7 Takagi Japan
61 O9 Takahagi Japan
61 J10 Takahama Japan
60 G11 Takahashi Japan
61 O8 Takahata Japan
60 E13 Takajō Japan
145 D4 Takaka New Zealand
46 E7 Taka, L Greece
83 K12 Takamaka Mahé I Indian Oc
60 H11 Takamatsu Japan
60 E13 Takamori Japan
60 O5 Takanosu Japan
52 H6 Takanysh U.S.S.R.
61 K9 Takaoka Japan
145 F4 Takapau New Zealand
145 F1 Takapuna New Zealand
60 H11 Takasago Japan
59 L4 Takasaki Japan
60 C12 Taka shima isld Saga Japan
60 E11 Taka shima isld Shimane Japan
61 J11 Takatsuki Japan
145 E2 Takatu Pt. New Zealand
88 G3 Takaungu Kenya
68 D2 Ta-Kaw Burma
60 D12 Takawa Japan
61 L9 Takayama Japan
60 E14 Takazaki Japan
69 F9 Tak Bai Thailand
60 E13 Takeda Japan
61 K10 Takefu Japan
60 F11 Takehara Japan
9 G4 Takeley England
68 G7 Takeo Cambodia
60 D12 Takeo Japan
60 C11 Takeshiki Japan
Take-shima see Tok-do
77 A1 Takestān Iran
60 E12 Taketazu Japan
71 C3 Takeum W Irian
78 K7 Takhadid Iraq
77 L1 Takhār reg Afghanistan
57 A4 Takhiatash U.S.S.R.
117 F5 Takhini R Yukon Terr
57 A4 Takhta U.S.S.R.
57 C6 Takhta-Bazar U.S.S.R.
55 E4 Takhtabrod U.S.S.R.
57 B3 Takhtakupyr U.S.S.R.
77 C5 Takht-e Jamshīd Iran
114 H4 Takijug L N W Terr
60 Q2 Takikawa Japan
100 B7 Takilma Oregon
69 C10 Takingeun Sumatra
60 R1 Takinoue Japan
119 R3 Takipy Manitoba
144 A6 Takitimu Mts New Zealand
86 G3 Takkaze R Ethiopia
117 L8 Takla Landing Br Col
Takla Makan see Taklimakan Shamo
66 B4 Taklimakan Shamo reg China
57 E5 Takob U.S.S.R.
85 D8 Takoradi Ghana
116 J5 Takotna Alaska
145 D1 Takou B New Zealand
116 F6 Takslesluk L Alaska
117 G6 Taku Br Col
117 F5 Taku Arm L Br Col/Yukon Terr
69 D8 Takua Thung Thailand
117 F6 Taku Glacier Br Col/Alaska
85 F7 Takum Nigeria
74 E2 Talagang Pakistan
133 D6 Talagapa Argentina
68 H7 Ta Lai Vietnam
83 J8 Talaimannar Sri Lanka
85 F5 Talak reg Niger
73 R8 Talakmau mt Sumatra
107 P5 Talala Oklahoma
16 E10 Talamagait Morocco
69 F14 Talang Akar Sumatra
70 K8 Talangbatu Sumatra
69 G14 Talangbetutu Sumatra
69 G14 Talang Djimar Sumatra
69 G14 Talangrimbo Sumatra
128 B4 Talara Peru
77 H7 Talar-i-Band mts Pakistan
57 F3 Talas U.S.S.R.
136 L3 Talasea New Britain
57 F4 Talasskiy Alatau, Khr mts U.S.S.R.
70 G5 Talatakoh isld Sulawesi
79 G4 Talat Mūsa mt Lebanon
16 D5 Talavera de la Reina Spain
130 C10 Talavera,I Paraguay
140 F4 Talawanta Queensland
71 G7 Talayan Philippines
65 G3 Talazhan China
143 E9 Talbot W Australia
142 F2 Talbot, C W Australia
113 F7 Talbot I Florida
115 M2 Talbot Inlet N W Terr
119 S4 Talbot L Manitoba
143 F7 Talbot, Mt W Australia
139 J4 Talbragar New S Wales
131 B5 Talca Chile
131 B5 Talca prov Chile
131 A6 Talcahuano Chile
131 B4 Talca,Pta Chile
109 M2 Talco Texas
94 G9 Talcott W Virginia
52 E6 Taldom U.S.S.R.
141 F4 Taldora Queensland
57 A3 Taldyk U.S.S.R.
57 J3 Taldy-Kurgan U.S.S.R.
77 B4 Tal-e Khosravī Iran
100 C7 Talent Oregon
8 C2 Talerddig Wales
8 C4 Talgarth Wales
76 B3 Talgupka India
138 C5 Talia S Australia
71 G5 Talibon Bohol Philippines
110 A7 Talihina Oklahoma
76 C2 Talikota India
71 G7 Talikua isld Mindanao Philippines
86 F4 Tali Post Sudan
71 F5 Talisay Cebu Philippines
71 G6 Talisayan Philippines
71 J4 Talisei isld Indonesia
55 D1 Talitsa Sverdlovsk U.S.S.R.
55 D3 Talitsa Sverdlovsk U.S.S.R.
54 M4 Talitskiy Chamlyk U.S.S.R.
33 N5 Talkau W Germany
116 N5 Talkeetna Mts Alaska
79 B7 Talkha Egypt
29 N3 Talkkunapää mt Finland
77 B3 Talkuncheh Iran
45 L4 Talla Italy
84 G5 Tallāb,At Libya
111 K8 Talladega Alabama
111 G10 Tallahala R Mississippi
111 M11 Tallahassee Florida
111 F7 Tallahatchie R Mississippi
139 H6 Tallangatta Victoria
111 L8 Tallapoosa Georgia
111 K9 Tallapoosa R Alabama
19 Q16 Tallard France
26 H10 Tallåsen Sweden
111 L9 Tallassee Alabama
143 B8 Tallering Pk W Australia
8 C4 Talley Wales
52 B5 Tallinn U.S.S.R.
26 M5 Talljäry Sweden
40 D6 Talloires France
14 C4 Tallow Irish Rep
119 P6 Tall Pines Sask
110 G2 Tallula Illinois
111 E9 Tallulah Louisiana
102 A2 Talmage California
107 N2 Talmage Kansas
99 L9 Talmage Nebraska
119 O9 Talmage Sask
40 B3 Talmay France
56 B4 Tal'menka U.S.S.R.
80 B7 Talmey Yafe Israel
18 D6 Talmont France
21 B9 Talmont France
74 F8 Taloda India
86 F3 Talodi Sudan
107 M5 Taloga Oklahoma
70 F4 Talok Kalimantan
68 D2 Ta-Long Burma
106 E5 Talpa New Mexico
108 H4 Talpa Texas
124 G7 Talpa de Allende Mexico
127 O2 Talparo R Trinidad
111 M11 Talquin,L Florida
80 C6 Tal Shahar Israel
52 B6 Talsi U.S.S.R.
26 L7 Tålsmark Sweden
133 C3 Taltal Chile
69 D12 Talu Sumatra
71 H4 Taludaä Sulawesi
71 E8 Talue isld Philippines
69 E13 Taluk Sumatra
68 G3 Ta Lus,C Vietnam
41 O4 Talvera R Italy
26 N1 Talvik Norway
141 J8 Talwood Queensland
139 G4 Talyawalka R New S Wales
8 C3 Talybont Wales
8 C1 Tal-y-cafn Wales
52 J3 Talyy U.S.S.R.
99 O8 Tama Iowa
61 M9 Tama Japan
61 N10 Tama R Japan
70 D3 Tamabo Ra Sarawak
68 B1 Tamadaw Burma
143 A7 Tamala W Australia
85 D7 Tamale Ghana
70 F6 Tamalea Sulawesi
16 C4 Tamames Spain
60 D13 Tamana Japan
130 J10 Tamandare Brazil
60 G11 Tamano Japan
85 F4 Tamanrasset Algeria
70 G5 Tamanusi Sulawesi
95 M6 Tamaqua Pennsylvania
45 L2 Tamara Italy
100 J5 Tamarack Idaho
99 N3 Tamarack Minnesota
60 E13 Tamarai Japan
17 H3 Tamarite de Litera Spain
110 G3 Tamaroa Illinois
41 J5 Tamaro,Mt Switzerland
8 B6 Tamar,R England
139 H8 Tamar R Tasmania
60 G11 Tamashima Japan
48 E4 Tamási Hungary
Tamatave see Toamasina
61 O9 Tamatsukuri Japan
128 D5 Tamaya R Peru
124 F5 Tamazula Mexico
124 H8 Tamazula de Gordiano Mexico
125 K7 Tamazunchale Mexiço
37 K2 Tambach Dietharz E Germany
85 B6 Tambacounda Senegal
70 D3 Tambalan Kalimantan
88 E10 Tambara Mozambique
130 J9 També Brazil
70 G7 Tambea Sulawesi
69 H12 Tambelan isld Indonesia
143 C10 Tambellup W Australia
87 E9 Tambero Zambia
131 B2 Tambillos,Nevado de los peak Chile
141 H6 Tambo Queensland
128 D7 Tambo R Peru
128 C6 Tambo de Mora Peru
71 G6 Tambog Pt Mindanao Philippines
71 K8 Tambolongang isld Indonesia
124 G5 Tambor Mexico
139 H6 Tamboritha,Mt Victoria
53 F7 Tambov U.S.S.R.
16 B2 Tambre,R Spain
142 C5 Tambrey W Australia
70 F5 Tambu Sulawesi
70 E2 Tambunan Sabah
86 E4 Tambura Sudan
70 F4 Tambu, Tk B Sulawesi
83 K9 Tambutta Sri Lanka
70 E1 Tambuyukon, G mt Sabah
58 B2 Tamch Mongolia
85 B5 Tamchakett Mauritania
55 C6 Tamdy U.S.S.R.
57 C4 Tamdybulak U.S.S.R.
57 C4 Tamdytau, Gory mt U.S.S.R.
128 D2 Tame Colombia
16 B3 Tâmega R Portugal
133 C7 Tamel Aike Argentina
85 F5 Tamgak, Mts Niger
57 E2 Tamgaly, Ozero L U.S.S.R.
125 L7 Tamiahua,L.de Mexico
113 F12 Tamiami Canal Florida
69 C10 Tamiang R Sumatra
76 C5 Tamil Nadu prov India
41 K4 Tamina R Switzerland
84 G3 Tamīnī,At Libya
41 K4 Tamins Switzerland
58 D2 Tamirin Gol R Mongolia
48 F5 Tamis R Yugoslavia
52 E3 Tamitsa U.S.S.R.
57 C1 Tamkamys U.S.S.R.
68 J5 Tam Ky Vietnam
71 F5 Tamlang Negros Philippines
45 R7 Tammaro R Italy
Tammerfors see Tampere
110 G4 Tamms Illinois
113 E10 Tampa Florida
107 N3 Tampa Kansas
70 K8 Tampang Sumatra
29 K10 Tampere Finland
99 R8 Tampico Illinois
125 L6 Tampico Mexico
101 T1 Tampico Montana
69 F11 Tampin Malaysia
68 J5 Tam Quam Vietnam
80 D2 Tamra Israel
58 G2 Tamsagbulag Mongolia
75 Q6 Tamu Burma
71 E7 Tamuk isld Philippines
9 E2 Tamworth England
95 Q3 Tamworth New Hampshire
139 K4 Tamworth New S Wales
121 O8 Tamworth Ontario
68 F6 Tamyong R Cambodia
57 H1 Tan U.S.S.R.
137 O5 Tana isld New Hebrides
116 Q6 Tana R Alaska
60 J12 Tanabe Japan
130 E7 Tanabi Brazil
116 Q5 Tanacross Alaska
116 Q5 Tanada L Alaska
26 Q1 Tanafjord inlet Norway
43 G8 Tanagro R Italy
61 O8 Tanagura Japan
69 D13 Tanahbala isld Indonesia
69 D12 Tanahbatu Sumatra
71 K8 Tanahdjampea isld Indonesia
70 E5 Tanahgrogot Kalimantan
73 Q9 Tanahmasa isld Indonesia
70 E3 Tanahmerah Kalimantan
69 F9 Tanah Merah Malaysia
26 R1 Tanahorn mt Norway
69 E12 Tanahputih Sumatra
70 M9 Tanah,Tg C Java
70 F7 Tanakeke isld Sulawesi
26 Q1 Tana Kirke Norway
86 G3 Tana, L Ethiopia
136 J3 Tanamerah W Irian
140 A4 Tanami N Terr Aust
68 H7 Tan An Vietnam
116 L4 Tanana Alaska
116 N4 Tanana R Alaska
Tananarive see Antananarivo
18 H8 Tanargue, Mt France
44 E2 Tanaro R Italy
84 E4 Tanārūt Libya
71 G5 Tanauan Leyte Philippines
141 F7 Tanbar Queensland
20 F3 Tancarville France
61 P13 Tancha Okinawa
65 D7 Tancheng China
59 J3 Tanch'ŏn N Korea
124 H8 Tancitario,Cerro de mt Mexico
125 K7 Tancuayalab Mexico
75 K5 Tanda India
71 G6 Tandag Mindanao Philippines
86 H3 Tandaho Ethiopia
48 L6 Țăndărei Romania
28 D6 Tanderup Denmark
131 F6 Tandil Argentina
131 F6 Tandil, Sa del ra Argentina
70 D6 Tandjung Kalimantan
70 E4 Tandjungbatu Kalimantan
70 F3 Tandjungbatu Kalimantan
70 F4 Tandjungbuajabuaja isld Kalimantan
70 K8 Tandjungkarang Sumatra
70 L9 Tandjungpriok Java
70 C5 Tandjungpusu Kalimantan
70 E3 Tandjungselor Kalimantan
70 B5 Tandjungwaringin Kalimantan
74 C6 Tando Adam Pakistan
74 C6 Tando Muhammad Khan Pakistan
138 F4 Tandou L New S Wales
55 G3 Tandovo, Oz L U.S.S.R.
14 E2 Tandragee N Ireland
27 G10 Tandsjöborg Sweden
28 D7 Tandslet Denmark
71 E8 Tandubatu isld Philippines
76 C2 Tandur India
145 F3 Taneatua New Zealand
59 K5 Tanega-shima isld Japan
61 P5 Taneichi Japan
Tanen mt see Taunggyi mt
70 F7 Tanete Sulawesi
71 A3 Taneti Halmahera Indonesia
31 O5 Tanew R Poland
95 K7 Taneytown Maryland
85 E4 Tanezrouft reg Algeria
85 G3 Tanezzuft watercourse Libya/Algeria
88 G4 Tanga Tanzania
75 N6 Tangail Bangladesh
137 L2 Tanga Is Bismarck Arch
83 K11 Tangalla Sri Lanka
Tanganyika see Tanzania
88 B5 Tanganyika,L E Africa
130 D10 Tangará Brazil
67 D3 Tangdukou China
28 D4 Tange Å R Denmark
16 D9 Tanger Morocco
33 P8 Tangerhütte E Germany
33 P7 Tangermünde E Germany
28 D4 Tange Sø L Denmark
58 G4 Tanggu China
66 D5 Tanggula Shan ra China
66 E5 Tanggula Shankou pass China
58 F5 Tang He China
65 C5 Tang He R China
Tangier see Tanger Morocco
122 K9 Tangier Nova Scotia
122 K9 Tangier Grand L Nova Scotia
95 M9 Tangier I Virginia
145 E4 Tangimoana New Zealand
111 F11 Tangipahoa R Louisiana
70 E3 Tangjungredeb Kalimantan
70 C5 Tangkahan Kalimantan
70 G6 Tangkeleboke, G mt Sulawesi
70 L9 Tangkuban Perahu mt Java
109 L5 Tanglewood Texas
Tanglha Range see Tanggula Shan
66 F5 Tangmai China
141 G5 Tangorin Queensland
145 D1 Tangowahine New Zealand
67 C6 Tangpeng China
66 D5 Tangra Yumco L China
69 B10 Tangse Sumatra
65 D5 Tangshan China
67 A3 Tangtang China
67 C3 Tangtou China
67 E5 Tangtouxia China
71 F5 Tangub Negros Philippines
85 E6 Tanguiéta Benin
59 J2 Tangwanghe China
67 F2 Tangxi China
65 C5 Tang Xian China
67 D1 Tangxianzhen China
68 D1 Tang-Yan Burma
67 C2 Tangyan He R China
65 C6 Tangyi China
65 H1 Tangyuan China
29 N4 Tanhua Finland
68 G7 Tani Cambodia
61 K10 Tanigumi Japan
40 E5 Taninges France
60 D14 Taniyama Japan
71 F6 Tanjay Philippines
70 L9 Tanjerang Java
69 F12 Tanjungbalai Kepulauan Riau Indonesia
69 D11 Tanjungbalai Sumatra
69 J11 Tanjung Blitung Indonesia
70 K7 Tanjungenim Sumatra
69 F14 Tanjung Luntar Sumatra
69 E11 Tanjungmengidan Sumatra
69 H14 Tanjung-pandan Indonesia
69 G12 Tanjungpinang Indonesia
69 D11 Tanjungpura Sumatra
69 G14 Tanjungraja Sumatra
69 H14 Tanjungrusa Indonesia
69 J13 Tanjungsaleh Indonesia
74 D2 Tank Pakistan
138 E3 Tankamarinna,L S Australia
29 N3 Tankapirtti Finland
108 G4 Tankersly Texas
56 G5 Tankhoy U.S.S.R.
55 D2 Tankovichi U.S.S.R.
68 B3 Tanlwe R Burma
68 J7 Tan My Vietnam
37 O7 Tann Bayern W Germany
37 J2 Tann Hessen W Germany
37 M3 Tanna E Germany
15 F4 Tannadice Scotland
22 H4 Tannay France
33 N9 Tanne E Germany
Tannenberg see Stębark
95 N4 Tannersville New York
95 M5 Tannersville Pennsylvania
37 N4 Tännesberg W Germany
37 J6 Tannhausen W Germany
41 M1 Tannheim W Germany
29 M6 Tannila Finland
119 N1 Tannin Ontario
80 C3 Tanninim Israel
28 E1 Tannis Bugt B Denmark
28 E1 Tannisby Denmark
37 L2 Tannroda E Germany
85 D7 Tano R Ghana
71 F5 Tañon Str Philippines
85 F6 Tanout Niger
103 P9 Tanque Arizona
124 H4 Tanque Alvarez Mexico
125 K7 Tanquian Mexico
75 K5 Tansing Nepal
79 A8 Tanta Egypt
68 B1 Tantabin Sagaing Burma
68 C3 Tantabin Tenasserim Burma
119 Q8 Tantallon Sask
85 B3 Tan-Tan Morocco
138 F6 Tantanoola S Australia
Tantung see Dandong
140 C3 Tanumbirini N Terr Aust
116 E6 Tanunak Alaska
138 E5 Tanunda S Australia
55 C3 Tanyp R U.S.S.R.
88 C4 Tanzania rep Africa
117 H6 Tanzilla R Br Col
65 E2 Tao'an China
67 G2 Taohua Dao isld China
Taohuaping see Longhui
67 D2 Taojiang China
68 D7 Tao,Ko isld Thailand
87 H13 Taolañaro Madagascar
65 D7 Taoluo China
Taonan see Tao'an
99 O6 Taopi Minnesota
43 G11 Taormina Sicily
106 E5 Taos New Mexico
85 D4 Taoudenni Mali
85 D2 Taourirt Morocco
85 D2 Taouz Morocco
67 D2 Taoyuan China
55 E3 Tap R U.S.S.R.
52 C5 Tapa U.S.S.R.
71 E8 Tapaan Passage Philippines
125 N10 Tapachula Mexico
69 E10 Tapah Malaysia
129 G5 Tapajós R Brazil
69 D11 Tapakkuda Sumatra
69 C11 Tapaktuan Sumatra
70 F6 Tapalang Sulawesi
133 E5 Tapalquén Argentina
69 E14 Tapan Sumatra
129 G3 Tapanahoni R Suriname
125 M9 Tapanatapec Mexico
144 B6 Tapanui New Zealand
128 F5 Tapauá Brazil
145 D4 Tapawera New Zealand
130 H9 Taperoá Brazil
131 H3 Tapes, Pta. de C Brazil
37 K6 Tapfheim W Germany
71 F7 Tapiantana isld Philippines
128 D5 Tapiche R Peru
29 L11 Tapiola Finland
128 E3 Tapirapeó, Sa mts Venezuela/Brazil
130 B4 Tapirapuã Brazil
69 F10 Tapis mt Malaysia
124 E4 Tapizuelas Mexico
75 M5 Taplejung Nepal
48 D4 Tapolca Hungary
68 D2 Ta-Pom Burma
95 L9 Tappahannock Virginia
94 F6 Tappan Res Ohio
98 G3 Tappen N Dakota
28 J6 Tappernøje Denmark
60 O4 Tappi zaki C Japan
60 P1 Tappu Japan
28 C6 Taps Denmark
55 D1 Tapsuy R U.S.S.R.
74 F8 Tapti R India
145 E2 Tapu New Zealand
145 D4 Tapuaenuku mt New Zealand
71 E8 Tapul Philippines
68 B3 Tapun Burma
128 F4 Tapurucuara Brazil
133 G3 Taquara Brazil
130 D7 Taquaraçu R Brazil
130 D4 Taquara,Sa.da mts Brazil
131 H2 Taquari R Brazil
130 C6 Taquari,Pantanal do swamp Brazil
112 K2 Tar R N Carolina
120 J8 Tara Ontario
141 K7 Tara Queensland
50 G3 Tara U.S.S.R.
71 E4 Tara isld Philippines
48 E7 Tara mt Yugoslavia
50 G3 Tara R U.S.S.R.
85 G7 Taraba R Nigeria
Tarābulus see Tripoli Libya
128 E3 Taracua Brazil
145 F3 Taradale New Zealand
139 J6 Tarago New S Wales
14 E3 Tara Hill Irish Rep
26 L5 Tårajaure Sweden
70 E3 Tarakan Kalimantan
60 D13 Taraki Japan
77 K3 Tarakki reg Afghanistan
47 L4 Taraklı Turkey
48 M4 Tarakliya U.S.S.R.
145 D4 Tarakohe New Zealand
139 J5 Taralga New S Wales
144 C5 Taramakau R New Zealand
71 M9 Taramana Indonesia
139 J5 Tarana New S Wales
145 E3 Taranaki stat area New Zealand
16 E4 Tarancón Spain
145 E1 Taranga I New Zealand
15 A3 Taransay isld Scotland
43 H8 Taranto Italy
43 H8 Taranto,G.di Italy
128 E7 Tarapacá prov Chile
145 F3 Taraponui mt New Zealand
128 C5 Tarapoto Peru
18 H7 Tarare France
145 E4 Tararua Range New Zealand
19 N17 Tarascon France
48 N1 Tarashcha U.S.S.R.
41 M4 Tarasp Switzerland
85 F3 Tarat Algeria
69 E12 Taratalbuluh Sumatra
17 F4 Taravilla Spain
145 F3 Tarawera New Zealand
145 F3 Tarawera, Mt New Zealand
17 F3 Tarazona Spain
17 F5 Tarazona de la Mancha Spain
28 K5 Tårbæk Denmark
57 K2 Tarbagatay, Khrebet mts U.S.S.R.
15 B3 Tarbert Harris Scotland
14 B4 Tarbert Irish Rep
12 C2 Tarbert Strathclyde Scotland
12 B2 Tarbert,L Scotland
18 F9 Tarbes France
12 D3 Tarbolton Scotland
112 K2 Tarboro N Carolina
141 F5 Tarbrax Queensland
48 K4 Tarcaului,Munţii mts Romania
141 F7 Tarco Queensland
138 C4 Tarcoola S Australia
139 H4 Tarcoon New S Wales
138 C2 Tarcoonyinna R S Australia
139 J6 Tarcutta New S Wales
18 E9 Tardets-Sorholus France
17 G3 Tardienta Spain
21 G10 Tardoire R France
143 B8 Tardun W Australia
139 L4 Taree New S Wales
139 G4 Tarella New S Wales
26 N4 Tärendö Sweden
40 E7 Tarentaise dist France
94 H6 Tarentum Pennsylvania
85 B3 Tarfaya Morocco
65 F1 Targan China
48 H6 Târgu Carbuneşti Romania
16 E10 Targuist Morocco
48 H3 Târgu Lăpus Romania
112 J3 Tarheel N Carolina
84 E3 Tarhūnah Libya
65 A4 Tarian Gol China
16 D8 Tarifa Spain
71 F2 Tarigtig Pt Philippines
133 E2 Tarija Bolivia
133 E2 Tarija prov Bolivia

99 N6 Thompson Iowa
119 U3 Thompson Manitoba
99 U4 Thompson Michigan
98 J2 Thompson N Dakota
95 M5 Thompson Pennsylvania
103 P3 Thompson Utah
117 N10 Thompson R Br Col
110 C1 Thompson R Missouri
100 K2 Thompson Falls Montana
142 B3 Thompson L W Australia
117 R4 Thompson Lake N W Terr
114 H5 Thompson Landing N W Terr
140 B6 Thompson, Mt N Terr Aust
138 B1 Thompson, Mt N Terr Australia
116 P6 Thompson Pass Alaska
109 M6 Thompsons Texas
144 A6 Thompson Sd New Zealand
Thompson's Falls see Nyahururu Falls
95 P4 Thompsonville Connecticut
99 V5 Thompsonville Michigan
99 Q8 Thomson Illinois
141 G6 Thomson R Queensland
143 B6 Thomson, Mt W Australia
144 B6 Thomson Mts New Zealand
68 E6 Thon Buri Thailand
40 D6 Thônes France
68 C4 Thongwa Burma
40 D5 Thonon France
21 G6 Thore France
18 G9 Thoré R France
106 B6 Thoreau New Mexico
21 F6 Thorée France
40 D5 Thorens les Glières France
Thorez see Torez
118 D4 Thorhild Alberta
141 G8 Thorlindah, L Queensland
13 G4 Thornaby England
9 H2 Thornage England
94 B4 Thornapple R Michigan
94 K8 Thornburg Virginia
8 D4 Thornbury England
144 B7 Thornbury New Zealand
120 K8 Thornbury Ontario
109 K5 Thorndale Texas
13 H6 Thorne England
102 F3 Thorne Nevada
9 F2 Thorney England
12 D1 Thornhill Central Scotland
12 E3 Thornhill Dumfries & Galloway Scotland
121 L9 Thornhill Ontario
109 P2 Thornton Arkansas
99 N7 Thornton Iowa
13 E1 Thornton Scotland
109 L4 Thornton Texas
100 H2 Thornton Washington
141 F4 Thorntonia Queensland
110 K1 Thorntown Indiana
121 L9 Thorold Ontario
Thorout see Torhout
100 E2 Thorp Washington
99 Q5 Thorp Wisconsin
145 D4 Thorpe New Zealand
9 H3 Thorpeness England
28 E4 Thorsager Denmark
118 C5 Thorsby Alberta
28 N2 Thorshavn Faeroes
146 A7 Thorshavnfjella Antarctica
28 D4 Thorsø Denmark
119 U1 Thorsteinson L Manitoba
146 G8 Thorvald Nilsen Mts Antarctica
8 C6 Thorverton England
68 G7 Thot Not Vietnam
21 E8 Thouars France
142 C5 Thouin Pt W Australia
46 E7 Thouría Greece
21 C6 Thourie France
22 D5 Thourotte France
95 L2 Thousand Is Ontario/New York
103 N3 Thousand Lake Mt Utah
101 L8 Thousand Spring Cr Nevada
101 L7 Thousand Springs Idaho
47 H3 Thrace Turkey
109 K5 Thrall Texas
100 E3 Thrall Washington
9 F3 Thrapston England
139 J6 Thredbo New S Wales
8 C3 Three Cocks Wales
101 K7 Three Creek Idaho
101 O4 Three Forks Montana
118 D7 Three Hills Alberta
139 G8 Three Hummock I Tasmania
110 J5 Three I.Res Tennessee
9 F2 Threekingham England
137 O8 Three Kings Basin Pacific Oc
145 D1 Three Kings Is New Zealand
140 D3 Three Knobs mt N Terr Aust
99 R4 Three Lakes Wisconsin
141 G2 Three Mile Opening, First & Second straits Gt Barrier Reef Aust
99 U8 Three Oaks Michigan
68 D5 Three Pagodas Pass Burma/Thailand
119 T3 Threepoint L Manitoba
85 D8 Three Points, C Ghana
102 F5 Three Rivers California
94 B5 Three Rivers Michigan
106 D8 Three Rivers New Mexico
109 J7 Three Rivers Texas
123 N5 Three Rock Cove Nfld
141 G1 Three Sisters islds Queensland
100 D5 Three Sisters mts Oregon
143 B8 Three Springs W Australia
13 E4 Threlkeld England
109 H2 Throckmorton Texas
68 F5 Throm Cambodia
143 E8 Throssell, L W Australia
143 E7 Throssell, Mt W Australia
142 D5 Throssel Ra W Australia
68 J5 Thu Bon R Vietnam
139 J5 Thuddungra New S Wales
18 H8 Thueyte France
40 E6 Thuile, la Italy
22 G3 Thuin Belgium
115 N2 Thule Greenland
146 A13 Thule I Antarctica
37 O2 Thum E Germany
101 P5 Thumb Wyoming
144 C5 Thumbs, The mt New Zealand
40 G4 Thun Switzerland
141 G7 Thunda Queensland
119 O2 Thunder Ontario
94 D2 Thunder B Michigan
99 R1 Thunder Bay Ontario
98 D4 Thunder Butte Cr S Dakota
120 G2 Thunderhouse Falls Ontario
126 D6 Thunder Knoll Caribbean
118 C4 Thunder L. Prov. Park Alberta
116 G2 Thunder Mt Alaska
36 H4 Thüngen W Germany
69 D8 Thung Maphrao Thailand
69 D8 Thung Song Thailand
69 D9 Thung Wa Thailand
75 O5 Thunkar Bhutan
40 B4 Thurey France
33 R5 Thürikow E Germany
41 L3 Thüringen Austria
37 J2 Thüringer Wald mts E Germany
19 N13 Thurins France
14 D4 Thurles Irish Rep
8 C7 Thurlestone England
139 G3 Thurloo Downs New S Wales
101 T3 Thurlow Montana
37 L3 Thurnau W Germany
28 F6 Thurø Denmark
13 E4 Thursby England
141 F1 Thursday I Queensland
121 P7 Thurso Quebec
15 E2 Thurso Scotland
15 E2 Thurso R Scotland
20 E4 Thury-Harcourt France
117 K7 Thutade L Br Col
28 A3 Thy reg Denmark
141 G7 Thylungra Queensland
87 G9 Thyolo Malawi
139 K4 Tia New S Wales
127 J9 Tía Juana Venezuela
65 G3 Tianboashan China
67 B5 Tiandeng China
67 B5 Tiandong China
67 B4 Tian'e China
67 C4 Tianhe China
65 D5 Tian in China
67 D1 Tianmen China
65 H3 Tianqiaoling China
Tianshan see Ar Horquin Qi
65 G1 Tiansheng China
58 E5 Tianshui China
67 G2 Tiantai China
67 B5 Tianyang China
Tianyi see Ningcheng
Tianzhen see Gaoqing
65 C4 Tianzhen China
67 C3 Tianzhu China
134 C11 Tiarei Tahiti I Pac Oc
85 E1 Tiaret Algeria
141 L7 Tiaro Queensland
85 D7 Tiassalé Ivory Coast
130 E9 Tibagi Brazil
86 B4 Tibati Cameroon
Tiber R see Tevere R
80 F2 Tiberias Israel
80 F2 Tiberias, L Israel
101 O1 Tiber Res Montana
86 C1 Tibesti reg Chad
84 F5 Tibesti, Sarir Libya
Tibet aut reg see Xizang Zizhiqu
66 C5 Tibet aut reg China
121 N4 Tiblemont Quebec
48 J3 Tiblesului Muntii Romania
138 F3 Tibooburra New S Wales
75 K4 Tibrikot Nepal
124 C3 Tiburón isld Mexico
71 F4 Ticao isld Philippines
9 G5 Ticehurst England
121 O8 Tichborne Ontario
85 C5 Tichitt Mauritania
85 B4 Tichla Mauritania
41 J5 Ticino canton Switzerland
44 E1 Ticino R Italy
13 G6 Tickhill England
9 E2 Ticknall England
95 O3 Ticonderoga New York
27 G13 Tidaholm Sweden
122 F6 Tide Hd New Brunswick
118 F8 Tide L Alberta
69 A9 Tiden Nicobar Is
100 B5 Tidewater Oregon
85 E3 Tidikelt reg Algeria
94 H5 Tidioute Pennsylvania
85 B5 Tidjikja Mauritania
138 E2 Tidna Hill S Australia
122 H8 Tidnish Nova Scotia
44 F2 Tidone R Italy
71 A2 Tidore Halmahera Indonesia
85 A5 Tidra, I Mauritania
9 E5 Tidworth England
85 C7 Tiébissou Ivory Coast
33 T7 Tiefensee E Germany
36 C6 Tieffenbach France
116 P6 Tiekel Alaska
25 D5 Tiel Netherlands
65 G1 Tieli China
65 F3 Tieling China
22 E1 Tielt Belgium
85 C7 Tiéme Ivory Coast
22 H2 Tienen Belgium
66 C3 Tien Shan ra China/U.S.S.R.
Tientsin see Tianjin
67 B6 Tien Yen Vietnam
89 D9 Tier Berg mt S Africa
27 J11 Tierp Sweden
106 D5 Tierra New Mexico
125 L8 Tierra Blanca Mexico
133 D8 Tierra del Fuego, I.Grande de Arg/Chile
101 U8 Tie Siding Wyoming
16 D4 Tiétar R Spain
130 F8 Tietê Brazil
130 E7 Tietê R Brazil
138 B2 Tietkens, Mt S Australia
100 E3 Tieton Washington
100 D3 Tieton Res Washington
138 C2 Tieyon S Australia
45 Q7 Tifata, M mt Italy
100 F1 Tiffany Mt Washington
86 G4 Tiffi Ethiopia
99 P8 Tiffin Iowa
94 D5 Tiffin Ohio
17 H10 Tiffrit Algeria
16 E9 Tifriste Morocco
112 D6 Tifton Georgia
70 D2 Tiga isld Sabah
116 E9 Tigalda I Aleutian Is
100 C4 Tigard Oregon
100 H1 Tiger Washington
112 F3 Tiger R S Carolina
99 R5 Tigerton Wisconsin
15 C5 Tighnabruaich Scotland
86 H5 Tigieglo Somalia
51 P3 Tigil U.S.S.R.
56 B5 Tigiretskiy Khrebet mts U.S.S.R.
112 E4 Tignall Georgia
86 B4 Tigneré Cameroon
42 A3 Tignes, Bge. de France
122 H7 Tignish Pr Edward I
128 C4 Tigre R Peru
127 N10 Tigre R Venezuela
125 K6 Tigre, Cerro del mt Mexico
131 B3 Tigre, Sa ra Argentina
78 J4 Tigris R Iraq
57 A3 Tigrovyy Khvost, Mys C U.S.S.R.
85 F3 Tiguentourine Algeria
86 C2 Tigui Chad
16 D9 Tiguisas Morocco
21 J6 Tigy France
79 D9 Tîh, Gebel el plat Egypt
145 E3 Tihoi New Zealand
28 B4 Tihøje hill Denmark
70 G6 Tiinampuu Sulawesi
106 D6 Tijeras New Mexico
124 A1 Tijuana Mexico
130 E10 Tijucas Brazil
122 G3 Tika Quebec
125 P9 Tikal anc site Guatemala
74 H6 Tikamgarh India
116 H6 Tikchik L Alaska
53 F10 Tikhoretsk U.S.S.R.
52 D5 Tikhvin U.S.S.R.
145 G2 Tikitiki New Zealand
145 F3 Tikokino New Zealand
137 O4 Tikopia isld Santa Cruz Is
78 J4 Tikrit Iraq
52 D3 Tiksha U.S.S.R.
52 D2 Tikshozero, Oz L U.S.S.R.
51 M1 Tiksi U.S.S.R.
71 H4 Tilamuta Sulawesi
141 H8 Tilbooroo Queensland
25 D5 Tilburg Netherlands
9 G5 Tilbury England
120 H10 Tilbury Ontario
133 D2 Tilcara Argentina
138 F3 Tilcha S Australia
110 G3 Tilden Illinois
98 J7 Tilden Nebraska
109 J7 Tilden Texas
48 G3 Tileagd Romania
85 D3 Tilemsï el Fasi Algeria
85 E5 Tilemsi, Vallée du Mali
98 C5 Tilford S Dakota
74 H5 Tilhar India
51 Q2 Tilichiki U.S.S.R.
68 B2 Tilin Burma
85 E6 Tillabéri Niger
100 B4 Tillamook Oregon
100 A4 Tillamook Rock Oregon
69 A8 Tillanchong I Nicobar Is
20 J5 Tillay-le-Peneux France
27 J12 Tillberga Sweden
40 B3 Tille R France
112 G2 Tillery, L N Carolina
118 F8 Tilley Alberta
85 E5 Tillia Niger
12 E1 Tillicoultry Scotland
20 H4 Tillières-sur-Avre France
28 G7 Tillitse Denmark
112 F5 Tillman S Carolina
113 L11 Tilloo Cay isld Bahamas
13 G2 Till, R England
120 K10 Tillsonburg Ontario
21 H9 Tilly France
20 D3 Tilly-sur-Seulles France
71 M9 Tilomar Timor
47 J8 Tílos isld Greece
139 G4 Tilpa New S Wales
85 E2 Tilrhemt Algeria
9 E5 Tilshead England
119 Q9 Tilston Manitoba
123 S4 Tilting Nfld
110 J1 Tilton Illinois
95 Q3 Tilton New Hampshire
70 G5 Tily mt Sulawesi
28 A4 Tim Denmark
54 J5 Tim U.S.S.R.
121 L5 Timagami Ontario
52 G2 Timanskiy Kryazh ra U.S.S.R.
144 C6 Timaru New Zealand
47 G9 Timbákion Crete Greece
111 F12 Timbalier I Louisiana
70 F2 Timbang isld Sabah
130 J9 Timbaúba Brazil
85 C5 Timbédra Mauritania
100 B4 Timber Oregon
140 B3 Timber Creek N Terr Aust
98 E4 Timber L S Dakota
112 J1 Timberlake N Carolina
102 H4 Timber Mt Nevada
139 G7 Timboon Victoria
130 E10 Timbo, R Brazil
Timbuktu see Tombouctou
70 F2 Timbun Mata Sabah
85 F3 Timellouline Algeria
85 D5 Timetrine Mts Mali
46 D5 Tímfi, Óros mt Greece
46 E6 Timfristós mt Greece
85 F5 Timia Niger
85 E3 Timimoun Algeria
Timiris, C see Mirik, C
56 B3 Timiryazevskiy U.S.S.R.
121 L5 Timiskaming, L Quebec
48 G5 Timişoara Romania
48 G5 Timişul R Romania
55 D1 Timkapaul' U.S.S.R.
33 N5 Timmendorfer Strand W Germany
27 G13 Timmersdala Sweden
85 F5 Timmersoi watercourse Niger
120 J4 Timmins Ontario
112 H3 Timmonsville S Carolina
46 E1 Timok R Yugoslavia
129 K5 Timon Brazil
71 M9 Timor isld E Indies
136 E4 Timor Trough Timor Sea
52 E4 Timoshino U.S.S.R.
133 E5 Timote Argentina
127 J10 Timotes Venezuela
70 D5 Timpah Kalimantan
103 J4 Timpahute Ra Nevada
101 O9 Timpanogos Cave Nat. Mon Utah
143 E7 Timperley Ra W Australia
101 N9 Timpie Utah
109 N4 Timpson Texas
26 J9 Timrå Sweden
28 B4 Timring Denmark
112 A2 Tims Ford L Tennessee
52 H4 Timsher U.S.S.R.
57 E3 Timur U.S.S.R.
70 O9 Timur, Jawa prov Java
144 D5 Timutimu Headland New Zealand
89 F8 Tina R S Africa
71 G8 Tinaca Pt Mindanao Philippines
127 K10 Tinaco Venezuela
71 F3 Tinaga isld Philippines
71 G5 Tinago Leyte Philippines
14 E4 Tinahely Irish Rep
124 J5 Tinaja Mexico
137 O4 Tinakula isld Santa Cruz Is
85 G4 Tin Alkoum Algeria
70 F6 Tinambung Sulawesi
127 K10 Tinaquillo Venezuela
48 G4 Tinca Romania
20 D4 Tinchebray France
22 C3 Tincques France
100 K7 Tindall Idaho
76 D4 Tindivanam India
70 K9 Tindjil isld Java
85 C3 Tindouf Algeria
28 N2 Tindur mt Faeroes
86 D2 Tine Sudan
85 E4 Tinef Algeria
102 F4 Tinemaha Res California
16 C1 Tineo Spain
85 C3 Tinfouchy Algeria
85 F3 Tin Fouye Algeria
141 L1 Tingalpa dist Brisbane, Qnsld
69 G11 Tinggi isld Malaysia
139 K3 Tingha New S Wales
75 K4 Tingjegaon Nepal
28 C7 Tinglev Denmark
99 M9 Tingley Iowa
115 P5 Tingmiarmiut Greenland
128 C5 Tingo María Peru
67 C3 Tingping China
85 C6 Tingrela Ivory Coast
66 D6 Tingri China
67 E2 Tingsiqiao China
27 G15 Tingsryd Sweden
133 D4 Tinguiririca mt Chile/Arg
26 C9 Tingvoll Norway
121 T7 Tingwick Quebec
Tingzhou see Changting
129 L6 Tinharé, I.de Brazil
67 B7 Tinh Gia Vietnam
145 F3 Tiniroto New Zealand
70 D3 Tinjar R Sarawak
144 D5 Tinline, Mt New Zealand
27 C11 Tinn Norway
141 H8 Tinnenburra Queensland
27 D12 Tinnoset Norway
27 D12 Tinnsjö L Norway
44 G3 Tino, I.di Italy
70 G4 Tinombo Sulawesi
69 E14 Tinopo isld Indonesia
47 G7 Tínos isld Greece
85 E4 Ti-n Rerhoh Algeria
111 D8 Tinsman Arkansas
142 C5 Tinstane, Mt W Australia
75 Q5 Tinsukia India
8 B6 Tintagel England
98 K3 Tintah Minnesota
85 F4 Tin Tarabine watercourse Algeria
20 B5 Tinténiac France
8 D4 Tintern England
22 K4 Tintigny Belgium
133 E3 Tintina Argentina
138 F6 Tintinara S Australia
16 C7 Tinto R Spain
15 E5 Tinto, Mt Scotland
145 F4 Tinui New Zealand
144 C5 Tinwald New Zealand
85 E4 Tin Zaouaten Algeria
111 D10 Tioga Louisiana
98 D1 Tioga N Dakota
95 K5 Tioga Pennsylvania
109 L2 Tioga Texas
94 G8 Tioga W Virginia
69 G11 Tioman isld Malaysia
120 H4 Tionaga Ontario
41 N5 Tione Italy
42 D2 Tione di Trento Italy
100 D8 Tionesta California
94 H5 Tionesta Pennsylvania
71 H7 Tioro Indonesia
71 C3 Tipin W Irian
94 A5 Tippecanoe Indiana
99 U9 Tippecanoe R Indiana
14 C4 Tipperary Irish Rep
14 D4 Tipperary co Irish Rep
111 F8 Tippo Mississippi
102 E5 Tipton California
110 K1 Tipton Indiana
107 M2 Tipton Kansas
110 D3 Tipton Missouri
109 H1 Tipton Oklahoma
103 K6 Tipton, Mt Arizona
110 G5 Tiptonville Tennessee
120 D4 Tip Top Hill Ontario
9 G4 Tiptree England
76 C4 Tiptur India
128 E3 Tiquié R Brazil
80 C5 Tira Israel
129 J4 Tiracambu, Sa.do mts Brazil
79 E11 Tirān isld Saudi Arabia
46 D3 Tiranë Albania
41 M5 Tirano Italy
83 K9 Tirappane Sri Lanka
53 C10 Tiraspol' U.S.S.R.
80 C2 Tirat Karmel Israel
80 F4 Tirat Zevi Israel
145 E2 Tirau New Zealand
145 F4 Tiraumea New Zealand
47 J6 Tire Turkey
78 G1 Tirebolu Turkey
15 B4 Tiree isld Scotland
48 J6 Tîrgovişte Romania
48 L3 Tîrgu Frumos Romania
48 H5 Tîrgu Jiu Romania
48 J4 Tîrgu Mures Romania
48 K3 Tîrgu Neamt Romania
48 K4 Tîrgu Ocna Romania
48 K4 Tîrgu Secuesc Romania
47 K4 Tirilye Turkey
85 B4 Tiris reg Mauritania
145 E2 Tiritiri New Zealand
Tirlemont see Tienen
55 C4 Tirlyanskiy U.S.S.R.
48 J4 Tîrnava Mare R Romania
48 J4 Tîrnava Mică R Romania
48 J4 Tîrnăveni Romania
46 E5 Tírnavos Greece
94 E6 Tiro Ohio
70 G7 Tiro Sulawesi
38 F8 Tirol prov Austria
41 O4 Tirolo Italy
80 C6 Tirosh Israel
86 D4 Tiroungoulou Cent Afr Republic
45 H4 Tirrenia Italy
138 D3 Tirret Ra S Australia
37 N4 Tirschenreuth W Germany
43 B8 Tirso R Sardinia
43 B8 Tirso, L. del Sardinia
28 G7 Tirsted Denmark
131 A7 Tirua, Pta Chile
76 D6 Tiruchchendur India
76 D5 Tiruchirappalli India
76 C6 Tirunelveli India
128 D5 Tiruntán Peru
76 D4 Tirupati India
76 D4 Tiruppattur India
76 C5 Tiruppur India
76 D4 Tiruvannamalai India
142 F5 Tiru Well W Australia
119 N6 Tisdale Sask
111 H7 Tishomingo Mississippi
109 L1 Tishomingo Oklahoma
99 R8 Tiskilwa Illinois
28 C6 Tislund Denmark
27 H13 Tisnaren L Sweden
31 J6 Tišnov Czechoslovakia
48 F2 Tisovec Czechoslovakia
48 H2 Tissa R U.S.S.R.
83 L11 Tissamaharama Sri Lanka
9 E1 Tissington England
27 E12 Tistedal Norway
48 F3 Tisza R Hungary
31 N8 Tiszavasvari Hungary
85 E3 Tit Algeria
116 K2 Titaluk R Alaska
9 E6 Titchfield England
128 E7 Titicaca, L Peru/Bolivia
116 L4 Titna R Alaska
42 J6 Titograd Yugoslavia
99 M6 Titonka Iowa
48 F7 Titova Užice Yugoslavia
52 D1 Titovka R U.S.S.R.
46 E3 Titov Veles Yugoslavia
26 C8 Titran Norway
94 C3 Tittabawassee R Michigan
37 L6 Titting W Germany
38 G5 Tittmoning W Germany
48 K6 Titu Romania
86 E5 Titule Zaïre
113 G9 Titusville Florida
94 H5 Titusville Pennsylvania
85 A6 Tivaouane Senegal
27 G13 Tived Sweden
8 C6 Tiverton England
122 F9 Tiverton Nova Scotia
120 J8 Tiverton Ontario
95 Q5 Tiverton Rhode I
45 N6 Tivoli Italy
95 O4 Tivoli New York
109 L7 Tivoli Texas
144 B7 Tiwai Pt New Zealand
68 D6 Ti-ywa Burma
124 H7 Tizapán el Alto Mexico
17 H9 Tizi Algeria
16 E10 Tizi-Ifri Morocco
125 P7 Tizimín Mexico
85 C3 Tiznit Morocco
124 J5 Tizoc Mexico
16 E10 Tiztoutine Morocco
28 B6 Tjæreborg Denmark
28 G6 Tjæreby Denmark
27 H13 Tjällmo Sweden
70 L9 Tjamara Java
26 K5 Tjåmotis Sweden
71 L10 Tjamplong Timor Indonesia
70 K9 Tjankuang Tg C Java
26 L4 Tjårro Keble mt Sweden
26 J5 Tjeggelvas L Sweden
26 H3 Tjeldöy isld Norway
28 D3 Tjele Denmark
70 D4 Tjemaru, G mt Kalimantan
71 J9 Tjempi, Teluk B Sumbawa Indonesia
70 F6 Tjenrana Sulawesi
70 N9 Tjepu Java
70 M9 Tjereme mt Java
25 E3 Tjeuke Meer Netherlands
70 L9 Tjiandjur Java
70 L9 Tjibadak Java
70 L9 Tjibatu Java
70 L9 Tjibuni R Java
70 M9 Tjidjulang Java
70 L9 Tjidua Java
70 L9 Tjihara Java
70 L9 Tjikadjang Java
70 L9 Tjikampek Java
70 M9 Tjilatjap Java
70 M9 Tjiledug Java
70 L9 Tjimahi Java
70 G6 Tjimpu Sulawesi
70 K8 Tjina, Tg C Sumatra
70 M9 Tjipatudjah Java
70 M9 Tjirebon Java
70 L9 Tjitarum R Java
27 E12 Tjöme isld Norway
27 E13 Tjörn isld Sweden
28 M1 Tjørnevig Faeroes
28 B4 Tjørring Denmark
26 F6 Tjötta Norway
69 F14 Tjurup Sumatra
53 F11 Tkvarcheli U.S.S.R.
125 L9 Tlacolula de Matamoros Mexico
125 M8 Tlacotalpan Mexico
125 K8 Tlalnepantla Mexico
125 K8 Tlálpam Mexico
125 L8 Tlapacoyán Mexico
124 H7 Tlaquepaque Mexico
125 K8 Tlaxcala Mexico
85 D2 Tlemcen Algeria
85 E5 Tlemcès Niger
48 J2 Tlumach U.S.S.R.
31 N3 Tłuszcz Poland
52 E6 T'ma R U.S.S.R.
84 F4 Tmassah Libya
85 D4 Tni Haïa Algeria
68 C4 To R Burma
126 G4 Toa R Cuba
117 L6 Toad River Br Col
87 H11 Toamasina Madagascar
45 J3 Toano Italy
95 L9 Toano Virginia
101 L9 Toano mt ra Nevada
145 F3 Toatoa New Zealand
133 E5 Toay Argentina
61 K11 Toba Japan
69 D11 Toba, Danau L Sumatra
127 M1 Tobago isld W Indies
117 L10 Toba Inlet Br Col
77 K4 Toba & Kakar Ranges Pakistan
101 L9 Tobar Nevada
17 F6 Tobarra Spain
60 D12 Tobata Japan
14 C2 Tobbercurry Irish Rep
71 H7 Tobea isld Indonesia
140 E5 Tobermorey N Terr Aust
120 J7 Tobermory Ontario
141 G7 Tobermory Queensland
15 B4 Tobermory Scotland
60 P2 Tōbetsu Japan
98 J9 Tobias Nebraska
61 N14 Tobiishi-hana C Iwo Jima Japan
115 R3 Tobin, Kap C Greenland
119 O5 Tobin L Sask
142 F5 Tobin,L W Australia
102 G1 Tobin, Mt Nevada
122 E6 Tobique R New Brunswick
61 N6 Tobi-shima isld Japan
69 H14 Toboali Indonesia
55 D4 Tobol U.S.S.R.
70 G5 Toboli Sulawesi
55 E2 Tobol'sk U.S.S.R.
68 J6 To Bong Vietnam
71 F5 Toboso Negros Philippines
Tobruk see Tubruq
95 M5 Tobyhanna Pennsylvania
52 H3 Tobysh U.S.S.R.
52 H2 Tobysh R U.S.S.R.
141 G6 Tocal Queensland
129 J5 Tocantínia Brazil
129 J5 Tocantinópolis Brazil
129 J4 Tocantins R Brazil
112 D3 Toccoa Georgia
41 H5 Toce R Italy
61 N9 Tochigi Japan
61 M8 Tochio Japan
133 D2 Toco Chile
133 C2 Tocopilla Chile
133 D2 Tocorpuri mt Chile/Bolivia
139 H6 Tocumwal New S Wales
127 K9 Tocuyo R Venezuela
127 K9 Tocuyo de la Costa Venezuela
74 F5 Toda India
26 C9 Todal Norway
116 L3 Todatonten Alaska
122 F7 Todd Mt New Brunswick
140 B2 Todd,Mt N Terr Aust
140 C6 Todd R N Terr Aust
143 F7 Todd Ra W Australia
47 J1 Toder Ikonomovo Bulgaria
32 M5 Todesfelde W Germany
13 F1 Todhills Scotland
42 E6 Todi Italy
41 J4 Tödi mt Switzerland
70 G5 Todjo Sulawesi
13 F6 Todmorden England
138 C2 Todmorden S Australia
61 Q6 Todoga-saki C Japan
60 P4 Todohokke Japan
131 A8 Todos los Santos, L Chile
129 L6 Todos os Santos, B. de Brazil
124 D6 Todos Santos Mexico
56 E5 Todzha, Oz L U.S.S.R.
14 B5 Toe Hd Irish Rep
68 D5 Toe Jaga, Khao mt Burma/Thailand
144 B7 Toetoes B New Zealand
118 E5 Tofield Alberta
117 L11 Tofino Br Col
27 F14 Tofta Sweden
27 E12 Tofte Norway
28 C6 Toftlund Denmark
116 M4 Tofty Alaska
137 R5 Tofua isld Tonga
Tōfutsu see Sernovodsk
61 O10 Tōgane Japan
41 H5 Togano, Monte Italy
41 K3 Toggenburg mt Switzerland
61 K8 Togi Japan
116 G7 Togiak Alaska
70 G5 Togian Kep isld Sulawesi
37 O7 Töging W Germany
86 G2 Togni Sudan
119 Q7 Togo Sask
85 E7 Togo rep W Africa
Togrog Ul see Qahar Youyi Qianqi
65 B4 Togtoh China
61 P12 Toguchi Okinawa
56 B3 Toguchin U.S.S.R.
56 E4 Togul'skiy Khrebet mts U.S.S.R.
57 B2 Togyz U.S.S.R.
102 E1 Tohakum Pk Nevada
74 F4 Tohana India
106 B6 Tohatchi New Mexico
70 C4 Tohenbatu mt Sarawak
134 A11 Tohiea Tahiti I Pac Oc
29 P9 Tohmajärvi Finland
29 L8 Toholampi Finland
113 F9 Tohopekaliga, L Florida
61 M11 Toi Japan
68 A7 Toibalewe Andaman Is
29 K10 Toijala Finland
71 H5 Toili Sulawesi
99 P2 Toimi Minnesota
60 E14 Toi-misaki Japan
29 K9 Toisvesi L Finland
29 M9 Toivakka Finland
99 S3 Toivola Michigan
102 G2 Toiyabe Ra Nevada
60 G11 Tōjō Japan
30 H6 Tok mt Czechoslovakia
145 E3 Tokaanu New Zealand
60 R2 Tokachi prefect Japan
60 Q2 Tokachi dake mt Japan
48 G2 Tokajo Hungary
70 G5 Tokala, G mt Sulawesi
61 M8 Tōkamachi Japan
144 B7 Tokanui New Zealand
86 G2 Tokar Sudan
59 J5 Tokara-retto islds Japan
55 F5 Tokarevka U.S.S.R.
52 D4 Tokari U.S.S.R.
52 G5 Tokarikha U.S.S.R.
78 F1 Tokat Turkey
145 D2 Tokatoka New Zealand
65 F6 Tökchök-kundo B S Korea
59 K4 Tok-do isld Japan/Korea
70 G6 Toke Sulawesi
134 K9 Tokelau Is Pacific Oc
101 P9 Tokewanna Pk Utah
56 E1 Tokhoma R U.S.S.R.
57 G5 Tokhtamysh U.S.S.R.
61 L10 Toki Japan
98 H2 Tokio N Dakota
116 Q5 Tok Junc Alaska
27 D12 Tokke-Vatn L Norway
116 M4 Toklat Alaska
Tokmak see Esme
57 H3 Tokmak U.S.S.R.
145 E3 Toko New Zealand
70 G6 Tokolimbu Sulawesi
145 E4 Tokomaru New Zealand
145 G3 Tokomaru Bay New Zealand
60 S1 Tokoro Japan
145 E3 Tokoroa New Zealand
57 H1 Tokrau R U.S.S.R.
52 E3 Toksha-Kuznetsova U.S.S.R.
66 D3 Toksun China
57 G4 Toktogul Vdkhr U.S.S.R.
57 K2 Tokty U.S.S.R.
70 D5 Tokung Kalimantan
59 K1 Tokur U.S.S.R.
60 H11 Tokushima Japan
60 E11 Tokuyama Japan
89 G3 Tokwe R Zimbabwe
62 Tōkyō conurbation Japan
61 N10 Tōkyō-wan B Japan
145 G3 Tolaga Bay New Zealand
106 G7 Tolar New Mexico
109 K3 Tolar Texas
78 K1 Tolavi U.S.S.R.
55 C4 Tolbazy U.S.S.R.
47 J1 Tolbukhin Bulgaria
130 D9 Toledo Brazil
133 C3 Toledo Chile
110 H2 Toledo Illinois
99 O7 Toledo Iowa
94 D5 Toledo Ohio
100 B5 Toledo Oregon
16 E5 Toledo Spain
100 C3 Toledo Washington
16 E5 Toledo prov Spain
109 O4 Toledo Bend Res Louisiana
16 D5 Toledo, Montes de mts Spain
42 E5 Tolentino Italy
44 L5 Tolfa, Mt.della Italy
27 G14 Tolg Sweden
26 E9 Tolga Norway
87 G12 Toliara Madagascar
128 C3 Tolima div Colombia
70 G4 Tolitoli Sulawesi
27 G16 Tollarp Sweden
33 S5 Tollense R E Germany
33 S5 Tollensesee L E Germany
103 M8 Tolleson Arizona
98 E1 Tolley N Dakota
102 E4 Tollhouse California
28 H5 Tølløse Denmark
57 B3 Tolmacheva, Ozero L U.S.S.R.
52 C5 Tolmachevo U.S.S.R.
42 E2 Tolmezzo Italy
42 F2 Tolmin Yugoslavia
48 E4 Tolna Hungary
48 E4 Tolna co Hungary
28 E2 Tolne Denmark
86 C6 Tolo Zaïre
54 A2 Tolochin U.S.S.R.
110 H2 Tolono Illinois
17 F1 Tolosa Spain
70 G6 Tolo, Teluk B Sulawesi
116 N4 Tolovana R Alaska
65 G7 Tolsan isld S Korea
15 B2 Tolsta Head Scotland
48 K2 Tolstoe U.S.S.R.
103 N9 Toltec Arizona
133 C5 Toltén Chile
131 A7 Toltén, R Chile
126 G10 Tolú Colombia
99 R8 Toluca Illinois
125 K8 Toluca Mexico
29 P5 Tolvant, Oz L U.S.S.R.
52 D4 Tolvayarvi U.S.S.R.
52 E4 Tolvuya U.S.S.R.
55 A4 Tol'yatti U.S.S.R.
55 D5 Tolybay U.S.S.R.
56 B3 Tom' R U.S.S.R.
99 Q6 Tomah Wisconsin
99 R4 Tomahawk Wisconsin
60 P3 Tomakomai Japan
60 P1 Tomamae Japan
128 F4 Tomar Brazil
16 B5 Tomar Portugal
57 H2 Tomar U.S.S.R.
Tomari see Golovnino
60 N3 Tomari Japan
59 M2 Tomari U.S.S.R.
31 O4 Tomashevka U.S.S.R.
48 M2 Tomashpol U.S.S.R.
130 E8 Tomasina Brazil
31 O5 Tomaszów Lubelski Poland
31 M4 Tomaszów Mazowiecka Poland
15 D3 Tomatin Scotland
124 G8 Tomatlán Mexico
38 O9 Tomaz Yugoslavia
109 M5 Tomball Texas
60 F10 Tombara Japan
86 F4 Tombe Sudan
111 H8 Tombigbee R Mississippi
71 H5 Tombila mt Sulawesi
87 B7 Tomboco Angola
70 G6 Tomboli Sulawesi
130 G7 Tombos Brazil
85 D5 Tombouctou Mali
103 O10 Tombstone Arizona
131 A6 Tome Chile
71 J7 Tomea isld Indonesia
27 G16 Tomelilla Sweden
121 L6 Tomiko Ontario
139 J4 Tomingley New S Wales
70 G4 Tomini Sulawesi
70 G5 Tomini, Teluk B Sulawesi
15 E3 Tomintoul Scotland
61 O8 Tomioka Japan
143 G7 Tomkinson Ras S/W Australia
26 F5 Tomma isld Norway
28 C2 Tømmerby Denmark
28 E6 Tommerup Denmark
51 M3 Tommot U.S.S.R.
60 G11 Tomo Japan
128 E2 Tomo R Colombia
124 F3 Tomóchic Mexico
60 H11 Tomogashima-suidō str Japan
71 J4 Tomohon Sulawesi
70 G6 Tomori Tk B Sulawesi
118 J8 Tompkins Sask
94 C4 Tompkins Center Michigan
110 L5 Tompkinsville Kentucky
70 G4 Tompo Sulawesi
143 C6 Tom Price W Australia
142 C6 Tom Price,Mt W Australia
66 D5 Tomra China
86 H4 Tomsa Ethiopia
56 C3 Tomsk U.S.S.R.
56 B2 Tomskaya Oblast prov U.S.S.R.
83 M9 Tom's Ridge Christmas I Indian Oc
95 N6 Toms River New Jersey
60 Q2 Tomuraushi yama mt Japan
Tomur Feng see Pobedy, Pik
116 Q6 Tom White, Mt Alaska
124 F4 Tónachic Mexico
125 N9 Tonalá Mexico
103 O5 Tonalea Arizona
42 D2 Tonale, Pso. di Italy
61 K9 Tonami Japan
128 E4 Tonantins Brazil
100 F1 Tonasket Washington
121 M9 Tonawanda New York
9 G5 Tonbridge England
60 J12 Tonda Japan
71 J4 Tondano Sulawesi
16 B4 Tondela Portugal
28 B7 Tønder Denmark
Tønder co see Sønderjylland
120 E3 Tondern Ontario
85 E4 Tondjara watercourse Algeria
88 C10 Tondongwe mt Zimbabwe
36 B3 Tondorf W Germany
61 N9 Tone R Japan
61 O10 Tone-gawa R Japan
8 C5 Tone, R England
139 G4 Tonga New S Wales
86 F4 Tonga Sudan
88 B10 Tonga Zambia
137 S6 Tonga island kingdom Pacific Oc
89 G7 Tongaat S Africa
145 D4 Tonga I New Zealand
139 G4 Tonga L New S Wales
139 G6 Tongala Victoria
67 F4 Tong'an China
110 A2 Tonganoxie Kansas
145 E3 Tongaporutu New Zealand
145 E3 Tongariro mt New Zealand
137 R6 Tongatapu Group Tonga
58 F5 Tongbai Shan mt ra China
Tongcheng see Dong'e
58 G5 Tongcheng China
67 D2 Tongcheng China
67 E1 Tongcheng China
58 E4 Tongchuan China
67 C3 Tongdao China
22 J2 Tongeren Belgium
67 E2 Tonggu China
65 A7 Tongguan China
67 A4 Tonghai China
59 J2 Tonghe China
59 J3 Tonghua China
59 K2 Tongjiang China
67 B1 Tongjiang China
59 J2 Tongken He R China
67 B6 Tong King, G. of Vietnam
12 D4 Tongland Scotland
67 B2 Tongliang China
59 H3 Tongliao China
67 F1 Tongling China
67 F2 Tonglu China
67 B1 Tongnan China
68 H6 Tong Noy Cambodia
87 G12 Tongobory Madagascar
131 B3 Tongoi, Bahia Chile
133 C4 Tongoy Chile
Tongquan see Malong
71 E7 Tongquil isld Philippines
67 C3 Tongren China
Tongres see Tongeren
Tongshan see Xuzhou
67 E2 Tongshan China
68 D2 Tongta Burma
58 C5 Tongtian He R China
15 D2 Tongue Scotland
101 U3 Tongue R Montana
126 F2 Tongue of the Ocean chan Bahamas
101 T4 Tongue R.Res Montana
65 C5 Tong Xian China
67 G1 Tongxiang China
65 D3 Tongxing China
65 C7 Tongxu China
65 F2 Tongyu China
65 F4 Tongyuanpu China
67 B4 Tongzhou China
67 B2 Tongzi China
58 B2 Tonhil Mongolia
99 R8 Tonica Illinois
124 E3 Tónichi Mexico
124 H8 Tonila Mexico
86 E4 Tonj Sudan
74 F5 Tonk India
107 N5 Tonkawa Oklahoma
52 G6 Tonkino U.S.S.R.
68 G7 Tonle Sap R Cambodia
21 D10 Tonnay-Charente France
18 F8 Tonneins France
28 D5 Tønning Denmark
32 J4 Tönning W Germany
102 G3 Tonopah Nevada
60 H11 Tonoshō Japan
27 D12 Tönsberg Norway
27 B13 Tonstad Norway
131 B3 Tontal, Sa ra Argentina
103 N8 Tonto Basin Arizona
103 O8 Tonto Nat.Mon Arizona
116 L5 Tonzona R Alaska
141 J8 Toobeah Queensland
143 B9 Toodyay W Australia
101 N9 Tooele Utah
141 K7 Toogoolawah Queensland
139 G6 Tooleyone New S Wales
143 G9 Toolgana W Australia
138 D5 Tooligie S Australia
116 N2 Toolik R Alaska
138 F6 Toolondo Victoria
139 J6 Tooma R New S Wales
141 G7 Toompine Queensland
141 F5 Toorak Queensland
141 K2 Toowong dist Brisbane, Qnsld
141 K8 Toowoomba Queensland
116 J1 Topagoruk R Alaska
48 L6 Topalu Romania
17 F7 Topares, Sa.de mts Spain
103 N10 Topawa Arizona
102 E3 Topaz L California
33 T8 Töpchin E Germany
13 G5 Topcliffe England
94 B5 Topeka Indiana
107 P2 Topeka Kansas
124 F5 Topia Mexico
56 C3 Topki U.S.S.R.
48 G1 Topl'a R Czechoslovakia
118 C4 Topland Alberta
117 K8 Topley Lodge Br Col
46 E1 Toplica R Yugoslavia
42 G3 Toplice Yugoslavia
48 J4 Topliţa Romania
131 A5 Topocalma, Pta Chile
103 K7 Topock Arizona
48 F6 Topola Yugoslavia
46 E3 Topolčane Yugoslavia
48 E2 Topol'čany Czechoslovakia
29 O10 Topol'ki U.S.S.R.
47 G2 Topolnitsa R Bulgaria
124 E5 Topolobampo Mexico
48 J6 Topoloveni Romania
47 H2 Topolovgrad Bulgaria
38 L9 Topolšica Yugoslavia
106 D1 Toponas Colorado
52 E5 Topornya U.S.S.R.
100 E3 Toppenish Washington
47 J1 Topraisar Romania
57 B4 Toprak-kala U.S.S.R.
52 F3 Topsa U.S.S.R.
95 U1 Topsfield Maine
8 C6 Topsham England
95 R3 Topsham Maine
95 M6 Topton Pennsylvania
103 L4 Toquerville Utah
102 G3 Toquima Ra Nevada
17 H3 Torá Spain
71 J4 Torawitan, Tg B Sulawesi
123 L8 Tor B Nova Scotia
143 C11 Tor B W Australia
47 J6 Torbalı Turkey
77 F2 Torbat-e-Ḩeydarīyeh Iran
77 G2 Torbat-e Jām Iran
8 C7 Torbay England
123 U6 Torbay Nfld
123 L8 Torbay Nova Scotia
27 F10 Torberget Norway
116 L6 Torbert, Mt Alaska
52 D5 Torbino U.S.S.R.
94 B1 Torch L Michigan
8 C7 Torcross England
20 H2 Torcy-le-Grand France
16 D3 Tordesillas Spain
138 F5 Tor Downs New S Wales
26 N6 Töre Sweden
27 G13 Töreboda Sweden
28 H7 Toreby Denmark
28 K4 Torekov Sweden
145 F2 Torere New Zealand
27 J12 Toresund Sweden
17 F3 Torete R Spain
54 K8 Torez U.S.S.R.
21 C7 Torfou France
33 S9 Torgau E Germany
33 U5 Torgelow E Germany
26 F6 Torghatten isld Norway
53 G8 Torgun R U.S.S.R.
27 H15 Torhamn Sweden
22 E1 Torhout Belgium
86 F4 Tori Ethiopia
70 G5 Toribulu Sulawesi
61 O10 Toride Japan
20 D3 Torigny-sur-Vire France
44 C1 Torino Italy
86 F5 Torit Sudan
130 D5 Torixoreu Brazil
52 D5 Torkovichi U.S.S.R.
29 N3 Törmänen Finland
8 D5 Tormarton England
142 E3 Torment, Pt W Australia
16 D4 Tormes R Spain
117 Q11 Tornado Mt Alberta/Br Col
28 D1 Tornby Denmark
26 M4 Torne älv R Sweden
32 L5 Tornesch W Germany
26 L3 Torneträsk Sweden
26 K3 Torneträsk L Sweden
115 N6 Torngat Mts Quebec/Labrador
48 F7 Tornik mt Yugoslavia

78

Tornillo — Tuolumne

108 A4 Tornillo Texas
28 C4 Torning Denmark
29 L6 Tornio Finland
29 L6 Tornionjoki *R* Finland
33 S6 Tornow E Germany
133 E5 Tornquist Argentina
60 S2 Tōro Japan
16 D3 Toro Spain
28 D6 Torø *isld* Denmark
131 B2 Toro, Cerro de *peak* Arg/Chile
48 J3 Toroiaga *mt* Romania
48 F3 Törökszentmiklós Hungary
47 F4 Toronaíos Kólpos *gulf* Greece
107 P4 Toronto Kansas
139 K5 Toronto New S Wales
94 G6 Toronto Ohio
121 D9 Toronto Ontario
52 D6 Toropets U.S.S.R.
124 H5 Toro, Pico del *mt* Mexico
102 H8 Toro Pk California
131 B4 Toro, Pta Chile
88 E1 Tororo Uganda
78 D3 Toros Dağlari *mts* Turkey
26 H9 Torp Sweden
15 F3 Torphins Scotland
52 F6 Torpino U.S.S.R.
8 B7 Torpoint England
26 H9 Torpshammar Sweden
133 G4 Torquato Severo Brazil
8 C7 Torquay England
98 C1 Torquay Sask
121 L8 Torrance Ontario
16 B6 Torrão Portugal
45 Q8 Torre Annunziata Italy
41 O6 Torrebelvicino Italy
17 H4 Torreblanca Spain
17 F2 Torrecilla en Cameros Spain
45 Q8 Torre del Greco Italy
44 F1 Torre del Mangano Italy
16 C3 Torre de Moncorvo Portugal
44 H4 Torre di Lago Puccini Italy
16 E7 Torredonjimeno Spain
45 L1 Torréglia Italy
16 C5 Torrejoncillo Spain
16 E1 Torrelavega Spain
42 G7 Torremaggiore Italy
16 E8 Torremolinos Spain
141 H5 Torrens *R* Queensland
141 H5 Torrens Cr Queensland
138 E4 Torrens, L S Australia
17 G5 Torrente Spain
124 H5 Torreón Mexico
17 G7 Torre Pacheco Spain
133 H3 Tôrres Brazil
124 D3 Torres Mexico
16 E9 Torres de Alealá Morocco
137 O4 Torres Is New Hebrides
16 B5 Torres Novas Portugal
141 F1 Torres Strait Queensland
16 A5 Torres Vedras Portugal
17 G7 Torrevieja Spain
103 N3 Torrey Utah
45 N5 Torricella in Sabina Italy
8 B6 Torridge, R England
28 E5 Torrild Denmark
28 C5 Tørring Denmark
118 D7 Torrington Alberta
95 O5 Torrington Connecticut
139 K3 Torrington New S Wales
98 B7 Torrington Wyoming
98 B7 Torrington, S Wyoming
140 C1 Tor Rock *mt* N Terr Aust
26 F8 Torröjen *L* Sweden
16 E8 Torrox Spain
27 H11 Torsåker Sweden
27 H15 Torsås Sweden
27 G15 Torsås, V Sweden
26 F9 Torsborg Sweden
27 F11 Torsby Sweden
27 H12 Torshälla Sweden
26 J2 Torsken Norway
26 L1 Torsvåg Norway
57 E3 Tortkol' U.S.S.R.
55 F5 Tortkuduk U.S.S.R.
43 F11 Torto *R* Sicily
113 L7 Tortola *isld* Virgin Is
131 B2 Tortolas, Cerro las *peak* Arg/Chile
44 E2 Tortona Italy
17 H4 Tortosa Spain
127 H4 Tortue, Île de la Haiti
77 D2 Ţorūd Iran
70 G5 Torue Sulawesi
66 B3 Torugart Pass *pass* U.S.S.R.
31 L2 Toruń Poland
27 F15 Torup Sweden
52 C5 Tõrva U.S.S.R.
27 G13 Torved Sweden
13 E5 Torver England
26 J7 Torvsjö Sweden
121 M8 Tory Hill Ontario
14 C1 Tory I Irish Rep
48 G2 Torysa *R* Czechoslovakia
31 J3 Torzym Poland
60 G12 Tosa Japan
60 F13 Tosa-Shimizu Japan
60 G12 Tosa-wan *B* Japan
60 G12 Tosa-Yamada Japan
87 D11 Tosca S Africa
45 K4 Toscana *reg* Italy
42 C5 Toscano, Arch *islds* Italy
124 D5 Tosca, Pta *C* Mexico
26 F6 Tosen Norway
26 F6 Tosenfjord *inlet* Norway
41 N3 Tösens Austria
61 K11 Tōshi-jima *isld* Japan
61 N11 To-shima *isld* Japan
61 P5 Tōshima-yama *mt* Japan
52 D5 Tosno U.S.S.R.
58 C4 Toson Hu *L* China
58 C2 Tosontsengel Mongolia
26 F9 Tossåsen Sweden
45 L3 Tossignano Italy
133 E3 Tostado Argentina
101 O3 Toston Montana
60 D12 Tosu Japan
78 D1 Tosya Turkey
31 L5 Toszek Poland
70 G6 Totala Sulawesi
17 F7 Totana Spain
144 C5 Totara Flat New Zealand
145 D1 Totara North New Zealand
145 D4 Totaranui New Zealand
27 E11 Toten *reg* Norway
32 L6 Tötensen W Germany
20 H2 Tôtes France
38 J6 Totes Gebirge *mts* Austria
48 F4 Tótkomlós Hungary
9 E1 Totley England
8 C7 Totnes England
129 G2 Totness Suriname
89 C6 Toto *mt* S Africa
144 B6 Totoko Pk New Zealand
125 L9 Totolápam Mexico
131 B2 Totoralillo Chile
85 C7 Totota Liberia
146 C10 Tottanfjella *ra* Antarctica
146 G2 Totten Gl Antarctica
139 H4 Tottenham New S Wales
121 L8 Tottenham Ontario
9 E6 Totton England
59 K4 Tottori Japan
60 G10 Tottori *prefect* Japan
83 K11 Totupola *mt* Sri Lanka
119 M6 Totzke Sask
85 C7 Touba Ivory Coast
85 C2 Toubkal *mt* Morocco
146 D10 Touchdown Hills Antarctica
100 G3 Touchet Washington
119 N7 Touchwood Hills Sask
18 H5 Toucy France
65 G3 Toudao Jiang *R* China
65 D3 Toufendi China
85 D6 Tougan Upper Volta
85 F2 Touggourt Algeria
85 B6 Tougue Guinea
85 C3 Touila Mauritania
19 J4 Toul France
85 C7 Toulépleu Ivory Coast
122 E3 Toulnustouc R Quebec
19 P18 Toulon France
99 R8 Toulon Illinois
102 F1 Toulon Nevada
19 O17 Touloubre *R* France
18 F9 Toulouse France
84 E5 Toumma Niger
85 C7 Toumodi Ivory Coast
68 C3 Toungoo Burma
20 F3 Touques France
22 B2 Touquet-Paris Plage, le France
21 F7 Touraine *prov* France
68 F3 Tourakom Laos
Tourane *see* Da Nang
22 E2 Tourcoing France
16 A1 Touriñan, C Spain
85 B4 Tourine Mauritania
20 B2 Tourlaville France
18 F10 Tourmalet, Col du France
22 E2 Tournai Belgium
18 G4 Tournan St Brie France
128 D5 Tournavista Peru
18 F9 Tournay France
19 N14 Tournon France
40 A4 Tournus France
20 J3 Tourny France
130 J8 Touros Brazil
20 G4 Tourouvre France
21 G7 Tours France
40 E5 Tour Sallière *mt* Switzerland
22 H4 Tourteron France
19 P18 Tourves France
20 H3 Tourville-sur-Andelle France
20 J5 Toury France
86 C1 Toussidé Pic *mt* Chad
20 K1 Toutencourt France
119 S7 Toutes Aides Manitoba
100 C3 Toutle Washington
89 B9 Touws River S Africa
37 O3 Toužím Czechoslovakia
127 J10 Tovar Venezuela
54 K3 Tovarkovskiy U.S.S.R.
27 C13 Tovdal Norway
27 C13 Tovdalselv *R* Norway
9 F3 Tove, R England
61 O5 Towada-Hachimantai Nat. Park Japan
61 O5 Towada ko *L* Japan
145 E1 Towai New Zealand
128 G2 Towakaima Guyana
139 J6 Towamba New S Wales
110 H1 Towanda Illinois
107 O4 Towanda Kansas
95 L5 Towanda Pennsylvania
70 G7 Towari Sulawesi
9 F3 Towcester England
99 O2 Tower Minnesota
98 J3 Tower City N Dakota
95 L6 Tower City Pennsylvania
101 P5 Tower Falls Wyoming
110 H2 Tower Hill Illinois
141 G5 Tower Hill Queensland
144 A6 Towing Head New Zealand
106 H3 Towner Colorado
98 F1 Towner N Dakota
102 G5 Townes Pass California
111 J8 Townley Alabama
95 M7 Townsend Delaware
112 F6 Townsend Georgia
101 O3 Townsend Montana
112 D2 Townsend Tennessee
99 S4 Townsend Wisconsin
139 J6 Townsend, Mt Victoria
141 K5 Townshend I Queensland
141 H4 Townsville Queensland
94 H5 Townville Pennsylvania
86 F4 Towot Sudan
95 L7 Towson Maryland
70 G6 Towuti *L* Sulawesi
8 C3 Towy, R Wales
112 D2 Toxaway, L N Carolina
66 B3 Toxkan He *R* China
108 D4 Toyah L Texas
60 O3 Tōya-ko *L* Japan
61 L9 Toyama Japan
61 L8 Toyama wan *B* Japan
116 A3 Toygunen U.S.S.R.
61 L10 Toyo Japan
60 G11 Toyohama Japan
61 L11 Toyohashi Japan
61 L11 Toyokawa Japan
60 R3 Toyokoro Japan
61 J11 Toyonaka Japan
60 H10 Toyooka Japan
61 N8 Toyosaka Japan
61 L10 Toyota Japan
29 K9 Töysä Finland
85 F2 Tozeur Tunisia
116 M4 Tozitna *R* Alaska
36 C4 Traben-Trarbach W Germany
78 G1 Trabzon Turkey
122 H6 Tracadie New Brunswick
123 L8 Tracadie Nova Scotia
122 F8 Tracey New Brunswick
69 H8 Tra Cu Vietnam
102 C4 Tracy California
99 O8 Tracy Iowa
99 L5 Tracy Minnesota
110 L6 Tracy City Tennessee
22 E5 Tracy-le-Mont France
41 J6 Tradate Italy
119 O3 Trade L Sask
110 J4 Tradewater *R* Kentucky
Tradom *see* Zhongba
99 O7 Traer Iowa
98 F10 Traer Kansas
16 C8 Trafalgar, C Spain
111 K8 Trafford Alabama
113 F11 Trafford, L Florida
131 B8 Traful *R* Argentina
131 B8 Traful, L Argentina
84 E4 Trāghan Libya
38 L5 Tragwein Austria
48 L5 Traian Romania
130 J9 Traição, B. de Brazil
133 C5 Traiguén Chile
133 C7 Traiguén, I Chile
100 H1 Trail Br Col
100 C7 Trail Oregon
98 F4 Trail City S Dakota
115 R3 Traill Ø *isld* Greenland
143 D6 Trainor Hills W Australia
117 N5 Trainor L N W Terr
20 K6 Trainou France
130 H10 Traipu Brazil
130 J9 Trairi *R* Brazil
38 N5 Traismauer Austria
20 G3 Trait, le France
52 H3 Trakt U.S.S.R.
111 F8 Tralake Mississippi
14 B4 Tralee Irish Rep
68 J6 Tram Bo Vietnam
40 F3 Tramelan Switzerland
68 G7 Tram Kak Cambodia
68 G7 Tram Khnan Cambodia
14 D4 Tramore Irish Rep
118 J6 Tramping Sask
27 H13 Tranås Sweden
28 E4 Tranbjerg Denmark
133 D3 Trancas Argentina
124 G3 Trancas Mexico
18 E6 Tranche, la France
130 H5 Trancoso Brazil
16 C4 Trancoso Portugal
27 F14 Tranemo Sweden
13 F2 Tranent Scotland
69 D9 Trang Thailand
139 J4 Trangie New S Wales
28 N3 Trangisvåg Faeroes
69 H8 Tranh De, Cua *R* Vietnam
43 G7 Trani Italy
26 J2 Tranöy Norway
76 D5 Tranquebar India
102 D5 Tranquillity California
19 Q18 Trans France
118 C1 Transcona Manitoba
89 F8 Transkei *dist* S Africa
27 F11 Transtrand Sweden
89 E5 Transvaal *prov* S Africa
48 J4 Transylvania *reg* Romania
Transylvanian Alps *see* Carpaţii Meridionali *Mts*
68 G8 Tra On Vietnam
41 L5 Traona Italy
43 E10 Trapani Sicily
101 L4 Trapper Pk Montana
131 H3 Trapua *R* Brazil
13 E2 Traquair Scotland
139 H7 Traralgon Victoria
17 F9 Traras, Mt.des Algeria
27 G15 Traryd Sweden
85 A5 Trarza *reg* Mauritania
45 P6 Trasacco Italy
42 E5 Trasimeno, L Italy
26 L6 Träskholm Sweden
109 P1 Traskwood Arkansas
16 C3 Tras os Montes e Alto Douro *prov* Portugal
16 B1 Trasparga Spain
36 B4 Trassem W Germany
45 H3 Trassilico Italy
68 F6 Trat Thailand
38 K5 Traun Austria
99 U3 Traunik Michigan
38 J6 Traunsee *L* Austria
38 G6 Traunstein W Germany
38 J6 Traunstein *mt* Austria
33 M5 Trave *R* W Germany
138 F5 Travellers L New S Wales
112 E3 Travellers Rest S Carolina
33 N5 Travemünde W Germany
33 M5 Travenberg W Germany
118 E8 Travers Alberta
146 A14 Traversay I Antarctica
94 B1 Traverse B.Grand Michigan
94 B1 Traverse B.Little Michigan
94 B2 Traverse City Michigan
98 K4 Traverse, L S Dakota
116 H4 Traverse Pk Alaska
45 H2 Traversetolo Italy
122 B5 Travers, L Quebec
144 D5 Travers, Mt New Zealand
131 C5 Travesia Puntana *reg* Argentina
131 C4 Travesia Tunuyán *reg* Argentina
109 J5 Travis, L Texas
42 H4 Travnik Yugoslavia
55 G4 Travnoye U.S.S.R.
44 F2 Travo Italy
14 D1 Trawbreaga B Irish Rep
109 N4 Trawick Texas
143 C9 Trayning W Australia
42 G2 Trbovlje Yugoslavia
8 B1 Tre-Arddur B Wales
127 J3 Treasure Beach Jamaica
116 J3 Treat I Alaska
44 F2 Trebbia *R* Italy
33 S8 Trebbin E Germany
33 O7 Trebel W Germany
33 R4 Trebel *R* E Germany
18 G9 Trèbes France
31 J6 Třebíč Czechoslovakia
42 J6 Trebinje Yugoslavia
42 J6 Trebišnica *R* Yugoslavia
48 G2 Trebišov Czechoslovakia
42 H5 Trebižat *R* Yugoslavia
144 A7 Treble Mt New Zealand
42 G3 Trebnje Yugoslavia
31 H6 Třeboň Czechoslovakia
48 D1 Třebová Czechoslovakia
33 R10 Trebsen E Germany
36 E4 Trebur W Germany
8 C4 Trecastle Wales
44 E1 Trecate Italy
45 K1 Trecenta Italy
106 B7 Trechado New Mexico
8 C4 Tredegar Wales
41 N6 Tredici Comuni *reg* Italy
9 E3 Tredington England
45 L3 Tredozio Italy
73 L6 Tree I Lakshadweep Indian Ocean
21 C6 Treffieux France
40 B5 Treffort France
8 C1 Trefnant Wales
8 C1 Trefriw Wales
8 C3 Tregaron Wales
119 N8 Tregarva Sask
101 L1 Trego Montana
102 E1 Trego Nevada
99 P4 Trego Wisconsin
8 B7 Tregony England
141 K4 Tregosse Islets & Reefs Gt Barrier Reef Aust
18 C4 Treguier France
119 T9 Treherne Manitoba
68 G8 Tre, Hon *isld* Vietnam
26 K8 Trehörningsjö Sweden
15 D4 Treig, L Scotland
18 G7 Treignac France
131 G4 Treinta y Tres Uruguay
36 C3 Treis-Karden W Germany
140 E5 Trekelano Queensland
89 G1 Trelawney Zimbabwe
127 J2 Trelawney *parish* Jamaica
21 E7 Trélazé France
32 L6 Trelde W Germany
28 D5 Trelde Næs *C* Denmark
133 D6 Trelew Argentina
27 F16 Trelleborg Sweden
8 D4 Trelleck Wales
22 G3 Trélon France
8 B2 Tremadoc Wales
18 E7 Tremblade, la France
20 H4 Tremblay-le-Vicomte France
117 L8 Trembleur L Br Col
106 F6 Trementina New Mexico
21 D7 Trementines France
37 K3 Tremersdorf W Germany
42 G6 Tremiti, I.di Italy
110 G1 Tremont Illinois
111 H7 Tremont Mississippi
95 L6 Tremont Pennsylvania
101 N8 Tremonton Utah
37 P4 Třemošná Czechoslovakia
17 H2 Tremp Spain
99 P5 Trempealeau Wisconsin
33 M5 Tremsbüttel W Germany
69 G8 Trem Trem *R* Vietnam
99 U3 Trenary Michigan
121 S5 Trenche *R* Quebec
48 E2 Trenčín Czechoslovakia
28 C3 Trend Å *R* Denmark
32 K9 Trendelburg W Germany
133 E5 Trenel Argentina
27 A11 Trengereid Norway
70 N10 Trenggalek Java
131 E5 Trenque Lauquen Argentina
Trent *see* Trento
108 G3 Trent Texas
112 K2 Trent *R* N Carolina
121 L8 Trent Canal Ontario
41 N5 Trentino-Alto Adige *reg* Italy
41 O5 Trento Italy
45 Q8 Tréntola Italy
113 E8 Trenton Florida
94 D4 Trenton Michigan
110 C1 Trenton Missouri
98 C1 Trenton N Dakota
98 E9 Trenton Nebraska
95 N6 Trenton New Jersey
95 M3 Trenton New York
122 K8 Trenton Nova Scotia
110 M2 Trenton Ohio
121 N8 Trenton Ontario
112 F4 Trenton S Carolina
110 H6 Trenton Tennessee
13 H6 Trent, R England
20 H4 Tréon France
46 D2 Trepča Yugoslavia
20 H1 Tréport, le France
38 H8 Treppo Carnico Italy
120 C3 Treptow L Ontario
133 F4 Tres Arboles Uruguay
131 E7 Tres Arroyos Argentina
21 B6 Tresboeuf France
128 F5 Três Casas Brazil
19 P16 Trescléoux France
9 F7 Tresco *isld* Isles of Scilly England
130 F7 Três Corações Brazil
33 N9 Treseburg E Germany
85 D1 Tres Forcas, C Morocco
15 B4 Treshnish I Scotland
48 E7 Treskavica *mt* Yugoslavia
130 D7 Três Lagoas Brazil
130 F6 Três Marias *dam* Brazil
133 B7 Tres Montes, Pen Chile
16 E2 Trespaderne Spain
130 D10 Tres Passos Brazil
131 E7 Tres Picos, Cerro *peak* Argentina
106 E5 Tres Piedras New Mexico
102 C5 Tres Pinos California
130 F7 Três Pontas Brazil
133 C3 Tres Puentes Chile
130 G8 Três Rios Brazil
21 G6 Tresson France
31 J6 Třešť Czechoslovakia
15 G2 Tresta Shetland Scotland
125 M8 Tres Zapotes Mexico
8 C4 Tretower Wales
19 P18 Trets France
27 D10 Trettin Norway
Treuburg *see* Olecko
37 K6 Treuchtlingen W Germany
33 N2 Treuen W Germany
33 R8 Treuenbrietzen E Germany
27 C12 Treungen Norway
Treves *see* Trier
20 D3 Trévières France
41 L6 Treviglio Italy
17 F2 Treviño Spain
42 E3 Treviso Italy
8 A6 Trevose Head England
40 A6 Trévoux France
36 G2 Treysa W Germany
31 H7 Trhové Sviny Czechoslovakia
27 H14 Triabo Sweden
139 J8 Triabunna Tasmania
21 C9 Triaize France
140 D2 Trial B N Terr Aust
47 J8 Tríanda Rhodes Greece
117 P8 Triangle Alberta
100 J7 Triangle Idaho
47 H8 Tría Nisiá *isld* Greece
48 E2 Tribeč *R* Czechoslovakia
20 C3 Tribehou France
40 H1 Triberg W Germany
33 R4 Tribsees E Germany
141 H3 Tribulation, C Queensland
107 J3 Tribune Kansas
119 O9 Tribune Sask
43 G8 Tricarico Italy
43 J9 Tricase Italy
76 C5 Trichur India
9 E6 Trickett's Cross England
22 D4 Tricot France
139 H5 Trida New S Wales
100 G8 Trident Pk Nevada
38 K7 Trieben Austria
37 N2 Triebes E Germany
20 J3 Trie-Chateau France
37 P6 Triefenried W Germany
20 K4 Triel-sur-Seine France
131 G4 Trienta-y-Tres Uruguay
36 B4 Trier W Germany
37 K5 Triesdorf W Germany
42 F3 Trieste Italy
42 E3 Trieste, G.di Italy
22 K5 Trieux France
18 C4 Trieux *R* France
37 P7 Triftern W Germany
42 F2 Triglav *mt* Yugoslavia
42 F7 Trigno *R* Italy
16 C7 Triguerós Spain
47 F5 Tríkeri Greece
46 E6 Trikhonís, L Greece
46 E5 Tríkkala Greece
46 E6 Tríklinos Greece
79 D3 Trikomo Cyprus
113 E9 Trilby Florida
17 F4 Trillo Spain
120 G2 Trilsbeck L Ontario
14 E3 Trim Irish Rep
13 G4 Trimdon England
9 H4 Trimley England
99 M6 Trimont Minnesota
142 B5 Trimouille I W Australia
124 D2 Trincheras Mexico
106 F4 Trinchere Colorado
83 L9 Trincomalee Sri Lanka
90 G11 Trindade *isld* Atlantic Oc
9 F4 Tring England
46 E5 Tringía *mt* Greece
121 T6 Tring Junction Quebec
128 F6 Trinidad Bolivia
100 A8 Trinidad California
128 D2 Trinidad Colombia
106 F4 Trinidad Colorado
126 D4 Trinidad Cuba
130 C10 Trinidad Paraguay
71 G4 Trinidad Philippines
131 G4 Trinidad Uruguay
100 E2 Trinidad Washington
127 O2 Trinidad *isld* W Indies
133 B7 Trinidad, Canal Chile
131 E7 Trinidad, I Argentina
20 G4 Trinite de-Reville, la France
123 T5 Trinity Nfld
109 M5 Trinity Texas
109 L3 Trinity *R* Texas
141 H3 Trinity B Queensland
100 C8 Trinity Center California
127 P3 Trinity Hills Trinidad
116 K8 Trinity Is Alaska
102 F1 Trinity Ra Nevada
100 C9 Trinity Res California
69 A8 Trinkat I Nicobar Is
44 D1 Trino Italy
Trinquet, Fort *see* Bir Moghreim
112 B3 Trion Georgia
43 H9 Trionto, C Italy
99 O7 Tripoli Iowa
79 F4 Tripoli Lebanon
84 E3 Tripoli Libya
46 E7 Trípolis Greece
84 E3 Tripolitania *reg* Libya
98 H6 Tripp S Dakota
36 D5 Trippstadt W Germany
37 M2 Triptis E Germany
75 O7 Tripura *prov* India
123 N3 Triquet, L Quebec
32 J4 Trischen *isld* W Germany
37 O4 Tři Sekery Czechoslovakia
90 H12 Tristan da Cunha Atlantic Oc
68 G7 Tri Ton Vietnam
33 M5 Trittau W Germany
130 H9 Triunfo Brazil
76 C6 Trivandrum India
48 D2 Trnava Czechoslovakia
20 E3 Troarn France
36 G7 Trochtelfingen W Germany
26 F5 Troena *isld* Norway
28 F6 Troense Denmark
38 M7 Trofaiach Austria
147 Q9 Trofimovsk U.S.S.R.
42 H5 Troglav *mt* Yugoslavia
21 I9 Trois Cornes *hill* France
36 C2 Troisdorf W Germany
36 C6 Troisfontaines France
127 L4 Trois Ilets Martinique W Indies
122 C5 Trois Pistoles Quebec
22 K3 Trois Ponts Belgium
127 N5 Trois Rivières Guadeloupe W I
121 S6 Trois Rivières Quebec
83 M14 Trois Swains, Les *islds* Kerguelen Indian Ocean
22 K3 Trois Vierges Luxembourg
54 M2 Troitsa U.S.S.R.
55 D4 Troitsk U.S.S.R.
55 D3 Troitskiy U.S.S.R.
52 J3 Troitsko-Pechorsk U.S.S.R.
55 C4 Troitskoye Bashkirskaya U.S.S.R.
55 E1 Troitskoye Tyumenskaya U.S.S.R.
127 L2 Troja Jamaica
28 N1 Troldenæs Faeroes
28 B5 Troldhede Denmark
28 N2 Troldhoved *isld* Faeroes
27 F13 Trollhättan Sweden
26 D9 Trollheimen *mt* Norway
26 C9 Trolltindane *mt* Norway
129 G4 Trombetas *R* Brazil
133 C5 Tromen *mt* Argentina
131 B6 Tromen, V Argentina
41 M6 Trompia, V Italy
26 K2 Tromsö Norway
26 K2 Tromsöysund Norway
55 F1 Trom'yegan *R* U.S.S.R.
102 G6 Trona California
131 B8 Tronador *peak* Arg/Chile
124 G6 Troncón Mexico
26 J3 Trondenes Norway
26 D8 Trondheim Norway
26 D8 Trondheimsfjord *inlet* Norway
26 E9 Tronfjell *mt* Norway
27 J10 Trönödal Sweden
42 F6 Tronto *R* Italy
21 G6 Trôo France
79 C4 Troödos, Mt Cyprus
12 D3 Trool, L Scotland
12 D2 Troon Scotland
43 G10 Tropea Italy
130 G4 Tropeiros, Sa.dos *mts* Brazil
103 M4 Tropic Utah
46 D2 Tropojë Albania
27 J13 Trosa Sweden
52 J2 Trosh U.S.S.R.
98 K6 Trosky Minnesota
119 N9 Trossachs Sask
12 D1 Trossachs Scotland
14 E1 Trostan *mt* N Ireland
28 E6 Trøstrup Korup Denmark
48 M2 Trostyanets U.S.S.R.
33 P9 Trotha E Germany
98 C2 Trotters N Dakota
48 K4 Trotusul *R* Romania
101 T9 Troublesome Colorado
142 F2 Troughton I W Australia
68 G6 Troun Cambodia
109 M3 Troup Texas
107 L4 Trousdale Kansas
122 F6 Trousers, L New Brunswick
111 D10 Trout Louisiana
117 L6 Trout *R* Br Col
13 F5 Troutbeck England
103 L6 Trout Cr Arizona
100 E5 Trout Cr Oregon
99 R3 Trout Creek Michigan
100 K2 Trout Creek Montana
121 L7 Trout Creek Ontario
103 L2 Trout Creek Utah
117 P10 Trout L Br Col
99 R3 Trout L Wisconsin
117 N5 Trout Lake N W Terr
101 Q5 Trout Pk Wyoming
118 C2 Trout R Alberta
123 O4 Trout River Nfld
95 K5 Trout Run Pennsylvania
94 J5 Troutville Pennsylvania
94 H9 Troutville Virginia
20 F3 Trouville France
8 D5 Trowbridge England
139 H8 Trowutta Tasmania
111 L10 Troy Alabama
100 J3 Troy Idaho
110 K3 Troy Indiana
127 J2 Troy Jamaica
110 F3 Troy Missouri
100 K1 Troy Montana
112 H2 Troy N Carolina
95 P4 Troy New Hampshire
95 O4 Troy New York
110 M1 Troy Ohio
100 H4 Troy Oregon
95 L5 Troy Pennsylvania
109 K4 Troy Texas
47 H5 Troy Turkey
94 G7 Troy W Virginia
47 G2 Troyan Bulgaria
18 H4 Troyes France
95 P2 Troy, N Vermont
103 J3 Troy Pk Nevada
37 N3 Tršnice Czechoslovakia
48 F1 Trstená Czechoslovakia
46 D1 Trstenik Yugoslavia
140 D1 Truant I N Terr Aust
119 N9 Truax Sask
54 E4 Trubchevsk U.S.S.R.
54 C6 Trubezh *R* U.S.S.R.
68 H7 Truc Giang Vietnam
124 G5 Truchas Mexico
106 E5 Truchas New Mexico
36 D6 Truchtersheim France
Trucial States *see* United Arab Emirates
102 D2 Truckee California
102 E2 Truckee *R* Nevada
140 B5 Truer Ra N Terr Aust
143 E7 Truer Tableland W Australia
15 D4 Truim *R* Scotland
121 M5 Truite, L. la Quebec
125 L2 Trujillo Honduras
106 F6 Trujillo New Mexico
128 C5 Trujillo Peru
16 D5 Trujillo Spain
127 J10 Trujillo Venezuela
134 F7 Truk Is Caroline Is Pacific Oc
99 M6 Truman Minnesota
110 F6 Trumann Arkansas
95 L4 Trumansburg New York
98 H9 Trumbull Nebraska
103 L5 Trumbull, Mt Arizona
9 G3 Trumpington England
20 F4 Trun France
139 J5 Trundle New S Wales
67 B5 Trung Khanh Phu Vietnam
69 G8 Trung Lon,Hon *isld* Vietnam
69 G8 Trung Nho,Hon *isld* Vietnam
8 A7 Truro England
99 N8 Truro Iowa
95 R4 Truro Massachusetts
122 J8 Truro Nova Scotia
138 E5 Truro S Australia
70 D2 Trusan Sarawak
108 H2 Truscott Texas
48 K3 Truşeşti Romania
37 J2 Trusetal E Germany
14 C2 Truskmore *mt* Irish Rep
143 D10 Truslove W Australia
70 E2 Trus Madi, G *mt* Sabah
52 H2 Trusovo U.S.S.R.
111 K8 Trussville Alabama
28 F4 Trustrup Denmark
117 M7 Trutch Br Col
106 C8 Truth or Consequences New Mexico
31 J5 Trutnov Czechoslovakia
20 D4 Truttemer-le-Petit France
95 L4 Truxton New York
18 G8 Truyère *R* France
47 G2 Tryavna Bulgaria
98 F8 Tryon Nebraska
145 E2 Tryphena New Zealand
27 F10 Trysil Norway
27 E10 Trysilelv *R* Norway
52 B6 Tryškiai U.S.S.R.
31 J2 Trzcianka Poland
31 H2 Trzebiez Poland
31 K4 Trzebnica Poland
31 K3 Trzemeszno Poland
42 F2 Tržič Yugoslavia
58 C2 Tsagaain-uul Mongolia
Tsaidam *see* Ch'ai-ta-mu P'en-ti *reg* China
Tsaidam *basin see* Qaidam
46 D5 Tsamandás Greece
Tsamkong *see* Zhanjiang
Tsangpo *see* Yarlung Zangbo Jiang
Tsaochwang *see* Zaozhuang
87 H11 Tsaratanana Madagascar
87 H10 Tsaratanana, Massif du *mt* Madagascar
87 D10 Tsau Botswana
88 G3 Tsavo Kenya
88 G3 Tsavo Nat. Park Kenya
41 M4 Tschlin Switzerland
55 D5 Tselinnyy U.S.S.R.
55 F5 Tselinograd U.S.S.R.
54 F3 Tsementnyy U.S.S.R.
58 E2 Tsenhermandal Mongolia
52 G3 Tsenogora U.S.S.R.
56 C3 Tsentral'nyy U.S.S.R.
87 C11 Tses Namibia
58 C2 Tsetserleg Mongolia
58 D2 Tsetserleg Mongolia
85 E7 Tsevié Togo
87 D11 Tshabong Botswana
87 D7 Tshabuta Zaïre
87 D10 Tshane Botswana
87 E8 Tshangalele, L Zaïre
86 B7 Tshela Zaïre
87 D7 Tshibala Zaïre
86 B6 Tshibobo, Pte Gabon
86 D7 Tshikapa Zaïre
87 D7 Tshimbalanga Zaïre
87 E8 Tshinsenda Zaïre
89 C4 Tshkudu Botswana
86 E7 Tshofa Zaïre
86 D6 Tshuapa *R* Zaïre
87 D10 Tshwanne Botswana
48 M1 Tsibulev U.S.S.R.
87 H13 Tsihombe Madagascar
52 G2 Tsil'ma *R* U.S.S.R.
53 F10 Tsimlyansk U.S.S.R.
65 D6 Tsinan China
87 D11 Tsineng S Africa
47 G3 Tsínga *mt* Greece
Tsingtao *see* Qingdao
68 F1 Tsinh Ho Vietnam
Tsining *see* Jining Nei Monggol Zizhiqu
Tsin Ling *mt ra see* Qin Ling
46 E5 Tsiótion Greece
58 G1 Tsipa *R* U.S.S.R.
87 H11 Tsiroanomandidy Madagascar
Tsitsihar *see* Qiqihar
89 C9 Tsitsikamaberge *mts* S Africa
52 G6 Tsivilsk U.S.S.R.
87 H12 Tsivory Madagascar
52 D6 Tsna *R* U.S.S.R.
61 K11 Tsu Japan
61 M8 Tsubame Japan
61 K9 Tsubata Japan
61 O9 Tsuchiura Japan
60 O4 Tsugaru-kaikyō *str* Japan
61 N8 Tsugawa Japan
61 P13 Tsuha Okinawa
61 L10 Tsukechi Japan
61 P13 Tsuken-jima *isld* Okinawa
60 P2 Tsukigata Japan
61 J12 Tsukiji Japan
60 E12 Tsukumi Japan
87 C9 Tsumeb Namibia
87 C10 Tsumis Namibia
61 M10 Tsuru Japan
61 K10 Tsuruga Japan
61 K10 Tsuruga-wan *B* Japan
61 K9 Tsurugi Japan
60 H12 Tsurugi-san *mt* Japan
61 N7 Tsuruoka Japan
59 L4 Tsururga Japan
60 E12 Tsurusaki Japan
61 K10 Tsushima Japan
59 J5 Tsushima *isld* Japan
60 C11 Tsushima-kaikyō *str* Japan
60 C11 Tsutsu Japan
60 E11 Tsuwano Japan
60 H10 Tsuyama Japan
60 D12 Tsuyazaki Japan
55 E1 Tsyngaly U.S.S.R.
52 D1 Tsyp Navolok U.S.S.R.
54 K1 Tsyurupi, Im U.S.S.R.
16 C3 Tua *R* Portugal
145 G3 Tuahine Pt. New Zealand
145 F3 Tuai New Zealand
145 E2 Tuakau New Zealand
14 C3 Tuam Irish Rep
145 D4 Tuamarina New Zealand
135 N10 Tuamotu *arch* Pacific Oc
135 M10 Tuamotu Ridge Pacific Oc
70 D6 Tuanan Kalimantan
68 F2 Tuan Giao Vietnam
69 C11 Tuangku *isld* Sumatra
67 B3 Tuanxi China
144 B7 Tuapeka Mouth New Zealand
125 N2 Tuapi Nicaragua
53 E11 Tuapse U.S.S.R.
70 E1 Tuaran Sabah
144 A7 Tuatapere New Zealand
70 K8 Tua, Tg *C* Sumatra
56 D4 Tuba *R* U.S.S.R.
103 N10 Tubac Arizona
103 N5 Tuba City Arizona
71 B3 Tubalai *isld* Indonesia
78 H5 Tubal, Wadi Iraq
70 O9 Tuban Java
133 H3 Tubarão Brazil
80 E4 Tubas Jordan
70 C3 Tubau Sarawak
71 D6 Tubbataha Reefs Sulu Sea
118 J8 Tuberose Sask
71 E7 Tubigan *isld* Philippines
71 E8 Tubig Puti Philippines
71 E4 Tubile Pt Philippines
36 G7 Tübingen W Germany
55 C4 Tubinskiy U.S.S.R.
22 G2 Tubize Belgium
71 F6 Tubod Mindanao Philippines
142 A5 Tubridgi Pt W Australia
84 G3 Tubruq Libya
70 E3 Tubu *R* Kalimantan
135 M10 Tubuai Is Pacific Oc
124 D2 Tubutama Mexico
127 K9 Tucacas Venezuela
100 H3 Tucannon *R* Washington
129 L6 Tucano Brazil
128 G7 Tucavaca Bolivia
18 G10 Tuchan France
67 A3 Tucheng China
117 J5 Tuchitua Yukon Terr
117 L6 Tuchodi *R* Br Col
31 K2 Tuchola Poland
48 G1 Tuchów Poland
143 C7 Tuckanarra W Australia
142 E4 Tuckfield, Mt W Australia
103 O9 Tucson Arizona
103 N9 Tucson Mts Arizona
133 D3 Tucumán *prov* Argentina
106 G6 Tucumcari New Mexico
129 G5 Tucunaré Brazil
127 M10 Tucupido Venezuela
127 N10 Tucupita Venezuela
129 J4 Tucurui Brazil
31 J2 Tuczno Poland
71 L10 Tudameda Indonesia
25 E6 Tüddern W Germany
28 G6 Tudeå *R* Denmark
17 F2 Tudela Spain
16 D3 Tudela de Duero Spain
120 J3 Tudhope Ontario
102 C2 Tudor California
16 C3 Tuela *R* Portugal
28 H5 Tuelsø Denmark
141 H8 Tuen Queensland
129 H4 Tueré *R* Brazil
20 G5 Tuffe France
136 K3 Tufi Papua New Guinea
8 B4 Tufton Wales
112 D3 Tugaloo L S Carolina
118 L8 Tugaske Sask
89 G7 Tugela *R* S Africa
94 E9 Tug Fork *R* Kentucky
139 K5 Tuggerah L New S Wales
116 K8 Tugidak I Alaska
71 G5 Tugnug Pt Samar Philippines
55 D1 Tugrovskiy U.S.S.R.
115 O3 Tugssâq Greenland
70 F4 Tuguan Maputi *isld* Indonesia
71 G7 Tugubun Pt Philippines
71 E2 Tuguegarao Philippines
55 D3 Tugulym U.S.S.R.
59 L1 Tugur U.S.S.R.
145 D4 Tui New Zealand
125 P10 Tuila Guatemala
65 A4 Tui Lamin Sum China
56 C4 Tuim U.S.S.R.
Tujiabu *see* Yongxiu
69 D11 Tuka Sumatra
55 C4 Tukan U.S.S.R.
79 B8 Tûkh Egypt
145 F3 Tukituki R New Zealand
68 F6 Tuk Luy Cambodia
114 F4 Tuktoyaktuk N W Terr
52 B6 Tukums U.S.S.R.
70 B5 Tukung, Bt *mt* Kalimantan
87 F7 Tukuyu Tanzania
77 K2 Tukzar Afghanistan
125 K6 Tula Mexico
54 J2 Tula U.S.S.R.
119 O4 Tulabi Lake Sask
58 C4 Tulai Shan China
117 N11 Tulameen Br Col
125 K7 Tulancingo Mexico
70 K8 Tulangbawang *R* Sumatra
102 E5 Tulare California
98 H5 Tulare S Dakota
102 E6 Tulare L.Bed California
108 A2 Tularosa New Mexico
106 B8 Tularosa Mts New Mexico
106 D9 Tularosa V New Mexico
89 B8 Tulbagh *mt* S Africa
128 C3 Tulcán Ecuador
48 M5 Tulcea Romania
48 M2 Tulchin U.S.S.R.
127 H9 Tulé Venezuela
102 E5 Tule *R* California
Tuléar *see* Toliara
108 F1 Tule Cr Texas
100 D8 Tule L California
100 E8 Tule L.Res California
19 N16 Tulette France
89 F3 Tuli Zimbabwe
31 L3 Tuliszków Poland
52 D3 Tulivaara Finland
80 D4 Tulkarm Jordan
14 C4 Tulla Irish Rep
110 K6 Tullahoma Tennessee
14 D3 Tullamore Irish Rep
139 J5 Tullamore New S Wales
18 G7 Tulle France
28 F7 Tullebølle Denmark
139 H5 Tullibigeal New S Wales
40 B7 Tullins France
48 C2 Tulln Austria
38 N5 Tullnerfeld *reg* Austria
111 D10 Tullos Louisiana
14 E4 Tullow Irish Rep
95 L4 Tully New York
141 H4 Tully Queensland
141 H4 Tully Falls Queensland
140 E3 Tully Inlet Queensland
52 D1 Tuloma *R* U.S.S.R.
65 H1 Tulongshan China
29 P8 Tulos, Oz *L* U.S.S.R.
52 D3 Tulos, Oz *L* U.S.S.R.
47 H2 Tulovo Bulgaria
52 J4 Tulpan U.S.S.R.
107 P5 Tulsa Oklahoma
117 G6 Tulsequah Br Col
14 C3 Tulsk Irish Rep
28 D4 Tulstrup Denmark
128 C3 Tuluá Colombia
125 Q7 Tulum Mexico
131 C4 Tulumaya *R* Argentina
55 C2 Tulumbasy U.S.S.R.
131 C3 Tulum, V.de Argentina
56 F4 Tulun U.S.S.R.
70 N10 Tulungagung Java
71 D5 Tuluran Philippines
55 C3 Tulva *R* U.S.S.R.
54 M1 Tuma U.S.S.R.
103 N10 Tumacacori Nat.Mon Arizona
128 C3 Tumaco Colombia
71 G7 Tumadgo Pt Mindanao Philippines
100 D5 Tumalo Oregon
52 D6 Tumanovo U.S.S.R.
55 E2 Tuman, Oz *L* U.S.S.R.
51 P2 Tumany U.S.S.R.
56 E5 Tumat-Tayga, Khrebet *mts* U.S.S.R.
128 G2 Tumatumari Guyana
86 D6 Tumba Zaïre
71 G7 Tumbao Philippines
139 J6 Tumbarumba New S Wales
128 B4 Tumbes Peru
124 H8 Tumbiscatio Mexico
95 R1 Tumbledown Mt Maine
140 B2 Tumbling Waters N Terr Aust
130 B9 Tumburús Argentina
9 F1 Tumby England
138 D5 Tumby Bay S Australia
65 A4 Tumd Youqi China
65 B4 Tumd Zuoqi China
80 G4 Tumeira Jordan
65 H3 Tumen China
59 J3 Tumen *R* China/Korea
128 F2 Tumeremo Venezuela
70 F2 Tumindao *isld* Philippines
130 H6 Tumiritinga Brazil
76 C4 Tumkur India
15 D4 Tummel *R* Scotland
59 M2 Tumnin *R* U.S.S.R.
77 H6 Tump Pakistan
69 F9 Tumpat Malaysia
74 H8 Tumsar India
85 D6 Tumu Ghana
129 G3 Tumucamaque, Sa *mts* Brazil
139 J6 Tumut New S Wales
52 H6 Tumutuk U.S.S.R.
27 F13 Tun Sweden
26 J9 Tuna Sweden
71 G7 Tuna Bay Mindanao Philippines
127 O2 Tunapuna Trinidad
128 E7 Tunari *mt* Bolivia
126 E4 Tunas de Zaza Cuba
131 E5 Tunas, L Argentina
77 D6 Tunb Buzurg *isld* Iran
139 H8 Tunbridge Tasmania
9 G5 Tunbridge Wells, Royal England
78 G2 Tunceli Turkey
67 C7 Tunchang China
139 L4 Tuncurry New S Wales
52 F3 Tundra U.S.S.R.
87 F7 Tunduma Zambia
88 F7 Tunduru Tanzania
28 J5 Tune Denmark
70 F2 Tungku Sabah
29 P6 Tungozero U.S.S.R.
67 G5 Tung Shan Taiwan
102 F1 Tungsten Nevada
117 J5 Tungsten N W Terr
Tungting Lake *see* Dongting Ho
70 C4 Tungun, Bt *mt* Kalimantan
56 F1 Tunguska *R* U.S.S.R.
58 E2 Tünhel Mongolia
27 C11 Tunhovdfjord *L* Norway
76 F2 Tuni India
43 C12 Tunis Tunisia
43 D11 Tunis, G. de Tunisia
84 D3 Tunisia *rep* N Africa
128 D2 Tunja Colombia
56 F5 Tunkinskiye Gol'tsy *mts* U.S.S.R.
65 B6 Tunliu China
26 E9 Tunna *R* Norway
139 H8 Tunnack Tasmania
120 G6 Tunnel Dam Ontario
19 O18 Tunnel du Rove France
94 H7 Tunnelton W Virginia
26 F7 Tunnsjö *L* Norway
28 E5 Tunø Denmark
8 D1 Tunstall Stafford England
9 H3 Tunstall Suffolk England
115 N6 Tunungayualok I Labrador
131 C4 Tunuyán, R Argentina
131 C4 Tunuyán, Sa. de *mts* Argentina
67 F2 Tunxi China
67 D4 Tuojiang China
67 A1 Tuo Jiang *R* China
65 E5 Tuoji Dao *isld* China
68 G6 Tuol Khpos Cambodia
102 D4 Tuolumne California

Tuolumne Meadows — Uruguay, R 79

102 E4 Tuolumne Meadows California
29 L7 Tuomioja Finland
51 L2 Tuoy U.S.S.R.
130 E7 Tupá Brazil
130 E6 Tupaciguara Brazil
128 F4 Tupanaóca Brazil
145 G2 Tuparoa New Zealand
111 H7 Tupelo Mississippi
109 L1 Tupelo Oklahoma
52 D6 Tupik U.S.S.R.
128 G4 Tupinambaranas, I Brazil
130 E4 Tupiraçaba Brazil
133 D2 Tupiza Bolivia
102 E6 Tupman California
29 L7 Tupos Finland
117 N8 Tupper Br Col
95 N2 Tupper Lake New York
133 D4 Tupungato mt Arg/Chile
65 E2 Tuquan China
128 C3 Tuquerres Colombia
67 D7 Tuqu Wan B China
66 D4 Tura China
75 O6 Tura India
55 D2 Tura R U.S.S.R.
145 E4 Turakina New Zealand
145 E4 Turakirae Head New Zealand
141 K8 Turallin Queensland
56 D5 Turan U.S.S.R.
59 K1 Turana, Khrebet mt U.S.S.R.
145 E3 Turangi New Zealand
42 E6 Turano R Italy
45 N5 Turano, L.di Italy
126 G9 Turbaco Colombia
52 H4 Turbanovo U.S.S.R.
77 H7 Turbat Pakistan
41 J3 Turbenthal Switzerland
126 F10 Turbo Colombia
17 H2 Turbón mt Spain
48 M1 Turbov U.S.S.R.
48 H6 Turburea Romania
52 E3 Turchasovo U.S.S.R.
48 H4 Turda Romania
143 C6 Turee Cr W Australia
16 E3 Turégano Spain
31 L3 Turek Poland
79 D10 Tûr, El Egypt
127 K10 Turen Venezuela
66 D3 Turfan Depression China
57 C1 Turgay U.S.S.R.
57 B1 Turgay R U.S.S.R.
55 D5 Turgayskaya Stolovaya Strana dist U.S.S.R.
121 L3 Turgeon R Quebec
47 H1 Türgovishte Bulgaria
55 D3 Turgoyak U.S.S.R.
47 J6 Turgutlu Turkey
78 F1 Turhal Turkey
52 C5 Türi U.S.S.R.
17 G5 Turia R Spain
129 J4 Turiaçu Brazil
127 L9 Turiamo Venezuela
31 L7 Turiec R Czechoslovakia
126 E3 Turiguano, I Cuba
Turin see Torino
118 E9 Turin Alberta
95 M3 Turin New York
55 D2 Turinsk U.S.S.R.
55 D3 Turinskaya-Sloboda U.S.S.R.
59 K2 Turiy Rog U.S.S.R.
48 D3 Türje Hungary
48 H1 Turka U.S.S.R.
56 G4 Turka R U.S.S.R.
Turkana, L see Rudolf, L
47 J4 Türkeli isld Turkey
41 O1 Turkenfeld W Germany
57 E3 Turkestan U.S.S.R.
57 E5 Turkestanskiy Khr mts U.S.S.R.
48 F3 Túrkeve Hungary
108 G1 Turkey Texas
99 P7 Turkey R Iowa
78 D2 Turkey rep W Asia
142 G3 Turkey Cr W Australia
106 F6 Turkey Mts New Mexico
41 N1 Türkheim W Germany
36 C4 Türkismühle W Germany
47 L5 Turkmen Dağı mt Turkey
57 B5 Turkmen-Kala U.S.S.R.
57 B6 Turkmenkarakul' U.S.S.R.
50 E4 Turkmenskaya S.S.R U.S.S.R.
127 H4 Turks Is W Indies
29 J11 Turku Finland
27 M10 Turku Pori reg Finland
86 G5 Turkwel R Kenya
16 E5 Turleque Spain
102 D4 Turlock California
130 G5 Turmalina Brazil
117 J6 Turnagain R Br Col
145 F4 Turnagain, C New Zealand
38 M6 Turnau Austria
119 Q5 Turnberry Manitoba
15 D5 Turnberry Scotland
119 S4 Turnbull Manitoba
140 B5 Turnbull, Mt N Terr Aust
95 R2 Turner Maine
94 D2 Turner Michigan
101 R1 Turner Montana
100 C5 Turner Oregon
100 H3 Turner Washington
101 U6 Turnercrest Wyoming
142 B6 Turner, Mt W Australia
142 G4 Turner River W Australia
95 P4 Turners Falls Massachusetts
118 C8 Turner Valley Alberta
101 P7 Turnerville Wyoming
22 H1 Turnhout Belgium
38 M6 Turnitz Austria
31 J5 Turnov Czechoslovakia
47 G1 Turnu Măgurele Romania
48 J5 Turnu Roşu Romania
48 H6 Turnu Severin Romania
57 H1 Turobay U.S.S.R.
31 O5 Turobin Poland
107 M4 Turon Kansas
139 J5 Turon R New S Wales
139 J5 Tuross R New S Wales
66 D3 Turpan China
108 D7 Turpin Oklahoma
106 D9 Turquoise New Mexico
116 K6 Turquoise L Alaska
38 J8 Turrach Austria
110 F6 Turrell Arkansas
125 N5 Turrialba Costa Rica
19 Q16 Turriers France
15 F3 Turriff Scotland
55 D1 Tursuntskiy Tuman, Oz L U.S.S.R.
57 E5 Tursunzade U.S.S.R.
55 E2 Turtas R U.S.S.R.
57 B4 Turtkul' U.S.S.R.
99 O1 Turtle R Ontario
122 H8 Turtle Cr New Brunswick
118 J5 Turtleford Sask
141 G1 Turtlehead I Queensland
141 K3 Turtle I Gt Barrier Reef Aust
142 C5 Turtle I W Australia
85 B7 Turtle Is Sierra Leone
98 F2 Turtle L N Dakota
118 J5 Turtle L Sask
99 O4 Turtle L Wisconsin
98 F1 Turtle Mts Manitoba/N Dakota
29 K5 Turtola Finland
98 H4 Turton S Dakota
145 E2 Turua New Zealand
51 H2 Turukhansk U.S.S.R.
55 E1 Turumeyevo U.S.S.R.
129 G3 Turuna R Brazil
28 D6 Turup Denmark
9 F3 Turvey England
130 D10 Turvo R Brazil
53 B8 Tur'ya R U.S.S.R.
31 L6 Turzovka Czechoslovakia
111 J8 Tuscaloosa Alabama
42 D6 Tuscania Italy
94 F6 Tuscarawas R Ohio
100 J8 Tuscarora Nevada
94 K6 Tuscarora Mt Pennsylvania
110 H2 Tuscola Illinois
100 K2 Tuscor Montana
110 D3 Tuscumbia Missouri
28 H5 Tuse Denmark
14 E4 Tuskar Rock Irish Rep
111 L9 Tuskegee Alabama
122 G10 Tusket Nova Scotia
54 H5 Tuskor' R U.S.S.R.
48 K4 Tuşnad Romania
21 F10 Tusson France
102 G8 Tustin California
94 B2 Tustin Michigan
26 C8 Tustna isld Norway
116 M6 Tustumena L Alaska
31 M4 Tuszyn Poland
78 J2 Tutak Turkey
145 D1 Tutamoe Range New Zealand
52 E5 Tutayev U.S.S.R.
9 E2 Tutbury England
98 E6 Tuthill S Dakota
76 D6 Tuticorin India
46 D1 Tutin Yugoslavia
145 F3 Tutira L New Zealand
29 O5 Tutiyarvi U.S.S.R.
70 D3 Tutoh R Sarawak
129 K4 Tutóia Brazil
70 D2 Tutong Brunei
48 L4 Tutova R Romania
33 S5 Tutow E Germany
47 H1 Tutrakan Bulgaria
48 K6 Tutraken Romania
117 F5 Tutshi L Yukon Terr
101 L7 Tuttle Idaho
98 F2 Tuttle N Dakota
107 N6 Tuttle Oklahoma
37 K2 Tüttleben W Germany
107 O2 Tuttle Cr.Res Kansas
99 M6 Tuttle L Minnesota
41 J2 Tuttlingen W Germany
137 S4 Tutuila isld Amer Samoa
125 L9 Tututepec Mexico
71 O8 Tutuwawang Indonesia
111 F7 Tutwiler Mississippi
41 O2 Tutzing W Germany
58 D2 Tuul Gol R Mongolia
29 L10 Tuulos Finland
29 P9 Tuupovarra Finland
29 O9 Tuusniemi Finland
137 Q3 Tuvalu islds Pacific Oc
137 R6 Tuvana-i-Ra isld Pacific Oc
137 R6 Tuvana-i-Tholo isld Pacific Oc
56 E5 Tuvinskaya Aut.Obl A.S.S.R. U.S.S.R.
103 L5 Tuweep Arizona
65 A5 Tuwei He R China
116 L6 Tuxedni B Alaska
118 A1 Tuxedo Manitoba
112 E2 Tuxedo N Carolina
41 P3 Tuxer Gebirge mt Austria
9 F1 Tuxford England
119 M8 Tuxford Sask
67 C1 Tuxiang China
124 H8 Tuxpan Jalisco Mexico
125 L7 Tuxpan Mexico
124 G7 Tuxpan Nayarit Mexico
125 N9 Tuxtla Gutiérrez Mexico
16 B2 Tuy Spain
55 F2 Tuy R U.S.S.R.
117 H6 Tuya L Br Col
68 J6 Tuy An Vietnam
67 B6 Tuyen Quang Vietnam
68 J6 Tuy Hoa Vietnam
52 H6 Tuymazy U.S.S.R.
77 A2 Tüysarkān Iran
78 D2 Tuz Gölü L Turkey
103 N7 Tuzigoot Nat.Mon Arizona
57 D4 Tuzkan, Ozero L U.S.S.R.
78 K4 Tuz Khurmātū Iraq
48 E6 Tuzla Yugoslavia
78 H2 Tuzla R Turkey
48 N5 Tuzly U.S.S.R.
27 F14 Tvååker Sweden
28 N3 Tværa Faeroes
26 L7 Tvärålund Sweden
26 M6 Tvärån Sweden
28 E4 Tved Århus Denmark
28 F6 Tved Fyn Denmark
28 E3 Tvede Denmark
27 C13 Tvedestrand Norway
Tver see Kalinin
28 E1 Tversted Denmark
52 E6 Tvertsa R U.S.S.R.
27 H15 Tving Sweden
28 D5 Tvingstrup Denmark
28 B4 Tvis Denmark
47 H2 Tvŭrditsa Bulgaria
68 B4 Twante Burma
31 K4 Twardogóra Poland
85 F4 Twaret Niger
121 N8 Tweed Ontario
139 L3 Tweed Heads New S Wales
118 F4 Tweedie Alberta
13 E3 Tweed, R Scotland
13 E3 Tweedsmuir Scotland
117 K9 Tweedsmuir Prov.Park Br Col
87 D11 Twee Rivieren S Africa
118 L9 Twelvemile L Sask
116 P4 Twelvemile Summit Alaska
14 B3 Twelve Pins mt Irish Rep
103 H7 Twentynine Palms California
143 F9 Twilight Cove W Australia
123 S4 Twillingate Nfld
38 L8 Twimberg Austria
100 B1 Twin Washington
101 N4 Twin Bridges Montana
98 K4 Twin Brooks S Dakota
108 G4 Twin Buttes Res Texas
119 O2 Twin City Ontario
101 L7 Twin Falls Idaho
115 N7 Twin Falls Labrador
142 F5 Twin Heads mt W Australia
141 G2 Twin Humps peak Queensland
94 C2 Twin L Michigan
99 U6 Twin Lake Michigan
116 K6 Twin Lakes Alaska
117 P7 Twin Lakes Alberta
106 D2 Twin Lakes Colorado
101 L6 Twin Lakes Res Idaho
123 Q4 Twin L.,N Nfld
123 R4 Twin L.,S Nfld
95 Q2 Twin Mountain New Hampshire
102 D2 Twin Peaks California
101 L5 Twin Peaks Idaho
143 C10 Twin Pks W Australia
143 D10 Twin Rocks W Australia
138 E3 Twins Cr S Australia
138 D4 Twins, The S Australia
145 D4 Twins, The mt New Zealand
98 K2 Twin Valley Minnesota
100 E1 Twisp Washington
32 J7 Twistringen W Germany
108 D8 Twitty Texas
117 J4 Twitya R N W Terr
144 C6 Twizel New Zealand
106 H4 Two Buttes Colorado
119 R8 Two Creeks Manitoba
99 T5 Two Creeks Wisconsin
101 P3 Twodot Montana
139 K6 Twofold B New S Wales
99 P2 Two Harbors Minnesota
116 L8 Two Headed I Alaska
118 F5 Two Hills Alberta
101 P5 Two Ocean Pass Wyoming
99 T5 Two Rivers Wisconsin
108 C2 Two Rivers Res New Mexico
9 E2 Twycross England
9 F5 Twyford Berks England
9 E5 Twyford Hampshire England
12 D4 Twynholm Scotland
48 H2 Tyachevo U.S.S.R.
112 G5 Tybee Roads S Carolina
28 H6 Tybjerg Denmark
102 H3 Tybo Nevada
28 D6 Tybrind Vig B Denmark
56 E1 Tychany R U.S.S.R.
55 G3 Tychkino U.S.S.R.
31 J2 Tychowo Poland
31 L5 Tychy Poland
26 E8 Tydal Norway
59 J1 Tyeda U.S.S.R.
117 F7 Tyee Alaska
100 A1 Tyee Washington
94 J9 Tye River Virginia
94 H8 Tygart V W Virginia
101 N7 Tyhee Idaho
27 C10 Tyin L Norway
31 O2 Tykocin Poland
98 K5 Tyler Minnesota
94 J5 Tyler Pennsylvania
109 M3 Tyler Texas
100 H2 Tyler Washington
111 A9 Tyler, L Texas
111 F10 Tylertown Mississippi
28 D2 Tylstrup Denmark
56 C1 Tym R U.S.S.R.
48 F1 Tymbark Poland
59 M1 Tymovskoye U.S.S.R.
55 F2 Tynay U.S.S.R.
59 H1 Tynda U.S.S.R.
118 E1 Tyndall Manitoba
98 J6 Tyndall S Dakota
144 C5 Tyndall, Mt New Zealand
26 J9 Tynderö Sweden
13 G4 Tyne and Wear co England
13 G3 Tynemouth England
118 J7 Tyner Sask
122 J7 Tyne Valley Pr Edward I
27 G11 Tyngsjö Sweden
31 H6 Týn nad Vltava Czechoslovakia
26 E9 Tynset Norway
8 C2 Tyn-y-Groes Wales
116 O5 Tyone R Alaska
79 F5 Tyr Lebanon
Tyre see Tyr
27 D11 Tyrifjorden L Norway
27 G15 Tyringe Sweden
59 K1 Tyrma U.S.S.R.
48 L2 Tyrnovo U.S.S.R.
112 E2 Tyron N Carolina
106 B9 Tyrone New Mexico
94 J6 Tyrone Pennsylvania
14 D2 Tyrone co N Ireland
139 G6 Tyrrell R Victoria
43 D8 Tyrrhenian Sea S Europe
28 D5 Tyrsted Denmark
26 H3 Tysfjord Norway
27 A12 Tysnesöy isld Norway
27 B11 Tyssedal Norway
27 J13 Tystberga Sweden
28 H6 Tystrup Denmark
31 O5 Tyszowce Poland
55 F3 Tyukalinsk U.S.S.R.
57 H4 Tyulek U.S.S.R.
55 C4 Tyul'gan U.S.S.R.
55 E1 Tyuli U.S.S.R.
52 J5 Tyul'kino U.S.S.R.
55 E3 Tyumen U.S.S.R.
57 D3 Tyumen'-Aryk U.S.S.R.
50 F2 Tyumenskaya Oblast' prov U.S.S.R.
55 E4 Tyuntyugur U.S.S.R.
57 C2 Tyuratam U.S.S.R.
52 D1 Tyuva Guba U.S.S.R.
119 O8 Tyvan Sask
48 M1 Tyvrov U.S.S.R.
8 B2 Tywyn Wales
25 C3 t'Zand Netherlands
87 F10 Tzaneen S Africa
Tzepo see Zibo
46 E5 Tzoumérka mt Greece
67 G4 Tz'u-kao Shan peak Taiwan
25 E2 Tzummarum Netherlands
85 B3 Uad el Jat watercourse Morocco
116 H7 Ualik, L Alaska
141 G5 Uanda Queensland
86 H5 Uanle Uen Somalia
86 A2 Uargalo Somalia
142 B6 Uaroo W Australia
86 A3 Uarsciek Somalia
128 G4 Uatumá R Brazil
129 L5 Uaua Brazil
130 G10 Uauá Brazil
128 E4 Uaupés Brazil
145 G3 Uawa R New Zealand
125 P9 Uaxactún Guatemala
130 G7 Ubá Brazil
56 B5 Uba R U.S.S.R.
55 E4 Ubagan R U.S.S.R.
130 G5 Ubaí Brazil
129 L6 Ubaitaba Brazil
86 C5 Ubangi R Cent Afr Republic/Zaire
Ubari see Awbāri
78 H6 Ubayyid, Wadi al Saudi Arabia
28 G5 Ubby Denmark
59 K5 Ube Japan
60 E12 Ube Japan
16 E6 Ubeda Spain
115 O3 Ubekendt Ejland isld Greenland
38 M7 Übelbach Austria
133 H1 Uberaba Brazil
130 B5 Uberaba L Brazil/Bolivia
36 B5 Überherrn W Germany
130 E6 Uberlândia Brazil
41 K2 Überlingen Switzerland
85 F7 Ubiaja Nigeria
33 S9 Ubigau E Germany
133 D2 Ubina mt Bolivia
94 E3 Ubly Michigan
68 F4 Ubolratna res Thailand
87 F11 Ubombo S Africa
68 G5 Ubon Ratchathani Thailand
36 F5 Ubstadt-Weiher W Germany
70 P10 Ubud Indonesia
128 D5 Ucayali R Peru
22 G2 Uccle Belgium
16 E3 Ucero R Spain
55 C4 Uchaly U.S.S.R.
61 O8 Uchigō Japan
60 F12 Uchiko Japan
115 K7 Uchi Lake Ontario
60 O3 Uchiura wan B Japan
40 A4 Uchizy France
57 C4 Uch Kuduk U.S.S.R.
32 J7 Uchte W Germany
33 P7 Uchte R E Germany
51 N3 Uchur R U.S.S.R.
22 L5 Uckange France
30 H2 Ücker R E Germany
36 C2 Uckerath W Germany
33 U4 Uckeritz E Germany
9 G6 Uckfield England
33 T9 Uckro E Germany
117 L11 Ucluelet Br Col
101 O6 Ucon Idaho
101 T5 Ucross Wyoming
56 G5 Uda R U.S.S.R.
74 E6 Udaipur India
75 M5 Udaipur Garhi Nepal
76 C5 Udamalpet India
54 D6 Uday R U.S.S.R.
76 D3 Udayagiri India
42 G4 Udbina Yugoslavia
28 E3 Udby Århus Denmark
28 H5 Udby Denmark
28 D6 Udby Fyn Denmark
28 E3 Udbyhø Denmark
28 E3 Udbyneder Denmark
27 E13 Uddevalla Sweden
12 D2 Uddingston Scotland
26 J6 Uddjaur L Sweden
25 E5 Uden Netherlands
32 M10 Uder E Germany
76 C1 Udgir India
74 F2 Udhampur Kashmir
142 E4 Udialla W Australia
42 E2 Udine Italy
56 E4 Udinskiy Khrebet mts
76 B4 Udipi India
71 K8 Udjung Indonesia
70 F7 Udjunglamuru Sulawesi
37 P3 Udlice Czechoslovakia
51 K4 Udokan Mongolia
52 E5 Udomlya U.S.S.R.
61 N11 Udone-jima isld Japan
68 F4 Udon Thani Thailand
140 B6 Udor, Mt N Terr Aust
59 L1 Udskaya Guba B U.S.S.R.
47 H2 Udvoy mt Bulgaria
59 L1 Udyl, Oz L U.S.S.R.
51 L1 Udzha U.S.S.R.
70 G5 Uëbonti Sulawesi
33 U5 Uecker R E Germany
33 T6 Ueckermark reg E Germany
33 U5 Ueckermünde E Germany
61 M9 Ueda Japan
25 F5 Uedem W Germany
32 G8 Üeffeln W Germany
86 H5 Uegit Somalia
98 K8 Uehling Nebraska
60 D13 Ueki Japan
86 E5 Uele R Zaïre
32 E7 Uelsen W Germany
33 N7 Uelzen W Germany
61 K11 Ueno Japan
61 N10 Uenohara Japan
86 E5 Uere R Zaïre
36 B3 Uess R W Germany
32 L5 Uetersen W Germany
55 C4 Ufa U.S.S.R.
37 J4 Uffenheim W Germany
55 C3 Ufimka U.S.S.R.
87 C10 Ugab R Namibia
116 J8 Ugaiushak I Alaska
116 L8 Ugak I Alaska
88 C4 Ugalla R Tanzania
116 E9 Ugamak I Aleutian Is
86 F5 Uganda rep Africa
116 L8 Uganik I Alaska
116 J8 Ugashik B Alaska
116 J8 Ugashik Lakes Alaska
28 C7 Uge Denmark
43 J9 Ugento Italy
28 H5 Ugerløse Denmark
28 E4 Uggelhüse Denmark
28 E1 Uggerby Denmark
28 E5 Uggerslev Denmark
16 E8 Ugijar Spain
28 E2 Ugilt Denmark
19 Q13 Ugine France
59 M2 Uglegorsk U.S.S.R.
52 E6 Uglich U.S.S.R.
42 H5 Ugljane Yugoslavia
48 E6 Ugljevik Yugoslavia
52 D5 Uglovka U.S.S.R.
Ugoi see Ujiji
54 G2 Ugra R U.S.S.R.
55 F1 Ugut U.S.S.R.
83 L10 Uhana Sri Lanka
31 K6 Uherské Hradiště Czechoslovakia
36 H6 Uhingen W Germany
87 C10 Uhlenhorst Namibia
37 K4 Uhlfeld W Germany
119 T2 Uhlman L Manitoba
37 L2 Uhlstädt E Germany
28 C5 Uhre Denmark
94 F6 Uhrichsville Ohio
31 O4 Uhrusk Poland
15 B3 Uig Skye Scotland
55 B6 Uil U.S.S.R.
55 C6 Uil R U.S.S.R.
128 E7 Uiñamarco, L Peru/Bolivia
103 L5 Uinkaret Plat Arizona
55 C3 Uinskoye U.S.S.R.
101 P9 Uinta Mts Utah
89 D9 Uitenhage S Africa
25 C3 Uitgeest Netherlands
25 C4 Uithoorn Netherlands
25 G2 Uithuizen Netherlands
25 G2 Uithuizerwad Netherlands
31 L5 Ujazd Poland
61 J11 Uji Japan
74 F7 Ujiain India
61 N9 Ujiie Japan
88 B4 Ujiji Tanzania
48 E3 Újpest Hungary
31 K2 Ujście Poland
70 F7 Ujung Pandang Sulawesi
61 Q12 Uka Okinawa
61 L8 Ukawa Japan
88 D3 Ukerewe isld Tanzania
75 Q6 Ukhrul India
52 E4 Ukhtoma U.S.S.R.
100 G4 Ukiah Oregon
61 P13 Ukibaru-jima isld Okinawa
116 D4 Ukivok Alaska
Ukkel see Uccle
52 B6 Ukmerge U.S.S.R.
27 H13 Ukna Sweden
54 G7 Ukraina S.S.R rep U.S.S.R.
55 F4 Ukrainka Omsk U.S.S.R.
55 G3 Ukrainka U.S.S.R.
42 H4 Ukrina R Yugoslavia
55 D3 Uksyanskoye U.S.S.R.
31 N2 Ukta Poland
52 G3 Uktym U.S.S.R.
60 B12 Uku-shima isld Japan
47 J7 Ula Turkey
58 E2 Ulaanbaatar Mongolia
58 B2 Ulaangom Mongolia
139 J4 Ulan New S Wales
Ulan Bator see Ulaanbaatar
65 C2 Ulan Hobor China
Ulan Hot see Horqin Youyi Qianqi
65 E2 Ulan Hua China
48 L1 Ulanov U.S.S.R.
65 A4 Ulansuhai Nur L China
56 G5 Ulan-Ude U.S.S.R.
131 C3 Ulapes, Sa mts Argentina
139 H2 Ularunda Queensland
141 H7 Ularunda Queensland
56 B5 Ul'ba U.S.S.R.
51 N3 Ulbanskiy Zaliv B U.S.S.R.
28 C3 Ulbjerg Denmark
9 G1 Ulceby Cross England
42 J7 Ulcinj Yugoslavia
13 E4 Uldale England
28 D5 Uldum Denmark
Uleåborg see Oulu
27 D12 Ulefoss Norway
98 K2 Ulen Minnesota
52 C6 Ulena U.S.S.R.
138 F3 Ulenia, L New S Wales
58 F1 Ulety U.S.S.R.
28 A4 Ulfborg Denmark
28 A4 Ulfborg Kirke Denmark
37 J1 Ulfen W Germany
65 D2 Ulgai China
65 D2 Ulgain Gol R China
13 G3 Ulgham England
76 A1 Ulhasnagar India
Uliastai see Dong Ujimqin Qi
58 C2 Uliastay Mongolia
86 E6 Ulindi R Zaïre
42 G4 Uljan isld Yugoslavia
48 G5 Uljma Yugoslavia
57 C1 Ul'kayak R U.S.S.R.
28 D7 Ulkebøl Denmark
28 C5 Ulkind Denmark
56 G3 Ul'kon R U.S.S.R.
139 K6 Ulladulla New S Wales
137 L8 Ulladulla Trough Pacific Oc
26 K9 Ullånger Sweden
27 F14 Ullared Sweden
26 M4 Ullatti Sweden
29 K8 Ullava Finland
17 H4 Ulldecona Spain
27 B11 Ullensvang Norway
28 F6 Ullerslev Denmark
28 D7 Ullerup Denmark
110 G4 Ullin Illinois
28 C3 Ullits Denmark
26 L2 Ullsfjord Norway
13 F4 Ullswater L England
59 K4 Ullung Do isld S Korea
111 E7 Ulm Arkansas
36 H7 Ulm W Germany
101 T5 Ulm Wyoming
139 L3 Ulmarra New S Wales
36 B3 Ulmen W Germany
48 K5 Ulmeni Romania
38 L5 Ulmerfeld Austria
125 M2 Ulmukhuas Nicaragua
48 E7 Ulog Yugoslavia
88 E9 Ulongue Mozambique
138 E2 Uloowaranie, L S Australia
13 E5 Ulpha England
56 H1 Ulqkhan Botuobuya R U.S.S.R.
27 F14 Ulricehamn Sweden
143 E7 Ulrich Ra W Australia
36 G2 Ulrichstein W Germany
26 H8 Ulriksfors Sweden
25 F2 Ulrum Netherlands
59 J4 Ulsan S Korea
28 D7 Ulsby W Germany
15 G1 Ulsta Shetland Scotland
28 E2 Ulsted Denmark
26 A9 Ulstein Norway
95 L5 Ulster Pennsylvania
14 D2 Ulster prov N Ireland
14 D2 Ulster Canal N Ireland
28 F5 Ulstrup Denmark
26 K4 Ultevis mt Sweden
139 G6 Ultima Victoria
140 D6 Ultim, Mt N Terr Aust
41 O4 Ultimo.V.d' Italy
51 M2 Ulu U.S.S.R.
125 P10 Ulua R Honduras
47 K4 Ulubat Gölü L Turkey
47 K6 Ulubey Turkey
47 K4 Ulu Dağ mt Turkey
71 D5 Ulugan B Philippines
88 F5 Uluguru mts Tanzania
69 E11 Ulu Kali, Gunung Malaysia
78 E3 Ulukişla Turkey
70 C4 Ululselua, Bt mt Kalimantan
66 D2 Ulungur He R China
66 D2 Ulungur Hu L China
Ulun Hua see Siziwang Qi
58 F1 Ulunkhan U.S.S.R.
47 J5 Ulus Dağı mt Turkey
69 E10 Ulu Soh, Gunung mt Malaysia
57 D1 Ulutau U.S.S.R.
57 D2 Ulutau, Gory mts U.S.S.R.
56 C2 Ulu-Yul R U.S.S.R.
15 B4 Ulva isld Scotland
13 E5 Ulverston England
139 H8 Ulverstone Tasmania
27 B11 Ulvik Norway
27 M10 Ulvila Finland
26 K8 Ulvön isld Sweden
28 K6 Ulvshale pen Denmark
28 J7 Ulv Sund chan Denmark
52 G6 Ul'yankovo U.S.S.R.
53 G7 Ul'yanovsk U.S.S.R.
55 F5 Ul'yanovskoye U.S.S.R.
101 L4 Ulysses Idaho
107 J4 Ulysses Kansas
98 J8 Ulysses Nebraska
57 C1 Ulyzhilanshik R U.S.S.R.
Ulzburg see Henstedt-Ulzburg
48 N2 Uman' U.S.S.R.
115 O3 Umanak Greenland
131 C2 Umango, Cerro peak Argentina
74 J7 Umaria India
74 C6 Umarkot Pakistan
138 E2 Umaroona, L S Australia
113 F9 Umatilla Florida
100 F4 Umatilla Oregon
71 G6 Umayan R Philippines
95 Q2 Umbagog L New Hampshire
140 D2 Umbakumba Northern Territory
108 E1 Umbarger Texas
140 C7 Umbeara N Terr Australia
42 E5 Umbertide Italy
136 K3 Umboi isld Papua New Guinea
144 B6 Umbrella Mts New Zealand
127 J1 Umbrella Pt Jamaica
42 E6 Umbria prov Italy
26 G5 Umbukta Norway
130 J9 Umbuzeiro Brazil
26 L8 Umeå Sweden
26 K7 Ume älv R Sweden
80 G5 Um ed Dananir Jordan
80 G6 Um el 'Amad Jordan
80 G7 Um el Malid Jordan
80 G4 Um el Manabi Jordan
71 B3 Umera Indonesia
80 G7 Um er Risas Jordan
89 G7 Umfolozi R S Africa
26 H6 Umfors Sweden
118 L1 Umfreville Ontario
88 B10 Umfuli R Zimbabwe
89 G7 Umgeni R S Africa
26 K7 Umgransele Sweden
41 N3 Umhausen Austria
88 B10 Umi R Zimbabwe
116 L2 Umiat Alaska
147 G1 Umingmakkok U.S.A.
89 G8 Umkomaas R S Africa
84 F4 Umm al 'Abīd Libya
84 E4 Umm al Arānib Libya
77 D7 Umm al Qaywayn U.A.E.
86 E3 Umm Bel Sudan
79 D10 Umm Bugma Egypt
37 K3 Ummerstadt E Germany
86 G3 Umm Hagar Ethiopia
86 E3 Umm Keddada Sudan
86 E2 Umm Lahai Sudan
77 A4 Umm Qasr Iran
86 F3 Umm Ruwaba Sudan
77 B7 Umm Sa'id Qatar
86 F3 Umm Saiyala Sudan
79 D10 Umm Shomar, G mt Egypt
79 C10 Umm Tinâşşib,G mt Egypt
26 H6 Umnäs Sweden
88 B10 Umniati R Zimbabwe
52 D1 Umozero, Oz L U.S.S.R.
37 L2 Umpferstedt E Germany
100 B6 Umpqua R Oregon
87 C8 Umpulo Angola
80 G4 Um Qantara Jordan
80 F3 Um Qeis Jordan
80 G8 Um Quleib Jordan
80 G6 Um Quseir Jordan
74 H8 Umrer India
80 G7 Um Rummana Jordan
80 G7 Um Shujeira el Gharbiya Jordan
89 G2 Umsweswe R Zimbabwe
87 F9 Umtali Zimbabwe
89 F8 Umtata S Africa
86 A4 Umuahia Nigeria
47 H4 Umurbey Turkey
88 C10 Umvukwe Ra mts Zimbabwe
89 G2 Umvuma Zimbabwe
89 G8 Umzimkulu R S Africa
89 F8 Umzimvubu R S Africa
89 F3 Umzingwane R Zimbabwe
130 H4 Una Brazil
130 J10 Una R Brazil
42 G4 Una R Yugoslavia
60 S2 Unabetsu-dake mt Japan
128 F6 Unacurizal Brazil
112 D5 Unadilla Georgia
95 M4 Unadilla New York
130 F5 Unaí Brazil
116 G5 Unalakleet Alaska
116 D10 Unalaska I Aleutian Is
144 D5 Una, Mt New Zealand
15 C2 Unapool Scotland
128 E2 Unare R Venezuela
29 M4 Unari Finland
70 G5 Unauna isld Sulawesi
17 G2 Uncastillo Spain
133 D1 Uncia Bolivia
106 C3 Uncompahgre Pk Colorado
106 B3 Uncompahgre Plateau Colorado
27 G13 Unden L Sweden
27 G13 Undenäs Sweden
138 F6 Underbool Victoria
28 E2 Understed Denmark
27 K11 Understen lt ho Sweden
27 H10 Undersvik Sweden
28 D5 Underup Denmark
99 L8 Underwood Iowa
98 E2 Underwood N Dakota
28 H5 Undløse Denmark
71 K10 Undu,Tg C Sumba Indonesia
54 D4 Unecha U.S.S.R.
128 E4 Uneiuxi R Brazil
79 F8 Uneiza Jordan
37 P4 Uněšov Czechoslovakia
52 E3 Unezhma U.S.S.R.
116 G9 Unga I Alaska
116 G4 Ungalik Alaska
139 H5 Ungarie New S Wales
138 D5 Ungarra S Australia
115 N6 Ungava B Quebec
48 L3 Ungeny U.S.S.R.
41 M1 Ungerhausen W Germany
59 K3 Unggi N Korea
128 D5 União Brazil
130 D10 União da Vitória Brazil
128 F4 União do Marmará Brazil
130 J10 União dos Palmares Brazil
112 E1 Unicoi Tennessee
48 D1 Uničov Czechoslovakia
31 L4 Uniejów Poland
42 F4 Unije isld Yugoslavia
116 E9 Unimak Aleutian Is
116 E9 Unimak I Aleutian Is
85 C8 Uni,Mt Liberia
128 F4 Unini R Brazil
133 D5 Unión Argentina
98 C9 Union Colorado
99 N7 Union Iowa
111 F11 Union Louisiana
95 S2 Union Maine
111 G9 Union Mississippi
110 E3 Union Missouri
99 L9 Union Nebraska
107 N6 Union Oklahoma
100 H4 Union Oregon
130 C9 Unión Paraguay
112 F3 Union S Carolina
94 G9 Union W Virginia
127 O8 Union isld Lesser Antilles
131 E7 Unión, B Argentina
95 K7 Union Bridge Maryland
111 F10 Union Church Mississippi
110 M1 Union City Indiana
94 B4 Union City Michigan
94 C6 Union City Ohio/Indiana
94 H5 Union City Pennsylvania
110 G5 Union City Tennessee
100 C7 Union Creek Oregon
95 M5 Uniondale Pennsylvania
126 D3 Unión de Reyes Cuba
100 H3 Union Flat Cr Washington
100 E3 Union Gap Washington
17 G7 Unión,La Spain
112 F2 Union Mills N Carolina
103 M7 Union,Mt Arizona
50 Union of Soviet Socialist Republics
101 Q6 Union Pass Wyoming
112 D4 Union Point Georgia
118 D1 Union Pt Manitoba
111 L9 Union Springs Alabama
95 L4 Union Springs New York
99 M10 Union Star Missouri
109 M9 Union Stock Yards Texas
111 J9 Uniontown Alabama
110 J4 Uniontown Kentucky
94 H7 Uniontown Pennsylvania
99 O9 Unionville Iowa
94 D3 Unionville Michigan
99 N9 Unionville Missouri
102 F1 Unionville Nevada
94 K8 Unionville Virginia
48 H4 Unirea Romania
31 L2 Unisław Poland
77 C7 United Arab Emirates (UAE) fed
6 United Kingdom of Gt.Britain & N.Ireland (UK)
92 United States of America (USA)
52 D3 Unitsa U.S.S.R.
95 S2 Unity Maine
100 G5 Unity Oregon
118 H6 Unity Sask
17 G4 Universales mt Spain
111 G7 University Mississippi
110 F3 University City Missouri
111 K13 University City St Louis
109 O9 University Park Texas
36 C2 Unkel W Germany
38 G6 Unken Austria
55 C3 Unkurda U.S.S.R.
32 G9 Unna W Germany
74 J5 Unnao India
27 G14 Unnaryd Sweden
60 F12 Unomachi Japan
37 L6 Unsernherrn W Germany
52 E2 Unskaya Guba B U.S.S.R.
15 G1 Unst Shetland Scotland
33 O10 Unstrut R E Germany
61 P12 Unten Okinawa
38 N6 Unter Berg mt Austria
39 C2 Unterbrunn W Germany
Unter Deufstetten see Fichtenau
41 M4 Unter Engadin dist Switzerland
36 H4 Unterfranken dist W Germany
38 H8 Untergailtal V Austria
36 F5 Unter Grombach W Germany
36 H6 Untergröningen W Germany
37 M7 Unterhaching W Germany
38 E7 Unter inn-tal V Austria
33 M7 Unterlüss W Germany
37 K3 Untermerzbach W Germany
36 H5 Untermünkheim W Germany
37 K5 Untern-Bibert W Germany
36 F5 Unter Schwarzach W Germany
Untersteinbach see Rauhenebrach
38 J7 Untertal R Austria
38 J7 Unter Tavern Austria
41 H4 Unterwalden canton Switzerland
36 E2 Unterwilden W Germany
37 M7 Unter Zolling W Germany
55 E1 Untor, Oz L U.S.S.R.
27 G10 Untorp Sweden
128 E3 Unturán, Sa. de mts Venezuela
117 H7 Unuk R Alaska
20 H5 Unverre France
118 H6 Unwin Sask
78 F1 Ünye Turkey
60 D13 Unzen-Amakusa Nat. Park Japan
60 D13 Unzen dake mt Japan
52 F5 Unzha U.S.S.R.
38 K7 Unzmarkt Austria
61 L9 Uozu Japan
54 H3 Upa R U.S.S.R.
101 P9 Upalco Utah
127 N10 Upata Venezuela
9 E5 Upavon England
87 E7 Upemba, L Zaïre
115 O3 Upernavik Greenland
12 E2 Uphall Scotland
98 F1 Upham N Dakota
89 B7 Upington S Africa
102 G7 Upland California
94 B6 Upland Indiana
98 H9 Upland Nebraska
121 P7 Uplands airport Ontario
9 G4 Upminster England
116 H6 Upnuk L Alaska
52 D1 Upolaksha U.S.S.R.
137 S4 Upolu isld W Samoa
135 U4 Upolu Pt Hawaiian Is
117 P10 Upper Arrow L Br Col
122 G7 Upper Blackville New Brunswick
9 F2 Upper Broughton England
8 C3 Upper Chapel Wales
123 P4 Upper Humber R Nfld
145 E4 Upper Hutt New Zealand
99 P6 Upper Iowa R Iowa
122 E7 Upper Kent New Brunswick
100 D7 Upper Klamath L Oregon
102 B2 Upper L California
14 B5 Upper L Irish Rep
117 F5 Upper Laberge Yukon Terr
117 J5 Upper Liard Yukon Terr
118 J1 Upper Manitou L Ontario
127 P2 Upper Manzanilla Trinidad
95 L8 Upper Marlboro Maryland
145 D4 Upper Moutere New Zealand
122 K8 Upper Musquodoboit Nova Scotia
86 F4 Upper Nile prov Sudan
99 M1 Upper Red L Minnesota
101 O5 Upper Red Rock L Montana
94 D6 Upper Sandusky Ohio
95 N2 Upper Saranac L New York
122 J8 Upper Stewiacke Nova Scotia
94 H8 Upper Tract W Virginia
94 K7 Upperville Virginia
85 D6 Upper Volta rep W Africa
139 H7 Upper Yarra Dam Victoria
9 F2 Uppingham England
27 J12 Upplands Väsby Sweden
27 K12 Uppsala Sweden
27 J12 Uppsala county Sweden
116 C6 Upright,C St Matthew I Bering Sea
99 M4 Upsala Minnesota
119 N1 Upsala Ontario
122 F6 Upsalquitch New Brunswick
74 G2 Upshi Kashmir
99 Q3 Upson Wisconsin
141 J4 Upstart, C Queensland
9 H5 Upstreet England
8 D3 Upton England
94 B9 Upton Kentucky
98 B5 Upton Wyoming
84 F3 Uqaylah,Al Libya
126 F10 Urabá,G.de Colombia
36 G7 Urach W Germany
128 F2 Uracoa Venezuela
65 A4 Urad Qianqi China
65 A4 Urad Zhonghou Lianheqi China
61 N10 Uraga Japan
60 Q3 Urakawa Japan
100 K1 Ural Montana
139 H5 Ural mt New S Wales
55 C4 Ural R U.S.S.R.
139 K4 Uralla New S Wales
5 R4 Ural Mts U.S.S.R.
142 F5 Ural Well W Australia
88 D4 Urambo Tanzania
139 H6 Urana New S Wales
140 E5 Urandangie Queensland
130 G4 Urandi Brazil
141 L7 Urangan Queensland
111 D10 Urania Louisiana
114 J6 Uranium City Sask
83 L10 Uraniya Sri Lanka
140 C2 Urapunga N Terr Aust
128 F3 Uraricoera Brazil
143 E9 Uraryie W Australia
57 E5 Ura-Tyube U.S.S.R.
60 P2 Urausunai Japan
61 N10 Urawa Japan
55 C4 Urazmetova U.S.S.R.
52 G6 Urazovka U.S.S.R.
54 K6 Urazovo U.S.S.R.
99 S9 Urbana Illinois
94 B6 Urbana Indiana
99 P7 Urbana Iowa
110 C4 Urbana Missouri
94 D6 Urbana Ohio
45 N4 Urbania Italy
95 L9 Urbanna Virginia
129 K4 Urbano Santos Brazil
16 E2 Urbel R Spain
45 N4 Urbino Italy
17 F2 Urbión, Sa. de mts Spain
22 F5 Urcel France
128 D6 Urcos Peru
18 E10 Urdos France
52 H2 Urdyuzhskoye Oz L U.S.S.R.
57 K2 Urdzhar U.S.S.R.
55 F3 Urekhovo U.S.S.R.
52 G5 Uren U.S.S.R.
145 E3 Urenui New Zealand
137 O4 Ureparapara isld New Hebrides
13 G5 Ure,R England
124 D3 Ures Mexico
145 F3 Urewera Country New Zealand
55 G3 Urez U.S.S.R.
78 G3 Urfa Turkey
38 K5 Urfahr Austria
41 O2 Urfeld W Germany
52 G6 Urga R U.S.S.R.
58 B2 Urgamal Mongolia
57 B4 Urgench U.S.S.R.
77 L3 Urgun Afghanistan
41 J4 Uri canton Switzerland
111 J10 Uriah Alabama
144 C5 Uriah, Mt New Zealand
128 D3 Uribe Colombia
127 H9 Uribia Colombia
110 B3 Urich Missouri
101 P8 Urie Wyoming
128 F2 Urimán Venezuela
141 G8 Urimbin Queensland
124 F4 Urique Mexico
41 H4 Uri Rothstock mt Switzerland
139 G3 Urisino New S Wales
55 E4 Uritskoye U.S.S.R.
29 K10 Urjala Finland
25 E3 Urk Netherlands
47 H6 Urla Turkey
48 K6 Urlaţi Romania
28 D5 Urlev Denmark
55 C4 Urman U.S.S.R.
55 E1 Urmannyy U.S.S.R.
52 G6 Urmary U.S.S.R.
59 K2 Urmi R U.S.S.R.
5 O9 Urmia, L Iran
55 F2 Urninskoye Boloto U.S.S.R.
52 J5 Urolka R U.S.S.R.
46 E2 Uroševac Yugoslavia
131 D7 Urre Lauquen, L Argentina
12 E3 Urr,L Scotland
99 P9 Ursa Illinois
57 E4 Ursat'yevskaya U.S.S.R.
37 J7 Ursberg W Germany
25 C3 Ursem Netherlands
37 M5 Ursensollen W Germany
52 F6 Urshelskiy U.S.S.R.
103 K4 Ursine Nevada
56 C4 Ursk U.S.S.R.
36 H6 Urspring W Germany
26 M7 Ursviken Sweden
55 C4 Urtazym U.S.S.R.
58 B4 Urt Moron China
124 E4 Uruáchic Mexico
130 E4 Uruaçu Brazil
130 E4 Uruana Brazil
124 H8 Uruapan del Progreso Mexico
128 D6 Urubamba Peru
128 G4 Urubu R Brazil
129 G4 Urucará Brazil
127 N10 Urucoa Venezuela
128 F4 Urucu R Brazil
129 K5 Uruçuí Brazil
130 F5 Urucuia Brazil
130 B6 Urucum Brazil
129 G4 Urucurituba Brazil
131 F2 Uruguaiana Brazil
130 D10 Uruguai,R Brazil
131 G4 Uruguay rep S America
131 F4 Uruguay, R Argentina

Urumchi see Ürümqi
79 G2 Urum es Sughra Syria
66 D3 Ürümqi China
69 C11 Urung Indonesia
139 L4 Urunga New S Wales
88 B10 Urungwe Zimbabwe
128 F6 Urupe R Brazil
52 H6 Urussu U.S.S.R.
130 F4 Urutágua Brazil
130 E5 Urutaí Brazil
145 E3 Uruti New Zealand
77 K3 Uruzgan Afghanistan
77 J3 Uruzgan prov Afghanistan
20 B2 Urville France
136 H2 Urville, Tg. D' C W Irian
89 R4 Urwi Botswana
60 Q2 Uryū R Japan
60 Q1 Uryu-ko L Japan
58 G1 Uryum R U.S.S.R.
56 C3 Uryup R U.S.S.R.
53 F8 Uryupinsk U.S.S.R.
52 G6 Urzhum U.S.S.R.
48 K6 Urziceni Romania
36 B4 Urzig W Germany
60 E12 Usa Japan
71 E7 Usak Turkey
47 K6 Uşak Turkey
87 C10 Usakos Namibia
80 E5 Usarin Jordan
133 F8 Usborne hill Falkland Is
36 E3 Usedom E Germany
80 D2 Usha Israel
116 L7 Ushagat I Alaska
50 G1 Ushakova, Ostrova islds
55 E3 Ushakovo U.S.S.R.
60 D13 Ushibuka Japan
61 L8 Ushitsu Japan
60 D12 Ushizu Japan
57 J2 Ush-Tobe U.S.S.R.
133 D8 Ushuaia airport Argentina
129 H5 Usina Brazil
36 F3 Usingen W Germany
8 D4 Usk Wales
27 A12 Uskedal Norway
8 C4 Usk,R Wales
Üskub see Skopje
47 K3 Üsküdar Turkey
47 J3 Üsküp Turkey
32 L9 Uslar W Germany
54 L4 Usman U.S.S.R.
56 D3 Usolka R U.S.S.R.
52 J5 Usol'ye U.S.S.R.
55 G4 Uspenka U.S.S.R.
57 G1 Uspenskiy U.S.S.R.
40 F7 Usséglio Italy
18 G7 Ussel France
13 H6 Usselby England
32 J10 Usseln W Germany
28 K5 Usserød Denmark
18 F6 Usson du Poitou France
59 K2 Ussuri R U.S.S.R.
59 K3 Ussuriysk U.S.S.R.
20 E4 Ussy France
52 G6 Usta R U.S.S.R.
56 D5 Ust'-Abakan U.S.S.R.
52 G4 Ust' Alekseyevo U.S.S.R.
27 C11 Ustaoset Norway
55 D3 Ust-Bagaryak U.S.S.R.
52 H4 Ust' Chernaya U.S.S.R.
48 H2 Ustchorna U.S.S.R.
52 J5 Ust' Dolgaya U.S.S.R.
41 J3 Uster Switzerland
48 E10 Ustica isld Italy
56 F3 Ust'-Ilimsky Vdkhr U.S.S.R.
52 J3 Ust'-Ilych U.S.S.R.
30 H5 Ustí nad Czechoslovakia
55 F2 Ust'ishim U.S.S.R.
55 G3 Ust'Izsa U.S.S.R.
31 K1 Ustka Poland
56 B6 Ust'-Kamenogorsk U.S.S.R.
58 G1 Ust'Karenga U.S.S.R.
55 C3 Ust'Katav U.S.S.R.
55 C3 Ust Kishert U.S.S.R.
55 H3 Ust'Koin U.S.S.R.
52 H4 Ust'Kulom U.S.S.R.
56 G3 Ust'-Kut U.S.S.R.
55 D2 Ust' Loz'va U.S.S.R.
52 J2 Ust' Luga U.S.S.R.
51 L3 Ust' Lyzha U.S.S.R.
52 H4 Ust'Maya U.S.S.R.
51 L3 Ust'-Muya U.S.S.R.
52 H4 Ust'Nem U.S.S.R.
59 K1 Ust'Niman U.S.S.R.
56 F4 Ust'-Ordynsky U.S.S.R.
56 F4 Ust'Ordynsky Buryat Nats Okr dist U.S.S.R.
47 G3 Ustovo Bulgaria
52 H2 Ust' Paden'ga U.S.S.R.
52 F3 Ust' Pinega U.S.S.R.
50 H2 Ust'-Port U.S.S.R.
52 F4 Ust' Puya U.S.S.R.
52 G4 Ust' Reka U.S.S.R.
31 O6 Ustrzyki Dolne Poland
52 D4 Ust'Sara U.S.S.R.
52 J3 Ust'-Shchugor U.S.S.R.
55 D1 Ust'-Tapsuy U.S.S.R.
55 F3 Ust'Tara U.S.S.R.
55 G3 Ust'Tarka U.S.S.R.
55 F3 Ust' Tava U.S.S.R.
52 H2 Ust' Tsil'ma U.S.S.R.
59 K1 Ust'Tyrma U.S.S.R.
52 J4 Ust' Un'ya U.S.S.R.
52 F3 Ust'ura U.S.S.R.
59 H1 Ust'urov U.S.S.R.
57 J1 Ust' Usa U.S.S.R.
55 D4 Ust'-Uyskoye U.S.S.R.
52 G3 Ust' Vacherga U.S.S.R.
52 F4 Ust'Voya U.S.S.R.
53 G3 Ust' Vyyskaya U.S.S.R.
52 F4 Ust'ya R U.S.S.R.
52 E5 Ust'ye U.S.S.R.
52 E6 Ust'ye R U.S.S.R.
50 E4 Ustyurt,Plato U.S.S.R.
66 C3 Usu China
71 L10 Usu China
60 E12 Usuki Japan
125 P11 Usulután El Salvador
125 O9 Usumacinta R Mexico
70 D3 Usun Apau Plateau Sarawak
89 G6 Usutu R Swaziland
55 F8 Usvyaty U.S.S.R.
71 B2 Uta isld Indonesia
103 N2 Utah state U.S.A.
103 N1 Utah L Utah
29 M7 Utajärvi Finland
60 Q2 Utashinai Japan
99 L7 Ute Iowa
17 G3 Utebo Spain
106 G6 Ute Cr New Mexico
88 G6 Utenge,L Tanzania
106 E5 Ute Park New Mexico
37 P4 Utery Czechoslovakia
55 G4 Utes U.S.S.R.
88 G6 Utete Tanzania
74 K7 Uthal Pakistan
32 J6 Uthmann W Germany
Uthumphon Phisai Thailand
129 G6 Utiariti Brazil
107 K3 Utica Kansas
94 D4 Utica Michigan
99 P6 Utica Minnesota
110 C2 Utica Mississippi
101 P3 Utica Missouri
98 J3 Utica Nebraska
91 M3 Utica New York
94 B6 Utica Ohio
17 G5 Utiel Spain
36 K7 Utüfällan Sweden
119 W3 Utik L Manitoba
145 E3 Utiku New Zealand
118 B3 Utikuma L Alberta
27 H16 Utladalen Sweden
27 C10 Utne R Norway
27 H15 Utlängen isld Sweden
106 G4 Utleyville Colorado
74 D1 Utmanzai Pakistan
27 K13 Utö Sweden
27 M12 Utö is h no Finland

140 C5 Utopia N Terr Aust
109 H6 Utopia Texas
75 K5 Utraula India
25 D4 Utrecht Netherlands
89 G6 Utrecht S Africa
16 D7 Utrera Spain
27 A12 Utsira R h no Norway
29 N2 Utsjoki Finland
61 N9 Utsunomiya Japan
53 G10 Utta U.S.S.R.
68 E4 Uttaradit Thailand
74 H4 Uttar Pradesh prov India
27 H12 Uttersberg Sweden
28 G7 Uttersløv Denmark
36 H4 Üttingen W Germany
9 E2 Uttoxeter England
17 K4 Utukok R Alaska
137 O4 Utupua isld Santa Cruz Is
55 B5 Utva R U.S.S.R.
37 O3 Utvina Czechoslovakia
52 H6 Utyashkino U.S.S.R.
32 M8 Utze W Germany
33 S5 Utzedel E Germany
17 G3 uuadalope R Spain
29 L9 Uurainen Finland
Uukaarlepyy see Nykarleby
29 J11 Uusikaupunki Finland
29 L11 Uusimaa prov Finland
52 H6 Uva U.S.S.R.
48 F7 Uvac R Yugoslavia
103 K2 Uvada Nevada
128 D3 Uva, L Colombia
112 E5 Uvalda Georgia
109 H8 Uvalde Texas
84 B4 Uvarovichi U.S.S.R.
52 E6 Uvarovo U.S.S.R.
55 E2 Uvat U.S.S.R.
137 O6 Uvéa isld Îles Loyauté Pacific Oc
137 R4 Uvéa isld Îles Wallis Pacific Oc
55 D4 Uvel'skiy U.S.S.R.
55 D3 Uvil'dy, Oz L U.S.S.R.
88 C4 Uvinza Tanzania
88 B3 Uvira Zaïre
115 O3 Uvkusigssat Greenland
60 E13 Uwae Japan
60 F12 Uwajima Japan
84 H5 Uwainat,Jebel mt Sudan
20 C5 Uwi isld Indonesia
69 H12 Uwi isld Indonesia
125 P7 Uxmal Mexico
55 D4 Uy R U.S.S.R.
116 K8 Uyak B Alaska
57 B3 Uyaly, Ozero L U.S.S.R.
55 D3 Uyandina R U.S.S.R.
48 J3 Uyar U.S.S.R.
15 G1 Uyea isld Scotland
15 G1 Uyeasound Scotland
50 H1 Uyedineniya,Ostrov isld U.S.S.R.
52 H2 Uyo Nigeria
85 F7 Uyo Nigeria
47 K6 Uysal Dağ mt Turkey
55 D4 Uyskoye U.S.S.R.
57 F3 Uyuk R U.S.S.R.
127 K9 Uyuni Bolivia
133 D2 Uyuni Bolivia
48 G2 Už R Czechoslovakia
28 C8 Uzbekistan S.S.R rep U.S.S.R.
16 D2 Uzdin Yugoslavia
53 G8 Uzen', Malyy R U.S.S.R.
57 G4 Uzgen U.S.S.R.
48 G2 Uzhgorod U.S.S.R.
48 H2 Uzhok U.S.S.R.
56 C3 Uzhur U.S.S.R.
48 F7 Užicka Požega Yugoslavia
41 J3 Uznach Switzerland
52 F6 Uzola R U.S.S.R.
59 K3 Uzun Uzbekistan
47 H8 Uzun isld Turkey
88 E6 Uzungwa Tanzania
44 H3 Uzunköprü Turkey
57 B3 Uzynkair U.S.S.R.

137 Q3 Vaitupu isld Tuvalu
47 F2 Vakarel Bulgaria
27 G11 Vakern Sweden
56 B1 Vakh R U.S.S.R.
57 F6 Vakhanskiy Khrebet mts
73 K1 Vakhsh R U.S.S.R.
57 E5 Vakhstroy U.S.S.R.
52 G5 Vakhtan U.S.S.R.
52 D3 Vaknavolok U.S.S.R.
27 A11 Vaksdal Norway
26 E8 Vålådalen Sweden
76 E7 Välaichchenai Sri Lanka
40 F5 Valais canton Switzerland
52 H5 Valamaz U.S.S.R.
18 E3 Valatie New York
43 G3 Valax isld Greece
38 E8 Val Badia Italy
121 P6 Val Barrette Quebec
26 G3 Valberg Norway
19 P15 Valbonnais France
122 E5 Val Brillant Quebec
25 E5 Valburg Netherlands
133 D6 Valchets Argentina
121 S7 Valcourt Quebec
41 O6 Valdagno Italy
16 D2 Valdaira R Spain
52 D5 Valday U.S.S.R.
52 D6 Valdayskaya Vozvyshennost' uplands U.S.S.R.
17 G4 Valde Algorfa Spain
20 K3 Valdecañas, Embalse de res Spain
17 F5 Valdeganga Spain
52 B6 Valdemárpils U.S.S.R.
27 J13 Valdemarsvik Sweden
17 F4 Valdemoro Spain
17 F4 Valdemoro-Sierra Spain
16 E6 Valdepeñas Spain
16 D3 Valderaduey R Spain
16 C3 Valderrobres Spain
99 T5 Valders Wisconsin
121 P7 Val des Bois Quebec
99 T8 Valdese N Carolina
124 H6 Valdés, Pen Argentina
116 O6 Valdez Alaska
106 F4 Valdez Colorado
131 B4 Valdivia prov Chile
40 F6 Valdivia Italy
48 E5 Valdobbiadene Italy
40 G7 Valdotra Yugoslavia
122 A8 Val-Racine Quebec
19 N16 Valréas France
44 N3 Valdres dist Norway
89 E6 Vala R S Africa
28 H7 Valse Italy
100 B5 Valsetz Oregon
26 G2 Vaisjärd Denmark
26 K5 Varjosträsk Sweden
29 N9 Varkaus Finland
143 C10 Varley, L W Australia
27 F12 Varmland reg Sweden
47 J1 Varna Bulgaria
55 D4 Varna U.S.S.R.
111 G11 Varnado Louisiana
27 G14 Värnamo Sweden
55 F7 Varnavino U.S.S.R.
59 K2 Varnenskiy U.S.S.R.
112 F5 Varnville S Carolina
79 D3 Varosha Cyprus
27 G13 Väring Sweden
20 J5 Varize France
26 K5 Varjosträsk Sweden
29 N9 Varkaus Finland
143 C10 Varley, L W Australia

118 E8 Vauxhall Alberta
87 J11 Vavatenina Madagascar
137 S5 Vava'u Group islds Tonga
52 H6 Vavozh U.S.S.R.
83 K9 Vavuniya Sri Lanka
118 J5 Vawn R Alberta
27 K12 Vaxholm Sweden
27 G15 Växjö Sweden
78 D4 Vayalpad India
50 F1 Vaygach, Ostrov isld U.S.S.R.
52 F3 Vaymuga R U.S.S.R.
129 L5 Vazante Brazil
130 F5 Vazante Brazil
16 B6 Vázaro Spain
47 G2 Vazovgrad Bulgaria
129 J6 Veadeiros Brazil
26 D3 Vebbestrup Denmark
21 H6 Vebron France
21 H3 Vechta W Germany
28 D2 Vechta W Germany
32 M8 Vechelde W Germany
28 D5 Vecht R Netherlands
32 H7 Vechta W Germany
32 L10 Veckerhagen W Germany
54 K2 Venev U.S.S.R.
28 K5 Vedbæk Denmark
27 F14 Veddige Sweden
42 E3 Veddum Denmark
48 J6 Vedea Romania
128 E2 Vedea R Romania
26 D3 Vedersø Denmark
26 E8 Vedrången Sweden
17 H6 Vedra isld Balearic Is
22 H3 Vedrin Belgium
28 C6 Vedsted Denmark
28 G6 Vedsted Denmark
27 C13 Veddum Sweden
110 J1 Veedersburg Indiana
28 C5 Veelden Netherlands
26 E6 Vega isld Norway
27 D13 Vega de la Tera Spain
28 K4 Vegådal S Sweden
28 B3 Vegesack W Germany
28 D3 Veggerby Denmark

16 C3 Valgañón Spain
52 F3 Valganguzha U.S.S.R.
27 H5 Valgerola Italy
54 L4 Valguarnera Caropepe Sicily
28 E7 Vallé Aurina Italy
52 F5 Valle Cura,Rio Del Argentina
133 B2 Valle d'Aosta Italy
40 G8 Valle d'Aosta aut reg Italy
121 R5 Valle de Banderas Mexico
16 E1 Valle de Cabuérniga Spain
127 M10 Valle de la Pascua Venezuela
128 C3 Valle del Cauca div Colombia
124 F4 Valle de Olivos Mexico
124 F4 Valle de Rosario Mexico
124 G4 Valle de Zaragoza Mexico
86 J2 Vallée de Zgarat Mali
122 B7 Vallée Jonction Quebec
85 E5 Vallée L'Azawak Mali/Niger
137 M3 Valle Fértil, Sa. de mt Argentina
68 F8 Valle Grande Bolivia
98 D2 Vallejera France
103 B3 Vallejo California
108 C6 Valle Nacional Mexico
108 C6 Valle, Rio Del Argentina
16 A7 Vallehermoso Canary Is

116 K7 Valley of Ten Thousand Smokes Alaska
137 Q5 Vanua Levu isld Fiji
99 N9 Van Wert Iowa
94 C6 Van Wert Ohio
87 D12 Vanwyksvlei S Africa
67 A4 Van Yen Vietnam
26 A9 Vanyhven Norway
26 A9 Vanylvsgapet R Norway
20 G2 Vanzant Missouri
110 D5 Vanzylsrus S Africa
41 H8 Varallo Italy
42 B3 Varallo Italy
77 B2 Varamin Iran
75 K6 Varanasi India
26 R1 Varangerfjorden inlet Norway
26 R1 Varangerhalvöya mt Norway
à2 G7 Varano, L. di Italy
131 A8 Varas,Pto Chile
20 E3 Varaville France
27 F14 Varberg Sweden
111 G8 Vardaman Mississippi
26 S1 Vardø Norway
28 C6 Varde Denmark
27 F14 Várdö Finland
20 C3 Vareš Yugoslavia
40 A7 Vareze R France
27 F13 Várgárda Sweden
55 E3 Vargas Yates I. Norway
130 F7 Varginha Brazil
18 G9 Varilhes France
112 J2 Varina N Carolina
27 G13 Väring Sweden
22 E5 Varize France
26 K5 Varjosträsk Sweden
29 N9 Varkaus Finland

27 H14 Vena Sweden
27 D10 Venabygd Norway
12 D1 Venachar,L Scotland
131 E4 Vensado Tuerto Argentina
45 Q7 Venafro Italy
128 F2 Venamo,Cerro mt Venezuela/Guyana
98 E9 Venango Nebraska
141 F4 Vena Park Queensland
44 C1 Venaria Italy
100 G6 Venator Oregon
130 E8 Venceslau Bráz Brazil
Venda see Venda
45 L1 Venda mt Italy
16 B6 Venda Nova Portugal
21 C6 Vendée France
36 D6 Vendenheim France
21 H6 Vendôme France
21 H3 Vendrell Spain
28 D2 Vendresse France
45 M1 Veneta, Laguna Italy
116 P3 Venetie Landing Alaska
32 H7 Veneto reg Italy
32 L10 Veckerhagen W Germany
54 K2 Venev U.S.S.R.
45 R8 Venezia Italy
42 D3 Venezia-Euganea prov Italy
42 E3 Venézis,G.di Italy
128 E2 Venezuela rep S America
127 J9 Venezuela,G.de Venezuela
26 D3 Vang Denmark
55 G3 Vengerovo U.S.S.R.
78 A2 Vengurla India
118 E4 Venice Alberta
113 C10 Venice Florida
Venice Italy see Venezia
111 G12 Venice Louisiana
111 M12 Venice St Louis
19 N13 Vénissieux France
27 G11 Venjan Sweden
76 E1 Venkataguri India
76 E1 Venkatapuram India
98 J3 Venlo N Dakota
25 F6 Venlo Netherlands
119 M7 Venn Sask
28 D7 Vennebjerg Denmark
32 E7 Vennebrügge W Germany
25 F6 Vennesla Norway
28 B3 Vena Bugt Denmark
19 Q15 Vanoisc France
121 O7 Venosta Quebec
41 N4 Venosa Italy
41 N4 Venosta, Alpi Italy
25 E5 Venray Netherlands
41 M14 Venta R U.S.S.R.
124 E5 Ventana,Pta de la C Mexico
133 E5 Ventana,Se rs Argentina
16 E8 Ventas de Zafarraya Spain
28 C5 Ventosa Denmark
44 C4 Ventimiglia Italy
9 E8 Ventnor England
19 O16 Ventoux, Mt France
27 C13 Ventschow E Germany
28 A5 Vejers Denmark
128 E3 Ventuari R Venezuela
102 E7 Ventura California
98 G3 Venturia N Dakota
113 F10 Venus Florida
98 B5 Venus B S Australia
138 C6 Venus Bay S Australia
124 H8 Venustiano Carranza Mexico
52 D4 Vepsovskaya Vozvyshennost' uplands U.S.S.R.
133 E3 Vera Argentina
17 F7 Vera Spain
109 H2 Vera Texas
133 D6 Vera, B Argentina
130 E8 Vera Cruz Brazil
125 L8 Veracruz Mexico
74 D8 Veraval India
42 B3 Verbania Italy
111 K9 Verbena Alabama
22 D5 Verberie France
52 E6 Verbilki U.S.S.R.
41 H7 Vercelli Italy
28 E7 Vercheni E Germany
45 R8 Vercors reg France
19 O16 Verdaches France
26 E8 Verdal Norway
26 E8 Verdalsöra Norway
71 E4 Verde isld Philippines
32 F10 Velburg W Germany
130 D6 Verde R Arizona
103 N7 Verde R Arizona
132 B4 Verde R Brazil
133 F2 Verde R Paraguay
85 A6 Verds, C Senegal
16 D6 Verde, Cay isld Bahamas
130 G4 Verde Grande R Brazil
130 E8 Verdeli Brazil
109 J1 Verdon Oklahoma
32 K7 Verden W Germany
131 C6 Verde,Pen Argentina
130 D7 Verde R Brazil
21 H6 Verdon France
21 H6 Verdon France
21 J3 Verdun France
18 F9 Verdun-sur-Garonne France
19 J6 Verdun-sur-le-Doubs France
124 E5 Verdura Mexico
52 D6 Vereshchagino U.S.S.R.
55 O2 Vereshchagino U.S.S.R.
52 H5 Vereya U.S.S.R.
89 G6 Vereeniging S Africa
119 P7 Veregin Sask
98 O2 Verena Netherlands
121 N5 Vérendrye, Parc Prov. de la Quebec
52 H5 Verkhneye Kuyto, Oz L U.S.S.R.

Washington — White L 83

107 N2 Washington Kansas
111 D11 Washington Louisiana
110 E3 Washington Missouri
112 K2 Washington N Carolina
95 P3 Washington New Hampshire
95 N6 Washington New Jersey
94 G6 Washington Penn
109 L5 Washington Texas
103 L4 Washington Utah
94 J8 Washington Virginia
100 F2 Washington *state* U.S.A.
94 D7 Washington Court Ho Ohio
97 Washington D.C *conurbation*
99 U4 Washington I Wisconsin
113 G9 Washington,L Florida
115 N1 Washington Land Greenland
95 Q2 Washington, Mt New Hampshire
109 J1 Washita *R* Oklahoma
101 Q4 Washoe Montana
100 C4 Washougal Washington
119 V7 Washow B Manitoba
9 G2 Wash, The *gulf* England
100 G3 Washtucna Washington
22 G4 Wasigny France
79 E9 Wasit Egypt
98 F1 Waskada Manitoba
119 V2 Waskaiowaka L Manitoba
118 L5 Waskesiu L Sask
114 J7 Waskesiu Lake Sask
118 E4 Wasketenau Alberta
99 M1 Waskish Minnesota
109 N3 Waskom Texas
22 F3 Wasmes Belgium
31 K4 Wąsosz Poland
60 Q1 Wassamu Japan
112 F6 Wassaw Sd Georgia
36 C6 Wasselonne France
25 F6 Wassenberg W Germany
37 J6 Wasseralfingen W Germany
22 L4 Wasserbillig Luxembourg
37 K5 Wassermungenau W Germany
37 K5 Wassertrüdingen W Germany
22 F3 Wassigny France
102 F3 Wassuk Ra Nevada
19 J4 Wassy France
98 D5 Wasta S Dakota
79 B9 Wasta,El Egypt
13 E5 Wast Water *L* England
37 J2 Wasungen E Germany
121 O3 Waswanipi Quebec
120 K4 Watabeag L Ontario
99 Q8 Wataga Illinois
83 L11 Watagoda *mt* Sri Lanka
70 G7 Watampone Sulawesi
70 F7 Watansoppeng Sulawesi
98 E4 Watauga S Dakota
109 M9 Watauga Texas
8 C5 Watchet England
118 L1 Watcomb Ontario
9 G3 Waterbeach England
87 C10 Waterberg Namibia
95 R3 Waterboro Maine
95 O5 Waterbury Connecticut
95 P2 Waterbury Vermont
126 F3 Water Cays *islds* Bahamas
112 G3 Wateree Pond *L* S Carolina
102 D4 Waterford California
14 D4 Waterford Irish Rep
120 K10 Waterford Ontario
94 H5 Waterford Pennsylvania
14 D4 Waterford *co* Irish Rep
14 E4 Waterford Hbr Irish Rep
8 A7 Watergate B England
119 S6 Waterhan L Manitoba
118 J4 Waterhen L Sask
140 C2 Waterhouse *R* N Terr Aust
140 C6 Waterhouse Ra N Terr Aust
109 O2 Waterloo Arkansas
22 G2 Waterloo Belgium
110 F3 Waterloo Illinois
94 B5 Waterloo Indiana
99 O7 Waterloo Iowa
101 N4 Waterloo Montana
95 L4 Waterloo New York
140 A3 Waterloo N Terr Aust
121 S7 Waterloo Quebec
127 O2 Waterloo Trinidad
8 C6 Waterloo Cross England
99 S8 Waterman Illinois
111 E10 Waterproof Louisiana
94 C2 Waters Michigan
99 R3 Watersmeet Michigan
118 D9 Waterton Pk Alberta
99 N5 Watertown Minnesota
95 M3 Watertown New York
98 J5 Watertown S Dakota
110 K5 Watertown Tennessee
99 S6 Watertown Wisconsin
138 E5 Watervale S Australia
111 G7 Water Valley Mississippi
108 G4 Water Valley Texas
95 O4 Watervliet New York
95 S2 Waterville Maine
99 N5 Waterville Minnesota
95 M4 Waterville New York
122 H8 Waterville Nova Scotia
121 T7 Waterville Quebec
100 E2 Waterville Washington
118 F2 Waterways Alberta
70 N9 Wates Java
9 F4 Watford England
120 J10 Watford Ontario
98 C2 Watford City N Dakota
107 P2 Wathena Kansas
143 B9 Watheroo W Australia
117 P8 Watino Alberta
106 F2 Watkins Colorado
99 M4 Watkins Minnesota
115 R4 Watkins Bjerge *mts* Greenland
95 L4 Watkins Glen New York
112 D4 Watkinsville Georgia
107 M6 Watonga Oklahoma
70 K9 Waton,Tg *C* Java
22 D2 Watou Belgium
71 B2 Watowato,Bk *mt* Halmahera Indonesia
106 F6 Watrous New Mexico
119 M7 Watrous Sask
86 E5 Watsa Zaïre
99 T9 Watseka Illinois
86 D6 Watsi-Kengo Zaïre
111 E8 Watson Arkansas
99 L4 Watson Minnesota
99 L9 Watson Missouri
119 N6 Watson Sask
138 B4 Watson S Australia
101 Q10 Watson Utah
141 F2 Watson *R* Queensland
117 J5 Watson Lake Yukon Terr
95 L5 Watsontown Pennsylvania
83 J10 Wattala Sri Lanka
22 C2 Watten France
141 G5 Watten Queensland
15 E2 Watten Scotland
32 F10 Wattenscheid W Germany
138 D3 Wattiwarriganna *R* S Australia
139 G3 Wattle Vale New S Wales
117 P6 Watt,Mt Alberta
143 F7 Watt, Mt W Australia
9 F4 Watton England
9 G2 Watton England
107 Q5 Watts Oklahoma
112 C2 Watts Bar Lake Tennessee
94 H4 Wattsburg Pennsylvania
70 G5 Watukama Sulawesi
70 G5 Watukantjoa Sulawesi
70 G6 Watuwila,Bk *mt* Sulawesi
38 G6 Watzmann *mt* W Germany
136 K3 Wau Papua New Guinea
86 E4 Wau Sudan
120 K7 Waubamick Ontario
121 L8 Waubaushene Ontario
98 J4 Waubay S Dakota
98 J4 Waubay L S Dakota
139 L4 Wauchope New S Wales
140 C5 Wauchope N Terr Aust
119 Q9 Wauchope Sask
113 F10 Wauchula Florida
99 O6 Waucoma Iowa
100 G1 Wauconda Washington
118 F1 Waugh Manitoba
138 E4 Waukaringa S Australia
142 D5 Waukarlycarly, L W Australia
70 F5 Waukata, G *mt* Sulawesi
99 N8 Waukee Iowa
99 T7 Waukegan Illinois
99 S6 Waukesha Wisconsin
107 N5 Waukomis Oklahoma
99 P6 Waukon Iowa
98 E9 Wauneta Nebraska
99 R5 Waupaca Wisconsin
99 S6 Waupun Wisconsin
109 K1 Waurika Oklahoma
98 J7 Wausa Nebraska
99 R5 Wausau Wisconsin
99 T4 Wausaukee Wisconsin
94 C5 Wauseon Ohio
81 G8 W Australian Ridge Indian Oc
99 R5 Wautoma Wisconsin
99 S6 Wauwatosa Wisconsin
140 B3 Wave Hill N Terr Aust
110 J2 Waveland Indiana
141 K1 Wavell Heights *dist* Brisbane, Qnsld
9 H3 Waveney,R England
145 E3 Waverley New Zealand
122 J9 Waverley Nova Scotia
100 H2 Waverley Washington
112 F6 Waverly Georgia
110 G2 Waverly Illinois
99 O7 Waverly Iowa
107 P3 Waverly Kansas
110 C2 Waverly Missouri
98 K9 Waverly Nebraska
95 L4 Waverly New York
98 K4 Waverly S Dakota
110 J5 Waverly Tennessee
95 K9 Waverly Virginia
111 M9 Waverly Hall Georgia
141 F7 Waverney Queensland
22 C2 Wavrans-sur-l'Aa France
22 H2 Wavre Belgium
22 D2 Wavrin France
118 E6 Wavy L Alberta
68 C4 Waw Burma
120 F4 Wawa Ontario
121 M3 Wawagosic *R* Quebec
120 J4 Wawaitin Falls Ontario
119 S9 Wawanesa Manitoba
84 F5 Waw an Nāmūs Libya
94 B5 Wawasee,L Indiana
70 G6 Wawo Sulawesi
102 E4 Wawona California
119 Q9 Wawota Sask
70 G6 Wawotobi Sulawesi
109 L3 Waxahachie Texas
112 G3 Waxhaw N Carolina
111 F9 Way Mississippi
101 O7 Wayan Idaho
Wayaobu *see* Zichang
112 E6 Waycross Georgia
68 F8 Way,Ko *isld* G of Thailand
143 D7 Way, L W Australia
99 P8 Wayland Iowa
94 E9 Wayland Kentucky
94 B4 Wayland Michigan
99 P9 Wayland Missouri
94 K4 Wayland New York
118 E7 Wayne Alberta
95 R2 Wayne Maine
94 D4 Wayne Michigan
110 C5 Wayne Missouri
98 J7 Wayne Nebraska
107 N7 Wayne Oklahoma
94 E8 Wayne W Virginia
110 H3 Wayne City Illinois
112 F4 Waynesboro Georgia
111 H10 Waynesboro Mississippi
94 K7 Waynesboro Pennsylvania
110 J6 Waynesboro Tennessee
94 J8 Waynesboro Virginia
94 F6 Waynesburg Ohio
94 G7 Waynesburg Pennsylvania
99 R9 Waynesville Illinois
110 D4 Waynesville Missouri
112 E2 Waynesville N Carolina
94 C7 Waynesville Ohio
107 M5 Waynoka Oklahoma
98 C7 Wayside Nebraska
108 F1 Wayside Texas
77 L3 Wazi Khwa Afghanistan
77 K1 Wazirabad Afghanistan
74 F2 Wazirabad Pakistan
31 L2 Wda *R* Poland
7 L11 Weald, The *reg* England
13 F4 Wearhead England
140 D3 Wearyan *R* N Terr Aust
141 H3 Weary B Queensland
99 M10 Weatherby Missouri
107 M6 Weatherford Oklahoma
109 K3 Weatherford Texas
95 M6 Weatherly Pennsylvania
110 C4 Weaubleau Missouri
111 L8 Weaver Alabama
8 D1 Weaverham England
119 V6 Weaver L Manitoba
100 C9 Weaverville California
111 L10 Webb Alabama
111 F8 Webb Mississippi
118 J8 Webb Sask
109 H8 Webb Texas
110 B4 Webb City Missouri
107 Q6 Webbers Falls Oklahoma
142 G6 Webb, Mt W Australia
145 F4 Weber New Zealand
106 G7 Weber City New Mexico
106 E2 Webster Colorado
113 E9 Webster Florida
99 O8 Webster Iowa
107 L2 Webster Kansas
95 Q4 Webster Massachusetts
98 H1 Webster N Dakota
95 K3 Webster New York
98 J4 Webster S Dakota
99 O4 Webster Wisconsin
99 N7 Webster City Iowa
110 F3 Webster Groves Missouri
109 M4 Weches Texas
37 O2 Wechselburg E Germany
71 A2 Weda Halmahera Indonesia
83 L11 Wedagama Sri Lanka
71 B2 Weda,Teluk *B* Halmahera Indonesia
133 E8 Weddell I Falkland Is
146 D11 Weddell Sea Antarctica
32 L7 Weddemark W Germany
144 C6 Wedderburn New Zealand
100 A7 Wedderburn Oregon
32 K4 Weddinghusen W Germany
32 K4 Weddingstedt W Germany
32 L5 Wedel W Germany
140 B6 Wedge, Central Mt N Terr Aust
112 G4 Wedgefield S Carolina
117 M10 Wedge Mt Br Columbia
140 B6 Wedge, Mt N Terr Aust
122 G10 Wedgeport Nova Scotia
8 D5 Wedmore England
9 D3 Wednesbury England
111 L8 Wedowee Alabama
100 C8 Weed California
9 E3 Weedon England
121 T7 Weedon Quebec
95 L3 Weedsport New York
94 J5 Weedville Pennsylvania
71 C3 Weeim *isld* W Irian
119 P6 Weekes Sask
111 E12 Weeks Louisiana
94 E9 Weeksbury Kentucky
Weeks I *see* Puketutu I
112 L1 Weeksville N Carolina
9 H4 Weeley England
139 J3 Weemelah New S Wales
32 F6 Weener W Germany
98 K9 Weeping Water Nebraska
25 E6 Weert Netherlands
109 K7 Weesatche Texas
28 C7 Weesby W Germany
41 K3 Weesen Switzerland
25 D4 Weesp Netherlands
25 G1 Weestereems Netherlands
139 H5 Weethalle New S Wales
9 G3 Weeting England
32 L8 Weetzen W Germany
139 J4 Wee Waa New S Wales
25 F5 Weeze W Germany
33 O8 Wefensleben E Germany
33 O8 Weferlingen E Germany
33 O9 Wegeleben E Germany
33 O8 Wegenstedt E Germany
41 H3 Weggis Switzerland
32 J8 Wegholm W Germany
31 J4 Węgliniec Poland
31 N1 Wegorapa *R* Poland
31 N1 Węgorzewo Poland
31 J2 Węgorzyno Poland
31 N3 Węgrów Poland
38 M6 Wegscheid Austria
38 J4 Wegscheid W Germany
69 B10 Weh *isld* Sumatra
25 F2 Wehe Netherlands
40 G2 Wehr W Germany
32 K9 Wehrden W Germany
36 F3 Wehrheim W Germany
65 D4 Weichang China
37 L6 Weichering W Germany
38 M6 Weichselboden Austria
65 C7 Weichuan China
37 N2 Weida E Germany
37 N4 Weiden W Germany
36 E2 Weidenau W Germany
37 M4 Weidenberg W Germany
36 H6 Weidenstetten W Germany
37 L3 Weidhausen W Germany
94 C3 Weidman Michigan
65 D6 Weifang China
65 E6 Weihai China
65 G2 Weihe China
58 E5 Wei He *R* China
37 N6 Weihmichl W Germany
36 E3 Weilburg W Germany
36 F6 Weil-der-Stadt W Germany
36 B2 Weilerswist W Germany
36 H6 Weilheim W Germany
36 E3 Weilmünster W Germany
36 E3 Weilnau W Germany
37 J5 Weiltingen W Germany
65 B4 Weilu China
37 L2 Weimar E Germany
109 L6 Weimar Texas
58 E5 Weinan China
110 F6 Weiner Arkansas
41 K2 Weinfelden Switzerland
36 E5 Weingarten W Germany
36 F5 Weingarten W Germany
36 F4 Weinheim W Germany
67 A3 Weining China
36 G5 Weinsberg W Germany
36 G6 Weinstadt W Germany
141 F2 Weipa Queensland
100 K3 Weippe Idaho
110 B4 Weir Kansas
111 G8 Weir Mississippi
121 Q7 Weir Quebec
109 K5 Weir Texas
141 J8 Weir *R* Queensland
143 B7 Weiragoo Ra W Australia
107 Q4 Weir City Kansas
119 M5 Weirdale Sask
113 F9 Weirsdale Florida
94 G6 Weirton W Virginia
37 N3 Weischlitz E Germany
100 J5 Weiser Idaho
65 C7 Weishan Hu *L* China
65 C7 Weishi China
Weishui *see* Jingxing
36 B4 Weiskirchen W Germany
37 L3 Weismain W Germany
36 F6 Weissach W Germany
37 K5 Weissenburg W Germany
37 M1 Weissenfels E Germany
37 J7 Weissenhorn W Germany
33 T7 Weissensee E Berlin E Germany
37 L1 Weissensee Erfurt E Germany
37 M3 Weissenstadt W Germany
36 H6 Weissenstein W Germany
37 M3 Weisser Main *R* W Germany
37 O5 Weisser Regen *R* W Germany
40 G5 Weisshorn *mt* Switzerland
38 L7 Weisskirchen Austria
41 N4 Weisskugel *mt* Austria
89 A5 Weissrand Mts Namibia
41 K3 Weisstannen Switzerland
33 S4 Weitenhagen E Germany
41 M2 Weitnau W Germany
67 F4 Weitou China
31 H7 Weitra Austria
38 N8 Weixelbaum Austria
38 K8 Weixelsdorf Austria
65 C6 Wei Xian China
65 D6 Wei Xian China
67 A3 Weixin China
67 A2 Weiyuan China
38 N7 Weiz Austria
41 H2 Weizen W Germany
Weizhou *see* Wenchuan
68 J2 Weizhou Dao *isld* China
31 L1 Wejherowo Poland
119 S4 Wekusko Manitoba
113 F8 Welaka Florida
138 C2 Welbourn Hill S Australia
94 F9 Welch W Virginia
99 M6 Welcome Minnesota
141 G3 Welcome Queensland
89 A8 Welcome Kop *mt* S Africa
146 J5 Welcome Mt Antarctica
37 K7 Welden W Germany
143 D8 Weld, Mt W Australia
102 F6 Weldon California
99 S9 Weldon Illinois
99 N9 Weldon Iowa
112 L1 Weldon N Carolina
119 M6 Weldon Sask
109 M4 Weldon Texas
99 N9 Weldon *R* Missouri
106 G1 Weldona Colorado
13 G3 Weldon Br England
143 B7 Weld Ra W Australia
143 D6 Weld Spring W Australia
107 O6 Weleetka Oklahoma
70 N9 Weleri Java
141 G7 Welford Queensland
141 G7 Welford Downs Queensland
83 K12 Weligama Sri Lanka
83 L11 Weliwewa Sri Lanka
22 K2 Welkenraedt Belgium
89 E6 Welkom S Africa
121 L10 Welland Canal Ontario
9 F2 Welland, R England
142 A4 Wellard *dist* Perth, W Aust
83 L11 Wellawaya Sri Lanka
113 E7 Wellborn Florida
36 H1 Wellerode Wald W Germany
9 E3 Wellesbourne England
140 E3 Wellesley Is Queensland
117 D4 Wellesley L Yukon Terr
98 F9 Wellfleet Nebraska
37 L6 Wellheim W Germany
22 J3 Wellin Belgium
9 F3 Wellingborough England
111 L8 Wellington Alabama
106 E1 Wellington Colorado
99 T9 Wellington Illinois
107 N4 Wellington Kansas
102 E3 Wellington Nevada
139 J4 Wellington New S Wales
145 F4 Wellington New Zealand
123 S5 Wellington Nfld
122 J9 Wellington Nova Scotia
94 E5 Wellington Ohio
121 N9 Wellington Ontario
122 H7 Wellington Pr Edward I
89 A9 Wellington S Africa
8 D2 Wellington Salop England
138 E6 Wellington S Australia
8 C6 Wellington Somerset England
108 G1 Wellington Texas
103 O2 Wellington Utah
145 E3 Wellington *stat area* New Zealand
115 K2 Wellington Chan N W Terr
133 C7 Wellington, I Chile
139 H7 Wellington, L Victoria
143 D7 Wellington Ra W Australia
108 E2 Wellman Texas
9 F1 Wellow England
107 N2 Wells Kansas
99 N6 Wells Minnesota
101 L8 Wells Nevada
95 N3 Wells New York
9 G2 Wells Norfolk England
8 D5 Wells Somerset England
109 N4 Wells Texas
95 K5 Wellsboro Pennsylvania
99 O7 Wellsburg Iowa
95 L4 Wellsburg New York
94 G6 Wellsburg W Virginia
145 E2 Wellsford New Zealand
117 N9 Wells Gray Prov. Park Br Col
141 G6 Wellshot Queensland
119 R1 Wells L Manitoba
143 E7 Wells, L W Australia
142 F3 Wells, Mt W Australia
142 D6 Wells Ra W Australia
95 P2 Wells River Vermont
94 E7 Wellston Ohio
110 E2 Wellsville Missouri
94 K4 Wellsville New York
101 O8 Wellsville Utah
103 K9 Wellton Arizona
119 S8 Wellwood Manitoba
38 K5 Wels Austria
25 D6 Welschap Netherlands
36 B4 Welschbillig W Germany
36 E1 Welschenennest W Germany
122 F8 Welsford New Brunswick
109 P5 Welsh Louisiana
8 D2 Welshampton England
122 F9 Welshpool New Brunswick
8 C2 Welshpool Wales
142 B2 Welshpool *dist* Perth, W Aust
13 H6 Welton England
32 G9 Welver W Germany
119 Q8 Welwyn Sask
9 F4 Welwyn Garden City England
36 H6 Welzheim W Germany
8 D2 Wem England
86 D6 Wema Zaïre
117 O8 Wembley Alberta
142 A1 Wembley *dist* Perth, W Aust
142 A1 Wembley Downs *dist* Perth, W Aust
8 B7 Wembury England
37 K6 Wemding W Germany
25 A5 Wemeldinge Netherlands
12 D2 Wemyss B Scotland
126 F2 Wemyss Bight Eleuthera Bahamas
65 C5 Wen'an China
100 E2 Wenatchee Washington
67 C7 Wenchang China
67 G3 Wencheng China
85 D7 Wenchi Ghana
67 A1 Wenchuan China
102 D1 Wendel California
101 L7 Wendell Idaho
98 K3 Wendell Minnesota
112 J2 Wendell N Carolina
36 D4 Wendelsheim W Germany
37 L5 Wendelstein W Germany
103 L8 Wenden Arizona
9 G3 Wenden England
36 D2 Wenden W Germany
65 E6 Wendeng China
33 Q6 Wendisch Priborn E Germany
33 O7 Wendland *reg* W Germany
9 G2 Wendling England
100 C5 Wendling Oregon
33 O5 Wendorf E Germany
9 F4 Wendover England
101 M9 Wendover Utah
98 B7 Wendover Wyoming
98 F5 Wendte S Dakota
22 E1 Wenduine Belgium
120 G5 Wenebegon L Ontario
67 B3 Weng'an China
36 B4 Wengerohr W Germany
67 D2 Wengjiang China
67 E4 Wengyuan China
65 D7 Wen He *R* China
36 G3 Wenings W Germany
67 A1 Wenjiang China
68 K1 Wenli China
67 G2 Wenling China
141 G2 Wenlock Queensland
141 F1 Wenlock *R* Queensland
128 A7 Wenman *isld* Galapagos Is
32 L8 Wennigsen W Germany
41 N3 Wenns Austria
99 R8 Wenona Illinois
67 C1 Wenquan China
67 A5 Wenshan China
65 C7 Wenshang China
65 B6 Wenshui China
67 B2 Wenshui China
139 G7 Wensleydale Victoria
57 K4 Wensu China
13 G6 Wentbridge England
13 G6 Wentworth England
95 Q3 Wentworth New Hampshire
138 F5 Wentworth New S Wales
98 K6 Wentworth S Dakota
122 J8 Wentworth Centre Nova Scotia
110 F3 Wentzville Missouri
65 B7 Wenxi China
65 B7 Wen Xian China
37 N5 Wenzenbach W Germany
67 G3 Wenzhou China
113 F10 Weohyakapka L Florida
100 B9 Weott California
89 E7 Wepener S Africa
22 H3 Wepion Belgium
33 T7 Werbellin E Germany
33 T7 Werbellinsee *L* E Germany
33 P7 Werben E Germany
33 S9 Werbig E Germany
22 K3 Werbomont Belgium
87 D11 Werda Botswana
37 N2 Werdau E Germany
33 R8 Werder E Germany
32 G10 Werdohl W Germany
32 G9 Werl W Germany
32 G7 Werlte W Germany
36 C1 Wermelskirchen W Germany
33 R10 Wermsdorf E Germany
36 H4 Wern *R* W Germany
37 N4 Wernberg W Germany
32 G9 Werne W Germany
37 J4 Werneck W Germany
117 F3 Wernecke Mts Yukon Terr
98 D2 Werner N Dakota
33 T7 Werneuchen E Germany
36 H3 Wernfeld W Germany
119 U2 Wernham L Manitoba
25 C6 Wernhout Netherlands
33 N9 Wernigerode E Germany
37 J1 Werra *R* E & W Germany
139 G7 Werribee Victoria
138 F5 Werrimull Victoria
139 K4 Werris Cr New S Wales
32 G9 Werse *R* W Germany
37 K7 Wertach *R* W Germany
36 H4 Wertheim W Germany
37 K6 Wertingen W Germany
25 D3 Wervershoof Netherlands
71 O9 Werwaru Indonesia
32 E9 Wesel W Germany
36 D5 Weselberg W Germany
33 R6 Wesenberg E Germany
32 H5 Weser *est* W Germany
32 L9 Weser *R* W Germany
71 N8 Wesiri Indonesia
107 J3 Weskan Kansas
86 G4 Weska Weka Ethiopia
109 K9 Weslaco Texas
121 N8 Weslemkoon L Ontario
95 U2 Wesley Maine
123 T4 Wesleyville Nfld
94 G4 Wesleyville Pennsylvania
32 F5 Wesse W Germany
32 J4 Wesselburen W Germany
36 B2 Wesseling W Germany
140 D1 Wessel Is N Terr Aust
98 H5 Wessington S Dakota
98 H5 Wessington Springs S Dakota
111 D8 Wesson Arkansas
111 F10 Wesson Mississippi
111 G8 West Mississippi
109 K4 West Texas
139 G6 West Victoria
32 G8 West W Germany
94 C7 West Alexandria Ohio
140 B1 West Alligator *R* N Terr Aust
99 S7 West Allis Wisconsin
138 C5 Westall,Pt S Australia
141 K6 West Arm Pt Queensland
13 G4 West Auckland England
113 B7 West B Florida
111 G12 West B Louisiana
109 N6 West B Texas
140 A3 West Baines *R* N Terr Aust
8 D6 West Bay England
111 L11 Westbay Florida
99 M7 West Bend Iowa
119 O7 West Bend Sask
99 S6 West Bend Wisconsin
75 M7 West Bengal *prov* India
111 J8 West Blocton Alabama
99 L9 Westboro Missouri
99 Q4 Westboro Wisconsin
119 T8 Westbourne Manitoba
99 P8 West Branch Iowa
94 C2 West Branch Michigan
13 G6 West Bretton England
117 O11 Westbridge Br Columbia
9 E2 West Bridgford England
9 E2 West Bromwich England
95 R3 Westbrook Maine
99 L5 Westbrook Minnesota
108 F3 Westbrook Texas
95 Q2 West Burke Vermont
15 G2 West Burra Shetland Scotland
8 D5 Westbury England
139 H8 Westbury Tasmania
101 O1 West Butte *mt* Montana
98 C1 Westby N Dakota
139 H6 Westby New S Wales
99 Q6 Westby Wisconsin
144 A6 West C New Zealand
127 H4 West Caicos *isld* Turks & Caicos Is
12 E2 West Calder Scotland
85 F7 West Cameroon *prov* Cameroon
143 C11 West Cape Howe W Australia
99 S8 West Chicago Illinois
106 E3 Westcliffe Colorado
109 M6 West Columbia Texas
99 O5 West Concord Minnesota
102 G7 West Covina California
9 G6 Westdean England
99 S5 West De Pere Wisconsin
99 N8 West Des Moines Iowa
122 J9 West Dover Nova Scotia
102 G6 Westend California
126 E1 West End Grand Bahama I
112 H2 West End N Carolina
141 K2 West End *dist* Brisbane, Qnsld
22 D1 Westende Belgium
113 J11 West End Settlement Grand Bahama I
32 L4 Westensee *L* W Germany
25 G3 Westerbork Netherlands
144 C5 Westerfield New Zealand
9 G5 Westerham England
98 J9 Western Nebraska
86 E4 Western Equatoria *prov* Sudan
76 A1 Western Ghats *mts* India
122 H10 Western Hd Nova Scotia
120 K7 Western Is Ontario
15 A3 Western Isles *reg* Scotland
94 H7 Westernport Maryland
139 H7 Western Port Victoria
141 G5 Western R Queensland
85 B4 Western Sahara *reg* Africa
137 S4 Western Samoa *islds* Pacific Oc
32 M9 Westerode W Germany
32 G6 Westerstede W Germany
36 D2 Westerwald *reg* W Germany
107 M3 Westfall Kansas
100 H6 Westfall Oregon
8 D2 West Felton England
99 T10 Westfield Illinois
95 P4 Westfield Massachusetts
94 H4 Westfield New York
94 K5 Westfield Pennsylvania
99 R6 Westfield Wisconsin
142 B3 Westfield *dist* Perth, W Aust
122 F8 Westfield Beach New Brunswick
110 B6 West Fork Arkansas
99 M6 West Fork *R* Minnesota
98 A1 West Fork *R* Montana
110 H4 West Frankfort Illinois
9 H5 Westgate England
141 H7 Westgate Queensland
30 West Germany
8 C4 West Glamorgan *co* Wales
112 E6 West Green Georgia
9 F6 West Grinstead England
141 J7 Westgrove Queensland
9 E3 West Haddon England
9 G5 West Ham England
94 E8 West Hamlin W Virginia
95 P6 Westhampton Beach Long I, N Y
37 K7 Westheim W Germany
36 E4 West Hofen W Germany
109 K6 Westhoff Texas
36 C6 Westhoffen France
100 B1 Westholme Br Col
98 E1 Westhope N Dakota
68 A6 West I Andaman Is
83 M8 West I Cocos Is Indian Oc
146 C3 West Ice Shelf Antarctica
32 G10 Westig W Germany
93 West Indies Caribbean
94 F10 West Jefferson N Carolina
94 D7 West Jefferson Ohio
22 E1 Westkapelle Belgium
25 A6 Westkapelle Netherlands
15 D5 West Kilbride Scotland
100 F8 West L Nevada
110 J1 West Lafayette Indiana
94 F6 West Lafayette Ohio
100 A6 Westlake Oregon
141 G6 Westland Queensland
144 B5 Westland *stat area* New Zealand
140 E5 West Leichhardt Queensland
9 H3 Westleton England
99 P8 West Liberty Iowa
94 D9 West Liberty Kentucky
94 D6 West Liberty Ohio
13 E2 West Linton Scotland
118 D4 Westlock Alberta
120 J10 West Lorne Ontario
West Lothian *co see* Lothian and Central *regions*
122 H2 West Magpie R Quebec
9 G5 West Malling England
94 C7 West Manchester Ohio
121 O7 Westmeath Ontario
14 D3 Westmeath *co* Irish Rep
110 F6 West Memphis Arkansas
9 G4 West Mersea England
94 G5 West Middlesex Pennsylvania
9 E2 West Midlands *co* England
94 C7 West Milton Ohio
95 L7 Westminster Maryland
112 D3 Westminster S Carolina
95 P3 Westminster Vermont
107 O2 Westmoreland Kansas
95 P4 Westmoreland New Hampshire
140 E3 Westmoreland Queensland
110 K5 Westmoreland Tennessee
103 J8 Westmorland California
Westmorland *co see* Cumbria
127 H2 Westmorland *parish* Jamaica
87 E10 West Nicholson Zimbabwe
108 G6 West Nueces *R* Texas
8 D2 Weston England
101 O7 Weston Idaho
94 C5 Weston Michigan
110 B2 Weston Missouri
98 K8 Weston Nebraska
144 C6 Weston New Zealand
94 D5 Weston Ohio
100 G4 Weston Oregon
70 D2 Weston Sabah
94 G7 Weston W Virginia
98 A5 Weston Wyoming
89 E6 Westonaria S Africa
8 D5 Weston-super-Mare England
109 H2 Westover Texas
32 F6 Westoverledingen W Germany
113 G11 West Palm Beach Florida
95 R2 West Paris Maine
110 J3 Westphalia Indiana
107 P3 Westphalia Kansas
94 K5 West Pike Pennsylvania
110 E5 West Plains Missouri
102 D3 West Point California
112 B5 West Point Georgia
110 J1 Westpoint Indiana
99 P9 West Point Iowa
94 B9 West Point Kentucky
111 H8 West Point Mississippi
95 N5 West Point New York
122 H4 West Point Quebec
139 G8 West Point Tasmania
95 L9 West Point Virginia
116 P4 West Point *mt* Alaska
West Polder *see* Markerwaard
102 A2 Westport California
94 B7 Westport Indiana
14 B3 Westport Irish Rep
95 O2 Westport New York
144 C4 Westport New Zealand
123 Q4 Westport Nfld
100 B3 Westport Oregon
98 H4 Westport S Dakota
110 H6 Westport Tennessee
100 A3 Westport Washington
118 A3 West Prairie R Alberta
98 K8 West Pt Nebraska
123 M10 West Pt Nova Scotia
122 H7 West Pt Pr Edward I
122 G10 West Pubnico Nova Scotia
126 A1 Westpunt Curaçao
13 G4 West Rainton England
119 Q5 Westray Manitoba
15 F1 Westray Firth Orkney Scotland
120 J5 Westree Ontario
36 C5 Westrich *reg* W Germany
117 L9 West Road R Br Col
13 F2 Westruther Scotland
123 P2 West St. Modiste Quebec
110 H3 West Salem Illinois
94 E6 West Salem Ohio
99 P6 West Salem Wisconsin
9 E5 West Shefford England
145 F3 Westshore New Zealand
99 L7 Westside Iowa
100 E7 West Side Oregon
139 J7 West Sister I Tasmania
7 L9 West Sole *sea rig* North Sea
95 Q2 West Stewartstown New Hampshire
9 F6 West Sussex *co* England
13 G5 West Tanfield England
25 D2 West Terschelling Netherlands
110 J2 West Union Illinois
99 P7 West Union Iowa
94 D8 West Union Ohio
94 G7 West Union W Virginia
94 C5 West Unity Ohio
117 L11 Westview Br Col
111 L11 Westville Florida
99 T9 Westville Illinois
99 U8 Westville Indiana
122 K8 Westville Nova Scotia
107 Q6 Westville Oklahoma
94 G8 West Virginia *state* U.S.A.
22 D1 West Vlaanderen Belgium
8 B5 Westward Ho England
103 P2 Westwater Utah
111 F12 Westwego Louisiana
95 M4 West Winfield New York
102 D1 Westwood California
141 K6 Westwood Queensland
109 L9 Westworth Texas
139 H5 West Wyalong New S Wales
101 O5 West Yellowstone Montana
13 G6 West Yorkshire *co* England
71 O8 Wetan *isld* Indonesia
71 N8 Wetar *isld* Indonesia
71 N9 Wetar, Selat *str* Indonesia
118 D6 Wetaskiwin Alberta
88 G4 Wete Tanzania
121 O3 Wetetnagami *R* Quebec
37 M1 Wethau E Germany
13 G6 Wetherby England
68 B1 Wetlet Burma
106 E3 Wetmore Colorado
109 J6 Wetmore Texas
106 E3 Wet Mts Colorado
98 H4 Wetonka S Dakota
36 F2 Wetter W Germany
36 F3 Wetter *R* W Germany
36 F3 Wetterau *reg* W Germany
22 F1 Wetteren Belgium
41 M3 Wetter Spitze *mt* Austria
41 O3 Wetterstein Geb *mt* Austria
33 P9 Wettin E Germany
32 F8 Wettringen W Germany
107 O6 Wetumka Oklahoma
111 K9 Wetumpka Alabama
68 C1 Wetwun Burma
36 F2 Wetzlar W Germany
37 L3 Wetzstein *mt* E Germany
36 B1 Wevelinghoven W Germany
110 E1 Wever Iowa
113 B7 Wewahitchka Florida
136 J2 Wewak Papua New Guinea
107 O6 Wewoka Oklahoma
14 E4 Wexford Irish Rep
14 E4 Wexford *co* Irish Rep
14 E4 Wexford B Irish Rep
14 E4 Wexford Harb Irish Rep
118 L4 Weyakwin L Sask
99 S5 Weyauwega Wisconsin
9 H2 Weybourne England
9 F5 Weybridge England
119 O9 Weyburn Sask
38 L6 Weyer Austria
36 D2 Weyerbusch W Germany
99 P4 Weyerhauser Wisconsin
36 D6 Weyersheim France
33 M7 Weyhausen W Germany
9 E5 Weyhill England
8 D6 Weymouth England
95 R4 Weymouth Massachusetts
122 G9 Weymouth Nova Scotia
141 G1 Weymouth B Queensland
141 G2 Weymouth,C Queensland
9 F5 Wey, R England
25 F4 Wezep Netherlands
145 E3 Whakahora New Zealand
145 E3 Whakamaru New Zealand
145 E1 Whakapara New Zealand
145 F3 Whakapunaki New Zealand
145 F4 Whakataki New Zealand
145 F2 Whakatane New Zealand
145 F3 Whakatane *R* New Zealand
68 D7 Whale B Burma
143 C6 Whaleback,Mt W Australia
116 D10 Whalebone C Aleutian Is
113 K12 Whale Cay *isld* Bahamas
Whale I *see* Motuhora I
123 P2 Whale I Quebec
146 J8 Whales, B. of Antarctica
9 E1 Whaley Bridge England
95 L10 Whaleyville Virginia
139 J3 Whallan *R* New S Wales
13 F6 Whalley England
15 G2 Whalsay *isld* Shetland Scotland
13 G3 Whalton England
145 E4 Whangaehu New Zealand
145 E2 Whangamata New Zealand
145 E3 Whangamomona New Zealand
145 D4 Whanganui Inlet New Zealand
145 E2 Whangaparaoa Pen New Zealand
145 D1 Whangape New Zealand
145 E2 Whangape, L New Zealand
145 G2 Whangapuraoa New Zealand
145 E1 Whangarei New Zealand
145 D1 Whangaroa New Zealand
145 E1 Whangaruru Harbour New Zealand
145 E4 Wharanui New Zealand
145 F4 Whareama New Zealand
145 F3 Wharerata New Zealand
13 G6 Wharfe, R England
95 N6 Wharton New Jersey
94 J5 Wharton Pennsylvania
109 L6 Wharton Texas
144 C5 Whataroa New Zealand
145 F3 Whatatutu New Zealand
145 E2 Whatawhata New Zealand
99 O8 What Cheer Iowa
100 C1 Whatcom, L Washington
111 J10 Whatley Alabama
102 C2 Wheatland California
98 B7 Wheatland Wyoming
98 A8 Wheatland Res Wyoming
110 E7 Wheatley Arkansas
9 E4 Wheatley England
120 H10 Wheatley Ontario
99 S8 Wheaton Illinois
107 O2 Wheaton Kansas
98 K4 Wheaton Minnesota
110 B5 Wheaton Missouri
8 C5 Wheddon Cross England
107 J2 Wheeler Kansas
100 B4 Wheeler Oregon
108 D8 Wheeler Texas
117 Q4 Wheeler L N W Terr
103 K3 Wheeler Pk Nevada
106 E5 Wheeler Pk New Mexico
102 F6 Wheeler Ridge California
94 E8 Wheelersburg Ohio
102 E7 Wheeler Springs California
94 G6 Wheeling W Virginia
98 C1 Wheelock N Dakota
94 E9 Wheelwright Kentucky
140 E6 Whelan,Mt Queensland
13 F5 Whernside *mt* England
9 E5 Wherwell England
138 C5 Whidbey I S Australia
100 C1 Whidbey I Washington
111 M11 Whigham Georgia
142 C5 Whim Creek W Australia
138 B2 Whinham, Mt S Australia
99 M2 Whipholt Minnesota
122 F9 Whipple Pt Nova Scotia
9 F4 Whipsnade England
101 N1 Whiskey Gap Alberta
119 T4 Whiskey Jack Landing Manitoba
140 D5 Whistleduck Creek N Terr Aust
111 H11 Whistler Alabama
9 E2 Whitacre England
112 K1 Whitakers N Carolina
13 E5 Whitbeck England
123 T6 Whitbourne Nfld
13 G4 Whitburn England
12 E2 Whitburn Scotland
13 H5 Whitby England
121 M9 Whitby Ontario
9 F4 Whitchurch Bucks England
9 E5 Whitchurch Hampshire England
8 D2 Whitchurch Salop England
8 C4 Whitchurch Wales
144 C5 Whitcombe Pass New Zealand
98 K5 White S Dakota
111 E7 White *R* Arkansas
101 S10 White *R* Colorado
99 U6 White *R* Michigan
103 J3 White *R* Nevada
98 F6 White *R* S Dakota
108 F2 White *R* Texas
103 P2 White *R* Utah
100 D2 White *R* Washington
99 Q3 White *R* Wisconsin
123 Q3 White B Nfld
118 J8 White Bear Sask
99 O4 White Bear L Minnesota
123 P6 White Bear R Nfld
100 J4 White Bird Idaho
110 J5 White Bluff Tennessee
100 F3 White Bluffs Washington
122 E6 White Brook New Brunswick
98 D4 White Butte S Dakota
119 W2 Whitecap L Manitoba
111 E11 White Castle Louisiana
113 G10 White City Florida
107 O3 White City Kansas
106 F9 White City New Mexico
139 G4 White Cliffs New S Wales
99 L10 White Cloud Kansas
94 B3 White Cloud Michigan
118 B4 White Court Alberta
98 D1 White Earth N Dakota
108 E2 Whiteface Texas
95 O2 Whiteface Mt New York
117 Q11 Whitefish Idaho
101 L1 Whitefish Montana
120 J6 Whitefish Ontario
99 U4 Whitefish *R* Michigan
99 T6 Whitefish Bay Wisconsin
116 K6 Whitefish L Alaska
118 E4 Whitefish L Alberta
99 V3 Whitefish L Michigan
99 M3 Whitefish L Minnesota
101 L1 Whitefish L Montana
119 O2 Whitefish L Ontario
119 N5 White Fox Sask
115 N6 Whitegull L Quebec
110 F2 White Hall Illinois
99 U6 Whitehall Michigan
101 N4 Whitehall Montana
99 P5 Whitehall Wisconsin
12 E5 Whitehaven England
95 M5 White Haven Pennsylvania
14 F2 Whitehead N Ireland
12 D4 Whitehill Scotland
116 N2 White Hills Alaska
103 K6 White Hills Arizona
100 D8 White Horse California
117 F5 Whitehorse Yukon Terr
101 L9 White Horse Pass Nevada
127 M3 White Horses Jamaica
White I *see* Kvitöya
146 H7 White I Antarctica
145 F2 White I New Zealand
115 L4 White I N W Terr
13 F1 Whitekirk Scotland
111 D12 White L Louisiana
99 U6 White L Michigan
140 A5 White L N Terr/W Aust
98 H6 White L S Dakota

84 White, L — Wörth

142 G5 White, L W Australia
99 S4 White Lake Wisconsin
94 A7 Whiteland Indiana
139 J8 Whitemark Tasmania
116 F4 White Mountain Alaska
14 E4 White Mt Irish Rep
116 D4 White Mts Alaska
102 F4 White Mts California
95 Q2 White Mts New Hampshire
117 P7 Whitemud R Alberta
86 F3 White Nile prov Sudan
86 F3 White Nile R Sudan
86 F2 White Nile Dam Sudan
112 K3 White Oak N Carolina
109 M2 White Oak Cr Texas
109 O2 White Oak L Arkansas
118 K1 White Otter L Ontario
98 D5 White Owl S Dakota
9 E5 Whiteparish England
117 F6 White Pass Br Col/Alaska
100 D3 White Pass Washington
94 B5 White Pigeon Michigan
99 R3 White Pine Michigan
100 K2 Whitepine Montana
112 D1 White Pine Tennessee
103 J2 White Pine Ra Nevada
112 G1 White Plains N Carolina
95 N5 White Plains New York
123 R2 White Pt Belle I, Nfld
140 D6 White Quartz Hill mt N Terr Aust
118 B8 White R Br Col
94 B8 White R Indiana
127 L2 White R Jamaica
98 F6 White R S Dakota
120 E4 White River Ontario
95 P3 White River Junc Vermont
103 J3 White River Valley Nevada
100 J8 White Rock Nevada
109 O9 White Rock Texas
107 M2 White Rock Cr Kansas
103 K3 White Rock Peak Nevada
White Russia see Belorussiya S.S.R.
117 K9 Whitesail L Br Col
100 D4 White Salmon Washington
117 P6 Whitesand R Alberta
8 B7 Whitesand B England
119 P7 Whitesand R Sask
108 A3 White Sands Missile Ra New Mexico
108 A3 White Sands Nat. Mon New Mexico
95 M3 Whitesboro New York
109 L2 Whitesboro Texas
112 C4 Whitesburg Georgia
94 E9 Whitesburg Kentucky
White Sea see Beloye More
109 L9 White Settlement Texas
118 F1 Whiteshell Manitoba
100 B4 Whiteson Oregon
119 U2 Whitestone L Manitoba
101 P3 White Sulphur Springs Montana
110 K4 Whitesville Kentucky
95 K4 Whitesville New York
94 F9 Whitesville W Virginia
100 E3 White Swan Washington
119 M4 Whiteswan L Sask
98 A1 Whitetail Montana
112 J3 Whiteville N Carolina
110 G6 Whiteville Tennessee
85 D7 White Volta R Ghana
101 S1 Whitewater Montana
106 B9 Whitewater New Mexico
99 S7 Whitewater Wisconsin
94 B7 Whitewater R Indiana
113 F12 Whitewater B Florida
120 A2 Whitewater L Ontario
138 B4 White Well S Australia
141 G5 Whitewood Queensland
119 P8 Whitewood Sask
98 C5 Whitewood S Dakota
98 J5 Whitewood, L S Dakota
109 L2 Whitewright Texas
139 H6 Whitfield Victoria
13 F4 Whitfield Hall England
127 H2 Whithorn Jamaica
12 D4 Whithorn Scotland
145 E2 Whitianga New Zealand
107 P2 Whiting Kansas
95 N7 Whiting New Jersey
117 G6 Whiting R Br Col/Alaska
12 G3 Whiting B Scotland
95 P4 Whitingham Res Vermont
118 K6 Whitkow Sask
118 F9 Whitla Alberta
8 B4 Whitland Wales
101 O1 Whitlash Montana
13 G3 Whitley Bay England
94 C10 Whitley City Kentucky
98 F4 Whitlocks Crossing S Dakota
95 R4 Whitman Massachusetts
98 H1 Whitman N Dakota
98 E7 Whitman Nebraska
98 A2 Whitman Nat. Mon Washington
112 F3 Whitmire S Carolina
8 C3 Whitney England
98 C7 Whitney Nebraska
103 J5 Whitney Nevada
121 M7 Whitney Ontario
100 G5 Whitney Oregon
109 K4 Whitney, L Texas
102 F5 Whitney, Mt California
109 J7 Whitsett Texas
9 H5 Whitstable England
141 J5 Whitsunday I Queensland
109 J3 Whitt Texas
94 G7 Whittaker W Virginia
99 M6 Whittemore Iowa
94 D2 Whittemore Michigan
116 N6 Whittier Alaska
102 F8 Whittier California
13 G3 Whittingham England
139 H7 Whittlesea Victoria
9 F2 Whittlesey England
139 H5 Whitton New S Wales
8 C3 Whitton Wales
13 G4 Whittonstall England
141 F7 Whitula R Queensland
9 E1 Whitwell England
112 B2 Whitwell Tennessee
114 J5 Wholdaia L N W Terr
138 D5 Whyalla S Australia
123 L8 Whycocomagh Nova Scotia
139 G3 Whyjonta New S Wales
68 D3 Wiang Pa Pao Thailand
68 D2 Wiang Phrao Thailand
120 J8 Wiarton Ontario
31 K5 Wiązów Poland
98 B2 Wibaux Montana
13 G6 Wibsey England
107 N4 Wichita Kansas
109 J1 Wichita R Texas
109 J2 Wichita Falls Texas
109 J1 Wichita Mts Oklahoma
15 E2 Wick Scotland
32 G10 Wickede W Germany
103 M8 Wickenburg Arizona
122 J4 Wickenden L Quebec
143 C10 Wickepin W Australia
100 C1 Wickersham Washington
108 D4 Wickett Texas
9 G4 Wickford England
95 Q5 Wickford Rhode I
9 E6 Wickham England
139 G7 Wickham, C Tasmania
140 A3 Wickham Mt N Terr Aust
121 S7 Wickham West Quebec
100 D6 Wickiup Res Oregon
110 G5 Wickliffe Kentucky
14 E4 Wicklow Irish Rep
14 E4 Wicklow co Irish Rep
8 D4 Wickwar England
31 L4 Widawka R Poland
36 G5 Widdern W Germany
121 L6 Widdifield Ontario
90 A11 Wideawake Ascension I
116 J8 Wide B Alaska
141 L7 Wide B Queensland
8 C6 Widecombe-in-the-Moor England
138 B2 Wide Gum R S Australia
94 G8 Widen W Virginia
141 H8 Widgeegoara R Queensland
143 D9 Widgiemooltha W Australia
71 B3 Widi, Pulau Pulau islds Indonesia
36 F4 Wiebelsbach W Germany
36 C5 Wiebelskirchen W Germany
31 K2 Więcbork Poland
36 C2 Wied W Germany
Wiedenbrück see Rheda-Wiedenbrück
32 H6 Wiefelstede W Germany
33 O10 Wiehe E Germany
32 J8 Wiehengebirge hills W Germany
36 D2 Wiehl W Germany
31 M2 Wielbark Poland
31 J3 Wieleń Poland
31 M6 Wieliczka Poland
31 L4 Wieluń Poland
38 O5 Wien Austria
38 O6 Wiener Neustadt Austria
32 M7 Wienhausen W Germany
116 M4 Wien L Alaska
33 O7 Wiepke E Germany
31 O5 Wieprz R Poland
33 N7 Wieren W Germany
109 O4 Wiergate Texas
25 D3 Wieringen Netherlands
25 C3 Wieringermeer Netherlands
31 L4 Wieruszów Poland
31 N4 Wierzbnik Poland
31 L2 Wierzchucin Poland
31 L2 Wierzyca R Poland
38 M8 Wies Austria
37 N4 Wiesau W Germany
36 E3 Wiesbaden W Germany
40 G2 Wiese R W Germany
33 Q8 Wiesenburg E Germany
36 H6 Wiesensteig W Germany
37 L4 Wiesent R W Germany
37 J4 Wiesentheid W Germany
37 L4 Wiesenttal W Germany
36 F5 Wiesloch W Germany
32 G6 Wiesmoor W Germany
32 F7 Wietmarschen W Germany
32 L7 Wietze W Germany
32 K7 Wietzen W Germany
32 L7 Wietzendorf W Germany
13 F6 Wigan England
98 B9 Wiggins Colorado
111 G11 Wiggins Mississippi
9 E6 Wight, I. of England
8 D3 Wigmore England
31 O2 Wigry, Jezioro L Poland
9 E2 Wigston England
13 E4 Wigton England
12 D4 Wigtown Scotland
Wigtown co see Dumfries and Galloway reg
25 F4 Wijhe Netherlands
25 E7 Wijk Netherlands
25 C4 Wijk aan Zee Netherlands
103 L7 Wikieup Arizona
120 J7 Wikwemikong Ontario
41 K3 Wil Switzerland
83 L11 Wila Oya R Sri Lanka
98 K9 Wilber Nebraska
121 M7 Wilberforce Ontario
140 D1 Wilberforce, C N Terr Aust
144 C5 Wilberforce R New Zealand
101 N3 Wilborn Montana
100 B6 Wilbur Oregon
100 G2 Wilbur Washington
94 E10 Wilbur Dam Tennessee
110 A7 Wilburton Oklahoma
9 F3 Wilby England
139 G4 Wilcannia New S Wales
99 M9 Wilcox Missouri
98 G9 Wilcox Nebraska
94 J5 Wilcox Pennsylvania
119 N8 Wilcox Sask
33 T8 Wildau E Germany
36 F8 Wildbad W Germany
33 R7 Wildberg E Germany
36 F6 Wildberg W Germany
123 Q4 Wild Bight Nfld
102 H2 Wildcat Pk Nevada
119 V3 Wilde Manitoba
37 J2 Wildeck W Germany
33 O2 Wildenfels E Germany
94 B10 Wilder Tennessee
81 O4 Wilder Freiger mt Austria
117 O9 Wilderness Prov. Park Alberta
110 H6 Wildersville Tennessee
25 G2 Wildervank Netherlands
32 H7 Wildeshausen W Germany
36 H3 Wildflecken W Germany
120 A4 Wild Goose Ontario
40 F5 Wildhorn mt Switzerland
101 P1 Wild Horse Alberta
100 K8 Wildhorse Res Nevada
119 P4 Wildnest L Sask
108 B8 Wildorado Texas
33 R8 Wildpark E Germany
98 K2 Wild Rice R Minnesota
98 K3 Wild Rice R N Dakota
98 C1 Wildrose N Dakota
99 R6 Wild Rose Wisconsin
40 G5 Wildstrubel mt Switzerland
118 B5 Wildwood Alberta
113 E9 Wildwood Florida
95 N8 Wildwood New Jersey
118 B1 Wildwood Pk Manitoba
106 H3 Wiley Colorado
36 F6 Wilferdingen W Germany
120 E2 Wilgar Ontario
89 F6 Wilge R S Africa
138 C4 Wilgena S Australia
146 D3 Wilhelm II Land Antarctica
129 G3 Wilhelmina Geb mts Suriname
25 D5 Wilhelmina Kanal Netherlands
136 J3 Wilhelm, Mt Papua New Guinea
31 H4 Wilhelm-Pieck-Stadt East Germany
31 H4 Wilhelm Pieck Stadt E Germany
32 H5 Wilhelmshaven W Germany
36 F2 Wilhelmshütte W Germany
33 O5 Wiligrad E Germany
70 N9 Wilis mt Java
95 M5 Wilkes Barre Pennsylvania
112 F1 Wilkesboro N Carolina
146 H3 Wilkes Coast Antarctica
146 F3 Wilkes Land Antarctica
37 N2 Wilkhau Hasslau E Germany
118 J6 Wilkie Sask
146 E13 Wilkins Coast Antarctica
146 F13 Wilkins Ice Antarctica
138 C3 Wilkinson L S Australia
112 D6 Willacoochee Georgia
103 M6 Willaha Arizona
100 B4 Willamette R Oregon
139 G5 Willandra Billabong R New S Wales
100 B3 Willapa R Washington
139 G3 Willara New S Wales
138 E2 Willara, L S Australia
98 C9 Willard Colorado
124 D3 Willard Mexico
98 B3 Willard Montana
106 D7 Willard New Mexico
94 E5 Willard Ohio
101 N8 Willard Utah
95 M8 Willards Maryland
139 G4 Willaroy New S Wales
103 P9 Willcox Arizona
32 K9 Willebadessen W Germany
22 G1 Willebroek Belgium
22 E2 Willems France
25 C5 Willemsdorp Netherlands
126 B1 Willemstad Curaçao
25 B5 Willemstad Netherlands
140 B3 Willeroo N Terr Aust
8 D3 Willersley England
22 H4 Willerzie Belgium
9 F4 Willesden England
118 C6 Willesden Green Alberta
120 B2 Willet Ontario
143 B6 Williambury W Australia
138 D3 William Creek S Australia
119 S5 William L Manitoba
138 F6 William, Mt Victoria
143 B10 William,Mt W Australia
103 M6 Williams Arizona
102 B2 Williams California
110 K3 Williams Indiana
99 N7 Williams Iowa
99 L1 Williams Minnesota
143 B10 Williams W Australia
141 F5 Williams R Queensland
95 S7 Williams Bay Wisconsin
99 O8 Williamsburg Iowa
94 C10 Williamsburg Kentucky
95 P4 Williamsburg Massachusetts
94 C7 Williamsburg Ohio
94 J6 Williamsburg Pennsylvania
95 L9 Williamsburg Virginia
127 K2 Williamsfield Jamaica
120 K8 Williamsford Ontario
126 E2 Williams I Bahamas
117 M9 Williams Lake Br Columbia
99 N8 Williamson Iowa
95 K3 Williamson New York
94 E9 Williamson W Virginia
146 J10 Williamson Hd Antarctica
99 T9 Williamsport Indiana
94 K7 Williamsport Maryland
123 Q3 Williamsport Nfld
95 K5 Williamsport Pennsylvania
94 C4 Williamston Michigan
112 K2 Williamston N Carolina
112 E3 Williamston S Carolina
94 C8 Williamstown Kentucky
95 O4 Williamstown Massachusetts
95 P2 Williamstown Vermont
94 F7 Williamstown W Virginia
94 F5 Williamsville Missouri
141 G8 Willie's Ra Queensland
127 P4 Willikie's Antigua W Indies
95 P5 Willimantic Connecticut
118 E5 Willingdon Alberta
117 P10 Willingdon, Mt Alberta
32 J10 Willingen W Germany
9 G3 Willingham England
13 G4 Willington England
109 M5 Willis Texas
94 G10 Willis Virginia
40 G3 Willisau Switzerland
141 K3 Willis Grp islds Gt Barrier Reef Aust
146 B15 Willis I S Georgia
113 E8 Williston Florida
98 C1 Williston N Dakota
87 D12 Williston S Africa
112 F4 Williston S Carolina
117 M8 Williston L Br Col
110 G4 Willisville Illinois
8 C5 Williton England
102 A2 Willits California
99 L4 Willmar Minnesota
119 P9 Willmar Sask
94 F5 Willoughby Ohio
138 E6 Willoughby, C S Australia
116 M6 Willow Alaska
108 E8 Willow Oklahoma
117 M9 Willow R Br Col
119 P7 Willowbrook Sask
119 M9 Willow Bunch L Sask
98 F1 Willow City N Dakota
100 E9 Willow Cr California
100 H5 Willow Cr Oregon
118 D8 Willow Cr. Prov. Park Alberta
117 O4 Willow L N W Terr
98 J5 Willow L S Dakota
117 N4 Willowlake R N W Terr
89 C9 Willowmore S Africa
140 C5 Willowra N Terr Aust
100 E8 Willow Ranch California
99 R4 Willow Res Wisconsin
99 O3 Willow River Minnesota
94 D4 Willow Run Michigan
102 B2 Willows California
119 M9 Willows Sask
110 E5 Willow Springs Missouri
139 K4 Willow Tree New S Wales
95 O2 Willsboro New York
142 G5 Wills,L W Australia
109 L3 Wills Point Texas
138 E6 Willunga S Australia
111 H11 Wilmar Alabama
33 T6 Wilmersdorf E Germany
99 S8 Wilmette Illinois
95 M7 Wilmington Delaware
99 S8 Wilmington Illinois
112 K3 Wilmington N Carolina
94 D7 Wilmington Ohio
138 E4 Wilmington S Australia
95 O4 Wilmington Vermont
99 L6 Wilmont Minnesota
107 L4 Wilmore Kansas
94 C9 Wilmore Kentucky
111 E8 Wilmot Arkansas
94 F6 Wilmot Ohio
144 B6 Wilmot, L New Zealand
144 A6 Wilmot Pass New Zealand
25 C4 Wilnis Netherlands
121 N7 Wilno Ontario
36 E2 Wilnsdorf W Germany
83 J9 Wilpattu game reserve Sri Lanka
138 E4 Wilpena R S Australia
22 G1 Wilrijk Belgium
101 P3 Wilsall Montana
37 O1 Wilsdruff E Germany
32 L6 Wilseder Berg hill W Germany
110 F6 Wilson Arkansas
107 M3 Wilson Kansas
111 E11 Wilson Louisiana
112 K2 Wilson N Carolina
94 J3 Wilson New York
109 K1 Wilson Oklahoma
108 F2 Wilson Texas
101 P6 Wilson Wyoming
139 G3 Wilson R Queensland
138 A4 Wilson Bluff S Australia
115 L4 Wilson, C N W Terr
140 F5 Wilson Cliffs hill W Australia
100 F2 Wilson Creek Washington
103 K3 Wilson Cr. Ra Nevada
106 H3 Wilson Junc Colorado
138 A2 Wilson, L S Australia
102 G7 Wilson, Mt California
106 C4 Wilson, Mt Colorado
103 K3 Wilson, Mt Nevada
142 G5 Wilson,Mt W Australia
107 M3 Wilson Res Kansas
139 H7 Wilson's Promontory Victoria
12 E2 Wilsontown Scotland
98 F9 Wilsonville Nebraska
32 K6 Wilstedt W Germany
32 K5 Wilster W Germany
109 N2 Wilton Arkansas
9 E5 Wilton England
99 P8 Wilton Iowa
98 F2 Wilton N Dakota
95 Q4 Wilton New Hampshire
99 Q6 Wilton Wisconsin
140 C2 Wilton R N Terr Aust
9 E5 Wiltshire co England
22 K4 Wiltz Luxembourg
143 D7 Wiluna W Australia
22 L4 Wilwerwiltz Luxembourg
119 S3 Wimapedi L Manitoba
113 E10 Wimauma Florida
9 F5 Wimbledon England
98 H2 Wimbledon N Dakota
145 F4 Wimbledon New Zealand
118 D7 Wimborne Alberta
9 E6 Wimborne England
22 B2 Wimereux France
113 B8 Wimico, L Florida
22 B2 Wimille France
38 K8 Wimitz R Austria
36 C6 Wimmenau France
139 G6 Wimmera R Victoria
118 A3 Winagami L Alberta
94 A5 Winamac Indiana
88 E2 Winam Gulf Kenya
139 G4 Winbar New S Wales
141 G7 Winbin Queensland
87 E11 Winburg S Africa
8 D5 Wincanton England
12 E2 Winchburgh Scotland
9 E4 Winchcomb England
109 H4 Winchell Texas
9 G6 Winchelsea England
95 P4 Winchendon Massachusetts
9 E5 Winchester England
100 J3 Winchester Idaho
99 Q10 Winchester Illinois
94 C6 Winchester Indiana
94 C9 Winchester Kentucky
95 P4 Winchester New Hampshire
144 C6 Winchester New Zealand
94 D8 Winchester Ohio
121 P7 Winchester Ontario
110 K6 Winchester Tennessee
109 K5 Winchester Texas
94 H7 Winchester Virginia
101 R6 Winchester Wyoming
100 A6 Winchester Bay Oregon
101 R6 Wind R Wyoming
138 D4 Windabout, L S Australia
101 P2 Windam Montana
143 D8 Windarra W Australia
Windau see Ventspils
94 J6 Windber Pennsylvania
98 C6 Wind Cave Nat. Park S Dakota
36 F3 Windecken W Germany
36 E5 Winden W Germany
112 D4 Winder Georgia
141 K7 Windera Queensland
113 L12 Windermere Bahamas
13 F5 Windermere England
120 G5 Windermere L Ontario
8 B6 Windfall Indiana
95 M6 Wind Gap Pennsylvania
95 R3 Windham, S Maine
32 K8 Windheim W Germany
87 C10 Windhoek Namibia
143 D7 Windich Springs W Australia
121 R5 Windigo Quebec
107 P7 Winding Stair Mts Oklahoma
37 N4 Windischeschenbach W Germany
38 K6 Windischgarsten Austria
146 F2 Windmill I Antarctica
95 M9 Windmill Pt Virginia
107 N3 Windom Kansas
99 L6 Windom Minnesota
106 C4 Windom Pk Colorado
141 F7 Windorah Queensland
37 P6 Windorf W Germany
99 T7 Wind Point Wisconsin
101 Q7 Wind R. Ra Wyoming
37 K5 Windsbach W Germany
106 F1 Windsor Colorado
95 P5 Windsor Connecticut
9 F5 Windsor England
99 S10 Windsor Illinois
95 P4 Windsor Massachusetts
110 C3 Windsor Missouri
112 L2 Windsor N Carolina
139 K5 Windsor New S Wales
95 M4 Windsor New York
144 C6 Windsor New Zealand
123 R5 Windsor Nfld
122 H9 Windsor Nova Scotia
120 H10 Windsor Ontario
121 T7 Windsor Quebec
112 F4 Windsor S Carolina
94 K10 Windsor Virginia
141 K1 Windsor dist Brisbane, Qnsld
94 G6 Windsor Heights W Virginia
126 H4 Windsor L. Great Inagua I Bahamas
95 P5 Windsor Locks Connecticut
109 J2 Windthorst Texas
141 F7 Windula R Queensland
127 O7 Windward Is W Indies
126 H5 Windward Passage Cuba/Haiti
116 N5 Windy Alaska
116 K5 Windy Fork R Alaska
119 P4 Windy L Sask
117 Q5 Windy Pt N W Terr
118 G3 Winefred L Alberta
99 R3 Winegar Wisconsin
94 C3 Winegars Michigan
100 E2 Winesap Washington
111 J8 Winfield Alabama
118 C6 Winfield Alberta
107 O4 Winfield Kansas
109 M2 Winfield Texas
8 D6 Winfrith England
98 F2 Wing N Dakota
110 J1 Wingate Indiana
106 B6 Wingate New Mexico
138 B2 Wingate Mts N Terr Aust
139 K4 Wingen New S Wales
22 E1 Wingene Belgium
36 C6 Wingen-sur-Moder France
9 F5 Wingham England
139 L4 Wingham New S Wales
120 J9 Wingham Ontario
110 H5 Wingo Kentucky
32 K5 Wingst W Germany
71 M9 Wini Timor Indonesia
101 Q2 Winifred Montana
98 J6 Winifred S Dakota
142 F6 Winifred, L W Australia
115 L6 Winisk Ontario
68 D5 Winkana Burma
25 C3 Winkel Netherlands
103 O9 Winkelman Arizona
9 F5 Winkfield England
37 O5 Winklarn W Germany
8 C6 Winkleigh England
119 U9 Winkler Manitoba
38 G8 Winklern Austria
100 C3 Winlock Washington
95 T1 Winn Maine
94 C3 Winn Michigan
140 B6 Winnalls Ridge N Terr Aust
85 D7 Winneba Ghana
99 M6 Winnebago Minnesota
98 K7 Winnebago Nebraska
99 S5 Winnebago, L Wisconsin
142 G6 Winnecke Hills N Terr/W Aust
140 B4 Winnecke,Mt N Terr Aust
142 E6 Winnecke Rock hill W Australia
99 S5 Winneconne Wisconsin
100 H9 Winnemucca Nevada
102 E1 Winnemucca L Nevada
36 G6 Winnenden W Germany
98 G6 Winner S Dakota
99 T7 Winnetka Illinois
98 G7 Winnetoon Nebraska
101 R2 Winnett Montana
111 D9 Winnfield Louisiana
99 M2 Winnibigoshish L Minnesota
109 N6 Winnie Texas
118 F9 Winnifred Alberta
33 O9 Winningen E Germany
142 A6 Winning W Australia
36 D3 Winningen W Germany
138 E4 Winninnie S Australia
118 A1 Winnipeg Manitoba
119 V8 Winnipeg Beach Manitoba
119 T5 Winnipeg, L Manitoba
119 S7 Winnipegosis Manitoba
119 R6 Winnipegosis, L Manitoba
95 Q3 Winnipesaukee, L New Hampshire
111 E9 Winnsboro Louisiana
112 F3 Winnsboro S Carolina
109 M3 Winnsboro Texas
112 E6 Winokur Georgia
103 N6 Winona Arizona
107 J2 Winona Kansas
99 S3 Winona Michigan
99 P5 Winona Minnesota
110 E4 Winona Missouri
109 M3 Winona Texas
100 H3 Winona Washington
109 P1 Winona, L Arkansas
95 O3 Winooski Vermont
95 P2 Winooski R Vermont
25 H2 Winschoten Netherlands
32 L7 Winsen W Germany
32 M6 Winsen W Germany
8 D1 Winsford England
98 J7 Winside Nebraska
103 O6 Winslow Arizona
110 B6 Winslow Arkansas
9 F4 Winslow England
110 J3 Winslow Indiana
95 S2 Winslow Maine
100 C2 Winslow Washington
137 R2 Winslow Reef Phoenix Is Pacific Oc
101 N5 Winsper Idaho
95 O5 Winsted Connecticut
9 E1 Winster England
13 G4 Winston England
101 O3 Winston Montana
106 C8 Winston New Mexico
112 G1 Winston Salem N Carolina
25 G2 Winsum Netherlands
118 H6 Winter Sask
38 M6 Winterbach Austria
36 D4 Winterberg W Germany
36 F1 Winterberg W Germany
8 D6 Winterbourne Abbas England
9 E5 Winterbourne Stoke England
33 O7 Winterfeld E Germany
113 F9 Winter Garden Florida
114 J3 Winter Harb N W Terr
103 K9 Winterhaven California
113 F9 Winter Haven Florida
119 U3 Wintering L Manitoba
36 G7 Winterlingen W Germany
106 E2 Winter Park Colorado
113 F9 Winter Park Florida
95 T2 Winterport Maine
102 C3 Winters California
108 H4 Winters Texas
103 M8 Wintersburg Arizona
99 M8 Winterset Iowa
22 K2 Winterslag Belgium
25 G5 Winterswijk Netherlands
41 J3 Winterthur Switzerland
13 H6 Winterton England
123 T6 Winterton Nfld
95 S7 Winterville Maine
95 R4 Winthrop Massachusetts
99 N5 Winthrop Minnesota
95 N2 Winthrop New York
100 E1 Winthrop Washington
99 T7 Winthrop Harbor Illinois
138 C2 Wintinna S Australia
99 N4 Winton Minnesota
112 K1 Winton N Carolina
113 M9 Winton New Providence I Bahamas
144 B7 Winton New Zealand
94 J5 Winton Pennsylvania
141 G5 Winton Queensland
100 E2 Winton Washington
101 Q8 Winton Wyoming
40 F1 Wintzenheim France
112 H4 Winyah B S Carolina
37 P6 Winzer W Germany
98 M5 Wiota Iowa
33 N10 Wipper R E Germany
36 C1 Wipperfürth W Germany
33 O9 Wippra E Germany
41 O3 Wipp Tal Austria
83 K11 Wirakettiya Sri Lanka
25 E2 Wirdum Netherlands
32 F6 Wirdum W Germany
9 E1 Wirksworth England
145 F2 Wiroa I New Zealand
138 E5 Wirrabara S Australia
138 D4 Wirraminna S Australia
138 D4 Wirrappa S Australia
138 F6 Wirrega S Australia
138 C3 Wirrida, L S Australia
138 C4 Wirrulla S Australia
99 N2 Wirt Minnesota
19 P15 Wirwignes France
9 G2 Wisbech England
9 F5 Wisborough Green England
95 S2 Wiscasset Maine
32 K5 Wischhafen W Germany
99 R4 Wisconsin R Wisconsin
99 R5 Wisconsin state U.S.A.
99 R6 Wisconsin Dells Wisconsin
99 R6 Wisconsin, L Wisconsin
146 G9 Wisconsin Ra Antarctica
99 R5 Wisconsin Rapids Wisconsin
101 M4 Wisdom Montana
94 E9 Wise Virginia
116 M3 Wiseman Alaska
101 N4 Wise River Montana
118 K7 Wiseton Sask
119 O7 Wishart Sask
12 E2 Wishaw Scotland
98 G3 Wishek N Dakota
100 E4 Wishram Washington
48 E1 Wisla Poland
31 L2 Wisla R Poland
31 N6 Wisłok R Poland
33 O5 Wismar E Germany
33 O5 Wismarbucht E Germany
111 E10 Wisner Louisiana
98 K8 Wisner Nebraska
22 B2 Wissant France
136 H2 Wissel, Danau D L W Irian
36 D5 Wissembourg France
36 D2 Wissen W Germany
9 G2 Wissey, R England
32 H8 Wissingen W Germany
99 P5 Wissota L Wisconsin
31 N4 Wista Poland
117 K9 Wistaria Br Columbia
109 N1 Wister Oklahoma
89 F5 Witbank S Africa
89 E8 Witberge mts S Africa
119 U3 Witchai L Manitoba
143 B10 Witchcliffe W Australia
118 K5 Witchekan L Sask
87 D11 Witdraai S Africa
9 G4 Witham England
9 F1 Witham, R England
8 C6 Witheridge England
13 G6 Withern England
13 J6 Withernsea England
141 J6 Withersfield Queensland
106 C8 Withington, Mt New Mexico
113 E9 Withlacoochee R Florida
100 F2 Withrow Washington
31 K3 Witkowo Poland
123 U6 Witless B Nfld
9 E4 Witney England
22 K4 Witry Belgium
22 G5 Witry-les-Reims France
22 D2 Witschate Belgium
99 R10 Witt Illinois
28 A7 Wittdün W Germany
37 L7 Wittelsbach W Germany
98 F6 Witten S Dakota
32 F10 Witten W Germany
33 S7 Wittenau E Germany
33 R9 Wittenberg E Germany
99 R5 Wittenberg Wisconsin
33 P7 Wittenberge E Germany
33 O5 Wittenburg E Germany
142 C5 Wittenoom W Australia
142 G4 Wittenoom,Mt W Australia
37 O2 Wittgendorf E Germany
125 N2 Witties, The islds Nicaragua
36 H4 Wittighausen W Germany
33 N7 Wittingen W Germany
70 E2 Witti Ra Sabah
32 H8 Wittlage W Germany
36 B4 Wittlich W Germany
32 K7 Wittlohe W Germany
103 M8 Wittmann Arizona
32 G5 Wittmund W Germany
13 G4 Witton Gilbert England
13 G4 Witton-le-Wear England
30 G1 Witow pen E Germany
33 Q6 Wittstock E Germany
87 C10 Witvlei Namibia
89 E5 Witwatersberg ridge S Africa
89 C2 Witwatersrand S Africa
32 L10 Witzenhausen W Germany
8 C5 Wiveliscombe England
119 W2 Wivenhoe Manitoba
118 L8 Wiwa Sask
9 H4 Wix England
31 O1 Wizajny Poland
22 C2 Wizernes France
31 M3 Wkra R Poland
31 L1 Władysławowo Poland
31 J4 Wleń Poland
31 L3 Włocławek Poland
31 O4 Włodawa Poland
31 M5 Włoszczowa Poland
33 O6 Wöbbelin E Germany
9 F4 Woburn England
95 R4 Woburn Massachusetts
142 C5 Wodgina W Australia
139 H6 Wodonga Victoria
31 M5 Wodzisław Poland
25 B6 Woensdrecht Netherlands
25 C4 Woerden Netherlands
36 D6 Wœrth France
22 J5 Wœvre, Forêt de France
94 C10 Wofford Kentucky
25 D3 Wognum Netherlands
41 H3 Wohlen Switzerland
33 O5 Wohlenberg E Germany
40 F4 Wohlen See L Switzerland
36 F2 Wohratal W Germany
32 J4 Wöhrden W Germany
121 N7 Woito Ontario
143 A8 Wokarina W Australia
65 H1 Woken China
65 H1 Woken He R China
117 O8 Woking Alberta
9 F5 Woking England
9 F5 Wokingham England
141 G5 Wokingham R Queensland
33 S6 Wokuhl E Germany
31 L4 Wola Poland
98 H8 Wolbach Nebraska
32 G9 Wolbeck W Germany
101 T10 Wolcott Colorado
95 L3 Wolcott New York
32 E2 Woldbrunn W Germany
33 T6 Woldegk E Germany
141 J7 Woleebee Queensland
111 G11 Wolf R Mississippi
110 G6 Wolf R Tennessee
99 S4 Wolf R Wisconsin
117 G5 Wolf R Yukon Terr
36 E7 Wolfach W Germany
37 P6 Wolfachau W Germany
123 M3 Wolf Bay Quebec
108 D7 Wolf Cr Texas/Okla
94 B10 Wolf Cr. Dam Kentucky
101 N2 Wolf Creek Montana
100 B7 Wolf Creek Oregon
106 D4 Wolf Cr. Pass Colorado
118 J6 Wolfe Sask
95 Q3 Wolfeboro New Hampshire
109 L2 Wolfe City Texas
121 O8 Wolfe Island Ontario
118 G4 Wolfe L Alberta
33 Q9 Wolfen E Germany
33 N8 Wolfenbüttel W Germany
9 G2 Wolferton England
32 K10 Wolfhagen W Germany
103 L5 Wolf Hole Arizona
123 L6 Wolf I Madeleine Is, Quebec
117 H5 Wolf L Yukon Terr
101 S4 Wolf Mts Wyo/Mont
98 G1 Wolford N Dakota
98 A1 Wolf Pt Montana
140 B2 Wolfram Hill N Terr Aust
37 K5 Wolframs-Eschenbach W Germany
41 O2 Wolfratshausen W Germany
38 L8 Wolfsberg Austria
33 N8 Wolfsburg W Germany
37 N2 Wolfsgefärth E Germany
36 E4 Wolfskehlen W Germany
36 D4 Wolfstein W Germany
122 H8 Wolfville Nova Scotia
33 T4 Wolgast E Germany
33 T4 Wolgaster Fähre E Germany
31 H2 Wolin Poland
37 L3 Wolkendorf W Germany
37 P2 Wolkenstein E Germany
33 N10 Wolkramshausen E Germany
114 H3 Wollaston, C N W Terr
133 D9 Wollaston, Is Chile
114 J6 Wollaston Lake Post Sask
114 H4 Wollaston Pen N W Terr
36 B2 Wollersheim W Germany
139 K5 Wollongong New S Wales
36 D4 Wollstein W Germany
87 E11 Wolmaransstad S Africa
33 Q9 Wolmirsleben E Germany
33 P8 Wolmirstedt E Germany
37 M6 Wolnzach W Germany
70 G6 Wolo Sulawesi
31 N3 Wołomin Poland
31 K4 Wołów Poland
71 K9 Wolowaru Flores Indonesia
119 O8 Wolseley Sask
138 F6 Wolseley S Australia
98 H5 Wolsey S Dakota
36 B4 Wolsfeld W Germany
13 G4 Wolsingham England
115 M5 Wolstenholme, C Quebec
31 J3 Wolsztyn Poland
32 L7 Wolthausen W Germany
33 M8 Woltorf W Germany
25 F3 Wolvega Netherlands
8 D2 Wolverhampton England
94 C1 Wolverine Michigan
22 G2 Wolvertem Belgium
9 E3 Wolverton England
98 K3 Wolverton Minnesota
9 E3 Wolvey England
120 H5 Woman River Ontario
141 F7 Wombunderry R Queensland
13 G6 Wombwell England
95 L6 Womelsdorf Pennsylvania
138 F3 Wompah New S Wales
140 D4 Wonarah N Terr Aust
143 E10 Wonberna W Australia
141 K7 Wondai Queensland
22 F1 Wondelgem Belgium
100 B7 Wonder Oregon
116 M5 Wonder L Alaska
140 E6 Wonditti,L Queensland
86 G4 Wondo Ethiopia
138 C4 Wondoma, C S Australia
140 F4 Wondoola Queensland
139 G4 Wongalarroo L New S Wales
141 G5 Wongalee Queensland
143 B9 Wongan Hills W Australia
70 G4 Wonggarasi Sulawesi
59 J4 Wonju S Korea
70 N9 Wonogiri Java
70 O9 Wonokromo Java
138 F4 Wonominta R N S Wales
70 N9 Wonosari Java
70 M9 Wonosobo Java
71 N9 Wonreli Indonesia
59 J4 Wonsan N Korea
139 H7 Wonthaggi Victoria
143 C6 Wonyulgunna,Mt W Australia
138 D4 Woocalla S Australia
94 J6 Wood Pennsylvania
98 F6 Wood S Dakota
98 B3 Wood R Sask
140 D4 Woodah I N Terr Aust
146 J6 Wood B Antarctica
113 F7 Woodbine Georgia
99 L8 Woodbine Iowa
107 N3 Woodbine Kansas
94 C10 Woodbine Kentucky
95 N7 Woodbine New Jersey
9 H3 Woodbridge England
121 L9 Woodbridge Ontario
95 K8 Woodbridge Virginia
117 R6 Wood Buffalo Nat. Park Alberta
99 N8 Woodburn Iowa
110 K5 Woodburn Kentucky
139 L3 Woodburn New S Wales
100 C4 Woodburn Oregon
112 C5 Woodbury Georgia
95 M7 Woodbury New Jersey
110 K6 Woodbury Tennessee
112 F5 Woodcliff Georgia
140 C4 Woodcock,Mt N Terr Aust
139 L3 Wooded Bluff New S Wales
139 L3 Woodenbong New S Wales
144 B7 Woodend New Zealand
117 M11 Woodfibre Br Columbia
9 G4 Woodford England
127 P5 Woodford Grenada
14 C3 Woodford Irish Rep
140 C5 Woodforde R N Terr Aust
102 E3 Woodfords California
9 F4 Wood Green England
140 C5 Woodgreen N Terr Aust
9 F1 Woodhall Spa England
13 G6 Woodhead England
99 Q8 Woodhull Illinois
95 K4 Woodhull New York
100 C2 Woodinville Washington
122 K8 Wood Is Pr Edward I
119 U1 Wood L Manitoba
98 F7 Wood L Nebraska
119 O3 Wood L Sask
102 E5 Woodlake California
102 C3 Woodland California
110 J1 Woodland Illinois
94 J6 Woodland Pennsylvania
100 C4 Woodland Washington
109 N10 Woodland Hills Texas
106 E3 Woodland Park Colorado
119 U8 Woodlands Manitoba
137 L3 Woodlark isld Papua New Guinea
110 G3 Woodlawn Illinois
142 A3 Woodman Pt W Australia
101 Q4 Wood, Mt Montana
118 L9 Wood Mt Sask
117 C5 Wood, Mt Yukon Terr
117 M9 Woodpecker Br Columbia
118 E1 Woodridge Manitoba
140 E6 Woodridge,Mt N Terr Aust
110 F3 Wood River Illinois
98 H9 Wood River Nebraska
140 E5 Woodroffe R N Terr/Queensland
138 B2 Woodroffe, Mt S Australia
106 G2 Woodrow Colorado
118 L9 Woodrow Sask
103 O7 Woodruff Arizona
107 L2 Woodruff Kansas
101 O8 Woodruff Utah
101 Q4 Woods mt Montana
109 K7 Woodsboro Texas
94 F7 Woodsfield Ohio
122 G10 Woods Harbour Nova Scotia
145 E4 Woodside New Zealand
103 O2 Woodside Utah
139 H7 Woodside Victoria
140 C4 Woods,L N Terr Aust
118 H1 Woods, Lake of the Minn/Ontario
111 D7 Woodson Arkansas
99 Q10 Woodson Illinois
109 H2 Woodson Texas
139 H7 Woods Pt Victoria
9 E4 Woodstock England
99 S7 Woodstock Illinois
122 E7 Woodstock New Brunswick
141 G4 Woodstock Queensland
141 H4 Woodstock Queensland
95 P3 Woodstock Vermont
95 Q2 Woodstock, N New Hampshire
107 M2 Woodston Kansas
95 M7 Woodstown New Jersey
95 Q2 Woodsville New Hampshire
111 M11 Woodville Florida
111 E10 Woodville Mississippi
145 E4 Woodville New Zealand
94 D5 Woodville Ohio
121 M8 Woodville Ontario
109 N5 Woodville Texas
107 L5 Woodward Oklahoma
102 D4 Woodward Res California
122 F9 Woodwards Cove New Brunswick
109 P4 Woodworth Louisiana
98 G2 Woodworth N Dakota
8 C5 Woody B England
116 L8 Woody Island Alaska
123 P4 Woody Point Newfoundland
119 Q6 Woody R Manitoba
8 D3 Woofferton England
71 A3 Wool Indonesia
8 D6 Wool England
8 B5 Woolacombe England
110 D3 Wooldridge Missouri
13 F3 Wooler England
118 D9 Woolford Prov. Park Alberta
143 D9 Woolgangie W Australia
141 G4 Woolgar Queensland
143 C6 Woolgathara W Australia
139 L4 Woolgoolga New S Wales
143 D9 Woolibar W Australia
140 C5 Woolla Downs N Terr Aust
9 G3 Woolpit England
102 F1 Woolsey Nevada
138 E4 Woolundra S Australia
8 D5 Woolverton England
9 G5 Woolwich England
138 D4 Woomera S Australia
95 Q4 Woonsocket Rhode I
98 H5 Woonsocket S Dakota
13 G3 Wooperton England
141 J6 Woorabinda Queensland
143 A7 Woorarnel W Australia
143 A7 Wooramel R W Australia
8 D2 Woore England
138 C3 Woorong, L S Australia
94 F6 Wooster Ohio
9 E4 Wootton Bassett England
38 O6 Wopfing Austria
117 O7 Wor Alberta
71 B2 Wor isld Halmahera Indonesia
33 M10 Worbis E Germany
8 D3 Worcester England
95 Q4 Worcester Massachusetts
95 N4 Worcester New York
89 A9 Worcester S Africa
Worcester co see Hereford and Worcester co
110 G3 Worden Illinois
101 R4 Worden Montana
100 D7 Worden Oregon
146 F13 Wordie Ice Shelf Antarctica
119 P9 Wordsworth Sask
38 F7 Wörgl Austria
12 E4 Workington England
9 E1 Worksop England
25 D3 Workum Netherlands
101 S5 Worland Wyoming
8 D5 Worle England
33 Q9 Wörlitz E Germany
8 D4 Wormbridge England
25 C4 Wormerveer Netherlands
22 C2 Wormhoudt France
13 F1 Wormit Scotland
33 P10 Wormlitz E Germany
36 E4 Worms W Germany
8 B4 Worms Head Wales
37 K6 Wörnitz R W Germany
32 J6 Worpswede W Germany
36 B1 Worringen W Germany
36 E4 Wörrstadt W Germany
143 E7 Worsnop,Mt W Australia
38 G7 Wörth Austria

38 O7 Wörth Austria
37 N6 Wörth Bayern W Germany
99 M9 Worth Missouri
36 E5 Wörth Rheinland-Pfalz W Germany
109 L4 Wortham Texas
8 C2 Worthen England
38 K8 Wörther See L Austria
127 P6 Worthing Barbados
9 F6 Worthing England
110 K2 Worthington Indiana
99 L6 Worthington Minnesota
99 O9 Worthington Missouri
94 D6 Worthington Ohio
109 L9 Worth, L Texas
94 B8 Worthville Kentucky
13 G6 Wortley England
71 A3 Wosi Halmahera Indonesia
118 E5 Wostok Alberta
70 G6 Wosu Sulawesi
121 T7 Wotton Quebec
8 D4 Wotton under Edge England
70 G6 Wotu Sulawesi
25 D4 Woudenberg Netherlands
25 C5 Woudrichem Netherlands
98 D6 Wounded Knee S Dakota
25 B5 Wouw Netherlands
141 K6 Wowan Queensland Aust
71 H7 Wowoni isld Indonesia
69 C10 Woyla R Sumatra
31 L5 Woźniki Poland
9 F1 Wragby England
Wrangel I see Vrangelya, Os.
117 G7 Wrangell Alaska
116 Q6 Wrangell Mts Alaska/Yukon Terr
9 G1 Wrangle England
106 H1 Wray Colorado
9 F2 Wreak, R England
141 G1 Wreck B Gt Barrier Reef Aust
32 H5 Wremen W Germany
100 B5 Wren Oregon
112 E4 Wrens Georgia
118 E9 Wrentham Alberta
9 H3 Wrentham England
95 Q4 Wrentham Massachusetts
8 D1 Wrexham Wales
30 H3 Wriezen E Germany
107 L4 Wright Kansas
121 O6 Wright Quebec
71 G5 Wright Samar Philippines
112 M1 Wright Bros. Nat. Mem N Carolina
107 P7 Wright City Oklahoma
138 A3 Wright, L S Australia
138 F4 Wright, Mt N S Wales
68 A7 Wrightmyo Andaman Is
103 O10 Wrightson, Mt Arizona
112 E5 Wrightsville Georgia
95 L6 Wrightsville Pennsylvania
112 K3 Wrightsville Beach N Carolina
139 H4 Wrightville New S Wales
102 G7 Wrightwood California
117 M4 Wrigley N W Terr
146 J10 Wrigley G Antarctica
32 L5 Wrist W Germany
118 F9 Writing-on-Stone Prov. Park Alberta
31 K4 Wrocław Poland
119 V6 Wrong L Manitoba
31 J3 Wronki Poland
9 G5 Wrotham England
8 D2 Wroxeter England
9 H2 Wroxham England
9 E3 Wroxton England
119 Q7 Wroxton Sask
31 J4 Wschowa Poland
65 C6 Wu'an China
143 B9 Wubin W Australia
65 A6 Wubu China
65 E1 Wuchagou China
65 G2 Wuchang China
67 E1 Wuchang China
65 B6 Wucheng China
65 D6 Wucheng China
Wuchow see Wuzhou
65 B4 Wuchuan China
67 C2 Wuchuan China
67 B5 Wucun China
58 E4 Wuda China
65 E5 Wudao China
65 F3 Wudaogou China
67 C2 Wudaoshui China
65 D6 Wudi China
65 A6 Wuding He R China
138 D5 Wudinna S Australia
58 D5 Wudu China
67 A1 Wudu China
67 C1 Wufeng China
67 C3 Wugang China
58 E4 Wuhai China
67 E1 Wuhan China
58 G5 Wuhe China
32 J6 Wuhrden reg W Germany
67 F1 Wuhu China
65 C5 Wuji China
65 G2 Wujia China
67 C6 Wujia China
67 G1 Wujiang China
67 B3 Wu Jiang R China
67 C2 Wu Jiang R China
65 F2 Wujiazhan China
67 F1 Wukang China
85 F7 Wukari Nigeria
65 G2 Wulajie China
33 P9 Wulfen E Germany
32 F9 Wulfen W Germany
33 Q6 Wulfersdorf E Germany
32 F10 Wülfrath W Germany
32 M6 Wulfsen W Germany
32 M9 Wulften W Germany
68 J1 Wuli China
65 D7 Wulian China
67 B1 Wulian China
67 A3 Wulian Feng mts China
65 B8 Wulichuan China
67 C5 Wuli Jiang R China
116 F3 Wulik R Alaska
65 H2 Wulin China
67 C2 Wuling Shan mts China
67 C1 Wulingzhen China
67 B2 Wulong China
71 O8 Wulur Indonesia
37 K5 Wülzburg W Germany
85 G7 Wum Cameroon
139 H5 Wumbulgel New S Wales
67 A3 Wumeng Shan mts China
67 C5 Wuming China
32 K6 Wümme R W Germany
74 H8 Wun India
142 C3 Wungang R W Australia
88 D6 Wungu Tanzania
67 E2 Wuning China
138 F5 Wunkar S Australia
32 J9 Wünnenberg W Germany
33 S8 Wünsdorf East Germany
37 N3 Wunsiedel W Germany
32 K8 Wunstorf W Germany
75 Q7 Wuntho Burma
103 N6 Wupatki Nat. Mon Arizona
67 E4 Wuping China
32 F10 Wuppertal W Germany
66 A4 Wuqia China
65 C5 Wuqiang China
65 C6 Wuqiao China
65 D5 Wuqing China
143 B8 Wurarga W Australia
37 O7 Wurmannsquick W Germany
85 F6 Wurno Nigeria
25 F7 Würselen W Germany
95 N5 Wurtsboro New York
140 F4 Wurung Queensland
37 M3 Wurzbach E Germany
36 H4 Würzburg W Germany
33 R10 Wurzen E Germany
67 C1 Wushan China
67 D1 Wushan China
67 C1 Wu Shan mts China
67 B1 Wusheng China
67 F2 Wusheng China
67 D1 Wusheng Guan pass China
57 J4 Wushi China
68 J2 Wushi China
67 C3 Wu Shui R China
67 G1 Wusong China
36 H3 Wüstensachsen W Germany
33 Q7 Wusterhausen E Germany
33 R7 Wustermark E Germany
32 H6 Wüsting W Germany
33 R7 Wustrau E Germany
33 P4 Wustrow E Germany
33 O7 Wustrow W Germany
59 K2 Wusuli Jiang R China
41 H2 Wutach R W Germany
65 B5 Wutai China
58 F4 Wutai Shan mt ra China
65 D3 Wu-tan China
67 C4 Wutong China
67 A2 Wutongqiao China
22 H1 Wuustwezel Belgium
58 D4 Wuwei China
67 F1 Wuwei China
67 C1 Wuxi China
67 G1 Wuxi China
65 B6 Wuxiang China
67 G1 Wuxing China
67 C5 Wuxuan China
Wuxue see Guangji
Wuyang see Zhenyuan
65 B6 Wuyang China
65 C6 Wuyi China
67 F1 Wuyi China
67 F2 Wuyi China
67 E4 Wuyi Shan mts China
58 E3 Wuyuan China
67 F2 Wuyuan China
Wuyuanzhen see Haiyan
65 B5 Wuzhai China
65 G2 Wuzhan China
65 A6 Wuzhen China
67 D1 Wuzhen China
65 B7 Wuzhi China
67 C7 Wuzhi Shan pk China
58 E4 Wuzhong China
67 D5 Wuzhou China
141 F3 Wyaaba Cr Queensland
99 P9 Wyaconda R Missouri
143 B9 Wyalkatchem W Australia
139 H5 Wyalong New S Wales
94 D4 Wyandotte Michigan
141 H7 Wyandra Queensland
139 J5 Wyangala Res New S Wales
141 G8 Wyara L Queensland
101 T5 Wyarno Wyoming
110 G5 Wyatt Missouri
9 G5 Wych Cross England
139 G6 Wycheproof Victoria
9 G5 Wye England
143 C8 Wyemandoo mt W Australia
8 D4 Wye, R Wales/England
99 Q5 Wyeville Wisconsin
109 L2 Wylie Texas
142 B6 Wyloo W Australia
8 D5 Wylye, R England
95 S1 Wyman Dam Maine
118 K8 Wymark Sask
100 E3 Wymer Washington
9 H2 Wymondham England
98 K9 Wymore Nebraska
138 C4 Wynbring S Australia
144 B7 Wyndham New Zealand
136 F5 Wyndham W Australia
142 G3 Wyndham W Australia
142 E3 Wyndham Ra W Australia
98 J3 Wyndmere N Dakota
110 F6 Wynne Arkansas
142 E4 Wynne,Mt W Australia
107 N7 Wynnewood Oklahoma
114 H3 Wynniatt B N W Terr
141 L7 Wynnum Queensland
107 O5 Wynona Oklahoma
98 J7 Wynot Nebraska
119 N7 Wynyard Sask
139 H8 Wynyard Tasmania
99 R6 Wyocena Wisconsin
98 A5 Wyodak Wyoming
101 S4 Wyola Montana
138 B3 Wyola, L S Australia
95 M7 Wyoming Delaware
99 R8 Wyoming Illinois
99 N4 Wyoming Minnesota
94 J4 Wyoming New York
120 H10 Wyoming Ontario
95 Q5 Wyoming Rhode I
101 R6 Wyoming state U.S.A.
101 P7 Wyoming Pk Wyoming
101 P7 Wyoming Ra Wyoming
139 K5 Wyong New S Wales
13 F6 Wyre, R England
31 K2 Wyrzysk Poland
31 O5 Wysokie Poland
31 N3 Wysokie Mazowieckie Poland
31 N3 Wyszków Poland
31 M3 Wyszogrod Poland
13 E5 Wythburn England
94 F10 Wytheville Virginia
83 M14 Wyville-Thomson mt Kerguelen Indian Oc

66 B4 Xaidulla China
66 D5 Xainza China
87 F11 Xai-Xai Mozambique
125 P7 Xal, Cerro de mt Mexico
Xamba see Hanggin Houqi
129 J5 Xambioa Brazil
65 A3 Xangdin Hural China
66 C5 Xangdoring China
25 F5 Xanten W Germany
47 G3 Xánthi Greece
130 D10 Xanxerê Brazil
128 E6 Xapuri Brazil
65 C2 Xar Hudag China
65 B3 Xar Moron China
59 G3 Xar Moron He R China
65 B3 Xar Moron Sum China
Xauen see Chechaouen
87 D10 Xau, L Botswana
129 J6 Xavantes, Sa. dos mts Brazil
57 L4 Xayar China
Xêgar see Tingri
110 H3 Xenia Illinois
94 D7 Xenia Ohio
128 F4 Xeriuini R Brazil
46 D5 Xerovoúni R Greece
67 F3 Xiabaishi China
Xiabancheng see Chengde
65 D4 Xiabancheng China
65 H2 Xiachengzi China
65 B7 Xiachuan China
67 D6 Xiachuan Dao isld China
Xiacun see Rushan
65 C4 Xiahuayuan China
67 C4 Xiajiang China
67 E3 Xiajiang China
65 C6 Xiajin China
67 F4 Xiamen China
58 E5 Xi'an China
67 C2 Xianfeng China
58 C6 Xiangcheng China
65 B8 Xiangcheng China
67 D3 Xiangdong China
67 B5 Xiangdu China
58 F5 Xiangfan China
65 B7 Xiangfen China
65 D5 Xianghe China
65 B3 Xianghuang Qi China
67 D3 Xiang Jiang R China
65 H1 Xianglan China
65 A7 Xiangning China
66 B5 Xiangquan He R China
67 G2 Xiangshan China
67 G2 Xiangshan Gang B China
65 D7 Xiangshui China
67 D3 Xiangtan China
67 D3 Xiangxiang China
65 G2 Xiangyang China
67 D2 Xiangyin China
65 B6 Xiangyuan China
67 C5 Xiangzhou China
67 G2 Xianju China
58 F6 Xianning China
Xiannumiao see Jiangdu
Xiantaozhen see Mianyang
67 F3 Xianxia Ling mt ra China
58 E5 Xianyang China
67 F4 Xianyou China
65 G1 Xiaobai China
65 G2 Xiaocheng China
65 D3 Xiaochengzi China
65 D4 Xiaochengzi China
68 J1 Xiaodong China
Xiaofan see Wuqiang
67 D1 Xiaogan China
66 C2 Xiaoguai China
67 E1 Xiaohexi China
59 J1 Xiao Hinggan Ling mt ra China
Xiaojiang see Pubei
65 E3 Xiaojieji China
66 F4 Xiao Qaidam China
67 G1 Xiaoshan China
65 A7 Xiao Shan ra China
65 F4 Xiaoshi China
67 D4 Xiao Shui R China
65 A6 Xiaosuan China
65 C5 Xiaowutai Shan mt China
67 F2 Xiao Xi R China
65 D7 Xiao Xian China
Xiaoxita see Yichang
Xiaoyi see Gong Xian
65 B6 Xiaoyi China
67 F3 Xiapu China
Xiashi see Haining
65 B7 Xia Xian China
65 C7 Xiayi China
Xiayingpan see Luzhi
58 D6 Xichang China
67 C6 Xichang China
67 C2 Xiche China
Xicheng see Yangyuan
67 B1 Xichong China
67 A5 Xichou China
65 E2 Xi Dorolj China
67 D3 Xidu China
Xiedian see Wanrong
Xiejiaji see Qingyun
67 D1 Xiemahe China
68 F3 Xieng Khouang Laos
67 C6 Xieyang Dao isld China
65 A7 Xiezian China
65 F3 Xifeng China
67 B3 Xifeng China
65 D4 Xifengkou China
66 D6 Xigazê China
65 E4 Xi He R China
65 G1 Xiji China
67 D5 Xi Jiang R China
65 E1 Xikou China
67 C2 Xikou China
65 B3 Xil China
67 B4 Xilin China
62 C2 Xilin Gol R China
65 H2 Xilinhe China
65 B2 Xilin Qagan Obo China
46 F6 Xilókastron Greece
65 D3 Xiluga He R China
67 B3 Ximahe China
65 E5 Ximayi isld China
58 C3 Ximiao China
65 E4 Ximucheng China
65 B7 Xin'an China
67 F2 Xin'anjiang Shuiku res China
Xin'anzhen see Xinyi
65 F2 Xin'anzhen China
59 H3 Xinbin China
Xin Bulag see Xianghuang Qi
58 G5 Xincai China
67 D2 Xinchang China
59 H6 Xinchang Zhejiang China
65 C5 Xincheng China
65 H1 Xincheng China
67 C4 Xincheng China
65 F3 Xinchengzi China
67 C7 Xincun China
Xindeng see Chengyang
65 G2 Xindian China
67 C1 Xindianzi China
67 A1 Xindu China
67 D4 Xindu China
67 E3 Xinfeng China
67 E4 Xinfeng China
67 C4 Xing'an China
67 E3 Xingan China
65 E4 Xingcheng China
65 C5 Xingchi China
67 E3 Xingguo China
65 B4 Xinghe China
65 G1 Xinghua China
67 F4 Xinghua Wan B China
65 J2 Xingkai Hu L China
65 D4 Xinglong China
65 G1 Xinglongzhen China
67 E4 Xingning China
67 B3 Xingren China
67 B4 Xingren China
65 F1 Xingshan China
67 C1 Xingshan China
58 F4 Xingtai China
65 C5 Xingtang China
67 F3 Xingtian China
129 H4 Xingú R Brazil
67 A2 Xingwen China
65 B5 Xing Xian China
65 B7 Xingyang China
67 A4 Xingyi China
67 E2 Xingzi China
57 L4 Xinhe China
65 C6 Xinhe China
Xin Hot see Abag Qi
67 D3 Xinhua China
67 C3 Xinhuang China
Xinhui see Aohan Qi
67 D5 Xinhui China
46 E5 Xiniás, L Greece
58 D4 Xining China
Xinji see Shulu
67 E2 Xinjian China
65 B7 Xinjiang Shanxi China
67 E2 Xin Jiang R China
Xinjiangkou see Songzi
66 C3 Xinjiang Uygur Zizhiqu China
65 E5 Xinjin China
67 A1 Xinjin China
65 E3 Xinkai He R China
65 C5 Xinle China
65 G2 Xinli China
65 D3 Xinlin China
65 E3 Xinlitun China
65 A5 Xinminzhen China
67 C3 Xinning China
Xinpu see Lianyungang
67 D2 Xinqiang China
67 D3 Xinshao China
65 D7 Xintai China
67 D1 Xintankou China
67 D4 Xintian China
65 D7 Xinwen China
65 B5 Xin Xian China
67 E1 Xin Xian China
65 B7 Xinxiang China
67 D5 Xinxing China
68 J3 Xinxing China
58 F5 Xinyang China
67 E1 Xinyang China
65 D7 Xinyi China
67 C5 Xinyi China
65 D7 Xinyi He R China
67 C7 Xinying China
67 E3 Xinyu China
65 D6 Xinzhai China
65 F2 Xinzhan China
65 G3 Xinzhan China
65 B7 Xinzheng China
58 F5 Xinzhou China
67 E1 Xinzhou China
58 F5 Xiong'er Shan mt ra China
65 C5 Xiong Xian China
65 E4 Xiongyuecheng China
65 B4 Xiping China
58 D4 Xiqing Shan mt ra China
129 K6 Xique-Xique Brazil
Xishuanghe see Kenli
67 B2 Xishui Guizhou China
67 E1 Xishui Hubei China
65 D2 Xi Ujimqin Qi China
67 F2 Xiuning China
58 E6 Xiushan China
67 C2 Xiushan China
67 E2 Xiushui China
67 E2 Xiu Shui R China
65 B7 Xiuwu China
65 F4 Xiuyan China
Xiwanzi see Chongli
66 D6 Xixabangma Feng mt China
65 A6 Xi Xian China
65 B6 Xiyang China
67 F3 Xiyang China
67 G3 Xiyang Dao isld China
67 B5 Xiyang Jiang R China
67 B5 Xiyangjie China
66 C5 Xizang Zizhiqu aut reg China
65 E5 Xizhong Dao isld China
125 K8 Xochimilco Mexico
58 G5 Xuancheng China
67 C1 Xuan'en China
67 B1 Xuanhan China
58 F3 Xuanhua China
67 A3 Xuanwei China
58 F5 Xuchang China
67 G2 Xuedou Shan mt China
67 C3 Xuefeng Shan mts China
65 A7 Xuejiaying China
Xugezhuang see Fengnan
59 H2 Xuguit Qi China
67 E3 Xu Jiang R China
65 E4 Xujiatun China
Xulun Hobot Qagan see Zhengxiangbai Qi
Xulun Hoh see Zhenlan Qi
67 A4 Xundian China
59 J2 Xunhe China
58 E5 Xun He R China
67 E4 Xunwu China
65 C7 Xun Xian China
65 A7 Xunyi China
67 C3 Xupu China
65 C5 Xushui China
67 E3 Xuwan China
67 C6 Xuwen China
68 H7 Xuyen Moc Vietnam
58 E6 Xuyong China
58 G5 Xuzhou China

100 K1 Yaak Montana
141 K6 Yaamba Queensland
67 A2 Ya'an China
138 F6 Yaapeet Victoria
86 B5 Yabassi Cameroon
86 G5 Yabelo Ethiopia
80 F4 Yabis R Jordan
125 N2 Yablis Nicaragua
48 J2 Yablonitse, Pereval pass U.S.S.R.
48 J2 Yablonov U.S.S.R.
51 L3 Yablonovyy, Khrebet mts U.S.S.R.
79 G5 Yabrūd Syria
141 H4 Yabulu Queensland
141 H5 Yacamunda Queensland
Yacha see Baisha
100 A5 Yachats Oregon
67 C7 Yacheng China
60 D14 Yachi Japan
67 B3 Yachi He R China
130 C10 Yaciretá isld Paraguay
139 H6 Yackandandah Victoria
100 C4 Yacolt Washington
133 E2 Yacuiba Bolivia
128 E6 Yacuma R Bolivia
128 E3 Yacurai Venezuela
80 D4 Yad Hanna Israel
112 F1 Yadkin R N Carolina
112 G1 Yadkinville N Carolina
80 B7 Yad Mordekhay Israel
80 C6 Yad Rambam Israel
68 H6 Ya Drang R Cambodia
52 G6 Yadrin U.S.S.R.
80 C5 Yafo Israel
84 E3 Yafran Libya
61 Q12 Yagaji-jima isld Okinawa
60 C13 Yagami Japan
47 J5 Yağcılar Turkey
60 P1 Yagishiri-tō isld Japan
124 G7 Yago Mexico
55 E2 Yagodnyy U.S.S.R.
52 G4 Yagrysh U.S.S.R.
126 E3 Yaguajay Cuba
131 G3 Yaguari R Uruguay
128 D4 Yaguas R Peru
124 E4 Yagui Mexico
80 D3 Yagur Israel
69 E9 Yaha Thailand
61 L10 Yahagi-gawa R Japan
100 J1 Yahk Br Columbia
124 H7 Yahualica Mexico
86 D5 Yahuma Zaïre
78 E2 Yahyali Turkey
68 D6 Yai, Khao mt Burma/Thailand
61 N9 Yaita Japan
61 M11 Yaizu Japan
80 G5 Yajuz Jordan
116 Q6 Yakataga Alaska
Yakeshi see Xuguit Qi
80 B8 Yakhini Israel
54 J1 Yakhroma U.S.S.R.
55 E2 Yakhtur, Oz L U.S.S.R.
100 E3 Yakima Washington
74 C8 Yakmach Pakistan
85 D6 Yako Upper Volta
117 E6 Yakobi I Alaska
86 D5 Yakoma Zaïre
47 F2 Yakoruda Bulgaria
86 D4 Yakossi Cent Afr Republic
57 K4 Yakrik China
52 J4 Yaksha U.S.S.R.
52 G5 Yakshanga U.S.S.R.
52 H6 Yakshur-Bod'ya U.S.S.R.
101 L1 Yakt Montana
60 O3 Yakumo Japan
59 J5 Yaku-shima isld Japan
117 D6 Yakutat Alaska
117 C6 Yakutat B Alaska
51 M2 Yakutsk U.S.S.R.
69 E9 Yala Thailand
83 L11 Yala game reserve Sri Lanka
47 K4 Yalakdere Turkey
144 D5 Yaldhurst New Zealand
117 N11 Yale Br Columbia
110 H2 Yale Illinois
99 M8 Yale Iowa
94 E3 Yale Michigan
107 O5 Yale Oklahoma
98 H5 Yale S Dakota
86 D5 Yaleko Zaïre
100 C4 Yale L Washington
143 B8 Yalgoo W Australia
86 D4 Yalinga Cent Afr Republic
127 L3 Yallahs Jamaica
127 L2 Yallahs R Jamaica
141 H6 Yalleroi Queensland
143 B10 Yallingup W Australia
139 H7 Yallourn Victoria
111 F8 Yalobusha R Mississippi
143 C7 Yaloginda W Australia
86 C4 Yaloké Cent Afr Republic
66 F5 Yalong Jiang R China
47 K4 Yalova Turkey
48 M4 Yalpukh R U.S.S.R.
138 F3 Yalpunga New S Wales Australia
48 L1 Yaltushkov U.S.S.R.
65 E1 Yalu He R China
65 G4 Yalu River China/Korea
55 E4 Yalym U.S.S.R.
60 Q2 Yamabe Karikachi Pass Japan
61 Q6 Yamada wan B Japan
60 D12 Yamaga Japan
61 O7 Yamagata Japan
61 N7 Yamagata prefect Japan
60 D14 Yamagawa Japan
60 E11 Yamaguchi Japan
59 K1 Yam-Alin', Khrebet mt U.S.S.R.
50 F1 Yamal, Poluostrov pen U.S.S.R.
61 M10 Yamanaka ko L Japan
61 M10 Yamanashi prefect Japan
47 J6 Yamanlar Dağı mt Turkey
58 F1 Yamarovka U.S.S.R.
60 H10 Yamasaki Japan
121 S6 Yamaska Quebec
113 G11 Yamato Florida
139 L3 Yamba New S Wales
138 F5 Yamba S Australia
139 G7 Yambacoona Tasmania
86 D4 Yambala Cent Afr Republic
85 B6 Yambering Guinea
128 D3 Yambi, Mesa de Colombia
86 E5 Yambio Sudan
47 H2 Yambol Bulgaria
Yamdrok Tso see Yamzho Yumco
68 C2 Yamethin Burma
80 E8 Yam Hamelah Israel
52 D6 Yami U.S.S.R.
61 O9 Yamizo-san mt Japan
80 F2 Yam Kinneret Israel
52 C5 Yamm U.S.S.R.
141 F7 Yamma Yamma,L Queensland
79 E7 Yammit Israel
85 D7 Yamoussoukro Ivory Coast
101 T9 Yampa Colorado
101 R9 Yampa R Colorado
142 E3 Yampi Sound W Australia
48 L2 Yampol U.S.S.R.
100 D7 Yamsay Mt Oregon
52 G4 Yamskoye U.S.S.R.
73 M3 Yamuna R India
74 G3 Yamunanagar India
55 G4 Yamyshevo U.S.S.R.
66 E6 Yamzho Yumco L China
51 N2 Yana R U.S.S.R.
138 F6 Yanac Victoria
60 D12 Yanagawa Japan
61 O8 Yanagawa Japan
61 P12 Yanaha-jima isld Okinawa
76 F2 Yanam India
65 A6 Yan'an China
128 D6 Yanaoca Peru
56 D2 Yanashimskiy Polkan peak U.S.S.R.
139 G4 Yancannia New S Wales
109 H6 Yancey Texas
112 H1 Yanceyville N Carolina
65 A6 Yanchang China
77 B3 Yanchashmeh Iran
Yancheng see Qihe
59 H5 Yancheng China
67 F1 Yancheng China
143 B9 Yanchep W Australia
65 A6 Yanchuan China
139 H5 Yanco New S Wales
143 D8 Yandal W Australia
138 F3 Yandama R S Australia
65 A4 Yandian China
143 C7 Yandil W Australia
141 L7 Yandina Queensland
68 B4 Yandoon Burma
85 C6 Yanfolila Mali
86 D5 Yangambi Zaïre
66 E5 Yangbajain China
65 B7 Yangcheng China
Yangchuan see Suiyang
67 D5 Yangchun China
Yangcun see Wuqing
67 E5 Yangcun China
65 F3 Yangdachengzi China
142 A3 Yangebup L W Australia
65 J2 Yanggang China
58 F3 Yanggao China
65 C6 Yanggu China
57 F4 Yangibazar U.S.S.R.
77 B2 Yangi Emām Iran
67 D6 Yangjiang China
65 E4 Yangjiazhangzi China
67 F3 Yangkou China
67 A4 Yanglin China
67 D2 Yangloudong China
65 C7 Yangmiao China
67 D3 Yangming Shan mt China
52 E3 Yangory U.S.S.R.
67 D7 Yangpu Gang inlet China
65 B6 Yangquan China
67 D3 Yangquan China
65 C7 Yangshan China
67 D4 Yangshan China
Yangshe see Shazhou
67 C4 Yangshuo China
67 F1 Yangtan China
Yangtze Gorges see Qutang Xia Wu Xia
Yangtze Kiang R see Chang Jiang
67 G1 Yangtze Kiang, Mouths of the China
55 E2 Yangutumskiye U.S.S.R.
68 D6 Yangwa Burma
67 E2 Yangxin China
65 B4 Yangyuan China
67 F1 Yangzhou China
67 C2 Yanhe China
65 A6 Yan He R China
138 D5 Yaninee, L S Australia
52 D4 Yanis'yarvi, Oz L U.S.S.R.
65 H3 Yanji China
65 C7 Yanjin China
67 A2 Yanjin China
67 B2 Yanjing China
139 H6 Yanko R New S Wales
138 F4 Yanko Glen New S Wales
98 J7 Yankton S Dakota
65 C7 Yanling China
Yannina see Ioánnina
54 B1 Yanovichi U.S.S.R.
52 G6 Yanovo U.S.S.R.
83 K9 Yan Oya R Sri Lanka
66 D3 Yanqi China
65 C4 Yanqing China
142 A6 Yanrey W Australia
65 D5 Yanshan China
67 A5 Yanshan China
67 F2 Yanshan China
65 D4 Yan Shan mts China
65 B7 Yanshi China
67 F4 Yanshi China
59 J2 Yanshou China
51 N1 Yanskiy Zaliv B U.S.S.R.
139 H3 Yantabulla New S Wales
59 H4 Yantai China
138 F3 Yantara, L N S Wales
67 B1 Yanting China
65 G3 Yantongshan China
67 G2 Yantou China
47 H1 Yantra R Bulgaria
80 D2 Yanūh Israel
Yanwu see Yuanyang
57 D3 Yany Kurgan U.S.S.R.
65 C7 Yanzhou China
67 B3 Yanzikou China
86 C3 Yao Chad
61 J11 Yao Japan
Yaodu see Dongzhi
65 A6 Yaotou China
86 B5 Yaoundé Cameroon
65 D7 Yaowan China
65 A7 Yao Xian China
69 D9 Yao Yai, Ko isld Thailand
136 H2 Yapen isld W Irian
141 F4 Yappar R Queensland
Yaqian see Yuexi
127 J5 Yaque del Sur R Dom Rep
124 E3 Yaqui R Mexico
100 A5 Yaquina Head Oregon
80 C5 Yaqum Israel
52 H5 Yar U.S.S.R.
126 F4 Yara Cuba
128 E1 Yaracuy state Venezuela
141 G6 Yaraka Queensland
52 G6 Yaransk U.S.S.R.
47 K7 Yaraşlı Gölü L Turkey
47 K6 Yarbasan Turkey
8 C6 Yarcombe England
138 D4 Yardea S Australia
80 F3 Yardena Israel
52 H3 Yarega U.S.S.R.
48 J2 Yaremcha U.S.S.R.
52 G3 Yarenga U.S.S.R.
52 G4 Yarensk U.S.S.R.
9 H2 Yare, R England
128 D3 Yari R Colombia
47 L5 Yarimca Turkey
80 D1 Yârîne Lebanon
140 E5 Yaringa R Queensland
128 E1 Yaritagua Venezuela
Yarkand see Shache
Yarkand R see Yarkant He
66 B4 Yarkant He R China
55 E3 Yarkovo U.S.S.R.
138 B4 Yarle Lakes S Australia
66 D6 Yarlung Zangbo Jiang R China
13 G5 Yarm England
48 K1 Yarmolintsy U.S.S.R.
9 E6 Yarmouth England
95 R3 Yarmouth Maine
95 R5 Yarmouth Massachusetts
122 F10 Yarmouth Nova Scotia
80 F3 Yarmuk R Syria
103 M7 Yarnell Arizona
52 E5 Yaroslavl' U.S.S.R.
80 E1 Yâroûn Lebanon
54 J7 Yarovaya U.S.S.R.
80 C5 Yarqon Israel
139 H7 Yarra R Victoria
141 G2 Yarraden Queensland
142 B5 Yarraloola W Australia
139 H7 Yarram Victoria
141 K7 Yarraman Queensland
140 D4 Yarran Ra N Terr Aust
139 H6 Yarrawonga Victoria
143 B8 Yarra Yarra Ls W Australia
142 D5 Yarrie W Australia
141 H7 Yarronvale Queensland
15 E5 Yarrow R Scotland
141 H5 Yarrowmere Queensland
55 F1 Yarsomovy U.S.S.R.
54 D1 Yartsevo U.S.S.R.
128 C2 Yarumal Colombia
48 L2 Yaryshev U.S.S.R.
86 D5 Yasanyama Zaire
137 Q5 Yasawa Grp islds Fiji
85 F6 Yashi Nigeria
85 E7 Yashikera Nigeria
60 F12 Ya-shima Japan
61 O6 Yashima Japan
60 F12 Yashiro-jima Japan
55 B4 Yashkino U.S.S.R.
54 J8 Yasinovataya U.S.S.R.
48 J2 Yasinya U.S.S.R.
139 J5 Yass New S Wales
60 G12 Yasuda Japan
60 G10 Yasugi Japan
77 B4 Yasuj Iran
128 E6 Yata Bolivia
47 J7 Yatağan Turkey
85 E6 Yatakala Niger
106 G5 Yates New Mexico
94 H6 Yatesboro Pennsylvania
107 P4 Yates Center Kansas
115 K5 Yathkyed L N W Terr
80 D5 Yatma Jordan
86 D5 Yatolema Zaïre
Yatou see Rongcheng
61 M10 Yatsuga take mt Japan
61 L9 Yatsuo Japan
60 D13 Yatsushiro Japan
80 D8 Yatta Jordan
8 D5 Yatton England
141 J6 Yatton Queensland
128 E3 Yatua R Venezuela
128 D7 Yauca Peru
127 L5 Yauco Puerto Rico
112 H4 Yauhannah S Carolina
128 C6 Yauyos Peru
103 M7 Yava Arizona
57 E5 Yavan U.S.S.R.
124 E4 Yavaros Mexico
128 D6 Yavero R Peru
128 E8 Yavi Argentina
128 E2 Yavi, Co mt Venezuela
128 E3 Yavita Venezuela
55 E4 Yavlenka U.S.S.R.
80 B6 Yavne Israel
80 F3 Yavnee Israel
31 O6 Yavorov U.S.S.R.
29 O3 Yavra R U.S.S.R.
68 B2 Yaw R Burma
60 F12 Yawatahama Japan
68 C2 Yawng-hwe Burma
67 B3 Yaxi China
67 C7 Ya Xian China
56 C3 Yaya U.S.S.R.
52 J5 Yayva R U.S.S.R.
77 C3 Yazd Iran
77 C4 Yazd-e Khvāst Iran
57 F5 Yazgulemskiy Khr mts U.S.S.R.
55 C4 Yazikovo U.S.S.R.
111 F9 Yazoo City Mississippi
52 J4 Yaz'va R U.S.S.R.
38 M5 Ybbs Austria
38 L6 Ybbsitz Austria
130 C9 Ybycúi Paraguay
28 A3 Ydby Denmark
28 G5 Yderby Denmark
28 D5 Yding Skovhøj hill Denmark
52 J3 Ydzhid Parma U.S.S.R.
68 C5 Ye Burma
139 H6 Yea Victoria
8 B7 Yealmpton England
Yebaishou see Jianping
86 C1 Yebbi bou Chad
16 D9 Yebel Buhasen mt Morocco
20 G2 Yébleron France
68 D5 Yebyu Burma
66 B4 Yecheng China
17 G6 Yecla Spain
124 E3 Yécora Mexico
68 C3 Yedashe Burma
47 K8 Yedi Burun C Turkey
48 L2 Yedintsy U.S.S.R.
52 F3 Yedoma Arkhangelsk U.S.S.R.
52 H2 Yedoma Komi U.S.S.R.
84 F5 Yédri Chad
142 E4 Yeeda River W Australia
138 D5 Yeelanna S Australia
52 D5 Yefimovskiy U.S.S.R.
54 K3 Yefremov U.S.S.R.
55 G6 Yegendybulak U.S.S.R.
55 E5 Yegindykol' U.S.S.R.
53 F10 Yegorlyk R U.S.S.R.
54 L1 Yegor'yevsk U.S.S.R.
130 C10 Yegros Paraguay
109 K5 Yegua Cr Texas
16 D7 Yeguas, Sa. de mts Spain
131 B5 Yeguas, Vol Chile
50 F2 Yehzarovo U.S.S.R.
86 F5 Yei Sudan
67 E1 Yeji China
85 D7 Yeji Ghana
Yekaterinburg see Sverdlovsk
55 D1 Yekaterininka U.S.S.R.
55 F3 Yekaterininskoye U.S.S.R.
59 J1 Yekaterinoslavka U.S.S.R.
54 K4 Yekaterinovka U.S.S.R.
68 A3 Ye Kyun isld Burma
52 H6 Yelabuga U.S.S.R.
55 D2 Yelan' U.S.S.R.
53 F8 Yelan' R U.S.S.R.
54 N5 Yelan'-Koleno U.S.S.R.
141 K8 Yelarbon Queensland
58 F1 Yeleninskiy U.S.S.R.
54 J9 Yelenovka U.S.S.R.
54 G3 Yelenskiy U.S.S.R.
54 K4 Yelets U.S.S.R.
55 E1 Yelizarovo U.S.S.R.
55 C5 Yelizavetinka U.S.S.R.
59 M1 Yelizavety, Mys C U.S.S.R.
15 G1 Yell isld Scotland
76 E2 Yellandu India
111 K10 Yellow R Alabama
99 Q5 Yellow R Wisconsin
119 M6 Yellow Creek Sask
143 C9 Yellowdine W Australia
119 N9 Yellow Grass Sask
114 H7 Yellowhead Pass Alberta
114 H5 Yellowknife N W Terr
99 L5 Yellow Medicine R Minnesota
139 H4 Yellow Mt New S Wales
100 K5 Yellow Pine Idaho
Yellow R see Huang He
59 H4 Yellow Sea China/Korea
110 N2 Yellow Springs Ohio
98 B2 Yellowstone R Montana
101 P5 Yellowstone L Wyoming
101 P5 Yellowstone Nat. Park Wyoming
15 G1 Yell Sound Scotland
110 D5 Yellville Arkansas
54 E2 Yel'nya U.S.S.R.
56 C1 Yeloguy R U.S.S.R.
55 E3 Yeloshnoye U.S.S.R.
55 C3 Yelovo Barda U.S.S.R.
16 C4 Yeltes R Spain
52 D6 Yel'tsy U.S.S.R.
125 M2 Yelucá mt Nicaragua
52 H3 Yelva R U.S.S.R.
140 E5 Yelvertoft Queensland
8 B7 Yelverton England
115 L1 Yelverton B N W Terr
85 E6 Yelwa Nigeria
55 D4 Yemanzhelinsk U.S.S.R.
112 G5 Yemassee S Carolina
72 E5 Yemen, North rep Arabia
72 F5 Yemen, South rep Arabia
55 E3 Yemets R U.S.S.R.
52 F3 Yemetsk U.S.S.R.
52 F3 Yemtsa U.S.S.R.
52 D1 Yena U.S.S.R.
54 K8 Yenakiyevo U.S.S.R.
68 B2 Yenangyat Burma
68 B2 Yenangyaung Burma
68 B3 Yenanma Burma
67 A6 Yen Bai Vietnam
67 A6 Yen Chau Vietnam
139 H5 Yenda New S Wales
85 E7 Yendi Ghana
58 F1 Yendondin U.S.S.R.
55 E1 Yendra U.S.S.R.
55 E1 Yendyr' U.S.S.R.
68 C2 Yengan Burma
66 B4 Yengisar China
47 J5 Yenice Turkey
47 H6 Yenifoça Turkey
47 J5 Yeniköy Turkey
31 M1 Yenino U.S.S.R.
47 J7 Yenipazar Aydin Turkey
47 L4 Yenipazar Bilecik Turkey
47 K4 Yenişehir Turkey
56 D2 Yenisey R U.S.S.R.
56 D2 Yeniseysk U.S.S.R.
50 H1 Yeniseyskiy Zaliv gulf U.S.S.R.
68 G2 Yen Lap Vietnam
68 G1 Yen Minh Vietnam
19 P13 Yenne France
52 E1 Yenozero, Oz L U.S.S.R.
68 G3 Yen Thanh Vietnam
116 M5 Yentna R Alaska
143 E8 Yeo, L W Australia
74 F8 Yeola India
Yeóryios isld see Áyios I
74 H8 Yeotmal India
139 J5 Yeoval New S Wales
8 D6 Yeovil England
124 E3 Yepachic Mexico
54 K3 Yepifan U.S.S.R.
141 K6 Yeppoon Queensland
46 F7 Yeráki Greece
124 J6 Yerbabuena Mexico
56 G1 Yerbogachen U.S.S.R.
78 E2 Yercöy Turkey
138 C4 Yerda S Australia
20 H2 Yere R France
55 F5 Yerementau, Gy mt U.S.S.R.
78 K1 Yerevan U.S.S.R.
56 D4 Yergak-Targak-Tayga, Khrebet mts U.S.S.R.
53 F9 Yergeni hills U.S.S.R.
143 D8 Yerilla W Australia
102 E3 Yerington Nevada
47 J7 Yerkesik Turkey
55 G4 Yermak U.S.S.R.
55 F1 Yermakovo U.S.S.R.
56 D4 Yermakovskoye U.S.S.R.
55 F5 Yermentau U.S.S.R.
52 H2 Yermitsa U.S.S.R.
102 H7 Yermo California
124 G4 Yermo Mexico
55 C4 Yermolayevo U.S.S.R.
54 H1 Yermolino U.S.S.R.
59 H1 Yerofey Pavlovich U.S.S.R.
79 E8 Yeroham Israel
141 K2 Yeronga dist Brisbane, Qnsld
52 H2 Yersa R U.S.S.R.
25 B6 Yerseke Netherlands
52 F4 Yertsevo U.S.S.R.
128 C6 Yerupaja mt Peru
80 D6 Yerushalayim Israel
20 G2 Yerville France
68 B2 Yesagyo Burma
67 C1 Yesanguan China
52 D6 Yesenovichi U.S.S.R.
55 E5 Yesil' U.S.S.R.
47 K5 Yesil Dağı mt Turkey
47 K7 Yeşilova Turkey
108 C1 Yeso New Mexico
80 C6 Yesodot Israel
51 K2 Yessey U.S.S.R.
17 F6 Yeste Spain
80 F1 Yesud HaMa'ala Israel
13 F3 Yetholm Scotland
139 K3 Yetman New S Wales
68 B1 Yeu Burma
18 D6 Yeu, I d' France
55 F3 Yevgashchino U.S.S.R.
21 J7 Yèvre R France
59 K2 Yevreysk Aut. Oblast reg U.S.S.R.
65 D6 Ye Xian China
78 L1 Yeylakh U.S.S.R.
53 E10 Yeysk U.S.S.R.
52 D6 Yezerishche U.S.S.R.
52 G5 Yezhikha U.S.S.R.
52 G3 Yezhuga R U.S.S.R.
130 C9 Yguazu, R Paraguay
130 C9 Yhú Paraguay
47 J8 Yialí isld Greece
84 J3 Yi' Allaq, Gebel Egypt
79 E3 Yialousa Cyprus
47 H9 Yianisádhes isld Crete Greece
46 E4 Yiannitsá Greece
68 E1 Yibang China
Yibei see Minglun
67 A2 Yibin China
80 B6 Yibna Israel
58 F5 Yichang China
67 D1 Yichang China
65 B7 Yicheng China
65 D7 Yicheng China
67 D1 Yicheng China
65 A6 Yichuan China
65 B7 Yichuan China
59 J2 Yichun China
67 E3 Yichun China
58 F5 Yidu China
65 D6 Yidu China
67 E2 Yifeng China
80 F1 Yiftah Israel
65 B7 Yi He R China
65 D7 Yi He R China

67 E3 Yihuang China
65 A7 Yijun China
65 H1 Yilan China
78 F2 Yildizeli Turkey
67 A3 Yiliang China
67 A4 Yiliang China
143 B10 Yilliminning W Australia
67 B1 Yilong China
65 G2 Yimianpo China
68 B2 Yin R Burma
65 D7 Yinan China
68 C4 Yinbaing Burma
65 B7 Yincheng China
58 E4 Yinchuan China
143 D9 Yindarlgooda, L W Australia
67 D1 Yindian China
67 D1 Yingcheng China
67 F3 Yingchuan China
65 J1 Yingchun China
67 D4 Yingde China
65 F4 Ying'ebu China
141 J7 Yingerbay Queensland
Yinggen see Qiongzhong
65 B7 Ying He R China
59 H3 Yingkou China
65 E4 Yingkou China
67 B1 Yingshan China
67 D1 Yingshan China
67 E2 Yingtan China
65 B5 Ying Xian China
65 D3 Yin He R China
66 C3 Yining China
67 C2 Yinjiang China
138 F5 Yinkame S Australia
68 B1 Yinmabin Burma
65 F2 Yinma He R China
68 C4 Yinnyein Burma
65 A4 Yin Shan mts China
47 G5 Yioúra isld Greece
Yiquan see Meitan
131 G4 Yi, R Uruguay
86 G4 Yirga Alem Ethiopia
80 D2 Yirka Israel
86 F4 Yirol Sudan
80 E1 Yir'on Israel
59 G2 Yirshi China
67 C4 Yishan China
65 D6 Yi Shan mts China
65 D7 Yishui China
80 E6 Yitav Jordan
46 F6 Yithion Greece
65 F3 Yitong China
65 F2 Yitong He R China
66 E3 Yiwu China
67 G2 Yiwu China
68 E2 Yiwu China
Yixian see Yicheng
65 C5 Yi Xian China
65 E4 Yi Xian China
67 F2 Yi Xian China
67 F1 Yixing China
65 D4 Yixun He R China
65 B7 Yiyang China
67 D2 Yiyang Hunan China
67 F2 Yiyang Jiangxi China
65 D6 Yiyuan China
67 D4 Yizhang China
67 F1 Yizheng China
31 K6 Yizovice Czechoslovakia
29 N11 Ylämaa Finland
29 J11 Yläne Finland
29 K8 Ylihärmä Finland
29 M6 Ylikiiminki Finland
52 C2 Ylikitka L Finland
29 M6 Yli-li Finland
29 K9 Ylistaro Finland
29 K5 Ylitornio Finland
29 L7 Ylivieska Finland
29 L4 Yllästunturi mt Finland
29 K10 Ylöjärvi Finland
115 R3 Ymers Ø isld Greenland
20 J5 Ymonville France
52 J4 Yndin U.S.S.R.
27 J13 Yngaren L Sweden
57 F1 Yntaly U.S.S.R.
86 B3 Yo Nigeria
109 K6 Yoakum Texas
60 O2 Yobetsu Japan
60 C12 Yobuko Japan
128 E7 Yocalla Bolivia
107 L3 Yocemento Kansas
111 G7 Yocono R Mississippi
106 F3 Yoder Colorado
98 B8 Yoder Wyoming
60 J11 Yodo Japan
60 G10 Yodoe Japan
133 D8 Yogan mt Chile
70 N9 Yogyakarta Java
117 P10 Yoho Nat. Park Br Columbia
60 O2 Yoichi Japan
60 O2 Yoichi dake mt Japan
125 L2 Yojoa, L. de Honduras
60 H10 Yōka Japan
86 C5 Yokadouma Cameroon
61 O10 Yōkaichiba Japan
111 F9 Yokena Mississippi
61 K11 Yokkaichi Japan
86 B4 Yoko Cameroon
60 F12 Yokogawara Japan
62 Yokohama conurbation Japan
61 N10 Yokosuka Japan
61 O6 Yokote Japan
60 O4 Yokotsu-dake mt Japan
86 B4 Yola Nigeria
125 M4 Yolaina, Cord. de Nicaragua
57 B5 Yolbarsli U.S.S.R.
65 E2 Yolin Mod China
86 D6 Yolombo Zaïre
61 P13 Yomitan Airport Okinawa
61 Q12 Yona Okinawa
61 P13 Yonabaru Okinawa
60 G10 Yonago Japan
67 G4 Yonagunijima Japan
61 Q12 Yonaha-dake mt Okinawa
100 B6 Yoncalla Oregon
61 O5 Yoneshiro-gawa R Japan
61 O8 Yonezawa Japan
67 F4 Yong'an China
67 D2 Yong'anshi China
67 B2 Yongchuan China
67 F4 Yongchun China
67 C3 Yongcong China
67 A4 Yongding China
67 D3 Yongding He R China
59 J4 Yongdŭngpo S Korea
67 E3 Yongfeng China
67 C4 Yongfu China
65 A6 Yonghe China
59 J4 Yonghŭng N Korea
65 G5 Yonghŭng-man B N Korea
58 F5 Yongji China
65 G3 Yongji China
67 G2 Yongjia China
Yongjing see Xifeng
67 G2 Yongkang China
65 C6 Yongnian China
Yongning see Xuyong
58 D6 Yongning China
67 C5 Yongning China
65 C5 Yongqing China
67 A2 Yongshan China
65 A7 Yongshou China
67 C2 Yongshun China
67 E3 Yongtai China
67 F4 Yongtai China
67 E3 Yongxin China
67 D3 Yongxing China
67 E2 Yongxiu China
Yongyang see Weng'an
118 H6 Yonker Sask
95 O6 Yonkers New York
107 P5 Yonkers Oklahoma
18 H5 Yonne dep France
18 H5 Yonne R France
68 B2 Yonzingyi Burma
57 H5 Yopurga China
111 H9 York Alabama
13 G6 York England
101 O3 York Montana
98 G1 York N Dakota
98 J9 York Nebraska
95 L7 York Pennsylvania
112 F3 York S Carolina
143 B9 York W Australia
141 G1 York, C Queensland
141 F2 York Downs Queensland
138 D5 Yorke Pen S Australia
138 D6 Yorketown S Australia
115 K6 York Factory Manitoba
123 O4 York Harb Nfld
115 N2 York, Kap C Greenland
116 D4 York Mts Alaska
123 R2 York Pt Labrador
122 G5 York R Quebec
142 F2 York Sd W Australia
Yorkshire co see N., W. & S.Yorks, Cleveland, Humberside counties
136 F4 York Sound W Australia
119 P7 Yorkton Sask
109 K7 Yorktown Texas
95 L9 Yorktown Virginia
95 R3 York Village Maine
99 S8 Yorkville Illinois
95 M3 Yorkville New York
125 L2 Yoro Honduras
102 D4 Yosemite L California
102 D4 Yosemite Lodge California
102 E3 Yosemite National Park California
61 M8 Yoshida Japan
61 P6 Yoshihama-wan B Japan
60 F12 Yoshino Japan
60 H11 Yoshino R Japan
61 K11 Yoshino-Kumano Nat. Park Japan
52 G6 Yoshkar Ola U.S.S.R.
60 D12 Yoshu Japan
Yösönbulag see Altay
101 M8 Yost Utah
61 O8 Yotsukura Japan
79 F9 Yotvata Israel
143 C8 Youanmi W Australia
117 L11 Youbou Br Columbia
14 D5 Youghal Irish Rep
67 B5 You Jiang R China
85 B6 Youkounkoun Guinea
9 E1 Youlgreave England
103 O7 Young Arizona
139 J5 Young New S Wales
119 M7 Young Sask
138 D4 Younghusband, L S Australia
138 E6 Younghusband Pen S Australia
140 D3 Young, Mt N Terr Aust
144 B6 Young Range New Zealand
88 E7 Youngs B Malawi
118 F7 Youngstown Alberta
111 L11 Youngstown Florida
94 J3 Youngstown New York
94 G5 Youngstown Ohio
111 D11 Youngsville Louisiana
112 J1 Youngsville N Carolina
106 D5 Youngsville New Mexico
94 H5 Youngsville Pennsylvania
101 Q6 Younts Pk Wyoming
102 B3 Yountville California
67 C2 You Shui R China
65 F3 Youxi China
67 D3 You Xian China
67 C2 Youyang China
65 H1 Youyi China
65 B4 Youyu China
139 G3 Yowah R Queensland
143 C7 Yowereena Hill W Australia
78 E2 Yozgat Turkey
130 B9 Ypacaraí, L Paraguay
29 K11 Ypäjä Finland
130 C8 Ypané, R Paraguay
130 C8 Ypé-jhú Paraguay
130 B9 Ypoá L Paraguay
20 F2 Yport France
29 L7 Ypäjä Finland
Ypres see Ieper
94 D4 Ypsilanti Michigan
100 C8 Yreka California
8 C3 Yrfon R Wales
8 C3 Yspytty Ystwyth Wales
18 H7 Yssingeaux France
27 G16 Ystad Sweden
8 C4 Ystalyfera Wales
8 B3 Ystrad Wales
8 C3 Ystrad-ffin Wales
8 C3 Ystwyth, R Wales
15 F3 Ythan, R Scotland
26 G9 Ytterhogdal Sweden
27 J12 Ytterjärna Sweden
28 J8 Ytterlännäs Sweden
26 E8 Ytteröy Norway
26 L7 Yttersjön Sweden
67 D1 Yuan'an China
67 C4 Yuanbao Shan mt China
67 E1 Yuan Hu China
67 D2 Yuanjiang China
67 C2 Yuan Jiang R China
68 F1 Yuan Jiang R China
67 C2 Yuanling China
65 B5 Yuanping China
65 B7 Yuanqu China
65 C6 Yuanshi China
67 E3 Yuan Shui R China
65 B7 Yuanyang China
67 D3 Yuanyue China
60 J11 Yuasa Japan
102 C2 Yuba R California
102 C2 Yuba City California
60 P2 Yūbari Japan
60 Q2 Yūbari dake mt Japan
86 G4 Yubdo Ethiopia
60 R1 Yūbetsu Japan
60 S2 Yūbetsu Japan
85 B3 Yubi, C Morocco
61 M9 Yubiso Japan
58 G3 Yubla Jordan
80 G3 Yubla Jordan
128 D7 Yucamani mt Peru
125 P7 Yucatan state Mexico
90 A6 Yucatan Basin Atlantic Oc
126 A3 Yucatan Chan Caribbean
103 K7 Yucca Arizona
102 H6 Yucca Flat Nevada
106 B4 Yucca House Nat. Mon Colorado
65 C6 Yucheng China
65 C7 Yucheng China
65 B6 Yuci China
67 D3 Yudaokou China
52 H5 Yudino U.S.S.R.
51 N3 Yudoma R U.S.S.R.
67 E4 Yudu China
67 B1 Yuechi China
67 D3 Yuekou China
Yuelai see Huachuan
67 C1 Yuelai China
65 F2 Yueliang Pao L China
140 B5 Yuendumu Mission N Terr Aust
67 G2 Yueqing China
67 G2 Yueqing Wan B China
58 D6 Yuexi China
67 E1 Yuexi China
58 D6 Yuexi He R China
67 A2 Yuexi He R China
Yueyang see Gu Xian
67 D2 Yueyang China
60 E12 Yufu-dake mt Japan
52 G5 Yug R U.S.S.R.
51 K2 Yuga R U.S.S.R.
67 E2 Yugan China
55 F1 Yugan U.S.S.R.
42 H4 Yugoslavia rep S Europe
67 G1 Yuhang China
65 B4 Yu He R China
65 A5 Yuhebu China
67 B4 Yuhong China
67 D7 Yuhuan China
143 B8 Yuin W Australia
65 E2 Yujiang China
67 C2 Yu Jiang R China
67 C5 Yu Jiang R China
52 H5 Yukamenskoye U.S.S.R.
54 G2 Yukhnov U.S.S.R.
61 N9 Yuki Japan
116 J4 Yuki R Alaska
113 F7 Yukon Florida
107 N6 Yukon Oklahoma
117 E4 Yukon Crossing Yukon Terr
55 E1 Yukonda R U.S.S.R.
116 E5 Yukon Delta Alaska
116 M4 Yukon R Alaska/Yukon Terr
114 F5 Yukon Territory Canada
60 E12 Yukuhashi Japan
52 F3 Yula R U.S.S.R.
55 C4 Yuldybayevo U.S.S.R.
146 K5 Yule B Antarctica
141 J7 Yuleba Queensland
142 B2 Yule Brook Perth, W Aust
113 F7 Yulee Florida
142 C5 Yule R W Australia
65 A5 Yulin China
67 C5 Yulin China
67 C7 Yulin China
65 A6 Yulinqiao China
103 K9 Yuma Arizona
98 D9 Yuma Colorado
52 D2 Yuma U.S.S.R.
16 D9 Yumas el Tolba Morocco
127 K5 Yuma, B. de Dom Rep
103 K9 Yuma Desert Arizona
55 C4 Yumaguzino U.S.S.R.
86 E6 Yumbi Zaïre
58 C3 Yumen China
58 C3 Yü-men-chen China
58 C3 Yumenzhen China
58 F1 Yumurchen U.S.S.R.
143 A8 Yuna W Australia
127 K5 Yuna R Dom Rep
78 C2 Yunak Turkey
67 D5 Yunan China
67 C1 Yun'anzhen China
65 B7 Yuncheng China
65 C7 Yuncheng China
143 D8 Yundamindera W Australia
67 D5 Yunfu China
128 E7 Yungas, Las mts Bolivia
139 G5 Yungera Victoria
Yunhe see Pei Xian
67 F2 Yunhe China
67 C5 Yunkai Dashan mts China
67 D1 Yunmeng China
67 A5 Yunnan prov China
143 D8 Yunndaga W Australia
60 O4 Yunokawa Japan
60 D13 Yunomae Japan
60 F10 Yunotsu Japan
16 E4 Yunquera de H Spain
67 A4 Yunshang China
138 E4 Yunta S Australia
58 F5 Yun Xian China
67 F5 Yunxiao China
67 C1 Yunyang China
65 B5 Yunzhong Shan mts China
67 C3 Yuping China
67 B3 Yuqing China
Yuqingsi see Aoxi
60 O3 Yūrappu-dake mt Japan
124 H7 Yuréscharo Mexico
56 B3 Yurga U.S.S.R.
55 D3 Yurgamysh U.S.S.R.
55 E3 Yurginskoye U.S.S.R.
128 C5 Yurimaguas Peru
52 B6 Yurino U.S.S.R.
52 H5 Yurla U.S.S.R.
51 K3 Yurma mt U.S.S.R.
52 G2 Yuroma U.S.S.R.
55 E2 Yurovskoye U.S.S.R.
66 B4 Yurungkax He R China
60 T2 Yururi-tō isld Japan
52 G5 Yur'ya U.S.S.R.
52 J2 Yur'yakha R U.S.S.R.
52 F6 Yur'yevets U.S.S.R.
52 E6 Yur'yev Pol'skiy U.S.S.R.
52 E6 Yuryuzan' Katav-Ivanovsk U.S.S.R.
125 L3 Yuscarán Honduras
67 F2 Yushan China
67 C2 Yushanzhen China
65 B6 Yushe China
52 H1 Yushino U.S.S.R.
29 P11 Yushkelovo U.S.S.R.
52 D3 Yushkozero U.S.S.R.
59 J3 Yushu China
66 F5 Yushu China
65 G2 Yushugou China
Yushuwan see Huaihua
78 H1 Yusufeli Turkey
60 F12 Yusuhara Japan
52 H5 Yus'va U.S.S.R.
65 C7 Yutai China
98 K8 Yutan Nebraska
52 H6 Yutaza U.S.S.R.
128 F7 Yuti Bolivia
65 D5 Yutian Hebei China
66 C4 Yutian Xinjiang Uygur Zizhiqu China
130 C10 Yuty Paraguay
67 F5 Yü-weng Tao Taiwan
Yuxi see Daozhen
65 B5 Yu Xian China
65 C5 Yu Xian China
65 C6 Yu Xian China
67 G1 Yuyao China
60 D11 Yuya-wan B Japan
52 F5 Yuza R U.S.S.R.
61 M9 Yuzawa Japan
52 F6 Yuzha U.S.S.R.
57 G5 Yuzh Alichurskiy, Khrebet mts U.S.S.R.
55 D4 Yuzhno-Ural'sk U.S.S.R.
55 D4 Yuzhnoural'skiy U.S.S.R.
56 C6 Yuzhnyy Altay, Khrebet mts U.S.S.R.
48 M2 Yuzhnyy Bug R U.S.S.R.
55 C4 Yuzhnyy Ural reg U.S.S.R.
Yuzhou see Chongqing
55 G4 Yuzno Podol'skoye U.S.S.R.
20 J4 Yvelines dep France
40 E4 Yverdon Switzerland
20 G2 Yvetot France
22 H3 Yvoir Anhee Belgium
40 E4 Yvonand Switzerland
21 I6 Yvoy-le Marron France
20 F5 Yvré-l'Evêque France
59 F3 Ywamun Burma
68 C3 Ywathit Burma
27 H13 Yxviken Sweden
21 D7 Yzernay France
21 G8 Yzeures-sur-Creuse France
25 C4 Zaandam Netherlands
25 C4 Zaandijk Netherlands
42 H6 Zaba mt Yugoslavia
80 E4 Zababida Jordan
48 F5 Žabalj Yugoslavia
48 G6 Žabari Yugoslavia
55 C4 Zabaykal'sk U.S.S.R.
58 G2 Zabaykal'sk U.S.S.R.
80 F3 Zabda Jordan
86 E5 Zabituy U.S.S.R.
31 K5 Zabkowice Poland
31 O3 Zabłudów Poland
77 G4 Zabol Iran
77 G6 Zāboli Iran
48 J2 Zabolotov U.S.S.R.
31 K6 Zábřeh Czechoslovakia
31 L5 Zabrze Poland
77 H6 Zābul reg Afghanistan
125 K3 Zacatal Guatemala
125 N8 Zacatal Mexico
124 H6 Zacatecas Mexico
124 H6 Zacatecas state Mexico
125 L9 Zacatecoluca El Salvador
111 E11 Zacatepec Mexico
33 O6 Zachary Louisiana
125 L2 Zachun E Germany
42 G4 Zacualpa Honduras
Zadar Yugoslavia
68 C7 Zadetkale Kyun isld Burma
68 C8 Zadetkyi Burma
68 C5 Zadi Burma
80 C5 Zafriyya Israel
54 K4 Zadonsk U.S.S.R.
80 C5 Zafriyya Israel
31 J4 Żagań Poland
52 B6 Zagare U.S.S.R.
45 N6 Zagarolo Italy
79 B8 Zagazig Egypt
43 C12 Zaghouan Tunisia
46 F5 Zagorá Greece
85 C2 Zagora Morocco
54 K1 Zagorsk U.S.S.R.
42 G3 Zagreb Yugoslavia
77 A3 Zāgros Mountains Iran
48 G6 Zagubica Yugoslavia
Zagunao see Li Xian
77 G5 Zāhedān Iran
98 C1 Zahl N Dakota
79 F5 Zahle Lebanon
33 R9 Zahna E Germany
57 H3 Zailiyskiy Alatau, Khr mts U.S.S.R.
36 H7 Zainingen W Germany
86 D5 Zaïre R W Africa
86 B7 Zaire Central Zaïre
86 D6 Zaire, Rep. of Africa
80 D5 Zaita Jordan
46 E1 Zaječar Yugoslavia
56 F5 Zakamensk U.S.S.R.
78 L1 Zakataly U.S.S.R.
78 J3 Zākho Iraq
46 D7 Zákinthos isld Greece
31 N5 Zaklików Poland
31 L6 Zakopane Poland
31 M3 Zakroczym Poland
47 H9 Zákros Crete Greece
48 D4 Zala R Hungary
48 D4 Zalaegerszeg Hungary
16 C7 Zalamea la Real Spain
Zalantun see Butha Qi
48 D4 Zalaövo Hungary
48 H3 Zalău Romania
48 K2 Zaleshchiki U.S.S.R.
94 E7 Zaleski Ohio
31 N1 Zales'ye U.S.S.R.
31 M2 Zalewo Poland
31 H2 Zalew Szczecinski lagoon Poland/E Germany
86 D3 Zalingei Sudan
50 E4 Zaliv Kara Bogaz Gol B Turkmenia U.S.S.R.
59 K3 Zaliv Petra Velikogo B U.S.S.R.
110 F4 Zalma Missouri
37 O3 Zalmanov Czechoslovakia
25 D5 Zaltbommel Netherlands
52 D5 Zaluch'ye U.S.S.R.
68 B4 Zalun Burma
117 O6 Zama L Alberta
71 E3 Zambales Mts Luzon Philippines
31 J5 Žamberk Czechoslovakia
87 G9 Zambeze R E Africa
87 D8 Zambezi Zambia
88 F10 Zambézia Mozambique
88 C7 Zambia rep Cent Africa
71 F7 Zamboanga Mindanao Philippines
71 F6 Zamboanguita Negros Philippines
126 G10 Zambrano Colombia
31 N3 Zambrów Poland
85 F6 Zamfara R Nigeria
102 C3 Zamora California
128 C4 Zamora Ecuador
124 H8 Zamora Mexico
16 D3 Zamora Spain
16 C3 Zamora prov Spain
125 L3 Zamorano Honduras
31 O5 Zamość Poland
61 P13 Zampa-misaki C Okinawa
128 F3 Zamuro, Sa. del mts Venezuela
84 E3 Zamzam Libya
86 B6 Zanaga Congo
17 F5 Záncara R Spain
25 H3 Zandberg Netherlands
22 G1 Zandvliet Belgium
25 C4 Zandvoort Netherlands
116 J3 Zane Hills Alaska
94 E6 Zanesville Ohio
74 G2 Zangla Kashmir
65 C6 Zanhuang China
41 L6 Zanica Italy
77 A1 Zanjān Iran
131 C3 Zanjón, R Argentina
36 H4 Zannone isld Italy
Zante see Zákinthos
143 E9 Zanthus W Australia
88 G5 Zanzibar Tanzania
88 G5 Zanzibar Chan Tanzania
88 G5 Zanzibar, I Tanzania
65 C5 Zaolin China
65 C6 Zaoqiang China
17 F4 Zaorejas Spain
85 F3 Zaouatanlaz Algeria
67 F1 Zaoxi China
67 D1 Zaoyang China
65 D6 Zaoyang Zhan China
61 O7 Zao-zan vol Japan
56 D3 Zaozernyy U.S.S.R.
65 D7 Zaozhuang China
98 E2 Zap N Dakota
46 D1 Zapadna Morava R Yugoslavia
54 A1 Zapadnaya Dvina R U.S.S.R.
59 M1 Zapadno Sakhalinskiy Khrebet mt U.S.S.R.
56 B2 Zapadnosibirskaya Nizmennost' lowland U.S.S.R.
56 C5 Zapadnyy Sayan U.S.S.R.
37 O4 Západočeský Kraj reg Czechoslovakia
133 C5 Zapala Argentina
109 H9 Zapata Texas
126 D3 Zapata, Pen. de Cuba
125 M4 Zapatera, I Nicaragua
128 D2 Zapatosa Colombia
126 H10 Zapatoza, Ciénaga de Colombia
37 K3 Zapfendorf W Germany
26 S2 Zapoliarno U.S.S.R.
29 P2 Zapolyarnyy U.S.S.R.
54 G9 Zaporozh'ye U.S.S.R.
124 H8 Zapotiltic Mexico
124 F7 Zapotlán Mexico
Zara see Zadar
78 F2 Zara Turkey
77 F2 Zarafshan U.S.S.R.
108 A4 Zaragoza Chihuahua Mexico
108 G7 Zaragoza Coahuila Mexico
71 D2 Zaragoza Luzon Philippines
17 G3 Zaragoza Spain
17 G3 Zaragoza prov Spain
124 H4 Zaragoza, Tiahualilo de Mexico
88 G5 Zaramu Tanzania
77 E4 Zarand Kerman Iran
77 B2 Zarand Ostan-e Markazi Iran
48 G4 Zărandului, Muntii mts Romania
77 G4 Zaranj Afghanistan
52 C6 Zarasai U.S.S.R.
131 F5 Zárate Argentina
54 K2 Zaraysk U.S.S.R.
127 M10 Zaraza Venezuela
57 F5 Zardaly U.S.S.R.
77 B3 Zard Kuh mt Iran
117 G7 Zarembo I Alaska
85 F6 Zaria Nigeria
46 E5 Zárkon Greece
85 D5 Zarma reg Mali
48 J5 Zarnești Romania
31 M4 Żarnów Poland
33 T5 Zarow R E Germany
80 G3 Zarqa R Jordan
77 E5 Zarqān Iran
33 N5 Zarrentin E Germany
128 C4 Zaruma Ecuador
31 J4 Żary Poland
85 F3 Zarzaïtine Algeria
85 G2 Zarzis Tunisia
37 P1 Zaschwitz E Germany
52 D2 Zasheyek U.S.S.R.
31 H4 Zasieki Poland
48 K2 Zastavna U.S.S.R.
87 E8 Zastron S Africa
54 B1 Zasul'ye U.S.S.R.
79 H7 Zatab ash Shamah Saudi Arabia
37 Q3 Žatec Czechoslovakia
31 L6 Zator Poland
33 R8 Zauche reg E Germany
57 A4 Zaunguzskiye Karakumy U.S.S.R.
109 N4 Zavalla Texas
Zavelstein see Bad Teinach-Zavelstein
22 G2 Zaventem Belgium
48 E6 Zavidovići Yugoslavia
59 J1 Zavitinsk U.S.S.R.
146 A14 Zavodovskii I Antarctica
56 B4 Zavodskoy U.S.S.R.
68 C2 Zawgyi R Burma
89 G1 Zawi Zimbabwe
31 L5 Zawiercie Poland
84 F4 Zawilah Libya
80 D5 Zāwiyah, Az Libya
84 G3 Zawiyet Masus Libya
79 G3 Zāwiye, Jebel ez mts Syria
56 F3 Zayarsk U.S.S.R.
56 B6 Zaysan, Oz res U.S.S.R.
57 L1 Zaysan, Ozero L U.S.S.R.
48 K1 Zbarazh U.S.S.R.
31 J3 Zbąszyń Poland
48 J1 Zborov U.S.S.R.
48 K1 Zbruch R U.S.S.R.
48 G2 Zdaňa Czechoslovakia
48 D1 Ždánice Czechoslovakia
30 H6 Zdice Czechoslovakia
31 L4 Zduńska Poland
Zealand isld see Sjælland
118 K7 Zealandia Sask
99 N7 Zearing Iowa
57 F6 Zebak Afghanistan
117 K11 Zeballos Br Columbia
79 G5 Zebdāni Syria
112 J2 Zebulon N Carolina
33 R6 Zechlin E Germany
41 H5 Zeda, Monte Italy
22 E1 Zedelgem Belgium
22 E1 Zeebrugge Belgium
139 H8 Zeehan Tasmania
94 A4 Zeeland Michigan
98 G4 Zeeland N Dakota
25 A6 Zeeland Netherlands
79 E7 Ze'elim Israel
80 E8 Ze'elim, N R Israel
89 E5 Zeerust S Africa
80 E2 Zefat Israel
85 E1 Zegdou Algeria
85 E5 Zeggeren watercourse Mali
33 S7 Zehdenick E Germany
33 S8 Zehlendorf W Berlin
33 Q5 Zehna E Germany
37 P1 Zehren E Germany
110 G4 Zeigler Illinois
37 K3 Zeil W Germany
86 H3 Zeila Somalia
25 D4 Zeist Netherlands
33 S10 Zeithain E Germany
37 O7 Zeitlarn W Germany
37 N1 Zeitz E Germany
80 G3 Zeizun Syria
22 G1 Zele Belgium
31 N4 Zelechów Poland
37 P5 Zelená Lhota Czechoslovakia
29 O11 Zelenogorsk U.S.S.R.
31 M1 Zelenogradsk U.S.S.R.
54 E9 Zelenoye U.S.S.R.
53 F11 Zelenshuk R U.S.S.R.
94 G6 Zelienople Pennsylvania
48 E2 Želiezovce Czechoslovakia
46 D1 Zelijn mt Yugoslavia
36 E7 Zell Baden-Württemberg W Germany
36 H4 Zell Bayern W Germany
36 C3 Zell Rheinland-Pfalz W Germany
98 H5 Zell S Dakota
37 K2 Zella-Mehlis E Germany
38 H6 Zell-am-See Austria
38 G7 Zell-am-See Austria
38 E6 Zell-am-Ziller Austria
38 L5 Zell-bei-zellhof Austria
33 S9 Zellendorf E Germany
36 H4 Zellingen W Germany
119 M7 Zelma Sask
31 L4 Zelów Poland
84 G4 Zelten Libya
36 C4 Zeltingen-Rachtig W Germany
22 F1 Zelzate Belgium
43 D11 Zembra isld Tunisia
50 D1 Zemlya Frantsa Iosifa U.S.S.R.
50 D1 Zemlya Georga isld Franz Josef Land U.S.S.R.
50 F1 Zemlya Vil'cheka Franz Josef Land U.S.S.R.
38 E7 Zemm R Austria
48 G2 Zemplėni-Hory mt Hungary
48 F6 Zemun Yugoslavia
107 M4 Zenda Kansas
67 D5 Zengcheng China
100 B9 Zenia California
42 H4 Zenica Yugoslavia
54 C5 Zen'kov U.S.S.R.
56 C4 Zen'kov U.S.S.R.
37 K5 Zenn R W Germany
22 G2 Zenne R Belgium
119 O5 Zenon Park Sask
60 G11 Zentsuji Japan
125 L9 Zenzontepec Mexico
98 D4 Zeona S Dakota
109 J4 Zephyr Texas
113 E9 Zephyrhills Florida
143 D8 Zephyr,Mt W Australia
57 E5 Zerav'shanskiy Khr mts U.S.S.R.
33 Q9 Zerbst E Germany
36 B4 Zerf W Germany
31 K3 Żerków Poland
40 G5 Zermatt Switzerland
101 U3 Zero Montana
46 D3 Zerqan Albania
33 U6 Zerrenthin E Germany
80 C3 Zerufa Israel
66 E6 Zêtang China
32 G6 Zetel W Germany
Zetland co see Shetland reg
6 K2 Zetland isld Scotland
65 E6 Zetouji China
37 M2 Zeulenroda E Germany
33 T8 Zeuthen E Germany
32 K6 Zeven W Germany
25 C5 Zevenbergen Netherlands
25 C5 Zevenbergse Hoek Netherlands
45 K1 Zevio Italy
59 J1 Zeya Vdkhr U.S.S.R.
59 J1 Zeya R U.S.S.R.
25 F5 Zeyenaar Netherlands
59 H1 Zeysko Bureinskaya Ravnina U.S.S.R.
47 J6 Zeytindağ Turkey
16 B4 Zêzere R Portugal
79 F4 Zghorta Lebanon
31 L4 Zgierz Poland
38 N8 Zgornja Kungota Yugoslavia
31 J4 Zgorzelec Poland
48 L2 Zguritsa U.S.S.R.
48 J2 Zhabe U.S.S.R.
67 F3 Zhaili China
67 C5 Zhaixu China
57 E1 Zhaksykon R U.S.S.R.
57 G2 Zhaksylyk U.S.S.R.
57 F1 Zhaksy Sarysu R U.S.S.R.
57 E1 Zhalanash U.S.S.R.
57 C1 Zhamankkol', Ozero L U.S.S.R.
57 E1 Zhanabas U.S.S.R.
57 B2 Zhanakentkala U.S.S.R.
57 B2 Zhanakurylys U.S.S.R.
57 C3 Zhanala U.S.S.R.
57 C3 Zhanatalap U.S.S.R.
57 E3 Zhanatas U.S.S.R.
65 C4 Zhangbei China
Zhangde see Anyang
Zhangdian see Zibo
65 G3 Zhangguangcai Ling mt ra China
65 E3 Zhanggutai China
65 C6 Zhang He R China
67 C6 Zhanghuang China
65 C4 Zhangjiakou China
67 E1 Zhangjiapang China
67 E2 Zhangjiashan China
67 C5 Zhangmu China
67 F4 Zhangping China
67 F4 Zhangpu China
65 D6 Zhangqiu China
65 D4 Zhangsanying China
67 E4 Zhang Shui R China
Zhangshuzhen see Qingjiang
59 H3 Zhangwu China
58 D4 Zhangye China
67 F4 Zhangzhou Fujian China
65 B6 Zhangzi China
65 E5 Zhangzi Dao isld China
65 D6 Zhanhua China
67 C6 Zhanjiang China
67 C6 Zhanjiang Gang B China
51 P1 Zhannetty, Ostrov isld U.S.S.R.
57 E1 Zhanteli U.S.S.R.
67 A4 Zhanyi China
65 E2 Zhanyu China
67 F5 Zhao'an China
65 B6 Zhaocheng China
65 F1 Zhaodong China
Zhaoge see Qi Xian
67 C4 Zhaoping China
67 D5 Zhaoqing China
66 C3 Zhaosu China
67 A3 Zhaotong China
65 C6 Zhao Xian China
65 E6 Zhaoyuan China
65 F2 Zhaoyuan China
Zhaozhen see Jintang
59 J2 Zhaozhou China
67 G1 Zhapu China
52 D6 Zhari U.S.S.R.
54 D1 Zharkovskiy U.S.S.R.
57 K1 Zharma U.S.S.R.
57 G1 Zharyk U.S.S.R.
48 N1 Zhashkov U.S.S.R.
51 M2 Zhatay U.S.S.R.
Zhaxi see Weixin
66 B5 Zhaxigang China
54 J9 Zhdanov U.S.S.R.
48 M5 Zhebriyany U.S.S.R.
65 C7 Zhecheng China
67 F2 Zhejiang prov China
57 E1 Zhel'dyadyr U.S.S.R.
56 F3 Zheleznodorozhnyy Irkutskaya Oblast U.S.S.R.
31 N1 Zheleznodorozhnyy U.S.S.R.
56 F3 Zheleznogorsk-Ilimsky U.S.S.R.
Zhelou see Ceheng
54 E8 Zheltyye Vody U.S.S.R.
67 B4 Zhenfeng China
67 B2 Zheng'an China
58 F4 Zhengding China
67 F3 Zhenghe China
Zhengjiakou see Gucheng
67 D2 Zhengjiayi China
65 C3 Zhengxiangbai Qi China
65 B7 Zhengzhou China
67 F4 Zhenhai China
67 G2 Zhenhai China
67 F1 Zhenjiang China
65 F2 Zhenlai China
65 C3 Zhenlan Qi China
67 C5 Zhenlong China
67 B3 Zhenning China
67 C1 Zhenping China
Zhenwudong see Ansai
65 F1 Zhenxiang China
67 A3 Zhenxiong China
67 C3 Zhenyuan China
67 C1 Zhenziling China
67 A4 Zhetai China
67 D1 Zhicheng China
67 A5 Zhicun China
48 J1 Zhidachov U.S.S.R.
Zhifang see Wuchang
58 B3 Zhifang China
56 G4 Zhigalovo U.S.S.R.
51 M2 Zhigansk U.S.S.R.
57 E1 Zhigerli U.S.S.R.
67 C3 Zhijiang China
67 D1 Zhijiang China
67 B3 Zhijin China
54 H7 Zhilkhar' U.S.S.R.
67 B6 Zhilang China
67 B6 Zhitan China
53 C8 Zhitomir U.S.S.R.
54 F3 Zhizdra U.S.S.R.
54 G2 Zhizdra R U.S.S.R.
54 B4 Zhlobin U.S.S.R.
48 L1 Zhmerinka U.S.S.R.
77 L4 Zhob R Pakistan
51 P1 Zhokhova, Ostrov isld U.S.S.R.
Zhongba see Jiangyou
66 C6 Zhongba China
67 B5 Zhongdong China
67 C4 Zhongdu China
65 F1 Zhonghe China
67 A1 Zhongjiang China
65 B7 Zhongmou China
67 D4 Zhongshan China
Zhongshu see Renhuai
65 B7 Zhongtiao Shan ra China
67 B1 Zhongxian China
58 F5 Zhongxiang China
67 E4 Zhongxin China
65 B6 Zhongyang China
68 K3 Zhongyuan China
67 D2 Zhoujiadian China
58 F5 Zhoukouzhen China
67 F3 Zhouning China
67 G1 Zhoushan Dao isld China
59 H5 Zhoushan Qundao China
48 N3 Zhovten U.S.S.R.
59 H4 Zhuanghe China
63 G10 Zhucang China
65 D6 Zhucheng China
Zhuji see Shangqiu
67 G2 Zhuji China
67 G2 Zhujia Jian isld China
67 D6 Zhujiang Kou B China
Zhujing see Jinshan
54 E3 Zhukovka U.S.S.R.
65 C5 Zhulong He R China
65 D4 Zhuluke China
58 F5 Zhumadian China
58 G3 Zhuolu China
58 G4 Zhuo Xian China
65 B4 Zhuozi China
65 E6 Zhuqiao China
54 C6 Zhuravnaha, Step' U.S.S.R.
67 C1 Zhushan China
67 D3 Zhuting China
58 E5 Zhuxi China
65 A7 Zhuyangzhen China
67 A4 Zhuyuan China
57 G2 Zhuzagashskiy U.S.S.R.
67 D3 Zhuzhou China
78 J3 Zibar Iraq
65 D6 Zibo China
65 A6 Zichang China
22 H2 Zichem Belgium
47 J2 Zidarovo Bulgaria
33 R5 Ziddorf E Germany
54 H7 Zid'ki U.S.S.R.
31 K5 Ziębice Poland
37 N2 Ziegendorf E Germany
36 G2 Ziegenhain W Germany
37 M2 Ziegenrück E Germany
140 B6 Ziel,Mt N Terr Aust
31 J4 Zielona Góra Poland
32 K10 Ziemendorf W Germany
25 A5 Zierikzee Netherlands
38 N4 Ziersdorf Austria
33 Q8 Ziesar E Germany
31 P1 Žiežmariai U.S.S.R.
79 B8 Zifta Egypt
68 A2 Zigaing Burma
84 G4 Zighan Libya
68 B3 Zigon Burma
67 A2 Zigong China
58 F5 Zigui China
85 A6 Ziguinchor Senegal
52 C6 Žigure U.S.S.R.
65 D6 Zi He R China
37 P5 Žihle Czechoslovakia
65 C5 Zijingguan China
80 C3 Zikhron Ya'aqov Israel
78 E1 Zile Turkey
48 E1 Žilina Czechoslovakia
84 F4 Zillah Libya
38 E7 Zillertal R Austria
38 E7 Zillertaler Alpen mts Austria
Zilling Tso L see Siling Co
141 K1 Zillmere dist Brisbane, Qnsld
52 C6 Zilupe U.S.S.R.
56 F4 Zima U.S.S.R.
125 K7 Zimapán Mexico
125 L9 Zimatlán de Alvarez Mexico
87 E9 Zimba Zambia
89 G3 Zimbabwe Zimbabwe
87 E9 Zimbabwe rep Africa
87 F9 Zimbue Mozambique
99 N4 Zimmerman Minnesota
36 G1 Zimmersrode W Germany
47 H2 Zimnitsa Bulgaria
48 J7 Zimricea Romania
77 G2 Zindajan Afghanistan
85 F6 Zinder Niger
30 G1 Zingst pen E Germany
38 L7 Zinken mt Austria
37 Q5 Žinkovy Czechoslovakia
33 T4 Zinnowitz E Germany
99 T7 Zion Illinois
127 P4 Zion Nevis W I
103 M4 Zion Can Utah
103 M4 Zion Nat. Park Utah
94 A7 Zionsville Indiana
33 O5 Zippendorf E Germany
80 E3 Zippori Israel
80 D2 Zippori R Israel
80 F3 Ziqlab R Jordan
128 D2 Ziraquirá Colombia
38 L7 Zirbitz Kogel mt Austria
42 G5 Žirje isld Yugoslavia
101 T9 Zirkel, Mt Colorado
37 K5 Zirndorf W Germany
46 D3 Žirovnica Yugoslavia
67 D2 Zi Shui R China
125 J8 Zitácuaro Mexico
67 B1 Zitong China
46 E5 Zitsa Greece
31 H5 Zittau E Germany
41 L3 Zitterklapfen mt Austria
116 M4 Zitziana R Alaska
67 F3 Zixi China
67 D4 Zixing China
65 C5 Ziya He R China
67 A1 Ziyang China
67 C3 Ziyuan China
67 B4 Ziyun China
67 F4 Ziyundong Shan mt China
41 L4 Zizers Switzerland
58 D6 Zizhong China
65 A6 Zizhou China
47 H1 Zlatarista Bulgaria
31 L7 Zlaté Moravce Czechoslovakia
46 D1 Zlatibor mt Yugoslavia
47 G2 Zlatitsa Bulgaria
48 H4 Zlatna Romania
47 G3 Zlatograd Bulgaria
54 C8 Zlatopol' U.S.S.R.
50 E3 Zlatoust U.S.S.R.
46 E3 Zletovo Yugoslavia
84 E3 Zlitan Libya
31 J2 Zlocieniec Poland
31 L4 Złoczew Poland
30 H5 Zloniee Czechoslovakia
48 G6 Zlot Yugoslavia
31 J4 Złotoryja Poland
31 K2 Złotów Poland
37 P3 Žlutice Czechoslovakia
54 C4 Zlynka U.S.S.R.
56 B5 Zmeinogorsk U.S.S.R.
53 D10 Zmeinyy, Ostrov isld U.S.S.R.
31 K4 Żmigród Poland
Zmiyev see Gottvald
54 C2 Znamenityy U.S.S.R.
54 D8 Znamenka U.S.S.R.
54 D8 Znamenka Vtoraya U.S.S.R.
31 K3 Żnin Poland
31 J7 Znojmo Czechoslovakia
37 P2 Zöblitz E Germany
45 J3 Zocca Italy
40 G3 Zofingen Switzerland
80 C5 Zofit Israel
41 L6 Zogno Italy
31 K7 Zohor Czechoslovakia
77 B4 Zohreh Iran
25 G2 Zolder Belgium
113 F10 Zolfo Springs Florida
36 E3 Zollhaus W Germany
48 J1 Zolochev U.S.S.R.
59 J1 Zolotaya Gora U.S.S.R.
54 N1 Zolotkovo U.S.S.R.
56 C4 Zolotogorskiy U.S.S.R.
54 D7 Zolotonosha U.S.S.R.
88 E9 Zomba Malawi
Zongga see Gyirong
66 F4 Zongjiafangzi China
86 C5 Zongo Zaïre
78 C1 Zonguldak Turkey
67 F1 Zongyang China
22 J2 Zonhoven Belgium
33 P10 Zorbau E Germany
37 Q4 Zörbig E Germany
80 F5 Zor el Hanahina Jordan
33 N9 Zorge W Germany
33 N10 Zorge R E Germany
16 D5 Zorita Spain
48 L4 Zorleni Romania
36 D6 Zorn R France
101 R2 Zortman Montana
31 L5 Zory Poland
85 C7 Zorzor Liberia
33 Q10 Zöschen E Germany
33 S8 Zossen E Germany
22 F2 Zottegem Belgium
86 C1 Zouar Chad
85 B4 Zouerate Mauritania
16 D10 Zoumi Morocco
65 D6 Zouping China
58 F4 Zouquan China
25 F2 Zoutkamp Netherlands
22 J2 Zoutleeuw Belgium
65 D7 Zou Xian China
67 C5 Zouxu China
48 F5 Zrenjanin Yugoslavia
42 G4 Zrmanja R Yugoslavia
31 J6 Zruč Czechoslovakia
41 G3 Zsáka Hungary
33 R10 Zschepplin E Germany
37 P2 Zschopau E Germany
37 O1 Zschopau R E Germany
37 O2 Zschorlau E Germany
127 M10 Zuata Venezuela
128 E2 Zuata R Venezuela
113 E8 Zuber Florida
16 E7 Zubia Spain
54 F1 Zubtsov U.S.S.R.
80 D3 Zububa Israel
37 L6 Zuchering W Germany
41 O4 Zuckerhütl mt Austria
133 E1 Zudañez Bolivia
33 S4 Zudar E Germany
85 C7 Zuénoula Ivory Coast
41 H3 Zug canton Switzerland
58 F1 Zugdeli U.S.S.R.
41 H3 Zuger See L Switzerland
41 O3 Zugspitze mt W Germany
25 B5 Zuid Beijerland Netherlands
25 G2 Zuidbroek Netherlands

INDEX ADDENDA AND ERRATA

The index went to press before the maps and the following corrections should be noted for the Index. The maps are correct.

1. For *New Hebrides* read *Vanuatu*.
2. *Panama* has now assumed sovereignty over the *Panama Canal Zone*.
3. *Antigua and Barbuda* became independent in 1982.
4. *Salisbury* became *Harare* on 18 April 1982. Other names in Zimbabwe have been changed on the maps but the old names appear in brackets.

88

THE TRANSCRIPTION OF CHINESE PLACE-NAMES

Chinese is written in Han characters, a system of writing which has remained in use for more than 3,000 years. Its most conspicuous features are the large number of characters and the complexity of most of them. All told, there cannot be fewer than 50,000, of which perhaps 11,000 may be encountered in bibliographic or similar research. Up to 3,000 characters are used in everyday written communication.

Han characters are ideographs but since the language is a spoken language and not just written, each character can be represented by a syllable – a vowel or a vowel with one or more consonants. Because the spoken language evolves with time and pronunciation varies with dialect many different readings of a character are possible.

Compared with English and other European languages, Chinese has few syllables, in Modern Standard Chinese hardly more than 400. With thousands of characters in use, many are equated with the same syllable. The syllable **sên** is represented by only one character. In contrast **yi** can be expressed by over 215. Tone (the modulation of the voice) helps to distinguish meaning, but generally context alone determines what is meant.

So complex a system of writing is not well suited to a modern industrial society but rather to a peasant community where the literate few have unlimited time to study. Printing is a formidable matter compared with European languages. Learning to read and write involves mastery of a large number of characters, imposing a great demand on memory and requiring a considerable amount of time.

There are many romanization systems for Chinese. Four are widely used in English. Of these the Wade-Giles system is most familiar. All British and American official maps have used the system exclusively since 1942, and millions of references exist in Wade-Giles romanizations. The system was first published in 1859 by Sir Thomas Wade and it was the basis, slightly modified, for the Chinese-English Dictionary of H. A. Giles published in 1912.

Of all the dialects of China, Northern Chinese (formerly called Mandarin Chinese) is most widespread. Wade-Giles and all systems since have used the educated Peking dialect of Northern Chinese as the standard language and the preferred readings of characters are given in that dialect which has become the model for Modern Standard Chinese.

Chinese, as distinct from European, interest in romanization was stimulated by the desire to promote a national language as well as to assist in learning to read the characters. Romanization would also serve as a means of writing the non-Chinese languages spoken within China and to help to write them in Chinese. A further aim was to encourage foreigners to learn Chinese.

As a first step towards these goals the most commonly used characters were simplified. Much discussion has centred around the replacement of Han characters by an alphabet, but this can only happen in the very remote future. Romanized Chinese may increasingly exist side-by-side with the characters but that does not mean that the Han characters are about to be dropped from use.

In 1958, the Chinese government approved the system called **Pinyin zimu** (phonetic alphabet) for the romanization of Chinese. Teachers of Chinese prefer Pinyin to Wade-Giles. It is a better source for up-to-date idiom and vocabulary but a great amount of material is not yet available in Pinyin. Students of Chinese, therefore, have to deal with other systems of romanization. For geographical names almost nothing existed in Pinyin for many years. Everything worth considering was in Wade-Giles. Yet in spite of the fact that the letters **c**, **q** and **x** were used in a way totally alien to English usage, Pinyin was neater than Wade-Giles which, for example, produces **Wu-lu-mu-chi** for English conventional **Urumchi** where Pinyin gives **Urumqi**. **Harbin** is so spelled in Pinyin but becomes **Ha-erh-pin** in Wade-Giles.

Ever since Pinyin was launched in 1958, the publishers of The Times Atlas have contemplated but, until now, rejected the adoption of Pinyin for the map plates covering China. Among the factors considered were the availability of sources for Pinyin names, the extent to which Pinyin was used in China and the acceptance and use of Pinyin outside China, particularly for geographical names. In spite of a State Council directive of 1975 that Pinyin would be used as the standard and sole romanization system for geographical and personal names, little was done in China to follow the directive until 1977. Early in 1979 Pinyin was accepted by most nations of the world as the system to be employed officially for romanized Chinese names. Times Books of London, the publishers of the Atlas, therefore decided to adopt Pinyin in place of Wade-Giles for the names of Mainland China and the map plates in this atlas now contain Pinyin names in place of Wade-Giles.

By way of example Peking in conventional English is **Beijing** in Pinyin and appears in that form in this atlas as opposed to **Pei-ching** in Wade-Giles. **Guangzhou** (Canton) in Pinyin was **Kuang-chou** in Wade-Giles. Further examples are: **Chongqing** (Chungking), **Ch'ung-ch'ing**; **Fuzhou** (Foochow), **Fu-chou**; **Jilin** (Kirin), **Chi-lin**; **Xian** (Sian), **Hsi-an**.

In Taiwan, where Pinyin is not used, Wade-Giles has been retained to conform to local practice. In Hong Kong a romanization based on Cantonese is used. Pinyin would be in conflict with official practice in Hong Kong.

In order to facilitate reference to Wade-Giles names, the relationship of consonants and vowels in the two systems is shown on this page.

No attempt has been made in this atlas to fabricate Pinyin names by conversion from Wade-Giles or by other methods: all Pinyin names have been taken from official Chinese sources. There are several reasons why fabrication would be inadmissible. The name itself may have changed; the administrative status of the place may not be known; there may be errors in the Wade-Giles transcription; the reading of the Han character may have changed. In areas where the people are not Chinese, e.g. Sinkiang, Tibet, Inner Mongolia, guessing at the Pinyin spelling could produce nonsensical names. For example, the character **shen** in Chinese is used to produce **xain** in **xainza** but **sên** in **Sêndo**. Likewise, to convert **Pa-yen-wu-la** from Wade-Giles would give **Bayan Wula** for the place in Inner Mongolia which is shown on Plate 23 as **Xi Ujimqin Qi (Bayan Ul Hot)**.

COMPARATIVE TABLES OF PINYIN AND WADE-GILES

VOWELS

Wade-Giles	Pinyin	Approximate pronunciation	Pinyin	Wade-Giles
eh	e	e as in met	e (after h, g, k)	o
erh	er	er as in her	e (after i, u, y)	eh
i (when initial or standing alone)	yi	yea as in yeast	er	erh
		ie as in fiesta	i (after j, q, r, sh)	ih
ieh	ie		ian	ien
ien	ian	ean as in meander	ie	ieh
ih	i	e as in her	ong	ung
o (standing alone or after h, k, k')	e	e as in her	ou (after y)	u
			u (after j, q, x, y)	ü
o (after f, m, p, p', w)	o	o as in corn	ü (after l, n)	ü
o (after other consonants)	uo	uo as in duo	ui (after g, k')	uei
			uo (after g, h, k, sh)	uo
u (after y)	ou	ou as in you	uo (otherwise)	o
ü (after l, n)	ü	u as in tu (French) or ü as in dünn (German)	yan	yen
			yi	i
ü (after ch, ch', hs, y)	u	o as in do		
uei (occurs only after k, k')	ui	uai as in quaint	Certain syllables eg Wade-Giles **yai** cannot be converted mechanically from system to system
ung	ong	ung as in jung (German)		

Note
In both panels the first column gives the Wade-Giles in alphabetical order; the second gives the Pinyin equivalent; the third, the pronunciation. The fourth and fifth columns give the same information as the first and second, but in Pinyin alphabetical order, to enable the reader to refer back from Pinyin. Unless otherwise stated, consonants are pronounced as in English and vowels as in Italian.

CONSONANTS

Wade-Giles	Pinyin	Approximate pronunciation	Pinyin	Wade-Giles
ch (except when followed by i or ü)	zh	j as in jump	b	p
			c	ts'
ch' (except when followed by i or ü)	ch	ch as in church	ci	tz'u
			chi	ch'ih
chi; chü	ji; ju	j as in jam	ch	ch'
ch'i; ch'ü	qi; qu	ch as in church	d	t
chih	zhi		g	k
ch'ih	chi		j	ch (when followed by i or u)
hs	x	sh as in shoe		
j	r	r as in red or z as in azure	k	k'
k	g	g as in good	p	p
k'	k	k as in kin	q	ch' (when followed by i or u)
p	b	b as in bat		
p'	p	p as in pat	r	j
ssu (sze)	si	si as in sierra	si	ssu (sze)
t	d	d as in dog	t	t'
t'	t	t as in tot	x	hs
ts	z	z as in zulu	yi	i
ts'	c	ts as in sits	you	yu
tzu	zi	ze as in zero	z	ts
tz'u	ci	tsy as in Betsy	zi	tzu
yai	ya or ai	yea as in yea	zh	ch
			zhi	chih

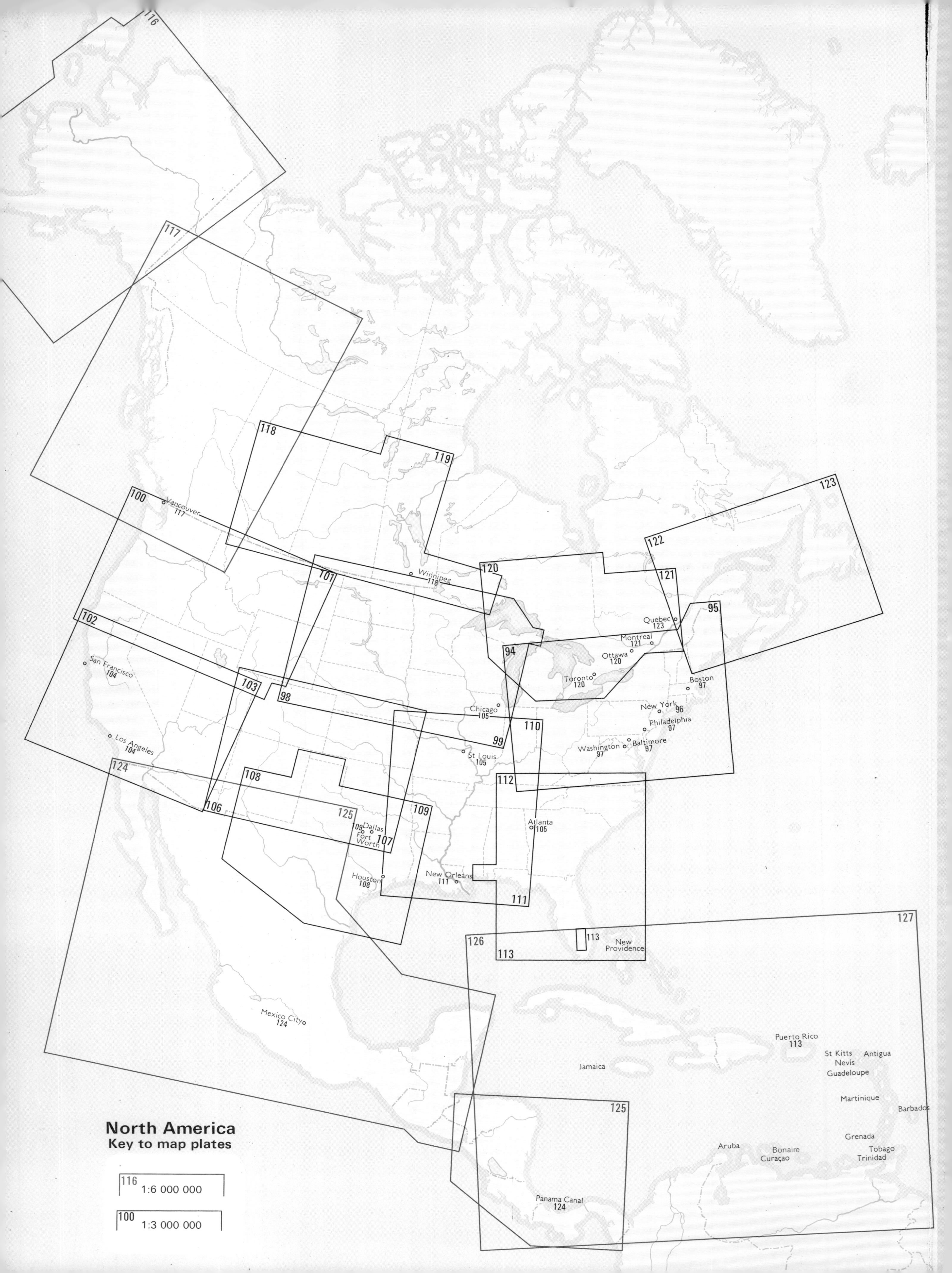
North America
Key to map plates
116 1:6 000 000
100 1:3 000 000
116
117
118
119
100
Vancouver 117
101
Winnipeg 118
120
121
122
123
95
Quebec 123
Montreal 121
Ottawa 120
Toronto 120
94
Boston 97
New York 96
Philadelphia 97
Baltimore 97
Washington 97
102
San Francisco 104
103
98
Chicago 105
99
110
St Louis 105
Los Angeles 104
124
108
106
125
109
Dallas
Fort Worth
107
112
Atlanta 105
Houston 108
New Orleans 111
111
113
New Providence
126
127
Mexico City 124
Puerto Rico 113
St Kitts
Nevis
Antigua
Guadeloupe
Jamaica
Martinique
Barbados
Grenada
Tobago
Trinidad
Aruba
Bonaire
Curaçao
Panama Canal 124